YOUTH BIBLE

YOUTH BIBLE

Contents

Old Testament

New Testament

Start Here

(Mainly for ministers and youth leaders, but worth reading anyway)

The Bible is God's message to humanity. He has spoken to all peoples and all generations. Of course, God first did this by directly addressing his people, the Israelites, in the Old Testament and the young church in the New Testament, in a language they could understand.

The original text of the Bible was written in Hebrew, Aramaic and Greek – languages of the people. Since God intends to speak to all people of all ages through his Word, each generation and language group must translate the Bible into its own language.

These facts, that the Bible is God's message and that it is ultimately addressed to all people in every age, require that a translation be both accurate and clear. These are the two overarching principles that stand behind the *New Century Version*.

An Accurate Translation

The first concern of the *New Century Version* is that the translation be faithful to the manuscripts in the original languages. A team composed of the World Bible Translation Centre and fifty additional, highly qualified and experienced Bible scholars and translators was assembled. This team included people with experience on the *New International Version*, the *New American Standard Bible*, and the *New King James Version*. The scholars came from a variety of theological colleges, universities, and seminaries in the United States, Canada, Australia, and Great Britain. These translators recognise that the most accurate translations are those which pay close attention to the meanings of words in their broader context, rather than those which simply treat words as isolated entities. They understand that a contemporary English translation must sometimes depart from the word order of the original languages to reflect accurately the meaning of God's Word to a modern English-speaking audience.

Further, it is true that translation involves interpretive decisions. With this in mind, it is important to note that the breadth of scholarship which stands behind the *New Century Version* ensures an unbiased translation.

Last, it should be mentioned that the best available Hebrew and Greek texts were used, principally the third edition of the United Bible Societies' Greek text and the latest edition of the Biblia Hebraica, along with the Septuagint.

A Clear Translation

The second concern was to make the language clear enough for all people to read the Bible and understand it for themselves. In maintaining clear language, several guidelines were followed. Vocabulary choice has been based upon *The Living Word Vocabulary* by Dr Edgar Dale and Dr Joseph O'Rourke (Worldbook-Childcraft International, 1981), which is the standard used by the editors of *The World Book Encyclopedia* to determine appropriate vocabulary. For difficult words that have no simpler synonyms, footnotes and dictionary references are provided. Footnotes appear at the bottom of the page and are indicated in the text by a raised letter (n) for "note". The dictionary/topical concordance is located at the back of the Bible with references indicated in the text by a raised letter (d).

The *New Century Version* aids understanding by using contemporary references for measurements and geographical locations when it is feasible. For instance, terms such as "shekels", "cubits", "omer" and "hin" have been converted to modern equivalents. Where geographical references are identical, the modern name has been used, such as the "Mediterranean Sea" instead of "Great Sea" or "Western Sea". Also, to minimise confusion, the most familiar name for a place is used consistently, instead of using variant names for the same place. "Lake Galilee" is used throughout rather than its variant forms, "Sea of Kinnereth", "Lake Gennesaret" and "Sea of Tiberias".

Ancient customs are often unfamiliar to modern readers. Customs such as shaving a man's beard to shame him or ritually walking between the halves of a dead animal to seal an agreement are meaningless to many modern-day readers. So these are clarified either in the text or in a footnote.

Since **meanings** of words change with time, care has been taken to avoid potential misunderstandings. To do so, the *New Century Version* uses contemporary language in place of the archaic language often found in translations. Frequently in the Old Testament God tells his people to "devote" something to him, as when he tells the Israelites to devote Jericho and everything in it to him. While we might understand this to mean he is telling them to keep it safe and holy, the exact opposite is true. He is telling them to destroy it totally as an offering to him. The *New Century Version* communicates the idea clearly by translating "devoted", in these situations, as "destroyed as an offering to the Lord".

Where there was potential for confusion, **rhetorical questions** have been stated according to their implied answer. The psalmist's question, "Who, O God, is like you?" has been stated more directly as, "God, there is no one like you."

Figures of speech have been translated according to their meanings. For instance, the expression, "the Virgin Daughter of Zion", which is frequently used in the Old Testament, is simply and accurately translated "the people of Jerusalem" so that the meaning is not obscured by the figure of speech.

Idiomatic expressions of the biblical languages are translated to communicate the same meaning to today's reader that would have been understood by the original audience. For example, the Hebrew idiom "he rested with his fathers" is translated by its meaning – "he died".

Obscure terms have been clarified. Terms are often obscure in the Bible because they are part of the ancient culture which God directly addressed in his revelation. In the Old Testament, for instance, God frequently condemns the people for their "high places" and "Asherah poles". The *New Century Version* translates these according to their meanings, which would have been understood by the Hebrews. "High places" is translated "places where gods were worshipped" and "Asherah poles" is translated "Asherah idols".

Gender language has also been translated with a concern for clarity. To avoid the misconception that "man", "mankind" and "he" are exclusively masculine when they are being used in a generic sense, this translation has chosen to use less ambiguous language, such as "people", "humans" and "human beings", and has carefully worked throughout to choose gender language that would accurately convey the intent of the original writers. Specifically and exclusively masculine and feminine references in the text have been retained.

Following in the tradition of other English versions, the *New Century Version* indicates the divine name YHWH, the Tetragrammaton, by putting LORD, and sometimes GOD, in capital letters. This is to distinguish it from Adonai, another Hebrew word that is translated "Lord".

Every attempt has been made to maintain proper English style, while clarifying concepts and communication. The beauty of Hebrew parallelism in poetry has been retained, and the images of the ancient languages have been captured in equivalent English images wherever possible, but in all cases, clarity of communication with the modern reader has taken precedence over preservation of the ancient form.

Study Aids

Other features to enhance understanding of the text include maps of Bible lands, subject headings throughout to identify speakers and topics, book introductions to give a summary of each book's theme, a dictionary/topical concordance of biblical words and concepts, and footnotes identifying Old Testament quotations in the New Testament.

Our Prayer

It is with great humility and prayerfulness that this Bible is presented. We acknowledge the infallibility of God's Word and yet our own human frailty. We pray that God has worked through us as his vessels so that we all might better learn his truth for ourselves and that it might richly grow in our lives. It is to his glory that this Bible is given.

The Publisher

Using the Youth Bible with Groups

• **Why is it that the Bible ends up on so many shelves – unopened, unread and covered in a thick coat of dust?** Many young people say that they find the Bible dull, boring, remote and difficult to understand. Numbers of the teenagers we work with have heard it all hundreds of times before. On the other hand we all deal with people from an unchurched background. They don't understand church "lingo" and struggle to see how the Bible and God are in any way relevant to their lives. It's our task to bring the Bible to life for both those who've never heard it and those who have grown tired of listening. So what can you do?

• **Keep your eyes on the real goal.** Jesus asked us to make disciples not academics. Sadly Bible study has often been more about learning Bible history than helping young people understand what God's Word is really saying about contemporary life. The *Youth Bible* is all about challenging this approach. Bible background is important but needs to be kept in the background which is why the **Sidelights** are short. The goal of Bible study is to help young people grow in their friendship with Jesus and discover more about how important that friendship is to everyday life. This is why the **Life Files** have been developed, with their focus on relating the unchanging truth of the Bible to rapidly changing culture. And it is why they take up so much of the book.

• **Make quality time for preparation.** Start by praying and asking for God's help – after all he inspired the Bible's authors in the first place and he can do the same for you. Then read and re-read the Bible passage that you are going to study. Try and summarise the main points in your own words to get hold of what you think the text is actually saying. Now use the **Topical Concordance and Dictionary** at the back of the *Youth Bible* to get a highly focused view. Use a full-scale concordance or commentaries to get the broader picture.

Use a book on Bible study methods to give you ideas on how to present your material. Do pinch ideas from books and magazines but adapt them rather than just swallowing them whole.

• **Use active learning approaches.** Outdated teaching methods have sometimes created a roadblock to making disciples and Bible studies based around a lecture will result in little Bible understanding and even less ability to apply it. The best learning methods are those that help your young people to discover the Bible's truths for themselves. Each **Life File** includes two active learning ideas under the heading "CONSIDER".

The Right Environment

• Use the smallest comfortable room. But remember 30 people in a crowded front room may make concentrating very difficult.

• Ensure that the phone will not ring at a vital moment.

• Never use a room which is being used for another activity at the same time.

• Avoid using a room which is on a through route to somewhere else.

• Use low chairs or cushions so people can put their bits on the floor.

• Get the temperature right. A stuffy room does not create a relaxed learning atmosphere.

• Leave space for latecomers so they don't feel awkward.

• Don't overrun and make sure people can get home on time.

• **See yourself as a facilitator rather than a lecturer.** Your aim should be to actively involve every group member. Let people express their thoughts and feelings. Having got healthy discussion going, your job is to occasionally steer it to keep it on target and moving, and to help group members to think through the implications of what they are discovering. You need to practise your listening as well as your speaking skills.

• **Questions are your basic tool to get the group thinking about the Bible passage.** Each **Life File** includes two questions to get the group going. Use extra questions that are clear and brief. Break long points down into a number of short statements and only then ask your question. Don't insult your group's intelligence by asking the obvious. Try to make your questions provocative to stir up reaction.

• **Bridge the cultural gap.** "The effective Christian is someone who holds the Bible in one hand, the newspaper in the other and reads both!" Use the newspaper or a video of the news to highlight issues like faith, drugs, alcohol, depression, death and poverty – the sort of subjects in the **Life File Guide** (starting on page 12). Get your youth group talking about what they think of the issue and introduce your biblical material from there.

• **Tie in to real-life experience.** The Bible is a practical guide to life today. Do things that encourage your members to put the Bible into practice, like visiting a prison or a soup kitchen or many of the other suggestions in the **Life Files.**

• **Always give page numbers.** Encourage people to use the list of contents to show where the books are. Don't give the impression that using the list of contents is second-rate.

• **Don't assume that all members of the group can read or write.** The *New Century Version* used in the *Youth Bible* is one of the most readable translations around (see **Start Here** p.6). But still be very careful before asking any group member to read aloud. You will never help people enjoy the Bible by intimidating or picking on them.

Using Life Files

• Always try and match the Life File to the situation of your group. Avoid using stories that are "too close for comfort".

• Ask the group whether they know of stories like the one that has been read.

• If you are working on a topic for an evening or at a weekend, break up into small groups each working on a different Life File.

• Dramatise the Life File stories.

• Get people to write alternative endings to the stories where appropriate. Have the group vote on the best/most realistic/most dramatic ending.

• Where the stories involve conflict, get people to role-play the characters and put them on trial as a way of discussing different points of view.

• Use stories as an opportunity to pray for people in situations like those in the story.

• Clip your own Life Files from newspapers, teen magazines or soap operas.

Getting to Know Your Bible

At times the Bible can feel like the most hard-going, difficult, confusing and boring book that has ever been written. The problem is that the Bible is very complicated.

- It isn't really a single book at all. The word "Bible" means "library" and that's exactly what it is – 66 books in all: 39 in the first section and 27 in the second.

- It was written by about 40 authors over a time period spanning more than 1,000 years and it contains 750,000 words. And if that's not enough, the Old Testament was written in Hebrew and the New Testament in Greek!

So why bother?

In a world where magazines, TV, radio, newspapers and other books bombard us with so many conflicting ideas about life, the Bible claims to be directly inspired by God himself – it's the Creator's message to his world. If that's true it means that the Bible is in a completely different league from any other advice you can find. If the Bible is God's guidebook to life, it makes sense to take it very, very seriously.

So, how do you make friends with the Bible and get the most out of reading it?
Here are ten dos and don'ts:

1. Do use a modern translation. It's very important that you read a version which captures the depth of the original language at the same time as expressing its truth in a clear up to date way. That's where the Youth Bible scores. See the notes down below.

2. Don't rush – read slowly. Think about what you are reading. Quality comes before quantity. Read it more than once. You'll find that you'll notice all sorts of things you missed first time round. Remember that it's better to understand one verse than read a whole chapter and forget the lot!

3. Do pray first. Ask God to speak to you. You might just pray, "Help me, God, to discover you and your will as I read my Bible." After you've finished reading it pray and talk to God about the things that he has said to you or if you have found it hard to understand, be honest with him about it.

Where The Youth Bible Scores

- It uses the *New Century Version* – a new translation, designed to be readable and reliable at the same time and the book itself is packed with all sorts of information that makes it user-friendly.

- If there is a particular problem or topic that you are thinking about you can look it up in the **Life File Guide** which lists over 400 topics on 80 important issues. Each **Life File** picks up on what the Bible has to say on that particular subject and then gives you a passage to read through or think about.

- Other relevant parts of the Bible are listed and because each reference comes with a page number beside it, you don't have to know where all those obscure books like Malachi, Jude and Esther are!

- Each individual book has a **Book Opener** – a short introduction to help you understand its purpose, with time charts and, in most cases, maps as well.

- **Sidelights** give you even more information about life in Bible times and the Bible itself.

4. Don't use it as a lucky dip. Don't open it at random and expect some magic word or phrase to leap out and solve all your problems. If you do, you are almost bound to end up getting confused. And don't try and read it from cover to cover right away. As we've already said it is a big and complicated book. Like with all other guidebooks the most sensible thing to do is to go to the issue you are thinking about at the time. Use a reading plan or the **Life File Guide** at the front of the Bible.

5. Do read it regularly. Just like food and exercise, "little and often" is best. If you can, set aside a short time every day to read a passage from the Bible and think it through. If your routine changes at the weekend, do something different then. Re-read what you have looked at during the week or talk it over with a friend. But remember that there is no right way to read the Bible. It's up to you to work out what suits you best.

6. Don't feel guilty if you miss a day. Why? Firstly, because everyone does. So you aren't odd. Life doesn't always work out quite according to plan for anybody. Secondly, the important point isn't to have your daily dose of Bible once every 24 hours but to take in its message.

7. Do ask yourself lots of questions. It's your job to find out what it's really saying rather than inventing your own meanings. Only when you have got to grips with its original meaning can you go on to discover what it's saying to you now. The box on this page gives you two sets of questions to ask your Bible passage. Copy them out onto a card or refer back to this page when you are reading.

8. Don't be put off when you have a boring week or more! It happens to everyone and you are probably gaining far more than you realise – though of course that will be easier to see looking back than at the time. The secret is to be disciplined and just keep on going.

9. Do read it responsibly. Having a time when you read the Bible each day isn't an end in itself, it is only a means to an end – understanding more about Jesus Christ, your Lord and friend, boss and brother. The biggest question isn't "How much have I read?" but "How much have I done about what I have read?" Once we have heard what God is saying about something we have a responsibility to act on it.

10. Don't be worried if you don't understand something. If you come across a difficult passage or anything that confuses you, get help. If you have a Bible commentary, concordance or Bible Dictionary, check it out there. If you can't solve it, ask your youth leader, minister or a friend – someone that you trust – to help you understand it.

What it meant then

(Use the **Sidelights** and **Book Openers** to help with these questions)

1. Who was the author and when and why was it written?
2. What kind of writing is it? Is it story or poetry and is the writer using symbols and pictures? If so, what do they mean?
3. Why did the author put it like this?
4. Was it written for a particular person or group of people?
5. What would the first readers have understood from these words?

What it means now

1. What is God saying to me through this passage?
2. What should I do?
3. What does it say about me or my situation?
4. What does it say about my relationships with God and with others?
5. Is there any special command, promise, warning or example that I should take notice of?

Life File Guide

This guide helps you find topics that interest or concern you. Refer to it when you are dealing with a particular problem or issue, or use it as a topical reading plan. Simply decide what topic you want to study and then read one Life File each day on that topic until you have read all the stories, thought about the issues and, most importantly, read the Bible passage.

Creation
Will We Ever Learn?	Genesis 2:4–17	4
Moment of Wonder	Proverbs 8:22–31	596
A Load of Rubbish!	Joel 2:21–27	867

Cults
Deadly Deception	Matthew 7:15–29	951
Good News, Bad News	Galatians 1:1–10	1257
Hazardous to Your Health	Ephesians 4:11–16	1274
Fatal Attraction	Colossians 2:1–15	1291
Knock Knock . . .	2 John 7–11	1379

Death
Breaking the Mould	Deuteronomy 34:1–12	199
Goodbye England's Rose	2 Samuel 1:17–27	285
Praise Beyond the Grave	Job 1:18–22	470
Welcomed Into Heaven	Isaiah 25:6–9	664
Old Before I Die	Isaiah 38:9–20	677
The Greatest Lesson	Mark 14:12–26	1026
Sharing Sadness	John 11:1–45	1115
Questions Unanswered	John 19:38–42	1132
Life After Death	1 Corinthians 15:12–28	1237
After AIDS	Philippians 1:21–27	1281
We Have Hope	1 Thessalonians 4:13–14	1300
Fear of Dying	Revelation 21:1–6	1403

Decision Making
Living With Deadlines	Deuteronomy 30:11–20	193
To Fly or Not	Job 28:20–28	487
What Do You Believe?	Jeremiah 17:5–8	736
Watch the Time	Matthew 25:1–13	986
Moving On	Luke 9:51–62	1056
But I Didn't Think . . .	Luke 16:19–31	1075
Different is OK!	Romans 14:5–12	1208
Who's Going to Know?	Ephesians 5:6–20	1276

Depression
Stirring Up Life	Job 7:1–8	474
The Wall Came Tumbling Down	Psalm 30	517
Positive	Isaiah 35	674

Discouragement
Counting	Genesis 15:1–6	17
Keep Your Chin Up	Numbers 21:4–9	149
Nothing Changes Round Here	Ecclesiastes 1:2–11	620
Is There Hope?	Habakkuk 1:1–3	904
Hope Breakers and Makers	1 John 5:1–15	1376

Doubt
Did God Really Say . . . ?	Genesis 17:15–19	20
Doubting David	Judges 6:33–40	233
Who Do You Believe?	Psalm 13	507
Having Confidence	Isaiah 7:10–16	648
Riding Out the Storm	John 14:1–14	1122
The Death of Doubt	John 20:19–31	1133

Drugs and Alcohol
Under the Influence	Esther 1:4–12	459
Not Alone . . .	Romans 7:14–25	1194

Life File Guide (14)

Life File Guide (22)

Have you ever known what you were looking for but didn't know where to find it in the Bible? A great event? A famous passage? A favourite story? Use this guide to help you find stories you remember but don't know where to find. The descriptions listed here are the common descriptions and are not always exactly the same as the descriptions in this Bible translation.

OLD
Testament

Genesis

Why Read This Book:

* Reflect on the beauty and wonder of God's creation (Genesis 1—2).
* Learn how God responds to rebellion against him (Genesis 3—11).
* Discover how God keeps his promises (Genesis 12—24).
* See how God works for good even during bad times (Genesis 37—50).

Behind the Scenes:

For weeks, you work tediously in art class creating a clay sculpture. You carefully shape the soft clay. One Friday, you leave the almost-finished sculpture to harden. On Monday you return. You find your clay twisted into a chaotic, unrecognisable blob. Rage and sadness swell up in you. You must begin the painstaking work all over again.

Genesis tells a similar story. It's the story of God's loving care in creating the world. But the story has a dark, twisted side. Genesis tells of human rebellion, murder and other human evil as people rebel against God.

Genesis falls naturally into two parts. Chapters 1—11 talk about the beginnings of the world. Here you'll read the famous stories of Adam and Eve, Cain and Abel, Noah and the tower of Babel. Each story shows how people often twist and destroy the gifts that God has given them.

Then chapters 12—50 talk specifically about the beginnings of the Hebrew people, later known as Israelites. You'll read about Abraham, the father of the nation, and his sons. And the book concludes with the story of Joseph, who God was able to use for great things even after his brothers had sold him into slavery.

Genesis is one of the most important books in the Bible. Not only does the rest of the Bible build on the foundation laid in this book, but the book shows how, from the beginning, God has used special people to play important roles in his world.

When?

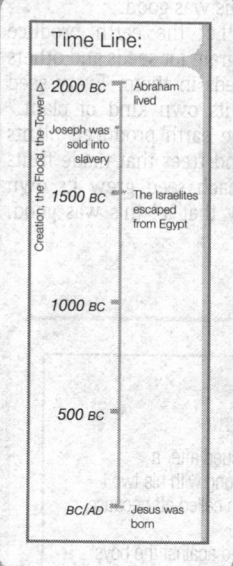

Time Line:

Creation, the Flood, the Tower

△ 2000 BC — Abraham lived

Joseph was sold into slavery

1500 BC — The Israelites escaped from Egypt

1000 BC

500 BC

BC/AD — Jesus was born

Where?

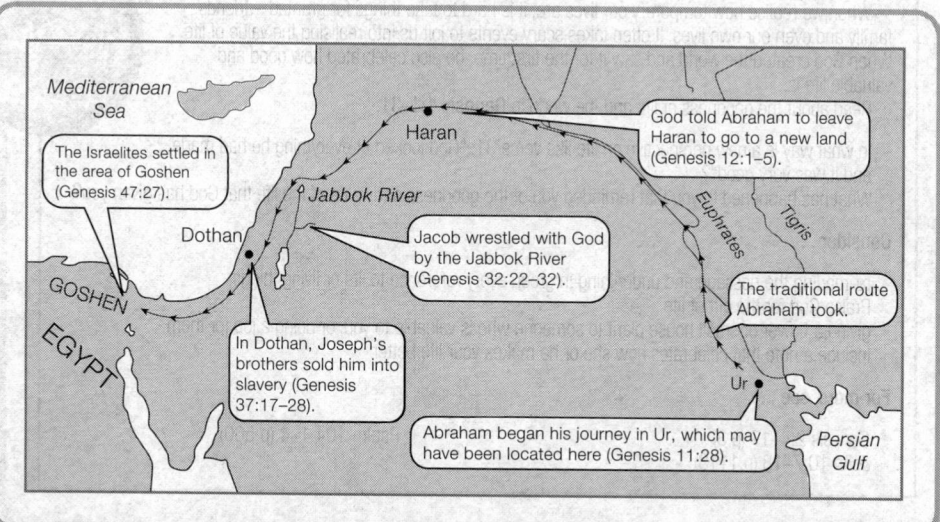

Mediterranean Sea

Haran

The Israelites settled in the area of Goshen (Genesis 47:27).

Jabbok River

Dothan

Jacob wrestled with God by the Jabbok River (Genesis 32:22–32).

GOSHEN

EGYPT

In Dothan, Joseph's brothers sold him into slavery (Genesis 37:17–28).

God told Abraham to leave Haran to go to a new land (Genesis 12:1–5).

Euphrates

Tigris

The traditional route Abraham took.

Ur

Abraham began his journey in Ur, which may have been located here (Genesis 11:28).

Persian Gulf

The Beginning of the World

1 In the beginning God created the sky and the earth. ²The earth was empty and had no form. Darkness covered the ocean, and God's Spirit *d* was moving over the water.

³Then God said, "Let there be light," and there was light. ⁴God saw that the light was good, so he divided the light from the darkness. ⁵God named the light "day" and the darkness "night". Evening passed, and morning came. This was the first day.

⁶Then God said, "Let there be something to divide the water in two." ⁷So God made the air and placed some of the water above the air and some below it. ⁸God named the air "sky". Evening passed, and morning came. This was the second day.

⁹Then God said, "Let the water under the sky be gathered together so the dry land will appear." And it happened. ¹⁰God named the dry land "earth" and the water that was gathered together "seas". God saw that this was good.

¹¹Then God said, "Let the earth produce plants—some to make grain for seeds and others to make fruits with seeds in them. Every seed will produce more of its own kind of plant." And it happened. ¹²The earth produced plants with grain for seeds, and trees that made fruits with seeds in them. Each seed grew its own kind of plant. God saw that all this was good.

LIFE

The Value of Life

After two terrifying days at sea, John Howes' eyes were filled with fear when he was rescued after a heroic swim ashore by his friend Peter Wells. Peter, fifteen, had been given up as dead along with his two companions after a 1,000 square kilometre search. The rescue team had eventually been called off because of stormy weather and because the three boys were probably already dead.

Two days of stormy seas and low night temperatures meant that the odds were stacked against the boys' survival. But Peter had managed to push back the levels of his endurance and had chosen to swim away from their boat and head for the shore. After his successful night swim, he scrabbled up a cliff-face and broke a window to get into an empty cottage, where he found a phone and rang 999. In a hoarse voice he told the emergency services what had happened and where his friend could be found and rescued too.

Prayers had gone up as the headmaster of their school asked God to return the boys. Peter's phone call showed that their prayers had already been answered.

True stories like this show us how fragile our hold on life is. They leave us reeling and stunned at what happens and can happen.

When we realise how temporary our lives are, it is hard to take things for granted – friends, family and even our own lives. It often takes scary events to jolt us into realising the value of life. When God created the world and saw it for the first time, he also celebrated how good and valuable life is.

Read about the goodness of life and the world in **Genesis 1:1–31**.

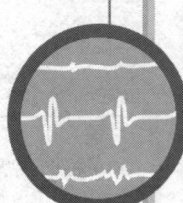

* In what way is a new perspective on life like verse 31: "God looked at everything he had made, and it was very good"?
* What has happened to you that reminded you of the goodness and value of the life that God has given you?

Consider . . .

* re-reading the passage and underlining in green every reference to life or living things.
  Praise God for the gift of life.
* giving a flower or small house plant to someone who is valuable to you, or doing a job for them.
  Include a note that celebrates how she or he makes your life better.

For more, see . . .

* Genesis 2:4–17 (p.3)   * Psalm 104:1–4 (p.560)
* John 10:7–18 (p.1113)

¹³Evening passed, and morning came. This was the third day.

¹⁴Then God said, "Let there be lights in the sky to separate day from night. These lights will be used for signs, seasons, days and years. ¹⁵They will be in the sky to give light to the earth." And it happened.

¹⁶So God made the two large lights. He made the brighter light to rule the day and the smaller light to rule the night. He also made the stars. ¹⁷God put all these in the sky to shine on the earth, ¹⁸to rule over the day and over the night, and to separate the light from the darkness. God saw that all these things were good. ¹⁹Evening passed, and morning came. This was the fourth day.

²⁰Then God said, "Let the water be filled with living things, and let birds fly in the air above the earth."

²¹So God created the large sea animals and every living thing that moves in the sea. The sea is filled with these living things, with each one producing more of its own kind. He also made every bird that flies, and each bird produced more of its own kind. God saw that this was good. ²²God blessed them and said, "Have many young ones so that you may grow in number. Fill the water of the seas, and let the birds grow in number on the earth." ²³Evening passed, and morning came. This was the fifth day.

²⁴Then God said, "Let the earth be filled with animals, each producing more of its own kind. Let there be tame animals and small crawling animals and wild animals, and let each produce more of its kind." And it happened.

²⁵So God made the wild animals, the tame animals, and all the small crawling animals to produce more of their own kind. God saw that this was good.

²⁶Then God said, "Let us make human beings in our image and likeness. And let them rule over the fish in the sea and the birds in the sky, over the tame animals, over all the earth, and over all the small crawling animals on the earth."

²⁷So God created human beings in his image. In the image of God he created them. He created them male and female. ²⁸God blessed them and said, "Have many children and grow in number. Fill the earth and be its master. Rule over the fish in the sea and over the birds in the sky and over every living thing that moves on the earth."

²⁹God said, "Look, I have given you all the plants that have grain for seeds and all the trees whose fruits have seeds in them. They will be food for you. ³⁰I have given all the green plants as food for every wild animal, every bird of the air,

and every small crawling animal." And it happened. ³¹God looked at everything he had made, and it was very good. Evening passed, and morning came. This was the sixth day.

The Seventh Day—Rest

2 So the sky, the earth, and all that filled them were finished. ²By the seventh day God finished the work he had been doing, so he rested from all his work. ³God blessed the seventh day and made it a holy day, because on that day he rested from all the work he had done in creating the world.

The First People

⁴This is the story of the creation of the sky and the earth. When the Lord God *d* first made the earth and the sky, ⁵there were still no plants on the earth. Nothing was growing in the fields because the Lord God had not yet made it rain on the land. And there was no person to care for the ground, ⁶but a mist would rise up from the earth and water all the ground.

⁷Then the Lord God took dust from the ground and formed a man from it. He breathed the breath of life into the man's nose, and the man became a living person. ⁸Then the Lord God planted a garden in the east, in a place called Eden, and put the man he had formed into it. ⁹The Lord God caused every beautiful tree and every tree that was good for food to grow out of the ground. In the middle of the garden, God put the tree that gives life and also the tree that gives the knowledge of good and evil.

¹⁰A river flowed through Eden and watered the garden. From there the river branched out to become four rivers. ¹¹The first river, named Pishon, flows around the whole land of Havilah, where there is gold. ¹²The gold of that land is excellent. Bdellium and onyx *n* are also found there. ¹³The second river, named Gihon, flows around the whole land of Cush. ¹⁴The third river, named Tigris, flows out of Assyria towards the east. The fourth river is the Euphrates.

¹⁵The Lord God put the man in the garden of Eden to care for it and work it. ¹⁶The Lord God commanded him, "You may eat the fruit from any tree in the garden, ¹⁷but you must not eat the fruit from the tree which gives the knowledge of good and evil. If you ever eat fruit from that tree, you will die!"

The First Woman

¹⁸Then the Lord God said, "It is not good for the man to be alone. I will make a helper who is right for him."

bdellium and onyx Bdellium is an expensive, sweet-smelling resin like myrrh, and onyx is a gem.

[19]From the ground God formed every wild animal and every bird in the sky, and he brought them to the man so the man could name them. Whatever the man called each living thing, that

became its name. [20]The man gave names to all the tame animals, to the birds in the sky, and to all the wild animals. But Adam [n] did not find a

helper that was right for him. [21]So the LORD God caused the man to sleep very deeply, and while he was asleep, God removed one of the man's ribs. Then God closed up the man's skin at the place where he took the rib. [22]The LORD God used the rib from the man to make a woman, and then he brought the woman to the man.

[23]And the man said,

"Now, this is someone whose bones came
　　from my bones,
　whose body came from my body.
I will call her 'woman',
　because she was taken out of man."

[24]So a man will leave his father and mother and be united with his wife, and the two will become one body.

[25]The man and his wife were naked, but they were not ashamed.

Adam　This is the name of the first man. It also means "humans", including men and women.

CREATION

Will We Ever Learn?

More than five hundred years ago, Christopher Columbus wrote about the forests on the Haitian island of La Gonave. He described "thousands of kinds of trees so tall that they seem to be scratching heaven". Today, its mountains are almost barren. When the rain comes, the rich topsoil is eroded away, causing floods.

One year, 33 people in the town of Anse-à-Galets on La Gonave died in a flood. Three years later, the people were ready for the flooding. No one died, but two churches, four homes, and a drinking-water system were destroyed.

Some say the floods are natural disasters. But they happen, in part, because the people don't care for the land. They cut down trees to make charcoal to cook with or to sell. It's the only way they know to survive.

But it hurts them. Without trees, the highlands aren't protected. When rainfall comes, the good soil washes away, and the lowlands flood. So cutting trees to survive actually makes survival more difficult.

The people of La Gonave are experiencing the problems that come when people don't take care of the environment. Read **Genesis 2:4–17**, particularly verse 15, to see how God expects us to care for his world.

* How well do you think the people of La Gonave are fulfilling the responsibility of caring for God's garden?
* In what ways have you taken responsibility for caring for the world or garden God has given you?

Consider . . .

* noting everything you throw away in a day or week. Decide which item you could avoid throwing away by recycling, reusing, or not purchasing.
* contributing to or getting involved with an organisation that plants trees to repair damage people have caused by cutting them down.

For more, see . . .

* Leviticus 25:1–7 (p.124)
* Colossians 1:15–20 (p.1290)
* Psalm 8:1–9 (p.503)

The Beginning of Sin

3 Now the snake was the most clever of all the wild animals the LORD God had made. One day the snake said to the woman, "Did God really say that you must not eat fruit from any tree in the garden?"

²The woman answered the snake, "We may eat fruit from the trees in the garden. ³But God told us, 'You must not eat fruit from the tree that is in the middle of the garden. You must not even touch it, or you will die.'"

⁴But the snake said to the woman, "You will not die. ⁵God knows that if you eat the fruit from that tree, you will learn about good and evil and you will be like God!"

⁶The woman saw that the tree was beautiful, that its fruit was good to eat, and that it would make her wise. So she took some of its fruit and ate it. She also gave some of the fruit to her husband, and he ate it.

⁷Then, it was as if their eyes were opened. They realised they were naked, so they sewed fig leaves together and made something to cover themselves.

⁸Then they heard the LORD God walking in the garden during the cool part of the day, and the man and his wife hid from the LORD God among the trees in the garden. ⁹But the LORD God called to the man and said, "Where are you?"

¹⁰The man answered, "I heard you walking in the garden, and I was afraid because I was naked, so I hid."

¹¹God asked, "Who told you that you were naked? Did you eat fruit from the tree from which I commanded you not to eat?"

¹²The man said, "You gave this woman to me and she gave me fruit from the tree, so I ate it."

¹³Then the LORD God said to the woman, "How could you have done such a thing?"

She answered, "The snake tricked me, so I ate the fruit."

MARRIAGE

So Lonely

Geoff and Samantha had been married for three years. They were mainly happy but Samantha's mother was an overbearing presence. Nothing could be decided outside the one-hour weekly phone call between Samantha and her mother. Geoff felt he had no power or authority to contribute to decisions in the relationship between him and Samantha. Things always needed her mum's approval, however obviously right they were. Samantha herself didn't seem to like this very much either, but she loved her mum who was very special to her – she was an only child. She didn't want to leave her mum out of things.

Geoff became frustrated and withdrawn. He had married Sam, not her mother, but somehow he never felt completely married to her. Then one day they took, jointly, a decision for themselves. Geoff's mother-in-law couldn't influence it because she was away travelling in India for a month. She couldn't be reached. Not that they tried that hard.

And it was a great decision – baby Alex is proof of that. And maybe Grandma sounds better than Mother-in-law does.

Marriage is about leaving as well as cleaving (joining).

Read **Genesis 2:18–24**. The story tells us that a human friend is the only cure for loneliness.

* What do you think this part of the creation story is trying to say about the relationship between God, man and woman?
* Does this passage teach us that the only answer to loneliness is a marriage partner?

Consider . . .

* what you are looking for in a life partner.
* listing, in order, all the things that would be important to you if you got married.

For more, see . . .

* Mark 10:7–8 (p.1016)
* Ephesians 5:21–33 (p.1275)

¹⁴The LORD God said to the snake,
"Because you did this,
    a curse will be put on you.
You will be cursed as no other animal,
      tame or wild, will ever be.
You will crawl on your stomach,
    and you will eat dust all the days of your life.
¹⁵I will make you and the woman
    enemies of each other.
Your descendants *d* and her descendants
    will be enemies.
One of her descendants will crush your head,
    and you will bite his heel."

¹⁶Then God said to the woman,
"I will cause you to have much trouble
    when you are pregnant,

and when you give birth to children,
    you will have great pain.
You will greatly desire your husband,
    but he will rule over you."

¹⁷Then God said to the man, "You listened to what your wife said, and you ate fruit from the tree from which I commanded you not to eat.
"So I will put a curse on the ground,
    and you will have to work very hard for
      your food.
In pain you will eat its food
    all the days of your life.
¹⁸The ground will produce thorns and weeds
    for you,
    and you will eat the plants of the field.
¹⁹You will sweat and work hard

SIN

An Expensive CD

Colin pulled the compact disc out from under his jacket as he sauntered out of the shopping centre. His cool exterior disguised his excitement. A track from the album had been at the top of the charts for five weeks now, and he couldn't get it out of his head. He'd never wanted a recording this much, and now he had it. He couldn't wait to listen to it.

Suddenly, a hand came down hard on the back of his neck and stopped him in his tracks.

"Back inside, you," the security guard growled, as Colin turned to face him. "I'll take that CD, thank you."

Colin felt humiliated as the guard escorted him back to the manager's office in the music store. Then he sat awkwardly while the manager finished talking to the police on the phone.

"A police officer will be here in a few minutes," he said as he put the receiver down. "I won't press charges if you're a first-timer, but I need your home phone number. Your mum or dad will have to come and get you."

Colin dictated the number as the manager dialled. "And, young man," the manager said as the phone rang, "I never want to see you in my shop again."

Colin dreaded seeing his mum. She'd be so disappointed. Her eyes would be glassy-wet and red. She wouldn't look at him. That was the hardest part. He laid his head back and waited.

Colin experienced shame as Adam and Eve experienced shame when God caught them disobeying him. Read **Genesis 3:8–24** to learn what happened.

* How does the shop manager's punishment for shoplifting compare with God's punishment of Adam and Eve? What resulted from Adam and Eve's sin? Was Colin's punishment – and Adam and Eve's – appropriate?
* In what ways do you, like Adam and Eve, try to hide from God when you disobey him?

Consider . . .

* interrupting the "blame chain" ("somebody else made me do it") by accepting responsibility for things you do.
* talking to someone you trust about a sin you've been hiding inside, then confessing the sin to God. Discover how the confession affects you.

For more, see . . .

* Psalm 119:9–16 (p.571)
* 1 John 1:5–10 (p.1371)

* John 8:1–11 (p.1109)

for your food.
Later you will return to the ground,
    because you were taken from it.
You are dust,
    and when you die, you will return to the
        dust."

[20]The man named his wife Eve,[n] because she is the mother of everyone who has ever lived.

[21]The LORD God made clothes from animal skins for the man and his wife and dressed them. [22]Then the LORD God said, "The man has become like one of us; he knows good and evil. We must keep him from eating some of the fruit from the tree of life, or he will live for ever." [23]So the LORD God forced the man out of the garden of Eden to work the ground from which he was taken. [24]After God forced the man out of the garden, he placed angels and a sword of fire that flashed around in every direction on its eastern border. This kept people from getting to the tree of life.

The First Family

4 Adam had sexual relations with his wife Eve, and she became pregnant and gave birth to Cain.[n] Eve said, "With the LORD's[d] help, I have given birth to a man." [2]After that, Eve gave birth to Cain's brother, Abel. Abel took care of flocks, and Cain became a farmer.

[3]Later, Cain brought some food from the ground as a gift to God. [4]Abel brought the best parts from some of the firstborn[d] of his flock. The LORD accepted Abel and his gift, [5]but he did not accept Cain and his gift. So Cain became very angry and felt rejected.

[6]The LORD asked Cain, "Why are you angry? Why do you look so unhappy? [7]If you do things well, I will accept you, but if you do not do them well, sin is ready to attack you. Sin wants you, but you must rule over it."

[8]Cain said to his brother Abel, "Let's go out into the field." While they were out in the field, Cain attacked his brother Abel and killed him.

[9]Later, the LORD said to Cain, "Where is your brother Abel?"

Cain answered, "I don't know. Is it my job to take care of my brother?"

[10]Then the LORD said, "What have you done? Your brother's blood is crying out to me from the ground. [11]And now you will be cursed in your work with the ground, the same ground where your brother's blood fell and where your hands killed him. [12]You will work the ground, but it will not grow good crops for you any more, and you will wander around on the earth."

[13]Then Cain said to the LORD, "This punishment is more than I can stand! [14]Today you have forced me to stop working the ground, and now I must hide from you. I must wander around on the earth, and anyone who meets me can kill me."

[15]The LORD said to Cain, "No! If anyone kills you, I will punish that person seven times more." Then the LORD put a mark on Cain warning anyone who met him not to kill him.

Cain's Family

[16]So Cain went away from the LORD and lived in the land of Nod,[n] east of Eden. [17]He had sexual relations with his wife, and she became pregnant and gave birth to Enoch. At that time Cain was building a city, which he named after his son Enoch. [18]Enoch had a son named Irad, Irad had a son named Mehujael, Mehujael had a son named Methushael and Methushael had a son named Lamech.

[19]Lamech married two women, Adah and

> ### Sidelight
> If one wife is a good idea, then two wives must be doubly wonderful, that is, twice as good. That's what Lamech thought (Genesis 4:19). The idea really caught on, and by the time it reached King Solomon, he ended up with seven hundred wives (1 Kings 11:3, p.325).

Zillah. [20]Adah gave birth to Jabal, who became the first person to live in tents and raise cattle. [21]Jabal's brother was Jubal, the first person to play the harp and flute. [22]Zillah gave birth to Tubal-Cain, who made tools out of bronze and iron. The sister of Tubal-Cain was Naamah.

[23]Lamech said to his wives:
"Adah and Zillah, hear my voice!
    You wives of Lamech, listen to what I say.
I killed a man for wounding me,
    a young man for hitting me.
[24]If Cain's killer is punished seven times,
    then Lamech's killer will be punished 77
        times."

Adam and Eve Have a New Son

[25]Adam had sexual relations with his wife Eve again, and she gave birth to a son. She named him Seth[n] and said, "God has given me another child. He will take the place of Abel, who was killed by Cain." [26]Seth also had a son, and they named him Enosh. At that time people began to pray to the LORD.

Eve   This name sounds like the Hebrew word for "alive".
Cain   This name sounds like the Hebrew word for "I have given birth".
Nod   This name sounds like the Hebrew word for "wander".
Seth   This name sounds like the Hebrew word for "to give".

Adam's Family History

5 This is the family history of Adam. When God created human beings, he made them in his own likeness. [2]He created them male and female, and on that day he blessed them and named them human beings.

[3]When Adam was 130 years old, he became the father of another son in his likeness and image, and Adam named him Seth. [4]After Seth was born, Adam lived 800 years and had other sons and daughters. [5]So Adam lived a total of 930 years, and then he died.

[6]When Seth was 105 years old, he had a son named Enosh. [7]After Enosh was born, Seth lived 807 years and had other sons and daughters. [8]So Seth lived a total of 912 years, and then he died.

[9]When Enosh was 90 years old, he had a son named Kenan. [10]After Kenan was born, Enosh lived 815 years and had other sons and daughters. [11]So Enosh lived a total of 905 years, and then he died.

[12]When Kenan was 70 years old, he had a son named Mahalalel. [13]After Mahalalel was born, Kenan lived 840 years and had other sons and daughters. [14]So Kenan lived a total of 910 years, and then he died.

[15]When Mahalalel was 65 years old, he had a son named Jared. [16]After Jared was born, Mahalalel lived 830 years and had other sons and daughters. [17]So Mahalalel lived a total of 895 years, and then he died.

[18]When Jared was 162 years old, he had a son named Enoch. [19]After Enoch was born, Jared lived 800 years and had other sons and daughters. [20]So Jared lived a total of 962 years, and then he died.

[21]When Enoch was 65 years old, he had a son named Methuselah. [22]After Methuselah was born, Enoch walked with God 300 years more and had other sons and daughters. [23]So Enoch lived a total of 365 years. [24]Enoch walked with God; one day Enoch could not be found, because God took him.

[25]When Methuselah was 187 years old, he had a son named Lamech. [26]After Lamech was born, Methuselah lived 782 years and had other sons and daughters. [27]So Methuselah lived a total of 969 years, and then he died.

[28]When Lamech was 182, he had a son. [29]Lamech named his son Noah [n] and said, "He will comfort us in our work, which comes from the ground the LORD has cursed." [30]After Noah was born, Lamech lived 595 years and had other sons and daughters. [31]So Lamech lived a total of 777 years, and then he died.

[32]After Noah was 500 years old, he became the father of Shem, Ham and Japheth.

> ### Sidelight
> If you think older adults tell too many stories about "When I was your age . . ." imagine what Methuselah's children must have thought. Genesis 5:27 says that he lived to be 969 years old. That means that, if he were born when Christopher Columbus discovered the Americas in 1492, he would only be middle-aged today!

The Human Race Becomes Evil

6 The number of people on earth began to grow, and daughters were born to them. [2]When the sons of God saw that these girls were beautiful, they married any of them they chose. [3]The LORD said, "My Spirit [d] will not remain in human beings for ever, because they are flesh. They will live only 120 years."

[4]The Nephilim [d] were on the earth in those days and also later. That was when the sons of God had sexual relations with the daughters of human beings. These women gave birth to children, who became famous and were the mighty warriors of long ago.

[5]The LORD saw that the human beings on the earth were very wicked and that everything they thought about was evil. [6]He was sorry he had made human beings on the earth, and his heart was filled with pain. [7]So the LORD said, "I will destroy all human beings that I made on the earth. And I will destroy every animal and everything that crawls on the earth and the birds of the air, because I am sorry I have made them." [8]But Noah pleased the LORD.

Noah and the Great Flood

[9]This is the family history of Noah. Noah was a good man, the most innocent man of his time, and he walked with God. [10]He had three sons: Shem, Ham and Japheth.

[11]People on earth did what God said was evil, and violence was everywhere. [12]When God saw that everyone on the earth did only evil, [13]he said to Noah, "Because people have made the earth full of violence, I will destroy all of them from the earth. [14]Build a boat of cypress wood for yourself. Make rooms in it and cover it inside and outside with tar. [15]This is how big I want you to build the boat: 150 metres long, 25 metres wide and 15 metres high. [16]Make an opening around the top of the boat that is 50 centimetres high from the

---

Noah　This name sounds like the Hebrew word for "rest".

edge of the roof down. Put a door in the side of the boat. Make an upper, middle and lower deck in it. [17]I will bring a flood of water on the earth to destroy all living things that live under the sky,

including everything that has the breath of life. Everything on the earth will die. [18]But I will make an agreement with you—you, your sons, your wife and your sons' wives will all go into the boat. [19]Also, you must bring into the boat two of every living thing, male and female. Keep them alive with you. [20]Two of every kind of bird,

animal and crawling thing will come to you to be kept alive. [21]Also, gather some of every kind of food and store it on the boat as food for you and the animals."

[22]Noah did everything that God commanded him.

The Flood Begins

7 Then the LORD said to Noah, "I have seen that you are the best person among the people of this time, so you and your family can go into the boat. [2]Take with you seven pairs, each male with its female, of every kind of clean [d] animal; and take one pair, each male with its female, of every kind of unclean animal. [3]Take seven pairs of all the birds of the sky, each male with its female. This will allow all these animals to continue living on the earth after the flood. [4]Seven days from now I will send rain on the earth. It will rain 40 days and 40 nights, and I will wipe from the earth every living thing that I have made."

Quiet Cancer

The symptoms don't seem too serious at first. You start to feel tired and short of breath. Your blood doesn't clot as well as it should, and you bruise easily.

But these minor problems can be symptoms of leukaemia, a deadly cancer.

Although the outward signs don't seem all that bad, inside the body is under attack. Cancer has invaded the bone marrow and bloodstream. The body no longer produces enough healthy white blood cells, taking away its ability to fight off infections. Suddenly, the body feels sick and needs immediate medical attention. Untreated, a person can die within six weeks. Treatment can involve injections of drugs that kill the cancer, but also kill normal cells.

The hope is that healthy cells will grow again after treatment, and that cancerous ones won't.

Like leukaemia, evil can spread without people really noticing it. Yet it's deadly and difficult to get rid of. See how God feels about evil in the world by reading **Genesis 6:5—7:24**.

* What similarities do you see between leukaemia and the evil described in the passage? How is God's response to that evil like the treatment for cancer?
* What kinds of evil described in the passage still exist today? How is God working in the world today to stop the spread of evil?

Consider . . .

* identifying a potential evil in your life and then talking to a parent or other trusted adult about how you can stop it before it grows into a bigger problem.
* cutting out newspaper articles that show evil in the world. Each day this week, pray for people who are trapped by that evil.

For more, see . . .

* Psalm 43:1–5 (p.525)
* 1 John 5:18–20 (p.1377)
* Romans 1:28–32 (p.1185)

⁵Noah did everything the LORD commanded him. ⁶Noah was 600 years old when the flood came. ⁷He and his wife and his sons and their wives went into the boat to escape the waters of the flood. ⁸The clean animals, the unclean animals, the birds and everything that crawls on the ground ⁹came to Noah. They went into the boat in groups of two, male and female, just as God had commanded Noah. ¹⁰Seven days later the flood started.

¹¹When Noah was 600 years old, the flood started. On the seventeenth day of the second month of that year the underground springs split open, and the clouds in the sky poured out rain. ¹²The rain fell on the earth for 40 days and 40 nights. ¹³On that same day Noah and his wife, his sons Shem, Ham and Japheth, and their wives went into the boat. ¹⁴They had every kind of wild and tame animal, every kind of animal that crawls on the earth and every kind of bird. ¹⁵Every creature that had the breath of life came to Noah in the boat in groups of two. ¹⁶One male and one female of every living thing came, just as God had commanded Noah. Then the LORD closed the door behind them.

¹⁷Water flooded the earth for 40 days, and as it rose it lifted the boat off the ground. ¹⁸The water continued to rise, and the boat floated on it above the earth. ¹⁹The water rose so much that even the highest mountains under the sky were covered by it. ²⁰It continued to rise until it was more than 7 metres above the mountains.

²¹All living things that moved on the earth died. This included all the birds, tame animals, wild animals and creatures that swarm on the earth, as well as all human beings. ²²So everything on dry land that had the breath of life in it died. ²³God destroyed from the earth every living thing that was on the land—every man, animal, crawling thing and bird of the sky. All that was left was Noah and what was there with him in the boat. ²⁴And the waters continued to cover the earth for 150 days.

The Flood Ends

8 But God remembered Noah and all the wild and tame animals with him in the boat. He made a wind blow over the earth, and the water went down. ²The underground springs stopped flowing, and the clouds in the sky stopped pouring down rain. ³⁻⁴The water that covered the earth began to go down. After 150 days it had gone down so much that the boat touched land again. It came to rest on one of the mountains of Ararat*ⁿ* on the seventeenth day of the seventh month. ⁵The water continued to go down so that by the first day of the tenth month the tops of the mountains could be seen.

⁶Forty days later Noah opened the window he had made in the boat, and ⁷he sent out a raven. It flew here and there until the water had dried up from the earth. ⁸Then Noah sent out a dove to find out if the water had dried up from the ground. ⁹The dove could not find a place to land because water still covered the earth, so it came back to the boat. Noah reached out his hand and took the bird and brought it back into the boat. ¹⁰After seven days Noah again sent out the dove from the boat, ¹¹and that evening it came back to him with a fresh olive leaf in its mouth. Then Noah knew that the ground was almost dry. ¹²Seven days later he sent the dove out again, but this time it did not come back.

¹³When Noah was 601 years old, in the first day of the first month of that year, the water was dried up from the land. Noah removed the covering of the boat and saw that the land was dry. ¹⁴By the twenty-seventh day of the second month the land was completely dry.

¹⁵Then God said to Noah, ¹⁶"You and your wife, your sons and their wives should go out of the boat. ¹⁷Bring every animal out of the boat with you—the birds, animals and everything that crawls on the earth. Let them have many young ones so that they might grow in number."

¹⁸So Noah went out with his sons, his wife and his sons' wives. ¹⁹Every animal, everything that crawls on the earth and every bird went out of the boat by families.

²⁰Then Noah built an altar to the LORD. He took some of all the clean *d* birds and animals, and he burned them on the altar as offerings to God. ²¹The LORD was pleased with these sacrifices and said to himself, "I will never again curse the ground because of human beings. Their thoughts are evil even when they are young, but I will never again destroy every living thing on the earth as I did this time.

²²"As long as the earth continues,
planting and harvest,
cold and hot,
summer and winter,
day and night
will not stop."

The New Beginning

9 Then God blessed Noah and his sons and said to them, "Have many children; grow in number and fill the earth. ²Every animal on earth, every bird in the sky, every animal that

Ararat   The ancient land of Urartu, an area in eastern Turkey.

crawls on the ground and every fish in the sea will respect and fear you. I have given them to you.

³"Everything that moves, everything that is alive, is yours for food. Earlier I gave you the green plants, but now I give you everything for food. ⁴But you must not eat meat that still has blood in it, because blood gives life. ⁵I will demand blood for life. I will demand the life of any animal that kills a person, and I will demand the life of anyone who takes another person's life.

⁶"Whoever kills a human being
    will be killed by a human being,
  because God made humans
    in his own image.

⁷"As for you, Noah, I want you and your family to have many children, to grow in number on the earth, and to become many."

⁸Then God said to Noah and his sons. ⁹"Now I am making my agreement with you and your people who will live after you, ¹⁰and with every living thing that is with you—the birds, the tame and the wild animals, and with everything that came out of the boat with you—with every living thing on earth. ¹¹I make this agreement with you: I will never again destroy all living things by a flood. A flood will never again destroy the earth."

¹²And God said, "This is the sign of the agreement between me and you and every living creature that is with you. ¹³I am putting my rainbow in the clouds as the sign of the agreement between me and the earth. ¹⁴When I bring clouds over the earth and a rainbow appears in them, ¹⁵I will remember my agreement between me and you and every living thing. Floods will never again destroy all life on the earth. ¹⁶When the rainbow appears in the clouds, I will see it and I will remember the agreement that continues for ever between me and every living thing on the earth."

¹⁷So God said to Noah, "The rainbow is a sign of the agreement that I made with all living things on earth."

Noah and His Sons

¹⁸The sons of Noah who came out of the boat

FUTURE

A Hope-Filled Dream

The future looked bleak for Miguel Rodriquez. Friends in his Brooklyn, New York neighbourhood used drugs, spent time in jail and dropped out of school. For them life seemed hopeless and the future bleak.

But Miguel had a friend who believed in him – Phill Carlos Archbold, his youth leader. Phill Carlos encouraged and supported Miguel, helped him with his homework and invited him over for meals. Sometimes he would even pay Miguel's bus fare so that he could get to school.

"He was a father-figure to me," Miguel says. "He was – and still is – always there for me." Phill Carlos' support and encouragement gave Miguel hope for the future. Though his friends dropped out of school, he completed his exams and went on to get a degree.

Because of Phill Carlos, Miguel looked forward to a bright future. God's promise to Noah also pointed to a bright future. Read about it in **Genesis 9:8–17**.

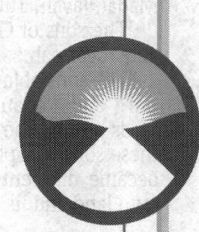

* How do you think God's promise to Noah gave him hope? How is that hope similar to the hope that Phill Carlos gave to Miguel?
* What signs – like the rainbow for Noah – do you see that give you hope and courage for the future?

Consider . . .

* drawing a rainbow on paper and putting it up where you can see it. Whenever something happens during the week that encourages you about your future, write it on the paper.
* watching the evening news to look for signs of hope. Thank God for those people who are working for a more positive future.

For more, see . . .

* Jeremiah 29:11 (p.749)
* 2 Corinthians 4:16–18 (p.1244)
* Matthew 6:25–34 (p.948)

with him were Shem, Ham and Japheth. (Ham was the father of Canaan.) ¹⁹These three men were Noah's sons, and all the people on earth came from these three sons.

²⁰Noah became a farmer and planted a vineyard. ²¹When he drank wine made from his grapes, he became drunk and lay naked in his tent. ²²Ham, the father of Canaan, looked at his naked father and told his brothers outside. ²³Then Shem and Japheth got a coat and, carrying it on both their shoulders, they walked backwards into the tent and covered their father. They turned their faces away so that they did not see their father's nakedness.

²⁴Noah was sleeping because of the wine. When he woke up and learned what his youngest son, Ham, had done to him, ²⁵he said,

"May there be a curse on Canaan!
    May he be the lowest slave to his
        brothers."

²⁶Noah also said,

"May the LORD, the God of Shem, be praised!
    May Canaan be Shem's slave.
²⁷May God give more land to Japheth.
    May Japheth live in Shem's tents,
    and may Canaan be their slave."

²⁸After the flood Noah lived 350 years. ²⁹He lived a total of 950 years, and then he died.

Nations Grow and Spread

10 This is the family history of Shem, Ham and Japheth, the sons of Noah. After the flood these three men had sons.

Japheth's Sons

²The sons of Japheth were Gomer, Magog, Madai, Javan, Tubal, Meshech and Tiras. ³The sons of Gomer were Ashkenaz, Riphath and Togarmah. ⁴The sons of Javan were Elishah, Tarshish, Kittim *n* and Rodanim. ⁵Those who lived in the lands around the Mediterranean Sea came from these sons of Japheth. All the families grew and became different nations, each nation with its own land and its own language.

Ham's Sons

⁶The sons of Ham were Cush, Mizraim, *n* Put and Canaan. ⁷The sons of Cush were Seba, Havilah, Sabtah, Raamah and Sabteca.

The sons of Raamah were Sheba and Dedan. ⁸Cush also had a descendant *d* named Nimrod, who became a very powerful man on earth.

⁹He was a great hunter before the LORD, which is why people say someone is "like Nimrod, a great hunter before the LORD." ¹⁰At first Nimrod's kingdom covered Babylon, Erech, Akkad and Calneh in the land of Babylonia. ¹¹From there he went to Assyria, where he built the cities of Nineveh, Rehoboth Ir and Calah. ¹²He also built Resen, the great city between Nineveh and Calah.

¹³Mizraim was the father of the Ludites, Anamites, Lehabites, Naphtuhites, ¹⁴Pathrusites, Casluhites and the people of Crete. (The Philistines came from the Casluhites.)

¹⁵Canaan was the father of Sidon, his first son, and of Heth. ¹⁶He was also the father of the Jebusites, Amorites, Girgashites, ¹⁷Hivites, Arkites, Sinites, ¹⁸Arvadites, Zemarites and Hamathites. The families of the Canaanites scattered. ¹⁹Their land reached from Sidon to Gerar as far as Gaza and then to Sodom, Gomorrah, Admah and Zeboiim, as far as Lasha.

²⁰All these people were the sons of Ham and all these families had their own languages, their own lands, and their own nations.

Shem's Sons

²¹Shem, Japheth's older brother, also had sons. One of his descendants *d* was the father of all the sons of Eber.

²²The sons of Shem were Elam, Asshur, Arphaxad, Lud and Aram. ²³The sons of Aram were Uz, Hul, Gether and Meshech. ²⁴Arphaxad was the father of Shelah, who was the father of Eber. ²⁵Eber was the father of two sons—one named Peleg, *n* because the earth was divided during his life, and the other was named Joktan.

²⁶Joktan was the father of Almodad, Sheleph, Hazarmaveth, Jerah, ²⁷Hadoram, Uzal, Diklah, ²⁸Obal, Abimael, Sheba, ²⁹Ophir, Havilah and Jobab. All these people were the sons of Joktan. ³⁰They lived in the area between Mesha and Sephar in the hill country in the east.

³¹These are the people from the family of Shem, arranged by families, languages, countries and nations.

³²This is the list of the families from the sons of Noah, arranged according to their nations. From these families came all the nations who spread across the earth after the flood.

The Languages Confused

11 At this time the whole world spoke one language, and everyone used the same words. ²As people moved from the east,

---

Kittim   His descendants were the people of Cyprus.
Mizraim   This is another name for Egypt.
Peleg   This name sounds like the Hebrew word for "divided".

they found a plain in the land of Babylonia and settled there.

³They said to each other, "Let's make bricks and bake them to make them hard." So they used bricks instead of stones, and tar instead of mortar. ⁴Then they said to each other, "Let's build a city and a tower for ourselves, whose top will reach high into the sky. We will become famous. Then we will not be scattered over all the earth."

⁵The Lord came down to see the city and the tower that the people had built. ⁶The Lord said, "Now, these people are united, all speaking the same language. This is only the beginning of what they will do. They will be able to do anything they want. ⁷Come, let us go down and confuse their language so they will not be able to understand each other."

⁸So the Lord scattered them from there over all the earth, and they stopped building the city. ⁹The place is called Babel ⁿ since that is where

Babel   This name sounds like the Hebrew word for "confused".

the Lord confused the language of the whole world. So the Lord caused them to spread out from there over the whole world.

Sidelight

The tower described in Genesis 11:1–9 was probably a ziggurat – a multi-storied temple built to worship Babylonian gods. The "temple towers", which looked like staircase pyramids, were built in most major Babylonian cities.

The Story of Shem's Family

¹⁰This is the family history of Shem. Two years after the flood, when Shem was 100 years old, his son Arphaxad was born. ¹¹After that, Shem lived 500 years and had other sons and daughters.

BOASTING

Pride Hurts

Everyone was sure Susan would get the lead role of Maria in the spring musical, *West Side Story*, especially Susan. She kept reminding everyone of her experience – having been in every production since she had started at the college.

"I can make Maria come to life on the stage," she proclaimed. "Besides, this is my last show. Lots of people will be disappointed if I'm not cast as Maria."

Audition day came, and Susan was ready.

She confidently sang, danced and acted. It felt great. "I was really good," she told her best friend Debbie on the phone that evening. "It's a great part. It'll really stretch me."

Next morning, Susan rushed to the drama room to see the cast list and confirm what she already knew. But she stared at the list in disbelief. Her name wasn't next to Maria. It was way down the page – a little part with just a few lines in Act Two. Humiliated, Susan left in tears.

Susan's problem was pride. And it was at the heart of the events in **Genesis 11:1–9**, where the people built a tower in disobedience to God.

* How did Susan's pride hurt her like pride hurt the tower builders?
* What "towers" of pride are you building in your own life?

Consider . . .

* giving a compliment to another person when you're tempted to boast about yourself.
* listing everything about yourself that makes you proud. Then put ticks beside items you think are appropriate forms of pride, and crosses beside those that aren't. Decide how you'll begin overcoming one of the crosses this week.

For more, see . . .

* Proverbs 16:18–19 (p.603)
* Philippians 2:1–11 (p.1282)
* Hosea 5:5–6 (p.854)

[12]When Arphaxad was 35 years old, his son Shelah was born. [13]After that, Arphaxad lived 403 years and had other sons and daughters.

[14]When Shelah was 30 years old, his son Eber was born. [15]After that, Shelah lived 403 years and had other sons and daughters.

[16]When Eber was 34 years old, his son Peleg was born. [17]After that, Eber lived 430 years and had other sons and daughters.

[18]When Peleg was 30 years old, his son Reu was born. [19]After that, Peleg lived 209 years and had other sons and daughters.

[20]When Reu was 32 years old, his son Serug was born. [21]After that, Reu lived 207 years and had other sons and daughters.

[22]When Serug was 30 years old, his son Nahor was born. [23]After that, Serug lived 200 years and had other sons and daughters.

[24]When Nahor was 29 years old, his son Terah was born. [25]After that, Nahor lived 119 years and had other sons and daughters.

[26]After Terah was 70 years old, his sons Abram, Nahor and Haran were born.

The Story of Terah's Family

[27]This is the family history of Terah. Terah was the father of Abram, Nahor and Haran. Haran was the father of Lot. [28]While his father, Terah, was still alive, Haran died in Ur in Babylonia, where he was born. [29]Abram and Nahor both married. Abram's wife was named Sarai, and Nahor's wife was named Milcah. She was the daughter of Haran, who was the father of both Milcah and Iscah. [30]Sarai was not able to have children.

[31]Terah took his son Abram, his grandson Lot (Haran's son), and his daughter-in-law Sarai (Abram's wife) and moved out of Ur of Babylonia. They had planned to go to the land of Canaan, but when they reached the city of Haran, they settled there.

[32]Terah lived to be 205 years old, and then he died in Haran.

God Calls Abram

12 The LORD said to Abram,[n] "Leave your country, your relatives and your father's family, and go to the land I will show you.

[2]I will make you a great nation,
 and I will bless you.
 I will make you famous,
 and you will be a blessing to others.
[3]I will bless those who bless you,
 and I will place a curse on those who harm you.

And all the people on earth
 will be blessed through you."

[4]So Abram left Haran as the LORD had told him, and Lot went with him. At this time Abram was 75 years old. [5]He took his wife Sarai, his nephew Lot, and everything they owned, as well as all the servants they had gained in Haran. They set out from Haran, planning to go to the land of Canaan, and in time they arrived there.

> **Sidelight**
> When Abram left Egypt, he lived in tents. It would have been a real change in lifestyle. They were probably made from animal skins and quite heavy, like those of modern Bedouins.

[6]Abram travelled through that land as far as the great tree of Moreh at Shechem. The Canaanites were living in the land at that time. [7]The LORD appeared to Abram and said, "I will give this land to your descendants."[d] So Abram built an altar there to the LORD, who had appeared to him. [8]Then he travelled from Shechem to the mountain east of Bethel and set up his tent there. Bethel was to the west, and Ai was to the east. There Abram built another altar to the LORD and worshipped him. [9]After this, he travelled on towards southern Canaan.

Abram Goes to Egypt

[10]At this time there was not much food in the land, so Abram went down to Egypt to live because there was so little food. [11]Just before they arrived in Egypt, he said to his wife Sarai,[n] "I know you are a very beautiful woman. [12]When the Egyptians see you, they will say, 'This woman is his wife.' Then they will kill me but let you live. [13]Tell them you are my sister so that things will go well with me and I may be allowed to live because of you."

[14]When Abram came to Egypt, the Egyptians saw that Sarai was very beautiful. [15]The Egyptian officers saw her and told the king of Egypt how beautiful she was. They took her to the king's palace, and [16]the king was kind to Abram because he thought Abram was her brother. He gave Abram sheep, cattle, male and female donkeys, male and female servants and camels.

[17]But the LORD sent terrible diseases on the king and all the people in his house because of Abram's wife Sarai. [18]So the king sent for Abram

---

Abram This name means "honoured father".
Sarai An Aramaic name meaning "princess".

and said, "What have you done to me? Why didn't you tell me Sarai was your wife? ¹⁹Why did you say, 'She is my sister' so that I made her my wife? Now, here is your wife. Take her and leave!" ²⁰Then the king commanded his men to make Abram leave Egypt; so Abram and his wife left with everything they owned.

Abram and Lot Separate

13 So Abram, his wife and Lot left Egypt, taking everything they owned, and travelled to southern Canaan. ²Abram was very rich in cattle, silver and gold.

³He left southern Canaan and went back to Bethel where he had camped before, between Bethel and Ai, ⁴and where he had built an altar. So he worshipped the LORD there.

⁵During this time Lot was travelling with Abram, and Lot also had flocks, herds and tents. ⁶Abram and Lot had so many animals that the land could not support both of them together, ⁷so Abram's herdsmen and Lot's herdsmen began to argue. The Canaanites and the Perizzites were living in the land at this time.

⁸Abram said to Lot, "There should be no arguing between you and me, or between your herdsmen and mine, because we are brothers. ⁹We should separate. The whole land is there in front of you. If you go to the left, I will go to the right. If you go to the right, I will go to the left."

GOD'S WILL

Unknown Outcomes

Although it was the 1950s, the Auca Indians of Ecuador, South America, were still a violent, Stone Age tribe.

But Jim Elliot felt God calling him to Ecuador to share the Gospel with the Aucas. Only one missionary had ever gone: a Jesuit priest who, in 1667, was murdered at his jungle outpost.

Jim didn't let history stop him from what he knew God wanted. "My going to Ecuador is God's counsel," Jim wrote in his diary.

So Jim and four other missionaries left their families and boarded the ship for Ecuador. They built a camp in Auca territory and began trying to befriend the Aucas. They would fly over their village in a small aeroplane, drop gifts and call out to the Indians in the Auca language.

On 6 January 1956, they finally befriended one Auca, a young man they called "George". Now, they hoped, they could make more contact with the tribe.

That weekend, the Aucas attacked, killing all the missionaries, including Jim Elliot.

But that wasn't the end of the story. Jim's wife, Elisabeth, refused to let the murder of her husband keep her from following God's call to Ecuador. She and other missionaries returned to Auca territory.

Less than three years later, Elisabeth wrote: "Today I sit in a tiny leaf-thatched hut . . . In another leaf house, just three metres away, sit two of the seven men who killed my husband."

Jim Elliot followed God's will, with seemingly tragic consequences. But God was at work even when his plan was difficult to see. And the missionary effort, started by Jim Elliot and continued by Elisabeth, prospered. Abram also left everything he knew to follow God to an unknown place. Read about his faith in **Genesis 12:1–9**.

* In what ways was Jim Elliot's call similar to Abram's call in the passage?
* Have you ever sensed that God wanted you to do something without your knowing what the result would be? How did you respond?

Consider . . .

* taking a step of faith by doing something you believe God wants you to do, such as sharing your faith with a friend or working on a bad habit.
* making a bookmark for your Bible with two big eyes on it to remind you to look for God's will as you read.

For more, see . . .

* Genesis 45:1–8 (p.51)   * Matthew 8:18–22 (p.952)
* James 4:13–17 (p.1352)

[10]Lot looked all around and saw the whole Jordan Valley and that there was much water there. It was like the LORD's garden, like the land of Egypt in the direction of Zoar. (This was before the LORD destroyed Sodom and Gomorrah.) [11]So Lot chose to move east and live in the Jordan Valley. In this way Abram and Lot separated. [12]Abram lived in the land of Canaan, but Lot lived among the cities in the Jordan Valley, very near to Sodom. [13]Now the people of Sodom were very evil and were always sinning against the LORD.

[14]After Lot left, the LORD said to Abram, "Look all around you—to the north and south and east and west. [15]All this land that you see I will give to you and your descendants *d* for ever. [16]I will make your descendants as many as the dust of the earth. If anyone could count the dust on the earth, he could count your people. [17]Get up! Walk through all this land because I am now giving it to you."

[18]So Abram moved his tents and went to live near the great trees of Mamre at the city of Hebron. There he built an altar to the LORD.

Lot is Captured

14 Now Amraphel was king of Babylonia, Arioch was king of Ellasar, Kedorlaomer was king of Elam and Tidal was king of Goiim. [2]All these kings went to war against several other kings: Bera, king of Sodom, Birsha, king of Gomorrah, Shinab, king of Admah, Shemeber, king of Zeboiim and the king of Bela. (Bela is also called Zoar.)

[3]These kings who were attacked united their armies in the Valley of Siddim (now the Dead Sea *d*). [4]They had served Kedorlaomer for twelve years, but in the thirteenth year, they all turned against him. [5]Then in the fourteenth year, Kedorlaomer and the kings with him came and defeated the Rephaites *d* in Ashteroth Karnaim, the Zuzites in Ham and the Emites in Shaveh Kiriathaim. [6]They also defeated the Horites in the mountains of Edom to El Paran (near the desert). [7]Then they turned back and went to En Mishpat (that is, Kadesh). They defeated all the Amalekites, as well as the Amorites who lived in Hazazon Tamar.

[8]At that time the kings of Sodom, Gomorrah, Admah, Zeboiim and Bela went out to fight in the Valley of Siddim. (Bela is called Zoar.) [9]They fought against Kedorlaomer, king of Elam, Tidal, king of Goiim, Amraphel, king of Babylonia and Arioch, king of Ellasar—four kings fighting against five. [10]There were many tar pits in the Valley of Siddim. When the kings of Sodom and Gomorrah and their armies ran away, some of the soldiers fell into the tar pits, but the others ran away to the mountains.

[11]Now Kedorlaomer and his armies took everything the people of Sodom and Gomorrah owned, including their food. [12]They took Lot, Abram's nephew, who was living in Sodom, and everything he owned. Then they left. [13]One of the men who was not captured went to Abram, the Hebrew, and told him what had happened. At that time Abram was camped near the great trees of Mamre the Amorite. Mamre was a brother of Eshcol and Aner, and they had all made an agreement to help Abram.

Abram Rescues Lot

[14]When Abram learned that Lot had been captured, he called out his 318 trained men who had been born in his camp. He led the men and chased the enemy all the way to the town of Dan. [15]That night he divided his men into groups, and they made a surprise attack against the enemy. They chased them all the way to Hobah, north of Damascus. [16]Then Abram brought back everything the enemy had stolen, the women and the other people and Lot and everything Lot owned.

[17]After defeating Kedorlaomer and the kings who were with him, Abram went home. As he was returning, the king of Sodom came out to meet him in the Valley of Shaveh (now called King's Valley).

[18]Melchizedek, king of Salem, brought out bread and wine. He was a priest for God Most High [19]and blessed Abram, saying,

"Abram, may you be blessed by God Most
    High,
    the God who made heaven and earth.
[20]And we praise God Most High,
    who has helped you to defeat your
      enemies."

Then Abram gave Melchizedek a tenth of everything he had brought back from the battle.

[21]The king of Sodom said to Abram, "You may keep all these things for yourself. Just give me my people who were captured."

[22]But Abram said to the king of Sodom, "I make a promise to the LORD, the God Most High, who made heaven and earth. [23]I promise that I will not keep anything that is yours. I will not keep even a thread or a sandal strap so that you cannot say, 'I made Abram rich.' [24]I will keep nothing but the food my young men have eaten. But give Aner, Eshcol and Mamre their share of what we won, because they went with me into battle."

God's Agreement with Abram

15 After these things happened, the LORD spoke his word to Abram in a vision: "Abram, don't be afraid. I will defend you, and I will give you a great reward."

²But Abram said, "Lord GOD, *d* what can you give me? I have no son, so my slave Eliezer from Damascus will get everything I own after I die." ³Abram said, "Look, you have given me no son, so a slave born in my house will inherit everything I have." ⁴Then the LORD spoke his word to Abram: "He will not be the one to inherit what you have. You will have a son of your own who will inherit what you have." ⁵Then God led Abram outside and said, "Look at the sky. There are so many stars you cannot count them. Your descendants *d* also will be too many to count."

⁶Abram believed the LORD. And the LORD accepted Abram's faith, and that faith made him acceptable to God.

⁷God said to Abram, "I am the LORD who led you out of Ur of Babylonia so that I could give you this land to own."

⁸But Abram said, "Lord GOD, how can I be sure that I will own this land?"

⁹The LORD said to Abram, "Bring me a three-year-old cow, a three-year-old goat, a three-year-old ram, a dove and a young pigeon."

¹⁰Abram brought them all to God. Then Abram killed the animals and cut each of them into two pieces, laying each half opposite the other half. But he did not cut the birds in half. ¹¹Later, large birds flew down to eat the animals, but Abram chased them away.

¹²As the sun was going down, Abram fell into a deep sleep. While he was asleep, a very terrible darkness came. ¹³Then the LORD said to Abram, "You can be sure that your descendants will be strangers and travel in a land they don't own. The people there will make them slaves and be cruel to them for 400 years. ¹⁴But I will punish the nation where they are slaves. Then your descendants will leave that land, taking great wealth with

DISCOURAGEMENT

Counting

Thomas wanted to create something to store electricity. Time after time – in fact, 50,000 times – he failed. But he kept trying, and eventually he succeeded. He had invented the first battery.

Someone asked him, "Don't you get discouraged when you have to try 50,000 experiments before you get any results?"

"Results?" Thomas replied. "Why, I've got lots of results. I now know 50,000 things that won't work."

Thomas didn't get discouraged when he didn't get instant results. Perhaps that's why Thomas Edison is credited with almost 1,300 inventions, including record players, films, microphones, light bulbs, and the transmitter that made telephones possible.

Just as Thomas Edison didn't expect instant results, so Abram also waited for God's promises to come true. Read **Genesis 15:1–6** to see how he didn't give in to discouragement.

* What kept Thomas Edison from giving in to discouragement? What kept Abram from giving in? What's similar and different about the two situations?
* When have you been discouraged and tempted to give up on God as Abram was tempted? What happened?

Consider . . .

* writing a letter of encouragement to yourself, then sealing the letter in an envelope to keep in your Bible. Open the letter and read it sometime when you're discouraged.
* visiting a hospital's physiotherapy department. Ask a therapist what characteristics keep people from getting discouraged in recovery. Apply those characteristics in your own life.

For more, see . . .

* Psalm 77:1–15 (p.545)
* Hebrews 6:13–19 (p.1335)
* Isaiah 40:27–31 (p.680)

them. [15]And you, Abram, will die in peace and will be buried at an old age. [16]After your great-great-grandchildren are born, your people will come to this land again. It will take that long, because I am not yet going to punish the Amorites for their evil behaviour."

[17]After the sun went down, it was very dark. Suddenly a smoking firepot and a blazing torch passed between the halves of the dead animals. [n] [18]So on that day the LORD made an agreement with Abram and said, "I will give to your descendants the land between the river of Egypt and the great river Euphrates. [19]This is the land of the Kenites, Kenizzites, Kadmonites, [20]Hittites, Perizzites, Rephaites, [d] [21]Amorites, Canaanites, Girgashites and Jebusites."

Ishmael is Born

16 Sarai, Abram's wife, had no children, but she had a slave girl from Egypt named Hagar. [2]Sarai said to Abram, "Look, the LORD has not allowed me to have children, so have sexual relations with my slave girl. If she has a child, maybe I can have my own family through her."

Abram did what Sarai said. [3]It was after he had lived ten years in Canaan that Sarai gave Hagar to her husband Abram. (Hagar was her slave girl from Egypt.)

[4]Abram had sexual relations with Hagar, and she became pregnant. When Hagar learned she was pregnant, she began to treat her mistress Sarai badly. [5]Then Sarai said to Abram, "This is your fault. I gave my slave girl to you, and when she became pregnant, she began to treat me badly. Let the LORD decide who is right—you or me."

[6]But Abram said to Sarai, "You are Hagar's mistress. Do anything you want to her." Then Sarai ill-treated Hagar, and Hagar ran away.

[7]The angel of the LORD found Hagar beside a spring of water in the desert, by the road to Shur. [8]The angel said, "Hagar, Sarai's slave girl, where have you come from? Where are you going?"

Hagar answered, "I am running away from my mistress Sarai."

[9]The angel of the LORD said to her, "Go home to your mistress and obey her." [10]The angel also said, "I will give you so many descendants [d] they will be too many to count."

[11]The angel added,

"You are now pregnant,
 and you will have a son.
You will name him Ishmael, [n]
because the LORD has heard your cries.

[12]Ishmael will be like a wild donkey.
He will be against everyone,
 and everyone will be against him.
He will attack all his brothers."

[13]The slave girl gave a name to the LORD who spoke to her: "You are 'God who sees me,'" because she said to herself, "Have I really seen God who sees me?" [14]So the well there, between Kadesh and Bered, was called Beer Lahai Roi. [n]

[15]Hagar gave birth to a son for Abram, and Abram named him Ishmael. [16]Abram was 86 years old when Hagar gave birth to Ishmael.

Proof of the Agreement

17 When Abram was 99 years old, the LORD appeared to him and said, "I am God Almighty. Obey me and do what is right. [2]I will make an agreement between us, and I will make you the ancestor of many people."

[3]Then Abram bowed face down on the ground. God said to him, [4]"I am making my agreement with you: I will make you the father of many nations. [5]I am changing your name from Abram [n] to Abraham [n] because I am making you

> **Sidelight** In the Bible, a change of name had great significance. That was certainly true when God changed Abram's name to Abraham (Genesis 17:5). Abram means "exalted father" in Hebrew, but Abraham means "father of a multitude" – a sign of God's promise.

a father of many nations. [6]I will give you many descendants. [d] New nations will be born from you, and kings will come from you. [7]And I will make an agreement between me and you and all your descendants from now on: I will be your God and the God of all your descendants. [8]You live in the land of Canaan now as a stranger, but I will give you and your descendants all this land for ever. And I will be the God of your descendants."

[9]Then God said to Abraham, "You and your descendants must keep this agreement from now on. [10]This is my agreement with you and all your descendants, which you must obey: every male among you must be circumcised. [d] [11]Cut away your foreskin to show that you are prepared to follow the agreement between me and you. [12]From now on when a baby boy is eight days old, you will circumcise him. This includes any boy born among your people or any who is your

---

passed . . . animals This showed that God sealed the agreement between himself and Abram.
Ishmael The Hebrew words for "Ishmael" and "has heard" sound similar.
Beer Lahai Roi This means "the well of the Living One who sees me".
Abram This name means "honoured father".
Abraham The end of the Hebrew word for "Abraham" sounds like the beginning of the Hebrew word for "many".

slave, who is not one of your descendants. [13]Circumcise every baby boy whether he is born in your family or bought as a slave. Your bodies will be marked to show that you are part of my agreement that lasts for ever. [14]Any male who is not circumcised will be cut off from his people, because he has broken my agreement."

Isaac—the Promised Son

[15]God said to Abraham, "I will change the name of Sarai,[n] your wife, to Sarah.[n] [16]I will bless her and give her a son, and you will be the father. She will be the mother of many nations. Kings of nations will come from her."

[17]Abraham bowed face down on the ground and laughed. He said to himself, "Can a man have a child when he is 100 years old? Can Sarah give birth to a child when she is 90?" [18]Then Abraham said to God, "Please let Ishmael be the son you promised."

[19]God said, "No, Sarah your wife will have a son, and you will name him Isaac.[n] I will make my agreement with him to be an agreement that continues for ever with all his descendants.[d]

[20]"As for Ishmael, I have heard you. I will bless him and give him many descendants. And I will cause their numbers to grow greatly. He will be the father of twelve great leaders, and I will make him into a great nation. [21]But I will make my agreement with Isaac, the son whom Sarah will have at this same time next year." [22]After God finished talking with Abraham, God rose and left him.

[23]Then Abraham gathered Ishmael, all the males born in his camp, and the slaves he had

---

Sarai   An Aramaic name meaning "princess".
Sarah   A Hebrew name meaning "princess".
Isaac   The Hebrew words for "he laughed" (v.17) and "Isaac" sound the same.

PROMISES

Silent Symbols

A wedding ring may just appear to be a little band of metal round someone's finger, but there's so much more to it than that.

Have you ever wondered why wedding rings are traditionally worn on the third finger of the left hand? It originates from the Egyptians who believed that the vein of that finger travelled directly to the heart. This belief was taken up by the Greeks when they conquered Egypt, and from them passed onto the Romans, who called this vein the *vena amoris*, which is Latin for "the vein of love". So, by wearing rings on the fourth finger of their left hands, a married couple symbolically declare their eternal love for each other.

Of course, every ring will symbolise something very individual from person to person. Who the ring was given by, the memories it triggers, how beautiful it is . . . all these things add up to making the humble wedding ring a very symbolic item. So, you can understand why the exchanging of the rings in a marriage service is such a big deal. When a man and woman promise before God to love one another, they want the rings to represent the relationship they'll have.

Read **Genesis 17:1–10**. God is talking about a promise between him and Abraham and all his descendants. God also asks Abraham to do something as a symbol of the promise between them.

* What was God asking the Israelites to do to symbolise their part of the promise?
* Why does it help to physically do something or have a symbol for a promise you've made?

Consider . . .

* what simple practical thing you could do to help you remember a promise God has made you.
* whenever you find promises in the Bible from God that apply to you, writing them down one side of a piece of paper. Then, when you want to commit to that promise, write your response down the other side.

For more, see . . .

* Numbers 23:19 (p.152)
* Matthew 28:16–20 (p.995)
* Joshua 4:15–24 (p.205)

bought. So that day Abraham circumcised every man and boy in his camp as God had told him to do. [24]Abraham was 99 years old when he was circumcised. [25]And Ishmael, his son, was thirteen years old when he was circumcised. [26]Abraham and his son were circumcised on the same day. [27]Also on that day all the men in Abraham's camp were circumcised, including all those born in his camp and all the slaves he had bought from other nations.

The Three Visitors

18 Later, the LORD again appeared to Abraham near the great trees of Mamre. Abraham was sitting at the entrance of his tent during the hottest part of the day. [2]He looked up and saw three men standing near him. When Abraham saw them, he ran from his tent to meet them. He bowed face down on the ground before them [3]and said, "Sir, if you think well of me, please stay awhile with me, your servant. [4]I will bring some water so all of you can wash your feet. You may rest under the tree, [5]and I will get some bread for you so you can regain your strength. Then you may continue your journey."

The three men said, "That is fine. Do as you said."

[6]Abraham hurried to the tent where Sarah was and said to her, "Hurry, prepare 22 litres of fine flour, and make it into loaves of bread." [7]Then Abraham ran to his herd and took one of his best calves. He gave it to a servant, who hurried to kill it and to prepare it for food. [8]Abraham gave the three men the calf that had been cooked, milk curds and milk. While they ate, he stood under the tree near them.

[9]The men asked Abraham, "Where is your wife, Sarah?"

"There, in the tent," said Abraham.

[10]Then the LORD said, "I will certainly return to you about this time a year from now. At that time your wife Sarah will have a son."

Sarah was listening at the entrance of the tent which was behind him. [11]Abraham and Sarah

---

DOUBT

Did God Really Say . . . ?

Craig was sure that God had told him that he was to move to Africa and tell people about Jesus. Only problem was, he didn't have the money to pay for the fare there or to live off! The more he prayed about it, the more he was convinced it was the right thing to do. He also believed God had said not to worry about the money because he would provide.

However, after just a few days, Craig began to doubt if he had really heard God. Maybe he had just been hoping that God would provide and God hadn't really spoken. Besides, why would God want to use someone like him anyway? Craig decided to try to find the money himself. He tried to get a personal loan, but the company refused. He even thought about selling some of his possessions, but in the end gave up. He'd obviously misheard God.

The next day Craig got a letter through the post from a great aunt he'd met once when he was a baby. He wasn't even sure if she was a Christian. She said in her letter that even though she didn't know what Craig was up to, she believed God had told her to give some of her savings to Craig to enable him to serve God as a missionary abroad. She sent Craig enough money to travel to Africa and to live off for three years!

Read **Genesis 17:15–19**.

* What do you think Craig and Abraham learnt from their experiences?
* Has God ever said something to you that seemed impossible? How did you react to it?

Consider . . .

* talking and praying through your doubts with someone whose friendship you respect.
* asking older Christians how they hear God.

For more, see . . .

* Matthew 21:18–22 (p.977)
* John 20:24–29 (p.1134)

were very old. Since Sarah was past the age when women normally have children, ¹²she laughed to herself, "My husband and I are too old to have a baby."

¹³Then the LORD said to Abraham, "Why did Sarah laugh? Why did she say, 'I am too old to have a baby'? ¹⁴Is anything too hard for the LORD? No! I will return to you at the right time a year from now, and Sarah will have a son."

¹⁵Sarah was afraid, so she lied and said, "I didn't laugh."

But the LORD said, "No. You did laugh."

¹⁶Then the men got up to leave and started out towards Sodom. Abraham walked along with them for a short time to send them on their way.

Abraham's Bargain with God

¹⁷The LORD said, "Should I tell Abraham what I am going to do now? ¹⁸Abraham's children will certainly become a great and powerful nation, and all nations on earth will be blessed through him. ¹⁹I have chosen him so he would command his children and his descendants *d* to live the way the LORD wants them to, to live right and be fair. Then I, the LORD, will give Abraham what I promised him."

²⁰Then the LORD said, "I have heard many complaints against the people of Sodom and Gomorrah. They are very evil. ²¹I will go down and see if they are as bad as I have heard. If not, I will know."

²²So the men turned and went towards Sodom, but Abraham stood there before the LORD. ²³Then Abraham approached him and asked, "Do you plan to destroy the good people along with the evil ones? ²⁴What if there are 50 good people in that city? Will you still destroy it? Surely you will save the city for the 50 good people living there. ²⁵Surely you will not destroy the good people along with the evil ones; then they would be treated the same. You are the judge of all the earth. Won't you do what is right?"

SERVICE

Gift For a Stranger

Unlike other leaders in India in the 1940s, V. P. Menon didn't have a university degree. He wasn't from a well-to-do or respected family. The oldest of thirteen children, he had to leave school at the age of thirteen to work in coal mines and factories.

As a young man, he went to Delhi to get a government job. On the way, everything he had – including his money and identification – was stolen at the railway station.

In desperation, he went to an elderly man standing nearby, explained his situation, and asked for a loan of fifteen rupees to buy food until he could get a job. The man gave him the money. Menon asked for his address so he could repay the loan, but the man said Menon didn't owe the debt to him, but to any stranger in need.

Menon never forgot his debt, and his life was marked by constant generosity to those in need. The day before Menon died, a beggar came to the family home asking for money to buy new sandals. Menon asked his daughter to take fifteen rupees out of his wallet to give to the man.

V. P. Menon served strangers selflessly, just as Abraham provided food for strangers in **Genesis 18:1–16**. Read how that incident affected Abraham.

* What attitudes cause people to share the way Menon and Abraham did?
* How do you need to become more like Abraham and Sarah? When have you served God by serving people you didn't know?

Consider . . .

* inviting someone who's new at your school, home to your house.
* trying V. P. Menon's approach. Give two pounds to a stranger in need, and ask that he or she repay it to another stranger in need.

For more, see . . .

* 1 Kings 17:10–16 (p.332)
* James 2:1–13 (p.1348)
* Hebrews 13:2 (p.1345)

²⁶The LORD said, "If I find 50 good people in the city of Sodom, I will save the whole city because of them."

²⁷Then Abraham said, "Though I am only dust and ashes, I have been brave to speak to the Lord. ²⁸What if there are only 45 good people in the city? Will you destroy the whole city for the lack of five good people?"

The LORD said, "If I find 45 there, I will not destroy the city."

²⁹Again Abraham said to him, "If you find only 40 good people there, will you destroy the city?"

The LORD said, "If I find 40, I will not destroy it."

³⁰Then Abraham said, "Lord, please don't be angry with me, but let me ask you this. If you find only 30 good people in the city, will you destroy it?"

He said, "If I find 30 good people there, I will not destroy the city."

³¹Then Abraham said, "I have been brave to speak to the Lord. But what if there are 20 good people in the city?"

He answered, "If I find 20 there, I will not destroy the city."

³²Then Abraham said, "Lord, please don't be angry with me, but let me bother you this one last time. What if you find ten there?"

He said, "If I find ten there, I will not destroy it."

³³When the LORD finished speaking to Abraham, he left, and Abraham returned home.

GOD'S LOVE

A Second Chance

Most girls would love to have Amy's looks. Her face. Her hair. Her figure. You would think she had it made.

But her good looks haven't kept her life from being a mess. At home, her alcoholic mum either neglected her or screamed at her. So she avoided home and hung about on street corners with other kids who didn't fit in.

At thirteen, Amy ran away from home for the fourth time and ended up being taken into care. It was then that she decided to turn her life round and make something of herself – to give herself a second chance.

When she returned to school, things went well. She made new friends who didn't drink or go to wild parties. Her life seemed to be coming together. But then a rumour started. "Amy sleeps around," people whispered at school. Nothing Amy said or did made any difference, and the rumour stuck. One by one, her new friends ditched her. Except Helen.

"I don't believe the rumour," she told Amy. "Besides, you deserve a second chance."

But Amy still felt rejected, so she went back to her old friends. She started dating Tim, who gave her expensive gifts bought with drug money. "I love you," he would tell Amy. But she soon discovered that he was only saying it to get her to have sex with him. When she wouldn't, he dropped her.

But Amy wasn't friendless. She still had Helen, and Helen's family took her in so that she would have a place to live. Now, three years later, she feels like part of the family. She knows what it's like to have a second chance.

Like Amy, the people of Sodom and Gomorrah were given a second chance. Read how they responded to it in **Genesis 18:20 – 19:25**.

* How are Amy's friend Helen and Abraham similar? different?
* If you were Abraham, when would you have given up begging for the lives of the people?

Consider . . .

* giving a friend a second chance when he or she does something that hurts you.
* keeping track of all the times when people give you second chances. Thank them by baking a cake or running an errand – and learning from your mistake.

For more, see . . .

* Joel 2:12–13 (p.865)
* Acts 26:9–18 (p.1179)

* Zephaniah 3:14–20 (p.914)

Lot Leaves Sodom

19 The two angels came to Sodom in the evening as Lot was sitting near the city gate. When he saw them, he got up and went to them and bowed face down on the ground. ²Lot said, "Sirs, please come to my house and spend the night. There you can wash your feet, and then tomorrow you may continue your journey."

The angels answered, "No, we will spend the night in the city's public square."

³But Lot begged them to come, so they agreed and went to his house. Then Lot prepared a meal for them. He baked bread without yeast, and they ate it.

⁴Before bedtime, men both young and old and from every part of Sodom surrounded Lot's house. ⁵They called to Lot, "Where are the two men who came to you tonight? Bring them out to us so we can have sexual relations with them."

⁶Lot went outside to them, closing the door behind him. ⁷He said, "No, my brothers! Do not do this evil thing. ⁸Look! I have two daughters who have never slept with a man. I will give them to you, and you may do anything you want with them. But please don't do anything to these men. They have come to my house, and I must protect them."

⁹The men around the house answered, "Move out of the way!" Then they said to each other, "This man Lot came to our city as a stranger, and now he wants to tell us what to do!" They said to Lot, "We will do worse things to you than to them." They started pushing him back and were ready to break down the door.

¹⁰But the two men staying with Lot opened the door, pulled him back inside the house, and then closed the door. ¹¹They struck those outside the door with blindness, so the men, both young and old, could not find the door.

¹²The two men said to Lot, "Do you have any other relatives in this city? Do you have any sons-in-law, sons, daughters or any other relatives? If you do, tell them to leave now, ¹³because we are about to destroy this city. The LORD has heard of all the evil that is here, so he has sent us to destroy it."

¹⁴So Lot went out and said to his future sons-in-law who were pledged to marry his daughters, "Hurry and leave this city! The LORD is about to destroy it!" But they thought Lot was joking.

¹⁵At dawn the next morning, the angels begged Lot to hurry. They said, "Go! Take your wife and your two daughters with you so you will not be destroyed when the city is punished."

¹⁶But Lot delayed. So the two men took the hands of Lot, his wife and his two daughters and led them safely out of the city. So the LORD was merciful to Lot and his family. ¹⁷After they brought them out of the city, one of the men said, "Run for your lives! Don't look back or stop anywhere in the valley. Run to the mountains, or you will be destroyed."

¹⁸But Lot said to one of them, "Sir, please don't force me to go so far! ¹⁹You have been merciful and kind to me and have saved my life. But I can't run to the mountains. The disaster will catch me, and I will die. ²⁰Look, that little town over there is not too far away. Let me run there. It's really just a little town, and I'll be safe there."

²¹The angel said to Lot, "Very well, I will allow you to do this also. I will not destroy that town. ²²But run there fast, because I cannot destroy Sodom until you are safely in that town." (That town is named Zoar,ⁿ because it is little.)

Sodom and Gomorrah are Destroyed

²³The sun had already come up when Lot entered Zoar. ²⁴The LORD sent a rain of burning sulphur down from the sky on Sodom and Gomorrah ²⁵and destroyed those cities. He also destroyed the whole Jordan Valley, everyone living in the cities, and even all the plants.

²⁶At that point Lot's wife looked back. When she did, she became a pillar of salt.

²⁷Early the next morning, Abraham got up and went to the place where he had stood before the LORD. ²⁸He looked down towards Sodom and Gomorrah and all the Jordan Valley and saw smoke rising from the land, like smoke from a furnace.

²⁹God destroyed the cities in the valley, but he remembered what Abraham had asked. So God saved Lot's life, but he destroyed the city where Lot had lived.

Lot and His Daughters

³⁰Lot was afraid to continue living in Zoar, so he and his two daughters went to live in the mountains in a cave. ³¹One day the older daughter said to the younger, "Our father is old. Everywhere on the earth women and men marry, but there are no men around here for us to marry. ³²Let's get our father drunk and have sexual relations with him. We can use him to have children and continue our family."

Sidelight

When God destroyed the cities of Sodom and Gomorrah (Genesis 19:23–29), he made sure they weren't built again. Archaeologists believe the two cities are now under water in a shallow part of the Dead Sea. The waters may have risen because of an earthquake around 2000 BC.

Zoar This name sounds like the Hebrew word for "little".

³³That night the two girls got their father drunk, and the older daughter went and had sexual relations with him. But Lot did not know when she lay down or when she got up. ³⁴The next day the older daughter said to the younger, "Last night I had sexual relations with my father. Let's get him drunk again tonight so you can go and have sexual relations with him, too. In this way we can use our father to have children to continue our family." ³⁵So that night they got their father drunk again, and the younger daughter went and had sexual relations with him. Again, Lot did not know when she lay down or when she got up.

³⁶So both of Lot's daughters became pregnant by their father. ³⁷The older daughter gave birth to a son and named him Moab. He is the ancestor of all the Moabite people who are still living today. ³⁸The younger daughter also gave birth to a son and named him Ben-Ammi. He is the father of all the Ammonite people who are still living today.

Abraham Tricks Abimelech

20 Abraham left Hebron and travelled to southern Canaan where he stayed awhile between Kadesh and Shur. When he moved to Gerar, ²he told people that his wife Sarah was his sister. Abimelech, king of Gerar, heard this, so he sent some servants to take her. ³But one night God spoke to Abimelech in a dream and said, "You will die. The woman you took is married."

⁴But Abimelech had not gone near Sarah, so he said, "Lord, would you destroy an innocent nation? ⁵Abraham himself told me, 'This woman is my sister,' and she also said, 'He is my brother.' I am innocent. I did not know I was doing anything wrong."

⁶Then God said to Abimelech in the dream, "Yes, I know you did not realise what you were doing. So I did not allow you to sin against me and touch her. ⁷Give Abraham his wife back. He is a prophet. *d* He will pray for you, and you will not die. But if you do not give Sarah back, you and all your family will surely die."

⁸So early the next morning, Abimelech called all his officers and told them everything that had happened in the dream. They were very afraid. ⁹Then Abimelech called Abraham to him and said, "What have you done to us? What wrong did I do against you? Why did you bring this trouble to my kingdom? You should not have done these things to me. ¹⁰What were you thinking that caused you to do this?"

¹¹Then Abraham answered, "I thought no one in this place respected God and that someone would kill me to get Sarah. ¹²And it is true that she is my sister. She is the daughter of my father, but she is not the daughter of my mother. ¹³When God told me to leave my father's house and wander in many different places, I told Sarah, 'You must do a special favour for me. Everywhere we go, tell people I am your brother.'"

¹⁴Then Abimelech gave Abraham some sheep, cattle and male and female slaves. He also gave Sarah, Abraham's wife, back to him ¹⁵and said, "Look around you at my land. You may live anywhere you want."

¹⁶Abimelech said to Sarah, "I gave your brother Abraham 1,000 pieces of silver to make up for any wrong that people may think about you. I want everyone to know that you are innocent."

¹⁷Then Abraham prayed to God, and God healed Abimelech, his wife and his servant girls so they could have children. ¹⁸The Lord had kept all the women in Abimelech's house from having children as a punishment to Abimelech for taking Abraham's wife, Sarah.

A Baby for Sarah

21 The Lord cared for Sarah as he had said, and did for her what he had promised. ²Sarah became pregnant and gave birth to a son for Abraham in his old age. Everything happened at the time God had said it would. ³Abraham named his son Isaac, the son Sarah gave birth to. ⁴He circumcised *d* Isaac when he was eight days old as God had commanded.

⁵Abraham was 100 years old when his son Isaac was born. ⁶And Sarah said, "God has made me laugh. *n* Everyone who hears about this will laugh with me. ⁷No one thought that I would be able to have Abraham's child, but even though Abraham is old I have given him a son."

Hagar and Ishmael Leave

⁸Isaac grew, and when he became old enough to eat food, Abraham gave a great feast. ⁹But Sarah saw Ishmael making fun of Isaac. (Ishmael was the son of Abraham by Hagar, Sarah's Egyptian slave.) ¹⁰So Sarah said to Abraham, "Throw out this slave woman and her son. Her son should not inherit anything; my son Isaac should receive it all."

¹¹This troubled Abraham very much because Ishmael was also his son. ¹²But God said to Abraham, "Don't be troubled about the boy and the slave woman. Do whatever Sarah tells you. The descendants *d* I promised you will be from Isaac. ¹³I will also make the descendants of Ishmael into a great nation because he is your son, too."

laugh The Hebrew words for "he laughed" and "Isaac" sound the same.

[14]Early the next morning Abraham took some food and a leather bag full of water. He gave them to Hagar and sent her away. Carrying these things and her son, Hagar went and wandered in the desert of Beersheba.

[15]Later, when all the water was gone from the bag, Hagar put her son under a bush. [16]Then she went away a short distance and sat down. She thought, "My son will die, and I cannot watch this happen." She sat there and began to cry.

[17]God heard the boy crying, and God's angel called to Hagar from heaven. He said, "What is wrong, Hagar? Don't be afraid! God has heard the boy crying there. [18]Help him up and take him by the hand. I will make his descendants into a great nation."

[19]Then God showed Hagar a well of water. So she went to the well and filled her bag with water and gave the boy a drink.

[20]God was with the boy as he grew up. Ishmael lived in the desert and became an archer. [21]He lived in the Desert of Paran, and his mother found a wife for him in Egypt.

Abraham's Bargain with Abimelech

[22]Then Abimelech came with Phicol, the commander of his army, and said to Abraham, "God is with you in everything you do. [23]So make a promise to me here before God that you will be fair with me and my children and my descendants. *d* Be kind to me and to this land where you have lived as a stranger—as kind as I have been to you."

[24]And Abraham said, "I promise." [25]Then Abraham complained to Abimelech about Abimelech's servants who had seized a well of water.

[26]But Abimelech said, "I don't know who did this. You never told me about this before today."

[27]Then Abraham gave Abimelech some sheep and cattle, and they made an agreement. [28]Abraham also put seven female lambs in front of Abimelech.

[29]Abimelech asked Abraham, "Why did you put these seven female lambs by themselves?"

[30]Abraham answered, "Accept these lambs from me to prove that you believe I dug this well."

[31]So that place was called Beersheba *n* because they made a promise to each other there.

[32]After Abraham and Abimelech made the agreement at Beersheba, Abimelech and Phicol, the commander of his army, went back to the land of the Philistines.

[33]Abraham planted a tamarisk tree at Beersheba and prayed to the LORD, the God who lives for ever. [34]And Abraham lived as a stranger in the land of the Philistines for a long time.

God Tests Abraham

22 After these things God tested Abraham's faith. God said to him, "Abraham!"

And he answered, "Here I am."

[2]Then God said, "Take your only son, Isaac, the son you love, and go to the land of Moriah. Kill him there and offer him as a whole burnt offering on one of the mountains I will tell you about."

[3]Abraham got up early in the morning and saddled his donkey. He took Isaac and two servants with him. After he cut the wood for the sacrifice, they went to the place to which God had told them to go. [4]On the third day Abraham looked up and saw the place in the distance. [5]He said to his servants, "Stay here with the donkey. My son and I will go over there and worship, and then we will come back to you."

[6]Abraham took the wood for the sacrifice and gave it to his son to carry, but he himself took the knife and the fire. So he and his son went on together.

[7]Isaac said to his father Abraham, "Father!"

Abraham answered, "Yes, my son."

Isaac said, "We have the fire and the wood, but where is the lamb we will burn as a sacrifice?"

[8]Abraham answered, "God will give us the lamb for the sacrifice, my son."

So Abraham and his son went on together [9]and came to the place God had told him about. Abraham built an altar there. He laid the wood on it and then tied up his son Isaac and laid him on the wood on the altar. [10]Then Abraham took his knife and was about to kill his son.

[11]But the angel of the LORD called to him from heaven and said, "Abraham! Abraham!"

Abraham answered, "Yes."

[12]The angel said, "Don't kill your son or hurt him in any way. Now I can see that you trust God and that you have not kept your son, your only son, from me."

[13]Then Abraham looked up and saw a ram caught in a bush by its horns. So Abraham went and took the ram and killed it. He offered it as a whole burnt offering to God, and his son was saved. [14]So Abraham named that place The LORD Provides. Even today people say, "On the mountain of the LORD it will be provided."

[15]The angel of the LORD called to Abraham from heaven a second time [16]and said, "The LORD says, 'Because you did not keep back your son, your only son, from me, I make you this promise by my own name: [17]I will surely bless you and give you many descendants. *d* They will be as many as the stars in the sky and the sand on the seashore, and they will capture the cities of their enemies. [18]Through your descendants all

---

Beersheba   This name means "well of the promise" or "well of seven".

the nations on the earth will be blessed, because you obeyed me.'"

¹⁹Then Abraham returned to his servants. They all travelled back to Beersheba and Abraham stayed there.

²⁰After these things happened, someone told Abraham: "Your brother Nahor and his wife Milcah have children now. ²¹The first son is Uz, and the second is Buz. The third son is Kemuel (the father of Aram). ²²Then there are Kesed, Hazo, Pildash, Jidlaph and Bethuel." ²³Bethuel became the father of Rebekah. Milcah was the mother of these eight sons, and Nahor, Abraham's brother, was the father. ²⁴Also Nahor had four other sons by his slave woman,ᵈ Reumah. Their names were Tebah, Gaham, Tahash and Maacah.

Sarah Dies

23 Sarah lived to be 127 years old. ²She died in Kiriath Arba (that is, Hebron) in

---

Sidelight

If his name matches his sleeping habits, you probably wouldn't want to spend the night at Nahor's. His name means "snorer" (Genesis 22:23–24).

---

the land of Canaan. Abraham was very sad and cried because of her. ³After a while he got up from the side of his wife's body and went to talk to the Hittites. He said, ⁴"I am only a stranger

---

PRIORITIES

Worth a Sacrifice

John couldn't sleep. He tossed restlessly in bed, wondering what to do. He had been planning to take a summer job at a local firm. The pay and hours looked great.

But then, last week at school, he had seen a poster about a camp for disabled children that needed someone to teach swimming. He loved water sports, and his youth leader had encouraged him to consider volunteering to help at the camp.

John wasn't prepared for the reaction when he mentioned the idea to his dad. "Why do you want to work for nothing when you could get paid?" his dad fumed. "It's not as if you're wealthy. And then you'll come running to me to pay your university fees."

His dad had a point, John reasoned as he stared up at the dark bedroom ceiling. But no matter how hard he tried, he couldn't forget about the camp – or those kids.

When John's alarm woke him the next morning, he knew what he had to do. "Dad," he explained at breakfast, "some things are worth sacrificing for. Helping at that camp is important to me." His dad didn't understand, but he agreed to let John stick with his priorities. So John phoned the camp organisers. Like John, Abraham had difficult decisions, but he also stuck with what he believed was right. Read **Genesis 22:1-18** to see what happened.

* What do John's and Abraham's decisions say about their priorities?
* When have you, like Abraham, had to make a difficult decision because of what you believed God wanted? What happened?

Consider . . .

* writing out the issues involved in a difficult decision. Keep the list by your bed or on your desk for a few days. Whenever you think of an option, benefit, or disadvantage, write it on the paper. Pray about your decision through the week and then make the decision, sticking to what you know to be right.
* having a "what if" discussion over lunch with friends in the school cafeteria. Brainstorm together several situations that test your priorities. Then discuss what you would do if you were in a particular situation.

For more, see . . .

* Proverbs 3 (p.592)
* Matthew 6:19–24 (p.948)

* Daniel 3:8–30 (p.835)

and a foreigner here. Sell me some of your land so that I can bury my dead wife."

[5]The Hittites answered Abraham, [6]"Sir, you are a great leader among us. You may have the best place we have to bury your dead. You may have any of our burying places that you want, and none of us will stop you from burying your dead wife."

[7]Abraham rose and bowed to the people of the land, the Hittites. [8]He said to them, "If you truly want to help me bury my dead wife here, speak to Ephron, the son of Zohar, for me. [9]Ask him to sell me the cave of Machpelah at the edge of his field. I will pay him the full price. You can be the witnesses that I am buying it as a burial place."

[10]Ephron was sitting among the Hittites at the city gate. He answered Abraham, [11]"No, sir. I will give you the land and the cave that is in it, with these people as witnesses. Bury your dead wife."

[12]Then Abraham bowed down before the Hittites. [13]He said to Ephron before all the people, "Please let me pay you the full price for the field. Accept my money, and I will bury my dead there."

[14]Ephron answered Abraham, [15]"Sir, the land is worth 400 pieces of silver, but I won't argue with you over the price. Take the land, and bury your dead wife."

[16]Abraham agreed and paid Ephron in front of the Hittite witnesses. He weighed out the full price, 400 pieces of silver, and they counted the weight as the traders normally did.

[17-18]So Ephron's field in Machpelah, east of Mamre, was sold. Abraham became the owner of the field, the cave in it, and all the trees that were in the field. The sale was made at the city gate, with the Hittites as witnesses. [19]After this, Abraham buried his wife Sarah in the cave in the field of Machpelah, near Mamre. (Mamre was later called Hebron in the land of Canaan.) [20]So Abraham bought the field and the cave in it from the Hittites to use as a burying place.

A Wife for Isaac

24 Abraham was now very old, and the LORD had blessed him in every way. [2]Abraham said to his oldest servant, who was in charge of everything he owned, "Put your hand under my leg.[n] [3]Make a promise to me before the LORD, the God of heaven and earth. Don't get a wife for my son from the Canaanite girls who live around here. [4]Instead, go back to my country, to the land of my relatives, and get a wife for my son Isaac."

[5]The servant said to him, "What if this woman does not want to return with me to this land? Then, should I take your son with me back to your homeland?"

[6]Abraham said to him, "No! Don't take my son back there. [7]The LORD, the God of heaven, brought me from the home of my father and the land of my relatives. And he promised me, 'I will give this land to your descendants.'[d] The LORD will send his angel before you to help you get a wife for my son there. [8]If the girl won't come back with you, you will be free from this promise. But you must not take my son back there." [9]So the servant put his hand under his master's leg and made a promise to Abraham about this.

[10]The servant took ten of Abraham's camels and left, carrying with him many different kinds of beautiful gifts. He went to North West Mesopotamia, to Nahor's city. [11]In the evening, when the women come out to get water, he made the camels kneel down at the well outside the city.

[12]The servant said, "LORD, God of my master Abraham, allow me to find a wife for his son today. Please show this kindness to my master Abraham. [13]Here I am, standing by the spring, and the girls from the city are coming out to get water. [14]I will say to one of them, 'Please put your jar down so I can drink.' Then let her say, 'Drink, and I will also give water to your camels.' If that happens, I will know she is the right one for your servant Isaac and that you have shown kindness to my master."

[15]Before the servant had finished praying, Rebekah, the daughter of Bethuel, came out of the city. (Bethuel was the son of Milcah and Nahor, Abraham's brother.) Rebekah was carrying her water jar on her shoulder. [16]She was very pretty, a virgin;[d] she had never had sexual relations with a man. She went down to the spring and filled her jar, then came back up. [17]The servant ran to her and said, "Please give me a little water from your jar."

[18]Rebekah said, "Drink, sir." She quickly lowered the jar from her shoulder and gave him a drink. [19]After he finished drinking, Rebekah said, "I will also pour some water for your camels." [20]So she quickly poured all the water from her jar into the drinking trough for the camels. Then she kept running to the well until she had given all the camels enough to drink.

Put . . . leg   This showed that a person would keep a promise.

²¹The servant quietly watched her. He wanted to be sure the LORD had made his trip successful. ²²After the camels had finished drinking, he gave Rebekah a gold ring weighing 5 grammes and two gold arm bracelets weighing about 110 grammes each. ²³He asked, "Who is your father? Is there a place in his house for me and my men to spend the night?"

²⁴Rebekah answered, "My father is Bethuel, the son of Milcah and Nahor." ²⁵Then she said, "And, yes, we have straw for your camels and a place for you to spend the night."

²⁶The servant bowed and worshipped the LORD ²⁷and said, "Blessed is the LORD, the God of my master Abraham. The LORD has been kind and truthful to him and has led me to my master's relatives."

²⁸Then Rebekah ran and told her mother's family about all these things. ²⁹She had a brother named Laban, who ran out to Abraham's servant, who was still at the spring. ³⁰Laban had heard what she had said and had seen the ring and the bracelets on his sister's arms. So he ran out to the well, and there was the man standing by the camels at the spring. ³¹Laban said, "Sir, you are welcome to come in; you don't have to stand outside. I have prepared the house for you and also a place for your camels."

³²So Abraham's servant went into the house. After Laban unloaded the camels and gave them straw and food, he gave water to Abraham's servant so he and the men with him could wash their feet. ³³Then Laban gave the servant food, but the servant said, "I will not eat until I have told you why I came."

So Laban said, "Then tell us."

³⁴He said, "I am Abraham's servant. ³⁵The LORD has greatly blessed my master in everything, and he has become a rich man. The LORD has given him many flocks of sheep, herds of cattle, silver and gold, male and female servants, camels and horses. ³⁶Sarah, my master's wife, gave birth to a son when she was old, and my master has given everything he owns to that son. ³⁷My master had me make a promise to him and said, 'Don't get a wife for my son from the Canaanite girls who live around here. ³⁸Instead, you must go to my father's people and to my family. There you must get a wife for my son.' ³⁹I said to my master, 'What if the woman will not come back with me?' ⁴⁰But he said, 'I serve the LORD, who will send his angel with you and will help you. You will get a wife for my son from my family and my father's people. ⁴¹Then you will be free from the promise. But if they will not give you a wife for my son, you will be free from this promise.'

⁴²Today I came to this spring. I said, 'LORD, God of my master Abraham, please make my trip successful. ⁴³I am standing by this spring. I will wait for a young woman to come out to get water, and I will say, "Please give me water from your jar to drink." ⁴⁴Then let her say, "Drink this water, and I will also get water for your camels." By this I will know the LORD has chosen her for my master's son.'

⁴⁵"Before I finished my silent prayer, Rebekah came out of the city with her water jar on her shoulder. She went down to the spring and got water. I said to her, 'Please give me a drink.' ⁴⁶She quickly lowered the jar from her shoulder and said, 'Drink this. I will also get water for your camels.' So I drank, and she gave water to my camels too. ⁴⁷When I asked her, 'Who is your father?' she answered, 'My father is Bethuel son of Milcah and Nahor.' Then I put the ring in her nose and the bracelets on her arms, ⁴⁸and I bowed my head and thanked the LORD. I praised the LORD, the God of my master Abraham, because he led me on the right road to get the granddaughter of my master's brother for his son. ⁴⁹Now, tell me, will you be kind and truthful to my master? And if not, tell me so. Then I will know what I should do."

⁵⁰Laban and Bethuel answered, "This is clearly from the LORD, and we cannot change what must happen. ⁵¹Rebekah is yours. Take her and go. Let her marry your master's son as the LORD has commanded."

⁵²When Abraham's servant heard these words, he bowed face down on the ground before the LORD. ⁵³Then he gave Rebekah gold and silver jewellery and clothes. He also gave expensive gifts to her brother and mother. ⁵⁴The servant and the men with him ate and drank and spent the night there. When they got up the next morning, the servant said, "Now let me go back to my master."

⁵⁵Rebekah's mother and her brother said, "Let Rebekah stay with us at least ten days. After that she may go."

⁵⁶But the servant said to them, "Do not make me wait, because the LORD has made my trip successful. Now let me go back to my master."

⁵⁷Rebekah's brother and mother said, "We will call Rebekah and ask her what she wants to do." ⁵⁸They called her and asked her, "Do you want to go with this man now?"

She said, "Yes, I do."

⁵⁹So they allowed Rebekah and her nurse to go with Abraham's servant and his men. ⁶⁰They blessed Rebekah and said,

"Our sister, may you be the mother of
        thousands of people,
    and may your descendants ᵈ capture the
        cities of their enemies."

⁶¹Then Rebekah and her servant girls got on the camels and followed the servant and his men. So the servant took Rebekah and left.

62At this time Isaac had left Beer Lahai Roi and was living in southern Canaan. 63One evening when he went out to the field to think, he looked up and saw camels coming. 64Rebekah also looked and saw Isaac. Then she jumped down from the camel 65and asked the servant, "Who is that man walking in the field to meet us?"

The servant answered, "That is my master." So Rebekah covered her face with her veil.

66The servant told Isaac everything that had happened. 67Then Isaac brought Rebekah into the tent of Sarah, his mother, and she became his wife. Isaac loved her very much, and so he was comforted after his mother's death.

Abraham's Family

25 Abraham married again, and his new wife was Keturah. 2She gave birth to Zimran, Jokshan, Medan, Midian, Ishbak and Shuah. 3Jokshan was the father of Sheba and Dedan. Dedan's descendants *d* were the people of Assyria, Letush and Leum. 4The sons of Midian were Ephah, Epher, Hanoch, Abida and Eldaah. All these were descendants of Keturah. 5Abraham left everything he owned to Isaac. 6But before Abraham died, he did give gifts to the sons of his other wives, then sent them to the east to be away from Isaac.

7Abraham lived to be 175 years old. 8He breathed his last breath and died at an old age, after a long and satisfying life. 9His sons Isaac and Ishmael buried him in the cave of Machpelah in the field of Ephron east of Mamre. (Ephron was the son of Zohar the Hittite.) 10So Abraham was buried with his wife Sarah in the same field that he had bought from the Hittites. 11After Abraham died, God blessed his son Isaac. Isaac was now living at Beer Lahai Roi.

12This is the family history of Ishmael, Abraham's son. (Hagar, Sarah's Egyptian servant, was Ishmael's mother.) 13These are the names of Ishmael's sons in the order they were born: Nebaioth, the first son, then Kedar, Adbeel, Mibsam, 14Mishma, Dumah, Massa, 15Hadad, Tema, Jetur,

FAMILY

Teen Rivalry

According to the American Chicle Youth Poll, most teenagers have one brother and one sister. Only 8 per cent of teenagers have no brothers or sisters. But 12 per cent have three or more brothers and sisters.

So how do they get along with their brothers and sisters? Only 62 per cent of young people in the poll say they're happy with their relationships with their brothers and sisters. It's the area of home life they're least satisfied with.

About 40 per cent say getting along better with their brothers and sisters would improve their home life more than anything else. Only 15 per cent of teenagers say they can talk about their problems with their brothers. And only 19 per cent say they can talk about their problems with their sisters.

Some tension between brothers and sisters is normal. Relationships have been tough for a long time. **Genesis 25:19–34** describes fierce rivalry between Esau and Jacob. Read how it made life difficult for them.

* If someone asked Jacob and Esau to respond to a survey about relationships, what do you think the two of them would say?
* How is your relationship with your brother and/or sister like or unlike the relationship between Jacob and Esau? Which of the two brothers do you most closely identify with?

Consider . . .

* sending your brother or sister a note – through the post – giving a compliment for something he or she did recently.
* asking a trusted adult for some help with your family conflicts.

For more, see . . .

* Judges 9:1–6 (p.235)
* 1 John 3:11–18 (p.1374)
* Luke 10:38–42 (p.1058)

Naphish and Kedemah. [16]These were Ishmael's sons, and these are the names of the tribal leaders listed according to their settlements and camps. [17]Ishmael lived for 137 years and then breathed his last breath and died. [18]His descendants lived from Havilah to Shur, which is east of Egypt stretching towards Assyria. They often attacked the descendants of his brothers.

Isaac's Family

[19]This is the family history of Isaac. [20]When Abraham's son, Isaac, was 40 years old, he married Rebekah, who came from North West Mesopotamia. She was Bethuel's daughter and the sister of Laban the Aramean. [21]Isaac's wife could not have children, so Isaac prayed to the LORD for her. The LORD heard Isaac's prayer, and Rebekah became pregnant.

[22]While she was pregnant, the babies struggled inside her. She asked, "Why is this happening to me?" Then she went to get an answer from the LORD.

[23]The LORD said to her,

"Two nations are in your body,
    and two groups of people will be taken
        from you.
One group will be stronger than the other,
    and the older will serve the younger."

[24]When the time came, Rebekah gave birth to twins. [25]The first baby was born red. Since his skin was like a hairy robe, he was named Esau.[n] [26]When the second baby was born, he was holding on to Esau's heel, so that baby was named Jacob.[n] Isaac was 60 years old when they were born.

[27]When the boys grew up, Esau became a skilled hunter. He loved to be out in the fields. But Jacob was a quiet man and stayed among the tents. [28]Isaac loved Esau because he hunted the wild animals that Isaac enjoyed eating. But Rebekah loved Jacob.

[29]One day Jacob was boiling a pot of vegetable soup. Esau came in from hunting in the fields, weak from hunger. [30]So Esau said to Jacob, "Let me eat some of that red soup, because I am weak with hunger." (That is why people call him Edom.[n])

[31]But Jacob said, "You must sell me your rights as the firstborn son."[n]

[32]Esau said, "I am almost dead from hunger. If I die, all of my father's wealth will not help me."

[33]But Jacob said, "First, promise me that you will give it to me." So Esau made a promise to Jacob and sold his part of their father's wealth to Jacob. [34]Then Jacob gave Esau bread and vegetable soup, and he ate and drank, and then left. So Esau showed how little he cared about his rights as the firstborn son.

Isaac Lies to Abimelech

26 Now there was a time of hunger in the land, besides the time of hunger that happened during Abraham's life. So Isaac went to the town of Gerar to see Abimelech king of the Philistines. [2]The LORD appeared to Isaac and said, "Don't go down to Egypt, but live in the land where I tell you to live. [3]Stay in this land, and I will be with you and bless you. I will give you and your descendants[d] all these lands, and I will keep the oath I made to Abraham your father. [4]I will give you many descendants, as hard to count as the stars in the sky, and I will give them all these lands. Through your descendants all the nations on the earth will be blessed. [5]I will do this because your father Abraham obeyed me. He did what I said and obeyed my commands, my teachings and my rules."

[6]So Isaac stayed in Gerar. [7]His wife Rebekah was very beautiful, and the men of that place asked Isaac about her. Isaac said, "She is my sister," because he was afraid to tell them she was his wife. He thought they might kill him so they could have her.

[8]Isaac lived there a long time. One day as Abimelech king of the Philistines looked out of his window, he saw Isaac holding his wife Rebekah tenderly. [9]Abimelech called for Isaac and said, "This woman is your wife. Why did you say she was your sister?"

Isaac said to him, "I was afraid you would kill me so you could have her."

[10]Abimelech said, "What have you done to us? One of our men might have had sexual relations with your wife. Then we would have been guilty of a great sin."

[11]So Abimelech warned everyone, "Anyone who touches this man or his wife will be put to death."

Isaac Becomes Rich

[12]Isaac planted seed in that land, and that year he gathered a great harvest. The LORD blessed

Esau This name may mean "hairy".
Jacob This name sounds like the Hebrew word for "heel". "Holding on to someone's heel" is a Hebrew saying for tricking someone.
Edom This name sounds like the Hebrew word for "red".
rights . . . son Usually the firstborn son had a high rank in the family. The firstborn son usually became the new head of the family.

him very much, [13]and he became rich. He gathered more wealth until he became a very rich man. [14]He had so many slaves and flocks and herds that the Philistines envied him. [15]So they stopped up all the wells the servants of Isaac's father Abraham had dug. (They had dug them when Abraham was alive.) The Philistines filled those wells with earth. [16]And Abimelech said to Isaac, "Leave our country because you have become much more powerful than we are."

[17]So Isaac left that place and camped in the Valley of Gerar and lived there. [18]Long before this time Abraham had dug many wells, but after he died, the Philistines filled them with earth. So Isaac dug those wells again and gave them the same names his father had given them. [19]Isaac's servants dug a well in the valley, from which a spring of water flowed. [20]But the herdsmen of Gerar argued with them and said, "This water is ours." So Isaac named that well Argue because they argued with him. [21]Then his servants dug another well. When the people also argued about it, Isaac named that well Fight. [22]He moved from there and dug another well. No one argued about this one, so he named it Room Enough. Isaac said, "Now the LORD has made room for us, and we will be successful in this land."

[23]From there Isaac went to Beersheba. [24]The LORD appeared to him that night and said, "I am the God of your father Abraham. Don't be afraid, because I am with you. I will bless you and give you many descendants[d] because of my servant Abraham." [25]So Isaac built an altar and

HONESTY

Getting Away With It

In sixties America, when it came to selling a particular make of television called RCA, one shop excelled. Everyone in the country town where the store was based who owned a TV owned that brand. A huge RCA store in Chicago was so impressed they sent one of their chief salesmen to find out if they could learn anything from the owners of the store about how to sell TVs.

When he arrived at the store in the late morning the salesman couldn't see anyone there. The salesman noticed a sign that said, "If you see a TV you like, take it home and try it out." Another sign instructed people bringing in a TV for repair to write down what was wrong with it and put the paper on the TV. Another sign said, "If you brought your TV in for repair and you see it here, it is fixed. The repair cost is on the tag. Leave the money in the box."

About an hour later, a customer from the town walked into the store. The Chicago salesman asked the customer where the store owners were.

The man replied, "Oh, they're out harvesting wheat. They should be back by 8 or 9 p.m. to close the store for the night."

The salesman realised with sadness that this type of honesty and trust wouldn't work back in his big city store.

Read **Genesis 26:1–11**.

- The salesman, like Isaac, wanted to get the best out of the situation. Both of them learned the value of honesty. Have you ever had to learn the hard way that "honesty is the best policy"?
- Read the passage and consider what God's reaction to Isaac's dishonesty might have been?

Consider . . .

- talking to a parent or trusted adult friend about situations when you might be tempted not to be honest. Ask what he or she would do in that situation.
- starting an honesty piggy bank. Each time you are honest when it's tough, put in a pound. Every time you are dishonest or tell a lie, take out a pound. Try to improve your "bank balance".

For more, see . . .

- Genesis 20:1–13 (p.24)
- Acts 5:1–11 (p.1145)
- Proverbs 3:3–4 (p.592)

worshipped the LORD there. He also made a camp there, and his servants dug a well.

²⁶Abimelech came from Gerar to see Isaac. He brought with him Ahuzzath, who advised him, and Phicol, the commander of his army. ²⁷Isaac asked them, "Why have you come to see me? You were my enemy and forced me to leave your country."

²⁸They answered, "Now we know that the LORD is with you. Let us swear an oath to each other. Let us make an agreement with you ²⁹that since we did not hurt you, you will not hurt us. We were good to you and sent you away in peace. Now the LORD has blessed you."

³⁰So Isaac prepared food for them, and they all ate and drank. ³¹Early the next morning the men swore an oath to each other. Then Isaac sent them away, and they left in peace.

³²That day Isaac's servants came and told him about the well they had dug, saying, "We found water in that well." ³³So Isaac named it Shibah *n* and that city is called Beersheba even now.

³⁴When Esau was 40 years old, he married two Hittite women—Judith daughter of Beeri and Basemath daughter of Elon. ³⁵These women brought much sorrow to Isaac and Rebekah.

Jacob Tricks Isaac

27 When Isaac was old, his eyes were poor, so he could not see clearly. One day he called his older son Esau to him and said, "Son."

Esau answered, "Here I am."

²Isaac said, "I am old and don't know when I might die. ³So take your bow and arrows and go hunting in the field for an animal for me to eat. ⁴When you prepare the tasty food that I love, bring it to me, and I will eat. Then I will bless you before I die." ⁵So Esau went out in the field to hunt.

Rebekah was listening as Isaac said this to his son Esau. ⁶She said to her son Jacob, "Listen, I heard your father saying to your brother Esau, ⁷'Kill an animal and prepare some tasty food for me to eat. Then I will bless you in the presence of the LORD before I die.' ⁸So obey me, my son, and do what I tell you. ⁹Go out to our goats and bring me two of the best young ones. I will prepare them just the way your father likes them. ¹⁰Then you will take the food to your father, and he will bless you before he dies."

¹¹But Jacob said to his mother Rebekah, "My brother Esau is a hairy man, and I am smooth! ¹²If my father touches me, he will know I am not Esau. Then he will not bless me but will place a curse on me because I tried to trick him."

¹³So Rebekah said to him, "If your father puts a curse on you, I will accept the blame. Just do what I said and go, get the goats for me."

¹⁴So Jacob went out and got two goats and brought them to his mother, and she cooked them in the special way Isaac enjoyed. ¹⁵She took the best clothes of her older son Esau that were in the house and put them on the younger son Jacob. ¹⁶She also took the skins of the goats and put them on Jacob's hands and neck. ¹⁷Then she gave Jacob the tasty food and the bread she had made.

> **Sidelight**
>
> Jacob was the world's first con man. With some help from his mother, Rebekah, and with the aid of goat skins, he fooled his father, Isaac, into thinking he was the older brother, Esau (Genesis 27:14–29). By mistakenly blessing Jacob instead of Esau, Isaac fulfilled God's promise to Rebekah in Genesis 25:23 (p.30).

¹⁸Jacob went in to his father and said, "Father."

And his father said, "Yes, my son. Who are you?"

¹⁹Jacob said to him, "I am Esau, your first son. I have done what you told me. Now sit up and eat some meat of the animal I hunted for you. Then bless me."

²⁰But Isaac asked his son, "How did you find and kill the animal so quickly?"

Jacob answered, "Because the LORD your God helped me to find it."

²¹Then Isaac said to Jacob, "Come near so I can touch you, my son. Then I will know if you are really my son Esau."

²²So Jacob came near to Isaac his father. Isaac touched him and said, "Your voice sounds like Jacob's voice, but your hands are hairy like the hands of Esau." ²³Isaac did not know it was Jacob, because his hands were hairy like Esau's hands, so Isaac blessed him. ²⁴Isaac asked, "Are you really my son Esau?"

Jacob answered, "Yes, I am."

²⁵Then Isaac said, "Bring me the food, and I will eat it and bless you." So Jacob gave him the food, and he ate. Jacob gave him wine, and he drank. ²⁶Then Isaac said to him, "My son, come near and kiss me." ²⁷So Jacob went to his father and kissed him. When Isaac smelled Esau's clothes, he blessed him and said,

"The smell of my son
 is like the smell of the field
 that the LORD has blessed.
²⁸May God give you plenty of rain
 and good soil
 so that you will have plenty of grain and
 new wine.

Shibah   This name sounds like the Hebrew words for "seven" and "promise."

[29]May nations serve you
 and peoples bow down to you.
May you be master over your brothers,
 and may your mother's sons bow down
   to you.
May everyone who curses you be cursed,
 and may everyone who blesses you be
   blessed."

[30]Isaac finished blessing Jacob. Then, just as Jacob left his father Isaac, Esau came in from hunting. [31]He also prepared some tasty food and brought it to his father. He said, "Father, rise and eat the food that your son killed for you and then bless me."

[32]Isaac asked, "Who are you?"

He answered, "I am your son—your firstborn *d* son—Esau."

[33]Then Isaac trembled greatly and said, "Then who was it that hunted the animals and brought me food before you came? I ate it, and I blessed him, and it is too late now to take back my blessing."

[34]When Esau heard the words of his father, he let out a loud and bitter cry. He said to his father, "Bless me—me, too, my father!"

[35]But Isaac said, "Your brother came and tricked me. He has taken your blessing."

[36]Esau said, "Jacob *n* is the right name for him. He has tricked me these two times. He took away my share of everything you own, and now he has taken away my blessing." Then Esau asked, "Haven't you saved a blessing for me?"

[37]Isaac answered, "I gave Jacob the power to be master over you, and all his brothers will be his servants. And I kept him strong with grain and new wine. There is nothing left to give you, my son."

[38]But Esau continued, "Do you have only one blessing, Father? Bless me, too, Father!" Then Esau began to cry out loud.

[39]Isaac said to him,

"You will live far away from the best land,
 far from the rain.
[40]You will live by using your sword,
 and you will be a slave to your brother.
But when you struggle,
 you will break free from him."

[41]After that Esau hated Jacob because of the blessing from Isaac. He thought to himself, "My father will soon die, and I will be sad for him. Then I will kill Jacob."

[42]Rebekah heard about Esau's plan to kill Jacob. So she sent for Jacob and said to him, "Listen, your brother Esau is comforting himself by planning to kill you. [43]So, my son, do what I say. My brother Laban is living in Haran. Go to him

at once! [44]Stay with him for a while, until your brother is not so angry. [45]In time, your brother will not be angry, and he will forget what you did to him. Then I will send a servant to bring you back. I don't want to lose both of my sons on the same day."

[46]Then Rebekah said to Isaac, "I am tired of Hittite women. If Jacob marries one of these Hittite women here in this land, I want to die."

Jacob Searches for a Wife

28 Isaac called Jacob and blessed him and commanded him, "You must not marry a Canaanite woman. [2]Go to the house of Bethuel, your mother's father, in North West Mesopotamia. Laban, your mother's brother, lives there. Marry one of his daughters. [3]May God Almighty bless you and give you many children, and may you become a group of many peoples. [4]May he give you and your descendants *d* the blessing of Abraham so that you may own the land where you are now living as a stranger, the land God gave to Abraham." [5]So Isaac sent Jacob to North West Mesopotamia, to Laban the brother of Rebekah. Bethuel the Aramean was the father of Laban and Rebekah, and Rebekah was the mother of Jacob and Esau.

[6]Esau learned that Isaac had blessed Jacob and sent him to North West Mesopotamia to find a wife there. He also learned that Isaac had commanded Jacob not to marry a Canaanite woman [7]and that Jacob had obeyed his father and mother and had gone to North West Mesopotamia. [8]So Esau saw that his father Isaac did not want his sons to marry Canaanite women. [9]Now Esau already had wives, but he went to Ishmael son of Abraham and he married Mahalath, Ishmael's daughter. Mahalath was the sister of Nebaioth.

Jacob's Dream at Bethel

[10]Jacob left Beersheba and set out for Haran. [11]When he came to a place, he spent the night there because the sun had set. He found a stone and laid his head on it to go to sleep. [12]Jacob dreamed that there was a ladder resting on the earth and reaching up into heaven, and he saw angels of God going up and coming down the ladder. [13]Then Jacob saw the LORD standing above the ladder, and he said, "I am the LORD, the God of Abraham your grandfather, and the God of Isaac. I will give you and your descendants *d* the land on which you are now sleeping. [14]Your descendants will be as many as the dust of the earth. They will spread west and east, north and south, and all the families of the earth will be blessed through you and your descendants. [15]I am with

---

Jacob This name sounds like the Hebrew word for "heel". "Holding on to someone's heel" is a Hebrew saying for tricking someone.

you and will protect you everywhere you go and will bring you back to this land. I will not leave you until I have done what I have promised you."

[16]Then Jacob woke from his sleep and said, "Surely the LORD is in this place, but I did not know it." [17]He was afraid and said, "This place frightens me! It is surely the house of God and the gate of heaven."

[18]Jacob rose early in the morning and took the stone he had slept on and set it up on its end. Then he poured olive oil on the top of it. [19]At first, the name of that city was Luz, but Jacob named it Bethel. [n]

[20]Then Jacob made a promise. He said, "I want God to be with me and to protect me on this journey. I want him to give me food to eat and clothes to wear [21]so I will be able to return in peace to my father's house. If the LORD does these things, he will be my God. [22]This stone which I have set up on its end will be the house of God. And I will give God one-tenth of all he gives me."

Jacob Arrives in North West Mesopotamia

29 Then Jacob continued his journey and came to the land of the people of the East. [2]He looked and saw a well in the field and three flocks of sheep lying nearby, because they drank water from this well. A large stone covered the mouth of the well. [3]When all the flocks gathered there, the shepherds would roll the stone away from the well and water the sheep. Then they would put the stone back in its place.

[4]Jacob said to the shepherds there, "My brothers, where are you from?"

They answered, "We are from Haran."

[5]Then Jacob asked, "Do you know Laban, grandson of Nahor?"

They answered, "We know him."

[6]Then Jacob asked, "How is he?"

They answered, "He is well. Look, his daughter Rachel is coming now with his sheep."

[7]Jacob said, "But look, it is still the middle of the day. It is not time for the sheep to be gathered for the night, so give them water and let them go back into the pasture."

[8]But they said, "We cannot do that until all the flocks are gathered. Then we will roll away the stone from the mouth of the well and water the sheep."

[9]While Jacob was talking with the shepherds, Rachel came with her father's sheep, because it was her job to care for the sheep. [10]When Jacob saw Laban's daughter Rachel and Laban's sheep, he went to the well and rolled the stone from its mouth and watered Laban's sheep. Now Laban

was the brother of Rebekah, Jacob's mother. [11]Then Jacob kissed Rachel and cried. [12]He told her that he was from her father's family and that he was the son of Rebekah. So Rachel ran home and told her father.

[13]When Laban heard the news about his sister's son Jacob, he ran to meet him. Laban hugged him and kissed him and brought him to his house, where Jacob told Laban everything that had happened.

[14]Then Laban said, "You are my own flesh and blood."

Jacob is Tricked

Jacob stayed there a month. [15]Then Laban said to Jacob, "You are my relative, but it is not right for you to work for me without pay. What would you like me to pay you?"

[16]Now Laban had two daughters. The older was Leah, and the younger was Rachel. [17]Leah had weak eyes, but Rachel was very beautiful. [18]Jacob loved Rachel, so he said to Laban, "Let me marry your younger daughter Rachel. If you will, I will work seven years for you."

[19]Laban said, "It would be better for her to marry you than someone else, so stay here with me." [20]So Jacob worked for Laban seven years so he could marry Rachel. But they seemed like just a few days to him because he loved Rachel very much.

[21]After seven years Jacob said to Laban, "Give me Rachel so that I may marry her. The time I promised to work for you is over."

[22]So Laban gave a feast for all the people there. [23]That evening he brought his daughter Leah to Jacob, and they had sexual relations. [24](Laban gave his slave girl Zilpah to his daughter to be her servant.) [25]In the morning when Jacob saw that he had had sexual relations with Leah, he said to Laban, "What have you done to me? I worked hard for you so that I could marry Rachel! Why did you trick me?"

[26]Laban said, "In our country we do not allow the younger daughter to marry before the older daughter. [27]But complete the full week of the

---

Sidelight   If you think it's hard to go out with the right boy or girl, imagine how Jacob felt. He worked for seven years to marry Rachel, only to be tricked into marrying her "weak-eyed" sister Leah. Then Jacob was given Rachel too, but he had to work for seven more years (Genesis 29:16–30). Jacob might have been fooled because the bride was brought to the wedding festivities wearing a veil.

Bethel   This name means "house of God".

marriage ceremony with Leah, and I will give you Rachel to marry also. But you must serve me another seven years."

[28]So Jacob did this, and when he had completed the week with Leah, Laban gave him his daughter Rachel as a wife. [29](Laban gave his slave girl Bilhah to his daughter Rachel to be her servant.) [30]So Jacob had sexual relations with Rachel also, and Jacob loved Rachel more than Leah. Jacob worked for Laban for another seven years.

Jacob's Family Grows

[31]When the LORD saw that Jacob loved Rachel more than Leah, he made it possible for Leah to have children, but not Rachel. [32]Leah became pregnant and gave birth to a son. She named him Reuben, [n] because she said, "The LORD has seen my troubles. Surely now my husband will love me."

[33]Leah became pregnant again and gave birth to another son. She named him Simeon [n] and said, "The LORD has heard that I am not loved, so he has given me this son."

[34]Leah became pregnant again and gave birth to another son. She named him Levi [n] and said, "Now, surely my husband will be close to me, because I have given him three sons."

[35]Then Leah gave birth to another son. She named him Judah, [n] because she said, "Now I will praise the LORD." Then Leah stopped having children.

30 When Rachel saw that she was not having children for Jacob, she envied her sister Leah. She said to Jacob, "Give me children, or I'll die!"

[2]Jacob became angry with her and said, "Can I do what only God can do? He is the one who has kept you from having children."

[3]Then Rachel said, "Here is my slave girl Bilhah. Have sexual relations with her so she can give birth to a child for me. Then I can have my own family through her."

[4]So Rachel gave Bilhah, her slave girl, to Jacob as a wife, and he had sexual relations with her. [5]She became pregnant and gave Jacob a son. [6]Rachel said, "God has judged me innocent. He has listened to my prayer and has given me a son," so she named him Dan. [n]

[7]Bilhah became pregnant again and gave Jacob a second son. [8]Rachel said, "I have struggled hard with my sister, and I have won." So she named that son Naphtali. [n]

[9]Leah saw that she had stopped having children, so she gave her slave girl Zilpah to Jacob as a wife. [10]When Zilpah had a son, [11]Leah said, "I am lucky," so she named him Gad. [n] [12]Zilpah gave birth to another son, [13]and Leah said, "I am very happy! Now women will call me happy," so she named him Asher. [n]

[14]During the wheat harvest Reuben went into the field and found some mandrake [n] plants and brought them to his mother Leah. But Rachel said to Leah, "Please give me some of your son's mandrakes."

[15]Leah answered, "You have already taken away my husband, and now you are trying to take away my son's mandrakes."

But Rachel answered, "If you will give me your son's mandrakes, you may sleep with Jacob tonight."

[16]When Jacob came in from the field that night, Leah went out to meet him. She said, "You will have sexual relations with me tonight because I have paid for you with my son's mandrakes." So Jacob slept with her that night.

[17]Then God answered Leah's prayer, and she became pregnant again. She gave birth to a fifth son [18]and said, "God has given me what I paid for, because I gave my slave girl to my husband." So Leah named her son Issachar. [n]

[19]Leah became pregnant again and gave birth to a sixth son. [20]She said, "God has given me a fine gift. Now surely Jacob will honour me, because I have given him six sons," so she named him Zebulun. [n]

[21]Later Leah gave birth to a daughter and named her Dinah.

[22]Then God remembered Rachel and answered her prayer, making it possible for her to have children. [23]When she became pregnant and gave birth to a son, she said, "God has taken away my shame," [24]and she named him Joseph. [n] Rachel said, "I wish the LORD would give me another son."

Reuben   This name sounds like the Hebrew word for "he has seen my troubles".
Simeon   This name sounds like the Hebrew word for "has heard".
Levi   This name sounds like the Hebrew word for "be close to".
Judah   This name sounds like the Hebrew word for "praise".
Dan   This name means "he has judged".
Naphtali   This name sounds like the Hebrew word for "my struggle".
Gad   This name may mean "lucky".
Asher   This name may mean "happy".
mandrake   A plant which was believed to cause a woman to become pregnant.
Issachar   This name sounds like the Hebrew word for "paid for".
Zebulun   This name sounds like the Hebrew word for "honour".
Joseph   This name sounds like the Hebrew word for "he adds".

Jacob Tricks Laban

25After the birth of Joseph, Jacob said to Laban, "Now let me go to my own home and country. 26Give me my wives and my children and let me go. I have earned them by working for you, and you know that I have served you well."

27Laban said to him, "If I have pleased you, please stay. I know the LORD has blessed me because of you. 28Tell me what I should pay you, and I will give it to you."

29Jacob answered, "You know that I have worked hard for you, and your flocks have grown while I cared for them. 30When I came, you had little, but now you have much. Every time I did something for you, the LORD blessed you. But when will I be able to do something for my own family?"

31Laban asked, "Then what should I give you?"

Jacob answered, "I don't want you to give me anything. Just do this one thing, and I will come back and take care of your flocks. 32Today let me go through all your flocks. I will take every speckled or spotted sheep, every black lamb and every spotted or speckled goat. That will be my pay. 33In the future you can easily see if I am honest. When you come to look at my flocks, if I have any goat that isn't speckled or spotted or any lamb that isn't black, you will know I stole it."

34Laban answered, "Agreed! We will do what you ask." 35But that day Laban took away all the male goats that had streaks or spots, all the speckled and spotted female goats (all those that had white on them), and all the black sheep. He told his sons to watch over them. 36Then he took these animals to a place that was three days' journey away from Jacob. Jacob took care of all the flocks that were left.

37So Jacob cut green branches from poplar, almond and plane trees, and peeled off some of the bark so that the branches had white stripes on them. 38He put the branches in front of the flocks at the watering places. When the animals came to drink, they also mated there, 39so the flocks mated in front of the branches. Then the young that were born were streaked, speckled or spotted. 40Jacob separated the young animals from the others, and he made them face the streaked and dark animals in Laban's flock. Jacob kept his animals separate from Laban's. 41When the stronger animals in the flock were mating, Jacob put the branches before their eyes so they would mate near the branches. 42But when the weaker animals mated, Jacob did not put the branches there. So the animals born from the weaker animals were Laban's, and those born from the stronger animals were Jacob's. 43In this way

Jacob became very rich. He had large flocks, many male and female servants, camels and donkeys.

Jacob Runs Away

31 One day Jacob heard Laban's sons talking. They said, "Jacob has taken everything our father owned, and in this way he has become rich." 2Then Jacob noticed that Laban was not as friendly as he had been before. 3The LORD said to Jacob, "Go back to the land where your ancestors lived, and I will be with you."

4So Jacob told Rachel and Leah to meet him in the field where he kept his flocks. 5He said to them, "I have seen that your father is not as friendly with me as he used to be, but the God of my father has been with me. 6You both know that I have worked as hard as I could for your father, 7but he cheated me and changed my pay ten times. But God has not allowed your father to harm me. 8When Laban said, 'You can have all the speckled animals as your pay,' all the animals gave birth to speckled young ones. But when he said, 'You can have all the streaked animals as your pay,' all the flocks gave birth to streaked babies. 9So God has taken the animals away from your father and has given them to me.

10"I had a dream during the season when the flocks were mating. I saw that the only male goats who were mating were streaked, speckled or spotted. 11The angel of God spoke to me in that dream and said, 'Jacob!' I answered, 'Yes!' 12The angel said, 'Look! Only the streaked, speckled or spotted male goats are mating. I have seen all the wrong things Laban has been doing to you. 13I am the God who appeared to you at Bethel, where you poured olive oil on the stone you set up on end and where you made a promise to me. Now I want you to leave here and go back to the land where you were born.' "

14Rachel and Leah answered Jacob, "Our father has nothing to give us when he dies. 15He has treated us like strangers. He sold us to you, and then he spent all of the money you paid for us. 16God took all this wealth from our father, and now it belongs to us and our children. So do whatever God has told you to do."

17So Jacob put his children and his wives on camels, 18and they began their journey back to Isaac, his father, in the land of Canaan. All the flocks of animals that Jacob owned walked ahead of them. He carried everything with him that he had gained while he lived in North West Mesopotamia.

19While Laban was gone to cut the wool from his sheep, Rachel stole the idols that belonged to him. 20And Jacob tricked Laban the Aramean by not telling him he was leaving. 21Jacob and his family left quickly, crossed the Euphrates

River, and travelled towards the mountains of Gilead.

[22] Three days later Laban learned that Jacob had run away, [23]so he gathered his relatives and began to chase him. After seven days Laban found him in the mountains of Gilead. [24]That night God came to Laban the Aramean in a dream and said, "Be careful! Do not say anything to Jacob, good or bad."

The Search for the Stolen Idols

[25]So Laban caught up with Jacob. Now Jacob had made his camp in the mountains, so Laban and his relatives set up their camp in the mountains of Gilead. [26]Laban said to Jacob, "What have you done? You cheated me and took my daughters as if you had captured them in a war. [27]Why did you run away secretly and trick me? Why didn't you tell me? Then I could have sent you away with joy and singing and with the music of tambourines [d] and harps. [28]You did not even let me kiss my grandchildren and my daughters goodbye. You were very foolish to do this! [29]I have the power to harm you, but last night the God of your father spoke to me and warned me not to say anything to you, good or bad. [30]I know you want to go back to your home, but why did you steal my idols?"

[31]Jacob answered Laban, "I left without telling you because I was afraid you would take your daughters away from me. [32]If you find anyone here who has taken your idols, that person will be killed! Your relatives will be my witnesses. You may look for anything that belongs to you and take anything that is yours." (Now Jacob did not know that Rachel had stolen Laban's idols.)

[33]So Laban looked in Jacob's tent, in Leah's tent, and in the tent where the two slave women stayed, but he did not find his idols. When he left Leah's tent, he went into Rachel's tent. [34]Rachel had hidden the idols inside her camel's saddle and was sitting on them. Although Laban looked through the whole tent, he did not find them.

[35]Rachel said to her father, "Father, don't be angry with me. I am not able to stand up before you because I am having my monthly period." So Laban looked through the camp, but he did not find his idols.

[36]Then Jacob became very angry and said, "What wrong have I done? What law have I broken to cause you to chase me? [37]You have looked through everything I own, but you have found nothing that belongs to you. If you have found anything, show it to everyone. Put it in front of your relatives and my relatives, and let them decide which one of us is right. [38]I have worked for you now for 20 years. During all that time none

of the lambs and kids died during birth, and I have not eaten any of the rams from your flocks. [39]Any time an animal was killed by wild beasts, I did not bring it to you, but made up for the loss myself. You made me pay for any animal that was stolen during the day or night. [40]In the daytime the sun took away my strength, and at night I was cold and could not sleep. [41]I worked like a slave for you for 20 years—the first fourteen to get your two daughters and the last six to earn your flocks. During that time you changed my pay ten times. [42]But the God of my father, the God of Abraham and the God of Isaac, was with me. Otherwise, you would have sent me away with nothing. But he saw the trouble I had and the hard work I did, and last night he corrected you."

Jacob and Laban's Agreement

[43]Laban said to Jacob, "These girls are my daughters. Their children belong to me, and these flocks are mine. Everything you see here belongs to me, but I can do nothing to keep my daughters and their children. [44]Let us make an agreement, and let us set up a pile of stones to remind us of it."

[45]So Jacob took a large rock and set it up on its end. [46]He told his relatives to gather rocks, so they took the rocks and piled them up; then they ate beside the pile. [47]Laban named that place in his language A Pile to Remind Us, and Jacob gave the place the same name in Hebrew.

[48]Laban said to Jacob, "This pile of rocks will remind us of the agreement between us." That is why the place was called A Pile to Remind Us. [49]It was also called Mizpah, [n] because Laban said, "Let the LORD watch over us while we are separated from each other. [50]Remember that God is our witness even if no one else is around us. He will know if you harm my daughters or marry other women. [51]Here is the pile of rocks that I have put between us and here is the rock I set up on end. [52]This pile of rocks and this rock set on end will remind us of our agreement. I will never go past this pile to hurt you, and you must never come to my side of them to hurt me. [53]Let the God of Abraham, who is the God of Nahor and the God of their fathers, punish either of us if we break this agreement."

So Jacob made a promise in the name of the God whom his father Isaac worshipped. [54]Then Jacob killed an animal and offered it as a sacrifice on the mountain, and he invited his relatives to share in the meal. After they finished eating, they spent the night on the mountain. [55]Early the next morning Laban kissed his grandchildren and his daughters and blessed them, and then he left to return home.

Mizpah   This name sounds like the Hebrew word for "watch".

Jacob Meets Esau

32 When Jacob also went his way, the angels of God met him. [2]When he saw them, he said, "This is the camp of God!" So he named that place Mahanaim. *n*

[3]Jacob's brother Esau was living in the area called Seir in the country of Edom. Jacob sent messengers to Esau, [4]telling them, "Give this message to my master Esau: 'This is what Jacob, your servant, says: I have lived with Laban and have remained there until now. [5]I have cattle, donkeys, flocks and male and female servants. I send this message to you and ask you to accept us.'"

[6]The messengers returned to Jacob and said, "We went to your brother Esau. He is coming to meet you and has 400 men with him."

[7]Then Jacob was very afraid and worried. He divided the people who were with him and all the flocks, herds and camels into two camps. [8]Jacob thought, "Esau might come and destroy one camp, but the other camp can run away and be saved."

[9]Then Jacob said, "God of my father Abraham! God of my father Isaac! LORD, you told me to return to my country and my family. You said that you would treat me well. [10]I am not worthy of the kindness and continual goodness you have shown me. The first time I travelled across the Jordan River, I had only my walking stick, but now I own enough to have two camps. [11]Please save me from my brother Esau. I am afraid he will come and kill all of us, even the mothers with the children. [12]You said to me, 'I will treat you well

Mahanaim This name means "two camps".

SPIRITUAL GROWTH

Smackdown: Wrestling With God

Steve's relationship with his parents wasn't always plain sailing during his teenage years, but now in his twenties it was good. Then one Sunday afternoon the phone rang and everything changed. It was Steve's brother: "It's Mum . . . she collapsed and has been rushed to hospital."

The next day, Steve drove to the hospital thinking he'd do his sonly duty, give the obligatory bunch of flowers and then tomorrow she'll be home. But something was wrong. Steve's mum grabbed his arm and said with tears in her eyes, "I want you to know that I love you very much . . . they've found out I've got an aneurysm, and I could die unless I have a brain operation tomorrow . . . and even then, the operation's really risky and there's a good chance I won't make it."

Steve's mind flooded with a million questions and fears. In tears, Steve cried out to God in prayer all night. He finally reached the point where he could leave it all in the Lord's hands and say, "Lord, even if you allow her to die, I'll still trust you."

The operation was a success. Thanks to God, after a long recovery period, she left hospital and life continued as it always had, only somehow better. Steve was now able to comfort others going through similar situations, as he understood their heartache.

In **Genesis 32:22–32** we read about how God took hold of Jacob and wrestled with him, reminding him that his life was in God's hands and not his own.

- Why did God pick a wrestling match with Jacob and then let him win?
- Some people say that it is never God's will for his people to be ill, or have struggles, or pain, or poverty. How does this passage show that isn't true?

Consider . . .

- whether you are persistent in prayer or give up too easily if nothing seems to be happening? Maybe God wants you to patiently keep praying, in order to develop your faith.
- making a list of any tough times you've had recently. Now think how God may have used them to make you stronger and trust him more.

For more, see . . .

- Job 1:8–22 (p.469)
- Philippians 3:7–16 (p.1283)
- Romans 8:18–28 (p.1195)
- James 1:2–8 (p.1348)

and will make your children as many as the sand of the seashore. There will be too many to count.' "

[13]Jacob stayed there for the night and prepared a gift for Esau from what he had with him: [14]200 female goats and 20 male goats, 200 female sheep and 20 rams, [15]30 female camels and their young, 40 cows and 10 bulls, 20 female donkeys and 10 male donkeys. [16]Jacob gave each separate flock of animals to one of his servants and said to them, "Go ahead of me and keep some space between each herd." [17]Jacob gave them their orders. To the servant with the first group of animals he said, "My brother Esau will come to you and ask, 'Whose servant are you? Where are you going and whose animals are these?' [18]Then you will answer, 'They belong to your servant Jacob. He sent them as a gift to you, my master Esau, and he also is coming behind us.' "

[19]Jacob ordered the second servant, the third servant, and all the other servants to do the same thing. He said, "Say the same thing to Esau when you meet him. [20]Say, 'Your servant Jacob is coming behind us.' " Jacob thought, "If I send these gifts ahead of me, maybe Esau will forgive me. Then when I see him, perhaps he will accept me." [21]So Jacob sent the gifts to Esau, but he himself stayed that night in the camp.

Jacob Wrestles with God

[22]During the night Jacob rose and crossed the Jabbok River at the crossing, taking with him his two wives, his two slave girls and his eleven sons. [23]He sent his family and everything he had across the river. [24]So Jacob was alone, and a man came and wrestled with him until the sun came up. [25]When the man saw he could not defeat Jacob, he struck Jacob's hip and put it out of joint. [26]Then he said to Jacob, "Let me go. The sun is coming up."

But Jacob said, "I will let you go if you will bless me."

[27]The man said to him, "What is your name?"

And he answered, "Jacob."

[28]Then the man said, "Your name will no longer be Jacob. Your name will now be Israel, [n] because you have wrestled with God and with people, and you have won."

[29]Then Jacob asked him, "Please tell me your name."

But the man said, "Why do you ask my name?" Then he blessed Jacob there.

[30]So Jacob named that place Peniel, [n] saying, "I have seen God face to face, but my life was saved." [31]Then the sun rose as he was leaving

that place, and Jacob was limping because of his leg. [32]So even today the people of Israel do not eat the muscle that is on the hip joint of animals, because Jacob was touched there.

> **Sidelight**   The first wrestling match in the Bible was more than a three-minute bout. It lasted all night. Jacob's opponent had supernatural strength, but Jacob still finished the fight undefeated – although he did sustain a sports-related injury and was given a fighter's name, Israel, which means "he wrestles with God" (Genesis 32:22–32).

Jacob Shows His Bravery

33 Jacob looked up and saw Esau coming, and with him were 400 men. So Jacob divided his children among Leah, Rachel and the two slave girls. [2]Jacob put the slave girls with their children first, then Leah and her children behind them, and Rachel and Joseph last. [3]Jacob himself went out in front of them and bowed down flat on the ground seven times as he was walking towards his brother.

[4]But Esau ran to meet Jacob and put his arms around him and hugged him. Then Esau kissed him, and they both cried. [5]When Esau looked up and saw the women and children, he asked, "Who are these people with you?"

Jacob answered, "These are the children God has given me. God has been good to me, your servant."

[6]Then the two slave girls and their children came up to Esau and bowed down flat on the earth before him. [7]Leah and her children also came up to Esau and also bowed down flat on the earth. Last of all, Joseph and Rachel came up to Esau, and they, too, bowed down flat before him.

[8]Esau said, "I saw many herds as I was coming here. Why did you bring them?"

Jacob answered, "They were to please you, my master."

[9]But Esau said, "I already have enough, my brother. Keep what you have."

[10]Jacob said, "No! Please! If I have pleased you, then accept the gift I give you. I am very happy to see your face again. It is like seeing the face of God, because you have accepted me. [11]So I beg you to accept the gift I give you. God has been very good to me, and I have more than I need." And because Jacob begged, Esau accepted the gift.

Israel This name means "he wrestles with God".
Peniel This name means "the face of God".

[12]Then Esau said, "Let us be going. I will travel with you."

[13]But Jacob said to him, "My master, you know that the children are weak. And I must be careful with my flocks and their young ones. If I force them to go too far in one day, all the animals will die. [14]So, my master, you go on ahead of me, your servant. I will follow you slowly and let the animals and the children set the speed at which we travel. I will meet you, my master, in Edom."

[15]So Esau said, "Then let me leave some of my people with you."

"No, thank you," said Jacob. "I only want to please you, my master." [16]So that day Esau started back to Edom. [17]But Jacob went to Succoth, where he built a house for himself and shelters for his animals. That is why the place was named Succoth. [n]

[18]Jacob left North West Mesopotamia and arrived safely at the city of Shechem in the land of Canaan. There he camped east of the city. [19]He bought a part of the field where he had camped from the sons of Hamor, father of Shechem, for 100 pieces of silver. [20]He built an altar there and named it after God, the God of Israel.

Dinah is Attacked

34 At this time Dinah, the daughter of Leah and Jacob, went out to visit the women of the land. [2]When Shechem, son of Hamor the Hivite, the ruler of the land, saw her, he took her and forced her to have sexual relations with him. [3]Shechem fell in love with Dinah, and he spoke kindly to her. [4]He told his father, Hamor, "Please get this girl for me so I can marry her."

[5]Jacob learned how Shechem had disgraced his daughter, but since his sons were out in the field with the cattle, Jacob said nothing until they came home. [6]While he waited, Hamor, father of Shechem, went to talk with Jacob.

[7]When Jacob's sons heard what had happened, they came in from the field. They were very angry that Shechem had done such a wicked thing to Israel. It was wrong for him to have sexual relations with Jacob's daughter; a thing like this should not be done.

[8]But Hamor talked to Dinah's brothers and said, "My son Shechem is deeply in love with Dinah. Please let him marry her. [9]Marry our people. Give your women to our men as wives and take our women for your men as wives. [10]You can live in the same land with us. You will be free to own land and to trade here."

[11]Shechem also talked to Jacob and to Dinah's brothers and said, "Please accept my offer. I will give anything you ask. [12]Ask as much as you want for the payment for the bride, and I will give it to you. Just let me marry Dinah."

[13]Jacob's sons answered Shechem and his father with lies, because Shechem had disgraced their sister Dinah. [14]The brothers said to them, "We cannot allow you to marry our sister, because you are not circumcised. [d] That would be a disgrace to us. [15]But we will allow you to marry her if you do this one thing: every man in your town must be circumcised like us. [16]Then your men can marry our women, and our men can marry your women, and we will live in your land and become one people. [17]If you refuse to be circumcised, we will take Dinah and leave."

[18]What they asked seemed fair to Hamor and Shechem. [19]So Shechem quickly went to be circumcised because he loved Jacob's daughter.

Now Shechem was the most respected man in his family. [20]So Hamor and Shechem went to the gate of their city and spoke to the men of their city, saying, [21]"These people want to be friends with us. So let them live in our land and trade here. There is enough land for all of us. Let us marry their women, and we can let them marry our women. [22]But we must agree to one thing: all our men must be circumcised as they are. Then they will agree to live in our land, and we will be one people. [23]If we do this, their cattle and their animals will belong to us. Let us do what they say, and they will stay in our land." [24]All the people who had come to the city gate heard this. They agreed with Hamor and Shechem and every man was circumcised.

[25]Three days later the men who were circumcised were still in pain. Two of Jacob's sons, Simeon and Levi (Dinah's brothers), took their swords and made a surprise attack on the city, killing all the men there. [26]They killed Hamor and his son Shechem and then took Dinah out of Shechem's house and left. [27]Jacob's sons came upon the dead bodies and stole everything that was in the city, to pay them back for what Shechem had done to their sister. [28]So the brothers took the flocks, herds and donkeys, and everything in city and in the fields. [29]They took every valuable thing the people owned, even their wives and children and everything in the houses.

[30]Then Jacob said to Simeon and Levi, "You have caused me a lot of trouble. Now the Canaanites and the Perizzites who live in the land will hate me. Since there are only a few of us, if they join together to attack us, my people and I will be destroyed."

[31]But the brothers said, "We will not allow our sister to be treated like a prostitute." [d]

Succoth   This name means "shelters".

Jacob in Bethel

35 God said to Jacob, "Go to the city of Bethel and live there. Make an altar to the God who appeared to you there when you were running away from your brother Esau."

2So Jacob said to his family and to all who were with him, "Put away the foreign gods you have, and make yourselves clean, *d* and change your clothes. 3We will leave here and go to Bethel. There I will build an altar to God, who has helped me during my time of trouble. He has been with me everywhere I have gone." 4So they gave Jacob all the foreign gods they had, and the earrings they were wearing, and he hid them under the great tree near the town of Shechem. 5Then Jacob and his sons left there. But God caused the people in the nearby cities to be afraid, so they did not follow them. 6And Jacob and all the people who were with him went to Luz, which is now called Bethel, in the land of Canaan. 7There Jacob built an altar and named the place Bethel, after God, because God had appeared to him there when he was running from his brother.

8Deborah, Rebekah's nurse, died and was buried under the oak tree at Bethel, so they named that place Oak of Crying.

Jacob's New Name

9When Jacob came back from North West Mesopotamia, God appeared to him again and blessed him. 10God said to him, "Your name is Jacob, but you will not be called Jacob any longer. Your new name will be Israel." So he called him Israel. 11God said to him, "I am God Almighty. Have many children and grow in number as a nation. You will be the ancestor of many nations and kings. 12The same land I gave to Abraham and Isaac I will give to you and your descendants." *d* 13Then God left him. 14Jacob set up a stone on edge in that place where God had talked to him, and he poured a drink offering and olive oil on it to make it special for God. 15And Jacob named the place Bethel.

Rachel Dies Giving Birth

16Jacob and his group left Bethel. Before they came to Ephrath, Rachel began giving birth to her baby, 17but she was having much trouble. When Rachel's nurse saw this, she said, "Don't be afraid, Rachel. You are giving birth to another son." 18Rachel gave birth to the son, but she herself died. As she lay dying, she named the boy Son of My Suffering, but Jacob called him Benjamin. *n*

19Rachel was buried on the road to Ephrath, a district of Bethlehem, 20and Jacob set up a rock on her grave to honour her. That rock is still there. 21Then Israel *n* continued his journey and camped just south of Migdal Eder.

22While Israel was there, Reuben had sexual relations with Israel's slave woman *d* Bilhah and Israel heard about it.

The Family of Israel

Jacob had twelve sons. 23He had six sons by his wife Leah: Reuben, his first son, then Simeon, Levi, Judah, Issachar and Zebulun.

24He had two sons by his wife Rachel: Joseph and Benjamin.

25He had two sons by Rachel's slave girl Bilhah: Dan and Naphtali.

26And he had two sons by Leah's slave girl Zilpah: Gad and Asher.

These are Jacob's sons who were born in North West Mesopotamia.

27Jacob went to his father Isaac at Mamre near Hebron, where Abraham and Isaac had lived. 28Isaac lived for 180 years. 29So Isaac breathed his last breath and died when he was very old, and his sons Esau and Jacob buried him.

Esau's Family

36 This is the family history of Esau (also called Edom).

2Esau married women from the land of Canaan: Adah daughter of Elon the Hittite; and Oholibamah daughter of Anah, the son of Zibeon the Hivite; 3and Basemath, Ishmael's daughter, the sister of Nebaioth.

4Adah gave birth to Eliphaz for Esau. Basemath gave him Reuel, 5and Oholibamah gave him Jeush, Jalam and Korah. These were Esau's sons who were born in the land of Canaan.

6Esau took his wives, his sons, his daughters and all the people who lived with him, his herds and other animals and all the belongings he had gained in Canaan, and he went to a land away from his brother Jacob. 7Esau's and Jacob's belongings were becoming too many for them to live in the same land. The land where they had lived could not support both of them, because they had too many herds. 8So Esau lived in the mountains of Edom. (Esau is also named Edom.)

Benjamin This name means "right-hand son" or "favourite son".
Israel Also called Jacob.

⁹This is the family history of Esau. He is the ancestor of the Edomites, who live in the mountains of Edom.

¹⁰Esau's sons were Eliphaz, son of Adah and Esau, and Reuel, son of Basemath and Esau. ¹¹Eliphaz had five sons: Teman, Omar, Zepho, Gatam and Kenaz. ¹²Eliphaz also had a slave woman *d* named Timna, and Timna and Eliphaz gave birth to Amalek. These were Esau's grandsons by his wife Adah.

¹³Reuel had four sons: Nahath, Zerah, Shammah and Mizzah. These were Esau's grandsons by his wife Basemath.

¹⁴Esau's third wife was Oholibamah the daughter of Anah. (Anah was the son of Zibeon.) Esau and Oholibamah gave birth to Jeush, Jalam and Korah.

¹⁵These were the leaders that came from Esau: Esau's first son was Eliphaz. From him came these leaders: Teman, Omar, Zepho, Kenaz, ¹⁶Korah, Gatam and Amalek. These were the leaders that came from Eliphaz in the land of Edom. They were the grandsons of Adah.

¹⁷Esau's son Reuel was the father of these leaders: Nahath, Zerah, Shammah and Mizzah. These were the leaders that came from Reuel in the land of Edom. They were the grandsons of Esau's wife Basemath.

¹⁸Esau's wife Oholibamah gave birth to these leaders: Jeush, Jalam and Korah. These are the leaders that came from Esau's wife Oholibamah the daughter of Anah. ¹⁹These were the sons of Esau (also called Edom), and these were their leaders.

²⁰These were the sons of Seir the Horite, who were living in the land: Lotan, Shobal, Zibeon, Anah, ²¹Dishon, Ezer and Dishan. These sons of Seir were the leaders of the Horites in Edom.

²²The sons of Lotan were Hori and Homam. (Timna was Lotan's sister.)

²³The sons of Shobal were Alvan, Manahath, Ebal, Shepho and Onam.

²⁴The sons of Zibeon were Aiah and Anah. Anah is the man who found the hot springs in the desert while he was caring for his father's donkeys.

²⁵The children of Anah were Dishon and Oholibamah, daughter of Anah.

²⁶The sons of Dishon were Hemdan, Eshban, Ithran and Keran.

²⁷The sons of Ezer were Bilhan, Zaavan and Akan.

²⁸The sons of Dishan were Uz and Aran.

²⁹These were the names of the Horite leaders: Lotan, Shobal, Zibeon, Anah, ³⁰Dishon, Ezer and Dishan.

These men were the leaders of the Horite families who lived in the land of Edom.

³¹These are the kings who ruled in the land of Edom before the Israelites ever had a king:

³²Bela son of Beor was the king of Edom. He came from the city of Dinhabah.

³³When Bela died, Jobab son of Zerah became king. Jobab was from Bozrah.

³⁴When Jobab died, Husham became king. He was from the land of the Temanites.

³⁵When Husham died, Hadad son of Bedad, who had defeated Midian in the country of Moab, became king. Hadad was from the city of Avith.

³⁶When Hadad died, Samlah became king. He was from Masrekah.

³⁷When Samlah died, Shaul became king. He was from Rehoboth on the Euphrates River.

³⁸When Shaul died, Baal-Hanan son of Acbor became king.

³⁹When Baal-Hanan son of Acbor died, Hadad became king. He was from the city of Pau. His wife's name was Mehetabel, daughter of Matred, who was the daughter of Me-Zahab.

⁴⁰These Edomite leaders, listed by their families and regions, came from Esau. Their names were Timna, Alvah, Jetheth, ⁴¹Oholibamah, Elah, Pinon, ⁴²Kenaz, Teman, Mibzar, ⁴³Magdiel and Iram. They were the leaders of Edom. (Esau was the father of the Edomites.) The area where each of these families lived was named after that family.

Joseph the Dreamer

37 Jacob lived in the land of Canaan, where his father had lived. ²This is the family history of Jacob:

Joseph was a young man, seventeen years old. He and his brothers, the sons of Bilhah and Zilpah, his father's wives, cared for the flocks. Joseph gave his father bad reports about his brothers. ³Since Joseph was born when his father Israel *n* was old, Israel loved him more than his other sons. He made Joseph a special robe with long sleeves. ⁴When Joseph's brothers saw that their father loved him more than he loved them, they hated their brother and could not speak to him politely.

⁵One time Joseph had a dream, and when he told his brothers about it, they hated him even more. ⁶Joseph said, "Listen to the dream I had. ⁷We were in the field tying bundles of wheat together. My bundle stood up, and your bundles of wheat gathered around it and bowed down to it."

⁸His brothers said, "Do you really think you will be king over us? Do you truly think you will rule over us?" His brothers hated him even more because of his dreams and what he had said.

Israel Also called Jacob.

[9]Then Joseph had another dream, and he told his brothers about it also. He said, "Listen, I had another dream. I saw the sun, moon and eleven stars bowing down to me."

[10]Joseph also told his father about this dream, but his father scolded him, saying, "What kind of dream is this? Do you really believe that your mother, your brothers and I will bow down to you?" [11]Joseph's brothers were jealous of him, but his father thought about what all these things could mean.

[12]One day Joseph's brothers went to Shechem to herd their father's flocks. [13]Israel said to Joseph, "Go to Shechem where your brothers are herding the flocks."

Joseph answered, "I will go."

[14]His father said, "Go and see if your brothers and the flocks are all right. Then come back and tell me." So Joseph's father sent him from the Valley of Hebron.

When Joseph came to Shechem, [15]a man found him wandering in the field and asked him, "What are you looking for?"

FAMILY

Family Feud

Another fight was brewing between Hannah and her sister. Usually Hannah was home from college for an hour or so before the anger boiled over. This time she hadn't even got her bag unpacked.

"How could you ruin my best jacket!" Hannah screamed as soon as she opened her wardrobe to hang up her clothes.

"I didn't fall off my bike on purpose," Naomi yelled from her room. "A car almost hit me. It's not my fault!"

"But you took my jacket," Hannah hissed, storming into her sister's room.

"Mum said I could wear anything in your wardrobe," Naomi retorted hotly.

"But you should've known I'd never let you wear this," Hannah shot back.

"It's just a stupid jacket," Naomi sneered sarcastically.

Hannah threw the torn jacket onto Naomi's bed. "Mum lets you get away with everything," she said, seething with anger. "But not this time. You're going to pay for this." And she stormed out of the room.

Naomi sat down on the bed, and her anger turned to tears. "Why do I have so much trouble with my sister?" she asked herself.

Naomi and Hannah's constant clashes are a lot like the clashes between Joseph and his brothers. Read **Genesis 37:1–36** to see what their bad relationship led to.

* What problems do you see in Hannah and Naomi's relationship that also show up in the relationship between Joseph and his brothers?
* Are you more like Joseph (the one who gets picked on) or his brothers (the ones who become jealous)?

Consider . . .

* writing an "I'm sorry" or "I forgive you" note to a family member and taping it to a mirror he or she uses.
* starting a "something nice" jar to collect notes about nice things other family members do for you. Look through the notes when you're angry at another family member.

For more, see . . .

* Genesis 27:1–41 (p.32)
* 1 John 2:9–11 (p.1372)
* Luke 10:38–41 (p.1058)

[16]Joseph answered, "I am looking for my brothers. Can you tell me where they are grazing the flocks?"

[17]The man said, "They have already gone. I heard them say they were going to Dothan." So Joseph went to look for his brothers and found them in Dothan.

Joseph Sold into Slavery

[18]Joseph's brothers saw him coming from far away. Before he reached them, they made a plan to kill him. [19]They said to each other, "Here comes that dreamer. [20]Let's kill him and throw his body into one of the wells. We can tell our father that a wild animal killed him. Then we will see what will become of his dreams."

[21]But Reuben heard their plan and saved Joseph, saying, "Let's not kill him. [22]Don't spill any blood. Throw him into this well here in the desert, but don't hurt him!" Reuben planned to save Joseph later and send him back to his father. [23]So when Joseph came to his brothers, they pulled off his robe with long sleeves [24]and threw him into the well. It was empty, and there was no water in it.

[25]While Joseph was in the well, the brothers sat down to eat. When they looked up, they saw a group of Ishmaelites travelling from Gilead to Egypt. Their camels were carrying spices, balm [d] and myrrh. [d]

[26]Then Judah said to his brothers, "What will we gain if we kill our brother and hide his death? [27]Let's sell him to these Ishmaelites. Then we will not be guilty of killing our own brother. After all, he is our brother, our own flesh and blood." And the other brothers agreed. [28]So when the Midianite traders came by, the brothers took Joseph out of the well and sold him to the Ishmaelites for 20 pieces of silver. And the Ishmaelites took him to Egypt.

[29]When Reuben came back to the well and Joseph was not there, he tore his clothes to show he was sad. [30]Then he went back to his brothers and said, "The boy is not there! What shall I do?" [31]The brothers killed a goat and dipped Joseph's robe in its blood. [32]Then they brought the long-sleeved robe to their father and said, "We found this robe. Look it over carefully and see if it is your son's robe."

[33]Jacob looked it over and said, "It is my son's robe! Some savage animal has eaten him. My son Joseph has been torn to pieces!" [34]Then Jacob tore his clothes and put on rough cloth to show that he was sad, and he continued to be sad about

his son for a long time. [35]All of his sons and daughters tried to comfort him, but he could not be comforted. He said, "I will be sad about my son until the day I die." So Jacob cried for his son Joseph.

[36]Meanwhile the Midianites who had bought Joseph had taken him to Egypt. There they sold him to Potiphar, an officer to the king of Egypt, and captain of the palace guard.

Judah and Tamar

38 About that time, Judah left his brothers and went to stay with a man named Hirah in the town of Adullam. [2]There Judah met a Canaanite girl, the daughter of a man named Shua and married her. Judah had sexual relations with her, [3]and she became pregnant and gave birth to a son, whom Judah named Er. [4]Later she gave birth to another son and named him Onan. [5]Still later she had another son and named him Shelah. She was at Kezib when this third son was born.

[6]Judah chose a girl named Tamar to be the wife of his first son Er. [7]But Er, Judah's oldest son, did what the LORD said was evil, so the LORD killed him. [8]Then Judah said to Er's brother Onan, "Go and have sexual relations with your dead brother's wife. [n] It is your duty to provide children for your brother in this way."

[9]But Onan knew that the children would not belong to him, so when he was supposed to have sexual relations with Tamar he did not complete the sex act. This made it impossible for Tamar to become pregnant and for Er to have descendants. [d] [10]The LORD was displeased by this wicked thing Onan had done, so the LORD killed Onan also. [11]Then Judah said to his daughter-in-law Tamar, "Go back to live in your father's house, and don't marry until my young son Shelah grows up." Judah was afraid that Shelah also would die like his brothers. So Tamar returned to her father's home.

[12]After a long time Judah's wife, the daughter of Shua, died. After Judah had got over his sorrow, he went to Timnah to his men who were cutting

---

Go . . . wife It was a custom in Israel that if a man died without children, one of his brothers would marry the widow. If a child was born, it would be considered the dead man's child.

the wool from his sheep. His friend Hirah from Adullam went with him. [13]Tamar learned that Judah, her father-in-law, was going to Timnah to cut the wool from his sheep. [14]So she took off the clothes that showed she was a widow and covered her face with a veil to hide who she was. Then she sat down by the gate of Enaim on the road to Timnah. She did this because Judah's younger son Shelah had grown up, but Judah had not made plans for her to marry him.

[15]When Judah saw her, he thought she was a prostitute,[d] because she had covered her face with a veil. [16]So Judah went to her and said, "Let me have sexual relations with you." He did not know that she was Tamar, his daughter-in-law.

She asked, "What will you give me if I let you have sexual relations with me?"

[17]Judah answered, "I will send you a young goat from my flock."

She answered, "First give me something to keep as a deposit until you send the goat."

[18]Judah asked, "What do you want me to give you as a deposit?"

Tamar answered, "Give me your seal and its cord,[n] and give me your walking stick." So Judah gave these things to her. Then Judah and Tamar had sexual relations, and Tamar became pregnant. [19]When Tamar went home, she took off the veil that covered her face and put on the clothes that showed she was a widow.

[20]Judah sent his friend Hirah with the young goat to find the woman and get back his seal and the walking stick he had given her, but Hirah could not find her. [21]He asked some of the people at the town of Enaim, "Where is the prostitute who was here by the road?"

They answered, "There has never been a prostitute here."

[22]So he went back to Judah and said, "I could not find the woman, and the people who lived there said, 'There has never been a prostitute here.'"

[23]Judah said, "Let her keep the things. I don't want people to laugh at us. I sent her the goat as I promised, but you could not find her."

[24]About three months later someone told Judah, "Tamar, your daughter-in-law, is guilty of acting like a prostitute, and now she is pregnant."

Then Judah said, "Bring her out and let her be burned to death."

[25]When the people went to bring Tamar out, she sent a message to her father-in-law that said,

"The man who owns these things has made me pregnant. Look at this seal and its cord and this walking stick, and tell me whose they are."

[26]Judah recognised them and said, "She is more in the right than I. She did this because I did not give her to my son Shelah as I promised." And Judah did not have sexual relations with her again.

[27]When the time came for Tamar to give birth, there were twins in her body. [28]While she was giving birth, one baby put his hand out. The nurse tied a red string on his hand and said, "This baby came out first." [29]But he pulled his hand back in, so the other baby was born first. The nurse said, "So you are able to break out first," and they named him Perez.[n] [30]After this, the baby with the red string on his hand was born, and they named him Zerah.

Joseph is Sold to Potiphar

39 Now Joseph had been taken down to Egypt. An Egyptian named Potiphar was an officer to the king of Egypt and the captain of the palace guard. He bought Joseph from the Ishmaelites who had brought him down there. [2]The LORD was with Joseph, and he became a successful man. He lived in the house of his master, Potiphar the Egyptian.

[3]Potiphar saw that the LORD was with Joseph and that the LORD made Joseph successful in everything he did. [4]So Potiphar was very happy with Joseph and allowed him to be his personal servant. He put Joseph in charge of the house, trusting him with everything he owned. [5]When Joseph was put in charge of the house and everything Potiphar owned, the LORD blessed the people in Potiphar's house because of Joseph. And the LORD blessed everything that belonged to Potiphar, both in the house and in the field. [6]So Potiphar left Joseph in charge of everything he owned and was not concerned about anything except the food he ate.

Joseph is Put into Prison

Now Joseph was well built and handsome. [7]After some time the wife of Joseph's master began to desire Joseph, and one day she said to him, "Have sexual relations with me."

[8]But Joseph refused and said to her, "My master trusts me with everything in his house. He has put me in charge of everything he owns. [9]There

---

seal . . . cord A seal was used like a rubber stamp, and people ran a string through it to tie around the neck. They wrote a contract, folded it, put wax or clay on the contract and pressed the seal onto it as a signature.
Perez This name means "breaking out".

is no one in his house greater than I. He has not kept anything from me except you, because you are his wife. How can I do such an evil thing? It is a sin against God."

¹⁰The woman talked to Joseph every day, but he refused to have sexual relations with her or even spend time with her.

¹¹One day Joseph went into the house to do his work as usual and was the only man in the house at that time. ¹²His master's wife grabbed his coat and said to him, "Come and have sexual relations with me." But Joseph left his coat in her hand and ran out of the house.

¹³When she saw that Joseph had left his coat in her hands and had run outside, ¹⁴she called to the servants in her house and said, "Look! This Hebrew slave was brought here to shame us. He came in and tried to have sex with me, but I screamed. ¹⁵My scream scared him and he ran away, but he left his coat with me." ¹⁶She kept his coat until her husband came home, ¹⁷and she told him the same story. She said, "This Hebrew slave you brought here came in to shame me! ¹⁸When he came near me, I screamed. He ran away, but he left his coat."

¹⁹When Joseph's master heard what his wife said Joseph had done, he became very angry. ²⁰So Potiphar arrested Joseph and put him into the prison where the king's prisoners were put. And Joseph stayed there in the prison.

²¹But the LORD was with Joseph and showed him kindness and caused the prison warden to like Joseph. ²²The prison warden chose Joseph to take care of all the prisoners, and he was responsible for whatever was done in the prison. ²³The warden paid no attention to anything that was in Joseph's care because the LORD was with Joseph and made him successful in everything he did.

Joseph Interprets Two Dreams

40 After these things happened, two of the king's officers displeased the king—the man who served wine to the king, and the king's baker. ²The king became angry with his officer who served him wine and his baker, ³so he put them in the prison of the captain of the guard, the same prison where Joseph was kept. ⁴The captain of the guard put the two prisoners in Joseph's care, and they stayed in prison for some time.

⁵One night both the king's officer who served him wine and the baker had a dream. Each had his own dream with its own meaning. ⁶When Joseph came to them the next morning, he saw they were worried. ⁷He asked the king's officers who were with him, "Why do you look so unhappy today?"

⁸The two men answered, "We both had dreams last night, but no one can explain their meaning to us."

Joseph said to them, "God is the only one who can explain the meaning of dreams. Tell me your dreams."

⁹So the man who served wine to the king told Joseph his dream. He said, "I dreamed I saw a vine, and ¹⁰on the vine were three branches. I watched the branches bud and blossom, and then the grapes ripened. ¹¹I was holding the king's cup, so I took the grapes and squeezed the juice into the cup. Then I gave it to the king."

¹²Then Joseph said, "I will explain the dream to you. The three branches stand for three days. ¹³Before the end of three days the king will free you, and he will allow you to return to your work. You will serve the king his wine just as you did before. ¹⁴But when you are free, remember me. Be kind to me, and tell the king about me so I can get out of this prison. ¹⁵I was taken by force from the land of the Hebrews, and I have done nothing here to deserve being put in prison."

¹⁶The baker saw that Joseph's explanation of the dream was good, so he said to him, "I also had a dream. I dreamed there were three bread baskets on my head. ¹⁷In the top basket were all kinds of baked food for the king, but the birds were eating this food out of the basket on my head."

¹⁸Joseph answered, "I will tell you what the dream means. The three baskets stand for three days. ¹⁹Before the end of three days, the king will cut off your head! He will hang your body on a pole, and the birds will eat your flesh."

²⁰Three days later, on his birthday, the king gave a feast for all his officers. In front of his officers, he released from prison the chief officer who served his wine and the chief baker. ²¹The king gave his chief officer who served wine his old position, and once again he put the king's cup of wine into the king's hand. ²²But the king hanged the baker on a pole. Everything happened just as Joseph had said it would, ²³but the officer who served wine did not remember Joseph. He forgot all about him.

The King's Dreams

41 Two years later the king dreamed he was standing on the bank of the Nile River. ²He saw seven fat and beautiful cows come up out of the river, and they stood there, eating the grass. ³Then seven more cows came up out of the river, but they were thin and ugly. They stood beside the seven beautiful cows on the bank of the Nile. ⁴The seven thin and ugly cows ate the seven beautiful fat cows. Then the king woke up.

[5]The king slept again and dreamed a second time. In his dream he saw seven full and good heads of grain growing on one stalk. [6]After that, seven more heads of grain sprang up, but they were thin and burned by the hot east wind. [7]The thin heads of grain ate the seven full and good heads. Then the king woke up again, and he realised it was only a dream. [8]The next morning the king was troubled about these dreams, so he sent for all the magicians and wise men of Egypt. The king told them his dreams, but no one could explain their meaning to him.

[9]Then the chief officer who served wine to the king said to him, "Now I remember something I promised to do, but I forgot about it. [10]There was a time when you were angry with the baker and me, and you put us in prison in the house of the captain of the guard. [11]In prison we each had a dream on the same night, and each dream had a different meaning. [12]A young Hebrew man, a servant of the captain of the guard, was in the prison with us. When we told him our dreams, he explained their meanings to us. He told each man the meaning of his dream, and [13]things happened exactly as he said they would: I was given back my old position, and the baker was hanged."

[14]So the king called for Joseph. The guards quickly brought him out of the prison, and he shaved, put on clean clothes and went before the king.

[15]The king said to Joseph, "I have had a dream, but no one can explain its meaning to me. I have heard that you can explain a dream when someone tells it to you."

[16]Joseph answered the king, "I am not able to explain the meaning of dreams, but God will do this for the king."

[17]Then the king said to Joseph, "In my dream I was standing on the bank of the Nile River. [18]I saw seven fat and beautiful cows that came up out of the river and ate the grass. [19]Then I saw seven more cows come out of the river that were thin and lean and ugly—the worst looking cows I have seen in all the land of Egypt. [20]And these thin and ugly cows ate the first seven fat cows, [21]but after they had eaten the seven cows, no one could tell they had eaten them. They looked just as thin and ugly as they did in the beginning. Then I woke up.

[22]"I had another dream. I saw seven full and good heads of grain growing on one stalk. [23]Then seven more heads of grain sprang up after them, but these heads were thin and ugly and were burned by the hot east wind. [24]Then the thin heads ate the seven good heads. I told this dream to the magicians, but no one could explain its meaning to me."

Joseph Tells the Dreams' Meaning

[25]Then Joseph said to the king, "Both of these dreams mean the same thing. God is telling you what he is about to do. [26]The seven good cows stand for seven years, and the seven good heads of grain stand for seven years. Both dreams mean the same thing. [27]The seven thin and ugly cows stand for seven years, and the seven thin heads of grain burned by the hot east wind stand for seven years of hunger. [28]This will happen as I told you. God is showing the king what he is about to do. [29]You will have seven years of good crops and plenty to eat in all the land of Egypt. [30]But after those seven years, there will come seven years of hunger, and all the food that grew in the land of Egypt will be forgotten. The time of hunger will eat up the land. [31]People will forget what it was like to have plenty of food, because the hunger that follows will be so great. [32]You had two dreams which mean the same thing. This shows that God has firmly decided that this will happen, and he will make it happen soon.

[33]"So let the king choose a man who is very wise and understanding and set him over the land of Egypt. [34]And let the king also appoint officers over the land, who should take one-fifth of all the food that is grown during the seven good years. [35]They should gather all the food that is produced during the good years that are coming, and under the king's authority they should store the grain in the cities and guard it. [36]That food should be saved to use during the seven years of hunger that will come on the land of Egypt. Then the people in Egypt will not die during the seven years of hunger."

Joseph is Made Ruler Over Egypt

[37]This seemed like a very good idea to the king, and all his officers agreed. [38]And the king asked them, "Can we find a better man than Joseph to take this job? God's Spirit is truly in him!"

[39]So the king said to Joseph, "God has shown you all this. There is no one as wise and understanding as you are, so [40]I will put you in charge of my palace. All the people will obey your orders, and only I will be greater than you."

[41]Then the king said to Joseph, "Look! I have put you in charge of all the land of Egypt." [42]Then the king took off from his own finger his ring with the royal seal on it, and he put it on Joseph's finger. He gave Joseph fine linen clothes to wear, and he put a gold chain around Joseph's neck. [43]The king had Joseph ride in the second royal chariot, and people walked ahead of his chariot calling, "Bow down!" By doing these things, the king put Joseph in charge of all of Egypt.

[44]The king said to him, "I am the king, and I say that no one in all the land of Egypt may lift a hand or a foot without your permission." [45]The king gave Joseph the name Zaphenath-Paneah. He also gave Joseph a wife named Asenath, who

---

Sidelight

In Old Testament times, Middle Easterners depended on rainfall to grow crops. If rain didn't come, people often went to Egypt, because the Nile River flooded each year, making the ground moist and rich. So famine in Egypt could mean disaster. That's why Joseph's prediction of seven years of famine was taken so seriously (Genesis 41:25–43).

---

was the daughter of Potiphera, priest of On. So Joseph travelled through all the land of Egypt.

[46]Joseph was 30 years old when he began serving the king of Egypt. And he left the king's court and travelled through all the land of Egypt. [47]During the seven good years, the crops in the land grew well. [48]And Joseph gathered all the food which was produced in Egypt during those seven years of good crops and stored the food in the cities. In every city he stored grain that had been grown in the fields around that city. [49]Joseph stored much grain, as much as the sand of the seashore—so much that he could not measure it.

[50]Joseph's wife was Asenath, daughter of Potiphera, the priest of On. Before the years of hunger came, Joseph and Asenath had two sons. [51]Joseph named the first son Manasseh [n] and said, "God has made me forget all the troubles I have had and all my father's family." [52]Joseph named the second son Ephraim [n] and said, "God has given me children in the land of my troubles."

[53]The seven years of good crops came to an end in the land of Egypt. [54]Then the seven years of hunger began, just as Joseph had said. In all the lands people had nothing to eat, but in Egypt there was food. [55]The time of hunger became terrible in all of Egypt, and the people cried to the king for food. He said to all the Egyptians, "Go to Joseph and do whatever he tells you."

[56]The hunger was everywhere in that part of the world. And Joseph opened the storehouses and sold grain to the people of Egypt, because the time of hunger became terrible in Egypt. [57]And all the people in that part of the world came to Joseph in Egypt to buy grain because the hunger was terrible everywhere in that part of the world.

The Dreams Come True

42 Jacob learned that there was grain in Egypt, so he said to his sons, "Why are you just sitting here looking at one another? [2]I have heard that there is grain in Egypt. Go down there and buy grain for us to eat, so that we will live and not die."

[3]So ten of Joseph's brothers went down to buy grain from Egypt. [4]But Jacob did not send Benjamin, Joseph's brother, with them, because he was afraid that something terrible might happen to him. [5]Along with many other people, the sons of Israel [n] went to Egypt to buy grain, because the people in the land of Canaan were also hungry.

[6]Now Joseph was governor over Egypt. He was the one who sold the grain to people who came to buy it. So Joseph's brothers came to him and bowed face down on the ground before him. [7]When Joseph saw his brothers, he knew who they were, but he acted as if he didn't know them. He asked unkindly, "Where do you come from?"

They answered, "We have come from the land of Canaan to buy food."

[8]Joseph knew they were his brothers, but they did not know who he was. [9]And Joseph remembered his dreams about his brothers bowing to him. He said to them, "You are spies! You came to learn where the nation is weak!"

[10]But his brothers said to him, "No, my master. We come as your servants just to buy food. [11]We are all sons of the same father. We are honest men, not spies."

[12]Then Joseph said to them, "No! You have come to learn where this nation is weak!"

[13]And they said, "We are ten of twelve brothers, sons of the same father, and we live in the land of Canaan. Our youngest brother is there with our father right now, and our other brother is gone."

[14]But Joseph said to them, "I can see I was right! You are spies! [15]But I will give you a way to prove you are telling the truth. As surely as the king lives, you will not leave this place until your youngest brother comes here. [16]One of you must go and get your brother. The rest of you will stay here in prison. We will see if you are telling the truth. If not, as surely as the king lives, you are spies." [17]Then Joseph put them all in prison for three days.

[18]On the third day Joseph said to them, "I am a God-fearing man. Do this and I will let you live: [19]if you are honest men, let one of your brothers stay here in prison while the rest of you go and

---

Manasseh   This name sounds like the Hebrew word for "made me forget".
Ephraim   This name sounds like the Hebrew word for "given me children".
Israel   Also called Jacob.

carry grain back to feed your hungry families. [20]Then bring your youngest brother back here to me. If you do this, I will know you are telling the truth, and you will not die."

The brothers agreed to this. [21]They said to each other, "We are being punished for what we did to our brother. We saw his trouble, and he begged us to save him, but we refused to listen. That is why we are in this trouble now."

[22]Then Reuben said to them, "I told you not to harm the boy, but you refused to listen to me. So now we are being punished for what we did to him."

[23]When Joseph talked to his brothers, he used an interpreter, so they did not know that Joseph understood what they were saying. [24]Then Joseph left them and cried. After a short time he went back and spoke to them. He took Simeon and tied him up while the other brothers watched. [25]Joseph told his servants to fill his brothers' bags with grain and to put the money the brothers had paid for the grain back in their bags. The servants were also to give them what they would need for their trip back home. And the servants did this.

[26]So the brothers put the grain on their donkeys and left. [27]When they stopped for the night, one of the brothers opened his sack to get food for his donkey. Then he saw his money in the top of the sack. [28]He said to the other brothers, "The money I paid for the grain has been put back. Here it is in my sack!"

The brothers were very frightened. They said to each other, "What has God done to us?"

The Brothers Return to Jacob

[29]The brothers went to their father Jacob in the land of Canaan and told him everything that had happened. [30]They said, "The master of that land spoke unkindly to us. He accused us of spying on his country, [31]but we told him that we were honest men, not spies. [32]We told him that we were ten of twelve brothers—sons of one father. We said that one of our brothers was gone and that our youngest brother was with our father in Canaan.

[33]"Then the master of the land said to us, 'Here is a way I can know you are honest men: leave one of your brothers with me, and take grain to feed your hungry families, and go. [34]And bring your youngest brother to me so I will know you are not spies but honest men. Then I will give you back your brother whom you leave with me, and you can move about freely in our land.'"

[35]As the brothers emptied their sacks, each of them found his money in his sack. When they and their father saw it, they were afraid.

[36]Their father Jacob said to them, "You are robbing me of all my children. Joseph is gone, Simeon is gone, and now you want to take Benjamin away, too. Everything is against me."

[37]Then Reuben said to his father, "You may put my two sons to death if I don't bring Benjamin back to you. Trust him to my care, and I will bring him back to you."

[38]But Jacob said, "I will not allow Benjamin to go with you. His brother is dead, and he is the only son left from my wife Rachel. I am afraid something terrible might happen to him during the trip to Egypt. Then I would be sad until the day I die."

The Brothers Go Back to Egypt

43 Still no food grew in the land of Canaan. [2]When Jacob's family had eaten all the grain they had brought from Egypt, Jacob said to them, "Go to Egypt again and buy a little more grain for us to eat."

[3]But Judah said to Jacob, "The governor of that country strongly warned us, 'If you don't bring your brother back with you, you will not be allowed to see me.' [4]If you will send Benjamin with us, we will go down and buy food for you. [5]But if you refuse to send Benjamin, we will not go. The governor of that country warned us that we would not see him if we didn't bring Benjamin with us."

[6]Israel [n] said, "Why did you tell the man you had another brother? You have caused me a lot of trouble."

[7]The brothers answered, "He questioned us carefully about ourselves and our family. He asked us, 'Is your father still alive? Do you have another brother?' We just answered his questions. How could we know he would ask us to bring our other brother to him?"

[8]Then Judah said to his father Jacob, "Send Benjamin with me, and we will go at once so that we, you, and our children may live and not die. [9]I will guarantee you that he will be safe, and I will be personally responsible for him. If I don't bring him back to you, you can blame me all my life. [10]If we had not wasted all this time, we could have already made two trips."

[11]Then their father Jacob said to them, "If it has to be that way, then do this: take some of the best foods in our land in your packs. Give them to the man as a gift: some balm, [d] some honey, spices, myrrh, [d] pistachio nuts and

---

Israel Also called Jacob.

almonds. [12]Take twice as much money with you this time, and take back the money that was returned to you in your sacks last time. Maybe it was a mistake. [13]And take Benjamin with you. Now leave and go to the man. [14]I pray that God Almighty will cause the governor to be merciful to you and that he will allow Simeon and Benjamin to come back with you. If I am robbed of my children, then I am robbed of them!"

[15]So the brothers took the gifts. They also took twice as much money as they had taken the first time, and they took Benjamin. They hurried down to Egypt and stood before Joseph.

[16]When Joseph saw Benjamin with them, he said to the servant in charge of his house, "Bring those men into my house. Kill an animal and prepare a meal. Those men will eat with me today at noon." [17]The servant did as Joseph told him and brought the men to Joseph's house.

[18]The brothers were afraid when they were brought to Joseph's house and thought, "We were brought here because of the money that was put in our sacks on the first trip. He wants to attack us, make us slaves, and take our donkeys." [19]So the brothers went to the servant in charge of Joseph's house and spoke to him at the door of the house. [20]They said, "Master, we came here once before to buy food. [21]While we were going home, we stopped for the night and when we opened our sacks each of us found all his money in his sack. We brought that money with us to give it back to you. [22]And we have brought more money to pay for the food we want to buy this time. We don't know who put that money in our sacks."

[23]But the servant answered, "It's all right. Don't be afraid. Your God, the God of your father, must have put the money in your sacks. I got the money you paid me for the grain last time." Then the servant brought Simeon out to them.

[24]The servant led the men into Joseph's house and gave them water, and they washed their feet. Then he gave their donkeys food to eat. [25]The men prepared their gift to give to Joseph when he arrived at noon, because they had heard they were going to eat with him there.

[26]When Joseph came home, the brothers gave him the gift they had brought into the house and bowed down to the ground in front of him. [27]Joseph asked them how they were. He said, "How is your aged father you told me about? Is he still alive?"

[28]The brothers answered, "Your servant, our father, is well. He is still alive." And they bowed low before Joseph to show him respect.

[29]When Joseph saw his brother Benjamin, who had the same mother as he, Joseph asked, "Is this your youngest brother you told me about?" Then he said to Benjamin, "God be good to you, my son!" [30]Then Joseph hurried off because he had to hold back the tears when he saw his brother Benjamin. So Joseph went into his room and cried there. [31]Then he washed his face and came out. He controlled himself and said, "Serve the meal."

[32]So they served Joseph at one table, his brothers at another table, and the Egyptians who ate with him at another table. This was because Egyptians did not like Hebrews and never ate with them. [33]Joseph's brothers were seated in front of him in order of their ages, from oldest to youngest. They looked at each other because they were so amazed. [34]Food from Joseph's table was taken to them, but Benjamin was given five times more food than the others. Joseph's brothers ate and drank freely with him.

Joseph Sets a Trap

44 Then Joseph gave a command to the servant in charge of his house. He said, "Fill the men's sacks with as much grain as they can carry, and put each man's money into his sack with the grain. [2]Put my silver cup in the sack of the youngest brother, along with his money for the grain." The servant did what Joseph told him.

[3]At dawn the brothers were sent away with their donkeys. [4]They were not far from the city when Joseph said to the servant in charge of his house, "Go after the men. When you catch up with them, say, 'Why have you paid back evil for good? [5]The cup you have stolen is the one my master uses for drinking and for explaining dreams. You have done a very wicked thing!' "

[6]So the servant caught up with the brothers and said to them what Joseph had told him to say.

[7]But the brothers said to the servant, "Why do you say these things? We would not do anything like that! [8]We brought back to you from the land of Canaan the money we found in our sacks. So surely we would not steal silver or gold from your master's house. [9]If you find that silver cup in the sack of one of us, then let him die, and we will be your slaves."

[10]The servant said, "We will do as you say, but only the man who has taken the cup will become my slave. The rest of you may go free."

[11]Then every brother quickly lowered his sack to the ground and opened it. [12]The servant searched the sacks, going from the oldest brother to the youngest, and found the cup in Benjamin's sack. [13]The brothers tore their clothes to show they were afraid. Then they put their sacks back on the donkeys and returned to the city.

[14]When Judah and his brothers went back to Joseph's house, Joseph was still there, so the brothers bowed face down on the ground before him. [15]Joseph said to them, "What have you

done? Didn't you know that a man like me can learn things by signs and dreams?"

¹⁶Judah said, "Master, what can we say? And how can we show we are not guilty? God has uncovered our guilt, so all of us will be your slaves, not just Benjamin."

¹⁷But Joseph said, "I will not make you all slaves! Only the man who stole the cup will be my slave. The rest of you may go back safely to your father."

¹⁸Then Judah went to Joseph and said, "Master, please let me speak plainly to you, and please don't be angry with me. I know that you are as powerful as the king of Egypt himself. ¹⁹When we were here before, you asked us, 'Do you have a father or a brother?' ²⁰And we answered you, 'We have an old father. And we have a younger brother, who was born when our father was old. This youngest son's brother is dead, so he is the only one of his mother's children left alive, and our father loves him very much.' ²¹Then you said to us, 'Bring that brother to me. I want to see him.' ²²And we said to you, 'That young boy cannot leave his father, because if he leaves him, his father would die.' ²³But you said to us, 'If you don't bring your youngest brother, you will not be allowed to see me again.' ²⁴So we went back to our father and told him what you had said.

²⁵"Later, our father said, 'Go again and buy us a little more food.' ²⁶We said to our father, 'We cannot go without our youngest brother. Without our youngest brother, we will not be allowed to see the governor.' ²⁷Then my father said to us, 'You know that my wife Rachel gave me two sons. ²⁸When one son left me, I thought, "Surely he has been torn apart by a wild animal," and I haven't seen him since. ²⁹Now you want to take this son away from me also. But something terrible might happen to him, and I would be miserable until the day I die.' ³⁰Now what will happen if we go home to our father without our youngest brother? He is so important in our father's life that ³¹when our father sees the young boy is not with us, he will die. And it will be our fault. We will cause the great sorrow that kills our father.

³²"I gave my father a guarantee that the young boy would be safe. I said to my father, 'If I don't bring him back to you, you can blame me all my life.' ³³So now, please allow me to stay here and be your slave, and let the young boy go back home with his brothers. ³⁴I cannot go back to my father if the boy is not with me. I couldn't stand to see my father that sad."

Joseph Reveals Who He Is

45 Joseph could not control himself in front of his servants any longer, so he cried out, "Have everyone leave me." When only the brothers were left with Joseph, he told them who he was. ²Joseph cried so loudly that the Egyptians heard him, and the people in the king's palace heard about it. ³He said to his brothers, "I am Joseph. Is my father still alive?" But the brothers could not answer him, because they were very afraid of him.

⁴So Joseph said to them, "Come close to me." When the brothers came close to him, he said to them, "I am your brother Joseph, whom you sold as a slave to go to Egypt. ⁵Now don't be worried or angry with yourselves because you sold me here. God sent me here ahead of you to save people's lives. ⁶No food has grown on the land for two years now, and there will be five more years without planting or harvest. ⁷So God sent me here ahead of you to make sure you have some descendants^d left on earth and to keep you alive in an amazing way. ⁸So it was not you who sent me here, but God. God has made me the highest officer of the king of Egypt. I am in charge of his palace, and I am the master of all the land of Egypt.

⁹"So leave quickly and go to my father. Tell him, 'Your son Joseph says: God has made me master over all Egypt. Come down to me quickly. ¹⁰Live in the land of Goshen where you will be near me. Your children, your grandchildren, your flocks and herds, and all that you have will also be near me. ¹¹I will care for you during the next five years of hunger so that you and your family and all that you have will not starve.'

¹²"Now you can see for yourselves, and so can my brother Benjamin, that the one speaking to you is really Joseph. ¹³So tell my father about how powerful I have become in Egypt. Tell him about everything you have seen. Now hurry and bring him back to me." ¹⁴Then Joseph hugged his brother Benjamin and cried, and Benjamin cried also. ¹⁵And Joseph kissed all his brothers and cried as he hugged them. After this, his brothers talked with him.

¹⁶When the king of Egypt and his officers learned that Joseph's brothers had come, they were very happy. ¹⁷So the king said to Joseph, "Tell your brothers to load their animals and go back to the land of Canaan ¹⁸and bring their father and their families back here to me. I will give them the best land in Egypt, and they will eat the best food we have here. ¹⁹Tell them to take some wagons from Egypt for their children and their wives and to bring their father back also. ²⁰Tell them not to worry about bringing any of their things with them, because we will give them the best of what we have in Egypt."

²¹So the sons of Israel did this. Joseph gave them wagons as the king had ordered and food

for their trip. [22]He gave each brother a change of clothes, but he gave Benjamin five changes of clothes and about 300 pieces of silver. [23]Joseph also sent his father ten donkeys loaded with the best things from Egypt and ten female donkeys loaded with grain, bread and other food for his father on his trip back. [24]Then Joseph told his brothers to go. As they were leaving, he said to them, "Don't quarrel on the way home."

[25]So the brothers left Egypt and went to their father Jacob in the land of Canaan. [26]They told him, "Joseph is still alive and is the ruler over all the land of Egypt." Their father was shocked and did not believe them. [27]But when the brothers told him everything Joseph had said, and when Jacob saw the wagons Joseph had sent to carry him back to Egypt, he felt better. [28]Israel [n] said, "Now I believe you. My son Joseph is still alive, and I will go and see him before I die."

Israel   Also called Jacob.

Jacob Goes to Egypt

46 So Israel [n] took all he had and started his trip. He went to Beersheba, where he offered sacrifices to the God of his father Isaac. [2]During the night God spoke to Israel in a vision and said, "Jacob, Jacob."

And Jacob answered, "Here I am."

[3]Then God said, "I am God, the God of your father. Don't be afraid to go to Egypt, because I will make your descendants [d] a great nation there. [4]I will go to Egypt with you, and I will bring you out of Egypt again. Joseph's own hands will close your eyes when you die."

[5]Then Jacob left Beersheba. The sons of Israel loaded their father, their children and their wives in the wagons the king of Egypt had sent. [6]They also took their farm animals and everything they had gained in Canaan. So Jacob went to Egypt with all his descendants— [7]his sons

REVENGE

Was it Worth it?

"Just good friends, right?" Anna smiled. Andrew and Anna had been going out through most of school, but now she had dumped him!

Everything suddenly became clear two weeks later when Andrew discovered that his best friend Neil was seeing Anna. He wasn't prepared to simply forgive and forget and he was going to get even!

He waited impatiently outside the main school gates that afternoon. When he saw Neil, he took a deep breath and threw a punch to his face.

"That's for taking Anna," he said, then turned and walked away. He smiled to himself. He had carried out his revenge quickly and effectively.

Gradually, it dawned on him that he had now not only lost his girlfriend, but also his best friend. Revenge had tasted sweet at first, but now it had turned bitter.

- Andrew's motive for revenge seemed fine in the heat of the moment. In **Genesis 45:3–8**, Joseph also had the motive and the opportunity to take revenge. Read about the different way he reacted.
- What difference can you see between the attitudes of Andrew and Joseph? How did their attitudes affect their responses?

Consider . . .

- thinking of how many people have done something to you out of revenge. Decide how you will respond to them the next time they get under your skin.
- how many films you have seen which rely on revenge to carry the plot. How would the story develop differently if the characters acted a little more like Joseph?

For more, see . . .

- Joshua 20:1–6 (p.218)
- Acts 7:51–60 (p.1149)

- Luke 6:27–36 (p.1048)

and grandsons, his daughters and granddaughters. He took all his family to Egypt with him.

Jacob's Family

[8]Now these are the names of the children of Israel who went into Egypt (Jacob and his descendants [d]).

Reuben was Jacob's first son. [9]Reuben's sons were Hanoch, Pallu, Hezron and Carmi.

[10]Simeon's sons were Jemuel, Jamin, Ohad, Jakin, Zohar and Shaul (Simeon's son by a Canaanite woman).

[11]Levi's sons were Gershon, Kohath and Merari.

[12]Judah's sons were Er, Onan, Shelah, Perez and Zerah (but Er and Onan had died in the land of Canaan). Perez's sons were Hezron and Hamul.

[13]Issachar's sons were Tola, Puah, Jashub and Shimron.

[14]Zebulun's sons were Sered, Elon and Jahleel.

[15]These are the sons of Leah and Jacob born in North West Mesopotamia, in addition to his daughter Dinah. There were 33 persons in this part of Jacob's family.

[16]Gad's sons were Zephon, Haggi, Shuni, Ezbon, Eri, Arodi and Areli.

[17]Asher's sons were Imnah, Ishvah, Ishvi and Beriah, and their sister was Serah. Beriah's sons were Heber and Malkiel.

[18]These are Jacob's sons by Zilpah, the slave girl whom Laban gave to his daughter Leah. There were sixteen persons in this part of Jacob's family.

[19]The sons of Jacob's wife Rachel were Joseph and Benjamin. [20]In Egypt, Joseph became the father of Manasseh and Ephraim by his wife Asenath, the daughter of Potiphera, priest of On.

[21]Benjamin's sons were Bela, Beker, Ashbel, Gera, Naaman, Ehi, Rosh, Muppim, Huppim and Ard.

[22]These are the sons of Jacob by his wife Rachel. There were fourteen persons in this part of Jacob's family.

[23]Dan's son was Hushim.

[24]Naphtali's sons were Jahziel, Guni, Jezer and Shillem.

[25]These are Jacob's sons by Bilhah, the slave girl whom Laban gave to his daughter Rachel. There were seven persons in this part of Jacob's family.

[26]So the total number of Jacob's direct descendants who went to Egypt was 66, not counting the wives of Jacob's sons. [27]Joseph had two sons born in Egypt, so the total number in the family of Jacob in Egypt was 70.

Jacob Arrives in Egypt

[28]Jacob sent Judah ahead of him to see Joseph in Goshen. When Jacob and his people came into the land of Goshen, [29]Joseph prepared his chariot and went to meet his father Israel in Goshen. As soon as Joseph saw his father, he hugged him, and cried there for a long time.

[30]Then Israel said to Joseph, "Now I am ready to die, because I have seen your face and I know you are still alive."

[31]Joseph said to his brothers and his father's family, "I will go and tell the king you are here. I will say, 'My brothers and my father's family have left the land of Canaan and have come here to me. [32]They are shepherds and take care of farm animals, and they have brought their flocks and their herds and everything they own with them.' [33]When the king calls you, he will ask, 'What work do you do?' [34]This is what you should tell him: 'We, your servants, have taken care of farm animals all our lives. Our ancestors did the same thing.' Then the king will allow you to settle in the land of Goshen, away from the Egyptians, because they don't like to be near shepherds."

Jacob Settles in Goshen

47 Joseph went in to the king and said, "My father and my brothers have arrived from Canaan with their flocks and herds and everything they own. They are now in the land of Goshen." [2]Joseph chose five of his brothers to introduce to the king.

[3]The king said to the brothers, "What work do you do?"

And they said to him, "We, your servants, are shepherds, just as our ancestors were." [4]They said to the king, "We have come to live in this land, because there is no grass in the land of Canaan for our animals to eat, and the hunger is terrible there. So please allow us to live in the land of Goshen."

[5]Then the king said to Joseph, "Your father and your brothers have come to you, [6]and you may choose any place in Egypt for them to live. Give your father and your brothers the best land; let them live in the land of Goshen. And if any of them are skilled shepherds, put them in charge of my sheep and cattle."

[7]Then Joseph brought in his father Jacob and introduced him to the king, and Jacob blessed the king.

[8]Then the king said to Jacob, "How old are you?"

[9]Jacob said to him, "My life has been spent wandering from place to place. It has been short and filled with trouble—only 130 years. My ancestors lived much longer than I." [10]Then Jacob blessed the king and left.

[11]Joseph obeyed the king and gave his father and brothers the best land in Egypt, near the city of Rameses. [12]And Joseph gave his father, his

brothers and everyone who lived with them the food they needed.

Joseph Buys Land for the King

[13]The hunger became worse, and since there was no food anywhere in the land, Egypt and Canaan became very poor. [14]Joseph collected all the money that was to be found in Egypt and Canaan. People paid for the grain they were buying, and he brought that money to the king's palace. [15]After some time, when the people in Egypt and Canaan had no money left, they went to Joseph and said, "Please give us food. Our money is gone, and if we don't eat, we will die here in front of you."

[16]Joseph answered, "Since you have no money, give me your farm animals, and I will give you food in return." [17]So people brought their farm animals to Joseph, and he gave them food in exchange for their horses, sheep, goats, cattle and donkeys. And he kept them alive by trading food for their farm animals that year.

[18]The next year the people came to Joseph and said, "You know we have no money left, and all our animals belong to you. We have nothing left except our bodies and our land. [19]Surely both we and our land will die here in front of you. Buy us and our land in exchange for food, and we will be slaves to the king, together with our land. Give us seed to plant so that we will live and not die, and the land will not become a desert."

[20]So Joseph bought all the land in Egypt for the king. Every Egyptian sold Joseph his field, because the hunger was very great. So the land became the king's, [21]and Joseph made the people slaves from one end of Egypt to the other. [22]The only land he did not buy was the land the priests owned. They did not need to sell their land because the king paid them for their work. So they had money to buy food.

[23]Joseph said to the people, "Now I have bought you and your land for the king, so I will give you seed and you can plant your fields. [24]At harvest time you must give one-fifth to the king. You may keep four-fifths for yourselves to use as seed for the field and as food for yourselves, your families and your children."

[25]The people said, "You have saved our lives. If you like, we will become slaves of the king."

[26]So Joseph made a law in Egypt, which continues today: one-fifth of everything from the land belongs to the king. The only land the king did not get was the priests' land.

"Don't Bury Me in Egypt"

[27]The Israelites continued to live in the land of Goshen in Egypt. There they gained possessions and had many children and grew in number. [28]Jacob[n] lived in Egypt seventeen years, so he lived to be 147 years old. [29]When Israel knew he soon would die, he called his son Joseph to him and said to him, "If you love me, put your hand under my leg.[n] Promise me you will not bury me in Egypt. [30]When I die, carry me out of Egypt, and bury me where my ancestors are buried."

Joseph answered, "I will do as you say."

[31]Then Jacob said, "Promise me." And Joseph promised him that he would do this. Then Israel worshipped as he leaned on the top of his walking stick.

Blessings for Manasseh and Ephraim

48 Some time later Joseph learned that his father was very sick, so he took his two sons Manasseh and Ephraim and went to his father. [2]When Joseph arrived, someone told Jacob,[n] "Your son Joseph has come to see you." Jacob was weak, so he used all his strength and sat up on his bed.

[3]Then Jacob said to Joseph, "God Almighty appeared to me at Luz in the land of Canaan and blessed me there. [4]He said to me, 'I will give you many children. I will make you the father of many peoples, and I will give your descendants[d] this land for ever.' [5]Your two sons, who were born here in Egypt before I came, will be counted as my own sons. Ephraim and Manasseh will be my sons just as Reuben and Simeon are my sons. [6]But if you have other children, they will be your own, and their land will be part of the land given to Ephraim and Manasseh. [7]When I came from North West Mesopotamia, Rachel died in the land of Canaan, as we were travelling towards Ephrath. This made me very sad, and I buried her there beside the road to Ephrath." (Today Ephrath is Bethlehem.)

[8]Then Israel saw Joseph's sons and said, "Who are these boys?"

[9]Joseph said to his father, "They are my sons that God has given me here in Egypt."

Israel said, "Bring your sons to me so I may bless them."

[10]At this time Israel's eyesight was bad because he was old. So Joseph brought the boys close to him, and Israel kissed the boys and put his arms around them. [11]He said to Joseph, "I thought I would never see you alive again, and now God has let me see you and also your children."

Jacob   Also called Israel.
put . . . leg   This showed that a person would keep a promise.

¹²Then Joseph moved his sons off Israel's lap and bowed face down to the ground. ¹³He put Ephraim on his right side and Manasseh on his left. (So Ephraim was near Israel's left hand, and Manasseh was near Israel's right hand.) Joseph brought the boys close to Israel. ¹⁴But Israel crossed his arms and put his right hand on the head of Ephraim, who was younger. He put

> **Sidelight**
>
> If you have older brothers and sisters and think they always get the best deal, take some comfort in Genesis 48:13–14. Though Israel blessed both Manasseh, the oldest, and Ephraim, the youngest, he crossed his hands and blessed Ephraim with his right hand. That made Ephraim's blessing more important.

his left hand on the head of Manasseh, the first-born *d* son. ¹⁵And Israel blessed Joseph and said,
"My ancestors Abraham and Isaac served
        our God,
    and like a shepherd God has led me all my
        life.
¹⁶He was the Angel who saved me from all my
        troubles.

Now I pray that he will bless these boys.
May my name be known through these boys,
    and may the names of my ancestors
        Abraham and Isaac be known through
        them.
May they have many descendants *d*
    on the earth."

¹⁷When Joseph saw that his father put his right hand on Ephraim's head, he didn't like it. So he took hold of his father's hand, wanting to move it from Ephraim's head to Manasseh's head. ¹⁸Joseph said to his father, "You are doing it wrong, Father. Manasseh is the firstborn son. Put your right hand on his head."

¹⁹But his father refused and said, "I know, my son, I know. Manasseh will be great and have many descendants. But his younger brother will be greater, and his descendants will be enough to make a nation."

²⁰So Israel blessed them that day and said,
"When a blessing is given in Israel, they
        will say:
    'May God make you like Ephraim and
        Manasseh.'"
In this way he made Ephraim greater than Manasseh.

²¹Then Israel said to Joseph, "Look at me; I am about to die. But God will be with you and will take you back to the land of your fathers. ²²I have

given you something that I did not give your brothers—the land of Shechem that I took from the Amorite people with my sword and my bow."

Jacob Blesses His Sons

49 Then Jacob called his sons to him. He said, "Come here to me, and I will tell you what will happen to you in the future.

²"Come together and listen, sons of Jacob.
    Listen to Israel, your father.

³"Reuben, my first son, you are my strength.
    Your birth showed I could be a father.
You have the highest position among my
        sons,
    and you are the most powerful.
⁴But you are uncontrolled like water,
    so you will no longer lead your brothers.
This is because you got into your father's bed
    and shamed me by having sexual relations
        with my slave girl.

⁵"Simeon and Levi are brothers
    who used their swords to do violence.
⁶I will not join their secret talks,
    and I will not meet with them to plan evil.
They killed men because they were angry,
    and they crippled oxen just for fun.
⁷May their anger be cursed, because it is too
        violent.
    May their violence be cursed, because it is
        too cruel.
I will divide them up among the tribes *d* of
        Jacob
    and scatter them through all the tribes of
        Israel.

⁸"Judah, your brothers will praise you.
    You will grab your enemies by the neck,
    and your brothers will bow down to you.
⁹Judah is like a young lion.
    You have returned from killing, my son.
Like a lion, he stretches out and lies down to
        rest,
    and no one is brave enough to wake him.
¹⁰Kings will come from Judah's family;
    someone from Judah will always be on the
        throne.
Judah will rule until Shiloh comes,
    and the nations will obey him.
¹¹He ties his donkey to a grapevine,
    his young donkey to the best branch.
He can afford to use wine to wash his
        clothes
    and the best wine to wash his robes.
¹²His eyes are dark like the colour of wine,
    and his teeth are as white as the colour of
        milk.

¹³"Zebulun will live near the sea.
His shore will be a safe place for ships,
and his land will reach as far as Sidon.

¹⁴"Issachar is like a strong donkey
who lies down while carrying his load.
¹⁵When he sees his resting place is good
and how pleasant his land is,
he will put his back to the load
and become a slave.

¹⁶"Dan will rule his own people
like the other tribes in Israel.
¹⁷Dan will be like a snake by the side of the
road,
a dangerous snake lying near the path.
That snake bites a horse's leg,
and the rider is thrown off backwards.

¹⁸"LORD, I wait for your salvation.

¹⁹"Robbers will attack Gad,
but he will defeat them and drive them
away.

²⁰"Asher's land will grow much good food;
he will grow food fit for a king.

²¹"Naphtali is like a female deer that runs free,
that has beautiful fawns.

²²"Joseph is like a grapevine that produces
much fruit,
a healthy vine watered by a spring,
whose branches grow over the wall.
²³Archers attack him violently
and shoot at him angrily,
²⁴but he aims his bow well.
His arms are made strong.
He gets his power from the Mighty God of
Jacob
and his strength from the Shepherd, the
Rock ᵈ of Israel.
²⁵Your father's God helps you.
God Almighty blesses you.
He blesses you with rain from above,
with water from springs below,
with many babies born to your wives,
and many young ones born to your
animals.
²⁶The blessings of your father are greater
than the blessings of the oldest mountains,
greater than the good things of the
long-lasting hills.
May these blessings rest on the head of
Joseph,
on the forehead of the one who was
separated from his brothers.

²⁷"Benjamin is like a hungry wolf.
In the morning he eats what he has caught,
and in the evening he divides what he has
taken."

²⁸These are the twelve tribes of Israel, and this is what their father said to them. He gave each son the blessing that was right for him. ²⁹Then Israel gave them a command and said, "I am about to die. Bury me with my ancestors in the cave in the field of Ephron the Hittite. ³⁰That cave is in the field of Machpelah, east of Mamre, in the land of Canaan. Abraham bought the field and cave from Ephron the Hittite for a burying place. ³¹Abraham and Sarah his wife are buried there. Isaac and Rebekah his wife are buried there, and I buried my wife Leah there. ³²The field and the cave in it were bought from the Hittite people." ³³After Jacob finished talking to his sons, he lay down. He put his feet back on the bed, took his last breath and died.

Jacob's Burial

50 When Jacob died, Joseph hugged his father and cried over him and kissed him. ²He commanded the doctors who served him to prepare his father's body, so the doctors prepared Jacob's body to be buried. ³It took the doctors 40 days to prepare his body (the usual time it took). And the Egyptians had a time of sorrow for Jacob that lasted 70 days.

⁴When this time of sorrow had ended, Joseph spoke to the king's officers and said, "If you think well of me, please tell this to the king: ⁵'When my father was near death, I made a promise to him that I would bury him in a cave in the land of Canaan, in a burial place that he cut out for himself. So please let me go and bury my father, and then I will return.'"

⁶The king answered, "Keep your promise. Go and bury your father."

⁷So Joseph went to bury his father. All the king's officers, the elders and all the leading men of Egypt went with Joseph. ⁸Everyone who lived with Joseph and his brothers went with him, as well as everyone who lived with his father. They left only their children, their flocks and their herds in the land of Goshen. ⁹They went with Joseph in chariots and on horses. It was a very large group.

¹⁰When they came to the threshing ᵈ floor of Atad, near the Jordan River, they cried loudly and bitterly for his father. Joseph's time of sorrow continued for seven days. ¹¹The people that lived in Canaan saw the sadness at the threshing floor of Atad and said, "Those Egyptians are showing great sorrow!" So now that place is named Sorrow of the Egyptians.

¹²So Jacob's sons did as their father commanded. ¹³They carried his body to the land of Canaan and buried it in the cave in the field of Machpelah near Mamre. Abraham had bought this cave and field from Ephron the Hittite to use

as a burial place. [14]After Joseph buried his father, he returned to Egypt, along with his brothers and everyone who had gone with him to bury his father.

The Brothers Fear Joseph

[15]After Jacob died, Joseph's brothers said, "What if Joseph is still angry with us? We did many wrong things to him. What if he plans to pay us back?" [16]So they sent a message to Joseph that said, "Your father gave this command before he died. [17]He said to us, 'You have done wrong and have sinned and done evil to Joseph. Tell Joseph to forgive you, his brothers.' So now, Joseph, we beg you to forgive our wrong. We are the servants of the God of your father." When Joseph received the message, he cried.

[18]And his brothers went to him and bowed low before him and said, "We are your slaves." [19]Then Joseph said to them, "Don't be afraid. Can I do what only God can do? [20]You meant to hurt me, but God turned your evil into good to save the lives of many people, which is being done. [21]So don't be afraid. I will take care of you and your children." So Joseph comforted his brothers and spoke kind words to them.

[22]Joseph continued to live in Egypt with all his father's family. He died when he was 110 years old. [23]During Joseph's lifetime Ephraim had children and grandchildren, and Joseph's son Manasseh had a son named Makir. Joseph accepted Makir's children as his own.

The Death of Joseph

[24]Joseph said to his brothers, "I am about to die, but God will take care of you. He will lead you out of this land to the land he promised to Abraham, Isaac and Jacob." [25]Then Joseph had the sons of Israel make a promise. He said, "Promise me that you will carry my bones with you out of Egypt."

[26]Joseph died when he was 110 years old. Doctors prepared his body for burial, and then they put him in a coffin in Egypt.

Exodus

Why Read This Book:

* Discover how God works in miraculous ways to set people free (Exodus 1—18).
* Learn guidelines for living as they are described in the Ten Commandments (Exodus 20).
* Compare ancient worship practices with worship today (Exodus 25—31, 35—40).

Behind the Scenes:

"Free at last, free at last; thank God Almighty, we are free at last."

This song celebrated freedom from slavery. And it became an important song in the American civil rights struggle in the 1950s and 1960s. But the song could also have been sung by the Israelites as they escaped from Egypt with Moses as their leader.

The Israelites had settled in Egypt about 400 years earlier when Joseph arranged for them to be Egypt's guests (see Genesis 47:1–12, p.53). But, in time, Egypt's rulers died, and the new rulers turned the Israelites into slaves.

The Israelites longed for freedom from the horrific slavery.

Exodus tells how God took the Hebrew people – descendants of Abraham – and shaped them into the free nation of Israel.

The book begins with the story of Moses being saved from death. Rescued by the king's daughter, Moses grew up in the king's palace. When Moses became an adult, God called him to lead the Israelites to freedom.

Though filled with uncertainty, Moses answered God's call and argued with the Egyptian king. ▷

When?

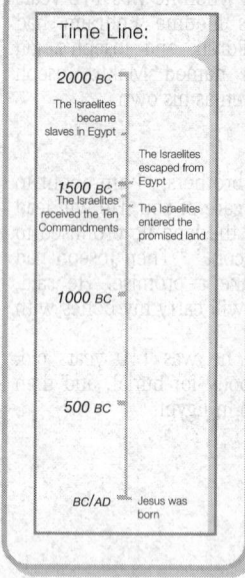

Time Line:

2000 BC
The Israelites became slaves in Egypt

The Israelites escaped from Egypt

1500 BC
The Israelites received the Ten Commandments

The Israelites entered the promised land

1000 BC

500 BC

BC/AD — Jesus was born

Where?

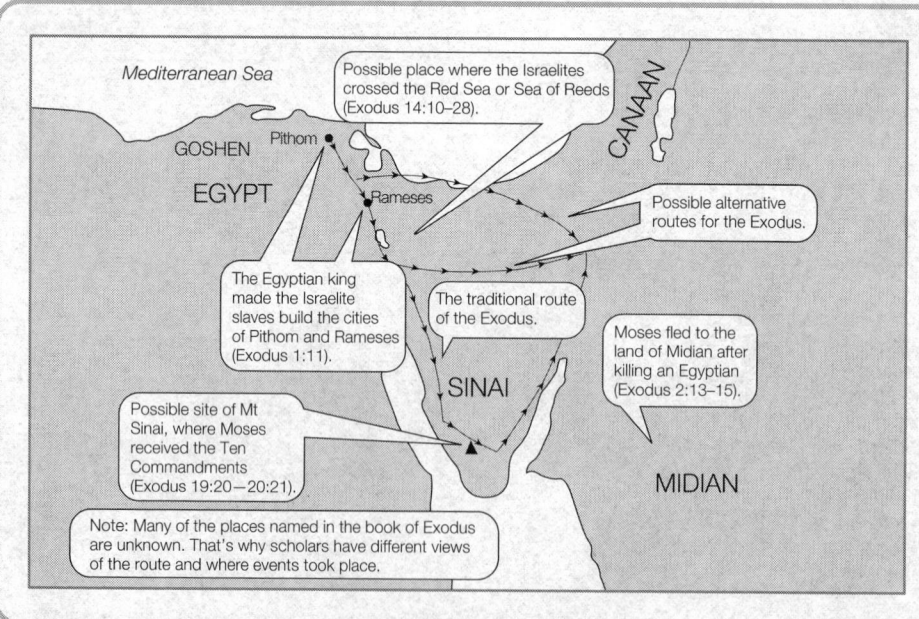

Mediterranean Sea

Possible place where the Israelites crossed the Red Sea or Sea of Reeds (Exodus 14:10–28).

CANAAN

GOSHEN   Pithom ●

EGYPT   ● Rameses

Possible alternative routes for the Exodus.

The Egyptian king made the Israelite slaves build the cities of Pithom and Rameses (Exodus 1:11).

The traditional route of the Exodus.

Moses fled to the land of Midian after killing an Egyptian (Exodus 2:13–15).

SINAI

Possible site of Mt Sinai, where Moses received the Ten Commandments (Exodus 19:20—20:21).

MIDIAN

Note: Many of the places named in the book of Exodus are unknown. That's why scholars have different views of the route and where events took place.

Behind the Scenes (cont.): Again and again the king resisted, but God's miraculous power convinced him to let Israel go. In excited celebration, the Israelites left promised land, Canaan, only to be chased by the king's army.

God's deliverance of Israel at the Red Sea is known as the Exodus.

Before reaching the promised land, however, the Israelites spent 40 ye the wilderness. There they learned more about what God wanted them to and be, as people and as a nation.

In Exodus 3:14, God reveals his name to Moses: I AM WHO I AM or YAHWEH. It means "The One Who Is Always Present". And, indeed, God was always with Moses and the Israelites in the desert. And he is always with us today.

Jacob's Family Grows Strong

1 When Jacob[n] went to Egypt, he took his sons, and each son took his own family with him. These are the names of the sons of Israel: [2]Reuben, Simeon, Levi, Judah, [3]Issachar, Zebulun, Benjamin, [4]Dan, Naphtali, Gad and Asher. [5]There was a total of 70 people who were descendants[d] of Jacob. Jacob's son Joseph was already in Egypt.

[6]Some time later, Joseph and his brothers died, along with all the people who had lived at that same time. [7]But the people of Israel had many children, and their number grew greatly. They became very strong, and the country of Egypt was filled with them.

Trouble for the People of Israel

[8]Then a new king began to rule Egypt, who did not know who Joseph was. [9]This king said to his people, "Look! The people of Israel are too many and too strong for us to handle! [10]If we don't make plans against them, the number of their people will grow even more. Then if there is a war, they might join our enemies and fight us and escape from the country!"

[11]So the Egyptians made life hard for the Israelites. They put slave masters over them, who forced the Israelites to build the cities Pithom and Rameses as supply centres for the king. [12]But the harder the Egyptians forced the Israelites to work, the more the Israelites grew in number and spread out. So the Egyptians became very afraid of them [13]and demanded even more of them. [14]They made their lives bitter. They forced the Israelites to work hard to make bricks and mortar and to do all kinds of work in the fields. The Egyptians were not merciful to them in all their painful work.

> **Sidelight** Making bricks in Egypt was a slow process for the Israelites (Exodus 1:14). Egyptian records show that a person could make about 65 bricks a day. A modern brickmaker turns out about 3,500 bricks daily.

[15]Two Hebrew nurses, named Shiphrah and Puah, helped the Israelite women give birth to their babies. The king of Egypt said to the nurses, [16]"When you are helping the Hebrew women give birth to their babies, watch! If the baby is a girl, let her live, but if it is a boy, kill him!" [17]But the nurses feared God, so they did not do as the king told them; they let all the boy babies live. [18]Then the king of Egypt sent for the nurses and said, "Why did you do this? Why did you let the boys live?"

[19]The nurses said to him, "The Hebrew women are much stronger than the Egyptian women. They give birth to their babies before we can get there." [20]God was good to the nurses. And the Hebrew people continued to grow in number, so they became even stronger. [21]Because the nurses feared God, he gave them families of their own.

[22]So the king commanded all his people, "Every time a boy is born to the Hebrews, you must throw him into the Nile River, but let all the girl babies live."

Baby Moses

2 Now a man from the family of Levi married a woman who was also from the family of Levi. [2]She became pregnant and gave birth to a son. When she saw how wonderful the baby was,

Jacob   Also called Israel.

im for three months. ³But after three she was not able to hide the baby any , so she got a basket and covered it with tar nat it would float. She put the baby in the sket. Then she put the basket among the tall stalks of grass at the edge of the Nile River. ⁴The baby's sister stood a short distance away to see what would happen to him.

⁵Then the daughter of the king of Egypt came to the river to take a bath, and her servant girls were walking beside the river. When she saw the basket in the tall grass, she sent her slave girl to get it. ⁶The king's daughter opened the basket and saw the baby boy. He was crying, so she felt sorry for him and said, "This is one of the Hebrew babies."

Sidelight

If you think waterbeds are something new, read Exodus 2:3, where Moses is given the first waterbed in the Bible. The tall grass he was placed in was probably papyrus, which the Egyptians used for making paper.

⁷Then the baby's sister asked the king's daughter, "Would you like me to go and find a Hebrew

SUFFERING

Running For His Life

Sydney Maree felt as though he didn't fit anywhere. A black in South Africa, he lived under harsh apartheid laws that restricted blacks in virtually all areas of life. He and his family could only live in black townships, and many things were denied them.

Sydney only felt at peace when he ran. There was something about running that gave him a sense of power in a world where he felt powerless because of unjust government. He'd run to school. He'd run more than a mile to the shop. He'd run everywhere he went.

When Sydney was sixteen, the high school athletics coach noticed his speed, and got him involved in running. Sydney trained tirelessly. "He was running for revenge," his trainer recalls, "running for liberation."

In 1976, his liberation began. He entered a major race in South Africa, with the help of a white businessman. The only high-schooler and the only black in the race, he won – and set a record for the fastest time ever by a high-schooler.

Sydney's life changed that day. He became a national hero and then went to school in the USA. He set records for his university and joined the US team in the 1984 Olympics.

The white businessman who helped Sydney to start racing in South Africa came to his college graduation. "Sydney started to tell me how he could never thank me enough," the supporter said. "I stopped him and said, 'No, it is I who must thank you.' Before I met him I'd only known blacks as people who did gardening for me. Now I know . . . that they too have goals and aspirations and can be like sons in my home."

Like Sydney, the Israelites faced extreme persecution as slaves in Egypt. Read about their situation in Exodus 1:6—2:10.

* How was Sydney's world like the world of the enslaved Israelites?
* How would you react if you faced the suffering the Israelites faced? How do you react to people suffering around you?

Consider . . .

* writing a story that describes a time you experienced suffering. Thank God for getting you through that tough time.
* talking to someone who has been through tremendous suffering (such as a refugee or a war veteran). What helped him or her survive?

For more, see . . .

* Psalm 57:1–11 (p.533)
* 1 John 3:16–18 (p.1374)
* Philippians 4:14–19 (p.1286)

woman to nurse the baby for you?"

8The king's daughter said, "Go!" So the girl went and got the baby's own mother.

9The king's daughter said to the woman, "Take this baby and nurse him for me, and I will pay you." So the woman took her baby and nursed him. 10When the child grew older, the woman took him to the king's daughter, and she adopted the baby as her own son. The king's daughter named him Moses, n because she had pulled him out of the water.

Moses Tries to Help

11Moses grew and became a man. One day he visited his people and saw that they were forced to work very hard. He saw an Egyptian beating a Hebrew man, one of Moses' own people. 12Moses looked all around and saw that no one was watching, so he killed the Egyptian and hid his body in the sand.

13The next day Moses returned and saw two Hebrew men fighting each other. He said to the one that was in the wrong, "Why are you hitting one of your own people?"

14The man answered, "Who made you our ruler and judge? Are you going to kill me as you killed the Egyptian?"

Moses was afraid and thought, "Now everyone knows what I did."

15When the king heard what Moses had done, he tried to kill him. But Moses ran away from the king and went to live in the land of Midian. There he sat down near a well.

Moses in Midian

16There was a priest in Midian who had seven daughters. His daughters went to that well to get water to fill the water troughs for their father's flock. 17Some shepherds came and chased the girls away, but Moses defended the girls and watered their flock.

18When they went back to their father Reuel, n he asked them, "Why have you come home early today?"

19The girls answered, "The shepherds chased us away, but an Egyptian defended us. He got water for us and watered our flock."

20He asked his daughters, "Where is this man? Why did you leave him? Invite him to eat with us."

21Moses agreed to stay with Jethro, and he gave his daughter Zipporah to Moses to be his wife. 22Zipporah gave birth to a son. Moses named him Gershom, n because Moses was a stranger in a land that was not his own.

23After a long time, the king of Egypt died. The people of Israel groaned, because they were forced to work very hard. When they cried for help, God heard them. 24God heard their cries, and he remembered the agreement he had made with Abraham, Isaac and Jacob. 25He saw the troubles of the people of Israel, and he was concerned about them.

The Burning Bush

3 One day Moses was taking care of Jethro's flock. (Jethro was the priest of Midian and also Moses' father-in-law.) When Moses led the flock to the west side of the desert, he came to Sinai, the mountain of God. 2There the angel of the LORD appeared to him in flames of fire coming out of a bush. Moses saw that the bush was on fire, but it was not burning up. 3So he said, "I will go closer to this strange thing. How can a bush continue burning without burning up?"

4When the LORD saw Moses was coming to look at the bush, God called to him from the bush, "Moses, Moses!"

And Moses said, "Here I am."

5Then God said, "Do not come any closer. Take off your sandals, because you are standing on holy ground. 6I am the God of your ancestors—the God of Abraham, the God of Isaac and the God of Jacob." Moses covered his face because he was afraid to look at God.

7The LORD said, "I have seen the troubles my people have suffered in Egypt, and I have heard their cries when the Egyptian slave masters hurt them. I am concerned about their pain, 8and I have come down to save them from the Egyptians. I will bring them out of that land and lead them to a good land with lots of room—a fertile land. It is the land of the Canaanites, Hittites, Amorites, Perizzites, Hivites and Jebusites. 9I have heard the cries of the people of Israel, and I have seen the way the Egyptians have made life hard for them. 10So now I am sending you to the king of Egypt. Go! Bring my people, the Israelites, out of Egypt!"

11But Moses said to God, "I am not a great man! How can I go to the king and lead the Israelites out of Egypt?"

12God said, "I will be with you. This will be the proof that I am sending you: after you lead the people out of Egypt, all of you will worship me on this mountain."

13Moses said to God, "When I go to the Israelites, I will say to them, 'The God of your fathers sent me to you.' What if the people say, 'What is his name?' What should I tell them?"

Moses   The name Moses sounds like the Hebrew word for "to pull out".

Reuel   He was also called Jethro.

Gershom   This name sounds like the Hebrew word for "a stranger there".

[14]Then God said to Moses, "I AM WHO I AM.[n] When you go to the people of Israel, tell them, 'I AM sent me to you.'"

[15]God also said to Moses, "This is what you should tell the people: 'The LORD is the God of your ancestors—the God of Abraham, the God of Isaac and the God of Jacob. He sent me to you.' This will always be my name, by which people from now on will know me.

[16]"Go and gather the elders and tell them this: 'The LORD, the God of your ancestors Abraham, Isaac and Jacob, has appeared to me. He said, I care about you, and I have seen what has happened to you in Egypt. [17]I promised I would take you out of your troubles in Egypt. I will lead you to the land of the Canaanites, Hittites, Amorites, Perizzites, Hivites and Jebusites—a fertile land.'

[18]"The elders will listen to you. And then you and the elders of Israel will go to the king of Egypt and tell him, 'The LORD, the God of the Hebrews, appeared to us. Let us travel three days into the desert to offer sacrifices to the LORD our God.'

I...I AM   The Hebrew words are like the name "Yahweh". This Hebrew name for God, usually called "LORD", shows that God always lives and is always with his people.

LEADERSHIP

Phone-a-Friend

The late 1980s saw a serious increase in cases of child abuse. Children of all ages were being abused emotionally and physically. The abuse took many forms, from school bullying to incest, and there seemed to be no one for desperate children to turn to for help.

Esther Rantzen, the British television presenter, enthusiastically volunteered to spearhead the launch of ChildLine – an organisation that exists to help children in desperate circumstances. All the victims have to do is to phone a special free telephone number for a friend to talk to – usually a professional counsellor who can arrange immediate help if necessary.

The ChildLine switchboard was jammed with calls as soon as it was officially opened. Children all over the country rang to get help and advice. Since then, ChildLine has firmly established itself as a helping hand – available to any child in need.

Because Esther saw the very real problem of child abuse in the United Kingdom, she took steps towards setting up an organisation which could help those in need. In a similar way, Moses heard about the Israelites' persecution in Egypt, and followed God's call to lead them to freedom. See **Exodus 3**.

* What are the differences between Esther's action and Moses' call to leadership?
* Have you, like Moses, felt called by God to take a leading role in fighting a particular problem? How have you responded to that call?

Consider . . .

* reading through a newspaper and identifying leaders and organisations who are fighting against suffering and injustice in the world. Pray for those leaders and organisations.
* making a list of the problems faced by the people around you – problems in your school, church, neighbourhood and country. Now think how you could help to solve one of those problems by taking a position of leadership.

For more, see . . .

* Psalm 22:1–12 (p.512)
* Luke 4:16–21 (p.1045)
* Micah 2:6–13 (p.892)

[19]"But I know that the king of Egypt will not let you go. Only a great power will force him to let you go, [20]so I will use my great power against Egypt. I will strike Egypt with all the miracles[d] that will happen in that land. After I do that, he will let you go. [21]I will cause the Egyptians to think well of the Israelites. So when you leave, they will give gifts to your people. [22]Each woman should ask her Egyptian neighbour and any Egyptian woman living in her house for gifts—silver, gold and clothing. You should put those gifts on your children when you leave Egypt. In this way you will take with you the riches of the Egyptians."

Proof for Moses

4 Then Moses answered, "What if the people of Israel do not believe me or listen to me? What if they say, 'The LORD did not appear to you?'"

[2]The LORD said to him, "What is that in your hand?"

Moses answered, "It's my walking stick."

[3]The LORD said, "Throw it on the ground."

So Moses threw it on the ground, and it became a snake. Moses ran from the snake, [4]but the LORD said to him, "Reach out and grab the snake by its tail." When Moses reached out and took hold of the snake, it again became a stick in his hand. [5]The LORD said, "This is so that the Israelites will believe that the LORD appeared to you. I am the God of their ancestors, the God of Abraham, the God of Isaac and the God of Jacob."

[6]Then the LORD said to Moses, "Put your hand inside your coat." So Moses put his hand inside his coat. When he took it out, it was white with a skin disease.

[7]Then he said, "Now put your hand inside your coat again." So Moses put his hand inside his coat again. When he took it out, his hand was healthy again, like the rest of his skin.

[8]Then the LORD said, "If the people do not believe you or pay attention to the first miracle,[d] they may believe you when you show them this second miracle. [9]After these two miracles, if they still do not believe or listen to you, take some water from the Nile River and pour it on the dry ground. The water will become blood when it touches the ground."

[10]But Moses said to the LORD, "Please, Lord, I have never been a skilled speaker. Even now, after talking to you, I cannot speak well. I speak slowly and can't find the best words."

[11]Then the LORD said to him, "Who made a person's mouth? And who makes someone deaf or not able to speak? Or who gives a person sight or blindness? It is I, the LORD. [12]Now go! I will help you speak, and I will teach you what to say."

[13]But Moses said, "Please, Lord, send someone else."

[14]The LORD became angry with Moses and said, "Your brother Aaron, from the family of Levi, is a skilled speaker. He is already coming to meet you, and he will be happy when he sees you. [15]You will speak to Aaron and tell him what to say. I will help both of you to speak and will teach you what to do. [16]Aaron will speak to the people for you. You will tell him what God says, and he will speak for you. [17]Take your walking stick with you, and use it to do the miracles."

Moses Returns to Egypt

[18]Moses went back to Jethro, his father-in-law, and said to him, "Let me go back to my people in Egypt. I want to see if they are still alive."

Jethro said to Moses, "Go! I wish you well."

[19]While Moses was still in Midian, the LORD said to him, "Go back to Egypt, because the men who wanted to kill you are dead now."

[20]So Moses took his wife and his sons, put them on a donkey, and started back to Egypt. He took with him the walking stick of God.

[21]The LORD said to Moses, "When you get back to Egypt, do all the miracles[d] I have given you the power to do. Show them to the king of Egypt. But I will make the king very stubborn, and he will not let the people go. [22]Then say to the king, 'This is what the LORD says: Israel is my firstborn[d] son. [23]I told you to let my son go so he may worship me. But you refused to let Israel go, so I will kill your firstborn son.'"

[24]As Moses was on his way to Egypt, he stopped at a resting place for the night. The LORD met him there and tried to kill him. [25]But Zipporah took a flint knife and circumcised[d] her son. Taking the skin, she touched Moses' feet with it and said to him, "You are a bridegroom of blood to me." [26]She said, "You are a bridegroom of blood," because she had to circumcise her son. So the LORD let Moses alone.

[27]Meanwhile the LORD said to Aaron, "Go out into the desert to meet Moses." When Aaron went, he met Moses at Sinai, the mountain of God, and kissed him. [28]Moses told Aaron everything the LORD had said to him when he sent him to Egypt. He also told him about the miracles which the LORD had commanded him to do.

[29]Moses and Aaron gathered all the elders of the Israelites, [30]and Aaron told them everything that the LORD had told Moses. Then Moses did the miracles for all the people to see, [31]and the Israelites believed. When they heard that the LORD was concerned about them and had seen their troubles, they bowed down and worshipped him.

Moses and Aaron Before the King

5 After Moses and Aaron talked to the people, they went to the king of Egypt and said, "This is what the LORD, the God of Israel, says: 'Let my people go so they may hold a feast for me in the desert.' "

²But the king of Egypt said, "Who is the LORD? Why should I obey him and let Israel go? I do not know the LORD, and I will not let Israel go."

³Then Aaron and Moses said, "The God of the Hebrews has met with us. Now let us travel three days into the desert to offer sacrifices to the LORD our God. If we don't do this, he may kill us with a disease or in war."

⁴But the king said to them, "Moses and Aaron, why are you taking the people away from their work? Go back to your work! ⁵There are very many Hebrews, and now you want them to stop working!"

⁶That same day the king gave a command to the slave masters and foremen. ⁷He said, "Don't give the people straw to make bricks as you used to do. Let them gather their own straw. ⁸But they must still make the same number of bricks as they did before. Do not accept fewer. They have become lazy, and that is why they are asking me, 'Let us go to offer sacrifices to our God.' ⁹Make these people work harder and keep them busy; then they will not have time to listen to the lies of Moses."

¹⁰So the slave masters and foremen went to the Israelites and said, "This is what the king says: 'I will no longer give you straw. ¹¹Go and get your own straw wherever you can find it. But you must make as many bricks as you made before.' " ¹²So the people went everywhere in Egypt looking for dry stalks to use for straw. ¹³The slave masters kept forcing the people to work harder. They said, "You must make just as many bricks as you did when you were given straw." ¹⁴The king's slave masters had made the Israelite foremen responsible for the work the people did. The Egyptian slave masters beat these men and asked them, "Why aren't you making as many bricks as you made in the past?"

¹⁵Then the Israelite foremen went to the king and complained, "Why are you treating us, your servants, this way? ¹⁶You give us no straw, but we are commanded to make bricks. Our slave masters beat us, but it is your own people's fault."

¹⁷The king answered, "You are lazy! You don't want to work! That is why you ask to leave here and make sacrifices to the LORD. ¹⁸Now, go back to work! We will not give you any straw, but you must make just as many bricks as you did before."

¹⁹The Israelite foremen knew they were in trouble, because the king had told them, "You must make just as many bricks each day as you did before." ²⁰As they were leaving the meeting with the king, they met Moses and Aaron, who were waiting for them. ²¹So they said to Moses and Aaron, "May the LORD punish you. You caused the king and his officers to hate us. You have given them an excuse to kill us."

Moses Complains to God

²²Then Moses returned to the LORD and said, "Lord, why have you brought this trouble on your people? Is this why you sent me here? ²³I went to the king and said what you told me to say, but ever since that time he has made the people suffer. And you have done nothing to save them."

6 Then the LORD said to Moses, "Now you will see what I will do to the king of Egypt. I will use my great power against him, and he will let my people go. Because of my power, he will force them out of his country."

²Then God said to Moses, "I am the LORD. ³I appeared to Abraham, Isaac and Jacob by the name God Almighty, but they did not know me by my name, the LORD. ⁴I also made my agreement with them to give them the land of Canaan. They lived in that land, but it was not their own. ⁵Now I have heard the cries of the Israelites, whom the Egyptians are treating as slaves, and I remember my agreement. ⁶So tell the people of Israel that I say to them, 'I am the LORD. I will save you from the hard work the Egyptians force you to do. I will make you free, so you will not be slaves to the Egyptians. I will free you by my great power, and I will punish the Egyptians terribly. ⁷I will make you my own people, and I will be your God. You will know that I am the LORD your God, the One who saves you from the hard work the Egyptians force you to do. ⁸I will lead you to the land that I promised to Abraham, Isaac and Jacob, and I will give you that land to own. I am the LORD.' "

⁹So Moses told this to the Israelites, but they would not listen to him. They were discouraged, and their slavery was hard.

¹⁰Then the LORD said to Moses, ¹¹"Go and tell the king of Egypt that he must let the Israelites leave his land."

¹²But Moses answered, "The Israelites will not listen to me, so surely the king will not listen to me either. I am not a good speaker."

¹³But the LORD spoke to Moses and Aaron and gave them orders about the Israelites and the king of Egypt. He commanded them to lead the Israelites out of Egypt.

Families of Israel

¹⁴These are the leaders of the families of Israel:

Israel's first son, Reuben, had four sons: Hanoch, Pallu, Hezron and Carmi. These are the family groups of Reuben.

¹⁵Simeon's sons were Jemuel, Jamin, Ohad, Jakin, Zohar and Shaul, the son of a Canaanite woman. These are the family groups of Simeon.

¹⁶Levi lived 137 years. These are the names of his sons according to their family history: Gershon, Kohath and Merari.

¹⁷Gershon had two sons, Libni and Shimei, with their families.

¹⁸Kohath lived for 133 years. The sons of Kohath were Amram, Izhar, Hebron and Uzziel.

¹⁹The sons of Merari were Mahli and Mushi.

These are the family groups of Levi, according to their family history.

²⁰Amram married his father's sister Jochebed, who gave birth to Aaron and Moses. Amram lived for 137 years.

²¹Izhar's sons were Korah, Nepheg and Zicri.

²²Uzziel's sons were Mishael, Elzaphan and Sithri.

²³Aaron married Elisheba, the daughter of Amminadab and the sister of Nahshon. Elisheba gave birth to Nadab, Abihu, Eleazar and Ithamar.

²⁴The sons of Korah were Assir, Elkanah and Abiasaph. These are the family groups of the Korahites.

²⁵Eleazar, son of Aaron, married a daughter of Putiel and she gave birth to Phinehas.

These are the leaders of the family groups of the Levites.

²⁶This was the Aaron and Moses to whom the LORD said, "Lead the people of Israel out of Egypt by their divisions." ²⁷Aaron and Moses are the ones who talked to the king of Egypt and told him to let the Israelites leave Egypt.

God Repeats His Call to Moses

²⁸The LORD spoke to Moses in the land of Egypt ²⁹and said, "I am the LORD. Tell the king of Egypt everything I tell you."

³⁰But Moses answered, "I am not a good speaker. The king will not listen to me."

7 The LORD said to Moses, "I have made you like God to the king of Egypt, and your brother Aaron will be like a prophet *d* for you. ²Tell Aaron your brother everything that I command you, and let him tell the king of Egypt to let the Israelites leave his country. ³But I will make the king stubborn. I will do many miracles *d* in Egypt, ⁴but he will still refuse to listen. So then I will punish Egypt terribly, and I will lead my divisions, my people the Israelites, out of that land. ⁵I will punish Egypt with my power, and I will bring the Israelites out of that land. Then they will know I am the LORD."

⁶Moses and Aaron did just as the LORD had commanded them. ⁷Moses was 80 years old and Aaron was 83 when they spoke to the king.

Aaron's Walking Stick Becomes a Snake

⁸The LORD said to Moses and Aaron, ⁹"Moses, when the king asks you to do a miracle, *d* tell Aaron to throw his walking stick down in front of the king, and it will become a snake."

¹⁰So Moses and Aaron went to the king as the LORD had commanded. Aaron threw his walking stick down in front of the king and his officers, and it became a snake.

¹¹So the king called in his wise men and his magicians, and with their tricks the Egyptian magicians were able to do the same thing. ¹²They threw their walking sticks on the ground, and their sticks became snakes. But Aaron's stick swallowed theirs. ¹³Still the king was stubborn and refused to listen to Moses and Aaron, just as the LORD had said.

The Water Becomes Blood

¹⁴Then the LORD said to Moses, "The king is being stubborn and refuses to let the people go. ¹⁵In the morning the king will go out to the Nile River. Go and meet him by the edge of the river, and take with you the walking stick that became a snake. ¹⁶Tell him: the LORD, the God of the Hebrews, sent me to you. He said, 'Let my people go and worship me in the desert.' Until now you have not listened. ¹⁷This is what the LORD says: 'This is how you will know that I am the LORD. I will strike the water of the Nile River with this stick in my hand, and the water will change into blood. ¹⁸Then the fish in the Nile will die, and the river will begin to stink. The Egyptians will not be able to drink the water from the Nile.' "

¹⁹The LORD said to Moses, "Tell Aaron: 'Take the walking stick in your hand and stretch your hand over the rivers, canals, ponds and pools in Egypt.' The water will become blood everywhere in Egypt, both in wooden buckets and in stone jars."

²⁰So Moses and Aaron did just as the LORD had commanded. In front of the king and his officers, Aaron raised his walking stick and struck the water in the Nile River. So all the water in the Nile changed into blood. ²¹The fish in the Nile died, and the river began to stink, so the Egyptians could not drink water from it. Blood was everywhere in the land of Egypt.

²²Using their tricks, the magicians of Egypt did the same thing. So the king was stubborn and refused to listen to Moses and Aaron, just as the LORD had said. ²³The king turned and went into his palace and ignored what Moses and Aaron had done. ²⁴The Egyptians could not drink the

water from the Nile, so all of them dug along the bank of the river, looking for water to drink.

The Frogs

²⁵Seven days passed after the LORD changed the Nile River into blood.

8 Then the LORD told Moses, "Go to the king of Egypt and tell him, 'This is what the LORD says: let my people go to worship me. ²If you refuse, I will punish Egypt with frogs. ³The Nile River will be filled with frogs. They will come up into your palace, into your bedroom, on your bed, into the houses of your officers and onto your people. They will come into your ovens and into your baking pans. ⁴The frogs will jump all over you, your people and your officers.'"

⁵Then the LORD said to Moses, "Tell Aaron to hold his walking stick in his hand over the rivers, canals and ponds. Make frogs come up out of the water onto the land of Egypt."

⁶So Aaron held his hand over all the waters of Egypt, and the frogs came up out of the water and covered the land of Egypt. ⁷The magicians used their tricks to do the same thing, so even more frogs came up onto the land of Egypt.

⁸The king called for Moses and Aaron and said, "Pray to the LORD to take the frogs away from me and my people. I will let your people go to offer sacrifices to the LORD."

⁹Moses said to the king, "Please set the time when I should pray for you, your people and your officers. Then the frogs will leave you and your houses and will remain only in the Nile."

¹⁰The king answered, "Tomorrow."

Moses said, "What you want will happen. By this you will know that there is no one like the LORD our God. ¹¹The frogs will leave you, your houses, your officers and your people. They will remain only in the Nile."

¹²After Moses and Aaron left the king, Moses asked the LORD about the frogs he had sent to the king. ¹³And the LORD did as Moses asked. The frogs died in the houses, in the yards and in the fields. ¹⁴The Egyptians put them in piles, and the whole country began to stink. ¹⁵But when the king saw that they were free of the frogs, he became stubborn again. He did not listen to Moses and Aaron, just as the LORD had said.

The Gnats

¹⁶Then the LORD said to Moses, "Tell Aaron to raise his walking stick and strike the dust on the ground. Then everywhere in Egypt the dust will change into gnats." ¹⁷They did this, and when Aaron raised the walking stick that was in his hand and struck the dust on the ground, everywhere in Egypt the dust changed into gnats. The gnats got on the people and animals. ¹⁸Using their tricks, the magicians tried to do the same thing, but they could not make the dust change into gnats. The gnats remained on the people and animals. ¹⁹So the magicians told the king that the power of God had done this. But the king was stubborn and refused to listen to them, just as the LORD had said.

The Flies

²⁰The LORD told Moses, "Get up early in the morning, and meet the king of Egypt as he goes out to the river. Tell him, 'This is what the LORD says: let my people go so they can worship me. ²¹If you don't let them go, I will send swarms of flies into your houses. The flies will be on you, your officers and your people. The houses of Egypt will be full of flies, and they will be all over the ground, too. ²²But I will not treat the Israelites the same as the Egyptian people. There will not be any flies in the land of Goshen, where my people live. By this you will know that I, the LORD, am in this land. ²³I will treat my people differently from your people. This miracle *d* will happen tomorrow.'"

²⁴So the LORD did as he had said, and great swarms of flies came into the king's palace and his officers' houses. All over Egypt flies were ruining the land. ²⁵The king called for Moses and Aaron and told them, "Offer sacrifices to your God here in this country."

²⁶But Moses said, "It wouldn't be right to do that, because the Egyptians hate the sacrifices we offer to the LORD our God. If they see us offering sacrifices they hate, they will throw stones at us and kill us. ²⁷Let us make a three-day journey into the desert. We must offer sacrifices to the LORD our God there, as the LORD told us to do."

²⁸The king said, "I will let you go so that you may offer sacrifices to the LORD your God in the desert, but you must not go very far away. Now go and pray for me."

²⁹Moses said, "I will leave and pray to the LORD, and he will take the flies away from you, your officers and your people tomorrow. But do not try to trick us again. Do not stop the people from going to offer sacrifices to the LORD."

³⁰So Moses left the king and prayed to the LORD, ³¹and the LORD did as he asked. He removed the flies from the king, his officers and his people so that not one fly was left. ³²But the king became stubborn again and did not let the people go.

The Disease on the Farm Animals

9 Then the LORD told Moses, "Go to the king of Egypt and tell him, 'This is what the LORD, the God of the Hebrews, says: let my people go to worship me. ²If you refuse to let them go and continue to hold them, ³the LORD will punish you.

He will send a terrible disease on your farm animals that are in the fields. He will cause your horses, donkeys, camels, cattle, goats and sheep to become sick. 4But the LORD will treat Israel's animals differently from the animals of Egypt. None of the animals that belong to the Israelites will die. 5The LORD has set tomorrow as the time he will do this in the land.' " 6The next day the LORD did as he promised. All the farm animals in Egypt died, but none of the animals belonging to the Israelites died. 7The king sent people to see what had happened to the animals of Israel, and they found that not one of them had died. But the king was still stubborn and did not let the people go.

The Boils

8The LORD said to Moses and Aaron, "Fill your hands with ashes from a furnace. Moses, throw the ashes into the air in front of the king of Egypt. 9The ashes will spread like dust through all the land of Egypt. They will cause boils to break out and become sores on the skin of people and animals everywhere in the land."

10So Moses and Aaron took ashes from a furnace and went and stood before the king. Moses threw ashes into the air, which caused boils to break out and become sores on people and animals. 11The magicians could not stand before Moses, because all the Egyptians had boils, even the magicians. 12But the LORD made the king stubborn, so he refused to listen to Moses and Aaron, just as the LORD had said.

The Hail

13Then the LORD said to Moses, "Get up early in the morning and go to the king of Egypt. Tell him, 'This is what the LORD, the God of the Hebrews, says: let my people go to worship me. 14If you don't, this time I will punish you, your officers and your people, with all my power. Then you will know there is no one in the whole land like me. 15By now I could have used my power and caused a terrible disease that would have destroyed you and your people from the earth. 16But I have let you live for this reason: to show you my power so that my name will be talked about in all the earth. 17You are still against my people and do not want to let them go. 18So at this time tomorrow, I will send a terrible hail-storm, the worst in Egypt since it became a nation. 19Now send for your animals and whatever you have in the fields, and bring them into a safe place. The hail will fall on every person or animal that is still in the fields. If they have not been brought in, they will die.' " 20Some of the king's officers respected the word of the LORD and hurried to bring their slaves and animals inside.

21But others ignored the LORD's message and left their slaves and animals in the fields.

22The LORD told Moses, "Raise your hand towards the sky. Then the hail will start falling in all the land of Egypt. It will fall on people, animals and on everything that grows in the fields of Egypt." 23When Moses raised his walking stick towards the sky, the LORD sent thunder and hail, and lightning flashed down to the earth. So he caused hail to fall upon the land of Egypt. 24There was hail, and lightning flashed as it hailed—the worst hailstorm in Egypt since it had become a nation. 25The hail destroyed all the people and animals that were in the fields in all the land of Egypt. It also destroyed everything that grew in the fields and broke all the trees in the fields. 26The only place it did not hail was in the land of Goshen, where the Israelites lived.

27The king sent for Moses and Aaron and told them, "This time I have sinned. The LORD is in the right, and I and my people are in the wrong. 28Pray to the LORD. We have had enough of God's thunder and hail. I will let you go; you do not have to stay here any longer."

29Moses told the king, "When I leave the city, I will raise my hands to the LORD in prayer, and the thunder and hail will stop. Then you will know that the earth belongs to the LORD. 30But I know that you and your officers do not yet fear the LORD God."

31The flax was in bloom, and the barley had ripened, so these crops were destroyed. 32But both wheat crops ripen later, so they were not destroyed.

33Moses left the king and went outside the city. He raised his hands to the LORD, and the thunder and hail stopped. The rain also stopped falling to the ground. 34When the king saw that the rain, hail and thunder had stopped, he sinned again, and he and his officers became stubborn. 35So the king became stubborn and refused to let the Israelites go, just as the LORD had said through Moses.

The Locusts

10 The LORD said to Moses, "Go to the king of Egypt. I have made him and his officers stubborn so I could show them my powerful miracles. d 2I also did this so you could tell your children and your grandchildren how I was hard on the Egyptians. Tell them about the miracles I did among them so that all of you will know that I am the LORD."

3So Moses and Aaron went to the king and told him, "This is what the LORD, the God of the Hebrews, says: 'How long will you refuse to be sorry for what you have done? Let my people go to worship me. 4If you refuse to let my people go, tomorrow I will bring locusts *d* into your country. [5]They will cover the land so that no one will be able to see the ground. They will eat anything that was left from the hailstorm and the leaves from every tree growing in the field. [6]They will fill your palaces and all your officers' houses, as well as the houses of all the Egyptians. There will be more locusts than your fathers or ancestors have ever seen—more than there have been since people began living in Egypt.' " Then Moses turned and walked away from the king.

[7]The king's officers asked him, "How long will this man make trouble for us? Let the Israelites go to worship the LORD their God. Don't you know that Egypt is ruined?"

[8]So Moses and Aaron were brought back to the king. He said to them, "Go and worship the LORD your God. But tell me, just who is going?"

[9]Moses answered, "We will go with our young and old people, our sons and daughters, and our flocks and herds, because we are going to have a feast to honour the LORD."

[10]The king said to them, "The LORD will really have to be with you if ever I let you and all of your children leave Egypt. See, you are planning something evil! [11]No! Only the men may go and worship the LORD, which is what you have been asking for." Then the king forced Moses and Aaron out of his palace.

[12]The LORD told Moses, "Raise your hand over the land of Egypt, and the locusts will come. They will spread all over the land of Egypt and will eat all the plants the hail did not destroy."

[13]So Moses raised his walking stick over the land of Egypt, and the LORD caused a strong wind to blow from the east. It blew across the land all that day and night, and when morning came, the east wind had brought the locusts. [14]Swarms of locusts covered all the land of Egypt and settled everywhere. There were more locusts than ever before or after, [15]and they covered the whole land so that it was black. They ate everything that was left after the hail—every plant in the field and all the fruit on the trees. Nothing green was left on any tree or plant anywhere in Egypt.

[16]The king quickly called for Moses and Aaron. He said, "I have sinned against the LORD your God and against you. [17]Now forgive my sin this time. Pray to the LORD your God, and ask him to stop this punishment that kills."

[18]Moses left the king and prayed to the LORD. [19]So the LORD changed the wind. He made a very strong wind blow from the west, and it blew the locusts away into the Red Sea. *d* Not one locust was left anywhere in Egypt. [20]But the LORD caused the king to be stubborn again, and he did not let the Israelites go.

The Darkness

[21]Then the LORD told Moses, "Raise your hand towards the sky, and darkness will cover the land of Egypt. It will be so dark you will be able to feel it." [22]Moses raised his hand towards the sky, and total darkness was everywhere in Egypt for three days. [23]No one could see anyone else, and no one could go anywhere for three days. But the Israelites had light where they lived.

[24]Again the king of Egypt called for Moses. He said, "All of you may go and worship the LORD. You may take your women and children with you, but you must leave your flocks and herds here."

[25]Moses said, "You must let us have animals to use as sacrifices and burnt offerings, because we have to offer them to the LORD our God. [26]So we must take our animals with us; not a hoof will be left behind. We have to use some of the animals to worship the LORD our God. We won't know exactly what we will need to worship the LORD until we get there."

[27]But the LORD made the king stubborn again, so he refused to let them go. [28]Then he told Moses, "Get out of here, and don't come again! The next time you see me, you will die."

[29]Then Moses told the king, "I'll do what you say. I will not come to see you again."

The Death of the Firstborn

11 Now the LORD had told Moses, "I have one more way to punish the king and the people of Egypt. After this, the king will send all of you away from Egypt. When he does, he will force you to leave completely. [2]Tell the men and women of Israel to ask their neighbours for things made of silver and gold." [3]The LORD had caused the Egyptians to respect the Israelites, and both the king's officers and the Egyptian people considered Moses to be a great man.

[4]So Moses said to the king, "This is what the LORD says: 'About midnight tonight I will go through all Egypt. [5]Every firstborn *d* son in the land of Egypt will die—from the firstborn son of the king, who sits on his throne, to the firstborn of the slave girl grinding grain. Also the firstborn farm animals will die. [6]There will be loud crying everywhere in Egypt, worse than at any time before or after this. [7]But not even a dog will bark at the Israelites or their animals.' Then you will know that the LORD treats Israel differently from Egypt. [8]All your officers will come to me. They will bow face down to the ground before me and say, 'Leave and take all your people with you.' After that, I will leave." Then Moses very angrily left the king.

[9]The LORD had told Moses, "The king will not listen to you and Aaron so that I may do many miracles *d* in the land of Egypt." [10]Moses and

Aaron did all these great miracles in front of the king. But the LORD made him stubborn, and the king would not let the Israelites leave his country.

The First Passover

12 The LORD spoke to Moses and Aaron in the land of Egypt: [2]"This month will be the beginning of months, the first month of the year for you. [3]Tell the whole community of Israel that on the tenth day of this month each man must get one lamb for the people in his house. [4]If there are not enough people in his house to eat a whole lamb, he must share it with his closest neighbour, considering the number of people. There must be enough lamb for everyone to eat. [5]The lamb must be a one-year-old male that has nothing wrong with it. This animal can be either a young sheep or a young goat. [6]Take care of the animals until the fourteenth day of the month. On that day all the people of the community of Israel will kill them in the evening before dark. [7]The people must take some of the blood and put it on the sides and tops of the doorframes of the houses where they eat the lambs. [8]On this night they must roast the lamb over a fire. They must eat it with bitter herbs and bread made without yeast. [9]Do not eat the lamb raw or boiled in water. Roast the whole lamb over a fire—with its head, legs and inner organs. [10]You must not leave any of it until morning, but if any of it is left over until morning, you must burn it with fire.

[11]"This is the way you must eat it: you must be fully dressed as if you were going on a trip. You must have your sandals on and your walking stick

GOD'S LOVE

Waiting For Miracles

When the children in George Muller's orphanage in Bristol ate dinner, they didn't know that the food on their plates was the only food in the orphanage. There was no food or money left for next morning's breakfast. George prayed that something would arrive that evening, but nothing did. He went to bed, committing the need to God.

The next morning, George went out for his early morning walk and prayer. For some reason, he took a different route than usual, and a friend saw him. "I'm glad to see you," his friend said. "Please accept five pounds for the orphans."

"Thank you," George said graciously, never mentioning that the money would provide the children's food for several days. "God bless you."

Because of his faith, George fed hundreds of homeless children in Bristol in the 1800s. But he never made public appeals for funds.

When the food ran out at the orphanage, George told no one but God. And, miraculously, God supplied it time and time again. When George was low on funds, only God knew. And the money arrived when George needed it.

George Muller would never have been able to help hundreds of orphans without God's love to provide for them. In the same way, the Israelites would never have escaped from Egypt without God's love to protect them. Read **Exodus 12:1–14** to see how God's love delivered them during the Passover.

* What similarities do you see between God's provision for George Muller's orphanages and his protection of the Israelites during the Passover?
* Has God's love helped you through a situation you could never have survived on your own? How did the experience make you feel about God?

Consider . . .

* thanking God for his love that has delivered you in the past from difficult situations.
* writing on a card a difficult situation you are experiencing. Put the card in a place where you will find it in a week or so to see how God has helped you through that difficult time.

For more, see . . .

* Psalm 34 (p.519)
* Romans 5:1–11 (p.1190)
* Hosea 14:1–8 (p.860)

in your hand. You must eat it in a hurry; this is the LORD's Passover. *d*

12"That night I will go through the land of Egypt and kill all the firstborn *d* animals and people in the land of Egypt. I will also punish all the gods of Egypt. I am the LORD. 13But the blood will be a sign on the houses where you are. When I see the blood, I will pass over you. Nothing terrible will hurt you when I punish the land of Egypt.

14"You are always to remember this day and celebrate it with a feast to the LORD. Your descendants *d* are to honour the LORD with this feast from now on. 15For this feast you must eat bread made without yeast for seven days. On the first day, you are to remove all the yeast from your houses. No one should eat any yeast for the full seven days of the feast, or that person will be cut off from Israel. 16You are to have holy meetings on the first and last days of the feast. You must not do any work on these days; the only work you may do is to prepare your meals. 17You must celebrate the Feast *d* of Unleavened Bread, because on this very day I brought your divisions of people out of Egypt. So all of your descendants must celebrate this day. This is a law that will last from now on. 18In the first month of the year you are to eat bread made without yeast, from the evening of the fourteenth day until the evening of the twenty-first day. 19For seven days there must not be any yeast in your houses. Anybody who eats yeast during this time, either an Israelite or non-Israelite, must be cut off from the community of Israel. 20During this feast you must not eat anything made with yeast. You must eat only bread made without yeast wherever you live."

21Then Moses called all the elders of Israel together and told them, "Get the animals for your families and kill the lamb for the Passover. 22Take a branch of the hyssop plant, dip it into the bowl filled with blood, and then wipe the blood on the sides and tops of the doorframes. No one may leave that house until morning. 23When the LORD goes through Egypt to kill the Egyptians, he will see the blood on the sides and tops of the doorframes, and he will pass over that house. He will not let the one who brings death come into your houses and kill you.

24"You must keep this command as a law for you and your descendants from now on. 25Do this when you go to the land the LORD has promised to give you. 26When your children ask you, 'Why are we doing these things?' 27you will say, 'This is the Passover sacrifice to honour the LORD. When we were in Egypt, the LORD passed over the houses of Israel, and when he killed the Egyptians, he saved our homes.'" Then the people bowed down and worshipped the LORD. 28They did just as the LORD commanded Moses and Aaron.

29At midnight the LORD killed all the firstborn sons in the land of Egypt—from the firstborn of the king who sat on the throne to the firstborn of the prisoner in jail. Also, all the firstborn farm animals died. 30The king, his officers and all the Egyptians got up during the night because someone had died in every house. So there was a loud outcry everywhere in Egypt.

Israel Leaves Egypt

31During the night the king called for Moses and Aaron and said, "Get up and leave my people. You and your people may do as you have asked; go and worship the LORD. 32Take all of your flocks and herds as you have asked, and go. And also bless me." 33The Egyptians also asked the Israelites to hurry and leave, saying, "If you don't leave, we will all die!"

34So the people took their dough before the yeast was added. They wrapped the bowls for making dough in clothing and carried them on their shoulders. 35The Israelites did what Moses told them to do and asked their Egyptian neighbours for things made of silver and gold and for clothing. 36The LORD caused the Egyptians to think well of them, and the Egyptians gave the people everything they asked for. So the Israelites took rich gifts from them.

37The Israelites travelled from Rameses to Succoth. There were about 600,000 men walking, not including the women and children. 38Many other people who were not Israelites went with them, as well as a large number of sheep, goats and cattle. 39The Israelites used the dough they had brought out of Egypt to bake loaves of bread without yeast. The dough had no yeast in it, because they had been rushed out of Egypt and had no time to get food ready for their trip.

40The people of Israel had lived in Egypt for 430 years; 41on the very day the 430 years ended, the LORD's divisions of people left Egypt. 42That night the LORD kept watch to bring them out of Egypt, and so on this same night the Israelites are to keep watch to honour the LORD from now on.

43The LORD told Moses and Aaron, "Here are the rules for Passover: *d* no foreigner is to eat the Passover. 44If someone buys a slave and circumcises *d* him, the slave may eat the Passover. 45But neither a person who lives for a short time in your country nor a hired worker may eat it.

46"The meal must be eaten inside a house; take none of the meat outside the house. Don't break any of the bones. 47The whole community of Israel must take part in this feast. 48A foreigner who lives with you may share in the LORD's Passover if all the males in his house become circumcised. Then, since he will be like a citizen of Israel, he may share in the meal. But a man who is not circumcised may not eat the Passover meal. ⁴⁹The same rules apply to an Israelite born in the country or to a foreigner living there."

⁵⁰So all the Israelites did just as the LORD had commanded Moses and Aaron. ⁵¹On that same day the LORD led the Israelites out of Egypt by their divisions.

The Law of the Firstborn

13 Then the LORD said to Moses, ²"Give every firstborn *d* male to me. Every firstborn male among the Israelites belongs to me, whether human or animal."

³Moses said to the people, "Remember this day, the day you left Egypt. You were slaves in that land, but the LORD with his great power brought you out of it. You must not eat bread made with yeast. ⁴Today, in the month of Abib, *d* you are leaving Egypt. ⁵The LORD will lead you to the land of the Canaanites, Hittites, Amorites, Hivites and Jebusites. This is the land he promised your ancestors he would give you, a fertile land. There you must celebrate this feast during the first month of every year. ⁶For seven days you must eat bread made without yeast, and on the seventh day there will be a feast to honour the LORD. ⁷So for seven days you must not eat any bread made with yeast. There must be no bread made with yeast anywhere in your land. ⁸On that day you should tell your son: 'We are having this feast because of what the LORD did for me when I came out of Egypt.' ⁹This feast will help you remember, like a mark on your hand or a reminder on your forehead. This feast will remind you to speak the LORD's teachings, because the LORD used his great power to bring you out of Egypt. ¹⁰So celebrate this feast every year at the right time.

¹¹"And when the LORD takes you into the land of the Canaanites, the land he promised to give you and your ancestors, ¹²you must give him every firstborn male. Also every firstborn male animal must be given to the LORD. ¹³Buy back every firstborn donkey by offering a lamb. But if you don't want to buy the donkey back, then break its neck. You must buy back from the LORD every firstborn of your sons.

¹⁴"From now on when your son asks you, 'What does this mean?' you will answer, 'With his great power, the LORD brought us out from Egypt, the land where we were slaves. ¹⁵The king of Egypt was stubborn and refused to let us leave. But the LORD killed every firstborn male in Egypt, both human and animal. That is why I sacrifice every firstborn male animal to the LORD, and that is why I buy back each of my firstborn sons from the LORD.' ¹⁶This feast is like a mark on your hand and a reminder

on your forehead to help you remember that the LORD brought us out of Egypt with his great power."

The Way Out of Egypt

¹⁷When the king sent the people out of Egypt, God did not lead them on the road through the Philistine country, though that was the shortest way. God said, "If they have to fight, they might change their minds and go back to Egypt." ¹⁸So God led them through the desert towards the Red Sea. *d* The Israelites were dressed for fighting when they left the land of Egypt.

¹⁹Moses carried the bones of Joseph with him, because before Joseph died, he had made the Israelites promise to do this. He had said, "When God saves you, remember to carry my bones with you out of Egypt."

²⁰The Israelites left Succoth and camped at Etham, on the edge of the desert. ²¹The LORD showed them the way; during the day he went ahead of them in a pillar of cloud, and during the night he was in a pillar of fire to give them light. In this way they could travel during the day or night. ²²The pillar of cloud was always with them during the day, and the pillar of fire was always with them at night.

14 Then the LORD said to Moses, ²"Tell the Israelites to turn back to Pi Hahiroth and to camp between Migdol and the Red Sea. Camp across from Baal Zephon, on the shore of the sea. ³The king will think, 'The Israelites are lost, trapped by the desert.' ⁴I will make the king stubborn again so he will chase after them, but I will defeat the king and his army. This will bring honour to me, and the Egyptians will know that I am the LORD." The Israelites did just as they were told.

The King Chases the Israelites

⁵When the king of Egypt was told that the Israelites had left, he and his officers changed their minds about them. They said, "What have we done? We have let the Israelites leave. We have lost our slaves!" ⁶So the king prepared his war chariot and took his army with him. ⁷He took 600 of his best chariots, together with all the other chariots of Egypt, each with an officer in it. ⁸The LORD made the king of Egypt stubborn, so he chased the Israelites, who were leaving victoriously. ⁹The Egyptians—with all the king's horses, chariot drivers and army—chased the Israelites. They caught up with them while they were camped by the Red Sea, *d* near Pi Hahiroth and Baal Zephon.

¹⁰When the Israelites saw the king and his army coming after them, they were very frightened and cried to the LORD for help. ¹¹They said

to Moses, "What have you done to us? Why did you bring us out of Egypt to die in the desert? There were plenty of graves for us in Egypt. 12We told you in Egypt, 'Let us alone; we will stay and serve the Egyptians.' Now we will die in the desert."

13But Moses answered, "Don't be afraid! Stand still and you will see the LORD save you today. You will never see these Egyptians again after today. 14You only need to remain calm; the LORD will fight for you."

15Then the LORD said to Moses, "Why are you crying out to me? Command the Israelites to start moving. 16Raise your walking stick and hold it over the sea so that the sea will split and the people can cross it on dry land. 17I will make the Egyptians stubborn so they will chase the Israelites, but I will be honoured when I defeat the king and all of his chariot drivers and chariots. 18When I defeat the king, his chariot drivers and

chariots, the Egyptians will know that I am the LORD."

19Now the angel of God who usually travelled in front of Israel's army moved behind them. Also, the pillar of cloud moved from in front of the people and stood behind them. 20So the cloud came between the Egyptians and the Israelites. This made it dark for the Egyptians but gave light to the Israelites. So the cloud kept the two armies apart all night.

21Then Moses held his hand over the sea. All that night the LORD drove back the sea with a strong east wind, making the sea become dry ground. The water was split, 22and the Israelites went through the sea on dry land, with a wall of water on their right and on their left.

23Then all the king's horses, chariots and chariot drivers followed them into the sea. 24When morning came, the LORD looked down from the pillar of cloud and fire at the Egyptian army and

FREEDOM

A Place to Call Home

The hot August night made it too stuffy to sleep. Elizabeth looked at her four children lying in the boxes in the back of her old car – the family's only home. She felt trapped with nowhere to go and no one to turn to.

"Oh God, my God," she cried and prayed silently. "Where are you, God? Have you forsaken me?" And she fell into a restless sleep.

For the next week, she went from hostel to hostel, hoping to find a place to live. One shelter took only children, and her four children wanted to be with their mum. When a hostel finally had room for all of them, it still wasn't a home.

Then a Christian friend gave Elizabeth hope. She arranged for the family to rent a house without having to pay a deposit first – and the first month was free. "God has told me to help you," the owner explained.

The new home gave Elizabeth a freedom from poverty that she had never known. "As a family, we've never been more secure," she says. "God solved my problem by using his people."

Elizabeth experienced new freedom from poverty and hopelessness as God worked through his people. The Israelites gained freedom from slavery in Egypt through Moses' leadership and God's work. Read about how they gained their freedom in **Exodus 14:19–31**.

* What feelings do you think Elizabeth would have if she read the story of the Israelites' new freedom? What parts would be most meaningful to her?
* As God led the Israelites to freedom, when has he freed you from a difficult situation? How did you celebrate?

Consider . . .

* finding someone in your school or church who's trapped by poverty, prejudice, or some other form of captivity. Talk to the person to find a way you can help him or her gain freedom.
* contacting a branch of Shelter in your area and volunteering to help repair homes.

For more, see . . .

* Exodus 15:1–11 (p.73)
* Galatians 5:1–15 (p.1263)
* John 8:31–38 (p.1110)

made them panic. ²⁵He kept the wheels of the chariots from turning, making it hard to drive the chariots. The Egyptians shouted, "Let's get away from the Israelites! The LORD is fighting for them and against Egypt."

²⁶Then the LORD told Moses, "Hold your hand over the sea so that the water will come back over the Egyptians, their chariots and chariot drivers." ²⁷So Moses raised his hand over the sea, and at dawn the sea returned to its place. The Egyptians tried to run from it, but the LORD swept them away into the sea. ²⁸The water returned, covering the chariots, chariot drivers and all the king's army that had followed the Israelites into the sea. Not one of them survived.

²⁹But the Israelites crossed the sea on dry land, with a wall of water on their right and on their left. ³⁰So that day the LORD saved the Israelites from the Egyptians, and the Israelites saw the Egyptians lying dead on the seashore. ³¹When the Israelites saw the great power the LORD had used against the Egyptians, they feared the LORD, and they trusted him and his servant Moses.

The Song of Moses

15 Then Moses and the Israelites sang this song to the LORD:

"I will sing to the LORD,
  because he is worthy of great honour.
He has thrown the horse and its rider
  into the sea.
²The LORD gives me strength and makes me
      sing;
  he has saved me.
He is my God,
  and I will praise him.
He is the God of my fathers,
  and I will honour him.
³The LORD is a warrior;
  the LORD is his name.
⁴The chariots and soldiers of the king of Egypt
  he has thrown into the sea.
The king's best officers
  are drowned in the Red Sea. *d*
⁵The deep waters covered them,
  and they sank to the bottom like a rock.
⁶Your right hand, LORD,
  is amazingly strong.
LORD, your right hand
  broke the enemy to pieces.
⁷In your great victory
  you destroyed those who were against you.
Your anger destroyed them,
  like fire burning straw.
⁸Just a blast of your breath,
  and the waters piled up.
The moving waters stood like a wall;

the deep waters became solid in the middle
  of the sea.

⁹"The enemy boasted,
  'I'll chase them and catch them.
I'll take all their riches;
  I'll take all I want.
I'll pull out my sword,
  and my hand will destroy them.'
¹⁰But you blew on them with your breath
  and covered them with the sea.
They sank like lead
  in the raging water.

¹¹"Are there any gods like you, LORD?
  There are no gods like you.
You are wonderfully holy,
  amazingly powerful,
  a worker of miracles. *d*
¹²You reached out with your right hand,
  and the earth swallowed our enemies.
¹³You keep your loving promise
  and lead the people you have saved.
With your strength you will guide them
  to your holy place.

¹⁴"The other nations will hear this and tremble
      with fear;
  terror will take hold of the Philistines.
¹⁵The leaders of the tribes *d* of Edom will be
      very frightened;
  the powerful men of Moab will shake with fear;
  the people of Canaan will lose all their
      courage.
¹⁶Terror and fear will fall on them.
When they see your strength,
  they will be as still as a rock.
They will be still until your people pass by, LORD.
  They will be still until the people you have
      taken as your own pass by.
¹⁷You will lead your people and place them
  on your very own mountain,
  the place that you, LORD, made for yourself to
      live,
  the temple, Lord, that your hands have made.
¹⁸The LORD will be king for ever!"

¹⁹The horses, chariot drivers and chariots of the king of Egypt went into the sea, and the LORD covered them with water from the sea. But the Israelites walked through the sea on dry land. ²⁰Then Aaron's sister, Miriam, a prophetess, *d* took a tambourine *d* in her hand. All the women followed her, playing tambourines and dancing. ²¹Miriam told them:

"Sing to the LORD,
  because he is worthy of great honour;
he has thrown the horse and its rider
  into the sea."

Bitter Water Becomes Good

[22]Moses led the Israelites away from the Red Sea [d] into the Desert of Shur. They travelled for three days in the desert but found no water. [23]Then they came to Marah, where there was water, but they could not drink it because it was too bitter. (That is why the place was named Marah. [n]) [24]The people grumbled to Moses and asked, "What will we drink?"

[25]So Moses cried out to the LORD, and the LORD showed him a tree. When Moses threw the tree into the water, the water became good to drink.

There the LORD gave the people a rule and a law to live by, and there he tested their loyalty to him. [26]He said, "You must obey the LORD your God and do what he says is right. If you obey all his commands and keep his rules, I will not bring on you any of the sicknesses I brought on the Egyptians. I am the LORD who heals you."

[27]Then the people travelled to Elim, where there were twelve springs of water and 70 palm trees. So the people camped there near the water.

The People Demand Food

16 The whole Israelite community left Elim and came to the Desert of Sin, which was between Elim and Sinai; they arrived there on the fifteenth day of the second month after they had left Egypt. [2]Then the whole Israelite community grumbled to Moses and Aaron in the desert. [3]They said to them, "It would have been

Marah   This name means "bitter".

WORRYING

A Little Hope

Jimmy, fifteen, has a lot to worry about. Born with cystic fibrosis, a lung disease, he has been in hospital five or six times a year since he was six. Every day he takes 25 pills and spends 20 minutes in physiotherapy.

Whenever he has a cold, he has to have injections. And if he feels a little sick, he has to go to the hospital immediately. As a result, he misses 50 to 60 days of school each year.

"My body is a bit like a car that everyone wants to keep in tip-top shape," he explains.

Jimmy also has a future to worry about. "I have to realise that, no matter what, I'll never be totally independent," he says. "There's always going to have to be someone there for me."

Yet Jimmy doesn't worry. "There are some things in life you have choices about and there are things you don't," he explains. "God will take care of whatever is going to happen."

So instead of worrying, Jimmy has hope and faith in God. "You always have to have a little hope," he says, "because if you run out of that, there's nothing worth anything. You might as well give up right then and there."

Jimmy has learned how faith helps us to overcome worries. In contrast, the Israelites in the desert worried about how to find food. Read **Exodus 16:2–15** to learn how God took care of their worries.

* How does Jimmy's faith in God contrast with the Israelites' worries about how to survive?
* What in the passage comforts you in an area of life that's had you worried lately?

Consider . . .

* asking someone with a disability how God has helped him or her overcome the worries that come with the disability.
* writing a list of your worries about the future. Then fold the sheet in half and write one of the Bible verses below on the back. Keep the sheet in your Bible as a reminder of God's promises.

For more, see . . .

* Joshua 1:9 (p.203)
* James 4:13–15 (p.1352)
* Luke 12:22–31 (p.1064)

better if the Lord had killed us in the land of Egypt. There we had meat to eat and all the food we wanted. But you have brought us into this desert to starve us to death."

⁴Then the Lord said to Moses, "I will cause food to fall like rain from the sky for all of you. Every day the people must go out and gather what they need for that day. I want to see if the people will do what I teach them. ⁵On the sixth day of each week, they are to gather twice as much as they gather on other days. Then they are to prepare it."

⁶So Moses and Aaron said to all the Israelites: "This evening you will know that the Lord is the one who brought you out of Egypt. ⁷Tomorrow morning you will see the glory of the Lord, because he has heard you grumble against him. We are nothing, so you are not grumbling against us, but against the Lord." ⁸And Moses said, "Each evening the Lord will give you meat to eat, and every morning he will give you all the bread you want, because he has heard you grumble against him. You are not grumbling against Aaron and me, because we are nothing; you are grumbling against the Lord."

⁹Then Moses said to Aaron, "Speak to the whole community of the Israelites, and say to them, 'Meet together in the presence of the Lord, because he has heard your grumblings.'"

¹⁰While Aaron was speaking to the whole community of the Israelites, they looked towards the desert. There the glory of the Lord appeared in a cloud.

¹¹The Lord said to Moses, ¹²"I have heard the grumblings of the people of Israel. So tell them, 'At twilight you will eat meat, and every morning you will eat all the bread you want. Then you will know I am the Lord your God.'"

¹³That evening quail came and covered the camp, and in the morning dew lay around the camp. ¹⁴When the dew was gone, thin flakes like frost were on the desert ground. ¹⁵When the Israelites saw it, they asked each other, "What is it?" because they did not know what it was.

So Moses told them, "This is the bread the Lord has given you to eat. ¹⁶The Lord has commanded, 'Each one of you must gather what he needs, about 2 litres for every person in your family.'"

¹⁷So the people of Israel did this; some people gathered much, and some gathered little. ¹⁸Then they measured it. The person who gathered more did not have too much, nor did the person who gathered less have too little. Each person gathered just as much as he needed.

¹⁹Moses said to them, "Don't keep any of it to eat the next day." ²⁰But some of the people did

not listen to Moses and kept part of it to eat the next morning. It became full of worms and began to stink, so Moses was angry with those people.

²¹Every morning each person gathered as much food as he needed, but when the sun became hot, it melted away.

²²On the sixth day the people gathered twice as much food—4 litres for every person. When all the leaders of the community came and told this to Moses, ²³he said to them, "This is what the Lord commanded, because tomorrow is the Sabbath, ᵈ the Lord's holy day of rest. Bake what you want to bake, and boil what you want to boil today. Save the rest of the food until tomorrow morning."

²⁴So the people saved it until the next morning, as Moses had commanded, and none of it began to stink or have worms in it. ²⁵Moses told the people, "Eat the food you gathered yesterday. Today is a Sabbath, the Lord's day of rest; you will not find any out in the field today. ²⁶You should gather the food for six days, but the seventh day is a Sabbath day. On that day there will not be any food on the ground."

²⁷On the seventh day some of the people went out to gather food, but they couldn't find any. ²⁸Then the Lord said to Moses, "How long will you people refuse to obey my commands and teachings? ²⁹Look, the Lord has made the Sabbath a day of rest for you. So on the sixth day he will give you enough food for two days, but on the seventh day each of you must stay where you are. Do not go anywhere." ³⁰So the people rested on the seventh day.

³¹The people of Israel called the food manna. ᵈ It was like small white seeds and tasted like wafers made with honey.

³²Then Moses said, "The Lord said, 'Save 2 litres of this food for your descendants. ᵈ Then they can see the food I gave you to eat in the desert when I brought you out of Egypt.'"

³³Moses told Aaron, "Take a jar and fill it with 2 litres of manna. Then place it before the Lord, and save it for your descendants." ³⁴So Aaron did what the Lord had commanded Moses. He put the jar of manna in front of the Agreement to keep it safe. ³⁵The Israelites ate manna for 40 years, until they came to the land where they settled—the edge of the land of Canaan. ³⁶The measure they used for the manna was about 2 litres, or one-tenth of an ephah. ⁿ

Water from a Rock

17 The whole Israelite community left the Desert of Sin and travelled from place to place, as the Lord commanded. They camped at Rephidim, but there was no water there for the

---

ephah   An ephah was a measure that equalled 20 litres.

people to drink. [2]So they quarrelled with Moses and said, "Give us water to drink."

Moses said to them, "Why do you quarrel with me? Why are you testing the LORD?"

[3]But the people were very thirsty for water, so they grumbled against Moses. They said, "Why did you bring us out of Egypt? Was it to kill us, our children and our farm animals with thirst?"

[4]So Moses cried to the LORD, "What can I do with these people? They are almost ready to stone me to death."

[5]The LORD said to Moses, "Go ahead of the people, and take some of the elders of Israel with you. Carry with you the walking stick that you used to strike the Nile River. Now go! [6]I will

Massah   This name is the Hebrew word for "testing".
Meribah   This name is the Hebrew word for "quarrel".

stand in front of you on a rock at Mount Sinai. Hit that rock with the stick, and water will come out of it so that the people can drink." Moses did these things as the elders of Israel watched. [7]He named that place Massah,[n] because the Israelites tested the LORD when they asked, "Is the LORD with us or not?" He also named it Meribah,[n] because they quarrelled.

The Amalekites Fight Israel

[8]At Rephidim the Amalekites came and fought the Israelites. [9]So Moses said to Joshua, "Choose some men and go and fight the Amalekites. Tomorrow I will stand on the top of the hill, holding the walking stick of God in my hands."

PATIENCE

A Lesson in Trust

Dave had become captain of the football team. He couldn't believe it when all his team mates had voted him in; he was so honoured to lead the team in the year of the Schools Cup. Saturday was their first big game and, as captain, he was to provide the oranges at half time. The night before, Dave reminded his mum for the tenth time.

The next morning Dave was at school bright and early to make sure everything was organised for their first big game. He gave his team the carefully prepared speech and reached in his bag to give the oranges to his coach. The only thing Dave could find were his spare socks!

Dave couldn't believe it; he was furious. He couldn't believe his mum could forget on the very first game he had as captain. He rang her.

"Mum, the game starts in ten minutes and I have no oranges! I reminded you last night; I can't believe you forgot. I'm the captain and it's our first big game. I'm so embarrassed."

While Dave paused for breath, his mum asked if he had checked his lunch bag.

"No. Why?" he replied.

His mum sighed, "Because the oranges are in there."

Dave became very impatient when he needed the oranges for his game and in **Exodus 17:1–7** we see the Israelites responding in the same way when they need water.

* How hard would it have been for the Israelites to be patient when they were thirsty and needed water in the desert?
* Should the Israelites have trusted God to provide for them, just as Dave should've trusted his mum?

Consider . . .

* ways in which you could be more patient? Trusting God may be difficult sometimes but we know that when we do he always provides for us.
* trying to talk to God more about the things that you struggle with and praying first before chatting with others.

For more, see . . .

* Proverbs 3:5–6 (p.592)
* Matthew 7:7–11 (p.950)
* Proverbs 14:29 (p.602)
* Luke 12:22–31 (p.1064)

¹⁰Joshua obeyed Moses and went to fight the Amalekites, while Moses, Aaron and Hur went to the top of the hill. ¹¹As long as Moses held his hands up, the Israelites were winning the fight, but when Moses put his hands down, the Amalekites were winning. ¹²Later, when Moses' arms became tired, the men put a large rock under him, and he sat on it. Then Aaron and Hur held up Moses' hands— Aaron on one side and Hur on the other. They kept his hands steady until the sun went down. ¹³So Joshua defeated the Amalekites in this battle.

¹⁴Then the LORD said to Moses, "Write about this battle in a book so people will remember. And be sure to tell Joshua, because I will completely destroy the Amalekites from the earth." ¹⁵Then Moses built an altar and named it The

> ### Sidelight
> Have you ever done the Mexican wave at a large event? Every time Moses raised his hands, God's power helped the Israelites to win the battle.

LORD is my Banner. ¹⁶Moses said, "I lifted my hands towards the LORD's throne. The LORD will fight against the Amalekites for ever."

Jethro Visits Moses

18 Jethro, Moses' father-in-law, was the priest of Midian. He heard about everything that God had done for Moses and his people, the Israelites, and how the LORD had led the Israelites out of Egypt. ²Now Moses had sent his wife Zipporah to Jethro, his father-in-law, ³along with his two sons. The first son was named Gershom, *ⁿ* because when he was born, Moses said, "I am a stranger in a foreign country." ⁴The other son was named Eliezer, *ⁿ* because when he was born, Moses said, "The God of my father is my help. He saved me from the king of Egypt."

⁵So Jethro, Moses' father-in-law, took Moses' wife and his two sons and went to Moses. He was camped in the desert near the mountain of God.

> ### Sidelight
> The book of Exodus is quoted 250 times in the New Testament, making it the fourth most quoted book. Only Isaiah, Psalms and Genesis are quoted more.

⁶Jethro had sent a message ahead to Moses that said, "I, Jethro, your father-in-law, am coming to you with your wife and her two sons."

⁷So Moses went out to meet his father-in-law and bowed down and kissed him. After the two men asked about each other's health, they went into Moses' tent. ⁸Moses told his father-in-law everything the LORD had done to the king and the Egyptians to help Israel. He told about all the problems they had faced along the way and how the LORD had saved them.

⁹Jethro was very happy to hear all the good things the LORD had done for Israel when he had saved them from the Egyptians. ¹⁰He said, "Praise the LORD. He has saved you from the Egyptians and their king, and he has saved the people from the power of the Egyptians. ¹¹Now I know the LORD is greater than all gods, because he did this to those who looked down on Israel." ¹²Then Jethro, Moses' father-in-law, gave a whole burnt offering and other sacrifices to God. Aaron and all the elders of Israel came to Moses' father-in-law to eat the holy meal together before God.

¹³The next day Moses solved disagreements among the people, and the people stood around him from morning until night. ¹⁴When Moses' father-in-law saw all that Moses was doing for the people, he asked, "What is all this you are doing for the people? Why are you the only one to solve disagreements? All the people are standing around you from morning until night!"

¹⁵Then Moses said to his father-in-law, "It is because the people come to me for God's help in solving their disagreements. ¹⁶When people have a disagreement, they come to me, and I decide who is right. I tell them God's laws and teachings."

¹⁷Moses' father-in-law said to him, "You are not doing this right. ¹⁸You and the people who come to you will get too tired. This is too much work for you; you can't do it by yourself. ¹⁹Now listen to me, and I will give you some advice. I want God to be with you. You must speak to God for the people and tell him about their disagreements. ²⁰Tell them about the laws and teachings, and teach them the right way to live and what they should do. ²¹But choose some capable men from among the people—men who respect God, who can be trusted, and who will not change their decisions for money. Make these men officers over the people, to rule over groups of thousands, hundreds, fifties and tens. ²²Let these officers solve the disagreements among the people all the time. They can bring the hard cases to you, but they can decide the simple cases themselves. That will make it easier for you, because

---

Gershom   This name sounds like the Hebrew word for "a stranger there".
Eliezer   This name sounds like the Hebrew words "My God is my help".

they will share the work with you. ²³If you do this as God commands you, then you will be able to do your job, and all the people will go home with their disagreements solved."

²⁴So Moses listened to his father-in-law and did everything he said. ²⁵He chose capable men from all the Israelites and made them leaders over the people; they were officers over groups of thousands, hundreds, fifties and tens. ²⁶These officers solved disagreements among the people all the time. They brought the hard cases to Moses, but they decided the simple cases themselves.

²⁷So Moses sent his father-in-law on his way, and Jethro went back to his own home.

Israel Camps at Sinai

19 Exactly three months after the Israelites had left Egypt, they reached the Desert of Sinai. ²When they left Rephidim, they came to the Desert of Sinai and camped in the desert in front of the mountain. ³Then Moses went up on the mountain to God. The LORD called to him from the mountain and said, "Say this to the family of Jacob, and tell the people of Israel: ⁴'Every one of you has seen what I did to the people of Egypt. You saw how I carried you out of Egypt, as if on eagle's wings. And I brought you here to me. ⁵So now if you obey me and keep my agreement, you will be my own possession, chosen

FOLLOWING GOD

A Trusted Leader

The whole drama class sniggered when it was announced that Adrian would be the student director for the spring production of *How to Succeed in Business*.

Adrian? He was a tall, thin student with a squeaky voice. The only reason classmates liked him was because he was a natural clown. He was hardly someone they would look up to.

But no matter. Mr Hall would be directing, and having Adrian as the assistant wouldn't hurt.

Then one evening the cast arrived for rehearsal to find Adrian sitting in Mr Hall's chair.

"Mr Hall is ill," Adrian announced. "He'll be all right, but he won't be back for a couple of weeks."

Groans echoed across the stage. "There goes our big hit," someone on stage laughed. "Kiss that Oscar goodbye." And everyone laughed.

The rehearsal was a disaster. People joked with their lines, missed their entrances, and talked to Adrian with mock respect.

Suddenly, he threw his clipboard on the stage. "All right," he said. "I know I'm just a second-year, and I know you lot don't think I can do this. But we've got to do it together – for Mr Hall."

Surprised by his honesty, the cast started paying attention, and they discovered Adrian was a natural. In his quiet way, he turned the school play into a big success.

The cast members began following Adrian when they realised that he could lead them. The Israelites made a bigger commitment and trusted God because they had seen his work before. Read about their agreement to follow God in **Exodus 19:1–8**.

* What similarities and differences do you see between Adrian's speech to the cast and God's declaration to Moses? Which parts of what they said provide the most motivation?
* How does God's leadership of the Israelites give you faith that you too can follow God?

Consider . . .

* finding a calendar from the past month and writing ways God was with you through the month. Keep the calendar handy to remind you of God's guidance when you have trouble following him.
* memorising Exodus 19:4 to boost your faith when you're discouraged.

For more, see . . .

* Jeremiah 2:1–11 (p.717)
* John 9:1–25 (p.1111)
* Ezekiel 16:59–63 (p.800)

from all nations. Even though the whole earth is mine, 6you will be my kingdom of priests and a holy nation.' You must tell the Israelites these words."

7So Moses went down and called the elders of the people together. He told them all the words the LORD had commanded him to say. 8All the people answered together, "We will do everything he has said." Then Moses took their answer back to the LORD.

9And the LORD said to Moses, "I will come to you in a thick cloud and speak to you. The people will hear me speaking with you and will always trust you." Then Moses told the LORD what the people had said.

10The LORD said to Moses, "Go to the people and have them spend today and tomorrow preparing themselves. They must wash their clothes 11and be ready by the day after tomorrow. On that day I, the LORD, will come down on Mount Sinai, and all the people will see me. 12But you must set a limit around the mountain that the people are not to cross. Tell them not to go up on the mountain and not to touch the foot of it. Anyone who touches the mountain must be put to death 13with stones or shot with arrows. No one is allowed to touch him. Whether it is a person or an animal, he will not live. But the trumpet will make a long blast, and only then may the people go up on the mountain."

14After Moses went down from the mountain to the people, he made them prepare themselves for service to God, and they washed their clothes. 15Then Moses said to the people, "Be ready in three days. Do not have sexual relations during this time."

16On the morning of the third day, there was thunder and lightning with a thick cloud on the mountain. There was a very loud blast from a trumpet, and all the people in the camp trembled. 17Then Moses led the people out of the camp to meet God, and they stood at the foot of the mountain. 18Mount Sinai was covered with smoke, because the LORD came down on it in fire. The smoke rose from the mountain like smoke from a furnace, and the whole mountain shook wildly. 19The sound from the trumpet became louder. Then Moses spoke, and the voice of God answered him.

20When the LORD came down on top of Mount Sinai, he called Moses to come up to the top of the mountain, and Moses went up. 21The LORD said to Moses, "Go down and warn the people that they must not force their way through to see me. If they do, many of them will die. 22Even the priests, who may come near me, must first prepare themselves. If they don't, I, the LORD, will punish them."

23Moses told the LORD, "The people cannot come up on Mount Sinai, because you yourself told us, 'Set a limit around the mountain, and set it apart as holy.' "

24The LORD said to him, "Go down and bring Aaron up with you, but don't allow the priests or the people to force their way through. They must not come up to the LORD, or I will punish them."

25So Moses went down to the people and told them these things.

The Ten Commandments

20 Then God spoke all these words: 2"I am the LORD your God, who brought you out of the land of Egypt where you were slaves.

3"You must not have any other gods except me.

4"You must not make for yourselves an idol that looks like anything in the sky above or on the earth below or in the water below the land. 5You must not worship or serve any idol, because I, the LORD your God, am a jealous God. If you hate me, I will punish your children, and even your grandchildren and great-grandchildren. 6But I show kindness to thousands who love me and obey my commands.

7"You must not use the name of the LORD your God thoughtlessly; the LORD will punish anyone who misuses his name.

8"Remember to keep the Sabbath d holy. 9Work and get everything done during six days each week, 10but the seventh day is a day of rest to honour the LORD your God. On that day no one may do any work: not you, your son or

---

Sidelight   The Ten Commandments (Exodus 20:2–17) are twice as easy to find as most famous Bible passages. They're also listed in Deuteronomy 5:6–21 (p.170), with only slight variations.

---

daughter, your male or female slaves, your animals, or the foreigners living in your cities. 11The reason is that in six days the LORD made everything—the sky, the earth, the sea and everything in them. On the seventh day he rested. So the LORD blessed the Sabbath day and made it holy.

12"Honour your father and your mother so that you will live a long time in the land that the LORD your God is going to give you.

13"You must not murder anyone.

14"You must not be guilty of adultery. d

15"You must not steal.

¹⁶"You must not tell lies about your neighbour. ¹⁷"You must not want to take your neighbour's house. You must not want his wife or his male or female slaves, or his ox or his donkey, or anything that belongs to your neighbour."

¹⁸When the people heard the thunder and the trumpet, and when they saw the lightning and the smoke rising from the mountain, they shook with fear and stood far away from the mountain. ¹⁹Then they said to Moses, "Speak to us yourself, and we will listen. But don't let God speak to us, or we will die."

²⁰Then Moses said to the people, "Don't be afraid, because God has come to test you. He wants you to respect him so you will not sin."

²¹The people stood far away from the mountain while Moses went near the dark cloud where God was. ²²Then the LORD told Moses to say these things to the Israelites: "You yourselves have seen that I talked with you from heaven. ²³You must not use gold or silver to make idols for yourselves; do not worship these gods in addition to me.

²⁴"Make an altar of earth for me, and sacrifice on it your whole burnt offerings and fellowship offerings, your sheep and your cattle. Worship me in every place that I choose, and I will come and bless you. ²⁵If you use stones to make an altar for me, don't use stones that you have shaped with tools. When you use any tools on them, you make them unsuitable for use in worship. ²⁶And you must not go up to my altar on steps, or people will be able to see under your clothes."

Laws for Living

21 Then God said to Moses, "These are the laws for living that you will give to the Israelites:

²"If you buy a Hebrew slave, he will serve you for six years. In the seventh year you are to set him free, and he will have to pay nothing. ³If he is not married when he becomes your slave, he must leave without a wife. But if he is married when he becomes your slave, he may take his wife with him. ⁴If the slave's master gives him a

GOD'S WILL

Picture This

At a large football game, a man arrived to find a large piece of card by his seat. He'd been asked to hold up the card to show the crowd. "That's ridiculous," the man thought, "it's a white card. There's nothing on it, no picture, nothing worth showing to anyone. I won't do it." And he threw the card away.

At the appropriate time, the crowd were told to raise their cards. The entire side of the stadium held up their piece of the image, revealing an enormous picture of a face – the star player. The man hadn't realised his card was just one piece of a giant jigsaw. Suddenly the supporters in the other stand began to laugh. There was a gap, right in the middle of the smile. The handsome star player suddenly had a tooth missing. All because one man didn't recognise his part.

Read **Exodus 20:1–20**. God can see the bigger picture, and we've all got a role to play. We've got a choice as to whether we do as we're asked, lift our card and become part of the bigger picture, or throw it away. By disobeying God's rules, you're telling him he doesn't know what's best and that you will do it your own way.

God does know what's best. He's no spoilsport – he created fun and laughter. God's rules are just an instruction manual on how to get the absolute best out of life.

* Look at the Ten Commandments: can you think of good reasons why God would make each one?
* Which of the commandments do you think are most important and why?

Consider . . .

* how you can know what God's will for your life is. Discuss this with your friends.
* whether you are following God's will or his best plan for you. If not, what will you do about this?

For more, see . . .

* Psalm 139:16 (p.582)
* 1 John 5:14 (p.1376)
* Proverbs 2:3–5 (p.590)

wife, and she gives birth to sons or daughters, the woman and her children will belong to the master. When the slave is set free, only he may leave.

⁵"But if the slave says, 'I love my master, my wife and my children, and I don't want to go free,' ⁶then the slave's master must take him to God. The master is to take him to a door or doorframe and punch a hole through the slave's ear using a sharp tool. Then the slave will serve that master all his life.

⁷"If a man sells his daughter as a slave, the rules for setting her free are different from the rules for setting the male slaves free. ⁸If the master wants to marry her but then decides he is not pleased with her, he must let one of her close relatives buy her back. He has no right to sell her to foreigners, because he has treated her unfairly. ⁹If the man who bought her promises to let the woman marry his son, he must treat her as a daughter. ¹⁰If the man who bought her marries another woman, he must not keep his first wife from having food or clothing or sexual relations. ¹¹If he does not give her these three things, she may go free, and she owes him no money.

Laws About Injuries

¹²"Anyone who hits a person and kills him must be put to death. ¹³But if a person kills someone accidentally, God allowed that to happen, so the person must go to a place I will choose. ¹⁴But if someone plans and murders another person on purpose, put him to death, even if he has run to my altar for safety.

¹⁵"Anyone who hits his father or his mother must be put to death.

¹⁶"Anyone who kidnaps someone and either sells him as a slave or still has him when he is caught must be put to death.

¹⁷"Anyone who says cruel things to his father or mother must be put to death.

¹⁸"If two men argue, and one hits the other with a rock or with his fist, the one who is hurt but not killed might have to stay in bed. ¹⁹Later

if he is able to get up and walk around outside with his walking stick, the one who hit him is not to be punished. But he must pay the injured man for the loss of his time, and he must support the injured man until he is completely healed.

²⁰"If a man beats his male or female slave with a stick, and the slave dies on the spot, the owner must be punished. ²¹But if the slave gets well after a day or two, the owner will not be punished since the slave belongs to him.

²²"Suppose two men are fighting and hit a pregnant woman, causing the baby to come out. If there is no further injury, the man who caused the accident must pay money—whatever amount the woman's husband says and the court allows. ²³But if there is further injury, then the punishment that must be paid is life for life, ²⁴eye for eye, tooth for tooth, hand for hand, foot for foot, ²⁵burn for burn, wound for wound and bruise for bruise.

²⁶"If a man hits his male or female slave in the eye, and the eye is blinded, the man is to free the slave to pay for the eye. ²⁷If a master knocks out a tooth of his male or female slave, the man is to free the slave to pay for the tooth.

²⁸"If a man's bull kills a man or woman, you must kill that bull by throwing stones at it, and you should not eat the bull. But the owner of the bull is not guilty. ²⁹However, suppose the bull has hurt people in the past and the owner, though warned, did not keep it in a pen. Then if it kills a man or woman, the bull must be stoned to death, and the owner must also be put to death. ³⁰But if the family of the dead person accepts money, the one who owned the bull may buy back his life, but he must pay whatever is demanded. ³¹Use this same law if the bull kills a person's son or daughter. ³²If the bull kills a male or female slave, the owner must pay the master the price for a new slave, or 30 pieces of silver, and the bull must also be stoned to death.

³³"If a man takes the cover off a pit, or digs a pit and does not cover it, and another man's ox or donkey comes and falls into it, ³⁴the owner of the pit must pay the owner of the animal for the loss. The dead animal will belong to the one who pays.

³⁵"If a man's bull kills another man's bull, they must sell the bull that is alive. Both men will get half of the money and half of the bull that was killed. ³⁶But if a person's bull has hurt other animals in the past and the owner did not keep it in a pen, that owner must pay bull for bull, and the dead animal is his.

Property Laws

22 "If a man steals a bull or a sheep and kills or sells it, he must pay back five bulls for the one bull he stole and four sheep for the one sheep he stole.

2-4"The robber who is caught must pay back what he stole. If he owns nothing, he must be sold as a slave to pay for what he stole. If the stolen animal is found alive with the robber, he must give the owner two animals for every animal he stole, whether it was a bull, donkey or sheep.

"If a thief is killed while breaking into a house at night, the one who killed him is not guilty of murder. But if this happens during the day, he is guilty of murder.

5"If a man lets his farm animal graze in his field or vineyard, and it wanders into another man's field or vineyard, the owner of the animal must pay back the loss from the best of his crop.

6"Suppose a man starts a fire that spreads through the thorn bushes to his neighbour's field. If the fire burns his neighbour's growing grain or grain that has been stacked, or if it burns his whole field, the person who started the fire must pay for what was burned.

7"Suppose a man gives his neighbour money or other things to keep for him and those things are stolen from the neighbour's house. If the thief is caught, he must pay back twice as much as he stole. 8But if the thief is never found, the owner of the house must make a promise before God that he has not stolen his neighbour's things.

9"Suppose two men disagree about who owns something—whether ox, donkey, sheep, clothing or something else that is lost. If each says, 'This is mine,' each man must bring his case to God. God's judges will decide who is guilty, and that person must pay the other man twice as much as the object is worth.

10"Suppose a man asks his neighbour to keep his donkey, ox, sheep or some other animal for him, and that animal dies, gets hurt or is taken away, without anyone seeing what happened. 11That neighbour must promise before the LORD that he did not harm or kill the other man's animal, and the owner of the animal must accept his promise made before God. The neighbour does not have to pay the owner for the animal. 12But if the animal was stolen from the neighbour, he must pay the owner for it. 13If wild animals killed it, the neighbour must bring the body as proof, and he will not have to pay for the animal that was killed.

14"If a man borrows an animal from his neighbour, and it gets hurt or dies while the owner is not there, the one who borrowed it must pay the owner for the animal. 15But if the owner is with the animal, the one who borrowed it does not have to pay. If the animal was rented, the rental price covers the loss.

Laws and Relationships

16"Suppose a man finds a woman who is not pledged to be married and has never had sexual relations with a man. If he tricks her into having sexual relations with him, he must give her family the payment to marry her and she will become his wife. 17But if her father refuses to allow his daughter to marry him, the man must still give the usual payment for a bride who has never had sexual relations.

18"Put to death any woman who does evil magic.

19"Put to death anyone who has sexual relations with an animal.

20"Destroy completely any person who makes a sacrifice to any god except the LORD.

21"Do not cheat or hurt a foreigner, because you were foreigners in the land of Egypt.

22"Do not cheat a widow or an orphan. 23If you do, and they cry out to me for help, I certainly will hear their cry. 24And I will be very angry and kill you in war. Then your wives will become widows, and your children will become orphans.

25"If you lend money to one of my people who is poor, do not treat him as a moneylender would. Charge him nothing for using your money. 26If your neighbour gives you his coat as a promise for the money he owes you, you must give it back to him by sunset, 27because it is the only cover to keep his body warm. He has nothing else to sleep in. If he cries out to me for help, I will listen, because I am merciful.

28"You must not speak against God or curse a leader of your people.

29"Do not hold back your offering from the first of your harvest and the first wine that you make. Also, you must give me your firstborn d sons. 30You must do the same with your bulls and your sheep. Let the firstborn males stay with their mothers for seven days, and on the eighth day you must give them to me.

31"You are to be my holy people. You must not eat the meat of any animal that has been killed by wild animals. Instead, give it to the dogs.

Laws About Fairness

23 "You must not tell lies. If you are a witness in court, don't help a wicked person by telling lies.

2"You must not do wrong just because everyone else is doing it. If you are a witness in court, you must not ruin a fair trial. You must not tell lies just because everyone else does. 3If a poor person is in court, you must not take his side just because he is poor.

⁴"If you see your enemy's ox or donkey wandering away, you must return it to him. ⁵If you see that your enemy's donkey has fallen because its load is too heavy, do not leave it there. You must help your enemy get the donkey back on its feet.

⁶"You must not be unfair to a poor person when he is in court. ⁷You must not lie when you accuse someone in court. Never allow an innocent or honest person to be put to death as punishment, because I will not treat guilty people as if they were innocent.

⁸"You must not accept money from a person who wants you to lie in court, because such money will not let you see what is right. Such money makes good people tell lies.

⁹"You must not mistreat a foreigner. You know how it feels to be a foreigner, because you were foreigners in Egypt.

Laws for the Sabbath

¹⁰"For six years you are to plant and harvest crops on your land. ¹¹Then during the seventh year, do not plough or plant your land. If any food grows there, allow the poor people to have it, and let the wild animals eat what is left. You should do the same with your vineyards and your orchards of olive trees.

¹²"You should work six days a week, but on the seventh day you must rest. This lets your ox and your donkey rest, and it also lets the slave born in your house and the foreigner be refreshed.

¹³"Be sure to do all that I have said to you. You must not even say the names of other gods; those names must not come out of your mouth.

Three Yearly Feasts

¹⁴"Three times each year you must hold a feast to honour me. ¹⁵You must celebrate the Feast *d* of Unleavened Bread in the way I commanded you. For seven days you must eat bread that is made without yeast at the set time during the month of Abib, *d* the month when you came out of Egypt. No one is to come to worship me without bringing an offering.

¹⁶"You must celebrate the Feast *d* of Weeks. Offer to God the first things you harvest from the crops you planted in your fields.

"You must celebrate the Feast *d* of Shelters in the autumn, when you gather all the crops from your fields.

¹⁷"So three times during every year all your males must come to worship the LORD God.

¹⁸"You must not offer animal blood along with anything that has yeast in it.

"You must not save any of the fat from the sacrifice for the next day.

¹⁹"You must bring the best of the firstfruits *d* of your land to the Holy Tent *n* of the LORD your God.

"You must not cook a young goat in its mother's milk.

God Will Help Israel

²⁰"I am sending an angel ahead of you, who will protect you as you travel. He will lead you to the place I have prepared. ²¹Pay attention to the angel and obey him. Do not turn against him; he will not forgive such turning against him because my power is in him. ²²If you listen carefully to all he says and do everything that I tell you, I will be an enemy to your enemies. I will fight all who fight against you. ²³My angel will go ahead of you and take you into the land of the Amorites, Hittites, Perizzites, Canaanites, Hivites and Jebusites, and I will destroy them.

²⁴"You must not bow down to their gods or worship them. You must not live in the way those people live. You must destroy their idols, breaking into pieces the stone pillars they use in worship. ²⁵If you worship the LORD your God, I will bless your bread and your water. I will take away sickness from you. ²⁶None of your women will have her baby die before it is born, and all women will have children. I will allow you to live long lives.

²⁷"I will make your enemies afraid of me. I will confuse any people you fight against, and I will make all your enemies run away from you. ²⁸I will send terror ahead of you that will force the Hivites, Canaanites and Hittites out of your way. ²⁹But I will not force all those people out in only one year. If I did, the land would become a desert and the wild animals would become too many for you. ³⁰Instead, I will force those people out slowly, until there are enough of you to take over the land.

³¹"I will give you the land from the Red Sea to the Mediterranean Sea, and from the desert to the Euphrates River. I will give you power over the people who now live in the land, and you will force them out ahead of you. ³²You must not make an agreement with those people or with their gods. ³³You must not let them live in your land, or they will make you sin against me. If you worship their gods, you will be caught in a trap."

Holy Tent Literally, "house of the LORD your God". See Exodus 25:9.

God and Israel Make Their Agreement

24 The LORD told Moses, "You, Aaron, Nadab, Abihu and 70 of the elders of Israel must come up to me and worship me from a distance. ²Then Moses alone must come near me; the others must not come near. The rest of the people must not come up the mountain with Moses."

³Moses told the people all the LORD's words and laws for living. Then all of the people answered out loud together, "We will do all the things the LORD has said." ⁴So Moses wrote down all the words of the LORD. And he got up early the next morning and built an altar near the bottom of the mountain. He set up twelve stones, one stone for each of the twelve tribes*d* of Israel. ⁵Then Moses sent young Israelite men to offer whole burnt offerings and to sacrifice young bulls as fellowship offerings to the LORD. ⁶Moses put half of the blood of these animals in bowls, and he sprinkled the other half of the blood on the altar. ⁷Then he took the Book of the Agreement and read it so the people could hear him. And they said, "We will do everything that the LORD has said; we will obey."

⁸Then Moses took the blood from the bowls and sprinkled it on the people, saying, "This is the blood that begins the Agreement, the Agreement which the LORD has made with you about all these words."

⁹Moses, Aaron, Nadab, Abihu and 70 of the elders of Israel went up the mountain ¹⁰and saw the God of Israel. Under his feet was a surface that looked as if it were paved with blue sapphire stones and it was as clear as the sky! ¹¹These leaders of the Israelites saw God, but God did not destroy them. Then they ate and drank together.

God Promises Moses the Stone Tablets

¹²The LORD said to Moses, "Come up the mountain to me. Wait there, and I will give you two stone tablets. On these are the teachings and the commands I have written to teach the people."

¹³So Moses and his helper Joshua set out, and Moses went up to Sinai, the mountain of God. ¹⁴Moses said to the elders, "Wait here for us until we come back to you. Aaron and Hur are with you, and anyone who has a disagreement with others can take it to them."

Moses Meets with God

¹⁵When Moses went up on the mountain, the cloud covered it. ¹⁶The glory of the LORD came down on Mount Sinai, and the cloud covered it for six days. On the seventh day the LORD called to Moses from inside the cloud. ¹⁷To the Israelites the glory of the LORD looked like a fire burning on top of the mountain. ¹⁸Then Moses went into the cloud and went higher up the mountain. He was on the mountain for 40 days and 40 nights.

Gifts for the LORD

25 The LORD said to Moses, ²"Tell the Israelites to bring me gifts. Receive for me the gifts each person wants to give. ³These are the gifts that you should receive from them: gold, silver and bronze; ⁴blue, purple and red thread; fine linen, goat hair and ⁵rams' skins that are dyed red; fine leather; acacia wood; ⁶olive oil to burn in the lamps; spices for sweet-smelling incense, *d* and the special olive oil poured on a person's head to make him a priest; and ⁷onyx stones and other jewels to be put on the holy robe *d* and the chest covering.

⁸"The people must build a holy place for me so that I can live among them. ⁹Build this Holy Tent *d* and everything in it by the plan I will show you.

The Ark of the Agreement

¹⁰"Use acacia wood and build an Ark *d* 110 centimetres long, 70 centimetres wide and 70 centimetres high. ¹¹Cover the Ark inside and out with pure gold, and put a gold strip all around it. ¹²Make four gold rings for the Ark and attach them to its four feet, two rings on each side. ¹³Then make poles from acacia wood and cover them with gold. ¹⁴Put the poles through the rings on the sides of the Ark, and use these poles to carry it. ¹⁵These poles must always stay in the rings of the Ark. Do not take them out. ¹⁶Then put in the Ark the Agreement which I will make with you.

¹⁷"Then make a lid of pure gold for the Ark; this is the mercy seat. *d* Make it 110 centimetres long and 70 centimetres wide. ¹⁸Then hammer gold to make two creatures with wings, and put one on each end of the lid. ¹⁹Attach one creature on one end of the lid and the other creature on the other end. Make them to be one piece with the lid at the ends. ²⁰The creatures' wings should be spread upwards, covering the lid, and the creatures are to face each other across the lid. ²¹Put this lid on top of the Ark, and put in the Ark the Agreement which I will make with you. ²²I will meet with you there, above the lid between the two winged creatures on the Ark of the Agreement. There I will give you all my commands for the Israelites.

The Table

²³"Make a table out of acacia wood, 90 centimetres long, 50 centimetres wide and 70 centimetres high. ²⁴Cover it with pure gold, and

put a gold strip around it. ²⁵Make a frame 8 centimetres high that stands up all around the edge, and put a gold strip around it. ²⁶Then make four gold rings. Attach them to the four corners of the table where the four legs are. ²⁷Put the rings close to the frame around the top of the table, because they will hold the poles for carrying it. ²⁸Make the poles out of acacia wood, cover them with gold, and carry the table with these poles. ²⁹Make the plates and bowls for the table, as well as the jars and cups, out of pure gold. They will be used for pouring out the drink offerings. ³⁰On this table put the bread that shows you are in my presence so that it is always there in front of me.

The Lampstand

³¹"Hammer pure gold to make a lampstand. Its base, stand, flower-like cups, buds and petals must all be joined together in one piece. ³²The lampstand must have six branches going out from its sides—three on one side and three on the other. ³³Each branch must have three cups shaped like almond flowers on it. Each cup must have a bud and a petal. Each of the six branches going out from the lampstand must be the same. ³⁴And there must be four more cups made like almond flowers on the lampstand itself. These cups must also have buds and petals. ³⁵Put a bud under each pair of branches that goes out from the lampstand. Each of the six branches going out from the lampstand must be the same. ³⁶The branches, buds and lampstand must be made of one piece, hammered out of pure gold.

³⁷"Then make seven small oil lamps and put them on the lampstand so that they give light to the area in front of it. ³⁸The wick trimmers and trays must be made of pure gold. ³⁹Use 34 kilogrammes of pure gold to make the lampstand and everything with it. ⁴⁰Be very careful to make them by the plan I showed you on the mountain.

The Holy Tent

26 "Make for the Holy Tent ᵈ ten curtains of fine linen and blue, purple and red thread. Have a skilled craftsman sew designs of creatures with wings on the pieces of cloth. ²Make each curtain the same size—14 metres long and 2 metres wide. ³Sew five curtains together for one set, and sew the other curtains together for the second set. ⁴Make loops of blue cloth on the edge of the end curtain of one set, and do the same for the end curtain of the other set. ⁵Make 50 loops on the end curtain of the first set and 50 loops on the end curtain of the second set. These loops must be opposite each other. ⁶And make 50 gold hooks to join the two sets of curtains so that the Holy Tent is one piece.

⁷"Then make another tent that will cover the Holy Tent, using eleven curtains made from goat hair. ⁸All these curtains must be the same size—15 metres long and 2 metres wide. ⁹Sew five of the curtains together into one set. Then sew the other six curtains together into the second set. Fold the sixth curtain double over the front of the Tent. ¹⁰Make 50 loops down the edge of the end curtain of one set, and do the same for the end curtain of the other set. ¹¹Then make 50 bronze hooks and put them in the loops to join the tent together so that the covering is one piece. ¹²Let the extra half piece of cloth hang over the back of the Holy Tent. ¹³There will be 50 centimetres hanging over the sides of the Holy Tent, to protect it. ¹⁴Make a covering for the Holy Tent from ram's skins coloured red, and over that make a covering from fine leather.

¹⁵"Use acacia wood to make upright frames for the Holy Tent. ¹⁶Each frame must be 5 metres long and 70 centimetres wide, ¹⁷with two pegs side by side. Every frame must be made in this way. ¹⁸Make 20 frames for the south side of the Holy Tent. ¹⁹Each frame must have two silver bases to go under it, a peg fitting into each base. You must make 40 silver bases for the frames. ²⁰Make 20 more frames for the north side of the Holy Tent ²¹and 40 silver bases for them—two bases for each frame. ²²You must make six frames for the rear or west end of the Holy Tent ²³and two frames for each corner at the rear. ²⁴The two frames are to be doubled at the bottom and joined at the top with a metal ring. Both corner frames must be made in this way. ²⁵So there will be a total of eight frames at the rear of the Tent, and there will be sixteen silver bases—two bases under each frame.

²⁶"Make crossbars of acacia wood to connect the upright frames of the Holy Tent. Make five crossbars to hold the frames together on one side ²⁷and five to hold the frames together on the other side. Also make five crossbars to hold the frames together on the west end, at the rear. ²⁸The middle crossbar is to be set halfway up the frames, and it is to run along the entire length of each side and rear. ²⁹Make gold rings on the sides of the frames to hold the crossbars, and cover the frames and the crossbars with gold. ³⁰Set up the Holy Tent by the plan shown to you on the mountain.

³¹"Make a curtain of fine linen and blue, purple and red thread, and have a skilled craftsman sew designs of creatures with wings on it. ³²Hang the curtain by gold hooks on four posts of acacia wood that are covered with gold, and set them in four silver bases. ³³Hang the curtain from the hooks in the roof, and put the Ark ᵈ of the Agreement containing the two flat stones behind it.

This curtain will separate the Holy Place from the Most Holy Place. [34]Put the lid on the Ark of the Agreement in the Most Holy Place.

[35]"Outside the curtain, put the table on the north side of the Holy Tent. Put the lampstand on the south side of the Holy Tent across from the table.

The Entrance of the Holy Tent

[36]"Then, for the entrance of the Tent, [d] make a curtain with fine linen and blue, purple and red thread. Someone who can sew well is to sew designs on it. [37]Make five posts of acacia wood covered with gold. Make gold hooks for them on which to hang the curtain, and make five bronze bases for them.

The Altar for Burnt Offerings

27 "Make an altar of acacia wood, 1.5 metres high. It should be square—2.5 metres long and 2.5 metres wide. [2]Make each of the four corners of the altar stick out like a horn, in such a way that the corners with their horns are all one piece. Then cover the whole altar with bronze.

[3]"Use bronze to make all the tools and dishes that will be used on the altar: the pots to remove the ashes, the shovels, the bowls for sprinkling blood, the meat forks and the pans for carrying the burning wood.

[4]"Make a large bronze screen to hold the burning wood, and put a bronze ring at each of the four corners of it. [5]Put the screen inside the altar, under its rim, halfway up from the bottom.

[6]"Make poles of acacia wood for the altar, and cover them with bronze. [7]Put the poles through the rings on both sides of the altar to carry it. [8]Make the altar out of boards and leave the inside hollow. Make it as you were shown on the mountain.

The Courtyard of the Holy Tent

[9]"Make a wall of curtains to form a courtyard around the Holy Tent. [d] The south side should have a wall of fine linen curtains 50 metres long. [10]Hang the curtains with silver hooks and bands on 20 bronze posts with 20 bronze bases. [11]The north side must also be 50 metres long. Hang its curtains on silver hooks and bands on 20 bronze posts with 20 bronze bases.

[12]"The west end of the courtyard must have a wall of curtains 25 metres long, with ten posts and ten bases on that wall. [13]The east end of the courtyard must also be 25 metres long. [14]On one side of the entry, there is to be a wall of curtains 7.5 metres long, held up by three posts on three bases. [15]On the other side of the entry, there is also to be a wall of curtains 7.5 metres long, held up by three posts on three bases.

[16]"The entry to the courtyard is to be a curtain 10 metres wide, made of fine linen with blue, purple and red thread. Someone who can sew well is to sew designs on it. It is to be held up by four posts on four bases. [17]All the posts around the courtyard must have silver bands and hooks and bronze bases. [18]The courtyard must be 50 metres long and 25 metres wide, with a wall of curtains around it 2.5 metres high, made of fine linen. The bases in which the posts are set must be bronze. [19]All the things used in the Holy Tent and all the tent pegs for the Holy Tent and the wall around the courtyard must be made of bronze.

Oil for the Lamp

[20]"Command the people of Israel to bring you pure olive oil, made from pressed olives, to keep the lamps on the lampstand burning. [21]Aaron and his sons must keep the lamps burning before the LORD from evening till morning. This will be in the Meeting Tent, [d] outside the curtain which is in front of the Ark. [d] The Israelites and their descendants [d] must obey this rule from now on.

Clothes for the Priests

28 "Tell your brother Aaron to come to you, along with his sons Nadab, Abihu, Eleazar and Ithamar. Separate them from the other Israelites to serve me as priests. [2]Make holy clothes for your brother Aaron to give him honour and beauty. [3]Tell all the skilled craftsmen to whom I have given wisdom to make special clothes for Aaron—clothes to show that he belongs to me so that he may serve me as a priest. [4]These are the clothes they must make: a chest covering, a holy robe, [d] an outer robe, a woven inner robe, a turban and a cloth belt. The craftsmen must make these holy clothes for your brother Aaron and his sons. Then they may serve me as priests. [5]The craftsmen must use gold and blue, purple and red thread, and fine linen.

The Holy Robe

[6]"Use gold and blue, purple and red thread, and fine linen to make the holy robe; [d] skilled craftsmen are to make it. [7]At each top corner of this holy robe there will be a pair of shoulder straps tied together over each shoulder.

[8]"The craftsmen will very carefully weave a belt on the holy robe that is made with the same materials—gold and blue, purple and red thread, and fine linen.

[9]"Take two onyx stones and write the names of the twelve sons of Israel on them, [10]six on one

stone and six on the other. Write the names in order, from the oldest son to the youngest. ¹¹Carve the names of the sons of Israel on these stones in the same way that a person carves words and designs on a seal. *d* Put gold around the stones to hold them on the holy robe. ¹²Then put the two stones on the two straps of the holy robe as reminders of the twelve sons of Israel. Aaron is to wear their names on his shoulders in the presence of the LORD as reminders of the sons of Israel. ¹³Make two gold pieces to hold the stones ¹⁴and two chains of pure gold, twisted together like a rope. Attach the chains to the two gold pieces that hold the stones.

The Chest Covering

¹⁵"Make a chest covering to help in making decisions. The craftsmen should make it as they made the holy robe, *d* using gold and blue, purple and red thread, and fine linen. ¹⁶The chest covering must be square—23 centimetres long and 23 centimetres wide—and folded double to make a pocket. ¹⁷Put four rows of beautiful gems on the chest covering: the first row must have a ruby, a topaz and a yellow quartz; ¹⁸the second must have turquoise, a sapphire and an emerald; ¹⁹the third must have a jacinth, an agate and an amethyst; ²⁰the fourth must have a chrysolite, an onyx and a jasper. Put gold around these jewels to attach them to the chest covering. ²¹There must be twelve jewels on the chest covering—one jewel for each of the names of the sons of Israel. Carve the name of one of the twelve tribes *d* on each of the stones as you would carve a seal. *d*

²²"Make chains of pure gold, twisted together like rope, for the chest covering. ²³Make two gold rings and put them on the two upper corners of the chest covering. ²⁴Attach the two gold chains to the two rings at the upper corners of the chest covering. ²⁵Attach the other ends of the two chains to the two gold pieces on the shoulder straps in the front of the holy robe.

²⁶"Make two gold rings and put them at the two lower corners of the chest covering, on the inside edge next to the holy robe. ²⁷Make two more gold rings and attach them to the bottom of the shoulder straps in the front of the holy robe. Put them close to the seam above the woven belt of the holy robe. ²⁸Join the rings of the chest covering to the rings of the holy robe with blue ribbon, connecting it to the woven belt so the chest covering will not swing out from the holy robe.

²⁹"When Aaron enters the Holy Place, he will wear the names of the sons of Israel over his heart, on the chest covering that helps in making decisions. This will be a continual reminder before the LORD. ³⁰And put the Urim and Thummim *d* inside the chest covering so that they will be on Aaron's heart when he goes before the LORD. They will help in making decisions for the Israelites. So Aaron will always carry them with him when he is before the LORD.

³¹"Make the outer robe to be worn under the holy robe, using only blue cloth. ³²Make a hole in the centre for Aaron's head, with a woven collar around the hole so it will not tear. ³³Make balls like pomegranates *d* of blue, purple and red thread, and hang them around the bottom of the outer robe with gold bells between them. ³⁴All around the bottom of the outer robe there should be a gold bell and a pomegranate ball, a gold bell and a pomegranate ball. ³⁵Aaron must wear this robe when he serves as priest. The ringing of the bells will be heard when he enters and leaves the Holy Place before the LORD so that Aaron will not die.

³⁶"Make a strip of pure gold and carve these words on it as you would carve a seal: *d* 'Holy to the LORD'. ³⁷Use blue ribbon to tie it to the turban; put it on the front of the turban. ³⁸Aaron must wear this on his forehead. In this way, he will be blamed if anything is wrong with the gifts of the Israelites. Aaron must always wear this on his head so the LORD will accept the gifts of the people.

³⁹"Make the woven inner robe of fine linen, and make the turban of fine linen also. Make the cloth belt with designs sewn on it. ⁴⁰Also make woven inner robes, cloth belts and headbands for Aaron's sons, to give them honour and beauty. ⁴¹Put these clothes on your brother Aaron and his sons, and pour olive oil on their heads to appoint them as priests. Make them belong to me so they may serve me as priests.

⁴²"Make for them linen underclothes to cover them from the waist to the upper parts of the legs. ⁴³Aaron and his sons must wear these underclothes when they enter the Meeting Tent *d* and whenever they come near the altar to serve as priests in the Holy Place. If they do not wear these clothes, they will be guilty of wrong, and they will die. This will be a law that will last from now on for Aaron and all his descendants. *d*

Appointing the Priests

29 "This is what you must do to appoint Aaron and his sons to serve me as priests. Take one young bull and two rams that have nothing wrong with them. ²Use fine wheat flour without yeast to make bread, cakes mixed with olive oil, and wafers brushed with olive oil. ³Put these in one basket, and bring them along with the bull and two rams. ⁴Bring Aaron and his sons to the entrance of the Meeting Tent *d* and wash them with water. ⁵Take the clothes and dress

Aaron in the inner robe and the outer robe of the holy robe. *d* Then put on him the holy robe and the chest covering, and tie the holy robe on him with its skilfully woven belt. [6]Put the turban on his head, and put the holy crown on the turban. [7]Take the special olive oil and pour it on his head to make him a priest.

[8]"Then bring his sons and put the inner robes on them. [9]Put the headbands on their heads, and tie cloth belts around their waists. Aaron and his descendants *d* will be priests in Israel, according to a rule that will continue from now on. This is how you will appoint Aaron and his sons as priests.

[10]"Bring the bull to the front of the Meeting Tent, and Aaron and his sons must put their hands on the bull's head. [11]Then kill the bull before the LORD at the entrance to the Meeting Tent. [12]Use your finger to put some of the bull's blood on the corners of the altar, and then pour the blood that is left at the bottom of the altar. [13]Take all the fat that covers the inner organs, as well as the best part of the liver, both kidneys and the fat around them, and burn them on the altar. [14]Take the bull's meat, skin and intestines, and burn them outside the camp. This is an offering to take away sin.

[15]"Take one of the rams, and have Aaron and his sons put their hands on its head. [16]Kill it, and take its blood and sprinkle it on all four sides of the altar. [17]Then cut it into pieces and wash its inner organs and its legs, putting them with its head and its other pieces. [18]Burn the whole ram on the altar; it is a burnt offering made by fire to the LORD. Its smell is pleasing to the LORD.

[19]"Take the other ram, and have Aaron and his sons put their hands on its head. [20]Kill it and take some of its blood. Put the blood on the bottom of the right ears of Aaron and his sons and on the thumbs of their right hands and on the big toes of their right feet. Then sprinkle the rest of the blood against all four sides of the altar. [21]Take some of the blood from the altar, and mix it with the special oil used in appointing priests. Sprinkle this on Aaron and his clothes, and on his sons and their clothes. This will show that Aaron and his sons and their clothes are given to my service.

[22]"Then take the fat from the rams, the fat tail and the fat that covers the inner organs. In addition, take the best part of the liver, both kidneys, and the fat around them, and the right thigh. (This is the ram to be used in appointing priests.)

[23]"Then take the basket of bread that you made without yeast, which you put before the LORD. From it take a loaf of bread, a cake made with olive oil and a wafer. [24]Put all these in the hands of Aaron and his sons, and tell them to present them as an offering to the LORD. [25]Then take them from their hands and burn them on the altar with the whole burnt offering. This is an offering made by fire to the LORD; its smell is pleasing to the LORD. [26]Then take the breast of the ram used to appoint Aaron as priest, and present it before the LORD as an offering. This part of the animal will be your share. [27]Set aside the breast and the thigh of the sheep that were used to appoint Aaron and his sons as priests. These parts belong to them. [28]They are to be the regular share which the Israelites will always give to Aaron and his sons. It is the gift the Israelites must give to the LORD from their fellowship offerings.

[29]"The holy clothes made for Aaron will belong to his descendants so that they can wear these clothes when they are appointed as priests. [30]Aaron's son, who will become high priest after Aaron, will come to the Meeting Tent to serve in the Holy Place. He is to wear these clothes for seven days.

[31]"Take the ram used to appoint priests and boil its meat in a place that is holy. [32]Then at the entrance of the Meeting Tent, Aaron and his sons must eat the meat of the ram and the bread that is in the basket. [33]They should eat these offerings that were used to remove their sins and to make them holy when they were made priests. But no one else is to eat them, because they are holy things. [34]If any of the meat from that sheep or any of the bread is left the next morning, it must be burned. It must not be eaten, because it is holy.

[35]"Do all these things that I commanded you to do to Aaron and his sons, and spend seven days appointing them. [36]Each day you are to offer a bull to remove the sins of Aaron and his sons so they will be given for service to the LORD. Make the altar ready for service to the LORD, and pour oil on it to make it holy. [37]Spend seven days making the altar ready for service to God and making it holy. Then the altar will become very holy, and anything that touches it must be holy.

The Daily Sacrifices

[38]"Every day from now on, offer on the altar two lambs that are one year old. [39]Offer one lamb in the morning and the other in the evening before dark. [40]In the morning, when you offer the first lamb, offer also two litres of fine flour mixed with one litre of oil from pressed olives. Pour out one litre of wine as a drink offering. [41]Offer the second lamb in the evening with the same grain offering and drink offering as you did in the morning. This is an offering made by fire to the LORD, and its smell is pleasing to him.

[42]"You must burn these things as an offering to the LORD every day, from now on, at the entrance of the Meeting Tent *d* before the LORD. When you

make the offering, I, the LORD, will meet you there and speak to you. ⁴³I will meet with the people of Israel there, and that place will be holy because of my glory.

⁴⁴"So I will make the Meeting Tent and the altar holy; I will also make Aaron and his sons holy so they may serve me as priests. ⁴⁵I will live with the people of Israel and be their God. ⁴⁶And they will know that I am the LORD their God who led them out of Egypt so that I could live with them. I am the LORD their God.

The Altar for Burning Incense

30 "Make an altar out of acacia wood for burning incense. *d* ²Make it square—50 centimetres long and 50 centimetres wide—and make it 90 centimetres high. The corners that stick out like horns must be one piece with the altar. ³Cover its top, its sides and its corners with pure gold, and put a gold strip all around the altar. ⁴Make two gold rings beneath the gold strip on opposite sides of the altar, and slide poles through them to carry the altar. ⁵Make the poles from acacia wood and cover them with gold. ⁶Put the altar of incense in front of the curtain that is near the Ark *d* of the Agreement, in front of the lid that covers that Ark. There I will meet with you.

⁷"Aaron must burn sweet-smelling incense on the altar every morning when he comes to take care of the oil lamps. ⁸He must burn incense again in the evening when he lights the lamps, so incense will burn before the LORD every day from now on. ⁹Do not use this altar for offering any other incense or burnt offering, or any kind of grain offering or drink offering. ¹⁰Once a year Aaron must make the altar ready for service to God by putting blood on its corners—the blood of the animal offered to remove sins. He is to do this once a year from now on. This altar belongs completely to the LORD's service."

The Tax for the Meeting Tent

¹¹The LORD said to Moses, ¹²"When you count the people of Israel, every person must buy back his life from the LORD so that no terrible things will happen to the people when you number them. ¹³Every person who is counted must pay 6 grammes of silver. (This is set by using a half of the Holy Place measure, which weighs 11.5 grammes.) This amount is a gift to the LORD. ¹⁴Every person who is counted and is 20 years old or older must give this amount to the LORD. ¹⁵A rich person must not give more than 6 grammes, and a poor person must not give less. You are paying this to the LORD to buy back your lives. ¹⁶Gather from the people of Israel this money paid to buy back their lives, and spend it on things for the service in the Meeting Tent. *d* This payment will remind the LORD that the Israelites' lives have been bought back."

The Bronze Bowl

¹⁷The LORD said to Moses, ¹⁸"Make a bronze bowl, on a bronze stand, for washing. Put the bowl and stand between the Meeting Tent *d* and the altar, and put water in the bowl. ¹⁹Aaron and his sons must wash their hands and feet with the water from this bowl. ²⁰Each time they enter the Meeting Tent they must wash with water so they will not die. Each time they approach the altar to serve as priests and offer a sacrifice to the LORD by fire, ²¹they must wash their hands and their feet so that they will not die. This is a rule which Aaron and his descendants *d* are to keep from now on."

Oil for Appointing

²²Then the LORD said to Moses, ²³"Take the finest spices: 6 kilogrammes of liquid myrrh, *d* half that amount (that is, 3 kilogrammes) of sweet-smelling cinnamon, 3 kilogrammes of sweet-smelling cane ²⁴and 6 kilogrammes of cassia. *d* Weigh all these by the Holy Place measure. Also take 4 litres of olive oil, ²⁵and mix all these things like a perfume to make a holy olive oil. This special oil must be put on people and things to make them ready for service to God. ²⁶Put this oil on the Meeting Tent *d* and the Ark *d* of the Agreement, ²⁷on the table and all its dishes, on the lampstand and all its tools, and on the incense *d* altar. ²⁸Also, put the oil on the altar for burnt offerings and on all its tools, as well as on the bowl and the stand under the bowl. ²⁹You will prepare all these things for service to God, and they will be very holy. Anything that touches these things must be holy.

³⁰"Put the oil on Aaron and his sons to give them for service to me, that they may serve me as priests. ³¹Tell the Israelites, 'This is to be my holy olive oil from now on. It is to be put on people and things to make them ready for service to God. ³²Do not pour it on the bodies of ordinary people, and do not make perfume in the same way that you make this oil. It is holy, and you must treat it as holy. ³³If anyone makes perfume like it or puts it on someone who is not a priest, that person must be cut off from his people.'"

Incense

³⁴Then the LORD said to Moses, "Take these sweet-smelling spices: resin, onycha, galbanum and pure frankincense. *d* Be sure that you have equal amounts of each. ³⁵Make incense *d* as a person who makes perfume would do. Add salt to it

to keep it pure and holy. [36]Beat some of the incense into a fine powder, and put it in front of the Ark [d] of the Agreement in the Meeting Tent, [d] where I will meet with you. You must use this incense powder only for its very special purpose. [37]Do not make incense for yourselves in the same way that you make this incense. Treat it as holy to the LORD. [38]Whoever makes incense like this to use as perfume must be cut off from his people."

Sidelight

Kentucky Fried Chicken isn't the first company to have a secret recipe. In ancient Israel, priests had a secret recipe for the spices in the holy incense (Exodus 30:34–38). Three of the ingredients – resin, galbanum and frankincense – were extracted from plants or trees. Onycha came from a shellfish in the Red Sea.

Bezalel and Oholiab Help

31 Then the LORD said to Moses, [2]"See, I have chosen Bezalel, son of Uri, from the tribe [d] of Judah. (Uri was the son of Hur.) [3]I have filled Bezalel with the Spirit [d] of God and have given him the skill, ability and knowledge to do all kinds of work. [4]He is able to design pieces to be made from gold, silver and bronze, [5]to cut jewels and put them in metal, to carve wood, and to do all kinds of work. [6]I have also chosen Oholiab, son of Ahisamach, from the tribe of Dan to work with Bezalel. I have given skills to all the craftsmen, and they will be able to make all these things I have commanded you: [7]the Meeting Tent, [d] the Ark [d] of the Agreement, the lid that covers the Ark, and everything in the Tent. [8]This includes the table and everything on it, the pure gold lampstand and everything with it, the altar of incense, [d] [9]the altar for burnt offerings and everything used with it, and the bowl and the stand under it. [10]They will make the woven clothes and the holy clothes for Aaron and the clothes for his sons to wear when they serve as priests. [11]They will also make the special olive oil used in appointing people and things to the service of the LORD, and the sweet-smelling incense for the Holy Place.

"These workers will make all these things just as I have commanded you."

The Day of Rest

[12]Then the LORD said to Moses, [13]"Tell the Israelites, 'You must keep the rules about my Sabbaths, [d] because they will be a sign between you and me from now on. In this way you will know that I, the LORD, make you holy.

[14]" 'Make the Sabbath a holy day. If anyone treats the Sabbath like any other day, that person must be put to death; anyone who works on the Sabbath day must be cut off from his people. [15]There are six days for working, but the seventh day is a day of rest, a day holy for the LORD. Anyone who works during the Sabbath day must be put to death. [16]The Israelites must remember the Sabbath day as an agreement between them and me that will continue from now on. [17]The Sabbath day will be a sign between me and the Israelites for ever, because in six days I, the LORD, made the sky and the earth. On the seventh day I did not work: I rested.' "

[18]When the LORD finished speaking to Moses on Mount Sinai, he gave him the two stone tablets with the Agreement written on them, written by the finger of God.

The People Make a Gold Calf

32 The people saw that a long time had passed and Moses had not come down from the mountain. So they gathered around Aaron and said, "Moses led us out of Egypt, but we don't know what has happened to him. Make us gods who will lead us."

[2]Aaron said to the people, "Take off the gold earrings that your wives, sons and daughters are wearing, and bring them to me." [3]So all the people took their gold earrings and brought them to Aaron. [4]He took the gold from the people and formed it with a tool and made a statue of a calf. Then the people said, "Israel, these are your gods who brought you out of the land of Egypt!"

[5]When Aaron saw all this, he built an altar before the calf and announced, "Tomorrow there will be a special feast to honour the LORD." [6]The people got up early the next morning and offered whole burnt offerings and fellowship offerings. They sat down to eat and drink, and then they got up and sinned sexually.

[7]Then the LORD said to Moses, "Go down from this mountain, because your people, the people you brought out of the land of Egypt, have ruined themselves. [8]They have quickly turned away from the things I commanded them to do. They have made for themselves a calf covered with gold, and they have worshipped it and offered sacrifices to it. They have said, 'Israel, these are your gods who brought you out of Egypt.' "

[9]The LORD said to Moses, "I have seen these people, and I know that they are very stubborn. [10]So now do not stop me. I am so angry with them that I am going to destroy them. Then I will make you and your descendants [d] a great nation."

[11]But Moses begged the LORD his God and said, "LORD, don't let your anger destroy your people, whom you brought out of Egypt with your great

power and strength. ¹²Don't let the people of Egypt say, 'The LORD brought the Israelites out of Egypt for an evil purpose. He planned to kill them in the mountains and destroy them from the earth.' So stop being angry, and don't destroy your people. ¹³Remember the men who served you—Abraham, Isaac and Israel. You promised with an oath to them and said, 'I will make your descendants as many as the stars in the sky. I will give your descendants all this land that I have promised them, and it will be theirs for ever.'" ¹⁴So the LORD changed his mind and did not destroy the people as he had said he might.

¹⁵Then Moses went down the mountain, and in his hands he had the two stone tablets with the Agreement on them. The commands were written on both sides of each stone, front and back. ¹⁶God himself had made the tablets, and God himself had written the commands on the tablets.

¹⁷When Joshua heard the sound of the people shouting, he said to Moses, "It sounds like war down in the camp."

¹⁸Moses answered:

"It is not a shout of victory;
  it is not a cry of defeat.
It is the sound of singing that I hear."

¹⁹When Moses came close to the camp, he saw the gold calf and the dancing, and he became very angry. He threw down the stone tablets that he was carrying and broke them at the bottom of the mountain. ²⁰Then he took the calf the people had made and melted it in the fire.

SIN

I Told You So

Peter carefully laid the extra pillows on his bed, fluffing them up to make them look bigger. Then he covered them with the sheets and bedspread. "That should do it," he whispered as he switched the light off.

He slipped over to the window and opened it carefully. Climbing out, he stretched his legs to reach the porch roof below, tiptoed to the edge and climbed down the trellis, carefully avoiding the climbing roses.

Chris and Ben were waiting in the car around the corner. "No problem," Peter said, hopping into the back seat. "They'll never know I've gone. Let's go."

The three friends didn't plan to stay at Sam's too long, but they didn't want to miss his end-of-exams party altogether. Peter had tried to get permission to go, but his parents wouldn't give him a later curfew. So he decided to go without them knowing.

It would have worked, except that the trellis wasn't as strong as he thought. When he returned home four hours later, it gave way beneath his foot, and he yelled with pain as he tumbled into the roses.

When the light came on in his parents' room, Peter knew he was in trouble. What would happen now? he wondered as he sat on the lawn and waited for his dad to appear.

Peter knew what he was doing was wrong, but he did it anyway. In the same way, the Israelites knew that they shouldn't build an idol to worship.

Read **Exodus 32:1–14** to see what happened when they did it anyway.

* What lesson might Peter have learned from the passage if he had read it before climbing out of the window?
* When have you, like the Israelites, doubted God's leadership and disobeyed him? What did you learn about trusting God from that experience?

Consider . . .

* praying that God will give you strength next time you're tempted to do something you know is wrong.
* listening to popular songs on the radio to find out what things people trust instead of God. How is their misplaced trust sinful?

For more, see . . .

* Deuteronomy 32:15–22 (p.196)
* Romans 6:1–7 (p.1191)
* 1 Kings 18:22–39 (p.334)

He ground it into powder. Then he threw the powder into the water and forced the Israelites to drink it.

²¹Moses said to Aaron, "What did these people do to you? Why did you cause them to do such a terrible sin?"

²²Aaron answered, "Don't be angry, master. You know that these people are always ready to do wrong. ²³The people said to me, 'Moses led us out of Egypt, but we don't know what has happened to him. Make us gods who will lead us.' ²⁴So I told the people, 'Take off your gold jewellery.' When they gave me the gold, I threw it into the fire and out came this calf!"

²⁵Moses saw that the people were acting wildly. Aaron had let them get out of control and become fools in front of their enemies. ²⁶So Moses stood at the entrance to the camp and said, "Let anyone who wants to follow the LORD come to me." And all the people from the family of Levi gathered around Moses.

²⁷Then Moses said to them, "The LORD, the God of Israel, says this: 'Every man must put on his sword and go through the camp from one end to the other. Each man must kill his brother, his friend and his neighbour.' " ²⁸The people from the family of Levi obeyed Moses, and that day about 3,000 of the Israelites died. ²⁹Then Moses said, "Today you have been given for service to the LORD. You were willing to kill your own sons and brothers, and God has blessed you for this."

³⁰The next day Moses told the people, "You have done a terrible sin. But now I will go up to the LORD. Maybe I can do something so your sins will be removed." ³¹So Moses went back to the LORD and said, "How terribly these people have sinned! They have made for themselves gods from gold. ³²Now, please forgive them this sin. If you will not, then erase my name from the book in which you have written the names of your people."

³³But the LORD told Moses, "I will erase from my book the names of the people who sin against me. ³⁴So now, go. Lead the people where I have told you, and my angel will lead you. When the time comes to punish, I will punish them for their sin."

³⁵So the LORD caused terrible things to happen to the people because of what they did with the calf Aaron had made.

33 Then the LORD said to Moses, "You and the people you brought out of Egypt must leave this place. Go to the land that I promised with an oath to give to Abraham, Isaac and Jacob when I said, 'I will give that land to your descendants.' ²I will send an angel to lead you, and I will force these people out of the land: the Canaanites, Amorites, Hittites, Perizzites, Hivites and Jebusites. ³Go up to a fertile land. But I will not go with you, because I might destroy you on the way, since you are such a stubborn people."

⁴When the people heard this bad news, they became very sad, and none of them put on jewellery. ⁵This was because the LORD had said to Moses, "Tell the Israelites, 'You are a stubborn people. If I were to go with you even for a moment, I would destroy you. So take off all your jewellery, and I will decide what to do with you.' " ⁶So the people of Israel took off their jewellery at Mount Sinai.

The Meeting Tent

⁷Moses used to take a tent and set it up a long way outside the camp; he called it the "Meeting Tent". *d* Anyone who wanted to ask the LORD about something would go to the Meeting Tent outside the camp. ⁸Whenever Moses went out to the Tent, all the people would rise and stand at the entrances of their tents, watching him until he entered the Meeting Tent. ⁹When Moses went into the Tent, the pillar of cloud would always come down and stay at the entrance of the Tent while the LORD spoke with Moses. ¹⁰Whenever the people saw the pillar of cloud at the entrance of the Tent, they stood and worshipped, each person at the entrance of his own tent.

¹¹The LORD spoke to Moses face to face as a man speaks with his friend. Then Moses would return to the camp, but Moses' young helper, Joshua son of Nun, did not leave the Tent.

¹²Moses said to the LORD, "You have told me to lead these people, but you did not say whom you would send with me. You have said to me, 'I know you very well, and I am pleased with you.' ¹³If I have truly pleased you, show me your plans so that I may know you and continue to please you. Remember that this nation is your people."

¹⁴The LORD answered, "I myself will go with you, and I will give you victory."

¹⁵Then Moses said to him, "If you yourself don't go with us, then don't send us away from this place. ¹⁶If you don't go with us, no one will know that you are pleased with me and with your people. These people and I will be no different from any other people on earth."

¹⁷Then the LORD said to Moses, "I will do what you ask, because I know you very well, and I am pleased with you."

Moses Sees God's Glory

¹⁸Then Moses said, "Now, please show me your glory."

¹⁹The LORD answered, "I will cause all my goodness to pass in front of you, and I will announce my name, the LORD, so you can hear it. I will show kindness to anyone to whom

I want to show kindness, and I will show mercy to anyone to whom I want to show mercy. ²⁰But you cannot see my face, because no one can see me and live.

²¹"There is a place near me where you may stand on a rock. ²²When my glory passes that place, I will put you in a large crack in the rock and cover you with my hand until I have passed by. ²³Then I will take away my hand, and you will see my back. But my face must not be seen."

Moses Gets New Stone Tablets

34 The LORD said to Moses, "Cut two more stone tablets like the first two, and I will write the same words on them that were on the first two stones which you broke. ²Be ready tomorrow morning, and then come up on Mount Sinai. Stand before me there on the top of the mountain. ³No one may come with you or even be seen anywhere on the mountain. Not even the flocks or herds may eat grass near that mountain."

⁴So Moses cut two stone tablets like the first ones. Then early the next morning he went up Mount Sinai, just as the LORD had commanded him, carrying the two stone tablets with him. ⁵Then the LORD came down in the cloud and stood there with Moses, and the LORD called out his name: the LORD.

⁶The LORD passed in front of Moses and said, "I am the LORD. The LORD is a God who shows

FORGIVENESS

Sharing the Blame

It was the end of lunch-break at school and Paula's class were in their classroom waiting for the teacher to come and take registration. The game they played whilst waiting had become something of a ritual. The girls had to try and get from one side of the classroom to the other, without the boys catching them. If they got caught they were pelted with rolled up paper and left-over sandwiches. It was a stupid game, but one that they all enjoyed as it secretly gave the boys and girls a chance to seek out their favourites . . .

This particular time, Paula had been caught and was just in the throes of getting a bag of crisps emptied down her neck. The boys were laughing and chanting and the whole scene was quite chaotic. Unfortunately, Mrs Kendon chose that moment to walk through the door.

She blew a fuse! The result being that all the boys got detention. She left the room and went to report the whole incident to the headmaster.

While she was gone, the room became quiet and then one of the girls said: "That's not entirely fair. We were as much to blame as the boys."

The other girls agreed, and as one body, they ran to the headmaster's room and explained that they should be punished too. The head was amazed at the honesty of their confession, but, although he was delighted, he had no alternative but to write out a detention notice for the girls too!

The girls felt strangely relieved. The next day at school, the boys presented the girls with a huge box of chocolates to show their appreciation.

Confession really is good for the soul, read about it in **Exodus 34:4–8**.

* What happens when people confess their guilt, according to verse 7?
* When was the last time you owned up to something to defend someone else?

Consider . . .

* making a chart that shows the consequences of a particular sin, put the sin at the top and then list below it, everything that happens as a result. How does forgiving help the consequences?
* asking God's forgiveness for something you have done, while also asking him to guide you as you deal responsibly with the consequences.

For more, see . . .

* 2 Chronicles 6:24–31 (p.405)
* Luke 17:1–4 (p.1076)
* Psalm 51:1–13 (p.530)

mercy, who is kind, who doesn't become angry quickly, who has great love and faithfulness [7]and is kind to thousands of people. The LORD forgives people for evil, for sin and for turning against him, but he does not forget to punish guilty people. He will punish not only the guilty people, but also their children, their grandchildren, their great-grandchildren and their great-great-grandchildren."

[8]Then Moses quickly bowed to the ground and worshipped. [9]He said, "Lord, if you are pleased with me, please go with us. I know that these are stubborn people, but forgive our evil and our sin. Take us as your own people."

[10]Then the LORD said, "I am making this agreement with you. I will do miracles [d] in front of all your people—things that have never before been done for any other nation on earth—and the people with you will see my work. I, the LORD, will do wonderful things for you. [11]Obey the things I command you today, and I will force out the Amorites, Canaanites, Hittites, Perizzites, Hivites and Jebusites ahead of you. [12]Be careful that you don't make an agreement with the people who live in the land where you are going, because it will bring you trouble. [13]Destroy their altars, break their stone pillars and cut down their Asherah [d] idols. [14]Don't worship any other god, because I, the LORD, the Jealous One, am a jealous God.

[15]"Be careful that you don't make an agreement with the people who live in that land. When they worship their gods, they will invite you to join them. Then you will eat their sacrifices. [16]If you choose some of their daughters as wives for your sons and those daughters worship gods, they will lead your sons to do the same thing.

[17]"Do not make gods of melted metal.

[18]"Celebrate the Feast [d] of Unleavened Bread. For seven days you must eat bread made without yeast as I commanded you. Do this during the month I have chosen, the month of Abib, [d] because in that month you came out of Egypt.

[19]"The firstborn [d] of every mother belongs to me, including every firstborn male animal that is born in your flocks and herds. [20]You may buy back a donkey by paying for it with a lamb, but if you don't want to buy back a donkey, you must break its neck. You must buy back all your firstborn sons.

"No one is to come before me without a gift.

[21]"You must work for six days, but on the seventh day you must rest—even during the planting season and the harvest season.

[22]"Celebrate the Feast [d] of Weeks when you gather the first grain of the wheat harvest. And celebrate the Feast [d] of Shelters in the autumn.

[23]"Three times each year all your males must come before the Lord GOD, the God of Israel. [24]I will force out nations ahead of you and expand the borders of your land. You will go before the LORD your God three times each year, and at that time no one will try to take your land from you.

[25]"Do not offer the blood of a sacrifice to me with anything containing yeast, and do not leave any of the sacrifice of the Feast [d] of Passover until the next morning.

[26]"Bring the best first crops that you harvest from your ground to the Tent [d] of the LORD your God.

"You must not cook a young goat in its mother's milk."

[27]Then the LORD said to Moses, "Write down these words, because with these words I have made an agreement with you and Israel."

[28]Moses stayed there with the LORD 40 days and 40 nights, and during that time he did not eat food or drink water. And Moses wrote the words of the Agreement—the Ten Commandments—on the stone tablets.

The Face of Moses Shines

[29]Then Moses came down from Mount Sinai, carrying the two stone tablets of the Agreement in his hands. But he did not know that his face was shining because he had talked with the LORD. [30]When Aaron and all the people of Israel saw that Moses' face was shining, they were afraid to go near him. [31]But Moses called to them, so Aaron and all the leaders of the people returned to Moses, and he talked with them. [32]After that, all the people of Israel came near him, and he gave them all the commands that the LORD had given him on Mount Sinai.

[33]When Moses finished speaking to the people, he put a covering over his face. [34]Whenever Moses went before the LORD to speak with him, Moses took off the covering until he came out. Then Moses would come out and tell the Israelites what the LORD had commanded. [35]They would see that Moses' face was shining. So he would cover his face again until the next time he went in to speak with the LORD.

Rules About the Sabbath

35 Moses gathered all the Israelite community together and said to them, "These are the things the LORD has commanded you to do. [2]You are to work for six days, but the seventh day will be a holy day, a Sabbath [d] of rest to honour the LORD. Anyone who works on that day must be put to death. [3]On the Sabbath day you must not light a fire in any of your houses."

⁴Moses said to all the Israelites, "This is what the LORD has commanded: ⁵From what you have, take an offering for the LORD. Let everyone who is willing bring this offering to the LORD: gold, silver, bronze, ⁶blue, purple and red thread, and fine linen, goat hair ⁷and rams' skins that are coloured red. They may also bring fine leather, acacia wood, ⁸olive oil for the lamps, spices for the special olive oil used for appointing priests and for the sweet-smelling incense, *d* ⁹onyx stones and other jewels to be put on the holy robe *d* and chest covering of the priests.

¹⁰"Let all the skilled workers come and make everything the LORD commanded: ¹¹the Holy Tent, *d* its outer tent and its covering, the hooks, frames, crossbars, posts and bases; ¹²the Ark *d* of the Agreement, its poles, lid and the curtain in front of it; ¹³the table and its poles, all the things that go with the table, and the bread that shows we are in God's presence; ¹⁴the lampstand for the light and all the things that go with it, the lamps and olive oil for the light; ¹⁵the altar of incense and its poles, the special oil and the sweet-smelling incense, the curtain for the entrance of the Meeting Tent; ¹⁶the altar of burnt offering and its bronze screen, its poles and all its tools, the bronze bowl and its base; ¹⁷the curtains around the courtyard, their posts and bases, and the curtain at the entrance to the courtyard; ¹⁸the pegs of the Holy Tent and of the courtyard and their ropes; ¹⁹the special clothes that the priest will wear in the Holy Place. These are the holy clothes for Aaron the priest and his sons to wear when they serve as priests."

²⁰Then all the people of Israel went away from Moses. ²¹Everyone who wanted to give, came and brought a gift to the LORD for making the Meeting Tent, all the things in the Tent, and the special clothes. ²²All the men and women who wanted to give, brought gold jewellery of all kinds—pins, earrings, rings and bracelets. They all presented their gold to the LORD. ²³Everyone who had blue, purple and red thread, and fine linen, and anyone who had goat hair or ram's skins coloured red or fine leather brought them to the LORD. ²⁴Everyone who could give silver or bronze brought that as a gift to the LORD, and everyone who had acacia wood to be used in the work brought it. ²⁵Every skilled woman used her hands to make the blue, purple and red thread, and fine linen, and they brought what they had made. ²⁶All the women who were skilled and wanted to help made thread of the goat hair. ²⁷The leaders brought onyx stones and other jewels to put on the holy robe and chest covering for the priest. ²⁸They also brought spices and olive oil for the sweet-smelling incense, the special oil, and the oil to burn in the lamps. ²⁹All the men

and women of Israel who wanted to help brought gifts to the LORD for all the work the LORD had commanded Moses and the people to do.

³⁰Then Moses said to the Israelites, "Look, the LORD has chosen Bezalel, son of Uri, the son of Hur, from the tribe *d* of Judah. ³¹The LORD has filled Bezalel with the Spirit *d* of God and has given him the skill, ability and knowledge to do all kinds of work. ³²He is able to design pieces to be made of gold, silver and bronze, ³³to cut stones and jewels and put them in metal, to carve wood, and to do all kinds of work. ³⁴Also, the LORD has given Bezalel and Oholiab, the son of Ahisamach from the tribe of Dan, the ability to teach others. ³⁵The LORD has given them the skill to do all kinds of work. They are able to cut designs in metal and stone. They can plan and sew designs in the fine linen with the blue, purple and red thread. And they are also able to

36 weave things. ¹So Bezalel, Oholiab and every skilled person will do the work the LORD has commanded, because he gave them the wisdom and understanding to do all the skilled work needed to build the Holy Tent."

²Then Moses called Bezalel, Oholiab and all the other skilled people to whom the LORD had given skills, and they came because they wanted to help with the work. ³They received from Moses everything the people of Israel had brought as gifts to build the Holy Tent. The people continued to bring gifts each morning because they wanted to. ⁴So all the skilled workers left the work they were doing on the Holy Tent, ⁵and they said to Moses, "The people are bringing more than we need to do the work the LORD commanded."

⁶Then Moses sent this command throughout the camp: "No man or woman should make anything else as a gift for the Holy Tent." So the people were kept from giving more, ⁷because what they had was already more than enough to do all the work.

The Holy Tent

⁸Then the skilled workers made the Holy Tent. *d* They made the ten curtains of blue, purple and red cloth, and they sewed designs of creatures with wings on the curtains. ⁹Each curtain was the same size—14 metres long and 2 metres wide. ¹⁰Five of the curtains were fastened together to make one set, and the other five were fastened together to make another set. ¹¹Then they made loops of blue cloth along the edge of the end curtain on the first set of five, and they did the same thing with the other set of five. ¹²There were 50 loops on one curtain and 50 loops on the other curtain, with the loops opposite each other. ¹³They made 50 gold hooks to join

the two curtains together so that the Holy Tent was joined together as one piece.

[14]Then the workers made another tent of eleven curtains made of goat hair, to put over the

> ### Sidelight
>
> Goat hair was good material for building the Holy Tent (Exodus 36:14–19). When it's dry, it's open and airy, making it cooler inside. But when it rains, the goat hairs expand and keep the moisture out.

Holy Tent. [15]All eleven curtains were the same size—15 metres long and 2 metres wide. [16]The workers sewed five curtains together into one set and six together into another set. [17]They made 50 loops along the edge of the outside curtain of one set and 50 loops along the edge of the outside curtain of the other set. [18]Then they made 50 bronze rings to join the two sets of cloth together and make the tent one piece. [19]They made two more coverings for the outer tent—one made of ram's skins coloured red and the other made of fine leather.

[20]Then they made upright frames of acacia wood for the Holy Tent. [21]Each frame was 5 metres tall and 70 centimetres wide, [22]and there were two pegs side by side on each one. Every frame of the Holy Tent was made in this way. [23]They made 20 frames for the south side of the Tent, [24]and they made 40 silver bases that went under the 20 frames. There were two bases for every frame—one for each peg of each frame. [25]They also made 20 frames for the north side of the Holy Tent [26]and 40 silver bases—two to go under each frame. [27]They made six frames for the rear or west end of the Holy Tent [28]and two frames for the corners at the rear of the Holy Tent. [29]These two frames were doubled at the bottom and joined at the top with a metal ring. They did this for each of these corners. [30]So there were eight frames and sixteen silver bases—two bases under each frame.

[31]Then they made crossbars of acacia wood to connect the upright frames of the Holy Tent. Five crossbars held the frames together on one side of the Tent, [32]and five held the frames together on the other side. Also, five crossbars held the frames together on the west end, at the rear of the Tent. [33]They made the middle crossbar run along the entire length of each side and rear of the Tent. It was set halfway up the frames. [34]They made gold rings on the sides of the frames to hold the crossbars, and they covered the frames and the crossbars with gold.

[35]Then they made the curtain of blue, purple and red thread, and fine linen. A skilled craftsman sewed designs of creatures with wings on it. [36]They made four posts of acacia wood for it and covered them with gold. Then they made gold hooks for the posts, as well as four silver bases in which to set the posts. [37]For the entrance to the Tent, they made a curtain of blue, purple and red thread, and fine linen. A person who sewed well, sewed designs on it. [38]Then they made five posts and hooks for it. They covered the tops of the posts and their bands with gold, and they made five bronze bases for the posts.

The Ark of the Agreement

37 Bezalel made the Ark[d] of acacia wood; it was 110 centimetres long, 70 centimetres wide and 70 centimetres high. [2]He covered it, both inside and out, with pure gold, and he put a gold strip around it. [3]He made four gold rings for it and attached them to its four feet, with two rings on each side. [4]Then he made poles of acacia wood and covered them with gold. [5]He put the poles through the rings on each side of the Ark to carry it. [6]Then he made a lid of pure gold that was 110 centimetres long and 70 centimetres wide. [7]Then Bezalel hammered gold to make two creatures with wings and attached them to each end of the lid. [8]He made one creature on one end of the lid and the other creature on the other end. He attached them to the lid so that it would be one piece. [9]The creatures' wings were spread upwards, covering the lid, and the creatures faced each other across the lid.

The Table

[10]Then he made the table of acacia wood; it was 90 centimetres long, 50 centimetres wide and 70 centimetres high. [11]He covered it with pure gold and put a gold strip around it. [12]He made a frame 8 centimetres high that stood up all around the edge, and he put a gold strip around it. [13]Then he made four gold rings for the table and attached them to the four corners of the table where the four legs were. [14]The rings were put close to the frame around the top of the table, because they held the poles for carrying it. [15]The poles for carrying the table were made of acacia wood and were covered with gold. [16]He made of pure gold all the things that were used on the table: the plates, bowls, cups and jars used for pouring the drink offerings.

The Lampstand

[17]Then he made the lampstand of pure gold, hammering out its base and stand. Its flower-like cups, buds and petals were joined together in one piece with the base and stand. [18]Six branches

went out from the sides of the lampstand—three on one side and three on the other. [19]Each branch had three cups shaped like almond flowers, and each cup had a bud and a petal. Each of the six branches going out from the lampstand was the same. [20]There were four more cups shaped like almond flowers on the lampstand itself, each with its buds and petals. [21]Three pairs of branches went out from the lampstand. A bud was under the place where each pair was attached to the lampstand. Each of the six branches going out from the lampstand was the same. [22]The buds, branches and lampstand were all one piece of pure, hammered gold. [23]He made seven pure gold lamps for this lampstand, and he made pure gold wick trimmers and trays. [24]He used about 35 kilogrammes of pure gold to make the lampstand and all the things that went with it.

The Altar for Burning Incense

[25]Then he made the altar of incense [d] out of acacia wood. It was square—50 centimetres long and 50 centimetres wide—and it was 90 centimetres high. Each corner that stuck out like a horn was joined into one piece with the altar. [26]He covered the top and all the sides and the corners with pure gold, and he put gold trim around the altar. [27]He made two gold rings and put them below the trim on opposite sides of the altar; these rings held the poles for carrying it. [28]He made the poles of acacia wood and covered them with gold.

[29]Then he made the holy olive oil for appointing the priests and the pure, sweet-smelling incense. He made them like a person who mixes perfumes.

The Altar for Burnt Offerings

38 Then he built the altar for burnt offerings out of acacia wood. The altar was square—2.5 metres long and 2.5 metres wide—and it was 1.5 metres high. [2]He made each corner stick out like a horn so that the horns and the altar were joined together in one piece. Then he covered the altar with bronze. [3]He made all the tools of bronze to use on the altar: the pots, shovels, bowls for sprinkling blood, meat forks and pans for carrying the fire. [4]He made a large bronze screen to hold the burning wood for the altar and put it inside the altar, under its rim, halfway up from the bottom. [5]He made bronze rings to hold the poles for carrying the altar, and he put them at the four corners of the screen. [6]Then he made poles of acacia wood and covered them with bronze. [7]He put the poles through the rings on both sides of the altar, to carry it. He made the altar of boards and left the inside hollow.

The Bronze Bowl

[8]He made the bronze bowl for washing, and he built it on a bronze stand. He used the bronze from mirrors that belonged to the women who served at the entrance to the Meeting Tent. [d]

The Courtyard of the Holy Tent

[9]Then he made a wall of curtains to form a courtyard around the Holy Tent. [d] On the south side the curtains were 50 metres long and were made of fine linen. [10]The curtains hung on silver hooks and bands, placed on 20 bronze posts with 20 bronze bases. [11]On the north side the wall of curtains was also 50 metres long, and it hung on silver hooks and bands on 20 posts with 20 bronze bases.

[12]On the west side of the courtyard, the wall of curtains was 25 metres long. It was held up by silver hooks and bands on ten posts with ten bases. [13]The east side was also 25 metres long. [14]On one side of the entry there was a wall of curtains 7.5 metres long, held up by three posts and three bases. [15]On the other side of the entry there was also a wall of curtains 7.5 metres long, held up by three posts and three bases. [16]All the curtains around the courtyard were made of fine linen. [17]The bases for the posts were made of bronze. The hooks and the bands on the posts were made of silver, and the tops of the posts were covered with silver also. All the posts in the courtyard had silver bands.

[18]The curtain for the entrance of the courtyard was made of blue, purple and red thread, and fine linen, sewn by a person who could sew well. The curtain was 10 metres long and 2.5 metres high, the same height as the curtains around the courtyard. [19]It was held up by four posts and four bronze bases. The hooks and bands on the posts were made of silver, and the tops on the posts were covered with silver. [20]All the tent pegs for the Holy Tent and for the curtains around the courtyard were made of bronze.

[21]This is a list of the materials used to make the Holy Tent, where the Agreement was kept. Moses ordered the Levites to make this list, and Ithamar, son of Aaron, was in charge of keeping it. [22]Bezalel, son of Uri, the son of Hur, of the tribe [d] of Judah, made everything the LORD commanded Moses. [23]Oholiab, son of Ahisamach, of the tribe of Dan, helped him. He could cut designs into metal and stone; he was a designer and also skilled at sewing the blue, purple and red thread, and fine linen.

[24]The total amount of gold used to build the Holy Tent was presented to the LORD. It weighed about a tonne, as set by the Holy Place measure.

25The silver was given by the members of the community who were counted. It weighed 3.5 tonnes, as set by the Holy Place measure. 26All the men 20 years old or older were counted. There were 603,550 men, and each man had to pay 6 grammes of silver, as set by the Holy Place measure. 27Of this silver, 3.5 tonnes were used to make the 100 bases for the Holy Tent and for the curtain—35 kilogrammes of silver in each base. 28They used 20 kilogrammes of silver to make the hooks for the posts and to cover the tops of the posts and to make the bands on them.

29The bronze which was presented to the LORD weighed about 2.5 tonnes. 30They used the bronze to make the bases at the entrance of the Meeting Tent, to make the altar and the bronze screen, and to make all the tools for the altar. 31This bronze was also used to make bases for the wall of curtains around the courtyard and bases for curtains at the entry to the courtyard, as well as to make the tent pegs for the Holy Tent and the curtains that surrounded the courtyard.

Clothes for the Priests

39 They used blue, purple and red thread to make woven clothes for the priests to wear when they served in the Holy Place. They made the holy clothes for Aaron as the LORD had commanded Moses.

2They made the holy robe d of gold and blue, purple and red thread, and fine linen. 3They hammered the gold into sheets and then cut it into long, thin strips. They worked the gold into the blue, purple and red thread, and fine linen. This was done by skilled craftsmen. 4They made the shoulder straps for the holy robe, which were attached to the top corners of the robe and tied together over each shoulder. 5The skilfully woven belt was made in the same way; it was joined to the holy robe as one piece. It was made of gold and blue, purple and red thread, and fine linen, in the way the LORD commanded Moses.

6They put gold around the onyx stones and then wrote the names of the sons of Israel on these gems, as a person carves words and designs on a seal. d 7Then they attached the gems on the shoulder straps of the holy robe, as reminders of the twelve tribes of Israel. This was done just as the LORD had commanded Moses.

8The skilled craftsmen made the chest covering like the holy robe; it was made of gold and blue, purple and red thread, and fine linen. 9The chest covering was square—23 centimetres long and 23 centimetres wide—and it was folded double to make a pocket. 10Then they put four rows of beautiful jewels on it: in the first row there was a ruby, a topaz and a yellow quartz; 11in the second there was a turquoise, a sapphire and an emerald; 12in the third there was a jacinth, an agate and an amethyst; 13in the fourth there was a chrysolite, an onyx and a jasper. Gold was put around these jewels to attach them to the chest covering, 14and the names of the sons of Israel were carved on these twelve jewels as a person carves a seal. Each jewel had the name of one of the twelve tribes d of Israel.

15They made chains of pure gold, twisted together like a rope, for the chest covering. 16The workers made two gold pieces and two gold rings. They put the two gold rings on the two upper corners of the chest covering. 17Then they put two gold chains in the two rings at the ends of the chest covering, 18and they fastened the other two ends of the chains to the two gold pieces. They attached these gold pieces to the two shoulder straps in the front of the holy robe. 19They made two gold rings and put them at the lower corners of the chest covering on the inside edge next to the holy robe. 20They made two more gold rings on the bottom of the shoulder straps in front of the holy robe, near the seam, just above the woven belt of the holy robe. 21They used a blue ribbon and tied the rings of the chest covering to the rings of the holy robe, connecting it to the woven belt. So that the chest covering would not swing out from the holy robe. They did all these things in the way the LORD commanded.

22Then they made the outer robe to be worn under the holy robe. It was woven only of blue cloth. 23They made a hole in the centre of the outer robe, with a woven collar sewn around it so it would not tear. 24Then they made balls like pomegranates d of blue, purple and red thread, and fine linen, and hung them around the bottom of the outer robe. 25They also made bells of pure gold and hung these around the bottom of the outer robe between the balls. 26So around the bottom of the outer robe there was a bell and a pomegranate ball, a bell and a pomegranate ball. The priest wore this outer robe when he served as priest, just as the LORD had commanded Moses.

27They wove inner robes of fine linen for Aaron and his sons, 28and they made turbans, headbands and underclothes of fine linen. 29Then they made the cloth belt of fine linen, and blue, purple and red thread, and designs were sewn onto it, just as the LORD had commanded Moses.

30They made a strip of pure gold, which is the holy crown, and carved these words in the gold, as one might carve on a seal: "Holy to the LORD". 31Then they tied this flat piece to the turban with a blue ribbon, as the LORD had commanded Moses.

32So all the work on the Meeting Tent d was finished. The Israelites did everything just as the

LORD had commanded Moses. ³³Then they brought the Holy Tent to Moses: the Tent and all its furniture, hooks, frames, crossbars, posts and bases; ³⁴the covering made of rams' skins coloured red, the covering made of fine leather and the curtain that covered the entrance to the Most Holy Place; ³⁵the Ark *d* of the Agreement, its poles and lid; ³⁶the table, all its containers, and the bread that showed they were in God's presence; ³⁷the pure gold lampstand with its lamps in a row, all its tools and the olive oil for the light; ³⁸the gold altar, the special olive oil used for appointing priests, the sweet-smelling incense, *d* and the curtain that covered the entrance to the Tent; ³⁹the bronze altar and its screen, its poles and all its tools, the bowl and its stand; and ⁴⁰the curtains for the courtyard with their posts and bases, the curtain that covered the entrance to the courtyard, the cords, pegs, and all the things in the Meeting Tent. ⁴¹They brought the clothes for the priests to wear when they served in the Holy Tent—the holy clothes for Aaron the priest and the clothes for his sons, which they wore when they served as priests.

⁴²The Israelites had done all this work just as the LORD had commanded Moses. ⁴³Moses looked closely at all the work and saw they had done it just as the LORD had commanded. So Moses blessed them.

Setting Up the Holy Tent

40 Then the LORD said to Moses: ²"On the first day of the first month, set up the Holy Tent, *d* which is the Meeting Tent. ³Put the Ark *d* of the Agreement in it and hang the curtain in front of the Ark. ⁴Bring in the table and arrange everything on the table that should be there. Then bring in the lampstand and set up its lamps. ⁵Put the gold altar for burning incense *d* in front of the Ark of the Agreement, and put the curtain at the entrance to the Holy Tent.

⁶"Put the altar of burnt offerings in front of the entrance of the Holy Tent, the Meeting Tent. ⁷Put the bowl between the Meeting Tent and the altar, and put water in it. ⁸Set up the courtyard around the Holy Tent, and put the curtain at the entrance to the courtyard.

⁹"Use the special olive oil and pour it on the Holy Tent and everything in it, in order to give the Tent and all that is in it for service to the LORD. They will be holy. ¹⁰Pour the special oil on the altar for burnt offerings and on all its tools. Give the altar for service to God, and it will be very holy. ¹¹Then pour the special olive oil on the bowl and the base under it so that they will be given for service to God.

¹²"Bring Aaron and his sons to the entrance of the Meeting Tent, and wash them with water.

¹³Then put the holy clothes on Aaron. Pour the special oil on him, and give him for service to God so that he may serve me as a priest. ¹⁴Bring Aaron's sons and put the inner robes on them. ¹⁵Pour the special oil on them in the same way that you appointed their father as priest, so that they may also serve me as priests. Pouring oil on them will make them a family of priests, they and their descendants *d* from now on."

¹⁶Moses did everything that the LORD commanded him.

¹⁷So the Holy Tent was set up on the first day of the first month during the second year after they left Egypt. ¹⁸When Moses set up the Holy Tent, he put the bases in place, and he put the frames on the bases. Next he put the crossbars through the rings of the frames and set up the posts. ¹⁹After that, Moses spread the cloth over the Holy Tent and put the covering over it, just as the LORD commanded.

²⁰Moses put the stone tablets that had the Agreement written on them into the Ark. He put the poles through the rings of the Ark and put the lid on it. ²¹Next he brought the Ark into the Tent and hung the curtain to cover the Ark, just as the LORD commanded him.

²²Moses put the table in the Meeting Tent on the north side of the Holy Tent in front of the curtain. ²³Then he put the bread on the table before the LORD, just as the LORD commanded him. ²⁴Moses put the lampstand in the Meeting Tent on the south side of the Holy Tent across from the table. ²⁵Then he put the lamps on the lampstand before the LORD, just as the LORD commanded him.

²⁶Moses put the gold altar for burning incense in the Meeting Tent in front of the curtain. ²⁷Then he burned sweet-smelling incense on it, just as the LORD commanded him. ²⁸Then he hung the curtain at the entrance to the Holy Tent.

²⁹He put the altar for burnt offerings at the entrance to the Holy Tent, the Meeting Tent, and offered a whole burnt offering and grain offerings on it, just as the LORD commanded him. ³⁰Moses put the bowl between the Meeting Tent and the altar for burnt offerings, and he put water in it for washing. ³¹Moses, Aaron and Aaron's sons used this water to wash their hands and feet. ³²They washed themselves every time they entered the Meeting Tent and every time they went near the altar for burnt offerings, just as the LORD commanded Moses.

³³Then Moses set up the courtyard around the Holy Tent and the altar, and he put up the curtain at the entrance to the courtyard. So Moses finished the work.

The Cloud Over the Holy Tent

34Then the cloud covered the Meeting Tent, *d* and the glory of the LORD filled the Holy Tent. 35Moses could not enter the Meeting Tent, because the cloud had settled on it, and the glory of the LORD filled the Holy Tent.

36When the cloud rose from the Holy Tent, the Israelites would begin to travel, 37but as long as the cloud stayed on the Holy Tent, they did not travel. They stayed in that place until the cloud rose. 38So the cloud of the LORD was over the Holy Tent during the day, and there was a fire in the cloud at night. So all the Israelites could see the cloud while they travelled.

Leviticus

When?

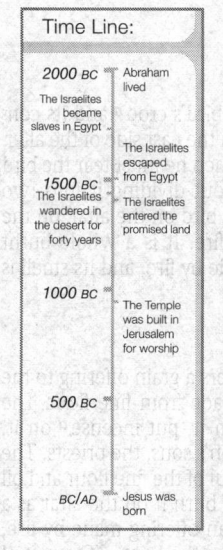

Time Line:

2000 BC	Abraham lived
The Israelites became slaves in Egypt	
	The Israelites escaped from Egypt
1500 BC The Israelites wandered in the desert for forty years	The Israelites entered the promised land
1000 BC	The Temple was built in Jerusalem for worship
500 BC	
BC/AD	Jesus was born

Where?

Why Read This Book:

- Discover how worshipping God today is different from how it used to be (Leviticus 1—7).
- Learn ancient laws people followed to obey God (Leviticus 18—20).
- Find out how people used to be punished for disobeying God's laws (Leviticus 24—26).

Behind the Scenes:

If you were a boy in ancient Israel and your great-great-great-grandfather was named Levi, you would be born with your career already planned. You would know where to live, what to wear, and exactly how to do your job. That's because the descendants of Levi – the Levites – were Israel's original priests. And Leviticus was the manual that they followed in leading people in worship.

The priests were the religious leaders in the Old Testament. They served God by preparing sacrifices to God from the people. People offered sacrifices to thank God and to ask for forgiveness for sins.

Priests were also responsible for maintaining the meeting place or "tabernacle". Many of the regulations in Leviticus deal with worship in the Meeting Tent – a portable sanctuary used as the Israelites wandered in the wilderness after being freed from slavery in Egypt. The worship regulations also applied to the Temple when it was built in Jerusalem about 350 years later.

This book is sometimes difficult for us to follow. It's filled with detailed (sometimes repulsive) instructions about animal sacrifices, building the Temple, and celebrating various religious festivals. It also contains explicit guidelines for all people about diet, sexuality, personal relationships and other areas of life. ▷

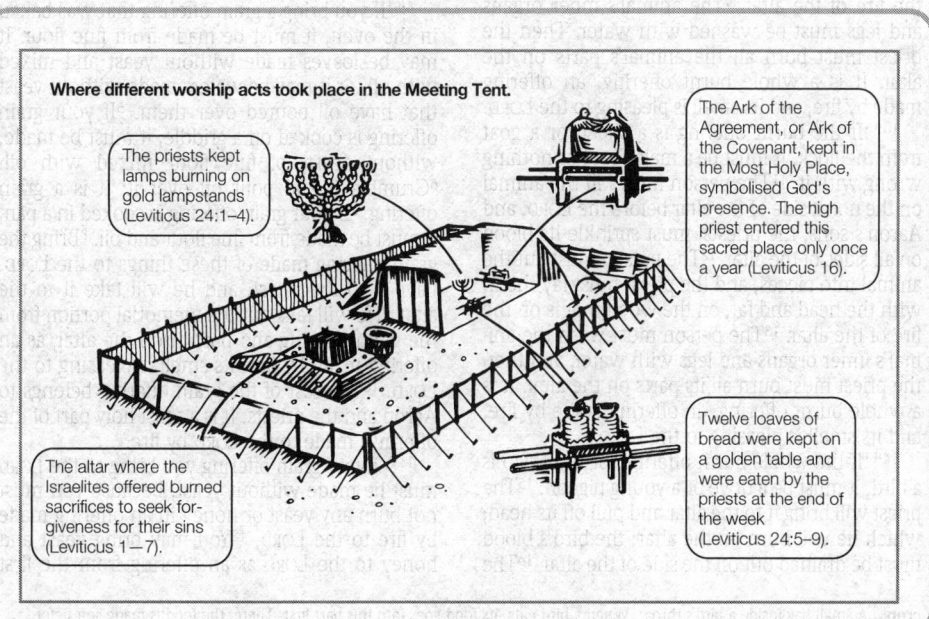

Where different worship acts took place in the Meeting Tent.

The priests kept lamps burning on gold lampstands (Leviticus 24:1–4).

The Ark of the Agreement, or Ark of the Covenant, kept in the Most Holy Place, symbolised God's presence. The high priest entered this sacred place only once a year (Leviticus 16).

The altar where the Israelites offered burned sacrifices to seek forgiveness for their sins (Leviticus 1—7).

Twelve loaves of bread were kept on a golden table and were eaten by the priests at the end of the week (Leviticus 24:5–9).

Behind the Scenes (cont.): Many of the guidelines seem irrelevant to us today. But behind all the details are themes that help us to understand what it means to follow God today. God wants a relationship with us, but we must first admit our sins and accept God's forgiveness. And God expects believers to live their lives in ways that are pleasing to him. As Leviticus 19:2 says: "I am the LORD your God. You must be holy because I am holy."

The Burnt Offering

1 The LORD called to Moses and spoke to him from the Meeting Tent, *d* saying, 2"Tell the people of Israel: 'When you bring an offering to the LORD, bring as your offering an animal from the herd or flock.

3" 'If the offering is a whole burnt offering from the herd, it must be a male that has nothing wrong with it. The person must take the animal to the entrance of the Meeting Tent so that the LORD will accept the offering. 4He must put his hand on the animal's head, and the LORD will accept it to remove the person's sin so that he will once again belong to God. 5He must kill the young bull before the LORD, and Aaron's sons, the priests, must bring its blood and sprinkle it on all sides of the altar at the entrance to the Meeting Tent. 6After that he will skin the animal and cut it into pieces. 7The priests, when they have put wood and fire on the altar, 8are to lay the head, the fat and other pieces on the wood that is on the fire of the altar. 9The animal's inner organs and legs must be washed with water. Then the priest must burn all the animal's parts on the altar. It is a whole burnt offering, an offering made by fire, and its smell is pleasing to the LORD.

10" 'If the burnt offering is a sheep or a goat from the flock, it must be a male that has nothing wrong with it. 11The person must kill the animal on the north side of the altar before the LORD, and Aaron's sons, the priests, must sprinkle its blood on all sides of the altar. 12The person must cut the animal into pieces, and the priest must lay them, with the head and fat, on the wood that is on the fire of the altar. 13The person must wash the animal's inner organs and legs with water, and then the priest must burn all its parts on the altar. It is a whole burnt offering, an offering made by fire, and its smell is pleasing to the LORD.

14" 'If the whole burnt offering for the LORD is a bird, it must be a dove or a young pigeon. 15The priest will bring it to the altar and pull off its head, which he will burn on the altar; the bird's blood must be drained out on the side of the altar. 16The priest must remove the bird's crop *n* and its contents and throw them on the east side of the altar, where the ashes are. 17Then he must tear the bird open by its wings without dividing it into two parts. He must burn the bird on the altar, on the wood which is on the fire. It is a whole burnt offering, an offering made by fire, and its smell is pleasing to the LORD.

The Grain Offering

2 " 'When anyone offers a grain offering to the LORD, it must be made from fine flour. The person must pour oil on it, put incense *d* on it, 2and then take it to Aaron's sons, the priests. The priest must take a handful of the fine flour and oil and all the incense, and burn it on the altar as a memorial portion. It is an offering made by fire, and its smell is pleasing to the LORD. 3The rest of the grain offering will belong to Aaron and the priests; it is a most holy part of the offerings made by fire to the LORD.

4" 'If you bring a grain offering that was baked in the oven, it must be made from fine flour. It may be loaves made without yeast and mixed with oil, or it may be wafers made without yeast that have oil poured over them. 5If your grain offering is cooked on a griddle, it must be made, without yeast, of fine flour mixed with oil. 6Crumble it and pour oil over it; it is a grain offering. 7If your grain offering is cooked in a pan, it must be made from fine flour and oil. 8Bring the grain offering made of these things to the LORD. Give it to the priest, and he will take it to the altar. 9He will take out the memorial portion from the grain offering and burn it on the altar, as an offering made by fire. Its smell is pleasing to the LORD. 10The rest of the grain offering belongs to Aaron and the priests. It is a most holy part of the offerings made to the LORD by fire.

11" 'Every grain offering you bring to the LORD must be made without yeast, because you must not burn any yeast or honey in an offering made by fire to the LORD. 12You may bring yeast and honey to the LORD as an offering from the first

---

crop   A small bag inside a bird's throat. When a bird eats, its food goes into this part first. There, the food is made soft before it goes into the stomach.

harvest, but they must not be burned on the altar as a pleasing smell. ¹³You must also put salt on all your grain offerings. Salt stands for your agreement with God that will last for ever; do not leave it out of your grain offering. You must add salt to all your offerings.

¹⁴" 'If you bring a grain offering from the first harvest to the Lord, bring crushed heads of new grain roasted in the fire. ¹⁵Put oil and incense on it; it is a grain offering. ¹⁶The priest will burn the memorial portion of the crushed grain and oil, with the incense on it. It is an offering by fire to the Lord.

The Fellowship Offering

3 " 'If a person's fellowship offering to the Lord is from the herd, it may be a male or female, but it must have nothing wrong with it. ²The person must put his hand on the animal's head and kill it at the entrance to the Meeting Tent. *d* Then Aaron's sons, the priests, must sprinkle the blood on all sides of the altar. ³From the fellowship offering he must make a sacrifice by fire to the Lord. He must offer the fat of the animal's inner organs (both the fat that is in them and that covers them), ⁴both kidneys with the fat that is on them near the lower back muscle, and the best part of the liver, which he will remove with the kidneys. ⁵Then the priests will burn these parts on the altar, on the whole burnt offering that is on the wood of the fire. It is an offering made by fire, and its smell is pleasing to the Lord.

⁶" 'If a person's fellowship offering to the Lord is a lamb or a goat, it may be a male or female, but it must have nothing wrong with it. ⁷If he offers a lamb, he must bring it before the Lord ⁸and put his hand on its head. Then he must kill the animal in front of the Meeting Tent, and the priests must sprinkle its blood on all sides of the altar. ⁹From the fellowship offering the person must make a sacrifice by fire to the Lord. He must bring the fat, the whole fat tail cut off close to the backbone, the fat of the inner organs (both the fat that is in them and that covers them), ¹⁰both kidneys with the fat that is on them, near the lower back muscle, and the best part of the liver, which he will remove with the kidneys. ¹¹Then the priest will burn these parts on the altar as food; it will be an offering made by fire to the Lord.

¹²" 'If a person's offering is a goat, he must offer it before the Lord ¹³and put his hand on its head. Then he must kill it in front of the Meeting Tent, and the priests must sprinkle its blood on all sides of the altar. ¹⁴From this offering the person must make a sacrifice by fire to the Lord. He must offer all the fat of the goat's inner organs (both the fat that is in them and that covers them), ¹⁵both kidneys with the fat that is on them near

the lower back muscle, and the best part of the liver, which he will remove with the kidneys. ¹⁶The priest will burn these parts on the altar as food. It is an offering made by fire, and its smell is pleasing to the Lord. All the fat belongs to the Lord.

¹⁷" 'This law will continue for people from now on, wherever you live: you must not eat any fat or blood.' "

The Sin Offering

4 The Lord said to Moses, ²"Tell the people of Israel this: 'When a person sins by accident and does some things the Lord has commanded not to be done, that person must do these things:

³" 'If the appointed priest sins so that he brings guilt on the people, then he must offer a young bull to the Lord, one that has nothing wrong with it, as a sin offering for the sin he has done. ⁴He will bring the bull to the entrance of the Meeting Tent *d* in front of the Lord, put his hand on its head, and kill it before the Lord. ⁵Then the appointed priest must bring some of the bull's blood into the Meeting Tent. ⁶The priest is to dip his finger into the blood and sprinkle it seven times before the Lord in front of the curtain of the Most Holy Place. ⁷The priest must also put some of the blood on the corners of the altar of incense *d* that stands before the Lord in the Meeting Tent. The rest of the blood he must pour out at the bottom of the altar of burnt offering, which is at the entrance of the Meeting Tent. ⁸He must remove all the fat from the bull of the sin offering—the fat on and around the inner organs, ⁹both kidneys with the fat that is on them near the lower back muscle, and the best part of the liver which he will remove with the kidneys. ¹⁰(He must do this in the same way that the fat is removed from the bull of the fellowship offering.) Then the priest must burn the animal parts on the altar of burnt offering. ¹¹But the priest must carry off the skin of the bull and all its meat, along with the rest of the bull—its head, legs, intestines and other inner organs. ¹²He must take it outside the camp to the special clean *d* place where the ashes are poured out. He must burn it on a wood fire on the pile of ashes.

13" 'If the whole nation of Israel sins accidentally without knowing it and does something the LORD has commanded not to be done, they are guilty. 14When they learn about the sin they have done, they must offer a young bull as a sin offering and bring it before the Meeting Tent. 15The elders of the group of people must put their hands on the bull's head before the LORD, and it must be killed before the LORD. 16Then the appointed priest must bring some of the bull's blood into the Meeting Tent. 17Dipping his finger in the blood, he must sprinkle it seven times before the LORD in front of the curtain. 18Then he must put some of the blood on the corners of the altar that is before the LORD in the Meeting Tent. The priest must pour out the rest of the blood at the bottom of the altar of burnt offering, which is at the entrance to the Meeting Tent. 19He must remove all the fat from the animal and burn it on the altar; 20he will do the same thing with this bull that he did with the first bull of the sin offering. In this way the priest removes the sins of the people so they will belong to the LORD and be forgiven. 21Then the priest must carry the bull outside the camp and burn it, just as he did with the first bull. This is the sin offering for the whole community.

22" 'If a ruler sins by accident and does something the LORD his God has commanded must not be done, he is guilty. 23When he learns about his sin, he must bring a male goat that has nothing wrong with it as his offering. 24The ruler must put his hand on the goat's head and kill it in the place where they kill the whole burnt offering before the LORD; it is a sin offering. 25The priest must take some of the blood of the sin offering on his finger and put it on the corners of the altar of burnt offering. He must pour out the rest of the blood at the bottom of the altar of burnt offering. 26He must burn all the goat's fat on the altar in the same way that he burns the fat of the fellowship offerings. In this way the priest removes the ruler's sin so that he belongs to the LORD, and the LORD will forgive him.

27" 'If any person in the community sins by accident and does something which the LORD has commanded must not be done, he is guilty. 28When the person learns about his sin, he must bring a female goat that has nothing wrong with it as an offering for his sin. 29He must put his hand on the animal's head and kill it at the place of the whole burnt offering. 30Then the priest must take some of the goat's blood on his finger and put it on the corners of the altar of burnt offering. He must pour out the rest of the goat's blood at the bottom of the altar. 31Then the priest must remove all the goat's fat in the same way the fat is removed from the fellowship offerings. He must burn it on the altar as a smell pleasing

to the LORD. In this way the priest will remove that person's sin so he will belong to the LORD, and the LORD will forgive him.

32" 'If this person brings a lamb as his offering for sin, he must bring a female that has nothing wrong with it. 33He must put his hand on the animal's head and kill it as a sin offering in the place where the whole burnt offering is killed. 34The priest must take some of the blood from the sin offering on his finger and put it on the corners of the altar of burnt offering. He must pour out the rest of the lamb's blood at the bottom of the altar. 35Then the priest must remove all the lamb's fat in the same way that the lamb's fat is removed from the fellowship offerings. He must burn the pieces on the altar on top of the offerings made by fire to the LORD. In this way the priest will remove that person's sins so he will belong to the LORD, and the LORD will forgive him.

Special Types of Accidental Sins

5 " 'If a person is ordered to tell in court what he has seen or what he knows and he does not tell the court, he is guilty of sin.

2" 'Or someone might touch something unclean, *d* such as the dead body of an unclean wild animal or an unclean farm animal or an unclean crawling animal. Even if he does not know that he touched it, he will still be unclean and guilty of sin.

3" 'Someone might touch human uncleanness— anything that makes someone unclean—and not know it. But when he learns about it, he will be guilty.

4" 'Or someone might make a promise before the LORD without thinking. It might be a promise to do something bad or something good; it might be about anything. Even if he forgets about it, when he remembers, he will be guilty.

5" 'When anyone is guilty of any of these things, he must tell how he sinned. 6He must bring an offering to the LORD as a penalty for sin; it must be a female lamb or goat from the flock. The priest will perform the acts to remove that person's sin so that he will once again belong to the LORD.

7" 'But if the person cannot afford a lamb, he must bring two doves or two young pigeons to the LORD as the penalty for his sin. One bird must be for a sin offering, and the other must be for a whole burnt offering. 8He must bring them to the priest, who will first offer the one for the sin offering. He will pull the bird's head from its neck, but he will not pull it completely off. 9He must sprinkle the blood from the sin offering on the side of the altar, and then he must pour the rest of the blood at the bottom of the altar; it is a sin offering. 10Then the priest must offer the second bird as a whole burnt offering, as the law says. In this way the priest will remove the person's sin so he will belong to the LORD, and the LORD will forgive him.

¹¹ "If the person cannot afford two doves or two pigeons, he must bring about 2 litres of fine flour as an offering for sin. He must not put oil or incense *d* on the flour, because it is a sin offering. ¹²He must bring the flour to the priest. The priest will take a handful of the flour as a memorial offering and burn it on the altar on top of the offerings made by fire to the LORD; it is a sin offering. ¹³In this way the priest will remove the person's sins so that he will belong to the LORD, and the LORD will forgive him. What is left of the sin offering belongs to the priest, like the grain offering.' "

The Penalty Offering

¹⁴The LORD said to Moses, ¹⁵"If a person accidentally sins and does something against the holy things of the LORD, he must bring from the flock a ram that has nothing wrong with it. This will be his penalty offering to the LORD. Its value in silver must be correct as set by the Holy Place measure. It is a penalty offering. ¹⁶That person must pay for the sin he did against the holy thing, adding one-fifth to its value. Then he must give it all to the priest. In this way the priest will remove the person's sin so he will belong to the LORD, by using the ram as the penalty offering. And the LORD will forgive the person.

¹⁷"If a person sins and does something the LORD has commanded not to be done, even if he does not know it, he is still guilty. He is responsible for his sin. ¹⁸He must bring the priest a ram from the flock, one that has nothing wrong with it and that is worth the correct amount. It will be a penalty offering. Though the person sinned without knowing it, with this offering the priest will remove the sin so that the person will belong to the LORD, and the LORD will forgive him. ¹⁹The person is guilty of doing wrong, so he must give the penalty offering to the LORD."

6 The LORD said to Moses, ²"A person might sin against the LORD by doing one of these sins: he might lie about what happened to something he was taking care of for someone else, or he might lie about a promise he made. He might steal something or cheat someone. ³He might find something that had been lost and then lie about it. He might make a promise before the LORD about something and not mean it, or he might do some other sin. ⁴If he does any of these things, he is guilty of sin. He must bring back whatever he stole or whatever he took by cheating. He must bring back the thing he took care of for someone else. He must bring back what he

found and lied about ⁵or what he made a false promise about. He must pay the full price plus an extra one-fifth of the value of what he took. He must give the money to the true owner on the day he brings his penalty offering. ⁶He must bring his penalty to the priest—a ram from the flock, one that does not have anything wrong with it and that is worth the correct amount. It will be a penalty offering to the LORD. ⁷Then the priest will perform the acts to remove that person's sin so that he will belong to the LORD, and the LORD will forgive him for the sins that made him guilty."

The Whole Burnt Offering

⁸The LORD said to Moses, ⁹"Give this command to Aaron and the priests: 'These are the teachings about the whole burnt offering: the burnt offering must stay on the altar all night until morning, and the altar's fire must be kept burning. ¹⁰The priest must put on his linen robe and linen underclothes next to his body. Then he will remove the ashes from the burnt offering on the altar and put them beside the altar. ¹¹Then he must take off those clothes and put on others and carry the ashes outside the camp to a special clean *d* place. ¹²But the fire must be kept burning on the altar; it must not be allowed to go out. The priest must put more firewood on the altar every morning, place the whole burnt offering on the fire, and burn the fat of the fellowship offerings. ¹³The fire must be kept burning on the altar all the time; it must not go out.

The Grain Offering

¹⁴" 'These are the teachings about the grain offering: the priests must bring it to the LORD in front of the altar. ¹⁵The priest must take a handful of fine flour, with the oil and all of the incense *d* on it, and burn the grain offering on the altar as a memorial offering to the LORD. Its smell is pleasing to him. ¹⁶Aaron and the priests may eat what is left, but it must be eaten without yeast in a holy place. They must eat it in the courtyard of the Meeting Tent. *d* ¹⁷It must not be cooked with yeast. I have given it as their share of the offerings made to me by fire; it is most holy, like the sin offering and the penalty offering. ¹⁸Any male descendant *d* of Aaron may eat it as his share of the offerings made to the LORD by fire, and this will continue from now on. Whatever touches these offerings shall become holy.' "

¹⁹The LORD said to Moses, ²⁰"This is the offering Aaron and the priests must bring to the LORD on the day they appoint Aaron as high priest: they must bring 2 litres of fine flour for a continual grain offering, half of it in the morning and half in the evening. ²¹The fine flour must be mixed with

oil and cooked on a griddle. Bring it when it is well mixed. Present the grain offering that is broken into pieces, and it will be a smell that is pleasing to the LORD. 22One of the priests appointed to take Aaron's place as high priest must make the grain offering. It is a rule for ever that the grain offering must be completely burned to the LORD. 23Every grain offering made by a priest must be completely burned; it must not be eaten."

The Sin Offering

24The LORD said to Moses, 25"Tell Aaron and the priests: 'These are the teachings about the sin offering: the sin offering must be killed in front of the LORD in the same place that the whole burnt offering is killed; it is most holy. 26The priest who offers the sin offering must eat it in a holy place, in the courtyard of the Meeting Tent. d 27Whatever touches the meat of the sin offering must be holy, and if the blood is sprinkled on any clothes, you must wash them in a holy place. 28The clay pot the meat is cooked in must be broken, or if a bronze pot is used, it must be scrubbed and rinsed with water. 29Any male in a priest's family may eat the offering; it is most holy. 30But if the blood of the sin offering is taken into the Meeting Tent and used to remove sin in the Holy Place, that sin offering must be burned with fire. It must not be eaten.

The Penalty Offering

7 " 'These are the teachings about the penalty offering, which is most holy: 2the penalty offering must be killed where the whole burnt offering is killed. Then the priest must sprinkle its blood on all sides of the altar. 3He must offer all the fat from the penalty offering—the fat tail, the fat that covers the inner organs, 4both kidneys with the fat that is on them near the lower back muscle, and the best part of the liver, which is to be removed with the kidneys. 5The priest must burn all these things on the altar as an offering made by fire to the LORD. It is a penalty offering. 6Any male in a priest's family may eat it. It is most holy, so it must be eaten in a holy place.

7" 'The penalty offering is like the sin offering in that the teachings are the same for both. The priest who offers the sacrifice to remove sins will get the meat for food. 8The priest who offers the burnt offering may also have the skin from it. 9Every grain offering that is baked in an oven, cooked on a griddle or baked in a dish belongs to the priest who offers it. 10Every grain offering, either dry or mixed with oil, belongs to the priests, and all priests will share alike.

The Fellowship Offering

11" 'These are the teachings about the fellowship offering a person may offer to the LORD: 12if he brings the fellowship offering to show his thanks, he should also bring loaves of bread made without yeast that are mixed with oil, wafers made without yeast that have oil poured over them, and loaves of fine flour that are mixed with oil. 13He must also offer loaves of bread made with yeast along with his fellowship offering, which he gives to show thanks. 14One of each kind of offering will be for the LORD; it will be given to the priest who sprinkles the blood of the fellowship offering. 15When the fellowship offering is given to thank the LORD, the meat from it must be eaten the same day it is offered; none of it must be left until morning.

16" 'If a person brings a fellowship offering just to give a gift to God or because of a special promise to him, the sacrifice should be eaten the same day he offers it. If there is any left, it may be eaten the next day. 17If any meat from this sacrifice is left on the third day, it must be burned up. 18Any meat of the fellowship offering eaten on the third day will not be accepted, nor will the sacrifice count for the person who offered it. It will become unclean, d and anyone who eats the meat will be guilty of sin.

19" 'People must not eat meat that touches anything unclean; they must burn this meat with fire. Anyone who is clean may eat other meat. 20But if anyone is unclean and eats the meat from the fellowship offering that belongs to the LORD, he must be cut off from his people.

21" 'If anyone touches something unclean—uncleanness that comes from people, from an animal or from some hated thing—touching it will make him unclean. If he then eats meat from the fellowship offering that belongs to the LORD, he must be cut off from his people.' "

22The LORD said to Moses, 23"Tell the people of Israel: 'You must not eat any of the fat from cattle, sheep or goats. 24If an animal is found dead or torn by wild animals, you may use its fat for other things, but you must not eat it. 25If someone eats fat from an animal offering made by fire to the LORD, he must be cut off from his people. 26No matter where you live, you must not eat blood from any bird or animal. 27Anyone who eats blood must be cut off from his people.' "

The Priests' Share

28The LORD said to Moses, 29"Tell the people of Israel: 'If someone brings a fellowship offering to the LORD, he must give part of it as his sacrifice to the LORD. 30He must carry that part of the gift in his own hands as an offering made by fire to the

Lord. He must bring the fat and the breast of the animal to the priest, to be presented to the Lord as the priests' share. ³¹Then the priest must burn the fat on the altar, but the breast of the animal will belong to Aaron and the priests. ³²You must also give the right thigh from the fellowship offering to the priest as a gift; ³³it will belong to the priest who offers the blood and fat of the fellowship offering. ³⁴I have taken the breast and the thigh from the fellowship offerings of the Israelites, and I have given these parts to Aaron and the priests as their share for all time from the Israelites.' "

³⁵This is the portion that belongs to Aaron and his sons from the offerings made by fire to the Lord. They were given this share on the day they were presented to the Lord as priests. ³⁶On the day the Lord appointed the priests, he commanded Israel to give this share to them, and it is to be given to the priests as their share from now on.

³⁷These are the teachings about the whole burnt offering, the grain offering, the sin offering, the penalty offering, the offering for the appointment of priests and the fellowship offering. ³⁸The Lord gave these teachings to Moses on Mount Sinai on the day he commanded the Israelites to bring their offerings to the Lord in the Sinai Desert.

Aaron and His Sons Appointed

8 The Lord said to Moses, ²"Bring Aaron and his sons and their clothes, the special olive oil used in appointing people and things to the service of the Lord, the bull of the sin offering and the two rams, and the basket of bread made without yeast. ³Then gather the people together at the entrance to the Meeting Tent." *d* ⁴Moses did as the Lord commanded him, and the people met together at the entrance to the Meeting Tent.

⁵Then Moses spoke to the people and said, "This is what the Lord has commanded to be done." ⁶Bringing Aaron and his sons forwards, Moses washed them with water. ⁷He put the inner robe on Aaron and tied the cloth belt around him. Then Moses put the outer robe on him and placed the holy robe *d* on him. He tied the skilfully woven belt around him so that the holy robe was tied to Aaron. ⁸Then Moses put the chest covering on him and put the Urim and the Thummim *d* in the chest covering. ⁹He also put the turban on Aaron's head. He put the strip of gold, the holy crown, on the front of the turban, as the Lord commanded him to do.

¹⁰Then Moses put the special oil on the Holy Tent *d* and everything in it, making them holy for the Lord. ¹¹He sprinkled some oil on the altar seven times, sprinkling the altar and all its tools and the large bowl and its base. In this way he made them holy for the Lord. ¹²He poured some of the special oil on Aaron's head to make Aaron holy for the Lord. ¹³Then Moses brought Aaron's sons forwards. He put the inner robes on them, tied cloth belts around them, and put headbands on them, as the Lord had commanded him.

¹⁴Then Moses brought the bull for the sin offering, and Aaron and his sons put their hands on its head. ¹⁵Moses killed the bull, took the blood, and with his finger put some of it on all the corners of the altar, to make it pure. Then he poured out the rest of the blood at the bottom of the altar. In this way he made it holy and ready for service to God. ¹⁶Moses took all the fat from the inner organs of the bull, the best part of the liver, and both kidneys with the fat that is on them, and he burned them on the altar. ¹⁷But he took the bull's skin, its meat and its intestines and burned them in a fire outside the camp, as the Lord had commanded him.

¹⁸Next Moses brought the ram of the burnt offering, and Aaron and his sons put their hands on its head. ¹⁹Then Moses killed it and sprinkled the blood on all sides of the altar. ²⁰He cut the ram into pieces and burned the head, the pieces and the fat. ²¹He washed the inner organs and legs with water and burned the whole ram on the altar as a burnt offering made by fire to the Lord; its smell was pleasing to the Lord. Moses did these things as the Lord had commanded him.

²²Then Moses brought the other ram, the one used in appointing Aaron and his sons as priests, and Aaron and his sons put their hands on its head. ²³Then Moses killed the sheep and put some of its blood on the bottom of Aaron's right ear, some on the thumb of Aaron's right hand, and some on the big toe of his right foot. ²⁴Then Moses brought Aaron's sons close to the altar. He put some of the blood on the bottom of their right ears, some on the thumbs of their right hands, and some on the big toes of their right feet. Then he sprinkled blood on all sides of the altar. ²⁵He took the fat, the fat tail, all the fat on the inner organs, the best part of the liver, both kidneys with their fat and the right thigh. ²⁶From the basket of bread made without yeast that is put before the Lord each day, Moses took a loaf of bread, a loaf made with oil and a wafer. He put these pieces of bread on the fat and right thigh of the ram. ²⁷All these things he put in the hands of Aaron and his sons and presented them as an offering before the Lord. ²⁸Then Moses took them from their hands and burned them on the altar on top of the burnt offering. So this was the offering for appointing Aaron and his sons as priests. It was an offering made by fire to the Lord, and its smell was pleasing to him. ²⁹Moses also took the

breast and presented it as an offering before the LORD. It was Moses' share of the ram used in appointing the priests, as the LORD had commanded him.

30Moses took some of the special oil and some of the blood which was on the altar, and he sprinkled them on Aaron and Aaron's clothes, and on Aaron's sons and their clothes. In this way Moses made Aaron, his clothes, his sons and their clothes holy for the LORD.

31Then Moses said to Aaron and his sons, "I gave you a command, saying, 'Aaron and his sons will eat these things.' So take the meat and basket of bread from the offering for appointing priests. Boil the meat at the door of the Meeting Tent, and eat it there with the bread. 32If any of the meat or bread is left, burn it. 33The time of appointing will last seven days; you must not go outside the entrance of the Meeting Tent until that time is up. Stay there until the time of your appointing is finished. 34The LORD commanded the things that were done today to remove your sins so you will belong to him. 35You must stay at the entrance of the Meeting Tent day and night for seven days. If you don't obey the LORD's commands, you will die. The LORD has given me these commands."

36So Aaron and his sons did everything the LORD had commanded through Moses.

Aaron and His Sons Offer Sacrifices

9 On the eighth day after the time of appointing, Moses called for Aaron and his sons and for the elders of Israel. 2He said to Aaron, "Take a bull calf and a ram that have nothing wrong with them, and offer them to the LORD. The calf will be a sin offering, and the ram will be a whole burnt offering. 3Tell the people of Israel, 'Take a male goat for a sin offering and a calf and a lamb for a whole burnt offering; each must be one year old, and it must have nothing wrong with it. 4Also take a bull and a ram for fellowship offerings, along with a grain offering mixed with oil. Offer all these things to the LORD, because the LORD will appear to you today.' "

5So all the people came to the front of the Meeting Tent, d bringing the things Moses had commanded them to bring, and they stood before the LORD. 6Moses said, "You have done what the LORD commanded, so you will see the LORD's glory."

7Then Moses told Aaron, "Go to the altar and offer sin offerings and whole burnt offerings. Do this to remove your sins and the people's sins so you will belong to God. Offer the sacrifices for the people and perform the acts to remove their sins for them so they will belong to the LORD, as the LORD has commanded."

8So Aaron went to the altar and killed the bull calf as a sin offering for himself. 9Then his sons brought the blood to him, and he dipped his finger in the blood and put it on the corners of the altar. He poured out the rest of the blood at the bottom of the altar. 10Aaron took the fat, the kidneys and the best part of the liver from the sin offering and burned them on the altar, in the way the LORD had commanded Moses. 11The meat and skin he burned outside the camp.

12Then Aaron killed the animal for the whole burnt offering. His sons brought the blood to him, and he sprinkled it on all sides of the altar. 13As they gave him the pieces and head of the burnt offering, Aaron burned them on the altar. 14He also washed the inner organs and the legs of the burnt offering and burned them on top of the burnt offering on the altar.

15Then Aaron brought the offering that was for the people. He took the goat of the people's sin offering and killed it and offered it for the sin offering, just as he had done for the first sin offering.

16Then Aaron brought the whole burnt offering and offered it in the way that the LORD had commanded. 17He also brought the grain offering to the altar. He took a handful of the grain and burned it on the altar, in addition to the morning's burnt offering.

18Aaron also killed the bull and the ram as the fellowship offerings for the people. His sons brought him the blood, and he sprinkled it on all sides of the altar. 19Aaron's sons also brought to Aaron the fat of the bull and the ram—the fat tail, the fat covering the inner organs, the kidneys and the best part of the liver. 20Aaron's sons put them on the breasts of the bull and the sheep. Then Aaron burned these fat parts on the altar. 21He presented the breasts and the right thigh before the LORD as the priests' share of the offering, as Moses had commanded.

22Then Aaron lifted his hands towards the people and blessed them. When he had finished offering the sin offering, the burnt offering and the fellowship offering, he stepped down from the altar.

23Moses and Aaron went into the Meeting Tent. Then they came out and blessed the people, and the LORD's glory came to all the people. 24Fire came out from the LORD and burned up the burnt offering and fat on the altar. When the people saw this, they shouted with joy and bowed face down on the ground.

God Destroys Nadab and Abihu

10 Aaron's sons Nadab and Abihu took their pans for burning incense, d put fire in them, and added incense; but they did not use

the special fire Moses had commanded them to use in the presence of the LORD. ²So fire came down from the LORD and destroyed Nadab and Abihu, and they died in front of the LORD. ³Then Moses said to Aaron, "This is what the LORD was speaking about when he said,

'I must be respected as holy
　by those who come near me;
　before all the people
　I must be given honour.' "

So Aaron did not say anything about the death of his sons.

⁴Aaron's uncle Uzziel had two sons named Mishael and Elzaphan. Moses said to them, "Come here and pick up your cousins' bodies. Carry them outside the camp away from the front of the Holy Place." ⁵So Mishael and Elzaphan obeyed Moses and carried the bodies of Nadab and Abihu, still clothed in the special priest's inner robes, outside the camp.

⁶Then Moses said to Aaron and his other sons, Eleazar and Ithamar, "Don't show sadness by tearing your clothes or leaving your hair uncombed. If you do, you will die, and the LORD will be angry with all the people. All the people of Israel, your relatives, may cry loudly about the LORD burning Nadab and Abihu, ⁷but you must not even leave the Meeting Tent. *d* If you go out of the entrance, you will die, because the LORD has appointed you to his service." So Aaron, Eleazar and Ithamar obeyed Moses.

⁸Then the LORD said to Aaron, ⁹"You and your sons must not drink wine or beer when you go into the Meeting Tent. If you do, you will die. This law will continue from now on. ¹⁰You must keep what is holy separate from what is not holy; you must keep what is clean *d* separate from what is unclean. ¹¹You must teach the people all the laws that the LORD gave to them through Moses."

¹²Moses said to Aaron and his remaining sons, Eleazar and Ithamar, "Eat the part of the grain offering that is left from the sacrifices offered by fire to the LORD, but do not add yeast to it. Eat it near the altar because it is most holy. ¹³You must eat it in a holy place, because this part of the offering made by fire to the LORD belongs to you and your sons. I have been commanded to tell you this. ¹⁴"Also, you and your sons and daughters may eat the breast and thigh of the fellowship offering that was presented to the LORD. You must eat them in a clean place; they are your share of the fellowship offerings given by the Israelites. ¹⁵The people must bring the fat from their animals that was part of the offering made by fire, and they must present it to the LORD along with the thigh and the breast of the fellowship offering. They will be the regular share of the offerings for you and your children, as the LORD has commanded."

¹⁶Moses looked for the goat of the sin offering, but it had already been burned up. So he became very angry with Eleazar and Ithamar, Aaron's remaining sons. He said, ¹⁷"Why didn't you eat that goat in a holy place? It is most holy, and the LORD gave it to you to take away the guilt of the people, to remove their sins so that they will belong to the LORD. ¹⁸You didn't bring the goat's blood inside the Holy Place. You were supposed to eat the goat in a holy place, as I commanded!"

¹⁹But Aaron said to Moses, "Today they brought their sin offering and burnt offering before the LORD, but these terrible things have still happened to me! Do you think the LORD would be any happier if I ate the sin offering today?" ²⁰When Moses heard this, he was satisfied.

Rules About What May Be Eaten

11 The LORD said to Moses and Aaron, ²"Tell the Israelites this: 'These are the land animals you may eat: ³you may eat any animal that has split hoofs completely divided and that chews the cud. *d*

⁴" 'Some animals only chew the cud or only have split hoofs, and you must not eat them. The camel chews the cud but does not have a split hoof; it is unclean *d* for you. ⁵The rock badger chews the cud but does not have a split hoof; it is unclean for you. ⁶The rabbit chews the cud but does not have a split hoof; it is unclean for you. ⁷Now the pig has a split hoof that is completely divided, but it does not chew the cud; it is unclean for you. ⁸You must not eat the meat from these animals or even touch their dead bodies; they are unclean for you.

⁹" 'Of the animals that live in the sea or in a river, if the animal has fins and scales, you may eat it. ¹⁰But whatever lives in the sea or in a river and does not have fins and scales—including the things that fill the water and all other things that live in it—you should hate. ¹¹You must not eat any meat from them or even touch their dead bodies, because you should hate them. ¹²You must hate any animal in the water that does not have fins and scales.

¹³" 'Also, these are the birds you are to hate. They are hateful and should not be eaten. You must not eat eagles, vultures, black vultures, ¹⁴kites, any kind of falcon, ¹⁵any kind of raven, ¹⁶horned owls, screech owls, sea gulls, any kind of hawk, ¹⁷little owls, cormorants, great owls, ¹⁸white owls, desert owls, ospreys, ¹⁹storks, any kind of heron, hoopoes or bats.

²⁰" 'Don't eat insects that have wings and walk on all four feet; they also are to be hated.

²¹" 'But you may eat certain insects that have wings and walk on four feet. You may eat those that have legs with joints above their feet so that

they can jump. ²²These are the insects you may eat: all kinds of locusts, winged locusts, crickets and grasshoppers. ²³But all other insects that have wings and walk on four feet you are to hate. ²⁴Those insects will make you unclean, and anyone who touches the dead body of one of these insects will become unclean until evening. ²⁵Anyone who picks up one of these dead insects must wash his clothes and be unclean until evening.

²⁶" 'Some animals have split hoofs, but the hoofs are not completely divided; others do not chew the cud. They are unclean for you, and anyone who touches the dead body of one of these animals will become unclean. ²⁷Of all the animals that walk on four feet, the animals that walk on their paws are unclean for you. Anyone who touches the dead body of one of these animals will become unclean until evening. ²⁸Anyone who picks up their dead bodies must wash his clothes and be unclean until evening; these animals are unclean for you.

²⁹" 'These crawling animals are unclean for you: moles, rats, all kinds of great lizards,

---

Sidelight   The Israelites' dietary law forbade eating moles, rats, lizards, crocodiles, chameleons and other reptiles (Leviticus 11:29–30). It seems to have been a sign to show that Israel was chosen and holy. Scholars have given health reasons as to which animals were clean and which transmitted disease, but above all the laws proved that God had the right to tell his people exactly what to eat.

---

³⁰geckos, crocodiles, lizards, sand reptiles and chameleons. ³¹These crawling animals are unclean for you; anyone who touches their dead bodies will be unclean until evening.

³²" 'If an unclean animal dies and falls on something, that thing will also become unclean. This includes anything made from wood, cloth, leather or rough cloth, regardless of its use. Whatever the animal falls on must be washed with water and be unclean until evening; then it will become clean again. ³³If the dead, unclean animal falls into a clay bowl, anything in the bowl will become unclean, and you must break the bowl. ³⁴If water from the unclean clay bowl gets on any food, that food will become unclean. ³⁵If any dead, unclean animal falls on something, it becomes unclean. If it is a clay oven or a clay baking pan, it must be broken into pieces. These things will be unclean; they are unclean for you. ³⁶" 'A spring or well that collects water will stay clean, but anyone who touches the dead

body of any unclean animal will become unclean. ³⁷If a dead, unclean animal falls on a seed to be planted, that seed is still clean. ³⁸But if you put water on some seeds and a dead, unclean animal falls on them, they are unclean for you.

³⁹" 'Also, if an animal which you use for food dies, anyone who touches its body will be unclean until evening. ⁴⁰Anyone who eats meat from this animal's dead body must wash his clothes and be unclean until evening. Anyone who picks up the animal's dead body must wash his clothes and be unclean until evening.

⁴¹" 'Every animal that crawls on the ground is to be hated; it must not be eaten. ⁴²You must not eat any of the animals that crawl on the ground, including those that crawl on their stomachs, that walk on all four feet, or on many feet. They are to be hated. ⁴³Do not make yourself unclean by these animals; you must not become unclean by them. ⁴⁴I am the LORD your God. Keep yourselves holy for me because I am holy. Don't make yourselves unclean with any of these crawling animals. ⁴⁵I am the LORD who brought you out of Egypt to be your God; you must be holy because I am holy.

⁴⁶" 'These are the teachings about all of the cattle, birds and other animals on earth, as well as the animals in the sea and those that crawl on the ground. ⁴⁷These teachings help people know the difference between unclean animals and clean animals; they help people know which animals may be eaten and which ones must not be eaten.' "

Rules for New Mothers

12 The LORD said to Moses, ²"Tell the people of Israel this: 'If a woman gives birth to a son, she will become unclean[d] for seven days, as she is unclean during her monthly period. ³On the eighth day the boy must be circumcised.[d] ⁴Then it will be 33 days before she becomes clean from her loss of blood. She must not touch anything that is holy or enter the Holy Tent until her time of cleansing is finished. ⁵But if she gives birth to a daughter, the mother will be unclean for two weeks, as she is unclean during her monthly period. It will be 66 days before she becomes clean from her loss of blood.

⁶" 'After she has a son or daughter and her days of cleansing are over, the new mother must bring certain sacrifices to the Meeting Tent.[d] She must give the priest at the entrance a year-old lamb for a burnt offering and a dove or young pigeon for a sin offering. ⁷He will offer them before the LORD to make her clean so she will belong to the LORD again; then she will be clean from her loss of blood. These are the teachings for a woman who gives birth to a boy or girl.

[8] " 'If she cannot afford a lamb, she is to bring two doves or two young pigeons, one for a burnt offering and one for a sin offering. In this way the priest will make her clean so she will belong to the LORD again, and she will be clean.' "

Rules About Skin Diseases

13 The LORD said to Moses and Aaron, [2]"Someone might have on his skin a swelling or a sore or a bright spot. If the sore looks like a harmful skin disease, the person must be brought to Aaron, the priest, or to one of Aaron's sons, the priests. [3]The priest must look at the sore on the person's skin. If the hair in the sore has become white, and the sore seems deeper than the person's skin, it is a harmful skin disease. When he has finished looking at the person, the priest must announce that the person is unclean. [d]

[4]"If there is a white spot on a person's skin, but the spot does not seem deeper than the skin, and if the hair from the spot has not turned white, the priest must separate that person from other people for seven days. [5]On the seventh day the priest must look at the person again. If he sees that the sore has not changed and it has not spread on the skin, the priest must keep the person separated for seven more days. [6]On the seventh day the priest must look at the person again. If the sore has faded and has not spread on the skin, the priest must announce that the person is clean. The sore is only a rash. The person must wash his clothes, and he will become clean again.

[7]"But if the sore spreads again after the priest has announced him clean, the person must come again to the priest. [8]The priest must look at him, and if the rash has spread on the skin, the priest must announce that the person is unclean; it is a harmful skin disease.

[9]"If a person has a harmful skin disease, he must be brought to the priest, [10]and the priest must look at him. If there is a white swelling in the skin, and the hair has become white, and the skin looks raw in the swelling, [11]it is a harmful skin disease. It is one he has had for a long time. The priest must announce that the person is unclean. He will not need to separate that person from other people, because everyone already knows that the person is unclean.

[12]"If the skin disease spreads all over a person's body, covering his skin from his head to his feet, as far as the priest can see, the priest must look at the person's whole body. [13]If the priest sees that the disease covers the whole body and has turned all of the person's skin white, he must announce that the person is clean.

[14]"But when the person has an open sore, he is unclean. [15]When the priest sees the open sore, he must announce that the person is unclean. The open sore is not clean; it is a harmful skin disease. [16]If the open sore becomes white again, the person must come to the priest. [17]The priest must look at him, and if the sores have become white, the priest must announce that the person with the sores is clean. Then he will be clean.

[18]"Someone may have a boil on his skin that is healed. [19]If in the place where the boil was, there is a white swelling or a bright red spot, this place on the skin must be shown to the priest. [20]And the priest must look at it. If the spot seems deeper than the skin and the hair on it has become white, the priest must announce that the person is unclean. The spot is a harmful skin disease that has broken out from inside the boil. [21]But if the priest looks at the spot and there are no white hairs in it and the spot is not deeper than the skin and it has faded, the priest must separate the person from other people for seven days. [22]If the spot spreads on the skin, the priest must announce that the person is unclean; it is a disease that will spread. [23]But if the bright spot does not spread or change, it is only the scar from the old boil. Then the priest must announce that the person is clean.

[24]"When a person gets a burn on his skin, if the open sore becomes white or red, [25]the priest must look at it. If the white spot seems deeper than the skin and the hair at that spot has become white, it is a harmful skin disease. The disease has broken out in the burn, and the priest must announce that the person is unclean. It is a harmful skin disease. [26]But if the priest looks at the spot and there is no white hair in the bright spot, and the spot is no deeper than the skin and has faded, the priest must separate the person from other people for seven days. [27]On the seventh day the priest must look at him again. If the spot has spread on the skin, the priest must announce that the person is unclean. It is a harmful skin disease. [28]But if the bright spot has not spread on the skin but has faded, it is the swelling from the burn. The priest must announce that the person is clean, because the spot is only a scar from the burn.

[29]"When a man or a woman gets a sore on the scalp or on the chin, [30]a priest must look at the sore. If it seems deeper than the skin and the hair around it is thin and yellow, the priest must announce that the person is unclean. It is an itch, a harmful skin disease of the head or chin. [31]But if the priest looks at it and it does not seem deeper than the skin and there is no black hair in it, the priest must separate the person from other people for seven days. [32]On the seventh day the priest must look at the sore. If it has not spread, and there are no yellow hairs growing in it, and the sore does not seem deeper than the skin, [33]the

person must shave himself, but he must not shave the sore place. The priest must separate that person from other people for seven more days. [34]On the seventh day the priest must look at the sore. If it has not spread on the skin and it does not seem deeper than the skin, the priest must announce that the person is clean. So the person must wash his clothes and become clean. [35]But if the sore spreads on the skin after the person has become clean, [36]the priest must look at him again. If the sore has spread on the skin, the priest doesn't need to look for the yellowish hair; the person is unclean. [37]But if the priest thinks the sore has stopped spreading, and black hair is growing in it, the sore has healed. The person is clean, and the priest must announce that he is clean.

[38]"When a man or a woman has white spots on the skin, [39]a priest must look at them. If the spots on the skin are dull white, the disease is only a harmless rash. That person is clean.

[40]"When anyone loses hair from his head and is bald, he is clean. [41]If he loses hair from the front of his head and has a bald forehead, he is clean. [42]But if there is a red-white sore on his bald head or forehead, it is a skin disease breaking out in those places. [43]A priest must look at that person. If the swelling of the sore on his bald head or forehead is red-white, like a skin disease that spreads, [44]that person has a skin disease. He is unclean. The priest must announce that the person is unclean because of the sore on his head.

[45]"If a person has a skin disease that spreads, he must warn other people by shouting, 'Unclean, unclean!' His clothes must be torn at the seams, he must let his hair stay uncombed, and he must cover his mouth. [46]That person will remain unclean while he has the disease; he is unclean. He must live alone outside the camp.

Rules About Mildew

[47]"Clothing might have mildew [d] on it. It might be clothing made of linen or wool [48](either woven or knitted), or of leather, or something made from leather. [49]If the mildew in the clothing, leather or woven or knitted material is green or red, it is a spreading mildew. It must be shown to the priest. [50]The priest must look at the mildew, and he must put that piece of clothing in a separate place for seven days. [51]On the seventh day he must look at the mildew again. If the mildew has spread on the cloth (either woven or knitted) or the leather, no matter what the leather was used for, it is a mildew that destroys; it is unclean. [52]The priest must burn the clothing. It does not matter if it is woven or knitted, wool or linen, or made of leather, because the mildew is spreading. It must be burned.

[53]"If the priest sees that the mildew has not spread in the cloth (either knitted or woven) or leather, [54]he must order the people to wash that piece of leather or cloth. Then he must separate the clothing for seven more days. [55]After the piece with the mildew has been washed, the priest must look at it again. If the mildew still looks the same, the piece is unclean, [d] even if the mildew has not spread. You must burn it in fire; it does not matter if the mildew is on one side or the other.

[56]"But when the priest looks at that piece of leather or cloth, the mildew might have faded after the piece has been washed. Then the priest must tear the mildew out of the piece of leather or cloth (either woven or knitted). [57]But if the mildew comes back to that piece of leather or cloth (either woven or knitted), the mildew is spreading. And whatever has the mildew must be burned with fire. [58]When the cloth (either woven or knitted) or the leather is washed and the mildew is gone, it must be washed again; then it will be clean.

[59]"These are the teachings about mildew on pieces of cloth (either woven or knitted) or leather, to decide if they are clean or unclean."

Rules for Cleansing from Skin Diseases

14 The LORD said to Moses, [2]"These are the teachings for the time at which people who had a harmful skin disease are made clean. [d]

"The person shall be brought to the priest, [3]and the priest must go outside the camp and look at the one who had the skin disease. If the skin disease is healed, [4]the priest will command that two living, clean birds, a piece of cedar wood, a piece of red string and a hyssop plant be brought for cleansing the person with the skin disease.

[5]"The priest must order one bird to be killed in a clay bowl containing fresh water. [6]Then he will take the living bird, the piece of cedar wood, the red string and the hyssop; all these he will dip into the blood of the bird that was killed over the fresh water. [7]The priest will sprinkle the blood seven times on the person being cleansed from the skin disease. He must announce that the person is clean and then go to an open field and let the living bird go free.

[8]"The person to be cleansed must wash his clothes, shave off all his hair, and bathe in water. Then he will be clean and may go into the camp, though he must stay outside his tent for the first seven days. [9]On the seventh day he must shave off all his hair—the hair from his head, his beard, his eyebrows and the rest of his hair. He must wash his clothes and bathe his body in water, and he will be clean.

¹⁰"On the eighth day the person who had the skin disease must take two male lambs that have nothing wrong with them and a year-old female lamb that has nothing wrong with it. He must also take 7 litres of fine flour mixed with oil for a grain offering and a third of a litre of olive oil. ¹¹The priest who is to announce that the person is clean must bring him and his sacrifices before the LORD at the entrance of the Meeting Tent.ᵈ ¹²The priest will take one of the male lambs and offer it with the olive oil as a penalty offering; he will present them before the LORD as an offering. ¹³Then he will kill the male lamb in the holy place, where the sin offering and the whole burnt offering are killed. The penalty offering is like the sin offering—it belongs to the priest and it is most holy.

¹⁴"The priest will take some of the blood of the penalty offering and put it on the bottom of the right ear of the person to be made clean. He will also put some of it on the thumb of the person's right hand and on the big toe of the person's right foot. ¹⁵Then the priest will take some of the oil and pour it into his own left hand. ¹⁶He will dip a finger of his right hand into the oil that is in his left hand, and with his finger he will sprinkle some of the oil seven times before the LORD. ¹⁷The priest will put some oil from his hand on the bottom of the right ear of the person to be made clean, some on the thumb of the person's right hand, and some on the big toe of the person's right foot. The oil will go on these places on top of the blood for the penalty offering. ¹⁸He will put the rest of the oil that is in his left hand on the head of the person to be made clean. In this way the priest will make that person clean so he can belong to the LORD again.

¹⁹"Next the priest will offer the sin offering to make that person clean so he can belong to the LORD again. After this the priest will kill the animal for the whole burnt offering, ²⁰and he will offer the burnt offering and grain offering on the altar. In this way he will make that person clean so he can belong to the LORD again.

²¹"But if the person is poor and unable to afford these offerings, he must take one male lamb for a penalty offering. It will be presented to the LORD to make him clean so he can belong to the LORD again. The person must also take 2.2 litres of fine flour mixed with oil for a grain offering. He must also take 0.3 litres of olive oil ²²and two doves or two young pigeons, which he can afford. One bird is for a sin offering and the other for a whole burnt offering. ²³On the eighth day the person will bring them for his cleansing to the priest at the entrance of the Meeting Tent, before the LORD. ²⁴The priest will take the lamb for the penalty offering and the oil, and he will present

them as an offering before the LORD. ²⁵Then he will kill the lamb of the penalty offering, take some of its blood, and put it on the bottom of the right ear of the person to be made clean. The priest will put some of this blood on the thumb of the person's right hand and some on the big toe of the person's right foot. ²⁶He will also pour some of the oil into his own left hand. ²⁷Then with a finger of his right hand, he will sprinkle some of the oil from his left hand seven times before the LORD. ²⁸The priest will take some of the oil from his hand and put it on the bottom of the right ear of the person to be made clean. He will also put some of it on the thumb of the person's right hand and some on the big toe of the person's right foot. The oil will go on these places on top of the blood from the penalty offering. ²⁹The priest must put the rest of the oil that is in his hand on the head of the person to be made clean, to make him clean so that he can belong to the LORD again. ³⁰Then the priest will offer one of the doves or young pigeons, which the person can afford. ³¹He must offer one of the birds for a sin offering and the other for a whole burnt offering, along with the grain offering. In this way the priest will make the person clean so that he can belong to the LORD again; he will become clean.

³²"These are the teachings for making a person clean after he has had a skin disease, if he cannot afford the regular sacrifices for becoming clean."

Rules for Cleaning Mildew

³³The LORD also said to Moses and Aaron, ³⁴"I am giving the land of Canaan to your people. When they enter that land, if I cause mildewᵈ to grow in someone's house in that land, ³⁵the owner of that house must come and tell the priest. He should say, 'I have seen something like mildew in my house.' ³⁶Then the priest must order the people to empty the house before he goes in to look at the mildew. This is so he will not have to say that everything in the house is unclean.ᵈ After this, the priest will go in to look at it. ³⁷He will look at the mildew, and if the mildew on the walls of the house is green or red and goes into the walls' surfaces, ³⁸he must go out and close up the house for seven days. ³⁹On the seventh day the priest must come back and check the house. If the mildew has spread on the walls of the house, ⁴⁰the priest must order the people to tear out the stones with the mildew on them. They should throw them away, at a certain unclean place outside the city. ⁴¹Then the priest must have all the inside of the house scraped. The people must throw away the plaster they scraped off the walls, at a certain unclean place outside the

city. ⁴²Then the owner must put new stones in the walls, and he must cover the walls with new clay plaster.

⁴³"Suppose a person has taken away the old stones and plaster and put in new stones and plaster. If mildew again appears in his house, ⁴⁴the priest must come back and check the house again. If the mildew has spread in the house, it is a mildew that destroys things; the house is unclean. ⁴⁵Then the owner must tear down the house, remove all its stones, plaster and wood, and take them to the unclean place outside the city. ⁴⁶Anyone who goes into that house while it is closed up will be unclean until

> ### Sidelight
> The bathroom's dirty, and it's your turn to clean it. But you cannot find the cleaning fluid. Leviticus 14:33–45 gives detailed instructions for cleaning mildew. You may find, however, that your parents are none too happy when you start tearing out all the mildewy bricks.

evening. ⁴⁷Anyone who eats in that house or lies down there must wash his clothes.

⁴⁸"Suppose after new stones and plaster have been put in a house, the priest checks it again and the mildew has not spread. Then the priest will announce that the house is clean, because the mildew is gone.

⁴⁹"Then, to make the house clean, the priest must take two birds, a piece of cedar wood, a piece of red string and a hyssop plant. ⁵⁰He will kill one bird in a clay bowl containing fresh water. ⁵¹Then he will take the bird that is still alive, the cedar wood, the hyssop and the red string, and he will dip them into the blood of the bird that was killed over the fresh water. The priest will sprinkle the blood on the house seven times. ⁵²He will use the bird's blood, the fresh water, the live bird, the cedar wood, the hyssop and the red string to make the house clean. ⁵³He will then go to an open field outside the city and let the living bird go free. This is how the priest makes the house clean and ready for service to the LORD."

⁵⁴These are the teachings about any kind of skin disease, ⁵⁵mildew on pieces of cloth or in a house, ⁵⁶swellings, rashes or bright spots on the skin; ⁵⁷they help people decide when things are unclean and when they are clean. These are the teachings about all these kinds of diseases.

Rules About a Person's Body

15 The LORD also said to Moses and Aaron, ²"Say to the people of Israel: 'When a fluid comes from a person's body, the fluid is unclean. *d* ³It doesn't matter if the fluid flows freely or if it is blocked from flowing; the fluid will make him unclean. This is the way the fluid makes him unclean:

⁴" 'If the person who discharges the body fluid lies on a bed, that bed becomes unclean, and everything he sits on becomes unclean. ⁵Anyone who touches his bed must wash his clothes and bathe in water, and the person will be unclean until evening. ⁶Whoever sits on something that the person who discharges the fluid sat on must wash his clothes and bathe in water; he will be unclean until evening. ⁷Anyone who touches the person who discharges the body fluid must wash his clothes and bathe in water; he will be unclean until evening.

⁸" 'If the person who discharges the body fluid spits on someone who is clean, that person must wash his clothes and bathe in water; he will be unclean until evening. ⁹Everything on which the person who is unclean sits when riding will become unclean. ¹⁰Anyone who touches something that was under him will be unclean until evening. And anyone who carries these things must wash his clothes and bathe in water; he will be unclean until evening.

¹¹" 'If the person who discharges a body fluid has not washed his hands in water and touches another person, that person must wash his clothes and bathe in water; he will be unclean until evening.

¹²" 'If a person who discharges a body fluid touches a clay bowl, that bowl must be broken. If he touches a wooden bowl, that bowl must be washed in water.

¹³" 'When a person who discharges a body fluid is made clean, he must count seven days for himself for his cleansing. He must wash his clothes and bathe his body in fresh water, and he will be clean. ¹⁴On the eighth day he must take two doves or two young pigeons before the LORD at the entrance of the Meeting Tent. *d* He will give the two birds to the priest. ¹⁵The priest will offer the birds, one for a sin offering and the other for a burnt offering. And the priest will make that person clean so he can belong to the LORD again.

¹⁶" 'If semen *n* goes out from a man, he must bathe in water; he will be unclean until evening. ¹⁷If the fluid gets on any clothing or leather, it must be washed with water; it will be unclean until evening.

semen   A man's body fluid by which he can make a woman pregnant.

18" 'If a man has sexual relations with a woman and semen comes out, both people must bathe in water; they will be unclean until evening.

Rules About a Woman's Body

19" 'When a woman has her monthly period, she is unclean *d* for seven days; anyone who touches her will be unclean until evening. 20Anything she lies on during this time will be unclean, and everything she sits on during this time will be unclean. 21Anyone who touches her bed must wash his clothes and bathe in water; that person will be unclean until evening. 22Anyone who touches something she has sat on must wash his clothes and bathe in water; that person will be unclean until evening. 23It does not matter if the person touched the woman's bed or something she sat on; he will be unclean until evening.

24" 'If a man has sexual relations with a woman and her monthly period touches him, he will be unclean for seven days; every bed he lies on will be unclean.

25" 'If a woman has a loss of blood for many days and it is not during her regular monthly period, or if she continues to have a loss of blood after her regular period, she will be unclean, as she is during her monthly period. She will be unclean for as long as she continues to bleed. 26Any bed she lies on during all the time of her bleeding will be like her bed during her regular monthly period. Everything she sits on will be unclean, as during her regular monthly period.

27" 'Whoever touches those things will be unclean and must wash his clothes and bathe in water; he will be unclean until evening. 28When the woman becomes clean from her bleeding, she must wait seven days, and after this she will be clean. 29Then on the eighth day she must take two doves or two young pigeons and bring them to the priest at the entrance of the Meeting Tent. *d* 30The priest must offer one bird for a sin offering and the other for a whole burnt offering. In this way the priest will make her clean so she can belong to the LORD again.

31" 'So you must warn the people of Israel to stay separated from things that make them unclean. If you don't warn the people, they might make my Holy Tent*d* unclean, and then they would have to die!' "

32These are the teachings for the person who discharges a body fluid and for the man who becomes unclean from semen *n* coming out of his body. 33These are the teachings for the woman who becomes unclean from her monthly period, for a man or woman who has a discharge, and for

a man who becomes unclean by having sexual relations with a woman who is unclean.

The Day of Cleansing

16 Now two of Aaron's sons had died while offering incense *d* to the LORD, and after that time the LORD spoke to Moses. 2The LORD said to him, "Tell your brother Aaron that there are times when he cannot go behind the curtain into the Most Holy Place where the Ark *d* is. If he goes in when I appear in a cloud over the lid on the Ark, he will die.

3"This is how Aaron may enter the Most Holy Place: before he enters, he must offer a bull for a sin offering and a ram for a whole burnt offering. 4He must put on the holy linen inner robe, with the linen underclothes next to his body. His belt will be the cloth belt, and he will wear the linen turban. These are holy clothes, so he must bathe his body in water before he puts them on.

5"Aaron must take from the people of Israel two male goats for a sin offering and one ram for a burnt offering. 6Then he will offer the bull for the sin offering for himself to remove sins from him and his family so that they will belong to the LORD.

7"Next Aaron will take the two goats and bring them before the LORD at the entrance to the Meeting Tent. *d* 8He will throw lots*d* for the two goats—one will be for the LORD and the other for the goat that removes sin. 9Then Aaron will take the goat that was chosen for the LORD by throwing the lot, and he will offer it as a sin offering. 10The other goat, which was chosen by lot to remove the sin, must be brought alive before the LORD. The priest will use it to perform the acts that remove Israel's sin so that they will belong to the LORD. Then this goat will be sent out into the desert as a goat that removes sin.

11"Then Aaron will offer the bull as a sin offering for himself, to remove the sins from him and his family so they will belong to the LORD; he will kill the bull for the sin offering for himself. 12Then he must take a pan full of burning coals from the altar before the LORD and two handfuls of sweet incense that has been ground into powder. He must bring it into the room behind the curtain. 13He must put the incense on the fire before the LORD so that the cloud of incense will cover the lid on the Ark. Then, when Aaron comes in, he will not die. 14Also, he must take some of the blood from the bull and sprinkle it with his finger on the front of the lid; with his finger he will sprinkle the blood seven times in front of the lid.

15"Then Aaron must kill the goat of the sin offering for the people and bring its blood into

semen   A man's body fluid by which he can make a woman pregnant.

the room behind the curtain. He must do with the goat's blood as he did with the bull's blood, sprinkling it on the lid and in front of the lid. ¹⁶Because the people of Israel have been unclean, *d* Aaron will perform the acts to make the Most Holy Place ready for service to the LORD. Then it will be clean from the sins and crimes of the Israelites. He must also do this for the Meeting Tent, because it stays in the middle of unclean people. ¹⁷When Aaron makes the Most Holy Place ready for service to the LORD, no one is allowed in the Meeting Tent until he comes out. So Aaron will perform the acts to remove sins from himself, his family and all the people of Israel, so that they will belong to the LORD. ¹⁸Afterwards he will go out to the altar that is before the LORD and will make it ready for service to the LORD. Aaron will take some of the bull's blood and some of the goat's blood and put it on the corners of the altar on all sides. ¹⁹Then, with his finger, he will sprinkle some of the blood on the altar seven times to make the altar holy for the LORD and clean from all the sins of the Israelites.

²⁰"When Aaron has finished making the Most Holy Place, the Meeting Tent and the altar ready for service to the LORD, he will offer the living goat. ²¹He will put both his hands on the head of the living goat, and he will confess over it all the sins and crimes of Israel. In this way Aaron will put the people's sins on the goat's head. Then he will send the goat away into the desert, and a man who has been appointed will lead the goat away. ²²So the goat will carry on itself all the people's sins to a lonely place in the desert. The man who leads the goat will let it loose there.

²³"Then Aaron will enter the Meeting Tent and take off the linen clothes he had put on before he went into the Most Holy Place; he must leave these clothes there. ²⁴He will bathe his body in water in a holy place and put on his regular clothes. Then he will come out and offer the whole burnt offering for himself and for the people, to remove sins from himself and the people so they will belong to the LORD. ²⁵Then he will burn the fat of the sin offering on the altar.

²⁶"The person who led the goat, the goat to remove sins, into the desert must wash his clothes and bathe his body in water. After that, he may come back into the camp.

²⁷"The bull and the goat for the sin offerings, whose blood was brought into the Most Holy Place to make it ready for service to the LORD, must be taken outside the camp; the animals' skins, bodies and intestines will be burned in the fire. ²⁸Then the one who burns them must wash his clothes and bathe his body in water. After that, he may come back into the camp.

²⁹"This law will always continue for you: on the tenth day of the seventh month, you must not eat and you must not do any work. The travellers or foreigners living with you must not work either. ³⁰It is on this day that the priests will make you clean so you will belong to the LORD again. All your sins will be removed. ³¹This is a very important day of rest for you, and you must not eat. This law will continue for ever.

³²"The priest appointed to take his father's place, on whom the oil was poured, will perform the acts for making things ready for service to the LORD. He must put on the holy linen clothes ³³and make the Most Holy Place, the Meeting Tent and the altar ready for service to the LORD. He must also remove the sins of the priests and all the people of Israel so that they will belong to the LORD. ³⁴That law for removing the sins of the Israelites so they will belong to the LORD will continue for ever. You will do these things once a year."

So they did the things the LORD had commanded Moses.

Offering Sacrifices

17 The LORD said to Moses, ²"Speak to Aaron, his sons and all the people of Israel. Tell them: 'This is what the LORD has commanded. ³If an Israelite kills an ox, a lamb or a goat either inside the camp or outside it, ⁴when he should have brought the animal to the entrance of the Meeting Tent *d* as a gift to the LORD in front of the LORD's Holy Tent, he is guilty of killing. He has killed, and he must be cut off from the people. ⁵This rule is so people will bring their sacrifices, which they have been sacrificing in the open fields, to the LORD. They must bring those animals to the LORD at the entrance of the Meeting Tent; they must bring them to the priest and offer them as fellowship offerings. ⁶Then the priest will sprinkle the blood from those animals on the LORD's altar near the entrance of the Meeting Tent. And he will burn the fat from those animals on the altar, as a smell pleasing to the LORD. ⁷They must not offer any more sacrifices to their goat idols, which they have chased like prostitutes. *d* These rules will continue for people from now on.'

⁸"Tell the people this: 'If any citizen of Israel or foreigner living with you offers a burnt offering or sacrifice, ⁹that person must take his sacrifice to the entrance of the Meeting Tent to offer it to the LORD. If he does not do this, he must be cut off from the people.

¹⁰" 'I will be against any citizen of Israel or foreigner living with you who eats blood. I will cut off that person from the people. ¹¹This is because the life of the body is in the blood, and I have given you rules for pouring that blood on the altar to remove your sins so that you will

belong to the LORD. It is the blood that removes the sins, because it is life. ¹²So I tell the people of Israel this: "None of you may eat blood, and no foreigner living among you may eat blood."

¹³" 'If any citizen of Israel or foreigner living among you catches a wild animal or bird that can be eaten, that person must pour the blood on the ground and cover it with earth. ¹⁴If blood is still in the meat, the animal's life is still in it. So I give this command to the people of Israel: "Don't eat meat that still has blood in it, because the animal's life is in its blood. Anyone who eats blood must be cut off."

¹⁵" 'If a person, either a citizen or a foreigner, eats an animal that died by itself or was killed by another animal, he must wash his clothes and bathe in water. He will be unclean until evening; then he will be clean. ¹⁶If he does not wash his clothes and bathe his body, he will be guilty of sin.' "

Rules About Sexual Relations

18 The LORD said to Moses, ²"Tell the people of Israel: 'I am the LORD your God. ³In the past you lived in Egypt, but you must not do what was done in that country. And you must not do as they do in the land of Canaan, where I am bringing you. Do not follow their customs. ⁴You must obey my rules and follow them. I am the LORD your God. ⁵Obey my laws and rules; a person who obeys them will live because of them. I am the LORD.

⁶" 'You must never have sexual relations with your close relatives. I am the LORD.

⁷" 'You must not shame your father by having sexual relations with your mother. She is your mother; do not have sexual relations with her. ⁸You must not have sexual relations with your father's wife; that would shame your father.

⁹" 'You must not have sexual relations with your sister, either the daughter of your father or

HOMOSEXUALITY

Be Holy As I Am Holy

Duncan was part of a group of guys who grew up together at school. As they grew older, he became aware that they were increasingly taking the mickey out of homosexual people. They would constantly use the word "gay" to describe something they didn't like or that was bad, and started abusing a few other guys they knew who were openly homosexual. While he didn't agree with homosexuality, Duncan didn't think it was right to pick on others or bully them.

He thought about what he had heard at church, but all they seemed to say was that homosexuality is wrong, without saying what that meant practically. In the end, he decided that Jesus wouldn't agree with picking on other people. He would have shown them love – the love that God shows everyone. So he stopped getting involved in the abuse and started trying to show glimpses of God's love to the homosexual guys.

Leviticus 18:1–24 warns the Israelites several times not to behave like the nations who occupied Canaan before them. The fundamental reason for this is simply stated: "I am the Lord your God". They are called to be holy because the Lord himself is holy.

The context of this is very similar to the modern world that we live in today. The ancient Near East was a world in which the practice of homosexuality was well known. Set against that background, the Old Testament laws are very striking. These laws ban every type of homosexual activity – not just rape as the Assyrians did, or sex with young people as the Egyptians did.

* Why should you obey the laws in Leviticus 18?
* How can you respond to God's challenge to be sexually pure?

Consider . . .

* how you would react if your best friend confessed to being homosexual.
* how you can reflect God's perfect love to homosexual people.

For more, see . . .

* Romans 1:18–27 (p.1185)
* 1 Thessalonians 4:1–8 (p.1298)
* 1 Corinthians 6 (p.1220)

your mother. It doesn't matter if she was born in your house or somewhere else.

¹⁰" 'You must not have sexual relations with your son's daughter or your daughter's daughter; that would bring shame on you.

¹¹" 'If your father and his wife have a daughter, she is your sister. You must not have sexual relations with her.

¹²" 'You must not have sexual relations with your father's sister; she is your father's close relative. ¹³You must not have sexual relations with your mother's sister; she is your mother's close relative. ¹⁴You must not have sexual relations with the wife of your father's brother, because this would shame him. She is your aunt.

¹⁵" 'You must not have sexual relations with your daughter-in-law; she is your son's wife. Do not have sexual relations with her.

¹⁶" 'You must not have sexual relations with your brother's wife. That would shame your brother.

¹⁷" 'You must not have sexual relations with both a woman and her daughter. And do not have sexual relations with this woman's grand-daughter, either the daughter of her son or her daughter; they are her close relatives. It is evil to do this.

¹⁸" 'While your wife is still living, you must not take her sister as another wife. Do not have sexual relations with her.

¹⁹" 'You must not go near a woman to have sexual relations with her during her monthly period, when she is unclean.ᵈ

²⁰" 'You must not have sexual relations with your neighbour's wife and make yourself unclean with her.

²¹" 'You must not give any of your children to be sacrificed to Molech,ᵈ because this would show that you do not respect your God. I am the LORD.

²²" 'You must not have sexual relations with a man as you would a woman. That is a hateful sin.

²³" 'You must not have sexual relations with an animal and make yourself unclean with it. Also a woman must not have sexual relations with an animal; it is not natural.

²⁴" 'Don't make yourself unclean by any of these wrong things. I am forcing nations out of their countries because they did these sins, and I am giving their land to you. ²⁵The land has become unclean, and I punished it for its sins, so the land is throwing out those people who live there.

²⁶" 'You must obey my laws and rules, and you must not do any of these hateful sins. These rules are for the citizens of Israel and for the people who live with you. ²⁷The people who lived in the land before you did all these hateful things and made the land unclean. ²⁸If you do these

things, you will also make the land unclean, and it will throw you out as it threw out the nations before you. ²⁹Anyone who does these hateful sins must be cut off from the people. ³⁰Keep my command not to do these hateful sins that were done by the people who lived in the land before you. Don't make yourself unclean by doing them. I am the LORD your God.' "

Other Laws

19 The LORD said to Moses, ²"Tell all the people of Israel: 'I am the LORD your God. You must be holy because I am holy.

³" 'You must respect your mother and father, and you must keep my Sabbaths. ᵈ I am the LORD your God.

⁴" 'Do not worship idols or make statues or gods for yourselves. I am the LORD your God.

⁵" 'When you sacrifice a fellowship offering to the LORD, offer it in such a way that it will be accepted. ⁶You may eat it on the same day you offer it or on the next day. But if any is left on the third day, you must burn it up. ⁷If any of it is eaten on the third day, it is unclean, ᵈ and it will not be accepted. ⁸Anyone who eats it then will be guilty of sin, because he did not respect the holy things that belong to the LORD. He must be cut off from the people.

⁹" 'When you harvest your crops on your land, do not harvest all the way to the corners of your fields. If grain falls onto the ground, don't gather it up. ¹⁰Don't pick all the grapes in your vine-yards, and don't pick up the grapes that fall to the ground. You must leave those things for poor people and for people travelling through your country. I am the LORD your God.

Sidelight They may not have had social security programmes to help the poor in Old Testament times, but the Israelites were careful to take care of the poor. Farmers were told to leave grain in their field so that poor people and travellers would have something to eat (Leviticus 19:9–10). The story of Ruth (Ruth 2:2–9, p.250) illustrates a time when someone used this law that provided for outsiders.

---

¹¹" 'You must not steal. You must not cheat people, and you must not lie to each other. ¹²You must not make a false promise by my name, or you will show that you don't respect your God. I am the LORD.

¹³" 'You must not cheat your neighbour or rob him. You must not keep a hired worker's salary all night until morning. ¹⁴You must not curse a

deaf person or put something in front of a blind person to make him fall. But you must respect your God. I am the LORD.

¹⁵ 'Be fair in your judging. You must not show special favour to poor people or great people, but be fair when you judge your neighbour. ¹⁶You must not spread false stories against other people, and you must not do anything that would put your neighbour's life in danger. I am the LORD.

¹⁷ 'You must not hate your fellow citizen in your heart. If your neighbour does something wrong, tell him about it, or you will be partly to blame. ¹⁸Forget about the wrong things people do to you, and do not try to get even. Love your neighbour as you love yourself. I am the LORD.

¹⁹ 'Obey my laws. You must not mate two different kinds of cattle or sow your field with two different kinds of seed. You must not wear clothing made from two different kinds of material mixed together.

²⁰ 'If a man has sexual relations with a slave girl of another man, but this slave girl has not been bought or given her freedom, there must be punishment. But they are not to be put to death, because the woman was not free. ²¹The man must bring a ram as his penalty offering to the LORD at the entrance to the Meeting Tent. *d* ²²The priest will offer the ram as a penalty offering before the LORD for the man's sin, to remove the sins of the man so that he will belong to the LORD. Then he will be forgiven for his sin.

²³ 'In the future, when you enter your country, you will plant many kinds of trees for food. After planting a tree, wait three years before using its fruit. ²⁴In the fourth year the fruit from the tree will be the LORD's, a holy offering of praise to him. ²⁵Then in the fifth year, you may eat the fruit from the tree. The tree will then produce more fruit for you. I am the LORD your God.

²⁶ 'You must not eat anything with the blood in it.

" 'You must not try to tell the future by signs or black magic.

²⁷ 'You must not cut the hair on the sides of your heads or cut the edges of your beard. ²⁸You must not cut your body to show sadness for

HONESTY

Help Yourself

"Don't take that!" Kerry was practically screaming at Michelle now.

"But my brother wants it for his room," came the reply as Michelle inched a little bit further up the pole. Michelle's target was the top of a crossing sign, one of the ones that beep and flash when it's safe to walk across the road.

"Just catch this," said Michelle as she pulled it from the top of the steel pole. "No one will miss it, and they'll put a new one up. And anyway, my dad pays his taxes; it's not like real stealing." Deep down, though, Michelle knew that Kerry thought it was wrong, and maybe she realised that too.

As Michelle dropped the sign, Kerry reached out her hands and caught it. It was broken now, no use – so they might as well take it. It wasn't as if they could fix it.

But after she left Michelle, Kerry began to think again. Why did they put those signs up? And then she remembered – it was so that people could cross the road safely, even those who are deaf or blind.

Like the council in Kerry's town, God put laws in place to make sure that people were protected. **Leviticus 19:1–18** shows us some of the rules that God wrote to protect people.

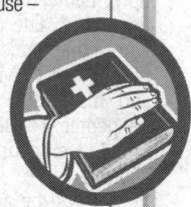

* Which parts of the passage can you see relate to what Kerry and Michelle were up to?
* Why do you think God put those rules in place? What happens when we break them?

Consider . . .

* going to a friend or family member and coming clean about something you've lied or misled others about.
* people less fortunate than you. How can you help them, as God says we should in verses 9 and 10?

For more, see . . .

* Proverbs 11:1–3 (p.599)   • Proverbs 24:26 (p.611)
* Acts 5:1–11 (p.1145)

someone who died or put tattoo marks on yourselves. I am the LORD.

²⁹" 'Do not dishonour your daughter by making her become a prostitute. *d* If you do this, the country will be filled with all kinds of sin.

³⁰" 'Obey the laws about Sabbaths, and respect my Most Holy Place. I am the LORD.

³¹" 'Do not go to mediums *d* or fortune-tellers for advice, or you will become unclean. I am the LORD your God.

³²" 'Show respect to old people; stand up in their presence. Show respect also to your God. I am the LORD.

³³" 'Do not mistreat foreigners living in your country, ³⁴but treat them just as you treat your own citizens. Love foreigners as you love yourselves, because you were once foreigners in Egypt. I am the LORD your God.

³⁵" 'Do not cheat when you measure the length or weight or amount of something. ³⁶Your weights and balances should weigh correctly, with your weighing baskets the right size and your jars holding the right amount of liquid. I am the LORD your God. I brought you out of the land of Egypt.

³⁷" 'Remember all my laws and rules, and obey them. I am the LORD.' "

Warnings About Various Sins

20 The LORD said to Moses, ²"You must also tell the people of Israel these things: 'If a person in your country gives one of his children to Molech, *d* that person must be killed. It doesn't matter if he is a citizen or a foreigner living in Israel; you must throw stones at him and kill him. ³I will be against him and cut him off from his people, because he gave his children to Molech. He showed that he did not respect my holy name, and he made my Holy Place unclean. *d* ⁴The people of the community might ignore that person and not kill the one who gave his children to Molech. ⁵But I will be against him and his family, and I will cut him off from his people. I will do this to anyone who follows him in being unfaithful to me by worshipping Molech.

⁶" 'I will be against anyone who goes to mediums *d* and fortune-tellers for advice, because that person is being unfaithful to me. So I will cut him off from his people.

⁷" 'Be my holy people. Be holy because I am the LORD your God. ⁸Remember and obey my laws. I am the LORD, and I have made you holy.

⁹" 'Anyone who curses his father or mother must be put to death. He has cursed his father or mother, so he has brought his own death on himself.

Punishments for Sexual Sins

¹⁰" 'If a man has sexual relations with his neighbour's wife, both the man and the woman are guilty of adultery *d* and must be put to death. ¹¹If a man has sexual relations with his father's wife, he has shamed his father, and both the man and his father's wife must be put to death. They have brought it on themselves.

¹²" 'If a man has sexual relations with his daughter-in-law, both of them must be put to death. What they have done is not natural. They have brought their own deaths on themselves.

¹³" 'If a man has sexual relations with another man as a man does with a woman, these two men have done a hateful sin. They must be put to death. They have brought it on themselves.

¹⁴" 'If a man has sexual relations with both a woman and her mother, this is evil. The people must burn that man and the two women in fire so that your people will not be evil.

¹⁵" 'If a man has sexual relations with an animal, he must be put to death. You must also kill the animal. ¹⁶If a woman approaches an animal and has sexual relations with it, you must kill the woman and the animal. They must be put to death. They have brought it on themselves.

¹⁷" 'It is shameful for a brother to marry his sister, the daughter of either his father or his mother, and to have sexual relations with her. In front of everyone they must both be cut off from their people. The man has shamed his sister, and he is guilty of sin.

¹⁸" 'If a man has sexual relations with a woman during her monthly period, both the woman and the man must be cut off from their people. They have sinned because they have showed the source of her blood.

¹⁹" 'Do not have sexual relations with your mother's sister or your father's sister, because that would shame a close relative. Both of you are guilty of this sin.

²⁰" 'If a man has sexual relations with his uncle's wife, he has shamed his uncle. That man and his uncle's wife will die without children; they are guilty of sin.

²¹" 'It is unclean for a man to marry his brother's wife. That man has shamed his brother, and they will have no children.

²²" 'Remember all my laws and rules, and obey them. I am leading you to your own land, and if you obey my laws and rules, that land will not throw you out. ²³I am forcing out ahead of you the people who live there. Because they did all these sins, I have hated them. Do not live the way those people lived.

²⁴" 'I have told you that you will get their land, which I will give to you as your very own; it is a fertile land. I am the LORD your God, and I have

set you apart from other people and made you my own. ²⁵So you must treat clean animals and birds differently from unclean animals and birds. Do not make yourselves unclean by any of these unclean birds or animals or things that crawl on the ground, which I have made unclean for you. ²⁶So you must be holy to me because I, the LORD, am holy, and I have set you apart from other people to be my own.

²⁷" 'A man or woman who is a medium *d* or a fortune-teller must be put to death. You must stone them to death; they have brought it on themselves.' "

How Priests Must Behave

21 The LORD said to Moses, "Tell these things to Aaron's sons, the priests: 'A priest must not make himself unclean *d* by touching a dead person. ²But if the dead person was one of his close relatives, he may touch him. The priest may make himself unclean if the dead person is his mother or father, son or daughter, brother or ³unmarried sister who is close to him because she has no husband. The priest may make himself unclean for her if she dies. ⁴But a priest must not make himself unclean if the dead person was only related to him by marriage.

⁵" 'Priests must not shave their heads, or shave off the edges of their beards, or cut their bodies. ⁶They must be holy to their God and show respect for God's name, because they present the offerings made by fire to the LORD, which is the food of their God. So they must be holy.

⁷" 'A priest must not marry an unclean prostitute *d* or a divorced woman, because he is holy to his God. ⁸Treat him as holy, because he offers up the food of your God. Think of him as holy; I am the LORD who makes you holy, and I am holy.

⁹" 'If a priest's daughter makes herself unclean by becoming a prostitute, she shames her father. She must be burned with fire.

¹⁰" 'The high priest, who was chosen from among his brothers, had the special olive oil poured on his head. He was also appointed to wear the priestly clothes. So he must not show his sadness by letting his hair go uncombed or tearing his clothes. ¹¹He must not go into a house where there is a dead body. He must not make himself unclean, even if it is for his own father or mother. ¹²The high priest must not go out of the Holy Place, because if he does and becomes unclean, he will make God's Holy Place unclean. The special oil used in appointing priests was poured on his head to separate him from the rest of the people. I am the LORD.

¹³" 'The high priest must marry a woman who is a virgin. *d* ¹⁴He must not marry a widow, a divorced woman or a prostitute. He must marry a virgin from his own people ¹⁵so the people will respect his children as his own. I am the LORD. I have set the high priest apart for his special job.' "

¹⁶The LORD said to Moses, ¹⁷"Tell Aaron: 'If any of your descendants *d* have something wrong with them, they must never come near to offer the special food of their God. ¹⁸Anyone who has something wrong with him must not come near: blind men, crippled men, men with damaged faces, deformed men, ¹⁹men with a crippled foot or hand, ²⁰hunchbacks, dwarfs, men who have something wrong with their eyes, men who have an itching disease or a skin disease or men who have damaged sex glands.

²¹" 'If one of Aaron's descendants *d* has something wrong with him, he cannot come near to make the offerings made by fire to the LORD. He has something wrong with him; he cannot offer the food of his God. ²²He may eat the most holy food and also the holy food. ²³But he may not go through the curtain into the Most Holy Place, and he may not go near the altar, because he has something wrong with him. He must not make my Holy Place unfit. I am the LORD who makes these places holy.' "

²⁴So Moses told these things to Aaron, Aaron's sons and all the people of Israel.

22 The LORD said to Moses, ²"Tell Aaron and his sons: 'The people of Israel will give offerings to me. These offerings are holy, and they are mine, so you must respect them to show that you respect my holy name. I am the LORD. ³Say to them: if any one of your descendants *d* from now on is unclean *d* and comes near the offerings that the Israelites made holy for me, that person must be cut off from appearing before me. I am the LORD.

⁴" 'If one of Aaron's descendants has a harmful skin disease, or if he discharges a body fluid, he cannot eat the holy offerings until he becomes clean. He could also become unclean from touching a dead body, from his own semen, *n* ⁵from touching any unclean crawling animal or from touching an unclean person (no matter what made the person unclean). ⁶Anyone who touches those things will become unclean until evening. That person must not eat the holy offerings unless he washes with water. ⁷He will be clean only after the sun goes down. Then he may eat the holy offerings; the offerings are his food.

⁸" 'If a priest finds an animal that died by itself or that was killed by some other animal, he must

---

semen   A man's body fluid by which he can make a woman pregnant.

not eat it. If he does, he will become unclean. I am the LORD.

9" 'If the priests keep all the rules I have given, they will not become guilty; if they are careful, they will not die. I am the LORD who has made them holy. ¹⁰Only people in a priest's family may eat the holy offering. A visitor staying with the priest or a hired worker must not eat it. ¹¹But if the priest buys a slave with his own money, that slave may eat the holy offerings; slaves who were born in his house may also eat his food. ¹²If a priest's daughter marries a person who is not a priest, she must not eat any of the holy offerings. ¹³But if the priest's daughter becomes widowed or divorced, with no children to support her, and if she goes back to her father's house where she lived as a child, she may eat some of her father's food. But only people from a priest's family may eat this food.

¹⁴" 'If someone eats some of the holy offering by mistake, that person must pay back the priest for that holy food, adding another one-fifth of the price of that food.

¹⁵" 'When the Israelites give their holy offerings to the LORD, the priest must not treat these holy things as though they were not holy. ¹⁶The priests must not allow those who are not priests to eat the holy offerings. If they do, they cause the ones who eat the holy offerings to become guilty, and they will have to pay for it. I am the LORD, who makes them holy.' "

¹⁷The LORD said to Moses, ¹⁸"Tell Aaron and his sons and all the people of Israel: 'A citizen of Israel or a foreigner living in Israel might want to bring a whole burnt offering, either for some special promise he has made or for a special gift he wants to give to the LORD. ¹⁹If he does, he must bring a male animal that has nothing wrong with it—a bull, a sheep or a goat—so it might be accepted for him. ²⁰He must not bring an animal that has something wrong with it, or it will not be accepted for him.

²¹" 'If someone brings a fellowship offering to the LORD, either as payment for a special promise the person has made or as a special gift the person wants to give the LORD, it might be from the herd or from the flock. But it must be healthy, with nothing wrong with it, so that it will be accepted. ²²You must not offer to the LORD any animal that is blind, that has broken bones or is crippled, that has running sores or any sort of skin disease. You must not offer any animals like these on the altar as an offering by fire to the LORD.

²³" 'If an ox or lamb is smaller than normal or is not perfectly formed, you may give it as a special gift to the LORD; it will be accepted. But it will not be accepted as payment for a special promise you have made.

²⁴" 'If an animal has bruised, crushed, torn or cut sex glands, you must not offer it to the LORD. You must not do this in your own land, ²⁵and you must not take such animals from foreigners as sacrifices to the LORD. Because the animals have been hurt in some way and have something wrong with them, they will not be accepted for you.' "

²⁶The LORD said to Moses, ²⁷"When an ox, a sheep or a goat is born, it must stay seven days with its mother. But from the eighth day on, this animal will be accepted as a sacrifice by fire to the LORD. ²⁸But you must not kill the animal and its mother on the same day, either an ox or a sheep.

²⁹"If you want to offer some special offering of thanks to the LORD, you must do it in a way that pleases him. ³⁰You must eat the whole animal that same day and not leave any of the meat for the next morning. I am the LORD.

³¹"Remember my commands and obey them; I am the LORD. ³²Show respect for my holy name. You Israelites must remember that I am holy; I am the LORD, who has made you holy. ³³I brought you out of Egypt to be your God. I am the LORD."

Special Holidays

23 The LORD said to Moses, ²"Tell the people of Israel: 'You will announce the LORD's appointed feasts as holy meetings. These are my special feasts.

The Sabbath

³" 'There are six days for you to work, but the seventh day will be a special day of rest. It is a day for a holy meeting; you must not do any work. It is a Sabbath *d* to the LORD in all your homes.

The Passover and Unleavened Bread

⁴" 'These are the LORD's appointed feasts, the holy meetings, which you will announce at the times set for them. ⁵The LORD's Passover *d* is on the fourteenth day of the first month, beginning at twilight. ⁶The Feast *d* of Unleavened Bread begins on the fifteenth day of the same month. You will eat bread made without yeast for seven days. ⁷On the first day of this feast you will have a holy meeting, and you must not do any work. ⁸For seven days you will bring an offering made by fire to the LORD. There will be a holy meeting on the seventh day, and on that day you must not do any regular work.' "

The First of the Harvest

⁹The LORD said to Moses, ¹⁰"Tell the people of Israel: 'You will enter the land I will give you and gather its harvest. At that time you must bring the first bundle of grain from your harvest to the

priest. ¹¹The priest will present the bundle before the LORD, and it will be accepted for you; he will present the bundle on the day after the Sabbath. *d*

¹²" 'On the day when you present the bundle of grain, offer a male lamb, one year old, that has nothing wrong with it, as a burnt offering to the LORD. ¹³You must also offer a grain offering—4 litres of fine flour mixed with olive oil as an offering made by fire to the LORD; its smell will be pleasing to him. You must also offer a litre of wine as a drink offering. ¹⁴Until the day you bring your offering to your God, do not eat any new grain, roasted grain or bread made from new grain. This law will always continue for people from now on, wherever you live.

The Feast of Weeks

¹⁵" 'Count seven full weeks from the morning after the Sabbath. *d* (This is the Sabbath on which you bring the bundle of grain to present as an offering.) ¹⁶On the fiftieth day, the first day after the seventh week, you will bring a new grain offering to the LORD. ¹⁷On that day bring two loaves of bread from your homes to be presented as an offering. Use yeast and 4 litres of flour to make those loaves of bread; they will be your gift to the LORD from the first wheat of your harvest.

¹⁸" 'Offer with the bread one young bull, two rams and seven male lambs that are one year old and have nothing wrong with them. Offer them with their grain offerings and drink offerings, as a burnt offering to the LORD. They will be an offering made by fire, and the smell will be pleasing to the LORD. ¹⁹You must also offer one male goat for a sin offering and two male, one-year-old lambs as a fellowship offering.

²⁰" 'The priest will present the two lambs as an offering before the LORD, along with the bread from the first wheat of the harvest. They are holy to the LORD, and they will belong to the priest. ²¹On that same day you will call a holy meeting; you must not do any work on that day. This law will continue for you from now on, wherever you live.

²²" 'When you harvest your crops on your land, do not harvest all the way to the corners of your field. If grain falls onto the ground, don't gather it up. Leave it for poor people and foreigners in your country. I am the LORD your God.' "

The Feast of Trumpets

²³Again the LORD said to Moses, ²⁴"Tell the people of Israel: 'On the first day of the seventh month you must have a special day of rest, a holy meeting, when you blow the trumpet for a special time of remembering. ²⁵Do not do any work, and bring an offering made by fire to the LORD.' "

The Day of Cleansing

²⁶The LORD said to Moses, ²⁷"The Day of Cleansing will be on the tenth day of the seventh month. There will be a holy meeting, and you will give up eating and bring an offering made by fire to the LORD. ²⁸Do not do any work on that day, because it is the Day of Cleansing. On that day the priests will go before the LORD and perform the acts to make you clean *d* so that you will belong to the LORD.

²⁹"Anyone who refuses to give up food on this day must be cut off from the people. ³⁰If anyone works on this day, I will destroy that person from among the people. ³¹You must not do any work at all; this law will continue for people from now on wherever you live. ³²It will be a special day of rest for you, and you must not eat. You will start this special day of rest on the evening after the ninth day of the month, and it will continue from that evening until the next evening."

The Feast of Shelters

³³Again the LORD said to Moses, ³⁴"Tell the people of Israel: 'On the fifteenth day of the seventh month is the Feast *d* of Shelters. This feast to the LORD will continue for seven days. ³⁵There will be a holy meeting on the first day; do not do any work. ³⁶You will bring an offering made by fire to the LORD each day for seven days. On the eighth day you will have another holy meeting, and you will bring an offering made by fire to the LORD. This will be a holy meeting; do not do any work.

³⁷(" 'These are the LORD's special feasts, when there will be holy meetings and when you bring offerings made by fire to the LORD. You will bring whole burnt offerings, grain offerings, sacrifices and drink offerings—each at the right time. ³⁸These offerings are in addition to those for the LORD's Sabbath *d* days, in addition to offerings you give as payment for special promises, and in addition to special offerings you want to give to the LORD.)

³⁹" 'So on the fifteenth day of the seventh month, after you have gathered in the crops of the land, celebrate the LORD's festival for seven days. You must rest on the first day and the eighth day. ⁴⁰On the first day you will take good fruit from the fruit trees, as well as branches from palm trees, poplars and other leafy trees. You will celebrate before the LORD your God for seven days. ⁴¹Celebrate this festival to the LORD for seven days each year. This law will continue from now on; you will celebrate it in the seventh month. ⁴²Live in shelters for seven days. All the people born in Israel must live in shelters ⁴³so that all your descendants *d* will know I made Israel live in shelters during the time I brought them out of Egypt. I am the LORD your God.' "

[44]So Moses told the people of Israel about all of the LORD's appointed feast days.

The Lampstand and the Holy Bread

24 The LORD said to Moses, [2]"Command the people of Israel to bring you pure oil from crushed olives. That oil is for the lamps so that these lamps may never go out. [3]Aaron will keep the lamps burning in the Meeting Tent[d] from evening until morning before the LORD; this is in front of the curtain of the Ark[d] of the Agreement. This law will continue from now on. [4]Aaron must always keep the lamps burning on the lampstands of pure gold before the LORD.

[5]"Take fine flour and bake twelve loaves of bread with it, using 4 litres of flour for each loaf. [6]Put them in two rows on the golden table before the LORD, six loaves in each row. [7]Put pure incense[d] on each row as the memorial portion to take the place of the bread. It is an offering made by fire to the LORD. [8]Every Sabbath[d] day Aaron will put the bread in order before the LORD, as an agreement with the people of Israel that will continue for ever. [9]That bread will belong to Aaron and his sons. They will eat it in a holy place, because it is a most holy part of the offerings made by fire to the LORD. That bread is their share for ever."

The Man Who Cursed God

[10]Now there was a son of an Israelite woman and an Egyptian father who was walking among the Israelites. A fight broke out in the camp between him and an Israelite. [11]The son of the Israelite woman began cursing and speaking against the LORD, so the people took him to Moses. (The mother's name was Shelomith, the daughter of Debri from the family of Dan.) [12]The people held him as a prisoner while they waited for the LORD's command to be made clear to them.

[13]Then the LORD said to Moses, [14]"Take the one who spoke against me outside the camp. Then all the people who heard him must put their hands on his head, and all the people must throw stones at him and kill him. [15]Tell the people of Israel this: 'If anyone curses his God, he is guilty of sin. [16]Anyone who speaks against the LORD must be put to death; all the people must kill him by throwing stones at him. Foreigners must be punished just like the people born in Israel; if they speak against the LORD, they must be put to death.

[17]" 'Whoever kills another person must be put to death. [18]Whoever kills an animal that belongs to another person must give that person another animal to take its place. [19]And whoever causes an injury to a neighbour must receive the same kind of injury in return: [20]broken bone for broken bone, eye for eye, tooth for tooth. Anyone who injures another person must be injured in the same way in return. [21]Whoever kills another person's animal must give that person another animal to take its place. But whoever kills another person must be put to death.

[22]" 'The law will be the same for the foreigner as for those from your own country. I am the LORD your God.' "

[23]Then Moses spoke to the people of Israel, and they took the person who had cursed outside the camp and killed him by throwing stones at him. So the people of Israel did as the LORD had commanded Moses.

The Time of Rest for the Land

25 The LORD said to Moses at Mount Sinai, [2]"Tell the people of Israel this: 'When you enter the land I will give you, let it have a special time of rest, to honour the LORD. [3]You may plant seed in your field for six years, and you may trim your vineyards for six years and bring in their fruits. [4]But during the seventh year, you must let the land rest. This will be a special time to honour the LORD. You must not plant seed in your field or trim your vineyards. [5]You must not cut the crops that grow by themselves after harvest, or gather the grapes from your vines that are not trimmed. The land will have a year of rest.

[6]" 'You may eat whatever the land produces during that year of rest. It will be food for your men and women servants, for your hired workers and for the foreigners living in your country. [7]It will also be food for your cattle and the wild animals of your land. Whatever the land produces may be eaten.

The Year of Jubilee

[8]" 'Count off seven groups of seven years, or 49 years. During that time there will be seven years of rest for the land. [9]On the Day of Cleansing,[d] you must blow the horn of a ram; this will be on the tenth day of the seventh month. You must blow the horn through the whole country. [10]Make the fiftieth year a special year, and announce freedom for all the people living in your country. This time will be called Jubilee.[n] You will each go back to your own property, each to your own family and family group. [11]The fiftieth year will be a special time for you to celebrate. Don't plant seeds, or harvest the crops that grow

---

Jubilee   This word comes from the Hebrew word for a horn of a ram.

by themselves, or gather grapes from the vines that are not trimmed. [12]That year is Jubilee; it will be a holy time for you. You may eat only the crops that come from the field. [13]In the year of Jubilee you each must go back to your own property.

[14]" 'If you sell your land to your neighbour, or if you buy land from your neighbour, don't cheat each other. [15]If you want to buy your neighbour's land, count the number of years since the last Jubilee, and use that number to decide the right price. If your neighbour sells the land to you, count the number of years left for harvesting crops, and use that number to decide the right price. [16]If there are many years, the price will be high. But if there are only a few years, lower the price, because your neighbour is really selling only a few crops to you. [17]You must not cheat each other, but you must respect your God. I am the LORD your God.

[18]" 'Remember my laws and rules, and obey them so that you will live safely in the land. [19]The land will give good crops to you, and you will eat as much as you want and live safely in the land.

> ## Sidelight
>
> The start of the year of Jubilee fell once every 50 years. Debts and grievances were forgiven and prisoners released in that year. Christ's birth signified a new age of Jubilee in which, when we call on his name, our debts and sins are cancelled and we can declare a new birth of caring, forgiveness and freedom – a lifetime of Jubilee.

[20]" 'But you might ask, "If we don't plant seeds or gather crops, what will we eat during the seventh year?" [21]I will send you such a great blessing during the sixth year that the land will produce enough crops for three years. [22]When you plant in the eighth year, you will still be eating from the old crop; you will eat the old crop until the harvest of the ninth year.

Property Laws

[23]" 'The land really belongs to me, so you can't sell it for all time. You are only foreigners and travellers living for a while on my land. [24]People might sell their land, but it must always be possible for the family to get its land back. [25]If a person in your country becomes very poor and sells some land, then close relatives must come and buy it back. [26]If there is not a close relative to buy the land back, but if the person makes enough money to be able to buy it back, [27]the years must be counted since the land was sold. That number must be used to decide how much the first owner

should pay back the one who bought it. Then the land will belong to the first owner again. [28]But if there is not enough money to buy it back, the one who bought it will keep it until the year of Jubilee. *d* During that celebration, the land will go back to the first owner's family.

[29]" 'If someone sells a home in a walled city, for a full year after it is sold the person has the right to buy it back. [30]But if the owner does not buy back the house before a full year has passed, it will belong to the one who bought it and to his future sons. The house will not go back to the first owner at Jubilee. [31]But houses in small towns without walls are like open country; they can be bought back, and they must be returned to their first owner at Jubilee.

[32]" 'The Levites may always buy back their houses in the cities that belong to them. [33]If someone buys a house from a Levite, that house in the Levites' city will again belong to the Levites in the Jubilee. This is because houses in Levite cities belong to the people of Levi; the Israelites gave these cities to them. [34]Also the fields and pastures around the Levites' cities cannot be sold, because those fields belong to the Levites for ever.

Rules for Slave Owners

[35]" 'If anyone from your country becomes too poor to support himself, help him to live among you as you would a stranger or foreigner. [36]Do not charge him any interest on money you loan to him, but respect your God; let the poor live among you. [37]Don't lend him money for interest, and don't try to make a profit from the food he buys. [38]I am the LORD your God, who brought you out of the land of Egypt to give the land of Canaan to you and to become your God.

[39]" 'If anyone from your country becomes very poor and sells himself as a slave to you, you must not make him work like a slave. [40]He will be like a hired worker and a visitor with you until the year of Jubilee. *d* [41]Then he may leave you, take his children, and go back to his family and the land of his ancestors. [42]This is because the Israelites are my servants, and I brought them out of slavery in Egypt. They must not become slaves again. [43]You must not rule this person cruelly, but you must respect your God.

[44]" 'Your men and women slaves must come from other nations around you; from them you may buy slaves. [45]Also you may buy as slaves children from the families of foreigners living in your land. These child slaves will belong to you, [46]and you may even pass them on to your children after you die; you can make them slaves for ever. But you must not rule cruelly over your own people, the Israelites.

47" 'Suppose a foreigner or visitor among you becomes rich. If someone in your country becomes so poor that he has to sell himself as a slave to the foreigner living among you or to a member of the foreigner's family, 48the poor person has the right to be bought back and become free. One of his relatives may buy him back: 49His uncle, his uncle's son, or any one of his close relatives may buy him back. Or, if he gets enough money, he may pay the money to free himself.

50" 'He and the one who bought him must count the time from when he sold himself up to the next year of Jubilee. Use that number to decide the price, because the person really only hired himself out for a certain number of years. 51If there are still many years before the year of Jubilee, the person must pay back a large part of the price. 52If there are only a few years left until Jubilee, the person must pay a small part of the first price. 53But he will live like a hired person with the foreigner every year; don't let the foreigner rule cruelly over him.

54" 'Even if no one buys him back, at the year of Jubilee, he and his children will become free. 55This is because the people of Israel are servants to me. They are my servants, whom I brought out of Egypt. I am the LORD your God.

Rewards for Obeying God

26 " 'Don't make idols for yourselves or set up statues or memorials. Don't put stone statues in your land to bow down to, because I am the LORD your God.

2" 'Remember my Sabbaths, *d* and respect my Holy Place. I am the LORD.

3" 'If you remember my laws and commands and obey them, 4I will give you rains at the right season; the land will produce crops, and the trees of the field will produce their fruit. 5Your threshing *d* will continue until the grape harvest, and your grape harvest will continue until it is time to plant. Then you will have plenty to eat and live safely in your land. 6I will give peace to your country; you will lie down in peace, and no one will make you afraid. I will keep harmful animals out of your country, and armies will not pass through it.

7" 'You will chase your enemies and defeat them, killing them with your sword. 8Five of you will chase 100 men; 100 of you will chase 10,000 men. You will defeat your enemies and kill them with your sword.

9" 'Then I will show kindness to you and let you have many children; I will keep my agreement with you. 10You will have enough crops to last for more than a year. When you harvest the new crops, you will have to throw out the old ones to make room for them. 11Also I will place my Holy Tent *d* among you, and I will not turn away from you. 12I will walk with you and be your God, and you will be my people. 13I am the LORD your God, who brought you out of Egypt, where you were slaves. I broke the heavy weights that were on your shoulders and let you walk proudly again.

Punishment for Not Obeying God

14" 'But if you do not obey me and keep all my commands, 15and if you turn away from my rules and hate my laws, refusing to obey all my commands, you have broken our agreement. 16As a result, I will do this to you: I will cause terrible things to happen to you. I will cause you to have disease and fever that will destroy your eyes and slowly kill you. You will not have success when you plant your seed, and your enemy will eat your crops. 17I will be against you, and your enemies will defeat you. These people who hate you will rule over you, and you will run away even when no one is chasing you.

18" 'If after all this you still do not obey me, I will punish you seven times more for your sins. 19I will break your great pride, and I will make the sky like iron and the earth like bronze. *n* 20You will work hard, but it will not help. Your land will not grow any crops, and your trees will not give their fruit.

21" 'If you still turn against me and refuse to obey me, I will beat you seven times harder. The more you sin, the more you will be punished. 22I will send wild animals to attack you, and they will take your children away from you and destroy your cattle. They will make you so few in number the roads will be empty.

23" 'If you don't learn your lesson after all these things, and if you still turn against me, 24I will also turn against you. I will punish you seven more times for your sins. 25You broke my agreement, and I will punish you. I will bring armies against you, and if you go into your cities for safety, I will cause diseases to spread among you so that your enemy will defeat you. 26There will be very little bread to eat; ten women will be able to cook all your bread in one oven. They will measure each piece of bread, and you will eat, but you will still be hungry.

27" 'If you still refuse to listen to me and still turn against me, 28I will show my great anger; I will punish you seven more times for your sins. 29You will eat the bodies of your sons and daughters. 30I will destroy your places where gods are worshipped and cut down your incense *d* altars.

---

sky . . . bronze   This means the sky will give no rain and the earth will produce no crops.

I will pile your dead bodies on the lifeless forms of your idols. I will hate you. ³¹I will destroy your cities and make your holy places empty, and I will not smell the pleasing smell of your offerings. ³²I will make the land empty so that your enemies who come to live in it will be shocked at it. ³³I will scatter you among the nations, and I will pull out my sword and destroy you. Your land will become empty, your cities a waste. ³⁴When you are taken to your enemy's country, your land will finally get its rest. It will enjoy its time of rest all the time it lies empty. ³⁵During the time the land is empty, it will have the rest you should have given it while you lived in it.

³⁶ 'Those of you who are left alive will lose their courage in the land of their enemies. They will be frightened by the sound of a leaf being blown by the wind. They will run as if someone were chasing them with a sword, and they will fall even when no one is chasing them. ³⁷They will fall over each other, as if someone were chasing them with a sword, even though no one is chasing them. You will not be strong enough to stand up against your enemies. ³⁸You will die among other nations and disappear in your enemies' countries. ³⁹So those who are left alive will rot away in their enemies' countries because of their sins. They will also rot away because of their ancestors' sins.

There is Always Hope

⁴⁰ 'But perhaps the people will confess their sins and the sins of their ancestors; maybe they will admit they turned against me and sinned against me, ⁴¹which made me turn against them and send them into the land of their enemies. If these disobedient people are sorry for what they did and accept punishment for their sin, ⁴²I will remember my agreement with Jacob, my agreement with Isaac and my agreement with Abraham, and I will remember the land. ⁴³The land will be left empty by its people, and it will enjoy its time of rest as it lies bare without them. Then those who are left alive will accept the punishment for their sins. They will learn that they were punished because they hated my laws and refused to obey my rules. ⁴⁴But even though this is true, I will not turn away from them when they are in the land of their enemies. I will not hate them so much that I completely destroy them and break my agreement with them, because I am the LORD their God. ⁴⁵For their good I will remember the agreement with their ancestors, whom I brought out of the land of Egypt so I could become their God; the other nations saw these things. I am the LORD.' "

⁴⁶These are the laws, rules and teachings the LORD made between himself and the Israelites through Moses at Mount Sinai.

Promises are Important

27 The LORD said to Moses, ²"Speak to the people of Israel and tell them: 'If someone makes a special promise to give a person as a servant to the LORD by paying a price that is the same value as that person, ³the price for a man 20 to 60 years old is about 50 pieces of silver. (You must use the measure as set by the Holy Place.) ⁴The price for a woman 20 to 60 years old is about 30 pieces of silver. ⁵The price for a man five to 20 years old is about 20 pieces of silver; for a woman it is about 10 pieces of silver. ⁶The price for a baby boy one month to five years old is about 5 pieces of silver; for a baby girl the price is about 3 pieces of silver. ⁷The price for a man 60 years old or older is about 15 pieces of silver; for a woman it is about 10 pieces of silver.

⁸ 'If anyone is too poor to pay the price, bring him to the priest, and the priest will set the price. The priest will decide how much money the person making the vow can afford to pay.

Gifts to the LORD

⁹ 'Some animals may be used as sacrifices to the LORD. If someone promises to bring one of these to the LORD, it will become holy. ¹⁰That person must not try to put another animal in its place or exchange it, a good animal for a bad one, or a bad animal for a good one. If this happens, both animals will become holy.

¹¹ 'Unclean ^d animals cannot be offered as sacrifices to the LORD, and if someone brings one of them to the LORD, that animal must be brought to the priest. ¹²The priest will decide a price for the animal, according to whether it is good or bad; as the priest decides, that is the price for the animal. ¹³If the person wants to buy back the animal, an additional one-fifth must be added to the price.

Value of a House

¹⁴ 'If a person gives a house as holy to the LORD, the priest must decide its value, according to whether the house is good or bad; as the priest decides, that is the price for the house. ¹⁵But if the person who gives the house wants to buy it back, an additional one-fifth must be added to the price. Then the house will belong to that person again.

Value of Land

¹⁶ 'If a person gives some family property to the LORD, the value of the fields will depend on how much seed is needed to plant them. It will cost about 50 pieces of silver for each 100 kilogrammes of barley seed needed. ¹⁷If the person gives a field at the year of Jubilee, ^d its value will stay at what the priest has decided. ¹⁸But if the

person gives the field after the Jubilee, the priest must decide the exact price by counting the number of years to the next year of Jubilee. Then he will subtract that number from its value. [19]If the person who gave the field wants to buy it back, one-fifth must be added to that price, and the field will belong to the first owner again.

[20]" 'If the person does not buy back the field, or if it is sold to someone else, the first person cannot ever buy it back. [21]When the land is released at the year of Jubilee, it will become holy to the LORD, like land specially given to him. It will become the property of the priests.

[22]" 'If someone gives to the LORD a field he has bought, which is not a part of his family land, [23]the priest must count the years to the next Jubilee. He must decide the price for the land, and the price must be paid on that day. Then that land will be holy to the LORD. [24]At the year of Jubilee, the land will go back to its first owner, to the family who sold the land.

[25]" 'You must use the measure as set by the Holy Place in paying these prices; it weighs 11.5 grammes.

Value of Animals

[26]" 'If an animal is the first one born to its parent, it already belongs to the LORD, so people may not give it again. If it is a cow or a sheep, it is the LORD's. [27]If the animal is unclean, [d] the person must buy it back for the price set by the priest, and the person must add one-fifth to that price. If it is not bought back, the priest must sell it for the price he had decided.

[28]" 'There is a special kind of gift that people set apart to give to the LORD; it may be a person, animal or field from the family property. That gift cannot be bought back or sold. Every special kind of gift is most holy to the LORD.

[29]" 'If anyone is given for the purpose of being destroyed, he cannot be bought back; he must be put to death.

[30]" 'One-tenth of all crops belongs to the LORD, including the crops from fields and the fruit from trees. That one-tenth is holy to the LORD. [31]If a person wants to get back that tenth, one-fifth must be added to its price.

[32]" 'The priest will take every tenth animal from a person's herd or flock, and it will be holy to the LORD. [33]The owner should not pick out the good animals from the bad or exchange one animal for another. If that happens, both animals will become holy; they cannot be bought back.' "

[34]These are the commands the LORD gave to Moses at Mount Sinai for the people of Israel.

Numbers

Why Read This Book:
- Learn what can happen when you don't trust God's power (Numbers 13—14).
- See that God plans to be good to his people (Numbers 22—24).
- Read about the first equal rights for women (Numbers 27:1-11).

When?

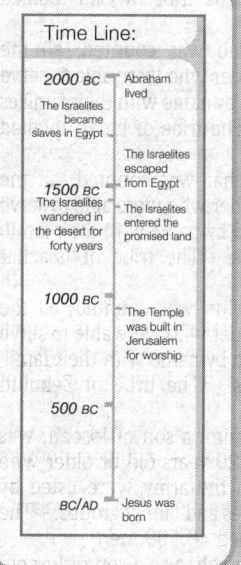

Time Line:

2000 BC	Abraham lived
The Israelites became slaves in Egypt	
	The Israelites escaped from Egypt
1500 BC The Israelites wandered in the desert for forty years	The Israelites entered the promised land
1000 BC	The Temple was built in Jerusalem for worship
500 BC	
BC/AD	Jesus was born

Behind the Scenes:

It's an important rugby match and there is just the chance for a try. You go for it and lose the ball. Within seconds the opposition are another five points up. Your discouraged team faces a long struggle if they are to turn the score in their favour.

On a far greater scale, the book of Numbers tells a similar story. The Hebrew people had been delivered from slavery in Egypt and were on their way to God's promised land. But they disobeyed God and spent 40 years wandering a hostile desert.

Numbers tells how God punished his people who had lost faith both in themselves and in him. It teaches us the importance of obeying and following God with all of our heart, and shows how God patiently and persistently disciplines his stubborn children.

Numbers gets its name from the census taken both at the beginning and at the end of the book. However, its original name "In the Desert" is more accurate.

Where?

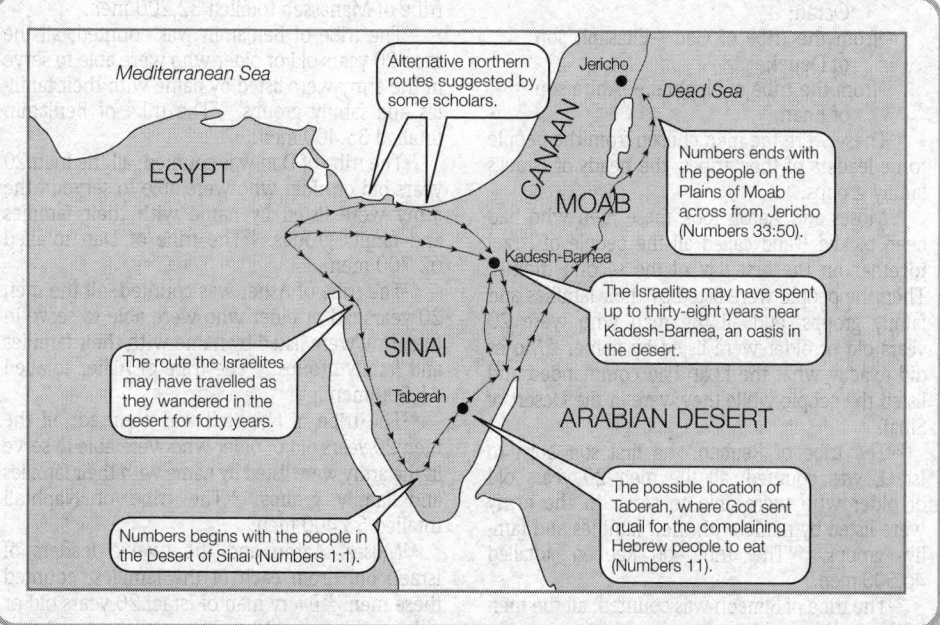

Alternative northern routes suggested by some scholars.

Numbers ends with the people on the Plains of Moab across from Jericho (Numbers 33:50).

The Israelites may have spent up to thirty-eight years near Kadesh-Barnea, an oasis in the desert.

The route the Israelites may have travelled as they wandered in the desert for forty years.

The possible location of Taberah, where God sent quail for the complaining Hebrew people to eat (Numbers 11).

Numbers begins with the people in the Desert of Sinai (Numbers 1:1).

The People of Israel are Counted

1 The LORD spoke to Moses in the Meeting Tent in the Desert of Sinai. This was on the first day of the second month in the second year after the Israelites left Egypt. He said to Moses: 2"You and Aaron must count all the people of Israel by families and family groups, listing the name of each man. 3You and Aaron must count every man 20 years old or older who will serve in the army of Israel, and list them by their divisions. 4One man from each tribe, the leader of his family, will help you. 5These are the names of the men who will help you:

> from the tribe of Reuben—Elizur son of Shedeur;
> 6from the tribe of Simeon—Shelumiel son of Zurishaddai;
> 7from the tribe of Judah—Nahshon son of Amminadab;
> 8from the tribe of Issachar—Nethanel son of Zuar;
> 9from the tribe of Zebulun—Eliab son of Helon;
> 10from the tribe of Ephraim son of Joseph—Elishama son of Ammihud;
> from the tribe of Manasseh son of Joseph—Gamaliel son of Pedahzur;
> 11from the tribe of Benjamin—Abidan son of Gideoni;
> 12from the tribe of Dan—Ahiezer son of Ammishaddai;
> 13from the tribe of Asher—Pagiel son of Ocran;
> 14from the tribe of Gad—Eliasaph son of Deuel;
> 15from the tribe of Naphtali—Ahira son of Enan."

16These were the men chosen from the people to be leaders of their tribes, the heads of Israel's family groups.

17Moses and Aaron took these men who had been picked 18and called all the people of Israel together on the first day of the second month. Then the people were listed by their families and family groups, and all the men who were 20 years old or older were listed by name. 19Moses did exactly what the LORD had commanded and listed the people while they were in the Desert of Sinai.

20The tribe of Reuben, the first son born to Israel, was counted; all the men 20 years old or older who were able to serve in the army were listed by name with their families and family groups. 21The tribe of Reuben totalled 46,500 men.

22The tribe of Simeon was counted; all the men 20 years old or older who were able to serve in the army were listed by name with their families and family groups. 23The tribe of Simeon totalled 59,300 men.

24The tribe of Gad was counted; all the men 20 years old or older who were able to serve in the army were listed by name with their families and family groups. 25The tribe of Gad totalled 45,650 men.

26The tribe of Judah was counted; all the men 20 years old or older who were able to serve in the army were listed by name with their families and family groups. 27The tribe of Judah totalled 74,600 men.

28The tribe of Issachar was counted; all the men 20 years old or older who were able to serve in the army were listed by name with their families and family groups. 29The tribe of Issachar totalled 54,400 men.

30The tribe of Zebulun was counted; all the men 20 years old or older who were able to serve in the army were listed by name with their families and family groups. 31The tribe of Zebulun totalled 57,400 men.

32The tribe of Ephraim, a son of Joseph, was counted; all the men 20 years old or older who were able to serve in the army were listed by name with their families and family groups. 33The tribe of Ephraim totalled 40,500 men.

34The tribe of Manasseh, also a son of Joseph, was counted; all the men 20 years old or older who were able to serve in the army were listed by name with their families and family groups. 35The tribe of Manasseh totalled 32,200 men.

36The tribe of Benjamin was counted; all the men 20 years old or older who were able to serve in the army were listed by name with their families and family groups. 37The tribe of Benjamin totalled 35,400 men.

38The tribe of Dan was counted; all the men 20 years old or older who were able to serve in the army were listed by name with their families and family groups. 39The tribe of Dan totalled 62,700 men.

40The tribe of Asher was counted; all the men 20 years old or older who were able to serve in the army were listed by name with their families and family groups. 41The tribe of Asher totalled 41,500 men.

42The tribe of Naphtali was counted; all the men 20 years old or older who were able to serve in the army were listed by name with their families and family groups. 43The tribe of Naphtali totalled 53,400 men.

44Moses, Aaron and the twelve leaders of Israel, one from each of the families, counted these men. 45Every man of Israel 20 years old or older who was able to serve in the army was counted and listed with his family. ⁴⁶The total number of men was 603,550.

⁴⁷The families from the tribe of Levi were not listed with the others, because ⁴⁸the LORD had

told Moses: ⁴⁹"Do not count the tribe of Levi or include them with the other Israelites. ⁵⁰Instead put the Levites in charge of the Holy Tent *d* of the Agreement and everything that is with it. They must carry the Holy Tent and everything in it, and they must take care of it and make their camp around it. ⁵¹Any time the Holy Tent is moved, the Levites must take it down, and any time it is set up, the Levites must do it. Anyone else who goes near the Holy Tent will be put to death. ⁵²The Israelites will make their camps in separate divisions, each family near its flag. ⁵³But the Levites must make their camp around the Holy Tent of the Agreement so that I will not be angry with the Israelites. The Levites will take care of the Holy Tent of the Agreement."

⁵⁴So the Israelites did everything just as the LORD commanded Moses.

The Camp Arrangement

2 The LORD said to Moses and Aaron: ²"The Israelites should make their camps around the Meeting Tent, *d* but they should not camp too close to it. They should camp under their family flag and banners."

³The camp of Judah will be on the east side, where the sun rises, and they will camp by divisions there under their flag. The leader of the people of Judah is Nahshon son of Amminadab. ⁴There are 74,600 men in his division.

⁵Next to them the tribe *d* of Issachar will camp. The leader of the people of Issachar is Nethanel son of Zuar. ⁶There are 54,400 men in his division.

⁷Next is the tribe of Zebulun. The leader of the people of Zebulun is Eliab son of Helon. ⁸There are 57,400 men in his division.

⁹There are a total of 186,400 men in the camps of Judah and its neighbours, in all their divisions. They will be the first to march out of camp.

¹⁰The divisions of the camp of Reuben will be on the south side, where they will camp under their flag. The leader of the people of Reuben is Elizur son of Shedeur. ¹¹There are 46,500 men in his division.

¹²Next to them the tribe of Simeon will camp. The leader of the people of Simeon is Shelumiel son of Zurishaddai. ¹³There are 59,300 men in his division.

¹⁴Next is the tribe of Gad. The leader of the people of Gad is Eliasaph son of Deuel. ¹⁵There are 45,650 men in his division.

¹⁶There are a total of 151,450 men in the camps of Reuben and its neighbours, in all their divisions. They will be the second group to march out of camp.

¹⁷When the Levites march out with the Meeting Tent, they will be in the middle of the other camps. The tribes will march out in the same order as they camp, each in its place under its flag.

¹⁸The divisions of the camp of Ephraim will be on the west side, where they will camp under their flag. The leader of the people of Ephraim is Elishama son of Ammihud. ¹⁹There are 40,500 men in his division.

²⁰Next to them the tribe of Manasseh will camp. The leader of the people of Manasseh is Gamaliel son of Pedahzur. ²¹There are 32,200 men in his division.

²²Next is the tribe of Benjamin. The leader of the people of Benjamin is Abidan son of Gideoni. ²³There are 35,400 men in his division.

²⁴There are a total of 108,100 men in the camps of Ephraim and its neighbours, in all their divisions. They will be the third group to march out of camp.

²⁵The divisions of the camp of Dan will be on the north side, where they will camp under their flag. The leader of the people of Dan is Ahiezer son of Ammishaddai. ²⁶There are 62,700 men in his division.

²⁷Next to them the tribe of Asher will camp. The leader of the people of Asher is Pagiel son of Ocran. ²⁸There are 41,500 men in his division.

²⁹Next is the tribe of Naphtali. The leader of the people of Naphtali is Ahira son of Enan. ³⁰There are 53,400 men in his division.

³¹There are 157,600 men in the camps of Dan and its neighbours. They will be the last to march out of camp, and they will travel under their own flag.

³²These are the Israelites who were counted by families. The total number of Israelites in the camps, counted by divisions, is 603,550. ³³Moses obeyed the LORD and did not count the Levites among the other people of Israel.

³⁴So the Israelites obeyed everything the LORD commanded Moses. They camped under their

flags and marched out by families and family groups.

Aaron's Family, the Priests

3 This is the family history of Aaron and Moses at the time the LORD talked to Moses on Mount Sinai.

²Aaron had four sons: Nadab, the oldest, Abihu, Eleazar and Ithamar. ³These were the names of Aaron's sons, who were appointed to serve as priests. ⁴But Nadab and Abihu died in the presence of the LORD when they offered the wrong kind of fire before the LORD in the Desert of Sinai. They had no sons. So Eleazar and Ithamar served as priests during the lifetime of their father Aaron.

⁵The LORD said to Moses, ⁶"Bring the tribe ᵈ of Levi and present them to Aaron the priest to help him. ⁷They will help him and all the Israelites at the Meeting Tent, ᵈ doing the work in the Holy Tent. ⁸The Levites must take care of everything in the Meeting Tent and serve the people of Israel by doing the work in the Holy Tent. ⁹Give the Levites to Aaron and his sons; of all the Israelites, the Levites are given completely to him. ¹⁰Appoint Aaron and his sons to serve as priests, but anyone else who comes near the holy things must be put to death."

¹¹The LORD also said to Moses, ¹²"I am choosing the Levites from all the Israelites to take the place of all the firstborn ᵈ children of Israel. The Levites will be mine, ¹³because the firstborn are mine. When you were in Egypt, I killed all the firstborn children of the Egyptians and took all the firstborn of Israel to be mine, both animals and children. They are mine. I am the LORD."

¹⁴The LORD again said to Moses in the Desert of Sinai, ¹⁵"Count the Levites by families and family groups. Count every male one month old or older." ¹⁶So Moses obeyed the LORD and counted them all.

¹⁷Levi had three sons, whose names were Gershon, Kohath and Merari.
¹⁸The Gershonite family groups were Libni and Shimei.
¹⁹The Kohathite family groups were Amram, Izhar, Hebron and Uzziel.
²⁰The Merarite family groups were Mahli and Mushi.

These were the family groups of the Levites.
²¹The family groups of Libni and Shimei belonged to Gershon; they were the Gershonite family groups. ²²The number that was counted was 7,500 males one month old or older. ²³The Gershonite family groups camped on the west side, behind the Holy Tent. ²⁴The leader of the families of Gershon was Eliasaph son of Lael. ²⁵In the Meeting Tent the Gershonites were in charge

of the Holy Tent, its covering, the curtain at the entrance to the Meeting Tent, ²⁶the curtains in the courtyard, the curtain at the entrance to the courtyard around the Holy Tent and the altar, the ropes and all the work connected with these things.

²⁷The family groups of Amram, Izhar, Hebron and Uzziel belonged to Kohath; they were the Kohathite family groups. ²⁸They had 8,600 males one month old or older, and they were responsible for taking care of the Holy Place. ²⁹The Kohathite family groups camped south of the Holy Tent. ³⁰The leader of the Kohathite families was Elizaphan son of Uzziel. ³¹They were responsible for the Ark, ᵈ the table, the lampstand, the altars, the tools of the Holy Place which they were to use, the curtain and all the work connected with these things. ³²The main leader of the Levites was Eleazar son of Aaron, the priest, who was in charge of all those responsible for the Holy Place.

³³The family groups of Mahli and Mushi belonged to Merari; they were the Merarite family groups. ³⁴The number that was counted was 6,200 males one month old or older. ³⁵The leader of the Merari families was Zuriel son of Abihail, and they were to camp north of the Holy Tent. ³⁶The Merarites were responsible for the frames of the Holy Tent, the braces, the posts, the bases and all the work connected with these things. ³⁷They were also responsible for the posts in the courtyard around the Holy Tent and their bases, tent pegs and ropes.

³⁸Moses, Aaron and his sons camped east of the Holy Tent, towards the sunrise, in front of the Meeting Tent. They were responsible for the Holy Place for the Israelites. Anyone else who came near the Holy Place was to be put to death.

³⁹Moses and Aaron counted the Levite men by their families, as the LORD commanded, and there were 22,000 males one month old or older.

Levites Take the Place of the Firstborn Sons

⁴⁰The LORD said to Moses, "Count all the firstbornᵈ sons in Israel one month old or older, and list their names. ⁴¹Take the Levites for me instead of the firstborn sons of Israel; take the animals of the Levites instead of the firstborn animals from the rest of Israel. I am the LORD."

⁴²So Moses did what the LORD commanded and counted all the firstborn sons of the Israelites. ⁴³When he listed all the firstborn sons one month old or older, there were 22,273 names.

⁴⁴The LORD also said to Moses, ⁴⁵"Take the Levites instead of all the firstborn sons of the Israelites, and take the animals of the Levites instead of the animals of the other people. The Levites are mine. I am the LORD. ⁴⁶Since there are 273 more

firstborn sons than Levites, [47]collect 5 pieces of silver for each of the 273 sons. Use the measure as set by the Holy Place, which is 11.5 grammes. [48]Give the silver to Aaron and his sons as the payment for the 273 Israelites."

[49]So Moses collected the money for the people the Levites could not replace. [50]From the first-born of the Israelites, he collected 1,365 pieces of silver, using the measure set by the Holy Place. [51]Moses obeyed the command of the LORD and gave the silver to Aaron and his sons.

The Jobs of the Kohath Family

4 The LORD said to Moses and Aaron, [2]"Count the Kohathites among the Levites by family groups and families. [3]Count the men from 30 to 50 years old, all who come to serve in the Meeting Tent. [d]

[4]"The Kohathites are responsible for the most holy things in the Meeting Tent. [5]When the Israelites are ready to move, Aaron and his sons must go into the Holy Tent, take down the curtain, and cover the Ark [d] of the Agreement with it. [6]Over this they must put a covering made from fine leather, then spread the solid blue cloth over that, and put the poles in place.

[7]"Then they must spread a blue cloth over the table for the bread that shows a person is in God's presence. They must put the plates, pans, bowls and the jars for drink offerings on the table; they must leave the bread that is always there on the table. [8]Then they must put a red cloth over all of these things, cover everything with fine leather, and put the poles in place.

[9]"With a blue cloth they must cover the lamp-stand, its lamps, its wick trimmers, its trays and all the jars for the oil used in the lamps. [10]Then they must wrap everything in fine leather and put all these things on a frame for carrying them.

[11]"They must spread a blue cloth over the gold altar, cover it with fine leather and put the poles in place.

[12]"They must gather all the things used for serving in the Holy Place and wrap them in a blue cloth. Then they must cover that with fine leather and put these things on a frame for carrying them.

[13]"They must clean the ashes off the bronze altar and spread a purple cloth over it. [14]They must gather all the things used for serving at the altar—the pans for carrying the fire, the meat forks, the shovels and the bowls—and put them on the bronze altar. Then they must spread a covering of fine leather over it and put the poles in place.

[15]"When the Israelites are ready to move, and when Aaron and his sons have covered the holy furniture and all the holy things, the Kohathites may go in and carry them away. In this way they won't touch the holy things and die. It is the Kohathites' job to carry the things that are in the Meeting Tent.

[16]"Eleazar son of Aaron, the priest, will be responsible for the Holy Tent and for everything in it, for all the holy things it has: the oil for the lamp, the sweet-smelling incense, [d] the continual grain offering and the oil used to appoint priests and things to the LORD's service."

[17]The LORD said to Moses and Aaron, [18]"Don't let the Kohathites be cut off from the Levites. [19]Do this for the Kohathites so that they may go near the Most Holy Place and not die: Aaron and his sons must go in and show each Kohathite what to do and what to carry. [20]The Kohathites must not enter and look at the holy things, even for a second, or they will die."

The Jobs of the Gershon Family

[21]The LORD said to Moses, [22]"Count the Gershonites by families and family groups. [23]Count the men from 30 to 50 years old, all who have a job to do in the Meeting Tent. [d]

[24]"This is what the Gershonite family groups must do and what they must carry: [25]They must carry the curtains of the Holy Tent, [d] the Meeting Tent, its covering and its outer covering made from fine leather. They must also carry the curtains for the entrance to the Meeting Tent, [26]the curtains of the courtyard that go around the Holy Tent and the altar, the curtain for the entrance to the courtyard, the ropes and all the things used with the curtains. They must do everything connected with these things. [27]Aaron and his sons are in charge of what the Gershonites do or carry; you tell them what they are responsible for carrying. [28]This is the work of the Gershonite family group at the Meeting Tent. Ithamar son of Aaron, the priest, will direct their work.

The Jobs of the Merari Family

[29]"Count the Merarite families and family groups. [30]Count the men from 30 to 50 years old, all who work at the Meeting Tent. [d] [31]It is their job to carry the following as they serve in the Meeting Tent: the frames of the Holy Tent, the crossbars, the posts and bases, [32]in addition to the posts that go around the courtyard, their bases, tent pegs, ropes and everything that is used with the poles around the courtyard. Tell each man exactly what to carry. [33]This is the work the Merarite family group will do for the Meeting Tent. Ithamar son of Aaron, the priest, will direct their work."

The Levite Families

[34]Moses, Aaron and the leaders of Israel counted the Kohathites by families and family groups,

35the men from 30 to 50 years old who were to work at the Meeting Tent. *d* 36There were 2,750 men in the family groups. 37This was the total of the Kohath family groups who worked at the Meeting Tent, whom Moses and Aaron counted as the LORD had commanded Moses.

38Also, the Gershonites were counted by families and family groups, 39the men from 30 to 50 years old who were given work at the Meeting Tent. 40The families and family groups had 2,630 men. 41This was the total of the Gershon family groups who worked at the Meeting Tent, whom Moses and Aaron counted as the LORD had commanded.

42Also, the men in the families and family groups of the Merari family were counted, 43the men from 30 to 50 years old who were to work at the Meeting Tent. 44The family groups had 3,200 men. 45This was the total of the Merari family groups, whom Moses and Aaron counted as the LORD had commanded Moses.

46So Moses, Aaron and the leaders of Israel counted all the Levites by families and family groups. 47They counted the men from 30 to 50 years old who were given work at the Meeting Tent and who carried the Tent. 48The total number of these men was 8,580. 49Each man was counted as the LORD had commanded Moses; each man was given his work and told what to carry as the LORD had commanded Moses.

Rules About Cleanliness

5 The LORD said to Moses, 2"Command the Israelites to send away from camp anyone with a harmful skin disease. Send away anyone who gives off body fluid or who has become unclean by touching a dead body. 3Send both men and women outside the camp so that they won't spread the disease there, where I am living among you." 4So Israel obeyed the LORD's command and sent those people outside the camp. They did just as the LORD had told Moses.

Paying for Doing Wrong

5The LORD said to Moses, 6"Tell the Israelites: 'When a man or woman does something wrong to another person, that is really sinning against the LORD. That person is guilty 7and must admit the wrong that has been done. The person must fully pay for the wrong that has been done, adding one-fifth to it, and giving it to the person who was wronged. 8But if that person is dead and does not have any close relatives to receive the payment, the one who did wrong owes the LORD and must pay the priest. In addition, the priest must sacrifice a ram to remove the wrong so that the person will belong to the LORD. 9When an Israelite

brings a holy gift, it should be given to the priest. 10No one has to give these holy gifts, but if someone does give them, they belong to the priest.' "

Suspicious Husbands

11Then the LORD said to Moses, 12"Tell the Israelites: 'A man's wife might be unfaithful to him 13and have sexual relations with another man. Her sin might be kept hidden from her husband so that he does not know about the wrong she did. Perhaps no one saw it, and she wasn't caught. 14But if her husband has feelings of jealousy and suspects she has sinned—whether she has or not— 15he should take her to the priest. The husband must also take an offering for her of 2 litres of barley flour. He must not pour oil or incense *d* on it, because this is a grain offering for jealousy, an offering of remembrance. It is to find out if she is guilty.

16" 'The priest will bring in the woman and make her stand before the LORD. 17He will take some holy water in a clay jar, and he will put some earth from the floor of the Holy Tent into the water. 18The priest will make the woman stand before the LORD, and he will loosen her hair. He will hand her the offering of remembrance, the grain offering for jealousy; he will hold the bitter water that brings a curse. 19The priest will make her take an oath and ask her, "Has another man had sexual relations with you? Have you been unfaithful to your husband? If you haven't, this bitter water that brings a curse won't hurt you. 20But if you have been unfaithful to your husband and have had sexual relations with a man besides him"— 21the priest will then put on her the curse that the oath will bring—"the LORD will make the people curse and reject you. He will make your stomach get big, and he will make your body unable to give birth to another baby. 22This water that brings a curse will go inside you and make your body unable to give birth to another baby."

" 'The woman must say, "I agree."

23" 'The priest should write these curses on a scroll, wash the words off into the bitter water, 24and make the woman drink the bitter water that brings a curse. If she is guilty, the water will make her sick. 25Then the priest will take the grain offering for jealousy from her. He will present it before the LORD and bring it to the altar. 26He will take a handful of the grain, which is a memorial offering, and burn it on the altar. After that he will make the woman drink the water 27to see if she is not pure and if she has sinned against her husband. When it goes into her, if her stomach gets big so that she is not able to have another baby, her people will reject her. 28But if the woman has not sinned, she is pure. She is not guilty, and she will be able to have babies.

²⁹" 'So this is the teaching about jealousy. This is what to do when a woman does wrong and is unfaithful while she is married to her husband. ³⁰It also should be done if the man gets jealous because he suspects his wife. The priest will have her stand before the LORD, and he will do all these things, just as the teaching commands. ³¹In this way the husband can be proven correct, and the woman will suffer if she has done wrong.' "

Rules for the Nazirites

6 The LORD said to Moses, ²"Tell the Israelites: 'If men or women want to promise to belong to the LORD in a special way, they will be called Nazirites. ³During this time, they must not drink wine or beer, or vinegar made from wine or beer. They must not even drink grape juice or eat grapes or raisins. ⁴While they are Nazirites, they must not eat anything that comes from the grapevine, even the seeds or the skin.

⁵" 'During the time they have promised to belong to the LORD, they must not cut their hair. They must be holy until this special time is over. They must let their hair grow long. ⁶During their special time of belonging to the LORD, Nazirites must not go near a dead body. ⁷Even if their own father, mother, brother or sister dies, they must not touch them, or they will become unclean. ᵈ They must still keep their promise to belong to God in a special way. ⁸While they are Nazirites, they belong to the LORD in a special way.

> ### Sidelight
>
> What do you call a person who grows a beard, watches what he eats, and never cuts his hair? A Nazirite. Nazirites were men who took a special vow to dedicate their lives to God (Numbers 6:2–8). Samson, whose story is in Judges 13—16 (p.239), was probably the most famous of these Nazirites.

⁹" 'If they are next to someone who dies suddenly, their hair, which was part of their promise, has been made unclean. So they must shave their head seven days later to be clean. ¹⁰Then on the eighth day, they must bring two doves or two young pigeons to the priest at the entrance to the Meeting Tent. ᵈ ¹¹The priest will offer one as a sin offering and the other as a burnt offering. This removes sin so they will belong to the LORD. (They had sinned because they were near a dead body.) That same day they will again promise to let their hair grow ¹²and give themselves to the LORD for another special time. They must bring a male lamb a year old as a penalty offering. The

days of the special time before don't count, because they became unclean during their first special time.

¹³" 'This is the teaching for the Nazirites. When the promised time is over, they must go to the entrance of the Meeting Tent ᵈ ¹⁴and give their offerings to the LORD. They must offer a year-old male lamb that has nothing wrong with it, as a burnt offering, a year-old female lamb that has nothing wrong with it, as a sin offering, and a ram that has nothing wrong with it, for a fellowship offering. ¹⁵They must also bring the grain offerings and drink offerings that go with them. And they must bring a basket of bread made without yeast, loaves made with fine flour mixed with oil, and wafers made without yeast, spread with oil.

¹⁶" 'The priest will give these offerings to the LORD and make the sin offering and the burnt offering. ¹⁷Then he will kill the ram as a fellowship offering to the LORD; along with it, he will present the basket of bread made without yeast, the grain offering and the drink offering.

¹⁸" 'The Nazirites must go to the entrance of the Meeting Tent and shave off their hair that they grew for their promise. The hair will be put in the fire that is under the sacrifice of the fellowship offering.

¹⁹" 'After the Nazirites cut off their hair, the priest will give them a boiled shoulder from the ram. From the basket he will also give a loaf and a wafer, both made without yeast. ²⁰Then the priest will present them to the LORD. They are holy and belong to the priest. Also, he is to present the breast and the thigh from the ram. After that, the Nazirites may drink wine.

²¹" 'This is the teaching for the Nazirites who make a promise. Everyone who makes the Nazirite promise must give all these gifts to the LORD. If they promised to do more, they must keep their promise, according to the teaching of the Nazirites.' "

The Priests' Blessings

²²The LORD said to Moses, ²³"Tell Aaron and his sons, 'This is how you should bless the Israelites. Say to them:
²⁴"May the LORD bless you and keep you.
²⁵May the LORD show you his kindness
    and have mercy on you.
²⁶May the LORD watch over you
    and give you peace." '
²⁷"So Aaron and his sons will bless the Israelites with my name, and I will bless them."

The Holy Tent

7 When Moses finished setting up the Holy Tent, ᵈ he gave it for service to the LORD by

pouring olive oil on the Tent and on everything used in it. He also poured oil on the altar and all its tools to prepare them for service to the LORD. [2]Then the leaders of Israel made offerings. These were the heads of the families, the leaders of each tribe *d* who counted the people. [3]They brought to the LORD six covered carts and twelve oxen— each leader giving an ox, and every two leaders giving a cart. They brought these to the Holy Tent.

[4]The LORD said to Moses, [5]"Accept these gifts from the leaders and use them in the work of the Meeting Tent. Give them to the Levites as they need them."

[6]So Moses accepted the carts and the oxen and gave them to the Levites. [7]He gave two carts and four oxen to the Gershonites, which they needed for their work. [8]Then Moses gave four carts and eight oxen to the Merarites, which they needed for their work. Ithamar son of Aaron, the priest, directed the work of all of them. [9]Moses did not give any oxen or carts to the Kohathites, because their job was to carry the holy things on their shoulders.

[10]When the oil was poured on the altar, the leaders brought their offerings to it to give it to the LORD's service; they presented them in front of the altar. [11]The LORD told Moses, "Each day one leader must bring his gift to make the altar ready for service to me."

[12-83]Each of the twelve leaders brought these gifts. Each leader brought one silver plate that weighed about 1,500 grammes, and one silver bowl that weighed about 800 grammes. These weights were set by the Holy Place measure. The bowl and the plate were filled with fine flour mixed with oil for a grain offering. Each leader also brought a large gold dish that weighed about 110 grammes and was filled with incense. *d*

In addition, each of the leaders brought one young bull, one ram and one male lamb a year old for a burnt offering; one male goat for a sin offering; and two oxen, five rams, five male goats and five male lambs a year old for a fellowship offering.

On the first day Nahshon son of Amminadab brought his gifts. He was the leader of the tribe of Judah.

PEACE

An Unlikely Gift

Adam, twenty-five, lives in a home with six handicapped people and four assistants. He can't speak, walk, or eat without help. His back is deformed, his movements are uncoordinated, and seizures grip his body daily.

But Adam's dependence on others has taught valuable lessons to those who know him. As people help Adam with things he can't do alone, they discover that Adam never hurries or worries. Without ever speaking, Adam communicates inner peace.

Some people would consider Adam worthless. But after being with Adam, people feel affected by that inner peace. As people help him, they are touched with a sense of affection that's much deeper than words. Though totally dependent on them, his gift is simply to be there with them. The peace Adam shares by his being with others far outweighs anything Adam can't do.

Adam shows that peace is a gift from God that's deeper than the things we do. Consider the source of Adam's peace as you read **Numbers 6:22–27**.

* How is the peace talked about in this passage like the peace that Adam shows in his life?
* Are you experiencing these things in your life? If not, how can you begin to experience them?

Consider . . .

* reading dictionary definitions of peace. Write the ones that apply to God's peace on a postcard and place it where you can see it every day.
* sitting silently for ten minutes in prayer, inviting God to give you inner peace. Think about how the experience affects the rest of your day.

For more, see . . .

* Psalm 119:165 (p.574)
* Romans 12:14–21 (p.1205)
* John 14:27 (p.1124)

On the second day Nethanel son of Zuar brought his gifts. He was the leader of the tribe of Issachar.

On the third day Eliab son of Helon brought his gifts. He was the leader of the tribe of Zebulun.

On the fourth day Elizur son of Shedeur brought his gifts. He was the leader of the tribe of Reuben.

On the fifth day Shelumiel son of Zurishaddai brought his gifts. He was the leader of the tribe of Simeon.

On the sixth day Eliasaph son of Deuel brought his gifts. He was the leader of the tribe of Gad.

On the seventh day Elishama son of Ammihud brought his gifts. He was the leader of the tribe of Ephraim.

On the eighth day Gamaliel son of Pedahzur brought his gifts. He was the leader of the tribe of Manasseh.

On the ninth day Abidan son of Gideoni brought his gifts. He was the leader of the tribe of Benjamin.

On the tenth day Ahiezer son of Ammishaddai brought his gifts. He was the leader of the tribe of Dan.

On the eleventh day Pagiel son of Ocran brought his gifts. He was the leader of the tribe of Asher.

On the twelfth day Ahira son of Enan brought his gifts. He was the leader of the tribe of Naphtali.

84So these were the gifts from the Israelite leaders when oil was poured on the altar and it was given for service to the LORD: twelve silver plates, twelve silver bowls and twelve gold dishes. 85Each silver plate weighed about 1,500 grammes, and each bowl weighed about 800 grammes. All the silver plates and silver bowls together weighed about 27 kilogrammes according to a weight set by the Holy Place measure. 86The twelve gold dishes filled with incense weighed 110 grammes each, according to the weight set by the Holy Place measure. Together the gold dishes weighed about 1,400 grammes. 87The total number of animals for the burnt offering was twelve bulls, twelve rams and twelve male lambs a year old. There was also a grain offering, and there were twelve male goats for a sin offering. 88The total number of animals for the fellowship offering was 24 bulls, 60 male goats and 60 male lambs a year old. All these offerings were for giving the altar to the service of the LORD after the oil had been poured on it.

89When Moses went into the Meeting Tent to speak with the LORD, he heard the LORD speaking to him. The voice was coming from between the two gold creatures with wings that were above the lid of the Ark *d* of the Agreement. In this way the LORD spoke with him.

The Lampstand

8 The LORD said to Moses, 2"Speak to Aaron and tell him, 'Put the seven lamps where they can light the area in front of the lampstand.'"

3Aaron did this, placing the lamps so that they lighted the area in front of the lampstand; he obeyed the command the LORD gave Moses. 4The lampstand was made from hammered gold, from its base to the flowers. It was made in exactly the way the LORD had showed Moses.

The Levites are Given to God

5The LORD said to Moses, 6"Take the Levites away from the other Israelites and make them clean. *d* 7This is what you should do to make them clean: sprinkle the cleansing water on them, and make them shave their bodies and wash their clothes so that they are clean. 8They must take a young bull and the grain offering of flour mixed with oil that goes with it. Then take a second young bull for a sin offering. 9Bring the Levites to the front of the Meeting Tent, *d* and gather all the Israelites around. 10When you bring the Levites before the LORD, the Israelites should put their hands on them. *n* 11Aaron will present the Levites before the LORD as an offering presented from the Israelites. Then the Levites will be ready to do the work of the LORD.

12"The Levites will put their hands on the bulls' heads—one bull will be a sin offering to the LORD, and the other will be a burnt offering, to remove the sins of the Levites so they will belong to the LORD. 13Make the Levites stand in front of Aaron and his sons and present the Levites as an offering to the LORD. 14In this way you must set apart the Levites from the other Israelites; the Levites will be mine.

15"Make the Levites pure, and present them as an offering so that they may come to work at the Meeting Tent. 16They will be given completely to me from the Israelites; I have taken them for myself instead of the firstborn *d* of every Israelite woman. 17All the firstborn in Israel—people or animals—are mine. When I killed all the firstborn in Egypt, I set the firstborn in Israel aside for myself. 18But I have taken the Levites instead of all the firstborn in Israel. 19From all the Israelites I have given the Levites to Aaron and his sons so that they may serve the Israelites at the Meeting Tent. They will help remove the Israelites' sins so that they belong to the LORD and so that no

---

put . . . them   This showed that the people had a part in giving the Levites their special work.

disaster strikes the Israelites when they approach the Holy Place."

[20]So Moses, Aaron and all the Israelites obeyed and did with the Levites what the LORD commanded Moses. [21]The Levites made themselves clean and washed their clothes. Then Aaron presented them as an offering to the LORD. He also removed their sins so they would be pure. [22]After that, the Levites came to the Meeting Tent to work, and Aaron and his sons told them what to do. They did with the Levites what the LORD commanded Moses.

[23]The LORD said to Moses, [24]"This command is for the Levites. Everyone 25 years old or older must come to the Meeting Tent, because they all have jobs to do there. [25]At the age of 50, they must retire from their jobs and not work again. [26]They may help their fellow Levites with their work at the Meeting Tent, but they must not do the work themselves. This is how you are to give the Levites their jobs."

The Passover is Celebrated

9 The LORD spoke to Moses in the Desert of Sinai in the first month of the second year after the Israelites left Egypt. He said, [2]"Tell the Israelites to celebrate the Passover[d] at the appointed time. [3]That appointed time is the fourteenth day of this month at twilight; they must obey all the rules about it."

[4]So Moses told the Israelites to celebrate the Passover, [5]and they did; it was in the Desert of Sinai at twilight on the fourteenth day of the first month. The Israelites did everything just as the LORD commanded Moses.

[6]But some of the people could not celebrate the Passover on that day because they were unclean[d] from touching a dead body. So they went to Moses and Aaron that day and [7]said to Moses, "We are unclean because of touching a dead body. But why should we be kept from offering gifts to the LORD at this appointed time? Why can't we join the other Israelites?"

[8]Moses said to them, "Wait, and I will find out what the LORD says about you."

[9]Then the LORD said to Moses, [10]"Tell the Israelites this: 'If you or your descendants[d] become unclean because of a dead body, or if you are away on a trip during the Passover, you must still celebrate the LORD's Passover. [11]But celebrate it at twilight on the fourteenth day of the second month. Eat the lamb with bitter herbs and bread made without yeast. [12]Don't leave any of it until the next morning or break any of its bones. When you celebrate the Passover, follow all the rules. [13]Anyone who is clean and is not away on a trip but does not eat the Passover must be cut off from the people. That person did not give an offering

to the LORD at the appointed time and must be punished for the sin.

[14]" 'Foreigners among you may celebrate the LORD's Passover, but they must follow all the rules. You must have the same rules for foreigners as you have for yourselves.' "

The Cloud Above the Tent

[15]On the day the Holy Tent,[d] the Tent of the Agreement, was set up, a cloud covered it. From dusk until dawn the cloud above the Tent looked like fire. [16]The cloud stayed above the Tent, and at night it looked like fire. [17]When the cloud moved from its place over the Tent, the Israelites moved, and wherever the cloud stopped, the Israelites camped. [18]So the Israelites moved at the LORD's command, and they camped at his command. While the cloud stayed over the Tent, they remained camped. [19]Sometimes the cloud stayed over the Tent for a long time, but the Israelites obeyed the LORD and did not move. [20]Sometimes the cloud was over it only a few days. At the LORD's command the people camped, and at his command they moved. [21]Sometimes the cloud stayed only from dusk until dawn; when the cloud lifted the next morning, the people moved. When the cloud lifted, day or night, the people moved. [22]The cloud might stay over the Tent for two days, a month or a year. As long as it stayed, the people camped, but when it lifted, they moved. [23]At the LORD's command the people camped, and at his command they moved. They obeyed the LORD's order that he commanded through Moses.

The Silver Trumpets

10 The LORD said to Moses, [2]"Make two trumpets of hammered silver, and use them to call the people together and to march out of camp. [3]When both trumpets are blown, the people should gather before you at the entrance to the Meeting Tent.[d] [4]If you blow only one trumpet, the leaders, the heads of the family groups of Israel, should meet before you. [5]When you loudly blow the trumpets, the tribes[d] camping on the east should move. [6]When you loudly blow them again, the tribes camping on the south should move; the loud sound will tell them to move. [7]When you want to gather the people, blow the trumpets, but don't blow them as loudly.

[8]"Aaron's sons, the priests, should blow the trumpets. This is a law for you and your descendants[d] from now on. [9]When you are fighting an enemy who attacks you in your own land, blow the trumpets loudly. The LORD your God will take notice of you and will save you from your enemies. [10]Also blow your trumpets at happy times and

during your feasts and at New Moon *d* festivals. Blow them over your burnt offerings and fellowship offerings, because they will help you remember your God. I am the LORD your God."

The Israelites Move Camp

¹¹The cloud lifted from the Tent *d* of the Agreement on the twentieth day of the second month of the second year. ¹²So the Israelites moved from the Desert of Sinai and continued until the cloud stopped in the Desert of Paran. ¹³This was their first time to move, and they did it as the LORD had commanded Moses.

¹⁴The divisions from the camp of Judah moved first under their flag. Nahshon son of Amminadab was the commander. ¹⁵Nethanel son of Zuar was over the division of the tribe *d* of Issachar. ¹⁶Eliab son of Helon was over the division of the tribe of Zebulun. ¹⁷Then the Holy Tent was taken down, and the Gershonites and Merarites, who carried it, moved next.

¹⁸Then came the divisions from the camp of Reuben under their flag, and Elizur son of Shedeur was the commander. ¹⁹Shelumiel son of Zurishaddai was over the division of the tribe of Simeon. ²⁰Eliasaph son of Deuel was over the division of the tribe of Gad. ²¹Then came the Kohathites, who carried the holy things; the Holy Tent was to be set up before they arrived.

²²Next came the divisions from the camp of Ephraim under their flag, and Elishama son of Ammihud was the commander. ²³Gamaliel son of Pedahzur was over the division of the tribe of Manasseh, ²⁴and Abidan son of Gideoni was over the division of the tribe of Benjamin.

²⁵The last ones were the rearguard for all the tribes. These were the divisions from the camp of Dan under their flag, and Ahiezer son of Ammishaddai was the commander. ²⁶Pagiel son of Ocran was over the division of the tribe of Asher; ²⁷Ahira son of Enan was over the division of the tribe of Naphtali. ²⁸This was the order the Israelite divisions marched in when they moved.

²⁹Hobab was the son of Reuel the Midianite, *n* who was Moses' father-in-law. Moses said to Hobab, "We are moving to the land the LORD promised to give us. Come with us and we will be good to you, because the LORD has promised good things to Israel."

³⁰But Hobab answered, "No, I will not go. I will go back to my own land where I was born." ³¹But Moses said, "Please don't leave us. You know where we can camp in the desert, and you can be our guide. ³²Come with us. We will share

with you all the good things the LORD gives us." ³³So they left the mountain of the LORD and travelled for three days. The Ark *d* of the LORD's Agreement went in front of the people for those three days, as they looked for a place to camp. ³⁴The LORD's cloud was over them during the day when they left their camp.

³⁵When the Ark left the camp, Moses said, "Rise up, LORD!
　Scatter your enemies:
　make those who hate you run from you."
³⁶And when the Ark was set down, Moses said, "Return, LORD,
　to the thousands of people of Israel."

Fire from the LORD

11 Now the people complained to the LORD about their troubles, and when he heard them, he became angry. Then fire from the LORD burned among the people at the edge of the camp. ²The people cried out to Moses, and when he prayed to the LORD, the fire stopped burning. ³So that place was called Taberah, *n* because the LORD's fire had burned among them.

Seventy Elders Help Moses

⁴Some troublemakers among them wanted better food, and soon all the Israelites began complaining. They said, "We want meat! ⁵We remember the fish we ate for free in Egypt. We also had cucumbers, melons, leeks, onions and garlic. ⁶But now we have lost our appetite; we never see anything but this manna!"

⁷The manna was like small white seeds. ⁸The people would go to gather it, and then grind it in handmills, or crush it between stones. After they cooked it in a pot or made cakes with it, it tasted like bread baked with olive oil. ⁹When the dew fell on the camp each night, so did the manna.

¹⁰Moses heard every family crying as they stood in the entrances of their tents. Then the LORD became very angry, and Moses got upset. ¹¹He asked the LORD, "Why have you brought me, your servant, this trouble? What have I done wrong that you made me responsible for all these people? ¹²I am not the father of all these people, and I didn't give birth to them. So why do you make me carry them to the land you promised to our ancestors? Must I carry them in my arms as a nurse carries a baby? ¹³Where can I get meat for all these people? They keep crying to me, 'We want meat!' ¹⁴I can't take care of all these people alone. It's too much for me. ¹⁵If you are going to continue doing this to me, then kill me now.

Reuel the Midianite　Also called Jethro.
Taberah　This name means "burning".

If you care about me, put me to death, and then I won't have any more troubles."

¹⁶The LORD said to Moses, "Bring me 70 of Israel's elders, men that you know are leaders among the people. Bring them to the Meeting Tent, *d* and have them stand there with you. ¹⁷I will come down and speak with you there. I will take some of the Spirit *d* that is in you, and I will give it to them. They will help you care for the people so that you will not have to care for them alone.

¹⁸"Tell the people this: 'Make yourselves holy for tomorrow, and you will eat meat. You cried to the LORD, "We want meat! We were better off in Egypt!" So now the LORD will give you meat to eat. ¹⁹You will eat it not for just one, two, five, ten or even twenty days, ²⁰but you will eat that meat for a whole month. You will eat it until it comes out your nose, and you will grow to hate it. This is because you have rejected the LORD, who is with you. You have cried to him, saying, "Why did we ever leave Egypt?" ' "

²¹Moses said, "LORD, here are 600,000 people standing around me, and you say, 'I will give them enough meat to eat for a month!' ²²If we killed all the flocks and herds, that would not be enough. If we caught all the fish in the sea, that would not be enough."

²³But the LORD said to Moses, "Do you think I'm weak? Now you will see if I can do what I say."

²⁴So Moses went out to the people and told them what the LORD had said. He gathered 70 of the elders together and had them stand around the Tent. ²⁵Then the LORD came down in the cloud and spoke to Moses. The LORD took some of the Spirit Moses had, and he gave it to the 70 leaders. With the Spirit in them, they prophesied, *d* but just that one time.

STRESS

Exam Stress

Claire was very stressed. Her GCSEs were later that summer and her parents were fighting all the time now. They had all stopped going to church. There was nowhere calm for her to revise. Her parents finally agreed that she could go to a friend's house to stay, just until the exams were over.

Poor Claire was so wound up and worried that from the start things went horribly wrong. The first exam was her French oral. Claire was dreading it but hoped she would remember what she'd written down about her hobbies and interests. It started off well enough. Mrs Hixon asked Claire to tell her about the things she liked to do, and Claire began to say what she'd memorised. But suddenly she stopped. Her mind was a total blank. She froze in horror, completely forgetting what she was supposed to say. Mrs Hixon tried to help by asking her something in French, but Claire couldn't understand and started to get upset. She begged Mrs Hixon to turn off the tape and help her, but when Mrs Hixon replied in French, Claire blew up.

It was all a blur from then on, but Claire remembers swearing at her teacher, kicking her chair over and running from the room in tears, slamming the door behind her. Everything had got on top of her and she just couldn't cope.

In **Numbers 11:10–15** Moses got very upset too. But Moses asked God to help him with his stress so that he wouldn't react in a way he would regret.

* How do you think God wants us to deal with stress?
* When do you think you should ask for God's help – right at the beginning or just before you're about to lose it? Why?

Consider . . .

* when you have exams coming up, asking God to help you all the way through – from your coursework, to the revision, and the exam itself.
* giving your stressful situations to God and asking him to fill you with his peace and patience.

For more, see . . .

* Matthew 11:28–30 (p.960)
* 1 Peter 5:7 (p.1362)
* Galatians 5:22–23 (p.1264)

26Two men named Eldad and Medad were also listed as leaders, but they did not go to the Tent. They stayed in the camp, but the Spirit was also given to them, and they prophesied in the camp. 27A young man ran to Moses and said, "Eldad and Medad are prophesying in the camp."

28Joshua son of Nun said, "Moses, my master, stop them!" (Ever since he was a young boy, Joshua had been Moses' assistant.)

29But Moses answered, "Are you jealous for me? I wish all the LORD's people could prophesy. I wish the LORD would give his Spirit to all of them!" 30Then Moses and the leaders of Israel went back to the camp.

The LORD Sends Quail

31The LORD sent a strong wind from the sea, and it blew quail into the area all around the camp. The quail were about a metre deep on the ground, and there were quail a day's walk in any direction. 32The people went out and gathered quail all that day, that night and the next day. Everyone gathered at least a tonne, and they

---

Sidelight

If you get sick of Christmas leftovers, try to imagine having 180 turkeys left over! That's roughly the number of quail that each Israelite gathered after complaining that God hadn't provided them with meat in the desert (Numbers 11:31–32).

---

spread them around the camp. 33But the LORD became very angry, and he gave the people a terrible sickness that came while the meat was still in their mouths. 34So the people named that place Kibroth Hattaavah,^{n} because there they buried those who wanted other food.

35From Kibroth Hattaavah the people went to stay at Hazeroth.

Miriam and Aaron Speak Against Moses

12 Miriam and Aaron began to talk against Moses because of his Cushite wife (he had married a Cushite). 2They said, "Is Moses the only one the LORD speaks through? Doesn't he also speak through us?" And the LORD heard this.

3(Now Moses was very humble. He was the least proud person on earth.)

4So the LORD suddenly spoke to Moses, Aaron and Miriam and said, "All three of you come to the Meeting Tent."^{d} So they went. 5The LORD came down in a pillar of cloud and stood at the

entrance to the Tent. He called to Aaron and Miriam, and they both came near. 6He said, "Listen to my words:

When a prophet^d is among you,
I, the LORD, will show myself to him in visions;
I will speak to him in dreams.
7But this is not true with my servant Moses.
I trust him to lead all my people.
8I speak face to face with him—
clearly, not with hidden meanings.
He has even seen the form of the LORD.
You should be afraid
to speak against my servant Moses."

9The LORD was very angry with them, and he left.

10When the cloud lifted from the Tent and Aaron turned towards Miriam, she was as white as snow; she had a skin disease. 11Aaron said to Moses, "Please, my master, forgive us for our foolish sin. 12Don't let her be like a baby who is born dead. (Sometimes a baby is born with half of its flesh eaten away.)"

13So Moses cried out to the LORD, "God, please heal her!"

14The LORD answered Moses, "If her father had spat in her face, she would have been shamed for seven days, so put her outside the camp for seven days. After that, she may come back." 15So Miriam was put outside the camp for seven days, and the people did not move on until she came back.

16After that, the people left Hazeroth and camped in the Desert of Paran.

The Spies Explore Canaan

13 The LORD said to Moses, 2"Send men to explore the land of Canaan, which I will give to the Israelites. Send one leader from each tribe."^{d}

3So Moses obeyed the LORD's command and sent the Israelite leaders out from the Desert of Paran. 4These are their names: from the tribe of Reuben, Shammua son of Zaccur; 5from the tribe of Simeon, Shaphat son of Hori; 6from the tribe of Judah, Caleb son of Jephunneh; 7from the tribe of Issachar, Igal son of Joseph; 8from the tribe of Ephraim, Hoshea son of Nun; 9from the tribe of Benjamin, Palti son of Raphu; 10from the tribe of Zebulun, Gaddiel son of Sodi; 11from the tribe of Manasseh (a tribe of Joseph), Gaddi son of Susi; 12from the tribe of Dan, Ammiel son of Gemalli; 13from the tribe of Asher, Sethur son of Michael; 14from the tribe of Naphtali, Nahbi son of Vophsi; 15from the tribe of Gad, Geuel son of Maki.

Kibroth Hattaavah   This name in Hebrew means "graves of wanting".

¹⁶These are the names of the men Moses sent to explore the land. (Moses gave Hoshea son of Nun the new name Joshua.)

¹⁷Moses sent them to explore Canaan and said, "Go through southern Canaan and then into the mountains. ¹⁸See what the land looks like. Are the people who live there strong or weak? Are there a few or many? ¹⁹What kind of land do they live in? Is it good or bad? What about the towns they live in—are they open like camps, or do they have walls? ²⁰What about the soil? Is it fertile or poor? Are there trees there? Try to bring back some of the fruit from that land." (It was the season for the first grapes.)

²¹So they went up and explored the land, from the Desert of Zin all the way to Rehob by Lebo Hamath. ²²They went through the southern area to Hebron, where Ahiman, Sheshai and Talmai, the descendants ^d of Anak lived. ^d (The city of Hebron had been built seven years before Zoan in Egypt.) ²³In the Valley of Eshcol, they cut off a branch of a grapevine that had one bunch of grapes on it and carried that branch on a pole between two of them. They also got some pomegranates ^d and figs. ²⁴That place was called the Valley of Eshcol, ⁿ because the Israelites cut off the bunch of grapes there. ²⁵After 40 days of exploring the land, the men returned to the camp.

²⁶They came back to Moses and Aaron and all the Israelites at Kadesh, in the Desert of Paran. The men reported to them and showed everybody the fruit from the land. ²⁷They told Moses, "We went to the land where you sent us, and it is a fertile land! Here is some of its fruit. ²⁸But the people who live there are strong. Their cities are walled and very large. We even saw some Anakites there. ²⁹The Amalekites live in the southern area; the Hittites, Jebusites and Amorites live in the mountains; and the Canaanites live near the sea and along the Jordan River."

³⁰Then Caleb told the people near Moses to be quiet, and he said, "We should certainly go up and take the land for ourselves. We can certainly do it."

³¹But the men who had gone with him said, "We can't attack those people; they are stronger than we are." ³²And those men gave the Israelites a bad report about the land they explored, saying, "The land that we explored is too large to conquer. All the people we saw are very tall. ³³We saw the Nephilim ^d people there. (The Anakites come from the Nephilim people.) We felt like grasshoppers, and we looked like grasshoppers to them."

The People Complain Again

14 That night all the people in the camp began crying loudly. ²All the Israelites complained against Moses and Aaron, and all the people said to them, "We wish we had died in Egypt or in this desert. ³Why is the LORD bringing us to this land to be killed with swords? Our wives and children will be taken away. We would be better off going back to Egypt." ⁴They said to each other, "Let's choose a leader and go back to Egypt."

⁵Then Moses and Aaron bowed face down in front of all the Israelites gathered there. ⁶Joshua son of Nun and Caleb son of Jephunneh, who had explored the land, tore their clothes. ⁷They said to all of the Israelites, "The land we explored is very good. ⁸If the LORD is pleased with us, he will lead us into that land and give us that fertile land. ⁹Don't turn against the LORD! Don't be afraid of the people in that land! We will chew them up. They have no protection, but the LORD is with us. So don't be afraid of them."

¹⁰Then all the people talked about killing them with stones. But the glory of the LORD appeared at the Meeting Tent ^d to all the Israelites. ¹¹The LORD said to Moses, "How long will these people ignore me? How long will they not believe me in spite of the miracles ^d I have done among them? ¹²I will give them a terrible sickness and get rid of them. But I will make you into a great nation that will be stronger than they are."

¹³Then Moses said to the LORD, "The Egyptians will hear about it! You brought these people from there by your great power, ¹⁴and the Egyptians will tell this to those who live in this land. They have already heard about you, LORD. They know that you are with your people and that you were seen face to face. They know that your cloud stays over your people and that you lead your people with that cloud during the day and with fire at night. ¹⁵If you put these people to death all at once, the nations who have heard about your power will say, ¹⁶'The LORD was not able to bring them into the land he promised them. So he killed them in the desert.'

¹⁷"So show your strength now, Lord. Do what you said: ¹⁸'The LORD doesn't become angry quickly, but he has great love. He forgives sin and law breaking. But the LORD never forgets to punish guilty people. When parents sin, he will also punish their children, their grandchildren, their great-grandchildren and their great-great-grandchildren.' ¹⁹By your great love, forgive these people's sin, just as you have forgiven them from the time they left Egypt until now."

Eshcol   This name in Hebrew means "bunch".

20The LORD answered, "I have forgiven them as you asked. 21But, as surely as I live and as surely as my glory fills the whole earth, I make this promise: 22all these men saw my glory and the miracles I did in Egypt and in the desert, but they disobeyed me and tested me ten times. 23So not one of them will see the land I promised to their ancestors. No one who rejected me will see that land. 24But my servant Caleb thinks differently and follows me completely. So I will bring him into the land he has already seen, and his children will own that land. 25Since the Amalekites and the Canaanites are living in the valleys, leave tomorrow and follow the desert road towards the Red Sea."

The LORD Punishes the People

26The LORD said to Moses and Aaron, 27"How long will these evil people complain about me? I have heard the grumbling and complaining of these Israelites. 28So tell them, 'This is what the LORD says. I heard what you said, and as surely as I live, I will do those very things to you: 29you will die in this desert. Every one of you who is 20 years old or older and who was counted with the people—all of you who complained against me—will die. 30Not one of you will enter the land where I promised you would live; only Caleb son of Jephunneh and Joshua son of Nun will go in. 31You said that your children would be taken away, but I will bring them into the land to enjoy what you refused. 32As for you, you will die in this desert. 33Your children will be shepherds here for 40 years. Because you were not loyal, they will suffer until you lie dead in the desert. 34For 40 years you will suffer for your sins—a year for each of the 40 days you explored the land. You will know me as your enemy.' 35I, the LORD, have spoken, and I will certainly do these things to all these evil people who have come together against me. So they will all die here in this desert."

36The men Moses had sent to explore the land had returned and spread complaints among all the people. They had given a bad report about the land. 37The men who gave a very bad report died; the LORD killed them with a terrible sickness. 38Only two of the men who explored the land did not die—Joshua son of Nun and Caleb son of Jephunneh.

39When Moses told these things to all the Israelites, they were very sad. 40Early the next morning they started to go towards the top of the mountains, saying, "We have sinned. We will go where the LORD told us."

41But Moses said, "Why are you disobeying the LORD's command? You will not win! 42Don't go, because the LORD is not with you and you will be beaten by your enemies. 43You will run into the Amalekites and Canaanites, who will kill you with swords. You have turned away from the LORD, so the LORD will not be with you."

44But they were proud. They went towards the top of the mountains, but Moses and the Ark *d* of the Agreement with the LORD did not leave the camp. 45The Amalekites and the Canaanites who lived in those mountains came down and attacked the Israelites and beat them back all the way to Hormah.

Rules About Sacrifices

15 The LORD said to Moses, 2"Speak to the Israelites and say to them, 'When you enter the land that I am giving you as a home, 3give the LORD offerings made by fire. These may be from your herds or flocks, as a smell pleasing to the LORD. These may be burnt offerings or sacrifices for special promises, or as gifts to him, or as festival offerings. 4The one who brings the offering shall also give the LORD a grain offering. It should be 2 litres of fine flour mixed with 1 litre of olive oil. 5Each time you offer a lamb as a burnt offering or sacrifice, also prepare 1 litre of wine as a drink offering.

6" 'If you are giving a ram, also prepare a grain offering of 4 litres of fine flour mixed with one and a half litres of olive oil. 7Also prepare one and a half litres of wine as a drink offering. Its smell will be pleasing to the LORD.

8" 'If you prepare a young bull as a burnt offering or sacrifice, whether it is for a special promise or a fellowship offering to the LORD, 9bring a grain offering with the bull. It should be 7 litres of fine flour mixed with 2 litres of olive oil. 10Also bring 2 litres of wine as a drink offering. This offering is made by fire, and its smell will be pleasing to the LORD. 11Prepare each bull or ram, lamb or young goat in this way. 12Do this for every one of the animals you bring.

13" 'All citizens must do these things in this way, and the smell of their offerings by fire will be pleasing to the LORD. 14From now on if foreigners who live among you want to make offerings by fire so the smell will be pleasing to the LORD, they must offer them in the same way that you do. 15The law is the same for you and for foreigners, and it will be from now on; you and the foreigners are alike before the LORD. 16The teachings and rules are the same for you and for the foreigners among you.' "

17The LORD said to Moses, 18"Tell the Israelites: 'You are going to another land, where I am taking you. 19When you eat the food there, offer part of it to the LORD. 20Offer a loaf of bread from the first of your grain, which will be your offering from the threshing *d* floor. ²¹From now on offer to the LORD the first part of your grain.

²²" 'Now what if you forget to obey any of these commands the LORD gave Moses? ²³These are the LORD's commands given to you through Moses, which began the day the LORD gave them to you and will continue from now on. ²⁴If the people forget to obey one of these commands, all the people must offer a young bull as a burnt offering, a smell pleasing to the LORD. By law you must also give the grain offering and the drink offering with it, and you must bring a male goat as a sin offering.

²⁵" 'The priest will remove that sin for all the Israelites so they will belong to the LORD. They are forgiven, because they didn't know they were sinning. For the wrong they did they brought offerings to the LORD, an offering by fire and a sin offering. ²⁶So all of the people of Israel and the foreigners living among them will be forgiven. No one meant to do wrong.

²⁷" 'If just one person sins without meaning to, a year-old female goat must be brought for a sin offering. ²⁸The priest will remove the sin of the person who sinned accidentally. He will remove it before the LORD, and the person will be forgiven. ²⁹The same teaching is for everyone who sins accidentally—for those born Israelites and for foreigners living among you.

³⁰" 'But anyone who sins on purpose is against the LORD and must be cut off from the people, whether it is someone born among you or a foreigner. ³¹That person has turned against the LORD's word and has not obeyed his commands. Such a person must surely be cut off from the others. He is guilty.' "

A Man Worked on the Sabbath

³²When the Israelites were still in the desert, they found a man gathering wood on the Sabbath *d* day. ³³Those who found him gathering wood brought him to Moses and Aaron and all the people. ³⁴They held the man under guard, because they did not know what to do with him. ³⁵Then the LORD said to Moses, "The man must surely die. All the people must kill him by throwing stones at him outside the camp." ³⁶So all the people took him outside the camp and stoned him to death, as the LORD commanded Moses.

The Tassels

³⁷The LORD said to Moses, ³⁸"Speak to the Israelites and tell them this: 'Tie several pieces of thread together and attach them to the corners of your clothes. Put a blue thread in each one of these tassels. Wear them from now on. ³⁹You will have these tassels to look at to remind you of

all the LORD's commands. Then you will obey them and not be disloyal by following what your bodies and eyes want. ⁴⁰Then you will remember to obey all my commands, and you will be God's holy people. ⁴¹I am the LORD your God, who brought you out of Egypt to be your God. I am the LORD your God.' "

Korah, Dathan, Abiram and On

16 Korah, Dathan, Abiram and On turned against Moses. (Korah was the son of Izhar, the son of Kohath, the son of Levi; Dathan and Abiram were brothers, the sons of Eliab; and On was the son of Peleth; Dathan, Abiram and On were from the tribe *d* of Reuben.) ²These men gathered 250 other Israelite men, well-known leaders chosen by the community, and challenged Moses. ³They came as a group to speak to Moses and Aaron and said, "You have gone too far. All the people are holy, every one of them, and the LORD is among them. So why do you put yourselves above all the people of the LORD?"

⁴When Moses heard this, he bowed face down. ⁵Then he said to Korah and all his followers: "Tomorrow morning the LORD will show who belongs to him. He will bring the one who is holy near to him; he will bring to himself the person he chooses. ⁶So Korah, you and all your followers do this: get some pans for burning incense. *d* ⁷Tomorrow put fire and incense in them and take them before the LORD. He will choose the man who is holy. You Levites have gone too far."

⁸Moses also said to Korah, "Listen, you Levites. ⁹The God of Israel has separated you from the rest of the Israelites. He brought you near to himself to do the work in the LORD's Holy Tent *d* and to stand before all the Israelites and serve them. Isn't that enough? ¹⁰He has brought you and all your fellow Levites near to himself, yet now you want to be priests. ¹¹You and your followers have joined together against the LORD. Your complaint is not against Aaron."

¹²Then Moses called Dathan and Abiram, the sons of Eliab, but they said, "We will not come! ¹³You have brought us out of a fertile land to this desert to kill us, and now you want to order us around. ¹⁴You haven't brought us into a fertile land; you haven't given us any land with fields and vineyards. Will you put out the eyes of these men? No! We will not come!"

¹⁵Then Moses became very angry and said to the LORD, "Don't accept their gifts. I have not taken anything from them, not even a donkey, and I have not done wrong to any of them."

¹⁶Then Moses said to Korah, "You and all your followers must stand before the LORD tomorrow. And Aaron will stand there with you and them.

¹⁷Each of you must take your pan and put incense in it; present these 250 pans before the LORD. You and Aaron must also present your pans." ¹⁸So each man got his pan and put burning incense in it and stood with Moses and Aaron at the entrance to the Meeting Tent. ¹⁹Korah gathered all his followers who were against Moses and Aaron, and they stood at the entrance to the Meeting Tent. Then the glory of the LORD appeared to everyone.

²⁰The LORD said to Moses and Aaron, ²¹"Move away from these men so I can destroy them quickly."

²²But Moses and Aaron bowed face down and cried out, "God, you are the God over the spirits of all people. Please don't be angry with this whole group. Only one man has really sinned."

²³Then the LORD said to Moses, ²⁴"Tell everyone to move away from the tents of Korah, Dathan and Abiram."

²⁵Moses stood and went to Dathan and Abiram; the elders of Israel followed him. ²⁶Moses warned the people, "Move away from the tents of these evil men! Don't touch anything of theirs, or you will be destroyed because of their sins." ²⁷So they moved away from the tents of Korah, Dathan and Abiram. Dathan and Abiram were standing outside their tents with their wives, children and little babies.

²⁸Then Moses said, "Now you will know that the LORD has sent me to do all these things; it was not my idea. ²⁹If these men die a normal death—the way men usually die—then the LORD did not really send me. ³⁰But if the LORD does something new, you will know they have insulted the LORD. The ground will open and swallow them. They will be buried alive and will go to the place of the dead, and everything that belongs to them will go with them."

³¹When Moses finished saying these things, the ground under the men split open. ³²The earth opened and swallowed them and all their families. All Korah's men and everything they owned went down. ³³They were buried alive, going to the place of the dead, and everything they owned went with them. Then the earth covered them. They died and were gone from the community. ³⁴The people of Israel around them heard their screams and ran away, saying, "The earth will swallow us, too!"

³⁵Then a fire came down from the LORD and destroyed the 250 men who had presented the incense.

³⁶The LORD said to Moses, ³⁷"Tell Eleazar son of Aaron, the priest, to take all the incense pans out of the fire. Have him scatter the coals a long distance away. But the incense pans are still holy.

³⁸Take the pans of these men who sinned and lost their lives, and hammer them into flat sheets that will be used to cover the altar. They are holy, because they were presented to the LORD, and they will be a sign to the Israelites."

³⁹So Eleazar the priest gathered all the bronze pans that had been brought by the men who were burned up. He had the pans hammered into flat sheets to put on the altar, ⁴⁰as the LORD had commanded him through Moses. These sheets were to remind the Israelites that only descendants ᵈ of Aaron should burn incense before the LORD. Anyone else would die like Korah and his followers.

Aaron Saves the People

⁴¹The next day all the Israelites complained against Moses and Aaron and said, "You have killed the LORD's people."

⁴²When the people gathered to complain against Moses and Aaron, they turned towards the Meeting Tent, ᵈ and the cloud covered it. The glory of the LORD appeared. ⁴³Then Moses and Aaron went in front of the Meeting Tent.

⁴⁴The LORD said to Moses, ⁴⁵"Move away from these people so I can destroy them quickly." So Moses and Aaron bowed face down.

⁴⁶Then Moses said to Aaron, "Get your pan, and put fire from the altar and incense ᵈ in it. Hurry to the people and remove their sin. The LORD is angry with them; the sickness has already started." ⁴⁷So Aaron did as Moses said. He ran to the middle of the people, where the sickness had already started among them. So Aaron offered the incense to remove their sin. ⁴⁸He stood between the dead and the living, and the sickness stopped there. ⁴⁹But 14,700 people died from that sickness, in addition to those who died because of Korah. ⁵⁰Then Aaron went back to Moses at the entrance to the Meeting Tent. The terrible sickness had been stopped.

Aaron's Walking Stick Buds

17 The LORD said to Moses, ²"Speak to the people of Israel and get twelve walking sticks from them—one from the leader of each tribe.ᵈ Write the name of each man on his stick, and ³on the stick from Levi, write Aaron's name. There must be one stick for the head of each tribe. ⁴Put them in the Meeting Tent ᵈ in front of the Ark ᵈ of the Agreement, where I meet with you. ⁵I will choose one man whose walking stick will begin to grow leaves; in this way I will stop the Israelites from always complaining against you."

⁶So Moses spoke to the Israelites. Each of the twelve leaders gave him a walking stick—one

from each tribe—and Aaron's walking stick was among them. [7]Moses put them before the LORD in the Tent of the Agreement.

[8]The next day, when Moses entered the Tent, he saw that Aaron's stick (which stood for the family of Levi) had grown leaves. It had even budded, blossomed and produced almonds. [9]So Moses brought out to the Israelites all the walking sticks from the LORD's presence. They all looked, and each man took back his stick.

[10]Then the LORD said to Moses, "Put Aaron's walking stick back in front of the Ark of the Agreement. It will remind these people who are always turning against me to stop their complaining against me so they won't die." [11]So Moses obeyed what the LORD commanded him.

[12]The people of Israel said to Moses, "We are going to die! We are destroyed. We are all destroyed! [13]Anyone who even comes near the Holy Tent of the LORD will die. Will we all die?"

The Work of the Priests and Levites

18 The LORD said to Aaron, "You, your sons and your family are now responsible for any wrongs done against the Holy Place; you and your sons are responsible for any wrongs done against the priests. [2]Bring with you your fellow Levites from your tribe, [d] and they will help you and your sons serve in the Tent [d] of the Agreement. [3]They are under your control, to do all the work that needs to be done in the Tent. But they must not go near the things in the Holy Place or near the altar. If they do, both you and they will die. [4]They will join you in taking care of the Meeting Tent. They must do the work at the Tent, and no one else may come near you.

[5]"You must take care of the Holy Place and the altar so that I won't become angry with the Israelites again. [6]I myself chose your fellow Levites from among the Israelites as a gift given for you to the LORD, to work at the Meeting Tent. [7]But only you and your sons may serve as priests. Only you may serve at the altar or go behind the curtain. I am giving you this gift of serving as a priest, and anyone else who comes near the Holy Place will be put to death."

[8]Then the LORD said to Aaron, "I myself make you responsible for the offerings given to me. All the holy offerings that the Israelites give to me, I give to you and your sons as your share, your continual portion. [9]Your share of the holy offerings is that part which is not burned. When the people bring me gifts as most holy offerings, whether they are grain or sin or penalty offerings, they will be set apart for you and your sons.

[10]You must eat the offering in a most holy place. Any male may eat it, but you must respect it as holy.

[11]"I also give you the offerings the Israelites present to me. I give these to you and your sons and daughters as your continual share. Anyone in your family who is clean [d] may eat it.

[12]"And I give you all the best olive oil and all the best new wine and grain. This is what the Israelites give to me, the LORD, from the first crops they harvest. [13]When they bring to the LORD all the first things they harvest, they will be yours. Anyone in your family who is clean may eat these things.

[14]"Everything in Israel that is given to the LORD is yours. [15]The first one born to any family, whether people or animals, will be offered to the LORD. And that will be yours. But you must make a payment for every firstborn [d] child and every firstborn animal that is unclean. [16]When they are one month old, you must make a payment for them of 5 pieces of silver, as set by the Holy Place measure.

> **Sidelight**   Your parents may say you're priceless, but the ancient Hebrews knew exactly how much a baby was worth. Numbers 18:15–16 tells how parents had to offer their child to God and then buy it back for about 60 grammes of silver when the baby was a month old.

[17]"But you must not make a payment for the firstborn ox or sheep or goat. Those animals are holy. Sprinkle their blood on the altar and burn their fat as an offering made by fire. The smell is pleasing to the LORD. [18]But the meat will be yours, just as the breast that is presented and the right thigh will be yours. [19]Anything the Israelites present as holy gifts I, the LORD, give to you, your sons and daughters as your continual portion. This is a lasting agreement of salt [n] before the LORD for you and your children for ever."

[20]The LORD also said to Aaron, "You will not inherit any of the land, and you will not own any land among the other people. I will be yours. Out of all the Israelites, only you will inherit me.

[21]"When the people of Israel give me a tenth of what they make, I will give that tenth to the Levites. This is their payment for the work they do serving at the Meeting Tent. [22]But the other Israelites must never go near the Meeting Tent, or they will die for their sin. [23]Only the Levites

---

agreement of salt   The meaning is not clear, but Leviticus 2:13 says, "Salt stands for your agreement with God that will last for ever."

should work in the Meeting Tent and be responsible for any sins against it. This is a rule from now on. The Levites will not inherit any land among the other Israelites, 24but when the Israelites give a tenth of everything they make to me, I will give that tenth to the Levites as a reward. That is why I said about the Levites: 'They will not inherit any land among the Israelites.'"

25The LORD said to Moses, 26"Speak to the Levites and tell them: 'You will receive a tenth of everything the Israelites make, which I will give to you. But you must give a tenth of that back to the LORD. 27I will accept your offering just as much as I accept the offerings from others, who give new grain or new wine. 28In this way you will present an offering to the LORD as the other Israelites do. When you receive a tenth from the Israelites, you will give a tenth of that to Aaron, the priest, as the LORD's share. 29Choose the best and holiest part from what you are given as the portion you must give to the LORD.'

30"Say to the Levites: 'When you present the best, it will be accepted as much as the grain and wine from the other people. 31You and your families may eat all that is left anywhere, because it is your pay for your work in the Meeting Tent. 32And if you always give the best part to the LORD, you will never be guilty. If you do not sin against the holy offerings of the Israelites, you will not die.'"

The Offering for Cleansing

19 The LORD said to Moses and Aaron, 2"These are the teachings that the LORD commanded. Tell the Israelites to get a young red cow that does not have anything wrong with it and that has never been worked. 3Give the cow to Eleazar the priest; he will take it outside the camp and kill it. 4Then Eleazar the priest must put some of its blood on his finger and sprinkle it seven times towards the front of the Meeting Tent. *d* 5The whole cow must be burned while he watches; the skin, the meat, the blood and the intestines must all be burned. 6Then the priest must take a cedar stick, a hyssop branch and a red string and throw them onto the burning cow. 7After the priest has washed himself and his clothes with water, he may come back into the camp, but he will be unclean *d* until evening. 8The man who burns the cow must wash himself and his clothes in water; he will be unclean until evening.

9"Then someone who is clean will collect the ashes from the cow and put them in a clean place outside the camp. The Israelites will keep these ashes to use in the cleansing water, in a special ceremony to cleanse away sin. 10The man who collected the cow's ashes must wash his clothes and be unclean until evening. This is a lasting rule for the Israelites and for the foreigners among them.

11"Those who touch a dead person's body will be unclean for seven days. 12They must wash themselves with the cleansing water on the third day and on the seventh day; then they will be clean. But if they do not wash themselves on the third day and the seventh day, they cannot be clean. 13If those who touch a dead person's body stay unclean and go to the LORD's Holy Tent, it becomes unclean; they must be cut off from Israel. If the cleansing water is not sprinkled on them, they are unclean and will stay unclean.

14"This is the teaching about someone who dies in a tent: anyone in the tent or anyone who enters it will be unclean for seven days. 15And every open jar or pot without a cover becomes unclean. 16If anyone is outside and touches someone who was killed by a sword or who died a natural death, or if anyone touches a human bone or a grave, that person will be unclean for seven days.

17"So you must use the ashes from the burnt offering to make that person clean again. Pour fresh water over the ashes into a jar. 18A clean person must take a hyssop branch and dip it into the water, and then he must sprinkle it over the Tent and all its objects. He must also sprinkle the people who were there, as well as anyone who touched a bone, or the body of someone who was killed, or a dead person, or a grave. 19The person who is clean must sprinkle this water on the unclean people on the third day and on the seventh day. On the seventh day they will become clean. They must wash their clothes and take a bath, and they will be clean that evening. 20If any who are unclean do not become clean, they must be cut off from the community. Since they were not sprinkled with the cleansing water, they stay unclean, and they could make the LORD's Holy Tent unclean. 21This is a lasting rule. Those who sprinkle the cleansing water must also wash their clothes, and anyone who touches the water will be unclean until evening. 22Anything an unclean person touches becomes unclean, and whoever touches it will be unclean until evening."

Moses Disobeys God

20 In the first month all the people of Israel arrived at the Desert of Zin, and they stayed at Kadesh. There Miriam died and was buried. 2There was no water for the people, so they came together against Moses and Aaron. 3They argued with Moses and said, "We should have died in front of the LORD as our brothers did. 4Why did you bring the LORD's people into this desert? Are we and our animals to die here?

⁵Why did you bring us from Egypt to this terrible place? It has no grain, figs, grapevines or pomegranates, *d* and there's no water to drink!"

⁶So Moses and Aaron left the people and went to the entrance of the Meeting Tent. *d* There they bowed face down, and the glory of the LORD appeared to them. ⁷The LORD said to Moses, ⁸"Take your walking stick, and you and your brother Aaron should gather the people. Speak to that rock in front of them so that its water will flow from it. When you bring the water out from that rock, give it to the people and their animals."

⁹So Moses took the stick from in front of the LORD, as he had said. ¹⁰Moses and Aaron gathered the people in front of the rock, and Moses said, "Now listen to me, you who turn against God! Do you want us to bring water out of this rock?" ¹¹Then Moses lifted his hand and hit the rock twice with his stick. Water began pouring out, and the people and their animals drank it.

¹²But the LORD said to Moses and Aaron, "Because you did not believe me, and because you did not honour me as holy before the people, you will not lead them into the land I will give them."

¹³These are the waters of Meribah, *n* where the Israelites argued with the LORD and where he showed them he was holy.

Edom will Not Let Israel Pass

¹⁴From Kadesh, Moses sent messengers to the king of Edom. He said, "Your brothers, the Israelites, say to you: you know about all the troubles we have had, ¹⁵how our ancestors went down into Egypt and we lived there for many years. The people of Egypt were cruel to us and our ancestors, ¹⁶but when we cried out to the LORD, he heard us and sent us an angel to bring us out of Egypt.

"Now we are here at Kadesh, a town on the edge of your land. ¹⁷Please let us pass through your country. We will not touch any fields of grain or vineyards, and will not drink water from the wells. We will travel only along the king's road, not turning right or left until we have passed through your country."

¹⁸But the king of Edom answered: "You may not pass through here. If you try, I will come and meet you with swords."

¹⁹The Israelites answered: "We will go along the main road, and if we or our animals drink any of your water, we will pay for it. We only want to walk through. That's all."

²⁰But he answered: "You may not pass through here."

Then the Edomites went out to meet the Israelites with a large and powerful army. ²¹The Edomites refused to let them pass through their country, so the Israelites turned back.

Aaron Dies

²²All the Israelites moved from Kadesh to Mount Hor, ²³near the border of Edom. There the LORD said to Moses and Aaron, ²⁴"Aaron will die. He will not enter the land that I'm giving to the Israelites, because you both acted against my command at the waters of Meribah. ²⁵Take Aaron and his son Eleazar up on Mount Hor, ²⁶and take off Aaron's special clothes and put them on his son Eleazar. Aaron will die there; he will join his ancestors."

²⁷Moses obeyed the LORD's command. They climbed up Mount Hor, and all the people saw them go. ²⁸Moses took off Aaron's clothes and put them on Aaron's son Eleazar. Then Aaron died there on top of the mountain. Moses and Eleazar came back down the mountain, ²⁹and when all the people learned that Aaron was dead, everyone in Israel cried for him for 30 days.

War with the Canaanites

21 The Canaanite king of Arad lived in the southern area. When he heard that the Israelites were coming on the road to Atharim, he attacked them and captured some of them. ²Then the Israelites made this promise to the LORD: "If you will help us defeat these people, we will completely destroy their cities." ³The LORD listened to the Israelites, and he let them defeat the Canaanites. The Israelites completely destroyed the Canaanites and their cities, so the place was named Hormah. *n*

The Bronze Snake

⁴The Israelites left Mount Hor and went on the road towards the Red Sea, in order to go around the country of Edom. But the people became impatient on the way ⁵and grumbled at God and Moses. They said, "Why did you bring us out of Egypt to die in this desert? There is no bread and no water, and we hate this terrible food!"

⁶So the LORD sent them poisonous snakes; they bit the people, and many of the Israelites died. ⁷The people came to Moses and said, "We sinned when we grumbled at you and the LORD. Pray that the LORD will take away these snakes." So Moses prayed for the people.

⁸The LORD said to Moses, "Make a bronze snake, and put it on a pole. When anyone who is

---

Meribah This name in Hebrew means "argument".
Hormah This name in Hebrew means "completely destroyed".

bitten looks at it, that person will live." ⁹So Moses made a bronze snake and put it on a pole. Then when a snake bit anyone, that person looked at the bronze snake and lived.

The Journey to Moab

¹⁰The Israelites went and camped at Oboth. ¹¹They went from Oboth to Iye Abarim, in the desert east of Moab. ¹²From there they went and camped in the Zered Valley. ¹³From there they went and camped across the Arnon, in the desert just inside the Amorite country. The Arnon is the border between the Moabites and the Amorites. ¹⁴That is why the Book of the Wars of the LORD says:

". . . and Waheb in Suphah, and the ravines,
    the Arnon, ¹⁵and the slopes of the ravines
    that lead to the settlement of Ar.
These places are at the border of Moab."

¹⁶The Israelites went from there to Beer; a well is there where the LORD said to Moses, "Gather the people and I will give them water."

¹⁷Then the Israelites sang this song:
"Pour out water, well!
    Sing about it.
¹⁸Princes dug this well.
    Important men made it.
    With their sceptres ᵈ and poles, they
        dug it."

The people went from the desert to Mattanah. ¹⁹From Mattanah they went to Nahaliel and on to Bamoth. ²⁰From Bamoth they went to the valley of Moab where the top of Mount Pisgah looks over the desert.

Israel Kills Sihon and Og

²¹The Israelites sent messengers to Sihon, king of the Amorites, saying, ²²"Let us pass through

DISCOURAGEMENT

Keep Your Chin Up

People can be very annoying. Just when you are feeling your absolute worst, one really insensitive comment from a friend can leave you even more discouraged than you were before they tried to help! But comments like "Keep your chin up!" from well-meaning mates probably speak a lot more truth and wisdom than we may be willing to admit or even accept.

The Israelites were getting fed up with wandering around in the desert (**Numbers 21:4–9**). Despite the fact that God was providing all they needed, they were getting really discouraged. They were finding it hard to see the positive side of life and then, when they thought it couldn't get any worse, they were plagued by poisonous snakes!

But Moses offered them, and us, a simple God-inspired suggestion: "Keep your chin up!" By looking up at the bronze snake, the poison from the snakebites would be stopped and their bites would be healed. However, it wasn't so much the act of looking at a bronze snake on a pole that was important. It was the act of looking up to God – the encourager – that brought healing.

Feeling down about life can be a poison too. As the venom of depression, hurtful comments or stress hits, it might be worth listening to the advice of your mates and of Moses: "Keep your chin up!"

* What are the snakebite-type problems that are getting at you at the moment?
* What could the "keep your chin up" approach to your problems do to change the way you deal with the tough stuff life throws at you?

Consider . . .

* making a list of all the things that are getting you down at the moment. Now play the "Glad Game". For every thing you have listed that is getting you down, match it with something that is positive in your life.
* finding ways to support someone who is worse off than you.

For more, see . . .

* Psalm 56 (p.532)
* Hebrews 12:2–3 (p.1343)
* Philippians 4:8 (p.1286)

your country. We will not go through any fields of grain or vineyards, or drink water from the wells. We will travel only along the king's road until we have passed through your country."

23But King Sihon would not let the Israelites pass through his country. He gathered his whole army together, and they marched out to meet Israel in the desert. At Jahaz they fought the Israelites. 24Israel killed the king and captured his land from the Arnon River to the Jabbok River. They took the land as far as the Ammonite border, which was strongly defended. 25Israel captured all the Amorite cities and lived in them, taking Heshbon and all the towns around it. 26Heshbon was the city where Sihon, the Amorite king, lived. In the past he had fought with the king of Moab and had taken all the land as far as the Arnon.

27That is why the poets say:
"Come to Heshbon
   and rebuild it;
   rebuild Sihon's city.
28A fire began in Heshbon;
   flames came from Sihon's city.
It destroyed Ar in Moab,
   and it burned the Arnon highlands.
29How terrible for you, Moab!
   The people of Chemosh *d* are ruined.
His sons ran away
   and his daughters were captured
   by Sihon, king of the Amorites.
30But we defeated those Amorites.
   We ruined their towns from Heshbon to
      Dibon,
   and we destroyed them as far as Nophah,
      near Medeba."

31So Israel lived in the land of the Amorites.

32After Moses sent spies to the town of Jazer, they captured the towns around it, forcing out the Amorites who lived there.

33Then the Israelites went up the road towards Bashan. Og king of Bashan and his whole army marched out to meet the Israelites, and they fought at Edrei.

34The LORD said to Moses, "Don't be afraid of him. I will hand him, his whole army and his land over to you. Do to him what you did to Sihon, the Amorite king who lived in Heshbon."

35So the Israelites killed Og and his sons and all his army; no one was left alive. And they took his land.

Balak Sends for Balaam

22 Then the people of Israel went to the plains of Moab, and they camped near the Jordan River across from Jericho.

2Balak son of Zippor saw everything the Israelites had done to the Amorites. 3And Moab was scared of so many Israelites; truly, Moab was terrified by them.

4The Moabites said to the elders of Midian, "These people will take everything around us like an ox eating grass."

Balak son of Zippor was the king of Moab at this time. 5He sent messengers to Balaam son of Beor at Pethor, near the Euphrates River in his native land. Balak said, "A nation has come out of Egypt that covers the land. They have camped next to me, 6and they are too powerful for me. So come and put a curse on them. Maybe then I can defeat them and make them leave the area. I know that if you bless someone, the blessings happen, and if you put a curse on someone, it happens."

7The elders of Moab and Midian went with payment in their hands. When they found Balaam, they told him what Balak had said.

8Balaam said to them, "Stay here for the night, and I will tell you what the LORD tells me." So the Moabite leaders stayed with him.

9God came to Balaam and asked, "Who are these men with you?"

10Balaam said to God, "The king of Moab, Balak son of Zippor, sent them to me with this message: 11'A nation has come out of Egypt that covers the land. So come and put a curse on them, and maybe I can fight them and force them out of my land.'"

12But God said to Balaam, "Do not go with them. Don't put a curse on those people, because I have blessed them."

13The next morning Balaam awoke and said to Balak's leaders, "Go back to your own country; the LORD has refused to let me go with you."

14So the Moabite leaders went back to Balak and said, "Balaam refused to come with us."

15So Balak sent other leaders—this time there were more of them, and they were more important. 16They went to Balaam and said, "Balak son of Zippor says this: Please don't let anything stop you from coming to me. 17I will pay you very well, and I will do what you say. Come and put a curse on these people for me."

18But Balaam answered Balak's servants, "King Balak could give me his palace full of silver and gold, but I cannot disobey the LORD my God in anything, great or small. 19You stay here tonight as the other men did, and I will find out what more the LORD tells me."

20That night God came to Balaam and said, "These men have come to ask you to go with them. Go, but only do what I tell you."

Balaam's Donkey Speaks

21Balaam got up the next morning and put a saddle on his donkey. Then he went with the

Moabite leaders. ²²But God became angry because Balaam went, so the angel of the LORD stood in the road to stop Balaam. Balaam was riding his donkey, and he had two servants with him. ²³When the donkey saw the angel of the LORD standing in the road with a sword in his hand, the donkey left the road and went into the field. Balaam hit the donkey to force her back on the road.

²⁴Later, the angel of the LORD stood on a narrow path between two vineyards, with walls on both sides. ²⁵Again the donkey saw the angel of the LORD, and she walked close to one wall, crushing Balaam's foot against it. So he hit her again.

²⁶The angel of the LORD went ahead again and stood at a narrow place, too narrow to turn left or right. ²⁷When the donkey saw the angel of the LORD, she lay down under Balaam. This made him so angry that he hit her with his stick. ²⁸Then the LORD made the donkey talk, and she said to Balaam, "What have I done to make you hit me three times?"

²⁹Balaam answered the donkey, "You have made me look foolish! I wish I had a sword in my hand! I would kill you right now!"

³⁰But the donkey said to Balaam, "I am your very own donkey, which you have ridden for years. Have I ever done this to you before?"

"No," Balaam said.

> ### Sidelight
>
> When pets talk, people listen. At least, Balaam listened when his donkey talked (Numbers 22:21–30). And it's good that he listened, because the donkey's advice kept him out of some serious trouble. But Balaam later led the Israelites to sin (Numbers 31:16, p.159), which is why Bible writers consider him evil (see, for example, 2 Peter 2:15–16, p.1366, and Revelation 2:14, p.1390).

³¹Then the LORD let Balaam see the angel of the LORD, who was standing in the road with his sword drawn. Then Balaam bowed face down on the ground.

³²The angel of the LORD asked Balaam, "Why have you hit your donkey three times? I have stood here to stop you, because what you are doing is wrong. ³³The donkey saw me and turned away from me three times. If she had not turned away, I would have killed you by now, but I would have let her live."

³⁴Then Balaam said to the angel of the LORD, "I have sinned; I did not know you were standing in the road to stop me. If I am wrong, I will go back."

³⁵The angel of the LORD said to Balaam, "Go with these men, but say only what I tell you." So Balaam went with Balak's leaders.

³⁶When Balak heard that Balaam was coming, he went out to meet him at Ar in Moab, which was beside the Arnon, at the edge of his country. ³⁷Balak said to Balaam, "I had asked you before to come quickly. Why didn't you come to me? I am able to reward you well."

³⁸But Balaam answered, "I have come to you now, but I can't say just anything. I can only say what God tells me to say."

³⁹Then Balaam went with Balak to Kiriath Huzoth. ⁴⁰Balak offered cattle and sheep as a sacrifice and gave some meat to Balaam and the leaders with him.

⁴¹The next morning Balak took Balaam to Bamoth Baal; from there he could see the edge of the Israelite camp.

Balaam's First Message

23 Balaam said to Balak, "Build me seven altars here, and prepare seven bulls and seven rams for me." ²Balak did what Balaam asked, and they offered a bull and a ram on each of the altars.

³Then Balaam said to Balak, "Stay here beside your burnt offering and I will go. If the LORD comes to me, I will tell you whatever he shows me." Then Balaam went to a higher place.

⁴God came to Balaam there, and Balaam said to him, "I have prepared seven altars, and I have offered a bull and a ram on each altar."

⁵The LORD told Balaam what he should say. Then the LORD said, "Go back to Balak and give him this message."

⁶So Balaam went back to Balak. Balak and all the leaders of Moab were still standing beside his burnt offering ⁷when Balaam gave them this message:

"Balak brought me here from Aram;
　　the king of Moab brought me from the
　　　eastern mountains.
Balak said, 'Come, put a curse on the people
　　of Jacob for me.
　Come, call down evil on the people of
　　Israel.'
⁸But God has not cursed them,
　　so I cannot curse them.
The LORD has not called down evil on them,
　　so I cannot call down evil on them.
⁹I see them from the top of the mountains;
　　I see them from the hills.
I see a people who live alone,
　　who think they are different from other
　　　nations.
¹⁰No one can number the many people of
　　Jacob,

and no one can count a fourth of Israel.
Let me die like good men,
    and let me end up like them!"

¹¹Balak said to Balaam, "What have you done to me? I brought you here to curse my enemies, but you have only blessed them!"

¹²But Balaam answered, "I must say what the LORD tells me to say."

Balaam's Second Message

¹³Then Balak said to him, "Come with me to another place, where you can also see the people. But you can only see part of them, not all of them. Curse them for me from there." ¹⁴So Balak took Balaam to the field of Zophim, on top of Mount Pisgah. There Balak built seven altars and offered a bull and a ram on each altar.

¹⁵So Balaam said to Balak, "Stay here by your burnt offering, and I will meet with God over there."

¹⁶So the LORD came to Balaam and told him what to say. Then he said, "Go back to Balak and say such and such."

¹⁷So Balaam went to Balak, where he and the leaders of Moab were standing beside his burnt offering. Balak asked him, "What did the LORD say?"

¹⁸Then Balaam gave this message:
"Stand up, Balak, and listen.
    Hear me, son of Zippor.
¹⁹God is not a human being, and he will
        not lie.
    He is not a human, and he does not
        change his mind.
    What he says he will do, he does.
    What he promises, he makes come true.
²⁰He told me to bless them,
    so I cannot change the blessing.
²¹He has found no wrong in the people of
        Jacob;
    he saw no fault in Israel.
    The LORD their God is with them,
        and they praise their King.
²²God brought them out of Egypt;
    they are as strong as a wild ox.
²³No tricks will work on the people of Jacob,
    and no magic will work against Israel.
    People now say about them,
    'Look what God has done for Israel!'
²⁴The people rise up like a lioness;
    they get up like a lion.
    Lions don't rest until they have eaten,
        until they have drunk their enemies'
            blood."

²⁵Then Balak said to Balaam, "You haven't cursed these people, so at least, don't bless them!"

²⁶Balaam answered Balak, "I told you before that I can only do what the LORD tells me."

Balaam's Third Message

²⁷Then Balak said to Balaam, "Come, I will take you to another place. Maybe God will be pleased to let you curse them from there." ²⁸So Balak took Balaam to the top of Peor, the mountain that looks over the desert.

²⁹Balaam told Balak, "Build me seven altars here and prepare for me seven bulls and seven rams." ³⁰Balak did what Balaam asked, and he offered a bull and a ram on each altar.

24 Balaam saw that the LORD wanted to bless Israel, so he did not try to use any magic but looked towards the desert. ²When Balaam saw the Israelites camped in their tribes, *d* the Spirit *d* of God took control of him, ³and he gave this message:
"This is the message of Balaam son of Beor,
    the message of a man who sees clearly;
⁴this is the message of a man who hears the
        words of God.
    I see a vision from the Almighty,
        and my eyes are open as I fall before him.
⁵Your tents are beautiful, people of Jacob!
    So are your homes, Israel!
⁶Your tents spread out like valleys,
    like gardens beside a river.
    They are like spices planted by the LORD,
        like cedar trees growing by the water.
⁷Israel's water buckets will always be full,
    and their crops will have plenty of water.
    Their king will be greater than Agag;
        their kingdom will be very great.
⁸God brought them out of Egypt;
    they are as strong as a wild ox.
    They will defeat their enemies
        and break their enemies' bones;
        they will shoot them with arrows.
⁹Like a lion, they lie waiting to attack;
    like a lioness, no one would be brave
        enough to wake them.
    Anyone who blesses you will be blessed,
        and anyone who curses you will be cursed."

¹⁰Then Balak was angry with Balaam, and he pounded his fist. He said to Balaam, "I called you here to curse my enemies, but you have continued to bless them three times. ¹¹Now go home! I said I would pay you well, but the LORD has made you lose your reward."

¹²Balaam said to Balak, "When you sent messengers to me, I told them, ¹³'Balak could give me his palace filled with silver and gold, but I still cannot go against the LORD's commands. I could not do anything, good or bad, on my own, but I must say what the LORD says.' ¹⁴Now I am going

back to my own people, but I will tell you what these people will do to your people in the future."

Balaam's Final Message

¹⁵Then Balaam gave this message:
"This is the message of Balaam son of Beor,
   the message of a man who sees clearly;
¹⁶this is the message of a man who hears the
      words of God.
I know well the Most High God.
I see a vision from the Almighty,
   and my eyes are open as I fall before him.
¹⁷I see someone who will come some day,
   someone who will come, but not soon.
A star will come from Jacob;
   a ruler will rise from Israel.
He will crush the heads of the Moabites
   and smash the skulls of the sons of Sheth.
¹⁸Edom will be conquered;
   his enemy Edom will be conquered,
   but Israel will grow wealthy.
¹⁹A ruler will come from the descendants *d* of
      Jacob
   and will destroy those left in the city."

²⁰Then Balaam saw Amalek and gave this message:
"Amalek was the most important nation,
   but Amalek will be destroyed at last."

²¹Then Balaam saw the Kenites and gave this message:
"Your home is safe,
   like a nest on a cliff.
²²But you Kenites will be burned up;
   Assyria will keep you captive."

²³Then Balaam gave this message:
"No one can live when God does this.
²⁴   Ships will sail from the shores of Cyprus
   and defeat Assyria and Eber,
   but they will also be destroyed."

²⁵Then Balaam got up and returned home, and Balak also went on his way.

Israel Worships Baal at Peor

25 While the people of Israel were still camped at Acacia, the men began sinning sexually with Moabite women. ²The women invited them to their sacrifices to their gods, and the Israelites ate food there and worshipped these gods. ³So the Israelites began to worship Baal *d* of Peor, and the LORD was very angry with them.
⁴The LORD said to Moses, "Get all the leaders of the people and kill them in open daylight in the presence of the LORD. Then the LORD will not be angry with the people of Israel."

⁵So Moses said to Israel's judges, "Each of you must put to death your people who have become worshippers of Baal of Peor."

⁶Moses and the Israelites were gathered at the entrance to the Meeting Tent, *d* crying there. Then an Israelite man brought a Midianite woman to his brothers in plain sight of Moses and all the people. ⁷Phinehas son of Eleazar, the son of Aaron, the priest, saw this, so he left the meeting and got his spear. ⁸He followed the Israelite into his tent and drove his spear through both the Israelite man and the Midianite woman. Then the terrible sickness among the Israelites stopped. ⁹This sickness had killed 24,000 people.

¹⁰The LORD said to Moses, ¹¹"Phinehas son of Eleazar, the son of Aaron, the priest, has saved the Israelites from my anger. He hates sin as much as I do. Since he tried to save my honour among them, I will not kill them. ¹²So tell Phinehas that I am making my peace agreement with him. ¹³He and his descendants *d* will always be priests, because he had great concern for the honour of his God. He removed the sins of the Israelites so that they would belong to God."

¹⁴The Israelite man who was killed with the Midianite woman was named Zimri son of Salu. He was the leader of a family in the tribe *d* of Simeon. ¹⁵And the name of the Midianite woman who was put to death was Cozbi daughter of Zur, who was the chief of a Midianite family.

¹⁶The LORD said to Moses, ¹⁷"The Midianites are your enemies, and you should kill them. ¹⁸They have already made you their enemies, because they tricked you at Peor and because of their sister Cozbi, the daughter of a Midianite leader. She was the woman who was killed when the sickness came because the people sinned at Peor."

The People are Counted

26 After the great sickness, the LORD said to Moses and Eleazar son of Aaron, the priest, ²"Count all the people of Israel by families. Count all the men who are 20 years old or older who will serve in the army of Israel." ³Moses and Eleazar the priest spoke to the people on the plains of Moab near the Jordan River, across from Jericho. They said, ⁴"Count the men 20 years old or older, as the LORD commanded Moses."

Here are the Israelites who came out of Egypt:
⁵The tribe *d* of Reuben, the first son born to Israel, was counted. From Hanoch came the Hanochite family group; from Pallu came the Palluite family group; ⁶from Hezron came the Hezronite family group; from Carmi came the Carmite family group. ⁷These were the family groups of Reuben, and the total number of men was 43,730.

⁸The son of Pallu was Eliab, ⁹and Eliab's sons were Nemuel, Dathan and Abiram. Dathan and Abiram were the leaders who turned against Moses and Aaron and followed Korah when he turned against the LORD. ¹⁰The earth opened up and swallowed them and Korah; they died at the same time the fire burned up the 250 men. This was a warning, ¹¹but the children of Korah did not die.

¹²These were the family groups in the tribe of Simeon: from Nemuel came the Nemuelite family group; from Jamin came the Jaminite family group; from Jakin came the Jakinite family group; ¹³from Zerah came the Zerahite family group; from Shaul came the Shaulite family group. ¹⁴These were the family groups of Simeon, and the total number of men was 22,200.

¹⁵These were the family groups in the tribe of Gad: from Zephon came the Zephonite family group; from Haggi came the Haggite family group; from Shuni came the Shunite family group; ¹⁶from Ozni came the Oznite family group; from Eri came the Erite family group; ¹⁷from Arodi came the Arodite family group; from Areli came the Arelite family group. ¹⁸These were the family groups of Gad, and the total number of men was 40,500.

¹⁹Two of Judah's sons, Er and Onan, died in Canaan.

²⁰These were the family groups in the tribe of Judah: from Shelah came the Shelanite family group; from Perez came the Perezite family group; from Zerah came the Zerahite family group. ²¹These were the family groups from Perez: from Hezron came the Hezronite family group; from Hamul came the Hamulite family group. ²²These were the family groups of Judah, and the total number of men was 76,500.

²³These were the family groups in the tribe of Issachar: from Tola came the Tolaite family group; from Puah came the Puthite family group; ²⁴from Jashub came the Jashubite family group; from Shimron came the Shimronite family group. ²⁵These were the family groups of Issachar, and the total number of men was 64,300.

²⁶These were the family groups in the tribe of Zebulun: from Sered came the Seredite family group; from Elon came the Elonite family group; from Jahleel came the Jahleelite family group. ²⁷These were the family groups of Zebulun, and the total number of men was 60,500.

²⁸These were the family groups of Joseph through Manasseh and Ephraim.

²⁹These were the family groups of Manasseh: from Makir came the Makirite family group (Makir was the father of Gilead); from Gilead came the Gileadite family group. ³⁰These were the family groups that came from Gilead: from Iezer

came the Iezerite family group; from Helek came the Helekite family group; ³¹from Asriel came the Asrielite family group; from Shechem came the Shechemite family group; ³²from Shemida came the Shemidaite family group; from Hepher came the Hepherite family group. ³³(Zelophehad son of Hepher had no sons; he had only daughters, and their names were Mahlah, Noah, Hoglah, Milcah and Tirzah.) ³⁴These were the family groups of Manasseh, and the total number of men was 52,700.

³⁵These were the family groups in the tribe of Ephraim: from Shuthelah came the Shuthelahite family group; from Beker came the Bekerite family group; from Tahan came the Tahanite family group. ³⁶This was the family group from Shuthelah: from Eran came the Eranite family group. ³⁷These were the family groups of Ephraim, and the total number of men was 32,500. These are the family groups that came from Joseph.

³⁸These were the family groups in the tribe of Benjamin: from Bela came the Belaite family group; from Ashbel came the Ashbelite family group; from Ahiram came the Ahiramite family group; ³⁹from Shupham came the Shuphamite family group; from Hupham came the Huphamite family group. ⁴⁰These were the family groups from Bela through Ard and Naaman: from Ard came the Ardite family group; from Naaman came the Naamite family group. ⁴¹These were the family groups of Benjamin, and the total number of men was 45,600.

⁴²This was the family group in the tribe of Dan: from Shuham came the Shuhamite family group. That was the family of Dan, ⁴³and the total number of men in the Shuhamite family group of Dan was 64,400.

⁴⁴These were the family groups in the tribe of Asher: from Imnah came the Imnite family group; from Ishvi came the Ishvite family group; from Beriah came the Beriite family group. ⁴⁵These were the family groups that came from Beriah: from Heber came the Heberite family group; from Malkiel came the Malkielite family group. ⁴⁶(Asher also had a daughter named Serah.) ⁴⁷These were the family groups of Asher, and the total number of men was 53,400.

⁴⁸These were the family groups in the tribe of Naphtali: from Jahzeel came the Jahzeelite family group; from Guni came the Gunite family group; ⁴⁹from Jezer came the Jezerite family group; from Shillem came the Shillemite family group. ⁵⁰These were the family groups of Naphtali, and the total number of men was 45,400.

⁵¹So the total number of the men of Israel was 601,730.

⁵²The LORD said to Moses, ⁵³"Divide the land among these people by the number of names.

54A large tribe will get more land, and a small tribe will get less land; the amount of land each tribe gets will depend on the number of its people. 55Divide the land by drawing lots, *d* and the land each tribe gets will be named after that tribe. 56Divide the land between large and small groups by drawing lots."

57The tribe of Levi was also counted. These were the family groups of Levi: from Gershon came the Gershonite family group; from Kohath came the Kohathite family group; from Merari came the Merarite family group. 58These also were Levite family groups: the Libnite family group, the Hebronite family group, the Mahlite family group, the Mushite family group and the Korahite family group. (Kohath was the ancestor of Amram, 59whose wife was named Jochebed. She was from the tribe of Levi and she was born in Egypt. She and Amram had two sons, Aaron and Moses, and their sister Miriam. 60Aaron was the father of Nadab, Abihu, Eleazar and Ithamar. 61But Nadab and Abihu died because they made an offering before the LORD with the wrong kind of fire.)

62The total number of male Levites one month old or older was 23,000. But these men were not counted with the other Israelites, because they were not given any of the land among the other Israelites.

63Moses and Eleazar the priest counted all these people. They counted the Israelites on the plains of Moab across the Jordan River from Jericho. 64Moses and Aaron the priest had counted the Israelites in the Desert of Sinai, but no one Moses counted on the plains of Moab was in the first counting. 65The LORD had told the Israelites they would all die in the desert, and the only two left were Caleb son of Jephunneh and Joshua son of Nun.

Zelophehad's Daughters

27 Then the daughters of Zelophehad came near. Zelophehad was the son of Hepher, the son of Gilead, the son of Makir, the son of Manasseh. Zelophehad's daughters belonged to the family groups of Manasseh son of Joseph. The daughters' names were Mahlah, Noah, Hoglah, Milcah and Tirzah. 2They went to the entrance of the Meeting Tent *d* and stood before Moses, Eleazar the priest, the leaders and all the people. They said, 3"Our father died in the desert. He was not one of Korah's followers who came together against the LORD, but he died because of his own sin, and he had no sons. 4Our father's name will die out because he had no sons. Give us property among our father's relatives."

5So Moses brought their case to the LORD, 6and the LORD said to him, 7"The daughters of Zelophehad are right; they should certainly get what their father owned. Give them property among their father's relatives.

8"Tell the Israelites, 'If a man dies and has no son, then everything he owned should go to his daughter. 9If he has no daughter, then everything he owned should go to his brothers. 10If he has no brothers, then everything he owned should go to his father's brothers. 11And if his father had no brothers, then everything he owned should go to the nearest relative in his family group. This should be a rule among the people of Israel, as the LORD has given this command to Moses.' "

Joshua is the New Leader

12Then the LORD said to Moses, "Climb this mountain in the Abarim Mountains, and look at the land I have given to the Israelites. 13After you have seen it, you will die and join your ancestors as your brother Aaron did, 14because you both acted against my command in the Desert of Zin. You did not honour me as holy before the people at the waters of Meribah." (This was at Meribah in Kadesh in the Desert of Zin.)

15Moses said to the LORD, 16"The LORD is the God of the spirits of all people. May he choose a leader for these people, 17who will go in and out before them. He must lead them out like sheep and bring them in; the LORD's people must not be like sheep without a shepherd."

18So the LORD said to Moses, "Take Joshua son of Nun, because my Spirit *d* is in him. Put your hand on him, 19and have him stand before Eleazar the priest and all the people. Then give him his orders as they watch. 20Let him share your honour so that all the Israelites will obey him. 21He must stand before Eleazar the priest, and Eleazar will get advice from the LORD by using the Urim. *d* At his command all the Israelites will go out, and at his command they will all come in."

22Moses did what the LORD told him. He took Joshua and had him stand before Eleazar the priest and all the people, 23and he put his hands on him and gave him orders, just as the LORD had told him.

Daily Offerings

28 The LORD said to Moses, 2"Give this command to the Israelites. Tell them: 'Bring me food offerings made by fire, for a smell that is pleasing to me, and be sure to bring them at the right time.' 3Say to them, 'These are the offerings you must bring to the LORD: two male lambs, a year old, as a burnt offering each day. They must have nothing wrong with them. 4Offer one lamb in the morning and the other lamb at twilight.

5Also bring a grain offering of 2 litres of fine flour, mixed with 1 litre of oil from pressed olives. 6This is the daily burnt offering which began at Mount Sinai; its smell is pleasing to the LORD. 7Offer 1 litre of wine with each lamb as a drink offering; pour it out to the LORD at the Holy Place. 8Offer the second lamb at twilight. As in the morning, also give a grain offering and a drink offering. This offering is made by fire, and its smell is pleasing to the LORD.

Sabbath Offerings

9" 'On the Sabbath *d* day you must give two male lambs, a year old, that have nothing wrong with them. Also give a drink offering and a grain offering; the grain offering must be 4 litres of fine flour mixed with olive oil. 10This is the burnt offering for every Sabbath, in addition to the daily burnt offering and drink offering.

Monthly Offerings

11" 'On the first day of each month bring a burnt offering to the LORD. This will be two young bulls, one ram and seven male lambs a year old, and they must have nothing wrong with them. 12Give a grain offering with each bull of 6.6 litres of fine flour mixed with olive oil. Also give a grain offering with the ram. It must be 4 litres of fine flour mixed with olive oil. 13And give a grain offering with each lamb of 2 litres of fine flour mixed with olive oil. This is a burnt offering, and its smell is pleasing to the LORD. 14The drink offering with each bull will be 2 litres of wine, with the ram it will be one and a half litres, and with each lamb it will be 1 litre of wine. This is the burnt offering that must be offered each month of the year. 15Besides the daily burnt offerings and drink offerings, bring a sin offering of one goat to the LORD.

LEADERSHIP

Taking the Stage

"Sam is in hospital," Mr Taylor told his class of drama students.

"But what about the play? Tonight's the first performance! What are we going to do?"

That was the question that was on the mind of everyone in the cast. For months Sam had been rehearsing his lead role. Without him the play would have to be cancelled.

"Someone will have to take Sam's place," Mr Taylor told them. "Someone who knows his lines off by heart."

The students looked at each other. "There's no one," they told him.

"I've got it!" Katie screamed excitedly. "What about Daniel!?"

Daniel was one of Sam's closest friends and had accompanied him to all the rehearsals. It was Daniel who had helped Sam to learn his lines.

Daniel swallowed nervously, then nodded slowly. "OK," he said, "I'll do it."

Sam had prepared the way to making the play a success, but it was Daniel who had to perform on stage in the end.

Similarly, when Moses died, it was Joshua who had to step in and face the next challenge. Read about him in **Numbers 27:12–23**.

* How was Daniel's training similar to the 40 years of preparation that Joshua went through?
* According to the passage, what is the best way to become a leader? How could you do it?

Consider . . .

* asking your parents what skills they have that they would like to teach you, then decide together how to go about it.
* talking to a leader in your church or fellowship and asking how they got to be in their position. Then write a short biography of that leader in your church newsletter.

For more, see . . .

* Judges 6:11–16 (p.231)
* 2 Timothy 2:1–7 (p.1317)
* John 21:15–22 (p.1134)

The Passover

16" 'The LORD's Passover *d* will be on the fourteenth day of the first month. 17The Feast *d* of Unleavened Bread begins on the fifteenth day of that month. For seven days, you may eat only bread made without yeast. 18Have a holy meeting on the first day of the festival, and don't work that day. 19Bring to the LORD an offering made by fire, a burnt offering of two young bulls, one ram and seven male lambs a year old. They must have nothing wrong with them. 20With each bull give a grain offering of 6 litres of fine flour mixed with olive oil. With the ram it must be 4 litres of fine flour mixed with oil. 21With each of the seven lambs, it must be 2 litres of fine flour mixed with oil. 22Bring one goat as a sin offering, to remove your sins so you will belong to God. 23Bring these offerings in addition to the burnt offerings you give every morning. 24So bring food for the offering made by fire each day for seven days, for a smell that is pleasing to the LORD. Do it in addition to the daily burnt offering and its drink offering. 25On the seventh day have a holy meeting, and don't work that day.

The Feast of Weeks

26" 'On the day of firstfruits *d* when you bring new grain to the LORD during the Feast *d* of Weeks, have a holy meeting. Don't work that day. 27Bring this burnt offering to the LORD: two young bulls, one ram and seven male lambs a year old. This smell is pleasing to the LORD. 28Also, with each bull give a grain offering of 6 litres of fine flour mixed with oil. With the ram, it must be 4 litres of flour, 29and with each of the seven lambs offer 2 litres of flour. 30Offer one male goat to remove your sins so that you will belong to God. 31Bring these offerings and their drink offerings in addition to the daily burnt offering and its grain offering. The animals must have nothing wrong with them.

The Feast of Trumpets

29 " 'Have a holy meeting on the first day of the seventh month, and don't work on that day. That is the day you blow the trumpets. 2Bring these burnt offerings as a smell pleasing to the LORD: one young bull, one ram and seven male lambs a year old. They must have nothing wrong with them. 3With the bull give a grain offering of 7 litres of fine flour mixed with oil. With the ram offer 4 litres, 4and with each of the seven lambs offer 2 litres. 5Offer one male goat for a sin offering to remove your sins so that you will belong to God. 6These offerings are in addition to the monthly and daily burnt offerings. Their grain offerings and drink offerings must be

done as you have been told. These offerings are made by fire to the LORD, and their smell is pleasing to him.

The Day of Cleansing

7" 'Have a holy meeting on the tenth day of the seventh month. On that day do not eat and do not work. 8Bring these burnt offerings as a smell pleasing to the LORD: one young bull, one ram and seven male lambs a year old. They must have nothing wrong with them. 9With the bull give a grain offering of 7 litres of fine flour mixed with oil. With the ram it must be 4 litres, 10and with each of the seven lambs it must be 2 litres. 11Offer one male goat as a sin offering. This will be in addition to the sin offering which removes your sins, the daily burnt offering with its grain offering and the drink offerings.

The Feast of Shelters

12" 'Have a holy meeting on the fifteenth day of the seventh month, and do not work on that day. Celebrate a festival to the LORD for seven days. 13Bring these burnt offerings, made by fire, as a smell pleasing to the LORD: thirteen young bulls, two rams and fourteen male lambs a year old. They must have nothing wrong with them. 14With each of the thirteen bulls offer a grain offering of 7 litres of fine flour mixed with oil. With each of the two rams it must be 4 litres, 15and with each of the fourteen lambs it must be 2 litres. 16Offer one male goat as a sin offering in addition to the daily burnt offering with its grain and drink offerings.

17" 'On the second day of this festival give an offering of twelve bulls, two rams and fourteen male lambs a year old. They must have nothing wrong with them. 18Bring the grain and drink offerings for the bulls, rams and lambs, according to the number required. 19Offer one male goat as a sin offering, in addition to the daily burnt offering with its grain and drink offerings.

20" 'On the third day offer eleven bulls, two rams and fourteen male lambs a year old. They must have nothing wrong with them. 21Bring the grain and drink offerings for the bulls, rams and lambs, according to the number required. 22Offer one male goat as a sin offering, in addition to the daily burnt offering with its grain and drink offerings.

23" 'On the fourth day offer ten bulls, two rams and fourteen male lambs a year old. They must have nothing wrong with them. 24Bring the grain and drink offerings for the bulls, rams and lambs, according to the number required. 25Offer one male goat as a sin offering, in addition to the daily burnt offering with its grain and drink offerings.

26" 'On the fifth day offer nine bulls, two rams and fourteen male lambs a year old. They must have nothing wrong with them. 27Bring the grain and drink offerings for the bulls, rams and lambs, according to the number required. 28Offer one male goat as a sin offering, in addition to the daily burnt offering with its grain and drink offerings.

29" 'On the sixth day offer eight bulls, two rams and fourteen male lambs a year old. They must have nothing wrong with them. 30Bring the grain and drink offerings for the bulls, rams and lambs, according to the number required. 31Offer one male goat as a sin offering, in addition to the daily burnt offering with its grain and drink offerings.

32" 'On the seventh day offer seven bulls, two rams and fourteen male lambs a year old. They must have nothing wrong with them. 33Bring the grain and drink offerings for the bulls, rams and lambs, according to the number required. 34Offer one male goat as a sin offering, in addition to the daily burnt offering with its grain and drink offerings.

35" 'On the eighth day have a closing meeting and do not work on that day. 36Bring an offering made by fire, a burnt offering, as a smell pleasing to the LORD. Offer one bull, one ram and seven male lambs a year old. They must have nothing wrong with them. 37Bring the grain and drink offerings for the bull, the rams and the lambs, according to the number required. 38Offer one male goat as a sin offering, in addition to the daily burnt offering with its grain and drink offerings.

39" 'At your festivals you should bring these to the LORD: your burnt offerings, grain offerings, drink offerings and fellowship offerings. These are in addition to other promised offerings and special gifts you want to give to the LORD.' "

40Moses told the Israelites everything the LORD had commanded him.

Rules About Special Promises

30 Moses spoke with the leaders of the Israelite tribes. *d* He told them these commands from the LORD.

2"If a man makes a promise to the LORD or says he will do something special, he must keep his promise. He must do what he said. 3If a young woman still living at home makes a promise to the LORD or pledges to do something special, 4and if her father hears about the promise or pledge and says nothing, she must do what she promised. She must keep her pledge. 5But if her father hears about the promise or pledge and does not allow it, then the promise or pledge does not have to be kept. Her father would not allow it, so the LORD will free her from her promise.

6"If a woman makes a pledge or a careless promise and then gets married, 7and if her husband hears about it and says nothing, she must keep her promise or the pledge she made. 8But if her husband hears about it and does not allow it, he cancels her pledge or the careless promise she made. The LORD will free her from keeping it.

9"If a widow or divorced woman makes a promise, she must do whatever she promised.

10"If a woman makes a promise or pledge while she is married, 11and if her husband hears about it but says nothing and does not stop her, she must keep her promise or pledge. 12But if her husband hears about it and cancels it, she does not have to do what she said. Her husband has cancelled it, so the LORD will free her from it. 13A woman's husband may make her keep or cancel any promise or pledge she has made. 14If he says nothing to her about it for several days, she must keep her promises. If he hears about them and says nothing, she must keep her promises. 15But if he cancels them long after he heard about them, he is responsible if she breaks her promise."

16These are commands that the LORD gave to Moses for husbands and wives, and for fathers with daughters living at home.

Israel Attacks the Midianites

31 The LORD spoke to Moses and said, 2"Pay back the Midianites for what they did to the Israelites; after that you will die."

3So Moses said to the people, "Get some men ready for war. The LORD will use them to pay back the Midianites. 4Send to war 1,000 men from each of the tribes *d* of Israel." 5So 12,000 men got ready for war, 1,000 men from each tribe. 6Moses sent those men to war; Phinehas son of Eleazar the priest was with them. He took with him the holy things and the trumpets for giving the alarm. 7They fought the Midianites as the LORD had commanded Moses, and they killed every Midianite man. 8Among those they killed were Evi, Rekem, Zur, Hur and Reba, who were the five kings of Midian. They also killed Balaam son of Beor with a sword.

9The Israelites captured the Midianite women and children, and they took all their flocks, herds and goods. 10They burned all the Midianite towns where they had settled and all their camps, 11but they took all the people and animals and goods. 12Then they brought the captives, the animals and the goods back to Moses and Eleazar the priest and all the Israelites. Their camp was on the plains of Moab near the Jordan River, across from Jericho.

[13]Moses, Eleazar the priest, and all the leaders of the people went outside the camp to meet them. [14]Moses was angry with the army officers, the commanders over 1,000 men and those over 100 men, who returned from war.

[15]He asked them, "Why did you let the women live? [16]They were the ones who followed Balaam's advice and turned the Israelites from the LORD at Peor. Then a terrible sickness struck the LORD's people. [17]Kill all the Midianite boys, and kill all the Midianite women who have had sexual relations. [18]But save for yourselves the girls who have not had sexual relations with a man.

[19]"All you men who killed anyone or touched a dead body must stay outside the camp for seven days. On the third and seventh days you and your captives must make yourselves clean. [d] [20]You must clean all your clothes and anything made of leather, goat hair or wood."

[21]Then Eleazar the priest said to the soldiers who had gone to war, "These are the teachings that the LORD gave to Moses. [22]Put any gold, silver, bronze, iron, tin or lead— [23]anything that will not burn—into the fire, and then it will be clean. But also purify those things with the cleansing water. Then they will be clean. If something cannot stand the fire, wash it with the water. [24]On the seventh day wash your clothes, and you will be clean. After that you may come into the camp."

Dividing the Goods

[25]The LORD said to Moses, [26]"You, Eleazar the priest, and the leaders of the family groups should take a count of the goods, the men and the animals that were taken. [27]Then divide those possessions between the soldiers who went to war and the rest of the people. [28]From the soldiers who went to war, take a tax for the LORD of one thing out of every 500. This includes people, cattle, donkeys or sheep. [29]Take it from the soldiers' half, and give it to Eleazar the priest as the LORD's share. [30]And from the people's half, take one thing out of every 50. This includes people, cattle, donkeys, sheep or other animals. Give that to the Levites, who take care of the LORD's Holy Tent." [d] [31]So Moses and Eleazar did as the LORD commanded Moses.

[32]There remained from what the soldiers had taken 675,000 sheep, [33]72,000 cattle, [34]61,000 donkeys [35]and 32,000 women who had not had sexual relations with a man. [36]The soldiers who went to war got 337,500 sheep [37]and they gave 675 of them to the LORD. [38]They got 36,000 cattle and they gave 72 of them to the LORD. [39]They got 30,500 donkeys and they gave 61 of them to the LORD. [40]They got 16,000 people, and they gave 32 of them to the LORD. [41]Moses gave the LORD's share to Eleazar the priest, as the LORD had commanded him.

[42]Moses separated the people's half from the soldiers' half. [43]The people got 337,500 sheep, [44]36,000 cattle, [45]30,500 donkeys [46]and 16,000 people. [47]From the people's half Moses took one thing out of every 50 for the LORD. This included the animals and the people. Then he gave them to the Levites, who took care of the LORD's Holy Tent. This was what the LORD had commanded Moses.

[48]Then the officers of the army, the commanders of 1,000 men and commanders of 100 men, came to Moses. [49]They told Moses, "We, your servants, have counted our soldiers under our command, and not one of them is missing. [50]So we have brought the LORD a gift of the gold things that each of us found: arm bands, bracelets, signet [d] rings, earrings and necklaces. These are to remove our sins so we will belong to the LORD."

[51]So Moses and Eleazar the priest took the gold from them, which had been made into all kinds of objects. [52]The commanders of 1,000 men and the commanders of 100 men gave the LORD the gold, and all of it together weighed about 190 kilogrammes; [53]each soldier had taken something for himself. [54]Moses and Eleazar the priest took the gold from the commanders of 1,000 men and the commanders of 100 men. Then they put it in the Meeting Tent [d] as a memorial before the LORD for the people of Israel.

The Tribes East of the Jordan

32 The people of Reuben and Gad had large flocks and herds. When they saw that the lands of Jazer and Gilead were good for the animals, [2]they came to Moses, Eleazar the priest and the leaders of the people. [3-4]They said, "We, your servants, have flocks and herds. The LORD has captured for the Israelites a land that is good for animals—the land around Ataroth, Dibon, Jazer, Nimrah, Heshbon, Elealeh, Sebam, Nebo and Beon. [5]If it pleases you, we would like this land to be given to us. Don't make us cross the Jordan River."

[6]Moses told the people of Gad and Reuben, "Shall your brothers go to war while you stay behind? [7]You will discourage the Israelites from going over to the land the LORD has given them. [8]Your ancestors did the same thing. I sent them from Kadesh Barnea to look at the land. [9]They went as far as the Valley of Eshcol, and when they saw the land, they discouraged the Israelites from going into the land the LORD had given them. [10]The LORD became very angry that day

and made this promise: [11]'None of the people who came from Egypt and who are 20 years old or older will see the land that I promised to Abraham, Isaac and Jacob. These people have not followed me completely. [12]Only Caleb son of Jephunneh the Kenizzite and Joshua son of Nun followed the LORD completely.'

[13]"The LORD was angry with Israel, so he made them wander in the desert for 40 years. Finally all the people who had sinned against the LORD died, [14]and now you are acting just like your ancestors! You sinful people are making the LORD even more angry with Israel. [15]If you stop following him, it will add to their stay in the desert, and you will destroy all these people."

[16]Then the Reubenites and Gadites came up to Moses and said, "We will build pens for our animals and cities for our children here. [17]Then our children will be in fortified cities, safe from the people who live in this land. Then we will prepare for war. We will help the other Israelites get their land, [18]and we will not return home until every Israelite has received his land. [19]We won't take any of the land west of the Jordan River; our part of the land is east of the Jordan."

[20]So Moses told them, "You must do these things. You must go before the LORD into battle [21]and cross the Jordan River armed, until the LORD forces out the enemy. [22]After the LORD helps us take the land, you may return home. You will have done your duty to the LORD and Israel, and you may have this land as your own.

[23]"But if you don't do these things, you will be sinning against the LORD; know for sure that you will be punished for your sin. [24]Build cities for your children and pens for your animals, but then you must do what you promised."

[25]The Gadites and Reubenites said to Moses, "We are your servants, and we will do what you, our master, command. [26]Our children, wives and all our cattle will stay in the cities of Gilead, [27]but we, your servants, will prepare for battle. We will go over and fight for the LORD, as you, our master, have said."

[28]So Moses gave orders about them to Eleazar the priest, to Joshua son of Nun, and to the leaders of the tribes [d] of Israel. [29]Moses said to them, "If the Gadites and Reubenites prepare for battle and cross the Jordan River with you, to go before the LORD and help you take the land, give them the land of Gilead for their own. [30]But if they do not go over armed, they will not receive it; their land will be in Canaan with you."

[31]The Gadites and Reubenites answered, "We are your servants, and we will do as the LORD said. [32]We will cross over into Canaan and go before the LORD ready for battle. But our land will be east of the Jordan River."

[33]So Moses gave that land to the tribes of Gad, Reuben and East Manasseh. (Manasseh was Joseph's son.) That land had been the kingdom of Sihon, king of the Amorites, and the kingdom of Og, king of Bashan, as well as all the cities and the land around them.

[34]The Gadites rebuilt the cities of Dibon, Ataroth, Aroer, [35]Atroth Shophan, Jazer, Jogbehah, [36]Beth Nimrah and Beth Haran. These were fortified cities. And they built sheep pens.

[37]The Reubenites rebuilt Heshbon, Elealeh, Kiriathaim, [38]Nebo, Baal Meon and Sibmah. They renamed Nebo and Baal Meon when they rebuilt them.

[39]The descendants [d] of Makir son of Manasseh went and captured Gilead and forced out the Amorites who were there. [40]So Moses gave Gilead to the family of Makir son of Manasseh and they settled there. [41]Jair son of Manasseh went out and captured the small towns there, and he called them the Towns of Jair. [42]Nobah went and captured Kenath and the small towns around it; then he named it Nobah after himself.

Israel's Journey from Egypt

33 These are the places where the Israelites went as Moses and Aaron led them out of Egypt in divisions. [2]At the LORD's command Moses recorded the places where they went, and these are the places they went.

[3]On the fifteenth day of the first month, the day after the Passover, [d] the Israelites left Rameses and marched out boldly in front of all the Egyptians. [4]The Egyptians were burying their firstborn [d] sons, whom the LORD had killed; the LORD showed that the gods of Egypt were false.

[5]The Israelites left Rameses and camped at Succoth.

[6]They left Succoth and camped at Etham, at the edge of the desert.

[7]They left Etham and went back to Pi Hahiroth, to the east of Baal Zephon, and camped near Migdol.

[8]They left Pi Hahiroth and walked through the sea into the desert. After going three days through the Desert of Etham, they camped at Marah.

[9]They left Marah and went to Elim; there were twelve springs of water and 70 palm trees where they camped.

[10]They left Elim and camped near the Red Sea. [d]

[11]They left the Red Sea and camped in the Desert of Sin.

[12]They left the Desert of Sin and camped at Dophkah.

[13]They left Dophkah and camped at Alush.

[14]They left Alush and camped at Rephidim, where the people had no water to drink.

¹⁵They left Rephidim and camped in the Desert of Sinai.

¹⁶They left the Desert of Sinai and camped at Kibroth Hattaavah.

¹⁷They left Kibroth Hattaavah and camped at Hazeroth.

¹⁸They left Hazeroth and camped at Rithmah.

¹⁹They left Rithmah and camped at Rimmon Perez.

²⁰They left Rimmon Perez and camped at Libnah.

²¹They left Libnah and camped at Rissah.

²²They left Rissah and camped at Kehelathah.

²³They left Kehelathah and camped at Mount Shepher.

²⁴They left Mount Shepher and camped at Haradah.

²⁵They left Haradah and camped at Makheloth.

²⁶They left Makheloth and camped at Tahath.

²⁷They left Tahath and camped at Terah.

²⁸They left Terah and camped at Mithcah.

²⁹They left Mithcah and camped at Hashmonah.

³⁰They left Hashmonah and camped at Moseroth.

³¹They left Moseroth and camped at Bene Berak Jaakan.

³²They left Bene Berak Jaakan and camped at Hor Haggidgad.

³³They left Hor Haggidgad and camped at Jotbathah.

³⁴They left Jotbathah and camped at Abronah.

³⁵They left Abronah and camped at Ezion Geber.

³⁶They left Ezion Geber and camped at Kadesh in the Desert of Zin.

³⁷They left Kadesh and camped at Mount Hor, on the border of Edom. ³⁸Aaron the priest obeyed the Lord and went up Mount Hor. There he died on the first day of the fifth month in the fortieth year after the Israelites left Egypt. ³⁹Aaron was 123 years old when he died on Mount Hor.

⁴⁰The Canaanite king of Arad, who lived in the southern area of Canaan, heard that the Israelites were coming.

⁴¹The people left Mount Hor and camped at Zalmonah.

⁴²They left Zalmonah and camped at Punon.

⁴³They left Punon and camped at Oboth.

⁴⁴They left Oboth and camped at Iye Abarim, on the border of Moab.

⁴⁵They left Iye Abarim and camped at Dibon Gad.

⁴⁶They left Dibon Gad and camped at Almon Diblathaim.

⁴⁷They left Almon Diblathaim and camped in the mountains of Abarim, near Nebo.

⁴⁸They left the mountains of Abarim and camped on the plains of Moab near the Jordan River across from Jericho. ⁴⁹They camped along the Jordan on the plains of Moab, and their camp went from Beth Jeshimoth to Abel Acacia.

⁵⁰On the plains of Moab by the Jordan River across from Jericho, the Lord spoke to Moses. He said, ⁵¹"Speak to the Israelites and tell them, 'When you cross the Jordan River and go into Canaan, ⁵²force out all the people who live there. Destroy all of their carved statues and metal idols. Wreck all of their places of worship. ⁵³Take over the land and settle there, because I have given this land to you to own. ⁵⁴Throw lots *d* to divide up the land by family groups, giving larger portions to larger family groups and smaller portions to smaller family groups. The land will be given as the lots decide; each tribe *d* will get its own land.

⁵⁵" 'But if you don't force those people out of the land, they will bring you trouble. They will be like sharp hooks in your eyes and thorns in your sides. They will bring trouble to the land where you live. ⁵⁶Then I will punish you as I had planned to punish them.' "

The Borders of Canaan

34 The Lord said to Moses, ²"Give this command to the people of Israel: 'You will soon enter Canaan and it will be yours. These shall be the borders: ³On the south you will get part of the Desert of Zin near the border of Edom. On the east side your southern border will start at the south end of the Dead Sea, *d* ⁴cross south of Scorpion Pass, and go through the Desert of Zin and south of Kadesh Barnea. Then it will go to Hazar Addar and over to Azmon. ⁵From Azmon it will go to the brook of Egypt, and it will end at the Mediterranean Sea.

⁶" 'Your western border will be the Mediterranean Sea.

⁷" 'Your northern border will begin at the Mediterranean Sea and go to Mount Hor. ⁸From Mount Hor it will go to Lebo Hamath, and on to Zedad. ⁹Then the border will go to Ziphron, and it will end at Hazar Enan. This will be your northern border.

¹⁰" 'Your eastern border will begin at Hazar Enan and go to Shepham. ¹¹From Shepham the border will go east of Ain to Riblah and along the hills east of Lake Galilee. ¹²Then the border will go down along the Jordan River and end at the Dead Sea.

" 'These are the borders around your country.' "

¹³So Moses gave this command to the Israelites: "This is the land you will receive. Throw lots *d* to divide it among the nine and a half tribes, *d* because the Lord commanded that it should be theirs. ¹⁴The tribes of Reuben, Gad and East Manasseh have already received their land.

[15] These two and a half tribes received land east of the Jordan River, across from Jericho."

[16] Then the LORD said to Moses, [17] "These are the men who will divide the land: Eleazar the priest and Joshua son of Nun. [18] Also take one leader from each tribe to help divide the land. [19] These are the names of the leaders: from the tribe of Judah, Caleb son of Jephunneh; [20] from the tribe of Simeon, Shemuel son of Ammihud; [21] from the tribe of Benjamin, Elidad son of Kislon; [22] from the tribe of Dan, Bukki son of Jogli; [23] from the tribe of Manasseh son of Joseph, Hanniel son of Ephod; [24] from the tribe of Ephraim son of Joseph, Kemuel son of Shiphtan; [25] from the tribe of Zebulun, Elizaphan son of Parnach; [26] from the tribe of Issachar, Paltiel son of Azzan; [27] from the tribe of Asher, Ahihud son of Shelomi; [28] from the tribe of Naphtali, Pedahel son of Ammihud."

[29] The LORD commanded these men to divide the land of Canaan among the Israelites.

The Levites' Towns

35 The LORD spoke to Moses on the plains of Moab across from Jericho by the Jordan River. He said, [2] "Command the Israelites to give the Levites cities to live in from the land they receive. Also give the Levites the pastureland around these cities. [3] Then the Levites will have cities where they may live and pastureland for their cattle, flocks and other animals. [4] The pastureland you give the Levites will extend 500 metres from the city wall. [5] Also measure 1,000 metres in each direction outside the city wall— 1,000 metres east of the city, 1,000 metres south of the city, 1,000 metres west of the city and 1,000 metres north of the city, with the city in the centre. This will be pastureland for the Levites' cities.

Cities of Safety

[6] "Six of the cities you give the Levites will be cities of safety. [d] A person who accidentally kills someone may run to one of those cities for safety. You must also give 42 other cities to the Levites; [7] give the Levites a total of 48 cities and their pastures. [8] The larger tribes [d] of Israel must give more cities, and the smaller tribes must give fewer cities. Each tribe must give some of its cities to the Levites, but the number of cities they give will depend on the size of their land."

[9] Then the LORD said to Moses, [10] "Tell the Israelites these things: 'When you cross the Jordan River and go into Canaan, [11] you must choose cities to be cities of safety, so that a person who accidentally kills someone may run to them for safety. [12] There the person will be safe from the dead person's relative who has the duty of punishing the killer. He will not die before he receives a fair trial in court. [13] The six cities you give will be cities of safety. [14] Give three cities east of the Jordan River and three cities in Canaan as cities of safety. [15] These six cities will be places of safety for citizens of Israel, as well as for foreigners and other people living with you. Any of these people who accidentally kills someone may run to one of these cities.

[16] " 'Anyone who uses an iron weapon to kill someone is a murderer. He must be put to death. [17] Anyone who takes a rock and kills a person with it is a murderer. He must be put to death. [18] Anyone who picks up a piece of wood and kills someone with it is a murderer. He must be put to death. [19] A relative of the dead person must put the murderer to death; when they meet, the relative must kill the murderer. [20] A person might shove someone or throw something at someone and cause death. [21] Or a person might hit someone with his hand and cause death. If it were done from hate, the person is a murderer and must be put to death. A relative of the dead person must kill the murderer when they meet.

[22] " 'But a person might suddenly push someone, and not from hatred. Or a person might accidentally throw something and hit someone. [23] Or a person might drop a rock on someone he couldn't see and kill that person. There was no plan to hurt anyone and no hatred for the one who was killed. [24] If that happens, the community must judge between the relative of the dead person and the killer, according to these rules. [25] They must protect the killer from the dead person's relative, sending the killer back to the original city of safety, to stay there until the high priest dies (the high priest had the holy oil poured on him).

Sidelight   Today, if a person kills someone, a trial is held. In Old Testament times, such a person could be killed by the victim's family. To protect people who accidentally killed someone, Numbers 35:6–28 tells of six cities of safety, where someone could go to be safe. But if the killer left the city, the dead person's family could take revenge.

---

[26] " 'Such a person must never go outside the limits of the city of safety. [27] If a relative of the dead person finds the killer outside the city, the relative may kill that person and not be guilty of murder. [28] The killer must stay in the city of safety until the high priest dies. After the high priest dies, the killer may go home.

[29] " 'These laws are for you from now on, wherever you live.

[30] " 'If anyone kills a person, the murderer may be put to death only if there are witnesses. No one may be put to death with only one witness. [31] " 'Don't take money to spare the life of a murderer who should be put to death. A murderer must be put to death. [32] " 'If someone has run to a city of safety, don't take money to let the person go back home before the high priest dies. [33] " 'Don't let murder spoil your land. The only way to remove the sin of killing an innocent person is for the murderer to be put to death. [34] I am the LORD, and I live among the Israelites. I live in that land with you, so do not spoil it with murder.' "

Land for Zelophehad's Daughters

36 The leaders of Gilead's family group went to talk to Moses and the leaders of the families of Israel. (Gilead was the son of Makir, the son of Manasseh, the son of Joseph.) [2] They said, "The LORD commanded you, our master, to give the land to the Israelites by throwing lots, [d] and the LORD commanded you to give the land of Zelophehad, our brother, to his daughters. [3] But if his daughters marry men from other tribes [d] of Israel, then that land will leave our family, and the people of the other tribes will get that land. So we will lose some of our land. [4] When the time of Jubilee [d] comes for the Israelites, their land will go to the tribes of the people they marry; their land will be taken away from us, the land we received from our fathers."

[5] Then Moses gave the Israelites this command from the LORD: "These men from the tribe of Joseph are right. [6] This is the LORD's command to Zelophehad's daughters: you may marry anyone you wish, as long as the person is from your own tribe. [7] In this way the Israelites' land will not pass from tribe to tribe, and each Israelite will keep the land in the tribe that belonged to his ancestors. [8] A woman who inherits her father's land may marry, but she must marry someone from her own tribe. In this way every Israelite will keep the land that belonged to his ancestors. [9] The land must not pass from tribe to tribe, and each Israelite tribe will keep the land it received from its ancestors."

[10] Zelophehad's daughters obeyed the LORD's command to Moses.

[11] So Zelophehad's daughters—Mahlah, Tirzah, Hoglah, Milcah and Noah—married their cousins, their father's relatives. [12] Their husbands were from the tribe of Manasseh son of Joseph, so their land stayed in their father's family group and tribe.

[13] These were the laws and commands that the LORD gave to the Israelites through Moses on the plains of Moab by the Jordan River, across from Jericho.

Deuteronomy

Why Read This Book:

- Be reminded of all the good things that God has done for his people (Deuteronomy 1—4).
- Find out what God requires of people because of his special relationship with them (Deuteronomy 5—28).
- See what God has in store for his people, when they do right and when they do wrong (Deuteronomy 29—30).

Behind the Scenes:

You've spent months reading books, listening in lessons and doing homework. You have learned lots of important information that will help you in the future. Then the week before the final exam, your teacher goes over what you've learned and urges you to remember everything that has happened.

The book of Deuteronomy is a lot like that final revision week. The Israelites, after wandering around the desert for 40 years, were preparing for the "final test" – about to enter God's promised land. But before that happened, their leader, Moses, made a point of delivering three "revision lesson" sermons.

In these sermons, Moses reminded God's people of all that he had done for them, and warned them against turning away from him as they entered the new land. ▷

When?

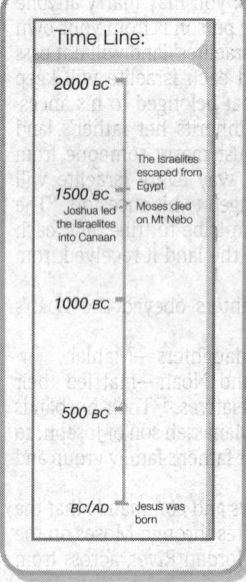

Time Line:

2000 BC

1500 BC
The Israelites escaped from Egypt
Joshua led the Israelites into Canaan
Moses died on Mt Nebo

1000 BC

500 BC

BC/AD
Jesus was born

Where?

Joshua became Israel's leader after Moses (Deuteronomy 34:9). He led the Israelites into the promised land.

Moses preached to the Israelites in the Jordan Valley in the desert east of the Jordan River (Deuteronomy 1:1).

Jordan River

Mediterranean Sea

CANAAN

Moses saw the promised land from Mt Nebo, where he died (Deuteronomy 34:1–5).

Dead Sea

Possible route out of the desert.

ARABIAN DESERT

SINAI

Deuteronomy recounts the forty years of wandering in the desert.

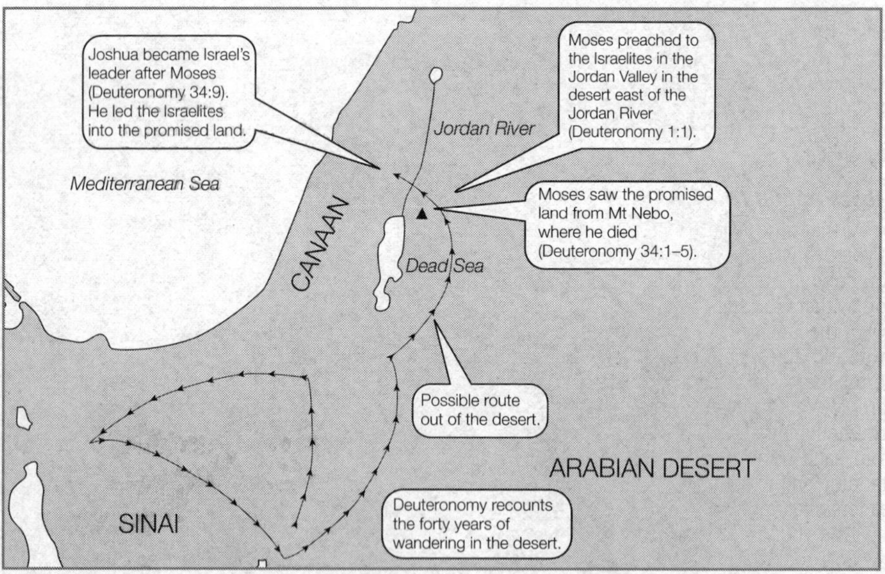

Behind the   The name "Deuteronomy" means "second law". It summarises the laws
Scenes (cont.):   which the Israelites received during their time in the desert.
                         Moses encourages God's people to obey the laws – not because of
                  some empty sense of "duty", but out of gratitude for God's unlimited love.

Moses Talks to the Israelites

1 This is the message Moses gave to all the people of Israel in the desert east of the Jordan River. They were in the desert area near Suph, between Paran and the towns of Tophel, Laban, Hazeroth and Dizahab. ²(The trip from Mount Sinai to Kadesh Barnea on the Mount Seir road takes eleven days.) ³40 years after the Israelites had left Egypt, on the first day of the eleventh month, Moses told the people of Israel everything the LORD had commanded him to tell them. ⁴This was after the LORD had defeated Sihon and Og. Sihon was king of the Amorite people and lived in Heshbon. Og was king of Bashan and lived in Ashteroth and Edrei. ⁵Now the Israelites were east of the Jordan River in the land of Moab, and there Moses began to explain what God had commanded. He said:

⁶The LORD our God spoke to us at Mount Sinai and said, "You have stayed long enough at this mountain. ⁷Get ready, and go to the mountain country of the Amorites, and to all the places around there—the Jordan Valley, the mountains, the western hills, the southern area, the sea coast, the land of Canaan and Lebanon. Go as far as the great river, the Euphrates. ⁸See, I have given you this land, so go in and take it for yourselves. The LORD promised it to your ancestors—Abraham, Isaac and Jacob and their descendants." ᵈ

Moses Appoints Leaders

⁹At that time I said, "I am not able to take care of you by myself. ¹⁰The LORD your God has made you grow in number so that there are as many of you as there are stars in the sky. ¹¹I pray that the LORD, the God of your ancestors, will give you a thousand times more people and do all the wonderful things he promised. ¹²But I cannot take care of your problems, your troubles and your arguments by myself. ¹³So choose some men from each tribe ᵈ—wise men who have understanding and experience—and I will make them leaders over you."

¹⁴And you said, "That's a good thing to do."

¹⁵So I took the wise and experienced leaders of your tribes, and I made them your leaders. I appointed commanders over 1,000 people, over 100 people, over 50 people and over ten people and made them officers over your tribes. ¹⁶Then I told your leaders, "Listen to the arguments between your people. Judge fairly between two Israelites or between an Israelite and a foreigner. ¹⁷When you judge, be fair to everyone; don't act as if one person is more important than another, and don't be afraid of anyone, because your decision comes from God. Bring the hard cases to me, and I will judge them." ¹⁸At that time I told you everything you must do.

Spies Enter the Land

¹⁹Then, as the LORD our God commanded us, we left Mount Sinai and went towards the mountain country of the Amorite people. We went through that large and terrible desert you saw, and then we came to Kadesh Barnea. ²⁰I said to you, "You have now come to the mountain country of the Amorites, to the land the LORD our God will give us. ²¹Look, here it is! Go up and take it. The LORD, the God of your ancestors, told you to do this, so don't be afraid and don't worry."

²²Then all of you came to me and said, "Let's send men before us to spy out the land. They can come back and tell us about the way we should go and the cities we will find."

²³I thought that was a good idea, so I chose twelve of your men, one for each tribe. ᵈ ²⁴They left and went up to the mountains, and when they came to the Valley of Eshcol they explored it. ²⁵They took some of the fruit from that land and brought it down to us, saying, "It is a good land that the LORD our God is giving us."

Israel Refuses to Enter

²⁶But you refused to go. You would not obey the command of the LORD your God, ²⁷but grumbled in your tents, saying, "The LORD hates us. He brought us out of Egypt just to give us to the Amorites, who will destroy us. ²⁸Where can we go now? The spies we sent have made us afraid, because they said, 'The people there are stronger and taller than we are. The cities are big, with walls up to the sky. And we saw the Anakites ᵈ there!'"

[29]Then I said to you, "Don't be frightened; don't be afraid of those people. [30]The LORD your God will go ahead of you and fight for you as he did in Egypt; you saw him do it. [31]And in the desert you saw how the LORD your God carried you, as one carries a child. And he has brought you safely all the way to this place."

[32]But you still did not trust the LORD your God, even though [33]he had always gone before you to find places for you to camp. In a fire at night and in a cloud during the day, he showed you which way to go.

[34]When the LORD heard what you said, he was angry and made an oath, saying, [35]"I promised a good land to your ancestors, but none of you evil people will see it. [36]Only Caleb son of Jephunneh will see it. I will give him and his descendants[d] the land he walked on, because he followed the LORD completely."

[37]Because of you, the LORD was also angry with me and said, "You won't enter the land either, [38]but your assistant, Joshua son of Nun, will enter it. Encourage him, because he will lead Israel to take the land for their own.

[39]"Your little children that you said would be captured, who do not know right from wrong at this time, will go into the land. I will give the land to them, and they will take it for their own. [40]But you must turn round and follow the desert road towards the Red Sea."

[41]Then you said to me, "We have sinned against the LORD, but now we will go up and fight, as the LORD our God commanded us." Then all of you put on weapons, thinking it would be easy to go into the mountains.

[42]But the LORD said to me, "Tell the people, 'You must not go up there and fight. I will not be with you, and your enemies will defeat you.'"

[43]So I told you, but you would not listen. You would not obey the LORD's command. You were proud, so you went on up into the mountains, [44]and the Amorites who lived in those mountains came out and fought you. They chased you like bees and defeated you from Edom to Hormah. [45]So you came back and cried before the LORD, but the LORD did not listen to you; he refused to pay attention to you. [46]So you stayed in Kadesh a long time.

Israel Wanders in the Desert

2 Then we turned round, and we travelled on the desert road towards the Red Sea, as the LORD had told me to do. We travelled through the mountains of Edom for many days.

[2]Then the LORD said to me, [3]"You have travelled through these mountains long enough. Turn north [4]and give the people this command: 'You will soon go through the land that belongs to your relatives, the descendants[d] of Esau who live in Edom. They will be afraid of you, but be very careful. [5]Do not go to war against them. I will not give you any of their land—not even a foot of it—because I have given the mountains of Edom to Esau as his own. [6]You must pay them in silver for any food you eat or water you drink.'"

[7]The LORD your God has blessed everything you have done; he has protected you while you travelled through this great desert. The LORD your God has been with you for the past 40 years, and you have had everything you needed.

[8]So we passed by our relatives, the descendants of Esau who lived in Edom. We turned off the Jordan Valley road that comes from the towns of Elath and Ezion Geber and travelled along the desert road to Moab.

The Land of Ar

[9]Then the LORD said to me, "Don't bother the people of Moab. Don't go to war against them, because I will not give you any of their land as your own; I have given Ar to the descendants[d] of Lot as their own." [10](The Emites, who lived in Ar before, were strong people, and there were many of them. They were very tall, like the Anakites. [d] [11]The Emites were thought to be Rephaites, [d] like the Anakites, but the Moabite people called them Emites. [12]The Horites also lived in Edom before, but the descendants of Esau forced them out and destroyed them, taking their place as Israel did in the land the LORD gave them as their own.)

[13]And the LORD said to me, "Now get up and cross the Zered Valley." So we crossed the valley. [14]It had been 38 years from the time we left Kadesh Barnea until we crossed the Zered Valley. By then, all the fighting men from that time had died, as the LORD had promised would happen. [15]The LORD continued to work against them to remove them from the camp until they were all dead.

[16]When the last of those fighting men had died, [17]the LORD said to me, [18]"Today you will pass by Ar, on the border of Moab. [19]When you come near the people of Ammon, don't bother them or go to war against them, because I will not give you any of their land as your own. I have given it to the descendants of Lot for their own."

[20](That land was also thought to be a land of the Rephaites, because those people used to live there, but the Ammonites called them Zamzummites. [21]They were strong people, and there were many of them; they were very tall, like the Anakites. The LORD destroyed the Zamzummites and the Ammonites forced them out of the land and took their place. [22]The LORD did the same thing for the descendants of Esau, who lived in Edom, when he destroyed the Horites.

The Edomites forced them out of the land and took their place, and they live there to this day. 23The Cretan people came from Crete and destroyed the Avvites, who lived in towns all the way to Gaza; the Cretan people destroyed them and took their place.)

Fighting the Amorites

24The LORD said, "Get up and cross the Arnon Ravine. See, I am giving you the power to defeat Sihon the Amorite, king of Heshbon, and I am giving you his land. So fight against him and begin taking his land. 25Today I will begin to make all the people in the world afraid of you. When they hear reports about you, they will shake with fear, and they will be terrified of you."

26I sent messengers from the desert of Kedemoth to Sihon king of Heshbon. They offered him peace, saying, 27"If you let us pass through your country, we will stay on the road and not turn right or left. 28We will pay you in silver for any food we eat or water we drink. We only want to walk through your country. 29The descendants d of Esau in Edom let us go through their land, and so did the Moabites in Ar. We want to cross the Jordan River into the land the LORD our God has given us." 30But Sihon king of Heshbon would not let us pass, because the LORD your God had made him stubborn. The LORD wanted you to defeat Sihon, and now this has happened.

31The LORD said to me, "See, I have begun to give Sihon and his country to you. Begin taking the land as your own."

32Then Sihon and all his army came out and fought us at Jahaz, 33but the LORD our God gave Sihon to us. We defeated him, his sons and all his army. 34We captured all his cities at that time and completely destroyed them, as well as the men, women and children. We left no one alive. 35But we kept the cattle and valuable things from the cities for ourselves. 36We defeated Aroer on the edge of the Arnon Ravine, and we defeated the town in the ravine, and even as far as Gilead. No town was too strong for us; the LORD our God gave us all of them. 37But you did not go near the land of the Ammonites, on the shores of the Jabbok River, or the towns in the mountains, as the LORD our God had commanded.

The Battle at Bashan

3 When we turned and went up the road towards Bashan, Og king of Bashan and all his army came out to fight us at Edrei. 2The LORD said to me, "Don't be afraid of Og, because I will hand him, his whole army and his land over to you. Do to him what you did to Sihon king of the Amorites, who ruled in Heshbon."

3So the LORD our God gave us Og king of Bashan and all his army; we defeated them and left no one alive. 4Then we captured all of Og's cities, all 60 of them, and took the whole area of Argob, Og's kingdom in Bashan. 5All these were strong cities, with high walls and gates with bars. And there were also many small towns with no walls. 6We completely destroyed them, just like the cities of Sihon king of Heshbon. We killed all the men, women and children, 7but we kept all the cattle and valuable things from the cities for ourselves.

8So at that time we took the land east of the Jordan River, from the Arnon Ravine to Mount Hermon, from these two Amorite kings. 9(Hermon is called Sirion by the Sidonian people, but the Amorites call it Senir.) 10We captured all the cities on the high plain and all of Gilead, and we took all of Bashan as far as Salecah and Edrei, towns in Og's kingdom of Bashan. 11(Only Og king of Bashan was left of the few Rephaites. d His bed was made of iron, and it was more than 4 metres long and 2 metres wide! It is still in the Ammonite city of Rabbah.)

The Land is Divided

12At that time we took this land to be our own. I gave the people of Reuben and Gad the land from Aroer by the Arnon Ravine, as well as half of the mountain country of Gilead and the cities in it. 13To the people of East Manasseh I gave the rest of Gilead and all of Bashan, the kingdom of Og. (The area of Argob in Bashan was called the land of the Rephaites. d 14Jair, a descendant d of Manasseh, took the whole area of Argob, all the way to the border of the Geshurites and Maacathites. So that land was named for Jair, and even today Bashan is called the Towns of Jair.) 15I gave Gilead to Makir. 16I gave the Reubenites and the Gadites the land that begins at Gilead and goes from the Arnon Ravine (the middle of the Arnon is the border) to the Jabbok River, which is the Ammonite border. 17The border on the west was the Jordan River in the Jordan Valley, and it goes from Lake Galilee to the Dead Sea d west of Mount Pisgah.

18At that time I gave you this command: "The LORD your God has given you this land as your own. Now your fighting men must take their weapons, and you must lead the other Israelites across the river. 19Your wives, your young children and your cattle may stay here. I know you have many cattle, and they may stay here in the cities I have given you, 20until the LORD also gives your Israelite relatives a place to rest. They will receive the land the LORD your God has given them on the other side of the Jordan River. After that, you may each return to the land I have given you."

21Then I gave this command to Joshua: "You have seen for yourself all that the LORD your God has done to these two kings. The LORD will do the same thing to all the kingdoms where you are going. 22Don't be afraid of them, because the LORD your God will fight for you."

Moses Cannot Enter the Land

23Then I begged the LORD: 24"Lord GOD, you have begun to show me, your servant, how great you are. You have great strength, and no other god in heaven or on earth can do the powerful things you do. There is no other god like you. 25Please let me cross the Jordan River so that I may see the good land by the Jordan. I want to see the beautiful mountains and Lebanon."

26But the LORD was angry with me because of you, and he would not listen to me. The LORD said to me, "That's enough. Don't talk to me any more about it. 27Climb to the top of Mount Pisgah and look west, north, south and east. You can look at the land, but you will not cross the Jordan River. 28Appoint Joshua and help him be brave and strong. He will lead the people across the river and give them the land that they are to inherit, but you can only look at it." 29So we stayed in the valley opposite Beth Peor.

Moses Tells Israel to Obey

4 Now, Israel, listen to the laws and commands I will teach you. Obey them so that you will live and so that you will go over and take the land the LORD, the God of your ancestors, is giving to you. 2Don't add to these commands, and don't leave anything out, but obey the commands of the LORD your God that I give you.

3You have seen for yourselves what the LORD did at Baal Peor, how the LORD your God destroyed everyone among you who followed Baal d in Peor. 4But all of you who continued following the LORD your God are still alive today.

5Look, I have taught you the laws and rules the LORD my God commanded me. Now you can obey the laws in the land you are entering, in the land you will take. 6Obey these laws carefully, in order to show the other nations that you have wisdom and understanding. When they hear about these laws, they will say, "This great nation of Israel is wise and understanding." 7No other nation is as great as we are. Their gods do not come near them, but the LORD our God comes near when we pray to him. 8And no other nation has such good teachings and commands as those I am giving to you today.

9But be careful! Watch out and don't forget the things you have seen. Don't forget them as long as you live, but teach them to your children and grandchildren. 10Remember the day you stood before the LORD your God at Mount Sinai. He said to me, "Bring the people together so I can tell them what I have to say. Then they will respect me as long as they live in the land, and they will teach these things to their children." 11When you came and stood at the bottom of the mountain, it blazed with fire that reached to the sky, and black clouds made it very dark. 12The LORD spoke to you from the fire. You heard the sound of words, but you did not see him; there was only a voice. 13The LORD told you about his Agreement, the Ten Commandments. He told you to obey them, and he wrote them on two stone tablets. 14Then the LORD commanded me to teach you the laws and rules that you must obey in the land you will take when you cross the Jordan River.

Laws About Idols

15Since the LORD spoke to you from the fire at Mount Sinai, but you did not see him, watch yourselves carefully! 16Don't sin by making idols of any kind, and don't make statues—of men or women, 17of animals on earth or birds that fly in the air, 18of anything that crawls on the ground or of fish in the water below. 19When you look up at the sky, you see the sun, moon and stars and everything in the sky. But don't bow down and worship them, because the LORD your God has made these things for all people everywhere. 20But the LORD brought you out of Egypt, which tested you like a furnace for melting iron, and he made you his very own people, as you are now.

21The LORD was angry with me because of you, and he swore that I would not cross the Jordan River to go into the good land the LORD your God is giving you as your own. 22I will die here in this land and not cross the Jordan, but you will soon go across and take that good land. 23Be careful. Don't forget the Agreement of the LORD your God that he made with you, and don't make any idols for yourselves, as the LORD your God has commanded you not to do. 24The LORD your God is a jealous God, like a fire that burns things up.

25Even after you have lived in the land a long time and have had children and grandchildren, don't do evil things. Don't make any kind of idol, and don't do what the LORD your God says is evil, because that will make him angry. 26If you do, I ask heaven and earth to speak against you this day that you will quickly be removed from this land that you are crossing the Jordan River to take. You will not live there long after that, but you will be completely destroyed. 27The LORD will scatter you among the other nations. Only a few of you will be left alive, and those few will be in other nations where the LORD will send you. [28]There you will worship gods made by people, gods made of wood and stone, that cannot see, hear, eat or smell. [29]But even there you can look for the LORD your God, and you will find him if you look for him with your whole being. [30]It will be hard when all these things happen to you. But after that you will come back to the LORD your God and obey him, [31]because the LORD your God is a merciful God. He will not leave you or destroy you. He will not forget the Agreement with your ancestors, which he swore to them.

The LORD is Great

[32]Nothing like this has ever happened before! Look at the past, long before you were even born. Go all the way back to when God made man on the earth, and look from one end of heaven to the other. Nothing like this has ever been heard of! [33]No other people have ever heard God speak from a fire and have still lived. But you have. [34]No other god has ever taken for himself one nation out of another. But the LORD your God did this for you in Egypt, right before your own eyes. He did it with tests, signs, miracles, [d] war and great sights, by his great power and strength.

[35]He showed you things so you would know that the LORD is God, and there is no other God besides him. [36]He spoke to you from heaven to teach you. He showed you his great fire on earth, and you heard him speak from the fire. [37]Because the LORD loved your ancestors, he chose you, their descendants, [d] and he brought you out of Egypt himself by his great strength. [38]He forced

---

GOD'S LOVE

Persistent Love

According to most people, Martha Henry should have hated Edward Henderson. After all, he had shot her son Calvin twice – once between the eyes and once in the neck.

Martha got the details of the shooting from Edward, who said he had intended to fire warning shots over the car, not into the car. He called the hospital almost every hour to see how Calvin was doing. Calvin died five days after the shooting, never having regained consciousness.

Martha believed Edward when he said the shooting was accidental. But the court didn't; he was sentenced to life in prison without any chance of being let out.

Then Martha felt God nudging her to share God's love with Edward. "I had a lot to think about while the Lord was pushing me to love Edward and not hold any bitterness against him," Martha says. "But, I'd learned from experience that when God tells you to do something, he means what he says."

On Martha's first visit, Edward was suspicious of her motives and didn't want to see her again. "I'm praying for you," she told him as she left. But each succeeding visit helped him open up. Eventually, he committed his life to Christ and began calling Martha "Mother Henry".

When Edward began appealing for parole, Martha pleaded his case. Though he hasn't been released, Martha believes he eventually will be. "He's not staying in there for ever," she says confidently. "The Lord has things for him to do!"

Martha reached out to Edward and believed he had a special role to play. God also reached out to the Israelites and chose them for a special role, revealing his incredible love in **Deuteronomy 4:32–40.**

* According to the passage, how were the Israelites like Edward?
* How did God make himself known to the Israelites? How are the reasons God worked in them similar to the reasons he has worked in you?

Consider . . .

* writing a love letter to God, thanking him for the many things he's done for you.
* becoming a pen pal with a prison inmate. Offer God's love and encouragement in your letters.

For more, see . . .

* Psalm 91:14–16 (p.555)
* Romans 5:6–8 (p.1190)
* Isaiah 43:1–4 (p.683)

nations out of their land ahead of you, nations that were bigger and stronger than you were. The LORD did this so he could bring you into their land and give it to you as your own, and this land is yours today.

³⁹Know and believe today that the LORD is God. He is God in heaven above and on the earth below. There is no other god! ⁴⁰Obey his laws and commands that I am giving you today so that things will go well for you and your children. Then you will live a long time in the land that the LORD your God is giving to you for ever.

Cities of Safety

⁴¹Moses chose three cities east of the Jordan River, ⁴²where a person who accidentally killed someone could go. If the person was not killed because of hatred, the murderer's life could be saved by running to one of these cities. ⁴³These were the cities: Bezer in the desert high plain was for the Reubenites; Ramoth in Gilead was for the Gadites; and Golan in Bashan was for the Manassites.

The Laws Moses Gave

⁴⁴These are the teachings Moses gave to the people of Israel. ⁴⁵They are the rules, commands and laws he gave them when they came out of Egypt. ⁴⁶They were in the valley near Beth Peor, east of the Jordan River, in the land of Sihon. Sihon king of the Amorites ruled in Heshbon and was defeated by Moses and the Israelites as they came out of Egypt. ⁴⁷The Israelites took his land and the land of Og king of Bashan, the two Amorite kings east of the Jordan River. ⁴⁸This land went from Aroer, on the edge of the Arnon Ravine, to Mount Hermon. ⁴⁹It included all the Jordan Valley east of the Jordan River, and it went as far as the Dead Sea*d* below Mount Pisgah.

The Ten Commandments

5 Moses called all the people of Israel together and said: Listen, Israel, to the commands and laws I am giving you today. Learn them and obey them carefully. ²The LORD our God made an Agreement with us at Mount Sinai. ³He did not make this Agreement with our ancestors, but he made it with us, with all of us who are alive here today. ⁴The LORD spoke to you face to face from the fire on the mountain. ⁵(At that time I stood between you and the LORD in order to tell you what the LORD said; you were afraid of the fire, so you would not go up on the mountain.) The LORD said:

⁶"I am the LORD your God; I brought you out of the land of Egypt where you were slaves.

⁷"You must not have any other gods except me.

⁸"You must not make for yourselves any idols or anything to worship that looks like something in the sky above or on the earth below or in the water below the land. ⁹You must not worship or serve any idol, because I, the LORD your God, am a jealous God. If people sin against me and hate me, I will punish their children, even their grand-children and great-grandchildren. ¹⁰But I will be very kind for 1,000 lifetimes to those who love me and obey my commands.

¹¹"You must not use the name of the LORD your God thoughtlessly, because the LORD will punish anyone who uses his name in this way.

¹²"Keep the Sabbath *d* as a holy day, as the LORD your God has commanded you. ¹³You may work and get everything done during six days each week, ¹⁴but the seventh day is a day of rest to honour the LORD your God. On that day no one may do any work: not you, your son or daughter, your male or female slaves, your ox, your donkey or any of your animals, or the foreigners living in your cities. That way your servants may rest as you do. ¹⁵Remember that you were slaves in Egypt and that the LORD your God brought you out of there by his great power and strength. So the LORD your God has commanded you to rest on the Sabbath day.

¹⁶"Honour your father and your mother as the LORD your God has commanded you. Then you will live a long time, and things will go well for you in the land that the LORD your God is going to give you.

¹⁷"You must not murder anyone.

¹⁸"You must not be guilty of adultery. *d*

¹⁹"You must not steal.

²⁰"You must not tell lies about your neighbour.

²¹"You must not want to take your neighbour's wife. You must not want to take your neighbour's house or land, his male or female slaves, his ox or his donkey, or anything that belongs to your neighbour."

²²The LORD spoke these commands to all of you on the mountain in a loud voice out of the fire, the cloud and the deep darkness; he did not say anything else. Then he wrote them on two stone tablets, and he gave them to me.

²³When you heard the voice from the darkness, as the mountain was blazing with fire, all your elders and leaders of your tribes *d* came to me. ²⁴And you said, "The LORD our God has shown us his glory and majesty, and we have heard his voice from the fire. Today we have seen that a person can live even if God speaks to him. ²⁵But now, we will die! This great fire will burn us up, and we will die if we hear the LORD our God speak any more. ²⁶No human being has ever heard the living God speaking from a fire and still lived, but we have. ²⁷Moses, you go near and listen to everything the LORD our God says. Then

you tell us what the LORD our God tells you, and we will listen and obey."

28The LORD heard what you said to me, and he said to me, "I have heard what the people said to you. Everything they said was good. 29I wish their hearts would always respect me and that they would always obey my commands so that things would go well for them and their children for ever!

30"Go and tell the people to return to their tents, 31but you stay here with me so that I may give you all the commands, rules and laws that you must teach the people to obey in the land I am giving them as their own."

32So be careful to do what the LORD your God has commanded you, and follow the commands exactly. 33Live the way the LORD your God has commanded you so that you may live and have what is good and have a long life in the land you will take.

The Command to Love God

6 These are the commands, rules and laws that the LORD your God told me to teach you to obey in the land you are crossing the Jordan River to take. 2You, your children and your grandchildren must respect the LORD your God as long as you live. Obey all his rules and commands I give you so that you will live a long time. 3Listen, Israel, and carefully obey these laws. Then all will go well for you, and you will become a great nation in a fertile land, just as the LORD, the God of your ancestors, has promised you.

FOLLOWING GOD

Walk and Talk

Peter was a birdwatcher. Some may say that's a very boring hobby, but he was an expert. When you went out with him, he made you aware of birds you'd never seen.

"Stand still," he'd say. "Now, listen."

Somewhere in the distance you heard a small cry.

"A Stone Curlew!" he would remark in triumph.

And before you knew what was happening, you were following him through bracken and long grass, getting scratched to pieces until suddenly, there in front of you was the bird in question. It made you feel almost as good as him.

Peter and his wife Miranda often felt that they should start a Bird Reserve. Somewhere where people could enjoy watching the beautiful creatures that God had made.

So they made their home in the Algarve, Portugal. A magnificent place for birdwatching. Gradually people came to stay at the A Rocha Reserve, and Peter took them out into the wilds and showed them Bee Eaters up close. It was the most natural thing for him to remark, "Isn't God fantastic? Just look at the colours on that one!" And as the sun came down, he would say, "The Lord seems to make a different sunset every night, have you noticed?"

Without really knowing it, Peter was doing exactly what it says in Deuteronomy 6:7. Talking about the Lord at home and walking down the road.

Deuteronomy 6:1–9 tells us about God's laws and how following them results in a better life.

* What promises did God give in this passage? How would they affect Peter's life?
* What could you do in your life to help fulfil these commands?

Consider . . .

* taking some time out to talk to God whilst enjoying a walk in the park or on the beach, appreciating God's creation.
* re-writing what Deuteronomy 6:5 means to you, in your own words.

For more, see . . .

* Deuteronomy 10:12–22 (p.175)
* Philippians 3:12–16 (p.1284)
* Psalm 119:9–16 (p.571)

⁴Listen, people of Israel! The LORD our God is the only LORD. ⁵Love the LORD your God with all your heart, all your soul and all your strength. ⁶Always remember these commands I give you today. ⁷Teach them to your children, and talk about them when you sit at home and walk along

---

Sidelight   Deuteronomy 6:4–9 is as important to the Jews as the Lord's Prayer (Matthew 6:9–13, p.948) is to Christians. The Deuteronomy passage is the basis for the Jewish Shema, which is recited morning and evening by many Jews. This classic declaration of faith is also recited just before death and in times of martyrdom.

---

the road, when you lie down and when you get up. ⁸Write them down and tie them to your hands as a sign. Tie them on your forehead to remind you, ⁹and write them on your doors and gates.

¹⁰The LORD your God will bring you into the land he promised to your ancestors, to Abraham, Isaac and Jacob, and he will give it to you. The land has large, growing cities you did not build, ¹¹houses full of good things you did not buy, wells you did not dig and vineyards and olive trees you did not plant. You will eat as much as you want. ¹²But be careful! Do not forget the LORD, who brought you out of the land of Egypt where you were slaves.

¹³Respect the LORD your God. You must worship him and make your promises only in his name. ¹⁴Do not worship other gods as the people around you do, ¹⁵because the LORD your God is a jealous God. He is present with you, and if you worship other gods, he will become angry with you and destroy you from the earth. ¹⁶Do not test the LORD your God as you did at Massah. ¹⁷Be sure to obey the commands of the LORD your God and the rules and laws he has given you. ¹⁸Do what the LORD says is good and right so that things will go well for you. Then you may go in and take the good land the LORD promised to your ancestors. ¹⁹He will force all your enemies out as you go in, as the LORD has said.

²⁰In the future when your children ask you, "What is the meaning of the laws, commands and rules the LORD our God gave us?" ²¹tell them, "We were slaves to the king of Egypt, but the LORD brought us out of Egypt by his great power. ²²The LORD showed us great and terrible signs and miracles, *d* which he did to Egypt, the king and his whole family. ²³The LORD brought us out of Egypt to lead us here and to give us the land he promised our ancestors. ²⁴The LORD ordered us to obey all these commands and to respect the LORD our

God so that we will always do well and stay alive, as we are today. ²⁵The right thing for us to do is this: obey all these rules in the presence of the LORD our God, as he has commanded."

You are God's People

7 The LORD your God will bring you into the land that you are entering and that you will have as your own. As you go in, he will force out these nations: the Hittites, Girgashites, Amorites, Canaanites, Perizzites, Hivites and Jebusites— seven nations that are stronger than you. ²The LORD your God will hand these nations over to you, and when you defeat them, you must destroy them completely. Do not make a peace treaty with them or show them any mercy. ³Do not marry any of them, or let your daughters marry their sons, or let your sons marry their daughters. ⁴If you do, those people will turn your children away from me, to begin serving other gods. Then the LORD will be very angry with you, and he will quickly destroy you. ⁵This is what you must do to those people: tear down their altars, smash their holy stone pillars, cut down their Asherah *d* idols and burn their idols in the fire. ⁶You are holy people who belong to the LORD your God. He has chosen you from all the people on earth to be his very own.

⁷The LORD did not care for you and choose you because there were many of you—you are the smallest nation of all. ⁸But the LORD chose you because he loved you, and he kept his promise to your ancestors. So he brought you out of Egypt by his great power and freed you from the land of slavery, from the power of the king of Egypt. ⁹So know that the LORD your God is God, the faithful God. He will keep his agreement of love for 1,000 lifetimes for people who love him and obey his commands. ¹⁰But he will pay back those people who hate him. He will destroy them, and he will not be slow to pay back those who hate him. ¹¹So be careful to obey the commands, rules and laws I give you today.

¹²If you pay attention to these laws and obey them carefully, the LORD your God will keep his agreement and show his love to you, as he promised your ancestors. ¹³He will love and bless you. He will make the number of your people grow; he will bless you with children. He will bless your fields with good crops and will give you grain, new wine and oil. He will bless your herds with calves and your flocks with lambs in the land he promised your ancestors he would give you. ¹⁴You will be blessed more than any other people. Every husband and wife will have children, and all your cattle will have calves. ¹⁵The LORD will take away all disease from you; you will not have the terrible diseases that were in Egypt, but he

will give them to all the people who hate you. [16]You must destroy all the people the LORD your God hands over to you. Do not feel sorry for them, and do not worship their gods, or they will trap you.

[17]You might say to yourselves, "Because these nations are stronger than we are, we can't force them out." [18]But don't be afraid of them. Remember what the LORD your God did to all of Egypt and its king. [19]You saw for yourselves the troubles, signs and miracles[d] he did, how the LORD's great power and strength brought you out of Egypt. The LORD your God will do the same thing to all the nations you now fear. [20]The LORD your God will also send terror among them so that even those who are alive and hiding from you will die. [21]Don't be afraid of them, because the LORD your God is with you; he is a great God and people are afraid of him. [22]When the LORD your God forces those nations out of the land, he will do it little by little ahead of you. You won't be able to destroy them all at once; otherwise, the wild animals will grow too many in number. [23]But the LORD your God will hand those nations over to you, confusing them until they are destroyed. [24]The LORD will help you defeat their kings, and the world will forget who they were. No one will be able to stop you; you will destroy them all. [25]Burn up their idols in the fire. Do not wish for the silver and gold they have, and don't take it for yourselves, or you will be trapped by it. The LORD your God hates it. [26]Do not bring one of those hateful things into your house, or you will be completely destroyed along with it. Hate and reject those things; they must be completely destroyed.

Remember the LORD

8 Carefully obey every command I give you today. Then you will live and grow in number, and you will enter and take the land the LORD promised your ancestors. [2]Remember how the LORD your God has led you in the desert for these 40 years, taking away your pride and testing you, because he wanted to know what was in your heart. He wanted to know if you would obey his commands. [3]He took away your pride when he let you get hungry, and then he fed you with manna,[d] which neither you nor your ancestors had ever seen. This was to teach you that a person does not live by eating only bread, but by everything the LORD says. [4]During these 40 years, your clothes did not wear out, and your feet did not swell. [5]Know in your heart that the LORD your God corrects you as a parent corrects a child.

[6]Obey the commands of the LORD your God,

living as he has commanded you, and respect him. [7]The LORD your God is bringing you into a good land, a land with rivers and pools of water, with springs that flow in the valleys and hills, [8]a land that has wheat and barley, vines, fig trees, pomegranates,[d] olive oil and honey. [9]It is a land where you will have plenty of food, where you will have everything you need, where the rocks are iron, and where you can dig copper out of the hills.

> ### Sidelight
> Most Christians pray or say grace before they eat a meal. But the ancient Israelites didn't just pray before they ate. They prayed afterwards as well (Deuteronomy 8:10).

[10]When you have all you want to eat, then praise the LORD your God for giving you a good land. [11]Be careful not to forget the LORD your God so that you fail to obey his commands, laws and rules that I am giving to you today. [12]When you eat all you want and build nice houses and live in them, [13]when your herds and flocks grow large and your silver and gold increase, when you have more of everything, [14]then your heart will become proud. You will forget the LORD your God, who brought you out of the land of Egypt, where you were slaves. [15]He led you through the large and terrible desert that was dry and had no water, and that had poisonous snakes and stinging insects. He gave you water from a solid rock [16]and manna to eat in the desert. Manna was something your ancestors had never seen. He did this to take away your pride and to test you, so things would go well for you in the end. [17]You might say to yourself, "I am rich because of my own power and strength," [18]but remember the LORD your God! It is he who gives you the power to become rich, keeping the agreement he promised to your ancestors, as it is today.

[19]If you ever forget the LORD your God and follow other gods and worship them and bow down to them, I warn you today that you will be destroyed. [20]Just as the LORD destroyed the other nations for you, you can be destroyed if you do not obey the LORD your God.

The LORD Will be With Israel

9 Listen, Israel. You will soon cross the Jordan River to go in and force out nations that are bigger and stronger than you. They have large cities with walls up to the sky. [2]The people there are Anakites,[d] who are strong and tall. You know about them, and you have heard it said: "No one can stop the Anakites." [3]But today remember that the LORD your God goes in before you to destroy them like a fire that burns things up. He will defeat them ahead of you, and you will force them out and destroy them quickly, just as the LORD has said.

[4]After the LORD your God has forced those nations out ahead of you, don't say to yourself, "The LORD brought me here to take this land because I am so good." No! It is because these nations are evil that the LORD will force them out ahead of you. [5]You are going in to take the land, not because you are good and honest, but because these nations are evil. That is why the LORD your God will force them out ahead of you, to keep his promise to your ancestors, to Abraham, Isaac and Jacob. [6]The LORD your God is giving you this good land to take as your own. But know this: it is not because you are good; you are a stubborn people.

Remember the LORD's Anger

[7]Remember this and do not forget it: you made the LORD your God angry in the desert. You would not obey the LORD from the day you left Egypt until you arrived here. [8]At Mount Sinai you made the LORD angry—angry enough to destroy you. [9]When I went up on the mountain to receive the stone tablets, the tablets with the Agreement the LORD had made with you, I stayed on the mountain for 40 days and 40 nights; I did not eat bread or drink water. [10]The LORD gave me two stone tablets, which God had written on with his own finger. On them were all the commands that the LORD gave to you on the mountain out of the fire, on the day you were gathered there.

[11]When the 40 days and 40 nights were over, the LORD gave me the two stone tablets, the tablets with the Agreement on them. [12]Then the

THANKFULNESS

Cinderella Story

Beth had grown up being passed from one foster home to the next. More often than not, she was sharing a room with at least one other child. Finally, when she was eighteen, a middle-aged couple called Rita and Paul agreed to adopt her permanently. She had a room of her own, clothes that were bought for her and not just cast-offs and, most importantly for her, Beth had people who loved her unconditionally and who were willing to accept her just as she was.

When college finished, her employers took her on full time, and by working hard Beth slowly but surely climbed her way up until she got the point where she was earning enough to buy her own place and provide for herself.

Things were amazing for a while, until one day she got a phone call from the hospital saying that her adoptive mum, Rita, had suffered a serious fall. She would be in hospital for a few weeks and then would need help around the house for a while.

Knowing that Rita's husband Paul wouldn't be able to cope by himself, Beth did as much as she could for the couple who had provided for her over the years. She also went to visit Rita in hospital every day until she was allowed to go home.

Read **Deuteronomy 8:10–18**.

- In what way is Beth's story similar to that of the Israelites mentioned in this passage?
- What pitfalls mentioned in this passage did Beth manage to avoid?

Consider . . .

- whether there are any situations where you didn't express proper thankfulness.
- making a list of all the things you have which you have to be thankful for. Take time to thank God properly for them – write a song, do it in prayer, etc.

For more, see . . .

- Psalm 92:1–5 (p.555)
- 2 Corinthians 9:6–15 (p.1248)
- Psalm 106:1–3 (p.562)

LORD told me, "Get up and go down quickly from here, because the people you brought out from Egypt are ruining themselves. They have quickly turned away from what I commanded and have made an idol for themselves."

[13]The LORD said to me, "I have watched these people, and they are very stubborn! [14]Get away so that I may destroy them and make the whole world forget who they are. Then I will make another nation from you that will be bigger and stronger than they are."

[15]So I turned and came down the mountain that was burning with fire and the two stone tablets with the Agreement were in my hands. [16]When I looked, I saw you had sinned against the LORD your God and had made an idol in the shape of a calf. You had quickly turned away from what the LORD had told you to do. [17]So I took the two stone tablets and threw them down, breaking them into pieces right in front of you.

[18]Then I again bowed face down on the ground before the LORD for 40 days and 40 nights; I did not eat bread or drink water. You had sinned by doing what the LORD said was evil, and you made him angry. [19]I was afraid of the LORD's anger and rage, because he was angry enough with you to destroy you, but the LORD listened to me again. [20]And the LORD was angry enough with Aaron to destroy him, but then I prayed for Aaron too. [21]I took that sinful calf idol you had made and burned it in the fire. I crushed it into a powder like dust and threw the dust into a stream that flowed down the mountain.

[22]You also made the LORD angry at Taberah, Massah and Kibroth Hattaavah.

[23]Then the LORD sent you away from Kadesh Barnea and said, "Go up and take the land I have given you." But you rejected the command of the LORD your God. You did not trust him or obey him. [24]You have refused to obey the LORD as long as I have known you.

[25]The LORD had said he would destroy you, so I threw myself down in front of him for those 40 days and 40 nights. [26]I prayed to the LORD and said, "Lord GOD, do not destroy your people, your own people, whom you freed and brought out of Egypt by your great power and strength. [27]Remember your servants Abraham, Isaac and Jacob. Don't look at how stubborn these people are, and don't look at their sin and evil. [28]Otherwise, Egypt will say, 'It was because the LORD was not able to take his people into the land he promised them, and it was because he hated them that he took them into the desert to kill them.' [29]But they are your people, LORD, your own people, whom you brought out of Egypt with your great power and strength."

New Stone Tablets

10 At that time the LORD said to me, "Cut two stone tablets like the first ones and come up to me on the mountain. Also make a wooden Ark. *d* [2]I will write on the tablets the same words that were on the first tablets, which you broke, and you will put the new tablets in the Ark."

[3]So I made the Ark out of acacia wood, and I cut out two stone tablets like the first ones. Then I went up on the mountain with the two tablets in my hands. [4]The LORD wrote the same things on these tablets he had written before—the Ten Commandments that he had told you on the mountain from the fire, on the day you were gathered there. And the LORD gave them to me. [5]Then I turned and came down the mountain; I put the tablets in the Ark I had made, as the LORD had commanded, and they are still there.

[6](The people of Israel went from the wells of the Jaakanites to Moserah. Aaron died there and was buried; his son Eleazar became priest in his place. [7]From Moserah they went to Gudgodah, and from Gudgodah they went to Jotbathah, a place with streams of water. [8]At that time the LORD chose the tribe *d* of Levi to carry the Ark of the Agreement with the LORD. They were to serve the LORD and to bless the people in his name, which they still do today. [9]That is why the Levites did not receive any land of their own; instead, they received the LORD himself as their gift, as the LORD your God told them.)

[10]I stayed on the mountain 40 days and 40 nights just like the first time, and the LORD listened to me this time also. He did not want to destroy you. [11]The LORD said to me, "Go and lead the people so that they will go in and take the land I promised their ancestors."

What the LORD Wants You to Do

[12]Now, Israel, this is what the LORD your God wants you to do: respect the LORD your God, and do what he has told you to do. Love him. Serve the LORD your God with your whole being, [13]and obey the LORD's commands and laws that I am giving you today for your own good.

[14]The LORD owns the world and everything in it—the heavens, even the highest heavens, are his. [15]But the LORD cared for and loved your ancestors, and he chose you, their descendants, *d* over all the other nations, just as it is today. [16]Give yourselves completely to serving him, and do not be stubborn any longer. [17]The LORD your God is God of all gods and Lord of all lords. He is the great God, who is strong and wonderful. He does not take sides, and he will not be talked into doing evil. [18]He helps orphans and widows, and he loves foreigners and gives them food and

clothes. [19]You also must love foreigners, because you were foreigners in Egypt. [20]Respect the LORD your God and serve him. Be loyal to him and make your promises in his name. [21]He is the one you should praise; he is your God, who has done great and wonderful things for you, which you have seen with your own eyes. [22]There were only 70 of your ancestors when they went down to Egypt, and now the LORD your God has made you as many as the stars in the sky.

Great Things Israel Saw

11 Love the LORD your God and always obey his orders, rules, laws and commands. [2]Remember today it was not your children who saw and felt the correction of the LORD your God. They did not see his majesty, his power, his strength [3]or his signs and the things he did in Egypt to the king and his whole country. [4]They did not see what he did to the Egyptian army, its horses and chariots, when he drowned them in the Red Sea[d] as they were chasing you. The LORD ruined them for ever. [5]They did not see what he did for you in the desert until you arrived here. [6]They did not see what he did to Dathan and Abiram, the sons of Eliab the Reubenite, when the ground opened up and swallowed them, their families, their tents and everyone who stood with them in Israel. [7]It was you who saw all these great things the LORD has done.

[8]So obey all the commands I am giving you today so that you will be strong and can go in and take the land you are going to take as your own. [9]Then you will live a long time in the land that the LORD promised to give to your ancestors and their descendants, [d] a fertile land. [10]The land you are going to take is not like Egypt, where you were. There you had to plant your seed and water it, like a vegetable garden, by using your feet. [11]But the land that you will soon cross the Jordan River to take is a land of hills and valleys, a land that drinks rain from heaven. [12]It is a land the LORD your God cares for. His eyes are on it continually, and he watches it from the beginning of the year to the end.

[13]If you carefully obey the commands I am giving you today and love the LORD your God and serve him with your whole being, [14]then he will send rain on your land at the right time, in the autumn and spring, and you will be able to gather your grain, new wine and oil. [15]He will put grass in the fields for your cattle, and you will have plenty to eat.

[16]Be careful, or you will be fooled and will turn away to serve and worship other gods. [17]If you do, the LORD will become angry with you and will shut the heavens so it will not rain.

Then the land will not grow crops, and you will soon die in the good land the LORD is giving you. [18]Remember my words with your whole being. Write them down and tie them to your hands as a sign; tie them on your foreheads to remind you. [19]Teach them well to your children, talking about them when you sit at home and walk along the road, when you lie down and when

---

Sidelight

If you have trouble remembering scripture passages, you are not alone. The Israelites apparently did too. So God told his people to write down his words and tie them to their hands so that they wouldn't forget them (Deuteronomy 11:18). This might get heavy if you memorised the whole Bible!

---

you get up. [20]Write them on your doors and gates [21]so that both you and your children will live a long time in the land the LORD promised your ancestors, as long as the skies are above the earth.

[22]If you are careful to obey every command I am giving you to follow, and love the LORD your God, and do what he has told you to do, and are loyal to him, [23]then the LORD will force all those nations out of the land ahead of you, and you will take the land from nations that are bigger and stronger than you. [24]Everywhere you step will be yours. Your land will go from the desert to Lebanon and from the Euphrates River to the Mediterranean Sea. [25]No one will be able to stop you. The LORD your God will do what he promised and will make the people afraid everywhere you go.

[26]See, today I am letting you choose a blessing or a curse. [27]You will be blessed if you obey the commands of the LORD your God that I am giving you today. [28]But you will be cursed if you disobey the commands of the LORD your God. So do not disobey the commands I am giving you today, and do not worship other gods you do not know. [29]When the LORD your God brings you into the land you will take as your own, you are to announce the blessings from Mount Gerizim and the curses from Mount Ebal. [30](These mountains are on the other side of the Jordan River, to the west, towards the sunset. They are near the great trees of Moreh in the land of the Canaanites who live in the Jordan Valley opposite Gilgal.) [31]You will soon cross the Jordan River to enter and take the land the LORD your God is giving you. When you take it over and live there, [32]be careful to obey all the commands and laws I am giving you today.

The Place for Worship

12 These are the commands and laws you must carefully obey in the land the LORD, the God of your ancestors, is giving you. Obey them as long as you live in the land. ²When you inherit the lands of these nations, you must completely destroy all the places where they serve their gods, on high mountains and hills and under every green tree. ³Tear down their altars, smash their holy stone pillars and burn their Asherah *d* idols in the fire. Cut down their idols and destroy their names from those places.

⁴Don't worship the LORD your God that way, ⁵but look for the place the LORD your God will choose—a place among your tribes *d* where he is to be worshipped. Go there, ⁶and bring to that place your burnt offerings and sacrifices; bring a tenth of what you gain and your special gifts; bring what you have promised and the special gifts you want to give the LORD, and bring the first animals born to your herds and flocks.

⁷There you will be together with the LORD your God. There you and your families will eat, and you will enjoy all the good things for which you have worked, because the LORD your God has blessed you.

⁸Do not worship the way we have been doing today, each person doing what he thinks is right. ⁹You have not yet come to a resting place, to the land the LORD your God will give you as your own. ¹⁰But soon you will cross the Jordan River to live in the land the LORD your God is giving you as your own, where he will give you rest from all your enemies and you will live in safety. ¹¹Then the LORD your God will choose a place where he is to be worshipped. To that place you must bring everything I tell you: your burnt offerings and sacrifices, your offerings of a tenth of what you gain, your special gifts and all your best things you promised to the LORD. ¹²There rejoice before the LORD your God. Everyone should rejoice: you, your sons and daughters, your male and female servants and the Levites from your towns who have no land of their own. ¹³Be careful that you don't sacrifice your burnt offerings just anywhere you please. ¹⁴Offer them only in the place the LORD will choose. He will choose a place in one of your tribes, and there you must do everything I am commanding you.

¹⁵But you may kill your animals in any of your towns and eat as much of the meat as you want, as if it were a deer or a gazelle; this is the blessing the LORD your God is giving you. Anyone, clean *d* or unclean, may eat this meat, ¹⁶but do not eat the blood. Pour it out on the ground like water.

¹⁷Do not eat in your own towns what belongs to the LORD: one-tenth of your grain, new wine or oil; the first animals born to your herds or flocks; whatever you have promised to give; the special gifts you want to give to the LORD, or any other gifts. ¹⁸Eat these things when you are together with the LORD your God, in the place the LORD your God chooses to be worshipped. Everyone must do this: you, your sons and daughters, your male and female servants and the Levites from your towns. Rejoice in the LORD your God's presence about the things you have worked for. ¹⁹Be careful not to forget the Levites as long as you live in the land.

²⁰When the LORD your God enlarges your country as he has promised, and you want some meat so you say, "I want some meat," you may eat as much meat as you want. ²¹If the LORD your God chooses a place where he is to be worshipped that is too far away from you, you may kill animals from your herds and flocks, which the LORD has given to you. I have commanded that you may do this. You may eat as much of them as you want in your own towns, ²²as you would eat gazelle or deer meat. Both clean and unclean people may eat this meat, ²³but be sure you don't eat the blood, because the life is in the blood. Don't eat the life with the meat. ²⁴Don't eat the blood, but pour it out on the ground like water. ²⁵If you don't eat it, things will go well for you and your children, because you will be doing what the LORD says is right.

²⁶Take your holy things and the things you have promised to give, and go to the place the LORD will choose. ²⁷Present your burnt offerings on the altar of the LORD your God, both the meat and the blood. The blood of your sacrifices should be poured beside the altar of the LORD your God, but you may eat the meat. ²⁸Be careful to obey all the rules I am giving you so that things will always go well for you and your children, and you will be doing what the LORD your God says is good and right.

²⁹You will enter the land and take it away from the nations that the LORD your God will destroy ahead of you. When you force them out and live in their land, ³⁰they will be destroyed for you, but be careful not to be trapped by asking about their gods. Don't say, "How do these nations worship? I will do the same." ³¹Don't worship the LORD your God that way, because the LORD hates the evil ways they worship their gods. They even burn their sons and daughters as sacrifices to their gods!

³²Be sure to do everything I have commanded you. Do not add anything to it, and do not take anything away from it.

False Prophets

13 Prophets *d* or those who tell the future with dreams might come to you and say they will show you a miracle *d* or a sign. ²The miracle or sign might even happen, and then they might say, "Let's serve other gods" (gods you have not known) "and let's worship them." ³But you must not listen to those prophets or dreamers. The LORD your God is testing you, to find out if you love him with your whole being. ⁴Serve only the LORD your God. Respect him, keep his commands and obey him. Serve him and be loyal to him. ⁵The prophets or dreamers must be killed, because they said you should turn against the LORD your God, who brought you out of Egypt and saved you from the land where you were slaves. They tried to turn you from doing what the LORD your God commanded you to do. You must get rid of the evil among you.

⁶Someone might try to lead you to serve other gods—it might be your brother, your son or daughter, the wife you love or a close friend. The person might say, "Let's go and worship other gods." (These are gods that neither you nor your ancestors have known, ⁷gods of the people who live around you, either nearby or far away, from one end of the land to the other.) ⁸Do not give in to such people. Do not listen or feel sorry for them, and do not let them go free or protect them. ⁹You must put them to death. You must be the first one to start to kill them, and then everyone else must join in. ¹⁰You must throw stones at them until they die, because they tried to turn you away from the LORD your God, who brought you out of the land of Egypt, where you were slaves. ¹¹Then everyone in Israel will hear about this and be afraid, and no one among you will ever do such an evil thing again.

Cities to Destroy

¹²The LORD your God is giving you cities in which to live, and you might hear something about one of them. Someone might say ¹³that evil people have moved in among you. And they might lead the people of that city away from God, saying, "Let's go and worship other gods." (These are gods you have not known.) ¹⁴Then you must ask about it, looking into the matter and checking carefully whether it is true. If it is proved that a hateful thing has happened among you, ¹⁵you must kill with a sword everyone who lives in that city. Destroy the city completely and kill everyone in it, as well as the animals, with a sword. ¹⁶Gather up everything those people owned, and put it in the middle of the city square. Then completely burn the city and everything they owned as a burnt offering to the LORD your God. That city should never be rebuilt; let it be ruined for ever. ¹⁷Don't keep for yourselves any of the things found in that city, so the LORD will not be angry any more. He will give you mercy and feel sorry for you, and he will make your nation grow larger, as he promised to your ancestors. ¹⁸You will have obeyed the LORD your God by keeping all his commands that I am giving to you today, and you will be doing what the LORD says is right.

God's Special People

14 You are the children of the LORD your God. When someone dies, do not cut yourselves or shave your heads to show your sadness. ²You are holy people, who belong to the LORD your God. He has chosen you from all the people on earth to be his very own.

³Do not eat anything the LORD hates. ⁴These are the animals you may eat: oxen, sheep, goats, ⁵deer, gazelle, roe deer, wild goats, ibex, antelope and mountain sheep. ⁶You may eat any animal that has a split hoof and chews the cud, *d* ⁷but you may not eat camels, rabbits or rock badgers. These animals chew the cud, but they do not have split hoofs, so they are unclean *d* for you. ⁸Pigs are also unclean for you; they have split hoofs, but they do not chew the cud. Do not eat their meat or touch their dead bodies.

⁹There are many things that live in the water. You may eat anything that has fins and scales, ¹⁰but do not eat anything that does not have fins and scales. It is unclean for you.

¹¹You may eat any clean bird. ¹²But do not eat these birds: eagles, vultures, black vultures, ¹³red kites, falcons, any kind of kite, ¹⁴any kind of raven, ¹⁵horned owls, screech owls, sea gulls, any kind of hawk, ¹⁶little owls, great owls, white owls, ¹⁷desert owls, ospreys, cormorants, ¹⁸storks, any kind of heron, the hoopoes or bats.

¹⁹All insects with wings are unclean for you; do not eat them. ²⁰Other things with wings are clean, and you may eat them.

²¹Do not eat anything you find that is already dead. You may give it to a foreigner living in your town, and he may eat it, or you may sell it to a foreigner. But you are holy people, who belong to the LORD your God.

Do not cook a baby goat in its mother's milk.

Sidelight | Throughout the Old Testament God is rarely spoken of as "Father" – in fact there are only fourteen such times. Mostly God is referred to as the Creator with a special relationship with Israel, his special people.

Giving One-Tenth

[22]Be sure to save one-tenth of all your crops each year. [23]Take it to the place the LORD your God will choose where he is to be worshipped. There, where you will be together with the LORD, eat the tenth of your grain, new wine and oil, and eat the animals born first to your herds and flocks. Do this so that you will learn to respect the LORD your God always. [24]But if the place the LORD will choose to be worshipped is too far away and he has blessed you so much you cannot carry a tenth, [25]exchange your one-tenth for silver. Then take the silver with you to the place the LORD your God shall choose. [26]Use the silver to buy anything you wish—cattle, sheep, wine, beer or anything you wish. Then you and your family will eat and celebrate there before the LORD your God. [27]Do not forget the Levites in your town, because they have no land of their own among you.

[28]At the end of every third year, everyone should bring one-tenth of that year's crop and store it in your towns. [29]This is for the Levites so they may eat and be full. (They have no land of their own among you.) It is also for strangers, orphans and widows who live in your towns so that all of them may eat and be full. Then the LORD your God will bless you and all the work you do.

The Special Seventh Year

15 At the end of every seven years, you must tell those who owe you anything that they do not have to pay you back. [2]This is how you must do it: everyone who has loaned money must cancel the loan and not make a neighbour or relative pay it back. This is the LORD's time for cancelling what people owe. [3]You may make a foreigner pay what is owed to you, but you must not collect what another Israelite owes you. [4]But there should be no poor people among you, because the LORD your God will richly bless you in the land he is giving you as your own. [5]He will bless you if you obey the LORD your God completely, but you must be careful to obey all the commands I am giving you today. [6]The LORD your God will bless you as he promised, and you will lend to other nations, but you will not need to borrow from them. You will rule over many nations, but none will rule over you.

[7]If there are poor among you, in one of the towns of the land the LORD your God is giving you, do not be selfish or greedy towards them. [8]But give freely to them, and freely lend them whatever they need. [9]Beware of evil thoughts. Don't think, "The seventh year is near, the year to cancel what people owe." You might be mean to the needy and not give them anything. Then they will complain to the LORD about you, and he will find you guilty of sin. [10]Give freely to the poor person, and do not wish that you didn't have to give. The LORD your God will bless your work and everything you touch. [11]There will always be poor people in the land, so I command you to give freely to your neighbours and to the poor and needy in your land.

Letting Slaves Go Free

[12]If one of your own people sells himself to you as a slave, whether it is a Hebrew man or woman, that person will serve you for six years. But in the seventh year you must let the slave go free. [13]When you let slaves go, don't send them away without anything. [14]Give them some of your flock, your grain and your wine, giving to them as the LORD has given to you. [15]Remember that you were slaves in Egypt, and the LORD your God saved you. That is why I give you this command today.

[16]But if your slave says to you, "I don't want to leave you," because he loves you and your family and has a good life with you, [17]stick an awl[n] through his ear into the door; he will be your slave for life. Also do this to a female slave.

[18]Do not think of it as a hard thing when you let your slaves go free. After all, they served you six years and did twice the work of a hired person. The LORD your God will bless you in everything you do.

Rules About Firstborn Animals

[19]Save all the first male animals born to your herds and flocks. They are for the LORD your God. Do not work the first calf born to your oxen, and do not cut off the wool from the first lamb born to your sheep. [20]Each year you and your family are to eat these animals in the presence of the LORD your God, in the place he will choose to be worshipped. [21]If an animal is crippled or blind or has something else wrong, do not sacrifice it to the LORD your God. [22]But you may eat that animal in your own town. Both clean[d] and unclean people may eat it, as they would eat a gazelle or a deer. [23]But don't eat its blood; pour it out on the ground like water.

The Passover

16 Celebrate the Passover[d] of the LORD your God during the month of Abib,[d] because it was during Abib that he brought you out

---

awl A tool like a big needle with a handle at one end.

of Egypt at night. [2]As the sacrifice for the Passover to the LORD your God, offer an animal from your flock or herd at the place the LORD will choose to be worshipped. [3]Do not eat it with bread made with yeast. But for seven days eat bread made without yeast, the bread of suffering, because you left Egypt in a hurry. So all your life you will remember the time you left Egypt. [4]There must be no yeast anywhere in your land for seven days. Offer the sacrifice on the evening of the first day, and eat all the meat before morning; do not leave it overnight.

[5]Do not offer the Passover sacrifice in just any town the LORD your God gives you, [6]but offer it in the place he will choose to be worshipped. Offer it in the evening as the sun goes down, which is when you left Egypt. [7]Roast the meat and eat it at the place the LORD your God will choose. The next morning go back to your tents. [8]Eat bread made without yeast for six days. On the seventh day have a special meeting for the LORD your God, and do not work that day.

The Feast of Weeks

[9]Count seven weeks from the time you begin to harvest the grain, [10]and then celebrate the Feast[d] of Weeks for the LORD your God. Bring an offering as a special gift to him, giving to him just as he has blessed you. [11]Rejoice before the LORD your God at the place he will choose to be worshipped. Everybody should rejoice: you, your sons and daughters, your male and female servants, the Levites in your town, the strangers, orphans and widows living among you. [12]Remember that you were slaves in Egypt, and carefully obey all these laws.

The Feast of Shelters

[13]Celebrate the Feast[d] of Shelters for seven days, after you have gathered your harvest from the threshing[d] floor and winepress. [d] [14]Everybody should rejoice at your Feast: you, your sons and daughters, your male and female servants, the Levites, strangers, orphans and widows who live in your towns. [15]Celebrate the Feast to the LORD your God for seven days at the place he will choose, because the LORD your God will bless all your harvest and all the work you do, and you will be completely happy.

[16]All your men must come before the LORD three times a year to the place he will choose. They must come at these times: the Feast[d] of Unleavened Bread, the Feast[d] of Weeks and the Feast of Shelters. No man should come before the LORD without a gift. [17]Each of you must bring a gift that will show how much the LORD your God has blessed you.

Judges for the People

[18]Appoint judges and officers for your tribes[d] in every town the LORD your God is giving you; they must judge the people fairly. [19]Do not judge unfairly or take sides. Do not let people pay you to make wrong decisions, because that kind of payment makes wise people seem blind, and it changes the words of good people. [20]Always do what is right so that you will live and always have the land the LORD your God is giving you.

God Hates Idols

[21]Do not set up a wooden Asherah [d] idol next to the altar you build for the LORD your God, [22]and do not set up holy stone pillars. The LORD your God hates them.

17 If an ox or sheep has something wrong with it, do not offer it as a sacrifice to the LORD your God. He would hate that.

[2]A man or woman in one of the towns the LORD gave you might be found doing something evil and breaking the Agreement. [3]That person may have served other gods and bowed down to them or to the sun or moon or stars of the sky, which I have commanded should not be done. [4]If someone has told you about it, you must look into the matter carefully. If it is true that such a hateful thing has happened in Israel, [5]take the man or woman who has done the evil thing to the city gates and throw stones at that person until he dies. [6]There must be two or three witnesses that it is true before the person is put to death; if there is only one witness, the person should not be put to death. [7]The witnesses must be the first to throw stones at the person, and then everyone else will follow. You must get rid of the evil among you.

Courts of Law

[8]Some cases that come before you, such as murder, quarrelling or attack, may be too difficult to judge. Take these cases to the place the LORD your God will choose. [9]Go to the priests who are Levites and to the judge who is on duty at that time. Ask them about the case, and they will decide. [10]You must follow the decision they give you at the place the LORD your God will choose. Be careful to do everything they tell you. [11]Follow the teachings they give you, and do whatever they decide, exactly as they tell you. [12]The person who does not show respect for the judge or priest who is there serving the LORD your God must be put to death. You must get rid of that evil from Israel. [13]Then everyone will hear about this and will be afraid, and they will not show disrespect any more.

Choosing a King

[14]When you enter the land the LORD your God is giving you, taking it as your own and living in it, you will say, "Let's appoint a king over us like the nations all around us." [15]Be sure to appoint over you the king the LORD your God chooses. He must be one of your own people. Do not appoint as your king a foreigner who is not a fellow Israelite. [16]The king must not have too many horses for himself, and he must not send people to Egypt to get more horses, because the LORD has told you, "Don't return that way again." [17]The king must not have many wives, or his heart will be led away from God. He must not have too much silver and gold.

[18]When he becomes king, he should write a copy of the teachings on a scroll for himself, a copy taken from the priests and Levites. [19]He should keep it with him all the time and read from it every day of his life. Then he will learn to respect the LORD his God, and he will obey all the teachings and commands. [20]He should not think he is better than his fellow Israelites, and he must not stop obeying the law in any way so that he and his descendants [d] may rule the kingdom for a long time.

Shares for Priests and Levites

18 The priests are from the tribe [d] of Levi, and that tribe will not receive a share of the land with the Israelites. They will eat the offerings made to the LORD by fire, which is their share. [2]They will not inherit any of the land like their brothers, but they will inherit the LORD himself, as he has promised them.

[3]When you offer a bull or sheep as a sacrifice, you must share with the priests, giving them the shoulder, the cheeks and the inner organs. [4]Give them the first of your grain, new wine and oil, as well as the first wool you cut from your sheep. [5]The LORD your God has chosen the priests and their descendants [d] out of all your tribes to stand and serve the LORD always.

[6]If a Levite moves from one of your towns anywhere in Israel where he lives and comes to the place the LORD will choose, because he wants to serve the LORD there, [7]he may serve the LORD his God. He will be like his fellow Levites who serve there before the LORD. [8]They all will have an equal share of the food. That is separate from what he has received from the sale of family possessions.

Do Not Follow Other Nations

[9]When you enter the land the LORD your God is giving you, don't learn to do the hateful things the other nations do. [10]Don't let anyone among you offer a son or daughter as a sacrifice in the fire. Don't let anyone use magic or witchcraft, [d] or try to explain the meaning of signs. [11]Don't let anyone try to control others with magic, and don't let them be mediums [d] or try to talk with the spirits of dead people. [12]The LORD hates anyone who does these things. Because the other nations do these things, the LORD your God will force them out of the land ahead of you. [13]But you must be innocent in the presence of the LORD your God.

The LORD's Special Prophet

[14]The nations you will force out listen to people who use magic and witchcraft, [d] but the LORD your God will not let you do those things. [15]The LORD your God will give you a prophet [d] like me, who is one of your own people. Listen to him. [16]This is what you asked the LORD your God to do when you were gathered at Mount Sinai. You said, "Don't make us listen to the voice of the LORD our God again, and don't make us look at this terrible fire any more, or we will die."

[17]So the LORD said to me, "What they have said is good. [18]So I will give them a prophet like you, who is one of their own people. I will tell him what to say, and he will tell them everything I command. [19]This prophet will speak for me; anyone who does not listen when he speaks will answer to me. [20]But if a prophet says something I did not tell him to say as though he were speaking for me, or if a prophet speaks in the name of other gods, that prophet must be killed."

[21]You might be thinking, "How can we know if a message is not from the LORD?" [22]If what a prophet says in the name of the LORD does not happen, it is not the LORD's message. That prophet was speaking his own ideas. Don't be afraid of him.

Cities of Safety

19 When the LORD your God gives you land that belongs to the other nations, nations that he will destroy, you will force them out and live in their cities and houses. [2]Then choose three cities in the middle of the land the LORD your God is giving you as your own. [3]Build roads to these cities, and divide the land the LORD is giving you into three parts so that someone who kills another person may run to these cities.

[4]This is the rule for someone who kills another person and runs to one of these cities in order to save his life. But the person must have killed a neighbour without meaning to, not out of hatred.

⁵For example, suppose someone goes into the forest with a neighbour to cut wood and swings an axe to cut down a tree. If the axe head flies off the handle, hitting and killing the neighbour, the one who killed him may run to one of these cities to save his life. ⁶Otherwise, the dead person's relative who has the duty of punishing a murderer might be angry and chase him. If the city is far away, the relative might catch and kill the person, even though he should not be killed because there was no intent to kill his neighbour. ⁷This is why I command you to choose these three cities.

⁸⁻⁹Carefully obey all these laws I'm giving you today. Love the LORD your God, and always do what he wants you to do. Then the LORD your God will enlarge your land as he promised your ancestors, giving you the whole land he promised to them. After that, choose three more cities of safety ¹⁰so that innocent people will not be killed in your land, the land that the LORD your God is giving you as your own. By doing this you will not be guilty of allowing the death of innocent people.

¹¹But if a person hates his neighbour and, after hiding and waiting, attacks and kills him and then runs to one of these cities for safety, ¹²the elders of his own city should send for the murderer. They should bring the person back from the city of safety and hand him over to the relative who has the duty of punishing the murderer. ¹³Show no mercy. You must remove from Israel

LEADERSHIP

Standing For Right

George Fox had a message from God, and he was not going to let anyone stop him from preaching it. In the 1600s, he urged people to listen to Christ, to be honest in business, and to care for the poor. He believed in religious liberty and that God worked through individual people, not just through the established church.

Though many people believed him and were converted, others opposed him. On many occasions, he was thrown down church steps or beaten. Once he was put in prison for six months. But he would not change his beliefs and so was sentenced to six more months as a result. "Truth can live in the jails," he wrote. "Be valiant for Truth upon the earth and tread upon deceit."

Despite the government's efforts to stop him from challenging the official church, Fox's message got through to people because of his conviction and honesty. Within eight years of beginning his ministry, 50,000 people had heard his message and had become followers.

Young followers, known as "the valiant 60", joined Fox in preaching at fairs, in markets, in fields, in prisons, and in courts.

When he died in 1691, about 100,000 people had joined Fox's movement, which became known as the Society of Friends. Today the Friends (or Quakers) span the world, spreading a message of peace, holiness, service, and religious liberty.

George Fox's ministry had a long-term impact because his message was a true message from God. In his farewell speech, Moses urged the Israelites to listen carefully to prophets' messages to learn if they are true or not. Read **Deuteronomy 18:15–20** to see the guidelines he established.

* In what ways did George Fox's message fit with the message of the prophets as described in this passage?
* How can this passage help you evaluate messages you hear from people who have leadership roles?

Consider . . .

* choosing key words from this passage to make a checklist for evaluating leaders. Use it whenever you wonder whether to believe what someone tells you.
* praying for Christian leaders around the world who sometimes have to risk their lives to speak God's truth.

For more, see . . .

* Jeremiah 37:1–21 (p.760)
* Luke 4:23–30 (p.1046)
* Hebrews 11:32–40 (p.1342)

the guilt of murdering innocent people so that things will go well for you.

¹⁴Do not move the stone that marks the border of your neighbour's land, which people long ago set in place. It marks what you inherit in the land the LORD your God is giving you as your own.

Rules About Witnesses

¹⁵One witness is not enough to accuse a person of a crime or sin. A case must be proved by two or three witnesses.

¹⁶If a witness lies and accuses a person of a crime, ¹⁷the two people who are arguing must stand in the presence of the LORD before the priests and judges who are on duty. ¹⁸The judges must check the matter carefully. The witness who is a liar, lying about a fellow Israelite, ¹⁹must be punished. He must be punished in the same way the other person would have been punished. You must get rid of the evil among you. ²⁰The rest of the people will hear about this and be afraid, and no one among you will ever do such an evil thing again. ²¹Show no mercy. A life must be paid for a life, an eye for an eye, a tooth for a tooth, a hand for a hand, a foot for a foot.

Laws for War

20 When you go to war against your enemies and you see horses and chariots and an army that is bigger than yours, don't be afraid of them. The LORD your God, who brought you out of Egypt, will be with you. ²The priest must come and speak to the army before you go into battle. ³He will say, "Listen, Israel! Today you are going into battle against your enemies. Don't lose your courage or be afraid. Don't panic or be frightened, ⁴because the LORD your God goes with you, to fight for you against your enemies and to save you."

⁵The officers should say to the army, "Has anyone built a new house but not given it to God? He may go home, because he might die in battle and someone else would get to give his house to God. ⁶Has anyone planted a vineyard and not begun to enjoy it? He may go home, because he might die in battle and someone else would enjoy his vineyard. ⁷Is any man engaged to a woman and not

yet married to her? He may go home, because he might die in battle and someone else would marry her." ⁸Then the officers should also say, "Is anyone here afraid? Has anyone lost his courage? He may go home so that he will not cause others to lose their courage too." ⁹When the officers finish speaking to the army, they should appoint commanders to lead it.

¹⁰When you march up to attack a city, first make them an offer of peace. ¹¹If they accept your offer and open their gates to you, all the people of that city will become your slaves and work for you. ¹²But if they do not make peace with you and fight you in battle, you should surround that city. ¹³The LORD your God will give it to you. Then kill all the men with your swords, ¹⁴and you may take everything else in the city for yourselves. Take the women, children and animals, and you may use these things the LORD your God gives you from your enemies. ¹⁵Do this to all the cities that are far away, that do not belong to the nations nearby.

¹⁶But leave nothing alive in the cities of the land the LORD your God is giving you. ¹⁷Completely destroy these people: the Hittites, Amorites, Canaanites, Perizzites, Hivites and Jebusites, as the LORD your God has commanded. ¹⁸Otherwise, they will teach you what they do for their gods, and if you do these hateful things, you will sin against the LORD your God.

¹⁹If you surround and attack a city for a long time, trying to capture it, do not destroy its trees with an axe. You can eat the fruit from the trees, but do not cut them down. These trees are not the enemy, so don't make war against them. ²⁰But you may cut down trees that you know are not fruit trees and use them to build devices to attack the city walls, until the city is captured.

A Person Found Murdered

21 Suppose someone is found murdered, lying in a field in the land the LORD your God is giving you as your own, and no one knows who killed the person. ²Your elders and judges should go to where the body was found, and they should measure how far it is to the nearby cities. ³The elders of the city nearest the body must take a young cow that has never worked or worn a yoke, ᵈ ⁴and they must lead her down to a valley that has never been ploughed or planted, with a stream flowing through it. There they must break the young cow's neck. ⁵The priests, the sons of Levi, should come forward, because they have been chosen by the LORD your God to serve him and to give blessings in the LORD's name. They are the ones who decide cases of quarrelling and attacks. ⁶Then all the elders of the city nearest the murdered person should wash their hands over the young cow whose neck was broken in the valley. [7]They should declare: "We did not kill this person, and we did not see it happen. [8]LORD, remove this sin from your people Israel, whom you have saved. Don't blame your people, the Israelites, for the murder of this innocent person." And so the murder will be paid for. [9]Then you will have removed from yourselves the guilt of murdering an innocent person, because you will be doing what the LORD says is right.

Captive Women as Wives

[10]When you go to war against your enemies, the LORD will help you defeat them so that you will take them captive. [11]If you see a beautiful woman among the captives and are attracted to her, you may take her as your wife. [12]Bring her into your home, where she must shave her head and cut her nails [13]and change the clothes she was wearing when you captured her. After she has lived in your house and cried for her parents for a month, you may marry her. You will be her husband, and she will be your wife. [14]But if you are not pleased with her, you must let her go anywhere she wants. You must not sell her for money or make her a slave, because you have taken away her honour.

The Oldest Son

[15]A man might have two wives, one he loves and one he doesn't. Both wives might have sons by him. If the older son belongs to the wife he does not love, [16]when that man wills his property to his sons he must not give the son of the wife he loves what belongs to the older son, the son of the wife he does not love. [17]He must agree to give the older son two shares of everything he owns, even though the older son is from the wife he does not love. That son was the first to prove his father could have children, so he has the rights that belong to the older son.

Sons Who Refuse to Obey

[18]If someone has a son who is stubborn, who turns against his father and mother and doesn't obey them or listen when they correct him, [19]his parents must take him to the elders at the city gate. [20]They will say to the leaders, "Our son is stubborn and turns against us. He will not obey us. He eats too much, and he is always drunk." [21]Then all the men in his town must throw stones at him until he dies. Get rid of the evil among you, because then all the people of Israel will hear about this and be afraid.

Other Laws

[22]If someone is guilty of a sin worthy of death, he must be put to death and his body displayed on a tree. [23]But don't leave his body hanging on the tree overnight; be sure to bury him that same day, because anyone whose body is displayed on a tree is cursed by God. You must not ruin the land the LORD your God is giving you as your own.

22

If you see your fellow Israelite's ox or sheep wandering away, don't ignore it. Take it back to its owner. [2]If the owner does not live close to you, or if you do not know who the owner is, take the animal home with you. Keep it until the owner comes looking for it; then give it back. [3]Do the same thing if you find a donkey or coat or anything someone lost. Don't just ignore it.

[4]If you see your fellow Israelite's donkey or ox fallen on the road, don't ignore it. Help the owner get it up.

[5]A woman must not wear men's clothes, and a man must not wear women's clothes. The LORD your God hates anyone who does that.

[6]If you find a bird's nest by the road, either in a tree or on the ground, and the mother bird is sitting on the young birds or eggs, do not take the mother bird with the young birds. [7]You may take the young birds, but you must let the mother bird go free. Then things will go well for you, and you will live a long time.

[8]When you build a new house, build a low wall around the edge of the roof [n] so you will not be guilty if someone falls off the roof.

[9]Don't plant two different kinds of seeds in your vineyard. Otherwise, both crops will be ruined.

[10]Don't plough with an ox and a donkey tied together.

[11]Don't wear clothes made of wool and linen woven together.

[12]Tie several pieces of thread together; then put these tassels on the four corners of your coat.

Marriage Laws

[13]If a man marries a girl and has sexual relations with her but then decides he does not like her, [14]he might talk badly about her and give her a bad name. He might say, "I married this woman, but when I had sexual relations with her, I did not find that she was a virgin." [d] [15]Then the girl's parents must bring proof that she was a virgin to the elders at the city gate. [16]The girl's father will say to the leaders, "I gave my daughter to this man to be his wife, but now he does not want her. [17]This man has told lies about my

---

roof   In Bible times houses were built with flat roofs. The roof was used for drying things such as flax and fruit. And it was used as an extra room, as a place for worship and as a place to sleep in the summer.

daughter. He has said, 'I did not find your daughter to be a virgin,' but here is the proof that my daughter was a virgin." Then her parents are to show the sheet to the city leaders, [18]and the leaders must take the man and punish him. [19]They must make him pay about a kilogramme of silver to the girl's father, because the man has given an Israelite virgin a bad name. The girl will continue to be the man's wife, and he may not divorce her as long as he lives.

[20]But if the things the husband said about his wife are true, and there is no proof that she was a virgin, [21]the girl must be brought to the door of her father's house. Then the men of the town must put her to death by throwing stones at her. She has done a disgraceful thing in Israel by having sexual relations before she was married. You must get rid of the evil among you.

[22]If a man is found having sexual relations with another man's wife, both the woman and the man who had sexual relations with her must die. Get rid of this evil from Israel.

[23]If a man meets a virgin in a city and has sexual relations with her, but she is engaged to another man, [24]you must take both of them to the city gate and put them to death by throwing stones at them. Kill the girl, because she was in a city and did not scream for help. And kill the man for having sexual relations with another man's wife. You must get rid of the evil among you.

[25]But if a man meets an engaged girl out in the country and forces her to have sexual relations with him, only the man who had sexual relations with her must be put to death. [26]Don't do anything to the girl, because she has not done a sin worthy of death. This is like the person who attacks and murders a neighbour; [27]the man found the engaged girl in the country and she screamed, but no one was there to save her.

PARENTS

Seaside Trouble

Rachel had her armbands on and was ready for action; it was perfect swimming conditions. She was only six, but as far as she was concerned, she was brilliant at swimming and would win medals when she was older! She was told by her parents not to swim out to sea – only to paddle. But she stomped off away from them. What did they know?

She waded in past her waist, and then launched out – doggy-paddling away.

After a while she turned back, and couldn't believe what she saw – everyone was very small and getting smaller. The current was taking her out to sea.

Thankfully, someone swam out to rescue Rachel and brought her safely to shore. As they stood on the beach, she caught sight of her mum – she looked so worried and upset. At that moment, Rachel realised two things – that her swimming career would have to wait for a bit and that next time she would listen to her parents.

Read **Deuteronomy 21:18–21**.

* Rachel was determined not to listen to her parents, but what was behind their rule and the ones in the Bible passage?
* The Bible passage seems pretty harsh about disobedience. Why do you think that is?

Consider . . .

* whether you need to say sorry to your parents if you know that you have had a bad attitude towards them.
* looking at baby photos of yourself. See how much effort it has taken for your parents to bring you up. Does this help you understand some of the rules they make for you?

For more, see . . .

* Exodus 20:12 (p.79)
* Luke 15:11–32 (p.1071)

* Proverbs 3:11–18 (p.592)

28If a man meets a virgin who is not engaged to be married and forces her to have sexual relations with him and people find out about it, 29the man must pay the girl's father about 50 pieces of silver. He must also marry the girl, because he has dishonoured her, and he may never divorce her for as long as he lives.

30A man must not marry his father's wife; he must not dishonour his father in this way.

The LORD's People

23 No man who has had part of his sex organ cut off may come into the meeting to worship the LORD.

2No one born to parents who were forbidden by law to marry may come into the meeting to worship the LORD. The descendants for ten generations may not come in either.

3No Ammonite or Moabite may come into the meeting to worship the LORD, and none of their descendants for ten generations may come in. 4This is because the Ammonites and Moabites did not give you bread and water when you came out of Egypt. And they hired Balaam son of Beor, from Pethor in North West Mesopotamia, to put a curse on you. 5But the LORD your God would not listen to Balaam. He turned the curse into a blessing for you, because the LORD your God loves you. 6Don't wish for their peace or success as long as you live.

7Don't hate Edomites; they are your close relatives. Don't hate Egyptians, because you were foreigners in their country. 8The great-grandchildren of these two peoples may come into the meeting to worship the LORD.

Keeping the Camp Clean

9When you are camped in time of war, keep away from unclean d things. 10If a man becomes unclean during the night, he must go outside the camp and not come back. 11But when evening comes, he must wash himself, and at sunset he may come back into the camp.

12Choose a place outside the camp where people may go to relieve themselves. 13Carry a tent peg with you, and when you relieve yourself, dig a hole and cover up your dung. 14The LORD your God moves around through your camp to protect you and to defeat your enemies for you, so the camp must be holy. He must not see anything unclean among you so that he will not leave you.

Other Laws

15If an escaped slave comes to you, do not hand over the slave to his master. 16Let the slave live with you anywhere he likes, in any town he chooses. Do not mistreat him.

17No Israelite man or woman must ever become a temple prostitute. d 18Do not bring a male or female prostitute's pay to the Temple d of the LORD your God to pay what you have promised to the LORD, because the LORD your God hates prostitution.

19If you loan your fellow Israelites money or food or anything else, don't make them pay back more than you loaned them. 20You may charge foreigners, but not fellow Israelites. Then the LORD your God will bless everything you do in the land you are entering to take as your own.

21If you make a promise to give something to the LORD your God, do not be slow to pay it, because the LORD your God demands it from you. Do not be guilty of sin. 22But if you do not make the promise, you will not be guilty. 23You must do whatever you say you will do, because you chose to make the promise to the LORD your God.

24If you go into your neighbour's vineyard, you may eat as many grapes as you wish, but do not put any grapes into your basket. 25If you go into your neighbour's grainfield, you may pick grain with your hands, but you must not cut down your neighbour's grain with your sickle.

24 A man might marry a woman but later decide she doesn't please him because he has found something bad about her. He writes out divorce papers for her, gives them to her and sends her away from his house. 2After she leaves his house, she goes and marries another man, 3but her second husband does not like her either. So he writes out divorce papers for her, gives them to her and sends her away from his house. Or the second husband might die. 4In either case, her first husband who divorced her must not marry her again, because she has become unclean. d The LORD would hate this. Don't bring this sin into the land the LORD your God is giving you as your own.

5A man who has just married must not be sent to war or be given any other duty. He should be free to stay home for a year to make his new wife happy.

6If someone owes you something, do not take his two stones for grinding grain—not even the upper one—in place of what he owes, because this is how the person makes a living.

7If someone kidnaps a fellow Israelite, either to make him a slave or sell him, the kidnapper must be killed. You must get rid of the evil among you.

8Be careful when someone has a skin disease. Do exactly what the priests, the Levites, teach you, being careful to do what I have commanded them. 9Remember what the LORD your God did to Miriam on your way out of Egypt.

10When you make a loan to your neighbours, don't go into their homes to get something in place of it. 11Stay outside and let them go in and get what they promised you. 12If a poor person gives you a coat to show he will pay the loan back, don't keep it overnight. 13Give the coat back at sunset, because your neighbour needs that coat to sleep in, and he will thank you. And the LORD your God will see that you have done a good thing.

14Don't cheat hired servants who are poor and needy, whether they are fellow Israelites or foreigners living in one of your towns. 15Pay them each day before sunset, because they are poor and need the money. Otherwise, they may complain to the LORD about you, and you will be guilty of sin.

16Parents must not be put to death if their children do wrong, and children must not be put to death if their parents do wrong. Each person must die for his own sin.

17Do not be unfair to a foreigner or an orphan. Don't take a widow's coat to make sure she pays you back. 18Remember that you were slaves in Egypt, and the LORD your God saved you from there. That is why I am commanding you to do this.

19When you are gathering your harvest in the field and leave behind a bundle of grain, don't go back and get it. Leave it there for foreigners, orphans and widows so that the LORD your God can bless everything you do. 20When you beat your olive trees to knock the olives off, don't beat the trees a second time. Leave what is left for foreigners, orphans and widows. 21When you harvest the grapes in your vineyard, don't pick the vines a second time. Leave what is left for foreigners, orphans and widows. 22Remember that you were slaves in Egypt; that is why I am commanding you to do this.

25 If two people have an argument and go to court, the judges will decide the case. They will declare one person right and the other guilty. 2If the guilty person has to be punished with a beating, the judge will make that person lie down and be beaten in front of him. The number of lashes should match the crime. 3But don't hit a person more than 40 times, because more than that would disgrace him before others.

4When an ox is working in the grain, do not cover its mouth to keep it from eating.

5If two brothers are living together, and one of them dies without having a son, his widow must not marry someone outside her husband's family.

Her husband's brother must marry her, which is his duty to her as a brother-in-law. 6The first son

> **Sidelight**
> This chapter shows how to respect and treat other people. It is wrong to humiliate or take advantage of others – even when they are family. The law about marrying a brother-in-law's widow helped make sure she was looked after (Deuteronomy 25:5–9).

she has counts as the son of the dead brother so that his name will not be forgotten in Israel.

7But if a man does not want to marry his brother's widow, she should go to the elders at the town gate. She should say, "My brother-in-law will not carry on his brother's name in Israel. He refuses to do his duty for me."

8Then the elders of the town must call for the man and talk to him. But if he is stubborn and says, "I don't want to marry her," 9the woman must go up to him in front of the elders. She must take off one of his sandals and spit in his face and say, "This is for the man who won't continue his brother's family!" 10Then that man's family shall be known in Israel as the Family of the Unsandalled.

11If two men are fighting and one man's wife comes to save her husband from his attacker, grabbing the attacker by his sex organs, 12you must cut off her hand. Show her no mercy.

13Don't carry two sets of weights with you, one heavy and one light. 14Don't have two different sets of measures in your house, one large and one small. 15You must have true and honest weights and measures so that you will live a long time in the land the LORD your God is giving you. 16The LORD your God hates anyone who is dishonest and uses dishonest measures.

17Remember what the Amalekites did to you when you came out of Egypt. 18When you were tired and worn out, they met you on the road and attacked all those lagging behind. They were not afraid of God. 19When the LORD your God gives you rest from all the enemies around you in the land he is giving you as your own, you shall destroy any memory of the Amalekites on the earth. Do not forget!

The First Harvest

26 When you go into the land the LORD your God is giving you as your own, to take it over and live in it, 2you must take some of the first harvest of crops that grow from the land the

LORD your God is giving you. Put the food in a basket and go to the place where the LORD your God will choose to be worshipped. [3]Say to the priest on duty at that time, "Today I declare before the LORD your God that I have come into the land the LORD promised our ancestors that he would give us." [4]The priest will take your basket and set it down in front of the altar of the LORD your God. [5]Then you shall announce before the LORD your God: "My father was a wandering Aramean. He went down to Egypt with only a few people, but they became a great, powerful and large nation there. [6]But the Egyptians were cruel to us, making us suffer and work very hard. [7]So we prayed to the LORD, the God of our ancestors, and he heard us. When he saw our trouble, hard work and suffering, [8]the LORD brought us out of Egypt with his great power and strength, using great terrors, signs and miracles.[d] [9]Then he brought us to this place and gave us this fertile land. [10]Now I bring part of the first harvest from this land that you, LORD, have given me." Place the basket before the LORD your God and bow down before him. [11]Then you and the Levites and foreigners among you should rejoice, because the LORD your God has given good things to you and your family.

[12]Bring a tenth of all your harvest the third year (the year to give a tenth of your harvest). Give it to the Levites, foreigners, orphans and widows so that they may eat in your towns and be full. [13]Then say to the LORD your God, "I have taken out of my house the part of my harvest that belongs to God, and I have given it to the Levites, foreigners, orphans and widows. I have done everything you commanded me; I have not broken your commands, and I have not forgotten any of them. [14]I have not eaten any of the holy part while I was in sorrow. I have not removed any of it while I was unclean,[d] and I have not

GIVING

First Harvest

Sue had never had so much money in her life. A distant relative had died and left £2,500 to Sue and each of her three brothers. Matthew was planning to buy a new guitar. Simon was a full-time youth worker. He wanted to buy a notebook computer and printer. Her youngest brother, Luke, had bought a set of drums. But as he was only thirteen, their parents had said that the rest had to be put into the bank.

Sue had lots of plans for her money, too. In a year she would be going to university. It would give her a "safety net". The money from her Saturday job never seemed to go far enough. She might even be able to buy a small car.

However, before any of those things she needed to decide how she was going to give away some of her legacy. There were so many needs. A friend was going to work for a mission and needed support. Sue was committed to a project for homeless young people.

The needs were limitless. But she knew that there was some way she could give – to share her "harvest" with others and show her thankfulness to God.

In **Deuteronomy 26:1–11** the Israelites were challenged to give to God because of all that he had given to them.

* Compare Sue's actions with the encouragement to give in the passage.
* What can you bring to God from your "first harvest" as a thank-offering?

Consider . . .

* participating in a project at your church as a way of giving back to God part of the love and time that he has given to you.
* taking 10 per cent of the money in your purse or wallet and giving it to God as a "tithe".

For more, see . . .

* Genesis 28:22 (p.34)
* Luke 11:42 (p.1062)
* Malachi 3:8–10 (p.930)

offered it for dead people. I have obeyed you, the LORD my God, and have done everything you commanded me. ¹⁵So look down from heaven, your holy home. Bless your people Israel and bless the land you have given us, which you promised to our ancestors—a fertile land."

Obey the LORD's Commands

¹⁶Today the LORD your God commands you to obey all these rules and laws; be careful to obey them with your whole being. ¹⁷Today you have said that the LORD is your God, and you have promised to do what he wants you to do—to keep his rules, commands and laws. You have said you will obey him. ¹⁸And today the LORD has said that you are his very own people, as he has promised you. But you must obey his commands. ¹⁹He will make you greater than all the other nations he made. He will give you praise, fame and honour, and you will be a holy people to the LORD your God, as he has said.

The Law Written on Stones

27 Then Moses, along with the elders of Israel, commanded the people, saying, "Keep all the commands I have given you today. ²Soon you will cross the Jordan River to go into the land the LORD your God is giving you. On that day set up some large stones and cover them with plaster. ³When you cross over, write all the words of these teachings on them. Then you may enter the land the LORD your God is giving you, a fertile land, just as the LORD, the God of your ancestors, promised. ⁴After you have crossed the Jordan River, set up these stones on Mount Ebal, as I command you today, and cover them with plaster. ⁵Build an altar of stones there to the LORD your God, but don't use any iron tool to cut the stones; ⁶build the altar of the LORD your God with stones from the field. Offer burnt offerings on it to the LORD your God, ⁷and offer fellowship offerings there, and eat them and rejoice before the LORD your God. ⁸Then write clearly all the words of these teachings on the stones."

Curses of the Law

⁹Then Moses and the Levites who were priests spoke to all Israel and said, "Be quiet, Israel. Listen! Today you have become the people of the LORD your God. ¹⁰Obey the LORD your God, and keep his commands and laws that I give you today."

¹¹That day Moses also gave the people this command:

¹²When you cross the Jordan River, these tribes *d* must stand on Mount Gerizim to bless the people: Simeon, Levi, Judah, Issachar, Joseph and Benjamin. ¹³And these tribes must stand on Mount Ebal to announce the curses: Reuben, Gad, Asher, Zebulun, Dan and Naphtali.

¹⁴The Levites will say to all the people of Israel in a loud voice:

¹⁵"Anyone will be cursed who makes an idol or statue and secretly sets it up, because the LORD hates the idols people make."

Then all the people will say, "Amen!"

¹⁶"Anyone will be cursed who dishonours his father or mother."

Then all the people will say, "Amen!"

¹⁷"Anyone will be cursed who moves the stone that marks a neighbour's border."

Then all the people will say, "Amen!"

¹⁸"Anyone will be cursed who sends a blind person down the wrong road."

Then all the people will say, "Amen!"

¹⁹"Anyone will be cursed who is unfair to foreigners, orphans or widows."

Then all the people will say, "Amen!"

²⁰"A man will be cursed who has sexual relations with his father's wife, because it is a dishonour to his father."

Then all the people will say, "Amen!"

²¹"Anyone will be cursed who has sexual relations with an animal."

Then all the people will say, "Amen!"

²²"A man will be cursed who has sexual relations with his sister, whether she is his father's daughter or his mother's daughter."

Then all the people will say, "Amen!"

²³"A man will be cursed who has sexual relations with his mother-in-law."

Then all the people will say, "Amen!"

²⁴"Anyone will be cursed who kills a neighbour secretly."

Then all the people will say, "Amen!"

²⁵"Anyone will be cursed who takes money to murder an innocent person."

Then all the people will say, "Amen!"

²⁶"Anyone will be cursed who does not agree with the words of these teachings and does not obey them."

Then all the people will say, "Amen!"

Blessings for Obeying

28 You must completely obey the LORD your God, and you must carefully follow all his commands I am giving you today. Then the LORD your God will make you greater than any other nation on earth. ²Obey the LORD your God so that all these blessings will come and stay with you:

³You will be blessed in the city and blessed in the country.

⁴Your children will be blessed, as well as your crops; your herds will be blessed with calves and your flocks with lambs.

[5]Your basket and your kitchen will be blessed. [6]You will be blessed when you come in and when you go out.

[7]The LORD will help you defeat the enemies that come to fight you. They will attack you from one direction, but they will run from you in seven directions.

[8]The LORD your God will bless you with full barns, and he will bless everything you do. He will bless the land he is giving you.

[9]The LORD will make you his holy people, as he promised. But you must obey his commands and do what he wants you to do. [10]Then everyone on earth will see that you are the LORD's people, and they will be afraid of you. [11]The LORD will make you rich: you will have many children, your animals will have many young, and your land will give good crops. It is the land that the LORD promised your ancestors he would give to you.

[12]The LORD will open up his heavenly storehouse so that the skies send rain on your land at the right time, and he will bless everything you do. You will lend to other nations, but you will not need to borrow from them. [13]The LORD will make you like the head and not like the tail; you will be on top and not on the bottom. But you must obey the commands of the LORD your God that I am giving you today, being careful to keep them. [14]Do not disobey anything I command you today. Do exactly as I command, and do not follow other gods or serve them.

Curses for Disobeying

[15]But if you do not obey the LORD your God and carefully follow all his commands and laws I am giving you today, all these curses will come upon you and stay:

[16]You will be cursed in the city and cursed in the country.

[17]Your basket and your kitchen will be cursed. [18]Your children will be cursed, as well as your crops; the calves of your herds and the lambs of your flocks will be cursed. [19]You will be cursed when you go in and when you go out.

[20]The LORD will send you curses, confusion and punishment in everything you do. You will be destroyed and suddenly ruined because you did wrong when you left him. [21]The LORD will give you terrible diseases and destroy you from the land you are going to take. [22]The LORD will punish you with disease, fever, swelling, heat, lack of rain, plant diseases and mildew, [d] until you die. [23]The sky above will be like bronze, and the ground below will be like iron. [n] [24]The LORD will turn the rain into dust and sand, which will fall from the skies until you are destroyed.

[25]The LORD will help your enemies defeat you. You will attack them from one direction, but you will run from them in seven directions. And you will become a thing of horror among all the kingdoms on earth. [26]Your dead bodies will be food for all the birds and wild animals, and there will be no one to scare them away. [27]The LORD will punish you with boils like those the Egyptians had. You will have bad growths, sores and itches that can't be cured. [28]The LORD will give you madness, blindness and a confused mind. [29]You will have to feel around in the daylight like a blind person. You will fail in everything you do. People will hurt you and steal from you every day, and no one will save you.

[30]You will be engaged to a woman, but another man will force her to have sexual relations with him. You will build a house, but you will not live in it. You will plant a vineyard, but you will not get its grapes. [31]Your ox will be killed before your eyes, but you will not eat any of it. Your donkey will be taken away from you, and it will not be brought back. Your sheep will be given to your enemies, and no one will save you. [32]Your sons and daughters will be given to another nation, and you will grow tired looking for them every day, but there will be nothing you can do. [33]People you don't know will eat the crops your land and hard work have produced. You will be mistreated and abused all your life. [34]The things you see will cause you to go mad. [35]The LORD will give you sore boils on your knees and legs that cannot be cured, and they will go from the soles of your feet to the tops of your heads.

[36]The LORD will send you and your king away to a nation neither you nor your ancestors know, where you will serve other gods made of wood and stone. [37]You will become a hated thing to the nations where the LORD sends you; they will laugh at you and make fun of you.

[38]You will plant much seed in your field, but your harvest will be small, because locusts [d] will eat the crop. [39]You will plant vineyards and work hard in them, but you will not pick the grapes or drink the wine, because the worms will eat them. [40]You will have olive trees in all your land, but you will not get any olive oil, because the olives will drop off the trees. [41]You will have sons and daughters, but you will not be able to keep them, because they will be taken captive. [42]Locusts will destroy all your trees and crops.

[43]The foreigners who live among you will get stronger and stronger, and you will get weaker and weaker. [44]Foreigners will lend money to you, but you will not be able to lend to them. They will be like the head, and you will be like the tail.

---

sky . . . iron   This means the sky will give no rain and the earth will produce no crops.

45All these curses will come upon you. They will chase you and catch you and destroy you, because you did not obey the LORD your God and keep the commands and laws he gave you. 46The curses will be signs and miracles*d* to you and your descendants *d* for ever. 47You had plenty of everything, but you did not serve the LORD your God with joy and a pure heart, 48so you will serve the enemies the LORD sends against you. You will be hungry, thirsty, naked and poor, and the LORD will put a load on you until he has destroyed you.

The Curse of an Enemy Nation

49The LORD will bring a nation against you from far away, from the end of the world, and it will swoop down like an eagle. You won't understand their language, 50and they will look fierce. They will not respect old people or feel sorry for the young. 51They will eat the calves from your herds and the harvest of your field, and you will be destroyed. They will not leave you any grain, new wine or oil, or any calves from your herds or lambs from your flocks. You will be ruined. 52That nation will surround and attack all your cities. You trust in your high, strong walls, but they will fall down. That nation will surround all your cities everywhere in the land the LORD your God is giving you.

53Your enemy will surround you. Those people will make you starve so that you will eat your own babies, the bodies of the sons and daughters the LORD your God gave you. 54Even the most gentle and kind man among you will become cruel to his brother, his wife whom he loves and his children who are still alive. 55He will not even give them any of the flesh of his children he is eating, because it will be all he has left. Your enemy will surround you and make you starve in all your cities. 56The most gentle and kind woman among you, so gentle and kind she would hardly even walk on the ground, will be cruel to her husband whom she loves and to her son and daughter. 57She will give birth to a baby, but she will plan to eat the baby and what comes after the birth itself. She will eat them secretly while the enemy surrounds the city. Those people will make you starve in all your cities.

58Be careful to obey everything in these teachings that are written in this book. You must respect the glorious and wonderful name of the LORD your God, 59or the LORD will give terrible diseases to you and your descendants. *d* You will have long and serious diseases, and long and miserable sicknesses. 60He will give you all the diseases of Egypt that you dread, and the diseases will stay with you. 61The LORD will also give you every disease and sickness not written in this Book of the Teachings, until you are destroyed.

62You people may have outnumbered the stars, but only a few of you will be left, because you did not obey the LORD your God. 63Just as the LORD was once happy with you and gave you good things and made you grow in number, so then the LORD will be happy to ruin and destroy you, and you will be removed from the land you are entering to take as your own.

64Then the LORD will scatter you among the nations—from one end of the earth to the other. There you will serve other gods of wood and stone, gods that neither you nor your ancestors have known. 65You will have no rest among those nations and no place that is yours. The LORD will make your mind worried, your sight weak and your soul sad. 66You will live with danger and be afraid night and day. You will not be sure that you will live. 67In the morning you will say, "I wish it were evening," and in the evening you will say, "I wish it were morning." Terror will be in your heart, and the things you have seen will scare you. 68The LORD will send you back to Egypt in ships, even though I, Moses, said you would never go back to Egypt. And there you will try to sell yourselves as slaves to your enemies, but no one will buy you.

The Agreement in Moab

29 The LORD commanded Moses to make an agreement with the Israelites in Moab in addition to the agreement he had made with them at Mount Sinai. These are the words of that agreement.

2Moses called all the Israelites together and said to them:

You have seen everything the LORD did before your own eyes to the king of Egypt and to the king's leaders and to the whole country. 3With your own eyes you saw the great troubles, signs and miracles. *d* 4But to this day the LORD has not given you a mind that understands; you don't really understand what you see with your eyes or hear with your ears. 5I led you through the desert for 40 years, and during that time neither your clothes nor sandals wore out. 6You ate no bread and drank no wine or beer. This was so you would understand that I am the LORD your God.

7When you came to this place, Sihon king of Heshbon and Og king of Bashan came out to fight us, but we defeated them. 8We captured their land and gave it to the tribes *d* of Reuben, Gad and East Manasseh to be their own.

9You must carefully obey everything in this agreement so that you will succeed in everything you do. 10Today you are all standing here before the LORD your God—your leaders and important men, your elders, officers and all the other men of Israel, 11your wives and children and the foreigners who live among you, who chop your wood and carry your water. 12You are all here to enter into an agreement and a promise with the LORD your God, an agreement the LORD your God is making with you today. 13This will make you today his own people. He will be your God, as he told you and as he promised your ancestors Abraham, Isaac and Jacob. 14But I am not just making this agreement and its promises with you 15who are standing here before the LORD your God today, but also with those who are not here today.

16You know how we lived in Egypt and how we passed through the countries when we came here. 17You saw their hateful idols made of wood, stone, silver and gold. 18Make sure no man, woman, family group or tribe among you leaves the LORD our God to go and serve the gods of those nations. They would be to you like a plant that grows bitter, poisonous fruit.

19These are the kind of people who hear these curses but bless themselves, thinking, "We will be safe even though we continue doing what we want to do." Those people may destroy all of your land, both wet and dry. 20The LORD will not forgive them. His anger will be like a burning fire against those people, and all the curses written in this book will come on them. The LORD will destroy any memory of them on the earth. 21He will separate them from all the tribes of Israel for punishment. All the curses of the Agreement that are written in this Book of the Teachings will happen to them.

22Your children who will come after you, as well as foreigners from faraway lands, will see the disasters that come to this land and the diseases the LORD will send on it. They will say, 23"The land is nothing but burning cinders and salt. Nothing is planted, nothing grows and nothing blooms. It is like Sodom and Gomorrah, and Admah and Zeboiim, which the LORD destroyed because he was very angry." 24All the other nations will ask, "Why has the LORD done this to the land? Why is he so angry?"

25And the answer will be, "It is because the people broke the Agreement of the LORD, the God of their ancestors, which he made with them when he brought them out of Egypt. 26They went and served other gods and bowed down to gods they did not even know. The LORD did not allow that, 27so he became very angry at the land and brought all the curses on it that are written in this book. 28Since the LORD became angry and furious with them, he took them out of their land and put them in another land where they are today."

29There are some things the LORD our God has kept secret, but there are some things he has let us know. These belong to us and our children for ever so that we will do everything in these teachings.

The Israelites Will Return

30 When all these blessings and curses I have described happen to you, and the LORD your God has sent you away to other nations, think about these things. 2Then you and your children will return to the LORD your God, and you will obey him with your whole being in everything I am commanding you today. 3Then the LORD your God will give you back your freedom. He will feel sorry for you, and he will bring you back again from the nations where he scattered you. 4He may send you to the ends of the earth, but he will gather you and bring you back from there, 5back to the land that belonged to your ancestors. It will be yours. He will give you success, and there will be more of you than there were of your ancestors. 6The LORD your God will prepare you and your descendants *d* to love him with your whole being so that you will live. 7The LORD your God will put all these curses on your enemies, who hate you and are cruel to you. 8And you will again obey the LORD, keeping all his commands that I give you today. 9The LORD your God will make you successful in everything you do. You will have many children, your cattle will have many calves, and your fields will produce good crops, because the LORD will again be happy with you, just as he was with your ancestors. 10But you must obey the LORD your God by keeping all his commands and rules that are written in this Book of the Teachings. You must return to the LORD your God with your whole being.

Choose Life or Death

11This command I give you today is not too hard for you; it is not beyond what you can do. 12It is not up in heaven. You do not have to ask, "Who will go up to heaven and get it for us so we can obey it and keep it?" 13It is not on the other side of the sea. You do not have to ask, "Who will go across the sea and get it? Who will tell it to us so we can keep it?" 14No, the word is very near you. It is in your mouth and in your heart so you may obey it.

15Look, today I offer you life and success, death and destruction. 16I command you today to love the LORD your God, to do what he wants you to do, and to keep his commands, his rules and his laws. Then you will live and grow in number, and the LORD your God will bless you in the land you are entering to take as your own.

17But if you turn away from the LORD and do not obey him, if you are led to bow and serve other gods, 18I tell you today that you will surely be destroyed. And you will not live long in the land you are crossing the Jordan River to enter and take as your own.

¹⁹Today I ask heaven and earth to be witnesses. I am offering you life or death, blessings or curses. Now, choose life! Then you and your children may live. ²⁰To choose life is to love the LORD your God, obey him and stay close to him. He is your life, and he will let you live many years in the land, the land he promised to give your ancestors Abraham, Isaac and Jacob.

Joshua Takes Moses' Place

31 Then Moses went and spoke these words to all the Israelites: ²"I am now 120 years old, and I cannot lead you any more. The LORD told me I would not cross the Jordan River; ³the LORD your God will lead you across himself. He will destroy those nations for you, and you will take over their land. Joshua will also lead you across, as the LORD has said. ⁴The LORD will do to those nations what he did to Sihon and Og, the kings of the Amorites, when he destroyed them and their land. ⁵The LORD will give those nations to you; do to them everything I told you. ⁶Be strong and brave. Don't be afraid of them and don't be frightened, because the LORD your God will go with you. He will not leave you or forget you."

⁷Then Moses called Joshua and said to him in front of the people, "Be strong and brave, because you will lead these people into the land the LORD promised to give their ancestors, and help them take it as their own. ⁸The LORD himself will go before you. He will be with you; he will not leave you or forget you. Don't be afraid and don't worry."

Moses Writes the Teachings

⁹So Moses wrote down these teachings and gave them to the priests and all the elders of Israel. (The priests are the sons of Levi, who carry the Ark *d* of the Agreement with the LORD.) ¹⁰⁻¹¹Then Moses commanded them: "Read these teachings for all Israel to hear at the end of every seven years, which is the year to cancel what

---

DECISION MAKING

Living With Deadlines

Luke had never kissed a girl – until he met Rachel at youth camp. It was love at first sight. Rachel and Luke were good for each other, and they encouraged each other in their faith.

But there was Eve to think about – Luke's girlfriend back home. She was cynical about the church, and she made fun of Luke's efforts to grow in his faith. Luke decided that he needed to end this unhealthy relationship.

When Luke got back home at the end of July, he had mixed emotions. It was hard breaking away from the past. So he decided that he would go back to his old girlfriend if he didn't get a letter from Rachel by 15 August. Each day, he checked his post. No letters.

On 15 August, he nervously flipped through the post. Nothing.

So he phoned Eve.

On 16 August, Rachel's letter came, but Luke had already made his choice.

Luke had to decide what to do. In the same way, the Israelites had a choice to make in **Deuteronomy 30:11–20**. Theirs was a much more important choice: whether or not to follow God.

* With this passage in mind, how would you advise Luke if he came to you for advice about his dilemma?
* What principles from this passage can help you to make wise choices?

Consider . . .

* circling the things in the passage that God asks people to do. Underline the "not to do" items.
* writing out an important decision you face. List all the pros and cons of your choices. Then circle any reasons that fit the scripture passage. Cross out any that contradict it. Your decision may be easier now.

For more, see . . .

* Genesis 39:6–23 (p.45)
* Matthew 25:1–13 (p.985)
* Joshua 24:14–15 (p.222)

people owe. Do it during the Feast *d* of Shelters, when all the Israelites will come to appear before the LORD your God and stand at the place he will choose. ¹²Gather all the people: the men, women, children and foreigners living in your towns so that they can listen and learn to respect the LORD your God and carefully obey everything in this law. ¹³Since their children do not know this law, they must hear it. They must learn to respect the LORD your God for as long as they live in the land you are crossing the Jordan River to take for your own."

The Lord Calls Moses and Joshua

¹⁴The LORD said to Moses, "Soon you will die. Get Joshua and come to the Meeting Tent *d* so that I may command him." So Moses and Joshua went to the Meeting Tent.

¹⁵The LORD appeared at the Meeting Tent in a cloud; the cloud stood over the entrance of the Tent. ¹⁶And the LORD said to Moses, "You will soon die. Then these people will not be loyal to me but will worship the foreign gods of the land they are entering. They will leave me, breaking the Agreement I made with them. ¹⁷Then I will

ABORTION

Choose Life

When Clarissa was asked to talk to the girls at her local High School, she assumed they wanted her to give a testimony. After all, it was an RE lesson and she was the local youth leader of her church.

However, when she arrived, the teacher Mrs Holloway had other ideas.

"My girls have been looking at the whole issue of 'life', what it's worth, etc. and they still have many questions they need to discuss. We have looked at the sacrifice that Jesus made in dying for the world and now they want to make the whole thing a bit more personal, I hope you don't mind. It's a bit like being thrown to the lions I'm afraid." Mrs Holloway smiled hopefully and Clarissa nodded and followed her down the hallway.

When she arrived in the room she was met by a sea of girls' faces. They looked at her quizzically as their teacher introduced her. The questions started almost immediately: "Would you die for anybody?" "Why do undeserving people die so young?"

Everything was fine, Clarissa managed to answer clearly, until she was asked:

"If you were raped, would you keep the baby?"

"Yes," replied Clarissa. There was a stunned silence and a wave of horror.

"How could you?" asked the same girl.

It was the youth leader's turn to look puzzled. "Well, it's hardly the baby's fault is it?" she answered. There were hushed whispers as most of the girls took in what was being said.

"But how could you keep a reminder of a rape?" asked another girl.

Clarissa looked at them with understanding. "I've never been raped, so I don't have an experienced answer. All I know is that I would value the life of the child above the horror of the crime. I couldn't condemn an innocent baby to death."

Slowly the girls accepted her answer and a new respect shone in their eyes.

Deuteronomy 30:15–20 offers the choices of life or death.

* How was Clarissa's answer similar to the words in this passage?
* What instructions could the girls have learnt from reading this passage?

Consider . . .

* the value of human life. How does that affect your views on abortion?
* talking to a Christian counsellor or minister if you have emotionally upsetting feelings after experiencing an abortion.

For more, see . . .

* Psalm 139:13–16 (p.581)
* 1 Peter 5:7 (p.1362)
* Isaiah 44:1–4 (p.685)

become very angry at them, and I will leave them. I will turn away from them, and they will be destroyed. Many terrible things will happen to them. Then they will say, 'It is because God is not with us that these terrible things are happening.' [18]I will surely turn away from them then, because they have done wrong and have turned to other gods.

[19]"Now write down this song and teach it to the Israelites. Then have them sing it, because it will be my witness against them. [20]When I bring them into the land I promised to their ancestors, a fertile land, they will eat as much as they want and get fat. Then they will turn to other gods and serve them. They will reject me and break my Agreement. [21]Then when many troubles and terrible things happen to them, this song will testify against them, because the song will not be forgotten by their descendants. [d] I know what they plan to do, even before I take them into the land I promised them." [22]So Moses wrote down the song that day, and he taught it to the Israelites.

[23]Then the LORD gave this command to Joshua son of Nun: "Be strong and brave, because you will lead the people of Israel to the land I promised them, and I will be with you."

[24]After Moses finished writing all the words of the teachings in a book, [25]he gave a command to the Levites, who carried the Ark [d] of the Agreement with the LORD. [26]He said, "Take this Book of the Teachings and put it beside the Ark of the Agreement with the LORD your God. It must stay there as a witness against you. [27]I know how stubborn and disobedient you are. You have disobeyed the LORD while I am alive and with you, and you will disobey even more after I die! [28]Gather all the elders of your tribes [d] and all your officers to me so that I may say these things for them to hear, and so that I may ask heaven and earth to testify against them. [29]I know that after I die you will become completely evil. You will turn away from the commands I have given you. Terrible things will happen to you in the future when you do what the LORD says is evil, and you

will make him angry with the idols you have made."

Moses' Song

[30]And Moses spoke this whole song for all the people of Israel to hear:

32 Hear, heavens, and I will speak.
        Listen, earth, to what I say.
[2]My teaching will drop like rain;
    my words will fall like dew.
They will be like showers on the grass;
    they will pour down like rain on young
        plants.
[3]I will announce the name of the LORD.
    Praise God because he is great!
[4]He is like a rock; what he does is perfect,
    and he is always fair.
He is a faithful God who does no wrong,
    who is right and fair.

[5]They have done evil against him.
    To their shame they are no longer his
        children;
    they are an evil and lying people.
[6]This is not the way to repay the LORD,
    you foolish and unwise people.
He is your Father and Maker,
    who made you and formed you.

[7]Remember the old days.
    Think of the years already passed.
Ask your father and he will tell you;
    ask your elders and they will inform
        you.
[8]God Most High gave the nations their
        lands,
    dividing up the human race.
He set up borders for the people
    and even numbered the Israelites.
[9]The LORD took his people as his share,
    the people of Jacob as his very own.

[10]He found them in a desert,
    a windy, empty land.
He surrounded them and brought them up,
    guarding them as those he loved very
        much.
[11]He was like an eagle building its nest
    that flutters over its young.
It spreads its wings to catch them
    and carries them on its feathers.
[12]The LORD alone led them,
    and there was no foreign god helping him.

[13]The LORD brought them to the heights of the
        land

and fed them the fruit of the fields.
He gave them honey from the rocks,
  bringing oil from the solid rock.
[14]There were milk curds from the cows and
    milk from the flock;
  there were fat sheep and goats.
There were rams and goats from Bashan
  and the best of the wheat.
You drank the juice of grapes.

[15]Israel grew fat and kicked;
  they were fat and full and firm.
They left the God who made them
  and rejected the Rock *d* who saved them.
[16]They made God jealous with foreign gods
  and angry with hateful idols.
[17]They made sacrifices to demons, *d* not God,
  to gods they had never known,
  new gods from nearby,
  gods your ancestors did not fear.

[18]You left God who is the Rock, your Father,
  and you forgot the God who gave you
    birth.

[19]The LORD saw this and rejected them;
  his sons and daughters had made him
    angry.
[20]He said, "I will turn away from them
  and see what will happen to them.
They are evil people,
  unfaithful children.
[21]They used things that are not gods to make
    me jealous
  and worthless idols to make me angry.
So I will use those who are not a nation to
    make them jealous;
  I will use a nation that does not understand
    to make them angry.
[22]My anger has started a fire
  that burns down to the place of the dead.

ENVIRONMENT

On Yer Bike!

Steve was a good minister and he tried hard to encompass the whole of God's teaching in his church. Lately, he had been concerned about the environment. He was aware that when God made the earth it was perfect, and that gradually so many things were being destroyed.

So, when one of the young people spoke to him on that very issue, he was all ears. Matthew's plan was that just for one Sunday, as many people as possible should come to church on bikes instead of in their cars. Some might even go as far as to walk instead!

Steve thought it was a great idea and announced it in church the following week. He let Matthew explain to the congregation that the air was getting so badly polluted by petrol fumes amongst a great deal of other things, that it would be good to do something about it. Things were far from the way God had made them.

The people were very enthusiastic and a few weeks later a very amusing sight hit the local town. Church members ranging from eight years to eighty years came whistling down the road on bicycles! They were wearing an assortment of shorts and coloured tops and the church looked very different.

Matthew's idea was a great success, and some of the people at his church still come on their bikes instead of cars, and others are more aware that sharing a car is better than nothing.

Deuteronomy 32:1–6 reminds us that we need to be wise with our world.

- How did Matthew's idea help to repay the Lord?
- What is our responsibility to God and to his creation?

Consider . . .

- whether you have done things to help reverse the pollution problem such as walking or cycling if your journey is less than two kilometres.
- making a list of plants and animals you see in your garden. Thank God for what he has made.

For more, see . . .

- Genesis 1:6–8 (p.2)
- Psalm 104 (p.560)

It will burn up the ground and its crops,
  and it will set fire to the base of the
    mountains.

23"I will pile troubles upon them
  and shoot my arrows at them.
24They will be starved and sick,
  destroyed by terrible diseases.
I will send them vicious animals
  and gliding, poisonous snakes.
25In the streets the sword will kill;
  in their homes there will be terror.
Young men and women will die,
  and so will babies and grey-haired men.
26I will scatter them as I said,
  and no one will remember them.
27But I didn't want their enemy to boast;
  their enemy might misunderstand

and say, 'We have won!
  The LORD has done none of this.' "

28Israel has no sense;
  they do not understand.
29I wish they were wise and understood this;
  I wish they could see what will happen to
    them.
30One person cannot chase 1,000 people,
  and two people cannot fight 10,000
unless their Rock has sold them,
  unless the LORD has given them up.
31The rock of these people is not like our Rock;
  our enemies agree to that.
32Their vine comes from Sodom,
  and their fields are like Gomorrah.
Their grapes are full of poison;
  their bunches of grapes are bitter.

GOD'S POWER

Stronger Than Hatred

Andrew was livid. He had come to pick up his son Rob from church camp. While waiting for the last session to end, he had overheard his son telling other campers how he hated his dad because of abuse. But Christ had changed Rob's life that week. "And I know Christ can change my dad, too," he had concluded.

Andrew stormed to camp director Ivor's office and verbally abused the director for what he had overheard. Ivor calmed Andrew down and responded, "If your son is worse because of this camp experience, call me. I'll personally apologise. But, if your son is better, write to thank me."

Andrew picked up his son, still steaming with anger. The two drove silently in the car listening to the radio. About a hundred miles from camp, Rob's dad pulled into a service area. As they looked at the view, Rob awkwardly put his arms around his dad and said, "Dad, I've hated you ever since I can remember. Will you forgive me?"

Two hours later, Ivor found Rob's dad back at the camp. "Christ made my son better," he told Ivor. "Can he do it in my life too?"

That day, Rob's father began the long process of healing and recovery.

It was not easy for either Rob or his father to let go of the feelings of anger and hatred. But, in the process, they discovered God's power in the world and in their own lives. Read a description of God's power in **Deuteronomy 32:36—33:4**.

* How might Rob's father have responded to this passage in the first part of the story? How might he have responded at the end?
* What characteristic of God in the passage helps you to understand God's power the most? What comfort do you gain from knowing that power?

Consider . . .

* confessing a way in which you've tried to escape from God (such as making decisions for selfish reasons), then letting God's power work in that area of your life.
* sharing your faith in God's power with someone who has no hope.

For more, see . . .

* Job 9:4–10 (p.475)
* Ephesians 1:19–22 (p.1270)
* Isaiah 46:8–12 (p.689)

³³Their wine is like snake poison,
  like the deadly poison of cobras.

³⁴"I have been saving this,
  and I have it locked in my storehouses.
³⁵I will punish those who do wrong; I will
    repay them.
  Soon their foot will slip,
  because their day of trouble is near,
    and their punishment will come quickly."

³⁶The LORD will defend his people
  and have mercy on his servants.
He will see that their strength is gone,
  that nobody is left, slaves or free.
³⁷Then he will say, "Where are their gods?
  Where is the rock they trusted?
³⁸Who ate the fat from their sacrifices,
  and who drank the wine of their drink
    offerings?
Let those gods come to help you!
  Let them protect you!

³⁹"Now you will see that I am the one God!
  There is no god but me.
I send life and death;
  I can hurt, and I can heal.
  No one can escape from me.
⁴⁰I raise my hand towards heaven and make
    this promise:
  As surely as I live for ever,
⁴¹I will sharpen my flashing sword,
  and I will take it in my hand to judge.
I will punish my enemies
  and pay back those who hate me.
⁴²My arrows will be covered with their blood;
  my sword will eat their flesh.
The blood will flow from those who are
    killed and the captives.
The heads of the enemy leaders will be
    cut off."

⁴³Be happy, nations, with his people,
  because he will repay you for the blood of
    his servants.
He will punish his enemies,
  and he will remove the sin of his land and
    people.

⁴⁴Moses came with Joshua son of Nun, and they spoke all the words of this song for the people to hear. ⁴⁵When Moses finished speaking these words to all Israel, ⁴⁶he said to them: "Pay careful attention to all the words I have said to you today, and command your children to obey carefully everything in these teachings. ⁴⁷These should not be unimportant words for you, but rather they mean life for you! By these words you will live a long time in the land you are crossing the Jordan River to take as your own."

Moses Goes Up to Mount Nebo

⁴⁸The LORD spoke to Moses again that same day and said, ⁴⁹"Go up the Abarim Mountains, to Mount Nebo in the country of Moab, across from Jericho. Look at the land of Canaan that I am giving to the Israelites as their own. ⁵⁰On that mountain that you climb, you will die and join your ancestors, just as your brother Aaron died on Mount Hor and joined his ancestors. ⁵¹You both sinned against me at the waters of Meribah Kadesh in the Desert of Zin, and you did not honour me as holy there among the Israelites. ⁵²So now you will only look at the land from far away. You will not enter the land I am giving the people of Israel."

Moses Blesses the People

33 Moses, the man of God, gave this blessing to the Israelites before he died. ²He said:

"The LORD came from Mount Sinai
  and rose like the sun from Edom;
  he showed his greatness from Mount Paran.
He came with thousands of angels
  from the southern mountains.
³The LORD surely loves his people
  and takes care of all those who belong to him.
They bow down at his feet,
  and they are taught by him.
⁴Moses gave us the teachings
  that belong to the people of Jacob.
⁵The LORD became king of Israel
  when the leaders of the people gathered,
  when the tribes ^d of Israel came together.

⁶"Let the people of Reuben live and not die,
  but let the people be few."

⁷Moses said this about the people of Judah:
"LORD, listen to Judah's prayer;
  bring them back to their people.
They defend themselves with their hands.
  Help them fight their enemies!"

⁸Moses said this about the people of Levi:
"LORD, your Thummim and Urim ^d belong
  to Levi, whom you love.
LORD, you tested him at Massah
  and argued with him at the waters of
    Meribah.
⁹He said about his father and mother,
  'I don't care about them.'
He did not treat his brothers as favourites
  or give special favours to his children,
but he protected your word
  and guarded your agreement.
¹⁰He teaches your laws to the people of Jacob
  and your teachings to the people of Israel.
He burns incense ^d before you

and makes whole burnt offerings on your
    altar.
[11]LORD, make them strong;
    be pleased with the work they do.
Defeat those who attack them,
    and don't let their enemies rise up again."

[12]Moses said this about the people of Benjamin:
"The LORD's loved ones will lie down in
    safety,
because he protects them all day long.
The ones he loves rest with him."

[13]Moses said this about the people of Joseph:
"May the LORD bless their land with
    wonderful dew from heaven,
with water from the springs below,
[14]with the best fruits that the sun brings,
    and with the best fruits that the moon
    brings.
[15]Let the old mountains give the finest crops,

and let the everlasting hills give the best
    fruits.
[16]Let the full earth give the best fruits,
    and let the LORD who lived in the burning
    bush be pleased.
May these blessings rest on the head of Joseph,
    on the forehead of the one who was
    blessed among his brothers.
[17]Joseph has the majesty of a firstborn [d] bull;
    he is as strong as a wild ox.
He will stab other nations,
    even those nations far away.
These are the ten thousands of Ephraim,
    and these are the thousands of Manasseh."

[18]Moses said this about the people of Zebulun:
"Be happy when you go out, Zebulun,
    and be happy in your tents, Issachar.
[19]They will call the people to the mountain,
    and there they will offer the right sacrifices.
They will do well from all that is in the sea,

DEATH

Breaking the Mould

"One Michael Owen! There's only one Michael Owen!" The England Football fans sang this at the top of their voices. The flags were raised high and scarves were waved from end to end of the stadium. And they were right. There is only one Michael Owen. We are all unique in God's eyes.

People often say, when talking of someone great – "God broke the mould after he made him!" And it's true! No two people are the same.

When we look back on the life of a friend who has died, we remember all the good things, all the unique things about that person and we realise that there will never be another person quite like them. When we understand this, we can start to understand how precious we are to God.

It makes the loss of a friend even more poignant as we realise we will never hear that voice or see that smile, for a long long time. It's an empty time, because no one will fill that space in the same way ever again. That's what grieving is all about. We need time to remember and mourn.

In **Deuteronomy 34:1–12** we find the same predicament.

* How did the Israelites grieve over Moses?
* When have you experienced the loss of someone close? How was your experience like that of the Israelites?

Consider . . .

* talking to a friend and a family member about times when they lost someone close. Ask what emotions they felt and how long they grieved.
* comforting someone who's facing death or grieving, by making a phone call, sending a card, visiting, or giving a hug.

For more, see . . .

* 2 Samuel 1:17–27 (p.284)
* Revelation 21:1–4 (p.1403)
* John 11:28–44 (p.1116)

and they will do well from the treasures
hidden in the sand on the shore."

20Moses said this about the people of Gad:
"Praise God who gives Gad more land!
  Gad lives there like a lion,
  who tears off arms and heads.
21They chose the best land for themselves.
  They received a large share, like that given
    to an officer.
When the leaders of the people gathered,
  the people of Gad did what the LORD
    said was right,
  and they judged Israel fairly."

22Moses said this about the people of Dan:
"Dan is like a lion's cub,
  who jumps out of Bashan."

23Moses said this about the people of Naphtali:
"Naphtali enjoys special kindnesses,
  and they are full of the LORD's blessings.
Take as your own the west and south."

24Moses said this about the people of Asher:
"Asher is the most blessed of the sons;
  let him be his brothers' favourite.
Let him bathe his feet in olive oil.
25Your gates will have locks of iron and
    bronze,
  and you will be strong as long as you live.

26"There is no one like the God of Israel,
  who rides through the skies to help you,
  who rides on the clouds in his majesty.
27The everlasting God is your place of safety,
  and his arms will hold you up for ever.
He will force your enemy out ahead of you,
  saying, "Destroy the enemy!'
28The people of Israel will lie down in safety.
  Jacob's spring is theirs alone.
Theirs is a land full of grain and new wine,
  where the skies drop their dew.
29Israel, you are blessed!
  No one else is like you,

because you are a people saved by the
  LORD.
He is your shield and helper,
  your glorious sword.
Your enemies will be afraid of you,
  and you will walk all over their holy places."

Moses Dies

34 Then Moses climbed Mount Nebo from the plains of Moab to the top of Mount Pisgah, across from Jericho. From there the LORD showed him all the land from Gilead to Dan, 2all of Naphtali and the lands of Ephraim and Manasseh, all the land of Judah as far as the Mediterranean Sea, 3as well as the southern desert and the whole Valley of Jericho up to Zoar. (Jericho is called the city of palm trees.) 4Then the LORD said to Moses, "This is the land I promised to Abraham, Isaac and Jacob when I said to them, 'I will give this land to your descendants.' *d* I have let you look at it, Moses, but you will not cross over there."

5Then Moses, the servant of the LORD, died there in Moab, as the LORD had said. 6He buried Moses in Moab in the valley opposite Beth Peor, but even today no one knows where his grave is. 7Moses was 120 years old when he died. His eyes were not weak, and he was still strong. 8The Israelites cried for Moses for 30 days, staying in the plains of Moab until the time of sadness was over.

9Joshua son of Nun was then filled with wisdom, because Moses had put his hands on him. So the Israelites listened to Joshua, and they did what the LORD had commanded Moses.

10There has never been another prophet *d* in Israel like Moses. The LORD knew Moses face to face 11and sent him to do signs and miracles *d* in Egypt—to the king, to all his officers and to the whole land of Egypt. 12Moses had great power, and he did great and wonderful things for all the Israelites to see.

Joshua

Why Read This Book:

* See how God leads people to victory when they are faithful (Joshua 1—12).
* Learn how God takes care of people's needs (Joshua 13—21).
* Be challenged to stay faithful to God (Joshua 22—24).

When?

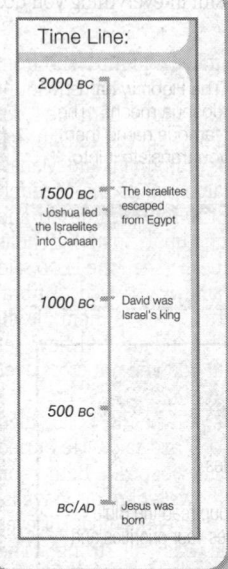

Time Line:

2000 BC

1500 BC — The Israelites escaped from Egypt
Joshua led the Israelites into Canaan

1000 BC — David was Israel's king

500 BC

BC/AD — Jesus was born

Behind the Scenes:

The book of Joshua could be a great script for an action-packed film. It's filled with spies, surprise attacks, warfare, leaders and unusual battles.

The central hero is Joshua, a creative military mind with great organisational skills. But above all, he is absolutely loyal to and dependent on God.

The plot tells how the Israelites conquered land that God promised to their ancestor Abram (Genesis 12:7, p.14). Their parents had escaped from Egypt but had not followed God.

So the whole generation that left Egypt had died in the desert, leaving the children – under Joshua's leadership – to conquer the land of Canaan.

Canaan consisted of many independent cities, each with its own king and army, and many had strong, high walls. So the Israelites had to defeat the cities one by one, beginning with the famous battle of Jericho (Joshua 6).

The books shows how God works through people and why obedience matters.

Where?

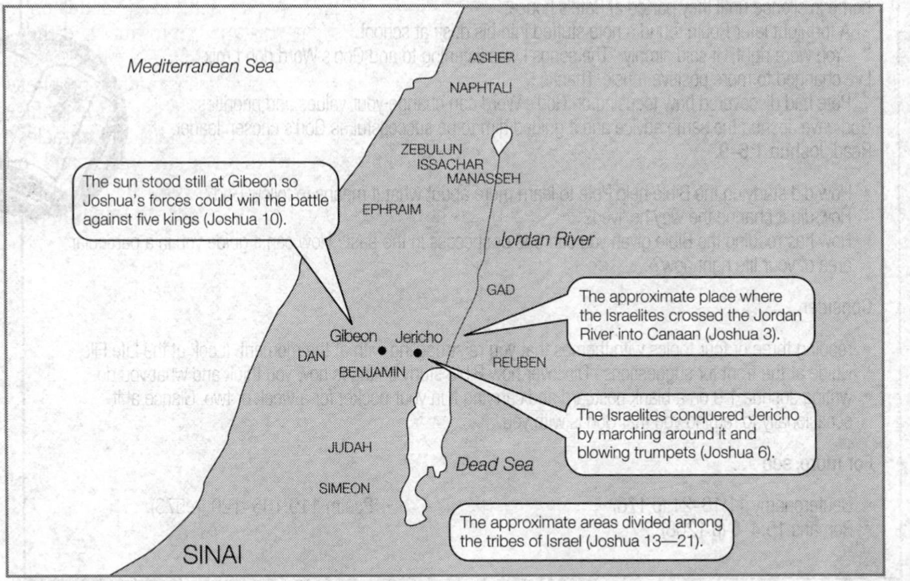

Mediterranean Sea

ASHER
NAPHTALI
ZEBULUN
ISSACHAR
MANASSEH
EPHRAIM
Jordan River
GAD
Gibeon   Jericho
DAN
BENJAMIN   REUBEN
JUDAH   Dead Sea
SIMEON
SINAI

The sun stood still at Gibeon so Joshua's forces could win the battle against five kings (Joshua 10).

The approximate place where the Israelites crossed the Jordan River into Canaan (Joshua 3).

The Israelites conquered Jericho by marching around it and blowing trumpets (Joshua 6).

The approximate areas divided among the tribes of Israel (Joshua 13—21).

God's Command to Joshua

1 After Moses, the servant of the LORD, died, the LORD spoke to Joshua son of Nun, Moses' assistant. ²The LORD said, "My servant Moses is dead. Now you and all these people go across the Jordan River into the land I am giving to the Israelites. ³I promised Moses I would give you this land, so I will give you every place you go in the land. ⁴All the land from the desert in the south to Lebanon in the north will be yours. All the land from the great river, the Euphrates, in the east, to the Mediterranean Sea in the west will be yours too, including the land of the Hittites. ⁵No one will be able to defeat you all your life. Just as I was with Moses, so I will be with you. I will not leave you or forget you.

⁶"Joshua, be strong and brave! You must lead these people so they can take the land that I promised their fathers I would give them. ⁷Be strong and brave. Be sure to obey all the teachings my servant Moses gave you. If you follow them exactly, you will be successful in everything you do.

> **Sidelight** The Hebrew name for Joshua means "The Lord saves". It's a more famous name than you might think. When you translate it into English, it's Jesus.

BIBLE STUDY

Where's the Focus?

Robin was appalled when he saw the CDs in his friend Pete's room.

"How can you listen to this rubbish?" he asked as he read the sexually explicit song titles.

"Give me a break," Pete shot back. "Who cares about the words?"

The conversation came back to Robin the next Wednesday night in Bible study. The group read the Bible and tried to apply its principles to their lives. They focused on how being a Christian shapes your priorities and interests in life and how it affects everything you do.

Robin was challenged by the discussion and wanted to talk about it with Pete. On the way home from the Bible study, they talked about friendships and being honest. Then Robin asked, "What does all this say about your music, Pete?"

Pete was furious. "Nothing. It's fine!" he shouted, hoping Robin would back off. Which he did. They walked home in silence until they parted at Pete's house.

A fortnight later Robin found a note stuffed into his desk at school.

"You were right," it said simply. "The songs I was listening to and God's Word don't mix. I've changed to more positive music. Thanks."

Pete had discovered how focusing on God's Word can change your values and priorities. God gave Joshua the same advice and it guided him to be successful as God's chosen leader. Read **Joshua 1:6–9**.

* How did studying the Bible help Pete to learn more about what it means to follow God? How did it change the way he lived?
* How has reading the Bible given you courage or success in the past? How can it guide you in a particular area of your life right now?

Consider . . .

* reading three or four topics with themes that you're struggling with at the moment. (Look at the Life File Guide at the front for suggestions.) Discover how Bible study changes how you think and what you do.
* writing Joshua 1:9 on a blank postcard and carrying it in your pocket for a week or two. Glance at it occasionally to remind you that God is with you.

For more, see . . .

* Deuteronomy 11:16–21 (p.176)
* Romans 15:4–6 (p.1208)
* Psalm 119:105–120 (p.573)

[8]Always remember what is written in the Book of the Teachings. Study it day and night to be sure to obey everything that is written there. If you do this, you will be wise and successful in everything. [9]Remember that I commanded you to be strong and brave. Don't be afraid, because the LORD your God will be with you everywhere you go."

Joshua's Orders to the People

[10]Then Joshua gave orders to the officers of the people: [11]"Go through the camp and tell the people, 'Get your supplies ready. Three days from now you will cross the Jordan River and take the land the LORD your God is giving you.' "

[12]Then Joshua said to the people of Reuben, Gad and East Manasseh, [13]"Remember what Moses, the servant of the LORD, told you. He said the LORD your God would give you rest and would give you this land. [14]Now the LORD has given you this land east of the Jordan River. Your wives, children and animals may stay here, but your fighting men must dress for war and cross the Jordan River ahead of your brothers to help them. [15]The LORD has given you a place to rest and will do the same for your brothers. But you must help them until they take the land the LORD their God is giving them. Then you may return to your own land east of the Jordan River, the land that Moses, the servant of the LORD, gave you."

[16]Then the people answered Joshua, "Whatever you command us to do, we will do. Wherever you send us, we will go. [17]Just as we fully obeyed Moses, we will obey you. We ask only that the LORD your God be with you just as he was with Moses. [18]Whoever refuses to obey your commands or turns against you will be put to death. Just be strong and brave!"

Spies Sent to Jericho

2 Joshua son of Nun secretly sent out two spies from Acacia and said to them, "Go and look at the land, particularly at the city of Jericho."

So the men went to Jericho and stayed at the house of a prostitute [d] named Rahab.

[2]Someone told the king of Jericho, "Some men from Israel have come here tonight to spy out the land."

[3]So the king of Jericho sent this message to Rahab: "Bring out the men who came to you and entered your house. They have come to spy out our whole land."

[4]But the woman had hidden the two men. She said, "They did come here, but I didn't know where they came from. [5]In the evening, when it was time to close the city gate, they left. I don't know where they went, but if you go quickly, maybe you can catch them." [6](The woman had taken the men up to the roof [n] and had hidden them there under stalks of flax [d] that she had spread out.) [7]So the king's men went out looking for the spies on the road that leads to the crossings of the Jordan River. The city gate was closed just after the king's men left the city.

[8]Before the spies went to sleep for the night, Rahab went up to the roof. [9]She said to them, "I know the LORD has given this land to your people. You frighten us very much. Everyone living in this land is terribly afraid of you [10]because we have heard how the LORD dried up the Red Sea [d] when you came out of Egypt. We have heard how you destroyed Sihon and Og, two Amorite kings who lived east of the Jordan. [11]When we heard this, we were very frightened. Now our men are afraid to fight you because the LORD your God rules the heavens above and the earth below! [12]So now, promise me before the LORD that you will show kindness to my family just as I showed kindness to you. Give me some proof that you will do this. [13]Allow my father, mother, brothers, sisters and all of their families to live. Save us from death."

[14]The men agreed and said, "It will be our lives for your lives if you don't tell anyone what we are doing. When the LORD gives us the land, we will be kind and true to you."

[15]The house Rahab lived in was built on the city wall, so she used a rope to let the men down through a window. [16]She said to them, "Go into the hills so the king's men will not find you. Hide there for three days. After the king's men return, you may go on your way."

[17]The men said to her, "You must do as we say. If not, we cannot be responsible for keeping this oath you have made us swear. [18]When we return to this land, you must tie this red rope in the window through which you let us down. Bring your father, mother, brothers and all your family into your house. [19]If anyone leaves your house and is killed, it is his own fault. We cannot be responsible for him. If anyone in your house is hurt, we will be responsible. [20]But if you tell anyone about this, we will be free from the oath you made us swear."

[21]Rahab answered, "I agree to this." So she sent them away, and they left. Then she tied the red rope in the window.

[22]The men left and went into the hills where they stayed for three days. The king's men looked for them all along the road, but after three days, they returned to the city without finding them.

---

roof In Bible times houses were built with flat roofs. The roof was used for drying things such as flax and fruit. And it was used as an extra room, as a place for worship and as a place to sleep in the summer.

23Then the two men started back. They left the hills and crossed the river and came to Joshua son of Nun and told him everything that had happened to them. 24They said, "The LORD surely has given us all of the land. All the people in that land are terribly afraid of us."

Crossing the Jordan

3 Early the next morning Joshua and all the Israelites left Acacia. They travelled to the Jordan River and camped there before crossing it. 2After three days the officers went through the camp 3and gave orders to the people: "When you see the priests and Levites carrying the Ark d of the Agreement with the LORD your God, leave where you are and follow it. 4That way you will know which way to go since you have never been here before. But do not follow too closely. Stay about a kilometre behind the Ark."

5Then Joshua told the people, "Make yourselves holy, because tomorrow the LORD will do amazing things among you."

6Joshua said to the priests, "Take the Ark of the Agreement and go ahead of the people." So the priests lifted the Ark and carried it ahead of the people.

7Then the LORD said to Joshua, "Today I will begin to make you great in the opinion of all the Israelites so the people will know I am with you just as I was with Moses. 8Tell the priests who carry the Ark of the Agreement to go to the edge of the Jordan River and stand in the water."

9Then Joshua said to the Israelites, "Come here and listen to the words of the LORD your God. 10Here is proof that the living God is with you and that he will force out the Canaanites, Hittites, Hivites, Perizzites, Girgashites, Amorites and Jebusites. 11The Ark of the Agreement with the Lord of the whole world will go ahead of you into the Jordan River. 12Now choose twelve men from among you, one from each of the twelve tribes d of Israel. 13The priests will carry the Ark of the LORD, the Master of the whole world, into the Jordan ahead of you. When they step into the water, it will stop. The river will stop flowing and will stand up in a heap."

14So the people left the place where they had camped, and they followed the priests who carried the Ark of the Agreement across the Jordan River. 15During harvest the Jordan overflows its banks. When the priests carrying the Ark came to the edge of the river and stepped into the water, 16the water a great distance away stopped flowing. It stood up in a heap a great distance away at Adam, a town near Zarethan. The water flowing down to the Sea of Arabah (the Dead Sea d) was completely cut off. So the people crossed the river near Jericho. 17The priests carried the Ark of the Agreement with the LORD to the middle of the river and stood there on dry ground. They waited there while all the people of Israel walked across the Jordan River on dry land.

Rocks to Remind the People

4 After all the people had finished crossing the Jordan, the LORD said to Joshua, 2"Choose twelve men from among the people, one from each tribe. d 3Tell them to get twelve rocks from the middle of the river, from where the priests stood. Carry the rocks and put them down where you stay tonight."

4So Joshua chose one man from each tribe. Then he called the twelve men together 5and said to them, "Go out into the river where the Ark d of the LORD your God is. Each of you bring back one rock, one for each tribe of Israel, and carry it on your shoulder. 6They will be a sign among you. In the future your children will ask you, 'What do these rocks mean?' 7Tell them the water stopped flowing in the Jordan when the Ark of the Agreement with the LORD crossed the river. These rocks will always remind the Israelites of this."

8So the Israelites obeyed Joshua and carried twelve rocks from the middle of the Jordan River, one rock for each of the twelve tribes of Israel, just as the LORD had commanded Joshua. They carried the rocks with them and put them down where they made their camp. 9Joshua also put twelve rocks in the middle of the Jordan River where the priests had stood while carrying the Ark of the Agreement. These rocks are still there today.

10The priests carrying the Ark continued standing in the middle of the river until everything was done that the LORD had commanded Joshua to tell the people, just as Moses had told Joshua. The people hurried across the river. 11After they finished crossing the river, the priests carried the Ark of the LORD to the other side as the people watched. 12The men from the tribes of Reuben, Gad and East Manasseh obeyed what Moses had told them. They were dressed for war, and they crossed the river ahead of the other people. 13About 40,000 soldiers, prepared for war, passed before the LORD as they marched across the river, going towards the plains of Jericho.

[14]That day the LORD made Joshua great in the opinion of all the Israelites. They respected Joshua all his life, just as they had respected Moses.

[15]Then the LORD said to Joshua, [16]"Command the priests to bring the Ark of the Agreement out of the river."

[17]So Joshua commanded the priests, "Come up out of the Jordan."

[18]Then the priests carried the Ark of the Agreement with the LORD out of the river. As soon as their feet touched dry land, the water began flowing again. The river again overflowed its banks, just as it had before they crossed.

[19]The people crossed the Jordan on the tenth day of the first month and camped at Gilgal, east of Jericho. [20]They carried with them the twelve rocks taken from the Jordan, and Joshua set them up at Gilgal. [21]Then he spoke to the Israelites: "In the future your children will ask you, 'What do these rocks mean?' [22]Tell them, 'Israel crossed the Jordan River on dry land. [23]The LORD your God caused the water to stop flowing until you finished crossing it, just as the LORD did to the Red Sea. [d] He stopped the water until we crossed it. [24]The LORD did this so all people would know he has great power and so you would always respect the LORD your God.'"

5 All the kings of the Amorites west of the Jordan and the Canaanite kings living by the Mediterranean Sea heard that the LORD dried up the Jordan River until the Israelites had crossed it. After that they were scared and too afraid to face the Israelites.

The Israelites are Circumcised

[2]At that time the LORD said to Joshua, "Make knives from flint stones and circumcise [d] the Israelites." [3]So Joshua made knives from flint stones and circumcised the Israelites at Gibeath Haaraloth.

[4]This is why Joshua circumcised the men: after the Israelites left Egypt, all the men old enough to serve in the army died in the desert on the way out of Egypt. [5]The men who had come out of Egypt had been circumcised, but none of those who were born in the desert on the trip from Egypt had been circumcised. [6]The Israelites had moved about in the desert for 40 years. During that time all the fighting men who had left Egypt had died because they had not obeyed the LORD. So the LORD swore they would not see the land he had promised their ancestors to give them, a fertile land. [7]Their sons took their places. But none of the sons born on the trip from Egypt had been circumcised, so Joshua circumcised them. [8]After all the Israelites had been circumcised, they stayed in camp until they were healed.

[9]Then the LORD said to Joshua, "As slaves in Egypt you were ashamed, but today I have removed that shame." So Joshua named that place Gilgal, which it is still named today.

[10]The people of Israel were camped at Gilgal on the plains of Jericho. It was there, on the evening of the fourteenth day of the month, they celebrated the Passover [d] Feast. [11]The day after the Passover, the people ate food grown on that land: bread made without yeast and roasted grain. [12]The day they ate this food, the manna [d] stopped coming. The Israelites no longer got the manna from heaven. They ate the food grown in the land of Canaan that year.

[13]Joshua was near Jericho when he looked up and saw a man standing in front of him with a sword in his hand. Joshua went to him and asked, "Are you a friend or an enemy?"

[14]The man answered, "I am neither. I have come as the commander of the LORD's army."

Then Joshua bowed face down on the ground and asked, "Does my master have a command for me, his servant?"

[15]The commander of the LORD's army answered, "Take off your sandals, because the place where you are standing is holy." So Joshua did.

The Fall of Jericho

6 The people of Jericho were afraid because the Israelites were near. They closed the city gates and guarded them. No one went into the city, and no one came out.

[2]Then the LORD said to Joshua, "Look, I have given you Jericho, its king, and all its fighting men. [3]March around the city with your army once a day for six days. [4]Have seven priests carry trumpets made from horns of rams and have them march in front of the Ark. [d] On the seventh day march around the city seven times and have the priests blow the trumpets as they march. [5]They will make one long blast on the trumpets. When you hear that sound, have all the people give a loud shout. Then the walls of the city will fall so the people can go straight into the city."

[6]So Joshua son of Nun called the priests together and said to them, "Carry the Ark of the Agreement. Tell seven priests to carry trumpets and march in front of it." [7]Then Joshua ordered the people, "Now go! March around the city. The soldiers with weapons should march in front of the Ark of the Agreement with the LORD."

[8]When Joshua finished speaking to the people, the seven priests began marching before the LORD. They carried the seven trumpets and blew them as they marched. The priests carrying the Ark of the Agreement with the LORD followed them. [9]Soldiers with weapons marched in front of the priests, and armed men walked behind the Ark. The priests were blowing their trumpets. [10]But Joshua had told the people not to give a war cry.

He said, "Don't shout. Don't say a word until the day I tell you. Then shout." ¹¹So Joshua had the Ark of the LORD carried around the city once. Then they went back to camp for the night.

¹²Early the next morning Joshua got up, and the priests carried the Ark of the LORD again. ¹³The seven priests carried the seven trumpets and marched in front of the Ark of the LORD, blowing their trumpets. Soldiers with weapons marched in front of them, and other soldiers walked behind the Ark of the LORD. All this time the priests were blowing their trumpets. ¹⁴So on the second day they marched around the city once and then went back to camp. They did this every day for six days.

¹⁵On the seventh day they got up at dawn and marched around the city, just as they had on the days before. But on that day they marched around the city seven times. ¹⁶The seventh time around the priests blew their trumpets. Then Joshua gave the command: "Now, shout! The LORD has given you this city! ¹⁷The city and everything in it are to be destroyed as an offering to the LORD. Only Rahab the prostitute *d* and everyone in her house should remain alive. They must not be killed, because Rahab hid the two spies we sent out. ¹⁸Don't take any of the things that are to be destroyed as an offering to the LORD. If you take them and bring them into

MUSIC

God's Powerful Gift

Music has huge power – it can divide or unite people. It is one of the biggest ways in which people nowadays are defined, be it liking rap, alternative, dance, rock, pop, indie, classical, metal, experimental or punk to name a few. This can lead to whole sub-cultures being created – fashion styles, places to hang out, and other activities, such as skating, are all tied to genres of music. It can even lead to tensions between the sub-cultures – over the years, many different gangs have grown from these groups.

However, music is also often part of bringing people together. It has played a large part in many of the big campaigns for justice and peace alongside annual events such as Comic Relief and Children in Need. Several of the campaigns have used concerts with huge impact, both in the amount of money they raised to help deal with issues such as famine and starvation in Africa, and in the way that it brought those issues to our attention.

A number of music stars use their fame to encourage others to make a difference. They may support a particular charity, organisation or cause, and use their music and status to help provide funding and publicity for that cause.

In **Joshua 6:2–5** we read how God brought the Israelites together and showed how music truly is a powerful gift – one that can make huge physical differences – even knocking down a city's walls!

* Has the power of creativity, especially music, had an impact on your life?
* How could you and your friends use music to make a difference for God?

Consider . . .

* writing a paraphrase of some of the old hymns that you know. Take the lyrics and try to rewrite them in everyday language. Spend time looking at the meaning of the words you sing in church and be blessed by the creativity of the poetic words. Some good songs to look at include "Praise My Soul the King of Heaven", "To God Be the Glory", and "Tell Out My Soul".
* going to your music collection and listening to the lyrics of your secular music. Check out the themes within the lyrics.

For more, see . . .

* 2 Chronicles 5:12–14 (p.404)
* Psalm 147:1 (p.586)

* Psalm 81:2–4 (p.549)

our camp, you yourselves will be destroyed, and you will bring trouble to all of Israel. ¹⁹All the silver and gold and things made from bronze and iron belong to the LORD and must be saved for him."

²⁰When the priests blew the trumpets, the people shouted. At the sound of the trumpets and the people's shout, the walls fell, and everyone ran straight into the city. So the Israelites defeated that city. ²¹They completely destroyed with the sword every living thing in the city—men and women, young and old, cattle, sheep and donkeys.

²²Joshua said to the two men who had spied out the land, "Go into the prostitute's house. Bring her out and bring out those who are with her, because of the promise you made to her." ²³So the two men went into the house and brought out Rahab, her father, mother, brothers and all those with her. They put all of her family in a safe place outside the camp of Israel.

²⁴Then Israel burned the whole city and everything in it, but they did not burn the things made from silver, gold, bronze and iron. These were saved for the LORD. ²⁵Joshua saved Rahab the prostitute, her family and all who were with her, because Rahab had helped the men he had sent to spy out Jericho. Rahab still lives among the Israelites today.

²⁶Then Joshua made this oath:
"Anyone who tries to rebuild this city of
        Jericho
   will be cursed by the LORD.
The one who lays the foundation of this city
   will lose his oldest son,
and the one who sets up the gates
   will lose his youngest son."

²⁷So the LORD was with Joshua, and Joshua became famous through all the land.

The Sin of Achan

7 But the Israelites did not obey the LORD. There was a man from the tribe*d* of Judah named Achan. (He was the son of Carmi and grandson of Zabdi, who was the son of Zerah.) Because Achan kept some of the things that were to be given to the LORD, the LORD became very angry at the Israelites.

²Joshua sent some men from Jericho to Ai, which was near Beth Aven, east of Bethel. He told them, "Go to Ai and spy out the area." So the men went to spy on Ai.

³Later they came back to Joshua and said, "There are only a few people in Ai, so we will not need all our people to defeat them. Send only 2,000 to 3,000 men to fight. There is no need to send all of our people." ⁴So about 3,000 men went up to Ai, but the people of Ai beat them badly. ⁵The people of Ai killed about 36 Israelites and then chased the rest from the city gate all the way down to the quarry, killing them as they went down the hill. When the Israelites saw this, they lost their courage.

⁶Then Joshua tore his clothes in sorrow. He bowed face down on the ground before the Ark *d* of the LORD and stayed there until evening. The elders of Israel did the same thing. They also threw dust on their heads to show their sorrow. ⁷Then Joshua said, "Lord GOD, you brought our people across the Jordan River. Why did you bring us this far and then let the Amorites destroy us? We would have been happy to stay on the other side of the Jordan. ⁸Lord, there is nothing I can say now. Israel has been beaten by the enemy. ⁹The Canaanites and all the other people in this country will hear about this and will surround and kill us all! Then what will you do for your own great name?"

¹⁰The LORD said to Joshua, "Stand up! Why are you down on your face? ¹¹The Israelites have sinned; they have broken the agreement I commanded them to obey. They took some of the things I commanded them to destroy. They have stolen and lied and have taken those things for themselves. ¹²That is why the Israelites cannot face their enemies. They turn away from the fight and run, because I have commanded that they be destroyed. I will not help you any more unless you destroy everything as I commanded you.

¹³"Now go! Make the people holy. Tell them, 'Set yourselves apart to the LORD for tomorrow. The LORD, the God of Israel, says some of you are keeping things he commanded you to destroy. You will never defeat your enemies until you throw away those things.

¹⁴" 'Tomorrow morning you must be present with your tribes. The LORD will choose one tribe to stand alone before him. Then the LORD will choose one family group from that tribe to stand before him. Then the LORD will choose one family from that family group to stand before him, person by person. ¹⁵The one who is keeping what should have been destroyed will himself be destroyed by fire. Everything he owns will be

destroyed with him. He has broken the agreement with the LORD and has done a disgraceful thing among the people of Israel!' "

16Early the next morning Joshua led all of Israel to present themselves in their tribes, and the LORD chose the tribe of Judah. 17So the family groups of Judah presented themselves, and the LORD then chose the family group of Zerah. When all the families of Zerah presented themselves, the family of Zabdi was chosen. 18And Joshua told all the men in that family to present themselves. The LORD chose Achan son of Carmi. (Carmi was the son of Zabdi, who was the son of Zerah.)

19Then Joshua said to Achan, "My son, tell the truth. Confess to the LORD, the God of Israel. Tell me what you did, and don't try to hide anything from me."

20Achan answered, "It is true! I have sinned against the LORD, the God of Israel. This is what I did: 21among the things I saw was a beautiful coat from Babylonia and about 2 kilogrammes of silver and more than half a kilogramme of gold. I wanted these things very much for myself, so I took them. You will find them buried in the ground under my tent, with the silver underneath."

22So Joshua sent men who ran to the tent and found the things hidden there, with the silver. 23The men brought them out of the tent, took them to Joshua and all the Israelites, and spread them out on the ground before the LORD. 24Then Joshua and all the people led Achan son of Zerah to the Valley of Trouble. They also took the silver, the coat, the gold, Achan's sons, daughters, cattle, donkeys, sheep, tent and everything he owned. 25Joshua said, "I don't know why you caused so much trouble for us, but now the LORD will bring trouble to you." Then all the people threw stones at Achan and his family until they died. Then the people burned them. 26They piled rocks over Achan's body, and they are still there today. That is why it is called the Valley of Trouble. After this the LORD was no longer angry.

Ai is Destroyed

8 Then the LORD said to Joshua, "Don't be afraid or give up. Lead all your fighting men to Ai. I will help you defeat the king of Ai, his people, his city and his land. 2You will do to Ai and its king what you did to Jericho and its king. Only this time you may take all the wealth and keep it for yourselves. Now tell some of your soldiers to set up an ambush behind the city."

3So Joshua led his whole army towards Ai. Then he chose 30,000 of his best fighting men and sent them out at night. 4Joshua gave them these orders: "Listen carefully. You must set up an ambush behind the city. Don't go far from it,

but continue to watch and be ready. 5I and the men who are with me will march towards the city, and the men in the city will come out to fight us, just as they did before. Then we will turn and run away from them. 6They will chase us away from the city, thinking we are running away from them as we did before. When we run away, 7come out from your ambush and take the city. The LORD your God will give you the power to win. 8After you take the city, burn it. See to it! You have your orders."

9Then Joshua sent them to wait in ambush between Bethel and Ai, to the west of Ai. But Joshua stayed the night with his people.

10Early the next morning Joshua gathered his men together. He and the elders of Israel led them up to Ai. 11All of the soldiers who were with Joshua marched up to Ai and stopped in front of the city and made camp north of it. There was a valley between them and the city. 12Then Joshua chose about 5,000 men and set them in ambush in the area west of the city between Bethel and Ai. 13So the people took their positions; the main camp was north of the city, and the other men were hiding to the west. That night Joshua went down into the valley.

14Now when the king of Ai saw the army of Israel, he and his people got up early the next morning and hurried out to fight them. They went out to a place east of the city, but the king did not know soldiers were waiting in ambush behind the city. 15Joshua and all the men of Israel let the army of Ai push them back. Then they ran towards the desert. 16The men in Ai were called to chase Joshua and his men, so they left the city and went after them. 17All the men of Ai and Bethel chased the army of Israel. The city was left open; not a man stayed to protect it.

18Then the LORD said to Joshua, "Hold your spear towards Ai, because I will give you that city." So Joshua held his spear towards the city of Ai. 19When the Israelites who were in ambush saw this, they quickly came out of their hiding place and hurried towards the city. They entered the city, took control of it, and quickly set it on fire.

20When the men of Ai looked back, they saw smoke rising from their city. At the same time the Israelites stopped running and turned against the men of Ai, who could not escape in any direction. 21When Joshua and all his men saw that the army had taken control of the city and saw the smoke rising from it, they stopped running and turned to fight the men of Ai. 22The men who were in ambush also came out of the city to help with the fight. So the men of Ai were caught between the armies of Israel. None of the enemy escaped. The Israelites fought until not one of the men of Ai was left alive, except 23the king of Ai, and they brought him to Joshua.

A Review of the Fighting

24During the fighting the army of Israel chased the men of Ai into the fields and desert and killed all of them. Then they went back to Ai and killed everyone there. 25All the people of Ai died that day, 12,000 men and women. 26Joshua had held his spear towards Ai, as a sign to destroy the city, and did not draw it back until all the people of Ai were destroyed. 27The people of Israel kept for themselves the animals and the other things the people of Ai had owned, as the LORD had commanded Joshua to do.

28Then Joshua burned the city of Ai and made it a pile of ruins. And it is still like that today. 29Joshua hanged the king of Ai on a tree and left him there until evening. At sunset Joshua told his men to take the king's body down from the tree and to throw it down at the city gate. Then they covered it with a pile of rocks, which is still there today.

30Joshua built an altar for the LORD, the God of Israel, on Mount Ebal, as 31Moses, the LORD's servant, had commanded. Joshua built the altar as it was explained in the Book of the Teachings of Moses. It was made from uncut stones; no tool was ever used on them. On that altar the Israelites offered burnt offerings to the LORD and fellowship offerings. 32There Joshua wrote the teachings of Moses on stones for all the people of Israel to see. 33The elders, officers, judges and all the Israelites were there; Israelites and non-Israelites were all standing around the Ark *d* of the Agreement with the LORD in front of the priests, the Levites who had carried the Ark. Half of the people stood in front of Mount Ebal, and half stood in front of Mount Gerizim. This was the way the LORD's servant Moses had earlier commanded the people to be blessed.

34Then Joshua read all the words of the teachings, the blessings and the curses, exactly as they were written in the Book of the Teachings. 35All the Israelites were gathered together—men, women and children—along with the non-Israelites who lived among them. Joshua read every command that Moses had given.

The Gibeonite Trickery

9 All the kings west of the Jordan River heard about these things: the kings of the Hittites, Amorites, Canaanites, Perizzites, Hivites and Jebusites. They lived in the mountains and on the western hills and along the whole Mediterranean Sea coast. 2So all these kings gathered to fight Joshua and the Israelites.

3When the people of Gibeon heard how Joshua had defeated Jericho and Ai, 4they decided to trick the Israelites. They gathered old sacks and old leather wine bags that were cracked and mended, and they put them on the backs of their donkeys. 5They put old sandals on their feet and wore old clothes, and they took some dry, mouldy bread. 6Then they went to Joshua in the camp near Gilgal.

The men said to Joshua and the Israelites, "We have travelled from a faraway country. Make a peace agreement with us."

7The Israelites said to these Hivites, "Maybe you live near us. How can we make a peace agreement with you?"

8The Hivites said to Joshua, "We are your servants."

But Joshua asked, "Who are you? Where do you come from?"

9The men answered, "We are your servants who have come from a far country, because we heard of the fame of the LORD your God. We heard about what he has done and everything he did in Egypt. 10We heard that he defeated the two kings of the Amorites from the east side of the Jordan River—Sihon king of Heshbon and Og king of Bashan who ruled in Ashtaroth. 11So our elders and our people said to us, 'Take food for your journey and go and meet the Israelites. Tell them, "We are your servants. Make a peace agreement with us."'

12"Look at our bread. On the day we left home to come to you it was warm and fresh, but now it is dry and mouldy. 13Look at our leather wine bags. They were new and filled with wine, but now they are cracked and old. Our clothes and sandals are worn out from the long journey."

14The men of Israel tasted the bread, but they did not ask the LORD what to do. 15So Joshua agreed to make peace with the Gibeonites and to let them live. And the leaders of the Israelites swore an oath to keep the agreement.

16Three days after they had made the agreement, the Israelites learned that the Gibeonites lived nearby. 17So the Israelites went to where they lived and on the third day came to their cities: Gibeon, Kephirah, Beeroth and Kiriath Jearim. 18But the Israelites did not attack those cities, because they had made a promise to them before the LORD, the God of Israel.

All the Israelites grumbled against the leaders. 19But the leaders answered, "We have given our promise before the LORD, the God of Israel, so we cannot attack them now. 20This is what we must do. We must let them live. Otherwise, God's anger will be against us for breaking the oath we swore to them. 21So let them live, but they will cut wood and carry water for our people." So the leaders kept their promise to them.

²²Joshua called for the Gibeonites and asked, "Why did you lie to us? Your land was near our camp, but you told us you were from a far country. ²³Now, you will be placed under a curse to be our slaves. You will have to cut wood and carry water for the house of my God."

²⁴The Gibeonites answered Joshua, "We lied to you because we were afraid you would kill us. We heard that the LORD your God commanded his servant Moses to give you all of this land and to kill all the people who lived in it. That is why we did this. ²⁵Now you can decide what to do with us, whatever you think is right."

²⁶So Joshua saved their lives by not allowing the Israelites to kill them, ²⁷but he made the Gibeonites slaves. They cut wood and carried water for the Israelites, and they did it for the altar of the LORD—wherever he chose it to be. They are still doing this today.

The Sun Stands Still

10 At this time Adoni-Zedek king of Jerusalem heard that Joshua had defeated Ai and completely destroyed it, as he had also done to Jericho and its king. The king also learned that the Gibeonites had made a peace agreement with Israel and that they lived nearby. ²Adoni-Zedek and his people were very afraid because of this. Gibeon was not a little town like Ai; it was a large city, as big as a city that had a king, and all its men were good fighters. ³So Adoni-Zedek king of Jerusalem sent a message to Hoham king of Hebron, Piram king of Jarmuth, Japhia king of Lachish and Debir king of Eglon. He begged them, ⁴"Come with me and help me attack Gibeon, which has made a peace agreement with Joshua and the Israelites."

⁵Then these five Amorite kings—the kings of Jerusalem, Hebron, Jarmuth, Lachish and Eglon—gathered their armies, went to Gibeon, surrounded it and attacked it.

⁶The Gibeonites sent this message to Joshua in his camp at Gilgal: "Don't let us, your servants, be destroyed. Come quickly and help us! Save us! All the Amorite kings from the mountains have joined their armies and are fighting against us."

⁷So Joshua marched out of Gilgal with his whole army, including his best fighting men. ⁸The LORD said to Joshua, "Don't be afraid of those armies, because I will hand them over to you. None of them will be able to stand against you."

⁹Joshua and his army marched all night from Gilgal for a surprise attack. ¹⁰The LORD confused those armies when Israel attacked, so Israel defeated them in a great victory at Gibeon. They chased them along the road going up to Beth Horon and killed men all the way to Azekah and Makkedah. ¹¹As they chased the enemy down the Beth Horon Pass to Azekah, the LORD threw large hailstones on them from the sky and killed them. More people were killed by the hailstones than by the Israelites' swords.

¹²On the day that the LORD gave up the Amorites to the Israelites, Joshua stood before all the people of Israel and said to the LORD:

"Sun, stand still over Gibeon.
   Moon, stand still over the Valley of
      Aijalon."
¹³So the sun stood still,
   and the moon stopped
      until the people defeated their enemies.
These words are written in the Book of Jashar. *d*

The sun stopped in the middle of the sky and waited to go down for a full day. ¹⁴That has never happened at any time before that day or since. That was the day the LORD listened to a human being. Truly the LORD was fighting for Israel!

¹⁵After this, Joshua and his army went back to the camp at Gilgal.

¹⁶During the fight the five kings ran away and hid in a cave near Makkedah, ¹⁷but someone found them hiding in the cave at Makkedah and told Joshua. ¹⁸So he said, "Cover the opening of the cave with large rocks. Put some men there to guard it, ¹⁹but don't stay there yourselves. Continue chasing the enemy and attacking them from behind. Don't let them get to their cities, because the LORD your God will hand them over to you."

²⁰So Joshua and the Israelites killed the enemy, but a few were able to get back to their fortified cities. ²¹After the fighting, Joshua's men came back safely to him at Makkedah. No one was brave enough to say a word against the Israelites.

²²Joshua said, "Move the rocks that are covering the opening of the cave and bring those five kings out to me." ²³So Joshua's men brought the five kings out of the cave—the kings of Jerusalem, Hebron, Jarmuth, Lachish and Eglon. ²⁴When they brought the five kings out to Joshua, he called for all his men. He said to the commanders of his army, "Come here! Put your feet on the necks of these kings." So they came close and put their feet on their necks.

²⁵Joshua said to his men, "Be strong and brave! Don't be afraid, because I will show you what the LORD will do to the enemies you will fight in the future." ²⁶Then Joshua killed the five kings and hung their bodies on five trees, where he left them until evening.

²⁷At sunset Joshua told his men to take the bodies down from the trees. Then they threw them into the same cave where they had been

hiding and covered the opening of the cave with large rocks, which are still there today.

²⁸That day Joshua defeated Makkedah. He killed the king and completely destroyed all the people in that city as an offering to the LORD; no one was left alive. He did the same thing to the king of Makkedah that he had done to the king of Jericho.

Defeating Southern Cities

²⁹Joshua and all the Israelites travelled from Makkedah to Libnah and attacked it. ³⁰The LORD handed over the city and its king. They killed every person in the city; no one was left alive. And they did the same thing to that king that they had done to the king of Jericho.

³¹Then Joshua and all the Israelites left Libnah and went to Lachish, which they surrounded and attacked. ³²The LORD handed over Lachish on the second day. The Israelites killed everyone in that city just as they had done to Libnah. ³³During this same time Horam king of Gezer came to help Lachish, but Joshua also defeated him and his army; no one was left alive.

³⁴Then Joshua and all the Israelites went from Lachish to Eglon. They surrounded Eglon, attacked it and ³⁵captured it the same day. They killed all its people and completely destroyed everything in it as an offering to the LORD, just as they had done to Lachish.

³⁶Then Joshua and the Israelites went from Eglon to Hebron and attacked it, ³⁷capturing it and all the little towns near it. The Israelites killed everyone in Hebron; no one was left alive there. Just as they had done to Eglon, they completely destroyed the city and all its people as an offering to the LORD.

³⁸Then Joshua and the Israelites went back to Debir and attacked it. ³⁹They captured that city, its king and all the little towns near it, completely destroying everyone in Debir as an offering to the LORD; no one was left alive there. Israel did to Debir and its king just as they had done to Libnah and its king, just as they had done to Hebron.

GOD'S POWER

The Ability and the Authority

The cars on the roads today are much more powerful than they used to be. Advances in aerodynamics and turbocharging mean that the speed limits which were set forty years ago don't seem to make much sense any more. But drivers still cannot drive down the motorway at 100 mph unless they have a flashing blue light and a shiny badge that says "Police". You see, there are two kinds of power: ability and authority.

It works the other way round too. That same policeman might be patrolling the community on a mountain bike when he comes across an armed robbery in progress. He has the power (authority) to arrest the criminal but doesn't have the power (ability) in his legs to chase the getaway car on his bike.

Read **Joshua 10:5–14** with this in mind. Can you see how both kinds of power are at work?

The people of Israel who were being led by Joshua understood God by giving him various names. One of their favourites was "El-Shaddai", which means "All-Powerful God". They had seen loads of amazing things taking place, things that made it clear to them that with God, nothing is impossible.

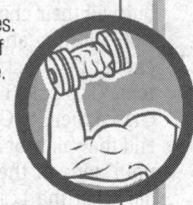

* Who can call themselves God's chosen people now? (You'll find clues in John 15:16, Colossians 3:12 and 1 Peter 2:9.)
* And now, in what ways might God's power – the ability and the authority – be made available?

Consider . . .

* doing some more study into the different names of God and what they reveal about his character.
* in what everyday situations you might need ability and authority.

For more, see . . .

* John 17:1–3 (p.1128)   * Acts 2:1–4 (p.1138)
* Colossians 1:15–17 (p.1290)

[40]So Joshua defeated all the kings of the cities of these areas: the mountains, southern Canaan, the western hills and the slopes. The LORD, the God of Israel, had told Joshua to completely destroy all the people as an offering to the LORD, so he left no one alive in those places. [41]Joshua captured all the cities from Kadesh Barnea to Gaza, and from Goshen to Gibeon. [42]He captured all these cities and their kings on one trip, because the LORD, the God of Israel, was fighting for Israel. [43]Then Joshua and all the Israelites returned to their camp at Gilgal.

Defeating Northern Kings

11 When Jabin king of Hazor heard about all that had happened, he sent messages to Jobab king of Madon, to the king of Shimron and to the king of Achshaph. [2]He sent messages to the kings in the northern mountains and also to the kings in the Jordan Valley south of Lake Galilee and in the western hills. He sent a message to the king of Naphoth Dor in the west [3]and to the kings of the Canaanites in the east and in the west. He sent messages to the Amorites, Hittites, Perizzites and Jebusites in the mountains. Jabin also sent one to the Hivites, who lived below Mount Hermon in the area of Mizpah. [4]So the armies of all these kings came together with their horses and chariots. There were as many soldiers as grains of sand on the seashore.

[5]All of these kings met together at the waters of Merom, joined their armies together into one camp, and made plans to fight against the Israelites.

[6]Then the LORD said to Joshua, "Don't be afraid of them, because at this time tomorrow I will give them to you. You will cripple their horses and burn all their chariots."

[7]So Joshua and his whole army surprised the enemy by attacking them at the waters of Merom. [8]The LORD handed them over to Israel. They chased them to Greater Sidon, Misrephoth Maim and the Valley of Mizpah in the east. Israel fought until none of the enemy was left alive. [9]Joshua did what the LORD said to do: he crippled their horses and burned their chariots.

[10]Then Joshua went back and captured the city of Hazor and killed its king. (Hazor had been the leader of all the kingdoms that fought against Israel.) [11]Israel killed everyone in Hazor, completely destroying them; no one was left alive. Then they burned Hazor itself.

[12]Joshua captured all of these cities, killed all of their kings, and completely destroyed everything in these cities. He did this just as Moses, the servant of the LORD, had commanded. [13]But the Israelites did not burn any cities that were built on their hills, except Hazor; only that city was burned by Joshua. [14]The people of Israel kept for themselves everything they found in the cities,

> **Sidelight**   Joshua's victory over Hazor was remarkable, considering that the city was huge for its day (Joshua 11:10). It had 40,000 residents, and its walls were about seventeen metres high – roughly four or five storeys. But despite the city's size and strength, it was never rebuilt after Israel destroyed it.

including all the animals. But they killed all the people there; they left no one alive. [15]Long ago the LORD had commanded his servant Moses to

> **Sidelight**   Joshua 11:13 tells us "the Israelites did not burn any cities that were built on their mounds". These mounds formed after war had destroyed a city – the people never cleared away the rubble, simply rebuilding on top of it. Soon the cities looked as if they were built on mounds. As many as 5,000 of these hills (which archeologists call "tells") exist today.

do this, and then Moses had commanded Joshua to do it. Joshua did everything the LORD had commanded Moses.

[16]So Joshua defeated all the people in the land. He had control of the mountains and the area of southern Canaan, all the areas of Goshen, the western hills and the Jordan Valley. He controlled the mountains of Israel and all the hills near them. [17]Joshua controlled all the land from Mount Halak near Edom to Baal Gad in the Valley of Lebanon, below Mount Hermon. Joshua also captured all the kings in the land and killed them. [18]He fought against them for many years. [19]The people of only one city in all the land had made a peace agreement with Israel—the Hivites living in Gibeon. All the other cities were defeated in war. [20]The LORD made those people stubborn so they would fight against Israel and he could completely destroy them without mercy. This is what the LORD had commanded Moses to do.

[21]Now Joshua fought the Anakites [d] who lived in the mountains of Hebron, Debir, Anab, Judah and Israel, and he completely destroyed them and their towns. [22]There were no Anakites left living in the land of the Israelites and only a few were left in Gaza, Gath and Ashdod. [23]Joshua took

control of all the land of Israel as the LORD had told Moses to do long ago. He gave the land to Israel, because he had promised it to them. Then Joshua divided the land among the tribes *d* of Israel, and there was peace in the land.

Kings Defeated by Israel

12 The Israelites took control of the land east of the Jordan River from the Arnon Ravine to Mount Hermon and all the land along the eastern side of the Jordan Valley. These lands belonged to the kings whom the Israelites defeated.

²Sihon king of the Amorites lived in the city of Heshbon and ruled the land from Aroer at the Arnon Ravine to the Jabbok River. His land started in the middle of the ravine, which was their border with the Ammonites. Sihon ruled over half the land of Gilead ³and over the eastern side of the Jordan Valley from Lake Galilee to the Dead Sea. *d* And he ruled from Beth Jeshimoth south to the slopes of Pisgah.

⁴Og king of Bashan was one of the last of the Rephaites. *d* He ruled the land in Ashtaroth and Edrei. ⁵He ruled over Mount Hermon, Salecah and all the area of Bashan up to where the people of Geshur and Maacah lived. Og also ruled half the land of Gilead up to the border of Sihon king of Heshbon.

⁶The LORD's servant Moses and the Israelites defeated all these kings, and Moses gave that land to the tribes *d* of Reuben and Gad and to East Manasseh as their own.

⁷Joshua and the Israelites also defeated kings in the land west of the Jordan River. He gave the people the land and divided it among the twelve tribes to be their own. It was between Baal Gad in the Valley of Lebanon and Mount Halak near Edom. ⁸This included the mountains, the western hills, the Jordan Valley, the slopes, the desert and southern Canaan. This was the land where the Hittites, Amorites, Canaanites, Perizzites, Hivites and Jebusites had lived. The Israelites defeated the king of each of the following cities: ⁹Jericho, Ai (near Bethel), ¹⁰Jerusalem, Hebron, ¹¹Jarmuth, Lachish, ¹²Eglon, Gezer, ¹³Debir, Geder, ¹⁴Hormah, Arad, ¹⁵Libnah, Adullam, ¹⁶Makkedah, Bethel, ¹⁷Tappuah, Hepher, ¹⁸Aphek, Lasharon, ¹⁹Madon, Hazor, ²⁰Shimron Meron, Achshaph, ²¹Taanach, Megiddo, ²²Kedesh, Jokneam in Carmel, ²³Dor (in Naphoth Dor), Goyim in Gilgal and ²⁴Tirzah.

The total number of kings was 31.

Land Still to be Taken

13 When Joshua was very old, the LORD said to him, "Joshua, you have grown old, but there is still much land for you to take. ²This is what is left: the regions of Geshur and of the Philistines; ³the area from the Shihor River at the border of Egypt to Ekron in the north, which belongs to the Canaanites; the five Philistine leaders at Gaza, Ashdod, Ashkelon, Gath and Ekron; the Avvites, ⁴who live south of the Canaanite land; ⁵the Gebalites, and the area of Lebanon east of Baal Gad below Mount Hermon to Lebo Hamath.

⁶"The Sidonians are living in the hill country from Lebanon to Misrephoth Maim, but I will force all of them out ahead of the Israelites. Be sure to remember this land when you divide the land among the Israelites, as I told you.

⁷"Now divide the land among the nine tribes *d* and West Manasseh."

Dividing the Land

⁸East Manasseh and the tribes of Reuben and Gad had received their land. The LORD's servant Moses had given them the land east of the Jordan River. ⁹Their land started at Aroer at the Arnon Ravine and continued to the town in the middle of the ravine, and it included the whole plain from Medeba to Dibon. ¹⁰All the towns ruled by Sihon king of the Amorites, who ruled in the city of Heshbon, were in that land. The land continued to the area where the Ammonites lived. ¹¹Gilead was also there, as well as the area where the people of Geshur and Maacah lived, and all of Mount Hermon and Bashan as far as Salecah. ¹²All the kingdom of Og king of Bashan was in the land. Og was one of the last of the Rephaites, and in the past he had ruled in Ashtaroth and Edrei. Moses had defeated them and had taken their land. ¹³Because the Israelites did not force out the people of Geshur and Maacah, they still live among the Israelites today.

¹⁴The tribe of Levi was the only one that did not get any land. Instead, they were given all the burned sacrifices made to the LORD, the God of Israel, as he had promised them.

¹⁵Moses had given each family group from the tribe of Reuben some land: ¹⁶theirs was the land from Aroer near the Arnon Ravine to the town of Medeba, including the whole plain and the town in the middle of the ravine; ¹⁷Heshbon and all the towns on the plain: Dibon, Bamoth Baal and Beth Baal Meon, ¹⁸Jahaz, Kedemoth, Mephaath, ¹⁹Kiriathaim, Sibmah, Zereth Shahar on the hill in the valley, ²⁰Beth Peor, the hills of Pisgah and Beth Jeshimoth. ²¹So that land included all the towns on the plain and all the area that Sihon king of the Amorites had ruled from the town of Heshbon. Moses had defeated him along with the leaders of the Midianites, including Evi, Rekem, Zur, Hur and Reba. All these leaders fought together with Sihon and lived in that country. ²²The Israelites

killed many people during the fighting, including Balaam of Beor, who tried to use magic to tell the future. 23The land given to Reuben stopped at the shore of the Jordan River. So the land given to the family groups of Reuben included all these towns and their villages that were listed.

24This is the land Moses gave to the tribe of Gad, to all its family groups: 25the land of Jazar and all the towns of Gilead; half the land of the Ammonites that went as far as Aroer near Rabbah; 26the area from Heshbon to Ramath Mizpah and Betonim; the area from Mahanaim to the land of Debir; 27in the valley, Beth Haram, Beth Nimrah, Succoth and Zaphon with the other land that Sihon king of Heshbon had ruled east of the Jordan River and continuing to the end of Lake Galilee. 28All this land went to the family groups of Gad, including all these towns and their villages.

29This is the land Moses had given to East Manasseh. Half of all the family groups in the tribe of Manasseh were given this land: 30the land started at Mahanaim and included all of Bashan and the land ruled by Og king of Bashan; all the towns of Jair in Bashan, 60 cities in all; 31half of Gilead, Ashtaroth and Edrei, the cities where Og king of Bashan had ruled. All this went to the family of Makir son of Manasseh, and half of all his sons were given this land.

32Moses had given this land to these tribes on the plains of Moab across the Jordan River east of Jericho. 33But Moses had given no land to the tribe of Levi because the LORD, the God of Israel, promised that he himself would be the gift for the Levites.

14 Eleazar the priest, Joshua son of Nun, and the leaders of all the tribes of Israel decided what land to give to the people in the land of Canaan. 2The LORD had commanded Moses long ago how he wanted the people to choose their land. The people of the nine-and-a-half tribes threw lots *d* to decide which land they would receive. 3Moses had already given the two-and-a-half tribes their land east of the Jordan River. But the tribe of Levi was not given any land like the others. 4The sons of Joseph had divided into two tribes—Manasseh and Ephraim. The tribe of Levi was not given any land. It was given only some towns in which to live and pastures for its animals. 5The LORD had told Moses how to give the land to the tribes of Israel, and the Israelites divided the land.

Caleb's Land

6One day some men from the tribe *d* of Judah went to Joshua at Gilgal. Among them was Caleb son of Jephunneh the Kenizzite. He said to Joshua, "You remember what the LORD said at Kadesh Barnea when he was speaking to the prophet Moses about you and me. 7Moses, the LORD's servant, sent me to look at the land where we were going. I was 40 years old then. When I came back, I told Moses what I thought about the land. 8The other men who went with me frightened the people, but I fully believed the LORD would allow us to take the land. 9So that day Moses promised me, 'The land where you went will become your land, and your children will own it for ever. I will give you that land because you fully believed in the LORD, my God.'

10"Now then, the LORD has kept his promise. He has kept me alive for 45 years from the time he said this to Moses during the time we all wandered in the desert. Now here I am, 85 years old. 11I am still as strong today as I was the day Moses sent me out, and I am just as ready to fight now as I was then. 12So give me the mountain country the LORD promised me that day long ago. Back then you heard that the Anakite *d* people lived there and the cities were large and well protected. But now with the LORD helping me, I will force them out, just as the LORD said."

13Joshua blessed Caleb son of Jephunneh and gave him the city of Hebron as his own. 14Hebron still belongs to the family of Caleb son of Jephunneh the Kenizzite because he had faith and obeyed the LORD, the God of Israel. 15(In the past it was called Kiriath Arba, named after Arba, the greatest man among the Anakites.)

After this there was peace in the land.

Land for Judah

15 The land that was given to the tribe *d* of Judah was divided among all the family groups. It went all the way to the Desert of Zin in the far south, at the border of Edom.

2The southern border of Judah's land started at the south end of the Dead Sea *d* 3and went south of Scorpion Pass to Zin. From there it passed to the south of Kadesh Barnea and continued past Hezron to Addar. From Addar it turned and went to Karka. 4It continued to Azmon, the brook of Egypt, and then to the Mediterranean Sea. This was the southern border.

5The eastern border was the shore of the Dead Sea, as far as the mouth of the Jordan River.

The northern border started at the shore of the sea at the mouth of the Jordan River. 6Then it went to Beth Hoglah and continued north of Beth Arabah to the stone of Bohan son of Reuben. 7Then the northern border went through the Valley of Achor to Debir where it turned towards the north and went to Gilgal. Gilgal is across from the road that goes through Adummim Pass, on the south side of the ravine. The border continued to the waters of En Shemesh and stopped at En Rogel. [8]Then it went through the Valley of Ben Hinnom, next to the southern side of the Jebusite city (which is called Jerusalem). There the border went to the top of the hill on the west side of Hinnom Valley, at the northern end of the Valley of Giants. [9]From there it went to the spring of the waters of Nephtoah and then it went to the cities near Mount Ephron. There it turned and went towards Baalah, which is called Kiriath Jearim. [10]At Baalah the border turned west and went towards Mount Seir. It continued along the north side of Mount Jearim (also called Kesalon) and came to Beth Shemesh. From there it went past Timnah [11]to the hill north of Ekron. Then it turned towards Shikkeron and went past Mount Baalah and continued on to Jabneel, ending at the sea.

[12]The Mediterranean Sea was the western border. Inside these borders lived the family groups of Judah.

[13]The Lord had commanded Joshua to give Caleb son of Jephunneh part of the land in Judah, so he gave Caleb the town of Kiriath Arba, also called Hebron. (Arba was the father of Anak. [d]) [14]Caleb forced out the three Anakite families living in Hebron: Sheshai, Ahiman and Talmai, the descendants [d] of Anak. [15]Then he left there and went to fight against the people living in Debir. (In the past Debir had been called Kiriath Sepher.) [16]Caleb said, "I will give Achsah, my daughter, as a wife to the man who attacks and captures the city of Kiriath Sepher." [17]Othniel son of Kenaz, Caleb's brother, captured the city, so Caleb gave his daughter Achsah to Othniel to be his wife. [18]When Achsah came to Othniel, she told him to ask her father for a field.

So Achsah went to her father. When she got down from her donkey, Caleb asked her, "What do you want?"

[19]Achsah answered, "Do me a special favour. Since you have given me land in southern Canaan, also give me springs of water." So Caleb gave her the upper and lower springs.

[20]The tribe of Judah got the land God had promised them. Each family group got part of the land.

[21]The tribe of Judah got all these towns in the southern part of Canaan near the border of Edom: Kabzeel, Eder, Jagur, [22]Kinah, Dimonah, Adadah, [23]Kedesh, Hazor, Ithnan, [24]Ziph, Telem, Bealoth, [25]Hazor Hadattah, Kerioth Hezron (also called Hazor), [26]Amam, Shema, Moladah, [27]Hazar Gaddah, Heshmon, Beth Pelet, [28]Hazar Shual, Beersheba, Biziothiah, [29]Baalah, Iim, Ezem, [30]Eltolad, Kesil, Hormah, [31]Ziklag, Madmannah, Sansannah, [32]Lebaoth, Shilhim, Ain and Rimmon. There were 29 towns and their villages.

[33]The tribe of Judah got these towns in the western hills: Eshtaol, Zorah, Ashnah, [34]Zanoah, En Gannim, Tappuah, Enam, [35]Jarmuth, Adullam, Socoh, Azekah, [36]Shaaraim, Adithaim and Gederah (also called Gederothaim). There were fourteen towns and their villages.

[37]Judah was also given these towns in the western hills: Zenan, Hadashah, Migdal Gad, [38]Dilean, Mizpah, Joktheel, [39]Lachish, Bozkath, Eglon, [40]Cabbon, Lahmas, Kitlish, [41]Gederoth, Beth Dagon, Naamah and Makkedah. There were sixteen towns and their villages.

[42]Judah was also given these towns in the western hills: Libnah, Ether, Ashan, [43]Iphtah, Ashnah, Nezib, [44]Keilah, Achzib and Mareshah. There were nine towns and their villages.

[45]The tribe of Judah was also given these towns: Ekron and all the small towns and villages near it; [46]the area west of Ekron and all the villages and small towns near Ashdod; [47]Ashdod and the small towns and villages around it; the villages and small towns around Gaza as far as the brook of Egypt and along the coast of the Mediterranean Sea.

[48]The tribe of Judah was also given these towns in the mountains: Shamir, Jattir, Socoh, [49]Dannah, Kiriath Sannah (also called Debir), [50]Anab, Eshtemoh, Anim, [51]Goshen, Holon and Giloh. There were eleven towns and their villages.

[52]They were also given these towns in the mountains: Arab, Dumah, Eshan, [53]Janim, Beth Tappuah, Aphekah, [54]Humtah, Kiriath Arba (also called Hebron) and Zior. There were nine towns and their villages.

[55]Judah was also given these towns in the mountains: Maon, Carmel, Ziph, Juttah, [56]Jezreel, Jokdeam, Zanoah, [57]Kain, Gibeah and Timnah. There were ten towns and their villages.

[58]They were also given these towns in the mountains: Halhul, Beth Zur, Gedor, [59]Maarath, Beth Anoth and Eltekon. There were six towns and their villages.

[60]The people of Judah were also given the two towns of Rabbah and Kiriath Baal (also called Kiriath Jearim) and their villages.

[61]Judah was given these towns in the desert: Beth Arabah, Middin, Secacah, [62]Nibshan, the City of Salt and En Gedi. There were six towns and all their villages.

[63]The army of Judah was not able to force out the Jebusites living in Jerusalem, so the Jebusites still live among the people of Judah to this day.

Land for Ephraim and Manasseh

16 This is the land the tribe *d* of Joseph received. It started at the Jordan River near Jericho and continued to the waters of Jericho, just east of the city. The border went up from Jericho to the mountains of Bethel. ²Then it continued from Bethel (also called Luz) to the Arkite border at Ataroth. ³From there it went west to the border of the Japhletites and continued to the area of the Lower Beth Horon. Then it went to Gezer and ended at the sea.

⁴So Manasseh and Ephraim, sons of Joseph, received their land.

⁵This is the land that was given to the family groups of Ephraim: their border started at Ataroth Addar in the east, went to Upper Beth Horon, ⁶and then to the sea. From Micmethath it turned eastwards towards Taanath Shiloh and continued eastwards to Janoah. ⁷Then it went down from Janoah to Ataroth and to Naarah. It continued until it touched Jericho and stopped at the Jordan River. ⁸The border went from Tappuah west to Kanah Ravine and ended at the sea. This is all the land that was given to each family group in the tribe of the Ephraimites. ⁹Many of the towns were actually within Manasseh's borders, but the people of Ephraim got those towns and their villages. ¹⁰The Ephraimites could not force the Canaanites to leave Gezer, so the Canaanites still live among the Ephraimites today, but they became slaves of the Ephraimites.

17 Then land was given to the tribe of Manasseh, Joseph's first son. Manasseh's first son was Makir, the father of Gilead. Makir was a great soldier, so the lands of Gilead and Bashan were given to his family. ²Land was also given to the other family groups of Manasseh—Abiezer, Helek, Asriel, Shechem, Hepher and Shemida. These were all the other sons of Manasseh son of Joseph.

³Zelophehad was the son of Hepher, who was the son of Gilead, who was the son of Makir, who was the son of Manasseh. Zelophehad had no sons, but he had five daughters, named Mahlah, Noah, Hoglah, Milcah and Tirzah. ⁴They went to Eleazar the priest and to Joshua son of Nun and all the leaders. They said, "The LORD told Moses to give us land like the men received." So Eleazar obeyed the LORD and gave the daughters some land, just like the brothers of their father. ⁵So the tribe of Manasseh had ten sections of land west of the Jordan River and two more sections, Gilead and Bashan, on the east side of the Jordan River. ⁶The daughters of Manasseh received land just as the sons did. Gilead was given to the rest of the families of Manasseh.

⁷The lands of Manasseh were in the area between Asher and Micmethath, near Shechem.

The border went south to the En Tappuah area, ⁸which belonged to Manasseh, except for the town of Tappuah. It was along the border of Manasseh's land and belonged to the sons of Ephraim. ⁹The border of Manasseh continued south to Kanah Ravine. The cities in this area of Manasseh belonged to Ephraim. Manasseh's border was on the north side of the ravine and went to the sea. ¹⁰The land to the south belonged to Ephraim, and the land to the north belonged to Manasseh. The Mediterranean Sea was the western border. The border touched Asher's land on the north and Issachar's land on the east.

¹¹In the areas of Issachar and Asher, the people of Manasseh owned these towns: Beth Shan and its small towns; Ibleam and its small towns; the people who lived in Dor and its small towns; the people in Naphoth Dor and its small towns; the people who lived in Taanach and its small towns; the people in Megiddo and its small towns. ¹²Manasseh was not able to defeat those cities, so the Canaanites continued to live there. ¹³When the Israelites grew strong, they forced the Canaanites to work for them, although they did not force them to leave the land.

Sidelight   When we think of nations, we think of united territory. But when the Israelites conquered Canaan, they really only conquered parts of it at first. So they divided the land among the twelve tribes before they really controlled it (Joshua 17:11–13). Later, individual tribes would conquer cities to unite their areas.

---

¹⁴The people from the tribes of Joseph said to Joshua, "You gave us only one area of land, but we are many people. Why did you give us only one part of all the land the LORD gave his people?"

¹⁵And Joshua answered them, "If you have too many people, go up to the forest and make a place for yourselves to live there in the land of the Perizzites and the Rephaites. *d* The mountain country of Ephraim is too small for you."

¹⁶The people of Joseph said, "It is true. The mountain country of Ephraim is not enough for us, but the land where the Canaanites live is dangerous. They are skilled fighters. They have powerful weapons in Beth Shan and all the small towns in that area, and they are also in the Valley of Jezreel."

¹⁷Then Joshua said to the people of Joseph—to Ephraim and Manasseh, "There are many of you, and you have great power. You should be given more than one share of land. ¹⁸You also will have the mountain country. It is a forest, but you can

cut down the trees and make it a good place to live. You will own all of it because you will force the Canaanites to leave the land even though they have powerful weapons and are strong."

The Rest of the Land Divided

18 All of the Israelites gathered together at Shiloh where they set up the Meeting Tent. *d* The land was now under their control. ²But there were still seven tribes *d* of Israel that had not yet received their land.

³So Joshua said to the Israelites: "Why do you wait so long to take your land? The LORD, the God of your ancestors, has given this land to you. ⁴Choose three men from each tribe, and I will send them out to study the land. They will describe in writing the land their tribe wants as its share, and then they will come back to me. ⁵They will divide the land into seven parts. The people of Judah will keep their land in the south, and the people of Joseph will keep their land in the north. ⁶You should describe the seven parts of land in writing and bring what you have written to me. Then I will throw lots *d* in the presence of the LORD our God. ⁷But the Levites do not get any part of these lands, because they are priests, and their work is to serve the LORD. Gad, Reuben and East Manasseh have received the land promised to them, which is east of the Jordan River. Moses, the servant of the LORD, gave it to them."

⁸So the men who were chosen to map the land started out. Joshua told them, "Go and study the land and describe it in writing. Then come back to me, and I will throw lots in the presence of the LORD here in Shiloh." ⁹So the men left and went into the land. They described in a scroll each town in the seven parts of the land. Then they came back to Joshua, who was still at the camp at Shiloh. ¹⁰There Joshua threw lots in the presence of the LORD to choose the lands that should be given to each tribe.

Land for Benjamin

¹¹The first part of the land was given to the tribe *d* of Benjamin. Each family group received some land between the land of Judah and the land of Joseph. This is the land chosen for Benjamin: ¹²the northern border started at the Jordan River and went along the northern edge of Jericho, and then it went west into the mountains. That boundary continued until it was just east of Beth Aven. ¹³From there it went south to Luz (also called Bethel) and then down to Ataroth Addar, which is on the hill south of Lower Beth Horon.

¹⁴At the hill to the south of Beth Horon, the border turned and went south near the western side of the hill. It went to Kiriath Baal (also called

Kiriath Jearim), a town where people of Judah lived. This was the western border.

¹⁵The southern border started near Kiriath Jearim and went west to the waters of Nephtoah. ¹⁶Then it went down to the bottom of the hill, which was near the Valley of Ben Hinnom, on the north side of the Valley of Rephaim. The border continued down the Hinnom Valley just south of the Jebusite city to En Rogel. ¹⁷There it turned north and went to En Shemesh. It continued to Geliloth near the Adummim Pass. Then it went down to the great Stone of Bohan son of Reuben. ¹⁸The border continued to the northern part of Beth Arabah and went down into the Jordan Valley. ¹⁹From there it went to the northern part of Beth Hoglah and ended at the north shore of the Dead Sea, *d* where the Jordan River flows into the sea. This was the southern border.

²⁰The Jordan River was the border on the eastern side. So this was the land given to the family groups of Benjamin with the borders on all sides.

²¹The family groups of Benjamin received these cities: Jericho, Beth Hoglah, Emek Keziz, ²²Beth Arabah, Zemaraim, Bethel, ²³Avvim, Parah, Ophrah, ²⁴Kephar Ammoni, Ophni and Geba. There were twelve towns and all their villages.

²⁵The tribe of Benjamin also received Gibeon, Ramah, Beeroth, ²⁶Mizpah, Kephirah, Mozah, ²⁷Rekem, Irpeel, Taralah, ²⁸Zelah, Haeleph, the Jebusite city (Jerusalem), Gibeah and Kiriath. There were fourteen towns and their villages. All these areas are the lands the family groups of Benjamin were given.

Land for Simeon

19 The second part of the land was given to the tribe *d* of Simeon. Each family group received some of the land inside the area of Judah. ²They received Beersheba (also called Sheba), Moladah, ³Hazar Shual, Balah, Ezem, ⁴Eltolad, Bethul, Hormah, ⁵Ziklag, Beth Marcaboth, Hazar Susah, ⁶Beth Lebaoth and Sharuhen. There were thirteen towns and their villages.

⁷They received the towns of Ain, Rimmon, Ether and Ashan, four towns and their villages. ⁸They also received all the very small areas with people living in them as far as Baalath Beer (this is the same as Ramah in southern Canaan). So these were the lands given to the family groups in the tribe of Simeon. ⁹The land of the Simeonites was taken from part of the land of Judah. Since Judah had much more land than they needed, the Simeonites received part of their land.

Land for Zebulun

¹⁰The third part of the land was given to the tribe *d* of Zebulun. Each family group of Zebulun received some of the land. The border of Zebulun

went as far as Sarid. [11]Then it went west to Mara- lah and came near Dabbesheth and then near Jokneam. [12]Then it turned to the east. It went from Sarid to the area of Kisloth Tabor and on to Daberath and to Japhia. [13]It continued eastwards to Gath Hepher and Eth Kazin, ending at Rim- mon. There the border turned and went towards Neah. [14]At Neah it turned again and went to the north to Hannathon and continued to the Valley of Iphtah El. [15]Inside this border were the cities of Kattath, Nahalal, Shimron, Idalah and Bethle- hem. There were twelve towns and their villages.

[16]So these are the towns and the villages that were given to the family groups of Zebulun.

Land for Issachar

[17]The fourth part of the land was given to the tribe [d] of Issachar. Each family group of Issachar received some of the land. [18]Their land included Jezreel, Kesulloth, Shunem, [19]Hapharaim, Shion, Anaharath, [20]Rabbith, Kishion, Ebez, [21]Remeth, En Gannim, En Haddah and Beth Pazzez.

[22]The border of their land touched the area called Tabor, Shahazumah and Beth Shemesh and stopped at the Jordan River. There were six- teen towns and their villages.

[23]These cities and towns were part of the land that was given to the family groups of Issachar.

Land for Asher

[24]The fifth part of the land was given to the tribe [d] of Asher. Each family group of Asher re- ceived some of the land. [25]Their land included Helkath, Hali, Beten, Achshaph, [26]Allammelech, Amad and Mishal.

The western border touched Mount Carmel and Shihor Libnath. [27]Then it turned east and went to Beth Dagon, touching Zebulun and the Valley of Iphtah El. Then it went north of Beth Emek and Neiel and passed north to Cabul. [28]From there it went to Abdon, Rehob, Hammon and Kanah and continued to Greater Sidon. [29]Then the border went back south towards Ra- mah and continued to the fortified city of Tyre. There it turned and went towards Hosah, ending at the sea. This was in the area of Achzib, [30]Um- mah, Aphek and Rehob. There were 22 towns and their villages.

[31]These cities and their villages were part of the land that was given to the family groups of Asher.

Land for Naphtali

[32]The sixth part of the land was given to the tribe [d] of Naphtali. Each family group of Naphtali received some of the land. [33]The border of their land started at the large tree in Zaanannim, which is near Heleph. Then it went through Ad- ami Nekeb and Jabneel, as far as Lakkum, and ended at the Jordan River. [34]Then it went to the west through Aznoth Tabor and stopped at Huk- kok. It went to the area of Zebulun on the south, Asher on the west, and Judah, at the Jordan River, on the east. [35]The fortified cities inside these borders were called Ziddim, Zer, Hammath, Rakkath, Kinnereth, [36]Adamah, Ramah, Hazor, [37]Kedesh, Edrei, En Hazor, [38]Iron, Migdal El, Horem, Beth Anath and Beth Shemesh. There were nineteen towns and all their villages.

[39]The towns and the villages around them were in the land that was given to the family groups of Naphtali.

Land for Dan

[40]The seventh part of the land was given to the tribe [d] of Dan. Each family group of Dan received some of the land. [41]Their land included Zorah, Eshtaol, Ir Shemesh, [42]Shaalabbin, Aijalon, Ithlah, [43]Elon, Timnah, Ekron, [44]Eltekeh, Gibbethon, Baalath, [45]Jehud, Bene Berak, Gath Rimmon, [46]Me Jarkon, Rakkon and the area near Joppa.

[47](But the Danites had trouble taking their land. They went and fought against Leshem, de- feated it, and killed the people who lived there. So the Danites moved into the town of Leshem and changed its name to Dan, because he was the father of their tribe.) [48]All of these towns and villages were given to the family groups of Dan.

Land for Joshua

[49]After the leaders finished dividing the land and giving it to the different tribes, [d] the Israelites gave Joshua son of Nun his land also. [50]They gave Joshua the town he asked for, Timnath Serah in the mountains of Ephraim, just as the LORD com- manded. He built up the town and lived there.

[51]So these lands were given to the different tribes of Israel. Eleazar the priest, Joshua son of Nun and the leaders of each tribe divided up the land by lots at Shiloh. They met in the presence of the LORD at the entrance to the Meeting Tent. [d] Now they had finished dividing the land.

Cities of Safety

20 Then the LORD said to Joshua: [2]"Tell the Israelites to choose the special cities of safety, [n] as I had Moses command you to do. [3]If a person kills someone accidentally and without meaning to kill him, that person may go to a city of safety [n] to hide. There the killer will be safe from the relative who has the duty of punishing a murderer.

---

cities of safety   A person who had accidentally killed someone could go to one of the six cities of safety to receive protection and a fair trial.

4"When the killer runs to one of those cities, he must stop at the entrance gate, stand there, and tell the elders of the people what happened. Then that person will be allowed to enter the city and will be given a place to live among them. 5But if the one who is chasing him follows him to that city, the leaders of the city must not hand over the killer. It was an accident. He did not hate him beforehand or kill him on purpose. 6The killer must stay in the city until a court comes to a decision and until the high priest dies. Then he may go back home to the town from which he ran away."

7So the Israelites chose these cities to be cities of safety: Kedesh in Galilee in the mountains of Naphtali; Shechem in the mountains of Ephraim; Kiriath Arba (also called Hebron) in the mountains of Judah; 8Bezer on the east side of the Jordan River near Jericho in the desert in the land of Reuben; Ramoth in Gilead in the land of Gad; and Golan in Bashan in the land of Manasseh. 9Any Israelite or anyone living among them who killed someone accidentally was to be allowed to run to one of these cities of safety. There he would not be killed, before he was judged, by the relative who had the duty of punishing a murderer.

Towns for the Levites

21 The heads of the Levite families went to talk to Eleazar the priest, to Joshua son of Nun and to the heads of the families of all the tribes d of Israel. 2At Shiloh in the land of Canaan, the heads of the Levite families said to them, "The LORD commanded Moses that you give us towns where we may live and pastures for our animals." 3So the Israelites obeyed this command of the LORD and gave the Levite people these towns and pastures for their own land: 4the Kohath family groups were part of the tribe of Levi. Some of the Levites in the Kohath family groups were from the family of Aaron the priest. To these Levites were given thirteen towns in the areas of Judah, Simeon and Benjamin. 5The other family groups of Kohath were given ten towns in the areas of Ephraim, Dan and West Manasseh.

6The people from the Gershon family groups were given thirteen towns in the land of Issachar, Asher, Naphtali and East Manasseh in Bashan.

7The family groups of Merari were given twelve towns in the areas of Reuben, Gad and Zebulun.

8So the Israelites gave the Levites these towns and the pastures around them, just as the LORD had commanded Moses.

9These are the names of the towns that came from the lands of Judah and Simeon. 10The first choice of towns was given to the Kohath family groups of the Levites. 11They gave them Kiriath Arba, also called Hebron, and all its pastures in the mountains of Judah. (Arba was the father of Anak. d) 12But the fields and the villages around Kiriath Arba had been given to Caleb son of Jephunneh.

13So they gave the city of Hebron to the descendants d of Aaron (Hebron was a city of safety n). They also gave them the towns of Libnah, 14Jattir, Eshtemoa, 15Holon, Debir, 16Ain, Juttah and Beth Shemesh, and all the pastures around them. Nine towns were given from these two tribes.

17They also gave the people of Aaron these cities that belonged to the tribe of Benjamin: Gibeon, Geba, 18Anathoth and Almon. They gave them these four towns and the pastures around them.

19So these thirteen towns with their pastures were given to the priests, who were from the family of Aaron.

20The other Kohathite family groups of the Levites were given these towns from the tribe of Ephraim: 21Shechem in the mountains of Ephraim (which was a city of safety), Gezer, 22Kibzaim and Beth Horon. There were four towns and their pastures.

23The tribe of Dan gave them Eltekeh, Gibbethon, 24Aijalon and Gath Rimmon. There were four towns and their pastures.

25West Manasseh gave them Taanach and Gath Rimmon and the pastures around these two towns.

26So these ten towns and the pastures around them were given to the rest of the Kohathite family groups.

27The Gershonite family groups of the Levite tribe were given these towns: East Manasseh gave them Golan in Bashan, which was a city of safety, and Be Eshtarah, and the pastures around these two towns.

28The tribe of Issachar gave them Kishion, Daberath, 29Jarmuth and En Gannim, and the pastures around these four towns.

30The tribe of Asher gave them Mishal, Abdon, 31Helkath and Rehob, and the pastures around these four towns.

32The tribe of Naphtali gave them Kedesh in Galilee (a city of safety n), Hammoth Dor and Kartan, and the pastures around these three towns.

33So the Gershonite family groups received thirteen towns and the pastures around them.

34The Merarite family groups (the rest of the Levites) were given these towns: the tribe of

---

cities of safety   A person who had accidentally killed someone could go to one of the six cities of safety to receive protection and a fair trial.

Zebulun gave them Jokneam, Kartah, [35]Dimnah and Nahalal, and the pastures around these four towns.

[36]The tribe of Reuben gave them Bezer, Jahaz, [37]Kedemoth and Mephaath, along with the pastures around these four towns.

[38]The tribe of Gad gave them Ramoth in Gilead (a city of safety [n]), Mahanaim, [39]Heshbon and Jazer, and the pastures around these four towns.

[40]So the total number of towns given to the Merarite family groups was twelve.

[41]A total of 48 towns with their pastures in the land of Israel were given to the Levites. [42]Each town had pastures around it.

[43]So the LORD gave the people all the land he had promised their ancestors. The people took the land and lived there. [44]The LORD gave them peace on all sides, as he had promised their ancestors. None of their enemies defeated them; the LORD handed all their enemies over to them. [45]He kept every promise he had made to the Israelites; each one came true.

Three Tribes Go Home

22 Then Joshua called a meeting of all the people from the tribes [d] of Reuben, Gad and East Manasseh. [2]He said to them, "You have done everything Moses, the LORD's servant, told you to do. You have also obeyed all my commands. [3]For a long time you have supported the other Israelites. You have been careful to obey the commands the LORD your God gave you. [4]The LORD your God promised to give the Israelites peace, and he has kept his promise. Now you may go back to your homes, to the land that Moses, the LORD's servant, gave you, on the east side of the Jordan River. [5]But be careful to obey the teachings and laws Moses, the LORD's servant, gave you: to love the LORD your God and obey his commands, to continue to follow him and serve him the very best you can."

[6]Then Joshua said goodbye to them, and they left and went away to their homes. [7]Moses had given the land of Bashan to East Manasseh. Joshua gave land on the west side of the Jordan River to West Manasseh. And he sent them to their homes and he blessed them. [8]He said, "Go back to your homes and your riches. You have many animals, silver, gold, bronze and iron, and many beautiful clothes. Also, you have taken many things from your enemies that you should divide among yourselves."

[9]So the people from the tribes of Reuben, Gad and East Manasseh left the other Israelites at Shiloh in Canaan and went back to Gilead. It was their own land, given to them by Moses as the LORD had commanded.

[10]The people of Reuben, Gad and East Manasseh went to Geliloth, near the Jordan River in the land of Canaan. There they built a beautiful altar. [11]The other Israelites still at Shiloh heard about the altar these three tribes built at the border of Canaan at Geliloth, near the Jordan River on Israel's side. [12]All the Israelites became very angry at these three tribes, so they met together and decided to fight them.

[13]The Israelites sent Phinehas son of Eleazar the priest to Gilead to talk to the people of Reuben, Gad and East Manasseh. [14]They also sent one leader from each of the ten tribes at Shiloh. Each of them was a leader of his family group of Israelites.

[15]These leaders went to Gilead to talk to the people of Reuben, Gad and East Manasseh. They said: [16]"All the Israelites ask you: "Why did you turn against the God of Israel by building an altar for yourselves? You know that this is against God's law. [17]Remember what happened at Peor? We still suffer today because of that sin, for which God made many Israelites very sick. [18]And now are you turning against the LORD and refusing to follow him?

" 'If you don't stop what you're doing today, the LORD will be angry with everyone in Israel tomorrow. [19]If your land is unclean, [d] come over into our land where the LORD's Tent is. Share it with us. But don't turn against the LORD and us by building another altar for the LORD our God. [20]Remember how Achan son of Zerah refused to obey the command about what must be completely destroyed. That one man broke God's law, but all the Israelites were punished. Achan died because of his sin, but others also died.' "

[21]The people from Reuben, Gad and East Manasseh answered, [22]"The LORD is God of gods! The LORD is God of gods! God knows, and we want you to know also. If we have done something wrong, you may kill us. [23]If we broke God's law, we ask the LORD himself to punish us. We did not build this altar to offer burnt offerings or grain and fellowship offerings.

[24]"We did not build it for that reason. We feared that some day your people would not accept us as part of your nation. Then they might say, 'You cannot worship the LORD, the God of Israel. [25]The LORD made the Jordan River a border between us and you people of Reuben and Gad. You cannot worship the LORD.' So we feared that your children might make our children stop worshipping the LORD.

---

cities of safety   A person who had accidentally killed someone could go to one of the six cities of safety to receive protection and a fair trial.

26"That is why we decided to build this altar. But it is not for burnt offerings and sacrifices. 27This altar is proof to you and us and to all our children who will come after us that we worship the LORD with our whole burnt offerings, grain and fellowship offerings. This was so your children would not say to our children, "You are not the LORD's.'

28"In the future if your children say that, our children can say, 'See the altar made by our ancestors. It is exactly like the LORD's altar, but we do not use it for sacrifices. It shows that we are part of Israel.'

29"Truly, we don't want to be against the LORD or to stop following him by building an altar for burnt offerings, grain offerings or sacrifices. We know the only true altar to the LORD our God is in front of the Holy Tent." *d*

30When Phinehas the priest and the ten leaders heard the people of Reuben, Gad and East Manasseh, they were pleased. 31So Phinehas, son of Eleazar the priest, said, "Now we know the LORD is with us and that you didn't turn against him. Now the Israelites will not be punished by the LORD."

Sidelight

Today we may worship God wherever we want. But that hasn't always been the case. In Joshua's time, Israel only presented its sacrifices at the Tabernacle. When three tribes built an altar by the Jordan River, the other tribes thought they might make sacrifices to a pagan God. They almost went to war, but talked through their differences instead (Joshua 22:9–34).

32Then Phinehas and the leaders left the people of Reuben and Gad in Gilead and went back to Canaan where they told the Israelites what had happened. 33They were pleased and thanked God. So they decided not to fight the people of Reuben and Gad and destroy those lands.

34And the people of Reuben and Gad named the altar Proof that We Believe the LORD Is God.

The Last Words of Joshua

23 The LORD gave Israel peace from their enemies around them. Many years passed, and Joshua grew very old. 2He called a meeting of all the elders, heads of families, judges and officers of Israel. He said, "I am now very old. 3You have seen what the LORD has done to our enemies to help us. The LORD your God fought for you. 4Remember that your people have been given

their land between the Jordan River and the Mediterranean Sea in the west, the land I promised to give you. 5The LORD your God will force out the people living there. The LORD will push them out ahead of you. And you will own the land, as he has promised you.

6"Be strong. You must be careful to obey everything commanded in the Book of the Teachings of Moses. Do exactly as it says. 7Don't become friends with the people living among us who are not Israelites. Don't say the names of their gods or make anyone swear by them. Don't serve or worship them. 8You must continue to follow the LORD your God, as you have done in the past.

9"The LORD has forced many great and powerful nations to leave ahead of you. No nation has been able to defeat you. 10With his help, one Israelite could defeat 1,000, because the LORD your God fights for you, as he promised to do. 11So you must be careful to love the LORD your God.

12"If you turn away from the way of the LORD and become friends with these people who are not part of Israel and marry them, 13the LORD your God will not help you defeat your enemies. They will be like traps for you, like whips on your back and thorns in your eyes, and none of you will be left in this good land the LORD your God has given you.

14"It's almost time for me to die. You know and fully believe that the LORD has done great things for you. You know that he has not failed to keep any of his promises. 15Every good promise that the LORD your God made has come true, and in the same way, his other promises will come true. He promised that evil will come to you and that he will destroy you from this good land that he gave you. 16This will happen if you don't keep your agreement with the LORD your God. If you go and serve other gods and worship them, the LORD will become very angry with you. Then none of you will be left in this good land he has given you."

24 Joshua gathered all the tribes *d* of Israel together at Shechem. He called the elders, heads of families, judges and officers of Israel to stand before God.

2Then Joshua said to all the people, "Here's what the LORD, the God of Israel, says to you: "A long time ago your ancestors lived on the other side of the Euphrates River. Terah, the father of Abraham and Nahor, worshipped other gods. 3But I, the LORD, took your ancestor Abraham from the other side of the river and led him through the land of Canaan. And I gave him many children, including his son Isaac. 4I gave Isaac two sons named Jacob and Esau. I gave the land around the mountains of Edom to Esau, but Jacob and his sons went down to Egypt. ⁵Then I sent Moses and Aaron to Egypt, where I brought many disasters on the Egyptians. Afterwards I brought you out. ⁶When I brought your ancestors out of Egypt, they came to the Red Sea, *d* and the Egyptians chased them with chariots and men on horses. ⁷So the people called out to the LORD. And I brought darkness between you and the Egyptians and created the sea to cover them. You yourselves saw what I did to the army of Egypt. After that, you lived in the desert for a long time.

⁸" 'Then I brought you to the land of the Amorites, east of the Jordan River. They fought against you, but I handed them over to you. I destroyed them before you, and you took control of that land. ⁹But the king of Moab, Balak son of Zippor, prepared to fight against the Israelites. The king sent for Balaam son of Beor to curse you, ¹⁰but I refused to listen to Balaam. So he asked for good things to happen to you! I saved you and brought you out of his power.

¹¹" 'Then you crossed the Jordan River and came to Jericho, where the people of Jericho fought against you. Also, the Amorites, Perizzites, Canaanites, Hittites, Girgashites, Hivites and Jebusites fought against you. But I handed them over to you. ¹²I sent terror ahead of you to force out two Amorite kings. You took the land without using swords and bows. ¹³I gave you that land where you did not have to work. I gave you cities that you did not have to build. And now you live in that land and in those cities, and you eat from vineyards and olive trees that you did not plant.' "

¹⁴Then Joshua said to the people, "Now respect the LORD and serve him fully and sincerely. Throw away the gods that your ancestors worshipped on the other side of the Euphrates River and in Egypt. Serve the LORD. ¹⁵But if you don't want to serve the LORD, you must choose for yourselves today whom you will serve. You may serve the gods that your ancestors worshipped when they lived on the other side of the Euphrates River, or you may serve the gods of the Amorites who lived in this land. As for me and my family, we will serve the LORD."

¹⁶Then the people answered, "We will never stop following the LORD to serve other gods! ¹⁷It was the LORD our God who brought our ancestors out of Egypt. We were slaves in that land, but the LORD did great things for us there. He brought us out and protected us while we travelled through other lands. ¹⁸Then he forced out all the people living in these lands, even the Amorites. So we will serve the LORD, because he is our God."

¹⁹Then Joshua said, "You are not able to serve the LORD, because he is a holy God and a jealous God. If you turn against him and sin, he will not forgive you. ²⁰If you leave the LORD and serve other gods, he will send you great trouble. The LORD may have been good to you, but if you turn against him, he will destroy you."

²¹But the people said to Joshua, "No! We will serve the LORD."

²²Then Joshua said, "You are your own witnesses that you have chosen to serve the LORD."

The people said, "Yes, we are."

²³Then Joshua said, "Now throw away the gods that you have. Love the LORD, the God of Israel, with all your heart."

²⁴Then the people said to Joshua, "We will serve the LORD our God, and we will obey him."

²⁵On that day at Shechem, Joshua made an agreement for the people. He made rules and laws for them to follow. ²⁶Joshua wrote these things in the Book of the Teachings of God. Then he took a large stone and set it up under the oak tree near the LORD's Holy Tent.*d*

²⁷Joshua said to all the people, "See this stone! It will remind you of what we did today. It was here the LORD spoke to us today. It will remind you of what happened so you will not turn against your God."

Joshua Dies

²⁸Then Joshua sent the people back to their land.

²⁹After that, Joshua son of Nun died at the age of 110. ³⁰They buried him in his own land at Timnath Serah, in the mountains of Ephraim, north of Mount Gaash.

> ### Sidelight
> When Joseph's bones were buried (Joshua 24:32), the people didn't dig a grave as we do today. Rather, the bones were probably placed in a family cave or a tomb cut from rock, large enough for several family members.

³¹The Israelites served the LORD during the lifetime of Joshua and during the lifetimes of the elders who lived after Joshua who had seen what the LORD had done for Israel.

Joseph Comes Home

³²When the Israelites left Egypt, they carried the bones of Joseph with them. They buried them at Shechem, in the land Jacob had bought for 100

pieces of silver from the sons of Hamor (Hamor was the father of Shechem). This land now belonged to Joseph's children.

33And Eleazar son of Aaron died and was buried at Gibeah in the mountains of Ephraim, which had been given to Eleazar's son Phinehas.

Judges

Why Read This Book:

* See how God does not want his people to follow the crowd (Judges 1—2).
* Discover how sin can capture people, but how God can set them free if they ask for forgiveness (Judges 3—16).
* Understand how people can become corrupt when they don't follow God (Judges 17—21).

Behind the Scenes:

Working in a fast food restaurant can be a disaster if the work isn't organised. Fries aren't ready when the burgers are done. The whipped ice cream runs empty. Customers receive the wrong orders. During the dinner-hour rush, lettuce can fly, mayonnaise can spill, and tempers flare as each person tries frantically to catch up.

The chaos of an unorganised fast food restaurant is similar to the chaos in Israel during the book of Judges. The last verse of the book summarises what it was like: "In those days Israel did not have a king. Everyone did what seemed right" (Judges 21:25).

Under the leadership of Joshua (see the book of Joshua, p.201), the Israelites had conquered major Canaanite cities and divided the land among the twelve Israelite tribes. But many Canaanites and other people still remained. They didn't believe in God, but worshipped idols and pagan gods.

These other people threatened the Israelites in two ways. First, they wanted the land back that the Israelites had taken away. So the Israelites had constantly to defend themselves. ▷

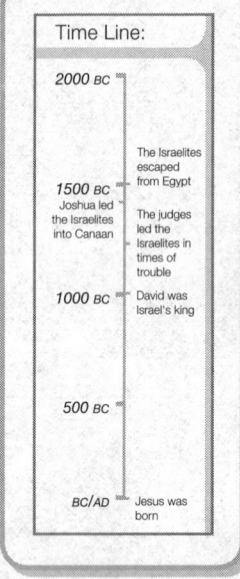

Time Line:

2000 BC	
	The Israelites escaped from Egypt
1500 BC	
Joshua led the Israelites into Canaan	The judges led the Israelites in times of trouble
1000 BC	David was Israel's king
500 BC	
BC/AD	Jesus was born

Where?

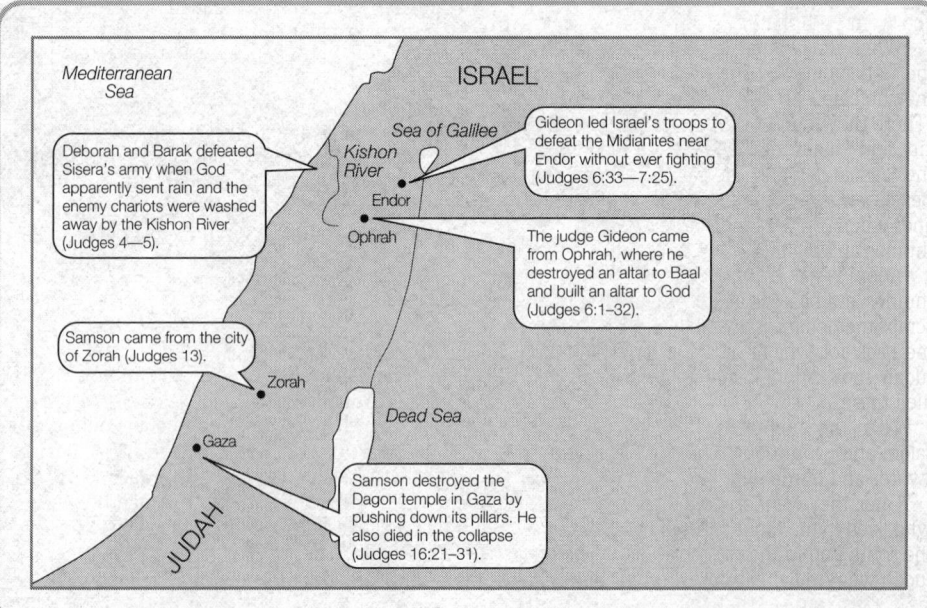

Mediterranean Sea

ISRAEL

Sea of Galilee

Kishon River

Gideon led Israel's troops to defeat the Midianites near Endor without ever fighting (Judges 6:33—7:25).

Deborah and Barak defeated Sisera's army when God apparently sent rain and the enemy chariots were washed away by the Kishon River (Judges 4—5).

Endor

Ophrah

The judge Gideon came from Ophrah, where he destroyed an altar to Baal and built an altar to God (Judges 6:1–32).

Samson came from the city of Zorah (Judges 13).

Zorah

Dead Sea

Gaza

Samson destroyed the Dagon temple in Gaza by pushing down its pillars. He also died in the collapse (Judges 16:21–31).

JUDAH

Behind the   Second, the Israelites married Canaanites, which God had said not to do;
Scenes (cont.):   then they accepted the Canaanites' religious practices, forgetting God.
                    Like workers in fast food restaurants, the Israelites needed leaders to
organise them and keep them on track. So in times of crisis, God chose
different judges to bring the twelve tribes together to fight their enemies.
These judges – such as Deborah, Samson and Gideon – became national
heroes for the Israelites.
                    Judges illustrates a common theme in the Old Testament. When a judge
or leader was faithful to God, the people remained loyal to God and
prospered. But when the judge died, the people sinned and were conquered.
Then in their suffering, they confessed their sin, and God called a new judge
to deliver them.
                    Judges reminds us of the importance of always following God – and the
dangers of ignoring God. At the same time, it shows that God is always willing
to forgive us when we come back to him.

Judah Fights the Canaanites

1 After Joshua died, the Israelites asked the
LORD, "Who will be first to go and fight for
us against the Canaanites?"

[2]The LORD said to them, "The tribe *d* of Judah
will go. I have handed the land over to them."

[3]The men of Judah said to the men of Simeon,
their relatives, "Come and help us fight the Canaanites for our land. If you do, we will go and
help you fight for your land." So the men of Simeon went with them.

[4]When Judah attacked, the LORD handed over
the Canaanites and the Perizzites to them, and
they defeated 10,000 men at the city of Bezek.
[5]There they found Adoni-Bezek, the ruler of the
city, and fought him. The men of Judah defeated
the Canaanites and the Perizzites, [6]but Adoni-
Bezek ran away. The men of Judah chased him,
and when they caught him, they cut off his
thumbs and big toes.

[7]Adoni-Bezek said, "Seventy kings whose
thumbs and big toes had been cut off used to eat
scraps that fell from my table. Now God has paid
me back for what I did to them." The men of
Judah took Adoni-Bezek to Jerusalem, and he
died there.

[8]Then the men of Judah fought against Jerusalem and captured it. They attacked with their
swords and burned the city.

[9]Later, they went down to fight the Canaanites
who lived in the mountains, in the dry country to
the south and in the western hills. [10]The men of
Judah went to fight against the Canaanites in the
city of Hebron (which used to be called Kiriath
Arba). And they defeated Sheshai, Ahiman and
Talmai.

Caleb and His Daughter

[11]Then they left there and went to fight against
the people living in Debir. (In the past Debir had
been called Kiriath Sepher.) [12]Before attacking
the city, Caleb said, "I will give Achsah, my
daughter, as a wife to the man who attacks and
captures the city of Kiriath Sepher." [13]Othniel son
of Kenaz, Caleb's younger brother, captured the
city, so Caleb gave his daughter Achsah to Othniel to be his wife. [14]When Achsah came to Othniel, she told him to ask her father for a field.
When she got down from her donkey, Caleb
asked her, "What do you want?"

[15]Achsah answered him, "Do me a special favour. Since you have given me land in southern
Canaan, also give me springs of water." So Caleb
gave her the upper and lower springs.

Fights with the Canaanites

[16]The Kenite people, who were from the family
of Moses' father-in-law, left Jericho, the city of
palm trees. They went with the men of Judah to
the Desert of Judah to live with them there in
southern Judah near the city of Arad.

[17]The men of Judah and the men of Simeon,
their relatives, defeated the Canaanites who lived
in Zephath. They completely destroyed the city,
so they called it Hormah. *n* [18]The men of Judah

Hormah   Hormah sounds like the Hebrew word meaning "to destroy completely".

captured Gaza, Ashkelon, Ekron and the lands around them.

[19]The LORD was with the men of Judah. They took the land in the mountains, but they could not force out the people living on the plain, because they had iron chariots. [20]As Moses had promised, Hebron was given to Caleb, and Caleb forced out the three sons of Anak. [d] [21]But the people of Benjamin could not make the Jebusite people leave Jerusalem. Since that time the Jebusites have lived with the people of Benjamin in Jerusalem.

[22]The men of Joseph went to fight against the city of Bethel, and the LORD was with them. [23]They sent some spies to Bethel (which used to be called Luz). [24]The spies saw a man coming out of the city and said to him, "Show us a way into the city, and we will be kind to you." [25]So the man showed them the way into the city. The men of Joseph attacked with swords the people in Bethel, but they let the man and his family go free. [26]He went to the land where the Hittites lived and built a city. He named it Luz, which it is called even today.

[27]There were Canaanites living in the cities of Beth Shan, Taanach, Dor, Ibleam, Megiddo and the small towns around them. The people of Manasseh did not force those people out of their towns, because the Canaanites were determined to stay there. [28]Later, the Israelites grew strong and forced the Canaanites to work as slaves, but they did not make all the Canaanites leave their land. [29]The people of Ephraim did not force out all of the Canaanites living in Gezer. So the Canaanites continued to live in Gezer with the people of Ephraim. [30]The people of Zebulun did not force out the Canaanites living in the cities of Kitron and Nahalol. They stayed and lived with the people of Zebulun, but Zebulun made them work as slaves.

[31]The people of Asher did not force the Canaanites from the cities of Acco, Sidon, Ahlab, Achzib, Helbah, Aphek and Rehob. [32]Since the people of Asher did not force them out, the Canaanites continued to live with them. [33]The people of Naphtali did not force out the people of the cities of Beth Shemesh and Beth Anath. So they continued to live with the Canaanites in those cities, and the Canaanites worked as slaves. [34]The Amorites forced the Danites back into the mountains and would not let them come down to live in the plain. [35]The Amorites were determined to stay in Mount Heres, Aijalon and Shaalbim. But when the Israelites grew stronger, they made the Amorites work as slaves. [36]The land of the Amorites was from Scorpion Pass to Sela and beyond.

The Angel of the LORD at Bokim

2 The angel of the LORD went up from Gilgal to Bokim [n] and said, "I brought you up from Egypt and led you to the land I promised to give your ancestors. I said, 'I will never break my agreement with you. [2]But you must not make an agreement with the people who live in this land. You must destroy their altars.' But you did not obey me. How could you do this? [3]Now I tell you, 'I will not force out the people in this land. They will be your enemies, and their gods will be a trap for you.'"

[4]After the angel gave Israel this message from the LORD, they cried loudly. [5]So they named the place Bokim. There they offered sacrifices to the LORD.

Joshua Dies

[6]Then Joshua sent the people back to their land. [7]The people served the LORD during the lifetime of Joshua and during the lifetimes of the elders who lived after Joshua and who had seen what great things the LORD had done for Israel. [8]Joshua son of Nun, the servant of the LORD, died at the age of 110. [9]They buried him in his own land at Timnath Serah in the mountains of Ephraim, north of Mount Gaash.

The People Disobey

[10]After those people had died, their children grew up and did not know the LORD or what he had done for Israel. [11]So they did what the LORD

> **Sidelight**   The Israelites sinned when they worshipped Baal (Judges 2:11), not only because Baal was a false god, but also because of the religion's worship practices. Archaeologists have found that the Canaanites practised infant sacrifice and prostitution in their temples. Baal worship included sexual elements intended to make the gods bring rain and fertility.

said was wrong, and they worshipped the Baal [d] idols. [12]They stopped following the LORD, the God of their ancestors who had brought them out of Egypt. They began to worship the gods of the people who lived around them, and that made the LORD angry. [13]The Israelites stopped following the LORD and worshipped Baal and Ashtoreth. [d] [14]The LORD was angry with the people of Israel, so he handed them over to robbers who took their possessions. He let their enemies who lived around them defeat them; they could not protect

Bokim   This name means "crying".

themselves. [15]When the Israelites went out to fight, they always lost, because the LORD was not with them. The LORD had sworn to them this would happen. So the Israelites suffered very much.

God Chooses Judges

[16]Then the LORD chose leaders called judges, [n] who saved the Israelites from the robbers. [17]But the Israelites did not listen to their judges. They were not faithful to God but worshipped other gods instead. Their ancestors had obeyed the LORD's commands, but they quickly turned away and did not obey. [18]When their enemies hurt them, the Israelites cried for help. So the LORD felt sorry for them and sent judges to save them from their enemies. The LORD was with those judges all their lives. [19]But when the judges died, the Israelites again sinned and worshipped other gods. They became worse than their ancestors. The Israelites were very stubborn and refused to change their evil ways.

[20]So the LORD became angry with the Israelites. He said, "These people have broken the agreement I made with their ancestors. They have not listened to me. [21]I will no longer defeat the nations who were left when Joshua died. [22]I will use them to test Israel, to see if Israel will keep the LORD's commands as their ancestors did." [23]In the past the LORD had permitted those nations to stay in the land. He did not quickly force them out or help Joshua's army defeat them.

3 These are the nations the LORD did not force to leave. He wanted to test the Israelites who had not fought in the wars of Canaan. [2](The only reason the LORD left those nations in the land was to teach the descendants [d] of the Israelites who had not fought in those wars how to fight.) [3]These are the nations: the five rulers of the Philistines, all the Canaanites, the people of Sidon and the Hivites who lived in the Lebanon mountains from Mount Baal Hermon to Lebo Hamath. [4]Those nations were in the land to test the Israelites—to see if they would obey the commands the LORD had given to their ancestors by Moses.

[5]The people of Israel lived with the Canaanites, Hittites, Amorites, Perizzites, Hivites and Jebusites. [6]The Israelites began to marry the daughters of those people, and they allowed their daughters to marry the sons of those people. Israel also served their gods.

Othniel, the First Judge

[7]The Israelites did what the LORD said was wrong. They forgot about the LORD their God and served the idols of Baal [d] and Asherah. [d] [8]So the LORD was angry with Israel and allowed Cushan-Rishathaim king of North West Mesopotamia to rule over the Israelites for eight years. [9]When Israel cried to the LORD, the LORD sent someone to save them. Othniel son of Kenaz, Caleb's younger brother, saved the Israelites. [10]The Spirit [d] of the LORD entered Othniel, and he became Israel's judge. When he went to war, the LORD handed over to him Cushan-Rishathaim, king of North West Mesopotamia. [11]So the land was at peace for 40 years. Then Othniel son of Kenaz died.

Ehud, the Judge

[12]Again the people of Israel did what the LORD said was wrong. So the LORD gave Eglon king of Moab power to defeat Israel because of the evil Israel did. [13]Eglon got the Ammonites and the Amalekites to join him. Then he attacked Israel and took Jericho, the city of palm trees. [14]So the people of Israel were ruled by Eglon king of Moab for eighteen years.

[15]When the people cried to the LORD, he sent someone to save them. He was Ehud, son of Gera from the people of Benjamin, who was left-handed. Israel sent Ehud to give Eglon king of Moab the payment he demanded. [16]Ehud made himself a sword with two edges, about half a metre long, and he tied it to his right hip under his clothes. [17]Ehud gave Eglon king of Moab the payment he demanded. Now Eglon was a very fat man. [18]After he had given Eglon the payment, Ehud sent away the people who had carried it. [19]When he passed the statues near Gilgal, he turned around and said to Eglon, "I have a secret message for you, King Eglon."

The king said, "Be quiet!" Then he sent all of his servants out of the room. [20]Ehud went to King Eglon, as he was sitting alone in the room above his summer palace.

Ehud said, "I have a message from God for you." As the king stood up from his chair, [21]Ehud reached with his left hand and took out the sword that was tied to his right hip. Then he stabbed the sword deep into the king's belly! [22]Even the handle sank in, and the blade came out of his back. The king's fat covered the whole sword, so Ehud left the sword in Eglon. [23]Then he went out of the room and closed and locked the doors behind him.

²⁴When the servants returned just after Ehud left, they found the doors to the room locked. So they thought the king was relieving himself. ²⁵They waited for a long time. Finally they became worried because he still had not opened the doors. So they got the key and unlocked them and saw their king lying dead on the floor!

²⁶While the servants were waiting, Ehud had escaped. He passed by the statues and went to Seirah. ²⁷When he reached the mountains of Ephraim he blew the trumpet. The people of Israel heard it and went down from the hills with Ehud leading them.

²⁸He said to them, "Follow me! The LORD has helped you to defeat your enemies, the Moabites." So Israel followed Ehud and captured the crossings of the Jordan River. They did not allow the Moabites to cross the Jordan River. ²⁹Israel killed about 10,000 strong and able men from Moab; not one escaped. ³⁰So that day Moab was forced to be under the rule of Israel, and there was peace in the land for 80 years.

Shamgar, the Judge

³¹After Ehud, Shamgar son of Anath saved Israel. Shamgar killed 600 Philistines with a sharp stick used to guide oxen.

Deborah, the Woman Judge

4 After Ehud died, the Israelites again did what the LORD said was wrong. ²So he let Jabin, a king of Canaan who ruled in the city of Hazor, defeat Israel. Sisera, who lived in Harosheth Haggoyim, was the commander of Jabin's army. ³Because he had 900 iron chariots and was very cruel to the people of Israel for 20 years, they cried to the LORD for help.

⁴A prophetess ᵈ named Deborah, the wife of Lappidoth, was judge of Israel at that time. ⁵Deborah would sit under the Palm Tree of Deborah, which was between the cities of Ramah and Bethel, in the mountains of Ephraim. And the people of Israel would come to her to settle their arguments.

⁶Deborah sent a message to Barak son of Abinoam. Barak lived in the city of Kedesh, which is in the area of Naphtali. Deborah said to Barak, "The

LEADERSHIP

Pass the Paintbrush

Leonardo da Vinci was one of the greatest artists who has ever lived. Almost six hundred years ago he came up with designs for a flying machine and other inventions, as well as his famous painting and sculpture.

One day a student walked into da Vinci's studio to find the master working on a huge canvas. He had chosen the subject and begun work. Then, suddenly, he stopped and asked the student to finish the painting.

The student protested, saying he could never do justice to the great painter's work. He felt he was unworthy to complete such an important job.

Da Vinci cut him off. "Will not what I have done inspire you to do your best?" he asked.

In the same way that da Vinci hoped to encourage his student, Deborah wanted to motivate Barak and the Israelites in battle. Read how she challenged Barak in **Judges 4:4–16.**

* How was da Vinci's challenge similar to Deborah's challenge to Barak?
* How can you use God's power to help you inspire others the way Deborah inspired Barak?

Consider . . .

* asking someone you admire for help to deal with a challenge you're facing.
* sending a thank-you note to someone – a parent, a friend, someone at church – who has inspired you in your faith in recent months.

For more, see . . .

* Judges 5:1–31 (p.229)
* Hebrews 12:1–3 (p.1343)

* 1 Corinthians 1:10–17 (p.1215)

L<small>ORD</small>, the God of Israel, commands you: 'Go and gather 10,000 men of Naphtali and Zebulun and lead them to Mount Tabor. ⁷I will make Sisera, the commander of Jabin's army, and his chariots, and his army meet you at the Kishon River. I will hand Sisera over to you.'"

⁸Then Barak said to Deborah, "I will go if you will go with me, but if you won't go with me, I won't go."

⁹"Of course I will go with you," Deborah answered, "but you will not get credit for the victory. The L<small>ORD</small> will let a woman defeat Sisera." So Deborah went with Barak to Kedesh. ¹⁰At Kedesh, Barak called the people of Zebulun and Naphtali together. From them, he gathered 10,000 men to follow him, and Deborah went with him also.

¹¹Now Heber the Kenite had left the other Kenites, the descendants *d* of Hobab, Moses' brother-in-law. Heber had put up his tent by the great tree in Zaanannim, near Kedesh.

¹²When Sisera was told that Barak son of Abinoam had gone to Mount Tabor, ¹³Sisera gathered his 900 iron chariots and all the men with him, from Harosheth Haggoyim to the Kishon River.

¹⁴Then Deborah said to Barak, "Get up! Today is the day the L<small>ORD</small> will hand over Sisera. The L<small>ORD</small> has already cleared the way for you." So Barak led 10,000 men down Mount Tabor. ¹⁵As Barak approached, the L<small>ORD</small> confused Sisera and his army and chariots. The L<small>ORD</small> defeated them with the sword, but Sisera left his chariot and ran away on foot. ¹⁶Barak and his men chased Sisera's chariots and army to Harosheth Haggoyim. With their swords they killed all of Sisera's men; not one of them was left alive.

¹⁷But Sisera himself ran away to the tent where Jael lived. She was the wife of Heber, one of the Kenite family groups. Heber's family was at peace with Jabin king of Hazor. ¹⁸Jael went out to meet Sisera and said to him, "Come into my tent, master! Come in. Don't be afraid." So Sisera went into Jael's tent, and she covered him with a rug.

¹⁹Sisera said to Jael, "I am thirsty. Please give me some water to drink." So she opened a leather bag of milk and gave him a drink. Then she covered him up.

²⁰He said to her, "Go and stand at the entrance to the tent. If anyone comes and asks you, 'Is anyone here?' say, 'No.'"

²¹But Jael, the wife of Heber, took a tent peg and a hammer and quietly went to Sisera. Since he was very tired, he was in a deep sleep. She hammered the tent peg through the side of Sisera's head and into the ground. And so Sisera died.

²²At that very moment Barak came by Jael's tent, chasing Sisera. Jael went out to meet him and said, "Come. I will show you the man you are looking for." So Barak entered her tent, and there Sisera lay dead, with the tent peg in his head.

²³On that day God defeated Jabin king of Canaan in the sight of Israel.

²⁴Israel became stronger and stronger against Jabin king of Canaan until finally they destroyed him.

The Song of Deborah

5 On that day Deborah and Barak son of Abinoam sang this song:

²"The leaders led Israel.
  The people volunteered to go to battle.
  Praise the L<small>ORD</small>!
³Listen, kings.
  Pay attention, rulers!
I myself will sing to the L<small>ORD</small>.
  I will make music to the L<small>ORD</small>, the God of
    Israel.

⁴"L<small>ORD</small>, when you came from Edom,
  when you marched from the land of Edom,
the earth shook,
  the skies rained,
  and the clouds dropped water.
⁵The mountains shook before the L<small>ORD</small>, the
    God of Mount Sinai,
  before the L<small>ORD</small>, the God of Israel!

⁶"In the days of Shamgar son of Anath,
  in the days of Jael, the main roads were
    empty.
  Travellers went on the back roads.
⁷There were no warriors in Israel
  until I, Deborah, arose,
  until I arose to be a mother to Israel.
⁸At that time they chose to follow new gods.
  Because of this, enemies fought us at our
    city gates.
No one could find a shield or a spear
  among the 40,000 people of Israel.
⁹My heart is with the commanders of Israel.
  They volunteered freely from among the
    people.
  Praise the L<small>ORD</small>!

Sidelight   When Jael gave Sisera milk to drink, it probably wasn't ice-cold (Judges 4:19). Because of the hot climate, people often curdled milk to preserve it. The nutritious result (known as kefir) is similar to yogurt. Unfortunately, you couldn't get it with strawberries and bananas mixed in.

¹⁰"You who ride on white donkeys
    and sit on saddle blankets,
    and you who walk along the road, listen!
¹¹Listen to the sound of the singers
    at the watering holes.
There they tell about the victories of the LORD,
    the victories of the LORD's warriors in Israel.
Then the LORD's people went down to the
    city gates.

¹²"Wake up, wake up, Deborah!
    Wake up, wake up, sing a song!
    Get up, Barak!
    Go and capture your enemies, son of
        Abinoam!

¹³"Then those who were left came down to the
    important leaders.
The LORD's people came down to me with
    strong men.
¹⁴They came from Ephraim in the mountains of
    Amalek.

Benjamin was among the people who
    followed you.
From the family group of Makir, the
    commanders came down.
And from Zebulun came those who lead.
¹⁵The princes of Issachar were with Deborah.
    The people of Issachar were loyal to Barak
    and followed him into the valley.
The Reubenites thought hard
    about what they would do.
¹⁶Why did you stay by the sheepfold?
    Was it to hear the music played for your
        sheep?
The Reubenites thought hard
    about what they would do.
¹⁷The people of Gilead stayed east of the
    Jordan River.
People of Dan, why did you stay by the
    ships?
The people of Asher stayed at the seashore,
    at their safe harbours.

MUSIC

Which Came First?

"I have this great tune running round in my head, but I'm just hopeless at lyrics," said James sadly to
his music teacher.

"That's because you're concentrating on the music all the time," Mr Bradley replied.

"But the music's so much easier, listen to this . . ." James played some chords on his guitar.
He started to sing "Yeah, yeah, I know it. Yeah yeah."

"But what are you trying to say?" asked his teacher.

"What do you mean?" James was puzzled.

"Well, if you want to write a song, first you must know what you want to sing about. Is it a love
song? Is it a sad song? Is it about personal feelings?" he asked.

"First you have to write down how you feel. Then put those words into a form of a poem and
then say them out loud until you can hear a melody or a rhythm."

James grinned. "You're a good teacher you know. That sounds like an excellent idea!"

Many songs have wonderful melodies and hopeless words.

Judges 5:2–5 talks of making music.

- How do the words of the song in Judges compare with the word James was singing?
- When was the last time you felt inspired to worship God with a song?

Consider . . .

- writing out a favourite Bible passage in your own words. Find a musical friend to help you
  compose some music for it.
- praying for your church musicians, thanking God for the talent he has given them.

For more, see . . .

- Exodus 15:1–8 (p.73)
- Revelation 15:3–4 (p.1399)
- Psalm 33:1–3 (p.519)

¹⁸But the people of Zebulun risked their lives,
  as did the people of Naphtali on the
    battlefield.

¹⁹"The kings came, and they fought.
  At that time the kings of Canaan fought
  at Taanach, by the waters of Megiddo.
  But they took away no silver or possessions
    of Israel.
²⁰The stars fought from heaven;
  from their paths, they fought Sisera.
²¹The Kishon River swept Sisera's men away,
  that old river, the Kishon River.
March on, my soul, with strength!
²²Then the horses' hoofs beat the ground.
  Galloping, galloping go Sisera's mighty
    horses.
²³'May the town of Meroz be cursed,' said the
    angel of the LORD.
  'Bitterly curse its people,
because they did not come to help the LORD.
  They did not fight the strong enemy.'

²⁴"May Jael, the wife of Heber the Kenite,
  be blessed above all women who live in
    tents.
²⁵Sisera asked for water,
  but Jael gave him milk.
In a bowl fit for a ruler,
  she brought him cream.
²⁶Jael reached out and took the tent peg.
  Her right hand reached for the workman's
    hammer.
She hit Sisera! She smashed his head!
  She crushed and pierced the side of
    his head!
²⁷At Jael's feet he sank.
  He fell, and he lay there.
  At her feet he sank. He fell.
Where Sisera sank, there he fell, dead!

²⁸"Sisera's mother looked out through the win-
    dow.
  She looked through the curtains and cried
    out,
  'Why is Sisera's chariot so late in coming?
  Why are sounds of his chariots' horses
    delayed?'
²⁹The wisest of her servant ladies answer her,
  and Sisera's mother says to herself,
³⁰'Surely they are robbing the people they
    defeated!
  Surely they are dividing those things among
    themselves!
Each soldier is given a girl or two.
  Maybe Sisera is taking pieces of dyed cloth.
Maybe they are even taking
  pieces of dyed, embroidered cloth for the
    necks of the victors!'

³¹"Let all your enemies die this way, LORD!
  But let all the people who love you
  be as strong as the rising sun!"

Then there was peace in the land for 40 years.

The Midianites Attack Israel

6 Again the Israelites did what the LORD said was wrong. So for seven years the LORD handed them over to Midian. ²Because the Midianites were very powerful and were cruel to Israel, the Israelites made hiding places in the mountains, in caves and in safe places. ³Whenever the Israelites planted crops, the Midianites, Amalekites and other peoples from the east would come and attack them. ⁴They camped in the land and destroyed the crops that the Israelites had planted as far away as Gaza. They left nothing for Israel to eat, and no sheep, cattle or donkeys. ⁵The Midianites came with their tents and their animals like swarms of locusts *d* to ruin the land. There were so many people and camels they could not be counted. ⁶Israel became very poor because of the Midianites, so they cried out to the LORD.

⁷When the Israelites cried out to the LORD against the Midianites, ⁸the LORD sent a prophet *d* to them. He said, "This is what the LORD, the God of Israel, says: I brought you out of Egypt, the land of slavery. ⁹I saved you from the Egyptians and from all those who were against you. I forced the Canaanites out of their land and gave it to you. ¹⁰Then I said to you, 'I am the LORD your God. Live in the land of the Amorites, but do not worship their gods.' But you did not obey me."

The Angel of the LORD Visits Gideon

¹¹The angel of the LORD came and sat down under the oak tree at Ophrah that belonged to Joash, one of the Abiezrite people. Gideon, Joash's son, was separating some wheat from the chaff *d* in a winepress *d* to keep the wheat from the Midianites. ¹²The angel of the LORD appeared to Gideon and said, "The LORD is with you, mighty warrior!"

¹³Then Gideon said, "Sir, if the LORD is with us, why are we having so much trouble? Where are the miracles *d* our ancestors told us he did when the LORD brought them out of Egypt? But now he has left us and has handed us over to the Midianites."

¹⁴The LORD turned to Gideon and said, "Go with your strength and save Israel from the Midianites. I am the one who is sending you."

¹⁵But Gideon answered, "Lord, how can I save Israel? My family group is the weakest in Manasseh, and I am the least important member of my family."

[16]The LORD answered him, "I will be with you. It will seem as if the Midianites you are fighting are only one man."

[17]Then Gideon said to the LORD, "If you are pleased with me, give me proof that it is really you talking with me. [18]Please wait here until I come back to you. Let me bring my offering and set it in front of you."

And the LORD said, "I will wait until you return."

[19]So Gideon went in and cooked a young goat, and with 10 kilogrammes of flour, made bread without yeast. Then he put the meat into a basket and the broth into a pot. He brought them out and gave them to the angel under the oak tree.

[20]The angel of God said to Gideon, "Put the meat and the bread without yeast on that rock over there. Then pour the broth on them." And Gideon did as he was told. [21]The angel of the LORD touched the meat and the bread with the end of the stick that was in his hand. Then fire jumped up from the rock and completely burned up the meat and the bread! And the angel of the LORD disappeared! [22]Then Gideon understood he had been talking to the angel of the LORD. So Gideon cried out, "Lord GOD! I have seen the angel of the LORD face to face!"

[23]But the LORD said to Gideon, "Calm down! Don't be afraid! You will not die!"

[24]So Gideon built an altar there to worship the LORD and named it The LORD Is Peace. It still stands at Ophrah, where the Abiezrites live.

Gideon Tears Down the Altar of Baal

[25]That same night the LORD said to Gideon, "Take the bull that belongs to your father and a second bull seven years old. Pull down your father's altar to Baal, [d] and cut down the Asherah[d] idol beside it. [26]Then build an altar to the LORD your God with its stones in the right order on this high ground. Kill and burn a second bull on this altar, using the wood from the Asherah idol."

[27]So Gideon got ten of his servants and did what the LORD had told him to do. But Gideon was afraid that his family and the men of the city might see him, so he did it at night, not in the daytime.

[28]When the men of the city got up the next morning, they saw that the altar for Baal had been destroyed and that the Asherah idol beside it had been cut down! They also saw the altar Gideon had built and the second bull that had been sacrificed on it. [29]The men of the city asked each other, "Who did this?"

After they asked many questions, someone told them, "Gideon son of Joash did this."

[30]So they said to Joash, "Bring your son out. He has pulled down the altar of Baal and cut down the Asherah idol beside it. He must die!"

[31]But Joash said to the angry crowd around him, "Are you going to take Baal's side? Are you going to defend him? Anyone who takes Baal's side will be killed by morning! If Baal is a god, let him fight for himself. It's his altar that has been pulled down." [32]So on that day Gideon got the name Jerub-Baal, which means "let Baal fight against him," because Gideon pulled down Baal's altar.

Gideon Defeats Midian

[33]All the Midianites, the Amalekites and other peoples from the east joined together and came across the Jordan River and camped in the Valley of Jezreel. [34]But the Spirit [d] of the LORD entered Gideon, and he blew a trumpet to call the Abiezrites to follow him. [35]He sent messengers to all of Manasseh, calling them to follow him. He also sent messengers to the people of Asher, Zebulun and Naphtali. So they also went up to meet Gideon and his men.

[36]Then Gideon said to God, "You said you would help me save Israel. [37]I will put some wool on the threshing [d] floor. If there is dew only on the wool but all of the ground is dry, then I will know that you will use me to save Israel, as you said." [38]And that is just what happened. When Gideon got up early the next morning and squeezed the wool, he got a full bowl of water from it.

[39]Then Gideon said to God, "Don't be angry with me if I ask just one more thing. Please let me make one more test. Let only the wool be dry while the ground around it gets wet with dew." [40]That night God did that very thing. Just the wool was dry, but the ground around it was wet with dew.

7 Early in the morning Jerub-Baal (also called Gideon) and all his men set up their camp at the spring of Harod. The Midianites were camped north of them in the valley at the bottom of the hill called Moreh. [2]Then the LORD said to Gideon, "You have too many men to defeat the Midianites. I don't want the Israelites to boast that they saved themselves. [3]So now, announce to the people, 'Anyone who is afraid may leave Mount Gilead and go back home.'" So 22,000 men returned home, but 10,000 remained.

[4]Then the LORD said to Gideon, "There are still too many men. Take the men down to the water, and I will test them for you there. If I say, 'This man will go with you,' he will go. But if I say, 'That one will not go with you,' he will not go."

[5]So Gideon led the men down to the water. There the LORD said to him, "Separate them into those who drink water by lapping it up like a dog and those who bend down to drink." [6]There were 300 men who used their hands to bring water to their mouths, lapping it as a dog does. All the rest got down on their knees to drink.

[7]Then the LORD said to Gideon, "Using the 300 men who lapped the water, I will save you and hand Midian over to you. Let all the others go home." [8]So Gideon sent the rest of Israel to their homes. But he kept the 300 men and took the jars and the trumpets of those who left.

Now the camp of Midian was in the valley below Gideon. [9]That night the LORD said to Gideon, "Get up. Go down and attack the camp of the Midianites, because I will give them to you. [10]But if you are afraid to go down, take your servant Purah with you. [11]When you come to the camp of Midian, you will hear what they are saying. Then you will not be afraid to attack the camp."

Gideon is Encouraged

So Gideon and his servant Purah went down to the edge of the enemy camp. [12]The Midianites, the Amalekites and all the peoples from the east were camped in that valley. There were so many of them they seemed like locusts. [d] Their camels could not be counted because they were as many as the grains of sand on the seashore!

[13]When Gideon came to the enemy camp, he heard a man telling his friend about a dream. He was saying, "I dreamed that a loaf of barley bread rolled into the camp of Midian. It hit the tent so hard that the tent turned over and fell flat!"

[14]The man's friend said, "Your dream is about the sword of Gideon son of Joash, a man of Israel. God will hand Midian and the whole army over to him!"

[15]When Gideon heard about the dream and what it meant, he worshipped God. Then Gideon went back to the camp of Israel and called out to them, "Get up! The LORD has handed the army

DOUBT

Doubting David

The big story of the 2002 football World Cup was David Beckham's metatarsal injury. Just one month before the biggest tournament in world football, England's golden boy and captain slid into a tackle and . . . snap . . . he'd broken a tiny bone in his foot. Things looked decidedly dodgy as to his participation.

To every football fan's delight, David made an amazingly swift recovery. The medical team duly announced he was fit to play and the good wishes of a nation were behind him.

It was pretty obvious, however, as the tournament progressed, that David himself was a little more doubtful about his recovery. Rather than his usual gutsy commitment, he was jumping out of tackles seemingly to protect his foot. One such missed challenge led to Brazil scoring a winner against England in the quarter finals.

In some ways, this is not unlike the story of Gideon in **Judges 6:33–40**. Gideon had all the promises – not from the England medical team but from the Lord himself – that he was a mighty man of valour and that he was going to defeat the Midianites. Yet he still wasn't convinced and doubted the Lord, looking for more signs from his fleeces on the ground.

- How did the doubt Gideon felt affect his behaviour?
- Was Gideon right to test God? Why did God not mind?

Consider . . .

- when it is and when it is not a good idea to test the Lord over his direction for our lives.
- whether there have ever been times when you have wanted to test God before trusting him. If so, what happened?

For more, see . . .

- Genesis 18:1–15 (p.20)
- John 20:24–29 (p.1134)
- Matthew 14:22–33 (p.966)

of Midian over to you!" [16]Gideon divided the 300 men into three groups. He gave each man a trumpet and an empty jar with a burning torch inside.

[17]Gideon told the men, "Watch me and do what I do. When I get to the edge of the camp, do what I do. [18]Surround the enemy camp. When I and everyone with me blow our trumpets, you blow your trumpets too. Then shout, 'For the LORD and for Gideon!' "

Midian is Defeated

[19]So Gideon and the 100 men with him came to the edge of the enemy camp just after they had changed guards. It was during the middle watch of the night. Then Gideon and his men blew their trumpets and smashed their jars. [20]All three groups of Gideon's men blew their trumpets and smashed their jars. They held the torches in their left hands and the trumpets in their right hands. Then they shouted, "A sword for the LORD and for Gideon!" [21]Each of Gideon's men stayed in his place around the camp, but the Midianites began shouting and running to escape.

[22]When Gideon's 300 men blew their trumpets, the LORD made all the Midianites fight each other with their swords! The enemy army ran away to the city of Beth Shittah towards Zererah. They ran as far as the border of Abel Meholah, near the city of Tabbath. [23]Then men of Israel from Naphtali, Asher and all of Manasseh were called out to chase the Midianites. [24]Gideon sent messengers through all the mountains of Ephraim, saying, "Come down and attack the Midianites. Take control of the Jordan River as far as Beth Barah before the Midianites can get to it."

So they called out all the men of Ephraim, who took control of the Jordan River as far as Beth Barah. [25]The men of Ephraim captured two princes of Midian named Oreb and Zeeb. They killed Oreb at the rock of Oreb and Zeeb at the winepress *d* of Zeeb, and they continued chasing the Midianites. They brought the heads of Oreb and Zeeb to Gideon, who was east of the Jordan River.

8 The men of Ephraim asked Gideon, "Why did you treat us this way? Why didn't you call us when you went to fight against Midian?" They argued angrily with Gideon.

[2]But he answered them, "I have not done as well as you! The small part you did was better than all that my people of Abiezer did. [3]God let you capture Oreb and Zeeb, the princes of Midian. How can I compare what I did with what you did?" When the men of Ephraim heard Gideon's answer, they were not as angry any more.

Gideon Captures Two Kings

[4]When Gideon and his 300 men came to the Jordan River, they were tired, but they chased the enemy across to the other side. [5]Gideon said to the men of Succoth, "Please give my soldiers some bread because they are very tired. I am chasing Zebah and Zalmunna, the kings of Midian."

[6]But the leaders of Succoth said, "Why should we give your soldiers bread? You haven't caught Zebah and Zalmunna yet."

[7]Then Gideon said, "The LORD will surrender Zebah and Zalmunna to me. After that, I will whip your skin with thorns and briers from the desert."

[8]Gideon left Succoth and went to the city of Peniel and asked them for food. But the people of Peniel gave him the same answer as the people of Succoth. [9]So Gideon said to the men of Peniel, "After I win the victory, I will return and pull down this tower."

[10]Zebah and Zalmunna and their army were in the city of Karkor. About 15,000 men were left of the armies of the peoples of the east. Already 120,000 soldiers had been killed. [11]Gideon went up the road of those who live in tents east of Nobah and Jogbehah, and he attacked the enemy army when they did not expect it. [12]Zebah and Zalmunna, the kings of Midian, ran away, but Gideon chased and captured them and frightened away their army.

[13]Then Gideon son of Joash returned from the battle by the Pass of Heres. [14]Gideon captured a young man from Succoth and asked him some questions. So the young man wrote down for Gideon the names of 77 officers and elders of Succoth.

Gideon Punishes Succoth

[15]When Gideon came to Succoth, he said to the people of that city, "Here are Zebah and Zalmunna. You made fun of me by saying, 'Why should we give bread to your tired men? You have not caught Zebah and Zalmunna yet.' " [16]So Gideon took the elders of the city and punished them with thorns and briers from the desert. [17]He also pulled down the tower of Peniel and killed the people in that city.

[18]Gideon asked Zebah and Zalmunna, "What were the men like that you killed on Mount Tabor?"

They answered, "They were like you. Each one of them looked like a prince."

[19]Gideon said, "Those were my brothers, my mother's sons. As surely as the LORD lives, I would not kill you if you had spared them." [20]Then Gideon said to Jether, his oldest son, "Kill

them." But Jether was only a boy and was afraid, so he did not take out his sword.

²¹Then Zebah and Zalmunna said to Gideon, "Come on. Kill us yourself. As the saying goes, 'It takes a man to do a man's job.'" So Gideon got up and killed Zebah and Zalmunna and took the decorations off their camels' necks.

Gideon Makes an Idol

²²The people of Israel said to Gideon, "You saved us from the Midianites. Now, we want you and your son and your grandson to rule over us."

²³But Gideon told them, "The LORD will be your ruler. I will not rule over you, nor will my son rule over you." ²⁴He said, "I want you to do this one thing for me. I want each of you to give me a gold earring from the things you took in the fighting." (The Ishmaelites[n] wore gold earrings.)

²⁵They said, "We will gladly give you what you want." So they spread out a coat, and everyone threw down an earring from what he had taken. ²⁶The gold earrings weighed about 20 kilogrammes. This did not include the decorations, necklaces and purple robes worn by the kings

> **Sidelight** People today wear earrings for decoration, but that has not always been the only reason. Three thousand years ago, people also wore earrings because they thought that they had magical power – which may be one reason why the Israelites took away the Ishmaelites' earrings in battle (Judges 8:23–27).

of Midian, nor the chains from the camels' necks. ²⁷Gideon used the gold to make a holy robe, which he put in his home town of Ophrah. But all the Israelites were unfaithful to God and worshipped it, so it became a trap for Gideon and his family.

The Death of Gideon

²⁸So Midian was under the rule of Israel; they did not cause trouble any more. And the land had peace for 40 years, as long as Gideon was alive.

²⁹Gideon[n] son of Joash went to his home to live. ³⁰He had 70 sons of his own, because he had many wives. ³¹He had a slave woman[d] who lived in Shechem, and he had a son by her, whom he named Abimelech. ³²So Gideon son of

Joash died at a good old age. He was buried in the tomb of Joash, his father, in Ophrah, where the Abiezrites live.

³³As soon as Gideon died, the people of Israel were again unfaithful to God and followed the Baals.[d] They made Baal-of-the-Agreement their god. ³⁴The Israelites did not remember the LORD their God, who had saved them from all their enemies living all around them. ³⁵And they were not kind to the family of Jerub-Baal, also called Gideon, for all the good he had done for Israel.

Abimelech Becomes King

9 Abimelech son of Gideon[n] went to his uncles in the city of Shechem. He said to his uncles and all of his mother's family group, ²"Ask the leaders of Shechem, 'Is it better for the 70 sons of Gideon to rule over you or for one man to rule?' Remember, I am your relative."

³Abimelech's uncles spoke to all the leaders of Shechem about this. And they decided to follow Abimelech, because they said, "He is our relative." ⁴So the leaders of Shechem gave Abimelech about 70 pieces of silver from the temple of the god Baal-of-the-Agreement. Abimelech used the silver to hire some worthless, reckless men, who followed him wherever he went. ⁵He went to Ophrah, the home town of his father, and murdered his 70 brothers, the sons of Gideon. He killed them all on one stone. But Gideon's youngest son, Jotham, hid from Abimelech and escaped. ⁶Then all of the leaders of Shechem and Beth Millo gathered beside the great tree standing in Shechem. There they made Abimelech their king.

Jotham's Story

⁷When Jotham heard this, he went and stood on the top of Mount Gerizim. He shouted to the people: "Listen to me, you leaders of Shechem, so that God will listen to you! ⁸One day the trees decided to appoint a king to rule over them. They said to the olive tree, 'You be king over us!'

⁹"But the olive tree said, 'Men and gods are honoured by my oil. Should I stop making it and go and sway over the other trees?'

¹⁰"Then the trees said to the fig tree, 'Come and be king over us!'

¹¹"But the fig tree answered, 'Should I stop making my sweet and good fruit and go and sway over the other trees?'

¹²"Then the trees said to the vine, 'Come and be king over us!'

Ishmaelites   Another name for the Midianites. See Genesis 37:25–28.
Gideon   Also called Jerub-Baal.

[13]"But the vine answered, 'My new wine makes men and gods happy. Should I stop making it and go and sway over the trees?'

[14]"Then all the trees said to the thornbush, 'Come and be king over us.'

[15]"But the thornbush said to the trees, 'If you really want to appoint me king over you, come and find shelter in my shade! But if not, let fire come out of the thornbush and burn up the cedars of Lebanon!'

[16]"Now, were you completely honest and sincere when you made Abimelech king? Have you been fair to Gideon [n] and his family? Have you treated Gideon as you should? [17]Remember, my father fought for you and risked his life to save you from the power of the Midianites. [18]But now you have turned against my father's family and have killed his 70 sons on one stone. You have made Abimelech, the son of my father's slave girl, king over the leaders of Shechem just because he is your relative! [19]So then, if you have been honest and sincere to Gideon and his family today, be happy with Abimelech as your king. And may he be happy with you! [20]But if not, may fire come out of Abimelech and completely burn you leaders of Shechem and Beth Millo! Also may fire come out of the leaders of Shechem and Beth Millo and burn up Abimelech!"

[21]Then Jotham ran away and escaped to the city of Beer. He lived there because he was afraid of his brother Abimelech.

Abimelech Fights Against Shechem

[22]Abimelech ruled Israel for three years. [23]Then God sent an evil spirit to make trouble between Abimelech and the leaders of Shechem so that the leaders of Shechem turned against him. [24]Abimelech had killed Gideon's [n] 70 sons, his own brothers, and the leaders of Shechem had helped him. So God sent the evil spirit to punish them. [25]The leaders of Shechem were against Abimelech then. They put men on the hilltops in ambush who robbed everyone going by. And Abimelech was told.

[26]A man named Gaal son of Ebed and his brothers moved into Shechem, and the leaders of Shechem trusted him. [27]They went out to the vineyards to pick grapes, and they squeezed the grapes. Then they had a feast in the temple of their god, where they ate and drank and cursed Abimelech. [28]Gaal son of Ebed said, "We are the men of Shechem. Who is Abimelech that we should serve him? Isn't he one of Gideon's sons, and isn't Zebul his officer? We should serve the men of Hamor, Shechem's father. Why should we serve Abimelech? [29]If you made me commander of these people, I would get rid of Abimelech. I would say to him, 'Get your army ready and come out to battle.'"

[30]Now when Zebul, the ruler of Shechem, heard what Gaal son of Ebed said, he was very angry. [31]He sent secret messengers to Abimelech, saying, "Gaal son of Ebed and Gaal's brothers have come to Shechem, and they are turning the city against you! [32]You and your men should get up during the night and hide in the fields outside the city. [33]As soon as the sun comes up in the morning, attack the city. When Gaal and his men come out to fight you, do what you can to them."

[34]So Abimelech and all his soldiers got up during the night and hid near Shechem in four groups. [35]Gaal son of Ebed went out and was standing at the entrance to the city gate. As he was standing there, Abimelech and his soldiers came out of their hiding places.

[36]When Gaal saw the soldiers, he said to Zebul, "Look! There are people coming down from the mountains!"

But Zebul said, "You are seeing the shadows of the mountains. The shadows just look like people."

[37]But again Gaal said, "Look, there are people coming down from the centre of the land, and there is a group coming from the fortune-tellers' tree!"

[38]Zebul said to Gaal, "Where is your boasting now? You said, 'Who is Abimelech that we should serve him?' You made fun of these men. Now go out and fight them."

[39]So Gaal led the men of Shechem out to fight Abimelech. [40]Abimelech and his men chased them, and many of Gaal's men were killed before they could get back to the city gate. [41]While Abimelech stayed at Arumah, Zebul forced Gaal and his brothers to leave Shechem.

[42]The next day the people of Shechem went out to the fields. When Abimelech was told about it, [43]he separated his men into three groups and hid them in the fields. When he saw the people coming out of the city, he jumped up and attacked them. [44]Abimelech and his group ran to the entrance gate to the city. The other two groups ran out to the people in the fields and struck them down. [45]Abimelech and his men fought the city of Shechem all day until they captured it and killed its people. Then he tore it down and threw salt [n] over the ruins.

Gideon Also called Jerub-Baal.
salt The salt would stop crops from growing there.

The Tower of Shechem Burns

[46]When the leaders who were in the Tower of Shechem heard what had happened to Shechem, they gathered in the safest room of the temple of El Berith. [47]Abimelech heard that all the leaders of the Tower of Shechem had gathered there. [48]So he and all his men went up Mount Zalmon, near Shechem. Abimelech took an axe and cut some branches and put them on his shoulders. He said to all those with him, "Hurry! Do what I have done!" [49]So all those men cut branches and followed Abimelech and piled them against the safest room of the temple. Then they set them on fire and burned the people inside. So all the people who were at the Tower of Shechem also died—about 1,000 men and women.

Abimelech's Death

[50]Then Abimelech went to the city of Thebez. He surrounded the city, attacked it and captured it. [51]But inside the city was a strong tower, so all the men, women and leaders of that city ran to the tower. When they got inside, they locked the door behind them. Then they climbed up to the roof of the tower. [52]Abimelech came to the tower to attack it. He approached the door of the tower to set it on fire, [53]but as he came near, a woman dropped a grinding stone on his head, crushing his skull.

[54]He quickly called to the officer who carried his armour and said, "Take out your sword and kill me. I don't want people to say, 'A woman killed Abimelech.' " So the officer stabbed Abimelech, and he died. [55]When the people of Israel saw Abimelech was dead, they all returned home.

[56]In that way God punished Abimelech for all the evil he had done to his father by killing his 70 brothers. [57]God also punished the men of Shechem for the evil they had done. So the curse spoken by Jotham, the youngest son of Gideon, [n] came true.

Tola, the Judge

10 After Abimelech died, another judge came to save Israel. He was Tola son of Puah, the son of Dodo. Tola was from the people of Issachar and lived in the city of Shamir in the mountains of Ephraim. [2]Tola was a judge for Israel for 23 years. Then he died and was buried in Shamir.

Jair, the Judge

[3]After Tola died, Jair from the region of Gilead became judge. He was a judge for Israel for 22 years. [4]Jair had 30 sons, who rode 30 donkeys. These 30 sons controlled 30 towns in Gilead, which are called the Towns of Jair to this day. [5]Jair died and was buried in the city of Kamon.

The Ammonites Trouble Israel

[6]Again the Israelites did what the LORD said was wrong. They worshipped Baal [d] and Ashtoreth, [d] the gods of Aram, Sidon, Moab and Ammon, and the gods of the Philistines. The Israelites left the LORD and stopped serving him. [7]So the LORD was angry with them and handed them over to the Philistines and the Ammonites. [8]In the same year those people destroyed the Israelites who lived east of the Jordan River in the region of Gilead, where the Amorites lived. So the Israelites suffered for eighteen years. [9]The Ammonites then crossed the Jordan River to fight the people of Judah, Benjamin and Ephraim, causing much trouble to the people of Israel. [10]So the Israelites cried out to the LORD, "We have sinned against you. We left our God and worshipped the Baal idols."

[11]The LORD answered the Israelites, "When the Egyptians, Amorites, Ammonites, Philistines, [12]Sidonians, Amalekites and Maonites were cruel to you, you cried out to me, and I saved you. [13]But now you have left me again and have worshipped other gods. So I refuse to save you again. [14]You have chosen those gods. So go and call to them for help. Let them save you when you are in trouble."

[15]But the people of Israel said to the LORD, "We have sinned. Do to us whatever you want, but please save us today!" [16]Then the Israelites threw away the foreign gods among them, and they worshipped the LORD again. So he felt sorry for them when he saw their suffering.

[17]The Ammonites gathered for war and camped in Gilead. The Israelites gathered and camped at Mizpah. [18]The leaders of the people of Gilead said, "Who will lead us to attack the Ammonites? He will become the head of all those who live in Gilead."

Jephthah Is Chosen as Leader

11 Jephthah was a strong soldier from Gilead. His father was named Gilead, and his mother was a prostitute. [d] [2]Gilead's wife had several sons. When they grew up, they forced Jephthah to leave his home, saying to him, "You will not get any of our father's property, because you are the son of another woman." [3]So Jephthah ran away from his brothers and lived in the land of Tob. There some worthless men began to follow him.

Gideon   Also called Jerub-Baal.

4After a time the Ammonites fought against Israel. 5When the Ammonites made war against Israel, the elders of Gilead went to Jephthah to bring him back from Tob. 6They said to him, "Come and lead our army so we can fight the Ammonites."

7But Jephthah said to them, "Didn't you hate me? You forced me to leave my father's house. Why are you coming to me now that you are in trouble?"

8The elders of Gilead said to Jephthah, "It is because of those troubles that we come to you now. Please come with us and fight against the Ammonites. You will be the ruler over everyone who lives in Gilead."

9Then Jephthah answered, "If you take me back to Gilead to fight the Ammonites and the LORD helps me win, I will be your ruler."

10The elders of Gilead said to him, "The LORD is listening to everything we are saying. We promise to do all that you tell us to do." 11So Jephthah went with the elders of Gilead, and the people made him their leader and commander of their army. Jephthah repeated all of his words in front of the LORD at Mizpah.

Jephthah Sends Messengers to the Ammonite King

12Jephthah sent messengers to the king of the Ammonites, asking, "What have you got against Israel? Why have you come to attack our land?"

13The king of the Ammonites answered the messengers of Jephthah, "We are fighting Israel because you took our land when you came up from Egypt. You took our land from the Arnon River to the Jabbok River to the Jordan River. Now give our land back to us peacefully."

14Jephthah sent the messengers to the Ammonite king again. 15They said:

"This is what Jephthah says: Israel did not take the land of the people of Moab or Ammon. 16When the Israelites came out of Egypt, they went into the desert to the Red Sea and then to Kadesh. 17Israel sent messengers to the king of Edom, saying, 'Let the people of Israel go across your land.' But the king of Edom refused. We sent the same message to the king of Moab, but he also refused. So the Israelites stayed at Kadesh.

18"Then the Israelites went into the desert around the borders of the lands of Edom and Moab. Israel went east of the land of Moab and camped on the other side of the Arnon River, the border of Moab. They did not cross it to go into the land of Moab.

19"Then Israel sent messengers to Sihon king of the Amorites, king of the city of Heshbon, asking, 'Let the people of Israel pass through your land to go to our land.' 20But Sihon did not trust the Israelites to cross his land. So he gathered all of his people and camped at Jahaz and fought with Israel.

21"But the LORD, the God of Israel, handed Sihon and his army over to Israel. All the land of the Amorites became the property of Israel. 22So Israel took all the land of the Amorites from the Arnon River to the Jabbok River, from the desert to the Jordan River.

23"It was the LORD, the God of Israel, who forced out the Amorites ahead of the people of Israel. So do you think you can make them leave? 24Take the land that your god Chemosh *d* has given you. We will live in the land the LORD our God has given us!

25"Are you any better than Balak son of Zippor, king of Moab? Did he ever quarrel or fight with the people of Israel? 26For 300 years the Israelites have lived in Heshbon and Aroer and the towns around them and in all the cities along the Arnon River. Why have you not taken these cities back in all that time? 27I have not sinned against you, but you are sinning against me by making war on me. May the LORD, the Judge, decide whether the Israelites or the Ammonites are right."

28But the king of the Ammonites ignored this message from Jephthah.

Jephthah's Promise

29Then the Spirit *d* of the LORD entered Jephthah. Jephthah passed through Gilead and Manasseh and the city of Mizpah in Gilead to the land of the Ammonites. 30Jephthah made a promise to the LORD, saying, "If you will hand over the Ammonites to me, 31I will give you as a burnt offering the first thing that comes out of my house to meet me when I return from the victory. It will be the LORD's."

32Then Jephthah went over to fight the Ammonites, and the LORD handed them over to him. 33In a great defeat Jephthah struck them down from the city of Aroer to the area of Minnith, and 20 cities as far as the city of Abel Keramim. So the Ammonites were defeated by the Israelites.

34When Jephthah returned to his home in Mizpah, his daughter was the first one to come out to meet him, playing a tambourine *d* and dancing. She was his only child; he had no other sons or daughters. 35When Jephthah saw his daughter, he tore his clothes to show his sorrow. He said, "My daughter! You have made me so sad because I made a promise to the LORD, and I cannot break it!"

36Then his daughter said, "Father, you made a promise to the LORD. So do to me just what you promised, because the LORD helped you defeat your enemies, the Ammonites." 37She also said, "But let me do one thing. Let me be alone for two months to go to the mountains. Since I will never marry, let me and my friends go and cry together."

³⁸Jephthah said, "Go." So he sent her away for two months. She and her friends stayed in the mountains and cried for her because she would

never marry. ³⁹After two months she returned to her father, and Jephthah did to her what he had promised. Jephthah's daughter never had a husband.

From this came a custom in Israel that ⁴⁰every year the young women of Israel would go out for four days to remember the daughter of Jephthah from Gilead.

Jephthah and Ephraim

12 The men of Ephraim called all their soldiers together and crossed the river to the town of Zaphon. They said to Jephthah, "Why didn't you call us to help you fight the Ammonites? We will burn your house down with you in it."

²Jephthah answered them, "My people and I fought a great battle against the Ammonites. I called you, but you didn't come to help me. ³When I saw that you would not help me, I risked my own life and went against the Ammonites. The LORD handed them over to me. So why have you come to fight against me today?"

⁴Then Jephthah called the men of Gilead together and fought the men of Ephraim. The men of Gilead struck them down because the Ephraimites had said, "You men of Gilead are nothing but deserters from Ephraim—living between Ephraim and Manasseh." ⁵The men of Gilead captured the crossings of the Jordan River that led to the country of Ephraim. A person from Ephraim trying to escape would say, "Let me cross the river." Then the men of Gilead would ask him, "Are you from Ephraim?" If he replied "No," ⁶they would say to him, "Say the word 'Shibboleth'." The men of Ephraim could not say that word correctly. So if the person from Ephraim said, "Sibboleth," the men of Gilead would kill him at the crossing. So 42,000 people from Ephraim were killed at that time.

⁷Jephthah was a judge for Israel for six years. Then Jephthah, the man from Gilead, died and was buried in a town in Gilead.

Ibzan, the Judge

⁸After Jephthah died, Ibzan from Bethlehem was a judge for Israel. ⁹He had 30 sons and 30 daughters. He let his daughters marry men who were not in his family group, and he brought 30 women who were not in his tribe *d* to be wives for his sons. Ibzan judged Israel for seven years. ¹⁰Then he died and was buried in Bethlehem.

Elon, the Judge

¹¹After Ibzan died, Elon from the tribe *d* of Zebulun was a judge for Israel. He judged Israel for ten years. ¹²Then Elon, the man of Zebulun, died and was buried in the city of Aijalon in the land of Zebulun.

Abdon, the Judge

¹³After Elon died, Abdon son of Hillel from the city of Pirathon was a judge for Israel. ¹⁴He had 40 sons and 30 grandsons, who rode on 70 donkeys. He judged Israel for eight years. ¹⁵Then Abdon son of Hillel died and was buried in Pirathon in the land of Ephraim, in the mountains where the Amalekites lived.

The Birth of Samson

13 Again the people of Israel did what the LORD said was wrong. So he handed them over to the Philistines for 40 years.

²There was a man named Manoah from the tribe *d* of Dan, who lived in the city of Zorah. He had a wife, but she could not have children. ³The angel of the LORD appeared to Manoah's wife and said, "You have not been able to have children, but you will become pregnant and give birth to a son. ⁴Be careful not to drink wine or beer or eat anything that is unclean, *d* ⁵because you will become pregnant and have a son. You must never cut his hair, because he will be a Nazirite, *d* given to God from birth. He will begin to save Israel from the power of the Philistines."

⁶Then Manoah's wife went to him and told him what had happened. She said, "A man from God came to me. He looked like an angel from God; his appearance was frightening. I didn't ask him where he was from, and he didn't tell me his name. ⁷But he said to me, 'You will become pregnant and will have a son. Don't drink wine or beer or eat anything that is unclean, because the boy will be a Nazirite to God from his birth until the day of his death.'"

⁸Then Manoah prayed to the LORD: "Lord, I beg you to let the man of God come to us again. Let

him teach us what we should do for the boy who will be born to us."

[9]God heard Manoah's prayer, and the angel of God came to Manoah's wife again while she was sitting in the field. But her husband Manoah was not with her. [10]So she ran to tell him, "He is here! The man who appeared to me the other day is here!"

[11]Manoah got up and followed his wife. When he came to the man, he said, "Are you the man who spoke to my wife?"

The man said, "I am."

[12]So Manoah asked, "When what you say happens, what kind of life should the boy live? What should he do?"

[13]The angel of the LORD said, "Your wife must be careful to do everything I told her to do. [14]She must not eat anything that grows on a grapevine, or drink any wine or beer, or eat anything that is unclean. She must do everything I have commanded her."

[15]Manoah said to the angel of the LORD, "We would like you to stay awhile so we can cook a young goat for you."

[16]The angel of the LORD answered, "Even if I stay awhile, I would not eat your food. But if you want to prepare something, offer a burnt offering to the LORD." (Manoah did not understand that the man was really the angel of the LORD.)

[17]Then Manoah asked the angel of the LORD, "What is your name? Then we will honour you when what you have said really happens."

[18]The angel of the LORD said, "Why do you ask my name? It is too amazing for you to understand." [19]So Manoah sacrificed a young goat on a rock and offered some grain as a gift to the LORD. Then an amazing thing happened as Manoah and his wife watched. [20]The flames went up to the sky from the altar. As the fire burned, the angel of the LORD went up to heaven in the flame. When Manoah and his wife saw that, they bowed face down on the ground. [21]The angel of the LORD did not appear to them again. Then Manoah understood that the man was really the angel of the LORD. [22]Manoah said, "We have seen God, so we will surely die."

[23]But his wife said to him, "If the LORD wanted to kill us, he would not have accepted our burnt offering or grain offering. He would not have shown us all these things or told us all this."

[24]So the woman gave birth to a boy and named him Samson. He grew, and the LORD blessed him. [25]The Spirit [d] of the LORD began to work in Samson while he was in the city of Mahaneh Dan, between the cities of Zorah and Eshtaol.

Samson's First Marriage

14 Samson went down to the city of Timnah where he saw a Philistine woman. [2]When he returned home, he said to his father and mother, "I saw a Philistine woman in Timnah. I want you to get her for me so I can marry her."

[3]His father and mother answered, "Surely there is a woman from Israel you can marry. Do you have to marry a woman from the Philistines, who are not circumcised?" [d]

But Samson said, "Get that woman for me! She is the one I want!" [4](Samson's parents did not know that the LORD wanted this to happen because he was looking for a way to challenge the Philistines, who were ruling over Israel at this time.) [5]Samson went down with his father and mother to Timnah, as far as the vineyard near there. Suddenly, a young lion came roaring towards Samson! [6]The Spirit [d] of the LORD entered Samson with great power, and he tore the lion apart with his bare hands. For him it was as easy as tearing apart a young goat. But Samson did not tell his father or mother what he had done. [7]Then he went down to the city and talked to the Philistine woman, and he liked her.

[8]Several days later Samson went back to marry her. On his way he went over to look at the body of the dead lion and found a swarm of bees and honey in it. [9]Samson got some of the honey with his hands and walked along eating it. When he came to his parents, he gave some to them. They ate it, too, but Samson did not tell them he had taken the honey from the body of the dead lion.

[10]Samson's father went down to see the Philistine woman. And Samson gave a feast, as was the custom for the bridegroom. [11]When the people saw him, they sent 30 friends to be with him.

Samson's Riddle

[12]Samson said to them, "Let me tell you a riddle. Try to find the answer during the seven days of the feast. If you can, I will give you 30 linen shirts and 30 changes of clothes. [13]But if you can't, you must give me 30 linen shirts and 30 changes of clothes."

So they said, "Tell us your riddle so we can hear it."

[14]Samson said,

"Out of the eater comes something to eat.

Out of the strong comes something sweet."
After three days, they had not found the
answer.

[15]On the fourth [n] day they said to Samson's wife, "Did you invite us here to make us poor?

---

fourth The Hebrew word is "seventh". Some old translations say "fourth", which fits the order of events better.

Trick your husband into telling us the answer to the riddle. If you don't, we will burn you and everyone in your father's house."

16So Samson's wife went to him, crying, and said, "You hate me! You don't really love me! You told my people a riddle, but you won't tell me the answer."

Samson said, "I haven't even told my father or mother. Why should I tell you?"

17Samson's wife cried for the rest of the seven days of the feast. So he finally gave her the answer on the seventh day, because she kept bothering him. Then she told her people the answer to the riddle.

18Before sunset on the seventh day of the feast, the Philistine men had the answer. They came to Samson and said,

"What is sweeter than honey?
  What is stronger than a lion?"

Then Samson said to them,

"If you had not ploughed with my young cow,
  you would not have solved my riddle!"

19Then the Spirit *d* of the LORD entered Samson and gave him great power. Samson went down to the city of Ashkelon and killed 30 of its men and took all that they had and gave the clothes to the men who had answered his riddle. Then he went to his father's house very angry. 20And Samson's wife was given to his best man.

Samson Troubles the Philistines

15 At the time of the wheat harvest, Samson went to visit his wife, taking a young goat with him. He said, "I'm going to my wife's room," but her father would not let him go in.

2He said to Samson, "I thought you really hated your wife, so I gave her to your best man. Her younger sister is more beautiful. Take her instead."

3But Samson said to them, "This time no one will blame me for hurting you Philistines!" 4So Samson went out and caught 300 foxes. He took two foxes at a time, tied their tails together and then tied a torch to the tails of each pair of foxes. 5After he lit the torches, he let the foxes loose in the grain fields of the Philistines so that he burned up their standing grain, the piles of grain, their vineyards and their olive trees.

6The Philistines asked, "Who did this?"

Someone told them, "Samson, the son-in-law of the man from Timnah, did because his father-in-law gave his wife to his best man."

So the Philistines burned Samson's wife and her father to death. 7Then Samson said to the Philistines, "Since you did this, I won't stop until I pay you back!" 8Samson attacked the Philistines

and killed many of them. Then he went down and stayed in a cave in the rock of Etam.

9The Philistines went up and camped in the land of Judah, near a place named Lehi. 10The men of Judah asked them, "Why have you come here to fight us?"

They answered, "We have come to make Samson our prisoner, to pay him back for what he did to our people."

11Then 3,000 men of Judah went to the cave in the rock of Etam and said to Samson, "What have you done to us? Don't you know that the Philistines rule over us?"

Samson answered, "I only paid them back for what they did to me."

12Then they said to him, "We have come to tie you up and to hand you over to the Philistines."

Samson said to them, "Promise me you will not hurt me yourselves."

13The men from Judah said, "We agree. We will just tie you up and give you to the Philistines. We will not kill you." So they tied Samson with two new ropes and led him up from the cave in the rock. 14When Samson came to the place named Lehi, the Philistines came to meet him, shouting for joy. Then the Spirit *d* of the LORD entered Samson and gave him great power. The ropes on him weakened like burned strings and fell off his hands! 15Samson found the jawbone of a dead donkey, took it, and killed 1,000 men with it!

16Then Samson said,

"With a donkey's jawbone
  I made donkeys out of them.
With a donkey's jawbone
  I killed 1,000 men!"

17When he finished speaking, he threw away the jawbone. So that place was named Ramath Lehi. *n*

18Samson was very thirsty, so he cried out to the LORD, "You gave me, your servant, this great victory. Do I have to die of thirst now? Do I have to be captured by people who are not circumcised?" *d* 19Then God opened up a hole in the ground at Lehi, and water came out. When Samson drank, he felt better; he felt strong again.

Ramnath Lehi   This name means "Jawbone Hill".

So he named that spring Caller's Spring, which is still in Lehi.

[20]Samson judged Israel for 20 years in the days of the Philistines.

Samson Goes to the City of Gaza

16 One day Samson went to Gaza and saw a prostitute *d* there. He went in to spend the night with her. [2]When the people of Gaza heard, "Samson has come here!" they surrounded the place and waited for him near the city gate all night. They said to each other, "When dawn comes, we will kill Samson!"

[3]But Samson only stayed with the prostitute until midnight. Then he got up and took hold of the doors and the two posts of the city gate and tore them loose, along with the bar. He put them on his shoulders and carried them to the top of the hill that faces the city of Hebron.

Samson and Delilah

[4]After this, Samson fell in love with a woman named Delilah, who lived in the Valley of Sorek. [5]The Philistine rulers went to Delilah and said, "Find out what makes Samson so strong. Trick him into telling you how we can overpower him, capture him and tie him up. If you do this, each one of us will give you 1,100 pieces of silver."

[6]So Delilah said to Samson, "Tell me why you are so strong. How can someone tie you up and capture you?"

[7]Samson answered, "Someone would have to tie me up with seven new bowstrings that have not been dried. Then I would be as weak as any other man."

[8]The Philistine rulers brought Delilah seven new bowstrings that had not been dried, and she tied Samson with them. [9]Some men were hiding in another room. Delilah said to him, "Samson, the Philistines are here!" But Samson broke the bowstrings like pieces of burned string. So the Philistines did not find out the secret of Samson's strength.

[10]Then Delilah said to Samson, "You made a fool of me. You lied to me. Now tell me how someone can tie you up."

[11]Samson said, "They would have to tie me with new ropes that have not been used before. Then I would become as weak as any other man."

[12]So Delilah took new ropes and tied Samson. Some men were hiding in another room. She called out to him, "Samson, the Philistines are here!" But he broke the ropes as easily as if they were threads.

[13]Then Delilah said to Samson, "Again you have made a fool of me. You lied to me. Tell me how someone can tie you up."

He said, "Using the loom, *n* weave the seven plaits of my hair into the cloth, and tighten it with a pin. Then I will be as weak as any other man."

While Samson slept, Delilah wove the seven plaits of his hair into the cloth. [14]Then she fastened it with a pin.

Again she said to him, "Samson, the Philistines are here!" Samson woke up and pulled out the pin and the loom with the cloth.

[15]Then Delilah said to him, "How can you say, 'I love you,' when you don't even trust me? This is the third time you have made a fool of me. You haven't told me the secret of your great strength." [16]She kept bothering Samson about his secret day after day until he felt he was going to die!

[17]So he told her everything. He said, "I have never had my hair cut, because I have been set apart to God as a Nazirite *d* since I was born. If someone shaved my head, I would lose my strength and be as weak as any other man."

[18]When Delilah saw that he had told her everything sincerely, she sent a message to the Philistine rulers. She said, "Come back one more time, because he has told me everything." So the Philistine rulers came back to Delilah and brought the silver with them. [19]Delilah got Samson to sleep, lying in her lap. Then she called in a man to shave off the seven plaits of Samson's hair. In this way she began to make him weak, and his strength left him.

[20]Then she said, "Samson, the Philistines are here!"

He woke up and thought, "I'll leave as I did before and shake myself free." But he did not know that the LORD had left him.

> **Sidelight** When Samson was forced to grind grain as a prisoner, the punishment was severe (Judges 16:21). The millstone he would have turned was probably made of limestone and was at least 60 centimetres across with a hole in the middle. Only large animals and extremely strong people could operate the grinding mills.

[21]Then the Philistines captured Samson and tore out his eyes. They took him down to Gaza, where they put bronze chains on him and made him grind grain in the prison. [22]But his hair began to grow again.

---

loom   A machine for making cloth from thread.

Samson Dies

23The Philistine rulers gathered to celebrate and to offer a great sacrifice to their god Dagon. *d* They said, "Our god has handed Samson our enemy over to us." 24When the people saw him, they praised their god, saying,

"This man destroyed our country.
He killed many of us!
But our god handed over
   our enemy to us."

25While the people were enjoying the celebration, they said, "Bring Samson out to perform for us." So they brought Samson from the prison, and he performed for them. They made him stand between the pillars. 26Samson said to the servant holding his hand, "Let me feel the pillars that hold up the temple so I can lean against them." 27Now the temple was full of men and women. All the Philistine rulers were there, and about 3,000 men and women were on the roof *n* watching Samson perform. 28Then Samson prayed to the LORD, "Lord GOD, remember me. God, please give me strength one more time so I can pay these Philistines back for putting out my two eyes!" 29Then Samson turned to the two centre pillars that supported the whole temple. He braced himself between the two pillars, with his right hand on one and his left hand on the other. 30Samson said, "Let me die with these Philistines!" Then he pushed as hard as he could, causing the temple to fall on the rulers and all the people in it. So Samson killed more of the Philistines when he died than when he was alive.

31Samson's brothers and his whole family went down to get his body. They brought him back and buried him in the tomb of Manoah, his father, between the cities of Zorah and Eshtaol. Samson was a judge for the people of Israel for 20 years.

Micah's Idols

17 There was a man named Micah who lived in the mountains of Ephraim. 2He said to his mother, "I heard you speak a curse about the 1,100 pieces of silver that were taken from you. I have the silver with me; I took it."

His mother said, "The LORD bless you, my son!"

3Micah gave the 1,100 pieces of silver to his mother. Then she said, "I will give this silver to the LORD. I will have my son make an idol and a statue. So I will give the silver back to you."

4When he gave the silver back to his mother, she took about 200 pieces and gave it to a silversmith. With it he made an idol and a statue, which stood in Micah's house. 5Micah had a special holy place, and he made a holy robe *d* and some household idols. Then Micah chose one of his sons to be his priest. 6At that time Israel did not have a king, so everyone did what seemed right.

7There was a young man who was a Levite *n* from the city of Bethlehem in Judah who was from the people of Judah. 8He left Bethlehem to look for another place to live, and on his way he came to Micah's house in the mountains of Ephraim. 9Micah asked him, "Where are you from?"

He answered, "I'm a Levite from Bethlehem in Judah. I'm looking for a place to live."

10Micah said to him, "Live with me and be my father and my priest. I will give you 10 pieces of silver each year and clothes and food." So the Levite went in. 11He agreed to live with Micah and became like one of Micah's own sons. 12Micah made him a priest, and he lived in Micah's house. 13Then Micah said, "Now I know the LORD will be good to me, because I have a Levite as my priest."

Dan's Family Captures Laish

18 At that time Israel did not have a king. And at that time the tribe *d* of Dan was still looking for a land where they could live, a land of their own. The Danites had not yet been given their own land among the tribes of Israel. 2So, from their family groups, they chose five soldiers from the cities of Zorah and Eshtaol to spy out and explore the land. They were told, "Go, explore the land."

They came to the mountains of Ephraim, to Micah's house, where they spent the night. 3When they came near Micah's house, they recognised the voice of the young Levite. *n* So they stopped there and asked him, "Who brought you here? What are you doing here? Why are you here?"

4He told them what Micah had done for him, saying, "He hired me. I am his priest."

5They said to him, "Please ask God if our journey will be successful."

6The priest said to them, "Go in peace. The LORD is pleased with your journey."

7So the five men left. When they came to the city of Laish, they saw that the people there lived in safety, like the people of Sidon. They thought they were safe and had plenty of everything. They lived a long way from the Sidonians and had no dealings with anyone else.

---

roof   In Bible times houses were built with flat roofs. The roof was used for drying things such as flax and fruit. And it was used as an extra room, as a place for worship and as a place to sleep in the summer.

Levite   The Levites were the only ones God had appointed as priests.

8When the five men returned to Zorah and Eshtaol, their relatives asked them, "What did you find?"

9They answered, "We have seen the land, and it is very good. We should attack them. Aren't you going to do something? Don't wait! Let's go and take that land! 10When you go, you will see there is plenty of land—plenty of everything! The people are not expecting an attack. Surely God has handed that land over to us!"

11So 600 Danites left Zorah and Eshtaol ready for war. 12On their way they set up camp near the city of Kiriath Jearim in Judah. That is why the place west of Kiriath Jearim is named Mahaneh Dan *n* to this day. 13From there they travelled on to the mountains of Ephraim. Then they came to Micah's house.

14The five men who had explored the land around Laish said to their relatives, "Do you know, in one of these houses there are a holy robe, *d* household gods, an idol and a statue? You know what to do." 15So they stopped at the Levite's house, which was also Micah's house, and greeted the Levite. 16The 600 Danites stood at the entrance gate, wearing their weapons of war. 17The five spies went into the house and took the idol, the holy robe, the household idols and the statue. The priest and the 600 men armed for war stood by the entrance gate.

18When the spies went into Micah's house and took the image, the holy robe, the household idols and the statue, the priest asked them, "What are you doing?"

19They answered, "Be quiet! Don't say a word. Come with us and be our father and priest. Is it better for you to be a priest for one man's house or for a tribe and family group in Israel?" 20This made the priest happy. So he took the holy robe, the household idols and the idol and went with the Danites. 21They left Micah's house, putting their little children, their animals and everything they owned in front of them.

22When they had gone a little way from Micah's house, the men who lived near Micah were called out and caught up with them. 23The men with Micah shouted at the Danites, who turned round and said to Micah, 'What's the matter with you? Why have you been called out to fight?"

24Micah answered, "You took my gods that I made and my priest. What do I have left? How can you ask me, 'What's the matter?' "

25The Danites answered, "You should not argue with us. Some of our angry men might attack you, killing you and your family." 26Then the Danites went on their way. Micah knew they

were too strong for him, so he turned and went back home.

27Then the Danites took what Micah had made and his priest and went on to Laish. They attacked those peaceful people and killed them with their swords and then burned the city. 28There was no one to save the people of Laish. They lived too far from Sidon, and they had no dealings with anyone else. Laish was in a valley near Beth Rehob.

The people of Dan rebuilt the city and lived there. 29They changed the name of Laish to Dan, naming it after their ancestor Dan, one of the sons of Israel.

30The people of Dan set up the idols in the city of Dan. Jonathan son of Gershom, Moses' son, and his sons served as priests for the tribe of Dan until the land was captured. 31The people of Dan set up the idols Micah had made as long as the Holy Tent*d* of God was in Shiloh.

A Levite and His Servant

19 At that time Israel did not have a king. There was a Levite who lived in the faraway mountains of Ephraim. He had taken a slave woman*d* from the city of Bethlehem in the land of Judah to live with him, 2but she was unfaithful to him. She left him and went back to her father's house in Bethlehem in Judah and stayed there for four months. 3Then her husband went to ask her to come back to him, taking with him his servant and two donkeys. When the Levite came to her father's house, she invited him to come in, and her father was happy to see him. 4The father-in-law, the young woman's father, asked him to stay. So he stayed for three days and ate, drank and slept there.

5On the fourth day they got up early in the morning. The Levite was getting ready to leave, but the woman's father said to his son-in-law, "Refresh yourself by eating something. Then go." 6So the two men sat down to eat and drink together. After that, the father said to him, "Please stay tonight. Relax and enjoy yourself." 7When the man got up to go, his father-in-law asked him to stay. So he stayed again that night. 8On the fifth day the man got up early in the morning to leave. The woman's father said, "Refresh yourself. Wait until this afternoon." So the two men ate together.

9When the Levite, his slave woman, and his servant got up to leave, the father-in-law, the young woman's father, said, "It's almost night. The day is almost gone. Spend the night here and enjoy yourself. Tomorrow morning you can get up early and go home." 10But the Levite did not

Mahaneh Dan   This name means "the camp of Dan".

want to stay another night. So he took his two saddled donkeys and his slave woman and travelled towards the city of Jebus (also called Jerusalem).

¹¹As the day was almost over, they came near Jebus. So the servant said to his master, "Let's stop at this city of the Jebusites, and spend the night here."

¹²But his master said, "No. We won't go inside a foreign city. Those people are not Israelites. We will go on to the city of Gibeah." ¹³He said, "Come on. Let's try to make it to Gibeah or Ramah so we can spend the night in one of those cities." ¹⁴So they went on. The sun went down as they came near Gibeah, which belongs to the tribe *d* of Benjamin. ¹⁵They stopped there to spend the night. They came to the public square of the city and sat down, but no one invited them home to spend the night.

¹⁶Late in the evening an old man came in from his work in the fields. His home was in the mountains of Ephraim, but now he was living in Gibeah. (The people of Gibeah were from the tribe of Benjamin.) ¹⁷He saw the traveller in the public square and asked, "Where are you going? Where did you come from?"

¹⁸The Levite answered, "We are travelling from Bethlehem in Judah to my home in the mountains of Ephraim. I have been to Bethlehem in Judah, but now I am going to the Holy Tent *d* of the LORD. No one has invited me to stay in his house. ¹⁹We already have straw and food for our donkeys and bread and wine for me, the young woman and my servant. We don't need anything."

²⁰The old man said, "You are welcome to stay at my house. Let me give you anything you need, but don't spend the night in the public square." ²¹So the old man took the Levite into his house, and he fed their donkeys. They washed their feet and had something to eat and drink.

²²While they were enjoying themselves, some wicked men of the city surrounded the house and beat on the door. They shouted to the old man who owned the house, "Bring out the man who came to your house. We want to have sexual relations with him."

²³The owner of the house went outside and said to them, "No, my friends. Don't be so evil. This man is a guest in my house. Don't do this terrible thing! ²⁴Look, here is my daughter, who has never had sexual relations before, and also the man's slave woman. I will bring them out to you now. Do anything you want with them, but don't do such a terrible thing to this man."

²⁵But the men would not listen to him. So the Levite took his slave woman and sent her outside to them. They forced her to have sexual relations with them, and they abused her all night long. Then, at dawn, they let her go. ²⁶She came back to the house where her master was staying and fell down at the door and lay there until daylight.

²⁷In the morning when the Levite got up, he opened the door of the house and went outside to go on his way. But his slave woman was lying at the doorway of the house, with her hands on the doorsill. ²⁸The Levite said to her, "Get up; let's go." But she did not answer. So he put her on his donkey and went home.

²⁹When the Levite got home, he took a knife and cut his slave woman into twelve parts, limb by limb. Then he sent a part to each area of Israel. ³⁰Everyone who saw this said, "Nothing like this has ever happened before, not since the people of Israel came out of Egypt. Think about it. Tell us what to do."

The War Between Israel and Benjamin

20 So all the Israelites from Dan to Beersheba, *n* including the land of Gilead, joined together before the LORD in the city of Mizpah. ²The leaders of all the tribes *d* of Israel took their places in the meeting of the people of God. There were 400,000 soldiers with swords. ³(The people of Benjamin heard that the Israelites had gone up to Mizpah.) Then the Israelites said to the Levite, "Tell us how this evil thing happened."

⁴So the husband of the murdered woman answered, "My slave woman *d* and I came to Gibeah in Benjamin to spend the night. ⁵During the night the men of Gibeah came after me. They surrounded the house and wanted to kill me. They forced my slave woman to have sexual relations and she died. ⁶I took her and cut her into parts and sent one part to each area of Israel because the people of Benjamin did this wicked and terrible thing in Israel. ⁷Now, all you Israelites, speak up. What is your decision?"

⁸Then all the people stood up at the same time, saying, "None of us will go home. Not one of us will go back to his house! ⁹Now this is what we will do to Gibeah. We will throw lots. *d* ¹⁰That way we will choose ten men from every 100 men from all the tribes of Israel, and we will choose 100 men from every 1,000, and 1,000 men from every 10,000. These will find supplies for the army. Then the army will go to the city of Gibeah of Benjamin to repay them for the terrible thing they have done in Israel." ¹¹So all the men of Israel were united and gathered against the city.

Dan to Beersheba   Dan was the city farthest north in Israel and Beersheba was the city farthest south. So this means all the people of Israel.

¹²The tribes of Israel sent men throughout the tribe of Benjamin demanding, "What is this evil thing some of your men have done? ¹³Hand over the wicked men in Gibeah so that we can put them to death. We must remove this evil from Israel."

But the Benjaminites would not listen to their fellow Israelites. ¹⁴The Benjaminites left their own cities and met at Gibeah to fight the Israelites. ¹⁵In only one day the Benjaminites got 26,000 soldiers together who were trained with swords. They also had 700 chosen men from Gibeah. ¹⁶Seven hundred of these trained soldiers were left-handed, each of whom could sling a stone at a hair and not miss!

Sidelight

Looking for a left-handed bowler? Try Judges 20:16 which tells how people with unusual skills were important in the Benjaminite army. They could hit a hair with a stone, and would have earned their place in anybody's cricket team.

¹⁷The Israelites, except for the Benjaminites, gathered 400,000 soldiers with swords.

¹⁸The Israelites went up to the city of Bethel and asked God, "Which tribe shall be first to attack the Benjaminites?"

The LORD answered, "Judah shall go first."

¹⁹The next morning the Israelites got up and made a camp near Gibeah. ²⁰The men of Israel went out to fight the Benjaminites and took their battle position at Gibeah. ²¹Then the Benjaminites came out of Gibeah and killed 22,000 Israelites during the battle that day. ²²⁻²³The Israelites went before the LORD and cried until evening. They asked the LORD, "Shall we go to fight our relatives, the Benjaminites, again?"

The LORD answered, "Go up and fight them." The men of Israel encouraged each other. So they took the same battle positions as they had taken on the first day.

²⁴The Israelites came to fight the Benjaminites on the second day. ²⁵The Benjaminites came out of Gibeah to attack the Israelites. This time, the Benjaminites killed 18,000 Israelites, all of whom carried swords.

²⁶Then the Israelites went up to Bethel. There they sat down and cried to the LORD and went without food all day until evening. They also brought burnt offerings and fellowship offerings to the LORD. ²⁷The Israelites asked the LORD a question. (In those days the Ark ᵈ of the Agreement with God was there at Bethel. ²⁸A priest named Phinehas son of Eleazar, the son of Aaron, served before the Ark of the Agreement.) They asked, "Shall we go to fight our relatives, the Benjaminites, again, or shall we stop fighting?"

The LORD answered, "Go, because tomorrow I will hand them over to you."

²⁹Then the Israelites set up ambushes all around Gibeah. ³⁰They went to fight against the Benjaminites at Gibeah on the third day, getting into position for battle as they had done before. ³¹When the Benjaminites came out to fight them, the Israelites backed up and led the Benjaminites away from the city. The Benjaminites began to kill some of the Israelites as they had done before. About 30 Israelites were killed—some in the fields and some on the roads leading to Bethel and to Gibeah.

³²The Benjaminites said, "We are winning as before!"

But the Israelites said, "Let's run. Let's trick them into going farther away from their city and onto the roads."

³³All the Israelites moved from their places and got into battle positions at a place named Baal Tamar. Then the Israelites ran out from their hiding places west of Gibeah. ³⁴Ten thousand of the best trained soldiers from all of Israel attacked Gibeah. The battle was very hard. The Benjaminites did not know disaster was about to come to them. ³⁵The LORD used the Israelites to defeat the Benjaminites. On that day the Israelites killed 25,100 Benjaminites, all armed with swords. ³⁶Then the Benjaminites saw that they were defeated.

The Israelites had moved back because they were depending on the surprise attack they had set up near Gibeah. ³⁷The men in hiding rushed into Gibeah, spread out and killed everyone in the city with their swords. ³⁸Now the Israelites had set up a signal with the men in hiding. The men in the surprise attack were to send up a cloud of smoke from the city. ³⁹Then the army of Israel turned round in the battle.

The Benjaminites had killed about 30 Israelites. They were saying, "We are winning, as in the first battle!" ⁴⁰But then a cloud of smoke began to rise from the city. The Benjaminites turned round and saw that the whole city was going up in smoke. ⁴¹Then the Israelites turned and began to fight. The Benjaminites were terrified because they knew that disaster was coming to them. ⁴²So the Benjaminites ran away from the Israelites towards the desert, but they could not escape the battle. And the Israelites who came out of the cities killed them. ⁴³They surrounded the Benjaminites and chased them and caught them in the area east of Gibeah. ⁴⁴So 18,000 brave Benjaminite fighters were killed. ⁴⁵The Benjaminites ran towards the desert to the rock of Rimmon, but the Israelites killed 5,000 Benjaminites along the roads. They chased them as far as Gidom and killed 2,000 more Benjaminites there.

⁴⁶On that day 25,000 Benjaminites were killed, all of whom had fought bravely with swords. ⁴⁷But 600 Benjaminites ran to the rock of Rimmon in the desert, where they stayed for four months. ⁴⁸Then the Israelites went back to the land of Benjamin and killed the people in every city and also the animals and everything they could find. And they burned every city they found.

Wives for the Men of Benjamin

21 At Mizpah the men of Israel had sworn, "Not one of us will let his daughter marry a man from the tribe^d of Benjamin."

²The people went to the city of Bethel and sat before God until evening, crying loudly. ³They said, "LORD, God of Israel, why has this terrible thing happened to us so that one tribe of Israel is missing today?"

⁴Early the next day the people built an altar and put burnt offerings and fellowship offerings to God on it.

⁵Then the Israelites asked, "Did any tribe of Israel not come here to meet with us in the presence of the LORD?" They asked this question because they had sworn that anyone who did not meet with them at Mizpah would be killed.

⁶The Israelites felt sorry for their relatives, the Benjaminites. They said, "Today one tribe has been cut off from Israel. ⁷We swore before the LORD that we would not allow our daughters to marry a Benjaminite. How can we make sure that the remaining men of Benjamin will have wives?" ⁸Then they asked, "Which one of the tribes of Israel did not come here to Mizpah?" They found that no one from the city of Jabesh Gilead had come. ⁹The people of Israel counted everyone, but there was no one from Jabesh Gilead.

¹⁰So the whole group of Israelites sent 12,000 soldiers to Jabesh Gilead to kill the people with their swords, even the women and children.

¹¹"This is what you must do," they said. "Kill every man in Jabesh Gilead and every married woman." ¹²The soldiers found 400 young unmarried women in Jabesh Gilead, so they brought them to the camp at Shiloh in Canaan.

¹³Then the whole group of Israelites sent a message to the men of Benjamin, who were at the rock of Rimmon, offering to make peace with them. ¹⁴So the men of Benjamin came back at that time. The Israelites gave them the women from Jabesh Gilead who had not been killed, but there were not enough women.

¹⁵The people of Israel felt sorry for the Benjaminites because the LORD had separated the tribes of Israel. ¹⁶The elders of the Israelites said, "The women of Benjamin have been killed. Where can we get wives for the men of Benjamin who are still alive? ¹⁷These men must have children to continue their families so a tribe in Israel will not die out. ¹⁸But we cannot allow our daughters to marry them, because we swore, 'Anyone who gives a wife to a man of Benjamin is cursed.' ¹⁹We have an idea! There is a yearly festival of the LORD at Shiloh, which is north of the city of Bethel, east of the road that goes from Bethel to Shechem, and south of the city of Lebonah."

²⁰So the elders told the men of Benjamin, "Go and hide in the vineyards. ²¹Watch for the young women from Shiloh to come out to join the dancing. Then run out from the vineyards and take one of the young Shiloh women and return to the land of Benjamin. ²²If their fathers or brothers come to us and complain, we will say: 'Be kind to the men of Benjamin. We did not get wives for Benjamin during the war, and you did not give the women to the men from Benjamin. So you are not guilty.'"

²³So that is what the Benjaminites did. While the young women were dancing, each man caught one of them, took her away and married her. Then they went back to the land God had given them and rebuilt their cities and lived there.

²⁴Then the Israelites went home to their own tribes and family groups, to their own land that God had given them.

²⁵In those days Israel did not have a king. Everyone did what seemed right.

Ruth

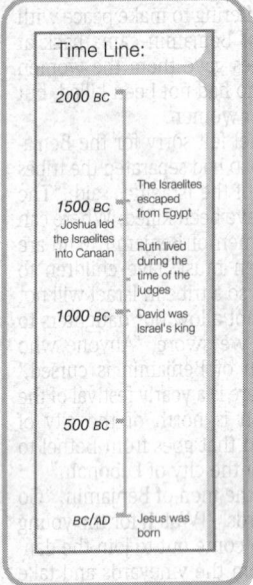

Why Read This Book:
* See how relationships grow strong (Ruth 1—2).
* Discover the importance of keeping agreements (Ruth 3—4).

Behind the Scenes:

The story of Ruth would never have made the evening news. There are no wars, no twisted plots, no villains. In fact, much more "important" things were happening at the time. The story took place during the period of the judges (see Judges, p.224), and Israel faced moral decline, foreign attacks and national chaos.

But in the midst of other seemingly important events, the Bible tells the simple, beautiful story of Ruth. It's a story of loyalty and faithfulness, a story of how ordinary people kept following God even when the nation of Israel was abandoning God.

The story opens in Moab, a non-Jewish area, where Naomi had gone to live. Her son had married a Moabite woman, Ruth. After only ten years, Ruth's husband died. Even though Naomi could have left Ruth, she took her in, and the two became close friends.

Then Ruth and Naomi moved to Israel, Naomi's homeland, where Ruth was a foreigner. There Ruth met Boaz, who married her so that Ruth's family name could continue. Years later, one of Ruth's descendants, David, became the greatest king of Israel. ▷

When?

Time Line:

2000 BC

1500 BC — The Israelites escaped from Egypt
Joshua led the Israelites into Canaan

Ruth lived during the time of the judges

1000 BC — David was Israel's king

500 BC

BC/AD — Jesus was born

Where?

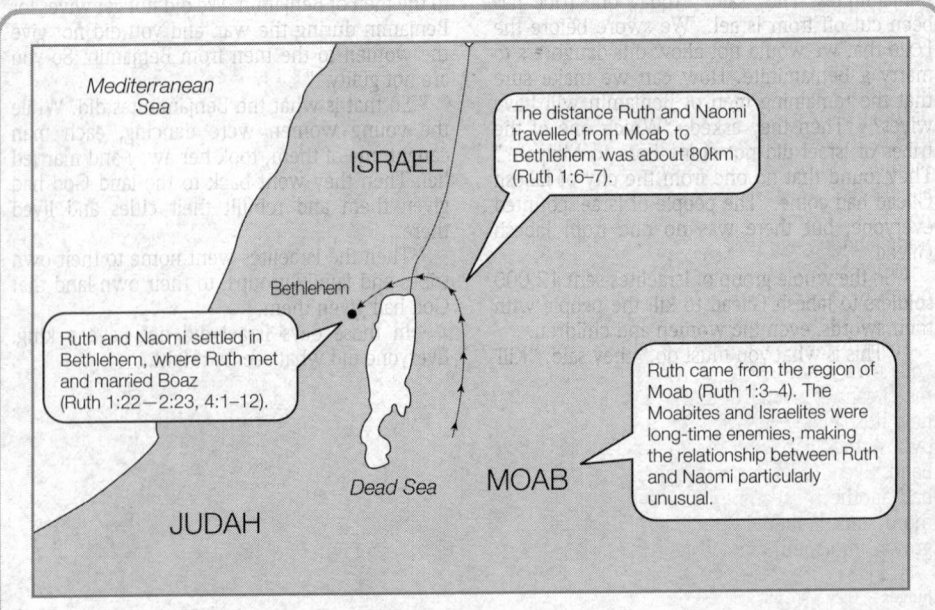

Mediterranean Sea

ISRAEL

Bethlehem

Dead Sea

JUDAH

MOAB

The distance Ruth and Naomi travelled from Moab to Bethlehem was about 80km (Ruth 1:6–7).

Ruth and Naomi settled in Bethlehem, where Ruth met and married Boaz (Ruth 1:22—2:23, 4:1–12).

Ruth came from the region of Moab (Ruth 1:3–4). The Moabites and Israelites were long-time enemies, making the relationship between Ruth and Naomi particularly unusual.

Behind the
Scenes (cont.):
Even more important, because of her marriage Ruth was included in the family of Jesus Christ (see Matthew 1:5, p.936).

The story of Ruth emphasises the importance of faithfulness and loyalty – of one person to another and to God. Each main character – Ruth, Naomi, Boaz – shows a loyalty beyond what's required.

The story also reminds us that we don't have to be famous or do great things to be important to God. What is most important to God is that people are faithful in whatever they do, whether or not they are famous.

---

1 1-2Long ago when the judges *n* ruled Israel, there was a shortage of food in the land. So a man named Elimelech left the town of Bethlehem in Judah to live in the country of Moab with his wife and his two sons. His wife was named Naomi, and his two sons were named Mahlon and Kilion. They were from the Ephrathah district from Bethlehem in Judah. When they came to Moab, they settled there.

3Then Naomi's husband, Elimelech, died, and she was left with her two sons. 4These sons married women from Moab. One was named Orpah and the other was named Ruth. Naomi and her sons had lived in Moab about ten years 5when Mahlon and Kilion also died. So Naomi was left alone without her husband or her two sons.

6While Naomi was in Moab, she heard that the LORD had come to help his people and had given them food again. So she and her daughters-in-law got ready to leave Moab and return home. 7Naomi and her daughters-in-law left the place where they had lived and started back to the land of Judah. 8But Naomi said to her two daughters-in-law, "Go back home, each of you to your own mother's house. May the LORD be as kind to you as you have been to me and my sons who are now dead. 9May the LORD give you another happy home and a new husband."

When Naomi kissed the women goodbye, they began to cry out loud. 10They said to her, "No, we want to go with you to your people."

11But Naomi said, "My daughters, return to your own homes. Why do you want to go with me? I cannot give birth to more sons to give you new husbands; 12go back, my daughters, to your own homes. I am too old to have another husband. Even if I told myself, 'I still have hope' and had another husband tonight, and even if I had more sons, 13should you wait until they were grown into men? Should you live for so many

years without husbands? Don't do that, my daughters. My life is much too sad for you to share, because the LORD has been against me!"

14The women cried together out loud again. Then Orpah kissed her mother-in-law Naomi goodbye, but Ruth held on to her tightly.

15Naomi said to Ruth, "Look, your sister-in-law is going back to her own people and her own gods. Go back with her."

Ruth Stays with Naomi

16But Ruth said, "Don't beg me to leave you or to stop following you. Where you go, I will go. Where you live, I will live. Your people will be my people, and your God will be my God. 17And where you die, I will die, and there I will be buried. I ask the LORD to punish me terribly if I do not keep this promise: not even death will separate us."

18When Naomi saw that Ruth had firmly made up her mind to go with her, she stopped arguing with her. 19So Naomi and Ruth went on until they came to the town of Bethlehem. When they entered Bethlehem, all the people became very excited. The women of the town said, "Is this really Naomi?"

20Naomi answered the people, "Don't call me Naomi. *n* Call me Mara, *n* because the Almighty has made my life very sad. 21When I left, I had all I wanted, but now, the LORD has brought me home with nothing. Why should you call me Naomi when the LORD has spoken against me and the Almighty has given me so much trouble?"

22So Naomi and her daughter-in-law Ruth, the Moabite, returned from Moab and arrived at Bethlehem at the beginning of the barley harvest.

Ruth Meets Boaz

2 Now Naomi had a rich relative named Boaz, from Elimelech's family.

---

judges They were not judges in courts of law, but leaders of the people in times of emergency.
Naomi This name means "happy" or "pleasant".
Mara This name means "bitter" or "sad".

²One day Ruth, the Moabite, said to Naomi, "I am going to the fields. Maybe someone will be kind enough to let me gather the grain he leaves behind."

Naomi said, "Go, my daughter."

³So Ruth went to the fields and gathered the grain that the workers cutting the grain had left behind. It just so happened that the field belonged to Boaz, from Elimelech's family.

Sidelight

When Ruth went to Boaz's field to harvest barley (Ruth 2:1–3), she wasn't stealing. Deuteronomy 24:19–21 (p.187) commanded farmers to leave some of the grain in the field so that the poor could harvest it.

⁴Soon Boaz came from Bethlehem and greeted his workers, "The Lord be with you!"

And the workers answered, "May the Lord bless you!"

⁵Then Boaz asked his servant in charge of the workers, "Whose girl is that?"

⁶The servant answered, "She is the young Moabite woman who came back with Naomi from the country of Moab. ⁷She said, 'Please let me follow the workers cutting grain and gather what they leave behind.' She came and has remained here, from morning until just now. She has stopped only a few moments to rest in the shelter."

⁸Then Boaz said to Ruth, "Listen, my daughter. Don't go to gather grain for yourself in another field. Don't even leave this field at all, but continue following closely behind my women workers. ⁹Watch to see into which fields they go to cut grain and follow them. I have warned the young men not to bother you. When you are thirsty, you may go and drink from the water jugs that the young men have filled."

¹⁰Then Ruth bowed low with her face to the ground and said to him, "I am not an Israelite. Why have you been so kind to notice me?"

¹¹Boaz answered her, "I know about all the help you have given your mother-in-law after your husband died. You left your father and mother and your own country to come to a nation where you did not know anyone. ¹²May the

FRIENDS

A Little Encouragement

Bruce would lie awake at night waiting to hear the sound of a car driving up. When he did, he would run to the front door to unlock it. Then he would cry with fear as his stepfather stumbled in, reeking of alcohol. Doors slammed. Dishes broke in the kitchen. The horrible yelling at his mother made Bruce wish his alcoholic stepfather would die.

Bruce might have gone mad if it hadn't been for friends like Tom. Tom was a year older than Bruce. The two laughed a lot together, and Tom taught Bruce how to fix cars. Whenever Tom gave Bruce a lift somewhere, he would end the trip by saying, "Stay cool, Bruce." Bruce knew he meant, "Hang on in there."

Those were hard times for Bruce, but he survived because of his friends – people like Tom.

Ruth and Naomi also faced hard times. Both lost their husbands, and Naomi also lost both her sons. But because of their friendship with each other, they got through it all. Read about their relationship in **Ruth 1:1–19**.

• How were Bruce's and Ruth's situations made better by friends?
• How can Ruth's example help you be a more committed friend?

Consider . . .

• befriending a newcomer at school or someone with a different background from you.
• being a committed friend to someone who is facing hard times by letting him or her talk openly about their problems.

For more, see . . .

• Leviticus 19:9–10 (p.118)
• 1 John 3:11–18 (p.1374)
• 1 Samuel 20:11–17 (p.274)

Lᴏʀᴅ reward you for all you have done. May your wages be paid in full by the Lᴏʀᴅ, the God of Israel, under whose wings you have come for shelter."

¹³Then Ruth said, "I hope I can continue to please you, sir. You have said kind and encouraging words to me, your servant, though I am not one of your servants."

¹⁴At mealtime Boaz told Ruth, "Come here. Eat some of our bread and dip it in our vinegar."

So Ruth sat down beside the workers. Boaz handed her some roasted grain, and she ate until she was full; she even had some food left over. ¹⁵When Ruth rose and went back to work, Boaz commanded his workers, "Let her gather even around the piles of cut grain. Don't tell her to go away. ¹⁶In fact, drop some full heads of grain for her from what you have in your hands, and let her gather them. Don't tell her to stop."

¹⁷So Ruth gathered grain in the field until evening. Then she separated the grain from the chaff, ᵈ and there was about 10 kilogrammes of barley. ¹⁸Ruth carried the grain into town, and her mother-in-law saw how much she had gathered. Ruth also took out the food that was left over from lunch and gave it to Naomi.

¹⁹Naomi asked her, "Where did you gather all this grain today? Where did you work? Blessed be whoever noticed you!"

Ruth told her mother-in-law whose field she had worked in. She said, "The man I worked with today is named Boaz."

²⁰Naomi told her daughter-in-law, "The Lᴏʀᴅ bless him! He continues to be kind to us—both the living and the dead!" Then Naomi told Ruth, "Boaz is one of our close relatives, ⁿ one who should take care of us."

²¹Then Ruth, the Moabite, said, "Boaz also told me, 'Keep close to my workers until they have finished my whole harvest.'"

²²But Naomi said to her daughter-in-law Ruth, "It is better for you to continue working with his women workers. If you work in another field, someone might hurt you." ²³So Ruth continued working closely with the workers of Boaz, gathering grain until the barley harvest and the wheat harvest were finished. And she continued to live with Naomi, her mother-in-law.

Naomi's Plan

3 Then Naomi, Ruth's mother-in-law, said to her, "My daughter, I must find a suitable home for you, one that will be good for you.

²Now Boaz, whose young women you worked with, is our close relative. ⁿ Tonight he will be working at the threshing ᵈ floor. ³Wash yourself, put on perfume, change your clothes and go down to the threshing floor. But don't let him know you're there until he has finished his dinner. ⁴Watch him so you will know where he lies down to sleep. When he lies down, go and lift the cover off his feet ⁿ and lie down. He will tell you what you should do."

⁵Then Ruth answered, "I will do everything you say."

⁶So Ruth went down to the threshing floor and did all her mother-in-law told her to do. ⁷After his evening meal, Boaz felt good and went to sleep lying beside the pile of grain. Ruth went to him quietly and lifted the cover from his feet and lay down.

⁸About midnight Boaz was startled and rolled over. There was a woman lying near his feet! ⁹Boaz asked, "Who are you?"

She said, "I am Ruth, your servant girl. Spread your cover over me, because you are a relative who is supposed to take care of me." ⁿ

¹⁰Then Boaz said, "The Lᴏʀᴅ bless you, my daughter. This act of kindness is greater than the kindness you showed to Naomi in the beginning. You didn't look for a young man to marry, either rich or poor. ¹¹Now, my daughter, don't be afraid. I will do everything you ask, because all the people in our town know you are a good woman. ¹²It is true that I am a relative who is to take care of you, but you have a closer relative than I. ¹³Stay here tonight, and in the morning we will see if he will take care of you. If he decides to take care of you, that is fine. But if he refuses, I will take care of you myself, as surely as the Lᴏʀᴅ lives. So stay here until morning."

¹⁴So Ruth stayed near his feet until morning but got up while it was still too dark to recognise anyone. Boaz thought, "People in town must not know that the woman came here to the threshing floor." ¹⁵So Boaz said to Ruth, "Bring me your shawl and hold it open."

So Ruth held her shawl open, and Boaz poured six portions of barley into it. Boaz then put it on her head and went back to the city.

¹⁶When Ruth went back to her mother-in-law, Naomi asked, "How did you do, my daughter?"

Ruth told Naomi everything that Boaz did for her. ¹⁷She said, "Boaz gave me these six portions of barley, saying, 'You must not go home without a gift for your mother-in-law.'"

---

close relatives In Bible times the closest relative could marry a widow without children so she could have children. He would care for this family, but they and their property would not belong to him. They would belong to the dead husband.
lift . . . feet This showed Ruth was asking him to be her husband.
Spread . . . me By this, Ruth was asking Boaz to marry her.

¹⁸Naomi answered, "Ruth, my daughter, wait here until you see what happens. Boaz will not rest until he has finished doing what he should do today."

Boaz Marries Ruth

4 Boaz went to the city gate and sat there until the close relative he had mentioned passed by. Boaz called to him, "Come here, friend, and sit down." So the man came over and sat down. ²Boaz gathered ten of the elders of the city and told them, "Sit down here!" So they sat down.

³Then Boaz said to the close relative, "Naomi, who has come back from the country of Moab, wants to sell the piece of land that belonged to our relative Elimelech. ⁴So I decided to tell you about it. If you want to buy back the land, then buy it in front of the people who are sitting here and in front of the elders of my people. But if you don't want to buy it, tell me, because you are the only one who can buy it, and I am next after you."

The close relative answered, "I will buy back the land."

⁵Then Boaz explained, "When you buy the land from Naomi, you must also marry Ruth, the Moabite, the dead man's wife. That way, the land will stay in the dead man's name."

⁶The close relative answered, "I can't buy back the land. If I did, I might harm what I can pass on to my own sons. I cannot buy the land back, so buy it yourself."

⁷Long ago in Israel when people traded or bought back something, one person took off his sandal and gave it to the other person. This was the proof of purchase in Israel.

⁸So the close relative said to Boaz, "Buy the land yourself," and he took off his sandal.

MARRIAGE

What a Drag!

Fran was nervous – she always was when she was watching her fiancé Andrew prepare for a race. It wasn't that he was a bad driver – but even some of the best drag racers had been killed. All she could do was to watch and pray.

His team closed the cockpit of the dragster and Andrew nudged it forwards to the starting line. The flag came down and his foot slammed down hard on the accelerator. A drag race only lasted a few seconds, so there was never any time to think about anything.

And then it happened. Fran screamed as Andrew's car flipped over and rolled under the crash barrier. The emergency team ran to the overturned racer and helped Andrew out; he was badly shaken, but not hurt. Fran ran to him, with tears running down her face, relieved that he was all right.

Andrew removed his helmet and took a hard look, first at his wrecked racer, and then at his fiancée. Taking a breath he said, "This is no good. I hate seeing you hurt so much every time I race. I've decided to quit. If nothing else, it will show you how much you mean to me."

Andrew showed his commitment to Fran by giving up the sport that he loved. When Boaz married Ruth, he also demonstrated his commitment to her. Read all about it in **Ruth 4:7–17**.

- How did Boaz demonstrate his commitment to Ruth? How does this compare with the way Andrew showed his commitment to Fran?
- What can you learn from this passage about what is most important when choosing a husband or wife?

Consider . . .

- writing a list of characteristics that you would hope to find in a marriage partner. Review this list, bearing in mind your faith and commitments.
- asking a married couple that you know about their commitment to each other and how it maintains a strong relationship.

For more, see . . .

- Genesis 29:15–30 (p.34)
- Ephesians 5:21–33 (p.1275)
- Matthew 19:4–6 (p.974)

[9]Then Boaz said to the elders and to all the people, "You are witnesses today. I am buying from Naomi everything that belonged to Elimelech and Kilion and Mahlon. [10]I am also taking Ruth, the Moabite who was the wife of Mahlon, as my wife. I am doing this so her dead husband's

---

Sidelight   Once Ruth had chosen God (Ruth 1:16) and remained faithful to him, her life changed – from having nothing in Chapter 1, she slowly reaped God's blessings. Once she was married to Boaz, she came to be the great-grandmother of King David and an ancestor of Jesus.

---

property will stay in his name and his name will not be separated from his family and his home town. You are witnesses today."

[11]So all the people and elders who were at the city gate said, "We are witnesses. May the LORD make this woman, who is coming into your home, like Rachel and Leah, who had many children and built up the people of Israel. May you become powerful in the district of Ephrathah and famous in Bethlehem. [12]As Tamar gave birth to Judah's son Perez,[n] may the LORD give you many children through Ruth. May your family be great like his."

[13]So Boaz took Ruth home as his wife and had sexual relations with her. The LORD let her become pregnant, and she gave birth to a son. [14]The women told Naomi, "Praise the LORD who gave you this grandson. May he become famous in Israel. [15]He will give you new life and will take care of you in your old age because of your daughter-in-law who loves you. She is better for you than seven sons, because she has given birth to your grandson."

[16]Naomi took the boy, held him in her arms and cared for him. [17]The neighbours gave the boy his name, saying, "This boy was born for Naomi." They named him Obed. Obed was the father of Jesse, and Jesse was the father of David.

[18]This is the family history of Perez, the father of Hezron. [19]Hezron was the father of Ram, who was the father of Amminadab. [20]Amminadab was the father of Nahshon, who was the father of Salmon. [21]Salmon was the father of Boaz, who was the father of Obed. [22]Obed was the father of Jesse, and Jesse was the father of David.

Perez   One of Boaz's ancestors.

1 Samuel

Why Read This Book:

- See how God uses great leaders (1 Samuel 1—7).
- Discover what can happen when leaders don't obey God (1 Samuel 8—15).
- Find out how God can unite a nation under a holy leader (1 Samuel 16—31).

When?

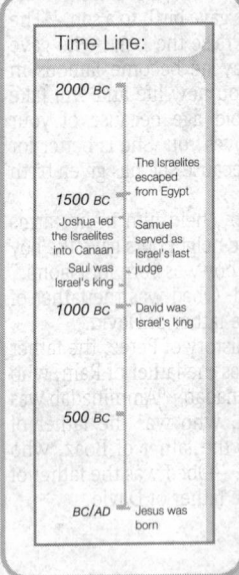

Time Line:

2000 BC

The Israelites escaped from Egypt

1500 BC

Joshua led the Israelites into Canaan

Samuel served as Israel's last judge

Saul was Israel's king

1000 BC

David was Israel's king

500 BC

BC/AD — Jesus was born

Behind the Scenes:

The pupils of the comprehensive school didn't get along very well with the pupils from the neighbouring school. There wasn't any reason for their dislike. The simple fact was that they preferred to keep themselves to themselves.

But when the local council announced that it was going to close the nearby sports centre, the pupils forgot their differences and united to fight the closure. The sports centre was an important facility which both schools used on a regular basis, and so the pupils got together and organised a protest march. A week later, the local council announced that they had changed their minds about the sports centre, and reassured both schools that it would remain open for their use.

At the time of Samuel, the Israelites lived in a similar situation. The twelve tribes existed independently, but always in fear of the Philistines who possessed superior iron weapons and controlled the fertile plains along the Mediterranean Sea – but wanted more. They wanted to conquer the Israelites and take their land too. ▷

Where?

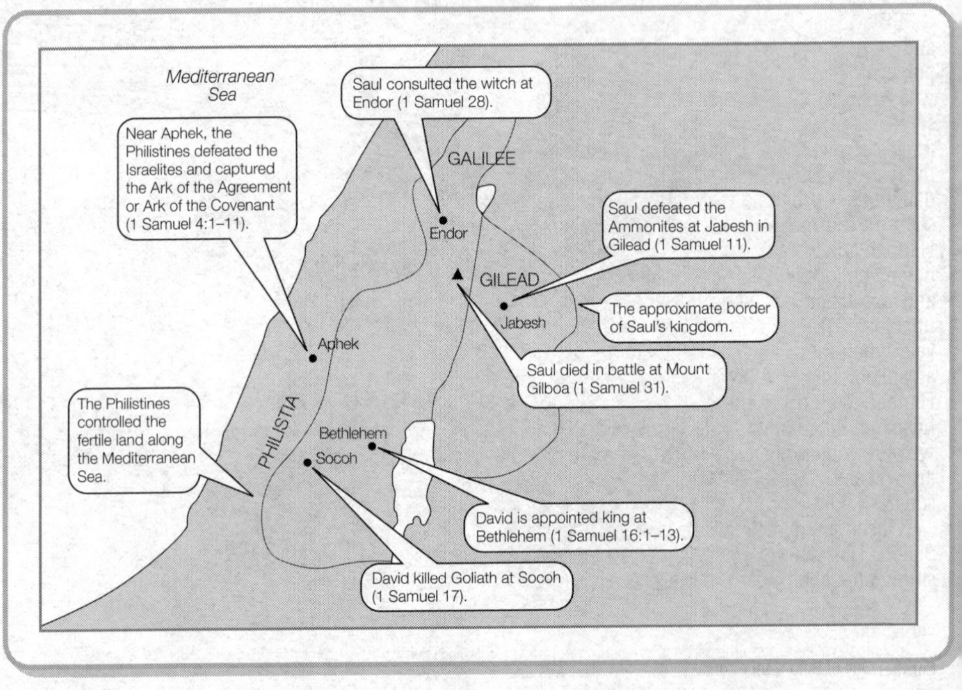

Mediterranean Sea

Saul consulted the witch at Endor (1 Samuel 28).

Near Aphek, the Philistines defeated the Israelites and captured the Ark of the Agreement or Ark of the Covenant (1 Samuel 4:1–11).

GALILEE

Endor

Saul defeated the Ammonites at Jabesh in Gilead (1 Samuel 11).

GILEAD

Jabesh

The approximate border of Saul's kingdom.

Aphek

Saul died in battle at Mount Gilboa (1 Samuel 31).

The Philistines controlled the fertile land along the Mediterranean Sea.

PHILISTIA

Bethlehem

Socoh

David is appointed king at Bethlehem (1 Samuel 16:1–13).

David killed Goliath at Socoh (1 Samuel 17).

**Behind the
Scenes (cont.):** In order to survive, the twelve tribes united and elected Samuel as their common leader. Samuel changed Israel's history. He stopped the Philistines from advancing, and then went on to appoint Israel's first two kings: King Saul and King David.

1 Samuel contains some of the most exciting stories in the Bible, including Saul's spectacular victories over the Philistines, David's famous battle with Goliath, and David's friendship with Jonathan. Through the stories 1 Samuel teaches us about the importance of having leaders who follow God.

Samuel's Birth

1 There was a man named Elkanah son of Jeroham from Ramathaim in the mountains of Ephraim. Elkanah was from the family of Zuph. (Jeroham was Elihu's son. Elihu was Tohu's son, and Tohu was the son of Zuph from the family group of Ephraim.) ²Elkanah had two wives named Hannah and Peninnah. Peninnah had children, but Hannah had none.

> **Sidelight**
> 1 and 2 Samuel
> were originally one book.
> The prophet Samuel – after whom the books were named – doesn't actually appear in 2 Samuel.

³Every year Elkanah left his town of Ramah and went up to Shiloh to worship the LORD All-powerful *d* and to offer sacrifices to him. Shiloh was where Hophni and Phinehas, the sons of Eli, served as priests of the LORD. ⁴When Elkanah offered sacrifices, he always gave a share of the meat to his wife Peninnah and to her sons and daughters. ⁵But Elkanah always gave a special share of the meat to Hannah, because he loved Hannah and because the LORD had kept her from having children. ⁶Peninnah would tease Hannah and upset her, because the LORD had made her unable to have children. ⁷This happened every year when they went up to the house of the LORD at Shiloh. Peninnah would upset Hannah until Hannah would cry and not eat anything. ⁸Her husband Elkanah would say to her, "Hannah, why are you crying and why won't you eat? Why are you sad? Don't I mean more to you than ten sons?"

⁹Once, after they had eaten their meal in Shiloh, Hannah got up. Now Eli the priest was sitting on a chair near the entrance to the LORD's house. ¹⁰Hannah was so sad that she cried and prayed to the LORD. ¹¹She made a promise, saying, "LORD All-powerful, see how sad I am. Remember me and don't forget me. If you will give me a son, I will give him back to you all his life, and no one will ever cut his hair with a razor."*n*

¹²While Hannah kept praying, Eli watched her mouth. ¹³She was praying in her heart so her lips moved, but her voice was not heard. Eli thought she was drunk ¹⁴and said to her, "Stop getting drunk! Throw away your wine!"

¹⁵Hannah answered, "No, sir, I have not drunk any wine or beer. I am a deeply troubled woman, and I was telling the LORD about all my problems. ¹⁶Don't think I am an evil woman. I have been praying because I have many troubles and am very sad."

¹⁷Eli answered, "Go! I wish you well. May the God of Israel give you what you asked of him."

¹⁸Hannah said, "May I always please you." When she left and ate something, she was not sad any more.

¹⁹Early the next morning Elkanah's family got up and worshipped the LORD. Then they went back home to Ramah. Elkanah had sexual relations with his wife Hannah, and the LORD remembered her. ²⁰So Hannah became pregnant, and in time she gave birth to a son. She named him Samuel, *n* saying, "His name is Samuel because I asked the LORD for him."

Hannah Gives Samuel to God

²¹Every year Elkanah went with his whole family to Shiloh to offer sacrifices and to keep the promise he had made to God. ²²But one year Hannah did not go with him. She told him, "When the boy is old enough to eat solid food, I will take him to Shiloh. Then I will give him to the LORD, and he will always live there."

---

cut . . . razor People who made special promises not to cut their hair or to drink wine or beer were called Nazirites. These people gave a specific time in their lives, or sometimes their entire lives, to the LORD. See Numbers 6:1–5.
Samuel This name sounds like the Hebrew word for "God heard".

²³Elkanah, Hannah's husband, said to her, "Do what you think is best. You may stay home until the boy is old enough to eat. May the LORD do what you have said." So Hannah stayed at home to nurse her son until he was old enough to eat.

²⁴When Samuel was old enough to eat, Hannah took him to the house of the LORD at Shiloh, along with a three-year-old bull, ten kilogrammes of flour, and a leather bag filled with wine. ²⁵After they had killed the bull for the sacrifice, Hannah brought Samuel to Eli. ²⁶She said to Eli, "As surely as you live, sir, I am the same woman who stood near you praying to the LORD. ²⁷I prayed for this child, and the LORD answered my prayer and gave him to me. ²⁸Now I give him back to the LORD. He will belong to the LORD all his life." And he worshipped the LORD there.

Hannah Gives Thanks

2 Hannah prayed:

"The LORD has filled my heart with joy;
I feel very strong in the LORD.
I can laugh at my enemies;
I am glad because you have helped me!

²"There is no one holy like the LORD.
There is no God but you;
there is no Rock *d* like our God.

³"Don't continue boasting,
don't speak proud words.
The LORD is a God who knows everything,
and he judges what people do.

⁴"The bows of warriors break,
but weak people become strong.
⁵Those who once had plenty of food now
must work for food,
but people who were hungry are hungry no
more.
The woman who could not have children
now has seven,
but the woman who had many children
now is sad.

BOASTING

She Spoke Too Soon

Elaine knew she was good looking. Stylish hair. Perfect complexion. Long eyelashes. Flawless figure. Whenever she had a chance, she would point out her own beauty and ridicule the "plain" girls. "Don't you care how you look?" she would say if someone's hair wasn't carefully curled or if make-up didn't hide every spot. "You really should take care of yourself . . . like I do."

When it was time for the local beauty contest, everyone knew Elaine would enter. And Elaine knew she would win. "Who round here can compete with me?" she would sneer.

As it turned out, Laura could. Laura entered the pageant because she wanted extra cash to eke out her college grant. And although she wasn't as strikingly beautiful as Elaine, her personality and smile gave her the edge.

When Laura was crowned, Elaine didn't even congratulate her. She burst into tears and stormed off the stage. "The judges are just stupid!" she cried, alone in the dressing room. "This whole thing is stupid!"

Elaine discovered how dangerous and humiliating boasting can be. Read **1 Samuel 2:1–10** to see what God thinks of people who boast.

- How does the passage describe what happened to Elaine? What does it say about Laura?
- What caution about events like beauty contests do you see?

Consider . . .

- stopping yourself next time you're tempted to boast about a high score or success. Instead, use your gifts to help others.
- thanking God for the gifts you have, instead of boasting about them.

For more, see . . .

- Proverbs 16:18–20 (p.603)   • Jeremiah 9:23–24 (p.728)
- Luke 1:46–55 (p.1037)

⁶"The Lord sends death,
   and he brings to life.
He sends people to the grave,
   and he raises them to life again.
⁷The Lord makes some people poor,
   and others he makes rich.
He makes some people humble,
   and others he makes great.
⁸The Lord raises the poor up from the dust,
   and he lifts the needy from the ashes.
He lets the poor sit with princes
   and receive a throne of honour.

"The foundations of the earth belong to the
   Lord,
   and the Lord set the world upon them.
⁹He protects those who are loyal to him,
   but evil people will be silenced in darkness.
Power is not the key to success.
¹⁰The Lord destroys his enemies;
   he will thunder in heaven against them.
The Lord will judge all the earth.
He will give power to his king
   and make his appointed king strong."

Eli's Evil Sons

¹¹Then Elkanah went home to Ramah, but the boy continued to serve the Lord under Eli the priest.

¹²Now Eli's sons were evil men; they did not care about the Lord. ¹³This is what the priests would normally do to the people: every time someone brought a sacrifice, the meat would be cooked in a pot. The priest's servant would then come carrying a fork that had three prongs. ¹⁴He would plunge the fork into the pot or the kettle. Whatever the fork brought out of the pot belonged to the priest. But this is how they treated all the Israelites who came to Shiloh to offer sacrifices. ¹⁵Even before the fat was burned, the priest's servant would come to the person offering sacrifices and say, "Give the priest some meat to roast. He won't accept boiled meat from you, only raw meat."

¹⁶If the one who offered the sacrifice said, "Let the fat be burned up first as usual, and then take anything you want," the priest's servant would answer, "No, give me the meat now. If you don't, I'll take it by force."

¹⁷The Lord saw that the sin of the servants was very great because they did not show respect for the offerings made to the Lord.

Samuel Grows Up

¹⁸But Samuel obeyed the Lord. As a boy he wore a linen holy robe.^d ¹⁹Every year Samuel's mother made a little coat for him and took it to

him when she went with her husband to Shiloh for the sacrifice. ²⁰When Eli blessed Elkanah and his wife, he would say, "May the Lord repay you with children through Hannah to take the place of the boy Hannah prayed for and gave back to the Lord." Then Elkanah and Hannah would go home. ²¹The Lord was kind to Hannah, so she became the mother of three sons and two daughters. And the boy Samuel grew up serving the Lord.

²²Now Eli was very old. He heard about everything his sons were doing to all the Israelites and how his sons had sexual relations with the women who served at the entrance to the Meeting Tent. ^d ²³Eli said to his sons, "Why do you do these evil things that the people tell me about? ²⁴No, my sons. The Lord's people are spreading a bad report about you. ²⁵If you sin against someone, God can help you. But if you sin against the Lord himself, no one can help you!" But Eli's sons would not listen to him, because the Lord had decided to put them to death.

²⁶The boy Samuel grew physically. He pleased the Lord and the people.

²⁷A man of God came to Eli and said, "This is what the Lord says: 'I clearly showed myself to the family of your ancestor Aaron when they were slaves to the king of Egypt. ²⁸I chose them from all the tribes ^d of Israel to be my priests. I wanted them to go up to my altar, to burn incense ^d and to wear the holy robe. I also let the family of your ancestor have part of all the offerings sacrificed by the Israelites. ²⁹So why don't you respect the sacrifices and gifts? You honour your sons more than me. You grow fat on the best parts of the meat the Israelites bring to me.'

³⁰"So the Lord, the God of Israel, says: 'I promised that your family and your ancestor's family would serve me always.' But now the Lord says: 'This must stop! I will honour those who honour me, but I will dishonour those who ignore me. ³¹The time is coming when I will destroy the descendants ^d of both you and your ancestors. No man will grow old in your family. ³²You will see trouble in my house. No matter what good things happen to Israel, there will never be an old man in your family. ³³I will not totally cut off your family from my altar. But your eyes will cry and your heart will be sad, because all your descendants will die.

³⁴" 'I will give you a sign. Both your sons, Hophni and Phinehas, will die on the same day. ³⁵I will choose a loyal priest for myself who will listen to me and do what I want. I will make his family continue, and he will always serve before my appointed king. ³⁶Then everyone left in your family will come and bow down before him.

They will beg for a little money or a little food and say, "Please give me a job as priest so I can have food to eat." ' "

God Calls Samuel

3 The boy Samuel served the LORD under Eli. In those days the LORD did not speak directly to people very often; there were very few visions.

2Eli's eyes were so weak he was almost blind. One night he was lying in bed. 3Samuel was also in bed in the LORD's house, where the Ark *d* of the Agreement was. God's lamp was still burning.

4Then the LORD called Samuel, and Samuel answered, "I am here!" 5He ran to Eli and said, "I am here. You called me."

But Eli said, "I didn't call you. Go back to bed." So Samuel went back to bed.

6The LORD called again, "Samuel!"

Samuel again went to Eli and said, "I am here. You called me."

Again Eli said, "I didn't call you. Go back to bed."

7Samuel did not yet know the LORD, and the LORD had not spoken directly to him yet.

8The LORD called Samuel for the third time. Samuel got up and went to Eli and said, "I am here. You called me."

Then Eli realised the LORD was calling the boy. 9So he told Samuel, "Go to bed. If he calls you again, say, 'Speak, LORD. I am your servant and I am listening.' " So Samuel went and lay down in bed.

10The LORD came and stood there and called as he had before, "Samuel, Samuel!"

Samuel said, "Speak, LORD. I am your servant and I am listening."

FOLLOWING GOD

Did Someone Call?

From the time she learned to play the flute, Jessica wanted to be a musician. She spent hours practising her flute for the school orchestra.

When Jessica wasn't practising her music, she was working on the school magazine. She hadn't planned on doing it, but her teacher had asked her to be magazine editor.

"I know you love music," her teacher told her, "but maybe you're overlooking your writing gifts."

Jessica dismissed the thought and kept concentrating on music. She regularly entered music competitions, hoping to get into a good music college. She did well in regional competitions, but never at national level. However, when the school magazine was entered in a national competition, it won first place.

"What's going on?" Jessica wondered, as she filled out applications for music schools. Her teacher's words came to mind: "Maybe you're overlooking your writing gifts."

Jessica went to music college, but didn't do well. She didn't enjoy all the theory and hours of practise. To lift her spirits, she went to work at the college newspaper. Now that was fun!

After the first term, she knew what she had to do. She dropped music and switched to English and communications.

"It took me a while to figure out what to do," she recalls. "I'm glad I finally paid attention to the gifts God gave me."

It took several years for Jessica to understand how God wanted her to use her gifts. Similarly, Samuel didn't recognise God's call right away in **1 Samuel 3:1–20**. But by listening to the advice of Eli the priest, Samuel heard and followed God's call.

- What signs did Jessica see that were similar to the calls Samuel heard?
- When have you, like Samuel, had trouble knowing what God wanted you to do?

Consider . . .

- silently listening for God's direction when you pray.
- asking someone you respect to help you figure out ways God might want you to follow him.

For more, see . . .

- Isaiah 6:1–8 (p.645)
- Acts 9:1–19 (p.1152)
- Mark 1:16–20 (p.997)

[11]The LORD said to Samuel, "Watch, I am going to do something in Israel that will shock those who hear about it. [12]At that time I will do to Eli and his family everything I promised, from beginning to end. [13]I told Eli I would punish his family always, because he knew his sons were evil. They acted without honour, but he did not stop them. [14]So I swore to Eli's family, 'Your guilt will never be removed by sacrifice or offering.'"

[15]Samuel lay down until morning. Then he opened the doors of the house of the LORD. He was afraid to tell Eli about the vision, [16]but Eli called to him, "Samuel, my son!"

Samuel answered, "I am here."

[17]Eli asked, "What did the LORD say to you? Don't hide it from me. May God punish you terribly if you hide from me anything he said to you."

[18]So Samuel told Eli everything and did not hide anything from him. Then Eli said, "He is the LORD. Let him do what he thinks is best."

[19]The LORD was with Samuel as he grew up; he did not let any of Samuel's messages fail to come true. [20]Then all Israel, from Dan to Beersheba, [n] knew Samuel was a true prophet [d] of the LORD. [21]And the LORD continued to show himself at Shiloh, and he showed himself to Samuel through his word.

4 So, news about Samuel spread through all of Israel.

The Philistines Capture the Ark of the Agreement

At that time the Israelites went out to fight the Philistines. The Israelites camped at Ebenezer and the Philistines at Aphek. [2]The Philistines went to meet the Israelites in battle. And as the battle spread, they defeated the Israelites, killing about 4,000 soldiers on the battlefield. [3]When some Israelite soldiers went back to their camp, the elders of Israel asked, "Why did the LORD let the Philistines defeat us? Let's bring the Ark [d] of the Agreement with the LORD here from Shiloh and take it with us into battle. Then God will save us from our enemies."

[4]So the people sent men to Shiloh. They brought back the Ark of the Agreement with the LORD All-powerful, who sits between the gold creatures with wings. Eli's two sons, Hophni and Phinehas, were there with the Ark.

[5]When the Ark of the Agreement with the LORD came into the camp, all the Israelites gave a great shout of joy that made the ground shake. [6]When the Philistines heard Israel's shout, they asked, "What's all this shouting in the Hebrew camp?"

Then the Philistines found out that the Ark of the LORD had come into the Hebrew camp. [7]They were afraid and said, "A god has come into the Hebrew camp! We're in trouble! This has never happened before! [8]How terrible it will be for us! Who can save us from these powerful gods? They are the ones who struck the Egyptians with all kinds of disasters in the desert. [9]Be brave, Philistines! Fight like men! In the past they were our slaves. So fight like men, or we will become their slaves."

[10]So the Philistines fought hard and defeated the Israelites, and every Israelite soldier ran away to his own home. It was a great defeat for Israel, because 30,000 Israelite soldiers were killed. [11]The Ark of God was taken by the Philistines, and Eli's two sons, Hophni and Phinehas, died.

[12]That same day a man from the tribe [d] of Benjamin ran from the battle. He tore his clothes and put dust on his head to show his great sadness. [13]When he arrived in Shiloh, Eli was by the side of the road. He was sitting there in a chair, watching, because he was worried about the Ark of God. When the Benjaminite entered Shiloh, he told the bad news. Then all the people in town cried loudly. [14]Eli heard the crying and asked, "What's all this noise?"

The Benjaminite ran to Eli and told him what had happened. [15]Eli was now 98 years old, and he was blind. [16]The Benjaminite told him, "I have come from the battle. I ran all the way here today."

Eli asked, "What happened, my son?"

[17]The Benjaminite answered, "Israel ran away from the Philistines, and the Israelite army has lost many soldiers. Your two sons are both dead, and the Philistines have taken the Ark of God."

[18]When he mentioned the Ark of God, Eli fell backwards off his chair. He fell beside the gate, broke his neck, and died, because he was old and fat. He had led Israel for 40 years.

> **Sidelight** Have you ever been told not to lean back on your chair? You could fall over backwards. Eli did . . . and died (1 Samuel 4:18).

The Glory is Gone

[19]Eli's daughter-in-law, the wife of Phinehas, was pregnant and was about to give birth. When she heard the news that the Ark [d] of God had been taken and that Eli, her father-in-law, and Phinehas, her husband, were both dead, she

Dan to Beersheba Dan was the city farthest north in Israel, and Beersheba was the city farthest south. So this means all the people of Israel.

began to give birth to her child. The child was born, but the mother had much trouble in giving birth. [20]As she was dying, the women who helped her said, "Don't worry! You've given birth to a son!" But she did not answer or pay attention. [21]She named the baby Ichabod, [n] saying, "Israel's glory is gone." She said this because the Ark of God had been taken and her father-in-law and husband were dead. [22]She said, "Israel's glory is gone, because the Ark of God has been taken away."

Trouble for the Philistines

5 After the Philistines had captured the Ark [d] of God, they took it from Ebenezer to Ashdod. [2]They carried it into Dagon's [d] temple and put it next to Dagon. [3]When the people of Ashdod rose early the next morning, they found that Dagon had fallen on his face on the ground before the Ark of the LORD. So they put Dagon back in his place. [4]The next morning when they rose, they again found Dagon fallen on the ground before the Ark of the LORD. His head and hands had broken off and were lying in the doorway. Only his body was still in one piece. [5]So, even today, Dagon's priests and others who enter his temple at Ashdod refuse to step on the doorsill.

[6]The LORD was hard on the people of Ashdod and their neighbours. He caused them to suffer and gave them growths on their skin. [7]When the people of Ashdod saw what was happening, they said, "The Ark of the God of Israel can't stay with us. God is punishing us and Dagon our god." [8]The people of Ashdod called all five Philistine kings together and asked them, "What should we do with the Ark of the God of Israel?"

The rulers answered, "Move the Ark of the God of Israel to Gath." So the Philistines moved it to Gath.

[9]But after they moved it to Gath, there was a great panic. The LORD was hard on that city also, and he gave both old and young people in Gath growths on their skin. [10]Then the Philistines sent the Ark of God to Ekron.

But when it came into Ekron, the people of Ekron yelled, "Why are you bringing the Ark of the God of Israel to our city? Do you want to kill us and our people?" [11]So they called all the kings of the Philistines together and said, "Send the Ark of the God of Israel back to its place before it kills us and our people!" All the people in the city were struck with terror because God was so hard on them there. [12]The people who did not die were troubled with growths on their skin. So the people of Ekron cried loudly to heaven.

The Ark of God is Sent Home

6 The Philistines kept the Ark [d] of God in their land seven months. [2]Then they called for their priests and magicians and said, "What should we do with the Ark of the LORD? Tell us how to send it back home!"

[3]The priests and magicians answered, "If you send back the Ark of the God of Israel, don't send it back empty. You must give a penalty offering. If you are then healed, you will know that it was because of the Ark that you had such trouble."

[4]The Philistines asked, "What kind of penalty offering should we send to Israel's God?"

They answered, "Make five gold models of the growths on your skin and five gold models of rats. The number of models must match the number of Philistine kings, because the same sickness has come on you and your kings. [5]Make models of the growths and the rats that are ruining the country, and give honour to Israel's God. Then maybe he will stop being so hard on you, your gods and your land. [6]Don't be stubborn like the king of Egypt and the Egyptians. God punished them terribly until they let the Israelites leave Egypt.

[7]"You must build a new cart and get two cows that have just had calves. These must be cows that have never had yokes [d] on their necks. Hitch the cows to the cart, and take the calves home, away from their mothers. [8]Put the Ark of the LORD on the cart and the gold models for the penalty offering in a box beside the Ark. Then send the cart straight on its way. [9]Watch the cart. If it goes towards Beth Shemesh in Israel's own land, the LORD has given us this great sickness. But if it doesn't, we will know that Israel's God has not punished us. Our sickness just happened by chance."

[10]The Philistines did what the priests and magicians said. They took two cows that had just had calves and hitched them to the cart, but they kept their calves at home. [11]They put the Ark of the LORD and the box with the gold rats and models of growths on the cart. [12]Then the cows went straight towards Beth Shemesh. They stayed on the road, mooing all the way, and did not turn right or left. The Philistine kings followed the cows as far as the border of Beth Shemesh.

[13]Now the people of Beth Shemesh were harvesting their wheat in the valley. When they looked up and saw the Ark of the LORD, they were very happy. [14]The cart came to the field belonging to Joshua of Beth Shemesh and stopped near a large rock. The people of Beth Shemesh chopped up the wood of the cart. Then they sacrificed the cows as burnt offerings to the LORD.

Ichabod   This name means "no glory".

15The Levites took down the Ark of the LORD and the box that had the gold models, and they put both on the large rock. That day the people of Beth Shemesh offered whole burnt offerings and made sacrifices to the LORD. 16After the five Philistine kings saw this, they went back to Ekron the same day.

17The Philistines had sent these gold models of the growths as penalty offerings to the LORD. They sent one model for each Philistine town: Ashdod, Gaza, Ashkelon, Gath and Ekron. 18And the Philistines also sent gold models of rats. The number of rats matched the number of towns belonging to the Philistine kings, including both fortified cities and country villages. The large rock on which they put the Ark of the LORD is still there in the field of Joshua of Beth Shemesh.

19But some of the men of Beth Shemesh looked into the Ark of the LORD. So God killed 70 of them. The people of Beth Shemesh cried because the LORD had struck them down. 20They said, "Who can stand before the LORD, this holy God? Whom will he strike next?"

21Then they sent messengers to the people of Kiriath Jearim, saying, "The Philistines have brought back the Ark of the LORD. Come down and take it to your city."

7 The men of Kiriath Jearim came and took the Ark of the LORD to Abinadab's house on a hill. There they made Abinadab's son Eleazar holy for the LORD so he could guard the Ark of the LORD.

The LORD Saves the Israelites

2The Ark*d* stayed at Kiriath Jearim a long time—20 years in all. And the people of Israel began to follow the LORD again. 3Samuel spoke to the whole group of Israel, saying, "If you're turning back to the LORD with all your hearts, you must remove your foreign gods and your idols of Ashtoreth.*d* You must give yourselves fully to the LORD and serve only him. Then he will save you from the Philistines."

4So the Israelites put away their idols of Baal*d* and Ashtoreth, and they served only the LORD.

5Samuel said, "All Israel must meet at Mizpah, and I will pray to the LORD for you." 6So the Israelites met together at Mizpah. They drew water from the ground and poured it out before the LORD and did not eat that day. They confessed, "We have sinned against the LORD." And Samuel served as judge of Israel at Mizpah.

7The Philistines heard the Israelites were meeting at Mizpah, so the Philistine kings came up to attack them. When the Israelites heard they were coming, they were afraid. 8They said

to Samuel, "Don't stop praying to the LORD our God for us! Ask him to save us from the Philistines!" 9Then Samuel took a baby lamb and offered it to the LORD as a whole burnt offering. He called to the LORD for Israel's sake, and the LORD answered him.

10While Samuel was burning the offering, the Philistines came near to attack Israel. But the LORD thundered against them with loud thunder. They were so frightened they became confused. So the Israelites defeated the Philistines in battle. 11The men of Israel ran out of Mizpah and chased the Philistines almost to Beth Car, killing the Philistines along the way.

Peace Comes to Israel

12After this happened Samuel took a stone and set it up between Mizpah and Shen. He named the stone Ebenezer, *n* saying, "The LORD has helped us to this point." 13So the Philistines were defeated and did not enter the Israelites' land again.

The LORD was against the Philistines all Samuel's life. 14Earlier the Philistines had taken towns from the Israelites, but the Israelites won them back, from Ekron to Gath. They also took back from the Philistines the lands near these towns. There was peace also between Israel and the Amorites.

15Samuel continued as judge of Israel all his life. 16Every year he went from Bethel to Gilgal to Mizpah and judged the Israelites in all these towns. 17But Samuel always went back to Ramah, where his home was. There he judged Israel and built an altar to the LORD.

Israel Asks for a King

8 When Samuel was old, he made his sons judges for Israel. 2His first son was named Joel, and his second son was named Abijah. Joel and Abijah were judges in Beersheba. 3But Samuel's sons did not live as he did. They tried to get money dishonestly, and they accepted money secretly to make wrong judgements.

4So all the elders came together and met Samuel at Ramah. 5They said to him, "You're old, and your sons don't live as you do. Give us a king to rule over us like all the other nations."

6When the elders said that, Samuel was not pleased. He prayed to the LORD, 7and the LORD told Samuel, "Listen to whatever the people say to you. They have not rejected you. They have rejected me from being their king. 8They are doing as they have always done. When I took them out of Egypt, they left me and served other gods. They are doing the same to you. 9Now listen to

---

Ebenezer   This name means "stone of help".

the people, but warn them what the king who rules over them will do."

¹⁰So Samuel told those who had asked him for a king what the LORD had said. ¹¹Samuel said, "If you have a king ruling over you, this is what he will do: he will take your sons and make them serve with his chariots and his horses, and they will run in front of the king's chariot. ¹²The king will make some of your sons commanders over thousands or over fifties. He will make some of your other sons plough his ground and reap his harvest. He will take others to make weapons of war and equipment for his chariots. ¹³He will take your daughters to make perfume and cook and bake for him. ¹⁴He will take your best fields, vineyards and olive groves and give them to his servants. ¹⁵He will take one-tenth of your grain and grapes and give it to his officers and servants. ¹⁶He will take your male and female servants, your best cattle and your donkeys and use them all for his own work. ¹⁷He will take one-tenth of your flocks, and you yourselves will become his slaves. ¹⁸When that time comes, you will cry out because of the king you chose. But the LORD will not answer you then."

¹⁹But the people would not listen to Samuel. They said, "No! We want a king to rule over us. ²⁰Then we will be the same as all the other nations. Our king will judge for us and go with us and fight our battles."

²¹After Samuel heard all that the people said, he repeated their words to the LORD. ²²The LORD answered, "You must listen to them. Give them a king."

Then Samuel told the people of Israel, "Go back to your towns."

Saul Looks for His Father's Donkeys

9 Kish, son of Abiel from the tribe *d* of Benjamin, was an important man. (Abiel was the son of Zeror, who was the son of Becorath, who was the son of Aphiah of Benjamin.) ²Kish had a son named Saul, who was a fine young man. There was no Israelite better than he. Saul stood a head taller than any other man in Israel.

³Now the donkeys of Saul's father, Kish, were lost. So Kish said to Saul, his son, "Take one of the servants, and go and look for the donkeys." ⁴Saul went through the mountains of Ephraim and the land of Shalisha, but he and the servant could not find the donkeys. They went into the land of Shaalim, but the donkeys were not there. They went through the land of Benjamin, but they still did not find them. ⁵When they arrived in the area of Zuph, Saul said to his servant, "Let's go back or my father will stop thinking about the donkeys and will start worrying about us."

⁶But the servant answered, "A man of God is in this town. People respect him because everything he says comes true. Let's go into the town now. Maybe he can tell us something about the journey we have taken."

⁷Saul said to his servant, "If we go into the town, what can we give him? The food in our bags is gone. We have no gift to give him. Do we have anything?"

⁸Again the servant answered Saul. "Look, I have nearly a piece of silver. Give it to the man of God. Then he will tell us about our journey." ⁹(In the past, if someone in Israel wanted to ask something from God, he would say, "Let's go to the seer." *d* We call the person a prophet *d* today, but in the past he was called a seer.)

¹⁰Saul said to his servant, "That's a good idea. Come, let's go." So they went towards the town where the man of God was.

¹¹As Saul and the servant were going up the hill to the town, they met some young women coming out to get water. Saul and the servant asked them, "Is the seer here?"

¹²The young women answered, "Yes, he's here. He's ahead of you. Hurry now. He has just come to our town today, because the people will offer a sacrifice at the place of worship. ¹³As soon as you enter the town, you will find him before he goes up to the place of worship to eat. The people will not begin eating until the seer comes, because he must bless the sacrifice. After that, the guests will eat. Go now, and you should find him."

Saul Meets Samuel

¹⁴Saul and the servant went up to the town. Just as they entered it, they saw Samuel coming towards them on his way up to the place of worship.

¹⁵The day before Saul came, the LORD had told Samuel: ¹⁶"About this time tomorrow I will send you a man from the land of Benjamin. Appoint him to lead my people Israel. He will save my people from the Philistines. I have seen the suffering of my people, and I have listened to their cry."

¹⁷When Samuel first saw Saul, the LORD said to Samuel, "This is the man I told you about. He will organise my people."

¹⁸Saul approached Samuel at the gate and said, "Please tell me where the seer's *d* house is."

¹⁹Samuel answered, "I am the seer. Go with me to the place of worship. Today you and your servant are to eat with me. Tomorrow morning I will answer all your questions and send you home. ²⁰Don't worry about the donkeys you lost three days ago, because they have been found.

Soon all the wealth of Israel will belong to you and your family."

[21]Saul answered, "But I am from the tribe *d* of Benjamin, the smallest tribe in Israel. And my family group is the smallest in the tribe of Benjamin. Why are you saying such things?"

[22]Then Samuel took Saul and his servant into a large room and gave them a choice place at the table. About 30 guests were there. [23]Samuel said to the cook, "Bring the meat I gave you, the portion I told you to set aside."

[24]So the cook took the thigh and put it on the table in front of Saul. Samuel said, "This is the meat saved for you. Eat it, because it was set aside for you for this special time. As I said, 'I had invited the people.'" So Saul ate with Samuel that day.

[25]After they finished eating, they came down from the place of worship and went to the town. Then Samuel talked with Saul on the roof *n* of his house. [26]At dawn they got up, and Samuel called to Saul on the roof. He said, "Get up, and I will send you on your way." So Saul got up and went out of the house with Samuel. [27]As Saul, his servant and Samuel were getting near the edge of the city, Samuel said to Saul, "Tell the servant to go on ahead of us, but you stay, because I have a message from God for you."

Samuel Appoints Saul

10 Samuel took a jar of olive oil and poured it on Saul's head. He kissed Saul and said, "The LORD has appointed you to lead his people. [2]After you leave me today, you will meet two men near Rachel's tomb on the border of Benjamin at Zelzah. They will say to you, 'The donkeys you were looking for have been found. But now your father has stopped thinking about his donkeys and is worrying about you. He is asking, "What will I do about my son?"'

[3]"Then you will go on until you reach the big tree at Tabor. Three men on their way to worship God at Bethel will meet you there. One man will be carrying three goats. Another will be carrying three loaves of bread. And the third will have a leather bag full of wine. [4]They will greet you and offer you two loaves of bread, which you must accept. [5]Then you will go to Gibeah of God, where a Philistine camp is. When you approach this town, a group of prophets *d* will come down from the place of worship. They will be playing harps, tambourines, *d* flutes and lyres, *d* and they will be prophesying. [6]Then the Spirit *d* of the LORD will rush upon you with power. You will prophesy with these prophets, and you will be changed

into a different man. [7]After these signs happen, do whatever you find to do, because God is with you.

[8]"Go ahead of me to Gilgal. I will come down to you to offer whole burnt offerings and fellowship offerings. But you must wait seven days. Then I will come and tell you what to do."

Saul Made King

[9]When Saul turned to leave Samuel, God changed Saul's heart. All these signs came true that day. [10]When Saul and his servant arrived at Gibeah, Saul met a group of prophets. *d* The Spirit *d* of God rushed upon him, and he prophesied with the prophets. [11]When people who had known Saul before saw him prophesying with the prophets, they asked each other, "What has happened to Kish's son? Is even Saul one of the prophets?"

[12]A man who lived there said, "Who is the father of these prophets?" So this became a famous saying: "Is even Saul one of the prophets?" [13]When Saul finished prophesying, he went to the place of worship.

[14]Saul's uncle asked him and his servant, "Where have you been?"

Saul said, "We were looking for the donkeys. When we couldn't find them, we went to talk to Samuel."

[15]Saul's uncle asked, "Please tell me. What did Samuel say to you?"

[16]Saul answered, "He told us the donkeys had already been found." But Saul did not tell his uncle what Samuel had said about his becoming king.

[17]Samuel called all the people of Israel to meet with the LORD at Mizpah. [18]He said, "This is what the LORD, the God of Israel, says: 'I led Israel out of Egypt. I saved you from Egypt's control and from other kingdoms that were troubling you.' [19]But now you have rejected your God. He saves you from all your troubles and problems, but you said, 'No! We want a king to rule over us.' Now come, stand before the LORD in your tribes *d* and family groups."

[20]When Samuel gathered all the tribes of Israel, the tribe of Benjamin was picked. [21]Samuel had them pass by in family groups, and Matri's family was picked. Then he had each man of Matri's family pass by, and Saul son of Kish was picked. But when they looked for Saul, they could not find him. [22]They asked the LORD, "Has Saul come here yet?"

The LORD said, "Yes. He's hiding behind the baggage."

---

roof In Bible times houses were built with flat roofs. The roof was used for drying things such as flax and fruit. And it was used as an extra room, as a place for worship and as a place to sleep in the summer.

23So they ran and brought him out. When Saul stood among the people, he was a head taller than anyone else. 24Then Samuel said to the people, "See the man the LORD has chosen. There is no one like him among all the people."

Then the people shouted, "Long live the king!"

Sidelight Even if you're shy, you could still hit the headlines. Saul, Israel's first king, was so shy that when the people tried to crown him, he hid behind some baggage (1 Samuel 10:20–24).

25Samuel explained the rights and duties of the king and then wrote them in a book and put it before the LORD. Then he told the people to go to their homes.

26Saul also went to his home in Gibeah. God touched the hearts of certain brave men who went along with him. 27But some troublemakers said, "How can this man save us?" They disapproved of Saul and refused to bring gifts to him. But Saul kept quiet.

Nahash Troubles Jabesh Gilead

11 About a month later Nahash the Ammonite and his army surrounded the city of Jabesh in Gilead. All the people of Jabesh said to Nahash, "Make a treaty with us, and we will serve you."

2But he answered, "I will make a treaty with you only if I'm allowed to tear out the right eye of each of you. Then all Israel will be ashamed!"

3The elders of Jabesh said to Nahash, "Give us seven days to send messengers through all Israel. If no one comes to help us, we will give ourselves up to you."

4When the messengers came to Gibeah where Saul lived and told the people the news, they cried loudly. 5Saul was coming home from ploughing the fields with his oxen when he heard the people crying. He asked, "What's wrong with the people that they are crying?" Then they told Saul what the messengers from Jabesh had said. 6When Saul heard their words, God's Spirit *d* rushed upon him with power, and he became very angry. 7So he took a pair of oxen and cut them into pieces. Then he gave the pieces of the oxen to messengers and ordered them to carry them through all the land of Israel.

The messengers said, "This is what will happen to the oxen of anyone who does not follow Saul and Samuel." So the people became very afraid of the LORD. They all came together as if they were one person. 8Saul gathered the people together at Bezek. There were 300,000 men from Israel and 30,000 men from Judah.

9They said to the messengers who had come, "Tell the people at Jabesh Gilead this: 'Before the day warms up tomorrow, you will be saved.'" So the messengers went and reported this to the people at Jabesh, and they were very happy. 10The people said to Nahash the Ammonite, "Tomorrow we will come out to meet you. Then you can do anything you want to us."

11The next morning Saul divided his soldiers into three groups. At dawn they entered the Ammonite camp and defeated them before the heat of the day. The Ammonites who escaped were scattered; no two of them were still together.

12Then the people said to Samuel, "Who didn't want Saul as king? Bring them here and we will kill them!"

13But Saul said, "No! No one will be put to death today. Today the LORD has saved Israel!"

14Then Samuel said to the people, "Come, let's go to Gilgal. There we will again promise to obey the king." 15So all the people went to Gilgal, and there, before the LORD, the people made Saul king. They offered fellowship offerings to the LORD, and Saul and all the Israelites had a great celebration.

Samuel's Farewell Speech

12 Samuel said to all Israel, "I have done everything you wanted me to do and have put a king over you. 2Now you have a king to lead you. I am old and grey, and my sons are here with you. I have been your leader since I was young. 3Here I am. If I have done anything wrong, you must testify against me before the LORD and his appointed king. Did I steal anyone's ox or donkey? Did I hurt or cheat anyone? Did I ever secretly accept money to pretend not to see something wrong? If I did any of these things, I will make it right."

4The Israelites answered, "You have not cheated us, or hurt us or taken anything unfairly from anyone."

5Samuel said to them, "The LORD is a witness to what you have said. His appointed king is also a witness today that you did not find anything wrong in me."

"He is our witness," they said.

6Then Samuel said to the people, "It is the LORD who chose Moses and Aaron and brought your ancestors out of Egypt. 7Now, stand there, and I will remind you of all the good things the LORD did for you and your ancestors.

[8]"After Jacob entered Egypt, his descendants [d] cried to the LORD for help. So the LORD sent Moses and Aaron, who took your ancestors out of Egypt and brought them to live in this place.

[9]"But they forgot the LORD their God. So he handed them over as slaves to Sisera, the commander of the army of Hazor, and as slaves to the Philistines and the king of Moab. They all fought against your ancestors. [10]Then your ancestors

---

Sidelight   The Israelites wanted to be like everyone else, so they chose a king to lead and fight for them. In asking for a king they chose to disobey God, who had promised to fight for them. Saul started well, and gave God the credit, but he later became disobedient (1 Samuel 13:1–23) and impatient. He was rejected from leadership to make way for David's success.

---

cried to the LORD and said, 'We have sinned. We have left the LORD and served the Baals [d] and the Ashtoreths.[d] But now save us from our enemies, and we will serve you.' [11]So the LORD sent Gideon, [n] Barak, Jephthah and Samuel. He saved you from your enemies around you, and you lived in safety. [12]But when you saw Nahash king of the Ammonites coming against you, you said, 'No! We want a king to rule over us!'—even though the LORD your God was your king. [13]Now here is the king you chose, the one you asked for. The LORD has put him over you. [14]You must honour the LORD and serve him. You must obey his word and not turn against his commands. Both you and the king ruling over you must follow the LORD your God. If you do, it will be well with you. [15]But if you don't obey the LORD, and if you turn against his commands, he will be against you. He will do to you what he did to your ancestors.

[16]"Now stand still and see the great thing the LORD will do before your eyes. [17]It is now the time of the wheat harvest.[n] I will pray for the LORD to send thunder and rain. Then you will know what an evil thing you did against the LORD when you asked for a king."

[18]Then Samuel prayed to the LORD, and that same day the LORD sent thunder and rain. So the people were very afraid of the LORD and Samuel. [19]They said to Samuel, "Pray to the LORD your God for us, your servants! Don't let us die! We've added to all our sins the evil of asking for a king."

[20]Samuel answered, "Don't be afraid. It's true that you did wrong, but don't turn away from the LORD. Serve the LORD with all your heart. [21]Idols are of no use, so don't worship them. They can't help you or save you. They are useless! [22]For his own sake, the LORD won't leave his people. Instead, he was pleased to make you his own people. [23]I will surely not stop praying for you, because that would be sinning against the LORD. I will teach you what is good and right. [24]You must honour the LORD and truly serve him with all your heart. Remember the wonderful things he did for you! [25]But if you are stubborn and do evil, he will sweep you and your king away."

13 Saul was 30 years old when he became king, and he was king over Israel for 42 years.[n] [2]Saul chose 3,000 men from Israel. 2,000 men stayed with him at Michmash in the mountains of Bethel, and 1,000 men stayed with Jonathan at Gibeah in Benjamin. Saul sent the other men in the army back home.

[3]Jonathan attacked the Philistine camp in Geba, and the other Philistines heard about it. Saul said, "Let the Hebrews hear what happened." So he told the men to blow trumpets through all the land of Israel. [4]All the Israelites heard the news. The men said, "Saul has defeated the Philistine camp. Now the Philistines will really hate us!" Then the Israelites were called to join Saul at Gilgal.

[5]The Philistines gathered to fight Israel with 3,000[n] chariots and 6,000 men to ride in them. Their soldiers were as many as the grains of sand on the seashore. The Philistines went and camped at Michmash, which is east of Beth Aven. [6]When the Israelites saw that they were in trouble, they went to hide in caves and bushes, among the rocks and in pits and wells. [7]Some Hebrews even went across the Jordan River to the land of Gad and Gilead.

But Saul stayed at Gilgal, and all the men in his army were shaking with fear. [8]Saul waited seven days, because Samuel had said he would meet him then. But Samuel did not come to Gilgal, and the soldiers began to leave. [9]So Saul said, "Bring me the whole burnt offering and the fellowship offerings." Then Saul offered the whole burnt offering. [10]Just as he finished, Samuel arrived, and Saul went to greet him.

[11]Samuel asked, "What have you done?"

Saul answered, "I saw the soldiers leaving me, and you were not here when you said you would

---

Gideon   Also called Jerub-Baal.
time . . . harvest   This was a dry time in the summer when no rains fell.
Saul . . . years   This is how the verse is worded in some early Greek copies. The Hebrew is not clear here.
3,000   Some Greek copies say 3,000. The Hebrew copies say 30,000.

be. The Philistines were gathering at Michmash. [12]Then I thought, 'The Philistines will come against me at Gilgal, and I haven't asked for the LORD's approval.' So I forced myself to offer the whole burnt offering."

[13]Samuel said, "You acted foolishly! You haven't obeyed the command of the LORD your God. If you had obeyed him, the LORD would have made your kingdom continue in Israel always, [14]but now your kingdom will not continue. The LORD has looked for the kind of man he wants. He has appointed him to rule his people, because you haven't obeyed his command."

[15]Then Samuel left Gilgal and went to Gibeah in Benjamin. Saul counted the men who were still with him, and there were about 600.

Hard Times for Israel

[16]Saul and his son Jonathan and the soldiers with him stayed in Gibeah in the land of Benjamin. The Philistines made their camp at Michmash. [17]Three groups went out from the Philistine camp to make attacks. One group went on the Ophrah road in the land of Shual. [18]The second group went on the Beth Horon road. The third group went on the border road that overlooks the Valley of Zeboim towards the desert.

[19]The whole land of Israel had no blacksmith because the Philistines had said, "The Hebrews might make swords and spears." [20]So all the Israelites had to go down to the Philistines to have their ploughs, hoes, axes and sickles sharpened. [21]The Philistine blacksmiths charged about 8 grammes of silver for sharpening ploughs and hoes. And they charged 4 grammes of silver for sharpening picks, axes and the sticks used to guide oxen.

[22]So when the battle came, the soldiers with Saul and Jonathan had no swords or spears. Only Saul and his son Jonathan had them.

> **Sidelight** The Philistines were such a threat to the Israelites partly because they were the only ones with iron weapons. Only Israelite royalty had swords (1 Samuel 13:19–22), and they were probably smuggled in from other countries.

Israel Defeats the Philistines

[23]A group from the Philistine army had gone out to the pass at Michmash.

14 One day Jonathan, Saul's son, said to the officer who carried his armour, "Come, let's go over to the Philistine camp on the other side." But Jonathan did not tell his father.

[2]Saul was sitting under a pomegranate[d] tree at the threshing[d] floor near Gibeah. He had about 600 men with him. [3]One man was Ahijah who was wearing the holy robe.[d] (Ahijah was a son of Ichabod's brother Ahitub. Ichabod was the son of Phinehas, the son of Eli, the LORD's priest in Shiloh.) No one knew Jonathan had left.

[4]There was a steep slope on each side of the pass that Jonathan planned to go through to reach the Philistine camp. The cliff on one side was named Bozez, and the cliff on the other side was named Seneh. [5]One cliff faced north towards Michmash. The other faced south towards Geba.

[6]Jonathan said to his officer who carried his armour, "Come. Let's go to the camp of those men who are not circumcised.[d] Maybe the LORD will help us. The LORD can give us victory if we have many people, or just a few."

[7]The officer who carried Jonathan's armour said to him, "Do whatever you think is best. Go ahead. I'm with you."

[8]Jonathan said, "Then come. We will cross over to the Philistines and let them see us. [9]If they say to us, 'Stay there until we come to you,' we will stay where we are. We won't go up to them. [10]But if they say, 'Come up to us,' we will climb up, and the LORD will let us defeat them. This will be the sign for us."

[11]When both Jonathan and his officer let the Philistines see them, the Philistines said, "Look! The Hebrews are crawling out of the holes they were hiding in!" [12]The Philistines in the camp shouted to Jonathan and his officer, "Come up to us. We'll teach you a lesson!"

Jonathan said to his officer, "Climb up behind me, because the LORD has given the Philistines to Israel!" [13]So Jonathan climbed up, using his hands and feet, and his officer climbed just behind him. Jonathan struck down the Philistines as he went, and his officer killed them as he followed behind him. [14]In that first fight Jonathan and his officer killed about 20 Philistines over a fifth of a hectare of ground.

[15]All the Philistine soldiers panicked—those in the camp and those in the raiding party. The ground itself shook! God had caused the panic.

[16]Saul's guards were at Gibeah in the land of Benjamin when they saw the Philistine soldiers running in every direction. [17]Saul said to his army, "Check to see who has left our camp." When they checked, they learned that Jonathan and his officer were gone.

[18]So Saul said to Ahijah the priest, "Bring the Ark[d] of God." (At that time it was with the Israelites.) [19]While Saul was talking to the priest, the confusion in the Philistine camp was growing. Then Saul said to Ahijah, "Put your hand down!"

²⁰Then Saul gathered his army and entered the battle. They found the Philistines confused, striking each other with their swords! ²¹Earlier, there were Hebrews who had served the Philistines and had stayed in their camp, but now they joined the Israelites with Saul and Jonathan. ²²When all the Israelites hidden in the mountains of Ephraim heard that the Philistine soldiers were running away, they also joined the battle and chased the Philistines. ²³So the LORD saved the Israelites that day, and the battle moved on past Beth Aven.

Saul Makes Another Mistake

²⁴The men of Israel were miserable that day because Saul had made an oath for all of them. He had said, "No one should eat food before evening and before I finish defeating my enemies. If he does, he will be cursed!" So no Israelite soldier ate food.

²⁵Now the army went into the woods, where there was some honey on the ground. ²⁶They came upon some honey, but no one took any because they were afraid of the oath. ²⁷Jonathan had not heard the oath Saul had put on the army, so he dipped the end of his stick into the honey and lifted some out and ate it. Then he felt better. ²⁸Then one of the soldiers told Jonathan, "Your father made an oath for all the soldiers. He said any man who eats today will be cursed! That's why they are so weak."

²⁹Jonathan said, "My father has made trouble for the land! See how much better I feel after just tasting a little of this honey! ³⁰It would have been much better for the men to eat the food they took from their enemies today. We could have killed many more Philistines!"

³¹That day the Israelites defeated the Philistines from Michmash to Aijalon. After that, they were very tired. ³²They had taken sheep, cattle and calves from the Philistines. Now they were so hungry they killed the animals on the ground and ate them, without draining the blood from them! ³³Someone said to Saul, "Look! The men are sinning against the LORD. They're eating meat without draining the blood from it!"

Saul said, "You have sinned! Roll a large stone over here now!" ³⁴Then he said, "Go to the men and tell them that each person must bring his ox and sheep to me and kill it here and eat it. Don't sin against the LORD by eating meat without draining the blood from it."

That night everyone brought his animals and killed them there. ³⁵Then Saul built an altar to the LORD. It was the first altar he had built to the LORD. ³⁶Saul said, "Let's go after the Philistines tonight and rob them. We won't let any of them live!"

The men answered, "Do whatever you think is best."

But the priest said, "Let's ask God."

³⁷So Saul asked God, "Should I chase the Philistines? Will you let us defeat them?" But God did not answer Saul at that time. ³⁸Then Saul said to all the leaders of his army, "Come here. Let's find out what sin has been done today. ³⁹As surely as the LORD lives who has saved Israel, even if my son Jonathan did the sin, he must die." But no one in the army spoke.

⁴⁰Then Saul said to all the Israelites, "You stand on this side. I and my son Jonathan will stand on the other side."

The men answered, "Do whatever you think is best."

⁴¹Then Saul prayed to the LORD, the God of Israel, "Give me the right answer."

And Saul and Jonathan were picked; the other men went free. ⁴²Saul said, "Now let us discover if it is I or Jonathan my son who is guilty." And Jonathan was picked.

⁴³Saul said to Jonathan, "Tell me what you have done."

So Jonathan told Saul, "I only tasted a little honey from the end of my stick. And must I die now?"

⁴⁴Saul said, "Jonathan, if you don't die, may God punish me terribly."

⁴⁵But the soldiers said to Saul, "Must Jonathan die? Never! He is responsible for saving Israel today! As surely as the LORD lives, not even a hair of his head will fall to the ground! Today Jonathan fought against the Philistines with God's help!" So the army saved Jonathan, and he did not die.

⁴⁶Then Saul stopped chasing the Philistines, and they went back to their own land.

Saul Fights Israel's Enemies

⁴⁷When Saul became king over Israel, he fought against Israel's enemies all around. He fought Moab, the Ammonites, Edom, the king of Zobah and the Philistines. Everywhere Saul went he defeated Israel's enemies. ⁴⁸He fought bravely and defeated the Amalekites. He saved the Israelites from their enemies who had robbed them.

⁴⁹Saul's sons were Jonathan, Ishvi and Malki-Shua. His older daughter was named Merab, and his younger daughter was named Michal. ⁵⁰Saul's wife was Ahinoam, daughter of Ahimaaz. The commander of his army was Abner son of Ner, Saul's uncle. ⁵¹Saul's father Kish and Abner's father Ner were sons of Abiel.

⁵²All Saul's life he fought hard against the Philistines. When he saw strong or brave men, he took them into his army.

Saul Rejected as King

15 Samuel said to Saul, "The LORD sent me to appoint you king over Israel. Now listen to his message. ²This is what the LORD All-powerful says: 'When the Israelites came out of Egypt, the Amalekites tried to stop them from going to Canaan. So I will punish them. ³Now go, attack the Amalekites and destroy everything they own as an offering to the LORD. Don't let anything live. Put to death men and women, children and small babies, cattle and sheep, camels and donkeys.' "

⁴So Saul called the army together at Telaim. There were 200,000 foot soldiers and 10,000 men from Judah. ⁵Then Saul went to the city of Amalek and set up an ambush in the ravine. ⁶He said to the Kenites, "Go away. Leave the Amalekites so that I won't destroy you with them, because you showed kindness to the Israelites when they came out of Egypt." So the Kenites moved away from the Amalekites.

⁷Then Saul defeated the Amalekites. He fought them all the way from Havilah to Shur, at the border of Egypt. ⁸He took King Agag of the Amalekites alive, but he killed all of Agag's army with the sword. ⁹Saul and the army let Agag live, along with the best sheep, fat cattle and lambs. They let every good animal live, because they did not want to destroy them. But when they found an animal that was weak or useless, they killed it.

¹⁰Then the LORD spoke his word to Samuel: ¹¹"I am sorry I made Saul king, because he has stopped following me and has not obeyed my commands." Samuel was upset, and he cried out to the LORD all night long.

¹²Early the next morning Samuel got up and went to meet Saul. But the people told Samuel, "Saul has gone to Carmel, where he has put up a monument in his own honour. Now he has gone down to Gilgal."

¹³When Samuel came to Saul, Saul said, "May the LORD bless you! I have obeyed the LORD's commands."

¹⁴But Samuel said, "Then why do I hear cattle mooing and sheep bleating?"

¹⁵Saul answered, "The soldiers took them from the Amalekites. They saved the best sheep and cattle to offer as sacrifices to the LORD your God, but we destroyed all the other animals."

¹⁶Samuel said to Saul, "Stop! Let me tell you what the LORD said to me last night."

Saul answered, "Tell me."

¹⁷Samuel said, "Once you didn't think much of yourself, but now you have become the leader of the tribes *d* of Israel. The LORD appointed you to be king over Israel. ¹⁸And he sent you on a mission. He said, 'Go and destroy those evil people, the Amalekites. Make war on them until all of them are dead.' ¹⁹Why didn't you obey the LORD? Why did you take the best things? Why did you do what the LORD said was wrong?"

²⁰Saul said, "But I did obey the LORD. I did what the LORD told me to do. I destroyed all the Amalekites, and I brought back Agag their king. ²¹The soldiers took the best sheep and cattle to sacrifice to the LORD your God at Gilgal."

²²But Samuel answered,

"What pleases the LORD more:
 burnt offerings and sacrifices
 or obedience to his voice?
It is better to obey than to sacrifice.
 It is better to listen to God than to offer the
  fat of rams.
²³Refusing to obey is as bad as the sin of sorcery. *d*
 Pride is as bad as the sin of worshipping idols.
You have rejected the LORD's command.
 Now he rejects you as king."

²⁴Then Saul said to Samuel, "I have sinned. I didn't obey the LORD's commands and your words. I was afraid of the people, and I did what they said. ²⁵Now, I beg you, forgive my sin. Come back with me so I may worship the LORD."

²⁶But Samuel said to Saul, "I won't go back with you. You rejected the LORD's command, and now he rejects you as king of Israel."

²⁷As Samuel turned to leave, Saul caught his robe, and it tore. ²⁸Samuel said to him, "The LORD has torn the kingdom of Israel from you today and has given it to one of your neighbours who is better than you. ²⁹The LORD is the Eternal One of Israel. He does not lie or change his mind. He is not a human being, so he does not change his mind."

³⁰Saul answered, "I have sinned. But please honour me in front of the elders of my people and in front of the Israelites. Come back with me so that I can worship the LORD your God." ³¹So Samuel went back with Saul, and Saul worshipped the LORD.

³²Then Samuel said, "Bring me King Agag of the Amalekites."

Agag came to Samuel in chains, but Agag thought, "Surely the threat of death has passed."

³³Samuel said to him, "Your sword made other mothers lose their children. Now your mother will have no children." And Samuel cut Agag to pieces before the LORD at Gilgal.

³⁴Then Samuel left and went to Ramah, but Saul went up to his home in Gibeah. ³⁵And Samuel never saw Saul again for the rest of his life, but he was sad for Saul. And the LORD was very sorry he had made Saul king of Israel.

Samuel Goes to Bethlehem

16 The LORD said to Samuel, "How long will you continue to feel sorry for Saul? I have rejected him as king of Israel. Fill your container with olive oil and go. I am sending you to Jesse who lives in Bethlehem, because I have chosen one of his sons to be king."

²But Samuel said, "If I go, Saul will hear the news and will try to kill me."

The LORD said, "Take a young calf with you. Say, 'I have come to offer a sacrifice to the LORD.' ³Invite Jesse to the sacrifice. Then I will tell you what to do. You must appoint the one I show you."

⁴Samuel did what the LORD told him to do. When he arrived at Bethlehem, the elders of Bethlehem shook with fear. They met him and asked, "Are you coming in peace?"

⁵Samuel answered, "Yes, I come in peace. I have come to make a sacrifice to the LORD. Set yourselves apart to the LORD and come to the sacrifice with me." Then he set Jesse and his sons apart to the LORD, and he invited them to come to the sacrifice.

⁶When they arrived, Samuel saw Eliab, and he thought, "Surely the LORD has appointed this person standing here before him."

⁷But the LORD said to Samuel, "Don't look at how handsome Eliab is or how tall he is, because I have not chosen him. God does not see the same way people see. People look at the outside of a person, but the LORD looks at the heart."

⁸Then Jesse called Abinadab and told him to pass by Samuel. But Samuel said, "The LORD has not chosen this man either." ⁹Then Jesse had Shammah pass by. But Samuel said, "No, the LORD has not chosen this one." ¹⁰Jesse had seven of his sons pass by Samuel. But Samuel said to him, "The LORD has not chosen any of these."

SELF-ESTEEM

Go For It!

At fifteen years old Matthew had the spelling age of a much younger person. He was seriously dyslexic and so had real trouble in reading, too. "Why not think about something like catering," the careers staff told him. "It's best to go for something you know you can achieve."

But then he had a session with a psychologist who was trying to get him extra time in exams. "What would you like to do?" the psychologist asked. Matthew replied that he would like to work professionally with people – perhaps be a psychologist himself. The psychologist was really encouraging. He knew that Matthew had a high IQ and could make it.

Matthew knew where he wanted to go. Even when he did poorly in his exams he still kept trying and his determination got him onto a good college course with fewer examinations – more course assessment. Sometimes, like David, Matthew was not sure how things would turn out and wondered if he should make other plans. Eventually he found one university which understood his problems and was willing to take him on. Today Matthew is close to the top of his class and well on target.

David knew what it was like to be put in his place. He wasn't the biggest, the strongest or the most heroic, but God still chose him. **1 Samuel 16:1–13** tells us why.

* What might have happened if Matthew and David had believed the negative things other people had said?
* What qualities did David have that you can see in yourself?

Consider . . .

* making a list of your good points that some people might overlook. Decide how you can use these gifts in serving God.
* talking to someone who is looked down upon at your school or church. Find out what areas they excel in, then encourage him or her to develop those skills even further.

For more, see . . .

* Psalm 147:10–11 (p.587)
* Ephesians 1:3–6 (p.1268)
* Galatians 2:6 (p.1258)

[11]Then he asked Jesse, "Are these all the sons you have?"

Jesse answered, "I still have the youngest son. He is out taking care of the sheep."

Samuel said, "Send for him. We will not sit down to eat until he arrives."

[12]So Jesse sent and had his youngest son brought in. He was a fine boy, tanned and handsome.

The LORD said to Samuel, "Go, appoint him, because he is the one."

[13]So Samuel took the container of olive oil and poured it on Jesse's youngest son to appoint him in front of his brothers. From that day on, the LORD's Spirit[d] worked in David. Samuel then went back to Ramah.

David Serves Saul

[14]But the LORD's Spirit[d] had left Saul, and an evil spirit from the LORD troubled him.

[15]Saul's servants said to him, "See, an evil spirit from God is troubling you. [16]Give us the command to look for someone who can play the harp. When the evil spirit from God troubles you, he will play, and you will feel better."

[17]So Saul said to his servants, "Find someone who can play well and bring him to me."

[18]One of the servants said, "I have seen a son of Jesse of Bethlehem play the harp. He is brave and courageous. He is a good speaker and handsome, and the LORD is with him."

[19]Then Saul sent messengers to Jesse, saying, "Send me your son David, who is with the sheep." [20]So Jesse loaded a donkey with bread, a leather bag full of wine and a young goat, and he sent them with his son David to Saul.

[21]When David came to Saul, he began to serve him. Saul liked David and made him the officer who carried his armour. [22]Saul sent a message to Jesse, saying, "Let David stay and serve me because I like him."

[23]When the evil spirit from God troubled Saul, David would take his harp and play. Then the evil spirit would leave him, and Saul would feel better.

David and Goliath

17 The Philistines gathered their armies for war. They met at Socoh in Judah and camped at Ephes Dammim between Socoh and

MUSIC

Musicianaries

One of the big bosses at MTV was quoted as saying, "We don't just influence this generation. We own this generation." And in some ways, he's right. Nothing has been as successful in recent times at shaping the minds and attitudes of the world's young people as music television. Nowadays, everyone wants to look, think and feel like a celebrity – even if it means "selling their soul to the devil" by compromising their faith in God.

However, there is a new breed of music missionaries – musicianaries – who refuse to believe that MTV owns this generation. They're the ones who allow Jesus to shape their destiny. Like young David in **1 Samuel 16:17–23**, they actually allow God to use their music to combat evil.

When confronted by sceptics who claimed that all rock music was evil, one famous Christian rocker wrote, "Why should the devil have all the good music?" Today, these musicianaries carry that same DNA. They'll use whatever style of music it takes to bring the message of Jesus' salvation to a broken, dying, celebrity-soaked world.

* Besides musical skills, what else did David have that made him so popular with King Saul?
* What skills have you been blessed with? Are you allowing God to use them to combat evil?

Consider . . .

* joining the ranks of musicianaries who would prefer to be shaped by the Word of God than by MTV.
* sponsoring a ministry you believe to be supporting true musicianaries. And don't forget to pray for them.

For more, see . . .

* 2 Chronicles 20:15–20 (p.414)
* Ephesians 6:10–20 (p.1277)
* 1 Corinthians 9:22–23 (p.1227)

Azekah. [2]Saul and the Israelites gathered in the Valley of Elah and camped there and took their positions to fight the Philistines. [3]The Philistines controlled one hill while the Israelites controlled another. The valley was between them.

[4]The Philistines had a champion fighter from Gath named Goliath. He was about 3 metres tall. He came out of the Philistine camp [5]with a bronze helmet on his head and a coat of bronze armour that weighed about 60 kilogrammes. [6]He wore bronze protectors on his legs, and he had a bronze spear on his back. [7]The wooden part of his larger spear was like a weaver's rod, and its blade weighed about 7 kilogrammes. The officer who carried his shield walked in front of him.

[8]Goliath stood and shouted to the Israelite soldiers, "Why have you taken positions for battle? I am a Philistine, and you are Saul's servants! Choose a man and send him to fight me. [9]If he can fight and kill me, we will be your servants. But if I can kill him, you will be our servants." [10]Then he said, "Today I stand and challenge the army of Israel! Send one of your men to fight me!" [11]When Saul and the Israelites heard the Philistine's words, they were very scared.

[12]Now David was the son of Jesse, an Ephrathite from Bethlehem in Judah. Jesse had eight sons. In Saul's time Jesse was an old man. [13]His three oldest sons followed Saul to the war. The first son was Eliab, the second was Abinadab, and the third was Shammah. [14]David was the youngest. Jesse's three oldest sons followed Saul, [15]but David went back and forth from Saul to Bethlehem, where he took care of his father's sheep.

[16]For 40 days the Philistine came out every morning and evening and stood before the Israelite army.

[17]Jesse said to his son David, "Take this 10 kilogrammes of cooked grain and ten loaves of bread to your brothers in the camp. [18]Also take ten pieces of cheese to the commander and to your brothers. See how your brothers are and bring back some proof to show me that they are all right. [19]Your brothers are with Saul and the army in the Valley of Elah, fighting against the Philistines."

[20]Early in the morning David left the sheep with another shepherd. He took the food and left as Jesse had told him. When David arrived at the camp, the army was going out to their battle positions, shouting their war cry. [21]The Israelites and Philistines were lining up their men to face each other in battle.

[22]David left the food with the man who kept the supplies and ran to the battle line to talk to his brothers. [23]While he was talking with them, Goliath, the Philistine champion from Gath, came out. He shouted things against Israel as usual,

and David heard him. [24]When the Israelites saw Goliath, they were very much afraid and ran away.

[25]They said, "Look at this man! He keeps coming out to challenge Israel. The king will give much money to whoever kills him. He will also let whoever kills him marry his daughter. And his father's family will not have to pay taxes in Israel."

[26]David asked the men who stood near him, "What will be done to reward the man who kills this Philistine and takes away the shame from Israel? Who does this uncircumcised *d* Philistine think he is? Does he think he can speak against the armies of the living God?"

[27]The Israelites told David what would be done for the man who would kill Goliath.

[28]When David's oldest brother Eliab heard David talking with the soldiers, he was angry with David. He asked David, "Why did you come here? Who's taking care of those few sheep of yours in the desert? I know you are proud and wicked at heart. You came down here just to watch the battle."

[29]David asked, "Now what have I done wrong? Can't I even talk?" [30]When he turned to other people and asked the same questions, they gave him the same answer as before. [31]Yet what David said was told to Saul, and he sent for David.

[32]David said to Saul, "Don't let anyone be discouraged. I, your servant, will go and fight this Philistine!"

[33]Saul answered, "You can't go out against this Philistine and fight him. You're only a boy. Goliath has been a warrior since he was a young man."

[34]But David said to Saul, "I, your servant, have been keeping my father's sheep. When a lion or bear came and took a sheep from the flock, [35]then I would chase it. I would attack it and save the sheep from its mouth. When it attacked me, I caught it by its fur and hit it and killed it. [36]I, your servant, have killed both a lion and a bear! This uncircumcised Philistine will be like them, because he has spoken against the armies of the living God. [37]The LORD who saved me from a lion and a bear will save me from this Philistine."

Saul said to David, "Go, and may the LORD be with you." [38]Saul put his own clothes on David. He put a bronze helmet on his head and dressed him in armour. [39]David put on Saul's sword and tried to walk around, but he was not used to all the armour Saul had put on him.

He said to Saul, "I can't go in this, because I'm not used to it." Then David took it all off. [40]He took his stick in his hand and chose five smooth stones from a stream. He put them in his shepherd's bag. With his sling in his hand, he went to meet the Philistine.

⁴¹At the same time, the Philistine was coming closer to David. The man who held his shield walked in front of him. ⁴²When Goliath looked at David and saw that he was only a boy, tanned and handsome, he looked down on David with disgust. ⁴³He said, "Do you think I am a dog, that you come at me with a stick?" He used his gods' names to curse David. ⁴⁴He said to David, "Come here. I'll feed your body to the birds of the air and the wild animals!"

⁴⁵But David said to him, "You come to me using a sword and two spears. But I come to you in the name of the LORD All-powerful, the God of the armies of Israel! You have spoken against him. ⁴⁶Today the LORD will hand you over to me,

---

Sidelight

Slam-dunking would have been easy for Goliath. At almost three metres tall he would have been just a few centimetres below the basketball rim. But he was no match for David who was good at "long shots" (1 Samuel 17:45–47).

---

and I'll kill you and cut off your head. Today I'll feed the bodies of the Philistine soldiers to the birds of the air and the wild animals. Then all the world will know there is a God in Israel! ⁴⁷Everyone gathered here will know the LORD does not need swords or spears to save people. The battle belongs to him, and he will hand you over to us."

⁴⁸As Goliath came near to attack him, David ran quickly to meet him. ⁴⁹He took a stone from his bag, put it into his sling, and slung it. The stone hit the Philistine and went deep into his forehead, and Goliath fell face down on the ground.

⁵⁰So David defeated the Philistine with only a sling and a stone. He hit him and killed him. He did not even have a sword in his hand. ⁵¹Then David ran and stood beside him. He took Goliath's sword out of its holder and killed him by cutting off his head.

When the Philistines saw that their champion was dead, they turned and ran. ⁵²The men of Israel and Judah shouted and chased the Philistines all the way to the entrance of the city of Gath and to the gates of Ekron.

The Philistines' bodies lay on the Shaaraim road as far as Gath and Ekron. ⁵³The Israelites returned after chasing the Philistines and robbed

their camp. ⁵⁴David took Goliath's head to Jerusalem and put Goliath's weapons in his own tent.

⁵⁵When Saul saw David go out to meet Goliath, Saul asked Abner, commander of the army, "Abner, who is that young man's father?"

Abner answered, "As surely as you live, my king, I don't know."

⁵⁶The king said, "Find out whose son he is."

⁵⁷When David came back from killing Goliath, Abner brought him to Saul. David was still holding Goliath's head.

⁵⁸Saul asked him, "Young man, who is your father?"

David answered, "I am the son of your servant Jesse of Bethlehem."

Saul Fears David

18 When David finished talking with Saul, Jonathan felt very close to David. He loved David as much as he loved himself. ²Saul kept David with him from that day on and did not let him go home to his father's house. ³Jonathan made an agreement with David, because he loved David as much as himself. ⁴He took off his coat and gave it to David, along with his armour, including his sword, bow and belt.

⁵Saul sent David to fight in different battles, and David was very successful. Then Saul put David over the soldiers, which pleased Saul's officers and all the other people.

⁶After David had killed the Philistine, he and the men returned home. Women came out from all the towns of Israel to meet King Saul. They sang songs of joy, danced, and played tambourines ᵈ and stringed instruments. ⁷As they played, they sang,

"Saul has killed thousands of his enemies,
but David has killed tens of thousands."

⁸The women's song upset Saul, and he became very angry. He thought, "The women say David has killed tens of thousands, but they say I have killed only thousands. The only thing left for him to have is the kingdom!" ⁹So Saul watched David closely from then on, because he was jealous.

¹⁰The next day an evil spirit from God rushed upon Saul, and he prophesied ᵈ in his house. David was playing the harp as he usually did, but Saul had a spear in his hand. ¹¹He threw the spear, thinking, "I'll pin David to the wall." But David escaped from him twice.

¹²The LORD was with David but had left Saul. So Saul was afraid of David. ¹³He sent David away and made him commander of 1,000 soldiers. So David led them in battle. ¹⁴He had great success in everything he did because the LORD was with him. ¹⁵When Saul saw that David was very successful, he feared David even more.

16But all the people of Israel and Judah loved David because he led them well in battle.

Saul's Daughter Marries David

17Saul said to David, "Here is my older daughter Merab. I will let you marry her. All I ask is that you remain brave and fight the LORD's battles." Saul thought, "I won't have to kill David. The Philistines will do that."

18But David answered Saul, saying, "Who am I? My family is not important enough for me to become the king's son-in-law." 19So, when the time came for Saul's daughter Merab to marry David, Saul gave her instead to Adriel of Meholah.

20Now Saul's other daughter, Michal, loved David. When they told Saul, he was pleased. 21He thought, "I will let her marry David. Then she will be a trap for him, and the Philistines will defeat him." So Saul said to David a second time, "You may become my son-in-law."

22And Saul ordered his servants to talk with David in private and say, "Look, the king likes you. His servants love you. You should be his son-in-law."

23Saul's servants said these words to David, but David answered, "Do you think it is easy to become the king's son-in-law? I am poor and unimportant."

24When Saul's servants told him what David had said, 25Saul said, "Tell David, 'The king doesn't want money for the bride. All he wants is 100 Philistine foreskins to get even with his enemies.' " Saul planned to let the Philistines kill David.

26When Saul's servants told this to David, he was pleased to become the king's son-in-law. 27So he and his men went out and killed 200 Philistines. David brought all their foreskins to Saul so he could be the king's son-in-law. Then Saul gave him his daughter Michal for his wife. 28Saul saw that the LORD was with David and that his daughter Michal loved David. 29So he grew even more afraid of David, and he was David's enemy all his life.

30The Philistine commanders continued to go out to fight the Israelites, but every time, David was more skilful than Saul's officers. So he became famous.

Saul Tries to Kill David

19 Saul told his son Jonathan and all his servants to kill David, but Jonathan liked David very much. 2So he warned David, "My father Saul is looking for a chance to kill you. Watch out in the morning. Hide in a secret place. 3I will go out and stand with my father in the field where you are hiding, and I'll talk to him about you. Then I'll let you know what I find out."

4When Jonathan talked to Saul his father, he said good things about David. Jonathan said, "The king should do no wrong to your servant David since he has done nothing wrong to you. What he has done has helped you greatly. 5David risked his life when he killed Goliath the Philistine, and the LORD won a great victory for all Israel. You saw it and were happy. Why would you do wrong against David? He's innocent. There's no reason to kill him!"

6Saul listened to Jonathan and then made this promise: "As surely as the LORD lives, David won't be put to death."

7So Jonathan called to David and told him everything that had been said. He brought David to Saul, and David was with Saul as before.

8When war broke out again, David went out to fight the Philistines. He defeated them, and they ran away from him.

9But once again an evil spirit from the LORD rushed upon Saul as he was sitting in his house with his spear in his hand. David was playing the harp. 10Saul tried to pin David to the wall with his spear, but David jumped out of the way. So Saul's spear went into the wall, and David ran away that night.

11Saul sent messengers to David's house to watch him and to kill him in the morning. But Michal, David's wife, warned him, saying, "Tonight you must run for your life. If you don't, you will be dead in the morning." 12So she let David down out of a window, and he ran away and escaped. 13Then Michal took an idol, laid it on the bed, covered it with clothes and put goats' hair on its head.

14Saul sent messengers to take David prisoner, but Michal said, "He is sick."

15Saul sent them back to see David, saying, "Bring him to me on his bed so I can kill him."

16When the messengers entered David's house, they found just an idol on the bed with goats' hair on its head.

17Saul said to Michal, "Why did you trick me this way? You let my enemy go so he could run away!"

Michal answered Saul, "David told me if I did not help him escape, he would kill me."

18After David had escaped from Saul, he went to Samuel at Ramah and told him everything Saul had done to him. Then David and Samuel went to Naioth and stayed there. 19Saul heard that David was in Naioth at Ramah. 20So he sent messengers to capture him. But they met a group of prophets *d* prophesying *d*, with Samuel standing there leading them. So the Spirit *d* of God entered Saul's men, and they also prophesied.

21When Saul heard the news, he sent more messengers, but they also prophesied. Then he sent messengers a third time, but they also prophesied. 22Finally, Saul himself went to Ramah, to the well at Secu. He asked, "Where are Samuel and David?"

The people answered, "In Naioth at Ramah."

23When Saul went to Naioth at Ramah, the Spirit of God also rushed upon him. And he walked on, prophesying until he came to Naioth at Ramah. 24He took off his robes and prophesied in front of Samuel. He lay that way all day and all night. That is why people ask, "Is even Saul one of the prophets?"

Jonathan Helps David

20 Then David ran away from Naioth in Ramah. He went to Jonathan and asked, "What have I done? What is my crime? How did I sin against your father? Why is he trying to kill me?"

2Jonathan answered, "No! You won't die! See, my father doesn't do anything great or small without first telling me. Why would he keep this from me? It's not true!"

3But David took an oath, saying, "Your father knows very well that you like me. He says to himself, 'Jonathan must not know about it, or he will tell David.' As surely as the LORD lives and as you live, I am only a step away from death!"

4Jonathan said to David, "I'll do anything you want me to do."

5So David said, "Look, tomorrow is the New Moon d festival. I am supposed to eat with the king, but let me hide in the field until the third evening. 6If your father notices I am gone, tell him, 'David begged me to let him go to his home town of Bethlehem. Every year at this time his family group offers a sacrifice.' 7If your father says, 'Fine,' I am safe. But if he becomes angry, you will know that he wants to hurt me. 8Jonathan, be loyal to me, your servant. You have made an agreement with me before the LORD. If I am guilty, you may kill me yourself! Why hand me over to your father?"

9Jonathan answered, "No, never! If I learn that my father plans to hurt you, I will warn you!"

10David asked, "Who will let me know if your father answers you unkindly?"

11Then Jonathan said, "Come, let's go out into the field." So the two of them went out into the field.

12Jonathan said to David, "I promise this before the LORD, the God of Israel: at this same time the day after tomorrow, I will find out how my father feels. If he feels good towards you, I will send word to you and let you know. 13But if my father plans to hurt you, I will let you know and send

you away safely. May the LORD punish me terribly if I don't do this. And may the LORD be with you as he has been with my father. 14But show me the kindness of the LORD as long as I live so that I may not die. 15You must never stop showing your kindness to my family, even when the LORD has destroyed all your enemies from the earth."

16So Jonathan made an agreement with David. He said, "May the LORD hold David's enemies responsible." 17And Jonathan asked David to repeat his promise of love for him, because he loved David as much as he loved himself.

18Jonathan said to David, "Tomorrow is the New Moon festival. Your seat will be empty, so my father will miss you. 19On the third day go to the place where you hid when this trouble began. Wait by the rock Ezel. 20On the third day I will shoot three arrows to the side of the rock as if I am shooting at a target. 21Then I will send a boy to find the arrows. If I say to him, 'The arrows are near you; bring them here,' you may come out of hiding. You are safe. As the LORD lives, there is no danger. 22But if I say to the boy, 'Look, the arrows are beyond you,' you must go, because the LORD is sending you away. 23Remember what we talked about. The LORD is a witness between you and me for ever."

24So David hid in the field. When the New Moon festival came, the king sat down to eat. 25He sat where he always sat, near the wall. Jonathan sat across from him, and Abner sat next to Saul, but David's place was empty. 26That day Saul said nothing. He thought, "Maybe something has happened to David so that he is unclean." d 27But the next day was the second day of the month, and David's place was still empty. So Saul said to Jonathan, "Why hasn't the son of Jesse come to the feast yesterday or today?"

28Jonathan answered, "David begged me to let him go to Bethlehem. 29He said, 'Let me go, because our family has a sacrifice in the town, and my brother has ordered me to be there. Now if I am your friend, please let me go to see my brothers.' That is why he has not come to the king's table."

30Then Saul became very angry with Jonathan. He said, "You son of a wicked, worthless woman! I know you are on the side of David son of Jesse! You bring shame on yourself and on your mother who gave birth to you. 31As long as Jesse's son lives, you will never be king or have a kingdom. Now send for David and bring him to me. He must die!"

32Jonathan asked his father, "Why should David be killed? What wrong has he done?" 33Then Saul threw his spear at Jonathan, trying to kill him. So Jonathan knew that his father really wanted to kill David. 34Jonathan was very angry and left the table. That second day of the month he refused to eat. He was ashamed of his father and upset over David.

[35]The next morning Jonathan went out to the field to meet David as they had agreed. He had a young boy with him. [36]Jonathan said to the boy, "Run and find the arrows I shoot." When he ran, Jonathan shot an arrow beyond him. [37]The boy ran to the place where Jonathan's arrow fell, but Jonathan called, "The arrow is beyond you!" [38]Then he shouted, "Hurry! Go quickly! Don't stop!" The boy picked up the arrow and brought it back to his master. [39](The boy knew nothing about what this meant; only Jonathan and David knew.) [40]Then Jonathan gave his weapons to the boy and told him, "Go back to town."

[41]When the boy left, David came out from the south side of the rock. He bowed face down on the ground before Jonathan three times. Then David and Jonathan kissed each other and cried together, but David cried the most.

[42]Jonathan said to David, "Go in peace. We have promised by the LORD that we will be friends. We said, 'The LORD will be a witness between you and me, and between our descendants[d] always.' " Then David left, and Jonathan went back to town.

David Goes to See Ahimelech

21 David went to Nob to see Ahimelech the priest. Ahimelech shook with fear when he saw David, and he asked, "Why are you alone? Why is no one with you?"

[2]David answered him, "The king gave me a special order. He told me, 'No one must know what I am sending you to do or what I told you to do.' I told my men where to meet me. [3]Now, what food do you have with you? Give me five loaves of bread or anything you find."

[4]The priest said to David, "I don't have any plain bread here, but I do have some holy bread. [n] You may eat it if your men have kept themselves from women."

[5]David answered, "No women have been near us for days. My men always keep themselves holy, even when we do ordinary work. And this is especially true when the work is holy."

[6]So the priest gave David the holy bread from the presence of God because there was no other. Each day the holy bread was replaced with hot bread.

[7]One of Saul's servants happened to be there that day. He had been held there before the LORD. He was Doeg the Edomite, the chief of Saul's shepherds.

[8]David asked Ahimelech, "Do you have a spear or sword here? The king's business was very important, so I left without my sword or any other weapon."

[9]The priest answered, "The sword of Goliath the Philistine, the one you killed in the Valley of Elah, is here. It is wrapped in a cloth behind the holy robe. [d] If you want it, you may take it. There's no other sword here but that one."

David said, "There is no other sword like it. Give it to me."

David Goes to Gath

[10]That day David ran away from Saul and went to Achish king of Gath. [11]But the servants of Achish said to him, "This is David, the king of the Israelites. He's the man they dance and sing about, saying:

'Saul has killed thousands of his enemies,
    but David has killed tens of thousands.' "

> ### Sidelight
> Most people know that David was a musician. Did you know he was an actor too? When he was afraid of being captured by the Philistine King Achish, he dribbled in his beard and acted crazy. He must have been good because the king let him go (1 Samuel 21:12–15).

[12]David paid attention to these words and was very much afraid of Achish king of Gath. [13]So he pretended to be insane in front of Achish and his servants. While he was with them, he acted like a madman and made marks on the doors of the gate and let spit run down his beard.

[14]Achish said to his servants, "Look at the man! He's insane! Why do you bring him to me? [15]I have enough madmen. I don't need you to bring him here to act like this in front of me! Don't let him in my house!"

David at Adullam and Mizpah

22 David left Gath and escaped to the cave of Adullam. When his brothers and other relatives heard that he was there, they went to see him. [2]Everyone who was in trouble, or who owed money, or who was unsatisfied gathered around David, and he became their leader. About 400 men were with him.

[3]From there David went to Mizpah in Moab and spoke to the king of Moab. He said, "Please let my father and mother come and stay with you until I learn what God is going to do for me."

---

holy bread   This was the bread that showed the people were in the presence of God. Normally only the priests ate this bread.

⁴So he left them with the king of Moab, and they stayed with him as long as David was hiding in the stronghold.*d*

⁵But the prophet *d* Gad said to David, "Don't stay in the stronghold. Go to the land of Judah." So David left and went to the forest of Hereth.

Saul Destroys Ahimelech's Family

⁶Saul heard that David and his men had been seen. Saul was sitting under the tamarisk tree on the hill at Gibeah, and all his officers were standing around him. He had a spear in his hand. ⁷Saul said to them, "Listen, men of Benjamin! Do you think the son of Jesse will give all of you fields and vineyards? Will David make you commanders over thousands of men or hundreds of men? ⁸You have all made plans against me! No one tells me when my son makes an agreement with the son of Jesse! No one cares about me! No one tells me when my son has encouraged my servant to ambush me this very day!"

⁹Doeg the Edomite, who was standing there with Saul's officers, said, "I saw the son of Jesse. He came to see Ahimelech son of Ahitub at Nob. ¹⁰Ahimelech prayed to the LORD for David and gave him food and gave him the sword of Goliath the Philistine."

¹¹Then the king sent for the priest Ahimelech son of Ahitub and for all of Ahimelech's relatives who were priests at Nob. And they all came to the king. ¹²Saul said to Ahimelech, "Listen now, son of Ahitub."

Ahimelech answered, "Yes, master."

¹³Saul said, "Why are you and Jesse's son against me? You gave him bread and a sword! You prayed to God for him. David has turned against me and is waiting to attack me even now!"

¹⁴Ahimelech answered, "You have no other servant who is as loyal as David, your own son-in-law and captain of your bodyguards. Everyone in your house respects him. ¹⁵That was not the first time I prayed to God for David. Don't blame me or any of my relatives. I, your servant, know nothing about what is going on."

¹⁶But the king said, "Ahimelech, you and all your relatives must die!" ¹⁷Then he told the guards at his side, "Go and kill the priests of the LORD, because they are on David's side. They knew he was running away, but they didn't tell me."

But the king's officers refused to kill the priests of the LORD.

¹⁸Then the king ordered Doeg, "Go and kill the priests." So Doeg the Edomite went and killed the priests. That day he killed 85 men who wore the linen holy robe.*d* ¹⁹He also killed the people of Nob, the city of the priests. With the sword he killed men, women, children, babies, cattle, donkeys and sheep.

²⁰But Abiathar, a son of Ahimelech, who was the son of Ahitub, escaped. He ran away and joined David. ²¹He told David that Saul had killed the LORD's priests. ²²Then David told him, "Doeg the Edomite was there at Nob that day. I knew he would surely tell Saul. So I am responsible for the death of all your father's family. ²³Stay with me. Don't be afraid. The man who wants to kill you also wants to kill me. You will be safe with me."

David Saves the People of Keilah

23 Someone told David, "Look, the Philistines are fighting against Keilah and stealing grain from the threshing *d* floors."

²David asked the LORD, "Should I go and fight these Philistines?"

The LORD answered him, "Go. Attack them, and save Keilah."

³But David's men said to him, "We're afraid here in Judah. We will be more afraid if we go to Keilah where the Philistine army is."

⁴David again asked the LORD, and the LORD answered, "Go down to Keilah. I will help you defeat the Philistines." ⁵So David and his men went to Keilah and fought the Philistines and took their cattle. David killed many Philistines and saved the people of Keilah. ⁶(Now Abiathar son of Ahimelech had brought the holy robe *d* with him when he came to David at Keilah.)

Saul Chases David

⁷Someone told Saul that David was now at Keilah. Saul said, "God has handed David over to me! He has trapped himself, because he has entered a town with gates and bars." ⁸Saul called all his army together for battle, and they prepared to go down to Keilah to attack David and his men.

⁹David learned Saul was making evil plans against him. So he said to Abiathar the priest, "Bring the holy robe." *d* ¹⁰David prayed, "LORD, God of Israel, I have heard that Saul plans to come to Keilah to destroy the town because of me. ¹¹Will the leaders of Keilah hand me over to Saul? Will Saul come down to Keilah, as I heard? LORD, God of Israel, tell me, your servant!"

The LORD answered, "Saul will come down."

¹²Again David asked, "Will the leaders of Keilah hand me and my men over to Saul?"

The LORD answered, "They will."

¹³So David and his 600 men left Keilah and kept moving from place to place. When Saul found out that David had escaped from Keilah, he did not go there.

[14]David stayed in the desert hideouts and in the hills of the Desert of Ziph. Every day Saul looked for David, but the LORD did not surrender David to him.

[15]While David was at Horesh in the Desert of Ziph, he learned that Saul was coming to kill him. [16]But Saul's son Jonathan went to David at Horesh and strengthened his faith in God. [17]Jonathan told him, "Don't be afraid, because my father won't touch you. You will be king of Israel, and I will be second to you. Even my father Saul knows this." [18]The two of them made an agreement before the LORD. Then Jonathan went home, but David stayed at Horesh.

[19]The people from Ziph went to Saul at Gibeah and told him, "David is hiding in our land. He's at the protected places of Horesh, on the hill of Hakilah, south of Jeshimon. [20]Now, our king, come down any time you want. It's our duty to hand David over to you."

[21]Saul answered, "The LORD bless you for helping me. [22]Go and learn more about him. Find out where he is staying and who has seen him there. I have heard that he is clever. [23]Find all the hiding places he uses, and come back and tell me everything. Then I'll go with you. If David is in the area, I will track him down among all the families in Judah."

[24]So they went back to Ziph ahead of Saul. Now David and his men were in the Desert of Maon[n] in the desert area south of Jeshimon. [25]Saul and his men went to look for David, but David heard about it and went down to a rock and stayed in the Desert of Maon. When Saul heard that, he followed David into the Desert of Maon.

[26]Saul was going along one side of the mountain, and David and his men were on the other side. They were hurrying to get away from Saul, because Saul and his men were closing in on them. [27]But a messenger came to Saul, saying, "Come quickly! The Philistines are attacking our land!" [28]So Saul stopped chasing David and went to challenge the Philistines. That is why people call this place Rock of Parting. [29]David also left the Desert of Maon and stayed in the protected places of En Gedi.

David Shames Saul

24 After Saul returned from chasing the Philistines, he was told, "David is in the Desert of En Gedi." [2]So he took 3,000 chosen men from all Israel and began looking for David and his men near the Rocks of the Wild Goats.

[3]Saul came to the sheep pens beside the road. A cave was there, and he went in to relieve himself. Now David and his men were hiding far back in the cave. [4]The men said to David, "Today is the day the LORD spoke of when he said, 'I will give your enemy over to you. Do anything you want with him.'"

Then David crept up to Saul and quietly cut off a corner of Saul's robe. [5]Later David felt guilty because he had cut off a corner of Saul's robe. [6]He said to his men, "May the LORD keep me from doing such a thing to my master! Saul is the LORD's appointed king. I should not do anything against him, because he is the LORD's appointed king!" [7]David used these words to stop his men; he did not let them attack Saul. Then Saul left the cave and went on his way.

[8]When David came out of the cave, he shouted to Saul, "My master and king!" Saul looked back, and David bowed face down on the ground. [9]He said to Saul, "Why do you listen when people say, 'David wants to harm you'? [10]You have seen something with your own eyes today. The LORD put you in my power in the cave. They said I should kill you, but I was merciful. I said, 'I won't harm my master, because he is the LORD's appointed king.' [11]My father, look at this piece of your robe in my hand! I cut off the corner of your robe, but I didn't kill you. Now understand and know I am not planning any evil against you. I did nothing wrong to you, but you are hunting me to kill me. [12]May the LORD judge between us, and may he punish you for the wrong you have done to me! But I am not against you. [13]There is an old saying: 'Evil things come from evil people.' But I am not against you. [14]Whom is the king of Israel coming out against? Whom are you chasing? It's as if you are chasing a dead dog or a flea. [15]May the LORD be our judge and decide between you and me. May he support me and show that I am right. May he save me from you!"

[16]When David finished saying these words, Saul asked, "Is that your voice, David my son?" And he cried loudly. [17]He said, "You are a better man than I am. You have been good to me, but I have done wrong to you. [18]You told me what good things you did. The LORD handed me over to you, but you did not kill me. [19]If a person finds his enemy, he doesn't just send him on his way, does he? May the LORD reward you because you were good to me today. [20]I know you will surely be king, and you will rule the kingdom of Israel. [21]Now swear to me by the LORD that you will not kill my descendants[d] and that you won't wipe out my name from my father's family."

Maon   Some early Greek copies say "Maon". The Hebrew copies say "Paran".

²²So David made the promise to Saul. Then Saul went back home, and David and his men went up to their protected place.

Nabal Insults David

25 Now Samuel died, and all the Israelites met and had a time of sadness for him. Then they buried him at his home in Ramah.

David moved to the Desert of Maon. ²A man in Maon who had land at Carmel was very rich. He had 3,000 sheep and 1,000 goats. He was cutting the wool off his sheep at Carmel. ³His name was Nabal, and he was a descendant *d* of Caleb. His wife was named Abigail. She was wise and beautiful, but Nabal was cruel and mean.

⁴While David was in the desert, he heard that Nabal was cutting the wool from his sheep. ⁵So he sent ten young men and told them, "Go to Nabal at Carmel, and greet him for me. ⁶Say to Nabal, 'May you and your family and all who belong to you have good health! ⁷I have heard that you are cutting the wool from your sheep. When your shepherds were with us, we did not harm them. All the time your shepherds were at Carmel, we stole nothing from them. ⁸Ask your servants, and they will tell you. We come at a happy time, so be kind to my young men. Please give anything you can find for them and for your son David.' "

⁹When David's men arrived, they gave the message to Nabal, but Nabal insulted them. ¹⁰He answered them, "Who is David? Who is this son of Jesse? Many slaves are running away from their masters today! ¹¹I have bread and water, and I have meat that I killed for my servants who cut the wool. But I won't give it to men I don't know."

¹²David's men went back and told him all Nabal had said. ¹³Then David said to them, "Put on your swords!" So they put on their swords, and David put on his also. About 400 men went with David, but 200 men stayed with the supplies.

¹⁴One of Nabal's servants said to Abigail, Nabal's wife, "David sent messengers from the desert to greet our master, but Nabal insulted them. ¹⁵These men were very good to us. They did not harm us. They stole nothing from us during all the time we were out in the field with them. ¹⁶Night and day they protected us. They were like a wall around us while we were with them caring for the sheep. ¹⁷Now think about it, and decide what you can do. Terrible trouble is coming to our master and all his family. Nabal is such a wicked man that no one can even talk to him."

¹⁸Abigail hurried. She took 200 loaves of bread, two leather bags full of wine, five cooked sheep, 15 kilogrammes of cooked grain, 100 cakes of raisins and 200 cakes of pressed figs and put all these on donkeys. ¹⁹Then she told her servants, "Go on. I'll follow you." But she did not tell her husband.

²⁰Abigail rode her donkey and came down towards the mountain ravine. There she met David and his men coming down towards her. ²¹David had just said, "It's been useless! I watched over Nabal's property in the desert. I made sure none of his sheep was missing. I did good to him, but he has paid me back with evil. ²²May God punish my enemies even more. I will not leave one of Nabal's men alive until morning."

²³When Abigail saw David, she quickly got off her donkey and bowed face down on the ground before him. ²⁴She fell at David's feet and said, "My master, let the blame be on me! Please let me talk to you. Listen to what I say. ²⁵My master, don't pay attention to this worthless man Nabal. He is like his name. His name means 'fool', and he is truly a fool. But I, your servant, didn't see the men you sent. ²⁶The LORD has kept you from killing and punishing anyone. As surely as the LORD lives and as surely as you live, may your enemies become like Nabal! ²⁷I have brought a gift to you for the men who follow you. ²⁸Please forgive my wrong. The LORD will certainly let your family have many kings, because you fight his battles. As long as you live, may you do nothing bad. ²⁹Someone might chase you to kill you, but the LORD your God will keep you alive. He will throw away your enemies' lives as he would throw a stone from a sling. ³⁰The LORD will keep all his promises of good things for you. He will make you leader over Israel. ³¹Then you won't feel guilty or troubled because you killed innocent people and punished them. Please remember me when the LORD brings you success."

³²David answered Abigail, "Praise the LORD, the God of Israel, who sent you to meet me. ³³May you be blessed for your wisdom. You have kept me from killing or punishing people today. ³⁴As surely as the LORD, the God of Israel, lives, he has kept me from hurting you. If you hadn't come quickly to meet me, not one of Nabal's men would have lived until morning."

³⁵Then David accepted Abigail's gifts. He told her, "Go home in peace. I have heard your words, and I will do what you have asked."

Nabal's Death

³⁶When Abigail went back to Nabal, he was in the house, eating like a king. He was very drunk and in a good mood. So she told him nothing until the next morning. ³⁷In the morning when he was not drunk, his wife told him everything. His heart stopped, and he became like stone. ³⁸About ten days later the LORD struck Nabal and he died.

³⁹When David heard that Nabal was dead, he said, "Praise the LORD! Nabal insulted me, but the LORD has supported me! He has kept me from doing wrong. The LORD has punished Nabal for his wrong."

Then David sent a message to Abigail, asking her to be his wife. ⁴⁰His servants went to Carmel and said to Abigail, "David sent us to take you so you can become his wife."

⁴¹Abigail bowed face down on the ground and said, "I am your servant. I'm ready to serve you and to wash the feet of my master's servants." ⁴²Abigail quickly got on a donkey and went with David's messengers, with her five maids following her. And she became David's wife.

⁴³David also had married Ahinoam of Jezreel. So they were both David's wives. ⁴⁴Saul's daughter Michal was also David's wife, but Saul had given her to Paltiel son of Laish, who was from Gallim.

David Shames Saul Again

26 The people of Ziph went to Saul at Gibeah and said to him, "David is hiding on the hill of Hakilah opposite Jeshimon."

²So Saul went down to the Desert of Ziph with 3,000 chosen men of Israel to look for David there. ³Saul made his camp beside the road on the hill of Hakilah opposite Jeshimon, but David stayed in the desert. When he heard Saul had followed him, ⁴he sent out spies and learned for certain that Saul had come to Hakilah.

⁵Then David went to the place where Saul had camped. He saw where Saul and Abner son of Ner, the commander of Saul's army, were sleeping. Saul was sleeping in the middle of the camp with all the army around him.

⁶David asked Ahimelech the Hittite and Abishai son of Zeruiah, Joab's brother, "Who will go down into Saul's camp with me?"

Abishai answered, "I'll go with you."

⁷So that night David and Abishai went into Saul's camp. Saul was asleep in the middle of the camp with his spear stuck in the ground near his head. Abner and the army were sleeping around Saul. ⁸Abishai said to David, "Today God has handed your enemy over to you. Let me pin Saul to the ground with my spear. I'll only have to do it once. I won't need to hit him twice."

⁹But David said to Abishai, "Don't kill Saul! No one can harm the LORD's appointed king and still be innocent! ¹⁰As surely as the LORD lives, the LORD himself will punish Saul. Maybe Saul will die naturally, or maybe he will go into battle and be killed. ¹¹But may the LORD keep me from harming his appointed king! Take the spear

and water jug that are near Saul's head. Then let's go."

¹²So David took the spear and water jug that were near Saul's head, and they left. No one saw them or knew about it or woke up, because the LORD had put them into a deep sleep.

¹³David crossed over to the other side of the hill and stood on top of the mountain far from Saul's camp. They were a long way away from each other. ¹⁴David shouted to the army and to Abner son of Ner, "Won't you answer me, Abner?"

Abner answered, "Who is calling for the king? Who are you?"

¹⁵David said, "You're the greatest man in Israel. Isn't that true? Why didn't you guard your master the king? Someone came into your camp to kill your master the king! ¹⁶You have not done well. As surely as the LORD lives, you and your men should die. You haven't guarded your master, the LORD's appointed king. Look! Where are the king's spear and water jug that were near his head?"

¹⁷Saul knew David's voice. He said, "Is that your voice, David my son?"

David answered, "Yes, it is, my master and king." ¹⁸David also said, "Why are you chasing me, my master? What wrong have I done? What evil am I guilty of? ¹⁹My master and king, listen to me. If the LORD made you angry with me, let him accept an offering. But if people did it, may the LORD curse them! They have made me leave the land the LORD gave me. They have told me, 'Go and serve other gods.' ²⁰Now don't let me die far away from the LORD's presence. The king of Israel has come out looking for a flea! You're just hunting a bird in the mountains!"

²¹Then Saul said, "I have sinned. Come back, David my son. Today you respected my life, so I will not try to hurt you. I have been very stupid and foolish."

²²David answered, "Here is your spear. Let one of your young men come here and get it. ²³The LORD rewards us for the things we do right and for our loyalty to him. The LORD handed you over to me today, but I wouldn't harm the LORD's appointed king. ²⁴As I respected your life today, may the LORD also respect my life and save me from all trouble."

²⁵Then Saul said to David, "You are blessed, my son David. You will do great things and succeed."

So David went on his way, and Saul went back home.

David Lives with the Philistines

27 But David thought to himself, "Saul will catch me some day. The best thing I can do is escape to the land of the Philistines. Then he will give up looking for me in Israel, and I can get away from him."

2So David and his 600 men left Israel and went to Achish son of Maoch, king of Gath. 3David, his men and their families made their home in Gath with Achish. David had his two wives with him—Ahinoam of Jezreel and Abigail of Carmel, the widow of Nabal. 4When Saul heard that David had run away to Gath, he stopped looking for him.

5Then David said to Achish, "If you are pleased with me, give me a place in one of the country towns where I can live. I don't need to live in the royal city with you."

6That day Achish gave David the town of Ziklag, and Ziklag has belonged to the kings of Judah ever since. 7David lived in the Philistine land a year and four months.

8David and his men went to raid the people of Geshur, Girzi and Amalek. (These people had lived for a long time in the land that reached to Shur and Egypt.) 9When David fought them, he killed all the men and women and took their sheep, cattle, donkeys, camels and clothes. Then he returned to Achish.

10Achish would ask David, "Where did you go raiding today?" And David would tell him that he had gone to the southern part of Judah, or Jerahmeel, or to the land of the Kenites. 11David never brought a man or woman alive to Gath. He thought, "If we bring people alive, they may tell Achish, 'This is what David really did.' " David did this all the time he lived in the Philistine land. 12So Achish trusted David and said to himself, "David's own people, the Israelites, now hate him very much. He will serve me for ever."

Saul and the Witch of Endor

28 Later, the Philistines gathered their armies to fight against Israel. Achish said to David, "You understand that you and your men must join my army."

2David answered, "You will see for yourself what I, your servant, can do!"

Achish said, "Fine, I'll make you my bodyguard for life."

3Now Samuel was dead, and all the Israelites had shown their sadness for him. They had buried Samuel in his home town of Ramah.

And Saul had forced out the mediums d and fortune-tellers from the land.

4The Philistines came together and made camp at Shunem. Saul gathered all the Israelites and made camp at Gilboa. 5When he saw the Philistine army, he was afraid, and his heart pounded with fear. 6He prayed to the LORD, but the LORD did not answer him through dreams, Urim d or prophets. d 7Then Saul said to his servants, "Find me a woman who is a medium so I may go and ask her what will happen."

His servants answered, "There is a medium in Endor."

8Then Saul put on other clothes to disguise himself, and at night he and two of his men went to see the woman. Saul said to her, "Talk to a spirit for me. Bring up the person I name."

9But the woman said to him, "Surely you know what Saul has done. He has forced the mediums and fortune-tellers from the land. You are trying to trap me and get me killed."

10Saul made a promise to the woman in the name of the LORD. He said, "As surely as the LORD lives, you won't be punished for this."

11The woman asked, "Whom do you want me to bring up?"

He answered, "Bring up Samuel."

12When the woman saw Samuel, she screamed. She said, "Why have you tricked me? You are Saul!"

13The king said to the woman, "Don't be afraid! What do you see?"

The woman said, "I see a spirit coming up out of the ground."

14Saul asked, "What does he look like?"

The woman answered, "An old man wearing a coat is coming up."

Then Saul knew it was Samuel, and he bowed face down on the ground.

15Samuel asked Saul, "Why have you disturbed me by bringing me up?"

Saul said, "I am greatly troubled. The Philistines are fighting against me, and God has left me. He won't answer me any more, either by prophets or in dreams. That's why I called for you. Tell me what to do."

16Samuel said, "The LORD has left you and has become your enemy. So why do you call on me? 17He has done what he said he would do—the things he said through me. He has torn the kingdom out of your hands and given it to one of your neighbours, David. 18You did not obey the LORD; you did not show the Amalekites how angry he was with them. That's why he has done this to you today. 19The LORD will hand over both Israel and you to the Philistines. Tomorrow you and your sons will be with me. The LORD will hand over the army of Israel to the Philistines."

20Saul quickly fell flat on the ground and was afraid of what Samuel had said. He was also very weak because he had eaten nothing all that day and night.

²¹Then the woman came to Saul and saw that he was really frightened. She said, "Look, I, your servant, have obeyed you. I have risked my life and done what you told me to do. ²²Now please listen to me. Let me give you some food so you may eat and have enough strength to go on your way."

²³But Saul refused, saying, "I won't eat."

His servants joined the woman in asking him to eat, and he listened to them. So he got up from the ground and sat on the bed.

²⁴At the house the woman had a fat calf, which she quickly killed. She took some flour and mixed dough with her hands. Then she baked some bread without yeast. ²⁵She put the food before them, and they ate. That same night they got up and left.

David Goes Back to Ziklag

29 The Philistines gathered all their soldiers at Aphek. Israel camped by the spring at Jezreel. ²The Philistine kings were marching with their groups of 100 and 1,000 men. David and his men were marching behind Achish. ³The Philistine commanders asked, "What are these Hebrews doing here?"

Achish told them, "This is David. He served Saul king of Israel, but he has been with me for over a year now. I have found nothing wrong in David since the time he left Saul."

⁴But the Philistine commanders were angry with Achish and said, "Send David back to the city you gave him. He cannot go with us into battle. If he does, we'll have an enemy in our own camp. He could please his king by killing our own men. ⁵David is the one the Israelites dance and sing about, saying:

'Saul has killed thousands of his enemies,
    but David has killed tens of thousands.' "

⁶So Achish called David and said to him, "As surely as the LORD lives, you are loyal. I would be pleased to have you serve in my army. Since the day you came to me, I have found no wrong in you. But the other kings don't trust you. ⁷Go back in peace. Don't do anything to displease the Philistine kings."

⁸David asked, "What wrong have I done? What evil have you found in me from the day I came to you until now? Why can't I go and fight your enemies, my lord and king?"

⁹Achish answered, "I know you are as good as an angel from God. But the Philistine commanders have said, 'David must not go with us into battle.' ¹⁰Early in the morning you and your master's servants should leave. Get up as soon as it is light and go."

¹¹So David and his men got up early in the morning and went back to the country of the Philistines. And the Philistines went up to Jezreel.

David's War with the Amalekites

30 On the third day, when David and his men arrived at Ziklag, he found that the Amalekites had raided southern Judah and Ziklag, attacking Ziklag and burning it. ²They captured the women and everyone, young and old, but they had not killed anyone. They had only taken them away.

³When David and his men came to Ziklag, they found the town had been burned and their wives, sons and daughters had been taken as prisoners. ⁴Then David and his army cried loudly until they were too weak to cry any more. ⁵David's two wives had also been taken—Ahinoam of Jezreel and Abigail the widow of Nabal from Carmel. ⁶The men in the army were threatening to kill David with stones, which greatly upset David. Each man was sad and angry because his sons and daughters had been captured, but David found strength in the LORD his God. ⁷David said to Abiathar the priest, "Bring me the holy robe." *d*

⁸Then David asked the LORD, "Should I chase the people who took our families? Will I catch them?"

The LORD answered, "Chase them. You will catch them, and you will succeed in saving your families."

⁹David and the 600 men with him came to the Besor Ravine, where some of the men stayed. ¹⁰David and 400 men kept up the chase. The other 200 men stayed behind because they were too tired to cross the ravine.

¹¹They found an Egyptian in a field and brought him to David. They gave the Egyptian some water to drink and some food to eat. ¹²And they gave him a piece of a fig cake and two clusters of raisins. Then he felt better, because he had not eaten any food or drunk any water for three days and nights.

¹³David asked him, "Who is your master? Where do you come from?"

He answered, "I'm an Egyptian, the slave of an Amalekite. Three days ago my master left me, because I was sick. ¹⁴We had attacked the southern area of the Kerethites, the land of Judah and the southern area of Caleb. We burned Ziklag, as well.

¹⁵David asked him, "Can you lead me to the people who took our families?"

He answered, "Yes, if you promise me before God that you won't kill me or give me back to my master. Then I will take you to them."

¹⁶So the Egyptian led David to the Amalekites. They were lying around on the ground, eating and drinking and celebrating with the things they had taken from the land of the Philistines and from Judah. ¹⁷David fought them from sunset until the evening of the next day. None of them escaped, except 400 young men who rode off on their camels. ¹⁸David got his two wives back and everything the Amalekites had taken. ¹⁹Nothing was missing. David brought back everyone, young and old, sons and daughters. He recovered the valuable things and everything the Amalekites had taken. ²⁰David took all the sheep and cattle, and his men made these animals go in front, saying, "They are David's prize."

²¹Then David came to the 200 men who had been too tired to follow him, who had stayed at the Besor Ravine. They came out to meet David and the people with him. When he came near, David greeted the men at the ravine.

²²But the evil men and troublemakers among those who followed David said, "Since these 200 men didn't go with us, we shouldn't give them any of the things we recovered. Just let each man take his wife and children and go."

²³David answered, "No, my brothers. Don't do that after what the LORD has given us. He has protected us and given us the enemy who attacked us. ²⁴Who will listen to what you say? The share will be the same for the one who stayed with the supplies as for the one who went into battle. All will share alike." ²⁵David made this an order and rule for Israel, which continues even today.

²⁶When David arrived in Ziklag, he sent some of the things he had taken from the Amalekites to his friends, the elders of Judah. He said, "Here is a present for you from the things we took from the LORD's enemies."

²⁷David also sent some things to the leaders in Bethel, Ramoth in the southern part of Judah,

Jattir, ²⁸Aroer, Siphmoth, Eshtemoa, ²⁹Racal, the cities of the Jerahmeelites and the Kenites, ³⁰Hormah, Bor Ashan, Athach, ³¹Hebron and to the people in all the other places where he and his men had been.

The Death of Saul

31 The Philistines fought against Israel, and the Israelites ran away from them. Many Israelites were killed on Mount Gilboa. ²The Philistines fought hard against Saul and his sons, killing his sons Jonathan, Abinadab and Malki-Shua. ³The fighting was heavy around Saul. The archers shot him, and he was badly wounded. ⁴He said to the officer who carried his armour, "Pull out your sword and kill me. Then those uncircumcised *d* men won't make fun of me and kill me." But Saul's officer refused, because he was afraid. So Saul took his own sword and threw himself on it. ⁵When the officer saw that Saul was dead, he threw himself on his own sword, and he died with Saul. ⁶So Saul, his three sons and the officer who carried his armour died together that day.

⁷When the Israelites who lived across the Jezreel Valley and those who lived across the Jordan River saw how the Israelite army had run away, and that Saul and his sons were dead, they left their cities and ran away. Then the Philistines came and lived there.

⁸The next day when the Philistines came to take all the valuable things from the dead soldiers, they found Saul and his three sons dead on Mount Gilboa. ⁹They cut off Saul's head and took off his armour. Then they sent messengers through all the land of the Philistines to tell the news in the temple of their idols and to their people. ¹⁰They put Saul's armour in the temple of the Ashtoreths *d* and hung his body on the wall of Beth Shan.

¹¹When the people living in Jabesh Gilead heard what the Philistines had done to Saul, ¹²the brave men of Jabesh marched all night and came to Beth Shan. They removed the bodies of Saul and his sons from the wall of Beth Shan and brought them to Jabesh. There they burned the bodies. ¹³They took their bones and buried them under the tamarisk tree in Jabesh. Then the people of Jabesh gave up eating for seven days.

2 Samuel

Why Read This Book:

* Learn how leaders can encourage people to follow God (2 Samuel 1—6).
* Discover how God can use people for good in spite of their faults (2 Samuel 7—12).
* See how family problems can hurt leaders (2 Samuel 13—20).

Behind the Scenes:

If 1 Samuel tells the story of David's youth (and it does), then 2 Samuel tells the story of his life as a king. David was first crowned as the king of Judah, and then later as the king of all Israel. He is without doubt one of the greatest role models in the Old Testament, and God himself referred to him as " . . . the kind of man I want. He will do all I want him to do" (Acts 13:22, p.1160).

But despite the fact that David achieved so much in his life, he wasn't perfect.

2 Samuel tells of his affair with Bathsheba, and then of the way that he had her husband murdered in order to try and cover up his sin. The book tells us about his struggle with family problems which led to the death of his precious son Absalom.

Yet throughout all these problems, hang-ups and sins, David never stopped trying to follow God. When God's prophet confronted the king about his sin, David repented without hesitation. When his family was falling apart, he cried out to God for help. ▷

When?

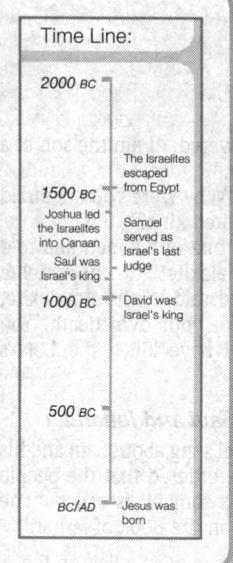

Time Line:

2000 BC

The Israelites escaped from Egypt

1500 BC
Joshua led the Israelites into Canaan
Saul was Israel's king

Samuel served as Israel's last judge

1000 BC
David was Israel's king

500 BC

BC/AD
Jesus was born

Where?

Outlined area is where the twelve tribes of Israel lived.

ARAM

Mediterranean Sea

David's army defeated the Israelite forces of Absalom, David's son, in the forest of Ephraim (2 Samuel 18:6–8).

When he became king, David had the Ark of God moved from Baalah to Jerusalem (2 Samuel 6:1–2).

ISRAEL

AMMON

• Baalah

Jerusalem •

David moved the capital of Israel to Jerusalem after he united the nation (2 Samuel 5:4–7).

Hebron •

Dead Sea   MOAB

David became king and started his rule in Hebron (2 Samuel 2:2–4).

EDOM

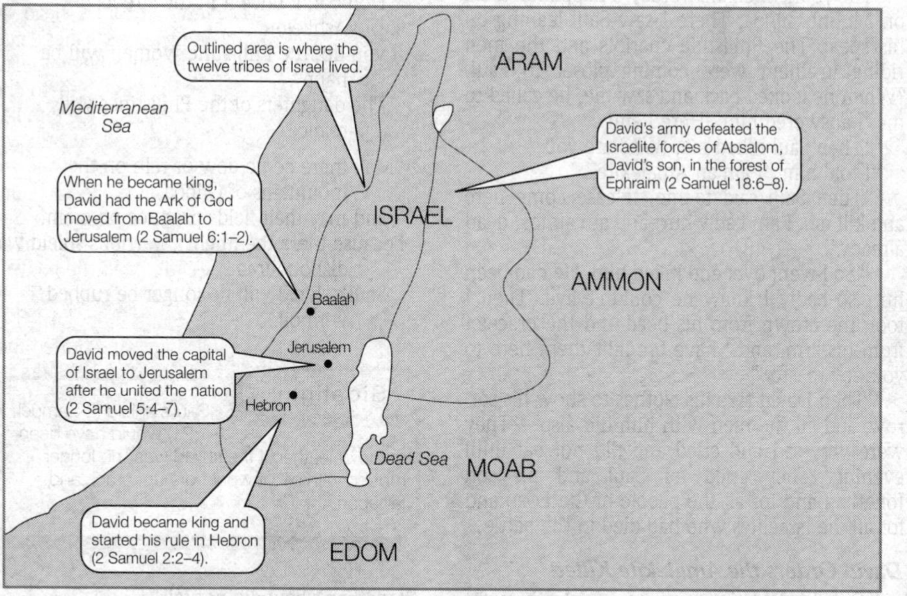

Behind the
Scenes (cont.):　Because David always relied on God, he became known as Israel's greatest king. He learned that God is a God of second chances, and that even when we fail, he is always prepared to pick us up, brush the dust from our clothes, and help us to continue following him.

David Learns About Saul's Death

1 Now Saul was dead. After David had defeated the Amalekites, he returned to Ziklag and stayed there for two days. [2]On the third day a young man from Saul's camp came to Ziklag. To show his sadness, his clothes were torn and he had dust on his head. He came and bowed face down on the ground before David.

[3]David asked him, "Where did you come from?"

The man answered, "I escaped from the Israelite camp."

[4]David asked him, "What happened? Please tell me!"

The man answered, "The people have run away from the battle, and many of them have fallen and are dead. Saul and his son Jonathan are dead also."

[5]David asked him, "How do you know Saul and his son Jonathan are dead?"

[6]The young man answered, "I happened to be on Mount Gilboa. There I saw Saul leaning on his spear. The Philistine chariots and the men riding in them were coming closer to Saul. [7]When he looked back and saw me, he called to me. I answered him, 'Here I am!'

[8]"Then Saul asked me, 'Who are you?'

"I told him, 'I am an Amalekite.'

[9]"Then Saul said to me, 'Please come here and kill me. I am badly hurt and am almost dead already.'

[10]"So I went over and killed him. He had been hurt so badly I knew he couldn't live. Then I took the crown from his head and the bracelet from his arm, and I have brought them here to you, my master."

[11]Then David tore his clothes to show his sorrow, and all the men with him did also. [12]They were very sad and cried and did not eat until evening. They cried for Saul and his son Jonathan and for all the people of the LORD and for all the Israelites who had died in the battle.

David Orders the Amalekite Killed

[13]David asked the young man who brought the report, "Where are you from?"

The young man answered, "I am the son of a foreigner, an Amalekite."

[14]David asked him, "Why were you not afraid to kill the LORD's appointed king?"

[15]Then David called one of his men and told him, "Go! Kill the Amalekite!" So the Israelite killed him. [16]David had said to the Amalekite, "You are responsible for your own death. You confessed by saying, 'I have killed the LORD's appointed king.' "

David's Song About Saul and Jonathan

[17]David sang a funeral song about Saul and his son Jonathan, [18]and he ordered that the people of Judah be taught this song. It is called "The Bow", and it is written in the Book of Jashar:

[19]"Israel, your leaders have been killed on the hills.
　How the mighty have fallen in battle!
[20]Don't tell it in Gath.
　Don't announce it in the streets of Ashkelon.
If you do, the Philistine women will be happy.
　The daughters of the Philistines will rejoice.

[21]"May there be no dew or rain on the mountains of Gilboa,
　and may their fields produce no grain,
because there the mighty warrior's shield was dishonoured.
　Saul's shield will no longer be rubbed with oil.

> **Sidelight**　Saul's shield (2 Samuel 1:21) would have been made of leather. If the shield was "no longer rubbed with oil", it would dry up, crack and fall apart.

[22]Jonathan's bow did not fail
　to kill many soldiers.

Saul's sword did not fail
  to wound many strong men.

23"We loved Saul and Jonathan
  and enjoyed them while they lived.
They are together even in death.
They were faster than eagles.
  They were stronger than lions.

24"You daughters of Israel, cry for Saul.
Saul clothed you with red dresses
  and put gold decorations on them.

25"How the mighty have fallen in battle!
  Jonathan is dead on Gilboa's hills.
26I cry for you, my brother Jonathan.
  I enjoyed your friendship so much.
Your love to me was wonderful,
  better than the love of women.
27"How the mighty have fallen!
  The weapons of war are gone."

David is Made King of Judah

2 Later, David prayed to the LORD, saying, "Should I go up to any of the cities of Judah?"

The LORD said to David, "Go."

David asked, "Where should I go?"

The LORD answered, "To Hebron."

2So David went up to Hebron with his two wives: Ahinoam from Jezreel and Abigail, the widow of Nabal from Carmel. 3David also brought his men and their families, and they all made their homes in the cities of Hebron. 4Then the men of Judah came to Hebron and appointed David king over Judah.

They told David that the men of Jabesh Gilead had buried Saul. 5So David sent messengers to the men of Jabesh Gilead and said to them, "The LORD bless you. You have shown loyalty to your master Saul by burying him. 6May the LORD now

DEATH

Goodbye England's Rose

The death of Diana, Princess of Wales, stunned our nation and the world. Everyone remembers where they were when they heard the news. Young and old, we joined together to grieve over a much loved lady. The three million flowers outside the palaces were a sign that people needed to do more than sit at home and mourn. They signed books, they threw bouquets into the path of the hearse as it made its way through England. It was obvious that something had to happen nationally to calm the people down and give them something to hold on to.

Elton John wrote a song for the funeral. Over thirty million people bought the record and felt strangely consoled by it.

When Saul and his son Jonathan died, David felt compelled to write a song. He saw the nation's grief and knew that he himself needed to do something. The funeral song that David wrote was given to the people of Judah. In fact, he ordered the nation to learn the song! There were no CDs in those days, so the song had to be taught.

Often we find it hard to express ourselves by speaking words alone, but to sing, to listen to music, to write it down maybe poetically is consolation itself.

Look at the words of David's song "The Bow" in **2 Samuel 1:17–27**, particularly the lines "We enjoyed them while they lived" and "I enjoyed your friendship so much".

* Do you feel helped by remembering the good things?
* Have you ever lost anyone close to you? How did you cope?

Consider . . .

* writing things down when you are sad about the loss of someone you love, and reading them later.
* telling the Lord how you feel, in a song or poem.

For more, see . . .

* Deuteronomy 34:1–12 (p.200)
* Matthew 5:4 (p.942)

* Isaiah 61:1–11 (p.705)

be loyal and true to you. I will also treat you well because you have done this. 7Now be strong and brave. Saul your master is dead, and the people of Judah have appointed me their king."

War Between Judah and Israel

8Abner son of Ner was the commander of Saul's army. Abner took Saul's son Ish-Bosheth to Mahanaim 9and made him king of Gilead, Ashuri, Jezreel, Ephraim, Benjamin and all Israel. 10Saul's son Ish-Bosheth was 40 years old when he became king over Israel, and he ruled two years. But the people of Judah followed David. 11David was king in Hebron for seven years and six months.

12Abner son of Ner and the servants of Ish-Bosheth son of Saul left Mahanaim and went to Gibeon. 13Joab son of Zeruiah and David's men also went there and met Abner and Ish-Bosheth's men at the pool of Gibeon. Abner's group sat on one side of the pool; Joab's group sat on the other.

14Abner said to Joab, "Let the young men have a contest here."

Joab said, "Yes, let them have a contest."

15Then the men got up and were counted—twelve from the people of Benjamin for Ish-Bosheth son of Saul, and twelve from David's men. 16Each man grabbed the one opposite him by the head and stabbed him in the side with a knife. So the men fell down together. For that reason, that place in Gibeon is called the Field of Knives. 17That day there was a terrible battle, and David's men defeated Abner and the Israelites.

Sidelight
The pool of Gibeon – where Saul's and David's armies fought – was a huge well (2 Samuel 2:8–17). Archaeologists have discovered what was probably the pool. It is 11½ metres in diameter, and has a 79-step winding stairway down to the water level, which is roughly 10 metres below the ground.

Abner Kills Asahel

18Zeruiah's three sons, Joab, Abishai and Asahel, were there. Now Asahel was a fast runner, as fast as a deer in the field. 19Asahel chased Abner, going straight towards him. 20Abner looked back and asked, "Is that you, Asahel?"

Asahel said, "Yes, it is."

21Then Abner said to Asahel, "Turn to your right or left and catch one of the young men and take his armour." But Asahel refused to stop chasing him.

22Abner again said to Asahel, "Stop chasing me! If you don't stop, I'll have to kill you! Then I won't be able to face your brother Joab again!"

23But Asahel refused to stop chasing Abner. So using the back end of his spear, Abner stabbed Asahel in the stomach, and the spear came out of his back. Asahel died right there, and everyone stopped when they came to the place where Asahel's body lay.

24But Joab and Abishai continued chasing Abner. As the sun was going down, they arrived at the hill of Ammah, near Giah on the way to the desert near Gibeon. 25The men of Benjamin came to Abner, and all stood together at the top of the hill.

26Abner shouted to Joab, "Must the sword kill for ever? Surely you must know this will only end in sadness! Tell the people to stop chasing their own brothers!"

27Then Joab said, "As surely as God lives, if you had not said anything, the people would have chased their brothers until morning." 28Then Joab blew a trumpet, and his people stopped chasing the Israelites. They did not fight them any more.

29Abner and his men marched all night through the Jordan Valley. They crossed the Jordan River, and after marching all day, arrived at Mahanaim.

30After he had stopped chasing Abner, Joab came back and gathered the people together. Asahel and nineteen of David's men were missing. 31But David's men had killed 360 Benjaminites who had followed Abner. 32David's men took Asahel and buried him in the tomb of his father at Bethlehem. Then Joab and his men marched all night. The sun came up as they reached Hebron.

3 There was a long war between the people who supported Saul's family and those who supported David's family. The supporters of David's family became stronger and stronger, but the supporters of Saul's family became weaker and weaker.

David's Sons

2Sons were born to David at Hebron. The first was Amnon, whose mother was Ahinoam from Jezreel. 3The second son was Kileab, whose mother was Abigail, the widow of Nabal from Carmel. The third son was Absalom, whose mother was Maacah daughter of Talmai, the king of Geshur. 4The fourth son was Adonijah, whose mother was Haggith. The fifth son was Shephatiah, whose mother was Abital. 5The sixth son was Ithream, whose mother was Eglah, David's wife. These sons were born to David at Hebron.

Abner Joins David

[6]During the war between the supporters of Saul's family and the supporters of David's family, Abner made himself a main leader among the supporters of Saul.

[7]Saul once had a slave woman [d] named Rizpah, who was the daughter of Aiah. Ish-Bosheth said to Abner, "Why did you have sexual relations with my father's slave woman?"

[8]Abner was very angry because of what Ish-Bosheth said, and he replied, "I have been loyal to Saul and his family and friends! I didn't hand you over to David. I am not a traitor working for Judah! But now you are saying I did something wrong with this woman! [9]May God help me if I don't join David! I will make sure that what the Lord promised does happen! [10]I will take the kingdom from the family of Saul and make David king of Israel and Judah, from Dan to Beersheba!"[n]

[11]Ish-Bosheth couldn't say anything to Abner, because he was afraid of him.

[12]Then Abner sent messengers to ask David, "Who is going to rule the land? Make an agreement with me, and I will help you unite all Israel."

[13]David answered, "Good! I will make an agreement with you, but I ask you one thing. I will not meet with you unless you bring Saul's daughter Michal to me." [14]Then David sent messengers to Saul's son Ish-Bosheth, saying, "Give me my wife Michal. She was promised to me, and I killed 100 Philistines to get her."

[15]So Ish-Bosheth sent men to take Michal from her husband Paltiel son of Laish. [16]Michal's husband went with her, crying as he followed her to Bahurim. But Abner said to Paltiel, "Go back home." So he went home.

Sidelight

Have you ever felt that your parents interfere with your choice of who to go out with? Think how David felt – he married Saul's daughter, Michal (1 Samuel 18:20–29, p.273) but when Saul fell out with David, he took his daughter away and gave her to someone else to marry (1 Samuel 25:44, p.279). Later, she was returned to David as part of a political bargain (2 Samuel 3:12–16).

---

[17]Abner sent this message to the elders of Israel: "You have been wanting to make David your king. [18]Now do it! The Lord said of David, 'Through my servant David, I will save my people Israel from the Philistines and all their enemies.' "

[19]Abner also said these things to the people of Benjamin. He then went to Hebron to tell David what the Benjaminites and Israel wanted to do. [20]Abner came with 20 men to David at Hebron. There David prepared a feast for them. [21]Abner said to David, "My master and king, I will go and bring all the Israelites to you. Then they will make an agreement with you so you will rule over all Israel as you wanted." So David let Abner go, and he left in peace.

Abner's Death

[22]Just then Joab and David's men came from a battle, bringing many valuable things they had taken from the enemy. David had let Abner leave in peace, so he was not with David at Hebron. [23]When Joab and all his army arrived at Hebron, the army said to Joab, "Abner son of Ner came to King David, and David let him leave in peace."

[24]Joab came to the king and said, "What have you done? Abner came to you. Why did you let him go? Now he's gone. [25]You know Abner son of Ner! He came to trick you! He came to learn about everything you are doing!"

[26]After Joab left David, he sent messengers after Abner, and they brought him back from the well of Sirah. But David did not know this. [27]When Abner arrived at Hebron, Joab took him aside into the gateway. He acted as though he wanted to talk with Abner in private, but Joab stabbed him in the stomach, and Abner died. Abner had killed Joab's brother Asahel, so Joab killed Abner to pay him back.

[28]Later when David heard the news, he said, "My kingdom and I are innocent for ever of the death of Abner son of Ner. The Lord knows this. [29]Joab and his family are responsible for this. May his family always have someone with sores or with a skin disease. May they always have someone who must lean on a crutch. May some of his family be killed in war. May they always have someone without food to eat."

[30](Joab and his brother Abishai killed Abner, because he had killed their brother Asahel in the battle at Gibeon.)

[31]Then David said to Joab and to all the people with Joab, "Tear your clothes and put on rough cloth to show how sad you are. Cry for Abner." King David himself followed the body of Abner. [32]They buried Abner in Hebron, and David and all the people cried at Abner's grave.

[33]King David sang this funeral song for Abner.

"Did Abner die like a fool?

Dan to Beersheba   Dan was the city farthest north in Israel, and Beersheba was the city farthest south. So this means all the people of Israel.

34 His hands were not tied.
　His feet were not in chains.
　He fell at the hands of evil men."

Then all the people cried again for Abner. 35They came to encourage David to eat while it was still day. But he made a promise, saying, "May God punish me terribly if I eat bread or anything else before the sun sets!"

36All the people saw what happened, and they agreed with what the king was doing, just as they agreed with everything he did. 37That day all the people of Judah and Israel understood that David did not order the killing of Abner son of Ner.

38David said to his officers, "You know that a great man died today in Israel. 39Even though I am the appointed king, I feel empty. These sons of Zeruiah are too much for me. May the LORD give them the punishment they should have."

Ish-Bosheth's Death

4 When Ish-Bosheth son of Saul heard that Abner had died at Hebron, he was shocked and all Israel became frightened. 2Two men who were captains in Saul's army came to Ish-Bosheth. One was named Baanah, and the other was named Recab. They were the sons of Rimmon of Beeroth, who was a Benjaminite. (The town Beeroth belonged to the tribe *d* of Benjamin. 3The people of Beeroth ran away to Gittaim, and they still live there as foreigners today.)

4(Saul's son Jonathan had a son named Mephibosheth, who was crippled in both feet. He was five years old when the news came from Jezreel that Saul and Jonathan were dead. Mephibosheth's nurse had picked him up and run away. But as she hurried to leave, she dropped him, and now he was lame.)

5Recab and Baanah, sons of Rimmon from Beeroth, went to Ish-Bosheth's house in the afternoon while he was having his midday rest. 6-7They went into the middle of the house as if to get some wheat. Ish-Bosheth was lying on his bed in his bedroom. Then Recab and Baanah stabbed him in the stomach, killed him, cut off his head and took it with them. They escaped and travelled all night through the Jordan Valley. 8When they arrived at Hebron, they gave his head to David and said to the king, "Here is the head of Ish-Bosheth son of Saul, your enemy. He tried to kill you! Today the LORD has paid back Saul and his family for what they did to you!"

9David answered Recab and his brother Baanah, the sons of Rimmon of Beeroth, "As surely as the LORD lives, he has saved me from all trouble! 10Once a man thought he was bringing me good news. When he told me, 'Saul is dead!' I seized him and killed him at Ziklag. That was the reward I gave him for his news! 11So even more I must put you evil men to death because you have killed an innocent man on his own bed in his own house!"

12So David commanded his men to kill Recab and Baanah. They cut off the hands and feet of Recab and Baanah and hung them over the pool of Hebron. Then they took Ish-Bosheth's head and buried it in Abner's tomb at Hebron.

David is Made King of Israel

5 Then all the tribes*d* of Israel came to David at Hebron and said to him, "Look, we are your own family. 2Even when Saul was king, you were the one who led Israel in battle. The LORD said to you, 'You will be a shepherd for my people Israel. You will be their leader.' "

3So all the elders of Israel came to King David at Hebron, and he made an agreement with them in Hebron in the presence of the LORD. Then they poured oil on David to make him king over Israel.

4David was 30 years old when he became king, and he ruled 40 years. 5He was king over Judah in Hebron for seven years and six months, and he was king over all Israel and Judah in Jerusalem for 33 years.

6When the king and his men went to Jerusalem to attack the Jebusites who lived there, the Jebusites said to David, "You can't get inside our city. Even the blind and the crippled can stop you." They thought David could not enter their city. 7But David did take the city of Jerusalem with its strong walls, and it became the City of David.

8That day David said to his men, "To defeat the Jebusites you must go through the water tunnel. Then you can reach those 'crippled' and 'blind' enemies. This is why people say, 'The blind and the crippled may not enter the palace.' "

9So David lived in the fortified city and called it the City of David. David built more buildings around it, beginning where the land was filled in. He also built more buildings inside the city. 10He became stronger and stronger, because the LORD God All-powerful was with him.

11Hiram king of the city of Tyre sent messengers to David, along with cedar logs, carpenters and stonecutters. They built a palace for David.

> **Sidelight** Although Jerusalem wasn't very big by modern standards it was a well-protected fortress city. David captured it and became king of the nation, "because the LORD God All-powerful was with him" (2 Samuel 5:10).

¹²Then David knew that the LORD really had made him king of Israel and that the LORD had made his kingdom great because the LORD loved his people Israel.

¹³After he came from Hebron, David took for himself more slave women *d* and wives in Jerusalem. More sons and daughters were born to David. ¹⁴These are the names of the sons born to David in Jerusalem: Shammua, Shobab, Nathan, Solomon, ¹⁵Ibhar, Elishua, Nepheg, Japhia, ¹⁶Elishama, Eliada and Eliphelet.

David Defeats the Philistines

¹⁷When the Philistines heard that David had been made king over Israel, all the Philistines went to look for him. But when David heard the news, he went down to the stronghold. *d* ¹⁸The Philistines came and camped in the Valley of Rephaim. ¹⁹David asked the LORD, "Should I attack the Philistines? Will you hand them over to me?"

The LORD said to David, "Go! I will certainly hand them over to you."

²⁰So David went to Baal Perazim and defeated the Philistines there. David said, "Like a flood of water, the LORD has broken through my enemies in front of me." So David named the place Baal Perazim. *n* ²¹The Philistines left their idols behind at Baal Perazim, so David and his men carried them away.

²²Once again the Philistines came and camped at the Valley of Rephaim. ²³When David prayed to the LORD, he answered, "Don't attack the Philistines from the front. Instead, go around and attack them in front of the balsam trees. ²⁴When you hear the sound of marching in the tops of the balsam trees, act quickly. I, the LORD, will have gone ahead of you to defeat the Philistine army."

Baal Perazim   This name means "the LORD breaks through".

LEADERSHIP

Earned Respect

The other athletics team members didn't know what to think when Anne walked into the changing room. She was a first year, and everyone else on the team was in their second or third year at college. "How's everybody doing?" she said cheerfully.

Within weeks, Anne had become a star, beating the county record in the 400 metres. But when the local newspaper reporter asked her about it, she replied: "I'm glad the team did well. The whole team encouraged me in that race. We work hard together."

Anne would never take glory for her performance. And, gradually, the older girls began asking her for coaching. By the end of the season, the whole team had become one of the best in the county.

When it came to picking a captain for the next year, no one questioned whom to pick. She might only be in her second year, and usually a final-year student led the team, but Anne was the team's natural leader.

Like Anne, David had proved his leadership skills for years. So when it came time to find a new king, he was a natural choice, even though he was young. Read how the country chose him in **2 Samuel 5:1–5**.

* How did both Anne and David earn respect so that they were chosen as leaders?
  How did their humility help them both as leaders?
* How can you, like David, work to earn people's respect so that you can be a leader?

Consider . . .

* talking to a leader you respect about how he or she became a leader. Then put into practise one tip you have learned.
* working to be a team player at church, school and work, then watching to see what leadership role you might play.

For more, see . . .

* Jeremiah 1:4–10 (p.716)
* 1 Corinthians 3:5–9 (p.1216)
* Matthew 20:20–28 (p.976)

²⁵So David did what the LORD commanded. He defeated the Philistines and chased them all the way from Gibeon to Gezer.

The Ark is Brought to Jerusalem

6 David again gathered all the chosen men of Israel—30,000 of them. ²Then he and all his people went to Baalah in Judahⁿ to bring back the Ark^d of God. The Ark is called by the Name, the name of the LORD All-powerful, whose throne is between the gold creatures with wings. ³They put the Ark of God on a new cart and brought it out of Abinadab's house on the hill. Uzzah and Ahio, sons of Abinadab, led the new cart ⁴which had the Ark of God on it. Ahio was walking in front of it. ⁵David and all the Israelites were celebrating in the presence of the LORD. They were playing wooden instruments: lyres,^d harps, tambourines,^d rattles and cymbals.

⁶When David's men came to the threshing^d floor of Nacon, the oxen stumbled. So Uzzah reached out to steady the Ark of God. ⁷The LORD was angry with Uzzah and killed him because of what he did. So Uzzah died there beside the Ark of God. ⁸David was angry because the LORD had killed Uzzah. Now that place is called the Punishment of Uzzah.

⁹David was afraid of the LORD that day, and he said, "How can the Ark of the LORD come to me now?" ¹⁰So David would not move the Ark of the LORD to be with him in Jerusalem. Instead, he took it to the house of Obed-Edom, a man from Gath. ¹¹The Ark of the LORD stayed in Obed-Edom's house for three months, and the LORD blessed Obed-Edom and all his family.

¹²The people told David, "The LORD has blessed the family of Obed-Edom and all that belongs to him, because the Ark of God is there." So David went and brought it up from Obed-Edom's house to Jerusalem with joy. ¹³When the men carrying the Ark of the LORD had walked six steps, David sacrificed a bull and a fat calf. ¹⁴Then David danced with all his might before the LORD. He had on a holy linen robe.^d ¹⁵David and all the Israelites shouted with joy and blew the trumpets as they brought the Ark of the LORD to the city.

¹⁶As the Ark of the LORD came into the city, Saul's daughter Michal looked out of the window. When she saw David jumping and dancing in the presence of the LORD, she hated him.

¹⁷David put up a tent for the Ark of the LORD, and then the Israelites put it in its place inside the tent. David offered whole burnt offerings and fellowship offerings before the LORD. ¹⁸When David finished offering the whole burnt offerings and the fellowship offerings, he blessed the people in the name of the LORD All-powerful. ¹⁹David gave a loaf of bread, a cake of dates and a cake of raisins to every Israelite, both men and women. Then all the people went home.

²⁰David went back to bless the people in his home, but Saul's daughter Michal came out to meet him. She said, "With what honour the king of Israel acted today! You took off your clothes in front of the servant girls of your officers like one who takes off his clothes without shame!"

²¹Then David said to Michal, "I did it in the presence of the LORD. The LORD chose me, not your father or anyone from Saul's family. The LORD appointed me to be over Israel. So I will celebrate in the presence of the LORD. ²²Maybe I will lose even more honour, and maybe I will be brought down in my own opinion, but the girls you talk about will honour me!"

²³And Saul's daughter Michal had no children to the day she died.

David Wants to Build a Temple

7 King David was living in his palace, and the LORD had given him peace from all his enemies around him. ²Then David said to Nathan the prophet,^d "Look, I am living in a palace made of cedar wood, but the Ark^d of God is in a tent!"

³Nathan said to the king, "Go and do what you really want to do, because the LORD is with you."

⁴But that night the LORD spoke his word to Nathan, ⁵"Go and tell my servant David, 'This is what the LORD says: will you build a house for me to live in? ⁶From the time I brought the Israelites out of Egypt until now I have not lived in a house. I have been moving around all this time with a tent as my home. ⁷As I have moved with the Israelites, I have never said to the tribes,^d whom I commanded to take care of my people Israel, "Why haven't you built me a house of cedar?" '

⁸"You must tell my servant David, 'This is what the LORD All-powerful says: I took you from the pasture and from tending the sheep and made you leader of my people Israel. ⁹I have been with you everywhere you have gone and have defeated your enemies for you. I will make you as famous as any of the great people on the earth. ¹⁰Also I will choose a place for my people Israel, and I will plant them so they can live in their own homes. They will not be bothered any more. Wicked people will no longer bother them as they have in the past ¹¹when I chose judges for my people Israel. But I will give you peace from all your enemies. I also tell you that I will make your descendants^d kings of Israel after you.

Baalah in Judah　Another name for Kiriath Jearim.

¹²" 'When you die and join your ancestors, I will make one of your sons the next king, and I will set up his kingdom. ¹³He will build a house for me, and I will let his kingdom rule always. ¹⁴I will be his father, and he will be my son. When he sins, I will use other people to punish him. They will be my whips. ¹⁵I took away my love from Saul, whom I removed before you, but I will never stop loving your son. ¹⁶But your family and your kingdom will continue always before me. Your throne will last for ever.' "

¹⁷Nathan told David everything God had said in this vision.

David Prays to God

¹⁸Then King David went in and sat in front of the LORD. David said, "Lord GOD, who am I? What is my family? Why did you bring me to this point? ¹⁹But even this is not enough for you, Lord GOD. You have also made promises about my future family. This is not normal, Lord GOD.

²⁰"What more can I say to you, Lord GOD, since you know me, your servant, so well! ²¹You have done this great thing because you said you would and because you wanted to, and you have let me know about it. ²²This is why you are great, Lord GOD! There is no one like you. There is no God except you. We have heard all this ourselves! ²³There is no nation like your people Israel. They are the only people on earth that God chose to be his own. You made your name well known. You did great and wonderful miracles*d* for them. You went ahead of them and forced other nations and their gods out of the land. You freed your people from slavery in Egypt. ²⁴You made the people of Israel your very own people for ever, and, LORD, you are their God.

²⁵"Now, LORD God, keep the promise for ever that you made about my family and me, your servant. Do what you have said. ²⁶Then you will be honoured always, and people will say, 'The LORD All-powerful is God over Israel!' And the family of your servant David will continue before you.

²⁷"LORD All-powerful, the God of Israel, you have said to me, 'I will make your family great.' So I, your servant, am brave enough to pray to you. ²⁸Lord GOD, you are God, and your words

THANKFULNESS

Unnoticed Gifts

If you have trouble thinking of things to thank God for, start with this list of things:

* A defence against tiny bacteria and larger creatures such as fleas, wasps and jellyfish.
* A radiator to cool you.
* Padding that takes the shape of objects it touches.
* Half a million transmitters that send messages through your body.
* A unique pattern that identifies you.

All these things are in just one part of your body: your skin. Imagine how much else you have to be thankful for in your life and world! David recognised the gifts that God had given to him and his family. Read his prayer of thanksgiving in **2 Samuel 7:18–29**.

Thank you!

* Why does God say that God gives good things? What is David's response?
* What has God given to you that reminds you of how important you are? How have you thanked God for that?

Consider . . .

* making a list of people and things for which you are most thankful. Thank God for each of these people or things this week, and write each person a thank-you message.
* tracing your family tree back as far as you can. Then talk to your parents about the strengths of each generation. Pray that God will guide and bless you and future generations.

For more, see . . .

* Psalm 98:1–9 (p.557)
* Colossians 1:9–13 (p.1289)
* Isaiah 63:7–9 (p.709)

are true. And you have promised these good things to me, your servant. [29]Please, bless my family. Let it continue before you always. Lord GOD, you have said so. With your blessing let my family always be blessed."

David Wins Many Wars

8 Later, David defeated the Philistines, conquered them, and took the city of Metheg Ammah.

[2]He also defeated the people of Moab. He made them lie on the ground, and then he used a rope to measure them. Those who were measured within two rope lengths were killed, but those who were within the next rope length were allowed to live. So the people of Moab became servants of David and gave him the payment he demanded.

[3]David also defeated Hadadezer son of Rehob, king of Zobah, as he went to take control again at the Euphrates River. [4]David captured 1,000 chariots, 7,000 men who rode in chariots, and 20,000 foot soldiers. He crippled all but 100 of the chariot horses.

[5]Arameans from Damascus came to help Hadadezer king of Zobah, but David killed 22,000 of them. [6]Then David put groups of soldiers in Damascus in Aram. The Arameans became David's servants and gave him the payment he demanded. The LORD gave David victory everywhere he went.

[7]David took the shields of gold that had belonged to Hadadezer's officers and brought them to Jerusalem. [8]David also took many things made of bronze from Tebah and Berothai, which had been cities under Hadadezer's control.

[9]Toi king of Hamath heard that David had defeated all the army of Hadadezer. [10]So Toi sent his son Joram to greet and congratulate King David for defeating Hadadezer. (Hadadezer had been at war with Toi.) Joram brought things made of silver, gold and bronze. [11]King David gave them to the LORD, along with the silver and gold he had taken from the other nations he had defeated. [12]These nations were Edom, Moab, Ammon, Philistia and Amalek. David also gave the LORD what he had taken from Hadadezer son of Rehob, king of Zobah.

[13]David was famous after he returned from defeating 18,000 Arameans in the Valley of Salt. [14]He put groups of soldiers all over Edom, and all the Edomites became his servants. The LORD gave David victory everywhere he went.

[15]David was king over all Israel, and he did what was fair and right for all his people. [16]Joab son of Zeruiah was commander over the army. Jehoshaphat son of Ahilud was the recorder. [17]Zadok son of Ahitub and Abiathar son of Ahimelech were priests. Seraiah was the royal secretary. [18]Benaiah son of Jehoiada was over the Kerethites and Pelethites.[n] And David's sons were priests.

David Helps Saul's Family

9 David asked, "Is anyone still left in Saul's family? I want to show kindness to that person for Jonathan's sake!"

[2]Now there was a servant named Ziba from Saul's family. So David's servants called Ziba to him. King David said to him, "Are you Ziba?"

He answered, "Yes, I am your servant."

[3]The king asked, "Is anyone left in Saul's family? I want to show God's kindness to that person."

Ziba answered the king, "Jonathan has a son still living who is crippled in both feet."

[4]The king asked Ziba, "Where is this son?"

Ziba answered, "He is at the house of Makir son of Ammiel in Lo Debar."

[5]Then King David had servants bring Jonathan's son from the house of Makir son of Ammiel in Lo Debar. [6]Mephibosheth, Jonathan's son, came before David and bowed face down on the floor.

David said, "Mephibosheth!"

Mephibosheth said, "I am your servant."

[7]David said to him, "Don't be afraid. I will be kind to you for your father Jonathan's sake. I will give you back all the land of your grandfather Saul, and you will always eat at my table."

[8]Mephibosheth bowed to David again and said, "You are being very kind to me, your servant! And I am no better than a dead dog!"

[9]Then King David called Saul's servant Ziba. David said to him, "I have given your master's grandson everything that belonged to Saul and his family. [10]You, your sons and your servants will farm the land and harvest the crops. Then your family will have food to eat. But Mephibosheth, your master's grandson, will always eat at my table."

(Now Ziba had fifteen sons and 20 servants.) [11]Ziba said to King David, "I, your servant, will do everything my master, the king, commands me."

So Mephibosheth ate at David's table as if he were one of the king's sons. [12]Mephibosheth had a young son named Mica. Everyone in Ziba's family became Mephibosheth's servants. [13]Mephibosheth lived in Jerusalem, because he always ate at the king's table. And he was crippled in both feet.

Kerethites and Pelethites   These were probably special units of the army that were responsible for the king's safety, a kind of palace guard.

War with the Ammonites and Arameans

10 When Nahash king of the Ammonites died, his son Hanun became king after him. [2]David said, "Nahash was loyal to me, so I will be loyal to his son Hanun." So David sent his messengers to comfort Hanun about his father's death.

David's officers went to the land of the Ammonites. [3]But the Ammonite leaders said to Hanun, their master, "Do you think David wants to honour your father by sending men to comfort you? No! David sent them to study the city and spy it out and capture it!" [4]So Hanun arrested David's officers. To shame them he shaved off half their beards and cut off their clothes at the hips. Then he sent them away.

[5]When the people told David, he sent messengers to meet his officers because they were very ashamed. King David said, "Stay in Jericho until your beards have grown back. Then come home."

[6]The Ammonites knew that they had insulted David. So they hired 20,000 Aramean foot soldiers from Beth Rehob and Zobah. They also hired the king of Maacah with 1,000 men and 12,000 men from Tob.

[7]When David heard about this, he sent Joab with the whole army. [8]The Ammonites came out and prepared for battle at the city gate. The Arameans from Zobah and Rehob and the men from Tob and Maacah were out in the field by themselves.

[9]Joab saw that there were enemies both in front of him and behind him. So he chose some of the best soldiers of Israel and sent them out to fight the Arameans. [10]Joab put the rest of the army under the command of Abishai, his brother. Then he sent them out to fight the Ammonites. [11]Joab said to Abishai, "If the Arameans are too strong for me, you must help me. Or, if the Ammonites are too strong for you, I will help you. [12]Be strong. We must fight bravely for our people and the cities of our God. The LORD will do what he thinks is right."

[13]Then Joab and the army with him went to attack the Arameans, and the Arameans ran away. [14]When the Ammonites saw that the Arameans were running away, they also ran away from Abishai and went back to their city. So Joab returned from the battle with the Ammonites and came to Jerusalem.

[15]When the Arameans saw that Israel had defeated them, they came together into one big army. [16]Hadadezer sent messengers to bring the Arameans from east of the Euphrates River, and they went to Helam. Their leader was Shobach, the commander of Hadadezer's army.

[17]When David heard about this, he gathered all the Israelites together. They crossed over the Jordan River and went to Helam. There the Arameans prepared for battle and attacked him. [18]But the Arameans ran away from the Israelites. David killed 700 Aramean chariot drivers and 40,000 Aramean horsemen. He also killed Shobach, the commander of the Aramean army.

[19]When the kings who served Hadadezer saw that the Israelites had defeated them, they made peace with the Israelites and served them. And the Arameans were afraid to help the Ammonites again.

> **Sidelight** If you wanted to shame a man in ancient Israel, you could shave off his beard. But if you did it, you had to be prepared for him to strike back in revenge. In 2 Samuel 10:1–19, such an act resulted in a war that took about 40,700 lives.

David Sins with Bathsheba

11 In the spring, when the kings normally went out to war, David sent out Joab, his servants and all the Israelites. They destroyed the Ammonites and attacked the city of Rabbah. But David stayed in Jerusalem. [2]One evening David got up from his bed and walked around on the roof[n] of his palace. While he was on the roof, he saw a woman bathing. She was very beautiful. [3]So David sent his servants to find out who she was. A servant answered, "That woman is Bathsheba daughter of Eliam. She is the wife of Uriah the Hittite." [4]So David sent messengers to bring Bathsheba to him. When she came to him, he had sexual relations with her. (Now Bathsheba had purified herself from her monthly period.) Then she went back to her house. [5]But Bathsheba became pregnant and sent word to David, saying, "I am pregnant."

[6]So David sent a message to Joab: "Send Uriah the Hittite to me." And Joab sent Uriah to David. [7]When Uriah came to him, David asked him how Joab was, how the soldiers were and how the war was going. [8]Then David said to Uriah, "Go home and rest."

So Uriah left the palace, and the king sent a gift to him. [9]But Uriah did not go home. Instead, he slept outside the door of the palace as all the king's officers did.

---

roof In Bible times houses were built with flat roofs. The roof was used for drying things such as flax and fruit. And it was used as an extra room, as a place for worship and as a place to sleep in the summer.

[10]The officers told David, "Uriah did not go home."

Then David said to Uriah, "You came from a long trip. Why didn't you go home?"

[11]Uriah said to him, "The Ark[d] and the soldiers of Israel and Judah are staying in tents. My master Joab and his officers are camping out in the fields. It isn't right for me to go home to eat and drink and have sexual relations with my wife!"

[12]David said to Uriah, "Stay here today. Tomorrow I'll send you back to the battle." So Uriah stayed in Jerusalem that day and the next. [13]Then David called Uriah to come to see him, so Uriah ate and drank with David. David made Uriah drunk, but he still did not go home. That evening Uriah again slept with the king's officers.

[14]The next morning David wrote a letter to Joab and sent it by Uriah. [15]In the letter David wrote, "Put Uriah on the front lines where the fighting is worst and leave him there alone. Let him be killed in battle."

[16]Joab watched the city and saw where its strongest defenders were and put Uriah there. [17]When the men of the city came out to fight against Joab, some of David's men were killed. And Uriah the Hittite was one of them.

[18]Then Joab sent David a complete account of the war. [19]Joab told the messenger, "Tell King David what happened in the war. [20]After you finish, the king may be angry and ask, 'Why did you go so near the city to fight? Didn't you know they would shoot arrows from the city wall? [21]Do you remember who killed Abimelech son of Jerub-Besheth?[n] It was a woman on the city wall. She threw a large stone for grinding grain on Abimelech and killed him there in Thebez. Why did you go so near the wall?' If

---

Jerub-Besheth   Another name for Gideon.

SEXUALITY

Risking Everything

Something about Louise turned Alan's head. Perhaps it was her figure . . . or her playful smile . . . or her piercing eyes. Whatever it was, Alan couldn't get her out of his mind.

After two weeks of nervous planning, he finally found the courage to ask her out. He did everything he could to impress her. He polished his motorbike and took her to the best restaurant in town. He turned on his charm, making sure she knew how important he was.

After that first date, they kissed at the door. But over the next few weeks, Alan wanted more. Each time, he would try to go a little further. Each time she would resist.

As their dizzying romance continued, Alan became more aggressive. Louise continued to resist, but Alan applied even more pressure. "If you really loved me," he said, "you wouldn't make me stop."

"But I do love you, Alan," she replied.

"Well, I can't be sure unless you show me."

Frightened at the prospect of losing Alan, Louise finally gave in. Three months later, she discovered she was pregnant.

Like Louise, David risked everything to have Bathsheba. And it nearly cost him everything. Read **2 Samuel 11:1–15** to see what happened.

- How did Alan and David abuse their power? What choices did Louise and Bathsheba have?
- What would you have done if you had been in David's situation? What about Bathsheba's?

Consider . . .

- writing on a small card three things you could say to someone who pressures you to have sex. Keep the card in your wallet or purse.
- praying regularly that God will give you strength to resist sexual temptation.

For more, see . . .

- 2 Samuel 12:1–14 (p.295)
- 1 Thessalonians 4:3–8 (p.1298)
- Matthew 5:27–30 (p.944)

King David asks that, tell him, 'Your servant Uriah the Hittite also died.' "

²²The messenger left and went to David and told him everything Joab had told him to say. ²³The messenger told David, "The men of Ammon were winning. They came out and attacked us in the field, but we fought them back to the city gate. ²⁴The archers on the city wall shot at your servants, and some of your men were killed. Your servant Uriah the Hittite also died."

²⁵David said to the messenger, "Say this to Joab: 'Don't be upset about this. The sword kills everyone the same. Make a stronger attack against the city and capture it.' Encourage Joab with these words."

²⁶When Bathsheba heard that her husband was dead, she cried for him. ²⁷After she finished her time of sadness, David sent servants to bring her to his house. She became David's wife and gave birth to his son, but the LORD did not like what David had done.

David's Son Dies

12 The LORD sent Nathan to David. When he came to David, he said, "There were two men in a city. One was rich, but the other was poor. ²The rich man had many sheep and cattle. ³But the poor man had nothing except one little female lamb he had bought. The poor man fed the lamb, and it grew up with him and his children. It shared his food and drank from his cup and slept in his arms. The lamb was like a daughter to him.

⁴"Then a traveller stopped to visit the rich man. The rich man wanted to feed the traveller, but he didn't want to take one of his own sheep or cattle. Instead, he took the lamb from the poor man and cooked it for his visitor."

⁵David became very angry at the rich man. He said to Nathan, "As surely as the LORD lives, the man who did this should die! ⁶He must pay for the lamb four times for doing such a thing. He had no mercy!"

SIN

Hidden Sins

* It wasn't a big crash. Just a little nudge in the car park. From what Trudy could see, just a rear light was broken. She would get it fixed before her parents returned from their weekend away, and they would never know she had taken the car without permission.
* When Justin Ball's parents asked him if he smoked, he was furious. "Of course not!" he shouted. "Don't you trust me?"
* It would be harmless. No one would know that Terri Walker's English test paper was just like Amy Woods's paper from four years ago. Amy had got an 'A' on it, so Terri figured she could too – with a lot less work.
* The lawn in front of the school looked like a moonscape. The tyres had torn the turf so badly that the whole lawn would have to be replaced. The head teacher demanded that anyone who knew what had happened report it. Almost everyone knew who it was. But no one said anything.

Just as people try to hide their sins today, David tried to hide his sin when he committed adultery with Bathsheba. But, as **2 Samuel 12:1–25** reveals, God saw the sin.

* What might the prophet Nathan say to the teenagers who tried to hide their sins?
* Just as David suffered the consequences of his sin, how have you suffered the consequences of something you've done wrong?

Consider . . .

* confessing to a parent or friend something you've done wrong but have kept hidden. Also confess it to God and accept his forgiveness.
* being honest and open next time you're confronted about something you did. See how the approach affects what happens.

For more, see . . .

* Psalm 51:1–13 (p.530)
* 1 John 1:8–10 (p.1371)
* Isaiah 29:15–16 (p.668)

7Then Nathan said to David, "You are the man! This is what the Lord, the God of Israel, says: 'I appointed you king of Israel and saved you from Saul. 8I gave you his kingdom and his wives. And I made you king of Israel and Judah. And if that had not been enough, I would have given you even more. 9So why did you ignore the Lord's command? Why did you do what he says is wrong? You killed Uriah the Hittite with the sword of the Ammonites and took his wife to be your wife! 10Now there will always be people in your family who will die by a sword, because you did not respect me; you took the wife of Uriah the Hittite for yourself!'

11"This is what the Lord says: 'I am bringing trouble to you from your own family. While you watch, I will take your wives from you and give them to someone who is very close to you. He will have sexual relations with your wives, and everyone will know it. 12You had sexual relations with Bathsheba in secret, but I will do this so all the people of Israel can see it.' "

13Then David said to Nathan, "I have sinned against the Lord."

Nathan answered, "The Lord has taken away your sin. You will not die. 14But what you did caused the Lord's enemies to lose all respect for him. For this reason the son who was born to you will die."

15Then Nathan went home. And the Lord caused the son of David and Bathsheba, Uriah's widow, to be very sick. 16David prayed to God for the baby. David refused to eat or drink. He went into his house and stayed there, lying on the ground all night. 17The elders of David's family came to him and tried to pull him up from the ground, but he refused to get up or to eat food with them.

18On the seventh day the baby died. David's servants were afraid to tell him that the baby was dead. They said, "Look, we tried to talk to David while the baby was alive, but he refused to listen to us. If we tell him the baby is dead, he may do something awful."

19When David saw his servants whispering, he knew that the baby was dead. So he asked them, "Is the baby dead?"

They answered, "Yes, he is dead."

20Then David got up from the floor, washed himself, put lotions on and changed his clothes. Then he went into the Lord's house to worship. After that, he went home and asked for something to eat. His servants gave him some food, and he ate.

21David's servants said to him, "Why are you doing this? When the baby was still alive, you refused to eat and you cried. Now that the baby is dead, you get up and eat food."

22David said, "While the baby was still alive, I refused to eat, and I cried. I thought, 'Who knows? Maybe the Lord will feel sorry for me and let the baby live.' 23But now that the baby is dead, why should I go without food? I can't bring him back to life. Some day I will go to him, but he cannot come back to me."

24Then David comforted Bathsheba his wife. He slept with her and had sexual relations with her. She became pregnant again and had another son, whom David named Solomon. The Lord loved Solomon. 25The Lord sent word through Nathan the prophet[d] to name the baby Jedidiah,[n] because the Lord loved the child.

David Captures Rabbah

26Joab fought against Rabbah, a royal city of the Ammonites, and he was about to capture it. 27Joab sent messengers to David and said, "I have fought against Rabbah and have captured its water supply. 28Now bring the other soldiers together and attack this city. Capture it before I capture it myself and call it by my name!"

29So David gathered all the army and went to Rabbah and fought against it and captured it. 30David took the crown off their king's head and had it placed on his own head. That gold crown weighed about 35 kilogrammes, and it had valuable gems in it. And David took many valuable things from the city. 31He also brought out the people of the city and forced them to work with saws, iron picks and axes. He also made them build with bricks. David did this to all the Ammonite cities. Then David and all his army returned to Jerusalem.

Amnon and Tamar

13 David had a son named Absalom and a son named Amnon. Absalom had a beautiful sister named Tamar, and Amnon loved her. 2Tamar was a virgin.[d] Amnon made himself sick just thinking about her, because he could not find any chance to be alone with her.

3Amnon had a friend named Jonadab son of Shimeah, David's brother. Jonadab was a very clever man. 4He asked Amnon, "Son of the king, why do you look so sad day after day? Tell me what's wrong!"

Amnon told him, "I love Tamar, the sister of my half-brother Absalom."

5Jonadab said to Amnon, "Go to bed and act

Jedidiah   This name means "loved by the Lord".

as if you are sick. Then your father will come to see you. Tell him, 'Please let my sister Tamar come in and give me food to eat. Let her make the food in front of me so I can watch and eat it from her hand.' "

⁶So Amnon went to bed and acted sick. When King David came in to see him, Amnon said to him, "Please let my sister Tamar come in. Let her make two of her special cakes for me while I watch. Then I will eat them from her hands."

⁷David sent for Tamar in the palace, saying, "Go to your brother Amnon's house and make some food for him." ⁸So Tamar went to her brother Amnon's house, and he was in bed. Tamar took some dough and pressed it together with her hands. She made some special cakes while Amnon watched. Then she baked them. ⁹Next she took the pan and served him, but he refused to eat.

He said to his servants, "All of you, leave me alone!" So they all left him alone. ¹⁰Amnon said to Tamar, "Bring the food into the bedroom so I may eat from your hand."

Tamar took the cakes she had made and brought them to her brother Amnon in the bedroom. ¹¹She went to him so he could eat from her hands, but Amnon grabbed her. He said, "Sister, come to bed with me."

¹²Tamar said to him, "No, brother! Don't force me! This should never be done in Israel! Don't do this shameful thing! ¹³I could never get rid of my shame! And you will be like the shameful fools in Israel! Please talk with the king, and he will let you marry me."

¹⁴But Amnon refused to listen to her. He was stronger than she was, so he forced her to have sexual relations with him. ¹⁵After that, Amnon hated Tamar. He hated her more than he had loved her before. Amnon said to her, "Get up and leave!"

¹⁶Tamar said to him, "No! Sending me away would be worse than what you've already done!"

But he refused to listen to her. ¹⁷He called his young servant back in and said, "Get this woman out of here and away from me! Lock the door after her." ¹⁸So his servant led her out of the room and bolted the door after her.

Tamar was wearing a special robe with long sleeves, because the king's virgin daughters wore this kind of robe. ¹⁹To show how upset she was, Tamar put ashes on her head and tore her special robe and put her hand on her head. Then she went away, crying loudly.

²⁰Absalom, Tamar's brother, said to her, "Has Amnon, your brother, forced you to have sexual relations with him? For now, sister, be quiet. He is your half-brother. Don't let this upset you so much!" So Tamar lived in her brother Absalom's house and was sad and lonely.

²¹When King David heard the news, he was very angry. ²²Absalom did not say a word, good or bad, to Amnon. But he hated Amnon for disgracing his sister Tamar.

Absalom's Revenge

²³Two years later Absalom had some men come to Baal Hazor, near Ephraim, to cut the wool from his sheep. Absalom invited all the king's sons to come also. ²⁴Absalom went to the king and said, "I have men coming to cut the wool. Please come with your officers and join me."

²⁵King David said to Absalom, "No, my son. We won't all go, because it would be too much trouble for you." Although Absalom begged David, he would not go, but he did give him his blessing.

²⁶Absalom said, "If you don't want to come, then please let my brother Amnon come with us."

King David asked, "Why should he go with you?"

²⁷Absalom kept begging David until he let Amnon and all the king's sons go with Absalom.

²⁸Then Absalom commanded his servants, "Watch Amnon. When he is drunk, I will tell you, 'Kill Amnon.' Right then, kill him! Don't be afraid, because I have commanded you! Be strong and brave!" ²⁹So Absalom's young men killed Amnon as Absalom commanded, but all of David's other sons got on their mules and escaped.

³⁰While the king's sons were on their way, the news came to David, "Absalom has killed all of the king's sons! Not one of them is left alive!" ³¹King David tore his clothes and lay on the ground to show his sadness. All his servants standing nearby tore their clothes also.

³²Jonadab son of Shimeah, David's brother, said to David, "Don't think all the young men, your sons, are killed. No, only Amnon is dead! Absalom has planned this ever since Amnon forced his sister Tamar to have sexual relations with him. ³³My master and king, don't think that all of the king's sons are dead. Only Amnon is dead!"

³⁴In the meantime Absalom had run away.

A guard standing on the city wall saw many people coming from the other side of the hill. ³⁵So Jonadab said to King David, "Look, I was right! The king's sons are coming!"

³⁶As soon as Jonadab had said this, the king's sons arrived, crying loudly. David and all his servants began crying also. ³⁷David cried for his son every day.

But Absalom ran away to Talmai[n] son of Ammihud, the king of Geshur. [38]After Absalom ran away to Geshur, he stayed there for three years. [39]When King David got over Amnon's death, he missed Absalom greatly.

Joab Sends a Wise Woman to David

14 Joab son of Zeruiah knew that King David missed Absalom very much. [2]So Joab sent messengers to Tekoa to bring a wise woman from there. He said to her, "Pretend to be very sad. Put on funeral clothes and don't put lotion on yourself. Act like a woman who has been crying many days for someone who died. [3]Then go to the king and say these words." Then Joab told her what to say.

[4]So the woman from Tekoa spoke to the king. She bowed face down on the ground to show respect and said, "My king, help me!"

[5]King David asked her, "What is the matter?"

The woman said, "I am a widow; my husband is dead. [6]I had two sons. They were out in the field fighting, and no one was there to stop them. So one son killed the other son. [7]Now all the family group is against me. They said to me, 'Bring the son who killed his brother so we may kill him for killing his brother. That way we will also get rid of the one who would receive what belonged to his father.' My son is like the last spark of a fire. He is all I have left. If they kill him, my husband's name and property will be gone from the earth."

[8]Then the king said to the woman, "Go home. I will take care of this for you."

[9]The woman of Tekoa said to him, "Let the blame be on me and my father's family. My master and king, you and your throne are innocent."

[10]King David said, "Bring me anyone who says anything bad to you. Then he won't bother you again."

[11]The woman said, "Please promise in the name of the LORD your God. Then my relative who has the duty of punishing a murderer won't add to the destruction by killing my son."

David said, "As surely as the LORD lives, no one will hurt your son. Not one hair from his head will fall to the ground."

[12]The woman said, "Let me say something to you, my master and king."

The king said, "Speak."

[13]Then the woman said, "Why have you decided this way against the people of God? When you judge this way, you show that you are guilty for not bringing back your son who was forced to leave home. [14]We will all die some day. We're like water spilled on the ground; no one can gather it back. But God doesn't take away life. Instead, he plans ways that those who have been sent away will not have to stay away from him! [15]My master and king, I came to say this to you because the people have made me afraid! I thought, 'Let me talk to the king. Maybe he will do what I ask. [16]Maybe he will listen. Perhaps he will save me from those who want to keep both me and my son from getting what God gave us.'

[17]"Now I say, 'May the words of my master the king give me rest. Like an angel of God, you know what is good and what is bad. May the LORD your God be with you!' "

[18]Then King David said, "Do not hide the truth. Answer me one question."

The woman said, "My master the king, please ask your question."

[19]The king said, "Did Joab tell you to say all these things?"

The woman answered, "As you live, my master the king, no one could avoid that question. You are right. Your servant Joab did tell me to say these things. [20]Joab did it so you would see things differently. My master, you are wise like an angel of God who knows everything that happens on earth."

Absalom Returns to Jerusalem

[21]The king said to Joab, "Look, I will do what I promised. Bring back the young man Absalom."

[22]Joab bowed face down on the ground and blessed the king. Then he said, "Today I know you are pleased with me, because you have done what I asked."

[23]Then Joab got up and went to Geshur and brought Absalom back to Jerusalem. [24]But King David said, "Absalom must go to his own house. He may not come to see me." So Absalom went to his own house and did not go to see the king.

[25]Absalom was greatly praised for his handsome appearance. No man in Israel was as handsome as he. No blemish was on him from his head to his foot. [26]At the end of every year, Absalom would cut his hair, because it became too heavy. When he weighed it, it would weigh about 2 kilogrammes by the royal measure.

[27]Absalom had three sons and one daughter. His daughter's name was also Tamar, and she was a beautiful woman.

[28]Absalom lived in Jerusalem for two full years without seeing King David. [29]Then Absalom sent for Joab so he could send him to the king, but Joab would not come. Absalom sent a message a second time, but Joab still refused to come. [30]Then Absalom said to his servants, "Look,

---

Talmai   He was Absalom's grandfather.

Joab's field is next to mine, and he has barley growing there. Go and burn it." So Absalom's servants set fire to Joab's field.

[31]Then Joab went to Absalom's house and said to him, "Why did your servants burn my field?"

[32]Absalom said to Joab, "I sent a message to you, asking you to come here. I wanted to send you to the king to ask him why he brought me home from Geshur. It would have been better for me to stay there! Now let me see the king. If I have sinned, he can put me to death!"

[33]So Joab went to the king and told him Absalom's words. Then the king called for Absalom. Absalom came and bowed face down on the ground before the king, and the king kissed him.

Absalom Plans to Take David's Kingdom

15 After this, Absalom got a chariot and horses for himself and 50 men to run before him. [2]Absalom would get up early and stand near the city gate.[n] Anyone who had a problem for the king to settle would come here. When someone came, Absalom would call out and say, "What city are you from?"

The person would answer, "I'm from one of the tribes[d] of Israel."

[3]Then Absalom would say, "Look, your claims are right, but the king has no one to listen to you." [4]Absalom would also say, "I wish someone would make me judge in this land! Then people with problems could come to me, and I could help them get justice."

> **Sidelight** Do you have a complaint about your local government? In ancient Israel, you wouldn't take your problem to the Town Hall. You would go to the city's gates, where people made business and legal deals. That's where Absalom took his complaints about his father, King David, and plotted to overthow him (2 Samuel 15:2–4).

[5]People would come near Absalom to bow to him. When they did, Absalom would reach out his hand and take hold of them and kiss them. [6]Absalom did that to all the Israelites who came to King David for decisions. In this way, Absalom stole the hearts of all Israel.

[7]After four years Absalom said to King David, "Please let me go to Hebron. I want to carry out my promise that I made to the LORD [8]while I was living in Geshur in Aram. I said, 'If the LORD takes

me back to Jerusalem, I will worship him in Hebron.'"

[9]The king said, "Go in peace."

So Absalom went to Hebron. [10]But he sent secret messengers through all the tribes of Israel. They told the people, "When you hear the trumpets, say this: 'Absalom is the king at Hebron!'"

[11]Absalom had invited 200 men to go with him. So they went from Jerusalem with him, but they didn't know what he was planning. [12]While Absalom was offering sacrifices, he sent for Ahithophel, one of the people who advised David, to come from his home town of Giloh. So Absalom's plans were working very well. More and more people began to support him.

[13]A messenger came to David, saying, "The Israelites are giving their loyalty to Absalom."

[14]Then David said to all his officers who were with him in Jerusalem, "We must leave quickly! If we don't, we won't be able to get away from Absalom. We must hurry before he catches us and destroys us and kills the people of Jerusalem."

[15]The king's officers said to him, "We will do anything you say."

[16]The king set out with everyone in his house, but he left ten slave women[d] to take care of the palace. [17]The king left with all his people following him, and they stopped at a house far away. [18]All the king's servants passed by him—the Kerethites and Pelethites,[n] all those from Gath, and the 600 men who had followed him.

[19]The king said to Ittai, a man from Gath, "Why are you also going with us? Turn back and stay with King Absalom because you are a foreigner. This is not your homeland. [20]You joined me only a short time ago. Should I make you wander with us when I don't even know where I'm going? Turn back and take your brothers with you. May kindness and loyalty be shown to you."

[21]But Ittai said to the king, "As surely as the LORD lives and as you live, I will stay with you, whether it means life or death."

[22]David said to Ittai, "Go, march on." So Ittai from Gath and all his people with their children marched on. [23]All the people cried loudly as everyone passed by. King David crossed the Kidron Valley, and then all the people went on to the desert. [24]Zadok and all the Levites with him carried the Ark[d] of the Agreement with God. They set it down, and Abiathar offered sacrifices until all the people had left the city.

[25]The king said to Zadok, "Take the Ark of God back into the city. If the LORD is pleased

---

city gate   People came here to conduct business. Public meetings and court cases were also held here.
Kerethites and Pelethites   These were probably special units of the army that were responsible for the king's safety, a kind of palace guard.

with me, he will bring me back and will let me see both it and Jerusalem again. [26]But if the LORD says he is not pleased with me, I am ready. He can do what he wants with me."

[27]The king also said to Zadok the priest, "Aren't you a seer? [d] Go back to the city in peace and take your son Ahimaaz and Abiathar's son Jonathan with you. [28]I will wait near the crossings into the desert until I hear from you." [29]So Zadok and Abiathar took the Ark of God back to Jerusalem and stayed there.

[30]David went up the Mount of Olives, [d] crying as he went. He covered his head and went barefoot. All the people with David covered their heads also and cried as they went. [31]Someone told David, "Ahithophel is one of the people with Absalom who made secret plans against you."

So David prayed, "LORD, please make Ahithophel's advice foolish."

[32]When David reached the top of the mountain where people used to worship God, Hushai the Arkite came to meet him. Hushai's coat was torn, and there was dust on his head to show how sad he was. [33]David said to Hushai, "If you go with me, you will be just one more person for me to take care of. [34]But if you return to the city, you can make Ahithophel's advice useless. Tell Absalom, 'I am your servant, my king. In the past I served your father, but now I will serve you.' [35]The priests Zadok and Abiathar will be with you. Tell them everything you hear in the royal palace. [36]Zadok's son Ahimaaz and Abiathar's son Jonathan are with them. Send them to tell me everything you hear." [37]So David's friend Hushai entered Jerusalem just as Absalom arrived.

Ziba Meets David

16 When David had passed a short way over the top of the Mount of Olives, [d] Ziba, Mephibosheth's servant, met him. Ziba had a row of donkeys loaded with 200 loaves of bread, 100 cakes of raisins, 100 cakes of figs and leather bags full of wine. [2]The king asked Ziba, "What are these things for?"

Ziba answered, "The donkeys are for your family to ride. The bread and cakes of figs are for the servants to eat. And the wine is for anyone to drink who might become weak in the desert."

[3]The king asked, "Where is Mephibosheth?"

Ziba answered him, "Mephibosheth is staying in Jerusalem because he thinks, 'Today the Israelites will give my father's kingdom back to me!'"

[4]Then the king said to Ziba, "All right. Everything that belonged to Mephibosheth, I now give to you!"

Ziba said, "I bow to you. I hope I will always be able to please you."

Shimei Curses David

[5]As King David came to Bahurim, a man came out and cursed him. He was from Saul's family group, and his name was Shimei son of Gera. [6]He threw stones at David and his officers, but the people and soldiers gathered all around David. [7]Shimei cursed David, saying, "Get out, get out, you murderer, you troublemaker. [8]The LORD is punishing you for the people in Saul's family you killed! You took Saul's place as king, but now the LORD has given the kingdom to your son Absalom! Now you are ruined because you are a murderer!"

[9]Abishai son of Zeruiah said to the king, "Why should this dead dog curse you, the king? Let me go over and cut off his head!"

[10]But the king answered, "This does not concern you, sons of Zeruiah! If he is cursing me because the LORD told him to, who can question him?"

[11]David also said to Abishai and all his officers, "My own son is trying to kill me! This man is a Benjaminite and has more right to kill me! Leave him alone, and let him curse me because the LORD told him to do this. [12]Maybe the LORD will see my misery and repay me with something good for Shimei's curses today!"

[13]So David and his men went on down the road, but Shimei followed on the nearby hillside. He kept cursing David and throwing stones and earth at him. [14]When the king and all his people arrived at the Jordan, they were very tired, so they rested there.

[15]Meanwhile, Absalom, Ahithophel and all the Israelites arrived at Jerusalem. [16]David's friend Hushai the Arkite came to Absalom and said to him, "Long live the king! Long live the king!"

[17]Absalom asked, "Why are you not loyal to your friend David? Why didn't you leave Jerusalem with your friend?"

[18]Hushai said, "I belong to the one chosen by the LORD and by these people and everyone in Israel. I will stay with you. [19]In the past I served your father. So whom should I serve now? David's son! I will serve you as I served him."

Ahithophel's Advice

[20]Absalom said to Ahithophel, "Tell us what we should do."

[21]Ahithophel said, "Your father left behind some of his slave women [d] to take care of the palace. Have sexual relations with them. Then all Israel will hear that your father is your enemy, and all your people will be encouraged to give you more support." [22]So they put up a tent for

Absalom on the roof[n] of the palace where everyone in Israel could see it. And Absalom had sexual relations with his father's slave women.

23At that time people thought Ahithophel's advice was as reliable as God's own word. Both David and Absalom thought it was that reliable.

17 Ahithophel said to Absalom, "Let me choose 12,000 men and chase David tonight. 2I'll catch him while he is tired and weak, and I'll frighten him so all his people will run away. But I'll kill only King David. 3Then I'll bring everyone back to you. If the man you are looking for is dead, everyone else will return safely." 4This plan seemed good to Absalom and to all the leaders of Israel.

5But Absalom said, "Now call Hushai the Arkite, so I can hear what he says." 6When Hushai came to Absalom, Absalom said to him, "This is the plan Ahithophel gave. Should we follow it? If not, tell us."

7Hushai said to Absalom, "Ahithophel's advice is not good this time." 8Hushai added, "You know your father and his men are strong. They are as angry as a bear that is robbed of its cubs. Your father is a skilled fighter. He won't stay all night with the army. 9He is probably already hiding in a cave or some other place. If the first attack fails, people will hear the news and think, 'Absalom's followers are losing!' 10Then even the men who are as brave as lions will be frightened, because all the Israelites know your father is a fighter. They know his men are brave!

11"This is what I suggest: gather all the Israelites from Dan to Beersheba.[n] There will be as many people as grains of sand by the sea. Then you yourself must go into the battle. 12We will go to David wherever he is hiding. We will fall on him as dew falls on the ground. We will kill him and all of his men so that no one will be left alive. 13If David escapes into a city, all the Israelites will bring ropes to that city and pull it into the valley. Not a stone will be left!"

14Absalom and all the Israelites said, "The advice of Hushai the Arkite is better than that of Ahithophel." (The LORD had planned to destroy the good advice of Ahithophel so the LORD could bring disaster on Absalom.)

15Hushai told Zadok and Abiathar, the priests, what Ahithophel had suggested to Absalom and the elders of Israel. He also reported to them what he himself had suggested. Hushai said, 16"Quickly! Send a message to David. Tell him not to stay tonight at the crossings into the desert but to cross over the Jordan River at once. If he crosses the river, he and all his people won't be destroyed."

17Jonathan and Ahimaaz were waiting at En Rogel. They did not want to be seen going into the city, so a servant girl would go out to them and give them messages. Then Jonathan and Ahimaaz would go and tell King David. 18But a boy saw Jonathan and Ahimaaz and told Absalom. So Jonathan and Ahimaaz left quickly and went to a man's house in Bahurim. He had a well in his courtyard, and they climbed down into it. 19The man's wife spread a sheet over the opening of the well and covered it with grain. No one could tell that anyone was hiding there.

20Absalom's servants came to the woman at the house and asked, "Where are Ahimaaz and Jonathan?"

She said to them, "They have already crossed the brook."

Absalom's servants then went to look for Jonathan and Ahimaaz, but they could not find them. So they went back to Jerusalem.

21After Absalom's servants left, Jonathan and Ahimaaz climbed out of the well and went to tell King David. They said, "Hurry, cross over the river! Ahithophel has said these things against you!" 22So David and all his people crossed the Jordan River. By dawn, everyone had crossed the Jordan.

23When Ahithophel saw that the Israelites did not accept his advice, he saddled his donkey and went to his home town. He left orders for his family and property, and then he hanged himself. He died and was buried in his father's tomb.

War Between David and Absalom

24David arrived at Mahanaim. And Absalom and all his Israelites crossed over the Jordan River. 25Absalom had made Amasa captain of the army instead of Joab. Amasa was the son of a man named Jether the Ishmaelite. Amasa's mother was Abigail daughter of Nahash and sister of Zeruiah, Joab's mother. 26Absalom and the Israelites camped in the land of Gilead.

27Shobi, Makir and Barzillai were at Mahanaim when David arrived. Shobi son of Nahash was from the Ammonite town of Rabbah. Makir son of Ammiel was from Lo Debar, and Barzillai was from Rogelim in Gilead. 28They brought beds, bowls, clay pots, wheat, barley, flour, roasted grain, beans, small peas, 29honey,

---

roof　In Bible times houses were built with flat roofs. The roof was used for drying things such as flax and fruit. And it was used as an extra room, as a place for worship and as a place to sleep in the summer.

Dan to Beersheba　Dan was the city farthest north in Israel, and Beersheba was the city farthest south. So this means all the people of Israel.

milk curds, sheep and cheese made from cows' milk for David and his people. They said, "The people are hungry and tired and thirsty in the desert."

18 David counted his men and placed over them commanders of thousands and commanders of hundreds. ²He sent the troops out in three groups. Joab commanded one-third of the men. Joab's brother Abishai son of Zeruiah commanded another third. And Ittai from Gath commanded the last third. King David said to them, "I will also go with you."

³But the men said, "You must not go with us! If we run away in the battle, Absalom's men won't care. Even if half of us are killed, Absalom's men won't care. But you're worth 10,000 of us! You can help us most by staying in the city."

⁴The king said to his people, "I will do what you think is best." So the king stood at the side of the gate as the army went out in groups of 100 and 1,000.

⁵The king commanded Joab, Abishai and Ittai, "Be gentle with young Absalom for my sake." Everyone heard the king's orders to the commanders about Absalom.

⁶David's army went out into the field against Absalom's Israelites, and they fought in the forest of Ephraim. ⁷There David's army defeated the Israelites. Many died that day—20,000 men. ⁸The battle spread through all the country, but that day more men died in the forest than in the fighting.

Absalom Dies

⁹Then Absalom happened to meet David's troops. As Absalom was riding his mule, it went under the thick branches of a large oak tree. Absalom's head got caught in the tree, and his mule ran out from under him. So Absalom was left hanging above the ground.

¹⁰When one of the men saw it happen, he told Joab, "I saw Absalom hanging in an oak tree!"

¹¹Joab said to him, "You saw him? Why didn't you kill him and let him fall to the ground? I would have given you a belt and ten pieces of silver!"

¹²The man answered, "I wouldn't touch the king's son even if you gave me 1,000 pieces of silver. We heard the king command you, Abishai and Ittai, 'Be careful not to hurt young Absalom.' ¹³If I had killed him, the king would have found out, and you would not have protected me!"

¹⁴Joab said, "I won't waste time here with you!" Absalom was still alive in the oak tree, so Joab took three spears and stabbed him in the heart. ¹⁵Ten young men who carried Joab's armour also gathered around Absalom and struck him and killed him.

¹⁶Then Joab blew the trumpet, so the troops stopped chasing the Israelites. ¹⁷Then Joab's men took Absalom's body and threw it into a large pit in the forest and filled the pit with many stones. All the Israelites ran away to their homes.

> **Sidelight** If you haven't had your hair cut recently, take care – Absalom's long hair got caught in a tree when his mule walked under it, leaving Absalom hanging there. It's no wonder, either. He only cut it once a year when it became too heavy – weighing about 2¹/₂ kilogrammes.

¹⁸When Absalom was alive, he had set up a pillar for himself in the King's Valley. He said, "I have no son to keep my name alive." So he named the pillar after himself, and it is called Absalom's Monument even today.

¹⁹Ahimaaz son of Zadok said to Joab, "Let me run and take the news to King David. I'll tell him the LORD has saved him from his enemies."

²⁰Joab answered Ahimaaz, "No, you are not the one to take the news today. You may do it another time, but do not take it today, because the king's son is dead."

²¹Then Joab said to a man from Cush, "Go, tell the king what you have seen." The Cushite bowed to Joab and ran to tell David.

²²But Ahimaaz son of Zadok begged Joab again, "No matter what happens, please let me go along with the Cushite!"

Joab said, "Son, why do you want to carry the news? You won't get any reward."

²³Ahimaaz answered, "No matter what happens, I will run."

So Joab said to Ahimaaz, "Run!" Then Ahimaaz ran by way of the Jordan Valley and passed the Cushite.

²⁴David was sitting between the inner and outer gates of the city. The watchman went up to the roof of the gate by the walls, and as he looked up, he saw a man running alone. ²⁵He shouted the news to the king.

The king said, "If he is alone, he is bringing good news!"

The man came nearer and nearer to the city. ²⁶Then the watchman saw another man running, and he called to the gatekeeper, "Look! Another man is running alone!"

The king said, "He is also bringing good news!"

²⁷The watchman said, "I think the first man runs like Ahimaaz son of Zadok."

The king said, "Ahimaaz is a good man. He must be bringing good news!"

²⁸Then Ahimaaz called a greeting to the king. He bowed face down on the ground before the king and said, "Praise the LORD your God! The LORD has defeated those who were against you, my king."

²⁹The king asked, "Is young Absalom all right?"

Ahimaaz answered, "When Joab sent me, I saw some great excitement, but I don't know what it was."

³⁰The king said, "Step over here and wait." So Ahimaaz stepped aside and stood there.

³¹Then the Cushite arrived. He said, "Master and king, hear the good news! Today the LORD has punished those who were against you!"

³²The king asked the Cushite, "Is young Absalom all right?"

The Cushite answered, "May your enemies and all who come to hurt you be like that young man!"

³³Then the king was very upset, and he went to the room over the city gate and cried. As he went, he cried out, "My son Absalom, my son Absalom! I wish I had died and not you. Absalom, my son, my son!"

Joab Scolds David

19 People told Joab, "Look, the king is sad and crying because of Absalom." ²David's army had won the battle that day. But it

REBELLION

Bad Boy

Pete and Julie wondered where a sick young man stopped and a stupid, self-destructive idiot started. It was especially painful for them as the sick young man was their son.

Tim had grown up in a happy family. He was a bright child, eager to learn and always laughing. He loved his brother and sister who were both doing fine at school and expected to go on to good universities.

But in his early teens, Tim turned into a rebel. He was rude to teachers and was regularly suspended from school. He did no homework. He fell in with a bad crowd.

Tim suffered from depression – although it was a while before it was properly diagnosed. His folks now knew that and wished they had taken action earlier. Everything seemed so clear with hindsight.

But now Tim, working in odd jobs here and there to make ends meet, regularly squandered his wages on alcohol and drugs. He lived in a succession of grimy squats. Sometimes he sneaked into the house and took money from his parents.

It was almost impossible to persuade him to see a doctor. Even when he did and got medication he forgot to take it, lost it or took drugs too which caused terrible mood swings as a side effect. How could Pete and Julie best show their love for their son?

2 Samuel 18:24–33 is about the immense human love between a father and son despite the son's dreadful rebellion.

* What do you think David hoped for as he waited for news of his son and the battle? How do you think he felt?
* Despite everything that Absalom had done, how did David react to the news of his death? Does this make sense to you?

Consider . . .

* praying for families that are torn apart by rebellion. Ask God to help the families to communicate and come back together.
* what you should do if you become aware of a friend's law breaking. Would it be better friendship to protect them or shop them?

For more, see . . .

* Hosea 11:1–11 (p.858)
* Romans 3:23 (p.1187)

* Luke 15:11–32 (p.1071)

became a very sad day for all the people, because they heard that the king was very sad for his son. [3]The people came into the city quietly that day. They were like an army that had been defeated in battle and had run away. [4]The king covered his face and cried loudly, "My son Absalom! Absalom, my son, my son!"

[5]Joab went into the king's house and said, "Today you have shamed all your men. They saved your life and the lives of your sons, daughters, wives and slave women.[d] [6]You have shamed them because you love those who hate you, and you hate those who love you. Today you have made it clear that your commanders and men mean nothing to you. What if Absalom had lived and all of us were dead? I can see you would be pleased. [7]Now go out and encourage your servants. I swear by the LORD that if you don't go out, no man will be left with you by tonight! That will be worse than all the troubles you have had from your youth until today."

[8]So the king went to the city gate.[n] When the news spread that the king was at the gate, everyone came to see him.

David Goes Back to Jerusalem

All the Israelites who had followed Absalom had run away to their homes. [9]People in all the tribes[d] of Israel began to argue, saying, "The king saved us from the Philistines and our other enemies, but he left the country because of Absalom. [10]We appointed Absalom to rule us, but now he has died in battle. We should make David the king again."

[11]King David sent a message to Zadok and Abiathar, the priests, that said, "Speak to the elders of Judah. Say, 'Even in my house I have heard what all the Israelites are saying. So why are you the last tribe to bring the king back to his palace? [12]You are my brothers, my own family. Why are you the last tribe to bring back the king?' [13]And say to Amasa, 'You are part of my own family. May God punish me terribly if I don't make you commander of the army in Joab's place!' "

[14]David touched the hearts of all the people of Judah at once. They sent a message to the king that said, "Return with all your men." [15]Then the king returned as far as the Jordan River. The men of Judah came to Gilgal to meet him and to bring him across the Jordan.

[16]Shimei son of Gera, a Benjaminite who lived in Bahurim, hurried down with the men of Judah to meet King David. [17]With Shimei came 1,000 Benjaminites. Ziba, the servant from Saul's family, also came, bringing his fifteen sons and 20 servants with him. They all hurried to

the Jordan River to meet the king. [18]The people went across the Jordan to help bring the king's family back to Judah and to do whatever the king wanted. As the king was crossing the river, Shimei son of Gera came to him and bowed face down on the ground in front of the king. [19]He said to the king, "My master, don't hold me guilty. Don't remember the wrong I did when you left Jerusalem! Don't hold it against me. [20]I know I have sinned. That is why I am the first person from Joseph's family to come down and meet you today, my master and king!"

[21]But Abishai son of Zeruiah said, "Shimei should die because he cursed you, the LORD's appointed king!"

[22]David said, "This does not concern you, sons of Zeruiah! Today you're against me! No one will be put to death in Israel today. Today I know I am king over Israel!" [23]Then the king promised Shimei, "You won't die."

[24]Mephibosheth, Saul's grandson, also went down to meet King David. Mephibosheth had not cared for his feet, cut his beard or washed his clothes from the time the king had left Jerusalem until he returned safely. [25]When Mephibosheth came from Jerusalem to meet the king, the king asked him, "Mephibosheth, why didn't you go with me?"

[26]He answered, "My master, my servant Ziba tricked me! I said to Ziba, 'I am crippled, so saddle a donkey. Then I will ride it so I can go with the king.' [27]But he lied about me to you. You, my master and king, are like an angel from God. Do what you think is good. [28]You could have killed all my grandfather's family. Instead, you put me with those people who eat at your own table. So I don't have a right to ask anything more from the king!"

[29]The king said to him, "Don't say anything more. I have decided that you and Ziba will divide the land."

[30]Mephibosheth said to the king, "Let Ziba take all the land now that my master the king has arrived safely home."

[31]Barzillai of Gilead came down from Rogelim to cross the Jordan River with the king. [32]Barzillai was a very old man, 80 years old. He had taken care of the king when David was staying at Mahanaim, because Barzillai was a very rich man. [33]David said to Barzillai, "Cross the river with me. Come with me to Jerusalem, and I will take care of you."

[34]But Barzillai answered the king, "Do you know how old I am? Do you think I can go with you to Jerusalem? [35]I am 80 years old! I am too

---

city gate   People came here to conduct business. Public meetings and court cases were also held here.

old to taste what I eat or drink. I am too old to hear the voices of men and women singers. Why should you be bothered with me? ³⁶I am not worthy of a reward from you, but I will cross the Jordan River with you. ³⁷Then let me go back so I may die in my own city near the grave of my father and mother. But here is Kimham, your servant. Let him go with you, my master and king. Do with him whatever you want."

³⁸The king answered, "Kimham will go with me. I will do for him anything you wish, and I will do anything for you that you wish." ³⁹The king kissed Barzillai and blessed him. Then Barzillai returned home, and the king and all the people crossed the Jordan.

⁴⁰When the king crossed over to Gilgal, Kimham went with him. All the troops of Judah and half the troops of Israel led David across the river.

⁴¹Soon all the Israelites came to the king and said to him, "Why did our relatives, the people of Judah, steal you away? Why did they bring you and your family across the Jordan River with your men?"

⁴²All the people of Judah answered the Israelites, "We did this because the king is our close relative. Why are you angry about it? We have not eaten food at the king's expense or taken anything for ourselves!"

⁴³The Israelites answered the people of Judah, "We have ten tribes in the kingdom, so we have more right to David than you do! But you ignored us! We were the first ones to talk about bringing our king back!"

But the people of Judah spoke even more unkindly than the people of Israel.

Sheba Leads Israel Away from David

20 It happened that a troublemaker named Sheba son of Bicri from the tribe*d* of Benjamin was there. He blew the trumpet and said:

"We have no share in David!
We have no part in the son of Jesse!
People of Israel, let's go home!"

²So all the Israelites left David and followed Sheba son of Bicri. But the people of Judah stayed with their king all the way from the Jordan River to Jerusalem.

³David came back to his palace in Jerusalem. He had left ten of his slave women *d* there to take care of the palace. Now he put them in a locked house. He gave them food, but he did not have sexual relations with them. So they lived like widows until they died.

⁴The king said to Amasa, "Tell the men of Judah to meet with me in three days, and you must also be here." ⁵So Amasa went to call the men of Judah together, but he took more time than the king had said.

⁶David said to Abishai, "Sheba son of Bicri is more dangerous to us than Absalom was. Take my men and chase him before he finds walled cities and escapes from us." ⁷So Joab's men, the Kerethites and the Pelethites, *n* and all the soldiers went with Abishai. They went out from Jerusalem to chase Sheba son of Bicri.

⁸When Joab and the army came to the great rock at Gibeon, Amasa came out to meet them. Joab was wearing his uniform, and at his waist he wore a belt that held his sword in its case. As Joab stepped forwards, his sword fell out of its case. ⁹Joab asked Amasa, "Brother, is everything all right with you?" Then with his right hand he took Amasa by the beard to kiss him. ¹⁰Amasa was not watching the sword in Joab's hand. So Joab pushed the sword into Amasa's stomach, causing Amasa's insides to spill onto the ground. Joab did not have to stab Amasa again; he was already dead. Then Joab and his brother Abishai continued to chase Sheba son of Bicri.

¹¹One of Joab's young men stood by Amasa's body and said, "Everyone who is for Joab and David should follow Joab!" ¹²Amasa lay in the middle of the road, covered with his own blood. When the young man saw that everyone was stopping to look at the body, he dragged it from the road, laid it in a field and put a cloth over it. ¹³After Amasa's body was taken off the road, all the men followed Joab to chase Sheba son of Bicri.

¹⁴Sheba went through all the tribes of Israel to Abel Beth Maacah. All the Berites also came together and followed him. ¹⁵So Joab and his men came to Abel Beth Maacah and surrounded it. They piled earth up against the city wall, and they began digging under the walls to bring them down.

¹⁶But a wise woman shouted out from the city, "Listen! Listen! Tell Joab to come here. I want to talk to him!"

¹⁷So Joab came near her. She asked him, "Are you Joab?"

He answered, "Yes, I am."

Then she said, "Listen to what I say."

Joab said, "I'm listening."

¹⁸Then the woman said, "In the past people would say, 'Ask for advice at Abel,' and the problem would be solved. ¹⁹I am one of the peaceful, loyal people of Israel. You are trying to destroy an important city of Israel. Why must you destroy what belongs to the LORD?"

Kerethites and Pelethites These were probably special units of the army that were responsible for the king's safety, a kind of palace guard.

²⁰Joab answered, "I would prefer not to destroy or ruin anything! ²¹That is not what I want. But there is a man here from the mountains of Ephraim, who is named Sheba son of Bicri. He has turned against King David. If you bring him to me, I will leave the city alone."

The woman said to Joab, "His head will be thrown over the wall to you."

²²Then the woman spoke very wisely to all the people of the city. They cut off the head of Sheba son of Bicri and threw it over the wall to Joab. So he blew the trumpet, and the army left the city. Every man returned home, and Joab went back to the king in Jerusalem.

²³Joab was commander of all the army of Israel. Benaiah son of Jehoiada led the Kerethites and Pelethites. ²⁴Adoniram was in charge of the men who were forced to do hard work. Jehoshaphat son of Ahilud was the recorder. ²⁵Sheba was the royal secretary. Zadok and Abiathar were the priests, ²⁶and Ira the Jairite was David's priest.

The Gibeonites Punish Saul's Family

21 During the time David was king, there was a shortage of food that lasted for three years. So David prayed to the LORD.

The LORD answered, "Saul and his family of murderers are the reason for this shortage, because he killed the Gibeonites." ²(Now the Gibeonites were not Israelites; they were a group of Amorites who were left alive. The Israelites had promised not to hurt the Gibeonites, but Saul had tried to kill them, because he was eager to help the people of Israel and Judah.)

King David called the Gibeonites together and spoke to them. ³He asked, "What can I do for you? How can I make up for the harm done so you can bless the LORD's people?"

⁴The Gibeonites said to David, "We cannot demand silver or gold from Saul or his family. And we don't have the right to kill anyone in Israel."

Then David asked, "What do you want me to do for you?"

⁵The Gibeonites said, "Saul made plans against us and tried to destroy all our people who are left in the land of Israel. ⁶So bring seven of his sons to us. Then we will kill them and hang them on stakes in the presence of the LORD at Gibeah, the home town of Saul, the LORD's chosen king."

The king said, "I will give them to you." ⁷But the king protected Mephibosheth, the son of Jonathan, the son of Saul, because of the promise he had made to Jonathan in the LORD's name. ⁸The king did take Armoni and Mephibosheth,ⁿ sons of Rizpah and Saul. (Rizpah was the daughter of Aiah.) And the king took the five sons of Saul's daughter Merab. (Adriel son of Barzillai the Meholathite was the father of Merab's five sons.) ⁹David gave these seven sons to the Gibeonites. Then the Gibeonites killed them and hung them on stakes on a hill in the presence of the LORD. All seven sons died together. They were put to death during the first days of the harvest season at the beginning of barley harvest.

¹⁰Aiah's daughter Rizpah took the rough cloth that was worn to show sadness and put it on a rock for herself. She stayed there from the beginning of the harvest until the rain fell on her sons' bodies. During the day she did not let the birds of the sky touch her sons' bodies, and during the night she did not let the wild animals touch them.

¹¹People told David what Aiah's daughter Rizpah, Saul's slave woman,ᵈ was doing. ¹²Then David took the bones of Saul and Jonathan from the men of Jabesh Gilead. (The Philistines had hung the bodies of Saul and Jonathan in the public square of Beth Shan after they had killed Saul at Gilboa. Later the men of Jabesh Gilead had secretly taken them from there.) ¹³David brought the bones of Saul and his son Jonathan from Gilead. Then the people gathered the bodies of Saul's seven sons who were hanged on stakes. ¹⁴The people buried the bones of Saul and his son Jonathan at Zela in Benjamin in the tomb of Saul's father Kish. The people did everything the king commanded.

Then God answered the prayers for the land.

Wars with the Philistines

¹⁵Again there was war between the Philistines and Israel. David and his men went out to fight the Philistines, but David became tired. ¹⁶Ishbi-Benob, one of the sons of Rapha,ᵈ had a bronze spearhead weighing about 3.5 kilogrammes and a new sword. He planned to kill David, ¹⁷but Abishai son of Zeruiah killed the Philistine and saved David's life.

Then David's men made a promise to him, saying, "Never again will you go out with us to battle. If you were killed, Israel would lose its greatest leader."

¹⁸Later, at Gob, there was another battle with the Philistines. Sibbecai the Hushathite killed Saph, another one of the sons of Rapha.

¹⁹Later, there was another battle at Gob with the Philistines. Elhanan son of Jaare-Oregim from Bethlehem killed Goliathⁿ from Gath. His spear was as large as a weaver's rod.

Mephibosheth   This is not Jonathan's son but another man with the same name.
Goliath   In 1 Chronicles 20:5 he is called Lahmi brother of Goliath.

²⁰At Gath another battle took place. A very large man was there; he had six fingers on each hand and six toes on each foot—24 fingers and toes in all. This man also was one of the sons of Rapha. ²¹When he challenged Israel, Jonathan son of Shimeah, David's brother, killed him.

Sidelight   David was again faced in battle by a giant, but he realised (probably with some sadness) that this was not his fight. He laid aside his armour and weaponry to allow Jonathan to bring the giant down (2 Samuel 21:21).

---

²²These four sons of Rapha from Gath were killed by David and his men.

David's Song of Praise

22 David sang this song to the LORD when the LORD saved him from Saul and all his other enemies. ²He said:

"The LORD is my rock, my protection, my
    Saviour.
³My God is my rock.
  I can run to him for safety.
He is my shield and my saving strength,
  my defender and my place of safety.
The LORD saves me from those who want to
    harm me.
⁴I will call to the LORD, who is worthy of
    praise,
  and I will be saved from my enemies.

⁵"The waves of death came around me;
  the deadly rivers overwhelmed me.
⁶The ropes of death wrapped around me.
  The traps of death were before me.
⁷In my trouble I called to the LORD;
  I cried out to my God.
From his temple he heard my voice;
  my call for help reached his ears.

⁸"The earth trembled and shook.
  The foundations of heaven began to shake.
  They trembled because the LORD was angry.
⁹Smoke came out of his nose,
  and burning fire came out of his mouth.
  Burning coals went before him.
¹⁰He tore open the sky and came down
  with dark clouds under his feet.
¹¹He rode a creature with wings and flew.
  He raced on the wings of the wind.
¹²He made darkness his shelter,
  surrounded by fog and clouds.
¹³Out of the brightness of his presence
  came flashes of lightning.
¹⁴The LORD thundered from heaven;
  the Most High raised his voice.
¹⁵He shot his arrows and scattered his enemies.
  His bolts of lightning confused them with
    fear.
¹⁶The LORD spoke strongly.
  The wind blew from his nose.
Then the valleys of the sea appeared,
  and the foundations of the earth were seen.

¹⁷"The LORD reached down from above and
    took me;
  he pulled me from the deep water.
¹⁸He saved me from my powerful enemies,
  from those who hated me, because they
    were too strong for me.
¹⁹They attacked me at my time of trouble,
  but the LORD supported me.
²⁰He took me to a safe place.
  Because he delights in me, he saved me.

²¹"The LORD spared me because I did what was
    right.
  Because I have not done evil, he has
    rewarded me.
²²I have followed the ways of the LORD;
  I have not done evil by turning from
    my God.
²³I remember all his laws
  and have not broken his rules.
²⁴I am innocent before him;
  I have kept myself from doing evil.
²⁵The LORD rewarded me because I did what
    was right,
  because I did what the LORD said was right.

²⁶"LORD, you are loyal to those who are loyal,
  and you are good to those who are good.
²⁷You are pure to those who are pure,
  but you are against those who are evil.
²⁸You save the humble,
  but you bring down those who are proud.
²⁹LORD, you give light to my lamp.
  The LORD brightens the darkness
    around me.
³⁰With your help I can attack an army.
  With God's help I can jump over a wall.

³¹"The ways of God are without fault;
  the LORD's words are pure.
He is a shield to those who trust him.
³²Who is God? Only the LORD.
  Who is the Rock? ^d Only our God.
³³God is my protection.
  He makes my way free from fault.
³⁴He makes me like a deer that does not
    stumble;
  he helps me stand on the steep mountains.
³⁵He trains my hands for battle
  so my arms can bend a bronze bow.
³⁶You protect me with your saving shield.

You have stooped to make me great.
37You give me a better way to live,
    so I live as you want me to.
38I chased my enemies and destroyed them.
    I did not stop till they were destroyed.
39I destroyed and crushed them
    so they couldn't rise up again.
    They fell beneath my feet.
40You gave me strength in battle.
    You made my enemies bow before me.
41You made my enemies turn back,
    and I destroyed those who hated me.
42They called for help,
    but no one came to save them.
They called to the LORD,
    but he did not answer them.
43I beat my enemies into pieces,
    like dust on the ground.
I poured them out and walked on them
    like mud in the streets.

44"You saved me when my people attacked me.
    You kept me as the leader of nations.
People I never knew serve me.
45Foreigners obey me.
    As soon as they hear me, they obey me.
46They all become afraid
    and tremble in their hiding places.

47"The LORD lives!
    May my Rock be praised!
Praise God, the Rock, who saves me!
48God gives me victory over my enemies
    and brings people under my rule.
49He frees me from my enemies.

"You set me over those who hate me.
    You saved me from cruel men.
50So I will praise you, LORD, among the nations.
    I will sing praises to your name.
51The LORD gives great victories to his king.
    He is loyal to his appointed king,
    to David and his descendants *d* for ever."

David's Last Words

23 These are the last words of David.

This is the message of David son of Jesse.
    The man made great by the Most High
        God speaks.
He is the appointed king of the God of Jacob;
    he is the sweet singer of Israel:

2"The LORD's Spirit *d* spoke through me,
    and his word was on my tongue.
3The God of Israel spoke;
    the Rock *d* of Israel said to me:
'Whoever rules fairly over people,

who rules with respect for God,
4is like the morning light at dawn,
    like a morning without clouds.
He is like sunshine after a rain
    that makes the grass grow from the
        ground.'

5"This is how God has cared for my family.
    God made a lasting agreement with me,
    right and sure in every way.
He will accomplish my salvation
    and satisfy all my desires.

6"But all evil people will be thrown away like
    thorns
    that cannot be held in a hand.
7No one can touch them
    except with a tool of iron or wood.
They will be thrown in the fire and burned
    where they lie."

David's Army

8These are the names of David's warriors:
Josheb-Basshebeth, the Tahkemonite, was head of the Three. *n* He killed 800 men at one time.
9Next was Eleazar son of Dodai the Ahohite. Eleazar was one of the three soldiers who were with David when they challenged the Philistines. The Philistines were gathered for battle, and the Israelites drew back. 10But Eleazar stayed where he was and fought the Philistines until he was so tired his hand stuck to his sword. The LORD gave a great victory for the Israelites that day. The troops came back after Eleazar had won the battle, but only to take weapons and armour from the enemy.
11Next there was Shammah son of Agee the Hararite. The Philistines came together to fight in a vegetable field. Israel's troops ran away from the Philistines, 12but Shammah stood in the middle of the field and fought for it and killed the Philistines. And the LORD gave a great victory.
13Once, three of the Thirty, David's chief soldiers, came down to him at the cave of Adullam during harvest. The Philistine army had camped in the Valley of Rephaim. 14At that time David was in the stronghold, *d* and some of the Philistines were in Bethlehem. 15David had a strong desire for some water. He said, "Oh, I wish someone would get me water from the well near the city gate of Bethlehem!" 16So the three warriors broke through the Philistine army and took water from the well near the city gate of Bethlehem. Then they brought it to David, but he refused to drink it. He poured it out before the LORD, 17saying, "May the LORD

Three, or maybe "Thirty"   These were David's most powerful soldiers. See 1 Chronicles 11:11.

keep me from drinking this water! It would be like drinking the blood of the men who risked their lives!" So David refused to drink it. These were the brave things that the three warriors did.

¹⁸Abishai, brother of Joab son of Zeruiah, was captain of the Three. Abishai fought 300 soldiers with his spear and killed them. He became as famous as the Three ¹⁹and was more honoured than the Three. He became their commander even though he was not one of them.

²⁰Benaiah son of Jehoiada was a brave fighter from Kabzeel who did mighty things. He killed two of the best warriors from Moab. He also went down into a pit and killed a lion on a snowy day. ²¹Benaiah killed a large Egyptian who had a spear in his hand. Benaiah had a club, but he grabbed the spear from the Egyptian's hand and killed him with his own spear. ²²These were the things Benaiah son of Jehoiada did. He was as famous as the Three. ²³He received more honour than the Thirty, but he did not become a member of the Three. David made him leader of his bodyguards.

The Thirty Chief Soldiers

²⁴The following men were among the Thirty:
Asahel brother of Joab;
Elhanan son of Dodo from Bethlehem;
²⁵Shammah the Harodite;
Elika the Harodite;
²⁶Helez the Paltite;
Ira son of Ikkesh from Tekoa;
²⁷Abiezer the Anathothite;
Mebunnai the Hushathite;
²⁸Zalmon the Ahohite;
Maharai the Netophathite;
²⁹Heled son of Baanah the Netophathite;
Ithai son of Ribai from Gibeah in Benjamin;
³⁰Benaiah the Pirathonite;
Hiddai from the ravines of Gaash;
³¹Abi-Albon the Arbathite;
Azmaveth the Barhumite;
³²Eliahba the Shaalbonite;
the sons of Jashen;
Jonathan ³³son of Shammah the Hararite;
Ahiam son of Sharar the Hararite;

GOVERNMENT

Respected Leaders

Bill Logue was a well-liked judge in the USA. He was respected by lawyers, by the police and convicted criminals alike. Even with his back-breaking load of court cases, Judge Logue found time to help underprivileged kids who had criminal records. He helped them start constructive lives so they wouldn't get into trouble again.

When Judge Logue was found to have throat cancer, cards, letters, flowers and presents swamped the hospital.

But nothing touched the judge as much as the fistful of letters he received from prisoners – prisoners he had sent to jail. "You helped me get my life back on track," they told him. "I'll never forget you. Thanks."

Judge Logue showed how God's followers can make a difference for good in government. When King David was dying, he celebrated how God had worked in his life for good. Read about it in **2 Samuel 23:1–7**.

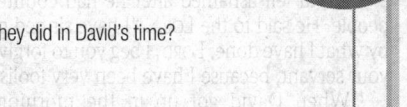

* How do verses 3 and 4 describe Judge Logue and other Christians like him who serve in government?
* Do leaders today have the same opportunities to serve God as they did in David's time? How can you support and encourage them to do good?

Consider . . .

* praying that God will guide your country's leaders as they make important decisions.
* writing a letter to local leaders to express your opinion on an important issue they are confronting.

For more, see . . .

* Psalm 2:1–11 (p.500)
* 1 Timothy 2:1–3 (p.1308)
* Proverbs 16:10–15 (p.603)

[34]Eliphelet son of Ahasbai the Maacathite;
Eliam son of Ahithophel the Gilonite;
[35]Hezro the Carmelite;
Paarai the Arbite;
[36]Igal son of Nathan of Zobah;
the son of Hagri;
[37]Zelek the Ammonite;
Naharai the Beerothite, who carried
the armour of Joab son of Zeruiah;
[38]Ira the Ithrite;
Gareb the Ithrite,
[39]and Uriah the Hittite.

There were 37 in all.

David Counts His Army

24 The LORD was angry with Israel again, and he caused David to turn against the Israelites. He said, "Go, count the people of Israel and Judah."

[2]So King David said to Joab, the commander of the army, "Go through all the tribes [d] of Israel, from Dan to Beersheba, [n] and count the people. Then I will know how many there are."

[3]But Joab said to the king, "May the LORD your God give you 100 times more people, and may my master the king live to see this happen. Why do you want to do this?"

[4]But the king commanded Joab and the commanders of the army, so they left the king to count the Israelites.

[5]After crossing the Jordan River, they camped near Aroer on the south side of the city in the ravine. They went through Gad and on to Jazer. [6]Then they went to Gilead and the land of Tahtim Hodshi and to Dan Janai and around to Sidon. [7]They went to the fortified city of Tyre and to all the cities of the Hivites and Canaanites. Finally, they went to southern Judah, to Beersheba. [8]After nine months and 20 days, they had gone through all the land. Then they came back to Jerusalem.

[9]Joab gave the list of the people to the king. There were 800,000 men in Israel who could use the sword and 500,000 men in Judah.

[10]David felt ashamed after he had counted the people. He said to the LORD, "I have sinned greatly by what I have done. LORD, I beg you to forgive me, your servant, because I have been very foolish."

[11]When David got up in the morning, the LORD spoke his word to Gad, who was a prophet [d] and David's seer. [d] [12]The LORD told Gad, "Go and tell David, 'This is what the LORD says: I offer you three choices. Choose one of them and I will do it to you.' "

[13]So Gad went to David and said to him, "Should three years of hunger come to you and your land? Or should your enemies chase you for three months? Or should there be three days of disease in your land? Think about it. Then decide which of these things I should tell the LORD who sent me."

[14]David said to Gad, "I am in great trouble. Let the LORD punish us, because the LORD is very merciful. Don't let my punishment come from human beings!"

[15]So the LORD sent a terrible disease on Israel. It began in the morning and continued until the chosen time to stop. From Dan to Beersheba 70,000 people died. [16]When the angel raised his arm towards Jerusalem to destroy it, the LORD felt very sorry about the terrible things that had happened. He said to the angel who was destroying the people, "That is enough! Put down your arm!" The angel of the LORD was then by the threshing[d] floor of Araunah the Jebusite.

[17]When David saw the angel that killed the people, he said to the LORD, "I am the one who sinned and did wrong. These people only followed me like sheep. They did nothing wrong. Please punish me and my family."

[18]That day Gad came to David and said, "Go and build an altar to the LORD on the threshing floor of Araunah the Jebusite." [19]So David did what Gad told him to do, just as the LORD commanded.

[20]Araunah looked and saw the king and his servants coming to him. So he went out and bowed face down on the ground before the king. [21]He said, "Why has my master the king come to me?"

David answered, "To buy the threshing floor from you so I can build an altar to the LORD. Then the terrible disease will stop."

[22]Araunah said to David, "My master and king, you may take anything you want for a sacrifice. Here are some oxen for the whole burnt offering and the threshing boards and the yokes[d] for the wood. [23]My king, I give everything to you." Araunah also said to the king, "May the LORD your God be pleased with you."

[24]But the king answered Araunah, "No, I will pay you for the land. I won't offer to the LORD my God burnt offerings that cost me nothing."

So David bought the threshing floor and the oxen for 50 pieces of silver. [25]He built an altar to the LORD there and offered whole burnt offerings and fellowship offerings. Then the LORD answered his prayer for the country, and the disease in Israel stopped.

Dan to Beersheba   Dan was the city farthest north in Israel, and Beersheba was the city farthest south. So this means all the people of Israel.

1 Kings

Why Read This Book:

* See how God blesses those who follow him (1 Kings 1—11).
* Recognise how faithfulness can help all parts of life (1 Kings 12—16).
* Discover what can happen to a country that turns away from God (1 Kings 17—22).

When?

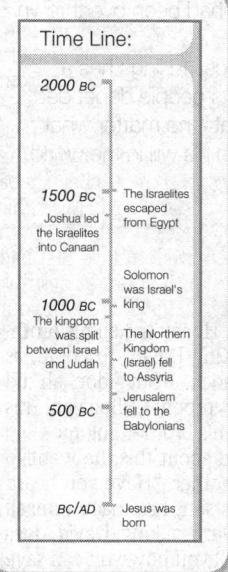

Time Line:

2000 BC

1500 BC — The Israelites escaped from Egypt

Joshua led the Israelites into Canaan

Solomon was Israel's king

1000 BC — The kingdom was split between Israel and Judah

The Northern Kingdom (Israel) fell to Assyria

Jerusalem fell to the Babylonians

500 BC

BC/AD — Jesus was born

Behind the Scenes:

Imagine how different history books would be if they evaluated presidents and other world leaders on whether or not they followed God. Their political, economic and military feats would only be important when they showed obedience to God. Which presidents, kings and leaders would be judged good and which ones bad?

That's the kind of history we find in 1 and 2 Kings, which were one continuous book in the original text. The story begins with King David turning over the country to his son Solomon. Solomon inherited a strong and united nation, exploding with energy. Through political and economic manoeuvring, Solomon made the country – and himself – rich and powerful.

Solomon seemed headed for greatness. But in the end, the writer says, "Solomon did what the Lord said was wrong and did not follow the Lord completely as his father David had done" (1 Kings 11:6).

What happened? He began seeing the wealth and power as his own, not as gifts from God. Though he spent seven years building a beautiful temple for God (1 Kings 6), he spent thirteen years building his own palace. ▷

Where?

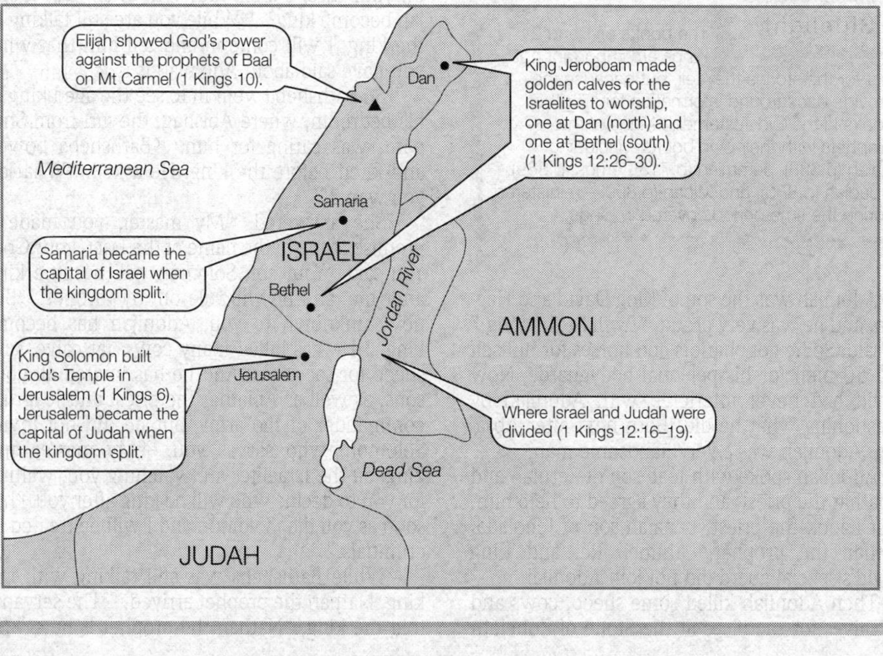

Elijah showed God's power against the prophets of Baal on Mt Carmel (1 Kings 10).

King Jeroboam made golden calves for the Israelites to worship, one at Dan (north) and one at Bethel (south) (1 Kings 12:26–30).

Dan

Mediterranean Sea

Samaria

ISRAEL

Samaria became the capital of Israel when the kingdom split.

Bethel

Jordan River

AMMON

King Solomon built God's Temple in Jerusalem (1 Kings 6). Jerusalem became the capital of Judah when the kingdom split.

Jerusalem

Where Israel and Judah were divided (1 Kings 12:16–19).

Dead Sea

JUDAH

Behind the Scenes (cont.):

Soon his power and prestige became more important than following God. He began worshipping false gods.

The kingdom started to crumble. First it split between Israel (in the north) and Judah (in the south). Then one king after another didn't follow God, and the people suffered as a result. When kings did follow God, the people prospered. But by the end of 2 Kings, both kingdoms had been overthrown and the people taken as slaves.

In telling about the rise and fall of good and bad kings, 1 Kings has a consistent theme: the long-term welfare of Israel and its people depended on obedience to God. And these stories remind us that – no matter what other forces are at play – God still works to accomplish his will in the world.

Adonijah Tries to Become King

1 At this time King David was very old, and although his servants covered him with blankets, he could not keep warm. ²They said to him, "We will look for a young woman to care for you. She will lie close to you and keep you warm." ³After searching everywhere in Israel for a beautiful young woman, they found a girl named Abishag from Shunam and brought her to the king. ⁴The girl was very beautiful, and she cared for the king and served him. But the king did not have sexual relations with her.

Sidelight   The books of 1 and 2 Kings are important not just for the stories they tell, but because they provide background information for 17 other books in the Old Testament. Many of the prophets with their own books – including Isaiah (p.638), Jeremiah (p.715), Amos (p.869), Obadiah (p.880), and Micah (p.890) – ministered during the time period covered in Kings.

---

⁵Adonijah was the son of King David and Haggith, and he was very proud. "I will be the king," he said. So he got chariots and horses for himself and 50 men as his personal bodyguard. ⁶Now David had never interfered with Adonijah by questioning what he did. Born next after Absalom, Adonijah was a very handsome man.

⁷Adonijah spoke with Joab son of Zeruiah and Abiathar the priest, and they agreed to help him. ⁸But Zadok the priest, Benaiah son of Jehoiada, Nathan the prophet,*d* Shimei, Rei and King David's special guard did not join Adonijah.

⁹Then Adonijah killed some sheep, cows and fat calves for sacrifices at the Stone of Zoheleth near the spring of Rogel. He invited all his brothers, the other sons of King David, to come, as well as all the men of Judah. ¹⁰But Adonijah did not invite Nathan the prophet, Benaiah, his father's special guard or his brother Solomon.

¹¹When Nathan heard about this, he went to Bathsheba, Solomon's mother. "Have you heard that Adonijah, Haggith's son, has made himself king?" Nathan asked. "Our real king, David, does not know it. ¹²Let me tell you how you can save yourself and your sons. ¹³Go to King David and tell him, 'My master and king, you promised that my son Solomon would be king and would rule on your throne after you. Why then has Adonijah become king?' ¹⁴While you are still talking to the king, I will come in and tell him that what you have said about Adonijah is true."

¹⁵So Bathsheba went in to see the aged king in his bedroom, where Abishag, the girl from Shunam, was caring for him. ¹⁶Bathsheba bowed and knelt before the king. He asked, "What do you want?"

¹⁷She answered, "My master, you made a promise to me in the name of the LORD your God. You said, 'Your son Solomon will become king after me, and he will rule on my throne.' ¹⁸But now, unknown to you, Adonijah has become king. ¹⁹He has killed many cows, fat calves and sheep for sacrifices. And he has invited all your sons, as well as Abiathar the priest and Joab the commander of the army, but he did not invite Solomon, who serves you. ²⁰My master and king, all the Israelites are watching you, waiting for you to decide who will be king after you. ²¹As soon as you die, Solomon and I will be treated as criminals."

²²While Bathsheba was still talking with the king, Nathan the prophet arrived. ²³The servants told the king, "Nathan the prophet is here." So

Nathan went to the king and bowed face down on the ground before him.

²⁴Nathan said, "My master and king, have you said that Adonijah will be the king after you and that he will rule on your throne? ²⁵Today he has sacrificed many cows, fat calves and sheep, and he has invited all your other sons, the commanders of the army, and Abiathar the priest. Right now they are eating and drinking with him. They are saying, 'Long live King Adonijah!' ²⁶But he did not invite me, your own servant, or Zadok the priest, or Benaiah son of Jehoiada or your son Solomon. ²⁷Did you do this? Since we are your servants, why didn't you tell us who should be king after you?"

David Makes Solomon King

²⁸Then the king said, "Tell Bathsheba to come in!" So she came in and stood before the king.

²⁹Then the king made this promise, "The LORD has saved me from all trouble. As surely as he lives, ³⁰I will do today what I have promised you in the name of the LORD, the God of Israel. I promised that your son Solomon would be king after me and rule on my throne in my place."

³¹Then Bathsheba bowed face down on the ground and knelt before the king and said, "Long live my master King David!"

³²Then King David said, "Tell Zadok the priest, Nathan the prophet^d and Benaiah son of Jehoiada to come in." When they came before the king, ³³he said to them, "Take my servants with you and put my son Solomon on my own mule. Take him down to the spring called Gihon. ³⁴There Zadok the priest and Nathan the prophet should pour olive oil on him and make him king over Israel. Blow the trumpet and shout, 'Long live King Solomon!' ³⁵Then come back up here with him. He will sit on my throne and rule in my place, because he is the one I have chosen to be the ruler over Israel and Judah."

³⁶Benaiah son of Jehoiada answered the king, "Amen! This is what the LORD, the God of my master, has declared! ³⁷The LORD has always helped you, our king. May he also help Solomon and make King Solomon's throne an even greater throne than yours."

³⁸So Zadok the priest, Nathan the prophet, and Benaiah son of Jehoiada left with the Kerethites and Pelethites.ⁿ They put Solomon on King David's mule and took him to the spring called Gihon. ³⁹Zadok the priest took the container of olive oil from the Holy Tent^d and poured the oil on Solomon's head to show he was the king. Then they blew the trumpet, and all the people shouted, "Long live King Solomon!" ⁴⁰All the people followed Solomon into the city. Playing flutes and shouting for joy, they made so much noise the ground shook.

⁴¹At this time Adonijah and all the guests with him were finishing their meal. When he heard the sound from the trumpet, Joab asked, "What does all that noise from the city mean?"

⁴²While Joab was speaking, Jonathan son of Abiathar the priest arrived. Adonijah said, "Come in! You are an important man, so you must be bringing good news."

⁴³But Jonathan answered, "No! Our master King David has made Solomon the new king. ⁴⁴King David sent Zadok the priest, Nathan the prophet, Benaiah son of Jehoiada, and all the king's bodyguards with him, and they have put Solomon on the king's own mule. ⁴⁵Then Zadok the priest and Nathan the prophet poured olive oil on Solomon at Gihon to make him king. After that they went into the city, shouting with joy. Now the whole city is excited, and that is the noise you hear. ⁴⁶Solomon has now become the king. ⁴⁷All the king's officers have come to tell King David that he has done a good thing. They are saying, 'May your God make Solomon even more famous than you and an even greater king than you.' " Jonathan continued, "And King David bowed down on his bed to worship God, ⁴⁸saying, 'Bless the LORD, the God of Israel. Today he has made one of my sons the king and allowed me to see it.' "

⁴⁹Then all of Adonijah's guests were afraid, and they left quickly and scattered. ⁵⁰Adonijah was also afraid of Solomon, so he went and took hold of the corners of the altar. ⁿ ⁵¹Then someone told Solomon, "Adonijah is afraid of you, so he is at the altar, holding on to its corners. He says, 'Tell King Solomon to promise me today that he will not kill me.' "

⁵²So Solomon answered, "Adonijah must show that he is a man of honour. If he does that, I promise he will not lose even a single hair from his head. But if he does anything wrong, he will die." ⁵³Then King Solomon sent some men to get Adonijah. When he was brought from the altar, he came before King Solomon and bowed down. Solomon told him, "Go home."

Kerethites and Pelethites   These were probably special units of the army that were responsible for the king's safety, a kind of palace guard.

corners of the altar   If a person were innocent of a crime, he could run into the Holy Place where the altar was. If he held on to the corners of the altar, which looked like horns, he would be safe.

The Death of David

2 Since it was almost time for David to die, he gave his son Solomon his last commands. [2]David said, "My time to die is near. Be a good and strong leader. [3]Obey the LORD your God. Follow him by obeying his demands, his commands, his laws and his rules that are written in the teachings of Moses. If you do these things, you will be successful in all you do and wherever you go. [4]And if you obey the LORD, he will keep the promise he made to me. He said: 'If your descendants[d] live as I tell them and have complete faith in me, a man from your family will always be king over the people of Israel.'

[5]"Also, you remember what Joab son of Zeruiah did to me. He killed the two commanders of Israel's armies: Abner son of Ner and Amasa son of Jether. He did this as if he and they were at war, although it was a time of peace. He put their blood on the belt around his waist and on his sandals on his feet. [6]Punish him in the way you think is wisest, but do not let him die peacefully of old age.

[7]"Be kind to the children of Barzillai of Gilead, and allow them to eat at your table. They welcomed me when I ran away from your brother Absalom.

[8]"And remember, Shimei son of Gera, the Benjaminite, is here with you. He cursed me the day I went to Mahanaim. But when he came down to meet me at the Jordan River, I promised him before the LORD, 'Shimei, I will not kill you.' [9]But you should not leave him unpunished. You are a wise man, and you will know what to do to him, but you must be sure he is killed."

[10]Then David died and was buried with his ancestors in Jerusalem. [11]He had ruled over

LEADERSHIP

The Mark of a Leader

Selwyn Hughes (who blessed millions through his *Everyday with Jesus* notes) was, like David, a Christian leader and was another man who knew how to die. He had cancer and, after ten years, when the doctors told him things didn't look great, he told people that he didn't know how long he had to live but asked them to pray that he would finish the work God wanted him to do and that he would die well.

He carried on writing and preaching until the cancer made it impossible and he went into a hospice. He was told that he had a matter of days to live and responded with eagerness and confidence by saying, "That's wonderful; I'm ready to meet Jesus."

Over those few days, his close friends and family visited him and he encouraged them by telling them he was ready for eternity. After a few days, he went into a peaceful sleep, with his friends praying at his bedside, and woke up in heaven.

Mick Brooks was one of Selwyn's friends. In the days that followed lots of people said to him, "Isn't it sad that Selwyn has died?" to which Mick answered, "Yes it is sad, but it's also joyful too; it's the best advert for dying that I've ever seen; it's great, it's orderly, it's godly. I hope I can do that."

Read **1 Kings 2:1–12**.

* How was what Selwyn did similar to what David says in the passage?
* How do you think you would have felt being an Israelite under David's leadership hearing those words?

Consider . . .

* what you would do for Jesus if you knew you only had a few days to live. Why not go ahead and do it anyway?
* what words of wisdom you would pass on to your friends. Write them down and keep them in your Bible.

For more, see . . .

* Psalm 132:11–18 (p.578)
* 2 Timothy 4:1–5 (p.1319)

* John 16:4–15 (p.1125)

Israel 40 years—seven years in Hebron and 33 years in Jerusalem.

Solomon Takes Control as King

¹²Solomon became king after David, his father, and he was in firm control of his kingdom.

¹³At this time Adonijah son of Haggith went to Bathsheba, Solomon's mother. "Do you come in peace?" Bathsheba asked.

"Yes. This is a peaceful visit," Adonijah answered. ¹⁴"I have something to say to you."

"You may speak," she said.

¹⁵"You remember that at one time the kingdom was mine," Adonijah said. "All the people of Israel recognised me as their king, but things have changed. Now my brother is the king, because the LORD chose him. ¹⁶Now I have one thing to ask you; please do not refuse me."

Bathsheba answered, "What do you want?"

¹⁷"I know King Solomon will do anything you ask him," Adonijah continued. "Please ask him to give me Abishag the Shunammite to be my wife."

¹⁸"Very well," she answered. "I will speak to the king for you."

¹⁹So Bathsheba went to King Solomon to speak to him for Adonijah. When Solomon saw her, he stood up to meet her, then bowed down and sat on the throne. He told some servants to bring another throne for his mother. Then she sat down at his right side.

²⁰Bathsheba said, "I have one small thing to ask you. Please do not refuse me."

"Ask, mother," the king answered. "I will not refuse you."

²¹So she said, "Allow Abishag the Shunammite to marry your brother Adonijah."

²²King Solomon answered his mother, "Why do you ask me to give him Abishag? Why don't you also ask for him to become the king since he is my older brother? Abiathar the priest and Joab son of Zeruiah would support him!"

²³Then King Solomon swore by the name of the LORD, saying, "May God punish me terribly if this doesn't cost Adonijah his life! ²⁴By the LORD who has given me the throne that belonged to my father David and who has kept his promise and given the kingdom to me and my people, Adonijah will die today!" ²⁵Then King Solomon gave orders to Benaiah son of Jehoiada, and he went and killed Adonijah.

²⁶King Solomon said to Abiathar the priest, "I should kill you too, but I will allow you to go back to your fields in Anathoth. I will not kill you at this time, because you helped carry the Ark *d* of the LORD GOD while marching with my father David. And I know you shared in all the hard times with him." ²⁷Then Solomon removed Abiathar from being the LORD's priest. This happened as the LORD had said it would, when he was speaking in Shiloh about the priest Eli and his descendants. *d*

²⁸When Joab heard about what had happened, he was afraid. He had supported Adonijah but not Absalom. So Joab ran to the Tent *d* of the LORD and took hold of the corners of the altar. *n* ²⁹Someone told King Solomon that Joab had run to the Tent of the LORD and was beside the altar. Then Solomon ordered Benaiah to go and kill him.

³⁰Benaiah went into the Tent of the LORD and said to Joab, "The king says, 'Come out!' "

But Joab answered, "No, I will die here."

So Benaiah went back to the king and told him what Joab had said. ³¹Then the king ordered Benaiah, "Do as he says! Kill him there and bury him. Then my family and I will be free of the guilt of Joab, who has killed innocent people. ³²Without my father knowing it, he killed two men who were much better than he was—Abner son of Ner, the commander of Israel's army, and Amasa son of Jether, the commander of Judah's army. So the LORD will pay him back for those deaths. ³³Joab and his family will be for ever guilty of their deaths, but there will be peace from the LORD for David, his descendants, his family and his throne for ever."

³⁴So Benaiah son of Jehoiada killed Joab, and he was buried near his home in the desert. ³⁵The king then made Benaiah son of Jehoiada commander of the army in Joab's place. He also made Zadok the new high priest in Abiathar's place.

³⁶Next the king sent for Shimei. Solomon said to him, "Build a house for yourself in Jerusalem and live there. Don't leave the city. ³⁷The very day you leave and cross the Kidron Valley, someone will kill you, and it will be your own fault."

³⁸So Shimei answered the king, "I agree with what you say. I will do what you say, my master and king." So Shimei lived in Jerusalem for a long time.

³⁹But three years later two of Shimei's slaves ran away to Achish king of Gath, who was the son of Maacah. Shimei heard that his slaves were in Gath, ⁴⁰so he put his saddle on his donkey and went to Achish at Gath to find them. Then he brought them back from Gath.

---

corners of the altar   If a person were innocent of a crime, he could run into the Holy Place where the altar was. If he held on to the corners of the altar, which looked like horns, he would be safe.

⁴¹Someone told Solomon that Shimei had gone from Jerusalem to Gath and had returned. ⁴²So Solomon sent for Shimei and said, "I made you promise in the name of the LORD not to leave Jerusalem. I warned you if you went out anywhere you would die, and you agreed to what I said. ⁴³Why did you break your promise to the LORD and disobey my command?" ⁴⁴The king also said, "You know the many wrong things you did to my father David, so now the LORD will punish you for those wrongs. ⁴⁵But the LORD will bless me and make the rule of David safe before the LORD for ever."

⁴⁶Then the king ordered Benaiah to kill Shimei, and he did. Now Solomon was in full control of his kingdom.

Solomon Asks for Wisdom

3 Solomon made an agreement with the king of Egypt by marrying his daughter and bringing her to Jerusalem. At this time Solomon was still building his palace and the Temple *d* of the LORD, as well as a wall around Jerusalem. ²The Temple for the worship of the LORD had not yet been finished, so people were still sacrificing at altars in many places of worship. ³Solomon showed he loved the LORD by following the commands his father David had given him, except many other places of worship were still used to offer sacrifices and to burn incense.*d*

⁴King Solomon went to Gibeon to offer a sacrifice, because it was the most important place of worship. He offered a thousand burnt offerings on that altar. ⁵While he was at Gibeon, the LORD appeared to him in a dream during the night. God said, "Ask for whatever you want me to give you."

⁶Solomon answered, "You were very kind to your servant, my father David. He obeyed you, and he was honest and lived right. You showed great kindness to him when you allowed his son to be king after him. ⁷LORD my God, now you have made me, your servant, king in my father's place. But I am like a little child; I don't know how to do what must be done. ⁸I, your servant, am here among your chosen people, and there are too many of them to count. ⁹I ask that you give me an obedient heart so I can rule the people in the right way and will know the difference between right and wrong. Otherwise, it is impossible to rule this great people of yours."

¹⁰The Lord was pleased that Solomon had asked this. ¹¹So God said to him, "You did not ask for a long life, or riches for yourself or the death of your enemies. Since you asked for wisdom to make the right decisions, ¹²I will do what you asked. I will give you wisdom and understanding that is greater than anyone has had in the past or

will have in the future. ¹³I will also give you what you did not ask for: riches and honour. During your life no other king will be as great as you. ¹⁴If you follow me and obey my laws and commands as your father David did, I will also give you a long life."

¹⁵After Solomon woke up from the dream, he went to Jerusalem. He stood before the Ark *d* of the Agreement with the Lord, where he made burnt offerings and fellowship offerings. After that, he gave a feast for all his leaders and officers.

Solomon Makes a Wise Decision

¹⁶One day two women who were prostitutes *d* came to Solomon. As they stood before him, ¹⁷one of the women said, "My master, this woman and I live in the same house. I gave birth to a baby while she was there with me. ¹⁸Three days later this woman also gave birth to a baby. No one else was in the house with us; it was just the two of us. ¹⁹One night this woman rolled over on her baby, and he died. ²⁰So she took my son from my bed during the night while I was asleep, and she carried him to her bed. Then she put the dead baby in my bed. ²¹The next morning when I got up to feed my baby, I saw that he was dead! When I looked at him more closely, I realised he was not my son."

²²"No!" the other woman cried. "The living baby is my son, and the dead baby is yours!"

But the first woman said, "No! The dead baby is yours, and the living one is mine!" So the two women argued before the king.

²³Then King Solomon said, "One of you says, 'My son is alive and your son is dead.' Then the other one says, 'No! Your son is dead and my son is alive.' "

²⁴The king sent his servants to get a sword. When they brought it to him, ²⁵he said, "Cut the living baby into two pieces, and give each woman half."

²⁶The real mother of the living child was full of love for her son. So she said to the king, "Please, my master, don't kill him! Give the baby to her!"

But the other woman said, "Neither of us will have him. Cut him into two pieces!"

Sidelight Many people have half-brothers or half-sisters these days because of stepfamilies. But Solomon suggested another approach: settling a dispute by cutting the baby in half and giving each mother half (1 Kings 3:16–28). Scholars have found 22 similar stories of wisdom in other cultures of ancient times.

27Then King Solomon said, "Don't kill him. Give the baby to the first woman, because she is the real mother."

28When the people of Israel heard about King Solomon's decision, they respected him very much. They saw he had wisdom from God to make the right decisions.

Solomon's Officers

4 King Solomon ruled over all Israel. 2These are the names of his leading officers:

Azariah son of Zadok was the priest;

3Elihoreph and Ahijah, sons of Shisha, recorded what happened in the courts;

Jehoshaphat son of Ahilud recorded the history of the people;

4Benaiah son of Jehoiada was commander of the army;

Zadok and Abiathar were priests;

5Azariah son of Nathan was in charge of the district governors;

Zabud son of Nathan was a priest and adviser to the king;

6Ahishar was responsible for everything in the palace;

Adoniram son of Abda was in charge of the slaves.

7Solomon placed twelve governors over the districts of Israel, who gathered food from their districts for the king and his family. Each governor was responsible for bringing food to the king for one month of each year. 8These are the names of the twelve governors:

Ben-Hur was governor of the mountain country of Ephraim;

9Ben-Deker was governor of Makaz, Shaalbim, Beth Shemesh and Elon Bethhanan;

10Ben-Hesed was governor of Arubboth, Socoh and all the land of Hepher;

11Ben-Abinadab was governor of Naphoth Dor (he was married to Taphath, Solomon's daughter);

12Baana son of Ahilud was governor of Taanach, Megiddo and all of Beth Shan next to Zarethan, this was below Jezreel from Beth Shan to Abel Meholah across from Jokmeam;

13Ben-Geber was governor of Ramoth in Gilead (he was governor of all the towns of Jair in Gilead—Jair was the son of Manasseh; Ben-Geber was also over the district of Argob in Bashan, which had 60 large, walled cities with bronze bars on their gates);

14Ahinadab son of Iddo was governor of Mahanaim;

15Ahimaaz was governor of Naphtali (he was married to Basemath, Solomon's daughter);

16Baana son of Hushai was governor of Asher and Aloth;

17Jehoshaphat son of Paruah was governor of Issachar;

18Shimei son of Ela was governor of Benjamin;

19Geber son of Uri was governor of Gilead. Gilead had been the country of Sihon king of the Amorites and Og king of Bashan. But Geber was the only governor over this district.

Solomon's Kingdom

20There were as many people in Judah and Israel as grains of sand on the seashore. The people ate, drank and were happy. 21Solomon ruled over all the kingdoms from the Euphrates River to the land of the Philistines, as far as the border of Egypt. These countries brought Solomon the payments he demanded, and they were under his control all his life.

22Solomon needed much food each day to feed himself and all the people who ate at his table: 6,000 litres of fine flour, 12,000 litres of grain, 23ten cows that were fed on good grain, 20 cows that were raised in the fields, 100 sheep, three kinds of deer, and fattened birds.

> **Sidelight**
> Each day it took 30 cattle (plus lots of other food) to feed all the people at Solomon's table (1 Kings 4:23). That would be about 120,000 Big Macs a day.

24Solomon controlled all the countries west of the Euphrates River—the land from Tiphsah to Gaza. And he had peace on all sides of his kingdom. 25During Solomon's life Judah and Israel, from Dan to Beersheba,[n] also lived in peace; all of his people were able to sit under their own fig trees and grapevines.

26Solomon had 4,000 stalls for his chariot horses and 12,000 horses. 27Each month one of the district governors gave King Solomon all the food he needed—enough for every person who ate at the king's table. The governors made sure he had everything he needed. 28They also brought enough barley and straw for Solomon's chariot and work horses; each person brought this grain to the right place.

Dan to Beersheba   Dan was the city farthest north in Israel, and Beersheba was the city farthest south. So this means all the people of Israel.

Solomon's Wisdom

²⁹God gave Solomon great wisdom so he could understand many things. His wisdom was as hard to measure as the grains of sand on the seashore. ³⁰His wisdom was greater than any wisdom of the East, or any wisdom in Egypt. ³¹He was wiser than anyone on earth. He was even wiser than Ethan the Ezrahite, as well as Heman, Calcol and Darda—the three sons of Mahol. King Solomon became famous in all the surrounding countries. ³²During his life he spoke 3,000 wise sayings and also wrote 1,005 songs. ³³He taught about many kinds of plants—everything from the great cedar trees of Lebanon to the weeds that grow out of the walls. He also taught about animals, birds, crawling things and fish. ³⁴People from all nations came to listen to King Solomon's wisdom. The kings of all nations sent them to him, because they had heard of Solomon's wisdom.

Preparing to Build the Temple

5 Hiram, the king of Tyre, had always been David's friend. When Hiram heard that Solomon had been made king in David's place, he sent his messengers to Solomon. ²Solomon sent this message back to King Hiram: ³"You remember my father David had to fight many wars with the countries around him, so he was never able to build a temple for worshipping the LORD his God. David was waiting until the LORD allowed him to defeat all his enemies. ⁴But now the LORD my God has given me peace on all sides of my country. I have no enemies now, and no danger threatens my people.

⁵"The LORD promised my father David, 'I will make your son king after you, and he will build a temple for worshipping me.' Now, I plan to build that temple for worshipping the LORD my God. ⁶So send your men to cut down cedar trees for me from Lebanon. My servants will work with yours, and I will pay them whatever wages you decide. We don't have anyone who can cut down trees as well as the people of Sidon."

⁷When Hiram heard what Solomon asked, he was very happy. He said, "Praise the LORD today! He has given David a wise son to rule over this great nation!" ⁸Then Hiram sent back this message to Solomon: "I received the message you sent, and I will give you all the cedar and pine trees you want. ⁹My servants will bring them down from Lebanon to the sea. There I will tie them together and float them along the shore to the place you choose. Then I will separate the logs there, and you can take them away. In return it is my wish that you give food to all those who live with me." ¹⁰So Hiram gave Solomon as much cedar and pine as he wanted.

¹¹And Solomon gave Hiram about 2,000 tonnes of wheat each year to feed the people who lived with him. Solomon also gave him about 4,000 litres of pure olive oil every year.

¹²The LORD gave Solomon wisdom as he had promised. And there was peace between Hiram and Solomon; these two kings made a treaty between themselves.

¹³King Solomon forced 30,000 men of Israel to help in this work. ¹⁴He sent a group of 10,000 men each month to Lebanon. Each group worked in Lebanon for a month, then went home for two months. A man named Adoniram was in charge. ¹⁵Solomon forced 80,000 men to work in the hill country, cutting stone, and he had 70,000 men to carry the stones. ¹⁶There were also 3,300 men who directed the workers. ¹⁷King Solomon commanded them to cut large blocks of fine stone to be used for the foundation of the Temple. *d* ¹⁸Solomon's and Hiram's builders and the men from Byblos carved the stones and prepared the stones and the logs for building the Temple.

Solomon Builds the Temple

6 Solomon began to build the Temple *d* 480 years after the people of Israel had left Egypt. This was during the fourth year of King Solomon's rule over Israel. It was the second month, the month of Ziv.

²The Temple was 30 metres long, 10 metres wide and 15 metres high. ³The porch in front of the main room of the Temple was 5 metres deep and 10 metres wide. This room ran along the front of the Temple itself. Its width was equal to that of the Temple. ⁴The Temple also had windows that opened and closed. ⁵Solomon also built some side rooms against the walls of the main room and the inner room of the Temple. He built rooms all around. ⁶The rooms on the bottom floor were 2.5 metres wide. Those on the middle floor were 3 metres wide, and the rooms above them were 3.5 metres wide. The Temple wall

that formed the side of each room was thinner than the wall in the room below. These rooms were pushed against the Temple wall, but they did not have their main beams built into this wall.

⁷The stones were prepared at the same place where they were cut from the ground. Since these stones were the only ones used to build the Temple, there was no noise of hammers, axes or any other iron tools at the Temple.

⁸The entrance to the ground floor beside the Temple was on the south side. From there, stairs went up to the first floor. And from there, stairs went on to the second-floor rooms. ⁹Solomon put a roof made from beams and cedar boards on the Temple. So he finished building the Temple ¹⁰as well as the ground floor that was beside the Temple. This ground floor was 2.5 metres high and was attached to the Temple by cedar beams.

Sidelight

Solomon's Temple was one of the largest structures in Israel at the time, but it wasn't very big by today's standards. It only had about 250 square metres of floor space – smaller than a school gym (1 Kings 6:2–38).

¹¹The LORD said to Solomon: ¹²"If you obey all my laws and commands, I will do for you what I promised your father David. ¹³I will live among the Israelites in this Temple, and I will never leave my people Israel."

¹⁴So Solomon finished building the Temple. ¹⁵The inside walls were covered from floor to ceiling with cedar boards. The floor was made from pine boards. ¹⁶A room 10 metres long was built in the back part of the Temple. This room, called the Most Holy Place, was separated from the rest of the Temple by cedar boards which reached from floor to ceiling. ¹⁷The main room, the one in front of the Most Holy Place, was 20 metres long. ¹⁸Everything inside the Temple was covered with cedar, which was carved with pictures of flowers and plants. A person could not see the stones of the wall, only the cedar.

¹⁹Solomon prepared the inner room at the back of the Temple to keep the Ark ᵈ of the Agreement with the LORD. ²⁰This inner room was 10 metres long, 10 metres wide and 10 metres high. He covered this room with pure gold, and he also covered the altar of cedar. ²¹He covered the inside of the Temple with pure gold, placing gold chains across the front of the inner room, which

was also covered with gold. ²²So all the inside of the Temple, as well as the altar of the Most Holy Place, was covered with gold.

²³Solomon made two creatures from olive wood and placed them in the Most Holy Place.

Sidelight

Building Solomon's Temple would ruin any church's budget (1 Kings 6:21). Just the gold overlay in the Temple would make it one of the most valuable buildings in the world if it were around today.

Each creature was 5 metres tall ²⁴and had two wings. Each wing was 2.5 metres long, so it was 5 metres from the end of one wing to the end of the other. ²⁵The creatures were the same size and shape; ²⁶each was 5 metres tall. ²⁷These creatures were put beside each other in the Most Holy Place with their wings spread out. One creature's wing touched one wall, and the other creature's wing touched the other wall with their wings touching each other in the middle of the room. ²⁸These two creatures were covered with gold.

²⁹All the walls around the Temple were carved with pictures of creatures with wings, as well as palm trees and flowers. This was true for both the main room and the inner room. ³⁰The floors of both rooms were covered with gold.

³¹Doors made from olive wood were placed at the entrance to the Most Holy Place. These doors had frames with five sides. ³²Creatures with wings, as well as palm trees and flowers, were also carved on the two olive wood doors that were covered with gold. The creatures and the palm trees on the doors were covered with gold as well. ³³At the entrance to the main room there was a square door frame made of olive wood. ³⁴Two doors were made from pine. Each door had two parts so the doors folded. ³⁵The doors were covered with pictures of creatures with wings, as well as palm trees and flowers. All of the carvings were covered with gold, which was evenly spread over them.

³⁶The inner courtyard was enclosed by walls, which were made of three rows of cut stones and one row of cedar boards.

³⁷Work began on the Temple in Ziv, the second month, during the fourth year Solomon was king over Israel. ³⁸The Temple was finished during the eleventh year he was king, in the eighth month, the month of Bul. It was built exactly as it was planned. Solomon had spent seven years building it.

Solomon's Palace

7 King Solomon also built a palace for himself; it took him thirteen years to finish it. ²Built of cedars from the Forest of Lebanon, it was 50 metres long, 25 metres wide and 15 metres high. It had four rows of cedar columns which supported the cedar beams. ³There were 45 beams on the roof, with 15 beams in each row, and the ceiling was covered with cedar above the beams. ⁴Windows were placed in three rows facing each other. ⁵All the doors were square, and the three doors at each end faced each other.

⁶Solomon also built the porch that had pillars. This porch was 25 metres long and 15 metres wide. Along the front of the porch was a roof supported by pillars.

⁷Solomon also built a throne room where he judged people, called the Hall of Justice. This room was covered with cedar from the floor to the ceiling. ⁸The palace where Solomon lived was built like the Hall of Justice, and it was behind this hall. Solomon also built the same kind of palace for his wife, who was the daughter of the king of Egypt.

⁹All these buildings were made with blocks of fine stone. First they were carefully cut. Then they were trimmed with a saw in the front and back. These fine stones went from the foundations of the buildings to the top of the walls. Even the courtyard was made with blocks of stone. ¹⁰The foundations were made with large blocks of fine stone, some as long as 5 metres. Others were 4 metres long. ¹¹On top of these foundation stones were other blocks of fine stone and cedar beams. ¹²The palace courtyard, the courtyard inside the Temple *d* and the porch of the Temple were surrounded by walls. All of these walls had three rows of stone blocks and one row of cedar beams.

The Temple is Completed Inside

¹³King Solomon sent to Tyre and had Huram brought to him. ¹⁴Huram's mother was a widow from the tribe *d* of Naphtali. His father was from Tyre and had been skilled in making things from bronze. Huram was also very skilled and experienced in bronze work. So he came to King Solomon and did all the bronze work.

¹⁵He made two bronze pillars, each one 9 metres tall and 6 metres around. ¹⁶He also made two bronze capitals *d* that were 2.5 metres tall, and he put them on top of the pillars. ¹⁷Then he made a net of seven chains for each capital, which covered the capitals on top of the two pillars. ¹⁸He made two rows of bronze pomegranates *d* to go on the nets. These covered the capitals at the top of the pillars. ¹⁹The capitals on top of the pillars in the porch were shaped like lilies, and they were 2 metres tall. ²⁰The capitals were on top of both pillars, above the bowl-shaped section and next to the nets. At that place there were 200 pomegranates in rows all around the capitals. ²¹Huram put these two bronze pillars at the porch of the Temple. *d* He named the south pillar He Establishes and the north pillar In Him Is Strength. ²²The capitals on top of the pillars were shaped like lilies. So the work on the pillars was finished.

²³Then Huram made from bronze a large round bowl, which was called the Sea. It was 15 metres around, 5 metres across and 2.5 metres deep. ²⁴Around the outer edge of the bowl was a rim. Under this rim were two rows of bronze plants which surrounded the bowl. There were ten plants every 50 centimetres, and these plants were made in one piece with the bowl. ²⁵The bowl rested on the backs of twelve bronze bulls that faced outwards from the centre of the bowl. Three bulls faced north, three faced west, three faced south and three faced east. ²⁶The sides of the bowl were 10 centimetres thick, and it held about 40,000 litres. The rim of the bowl was like the rim of a cup or like a lily blossom.

²⁷Then Huram made ten bronze stands, each one 2 metres long, 2 metres wide and 1.5 metres high. ²⁸The stands were made from square sides, which were put on frames. ²⁹On the sides were bronze lions, bulls and creatures with wings. On the frames above and below the lions and bulls were designs of flowers hammered into the bronze. ³⁰Each stand had four bronze wheels with bronze axles. At the corners there were bronze supports for a large bowl, and the supports had designs of flowers. ³¹There was a frame on top of the bowls, 50 centimetres high above the bowls. The opening of the bowl was round, 75 centimetres deep. Designs were carved into the bronze on the frame, which was square, not round. ³²The four wheels, placed under the frame, were 75 centimetres high. The axles between the wheels were made as one piece with the stand. ³³The wheels were like a chariot's wheels. Everything on the wheels—the axles, rims, spokes and hubs—was made of bronze.

³⁴The four supports were on the four corners of each stand. They were made as one piece with the stand. ³⁵A strip of bronze around the top of each stand was 25 centimetres deep. It was also made as one piece with the stand. ³⁶The sides of the stand and the frames were covered with carvings of creatures with wings, as well as lions, palm trees and flowers. ³⁷This is the way Huram made the ten stands. The bronze for each stand was melted and poured into a mould, so all the stands were the same size and shape.

38Huram also made ten bronze bowls, one bowl for each of the ten stands. Each bowl was 2 metres across and could hold about 800 litres. 39Huram put five stands on the south side of the Temple and five on the north side. He put the large bowl in the south-east corner of the Temple. 40Huram also made bowls, shovels and small bowls.

So Huram finished all his work for King Solomon on the Temple of the LORD:

41two pillars;

two large bowls for the capitals on top of the pillars;

two nets to cover the two large bowls for the capitals on top of the pillars;

42400 pomegranates for the two nets (there were two rows of pomegranates for each net covering the bowls for the capitals on top of the pillars);

43ten stands with a bowl on each stand;

44the large bowl with twelve bulls under it;

45the pots, shovels, small bowls and all the dishes for the Temple of the LORD.

Huram made everything King Solomon wanted from polished bronze. 46The king had these things poured into clay moulds that were made in the plain of the Jordan River between Succoth and Zarethan. 47Solomon never weighed the bronze used to make these things, because there was too much to weigh. So the total weight of all the bronze was never known.

48Solomon also made all the things for the Temple of the LORD:

the golden altar;

the golden table which held the bread that shows God's people are in his presence;

49the lampstands of pure gold (five on the right side and five on the left side in front of the Most Holy Place);

the flowers, lamps and tongs of gold;

50the pure gold bowls, wick trimmers, small bowls, pans and dishes used to carry coals;

the gold hinges for the doors of the Most Holy Place and the main room of the Temple.

51Finally the work King Solomon did for the Temple of the LORD was finished. Solomon brought in everything his father David had set apart for the Temple—silver, gold and other articles. He put everything in the treasuries of the Temple of the LORD.

The Ark is Brought into the Temple

8 King Solomon called for the elders of Israel, the heads of the tribes *d* and the leaders of the families to come to him in Jerusalem. He wanted them to bring the Ark *d* of the Agreement with the LORD from the older part of the city. 2So all the Israelites came together with King Solomon during the festival in the month of Ethanim, the seventh month.

3When all the elders of Israel arrived, the priests lifted up the Ark. 4They carried the Ark of the LORD, the Meeting Tent *d* and the holy things; the priests and the Levites brought them up. 5King Solomon and all the Israelites gathered before the Ark and sacrificed so many sheep and cattle no one could count them all. 6Then the priests put the Ark of the Agreement with the LORD in its place inside the Most Holy Place in the Temple, *d* under the wings of the golden creatures. 7The wings of these creatures were spread out over the place for the Ark, covering it and its carrying poles. 8The carrying poles were so long that anyone standing in the Holy Place in front of the Most Holy Place could see the ends of the poles, but no one could see them from outside the Holy Place. The poles are still there today. 9The only things inside the Ark were two stone tablets *n* that Moses had put in the Ark at Mount Sinai. That was where the LORD made his agreement with the Israelites after they came out of Egypt. 10When the priests left the Holy Place, a cloud filled the Temple of the LORD. 11The priests could not continue their work, because the Temple was filled with the glory of the LORD.

Solomon Speaks to the People

12Then Solomon said, "The LORD said he would live in a dark cloud. 13LORD, I have truly built a wonderful Temple *d* for you—a place for you to live for ever."

14While all the Israelites were standing there, King Solomon turned to them and blessed them. 15Then he said, "Praise the LORD, the God of Israel. He has done what he promised to my father David. The LORD said, 16'Since the time I brought my people Israel out of Egypt, I have not chosen a city in any tribe *d* of Israel where a temple will be built for me. But I have chosen David to lead my people Israel.'

17"My father David wanted to build a temple for the LORD, the God of Israel. 18But the LORD said to my father David, 'It was good that you wanted to build a temple for me. 19But you are not the one to build it. Your son, who comes from your own body, is the one who will build my temple.'

---

stone tablets   They were the two tablets on which God wrote the Ten Commandments.

²⁰"Now the LORD has kept his promise. I am the king now in place of David my father. Now I rule Israel as the LORD promised, and I have built the Temple for the LORD, the God of Israel. ²¹I have made a place there for the Ark, in which is the Agreement the LORD made with our ancestors when he brought them out of Egypt."

Solomon's Prayer

²²Then Solomon stood facing the LORD's altar, and all the Israelites were standing behind him. He spread out his hands towards the sky ²³and said:

"LORD, God of Israel, there is no god like you in heaven above or on earth below. You keep your agreement of love with your servants who truly follow you. ²⁴You have kept the promise you made to your servant David, my father. You spoke it with your own mouth and finished it with your hands today. ²⁵Now LORD, God of Israel, keep the promise you made to your servant David, my father. You said, 'If your sons are careful to obey me as you have obeyed me, there will always be someone from your family ruling Israel.' ²⁶Now, God of Israel, please continue to keep that promise you made to your servant David, my father.

²⁷"But, God, can you really live here on the earth? The sky and the highest place in heaven cannot contain you. Surely this house which

PRAYER

Praying About Real Life

When fifteen-year-old Linda and her mum talked about Linda's ex-boyfriend one evening, the conversation quickly escalated into a fight.

"Tony seems such a nice boy, Linda," Mum complained. "I really think you handled the whole thing badly."

"I didn't ask your opinion, Mum, but thanks anyway." Linda's words dripped with sarcasm. She felt as if she were about to explode. "I'm tired of your constant meddling. I can't even put my shoes on without getting your approval first. I have a life, Mother. Why don't you let me live it by myself?"

Then Linda stormed away. She didn't know or care what her mother thought – she just wanted to leave.

Linda ended up at a nearby park for the next few hours. There, she discovered how much prayer can help. At first, she was angry with God. "Why does all this happen to me?" she asked God. "I shouldn't be having so much trouble with this! I'm a Christian." Linda felt that she ought to be able to deal with her family problems. Soon, Linda asked God to help her. She spent some time worshipping and concentrating on God's power and goodness. Once she had calmed down, Linda asked God to help her to understand her mum's side of the argument.

Linda got home late, but in the morning, she and her mother apologised. That evening, they talked about how they could have dealt with their feelings better. And Linda decided to talk to Tony.

"It'll give me the chance to let him know I still care," she told her mum, smiling.

Linda's relationship with her mum isn't perfect, but she knows that she can turn to God in prayer for real-life issues like this one.

King Solomon also turned to God and prayed about real-life issues. Read his prayer after God's Temple was built in **1 Kings 8:22–30**.

* What elements do Linda's prayer and King Solomon's prayer have in common? What's different?
* How does King Solomon's prayer compare with the kind of prayers you usually pray?

Consider . . .

* listing all the concerns of your life on paper and then talking to God about each one.
* offering to pray with others who are going through rough times.

For more, see . . .

* 2 Samuel 22:1–51 (p.307)
* John 17:20–26 (p.1128)
* Luke 1:46–55 (p.1037)

I have built cannot contain you. 28But please listen to my prayer and my request, because I am your servant. LORD my God, hear this prayer your servant prays to you today. 29Night and day please watch over this Temple *d* where you have said, 'I will be worshipped there.' Hear the prayer I pray facing this Temple. 30Hear my prayers and the prayers of your people Israel when we pray facing this place. Hear from your home in heaven, and when you hear, forgive us.

31"If someone wrongs another person, he will be brought to the altar in this Temple. If he swears an oath that he is not guilty, 32then hear in heaven. Judge the case, punish the guilty, but declare that the innocent person is not guilty.

33"When your people, the Israelites, sin against you, their enemies will defeat them. But if they come back to you and praise you and pray to you in this Temple, 34then hear them in heaven. Forgive the sins of your people Israel, and bring them back to the land you gave to their ancestors.

35"When they sin against you, you will stop the rain from falling on their land. Then they will pray, facing this place and praising you; they will stop sinning when you make them suffer. 36When this happens, please hear their prayer in heaven, and forgive the sins of your servants, the Israelites. Teach them to do what is right. Then please send rain to this land you have given particularly to them.

37"At times the land will become so dry that no food will grow, or a great sickness will spread among the people. Sometimes all the crops will be destroyed by locusts *d* or grasshoppers. Your people will be attacked in their cities by their enemy or will become sick. 38When any of these things happen, the people will become truly sorry. If your people spread their hands in prayer towards this Temple, 39then hear their prayers from your home in heaven. Forgive and treat each person as he should be treated because you know what is in a person's heart. Only you know what is in everyone's heart. 40Then your people will respect you as long as they live in this land you gave to our ancestors.

41–42"People who are not Israelites, foreigners from other lands, will hear about your greatness and power. They will come from far away to pray at this Temple. 43Then hear from your home in heaven, and do whatever they ask you. Then people everywhere will know you and respect you, just as your people in Israel do. Then everyone will know I built this Temple as a place to worship you.

44"When your people go out to fight their enemies along some road on which you send them, your people will pray to you, facing the city which you have chosen and the Temple I have built for you. 45Then hear in heaven their prayers, and do what is right.

46"Everyone sins, so your people will also sin against you. You will become angry with them and hand them over to their enemies. Their enemies will capture them and take them away to their countries far or near. 47Your people will be sorry for their sins when they are held as prisoners in another country. They will be sorry and pray to you in the land where they are held as prisoners, saying, 'We have sinned. We have done wrong and acted wickedly.' 48They will truly turn back to you in the land of their enemies. They will pray to you, facing this land you gave their ancestors, this city you have chosen and the Temple I have built for you. 49Then hear their prayers from your home in heaven, and do what is right. 50Forgive your people for all their sins and for turning against you. Make those who have captured them show them mercy. 51Remember, they are your special people. You brought them out of Egypt, as if you were pulling them out of a blazing furnace.

52"Give your attention to my prayers and the prayers of your people Israel. Listen to them whenever they ask you for help. 53You chose them from all the nations on earth to be your very own people. This is what you promised through Moses your servant when you brought our ancestors out of Egypt, Lord GOD."

54Solomon prayed this prayer to the LORD, kneeling in front of the altar with his arms raised towards heaven. When he finished praying, he got up. 55Then, in a loud voice, he stood and blessed all the people of Israel, saying: 56"Praise the LORD! He promised he would give rest to his people Israel, and he has given us rest. The LORD has kept all the good promises he gave through his servant Moses. 57May the LORD our God be with us as he was with our ancestors. May he never leave us, 58and may he turn us to himself so we will follow him. Let us obey all the laws and commands he gave our ancestors. 59May the LORD our God remember this prayer day and night and do what is right for his servant and his people Israel day by day. 60Then all the people of the world will know the LORD is the only true God. 61You must fully obey the LORD our God and follow all his laws and commands. Continue to obey in the future as you do now."

Sacrifices are Offered

62Then King Solomon and all Israel with him offered sacrifices to the LORD. 63Solomon killed 22,000 cattle and 120,000 sheep as fellowship offerings. So the king and all the people gave the Temple *d* to the LORD.

⁶⁴On that day King Solomon made holy the middle part of the courtyard which is in front of the Temple of the LORD. There he offered whole burnt offerings, grain offerings and the fat of the fellowship offerings. He offered them in the courtyard, because the bronze altar before the LORD was too small to hold all the burnt offerings, the grain offerings and the fat of the fellowship offerings.

⁶⁵Solomon and all the Israelites celebrated the other festival that came at that time. People came from as far away as Lebo Hamath and the brook of Egypt. A great many people celebrated before the LORD for seven days, then seven more days, for a total of fourteen days. ⁶⁶On the following day Solomon sent the people home. They blessed the king as they went, happy because of all the good things the LORD had done for his servant David and his people Israel.

The LORD Appears to Solomon Again

9 Solomon finished building the Temple *d* of the LORD and his royal palace and everything he wanted to build. ²Then the LORD appeared to him again just as he had done before, in Gibeon. ³The LORD said to him: "I have heard your prayer and what you have asked me to do. You built this Temple, and I have made it a holy place. I will be worshipped there for ever and will watch over it and protect it always.

⁴"But you must serve me as your father David did; he was fair and sincere. You must obey all I have commanded and keep my laws and rules. ⁵If you do, I will make your kingdom strong. This is the promise I made to your father David—that someone from his family would always rule Israel.

⁶"But you and your children must follow me and obey the laws and commands I have given you. You must not serve or worship other gods. ⁷If you do, I will force Israel to leave the land I have given them, and I will leave this Temple that I have made holy. All the nations will make fun of Israel and speak evil about them. ⁸If the Temple is destroyed, everyone who passes by will be shocked. They will make fun of you and ask, 'Why did the LORD do this terrible thing to this land and this Temple?' ⁹People will answer, 'This happened because they left the LORD their God. This was the God who brought their ancestors out of Egypt, but they decided to follow other gods. They worshipped and served those gods, so the LORD brought all this disaster on them.' "

Solomon's Other Achievements

¹⁰By the end of 20 years, King Solomon had built two buildings—the Temple *d* of the LORD and the royal palace. ¹¹At that time King Solomon gave 20 towns in Galilee to Hiram king of Tyre, because Hiram had helped with the buildings. Hiram had given Solomon all the cedar, pine and gold he wanted. ¹²So Hiram travelled from Tyre to see the towns Solomon had given him, but when he saw them, he was not pleased. ¹³He asked, "What good are these towns you have given me, my brother?" So he named them the Land of Cabul,ⁿ and they are still called that today. ¹⁴Hiram had sent Solomon about 4 tonnes of gold.

¹⁵This is the account of the forced labour Solomon used to build the Temple and the palace. He had them fill in the land and build the wall around Jerusalem. He also had them rebuild the cities of Hazor, Megiddo and Gezer. ¹⁶(In the past the king of Egypt had attacked and captured Gezer. After burning it, he killed the Canaanites who lived there. Then he gave it as a wedding present to his daughter, who married Solomon. ¹⁷So Solomon rebuilt it.) He also built the cities of Lower Beth Horon ¹⁸and Baalath, as well as Tadmor, which is in the desert. ¹⁹King Solomon also built cities for storing grain and supplies and cities for his chariots and horses. He built whatever he wanted in Jerusalem, Lebanon and everywhere he ruled.

²⁰There were other people in the land who were not Israelites—Amorites, Hittites, Perizzites, Hivites and Jebusites. ²¹They were descendants *d* of people that the Israelites had not destroyed. Solomon forced them to work for him as slaves, as is still true today. ²²But Solomon did not make slaves of the Israelites. They were his soldiers, government leaders, officers, captains, chariot commanders and drivers.

²³These were his most important officers over the work. There were 550 supervisors over the people who did the work on Solomon's projects. ²⁴The daughter of the king of Egypt moved from the old part of Jerusalem to the palace that Solomon had built for her. Then Solomon filled in the surrounding land.

²⁵Three times each year Solomon offered whole burnt offerings and fellowship offerings on the altar he had built for the LORD. He also burned incense *d* before the LORD. So he finished the work on the Temple.

²⁶King Solomon also built ships at Ezion Geber, a town near Elath on the shore of the Red Sea, in the land of Edom. ²⁷Hiram had skilled sailors, so he sent them to serve in these ships with

Solomon's men. ²⁸The ships sailed to Ophir and brought back about 14 tonnes of gold to King Solomon.

The Queen of Sheba Visits Solomon

10 When the queen of Sheba heard about Solomon, she came to test him with hard questions. ²She travelled to Jerusalem with a large group of servants and camels carrying spices, jewels and much gold. When she came to Solomon, she talked with him about all she had in mind, ³and Solomon answered all her questions. Nothing was too hard for him to explain to her. ⁴The queen of Sheba learned that Solomon was very wise. She saw the palace he had built, ⁵the food on his table, his many officers, the palace servants and their good clothes. She saw the servants who served him at feasts and the whole burnt offerings he made in the Temple *d* of the LORD. All these things amazed her.

⁶So she said to King Solomon, "What I heard in my own country about your achievements and wisdom is true. ⁷I could not believe it then, but now I have come and seen it with my own eyes. I was not told even half of it! Your wisdom and wealth are much greater than I had heard. ⁸Your men and officers are very happy, because in always serving you, they are able to hear your wisdom. ⁹Praise the LORD your God, who was pleased to make you king of Israel. The LORD has constant love for Israel, so he made you king to keep justice and to rule fairly."

¹⁰Then she gave the king about 4 tonnes of gold and many spices and jewels. No one since that time has brought more spices than the queen of Sheba gave to King Solomon.

¹¹(Hiram's ships brought gold from Ophir, as well as much juniper wood and jewels. ¹²Solomon used the juniper wood to build supports for the Temple of the LORD and the palace, and to make harps and lyres *d* for the musicians. Such fine juniper wood has not been brought in or been seen since that time.)

¹³King Solomon gave the queen of Sheba everything she wanted and asked for, in addition to what he had already given her of his wealth. Then she and her servants returned to her own country.

Solomon's Wealth

¹⁴Every year King Solomon received about 23 tonnes of gold. ¹⁵Besides that, he also received gold from the traders and merchants, as well as from the kings of Arabia and governors of the land.

¹⁶King Solomon made 200 large shields of hammered gold, each of which contained about 7 kilogrammes of gold. ¹⁷He also made 300 smaller shields of hammered gold, each of which contained about 2 kilogrammes of gold. The king put them in the Palace of the Forest of Lebanon.

¹⁸The king built a large throne of ivory and covered it with fine gold. ¹⁹The throne had six steps on it, and its back was round at the top. There were armrests on both sides of the chair, and each armrest had a lion beside it. ²⁰Twelve lions stood on the six steps, one lion at each end of each step. Nothing like this had ever been made for any other kingdom. ²¹All of Solomon's drinking cups, as well as the dishes in the Palace of the Forest of Lebanon, were made of pure gold. Nothing was made from silver, because silver was not so valuable in Solomon's time.

²²King Solomon also had many trading ships at sea, along with Hiram's ships. Every three years the ships returned, bringing back gold, silver, ivory, apes and baboons.

²³So Solomon had more riches and wisdom than all the other kings on earth. ²⁴People everywhere wanted to see King Solomon and listen to the wisdom God had given him. ²⁵Every year those who came brought gifts of silver and gold, clothes, weapons, spices, horses and mules.

²⁶Solomon had 1,400 chariots and 12,000 horses. He kept some in special cities for the chariots, and others he kept with him in Jerusalem. ²⁷In Jerusalem Solomon made silver as common as stones and cedar trees as common as the fig trees on the western hills. ²⁸He brought in horses from Egypt and Kue. His traders bought them in Kue. ²⁹A chariot from Egypt cost about 600 pieces of silver, and a horse cost nearly 150 pieces of silver. Solomon's traders also sold horses and chariots to all the kings of the Hittites and the Arameans.

Solomon's Many Wives

11 King Solomon loved many women who were not from Israel. He loved the daughter of the king of Egypt, as well as women of the Moabites, Ammonites, Edomites, Sidonians and Hittites. ²The LORD had told the Israelites, "You must not marry people of other nations. If you do, they will cause you to follow their gods." But Solomon fell in love with these women. ³He had 700 wives who were from royal families and 300 slave women *d* who gave birth to his children. His wives caused him to turn away from God. ⁴As Solomon grew old, his wives caused him to follow other gods. He did not follow the LORD completely as his father David had done. ⁵Solomon worshipped Ashtoreth, *d* the goddess of the people of Sidon, and Molech, *d* the hated god of the Ammonites. ⁶So Solomon did what the LORD said was wrong and did not follow the LORD completely as his father David had done.

[7]On a hill east of Jerusalem, Solomon built two places for worship. One was a place to worship Chemosh,[d] the hated god of the Moabites, and the other was a place to worship Molech, the hated god of the Ammonites. [8]Solomon did the same thing for all his foreign wives so they could burn incense [d] and offer sacrifices to their gods.

[9]The LORD had appeared to Solomon twice, but the king turned away from following the LORD, the God of Israel. The LORD was angry with Solomon, [10]because he had commanded Solomon not to follow other gods. But Solomon did not obey the LORD's command. [11]So the LORD said to Solomon, "Because you have chosen to break your agreement with me and have not obeyed my commands, I will tear your kingdom away from you and give it to one of your officers. [12]But I will not take it away while you are alive because of my love for your father David. I will tear it away from your son when he becomes king. [13]I will not tear away all the kingdom from him, but I will leave him one tribe [d] to rule. I will do this because of David, my servant, and because of Jerusalem, the city I have chosen."

Solomon's Enemies

[14]The LORD caused Hadad the Edomite, a member of the family of the king of Edom, to become Solomon's enemy. [15]Earlier, David had defeated Edom. When Joab, the commander of David's army, went into Edom to bury the dead, he killed all the males. [16]Joab and all the Israelites stayed in Edom for six months and killed every male in Edom. [17]At that time Hadad was only a young boy, so he ran away to Egypt with some of his father's officers. [18]They left Midian and went to Paran, where they were joined by other men. Then they all went to Egypt to see the king, who gave Hadad a house, some food and some land.

[19]The king liked Hadad so much he gave Hadad a wife—the sister of Tahpenes, the king's wife. [20]They had a son named Genubath. Queen Tahpenes brought him up in the royal palace with the king's own children.

[21]While he was in Egypt, Hadad heard that David had died and that Joab, the commander of the army, was dead also. So Hadad said to the king, "Let me go; I will return to my own country."

[22]"Why do you want to go back to your own country?" the king asked. "What haven't I given you here?"

"Nothing," Hadad answered, "but please, let me go."

[23]God also caused another man to be Solomon's enemy—Rezon son of Eliada. Rezon had run away from his master, Hadadezer king of Zobah. [24]After David defeated the army of Zobah, Rezon gathered some men and became the leader of a small army. They went to Damascus and settled there, and Rezon became king of Damascus. [25]Rezon ruled Aram, and he hated Israel. So he was an enemy of Israel all the time Solomon was alive. Both Rezon and Hadad made trouble for Israel.

[26]Jeroboam son of Nebat was one of Solomon's officers. He was an Ephraimite from the town of Zeredah, and he was the son of a widow named Zeruah. Jeroboam turned against the king.

[27]This is the story of how Jeroboam turned against the king. Solomon was filling in the land and repairing the wall of Jerusalem, the city of David, his father. [28]Jeroboam was a capable man, and Solomon saw that this young man was a good worker. So Solomon put him over all the workers from the tribes [d] of Ephraim and Manasseh.

[29]One day as Jeroboam was leaving Jerusalem, Ahijah, the prophet [d] from Shiloh, who was wearing a new coat, met him on the road. The two men were alone out in the country. [30]Ahijah took his new coat and tore it into twelve pieces. [31]Then he said to Jeroboam, "Take ten pieces of this coat for yourself. The LORD, the God of Israel, says: 'I will tear the kingdom away from Solomon and give you ten tribes. [32]But I will allow him to control one tribe. I will do this for the sake of my servant David and for Jerusalem, the city I have chosen from all the tribes of Israel. [33]I will do this because Solomon has stopped following me and has worshipped the Sidonian god Ashtoreth,[d] the Moabite god Chemosh,[d] and the Ammonite god Molech. Solomon has not obeyed me by doing what I said is right and obeying my laws and commands, as his father David did.

[34]" 'But I will not take all the kingdom away from Solomon. I will let him rule all his life because of my servant David, whom I chose, who obeyed all my commands and laws. [35]But I will take the kingdom away from his son, and I will allow you to rule over the ten tribes. [36]I will allow Solomon's son to continue to rule over one tribe so that there will always be a descendant of David, my servant, in Jerusalem, the city where I chose to be worshipped. [37]But I will make you rule over everything you want. You will rule over all of Israel, [38]and I will always be with you if you do what I say is right. You must obey all my commands. If you obey my laws and commands as David did, I will be with you. I will make your family a lasting family of kings, as I did for David, and give Israel to you. [39]I will punish David's children because of this, but I will not punish them for ever.' "

Solomon's Death

⁴⁰Solomon tried to kill Jeroboam, but he ran away to Egypt, to Shishak king of Egypt, where he stayed until Solomon died.

⁴¹Everything else King Solomon did, and the wisdom he showed, is written in the book of the history of Solomon. ⁴²Solomon ruled in Jerusalem over all Israel for 40 years. ⁴³Then he died and was buried in Jerusalem, the city of David, his father. And his son Rehoboam became king in his place.

Israel Turns Against Rehoboam

12 Rehoboam went to Shechem, where all the Israelites had gone to make him king. ²Jeroboam son of Nebat was still in Egypt, where he had gone to escape from Solomon. When Jeroboam heard about Rehoboam being made king, he was living in Egypt. ³After the people sent for him, he and the people went to Rehoboam and said to him, ⁴"Your father forced us to work very hard. Now, make it easier for us, and don't make us work as hard as he did. Then we will serve you."

⁵Rehoboam answered, "Go away for three days, and then come back to me." So the people left.

⁶King Rehoboam asked the elders who had advised Solomon during his lifetime, "How do you think I should answer these people?"

⁷They said, "You should be like a servant to them today. If you serve them and give them a kind answer, they will serve you always."

⁸But Rehoboam rejected this advice. Instead, he asked the young men who had grown up with him and who served as his advisers. ⁹Rehoboam asked them, "What is your advice? How should we answer these people who said, 'Don't make us work as hard as your father did'?"

¹⁰The young men who had grown up with him answered, "Those people said to you, 'Your father forced us to work very hard. Now make our work easier.' You should tell them, 'My little finger is bigger than my father's legs. ¹¹He forced you to work hard, but I will make you work even harder. My father beat you with whips, but I will beat you with whips that have sharp points.' "

¹²Rehoboam had told the people, "Come back to me in three days." So after three days Jeroboam and all the people returned to Rehoboam. ¹³King Rehoboam spoke cruel words to them, because he had rejected the advice the elders had given him. ¹⁴He followed the advice of the young men and said to the people, "My father forced you to work hard, but I will make you work even harder. My father beat you with whips, but I will beat you with whips that have

sharp points." ¹⁵So the king did not listen to the people. The LORD caused this to happen to keep the promise he had made to Jeroboam son of Nebat through Ahijah, a prophet *d* from Shiloh.

¹⁶When all the Israelites saw that the new king refused to listen to them, they said to the king,

"We have no share in David!
   We have no part in the son of Jesse!
People of Israel, let's go to our own homes!
   Let David's son rule his own people!"

So the Israelites went home. ¹⁷But Rehoboam still ruled over the Israelites who lived in the towns of Judah.

¹⁸Adoniram was in charge of the people who were forced to work. When Rehoboam sent him to the people of Israel, they threw stones at him until he died. But King Rehoboam ran to his chariot and escaped to Jerusalem. ¹⁹Since then, Israel has been against the family of David.

> **Sidelight**
>
> When the kingdom was divided (1 Kings 12:16–19), Israel (the Northern Kingdom) was stronger economically, had more people, controlled major roads, and possessed the best land. Judah was smaller and had fewer resources. Yet Judah survived about 150 years longer than Israel. It didn't face as many attacks from hostile nations, and more of the kings followed God's leadership.

²⁰When all the Israelites heard that Jeroboam had returned, they called him to a meeting and made him king over all Israel. Only the tribe *d* of Judah continued to follow the family of David.

²¹When Rehoboam arrived in Jerusalem, he gathered 180,000 of the best soldiers from the tribes of Judah and Benjamin. As son of Solomon, Rehoboam wanted to fight the people of Israel to take back his kingdom.

²²But God spoke his word to Shemaiah, a man of God, saying, ²³"Speak to Solomon's son Rehoboam, the king of Judah, and to all the people of Judah and Benjamin and the rest of the people. Say to them, ²⁴'The LORD says you must not go to war against your brothers, the Israelites. Every one of you should go home, because I made all these things happen.' " So they obeyed the LORD's command and went home as the LORD had commanded.

²⁵Then Jeroboam made Shechem in the mountains of Ephraim a very strong city, and he lived there. He also went to the city of Peniel and made it stronger.

Jeroboam Builds Golden Calves

26Jeroboam said to himself, "The kingdom will probably go back to David's family. 27If the people continue going to the Temple*d* of the LORD in Jerusalem to offer sacrifices, they will want to be ruled again by Rehoboam. Then they will kill me and follow Rehoboam king of Judah."

28King Jeroboam asked for advice. Then he made two golden calves. "It is too long a journey for you to go to Jerusalem to worship," he said to the people. "Israel, here are your gods who brought you out of Egypt." 29Jeroboam put one golden calf in the city of Bethel and the other in the city of Dan. 30This became a very great sin, because the people travelled as far as Dan to worship the calf there.

31Jeroboam built temples on the places of worship. He also chose priests from all the people, not just from the tribe*d* of Levi. 32And he started a new festival on the fifteenth day of the eighth month, just like the festival in Judah. During that time the king offered sacrifices on the altar, along with sacrifices to the calves in Bethel he had made. He also chose priests in Bethel to serve at the places of worship he had made. 33So Jeroboam chose his own time for a festival for the Israelites—the fifteenth day of the eighth month. During that time he offered sacrifices on the altar he had built in Bethel. He set up a festival for the Israelites and offered sacrifices on the altar.

The Man of God Speaks Against Bethel

13 The LORD commanded a man of God from Judah to go to Bethel. When he arrived, Jeroboam was standing by the altar to offer a sacrifice. 2The LORD had commanded the man of God to speak against the altar. The man said, "Altar, altar, the LORD says to you: 'David's family will have a son named Josiah. The priests for the places of worship now make their sacrifices on you, but Josiah will sacrifice those priests on you. Human bones will be burned on you.' " 3That same day the man of God gave proof that these things would happen. "This is the LORD's sign that this will happen," he said. "This altar will break apart, and the ashes on it will fall to the ground."

4When King Jeroboam heard what the man of God said about the altar in Bethel, the king raised his hand from the altar and pointed at the man. "Take him!" he said. But when the king said this, his arm was paralysed, and he could not move it. 5The altar also broke into pieces, and its ashes fell to the ground. This was the sign the LORD had told the man of God to give.

6Then the king said to the man of God, "Please pray to the LORD your God for me, and ask him to heal my arm."

So the man of God prayed to the LORD, and the king's arm was healed, becoming as it was before.

7Then the king said to the man of God, "Please come home and eat with me, and I will give you a gift."

8But the man of God answered the king, "Even if you gave me half of your kingdom, I would not go with you. I will not eat or drink anything in this place. 9The LORD commanded me not to eat or drink anything nor to return on the same road by which I came." 10So he took a different road and did not return on the same road by which he had come to Bethel.

11Now an old prophet*d* was living in Bethel. His sons came and told him what the man of God had done there that day. They also told their father what he had said to King Jeroboam. 12The father asked, "Which road did he use when he left?" So his sons showed him the road the man of God from Judah had taken. 13Then the prophet told his sons to put a saddle on his donkey. So they saddled the donkey, and he left.

14He went after the man of God and found him sitting under an oak tree. The prophet asked, "Are you the man of God who came from Judah?"

The man answered, "Yes, I am."

15The prophet said, "Please come home and eat with me."

16"I can't go home with you," the man of God answered. "I can't eat or drink with you in this place. 17The LORD said to me, 'Don't eat or drink anything there or return on the same road by which you came.' "

18Then the old prophet said, "But I also am a prophet like you." Then he told a lie. He said, "An angel from the LORD came to me and told me to bring you to my home. He said you should eat and drink with me." 19So the man of God went to the old prophet's house, and he ate and drank with him there.

20While they were sitting at the table, the LORD spoke his word to the old prophet. 21The old prophet cried out to the man of God from Judah, "The LORD said you did not obey him! He said you did not do what the LORD your God commanded you. 22The LORD commanded you not to eat or drink anything in this place, but you came back and ate and drank. So your body will not be buried in your family grave."

23After the man of God finished eating and drinking, the prophet put a saddle on his donkey for him, and the man left. 24As he was travelling home, a lion attacked and killed him. His body lay on the road, with the donkey and the lion standing nearby. 25Some men who were travelling on that road saw the body and the lion standing nearby. So they went to the city where the old prophet lived and told what they had seen.

26The old prophet who had brought back the man of God heard what had happened. "It is the man of God who did not obey the LORD's command," he said. "So the LORD sent a lion to kill him, just as he said he would."

27Then the prophet said to his sons, "Put a saddle on my donkey," which they did. 28The old prophet went out and found the body lying on the road, with the donkey and the lion still standing nearby. The lion had not eaten the body or hurt the donkey. 29The prophet put the body on his donkey and carried it back to the city to have a time of sadness for him and to bury him. 30The prophet buried the body in his own family grave, and they were sad for the man of God and said, "Oh, my brother."

31After the prophet buried the body, he said to his sons, "When I die, bury me in this same grave. Put my bones next to his. 32Through him the LORD spoke against the altar at Bethel and against the places of worship in the towns of Samaria. What the LORD spoke through him will certainly come true."

33After this incident King Jeroboam did not stop doing evil. He continued to choose priests for the places of worship from among all the people. Anyone who wanted to be a priest for the places of worship was allowed to be one. 34In this way the family of Jeroboam sinned, and this sin caused its ruin and destruction from the earth.

Jeroboam's Son Dies

14 At that time Jeroboam's son Abijah became very sick. 2So Jeroboam said to his wife, "Go to Shiloh to see the prophet *d* Ahijah. He is the one who said I would become king of Israel. But dress yourself so people won't know you are my wife. 3Take the prophet ten loaves of bread, some cakes and a jar of honey. Then ask him what will happen to our son, and he will tell you." 4So the king's wife did as he said and went to Ahijah's home in Shiloh.

Now Ahijah was very old and blind. 5The LORD said to him, "Jeroboam's son is sick, and Jeroboam's wife is coming to ask you about him. When she arrives, she will pretend to be someone else." Then the LORD told Ahijah what to say.

6When Ahijah heard her walking to the door, he said, "Come in, wife of Jeroboam. Why are you pretending to be someone else? I have bad news for you. 7Go back and tell Jeroboam that this is what the LORD, the God of Israel, says: 'Jeroboam, I chose you from among all the people and made you the leader of my people Israel. 8I tore the kingdom away from David's family,

and I gave it to you. But you are not like my servant David, who always obeyed my commands and followed me with all his heart. He did only what I said was right. 9But you have done more evil than anyone who ruled before you. You have stopped following me and have made other gods and idols of metal. This has made me very angry, 10so I will soon bring disaster to your family. I will kill all the men in your family, both slaves and free men. I will destroy your family as completely as fire burns up manure. 11Anyone from your family who dies in the city will be eaten by dogs, and those who die in the fields will be eaten by the birds. The LORD has spoken.' "

12Then Ahijah said to Jeroboam's wife, "Go home now. As soon as you enter your city, your son will die, 13and all Israel will be sad for him and bury him. He is the only one of Jeroboam's family who will be buried, because he is the only one in the king's family who pleased the LORD, the God of Israel.

14"The LORD will put a new king over Israel, who will destroy Jeroboam's family, and this will happen soon. 15Then the LORD will punish Israel, which will be like grass moving in the water. The LORD will pull up Israel from this good land, the land he gave their ancestors. He will scatter Israel beyond the Euphrates River, because he is angry with the people. They made the LORD angry when they set up idols to worship Asherah.*d* 16Jeroboam sinned, and then he made the people of Israel sin. So the LORD will let the people of Israel be defeated."

17Then Jeroboam's wife left and returned to Tirzah. As soon as she entered her home, the boy died. 18After they buried him, all Israel had a time of sadness for him, just as the LORD had said through his servant, the prophet Ahijah.

19Everything else Jeroboam did is written in the book of the history of the kings of Israel. He fought wars and continued to rule the people, 20serving as king for 22 years. Then he died, and his son Nadab became king in his place.

The Death of Rehoboam

21Solomon's son Rehoboam was 41 years old when he became king of Judah. His mother was Naamah from Ammon. Rehoboam ruled in Jerusalem for seventeen years. (The LORD had chosen that city from all the land of Israel as the place where he would be worshipped.)

22The people of Judah did what the LORD said was wrong. Their sins made the LORD very angry, even more angry than he had been at their ancestors. 23The people built stone pillars and places to worship gods and Asherah *d* idols on every high hill and under every green tree. 24There were even male prostitutes *d* in the land. They acted like the people who had lived in the land before the Israelites. They had done many evil things, and God had taken the land away from them. ²⁵During the fifth year Rehoboam was king, Shishak king of Egypt attacked Jerusalem. ²⁶He took the treasures from the Temple *d* of the LORD and the king's palace. He took everything, even the gold shields Solomon had made. ²⁷So King Rehoboam made bronze shields to put in their place and gave them to the commanders of the guards for the palace gates. ²⁸Whenever the king went to the Temple of the LORD, the guards carried the shields. Later, they would put them back in the guardroom.

²⁹Everything else King Rehoboam did is written in the book of the history of the kings of Judah. ³⁰There was hostility between Rehoboam and Jeroboam continually. ³¹Rehoboam, son of Naamah from Ammon, died and was buried with his ancestors in Jerusalem, and his son Abijah became king in his place.

Abijah King of Judah

15 Abijah became king of Judah during the eighteenth year Jeroboam son of Nebat was king of Israel. ²Abijah ruled in Jerusalem for three years. His mother was Maacah daughter of Abishalom. ³He did all the same sins his father before him had done. Abijah was not faithful to the LORD his God as David, his great-grandfather, had been. ⁴Because the LORD loved David, the LORD gave him a kingdom in Jerusalem and allowed him to have a son to be king after him. The LORD also kept Jerusalem safe. ⁵David always did what the LORD said was right and obeyed his commands all his life, except the one time when David sinned against Uriah the Hittite.

⁶There was war between Abijah and Jeroboam during Abijah's lifetime. ⁷Everything else Abijah did is written in the book of the history of the kings of Judah. During the time Abijah ruled, there was war between Abijah and Jeroboam. ⁸Abijah died and was buried in Jerusalem, and his son Asa became king in his place.

Asa King of Judah

⁹During the twentieth year Jeroboam was king of Israel, Asa became king of Judah. ¹⁰His grandmother's name was Maacah, the daughter of Abishalom. Asa ruled in Jerusalem for 41 years.

¹¹Asa did what the LORD said was right, as his ancestor David had done. ¹²He forced the male prostitutes *d* at the worship places to leave the country. He also took away the idols that his ancestors had made. ¹³His grandmother Maacah had made a terrible Asherah *d* idol, so Asa removed her from being queen mother. He cut down that idol and burned it in the Kidron Valley.

¹⁴The places of worship to gods were not removed. Even so, Asa was faithful to the LORD all his life. ¹⁵Asa brought into the Temple *d* of the LORD the gifts he and his father had given: gold, silver and utensils.

¹⁶There was war between Asa and Baasha king of Israel all the time they were kings. ¹⁷Baasha attacked Judah, and he made the town of Ramah strong so he could keep people from leaving or entering Judah, Asa's country.

¹⁸Asa took the rest of the silver and gold from the treasuries of the Temple of the LORD and his own palace and gave it to his officers. Then he sent them to Ben-Hadad son of Tabrimmon, who was the son of Hezion. Ben-Hadad was the king of Aram and ruled in the city of Damascus. Asa said, ¹⁹"Let there be a treaty between you and me as there was between my father and your father. I am sending you a gift of silver and gold. Break your treaty with Baasha king of Israel so he will leave my land."

²⁰Ben-Hadad agreed with King Asa, so he sent the commanders of his armies to attack the towns of Israel. They defeated the towns of Ijon, Dan and Abel Beth Maacah, as well as all Galilee and the area of Naphtali. ²¹When Baasha heard about these attacks, he stopped building up Ramah and returned to Tirzah. ²²Then King Asa gave an order to all the people of Judah; everyone had to help. They carried away all the stones and wood Baasha had been using in Ramah, and they used them to build up Geba and Mizpah in the land of Benjamin.

²³Everything else Asa did—his victories and the cities he built—is written in the book of the history of the kings of Judah. When he became old, he got a disease in his feet. ²⁴After Asa died, he was buried with his ancestors in Jerusalem, the city of David, his ancestor. Then Jehoshaphat, Asa's son, became king in his place.

Nadab King of Israel

²⁵Nadab son of Jeroboam became king of Israel during the second year Asa was king of Judah. Nadab was king of Israel for two years, ²⁶and he did what the LORD said was wrong. Jeroboam had led the people of Israel to sin, and Nadab sinned in the same way as his father Jeroboam.

²⁷Baasha son of Ahijah, from the tribe *d* of Issachar, made plans to kill Nadab. Nadab and all Israel were attacking the Philistine town of Gibbethon, so Baasha killed Nadab there. ²⁸This happened during Asa's third year as king of Judah, and Baasha became the next king of Israel.

Baasha King of Israel

²⁹As soon as Baasha became king, he killed all of Jeroboam's family, leaving no one in Jeroboam's

family alive. He destroyed them all as the Lord had said would happen through his servant Ahijah from Shiloh. ³⁰King Jeroboam had sinned very much and had led the people of Israel to sin, so he made the Lord, the God of Israel, very angry.

³¹Everything else Nadab did is written in the book of the history of the kings of Israel. ³²There was war between Asa king of Judah and Baasha king of Israel all the time they ruled.

³³Baasha son of Ahijah became king of Israel during Asa's third year as king of Judah. Baasha ruled in Tirzah for 24 years, ³⁴and he did what the Lord said was wrong. Jeroboam had led the people of Israel to sin, and Baasha sinned in the same way as Jeroboam.

16 Jehu son of Hanani spoke the word of the Lord against King Baasha. ²The Lord said, "You were nothing, but I took you and made you a leader over my people Israel. But you have followed the ways of Jeroboam and have led my people Israel to sin. Their sins have made me angry, ³so, Baasha, I will soon destroy you and your family. I will do to you what I did to the family of Jeroboam son of Nebat. ⁴Anyone from your family who dies in the city will be eaten by dogs, and anyone from your family who dies in the fields will be eaten by birds."

⁵Everything else Baasha did and all his victories are written down in the book of the history of the kings of Israel. ⁶So Baasha died and was buried in Tirzah, and his son Elah became king in his place.

⁷The Lord spoke his word against Baasha and his family through the prophet *d* Jehu son of Hanani. Baasha had done many things the Lord said were wrong, which made the Lord very angry. He did the same evil deeds that Jeroboam's family had done before him. The Lord also spoke against Baasha because he killed all of Jeroboam's family.

Elah King of Israel

⁸Elah son of Baasha became king of Israel during Asa's twenty-sixth year as king of Judah, and Elah ruled in Tirzah for two years.

⁹Zimri, one of Elah's officers, commanded half of Elah's chariots. Zimri made plans against Elah while the king was in Tirzah, getting drunk at Arza's home. (Arza was in charge of the palace at Tirzah.) ¹⁰Zimri went into Arza's house and killed Elah during Asa's twenty-seventh year as king of Judah. Then Zimri became king of Israel in Elah's place.

Zimri King of Israel

¹¹As soon as Zimri became king, he killed all of Baasha's family, not allowing any of Baasha's family or friends to live. ¹²So Zimri destroyed all of Baasha's family just as the Lord had said it would

happen through the prophet*d* Jehu. ¹³Baasha and his son Elah sinned and led the people of Israel to sin, and they made the Lord, the God of Israel, angry because of their worthless idols.

¹⁴Everything else Elah did is written in the book of the history of the kings of Israel.

¹⁵So during Asa's twenty-seventh year as king of Judah, Zimri became king of Israel and ruled in Tirzah seven days.

The army of Israel was camped near Gibbethon, a Philistine town. ¹⁶The men in the camp heard that Zimri had made secret plans against King Elah and had killed him. So that day in the camp they made Omri, the commander of the army, king over Israel. ¹⁷So Omri and all the Israelite army left Gibbethon and attacked Tirzah. ¹⁸When Zimri saw that the city had been captured, he went into the palace and set it on fire, burning the palace and himself with it. ¹⁹So Zimri died because he had sinned by doing what the Lord said was wrong. Jeroboam had led the people of Israel to sin, and Zimri sinned in the same way as Jeroboam.

²⁰Everything else Zimri did and the story of how he turned against King Elah are written down in the book of the history of the kings of Israel.

Omri King of Israel

²¹The people of Israel were divided into two groups. Half of the people wanted Tibni son of Ginath to be king, while the other half wanted Omri. ²²Omri's followers were stronger than the followers of Tibni son of Ginath, so Tibni died and Omri became king.

²³Omri became king of Israel during the thirty-first year Asa was king of Judah. Omri ruled Israel for twelve years, six of those years in the city of Tirzah. ²⁴He bought the hill of Samaria from Shemer for about 6,000 pieces of silver. Omri built a city on that hill and called it Samaria after the name of its earlier owner, Shemer.

Sidelight King Omri doesn't get much press in the Bible (1 Kings 16:23–28), but he probably was one of the most powerful leaders of the Northern Kingdom. According to other sources, he established a strong rule and conquered the Moabites, long-term enemies. But, the Bible says, "he did more evil than all the kings who came before him".

---

²⁵But Omri did what the Lord said was wrong; he did more evil than all the kings who came before him. ²⁶Jeroboam son of Nebat had led the people of Israel to sin, and Omri sinned in the

same way as Jeroboam. The Israelites made the LORD, the God of Israel, very angry because they worshipped worthless idols.

[27]Everything else Omri did and all his successes are written in the book of the history of the kings of Israel. [28]So Omri died and was buried in Samaria, and his son Ahab became king in his place.

Ahab King of Israel

[29]Ahab son of Omri became king of Israel during Asa's thirty-eighth year as king of Judah, and Ahab ruled Israel in the city of Samaria for 22 years. [30]More than any king before him, Ahab son of Omri did many things the LORD said were wrong. [31]He sinned in the same ways as Jeroboam son of Nebat, but he did even worse things. He married Jezebel daughter of Ethbaal, the king of Sidon. Then Ahab began to serve Baal[d] and worship him. [32]He built a temple in Samaria for worshipping Baal and put an altar there for Baal. [33]Ahab also made an idol for worshipping Asherah.[d] He did more things to make the LORD, the God of Israel, angry than all the other kings before him.

[34]During the time of Ahab, Hiel from Bethel rebuilt the city of Jericho. It cost Hiel the life of Abiram, his oldest son, to begin work on the city, and it cost the life of Segub, his youngest son, to build the city gates.[n] This happened just as the LORD, speaking through Joshua son of Nun, said it would happen.[n]

Elijah Stops the Rain

17 Now Elijah the Tishbite was a prophet[d] from the settlers in Gilead. "I serve the LORD, the God of Israel," Elijah said to Ahab. "As surely as the LORD lives, no rain or dew will fall during the next few years unless I command it."

[2]Then the LORD spoke his word to Elijah: [3]"Leave this place and go east and hide near Kerith Ravine east of the Jordan River. [4]You may drink from the stream, and I have commanded ravens to bring you food there." [5]So Elijah did what the LORD said; he went to Kerith Ravine, east of the Jordan, and lived there. [6]The birds brought Elijah bread and meat every morning and evening, and he drank water from the stream.

[7]After a while the stream dried up because there was no rain. [8]Then the LORD spoke his word to Elijah, [9]"Go to Zarephath in Sidon and live there. I have commanded a widow there to take care of you."

[10]So Elijah went to Zarephath. When he reached the town gate, he saw a widow gathering wood for a fire. Elijah asked her, "Would you bring me a little water in a cup so I may have a drink." [11]As she was going to get his water, Elijah said, "Please bring me a piece of bread, too."

[12]The woman answered, "As surely as the LORD your God lives, I have no bread. I have only a handful of flour in a jar and only a little olive oil in a jug. I came here to gather some wood so I could go home and cook our last meal. My son and I will eat it and then die from hunger."

[13]"Don't worry," Elijah said to her. "Go home and cook your food as you have said. But first make a small loaf of bread from the flour you have, and bring it to me. Then cook something for yourself and your son. [14]The LORD, the God of Israel, says, 'That jar of flour will never be empty, and the jug will always have oil in it, until the day the LORD sends rain to the land.' "

[15]So the woman went home and did what Elijah told her to do. And the woman and her son and Elijah had enough food every day. [16]The jar of flour and the jug of oil were never empty, just as the LORD, through Elijah, had promised.

Elijah Brings a Boy Back to Life

[17]Some time later the son of the woman who owned the house became sick. He grew worse and worse and finally stopped breathing. [18]The woman said to Elijah, "Man of God, what have you done to me? Did you come here to remind me of my sin and to kill my son?"

[19]Elijah said to her, "Give me your son." Elijah took the boy from her, carried him upstairs and laid him on the bed in the room where he was staying. [20]Then he prayed to the LORD: "LORD my God, this widow is letting me stay in her house. Why have you done this terrible thing to her and caused her son to die?" [21]Then Elijah lay on top of the boy three times. He prayed to the LORD, "LORD my God, let this boy live again!"

[22]The LORD answered Elijah's prayer; the boy began breathing again and was alive. [23]Elijah carried the boy downstairs and gave him to his mother and said, "See! Your son is alive!"

[24]"Now I know you really are a man from God," the woman said to Elijah. "I know that the LORD truly speaks through you!"

Elijah Kills the Prophets of Baal

18 During the third year without rain, the LORD spoke his word to Elijah: "Go and meet King Ahab, and I will soon send rain." [2]So Elijah went to meet Ahab.

---

city gate   People came here to conduct business. Public meetings and court cases were also held here.
the LORD . . . happen   When Joshua destroyed Jericho, he said whoever rebuilt the city would lose his oldest and youngest sons. See Joshua 6:26.

By this time there was no food in Samaria. ³King Ahab sent for Obadiah, who was in charge of the king's palace. (Obadiah was a true follower of the LORD. ⁴When Jezebel was killing all the LORD's prophets,*d* Obadiah hid 100 of them in two caves, 50 in one cave and 50 in another. He also brought them food and water.) ⁵Ahab said to Obadiah, "Let's check every spring and valley in the land. Maybe we can find enough grass to keep our horses and mules alive and not have to kill our animals." ⁶So each one chose a part of the country to search; Ahab went in one direction and Obadiah in another.

⁷While Obadiah was on his way, Elijah met him. Obadiah recognised Elijah, so he bowed down to the ground and said, "Elijah? Is it really you, master?"

⁸"Yes," Elijah answered. "Go and tell your master that I am here."

⁹Then Obadiah said, "What wrong have I done for you to hand me over to Ahab like this? He will put me to death. ¹⁰As surely as the LORD your God lives, the king has sent people to every country to search for you. If the ruler said you were not there, Ahab forced the ruler to swear you could not be found in his country. ¹¹Now you want me to go to my master and tell him, 'Elijah is here'? ¹²The Spirit *d* of the LORD may carry you to some other place after I leave. If I go and tell King Ahab you are here, and he comes and doesn't find you, he will kill me! I have followed the LORD since I was a boy. ¹³Haven't you been told what I did? When Jezebel was killing the LORD's prophets, I hid 100 of them, 50 in one cave and 50 in another. I brought them food and water. ¹⁴Now you want me to go and tell my master you are here? He will kill me!"

HUNGER AND POVERTY

Letting God Use You

John went to help at the rescue mission mainly because someone had asked him to go. He had never done anything like this before in all of his fifteen years. But a friend had asked him to help out this Sunday, and John couldn't think of any reason not to. So he went.

When they got there, John and his friends did simple tasks – preparing food, setting places, washing dishes, cleaning tables. They just helped where they were needed.

The rescue mission was run-down and dirty. The people they served were dirty from sleeping rough on the streets, and they didn't seem to appreciate what John and his friends were doing for them. Some of John's friends didn't go back when they were asked to help out again.

But John went back. And he would go again.

He felt that he was needed there, and it was rewarding to give to people when you knew that they couldn't pay you back.

John was impressed with the staff at the rescue mission, and with their attitude towards the people they served. Even though they acted hard at times, they really cared for the people who came there.

Hunger and poverty have existed in the world almost since the beginning of time. God wants Christians – every Christian – to offer help and God's love to the poor and hungry. God even used the great prophet Elijah to help a widow and her son in **1 Kings 17:8–16**.

* What's the difference between the widow in this passage and the people John helped?
  What motives did John have for helping the poor? What motives did Elijah have for helping the widow?
* How does God keep the "jars of flour and jugs of oil" full for poor and hungry people today?
  What role can you play in providing food for hungry people?

Consider . . .

* skipping dinner tonight and spending that time praying for poor and hungry people.
* following John's example by volunteering to work in a soup kitchen or a homeless shelter.

For more, see . . .

* Exodus 16:1–15 (p.74)
* John 6:30–35 (p.1105)
* Mark 6:34–44 (p.1007)

¹⁵Elijah answered, "As surely as the LORD All-powerful lives, whom I serve, I will be seen by Ahab today."

¹⁶So Obadiah went to Ahab and told him where Elijah was. Then Ahab went to meet Elijah.

¹⁷When he saw Elijah, he asked, "Is it you—the biggest troublemaker in Israel?"

¹⁸Elijah answered, "I have not made trouble in Israel. You and your father's family have made all this trouble by not obeying the LORD's commands. You have gone after the Baals.*d* ¹⁹Now tell all Israel to meet me at Mount Carmel. Also bring the 450 prophets of Baal and the 400 prophets of Asherah,*d* who eat at Jezebel's table."

²⁰So Ahab called all the Israelites and those prophets to Mount Carmel. ²¹Elijah approached the people and said, "How long will you not decide between two choices? If the LORD is the true God, follow him, but if Baal is the true God, follow him!" But the people said nothing.

²²Elijah said, "I am the only prophet of the LORD here, but there are 450 prophets of Baal. ²³Bring two bulls. Let the prophets of Baal choose one bull and kill it and cut it into pieces. Then let them put the meat on the wood, but they are not to set fire to it. I will prepare the other bull, putting the meat on the wood but not setting fire to it. ²⁴You prophets of Baal, pray to your god, and I will pray to the LORD. The god who answers by setting fire to his wood is the true God."

All the people agreed that this was a good idea.

²⁵Then Elijah said to the prophets of Baal, "There are many of you, so you go first. Choose a bull and prepare it. Pray to your god, but don't start the fire."

Sidelight

The 450 prophets of Baal had a home team advantage in the contest against Elijah and God (1 Kings 18:20–46). Baal was considered the god of Mt Carmel, and he was also the rain-giving god. When Elijah was the one who prayed and brought fire and ended the drought, the false prophets might have died of embarrassment if Elijah hadn't executed them first.

SUFFERING

What am I Doing Wrong?

For as long as she could remember, Louise had believed in God. Her whole family were very involved in the church, and at home God was a huge part of their lives.

Then, things began to change in Louise's house. Her parents started arguing, and eventually they told Louise and her brother they were getting a divorce. Louise was devastated; she didn't understand what was happening. The following month Louise's gran died and it felt like things couldn't get any worse. But soon Louise found out that her dad had a gambling problem and that they were thousands of pounds in debt. Her mum seemed to be getting sick all the time and Louise and her brother spent a lot of time visiting her in hospital.

Although the rest of her family didn't seem to care about God any more, Louise did. She still went to church and youth group; she really tried to read her Bible and she certainly prayed lots. Sometimes though, Louise couldn't help being angry with God. Why were all these awful things happening to her? Why had it all gone so wrong? Was it something she had done?

In **1 Kings 17:17–24** a widow was also going through a really hard time when her son fell ill and died.

- Why did the widow think her son was ill? Did Louise feel the same way?
- What did the widow learn from her son coming back to life?

Consider . . .

- whether there are any difficult situations in your life that you need to trust God with.
- keeping a journal and writing down all that is happening in your life. You'll be amazed, when you look back, at how much God was working in your life, even through the hard times.

For more, see . . .

- Isaiah 53 (p.697)
- Romans 5:1–5 (p.1190)
- John 9:1–7 (p.1111)

²⁶So they took the bull that was given to them and prepared it. They prayed to Baal from morning until noon, shouting, "Baal, answer us!" But there was no sound, and no one answered. They danced around the altar they had built. ²⁷At noon Elijah began to make fun of them. "Pray louder!" he said. "If Baal really is a god, maybe he is thinking, or busy, or travelling! Maybe he is sleeping so you will have to wake him!" ²⁸The prophets prayed louder, cutting themselves with swords and spears until their blood flowed, which was the way they worshipped. ²⁹The afternoon passed, and the prophets continued to act like this until it was time for the evening sacrifice. But no voice was heard; Baal did not answer, and no one paid attention.

³⁰Then Elijah said to all the people, "Now come to me." So they gathered around him, and Elijah rebuilt the altar of the LORD, which had been torn down. ³¹He took twelve stones, one stone for each of the twelve tribes,ᵈ the number of Jacob's sons. (The LORD changed Jacob's name to Israel.) ³²Elijah used these stones to rebuild the altar in honour of the LORD. Then he dug a ditch around the altar that was big enough to hold about 14 litres of seed. ³³Elijah put the wood on the altar, cut the bull into pieces and laid the pieces on the wood. ³⁴Then he said, "Fill four jars with water, and pour it on the meat and on the wood." Then Elijah said, "Do it again," and they did it again. Then he said, "Do it a third time," and they did it the third time. ³⁵So the water ran off the altar and filled the ditch.

³⁶At the time for the evening sacrifice, the prophet Elijah went near the altar. "LORD, you are the God of Abraham, Isaac and Israel," he prayed. "Prove that you are the God of Israel and that I am your servant. Show these people that you commanded me to do all these things. ³⁷LORD, answer my prayer so these people will know that you, LORD, are God and that you will change their minds."

³⁸Then fire from the LORD came down and burned the sacrifice, the wood, the stones and the ground around the altar. It also dried up the water in the ditch. ³⁹When all the people saw this, they fell down to the ground, crying, "The LORD is God! The LORD is God!"

⁴⁰Then Elijah said, "Capture the prophets of Baal! Don't let any of them run away!" The people captured all the prophets. Then Elijah led them down to the Kishon Valley, where he killed them.

The Rain Comes Again

⁴¹Then Elijah said to Ahab, "Now, go, eat and drink, because a heavy rain is coming." ⁴²So King Ahab went to eat and drink. At the same time Elijah climbed to the top of Mount Carmel,

where he bent down to the ground with his head between his knees.

⁴³Then Elijah said to his servant, "Go and look towards the sea."

The servant went and looked. "I see nothing," he said.

Elijah told him to go and look again. This happened seven times. ⁴⁴The seventh time, the servant said, "I see a small cloud, the size of a human fist, coming from the sea."

Elijah told the servant, "Go to Ahab and tell him to get his chariot ready and go home now. Otherwise, the rain will stop him."

> **Sidelight** For a short time, Elijah may have been the fastest runner in the world. Fearing the rain would start while he was on the mountains, Elijah received God's power and ran from Mt Carmel to Jezreel – about ten miles – faster then the king's chariots (1 Kings 18:46). Some people will do anything to keep from getting their hair wet!

⁴⁵After a short time the sky was covered with dark clouds. The wind began to blow, and soon a heavy rain began to fall. Ahab got in his chariot and started back to Jezreel. ⁴⁶The LORD gave his power to Elijah, who tightened his clothes around him and ran ahead of King Ahab all the way to Jezreel.

Elijah Runs Away

19 King Ahab told Jezebel everything Elijah had done and how Elijah had killed all the prophetsᵈ with a sword. ²So Jezebel sent a messenger to Elijah, saying, "May the gods punish me terribly if by this time tomorrow I don't kill you just as you killed those prophets."

³When Elijah heard this, he was afraid and ran for his life, taking his servant with him. When they came to Beersheba in Judah, Elijah left his servant there. ⁴Then Elijah walked for a whole day into the desert. He sat down under a bush and asked to die. "I have had enough, LORD," he prayed. "Let me die. I am no better than my ancestors." ⁵Then he lay down under the tree and slept.

Suddenly an angel came to him and touched him. "Get up and eat," the angel said. ⁶Elijah saw near his head a loaf baked over coals and a jar of water, so he ate and drank. Then he went back to sleep.

⁷Later the LORD's angel came to him a second time. The angel touched him and said, "Get up and eat. If you don't, the journey will be too hard for you." ⁸So Elijah got up and ate and drank.

The food made him strong enough to walk for 40 days and nights to Mount Sinai, the mountain of God. ⁹There Elijah went into a cave and stayed all night.

Then the LORD spoke his word to him: "Elijah! Why are you here?"

¹⁰He answered, "LORD God All-powerful, I have always served you as well as I could. But the people of Israel have broken their agreement with you, destroyed your altars and killed your prophets with swords. I am the only prophet left, and now they are trying to kill me, too."

¹¹The LORD said to Elijah, "Go, stand in front of me on the mountain, and I will pass by you." Then a very strong wind blew until it caused the mountains to fall apart and large rocks to break in front of the LORD. But the LORD was not in the wind. After the wind, there was an earthquake, but the LORD was not in the earthquake. ¹²After the earthquake, there was a fire, but the LORD was not in the fire. After the fire, there was a quiet, gentle sound. ¹³When Elijah heard it, he covered his face with his coat and went out and stood at the entrance to the cave.

Then a voice said to him, "Elijah! Why are you here?"

¹⁴He answered, "LORD God All-powerful, I have always served you as well as I could. But the people of Israel have broken their agreement with you, destroyed your altars and killed your prophets with swords. I am the only prophet left, and now they are trying to kill me, too."

STRESS

I'll Get You For That!

Bullying is a terrible thing. It's more frightening than you can imagine. Let me tell you about Dan . . .

He was fourteen years old and went to the local secondary school. He wasn't particularly strong and his blond hair and blue eyes caught the attention of the tough guys. They started cornering him at break and asking for money. They threatened to beat him up if he didn't bring things to school for them. Dan was fearful, but also angry that people like them existed. But what could he do?

Most days he managed to get some money, or give them his lunch.

One day he had had enough.

A week later, one of his classmates called at his house and asked his mother if Dan was OK.

"What do you mean, 'How is he?'" she replied.

"Well, he hasn't been to school for most of the week and I assumed he was ill," stated his friend.

Dan's mother was shocked and when he came home that night, both his mother and father challenged him.

"Just tell us where you've been? We can't believe you've been playing truant."

Neither of them were angry, just very very concerned.

In the end, Dan explained, in tears, that he'd been standing on the corner of the High Street, trying to pluck up enough courage to jump in front of a car.

"My friend Matt had an accident a while back and it kept him off school for months," he explained.

Dan's parents had no idea of the stress put on an ordinary teenager. They were horrified and soon sorted the situation out.

Read **1 Kings 19:1–5** and see how Elijah was in a similar situation.

* Elijah was no weakling, but how did he cope with the stressful time in the passage?
* How is bullying approached at your school?

Consider . . .

* telling a close friend or respected teacher if you are being bullied.
* making a "loner" at school part of your close group of friends.

For more, see . . .

* Isaiah 51:12–16 (p.695)

* 2 Corinthians 12:8–10 (p.1252)

15The LORD said to him, "Go back on the road that leads to the desert around Damascus. Enter that city, and pour olive oil on Hazael to make him king over Aram. 16Then pour oil on Jehu son of Nimshi to make him king over Israel. Next, pour oil on Elisha son of Shaphat from Abel Meholah to make him a prophet in your place. 17Jehu will kill anyone who escapes from Hazael's sword, and Elisha will kill anyone who escapes from Jehu's sword. 18I have 7,000 people left in Israel who have never bowed down before Baal *d* and whose mouths have never kissed his idol."

Elisha Becomes a Prophet

19So Elijah left that place and found Elisha son of Shaphat ploughing a field with a team of oxen.

He owned twelve teams of oxen and was ploughing with the twelfth team. Elijah came up to Elisha, took off his coat and put it on Elisha. 20Then Elisha left his oxen and ran to follow Elijah. "Let me kiss my father and my mother goodbye," Elisha said. "Then I will go with you."

Elijah answered, "Go back. It does not matter to me."

21So Elisha went back and took his pair of oxen and killed them. He used their wooden yoke *d* for a fire. Then he cooked the meat and gave it to the people. After they ate it, Elisha left and followed Elijah and became his helper.

Ben-Hadad and Ahab Go to War

20 Ben-Hadad king of Aram gathered together all his army. There were 32 kings

LONELINESS

Better Do it Yourself

Struck by the constant news of suffering, poverty and ill health in Africa, Kerry and three of her mates decided that they should do something to help make a difference.

A national charity was holding a postcard campaign to petition the government to help the crisis. This would be the perfect opportunity to raise awareness in the school and do something productive at the same time. The four friends got together to divide up jobs and plan the event.

Kerry would contact the charity and get the info, posters and postcards. Mark would speak to the head teacher and ask permission to speak in assemblies, hand out postcards and put up collection points. Siobhan would organise student volunteers to hand out postcards around the school over the week. Dave would contact the local press to let the community know what was happening at the school and why.

With a week to go, Mark called Kerry and said he hadn't had time to speak to the head. Next was Dave – he hadn't called the paper. And, no surprise to Kerry, it soon came to light that Siobhan hadn't fulfilled her part of the bargain either.

Kerry had only been trying to do a good thing – putting herself out to make a difference. And her mates had just let her down, one by one. Why did no one else care? Frustration, betrayal, anger, but most of all, a total sense of loneliness came over Kerry as she struggled to work out what on earth to do now.

Take a look at **1 Kings 19:11–18**.

* Compare Kerry with Elijah. Why do you think Elijah felt let down and alone?
* God comforted Elijah – not with a big show of awesome power, but with a quiet, gentle sound. How often do you think of God as close and comforting?

Consider . . .

* writing a card of encouragement to someone who you've noticed doing a good job.
* spending time reading the Bible and praying about what God thinks about you. Look up every time God is called "Father" and what the Bible says about his children.

For more, see . . .

* Joshua 1:1–9 (p.202)
* Philippians 4:10–13 (p.1286)
* 2 Kings 6:13–17 (p.351)

with their horses and chariots who went with him and surrounded Samaria and attacked it. [2]The king sent messengers into the city to Ahab king of Israel.

This was his message: "Ben-Hadad says, [3]'Your silver and gold belong to me, as well as the best of your wives and children.' "

[4]Ahab king of Israel answered, "My master and king, I agree to what you say. I and everything I have belong to you."

[5]Then the messengers came to Ahab again. They said, "Ben-Hadad says, 'I told you before that you must give me your silver and gold, your wives and your children. [6]About this time tomorrow I will send my men, who will search everywhere in your palace and in the homes of your officers. Whatever they want they will take and carry off.' "

[7]Then Ahab called a meeting of all the elders of his country. He said, "Ben-Hadad is looking for trouble. First he said I had to give him my wives, my children, my silver and my gold, and I have not refused him."

[8]The elders and all the people said, "Don't listen to him or agree to this."

[9]So Ahab said to Ben-Hadad's messengers, "Tell my master the king: 'I will do what you said at first, but I cannot allow this second command.' " And King Ben-Hadad's men carried the message back to him.

[10]Then Ben-Hadad sent another message to Ahab: "May the gods punish me terribly if I don't completely destroy Samaria. There won't be enough left for each of my men to get a handful of dust!"

[11]Ahab answered, "Tell Ben-Hadad, 'The man who puts on his armour should not boast. It's the man who lives to take it off who has the right to boast.' "

[12]Ben-Hadad was drinking in his tent with the other rulers when the message came from Ahab. Ben-Hadad commanded his men to prepare to attack the city, and they moved into place for battle.

[13]At the same time a prophet [d] came to Ahab king of Israel. The prophet said, "Ahab, the LORD says to you, 'Do you see that big army? I will hand it over to you today so you will know I am the LORD.' "

[14]Ahab asked, "Who will you use to defeat them?"

The prophet answered, "The LORD says, 'The young officers of the district governors will defeat them.' "

Then the king asked, "Who will command the main army?"

The prophet answered, "You will."

[15]So Ahab gathered the young officers of the district governors, 232 of them. Then he called together the army of Israel, about 7,000 people in all.

[16]They marched out at noon, while Ben-Hadad and the 32 rulers helping him were getting drunk in their tents. [17]The young officers of the district governors attacked first. Ben-Hadad sent out scouts who told him that soldiers were coming from Samaria. [18]Ben-Hadad said, "They may be coming to fight, or they may be coming to ask for peace. In either case capture them alive."

[19]The young officers of the district governors led the attack, followed by the army of Israel. [20]Each officer of Israel killed the man who came against him. The men from Aram ran away as Israel chased them, but Ben-Hadad king of Aram escaped on a horse with some of his horsemen. [21]Ahab king of Israel led the army and destroyed the Arameans' horses and chariots. King Ahab thoroughly defeated the Aramean army.

[22]Then the prophet went to Ahab king of Israel and said, "The king of Aram will attack you again next spring. So go home now and strengthen your army and see what you need to do."

[23]Meanwhile the officers of Ben-Hadad king of Aram said to him, "The gods of Israel are mountain gods. Since we fought in a mountain area, Israel won. Let's fight them on the flat land, and then we will win. [24]This is what you should do. Don't allow the 32 rulers to command the armies, but put other commanders in their places. [25]Gather an army like the one that was destroyed and as many horses and chariots as before. We will fight the Israelites on flat land, and then we will win." Ben-Hadad agreed with their advice and did what they said.

[26]The next spring Ben-Hadad gathered the army of Aram and went up to Aphek to fight against Israel.

[27]The Israelites also had prepared for war. They marched out to meet the Arameans and camped opposite them. The Israelites looked like two small flocks of goats, but the Arameans covered the area.

[28]A man of God came to the king of Israel with this message: "The LORD says, 'The people of Aram say that I, the LORD, am a god of the mountains, not a god of the valleys. So I will allow you to defeat this big army, and then you will know I am the LORD.' "

[29]The armies were camped across from each other for seven days. On the seventh day the battle began. The Israelites killed 100,000 Aramean soldiers in one day. [30]The rest of them

ran away to the city of Aphek, where a city wall fell on 27,000 of them. Ben-Hadad also ran away to the city and hid in a room.

³¹His officers said to him, "We have heard that the kings of Israel are trustworthy. Let's dress in rough cloth to show our sadness, and wear ropes on our heads. Then we will go to the king of Israel, and perhaps he will let you live."

³²So they dressed in rough cloth and wore ropes on their heads and went to the king of Israel. They said, "Your servant Ben-Hadad says, 'Please let me live.' "

Ahab answered, "Is he still alive? He is my brother."

³³Ben-Hadad's men had wanted a sign from Ahab. So when Ahab called Ben-Hadad his brother, they quickly said, "Yes! Ben-Hadad is your brother."

Ahab said, "Bring him to me." When Ben-Hadad came, Ahab asked him to join him in the chariot.

³⁴Ben-Hadad said to him, "Ahab, I will give you back the cities my father took from your father. And you may put shops in Damascus, as my father did in Samaria."

Ahab said, "If you agree to this, I will allow you to go free." So the two kings made a peace agreement. Then Ahab let Ben-Hadad go free.

A Prophet Speaks Against Ahab

³⁵One prophet from one of the groups of prophets *d* told another, "Hit me!" He said this because the Lord had commanded it, but the other man refused. ³⁶The prophet said, "You did not obey the Lord's command, so a lion will kill you as soon as you leave me." When the man left, a lion found him and killed him.

³⁷The prophet went to another man and said, "Hit me, please!" So the man hit him and hurt him. ³⁸The prophet wrapped his face in a cloth so no one could tell who he was. Then he went and waited by the road for the king. ³⁹As Ahab king of Israel passed by, the prophet called out to him. "I went to fight in the battle," the prophet

said. "One of our men brought an enemy soldier to me. Our man said, 'Guard this man. If he runs away, you will have to give your life in his place. Or, you will have to pay a fine of 3,000 pieces of silver.' ⁴⁰But I was busy doing other things, so the man ran away."

The king of Israel answered, "You have already said what the punishment is. You must do what the man said."

⁴¹Then the prophet quickly took the cloth from his face. When the king of Israel saw him, he knew he was one of the prophets. ⁴²The prophet said to the king, "This is what the Lord says: 'You freed the man I said should die, so your life will be taken instead of his. The lives of your people will also be taken instead of the lives of his people.' "

⁴³Then King Ahab went back to his palace in Samaria, angry and upset.

Ahab Takes Naboth's Vineyard

21 After these things had happened, this is what followed. A man named Naboth owned a vineyard in Jezreel, near the palace of Ahab king of Israel. ²One day Ahab said to Naboth, "Give me your vineyard. It is near my palace, and I want to make it into a vegetable garden. I will give you a better vineyard in its place, or, if you prefer, I will pay you what it is worth."

³Naboth answered, "May the Lord keep me from ever giving my land to you. It belongs to my family."

⁴Ahab went home angry and upset, because he did not like what Naboth from Jezreel had said. (Naboth had said, "I will not give you my family's land.") Ahab lay down on his bed, turned his face to the wall and refused to eat.

⁵His wife, Jezebel, came in and asked him, "Why are you so upset that you refuse to eat?"

⁶Ahab answered, "I talked to Naboth, the man from Jezreel. I said, 'Sell me your vineyard, or, if you prefer, I will give you another vineyard for it.' But Naboth refused."

⁷Jezebel answered, "Is this how you rule as king over Israel? Get up, eat something, and cheer up. I will get Naboth's vineyard for you."

⁸So Jezebel wrote some letters, signed Ahab's name to them, and used his own seal *d* to seal them. Then she sent them to the elders and important men who lived in Naboth's town. ⁹The letter she wrote said: "Declare a day during which the people are to give up eating. Call the people together, and give Naboth a place of honour among them. ¹⁰Seat two troublemakers across from him, and have them say they heard Naboth speak against God and the king. Then

take Naboth out of the city and kill him with stones."

¹¹The elders and important men of Jezreel obeyed Jezebel's command, just as she wrote in the letters. ¹²They declared a special day on which the people were to give up eating. And they put Naboth in a place of honour before the people. ¹³Two troublemakers sat across from Naboth and said in front of everybody that they had heard him speak against God and the king. So the people carried Naboth out of the city and killed him with stones. ¹⁴Then the leaders sent a message to Jezebel, saying, "Naboth has been killed."

¹⁵When Jezebel heard that Naboth had been killed, she told Ahab, "Naboth of Jezreel is dead. Now you may go and take for yourself the vineyard he would not sell to you." ¹⁶When Ahab heard that Naboth of Jezreel was dead, he got up and went to the vineyard to take it for his own.

¹⁷At this time the LORD spoke his word to the prophet Elijah the Tishbite. The LORD said, ¹⁸"Go to Ahab king of Israel in Samaria. He is at Naboth's vineyard, where he has gone to take it as his own. ¹⁹Tell Ahab that I, the LORD, say to him, 'You have murdered Naboth and taken his land. So I tell you this: in the same place the dogs licked up Naboth's blood, they will also lick up your blood!' "

²⁰When Ahab saw Elijah, he said, "So you have found me, my enemy!"

Elijah answered, "Yes, I have found you. You have always chosen to do what the LORD says is wrong. ²¹So the LORD says to you, 'I will soon destroy you. I will kill you and every male in your family, both slave and free. ²²Your family will be like the family of King Jeroboam son of Nebat and like the family of King Baasha son of Ahijah. I will destroy you, because you have made me angry and have led the people of Israel to sin.'

²³"And the LORD also says, 'Dogs will eat the body of Jezebel in the city of Jezreel.'

²⁴"Anyone in your family who dies in the city will be eaten by dogs, and anyone who dies in the fields will be eaten by birds."

²⁵There was no one like Ahab who had chosen so often to do what the LORD said was wrong, because his wife Jezebel influenced him to do evil. ²⁶Ahab sinned terribly by worshipping idols, just as the Amorite people did. And the LORD had taken away their land and given it to the people of Israel.

²⁷After Elijah finished speaking, Ahab tore his clothes. He put on rough cloth, refused to eat and even slept in the rough cloth to show how sad and upset he was.

²⁸The LORD spoke his word to Elijah the Tishbite: ²⁹"I see that Ahab is now sorry for what he has done. So I will not cause the trouble to come to him during his life, but I will wait until his son is king. Then I will bring this trouble to Ahab's family."

The Death of Ahab

22 For three years there was peace between Israel and Aram. ²During the third year Jehoshaphat king of Judah went to visit Ahab king of Israel.

³At that time Ahab asked his officers, "Do you remember that the king of Aram took Ramoth in Gilead from us? Why have we done nothing to get it back?" ⁴So Ahab asked King Jehoshaphat, "Will you go with me to fight at Ramoth in Gilead?"

"I will go with you," Jehoshaphat answered. "My soldiers are yours, and my horses are yours." ⁵Jehoshaphat also said to Ahab, "But first we should ask if this is the LORD's will."

⁶Ahab called about 400 prophets *d* together and asked them, "Should I go to war against Ramoth in Gilead or not?"

They answered, "Go, because the Lord will hand them over to you."

⁷But Jehoshaphat asked, "Isn't there a prophet of the LORD here? Let's ask him what we should do."

⁸Then King Ahab said to Jehoshaphat, "There is one other prophet. We could ask the LORD through him, but I hate him. He never prophesies anything good about me, but something bad. He is Micaiah son of Imlah."

Jehoshaphat said, "King Ahab, you shouldn't say that!"

⁹So Ahab king of Israel told one of his officers to bring Micaiah to him at once.

¹⁰Ahab king of Israel and Jehoshaphat king of Judah had on their royal robes and were sitting on their thrones at the threshing *d* floor, near the entrance to the gate of Samaria. All the prophets were standing before them, speaking their messages. ¹¹Zedekiah son of Kenaanah had made some iron horns. He said to Ahab, "This is what the LORD says, 'You will use these horns to fight the Arameans until they are destroyed.' "

¹²All the other prophets said the same thing. "Attack Ramoth in Gilead and win, because the LORD will hand the Arameans over to you."

¹³The messenger who had gone to get Micaiah said to him, "All the other prophets are saying King Ahab will succeed. You should agree with them and give the king a good answer."

¹⁴But Micaiah answered, "As surely as the

LORD lives, I can tell him only what the LORD tells me."

15When Micaiah came to Ahab, the king asked him, "Micaiah, should we attack Ramoth in Gilead or not?"

Micaiah answered, "Attack and win! The LORD will hand them over to you."

16But Ahab said to Micaiah, "How many times do I have to tell you to speak only the truth to me in the name of the LORD?"

17So Micaiah answered, "I saw the army of Israel scattered over the hills like sheep without a shepherd. The LORD said, 'They have no leaders. They should go home and not fight.' "

18Then Ahab king of Israel said to Jehoshaphat, "I told you! He never prophesies anything good about me, but only bad."

19But Micaiah said, "Hear the message from the LORD: I saw the LORD sitting on his throne with his heavenly army standing near him on his right and on his left. 20The LORD said, 'Who will trick Ahab into attacking Ramoth in Gilead where he will be killed?'

"Some said one thing; some said another. 21Then one spirit came and stood before the LORD and said, 'I will trick him.'

22"The LORD asked, 'How will you do it?'

"The spirit answered, 'I will go to Ahab's prophets and make them tell lies.'

"So the LORD said, 'You will succeed in tricking him. Go and do it.' "

23Micaiah said, "Ahab, the LORD has made your prophets lie to you, and the LORD has decided that disaster should come to you."

24Then Zedekiah son of Kenaanah went up to Micaiah and slapped him in the face. Zedekiah said, "Has the LORD's spirit left me to speak through you?"

25Micaiah answered, "You will find out on the day you go to hide in an inside room."

26Then Ahab king of Israel ordered, "Take Micaiah and send him to Amon, the governor of the city, and to Joash, the king's son. 27Tell them I said to put this man in prison and give him only bread and water until I return safely from the battle."

28Micaiah said, "Ahab, if you come back safely from battle, the LORD has not spoken through me. Remember my words, all you people!"

29So Ahab king of Israel and Jehoshaphat king of Judah went to Ramoth in Gilead. 30King Ahab said to Jehoshaphat, "I will go into battle, but I will wear other clothes so no one will recognise me. But you wear your royal clothes." So Ahab wore other clothes and went into battle.

31The king of Aram had ordered his 32 chariot commanders, "Don't fight with anyone—impor-

tant or unimportant—except the king of Israel." 32When these commanders saw Jehoshaphat, they thought he was certainly the king of Israel, so they turned to attack him. But Jehoshaphat began shouting. 33When they saw he was not King Ahab, they stopped chasing him.

34By chance, a soldier shot an arrow, but he hit Ahab king of Israel between the pieces of his armour. King Ahab said to his chariot driver, "Turn round and get me out of the battle, because I am hurt!" 35The battle continued all day. King Ahab was held up in his chariot and faced the Arameans. His blood flowed down to the bottom of the chariot. That evening he died. 36Near sunset a cry went out through the army of Israel: "Each man go back to his own city and land."

37In that way King Ahab died. His body was carried to Samaria and buried there. 38The men cleaned Ahab's chariot at a pool in Samaria where prostitutes d bathed, and the dogs licked his blood from the chariot. These things happened as the LORD had said they would.

39Everything else Ahab did is written in the book of the history of the kings of Israel. It tells about the palace Ahab built and decorated with ivory and the cities he built. 40So Ahab died, and his son Ahaziah became king in his place.

Jehoshaphat King of Judah

41Jehoshaphat son of Asa became king of Judah during Ahab's fourth year as king of Israel. 42Jehoshaphat was 35 years old when he became king, and he ruled in Jerusalem for 25 years. His mother's name was Azubah daughter of Shilhi. 43Jehoshaphat was good, like his father Asa, and he did what the LORD said was right. But Jehoshaphat did not destroy the places where gods were worshipped, so the people continued offering sacrifices and burning incense d there. 44Jehoshaphat was at peace with the king of Israel. 45Jehoshaphat fought many wars, and these wars and his successes are written in the book of the history of the kings of Judah. 46There were male prostitutes d still in the places of worship from the days of his father, Asa. So Jehoshaphat forced them to leave.

47During this time the land of Edom had no king; it was ruled by a governor.

48King Jehoshaphat built trading ships to sail to Ophir for gold. But the ships were destroyed at Ezion Geber, so they never set sail. 49Ahaziah son of Ahab went to help Jehoshaphat, offering to give Jehoshaphat some men to sail with his men, but Jehoshaphat refused.

50Jehoshaphat died and was buried with his ancestors in Jerusalem, the city of David, his ancestor. Then his son Jehoram became king in his place.

Ahaziah King of Israel

[51]Ahaziah son of Ahab became king of Israel in Samaria during Jehoshaphat's seventeenth year as king over Judah. Ahaziah ruled Israel for two years, [52]and he did what the LORD said was wrong. He did the same evil his father Ahab, his mother Jezebel and Jeroboam son of Nebat had done. All these rulers led the people of Israel into more sin. [53]Ahaziah worshiped and served the god Baal, [d] and this made the LORD, the God of Israel, very angry. In these ways Ahaziah did what his father had done.

2 Kings

Why Read This Book:

* See how God uses leaders to encourage people to follow him (2 Kings 1—8).
* Learn how unfaithfulness to God can destroy a nation (2 Kings 9—17).
* Be encouraged that God keeps his promises even when people don't keep theirs (2 Kings 18—23).

Behind the Scenes:

The land was in mess. The kingdom that David and Solomon built had split into Israel (in the north) and Judah (in the south), and both countries faced attack from the outside and unrest from within. Making matters worse, the people kept turning to the false god Baal for help, ignoring and forgetting the true God.

But even in this difficult situation, God hadn't forgotten his people. He sent the prophet Elisha to challenge them to turn back to God. Unlike his combative predecessor Elijah (1 Kings 16—19, p.331), Elisha was more of a healer and comforter. He performed numerous miracles to ease people's pain (2 Kings 4), and he also performed miracles on behalf of the nation (2 Kings 5). He showed that God hadn't given up on his people and would accept the Israelites if they would come back to him.

The Northern Kingdom did experience a brief revival under King Jeroboam II. But the overall decline continued, until Samaria – the northern capital – was destroyed and the people were taken into exile. ▷

When?

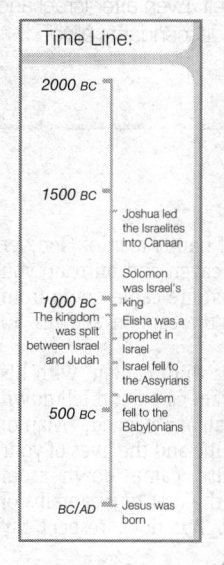

Time Line:

2000 BC

1500 BC
- Joshua led the Israelites into Canaan
- Solomon was Israel's king

1000 BC
The kingdom was split between Israel and Judah
- Elisha was a prophet in Israel
- Israel fell to the Assyrians
- Jerusalem fell to the Babylonians

500 BC

BC/AD
- Jesus was born

Where?

The Assyrians defeated Israel and took the people into captivity (2 Kings 17:3–6).

Mediterranean Sea

ASSYRIA

Samaria, the capital of Israel.

Euphrates

Tigris

Samaria

ISRAEL

The people of Judah were taken into captivity in Babylon (2 Kings 25:18–21).

Jerusalem

MOAB

BABYLON

The Babylonians destroyed Jerusalem and the Temple (2 Kings 25:1–17).

With help from Elisha, Judah and Israel defeated Moab (2 Kings 3).

JUDAH

Persian Gulf

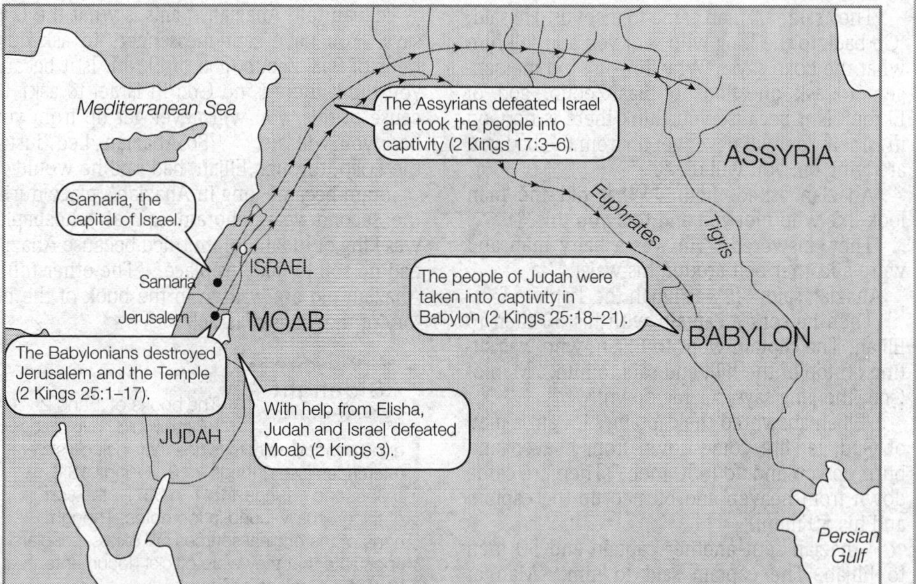

Behind the
Scenes (cont.): The Southern Kingdom also experienced some good years – under King Josiah, who repaired the Temple and led a religious revival in Judah. But in the end, Judah fell, the Temple was destroyed, and the Babylonians took the people into exile.

Despite the Israelites' unfaithfulness, God remained faithful. During this time he sent great prophets to call the people back to himself. Even after Israel and Judah fell, God kept his promise to keep King David's descendants alive. And from those descendants eventually came Jesus.

Elijah and King Ahaziah

1 After Ahab died, Moab broke away from Israel's rule. ²Ahaziah fell down through the wooden bars in his upstairs room in Samaria and was badly hurt. He sent messengers and told them, "Go, ask Baal-Zebub, god of Ekron, if I will recover from my injuries."

³But the LORD's angel said to Elijah the Tishbite, "Go up and meet the messengers sent by the king of Samaria. Ask them, 'Why are you going to ask questions of Baal-Zebub, god of Ekron? Is it because you think there is no God in Israel?' ⁴This is what the LORD says: 'You will never get up from the bed you are lying on; you will die.' " Then Elijah left.

⁵When the messengers returned to Ahaziah, he asked them, "Why have you returned?"

⁶They said, "A man came to meet us. He said, 'Go back to the king who sent you and tell him what the LORD says: "Why do you send messengers to ask questions of Baal-Zebub, god of Ekron? Is it because you think there is no God in Israel? You will never get up from the bed you are lying on; you will die." ' "

⁷Ahaziah asked them, "What did the man look like who met you and told you this?"

⁸They answered, "He was a hairy man and wore a leather belt around his waist."

Ahaziah said, "It was Elijah the Tishbite."

⁹Then he sent a captain with his 50 men to Elijah. The captain went to Elijah, who was sitting on top of the hill, and said to him, "Man of God, the king says, 'Come down!' "

¹⁰Elijah answered the captain, "If I am a man of God, let fire come down from heaven and burn up you and your 50 men." Then fire came down from heaven and burned up the captain and his 50 men.

¹¹Ahaziah sent another captain and 50 men to Elijah. The captain said to him, "Man of God, this is what the king says: 'Come down quickly!' "

¹²Elijah answered, "If I am a man of God, let fire come down from heaven and burn up you and your 50 men!" Then fire came down from heaven and burned up the captain and his 50 men.

¹³Ahaziah then sent a third captain with his 50 men. The third captain came and fell down on his knees before Elijah and begged, "Man of God, please respect my life and the lives of your 50 servants. ¹⁴See, fire came down from heaven and burned up the first two captains of 50 with all their men. But now, respect my life."

¹⁵The LORD's angel said to Elijah, "Go down with him and don't be afraid of him." So Elijah got up and went down with him to see the king.

¹⁶Elijah told Ahaziah, "This is what the LORD says: 'You have sent messengers to ask questions of Baal-Zebub, god of Ekron. Is it because you think there is no God in Israel to ask? Because of this, you will never get up from your bed; you will die.' " ¹⁷So Ahaziah died, just as the LORD, through Elijah, had said he would.

Joram became king in Ahaziah's place during the second year Jehoram son of Jehoshaphat was king of Judah. Joram ruled because Ahaziah had no son to take his place. ¹⁸The other things Ahaziah did are written in the book of the history of the kings of Israel.

Sidelight The books of 1 and 2 Kings would have made good school projects, since they include several references (see 2 Kings 1:18, 2 Kings 13:8, p.358, and 1 Kings 11:41, p.327) – the sort of thing usually found in footnotes. Though none of the original sources still exists, scholars speculate that they were official documents kept in the palace or Temple.

Elijah is Taken to Heaven

2 It was almost time for the LORD to take Elijah by a whirlwind up into heaven. While Elijah and Elisha were leaving Gilgal, ²Elijah said to Elisha, "Please stay here. The LORD has told me to go to Bethel."

But Elisha said, "As the LORD lives, and as you live, I won't leave you." So they went down to Bethel. ³The groups of prophets at Bethel came out to Elisha and said to him, "Do you know the LORD will take your master away from you today?"

Elisha said, "Yes, I know, but don't talk about it." ⁴Elijah said to him, "Stay here, Elisha, because the LORD has sent me to Jericho."

But Elisha said, "As the LORD lives, and as you live, I won't leave you."

So they went to Jericho. ⁵The groups of prophets at Jericho came to Elisha and said, "Do you know that the LORD will take your master away from you today?"

Elisha answered, "Yes, I know, but don't talk about it."

⁶Elijah said to Elisha, "Stay here. The LORD has sent me to the Jordan River."

Sidelight

The prophets Elijah and Elisha had similar names but different styles. Elijah – whose name means "the Lord is my God" – preached judgement and repentance, and lived alone. Elisha – whose name means "the Lord is salvation" – stressed hope and grace, and lived among the people, especially the poor. Yet God used these two different people to accomplish his work.

FRIENDS

Forever Friends

Steve and James had known each other for as long as they could remember. They lived across the street, went to the same primary school and would spend almost every waking moment together. On their first day at secondary school, the boys were given their new timetables. Steve, being brighter than James at most subjects, was placed in higher sets and as they read their timetables aloud they realised they had no classes together. James tried to pretend that it didn't matter, but he was gutted.

The first week went by and they still met up after school to walk home. Soon Steve started making new friends with people in his other classes and forgot to meet up with James. By the time the next school year came round, they had totally lost contact and didn't meet up at all.

One day after school, Steve was walking home with a group of his new friends when they started to shout abuse at a kid on the other side of the road. Steve thought it was really funny and began to join in until he realised that it was James, his old friend. James turned round to look at the gang of boys and saw that it was Steve and his new friends.

In that moment, Steve had a choice. Would he continue to pick on James and surely ruin their friendship forever or would he stand up for him? Steve chose to stand up for James, and told his friends to pack it in. Steve then walked home with James and they started hanging out again.

Read **2 Kings 2:1–12**.

* Elisha stuck by Elijah until he was taken to heaven, even when Elijah told him to leave him. What characteristics did it take for Elisha and Steve to stick with their friends?
* What were the rewards for Elisha and Steve for being faithful friends?

Consider . . .

* whether there are any situations when it isn't right to stand up for our friends.
* the reasons why we don't stand up for our friends when we should. Ask someone to pray with you to help you become a faithful friend.

For more, see . . .

* Ruth 1:14–18 (p.249)
* John 15:14–16 (p.1125)
* Job 42:7–10 (p.498)

Elisha answered, "As the LORD lives, and as you live, I won't leave you."

So the two of them went on. [7]Fifty men of the groups of prophets came and stood at a distance from where Elijah and Elisha were by the Jordan. [8]Elijah took off his coat, rolled it up, and hit the water. The water divided to the right and to the left, and Elijah and Elisha crossed over on dry ground.

[9]After they had crossed over, Elijah said to Elisha, "What can I do for you before I am taken from you?"

Elisha said, "Leave me a double share of your spirit."[n]

[10]Elijah said, "You have asked a hard thing. But if you see me when I am taken from you, it will be yours. If you don't, it won't happen."

[11]As they were walking and talking, a chariot and horses of fire appeared and separated Elijah from Elisha. Then Elijah went up to heaven in a

> ### Sidelight
> The prophet Elijah was whisked into heaven by a whirlwind, a chariot, and horses of fire – the first hot rod mentioned in the Bible (2 Kings 2:11). He is one of only two people mentioned in the Old Testament who never died. The other is Enoch (Genesis 5:24, p.8).

whirlwind. [12]Elisha saw it and shouted, "My father! My father! The chariots of Israel and their horsemen!" And Elisha did not see him any more. Then Elisha grabbed his own clothes and tore them to show how sad he was.

[13]He picked up Elijah's coat that had fallen from him. Then he returned and stood on the bank of the Jordan. [14]Elisha hit the water with Elijah's coat and said, "Where is the LORD, the God of Elijah?" When he hit the water, it divided to the right and to the left, and Elisha crossed over.

[15]The groups of prophets at Jericho were watching and said, "Elisha now has the spirit Elijah had." And they came to meet him, bowing down to the ground before him. [16]They said to him, "There are 50 strong men with us. Please let them go and look for your master. Maybe the Spirit[d] of the LORD has taken Elijah up and set him down on some mountain or in some valley."

But Elisha answered, "No, don't send them."

[17]When the groups of prophets had begged Elisha until he couldn't refuse them any more, he said, "Send them." So they sent 50 men who

looked for three days, but they could not find him. [18]Then they came back to Elisha at Jericho where he was staying. He said to them, "I told you not to go, didn't I?"

Elisha Makes the Water Pure

[19]The people of the city said to Elisha, "Look, master, this city is a nice place to live as you can see. But the water is so bad the land cannot grow crops."

[20]Elisha said, "Bring me a new bowl and put salt in it." So they brought it to him.

[21]Then he went out to the spring and threw the salt in it. He said, "This is what the LORD says: 'I have healed this water. From now on it won't cause death, and it won't keep the land from growing crops.'" [22]So the water has been healed to this day just as Elisha had said.

Boys Make Fun of Elisha

[23]From there Elisha went up to Bethel. On the way some boys came out of the city and made fun of him. They said to him, "Go up too, you baldhead! Go up too, you baldhead!" [24]Elisha turned around, looked at them and put a curse on them in the name of the LORD. Then two mother bears came out of the woods and tore 42 of the boys to pieces. [25]Elisha went to Mount Carmel and from there he returned to Samaria.

> ### Sidelight
> If you like making fun of people, be careful. Some young men made fun of the prophet Elisha's baldness, and they got mauled by bears (2 Kings 2:23–25). Why was their teasing so bad? Elisha had shaved his head to show his role as a prophet of God, and they were jeering him to "go up" to heaven like Elijah. So they were really making fun of his faith.

War Between Israel and Moab

3 Joram son of Ahab became king over Israel at Samaria in Jehoshaphat's eighteenth year as king of Judah. And Joram ruled twelve years. [2]He did what the LORD said was wrong, but he was not like his father and mother; he removed the stone pillars his father had made for Baal.[d] [3]But he continued to sin like Jeroboam son of Nebat who had led Israel to sin. Joram did not stop doing these same sins.

[4]Mesha king of Moab raised sheep. He paid the king of Israel 100,000 lambs and the wool of 100,000 sheep. [5]But when Ahab died, the king

---

Leave . . . spirit   By law, the first son in a family would inherit a double share of his father's possessions. Elisha is asking to inherit a share of his master's power as his follower. He is not asking for twice as much power as Elijah had.

of Moab turned against the king of Israel. [6]So King Joram went out from Samaria and gathered Israel's army. [7]He also sent messengers to Jehoshaphat king of Judah. "The king of Moab has turned against me," he said. "Will you go with me to fight Moab?"

Jehoshaphat replied, "I will go with you. My soldiers and my horses are yours."

[8]Jehoshaphat asked, "Which way should we attack?"

Joram answered, "Through the Desert of Edom."

[9]So the king of Israel went with the king of Judah and the king of Edom. After they had marched seven days, there was no more water for the army or for their animals that were with them. [10]The king of Israel said, "This is terrible! The LORD has called us three kings together to hand us over to the Moabites!"

[11]But Jehoshaphat asked, "Is there a prophet[d] of the LORD here? We can ask the LORD through him."

An officer of the king of Israel answered, "Elisha son of Shaphat is here. He was Elijah's servant."

[12]Jehoshaphat said, "He speaks the LORD's truth." So the king of Israel and Jehoshaphat and the king of Edom went down to see Elisha.

[13]Elisha said to the king of Israel, "I have nothing to do with you. Go to the prophets of your father and to the prophets of your mother!"

The king of Israel said to Elisha, "No, the LORD has called us three kings together to hand us over to the Moabites."

[14]Elisha said, "As surely as the LORD All-powerful lives, whom I serve, I tell you the truth. I wouldn't even look at you or notice you if Jehoshaphat king of Judah were not here. I respect him. [15]Now bring me someone who plays the harp."

While the harp was being played, the LORD gave Elisha power. [16]Then Elisha said, "The LORD says to dig holes in the valley. [17]The LORD says you won't see wind or rain, but the valley will be filled with water. Then you, your cattle and your other animals can drink. [18]This is easy for the LORD to do; he will also hand Moab over to you. [19]You will destroy every fortified city and every important town. You will cut down every good tree and stop up all springs. You will ruin every good field with rocks."

[20]The next morning, about the time the sacrifice was offered, water came from the direction of Edom and filled the valley.

[21]All the Moabites heard that the kings had come up to fight against them. So they gathered everyone old enough to put on armour and waited at the border. [22]But when the Moabites

got up early in the morning, the sun was shining on the water. They saw the water across from them, and it looked as red as blood. [23]Then they said, "This is blood! The kings must have fought and killed each other! Come, Moabites, let's take the valuable things from the dead bodies!"

[24]When the Moabites came to the camp of Israel, the Israelites came out and fought them until they ran away. Then the Israelites went on into the land, killing the Moabites. [25]They tore down the cities and threw rocks all over every good field. They stopped up all the springs and cut down all the good trees. Kir Hareseth was the only city with its stones still in place, but the men with slings surrounded it and conquered it too.

[26]When the king of Moab saw that the battle was too much for him, he took 700 men with swords to try to break through to the king of Edom. But they could not break through. [27]Then the king of Moab took his oldest son, who would have been king after him, and offered him as a burnt offering on the wall. So there was great anger against the Israelites, who left and went back to their own land.

A Widow Asks Elisha for Help

4 The wife of a man from the groups of prophets[d] said to Elisha, "Your servant, my husband, is dead. You know he honoured the LORD. But now the man he owes money to is coming to take my two boys as his slaves!"

[2]Elisha answered, "How can I help you? Tell me, what do you have in your house?"

The woman said, "I don't have anything there except a pot of oil."

[3]Then Elisha said, "Go and get empty jars from all your neighbours. Don't ask for just a few. [4]Then go into your house and shut the door behind you and your sons. Pour oil into all the jars, and set the full ones aside."

[5]So she left Elisha and shut the door behind her and her sons. As they brought the jars to her, she poured out the oil. [6]When the jars were all full, she said to her son, "Bring me another jar." But he said, "There are no more jars." Then the oil stopped flowing.

[7]She went and told Elisha. And the prophet said to her, "Go, sell the oil and pay what you owe. You and your sons can live on what is left."

The Shunammite Woman

[8]One day Elisha went to Shunem, where an important woman lived. She begged Elisha to stay and eat. So every time Elisha passed by, he stopped there to eat. [9]The woman said to her husband, "I know that this is a holy man of God who passes by our house all the time. [10]Let's make

a small room on the roof[n] and put a bed in the room for him. We can put a table, a chair and a lampstand there. Then when he comes by, he can stay there."

[11] One day Elisha came to the woman's house. After he went to his room and rested, [12] he said to his servant Gehazi, "Call the Shunammite woman."

When the servant had called her, she stood in front of him. [13] Elisha had told his servant, "Now say to her, 'You have gone to all this trouble for us. What can I do for you? Do you want me to speak to the king or the commander of the army for you?' "

She answered, "I live among my own people."

[14] Elisha said to Gehazi, "But what can we do for her?"

He answered, "She has no son, and her husband is old."

[15] Then Elisha said to Gehazi, "Call her." When he called her, she stood in the doorway. [16] Then Elisha said, "About this time next year, you will hold a son in your arms."

The woman said, "No, master, man of God, don't lie to me, your servant!"

[17] But the woman became pregnant and gave birth to a son at that time the next year, just as Elisha had told her.

[18] The boy grew up and one day went out to his father, who was with the men harvesting grain. [19] The boy said to his father, "My head! My head!"

The father said to his servant, "Take him to his mother!" [20] The servant took him to his mother, and he lay on his mother's lap until noon. Then he died. [21] So she took him up and laid him on Elisha's bed. Then she shut the door and left.

[22] She called to her husband, "Send me one of the servants and one of the donkeys. Then I can go quickly to the man of God and return."

[23] The husband said, "Why do you want to go to him today? It isn't the New Moon[d] or the Sabbath[d] day."

She said, "It will be all right."

[24] Then she saddled the donkey and said to her servant, "Lead on. Don't slow down for me unless I tell you." [25] So she went to Elisha, the man of God, at Mount Carmel.

When he saw her coming from far away, he said to his servant Gehazi, "Look, there's the Shunammite woman! [26] Run to meet her and ask, 'Are you all right? Is your husband all right? Is the boy all right?' "

She answered, "Everything is all right."

[27] Then she came to Elisha at the hill and grabbed his feet. Gehazi came near to pull her away, but Elisha said to him, "Leave her alone. She's very upset, and the LORD has not told me about it. He has hidden it from me."

[28] She said, "Master, did I ask you for a son? Didn't I tell you not to lie to me?"

[29] Then Elisha said to Gehazi, "Get ready. Take my walking stick in your hand and go quickly. If you meet anyone, don't say hello. If anyone greets you, don't answer. Lay my walking stick on the boy's face."

[30] The boy's mother said, "As surely as the LORD lives and as you live, I won't leave you!" So Elisha got up and followed her.

[31] Gehazi went on ahead and laid the walking stick on the boy's face, but the boy did not talk or move. Then Gehazi went back to meet Elisha. "The boy has not awakened," he said.

[32] When Elisha came into the house, the boy was lying dead on his bed. [33] Elisha entered the room and shut the door, so only he and the boy were in the room. Then he prayed to the LORD. [34] He went to the bed and lay on the boy, putting his mouth on the boy's mouth, his eyes on the boy's eyes, and his hands on the boy's hands. He stretched himself out on top of the boy. Soon the boy's skin became warm. [35] Elisha turned away and walked around the room. Then he went back and put himself on the boy again. The boy sneezed seven times and opened his eyes.

[36] Elisha called Gehazi and said, "Call the Shunammite!" So he did. When she came, Elisha said, "Pick up your son." [37] She came in and fell at Elisha's feet, bowing face down to the floor. Then she picked up her son and went out.

Elisha and the Stew

[38] When Elisha returned to Gilgal, there was a shortage of food in the land. While the groups of prophets[d] were sitting in front of him, he said to his servant, "Put the large pot on the fire, and boil some stew for these men."

[39] One of them went out into the field to gather plants. Finding a wild vine, he picked

---

roof   In Bible times houses were built with flat roofs. The roof was used for drying things such as flax and fruit. And it was used as an extra room, as a place for worship and as a place to sleep in the summer.

fruit from the vine and filled his robe with it. Then he came and cut up the fruit into the pot. But they didn't know what kind of fruit it was. [40]They poured out the stew for the others to eat. When they began to eat it, they shouted, "Man of God, there's death in the pot!" And they could not eat it.

[41]Elisha told them to bring some flour. He threw it into the pot and said, "Pour it out for the people to eat." This time there was nothing harmful in the pot.

Elisha Feeds the People

[42]A man from Baal Shalishah came to Elisha, bringing him 20 loaves of barley bread from the first harvest. He also brought fresh grain in his sack. Elisha said, "Give it to the people to eat."

[43]Elisha's servant asked, "How can I feed 100 people with so little?"

"Give the bread to the people to eat," Elisha said. "This is what the LORD says: 'They will eat and will have food left over.' " [44]After he gave it to them, the people ate and had food left over, as the LORD had said.

Naaman is Healed

5 Naaman was commander of the army of the king of Aram. He was honoured by his master, and he had much respect because the LORD used him to give victory to Aram. He was a mighty and brave man, but he had a skin disease.

[2]The Arameans had gone out to steal from the Israelites and had taken a little girl as a captive. This little girl served Naaman's wife. [3]She said to her mistress, "I wish my master would meet the prophet [d] who lives in Samaria. He would cure him of his disease."

[4]Naaman went to the king and told him what the girl from Israel had said. [5]The king of Aram said, "Go ahead, and I will send a letter to the king of Israel." So Naaman left and took with him about 30,000 pieces of silver, as well as 6,000 pieces of gold and ten changes of clothes. [6]He brought the letter to the king of Israel,

---

SICKNESS

Take Your Medicine

Although the lightweight brace could be worn under her clothes, Alison felt self-conscious about wearing it. She dreaded people's comments the first day she went to school with the "contraption". She thought that everyone would notice it and make fun.

But Alison knew that if she didn't wear the brace, she would probably need to have an operation. Alison had a curvature of the spine, a condition that could be stopped if she wore the back brace during her growing years. Without the brace, the curvature could have progressed so that she would not be able to stand up straight.

Alison wore the brace. And as it turned out, no one noticed. "No one even knew I had it," she recalls. That made the choice to wear the brace much easier. But it still seemed a nuisance. Every day over the next two years, Alison had to choose: should she wear her back brace or not?

Sometimes, people avoid medical treatment just because it's strange or embarrassing. But people won't get better if they don't follow the doctor's – or God's – orders. That was Naaman's predicament in **2 Kings 5:1–14**.

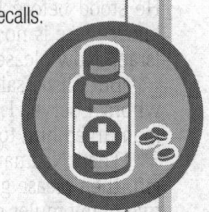

* What does God have to do with Alison's and Naaman's medical treatments?
* What kinds of thing can keep God from working in our lives?

Consider . . .

* talking to someone at school who has to wear some kind of medical device and finding out how he or she feels about wearing it.
* encouraging someone you know to participate in God's healing processes by following doctor's orders.

For more, see . . .

* Psalm 41 (p.525)
* Acts 3:1–10 (p.1142)
* John 9:1–11 (p.1111)

which read, "I am sending my servant Naaman to you so you can heal him of his skin disease."

7When the king of Israel read the letter, he tore his clothes to show how upset he was. He said, "I'm not God! I can't kill and make alive again! Why does this man send someone with a skin disease for me to heal? You can see that the king of Aram is trying to start trouble with me."

8When Elisha, the man of God, heard that the king of Israel had torn his clothes, he sent the king this message: "Why have you torn your clothes? Let Naaman come to me. Then he will know there is a prophet in Israel." 9So Naaman went with his horses and chariots to Elisha's house and stood outside the door.

10Elisha sent Naaman a messenger who said, "Go and wash in the Jordan River seven times. Then your skin will be healed, and you will be clean."

11Naaman became angry and left. He said, "I thought Elisha would surely come out and stand before me and call on the name of the LORD his God. I thought he would wave his hand over the place and heal the disease. 12The Abana and the Pharpar, the rivers of Damascus, are better than all the waters of Israel. Why can't I wash in them and become clean?" So Naaman went away very angry.

13Naaman's servants came near and said to him, "My father, if the prophet had told you to do some great thing, wouldn't you have done it? Doesn't it make more sense just to do it? After all, he only told you, 'Wash, and you will be clean.'" 14So Naaman went down and dipped in the Jordan seven times, just as Elisha had said. Then his skin became new again, like the skin of a child. And he was clean.

15Naaman and all his group returned to Elisha. He stood before Elisha and said, "Look, I now know there is no God in all the earth except in Israel. Now please accept a gift from me."

16But Elisha said, "As surely as the LORD lives whom I serve, I won't accept anything." Naaman urged him to take the gift, but he refused.

17Then Naaman said, "If you won't take the gift, then please give me some soil—as much as two of my mules can carry. From now on I'll not offer any burnt offering or sacrifice to any other gods but the LORD. 18But let the LORD pardon me for this: When my master goes into the temple of Rimmon*n* to worship, he leans on my arm. Then I must bow in that temple. May the LORD pardon me when I do that."

19Elisha said to him, "Go in peace."

Naaman left Elisha and went a short way. 20Gehazi, the servant of Elisha the man of God, thought, "My master has not accepted what Naaman the Aramean brought. As surely as the LORD lives, I'll run after him and get something from him." 21So Gehazi went after Naaman.

When Naaman saw someone running after him, he got off the chariot to meet Gehazi. He asked, "Is everything all right?"

22Gehazi said, "Everything is all right. My master has sent me. He said, 'Two young men from the groups of prophets in the mountains of Ephraim just came to me. Please give them 3,000 pieces of silver and two changes of clothes.'"

23Naaman said, "Please take 6,000 pieces," and he urged Gehazi to take it. He tied 68 kilogrammes of silver in two bags with two changes of clothes. Then he gave them to two of his servants to carry for Gehazi. 24When they came to the hill, Gehazi took these things from Naaman's servants and put them in the house. Then he let Naaman's servants go, and they left.

25When he came in and stood before his master, Elisha said to him, "Where have you been, Gehazi?"

"I didn't go anywhere," he answered.

26But Elisha said to him, "My spirit was with you. I knew when the man turned from his chariot to meet you. This isn't a time to take money, clothes, olives, grapes, sheep, oxen, male servants or female servants. 27So Naaman's skin disease will come on you and your children for ever." When Gehazi left Elisha, he had the disease and was as white as snow.

An Axehead Floats

6 The groups of prophets *d* said to Elisha, "The place where we meet with you is too small for us. 2Let's go to the Jordan River. There everyone can get a log, and let's build a place there to live."

Elisha said, "Go."

3One of them said, "Please go with us."

Elisha answered, "I will go," 4so he went with them. When they arrived at the Jordan, they cut down some trees. 5As one man was cutting down a tree, the head of his axe fell into the water. He yelled, "Oh, my master! I borrowed that axe!"

6Elisha asked, "Where did it fall?" The man showed him the place. Then Elisha cut down a stick and threw it into the water, and it made the

---

temple of Rimmon   The place where the Aramean people worshipped the god Rimmon.

iron head float. ⁷Elisha said, "Pick up the axe-head." Then the man reached out and took it.

Elisha and the Blinded Arameans

⁸The king of Aram was at war with Israel. He had a council meeting with his officers and said, "I will set up my camp in this place."

⁹Elisha, the man of God, sent a message to the king of Israel, saying, "Be careful! Don't pass that place, because the Arameans are going down there!"

¹⁰The king of Israel checked the place about which Elisha had warned him. Elisha warned him several times, so the king protected himself there.

¹¹The king of Aram was angry about this. He called his officers together and demanded, "Tell me who of us is working for the king of Israel."

¹²One of the officers said, "None, my master and king. It's Elisha, the prophet ᵈ from Israel. He can tell you what you speak in your bedroom."

¹³The king said, "Go and find him so I can send men and catch him."

The servants came back and reported, "He is in Dothan."

¹⁴Then the king sent horses, chariots and many troops to Dothan. They arrived at night and surrounded the city.

¹⁵Elisha's servant got up early, and when he went out, he saw an army with horses and chariots all around the city. The servant said to Elisha, "Oh, my master, what can we do?"

¹⁶Elisha said, "Don't be afraid. The army that fights for us is larger than the one against us."

¹⁷Then Elisha prayed, "LORD, open my servant's eyes, and let him see."

The LORD opened the eyes of the young man, and he saw that the mountain was full of horses and chariots of fire all around Elisha.

¹⁸As the enemy came down towards Elisha, he prayed to the LORD, "Make these people blind." So he made the Aramean army blind, as Elisha had asked.

¹⁹Elisha said to them, "This is not the right road or the right city. Follow me and I'll take you to the man you are looking for." Then Elisha led them to Samaria.

²⁰After they entered Samaria, Elisha said, "LORD, open these men's eyes so they can see." So the LORD opened their eyes, and the Aramean army saw that they were inside the city of Samaria!

²¹When the king of Israel saw the Aramean army, he said to Elisha, "My father, should I kill them? Should I kill them?"

²²Elisha answered, "Don't kill them. You wouldn't kill people whom you captured with your sword and bow. Give them food and water,

and let them eat and drink and then go home to their master." ²³So he prepared a great feast for the Aramean army. After they ate and drank, the king sent them away, and they went home to their master. The soldiers of Aram did not come any more into the land of Israel.

A Shortage of Food

²⁴Later, Ben-Hadad king of Aram gathered his whole army and surrounded and attacked Samaria. ²⁵There was a shortage of food in Samaria. It was so bad that a donkey's head sold for about 80 pieces of silver, and 8 litres of dove's dung sold for about 5 pieces of silver.

²⁶As the king of Israel was passing by on the wall, a woman yelled out to him, "Help me, my master and king!"

²⁷The king said, "If the LORD doesn't help you, how can I? Can I get help from the threshing ᵈ floor or from the winepress?" ᵈ ²⁸Then the king said to her, "What is your trouble?"

She answered, "This woman said to me, 'Give up your son so we can eat him today. Then we will eat my son tomorrow.' ²⁹So we boiled my son and ate him. Then the next day I said to her, 'Give up your son so we can eat him.' But she had hidden him."

³⁰When the king heard the woman's words, he tore his clothes in sadness. As he walked along the wall, the people looked and saw he had on rough cloth under his clothes to show his sadness. ³¹He said, "May God punish me terribly if the head of Elisha son of Shaphat isn't cut off from his body today!"

³²The king sent a messenger to Elisha, who was sitting in his house with the elders. But before the messenger arrived, Elisha said to them, "See, this murderer is sending men to cut off my head. When the messenger arrives, shut the door and hold it; don't let him in. The sound of his master's feet is behind him."

³³Elisha was still talking to the leaders when the messenger arrived. The king said, "This trouble has come from the LORD. Why should I wait for the LORD any longer?"

7 Elisha said, "Listen to the LORD's word. This is what the LORD says: 'About this time tomorrow 8 litres of fine flour will be sold for a piece of silver, and 6 kilogrammes of barley will be sold for a piece of silver. This will happen at the gate of Samaria.' "

²Then the officer who was close to the king answered Elisha, "Even if the LORD opened windows in the sky, that couldn't happen."

Elisha said, "You will see it with your eyes, but you will not eat any of it."

³There were four men with a skin disease at the entrance to the city gate. They said to each

other, "Why should we sit here until we die? ⁴There is no food in the city. So if we go into the city, we will die there. If we stay here, we will die. So let's go to the Aramean camp. If they let us live, we will live. If they kill us, we die."

⁵So they got up at twilight and went to the Aramean camp, but when they arrived, no one was there. ⁶The Lord had caused the Aramean army to hear the sound of chariots, horses and a large army. They had said to each other, "The king of Israel has hired the Hittite and Egyptian kings to attack us!" ⁷So they got up and ran away in the twilight, leaving their tents, horses and donkeys. They left the camp standing and ran for their lives.

⁸When the men with the skin disease came to the edge of the camp, they went into one of the tents and ate and drank. They carried silver, gold and clothes out of the camp and hid them. Then they came back and entered another tent. They carried things from this tent and hid them, as well. ⁹Then they said to each other, "We're doing wrong. Today we have good news, but we are silent. If we wait until the sun comes up, we'll be discovered. Let's go right now and tell the people in the king's palace."

¹⁰So they went and called to the gatekeepers of the city. They said, "We went to the Aramean camp, but no one is there; we didn't hear anyone. The horses and donkeys were still tied up, and the tents were still standing." ¹¹Then the gatekeepers shouted out and told the people in the palace.

¹²The king got up in the night and said to his officers, "I'll tell you what the Arameans are doing to us. They know we are starving. They have gone out of the camp to hide in the field. They're saying, 'When the Israelites come out of the city, we'll capture them alive. Then we'll enter the city.' "

¹³One of his officers answered, "Let some men take five of the horses that are still left in the city. These men are like all the Israelites who are left; they are also about to die. Let's send them to see what has happened."

¹⁴So the men took two chariots with horses. The king sent them after the Aramean army, saying, "Go and see what has happened." ¹⁵The men followed the Aramean army as far as the Jordan River. The road was full of clothes and equipment that the Arameans had thrown away as they had hurriedly left. So the messengers returned and told the king. ¹⁶Then the people went out and took valuable things from the Aramean camp. So 8 litres of fine flour were sold for a piece of silver, and 6 kilogrammes of barley were sold for a piece of silver, just as the Lord had said.

¹⁷The king chose the officer who was close to him to guard the gate, but the people trampled the officer to death. This happened just as Elisha had told the king when the king came to his house. ¹⁸He had said, "6 kilogrammes of barley and 8 litres of fine flour will each sell for a piece of silver about this time tomorrow at the gate of Samaria."

¹⁹But the officer had answered, "Even if the Lord opened windows in the sky, that couldn't happen." And Elisha had told him, "You will see it with your eyes, but you won't eat any of it." ²⁰It happened to the officer just that way. The people trampled him in the gateway, and he died.

The Shunammite Regains Her Land

8 Elisha spoke to the woman whose son he had brought back to life. He said, "Get up and go with your family. Stay wherever you can, because the Lord has called for a time without food that will last seven years." ²So the woman got up and did as the man of God had said. She left with her family, and they stayed in the land of the Philistines for seven years. ³After seven years she returned from the land of the Philistines and went to beg the king for her house and land. ⁴The king was talking with Gehazi, the servant of the man of God. The king had said, "Please tell me all the great things Elisha has done." ⁵Gehazi was telling the king how Elisha had brought a dead boy back to life. Just then the woman whose son Elisha had brought back to life came and begged the king for her house and land.

Gehazi said, "My master and king, this is the woman, and this is the son Elisha brought back to life."

⁶The king asked the woman, and she told him about it. Then the king chose an officer to help her. "Give the woman everything that is hers," the king said. "Give her all the money made from her land from the day she left until now."

Ben-Hadad is Killed

⁷Then Elisha went to Damascus, where Ben-Hadad king of Aram was sick. Someone told him, "The man of God has arrived."

⁸The king said to Hazael, "Take a gift in your hand and go and meet him. Ask the Lord through him if I will recover from my sickness."

⁹So Hazael went to meet Elisha, taking with him a gift of 40 camels loaded with every good thing in Damascus. He came and stood before Elisha and said, "Your son Ben-Hadad king of Aram sent me to you. He asks if he will recover from his sickness."

¹⁰Elisha said to Hazael, "Go and tell Ben-Hadad, 'You will surely recover,' but the Lord

has told me he will really die." [11]Hazael stared at Elisha until he felt ashamed. Then Elisha cried.

[12]Hazael asked, "Why are you crying, master?"

Elisha answered, "Because I know what evil you will do to the Israelites. You will burn their fortified cities with fire and kill their young men with swords. You will throw their babies to the ground and split open their pregnant women."

[13]Hazael said, "Am I a dog? How could I do such things?"

Elisha answered, "The LORD has shown me that you will be king over Aram."

[14]Then Hazael left Elisha and came to his master. Ben-Hadad said to him, "What did Elisha say to you?"

Hazael answered, "He told me that you will surely recover." [15]But the next day Hazael took a blanket and dipped it in water. Then he put it over Ben-Hadad's face, and he died. So Hazael became king in Ben-Hadad's place.

Jehoram King of Judah

[16]While Jehoshaphat was king in Judah, Jehoram son of Jehoshaphat became king of Judah. This was during the fifth year Joram son of Ahab was king of Israel. [17]Jehoram was 32 years old when he began to rule, and he ruled eight years in Jerusalem. [18]He followed the ways of the kings of Israel, just as the family of Ahab had done, because he married Ahab's daughter. Jehoram did what the LORD said was wrong. [19]But the LORD would not destroy Judah because of his servant David. The LORD had promised that one of David's descendants [d] would always rule.

[20]In Jehoram's time Edom broke away from Judah's rule and chose their own king. [21]So Jehoram and all his chariots went to Zair. The Edomites surrounded him and his chariot commanders. Jehoram got up and attacked the Edomites at night, but his army ran away to their tents. [22]From then until now the country of Edom has fought against the rule of Judah. At the same time Libnah also broke away from Judah's rule.

[23]The other acts of Jehoram and all the things he did are written in the book of the history of the kings of Judah. [24]Jehoram died and was buried with his ancestors in Jerusalem, and Jehoram's son Ahaziah ruled in his place.

[25]Ahaziah son of Jehoram became king of Judah during the twelfth year Joram son of Ahab was king of Israel. [26]Ahaziah was 22 years old when he became king, and he ruled one year in Jerusalem. His mother's name was Athaliah, a granddaughter of Omri king of Israel. [27]Ahaziah followed the ways of Ahab's family. He did what the LORD said was wrong, as Ahab's family had done, because he was a son-in-law to Ahab.

[28]Ahaziah went with Joram son of Ahab to Ramoth in Gilead, where they fought against Hazael king of Aram. The Arameans wounded Joram. [29]So King Joram returned to Jezreel to heal from the wound he had received from the Arameans at Ramoth when he fought Hazael king of Aram. Ahaziah son of Jehoram king of Judah went down to visit Joram son of Ahab at Jezreel, because he had been wounded.

Jehu is Chosen King

9 At the same time, Elisha the prophet [d] called a man from the groups of prophets. Elisha said, "Get ready, and take this small bottle of olive oil in your hand. Go to Ramoth in Gilead. [2]When you arrive, find Jehu son of Jehoshaphat, the son of Nimshi. Go in and make Jehu get up from among his brothers, and take him to an inner room. [3]Then take the bottle and pour the oil on Jehu's head and say, 'This is what the LORD says: I have appointed you king over Israel.' Then open the door and run away. Don't wait!"

[4]So the young man, the prophet, went to Ramoth in Gilead. [5]When he arrived, he saw the officers of the army sitting together. He said, "Commander, I have a message for you."

Jehu asked, "For which one of us?"

The young man said, "For you, commander."

[6]Jehu got up and went into the house. Then the young prophet poured the olive oil on Jehu's head and said to him, "This is what the LORD, the God of Israel says: 'I have appointed you king over the LORD's people Israel. [7]You must destroy the family of Ahab your master. I will punish Jezebel for the deaths of my servants the prophets and for all the LORD's servants who were murdered. [8]All of Ahab's family must die. I will not let any male child in Ahab's family live in Israel, whether slave or free. [9]I will make Ahab's family like the family of Jeroboam son of Nebat and like the family of Baasha son of Ahijah. [10]The dogs will eat Jezebel at Jezreel, and no one will bury her.' "

Then the young prophet opened the door and ran away.

[11]When Jehu went back to his master's officers, one of them said to Jehu, "Is everything all right? Why did this madman come to you?"

Jehu answered, "You know the man and how he talks."

[12]They answered, "That's not true. Tell us."

Jehu said, "He said to me, 'This is what the LORD says: I have appointed you to be king over Israel.' "

[13]Then the officers hurried, and each man took off his own coat and put it on the stairs for Jehu. They blew the trumpet and shouted, "Jehu is king!"

Joram and Ahaziah are Killed

[14]So Jehu son of Jehoshaphat, the son of Nimshi, made plans against Joram. Now Joram and all Israel had been defending Ramoth in Gilead from Hazael king of Aram. [15]But King Joram had to return to Jezreel to heal from the injuries the Arameans had given him when he fought against Hazael king of Aram.

Jehu said, "If you agree with this, don't let anyone leave the city. They might tell the news in Jezreel." [16]Then he got into his chariot and set out for Jezreel, where Joram was resting. Ahaziah king of Judah had gone down to see him.

[17]The look-out was standing on the watchtower in Jezreel when he saw Jehu's troops coming. He said, "I see some soldiers!"

Joram said, "Take a horseman and send him to meet them. Tell him to ask, 'Is all in order?'"

[18]The horseman rode out to meet Jehu, and he said, "This is what the king says: 'Is all in order?'"

Jehu said, "Why bother yourself with order? Come along behind me."

The look-out reported, "The messenger reached them, but he is not coming back."

[19]Then Joram sent out a second horseman. This rider came to Jehu's group and said, "This is what the king says: 'Is all in order?'"

Jehu answered, "Why bother yourself with order? Come along behind me."

[20]The look-out reported, "The second man reached them, but he is not coming back. The man in the chariot is driving like Jehu son of Nimshi. He drives as if he were mad!"

> ### Sidelight
> The first record of bad driving in the Bible is in 2 Kings 9:20. King Jehu was such a bad driver that people could recognise his chariot driving from a distance. They said he drove "as if he were crazy". But since he was a king, nobody could complain.

[21]Joram said, "Get my chariot ready." Then the servant got Joram's chariot ready. Joram king of Israel and Ahaziah king of Judah went out, each in his own chariot, to meet Jehu at the property of Naboth the Jezreelite.

[22]When Joram saw Jehu, he said, "Is all in order, Jehu?"

Jehu answered, "There will never be any order as long as your mother Jezebel worships idols and uses witchcraft." [d]

[23]Joram turned the horses to run away and yelled to Ahaziah, "It's a trick, Ahaziah!"

[24]Then Jehu drew his bow and shot Joram between his shoulders. The arrow went through Joram's heart, and he fell down in his chariot.

[25]Jehu ordered Bidkar, his chariot officer, "Pick up Joram's body, and throw it into the field of Naboth the Jezreelite. Remember when you and I rode together with Joram's father Ahab. The LORD made this prophecy [d] against him: [26]'Yesterday I saw the blood of Naboth and his sons, says the LORD, so I will punish Ahab in his field, says the LORD.' Take Joram's body and throw it into the field, as the LORD has said."

[27]When Ahaziah king of Judah saw this, he ran away towards Beth Haggan. Jehu chased him, saying, "Shoot Ahaziah, too!" Ahaziah was wounded in his chariot on the way up to Gur near Ibleam. He got as far as Megiddo but died there. [28]Ahaziah's servants carried his body in a chariot to Jerusalem and buried him with his ancestors in his tomb in Jerusalem. [29](Ahaziah had become king over Judah in the eleventh year Joram son of Ahab was king.)

Death of Jezebel

[30]When Jehu came to Jezreel, Jezebel heard about it. She put on her eye paint and fixed her hair. Then she looked out of the window. [31]When Jehu entered the city gate, Jezebel said, "Have you come in peace, you Zimri, [n] you who killed your master?"

[32]Jehu looked up at the window and said, "Who is on my side? Who?" Two or three servants looked out the window at Jehu. [33]He said to them, "Throw her down." So they threw Jezebel down, and the horses ran over her. Some of her blood splashed on the wall and on the horses.

> ### Sidelight
> When wicked Queen Jezebel put on make-up (2 Kings 9:30–33), it was probably quite elaborate. Women in those days used black eyeliner, blue eyeshadow, red lipstick and nail polish, powders and perfume. None of it did much good, though, when she was thrown out of the window and trampled by horses.

[34]Jehu went into the house and ate and drank. Then he said, "Now see about this cursed woman. Bury her, because she is a king's daughter." [35]The men went to bury Jezebel, but they could not find her. They found only her skull,

---

Zimri He was the man who killed Elah and the family of Baasha. Read 1 Kings 16:8–12.

feet and the palms of her hands. [36]When they came back and told Jehu, he said, "The LORD said this through his servant Elijah the Tishbite: 'The dogs will eat Jezebel at Jezreel. [37]Her body will be like manure on the field in the land at Jezreel. No one will be able to say that this is Jezebel.' "

Families of Ahab and Ahaziah Killed

10 Ahab had 70 sons in Samaria. Jehu wrote letters and sent them to Samaria to the officers and elders of Jezreel and to the guardians of the sons of Ahab. Jehu said, [2]"You have your master's sons with you, and you have chariots, horses, a city with strong walls and weapons. When you get this letter, [3]choose the best and most worthy person among your master's sons, and make him king. Then fight for your master's family."

[4]But the officers and leaders of Jezreel were frightened. They said, "Two kings could not stand up to Jehu, so how can we?"

[5]The palace manager, the city governor, the elders and the guardians sent a message to Jehu. "We are your servants," they said. "We will do everything you tell us to do. We won't make any man king, so do whatever you think is best."

[6]Then Jehu wrote a second letter, saying, "If you are on my side and will obey me, cut off the heads of your master's sons and come to me at Jezreel tomorrow about this time."

Now the 70 sons of the king's family were with the leading men of the city who were their guardians. [7]When the leaders received the letter, they took the king's sons and killed all 70 of them. They put their heads in baskets and sent them to Jehu at Jezreel. [8]The messenger came to Jehu and told him, "They have brought the heads of the king's sons."

Then Jehu said, "Lay the heads in two piles at the city gate [n] until morning."

[9]In the morning, Jehu went out and stood before the people and said to them, "You are innocent. Look, I made plans against my master and killed him. But who killed all these? [10]You should know that everything the LORD said about Ahab's family will come true. The LORD has spoken through his servant Elijah, and the LORD has done what he said." [11]So Jehu killed every one of Ahab's family in Jezreel who was still alive. He also killed all Ahab's leading men, close friends and priests. No one who had helped Ahab was left alive.

[12]Then Jehu left and went to Samaria by way of the road to Beth Eked of the Shepherds. [13]There Jehu met some relatives of Ahaziah king of Judah. Jehu asked, "Who are you?"

They answered, "We are relatives of Ahaziah. We have come down to get revenge for the families of the king and the king's mother."

[14]Then Jehu said, "Take them alive!" So they captured Ahaziah's relatives alive and killed them at the well near Beth Eked—42 of them. Jehu did not leave anyone alive.

[15]After Jehu left there, he met Jehonadab son of Recab, who was also on his way to meet Jehu. Jehu greeted him and said, "Are you as good a friend to me as I am to you?"

Jehonadab answered, "Yes, I am."

Jehu said, "If you are, then give me your hand." So Jehonadab gave him his hand, and Jehu pulled him into the chariot. [16]"Come with me," Jehu said. "You can see how strong my feelings are for the LORD." So Jehu had Jehonadab ride in his chariot.

[17]When Jehu came to Samaria, he killed all of Ahab's family in Samaria. He destroyed all those who were left, just as the LORD had told Elijah it would happen.

Baal Worshippers Killed

[18]Then Jehu gathered all the people together and said to them, "Ahab served Baal [d] a little, but Jehu will serve Baal much. [19]Now call for me all Baal's prophets and priests and all the people who worship Baal. Don't let anyone miss this meeting, because I have a great sacrifice for Baal. Anyone who is not there will not live." But Jehu was tricking them so he could destroy the worshippers of Baal. [20]He said, "Prepare a holy meeting for Baal." So they announced the meeting. [21]Then Jehu sent word through all Israel, and all the worshippers of Baal came; not one stayed at home. They came into the temple of Baal, and the temple was filled from one side to the other. [22]Jehu said to the man who kept the robes, "Bring out robes for all the worshippers of Baal." After he brought out robes for them, [23]Jehu and Jehonadab son of Recab went into the temple of Baal. Jehu said to the worshippers of Baal, "Look around, and make sure there are no servants of the LORD with you. Be sure there are only worshippers of Baal." [24]Then the worshippers of Baal went in to offer sacrifices and burnt offerings.

Jehu had 80 men waiting outside. He had told them, "Don't let anyone escape. If you do, you must pay with your own life."

[25]As soon as Jehu finished offering the burnt offering, he ordered the guards and the captains, "Go in and kill the worshippers of Baal. Don't let anyone come out." So the guards and captains

---

city gate   People came here to conduct business. Public meetings and court cases were also held here.

killed the worshippers of Baal with the sword and threw their bodies out. Then they went to the inner rooms of the temple [26]and brought out the pillars of the temple of Baal and burned them. [27]They tore down the stone pillar of Baal, as well as the temple of Baal. And they made it into a sewage pit, as it is today.

[28]So Jehu destroyed Baal worship in Israel, [29]but he did not stop doing the sins Jeroboam son of Nebat had done. Jeroboam had led Israel to sin by worshipping the golden calves in Bethel and Dan.

[30]The LORD said to Jehu, "You have done well in obeying what I said was right. You have done to the family of Ahab as I wanted. Because of this, your descendants [d] as far as your great-great-grandchildren will be kings of Israel." [31]But Jehu was not careful to follow the teachings of the LORD, the God of Israel, with all his heart. He did not stop doing the same sins Jeroboam had done, by which he had led Israel to sin.

[32]At that time the LORD began to make Israel smaller. Hazael defeated the Israelites in all the land of Israel, [33]taking all the land of the Jordan known as the land of Gilead. (It was the region of Gad, Reuben and Manasseh.) He took land from Aroer by the Arnon Ravine through Gilead to Bashan.

[34]The other things Jehu did—everything he did and all his victories—are recorded in the book of the history of the kings of Israel. [35]Jehu died and was buried in Samaria, and his son Jehoahaz became king in his place. [36]Jehu was king over Israel in Samaria for 28 years.

Athaliah and Joash

11 When Ahaziah's mother, Athaliah, saw that her son was dead, she killed all the royal family. [2]But Jehosheba, King Jehoram's daughter and Ahaziah's sister, took Joash, Ahaziah's son. She stole him from among the other sons of the king who were about to be murdered. She put Joash and his nurse in a bedroom to hide him from Athaliah, so he was not killed. [3]He hid with her in the Temple [d] of the LORD for six years. During that time Athaliah ruled the land.

> **Sidelight** It may seem like a modern idea to have a woman as Prime Minister, but one woman, Athaliah, ruled Judah for seven years (2 Kings 11:1–3). She didn't get her position by popular vote!

[4]In the seventh year Jehoiada sent for the commanders of groups of 100 men, as well as the Carites.[n] He brought them together in the Temple of the LORD and made an agreement with them. There, in the Temple of the LORD, he made them promise loyalty, and then he showed them the king's son. [5]He commanded them, "This is what you must do. A third of you who go on duty on the Sabbath [d] will guard the king's palace. [6]A third of you will be at the Sur Gate, and another third will be at the gate behind the guard. This way you will guard the Temple. [7]The two groups who go off duty on the Sabbath must protect the Temple of the LORD for the king. [8]All of you must stand around the king, each man with his weapons in his hand. If anyone comes near, kill him. Stay close to the king when he goes out and when he comes in."

[9]The commanders of groups of 100 men obeyed everything Jehoiada the priest had commanded. Each one took his men who came on duty on the Sabbath and those who went off duty on the Sabbath, and they came to Jehoiada the priest. [10]He gave the commanders the spears and shields that had belonged to King David and that were kept in the Temple of the LORD.

Joash Becomes King

[11]Then each guard took his place with his weapons in his hand. There were guards from the south side of the Temple [d] to the north side. They stood by the altar and the Temple and around the king. [12]Jehoiada brought out the king's son and put the crown on him and gave him a copy of the agreement. They appointed him king and poured olive oil on him. Then they clapped their hands and said, "Long live the king!"

[13]When Athaliah heard the noise of the guards and the people, she went to them at the Temple of the LORD. [14]She looked, and there was the king, standing by the pillar, as the custom was. The officers and trumpeters were standing beside him, and all the people of the land were very happy and were blowing trumpets. Then Athaliah tore her clothes and screamed, "Traitors! Traitors!"

[15]Jehoiada the priest gave orders to the commanders of the groups of 100 men, who led the army. He said, "Surround her with soldiers and kill with a sword anyone who follows her." He commanded this because he had said, "Don't put Athaliah to death in the Temple of the LORD." [16]So they caught her when she came to the horses' entrance near the palace. There she was put to death.

Carites This was probably a special unit of the army that was responsible for the king's safety, a kind of palace guard similar to the Kerethites and the Pelethites.

[17]Then Jehoiada made an agreement between the LORD and the king and the people that they would be the LORD's special people. He also made an agreement between the king and the people. [18]All the people of the land went to the temple of Baal *d* and tore it down, smashing the altars and idols. They also killed Mattan, the priest of Baal, in front of the altars.

Then Jehoiada the priest placed guards at the Temple of the LORD. [19]He took with him the commanders of 100 men and the Carites, the royal bodyguards, as well as the guards and all the people of the land. Together they took the king out of the Temple of the LORD and went into the palace through the gate of the guards. Then the king sat on the royal throne. [20]So all the people of the land were very happy, and Jerusalem had peace, because Athaliah had been put to death with the sword at the palace. [21]Joash was seven years old when he became king.

> **Sidelight**
> If anyone asked Joash if he had "grown up in the church" he could have easily said yes. In fact, he was hidden in the Temple for six years to keep from getting killed. At the age of seven, he became the youngest king in the Bible (2 Kings 11:1–3, 21).

12 Joash became king of Judah in Jehu's seventh year as king of Israel, and he ruled for 40 years in Jerusalem. His mother's name was Zibiah, and she was from Beersheba. [2]Joash did what the LORD said was right as long as Jehoiada the priest taught him. [3]But the places where gods were worshiped were not removed; the people still made sacrifices and burned incense*d* there.

Joash Repairs the Temple

[4]Joash said to the priests, "Take all the money brought as offerings to the Temple*d* of the LORD. This includes the money each person owes in taxes and the money each person promises or brings freely to the LORD. [5]Each priest will take the money from the people he serves. Then the priests must repair any damage they find in the Temple."

[6]But by the twenty-third year Joash was king, the priests still had not repaired the Temple. [7]So King Joash called for Jehoiada the priest and the other priests and said to them, "Why aren't you repairing the damage of the Temple? Don't take any more money from the people you serve, but hand over the money for the repair of the Temple." [8]The priests agreed not to take

any more money from the people and not to repair the Temple themselves.

[9]Jehoiada the priest took a box and made a hole in the top of it. Then he put it by the altar, on the right side as the people came into the Temple of the LORD. The priests guarding the doorway put all the money brought to the Temple of the LORD into the box. [10]Each time the priests saw that the box was full of money, the king's royal secretary and the high priest came. They counted the money that had been brought to the Temple of the LORD, and they put it into bags. [11]Next they weighed the money and gave it to the people in charge of the work on the Temple. With it they paid the carpenters and the builders who worked on the Temple of the LORD, [12]as well as the bricklayers and stonecutters. They also used the money to buy timber and cut stone to repair the damage of the Temple of the LORD. It paid for everything.

[13]The money brought into the Temple of the LORD was not used to make silver cups, wick trimmers, bowls, trumpets, or gold or silver vessels. [14]They paid the money to the workers, who used it to repair the Temple of the LORD. [15]They did not demand to know how the money was spent, because the workers were honest. [16]The money from the penalty offerings and sin offerings was not brought into the Temple of the LORD, because it belonged to the priests.

Joash Saves Jerusalem

[17]About this time Hazael king of Aram attacked Gath and captured it. Then he went to attack Jerusalem. [18]Joash king of Judah took all the holy things given by his ancestors, the kings of Judah—Jehoshaphat, Jehoram and Ahaziah. He also took his own holy things as well as the gold that was found in the treasuries of the Temple *d* of the LORD and the gold from the palace. Joash sent all this treasure to Hazael king of Aram, who turned away from Jerusalem.

[19]Everything else Joash did is written in the book of the history of the kings of Judah. [20]His officers made plans against him and killed him at Beth Millo on the road down to Silla. [21]The officers who killed him were Jozabad son of Shimeath and Jehozabad son of Shomer. Joash was buried with his ancestors in Jerusalem, and Amaziah, his son, became king in his place.

Jehoahaz King of Israel

13 Jehoahaz son of Jehu became king over Israel in Samaria during the twenty-third year Joash son of Ahaziah was king of Judah.

Jehoahaz ruled for seventeen years, ²and he did what the LORD said was wrong. Jehoahaz did the same sins Jeroboam son of Nebat had done. Jeroboam had led Israel to sin, and Jehoahaz did not stop doing these same sins. ³So the LORD was angry with Israel and handed them over to Hazael king of Aram and his son Ben-Hadad for a long time.

⁴Then Jehoahaz begged the LORD, and the LORD listened to him. The LORD had seen the troubles of Israel; he saw how terribly the king of Aram was treating them. ⁵He gave Israel a man to save them, and they escaped from the Arameans. The Israelites then lived in their own homes as they had before, ⁶but they still did not stop doing the same sins that the family of Jeroboam had done. He had led Israel to sin, and they continued doing those sins. The Asherah *d* idol also was left standing in Samaria. ⁷Nothing was left of Jehoahaz's army except 50 horsemen, ten chariots and 10,000 foot soldiers. The king of Aram had destroyed them and made them like chaff. *d*

⁸Everything else Jehoahaz did and all his victories are written in the book of the history of the kings of Israel. ⁹Jehoahaz died and was buried in Samaria, and his son Jehoash became king in his place.

Jehoash King of Israel

¹⁰Jehoash son of Jehoahaz became king of Israel in Samaria during Joash's thirty-seventh year as king of Judah. Jehoash ruled for sixteen years, ¹¹and he did what the LORD said was wrong. He did not stop doing the same sins Jeroboam son of Nebat had done. Jeroboam had led Israel to sin, and Jehoash continued to do the same thing. ¹²Everything else he did and all his victories, including his war against Amaziah king of Judah, are written in the book of the history of the kings of Israel. ¹³Jehoash died, and Jeroboam took his place on the throne. Jehoash was buried in Samaria with the kings of Israel.

The Death of Elisha

¹⁴At this time Elisha became sick. Before he died, Jehoash king of Israel went to Elisha and cried for him. Jehoash said, "My father, my father! The chariots of Israel and their horsemen!"

¹⁵Elisha said to Jehoash, "Take a bow and arrows." So he took a bow and arrows. ¹⁶Then Elisha said to him, "Put your hand on the bow." So Jehoash put his hand on the bow. Then Elisha put his hands on the king's hands. ¹⁷Elisha said, "Open the east window." So Jehoash opened the window. Then Elisha said, "Shoot," and Jehoash shot. Elisha said, "The LORD's arrow of victory over Aram! You will defeat the Arameans at Aphek until you destroy them."

¹⁸Elisha said, "Take the arrows." So Jehoash took them. Then Elisha said to him, "Strike the ground." So Jehoash struck the ground three times and stopped. ¹⁹The man of God was angry with him. "You should have struck five or six times!" Elisha said. "Then you would have struck Aram until you had completely destroyed it. But now you will defeat it only three times."

²⁰Then Elisha died and was buried.

At that time groups of Moabites would rob the land in the springtime. ²¹Once as some Israelites were burying a man, suddenly they saw a group of Moabites coming. The Israelites threw the dead man into Elisha's grave. When the man touched Elisha's bones, the man came back to life and stood on his feet.

War with Aram

²²During all the days Jehoahaz was king, Hazael king of Aram troubled Israel. ²³But the LORD was kind to the Israelites; he had mercy on them and helped them because of his agreement with Abraham, Isaac and Jacob. To this day he has never wanted to destroy them or reject them.

²⁴When Hazael king of Aram died, his son Ben-Hadad became king in his place. ²⁵During a war Hazael had taken some cities from Jehoahaz, Jehoash's father. Now Jehoash took back those cities from Hazael's son Ben-Hadad. He defeated Ben-Hadad three times and took back the cities of Israel.

Amaziah King of Judah

14 Amaziah son of Joash became king of Judah during the second year Jehoash son of Jehoahaz was king of Israel. ²Amaziah was 25 years old when he became king, and he ruled for 29 years in Jerusalem. His mother was named Jehoaddin, and she was from Jerusalem. ³Amaziah did what the LORD said was right. He did everything his father Joash had done, but he did not do as his ancestor David had done. ⁴The places where gods were worshipped were not removed, so the people still sacrificed and burned incense *d* there.

⁵As soon as Amaziah took control of the kingdom, he put to death the officers who had murdered his father the king. ⁶But he did not put to death the children of the murderers because of the rule written in the Book of the Teachings of Moses. The LORD had commanded: "Parents must not be put to death when their children do

wrong, and children must not be put to death when their parents do wrong. Each must die for his own sins." [n]

[7]In battle Amaziah killed 10,000 Edomites in the Valley of Salt. He also took the city of Sela. He called it Joktheel, as it is still called today.

[8]Amaziah sent messengers to Jehoash son of Jehoahaz, the son of Jehu, king of Israel. They said, "Come, let's meet face to face."

[9]Then Jehoash king of Israel answered Amaziah king of Judah, "A thornbush in Lebanon sent a message to a cedar tree in Lebanon. It said, 'Let your daughter marry my son.' But then a wild animal from Lebanon came by, walking on and crushing the thornbush. [10]You have defeated Edom, but you have become proud. Stay at home and boast. Don't ask for trouble, or you and Judah will be defeated."

[11]But Amaziah would not listen, so Jehoash king of Israel went to attack. He and Amaziah king of Judah faced each other in battle at Beth Shemesh in Judah. [12]Israel defeated Judah, and every man of Judah ran away to his home. [13]At Beth Shemesh Jehoash king of Israel captured Amaziah king of Judah. (Amaziah was the son of Joash, who was the son of Ahaziah.) Jehoash went up to Jerusalem and broke down the wall of Jerusalem from the Gate of Ephraim to the Corner Gate, which was about 200 metres. [14]He took all the gold and silver and everything in the Temple [d] of the LORD, and he took the treasuries of the palace and some hostages. Then he returned to Samaria.

[15]The other acts of Jehoash and his victories, including his war against Amaziah king of Judah, are written in the book of the history of the kings of Israel. [16]Jehoash died and was buried in Samaria with the kings of Israel, and his son Jeroboam became king in his place.

[17]Amaziah son of Joash, the king of Judah, lived fifteen years after the death of Jehoash son of Jehoahaz, the king of Israel. [18]The other things Amaziah did are written in the book of the history of the kings of Judah. [19]The people in Jerusalem made plans against him. So he ran away to the town of Lachish, but they sent men after him to Lachish and killed him. [20]They brought his body back on horses, and he was buried with his ancestors in Jerusalem, in the city of David.

[21]Then all the people of Judah made Uzziah [n] king in place of his father Amaziah. Uzziah was sixteen years old. [22]He rebuilt the town of Elath and made it part of Judah again after Amaziah died.

Jeroboam King of Israel

[23]Jeroboam son of Jehoash became king of Israel in Samaria during the fifteenth year Amaziah was king of Judah. (Amaziah was the son of Joash.) Jeroboam ruled for 41 years, [24]and he did what the LORD said was wrong. Jeroboam son of Nebat had led Israel to sin, and Jeroboam son of Jehoash did not stop doing the same sins. [25]Jeroboam won back Israel's border from Lebo Hamath to the Dead Sea. [d] This happened as the LORD, the God of Israel, had said through his servant Jonah son of Amittai, the prophet [d] from Gath Hepher. [26]The LORD had seen how the Israelites, both slave and free, were suffering terribly. No one was left who could help Israel. [27]The LORD had not said he would completely destroy Israel from the world, so he saved the Israelites through Jeroboam son of Jehoash.

[28]Everything else Jeroboam did is written down—all his victories and how he won back from Judah the towns of Damascus and Hamath for Israel. All this is written in the book of the history of the kings of Israel. [29]Jeroboam died and was buried with his ancestors, the kings of Israel. Jeroboam's son Zechariah became king in his place.

Uzziah King of Judah

15 Uzziah [n] son of Amaziah became king of Judah during Jeroboam's twenty-seventh year as king of Israel. [2]Uzziah was sixteen years old when he became king, and he ruled for 52 years in Jerusalem. His mother was named Jecoliah, and she was from Jerusalem. [3]He did what the LORD said was right, just as his father Amaziah had done. [4]But the places where gods were worshipped were not removed, so the people still made sacrifices and burned incense [d] there.

[5]The LORD struck Uzziah with a skin disease, which he had until the day he died. So he had to live in a separate house. Jotham, the king's son, was in charge of the palace, and he governed the people of the land.

[6]All the other things Uzziah did are written in the book of the history of the kings of Judah. [7]Uzziah died and was buried near his ancestors in Jerusalem, and his son Jotham became king in his place.

Zechariah King of Israel

[8]Zechariah son of Jeroboam was king over Israel in Samaria. He ruled for six months during Uzziah's [n] thirty-eighth year as king of Judah. [9]Zechariah did what the LORD said was wrong, just as his ancestors had done. Jeroboam son of

---

"Parents . . . sins." See Deuteronomy 24:16.
Uzziah Also called Azariah.

Nebat had led the people of Israel to sin, and Zechariah did not stop doing the same sins.

[10]Shallum son of Jabesh made plans against Zechariah and killed him in front of the people. Then Shallum became king in his place. [11]The other acts of Zechariah are written in the book of the history of the kings of Israel. [12]The LORD had told Jehu: "Your sons down to your great-great-grandchildren will be kings of Israel," and the LORD's word came true.

Shallum King of Israel

[13]Shallum son of Jabesh became king during Uzziah's[n] thirty-ninth year as king of Judah. Shallum ruled for a month in Samaria. [14]Then Menahem son of Gadi came up from Tirzah to Samaria and attacked Shallum son of Jabesh in Samaria. He killed him and became king in Shallum's place.

[15]The other acts of Shallum and his secret plans are written in the book of the history of the kings of Israel.

Menahem King of Israel

[16]Menahem started out from Tirzah and attacked Tiphsah, destroying the city and the area nearby. This was because the people had refused to open the city gate for him. He defeated them and ripped open all their pregnant women.

[17]Menahem son of Gadi became king over Israel during Uzziah's thirty-ninth year as king of Judah. Menahem ruled for ten years in Samaria, [18]and he did what the LORD said was wrong. Jeroboam son of Nebat had led Israel to sin, and all the time Menahem was king, he did not stop doing the same sins.

[19]Pul king of Assyria came to attack the land. Menahem gave him about 35 tonnes of silver so Pul would support him and make his hold on the kingdom stronger. [20]Menahem taxed Israel to pay about 50 pieces of silver to each soldier of the king of Assyria. So the king left and did not stay in the land.

[21]Everything else Menahem did is written in the book of the history of the kings of Israel. [22]Then Menahem died, and his son Pekahiah became king in his place.

Pekahiah King of Israel

[23]Pekahiah son of Menahem became king over Israel in Samaria during Uzziah's[n] fiftieth year as king of Judah. Pekahiah ruled for two years, [24]and he did what the LORD said was wrong. Jeroboam son of Nebat had led Israel to sin, and Pekahiah did not stop doing the same sins.

[25]Pekah son of Remaliah was one of Pekahiah's captains, and he made plans against Pekahiah. He took 50 men of Gilead with him and killed Pekahiah, as well as Argob and Arieh, in the palace at Samaria. Then Pekah became king in Pekahiah's place.

[26]Everything else Pekahiah did is written in the book of the history of the kings of Israel.

Pekah King of Israel

[27]Pekah son of Remaliah became king over Israel in Samaria during Uzziah's[n] fifty-second year as king of Judah. Pekah ruled for 20 years, [28]and he did what the LORD said was wrong. Jeroboam son of Nebat had led Israel to sin, and Pekah did not stop doing the same sins.

[29]Tiglath-Pileser[n] was king of Assyria. He attacked while Pekah was king of Israel, capturing the cities of Ijon, Abel Beth Maacah, Janoah, Kedesh and Hazor. He also captured Gilead and Galilee and all the land of Naphtali and carried the people away to Assyria. [30]Then Hoshea son of Elah made plans against Pekah son of Remaliah and attacked and killed him. Then Hoshea became king in Pekah's place during the twentieth year Jotham son of Uzziah was king.

[31]Everything else Pekah did is written in the book of the history of the kings of Israel.

Jotham King of Judah

[32]Jotham son of Uzziah became king of Judah during the second year Pekah son of Remaliah was king of Israel. [33]Jotham was 25 years old when he became king, and he ruled for sixteen years in Jerusalem. His mother's name was Jerusha, daughter of Zadok. [34]Jotham did what the LORD said was right, just as his father Uzziah had done. [35]But the places where gods were worshiped were not removed, and the people still made sacrifices and burned incense[d] there. Jotham rebuilt the Upper Gate of the Temple[d] of the LORD.

[36]The other things Jotham did while he was king are written in the book of the history of the kings of Judah. [37]At that time the LORD began to send Rezin king of Aram and Pekah son of Remaliah against Judah. [38]Jotham died and was buried with his ancestors in Jerusalem, the city of David, his ancestor. Then Jotham's son Ahaz became king in his place.

Ahaz King of Judah

16 Ahaz was the son of Jotham king of Judah. Ahaz became king of Judah in the seventeenth year Pekah son of Remaliah was

---

Uzziah Also called Azariah.
Tiglath-Pileser Also called Pul.

king of Israel. [2]Ahaz was 20 years old when he became king, and he ruled for sixteen years in Jerusalem. Unlike his ancestor David, he did not do what the LORD his God said was right. [3]Ahaz did the same things the kings of Israel had done. He even made his son pass through fire. He did the same hateful sins as the nations had done whom the LORD had forced out of the land ahead of the Israelites. [4]Ahaz offered sacrifices and burned incense [d] at the places where gods were worshipped, on the hills and under every green tree.

[5]Rezin king of Aram and Pekah son of Remaliah, the king of Israel, came up to attack Jerusalem. They surrounded Ahaz but could not defeat him. [6]At that time Rezin king of Aram took back the city of Elath for Aram, and he forced out all the people of Judah. Then Edomites moved into Elath, and they still live there today.

[7]Ahaz sent messengers to Tiglath-Pileser [n] king of Assyria, saying, "I am your servant and your friend. Come and save me from the king of Aram and the king of Israel, who are attacking me." [8]Ahaz took the silver and gold that was in the Temple [d] of the LORD and in the treasuries of the palace, and he sent these as a gift to the king of Assyria. [9]So the king of Assyria listened to Ahaz. He attacked Damascus and captured it and sent all its people away to Kir. And he killed Rezin.

[10]Then King Ahaz went to Damascus to meet Tiglath-Pileser king of Assyria. Ahaz saw an altar at Damascus, and he sent plans and a pattern of this altar to Uriah the priest. [11]So Uriah the priest built an altar, following the plans King Ahaz had sent him from Damascus. Uriah finished the altar before King Ahaz came back from Damascus. [12]When the king arrived from Damascus, he saw the altar and went near and offered sacrifices on it. [13]He burned his burnt offerings and grain offerings and poured out his drink offering. He also sprinkled the blood of his fellowship offerings on the altar.

[14]Ahaz moved the bronze altar that was before the LORD at the front of the Temple. It was between Ahaz's altar and the Temple of the LORD, but he put it on the north side of his altar. [15]King Ahaz commanded Uriah the priest, "On the large altar burn the morning burnt offering, the evening grain offering, the king's burnt offering and grain offering, and the whole burnt offering, the grain offering and the drink offering for all the people of the land. Sprinkle on the altar all the blood of the burnt offering and of the sacrifice. But I will use the bronze altar to ask questions of God." [16]So Uriah the priest did everything as King Ahaz commanded him.

[17]Then King Ahaz took off the side panels from the bases and removed the washing bowls from the top of the bases. He also took the large bowl, which was called the Sea, off the bronze bulls that held it up, and he put it on a stone base. [18]Ahaz took away the platform for the royal throne, which had been built at the Temple of the LORD. He also took away the outside entrance for the king. He did these things because of the king of Assyria.

[19]The other things Ahaz did as king are written in the book of the history of the kings of Judah. [20]Ahaz died and was buried with his ancestors in Jerusalem, and Ahaz's son Hezekiah became king in his place.

Hoshea, Last King of Israel

17 Hoshea son of Elah became king over Israel during Ahaz's twelfth year as king of Judah. Hoshea ruled in Samaria for nine years. [2]He did what the LORD said was wrong, but he was not as bad as the kings of Israel who had ruled before him.

[3]Shalmaneser king of Assyria came to attack Hoshea. Hoshea had been Shalmaneser's servant and had made the payments to Shalmaneser that he had demanded. [4]But the king of Assyria found out that Hoshea had made plans against him by sending messengers to So, the king of Egypt. Hoshea had also stopped giving Shalmaneser the payments, which he had paid every year in the past. For that, the king put Hoshea in prison. [5]Then the king of Assyria came and attacked all the land of Israel. He surrounded Samaria and attacked it for three years. [6]He defeated Samaria in the ninth year Hoshea was king, and he took the Israelites away to Assyria. He settled them in Halah, in Gozan on the Habor River and in the cities of the Medes.

Israelites Punished for Sin

[7]All these things happened because the Israelites had sinned against the LORD their God. He had brought them out of Egypt and had rescued them from the power of the king of Egypt, but the Israelites had honoured other gods. [8]They lived like the nations the LORD had forced out of the land ahead of them. They lived as their evil kings had shown them, [9]secretly sinning against the LORD their God. They built places to worship gods in all their cities, from the watchtower to the fortified city. [10]They put up stone pillars to gods and Asherah [d] idols on every high hill and under every green tree. [11]The Israelites burned incense [d] everywhere gods were worshipped, just as the nations who lived there before them

---

Tiglath-Pileser Also called Pul.

had done, whom the LORD had forced out of the land. The Israelites did wicked things that made the LORD angry. [12]They served idols when the LORD had said, "You must not do this." [13]The LORD used every prophet [d] and seer [d] to warn Israel and Judah. He said, "Stop your evil ways and obey my commands and laws. Follow all the teachings that I commanded your ancestors, the teachings that I gave you through my servants the prophets."

[14]But the people would not listen. They were stubborn, just as their ancestors had been who did not believe in the LORD their God. [15]They rejected the LORD's laws and the agreement he had made with their ancestors. And they refused to listen to his warnings. They worshipped useless idols and became useless themselves. They did what the nations around them did, which the LORD had warned them not to do.

[16]The people rejected all the commands of the LORD their God. They moulded statues of two calves, and they made an Asherah idol. They worshipped all the stars of the sky and served Baal. [d] [17]They made their sons and daughters pass through fire and tried to find out the future by magic and witchcraft. [d] They always chose to do what the LORD said was wrong, which made him angry. [18]Because he was very angry with the people of Israel, he removed them from his presence. Only the tribe [d] of Judah was left.

Judah is Also Guilty

[19]But even Judah did not obey the commands of the LORD their God. They did what the Israelites had done, [20]so the LORD rejected all the people of Israel. He punished them and let others destroy them; he threw them out of his presence. [21]When the LORD separated them from the family of David, the Israelites made Jeroboam son of Nebat their king. Jeroboam led the Israelites away from the LORD and led them to sin greatly. [22]So they continued to do all the sins Jeroboam did. They did not stop doing these sins [23]until the LORD removed the Israelites from his presence, just as he had said through all his servants the prophets. [d] So the Israelites were taken out of their land to Assyria, and they have been there to this day.

The Beginning of the Samaritan People

[24]The king of Assyria brought people from Babylon, Cuthah, Avva, Hamath and Sepharvaim and put them in the cities of Samaria to replace the Israelites. These people took over Samaria and lived in the cities. [25]At first they did not worship the LORD, so he sent lions among them which killed some of them. [26]The king of Assyria was told, "You sent foreigners into the cities of Samaria who do not know the law of the god of the land. This is why he has sent lions among them. The lions are killing them because they don't know what the god wants."

[27]Then the king of Assyria commanded, "Send back one of the priests you took away. Let him live there and teach the people what the god wants." [28]So one of the priests who had been carried away from Samaria returned to live in Bethel. And he taught the people how to honour the LORD.

[29]But each nation made gods of its own and put them in the cities where they lived and in the temples where gods were worshipped. These temples had been built by the Samaritans. [30]The people from Babylon made Succoth Benoth their god. The people from Cuthah worshipped Nergal. The people of Hamath worshipped Ashima. [31]The Avvites worshipped Nibhaz and Tartak. The Sepharvites burned their children in the fire, sacrificing them to Adrammelech and Anammelech, the gods of Sepharvaim. [32]They also honoured the LORD, but they chose priests for the places where gods were worshipped. The priests were chosen from among themselves, and they made sacrifices for the people. [33]The people honoured the LORD but also served their own gods, just as the nations did from which they had been brought. [34]Even today they do as they did in the past. They do not worship the LORD nor obey his rules and commands. They do not obey the teachings or the commands of the LORD, which he gave to the children of Jacob, whom he had named Israel. [35]The LORD had made an agreement with them and had commanded them, "Do not honour other gods. Do not bow down to them or worship them or offer sacrifices to them. [36]Worship the LORD who brought you up out of the land of Egypt with great power and strength. Bow down to him and offer sacrifices to him. [37]Always obey the rules, orders, teachings and commands he wrote for you. Do not honour other gods. [38]Do not forget the agreement I made with you, and do not honour other gods. [39]Instead worship the LORD your God, who will save you from all your enemies."

[40]But the Israelites did not listen. They kept on doing the same things they had done before. [41]So these nations honoured the LORD but also worshipped their idols, and their children and grandchildren still do as their ancestors did.

Hezekiah King of Judah

18 Hezekiah son of Ahaz king of Judah became king during the third year Hoshea son of Elah was king of Israel. [2]Hezekiah was 25 years old when he became king, and he ruled for 29 years in Jerusalem. His mother's name was Abijah daughter of Zechariah. [3]Hezekiah did what the LORD said was right, just as his ancestor David had done. ⁴He removed the places where gods were worshipped. He smashed the stone pillars and cut down the Asherah *d* idols. Also the Israelites had been burning incense *d* to Nehushtan, the bronze snake Moses had made. But Hezekiah broke it into pieces.

⁵Hezekiah trusted in the LORD, the God of Israel. There was no one like him among all the kings of Judah, either before him or after him. ⁶Hezekiah was loyal to the LORD and did not stop following him; he obeyed the commands the LORD had given Moses. ⁷And the LORD was with Hezekiah, so he had success in everything he did. He turned against the king of Assyria and stopped serving him. ⁸Hezekiah defeated the Philistines all the way to Gaza and its borders, including the watchtowers and the fortified cities.

The Assyrians Capture Samaria

⁹Shalmaneser king of Assyria surrounded Samaria and attacked it in the fourth year Hezekiah was king. This was the seventh year Hoshea son of Elah was king of Israel. ¹⁰After three years the Assyrians captured Samaria. This was in the sixth year Hezekiah was king, which was Hoshea's ninth year as king of Israel. ¹¹The king of Assyria took the Israelites away to Assyria and settled them in Halah, in Gozan on the Habor River and in the cities of the Medes. ¹²This happened because they did not obey the LORD their God. They broke his agreement and did not obey all that Moses, the LORD's servant, had commanded. They would not listen to the commands or do them.

Assyria Attacks Judah

¹³During Hezekiah's fourteenth year as king, Sennacherib king of Assyria attacked all the fortified cities of Judah and captured them. ¹⁴Then Hezekiah king of Judah sent a message to the king of Assyria at Lachish. He said, "I have done wrong. Leave me alone, and I will pay anything you ask." So the king of Assyria made Hezekiah pay about 10 tonnes of silver and 1 tonne of gold. ¹⁵Hezekiah gave him all the silver that was in the Temple *d* of the LORD and in the palace treasuries. ¹⁶Hezekiah stripped all the gold that covered the doors and doorposts of the Temple of the LORD. Hezekiah had put gold on these doors himself, but he gave it all to the king of Assyria.

¹⁷The king of Assyria sent out his supreme commander, his chief officer and his field commander. They went with a large army from Lachish to King Hezekiah in Jerusalem. When they came near the waterway from the upper pool on the road where people do their laundry, they stopped. ¹⁸They called for the king, so the king sent Eliakim, Shebna and Joah out to meet them. Eliakim son of Hilkiah was the palace manager, Shebna was the royal secretary and Joah son of Asaph was the recorder.

¹⁹The field commander said to them, "Tell Hezekiah this:

"'The great king, the king of Assyria, says: What can you trust in now? ²⁰You say you have battle plans and power for war, but your words mean nothing. Whom are you trusting for help so that you turn against me? ²¹Look, you are depending on Egypt to help you, but Egypt is like a splintered walking stick. If you lean on it for help, it will stab your hand and hurt you. The king of Egypt will hurt all those who depend on him. ²²You might say, "We are depending on the LORD our God," but Hezekiah destroyed the LORD's altars and the places of worship. Hezekiah told Judah and Jerusalem, "You must worship only at this one altar in Jerusalem."

²³"'Now make an agreement with my master, the king of Assyria: I will give you 2,000 horses if you can find enough men to ride them. ²⁴You cannot defeat one of my master's least important officers, so why do you depend on Egypt to give you chariots and horsemen? ²⁵I have not come to attack and destroy this place without an order from the LORD. The LORD himself told me to come to this country and destroy it.' "

²⁶Then Eliakim son of Hilkiah, Shebna and Joah said to the field commander, "Please speak to us in the Aramaic language. We understand it. Don't speak to us in Hebrew, because the people on the city wall can hear you."

²⁷"No," the commander said, "my master did not send me to tell these things only to you and your king. He sent me to speak also to those people sitting on the wall who will have to eat their own dung and drink their own urine like you."

²⁸Then the commander stood and shouted loudly in the Hebrew language, "Listen to what the great king, the king of Assyria, says! ²⁹The king says you should not let Hezekiah fool you, because he can't save you from my power. ³⁰Don't let Hezekiah talk you into trusting the LORD by saying, 'The LORD will surely save us. This city won't be handed over to the king of Assyria.'

³¹"Don't listen to Hezekiah. The king of Assyria says, 'Make peace with me, and come out of the city to me. Then everyone will be free to eat the fruit from his own grapevine and fig tree and to drink water from his own well. ³²After that I will come and take you to a land like your own—a land with grain and new wine, bread and vineyards, olives and honey. Choose to live and not to die!'

"Don't listen to Hezekiah. He is fooling you when he says, 'The LORD will save us.' [33]Has a god of any other nation saved his people from the power of the king of Assyria? [34]Where are the gods of Hamath and Arpad? Where are the gods of Sepharvaim, Hena and Ivvah? They did not save Samaria from my power. [35]Not one of all the gods of these countries has saved his people from me. Neither can the LORD save Jerusalem from my power."

[36]The people were silent. They didn't answer the commander at all, because King Hezekiah had ordered, "Don't answer him."

[37]Then Eliakim, Shebna and Joah tore their clothes to show how upset they were. (Eliakim son of Hilkiah was the palace manager, Shebna was the royal secretary and Joah son of Asaph was the recorder.) The three men went to Hezekiah and told him what the field commander had said.

> **Sidelight** The Assyrians' attack on Jerusalem led by Sennacherib isn't recorded only in the Bible (2 Kings 18:13–37). Archaeologists have found "Sennacherib's Prism", which gives the invaders' view of the situation. Another source tells how a plague of mice attacked Sennacherib's army to make the Assyrians retreat.

Jerusalem will Be Saved

19 When King Hezekiah heard the message, he tore his clothes and put on rough cloth to show how sad he was. Then he went into the Temple [d] of the LORD. [2]Hezekiah sent Eliakim, the palace manager and Shebna, the royal secretary, and the elders of the priests to Isaiah. They were all wearing rough cloth when they came to Isaiah the prophet, [d] the son of Amoz. [3]They told Isaiah, "This is what Hezekiah says: 'Today is a day of sorrow and punishment and disgrace, as when a child should be born, but the mother is not strong enough to give birth to it. [4]The king of Assyria sent his field commander to make fun of the living God. Maybe the LORD your God will hear what the commander said and will punish him for it. So pray for the few of us who are left alive.' "

[5]When Hezekiah's officers came to Isaiah, [6]he said to them, "Tell your master this: the LORD says, 'Don't be afraid of what you have heard. Don't be frightened by the words the servants of the king of Assyria have spoken against me. [7]Listen! I am going to put a spirit in the king of Assyria. He will hear a report that will make him return to his own country, and I will cause him to die by the sword there.' "

[8]The field commander heard that the king of Assyria had left Lachish. When he went back, he found the king fighting against the city of Libnah.

[9]The king received a report that Tirhakah, the Cushite king of Egypt, was coming to attack him. When the king of Assyria heard this, he sent messengers to Hezekiah, saying, [10]"Tell Hezekiah king of Judah: 'Don't be fooled by the god you trust. Don't believe him when he says Jerusalem will not be handed over to the king of Assyria. [11]You have heard what the kings of Assyria have done. They have completely defeated every country, so do not think you will be saved. [12]Did the gods of those people save them? My ancestors destroyed them, defeating the cities of Gozan, Haran and Rezeph, and the people of Eden living in Tel Assar. [13]Where are the kings of Hamath and Arpad? Where are the kings of Sepharvaim, Hena and Ivvah?' "

Hezekiah Prays to the LORD

[14]When Hezekiah received the letter from the messengers and read it, he went up to the Temple [d] of the LORD. He spread the letter out before the LORD [15]and prayed to the LORD: "LORD, God of Israel, whose throne is between the gold creatures with wings, only you are God of all the kingdoms of the earth. You made the heavens and the earth. [16]Hear, LORD, and listen. Open your eyes, LORD, and see. Listen to the words Sennacherib has said to insult the living God. [17]It is true, LORD, that the kings of Assyria have destroyed these countries and their lands. [18]They have thrown the gods of these nations into the fire, but they were only wood and rock statues that people made. So the kings have destroyed them. [19]Now, LORD our God, save us from the king's power so that all the kingdoms of the earth will know that you, LORD, are the only God."

God Answers Hezekiah

[20]Then Isaiah son of Amoz sent a message to Hezekiah that said, "This is what the LORD, the God of Israel, says: 'I have heard your prayer to me about Sennacherib king of Assyria.' [21]This is what the LORD has said against Sennacherib:

'The people of Jerusalem
  hate you and make fun of you.
The people of Jerusalem
  laugh at you as you run away.
[22]You have insulted me and spoken against me;
  you have raised your voice against me.
You have a proud look on your face,
  which is against me, the Holy One of
  Israel.

²³You have sent your messengers to insult the
  Lord.
  You have said, "With my many chariots
I have gone to the tops of the mountains,
  to the highest mountains of Lebanon.
I have cut down its tallest cedars
  and its best pine trees.
I have gone to its farthest places
  and to its best forests.
²⁴I have dug wells in foreign countries
  and drunk water there.
By the soles of my feet,
  I have dried up all the rivers of Egypt."

²⁵" 'King of Assyria, surely you have heard.
  Long ago I, the LORD, planned these
    things.
Long ago I designed them,
  and now I have made them happen.
I allowed you to turn those fortified cities
  into piles of rocks.
²⁶The people in those cities were weak;
  they were frightened and put to shame.
They were like grass in the field,
  like tender, young grass,
like grass on the housetop
  that is burned by the wind before it can
    grow.
²⁷" 'I know when you rest,
  when you come and go,
  and how you rage against me.
²⁸Because you rage against me,
  and because I have heard your proud
    words,
I will put my hook in your nose
  and my bit in your mouth.
Then I will force you to leave my country
  the same way you came.'

²⁹"Then the LORD said, 'Hezekiah, I will give
you this sign:
This year you will eat the grain that grows
  wild,
  and the second year you will eat what
    grows wild from that.
But in the third year, plant grain and
  harvest it.
Plant vineyards and eat their fruit.
³⁰Some of the people in the family of Judah
  will escape.
Like plants that take root,
  they will grow strong and have many
    children.
³¹A few people will come out of Jerusalem
  alive;
  a few from Mount Zion *d* will live.
The strong love of the LORD All-powerful
  will make this happen.'

³²"So this is what the LORD says about the king
of Assyria:
'He will not enter this city
  or even shoot an arrow here.
He will not fight against it with shields
  or build a ramp to attack the city walls.
³³He will return to his country the same way he
    came,
  and he will not enter this city,'
  says the LORD.
³⁴'I will defend and save this city
  for my sake and for the sake of David, my
    servant.' "

³⁵That night the angel of the LORD went out
and killed 185,000 men in the Assyrian camp.
When the people got up early the next morning,
they saw all the dead bodies. ³⁶So Sennacherib
king of Assyria left and went back to Nineveh
and stayed there.

³⁷One day as Sennacherib was worshipping in
the temple of his god Nisroch, his sons Adrammelech and Sharezer killed him with a sword. Then
they escaped to the land of Ararat. So Sennacherib's son Esarhaddon became king of Assyria.

Hezekiah's Illness

20 At that time Hezekiah became so sick he
almost died. The prophet *d* Isaiah son of
Amoz went to see him and told him, "This is
what the LORD says: 'Make arrangements because
you are not going to live, but die.' "

²Hezekiah turned towards the wall and
prayed to the LORD, ³"LORD, please remember
that I have always obeyed you. I have given myself completely to you and have done what you
said was right." Then Hezekiah cried loudly.

⁴Before Isaiah had left the middle courtyard,
the LORD spoke his word to Isaiah: ⁵"Go back
and tell Hezekiah, the leader of my people: 'This
is what the LORD, the God of your ancestor
David, says: I have heard your prayer and seen
your tears, so I will heal you. Three days from
now you will go up to the Temple *d* of the LORD.
⁶I will add fifteen years to your life. I will save
you and this city from the king of Assyria; I will
protect the city for my sake and for the sake of
my servant David.' "

⁷Then Isaiah said, "Make a paste from figs."
So they made it and put it on Hezekiah's boil,
and he got well.

⁸Hezekiah had asked Isaiah, "What will be
the sign that the LORD will heal me and that I
will go up to the Temple of the LORD on the third
day?"

⁹Isaiah said, "The LORD will do what he says.
This is the sign from the LORD to show you: do
you want the shadow to go forwards ten steps or
back ten steps?"

¹⁰Hezekiah answered, "It's easy for the shadow to go forwards ten steps. Instead, let it go back ten steps."

¹¹Then Isaiah the prophet called to the LORD, and the LORD brought the shadow ten steps back up the stairway of Ahaz that it had gone down.

Messengers from Babylon

¹²At that time Merodach-Baladan son of Baladan was king of Babylon. He sent letters and a gift to Hezekiah, because he had heard that Hezekiah was sick. ¹³Hezekiah listened to the messengers, so he showed them what was in his storehouses: the silver, gold, spices, expensive perfumes, his swords and shields, and all his wealth. He showed them everything in his palace and his kingdom.

¹⁴Then Isaiah the prophet *d* went to King Hezekiah and asked him, "What did these men say? Where did they come from?"

Hezekiah said, "They came from a faraway country—from Babylon."

¹⁵So Isaiah asked him, "What did they see in your palace?"

Hezekiah said, "They saw everything in my palace. I showed them all my wealth."

¹⁶Then Isaiah said to Hezekiah, "Listen to the words of the LORD: ¹⁷'In the future everything in your palace and everything your ancestors have stored up until this day will be taken away to Babylon. Nothing will be left,' says the LORD. ¹⁸'Some of your own children, those who will be born to you, will be taken away. And they will become servants in the palace of the king of Babylon.' "

¹⁹Hezekiah told Isaiah, "These words from the LORD are good." He said this because he thought, "There will be peace and security in my lifetime."

²⁰Everything else Hezekiah did—all his victories, his work on the pool, his work on the tun-

> ### Sidelight
> The tunnel King Hezekiah dug to provide water for Jerusalem during the Assyrian siege (2 Kings 20:20) was cut through 525 metres of solid limestone – a massive job completed without modern tunnelling machines. An inscription on "Hezekiah's Tunnel" says workers started digging at each end and met in the middle. People still walk through the tunnel today.

nel to bring water into the city—is written in the book of the history of the kings of Judah. ²¹Then Hezekiah died, and his son Manasseh became king in his place.

Manasseh King of Judah

21 Manasseh was twelve years old when he became king, and he was king for 55 years in Jerusalem. His mother's name was Hephzibah. ²He did what the LORD said was wrong. He did the hateful things the other nations had done—the nations that the LORD had forced out of the land ahead of the Israelites. ³Manasseh's father, Hezekiah, had destroyed the places where gods were worshipped, but Manasseh rebuilt them. He built altars for Baal, *d* and he made an Asherah *d* idol as Ahab king of Israel had done. Manasseh also worshipped all the

> ### Sidelight
> The longest reign in the Bible was that of Manasseh. He reigned 55 years (2 Kings 21:1). Despite his long rule, Manasseh was considered one of the most evil kings of Judah (2 Chronicles 33:9, p.426). The king with the shortest reign was Zimri (1 Kings 16:15, p.331), who lasted only seven days!

stars of the sky and served them. ⁴The LORD had said about the Temple, *d* "I will be worshipped in Jerusalem," but Manasseh built altars in the Temple of the LORD. ⁵He built altars to worship the stars in the two courtyards of the Temple of the LORD. ⁶He made his own son pass through fire. He practised magic and told the future by explaining signs and dreams, and he got advice from mediums *d* and fortune-tellers. He did many things the LORD said were wrong, which made the LORD angry.

⁷Manasseh carved an Asherah idol and put it in the Temple. The LORD had said to David and his son Solomon about the Temple, "I will be worshipped for ever in this Temple and in Jerusalem, which I have chosen from all the tribes *d* of Israel. ⁸I will never again make the Israelites wander out of the land I gave their ancestors. But they must obey everything I have commanded them and all the teachings my servant Moses gave them." ⁹But the people did not listen. Manasseh led them to do more evil than the nations the LORD had destroyed ahead of the Israelites.

¹⁰The LORD said through his servants the prophets, *d* ¹¹"Manasseh king of Judah has done these hateful things. He has done more evil than the Amorites before him. He has also led Judah to sin with his idols. ¹²So this is what the LORD, the God of Israel, says: 'I will bring so much trouble on Jerusalem and Judah that anyone who hears about it will be shocked. ¹³I will stretch the

measuring line of Samaria over Jerusalem, and the plumb line *d* used against Ahab's family will be used on Jerusalem. I will wipe out Jerusalem as a person wipes a dish and turns it upside down. ¹⁴I will throw away the rest of my people who are left. I will give them to their enemies, and they will be robbed by all their enemies, ¹⁵because my people did what I said was wrong. They have made me angry from the day their ancestors left Egypt until now.' "

¹⁶Manasseh also killed many innocent people, filling Jerusalem from one end to the other with their blood. This was besides the sin he led Judah to do; he led Judah to do what the LORD said was wrong.

¹⁷The other things Manasseh did as king, even the sin he did, are written in the book of the history of the kings of Judah. ¹⁸Manasseh died and was buried in the garden of his own palace, the garden of Uzza. Then Manasseh's son Amon became king in his place.

Amon King of Judah

¹⁹Amon was 22 years old when he became king, and he was king for two years in Jerusalem. His mother's name was Meshullemeth daughter of Haruz, who was from Jotbah. ²⁰Amon did what the LORD said was wrong, as his father Manasseh had done. ²¹He lived in the same way his father had lived: he worshipped the idols his father had worshipped, and he bowed down before them. ²²Amon rejected the LORD, the God of his ancestors, and did not follow the ways of the LORD.

²³Amon's officers made plans against him and killed him in his palace. ²⁴Then the people of the land killed all those who had made plans to kill King Amon, and they made his son Josiah king in his place.

²⁵Everything else Amon did is written in the book of the history of the kings of Judah. ²⁶He was buried in his grave in the garden of Uzza, and his son Josiah became king in his place.

Josiah King of Judah

22 Josiah was eight years old when he became king, and he ruled for 31 years in Jerusalem. His mother's name was Jedidah daughter of Adaiah, who was from Bozkath. ²Josiah did what the LORD said was right. He lived as his ancestor David had lived, and he did not stop doing what was right.

³In Josiah's eighteenth year as king, he sent Shaphan to the Temple *d* of the LORD. Shaphan son of Azaliah, the son of Meshullam, was the royal secretary. Josiah said, ⁴"Go up to Hilkiah the high priest, and have him empty out the money the gatekeepers have gathered from the people. This is the money they have brought into the Temple of the LORD. ⁵Have him give the money to the supervisors of the work on the Temple of the LORD. They must pay the workers who repair the Temple of the LORD— ⁶the carpenters, builders and bricklayers. Also use the money to buy timber and cut stone to repair the Temple. ⁷They do not need to report how they use the money given to them, because they are working honestly."

The Book of the Teachings is Found

⁸Hilkiah the high priest said to Shaphan the royal secretary, "I've found the Book of the Teachings in the Temple *d* of the LORD." He gave it to Shaphan, who read it.

⁹Then Shaphan the royal secretary went to the king and reported to Josiah, "Your officers have paid out the money that was in the Temple of the LORD. They have given it to the workers and supervisors at the Temple." ¹⁰Then Shaphan the royal secretary told the king, "Hilkiah the priest has given me a book." And Shaphan read from the book to the king.

¹¹When the king heard the words of the Book of the Teachings, he tore his clothes to show how upset he was. ¹²He gave orders to Hilkiah the priest, Ahikam son of Shaphan, Acbor son of Micaiah, Shaphan the royal secretary and Asaiah the king's servant. These were the orders: ¹³"Go and ask the LORD about the words in the book that was found. Ask for me, for all the people and for all Judah. The LORD's anger is burning against us, because our ancestors did not obey the words of this book; they did not do all the things written for us to do."

¹⁴So Hilkiah the priest, Ahikam, Acbor, Shaphan and Asaiah went to talk to Huldah the prophetess. *d* She was the wife of Shallum son of Tikvah, the son of Harhas, who took care of the king's clothes. Huldah lived in Jerusalem, in the new area of the city.

¹⁵She said to them, "This is what the LORD, the God of Israel, says: 'Tell the man who sent you to me, ¹⁶"This is what the LORD says: 'I will bring trouble to this place and to the people living here, as it is written in the book which the king of Judah has read. ¹⁷The people of Judah have left me and have burned incense *d* to other gods. They have made me angry by all that they have done. My anger burns against this place like a fire, and it will not be put out.' " ¹⁸Tell the king of Judah, who sent you to ask the LORD, "This is what the LORD, the God of Israel, says about the words you heard: ¹⁹When you heard my words against this place and its people, you became sorry for what you had done and upset yourself before me. I said they would be cursed

and would be destroyed. You tore your clothes to show how upset you were, and you cried in my presence. This is why I have heard you, says the LORD. [20]So I will let you die, and you will be buried in peace. You won't see all the trouble I will bring to this place.""

So they took her message back to the king.

The People Hear the Agreement

23 Then the king gathered all the elders of Judah and Jerusalem together. [2]He went up to the Temple [d] of the LORD, and all the people from Judah and Jerusalem went with him. The priests, prophets [d] and all the people—from the least important to the most important—went with him. He read to them all the words of the Book of the Agreement that was found in the Temple of the LORD. [3]The king stood by the pillar and made an agreement in the presence of the LORD to follow the LORD and obey his commands, rules and laws with his whole being, and to obey the words of the agreement written in this book. Then all the people promised to obey the agreement.

Josiah Destroys the Places for Idol Worship

[4]The king commanded Hilkiah the high priest and the priests of the next rank and the gatekeepers to bring out of the Temple [d] of the LORD everything made for Baal, [d] Asherah [d] and all the stars of the sky. Then Josiah burnt them outside Jerusalem in the open country of the Kidron Valley and carried their ashes to Bethel. [5]The kings of Judah had chosen priests for these gods. These priests burnt incense [d] in the places where gods were worshipped in the cities of Judah and the towns around Jerusalem. They burnt incense to Baal, the sun, the moon, the planets and all the stars of the sky. But Josiah took those priests away. [6]He removed the Asherah idol from the Temple of the LORD and took it outside Jerusalem to the Kidron Valley, where he burnt it and beat it into dust. Then he threw the ashes on the graves of the common people. [7]He also tore down the houses of the male prostitutes [d] who were in the Temple of the LORD, where the women did weaving for Asherah.

[8]King Josiah brought all the false priests from the cities of Judah. He ruined the places where gods were worshipped, where the priests had burnt incense, from Geba to Beersheba. He destroyed the places of worship at the entrance to the Gate of Joshua, the ruler of the city, on the left side of the city gate. [9]The priests at the places where gods were worshipped were not allowed to serve at the LORD's altar in Jerusalem. But they could eat bread made without yeast with their brothers.

[10]Josiah ruined Topheth, in the Valley of Ben Hinnom, so no one could sacrifice his son or daughter to Molech. [d] [11]Judah's kings had placed horses at the front door of the Temple of the LORD in the courtyard near the room of Nathan-Melech, an officer. These horses were for the worship of the sun. So Josiah removed them and burnt the chariots that were for sun worship also.

[12]The kings of Judah had built altars on the roof [n] of the upstairs room of Ahaz. Josiah broke down these altars and the altars Manasseh had made in the two courtyards of the Temple of the LORD. Josiah smashed them to pieces and threw their dust into the Kidron Valley. [13]King Josiah ruined the places where gods were worshipped east of Jerusalem, south of the Mount of Olives. [n] Solomon king of Israel had built these places. One was for Ashtoreth, [d] the hated goddess of the Sidonians. One was for Chemosh, [d] the hated god of Moab. And one was for Molech, the hated god of the Ammonites. [14]Josiah smashed to pieces the stone pillars they worshipped, and he cut down the Asherah idols. Then he covered the places with human bones.

[15]Josiah also broke down the altar at Bethel—the place of worship made by Jeroboam son of Nebat, who had led Israel to sin. Josiah burnt that place, broke the stones of the altar into pieces, then beat them into dust. He also burnt the Asherah idol. [16]When he turned round, he saw the graves on the mountain. He had the bones taken from the graves, and he burnt them on the altar to ruin it. This happened as the LORD had said it would through the man of God.

[17]Josiah asked, "What is that monument I see?"

The people of the city answered, "It's the grave of the man of God who came from Judah. This prophet announced the things you have done against the altar of Bethel."

[18]Josiah said, "Leave the grave alone. No one may move this man's bones." So they left his bones and the bones of the prophet who had come from Samaria.

[19]The kings of Israel had built temples for worshipping gods in the cities of Samaria, which had caused the LORD to be angry. Josiah removed all those temples and did the same things as he had done at Bethel. [20]He killed all the priests of those

---

roof   In Bible times houses were built with flat roofs. The roof was used for drying things such as flax and fruit. And it was used as an extra room, as a place for worship and as a place to sleep in the summer.
Mount of Olives   Literally, "The Mountain of Ruin".

places of worship; he killed them on the altars and burnt human bones on the altars. Then he went back to Jerusalem.

Josiah Celebrates the Passover

²¹The king commanded all the people, "Celebrate the Passover *d* to the LORD your God as it is written in this Book of the Agreement." ²²The Passover had not been celebrated like this since the judges led Israel. Nor had one like it happened while there were kings of Israel and kings of Judah. ²³This Passover was celebrated to the LORD in Jerusalem in the eighteenth year of King Josiah's rule.

²⁴Josiah destroyed the mediums, *d* fortune-tellers, house gods and idols. He also destroyed all the hated gods seen in the land of Judah and Jerusalem. This was to obey the words of the teachings written in the book Hilkiah the priest had found in the Temple *d* of the LORD.

²⁵There was no king like Josiah before or after him. He obeyed the LORD with all his heart, soul and strength, following all the Teachings of Moses.

²⁶Even so, the LORD did not stop his strong and terrible anger. His anger burned against Judah because of all Manasseh had done to make him angry. ²⁷The LORD said, "I will send Judah out of my sight, as I have sent Israel away. I will reject Jerusalem, which I chose. And I will take away the Temple about which I said, 'I will be worshipped there.'"

²⁸Everything else Josiah did is written in the book of the history of the kings of Judah.

²⁹While Josiah was king, Neco king of Egypt went to help the king of Assyria at the Euphrates River. King Josiah marched out to fight against Neco, but at Megiddo, Neco faced him and killed him. ³⁰Josiah's servants carried his body in a chariot from Megiddo to Jerusalem and buried him in his own grave. Then the people of Judah chose Josiah's son Jehoahaz and poured olive oil on him to make him king in his father's place.

Jehoahaz King of Judah

³¹Jehoahaz was 23 years old when he became king, and he was king in Jerusalem for three months. His mother's name was Hamutal, who was the daughter of Jeremiah from Libnah. ³²Jehoahaz did what the LORD said was wrong, just as his ancestors had done.

³³King Neco took Jehoahaz prisoner at Riblah in the land of Hamath so that Jehoahaz could not rule in Jerusalem. Neco made the people of Judah pay about 3.5 tonnes of silver and about 35 kilogrammes of gold.

³⁴King Neco made Josiah's son Eliakim the king in place of Josiah his father. Then Neco changed Eliakim's name to Jehoiakim. But Neco took Jehoahaz to Egypt, where he died. ³⁵Jehoiakim gave King Neco the silver and gold he demanded. Jehoiakim taxed the land and took silver and gold from the people of the land to give to King Neco. Each person had to pay his share.

Jehoiakim King of Judah

³⁶Jehoiakim was 25 years old when he became king, and he was king in Jerusalem for eleven years. His mother's name was Zebidah daughter of Pedaiah, who was from Rumah. ³⁷Jehoiakim did what the LORD said was wrong, just as his ancestors had done.

24 While Jehoiakim was king, Nebuchadnezzar king of Babylon attacked the land of Judah. So Jehoiakim became Nebuchadnezzar's servant for three years. Then he turned against Nebuchadnezzar and broke away from his rule. ²The LORD sent raiding men from Babylon, Aram, Moab and Ammon against Jehoiakim to destroy Judah. This happened as the LORD had said it would through his servants the prophets. *d*

³The LORD commanded this to happen to the people of Judah, to remove them from his presence, because of all the sins of Manasseh. ⁴He had killed many innocent people and had filled Jerusalem with their blood. And the LORD would not forgive these sins.

⁵The other things that happened while Jehoiakim was king and all he did are written in the book of the history of the kings of Judah. ⁶Jehoiakim died, and his son Jehoiachin became king in his place.

⁷The king of Egypt did not leave his land again, because the king of Babylon had captured all that belonged to the king of Egypt, from the brook of Egypt to the Euphrates River.

Jehoiachin King of Judah

⁸Jehoiachin was eighteen years old when he became king, and he was king for three months in Jerusalem. His mother's name was Nehushta daughter of Elnathan from Jerusalem. ⁹Jehoiachin did what the LORD said was wrong, just as his father had done.

¹⁰At that time the officers of Nebuchadnezzar king of Babylon came up to Jerusalem. When they reached the city, they attacked it. ¹¹Nebuchadnezzar himself came to the city while his officers were attacking it. ¹²Jehoiachin king of Judah surrendered to the king of Babylon, along with Jehoiachin's mother, servants, elders and officers. So Nebuchadnezzar made Jehoiachin a prisoner in the eighth year he was king of Babylon. ¹³Nebuchadnezzar took all the treasures from the Temple *d* of the LORD and from the palace.

He cut up all the gold objects Solomon king of Israel had made for the Temple of the LORD. This happened as the LORD had said it would. [14]Nebuchadnezzar took away all the people of Jerusalem, including all the leaders, all the wealthy people, and all the craftsmen and metal workers. There were 10,000 prisoners in all. Only the poorest people in the land were left. [15]Nebuchadnezzar carried away Jehoiachin to Babylon, as well as the king's mother and his wives, the officers and the leading men of the land. They were taken captive from Jerusalem to Babylon. [16]The king of Babylon also took all 7,000 soldiers, who were strong and able to fight in war, and about 1,000 craftsmen and metal workers. Nebuchadnezzar took them as prisoners to Babylon. [17]Then he made Mattaniah, Jehoiachin's uncle, king in Jehoiachin's place. He also changed Mattaniah's name to Zedekiah.

Zedekiah King of Judah

[18]Zedekiah was 21 years old when he became king, and he was king in Jerusalem for eleven years. His mother's name was Hamutal daughter of Jeremiah[n] from Libnah. [19]Zedekiah did what the LORD said was wrong, just as Jehoiakim had done. [20]All this happened in Jerusalem and Judah because the LORD was angry with them. Finally, he threw them out of his presence.

The Fall of Jerusalem

Zedekiah turned against the king of Babylon. **25** Nebuchadnezzar king of Babylon marched against Jerusalem with his whole army during Zedekiah's ninth year as king, on the tenth day of the tenth month. He made a camp around the city and piled earth against the city walls to attack it. [2]The city was under attack until Zedekiah's eleventh year as king. [3]By the ninth day of the fourth month, the hunger was terrible in the city. There was no food for the people to eat. [4]Then the city was broken into, and the whole army ran away at night through the gate between the two walls by the king's garden. While the Babylonians were still surrounding the city, Zedekiah and his men ran away towards the Jordan Valley. [5]But the Babylonian army chased King Zedekiah and caught up with him in the plains of Jericho. All of his army was scattered from him, [6]so they captured Zedekiah and took him to the king of Babylon at Riblah. There he passed sentence on Zedekiah. [7]They killed Zedekiah's sons as he watched. Then they put out his eyes and put bronze chains on him

and took him to Babylon.

[8]Nebuzaradan was the commander of the king's special guards. This officer of the king of Babylon came to Jerusalem on the seventh day of the fifth month, in Nebuchadnezzar's nineteenth year as king of Babylon. [9]Nebuzaradan set fire to the Temple[d] of the LORD and the palace and all the houses of Jerusalem. Every important building was burned.

[10]The whole Babylonian army, led by the commander of the king's special guards, broke down the walls around Jerusalem. [11]Nebuzaradan, the commander of the guards, captured the people left in Jerusalem, those who had surrendered to the king of Babylon and the rest of the people. [12]But the commander left behind some of the poorest people of the land to take care of the vineyards and fields.

[13]The Babylonians broke up the bronze pillars, the bronze stands and the large bronze bowl, which was called the Sea, in the Temple of the LORD. Then they carried the bronze to Babylon. [14]They also took the pots, shovels, wick trimmers, dishes and all the bronze objects used to serve in the Temple. [15]The commander of the king's special guards took away the pans for carrying hot coals, the bowls and everything made of pure gold or silver. [16]There were two pillars and the large bronze bowl and the movable stands which Solomon had made for the Temple of the LORD. There was so much bronze that it could not be weighed. [17]Each pillar was about 9 metres high. The bronze capital[d] on top of the pillar was about 1.5 metres high. It was decorated with a net design and bronze pomegranates[d] all around it. The other pillar also had a net design and was like the first pillar.

Judah is Taken Prisoner

[18]The commander of the guards took some prisoners—Seraiah the chief priest, Zephaniah the priest next in rank, and the three doorkeepers. [19]Of the people who were still in the city, he took the officer in charge of the fighting men, as well as five people who advised the king. He took the royal secretary who selected people for the army and 60 other men who were in the city. [20]Nebuzaradan, the commander, took all these people and brought them to the king of Babylon at Riblah. [21]There at Riblah, in the land of Hamath, the king had them killed. So the people of Judah were led away from their country as captives.

Jeremiah   This is not the prophet Jeremiah, but another man with the same name.

Gedaliah Becomes Governor

²²Nebuchadnezzar king of Babylon left some people in the land of Judah. He appointed Gedaliah son of Ahikam, the son of Shaphan, as governor.

²³The army captains and their men heard that the king of Babylon had made Gedaliah governor, so they came to Gedaliah at Mizpah. They were Ishmael son of Nethaniah, Johanan son of Kareah, Seraiah son of Tanhumeth the Netophathite, Jaazaniah son of the Maacathite, and their men. ²⁴Then Gedaliah promised these army captains and their men, "Don't be afraid of the Babylonian officers. Live in the land and serve the king of Babylon, and everything will go well for you."

²⁵In the seventh month Ishmael son of Nethaniah, son of Elishama from the king's family, came with ten men and killed Gedaliah. They also killed the men of Judah and Babylon who were with Gedaliah at Mizpah. ²⁶Then all the people, from the least important to the most important, along with the army leaders, ran away to Egypt, because they were afraid of the Babylonians.

Jehoiachin is Set Free

²⁷Jehoiachin king of Judah was held in Babylon for 37 years. In the thirty-seventh year Evil-Merodach became king of Babylon, and he let Jehoiachin out of prison on the twenty-seventh day of the twelfth month. ²⁸Evil-Merodach spoke kindly to Jehoiachin and gave him a seat of honour above the seats of the other kings who were with him in Babylon. ²⁹So Jehoiachin put away his prison clothes. For the rest of his life, he ate at the king's table. ³⁰Every day, for as long as Jehoiachin lived, the king gave him an allowance.

1 Chronicles

Why Read This Book:

* See God's faithfulness traced through history (1 Chronicles 1—9).
* Find out how David's relationship with God affected every area of his life (1 Chronicles 10—29).

When?

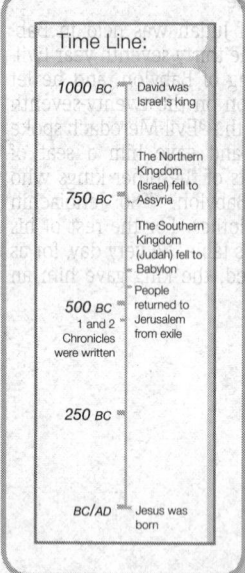

Time Line:

1000 BC	David was Israel's king
750 BC	The Northern Kingdom (Israel) fell to Assyria
	The Southern Kingdom (Judah) fell to Babylon
500 BC 1 and 2 Chronicles were written	People returned to Jerusalem from exile
250 BC	
BC/AD	Jesus was born

Behind the Scenes:

Most people – not just old people – like to understand about their "roots". They like to know which town their family came from and a little bit about their relatives and the way that older members of the family lived. Knowing about roots is less important for people who feel that they are part of a traditional society but, when life becomes a struggle, having something on which to base your feelings about yourself becomes a lifeline.

The books of 1 and 2 Chronicles (which were originally one book) are about roots. They were written hundreds of years after the events, to tell the Israelites where they had come from. The Israelites had been exiles – prisoners of war – in Babylon, where they had been taken because they did not follow God. They had returned to Jerusalem and were rebuilding their city, their history and their lives.

1 Chronicles was written to inspire these Israelites to return not only to Jerusalem but also to God. To do this, the author traced Israel's family roots and then told the story of the nation's greatest ruler, King David. Throughout the book one message is clear: the nation's success is directly linked to the people's relationship with God. ▷

Where?

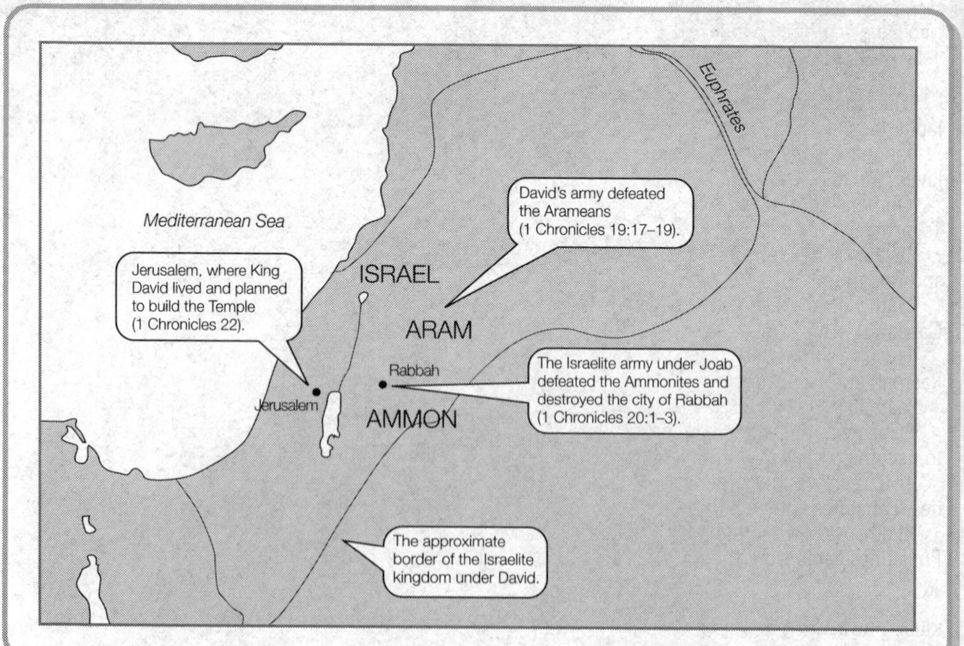

Mediterranean Sea

Euphrates

ISRAEL

ARAM

Rabbah

AMMON

Jerusalem

Jerusalem, where King David lived and planned to build the Temple (1 Chronicles 22).

David's army defeated the Arameans (1 Chronicles 19:17–19).

The Israelite army under Joab defeated the Ammonites and destroyed the city of Rabbah (1 Chronicles 20:1–3).

The approximate border of the Israelite kingdom under David.

Behind the
Scenes (cont.):

The two books of Chronicles weren't written to give a precise history of the Israelites. For example, the stories of David and Solomon leave out some of the negative stories found in 1 and 2 Samuel (p.254 and p.283), and in 1 and 2 Kings (p.311 and p.343) which cover the same period.

Instead, 1 and 2 Chronicles were written to point out how God had guided people in the past and to remind readers of the importance of following God.

From Adam to Abraham

1 Adam was the father of Seth. Seth was the father of Enosh. Enosh was the father of Kenan. ²Kenan was the father of Mahalalel. Mahalalel was the father of Jared. Jared was the father of Enoch. ³Enoch was the father of Methuselah. Methuselah was the father of Lamech and Lamech was the father of Noah.

> ### Sidelight
> Genealogies – family histories – like the one in 1 Chronicles 1–9 are common in the Old Testament. In fact, there are about 24 of them in the Old Testament, with the Chronicles genealogy being the longest. Unlike modern genealogies, Old Testament lists included only important people, not everyone who descended from the original person.

⁴The sons of Noah were Shem, Ham and Japheth.

⁵Japheth's sons were Gomer, Magog, Madai, Javan, Tubal, Meshech and Tiras.

⁶Gomer's sons were Ashkenaz, Riphath and Togarmah.

⁷Javan's sons were Elishah, Tarshish, Kittim *n* and Rodanim.

⁸Ham's sons were Cush, Mizraim, *n* Put and Canaan.

⁹Cush's sons were Seba, Havilah, Sabta, Raamah and Sabteca.

Raamah's sons were Sheba and Dedan.

¹⁰Cush was the father of Nimrod, who grew up to become a mighty warrior on the earth.

¹¹Mizraim was the father of the Ludites, Anamites, Lehabites and Naphtuhim,

¹²Pathrusites, Casluhites and Caphtorites. (The Philistines came from the Casluhites.)

¹³Canaan's first child was Sidon. He was also the father of the Hittites, ¹⁴Jebusites, Amorites, Girgashites, ¹⁵Hivites, Arkites, Sinites, ¹⁶Arvadites, Zemarites and Hamathites.

¹⁷Shem's sons were Elam, Asshur, Arphaxad, Lud and Aram.

Aram's sons were Uz, Hul, Gether and Meshech.

¹⁸Arphaxad was the father of Shelah, who was the father of Eber.

¹⁹Eber had two sons. One son was named Peleg, *n* because the people on the earth were divided into different languages during his life. Peleg's brother was named Joktan.

²⁰Joktan was the father of Almodad, Sheleph, Hazarmaveth, Jerah, ²¹Hadoram, Uzal, Diklah,

> ### Sidelight
> If you're looking for an easy Bible verse to memorise try 1 Chronicles 1:25. With just three words, it's the shortest verse in the Old Testament. But you might still have trouble remembering it; Eber, Peleg and Reu aren't common names.

²²Obal, Abimael, Sheba, ²³Ophir, Havilah and Jobab. All these were Joktan's sons. ²⁴The family line included Shem, Arphaxad, Shelah, ²⁵Eber, Peleg, Reu, ²⁶Serug, Nahor, Terah ²⁷and Abram, who was called Abraham.

Abraham's Family

²⁸Abraham's sons were Isaac and Ishmael.

²⁹These were the sons of Isaac and Ishmael. Ishmael's first son was Nebaioth. His other sons were Kedar, Adbeel, Mibsam, ³⁰Mishma, Dumah, Massa, Hadad, Tema, ³¹Jetur, Naphish

---

Kittim   His descendants were the people of Cyprus.
Mizraim   This is another name for Egypt.
Peleg   This name sounds like the Hebrew word for "divided".

and Kedemah. These were Ishmael's sons. [32]Keturah, Abraham's slave woman,[d] gave birth to Zimran, Jokshan, Medan, Midian, Ishbak and Shuah.

Jokshan's sons were Sheba and Dedan. [33]Midian's sons were Ephah, Epher, Hanoch, Abida and Eldaah. All these were descendants[d] of Keturah.

[34]Abraham was the father of Isaac and Isaac's sons were Esau and Israel.

[35]Esau's sons were Eliphaz, Reuel, Jeush, Jalam and Korah.

[36]Eliphaz's sons were Teman, Omar, Zepho, Gatam, Kenaz, Timna and Amalek.

[37]Reuel's sons were Nahath, Zerah, Shammah and Mizzah.

The Edomites from Seir

[38]Seir's sons were Lotan, Shobal, Zibeon, Anah, Dishon, Ezer and Dishan.

[39]Lotan's sons were Hori, Homam and his sister was Timna.

[40]Shobal's sons were Alvan, Manahath, Ebal, Shepho and Onam.

Zibeon's sons were Aiah and Anah. [41]Anah's son was Dishon.

Dishon's sons were Hemdan, Eshban, Ithran and Keran.

[42]Ezer's sons were Bilhan, Zaavan and Akan. Dishan's sons were Uz and Aran.

The Kings of Edom

[43]These kings ruled in Edom before there were kings in Israel. Bela son of Beor was king of Edom, and his city was named Dinhabah.

[44]When Bela died, Jobab son of Zerah became king. He was from Bozrah.

[45]When Jobab died, Husham became king. He was from the land of the Temanites.

[46]When Husham died, Hadad son of Bedad became king, and his city was named Avith. Hadad defeated Midian in the country of Moab.

[47]When Hadad died, Samlah became king. He was from Masrekah.

[48]When Samlah died, Shaul became king. He was from Rehoboth by the river.

[49]When Shaul died, Baal-Hanan son of Acbor became king.

[50]When Baal-Hanan died, Hadad became king, and his city was named Pau. Hadad's wife was named Mehetabel, and she was the daughter of Matred, who was the daughter of Me-Zahab. [51]Then Hadad died.

The leaders of the family groups of Edom were Timna, Alvah, Jetheth, [52]Oholibamah, Elah, Pinon, [53]Kenaz, Teman, Mibzar, [54]Magdiel and Iram. These were the leaders of Edom.

Israel's Family

2 The sons of Israel[n] were Reuben, Simeon, Levi, Judah, Issachar, Zebulun, [2]Dan, Joseph, Benjamin, Naphtali, Gad and Asher.

Judah's Family

[3]Judah's sons were Er, Onan and Shelah. A Canaanite woman, the daughter of Shua, was their mother. Judah's first son, Er, did what the LORD said was wicked, so the LORD put him to death. [4]Judah's daughter-in-law Tamar gave birth to Perez and Zerah. Judah was the father, so Judah had five sons.

[5]Perez's sons were Hezron and Hamul.

[6]Zerah had five sons: Zimri, Ethan, Heman, Calcol and Darda.

[7]Carmi's son was Achan, who caused trouble for Israel because he took things that had been given to the LORD to be destroyed.

[8]Ethan's son was Azariah.

[9]Hezron's sons were Jerahmeel, Ram and Caleb.

[10]Ram was Amminadab's father, and Amminadab was Nahshon's father. Nahshon was the leader of the people of Judah. [11]Nahshon was the father of Salmon, who was the father of Boaz. [12]Boaz was the father of Obed, and Obed was the father of Jesse.

[13]Jesse's first son was Eliab. His second son was Abinadab, his third was Shimea, [14]his fourth was Nethanel, his fifth was Raddai, [15]his sixth was Ozem and his seventh son was David. [16]Their sisters were Zeruiah and Abigail. Zeruiah's three sons were Abishai, Joab and Asahel. [17]Abigail was the mother of Amasa and his father was Jether, an Ishmaelite.

Caleb's Family

[18]Caleb son of Hezron had children by his wife Azubah and by Jerioth. Caleb and Azubah's sons were Jesher, Shobab and Ardon. [19]When Azubah died, Caleb married Ephrath. They had a son named Hur, [20]who was the father of Uri, who was the father of Bezalel.

[21]Later, when Hezron was 60 years old, he married the daughter of Makir, Gilead's father. Hezron had sexual relations with Makir's daughter, and she had a son named Segub. [22]Segub was the father of Jair. Jair controlled 23 cities in the country of Gilead. [23](But Geshur and Aram captured the towns of Jair, as well as Kenath and the small towns around it—60 towns in all.)

Israel   Another name for Jacob.

All these were descendants *d* of Makir, the father of Gilead.

²⁴After Hezron died in Caleb Ephrathah, his wife Abijah had his son, named Ashhur. Ashhur became the father of Tekoa.

Jerahmeel's Family

²⁵Hezron's first son was Jerahmeel. Jerahmeel's sons were Ram, Bunah, Oren, Ozem and Ahijah. Ram was Jerahmeel's first son. ²⁶Jerahmeel had another wife, named Atarah. She was the mother of Onam.

²⁷Jerahmeel's first son, Ram, had sons. They were Maaz, Jamin and Eker.

²⁸Onam's sons were Shammai and Jada. Shammai's sons were Nadab and Abishur. ²⁹Abishur's wife was named Abihail, and their sons were Ahban and Molid. ³⁰Nadab's sons were Seled and Appaim. Seled died without having children.

³¹Appaim's son was Ishi, who became the father of Sheshan.

Sheshan was the father of Ahlai.

³²Jada was Shammai's brother, and Jada's sons were Jether and Jonathan. Jether died without having children.

³³Jonathan's sons were Peleth and Zaza.

These were Jerahmeel's descendants. *d*

³⁴Sheshan did not have any sons, only daughters. He had a servant from Egypt named Jarha. ³⁵Sheshan let his daughter marry his servant Jarha, and she had a son named Attai.

³⁶Attai was the father of Nathan. Nathan was the father of Zabad. ³⁷Zabad was the father of Ephlal. Ephlal was the father of Obed. ³⁸Obed was the father of Jehu. Jehu was the father of Azariah. ³⁹Azariah was the father of Helez. Helez was the father of Eleasah. ⁴⁰Eleasah was the father of Sismai. Sismai was the father of Shallum. ⁴¹Shallum was the father of Jekamiah, and Jekamiah was the father of Elishama.

The Clans of Caleb

⁴²Caleb was Jerahmeel's brother. Caleb's first son was Mesha. Mesha was the father of Ziph, and his son Mareshah was the father of Hebron. ⁴³Hebron's sons were Korah, Tappuah, Rekem and Shema. ⁴⁴Shema was the father of Raham, who was the father of Jorkeam. Rekem was the father of Shammai. ⁴⁵Shammai was the father of Maon, and Maon was the father of Beth Zur.

⁴⁶Caleb's slave woman *d* was named Ephah and she was the mother of Haran, Moza and Gazez. Haran was the father of Gazez.

⁴⁷Jahdai's sons were Regem, Jotham, Geshan, Pelet, Ephah and Shaaph.

⁴⁸Caleb had another slave woman named Maacah. She was the mother of Sheber, Tirhanah, ⁴⁹Shaaph and Sheva. Shaaph was the father of Madmannah. Sheva was the father of Macbenah and Gibea. Caleb's daughter was Achsah.

⁵⁰⁻⁵¹These were Caleb's descendants: *d* Caleb's son Hur was the first son of his mother Ephrathah. Hur's sons were Shobal, Salma and Hareph. Shobal was the father of Kiriath Jearim. Salma was the father of Bethlehem. And Hareph was the father of Beth Gader.

⁵²Shobal was the father of Kiriath Jearim. Shobal's descendants were Haroeh, half the Manahathites, ⁵³and the family groups of Kiriath Jearim: the Ithrites, Puthites, Shumathites and Mishraites. The Zorathites and the Eshtaolites came from the Mishraite people.

⁵⁴Salma's descendants were Bethlehem, the Netophathites, Atroth Beth Joab, half the Manahathites and the Zorites. ⁵⁵His descendants included the families who lived at Jabez, who wrote and copied important papers. They were called the Tirathites, Shimeathites and Sucathites and were from the Kenite family group who came from Hammath. He was the father of the people living in Recab.

David's Family

3 These are David's sons who were born in Hebron. The first was Amnon, whose mother was Ahinoam from Jezreel. The second son was Daniel, whose mother was Abigail from Carmel. ²The third son was Absalom, whose mother was Maacah daughter of Talmai, the king of Geshur. The fourth son was Adonijah, whose mother was Haggith. ³The fifth son was Shephatiah, whose mother was Abital. The sixth son was Ithream, whose mother was Eglah. ⁴These six sons of David were born to him in Hebron, where David ruled for seven and a half years.

David ruled in Jerusalem for 33 years. ⁵These were his children who were born in Jerusalem: Shammua, Shobab, Nathan and Solomon—the four children of David and Bathsheba, Ammiel's daughter. ⁶⁻⁸David's other nine children were Ibhar, Elishua, Eliphelet, Nogah; Nepheg, Japhia, Elishama, Eliada and Eliphelet. ⁹These were all of David's sons, except for those born to his slave women. *d* David also had a daughter named Tamar.

The Kings of Judah

¹⁰Solomon's son was Rehoboam. Rehoboam's son was Abijah. Abijah's son was Asa. Asa's son was Jehoshaphat. ¹¹Jehoshaphat's son was Jehoram. Jehoram's son was Ahaziah. Ahaziah's son was Joash. ¹²Joash's son was Amaziah. Amaziah's son was Azariah. Azariah's son was Jotham. ¹³Jotham's son was Ahaz. Ahaz's son was Hezekiah. Hezekiah's son was Manasseh.

[14]Manasseh's son was Amon, and Amon's son was Josiah.

[15]These were Josiah's sons: his first son was Johanan, his second was Jehoiakim, his third was Zedekiah and his fourth was Shallum.

[16]Jehoiakim was followed by Jehoiachin, and he was followed by Zedekiah.

David's Descendants After the Babylonian Captivity

[17]Jehoiachin was taken as a prisoner. His sons were Shealtiel, [18]Malkiram, Pedaiah, Shenazzar, Jekamiah, Hoshama and Nedabiah.

[19]Pedaiah's sons were Zerubbabel and Shimei. Zerubbabel's sons were Meshullam and Hananiah, and their sister was Shelomith. [20]Zerubbabel also had five other sons: Hashubah, Ohel, Berekiah, Hasadiah and Jushab-Hesed.

[21]Hananiah's descendants [d] were Pelatiah and Jeshaiah, and the sons of Rephaiah, Arnan, Obadiah and Shecaniah.

[22]Shecaniah's son was Shemaiah. Shemaiah's sons were Hattush, Igal, Bariah, Neariah and Shaphat. There were six in all.

[23]Neariah had three sons: Elioenai, Hizkiah and Azrikam.

[24]Elioenai had seven sons: Hodaviah, Eliashib, Pelaiah, Akkub, Johanan, Delaiah and Anani.

Other Family Groups of Judah

4 Judah's descendants [d] were Perez, Hezron, Carmi, Hur and Shobal.

[2]Reaiah was Shobal's son. Reaiah was the father of Jahath, and Jahath was the father of Ahumai and Lahad. They were the family groups of the Zorathite people.

[3-4]Hur was the oldest son of Caleb and his wife Ephrathah. Hur was the leader of Bethlehem. His three sons were Etam, Penuel and Ezer. Etam's sons were Jezreel, Ishma and Idbash. They had a sister named Hazzelelponi. Penuel was the father of Gedor and Ezer was the father of Hushah.

[5]Tekoa's father was Ashhur. Ashhur had two wives named Helah and Naarah.

[6]The sons of Ashhur and Naarah were Ahuzzam, Hepher, Temeni and Haahashtari. These were the descendants of Naarah.

[7]Helah's sons were Zereth, Zohar, Ethnan [8]and Koz. Koz was the father of Anub, Hazzobebah and the Aharhel family group. Aharhel was the son of Harum.

[9]There was a man named Jabez, who was respected more than his brothers. His mother named him Jabez [n] because she said, "I was in much pain when I gave birth to him." [10]Jabez prayed to the God of Israel, "Please do good things for me and give me more land. Stay with me, and don't let anyone hurt me. Then I won't have any pain." And God did what Jabez had asked.

[11]Kelub, Shuhah's brother, was the father of Mehir. Mehir was the father of Eshton. [12]Eshton was the father of Beth Rapha, Paseah and Tehinnah. Tehinnah was the father of the people from the town of Nahash. These people were from Recah.

[13]The sons of Kenaz were Othniel and Seraiah. Othniel's sons were Hathath and Meonothai. [14]Meonothai was the father of Ophrah.

Seraiah was the father of Joab. Joab was the ancestor of the people from Craftsmen's Valley, named that because the people living there were craftsmen.

> **Sidelight** In Bible times most people worked from home and professions stuck together. One group lived in Craftsmen's Valley (1 Chronicles 4:14).

[15]Caleb was Jephunneh's son. Caleb's sons were Iru, Elah and Naam. Elah's son was Kenaz.

[16]Jehallelel's sons were Ziph, Ziphah, Tiria and Asarel.

[17-18]Ezrah's sons were Jether, Mered, Epher and Jalon. Mered married Bithiah, the daughter of the king of Egypt. The children of Mered and Bithiah were Miriam, Shammai and Ishbah. Ishbah was the father of Eshtemoa. Mered also had a wife from Judah, who gave birth to Jered, Heber and Jekuthiel. Jered became the father of Gedor. Heber became the father of Soco. And Jekuthiel became the father of Zanoah.

[19]Hodiah's wife was Naham's sister. The sons of Hodiah's wife were Eshtemoa and the father of Keilah. Keilah was from the Garmite people, and Eshtemoa was from the Maacathite people.

[20]Shimon's sons were Amnon, Rinnah, Ben-Hanan and Tilon.

Ishi's sons were Zoheth and Ben-Zoheth.

[21-22]Shelah was Judah's son. Shelah's sons were Er, Laadah, Jokim, the men from Cozeba, Joash and Saraph. Er was the father of Lecah. Laadah was the father of Mareshah and the family groups of linen workers at Beth Ashbea. Joash and Saraph ruled in Moab and Jashubi Lehem. The writings about this family are very old. [23]These sons of Shelah were potters. They lived in Netaim and Gederah and worked for the king.

Jabez   This name in Hebrew sounds like the word for "pain".

Simeon's Children

24Simeon's sons were Nemuel, Jamin, Jarib, Zerah and Shaul. 25Shaul's son was Shallum. Shallum's son was Mibsam. Mibsam's son was Mishma.

26Mishma's son was Hammuel. Hammuel's son was Zaccur. Zaccur's son was Shimei. 27Shimei had sixteen sons and six daughters, but his brothers did not have many children, so there were not as many people in their family group as there were in Judah.

28Shimei's children lived in Beersheba, Moladah, Hazar Shual, 29Bilhah, Ezem, Tolad, 30Bethuel, Hormah, Ziklag, 31Beth Marcaboth, Hazar Susim, Beth Biri and Shaaraim. They lived in these cities until David became king. 32The five villages near these cities were Etam, Ain, Rimmon, Token and Ashan. 33There were also other villages as far away as Baalath. This is where they lived. And they wrote the history of their family.

34-38The men in this list were leaders of their family groups: Meshobab, Jamlech, Joshah son of Amaziah, Joel, Jehu son of Joshibiah (Joshibiah was the son of Seraiah, who was the son of Asiel), Elioenai, Jaakobah, Jeshohaiah, Asaiah, Adiel, Jesimiel, Benaiah and Ziza. (Ziza was the son of Shiphi, who was the son of Allon. Allon was the son of Jedaiah, who was the son of Shimri. And Shimri was the son of Shemaiah.)

These families grew very large. 39They went outside the city of Gedor to the east side of the valley to look for pasture for their flocks. 40They found good pastures with plenty of grass, and the land was open country and peaceful and quiet. Ham's descendants *d* had lived there in the past.

41These men who were listed came to Gedor while Hezekiah was king of Judah. They fought against the Hamite people, destroying their tents, and also against the Meunites who lived there, and completely destroyed them. So there are no Meunites there even today. Then these men began to live there, because there was pasture for their flocks. 42Ishi's sons, Pelatiah, Neariah, Rephaiah and Uzziel, led 500 of the Simeonites and attacked the people living in the mountains of Edom. 43They killed the few Amalekites who were still alive. From that time until now these Simeonites have lived in Edom.

Reuben's Children

5 Reuben was Israel's first son. Reuben should have received the special privileges of the oldest son, but he had sexual relations with his father's slave woman. *d* So those special privileges were given to Joseph's sons. (Joseph was a son of Israel.) In the family history Reuben's name is not listed as the first son. 2Judah became stronger

than his brothers, and a leader came from his family. But Joseph's family received the privileges that belonged to the oldest son. 3Reuben was Israel's first son. Reuben's sons were Hanoch, Pallu, Hezron and Carmi.

4These were the children of Joel: Shemaiah was Joel's son. Gog was Shemaiah's son. Shimei was Gog's son. 5Micah was Shimei's son. Reaiah was Micah's son. Baal was Reaiah's son. 6Beerah was Baal's son. Beerah was a leader of the tribe *d* of Reuben. Tiglath-Pileser king of Assyria captured him and took him away.

7Joel's brothers and all his family groups are listed just as they are written in their family histories: Jeiel was the first, then Zechariah 8and Bela. (Bela was the son of Azaz. Azaz was the son of Shema, and Shema was the son of Joel.) They lived in the area of Aroer all the way to Nebo and Baal Meon. 9Bela's people lived to the east—as far as the edge of the desert, which is beside the Euphrates River—because they had too many cattle for the land of Gilead.

10When Saul was king, Bela's people fought a war against the Hagrite people and defeated them. Then Bela's people lived in the tents that had belonged to the Hagrites in all the area east of Gilead.

Gad's Children

11The people from the tribe *d* of Gad lived near the Reubenites. The Gadites lived in the area of Bashan all the way to Salecah. 12Joel was the main leader, Shapham was second, and then Janai and Shaphat were leaders in Bashan.

13The seven relatives in their families were Michael, Meshullam, Sheba, Jorai, Jacan, Zia and Eber. 14They were the descendants *d* of Abihail. Abihail was Huri's son. Huri was Jaroah's son. Jaroah was Gilead's son. Gilead was Michael's son. Michael was Jeshishai's son. Jeshishai was Jahdo's son, and Jahdo was the son of Buz. 15Ahi was Abdiel's son, and Abdiel was Guni's son. Ahi was the leader of their family.

16The Gadites lived in Gilead, Bashan and the small towns around it, and on all the pasturelands in the Plain of Sharon all the way to the borders. 17All these names were written in the family history of Gad during the time Jotham was king of Judah and Jeroboam was king of Israel.

Soldiers Skilled in War

18There were 44,760 soldiers from the tribes *d* of Reuben and Gad and East Manasseh who carried shields and swords and bows. They were skilled in war. 19They started a war against the Hagrites and the people of Jetur, Naphish and Nodab. 20The men from the tribes of Manasseh, Reuben and Gad prayed to God during the war, asking him to help them. So he helped them because they trusted him. He handed over to them the Hagrites and all those who were with them. [21]They took the animals that belonged to the Hagrites: 50,000 camels, 250,000 sheep and 2,000 donkeys. They also captured 100,000 people. [22]Many Hagrites were killed because God helped the people of Reuben, Gad and Manasseh. Then they lived there until Babylon captured them and took them away.

East Manasseh

[23]There were many people in East Manasseh, and they lived in the area of Bashan all the way to Baal Hermon, Senir and Mount Hermon. [24]These were the family leaders: Epher, Ishi, Eliel, Azriel, Jeremiah, Hodaviah and Jahdiel. They were all strong, brave and famous men, and leaders in their families. [25]But they sinned against the God that their ancestors had worshipped. They began worshipping the gods of the people in that land, and those were the people God was destroying. [26]So the God of Israel made Pul king of Assyria want to go to war. (Pul was also called Tiglath-Pileser.) He captured the people of Reuben, Gad and East Manasseh, and he took them away to Halah, Habor, Hara and near the Gozan River. They have lived there from that time until this day.

Levi's Children

6 Levi's sons were Gershon, Kohath and Merari. [2]Kohath's sons were Amram, Izhar, Hebron and Uzziel. [3]Amram's children were Aaron, Moses and Miriam.

Aaron's sons were Nadab, Abihu, Eleazar and Ithamar. [4]Eleazar was the father of Phinehas. Phinehas was the father of Abishua. [5]Abishua was the father of Bukki. Bukki was the father of Uzzi. [6]Uzzi was the father of Zerahiah. Zerahiah was the father of Meraioth. [7]Meraioth was the father of Amariah. Amariah was the father of Ahitub. [8]Ahitub was the father of Zadok. Zadok was the father of Ahimaaz. [9]Ahimaaz was the father of Azariah. Azariah was the father of Johanan. [10]Johanan was the father of Azariah. (Azariah was a priest in the Temple [d] Solomon built in Jerusalem.) [11]Azariah was the father of Amariah. Amariah was the father of Ahitub. [12]Ahitub was the father of Zadok. Zadok was the father of Shallum. [13]Shallum was the father of Hilkiah. Hilkiah was the father of Azariah. [14]Azariah was the father of Seraiah, and Seraiah was the father of Jehozadak. [15]Jehozadak was forced to leave his home when the LORD sent Judah and Jerusalem into captivity under the control of Nebuchadnezzar.

[16]Levi's sons were Gershon, Kohath and Merari. [17]The names of Gershon's sons were Libni and Shimei. [18]Kohath's sons were Amram, Izhar, Hebron and Uzziel. [19]Merari's sons were Mahli and Mushi.

This is a list of the family groups of Levi, listed by the name of the father of each group. [20]Gershon's son was Libni. Libni's son was Jehath. Jehath's son was Zimmah. [21]Zimmah's son was Joah. Joah's son was Iddo. Iddo's son was Zerah. And Zerah's son was Jeatherai. [22]Kohath's son was Amminadab. Amminadab's son was Korah. Korah's son was Assir. [23]Assir's son was Elkanah. Elkanah's son was Ebiasaph. Ebiasaph's son was Assir. [24]Assir's son was Tahath. Tahath's son was Uriel. Uriel's son was Uzziah, and Uzziah's son was Shaul. [25]Elkanah's sons were Amasai and Ahimoth. [26]Ahimoth's son was Elkanah. Elkanah's son was Zophai. Zophai's son was Nahath. [27]Nahath's son was Eliab. Eliab's son was Jeroham. Jeroham's son was Elkanah, and Elkanah's son was Samuel. [28]Samuel's sons were Joel, the first son, and Abijah, the second son. [29]Merari's son was Mahli. Mahli's son was Libni. Libni's son was Shimei. Shimei's son was Uzzah. [30]Uzzah's son was Shimea. Shimea's son was Haggiah, and Haggiah's son was Asaiah.

The Temple Musicians

[31]David chose some people to be in charge of the music in the house of the LORD. They began their work after the Ark [d] of the Agreement was put there. [32]They served by making music at the Holy Tent [d] (also called the Meeting Tent), and they served until Solomon built the Temple [d] of the LORD in Jerusalem. They followed the rules for their work.

> **Sidelight** According to 1 Chronicles 6:31–32, King David may have started the first professional Jerusalem Philharmonic Orchestra and Chorus to lead music in the Temple. Today the musicians would probably go on strike: 1 Chronicles 9:33 (p.382) says they were on duty "day and night".

[33]These are the musicians and their sons:
From Kohath's family there was Heman the singer. Heman was Joel's son. Joel was Samuel's son. [34]Samuel was Elkanah's son. Elkanah was Jeroham's son. Jeroham was Eliel's son. Eliel was Toah's son. [35]Toah was Zuph's son. Zuph was Elkanah's son. Elkanah was Mahath's son.

Mahath was Amasai's son. [36]Amasai was Elkanah's son. Elkanah was Joel's son. Joel was Azariah's son. Azariah was Zephaniah's son. [37]Zephaniah was Tahath's son. Tahath was Assir's son. Assir was Ebiasaph's son. Ebiasaph was Korah's son. [38]Korah was Izhar's son. Izhar was Kohath's son. Kohath was Levi's son. Levi was Israel's son.

[39]There was Heman's helper Asaph, whose group stood by Heman's right side. Asaph was Berekiah's son. Berekiah was Shimea's son. [40]Shimea was Michael's son. Michael was Baaseiah's son. Baaseiah was Malkijah's son. [41]Malkijah was Ethni's son. Ethni was Zerah's son. Zerah was Adaiah's son. [42]Adaiah was Ethan's son. Ethan was Zimmah's son. Zimmah was Shimei's son. [43]Shimei was Jahath's son. Jahath was Gershon's son, and Gershon was Levi's son.

[44]Merari's family were the helpers of Heman and Asaph, and they stood by Heman's left side. In this group was Ethan son of Kishi. Kishi was Abdi's son. Abdi was Malluch's son. [45]Malluch was Hashabiah's son. Hashabiah was Amaziah's son. Amaziah was Hilkiah's son. [46]Hilkiah was Amzi's son. Amzi was Bani's son. Bani was Shemer's son. [47]Shemer was Mahli's son. Mahli was Mushi's son. Mushi was Merari's son, and Merari was Levi's son.

[48]The other Levites served by doing their own special work in the Holy Tent, the house of God. [49]Aaron and his descendants [d] offered the sacrifices on the altar of burnt offering and burned the incense on the altar of incense. They offered the sacrifices that removed the Israelites' sins so they could belong to God. They did all the work in the Most Holy Place and followed all the laws that Moses, God's servant, had commanded.

[50]These were Aaron's sons: Eleazar was Aaron's son. Phinehas was Eleazar's son. Abishua was Phinehas' son. [51]Bukki was Abishua's son. Uzzi was Bukki's son. Zerahiah was Uzzi's son. [52]Meraioth was Zerahiah's son. Amariah was Meraioth's son. Ahitub was Amariah's son. [53]Zadok was Ahitub's son and Ahimaaz was Zadok's son.

Land for the Levites

[54]These are the places where Aaron's descendants [d] lived. His descendants from the Kohath family group received the first share of the land. [55]They were given the city of Hebron in Judah and the pastures around it, [56]but the fields farther from the city and the villages near Hebron were given to Caleb son of Jephunneh. [57]So the descendants of Aaron were given Hebron, one of the cities of safety. [n] They also received the towns and pastures of Libnah, Jattir, Eshtemoa, [58]Hilen,

Debir, [59]Ashan, Juttah and Beth Shemesh. [60]They also received these towns and pastures from the tribe of Benjamin: Gibeon, Geba, Alemeth and Anathoth.

The Kohath family groups received a total of thirteen towns.

[61]The rest of the Kohath family group was given ten towns from the family groups of West Manasseh. The towns were chosen by throwing lots. [d]

[62]The Gershon family group received thirteen towns from the tribes of Issachar, Asher, Naphtali and the part of Manasseh living in Bashan.

[63]The Merari family group received twelve towns from the tribes of Reuben, Gad and Zebulun. Those towns were chosen by throwing lots.

[64]So the Israelites gave these towns and their pastures to the Levites. [65]The towns from the tribes of Judah, Simeon and Benjamin, which were named, were chosen by throwing lots.

[66]Some of the Kohath family groups received towns and pastures from the tribe of Ephraim. [67]They received Shechem, one of the cities of safety, with its pastures in the mountains of Ephraim. They also received the towns and pastures of Gezer, [68]Jokmeam, Beth Horon, [69]Aijalon and Gath Rimmon.

[70]The rest of the people in the Kohath family group received the towns of Aner and Bileam and their pastures from West Manasseh.

[71]From East Manasseh, the Gershon family received the towns and pastures of Golan in Bashan and Ashtaroth.

[72-73]From the tribe of Issachar, the Gershon family received the towns and pastures of Kedesh, Daberath, Ramoth and Anem.

[74-75]From the tribe of Asher, the Gershon family received the towns and pastures of Mashal, Abdon, Hukok and Rehob.

[76]From the tribe of Naphtali, the Gershon family received the towns and pastures of Kedesh in Galilee, Hammon and Kiriathaim.

[77]The rest of the Levites, the people from the Merari family, received from the tribe of Zebulun the towns and pastures of Jokneam, Kartah, Rimmono and Tabor.

[78-79]From the tribe of Reuben, the Merari family received the towns and pastures of Bezer in the desert, Jahzah, Kedemoth and Mephaath. (The tribe of Reuben lived east of the Jordan River, across from Jericho.)

[80-81]From the tribe of Gad, the Merari family received the towns and pastures of Ramoth in Gilead, Mahanaim, Heshbon and Jazer.

---

cities of safety A person who had accidentally killed someone could go to one of the six cities of safety to receive protection and a fair trial.

Issachar's Children

7 Issachar had four sons: Tola, Puah, Jashub and Shimron.

[2]Tola's sons were Uzzi, Rephaiah, Jeriel, Jahmai, Ibsam and Samuel, and they were leaders of their families. In the family history of Tola's descendants,[d] 22,600 men were listed as fighting men during the time David was king.

[3]Uzzi's son was Izrahiah.

Izrahiah's sons were Michael, Obadiah, Joel and Isshiah. All five of them were leaders. [4]Their family history shows they had 36,000 men ready to serve in the army, because they had many wives and children.

[5]The records of the family groups of Issachar show there were 87,000 fighting men.

Benjamin's Children

[6]Benjamin had three sons: Bela, Beker and Jediael.

[7]Bela had five sons: Ezbon, Uzzi, Uzziel, Jerimoth and Iri, and they were leaders of their families. Their family history shows they had 22,034 fighting men.

[8]Beker's sons were Zemirah, Joash, Eliezer, Elioenai, Omri, Jeremoth, Abijah, Anathoth and Alemeth. They all were Beker's sons. [9]Their family history listed the family leaders and 20,200 fighting men.

[10]Jediael's son was Bilhan.

Bilhan's sons were Jeush, Benjamin, Ehud, Kenaanah, Zethan, Tarshish and Ahishahar. [11]All these sons of Jediael were leaders of their families. They had 17,200 fighting men ready to serve in the army.

[12]The Shuppites and Huppites were descendants[d] of Ir and the Hushites were descendants of Aher.

Naphtali's Children

[13]Naphtali's sons were Jahziel, Guni, Jezer and Shillem. They were Bilhah's grandsons.

Manasseh's Children

[14]These are Manasseh's descendants.[d] Manasseh had an Aramean slave woman,[d] who was the mother of Asriel and Makir. Makir was Gilead's father. [15]Makir took a wife from the Huppites and Shuppites. His sister was named Maacah. His second son was named Zelophehad, and he had only daughters. [16]Makir's wife Maacah had a son whom she named Peresh. Peresh's brother was named Sheresh. Sheresh's sons were Ulam and Rakem.

[17]Ulam's son was Bedan.

These were the sons of Gilead, who was the son of Makir. Makir was Manasseh's son. [18]Makir's sister Hammoleketh gave birth to Ishhod, Abiezer and Mahlah.

[19]The sons of Shemida were Ahian, Shechem, Likhi and Aniam.

Ephraim's Children

[20]These are the names of Ephraim's descendants.[d] Ephraim's son was Shuthelah. Shuthelah's son was Bered. Bered's son was Tahath. Tahath's son was Eleadah. Eleadah's son was Tahath. [21]Tahath's son was Zabad. Zabad's son was Shuthelah.

Ezer and Elead went to Gath to steal cows and sheep and were killed by some men who grew up in that city. [22]Their father Ephraim cried for them many days, and his family came to comfort him. [23]Then he had sexual relations with his wife again. She became pregnant and gave birth to a son whom Ephraim named Beriah[n] because of the trouble that had happened to his family. [24]Ephraim's daughter was Sheerah. She built Lower Beth Horon, Upper Beth Horon and Uzzen Sheerah.

[25]Rephah was Ephraim's son. Resheph was Rephah's son. Telah was Resheph's son. Tahan was Telah's son. [26]Ladan was Tahan's son. Ammihud was Ladan's son. Elishama was Ammihud's son. [27]Nun was Elishama's son, and Joshua was the son of Nun.

[28]Ephraim's descendants lived in these lands and towns: Bethel and the villages near it, Naaran on the east, Gezer and the villages near it on the west, and Shechem and the villages near it. These villages went all the way to Ayyah and its villages. [29]Along the borders of Manasseh's land were the towns of Beth Shan, Taanach, Megiddo, Dor and the villages near them. The descendants of Joseph son of Israel lived in these towns.

Asher's Children

[30]Asher's sons were Imnah, Ishvah, Ishvi and Beriah. Their sister was Serah.

[31]Beriah's sons were Heber and Malkiel. Malkiel was Birzaith's father.

[32]Heber was the father of Japhlet, Shomer, Hotham and their sister Shua.

[33]Japhlet's sons were Pasach, Bimhal and Ashvath. They were Japhlet's children.

[34]Japhlet's brother was Shomer. Shomer's sons were Rohgah, Hubbah and Aram.

[35]Shomer's brother was Hotham. Hotham's sons were Zophah, Imna, Shelesh and Amal.

[36]Zophah's sons were Suah, Harnepher, Shual, Beri, Imrah, [37]Bezer, Hod, Shamma, Shilshah, Ithran and Beera.

Beriah   This name sounds like the Hebrew word for "trouble".

38Jether's sons were Jephunneh, Pispah and Ara.

39Ulla's sons were Arah, Hanniel and Rizia.

40All these men were descendants of Asher and leaders of their families. They were powerful warriors and outstanding leaders. Their family history lists that they had 26,000 soldiers ready to serve in the army.

The Family History of King Saul

8 Benjamin was the father of Bela, his first son. Ashbel was his second son, Aharah was his third, 2Nohah was his fourth and Rapha was his fifth son.

3Bela's sons were Addar, Gera, Abihud, 4Abishua, Naaman, Ahoah, 5Gera, Shephuphan and Huram.

6These were the descendants d of Ehud and leaders of their families in Geba. They were forced to move to Manahath. 7Ehud's descendants were Naaman, Ahijah and Gera. Gera forced them to leave. He was the father of Uzza and Ahihud.

8-11Shaharaim and his wife Hushim had sons named Abitub and Elpaal. In Moab, Shaharaim divorced his wives Hushim and Baara. Shaharaim and his wife Hodesh had these sons: Jobab, Zibia, Mesha, Malcam, Jeuz, Sakia and Mirmah. They were leaders of their families.

12-13Elpaal's sons were Eber, Misham, Shemed, Beriah and Shema. Shemed built the towns of Ono and Lod and the villages around them. Beriah and Shema were leaders of the families living in Aijalon, and they forced out the people who lived in Gath.

14Beriah's sons were Ahio, Shashak, Jeremoth, 15Zebadiah, Arad, Eder, 16Michael, Ishpah and Joha.

17Elpaal's sons were Zebadiah, Meshullam, Hizki, Heber, 18Ishmerai, Izliah and Jobab.

19Shimei's sons were Jakim, Zicri, Zabdi, 20Elienai, Zillethai, Eliel, 21Adaiah, Beraiah and Shimrath.

22Shashak's sons were Ishpan, Eber, Eliel, 23Abdon, Zicri, Hanan, 24Hananiah, Elam, Anthothijah, 25Iphdeiah and Penuel.

26Jeroham's sons were Shamsherai, Shehariah, Athaliah, 27Jaareshiah, Elijah and Zicri.

28The family histories show that all these men were leaders of their families and lived in Jerusalem.

29Jeiel lived in the town of Gibeon, where he was the leader. His wife was named Maacah. 30Jeiel's first son was Abdon. His other sons were Zur, Kish, Baal, Ner, Nadab, 31Gedor, Ahio, Zeker 32and Mikloth. Mikloth was the father of Shimeah. These sons also lived near their relatives in Jerusalem.

33Ner was the father of Kish. Kish was the father of Saul, and Saul was the father of Jonathan, Malki-Shua, Abinadab and Esh-Baal.

34Jonathan's son was Merib-Baal, who was the father of Micah.

35Micah's sons were Pithon, Melech, Tarea and Ahaz. 36Ahaz was the father of Jehoaddah. Jehoaddah was the father of Alemeth, Azmaveth and Zimri. Zimri was the father of Moza. 37Moza was the father of Binea. Raphah was Binea's son. Eleasah was Raphah's son and Azel was Eleasah's son.

38Azel had six sons: Azrikam, Bokeru, Ishmael, Sheariah, Obadiah and Hanan. All these were Azel's sons.

39Azel's brother was Eshek. Eshek's first son was Ulam, his second was Jeush and Eliphelet was his third. 40Ulam's sons were mighty warriors and good archers. They had many sons and grandsons—150 of them in all.

All these men were Benjamin's descendants.

9 The names of all the people of Israel were listed in their family histories, and those family histories were put in the book of the kings of Israel.

The People in Jerusalem

The people of Judah were captured and forced to go to Babylon, because they were not faithful to God. 2The first people to come back and live in their own lands and towns were some Israelites, priests, Levites and Temple d servants.

3People from the tribes d of Judah, Benjamin, Ephraim and Manasseh lived in Jerusalem. This is a list of those people.

4There was Uthai son of Ammihud. (Ammihud was Omri's son. Omri was Imri's son. Imri was Bani's son. Bani was a descendant d of Perez, and Perez was Judah's son.)

5Of the Shilonite people there were Asaiah and his sons. Asaiah was the oldest son in his family.

6Of the Zerahite people there were Jeuel and other relatives of Zerah. There were 690 of them in all.

7From the tribe of Benjamin there was Sallu son of Meshullam. (Meshullam was Hodaviah's son, and Hodaviah was Hassenuah's son.) 8There was also Ibneiah son of Jeroham and Elah son of Uzzi. (Uzzi was Micri's son.) And there was Meshullam son of Shephatiah. (Shephatiah was Reuel's son, and Reuel was Ibnijah's son.) 9The family history of Benjamin lists 956 people living in Jerusalem, and all these were leaders of their families.

10Of the priests there were Jedaiah, Jehoiarib, Jakin and 11Azariah son of Hilkiah. (Hilkiah was Meshullam's son. Meshullam was Zadok's son.

Zadok was Meraioth's son. Meraioth was Ahitub's son. Ahitub was the officer responsible for the Temple of God.) [12]Also there was Adaiah son of Jeroham. (Jeroham was Pashhur's son, and Pashhur was Malkijah's son.) And there was Maasai son of Adiel. (Adiel was Jahzerah's son. Jahzerah was Meshullam's son. Meshullam was Meshillemith's son, and Meshillemith was Immer's son.) [13]There were 1,760 priests. They were leaders of their families, and they were responsible for serving in the Temple of God.

[14]Of the Levites there was Semaiah son of Hasshub. (Hasshub was Azrikam's son, and Azrikam was Hashabiah's son. Hashabiah was from the family of Merari.) [15]There were also Bakbakkar, Heresh, Galal and Mattaniah son of Mica. (Mica was Zicri's son, and Zicri was Asaph's son.) [16]There was also Obadiah son of Shemaiah. (Shemaiah was Galal's son and Galal was Jeduthun's son.) And there was Berekiah son of Asa. (Asa was the son of Elkanah, who lived in the villages of the Netophathites.)

[17]Of the gatekeepers there were Shallum, Akkub, Talmon, Ahiman and their relatives. Shallum was their leader. [18]These gatekeepers from the tribe of Levi still stand next to the King's Gate on the east side of the city. [19]Shallum was Kore's son. Kore was Ebiasaph's son, and Ebiasaph was Korah's son. Shallum and his relatives from the family of Korah were gatekeepers and were responsible for guarding the gates of the Temple. Their ancestors had also been responsible for guarding the entrance to the Temple of the LORD. [20]In the past Phinehas, Eleazar's son, was in charge of the gatekeepers, and the LORD was with Phinehas. [21]Zechariah son of Meshelemiah was the gatekeeper at the entrance to the Temple.

[22]In all, 212 men were chosen to guard the gates, and their names were written in their family histories in their villages. David and Samuel the seer[d] chose these men because they were dependable. [23]The gatekeepers and their descendants had to guard the gates of the Temple of the LORD. (The Temple took the place of the Holy Tent. [d]) [24]There were gatekeepers on all four sides of the Temple: east, west, north and south. [25]The gatekeepers' relatives who lived in the villages had to come and help them at times. Each time they came they helped the gatekeepers for seven days. [26]Because they were dependable, four gatekeepers were made the leaders of all the gatekeepers. They were Levites, and they were responsible for the rooms and treasures in the Temple of God. [27]They stayed up all night guarding the Temple of God, and they opened it every morning.

[28]Some of the gatekeepers were responsible for the dishes used in the Temple services. They counted these utensils when people took them out and when they brought them back. [29]Other gatekeepers were chosen to take care of the furniture and utensils in the Holy Place. They also took care of the flour, wine, oil, incense [d] and spices, [30]but some of the priests took care of mixing the spices. [31]There was a Levite named Mattithiah who was dependable and had the job of baking the bread used for the offerings. He was the first son of Shallum, who was from the family of Korah. [32]Some of the gatekeepers from the Kohath family had the job of preparing the special

> **Sidelight**
>
> If being a gatekeeper sounds like a cushy job, read 1 Chronicles 9:28–32 before applying. The Temple gatekeepers were probably priests who washed dishes, kept accounts, baked bread and mixed spices.

bread that was put on the table every Sabbath [d] day.

[33]Some of the Levites were musicians in the Temple. The leaders of these families stayed in the rooms of the Temple. Since they were on duty day and night, they did not do other work in the Temple.

[34]These are the leaders of the Levite families. Their names were listed in their family histories, and they lived in Jerusalem.

The Genealogy of King Saul

[35]Jeiel lived in the town of Gibeon, where he was the leader. His wife was named Maacah. [36]Jeiel's first son was Abdon. His other sons were Zur, Kish, Baal, Ner, Nadab, [37]Gedor, Ahio, Zechariah and Mikloth. [38]Mikloth was Shimeam's father. Jeiel's family lived near their relatives in Jerusalem.

[39]Ner was Kish's father. Kish was Saul's father. Saul was the father of Jonathan, Malki-Shua, Abinadab and Esh-Baal.

[40]Jonathan's son was Merib-Baal, who was the father of Micah.

[41]Micah's sons were Pithon, Melech, Tahrea and Ahaz. [42]Ahaz was Jadah's father. Jadah was the father of Alemeth, Azmaveth and Zimri. Zimri was Moza's father. [43]Moza was Binea's father. Rephaiah was Binea's son. Eleasah was Rephaiah's son, and Azel was Eleasah's son.

[44]Azel had six sons: Azrikam, Bokeru, Ishmael, Sheariah, Obadiah and Hanan. They were Azel's sons.

The Death of King Saul

10 The Philistines fought against Israel, and the Israelites ran away from them. Many Israelites were killed on Mount Gilboa. [2]The Philistines fought hard against Saul and his sons, killing his sons Jonathan, Abinadab and Malki-Shua. [3]The fighting was heavy around Saul, and the archers shot him with their arrows and wounded him.

[4]Then Saul said to the officer who carried his armour, "Pull out your sword and stab me. If you don't, these Philistines who are not circumcised will come and hurt me." But Saul's officer refused, because he was afraid. So Saul took his own sword and threw himself on it. [5]When the officer saw that Saul was dead, he threw himself on his own sword and died. [6]So Saul and three of his sons died; all his family died together.

[7]When the Israelites living in the valley saw that their army had run away and that Saul and his sons were dead, they left their towns and ran away. Then the Philistines came and settled in them.

[8]The next day when the Philistines came to strip the dead soldiers, they found Saul and his sons dead on Mount Gilboa. [9]The Philistines stripped Saul's body and took his head and his armour. Then they sent messengers through all their country to tell the news to their idols and to their people. [10]The Philistines put Saul's armour in the temple of their idols and hung his head in the temple of Dagon. [d]

[11]All the people in Jabesh Gilead heard what the Philistines had done to Saul. [12]So the brave men of Jabesh went and got the bodies of Saul and his sons and brought them to Jabesh. They buried their bones under the large tree in Jabesh. Then the people of Jabesh gave up eating for seven days.

[13]Saul died because he was not faithful to the LORD and did not obey the LORD. He even went to a medium [d] and asked her for advice [14]instead of asking the LORD. This is why the LORD put Saul to death and gave the kingdom to Jesse's son David.

David Becomes King

11 Then the people of Israel came to David at the town of Hebron and said, "Look, we are your own family. [2]Even when Saul was king, you were the one who led Israel in battle. The LORD your God said to you, 'You will be the shepherd for my people Israel. You will be their leader.'"

[3]So all the elders of Israel came to King David at Hebron. He made an agreement with them in Hebron in the presence of the LORD. Then they poured oil on David to make him king over Israel. The LORD had promised through Samuel that this would happen.

David Captures Jerusalem

[4]David and all the Israelites went to the city of Jerusalem. At that time Jerusalem was called Jebus, and the people living there were named Jebusites. [5]They said to David, "You can't get inside our city." But David did take the city of Jerusalem with its strong walls, and it became the City of David.

[6]David had said, "The person who leads the attack against the Jebusites will become the commander over all my army." Joab son of Zeruiah led the attack, so he became the commander of the army.

[7]Then David made his home in the fortified city, which is why it was named the City of David. [8]David rebuilt the city, beginning where the land was filled in and going to the wall that was around the city. Joab repaired the other parts of the city. [9]David became stronger and stronger, and the LORD All-powerful was with him.

David's Mighty Warriors

[10]This is a list of the leaders over David's warriors who helped make David's kingdom strong. All the people of Israel also supported David's kingdom. These heroes and all the people of Israel made David king, just as the LORD had promised.

[11]This is a list of David's warriors:

Jashobeam was from the Hacmonite people. He was the head of the Three, [n] David's most powerful soldiers. He used his spear to fight 300 men at one time, and he killed them all.

[12]Next was Eleazar, one of the Three. Eleazar was Dodai's son from the Ahohite people. [13]Eleazar was with David at Pas-Dammim when the Philistines came there to fight. There was a field of barley at that place. The Israelites ran away from the Philistines, [14]but they stopped in the middle of that field and fought for it and killed the Philistines. The LORD gave them a great victory.

[15]Once, three of the Thirty, David's chief soldiers, came down to him at the rock by the cave near Adullam. At the same time the Philistine army had camped in the Valley of Rephaim. [16]At that time David was in a stronghold, [d] and some of the Philistines were in Bethlehem. [17]David had a strong desire for some water. He said, "Oh, I wish someone would get me water from the well near the city gate [n] of Bethlehem!" [18]So

Three Or maybe "Thirty". These were David's most powerful soldiers. See 2 Samuel 23:8.
city gate People came here to conduct business. Public meetings and court cases were also held here.

the Three broke through the Philistine army and took water from the well near the city gate in Bethlehem. Then they brought it to David, but he refused to drink it. He poured it out before the LORD, [19]saying, "May God keep me from drinking this water! It would be like drinking the blood of the men who risked their lives to bring it to me!" So David refused to drink it.

These were the brave things that the three warriors did.

[20]Abishai brother of Joab was the captain of the Three. Abishai fought 300 soldiers with his spear and killed them. He became as famous as the Three [21]and was more honoured than the Three. He became their commander even though he was not one of them.

[22]Benaiah son of Jehoiada was a brave fighter from Kabzeel who did mighty things. He killed two of the best warriors from Moab. He also went down into a pit and killed a lion on a snowy day. [23]Benaiah killed an Egyptian who was about 2.5 metres tall and had a spear as large as a weaver's rod. Benaiah had a club, but he grabbed the spear from the Egyptian's hand and killed him with his own spear. [24]These were the things Benaiah son of Jehoiada did. He was as famous as the Three. [25]He received more honour than the Thirty, but he did not become a member of the Three. David made him leader of his bodyguards.

The Thirty Chief Soldiers

[26]These were also mighty warriors:
Asahel brother of Joab;
Elhanan son of Dodo from Bethlehem;
[27]Shammoth the Harorite;
Helez the Pelonite;
[28]Ira son of Ikkesh from Tekoa;
Abiezer the Anathothite;
[29]Sibbecai the Hushathite;
Ilai the Ahohite;
[30]Maharai the Netophathite;
Heled son of Baanah the Netophathite;
[31]Ithai son of Ribai from Gibeah in Benjamin;
Benaiah the Pirathonite;
[32]Hurai from the ravines of Gaash;
Abiel the Arbathite;
[33]Azmaveth the Baharumite;
Eliahba the Shaalbonite;
[34]the sons of Hashem the Gizonite;
Jonathan son of Shagee the Hararite;
[35]Ahiam son of Sacar the Hararite;
Eliphal son of Ur;
[36]Hepher the Mekerathite;
Ahijah the Pelonite;
[37]Hezro the Carmelite;
Naarai son of Ezbai;
[38]Joel brother of Nathan;

Mibhar son of Hagri;
[39]Zelek the Ammonite;
Naharai the Berothite, the officer who carried the armour for Joab son of Zeruiah;
[40]Ira the Ithrite;
Gareb the Ithrite;
[41]Uriah the Hittite;
Zabad son of Ahlai;
[42]Adina son of Shiza the Reubenite, who was the leader of the Reubenites, and his 30 soldiers;
[43]Hanan son of Maacah;
Joshaphat the Mithnite;
[44]Uzzia the Ashterathite;
Shama and Jeiel sons of Hotham the Aroerite;
[45]Jediael son of Shimri;
Joha, Jediael's brother, the Tizite;
[46]Eliel the Mahavite;
Jeribai and Joshaviah, Elnaam's sons;
Ithmah the Moabite;
[47]Eliel, Obed and Jaasiel the Mezobaites.

Warriors Join David

12 These were the men who came to David at Ziklag when David was hiding from Saul son of Kish. They were among the warriors who helped David in battle. [2]They came with bows for weapons and could use either their right or left hands to shoot arrows or to sling rocks. They were Saul's relatives from the tribe [d] of Benjamin. [3]Ahiezer was their leader, and there was Joash. (Ahiezer and Joash were sons of Shemaah, who was from the town of Gibeah.) There were also Jeziel and Pelet, the sons of Azmaveth. There were Beracah and Jehu from the town of Anathoth. [4]And there was Ishmaiah from the town of Gibeon; he was one of the Thirty. In fact, he was the leader of the Thirty. There were Jeremiah, Jahaziel, Johanan and Jozabad from Gederah. [5]There were Eluzai, Jerimoth, Bealiah and Shemariah. There was Shephatiah from Haruph. [6]There were Elkanah, Isshiah, Azarel, Joezer and Jashobeam from the family group of Korah. [7]And there were Joelah and Zebadiah, the sons of Jeroham, from the town of Gedor.

[8]Part of the people of Gad joined David at his stronghold [d] in the desert. They were brave warriors trained for war and skilled with shields and spears. They were as fierce as lions and as fast as gazelles [d] over the hills.

[9]Ezer was the leader of Gad's army, and Obadiah was second in command. Eliab was third, [10]Mishmannah was fourth, Jeremiah was fifth, [11]Attai was sixth, Eliel was seventh, [12]Johanan was eighth, Elzabad was ninth, [13]Jeremiah was tenth and Macbannai was eleventh in command.

[14]They were the commanders of the army from Gad. The least of these leaders was in charge of 100 soldiers, and the greatest was in charge of 1,000. [15]They crossed the Jordan River and chased away the people living in the valleys, to the east and to the west. This happened in the first month of the year when the Jordan floods the valley.

[16]Other people from the tribes of Benjamin and Judah also came to David at his stronghold. [17]David went out to meet them and said to them, "If you have come peacefully to help me, I welcome you. Join me. But if you have come to turn me over to my enemies, even though I have done nothing wrong, the God of our fathers will see this and punish you."

[18]Then the Spirit *d* entered Amasai, the leader of the Thirty, and he said:

"We belong to you, David.
  We are with you, son of Jesse.
  Success, success to you.
  Success to those who help you,
  because your God helps you."

So David welcomed these men and made them leaders of his army.

[19]Some of the men from Manasseh also joined David when he went with the Philistines to fight Saul. But David and his men did not really help the Philistines. After talking about it, the Philistine leaders decided to send David away. They said, "If David goes back to his master Saul, we will be killed." [20]These are the men from Manasseh who joined David when he went to Ziklag: Adnah, Jozabad, Jediael, Michael, Jozabad, Elihu and Zillethai. Each of them was a leader of 1,000 men from Manasseh. [21]All these men of Manasseh were brave soldiers, and they helped David fight against groups of men who went around the country robbing people. These soldiers became commanders in David's army. [22]Every day more men joined David, and his army became large, like the army of God.

Others Join David at Hebron

[23]These are the numbers of the soldiers ready for battle who joined David at Hebron. They came to help turn the kingdom of Saul over to David, just as the LORD had said.

[24]There were 6,800 men with their weapons from Judah. They carried shields and spears.

[25]There were 7,100 men from Simeon. They were warriors ready for war.

[26]There were 4,600 men from Levi. [27]Jehoiada, a leader from Aaron's family, was in that group. There were 3,700 with him. [28]Zadok was also in that group. He was a strong young warrior, and with him came 22 leaders from his family.

[29]There were 3,000 men from Benjamin, who were Saul's relatives. Most of them had remained loyal to Saul's family until then.

[30]There were 20,800 men from Ephraim. They were brave warriors and were famous men in their own family groups.

[31]There were 18,000 men from West Manasseh. Each one was especially chosen to make David king.

[32]There were 200 leaders from Issachar. They knew what Israel should do, and they knew the right time to do it. Their relatives were with them and under their command.

[33]There were 50,000 men from Zebulun. They were trained soldiers and knew how to use every kind of weapon of war. They followed David completely.

[34]There were 1,000 officers from Naphtali. They had 37,000 soldiers with them who carried shields and spears.

[35]There were 28,600 men from Dan, who were ready for war.

[36]There were 40,000 trained soldiers from Asher, who were ready for war.

[37]There were 120,000 soldiers from the east side of the Jordan River from the people of Reuben, Gad and East Manasseh. They had every kind of weapon.

[38]All these fighting men were ready to go to war. They came to Hebron fully agreed to make David king of all Israel. All the other Israelites also agreed to make David king. [39]They spent three days there with David, eating and drinking, because their relatives had prepared food for them. [40]Also, their neighbours came from as far away as Issachar, Zebulun and Naphtali, bringing food on donkeys, camels, mules and oxen. They brought much flour, fig cakes, raisins, wine, oil, cows and sheep, because the people of Israel were very happy.

Bringing Back the Ark

13 David talked with all the officers of his army, the commanders of 100 men and the commanders of 1,000 men. [2]Then David called the people of Israel together and said, "If you think it is a good idea, and if it is what the LORD our God wants, let's send a message. Let's tell our fellow Israelites in all the areas of Israel and the priests and Levites living with them in their towns and pastures to come and join us. [3]Let's bring the Ark*d* of our God back to us. We did not use it to ask God for help while Saul was king." [4]All the people agreed with David, because they all thought it was the right thing to do.

[5]So David gathered all the Israelites, from the Shihor River in Egypt to Lebo Hamath, to bring the Ark of God back from the town of Kiriath

Jearim. [6]David and all the Israelites with him went to Baalah of Judah, which is Kiriath Jearim, to get the Ark of God the LORD. God's throne is between the golden, winged creatures on the Ark, and the Ark is called by his name.

[7]The people carried the Ark of God from Abinadab's house on a new cart, and Uzzah and Ahio guided it. [8]David and all the Israelites were celebrating in the presence of God. With all their strength they were singing and playing lyres, [d] harps, tambourines, [d] cymbals and trumpets.

[9]When David's men came to the threshing[d] floor of Kidon, the oxen stumbled, and Uzzah reached out his hand to steady the Ark. [10]The LORD was angry with Uzzah and killed him, because he had touched the Ark. So Uzzah died there in the presence of God.

[11]David was angry because the LORD had punished Uzzah in his anger. Now that place is called The Punishment of Uzzah.

[12]David was afraid of God that day and asked, "How can I bring the Ark of God home to me?" [13]So David did not take the Ark with him to Jerusalem. Instead, he took it to the house of Obed-Edom who was from Gath. [14]The Ark of God stayed with Obed-Edom's family in his house for three months, and the LORD blessed Obed-Edom's family and everything he owned.

David's Kingdom Grows

14 Hiram king of the city of Tyre sent messengers to David. He also sent cedar logs, bricklayers and carpenters to build a palace for David. [2]Then David knew that the LORD really had made him king of Israel and that he had made his kingdom great. The LORD did this because he loved his people Israel.

[3]David married more women in Jerusalem and had more sons and daughters. [4]These are the names of David's children born in Jerusalem: Shammua, Shobab, Nathan, Solomon, [5]Ibhar, Elishua, Elpelet, [6]Nogah, Nepheg, Japhia, [7]Elishama, Beeliada and Eliphelet.

David Defeats the Philistines

[8]When the Philistines heard that David had been made king of all Israel, they went to look for him. But David heard about it and went out to fight them. [9]The Philistines had attacked and robbed the people in the Valley of Rephaim. [10]David asked God, "Should I go and attack the Philistines? Will you hand them over to me?"

The LORD answered him, "Go, I will hand them over to you."

[11]So David and his men went up to the town of Baal Perazim and defeated the Philistines.

David said, "Like a flood of water, God has broken through my enemies by using me." So that place was named Baal Perazim. [n] [12]The Philistines had left their idols there, so David ordered his men to burn them.

[13]Soon the Philistines attacked the people in the valley again. [14]David prayed to God again, and God answered him, saying, "Don't attack the Philistines from the front. Instead, go around them and attack them in front of the balsam trees. [15]When you hear the sound of marching in the tops of the balsam trees, then attack. I, God, will have gone out before you to defeat the Philistine army." [16]David did as God commanded, and he and his men defeated the Philistine army all the way from Gibeon to Gezer.

[17]So David became famous in all the countries, and the LORD made all nations afraid of him.

The Ark is Brought to Jerusalem

15 David built houses for himself in Jerusalem. Then he prepared a place for the Ark [d] of God, and he set up a tent for it. [2]David said, "Only the Levites may carry the Ark of God. The LORD chose them to carry the Ark of the LORD and to serve him for ever."

[3]David called all the people of Israel to come to Jerusalem. He wanted to bring the Ark of the LORD to the place he had made for it. [4]David called together the descendants [d] of Aaron and the Levites. [5]There were 120 people from Kohath's family group, with Uriel as their leader. [6]There were 220 people from Merari's family group, with Asaiah as their leader. [7]There were 130 people from Gershon's family group, with Joel as their leader. [8]There were 200 people from Elizaphan's family group, with Shemaiah as their leader. [9]There were 80 people from Hebron's family group, with Eliel as their leader. [10]And there were 112 people from Uzziel's family group, with Amminadab as their leader.

[11]Then David asked the priests Zadok and Abiathar and these Levites to come to him: Uriel, Asaiah, Joel, Shemaiah, Eliel and Amminadab. [12]David said to them, "You are the leaders of the families of Levi. You and the other Levites must give yourselves for service to the LORD. Bring up the Ark of the LORD, the God of Israel, to the place I have made for it. [13]The last time we did not ask the LORD how to carry it. You Levites didn't carry it, so the LORD our God punished us."

[14]Then the priests and Levites prepared themselves for service to the LORD so they could carry the Ark of the LORD, the God of Israel. [15]The Levites used special poles to carry the Ark of God on

Baal Perazim   This name means "the LORD breaks through".

their shoulders, as Moses had commanded, just as the LORD had said they should.

16David told the leaders of the Levites to appoint their brothers as singers to play their lyres, *d* harps and cymbals and to sing happy songs.

17So the Levites appointed Heman and his relatives Asaph and Ethan. Heman was Joel's son. Asaph was Berekiah's son. And Ethan, from the Merari family group, was Kushaiah's son. 18There was also a second group of Levites: Zechariah, Jaaziel, Shemiramoth, Jehiel, Unni, Eliab, Benaiah, Maaseiah, Mattithiah, Eliphelehu, Mikneiah, Obed-Edom and Jeiel. They were the Levite guards.

19The singers Heman, Asaph and Ethan played bronze cymbals. 20Zechariah, Jaaziel, Shemiramoth, Jehiel, Unni, Eliab, Maaseiah and Benaiah played the lyres. 21Mattithiah, Eliphelehu, Mikneiah, Obed-Edom, Jeiel and Azaziah played the harps. 22The Levite leader Kenaniah was in charge of the singing, because he was very good at it.

23Berekiah and Elkanah were two of the guards for the Ark of the Agreement. 24The priests Shebaniah, Joshaphat, Nethanel, Amasai, Zechariah, Benaiah and Eliezer had the job of blowing trumpets in front of the Ark of God. Obed-Edom and Jehiah were also guards for the Ark.

25David, the elders of Israel, and the commanders of 1,000 soldiers went to get the Ark of the Agreement with the LORD. They all went to bring the Ark from Obed-Edom's house with great joy. 26Because God helped the Levites who carried the Ark of the Agreement with the LORD, they sacrificed seven bulls and seven rams. 27All the Levites who carried the Ark, and Kenaniah, the man in charge of the singing, and all the singers wore robes of fine linen. David also wore a robe of fine linen and a holy robe *d* of fine linen. 28So all the people of Israel brought up the Ark of the Agreement with the LORD. They shouted, blew horns and trumpets and played cymbals, lyres and harps.

29As the Ark of the Agreement with the LORD entered Jerusalem, Saul's daughter Michal watched from a window. When she saw King David dancing and celebrating, she hated him.

16 They brought the Ark *d* of God and put it inside the tent that David had set up for it. Then they offered burnt offerings and fellowship offerings to God. 2When David had finished giving the burnt offerings and fellowship offerings, he blessed the people in the name of the LORD. 3He gave a loaf of bread, some dates and raisins to every Israelite man and woman.

4Then David appointed some of the Levites to serve before the Ark of the LORD. They had the job of leading the worship and giving thanks and praising the LORD, the God of Israel. 5Asaph, who played the cymbals, was the leader. Zechariah was second to him. The other Levites were Jaaziel, Shemiramoth, Jehiel, Mattithiah, Eliab, Benaiah, Obed-Edom and Jeiel. They played the lyres *d* and harps. 6Benaiah and Jahaziel were priests who blew the trumpets regularly before the Ark of the Agreement with God. 7That day David first gave Asaph and his relatives the job of singing praises to the LORD.

David's Song of Thanks

8Give thanks to the LORD and pray to him.
　　Tell the nations what he has done.
9Sing to him; sing praises to him.
　　Tell about all his miracles. *d*
10Be glad that you are his;
　　let those who seek the LORD be happy.
11Depend on the LORD and his strength;
　　always go to him for help.
12Remember the miracles he has done,
　　his wonders, and his decisions.
13You are the descendants *d* of his servant,
　　Israel;
　　you are the children of Jacob, his chosen
　　people.

14He is the LORD our God.
　　His laws are for all the world.
15He will keep his agreement for ever;
　　he will keep his promises always.
16He will keep the agreement he made with
　　Abraham
　　and the promise he made to Isaac.
17He made it a law for the people of Jacob;
　　he made it an agreement with Israel to last
　　for ever.
18He said, "I will give the land of Canaan
　　to you,
　　to belong to you."

19Then God's people were few in number,
　　and they were strangers in the land.
20They went from one nation to another,
　　from one kingdom to another.
21But he did not let anyone hurt them;
　　he warned kings not to harm them.
22He said, "Don't touch my chosen people,
　　and don't harm my prophets." *d*

23Sing to the LORD, all the earth.
　　Every day tell how he saves us.
24Tell the nations about his glory;
　　tell all peoples the miracles he does.
25The LORD is great; he should be praised.
　　He should be respected more than all the
　　gods.
26All the gods of the nations are only idols,
　　but the LORD made the skies.

²⁷He has glory and majesty;
he has power and joy in his Temple.*

²⁸Praise the LORD, all nations on earth.
Praise the Lord's glory and power;
²⁹ praise the glory of the LORD's name.
Bring an offering and come to him.
Worship the Lord because he is holy.
³⁰Tremble before him, everyone on earth.
The earth is set, and it cannot be moved.
³¹Let the skies rejoice and the earth be glad.
Let people everywhere say, "The LORD is king!"
³²Let the sea and everything in it shout;
let the fields and everything in them rejoice.
³³Then the trees of the forest will sing
for joy before the LORD.
They will sing because he is coming to judge the world.
³⁴Thank the LORD because he is good.
His love continues for ever.
³⁵Say to him, "Save us, God our Saviour,
and bring us back and save us from other nations.
Then we will thank you
and will gladly praise you."
³⁶Praise the LORD, the God of Israel.
He always was and always will be.

All the people said "Amen" and praised the Lord.

³⁷Then David left Asaph and the other Levites there in front of the Ark* of the Agreement with the LORD. They were to serve there every day. ³⁸David also left Obed-Edom and 68 other Levites to serve with them. Hosah and Obed-Edom son of Jeduthun were guards.

³⁹David left Zadok the priest and the other priests who served with him in front of the Tent of the LORD at the place of worship in Gibeon. ⁴⁰Every morning and evening they offered burnt offerings on the altar of burnt offerings, following the rules written in the Teachings of the LORD, which he had given Israel. ⁴¹With them were Heman and Jeduthun and other Levites. They were chosen by name to sing praises to the LORD because his love continues for ever. ⁴²Heman and Jeduthun also had the job of playing the trumpets and cymbals and other musical instruments when songs were sung to God. Jeduthun's sons guarded the gates.

⁴³Then all the people left. Each person went home, and David also went home to bless the people in his home.

God's Promise to David

17 When David moved into his palace, he said to Nathan the prophet, "Look, I am living in a palace made of cedar, but the Ark* of the Agreement with the LORD sits in a tent."

²Nathan said to David, "Do what you want to do, because God is with you."

³But that night God spoke his word to Nathan, saying, ⁴"Go and tell David my servant, 'This is what the LORD says: You are not the person to build a house for me to live in. ⁵From the time I brought Israel out of Egypt until now I have not lived in a house. I have moved from one tent site to another and from one place to another. ⁶As I have moved with the Israelites to different places, I have never said to the leaders, whom I commanded to take care of my people, "Why haven't you built me a house of cedar?"'

⁷"Now, tell my servant David: 'This is what the LORD All-powerful says: I took you from the pasture and from tending the sheep and made you king of my people Israel. ⁸I have been with you everywhere you have gone. I have defeated your enemies for you. I will make you as famous as any of the great people on the earth. ⁹I will choose a place for my people Israel, and I will plant them so they can live in their own homes. They will not be bothered any more. Wicked people will no longer hurt them as they have in the past ¹⁰when I chose judges for my people Israel. I will defeat all your enemies.

"'I tell you that the LORD will make your descendants* kings of Israel after you. ¹¹When you die and join your ancestors, I will make one of your sons the new king, and I will set up his kingdom. ¹²He will build a house for me, and I will let his kingdom rule always. ¹³I will be his father, and he will be my son. I took away my love from Saul, who ruled before you, but I will never stop loving your son. ¹⁴I will put him in charge of my house and kingdom for ever. His family will rule for ever.'"

¹⁵Nathan told David everything God had said in this vision.

David Prays to God

¹⁶Then King David went in and sat in front of the LORD. David said, "LORD God, who am I? What is my family? Why did you bring me to this point? ¹⁷But that was not enough for you, God. You have also made promises about my future family. LORD God, you have treated me like a very important person.

¹⁸"What more can I say to you for honouring me, your servant? You know me so well. ¹⁹LORD, you have done this wonderful thing for my sake and because you wanted to. You have made known all these great things.

²⁰"There is no one like you, LORD. There is no God except you. We have heard all this ourselves! ²¹There is no nation like your people

Israel. They are the only people on earth that God chose to be his own. You made your name well known by the great and wonderful things you did for them. You went ahead of them and forced other nations out of the land. You freed your people from slavery in Egypt. 22You made the people of Israel your very own people for ever, and, LORD, you are their God.

23"LORD, keep the promise for ever that you made about my family and me, your servant. Do what you have said. 24Then you will be honoured always, and people will say, 'The LORD All-powerful, the God over Israel, is Israel's God!' And the family of your servant David will continue before you.

25"My God, you have told me that you would make my family great. So I, your servant, am brave enough to pray to you. 26LORD, you are God, and you have promised these good things to me, your servant. 27You have chosen to bless my family. Let it continue before you always. LORD, you have blessed my family, so it will always be blessed."

David Defeats Nations

18 Later, David defeated the Philistines, conquered them, and took the city of Gath and the small towns around it.

2He also defeated the people of Moab. So the people of Moab became servants of David and gave him the payment he demanded.

3David also defeated Hadadezer king of Zobah all the way to the town of Hamath as he tried to spread his kingdom to the Euphrates River. 4David captured 1,000 of his chariots, 7,000 men who rode in chariots and 20,000 foot soldiers. He crippled all but 100 of the chariot horses.

5Arameans from Damascus came to help Hadadezer king of Zobah, but David killed 22,000 of them. 6Then David put groups of soldiers in Damascus in Aram. The Arameans became David's servants and gave him the payments he demanded. So the LORD gave David victory everywhere he went.

7David took the shields of gold that had belonged to Hadadezer's officers and brought them to Jerusalem. 8David also took many things made of bronze from Tebah and Cun, which had been cities under Hadadezer's control. Later, Solomon used this bronze to make things for the Temple: *d* the large bronze bowl, which was called the Sea, the pillars and other bronze utensils.

9Toi king of Hamath heard that David had defeated all the army of Hadadezer king of Zobah. 10So Toi sent his son Hadoram to greet and congratulate King David for defeating Hadadezer. (Hadadezer had been at war with Toi.) Hadoram brought things made of gold, silver and bronze. 11King David gave them to the LORD, along with the silver and gold he had taken from these nations: Edom, Moab, the Ammonites, the Philistines and Amalek.

12Abishai son of Zeruiah killed 18,000 Edomites in the Valley of Salt. 13David put groups of soldiers in Edom, and all the Edomites became his servants. The LORD gave David victory everywhere he went.

David's Important Officers

14David was king over all of Israel, and he did what was fair and right for all his people. 15Joab son of Zeruiah was commander over the army. Jehoshaphat son of Ahilud was the recorder. 16Zadok son of Ahitub and Abiathar son of Ahimelech were priests. Shavsha was the royal secretary. 17Benaiah son of Jehoiada was over the Kerethites and Pelethites. *n* And David's sons were important officers who served at his side.

War with the Ammonites and Arameans

19 When Nahash king of the Ammonites died, his son became king after him. 2David said, "Nahash was loyal to me, so I will be loyal to his son Hanun." So David sent messengers to comfort Hanun about his father's death.

David's officers went to the land of the Ammonites to comfort Hanun. 3But the Ammonite leaders said to Hanun, "Do you think David wants to honour your father by sending men to comfort you? No! David sent them to study the land and capture it and spy it out." 4So Hanun arrested David's officers. To shame them he shaved their beards and cut off their clothes at the hips. Then he sent them away.

5When the people told David what had happened to his officers, he sent messengers to meet them, because they were very ashamed. King David said, "Stay in Jericho until your beards have grown back. Then come home."

6The Ammonites knew that they had insulted David. So Hanun and the Ammonites sent about 35 tonnes of silver to hire chariots and chariot drivers from North West Mesopotamia, Aram Maacah and Zobah. 7The Ammonites hired 32,000 chariots and the king of Maacah and his army. So they came and set up camp near the town of Medeba. The Ammonites themselves came out of their towns and got ready for battle.

8When David heard about this, he sent Joab with the whole army. 9The Ammonites came out

---

Kerethites and Pelethites   These were probably special units of the army that were responsible for the king's safety, a kind of palace guard.

and prepared for battle at the city gate. *n* The kings who had come to help were out in the field by themselves.

[10]Joab saw that there were enemies both in front of him and behind him. So he chose some of the best soldiers of Israel and sent them out to fight the Arameans. [11]Joab put the rest of the army under the command of Abishai, his brother. Then they went out to fight the Ammonites. [12]Joab said to Abishai, "If the Arameans are too strong for me, you must help me. Or, if the Ammonites are too strong for you, I will help you. [13]Be strong. We must fight bravely for our people and the cities of our God. The LORD will do what he thinks is right."

[14]Then Joab and the army with him went to attack the Arameans, and the Arameans ran away. [15]When the Ammonites saw that the Arameans were running away, they also ran away from Joab's brother Abishai and went back to their city. So Joab went back to Jerusalem.

[16]When the Arameans saw that Israel had defeated them, they sent messengers to bring other Arameans from east of the Euphrates River. Their leader was Shophach, the commander of Hadadezer's army.

[17]When David heard about this, he gathered all the Israelites, and they crossed over the Jordan River. He prepared them for battle, facing the Arameans. The Arameans fought with him, [18]but they ran away from the Israelites. David killed 7,000 Aramean chariot drivers and 40,000 Aramean foot soldiers. He also killed Shophach, the commander of the Aramean army.

[19]When those who served Hadadezer saw that the Israelites had defeated them, they made peace with David and served him. So the Arameans refused to help the Ammonites again.

> **Sidelight**   In the ancient world even war depended on the weather. Apparently the right time for war in the Old Testament was springtime (1 Chronicles 20:1). Kings would go to war right after the spring harvest when there wasn't much to do on the farm and when the soldiers could live off the land.

Joab Destroys the Ammonites

20 In the spring, the time of year when kings normally went out to battle, Joab led out the army of Israel. But David stayed in Jerusalem. The army of Israel destroyed the land of Ammon and went to the city of Rabbah and attacked it. [2]David took the crown off the head of their king, *n* and had it placed on his own head. That gold crown weighed about 35 kilogrammes, and it had valuable gems in it. And David took many valuable things from the city. [3]He also brought out the people of the city and forced them to work with saws, iron picks and axes. David did this to all the Ammonite cities. Then David and all his army returned to Jerusalem.

Philistine Giants are Killed

[4]Later, at Gezer, war broke out with the Philistines. Sibbecai the Hushathite killed Sippai, who was one of the descendants *d* of the Rephaites. *d* So those Philistines were defeated.

[5]Later, there was another battle with the Philistines. Elhanan son of Jair killed Lahmi, the brother of Goliath, who was from the town of Gath. His spear was as large as a weaver's rod.

[6]At Gath another battle took place. A very large man was there; he had six fingers on each hand and six toes on each foot—24 fingers and toes in all. This man also was one of the sons of Rapha. *d* [7]When he spoke against Israel, Jonathan son of Shimea, David's brother, killed him.

[8]These descendants of Rapha from Gath were killed by David and his men.

David Counts the Israelites

21 Satan was against Israel, and he caused David to count the people of Israel. [2]So David said to Joab and the commanders of the troops, "Go and count all the Israelites from Beersheba to Dan. *n* Then tell me so I will know how many there are."

[3]But Joab said, "May the LORD give the nation a hundred times more people. My master the king, all the Israelites are your servants. Why do you want to do this, my master? You will make Israel guilty of sin."

[4]But the king commanded Joab, so Joab left and went through all Israel. Then he returned to Jerusalem. [5]Joab gave the list of the people to David. There were 1,100,000 men in all of Israel who could use the sword, and there were 470,000 men in Judah who could use the sword. [6]Joab did not count the tribes *d* of Levi and Benjamin, because he disliked King David's order. [7]David had done something God had said was wrong, so God punished Israel.

---

city gate   People came here to conduct business. Public meetings and court cases were also held here.
their king   Or, "Milcom", the god of the Ammonite people.
Beersheba to Dan   Beersheba was the city farthest south in Israel, and Dan was the city farthest north. So this means all the people of Israel.

8Then David said to God, "I have sinned greatly by what I have done! Now, I beg you to forgive me, your servant, because I have been very foolish."

9The LORD said to Gad, who was David's seer, *d* 10"Go and tell David, 'This is what the LORD says: I offer you three choices. Choose one of them and I will do it.'"

11So Gad went to David and said to him, "This is what the LORD says: 'Choose for yourself 12three years of hunger. Or choose three months of running from your enemies as they chase you with their swords. Or choose three days of punishment from the LORD, in which a terrible disease will spread through the country. The angel of the LORD will go through Israel destroying the people.' Now, David, decide which of these things I should tell the LORD who sent me."

13David said to Gad, "I am in great trouble. Let the LORD punish me, because the LORD is very merciful. Don't let my punishment come from human beings."

14So the LORD sent a terrible disease on Israel, and 70,000 people died. 15God sent an angel to destroy Jerusalem, but when the angel started to destroy it, the LORD saw it and felt very sorry about the terrible things that had happened. So he said to the angel who was destroying, "That is enough! Put down your arm!" The angel of the LORD was then standing at the threshing *d* floor of Araunah the Jebusite.

16David looked up and saw the angel of the LORD in the sky, holding his sword drawn and pointed at Jerusalem. Then David and the elders bowed face down on the ground. They were wearing rough cloth to show their grief. 17David said to God, "I am the one who sinned and did wrong. I gave the order for the people to be counted. These people only followed me like sheep. They did nothing wrong. LORD my God, please punish me and my family, but stop the terrible disease that is killing your people."

18Then the angel of the LORD told Gad to tell David that he should build an altar to the LORD on the threshing floor of Araunah the Jebusite. 19So David did what Gad told him to do, in the name of the LORD.

20Araunah was separating the wheat from the straw. When he turned round, he saw the angel. Araunah's four sons who were with him hid. 21David came to Araunah, and when Araunah saw him, he left the threshing floor and bowed face down on the ground before David.

22David said to him, "Sell me your threshing floor so I can build an altar to the LORD here. Then the terrible disease will stop. Sell it to me for the full price."

23Araunah said to David, "Take this threshing floor. My master the king, do anything you want. Look, I will also give you oxen for the whole burnt offerings, the threshing boards for the wood, and wheat for the grain offering. I give everything to you."

24But King David answered Araunah, "No, I will pay the full price for the land. I won't take anything that is yours and give it to the LORD. I won't offer a burnt offering that costs me nothing."

25So David paid Araunah about 7 kilogrammes of gold for the place. 26David built an altar to the LORD there and offered whole burnt offerings and fellowship offerings. David prayed to the LORD, and he answered him by sending down fire from heaven on the altar of burnt offering. 27Then the LORD commanded the angel to put his sword back into its holder.

28When David saw that the LORD had answered him on the threshing floor of Araunah, he offered sacrifices there. 29The Holy Tent *d* that Moses made while the Israelites were in the desert and the altar of burnt offerings were in Gibeon at the place of worship. 30But David could not go to the Holy Tent to speak with God, because he was afraid of the angel of the LORD and his sword.

22 David said, "The Temple *d* of the LORD God and the altar for Israel's burnt offerings will be built here."

David Makes Plans for the Temple

2So David ordered all foreigners living in Israel to gather together. From that group David chose stonecutters to cut stones to be used in building the Temple *d* of God. 3David supplied a large amount of iron to be used for making nails and hinges for the gate doors. He also supplied more bronze than could be weighed, 4and he supplied more cedar logs than could be counted. Much of the cedar had been brought to David by the people from Sidon and Tyre.

5David said, "We should build a great Temple for the LORD, which will be famous everywhere for its greatness and beauty. But my son Solomon is young. He hasn't yet learned what he needs to know, so I will prepare for the building of it." So David got many of the materials ready before he died.

6Then David called for his son Solomon and told him to build the Temple for the LORD, the God of Israel. 7David said to him, "My son, I wanted to build a temple for worshipping the LORD my God. 8But the LORD spoke his word to me, 'David, you have killed many people. You have fought many wars. You cannot build a temple for worship to me, because you have killed many people. 9But, you will have a son, a man of peace and rest. I will give him rest from all his enemies around him. His name will be Solomon,[n] and I will give Israel peace and quiet while he is king. [10]Solomon will build a temple for worship to me. He will be my son, and I will be his father. I will make his kingdom strong; someone from his family will rule Israel for ever.' "

[11]David said, "Now, my son, may the LORD be with you. May you build a temple for the LORD your God, as he said you would. [12]He will make you the king of Israel. May the LORD give you wisdom and understanding so you will be able to obey the teachings of the LORD your God. [13]Be careful to obey the rules and laws the LORD gave Moses for Israel. If you obey them, you will have success. Be strong and brave. Don't be afraid or discouraged.

[14]"Solomon, I have worked hard getting many of the materials for building the Temple of the LORD. I have supplied about 3,550 tonnes of gold, about 35,000 tonnes of silver, so much bronze and iron it cannot be weighed, and wood and stone. You may add to them. [15]You have many workmen—stonecutters, bricklayers, carpenters and people skilled in every kind of work. [16]They are skilled in working with gold, silver, bronze and iron. You have more craftsmen than can be counted. Now begin the work, and may the LORD be with you."

[17]Then David ordered all the leaders of Israel to help his son Solomon. [18]David said to them, "The LORD your God is with you. He has given you rest from our enemies. He has handed over to me the people living around us. The LORD and his people are in control of this land. [19]Now give yourselves completely to obeying the LORD your God. Build the holy place of the LORD God; build the Temple for worship to the LORD. Then bring the Ark[d] of the Agreement with the LORD and the holy things that belong to God into the Temple."

The Levites

23 After David had lived long and was old, he made his son Solomon the new king of Israel. [2]David gathered all the leaders of Israel, along with the priests and Levites. [3]He counted the Levites who were 30 years old and older. In all, there were 38,000 Levites. [4]David said, "Of these, 24,000 Levites will direct the work of the Temple[d] of the LORD, 6,000 Levites will be officers and judges, [5]4,000 Levites will be gatekeepers and 4,000 Levites will praise the LORD with musical instruments I made for giving praise."

[6]David separated the Levites into three groups that were led by Levi's three sons: Gershon, Kohath and Merari.

The People of Gershon

[7]From the people of Gershon, there were Ladan and Shimei.

[8]Ladan had three sons. His first son was Jehiel, and his other sons were Zetham and Joel.

[9]Shimei's sons were Shelomoth, Haziel and Haran. These three sons were leaders of Ladan's families. [10]Shimei had four sons: Jahath, Ziza, Jeush and Beriah. [11]Jahath was the first son, and Ziza was the second son. But Jeush and Beriah did not have many children, so they were counted as if they were one family.

The People of Kohath

[12]Kohath had four sons: Amram, Izhar, Hebron and Uzziel.

[13]Amram's sons were Aaron and Moses. Aaron and his descendants[d] were chosen to be special for ever. They were chosen to prepare the holy things for the LORD's service, to offer sacrifices before the LORD, and to serve him as priests. They were to give blessings in his name for ever.

[14]Moses was the man of God, and his sons were counted as part of the tribe[d] of Levi. [15]Moses' sons were Gershom and Eliezer. [16]Gershom's first son was Shubael. [17]Eliezer's first son was Rehabiah. Eliezer had no other sons, but Rehabiah had many sons.

[18]Izhar's first son was Shelomith.

[19]Hebron's first son was Jeriah, his second was Amariah, his third was Jahaziel, and his fourth was Jekameam.

[20]Uzziel's first son was Micah and his second was Isshiah.

The People of Merari

[21]Merari's sons were Mahli and Mushi. Mahli's sons were Eleazar and Kish. [22]Eleazar died without sons; he had only daughters. Eleazar's daughters married their cousins, the sons of Kish. [23]Mushi's three sons were Mahli, Eder and Jerimoth.

The Levites' Work

[24]These were Levi's descendants[d] listed by their families. They were the leaders of families. Each person who was 20 years old or older was listed. They served in the LORD's Temple. [d]

[25]David had said, "The LORD, the God of Israel, has given rest to his people. He has come to live in Jerusalem for ever. [26]So the Levites don't need to carry the Holy Tent[d] or any of the things used in its services any more." [27]David's last instructions were to count the Levites who were 20 years old and older.

Solomon   This name sounds like the Hebrew word for "peace".

²⁸The Levites had the job of helping Aaron's descendants in the service of the Temple of the LORD. They cared for the Temple courtyard and side rooms, and they made all the holy things pure. Their job was to serve in the Temple of God. ²⁹They were responsible for putting the holy bread on the table, for the flour in the grain offerings, for the bread made without yeast, for the baking and mixing, and for the measuring. ³⁰The Levites also stood every morning and gave thanks and praise to the LORD. They also did this every evening. ³¹The Levites offered all the burnt offerings to the LORD on the special days of rest, at the New Moon *d* festivals and at all appointed feasts. They served before the LORD every day. They were to follow the rules for how many Levites should serve each time. ³²So the Levites took care of the Meeting Tent and the Holy Place. And they helped their relatives, Aaron's descendants, with the services at the Temple of the LORD.

The Groups of the Priests

24 These were the groups of Aaron's sons: Aaron's sons were Nadab, Abihu, Eleazar and Ithamar. ²But Nadab and Abihu died before their father did, and they had no sons. So Eleazar and Ithamar served as the priests. ³David, with the help of Zadok, a descendant *d* of Eleazar, and Ahimelech, a descendant of Ithamar, separated their family groups into two different groups. Each group had certain duties. ⁴There were more leaders from Eleazar's family than from Ithamar's—sixteen leaders from Eleazar's family and eight leaders from Ithamar's family. ⁵Men were chosen from Eleazar's and Ithamar's families by throwing lots. *d* Some men from each family were chosen to be in charge of the Holy Place, and some were chosen to serve as priests.

⁶Shemaiah son of Nethanel, from the tribe *d* of Levi, was the secretary. He recorded the names of those descendants in front of King David, the officers, Zadok the priest, Ahimelech son of Abiathar, and the leaders of the families of the priests and Levites. The work was divided by lots among the families of Eleazar and Ithamar. The following men with their groups were chosen.

⁷The first one chosen was Jehoiarib. The second was Jedaiah. ⁸The third was Harim. The fourth was Seorim. ⁹The fifth was Malkijah. The sixth was Mijamin. ¹⁰The seventh was Hakkoz. The eighth was Abijah. ¹¹The ninth was Jeshua. The tenth was Shecaniah. ¹²The eleventh was Eliashib. The twelfth was Jakim. ¹³The thirteenth was Huppah. The fourteenth was Jeshebeab. ¹⁴The fifteenth was Bilgah. The sixteenth was Immer. ¹⁵The seventeenth was Hezir. The eighteenth was Happizzez. ¹⁶The nineteenth

was Pethahiah. The twentieth was Jehezkel. ¹⁷The twenty-first was Jakin. The twenty-second was Gamul. ¹⁸The twenty-third was Delaiah. The twenty-fourth was Maaziah.

¹⁹These were the groups chosen to serve in the Temple of the LORD. They obeyed the rules given them by Aaron, just as the LORD, the God of Israel, had commanded him.

The Other Levites

²⁰These are the names of the rest of Levi's descendants: *d*

Shubael was a descendant of Amram, and Jehdeiah was a descendant of Shubael. ²¹Isshiah was the first son of Rehabiah.

²²From the Izhar family group, there was Shelomoth, and Jahath was a descendant of Shelomoth. ²³Hebron's first son was Jeriah, Amariah was his second, Jahaziel was his third and Jekameam was his fourth.

²⁴Uzziel's son was Micah. Micah's son was Shamir. ²⁵Micah's brother was Isshiah and Isshiah's son was Zechariah.

²⁶Merari's descendants were Mahli and Mushi. Merari's son was Jaaziah. ²⁷Jaaziah son of Merari had sons named Shoham, Zaccur and Ibri. ²⁸Mahli's son was Eleazar, but Eleazar did not have any sons. ²⁹Kish's son was Jerahmeel. ³⁰Mushi's sons were Mahli, Eder and Jerimoth.

These are the Levites, listed by their families. ³¹They were chosen for special jobs by throwing lots *d* in front of King David, Zadok, Ahimelech, the leaders of the families of the priests and of the Levites. They did this just as their relatives, the priests, Aaron's descendants, had done. The families of the oldest brother and the youngest brother were treated the same.

> **Sidelight** It might seem strange if your minister started singing during a sermon. But 1 Chronicles 25:1 describes people who were chosen to preach – and play harps, lyres and cymbals. The cymbals must have helped if the sermon got boring.

The Music Groups

25 David and the commanders of the army chose some of the sons of Asaph, Heman and Jeduthun to preach and play harps, lyres *d* and cymbals. Here is a list of the men who served in this way:

²Asaph's sons who served were Zaccur, Joseph, Nethaniah and Asarelah. King David chose Asaph to preach, and Asaph directed his sons.

³Jeduthun's sons who served were Gedaliah, Zeri, Jeshaiah, Shimei, Hashabiah and Mattithiah. There were six of them, and Jeduthun directed them. He preached and used a harp to give thanks and praise to the LORD.

⁴Heman's sons who served were Bukkiah, Mattaniah, Uzziel, Shubael, Jerimoth, Hananiah, Hanani, Eliathah, Giddalti, Romamti-Ezer, Joshbekashah, Mallothi, Hothir and Mahazioth. ⁵All these were sons of Heman, David's seer. *d* God promised to make Heman strong, so Heman had many sons. God gave him fourteen sons and three daughters. ⁶Heman directed all his sons in making music for the Temple *d* of the LORD with cymbals, lyres and harps; that was their way of serving in the Temple of God. King David was in charge of Asaph, Jeduthun and Heman. ⁷These men and their relatives were trained and skilled in making music for the LORD. There were 288 of them. ⁸Everyone threw lots *d* to choose the time his family was to serve at the Temple. The young and the old, the teacher and the student, had to throw lots.

⁹First, the lot fell to Joseph, from the family of Asaph.

Second, twelve men were chosen from Gedaliah, his sons and relatives.

¹⁰Third, twelve men were chosen from Zaccur, his sons and relatives.

¹¹Fourth, twelve men were chosen from Izri, his sons and relatives.

¹²Fifth, twelve men were chosen from Nethaniah, his sons and relatives.

¹³Sixth, twelve men were chosen from Bukkiah, his sons and relatives.

¹⁴Seventh, twelve men were chosen from Jesarelah, his sons and relatives.

MUSIC

More Than Just a Song

Natalie was a very musical girl. She was one of those people who could just sit at a piano and play. Once she had heard a melody, she would play it straight back to you. When the youth pastor asked her if she would like to lead the worship at the Sunday evening service, she was flustered.

"Oh, I really don't think I could do that," she replied. "If you like, I could play along with the band, but I don't lead worship. You should ask Jason."

The youth pastor was puzzled. Natalie was far more musical than Jason. As far as he could remember, Jason didn't play anything, in fact, he could only recall him singing enthusiastically with his hands in the air. When he remarked on this to Natalie, she said:

"Oh but that's exactly what you want! To lead worship you have to have a ministry, you need to lead the people in praises to God. I can only play an instrument, but Jason could lead the people in worship."

The youth pastor was surprised at Natalie's insight into the situation and agreed to try Jason out. And she was right! Natalie took her place in the band and the music was wonderful, but the congregation followed Jason's lead and the worship was better than ever.

We all have gifts to use in our church, but there's a difference between playing music and leading worship. Natalie wisely understood this.

In **1 Chronicles 25:1–8** David chose some people who could play and some people who could preach to lead worship in the Temple.

* How did the men in verse 7 differ from Natalie?
* What gifts do you have that you've used in your church?

Consider . . .

* taking music lessons to develop any talents you have.
* approaching the church musicians and telling them you appreciate their help in worshipping the Lord.

For more, see . . .

* 1 Samuel 16:14–18 (p.270)
* Ephesians 5:19 (p.1275)
* Psalm 98:4–6 (p.558)

15Eighth, twelve men were chosen from Jeshaiah, his sons and relatives.

16Ninth, twelve men were chosen from Mattaniah, his sons and relatives.

17Tenth, twelve men were chosen from Shimei, his sons and relatives.

18Eleventh, twelve men were chosen from Azarel, his sons and relatives.

19Twelfth, twelve men were chosen from Hashabiah, his sons and relatives.

20Thirteenth, twelve men were chosen from Shubael, his sons and relatives.

21Fourteenth, twelve men were chosen from Mattithiah, his sons and relatives.

22Fifteenth, twelve men were chosen from Jerimoth, his sons and relatives.

23Sixteenth, twelve men were chosen from Hananiah, his sons and relatives.

24Seventeenth, twelve men were chosen from Joshbekashah, his sons and relatives.

25Eighteenth, twelve men were chosen from Hanani, his sons and relatives.

26Nineteenth, twelve men were chosen from Mallothi, his sons and relatives.

27Twentieth, twelve men were chosen from Eliathah, his sons and relatives.

28Twenty-first, twelve men were chosen from Hothir, his sons and relatives.

29Twenty-second, twelve men were chosen from Giddalti, his sons and relatives.

30Twenty-third, twelve men were chosen from Mahazioth, his sons and relatives.

31Twenty-fourth, twelve men were chosen from Romamti-Ezer, his sons and relatives.

The Gatekeepers

26 These are the groups of the gatekeepers. From the family of Korah, there was Meshelemiah son of Kore, who was from Asaph's family. 2Meshelemiah had sons. Zechariah was his first son, Jediael was second, Zebadiah was third, Jathniel was fourth, 3Elam was fifth, Jehohanan was sixth and Eliehoenai was seventh.

4Obed-Edom had sons. Shemaiah was his first son, Jehozabad was second, Joah was third, Sacar was fourth, Nethanel was fifth, 5Ammiel was sixth, Issachar was seventh and Peullethai was eighth. God blessed Obed-Edom with children.

6Obed-Edom's son Shemaiah also had sons. They were leaders in their father's family because they were capable men. 7Shemaiah's sons were Othni, Rephael, Obed, Elzabad, Elihu and Semakiah. Elihu and Semakiah were skilled workers. 8All these were Obed-Edom's descendants. d They and their sons and relatives were capable men and strong workers. Obed-Edom had 62 descendants in all.

9Meshelemiah had sons and relatives who were skilled workers. In all, there were eighteen.

10From the Merari family, Hosah had sons. Shimri was chosen to be in charge. Although he was not the oldest son, his father chose him to be in charge. 11Hilkiah was his second son, Tabaliah was third and Zechariah was fourth. In all, Hosah had thirteen sons and relatives.

12These were the leaders of the groups of gatekeepers, and they served in the Temple d of the Lord. Their relatives also worked in the Temple. 13By throwing lots, d each family chose a gate to guard. Young and old threw lots.

14Meshelemiah was chosen by lot to guard the East Gate. Then lots were thrown for Meshelemiah's son Zechariah. He was a wise counsellor and was chosen for the North Gate. 15Obed-Edom was chosen for the South Gate, and Obed-Edom's sons were chosen to guard the storehouse. 16Shuppim and Hosah were chosen for the West Gate and the Shalleketh Gate on the upper road.

Guards stood side by side with guards. 17Six Levites stood guard every day at the East Gate; four Levites stood guard every day at the North Gate; four Levites stood guard every day at the South Gate; and two Levites at a time guarded the storehouse. 18There were two guards at the western court and four guards on the road to the court.

19These were the groups of the gatekeepers from the families of Korah and Merari.

Other Leaders

20Other Levites were responsible for guarding the treasuries of the Temple d of God and for the places where the holy things were kept.

21Ladan was Gershon's son and the ancestor of several family groups. Jehiel was a leader of one of the family groups. 22His sons were Zetham and Joel his brother, and they were responsible for the treasuries of the Temple of the Lord.

23Other leaders were chosen from the family groups of Amram, Izhar, Hebron and Uzziel. 24Shubael, the descendant d of Gershom, who was Moses' son, was the leader responsible for the treasuries. 25These were Shubael's relatives from Eliezer: Eliezer's son Rehabiah, Rehabiah's son Jeshaiah, Jeshaiah's son Joram, Joram's son Zicri and Zicri's son Shelomith. 26Shelomith and his relatives were responsible for everything that had been collected for the Temple by King David, by the heads of families, by the commanders of 1,000 men and of 100 men, and by other army commanders. 27They also gave some of the things they had taken in wars to be used in repairing the Temple of the Lord. 28Shelomith and his relatives took care of all the holy things. Some had been given by Samuel the seer, *d* Saul son of Kish, Abner son of Ner and Joab son of Zeruiah.

²⁹Kenaniah was from the Izhar family. He and his sons worked outside the Temple as officers and judges in different places in Israel.

³⁰Hashabiah was from the Hebron family. He and his relatives were responsible for the Lord's work and the king's business in Israel west of the Jordan River. There were 1,700 skilled men in Hashabiah's group. ³¹The history of the Hebron family shows that Jeriah was their leader. In David's fortieth year as king, the records were searched, and some capable men of the Hebron family were found living at Jazer in Gilead. ³²Jeriah had 2,700 relatives who were skilled men and leaders of families. King David gave them the responsibility of directing the tribes *d* of Reuben, Gad and East Manasseh in God's work and the king's business.

Army Divisions

27 This is the list of the Israelites who served the king in the army. Each division was on duty one month each year. There were leaders of families, commanders of 100 men, commanders of 1,000 men, and other officers. Each division had 24,000 men.

²Jashobeam son of Zabdiel was in charge of the first division for the first month. There were 24,000 men in his division. ³Jashobeam, one of the descendants *d* of Perez, was leader of all the army officers for the first month.

⁴Dodai, from the Ahohites, was in charge of the division for the second month. Mikloth was a leader in the division. There were 24,000 men in Dodai's division.

⁵The third commander, for the third month, was Benaiah son of Jehoiada the priest. There were 24,000 men in his division. ⁶He was the Benaiah who was one of the Thirty *n* soldiers. Benaiah was a brave warrior who led those men. Benaiah's son Ammizabad was in charge of Benaiah's division.

⁷The fourth commander, for the fourth month, was Asahel, the brother of Joab. Later, Asahel's son Zebadiah took his place as commander. There were 24,000 men in his division.

⁸The fifth commander, for the fifth month, was Shamhuth, from Izrah's family. There were 24,000 men in his division.

⁹The sixth commander, for the sixth month, was Ira son of Ikkesh from the town of Tekoa. There were 24,000 men in his division.

¹⁰The seventh commander, for the seventh month, was Helez. He was from the Pelonites

and a descendant of Ephraim. There were 24,000 men in his division.

¹¹The eighth commander, for the eighth month, was Sibbecai. He was from Hushah and was from Zerah's family. There were 24,000 men in his division.

¹²The ninth commander, for the ninth month, was Abiezer. He was from Anathoth in Benjamin. There were 24,000 men in his division.

¹³The tenth commander, for the tenth month, was Maharai. He was from Netophah and was from Zerah's family. There were 24,000 men in his division.

¹⁴The eleventh commander, for the eleventh month, was Benaiah. He was from Pirathon in Ephraim. There were 24,000 men in his division.

¹⁵The twelfth commander, for the twelfth month, was Heldai. He was from Netophah and was from Othniel's family. There were 24,000 men in his division.

Leaders of the Tribes

¹⁶These were the leaders of the tribes *d* of Israel. Eliezer son of Zicri was over the tribe of Reuben. Shephatiah son of Maacah was over the tribe of Simeon. ¹⁷Hashabiah son of Kemuel was over the tribe of Levi. Zadok was over the people of Aaron. ¹⁸Elihu, one of David's brothers, was over the tribe of Judah. Omri son of Michael was over the tribe of Issachar. ¹⁹Ishmaiah son of Obadiah was over the tribe of Zebulun. Jerimoth son of Azriel was over the tribe of Naphtali. ²⁰Hoshea son of Azaziah was over the tribe of Ephraim. Joel son of Pedaiah was over West Manasseh. ²¹Iddo son of Zechariah was over East Manasseh. Jaasiel son of Abner was over the tribe of Benjamin. ²²Azarel son of Jeroham was over the tribe of Dan.

These were the leaders of the tribes of Israel.

²³The Lord had promised to make the Israelites as many as the stars in the sky. So David only counted the men who were 20 years old and older. ²⁴Joab son of Zeruiah began to count the people, but he did not finish. God became angry with Israel for counting the people, so the number of the people was not put in the history book about King David's rule.

The King's Directors

²⁵Azmaveth son of Adiel was in charge of the royal storehouses.

Jonathan son of Uzziah was in charge of the storehouses in the country, towns, villages and towers.

²⁶Ezri son of Kelub was in charge of the field workers who farmed the land.

Thirty These were David's most powerful soldiers. See 2 Samuel 23:20–39.

²⁷Shimei, from the town of Ramah, was in charge of the vineyards.

Zabdi, from Shapham, was in charge of storing the wine that came from the vineyards.

²⁸Baal-Hanan, from Geder, was in charge of the olive trees and sycamore trees in the western hills.

Joash was in charge of storing the olive oil.

²⁹Shitrai, from Sharon, was in charge of the herds that fed in the Plain of Sharon.

Shaphat son of Adlai was in charge of the herds in the valleys.

³⁰Obil, an Ishmaelite, was in charge of the camels.

Jehdeiah, from Meronoth, was in charge of the donkeys.

³¹Jaziz, from the Hagrites, was in charge of the flocks.

All these men were the officers who took care of King David's property.

³²Jonathan was David's uncle, and he advised David. Jonathan was a wise man and a teacher of the law. Jehiel son of Hacmoni took care of the king's sons. ³³Ahithophel advised the king. Hushai, from the Arkite people, was the king's friend. ³⁴Jehoiada and Abiathar later took Ahithophel's place in advising the king. Jehoiada was Benaiah's son. Joab was the commander of the king's army.

David's Plans for the Temple

28 David commanded all the leaders of Israel to come to Jerusalem. There were the leaders of the tribes, *d* commanders of the divisions serving the king, commanders of 1,000 men and of 100 men, leaders who took care of the property and animals that belonged to the king and his sons, men over the palace, the powerful men and all the brave warriors.

²King David stood up and said, "Listen to me, my relatives and my people. I wanted to build a place to keep the Ark *d* of the Agreement with the LORD. I wanted it to be God's footstool. So I made plans to build a temple. ³But God said to me, 'You must not build a temple for worshipping me, because you are a soldier and have killed many people.'

⁴"But the LORD, the God of Israel, chose me from my whole family to be king of Israel for ever. He chose the tribe of Judah to lead, and from the people of Judah, he chose my father's family. From that family God was pleased to make me king of Israel. ⁵The LORD has given me many sons, and from those sons he has chosen Solomon to be the new king of Israel. Israel is the LORD's kingdom. ⁶The LORD said to me, 'Your son Solomon will build my Temple *d* and its courtyards. I have chosen Solomon to be my son, and

I will be his father. ⁷He is obeying my laws and commands now. If he continues to obey them, I will make his kingdom strong for ever.'"

⁸David said, "Now, in front of all Israel, the assembly of the LORD, and in the hearing of God, I tell you these things: be careful to obey all the commands of the LORD your God. Then you will keep this good land and pass it on to your descendants *d* for ever.

⁹"And you, my son Solomon, accept the God of your father. Serve him completely and willingly, because the LORD knows what is in everyone's mind. He understands everything you think. If you go to him for help, you will get an answer. But if you turn away from him, he will leave you for ever. ¹⁰Solomon, you must understand this. The LORD has chosen you to build the Temple as his holy place. Be strong and finish the job."

¹¹Then David gave his son Solomon the plans for building the Temple and the courtyard around the Temple. They included its buildings, its storerooms, its upper rooms, its inside rooms and the place where the people's sins were cancelled. ¹²David gave him plans for everything he had in mind: the courtyards around the LORD's Temple and all the rooms around it, the Temple treasuries and the treasuries of the holy things used in the Temple. ¹³David gave Solomon directions for the groups of the priests and Levites. David told him about all the work of serving in the Temple of the LORD and about the things to be used in the Temple service ¹⁴that were made of gold or silver. David told Solomon how much gold or silver should be used to make each thing. ¹⁵David told him how much gold to use for each gold lampstand and its lamps and how much silver to use for each silver lampstand and its lamps. The different lampstands were to be used where needed. ¹⁶David told him how much gold should be used for each table that held the holy bread and how much silver should be used for the silver tables. ¹⁷He told how much pure gold should be used to make the forks, bowls and pitchers and how much gold should be used to make each gold dish. He told how much silver should be used to make each silver dish ¹⁸and how much pure gold should be used for the altar of incense. *d* He also gave Solomon the plans for the chariot of the golden creatures that spread their wings over the Ark of the Agreement with the LORD.

¹⁹David said, "All these plans were written with the LORD guiding me. He helped me understand everything in the plans."

²⁰David also said to his son Solomon, "Be strong and brave, and do the work. Don't be afraid or discouraged, because the LORD God, my God, is with you. He will not fail you or leave you

until all the work for the Temple of the LORD is finished. ²¹The groups of the priests and Levites are ready for all the work on the Temple of God. Every skilled worker is ready to help you with all the work. The leaders and all the people will obey every command you give."

Gifts for Building the Temple

29 King David said to all the Israelites who were gathered, "God chose my son Solomon, who is young and hasn't yet learned what he needs to know, but the work is important. This palace is not for people; it is for the LORD God. ²I have done my best to prepare for building the Temple*d* of God. I have given gold for the things made of gold and silver for the things made of silver. I have given bronze for the things made of bronze and iron for the things made of iron. I have given wood for the things made of wood and onyx for the settings. I have given turquoise gems of many different colours, valuable stones and white marble. I have given much of all these things. ³I have already given this for the Temple, but now I am also giving my own treasures of gold and silver, because I really want the Temple of my God to be built. ⁴I have given about 100 tonnes of pure gold from Ophir and about 236 tonnes of pure silver. They will be used to cover the walls of the buildings ⁵and for all the gold and silver work. Skilled men may use the gold and silver to make things for the Temple. Now, who is ready to give himself to the service of the LORD today?"

ENVIRONMENT

Promises, Promises

The phone was ringing. This meant a couple of things to Harry. One, in his line of work it would be some stress-relating public relations problem. Two, he needed a cigarette. The two things went together. Ever since he'd joined the PR company he had this routine. Dealing with journalists and the media in general was hard work. He'd seen a lot of his colleagues turn to drink at the end of a rough day and he didn't want to go down the same road. So, if he had a cigarette he felt that it calmed him down and he could cope.

The trouble was, Harry was a Christian. He was very involved in his church and dedicated to helping his youth group.

On this particularly stressful day, Harry took time out to pray.

"Lord, help me to cope . . . " he said, and then lit up his cigarette and answered the phone.

As he finished the phone call, a workmate walked into the room.

"Phew, Harry it's like a fiery furnace in here with all that smoke!" he wafted his hands around. "Can't be good for you, and it's not doing me much good either." He started coughing. "Ugh, what are you putting in your body?"

It was only then that Harry remembered last week's Bible study. It was about the body being like a temple for the Holy Spirit, but he thought that it meant things like drugs and booze . . .

For the first time, he realised that God was telling him that he was polluting his body, the body that Jesus had bought with a price.

He made a firm promise to God there and then that he would never damage his body this way again. And he didn't.

1 Chronicles 28:4–8 talks of cleansing.

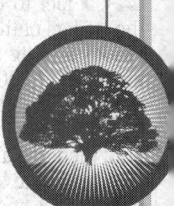

- How could Harry make himself ready, according to this passage?
- What impurities can you remove from your life to help you prepare for service?

Consider . . .

- embarking on a more healthy eating programme to help improve your physical well-being.
- writing down one thing that hinders your service to God. Ask God to help you put a stop to it.

For more, see . . .

- 1 Corinthians 3:16–17 (p.1218)
- Ephesians 5:26–27 (p.1276)
- 2 Corinthians 6:16–7:1 (p.1247)

⁶The family leaders and the leaders of the tribes of Israel, the commanders of 1,000 men and of 100 men, and the leaders responsible for the king's work gave their valuable things. ⁷They gave about 170 tonnes of gold, about 350 tonnes of silver, about 600 tonnes of bronze and about 3,500 tonnes of iron to the Temple of God. ⁸People who had valuable gems gave them to the treasury of the Temple of the LORD, and Jehiel, from the Gershon family, took care of the valuable gems. ⁹The leaders gave willingly and completely to the LORD. The people rejoiced to see their leaders give so gladly, and King David was also very happy.

David's Prayer

¹⁰David praised the LORD in front of all the people who were gathered. He said:

"We praise you, LORD,
   God of our father Israel.
We praise you for ever and ever.
¹¹LORD, you are great and powerful.
You have glory, victory and honour.
Everything in heaven and on earth belongs
   to you.

The kingdom belongs to you, LORD;
   you are the ruler over everything.
¹²Riches and honour come from you.
   You rule everything.
You have the power and strength
   to make anyone great and strong.
¹³Now, our God, we thank you
   and praise your glorious name.

¹⁴"These things did not really come from me
   and my people.
Everything comes from you;
   we have given you back what you gave us.
¹⁵We are like foreigners and strangers,
   as our ancestors were.
Our time on earth is like a shadow.
   There is no hope.
¹⁶LORD our God, we have gathered all this
   to build your Temple for worship of you.
But everything has come from you;
   everything belongs to you.
¹⁷I know, my God, that you test people's
   hearts.
You are happy when people do what is
   right.

THANKFULNESS

A Letter to Dad

Amanda was twenty when she moved away from home to work for the summer. While she was away she wrote this letter.

"Lately I've thought of you often and wanted to thank you for many things!

I suppose I've started seeing the simple things that you and Mum taught us. The basics – like manners and respect – but also contentment with what we have, finding joy in each other, listening, forgiving and understanding. You taught us that those things not only make life flow more smoothly, but that they also show Jesus to the world. Now I understand!

Dad, I miss being able to share things with you. You always listen and understand. Thank you for all your time, love and care. You've planted many seeds. I know I'll be reaping from this garden for a lifetime!"

Amanda showed her appreciation for her father through a letter. In **1 Chronicles 29:10–13**, King David thanked his heavenly father for all he had done for Israel.

* How are Amanda's letter and David's prayer alike?
* How can you, like David, express your praise to God?

Consider . . .

* writing a poem expressing your thanks to God for something.
* sending a card to thank someone for something he or she has done for you.

For more, see . . .

* Psalm 100 (p.558)
* Revelation 7:9–12 (p.1393)
* Ephesians 1:15–16 (p.1269)

I was happy to give all these things,
and I gave with an honest heart.
Your people gathered here are happy to give
to you,
and I rejoice to see their giving.
¹⁸LORD, you are the God of our ancestors,
the God of Abraham, Isaac and Jacob.
Make your people want to serve you always,
and make them want to obey you.
¹⁹Give my son Solomon a desire to serve you.
Help him always obey your commands,
laws and rules.
Help him build the Temple
for which I have prepared."

²⁰Then David said to all the people who were gathered, "Praise the LORD your God." So they all praised the LORD, the God of their ancestors, and they bowed to the ground to give honour to the LORD and the king.

Solomon Becomes King

²¹The next day the people sacrificed to the LORD. They offered burnt offerings to him of 1,000 bulls, 1,000 rams and 1,000 male lambs. They also brought drink offerings. Many sacrifices were made for all the people of Israel. ²²That day the people ate and drank with much joy, and the LORD was with them.

And they made David's son Solomon king for the second time. They poured olive oil on Solomon to appoint him king in the presence of the LORD. And they poured oil on Zadok to appoint him as priest. ²³Then Solomon sat on the LORD's throne as king and took his father David's place. Solomon was very successful, and all the people of Israel obeyed him. ²⁴All the leaders and soldiers and King David's sons accepted Solomon as king and promised to obey him. ²⁵The LORD made Solomon great before all the Israelites and gave Solomon much honour. No king of Israel before Solomon had such honour.

David's Death

²⁶David son of Jesse was king over all Israel. ²⁷He had ruled over Israel 40 years—seven years in Hebron and 33 years in Jerusalem. ²⁸David died when he was old. He had lived a good, long life and had received many riches and honours. His son Solomon became king after him.

²⁹Everything David did as king, from beginning to end, is recorded in the records of Samuel the seer, *d* the records of Nathan the prophet and the records of Gad the seer. ³⁰Those writings tell what David did as king of Israel. They tell about his power and what happened to him and to Israel and to all the kingdoms around them.

2 Chronicles

Why Read This Book:

* See how following God can unite people and help them to prosper (2 Chronicles 1—9).
* Learn what can happen when people turn away from God (2 Chronicles 10—36).

When?

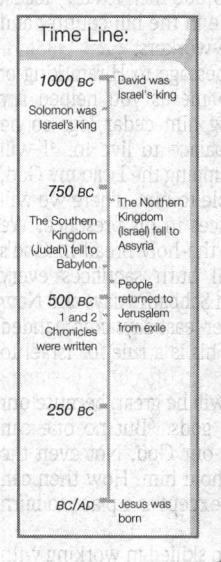

Time Line:

1000 BC	David was Israel's king
Solomon was Israel's king	
750 BC	The Northern Kingdom (Israel) fell to Assyria
The Southern Kingdom (Judah) fell to Babylon	
500 BC	People returned to Jerusalem from exile
1 and 2 Chronicles were written	
250 BC	
BC/AD	Jesus was born

Behind the Scenes:

If God offered to grant you a wish, what would you request? Popularity? Lots of money? Good looks? Fame? A new sports car?

When 2 Chronicles begins, Solomon had inherited Israel from his father, David, and God promised to give him whatever he asked for. Instead of asking for wealth or military power, Solomon requested wisdom to govern Israel the way that God wanted. His wish was granted. 2 Chronicles describes a glorious reign for Solomon. Central to Solomon's impact was the spectacular Temple that he built for God in Jerusalem. (See the introduction to 1 Kings for the rest of the story.)

Unfortunately, the nation struggled after Solomon's death. First, a civil war divided Israel into two kingdoms. The North – keeping the name Israel – rejected rule by David's descendants and chose its own king. The South – adopting the name Judah – kept David's descendants in power but had trouble maintaining a relationship with God.

2 Chronicles traces the history of the Israelites after King David, beginning with the united kingdom under Solomon and then focusing on Judah after the kingdom divided. The story is similar to the accounts in 1 and 2 Kings (p.311 and p.343).

2 Chronicles continues the message of 1 Chronicles, since they were originally one book (see 1 Chronicles introduction, p.372). The writer is retelling the history of Israel and Judah as a reminder and warning that the nation's success is directly linked to its relationship with God.

Where?

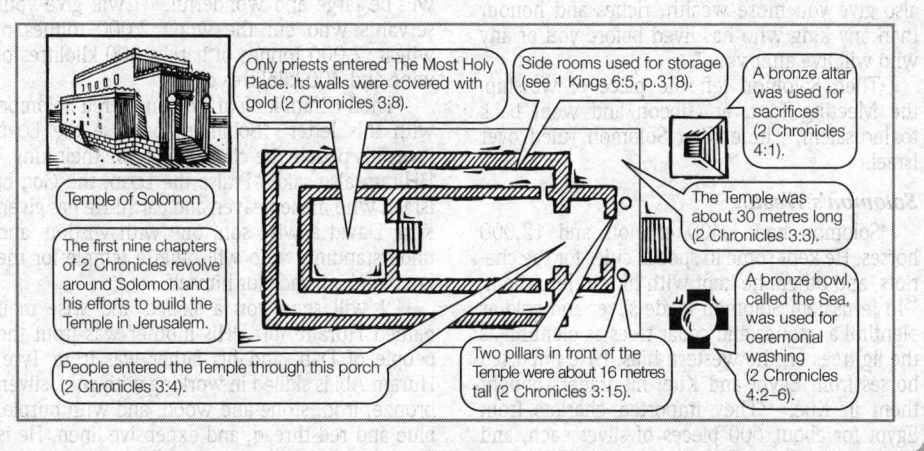

Temple of Solomon

The first nine chapters of 2 Chronicles revolve around Solomon and his efforts to build the Temple in Jerusalem.

Only priests entered The Most Holy Place. Its walls were covered with gold (2 Chronicles 3:8).

Side rooms used for storage (see 1 Kings 6:5, p.318).

A bronze altar was used for sacrifices (2 Chronicles 4:1).

The Temple was about 30 metres long (2 Chronicles 3:3).

A bronze bowl, called the Sea, was used for ceremonial washing (2 Chronicles 4:2–6).

People entered the Temple through this porch (2 Chronicles 3:4).

Two pillars in front of the Temple were about 16 metres tall (2 Chronicles 3:15).

Solomon Asks for Wisdom

1 Solomon, David's son, became a powerful king, because the LORD his God was with him and made him very great.

²Solomon spoke to all the people of Israel—the commanders of 100 men and of 1,000 men, the judges, every leader in all Israel and the leaders of the families. ³Then Solomon and all the people with him went to the place of worship at the town of Gibeon. God's Meeting Tent, *d* which Moses the LORD's servant had made in the desert, was there. ⁴David had brought the Ark *d* of God from Kiriath Jearim to Jerusalem, where he had made a place for it and had set up a tent for it. ⁵The bronze altar that Bezalel son of Uri, who was the son of Hur, had made was in Gibeon in front of the Holy Tent. So Solomon and the people worshipped there. ⁶Solomon went up to the bronze altar in the presence of the LORD at the Meeting Tent and offered 1,000 burnt offerings on it.

⁷That night God appeared to Solomon and said to him, "Ask for whatever you want me to give you."

⁸Solomon answered, "You have been very kind to my father David, and you have made me king in his place. ⁹Now, LORD God, may your promise to my father David come true. You have made me king of a people who are as many as the dust of the earth. ¹⁰Now give me wisdom and knowledge so that I can lead these people in the right way, because no one can rule them without your help."

¹¹God said to Solomon, "You have not asked for wealth or riches or honour, or for the death of your enemies, or for a long life. But since you have asked for wisdom and knowledge to lead my people, over whom I have made you king, ¹²I will give you wisdom and knowledge. I will also give you more wealth, riches and honour than any king who has lived before you or any who will live after you."

¹³Then Solomon left the place of worship, the Meeting Tent, at Gibeon and went back to Jerusalem. There King Solomon ruled over Israel.

Solomon's Wealth

¹⁴Solomon had 1,400 chariots and 12,000 horses. He kept some in special cities for the chariots, and others he kept with him in Jerusalem. ¹⁵In Jerusalem Solomon made silver and gold as plentiful as stones and cedar trees as plentiful as the fig trees on the western hills. ¹⁶He imported horses from Egypt and Kue; his traders bought them in Kue. ¹⁷They imported chariots from Egypt for about 600 pieces of silver each, and horses cost nearly 150 pieces of silver apiece.

Then they sold the horses and chariots to all the kings of the Hittites and the Arameans.

Solomon Prepares for the Temple

2 Solomon decided to build a temple *d* as a place to worship the LORD and also a palace for himself. ²He chose 70,000 men to carry loads, 80,000 men to cut stone in the hill country and 3,600 men to direct the workers.

³Solomon sent this message to Hiram king of the city of Tyre: "Help me as you helped my father David by sending him cedar logs so he could build himself a palace to live in. ⁴I will build a temple for worshipping the LORD my God, and I will give this temple to him. There we will burn sweet-smelling spices in his presence. We will continually set out the holy bread in God's presence. And we will burn sacrifices every morning and evening, on Sabbath *d* days and New Moons, *d* and on the other feast days commanded by the LORD our God. This is a rule for Israel to obey for ever.

⁵"The temple I build will be great, because our God is greater than all gods. ⁶But no one can really build a house for our God. Not even the highest of heavens can hold him. How then can I build a temple for him except as a place to burn sacrifices to him?

⁷"Now send me a man skilled in working with gold, silver, bronze and iron, and with purple, red and blue thread. He must also know how to make engravings. He will work with my skilled craftsmen in Judah and Jerusalem, whom my father David chose.

⁸"Also send me cedar, pine and juniper logs from Lebanon. I know your servants are experienced at cutting down the trees in Lebanon, and my servants will help them. ⁹Send me a lot of wood, because the temple I am going to build will be large and wonderful. ¹⁰I will give your servants who cut the wood 2,000 tonnes of wheat, 2,000 tonnes of barley, 400 kilolitres of wine and 400 kilolitres of oil."

¹¹Then Hiram king of Tyre answered Solomon with this letter: "Solomon, because the LORD loves his people, he chose you to be their king." ¹²Hiram also said: "Praise the LORD, the God of Israel, who made heaven and earth! He has given King David a wise son, one with wisdom and understanding, who will build a temple for the LORD and a palace for himself.

¹³"I will send you a skilled and wise man named Huram-Abi. ¹⁴His mother was from the people of Dan, and his father was from Tyre. Huram-Abi is skilled in working with gold, silver, bronze, iron, stone and wood, and with purple, blue and red thread, and expensive linen. He is skilled in making engravings and can make any

design you show him. He will help your crafts-men and the craftsmen of your father David.

[15]"Now send my servants the wheat, barley, oil and wine you promised. [16]We will cut as much wood from Lebanon as you need and will bring it on rafts by sea to Joppa. Then you may carry it to Jerusalem."

[17]Solomon counted all the foreigners living in Israel. (This was after the time his father David had counted the people.) There were 153,600 foreigners in the country. [18]Solomon chose 70,000 of them to carry loads, 80,000 of them to cut stone in the mountains and 3,600 of them to direct the workers and to keep the people working.

> ## Sidelight
>
> Mount Moriah, where Solomon built the Temple (2 Chronicles 3:1), is a highly sacred spot for modern-day Christians, Jews and Muslims. It is traditionally where Abraham offered his son Isaac as a sacrifice (Genesis 22:2, p.25) and where God came to David (2 Samuel 24:18, p.310). The Dome of the Rock, a Muslim shrine, has occupied this traditional spot since the seventh century AD.

Solomon Builds the Temple

3 Then Solomon began to build the Temple [d] of the Lord in Jerusalem on Mount Moriah. This was where the Lord had appeared to David, Solomon's father. Solomon built the Temple on the place David had prepared on the threshing [d] floor of Araunah the Jebusite. [2]Solomon began building in the second month of the fourth year he ruled Israel.

[3]Solomon used these measurements for build-ing the Temple of God. It was 30 metres long and 10 metres wide, using the old measurement. [4]The porch in front of the main room of the Tem-ple was 10 metres long and 10 metres high.

He covered the inside of the porch with pure gold. [5]He put panels of pine on the walls of the main room and covered them with pure gold. Then he put designs of palm trees and chains in the gold. [6]He decorated the Temple with gems and gold from Parvaim. [n] [7]He put gold on the Temple's ceiling beams, doorposts, walls and doors, and he carved creatures with wings on the walls.

[8]Then he made the Most Holy Place. It was 10 metres long and 10 metres wide, as wide as the Temple. He covered its walls with over 20 tonnes of pure gold. [9]The gold nails weighed over 500

grammes. He also covered the upper rooms with gold.

[10]He made two creatures with wings for the Most Holy Place and covered them with gold. [11]The wings of the gold creatures were 10 metres across. One wing of one creature was 2.5 metres long and touched the Temple wall. The crea-ture's other wing was also 2.5 metres long, and it touched a wing of the second creature. [12]One wing of the second creature touched the other side of the room and was also 2.5 metres long. The second creature's other wing touched the first creature's wing, and it was also 2.5 metres long. [13]Together, the creatures' wings were 10 metres across. The creatures stood on their feet, facing the main room.

[14]He made the curtain of blue, purple and red thread, and expensive linen, and he put designs of creatures with wings in it.

[15]He made two pillars to stand in front of the Temple. They were about 16 metres tall, and the capital [d] of each pillar was over 2 metres tall. [16]He made a net of chains and put them on the tops of the pillars. He made 100 pomegranates [d] and put them on the chains. [17]Then he put the pillars up in front of the Temple. One pillar stood on the south side, the other on the north. He named the south pillar He Establishes and the north pillar In Him Is Strength.

Things for the Temple

4 He made a bronze altar 10 metres long, 10 metres wide and 5 metres tall. [2]Then he made from bronze a large round bowl, which was called the Sea. It was 15 metres around, 5 metres across and 2.5 metres deep. [3]There were carvings of bulls under the rim of the bowl—ten bulls every 50 centimetres. They were in two rows and were made in one piece with the bowl.

[4]The bowl rested on the backs of twelve bronze bulls that faced outwards from the centre of the bowl. Three bulls faced north, three faced west, three faced south and three faced east. [5]The sides of the bowl were 8 centimetres thick, and it held about 60,000 litres. The rim of the bowl was like the rim of a cup or like a lily blossom.

[6]He made ten smaller bowls and put five on the south side and five on the north. They were for washing the animals for the burnt offerings, but the large bowl was for the priests to wash in.

[7]He made ten lampstands of gold, following the plans. He put them in the Temple, [d] five on the south side and five on the north.

[8]He made ten tables and put them in the Tem-ple, five on the south side and five on the north. And he used gold to make 100 other bowls.

Parvaim　There was a lot of gold there. It may have been in the country of Ophir.

⁹He also made the priests' courtyard and the large courtyard. He made the doors that opened to the courtyard and covered them with bronze. ¹⁰Then he put the large bowl in the south-east corner of the Temple.

¹¹Huram-Abi also made bowls, shovels and small bowls. So he finished his work for King Solomon on the Temple of God:

¹²two pillars;

two large bowls for the capitals on top of the pillars;

two nets to cover the two large bowls for the capitals on top of the pillars;

¹³400 pomegranates *d* for the two nets (there were two rows of pomegranates for each net covering the bowls for the capitals on top of the pillars);

¹⁴the stands with a bowl on each stand;

¹⁵the large bowl with twelve bulls under it;

¹⁶the pots, shovels, forks and all the objects to go with them.

All the things that Huram-Abi made for King Solomon for the Temple of the LORD were made of polished bronze. ¹⁷The king had these things poured into clay moulds that were made in the plain of the Jordan River between Succoth and Zarethan. ¹⁸Solomon had so many things made that the total weight of all the bronze was never known.

¹⁹Solomon also made all the things for God's Temple: the golden altar; tables which held the bread that shows God's people are in his presence; ²⁰the lampstands and their lamps of pure gold, to burn in front of the Most Holy Place as planned; ²¹the flowers, lamps and tongs of pure gold; ²²the pure gold wick trimmers, small bowls, pans and dishes used to carry coals; the gold doors for the Temple; and the inside doors of the Most Holy Place and of the main room.

5 Finally all the work Solomon did for the Temple *d* of the LORD was finished. He brought in everything his father David had set apart for the Temple—all the silver and gold and everything. And he put everything in the treasuries of God's Temple.

The Ark is Brought into the Temple

²Solomon called for the elders of Israel, the heads of the tribes *d* and the leaders of the families to come to him in Jerusalem. He wanted them to bring the Ark *d* of the Agreement with the LORD from the older part of the city. ³So all the Israelites came together with the king during the festival in the seventh month.

⁴When all the elders of Israel arrived, the Levites lifted up the Ark. ⁵They carried the Ark of the Agreement, the Meeting Tent *d* and the holy utensils in it; the priests and the Levites brought them up. ⁶King Solomon and all the Israelites gathered before the Ark of the Agreement and sacrificed so many sheep and bulls no one could count them.

⁷Then the priests put the Ark of the Agreement with the LORD in its place inside the Most Holy Place in the Temple, *d* under the wings of the

> **Sidelight** Imagine having services in the street outside your church. That's what the ancient Israelites did. The Temple was considered God's house, which was symbolised by putting the Ark of the Agreement in it (2 Chronicles 5:2, 7). It wasn't really a place to gather for worship or study. They had meetings outside the Temple. But they had the weather for it too!

golden creatures. ⁸The wings of these creatures were spread out over the place for the Ark, covering it and its carrying poles. ⁹The carrying poles were so long that anyone standing in the Holy Place in front of the Most Holy Place could see the ends of the poles. But no one could see them from outside the Holy Place. The poles are still there today. ¹⁰The only things inside the Ark were two stone tablets*n* that Moses had put in the Ark at Mount Sinai. That was where the LORD made his agreement with the Israelites after they came out of Egypt.

¹¹Then all the priests left the Holy Place. (All the priests from each group had made themselves ready to serve the LORD.) ¹²All the Levite musicians—Asaph, Heman, Jeduthun and all their sons and relatives—stood on the east side of the altar. They were dressed in white linen and played cymbals, harps and lyres.*d* With them were 120 priests who blew trumpets. ¹³Those who blew the trumpets and those who sang together sounded like one person as they praised and thanked the LORD. They sang as others played their trumpets, cymbals and other instruments. They praised the LORD with this song:

"He is good;

his love continues for ever."

Then the Temple of the LORD was filled with a cloud. ¹⁴The priests could not continue their work because of the cloud, because the LORD's glory filled the Temple of God.

---

stone tablets   They were the two stone tablets on which God wrote the Ten Commandments.

Solomon Speaks to the People

6 Then Solomon said, "The LORD said he would live in the dark cloud. ²LORD, I have built a wonderful Temple *d* for you—a place for you to live in for ever."

³While all the Israelites were standing there, King Solomon turned to them and blessed them. ⁴Then he said, "Praise the LORD, the God of Israel. He has done what he promised to my father David. The LORD said, ⁵'Since the time I brought my people out of Egypt, I have not chosen a city in any tribe *d* of Israel where a temple will be built for me. I did not choose a man to lead my people Israel. ⁶But now I have chosen Jerusalem as the place I am to be worshipped, and I have chosen David to lead my people Israel.'

⁷"My father David wanted to build a temple for the LORD, the God of Israel. ⁸But the LORD said to my father David, 'It was good that you wanted to build a temple for me. ⁹But you are not the one to build it. Your son, who comes from your own body, is the one who will build my temple.'

¹⁰"Now the LORD has kept his promise. I am the king now in place of David my father. Now I rule Israel as the LORD promised, and I have built the Temple for the LORD, the God of Israel. ¹¹There I have put the Ark, *d* in which is the Agreement the LORD made with the Israelites."

Solomon's Prayer

¹²Then Solomon stood facing the LORD's altar, and all the Israelites were standing behind him. He spread out his hands. ¹³He had made a bronze platform 2.5 metres long, 2.5 metres wide and 1.5 metres high, and he had placed it in the middle of the outer courtyard. Solomon stood on the platform. Then he kneeled in front of all the people of Israel gathered there, and he spread out his hands towards the sky. ¹⁴He said, "LORD, God of Israel, there is no god like you in heaven or on earth. You keep your agreement of love with your servants who truly follow you. ¹⁵You have kept the promise you made to your servant David, my father. You spoke it with your own mouth and finished it with your hands today.

¹⁶"Now, LORD, God of Israel, keep the promise you made to your servant David, my father. You said, 'If your sons are careful to obey my teachings as you have obeyed, there will always be someone from your family ruling Israel.' ¹⁷Now, LORD, God of Israel, please continue to keep that promise you made to your servant.

¹⁸"But, God, can you really live here on the earth with people? The sky and the highest place in heaven cannot contain you. Surely this house which I have built cannot contain you. ¹⁹But please listen to my prayer and my request, because I am your servant. LORD my God, hear this prayer your servant prays to you. ²⁰Day and night please watch over this Temple *d* where you have said you would be worshipped. Hear the prayer I pray facing this Temple. ²¹Hear my prayers and the prayers of your people Israel when we pray facing this place. Hear from your home in heaven, and when you hear, forgive us.

²²"If someone wrongs another person, he will be brought to the altar in this Temple. If he swears an oath that he is not guilty, ²³then hear in heaven. Judge the case, punish the guilty, but declare that the innocent person is not guilty.

²⁴"When your people, the Israelites, sin against you, their enemies will defeat them. But if they come back to you and praise you and pray to you in this Temple, ²⁵then listen from heaven. Forgive the sin of your people Israel, and bring them back to the land you gave to them and their ancestors.

²⁶"When they sin against you, you will stop the rain from falling on their land. Then they will pray, facing this place and praising you; they will stop sinning when you make them suffer. ²⁷When this happens, hear their prayer in heaven, and forgive the sins of your servants, the Israelites. Teach them to do what is right. Then please send rain to this land you have given particularly to them.

²⁸"At times the land will get so dry that no food will grow, or a great sickness will spread among the people. Sometimes the crops will be destroyed by locusts *d* or grasshoppers. Your people will be attacked in their cities by their enemies, or will become sick. ²⁹When any of these things happens, the people will become truly sorry. If your people spread their hands in prayer towards this Temple, ³⁰then hear their prayers from your home in heaven. Forgive and treat each person as he should be treated because you know what is in a person's heart. Only you know what is in people's hearts. ³¹Then the people will respect and obey you as long as they live in this land you gave our ancestors.

³²"People who are not Israelites, foreigners from other lands, will hear about your greatness and power. They will come from far away to pray at this Temple. ³³Then hear from your home in heaven, and do whatever they ask you. Then people everywhere will know you and respect you, just as your people Israel do. Then everyone will know that I built this Temple as a place to worship you.

³⁴"When your people go out to fight their enemies along some road on which you send them, your people will pray to you, facing this city which you have chosen and the Temple I have built for you. ³⁵Then hear in heaven their prayers and do what is right.

³⁶"Everyone sins, so your people will also sin against you. You will become angry with them and will hand them over to their enemies. Their enemies will capture them and take them away to a country far or near. ³⁷Your people will be sorry for their sins when they are held as prisoners in another country. They will be sorry and pray to you in the land where they are held as prisoners, saying, 'We have sinned. We have done wrong and acted wickedly.' ³⁸They will truly turn back to you in the land where they are captives. They will pray, facing this land you gave their ancestors, this city you have chosen and the Temple I have built for you. ³⁹Then hear their prayers from your home in heaven and do what is right. Forgive your people who have sinned against you.

⁴⁰"Now, my God, look at us. Listen to the prayers we pray in this place.

⁴¹Now, rise, Lord God, and come to your
resting place.
Come with the Ark ^d of the Agreement that
shows your strength.
Let your priests receive your salvation,
Lord God,
and may your holy people be happy
because of your goodness.
⁴²Lord God, do not reject your appointed one.
Remember your love for your servant
David."

The Temple is Given to the Lord

7 When Solomon finished praying, fire came down from the sky and burned up the burnt offering and the sacrifices. The Lord's glory filled the Temple. ^d ²The priests could not enter the Temple of the Lord, because the Lord's glory filled it. ³When all the people of Israel saw the fire come down from heaven and the Lord's glory on the Temple, they bowed down on the pavement with their faces to the ground. They worshipped and thanked the Lord, saying,

"He is good;
his love continues for ever."

⁴Then King Solomon and all the people offered sacrifices to the Lord. ⁵King Solomon offered a sacrifice of 22,000 cattle and 120,000 sheep. So the king and all the people gave the Temple to God. ⁶The priests stood ready to do their work. The Levites also stood with the instruments of the Lord's music that King David had made for praising the Lord. The priests and Levites were saying, "His love continues for ever." The priests, who stood across from the Levites, blew their trumpets, and all the Israelites were standing.

⁷Solomon made holy the middle part of the courtyard, which is in front of the Temple of the Lord. There he offered whole burnt offerings and the fat of the fellowship offerings. He offered them in the courtyard, because the bronze altar he had made could not hold the burnt offerings, grain offerings and fat.

⁸Solomon and all the Israelites celebrated the festival for seven days. There were many people, and they came from as far away as Lebo Hamath and the brook of Egypt. ⁹For seven days they celebrated giving the altar for the worship of God. Then they celebrated the festival for seven days. On the eighth day they had a meeting. ¹⁰On the twenty-third day of the seventh month Solomon sent the people home, full of joy. They were happy because the Lord had been so good to David, Solomon and his people Israel.

The Lord Appears to Solomon

¹¹Solomon finished the Temple ^d of the Lord and his royal palace. He had success in doing everything he planned in the Temple of the Lord and his own palace. ¹²Then the Lord appeared to Solomon at night and said to him, "I have heard your prayer and have chosen this place for myself to be a Temple for sacrifices.

¹³"I may stop the sky from sending rain. I may command the locusts ^d to destroy the land. I may send sicknesses to my people. ¹⁴Then if my people, who are called by my name, are sorry for what they have done, if they pray and obey me and stop their evil ways, I will hear them from heaven. I will forgive their sin, and I will heal their land. ¹⁵Now I will see them, and I will listen to the prayers prayed in this place. ¹⁶I have chosen this Temple and made it holy. So I will be worshipped there for ever. Yes, I will always watch over it and love it.

¹⁷"But you must serve me as your father David did. You must obey all I have commanded and keep my laws and rules. ¹⁸If you do, I will make your kingdom strong. This is the agreement I made with your father David, saying, 'Someone from your family will always rule in Israel.'

¹⁹"But you must follow me and obey the laws and commands I have given you. You must not serve or worship other gods. ²⁰If you do, I will take the Israelites out of my land, the land I have given them, and I will leave this Temple that I have made holy. All the nations will make fun of it and speak evil about it. ²¹This Temple is honoured now, but then, everyone who passes by will be shocked. They will ask, 'Why did the Lord do this terrible thing to this land and this Temple?' ²²People will answer, 'This happened because they left the Lord, the God of their ancestors, the God who brought them out of Egypt. They decided to follow other gods and worshipped and served them, so he brought all this disaster on them.'"

Solomon's Other Achievements

8 By the end of 20 years, Solomon had built the Temple *d* of the LORD and the royal palace. ²Solomon rebuilt the towns that Hiram had given him, and Solomon sent Israelites to live in them. ³Then he went to Hamath Zobah and captured it. ⁴Solomon also built the town of Tadmor in the desert, and he built all the towns in Hamath as towns for storing grain and supplies. ⁵He rebuilt the towns of Upper Beth Horon and Lower Beth Horon, protecting them with strong walls, gates and bars in the gates. ⁶He also rebuilt the town of Baalath. And he built all the other towns for storage and all the cities for his chariots and horses. He built all he wanted in Jerusalem, Lebanon and everywhere he ruled.

⁷There were other people in the land who were not Israelites—the Hittites, Amorites, Perizzites, Hivites and Jebusites. ⁸They were descendants *d* of the people that the Israelites had not destroyed. Solomon forced them to be slave workers, as is still true today. ⁹But Solomon did not make slaves of the Israelites. They were his soldiers, chief captains, commanders of his chariots and his chariot drivers. ¹⁰These were his most important officers. There were 250 of them to direct the people.

¹¹Solomon brought the daughter of the king of Egypt from the older part of Jerusalem to the palace he had built for her. Solomon said, "My wife must not live in King David's palace, because the places where the Ark *d* of the Agreement has been are holy."

¹²Then Solomon offered burnt offerings to the LORD on the altar he had built for the LORD in front of the Temple porch. ¹³He offered sacrifices every day as Moses had commanded. They were offered on the Sabbath *d* days, New Moons *d* and the three yearly feasts—the Feast *d* of Unleavened Bread, the Feast of Weeks and the Feast of Shelters. ¹⁴Solomon followed his father David's instructions and chose the groups of priests for their service and the Levites to lead the praise and to help the priests do their daily work. And he chose the gatekeepers by their groups to serve at each gate, as David, the man of God, had commanded. ¹⁵They obeyed all of Solomon's commands to the priests and Levites, as well as his commands about the treasuries.

¹⁶All Solomon's work was done as he had said from the day the foundation of the Temple of the LORD was begun, until it was finished. So the Temple was finished.

¹⁷Then Solomon went to the towns of Ezion Geber and Elath near the Red Sea *d* in the land of Edom. ¹⁸Hiram sent ships to Solomon that were commanded by his own men, who were skilled sailors. Hiram's men went with Solomon's men

to Ophir and brought back about 15 tonnes of gold to King Solomon.

The Queen of Sheba Visits

9 When the queen of Sheba heard about Solomon's fame, she came to Jerusalem to test him with hard questions. She had a large group of servants with her and camels carrying spices, jewels and much gold. When she came to Solomon, she talked with him about all she had in mind, ²and Solomon answered all her questions. Nothing was too hard for him to explain to her. ³The queen of Sheba saw that Solomon was very wise. She saw the palace he had built, ⁴the food on his table, his many officers, the palace servants and their good clothes, the servants who served Solomon his wine and their good clothes. She saw the whole burnt offerings he made in the Temple *d* of the LORD. All these things amazed her.

⁵So she said to King Solomon, "What I heard in my own country about your achievements and wisdom is true. ⁶I did not believe it then, but now I have come and seen it with my own eyes. I was not told even half of your great wisdom! You are much greater than I had heard. ⁷Your men and officers are very happy, because in always serving you, they are able to hear your wisdom. ⁸Praise the LORD your God who was pleased to make you king. He has put you on his throne to rule for the LORD your God, because your God loves the people of Israel and supports them for ever. He has made you king over them to keep justice and to rule fairly."

⁹Then she gave the king about 4 tonnes of gold and many spices and jewels. No one had ever given such spices as the queen of Sheba gave to King Solomon.

¹⁰Hiram's men and Solomon's men brought gold from Ophir, juniper wood and jewels. ¹¹King Solomon used the juniper wood to build steps for the Temple of the LORD and the palace and to make lyres *d* and harps for the musicians. No one in Judah had ever seen such beautiful things as these.

¹²King Solomon gave the queen of Sheba everything she wanted and asked for, even more than she had brought to him. Then she and her servants returned to her own country.

Solomon's Wealth

¹³Every year King Solomon received about 23 tonnes of gold. ¹⁴Besides that, he also received gold from traders and merchants. All the kings of Arabia and the governors of the land also brought gold and silver.

¹⁵King Solomon made 200 large shields of hammered gold, each of which contained about

7 kilogrammes of hammered gold. [16]He also made 300 smaller shields of hammered gold, each of which contained about 3 kilogrammes of gold. The king put them in the Palace of the Forest of Lebanon.

[17]The king built a large throne of ivory and covered it with pure gold. [18]The throne had six steps on it and a gold footstool. There were armrests on both sides of the chair, and each armrest had a lion beside it. [19]Twelve lions stood on the six steps, one lion at each end of each step. Nothing like this had ever been made for any other kingdom. [20]All of Solomon's drinking cups, as well as the dishes in the Palace of the Forest of Lebanon, were made of pure gold. In Solomon's time people did not think silver was valuable.

[21]King Solomon had many ships that he sent out to trade, with Hiram's men as the crews. Every three years the ships returned, bringing back gold, silver, ivory, apes and baboons.

[22]King Solomon had more riches and wisdom than all the other kings on earth. [23]All the kings of the earth wanted to see Solomon and listen to the wisdom God had given him. [24]Year after year everyone who came brought gifts of silver and gold, clothes, weapons, spices, horses and mules. [25]Solomon had 4,000 stalls for horses and chariots, and he had 12,000 horses. He kept some in special cities for the chariots, and others he kept with him in Jerusalem. [26]Solomon ruled over all the kingdoms from the Euphrates River to the land of the Philistines, as far as the border of Egypt. [27]In Jerusalem the king made silver as common as stones and cedar trees as plentiful as the fig trees on the western hills. [28]Solomon imported horses from Egypt and all other countries.

Solomon's Death

[29]Everything else Solomon did, from the beginning to the end, is written in the records of Nathan the prophet, [d] and in the prophecy of Ahijah the Shilonite and in the visions of Iddo the seer, [d] who wrote about Jeroboam, Nebat's son. [30]Solomon ruled in Jerusalem over all Israel for 40 years. [31]Then Solomon died and was buried in Jerusalem, the city of David, his father. And Solomon's son Rehoboam became king in his place.

Israel Turns Against Rehoboam

10 Rehoboam went to Shechem, where all the Israelites had gone to make him king. [2]Jeroboam son of Nebat was in Egypt, where he had gone to escape from King Solomon. When Jeroboam heard about Rehoboam being made king, he returned from Egypt. [3]After the people sent for him, he and the people went to Rehoboam and said to him, [4]"Your father forced us to work very hard. Now, make it easier for us, and don't make us work as he did. Then we will serve you."

> **Sidelight**   2 Chronicles 10–36 is a lot like a condensed version of 1 and 2 Kings (p.311 and p.343). In 2 Chronicles, the material on the divided kingdom takes up 27 chapters, but Kings devotes 36 chapters to the same period.

[5]Rehoboam answered, "Come back to me in three days." So the people left.

[6]King Rehoboam asked the elders who had advised Solomon during his lifetime, "How do you think I should answer these people?"

[7]They answered, "Be kind to these people. If you please them and give them a kind answer, they will serve you always."

[8]But Rehoboam rejected this advice. Instead, he asked the young men who had grown up with him and who served as his advisers. [9]Rehoboam asked them, "What is your advice? How should we answer these people who said, 'Don't make us work as hard as your father did'?"

[10]The young men who had grown up with him answered, "The people said to you, 'Your father forced us to work very hard. Now make our work easier.' You should tell them, 'My little finger is bigger than my father's legs. [11]He forced you to work hard, but I will make you work even harder. My father beat you with whips, but I will beat you with whips that have sharp points.'"

[12]Rehoboam had told the people, "Come back to me in three days." So after three days Jeroboam and all the people returned to Rehoboam. [13]King Rehoboam spoke cruel words to them, because he had rejected the advice of the older leaders. [14]He followed the advice of the young men and said, "My father forced you to work hard, but I will make you work even harder. My father beat you with whips, but I will beat you with whips that have sharp points." [15]So the king did not listen to the people. God caused this to happen so that the LORD could keep the promise he had made to Jeroboam son of Nebat through Ahijah, a prophet [d] from Shiloh.

[16]When all the Israelites saw that the king refused to listen to them, they said to the king,

"We have no share in David!

We have no part in the son of Jesse!

People of Israel, let's go to our own homes!

Let David's son rule his own people."

So all the Israelites went home. [17]But Rehoboam still ruled over the Israelites who lived in the towns of Judah.

18Adoniram was in charge of the people who were forced to work. When Rehoboam sent him to the people, they threw stones at him until he died. But King Rehoboam ran to his chariot and escaped to Jerusalem. 19Since then, Israel has been against the family of David.

11 When Rehoboam arrived in Jerusalem, he gathered 180,000 of the best soldiers from Judah and Benjamin. He wanted to fight Israel to take back his kingdom. 2But the LORD spoke his word to Shemaiah, a man of God, saying, 3"Speak to Solomon's son Rehoboam, the king of Judah, and to all the Israelites living in Judah and Benjamin. Say to them, 4'The LORD says you must not go to war against your brothers. Every one of you should go home, because I made all these things happen.'" So they obeyed the LORD's command and turned back and did not attack Jeroboam.

Rehoboam Makes Judah Strong

5Rehoboam lived in Jerusalem and built strong cities in Judah to defend it. 6He built up the cities of Bethlehem, Etam, Tekoa, 7Beth Zur, Soco, Adullam, 8Gath, Mareshah, Ziph, 9Adoraim, Lachish, Azekah, 10Zorah, Aijalon and Hebron. These were fortified cities in Judah and Benjamin. 11When Rehoboam made those cities strong, he put commanders and supplies of food, oil and wine in them. 12Also, Rehoboam put shields and spears in all the cities and made them very strong. Rehoboam kept the people of Judah and Benjamin under his control.

13The priests and the Levites from all over Israel joined Rehoboam. 14The Levites even left their pasturelands and property and came to Judah and Jerusalem, because Jeroboam and his sons refused to let them serve as priests to the LORD. 15Jeroboam chose his own priests for the places of worship and for the goat and calf idols he had made. 16There were people from all the tribes *d* of Israel who wanted to obey the LORD, the God of Israel. So they went to Jerusalem with the Levites to sacrifice to the LORD, the God of their fathers. 17These people made the kingdom of Judah strong, and they supported Solomon's son Rehoboam for three years. During this time they lived the way David and Solomon had lived.

Rehoboam's Family

18Rehoboam married Mahalath, the daughter of Jerimoth and Abihail. Jerimoth was David's son, and Abihail was the daughter of Eliab, Jesse's son. 19Mahalath gave Rehoboam these sons: Jeush, Shemariah and Zaham. 20Then Rehoboam married Absalom's daughter Maacah, and she gave Rehoboam these children: Abijah, Attai, Ziza and Shelomith. 21Rehoboam loved Maacah more than his other wives and slave women. *d* Rehoboam had eighteen wives and 60 slave women and was the father of 28 sons and 60 daughters. 22Rehoboam chose Abijah son of Maacah to be the leader of his own brothers, because he planned to make Abijah king. 23Rehoboam acted wisely. He spread his sons through all the areas of Judah and Benjamin, sending them to every fortified city. He gave plenty of supplies to his sons, and he also found wives for them.

Shishak Attacks Jerusalem

12 After Rehoboam's kingdom was set up and he became strong, he and the people of Judah stopped obeying the teachings of the LORD. 2During the fifth year Rehoboam was king, Shishak king of Egypt attacked Jerusalem, because Rehoboam and the people were unfaithful to the LORD. 3Shishak had 1,200 chariots and 60,000 horsemen. He brought troops of Libyans, Sukkites and Cushites from Egypt with him, so many they couldn't be counted. 4Shishak captured the fortified cities of Judah and came as far as Jerusalem.

5Then Shemaiah the prophet *d* came to Rehoboam and the leaders of Judah who had gathered in Jerusalem because they were afraid of Shishak. Shemaiah said to them, "This is what the LORD says: 'You have left me, so now I will leave you to face Shishak alone.'"

6Then the leaders of Judah and King Rehoboam were sorry for what they had done. They said, "The LORD does what is right."

7When the LORD saw they were sorry for what they had done, the LORD spoke his word to Shemaiah, saying, "The king and the leaders are sorry. So I will not destroy them but will save them soon. I will not use Shishak to punish Jerusalem in my anger. 8But the people of Jerusalem will become Shishak's servants so they may learn that serving me is different from serving the kings of other nations."

9Shishak king of Egypt attacked Jerusalem and took the treasures from the Temple *d* of the LORD and the king's palace. He took everything, even the gold shields Solomon had made. 10So King Rehoboam made bronze shields to take their place and gave them to the commanders of the guards for the palace gates. 11Whenever the king went to the Temple of the LORD, the guards went with him, carrying the shields. Later, they would put them back in the guardroom.

12When Rehoboam was sorry for what he had done, the LORD held his anger back and did not fully destroy Rehoboam. There was some good in Judah.

13King Rehoboam made himself a strong king in Jerusalem. He was 41 years old when he became king, and he was king in Jerusalem for seventeen years. Jerusalem is the city that the LORD chose from all the tribes*d* of Israel in which he was to be worshipped. Rehoboam's mother was Naamah from the country of Ammon. [14]Rehoboam did evil because he did not want to obey the LORD.

[15]The things Rehoboam did as king, from the beginning to the end, are written in the records of Shemaiah the prophet and Iddo the seer, *d* in the family histories. There were wars between Rehoboam and Jeroboam all the time they ruled. [16]Rehoboam died and was buried in Jerusalem, and his son Abijah became king in his place.

Abijah King of Judah

13 Abijah became the king of Judah during the eighteenth year Jeroboam was king of Israel. [2]Abijah ruled in Jerusalem for three years. His mother was Maacah daughter of Uriel from the town of Gibeah.

And there was war between Abijah and Jeroboam. [3]Abijah led an army of 400,000 capable soldiers into battle, and Jeroboam prepared to fight him with 800,000 capable soldiers.

[4]Abijah stood on Mount Zemaraim in the mountains of Ephraim and said, "Jeroboam and all Israel, listen to me! [5]You should know that the LORD, the God of Israel, gave David and his sons the right to rule Israel for ever by an agreement of salt. *n* [6]But Jeroboam son of Nebat, one of the officers of Solomon, David's son, turned against his master. [7]Then worthless, evil men joined Jeroboam against Rehoboam, Solomon's son. He was young and didn't know what to do, so he could not stop them.

[8]"Now you people are making plans against the LORD's kingdom, which belongs to David's sons. There are many of you, and you have the gold calves Jeroboam made for you as gods. [9]You have thrown out the Levites and the LORD's priests, Aaron's sons. You have chosen your own priests as people in other countries do. Anyone who comes with a young bull and seven rams can become a priest of idols that are not gods.

[10]"But as for us, the LORD is our God; we have not left him. The priests who serve the LORD are Aaron's sons, and the Levites help them. [11]They offer burnt offerings and sweet-smelling incense *d* to the LORD every morning and evening. They put the bread on the special table in the Temple. *d* And they light the lamps on the gold lampstand every evening. We obey the command of the LORD our God, but you have left him. [12]God himself is with us as our ruler. His priests blow the trumpet to call

us to war against you. Men of Israel, don't fight against the LORD, the God of your ancestors, because you won't succeed."

[13]But Jeroboam had sent some troops to sneak behind Judah's army. So while Jeroboam was in front of Judah's army, Jeroboam's soldiers were behind them. [14]When the soldiers of Judah turned around, they saw Jeroboam's army attacking both in front and at the back. So they cried out to the LORD, and the priests blew the trumpets. [15]Then the men of Judah gave a battle cry. When they shouted, God caused Jeroboam and the army of Israel to run away from Abijah and the army of Judah. [16]When the army of Israel ran away from the men of Judah, God handed them over to Judah. [17]Abijah's army struck Israel so that 500,000 of Israel's best men were killed. [18]So at that time the people of Israel were defeated. And the people of Judah won, because they depended on the LORD, the God of their ancestors.

[19]Abijah's army chased Jeroboam's army and captured from him the towns of Bethel, Jeshanah and Ephron, and the small villages near them. [20]Jeroboam never became strong again while Abijah was alive. The LORD struck Jeroboam, and he died.

[21]But Abijah became strong. He married fourteen women and was the father of 22 sons and sixteen daughters. [22]Everything else Abijah did—what he said and what he did—is recorded in the writings of the prophet Iddo.

14 Abijah died and was buried in Jerusalem. His son Asa became king in his place, and there was peace in the country for ten years during Asa's time.

Asa King of Judah

[2]Asa did what the LORD his God said was good and right. [3]He removed the foreign altars and the places where gods were worshipped. He smashed the stone pillars that honoured other gods, and he tore down the Asherah *d* idols. [4]Asa commanded the people of Judah to follow the LORD, the God of their ancestors, and to obey his teachings and commandments. [5]He also removed the places where gods were worshipped and the incense altars from every town in Judah. So the kingdom had peace while Asa was king. [6]Asa built fortified cities in Judah during the time of peace. He had no war in these years, because the LORD gave him peace.

[7]Asa said to the people of Judah, "Let's build up these towns and put walls around them. Let's make towers, gates and bars in the gates. This country is ours, because we have obeyed the LORD our God. We have followed him, and he has

---

an agreement of salt   An unbreakable agreement.

given us peace all around." So they built and had success.

8Asa had an army of 300,000 men from Judah and 280,000 men from Benjamin. The men from Judah carried large shields and spears. The men from Benjamin carried small shields and bows and arrows. All of them were brave fighting men. 9Then Zerah from Cush came out to fight them with an enormous army and 300 chariots. They came as far as the town of Mareshah. 10So Asa

Sidelight Today, Zerah from Cush (2 Chronicles 14:9) would be "Zerah from Ethiopia", a country south-east of Egypt in Africa.

went out to fight Zerah and prepared for battle in the Valley of Zephathah at Mareshah.

11Asa called out to the LORD his God, saying, "LORD, only you can help weak people against the strong. Help us, LORD our God, because we depend on you. We fight against this enormous army in your name. LORD, you are our God. Don't let anyone win against you."

12So the LORD defeated the Cushites when Asa's army from Judah attacked them, and the Cushites ran away. 13Asa's army chased them as far as the town of Gerar. So many Cushites were killed that the army could not fight again; they were crushed by the LORD and his army. Asa and his army carried many valuable things away from the enemy. 14They destroyed all the towns near Gerar, because the people living in these towns were afraid of the LORD. Since these towns had many valuable things, Asa's army took them away. 15Asa's army also attacked the camps where the shepherds lived and took many sheep and camels. Then they returned to Jerusalem.

Asa's Changes

15 The Spirit *d* of God entered Azariah son of Oded. 2Azariah went to meet Asa and said, "Listen to me, Asa and all you people of Judah and Benjamin. The LORD is with you when you are with him. If you obey him, you will find him, but if you leave him, he will leave you. 3For a long time Israel was without the true God and without a priest to teach them and without the teachings. 4But when they were in trouble, they turned to the LORD, the God of Israel. They looked for him and found him. 5In those days no one could travel safely. There was much trouble in all the nations. 6One nation would destroy another nation, and one city would destroy another city, because God troubled them with all kinds of distress. 7But you should be strong. Don't give up,

because you will get a reward for your good work."

8Asa felt brave when he heard these words and the message from Azariah son of Oded the prophet. *d* So he removed the hateful idols from all of Judah and Benjamin and from the towns he had captured in the hills of Ephraim. He repaired the LORD's altar that was in front of the porch of the Temple *d* of the LORD.

9Then Asa gathered all the people from Judah and Benjamin and from the tribes *d* of Ephraim, Manasseh and Simeon who were living in Judah. Many people came to Asa even from Israel, because they saw that the LORD, Asa's God, was with him.

10Asa and these people gathered in Jerusalem in the third month of the fifteenth year of Asa's rule. 11At that time they sacrificed to the LORD 700 bulls and 7,000 sheep and goats from the valuable things Asa's army had taken from their enemies. 12Then they made an agreement to obey the LORD, the God of their ancestors, with their whole being. 13Anyone who refused to obey the LORD, the God of Israel, was to be killed. It did not matter if that person was important or unimportant, a man or woman. 14Then Asa and the people made a promise before the LORD, shouting with a loud voice and blowing trumpets and sheep's horns. 15All the people of Judah were happy about the promise, because they had promised with all their heart. They looked for God and found him. So the LORD gave them peace in all the country.

16King Asa also removed Maacah, his grandmother, from being queen mother, because she had made a terrible Asherah *d* idol. Asa cut down that idol, smashed it into pieces and burned it in the Kidron Valley. 17But the places of worship to gods were not removed from Judah. Even so, Asa was faithful all his life.

18Asa brought into the Temple of God the gifts he and his father had given: silver, gold and utensils.

19There was no more war until the thirty-fifth year of Asa's rule.

Asa's Last Years

16 In the thirty-sixth year of Asa's rule, Baasha king of Israel attacked Judah. He made the town of Ramah strong so he could keep people from leaving or entering Judah, Asa's country.

2Asa took silver and gold from the treasuries of the Temple *d* of the LORD and out of his own palace. Then he sent it with messengers to Ben-Hadad king of Aram, who lived in Damascus. Asa said, 3"Let there be a treaty between you and me as there was between my father and your father.

I am sending you silver and gold. Break your treaty with Baasha king of Israel so he will leave my land."

⁴Ben-Hadad agreed with King Asa and sent the commanders of his armies to attack the towns of Israel. They defeated the towns of Ijon, Dan and Abel Beth Maacah, and all the towns in Naphtali where treasures were stored. ⁵When Baasha heard about this, he stopped building up Ramah and left his work. ⁶Then King Asa brought all the people of Judah to Ramah, and they carried away the rocks and wood that Baasha had used. And they used them to build up Geba and Mizpah.

⁷At that time Hanani the seer ᵈ came to Asa king of Judah and said to him, "You depended on the king of Aram to help you and not on the LORD your God. So the king of Aram's army escaped from you. ⁸The Cushites and Libyans had a large and powerful army and many chariots and horsemen. But you depended on the LORD to help you, so he handed them over to you. ⁹The LORD searches all the earth for people who have given themselves completely to him. He wants to make them strong. Asa, you did a foolish thing, so from now on you will have wars."

¹⁰Asa was angry with Hanani the seer because of what he had said; he was so angry that he put Hanani in prison. And Asa was cruel to some of the people at the same time.

¹¹Everything Asa did as king, from the beginning to the end, is written in the book of the kings of Judah and Israel. ¹²In the thirty-ninth year of his rule, Asa got a disease in his feet. Though his disease was very bad, he did not ask

---

Sidelight

Did King Asa have one of the world's first cases of athlete's foot (2 Chronicles 16:12)? Probably not. He may have had dropsy, which makes the feet swell like a tumour. Or the phrase may be a polite way to say he had a sexually transmitted disease.

---

for help from the LORD, but only from the doctors. ¹³Then Asa died in the forty-first year of his rule. ¹⁴The people buried Asa in the tomb he had made for himself in Jerusalem. They laid him on a bed filled with spices and different kinds of mixed perfumes, and they made a large fire to honour him.

Jehoshaphat King of Judah

17 Jehoshaphat, Asa's son, became king of Judah in his place. Jehoshaphat made

Judah strong so they could fight against Israel. ²He put troops in all the fortified cities of Judah, in the land of Judah and in the towns of Ephraim that his father Asa had captured.

³The LORD was with Jehoshaphat, because he lived as his ancestor David had lived when he first became king. Jehoshaphat did not ask for help from the Baal ᵈ idols, ⁴but from the God of his father. He obeyed God's commands and did not live as the people of Israel lived. ⁵The LORD made Jehoshaphat a strong king over Judah. All the people of Judah brought gifts to Jehoshaphat, so he had much wealth and honour. ⁶He wanted very much to obey the LORD. He also removed the places for worshipping gods and the Asherah ᵈ idols from Judah.

⁷During the third year of his rule, Jehoshaphat sent his officers to teach in the towns of Judah. These officers were Ben-Hail, Obadiah, Zechariah, Nethanel and Micaiah. ⁸Jehoshaphat sent with them these Levites: Shemaiah, Nethaniah, Zebadiah, Asahel, Shemiramoth, Jehonathan, Adonijah, Tobijah and Tob-Adonijah. He also sent the priests Elishama and Jehoram. ⁹These leaders, Levites and priests taught the people in Judah. They took the Book of the Teachings of the LORD and went through all the towns of Judah and taught the people.

¹⁰The nations near Judah were afraid of the LORD, so they did not start a war against Jehoshaphat. ¹¹Some of the Philistines brought gifts and silver to Jehoshaphat as he demanded. Some Arabs brought him flocks: 7,700 rams and 7,700 goats.

¹²Jehoshaphat grew more and more powerful. He built strong, walled cities and towns for storing supplies in Judah. ¹³He kept many supplies in the towns of Judah, and he kept trained soldiers in Jerusalem. ¹⁴These soldiers were listed by families. From the families of Judah, these were the commanders of groups of 1,000 men: Adnah was the commander of 300,000 soldiers; ¹⁵Jehohanan was the commander of 280,000 soldiers; ¹⁶Amasiah was the commander of 200,000 soldiers. Amasiah son of Zicri had volunteered to serve the LORD.

¹⁷These were the commanders from the families of Benjamin: Eliada, a brave soldier, had 200,000 soldiers who used bows and shields. ¹⁸And Jehozabad had 180,000 men armed for war.

¹⁹All these soldiers served King Jehoshaphat. The king also put other men in the fortified cities through all of Judah.

Micaiah Warns King Ahab

18 Jehoshaphat had much wealth and honour, and he made an agreement with

King Ahab through marriage. *n 2*A few years later Jehoshaphat went to visit Ahab in Samaria. Ahab sacrificed many sheep and cattle at a great feast to honour Jehoshaphat and the people with him. He encouraged Jehoshaphat to attack Ramoth in Gilead. 3Ahab king of Israel asked Jehoshaphat king of Judah, "Will you go with me to attack Ramoth in Gilead?"

Jehoshaphat answered, "I will go with you, and my soldiers are yours. We will join you in the battle." 4Jehoshaphat also said to Ahab, "But first we should ask if this is the LORD's will."

5So King Ahab called 400 prophets *d* together and asked them, "Should we go to war against Ramoth in Gilead or not?"

They answered, "Go, because God will hand them over to you."

6But Jehoshaphat asked, "Isn't there a prophet of the LORD here? Let's ask him what we should do."

7Then King Ahab said to Jehoshaphat, "There is one other prophet. We could ask the LORD through him, but I hate him. He never prophesies *d* anything good about me, but always something bad. He is Micaiah son of Imlah."

Jehoshaphat said, "King Ahab, you shouldn't say that!"

8So Ahab king of Israel told one of his officers to bring Micaiah to him at once.

9Ahab king of Israel and Jehoshaphat king of Judah had on their royal robes and were sitting on their thrones at the threshing *d* floor, near the entrance to the gate of Samaria. All the prophets were standing before them speaking their messages. 10Zedekiah son of Kenaanah had made some iron horns. He said to Ahab, "This is what the LORD says: 'You will use these horns to fight the Arameans until they are destroyed.'"

11All the other prophets said the same thing, "Attack Ramoth in Gilead and win, because the LORD will hand the Arameans over to you."

12The messenger who had gone to get Micaiah said to him, "All the other prophets are saying King Ahab will win. You should agree with them and give the king a good answer."

13But Micaiah answered, "As surely as the LORD lives, I can tell him only what my God says."

14When Micaiah came to Ahab, the king asked him, "Micaiah, should we attack Ramoth in Gilead or not?"

Micaiah answered, "Attack and win! They will be handed over to you."

15But Ahab said to Micaiah, "How many times do I have to tell you to speak only the truth to me in the name of the LORD?"

16So Micaiah answered, "I saw the army of Israel scattered over the hills like sheep without a shepherd. The LORD said, 'They have no leaders. They should go home and not fight.'"

17Then Ahab king of Israel said to Jehoshaphat, "I told you! He never prophesies anything good about me, but only bad."

18But Micaiah said, "Hear the message from the LORD: I saw the LORD sitting on his throne with his heavenly army standing on his right and on his left. 19The LORD said, 'Who will trick King Ahab of Israel into attacking Ramoth in Gilead where he will be killed?'

"Some said one thing; some said another. 20Then one spirit came and stood before the LORD and said, 'I will trick him.'

"The LORD asked, 'How will you do it?'

21"The spirit answered, 'I will go to Ahab's prophets and make them tell lies.'

"So the LORD said, 'You will succeed in tricking him. Go and do it.'"

22Micaiah said, "Ahab, the LORD has made your prophets lie to you, and the LORD has decided that disaster should come to you."

23Then Zedekiah son of Kenaanah went up to Micaiah and slapped him in the face. Zedekiah said, "Has the LORD's Spirit *d* left me to speak through you?"

24Micaiah answered, "You will find out on the day you go to hide in an inside room."

25Then Ahab king of Israel ordered, "Take Micaiah and send him to Amon, the governor of the city, and to Joash, the king's son. 26Tell them I said to put this man in prison and give him only bread and water until I return safely from the battle."

27Micaiah said, "Ahab, if you come back safely from the battle, the LORD has not spoken through me. Remember my words, all you people!"

Ahab is Killed

28So Ahab king of Israel and Jehoshaphat king of Judah went to Ramoth in Gilead. 29King Ahab said to Jehoshaphat, "I will go into battle, but I will wear other clothes so no one will recognise me. But you wear your royal clothes." So Ahab wore other clothes and they went into battle.

30The king of Aram ordered his chariot commanders, "Don't fight with anyone—important or unimportant—except the king of Israel." 31When these commanders saw Jehoshaphat, they thought he was the king of Israel, so they turned to attack him. But Jehoshaphat began shouting and the LORD helped him. God made the chariot commanders turn away from Jehoshaphat. 32When they saw he was not King Ahab, they stopped chasing him.

---

agreement . . . through marriage   Jehoshaphat's son Jehoram married Athaliah, Ahab's daughter. See 2 Chronicles 21:6.

33By chance, a soldier shot an arrow which hit Ahab king of Israel between the pieces of his armour. King Ahab said to his chariot driver, "Turn around and get me out of the battle, because I am hurt!" 34The battle continued all day. King Ahab held himself up in his chariot and faced the Arameans until evening. Then he died at sunset.

19 Jehoshaphat king of Judah came back safely to his palace in Jerusalem. 2Jehu son of Hanani, a seer, *d* went out to meet him and said to the king, "Why did you help evil people? Why do you love those who hate the LORD? That is the reason the LORD is angry with you. 3But there is some good in you. You took the Asherah *d* idols out of this country, and you have tried to obey God."

Jehoshaphat Chooses Judges

4Jehoshaphat lived in Jerusalem. He went out again to be with the people, from Beersheba to the mountains of Ephraim, and he turned them back to the LORD, the God of their ancestors. 5Jehoshaphat appointed judges in all the land, in each of the strong, walled cities of Judah. 6Jehoshaphat said to them, "Watch what you do, because you are not judging for people but for the LORD. He will be with you when you make a decision. 7Now let each of you fear the LORD. Watch what you do, because the LORD our God wants people to be fair. He wants all people to be treated the same, and he doesn't want decisions influenced by money."

8And in Jerusalem Jehoshaphat appointed some of the Levites, priests and leaders of Israelite families to be judges. They were to decide cases about the law of the LORD and settle problems between the people who lived in Jerusalem. 9Jehoshaphat commanded them, "You must always serve the LORD completely, and you must fear him. 10Your people living in the cities will bring you cases about killing, about the teachings, commands, rules or some other law. In all these cases you must warn the people not to sin against the LORD. If you don't, he will be angry with you and your people. But if you warn them, you won't be guilty. 11"Amariah, the leading priest, will be over you in all cases about the LORD. Zebadiah son of Ishmael, a leader in the tribe *d* of Judah, will be over you in all cases about the king. Also, the Levites will serve as officers for you. Have courage. May the LORD be with those who do what is right."

Jehoshaphat Faces War

20 Later the Moabites, Ammonites and some Meunites came to start a war with Jehoshaphat. 2Messengers came and told Jehoshaphat, "A large army is coming against you from Edom, from the other side of the Dead Sea. *d* They are already in Hazazon Tamar!" (Hazazon Tamar is also called En Gedi.) 3Jehoshaphat was afraid, so he decided to ask the LORD what to do. He announced that no one in Judah should eat during this special time of prayer to God. 4The people of Judah came together to ask the LORD for help; they came from every town in Judah.

5The people of Judah and Jerusalem met in front of the new courtyard in the Temple *d* of the LORD. Then Jehoshaphat stood up, 6and he said, "LORD, God of our ancestors, you are the God in heaven. You rule over all the kingdoms of the nations. You have power and strength, so no one can stand against you. 7Our God, you forced out the people who lived in this land as your people Israel moved in. And you gave this land for ever to the descendants *d* of your friend Abraham. 8They lived in this land and built a Temple for you. They said, 9'If trouble comes upon us, or war, punishment, sickness or hunger, we will stand before you and before this Temple where you have chosen to be worshipped. We will cry out to you when we are in trouble. Then you will hear and save us.'

10"But now here are men from Ammon, Moab and Edom. You wouldn't let the Israelites enter their lands when the Israelites came from Egypt. So the Israelites turned away and did not destroy them. 11But see how they repay us for not destroying them! They have come to force us out of your land, which you gave us as our own. 12Our God, punish those people. We have no power against this large army that is attacking us. We don't know what to do, so we look to you for help."

13All the men of Judah stood before the LORD with their babies, wives and children. 14Then the Spirit *d* of the LORD entered Jahaziel. (Jahaziel was Zechariah's son. Zechariah was Benaiah's son. Benaiah was Jeiel's son and Jeiel was Mattaniah's son.) Jahaziel, a Levite and a descendant of Asaph, stood up in the meeting. 15He said, "Listen to me, King Jehoshaphat and all you people living in Judah and Jerusalem. The LORD says this to you: 'Don't be afraid or discouraged because of this large army. The battle is not your battle, it is God's. 16Tomorrow go down there and fight those people. They will come up through the Pass of Ziz. You will find them at the end of the ravine that leads to the Desert of Jeruel. 17You won't need to fight in this battle. Just stand strong in your places and you will see the LORD save you. Judah and Jerusalem, don't be afraid or discouraged because the LORD is with you. So go out against those people tomorrow.' "

18Jehoshaphat bowed face down on the ground. All the people of Judah and Jerusalem bowed down before the LORD and worshipped him. [19]Then some Levites from the Kohathite and Korahite people stood up and praised the LORD, the God of Israel, with very loud voices.

[20]Jehoshaphat's army went out into the Desert of Tekoa early in the morning. As they were starting out, Jehoshaphat stood and said, "Listen to me, people of Judah and Jerusalem. Have faith in the LORD your God, and you will stand strong. Have faith in his prophets, [d] and you will succeed." [21]Jehoshaphat listened to the people's advice. Then he chose men to be singers to the LORD, to praise him because he is holy and wonderful. As they marched in front of the army, they said,

"Thank the LORD,
    because his love continues for ever."

[22]As they began to sing and praise God, the LORD set ambushes for the people of Ammon, Moab and Edom who had come to attack Judah. And they were defeated. [23]The Ammonites and Moabites attacked the Edomites, destroying them completely. After they had killed the Edomites, they killed each other.

[24]When the men from Judah came to a place where they could see the desert, they looked at the enemy's large army. But they only saw dead bodies lying on the ground; no one had escaped. [25]When Jehoshaphat and his army came to take their valuables, they found many supplies, much clothing and other valuable things. There was more than they could carry away; there was so much it took three days to gather it all. [26]On the fourth day Jehoshaphat and his army met in the Valley of Beracah and praised the LORD. That is why that place has been called the Valley of Beracah [n] to this day.

[27]Then Jehoshaphat led all the men from Judah and Jerusalem back to Jerusalem. The LORD had made them happy because their enemies were defeated. [28]They entered Jerusalem with harps, lyres [d] and trumpets and went to the Temple of the LORD.

[29]When all the kingdoms of the lands around them heard how the LORD had fought Israel's enemies, they feared God. [30]So Jehoshaphat's kingdom was not at war. His God gave him peace from all the countries around him.

Jehoshaphat's Rule Ends

[31]Jehoshaphat ruled over the country of Judah. He was 35 years old when he became king, and he ruled in Jerusalem for 25 years. His mother's name was Azubah daughter of Shilhi. [32]Jehoshaphat was good like his father Asa, and he did what the LORD said was right. [33]But the places where gods were worshipped were not removed, and the people did not really want to follow the God of their ancestors.

[34]The other things Jehoshaphat did as king, from the beginning to the end, are written in the records of Jehu son of Hanani, which are in the book of the kings of Israel.

[35]Later, Jehoshaphat king of Judah made a treaty with Ahaziah king of Israel, which was a wrong thing to do. [36]Jehoshaphat agreed with Ahaziah to build trading ships, which they built in the town of Ezion Geber. [37]Then Eliezer son of Dodavahu from the town of Mareshah spoke against Jehoshaphat. He said, "Jehoshaphat, because you joined with Ahaziah, the LORD will destroy what you have made." The ships were wrecked so they could not sail out to trade.

21 Jehoshaphat died and was buried with his ancestors in Jerusalem, the city of David. Then his son Jehoram became king in his place. [2]Jehoram's brothers were Azariah, Jehiel, Zechariah, Azariahu, Michael and Shephatiah. They were the sons of Jehoshaphat king of Judah. [3]Jehoshaphat gave his sons many gifts of silver, gold and valuable things, and he gave them fortified cities in Judah. But Jehoshaphat gave the kingdom to Jehoram, because he was the first son.

Jehoram King of Judah

[4]When Jehoram took control of his father's kingdom, he killed all his brothers with a sword and also killed some of the leaders of Judah. [5]He was 32 years old when he began to rule, and he ruled eight years in Jerusalem. [6]He followed in the ways of the kings of Israel, just as the family of Ahab had done, because he married Ahab's daughter. Jehoram did what the LORD said was wrong. [7]But the LORD would not destroy David's family because of the agreement he had made with David. He had promised that one of David's descendants [d] would always rule.

[8]In Jehoram's time, Edom broke away from Judah's rule and chose their own king. [9]So Jehoram went to Edom with all his commanders and chariots. The Edomites surrounded him and his chariot commanders, but Jehoram got up and attacked the Edomites at night. [10]From then until now the country of Edom has fought against the rule of Judah. At the same time the people of Libnah also broke away from Jehoram because Jehoram left the LORD, the God of his ancestors.

[11]Jehoram also built places to worship gods on the hills in Judah. He led the people of Jerusalem to sin, and he led the people of Judah away from

Beracah This name means "blessing" or "praise".

the LORD. ¹²Then Jehoram received this letter from Elijah the prophet:

This is what the LORD, the God of your ancestor David, says, "Jehoram, you have not lived as your father Jehoshaphat lived and as Asa king of Judah lived. ¹³But you have lived as the kings of Israel lived, leading the people of Judah and Jerusalem to sin against God, as Ahab and his family did. You have killed your brothers and they were better than you. ¹⁴So now the LORD is about to punish your people, your children, your wives and everything you own. ¹⁵You will have a terrible disease in your intestines that will become worse every day. Finally it will cause your intestines to come out."

Sidelight The "terrible disease in your intestines" that was prophesied for King Jehoram by Elijah (2 Chronicles 21:15) was probably dysentery, a common ailment in the Middle East and other parts of the world. The king's case may have been chronic, resulting in intestinal blockage and death.

¹⁶The LORD caused the Philistines and the Arabs who lived near the Cushites to be angry with Jehoram. ¹⁷So the Philistines and Arabs attacked Judah and carried away all the wealth of Jehoram's palace, as well as his sons and wives. Only Jehoram's youngest son, Ahaziah, was left.

¹⁸After these things happened, the LORD gave Jehoram a disease in his intestines that could not be cured. ¹⁹After he was sick for two years, Jehoram's intestines came out because of the disease, and he died in terrible pain. The people did not make a fire to honour Jehoram as they had done for his ancestors.

²⁰Jehoram was 32 years old when he became king, and he ruled for eight years in Jerusalem. No one was sad when he died. He was buried in Jerusalem, but not in the graves for the kings.

Ahaziah King of Judah

22 The people of Jerusalem chose Ahaziah, Jehoram's youngest son, to be king in his place. The robbers who had come with the Arabs to attack Jehoram's camp had killed all of Jehoram's older sons. So Ahaziah began to rule Judah. ²Ahaziah was 22 years old when he became king, and he ruled for a year in Jerusalem. His mother's name was Athaliah, a granddaughter of Omri. ³Ahaziah followed the ways of Ahab's family, because his mother encouraged him to do wrong.

⁴Ahaziah did what the LORD said was wrong, as Ahab's family had done. They gave advice to Ahaziah after his father died, and their bad advice led to his death. ⁵Following their advice, Ahaziah went with Joram son of Ahab to Ramoth in Gilead, where they fought against Hazael king of Aram. The Arameans wounded Joram. ⁶So Joram returned to Jezreel to heal from the wounds he received at Ramoth when he fought Hazael king of Aram.

Ahaziah son of Jehoram and king of Judah went down to visit Joram son of Ahab at Jezreel because he had been wounded.

⁷God caused Ahaziah's death when he went to visit Joram. Ahaziah arrived and went out with Joram to meet Jehu son of Nimshi, whom the LORD had appointed to destroy Ahab's family. ⁸While Jehu was punishing Ahab's family, he found the leaders of Judah and the sons of Ahaziah's relatives who served Ahaziah, and Jehu killed them all. ⁹Then Jehu looked for Ahaziah. Jehu's men caught him hiding in Samaria, so they brought him to Jehu. Then they killed and buried him. They said, "Ahaziah is a descendant *d* of Jehoshaphat, and Jehoshaphat obeyed the LORD with all his heart." No one in Ahaziah's family had the power to take control of the kingdom of Judah.

Athaliah and Joash

¹⁰When Ahaziah's mother, Athaliah, saw that her son was dead, she killed all the royal family in Judah. ¹¹But Jehosheba, King Jehoram's daughter, took Joash, Ahaziah's son. She stole him from among the other sons of the king who were going to be murdered and put him and his nurse in a bedroom. So Jehosheba, who was King Jehoram's daughter and Ahaziah's sister and the wife of Jehoiada the priest, hid Joash so Athaliah could not kill him. ¹²He hid with them in the Temple *d* of God for six years. During that time Athaliah ruled the land.

23 In the seventh year Jehoiada decided to do something. He made an agreement with the commanders of the groups of 100 men: Azariah son of Jeroham, Ishmael son of Jehohanan, Azariah son of Obed, Maaseiah son of Adaiah and Elishaphat son of Zicri. ²They went around in Judah and gathered the Levites from all the towns, and they gathered the leaders of the families of Judah. Then they went to Jerusalem. ³All the people together made an agreement with the king in the Temple *d* of God.

Jehoiada said to them, "The king's son will rule, as the LORD promised about David's descendants. *d* ⁴Now this is what you must do: you priests and Levites go on duty on the Sabbath. *d* A third of you will guard the doors. ⁵A third of you will be at the king's palace, and a third of you will be at the Foundation Gate. All the other people will stay in the courtyards of the Temple of the LORD. ⁶Don't let anyone come into the Temple of the LORD except the priests and Levites who serve. They may come because they have been made ready to serve the LORD, but all the others must do the job the LORD has given them. ⁷The Levites must stay near the king, each man with his weapon in his hand. If anyone tries to enter the Temple, kill him. Stay close to the king when he goes in and when he goes out."

Joash Becomes King

⁸The Levites and all the people of Judah obeyed everything Jehoiada the priest had commanded. He did not excuse anyone from the groups of the priests. So each commander took his men who came on duty on the Sabbath ᵈ with those who went off duty on the Sabbath. ⁹Jehoiada gave the commanders of 100 men the spears and the large and small shields that had belonged to King David and that were kept in the Temple ᵈ of God. ¹⁰Then Jehoiada told the men where to stand, each man with his weapon in his hand. There were guards from the south side of the Temple to the north side. They stood by the altar and the Temple and around the king.

¹¹Jehoiada and his sons brought out the king's son and put the crown on him and gave him a copy of the agreement. Then they appointed him king and poured olive oil on him and shouted, "Long live the king!"

¹²When Athaliah heard the noise of the people running and praising the king, she went to them at the Temple of the LORD. ¹³She looked, and there was the king standing by his pillar at the entrance. The officers and the trumpeters were standing beside him, and all the people of the land were happy and blowing trumpets. The singers were playing musical instruments and leading praises. Then Athaliah tore her clothes and screamed, "Traitors! Traitors!"

¹⁴Jehoiada the priest sent out the commanders of 100 men, who led the army. He said, "Surround her with soldiers and take her out of the Temple area. Kill with a sword anyone who follows her." He had said, "Don't put Athaliah to death in the Temple of the LORD." ¹⁵So they caught her when she came to the entrance of the Horse Gate near the palace. There they put her to death.

¹⁶Then Jehoiada made an agreement with the people and the king that they would be the LORD's special people. ¹⁷All the people went to the temple of Baal ᵈ and tore it down, smashing the altars and idols. They killed Mattan, the priest of Baal, in front of the altars.

¹⁸Then Jehoiada chose the priests, who were Levites, to be responsible for the Temple of the LORD. David had given them duties in the Temple of the LORD. They were to offer the burnt offerings to the LORD as the Teachings of Moses commanded, and they were to offer them with much joy and singing as David had commanded. ¹⁹Jehoiada put guards at the gates of the Temple of the LORD so that anyone who was unclean ᵈ in any way could not enter.

²⁰Jehoiada took with him the commanders of 100 men, the important men, the rulers of the people, and all the people of the land to take the king out of the Temple of the LORD. They went through the Upper Gate into the palace, and then they seated the king on the throne. ²¹So all the people of the land were very happy, and Jerusalem had peace, because Athaliah had been put to death with the sword.

Joash Repairs the Temple

24 Joash was seven years old when he became king, and he ruled for 40 years in Jerusalem. His mother's name was Zibiah, and she was from Beersheba. ²Joash did what the LORD said was right as long as Jehoiada the priest was alive. ³Jehoiada chose two wives for Joash, and Joash had sons and daughters.

⁴Later, Joash decided to repair the Temple ᵈ of the LORD. ⁵He called the priests and the Levites together and said to them, "Go to the towns of Judah and gather the money all the Israelites have to pay every year. Use it to repair the Temple of your God. Do this now." But the Levites did not hurry.

⁶So King Joash called for Jehoiada the leading priest and said to him, "Why haven't you made the Levites bring in from Judah and Jerusalem the tax money that Moses, the LORD's servant, and the people of Israel used for the Holy Tent?" ᵈ

⁷In the past the sons of wicked Athaliah had broken into the Temple of God and used its holy things for worshipping the Baal ᵈ idols.

⁸King Joash commanded that a box for contributions be made. They put it outside, at the gate of the Temple of the LORD. ⁹Then the Levites made an announcement in Judah and Jerusalem, telling people to bring to the LORD the tax money Moses, the servant of God, had made the Israelites give while they were in the desert. ¹⁰All the officers and people were happy to bring their money, and they put it in the box until the box was full. ¹¹When the Levites would take the box to the king's officers, they would see that it was full of money. Then the king's royal secretary and the leading priest's officer would come and take out the money and return the box to its place. They did this often and gathered much money.

¹²King Joash and Jehoiada gave the money to the people who worked on the Temple of the LORD. And they hired stoneworkers and carpenters to repair the Temple of the LORD. They also hired people to work with iron and bronze to repair the Temple.

¹³The people worked hard, and the work to repair the Temple went well. They rebuilt the Temple of God to be as it was before, but even stronger. ¹⁴When the workers finished, they brought the money that was left to King Joash and Jehoiada. They used that money to make utensils for the Temple of the LORD, utensils for the service in the Temple and for the burnt offerings, and bowls and other utensils from gold and silver. Burnt offerings were given every day in the Temple of the LORD while Jehoiada was alive.

¹⁵Jehoiada grew old and lived many years. Then he died when he was 130 years old.

¹⁶Jehoiada was buried in Jerusalem with the kings, because he had done much good in Judah for God and his Temple.

Joash Does Evil

¹⁷After Jehoiada died, the officers of Judah came and bowed down to King Joash, and he listened to them. ¹⁸The king and these leaders stopped worshipping in the Temple *d* of the LORD, the God of their ancestors. Instead, they began to worship the Asherah *d* idols and other idols. Because they did wrong, God was angry with the people of Judah and Jerusalem. ¹⁹Even though the LORD sent prophets *d* to the people to turn them back to him and even though the prophets warned them, they refused to listen.

²⁰Then the Spirit *d* of God entered Zechariah son of Jehoiada the priest. Zechariah stood before the people and said, "This is what God says: 'Why

---

REBELLION

This is My Life

"Eleven p.m. But I'm seventeen! Everyone's going to laugh at me! No one has to be home that early!" Brian couldn't believe that his parents could be so unfair. Perhaps he had ignored their rules lately, but he was old enough to run his own life.

"I'm leaving!" he yelled and stormed out of the house.

After spending the night with a friend, he came home, hoping his parents would be really worried. But his dad didn't yell or ask questions. He simply took away Brian's car keys.

Not to be beaten, Brian took out all his savings of £250 and bought an old car. It looked rough, but seemed to run OK, and he defiantly drove it home.

That night Brian decided to go cruising in his "new" car. Ten minutes away from home, the car ground to a painful halt – the clutch had gone. And Brian didn't have any money for repairs. He abandoned the car and walked home.

The car sat in the road until the police had it towed away.

Brian never saw his car or his £250 again. And he didn't drive the family car for two months.

By rebelling against his parents, Brian lost both money and privileges. Read **2 Chronicles 24:17–25** to learn how King Joash's rebellion against God affected his life.

* What were common factors in Brian's and Joash's rebellion?
* Joash's rebellion against God resulted in a murder. If you've ever rebelled against God, what has been a result of that rebellion?

Consider . . .

* evaluating your own life for signs of rebellion against God and then working on ways to get rid of the rebellion.
* visiting a prison or detention centre and sharing your experience of God's forgiveness.

For more, see . . .

* Proverbs 1:8–9 (p.590)
* 1 Peter 2:13–25 (p.1358)

* Romans 3:9–20 (p.1187)

do you disobey the LORD's commands? You will not be successful. Because you have left the LORD, he has also left you.' "

²¹But the king and his officers made plans against Zechariah. At the king's command they threw stones at him in the courtyard of the Temple of the LORD until he died. ²²King Joash did not remember Jehoiada's kindness to him, so Joash killed Zechariah, Jehoiada's son. Before Zechariah died, he said, "May the LORD see what you are doing and punish you."

²³At the end of the year, the Aramean army came against Joash. They attacked Judah and Jerusalem, killed all the leaders of the people, and sent all the valuable things to their king in Damascus. ²⁴The Aramean army came with only a small group of men, but the LORD handed over to them a very large army from Judah, because the people of Judah had left the LORD, the God of their ancestors. So Joash was punished. ²⁵When the Arameans left, Joash was badly wounded. His own officers made plans against him because he had killed Zechariah son of Jehoiada the priest. So they killed Joash in his own bed. He died and was buried in Jerusalem but not in the graves of the kings.

²⁶The officers who made plans against Joash were Jozabad and Jehozabad. Jozabad was the son of Shimeath, a woman from Ammon. And Jehozabad was the son of Shimrith, a woman from Moab. ²⁷The story of Joash's sons, the great prophecies[d] against him, and how he repaired the Temple of God are written in the book of the kings. Joash's son Amaziah became king in his place.

Amaziah King of Judah

25 Amaziah was 25 years old when he became king, and he ruled for 29 years in Jerusalem. His mother's name was Jehoaddin, and she was from Jerusalem. ²Amaziah did what the LORD said was right, but he did not really want to obey him. ³As soon as Amaziah took strong control of the kingdom, he put to death the officers who had murdered his father the king. ⁴But Amaziah did not put to death their children. He obeyed what was written in the Book of Moses, where the LORD commanded, "Parents must not be put to death when their children do wrong, and children must not be put to death when their parents do wrong. Each must die for his own sins." [n]

⁵Amaziah gathered the people of Judah together. He grouped all the people of Judah and Benjamin by families, and he put commanders over groups of 1,000 and over groups of 100. He counted the men who were 20 years old and older. In all there were 300,000 soldiers ready to fight and skilled with spears and shields.

⁶Amaziah also hired 100,000 soldiers from Israel for about 3.5 tonnes of silver. ⁷But a man of God came to Amaziah and said, "My king, don't let the army of Israel go with you. The LORD is not with Israel or the people from the tribe[d] of Ephraim. ⁸You can make yourself strong for war, but God will defeat you. He has the power to help you or to defeat you."

⁹Amaziah said to the man of God, "But what about the 3.5 tonnes of silver I paid to the Israelite army?"

The man of God answered, "The LORD can give you much more than that."

¹⁰So Amaziah sent the Israelite army back home to Ephraim. They were very angry with the people of Judah and went home angry.

¹¹Then Amaziah became very brave and led his army to the Valley of Salt in the country of Edom. There Amaziah's army killed 10,000 Edomites. ¹²The army of Judah also captured 10,000 and took them to the top of a cliff and threw them off so that they split open.

¹³At the same time the Israelite troops that Amaziah had not allowed to fight in the war were robbing towns in Judah. From Samaria to Beth Horon they killed 3,000 people and took many valuable things.

¹⁴When Amaziah came home after defeating the Edomites, he brought back the idols they worshipped and started to worship them himself. He bowed down to them and offered sacrifices to them. ¹⁵The LORD was very angry with Amaziah, so he sent a prophet[d] to him who said, "Why have you asked their gods for help? They could not even save their own people from you!"

¹⁶As the prophet spoke, Amaziah said to him, "We never gave you the job of advising the king. Stop, or you will be killed."

The prophet stopped speaking except to say, "I know that God has decided to destroy you because you have done this. You did not listen to my advice."

¹⁷Amaziah king of Judah talked with those who advised him. Then he sent a message to Jehoash son of Jehoahaz, who was the son of Jehu king of Israel. Amaziah said to Jehoash, "Come, let's meet face to face."

¹⁸Then Jehoash king of Israel answered Amaziah king of Judah, "A thornbush in Lebanon sent a message to a cedar tree in Lebanon. It said, 'Let your daughter marry my son.' But then a wild animal from Lebanon came by, walking on and crushing the thornbush. ¹⁹You say to yourself that you have defeated Edom, but you have become proud and you boast. But stay at home! Don't ask for trouble, or you and Judah will be defeated."

"Parents . . . sins." See Deuteronomy 24:16.

[20]But Amaziah would not listen. God caused this to happen so that Jehoash would defeat Judah, because Judah asked for help from the gods of Edom. [21]So Jehoash king of Israel went to attack. He and Amaziah king of Judah faced each other in battle at Beth Shemesh in Judah. [22]Israel defeated Judah, and every man of Judah ran away to his home. [23]At Beth Shemesh, Jehoash king of Israel captured Amaziah king of Judah. (Amaziah was the son of Joash, who was the son of Ahaziah.) Then Jehoash brought him to Jerusalem. Jehoash broke down the wall of Jerusalem, from the Gate of Ephraim to the Corner Gate, about 200 metres. [24]He took all the gold and silver and all the utensils from the Temple [d] of God that Obed-Edom had taken care of. He also took the treasures from the palace and some hostages. Then he returned to Samaria.

[25]Amaziah son of Joash, the king of Judah, lived fifteen years after the death of Jehoash son of Jehoahaz, the king of Israel. [26]The other things Amaziah did as king, from the beginning to the end, are written in the book of the kings of Judah and Israel. [27]When Amaziah stopped obeying the LORD, the people in Jerusalem made plans against him. So he ran away to the town of Lachish, but they sent men after him to Lachish and killed him. [28]They brought his body back on horses, and he was buried with his ancestors in Jerusalem, the city of David.

Uzziah King of Judah

26 Then all the people of Judah made Uzziah [n] king in place of his father Amaziah. Uzziah was sixteen years old. [2]He rebuilt the town of Elath and made it part of Judah again after Amaziah died.

[3]Uzziah was sixteen years old when he became king, and he ruled for 52 years in Jerusalem. His mother's name was Jecoliah, and she

> **Sidelight** Wouldn't it be nice if everyone obeyed your slightest command? Uzziah must have felt that way when he became king at the age of sixteen (2 Chronicles 26:3). Do you suppose his first decree was to outlaw homework?

was from Jerusalem. [4]He did what the LORD said was right, just as his father Amaziah had done. [5]Uzziah obeyed God while Zechariah was alive, because he taught Uzziah how to respect and obey God. And as long as Uzziah obeyed the LORD, God gave him success.

[6]Uzziah fought a war against the Philistines. He tore down the walls around their towns of Gath, Jabneh and Ashdod and built new towns near Ashdod and in other places among the Philistines. [7]God helped Uzziah fight the Philistines, the Arabs living in Gur Baal and the Meunites. [8]Also, the Ammonites made the payments Uzziah demanded. He was very powerful, so his name became famous all the way to the border of Egypt.

[9]Uzziah built towers in Jerusalem at the Corner Gate, the Valley Gate and where the wall turned, and he made them strong. [10]He also built towers in the desert and dug many wells, because he had many cattle on the western hills and in the plains. He had people who worked his fields and vineyards in the hills and in the fertile lands, because he loved the land.

[11]Uzziah had an army of trained soldiers. They were counted and put in groups by Jeiel the royal secretary and Maaseiah the officer. Hananiah, one of the king's commanders, was their leader. [12]There were 2,600 leaders over the soldiers. [13]They were in charge of an army of 307,500 men who fought with great power to help the king against the enemy. [14]Uzziah gave his army shields, spears, helmets, armour, bows and stones for their slings. [15]In Jerusalem Uzziah made devices that were invented by clever men. These devices on the towers and corners of the city walls were used to shoot arrows and large rocks. So Uzziah became famous in faraway places, because he had much help until he became powerful.

> **Sidelight** Modern military experts debate whether their weapons are offensive or defensive. But ancient city walls (2 Chronicles 26:15) served both purposes. Massive in size, the walls offered a strong defence against battering and invasion. They also gave people on the walls an offensive position from which to drop rocks, shoot arrows, or pour hot oil on attackers.

[16]But when Uzziah became powerful, his pride led to his ruin. He was unfaithful to the LORD his God; he went into the Temple [d] of the LORD to burn incense [d] on the altar for incense. [17]Azariah and 80 other brave priests who served the LORD followed Uzziah into the Temple. [18]They told him he was wrong and said to him, "You don't have the right to burn incense to the LORD. Only the priests, Aaron's descendants, [d] should burn

---

Uzziah Also called Azariah.

the incense, because they have been made holy. Leave this holy place. You have been unfaithful, and the LORD God will not honour you for this."

¹⁹Uzziah was standing beside the altar for incense in the Temple of the LORD, and in his hand was a pan for burning incense. He was very angry with the priests. As he was standing in front of the priests, a skin disease broke out on his forehead. ²⁰Azariah, the leading priest, and all the other priests looked at him and saw the skin disease on his forehead. So they hurried him out of the Temple. Uzziah also rushed out, because the LORD was punishing him. ²¹So King Uzziah had the skin disease until the day he died. He had to live in a separate house and could not enter the Temple of the LORD. His son Jotham was in charge of the palace, and he governed the people of the land.

²²The other things Uzziah did as king, from beginning to end, were written down by the prophet Isaiah son of Amoz. ²³Uzziah died and was buried near his ancestors in a graveyard that belonged to the kings. This was because people said, "He had a skin disease." And his son Jotham became king in his place.

Jotham King of Judah

27 Jotham was 25 years old when he became king, and he ruled for sixteen years in Jerusalem. His mother's name was Jerusha daughter of Zadok. ²Jotham did what the LORD said was right, just as his father Uzziah [n] had done. (But Jotham did not enter the Temple [d] of the LORD to burn incense [d] as his father had.) But the people continued doing wrong. ³Jotham rebuilt the Upper Gate of the Temple of the LORD and he added greatly to the wall at Ophel. ⁴He also built towns in the hill country of Judah, as well as walled cities and towers in the forests.

⁵Jotham also fought the king of the Ammonites and defeated them. So each year for three years they gave Jotham about 3.5 tonnes of silver, about 1,000 tonnes of wheat and about 1,000 tonnes of barley. ⁶Jotham became powerful, because he always obeyed the LORD his God.

⁷The other things Jotham did while he was king and all his wars are written in the book of the kings of Israel and Judah. ⁸Jotham was 25 years old when he became king, and he ruled for sixteen years in Jerusalem. ⁹Jotham died and was buried in Jerusalem, the city of David. Then Jotham's son Ahaz became king in his place.

Ahaz King of Judah

28 Ahaz was 20 years old when he became king, and he ruled for sixteen years in Jerusalem. Unlike his ancestor David, he did not do what the LORD said was right. ²Ahaz did the same things the kings of Israel had done. He made metal idols to worship Baal. [d] ³He burnt incense [d] in the Valley of Ben Hinnom and made his children pass [n] through the fire. He did the same hateful sins as the nations had done whom the LORD had forced out of the land ahead of the Israelites. ⁴Ahaz offered sacrifices and burnt incense at the places where gods were worshipped, and on the hills and under every green tree.

⁵So the LORD his God handed over Ahaz to the king of Aram. The Arameans defeated Ahaz and took many people of Judah as prisoners to Damascus.

He also handed over Ahaz to Pekah king of Israel, and Pekah's army killed many soldiers of Ahaz. ⁶The army of Pekah son of Remaliah killed 120,000 brave soldiers from Judah in one day. Pekah defeated them because they had left the LORD, the God of their ancestors. ⁷Zicri, a warrior from Ephraim, killed King Ahaz's son Maaseiah. He also killed Azrikam, the officer in charge of the palace and Elkanah, who was second in command to the king. ⁸The Israelite army captured 200,000 of their own relatives. They took women, sons and daughters and many valuable things from Judah and carried them back to Samaria. ⁹But a prophet [d] of the LORD named Oded was there. He met the Israelite army when it returned to Samaria and said to them, "The LORD, the God of your ancestors, handed Judah over to you, because he was angry with those people. But God has seen the cruel way you killed them. ¹⁰Now you plan to make the people of Judah and Jerusalem your slaves, but you also have sinned against the LORD your God. ¹¹Now listen to me. Send back your brothers and sisters whom you captured, because the LORD is very angry with you."

¹²Then some of the leaders in Ephraim—Azariah son of Jehohanan, Berekiah son of Meshillemoth, Jehizkiah son of Shallum and Amasa son of Hadlai—met the Israelite soldiers coming home from war. ¹³They warned the soldiers, "Don't bring the prisoners from Judah here. If you do, we will be guilty of sin against the LORD, and that will make our sin and guilt even worse. Our guilt is already so great that he is angry with Israel."

¹⁴So the soldiers left the prisoners and valuable things in front of the officers and people there. ¹⁵The leaders who were named took the prisoners and gave those who were naked the clothes that the Israelite army had taken. They gave the prisoners clothes, sandals, food, drink and medicine. They put the weak prisoners on donkeys

---

Uzziah   Also called Azariah.

pass   This means that Ahaz sacrificed his children in the fire.

and took them back to their families in Jericho, the city of palm trees. Then they returned home to Samaria.

¹⁶⁻¹⁷At that time the Edomites came again and attacked Judah and carried away prisoners. So King Ahaz sent to the king of Assyria for help. ¹⁸The Philistines also robbed the towns in the western hills and in southern Judah. They captured the towns of Beth Shemesh, Aijalon, Gederoth, Soco, Timnah and Gimzo, and the villages around them. Then the Philistines lived in those towns. ¹⁹The LORD brought trouble on Judah because Ahaz their king led the people of Judah to sin, and he was unfaithful to the LORD. ²⁰Tiglath-Pileser king of Assyria came to Ahaz, but he gave Ahaz trouble instead of help. ²¹Ahaz took some valuable things from the Temple ᵈ of the LORD, from the palace and from the princes, and he gave them to the king of Assyria, but it did not help.

²²During Ahaz's troubles he was even more unfaithful to the LORD. ²³He offered sacrifices to the gods of the people of Damascus, who had defeated him. He thought, "The gods of the kings of Aram helped them. If I offer sacrifices to them, they will help me also." But this brought ruin to Ahaz and all Israel.

²⁴Ahaz gathered the things from the Temple of God and broke them into pieces. Then he closed the doors of the Temple of the LORD. He made altars and put them on every street corner in Jerusalem. ²⁵In every town in Judah, Ahaz made places for burning sacrifices to worship other gods. So he made the LORD, the God of his ancestors, very angry.

²⁶The other things Ahaz did as king, from beginning to end, are written in the book of the kings of Judah and Israel. ²⁷Ahaz died and was buried in the city of Jerusalem, but not in the graves of the kings of Israel. Ahaz's son Hezekiah became king in his place.

Hezekiah Purifies the Temple

29 Hezekiah was 25 years old when he became king, and he ruled for 29 years in Jerusalem. His mother's name was Abijah daughter of Zechariah. ²Hezekiah did what the LORD said was right, just as his ancestor David had done.

³Hezekiah opened the doors of the Temple ᵈ of the LORD and repaired them in the first month of the first year he was king. ⁴Hezekiah brought in the priests and Levites and gathered them in the courtyard on the east side of the Temple. ⁵Hezekiah said, "Listen to me, Levites. Make yourselves ready for the LORD's service, and make holy the Temple of the LORD, the God of your ancestors. Remove from the Temple everything that

makes it impure. ⁶Our ancestors were unfaithful to God and did what the LORD said was wrong. They left the LORD and stopped worshipping at the Temple where he lives. They rejected him. ⁷They shut the doors of the porch of the Temple, and they let the fire go out in the lamps. They stopped burning incense ᵈ and offering burnt offerings in the holy place to the God of Israel. ⁸So the LORD became very angry with the people of Judah and Jerusalem, and he punished them. Other people are frightened and shocked by what he did to them. So they insult the people of Judah. You know these things are true. ⁹That is why our ancestors were killed in battle and our sons, daughters and wives were taken captive. ¹⁰Now I, Hezekiah, have decided to make an agreement with the LORD, the God of Israel, so he will not be angry with us any more. ¹¹My sons, don't waste any more time. The LORD chose you to stand before him, to serve him, to be his servants and to burn incense to him."

¹²These are the Levites who started to work. From the Kohathite family there were Mahath son of Amasai and Joel son of Azariah. From the Merarite family there were Kish son of Abdi and Azariah son of Jehallelel. From the Gershonite family there were Joah son of Zimmah and Eden son of Joah. ¹³From Elizaphan's family there were Shimri and Jeiel. From Asaph's family there were Zechariah and Mattaniah. ¹⁴From Heman's family there were Jehiel and Shimei. From Jeduthun's family there were Shemaiah and Uzziel.

¹⁵These Levites gathered their brothers together and made themselves holy for service in the Temple. Then they went into the Temple of the LORD to purify it. They obeyed the king's command that had come from the LORD. ¹⁶When the priests went into the Temple of the LORD to purify it, they took out all the unclean ᵈ things they found in the Temple of the LORD and put them in the Temple courtyard. Then the Levites took these things out to the Kidron Valley. ¹⁷Beginning on the first day of the first month, they made the Temple holy for the LORD's service. On the eighth day of the month, they came to the porch of the Temple, and for eight more days they made the Temple of the LORD holy. So they finished on the sixteenth day of the first month.

¹⁸Then they went to King Hezekiah and said, "We have purified the entire Temple of the LORD, the altar for burnt offerings and its utensils, and the table for the holy bread and all its utensils. ¹⁹When Ahaz was king, he was unfaithful to God and removed some things from the Temple. But we have put them back and made them holy for the LORD. They are now in front of the LORD's altar."

²⁰Early the next morning King Hezekiah gathered the leaders of the city and went up to the

Temple of the LORD. [21]They brought seven bulls, seven rams, seven lambs and seven male goats. These animals were an offering to remove the sin of the people and the kingdom of Judah and to make the Temple ready for service to God. King Hezekiah commanded the priests, the descendants [d] of Aaron, to offer these animals on the LORD's altar. [22]So the priests killed the bulls and sprinkled their blood on the altar. They killed the rams and sprinkled their blood on the altar. Then they killed the lambs and sprinkled their blood on the altar. [23]Then the priests brought the male goats for the sin offering before the king and the people there. After the king and the people put their hands on the goats, [24]the priests killed them. With the goats' blood they made an offering on the altar to remove the sins of the Israelites so they would belong to God. The king had said that the burnt offering and sin offering should be made for all Israel.

[25]King Hezekiah put the Levites in the Temple of the LORD with cymbals, harps and lyres, [d] as David, Gad and Nathan had commanded. (Gad was the king's seer [d] and Nathan was a prophet. [d]) This command came from the LORD through his prophets. [26]So the Levites stood ready with David's instruments of music, and the priests stood ready with their trumpets.

[27]Then Hezekiah gave the order to sacrifice the burnt offering on the altar. When the burnt offering began, the singing to the LORD also began. The trumpets were blown and the musical instruments of David king of Israel were played. [28]All the people worshipped, the singers sang and the trumpeters blew their trumpets until the burnt offering was finished.

[29]When the sacrifices were completed, King Hezekiah and everyone with him bowed down and worshipped. [30]King Hezekiah and his officers ordered the Levites to praise the LORD, using the words David and Asaph the seer had used. So they praised God with joy and bowed down and worshipped.

[31]Then Hezekiah said, "Now that you people of Judah have given yourselves to the LORD, come near to the Temple of the LORD. Bring sacrifices and offerings to show thanks to him." So the people brought sacrifices and thank offerings, and anyone who was willing also brought burnt offerings. [32]For burnt offerings they brought a total of 70 bulls, 100 rams and 200 lambs; all these animals were sacrificed as burnt offerings to the LORD. [33]The holy offerings totalled 600 bulls and 3,000 sheep and goats. [34]There were not enough priests to skin all the animals for the burnt offerings.

So their relatives the Levites helped them until the work was finished and other priests could be made holy. The Levites had been more careful to make themselves holy for the LORD's service than the priests. [35]There were many burnt offerings along with the fat of fellowship offerings and drink offerings. So the service in the Temple of the LORD began again. [36]And Hezekiah and the people were very happy that God had made it happen so quickly for his people.

The Passover Celebration

30 King Hezekiah sent messages to all the people of Israel and Judah, and he wrote letters to the people of Ephraim and Manasseh. Hezekiah invited all these people to come to the Temple [d] of the LORD in Jerusalem to celebrate the Passover [d] for the LORD, the God of Israel. [2]King Hezekiah, his officers and all the people in Jerusalem agreed to celebrate the Passover in the second month. [3]They could not celebrate it at the normal time, because not enough priests had made themselves ready to serve the LORD, and the people had not yet gathered in Jerusalem. [4]This plan satisfied King Hezekiah and all the people. [5]So they made an announcement everywhere in Israel, from Beersheba to Dan, [n] telling the people to come to Jerusalem to celebrate the Passover for the LORD, the God of Israel. For a long time most of the people had not celebrated the Passover as the law commanded. [6]At the king's command, the messengers took letters from him and his officers all through Israel and Judah. This is what the letters said:

> People of Israel, return to the LORD, the God of Abraham, Isaac and Israel. Then God will return to you who are still alive, who have escaped from the kings of Assyria. [7]Don't be like your ancestors or your relatives. They turned against the LORD, the God of their ancestors, so he caused other people to be disgusted with them. You know this is true. [8]Don't be stubborn as your ancestors were, but obey the LORD willingly. Come to the Temple, which he has made holy for ever. Serve the LORD your God so he will not be angry with you. [9]Come back to the LORD. Then the people who captured your relatives and children will be kind to them and will let them return to this land. The LORD your God is kind and merciful. He will not turn away from you if you return to him.

[10]The messengers went to every town in Ephraim and Manasseh, and all the way to Zebulun,

---

Beersheba to Dan   Dan was the city farthest north in Israel, and Beersheba was the city farthest south. So this means all the people of Israel.

but the people laughed at them and made fun of them. [11]But some men from Asher, Manasseh and Zebulun were sorry for what they had done and went to Jerusalem. [12]And God united all the people of Judah in obeying King Hezekiah and his officers, because their command had come from the LORD.

[13]In the second month a large crowd came together in Jerusalem to celebrate the Feast [d] of Unleavened Bread. [14]The people removed the altars and incense [d] altars to gods in Jerusalem and threw them into the Kidron Valley.

[15]They killed the Passover lamb on the fourteenth day of the second month. The priests and the Levites were ashamed, so they made themselves holy and brought burnt offerings into the Temple of the LORD. [16]They took their regular places in the Temple as the Teachings of Moses, the man of God, commanded. The Levites gave the blood of the sacrifices to the priests, who sprinkled it on the altar. [17]Since many people in the crowd had not made themselves holy, the Levites killed the Passover lambs for everyone who was not clean. [d] The Levites made each lamb holy for the LORD. [18-19]Although many people from Ephraim, Manasseh, Issachar and Zebulun had not purified themselves for the feast, they ate the Passover even though it was against the law. So Hezekiah prayed for them, saying, "LORD, you are good. You are the LORD, the God of our ancestors. Please forgive all those who try to obey you even if they did not make themselves clean as the rules of the Temple command." [20]The LORD listened to Hezekiah's prayer, and he healed the people. [21]The Israelites in Jerusalem celebrated the Feast of Unleavened Bread for seven days with great joy to the LORD. The Levites and priests praised the LORD every day with loud music. [22]Hezekiah encouraged all the Levites who showed they understood well how to do their service for the LORD. The people ate the feast for seven days, offered fellowship offerings and praised the LORD, the God of their ancestors.

[23]Then all the people agreed to stay seven more days, so they celebrated with joy for seven more days. [24]Hezekiah king of Judah gave 1,000 bulls and 7,000 sheep to the people. The officers gave 1,000 bulls and 10,000 sheep to the people. Many priests made themselves holy. [25]All the people of Judah, the priests, the Levites, those who came from Israel, the foreigners from Israel and the foreigners living in Judah were very happy. [26]There was much joy in Jerusalem, because there had not been a celebration like this since the time of Solomon son of David and king of Israel. [27]The priests and Levites stood up and blessed the people, and God heard them because their prayer reached heaven, his holy home.

The Collection for the Priests

31 When the Passover [d] celebration was finished, all the Israelites in Jerusalem went out to the towns of Judah. There they smashed the stone pillars used to worship gods. They cut down the Asherah [d] idols and destroyed the altars and places for worshipping gods in all of Judah, Benjamin, Ephraim and Manasseh. After they had destroyed all of them, the Israelites returned to their own towns and homes.

[2]King Hezekiah appointed groups of priests and Levites for their special duties. They were to offer burnt offerings and fellowship offerings, to worship and to give thanks and praise at the gates of the LORD's house. [3]Hezekiah gave some of his own animals for the burnt offerings, which were given every morning and evening on Sabbath [d] days, during New Moons [d] and at other feasts commanded in the LORD's Teachings.

[4]Hezekiah commanded the people living in Jerusalem to give the priests and Levites the portion that belonged to them. Then the priests and Levites could give all their time to the LORD's Teachings. [5]As soon as the king's command went out to the Israelites, they gave freely of the first portion of their grain, new wine, oil, honey and everything they grew in their fields. They brought a large amount, one-tenth of everything. [6]The people of Israel and Judah who lived in Judah also brought one-tenth of their cattle and sheep and one-tenth of the holy things that were given to the LORD their God, and they put all of them in piles. [7]The people began the piles in the third month and finished in the seventh month. [8]When Hezekiah and his officers came and saw the piles, they praised the LORD and his people, the people of Israel. [9]Hezekiah asked the priests and Levites about the piles. [10]Azariah, the leading priest from Zadok's family, answered Hezekiah, "Since the people began to bring their offerings to the Temple [d] of the LORD, we have had plenty to eat and plenty left over, because the LORD has blessed his people. So we have all this left over."

[11]Then Hezekiah commanded the priests to prepare the storerooms in the Temple of the LORD. So this was done. [12]Then the priests brought in the offerings and the things given to the LORD and a tenth of everything the people had given. Conaniah the Levite was in charge of these things, and his brother Shimei was second to him. [13]Conaniah and his brother Shimei were over these supervisors: Jehiel, Azaziah, Nahath, Asahel, Jerimoth, Jozabad, Eliel, Ismachiah, Mahath and Benaiah. King Hezekiah and Azariah the officer in charge of the Temple of God had chosen them.

¹⁴Kore, son of Imnah the Levite, was in charge of the special gifts the people wanted to give to God. He was responsible for giving out the contributions made to the LORD and the holy gifts. Kore was the guard at the East Gate. ¹⁵Eden, Miniamin, Jeshua, Shemaiah, Amariah and Shecaniah helped Kore in the towns where the priests lived. They gave from what was collected to the other groups of priests, both young and old.

¹⁶From what was collected, these men also gave to the males three years old and older who had their names in the Levite family histories. They were to enter the Temple of the LORD for their daily service, each group having its own responsibilities. ¹⁷The priests were given their part of the collection, by families, as listed in the family histories. The Levites 20 years old and older were given their part of the collection, based on their responsibilities and their groups. ¹⁸The Levites' babies, wives, sons and daughters also got part of the collection. This was done for all the Levites who were listed in the family histories, because they always kept themselves ready to serve the LORD.

¹⁹Some of Aaron's descendants, *d* the priests, lived on the farmlands near the towns or in the towns. Men were chosen by name to give part of the collection to these priests. All the males and those named in the family histories of the Levites received part of the collection.

²⁰This is what King Hezekiah did in Judah. He did what was good and right and obedient before the LORD his God. ²¹Hezekiah tried to obey God in his service of the Temple of God, and he tried to obey God's teachings and commands. He gave himself fully to his work for God. So he had success.

Assyria Attacks Judah

32 After Hezekiah did all these things to serve the LORD, Sennacherib king of Assyria came and attacked Judah. He and his army surrounded and attacked the fortified cities, hoping to take them for himself. ²Hezekiah knew that Sennacherib had come to Jerusalem to attack it. ³So Hezekiah and his officers and army commanders decided to cut off the water from the springs outside the city. So the officers and commanders helped Hezekiah. ⁴Many people came and cut off all the springs and the stream that flowed through the land. They said, "The king of Assyria will not find much water when he comes here." ⁵Then Hezekiah made Jerusalem stronger. He rebuilt all the broken parts of the wall and put towers on it. He also built another wall outside the first one and strengthened the area that was filled in on the east side of the old part of Jerusalem. He also made many weapons and shields.

⁶Hezekiah put army commanders over the people and met with them at the open place near the city gate. Hezekiah encouraged them, saying, ⁷"Be strong and brave. Don't be afraid or worried because of the king of Assyria or his large army. There is a greater power with us than with him. ⁸He only has men, but we have the LORD our God to help us and to fight our battles." The people were encouraged by the words of Hezekiah king of Judah.

⁹After this King Sennacherib of Assyria and all his army surrounded and attacked Lachish. Then he sent his officers to Jerusalem with this mes-

> **Sidelight**
> The Assyrian attack on Lachish (2 Chronicles 32:9) was horrible for its citizens. Archaeologists have found the bones of 1,500 bodies in a pit there, a sign of the terrible siege.

sage for King Hezekiah of Judah and all the people of Judah in Jerusalem:

¹⁰Sennacherib king of Assyria says this: "You have nothing to trust in to help you. It is no use for you to stay in Jerusalem under attack. ¹¹Hezekiah says to you, 'The LORD our God will save us from the king of Assyria,' but he is fooling you. If you stay in Jerusalem, you will die from hunger and thirst. ¹²Hezekiah himself removed your LORD's places of worship and altars. He told you people of Judah and Jerusalem that you must worship and burn incense *d* on only one altar.

¹³"You know what my ancestors and I have done to all the people in other nations. The gods of those nations could not save their people from my power. ¹⁴My ancestors destroyed those nations; none of their gods could save them from me. So your god cannot save you from my power. ¹⁵Do not let Hezekiah fool you or trick you, and do not believe him. No god of any nation or kingdom has been able to save his people from me or my ancestors. Your god is even less able to save you from me."

¹⁶Sennacherib's officers said worse things against the LORD God and his servant Hezekiah. ¹⁷King Sennacherib also wrote letters insulting the LORD, the God of Israel. They spoke against him, saying, "The gods of the other nations could not save their people from me. In the same way Hezekiah's God won't be able to save his people from me." ¹⁸Then the king's officers shouted in Hebrew, calling out to the people of Jerusalem who were on the city wall. The officers wanted to scare the people away so they could capture

Jerusalem. [19]They spoke about the God of Jerusalem as though he were like the gods the people of the world worshipped, which are made by human hands.

[20]King Hezekiah and the prophet[d] Isaiah son of Amoz prayed to heaven about this. [21]Then the LORD sent an angel who killed all the soldiers, leaders and officers in the camp of the king of Assyria. So the king went back to his own country in disgrace. When he went into the temple of his god, some of his own sons killed him with a sword.

[22]So the LORD saved Hezekiah and the people in Jerusalem from Sennacherib king of Assyria and from all other people. He took care of them on every side. [23]Many people brought gifts for the LORD to Jerusalem, and they also brought valuable gifts to King Hezekiah of Judah. From then on all the nations respected Hezekiah.

Hezekiah Dies

[24]At that time Hezekiah became so sick he almost died. When he prayed to the LORD, the LORD spoke to him and gave him a sign.[n] [25]But Hezekiah did not thank God for his kindness, because he was so proud. So the LORD was angry with him and the people of Judah and Jerusalem. [26]But later Hezekiah and the people of Jerusalem were sorry and stopped being proud, so the LORD did not punish them while Hezekiah was alive.

[27]Hezekiah had many riches and much honour. He made treasuries for his silver, gold, gems, spices, shields and other valuable things. [28]He built storage buildings for grain, new wine and oil, stalls for all the cattle and pens for the sheep. [29]He also built many towns. He had many flocks and herds, because God had given Hezekiah much wealth.

[30]It was Hezekiah who cut off the upper pool of the Gihon spring and made those waters flow straight down to the west side of the older part of Jerusalem. And Hezekiah was successful in everything he did. [31]But once the leaders of Babylon sent messengers to Hezekiah, asking him about a strange sign[n] that had happened in the land. When they came, God left Hezekiah alone to test him so he could know everything that was in Hezekiah's heart.[n]

[32]Hezekiah's love for God and the other things he did as king are written in the vision of the prophet[d] Isaiah son of Amoz. This is in the book of the kings of Judah and Israel. [33]Hezekiah died and was buried on a hill, where the graves of David's ancestors are. All the people of Judah and Jerusalem honoured Hezekiah when he died, and his son Manasseh became king in his place.

Manasseh King of Judah

33 Manasseh was twelve years old when he became king, and he was king for 55 years in Jerusalem. [2]He did what the LORD said was wrong. He did the hateful things the nations had done—the nations that the LORD had forced out of the land ahead of the Israelites. [3]Manasseh's father, Hezekiah, had torn down the places where gods were worshipped, but Manasseh rebuilt them. He also built altars for the Baal[d] gods, and he made Asherah[d] idols and worshipped all the stars of the sky and served them. [4]The LORD had said about the Temple,[d] "I will be worshipped in Jerusalem for ever," but Manasseh built altars in the Temple of the LORD. [5]He built altars to worship the stars in the two courtyards of the Temple of the LORD. [6]He made his children pass through fire in the Valley of Ben Hinnom. He practised magic and witchcraft[d] and told the future by explaining signs and dreams. He got advice from mediums[d] and fortune-tellers. He did many things the LORD said were wrong, which made the LORD angry.

[7]Manasseh carved an idol and put it in the Temple of God. God had said to David and his son Solomon about the Temple, "I will be worshipped for ever in this Temple and in Jerusalem, which I have chosen from all the tribes[d] of Israel. [8]I will never again make the Israelites leave the land I gave to their ancestors. But they must obey everything I have commanded them in all the teachings, rules and commands I gave them through Moses." [9]But Manasseh led the people of Judah and Jerusalem to do wrong. They did more evil than the nations the LORD had destroyed ahead of the Israelites.

[10]The LORD spoke to Manasseh and his people, but they did not listen. [11]So the LORD brought the king of Assyria's army commanders to attack Judah. They captured Manasseh, put hooks in him, placed bronze chains on his hands and took him to Babylon. [12]As Manasseh suffered, he begged the LORD his God for help and humbled himself before the God of his ancestors. [13]When Manasseh prayed, the LORD heard him and had pity on him. So the LORD let him return to Jerusalem and to his kingdom. Then Manasseh knew that the LORD is the true God.

[14]After that happened, Manasseh rebuilt the outer wall of Jerusalem and made it higher. It was in the valley on the west side of the Gihon spring and went to the entrance of the Fish Gate and around the hill of Ophel. Then he

---

sign See Isaiah 38:1–8. It tells the story about the sign and how the Lord gave Hezekiah fifteen more years to live.
God . . . heart See 2 Kings 20:12–19.

put commanders in all the fortified cities in Judah.

¹⁵Manasseh removed the idols of other nations, including the idol in the Temple of the LORD. He removed all the altars he had built on the Temple hill and in Jerusalem and threw them out of the city. ¹⁶Then he set up the LORD's altar and sacrificed on it fellowship offerings and offerings to show thanks to God. Manasseh commanded all the people of Judah to serve the LORD, the God of Israel. ¹⁷The people continued to offer sacrifices at the places of worship, but their sacrifices were only to the LORD their God. ¹⁸The other things Manasseh did as king, his prayer to his God, and what the seers*ᵈ* said to him in the name of the LORD, the God of Israel— all are recorded in the book of the history of the kings of Israel. ¹⁹Manasseh's prayer and God's pity for him, his sins, his unfaithfulness, the places he built for worshipping gods and the Asherah idols before he humbled himself—all are written in the book of the seers. ²⁰Manasseh died and was buried in his palace. Then Manasseh's son Amon became king in his place.

Amon King of Judah

²¹Amon was 22 years old when he became king, and he was king for two years in Jerusalem. ²²He did what the LORD said was wrong, as his father Manasseh had done. Amon worshipped and offered sacrifices to all the carved idols Manasseh had made. ²³Amon did not humble himself before the LORD as his father Manasseh had done. Instead, Amon sinned even more. ²⁴King Amon's officers made plans against him and killed him in his palace. ²⁵Then the people of the land killed all those who had made plans to kill King Amon, and they made his son Josiah king in his place.

Josiah King of Judah

34 Josiah was eight years old when he became king, and he ruled for 31 years in Jerusalem. ²He did what the LORD said was right. He lived as his ancestor David had lived, and he did not stop doing what was right.

³In his eighth year as king while he was still young, Josiah began to obey the God of his ancestor David. In his twelfth year as king, Josiah began to remove from Judah and Jerusalem the gods, the places for worshipping gods, the Asherah*ᵈ* idols, and the wooden and metal idols. ⁴The people tore down the altars for the Baal*ᵈ* gods as Josiah directed. Then Josiah cut down the incense*ᵈ* altars that were above them. He broke up the Asherah idols and the wooden and metal idols and beat them into powder. Then he sprinkled the powder on the graves

of the people who had offered sacrifices to these gods. ⁵He burned the bones of their priests on their own altars. So Josiah removed idol worship from Judah and Jerusalem, ⁶and from the towns in the areas of Manasseh, Ephraim and Simeon all the way to Naphtali, and in the ruins near these towns. ⁷Josiah broke down the altars and Asherah idols and beat the idols into powder. He cut down all the incense altars in all of Israel. Then he went back to Jerusalem.

⁸In Josiah's eighteenth year as king, he made Judah and the Temple*ᵈ* pure again. He sent Shaphan son of Azaliah, Maaseiah the city leader

> **Sidelight** The "places" or "high places" where people worshipped false gods weren't necessarily hills or mountains (2 Chronicles 34:3–7). They were sacred platforms on which idols stood. The only way to get people to stop worshipping at them was to destroy them completely as King Josiah did.

and Joah son of Joahaz the recorder to repair the Temple of the LORD, the God of Josiah. ⁹These men went to Hilkiah the high priest and gave him the money the Levite gatekeepers had gathered from the people of Manasseh, Ephraim and all the Israelites who were left alive, and also from all the people of Judah, Benjamin and Jerusalem. This is the money they had brought into the Temple of God. ¹⁰Then the Levites gave it to the supervisors of the work on the Temple of the LORD, and they paid the workers who rebuilt and repaired the Temple. ¹¹They gave money to carpenters and builders to buy cut stone and wood. The wood was used to rebuild the buildings and to make beams for them, because the kings of Judah had let the buildings fall into ruin. ¹²The men did their work well. Their supervisors were Jahath and Obadiah, who were Levites from the family of Merari, and Zechariah and Meshullam, who were from the family of Kohath. These Levites were all skilled musicians. ¹³They were also in charge of the workers who carried loads and all the other workers. Some Levites worked as secretaries, officers and gatekeepers.

The Book of the Teachings is Found

¹⁴The Levites brought out the money that was in the Temple*ᵈ* of the LORD. As they were doing this, Hilkiah the priest found the Book of the LORD's Teachings that had been given through Moses. ¹⁵Hilkiah said to Shaphan the

royal secretary, "I've found the Book of the Teachings in the Temple of the LORD!" Then he gave it to Shaphan.

[16]Shaphan took the book to the king and re-

Sidelight

If you don't think secretaries are important, read 2 Chronicles 34:13, which tells that the Levites served as honoured secretaries in the Temple. Do you think they had to take a typing test?

---

ported to Josiah, "Your officers are doing everything you told them to do. [17]They have paid out the money that was in the Temple of the LORD and have given it to the supervisors and the workers." [18]Then Shaphan the royal secretary told the king, "Hilkiah the priest has given me a book." And Shaphan read from the book to the king.

[19]When the king heard the words of the Teachings, he tore his clothes to show how upset he was. [20]He gave orders to Hilkiah, Ahikam son of Shaphan, Acbor son of Micaiah, Shaphan the royal secretary and Asaiah, the king's servant. These were the orders: [21]"Go and ask the LORD about the words in the book that was found. Ask for me and for the people who are left alive in Israel and Judah. The LORD is very angry with us, because our ancestors did not obey the LORD's word; they did not do everything this book says to do."

[22]So Hilkiah and those the king sent with him went to talk to Huldah the prophetess. [d] She was the wife of Shallum son of Tikvah, the son of Harhas, who took care of the king's clothes. Huldah lived in Jerusalem, in the new area of the city.

[23]She said to them, "This is what the LORD, the God of Israel, says: Tell the man who sent you to me, [24]'This is what the LORD says: I will bring trouble to this place and to the people living here. I will bring all the curses that are written in the book that was read to the king of Judah. [25]The people of Judah have left me and have burned incense [d] to other gods. They have made me angry by all the evil things they have made. So I will punish them in my anger, which will not be put out.' [26]Tell the king of Judah, who sent you to ask the LORD, 'This is what the LORD, the God of Israel, says about the words you heard: [27]When you heard my words against this place and its people, you became sorry for what you had done and you upset yourself before me. You tore your clothes to show how upset you were, and you cried in my presence. This is why I have heard you, says the LORD. [28]So I will let you die and be buried in peace. You won't see all the trouble I

will bring to this place and the people living here.'"

So they took her message back to the king.

[29]Then the king gathered all the elders of Judah and Jerusalem together. [30]He went up to the Temple of the LORD, and all the people from Judah and from Jerusalem went with him. The priests, the Levites and all the people—from the most important to the least important—went with him. He read to them all the words in the Book of the Agreement that was found in the Temple of the LORD. [31]The king stood by his pillar and made an agreement in the presence of the LORD to follow the LORD and obey his commands, rules and laws with his whole being and to obey the words of the agreement written in this book. [32]Then Josiah made all the people in Jerusalem and Benjamin promise to accept the agreement. So the people of Jerusalem obeyed the agreement of God, the God of their ancestors.

[33]And Josiah threw out the hateful idols from all the land that belonged to the Israelites. He led everyone in Israel to serve the LORD their God. While Josiah lived, the people obeyed the LORD, the God of their ancestors.

Josiah Celebrates the Passover

35 King Josiah celebrated the Passover [d] to the LORD in Jerusalem. The Passover lamb was killed on the fourteenth day of the first month. [2]Josiah chose the priests to do their duties, and he encouraged them as they served in the Temple [d] of the LORD. [3]The Levites taught the Israelites and were made holy for service to the LORD. Josiah said to them, "Put the Holy Ark [d] in the Temple that David's son Solomon, the king of Israel, built. Do not carry it from place to place on your shoulders any more. Now serve the LORD your God and his people Israel. [4]Prepare yourselves by your family groups for service, and do the jobs that King David and his son Solomon gave you to do.

[5]"Stand in the holy place with a group of the Levites for each family group of the people. [6]Kill the Passover lambs, and make yourselves holy to the LORD. Prepare the lambs for your relatives, the people of Israel, as the LORD through Moses commanded us to do."

[7]Josiah gave the Israelites 30,000 sheep and goats to kill for the Passover sacrifices, and he gave them 3,000 cattle. They were all his own animals.

[8]Josiah's officers also gave willingly to the people, the priests and the Levites. Hilkiah, Zechariah and Jehiel, the officers in charge of the Temple, gave the priests 2,600 lambs and goats and 300 cattle for Passover sacrifices. [9]Conaniah, his brothers Shemaiah and Nethanel, and Hashabiah,

Jeiel and Jozabad gave the Levites 5,000 sheep and goats and 500 cattle for Passover sacrifices. These men were leaders of the Levites.

[10]When everything was ready for the Passover service, the priests and Levites went to their places, as the king had commanded. [11]The Passover lambs were killed. Then the Levites skinned the animals and gave the blood to the priests, who sprinkled it on the altar. [12]Then they gave the animals for the burnt offerings to the different family groups so the burnt offerings could be offered to the LORD as was written in the book of Moses. They also did this with the cattle. [13]The Levites roasted the Passover sacrifices over the fire as they were commanded, and they boiled the holy offerings in pots, kettles and pans. Then they quickly gave the meat to the people. [14]After this was finished, the Levites prepared meat for themselves and for the priests, the descendants [d] of Aaron. The priests worked until night, offering the burnt offerings and burning the fat of the sacrifices.

[15]The Levite singers from Asaph's family stood in the places chosen for them by King David, Asaph, Heman and Jeduthun, the king's seer. [d] The gatekeepers at each gate did not have to leave their places, because their fellow Levites had prepared everything for them for the Passover.

[16]So everything was done that day for the worship of the LORD, as King Josiah commanded. The Passover was celebrated, and the burnt offerings were offered on the LORD's altar. [17]The Israelites who were there celebrated the Passover and the Feast [d] of Unleavened Bread for seven days. [18]The Passover had not been celebrated like this in Israel since the prophet [d] Samuel was alive. None of the kings of Israel had ever celebrated a Passover as did King Josiah, the priests, the Levites, the people of Judah and Israel who were there, and the people of Jerusalem. [19]This Passover was celebrated in the eighteenth year Josiah was king.

The Death of Josiah

[20]After Josiah did all this for the Temple, [d] Neco king of Egypt led an army to attack Carchemish, a town on the Euphrates River. And Josiah marched out to fight against Neco. [21]But Neco sent messengers to Josiah, saying, "King Josiah, there should not be war between us. I did not come to fight you, but my enemies. God told me to hurry and he is on my side. So don't fight God, or he will destroy you."

[22]But Josiah did not go away. He wore different clothes so no one would know who he was. Refusing to listen to what Neco said at God's command, Josiah went to fight on the plain of Megiddo. [23]In the battle King Josiah was shot by archers. He told his servants, "Take me away because I am badly wounded." [24]So they took him out of his chariot and put him in another chariot and carried him to Jerusalem. There he died and

> **Sidelight** If you want to buy a house on the plain of Megiddo (2 Chronicles 35:22), expect to pay high "war insurance". This plain may be one of the bloodiest battlegrounds in the world. Archaeologists have uncovered twenty cities – one on top of the other – that have been destroyed at this site.

was buried in the graves where his ancestors were buried. All the people of Judah and Jerusalem were very sad because he was dead.

[25]Jeremiah wrote some sad songs about Josiah. Even to this day all the men and women singers remember and honour Josiah with these songs. It became a custom in Israel to sing these songs that are written in the collection of sad songs.

[26–27]The other things Josiah did as king, from beginning to end, are written in the book of the kings of Israel and Judah. It tells how he loved what was written in the LORD's teachings.

Jehoahaz King of Judah

36 The people of Judah chose Josiah's son Jehoahaz and made him king in Jerusalem in his father's place.

[2]Jehoahaz was 23 years old when he became king, and he was king in Jerusalem for three months. [3]Then King Neco of Egypt removed Jehoahaz from being king in Jerusalem. Neco made the people of Judah pay about 3.5 tonnes of silver and about 35 kilogrammes of gold. [4]The king of Egypt made Jehoahaz's brother Eliakim the king of Judah and Jerusalem and changed his name to Jehoiakim. But Neco took his brother Jehoahaz to Egypt.

Jehoiakim King of Judah

[5]Jehoiakim was 25 years old when he became king, and he was king in Jerusalem for eleven years. He did what the LORD his God said was wrong. [6]King Nebuchadnezzar of Babylon attacked Judah, captured Jehoiakim, put bronze chains on him and took him to Babylon. [7]Nebuchadnezzar removed some of the things from the Temple [d] of the LORD, took them to Babylon and put them in his own palace.

[8]The other things Jehoiakim did as king, the hateful things he did and everything he was guilty of doing, are written in the book of the kings of

Israel and Judah. And Jehoiakim's son Jehoiachin became king in his place.

Jehoiachin King of Judah

⁹Jehoiachin was eighteen years old when he became king of Judah, and he was king in Jerusalem for three months and ten days. He did what the LORD said was wrong. ¹⁰In the spring King Nebuchadnezzar sent for Jehoiachin and brought him and some valuable treasures from the Temple *d* of the LORD to Babylon. Then Nebuchadnezzar made Jehoiachin's uncle Zedekiah the king of Judah and Jerusalem.

Zedekiah King of Judah

¹¹Zedekiah was 21 years old when he became king of Judah, and he was king in Jerusalem for eleven years. ¹²Zedekiah did what the LORD his God said was wrong. The prophet *d* Jeremiah spoke messages from the LORD, but Zedekiah did not obey. ¹³Zedekiah turned against King Nebuchadnezzar, who had forced him to swear in God's name to be loyal to him. But Zedekiah became stubborn and refused to obey the LORD,

the God of Israel. ¹⁴Also, all the leaders of the priests and the people of Judah became more wicked, following the evil example of the other nations. The LORD had made the Temple *d* in Jerusalem holy, but the leaders made it unholy.

The Fall of Jerusalem

¹⁵The LORD, the God of their ancestors, sent prophets *d* again and again to warn his people, because he had pity on them and on his Temple. *d* ¹⁶But they made fun of God's prophets and hated God's messages. They refused to listen to the prophets until, finally, the LORD became so angry with his people that he could not be stopped. ¹⁷So God brought the king of Babylon to attack them. The king killed the young men even when they were in the Temple. He had no mercy on the young men or women, the old men or those who were sick. God handed all of them over to Nebuchadnezzar. ¹⁸Nebuchadnezzar carried away to Babylon all the things from the Temple of God, both large and small, and all the treasures from the Temple of the LORD and from the king and his officers. ¹⁹Nebuchadnezzar and his army set

ANGER

One Mad Mum

Cari Lightner was only thirteen years old when a drunk driver swerved and killed her.

When the police arrested the driver, they discovered he had been arrested many times before for drunk driving. Still, they told Cari's mother, Candy, that this man would probably go free. There were no laws in the USA at that time that could keep him in prison.

How could someone kill her daughter and go free? In her anger, Candy declared to friends, "I'm going to start an organisation." She created Mothers Against Drunk Drivers (MADD), a group that would work to pass tough laws that would punish drunk drivers. And the work paid off. Within five years, every state in the United States had made its drink-driving laws more strict.

MADD has made people aware of the problem of drinking and driving, and its efforts have saved lives.

Candy Lightner and the thousands of MADD members put their anger to work and brought about change. In **2 Chronicles 36:14–21**, you can see changes that occurred when God became angry with his people.

* What part did anger play in Candy's – and God's – actions?
* Based on this passage, what kinds of things make God angry?

Consider . . .

* writing to politicians about an issue you think needs to be changed.
* thinking of an issue that makes you angry and then doing three things to change the situation.

For more, see . . .

* Exodus 32:19–35 (p.91)
* Luke 19:45–48 (p.1083)

* Psalm 103:8 (p.559)

fire to God's Temple and broke down Jerusalem's wall and burned all the palaces. They took or destroyed every valuable thing in Jerusalem.

²⁰Nebuchadnezzar took captive to Babylon the people who were left alive, and he forced them to be slaves for him and his descendants. *d* They remained there as slaves until the Persian kingdom defeated Babylon. ²¹And so what the LORD had told Israel through the prophet Jeremiah happened: the country was an empty wasteland for 70 years to make up for the years of Sabbath rest*n* that the people had not kept.

²²In the first year Cyrus was king of Persia, the LORD had Cyrus send an announcement to his whole kingdom. This happened so the LORD's message spoken by Jeremiah would come true. He wrote:

²³This is what Cyrus king of Persia says:

The Lord, the God of heaven, has given me all the kingdoms of the earth, and he has appointed me to build a Temple for him at Jerusalem in Judah. Now may the Lord your God be with all of you who are his people. You are free to go to Jerusalem.

Sabbath rest   The Law said that every seventh year the land was not to be farmed. See Leviticus 25:1–7.

Ezra

When?

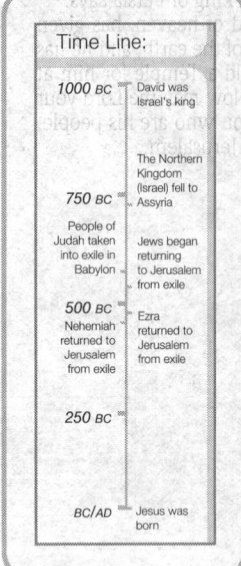

Time Line:

1000 BC	David was Israel's king
	The Northern Kingdom (Israel) fell to Assyria
750 BC	
People of Judah taken into exile in Babylon	Jews began returning to Jerusalem from exile
500 BC	Ezra returned to Jerusalem from exile
Nehemiah returned to Jerusalem from exile	
250 BC	
BC/AD	Jesus was born

Why Read This Book:

* See how God uses world events to help his people (Ezra 1).
* Learn how to trust God in the face of opposition (Ezra 4—6).
* Examine the cost of compromising beliefs (Ezra 7—10).

Behind the Scenes:

If you have moved from one community to another, you know what it's like to visit the old community. Nothing seems the same. Trees look larger, buildings older and people different. It's no longer home.

The people of Judah had been gone from Israel for many years, captives of the Babylonian Empire. The Persians had then conquered Babylon and let the captives go home. The Jews could return to Jerusalem and worship their God.

But things were different now. The people were different. Now they were called Jews, not Israelites. Many of them spoke primarily Aramaic, not the old Hebrew. They used to be rural people; now they lived in towns.

Instead of being an independent nation, the returning Jews were more like a religious community. The people who had stayed behind resented the exiles for wanting their land back. And Jerusalem, which the Babylonians had destroyed, lay in ruins. So, despite the excitement, home wasn't the way they had left it.

The books of Ezra and Nehemiah (p.443), which were originally one book, tell the story of these returning exiles. In general, the books focus on the rebuilding of the Temple (Ezra 1—7), the preserving of the faith (Ezra 8—10) and the rebuilding of Jerusalem's walls (Nehemiah).

Through it all, we often see people wanting to give up. We see leaders challenging them and renewing their energy. And we see the people's faithfulness even when the obstacles seem impossible. Their story can be a comfort and a challenge to help us to stick with our faith in tough times.

Where?

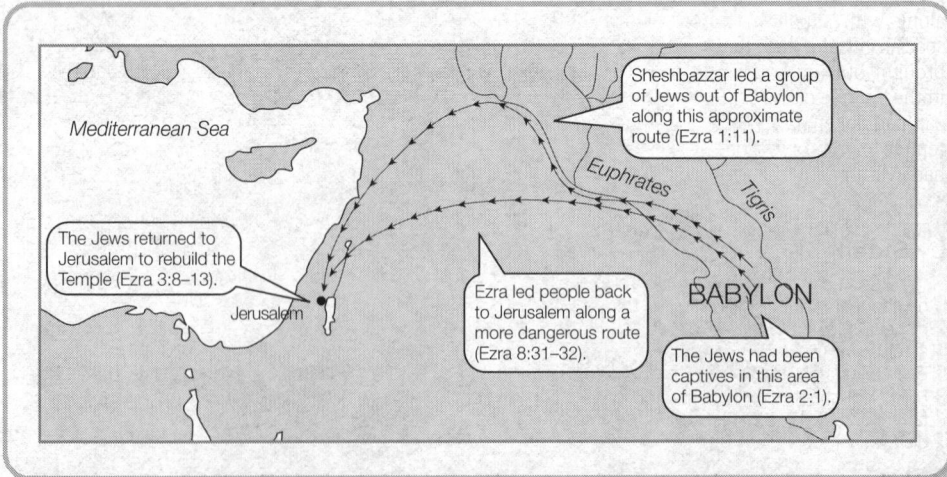

Sheshbazzar led a group of Jews out of Babylon along this approximate route (Ezra 1:11).

The Jews returned to Jerusalem to rebuild the Temple (Ezra 3:8–13).

Ezra led people back to Jerusalem along a more dangerous route (Ezra 8:31–32).

The Jews had been captives in this area of Babylon (Ezra 2:1).

Mediterranean Sea

Euphrates

Tigris

BABYLON

Jerusalem

Cyrus Helps the Captives Return

1 In the first year Cyrus was king of Persia, the LORD caused Cyrus to send an announcement to his whole kingdom and to put it in writing. This happened so the LORD's message spoken by Jeremiah would come true. He wrote:

²This is what Cyrus king of Persia says:

The LORD, the God of heaven, has given all the kingdoms of the earth to me, and he has appointed me to build a Temple *d* for him at Jerusalem in Judah. ³May God be with all of you who are his people. You are free to go to Jerusalem in Judah and build the Temple of the LORD, the God of Israel, who is in Jerusalem. ⁴Those who stay behind, wherever they live, should support those who want to go. Give them silver and gold, supplies and cattle, and special gifts for the Temple of God in Jerusalem.

> **Sidelight**
> King Cyrus's decree granting religious freedom to the Jews apparently wasn't a special privilege for them alone (Ezra 1:4). Archaeologists have unearthed The Cyrus Cylinder, which reveals that Cyrus's policy extended to all people who had been taken captive by Babylon.

⁵Then the family leaders of Judah and Benjamin and the priests and Levites got ready to go to Jerusalem—everyone God had caused to want to go to Jerusalem to build the Temple of the LORD. ⁶All their neighbours helped them, giving them things made of silver and gold, along with supplies, cattle, valuable gifts and special gifts for the Temple. ⁷Also, King Cyrus brought out the bowls and pans that belonged in the Temple of the LORD, which Nebuchadnezzar had taken from Jerusalem and put in the temple of his own god. ⁸Cyrus king of Persia had Mithredath the treasurer bring them and

> **Sidelight**
> When Cyrus sent the Jews back to Jerusalem, he had them take 30 gold dishes, 1,000 silver dishes, 29 silver pans, 30 gold bowls and 410 silver bowls (Ezra 1:9) – valuables that had been taken from the Temple in Jerusalem by King Nebuchadnezzar when he destroyed it (2 Kings 25:8–17, p.370). Hope he sent a dishwasher too!

count them out for Sheshbazzar, the prince of Judah.

⁹He listed 30 gold dishes, 1,000 silver dishes, 29 pans, ¹⁰30 gold bowls, 410 matching silver bowls and 1,000 other pieces.

¹¹There was a total of 5,400 pieces of gold and silver. Sheshbazzar brought all these things along when the captives went from Babylon to Jerusalem.

The Captives who Returned

2 These are the people of the area who returned from captivity, whom Nebuchadnezzar king of Babylon had taken away to Babylon. They returned to Jerusalem and Judah, each going back to his own town. ²These people returned with Zerubbabel, Jeshua, Nehemiah, Seraiah, Reelaiah, Mordecai, Bilshan, Mispar, Bigvai, Rehum and Baanah.

> **Sidelight**
> Not all the Jews returned from exile when the Persians let them leave (Ezra 2:1–2). According to Babylonian records, some Jews had become prominent bankers, business people and government officials in Babylon.

These are the people from Israel: ³the descendants *d* of Parosh—2,172; ⁴the descendants of Shephatiah—372; ⁵the descendants of Arah—775; ⁶the descendants of Pahath-Moab (through the family of Jeshua and Joab)—2,812; ⁷the descendants of Elam—1,254; ⁸the descendants of Zattu—945; ⁹the descendants of Zaccai—760; ¹⁰the descendants of Bani—642; ¹¹the descendants of Bebai—623; ¹²the descendants of Azgad—1,222; ¹³the descendants of Adonikam—666; ¹⁴the descendants of Bigvai—2,056; ¹⁵the descendants of Adin—454; ¹⁶the descendants of Ater (through the family of Hezekiah)—98; ¹⁷the descendants of Bezai—323; ¹⁸the descendants of Jorah—112; ¹⁹the descendants of Hashum—223; ²⁰the descendants of Gibbar—95.

²¹These are the people from the towns: of Bethlehem—123; ²²of Netophah—56; ²³of Anathoth—128; ²⁴of Azmaveth—42; ²⁵of Kiriath Jearim, Kephirah and Beeroth—743; ²⁶of Ramah and Geba—621; ²⁷of Michmash—122; ²⁸of Bethel and Ai—223; ²⁹of Nebo—52; ³⁰of Magbish—156; ³¹of the other town of Elam—1,254; ³²of Harim—320; ³³of Lod, Hadid and Ono—725; ³⁴of Jericho—345; ³⁵of Senaah—3,630.

³⁶These are the priests: the descendants of Jedaiah (through the family of Jeshua)—973; ³⁷the

descendants of Immer—1,052; ³⁸the descendants of Pashhur—1,247; ³⁹the descendants of Harim—1,017.

⁴⁰These are the Levites: the descendants of Jeshua and Kadmiel (through the family of Hodaviah)—74.

⁴¹These are the singers: the descendants of Asaph—128.

⁴²These are the gatekeepers of the Temple: *d* the descendants of Shallum, Ater, Talmon, Akkub, Hatita and Shobai—139.

⁴³These are the Temple servants: the descendants of Ziha, Hasupha, Tabbaoth, ⁴⁴Keros, Siaha, Padon, ⁴⁵Lebanah, Hagabah, Akkub, ⁴⁶Hagab, Shalmai, Hanan, ⁴⁷Giddel, Gahar, Reaiah, ⁴⁸Rezin, Nekoda, Gazzam, ⁴⁹Uzza, Paseah, Besai, ⁵⁰Asnah, Meunim, Nephussim, ⁵¹Bakbuk, Hakupha, Harhur, ⁵²Bazluth, Mehida, Harsha, ⁵³Barkos, Sisera, Temah, ⁵⁴Neziah and Hatipha.

⁵⁵These are the descendants of the servants of Solomon: the descendants of Sotai, Hassophereth, Peruda, ⁵⁶Jaala, Darkon, Giddel, ⁵⁷Shephatiah, Hattil, Pokereth-Hazzebaim and Ami.

⁵⁸The Temple servants and the descendants of the servants of Solomon numbered 392.

⁵⁹Some people came to Jerusalem from the towns of Tel Melah, Tel Harsha, Kerub, Addon and Immer, but they could not prove that their ancestors came from Israel. ⁶⁰They were the descendants of Delaiah, Tobiah and Nekoda—652.

⁶¹Also these priests: the descendants of Hobaiah, Hakkoz and Barzillai, who had married a daughter of Barzillai from Gilead and was called by her family name.

⁶²These people searched for their family records but could not find them. So they could not be priests, because they were thought to be unclean. ⁶³The governor ordered them not to eat any of the food offered to God until a priest had settled this matter by using the Urim and Thummim. *d*

⁶⁴The total number of those who returned was 42,360. ⁶⁵This is not counting their 7,337 male and female servants and the 200 male and female singers they had with them. ⁶⁶They had 736 horses, 245 mules, ⁶⁷435 camels and 6,720 donkeys.

⁶⁸When they arrived at the Temple of the LORD in Jerusalem, some of the leaders of families gave offerings to rebuild the Temple of God on the same site as before. ⁶⁹They gave as much as they could to the treasury to rebuild the Temple— about 500 kilogrammes of gold, about 2,800 kilogrammes of silver and 100 pieces of clothing for the priests.

⁷⁰All the Israelites settled in their home towns. The priests, Levites, singers, gatekeepers and Temple servants, along with some of the other people, settled in their own towns as well.

Rebuilding the Altar

3 In the seventh month, after the Israelites were settled in their home towns, they met together in Jerusalem. ²Then Jeshua son of Jozadak and his fellow priests joined Zerubbabel son of Shealtiel and began to build the altar of the God of Israel where they could offer burnt offerings, just as it is written in the Teachings of Moses, the man of God. ³Even though they were afraid of the people living around them, they built the altar where it had been before. And they offered burnt offerings on it to the LORD morning and evening. ⁴Then, to obey what was written, they celebrated the Feast *d* of Shelters. They offered the right number of sacrifices for each day of the festival. ⁵After the Feast of Shelters, they had regular sacrifices every day, as well as sacrifices for the New Moon*d* and all the festivals commanded by the LORD. Also there were special offerings brought as gifts to the LORD. ⁶On the first day of the seventh month they began to bring burnt offerings to the LORD, but the foundation of the LORD's Temple *d* had not yet been laid.

Rebuilding the Temple

⁷Then they gave money to the bricklayers and carpenters. They also gave food, wine and oil to the cities of Sidon and Tyre so they would float cedar logs from Lebanon to the seacoast town of Joppa. Cyrus king of Persia had given permission for this.

⁸In the second month of the second year after their arrival at the Temple*d* of God in Jerusalem, Zerubbabel son of Shealtiel, Jeshua son of Jozadak, their fellow priests and Levites, and all who had returned from captivity to Jerusalem began to work. They chose Levites 20 years old and older to be in charge of the building of the Temple of the LORD. ⁹These men were in charge of the work of building the Temple of God: Jeshua and his sons and brothers; Kadmiel and his sons who were the descendants of Hodaviah; and the sons of Henadad and their sons and brothers. They were all Levites.

¹⁰The builders finished laying the foundation of the Temple of the LORD. Then the priests, dressed in their robes, stood with their trumpets, and the Levites, the sons of Asaph, stood with their cymbals. They all took their places and praised the LORD just as David king of Israel had said to do. ¹¹With praise and thanksgiving, they sang to the LORD:

"He is good;

his love for Israel continues for ever."

And then all the people shouted loudly, "Praise the LORD! The foundation of his Temple has been laid." ¹²But many of the older priests, Levites and family leaders who had seen the first Temple cried when they saw the foundation of this Temple. Most of the other people were shouting with joy. [13]The people made so much noise it could be heard far away, and no one could tell the difference between the joyful shouting and the sad crying.

Enemies of the Rebuilding

4 When the enemies of the people of Judah and Benjamin heard that the returned captives were building a Temple [d] for the LORD, the God of Israel, [2]they came to Zerubbabel and the leaders of the families. The enemies said, "Let us help you build, because we are like you and want to worship your God. We have been offering sacrifices to him since the time of Esarhaddon king of Assyria, who brought us here."

[3]But Zerubbabel, Jeshua and the leaders of Israel answered, "You will not help us build a Temple to our God. We will build it ourselves for the LORD, the God of Israel, as King Cyrus, the king of Persia, commanded us to do."

[4]Then the people around them tried to discourage the people of Judah by making them afraid to build. [5]Their enemies hired others to delay the building plans during the time Cyrus was king of Persia. And it continued to the time Darius was king of Persia.

More Problems for the Builders

[6]When Xerxes first became king, those enemies wrote a letter against the people of Judah and Jerusalem.

[7]When Artaxerxes became king of Persia, Bishlam, Mithredath, Tabeel and those with them wrote a letter to Artaxerxes. It was written in the Aramaic language and translated.

[8]Rehum the governor and Shimshai the governor's secretary wrote a letter against Jerusalem to Artaxerxes the king. It said:

Sidelight
The Old Testament was originally written in Hebrew, right? Well, not all of it. Ezra 4:8—6:18 and 7:12—26 were written in Aramaic, which was the language Jesus would speak centuries later. Three other Old Testament passages were also written in Aramaic (Genesis 31:47, p.37; Jeremiah 10:11, p.729; and Daniel 2:4—7:28, p.834).

[9]This letter is from Rehum the governor, Shimshai the secretary and their fellow workers—the judges and important officers over the men who came from Tripolis, Persia, Erech and Babylon, the Elamite people of Susa, [10]and those whom the great and honourable Ashurbanipal forced out of their countries and settled in the city of Samaria and in other places of the west of the Euphrates River.

[11](This is a copy of the letter they sent to Artaxerxes.)

To King Artaxerxes.
From your servants who live west of the Euphrates River.

[12]King Artaxerxes, you should know that the Jewish people who came to us from you have gone to Jerusalem to rebuild that evil city that refuses to obey. They are fixing the walls and repairing the foundations of the buildings.

[13]Now, King Artaxerxes, you should know that if Jerusalem is built and its walls are fixed, Jerusalem will not pay taxes of any kind. Then the amount of money your government collects will be less. [14]Since we must be loyal to the government, we don't want to see the king dishonoured. So we are writing to let the king know. [15]We suggest you search the records of the kings who ruled before you. You will find out that the city of Jerusalem refuses to obey and makes trouble for kings and areas controlled by Persia. Since long ago it has been a place where disobedience has started. That is why it was destroyed. [16]We want you to know, King Artaxerxes, that if this city is rebuilt and its walls fixed, you will be left with nothing west of the Euphrates River.

[17]King Artaxerxes sent this answer:

To Rehum the governor and Shimshai the secretary, to all their fellow workers living in Samaria, and to those in other places west of the Euphrates River.

Greetings.
[18]The letter you sent to us has been translated and read to me. [19]I ordered the records to be searched, and it was done. We found that Jerusalem has a history of disobedience to kings and has been a place of problems and trouble. [20]Jerusalem has had powerful kings who have ruled over the whole area west of the Euphrates River, and taxes of all kinds have been paid to them. [21]Now, give an order for those men to stop work. The city of Jerusalem will not be rebuilt until I say so. [22]Make sure you do this, because if they continue, it will hurt the government.

[23]A copy of the letter that King Artaxerxes sent was read to Rehum and Shimshai the secretary and the others. Then they quickly went to the Jewish people in Jerusalem and forced them to stop building.

[24]So the work on the Temple *d* of God in Jerusalem stopped until the second year Darius was king of Persia.

Tattenai's Letter to Darius

5 The prophets Haggai and Zechariah, a descendant *d* of Iddo, prophesied *d* to the Jewish people in Judah and Jerusalem in the name of the God of Israel, who was over them. [2]Then Zerubbabel son of Shealtiel and Jeshua son of Jozadak started working again to rebuild the Temple *d* of God in Jerusalem. And the prophets of God were there, helping them.

[3]At that time Tattenai, who was the governor west of the Euphrates River, and Shethar-Bozenai and their fellow workers went to the Jewish people and asked, "Who gave you permission to rebuild this Temple and fix these walls?" [4]They also asked, "What are the names of the men working on this building?" [5]But their God was watching over the elders of the Jewish people. The builders were not stopped until a report could go to King Darius and his written answer could be received.

[6]This is a copy of the letter that was sent to King Darius by Tattenai, who was the governor of west of the Euphrates River, Shethar-Bozenai and the other important officers of west of the Euphrates River. [7]This is what was said in the report they sent to him:

To King Darius.

Greetings. May you have peace.

[8]King Darius, you should know that we went to the district of Judah where the Temple of the great God is. The people are building that Temple with large stones and they are putting timbers in the walls. They are working very hard and are building very fast.

[9]We asked their elders, "Who gave you permission to rebuild this Temple and these walls?" [10]We also asked for their names, and we wrote down the names of their leaders so you would know who they are.

[11]This is the answer they gave to us: "We are the servants of the God of heaven and earth. We are rebuilding the Temple that a great king of Israel built and finished many years ago. [12]But our ancestors made the God of heaven angry, so he handed them over to Nebuchadnezzar king of Babylon, who destroyed this Temple and took the people to Babylon as captives.

[13]"Later, in the first year Cyrus was king of Babylon, he gave a special order for this Temple to be rebuilt. [14]Cyrus brought out from the temple in Babylon the gold and silver bowls and pans that came from the Temple of God. Nebuchadnezzar had taken them from the Temple in Jerusalem and had put them in the temple in Babylon.

"Then King Cyrus gave them to Sheshbazzar, his appointed governor. [15]Cyrus said to him, 'Take these gold and silver bowls and pans, and put them back in the Temple in Jerusalem and rebuild the Temple of God where it was.' [16]So Sheshbazzar came and laid the foundations of the Temple of God in Jerusalem. From that day until now the work has been going on, but it is not yet finished."

[17]Now, if the king wishes, let a search be made in the royal records of Babylon. See if King Cyrus gave an order to rebuild this Temple in Jerusalem. Then let the king write to us and tell us what he has decided.

The Order of Darius

6 So King Darius gave an order to search the records kept in the treasury in Babylon. [2]A scroll was found in Ecbatana, the capital city of Media. This is what was written on it:

Note:

[3]King Cyrus gave an order about the Temple *d* of God in Jerusalem in the first year he was king. This was the order:

"Let the Temple be rebuilt as a place to present sacrifices. Let its foundations be laid; it should be 30 metres high and 30 metres wide. [4]It must have three layers of large stones and then one layer of timbers. The costs should be paid from the king's treasury. [5]The gold and silver utensils from the Temple of God should be put back in their places. Nebuchadnezzar took them from the Temple in Jerusalem and brought them to Babylon, but they are to be put back in the Temple of God in Jerusalem."

[6]Now then, Tattenai, governor of west of the Euphrates River, Shethar-Bozenai and all the officers of that area, stay away from there. [7]Do not bother the work on that Temple of God. Let the governor of the Jewish people and the Jewish elders rebuild this Temple where it was before.

[8]Also, I order you to do this for those elders of the Jewish people who are building this Temple: the cost of the building is to be fully paid from the royal treasury, from taxes collected from west of the Euphrates River.

Do this so the work will not stop. [9]Give those people anything they need—young bulls, rams or lambs for burnt offerings to the God of heaven, or wheat, salt, wine or olive oil. Give the priests in Jerusalem anything they ask for every day without fail. [10]Then they may offer sacrifices pleasing to the God of heaven, and they may pray for the life of the king and his sons.

[11]Also, I give this order: if anyone changes this order, a wooden beam is to be pulled from his house and driven through his body. Because of his crime, make his house a pile

Sidelight
King Darius didn't like his orders to be questioned. If you changed what he said, a wooden beam was to be taken from your house and driven through your body (Ezra 6:11). According to other sources, Darius impaled 3,000 Babylonians when he captured their city.

of ruins. [12]God has chosen Jerusalem as the place he is to be worshipped. May he punish any king or person who tries to change this order and destroy this Temple.

I, Darius, have given this order. Let it be obeyed quickly and carefully.

Completion of the Temple

[13]So, Tattenai, the governor west of the Euphrates River, Shethar-Bozenai and their fellow workers carried out King Darius' order quickly and carefully. [14]The Jewish elders continued to build and were successful because of the preaching of Haggai the prophet [d] and Zechariah, a descendant of Iddo. They finished building the Temple [d] as the God of Israel had commanded and as kings Cyrus, Darius and Artaxerxes of Persia had ordered. [15]The Temple was finished on the third day of the month of Adar in the sixth year Darius was king.

[16]Then the people of Israel celebrated and gave the Temple to God to honour him. Everybody was happy: the priests, the Levites and the rest of the Jewish people who had returned from captivity. [17]They gave the Temple to God by offering 100 bulls, 200 rams and 400 lambs as sacrifices. And as an offering to forgive the sins of all Israel, they offered twelve male goats, one goat for each tribe [d] in Israel. [18]Then they put the priests and the Levites into their separate groups. Each group had a certain time to serve God in the Temple at Jerusalem as it is written in the Book of Moses.

The Passover is Celebrated

[19]The Jewish people who returned from captivity celebrated the Passover [d] on the fourteenth day of the first month. [20]The priests and Levites had made themselves clean. [d] Then the Levites killed the Passover lambs for all the people who had returned from captivity, for their relatives the priests and for themselves. [21]So all the people of Israel who returned from captivity ate the Passover lamb. So did the people who had given up the unclean ways of their non-Jewish neighbours in order to worship the LORD, the God of Israel. [22]For seven days they celebrated the Feast [d] of Unleavened Bread in a very joyful way. The LORD had made them happy by changing the mind of the king of Assyria so that he helped them in the work on the Temple of the God of Israel.

Ezra Comes to Jerusalem

7 After these things [n] during the rule of Artaxerxes king of Persia, Ezra came up from Babylon. Ezra was the son of Seraiah, the son of Azariah, the son of Hilkiah, [2]the son of Shallum, the son of Zadok, the son of Ahitub, [3]the son of Amariah, the son of Azariah, the son of Meraioth, [4]the son of Zerahiah, the son of Uzzi, the son of Bukki, [5]the son of Abishua, the son of Phinehas, the son of Eleazar, the son of Aaron the high priest. [6]This Ezra came to Jerusalem from Babylon. He was a teacher and knew well the Teachings of Moses that had been given by the LORD, the God of Israel. Ezra received everything he asked for from the king, because the LORD his God was helping him. [7]In the seventh year of King Artaxerxes more Israelites came to Jerusalem. Among them were priests, Levites, singers, gatekeepers and Temple [d] servants.

[8]Ezra arrived in Jerusalem in the fifth month of Artaxerxes' seventh year as king. [9]Ezra had left Babylon on the first day of the first month, and he arrived in Jerusalem on the first day of the fifth

Sidelight
Ezra's journey from Babylon to Jerusalem was about 1,440 km – about two days' driving. But because there were no motorways or cars, the trip took about four months (Ezra 7:9).

month, because God was helping him. [10]Ezra had worked hard to know and obey the Teachings of the LORD and to teach his rules and commands to the Israelites.

After these things   There is a time period of about 60 years between chapters six and seven.

Artaxerxes' Letter to Ezra

[11]King Artaxerxes had given a letter to Ezra, a priest and teacher who taught about the commands and laws the LORD gave Israel. This is a copy of the letter:

Sidelight Ezra is known as the "Father of Judaism" for his role in preserving the faith (Ezra 7:10). Tradition credits him with dictating from memory 94 books (including 24 in the Old Testament) that might otherwise have been lost or burned during the Exile.

---

[12]From Artaxerxes, king of kings, to Ezra the priest, a teacher of the Law of the God of heaven.

Greetings.

[13]Now I give this order: Any Israelite in my kingdom who wishes may go with you to Jerusalem, including priests and Levites. [14]Ezra, you are sent by the king and the seven people who advise him to ask how Judah and Jerusalem are obeying the Law of your God, which you are carrying with you. [15]Also take with you the silver and gold that the king and those who advise him have given freely to the God of Israel, whose Temple [d] is in Jerusalem. [16]Also take the silver and gold you receive from the area of Babylon. Take the offerings the Israelites and their priests have given as gifts for the Temple of your God in Jerusalem. [17]With this money buy bulls, rams and lambs, and the grain offerings and drink offerings that go with those sacrifices. Then sacrifice them on the altar in the Temple of your God in Jerusalem.

[18]You and your fellow Jews may spend the silver and gold left over as you want and as God wishes. [19]Take to the God of Jerusalem all the utensils for worship in the Temple of your God, [20]which we have given you. Use the royal treasury to pay for anything else you need for the Temple of your God.

[21]Now I, King Artaxerxes, give this order to all the men in charge of the treasury of west of the Euphrates River: Give Ezra, a priest and a teacher of the Law of the God of heaven, whatever he asks for. [22]Give him up to 3.5 tonnes of silver, 10 tonnes of wheat, 2,000 litres of wine and 2,000 litres of olive oil. And give him as

much salt as he wants. [23]Carefully give him whatever the God of heaven wants for the Temple of the God of heaven. We do not want God to be angry with the king and his sons. [24]Remember, you must not make these people pay taxes of any kind: priests, Levites, singers, gatekeepers, Temple servants and other workers in this Temple of God.

[25]And you, Ezra, use the wisdom you have from your God to choose judges and lawmakers to rule the Jewish people, west of the Euphrates River. They know the laws of your God, and you may teach anyone who does not know them. [26]Whoever does not obey the law of your God or of the king must be punished. He will be killed, or sent away, or have his property taken away, or be put in jail.

[27]Praise the LORD, the God of our ancestors. He caused the king to want to honour the Temple of the LORD in Jerusalem. [28]The LORD has shown me, Ezra, his love in the presence of the king, those who advise the king and the royal officers. Because the LORD my God was helping me, I had courage, and I gathered the leaders of Israel to return with me.

Leaders Who Returned with Ezra

8 These are the leaders of the family groups and those who were listed with them who came back with me from Babylon during the rule of King Artaxerxes.

[2]From the descendants [d] of Phinehas: Gershom. From the descendants of Ithamar: Daniel. From the descendants of David: Hattush [3]of the descendants of Shecaniah.

From the descendants of Parosh: Zechariah, with 150 men.

[4]From the descendants of Pahath-Moab: Eliehoenai son of Zerahiah, with 200 men.

[5]From the descendants of Zattu: Shecaniah son of Jahaziel, with 300 men.

[6]From the descendants of Adin: Ebed son of Jonathan, with 50 men.

[7]From the descendants of Elam: Jeshaiah son of Athaliah, with 70 men.

[8]From the descendants of Shephatiah: Zebadiah son of Michael, with 80 men.

[9]From the descendants of Joab: Obadiah son of Jehiel, with 218 men.

[10]From the descendants of Bani: Shelomith son of Josiphiah, with 160 men.

[11]From the descendants of Bebai: Zechariah son of Bebai, with 28 men.

[12]From the descendants of Azgad: Johanan son of Hakkatan, with 110 men.

¹³From the descendants of Adonikam, these were the last ones: Eliphelet, Jeuel and Shemaiah, with 60 men. ¹⁴From the descendants of Bigvai: Uthai and Zaccur, with 70 men.

The Return to Jerusalem

¹⁵I called all those people together at the canal that flows towards Ahava, where we camped for three days. I checked all the people and the priests, but I did not find any Levites. ¹⁶So I called these leaders: Eliezer, Ariel, Shemaiah, Elnathan, Jarib, Elnathan, Nathan, Zechariah and Meshullam. And I called Joiarib and Elnathan, who were teachers. ¹⁷I sent these men to Iddo, the leader at Casiphia, and told them what to say to Iddo and his relatives, who are the Temple ᵈ servants in Casiphia. I sent them to bring servants to us for the Temple of our God. ¹⁸Our God was helping us, so Iddo's relatives gave us Sherebiah, a wise man from the descendants of Mahli son of Levi, who was the son of Israel. And they brought Sherebiah's sons and brothers, for a total of eighteen men. ¹⁹And they brought to us Hashabiah and Jeshaiah from the descendants of Merari, and his brothers and nephews. In all there were 20 men. ²⁰They also brought 220 of the Temple servants, a group David and the officers had set up to help the Levites. All of those men were listed by name.

²¹There by the Ahava Canal, I announced we would all give up eating and humble ourselves before our God. We would ask God for a safe trip for ourselves, our children and all our possessions. ²²I was ashamed to ask the king for soldiers and horsemen to protect us from enemies on the road. We had said to the king, "Our God helps everyone who obeys him, but he is very angry with all who reject him." ²³So we gave up eating and prayed to our God about our trip, and he answered our prayers.

²⁴Then I chose twelve of the priests who were leaders, Sherebiah, Hashabiah and ten of their relatives. ²⁵I weighed the offering of silver and gold and the utensils given for the Temple of our God, and I gave them to the twelve priests I had chosen. The king, the people who advised him, his officers and all the Israelites there with us had given these things for the Temple. ²⁶I weighed out and gave them about 22 tonnes of silver, about 14 tonnes of silver objects and about 14 tonnes of gold. ²⁷I gave them 20 gold bowls that weighed about 8.5 kilogrammes and two fine pieces of polished bronze that were as valuable as gold.

²⁸Then I said to the priests, "You and these utensils belong to the LORD for his service. The silver and gold are gifts to the LORD, the God of your ancestors. ²⁹Guard these things carefully. In Jerusalem, weigh them in front of the leading priests, Levites and the leaders of the family groups of Israel in the rooms of the Temple of the LORD." ³⁰So the priests and Levites accepted the silver, the gold and the utensils that had been weighed to take them to the Temple of our God in Jerusalem.

³¹On the twelfth day of the first month we left the Ahava Canal and started towards Jerusalem. Our God helped us and protected us from enemies and robbers along the way. ³²Finally we arrived in Jerusalem where we rested three days.

³³On the fourth day we weighed out the silver, the gold and the utensils in the Temple of our God. We handed them to the priest Meremoth son of Uriah. Eleazar son of Phinehas was with him, as were the Levites Jozabad son of Jeshua and Noadiah son of Binnui. ³⁴We checked everything by number and by weight, and the total weight was written down.

³⁵Then the captives who returned made burnt offerings to the God of Israel. They sacrificed twelve bulls for all Israel, 96 rams and 77 lambs. For a sin offering there were twelve male goats. All this was a burnt offering to the LORD. ³⁶They took King Artaxerxes' orders to the royal officers and to the governors, west of the Euphrates River. Then these men gave help to the people and the Temple of God.

Ezra's Prayer

9 After these things had been done, the leaders came to me and said, "Ezra, the Israelites, including the priests and Levites, have not kept themselves separate from the people around us. Those neighbours do evil things, as the Canaanites, Hittites, Perizzites, Jebusites, Ammonites, Moabites, Egyptians and Amorites did. ²The Israelite men and their sons have married these women. They have mixed the people who belong to God with the people around them. The leaders and officers of Israel have led the rest of the Israelites to do this unfaithful thing."

³When I heard this, I angrily tore my robe and coat, pulled hair from my head and beard, and sat

---

Sidelight When Ezra got upset, he tore his clothes and pulled hair out of his head and beard – the only person to do that in the Bible (Ezra 9:3). Nehemiah had a less painful approach – for him, at least. He pulled out the hair of people at whom he was angry (Nehemiah 13:25, p.457).

down in shock. [4]Everyone who trembled in fear at the word of the God of Israel gathered around me because of the unfaithfulness of the captives who had returned. I sat there in shock until the evening sacrifice.

[5]At the evening sacrifice I got up from where I had shown my shame. My robe and coat were torn, and I fell on my knees with my hands spread out to the LORD my God. [6]I prayed, "My God, I am too ashamed and embarrassed to lift up my face to you, my God, because our sins are so many. They are higher than our heads. Our guilt even reaches up to the sky. [7]From the days of our ancestors until now, our guilt has been great. Because of our sins, we, our kings and our priests have been punished by the sword and captivity. Foreign kings have taken away our things and shamed us, even as it is today.

[8]"But now, for a short time, the LORD our God has been kind to us. He has let some of us come back from captivity and has let us live in safety in his holy place. And so our God gives us hope and a little relief from our slavery. [9]Even though we are slaves, our God has not left us. He caused the kings of Persia to be kind to us and has given us new life. We can rebuild the Temple [d] and repair its ruins. And he has given us a wall to protect us in Judah and Jerusalem.

[10]"But now, our God, what can we say after you have done all this? We have disobeyed your commands [11]that you gave through your servants the prophets. [d] You said, 'The land you are entering to own is ruined; the people living there have spoiled it by the evil they do. Their evil filled the land with uncleanness [d] from one end to the other. [12]So do not let your daughters marry their sons, and do not let their daughters marry your sons. Do not wish for their peace or success. Then you will be strong and eat the good things of the land. Then you can leave this land to your descendants [d] for ever.'

[13]"What has happened to us is our own fault. We have done evil things, and our guilt is great. But you, our God, have punished us less than we deserve; you have left a few of us alive. [14]We should not again break your commands by allowing marriages with these wicked people. If we did, you would get angry enough to destroy us,

FORGIVENESS

An Unexpected Visitor

"The Pope has been shot!" These words echoed throughout the world on 13 May 1981. Pope John Paul II had been shot in the stomach by Mehmet Ali Agca.

It tooks hours of surgery and weeks of painful rehabilitation for the Pope to regain his health. Yet he survived and returned to his duties. The terrorist was captured and imprisoned. It seemed the end of a near-fatal story. But it wasn't.

Less than three years after the shooting, the Pope visited Agca in Rome's Rebibbia prison. Sitting in Agca's cell, John Paul held Agca's hand and spoke softly with him for twenty minutes.

What did the Pope say to the man who had tried to kill him? "I spoke to him as a brother whom I have pardoned, and who has my complete trust . . . I was able to meet my assailant and repeat to him the pardon I gave immediately."

Pope John Paul II showed love to Mehmet Ali Agca by forgiving him. **Ezra 9:1–9** tells how God showed love to his people by forgiving them.

- Did Agca or the Israelites deserve the love and forgiveness they received? Why or why not?
- When has God forgiven you when you felt you didn't deserve it?

Consider . . .

- making a list of people who have offended you and then forgiving them in the same way that God has forgiven you.
- doing one loving thing for someone who it has been hard for you to love.

For more, see . . .

- Isaiah 1:18–20 (p.640)
- Romans 5:6–11 (p.1190)
- Matthew 6:9–15 (p.948)

and none of us would be left alive. [15]LORD, God of Israel, by your goodness a few of us are left alive today. We admit that we are guilty and none of us should be allowed to stand before you."

The People Confess Sin

10 As Ezra was praying and confessing and crying and throwing himself down in front of the Temple, [d] a large group of Israelite men, women and children gathered around him who were also crying loudly. [2]Then Shecaniah son of Jehiel the Elamite said to Ezra, "We have been unfaithful to our God by marrying women from the peoples around us. But even so, there is still hope for Israel. [3]Now let us make an agreement before our God. We will send away all these women and their children as you and those who respect the commands of our God advise. Let it be done to obey God's Teachings. [4]Get up, Ezra. You are in charge, and we will support you. Have courage and do it."

[5]So Ezra got up and made the priests, Levites and all the people of Israel promise to do what was suggested; and they promised. [6]Then Ezra left the Temple and went to the room of Jehohanan son of Eliashib. While Ezra was there, he did not eat or drink, because he was still sad about the unfaithfulness of the captives who had returned.

[7]They sent out an order in Judah and Jerusalem for all the captives who had returned to meet together in Jerusalem. [8]Whoever did not come to Jerusalem within three days would lose his property and would no longer be a member of the community of the returned captives. That was the decision of the officers and elders.

[9]So within three days all the people of Judah and Benjamin gathered in Jerusalem. It was the twentieth day of the ninth month. All the people were sitting in the open place in front of the Temple and were upset because of the meeting and because it was raining. [10]Ezra the priest stood up and said to them, "You have been unfaithful and have married non-Jewish women. You have made Israel more guilty. [11]Now, confess it to the LORD, the God of your ancestors. Do his will and separate yourselves from the people living around you and from your non-Jewish wives."

[12]Then the whole group answered Ezra with a loud voice, "Ezra, you're right! We must do what you say. [13]But there are many people here, and it's the rainy season. We can't stand outside, and this problem can't be solved in a day or two, because we have sinned badly. [14]Let our officers make a decision for the whole group. Then let everyone in our towns who has married a non-Jewish woman meet with the elders and judges of each town at a planned time, until the hot anger of our God turns away from us." [15]Only Jonathan son of Asahel, Jahzeiah son of Tikvah, Meshullam and Shabbethai the Levite were against the plan.

[16]So the returned captives did what was suggested. Ezra the priest chose men who were leaders of the family groups and named one from each family division. On the first day of the tenth month they sat down to study each case. [17]By the first day of the first month, they dealt with all the men who had married non-Jewish women.

Those Guilty of Marrying Non-Jewish Women

[18]These are the descendants [d] of the priests who had married foreign women:

From the descendants of Jeshua son of Jozadak and Jeshua's brothers: Maaseiah, Eliezer, Jarib and Gedaliah. [19](They all promised to divorce their wives, and each one brought a ram from the flock as a penalty offering.)

[20]From the descendants of Immer: Hanani and Zebadiah.

[21]From the descendants of Harim: Maaseiah, Elijah, Shemaiah, Jehiel and Uzziah.

[22]From the descendants of Pashhur: Elioenai, Maaseiah, Ishmael, Nethanel, Jozabad and Elasah.

[23]Among the Levites: Jozabad, Shimei, Kelaiah (also called Kelita), Pethahiah, Judah and Eliezer.

[24]Among the singers: Eliashib.

Among the gatekeepers: Shallum, Telem and Uri.

[25]And among the other Israelites, these married non-Jewish women:

From the descendants of Parosh: Ramiah, Izziah, Malkijah, Mijamin, Eleazar, Malkijah and Benaiah.

[26]From the descendants of Elam: Mattaniah, Zechariah, Jehiel, Abdi, Jeremoth and Elijah.

[27]From the descendants of Zattu: Elioenai, Eliashib, Mattaniah, Jeremoth, Zabad and Aziza.

[28]From the descendants of Bebai: Jehohanan, Hananiah, Zabbai and Athlai.

[29]From the descendants of Bani: Meshullam, Malluch, Adaiah, Jashub, Sheal and Jeremoth.

[30]From the descendants of Pahath-Moab: Adna, Kelal, Benaiah, Maaseiah, Mattaniah, Bezalel, Binnui and Manasseh.

[31]From the descendants of Harim: Eliezer, Ishijah, Malkijah, Shemaiah, Shimeon, [32]Benjamin, Malluch and Shemariah.

[33]From the descendants of Hashum: Mattenai, Mattattah, Zabad, Eliphelet, Jeremai, Manasseh and Shimei.

[34]From the descendants of Bani: Maadai, Amram, Uel, [35]Benaiah, Bedeiah, Keluhi, [36]Vaniah,

Meremoth, Eliashib, 37Mattaniah, Mattenai and Jaasu.

38From the descendants of Binnui: Shimei, 39Shelemiah, Nathan, Adaiah, 40Macnadebai, Shashai, Sharai, 41Azarel, Shelemiah, Shemariah, 42Shallum, Amariah and Joseph.

43From the descendants of Nebo: Jeiel, Mattithiah, Zabad, Zebina, Jaddai, Joel and Benaiah.

44All these men had married non-Jewish women, and some of them had children by these wives.

Nehemiah

When?

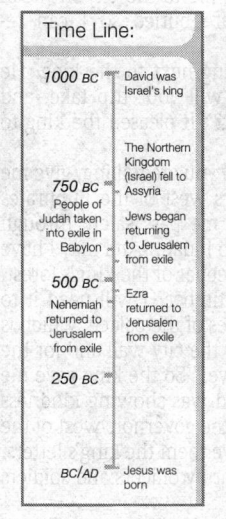

Time Line:

1000 BC	David was Israel's king
750 BC	The Northern Kingdom (Israel) fell to Assyria
People of Judah taken into exile in Babylon	Jews began returning to Jerusalem from exile
500 BC	Ezra returned to Jerusalem from exile
Nehemiah returned to Jerusalem from exile	
250 BC	
BC/AD	Jesus was born

Why Read This Book:

* Understand the importance of acting on what you believe (Nehemiah 1—5).
* Recognise how serving God sometimes means standing against those who don't serve him (Nehemiah 6—7).
* See the life-changing effects of believing God's word (Nehemiah 8—13).

Behind the Scenes:

Can you imagine a member of the government resigning in order to walk across a desert and rebuild his home town? If you can, then you have a fairly good idea of what Nehemiah did.

He held a high office in the kingdom of Persia, which ruled almost all of the Near East. He had money and power.

Unlike many leaders in biblical times, whose positions led them away from God, Nehemiah was not really happy in his important position. The book of Nehemiah reads like a private diary. In it we learn that, although Nehemiah was a powerful leader, he had not let his position come between him and God.

In this book, we learn about what makes a good leader. We learn about Nehemiah's prayer life, organisational skills and dependence on God. We also learn that it isn't good enough for us to moan about how bad a situation is – we need to stand on our feet and take action. Only then will the world around us begin to change.

Where?

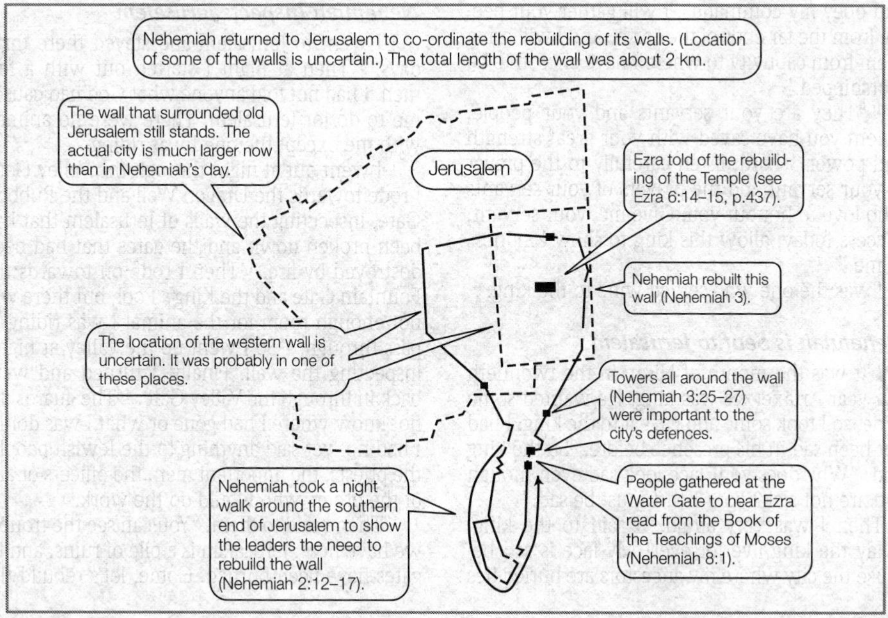

Nehemiah returned to Jerusalem to co-ordinate the rebuilding of its walls. (Location of some of the walls is uncertain.) The total length of the wall was about 2 km.

The wall that surrounded old Jerusalem still stands. The actual city is much larger now than in Nehemiah's day.

Jerusalem

Ezra told of the rebuilding of the Temple (see Ezra 6:14–15, p.437).

Nehemiah rebuilt this wall (Nehemiah 3).

The location of the western wall is uncertain. It was probably in one of these places.

Towers all around the wall (Nehemiah 3:25–27) were important to the city's defences.

Nehemiah took a night walk around the southern end of Jerusalem to show the leaders the need to rebuild the wall (Nehemiah 2:12–17).

People gathered at the Water Gate to hear Ezra read from the Book of the Teachings of Moses (Nehemiah 8:1).

Nehemiah's Prayer

1 These are the words of Nehemiah son of Hacaliah.

In the month of Kislev in the twentieth year,[n] I, Nehemiah, was in the capital city of Susa. [2]One of my brothers named Hanani came with some other men from Judah. I asked them about Jerusalem and the Jewish people who lived through the captivity.

[3]They answered me, "Those who are left from the captivity are back in Judah, but they are in much trouble and are full of shame. The wall around Jerusalem is broken down, and its gates have been burnt."

[4]When I heard these things, I sat down and cried for several days. I was sad and ate nothing. I prayed to the God of heaven, [5]"LORD, God of heaven, you are the great God who is to be respected. You are loyal, and you keep your agreement with those who love you and obey your commands. [6]Look and listen carefully. Hear the prayer that I, your servant, am praying to you day and night for your servants, the Israelites. I confess the sins we Israelites have done against you. My father's family and I have sinned against you. [7]We have been wicked towards you and have not obeyed the commands, rules and laws you gave your servant Moses.

[8]"Remember what you taught your servant Moses, saying, 'If you are unfaithful, I will scatter you among the nations. [9]But if you return to me and obey my commands, I will gather your people from the far ends of the earth. And I will bring them from captivity to where I have chosen to be worshipped.'

[10]"They are your servants and your people, whom you have saved with your great strength and power. [11]Lord, listen carefully to the prayer of your servant and the prayers of your servants who love to honour you. Give me, your servant, success today; allow this king to show kindness to me."

I was the one who served wine to the king.

Nehemiah is Sent to Jerusalem

2 It was the month of Nisan in the twentieth year Artaxerxes was king. He wanted some wine, so I took some and gave it to the king. I had not been sad in his presence before. [2]So the king said, "Why does your face look sad even though you are not sick? Your heart must be sad."

Then I was very afraid. [3]I said to the king, "May the king live for ever! My face is sad because the city where my ancestors are buried lies in ruins, and its gates have been destroyed by fire."

[4]Then the king said to me, "What do you want?"

First I prayed to the God of heaven. [5]Then I answered the king, "If you are willing and if I have pleased you, send me to the city in Judah where my ancestors are buried so I can rebuild it."

[6]The queen was sitting next to the king. He asked me, "How long will your trip take, and when will you get back?" It pleased the king to send me, so I set a time.

[7]I also said to him, "If you are willing, give me letters for the governors west of the Euphrates River. Tell them to let me pass safely through their lands on my way to Judah. [8]And may I have a letter for Asaph, the keeper of the king's forest, telling him to give me timber? I will need it to make boards for the gates of the palace, which is by the Temple,[d] and for the city wall and for the house in which I will live." So the king gave me the letters, because God was showing kindness to me. [9]Then I went to the governors west of the Euphrates River and gave them the king's letters. The king had also sent army officers and soldiers on horses with me.

[10]When Sanballat the Horonite and Tobiah the Ammonite officer heard about this, they were upset that someone had come to help the Israelites.

Nehemiah Inspects Jerusalem

[11]I went to Jerusalem and stayed there three days. [12]Then at night I started out with a few men. I had not told anyone what God had caused me to do for Jerusalem. There were no animals with me except the one I was riding.

[13]I went out at night through the Valley Gate. I rode towards the Dragon Well and the Rubbish Gate, inspecting the walls of Jerusalem that had been broken down and the gates that had been destroyed by fire. [14]Then I rode on towards the Fountain Gate and the King's Pool, but there was not enough room for the animal I was riding to pass through. [15]So I went up the valley at night, inspecting the wall. Finally, I turned and went back in through the Valley Gate. [16]The guards did not know where I had gone or what I was doing. I had not yet said anything to the Jewish people, the priests, the important men, the officers or any of the others who would do the work.

[17]Then I said to them, "You can see the trouble we have here. Jerusalem is a pile of ruins, and its gates have been burned. Come, let's rebuild the

twentieth year   This is probably referring to the twentieth year King Artaxerxes I ruled Persia.

wall of Jerusalem so we won't be full of shame any longer." [18]I also told them how God had been kind to me and what the king had said to me.

Then they answered, "Let's start rebuilding." So they began to work hard.

[19]But when Sanballat the Horonite, Tobiah the Ammonite officer and Geshem the Arab heard about it, they made fun of us and laughed at us. They said, "What are you doing? Are you turning against the king?"

[20]But I answered them, "The God of heaven will give us success. We, his servants, will start rebuilding, but you have no share, claim or memorial in Jerusalem."

Builders of the Wall

3 Eliashib the high priest and his fellow priests went to work and rebuilt the Sheep Gate. They gave it to the Lord's service and set its doors in place. They worked as far as the Tower of the Hundred and gave it to the Lord's service. Then they went on to the Tower of Hananel. [2]Next to them, the men of Jericho built part of the wall, and Zaccur son of Imri built next to them.

[3]The sons of Hassenaah rebuilt the Fish Gate, laying its boards and setting its doors, bolts and bars in place. [4]Meremoth son of Uriah, the son of Hakkoz, made repairs next to them. Meshullam son of Berekiah, the son of Meshezabel, made repairs next to Meremoth. And Zadok son of Baana made repairs next to Meshullam. [5]The men from Tekoa made repairs next to them, but the leading men of Tekoa would not work under their supervisors.

[6]Joiada son of Paseah and Meshullam son of Besodeiah repaired the Old Gate. They laid its boards and set its doors, bolts and bars in place. [7]Next to them, Melatiah from Gibeon, other men from Gibeon and Mizpah, and Jadon from Meronoth made repairs. These places were ruled by the governor west of the Euphrates River. [8]Next to them, Uzziel son of Harhaiah, a goldsmith, made repairs. And next to him, Hananiah, a perfume maker, made repairs. These men rebuilt Jerusalem as far as the Broad Wall. [9]The next part of the wall was repaired by Rephaiah son of Hur, the ruler of half of the district of Jerusalem. [10]Next to him, Jedaiah son of Harumaph made repairs opposite his own house. And next to him, Hattush son of Hashabneiah made repairs. [11]Malkijah son of Harim and Hasshub son of Pahath-Moab repaired another part of the wall and the Tower of the Ovens. [12]Next to them Shallum son of

Hallohesh, the ruler of half of the district of Jerusalem, and his daughters made repairs.

Sidelight Did you know that women held building jobs in Bible times (Nehemiah 3:12)?

[13]Hanun and the people of Zanoah repaired the Valley Gate, rebuilding it and setting its doors, bolts and bars in place. They also repaired the 500 metres of the wall to the Rubbish Gate.

[14]Malkijah son of Recab, the ruler of the district of Beth Hakkerem, repaired the Rubbish Gate. He rebuilt that gate and set its doors, bolts and bars in place.

[15]Shallun son of Col-Hozeh, the ruler of district of Mizpah, repaired the Fountain Gate. He rebuilt it, put a roof over it and set its doors, bolts and bars in place. He also repaired the wall of the Pool of Siloam next to the King's Garden all the way to the steps that went down from the older part of the city. [16]Next to Shallun was Nehemiah[n] son of Azbuk, the ruler of half of the district of Beth Zur. He made repairs opposite the tombs of David and as far as the man-made pool and the House of the Heroes.

[17]Next to him, the Levites made repairs, working under Rehum son of Bani. Next to him, Hashabiah, the ruler of half of the district of Keilah, for his district. [18]Next to him, Binnui son of Henadad and his Levites made repairs. Binnui was the ruler of the other half of the district of Keilah. [19]Next to them, Ezer son of Jeshua, the ruler of Mizpah, repaired another part of the wall. He worked across from the way up to the storehouse for weapons, as far as the bend. [20]Next to him, Baruch son of Zabbai worked hard on the wall that went from the bend to the entrance to the house of Eliashib, the high priest. [21]Next to him, Meremoth son of Uriah, the son of Hakkoz, repaired the wall that went from the entrance to Eliashib's house to the far end of it.

[22]Next to him worked the priests from the surrounding area. [23]Next to them, Benjamin and Hasshub made repairs in front of their own house. Next to them, Azariah son of Maaseiah, the son of Ananiah, made repairs beside his own house. [24]Next to him, Binnui son of Henadad repaired the wall that went from Azariah's house to the bend and on to the corner. [25]Palal son of Uzai worked across from the bend and by the tower on the upper palace, which is near the

Nehemiah   This is a different Nehemiah from the one who wrote this book.

courtyard of the king's guard. Next to Palal, Pedaiah son of Parosh made repairs. 26The Temple [d] servants who lived on the hill of Ophel made repairs as far as a point opposite the Water Gate. They worked towards the east and the tower that extends from the palace. 27Next to them, the people of Tekoa repaired the wall from the great tower that extends from the palace to the wall of Ophel.

28The priests made repairs above the Horse Gate, each working in front of his own house. 29Next to them, Zadok son of Immer made repairs across from his own house. Next to him, Shemaiah son of Shecaniah, the guard of the East Gate, made repairs. 30Next to him, Hananiah son of Shelemiah, and Hanun, the sixth son of Zalaph, made repairs on another part of the wall. Next to them, Meshullam son of Berekiah made repairs across from where he lived. 31Next to him, Malkijah, one of the goldsmiths, made repairs. He worked as far as the house of the Temple servants and the traders, which is across from the Inspection Gate, and as far as the room above the corner of the wall. 32The goldsmiths and the traders made repairs between the room above the corner of the wall and the Sheep Gate.

Those Against the Rebuilding

4 When Sanballat heard we were rebuilding the wall, he was very angry, even furious. He made fun of the Jewish people. 2He said to his friends and those with power in Samaria, "What are these weak Jews doing? Will they rebuild the wall? Will they offer sacrifices? Can they finish it in one day? Can they bring stones back to life from piles of rubbish and ashes?"

> ### Sidelight
>
> Rebuilding the walls may have seemed impossible to people who opposed the work (Nehemiah 4:2–3), partly because many of the stones had cracked when the city was burned by the Babylonians. The Jews did rebuild some existing walls with the old materials, but they had to build brand-new walls in some places.

3Tobiah the Ammonite, who was next to Sanballat, said, "If a fox climbed up on the stone wall they are building, it would break it down."

4I prayed, "Hear us, our God. We are hated. Turn the insults of Sanballat and Tobiah back on their own heads. Let them be captured and stolen like valuables. 5Do not hide their guilt or take away their sins so that you can't see them, because they have insulted the builders."

6So we rebuilt the wall to half its height, because the people were willing to work.

7But Sanballat, Tobiah, the Arabs, the Ammonites and the people from Ashdod were very angry when they heard that the repairs to Jerusalem's walls were continuing and that the holes in the wall were being closed. 8So they all made plans to come to Jerusalem and fight and stir up trouble. 9But we prayed to our God and appointed guards to watch for them day and night.

10The people of Judah said, "The workers are getting tired. There is so much rubbish we cannot rebuild the wall."

11And our enemies said, "The Jews won't know or see anything until we come among them and kill them and stop the work."

12Then the Jewish people who lived near our enemies came and told us ten times, "Everywhere you turn, the enemy will attack us." 13So I put people behind the lowest places along the wall—the open places—and I put families together with their swords, spears and bows. 14Then I looked around and stood up and said to the important men, the leaders and the rest of the people: "Don't be afraid of them. Remember the Lord, who is great and powerful. Fight for your brothers, your sons and daughters, your wives and your homes."

15Then our enemies heard that we knew about their plans and that God had ruined their plans. So we all went back to the wall, each to his own work.

16From that day on, half my people worked on the wall. The other half was ready with spears, shields, bows and armour. The officers stood behind the people of Judah 17who were building the wall. Those who carried materials did their work with one hand and carried a weapon with the other. 18Each builder wore his sword at his side as he worked. The man who blew the trumpet to warn the people stayed next to me.

19Then I said to the important men, the leaders and the rest of the people, "This is a very big job. We are spreading out along the wall so that we are far apart. 20Wherever you hear the sound of the trumpet, assemble there. Our God will fight for us."

21So we continued to work with half the men holding spears from sunrise till the stars came out. 22At that time I also said to the people, "Let every man and his helper stay inside Jerusalem at night. They can be our guards at night and workmen during the day." 23Neither I, my brothers, my workers nor the guards with me ever took off our clothes. Each person carried his weapon even when he went for water.

Nehemiah Helps Poor People

5 The men and their wives complained loudly against their fellow Jews. ²Some of them were saying, "We have many sons and daughters in our families. To eat and stay alive, we need grain."

³Others were saying, "We are borrowing money against our fields, vineyards and homes to get grain because there is not much food."

⁴And still others were saying, "We are borrowing money to pay the king's tax on our fields and vineyards. ⁵We are just like our fellow Jews, and our sons are like their sons. But we have to sell our sons and daughters as slaves. Some of our daughters have already been sold. But there is nothing we can do, because our fields and vineyards already belong to other people."

⁶When I heard their complaints about these things, I was very angry. ⁷After I thought about it, I accused the important people and the leaders,

"You are charging your own brothers too much interest." So I called a large meeting to deal with them. ⁸I said to them, "As much as possible, we have bought freedom for our fellow Jews who had been sold to foreigners. Now you are selling your fellow Jews to us!" The leaders were quiet and had nothing to say.

⁹Then I said, "What you are doing is not right. Don't you fear God? Don't let our foreign enemies shame us. ¹⁰I, my brothers and my men are also lending money and grain to the people. But stop charging them so much for this. ¹¹Give back their fields, vineyards, olive trees and houses right now. Also give back the extra amount you charged—the hundredth part of the money, grain, new wine and oil."

¹²They said, "We will give it back and not demand anything more from them. We will do as you say."

HUNGER AND POVERTY

A Blanket of Love

Eleven-year-old Trevor Ferrell learned that there were people living on the streets of Philadelphia, in the USA – not far from his suburban home. Curious, he talked his parents into taking him there. Trevor got out of the car and gave a homeless person a blanket.

When Trevor returned home, he searched for extra blankets and clothing, and he convinced his parents to take him downtown again and again with deliveries.

He talked to people at his church, and they donated food, clothing and even a van to take things to the homeless.

Soon Trevor was in the newspapers, on television, even meeting the President of the USA! Trevor wanted to tell others what they could do to help.

Now there is a home in Philadelphia called "Trevor's Place". People can live and be fed there. Trevor Ferrell began by giving a little of himself and was able to challenge others to do the same. "One person can make a difference," Trevor says. "Just do what you can and follow your heart."

Nehemiah was also a person who made a difference for the poor. See how he helped them in **Nehemiah 5:1–11**.

* How did Nehemiah use his political power as governor of Judah to help the poor? How were Trevor's actions like Nehemiah's?
* How can you, like Trevor and Nehemiah, help people who are hungry?

Consider . . .

* helping low-income people in your community by giving non-perishable food to a food bank that distributes supplies to people in need.
* encouraging your government to take care of the needs of the poor by joining an organisation which speaks out for the poor.

For more, see . . .

* Deuteronomy 15:7–8 (p.179)
* James 2:1–9 (p.1348)
* Matthew 25:31–46 (p.987)

Then I called for the priests, and I made the important men and leaders take an oath to do what they had said. [13]Also I shook out the folds of my robe and said, "In this way may God shake out everyone who does not keep his promise. May God shake him out of his house and out of the things that are his. Let that person be shaken out and emptied!"

Then the whole group said, "Amen," and they praised the Lord. So the people did what they had promised.

[14]I was appointed governor in the land of Judah in the twentieth year of King Artaxerxes' rule. I was governor of Judah for twelve years, until his thirty-second year. During that time neither my brothers nor I ate the food that was allowed for a governor. [15]But the governors before me had placed a heavy load on the people. They took about 40 pieces of silver from each person, along with food and wine. The governors' helpers before me also controlled the people, but I did not do that, because I feared God. [16]I worked on the wall, as did all my men who were gathered there. We did not buy any fields.

[17]Also, I fed 150 Jewish people and officers at my table, as well as those who came from the nations around us. [18]This is what was prepared every day: one ox, six good sheep, and birds. And every ten days there were all kinds of wine. But I never demanded the food that was allowed a governor, because the people were already working very hard.

[19]Remember to be kind to me, my God, for all the good I have done for these people.

More Problems for Nehemiah

6 Then Sanballat, Tobiah, Geshem the Arab and our other enemies heard that I had rebuilt the wall and that there was not one gap in it. But I had not yet set the doors in the gates. [2]So Sanballat and Geshem sent me this message: "Come, Nehemiah, let's meet together in Kephirim on the plain of Ono."

But they were planning to harm me. [3]So I sent messengers to them with this answer: "I am doing a great work and I can't come down. I don't want the work to stop while I leave to meet you." [4]Sanballat and Geshem sent the same message to me four times, and each time I sent back the same answer.

[5]The fifth time Sanballat sent his helper to me with the message, and in his hand was an unsealed letter. [6]This is what was written:

A report is going around to all the nations, and Geshem says it is true, that you and the

Jewish people are planning to turn against the king and that you are rebuilding the wall. They say you are going to be their king [7]and that you have appointed prophets[d] to announce in Jerusalem: "There is a king of Judah!" The king will hear about this. So come, let's discuss this together.

[8]So I sent him back this answer: "Nothing you are saying is really happening. You are just making it up in your own mind."

[9]Our enemies were trying to scare us, thinking, "They will get too weak to work. Then the wall will not be finished."

But I prayed, "God, make me strong."

[10]One day I went to the house of Shemaiah son of Delaiah, the son of Mehetabel. Shemaiah had to stay at home. He said, "Nehemiah, let's meet in the Temple[d] of God. Let's go inside the Temple and close the doors, because men are coming at night to kill you."

[11]But I said, "Should a man like me run away? Should I run for my life into the Temple? I will not go." [12]I knew that God had not sent him but that Tobiah and Sanballat had paid him to prophesy[d] against me. [13]They paid him to frighten me so I would do this and sin. Then they could give me a bad name to shame me.

[14]I prayed, "My God, remember Tobiah and Sanballat and what they have done. Also remember the prophetess Noadiah and the other prophets who have been trying to frighten me."

> **Sidelight**   Building the wall around Jerusalem took 52 days (Nehemiah 6:15). Some archaeologists believe that the wall would have been more secure if Nehemiah had slowed the work down. Portions of the wall that have been uncovered show signs of the hasty construction. Nehemiah kept up the pace because his enemies were getting ready to attack (Nehemiah 4:11–24, p.446).

The Wall is Finished

[15]The wall of Jerusalem was completed on the twenty-fifth day of the month of Elul. It took 52 days to rebuild. [16]When all our enemies heard about it and all the nations around us saw it, they were shamed. They then understood that the work had been done with the help of our God.

[17]Also in those days the important men of Judah sent many letters to Tobiah, and he answered them. [18]Many Jewish people had promised to be faithful to Tobiah, because he was the son-in-law of Shecaniah son of Arah. And Tobiah's son

Jehohanan had married the daughter of Meshullam son of Berekiah. [19]These important men kept telling me about the good things Tobiah was doing, and then they would tell Tobiah what I said about him. So Tobiah sent letters to frighten me.

7 After the wall had been rebuilt and I had set the doors in place, the gatekeepers, singers and Levites were chosen. [2]I put my brother Hanani, along with Hananiah, the commander of the palace, in charge of Jerusalem. Hananiah was honest and feared God more than most people. [3]I said to them, "The gates of Jerusalem should not be opened until the sun is hot. While the gatekeepers are still on duty, have them shut and bolt the doors. Appoint people who live in Jerusalem as guards, and put some at guard posts and some near their own houses."

> **Sidelight** Though Nehemiah thought that Jerusalem was large (Nehemiah 7:4), by our standards it was very small – almost a village. The ancient city took up only 30 or 40 acres – only a short run around the perimeter.

The Captives Who Returned

[4]The city was large and roomy, but there were few people in it, and the houses had not yet been rebuilt. [5]Then my God caused me to gather the important men, the leaders and the common people so I could register them by families. I found the family history of those who had returned first. This is what I found written there:

[6]These are the people of the area who returned from captivity, whom Nebuchadnezzar king of Babylon had taken away. They returned to Jerusalem and Judah, each going back to his own town. [7]These people returned with Zerubbabel, Jeshua, Nehemiah, Azariah, Raamiah, Nahamani, Mordecai, Bilshan, Mispereth, Bigvai, Nehum and Baanah.

These are the people from Israel: [8]the descendants[d] of Parosh—2,172; [9]the descendants of Shephatiah—372; [10]the descendants of Arah—652; [11]the descendants of Pahath-Moab (through the family of Jeshua and Joab)—2,818; [12]the descendants of Elam—1,254; [13]the descendants of Zattu—845; [14]the descendants of Zaccai—760; [15]the descendants of Binnui—648; [16]the descendants of Bebai—628; [17]the descendants of Azgad—2,322; [18]the descendants of Adonikam—667; [19]the descendants of Bigvai—2,067; [20]the descendants of Adin—655; [21]the descendants of Ater (through Hezekiah)—98; [22]the descendants of Hashum—328; [23]the descendants

of Bezai—324; [24]the descendants of Hariph—112; [25]the descendants of Gibeon—95.

[26]These are the people from the towns of Bethlehem and Netophah—188; [27]of Anathoth—128; [28]of Beth Azmaveth—42; [29]of Kiriath Jearim, Kephirah and Beeroth—743; [30]of Ramah and Geba—621; [31]of Michmash—122; [32]of Bethel and Ai—123; [33]of the other Nebo—52; [34]of the other Elam—1,254; [35]of Harim—320; [36]of Jericho—345; [37]of Lod, Hadid and Ono—721; [38]of Senaah—3,930.

[39]These are the priests: the descendants of Jedaiah (through the family of Jeshua)—973; [40]the descendants of Immer—1,052; [41]the descendants of Pashhur—1,247; [42]the descendants of Harim—1,017.

[43]These are the Levites: the descendants of Jeshua (through Kadmiel through the family of Hodaviah)—74.

[44]These are the singers: the descendants of Asaph—148.

[45]These are the gatekeepers: the descendants of Shallum, Ater, Talmon, Akkub, Hatita and Shobai—138.

[46]These are the Temple[d] servants: the descendants of Ziha, Hasupha, Tabbaoth, [47]Keros, Sia, Padon, [48]Lebana, Hagaba, Shalmai, [49]Hanan, Giddel, Gahar, [50]Reaiah, Rezin, Nekoda, [51]Gazzam, Uzza, Paseah, [52]Besai, Meunim, Nephussim, [53]Bakbuk, Hakupha, Harhur, [54]Bazluth, Mehida, Harsha, [55]Barkos, Sisera, Temah, [56]Neziah and Hatipha.

[57]These are the descendants of the servants of Solomon: the descendants of Sotai, Sophereth, Perida, [58]Jaala, Darkon, Giddel, [59]Shephatiah, Hattil, Pokereth-Hazzebaim and Amon.

[60]The Temple servants and the descendants of the servants of Solomon totalled 392 people.

[61]Some people came to Jerusalem from the towns of Tel Melah, Tel Harsha, Kerub, Addon and Immer, but they could not prove that their ancestors came from Israel. Here are their names and their number: [62]the descendants of Delaiah, Tobiah and Nekoda—642.

[63]And these priests could not prove that their ancestors came from Israel: the descendants of Hobaiah, Hakkoz and Barzillai. (He had married a daughter of Barzillai from Gilead and was called by her family name.)

[64]These people searched for their family records, but they could not find them. So they could not be priests, because they were thought to be unclean. [d] [65]The governor ordered them not to eat any of the holy food until a priest settled this matter by using the Urim and Thummim. [d]

[66]The total number of those who returned was 42,360. [67]This is not counting their 7,337 male

and female servants and the 245 male and female singers with them. ⁶⁸They had 736 horses, 245 mules, ⁶⁹435 camels and 6,720 donkeys.

⁷⁰Some of the family leaders gave to the work. The governor gave to the treasury about 8 kilogrammes of gold, 50 bowls and 530 pieces of clothing for the priests. ⁷¹Some of the family leaders gave about 170 kilogrammes of gold and about 1.3 tonnes of silver to the treasury for the work. ⁷²The total of what the other people gave was about 170 kilogrammes of gold, about a tonne of silver and 67 pieces of clothing for the priests. ⁷³So these people all settled in their own towns: the priests, the Levites, the gatekeepers, the singers, the Temple servants and all the other people of Israel.

Ezra Reads the Teachings

By the seventh month the Israelites were settled in their own towns.

8 All the people of Israel gathered together in the square by the Water Gate. They asked Ezra the teacher to bring out the Book of the Teachings of Moses, which the LORD had given to Israel.

²So on the first day of the seventh month, Ezra the priest brought out the Teachings for the crowd. Men, women and all who could listen and understand had gathered. ³At the square by the Water Gate Ezra read the Teachings out loud from early morning until noon to the men, women and everyone who could listen and understand. All the people listened carefully to the Book of the Teachings.

⁴Ezra the teacher stood on a high wooden platform that had been built just for this time. On his right were Mattithiah, Shema, Anaiah, Uriah, Hilkiah and Maaseiah. And on his left were Pedaiah, Mishael, Malkijah, Hashum, Hashbaddanah, Zechariah and Meshullam.

⁵Ezra opened the book in full view of everyone, because he was above them. As he opened it, all the people stood up. ⁶Ezra praised the LORD, the great God, and all the people held up their hands and said, "Amen! Amen!" Then they bowed down and worshipped the LORD with their faces to the ground.

⁷These Levites explained the Teachings to the people as they stood there: Jeshua, Bani, Sherebiah, Jamin, Akkub, Shabbethai, Hodiah, Maaseiah, Kelita, Azariah, Jozabad, Hanan and Pelaiah. ⁸They read from the Book of the Teachings of God and explained what it meant so the people understood what was being read.

⁹Then Nehemiah the governor, Ezra the priest and teacher, and the Levites who were teaching said to all the people, "This is a holy day to the LORD your God. Don't be sad or cry." All the people had been crying as they listened to the words of the Teachings.

¹⁰Nehemiah said, "Go and enjoy good food and sweet drinks. Send some to people who have none, because today is a holy day to the Lord. Don't be sad, because the joy of the LORD will make you strong."

¹¹The Levites helped calm the people, saying, "Be quiet, because this is a holy day. Don't be sad."

¹²Then all the people went away to eat and drink, to send some of their food to others and to celebrate with great joy. They finally understood what they had been taught.

¹³On the second day of the month, the leaders of all the families, the priests and the Levites met with Ezra the teacher. They gathered to study the words of the Teachings. ¹⁴This is what they found written in the Teachings: the LORD commanded through Moses that the people of Israel were to live in shelters during the feast of the seventh month. ¹⁵The people were supposed to preach this message and spread it through all their towns and in Jerusalem: "Go out into the mountains, and bring back branches from olive and wild olive trees, myrtle trees, palms and shade trees. Make shelters with them, as it is written."

¹⁶So the people went out and got tree branches. They built shelters on their roofs, **ⁿ** in their courtyards, in the courtyards of the Temple, **ᵈ** in the square by the Water Gate and in the square next to the Gate of Ephraim. ¹⁷The whole group that had come back from captivity built shelters and lived in them. The Israelites had not done this since the time of Joshua son of Nun. And they were very happy.

¹⁸Ezra read to them every day from the Book of the Teachings, from the first day to the last. The people of Israel celebrated the feast for seven days, and then on the eighth day the people gathered as the law said.

Israel Confesses Sins

9 On the twenty-fourth day of that same month, the people of Israel gathered. They did not eat, and they wore rough cloth and put dust on their heads to show their sadness. ²Those people whose ancestors were from Israel had separated themselves from all foreigners. They stood and confessed their sins and their ancestors' sins. ³For a quarter of the day they stood where they

---

roofs   In Bible times houses were built with flat roofs. The roof was used for drying things such as flax and fruit. And it was used as an extra room, as a place for worship and as a place to sleep in the summer.

were and read from the Book of the Teachings of the LORD their God. For another quarter of the day they confessed their sins and worshipped the LORD their God. 4These Levites were standing on the stairs: Jeshua, Bani, Kadmiel, Shebaniah, Bunni, Sherebiah, Bani and Kanani. They called out to the LORD their God with loud voices. 5Then these Levites spoke: Jeshua, Kadmiel, Bani, Hashabneiah, Sherebiah, Hodiah, Shebaniah and Pethahiah. They said, "Stand up and praise the LORD your God, who lives for ever and ever."

The People's Prayer

"Blessed be your wonderful name.
    It is more wonderful than all blessing and
        praise.
6You are the only LORD.
    You made the heavens, even the highest
        heavens,
    with all the stars.
You made the earth and everything on it,
    the seas and everything in them;
    you give life to everything.
The heavenly army worships you.

7"You are the LORD,
    the God who chose Abram
and brought him out of Ur in Babylonia
    and named him Abraham.
8You found him faithful to you,
    so you made an agreement with him
to give his descendants *d* the land of the
        Canaanites,
    Hittites, Amorites,
    Perizzites, Jebusites and Girgashites.
You have kept your promise,
    because you do what is right.

9"You saw our ancestors suffering in Egypt
    and heard them cry out at the Red Sea.*d*
10You did signs and miracles*d* against the king
        of Egypt,
    and against all his officers and all his people,
    because you knew how proud they were.
You became as famous as you are today.
11You divided the sea in front of our ancestors;
    they walked through on dry ground.
But you threw the people chasing them into
        the deep water,
    like a stone thrown into mighty waters.
12You led our ancestors with a pillar of cloud by
        day
    and with a pillar of fire at night.
It lit the way
    they were supposed to go.
13You came down to Mount Sinai
    and spoke from heaven to our ancestors.
You gave them fair rules and true teachings,
    good orders and commands.

14You told them about your holy Sabbath*d*
    and gave them commands, orders and
        teachings
    through your servant Moses.
15When they were hungry, you gave them
        bread from heaven.
When they were thirsty, you brought them
        water from the rock.
You told them to enter and take over
    the land you had promised to give them.

16"But our ancestors were proud and
        stubborn
    and did not obey your commands.
17They refused to listen;
    they forgot the miracles you did for them.
So they became stubborn and turned
        against you,
    choosing a leader to take them back to
        slavery.
But you are a forgiving God.
    You are kind and full of mercy.
You do not become angry quickly and you
        have great love.
    So you did not leave them.
18Our ancestors even made an idol of a calf for
        themselves.
    They said, 'This is your god, Israel,
    who brought you up out of Egypt.'
They spoke against you.

19"You have great mercy,
    so you did not leave them in the desert.
The pillar of cloud guided them by day,
    and the pillar of fire led them at night,
    lighting the way they were to go.
20You gave your good Spirit *d* to teach them.
    You gave them manna *d* to eat
    and water when they were thirsty.
21You took care of them for 40 years in the
        desert;
    they needed nothing.
Their clothes did not wear out,
    and their feet did not swell.

22"You gave them kingdoms and nations;
    you gave them more land.
They took over the country of Sihon king of
        Heshbon
    and the country of Og king of Bashan.
23You made their children as many as the stars
        in the sky,
    and you brought them into the land
    that you told their fathers to enter and take
        over.
24So their children went into the land and took
        over.
    The Canaanites lived there, but you
        defeated them for our ancestors.

You handed over to them the Canaanites,
    their kings and the people of the land.
Our ancestors could do what they wanted
    with them.
25They captured strong, walled cities and fertile
    land.
They took over houses full of good things,
    wells that were already dug,
vineyards, olive trees and many fruit trees.
They ate until they were full and grew fat;
    they enjoyed your great goodness.

26"But they were disobedient and turned
    against you
    and ignored your teachings.
Your prophets *d* warned them to come back
    to you,
but they killed those prophets
    and spoke against you.
27So you handed them over to their enemies,
    and their enemies treated them badly.
But in this time of trouble our ancestors cried
    out to you,
    and you heard from heaven.
You had great mercy
    and gave them saviours who saved them
    from the power of their enemies.
28But as soon as they had rest,
    they again did what was evil.
So you left them to their enemies
    who ruled over them.
When they cried out to you again,
    you heard from heaven.
Because of your mercy, you saved them
    again and again.
29You warned them to return to your
    teachings,
but they were proud and did not obey your
    commands.
If someone obeys your laws, he will live,
    but they sinned against your laws.
They were stubborn, unwilling and
    disobedient.
30You were patient with them for many years
    and warned them by your Spirit through
    the prophets,
but they did not pay attention.
So you handed them over to other
    countries.
31But because your mercy is great, you did not
    kill them all or leave them.
You are a kind and merciful God.

32"And so, our God, you are the great and
    mighty and wonderful God.
You keep your agreement of love.
Do not let all our trouble seem unimportant
    to you.

This trouble has come to us, to our kings and
    our leaders,
to our priests and prophets,
to our ancestors and all your people
from the days of the kings of Assyria
    until today.
33You have been fair in everything that has
    happened to us;
you have been loyal, but we have been
    wicked.
34Our kings, leaders, priests and ancestors did
    not obey your teachings;
they did not pay attention to the commands
    and warnings you gave them.
35Even when our ancestors were living in their
    kingdom,
enjoying all the good things you had given
    them,
enjoying the land that was fertile and full of
    room,
they did not stop their evil ways.

36"Look, we are slaves today
    in the land you gave our ancestors.
They were to enjoy its fruit and its good
    things,
but look, we are slaves here.
37The land's great harvest belongs to the kings
    you have put over us
because of our sins.
Those kings rule over us and our cattle as
    they please,
so we are in much trouble.

The People's Agreement

38"Because of all this, we are making an agreement in writing, and our leaders, Levites and priests are putting their seals *d* on it."

10 These are the men who sealed the agreement:
Nehemiah the governor, son of Hacaliah.
2Zedekiah, Seraiah, Azariah, Jeremiah, 3Pashhur, Amariah, Malkijah, 4Hattush, Shebaniah, Malluch, 5Harim, Meremoth, Obadiah, 6Daniel, Ginnethon, Baruch, 7Meshullam, Abijah, Mijamin, 8Maaziah, Bilgai and Shemaiah. These are the priests.
9These are the Levites who sealed it: Jeshua son of Azaniah, Binnui of the sons of Henadad, Kadmiel 10and their fellow Levites: Shebaniah, Hodiah, Kelita, Pelaiah, Hanan, 11Mica, Rehob, Hashabiah, 12Zaccur, Sherebiah, Shebaniah, 13Hodiah, Bani and Beninu.
14These are the leaders of the people who sealed the agreement: Parosh, Pahath-Moab, Elam, Zattu, Bani, 15Bunni, Azgad, Bebai, 16Adonijah, Bigvai, Adin, 17Ater, Hezekiah, Azzur, 18Hodiah, Hashum, Bezai, 19Hariph, Anathoth,

Nebai, ²⁰Magpiash, Meshullam, Hezir, ²¹Meshez-abel, Zadok, Jaddua, ²²Pelatiah, Hanan, Anaiah, ²³Hoshea, Hananiah, Hasshub, ²⁴Hallohesh, Pilha, Shobek, ²⁵Rehum, Hashabnah, Maaseiah, ²⁶Ahiah, Hanan, Anan, ²⁷Malluch, Harim and Baanah.

²⁸The rest of the people took an oath. They were the priests, Levites, gatekeepers, singers, Temple ^d servants, all those who separated them-selves from foreigners to keep the Teachings of God and also their wives and their sons and daughters who could understand. ²⁹They joined their fellow Israelites and their leading men in taking an oath, which was tied to a curse in case they broke the oath. They promised to follow the Teachings of God, which they had been given through Moses the servant of God, and to obey all the commands, rules and laws of the LORD our God.

³⁰They said:

We promise not to let our daughters marry foreigners nor to let our sons marry their daughters. ³¹Foreigners may bring goods or grain to sell on the Sabbath, ^d but we will not buy on the Sabbath or any holy day. Every seventh year we will not plant, and that year we will forget all that people owe us.

³²We will be responsible for the com-mands to pay for the service of the Temple of our God. We will give 4 grammes of silver each year. ³³It is for the bread that is set out on the table; the regular grain offerings and burnt offerings; the offerings on the Sab-baths, New Moon ^d festivals and special feasts; the holy offerings; the offerings to re-move the sins of the Israelites so they will belong to God; and for the work of the Tem-ple of our God.

³⁴We, the priests, the Levites and the peo-ple, have thrown lots^d to decide at what time of year each family must bring wood to the Temple. The wood is for burning on the altar of the LORD our God, and we will do this as it is written in the Teachings.

³⁵We also will bring the first fruits from our crops and the first fruits ^d of every tree to the Temple each year.

³⁶We will bring to the Temple our first-born ^d sons and cattle and the firstborn of our herds and flocks, as it is written in the Teachings. We will bring them to the priests who are serving in the Temple.

³⁷We will bring to the priests at the store-rooms of the Temple the first of our ground meal, our offerings, the fruit from all our trees and our new wine and oil. And we will

bring a tenth of our crops to the Levites, who will collect these things in all the towns where we work. ³⁸A priest of Aaron's family must be with the Levites when they receive the tenth of the people's crops. The Levites must bring a tenth of all they receive to the Temple of our God to put in the storerooms of the treasury. ³⁹The people of Israel and the Levites are to bring to the storerooms the gifts of grain, new wine and oil. That is where the utensils for the Temple are kept and where the priests who are serving, the gatekeepers and singers stay.

We will not ignore the Temple of our God.

New People Move into Jerusalem

11 The leaders of Israel lived in Jerusalem. But the rest of the people threw lots ^d to choose one person out of every ten to come and live in Jerusalem, the holy city. The other nine could stay in their own cities. ²The people blessed those who volunteered to live in Jerusalem.

³These are the area leaders who lived in Jerusalem. (Some people lived on their own land in the cities of Judah. These included Is-raelites, priests, Levites, Temple ^d servants and descendants ^d of Solomon's servants. ⁴Others from the families of Judah and Benjamin lived in Jerusalem.)

These are the descendants of Judah who moved into Jerusalem. There was Athaiah son of Uzziah. (Uzziah was the son of Zechariah, the son of Amariah. Amariah was the son of Shephatiah, the son of Mahalalel. Mahalalel was a descendant of Perez.) ⁵There was also Mas-seiah son of Baruch. (Baruch was the son of Col-Hozeh, the son of Hazaiah. Hazaiah was the son of Adaiah, the son of Joiarib. Joiarib was the son of Zechariah, a descendant of Shelah.) ⁶All the descendants of Perez who lived in Jerusalem to-talled 468 men. They were soldiers.

⁷These are descendants of Benjamin who moved into Jerusalem. There was Sallu son of Meshullam. (Meshullam was the son of Joed, the son of Pedaiah. Pedaiah was the son of Kola-iah, the son of Maaseiah. Maaseiah was the son of Ithiel, the son of Jeshaiah.) ⁸Following him were Gabbai and Sallai, for a total of 928 men. ⁹Joel son of Zicri was appointed over them, and Judah son of Hassenuah was second in charge of the new area of the city.

¹⁰These are the priests who moved into Jeru-salem. There was Jedaiah son of Joiarib, Jakin ¹¹and Seraiah son of Hilkiah, the supervisor in the Temple. (Hilkiah was the son of Meshullam, the son of Zadok. Zadok was the son of Meraioth, the son of Ahitub.) ¹²And there were others with

them who did the work for the Temple. Altogether there were 822 men. Also there was Adaiah son of Jeroham. (Jeroham was the son of Pelaliah, the son of Amzi. Amzi was the son of Zechariah, the son of Pashhur. Pashhur was the son of Malkijah.) [13]And there were family heads with him. Altogether there were 242 men. Also there was Amashsai son of Azarel. (Azarel was the son of Ahzai, the son of Meshillemoth. Meshillemoth was the son of Immer.) [14]And there were brave men with Amashsai. Altogether there were 128 men. Zabdiel son of Haggedolim was appointed over them.

[15]These are the Levites who moved into Jerusalem. There was Shemaiah son of Hasshub. (Hasshub was the son of Azrikam, the son of Hashabiah. Hashabiah was the son of Bunni.) [16]And there were Shabbethai and Jozabad, two of the leaders of the Levites who were in charge of the work outside the Temple. [17]There was Mattaniah son of Mica. (Mica was the son of Zabdi, the son of Asaph.) Mattaniah was the director who led the people in thanksgiving and prayer. There was Bakbukiah, who was second in charge over his fellow Levites. And there was Abda son of Shammua. (Shammua was the son of Galal, the son of Jeduthun.) [18]Altogether 284 Levites lived in the holy city of Jerusalem.

[19]The gatekeepers who moved into Jerusalem were Akkub, Talmon and others with them. There was a total of 172 men who guarded the city gates.

[20]The other Israelites, priests and Levites lived on their own land in all the cities of Judah.

[21]The Temple servants lived on the hill of Ophel, and Ziha and Gishpa were in charge of them.

[22]Uzzi son of Bani was appointed over the Levites in Jerusalem. (Bani was the son of Hashabiah, the son of Mattaniah. Mattaniah was the son of Mica.) Uzzi was one of Asaph's descendants, who were the singers responsible for the service of the Temple. [23]The singers were under the king's orders, which regulated them day by day.

[24]Pethahiah son of Meshezabel was the king's spokesman. (Meshezabel was a descendant of Zerah, the son of Judah.)

[25]Some of the people of Judah lived in villages with their surrounding fields. They lived in Kiriath Arba and its surroundings, in Dibon and its surroundings, in Jekabzeel and its surroundings, [26]in Jeshua, Moladah, Beth Pelet, [27]Hazar Shual, Beersheba and its surroundings, [28]in Ziklag and Meconah and its surroundings, [29]in En Rimmon, Zorah, Jarmuth, [30]Zanoah, Adullam and their villages, in Lachish and the fields around it, and in Azekah and its surroundings. So they settled from Beersheba all the way to the Valley of Hinnom.

[31]The descendants of the Benjaminites from Geba lived in Michmash, Aija, Bethel and its surroundings, [32]in Anathoth, Nob, Ananiah, [33]Hazor, Ramah, Gittaim, [34]Hadid, Zeboim, Neballat, [35]Lod, Ono and in the Valley of the Craftsmen.

[36]Some groups of the Levites from Judah settled in the land of Benjamin.

Priests and Levites

12 These are the priests and Levites who returned with Zerubbabel son of Shealtiel and with Jeshua. There were Seraiah, Jeremiah, Ezra, [2]Amariah, Malluch, Hattush, [3]Shecaniah, Rehum, Meremoth, [4]Iddo, Ginnethon, Abijah, [5]Mijamin, Moadiah, Bilgah, [6]Shemaiah, Joiarib, Jedaiah, [7]Sallu, Amok, Hilkiah and Jedaiah. They were the leaders of the priests and their relatives in the days of Jeshua.

[8]The Levites were Jeshua, Binnui, Kadmiel, Sherebiah, Judah and Mattaniah. Mattaniah and his relatives were in charge of the songs of thanksgiving. [9]Bakbukiah and Unni, their relatives, stood across from them in the services.

[10]Jeshua was the father of Joiakim. Joiakim was the father of Eliashib. Eliashib was the father of Joiada. [11]Joiada was the father of Jonathan and Jonathan was the father of Jaddua.

[12]In the days of Joiakim, these priests were the leaders of the families of priests: Meraiah, from Seraiah's family; Hananiah, from Jeremiah's family; [13]Meshullam, from Ezra's family; Jehohanan, from Amariah's family; [14]Jonathan, from Malluch's family; Joseph, from Shecaniah's family; [15]Adna, from Harim's family; Helkai, from Meremoth's family; [16]Zechariah, from Iddo's family; Meshullam, from Ginnethon's family; [17]Zicri, from Abijah's family; Piltai, from Miniamin's and Moadiah's families; [18]Shammua, from Bilgah's family; Jehonathan, from Shemaiah's family; [19]Mattenai, from Joiarib's family; Uzzi, from Jedaiah's family; [20]Kallai, from Sallu's family; Eber, from Amok's family; [21]Hashabiah, from Hilkiah's family; and Nethanel, from Jedaiah's family.

[22]The leaders of the families of the Levites and the priests were written down in the days of Eliashib, Joiada, Johanan and Jaddua, while Darius the Persian was king. [23]The family leaders among the Levites were written down in the history book, but only up to the time of Johanan son of Eliashib. [24]The leaders of the Levites were Hashabiah, Sherebiah, Jeshua son of Kadmiel and their relatives. Their relatives stood across from them and gave praise and thanksgiving to God. One group answered the other group, as David, the man of God, had commanded.

[25]These were the gatekeepers who guarded the storerooms next to the gates: Mattaniah,

Bakbukiah, Obadiah, Meshullam, Talmon and Akkub. [26]They served in the days of Joiakim son of Jeshua, the son of Jozadak. They also served in the days of Nehemiah the governor and Ezra the priest and teacher.

The Wall of Jerusalem

[27]When the wall of Jerusalem was offered as a gift to God, they asked the Levites to come from wherever they lived to Jerusalem to celebrate with joy the gift of the wall. They were to celebrate with songs of thanksgiving and with the music of cymbals, harps and lyres. *d* [28]They also brought together singers from all around Jerusalem, from the Netophathite villages, [29]from Beth Gilgal and from the areas of Geba and Azmaveth. The singers had built villages for themselves around Jerusalem. [30]The priests and Levites made themselves pure, and they also made the people, the gates and the wall of Jerusalem pure.

[31]I had the leaders of Judah go up on top of the wall, and I appointed two large choruses to give thanks. One chorus went to the right on top of the wall, towards the Rubbish Gate. [32]Behind them went Hoshaiah and half the leaders of Judah. [33]Azariah, Ezra, Meshullam, [34]Judah, Benjamin, Shemaiah and Jeremiah also went. [35]Some priests with trumpets also went, along with Zechariah son of Jonathan. (Jonathan was the son of Shemaiah, the son of Mattaniah. Mattaniah was the son of Micaiah, the son of Zaccur. Zaccur was the son of Asaph.) [36]Zechariah's relatives also went. They were Shemaiah, Azarel, Milalai, Gilalai, Maai, Nethanel, Judah and Hanani. These men played the musical instruments of David, the man of God, and Ezra the teacher walked in front of them. [37]They went from the Fountain Gate straight up the steps to the highest part of the wall by the older part of the city. They went on above the house of David to the Water Gate on the east.

[38]The second chorus went to the left, while I followed them on top of the wall with half the people. We went from the Tower of the Ovens to the Broad Wall, [39]over the Gate of Ephraim to the Old Gate and the Fish Gate, to the Tower of Hananel and the Tower of the Hundred. We went as far as the Sheep Gate and stopped at the Gate of the Guard.

MUSIC

Back of the Net

Jon was one of those quiet, unassuming kinds of guys who got on with life in his own way. But, even though Jon didn't say much, within a second of him walking into the room, you would notice something about him. Jon was a fanatic for his football team. Everyday he wore their scarf. He even wore their footy shirt under his school uniform, exposing it proudly at lunch during the daily kick around on the school field.

That wasn't all. Jon's most prized possession was his season ticket. Jon was a die-hard supporter and he'd be there, through thick and thin, rain or shine, home or away. This quiet guy, who rarely uttered a word, could be seen standing, hands raised, chest puffed out, singing at the top of his voice. And if they ever scored a goal (which wasn't that often), every fibre of his being exploded into jubilant adoration and ecstatic praise for those eleven men who had placed the ball in the back of the net.

Read **Nehemiah 12:27–43** and see how God's people celebrate what he's done for them.

* A wall doesn't sound that great, so why did the people go so crazy over a bunch of bricks?
* What's similar about Jon's footy enthusiasm and Israel with their new wall – and what's different?

Consider . . .

* making a list in five minutes of as many things as you can think of that God has done for you. Put the list in your Bible and take it with you next time you're going somewhere to sing songs to God. Get the list out and see how it fuels your worship.
* making up your own songs to praise God with.

For more, see . . .

* 1 Chronicles 13:8 (p.386)
* Romans 12:1–2 (p.1203)

* Psalm 98 (p.557)

⁴⁰The two choruses took their places at the Temple.*d* Half of the leaders and I did also. ⁴¹These priests were there with their trumpets: Eliakim, Maaseiah, Miniamin, Micaiah, Elioenai, Zechariah and Hananiah. ⁴²These people were also there: Maaseiah, Shemaiah, Eleazar, Uzzi, Jehohanan, Malkijah, Elam and Ezer. The choruses sang, led by Jezrahiah. ⁴³The people offered many sacrifices that day and were happy because God had given them great joy. The women and children were happy. The sound of happiness in Jerusalem could be heard far away.

Sidelight   When the Jews dedicated the completed wall around Jerusalem (Nehemiah 12:27–43), they didn't cut a ribbon or break a bottle of champagne. They probably offered an animal sacrifice and sprinkled blood or holy water on the wall.

⁴⁴At that time the leaders appointed men to be in charge of the storerooms. These rooms were for the gifts, the first fruits*d* and the tenth that the people brought. The Teachings said they should bring a share for the priests and Levites from the fields around the towns. The people of Judah were happy to do this for the priests and Levites who served. ⁴⁵They performed the service of their God in making things pure. The singers and gatekeepers also did their jobs, as David had commanded his son Solomon. ⁴⁶Earlier, in the time of David and Asaph, there was a leader of the singers and of the songs of praise and thanksgiving to God. ⁴⁷So it was in the days of Zerubbabel and Nehemiah. All the people of Israel gave something to the singers and gatekeepers, and they also set aside part for the Levites. Then the Levites set aside part for the descendants*d* of Aaron.

Foreign People are Sent Away

13 On that day they read the Book of Moses to the people, and they found that it said no Ammonite or Moabite should ever be allowed in the meeting to worship. ²The Ammonites and Moabites had not welcomed the Israelites with food and water. Instead, they had hired Balaam to put a curse on Israel. (But our God turned the curse into a blessing.) ³When the people heard this teaching, they separated all foreigners from Israel.

Nehemiah Returns to Jerusalem

⁴Before that happened, Eliashib the priest, who was in charge of the Temple*d* storerooms, was friendly with Tobiah. ⁵Eliashib let Tobiah use one of the large storerooms. Earlier it had been used for grain offerings, incense,*d* the utensils and the tenth offerings of grain, new wine and olive oil that belonged to the Levites, singers and gatekeepers. It had also been used for gifts for the priests.

⁶I was not in Jerusalem when this happened. I had gone back to Artaxerxes king of Babylon in the thirty-second year he was king. Finally I asked the king to let me leave. ⁷When I returned to Jerusalem, I found out the evil Eliashib had done by letting Tobiah have a room in the Temple courtyard. ⁸I was very upset at this, so I threw all of Tobiah's goods out of the room. ⁹I ordered the rooms to be purified, and I brought back the utensils for God's Temple, the grain offerings and the incense.

¹⁰Then I found out the people were not giving the Levites their shares. So the Levites and singers who served had gone back to their own farms. ¹¹I argued with the officers, saying, "Why haven't you taken care of the Temple?" Then I gathered the Levites and singers and put them back at their places.

¹²All the people of Judah then brought to the storerooms a tenth of their crops, new wine and olive oil. ¹³I put these men in charge of the storerooms: Shelemiah the priest, Zadok the teacher and Pedaiah a Levite. I made Hanan son of Zaccur, the son of Mattaniah, their helper. Everyone knew they were honest men. They gave out the portions that went to their relatives.

¹⁴Remember me, my God, for this. Do not ignore my love for the Temple and its service.

¹⁵In those days I saw people in Judah working in the winepresses*d* on the Sabbath*d* day. They were bringing in grain and loading it on donkeys. And they were bringing loads of wine, grapes and figs into Jerusalem on the Sabbath day. So I warned them about selling food on that day. ¹⁶People from the city of Tyre who were living in Jerusalem brought in fish and other things and sold them there on the Sabbath day to the people of Judah. ¹⁷I argued with the important men of Judah and said to them, "What is this evil thing you are doing? You are ruining the Sabbath day. ¹⁸This is just what your ancestors did. So our God did terrible things to us and this city. Now you are making him even more angry at Israel by ruining the Sabbath day."

¹⁹So I ordered that the doors be shut at sunset before the Sabbath and not be opened until the Sabbath was over. I put my servants at the gates so no load could come in on the Sabbath. ²⁰Once or twice traders and sellers of all kinds of goods spent the night outside Jerusalem. ²¹So I warned them, "Why are you spending the night by the wall? If you do it again, I will force you away."

After that, they did not come back on the Sabbath. [22]Then I ordered the Levites to purify themselves and to guard the city gates to make sure the Sabbath remained holy.

Remember me, my God, for this. Have mercy on me because of your great love.

[23]In those days I saw men of Judah who had married women from Ashdod, Ammon and Moab. [24]Half their children were speaking the language of Ashdod or some other place, and they couldn't speak the language of Judah. [25]I argued with those people, put curses on them, hit some of them and pulled out their hair. I forced them to make a promise to God, saying, "Do not let your daughters marry the sons of foreigners, and do not take the daughters of foreigners as wives for your sons or yourselves. [26]Foreign women made King Solomon of Israel sin. There was never a king like him in any of the nations. God loved Solomon and made him king over all Israel, but foreign women made him sin. [27]And now you are not obedient when you do this evil thing. You are unfaithful to our God when you marry foreign wives."

[28]Joiada was the son of Eliashib the high priest. One of Joiada's sons married a daughter of Sanballat the Horonite, so I sent him away from me.

[29]Remember them, my God, because they made the priesthood unclean *d* and the agreement of the priests and Levites unclean.

[30]So I purified them of everything that was foreign. I appointed duties for the priests and Levites, giving each man his own job. [31]I also made sure wood was brought for the altar at regular times and that the first fruits *d* were brought.

Remember me, my God; be kind to me.

Esther

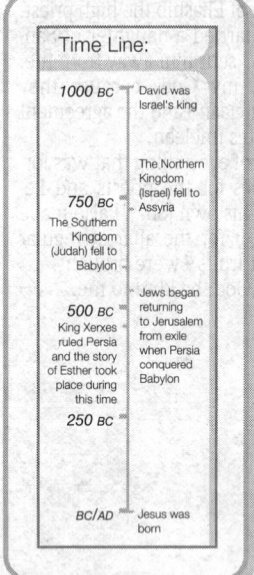

Time Line:

1000 BC	David was Israel's king
	The Northern Kingdom (Israel) fell to Assyria
750 BC	
The Southern Kingdom (Judah) fell to Babylon	
500 BC	Jews began returning to Jerusalem from exile when Persia conquered Babylon
King Xerxes ruled Persia and the story of Esther took place during this time	
250 BC	
BC/AD	Jesus was born

Why Read This Book:

* Recognise God's work in life's circumstances (Esther 1—2)
* Discover how an obedient person can have a major impact in the world (Esther 4—10).

Behind the Scenes:

How do you respond in a crisis? Does your fear make you freeze up so that you can't do anything to help? Or do you reveal far more strength than you would normally have?

Esther faced a tough situation. She might be able to save thousands of Jewish lives by stopping the decree of King Xerxes to exterminate all the Jews in the Persian Empire. But if she tried, she could lose her own life. Would she "freeze", or would she take heroic action? This book tells how Esther responded.

The story begins when King Xerxes got rid of Queen Vashti because she wouldn't obey him. Four years later, the king picked a new queen, Esther, not knowing that she was a Jew.

Then the plot thickens. Esther's cousin, Mordecai, refused to bow down to Haman, a court official. Haman became furious and convinced the king to order the killing of all the Jews. Through a messenger, Mordecai told Esther about the death decree and convinced her to use her influence to stop the order. Esther agreed, saying, "I will go to the king, even though it is against the law, and if I die, I die" (Esther 4:16). So she went to the king to plead for the Jews, including herself. She succeeded. Then Haman was executed and Mordecai honoured.

Esther is one of the most unusual books in the Bible. In some ways, it's a "secular" book; nowhere does it mention God, worship, prayer, or other religious practices. Yet God's protection is clear throughout. The number of "coincidences" in the book illustrate that God's hand is at work in events, even when we don't realise it.

Where?

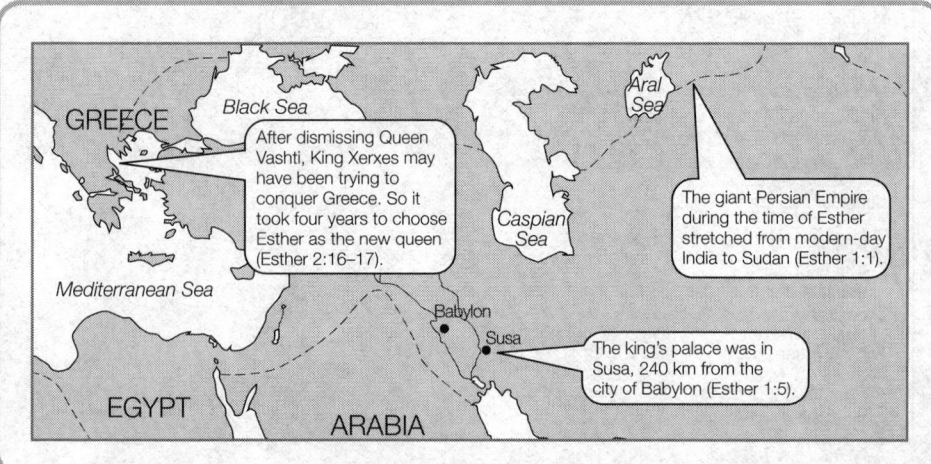

After dismissing Queen Vashti, King Xerxes may have been trying to conquer Greece. So it took four years to choose Esther as the new queen (Esther 2:16–17).

The giant Persian Empire during the time of Esther stretched from modern-day India to Sudan (Esther 1:1).

The king's palace was in Susa, 240 km from the city of Babylon (Esther 1:5).

Queen Vashti Disobeys the King

1 This is what happened during the time of King Xerxes, the king who ruled the 127 areas from India to Cush. ²In those days King Xerxes ruled from his capital city of Susa. ³In the third year of his rule, he gave a banquet for all his important men and royal officers. The army leaders from the countries of Persia and Media and the important men from all Xerxes' empire were there.

⁴The banquet lasted 180 days. All during that time King Xerxes was showing off the great wealth of his kingdom and his own great riches and glory. ⁵When the 180 days were over, the king gave another banquet. It was held in the courtyard of the palace garden for seven days, and it was for everybody in the palace at Susa, from the greatest to the least. ⁶The courtyard had fine white curtains and purple linen that were

DRUGS AND ALCOHOL

Under the Influence

"I wonder what it's like to drown," Scott Walters mused aloud. He quietly exhaled, then slipped under the water in his backyard pool.

Scott was from a wealthy family and was about eleven when he began trying drinks from his father's drinks cabinet. No one in the family seemed to notice or care, so he continued to drink occasionally – in small amounts.

One afternoon several of Scott's friends came over to swim in the family pool.

"My family lets me drink whenever I want to," Scott claimed. "In fact, my dad and I drink together all the time."

"You're lying," scowled Brett, one of Scott's friends. "Your dad doesn't let you drink."

"What do you know?" countered Scott. "You've probably never had anything stronger than milk."

"OK, then," Brett said, "prove it. Prove to us that you drink."

Scott didn't really want to drink right then, because he never knew when his dad would come home. But after repeated dares from his friends, Scott went to the cabinet and poured a little from each bottle into a large glass. Then he drank it all. Scott's friends let out a big "Whoop!" impressed by Scott's ability to "handle his booze".

Scott didn't feel anything happen right away. He thought he was OK, so he jumped into the pool with his friends. But the longer his friends played, the more quiet and distant Scott became.

No one noticed when Scott slipped quietly under the water.

After a minute or two, Brett asked, "Hey, where's Scott?"

The boys saw Scott's form on the bottom. They frantically pulled him from the pool, laid him on the concrete on his side and tried to revive him. Scott soon came around and began to cough up water.

After a few minutes, Scott sat up on the edge of the pool, so drunk he didn't even realise he had almost died.

Alcohol and drugs keep us from thinking clearly. In **Esther 1:4–12**, read how King Xerxes reacted after drinking a large amount of wine.

- What effect did alcohol have on Scott and King Xerxes?
- What does this passage say about using drugs and alcohol?

Consider . . .

- writing reasons you choose not to use alcohol or other drugs, and keeping that list in your Bible as a reminder.
- scanning the newspaper for articles that involved drink driving or violence resulting from drug or alcohol use, then consider asking God to help the people in each of those situations.

For more, see . . .

- Proverbs 23:29–35 (p.610)
- Ephesians 5:15–18 (p.1275)
- Galatians 5:19–23 (p.1264)

tied to silver rings on marble pillars by white and purple cords. And there were gold and silver couches on a floor set with tiles of white marble, shells and gems. [7]Wine was served in gold cups of various kinds. And there was plenty of the king's wine, because he was very generous. [8]The king commanded that the guests be permitted to drink as much as they wished. He told the wine servers to serve each person what he wanted.

> ### Sidelight
>
> Do you prefer sitting up or laying down? Did you realise that the very rich people in Esther's day spent their time lounged on gold and silver couches when they ate. Eating in bed was normal (Esther 1:4–8)! Ordinary folk had wooden beds with cord nets for mattresses and the poor slept on the ground covering themselves with their clothes.

[9]Queen Vashti also gave a banquet for the women in the royal palace of King Xerxes.

[10]On the seventh day of the banquet, King Xerxes was very happy, because he had been drinking much wine. He gave a command to the seven eunuchs [d] who served him—Mehuman, Biztha, Harbona, Bigtha, Abagtha, Zethar and Carcas. [11]He commanded them to bring him Queen Vashti, wearing her royal crown. She was to come to show her beauty to the people and important men, because she was very beautiful. [12]The eunuchs told Queen Vashti about the king's command, but she refused to come. Then the king became very angry; his anger was like a burning fire.

> ### Sidelight
>
> Some people in ancient times really knew how to party. King Xerxes threw one that lasted six months. Herodotus, the Greek historian, noted the lengthy banquets where Xerxes may have made a plot to exterminate the Jews and a disastrous plan to invade Greece.

[13]It was a custom for the king to ask advice from experts about law and order. So King Xerxes spoke with the wise men who would know the right thing to do. [14]The wise men the king usually talked to were Carshena, Shethar, Admatha, Tarshish, Meres, Marsena and Memucan, seven of the important men of Persia and Media. These seven had special privileges to see the king and had the highest rank in the kingdom. [15]The king asked them, "What does the law say must be done to Queen Vashti? She has not obeyed the command of King Xerxes, which the eunuchs took to her."

[16]Then Memucan said to the king and the other important men, "Queen Vashti has not done wrong to the king alone. She has also done wrong to all the important men and all the people in all the empire of King Xerxes. [17]All the wives of the important men of Persia and Media will hear about the queen's actions. Then they will no longer honour their husbands. They will say, 'King Xerxes commanded Queen Vashti to be brought to him, but she refused to come.' [18]Today the wives of the important men of Persia and Media have heard about the queen's actions. So they will speak in the same way to their husbands, and there will be no end to disrespect and anger.

[19]"So, our king, if it pleases you, give a royal order, and let it be written in the laws of Persia and Media, which cannot be changed. The law should say Vashti is never again to enter the presence of King Xerxes. Also let the king give her place as queen to someone who is better than she is. [20]And let the king's order be announced everywhere in his great kingdom. Then all the women will respect their husbands, from the greatest to the least."

[21]The king and his important men were happy with this advice, so King Xerxes did as Memucan suggested. [22]He sent letters to all the areas of the kingdom in the writing of each area and in the language of each group of people. These letters announced that each man was to be the ruler of his own family.

Esther is Made Queen

2 Later, when King Xerxes was not so angry, he remembered Vashti and what she had done and his order about her. [2]Then the king's personal servants suggested, "Let a search be made for beautiful young girls for the king. [3]Let the king choose supervisors in every area of his kingdom to bring every beautiful young girl to the palace at Susa. They should be taken to the women's quarters and put under the care of Hegai, the king's eunuch [d] in charge of the women. And let beauty treatments be given to them. [4]Then let the girl who most pleases the king become queen in place of Vashti." The king liked this idea, so he did as they said.

[5]Now there was a Jewish man in the palace of Susa whose name was Mordecai son of Jair. Jair was the son of Shimei, the son of Kish. Mordecai was from the tribe [d] of Benjamin, [6]which had been taken captive from Jerusalem by Nebuchadnezzar king of Babylon. They were part of the group taken into captivity with Jehoiachin king of Judah. [7]Mordecai had a cousin named Hadassah,

who had no father or mother, so Mordecai took care of her. Hadassah was also called Esther, and she had a very pretty figure and face. Mordecai had adopted her as his own daughter when her father and mother died.

⁸When the king's command and order had been heard, many girls had been brought to the palace in Susa and put under the care of Hegai. Esther was also taken to the king's palace and put under the care of Hegai, who was in charge of the women. ⁹Esther pleased Hegai, and he liked her. So Hegai quickly began giving Esther her beauty treatments and special food. He gave her seven servant girls chosen from the king's palace. Then he moved her and her seven servant girls to the best part of the women's quarters.

¹⁰Esther did not tell anyone about her family or who her people were, because Mordecai had told her not to. ¹¹Every day Mordecai walked back and forth near the courtyard where the king's women lived to find out how Esther was and what was happening to her.

¹²Before a girl could take her turn with King Xerxes, she had to complete twelve months of beauty treatments that were ordered for the women. For six months she was treated with oil and myrrh *d* and for six months with perfumes and cosmetics. ¹³Then she was ready to go to the king. Anything she asked for was given to her to take with her from the women's quarters to the

Sidelight   If you think somebody at home takes too long in the bathroom, just be glad she isn't Esther. It took Esther a year of beauty treatments to get ready for the king (Esther 2:12–13).

king's palace. ¹⁴In the evening she would go to the king's palace, and in the morning she would return to another part of the women's quarters. There she would be placed under the care of Shaashgaz, the king's eunuch in charge of the slave women. *d* The girl would not go back to the king again unless he was pleased with her and asked for her by name.

¹⁵The time came for Esther daughter of Abihail, Mordecai's uncle, who had been adopted by Mordecai, to go to the king. She asked for only what Hegai suggested she should take. (Hegai was the king's eunuch who was in charge of the women.) Everyone who saw Esther liked her. ¹⁶So Esther was taken to King Xerxes in the royal palace in the tenth month, the month of Tebeth, during Xerxes' seventh year as king.

¹⁷And the king was pleased with Esther more than with any of the other girls. He liked her more than any of the other girls, so he put a royal crown on her head and made her queen in place of Vashti. ¹⁸Then the king gave a great banquet for Esther and invited all his important men and royal officers. He announced a holiday for all the empire and had the government give away gifts.

Mordecai Discovers an Evil Plan

¹⁹Now Mordecai was sitting at the king's gate when the girls were gathered the second time. ²⁰Esther still had not told anyone about her family or who her people were, just as Mordecai had commanded her. She obeyed Mordecai just as she had done when she was under his care.

²¹Now Bigthana and Teresh were two of the king's officers who guarded the doorway. While Mordecai was sitting at the king's gate, they became angry and began to make plans to kill King Xerxes. ²²But Mordecai found out about their plans and told Queen Esther. Then Esther told the king how Mordecai had discovered the evil plan. ²³When the report was investigated, it was found to be true, and the two officers who had planned to kill the king were hanged. All this was written down in the daily court record in the king's presence.

Haman Plans to Destroy the Jewish People

3 After these things happened, King Xerxes honoured Haman son of Hammedatha the Agagite. He gave him a new rank that was higher than all the important men. ²All the royal officers at the king's gate would bow down and kneel before Haman, as the king had ordered. But Mordecai would not bow down or show him honour.

³Then the royal officers at the king's gate asked Mordecai, "Why don't you obey the king's command?" ⁴And they said this to him every day. When he did not listen to them, they told Haman about it. They wanted to see if Haman would accept Mordecai's behaviour because Mordecai had told them he was Jewish.

⁵When Haman saw that Mordecai would not bow down to him or honour him, he became very angry. ⁶He thought of himself as too important to try to kill only Mordecai. He had been told who the people of Mordecai were, so he looked for a way to destroy all of Mordecai's people, the Jews, in all of Xerxes' kingdom.

⁷It was in the first month of the twelfth year of King Xerxes' rule—the month of Nisan. Pur (that is, the lot *d*) was thrown before Haman to choose a day and a month. So the twelfth month, the month of Adar, was chosen.

⁸Then Haman said to King Xerxes, "There is a certain group of people scattered among the other people in all the areas of your kingdom. Their customs are different from those of all the other

people, and they do not obey the king's laws. It is not right for you to allow them to continue living in your kingdom. ⁹If it pleases the king, let an order be given to destroy those people. Then I will pay 350 tonnes of silver to those who do the king's business, and they will put it into the royal treasury."

¹⁰So the king took his signet *d* ring off and gave it to Haman son of Hammedatha, the Agagite, the enemy of the Jewish people. ¹¹Then the king said to Haman, "The money and the people are yours. Do with them as you please."

¹²On the thirteenth day of the first month, the royal secretaries were called, and they wrote out all of Haman's orders. They wrote to the king's governors and to the captains of the soldiers in each area and to the important men of each group of people. The orders were written in the writing of each area and in the language of each people. They were written in the name of King Xerxes and sealed with his signet ring. ¹³Letters were sent by messengers to all the king's empire ordering them to destroy, kill and completely wipe out all the Jewish people. That meant young and old, women and little children too. It was to happen on a single day—the thirteenth day of the twelfth month, which was Adar. And they could take everything the Jewish people owned. ¹⁴A copy of the order was given out as a law in every area so all the people would be ready for that day.

¹⁵The messengers set out, hurried by the king's command, as soon as the order was given in the palace at Susa. The king and Haman sat down to drink, but the city of Susa was in confusion.

Mordecai Asks Esther to Help

4 When Mordecai heard about all that had been done, he tore his clothes, put on rough cloth and ashes, and went out into the city crying loudly and painfully. ²But Mordecai went only as far as the king's gate, because no one was allowed to enter that gate dressed in rough cloth. ³As the king's order reached every area, there was great sadness and loud crying among the Jewish people. They gave up eating and cried out loudly, and many of them lay down on rough cloth and ashes to show how sad they were.

⁴When Esther's servant girls and eunuchs *d* came to her and told her about Mordecai, she was very upset and afraid. She sent clothes for Mordecai to put on instead of the rough cloth, but he would not wear them. ⁵Then Esther called for Hathach, one of the king's eunuchs chosen by the king to serve her. Esther ordered him to find out what was bothering Mordecai and why.

⁶So Hathach went to Mordecai, who was in the city square in front of the king's gate.

⁷Mordecai told Hathach everything that had happened to him, and he told Hathach about the amount of money Haman had promised to pay into the king's treasury for the killing of the Jewish people. ⁸Mordecai also gave him a copy of the order to kill the Jewish people, which had been given in Susa. He wanted Hathach to show it to Esther and to tell her about it. And Mordecai told him to order Esther to go into the king's presence to beg for mercy and to plead with him for her people.

⁹Hathach went back and reported to Esther everything Mordecai had said. ¹⁰Then Esther told Hathach to tell Mordecai, ¹¹"All the royal officers and people of the royal areas know that no man or woman may go to the king in the inner courtyard without being called. There is only one law about this: anyone who enters must be put to death unless the king holds out his gold sceptre. *d* Then that person may live. And I have not been called to go to the king for 30 days."

¹²Esther's message was given to Mordecai. ¹³Then Mordecai sent back word to Esther: "Just because you live in the king's palace, don't think that out of all the Jewish people you alone will escape. ¹⁴If you keep quiet at this time, someone else will help and save the Jewish people, but you and your father's family will all die. And who knows, you may have been chosen queen for just such a time as this."

¹⁵Then Esther sent this answer to Mordecai: ¹⁶"Go and get all the Jewish people in Susa together. For my sake, give up eating; do not eat or drink for three days, night and day. I and my servant girls will also give up eating. Then I will go to the king, even though it is against the law, and if I die, I die."

¹⁷So Mordecai went away and did everything Esther had told him to do.

Esther Speaks to the King

5 On the third day Esther put on her royal robes and stood in the inner courtyard of the king's palace, facing the king's hall. The king was sitting on his royal throne in the hall, facing the doorway. ²When the king saw Queen Esther standing in the courtyard, he was pleased. He held out to her the gold sceptre *d* that was in his hand, so Esther went forwards and touched the end of it.

³The king asked, "What is it, Queen Esther? What do you want to ask me? I will give you as much as half of my kingdom."

⁴Esther answered, "My king, if it pleases you, come today with Haman to a banquet that I have prepared for him."

⁵Then the king said, "Bring Haman quickly so we may do what Esther asks."

So the king and Haman went to the banquet Esther had prepared for them. [6]As they were drinking wine, the king said to Esther, "Now, what are you asking for? I will give it to you. What is it you want? I will give you as much as half of my kingdom."

[7]Esther answered, "This is what I want and what I ask for. [8]My king, if you are pleased with me and if it pleases you, give me what I ask for and do what I want. Come with Haman tomorrow to the banquet I will prepare for you. Then I will answer your question about what I want."

Haman's Plans Against Mordecai

[9]Haman left the king's palace that day happy and content. But when he saw Mordecai at the king's gate and saw that Mordecai did not stand up or tremble with fear before him, Haman became very angry with Mordecai. [10]But he controlled his anger and went home.

Then Haman called together his friends and his wife, Zeresh. [11]He told them how wealthy he was and how many sons he had. He also told them all the ways the king had honoured him and how the king had placed him higher than his important men and his royal officers. [12]He also said, "I'm the only person Queen Esther invited to come with the king to the banquet she gave. And tomorrow also the queen has asked me to be her guest with the king. [13]But all this does not really

HEROES

Risky Business

"They were chasing a little boy of about ten years old. They caught up with him, and one of them took his gun and smashed the child's head in. They killed him."

Those are the words of Giorgio Perlasca, who witnessed this murder in Hungary in 1944. It was World War II, and the Nazis were killing the Jews, regardless of their age.

Although he was Italian, Perlasca was able to masquerade as a top Spanish diplomat and help to save the Jews.

For three months, Perlasca distributed letters to all the Jews he could find. The letters stated that the Jews had been granted the protection of the Spanish government. When he saw Jews being herded onto to trains, headed for death, he confronted the Nazis and ordered them to return the people to him. He housed more than 5,000 Jews in eleven apartment buildings where he hung Spain's flag to protect the occupants.

Historians estimate that Perlasca helped to save more than 10,000 people before his cover was blown when Spain cut off diplomatic relations with Hungary at the end of 1944.

Queen Esther also put her life on the line for the Jews. Read her story in **Esther 4:9–16**.

* What risks did both Perlasca and Esther take to save the Jews?
* We may not all have the chance to save thousands of people from dying, but we can still make a difference. How can you be a hero for God?

Consider . . .

* reading a biography of a Christian man or woman who made major inroads for others through their life.
* who your heroes are and how well they measure up to the standards of Esther. Then decide if you need to change heroes.

For more, see . . .

* Exodus 14:5–31 (p.71)
* Hebrews 11:29–40 (p.1342)
* Joshua 2:1–22 (p.203)

make me happy when I see that Jew Mordecai sitting at the king's gate."

[14]Then Haman's wife, Zeresh, and all his friends said, "Have a 25-metre-high platform built, and in the morning ask the king to have Mordecai hanged on it. Then go to the banquet with the king and be happy." Haman liked this suggestion, so he ordered the platform to be built.

Mordecai is Honoured

6 That same night the king could not sleep. So he gave an order for the daily court record to be brought in and read to him. [2]It was found recorded that Mordecai had warned the king about Bigthana and Teresh, two of the king's officers who guarded the doorway and who had planned to kill the king.

[3]The king asked, "What honour and reward have been given to Mordecai for this?"

The king's personal servants answered, "Nothing has been done for Mordecai."

[4]The king said, "Who is in the courtyard?" Now Haman had just entered the outer court of the king's palace. He had come to ask the king about hanging Mordecai on the platform he had prepared.

[5]The king's personal servants said, "Haman is standing in the courtyard."

The king said, "Bring him in."

[6]So Haman came in. And the king asked him, "What should be done for a man whom the king wants very much to honour?"

And Haman thought to himself, "Whom would the king want to honour more than me?" [7]So he answered the king, "This is what you could do for the man you want very much to honour. [8]Have the servants bring a royal robe that the king himself has worn. And also bring a horse with a royal crown on its head, a horse that the king himself has ridden. [9]Let the robe and the horse be given to one of the king's most important men. Let the servants put the robe on the man the king wants to honour, and let them lead him on the horse through the city streets. As they are leading him, let them announce: 'This is what is done for the man whom the king wants to honour!'"

[10]The king commanded Haman, "Go quickly. Take the robe and the horse just as you have said, and do all this for Mordecai the Jew who sits at the king's gate. Do not leave out anything you have suggested."

[11]So Haman took the robe and the horse, and he put the robe on Mordecai. Then he led him on horseback through the city streets, announcing before Mordecai: "This is what is done for the man whom the king wants to honour!"

[12]Then Mordecai returned to the king's gate, but Haman hurried home with his head covered, because he was embarrassed and ashamed. [13]He told his wife, Zeresh, and all his friends everything that had happened to him.

Haman's wife and the men who gave him advice said, "You are starting to lose power to Mordecai. Since he is a Jew, you cannot win against him. You will surely be ruined." [14]While they were still talking, the king's eunuchs [d] came to Haman's house and made him hurry to the banquet Esther had prepared.

Haman is Hanged

7 So the king and Haman went in to eat with Queen Esther. [2]As they were drinking wine on the second day, the king asked Esther again, "What are you asking for? I will give it to you. What is it you want? I will give you as much as half of my kingdom."

[3]Then Queen Esther answered, "My king, if you are pleased with me, and if it pleases you, let me live. This is what I ask. And let my people live, too. This is what I want. [4]My people and I have been sold to be destroyed, to be killed and completely wiped out. If we had been sold as male and female slaves, I would have kept quiet, because that would not be enough of a problem to bother the king."

[5]Then King Xerxes asked Queen Esther, "Who is he, and where is he? Who has done such a thing?"

[6]Esther said, "Our enemy and foe is this wicked Haman!"

Then Haman was filled with terror before the king and queen. [7]The king was very angry, so he got up, left his wine and went out into the palace garden. But Haman stayed inside to beg Queen Esther to save his life. He could see that the king had already decided to kill him.

Sidelight Going to the palace garden to cool off was probably a good idea for the angry king (Esther 7:7). The palace at Susa was the king's winter palace because it was warmer than the government headquarters in Persepolis.

---

[8]When the king returned from the palace garden to the banquet hall, he saw Haman falling on the couch where Esther was lying. The king said, "Will he even attack the queen while I am in the house?"

As soon as the king said that, servants came in and covered Haman's face. [9]Harbona, one of the eunuchs [d] there serving the king, said, "Look, a

25-metre-high platform stands near Haman's house. This is the one Haman had prepared for Mordecai, who gave the warning that saved the king."

The king said, "Hang Haman on it!" [10]So they hanged Haman on the platform he had prepared for Mordecai. Then the king was not so angry any more.

> **Sidelight**   The execution planned by Haman for Mordecai, but carried out by the king on Haman (Esther 7:8–10), probably would not have been hanging in the modern sense, but may have involved impaling the victim on a sharp stake and then hanging the body in the city for display. Romans adapted this method to develop execution on crosses.

The King Helps the Jewish People

8 That same day King Xerxes gave Queen Esther everything Haman, the enemy of the Jewish people, had left when he died. And Mordecai came in to see the king, because Esther had told the king how he was related to her. [2]Then the king took off his signet [d] ring that he had taken back from Haman, and he gave it to Mordecai. Esther put Mordecai in charge of everything Haman left when he died.

[3]Once again Esther spoke to the king. She fell at the king's feet and cried and begged him to stop the evil plan that Haman the Agagite had planned against the Jews. [4]The king held out the gold sceptre [d] to Esther. So Esther got up and stood in front of him.

[5]She said, "My king, if you are pleased with me, and if it pleases you to do this, if you think it is the right thing to do, and if you are happy with me, let an order be written to cancel the letters Haman wrote. Haman the Agagite sent messages to destroy all the Jewish people in all of your kingdom. [6]I could not stand to see that terrible thing happen to my people. I could not stand to see my family killed."

[7]King Xerxes answered Queen Esther and Mordecai the Jew, "Because Haman was against the Jewish people, I have given his things to Esther and my soldiers have hanged him. [8]Now, in the king's name, write another order to the Jewish people as it seems best to you. Then seal the order with the king's signet ring, because no letter written in the king's name and sealed with his signet ring can be cancelled."

[9]At that time the king's secretaries were called. This was the twenty-third day of the third month, which is Sivan. The secretaries wrote out all of Mordecai's orders to the Jews, to the governors, to the captains of the soldiers in each area and to the important men of the 127 areas that reached from India to Cush. They wrote in the writing of each area and in the language of each people. They also wrote to the Jewish people in their own writing and language. [10]Mordecai wrote orders in the name of King Xerxes and sealed the letters with the king's signet ring. Then he sent the king's orders by messengers on fast horses, horses that were raised just for the king.

> **Sidelight**   The longest verse in the Bible is Esther 8:9. It's 88 words long.

[11]These were the king's orders: the Jewish people in every city have the right to gather together to protect themselves. They may destroy, kill and completely wipe out the army of any area or people who attack them. And they are to do the same to the women and children of that army. They may also take by force the property of their enemies. [12]The one day set for the Jewish people to do this in all the empire of King Xerxes was the thirteenth day of the twelfth month, the month of Adar. [13]A copy of the king's order was to be sent out as a law in every area. It was to be made known to the people of every nation living in the kingdom so the Jewish people would be ready on that set day to strike back at their enemies.

> **Sidelight**   The Persians may not have had Royal Mail, but they had an excellent postal system to deliver Mordecai's letter (Esther 8:10). The Persian Empire was divided into 20 satrapies (or provinces), which were interconnected by an efficient postal service begun by King Cyrus around 535 BC.

[14]The messengers hurried out, riding on the royal horses, because the king commanded those messengers to hurry. And the order was also given in the palace at Susa.

[15]Mordecai left the king's presence wearing royal clothes of blue and white and a large gold crown. He also had a purple robe made of the best linen. And the people of Susa shouted for joy. [16]It was a time of happiness, joy, gladness and honour for the Jewish people. [17]As the king's order went to every area and city, there was joy and gladness among the Jewish people. In every area

and city to which the king's order went, they were having feasts and celebrating. And many people through all the empire became Jews, because they were afraid of the Jewish people.

Victory for the Jewish People

9 The order the king had commanded was to be done on the thirteenth day of the twelfth month, the month of Adar. That was the day the enemies of the Jewish people had hoped to defeat them, but that was changed. So the Jewish people themselves defeated those who hated them. [2]The Jews met in their cities in all the empire of King Xerxes in order to attack those who wanted to harm them. No one was strong enough to fight against them, because all the other people living in the empire were afraid of them. [3]All the important men of the areas, the governors, captains of the soldiers, and the king's officers helped the Jewish people, because they were afraid of Mordecai. [4]Mordecai was very important in the king's palace. He was famous in all the empire, because he was becoming a leader of more and more people.

[5]And, with their swords, the Jewish people defeated all their enemies, killing and destroying them. And they did what they wanted with those people who hated them. [6]In the palace at Susa, they killed and destroyed 500 men. [7]They also killed: Parshandatha, Dalphon, Aspatha, [8]Poratha, Adalia, Aridatha, [9]Parmashta, Arisai, Aridai and Vaizatha, [10]the ten sons of Haman, son of Hammedatha, the enemy of the Jewish people. But the Jewish people did not take their belongings.

[11]On that day the number killed in the palace at Susa was reported to the king. [12]The king said to Queen Esther, "The Jewish people have killed and destroyed 500 people in the palace at Susa, and they have also killed Haman's ten sons. What have they done in the rest of the king's empire! Now what else are you asking? I will do it! What else do you want? It will be done!"

[13]Esther answered, "If it pleases the king, give the Jewish people who are in Susa permission to do again tomorrow what the king ordered for today. And let the bodies of Haman's ten sons be hanged on the platform."

[14]So the king ordered that it be done. A law was given in Susa, and the bodies of the ten sons of Haman were hanged. [15]The Jewish people in Susa came together on the fourteenth day of the month of Adar. They killed 300 people in Susa, but they did not take their belongings.

[16]At that same time, all the Jewish people in the king's empire also met to protect themselves and get rid of their enemies. They killed 75,000 of those who hated them, but they did not take their belongings. [17]This happened on the thirteenth day of the month of Adar. On the fourteenth day they rested and made it a day of joyful feasting.

The Feast of Purim

[18]But the Jewish people in Susa met on the thirteenth and fourteenth days of the month of Adar. Then they rested on the fifteenth day and made it a day of joyful feasting.

[19]This is why the Jewish people who live in the country and small villages celebrate on the fourteenth day of the month of Adar. It is a day of joyful feasting and a day for exchanging gifts.

[20]Mordecai wrote down everything that had happened. Then he sent letters to all the Jewish people in all the empire of King Xerxes, far and near. [21]He told them to celebrate every year on the fourteenth and fifteenth days of the month of Adar, [22]because that was when the Jewish people got rid of their enemies. They were also to celebrate it as the month their sadness was turned to joy and their crying for the dead was turned into celebration. He told them to celebrate those days as days of joyful feasting and as a time for giving food to each other and presents to the poor.

> ### Sidelight
> The two despised Jews rose to become very important, but they never forgot their roots. Because of Esther and Mordecai's faithfulness, Jews celebrate each year in February or March with parties, gifts and aid to the poor as part of the joyous Feast of Purim (Esther 9:8–32).

[23]So the Jewish people agreed to do what Mordecai had written to them, and they agreed to hold the celebration every year. [24]Haman son of Hammedatha, the Agagite, was the enemy of all the Jewish people. He had made an evil plan against the Jewish people to destroy them, and he had thrown the Pur (that is, the lot [d]) to choose a day to ruin and destroy them. [25]But when the king learned of the evil plan, he sent out written orders that the evil plans Haman had made against the Jewish people would be used against him. And those orders said that Haman and his sons should be hanged on the platform. [26]So these days were called Purim, which comes from the word "Pur" (the lot). Because of everything written in this letter and what they had seen and what happened to them, [27]the Jewish people set up this custom. They and their descendants [d] and all those who join them are always to celebrate these two days every year. They should do it in the right way and at the time Mordecai had

ordered them in the letter. [28]These two days should be remembered and celebrated from now on in every family, in every area and in every city. These days of Purim should always be celebrated by the Jewish people, and their descendants should always remember to celebrate them too.

[29]So Queen Esther daughter of Abihail, along with Mordecai the Jew, wrote this second letter about Purim. Using the power they had, they wrote to prove the first letter was true. [30]And Mordecai sent letters to all the Jewish people in the 127 areas of the kingdom of Xerxes, writing them a message of peace and truth. [31]He wrote to set up these days of Purim at the chosen times. Mordecai the Jew and Queen Esther had sent out the order for the Jewish people, just as they had set up things for themselves and their descendants: On these two days the people should give up eating and cry loudly. [32]Esther's letter set up the rules for Purim and they were written down in the records.

The Greatness of Mordecai

10 King Xerxes demanded taxes everywhere, even from the cities on the seacoast. [2]And all the great things Xerxes did by his power and strength are written in the record books of the kings of Media and Persia. Also written in those record books are all the things done by Mordecai, whom the king made great. [3]Mordecai the Jew was second in importance to King Xerxes, and he was the most important man among the Jewish people. His fellow Jews respected him very much, because he worked for the good of his people and spoke up for the safety of all the Jewish people.

Job

When?

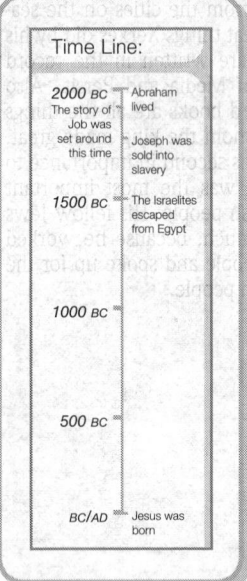

Time Line:

2000 BC — Abraham lived
The story of Job was set around this time
— Joseph was sold into slavery

1500 BC — The Israelites escaped from Egypt

1000 BC

500 BC

BC/AD — Jesus was born

Why Read This Book:

* Learn patience from someone who is suffering unfairly (Job 1:21—2:10; 16; 19).
* Realise it's OK to question God (Job 10, 13, 23).
* See how God is always there, even when he doesn't seem to be (Job 38—42).

Behind the Scenes:

Why do good people suffer? Why do bad people seem to get away with everything? How can God love us if he lets bad things happen to us? If you have ever asked those questions, you are not alone. For centuries, people have asked them and struggled with them.

The book of Job addresses those questions as it tells about Job, an upright and wealthy man. Like others of his day, he believed that all his blessings were the result of his goodness. He accepted traditional answers to life's questions.

Then his life fell apart. He lost everything – his family, his health and his belongings. Life wasn't supposed to work out this way. In his pain, he cried out angrily to God, "Why do innocent people suffer?"

Four friends made matters worse by telling Job the same old thing: God rewards the righteous and punishes sinners (Job 3—37). Job sincerely believed he was innocent, but he couldn't explain the suffering. He felt betrayed by God. Yet patiently he kept his faith in God and waited for God's answers to his questions. ▷

Where?

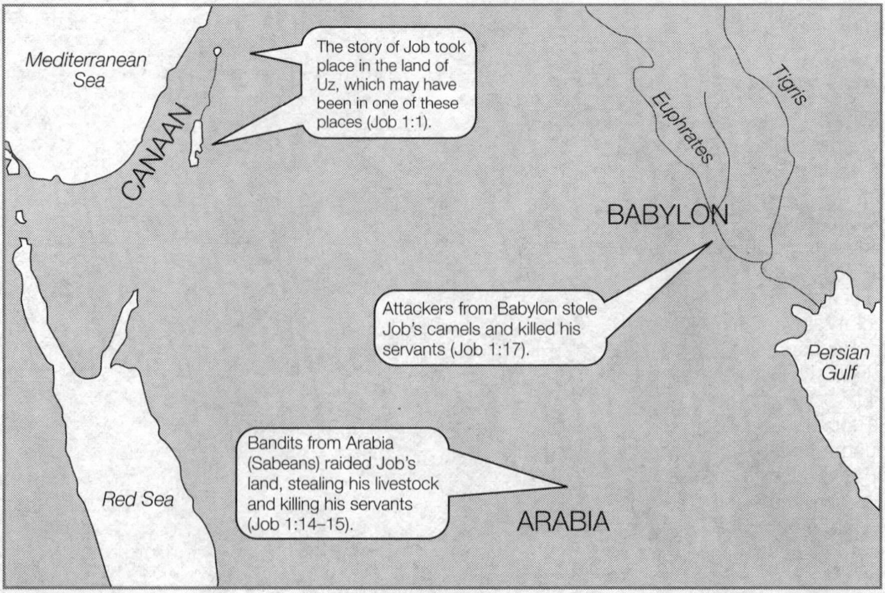

> The story of Job took place in the land of Uz, which may have been in one of these places (Job 1:1).

Mediterranean Sea

CANAAN

Euphrates

Tigris

BABYLON

> Attackers from Babylon stole Job's camels and killed his servants (Job 1:17).

Persian Gulf

> Bandits from Arabia (Sabeans) raided Job's land, stealing his livestock and killing his servants (Job 1:14–15).

Red Sea

ARABIA

Behind the
Scenes (cont.): Job and his friends never settled their debate. Suddenly God appeared
on the scene through a storm, in chapters 38—41. He didn't answer Job,
though he did speak to him. God reminded Job that his greatness and
wisdom are beyond human understanding. Job then realised that it wasn't
his place to try to understand God. Instead, he was to follow God faithfully
no matter what happened.

People continue to struggle with why good people suffer. The book of
Job tells us that it's OK to ask God tough questions. It also challenges us
to remain faithful in spite of suffering. In the end, we can trust in God's
goodness, justice and wisdom – even when we can't see it ourselves.

Job, the Good Man

1 A man named Job lived in the land of Uz. He
was an honest and innocent man; he honoured God and stayed away from evil. ²Job had
seven sons and three daughters. ³He owned
7,000 sheep, 3,000 camels, 500 teams of oxen
and 500 female donkeys. He also had a large
number of servants. He was the greatest man
among all the people of the East.

⁴Job's sons took turns holding feasts in their
homes and invited their sisters to eat and drink
with them. ⁵After a feast was over, Job would
send and have them made clean. *d* Early in the
morning Job would offer a burnt offering for each
of them, because he thought, "My children may
have sinned and cursed God in their hearts." Job
did this every time.

Satan Appears Before the Lord

⁶One day the angels came to show themselves
before the Lord, and Satan was with them. ⁷The
Lord said to Satan, "Where have you come
from?"

Satan answered the Lord, "I have been wandering around the earth, going back and forth
in it."

⁸Then the Lord said to Satan, "Have you noticed my servant Job? No one else on earth is like
him. He is an honest and innocent man, honouring God and staying away from evil."

⁹But Satan answered the Lord, "Job honours
God for a good reason. ¹⁰You have put a wall
around him, his family and everything he owns.
You have blessed the things he has done. His
flocks and herds are so large they almost cover
the land. ¹¹But reach out your hand and destroy
everything he has, and he will curse you to your
face."

¹²The Lord said to Satan, "All right, then.
Everything Job has is in your power, but you

must not touch Job himself." Then Satan left the
Lord's presence.

¹³One day Job's sons and daughters were eating and drinking wine together at the oldest
brother's house. ¹⁴A messenger came to Job and
said, "The oxen were ploughing and the donkeys
were eating grass nearby, ¹⁵when the Sabeans attacked and carried them away. They killed the
servants with swords, and I am the only one who
escaped to tell you!"

¹⁶The messenger was still speaking when another messenger arrived and said, "Lightning
from God fell from the sky. It burned up the
sheep and the servants, and I am the only one
who escaped to tell you!"

¹⁷The second messenger was still speaking
when another messenger arrived and said, "The
Babylonians sent three groups of attackers that
swept down and stole your camels and killed the
servants. I am the only one who escaped to
tell you!"

> **Sidelight** The theft of Job's camels
> is equivalent to stealing
> a Landrover today, as these amazing animals
> were prized for their swift and reliable transport
> abilities in the hot desert. A one-humped camel
> could reach a top speed of 16 kilometres
> an hour.

¹⁸The third messenger was still speaking when
another messenger arrived and said, "Your sons
and daughters were eating and drinking wine together at the oldest brother's house. ¹⁹Suddenly a
great wind came from the desert, hitting all four
corners of the house at once. The house fell in on
the young people, and they are all dead. I am the
only one who escaped to tell you!"

²⁰When Job heard this, he got up and tore his
robe and shaved his head to show how sad he was.

Then he bowed down to the ground to worship God. ²¹He said:

"I was naked when I was born,
  and I will be naked when I die.
The LORD gave these things to me,
  and he has taken them away.
  Praise the name of the LORD."

²²In all this Job did not sin or blame God.

Satan Appears Before the LORD Again

2 On another day the angels came to show themselves before the LORD, and Satan was with them again. ²The LORD said to Satan, "Where have you come from?"

Satan answered the LORD, "I have been wandering around the earth, going back and forth in it."

³Then the LORD said to Satan, "Have you noticed my servant Job? No one else on earth is like him. He is an honest and innocent man, honouring God and staying away from evil. You caused me to ruin him for no good reason, but he continues to be without blame."

⁴"One skin for another!" Satan answered. "A man will give all he has to save his own life. ⁵But reach out your hand and destroy his flesh and bones, and he will curse you to your face."

⁶The LORD said to Satan, "All right, then. Job is in your power, but you may not take his life."

⁷So Satan left the LORD's presence. He put painful sores on Job's body, from the top of his head to the soles of his feet. ⁸Job took a piece of broken pottery to scrape himself, and he sat in ashes in misery.

⁹Job's wife said to him, "Why are you trying to stay innocent? Curse God and die!"

¹⁰Job answered, "You are talking like a foolish woman. Should we take only good things from God and not trouble?" In spite of all this Job did not sin in what he said.

DEATH

Praise Beyond the Grave

The bomb detonated. In milliseconds, a ball of heat and fire exploded, filling the train with debris, bits of metal and shards of glass. There were no survivors.

A hundred miles away was Abi. She'd stayed at home that day to do some exam revision before a mate's party. Her family had caught the train and gone out shopping. They'd caught the train that had blown up.

As time passed, Abi experienced a vast range of emotions. Sometimes she could do nothing but cry – cry until it hurt. Other times she felt guilty for not being on the train too. Some days just breathing seemed difficult; others were almost normal. Initially, her friends called round and tried to cheer her up. After a while though, they visited less often. They started to say things like, "It is time you got over it now" and "Try not to get angry at God" – but time was not making it better, and Abi was furious with God.

Job is struck by an incredible disaster. He is overwhelmed with grief and throws his whole self into mourning. He gets angry, and dares to ask why. Then he does an incredible thing. He bows down and worships the Lord, who is always in control, who rules our yesterday, our today and our tomorrow and who gives us life everlasting. Maybe Job's response in **Job 1:18–22** is not a bad one to copy.

* How does this passage affect your view of God?
* What would you say to Abi if you were one of her friends?

Consider . . .

* making a list of all that God has given you. Look at the list and give thanks to him, then tell him it is his if he needs it back again one day.
* visiting someone you know who has had someone close to them die. Let them know you read this and thought of them – it may be difficult, but they will really appreciate it.

For more, see . . .

* Psalm 23 (p.513)
* 1 Corinthians 15:35–58 (p.1236)
* Romans 5 (p.1190)
* Revelation 21 (p.1403)

Job's Three Friends Come to Help

11Now Job had three friends: Eliphaz the Temanite, Bildad the Shuhite and Zophar the Naamathite. When these friends heard about Job's troubles, they agreed to meet and visit him. They wanted to show their concern and to comfort him. 12They saw Job from far away, but he looked so different they almost didn't recognise him. They began to cry loudly and tore their robes and put earth on their heads to show how sad they were. 13Then they sat on the ground with Job for seven days and seven nights. No one said a word to him because they saw how much he was suffering.

Job Curses His Birth

3 After seven days Job cried out and cursed the day he had been born, 2saying:

3"Let the day I was born be destroyed,
and the night it was said, 'A boy is born!'
4Let that day turn to darkness.
Don't let God care about it.
Don't let light shine on it.
5Let darkness and gloom have that day.
Let a cloud hide it.
Let thick darkness cover its light.
6Let thick darkness capture that night.
Don't count it among the days of the year
or put it in any of the months.
7Let that night be empty,
with no shout of joy to be heard.
8Let those who curse days curse that day.
Let them prepare to wake up the sea
monster Leviathan. *d*
9Let that day's morning stars never appear;
let it wait for daylight that never comes.
Don't let it see the first light of dawn,
10because it allowed me to be born
and did not hide trouble from my eyes.

11"Why didn't I die as soon as I was born?
Why didn't I die when I came out of the
womb?
12Why did my mother's lap receive me,
and my mother's breasts feed me?
13If they had not been there,
I would be lying dead in peace;
I would be asleep and at rest
14with kings and wise men of the earth
who built places for themselves that are
now ruined.
15I would be asleep with rulers
who filled their houses with gold and silver.
16Why was I not buried like a child born dead,
like a baby who never saw the light of day?
17In the grave the wicked stop making trouble,
and the tired workers are at rest.

18In the grave there is rest for the captives
who no longer hear the shout of the slave
driver.
19People great and small are in the grave,
and the slave is freed from his master.

20"Why is light given to those in misery?
Why is life given to those who are so unhappy?
21They want to die, but death does not come.
They search for death more than for hidden
treasure.
22They are very happy
when they get to the grave.
23They cannot see where they are going.
God has hidden the road ahead.
24I make sad sounds as I eat;
my groans pour out like water.
25Everything I feared and dreaded
has happened to me.
26I have no peace or quietness.
I have no rest, only trouble."

Eliphaz Speaks

4 Then Eliphaz the Temanite answered:

2"If someone tried to speak with you, would
you be upset?
I cannot keep from speaking.
3Think about the many people you have taught
and the weak hands you have made strong.
4Your words have comforted those who fell,
and you have strengthened those who
could not stand.
5But now trouble comes to you, and you are
discouraged;
trouble hits you, and you are terrified.
6You should have confidence because you
respect God;
you should have hope because you are
innocent.

7"Remember that the innocent will not die;
honest people will never be destroyed.
8I have noticed that people who plough evil
and plant trouble, harvest it.
9God's breath destroys them,
and a blast of his anger kills them.
10Lions may roar and growl,
but when the teeth of a strong lion are
broken,
11that lion dies of hunger.
The cubs of the mother lion are scattered.

12"A word was brought to me in secret,
and my ears heard a whisper of it.
13It was during a troublesome dream
when people are in deep sleep.
14I was trembling with fear;
all my bones were shaking.

15A spirit glided past my face,
and the hair on my body stood on end.
16The spirit stopped,
but I could not see what it was.
A shape stood before my eyes,
and I heard a quiet voice.
17It said, 'Can a human be more right
than God?
Can a person be pure before his maker?
18God does not trust his angels;
he blames them for mistakes.
19So he puts even more blame on people who
live in clay houses, *n*
whose foundations are made of dust,
who can be crushed like a moth.
20Between dawn and sunset many people are
broken to pieces;
without being noticed, they die and are
gone for ever.
21The ropes of their tents are pulled up,
and they die without wisdom.'

5 "Call if you want to, Job, but no one will
answer you.
You can't turn to any of the holy ones.
2Anger kills the fool,
and jealousy kills the stupid.
3I have seen a fool succeed,
but I cursed his home immediately.
4His children are far from safety
and are crushed in court with no defence.
5The hungry eat his harvest,
even taking what grew among the thorns,
and thirsty people want his wealth.
6Hard times do not come up from the ground,
and trouble does not grow from the earth.
7People produce trouble
as surely as sparks fly upwards.

8"But if I were you, I would call on God
and bring my problem before him.
9God does wonders that cannot be understood;
he does so many miracles *d* they cannot be
counted.
10He gives rain to the earth
and sends water on the fields.
11He makes the humble person important
and lifts the sad to places of safety.
12He ruins the plans of those who trick others
so they have no success.
13He catches the wise in their own clever traps
and sweeps away the plans of those who try
to trick others.
14Darkness covers them up in the daytime;
even at noon they feel around in the dark.
15God saves the needy from their lies
and from the harm done by powerful people.

16So the poor have hope,
while those who are unfair are silenced.

17"The one whom God corrects is happy,
so do not hate being corrected by the
Almighty.
18God hurts, but he also bandages up;
he injures, but his hands also heal.
19He will save you from six troubles;
even seven troubles will not harm you.
20God will buy you back from death in times of
hunger,
and in battle he will save you from the
sword.
21You will be protected from the tongue that
strikes like a whip,
and you will not be afraid when destruction
comes.
22You will laugh at destruction and hunger,
and you will not fear the wild animals,
23because you will have an agreement with the
stones in the field,
and the wild animals will be at peace with you.
24You will know that your tent is safe,
because you will check the things you own
and find nothing missing.
25You will know that you will have many
children,
and your descendants *d* will be like the grass
on the earth.
26You will come to the grave with all your
strength,
like bundles of grain gathered at the right
time.

27"We have checked this, and it is true,
so hear it and decide what it means to you."

Job Answers Eliphaz

6 Then Job answered:

2"I wish my suffering could be weighed
and my misery put on scales.
3My sadness would be heavier than the sand
of the seas.
No wonder my words seem careless.
4The arrows of the Almighty are in me;
my spirit drinks in their poison;
God's terrors are gathered against me.

Sidelight   There are many names for
God throughout the Bible;
the characters in Job referred to him as "God
Almighty". The literal translation from Hebrew
is "Lord of the Mountain" (Job 6:4).

---

clay houses   This is probably talking about people's bodies.

5A wild donkey does not bray when it has
    grass to eat,
    and an ox is quiet when it has food.
6Tasteless food is not eaten without salt,
    and there is no flavour in the white of
        an egg.
7I refuse to touch it;
    such food makes me sick.

8"How I wish that I might have what I ask for
    and that God would give me what I
        hope for.
9How I wish God would crush me
    and reach out his hand to destroy me.
10Then I would have this comfort
    and be glad even in this unending pain,
    because I would know I did not reject the
        words of the Holy One.

11"I do not have the strength to wait.
    There is nothing to hope for,
    so why should I be patient?
12I do not have the strength of stone;
    my flesh is not bronze.
13I have no power to help myself,
    because success has been taken away
        from me.

14"They say, 'A man's friends should be kind to
    him when he is in trouble,
    even if he stops fearing the Almighty.'
15But my brothers cannot be counted on.
    They are like streams that do not always
        flow,
    streams that sometimes run over.
16They are made dark by melting ice
    and rise with melting snow.
17But they stop flowing in the dry season;
    they disappear when it is hot.
18Travellers turn away from their paths
    and go into the desert and die.
19The groups of travellers from Tema look for
        water,
    and the traders of Sheba look hopefully.
20They are upset because they had been sure;
    when they arrive, they are disappointed.
21You also have been of no help.
    You see something terrible, and you are
        afraid.
22I have never said, 'Give me a gift.
    Use your wealth to pay my debt.
23Save me from the enemy's power.
    Buy me back from the clutches of cruel
        people.'

24"Teach me, and I will be quiet.
    Show me where I have been wrong.
25Honest words are painful,
    but your arguments prove nothing.

26Do you mean to correct what I say?
    Will you treat the words of a troubled man
        as if they were only wind?
27You would even gamble for orphans
    and would trade away your friend.

28"But now please look at me.
    I would not lie to your face.
29Change your mind; do not be unfair;
    think again, because my innocence is being
        questioned.
30What I am saying is not wicked;
    I can tell the difference between right and
        wrong.

7 "People have a hard task on earth,
    and their days are like those of a
        hired man.
2They are like a slave wishing for the evening
        shadows,
    like a labourer waiting to be paid.
3But I am given months that are empty,
    and nights of misery have been given to me.
4When I lie down, I think, 'How long until I
        get up?'
    The night is long, and I toss until dawn.
5My body is covered with worms and scabs,
    and my skin is broken and full of sores.

6"My days go by faster than a weaver's tool,
    and they come to an end without hope.
7Remember, God, that my life is only a breath.
    My eyes will never see happy times again.
8Those who see me now will see me no more;
    you will look for me, but I will be gone.
9As a cloud disappears and is gone,
    people go to the grave and never return.
10They will never come back to their houses
        again,
    and their places will not know them any
        more.
11So I will not stay quiet;
    I will speak out in the suffering of my spirit.
    I will complain because I am so unhappy.
12I am not the sea or the sea monster.
    So why have you set a guard over me?
13Sometimes I think my bed will comfort me
    or that my couch will stop my complaint.
14Then you frighten me with dreams
    and terrify me with visions.
15My throat prefers to be choked;
    my bones welcome death.
16I hate my life; I don't want to live for ever.
    Leave me alone, because my days have no
        meaning.

17"Why do you make people so important
    and give them so much attention?
18You examine them every morning
    and test them every moment.

¹⁹Will you never look away from me
    or leave me alone even long enough to
       swallow?
²⁰If I have sinned, what have I done to
    you,
    you watcher of men?
Why have you made me your target?
Have I become a heavy load for you?
²¹Why don't you pardon my wrongs
    and forgive my sins?
I will soon lie down in the dust of death.
    Then you will search for me, but I will be
       no more."

Bildad Speaks to Job

8 Then Bildad the Shuhite answered:

²"How long will you say such things?
    Your words are no more than wind.

³God does not twist justice;
    the Almighty does not make wrong what is
       right.
⁴Your children sinned against God,
    and he punished them for their sins.
⁵But you should ask God for help
    and pray to the Almighty for mercy.
⁶If you are good and honest,
    he will stand up for you
    and bring you back where you belong.
⁷Where you began will seem unimportant,
    because your future will be so successful.

⁸"Ask old people;
    find out what their ancestors learned,
⁹because we were only born yesterday and
      know nothing.
Our days on earth are only a shadow.
¹⁰Those people will teach you and tell you
    and speak about what they know.

DEPRESSION

Stirring Up Life

Mandy sat beside the swirling river that ran through town. Her fright and hurt had changed into a deadly heaviness. It stifled her. It dulled all hope.

Only last week everything had seemed all right. Then Stuart dumped her – just put his arm around her best friend and went off with her. It nearly killed Mandy. How could he . . . when he said he loved her? And how could Sheila?

Mandy tried to talk to her mum, but the whole house was a constant battlefield, with everyone yelling at each other. Her stepfather was out of work and there wasn't enough money to go round.

The water invited her into its depths. It offered an easy way out.

"Can I sit here with you?"

Mandy looked up at a tall girl. She had seen her a few times at school, always by herself, but self-assured, at ease.

"If you want."

"I'm nobody to you, but . . . I know what happened, and I care." The girl sat down. "I've been there. And even though it doesn't seem possible now, things will get better. Just hang on in there, OK?"

Mandy looked into the girl's brown eyes. Their sincerity stirred life inside Mandy.

Like Mandy, Job felt overwhelmed by a sense of loss and depression. Read his story in **Job 7:1–8**.

* How does Mandy's depression compare with Job's?
* When you feel the way Job did in verses 3 and 7, what do you need most?

Consider . . .

* talking to a trusted friend about a problem that's getting you down.
* organising a peer counselling programme at your church or school. Talk to your youth leader or school teacher for ideas.

For more, see . . .

* Psalm 139:1–24 (p.581)
* Philippians 2:1–4 (p.1282)

* 2 Corinthians 1:3–7 (p.1241)

¹¹Papyrus ^{d} plants cannot grow where there is
    no swamp,
  and reeds cannot grow tall without water.
¹²While they are still growing and not yet cut,
  they will dry up quicker than grass.
¹³That is what will happen to those who
    forget God;
  the hope of the wicked will be gone.
¹⁴What they hope in is easily broken;
  what they trust is like a spider's web.
¹⁵They lean on the spider's web, but it breaks.
  They hold on to it, but it does not hold up.
¹⁶They are like well-watered plants in the
    sunshine
  that spread their roots all through the
    garden.
¹⁷They wrap their roots around a pile of rocks
  and look for a place among the stones.
¹⁸But if a plant is torn from its place,
  then that place rejects it and says, 'I never
    saw you.'
¹⁹Now joy has gone away;
  other plants grow up from the same earth.

²⁰"Surely God does not reject the innocent
  or give strength to those who do evil.
²¹God will yet fill your mouth with laughter
  and your lips with shouts of joy.
²²Your enemies will be covered with shame,
  and the tents of the wicked will be gone."

Job Answers Bildad

9 Then Job answered:

²"Yes, I know that this is true,
  but how can anyone be right in the
    presence of God?
³Someone might want to argue with God,
  but no one could answer God,
  not even one out of a thousand.
⁴God's wisdom is deep, and his power
    is great;
  no one can fight him without getting hurt.
⁵God moves mountains without anyone
    knowing it
  and turns them over when he is angry.
⁶He shakes the earth out of its place
  and makes its foundations tremble.
⁷He commands the sun not to shine
  and shuts off the light of the stars.
⁸He alone stretches out the skies
  and walks on the waves of the sea.
⁹It is God who made the Bear, Orion and the
    Pleiades ^{n}
  and the groups of stars in the southern sky.

¹⁰He does wonders that cannot be understood;
  he does so many miracles ^{d} they cannot be
    counted.
¹¹When he passes me, I cannot see him;
  when he goes by me, I do not
    recognise him.
¹²If he snatches something away, no one can
    stop him
  or say to him, 'What are you doing?'
¹³God will not hold back his anger.
  Even the helpers of the monster Rahab ^{d} lie
    at his feet in fear.
¹⁴So how can I argue with God,
  or even find words to argue with him?
¹⁵Even if I were right, I could not answer him;
  I could only beg God, my Judge, for mercy.
¹⁶If I called to him and he answered,
  I still don't believe he would listen to me.
¹⁷He would crush me with a storm
  and multiply my wounds for no reason.
¹⁸He would not let me catch my breath
  but would overwhelm me with misery.
¹⁹When it comes to strength, God is stronger
    than I;
  when it comes to justice, no one can
    accuse him.
²⁰Even if I were right, my own mouth would
    say I was wrong;
  if I were innocent, my mouth would say I
    was guilty.

²¹"I am innocent,
  but I don't care about myself.
  I hate my own life.
²²It is all the same. That is why I say,
  'God destroys both the innocent and the
    guilty.'
²³If the whip brings sudden death,
  God will laugh at the suffering of the
    innocent.
²⁴When the land falls into the hands of evil
    people,
  he covers the judges' faces so they can't
    see it.
  If it is not God who does this, then who is
    it?

²⁵"My days go by faster than a runner;
  they fly away without my seeing any joy.
²⁶They glide past like paper boats.
  They attack like eagles swooping down to
    feed.
²⁷Even though I say, 'I will forget my
    complaint;
  I will change the look on my face and
    smile,'

Bear ... Pleiades   Names of well-known groups of stars.

²⁸I still dread all my suffering.
  I know you will hold me guilty.
²⁹I have already been found guilty,
  so why should I struggle for no reason?
³⁰I might wash myself with soap
  and scrub my hands with strong soap,
³¹but you would push me into a dirty pit,
  and even my clothes would hate me.

³²"God is not a man like me, so I cannot
    answer him.
  We cannot meet each other in court.
³³I wish there were someone to make peace
    between us,
  someone to decide our case.
³⁴Maybe he could remove God's punishment
  so his terror would no longer frighten me.
³⁵Then I could speak without being afraid,
  but I am not able to do that.

10

"I hate my life,
    so I will complain without holding
    back;
  I will speak because I am so unhappy.
²I will say to God: Do not hold me guilty,
  but tell me what you have against me.
³Does it make you happy to trouble me?
  Don't you care about me, the work of your
    hands?
  Are you happy with the plans of evil
    people?
⁴Do you have human eyes
  that see as we see?
⁵Are your days like the days of man,
  and your years like our years?
⁶You look for the evil I have done
  and search for my sin.
⁷You know I am not guilty,
  but no one can save me from your power.

⁸"Your hands shaped and made me.
  Do you now turn around and destroy me?
⁹Remember that you moulded me like a piece
    of clay.
  Will you now turn me back into dust?
¹⁰You formed me inside my mother
  like cheese formed from milk.
¹¹You dressed me with skin and flesh;
  you sewed me together with bones and
    muscles.
¹²You gave me life and showed me kindness,
  and in your care you watched over my life.

¹³"But in your heart you hid other plans.
  I know this was in your mind.
¹⁴If I sinned, you would watch me
  and would not let my sin go unpunished.
¹⁵How terrible it will be for me if I am guilty!
  Even if I am right, I cannot lift my head.

I am full of shame
  and experience only pain.
¹⁶If I hold up my head, you hunt me like a lion
  and again show your terrible power
    against me.
¹⁷You bring new witnesses against me
  and increase your anger against me.
  Your armies come against me.

¹⁸"So why did you allow me to be born?
  I wish I had died before anyone saw me.
¹⁹I wish I had never lived,
  but had been carried straight from birth to
    the grave.
²⁰The few days of my life are almost over.
  Leave me alone so I can have a moment
    of joy.
²¹Soon I will leave; I will not return
  from the land of darkness and gloom,
²²the land of darkest night,
  from the land of gloom and confusion,
  where even the light is darkness."

Zophar Speaks to Job

11

Then Zophar the Naamathite answered:

²"Should these words go unanswered?
  Is this talker in the right?
³Your lies do not make people quiet;
  people should correct you when you make
    fun of God.
⁴You say, 'My teachings are right,
  and I am clean ᵈ in God's sight.'
⁵I wish God would speak
  and open his lips against you
⁶and tell you the secrets of wisdom,
  because wisdom has two sides.
  Know this: God has even forgotten some of
    your sin.

⁷"Can you understand the secrets of God?
  Can you search the limits of the Almighty?
⁸His limits are higher than the heavens;
  you cannot reach them!
  They are deeper than the grave;
  you cannot understand them!
⁹His limits are longer than the earth
  and wider than the sea.

¹⁰"If God comes along and puts you in prison
  or calls you into court, no one can stop him.
¹¹God knows who is evil,
  and when he sees evil, he takes note of it.
¹²A fool cannot become wise
  any more than a wild donkey can be born
    tame.

¹³"You must give your whole heart to him
  and hold out your hands to him for help.

¹⁴Put away the sin that is in your hand;
    let no evil remain in your tent.
¹⁵Then you can lift up your face without shame,
    and you can stand strong without fear.
¹⁶You will forget your trouble
    and remember it only as water gone by.
¹⁷Your life will be as bright as the
        noonday sun,
    and darkness will seem like morning.
¹⁸You will feel safe because there is hope;
    you will look around and rest in safety.
¹⁹You will lie down and no one will scare you.
    Many people will want favours from you.
²⁰But the wicked will not be able to see,
    so they will not escape.
    Their only hope will be to die."

Job Answers Zophar

12 Then Job answered:

²"You really think you are the only wise people
    and that when you die, wisdom will die
        with you!
³But my mind is as good as yours;
    you are not better than I am.
    Everyone knows all these things.
⁴My friends all laugh at me
    when I call on God and expect him to
        answer me;
    they laugh at me even though I am right
        and innocent!
⁵Those who are comfortable don't care that
        others have trouble;
    they think it right that those people should
        have troubles.
⁶The tents of robbers are not bothered,
    and those who make God angry are safe.
    They have their god in their pocket.

⁷"But ask the animals, and they will teach you,
    or ask the birds of the air, and they will
        tell you.
⁸Speak to the earth, and it will teach you,
    or let the fish of the sea tell you.
⁹Every one of these knows
    that the hand of the LORD has done this.
¹⁰The life of every creature
    and the breath of all people are in God's
        hand.
¹¹The ear tests words
    as the tongue tastes food.
¹²Older people are wise,
    and long life brings understanding.

¹³"But only God has wisdom and power,
    good advice and understanding.
¹⁴What he tears down cannot be rebuilt;
    anyone he puts in prison cannot be let out.

¹⁵If God holds back the waters, there is no rain;
    if he lets the waters go, they flood the land.
¹⁶He is strong and victorious;
    both the one who fools others and the one
        who is fooled belong to him.
¹⁷God leads the wise away as captives
    and turns judges into fools.
¹⁸He takes off chains that kings put on
    and puts a cloth on their bodies.
¹⁹He leads priests away naked
    and destroys the powerful.
²⁰He makes trusted people be silent
    and takes away the wisdom of older leaders.
²¹He brings disgrace on important people
    and takes away the weapons of the strong.
²²He uncovers the deep things of darkness
    and brings dark shadows into the light.
²³He makes nations great and then destroys
        them;
    he makes nations large and then scatters
        them.
²⁴He takes understanding away from the
        leaders of the earth
    and makes them wander through a desert
        without paths.
²⁵They feel around in darkness with no light;
    he makes them stumble like drunkards.

13 "Now my eyes have seen all this;
        my ears have heard and
        understood it.
²What you know, I also know.
    You are not better than I am.
³But I want to speak to the Almighty
    and to argue my case with God.
⁴But you smear me with lies.
    You are worthless doctors, all of you!
⁵I wish you would just stop talking;
    then you would really be wise!
⁶Listen to my argument,
    and hear the pleading of my lips.
⁷You should not speak evil in the name of God;
    you cannot speak God's truth by telling lies.
⁸You should not unfairly choose his side against
        mine;
    you should not argue the case for God.
⁹You will not do well if he examines you;
    you cannot fool God as you might fool
        humans.
¹⁰God would surely scold you
    if you unfairly took one person's side.
¹¹His bright glory would scare you,
    and you would be very much afraid of him.
¹²Your wise sayings are worth no more than ashes,
    and your arguments are as weak as clay.

¹³"Be quiet and let me speak.
    Let things happen to me as they will.

¹⁴Why should I put myself in danger
and take my life in my own hands?
¹⁵Even if God kills me, I have hope in him;
I will still defend my ways to his face.
¹⁶This is my salvation.
The wicked cannot come before him.
¹⁷Listen carefully to my words;
let your ears hear what I say.
¹⁸See, I have prepared my case,
and I know I will be proved right.
¹⁹No one can accuse me of doing wrong.
If someone can, I will be quiet and die.

²⁰"God, please just give me these two things,
and then I will not hide from you:
²¹Take your punishment away from me,
and stop frightening me with your terrors.
²²Then call me, and I will answer,
or let me speak, and you answer.
²³How many evil things and sins have I done?
Show me my wrong and my sin.
²⁴Don't hide your face from me;
don't think of me as your enemy.
²⁵Don't punish a leaf that is blown by the
wind;
don't chase after straw.
²⁶You write down cruel things against me
and make me suffer for my boyhood sins.
²⁷You put my feet in chains
and keep close watch wherever I go.
You even mark the soles of my feet.

²⁸"Everyone wears out like something rotten,
like clothing eaten by moths.

14
"All of us born to women
live only a few days and have lots of
trouble.
²We grow up like flowers and then dry up
and die.
We are like a passing shadow that does not
last.
³Lord, do you need to watch me like this?
Must you bring me before you to be judged?
⁴No one can bring something clean from
something dirty.
⁵Our time is limited.
You have given us only so many months
to live
and have set limits we cannot go beyond.
⁶So look away from us and leave us alone
until we put in our time like a labourer.

⁷"If a tree is cut down,
there is hope that it will grow again
and will send out new branches.
⁸Even if its roots grow old in the ground,
and its stump dies in the earth,
⁹at the smell of water it will bud
and put out new shoots like a plant.

¹⁰But we die, and our bodies are laid in the
ground;
we take our last breath and are gone.
¹¹Water disappears from a lake,
and a river loses its water and dries up.
¹²In the same way, we lie down and do not
rise again;
we will not get up or be awakened
until the heavens disappear.

¹³"I wish you would hide me in the grave;
hide me until your anger is gone.
I wish you would set a time
and then remember me!
¹⁴If a person dies, will he live again?
All my days are a struggle;
I will wait until things change for me.
¹⁵You will call, and I will answer you;
you will desire the creature your hands
have made.
¹⁶Then you will count my steps,
but you will not keep track of my sin.
¹⁷My wrongs will be closed up in a bag,
and you will cover up my sin.

¹⁸"A mountain washes away and crumbles;
and a rock can be moved from its place.
¹⁹Water washes over stones and wears them
down,
and rushing waters wash away the earth.
In the same way, you destroy my hope.
²⁰You defeat a person for ever, and he is gone;
you change his appearance and send him
away.
²¹His sons are honoured, but he does not know it;
his sons are disgraced, but he does not see it.
²²He only feels the pain of his body
and feels sorry for himself."

Eliphaz Answers Job

15
Then Eliphaz the Temanite answered:
²"A wise person would not answer with
empty words
or fill his stomach with the hot east wind.
³He would not argue with useless words
or make speeches that have no value.
⁴But you even destroy respect for God
and limit the worship of him.
⁵Your sin teaches your mouth what to say;
you use words to trick others.
⁶It is your own mouth, not mine, that shows
you are wicked;
your own lips testify against you.

⁷"You are not the first man ever born;
you are not older than the hills.
⁸You did not listen in on God's secret advice.
But you limit wisdom to yourself.

⁹You don't know any more than we know.
  You don't understand any more than we
    understand.
¹⁰Old people with grey hair are on our side;
  they are even older than your father.

¹¹Is the comfort God gives you not enough
    for you,
  even when words are spoken gently to you?
¹²Has your heart carried you away from God?
  Why do your eyes flash with anger?
¹³Why do you speak out your anger
    against God?
  Why do these words pour out of your
    mouth?

¹⁴"How can anyone be pure?
  How can someone born to a woman be
    good?
¹⁵God places no trust in his holy ones,
  and even the heavens are not pure in his
    eyes.
¹⁶How much less pure is one who is terrible
    and rotten
  and drinks up evil as if it were water!

¹⁷"Listen to me, and I will tell you about it;
  I will tell you what I have seen.
¹⁸These are things wise men have told;
  their fathers told them, and they have
    hidden nothing.
¹⁹(The land was given to their fathers only,
  and no foreigner lived among them.)
²⁰The wicked suffer pain all their lives;
  the cruel suffer during all the years saved up
    for them.
²¹Terrible sounds fill their ears,
  and when things seem to be going well,
    robbers attack them.
²²Evil people give up trying to escape from the
    darkness;
  it has been decided that they will die by
    the sword.
²³They wander around and will become food
    for vultures.
  They know darkness will soon come.
²⁴Worry and suffering terrify them;
  they overwhelm them, like a king ready to
    attack,

²⁵because they shake their fists at God
  and try to get their own way against the
    Almighty.
²⁶They stubbornly charge at God
  with thick, strong shields.

²⁷"Although the faces of the wicked are heavy
    with fat,
  and their waists are fat with flesh,
²⁸they will live in towns that are ruined,
  in houses where no one lives,
  which are crumbling into ruins.
²⁹The wicked will no longer get rich,
  and the riches they have will not last;
  the things they own will no longer spread
    over the land.
³⁰They will not escape the darkness.
  A flame will dry up their branches;
  God's breath will carry the wicked away.
³¹The wicked should not fool themselves by
    trusting what is useless.
  If they do, they will get nothing in return.
³²Their branches will dry up before they finish
    growing
  and will never turn green.
³³They will be like a vine whose grapes are
    pulled off before they are ripe,
  like an olive tree that loses its blossoms.
³⁴People without God can produce nothing.
  Fire will destroy the tents of those who
    take money to do evil,
³⁵who plan trouble and give birth to evil,
  whose hearts plan ways to trick others."

Job Answers Eliphaz

16 Then Job answered:

²"I have heard many things like these.
  You are all painful comforters!
³Will your long speeches never end?
  What makes you keep on arguing?
⁴I also could speak as you do
  if you were in my place.
  I could make great speeches against you
    and shake my head at you.
⁵But, instead, I would encourage you,
  and my words would bring you relief.

⁶"Even if I speak, my pain is not less,
  and if I don't speak, it still does not go away.
⁷God, you have surely taken away
    my strength
  and destroyed my whole family.
⁸You have made me thin and weak,
  and this shows I have done wrong.
⁹God attacks me and tears me with anger;
  he grinds his teeth at me;
  my enemy stares at me with his angry eyes.

¹⁰People open their mouths to make fun of me
and slap my cheeks to insult me.
They unite against me.
¹¹God has turned me over to evil people
and has handed me over to the wicked.
¹²Everything was fine with me,
but God broke me into pieces;
he held me by the neck and crushed me.
He has made me his target;
¹³ his archers surround me.
He stabs my kidneys without mercy;
he spills my blood on the ground.
¹⁴Again and again God attacks me;
he runs at me like a soldier.

¹⁵"I have sewed rough cloth over my skin to
show my sadness
and have buried my face in the dust.
¹⁶My face is red from crying;
I have dark circles around my eyes.
¹⁷Yet my hands have never done anything cruel,
and my prayer is pure.

¹⁸"Earth, please do not cover up my blood.
Don't let my cry ever stop being heard!
¹⁹Even now I have one who speaks for me in
heaven;
the one who is on my side is high above.
²⁰The one who speaks for me is my friend.
My eyes pour out tears to God.
²¹He begs God on behalf of a human
as a person begs for his friend.

²²"Only a few years will pass
before I go on the journey of no return.

17 My spirit is broken;
the days of my life are almost gone.
The grave is waiting for me.
²Those who laugh at me surround me;
I watch them insult me.

³"God, make me a promise.
No one will make a pledge for me.
⁴You have closed their minds to
understanding.
Do not let them win over me.
⁵A person might speak against his friends for
money,
but if he does, the eyes of his children go
blind.

⁶"God has made my name a curse word;
people spit in my face.
⁷My sight has grown weak because of my
sadness,
and my body is as thin as a shadow.
⁸Honest people are upset about this;
innocent people are upset with those who
do wrong.

⁹But those who do right will continue to do
right,
and those whose hands are not dirty with
sin will grow stronger.

¹⁰"But, all of you, come and try again!
I do not find a wise person among you.
¹¹My days are gone, and my plans have been
destroyed,
along with the desires of my heart.
¹²These men think night is day;
when it is dark, they say, 'Light is near.'
¹³If the only home I hope for is the grave,
if I spread out my bed in darkness,
¹⁴if I say to the grave, 'You are my father,'
and to the worm, 'You are my mother' or
'You are my sister,'
¹⁵where, then, is my hope?
Who can see any hope for me?
¹⁶Will hope go down to the gates of death?
Will we go down together into the dust?"

Bildad Answers Job

18 Then Bildad the Shuhite answered:

²"When will you stop these speeches?
Be sensible, and then we can talk.
³You think of us as cattle,
as if we are stupid.
⁴You tear yourself to pieces in your anger.
Should the earth be vacant just for you?
Should the rocks move from their places?

⁵"The lamp of the wicked will be put out,
and the flame in their lamps will stop
burning.
⁶The light in their tents will grow dark,
and the lamps by their sides will go out.
⁷Their strong steps will grow weak;
they will fall into their own evil traps.
⁸Their feet will be caught in a net
when they walk into its web.
⁹A trap will catch them by the heel
and hold them tight.
¹⁰A trap for them is hidden on the ground,
right in their path.
¹¹Terrible things startle them from every side
and chase them at every step.
¹²Hunger takes away their strength,
and disaster is at their side.
¹³Disease eats away parts of their skin;
death eats away at their arms and legs.
¹⁴They are torn from the safety of their tents
and dragged off to Death, the King of
Terrors.
¹⁵Their tents are set on fire,
and sulphur is scattered over their homes.
¹⁶Their roots dry up below ground,
and their branches die above ground.

¹⁷People on earth will not remember them;
   their names will be forgotten in the land.
¹⁸They will be driven from light into darkness
   and chased out of the world.
¹⁹They have no children or descendants *d*
      among their people,
   and no one will be left alive where they
      once lived.
²⁰People of the west will be shocked at what
      has happened to them,
   and people of the east will be very
      frightened.
²¹Surely this is what will happen to the
      wicked;
   such is the place of one who does not
      know God."

Job Answers Bildad

19 Then Job answered:

²"How long will you hurt me
   and crush me with your words?
³You have insulted me ten times now
   and attacked me without shame.
⁴Even if I have sinned,
   it is my worry alone.
⁵If you want to make yourselves look better
      than I,
   you can blame me for my suffering.
⁶But know that God has wronged me
   and pulled his net around me.

⁷"I shout, 'I have been wronged!'
   But I get no answer.
 I scream for help
   but I get no justice.
⁸God has blocked my way so I cannot pass;
   he has covered my paths with darkness.
⁹He has taken away my honour
   and removed the crown from my head.
¹⁰He beats me down on every side until I am
      gone;
   he destroys my hope like a fallen tree.
¹¹His anger burns against me,
   and he treats me like an enemy.
¹²His armies gather;
   they prepare to attack me.
   They camp around my tent.

¹³"God has made my brothers my enemies,
   and my friends have become strangers.
¹⁴My relatives have gone away,
   and my friends have forgotten me.
¹⁵My guests and my female servants treat me
      like a stranger;
   they look at me as if I were a foreigner.
¹⁶I call for my servant, but he does not answer,
   even when I beg him with my own mouth.

¹⁷My wife can't stand my breath,
   and my own family dislikes me.
¹⁸Even the little boys hate me
   and talk about me when I leave.
¹⁹All my close friends hate me;
   even those I love have turned against me.
²⁰I am nothing but skin and bones;
   I have escaped by the skin of my teeth.
²¹Pity me, my friends, pity me,
   because the hand of God has hit me.
²²Why do you chase me as God does?
   Haven't you hurt me enough?

²³"How I wish my words were written down,
   written on a scroll.
²⁴I wish they were carved with an iron pen
      into lead,
   or carved into stone for ever.
²⁵I know that my Defender lives,
   and in the end he will stand upon the earth.
²⁶Even after my skin has been destroyed,
   in my flesh I will see God.
²⁷I will see him myself;
   I will see him with my very own eyes.
   How my heart wants that to happen!

²⁸"If you say, 'We will continue to trouble Job,
   because the problem lies with him,'
²⁹you should be afraid of the sword yourselves.
   God's anger will bring punishment by the
      sword.
   Then you will know there is judgement."

Zophar Answers

20 Then Zophar the Naamathite answered:

²"My troubled thoughts cause me to answer,
   because I am very upset.
³You correct me and I am insulted,
   but I understand how to answer you.

⁴"You know how it has been for a long time,
   ever since people were first put on the earth.
⁵The happiness of evil people is brief,
   and the joy of the wicked lasts only a
      moment.
⁶Their pride may be as high as the heavens,
   and their heads may touch the clouds,
⁷but they will be gone for ever, like their own
      dung.
   People who knew them will say, 'Where are
      they?'
⁸They will fly away like a dream
   and not be found again;
   they will be chased away like a vision in
      the night.
⁹Those who saw them will not see them again;
   the places where they lived will see them
      no more.

¹⁰Their children will have to pay back the poor,
and they will have to give up their wealth.
¹¹They had the strength of their youth in their
bones,
but it will lie with them in the dust of
death.
¹²"Evil may taste sweet in their mouths,
and they may hide it under their tongues.
¹³They cannot stand to let go of it;
they keep it in their mouths.
¹⁴But their food will turn sour in their
stomachs,
like the poison of a snake inside them.
¹⁵They have swallowed riches, but they will
spit them out;
God will make them vomit their riches up.
¹⁶They will suck the poison of snakes,
and the snake's fangs will kill them.

Sidelight

Snakes were dangerous desert residents in Bible times (Job 20:14–16). Numerous varieties of snake lived in the desert, and about half a dozen of the species were poisonous. In one instance, snakes invaded an Israelite camp (Numbers 21:6–8, p.148), and many of the Israelites died from the bites.

---

¹⁷They will not admire the sparkling streams
or the rivers flowing with honey and cream.
¹⁸They must give back what they worked for
without eating it;
they will not enjoy the money they made
from their trading,
¹⁹because they troubled the poor and left them
with nothing.
They have taken houses they did not build.

²⁰"Evil people never lack an appetite,
and nothing escapes their selfishness.
²¹But nothing will be left for them to eat;
their riches will not continue.
²²When they still have plenty, trouble will
catch up with them,
and great misery will come down on them.
²³When the wicked fill their stomachs,
God will send his burning anger against
them,
and blows of punishment will fall on them
like rain.
²⁴The wicked may run away from an iron
weapon,
but a bronze arrow will stab them.
²⁵They will pull the arrows out of their backs
and pull the points out of their livers.
Terrors will come over them;

²⁶ total darkness waits for their treasure.
A fire not fanned by people will destroy
them
and burn up what is left of their tents.
²⁷The heavens will show their guilt,
and the earth will rise up against them.
²⁸A flood will carry their houses away,
swept away on the day of God's anger.
²⁹This is what God plans for evil people;
this is what he has decided they will
receive."

Job Answers Zophar

21 Then Job answered:

²"Listen carefully to my words,
and let this be the way you comfort me.
³Be patient while I speak.
After I have finished, you may continue to
make fun of me.

⁴"My complaint is not just against people;
I have reason to be impatient.
⁵Look at me and be shocked;
put your hand over your mouth in shock.
⁶When I think about this, I am terribly afraid
and my body shakes.
⁷Why do evil people live a long time?
They grow old and become more
powerful.
⁸They see their children around them;
they watch them grow up.
⁹Their homes are safe and without fear;
God does not punish them.
¹⁰Their bulls never fail to mate;
their cows have healthy calves.
¹¹They send out their children like a flock;
their little ones dance about.
¹²They sing to the music of tambourines ᵈ and
harps,
and the sound of the flute makes them
happy.
¹³Evil people enjoy successful lives
and then go peacefully to the grave.
¹⁴They say to God, 'Leave us alone!
We don't want to know your ways.
¹⁵Who is the Almighty that we should
serve him?
What would we gain by praying to him?'
¹⁶The success of the wicked is not their own
doing.
Their way of thinking is different from
mine.
¹⁷Yet how often are the lamps of evil people
turned off?
How often does trouble come to them?
How often do they suffer God's angry
punishment?

¹⁸How often are they like straw in the wind
   or like chaff *d* that is blown away by a
      storm?
¹⁹It is said, 'God saves up a person's
      punishment for his children.'
   But God should punish the wicked
      themselves so they will know it.
²⁰Their eyes should see their own destruction,
   and they should suffer the anger of the
      Almighty.
²¹They do not care about the families they
      leave behind
   when their lives have come to an end.

²²"No one can teach knowledge to God;
   he is the one who judges even the most
      important people.
²³One person dies while he still has all his
      strength,
   feeling completely safe and comfortable.
²⁴His body was well fed,
   and his bones were strong and healthy.
²⁵But another person dies with an unhappy
      heart,
   never enjoying any happiness.
²⁶They are buried next to each other,
   and worms cover them both.

²⁷"I know very well your thoughts
   and your plans to wrong me.
²⁸You ask about me, 'Where is this great man's
      house?
   Where are the tents where the wicked
      live?'
²⁹Have you never asked those who travel?
   Have you never listened to their stories?
³⁰On the day of God's anger and punishment,
   it is the wicked who are spared.
³¹Who will accuse them to their faces?
   Who will pay them back for the evil they
      have done?
³²They are carried to their graves,
   and someone keeps watch over their
      tombs.
³³The earth in the valley seems sweet
      to them.
   Everybody follows after them,
   and many people go before them.

³⁴"So how can you comfort me with this
      nonsense?
   Your answers are only lies!"

Eliphaz Answers

22 Then Eliphaz the Temanite answered:

²"Can anyone be of real use to God?
   Can even a wise person do him good?

³Does it help the Almighty for you to be good?
   Does he gain anything if you are innocent?
⁴Does God punish you for respecting him?
   Does he bring you into court for this?
⁵No! It is because your evil is without limits
   and your sins have no end.
⁶You took your brothers' things for a debt
      they didn't owe;
   you took clothes from people and left them
      naked.
⁷You did not give water to tired people,
   and you kept food from the hungry.
⁸You were a powerful man who owned land;
   you were honoured and lived in the land.
⁹But you sent widows away empty-handed,
   and you mistreated orphans.
¹⁰That is why traps are all around you
   and sudden danger frightens you.
¹¹That is why it is so dark you cannot see
   and a flood of water covers you.

¹²"God is in the highest part of heaven.
   See how high the highest stars are!
¹³But you ask, 'What does God know?
   Can he judge us through the dark clouds?
¹⁴Thick clouds cover him so he cannot see us
   as he walks around high up in the sky.'
¹⁵Are you going to stay on the old path
   where evil people walk?
¹⁶They were carried away before their time
      was up,
   and their foundations were washed away
      by a flood.
¹⁷They said to God, 'Leave us alone!
   The Almighty can do nothing to us.'
¹⁸But it was God who filled their houses with
      good things.
   Their way of thinking is different from
      mine.

¹⁹"Good people can watch and be glad;
   the innocent can laugh at them and say,
²⁰'Surely our enemies are destroyed,
   and fire burns up their wealth.'

²¹"Obey God and be at peace with him;
   this is the way to happiness.
²²Accept teaching from his mouth,
   and keep his words in your heart.
²³If you return to the Almighty, you will be
      blessed again.
   So remove evil from your house.
²⁴Throw your gold nuggets into the dust
   and your fine gold among the rocks in the
      ravines.
²⁵Then the Almighty will be your gold
   and the best silver for you.
²⁶You will find pleasure in the Almighty,
   and you will look up to him.

²⁷You will pray to him, and he will hear you,
    and you will keep your promises to him.
²⁸Anything you decide will be done,
    and light will shine on your ways.
²⁹When people are made humble and you say,
    'Have courage,'
    then the humble will be saved.
³⁰Even a guilty person will escape
    and be saved because your hands are
    clean." *d*

Job Answers

23 Then Job answered:

²"My complaint is still bitter today.
    I am groaning because God's heavy hand is
    on me.
³I wish I knew where to find God
    so I could go to where he lives.
⁴I would present my case before him
    and fill my mouth with arguments.
⁵I would learn how he would answer me
    and would think about what he
    would say.
⁶Would he not argue strongly against me?
    No, he would really listen to me.
⁷Then an honest person could present his case
    to God,
    and I would be saved for ever by my judge.

⁸"If I go to the east, God is not there;
    if I go to the west, I do not see him.
⁹When he is at work in the north, I catch no
    sight of him;
    when he turns to the south, I cannot
    see him.
¹⁰But God knows the way that I take,
    and when he has tested me, I will come
    out like gold.
¹¹My feet have closely followed his steps;
    I have stayed in his way;
    I did not turn aside.
¹²I have never left the commands he has
    spoken;
    I have treasured his words more than
    my own.

¹³"But he is the only God.
    Who can come against him?
    He does anything he wants.
¹⁴He will do to me what he said he would do,
    and he has many plans like this.
¹⁵That is why I am frightened of him;
    when I think of this, I am afraid of him.
¹⁶God has made me afraid;
    the Almighty terrifies me.
¹⁷But I am not hidden by the darkness,
    by the thick darkness that covers my face.

24 "I wish the Almighty would set a time
    for judging.
    Those who know God do not see such
    a day.
²Wicked people take other people's land;
    they steal flocks and take them to new
    pastures.
³They chase away the orphan's donkey
    and take the widow's ox when she has no
    money.
⁴They push needy people off the path;
    all the poor of the land hide from them.
⁵The poor become like wild donkeys in the
    desert
    who go about their job of finding food.
    The desert gives them food for their
    children.
⁶They gather hay and straw in the fields
    and pick up leftover grapes from the
    vineyard of the wicked.
⁷They spend the night naked, because they
    have no clothes,
    nothing to cover themselves in the cold.
⁸They are soaked from mountain rains
    and stay near the large rocks because they
    have no shelter.
⁹The fatherless child is grabbed from its
    mother's breast;
    they take a poor mother's baby to pay for
    what she owes.
¹⁰So the poor go around naked without any
    clothes;
    they carry bundles of grain but still go
    hungry;
¹¹they crush olives to get oil
    and grapes to get wine, but they still go
    thirsty.
¹²Dying people groan in the city,
    and the injured cry out for help,
    but God accuses no one of doing wrong.

¹³"Those who fight against the light
    do not know God's ways
    or stay in his paths.
¹⁴When the day is over, the murderers get up
    to kill the poor and needy.
    At night they go about like thieves.
¹⁵Those who are guilty of adultery *d* watch for
    the night,
    thinking, 'No one will see us,'
    and they keep their faces covered.
¹⁶In the dark, evil people break into houses.
    In the daytime they shut themselves up in
    their own houses,
    because they want nothing to do with the
    light.
¹⁷Darkness is like morning to all these evil
    people

who make friends with the terrors of
darkness.

¹⁸"They are like foam floating on the water.
Their part of the land is cursed;
no one uses the road that goes by their
vineyards.
¹⁹As heat and dryness quickly melt the snow,
so the grave quickly takes away the sinners.
²⁰Their mothers forget them,
and worms will eat their bodies.
They will not be remembered,
so wickedness is broken in pieces like a
stick.
²¹These evil people abuse women who cannot
have children
and show no kindness to widows.
²²But God drags away the strong by his power.
Even though they seem strong, they do not
know how long they will live.
²³God may let these evil people feel safe,
but he is watching their ways.
²⁴For a little while they are important, and
then they die;
they are laid low and buried like everyone
else;
they are cut off like the heads of grain.
²⁵If this is not true, who can prove I am
wrong?
Who can show that my words are worth
nothing?"

Bildad Answers

25 Then Bildad the Shuhite answered:

²"God rules and he must be honoured;
he set up order in his high heaven.
³No one can count God's armies.
His light shines on all people.
⁴So no one can be good in the presence
of God,
and no one born to a woman can be pure.
⁵Even the moon is not bright
and the stars are not pure in his eyes.
⁶People are much less! They are like insects.
They are only worms!"

Job Answers Bildad

26 Then Job answered:

²"You are no help to the helpless!
You have not given help to the weak!
³Your advice lacks wisdom!
You have shown little understanding!
⁴Who has helped you say these words?
And where did you get these words?
⁵"The spirits of the dead tremble,
those who are beneath and in the waters.

⁶Death is naked before God;
destruction is uncovered before him.
⁷God stretches the northern sky out over
empty space
and hangs the earth on nothing.
⁸He wraps up the waters in his thick clouds,
but the clouds do not break under their
weight.
⁹He covers the face of the moon,
spreading his clouds over it.
¹⁰He draws the horizon like a circle on the
water
at the place where light and darkness meet.
¹¹Heaven's foundations shake
when he thunders at them.
¹²With his power he controls the sea;
by his wisdom he destroys Rahab,^d the sea
monster.
¹³He breathes, and the sky clears.
His hand stabs the fleeing snake.
¹⁴And these are only a small part of God's
works.
We only hear a small whisper of him.
Who could understand God's thundering
power?"

27 And Job continued speaking:

²"As surely as God lives, who has taken away
my rights,
the Almighty, who has made me unhappy,
³as long as I am alive
and God's breath of life is in my nose,
⁴my lips will not speak evil,
and my tongue will not tell a lie.
⁵I will never agree you are right;
until I die, I will never stop saying I am
innocent.
⁶I will insist that I am right; I will not back
down.
My sense of right and wrong will never
bother me.

⁷"Let my enemies be like evil people,
my foes like those who are wrong.
⁸What hope do the wicked have when
they die,
when God takes their life away?
⁹God will not listen to their cries
when trouble comes to them.
¹⁰They will not find joy in the Almighty,
even though they call out to God all the
time.
¹¹"I will teach you about the power of God
and will not hide the ways of the Almighty.
¹²You have all seen this yourselves.
So why are we having all this talk that
means nothing?

¹³"Here is what God has planned for evil
people,
and what the Almighty will give to cruel
people:
¹⁴They may have many children, but the sword
will kill them.
Their children who are left will never have
enough to eat.
¹⁵Then they will die of disease and be buried,
and the widows will not even cry for them.
¹⁶The wicked may heap up silver like piles of
earth
and have so many clothes they are like piles
of clay.
¹⁷But good people will wear what evil people
have gathered,
and the innocent will divide up their silver.
¹⁸The houses the wicked build are like a
spider's web,
like a hut that a guard builds.
¹⁹The wicked are rich when they go to bed,
but they are rich for the last time;
when they open their eyes, everything is
gone.
²⁰Fears come over them like a flood,
and a storm snatches them away in the
night.
²¹The east wind will carry them away, and then
they are gone,
because it sweeps them out of their place.
²²The wind will hit them without mercy
as they try to run away from its power.
²³It will be as if the wind is clapping its hands;
it will whistle at them as they run from
their place.

28 "There are mines where people dig
silver
and places where gold is made pure.
²Iron is taken from the ground,
and copper is melted out of rocks.
³Miners bring lights
and search deep into the mines
for metal in thick darkness.
⁴Miners dig a tunnel far from where people
live,
where no one has ever walked;
they work far from people, swinging and
swaying from ropes.
⁵Food grows on top of the earth,
but below ground things are changed as if
by fire.
⁶Sapphires are found in rocks,
and gold dust is also found there.
⁷No hawk knows that path;
the falcon has not seen it.
⁸Proud animals have not walked there,
and no lions cross over it.

⁹Miners hit the rocks of flint
and dig away at the bottom of the
mountains.
¹⁰They cut tunnels through the rock
and see all the treasures there.
¹¹They search for places where rivers begin
and bring things hidden out into the light.

¹²"But where can wisdom be found,
and where does understanding live?
¹³People do not understand the value of
wisdom;
it cannot be found among those who are
alive.
¹⁴The deep ocean says, 'It's not in me;'
the sea says, 'It's not in me.'
¹⁵Wisdom cannot be bought with gold,
and its cost cannot be weighed in silver.
¹⁶Wisdom cannot be bought with fine gold
or with valuable onyx or sapphire gems.
¹⁷Gold and crystal are not as valuable as
wisdom,
and you cannot buy it with jewels of gold.
¹⁸Coral and jasper are not worth talking about,
and the price of wisdom is much greater
than rubies.
¹⁹The topaz from Cush cannot compare with
wisdom;
it cannot be bought with the purest gold.

²⁰"So where does wisdom come from,
and where does understanding live?
²¹It is hidden from the eyes of every living
thing,
even from the birds of the air.
²²The places of destruction and death say,
'We have heard reports about it.'
²³Only God understands the way to wisdom,
and he alone knows where it lives,
²⁴because he looks to the farthest parts of the
earth
and sees everything under the sky.
²⁵When God gave power to the wind
and measured the water,
²⁶when he made rules for the rain
and set a path for a thunderstorm to follow,
²⁷then he looked at wisdom and decided its
worth;
he set wisdom up and tested it.
²⁸Then he said to humans,
'The fear of the Lord is wisdom;
to stay away from evil is understanding.'"

Job Continues

29 Job continued to speak:

²"How I wish for the months that have passed
and the days when God watched over me.

³God's lamp shone on my head,
 and I walked through darkness by his light.
⁴I wish for the days when I was strong,
 when God's close friendship blessed my house.
⁵The Almighty was still with me,
 and my children were all around me.
⁶It was as if my path were covered with cream
 and the rocks poured out olive oil for me.
⁷I would go to the city gate
 and sit in the public square.
⁸When the young men saw me, they would step aside,
 and the old men would stand up in respect.
⁹The leading men stopped speaking
 and covered their mouths with their hands.
¹⁰The voices of the important men were quiet,
 as if their tongues stuck to the roof of their mouths.

¹¹Anyone who heard me spoke well of me,
 and those who saw me praised me,
¹²because I saved the poor who called out
 and the orphan who had no one to help.
¹³The dying person blessed me,
 and I made the widow's heart sing.
¹⁴I put on right living as if it were clothing;
 I wore fairness like a robe and a turban.
¹⁵I was eyes for the blind
 and feet for the lame.
¹⁶I was like a father to needy people,
 and I took the side of strangers who were in trouble.
¹⁷I broke the fangs of evil people
 and snatched the captives from their teeth.

¹⁸"I thought, 'I will live for as many days as there are grains of sand,
 and I will die in my own house.

DECISION MAKING

To Fly or Not

Sixteen-year-old Neil stared at the model plane on his desk. He had loved planes all his life. Every penny he earned went on flying lessons, but now he wasn't sure.

The day before, Neil had watched helplessly as a friend's plane crashed before his eyes. He had rushed to the plane to try to help, but the crash was fatal. Neil could still remember cradling his friend's head in his lap; he remembered his dying breath.

What now? Should he go on with his own flying plans? He didn't want to die too.

For two days Neil sat in his bedroom. He analysed the risks, struggled through his fears and dreams, and recalled the conflicting advice given to him: "Follow your dream!" "Dreams are worthless when you're dead!" He didn't know what to do.

Then he took out an old Sunday school notebook he had made. On its cover was a picture of Jesus. Inside he had listed qualities of the Saviour: "He was sinless"; "He championed the poor"; "He was unselfish"; "He was close to God". Neil studied them closely and then closed his eyes in thanksgiving and made his choice.

"Mum," he said, "I hope you and Dad understand, but with God's help, I must go on flying."

Neil Armstrong's decision that day would eventually take him to the moon, to become the first human on its surface.

Neil learned that wisdom in making decisions is sometimes hard to find, as the writer said in **Job 28:20–28**.

* How did Neil and the writer of Job find wisdom?
* If wisdom is as difficult to find as verse 21 states, how do you find it?

Consider . . .

* asking God to give you wisdom concerning an important relationship in your life.
* listing the "fors" and "againsts" of decisions you must make soon. Pray that God will guide you.

For more, see . . .

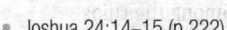

* Deuteronomy 30:11–20 (p.192)
* Matthew 26:36–45 (p.990)
* Joshua 24:14–15 (p.222)

¹⁹My roots will reach down to the water.
  The dew will lie on the branches all night.
²⁰New honours will come to me continually,
  and I will always have great strength.'

²¹"People listened to me carefully
  and waited quietly for my advice.
²²After I finished speaking, they spoke no
    more.
  My words fell very gently on their ears.
²³They waited for me as they would for rain
  and drank in my words like spring rain.
²⁴I smiled at them when they doubted,
  and my approval was important to them.
²⁵I chose the way for them and was their leader.
  I lived like a king among his army,
  like a person who comforts sad people.

30 "But now men who are younger than I
    make fun of me.
  I would not even have let their fathers
  sit with my sheep dogs.
²What use did I have for their strength
  since they had lost their strength to work?
³They were thin from hunger
  and wandered the dry and ruined land at
    night.
⁴They gathered desert plants among the brush
  and ate the root of the broom tree.
⁵They were forced to live away from people;
  people shouted at them as if they were
    thieves.
⁶They lived in dried up stream beds,
  in caves and among the rocks.
⁷They howled like animals among the bushes
  and huddled together in the brush.
⁸They are worthless people without names
  and were forced to leave the land.

⁹"Now they make fun of me with songs;
  my name is a joke among them.
¹⁰They hate me and stay far away from me,
  but they do not mind spitting in my face.
¹¹God has taken away my strength and made
    me suffer,
  so they attack me with all their anger.
¹²On my right side they rise up like a mob.
  They lay traps for my feet
  and prepare to attack me.
¹³They break up my road
  and work to destroy me,
  and no one helps me.
¹⁴They come at me as if through a hole in the
    wall,
  and they roll in among the ruins.
¹⁵Great fears overwhelm me.
  They blow my honour away as if by a great
    wind,
  and my safety disappears like a cloud.

¹⁶"Now my life is almost over;
  my days are full of suffering.
¹⁷At night my bones ache;
  gnawing pains never stop.
¹⁸In his great power God grabs hold of my
    clothing
  and chokes me with the collar of my coat.
¹⁹He throws me into the mud,
  and I become like earth and ashes.

²⁰"I cry out to you, God, but you do not
    answer;
  I stand up, but you just look at me.
²¹You have turned on me without mercy;
  with your powerful hand you attacked me.
²²You snatched me up and threw me into the
    wind
  and tossed me about in the storm.
²³I know you will bring me down to death,
  to the place where all living people
    must go.

²⁴"Surely no one would hurt a ruined man
  when he cries for help in his time of trouble.
²⁵I cried for those who were in trouble;
  I have been very sad for poor people.
²⁶But when I hoped for good, only evil came
    to me;
  when I looked for light, darkness came.
²⁷I never stop being upset;
  days of suffering are ahead of me.
²⁸I have turned black, but not by the sun.
  I stand up in public and cry for help.
²⁹I have become a brother to wild dogs
  and a friend to ostriches.
³⁰My skin has become black and peels off,
  as my body burns with fever.
³¹My harp is tuned to sing a sad song,
  and my flute is tuned to moaning.

31 "But I made an agreement with my
    eyes
  not to look with desire at a girl.
²What has God above promised for people?
  What has the Almighty planned from on
    high?
³It is ruin for evil people
  and disaster for those who do wrong.
⁴God sees my ways
  and counts every step I take.

⁵"If I have been dishonest
  or lied to others,
⁶then let God weigh me on honest scales.
  Then he will know I have done nothing
    wrong.
⁷If I have turned away from doing what is right,
  or my heart has been led by my eyes to do
    wrong,
  or my hands have been made unclean, ᵈ

8then let other people eat what I have planted,
  and let my crops be ploughed up.

9"If I have desired another woman
  or have waited at my neighbour's door for
    his wife,
10then let my wife grind another man's grain,
  and let other men have sexual relations
    with her.
11That would be shameful,
  a sin to be punished.
12It is like a fire that burns and destroys;
  all I have done would be ploughed up.

13"If I have been unfair to my male and female
    slaves
  when they had a complaint against me,
14how could I tell God what I did?
  What will I answer when he asks me to
    explain what I've done?
15God made me in my mother's womb, and he
    also made them;
  the same God formed both of us in our
    mothers' wombs.

16"I have never refused the appeals of the poor
  or let widows give up hope while looking
    for help.
17I have not kept my food to myself
  but have given it to the orphans.
18Since I was young, I have been like a father to
    the orphans.
  From my birth I guided the widows.
19I have not let anyone die for lack of clothes
  or let a needy person go without a coat.
20That person's heart blessed me,
  because I warmed him with the wool of
    my sheep.
21I have never hurt an orphan
  even when I knew I could win in court.
22If I have, then let my arm fall off my shoulder
  and be broken at the joint.
23I fear destruction from God,
  and I fear his majesty, so I could not do such
    things.

24"I have not put my trust in gold
  or said to pure gold, 'You are my security.'
25I have not celebrated my great wealth
  or the riches my hands had gained.
26I have not thought about worshipping the sun
    in its brightness
  nor admired the moon moving in glory
27so that my heart was pulled away from God.
  My hand has never offered the sun and
    moon a kiss of worship.
28If I had, these also would have been sins to be
    punished,
  because I would have been unfaithful to
    God.

29"I have not been happy when my enemy fell
  or laughed when he had trouble.
30I have not let my mouth sin
  by cursing my enemy's life.
31The men of my house have always said,
  'Everyone has eaten all he wants of Job's
    food.'
32No stranger ever had to spend the night in
    the street,
  because I always let travellers stay in my
    home.
33I have not hidden my sin as others do,
  secretly keeping my guilt to myself.
34I was not so afraid of the crowd
  that I kept quiet and stayed inside
  because I feared being hated by other
    families.

35("How I wish a court would hear my case!
  Here I sign my name to show I have told
    the truth.
  Now let the Almighty answer me;
  let the one who accuses me write it down.
36I would wear the writing on my shoulder;
  I would put it on like a crown.
37I would explain to God every step I took,
  and I would come near to him like a
    prince.)

38"If my land cries out against me
  and its ploughed rows are not wet with
    tears,
39if I have taken the land's harvest without
    paying
  or have broken the spirit of those who
    worked the land,
40then let thorns come up instead of wheat,
  and let weeds come up instead of barley."

The words of Job are finished.

Elihu Speaks

32 These three men stopped trying to answer Job, because he was so sure he was right. 2But Elihu son of Barakel the Buzite, from the family of Ram, became very angry with Job, because Job claimed he was right instead of God. 3Elihu was also angry with Job's three friends who had no answer to show that Job was wrong, yet continued to blame him. 4Elihu had waited before speaking to Job, because the three friends were older than he was. 5But when Elihu saw that the three men had nothing more to say, he became very angry.

6So Elihu son of Barakel the Buzite said this:

"I am young,
  and you are old.
That is why I was afraid
  to tell you what I know.

⁷I thought, 'Older people should speak,
　　and those who have lived many years
　　　should teach wisdom.'
⁸But it is the spirit in a person,
　　the breath of the Almighty, that gives
　　　understanding.
⁹It is not just older people who are wise;
　　they are not the only ones who understand
　　　what is right.
¹⁰So I say, listen to me.
　　I too will tell you what I know.
¹¹I waited while you three spoke,
　　and listened to your explanations.
　While you looked for words to use,
¹²　I paid close attention to you.
　　But not one of you has proved Job wrong;
　　　none of you has answered his arguments.
¹³Don't say, 'We have found wisdom;
　　only God will show Job to be wrong, not
　　　people.'
¹⁴Job has not spoken his words against me,
　　so I will not use your arguments to
　　　answer Job.

¹⁵"These three friends are defeated and have
　　　no more to say;
　　words have failed them.
¹⁶Now they are standing there with no answers
　　　for Job.
　　Now that they are quiet, must I wait to
　　　speak?
¹⁷No, I too will speak
　　and tell what I know.
¹⁸I am full of words,
　　and the spirit in me causes me to speak.
¹⁹I am like wine that has been bottled up;
　　I am ready to burst like a new leather
　　　wine bag.
²⁰I must speak so I will feel relief;
　　I must open my mouth and answer.
²¹I will be fair to everyone
　　and not flatter anyone.
²²I don't know how to flatter,
　　and if I did, my Maker would quickly take
　　　me away.

33 "Now, Job, listen to my words.
　　　Pay attention to everything I say.
²I open my mouth
　　and am ready to speak.
³My words come from an honest heart,
　　and I am sincere in saying what I know.
⁴The Spirit *d* of God created me,
　　and the breath of the Almighty gave me
　　　life.
⁵Answer me if you can;
　　get yourself ready and stand before me.
⁶I am just like you before God;
　　I too am made out of clay.

⁷Don't be afraid of me;
　　I will not be hard on you.

⁸"But I heard what you have said;
　　I heard every word.
⁹You said, 'I am pure and without sin;
　　I am innocent and free from guilt.
¹⁰But God has found fault with me;
　　he considers me his enemy.
¹¹He locks my feet in chains
　　and closely watches everywhere I go.'

¹²"But I tell you, you are not right in saying this,
　　because God is greater than we are.
¹³Why do you accuse God
　　of not answering anyone?
¹⁴God does speak—sometimes one way and
　　　sometimes another—
　　even though people may not understand it.
¹⁵He speaks in a dream or a vision of the night
　　when people are in a deep sleep,
　　　lying on their beds.
¹⁶He speaks in their ears
　　and frightens them with warnings
¹⁷to turn them away from doing wrong
　　and to keep them from being proud.
¹⁸God does this to save a person from death,
　　to keep him from dying.
¹⁹A person may be corrected while in bed in
　　　great pain;
　　he may have continual pain in his very
　　　bones.
²⁰He may be in such pain that he even hates
　　　food,
　　even the very best meal.
²¹His body becomes so thin there is almost
　　　nothing left of it,
　　and his bones that were hidden now stick out.
²²He is near death,
　　and his life is almost over.

²³"But there may be an angel to speak for him,
　　one out of a thousand, who will tell him
　　　what to do.
²⁴The angel will beg for mercy and say:
　　'Save him from death.
　　I have found a way to pay for his life.'
²⁵Then his body is made new like a child's.
　　It will return to the way it was when he
　　　was young.
²⁶That person will pray to God, and God will
　　　listen to him.
　　He will see God's face and will shout with
　　　happiness.
　　And God will set things right for him again.
²⁷Then he will say to others,
　　'I sinned and twisted what was right,
　　but I did not receive the punishment I should
　　　have received.

²⁸God bought my life back from death,
  and I will continue to enjoy life.'

²⁹"God does all these things to a person
  two or even three times
³⁰so he won't die as punishment for his sins
  and so he may still enjoy life.

³¹"Job, pay attention and listen to me;
  be quiet, and I will speak.
³²If you have anything to say, answer me;
  speak up, because I want to prove you
    right.
³³But if you have nothing to say, then listen
    to me;
  be quiet, and I will teach you wisdom."

34 Then Elihu said:

²"Hear my words, you wise men;
  listen to me, you who know a lot.

³The ear tests words
  as the tongue tastes food.
⁴Let's decide for ourselves what is right,
  and let's learn together what is good.

⁵"Job says, 'I am not guilty,
  and God has refused me a fair trial.
⁶Instead of getting a fair trial,
  I am called a liar.
I have been seriously hurt,
  even though I have not sinned.'
⁷There is no other man like Job;
  he takes insults as if he were drinking water.
⁸He keeps company with those who do evil
  and spends time with wicked men,
⁹because he says, 'It is no use
  trying to please God.'

¹⁰"So listen to me, you who can understand.
  God can never do wrong!
  It is impossible for the Almighty to do evil.

PERSISTENCE

Change of Plan

Sarah always knew that she wanted to be a doctor. At five years old, she'd play with stethoscopes. At eighteen, she was reading medical books instead of going to the cinema. While the rest of her friends had no idea what they wanted to be, Sarah passionately believed God had called her to be a doctor.

However, the summer just before Sarah was due to go to university, she got ill. She was in and out of hospital, yet the doctors had no idea what was wrong with her. Sarah managed to study whilst constantly trying new medication. But nothing worked. Finally, she got so ill that she had to move back in with her parents to be looked after.

Although never close to death, there were times when Sarah wanted to give up. She couldn't do the job that she loved, and although she still trusted God completely she had no idea why he was allowing her to go through this.

Then her church held a week of prayer. They committed themselves to pleading with God on her behalf, crying out to God to heal her. God answered their prayers and started to heal Sarah in his own time. She was able to start work with the benefit of seeing how much God used her when she thought she was useless. She could see how God was speaking to her in her suffering – teaching her, disciplining her and ultimately healing her.

Sarah still has days when she feels ill. But she no longer feels useless. She knows that our God is a God whose love and promises are constant, even when it may seem like there is no hope.
Read **Job 33:14–24**.

* What hope do we see in this passage?
* What does this say about how God teaches and speaks to us?

Consider . . .

* whether you have ever felt you were in a hopeless situation. How did God work in that time?
* reading Ecclesiastes 3:1–11 to see what it says about God's sense of time compared to ours?

For more, see . . .

* Psalm 73:21–28 (p.544)

* Hebrews 12:4–12 (p.1343)

¹¹God pays a person back for what he has done
and gives him what his actions deserve.
¹²Truly God will never do wrong;
the Almighty will never twist what is right.
¹³No one chose God to rule over the earth
or put him in charge of the whole world.
¹⁴If God should decide
to take away life and breath,
¹⁵then everyone would die together
and turn back into dust.

¹⁶"If you can understand, hear this;
listen to what I have to say.
¹⁷Can anyone govern who hates what is right?
How can you blame God who is both fair
and powerful?
¹⁸God is the one who says to kings, 'You are
worthless,'
or to important people, 'You are evil.'
¹⁹He is not nicer to princes than other people,
nor kinder to rich people than poor people,
because he made them all with his own
hands.
²⁰They can die in a moment, in the middle of
the night.
They are struck down, and then they pass
away;
powerful people die without help.

²¹"God watches where people go;
he sees every step they take.
²²There is no dark place or deep shadow
where those who do evil can hide from
him.
²³He does not set a time
for people to come before him for judging.
²⁴Without asking questions, God breaks
powerful people into pieces
and puts others in their place.
²⁵Because God knows what people do,
he defeats them in the night, and they are
crushed.
²⁶He punishes them for the evil they do
so that everyone else can watch,
²⁷because they stopped following God
and did not care about any of his ways.
²⁸The cry of the poor comes to God;
he hears the cry of the needy.
²⁹But if God keeps quiet, who can blame him?
If he hides his face, who can see him?
God still rules over both nations and persons
alike.
³⁰ He keeps the wicked from ruling
and from trapping others.

³¹"But suppose someone says to God,
'I am guilty, but I will not sin any more.
³²Teach me what I cannot see.
If I have done wrong, I will not do it again.'

³³So, Job, should God reward you as you want
when you refuse to change?
You must decide, not I,
so tell me what you know.

³⁴"Those who understand speak,
and the wise who hear me say,
³⁵'Job speaks without knowing what is true;
his words show he does not understand.'
³⁶I wish Job would be tested completely,
because he answered like an evil man!
³⁷Job now adds to his sin by turning
against God.
He claps his hands in protest,
speaking more and more against God."

35

Then Elihu said:

²"Do you think this is fair?
You say, 'God will show that I am right,'
³but you also ask, 'What's the use?
I don't gain anything by not sinning.'

⁴"I will answer you
and your friends who are with you.
⁵Look up at the sky
and see the clouds so high above you.
⁶If you sin, it does nothing to God;
even if your sins are many, they do nothing
to him.
⁷If you are good, you give nothing to God;
he receives nothing from your hand.
⁸Your evil ways only hurt a man like
yourself,
and the good you do only helps other
human beings.

⁹"People cry out when they are in trouble;
they beg for relief from powerful people.
¹⁰But no one asks, 'Where is God, my Maker,
who gives us songs in the night,
¹¹who teaches more to us than the animals of
the earth
and wiser than the birds of the air?'
¹²God does not answer evil people when they
cry out,
because the wicked are proud.
¹³God does not listen to their useless
begging;
the Almighty pays no attention to them.
¹⁴He will listen to you even less
when you say that you do not see him,
that your case is before him,
that you must wait for him,
¹⁵ that his anger never punishes,
and that he doesn't notice evil.
¹⁶So Job is only speaking nonsense,
saying many words without knowing what
is true."

Elihu's Speech Continues

36
Elihu continued:

2"Listen to me a little longer, and I will show you
that there is more to be said for God.
3What I know comes from far away.
I will show that my Maker is right.
4You can be sure that my words are not false;
one who really knows is with you.

5"God is powerful, but he does not hate people;
he is powerful and sure of what he wants
to do.
6He will not keep evil people alive,
but he gives the poor their rights.
7He always watches over those who do right;
he sets them on thrones with kings
and they are honoured for ever.
8If people are bound in chains,
or if trouble, like ropes, ties them up,
9God tells them what they have done,
that they have sinned in their pride.
10God makes them listen to his warning
and commands them to change from doing
evil.
11If they obey and serve him,
the rest of their lives will be successful,
and the rest of their years will be happy.
12But if they do not listen,
they will die by the sword,
and they will die without knowing why.

13"Those who have wicked hearts hold on to
anger.
Even when God punishes them, they do
not cry for help.
14They die while they are still young,
and their lives end in disgrace.
15But God saves those who suffer through their
suffering;
he gets them to listen through their pain.

16"God is gently calling you from the jaws of
trouble
to an open place of freedom
where he has set your table full of the best
food.
17But now you are being punished like the
wicked;
you are getting justice.
18Be careful! Don't be led away from God by
riches;
don't let much money turn you away.
19Neither your wealth nor all your great strength
will keep you out of trouble.
20Don't wish for the night
when people are taken from their homes.
21Be careful not to turn to evil,
which you seem to want more than suffering.

22"God is great and powerful;
no other teacher is like him.
23No one has planned his ways for him;
no one can say to God, 'You have done
wrong.'
24Remember to praise his work,
about which people have sung.
25Everybody has seen it;
people look at it from far off.
26God is so great, greater than we can
understand!
No one knows how old he is.

27"He takes up the drops of water from the
earth
and turns them into rain.
28The rain then pours down from the clouds,
and showers fall on people.
29No one understands how God spreads out
the clouds
or how he sends thunder from where he
lives.
30Watch how God scatters his lightning
around him,
lighting up the deepest parts of the sea.
31This is the way God governs the nations;
this is how he gives us enough food.
32God fills his hands with lightning
and commands it to strike its target.
33His thunder announces the coming storm,
and even the cattle know it is near.

37
"At the sound of his thunder, my heart
pounds
as if it will jump out of my chest.
2Listen! Listen to the thunder of God's voice
and to the rumbling that comes from his
mouth.
3He turns his lightning loose under the
whole sky
and sends it to the farthest parts of the
earth.
4After that you can hear the roar
when he thunders with a great sound.
He does not hold back the flashing
when his voice is heard.
5God's voice thunders in wonderful ways;
he does great things we cannot understand.
6He says to the snow, 'Fall on the earth,'
and to the shower, 'Be a heavy rain.'
7With it, he stops everyone from working
so everyone knows it is the work of God.
8The animals take cover from the rain
and stay in their dens.
9The storm comes from where it was stored;
the cold comes with the strong winds.
10The breath of God makes ice,
and the wide waters become frozen.

¹¹He fills the clouds with water
and scatters his lightning through them.
¹²At his command they swirl around
over the whole earth,
doing whatever he commands.
¹³He uses the clouds to punish people
or to water his earth and show his love.

¹⁴"Job, listen to this:
Stop and notice God's miracles. ᵈ
¹⁵Do you know how God controls the clouds
and makes his lightning flash?
¹⁶Do you know how the clouds hang in
the sky?
Do you know the miracles of God, who
knows everything?
¹⁷You suffer in your clothes
when the land is silenced by the hot, south
wind.
¹⁸You cannot stretch out the sky like God
and make it look as hard as polished bronze.
¹⁹Tell us what we should say to him;
we cannot get our arguments ready because
we do not have enough understanding.
²⁰Should God be told that I want to speak?
Would a person ask to be swallowed up?
²¹No one can look at the sun
when it is bright in the sky
after the wind has blown all the clouds away.
²²God comes out of the north in golden light,
in overwhelming greatness.
²³The Almighty is too high for us to reach.
He has great strength;
he is always right and never punishes unfairly.
²⁴That is why people honour him;
he does not respect those who say they are
wise."

The LORD Questions Job

38 Then the LORD answered Job from the
storm. He said:
²"Who is this that makes my purpose unclear
by saying things that are not true?
³Be strong like a man!
I will ask you questions,
and you must answer me.
⁴Where were you when I made the earth's
foundation?
Tell me, if you understand.
⁵Who marked off how big it should be?
Surely you know!
Who stretched a ruler across it?
⁶What were the earth's foundations set on,
or who put its cornerstone ᵈ in place
⁷while the morning stars sang together
and all the angels shouted with joy?

⁸"Who shut the doors to keep the sea in
when it broke through and was born,

⁹when I made the clouds like a coat for
the sea
and wrapped it in dark clouds,
¹⁰when I put limits on the sea

> **Sidelight** Ancient cultures
> envisaged the earth
> resting on everything from pillars to sea turtles
> (Job 38:4–6). The fear and speculation has
> gone, since Newton discovered gravity.

and put its doors and bars in place,
¹¹when I said to the sea, 'You may come this
far, but no farther;
this is where your proud waves must stop'?

¹²"Have you ever ordered the morning to begin,
or shown the dawn where its place was
¹³in order to take hold of the earth by its edges
and shake evil people out of it?
¹⁴At dawn the earth changes like clay being
pressed by a seal; ᵈ
the hills and valleys stand out like folds in
a coat.
¹⁵Light is not given to evil people;
their arm is raised to do harm, but it is
broken.

¹⁶"Have you ever gone to where the sea begins
or walked in the valleys under the sea?
¹⁷Have the gates of death been opened to you?
Have you seen the gates of the deep
darkness?
¹⁸Do you understand how wide the earth is?
Tell me, if you know all these things.

¹⁹"What is the path to the source of light,
and where does darkness live?
²⁰Can you take them to their places?
Do you know the way to their homes?
²¹Surely you know, if you were already born
when all this happened!
Have you lived that many years?

²²"Have you ever gone into the storehouse of
the snow
or seen the storehouses for hail,
²³which I save for times of trouble,
for days of war and battle?
²⁴Where is the place from which light comes?
Where is the place from which the east
winds blow over the earth?
²⁵Who cuts a waterway for the heavy rains
and sets a path for the thunderstorm?
²⁶Who waters the land where no one lives,
the desert that has no one in it?
²⁷Who sends rain to satisfy the empty land
so the grass begins to grow?

²⁸Does the rain have a father?
  Who is father to the drops of dew?
²⁹Who is the mother of the ice?
  Who gives birth to the frost from the sky
³⁰when the water becomes hard as stone,
  and even the surface of the ocean is
    frozen?

³¹"Can you tie up the stars of the Pleiades
  or loosen the ropes of the stars in Orion?
³²Can you bring out the stars on time
  or lead out the stars of the Bear with its
    cubs?
³³Do you know the laws of the sky
  and understand their rule over the earth?

³⁴"Can you shout an order to the clouds
  and cover yourself with a flood of water?
³⁵Can you send lightning bolts on their way?
  Do they come to you and say, 'Here
    we are'?
³⁶Who put wisdom inside the mind
  or understanding in the heart?
³⁷Who has the wisdom to count the clouds?
  Who can pour water from the jars of
    the sky
³⁸when the dust becomes hard
  and the clumps of earth stick together?

³⁹"Do you hunt food for the female lion
  to satisfy the hunger of the young lions
⁴⁰while they lie in their dens
  or hide in the bushes waiting to attack?
⁴¹Who gives food to the birds
  when their young cry out to God
  and wander about without food?

39 "Do you know when the mountain
        goats give birth?
  Do you watch when the deer gives birth to
    her fawn?
²Do you count the months until they give
    birth
  and know the right time for them to give
    birth?
³They lie down, their young are born,
  and then the pain of giving birth is over.
⁴Their young ones grow big and strong in the
    wild country.
  Then they leave their homes and do not
    return.

⁵"Who let the wild donkey go free?
  Who untied its ropes?
⁶I am the one who gave the donkey the desert
    as its home;
  I gave it the desert lands as a place to live.
⁷The wild donkey laughs at the confusion in
    the city,
  and it does not hear the drivers shout.

⁸It roams the hills looking for pasture,
  looking for anything green to eat.

⁹"Will the wild ox agree to serve you
  and stay by your feeding box at night?
¹⁰Can you hold it to the ploughed row with a
    harness
  so it will plough the valleys for you?
¹¹Will you depend on the wild ox for its great
    strength
  and leave your heavy work for it to do?
¹²Can you trust the ox to bring in your grain
  and gather it to your threshing ᵈ floor?

¹³"The wings of the ostrich flap happily,
  but they are not like the feathers of the
    stork.
¹⁴The ostrich lays its eggs on the ground
  and lets them warm in the sand.
¹⁵It does not stop to think that a foot might
    step on them and crush them;
  it does not care that some animal might
    walk on them.
¹⁶The ostrich is cruel to its young, as if they
    were not even its own.
  It does not care that its work is for
    nothing,
¹⁷because God did not give the ostrich
    wisdom;
  God did not give it a share of good sense.
¹⁸But when the ostrich gets up to run, it is so
    fast
  that it laughs at the horse and its rider.

¹⁹"Job, are you the one who gives the horse its
    strength
  or puts a flowing mane on its neck?
²⁰Do you make the horse jump like a locust? ᵈ
  It scares people with its proud snorting.
²¹It paws wildly, enjoying its strength,
  and charges into battle.
²²It laughs at fear and is afraid of nothing;
  it does not run away from the sword.
²³The bag of arrows rattles against the horse's
    side,
  along with the flashing spears and swords.
²⁴With great excitement, the horse races over
    the ground;
  and it cannot stand still when it hears the
    trumpet.
²⁵When the trumpet blows, the horse
    snorts, 'Aha!'
  It smells the battle from far away;
  it hears the shouts of commanders and the
    battle cry.

²⁶"Is it through your wisdom that the hawk
    flies
  and spreads its wings towards the south?

27Are you the one that commands the eagle
to fly
and build its nest so high?
28It lives on a high cliff and stays there at night;
the rocky peak is its protected place.
29From there it looks for its food;
its eyes can see it from far away.
30Its young eat blood,
and where there is something dead, the
eagle is there."

40

The LORD said to Job:

2"Will the person who argues with the
Almighty correct him?
Let the person who accuses God
answer him."

3Then Job answered the LORD:
4"I am not worthy; I cannot answer you
anything,
so I will put my hand over my mouth.
5I spoke once, but I will not answer again;
I even spoke twice, but I will say nothing
more."

6Then the LORD spoke to Job from the storm:
7"Be strong, like a man!
I will ask you questions,
and you must answer me.
8Would you say that I am unfair?
Would you blame me to make yourself look
right?
9Are you as strong as God?
Can your voice thunder like his?
10If so, then decorate yourself with glory and
beauty;
dress in honour and greatness as if they
were clothing.
11Let your great anger punish;
look at the proud and bring them down.
12Look at the proud and make them humble.
Crush the wicked wherever they are.
13Bury them all in the earth together;
cover their faces in the grave.
14If you can do that, then I myself will praise
you,
because you are strong enough to save
yourself.

15"Look at the behemoth, *n*
which I made just as I made you.
It eats grass like an ox.
16Look at the strength it has in its body;
the muscles of its stomach are powerful.
17Its tail moves like a cedar tree;
the muscles of its thighs are woven together.

18Its bones are like tubes of bronze;
its legs are like bars of iron.
19It is one of the first of God's works,
but its Maker can destroy it.
20The hills, where the wild animals play,
provide food for it.
21It lies under the lotus plants,
hidden by the tall grass in the swamp.
22The lotus plants hide it in their shadow;
the poplar trees by the streams surround it.
23If the river floods, it will not be afraid;
it is safe even if the Jordan River rushes to
its mouth.
24Can anyone blind its eyes and capture it?
Can anyone put hooks in its nose?

41

"Can you catch the leviathan *d* on a
fish-hook
or tie its tongue down with a rope?
2Can you put a cord through its nose
or a hook in its jaw?
3Will it keep begging you for mercy
and speak to you with gentle words?
4Will it make an agreement with you
and let you take it as your slave for life?
5Can you make a pet of the leviathan as you
would a bird
or put it on a leash for your girls?
6Will traders try to bargain with you for it?
Will they divide it up among the
merchants?
7Can you stick darts all over its skin
or fill its head with fishing spears?
8If you put one hand on it,
you will never forget the battle,
and you will never do it again!
9There is no hope of defeating it;
just seeing it overwhelms people.
10No one is brave enough to make it angry,
so who would be able to stand up
against me?
11No one has ever given me anything that I
must pay back,
because everything under the sky belongs
to me.
12"I will speak about Leviathan's arms and legs,
its great strength and well-formed body.
13No one can tear off its outer hide
or poke through its double armour.
14No one can force open its great jaws;
they are filled with frightening teeth.
15It has rows of shields on its back
that are tightly sealed together.
16Each shield is so close to the next one
that no air can go between them.

behemoth   A large land animal, meaning obscure.

¹⁷They are joined strongly to one another;
  they hold on to each other and cannot be
    separated.
¹⁸When it snorts, flashes of light are
    thrown out,
  and its eyes look like the light at dawn.
¹⁹Flames blaze from its mouth;
  sparks of fire shoot out.
²⁰Smoke pours out of its nose,
  as if coming from a large pot over a hot
    fire.
²¹Its breath sets coals on fire,
  and flames come out of its mouth.
²²There is great strength in its neck.
  People are afraid and run away.
²³The folds of its skin are tightly joined;
  they are set and cannot be moved.

²⁴Its chest is as hard as a rock,
  even as hard as a grinding stone.
²⁵The powerful fear its terrible looks
  and draw back in fear as it moves.
²⁶The sword that hits it does not hurt it,
  nor the arrows, darts and spears.
²⁷It treats iron as if it were straw
  and bronze metal as if it were
    rotten wood.
²⁸It does not run away from arrows;
  stones from slings are like chaff*d* to it.
²⁹Clubs feel like pieces of straw to it,
  and it laughs when they shake a spear at it.
³⁰The underside of its body is like broken
    pieces of pottery.
  It leaves a trail in the mud like a threshing*d*
    board.

FOLLOWING GOD

His Presence

"There came into my soul . . . a sense of the glory of the divine being; a new sense, quite different from anything I had ever experienced before."

Jonathan Edwards (1703–1758)

Edwards followed God by devoting his life to proclaiming and defending the gospel as one of the leaders of the Great Awakening in New England in the USA.

"Down in my deep well, shrouded with blackness, feeling helpless and devoid of hope, I cried out for help. Now, at last, I was ready to go to any length to achieve sobriety. And God heard my cry and answered."

Michael

Michael felt God's presence in his time of need and began the long road to recovery from alcoholism through Alcoholics Anonymous. He follows God day by day as a minister who helps others to recover from alcoholism.

"At this moment I feel something 'let go' inside and lo, God is here! It is a heart-melting 'here-ness', a lovely whispering of father to child."

Frank Laubauch (1884–1970)

Laubauch became a missionary and developed a worldwide method of teaching people to read.
  The experience of God's presence led these three to act on their faith. Job was also changed as he experienced God's presence. Read **Job 42:1–6**.

* How does Job's reaction to meeting God compare with these three people's sense of God's presence with them? How is it different?
* How would your faith change if you suddenly sensed God's presence, as in verses 4 and 5?

Consider . . .

* praying for God to give you a clear picture of what he wants you to do for him.
* writing down what you value most, why you value it, and how your feelings about it would change if you considered it as a loan from God.

For more, see . . .

* 1 Kings 19:11–13 (p.336)
* Acts 9:3–19 (p.1152)
* Psalm 63:1–8 (p.536)

[31]It makes the deep sea bubble like a
    boiling pot;
  it stirs up the sea like a pot of oil.
[32]When it swims, it leaves a shining path in the
    water
  that makes the sea look as if it had white
    hair.
[33]Nothing else on earth is equal to it;
  it is a creature without fear.
[34]It looks down on all those who are too proud;
  it is king over all proud creatures."

Job Answers the LORD

42 Then Job answered the LORD:

[2]"I know that you can do all things
  and that no plan of yours can be ruined.
[3]You asked, 'Who is this that made my
    purpose unclear by saying things that
    are not true?'
  Surely I spoke of things I did not
    understand;
  I talked of things too wonderful for me to
    know.

[4]"You said, 'Listen now, and I will speak.
  I will ask you questions,
  and you must answer me.'
[5]My ears had heard of you before,
  but now my eyes have seen you.
[6]So now I hate myself;
  I will change my heart and life.
  I will sit in the dust and ashes."

End of the Story

[7]After the LORD had said these things to Job, he said to Eliphaz the Temanite, "I am angry with you and your two friends, because you have not said what is right about me, as my servant Job did. [8]Now take seven bulls and seven rams, and go to my servant Job, and offer a burnt offering

for yourselves. My servant Job will pray for you, and I will listen to his prayer. Then I will not punish you for being foolish. You have not said what is right about me, as my servant Job did." [9]So Eliphaz the Temanite, Bildad the Shuhite and Zophar the Naamathite did as the LORD said, and the LORD listened to Job's prayer.

[10]After Job had prayed for his friends, the LORD gave him success again. The LORD gave Job twice as much as he had owned before. [11]Job's brothers and sisters came to his house, along with everyone who had known him before, and they all ate with him there. They comforted him and made him feel better about the trouble the LORD had brought on him, and each one gave Job a piece of silver and a gold ring.

[12]The LORD blessed the last part of Job's life even more than the first part. Job had 14,000 sheep, 6,000 camels, 1,000 teams of oxen and 1,000 female donkeys. [13]Job also had seven sons and three daughters. [14]He named the first daughter Jemimah, the second daughter Keziah and the third daughter Keren-Happuch. [15]There were no other women in all the land as beautiful as Job's daughters. And their father Job gave them land to own along with their brothers.

> **Sidelight** Unusual names were a source of pride in ancient times, and the names that Job gave his daughters were certainly unusual. Their Hebrew names translate as "dove", "cinnamon" and "container of eyeshadow" (Job 42:14).

[16]After this, Job lived 140 years. He lived to see his children, grandchildren, great-grandchildren and great-great-grandchildren. [17]Then Job died; he was old and had lived many years.

Psalms

When?

Time Line:

2000 BC

1500 BC

1000 BC

500 BC

BC/AD

The Israelites escaped from Egypt

King David ruled Israel and almost half the psalms refer to him

Jews began returning to Jerusalem from exile

Judah fell to the Babylonians

Final collection of psalms was probably completed

Jesus was born

Why Read This Book:

* Be inspired to express your feelings through songs about tough and joyful situations (such as Psalms 4, 27, 55, 147).
* Improve your prayer life by following the many models of prayer in the Psalms (such as Psalms 6, 32, 51, 102, 130, 143).
* Learn to praise and worship God through songs of praise (such as Psalms 8, 47, 81, 84, 108, 150).

Behind the Scenes:

If you flip through a hymn book, you see some upbeat songs, some quiet, some well known and others that are rarely sung.

The book of Psalms was the hymn book for Jews and Christians for many centuries. Each psalm is really a song for worship. Like modern hymn books, Psalms contains songs that express joy, sadness, celebration, loneliness and many other emotions. Different psalms were written by different people over several centuries, so the book is rich with diversity. The New Testament quotes from Psalms more than any other book in the Old Testament, except Isaiah. Psalms is also the longest book of the Bible and contains some of the most popular reading in the Bible. Through these poetic words we can understand better our own hearts' longings to be close to God.

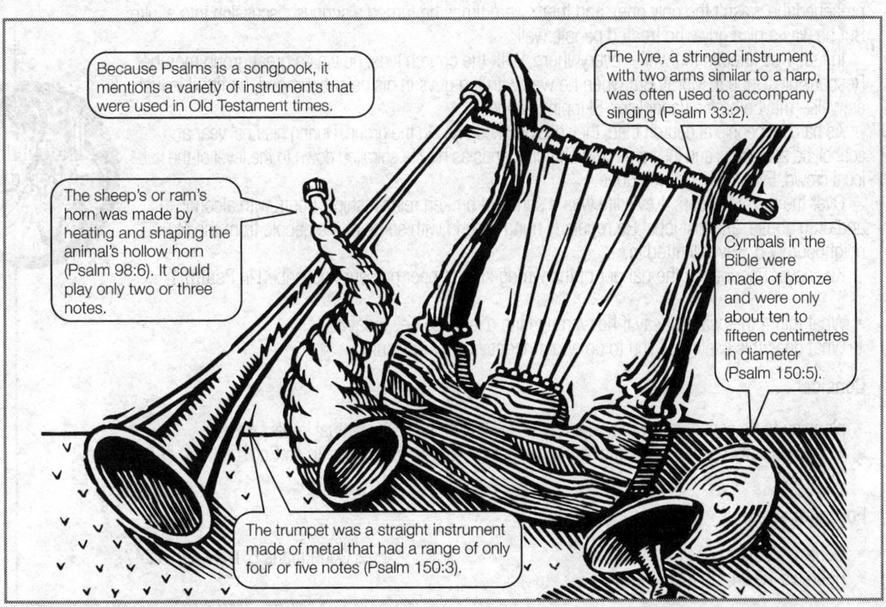

Where?

Because Psalms is a songbook, it mentions a variety of instruments that were used in Old Testament times.

The lyre, a stringed instrument with two arms similar to a harp, was often used to accompany singing (Psalm 33:2).

The sheep's or ram's horn was made by heating and shaping the animal's hollow horn (Psalm 98:6). It could play only two or three notes.

Cymbals in the Bible were made of bronze and were only about ten to fifteen centimetres in diameter (Psalm 150:5).

The trumpet was a straight instrument made of metal that had a range of only four or five notes (Psalm 150:3).

Book 1

Two Ways to Live

1 Happy are those who don't listen to the
   wicked,
   who don't go where sinners go,
   who don't do what evil people do.
²They love the LORD's teachings,
   and they think about those teachings day
      and night.
³They are strong, like a tree planted by a river.
   The tree produces fruit in season,
   and its leaves don't die.
Everything they do will succeed.

⁴But wicked people are not like that.
   They are like chaff*ᵈ* that the wind blows
      away.

⁵So the wicked will not escape God's
      punishment.
   Sinners will not worship with God's people.

⁶This is because the LORD takes care of his
      people,
   but the wicked will be destroyed.

The LORD's Chosen King

2 Why are the nations so angry?
   Why are the people making useless plans?
²The kings of the earth prepare to fight,
   and their leaders make plans together
against the LORD
   and his appointed one.
³They say, "Let's break the chains that hold us
      back
   and throw off the ropes that tie us down."

PEER PRESURE

The Laugh-a-Minute Kid

Kev Bennett was a riot. He could make more weird sounds, contort his face into more outrageous expressions and do more impressions than almost any other seventeen-year-old. He was so thin he could do tricks with his shoulder blades. People couldn't stop laughing when he tried playing "Chopsticks" on the piano with them!

And Kev was friendly. He seemed to relate to everyone. When he and his friends stopped at a fast food restaurant, in less than two minutes he would be charming the girl working the cash register and entertaining children three tables away.

Kev was great to have in the church youth group. Sure, he didn't always pay attention when the pastor preached (he wasn't the only one), and there were times he turned a serious discussion into a joke. But he was a nice guy who treated people well.

In fact, Kev fitted in too well – everywhere. With the church kids, he was a great group member. Responsible. Upbeat. Moral. But when he was with the guys in his neighbourhood, he fitted in just as well – maybe better. Vandalism. Skipping school.

As hard as people at church tried, they couldn't keep Kev in the group. During his final year at school, he spent less and less time with church friends as his life spiralled down to the level of the local crowd. Eventually, he was gone.

Over the next ten years, Kev's life was a series of broken relationships, bouts with alcohol and drug abuse, and lost jobs. He regularly hung around with some of the people from the old neighbourhood. Kev still fitted in.

Kev never understood the danger of the wrong kind of peer pressure described in **Psalm 1**.

* What might the psalmist say if he were writing a letter to Kev today?
* What does this psalm tell you to do about negative peer pressure?

Consider . . .

* planning to do something with a friend who will have a positive spiritual impact on you.
* writing your own psalm (a song or a poem) that expresses your desire to do God's will rather than follow the crowd.

For more, see . . .

* Genesis 26:1–11 (p.30)
* Hebrews 10:24–25 (p.1339)

* 2 Corinthians 6:14–18 (p.1247)

⁴But the one who sits in heaven laughs;
    the Lord makes fun of them.
⁵Then the LORD warns them
    and frightens them with his anger.

Sidelight

The book of Psalms is actually made up of five separate books (see heading above Psalm 1). Psalms 1—41 are Book One. Psalms 42—72 are Book Two. Psalms 73—89 are Book Three. Psalms 90—106 are Book Four. And Psalms 107—150 are Book Five. Each "book" may have been collected at a different time.

---

⁶He says, "I have appointed my own king
    to rule in Jerusalem on my holy mountain,
       Zion."

⁷Now I will tell you what the LORD has
    declared:

he said to me, "You are my son.
    Today I have become your father.
⁸If you ask me,
    I will give you the nations;
    all the people on earth will be yours.
⁹You will rule over them with an iron rod.
    You will break them into pieces like
       pottery."

¹⁰So, kings, be wise;
    rulers, learn this lesson.
¹¹Obey the LORD with great fear.
    Be happy, but tremble.
¹²Show that you are loyal to his son,
    or you will be destroyed by his anger,
because he can quickly become angry.
    But happy are those who trust him for
       protection.

Sidelight

The way citizens in Bible times showed their loyalty to royalty (Psalm 2:12) was by kissing the feet of the king or prince.

A Morning Prayer

David sang this when he ran away
from his son Absalom.

3 LORD, I have many enemies!
    Many people have turned against me.
²Many are saying about me,
    "God won't rescue him."   *Selah*ᵈ

³But, LORD, you are my shield,
    my wonderful God who gives me
       courage.
⁴I will pray to the LORD,
    and he will answer me from his holy
       mountain.   *Selah*

⁵I can lie down and go to sleep,
    and I will wake up again,
    because the LORD gives me strength.
⁶Thousands of troops may surround me,
    but I am not afraid.

⁷LORD, rise up!
    My God, come and save me!
You have struck my enemies on the cheek;
    you have broken the teeth of the wicked.

⁸The LORD can save his people.
    LORD, bless your people.   *Selah*

An Evening Prayer

For the director of music. With stringed instruments.
A psalm of David.

4 Answer me when I pray to you,
    my God who does what is right.
Make things easier for me when I am in
    trouble.
Have mercy on me and hear my prayer.

²People, how long will you turn my honour
    into shame?
How long will you love what is false and
    look for new lies?   *Selah*ᵈ
³You know that the LORD has chosen for
    himself those who are loyal to him.
    The LORD listens when I pray to him.

⁴When you are angry, do not sin.
    Think about these things quietly
    as you go to bed.   *Selah*

⁵Do what is right as a sacrifice to the LORD
    and trust the LORD.

⁶Many people ask,
    "Who will give us anything good?"
    LORD, be kind to us.
⁷But you have made me very happy,
    happier than they are,
    even with all their grain and new wine.
⁸I go to bed and sleep in peace,
    because, LORD, only you keep me safe.

A Morning Prayer for Protection

For the director of music. For flutes. A psalm of David.

5 LORD, listen to my words.
    Understand my sadness.

²Listen to my cry for help, my King and
my God,
because I pray to you.
³LORD, every morning you hear my voice.
Every morning, I tell you what I need,
and I wait for your answer.

⁴You are not a God who is pleased with the
wicked;
you do not live with those who do evil.
⁵Those people who make fun of you cannot
stand before you.
You hate all those who do evil.
⁶You destroy liars;

the LORD hates those who kill and trick
others.
⁷Because of your great love,
I can come into your Temple. *d*
Because I fear and respect you,
I can worship in your holy Temple.
⁸LORD, since I have many enemies,
show me the right thing to do.
Show me clearly how you want me to live.
⁹My enemies' mouths do not tell the truth;
in their hearts they want to destroy others.
Their throats are like open graves;
they use their tongues for telling lies.

ANGER

He Lost His Grip

The school paper's sports headline said it all: "Tom Harley Loses Tennis Tournament With a Smash".

Tom read the biting article and then let out a sigh. He had felt so stupid for letting his anger get to him at the tournament that day. But the deed was done. Nothing could repair his tennis racket. He had hurled the stringed beast at the fence in a spark of rage. And his brand new racket abruptly met the fence post. "Come on, Tom," his partner Jim had whispered intensely. "Relax. Your temper's going to lose this match for us."

"I'm fine," Tom had snapped. "Where's your extra racket?"

They probably would have lost anyway, but Tom was still furious about having to play with an unfamiliar racket. They only won three games in the next two sets.

The trainer didn't say a word that day, but Tom could tell he was furious. The next week at practise, he made Tom and Jim do extra "hate drills".

"Any doubles team with enough extra energy to waste on destroying tennis rackets," the coach said, "can surely handle a little extra running." So the twosome painfully ran the width of six tennis courts, forwards and backwards, again and again.

And then there was the teasing from Tom's team-mates.

"Hey, Tantrum Tom, fought off any marauding fence posts recently?"

"So, Tom, how many tennis rackets have you bought this month?"

Even with all this abuse, Tom hadn't learned his lesson. It took several more temper tantrums and broken rackets for him to learn the simple truth that anger wasn't going to make him play better tennis, or improve his life.

Anger can sometimes be constructive. But the psalmist reminds us how destructive anger can become. He warns us in **Psalm 4**, "When you are angry, do not sin." Hold on to the racket!

* Do you think throwing a tennis racket in a fit of anger is a sin? Why or why not?
* How can you avoid doing wrong things when you're angry?

Consider . . .

* seeking forgiveness from someone you've sinned against because of your anger.
* picturing the place or situation in which you get the angriest, and asking God to help you stay calm the next time you're there.

For more, see . . .

* Exodus 32 (p.90)
* Ephesians 4:26–27 (p.1274)

* Mark 11:15–19 (p.1020)

¹⁰God, declare them guilty!
Let them fall into their own traps.
Send them away because their sins are many;
they have turned against you.

¹¹But let everyone who trusts you be happy;
let them sing glad songs for ever.
Protect those who love you
and who are happy because of you.
¹²LORD, you bless those who do what is right;
you protect them like a soldier's shield.

A Prayer for Mercy in Troubled Times

For the director of music. With stringed instruments.
Upon the sheminith. ᵈ A psalm of David.

6 LORD, don't punish me when you are
angry;
don't punish me when you are very angry.
²LORD, have mercy on me because I am
weak.
Heal me, LORD, because my bones ache.
³I am very upset.
LORD, how long will it be?

⁴LORD, return and save me;
save me because of your love.
⁵Dead people don't remember you;
those in the grave don't praise you.

⁶I am tired of crying to you.
Every night my bed is wet with tears;
my bed is soaked from my crying.
⁷My eyes are weak from so much crying;
they are weak from crying about my
enemies.

⁸Get away from me, all you who do evil,
because the LORD has heard my crying.
⁹The LORD has heard my cry for help;
the LORD will answer my prayer.
¹⁰All my enemies will be ashamed and
troubled.
They will turn and suddenly leave in
shame.

A Prayer for Fairness

A shiggaion ᵈ of David which he sang to the LORD
about Cush, from the tribe of Benjamin.

7 LORD my God, I trust in you for protection.
Save me and rescue me
from those who are chasing me.
²Otherwise, like a lion they will tear me apart.
They will rip me to pieces, and no one can
save me.

³LORD my God, what have I done?
Have my hands done something wrong?
⁴Have I done wrong to my friend
or stolen without reason from my enemy?

⁵If I have, let my enemy chase me and
capture me.
Let him trample me into the dust
and bury me in the ground.   *Selah*ᵈ

⁶LORD, rise up in your anger;
stand up against my enemies' anger.
Get up and demand fairness.
⁷Gather the nations around you
and rule them from above.
⁸LORD, judge the people.
LORD, defend me because I am right,
because I have done no wrong, God Most
High.
⁹God, you do what is right.
You know our thoughts and feelings.
Stop those wicked actions done by evil
people,
and help those who do what is right.

¹⁰God protects me like a shield;
he saves those whose hearts are right.
¹¹God judges by what is right,
and God is always ready to punish the
wicked.
¹²If they do not change their lives,
God will sharpen his sword;
he will string his bow and take aim.
¹³He has prepared his deadly weapons;
he has made his flaming arrows.

¹⁴There are people who think up evil
and plan trouble and tell lies.
¹⁵They dig a hole to trap others,
but they will fall into it themselves.
¹⁶They will get themselves into trouble;
the violence they cause will hurt only
themselves.

¹⁷I praise the LORD because he does what is
right.
I sing praises to the LORD Most High.

The LORD's Greatness

For the director of music. On the gittith. ᵈ
A psalm of David.

8 LORD our Lord,
your name is the most wonderful name
in all the earth!

It brings you praise in heaven above.
²You have taught children and babies
to sing praises to you
because of your enemies.
And so you silence your enemies
and destroy those who try to take
revenge.

³I look at your heavens,
which you made with your fingers.

I see the moon and stars,
    which you created.
4But why are people important to you?
    Why do you take care of human beings?
5You made them a little lower than the
        angels
    and crowned them with glory and honour.

6You put them in charge of everything you
        made.
    You put all things under their control:
7all the sheep, the cattle
    and the wild animals,
8the birds in the sky,
    the fish in the sea
    and everything that lives underwater.

9LORD our Lord,
    your name is the most wonderful name in
        all the earth!

Thanksgiving for Victory

For the director of music. To the tune of "The Death
of the Son". A psalm of David.

9 I will praise you, LORD, with all my heart.
    I will tell of all the miracles *d* you have
        done.
2I will be happy because of you;
    God Most High, I will sing praises to your
        name.
3My enemies turn back;

SELF-ESTEEM

A Speck?

When you look up in the sky at night, it's easy to see that the Earth is little more than a tiny speck in a giant universe. And within our solar system are nine planets, each of them unique and wonderful.

Mercury, the closest planet to the Sun, is still 58 million kilometres from the sun. Venus, the next closest planet, is just a little smaller than the Earth and is covered by a layer of clouds that hide its surface.

Beyond Earth is Mars, which is like a red desert of rock, sand and soil. Jupiter, the largest planet, comes next. Its diameter is eleven times that of Earth. Saturn is next and is the last planet we can see with the unaided eye. The next planet, Uranus is 2.9 billion kilometres from the sun. Beyond it are Neptune and Pluto, which have eccentric rotation patterns, so they sometimes switch places, making Pluto closer to the sun than Neptune.

Overwhelming, isn't it? It makes us seem so insignificant.

But wait! Mercury's temperature can reach 1,440 degrees. Clouds on Venus drip pure sulphuric acid. The atmosphere on Mars is like car exhaust. A mixture of sulphur and phosphorus make Jupiter like a giant match head, ready to ignite.

On Saturn, raindrops are liquefied methane gas. Uranus is covered in radioactive smog. One hemisphere of Neptune will not see sunlight until the year 2030. And Pluto is frozen solid.

Makes you think God cares specially for us on Earth, doesn't it?

When the psalmist looked to the heavens he, too, was overwhelmed and felt insignificant. But he recognised how special the Earth and its people are to God.

* How do these facts about the solar system relate to Psalm 8?
* Do you ever struggle with the thought that God values you and finds you important?
    What's the message of Psalm 8 for you?

Consider . . .

* listing the different ways in which you strive to feel important and comparing them to the reasons you believe that God truly values you. The Bible passages listed below can get you started.
* doing something special for yourself – such as going to a concert or buying yourself flowers – as a way of recognising how special you are to God!

For more, see . . .

* Genesis 1:26–31 (p.3)
* Romans 5:6–8 (p.1190)

* John 3:16–17 (p.1100)

they are overwhelmed and die because
of you.
⁴You have heard my complaint;
you sat on your throne and judged by what
was right.
⁵You spoke strongly against the foreign nations
and destroyed the wicked;
you wiped out their names for ever and
ever.
⁶The enemy is gone for ever.
You destroyed their cities;
no one even remembers them.

⁷But the LORD rules for ever.
He sits on his throne to judge,
⁸and he will judge the world in fairness;
he will decide what is fair for the nations.
⁹The LORD defends those who suffer;
he defends them in times of trouble.
¹⁰Those who know the LORD trust him,
because he will not leave those who come
to him.

¹¹Sing praises to the LORD who is king on
Mount Zion. *d*
Tell the nations what he has done.
¹²He remembers who the murderers are;
he will not forget the cries of those who
suffer.

¹³LORD, have mercy on me.
See how my enemies hurt me.
Do not let me go through the gates of
death.
¹⁴Then, at the gates of Jerusalem, I will
praise you;
I will rejoice because you saved me.

¹⁵The nations have fallen into the pit they dug.
Their feet are caught in the nets they laid.
¹⁶The LORD has made himself known by his fair
decisions;
the wicked get trapped by what they do.

Higgaion. d Selah d

¹⁷Wicked people will go to the grave,
and so will all those who forget God.
¹⁸But those who have troubles will not be
forgotten.
The hopes of the poor will never die.

¹⁹LORD, rise up and judge the nations.
Don't let people think they are strong.
²⁰Teach them to fear you, LORD.
The nations must learn that they are only
human.   *Selah*

A Complaint About Evil People

10 LORD, why are you so far away?
Why do you hide when there is
trouble?

²Proudly the wicked chase down those who
suffer.
Let them be caught in their own traps.
³They boast about the things they want.
They bless the greedy but hate the LORD.
⁴The wicked people are too proud.
They do not look for God;
there is no room for God in their thoughts.
⁵They always succeed.
They are far from keeping your laws;
they make fun of their enemies.
⁶They say to themselves, "Nothing bad will
ever happen to me;
I will never be ruined."
⁷Their mouths are full of curses, lies and
threats;
they use their tongues for sin and evil.
⁸They hide near the villages.
They look for innocent people to kill;
they watch in secret for the helpless.
⁹They wait in hiding like a lion.
They wait to catch poor people;
they catch the poor in nets.
¹⁰The poor are thrown down and crushed;
they are defeated because the others are
stronger.
¹¹The wicked think, "God has forgotten us.
He doesn't see what is happening."

¹²LORD, rise up and punish the wicked.
Don't forget those who need help.
¹³Why do wicked people hate God?
They say to themselves, "God won't
punish us."
¹⁴LORD, surely you see these cruel and evil
things;
look at them and do something.
People in trouble look to you for help.
You are the one who helps the orphans.
¹⁵Break the power of wicked people.
Punish them for the evil they have done.

¹⁶The LORD is King for ever and ever.
Destroy from your land those nations that
do not worship you.
¹⁷LORD, you have heard what the poor people
want.
Do what they ask, and listen to them.
¹⁸Protect the orphans and put an end to
suffering
so they will no longer be afraid of evil
people.

Trust in the LORD

For the director of music. Of David.

11 I trust in the LORD for protection.
So why do you say to me,
"Fly like a bird to your mountain.

²Like hunters, the wicked string their bows;
    they set their arrows on the bowstrings.
They shoot from dark places
    at those who are honest.
³When all that is good falls apart,
    what can good people do?"

⁴The LORD is in his holy temple; *d*
    the LORD sits on his throne in heaven.
He sees what people do;
    he keeps his eye on them.
⁵The LORD tests those who do right,
    but he hates the wicked and those who
        love to hurt others.
⁶He will send hot coals and burning sulphur
    on the wicked.
    A whirlwind is what they will get.

⁷The LORD does what is right, and he loves
    justice,
    so honest people will see his face.

Sidelight

The psalmist refers to a whirlwind, which is all too common in the desert. The wind is called a sirocco and can last for many days, wreaking havoc and destruction.

A Prayer Against Liars

For the director of music. Upon the sheminith. *d*
A psalm of David.

12 Save me, LORD, because the good
    people are all gone;
    no true believers are left on earth.
²Everyone lies to his neighbours;
    they say one thing and mean another.

³The LORD will stop those flattering lips
    and cut off those boasting tongues.
⁴They say, "Our tongues will help us win.
    We can say what we wish; no one is our
        master."

⁵But the LORD says,
  "I will now rise up,
    because the poor are being hurt.
  Because of the moans of the helpless,
    I will give them the help they want."
⁶The LORD's words are pure,
    like silver purified by fire,
    like silver purified seven times over.

⁷LORD, you will keep us safe;
    you will always protect us from such
        people.
⁸But the wicked are all around us;
    everyone loves what is wrong.

A Prayer for God to be Near

For the director of music. A psalm of David.

13 How long will you forget me, LORD?
    For ever?
How long will you hide from me?
²How long must I worry
    and feel sad in my heart all day?
How long will my enemy win over me?

³LORD, look at me.
    Answer me, my God;
    tell me, or I will die.
⁴Otherwise my enemy will say, "I have won!"
    Those against me will rejoice that I've been
        defeated.

⁵I trust in your love.
    My heart is happy because you saved me.
⁶I sing to the LORD
    because he has taken care of me.

The Unbelieving Fool

For the director of music. Of David.

14 Fools say to themselves,
    "There is no God."
Fools are evil and do terrible things;
    there is no one who does anything good.

²The LORD looked down from heaven on all
    people
    to see if anyone understood,
    if anyone was looking to God for help.
³But all have turned away.
    Together, everyone has become evil.
There is no one who does anything good,
    not even one.

⁴Don't the wicked understand?
They destroy my people as if they were
        eating bread.
    They do not ask the LORD for help.
⁵But the wicked are filled with terror,
    because God is with those who do what is
        right.
⁶The wicked upset the plans of the poor,
    but the LORD will protect them.

⁷I pray that victory will come to Israel from
    Mount Zion! *d*
    May the LORD bring them back.
Then the people of Jacob will rejoice,
    and the people of Israel will be glad.

What the LORD Demands

A psalm of David.

15 LORD, who may enter your Holy Tent? *d*
    Who may live on your holy
        mountain?

²Only those who are innocent
    and who do what is right.
Such people speak the truth from their hearts
³ and do not tell lies about others.
They do no wrong to their neighbours
    and do not gossip.
⁴They do not respect hateful people
    but honour those who honour the
        LORD.
They keep their promises to their
        neighbours,
    even when it hurts.
⁵They do not charge interest on money they
        lend
    and do not take money to hurt innocent
        people.
Whoever does all these things will never be
        destroyed.

The LORD Takes Care of His People

A miktam *d* of David.

16 Protect me, God,
        because I trust in you.

²I said to the LORD, "You are my Lord.
    Every good thing I have comes from you."
³As for the godly people in the world,
    they are the wonderful ones I enjoy.
⁴But those who turn to idols
    will have much pain.
I will not offer blood to those idols
    or even speak their names.

⁵No, the LORD is all I need.
    He takes care of me.
⁶My share in life has been pleasant;
    my part has been beautiful.

DOUBT

Who Do You Believe?

The musicians that owned the studio were just about to go to bed when one of them decided to check downstairs again. He was thinking of making sure everything had been turned off. As soon as he walked down the stairs he gave a shout, and the rest of the guys ran towards the studio door. As they looked down the stairs they could see the water gushing in and flooding everything. It was rising fast and destroying keyboards and equipment as it went.

It actually took the Fire Brigade twenty-four hours to stem the flow. The culprit had been a burst water main just outside the studio.

The band that owned the studio sat and asked the Lord why this had happened.

Within a few days, many friends came around the studio with all kinds of advice . . . "Maybe God doesn't want you to have music in your house" . . . "The Lord is telling you that rock music is evil" . . . "He wants to bless you and start it up again" . . . "He wants you to see his provision."

The guys had many many doubts about the sense of it all, until the man from the water company came round and said:

"It is completely our fault. We will pay for all the instruments and for your studio to be completely rebuilt." The band were ecstatic!

In **Psalm 13** David didn't want the enemy to win over his doubts.

* What would the enemy have the band believe in this story? What was the truth?
* It's OK to doubt, but when was the last time you doubted God and what was the result?

Consider . . .

* sharing your doubts with a Christian leader that you respect. They may have been there and be able to help with some answers.
* visiting your local Christian bookshop to find a book that answers some of the difficult questions that Christians have to deal with.

For more, see . . .

* Jeremiah 1:4–10 (p.716)
* Romans 4:18–25 (p.1190)

* John 20:24–29 (p.1134)

7I praise the LORD because he advises me.
  Even at night, I feel his leading.
8I keep the LORD before me always.
  Because he is close by my side,
  I will not be hurt.

9So I rejoice and am glad.
  Even my body has hope,
10because you will not leave me in the grave.
  You will not let your holy one rot.
11You will teach me how to live a holy life.
  Being with you will fill me with joy;
  at your right hand I will find pleasure for ever.

A Prayer for Protection

A prayer of David.

17 LORD, hear me begging for fairness;
        listen to my cry for help.
Pay attention to my prayer,
  because I speak the truth.
2You will judge that I am right;
  your eyes can see what is true.

3You have examined my heart;
  you have tested me all night.

You questioned me without finding anything
    wrong;
  I have not sinned with my mouth.
4I have obeyed your commands,
  so I have not done what evil people do.
5I have done what you told me;
  I have not failed.

6I call to you, God,
  and you answer me.
 Listen to me now,
  and hear what I say.
7Your love is wonderful.
  By your power you save those who trust you
  from their enemies.
8Protect me as you would protect your
    own eye.
  Hide me under the shadow of your wings.
9Keep me from the wicked who attack me,
  from my enemies who surround me.

10They are selfish
  and boast about themselves.
11They have chased me until they have
    surrounded me.
  They plan to throw me to the ground.

REVENGE

Hate Stealer

I can't remember his name. I'm really not sure how old he was. I can hardly remember his face. His broken English was difficult to understand. But I have never forgotten his story.

Before being baptised, this Vietnamese refugee stood before our church to tell how Jesus Christ had changed his life. He spoke of the horrors of war – of escape through jungles and rivers and over the border into Thailand, of hunger and near starvation in overcrowded camps, and of the joy of coming to America.

But above all his captivating stories, one part of his testimony left a lasting impression.

"Brothers and sisters," he said. "I came to America alone, and I came with much hatred in my heart. But when Jesus came into my heart, he stole my hate away. Now I can say that I love even my enemies."

David faced circumstances similar to this Vietnamese refugee. Read **Psalm 17** to find David's response to his enemies.

* What did David have in common with this Vietnamese refugee? How were their responses to their enemies different?
* How can you leave matters in God's hands – as David did – when you are treated unfairly?

Consider . . .

* praying for someone who has treated you unfairly and whom you consider to be an "enemy".
* listing ways in which the world would be different if people and nations would turn away from revenge. Then pray for world peace – starting in your own home and area.

For more, see . . .

* 1 Samuel 24 (p.277)
* Romans 12:14–21 (p.1205)
* Matthew 5:38–48 (p.946)

Revenge

¹²They are like lions ready to kill;
    like lions, they sit in hiding.

¹³LORD, rise up, face the enemy and throw
      them down.
    Save me from the wicked with your sword.
¹⁴LORD, save me by your power
    from those whose reward is in this life.

  They have plenty of food.
  They have many sons
  and leave much money to their children.

¹⁵Because I have lived right, I will see your
      face.
    When I wake up, I will see your likeness
      and be satisfied.

A Song of Victory

For the director of music. By the LORD's servant, David.
David sang this song to the LORD when the LORD had
saved him from Saul and all his other enemies.

18
I love you, LORD. You are my strength.

²The LORD is my rock, my protection, my
    Saviour.
  My God is my rock.
  I can run to him for safety.
  He is my shield and my saving strength,
    my defender.
³I will call to the LORD, who is worthy of
    praise,
  and I will be saved from my enemies.

⁴The ropes of death came around me;
    the deadly rivers overwhelmed me.
⁵The ropes of death wrapped around me.
  The traps of death were before me.
⁶In my trouble I called to the LORD.
  I cried out to my God for help.
 From his temple ᵈ he heard my voice;
  my call for help reached his ears.

⁷The earth trembled and shook.
    The foundations of the mountains began to
      shake.
  They trembled because the LORD was angry.
⁸Smoke came out of his nose,
    and burning fire came out of his mouth.
  Burning coals went before him.
⁹He tore open the sky and came down
  with dark clouds under his feet.
¹⁰He rode a creature with wings and flew.
  He raced on the wings of the wind.
¹¹He made darkness his covering, his shelter
    around him,
  surrounded by fog and clouds.
¹²Out of the brightness of his presence came
    clouds
  with hail and lightning.

¹³The LORD thundered from heaven;
  the Most High raised his voice,
  and there was hail and lightning.
¹⁴He shot his arrows and scattered his enemies.
  His many bolts of lightning confused them
    with fear.
¹⁵LORD, you spoke strongly.
  The wind blew from your nose.
  Then the valleys of the sea appeared,
  and the foundations of the earth were seen.

¹⁶The LORD reached down from above and
    took me;
  he pulled me from the deep water.
¹⁷He saved me from my powerful enemies,
  from those who hated me, because they
    were too strong for me.
¹⁸They attacked me at my time of trouble,
  but the LORD supported me.
¹⁹He took me to a safe place.
  Because he delights in me, he saved me.

²⁰The LORD spared me because I did what was
    right.
  Because I have not done evil, he has
    rewarded me.
²¹I have followed the ways of the LORD;
  I have not done evil by turning away from
    my God.
²²I remember all his laws
  and have not broken his rules.
²³I am innocent before him;
  I have kept myself from doing evil.
²⁴The LORD rewarded me because I did what
    was right,
  because I did what the LORD said was right.

²⁵LORD, you are loyal to those who are loyal,
  and you are good to those who are good.
²⁶You are pure to those who are pure,
  but you are against those who are bad.
²⁷You save the humble,
  but you bring down those who are proud.
²⁸LORD, you give light to my lamp.
  My God brightens the darkness around me.
²⁹With your help I can attack an army.
  With God's help I can jump over a wall.

³⁰The ways of God are without fault.
  The LORD's words are pure.
  He is a shield to those who trust him.
³¹Who is God? Only the LORD.
  Who is the Rock? ᵈ Only our God.
³²God is my protection.
  He makes my way free from fault.
³³He makes me like a deer that does not
    stumble;
  he helps me stand on the steep mountains.
³⁴He trains my hands for battle
  so my arms can bend a bronze bow.

³⁵You protect me with your saving shield.
  You support me with your right hand.
  You have stooped to make me great.
³⁶You give me a better way to live,
  so I live as you want me to.

³⁷I chased my enemies and caught them.
  I did not stop until they were destroyed.
³⁸I crushed them so they couldn't rise up
    again.
  They fell beneath my feet.
³⁹You gave me strength in battle.
  You made my enemies bow before me.
⁴⁰You made my enemies turn back,
  and I destroyed those who hated me.
⁴¹They called for help,
  but no one came to save them.
  They called to the LORD,
  but he did not answer them.
⁴²I beat my enemies into pieces, like dust in
    the wind.
  I poured them out like mud in the streets.

⁴³You saved me when the people attacked me.
  You made me the leader of nations.
  People I never knew serve me.
⁴⁴As soon as they hear me, they obey me.
  Foreigners obey me.
⁴⁵They all become afraid
  and tremble in their hiding places.

⁴⁶The LORD lives!
  May my Rock be praised.
  Praise the God who saves me!
⁴⁷God gives me victory over my enemies
  and brings people under my rule.
⁴⁸He saves me from my enemies.

You set me over those who hate me.
  You saved me from cruel men.
⁴⁹So I will praise you, LORD, among the nations.
  I will sing praises to your name.
⁵⁰The LORD gives great victories to his king.
  He is loyal to his appointed king,
  to David and his descendants ^d for ever.

God's Works and Word

For the director of music. A psalm of David.

19 The heavens tell the glory of God,
    and the skies announce what his
      hands have made.
²Day after day they tell the story;
  night after night they tell it again.
³They have no speech or words;
  they have no voice to be heard.
⁴But their message goes out through all the
    world;
  their words go everywhere on earth.

The sky is like a home for the sun.

⁵ The sun comes out like a bridegroom from
    his bedroom.
  It rejoices like an athlete eager to run a
    race.
⁶The sun rises at one end of the sky
  and follows its path to the other end.
  Nothing hides from its heat.
⁷The teachings of the LORD are perfect;
  they give new strength.
  The LORD's rules can be trusted;
  they make plain people wise.
⁸The orders of the LORD are right;
  they make people happy.
  The commands of the LORD are pure;
  they light up the way.
⁹Respect for the LORD is good;
  it will last for ever.
  The judgements of the LORD are true;
  they are completely right.
¹⁰They are worth more than gold,
  even the purest gold.
  They are sweeter than honey,
  even the finest honey.
¹¹By them your servant is warned.
  Keeping them brings great reward.

¹²People cannot see their own mistakes.
  Forgive me for my secret sins.
¹³Keep me from the sins of pride;
  don't let them rule me.
  Then I can be pure
  and innocent of the greatest of sins.

¹⁴I hope my words and thoughts please you.
  LORD, you are my Rock, ^d the one who
    saves me.

A Prayer for the King

For the director of music. A psalm of David.

20 May the LORD answer you in times of
    trouble.
  May the God of Jacob protect you.
²May he send you help from his Temple ^d
  and support you from Mount Zion. ^d
³May he remember all your offerings
  and accept all your sacrifices.   *Selah*^d

⁴May he give you what you want
  and make all your plans succeed,
⁵and we will shout for joy when you
    succeed,
  and we will raise a flag in the name of our
    God.
  May the LORD give you all that you ask for.

⁶Now I know the LORD helps his appointed
    king.
  He answers him from his holy heaven

and saves him with his strong right hand.
⁷Some trust in chariots, others in horses,
  but we trust the LORD our God.
⁸They are overwhelmed and defeated,
  but we march forwards and win.

⁹LORD, save the king!
  Answer us when we call for help.

Thanksgiving for the King

For the director of music. A psalm of David.

21 LORD, the king rejoices because of your
       strength;
  he is so happy when you save him!
²You gave the king what he wanted
  and did not refuse what he asked for.   *Selah*^d
³You put good things before him
  and placed a gold crown on his head.
⁴He asked you for life,
  and you gave it to him,
  so his years go on and on.

⁵He has great glory because you gave him
    victories;
  you gave him honour and praise.
⁶You always gave him blessings;
  you made him glad because you were
    with him.
⁷The king truly trusts the LORD.
  Because God Most High always loves him,
  he will not be overwhelmed.

⁸Your hand is against all your enemies;
  those who hate you will feel your power.
⁹When you appear,
  you will burn them as in a furnace.
 In your anger you will swallow them up,
  and fire will burn them up.
¹⁰You will destroy their families from the earth;
  their children will not live.
¹¹They made evil plans against you,
  but their traps won't work.
¹²You will make them turn their backs
  when you aim your arrows at them.

BIBLE STUDY

What's the Use?

A Bible has many uses. You can get tiny versions that can be hung on a chain like a locket, and used for decoration. Many babies are presented with white Bibles to remind them of their Christening, as a memento. There are huge ones that lay open in big old churches.

On the other hand, you could use it as a doorstop. That what Sue's was for. It was a smallish black Bible with a gold pattern on it and it was just the right size to wedge in the bedroom door if you wanted some privacy. It was used this way for a number of years until one day everything changed.

Sue worked for a radio station and had been given a copy of the album *Jesus Christ Superstar* by its writer, Tim Rice. Sue immediately fell in love with the musical and played it for weeks on end. Then one day she was reading the lyric sheet and noticed that there was a text at the end of the last song. The song where Jesus was left dying on a cross. Out of curiosity, she picked up the Bible wedged in the door and started to read the account of Jesus' death. To her astonishment she read that when Jesus died, it wasn't the end of the story. She went on to read about the Resurrection, and soon afterwards Sue became a Christian.

She started to use the Bible as it was intended to be used, as a guideline for life.
Read in **Psalm 19** what the Bible is really for: that the Lord's teachings are perfect and give strength.

* What teachings in the psalm would help a young Christian?
* How can you use these truths in your life this week?

Consider . . .

* highlighting or underlining a verse in this psalm that has a special impact on you.
* finding a friend who will meet with you once a week to study the Bible.

For more, see . . .

* Psalm 119:1–48 (p.571)
* 2 Timothy 3:14–17 (p.1319)

* John 14:23–24 (p.1124)

¹³Be supreme, LORD, in your power.
We sing and praise your greatness.

The Prayer of a Suffering Man

For the director of music. To the tune of "The
Doe of Dawn". A psalm of David.

22 My God, my God, why have you
rejected me?
You seem far from saving me,
far from the words of my moans.
²My God, I call to you during the day,
but you do not answer.
I call at night;
I am not silent.

³You sit as the Holy One.
The praises of Israel are your throne.
⁴Our ancestors trusted you;
they trusted, and you saved them.
⁵They called to you for help
and were rescued.
They trusted you
and were not disappointed.

⁶But I am like a worm instead of a man.
People make fun of me and hate me.
⁷Those who look at me laugh.
They stick out their tongues and shake
their heads.
⁸They say, "Turn to the LORD for help.
Maybe he will save you.
If he likes you,
maybe he will rescue you."

⁹You had my mother give birth to me.
You made me trust you
while I was just a baby.
¹⁰I have leaned on you since the day I was
born;
you have been my God since my mother
gave birth to me.
¹¹So don't be far away from me.
Now trouble is near,
and there is no one to help.

¹²People have surrounded me like angry
bulls.
Like the strong bulls of Bashan, they are on
every side.
¹³Like hungry, roaring lions
they open their mouths at me.

¹⁴My strength is gone,
like water poured out onto the ground,
and my bones are out of joint.
My heart is like wax;
it has melted inside me.
¹⁵My strength has dried up like a clay pot,
and my tongue sticks to the top of my
mouth.
You laid me in the dust of death.
¹⁶Evil people have surrounded me;
like dogs they have trapped me.
They have bitten my arms and legs.
¹⁷I can count all my bones;
people look and stare at me.
¹⁸They divided my clothes among them,
and they threw lots ᵈ for my clothing.

¹⁹But, LORD, don't be far away.
You are my strength; hurry to help me.
²⁰Save me from the sword;
save my life from the dogs.
²¹Rescue me from the lion's mouth;
save me from the horns of the bulls.

²²Then I will tell my fellow Israelites
about you;
I will praise you in the public meeting.
²³Praise the LORD, all you who respect him.
All you descendants ᵈ of Jacob,
honour him;
fear him, all you Israelites.
²⁴He does not ignore those in trouble.
He doesn't hide from them
but listens when they call out to him.

²⁵LORD, I praise you in the great meeting of
your people;
these worshippers will see me do what I
promised.
²⁶Poor people will eat until they are full;
those who look to the LORD will
praise him.
May your hearts live for ever!
²⁷People everywhere will remember
and will turn to the LORD.
All the families of the nations
will worship him
²⁸because the LORD is King,
and he rules the nations.

²⁹All the powerful people on earth will eat and
worship.
Everyone will bow down to him,
all who will one day die.
³⁰The people in the future will serve him;
they will always be told about the Lord.
³¹They will tell that he does what is right.
People who are not yet born
will hear what God has done.

Sidelight   Travellers through the
region of Bashan, north-
east of Galilee, may have needed professional
bodyguards. In addition to "strong bulls" (Psalm
22:12), Bashan was notorious for fierce lions
and giant people.

The LORD the Shepherd

A psalm of David.

23 The LORD is my shepherd;
  I have everything I need.
[2]He lets me rest in green pastures.
  He leads me to calm water.
[3]He gives me new strength.

> **Sidelight** Psalm 23 has always been one of the favourite, most-quoted passages in the Old Testament. The early Christian church sang this song when people were baptised.

He leads me on paths that are right
  for the good of his name.
[4]Even if I walk through a very dark valley,
  I will not be afraid,
because you are with me.
  Your rod and your staff[n] comfort me.

[5]You prepare a meal for me
  in front of my enemies.
You pour oil on my head;[n]
  you fill my cup to overflowing.
[6]Surely your goodness and love will be
    with me
  all my life,
and I will live in the house of the LORD for
    ever.

staff   The stick a shepherd uses to guide and protect his sheep.
pour oil . . . head   This can mean that God gave him great wealth and blessed him.

HAPPINESS

Full of Joy . . . Always

Frank Gamble grew up wanting to be a missionary. His path to London Bible College was part of fulfilling God's will for his life. Frank proved himself to be a friendly extrovert and keen on football.

Following his graduation he married Glenda and became assistant pastor at Roxeth Green Free Church, where his spiritual and musical gifts came to the fore.

From 1977, however, Frank became increasingly disabled. He had a disease called ankylosing spondylitis – a disease that slowly spreads and paralyses every joint in the body.

The years of ill health took a toll on Frank's body, but in contrast they made his radiant face that much more evident. Anyone who visited him to bring comfort came away with far more than they had been able to give.

Although the disease imprisoned his body, his mind and spirit were free and he left others laughing and relaxed.

Frank said, "God is good, and his love fills my heart with joy and hope. As a family we enjoy his presence and provision. One day I will walk and run again. But right now I can rejoice in my sufferings because I believe that he is producing good things in me."

Despite awful pain, Frank held on to the truth that David declared in **Psalm 23**.

* What phrase in Psalm 23 best describes the reason for Frank's happiness despite such terrible circumstances?
* How can you make the truths of Psalm 23 the foundation of your happiness?

Consider . . .

* taking a personal inventory of the sources of your happiness, by writing as many responses as you can to this phrase: "Happiness, for me, is . . ."
* going for a walk and talking to God about a "dark valley" you are going through at the moment.

For more, see . . .

* Psalm 100 (p.558)
* Philippians 4:4–7 (p.1285)

* Matthew 5:1–12 (p.942)

A Welcome for God into the Temple

A psalm of David.

24 The earth belongs to the LORD, and
everything in it—
the world and all its people.
²He built it on the waters
and set it on the rivers.

³Who may go up on the mountain of the
LORD?
Who may stand in his holy Temple? *d*
⁴Only those with clean hands and pure hearts,
who have not worshipped idols,
who have not made promises in the name
of a false god.
⁵They will receive a blessing from the LORD;
the God who saves them will declare them
right.
⁶They try to follow God;
they look to the God of Jacob for help.

Selah d

⁷Gates, open all the way.
Open wide, aged doors
so the glorious King will come in.
⁸Who is this glorious King?
The LORD, strong and mighty.
The LORD, the powerful warrior.
⁹Gates, open all the way.
Open wide, aged doors
so the glorious King will come in.
¹⁰Who is this glorious King?
The LORD All-powerful—
he is the glorious King.

Selah

A Prayer for God to Guide

Of David.

25 LORD, I give myself to you;
²my God, I trust you.
Do not let me be disgraced;
do not let my enemies laugh at me.
³No one who trusts you will be disgraced,
but those who sin without excuse will be
disgraced.

⁴LORD, tell me your ways.
Show me how to live.
⁵Guide me in your truth,
and teach me, my God, my Saviour.
I trust you all day long.
⁶LORD, remember your mercy and love
that you have shown since long ago.
⁷Do not remember the sins
and wrong things I did when I was young.
But remember to love me always
because you are good, LORD.

⁸The LORD is good and right;
he points sinners to the right way.

⁹He shows those who are humble how to do
right,
and he teaches them his ways.
¹⁰All the LORD's ways are loving and true
for those who follow the demands of his
agreement.
¹¹For the sake of your name, LORD,
forgive my many sins.
¹²Are there those who respect the LORD?
He will point them to the best way.
¹³They will enjoy a good life,
and their children will inherit the land.
¹⁴The LORD tells his secrets to those who
respect him;
he tells them about his agreement.
¹⁵My eyes are always looking to the LORD for
help.
He will keep me from any traps.

¹⁶Turn to me and have mercy on me,
because I am lonely and hurting.
¹⁷My troubles have grown larger;
free me from my problems.
¹⁸Look at my suffering and troubles,
and take away all my sins.
¹⁹Look at how many enemies I have!
See how much they hate me!
²⁰Protect me and save me.
I trust you, so do not let me be disgraced.
²¹My hope is in you,
so may goodness and honesty guard me.
²²God, save Israel from all their troubles!

The Prayer of an Innocent Believer

Of David.

26 LORD, defend me because I have lived
an innocent life.
I have trusted the LORD and never doubted.
²LORD, try me and test me;
look closely into my heart and mind.
³I see your love,
and I live by your truth.
⁴I do not spend time with liars,
nor do I make friends with those who hide
their sin.
⁵I hate the company of evil people,
and I won't sit with the wicked.
⁶I wash my hands to show I am innocent,
and I come to your altar, LORD.
⁷I raise my voice in praise
and tell of all the miracles *d* you have done.
⁸LORD, I love the Temple *d* where you live,
where your glory is.

⁹Do not kill me with those sinners
or take my life with those murderers.
¹⁰Evil is in their hands,
and they do wrong for money.

[11]But I have lived an innocent life,
    so save me and have mercy on me.

[12]I stand in a safe place.
    LORD, I praise you in the great meeting.

A Song of Trust in God

Of David.

27 The LORD is my light and the one who
        saves me.
I fear no one.
The LORD protects my life;
    I am afraid of no one.
[2]Evil people may try to destroy my body.
    My enemies and those who hate me
        attack me,
but they are overwhelmed and defeated.

[3]If an army surrounds me,
    I will not be afraid.
If war breaks out,
    I will trust the LORD.

[4]I ask only one thing from the LORD.
    This is what I want:
let me live in the LORD's house
    all my life.
Let me see the LORD's beauty
    and look with my own eyes at his
        Temple. *d*
[5]During danger he will keep me safe in his
        shelter.
He will hide me in his Holy Tent, *d*
    or he will keep me safe on a high
        mountain.

FEAR

Evacuation

The station was packed full of children looking nervously at the big train as it pulled into the platform, smoke pouring out of the funnel. Each child clutched a small bag of their belongings and a little cardboard box containing their gas mask, and each wore a label around their neck, as if they were parcels, saying who they were and where they were going. The whistle sounded and slowly, with tears in their eyes, the children got onto the train and waved goodbye to their parents.

This is the frightening situation that many children found themselves in during the Second World War, as they became evacuees. The British Government knew that big towns and cities would be the target for bombs, so encouraged people to send their children to the countryside where they would be safer. This was called the Evacuation.

The countryside was a big shock for many of the children who had never been out of the town or city – some were petrified because they had never seen (or heard or smelled) animals like cows before! When they arrived at their destination, the adults of the small towns and villages would sometimes pick which children they wanted to come and live with them, so lined the children up and chose them one by one.

By the end of the Second World War, around 3.5 million people, mainly children, had experienced evacuation. At first, it must have been a terrifying experience, but it was much safer for them in the country, and many lives were saved.

Read **Psalm 27**.

* Imagine having to leave your family and go to live with strangers in another part of the country. How would that make you feel?
* Which verses in Psalm 27 would help you if you were an evacuee experiencing those feelings?

Consider . . .

* memorising the verse from Psalm 27 that you most want to remember next time you are afraid.
* circling in your Bible every time the word "will" is used in this psalm. What does that tell you about the confidence we can have in God when we are fearful?

For more, see . . .

* Joshua 1:1–9 (p.202)   • Luke 8:22–25 (p.1053)
* 1 John 4:18 (p.1374)

6My head is higher than my enemies
　　　around me.
I will offer joyful sacrifices in his
　　　Holy Tent.
　I will sing and praise the LORD.

7LORD, hear me when I call;
　　have mercy and answer me.
8My heart said of you, "Go, worship him."
　　So I come to worship you, LORD.
9Do not turn away from me.
　Do not turn your servant away in anger;
　　you have helped me.
　Do not push me away or leave me alone,
　　God, my Saviour.
10If my father and mother leave me,
　　the LORD will take me in.
11LORD, teach me your ways,
　　and guide me to do what is right
　　because I have enemies.
12Do not hand me over to my enemies,
　　because they tell lies about me
　　and say they will hurt me.

13I truly believe
　I will live to see the LORD's goodness.
14Wait for the LORD's help.
　Be strong and brave,
　and wait for the LORD's help.

A Prayer in Troubled Times

Of David.

28 LORD, my Rock,*d* I call out to you
　　　for help.
　Do not be deaf to me.
　If you are silent,
　　I will be like those in the grave.
2Hear the sound of my prayer,
　　when I cry out to you for help.
　I raise my hands
　　towards your Most Holy Place.

3Don't drag me away with the wicked,
　　with those who do evil.
　They say "Peace" to their neighbours,
　　but evil is in their hearts.
4Pay them back for what they have done,
　　for their evil deeds.
　Pay them back for what they have done;
　　give them their reward.
5They don't understand what the LORD has
　　done
　or what he has made.
　So he will knock them down
　　and not lift them up.

6Praise the LORD,
　because he heard my prayer for help.

7The LORD is my strength and shield.
　I trust him, and he helps me.
　I am very happy,
　　and I praise him with my song.

8The LORD is powerful;
　　he gives victory to his chosen one.
9Save your people
　　and bless those who are your own.
　Be their shepherd and carry them
　　for ever.

God in the Thunderstorm

A psalm of David.

29 Praise the LORD, you angels;
　　　praise the LORD's glory and power.
2Praise the LORD for the glory of his
　　　name;
　worship the LORD because he is holy.

3The LORD's voice is heard over the sea.
　The glorious God thunders;
　　the LORD thunders over the ocean.
4The LORD's voice is powerful;
　　the LORD's voice is majestic.
5The LORD's voice breaks the trees;
　　the LORD breaks the cedars of
　　　Lebanon.

> ### Sidelight
>
> God's power was indeed great to break the cedars of Lebanon (Psalm 29:5). These trees grew 20 to 25 metres tall, with trunks sometimes more than 4 metres in diameter. To cut them down and saw them up, even today, would be a mammoth task even with power saws.

6He makes the land of Lebanon dance like a
　　calf
　and Mount Hermon jump like a baby
　　bull.
7The LORD's voice makes the lightning
　　flash.
8The LORD's voice shakes the desert;
　　the LORD shakes the Desert of Kadesh.
9The LORD's voice shakes the oaks
　　and strips the leaves off the trees.
　In his Temple*d* everyone says, "Glory
　　to God!"

10The LORD controls the flood.
　　The LORD will be King for ever.
11The LORD gives strength to his people;
　　the LORD blesses his people with
　　　peace.

Thanksgiving for Escaping Death

A psalm of David. A song for giving
the Temple[d] to the LORD.

30 I will praise you, LORD,
    because you rescued me.
You did not let my enemies laugh at me.
[2]LORD, my God, I prayed to you,
    and you healed me.
[3]You lifted me out of the grave;
    you spared me from going down to the
        place of the dead.

[4]Sing praises to the LORD, you who belong
        to him;
    praise his holy name.

[5]His anger lasts only a moment,
    but his kindness lasts for a lifetime.
Crying may last for a night,
    but joy comes in the morning.

[6]When I felt safe, I said,
    "I will never fear."
[7]LORD, in your kindness you made my
        mountain safe.
But when you turned away, I was
        frightened.

[8]I called to you, LORD,
    and asked you to have mercy on me.
[9]I said, "What good will it do if I die
    or if I go down to the grave?

DEPRESSION

The Wall Came Tumbling Down

On 13 August 1961, at 2.30 a.m., with floodlights to illuminate their work and soldiers to ensure no interruptions, engineering crews began sinking posts in the pavement of Berlin. Then they attached massive sheets of barbed wire.

Many thought it was a farce, but from that middle-of-the-night beginning, the Berlin Wall was built. It divided families, friends and nations. About 10,000 East Germans attempted to cross the wall in the next 29 years, by tunnelling, flying, even blasting. At least 191 died trying.

The best-known defector, Peter Fechter, was shot down by border guards in front of photographers and TV crews in 1962. Others were imprisoned for trying to cross the wall.

Nothing portrayed the division of an entire country more dramatically than the Berlin Wall. And nothing else so well symbolised the broken people of this war-torn territory.

On 17 November 1989, Egon Krenz, the premier of East Germany, ordered that the wall be torn down. In no time, sledgehammers wielded by East and West Berliners broke through, opening the way for millions to cross back and forth in one joyous parade. No papers were checked. Even the border guards fought to keep from smiling.

"The wall is gone!" the people chanted. "The wall is gone." From both sides of the city they climbed on top of undamaged portions of the three-metre structure, laughing, crying, embracing, singing and dancing.

When David was delivered from his enemies, he expressed the same joyous feeling in his prayer, "You changed my sorrow into dancing." Read **Psalm 30** to find out how your sorrow and depression can be turned to joy.

* How was the destruction of the Berlin Wall like David's deliverance?
* What "walls" of sorrow and depression need to be broken down by God in your life? What sorrow in your life would you like God to turn into dancing?

Consider . . .

* expressing thanks to people you turn to when you're depressed.
* planning a personal "party" complete with your favourite cake to celebrate a victory God has gained in your life.

For more, see . . .

* Isaiah 61:3 (p.705)
* Luke 15:11–32 (p.1071)
* Jonah 2 (p.885)

Dust cannot praise you;
   it cannot speak about your truth.
¹⁰Lord, hear me and have mercy on me.
   Lord, help me."

¹¹You changed my sorrow into dancing.
   You took away my clothes of sadness,
   and clothed me in happiness.
¹²I will sing to you and not be silent.
   Lord, my God, I will praise you for ever.

A Prayer of Faith in Troubled Times

For the director of music. A psalm of David.

31 Lord, I trust in you;
        let me never be disgraced.
   Save me because you do what is right.
²Listen to me
   and save me quickly.
 Be my rock of protection,
   a strong city to save me.
³You are my rock and my protection.
   For the good of your name, lead me and
        guide me.
⁴Set me free from the trap they set for me,
   because you are my protection.
⁵I give you my life.
   Save me, Lord, God of truth.

⁶I hate those who worship false gods.
   I trust only in the Lord.
⁷I will be glad and rejoice in your love,
   because you saw my suffering;
   you knew my troubles.
⁸You have not handed me over to my enemies
   but have set me in a safe place.

⁹Lord, have mercy, because I am in misery.
   My eyes are weak from so much crying,
   and my whole being is tired from grief.
¹⁰My life is ending in sadness,
   and my years are spent in crying.
 My troubles are using up my strength,
   and my bones are getting weaker.
¹¹Because of all my troubles, my enemies
        hate me,
   and even my neighbours look down on me.
 When my friends see me,
   they are afraid and run.
¹²I am like a piece of a broken pot.
   I am forgotten as if I were dead.
¹³I have heard many insults.
   Terror is all around me.
 They make plans against me
   and want to kill me.

¹⁴Lord, I trust you.
   I have said, "You are my God."
¹⁵My life is in your hands.
   Save me from my enemies
   and from those who are chasing me.

¹⁶Show your kindness to me, your servant.
   Save me because of your love.
¹⁷Lord, I called to you,
   so do not let me be disgraced.
 Let the wicked be disgraced
   and lie silent in the grave.
¹⁸With pride and hatred
   they speak against those who do right.
 So silence their lying lips.

¹⁹How great is your goodness
   that you have stored up for those who
        fear you,
 that you have given to those who trust you.
   You do this for all to see.
²⁰You protect them by your presence
   from what people plan against them.
   You shelter them from evil words.
²¹Praise the Lord.
   His love to me was wonderful
   when my city was attacked.
²²In my distress, I said,
   "God cannot see me!"
 But you heard my prayer
   when I cried out to you for help.

²³Love the Lord, all you who belong to him.
   The Lord protects those who truly believe,
 but he punishes the proud as much as they
        have sinned.
²⁴All you who put your hope in the Lord
   be strong and brave.

It is Better to Confess Sin

A maskil **d** of David.

32 Happy is the person
        whose sins are forgiven,
   whose wrongs are pardoned.
²Happy is the person
   whom the Lord does not consider guilty
   and in whom there is nothing false.

³When I kept things to myself,
   I felt weak deep inside me.
   I moaned all day long.
⁴Day and night you punished me.
   My strength was gone as in the summer
        heat.   *Selah* **d**
⁵Then I confessed my sins to you
   and didn't hide my guilt.
 I said, "I will confess my sins to the Lord",
   and you forgave my guilt.   *Selah*

⁶For this reason, all who obey you
   should pray to you while they still can.
 When troubles rise like a flood,
   they will not reach them.
⁷You are my hiding place.
   You protect me from my troubles
   and fill me with songs of salvation.   *Selah*

8The LORD says, "I will make you wise and
show you where to go.
I will guide you and watch over you.
9So don't be like a horse or donkey
that doesn't understand.
They must be led with bits and reins,
or they will not come near you."

10Wicked people have many troubles,
but the LORD's love surrounds those who
trust him.

11Good people, rejoice and be happy in the LORD.
Sing all you whose hearts are right.

Praise God Who Creates and Saves

33 Sing to the LORD, you who do what is
right;
honest people should praise him.
2Praise the LORD on the harp;
make music for him on a ten-stringed lyre. *d*
3Sing a new song to him;
play well and joyfully.

4God's word is true,
and everything he does is right.
5He loves what is right and fair;
the LORD's love fills the earth.

6The sky was made at the LORD's command.
By the breath from his mouth, he made all
the stars.
7He gathered the water of the sea into a heap.
He made the great ocean stay in its place.
8All the earth should worship the LORD;
the whole world should fear him.
9He spoke, and it happened.
He commanded, and it appeared.
10The LORD upsets the plans of nations;
he ruins all their plans.
11But the LORD's plans will stand for ever;
his ideas will last from now on.

12Happy is the nation whose God is the LORD,
the people he chose for his very own.
13The LORD looks down from heaven
and sees every person.
14From his throne he watches
all who live on earth.
15He made their hearts
and understands everything they do.
16No king is saved by his great army.
No warrior escapes by his great strength.
17Horses can't bring victory;
they can't save by their strength.
18But the LORD looks after those who fear him,
those who put their hope in his love.
19He saves them from death
and spares their lives in times of hunger.

20So our hope is in the LORD.
He is our help, our shield to protect us.

21We rejoice in him,
because we trust his holy name.
22LORD, show your love to us
as we put our hope in you.

Praise God Who Judges and Saves

David's song from the time he pretended to be insane
so that Abimelech would send him away.

34 I will praise the LORD at all times;
his praise is always on my lips.
2My whole being praises the LORD.
The poor will hear and be glad.
3Praise the LORD with me,
and let us praise his name together.

4I asked the LORD for help, and he
answered me.
He saved me from all that I feared.
5Those who go to him for help are happy,
and they are never disgraced.
6This poor man called, and the LORD
heard him
and saved him from all his troubles.
7The angel of the LORD camps around those
who fear God,
and he saves them.

8Examine and see how good the LORD is.
Happy is the person who trusts him.
9You who belong to the LORD, fear him!
Those who fear him will have everything
they need.
10Even lions may get weak and hungry,
but those who look to the LORD will have
every good thing.

11Children, come and listen to me.
I will teach you to worship the LORD.
12You must do these things
to enjoy life and have many happy days.
13You must not say evil things,
and you must not tell lies.
14Stop doing evil and do good.
Look for peace and work for it.

15The LORD sees the good people
and listens to their prayers.
16But the LORD is against those who do evil;
he makes the world forget them.

17The LORD hears good people when they cry
out to him,
and he saves them from all their
troubles.
18The LORD is close to the broken-hearted,
and he saves those whose spirits have been
crushed.

19People who do what is right may have many
problems,
but the LORD will solve them all.

²⁰He will protect their very bones;
  not one of them will be broken.
²¹Evil will kill the wicked;
  those who hate good people will be judged
    guilty.
²²But the LORD saves his servants' lives;
  no one who trusts him will be judged
    guilty.

Sidelight Have you ever made an
acrostic in which you use
each letter of a word to start a new word or
phrase? Some psalms (such as Psalms 34, 37,
111 and 146) use this structure. In Hebrew,
each unit of those psalms begins with a
successive letter of the alphabet.

A Prayer for Help

Of David.

35 LORD, battle against those who battle
  with me.
  Fight against those who fight against me.
²Pick up the shield and armour.
  Rise up and help me.
³Lift up your spears, both large and small,
  against those who chase me.
  Tell me, "I will save you."

⁴Make those who want to kill me
  be ashamed and disgraced.
  Make those who plan to harm me
  turn back and run away.
⁵Make them like chaff *d* blown by the
  wind
  as the angel of the LORD forces them away.
⁶Let their road be dark and slippery
  as the angel of the LORD chases them.
⁷For no reason they spread out their net to
    trap me;
  for no reason they dug a pit for me.
⁸So let ruin strike them suddenly.
  Let them be caught in their own nets;
  let them fall into the pit and die.
⁹Then I will rejoice in the LORD;
  I will be happy when he saves me.
¹⁰Even my bones will say,
  "LORD, who is like you?
  You save the weak from the strong,
  the weak and poor from robbers."

¹¹Men without mercy stand up to testify.
  They ask me things I do not know.
¹²They repay me with evil for the good I have
    done,
  and they make me very sad.

¹³Yet when they were sick, I put on clothes of
    sadness
  and showed my sorrow by going without
    food.
  But my prayers were not answered.
¹⁴ I acted as if they were my friends or
    brothers.
  I bowed in sadness as if I were crying for my
    mother.
¹⁵But when I was in trouble, they gathered and
    laughed;
  they gathered to attack before I knew it.
  They insulted me without stopping.
¹⁶They made fun of me and were cruel to me
  and ground their teeth at me in anger.
¹⁷Lord, how long will you watch this happen?
  Save my life from their attacks;
  save me from these people who are like lions.
¹⁸I will praise you in the great meeting.
  I will praise you among crowds of people.

¹⁹Do not let my enemies laugh at me;
  they hate me for no reason.
  Do not let them make fun of me;
  they have no cause to hate me.
²⁰Their words are not friendly
  but are lies about peace-loving people.
²¹They speak against me
  and say, "Aha! We saw what you did!"

²²LORD, you have been watching. Do not keep
    quiet.
  Lord, do not leave me alone.
²³Wake up! Come and defend me!
  My God and Lord, fight for me!
²⁴LORD my God, defend me with your justice.
  Don't let them laugh at me.
²⁵Don't let them think, "Aha! We got what we
    wanted!"
  Don't let them say, "We destroyed him."

²⁶Let them be ashamed and embarrassed,
  because they were happy when I hurt.
  Cover them with shame and disgrace,
  because they thought they were better than
    I was.
²⁷May my friends sing and shout for joy.
  May they always say, "Praise the greatness
    of the LORD,
  who loves to see his servants do well."
²⁸I will tell of your goodness
  and will praise you every day.

Wicked People and a Good God

For the director of music. Of David,
the servant of the LORD.

36 Sin speaks to the wicked in their
  hearts.
  They have no fear of God.

²They think too much of themselves
    so they don't see their sin and hate it.
³Their words are wicked lies;
    they are no longer wise or good.
⁴At night they make evil plans;
    what they do leads to nothing good.
    They don't refuse things that are evil.

⁵LORD, your love reaches to the heavens,
    your loyalty to the skies.
⁶Your goodness is as high as the mountains.
    Your justice is as deep as the great
        ocean.
  LORD, you protect both people and
        animals.
⁷God, your love is so precious!
    You protect people in the shadow of your
        wings.
⁸They eat the rich food in your house,
    and you let them drink from your river of
        pleasure.

⁹You are the giver of life.
    Your light lets us enjoy life.
¹⁰Continue to love those who know you
    and to do good to those who are good.
¹¹Don't let proud people attack me
    and the wicked force me away.
¹²Those who do evil have been defeated.
    They are overwhelmed;
    they cannot do evil any longer.

God will Reward Fairly

Of David.

37 Don't be upset because of evil people.
    Don't be jealous of those who do
        wrong,
²because, like the grass, they will soon dry up.
    Like green plants, they will soon die away.

³Trust the LORD and do good.
    Live in the land and feed on truth.

JEALOUSY

Risky Business

Kevin was a thief – everyone knew that. After all, he didn't try to keep it much of a secret, did he? Every week he would boast that he had "done another job" with his elder brother – the same brother who had already been in jail.

But amazingly, his friends at school envied him. Oh no, they didn't envy the fact that if he got caught he would get a criminal record, but they did envy the fact that he could get anything.

Kevin would cycle to school on a brand new bike. He would always wear designer clothes and the latest trainers. His friends not only envied his bike and clothes, but also the fact that whatever he wanted was only another burglary away.

For days Kevin had been boasting that he was going to rob another house at the weekend, to get an MP3 player.

On Monday, Kevin wasn't at school. The expensive bike was not in the school shed. Someone had told the police which house was going to be robbed – and now he was at the police station facing charges that could ruin his entire life. All this, at the age of fourteen.

Now those who had envied Kevin laughed at him and enjoyed the fact that he was being punished. If these people had ever read **Psalm 37**, they wouldn't have been envious in the first place. Read it and see why.

* What does the psalm say our attitude should be towards people like Kevin?
* How does this psalm help you to stop feeling jealous of other people?

Consider . . .

* reading the psalm again and thinking of ten reasons why feeling jealous of someone is senseless.
* suggesting a group discussion about jealousy to your church youth leader.

For more, see . . .

* Proverbs 24:1–2 (p.610)
* James 1:9–11 (p.1348)

* Matthew 6:19–24 (p.948)

4Enjoy serving the LORD,
and he will give you what you want.

5Depend on the LORD;
trust him, and he will take care of you.
6Then your goodness will shine like the sun,
and your fairness like the noonday sun.

7Wait and trust the LORD.
Don't be upset when others get rich
or when someone else's plans succeed.

8Don't get angry.
Don't be upset; it only leads to trouble.
9Evil people will be sent away,
but those who trust the LORD will inherit
the land.

10In a little while the wicked will be no
more.
You may look for them, but they will be
gone.
11People who are not proud will inherit the
land
and will enjoy complete peace.

12The wicked make evil plans against good
people.
They grind their teeth at them in anger.
13But the Lord laughs at the wicked,
because he sees that their day is coming.
14The wicked draw their swords
and bend their bows
to kill the poor and helpless,
to kill those who are honest.
15But their swords will stab their own hearts,
and their bows will break.

16It is better to have little and be right
than to have much and be wrong.
17The power of the wicked will be broken,
but the LORD supports those who do right.

18The LORD watches over the lives of the
innocent,
and their reward will last for ever.
19They will not be ashamed when trouble
comes.
They will be full in times of hunger.

20But the wicked will die.
The LORD's enemies will be like the flowers
of the fields;
they will disappear like smoke.
21The wicked borrow and don't pay back,
but those who do right give freely to
others.
22Those whom the LORD blesses will inherit the
land,
but those he curses will be sent away.
23When a person's steps follow the LORD,
God is pleased with his ways.

24If he stumbles, he will not fall,
because the LORD holds his hand.

25I was young, and now I am old,
but I have never seen good people left
helpless
or their children begging for food.
26Good people always lend freely to others,
and their children are a blessing.

27Stop doing evil and do good,
so you will live for ever.
28The LORD loves justice
and will not leave those who worship him.
He will always protect them,
but the children of the wicked will die.
29Good people will inherit the land
and will live in it for ever.

30A good person speaks with wisdom,
and he says what is fair.
31The teachings of his God are in his heart,
so he does not fail to keep them.

32The wicked watch for good people
so that they may kill them.
33But the LORD will not take away his
protection
or let good people be judged guilty.

34Wait for the LORD's help
and follow him.
He will honour you and give you the land,
and you will see the wicked sent away.

35I saw a wicked and cruel man
who looked strong like a healthy tree in
good soil.
36But he died and was gone;
I looked for him, but he couldn't be found.

37Think of the innocent person,
and watch the honest one.
The man who has peace
will have children to live after him.
38But sinners will be destroyed;
in the end the wicked will die.

39The LORD saves good people;
he is their strength in times of trouble.
40The LORD helps them and saves them;
he saves them from the wicked,
because they trust in him for protection.

A Prayer in Time of Sickness

A psalm of David to remember.

38 LORD, don't punish me when you are
angry.
Don't punish me when you are furious.
2Your arrows have wounded me,
and your hand has come down on me.

³My body is sick from your punishment.
 Even my bones are not healthy because of
  my sin.
⁴My guilt has overwhelmed me;
 like a load it weighs me down.

⁵My sores stink and become infected
 because I was foolish.
⁶I am bent over and bowed down;
 I am sad all day long.
⁷I am burning with fever,
 and my whole body is sore.
⁸I am weak and faint.
 I moan from the pain I feel.

⁹Lord, you know everything I want;
 my cries are not hidden from you.
¹⁰My heart pounds, and my strength is gone.
 I am losing my sight.
¹¹Because of my wounds, my friends and
  neighbours avoid me,
 and my relatives stay far away.
¹²Some people set traps to kill me.
 Those who want to hurt me plan trouble;
 all day long they think up lies.

¹³I am like a deaf man; I cannot hear.
 Like a mute, I cannot speak.
¹⁴I am like a person who does not hear,
 who has no answer to give.
¹⁵I trust you, LORD.
 You will answer, my Lord and God.
¹⁶I said, "Don't let them laugh at me
 or boast when I am defeated."

¹⁷I am about to die,
 and I cannot forget my pain.
¹⁸I confess my guilt;
 I am troubled by my sin.
¹⁹My enemies are strong and healthy,
 and many hate me for no reason.
²⁰They repay me with evil for the good I did.
 They lie about me because I try to do good.

²¹LORD, don't leave me;
 my God, don't go away.
²²Quickly come and help me,
 my Lord and Saviour.

Life is Short

For the director of music. For Jeduthun.
A psalm of David.

39 I said, "I will be careful how I act
 and will not sin by what I say.
I will be careful what I say
 around wicked people."
²So I kept very quiet.
 I didn't even say anything good,
 but I became even more upset.

³I became very angry inside,
 and as I thought about it, my anger burned.
 So I spoke:

⁴"LORD, tell me when the end will come
 and how long I will live.
 Let me know how long I have.
⁵You have given me only a short life;
 my lifetime is like nothing to you.
 Everyone's life is only a breath. *Selah*^d
⁶People are like shadows moving about.
 All their work is for nothing;
 they collect things but don't know who will
  get them.

⁷"So, Lord, what hope do I have?
 You are my hope.
⁸Save me from all my sins.
 Don't let wicked fools make fun of me.
⁹I am quiet; I do not open my mouth,
 because you are the one who has done this.
¹⁰Stop punishing me;
 your beating is about to kill me.
¹¹You correct and punish people for their sins;
 like a moth, you destroy what they love.
 Everyone's life is only a breath. *Selah*

¹²"LORD, hear my prayer,
 and listen to my cry.
 Do not ignore my tears.
I am like a visitor with you.
 Like my ancestors, I'm only here for a short
  time.
¹³Leave me alone so I can be happy
 before I leave and am no more."

Praise and Prayer for Help

For the director of music. A psalm of David.

40 I waited patiently for the LORD.
 He turned to me and heard my cry.
²He lifted me out of the pit of destruction,
 out of the sticky mud.
He stood me on a rock
 and made my feet steady.
³He put a new song in my mouth,
 a song of praise to our God.
Many people will see this and worship him.
 Then they will trust the LORD.

⁴Happy is the person
 who trusts the LORD,
who doesn't turn to those who are proud
 or to those who worship false gods.
⁵LORD my God, you have done many miracles. ^d
 Your plans for us are many.
If I tried to tell them all,
 there would be too many to count.

⁶You do not want sacrifices and offerings.
 But you have made a hole in my ear
 to show that my body and life are yours.

You do not ask for burnt offerings
  and sacrifices to take away sins.
7Then I said, "Look, I have come.
  It is written about me in the book.
8My God, I want to do what you want.
  Your teachings are in my heart."

9I will tell about your goodness in the great
      meeting of your people.
  LORD, you know my lips are not silent.
10I do not hide your goodness in my heart;
  I speak about your loyalty and salvation.
  I do not hide your love and truth
  from the people in the great meeting.

11LORD, do not hold back your mercy
      from me;
  let your love and truth always protect me.
12Troubles have surrounded me;
  there are too many to count.

My sins have caught me
  so that I cannot see a way to escape.
I have more sins than hairs on my head,
  and I have lost my courage.

13Please, LORD, save me.
  Hurry, LORD, to help me.
14People are trying to kill me.
  Shame them and disgrace them.
People want to hurt me.
  Let them run away in disgrace.
15People are making fun of me.
  Let them be shamed into silence.
16But let those who follow you
  be happy and glad.
They love you for saving them.
  May they always say, "Praise the LORD!"

17Lord, because I am poor and helpless,
  please remember me.

GOD'S POWER

Against All Odds

It was 18 June 1940, one of Britain's grimmest historical moments. Hitler's army had already wiped out the French army – one of the largest in the world – in forty days. Russia had signed a pact with Hitler. The United States was not involved. Britain stood alone.

Hitler's air force, the Luftwaffe, was mercilessly pounding English cities. Germany had more than eleven hundred fighter planes and fifteen hundred light bombers facing fewer than seven hundred British Spitfires and Hurricanes. Before the Battle of Britain was over, forty-five thousand in London alone were killed or injured.

Sir Winston Churchill – the wartime Prime Minister – was never known to be a particularly religious man. But during the darkest hours of the battle, something in him seemed to understand that only God could save his country from the Nazi pounding: "If the Almighty God in his mercy should lighten or shorten our labours and the torment of all mankind, all his servants will be thankful. Let God defend the right; heed the call of duty and honour, and see that our policy and conduct are upon the highest level, and that honour should be our guide."

Against all odds, the British prevailed.

King David also called on God to save him from his enemies. Nowhere is David's cry for help expressed more strongly than in **Psalm 40**.

* How do you think Churchill would have responded to verses 1–3 if he had read them while Germany was bombing London?
* If you were writing a modern version of Psalm 40, what tough situations from your own life and the world would you include?

Consider . . .

* praying for God's deliverance in what you believe is the world's most pressing crisis.
* scanning news reports of current world crises and looking for references to dependence on God for help.

For more, see . . .

* Exodus 14:5–31 (p.71)
* 2 Peter 1:3–4 (p.1365)

* Daniel 6 (p.839)

You are my helper and saviour.
My God, do not wait.

A Prayer in Time of Sickness

For the director of music. A psalm of David.

41 Happy is the person who thinks about
the poor.
When trouble comes, the LORD will
save him.
[2] The LORD will protect him and spare his life
and will bless him in the land.
He will not let his enemies take him.
[3] The LORD will give him strength when he is
sick,
and he will make him well again.

[4] I said, "LORD, have mercy on me.
Heal me, because I have sinned against you."
[5] My enemies are saying evil things about me.
They say, "When will he die and be
forgotten?"
[6] Some people come to see me,
but they lie.
They just come to get bad news.
Then they go and gossip.
[7] All my enemies whisper about me
and think the worst about me.
[8] They say, "He has a terrible disease.
He will never get out of bed again."
[9] My best and truest friend, who ate at my table,
has even turned against me.

[10] LORD, have mercy on me.
Give me strength so I can pay them back.
[11] Because my enemies do not defeat me,
I know you are pleased with me.
[12] Because I am innocent, you support me
and will let me be with you for ever.

[13] Praise the LORD, the God of Israel.
He has always been,
and he will always be.
Amen and amen.

Book 2

Wishing to be Near God

For the director of music. A maskil [d]
of the sons of Korah.

42 As a deer thirsts for streams of water,
so I thirst for you, God.
[2] I thirst for the living God.
When can I go to meet with him?
[3] Day and night, my tears have been my food.
People are always saying,
"Where is your God?"
[4] When I remember these things,
I speak with a broken heart.

I used to walk with the crowd
and lead them to God's Temple [d]
with songs of praise.
[5] Why am I so sad?
Why am I so upset?
I should put my hope in God
and keep praising him,
my Saviour and [6] my God.

I am very sad.
So I remember you where the Jordan River
begins,
near the peaks of Hermon and Mount
Mizar.
[7] Troubles have come again and again,
sounding like waterfalls.
Your waves are crashing all around me.
[8] The LORD shows his true love every day.
At night I have a song,
and I pray to my living God.
[9] I say to God, my Rock, [d]
"Why have you forgotten me?
Why am I sad
and troubled by my enemies?"
[10] My enemies' insults make me feel
as if my bones were broken.
They are always saying,
"Where is your God?"
[11] Why am I so sad?
Why am I so upset?
I should put my hope in God
and keep praising him,
my Saviour and my God.

A Prayer for Protection

43 God, defend me.
Argue my case against those who
don't follow you.
Save me from liars and those who do evil.
[2] God, you are my strength.
Why have you rejected me?
Why am I sad
and troubled by my enemies?
[3] Send me your light and truth
to guide me.
Let them lead me to your holy mountain,
to where you live.
[4] Then I will go to the altar of God,
to God who is my joy and happiness.
I will praise you with a harp,
God, my God.

[5] Why am I so sad?
Why am I so upset?
I should put my hope in God
and keep praising him,
my Saviour and my God.

A Prayer for Help

For the director of music. A maskil[d]
of the sons of Korah.

44 God, we have heard about you.
Our ancestors told us
what you did in their days,
in days long ago.
[2]With your power you forced the nations out
of the land
and placed our ancestors here.
You destroyed those other nations,
but you made our ancestors grow strong.
[3]It wasn't their swords that took the land.
It wasn't their power that gave them
victory.
But it was your great power and strength.
You were with them because you loved
them.

[4]My God, you are my King.
Your commands led Jacob's people to
victory.
[5]With your help we pushed back our
enemies.
In your name we trampled those who came
against us.
[6]I don't trust my bow to help me,
and my sword can't save me.
[7]You saved us from our foes,
and you made our enemies ashamed.
[8]We will praise God every day;
we will praise your name for ever.   *Selah*[d]

[9]But you have rejected us and shamed us.
You don't march with our armies any
more.
[10]You let our enemies push us back,
and those who hate us have taken our
wealth.
[11]You gave us away like sheep to be eaten
and have scattered us among the nations.
[12]You sold your people for nothing
and made no profit on the sale.

[13]You made us a joke to our neighbours;
those around us laugh and make fun
of us.
[14]You made us a joke to the other nations;
people shake their heads.
[15]I am always in disgrace,
and I am covered with shame.
[16]My enemy is getting even
with insults and curses.

[17]All these things have happened to us,
but we have not forgotten you
or failed to keep our agreement with you.
[18]Our hearts haven't turned away from you,
and we haven't stopped following you.

[19]But you crushed us in this place where wild
dogs live,
and you covered us with deep darkness.
[20]If we had forgotten our God
or lifted our hands in prayer to foreign gods,
[21]God would have known,
because he knows what is in our hearts.
[22]But for you we are in danger of death all the
time.
People think we are worth no more than
sheep to be killed.

[23]Wake up, Lord! Why are you sleeping?
Get up! Don't reject us for ever.
[24]Why do you hide from us?
Have you forgotten our pain and troubles?

[25]We have been pushed down into the ground;
we are flat on the ground.
[26]Get up and help us.
Because of your love, save us.

A Song for the King's Wedding

For the director of music. To the tune of "Lilies".
A maskil. [d] A love song of the sons of Korah.

45 Beautiful words fill my mind.
I am speaking of royal things.
My tongue is like the pen of a skilled
writer.

[2]You are more handsome than anyone,
and you are an excellent speaker,
so God has blessed you for ever.
[3]Put on your sword, powerful warrior.
Show your glory and majesty.
[4]In your majesty win the victory
for what is true and right.
Your power will do amazing things.
[5]Your sharp arrows will enter
the hearts of the king's enemies.
Nations will be defeated before you.
[6]God, your throne will last for ever and ever.
You will rule your kingdom with fairness.
[7]You love right and hate evil,
so God has chosen you from among your
friends;
he has set you apart with much joy.
[8]Your clothes smell like myrrh,[d] aloes[d] and
cassia.[d]
From palaces of ivory
music comes to make you happy.
[9]Kings' daughters are among your honoured
women.
Your bride stands at your right side
wearing gold from Ophir.

[10]Listen to me, daughter; look and pay
attention.
Forget your people and your father's family.

¹¹The king loves your beauty.
Because he is your master, you should
obey him.

Sidelight With the rest of the
psalms we can gain a
unique understanding of all that God wants to
share with us; he cares and delights to hear
both our praise and our sorrows.

---

¹²People from the city of Tyre have brought a
gift.
Wealthy people will want to meet you.
¹³The princess is very beautiful.
Her gown is woven with gold.
¹⁴In her beautiful clothes she is brought to the
king.
Her bridesmaids follow behind her,
and they are also brought to him.
¹⁵They come with happiness and joy;
they enter the king's palace.
¹⁶You will have sons to replace your fathers.
You will make them rulers through all the
land.
¹⁷I will make your name famous from
now on,
so people will praise you for ever and ever.

God Protects His People

For the director of music. By alamoth. *d* A psalm of
the sons of Korah.

46 God is our protection and our strength.
He always helps in times of trouble.
²So we will not be afraid even if the earth
shakes,
or the mountains fall into the sea,
³even if the oceans roar and foam,
or the mountains shake at the raging sea. *Selah d*

⁴There is a river that brings joy to the city
of God,
the holy place where God Most High
lives.
⁵God is in that city, and so it will not be
shaken.
God will help her at dawn.
⁶Nations tremble and kingdoms shake.
God shouts and the earth crumbles.
⁷The LORD All-powerful is with us;
the God of Jacob is our defender. *Selah*
⁸Come and see what the LORD has done,
the amazing things he has done on the
earth.

⁹He stops wars everywhere on the earth.
He breaks all bows and spears
and burns up the chariots with fire.
¹⁰God says, "Be quiet and know that I
am God.
I will be supreme over all the nations;
I will be supreme in the earth."
¹¹The LORD All-powerful is with us;
the God of Jacob is our defender. *Selah*

God, the King of the World

For the director of music. A psalm
of the sons of Korah.

47 Clap your hands, all you people.
Shout to God with joy.
²The LORD Most High is wonderful.
He is the great King over all the earth!
³He defeated nations for us
and put them under our control.
⁴He chose the land we would inherit.
We are the children of Jacob, whom he
loved. *Selah d*
⁵God has risen with a shout of joy;
the LORD has risen as the trumpets
sounded.
⁶Sing praises to God. Sing praises.
Sing praises to our King. Sing praises.

⁷God is King of all the earth,
so sing a song of praise to him.
⁸God is King over the nations.
God sits on his holy throne.
⁹The leaders of the nations meet
with the people of the God of Abraham,
because the leaders of the earth belong to
God.
He is supreme.

Jerusalem, the City of God

A psalm of the sons of Korah.

48 The LORD is great; he should be praised
in the city of our God, on his holy
mountain.
²It is high and beautiful
and brings joy to the whole world.
Mount Zion *d* is like the high mountains of
the north;
it is the city of the Great King.
³God is within its palaces;
he is known as its defender.

⁴Kings joined together
and came to attack the city.
⁵But when they saw it, they were amazed.
They ran away in fear.
⁶Fear took hold of them;
they hurt like a woman having a baby.

7You destroyed the large trading ships
   with an east wind.

8First we heard
   and now we have seen
that God will always keep his city safe.
   It is the city of the LORD All-powerful,
   the city of our God.   *Selah* [d]

9God, we come into your Temple [d]
   to think about your love.
10God, your name is known everywhere;
   all over the earth people praise you.
   Your right hand is full of goodness.
11Mount Zion is happy
   and all the towns of Judah rejoice,
because your decisions are fair.

12Walk around Jerusalem
   and count its towers.
13Notice how strong they are.
   Look at the palaces.
   Then you can tell your children about them.
14This God is our God for ever and ever.
   He will guide us from now on.

Trusting Money is Foolish

For the director of music. A psalm
of the sons of Korah.

49 Listen to this, all you nations;
   listen, all you who live on earth.
2Listen, both great and small,
   rich and poor together.

WORSHIP

With All Your Heart *or* With All Your Mind?

As Lester (or "Lecture" as he was affectionately known by the youth group) walked into church, he spotted the drum kit being set up. Without a second's hesitation, he turned on his heels, walked out the door and headed across town for a more "reverent" worship experience! Like a few of the middle-aged men at church, he couldn't stand modern songs, with their simple words and overly emotional "pop" music. After all, "They're not crammed full of rich biblical truths and majestic imagery like the good old hymns, are they?" "La la la la. La la la la (x8)" followed by "Jesus, you're great" never really seemed to give God the praise Lester felt he deserved.

Josh, the church's young drummer, was Lester's opposite! He loved the freedom and emotion of the modern songs and played his heart out to God. During the old hymns, he simply switched off, finding them "like a boring poetry lesson with all the passion and joy of a maths exam".

Do you have a Josh or Lester in your church? Maybe you relate to one of them yourself.

Take a look at **Psalm 47** and notice how rich the language is, describing in great detail and with beautiful imagery the awesome power of God, and yet all sung to the backdrop of shouts and cries of joy, clapping hands and trumpets. It involves both our minds *and* our emotions.

* If Josh and Lester were to read Psalm 47, what do you think they could both learn about worship?
* Notice how Psalm 47 is a command to *all* nations to worship the Lord. There are so many different styles of music and expressions of worship all across the world. What can we learn from other Christians in how they worship?

Consider . . .

* ways in which you can worship God this week apart from just singing. Worship is so much more than just singing; it should be a lifestyle.
* next time you go to church or youth group, asking God to help you worship him with all your heart *and* with all your mind, even when it's not easy and the style is not your first choice.

For more, see . . .

* Habakkuk 3 (p.907)
* Ephesians 5:19–20 (p.1275)

* Matthew 22:34–40 (p.980)

³What I say is wise,
and my heart speaks with understanding.
⁴I will pay attention to a wise saying;
I will explain my riddle on the harp.

⁵Why should I be afraid of bad days?
Why should I fear when evil men
surround me?
⁶They trust in their money
and boast about their riches.
⁷No one can buy back the life of another.
No one can pay God for his own life,
⁸because the price of a life is high.
No payment is ever enough.
⁹Do people live for ever?
Don't they all face death?

¹⁰See, even wise people die.
Fools and stupid people also die
and leave their wealth to others.
¹¹Their graves will always be their homes.
They will live there from now on,
even though they named places after
themselves.

¹²Even rich people do not live for ever;
like the animals, people die.

¹³This is what will happen to those who trust
in themselves
and to their followers who believe them.

Selah*d*

¹⁴Like sheep, they must die,
and death will be their shepherd.
Honest people will rule over them in the
morning,
and their bodies will rot in a grave far from
home.
¹⁵But God will save my life
and will take me from the grave.   Selah

¹⁶Don't be afraid of rich people
because their houses are more beautiful.
¹⁷They don't take anything to the grave;
their wealth won't go down with them.
¹⁸Even though they were praised when they
were alive—
and people may praise you when you
succeed—
¹⁹they will go to where their ancestors are.
They will never see light again.

²⁰Rich people with no understanding
are just like animals that die.

God Wants True Worship

A psalm of Asaph.

50
The God of gods, the LORD, speaks.
He calls the earth from the rising to
the setting sun.

²God shines from Jerusalem,
whose beauty is perfect.
³Our God comes, and he will not be silent.
A fire burns in front of him,
and a powerful storm surrounds him.
⁴He calls to the sky above and to the earth
that he might judge his people.
⁵He says, "Gather around, you who
worship me,
who have made an agreement with me,
using a sacrifice."
⁶God is the judge,
and even the skies say he is right.   Selah*d*

⁷God says, "My people, listen to me;
Israel, I will testify against you.
I am God, your God.
⁸I do not scold you for your sacrifices.
You always bring me your burnt
offerings.
⁹But I do not need bulls from your stalls
or goats from your pens,
¹⁰because every animal of the forest is already
mine.
The cattle on a thousand hills are mine.
¹¹I know every bird on the mountains,
and every living thing in the fields
is mine.
¹²If I were hungry, I would not tell you,
because the earth and everything in it
are mine.
¹³I don't eat the meat of bulls
or drink the blood of goats.
¹⁴Give an offering to show thanks to God.
Give God Most High what you have
promised.
¹⁵Call to me in times of trouble.
I will save you, and you will
honour me."

¹⁶But God says to the wicked:

"Why do you talk about my laws?
Why do you mention my agreement?
¹⁷You hate my teachings
and turn your back on what I say.
¹⁸When you see a thief, you join him.
You take part in adultery. *d*
¹⁹You don't stop your mouth from
speaking evil,
and your tongue makes up lies.
²⁰You speak against your brother
and lie about your mother's son.
²¹I have kept quiet while you did these
things,
so you thought I was just like you.
But I will scold you
and accuse you to your face.

²²"Think about this, you who forget God.
　　Otherwise, I will tear you apart,
　　and no one will save you.
²³Those people honour me
　　who bring me offerings to show thanks.
　　And I, God, will save those who do that."

A Prayer for Forgiveness

For the director of music. A psalm of David when the
prophet ᵈ Nathan came to David after David's
sin with Bathsheba.

51
God, be merciful to me
　　because you are loving.
Because you are always ready to be
　　merciful,
wipe out all my wrongs.
²Wash away all my guilt
　　and make me clean again.

³I know about my wrongs,
　　and I can't forget my sin.

⁴You are the only one I have sinned
　　against;
　I have done what you say is wrong.
　You are right when you speak
　　and fair when you judge.
⁵I was brought into this world in sin.
　　In sin my mother gave birth to me.

⁶You want me to be completely truthful,
　　so teach me wisdom.

⁷Take away my sin, and I will be clean.
　　Wash me, and I will be whiter than
　　　snow.
⁸Make me hear sounds of joy and gladness;
　　let the bones you crushed be happy
　　　again.
⁹Turn your face from my sins
　　and wipe out all my guilt.

¹⁰Create in me a pure heart, God,
　　and make my spirit right again.

SEXUALITY

Fancy That

There was a family whose members always carried rucksacks. They lived in the strange belief that this was how normal people lived. They put a stone or pebble in their own rucksack every month if they felt they had been bad. After a while, the rucksacks became quite heavy, even though the load built up slowly.

Arriving at the especially self-conscious teenage years was often difficult: some covered up, choosing to wear baggy coats over their rucksacks; some just acted naturally, telling their friends it was something you could get used to or act as if it was not really there; others were paralysed with fear and never left their house.

Well that would be a bit stupid wouldn't it! No one carries their burdens round with them like that! Or do they?

Some people seem to operate in that way with guilt. They carry regrets and self-loathing around with them all the time. Some are good at hiding it. Some manage to pretend it's not there. Some are crushed by it. And the guilt of sexual sin appears worse than the rest. It sort of lives with you; sticks to you; clings – like a rucksack full of rocks you have to carry around with you.

Psalm 51 is the psalm David wrote when he was convicted of his sins of adultery and murder. You can read the whole story of what David did in 2 Samuel 11:1 – 12:25.

- What does David do?
- How does he hope life will be different in the future?

Consider . . .

- what your natural tendency is when dealing with guilt. Do you pretend it's not there, get crushed by it, hide it, confess?
- asking God to give you the strength to stay away from sexual sin. He says he will. Do you trust him?

For more, see . . .

- Isaiah 43:25 (p.684)
- 1 John 1:8–10 (p.1371)

- Isaiah 44:22 (p.687)

11Do not send me away from you
or take your Holy Spirit *d* away from me.
12Give me back the joy of your salvation.
Keep me strong by giving me a willing
spirit.
13Then I will teach your ways to those who do
wrong,
and sinners will turn back to you.
14God, save me from the guilt of murder,
God of my salvation,
and I will sing about your goodness.
15Lord, let me speak
so I may praise you.
16You are not pleased by sacrifices, or I would
give them.
You don't want burnt offerings.
17The sacrifice God wants is a broken spirit.
God, you will not reject a heart that is
broken and sorry for sin.
18Do whatever good you wish for
Jerusalem.
Rebuild the walls of Jerusalem.
19Then you will be pleased with right sacrifices
and whole burnt offerings,
and bulls will be offered on your altar.

God will Punish the Proud

For the director of music. A maskil *d* of David. When
Doeg the Edomite came to Saul and said to him,
"David is in Ahimelech's house."

52 Mighty warrior, why do you boast
about the evil you do?
God's love will continue for ever.
2You think up evil plans.
Your tongue is like a sharp razor,
making up lies.
3You love wrong more than right
and lies more than truth.   *Selah**d*
4You love words that bite
and tongues that lie.

5But God will ruin you for ever.
He will seize you and throw you out of
your tent;
he will tear you away from the land of
the living.   *Selah*
6Those who do right will see this and
fear God.
They will laugh at you and say,
7"Look what happened to the man
who did not depend on God
but depended on his money.
He grew strong by his evil plans."
8But I am like an olive tree
growing in God's Temple. *d*
I trust God's love
for ever and ever.

9God, I will thank you for ever for what you
have done.
With those who worship you, I will trust
you because you are good.

The Unbelieving Fool

For the director of music. By mahalath. *d*
A maskil *d* of David.

53 Fools say to themselves,
"There is no God."
Fools are evil and do terrible things;
none of them does anything good.

2God looked down from heaven on all
people
to see if anyone was wise,
if anyone was looking to God for help.
3But all have turned away.
Together, everyone has become evil;
none of them does anything good.
Not a single person.

4Don't the wicked understand?
They destroy my people as if they were
eating bread.
They do not ask God for help.
5The wicked are filled with terror
where there had been nothing to fear.
God will scatter the bones of your
enemies.
You will defeat them,
because God has rejected them.

6I pray that victory will come to Israel from
Mount Zion! *d*
May God bring them back.
Then the people of Jacob will rejoice,
and the people of Israel will be glad.

A Prayer for Help

For the director of music. With stringed instruments. A
maskil *d* of David when the Ziphites went to Saul and
said, "We think David is hiding among our people."

54 God, save me because of who you are.
By your strength show that I am
innocent.

Sidelight Feeling down? Then
praise God! That's the
attitude of even the saddest psalms, which
are called "laments". These laments (such as
Psalms 54—61) show individuals and the nation
of Israel praying in times of crisis. Of all the
types of psalm, the lament is most common.

2Hear my prayer, God;
listen to what I say.

³Strangers turn against me,
and cruel men want to kill me.
They do not care about God.   *Selah* ᵈ

⁴See, God will help me;
the Lord will support me.

⁵Let my enemies be punished with their own
evil.
Destroy them because you are loyal
to me.

⁶I will offer a sacrifice as a special gift
to you.
I will thank you, LORD, because you are
good.
⁷You have saved me from all my troubles,
and I have seen my enemies defeated.

A Prayer About a False Friend

For the director of music. With stringed instruments.
A maskil ᵈ of David.

55 God, listen to my prayer
and do not ignore my cry for help.
²Pay attention to me and answer me.
I am troubled and upset
³by what the enemy says
and how the wicked look at me.
They bring troubles down on me,
and in anger they attack me.

⁴I am frightened inside;
the terror of death has attacked me.
⁵I am scared and shaking,
and terror grips me.
⁶I said, "I wish I had wings like a dove.
Then I would fly away and rest.
⁷I would wander far away
and stay in the desert.   *Selah* ᵈ
⁸I would hurry to my place of escape,
far away from the wind and storm."

⁹Lord, destroy and confuse their words,
because I see violence and fighting in the
city.
¹⁰Day and night they are all around its
walls,
and evil and trouble are everywhere
inside.
¹¹Destruction is everywhere in the city;
trouble and lying never leave its streets.

¹²It was not an enemy insulting me.
I could stand that.
It was not someone who hated me.
I could hide from him.
¹³But it is you, a person like me,
my companion and good friend.

¹⁴We had a good friendship
and walked together to God's Temple. ᵈ

¹⁵Let death take away my enemies.
Let them die while they are still young
because evil lives with them.
¹⁶But I will call to God for help,
and the LORD will save me.
¹⁷Morning, noon and night I am troubled and
upset,
but he will listen to me.
¹⁸Many are against me,
but he keeps me safe in battle.
¹⁹God who lives for ever
will hear me and punish them.   *Selah*

But they will not change;
they do not fear God.

²⁰The one who was my friend attacks his
friends
and breaks his promises.
²¹His words are slippery like butter,
but war is in his heart.
His words are smoother than oil,
but they cut like knives.

²²Give your worries to the LORD,
and he will take care of you.
He will never let good people down.
²³But, God, you will bring down
the wicked to the grave.
Murderers and liars will live
only half a lifetime.

But I will trust in you.

Trusting God for Help

For the director of music. To the tune of "The Dove in
the Distant Oak". A miktam ᵈ of David when the
Philistines captured him in Gath.

56 God, be merciful to me because people
are chasing me;
the battle has pressed me all day long.
²My enemies have chased me all day;
there are many proud people
fighting me.

³When I am afraid,
I will trust you.
⁴I praise God for his word.
I trust God, so I am not afraid.
What can human beings do to me?

⁵All day long they twist my words;
all their evil plans are against me.
⁶They wait. They hide.
They watch my steps,
hoping to kill me.

⁷God, do not let them escape;
  punish the foreign nations in your
    anger.
⁸You have recorded my troubles.
  You have kept a list of my tears.
    Aren't they in your records?

⁹On the day I call for help, my enemies will
    be defeated.
  I know that God is on my side.
¹⁰I praise God for his word to me;
  I praise the LORD for his word.
¹¹I trust in God. I will not be afraid.
  What can people do to me?

¹²God, I must keep my promises to you.
  I will give you my offerings to
    thank you,
¹³because you have saved me from death.
  You have kept me from being
    defeated.
  So I will walk with God
    in the light among the living.

A Prayer in Troubled Times

For the director of music. To the tune of "Do Not
Destroy". A miktam ^d of David when he escaped from
Saul in the cave.

57 Be merciful to me, God; be merciful
      to me
  because I come to you for protection.
  Let me hide under the shadow of your
    wings
    until the trouble has passed.

²I cry out to God Most High,
  to the God who does everything
    for me.
³He sends help from heaven and saves me.
  He punishes those who chase me.   *Selah*^d

  God sends me his love and truth.

⁴Enemies, like lions, are all around me;
  I must lie down among them.
  Their teeth are like spears and arrows,
    their tongues as sharp as swords.

FRIENDS

Sisterly Love?

Vicky and her twin sister Sarah were like two peas in a pod to look at, but completely opposite in character. Vicky was the rebel, always staying out later than the deadline, up for the latest thrill, and into the latest extreme fashion or trend. Sarah, although not perfect, enjoyed school and studying, wasn't bothered about going to all the "cool" parties or being seen hanging around with the "right" group. In spite of their differences, Sarah and Vicky were close friends.

When she wasn't out shopping or hanging out with her sister, Vicky spent a lot of time with her boyfriend Blake, who had also become one of her best friends. After one particular spending spree, Vicky came home to find Blake and her sister, Sarah, kissing in the front room. Vicky couldn't believe her eyes and felt devastated, utterly betrayed by her two closest friends.

David was also betrayed by a close friend. Read **Psalm 55** to see how hurtful he found it.

* Why was the betrayal experienced by Vicky and David so hurtful?
* How can verse 22 help you deal with betrayal by a friend?

Consider . . .

* asking God to forgive you if you've betrayed a friend or allowing God to help you forgive a friend who has betrayed you.
* whether you can mend a friendship or relationship that has been broken by betrayal, by talking to the people concerned.

For more, see . . .

* Proverbs 17:9 (p.604)
* Luke 22:1–6 (p.1087)

* Matthew 26:69–75 (p.990)

⁵God is supreme over the skies;
   his majesty covers the earth.

⁶They set a trap for me.
   I am very worried.
 They dug a pit in my path,
   but they fell into it themselves.   *Selah*

⁷My heart is steady, God; my heart is steady.
   I will sing and praise you.
⁸Wake up, my soul.
   Wake up, harp and lyre! *d*
   I will wake up the dawn.

⁹Lord, I will praise you among the
      nations;
   I will sing songs of praise about you to all
      the nations.
¹⁰Your great love reaches to the skies,
   your truth to the clouds.
¹¹God, you are supreme above the skies.
   Let your glory be over all the earth.

Unfair Judges

For the director of music. To the tune of "Do Not
Destroy". A miktam *d* of David.

58 Do you rulers really say what is right?
      Do you judge people fairly?
²No, in your heart you plan evil;
   you think up violent crimes in the land.
³From birth, evil people turn away
      from God;
   they wander off and tell lies as soon as they
      are born.
⁴They are like poisonous snakes,
   like deaf cobras that stop up their ears
⁵so they cannot hear the music of the snake
      charmer
   no matter how well he plays.

⁶God, break the teeth in their mouths!
   Tear out the fangs of those lions, LORD!
⁷Let them disappear like water that
      flows away.
   Let them be cut short like a broken
      arrow.
⁸Let them be like snails that melt as they
      move.
   Let them be like a child born dead who
      never saw the sun.
⁹His anger will blow them away alive
   faster than burning thorns can heat
      a pot.
¹⁰Good people will be glad when they see him
      take revenge.
   They will wash their feet in the blood of
      the wicked.
¹¹Then people will say,
   "There really are rewards for doing what
      is right.

There really is a God who judges the
   world."

A Prayer for Protection

For the director of music. To the tune of "Do Not
Destroy". A miktam *d* of David when Saul sent men to
watch David's house to kill him.

59 God, save me from my enemies.
      Protect me from those who come
      against me.
²Save me from those who do evil
   and from murderers.

³Look, men are waiting to ambush me.
   Cruel men attack me,
   but I have not sinned or done wrong,
      LORD.
⁴I have done nothing wrong, but they are
      ready to attack me.
   Wake up to help me, and look.
⁵You are the LORD God All-powerful, the God
      of Israel.
   Arise and punish those people.
   Do not give those traitors any
      mercy.   *Selah* *d*

⁶They come back at night.
   Like dogs they growl and roam round the
      city.
⁷Notice what comes from their mouths.
   Insults come from their lips,
   because they say, "Who's listening?"
⁸But, LORD, you laugh at them;
   you make fun of all of them.
⁹God, my strength, I am looking to you,
   because God is my defender.
¹⁰My God loves me,
   and he goes in front of me.

He will help me defeat my enemies.
¹¹Lord, our protector, do not kill them, or my
      people will forget.
   With your power scatter them and defeat
      them.
¹²They sin by what they say;
   they sin with their words.
 They curse and tell lies,
   so let their pride trap them.
¹³Destroy them in your anger;
   destroy them completely!
 Then they will know
   that God rules over Israel
   and to the ends of the earth.   *Selah*

¹⁴They come back at night.
   Like dogs they growl
   and roam round the city.
¹⁵They wander about looking for food,
   and they howl if they do not find
      enough.

16But I will sing about your strength.
  In the morning I will sing about your
    love.
  You are my defender,
    my place of safety in times of trouble.

17God, my strength, I will sing praises to you.
  God, my defender, you are the God who
    loves me.

A Prayer After a Defeat

For the director of music. To the tune of "Lily of the
Agreement". A miktam *d* of David. For teaching. When
David fought the Arameans of North West
Mesopotamia and Zobah, and when Joab returned and
defeated 12,000 Edomites at the Valley of Salt.

60
God, you have rejected us and
  scattered us.
You have been angry, but please come back
  to us.
2You made the earth shake and crack.
  Heal its breaks because it is shaking.
3You have given your people trouble.
  You made us unable to walk straight, like
    people drunk with wine.

4You have raised a banner to gather those
    who fear you.
  Now they can stand up against the enemy.
                                        Selah *d*

5Answer us and save us by your power
  so the people you love will be rescued.
6God has said from his Temple, *d*
  "When I win, I will divide Shechem
    and measure off the Valley of Succoth.
7Gilead and Manasseh are mine.
  Ephraim is like my helmet.
  Judah holds my royal sceptre. *d*
8Moab is like my washbowl.
  I throw my sandals at Edom.
  I shout at Philistia."

9Who will bring me to the fortified city?
  Who will lead me to Edom?
10God, surely you have rejected us;
  you do not go out with our armies.
11Help us fight the enemy.
  Human help is useless,
12but we can win with God's help.
  He will defeat our enemies.

A Prayer for Protection

For the director of music. With stringed instruments.
Of David.

61
God, hear my cry;
  listen to my prayer.

2I call to you from the ends of the earth
  when I am afraid.

Carry me away to a high mountain.
3You have been my protection,
  like a strong tower against my enemies.

4Let me live in your Holy Tent *d* for ever.
  Let me find safety in the shelter of your
    wings.   *Selah* *d*
5God, you have heard my promises.
  You have given me what belongs to those
    who fear you.

6Give the king a long life;
  let him live many years.
7Let him rule in the presence of God
    for ever.
  Protect him with your love and truth.

8Then I will praise your name for ever,
  and every day I will keep my promises.

Trust Only in God

For the director of music. For Jeduthun.
A psalm of David.

62
I find rest in God;
  only he can save me.
2He is my rock and my salvation.
  He is my defender;
  I will not be defeated.

3How long will you attack someone?
  Will all of you kill that person?
  Who is like a leaning wall, like a fence
    ready to fall?
4They are planning to make that person
    fall.
  They enjoy telling lies.
  With their mouths they bless,
    but in their hearts they curse.   *Selah* *d*

5I find rest in God alone;
  only he gives me hope.
6He is my rock and my salvation.
  He is my defender;
  I will not be defeated.
7My honour and salvation come from God.
  He is my mighty rock and my protection.

8People, trust God all the time.
  Tell him all your problems,
  because God is our protection.   *Selah*

9The least of people are only a breath,
  and even the greatest are just a lie.
  On the scales, they weigh nothing;
    together they are only a breath.
10Do not trust in force.
  Stealing is of no use.
  Even if you gain more riches,
    don't put your trust in them.

11God has said this,
  and I have heard it over and over:

God is strong.

¹²The Lord is loving.
   You reward people for what they have
      done.

Wishing to be Near God

A psalm of David when he was in the Desert of Judah.

63 God, you are my God.
         I search for you.
I thirst for you
   like someone in a dry, empty land
   where there is no water.

²I have seen you in the Temple *d*
   and have seen your strength and glory.
³Because your love is better than life,
   I will praise you.
⁴I will praise you as long as I live.
   I will lift up my hands in prayer to your
      name.

⁵I will be content as if I had eaten the best
      foods.
   My lips will sing, and my mouth will
      praise you.

⁶I remember you while I'm lying in my
      bed;
   I think about you through the night.
⁷You are my help.
   Because of your protection, I sing.
⁸I stay close to you;
   you support me with your right hand.

⁹Some people are trying to kill me,
   but they will go down to the grave.
¹⁰They will be killed with swords
   and eaten by wild dogs.

¹¹But the king will rejoice in his God.
   All who make promises in his name will
      praise him,
   but the mouths of liars will be shut.

WORRYING

Not in My Hands

Millie wasn't a happy person. She wasn't "glass is half empty" so much as not really having a glass at all! She was draining to be around because every little thing that happened was, to her, just something else that could go wrong. She was always worrying about things that were due to happen the next day, the next week, the next month. And her mind took her off on wild imaginings as she daydreamed about the terrible things that could be around the corner. Millie often got into bed at night and couldn't really remember much about the day.

Leo Buscaglia writes, "Worry never robs tomorrow of its sorrow, it only saps today of its joy."

Worry is assuming responsibilities you can't handle. The truth is that God never intended you to handle certain situations or problems on your own, because they were his to start with.

You can learn to control what goes on in your mind. How? By filling it with God's Word, applying it to each situation as it arises and leaning on it in the hard times, as David does in **Psalm 62**.

* David went through some really hard times. Why do you think he was able to write these words to God even though he was struggling?
* Why is it a sin to worry about situations?

Consider . . .

* all the situations that you worry about and pray that God will help you imagine a better scenario.
* every time you feel yourself worrying, saying out loud or in your head "I take captive those thoughts and make them obedient to you Lord" (2 Corinthians 10:5).

For more, see . . .

* Matthew 6:25 (p.948)
* Philippians 4:6–9 (p.1285)
* John 14:27 (p.1124)

A Prayer Against Enemies

For the director of music. A psalm of David.

64 God, listen to my complaint.
I am afraid of my enemies;
protect my life from them.
2Hide me from those who plan wicked
things,
from that mob who does evil.

3They sharpen their tongues like swords
and shoot bitter words like arrows.
4From their hiding places they shoot at
innocent people;
they shoot suddenly and are not afraid.

5They encourage each other to do wrong.
They talk about setting traps,
thinking no one will see them.
6They plan wicked things and say,
"We have a perfect plan."
The mind of human beings is hard to
understand.

7But God will shoot them with arrows;
they will suddenly be struck down.
8Their own words will be used against
them.
All who see them will shake their
heads.

9Then everyone will fear God.
They will tell what God has done,
and they will learn from what he has
done.
10Good people will be happy in the LORD
and will find protection in him.
Let everyone who is honest praise the
LORD.

A Hymn of Thanksgiving

For the director of music. A psalm of David. A song.

65 God, you will be praised in Jerusalem.
We will keep our promises to you.
2You hear our prayers.
All people will come to you.
3Our guilt overwhelms us,
but you forgive our sins.
4Happy are the people you choose
and invite to stay in your court.
We are filled with good things in your
house,
your holy Temple. *d*

5You answer us in amazing ways,
God our Saviour.
People everywhere on the earth
and beyond the sea trust you.
6You made the mountains by your strength;

you are dressed in power.
7You stopped the roaring seas,
the roaring waves,
and the uproar of the nations.
8Even those people at the ends of the earth
fear your miracles. *d*
You are praised from where the sun rises to
where it sets.

9You take care of the land and water it;
you make it very fertile.
The rivers of God are full of water.
Grain grows because you make it grow.
10You send rain to the ploughed fields;
you fill the rows with water.
You soften the ground with rain,
and then you bless it with crops.
11You give the year a good harvest,
and you load the wagons with many
crops.
12The desert is covered with grass
and the hills with happiness.
13The pastures are full of flocks,
and the valleys are covered with grain.
Everything shouts and sings for joy.

Praise God for What He Has Done

For the director of music. A song. A psalm.

66 Everything on earth, shout with joy
to God!
2Sing about his glory!
Make his praise glorious!
3Say to God, "Your works are amazing!
Because your power is great,
your enemies fall before you.
4All the earth worships you
and sings praises to you.
They sing praises to your name."   *Selah* *d*

5Come and see what God has done,
the amazing things he has done for people.
6He turned the sea into dry land.
The people crossed the river on foot.
So let us rejoice because of what he has
done.
7He rules for ever with his power.
He keeps his eye on the nations,
so people should not turn against him.   *Selah*

8You people, praise our God;
loudly sing his praise.
9He protects our lives
and does not let us be defeated.
10God, you have tested us;
you have purified us like silver.
11You let us be trapped
and put a heavy load on us.
12You let our enemies walk on our heads.

We went through fire and flood,
  but you brought us to a place with good
    things.
[13]I will come to your Temple *d* with burnt
    offerings.
  I will give you what I promised,
[14] objects I promised to you when I was in
    trouble.
[15]I will bring you offerings of fat animals,
  and I will offer rams, bulls and goats.   *Selah*

[16]All of you who fear God, come and listen,
  and I will tell you what he has done
    for me.
[17]I cried out to him with my mouth
  and praised him with my tongue.
[18]If I had known of any sin in my heart,
  the Lord would not have listened to me.
[19]But God has listened;
  he has heard my prayer.
[20]Praise God,
  who did not ignore my prayer
  or hold back his love from me.

Everyone Should Praise God

For the director of music. With stringed instruments.
A psalm. A song.

67 God, have mercy on us and bless us
  and show us your kindness   *Selah**d*

[2]so the world will learn your ways,
  and all nations will learn that you can save.

[3]God, the people should praise you;
  all people should praise you.
[4]The nations should be glad and sing
  because you judge people fairly.
  You guide all the nations on earth.   *Selah*

[5]God, the people should praise you;
  all people should praise you.

[6]The land has given its crops.
  God, our God, blesses us.
[7]God blesses us
  so people all over the earth will fear him.

Praise God Who Saved the Nation

For the director of music. A psalm of David. A song.

68 Let God rise up and scatter his
      enemies;
  let those who hate him run away
    from him.
[2]Blow them away as smoke
  is driven away by the wind.
  As wax melts before a fire,
    let the wicked be destroyed before God.
[3]But those who do right should be glad

and should rejoice before God;
  they should be happy and glad.

[4]Sing to God; sing praises to his name.
  Prepare the way for him
    who rides through the desert,
  whose name is the LORD.
  Rejoice before him.
[5]God is in his holy Temple. *d*
  He is a father to orphans,
    and he defends the widows.
[6]God gives the lonely a home.
  He leads prisoners out with joy,
    but those who turn against God will live in
      a dry land.

Sidelight

Israelite con men should
have known better than
to harass orphans and widows, two groups of
people who had a special place in God's heart
(Psalm 68:5). Look up the penalty for cheating
the defenceless in Exodus 22:22–24, p.82.

---

[7]God, you led your people out
  when you marched through the desert.
                                          *Selah**d*
[8]The ground shook
  and the sky poured down rain
  before God, the God of Mount Sinai,
    before God, the God of Israel.
[9]God, you sent much rain;
  you refreshed your tired land.
[10]Your people settled there.
  God, in your goodness
    you took care of the poor.

[11]The Lord gave the command,
  and a great army told the news:
[12]"Kings and their armies run away.
  In camp they divide the wealth taken
    in war.
[13]Those who stayed by the campfires
  will share the riches taken in battle."
[14]The Almighty scattered kings
  like snow on Mount Zalmon.

[15]The mountains of Bashan are high;
  the mountains of Bashan have many
    peaks.
[16]Why do you mountains with many peaks
  look with envy
    on the mountain that God chose for his
      home?
  The LORD will live there for ever.
[17]God comes with millions of chariots;

the Lord comes from Mount Sinai to his
holy place.
18When you went up to the heights,
you led a parade of captives.
You received gifts from the people,
even from those who turned against you.
And the LORD God will live there.

19Praise the Lord, God our Saviour,
who helps us every day.   *Selah*
20Our God is a God who saves us;
the LORD God saves us from death.

21God will crush his enemies' heads,
the hairy skulls of those who continue to sin.
22The Lord said, "I will bring the enemy back
from Bashan;
I will bring them back from the depths of
the sea.
23Then you can stick your feet in their blood,
and your dogs can lick their share."

24God, people have seen your victory march;
God my King marched into the holy place.
25The singers are in front and the instruments
are behind.

In the middle are the girls with the
tambourines. *d*
26Praise God in the meeting place;
praise the LORD in the gathering of Israel.
27There is the smallest tribe,*d* Benjamin,
leading them.
And there are the leaders of Judah with
their group.
There also are the leaders of Zebulun and
of Naphtali.

28God, order up your power;
show the mighty power you have used for
us before.
29Kings will bring their wealth to you,
to your Temple in Jerusalem.
30Punish Egypt, the beast in the tall grass along
the river.
Punish the leaders of nations, those bulls
among the cows.
Defeated, they will bring you their silver.
Scatter those nations that love war.
31Messengers will come from Egypt;
the people of Cush will pray to God.

LONELINESS

On the Road Again

"Sometimes I think we're gypsies," Rebecca confesses, describing the way her family has moved seven times in four years. "When your father's in the army, you get used to it."

She laughs, but it sounds forced, and she looks away. There's a sadness in her voice, and she seems a little scared.

"You know, it's not that easy leaving friends and making new ones. When you're new, it helps a lot if people come up and introduce themselves," she says softly. "Or ask you to go to a club or church group meeting with them, or just to get a Coke. Loneliness must be one of the worst feelings in the world."

Everyone feels lonely sometimes. But, like Rebecca, we all have a home with God no matter how alone we may feel. Read **Psalm 68:1–10** to find God's assurance that he gives the lonely a place to belong.

* How do you think Rebecca would define the word "home" in this psalm?
* When you're feeling lonely, what sort of "home" do you think faith in God's love can help you to build?

Consider . . .

* organising a "welcome team" of kids to greet newcomers to your school or church.
* widening your circle of friends by making a list of talents that God has given you, including personality traits, such as a sense of humour, or the ability to listen, and using the list to guide you to new clubs and activities.

For more, see . . .

* Job 19:13–27 (p.481)   * Matthew 28:18–20 (p.995)
* 2 Timothy 4:16–18 (p.1321)

32Kingdoms of the earth, sing to God;
   sing praises to the Lord.   *Selah*
33Sing to the one who rides through the skies,
      which are from long ago.
   He speaks with a thundering voice.
34Announce that God is powerful.
   He rules over Israel,
   and his power is in the skies.
35God, you are wonderful in your Temple.
   The God of Israel gives his people strength
      and power.

   Praise God!

A Cry for Help

For the director of music. To the tune of "Lilies".
A psalm of David.

69 God, save me,
   because the water has risen to my
      neck.
2I'm sinking down into the mud,
   and there is nothing to stand on.
I am in deep water,
   and the flood covers me.
3I am tired from calling for help;
   my throat is sore.
My eyes are tired from waiting
   for God to help me.
4There are more people who hate me for no
      reason than hairs on my head;
   powerful enemies want to destroy me for
      no reason.
They make me pay back
   what I did not steal.

5God, you know what I have done wrong;
   I cannot hide my guilt from you.
6Lord GOD All-powerful,
   do not let those who hope in you be
      ashamed because of me.
God of Israel,
   do not let your worshippers be disgraced
      because of me.
7For you, I carry this shame,
   and my face is covered with disgrace.
8I am like a stranger to my closest relatives
   and a foreigner to my mother's children.
9My strong love for your Temple *d* completely
      controls me.
   When people insult you, it hurts me.
10When I cry and go without food,
   they make fun of me.
11When I wear clothes of sadness,
   they joke about me.
12They make fun of me in public places,
   and the drunkards make up songs about me.

13But I pray to you, LORD, for favour.
   God, because of your great love, answer me.

You are truly able to save.
14Pull me from the mud,
   and do not let me sink.
Save me from those who hate me
   and from the deep water.
15Do not let the flood drown me
   or the deep water swallow me
   or the grave close its mouth over me.
16LORD, answer me because your love is so good.
   Because of your great kindness, turn to me.
17Do not hide from me, your servant.
   I am in trouble. Hurry to help me!
18Come near and save me;
   rescue me from my enemies.
19You see my shame and disgrace.
   You know all my enemies and what they
      have said.
20Insults have broken my heart
   and left me weak.
   I looked for sympathy, but there was none;
   I found no one to comfort me.
21They put poison in my food
   and gave me vinegar to drink.

22Let their own feasts cause their ruin;
   let their feasts trap them and pay them back.
23Let their eyes be closed so they cannot see
   and their backs be for ever weak from
      troubles.
24Pour your anger out on them;
   let your anger catch up with them.
25May their place be empty;
   leave no one to live in their tents.
26They chase after those you have hurt,
   and they talk about the pain of those you
      have wounded.
27Charge them with crime after crime,
   and do not let them have anything good.
28Wipe their names from the book of life,
   and do not list them with those who do
      what is right.

29I am sad and hurting.
   God, save me and protect me.
30I will praise God in a song
   and will honour him by giving thanks.
31That will please the LORD more than offering
      him cattle,
   more than sacrificing a bull with horns and
      hoofs.
32Poor people will see this and be glad.
   Be encouraged, you who worship God.
33The LORD listens to those in need
   and does not look down on captives.

34Heaven and earth should praise him,
   the seas and everything in them.
35God will save Jerusalem
   and rebuild the cities of Judah.

Then people will live there and own the land.
36 The descendants *d* of his servants will
      inherit that land,
and those who love him will live there.

A Cry for God to Help Quickly

For the director of music. A psalm of David. To help
people remember.

70 God, come quickly and save me.
     Lᴏʀᴅ, hurry to help me.
2Let those who are trying to kill me
  be ashamed and disgraced.
Let those who want to hurt me
  run away in disgrace.
3Let those who make fun of me
  stop because of their shame.
4But let all those who worship you
  rejoice and be glad.

Let those who love your salvation
  always say, "Praise the greatness
    of God."

5I am poor and helpless;
  God, hurry to me.
You help me and save me.
  Lᴏʀᴅ, do not wait.

An Old Person's Prayer

71 In you, Lᴏʀᴅ, is my protection.
    Never let me be ashamed.
2Because you do what is right, save and
  rescue me;
listen to me and save me.
3Be my place of safety
  where I can always come.
Give the command to save me,

PERSISTENCE

Follow Your Dreams

Jane loved to dance. She had been doing it ever since she was little and now she was older she was starting to think that maybe she could make a career out of it. However, many of her school mates thought dancing was silly and would regularly make fun of her, her dancing and anything else they could in order to make her feel small. "It's a waste of time," they'd say, "you'll never be good enough." Though the comments really hurt Jane, she was determined to carry on because she knew how much fun dancing was for her and how good it was for keeping her fit.

After she finished school, she went to college to train as a dancer, and years later, after lots of hard work and dedication, she was asked to be the company's principal dancer. As the curtains opened on her first professional performance, she smiled with pride, knowing that all her hard work and perseverance had paid off. Thank goodness she hadn't given in to the taunts back in school, otherwise she would have missed out on all this.

Jane had to battle through people judging her and making fun of her because they didn't understand something that she was so passionate about.

* Jane's passion was dancing. What was it in **Psalm 69:6–15** that David was so passionate about?
* What is similar in the way that both Jane and King David coped with their situations?

Consider . . .

* how you'd feel if you were misunderstood and mocked by people around you because of something they didn't understand? Consider whether you've ever done the same to another person. If you have, go to them and say sorry.
* writing a list of things you are passionate about and that you would be prepared to persevere through difficult situations for.

For more, see . . .

* Romans 4:18–25 (p.1190)
* James 5:7–16 (p.1352)

* Hebrews 12:1–3 (p.1343)

because you are my rock and my fortified
 city.
⁴My God, save me from the power of the
 wicked
and from the hold of evil and cruel
 people.

⁵Lord, you are my hope.
 Lord, I have trusted you since I was
 young.
⁶I have depended on you since I was born;
 you helped me even on the day of my
 birth.
 I will always praise you.

⁷I am an example to many people,
 because you are my strong protection.
⁸I am always praising you;
 all day long I honour you.

⁹Do not reject me when I am old;
 do not leave me when my strength
 is gone.
¹⁰My enemies make plans against me,
 and they meet together to kill me.
¹¹They say, "God has left him.
 Go after him and take him,
 because no one will save him."
¹²God, don't be far off.
 My God, hurry to help me.
¹³Let those who accuse me
 be ashamed and destroyed.
 Let those who are trying to hurt me
 be covered with shame and disgrace.

¹⁴But I will always have hope
 and will praise you more and more.
¹⁵I will tell how you do what is right.
 I will tell about your salvation all day long,
 even though it is more than I can tell.
¹⁶I will come and tell about your powerful
 works, Lord God.
 I will remind people that only you do what
 is right.

¹⁷God, you have taught me since I was
 young.
 To this day I tell about the miracles *d*
 you do.
¹⁸Even though I am old and grey,
 do not leave me, God.
 I will tell the children about your power;
 I will tell those who live after me about
 your might.

¹⁹God, your justice reaches to the skies.
 You have done great things;
 God, there is no one like you.
²⁰You have given me many troubles and bad
 times,
 but you will give me life again.

When I am almost dead,
 you will keep me alive.
²¹You will make me greater than ever,
 and you will comfort me again.

²²I will praise you with the harp.
 I trust you, my God.
 I will sing to you with the lyre, *d*
 Holy One of Israel.
²³I will shout for joy when I sing praises
 to you.
 You have saved me.
²⁴I will tell about your justice all day long.
 And those who want to hurt me
 will be ashamed and disgraced.

A Prayer for the King

Of Solomon.

72 God, give the king your good
 judgement
and the king's son your goodness.
²Help him judge your people fairly
 and decide what is right for the poor.
³Let there be peace on the mountains
 and goodness on the hills for the
 people.
⁴Help him be fair to the poor
 and save the needy
 and punish those who hurt them.

⁵May they respect you as long as the sun
 shines
 and as long as the moon glows.
⁶Let him be like rain on the grass,
 like showers that water the earth.
⁷Let goodness be plentiful while he lives.
 Let peace continue as long as there is a
 moon.

⁸Let his kingdom go from sea to sea,
 and from the Euphrates River to the ends
 of the earth.
⁹Let the people of the desert bow down
 to him,
 and make his enemies lick the dust.
¹⁰Let the kings of Tarshish and the faraway
 lands
 bring him gifts.
 Let the kings of Sheba and Seba
 bring their presents to him.
¹¹Let all kings bow down to him
 and all nations serve him.

¹²He will help the poor when they cry out
 and will save the needy when no one else
 will help.
¹³He will be kind to the weak and poor,
 and he will save their lives.

[14]He will save them from cruel people who try
     to hurt them,
  because their lives are precious to him.

[15]Long live the king!
  Let him receive gold from Sheba.
Let people always pray for him
  and bless him all day long.
[16]Let the fields grow plenty of grain
  and the hills be covered with crops.
Let the land be as fertile as Lebanon,
  and let the cities grow like the grass in a
     field.
[17]Let the king be famous for ever;
  let him be remembered as long as the sun
     shines.

Let the nations be blessed because of him,
  and may they all bless him.

[18]Praise the LORD God, the God of Israel,
  who alone does such miracles. [d]

[19]Praise his glorious name for ever.
  Let his glory fill the whole world.
        Amen and amen.

[20]This ends the prayers of David son of Jesse.

Book 3

Should the Wicked Be Rich?

A psalm of Asaph.

73 God is truly good to Israel,
        to those who have pure hearts.

[2]But I had almost stopped believing;
  I had almost lost my faith
[3]because I was jealous of proud people.
  I saw wicked people doing well.

[4]They are not suffering;
  they are healthy and strong.
[5]They don't have troubles like the rest
  of us;

HUNGER AND POVERTY

Making Apathy History

Bob Geldolf and Bono were the figureheads for the huge "Make Poverty History" campaign in 2005 which included the amazing "Live8" gigs and led rich governments to release billions in debt relief. There is a long way to go, but their actions have played a part in making the world a fairer place.

If you trace the campaign back to its roots, you will find a small group of nameless, praying Christians who met in a flat in London, inspired by words like those in **Psalm 72**: "decide what is right for the poor" and "be fair to the poor". They launched the "Jubilee 2000" campaign. Their prayers and their actions clearly touched the heart of God, and a worldwide movement for change was born. Millions wore wristbands, marched, petitioned and wrote to governments urging them to "be kind to the weak and poor".

Bob and Bono did a great job, but all their ranting would have come to nothing without the army of anonymous caring people who birthed the movement and maintained it through their efforts.

On one occasion, Mother Theresa, the remarkable nun who devoted her life to caring for the poorest of the poor in India, was asked by a cynical journalist, "Surely your work is just a drop in the ocean of need." Her wonderful answer was, "Yes, but the ocean is made up of tiny drops."

* What would it mean for you to "be fair to the poor" in the way you act?
* What good work by non-Christian companies or groups could you support in prayer?

Consider . . .

* praying for your youth leaders and parents that God would give them his heart to "do what is right for the poor".
* putting aside some of your money every week, specifically for work amongst the poor. Ask God to guide you as to where you should send it.

For more, see . . .

* Deuteronomy 14:22–29 (p.179)
* 2 Corinthians 9:6–11 (p.1248)

* Proverbs 14:31 (p.602)

they don't have problems like other
people.
⁶They wear pride like a necklace
and put on violence as their clothing.
⁷They are looking for profits
and do not control their selfish desires.
⁸They make fun of others and speak evil;
proudly they speak of hurting others.
⁹They boast to the sky.
They say that they own the earth.
¹⁰So their people turn to them
and give them whatever they want.
¹¹They say, "How can God know?
What does God Most High know?"

¹²These people are wicked,
always at ease and getting richer.
¹³So why have I kept my heart pure?
Why have I kept my hands from doing
wrong?
¹⁴I have suffered all day long;
I have been punished every morning.

¹⁵God, if I had decided to talk like this,
I would have let your people down.
¹⁶I tried to understand all this,
but it was too hard for me to see
¹⁷until I went to the Temple *d* of God.
Then I understood what will happen to
them.

¹⁸You have put them in danger;
you cause them to be destroyed.
¹⁹They are destroyed in a moment;
they are swept away by terrors.
²⁰It will be like waking from a dream.
Lord, when you rise up, they will
disappear.

²¹When my heart was sad
and I was angry,
²²I was senseless and stupid.
I acted like an animal towards you.

²³But I am always with you;
you have held my hand.
²⁴You guide me with your advice,
and later you will receive me in honour.
²⁵I have no one in heaven but you;
I want nothing on earth besides you.
²⁶My body and my mind may become weak,
but God is my strength.
He is mine for ever.

²⁷Those who are far from God will die;
you destroy those who are unfaithful.
²⁸But I am close to God, and that is good.
The Lord GOD is my protection.
I will tell all that you have done.

A Nation in Trouble Prays

A maskil *d* of Asaph.

74 God, why have you rejected us for so
long?
Why are you angry with us, the sheep of
your pasture?
²Remember the people you bought long ago.
You saved us, and we are your very own.
After all, you live on Mount Zion. *d*
³Make your way through these old ruins;
the enemy wrecked everything in the
Temple. *d*

⁴Those who were against you shouted in your
meeting place
and raised their flags there.
⁵They came with axes raised
as if to cut down a forest of trees.
⁶They smashed the carved panels
with their axes and hatchets.
⁷They burned your Temple to the ground;
they have made the place where you live
unclean. *d*
⁸They thought, "We will completely crush
them!"
They burned every place where God was
worshipped in the land.
⁹We do not see any signs.
There are no more prophets, *d*
and no one knows how long this will last.

¹⁰God, how much longer will the enemy make
fun of you?
Will they insult you for ever?
¹¹Why do you hold back your power?
Bring your power out in the open and
destroy them!

¹²God, you have been our king for a long time.
You bring salvation to the earth.
¹³You split open the sea by your power
and broke the heads of the sea monster.
¹⁴You smashed the heads of the monster
Leviathan *d*
and gave him to the desert creatures as
food.
¹⁵You opened up the springs and streams
and made the flowing rivers run dry.
¹⁶Both the day and the night are yours;
you made the sun and the moon.
¹⁷You set all the limits on the earth;
you created summer and winter.

¹⁸LORD, remember how the enemy insulted you.
Remember how those foolish people made
fun of you.
¹⁹Do not give us, your doves, to those wild
animals.
Never forget your poor people.

20Remember the agreement you made
with us,
because violence fills every dark corner of
this land.
21Do not let your suffering people be disgraced.
Let the poor and helpless praise you.

22God, arise and defend yourself.
Remember the insults that come from those
foolish people all day long.
23Don't forget what your enemies said;
don't forget their roar as they rise against
you always.

God the Judge

For the director of music. To the tune of "Do Not
Destroy". A psalm of Asaph. A song.

75

God, we thank you;
we thank you because you are near.
We tell about the miracles *d* you do.

2You say, "I set the time for trial,
and I will judge fairly.
3The earth with all its people may shake,
but I am the one who holds it steady.   *Selah d*
4I say to those who are proud, 'Don't boast,'
and to the wicked, 'Don't show your
power.
5Don't try to use your power against
heaven.
Don't be stubborn.'"

6No one from the east or the west
or the desert can judge you.
7God is the judge;
he judges one person as guilty and another
as innocent.
8The LORD holds a cup of anger in his hand;
it is full of wine mixed with spices.
He pours it out even to the last drop,
and the wicked drink it all.

9I will tell about this for ever;
I will sing praise to the God of Jacob.
10He will take all power away from the
wicked,
but the power of the good people will
grow.

The God Who Always Wins

For the director of music. With stringed instruments.
A psalm of Asaph. A song.

76

People in Judah know God;
his fame is great in Israel.
2His Tent *d* is in Jerusalem;
his home is on Mount Zion. *d*
3There God broke the flaming arrows,
the shields, the swords and the weapons of
war.   *Selah d*

4God, how wonderful you are!
You are more wonderful than the hills full
of animals.
5The brave soldiers were stripped
as they lay asleep in death.
Not one warrior
had the strength to stop it.
6God of Jacob, when you spoke strongly,
horses and riders fell dead.
7You are feared;
no one can stand against you when you are
angry.
8From heaven you gave the decision,
and the earth was afraid and silent.
9God, you stood up to judge
and to save the needy people of the earth.
                                                              Selah
10People praise you for your anger against evil.
Those who live through your anger are
stopped from doing more evil.

11Make and keep your promises to the LORD
your God.
From all around, gifts should come to the
God we worship.
12God breaks the spirits of great leaders;
the kings on earth fear him.

Remembering God's Help

For the director of music. For Jeduthun.
A psalm of Asaph.

77

I cry out to God;
I call to God, and he will hear me.
2I look for the Lord on the day of trouble.
All night long I reach out my hands,
but I cannot be comforted.

3When I remember you God, I become
upset;
when I think, I become afraid.   *Selah d*

4You keep my eyes from closing.
I am too upset to say anything.
5I keep thinking about the old days,
the years of long ago.
6At night I remember my songs.
I think and I ask myself:

7"Will the Lord reject us for ever?
Will he never be kind to us again?
8Is his love gone for ever?
Has he stopped speaking for all time?
9Has God forgotten mercy?
Is he too angry to pity us?"   *Selah*

10Then I say, "This is what makes me sad:
for years the power of God Most High was
with us."

11I remember what the LORD did;
I remember the miracles *d* you did long ago.

¹²I think about all the things you did
and consider your deeds.
¹³God, your ways are holy.
No god is as great as our God.
¹⁴You are the God who does miracles;
you have shown people your power.
¹⁵By your great power you have saved your
people,
the descendants *d* of Jacob and Joseph. *Selah*

¹⁶God, the waters saw you;
they saw you and became afraid;
the deep waters shook with fear.
¹⁷The clouds poured down their rain.
The sky thundered.
Your lightning flashed back and forth like
arrows.
¹⁸Your thunder could be heard in the
whirlwind.
Lightning lit up the world.
The earth trembled and shook.
¹⁹You made a way through the sea
and paths through the deep waters,
but your footprints were not seen.

²⁰You led your people like a flock
by using Moses and Aaron.

God Saved Israel from Egypt

A maskil d of Asaph.

78 My people, listen to my teaching;
listen to what I say.
²I will speak using stories;
I will tell secret things from long ago.
³We have heard them and known them
by what our ancestors have told us.
⁴We will not keep them from our children;
we will tell those who come later
about the praises of the LORD.
We will tell about his power
and the miracles *d* he has done.
⁵The LORD made an agreement with Jacob
and gave the Teachings to Israel,
which he commanded our ancestors
to teach to their children.
⁶Then their children would know them,
even their children not yet born.
And they would tell their children.
⁷So they would all trust God
and would not forget what he had done
but would obey his commands.
⁸They would not be like their ancestors
who were stubborn and disobedient.
Their hearts were not loyal to God,
and they were not true to him.

⁹The men of Ephraim had bows for weapons,
but they ran away on the day of battle.

¹⁰They didn't keep their agreement with God
and refused to live by his teachings.
¹¹They forgot what he had done
and the miracles he had shown them.
¹²He did miracles while their ancestors
watched,
in the fields of Zoan in Egypt.
¹³He divided the Red Sea *d* and led them
through.
He made the water stand up like a wall.
¹⁴He led them with a cloud by day
and by the light of a fire by night.
¹⁵He split the rocks in the desert
and gave them more than enough water, as
if from the deep ocean.
¹⁶He brought streams out of the rock
and caused water to flow down like rivers.

¹⁷But the people continued to sin against him;
in the desert they turned against God Most
High.
¹⁸They decided to test God
by asking for the food they wanted.
¹⁹Then they spoke against God,
saying, "Can God prepare food in the
desert?
²⁰When he hit the rock, water poured out
and rivers flowed down.
But can he give us bread also?
Will he provide his people with meat?"
²¹When the LORD heard them, he was very
angry.
His anger was like fire to the people of
Jacob;
his anger grew against the people of Israel.
²²They had not believed God
and had not trusted him to save them.
²³But he gave a command to the clouds above
and opened the doors of heaven.
²⁴He rained manna *d* down on them to eat;
he gave them grain from heaven.
²⁵So they ate the bread of angels.
He sent them all the food they could eat.
²⁶He sent the east wind from heaven
and led the south wind by his power.
²⁷He rained meat on them like dust.
The birds were as many as the sand of
the sea.
²⁸He made the birds fall inside the camp,
all around the tents.
²⁹So the people ate and became very full.
God had given them what they wanted.
³⁰While they were still eating,
and while the food was still in their mouths,
³¹God became angry with them.
He killed some of the healthiest of them;
he struck down the best young men of
Israel.

32But they kept on sinning;
   they did not believe even with the
      miracles.
33So he ended their days without meaning
   and their years in terror.
34Any time he killed them, they would look to
      him for help;
   they would come back to God and
      follow him.
35They would remember that God was their
      Rock, *d*
   that God Most High had saved them.
36But their words were false,
   and their tongues lied to him.
37Their hearts were not really loyal to God;
   they did not keep his agreement.
38Still God was merciful.
   He forgave their sins
   and did not destroy them.
Many times he held back his anger
   and did not stir up all his anger.
39He remembered that they were only
      human,
   like a wind that blows and does not come
      back.
40They turned against God so often in the
      desert
   and made him very sad there.
41Again and again they tested God
   and brought pain to the Holy One of
      Israel.
42They did not remember his power
   or the time he saved them from the
      enemy.
43They forgot the signs he did in Egypt
   and his wonders in the fields of Zoan.
44He turned their rivers to blood
   so no one could drink the water.
45He sent flies that bit the people.
   He sent frogs that destroyed them.
46He gave their crops to grasshoppers
   and what they worked for to locusts. *d*
47He destroyed their vines with hail
   and their sycamore trees with sleet.
48He killed their animals with hail
   and their cattle with lightning.
49He showed them his hot anger.
   He sent his strong anger against them,
   his destroying angels.
50He found a way to show his anger.
   He did not keep them from dying
   but let them die by a terrible disease.
51God killed all the firstborn *d* sons in
      Egypt,
   the oldest son of each family of Ham. *n*

52But God led his people out like sheep
   and he guided them like a flock through
      the desert.
53He led them to safety so they had nothing to
      fear,
   but their enemies drowned in the sea.
54So God brought them to his holy land,
   to the mountain country he took with his
      own power.
55He forced out the other nations,
   and he had his people inherit the land.
   He let the tribes *d* of Israel settle there in
      tents.

56But they tested God
   and turned against God Most High;
   they did not keep his rules.
57They turned away and were disloyal just like
      their ancestors.
   They were like a crooked bow that does
      not shoot straight.
58They made God angry by building places to
      worship gods;
   they made him jealous with their idols.
59When God heard them, he became very
      angry
   and rejected the people of Israel completely.
60He left his dwelling at Shiloh,
   the Tent where he lived among the
      people.
61He let the Ark, *d* his power, be captured;
   he let the Ark, his glory, be taken by
      enemies.
62He let his people be killed;
   he was very angry with his children.
63The young men died by fire,
   and the young women had no one to
      marry.
64Their priests fell by the sword,
   but their widows were not allowed to cry.

65Then the Lord got up as if he had been
      asleep;
   he awoke like a man who had been drunk
      with wine.
66He struck down his enemies
   and disgraced them for ever.
67But God rejected the family of Joseph;
   he did not choose the tribe of Ephraim.
68Instead, he chose the tribe of Judah
   and Mount Zion, *d* which he loves.
69And he built his Temple *d* high like the
      mountains.
   Like the earth, he built it to last for ever.
70He chose David to be his servant
   and took him from the sheep pens.

Ham   The people in Egypt were descendants of Ham, one of Noah's sons. See Genesis 10:6.

71He brought him from tending the sheep
so he could lead the flock, the people of
Jacob,
his own people, the people of Israel.
72And David led them with an innocent
heart
and guided them with skilful hands.

The Nation Cries for Jerusalem

A psalm of Asaph.

79

God, nations have come against your
chosen people.
They have ruined your holy Temple. *d*
They have turned Jerusalem into ruins.
2They have given the bodies of your servants
as food to the wild birds.
They have given the bodies of those who
worship you to the wild animals.
3They have spilled blood like water all around
Jerusalem.
No one was left to bury the dead.
4We are a joke to the other nations;
they laugh and make fun of us.

5Lord, how long will this last?
Will you be angry for ever?
How long will your jealousy burn like a
fire?
6Be angry with the nations that do not
know you
and with the kingdoms that do not
honour you.
7They have destroyed the people of Jacob
and destroyed their land.
8Don't punish us for our past sins.
Show your mercy to us soon,
because we are helpless!

9God our Saviour, help us
so people will praise you.
Save us and forgive our sins
so people will honour you.
10Why should the nations say,
"Where is their God?"
Tell the other nations in our presence
that you punish those who kill your
servants.
11Hear the moans of the prisoners.
Use your great power
to save those sentenced to die.

12Repay those around us seven times over
for their insults to you, Lord.
13We are your people, the sheep of your
flock.
We will thank you always;
for ever and ever we will praise you.

A Prayer to Bring Israel Back

For the director of music. To the tune of "Lilies of the
Agreement". A psalm of Asaph.

80

Shepherd of Israel, listen to us.
You lead the people of Joseph like a
flock.
You sit on your throne between the gold
creatures with wings.
Show your greatness 2to the people of
Ephraim, Benjamin and Manasseh.
Use your strength,
and come to save us.

3God, take us back.
Show us your kindness so we can be saved.

4Lord God All-powerful,
how long will you be angry
at the prayers of your people?
5You have fed your people with tears;
you have made them drink many tears.
6You made those around us fight over us,
and our enemies make fun of us.

7God All-powerful, take us back.
Show us your kindness so we can be saved.

8You brought us out of Egypt as if we were a
vine.
You forced out other nations and planted
us in the land.
9You cleared the ground for us.
Like a vine, we took root and filled the
land.
10We covered the mountains with our shade.
We had limbs like the mighty cedar tree.
11Our branches reached the Mediterranean Sea,
and our shoots went to the Euphrates River.

12So why did you pull down our walls?
Now everyone who passes by steals
from us.
13Like wild pigs they walk over us;
like wild animals they feed on us.

14God All-powerful, come back.
Look down from heaven and see.
Take care of us, your vine.
15 You planted this shoot with your own
hands
and strengthened this child.

16Now it is cut down and burned with fire;
you destroyed us by your angry looks.
17With your hand,
strengthen the one you have chosen for
yourself.
18Then we will not turn away from you.
Give us life again, and we will call to you
for help.

[19]LORD God All-powerful, take us back.
Show us your kindness so we can be saved.

A Song for a Holiday

For the director of music. By the gittith. *d* A psalm of
AsAph.

81
Sing for joy to God, our strength;
shout out loud to the God of Jacob.
[2]Begin the music. Play the tambourines. *d*
Play pleasant music on the harps and lyres. *d*

[3]Blow the trumpet at the time of the New
Moon, *d*
when the moon is full, when our feast begins.

> ### Sidelight
> The sheep's horn
> was used like a trumpet
> (Psalm 81:3). It is the only ancient instrument
> mentioned in the Bible that's still used in Jewish
> synagogues. It's made by heating and shaping
> the animal's hollow horn.

[4]This is the law for Israel;
it is the command of the God of Jacob.
[5]He gave this rule to the people of Joseph
when they went out of the land of Egypt.

I heard a language I did not know, saying:
[6]"I took the load off their shoulders;
I let them put down their baskets.
[7]When you were in trouble, you called, and I
saved you.
I answered you with thunder.
I tested you at the waters of Meribah.   *Selah* *d*
[8]My people, listen. I am warning you.
Israel, please listen to me!
[9]You must not have foreign gods;
you must not worship any false god.
[10]I, the LORD, am your God,
who brought you out of Egypt.
Open your mouth and I will feed you.

[11]"But my people did not listen to me;
Israel did not want me.
[12]So I let them go their stubborn way
and follow their own advice.

CELEBRATING

Shout Out Loud!

Imagine . . .

* Christmas without Christmas carols
* a wedding without the "Wedding March"
* the Trooping of the Colour without a band
* a party without music

Now for a really hard one. Imagine going for the rest of your life without a group of friends and relatives
singing "Happy Birthday"!
It would be pretty miserable, wouldn't it?
People have used music to celebrate life's joys for centuries, dating all the way back to ancient
writings such as the Psalms. **Psalm 81:1–10** calls people to shout and "sing for joy to God,
our strength" for God's goodness and gifts.

* Why do you think the psalmist included a variety of methods for celebrating?
* What way of celebrating God do you enjoy most?

Consider . . .

* putting a simple prayer to music and singing it to God.
* learning a new song or joining a music group to find new ways to worship God.

For more, see . . .

* 1 Chronicles 13:6–8 (p.386)
* Psalm 149 (p.588)
* Ephesians 5:15–20 (p.1275)

¹³"I wish my people would listen to me;
    I wish Israel would live my way.
¹⁴Then I would quickly defeat their enemies
    and turn my hand against their foes.
¹⁵Those who hate the LORD would bow
        before him.
    Their punishment would continue for ever.
¹⁶But I would give you the finest wheat
    and fill you with honey from the rocks."

A Cry for Justice

A psalm of Asaph.

82 God is in charge of the great meeting;
    he judges among the "gods".

²He says, "How long will you defend evil
        people?
    How long will you show greater kindness
        to the wicked?   *Selah*^d

³Defend the weak and the orphans;
    defend the rights of the poor and suffering.
⁴Save the weak and helpless;
    free them from the power of the wicked.

⁵"You know nothing. You don't understand.
    You walk in the dark,
        while the world is falling apart.

⁶"I said, 'You are "gods".
    You are all sons of God Most High.'
⁷But you will die like any other person;
    you will fall like all the leaders."

⁸God, come and judge the earth,
    because you own all the nations.

A Prayer Against the Enemies

A song. A psalm of Asaph.

83 God, do not keep quiet;
    God, do not be silent or still.
²Your enemies are making noises;
    those who hate you are getting ready to
        attack.
³They are making secret plans against your
        people;
    they plot against those you love.
⁴They say, "Come, let's destroy them as a
        nation.
    Then no one will ever remember the name
        'Israel'."

⁵They are united in their plan.
    These have made an agreement against you:
⁶the families of Edom and the Ishmaelites,
    Moab and the Hagrites,
⁷the people of Byblos, Ammon, Amalek,
    Philistia and Tyre.
⁸Even Assyria has joined them
    to help Ammon and Moab, the
        descendants^d of Lot.   *Selah*^d

⁹God, do to them what you did to Midian,
    what you did to Sisera and Jabin at the
        Kishon River.
¹⁰They died at Endor,
    and their bodies rotted on the ground.
¹¹Do to their important leaders what you did to
        Oreb and Zeeb.
    Do to their princes what you did to Zebah
        and Zalmunna.
¹²They said, "Let's take for ourselves
    the pasturelands that belong to God."

¹³My God, make them like tumbleweed,
    like chaff^d blown away by the wind.
¹⁴Be like a fire that burns a forest
    or like flames that blaze through the
        hills.
¹⁵Chase them with your storm,
    and frighten them with your wind.
¹⁶Cover them with shame.
    Then people will look for you, LORD.

¹⁷Make them afraid and ashamed for ever.
    Disgrace them and destroy them.
¹⁸Then they will know that you are the
        LORD,
    that only you are God Most High over all
        the earth.

> **Sidelight** Psalms 84 and 122 –
> among others – are
> pilgrim songs, "songs for the road". Three times
> a year, faithful Jews packed and got ready for
> the journey to Jerusalem – joining crowds of
> other "praise marchers" on the way.

Wishing to Be in the Temple

For the director of music. On the gittith. ^d *A psalm
of the sons of Korah.*

84 LORD All-powerful,
    how lovely is your Temple!^d
²I want more than anything
    to be in the courtyards of the LORD's
        Temple.
    My whole being wants
        to be with the living God.

³The sparrows have found a home,
    and the swallows have nests.
    They raise their young near your altars,
        LORD All-powerful, my King and my God.
⁴Happy are the people who live at your
        Temple;
    they are always praising you.   *Selah*^d
⁵Happy are those whose strength comes
        from you,
    who want to travel to Jerusalem.

⁶As they pass through the Valley of Baca,
  they make it like a spring.
  The autumn rains fill it with pools of
      water.
⁷The people get stronger as they go,
  and everyone meets with God in Jerusalem.

⁸Lord God All-powerful, hear my prayer;
  God of Jacob, listen to me.   *Selah*
⁹God, look at our shield;
  be kind to your appointed king.

¹⁰One day in the courtyards of your Temple is
      better
  than a thousand days anywhere else.
  I would rather be a doorkeeper in the
      Temple of my God
  than live in the homes of the wicked.
¹¹The Lord God is like a sun and shield;
  the Lord gives us kindness and honour.
  He does not hold back anything good
  from those whose lives are innocent.

¹²Lord All-powerful,
  happy are the people who trust you!

A Prayer for the Nation

For the director of music. A psalm
of the sons of Korah.

85 Lord, you have been kind to your land;
  you brought back the people of
  Jacob.
²You forgave the guilt of the people
  and covered all their sins.   *Selah*[d]
³You stopped all your anger;
  you turned back from your strong
      anger.

⁴God our Saviour, bring us back again.
  Stop being angry with us.
⁵Will you be angry with us for ever?
  Will you stay angry from now on?
⁶Won't you give us life again?
  Your people would rejoice in you.

WORSHIP

Present of Presence

Natasha was known at the youth club for having a violent temper. If anyone annoyed her or said anything bad to her, she would fly off the handle. She was even known to lash out at people when she was in a rage.

One particular evening the talk was about spending time with God and being in his presence. This was new to Natasha, but it sounded good and she wanted to know more. The speaker said that when we are in God's presence he can change us from the inside out and make us new.

At the end of the talk, Natasha's heart was racing and she went to find the leader who had been speaking. "What is it that you want from God?" the leader asked.

"I don't know really," Natasha explained. "But I want to know more about his presence and to stop being so angry all the time!"

The youth leader explained that we can ask God to forgive us and he will fill us with his presence, then God can start changing us from the inside out. Natasha's heart was pounding really fast and she was excited and nervous at the same time. "I want that," she stammered . . . and they prayed together. As they did, Natasha felt a peace go through her body from the top of her head to the tips of her toes.

Since that day, whenever Natasha feels like she is going to get really angry and start going crazy, she starts to worship God and prays that his presence will fill her and help her be calm enough to sort out the situation. Read **Psalm 84**.

* Look at verse 10 and think about Natasha. What are the benefits of being with God?
* What are the things that stop us from being in God's presence and asking for his help?

Consider . . .

* encouraging your youth leader or minister when they help you worship God, by saying thank you to them.
* writing your own psalm to God telling him how he helps you and makes you feel.

For more, see . . .

* Luke 4:8 (p.1044)   * Romans 12:1 (p.1203)

[7]LORD, show us your love,
and save us.

[8]I will listen to God the LORD.
He has ordered peace for those who
worship him.
Don't let them go back to foolishness.
[9]God will soon save those who respect him,
and his glory will be seen in our land.

[10]Love and truth belong to God's people;
goodness and peace will be theirs.
[11]On earth people will be loyal to God,
and God's goodness will shine down from
heaven.
[12]The LORD will give his goodness,
and the land will give its crops.
[13]Goodness will go before God
and prepare the way for him.

A Cry for Help

A prayer of David.

86 LORD, listen to me and answer me.
I am poor and helpless.
[2]Protect me, because I worship you.
My God, save me, your servant who trusts
in you.
[3]Lord, have mercy on me,
because I have called to you all day.
[4]Give happiness to me, your servant,
because I give my life to you, Lord.

[5]Lord, you are kind and forgiving
and have great love for those who call
to you.
[6]LORD, hear my prayer,
and listen when I ask for mercy.
[7]I call to you in times of trouble,
because you will answer me.

[8]Lord, there is no god like you
and no works like yours.
[9]Lord, all the nations you have made
will come and worship you.
They will honour you.
[10]You are great and you do miracles. [d]
Only you are God.

[11]LORD, teach me what you want me to do,
and I will live by your truth.
Teach me to respect you completely.
[12]Lord, my God, I will praise you with all my
heart,
and I will honour your name for ever.
[13]You have great love for me.
You have saved me from death.
[14]God, proud men are attacking me;
a gang of cruel men is trying to kill me.
They do not respect you.

[15]But Lord, you are a God who shows mercy
and is kind.
You don't become angry quickly.
You have great love and faithfulness.
[16]Turn to me and have mercy.
Give me, your servant, strength.
Save me, the son of your female servant.
[17]Show me a sign of your goodness.
When my enemies look, they will be
ashamed.
You, LORD, have helped me and
comforted me.

God Loves Jerusalem

A song. A psalm of the sons of Korah.

87 The LORD built Jerusalem on the holy
mountain.
[2] He loves its gates
more than any other place in Israel.
[3]City of God,
wonderful things are said about you. *Selah* [d]
[4]God says, "I will put Egypt and Babylonia
on the list of nations that know me.
People from Philistia, Tyre and Cush
will be born there."

[5]They will say about Jerusalem,
"This one and that one were born there.
God Most High will strengthen her."
[6]The LORD will keep a list of the nations.
He will note, "This person was born there."
Selah

[7]They will dance and sing,
"All good things come from Jerusalem."

A Sad Complaint

A song. A psalm of the sons of Korah. For the director
of music. By the mahalath leannoth. [d] A maskil [d]
of Heman the Ezrahite.

88 LORD, you are the God who saves me.
I cry out to you day and night.
[2]Receive my prayer,
and listen to my cry.

[3]My life is full of troubles,
and I am nearly dead.
[4]They think I am on the way to my grave.
I am like a man with no strength.
[5]I have been left as dead,
like a body lying in a grave
whom you don't remember any more,
cut off from your care.

[6]You have brought me close to death;
I am almost in the dark place of the dead.
[7]You have been very angry with me;
all your waves crush me. *Selah* [d]

⁸You have taken my friends away from me
and have made them hate me.
I am trapped and cannot escape.
⁹ My eyes are weak from crying.
LORD, I have prayed to you every day;
I have lifted my hands in prayer to you.

¹⁰Do you show your miracles *d* for the dead?
Do their spirits rise up and praise you?   *Selah*
¹¹Will your love be told in the grave?
Will your loyalty be told in the place of death?
¹²Will your miracles be known in the dark grave?
Will your goodness be known in the land of
forgetfulness?

¹³But, LORD, I have called out to you for help;
every morning I pray to you.
¹⁴LORD, why do you reject me?
Why do you hide from me?

¹⁵I have been weak and dying since I was young.
I suffer from your terrors, and I am helpless.
¹⁶You have been angry with me,
and your terrors have destroyed me.
¹⁷They surround me daily like a flood;
they are all around me.
¹⁸You have taken away my loved ones and
friends.
Darkness is my only friend.

A Song About God's Loyalty

A maskil *d* of Ethan the Ezrahite.

89 I will always sing about the LORD's
love;
I will tell of his loyalty from now on.
²I will say, "Your love continues for ever;
your loyalty goes on and on like the sky."

³You said, "I made an agreement with the man
of my choice;
I made a promise to my servant David.
⁴I told him, 'I will make your family continue
for ever.
Your kingdom will go on and on.' "   *Selah d*

⁵LORD, the heavens praise you for your miracles *d*
and for your loyalty in the meeting of your
holy ones.
⁶Who in heaven is equal to the LORD?
None of the angels is like the LORD.
⁷When the holy ones meet, it is God they fear.
He is more frightening than all who
surround him.
⁸Lord GOD All-powerful, who is like you?
LORD, you are powerful and completely
trustworthy.

⁹You rule the mighty sea
and calm the stormy waves.
¹⁰You crushed the sea monster Rahab; *d*
by your power you scattered your enemies.

¹¹The skies and the earth belong to you.
You made the world and everything in it.
¹²You created the north and the south.
Mount Tabor and Mount Hermon sing for
joy at your name.
¹³Your arm has great power.
Your hand is strong; your right hand is
lifted up.

¹⁴Your kingdom is built on what is right and
fair.
Love and truth are in all you do.

¹⁵Happy are the people who know how to
praise you.
LORD, let them live in the light of your
presence.
¹⁶In your name they rejoice
and continually praise your goodness.
¹⁷You are their glorious strength,
and in your kindness you honour our king.
¹⁸Our king, our shield, belongs to the LORD,
to the Holy One of Israel.

¹⁹Once, in a vision, you spoke
to those who worship you.
You said, "I have given strength to a warrior;
I have raised up a young man from my
people.
²⁰I have found my servant David;
I appointed him by pouring holy oil
on him.
²¹I will steady him with my hand
and strengthen him with my arm.
²²No enemy will make him give forced
payments,
and wicked people will not defeat him.
²³I will crush his enemies in front of him;
I will defeat those who hate him.
²⁴My loyalty and love will be with him.
Through me he will be strong.
²⁵I will give him power over the sea
and control over the rivers.
²⁶He will say to me, 'You are my father,
my God, the Rock, *d* my Saviour.'
²⁷I will make him my firstborn *d* son,
the greatest king on earth.
²⁸My love will watch over him for ever,
and my agreement with him will
never end.
²⁹I will make his family continue,
and his kingdom will last as long as the
skies.

³⁰"If his descendants *d* reject my teachings
and do not follow my laws,
³¹if they ignore my demands
and disobey my commands,
³²then I will punish their sins with a rod
and their wrongs with a whip.

33But I will not hold back my love from David,
 nor will I stop being loyal.
34I will not break my agreement
 nor change what I have said.
35I have promised by my holiness,
 I will not lie to David.
36His family will go on for ever.
 His kingdom will last before me like the sun.
37It will continue for ever, like the moon,
 like a dependable witness in the sky."   *Selah*

38But now you have refused and rejected your
 appointed king.
 You have been angry with him.
39You have abandoned the agreement with
 your servant
 and thrown his crown to the ground.
40You have torn down all his city walls;
 you have turned his strong cities into
 ruins.
41Everyone who passes by steals from him.
 His neighbours insult him.
42You have given strength to his enemies
 and have made them all happy.
43You have made his sword useless;
 you did not help him stand in battle.
44You have kept him from winning
 and have thrown his throne to the ground.
45You have cut his life short
 and covered him with shame.   *Selah*

46LORD, how long will this go on?
 Will you ignore us for ever?
 How long will your anger burn like a fire?
47Remember how short my life is.
 Why did you create us? For nothing?
48What person alive will not die?
 Who can escape the grave?   *Selah*
49Lord, where is your love from times past,
 which in your loyalty you promised to
 David?
50Lord, remember how they insulted your
 servant;
 remember how I have suffered the insults
 of the nations.
51LORD, remember how your enemies
 insulted you
 and how they insulted your appointed king
 wherever he went.

52Praise the LORD for ever!
 Amen and amen.

Book 4

God is Eternal, and We are Not

A prayer of Moses, the man of God.

90 Lord, you have been our home
 since the beginning.

2Before the mountains were born
 and before you created the earth and the
 world,
 you are God.
 You have always been, and you will
 always be.
3You turn people back into dust.
 You say, "Go back into dust, human
 beings."
4To you, a thousand years
 is like the passing of a day,
 or like a few hours in the night.
5While people sleep, you take their lives.
 They are like grass that grows up in the
 morning.
6In the morning they are fresh and new,
 but by evening they dry up and die.

7We are destroyed by your anger;
 we are terrified by your hot anger.
8You have put the evil we have done right in
 front of you;
 you clearly see our secret sins.
9All our days pass while you are angry.
 Our years end with a moan.
10Our lifetime is 70 years
 or, if we are strong, 80 years.
 But the years are full of hard work and pain.
 They pass quickly, and then we are gone.

11Who knows the full power of your anger?
 Your anger is as great as our fear of you
 should be.
12Teach us how short our lives really are
 so that we may be wise.

13LORD, how long before you return
 and show kindness to your servants?
14Fill us with your love every morning.
 Then we will sing and rejoice all our lives.
15We have seen years of trouble.
 Now give us as much joy as you gave us
 sorrow.
16Show your servants the wonderful things
 you do;
 show your greatness to their children.
17Lord our God, treat us well.
 Give us success in what we do;
 yes, give us success in what we do.

Safe in the LORD

91 Those who go to God Most High for
 safety
 will be protected by the Almighty.
2I will say to the LORD, "You are my place of
 safety and protection.
 You are my God and I trust you."

3God will save you from hidden traps
 and from deadly diseases.

4He will cover you with his feathers,
and under his wings you can hide.
His truth will be your shield and protection.
5You will not fear any danger by night
or an arrow during the day.
6You will not be afraid of diseases that come
in the dark
or sickness that strikes at noon.
7At your side a thousand people may die,
or even ten thousand right beside you,
but you will not be hurt.
8You will only watch
and see the wicked punished.

9The LORD is your protection;
you have made God Most High your place
of safety.
10Nothing bad will happen to you;
no disaster will come to your home.
11He has put his angels in charge of you
to watch over you wherever you go.
12They will catch you in their hands
so that you will not hit your foot on a rock.
13You will walk on lions and cobras;
you will step on strong lions and snakes.

14The LORD says, "Whoever loves me, I will save.
I will protect those who know me.
15They will call to me, and I will answer them.
I will be with them in trouble;
I will rescue them and honour them.
16I will give them a long, full life,
and they will see how I can save."

Thanksgiving for God's Goodness

A psalm. A song for the Sabbath *d* day.

92 It is good to praise you, LORD,
to sing praises to God Most High.
2It is good to tell of your love in the morning
and of your loyalty at night.
3It is good to praise you with the ten-stringed
lyre *d*
and with the soft-sounding harp.

4LORD, you have made me happy by what you
have done;
I will sing for joy about what your hands
have done.
5LORD, you have done such great things!
How deep are your thoughts!
6Stupid people don't know these things,
and fools don't understand.
7Wicked people grow like the grass.
Evil people seem to do well,
but they will be destroyed for ever.

8But, LORD, you will be honoured for ever.

9LORD, surely your enemies,
surely your enemies will be destroyed,
and all who do evil will be scattered.

10But you have made me as strong as an ox.
You have poured fine oils on me.
11When I looked, I saw my enemies;
I heard the cries of those who are
against me.

12But good people will grow like palm trees;
they will be tall like the cedars of Lebanon.
13Like trees planted in the Temple of the
LORD,
they will grow strong in the courtyards of
our God.
14When they are old, they will still produce
fruit;
they will be healthy and fresh.
15They will say that the LORD is good.
He is my Rock, *d* and there is no wrong
in him.

The Majesty of the LORD

93 The LORD is king. He is clothed in
majesty.
The LORD is clothed in majesty
and armed with strength.
The world is set,
and it cannot be moved.
2LORD, your kingdom was set up long ago;
you are everlasting.

3LORD, the seas raise,
the seas raise their voice.
The seas raise up their pounding waves.
4The sound of the water is loud;
the ocean waves are powerful,
but the LORD above is much greater.

5LORD, your laws will stand for ever.
Your Temple *d* will be holy for ever.

God will Pay Back His Enemies

94 The LORD is a God who punishes.
God, show your greatness and
punish!
2Rise up, Judge of the earth,
and give the proud what they deserve.
3How long will the wicked be happy?
How long, LORD?
4They are full of proud words;
those who do evil boast about what they
have done.
5LORD, they crush your people
and make your children suffer.
6They kill widows and foreigners
and murder orphans.
7They say, "The LORD doesn't see;
the God of Jacob doesn't notice."

8You stupid ones among the people, pay
attention.
You fools, when will you understand?

⁹Can't the creator of ears hear?
　　Can't the maker of eyes see?
¹⁰Won't the one who corrects nations
　　　punish you?
　　Doesn't the teacher of people know
　　　everything?
¹¹The LORD knows what people think.
　　He knows their thoughts are just a puff of
　　　wind.

¹²LORD, those you correct are happy;
　　you teach them from your law.
¹³You give them rest from times of trouble
　　until a pit is dug for the wicked.
¹⁴The LORD won't leave his people
　　nor give up his children.
¹⁵Judgement will again be fair,
　　and all who are honest will follow it.

¹⁶Who will help me fight against the wicked?
　　Who will stand with me against those who
　　　do evil?
¹⁷If the LORD had not helped me,
　　I would have died in a minute.
¹⁸I said, "I am about to fall,"
　　but, LORD, your love kept me safe.
¹⁹I was very worried,
　　but you comforted me and made me
　　　happy.

²⁰Crooked leaders cannot be friends with you.
　　They use the law to cause suffering.
²¹They join forces against people who do right
　　and sentence to death the innocent.
²²But the LORD is my defender;
　　my God is the rock of my protection.
²³God will pay them back for their sins
　　and will destroy them for their evil.
　　The LORD our God will destroy them.

A Call to Praise and Obedience

95 Come, let's sing for joy to the LORD.
　　Let's shout praises to the Rock *d* who
　　　saves us.
²Let's come to him with thanksgiving.
　　Let's sing songs to him,

³because the LORD is the great God,
　　the great King over all gods.
⁴The deepest places on earth are his,
　　and the highest mountains belong to him.
⁵The sea is his because he made it,
　　and he created the land with his own
　　　hands.

⁶Come, let's worship him and bow down.
　　Let's kneel before the LORD who
　　　made us,
⁷because he is our God
　　and we are the people he takes care of
　　and the sheep that he tends.

Today listen to what he says:
⁸ "Do not be stubborn, as your ancestors were
　　　at Meribah,
　　as they were that day at Massah in the
　　　desert.
⁹There your ancestors tested me
　　and tried me even though they saw what
　　　I did.
¹⁰I was angry with those people for forty years.
　　I said, 'They are not loyal to me
　　and have not understood my ways.'
¹¹I was angry and made a promise,
　　'They will never enter my rest.' "

Praise for the LORD's Glory

96 Sing to the LORD a new song;
　　sing to the LORD, all the earth.
²Sing to the LORD and praise his name;
　　every day tell how he saves us.
³Tell the nations of his glory;
　　tell all peoples the miracles *d* he does,

⁴because the LORD is great; he should be
　　　praised at all times.
　　He should be honoured more than all the
　　　gods,
⁵because all the gods of the nations are only
　　　idols,
　　but the LORD made the heavens.
⁶The LORD has glory and majesty;
　　he has power and beauty in his Temple. *d*

⁷Praise the LORD, all nations on earth;
　　praise the LORD's glory and power.
⁸Praise the glory of the LORD's name.
　　Bring an offering and come into his Temple
　　　courtyards.
⁹Worship the LORD because he is holy.
　　Tremble before him, everyone on earth.

¹⁰Tell the nations, "The LORD is king."
　　The earth is set, and it cannot be moved.
　　He will judge the people fairly.
¹¹Let the skies rejoice and the earth be glad;
　　let the sea and everything in it shout.
¹² Let the fields and everything in them rejoice.
　　Then all the trees of the forest will sing
　　　for joy
¹³ before the LORD, because he is coming.
　　He is coming to judge the world;
　　he will judge the world with fairness
　　and the peoples with truth.

A Hymn About the LORD's Power

97 The LORD is king. Let the earth rejoice;
　　faraway lands should be glad.

²Thick, dark clouds surround him.
　　His kingdom is built on what is right and
　　　fair.

³A fire goes before him
and burns up his enemies all around.
⁴His lightning lights up the world;
when the people see it, they tremble.
⁵The mountains melt like wax before
the LORD,
before the Lord of all the earth.
⁶The heavens tell about his goodness,
and all the people see his glory.

⁷Those who worship idols should be ashamed;
they boast about their gods.
All the gods should worship the LORD.

⁸When Jerusalem hears this, she is glad,
and the towns of Judah rejoice.
They are happy because of your
judgements, LORD.
⁹You are the LORD Most High over all the earth;
you are supreme over all gods.

¹⁰People who love the LORD hate evil.
The LORD watches over those who follow him
and frees them from the power of the wicked.
¹¹Light shines on those who do right;
joy belongs to those who are honest.
¹²Rejoice in the LORD, you who do right.
Praise his holy name.

The LORD of Power and Justice

A psalm.

98 Sing to the LORD a new song,
because he has done miracles. *d*
By his right hand and holy arm
he has won the victory.
²The LORD has made known his power to save;
he has shown the other nations his victory
for his people.
³He has remembered his love
and his loyalty to the people of Israel.

EVIL

The Prowling Lion

Steve was worried about the person who used to be his best friend. This friend, Jake, had previously been quite a normal guy, but he'd recently got interested in mysterious symbols and claimed to be a follower of Satan (or the devil). Steve, who wasn't religious at all, tried to persuade Jake that this was all total rubbish – a load of superstitious mumbo-jumbo.

The writer C.S. Lewis, author of the Narnia stories, once wrote that there are two wrong attitudes to evil: one is to take an unhealthy interest in it, like Jake; the other is to just dismiss it is as nonsense, like Steve.

The Bible makes it clear that evil is constantly near us – always attacking God's creation and particularly trying to influence us. And it's a destructive influence. The Old Testament pictures evil as waiting outside our door, wanting to grab us. The New Testament says that the devil is like a lion prowling around, looking for someone to eat. We can't just laugh the devil and evil off as unimportant.

But we have God on our side, the God who created the universe and who is far more powerful than anything inside it. Although the devil is incredibly strong compared to us, he is nothing compared to God. God has sent his Son Jesus to die on the cross to defeat the devil. The devil hoped that human beings would all die and be punished for committing sin, but God's plan all along was that Jesus would die for our sin. So the devil's hopes will come to nothing. And now God has given us power so we can stand up to the devil: if we're Christians, the Holy Spirit in us will give us strength to fight against the temptations that the devil tries to put in our minds. So we know that the devil exists, and that we should take him seriously – though not too seriously. **Read Psalm 97**.

* How can we know when we're being tempted to do evil?
* How can we stand up to the devil?

Consider . . .

* writing down specific moments in the last week when you feel the devil has tried to lead you astray.
* praying for strength to resist the devil when he tempts you to do evil.

For more, see . . .

* Genesis 4:7 (p.7)
* 1 John 4:4 (p.1374)
* 1 Peter 5:8 (p.1363)

All the ends of the earth have seen
  God's power to save.

⁴Shout with joy to the LORD, all the earth;
  burst into songs and make music.
⁵Make music to the LORD with harps,
  with harps and the sound of singing.
⁶Blow the trumpets and the sheep's horns;
  shout for joy to the LORD the King.

⁷Let the sea and everything in it shout;
  let the world and everyone in it sing.
⁸Let the rivers clap their hands;
  let the mountains sing together for joy.
⁹Let them sing before the LORD,
  because he is coming to judge the world.
He will judge the world fairly;
  he will judge the peoples with fairness.

The LORD, the Fair and Holy King

99 The LORD is king.
    Let the peoples shake with fear.
He sits between the gold creatures with
  wings.
  Let the earth shake.
²The LORD in Jerusalem is great;
  he is supreme over all the peoples.
³Let them praise your name;
  it is great, holy and to be feared.

⁴The King is powerful and loves justice.
  LORD, you made things fair;
you have done what is fair and right
  for the people of Jacob.
⁵Praise the LORD our God,
  and worship at the Temple, *d* his footstool.
  He is holy.

⁶Moses and Aaron were among his priests,
  and Samuel was among his worshippers.
  They called to the LORD,
    and he answered them.
⁷He spoke to them from the pillar of cloud.
  They kept the rules and laws he gave them.

⁸LORD our God, you answered them.
  You showed them that you are a
    forgiving God,
  but you punished them for their wrongs.
⁹Praise the LORD our God,
  and worship at his holy mountain,
  because the LORD our God is holy.

A Call to Praise the LORD

A psalm of thanks.

100 Shout to the LORD, all the earth.
  ² Serve the LORD with joy;
  come before him with singing.
³Know that the LORD is God.
  He made us, and we belong to him;
  we are his people, the sheep he tends.

⁴Come into his city with songs of thanksgiving
  and into his courtyards with songs of praise.
  Thank him and praise his name.
⁵The LORD is good. His love is for ever,
  and his loyalty goes on and on.

A Promise to Rule Well

A psalm of David.

101 I will sing of your love and fairness;
  LORD, I will sing praises to you.
²I will be careful to live an innocent life.
  When will you come to me?

I will live an innocent life in my house.
³ I will not look at anything wicked.
I hate those who turn against you;
  they will not be found near me.

⁴Let those who want to do wrong stay away
    from me;
  I will have nothing to do with evil.

⁵If anyone secretly says things against his
    neighbour,
  I will stop him.
I will not allow people
  to be proud and look down on others.

⁶I will look for trustworthy people
  so I can live with them in the land.
Only those who live innocent lives
  will be my servants.

⁷No one who is dishonest will live in my house;
  no liars will stay around me.

Sidelight If you repeat yourself
too much, just tell people
you're making up Hebrew poetry. One
characteristic of this poetry – called parallelism –
was that two consecutive lines would each say
essentially the same thing in a different way.
(For example, see Psalm 101:7.)

---

⁸Every morning I will destroy the wicked in
    the land.
  I will rid the LORD's city of people who do
    evil.

A Cry for Help

A prayer of a person who is suffering when he is
discouraged and tells the Lord his complaints.

102 LORD, listen to my prayer;
  let my cry for help come to you.
²Do not hide from me
  in my time of trouble.
Pay attention to me.
  When I cry for help, answer me quickly.

3My life is passing away like smoke,
   and my bones are burned up with fire.
4My heart is like grass
   that has been cut and dried.
   I forget to eat.
5Because of my grief,
   my skin hangs on my bones.
6I am like a desert owl,
   like an owl living among the ruins.
7I lie awake.
   I am like a lonely bird on a housetop.
8All day long enemies insult me;
   those who make fun of me use my name
      as a curse.
9I eat ashes for food,
   and my tears fall into my drink.
10Because of your great anger,
   you have picked me up and thrown me away.
11My days are like a passing shadow;
   I am like dried grass.

12But, Lord, you rule for ever,
   and your fame goes on and on.
13You will come and have mercy on Jerusalem,
   because the time has now come to be kind
      to her;
   the right time has come.
14Your servants love even her stones;
   they even care about her dust.
15Nations will fear the name of the Lord,
   and all the kings on earth will honour you.
16The Lord will rebuild Jerusalem;
   there his glory will be seen.
17He will answer the prayers of the needy;
   he will not reject their prayers.

18Write these things for the future
   so that people who are not yet born will
      praise the Lord.
19The Lord looked down from his holy place
      above;
   from heaven he looked down at the earth.
20He heard the moans of the prisoners,
   and he freed those sentenced to die.
21The name of the Lord will be heard in
      Jerusalem;
   his praise will be heard there.
22People will come together,
   and kingdoms will serve the Lord.

23God has made me tired of living;
   he has cut short my life.
24So I said, "My God, do not take me in the
      middle of my life.
   Your years go on and on.
25In the beginning you made the earth,
   and your hands made the skies.
26They will be destroyed, but you will remain.
   They will all wear out like clothes.

And, like clothes, you will change them
   and throw them away.
27But you never change,
   and your life will never end.
28Our children will live in your presence,
   and their children will remain with you."

Praise to the Lord of Love

Of David.

103 My whole being, praise the Lord;
   all my being, praise his holy
      name.
2My whole being, praise the Lord
   and do not forget all his kindnesses.
3He forgives all my sins
   and heals all my diseases.
4He saves my life from the grave
   and loads me with love and mercy.
5He satisfies me with good things
   and makes me young again, like the eagle.

6The Lord does what is right and fair
   for all who are wronged by others.

7He showed his ways to Moses
   and his deeds to the people of Israel.
8The Lord shows mercy and is kind.
   He does not become angry quickly, and he
      has great love.
9He will not always accuse us,
   and he will not be angry for ever.
10He has not punished us as our sins should be
      punished;
   he has not repaid us for the evil we have
      done.
11As high as the sky is above the earth,
   so great is his love for those who
      respect him.
12He has taken our sins away from us
   as far as the east is from the west.
13The Lord has mercy on those who
      respect him,
   as a father has mercy on his children.
14He knows how we were made;
   he remembers that we are dust.
15Human life is like grass;
   we grow like a flower in the field.
16After the wind blows, the flower is gone,
   and there is no sign of where it was.
17But the Lord's love for those who
      respect him
   continues for ever and ever,
   and his goodness continues to their
      grandchildren
18and to those who keep his agreement
   and who remember to obey his orders.

19The Lord has set his throne in heaven,
   and his kingdom rules over everything.

²⁰You who are his angels, praise the LORD.
    You are the mighty warriors who do what
        he says
    and who obey his voice.
²¹You, his armies, praise the LORD;
    you are his servants who do what he wants.
²²Everything the LORD has made
    should praise him in all the places he rules.

My whole being, praise the LORD.

Praise to God Who Made the World

104   My whole being, praise the LORD.
        LORD my God, you are very great.
You are clothed with glory and majesty;
² you wear light like a robe.
You stretch out the skies like a tent.
³ You build your room above the clouds.
You make the clouds your chariot,
    and you ride on the wings of the wind.
⁴You make the winds your messengers,
    and flames of fire are your servants.

⁵You built the earth on its foundations
    so it can never be moved.

⁶You covered the earth with oceans;
    the water was above the mountains.
⁷But at your command, the water rushed away.
    When you thundered your orders, it
        hurried away.
⁸The mountains rose; the valleys sank.
    The water went to the places you made for it.
⁹You set borders for the seas that they cannot
        cross,
    so water will never cover the earth again.

¹⁰You make springs pour into the ravines;
    they flow between the mountains.
¹¹They water all the wild animals;
    the wild donkeys come there to drink.
¹²Wild birds make nests by the water;
    they sing among the tree branches.
¹³You water the mountains from above.
    The earth is full of the things you made.
¹⁴You make the grass for cattle
    and vegetables for the people.
    You make food grow from the earth.
¹⁵You give us wine that makes happy hearts
    and olive oil that makes our faces shine.
    You give us bread that gives us strength.

GOD'S LOVE

Easy to Take For Granted

It's invisible – easy to take for granted. Your hand will go right through it.

It combines with practically everything, and if it didn't, life couldn't exist. It's part of hundreds of thousands of things we use daily, and it makes up two-thirds of your body . . . nine-tenths of the oceans . . . one-fifth of the air you breathe.

Try living without it. You can't. Nothing can. It's invisible. You take it for granted and never think about it because it's everywhere.

You guessed it – it's oxygen.

In many ways, God's love is like oxygen. They're both invisible, and they're both everywhere. But God's love is even more essential for life than oxygen. The writer of **Psalm 103** knew the importance of God's love for living.

* What phrases in this psalm reflect God's active, assertive love for us?
* How is God's love alive in the attitudes and actions of people you know?

Consider . . .

* thinking about what God has done in your life and writing two-word sentences combining the word "God . . ." and an action word, such as "God strengthens" or "God listens".
* choosing three ways in which you can become more active in showing God's love to others, starting this week.

For more, see . . .

* Genesis 1:26–31 (p.3)
* John 3:16–21 (p.1100)

* Proverbs 3:11–12 (p.592)

¹⁶The LORD's trees have plenty of water;
    they are the cedars of Lebanon, which he
    planted.
¹⁷The birds make their nests there;
    the stork's home is in the fir trees.
¹⁸The high mountains belong to the wild
    goats.
    The rocks are hiding places for the
    badgers.

¹⁹You made the moon to mark the seasons,
    and the sun always knows when to set.
²⁰You make it dark, and it becomes night.
    Then all the wild animals creep around.
²¹The lions roar as they attack.
    They look to God for food.
²²When the sun rises, they leave
    and go back to their dens to lie down.
²³Then people go to work
    and work until evening.

²⁴LORD, you have made many things;
    with your wisdom you made them all.
    The earth is full of your riches.
²⁵Look at the sea, so big and wide,
    with creatures large and small that cannot
    be counted.
²⁶Ships travel over the ocean,
    and there is the sea monster Leviathan, ^d
    which you made to play there.

²⁷All these things depend on you
    to give them their food at the right time.
²⁸When you give it to them,
    they gather it up.
    When you open your hand,
    they are filled with good food.
²⁹When you turn away from them,
    they become frightened.
    When you take away their breath,
    they die and turn to dust.
³⁰When you breathe on them,
    they are created,
    and you make the land new again.

³¹May the glory of the LORD be for ever.
    May the LORD enjoy what he has made.
³²He just looks at the earth, and it shakes.
    He touches the mountains, and they
    smoke.
³³I will sing to the LORD all my life;
    I will sing praises to my God as long as I
    live.
³⁴May my thoughts please him;
    I am happy in the LORD.
³⁵Let sinners be destroyed from the earth,
    and let the wicked live no longer.

My whole being, praise the LORD.

Praise the LORD.

God's Love for Israel

105

¹Give thanks to the LORD and pray
    to him.
Tell the nations what he has done.
²Sing to him; sing praises to him.
    Tell about all his miracles. ^d
³Be glad that you are his;
    let those who seek the LORD be happy.
⁴Depend on the LORD and his strength;
    always go to him for help.

⁵Remember the miracles he has done;
    remember his wonders and his
    decisions.
⁶You are descendants ^d of his servant
    Abraham,
    the children of Jacob, his chosen
    people.
⁷He is the LORD our God.
    His laws are for all the world.

⁸He will keep his agreement for ever;
    he will keep his promises always.
⁹He will keep the agreement he made with
    Abraham
    and the promise he made to Isaac.
¹⁰He made it a law for the people of Jacob;
    he made it an agreement with Israel to last
    for ever.
¹¹The LORD said, "I will give you the land of
    Canaan,
    and it will belong to you."

¹²Then God's people were few in number.
    They were strangers in the land.
¹³They went from one nation to another,
    from one kingdom to another.
¹⁴But the LORD did not let anyone hurt
    them;
    he warned kings not to harm them.
¹⁵He said, "Don't touch my chosen people,
    and don't harm my prophets." ^d

¹⁶God ordered a time of hunger in the land,
    and he destroyed all the food.
¹⁷Then he sent a man ahead of them—
    Joseph, who was sold as a slave.
¹⁸They put chains around his feet
    and an iron ring around his neck.
¹⁹Then the time he had spoken of came,
    and the LORD's words proved that Joseph
    was right.
²⁰The king of Egypt sent for Joseph and
    freed him;
    the ruler of the people set him free.
²¹He made him the master of his house;
    Joseph was in charge of his riches.
²²He could order the princes as he wished.
    He taught the older men to be wise.

[23]Then his father Israel came to Egypt;
Jacob[n] lived in Egypt. [n]
[24]The LORD made his people grow in number,
and he made them stronger than their
enemies.
[25]He caused the Egyptians to hate his people
and to make plans against his servants.
[26]Then he sent his servant Moses,
and Aaron, whom he had chosen.
[27]They did many signs among the Egyptians
and worked wonders in Egypt.
[28]The LORD sent darkness and made the land
dark,
but the Egyptians turned against what he
said.
[29]So he changed their water into blood
and made their fish die.
[30]Then their country was filled with frogs,
even in the bedrooms of their rulers.
[31]The LORD spoke and flies came,
and gnats were everywhere in the country.
[32]He made hail fall like rain
and sent lightning through their land.
[33]He struck down their grapevines and fig trees,
and he destroyed every tree in the country.
[34]He spoke and grasshoppers came;
the locusts[d] were too many to count.
[35]They ate all the plants in the land
and everything the earth produced.
[36]The LORD also killed all the firstborn[d] sons in
the land,
the oldest son of each family.

[37]Then he brought his people out,
and they carried with them silver and gold.
Not one of his people stumbled.
[38]The Egyptians were glad when they left,
because the Egyptians were afraid of them.
[39]The LORD covered them with a cloud
and lit up the night with fire.
[40]When they asked, he brought them quail
and filled them with bread from heaven.
[41]God split the rock, and water flowed out;
it ran like a river through the desert.
[42]He remembered his holy promise
to his servant Abraham.

[43]So God brought his people out with joy,
his chosen ones with singing.
[44]He gave them the lands of other nations,
so they received what others had
worked for.
[45]This was so they would keep his orders
and obey his teachings.

Praise the LORD!

Israel's Failure to Trust God

106

Praise the LORD!
Thank the LORD because he is
good.
His love continues for ever.
[2]No one can tell all the mighty things the
LORD has done;
no one can speak all his praise.
[3]Happy are those who do right,
who do what is fair at all times.

[4]LORD, remember me when you are kind to
your people;
help me when you save them.
[5]Let me see the good things you do for your
chosen people.
Let me be happy along with your happy
nation;
let me join your own people in praising you.

[6]We have sinned just as our ancestors did.
We have done wrong; we have done evil.
[7]Our ancestors in Egypt
did not learn from your miracles. [d]
They did not remember all your kindnesses,
so they turned against you at the Red Sea. [d]
[8]But the LORD saved them for his own sake,
to show his great power.
[9]He commanded the Red Sea, and it dried up.
He led them through the deep sea as if it
were a desert.
[10]He saved them from those who hated them.
He saved them from their enemies,
[11]and the water covered their foes.
Not one of them escaped.
[12]Then the people believed what the LORD said,
and they sang praises to him.

[13]But they quickly forgot what he had done;
they did not wait for his advice.
[14]They became greedy for food in the desert,
and they tested God there.
[15]So he gave them what they wanted,
but he also sent a terrible disease among
them.

[16]The people in the camp were jealous of
Moses
and of Aaron, the holy priest of the LORD.
[17]Then the ground opened up and swallowed
Dathan
and closed over Abiram's group.
[18]A fire burned among their followers,
and flames burned up the wicked.

[19]The people made a gold calf at Mount Sinai
and worshipped a metal statue.

Jacob   Also called Israel.
Egypt   Literally, "the land of Ham". Also in verse 27. The people in Egypt were descendants of Ham, one of Noah's sons. See
Genesis 10:6.

²⁰They exchanged their glorious God
　　for a statue of a bull that eats grass.
²¹They forgot the God who saved them,
　　who had done great things in Egypt, *n*
²²who had done miracles in Egypt
　　and amazing things by the Red Sea.
²³So God said he would destroy them.
　　But Moses, his chosen one, stood
　　　before him
　　and stopped God's anger from destroying
　　　them.

²⁴Then they refused to go into the beautiful
　　　land of Canaan;
　　they did not believe what God promised.
²⁵They grumbled in their tents
　　and did not obey the LORD.
²⁶So he swore to them
　　that they would die in the desert.
²⁷He said their children would be killed by
　　　other nations
　　and that they would be scattered among
　　　other countries.

²⁸They joined in worshipping Baal *d* at Peor
　　and ate meat that had been sacrificed to
　　　lifeless statues.
²⁹They made the LORD angry by what they did,
　　so many people became sick with a terrible
　　　disease.
³⁰But Phinehas prayed to the LORD,
　　and the disease stopped.
³¹Phinehas did what was right,
　　and it will be remembered from now on.

³²The people also made the LORD angry at
　　　Meribah,
　　and Moses was in trouble because of them.
³³The people turned against the Spirit *d*
　　　of God,
　　so Moses spoke without stopping to think.

³⁴The people did not destroy the other nations
　　as the LORD had told them to do.
³⁵Instead, they mixed with the other nations
　　and learned their customs.
³⁶They worshipped other nations' idols
　　and were trapped by them.
³⁷They even killed their sons and daughters
　　as sacrifices to demons. *d*
³⁸They killed innocent people,
　　their own sons and daughters,
　　as sacrifices to the idols of Canaan.
　　So the land was made unholy by their
　　　blood.
³⁹The people became unholy by their sins;
　　they were unfaithful to God in what
　　　they did.

⁴⁰So the LORD became angry with his
　　　people
　　and hated his own children.
⁴¹He handed them over to other nations
　　and let their enemies rule over them.
⁴²Their enemies were cruel to them
　　and kept them under their power.
⁴³The LORD saved his people many times,
　　but they continued to turn against him.
　　So they became even more wicked.

⁴⁴But God saw their misery
　　when he heard their cry.
⁴⁵He remembered his agreement with them,
　　and he felt sorry for them because of his
　　　great love.
⁴⁶He caused them to be pitied
　　by those who held them captive.

⁴⁷LORD our God, save us
　　and bring us back from other nations.
　　Then we will thank you
　　and will gladly praise you.

⁴⁸Praise the LORD, the God of Israel.
　　He always was and always will be.
　　Let all the people say, "Amen!"

Praise the LORD!

Book 5

God Saves from Many Dangers

107 Thank the LORD because he is good.
　　　His love continues for ever.
²That is what those whom the LORD has saved
　　　should say.
　　He has saved them from the enemy
³and has gathered them from other lands,
　　from east and west, north and south.

⁴Some people had wandered in the desert
　　　lands.
　　They found no city in which to live.
⁵They were hungry and thirsty,
　　and they were discouraged.
⁶In their misery they cried out to the
　　　LORD,
　　and he saved them from their troubles.
⁷He led them on a straight road
　　to a city where they could live.
⁸Let them give thanks to the LORD for
　　　his love
　　and for the miracles *d* he does for people.
⁹He satisfies the thirsty
　　and fills up the hungry.

¹⁰Some sat in gloom and darkness;
　　they were prisoners suffering in chains.

Egypt　Literally, "the land of Ham". The people in Egypt were descendants of Ham, one of Noah's sons. See Genesis 10:6.

11They had turned against the words of God
  and had refused the advice of God Most
  High.
12So he broke their pride by hard work.
  They stumbled, and no one helped.
13In their misery they cried out to the LORD,
  and he saved them from their troubles.
14He brought them out of their gloom and
  darkness
  and broke their chains.
15Let them give thanks to the LORD for his love
  and for the miracles he does for people.
16He breaks down bronze gates
  and cuts apart iron bars.
17Some fools turned against God
  and suffered for the evil they did.
18They refused to eat anything,
  so they almost died.
19In their misery they cried out to the LORD,
  and he saved them from their troubles.
20God gave the command and healed them,
  so they were saved from dying.
21Let them give thanks to the LORD for his love
  and for the miracles he does for people.
22Let them offer sacrifices to thank him.
  With joy they should tell what he has done.

23Others went out to sea in ships
  and did business on the great oceans.
24They saw what the LORD could do,
  the miracles he did in the deep oceans.
25He spoke, and a storm came up,
  which blew up high waves.
26The ships were tossed as high as the sky and
  fell low to the depths.
  The storm was so bad that they lost their
  courage.
27They stumbled and fell like people who were
  drunk.
  They did not know what to do.
28In their misery they cried out to the LORD,
  and he saved them from their troubles.
29He stilled the storm
  and calmed the waves.
30They were happy that it was quiet,
  and God guided them to the port they
  wanted.
31Let them give thanks to the LORD for
  his love
  and for the miracles he does for people.
32Let them praise his greatness in the meeting
  of the people;
  let them praise him in the meeting of the
  elders.

33He changed rivers into a desert
  and springs of water into dry ground.
34He made fertile land salty,
  because the people there did evil.

35He changed the desert into pools of water
  and dry ground into springs of water.
36He had the hungry settle there
  so they could build a city in which to live.
37They planted seeds in the fields and
  vineyards,
  and they had a good harvest.
38God blessed them, and they grew in
  number.
  Their cattle did not become fewer.

39Because of disaster, troubles and sadness,
  their families grew smaller and weaker.
40He showed he was displeased with their
  leaders
  and made them wander in a pathless
  desert.
41But he lifted the poor out of their suffering
  and made their families grow like flocks of
  sheep.
42Good people see this and are happy,
  but the wicked say nothing.

43Whoever is wise will remember these
  things
  and will think about the love of the LORD.

A Prayer for Victory

A song. A psalm of David.

108

God, my heart is steady.
  I will sing and praise you with all
  my being.
2Wake up, harp and lyre! *d*
  I will wake up the dawn.
3LORD, I will praise you among the nations;
  I will sing songs of praise about you to all
  the nations.
4Your great love reaches to the skies,
  your truth to the heavens.
5God, you are supreme above the skies.
  Let your glory be over all the earth.

6Answer us and save us by your power
  so the people you love will be rescued.
7God has said from his Temple, *d*
  "When I win, I will divide Shechem
  and measure off the Valley of Succoth.
8Gilead and Manasseh are mine.
  Ephraim is like my helmet.
  Judah holds my royal sceptre. *d*
9Moab is like my washbowl.
  I throw my sandals at Edom.
  I shout at Philistia."

10Who will bring me to the fortified city?
  Who will lead me to Edom?
11God, surely you have rejected us;
  you do not go out with our armies.
12Help us fight the enemy.
  Human help is useless,

13but we can win with God's help.
  He will defeat our enemies.

A Prayer Against an Enemy

For the director of music. A psalm of David.

109
God, I praise you.
  Do not be silent.
2Wicked people and liars have spoken
    against me;
  they have told lies about me.

Sidelight

Not all the psalms are positive and upbeat. Psalm 109, for example, sounds downright nasty. Verses 6–20 are written in the form of ancient Near Eastern curses, which were said to try to speed justice upon enemies and guilty people. A curse was intended to go into effect only if the person was guilty (see Numbers 5:18–28, p.134 and Deuteronomy 27:15–26, p.189).

3They have said hateful things about me
  and attack me for no reason.
4They attacked me, even though I loved them
  and prayed for them.
5I was good to them, but they repay me with
    evil.
  I loved them, but they hated me in return.

6They say about me, "Have an evil person
    work against him,
  and let an accuser stand against him.
7When he is judged, let him be found guilty,
  and let even his prayers show his guilt.
8Let his life be cut short,
  and let another man replace him as leader.
9Let his children become orphans
  and his wife a widow.
10Make his children wander around, begging
    for food.
  Let them be forced out of the ruins in
    which they live.
11Let the people to whom he owes money take
    everything he owns,
  and let strangers steal everything he has
    worked for.
12Let no one show him love
  or have mercy on his orphaned children.
13Let all his descendants d die
  and be forgotten by those who live
    after him.
14LORD, remember how wicked his ancestors
    were,
  and don't let the sins of his mother be
    wiped out.

15LORD, always remember their sins.
  Then make people forget about them
    completely.
16"He did not remember to be loving.
  He hurt the poor, the needy and those who
    were sad
  until they were nearly dead.
17He loved to put curses on others,
  so let those same curses fall on him.
  He did not like to bless others,
  so do not let good things happen to him.
18He cursed others as often as he wore clothes.
  Cursing others filled his body and his life,
  like drinking water and using olive oil.
19So let curses cover him like clothes
  and wrap round him like a belt."
20May the LORD do these things to those who
    accuse me,
  to those who speak evil against me.
21But you, Lord GOD,
  be kind to me so others will know you are
    good.
  Because your love is good, save me.
22I am poor and helpless
  and very sad.
23I am dying like an evening shadow;
  I am shaken off like a locust. d
24My knees are weak from hunger,
  and I have grown thin.
25My enemies insult me;
  they look at me and shake their heads.

26LORD my God, help me;
  because you are loving, save me.
27Then they will know that your power has
    done this;
  they will know that you have done it, LORD.
28They may curse me, but you bless me.
  They may attack me, but they will be
    disgraced.
  Then I, your servant, will be glad.
29Let those who accuse me be disgraced
  and covered with shame like a coat.

30I will thank the LORD very much;
  I will praise him in front of many people.
31He defends the helpless
  and saves them from those who accuse
    them.

The LORD Appoints a King

A psalm of David.

110
The LORD said to my Lord,
  "Sit by me at my right side
until I put your enemies under your
    control."

²The LORD will enlarge your kingdom beyond
    Jerusalem,
and you will rule over your enemies.
³Your people will join you on your day of battle.
    You have been dressed in holiness from
        birth;
    you have the freshness of a child.

⁴The LORD has made a promise
    and will not change his mind.
He said, "You are a priest for ever,
    a priest like Melchizedek."

⁵The Lord is beside you to help you.
    When he becomes angry, he will crush kings.

ADDICTION

Every Other Word

James was a great DJ, one of the best and noted for his thorough professionalism. For Ben it was a fabulous opportunity to watch him at work. The young teenager had a great yearning to DJ for a living and took every chance that came his way to use his skills and watch others. But the opportunity to watch James in action was totally different. Ben had been asked along to the radio station by a neighbour who was engineering there.

When the day finally came and Ben walked into the studio, his eyes were everywhere, looking at the decks and the mixers, it was awe-inspiring.

James, his idol, came over and shook hands with him.

"So, you want to do this for a career eh? Then you'd better come and sit by me and I'll show you the tricks of the trade."

Ben couldn't believe it was happening. The show started live "on air" and James seemed to be able to do hundreds of things at once, changing jingles, cueing up newsflashes, sorting out the CDs, talking to his adoring public.

Then came the shock.

While the record was playing, the DJ took off his headphones to talk to the engineer and his producer. His sentences were absolutely littered with swear words! Not just one or two, but it seemed to Ben that it was every other word.

He was so taken aback that he said nothing and just carried on watching and listening to the programme. But there it was again, and again. Until finally during a break for the news, he dared to ask James about it.

"Oh my dear boy, it's nothing. Once you're on air you become a total professional, and off the air you are just yourself," he explained with a lazy smile.

"Aren't you afraid you're going to swear over the airwaves?" Ben asked, amazed.

"It's funny you should ask that, because I suppose once I'm doing the programme I'm concentrating, but once I'm off the air, I don't even notice I'm doing it!"

Ben went home with a totally different image in his head.

In **Psalm 109:17–21** David complains that people were trying to give him a false image, and one of the things they tried to do was to accuse him of the same sin as James in this story.

* According to Psalm 109:18, how natural can swearing become?
* Have you ever noticed some "habitual sin" in your life? What have you tried to do about it?

Consider . . .

* taking a deep breath the next time you're going to lose it . . . making sure you have control of your tongue, not the other way round!
* making a note of two things you struggle to control, then ask God to give you the power to control them.

For more, see . . .

* Psalm 141:3 (p.582)
* James 3:7–10 (p.1351)

* 1 Corinthians 10:12–13 (p.1228)

⁶He will judge those nations, filling them with
    dead bodies;
  he will defeat rulers all over the world.
⁷The king will drink from the brook on the way.
  Then he will be strengthened.

Praise the LORD's Goodness

111 Praise the LORD!

I will thank the LORD with all my heart
  in the meeting of his good people.

²The LORD does great things;
  those who enjoy them seek them.
³What he does is glorious and splendid,
  and his goodness continues for ever.
⁴His miracles *d* are unforgettable.
  The LORD is kind and merciful.
⁵He gives food to those who fear him.
  He remembers his agreement for ever.
⁶He has shown his people his power
  when he gave them the lands of other
    nations.
⁷Everything he does is good and fair;
  all his orders can be trusted.

⁸They will continue for ever.
  They were made true and right.
⁹He sets his people free.
  He made his agreement everlasting.
  He is holy and wonderful.
¹⁰Wisdom begins with respect for the LORD;
  those who obey his orders have good
    understanding.
  He should be praised for ever.

Honest People are Blessed

112 Praise the LORD!

Happy are those who respect the LORD,
  who want what he commands.

²Their descendants *d* will be powerful in the
    land;
  the children of honest people will be
    blessed.
³Their houses will be full of wealth and riches,
  and their goodness will continue for ever.
⁴A light shines in the dark for honest people,
  for those who are merciful and kind and
    good.

HONESTY

Slow But Sure

Almost everyone cheated in Mrs Young's algebra class. It was just so incredibly easy. The three class "brains" were generous with whispered answers on tests and would lend homework papers for copying. Mrs Young didn't seem to catch on, or else she ignored it, not knowing how to put a stop to it.

Robert didn't believe in cheating, though. He plodded along, doing his own work, scoring Cs or C+s. That's why everybody was surprised when he got the best maths results of anybody in the school – even better than the brains – and was accepted for university.

"How did you do it, Robert?" asked one of the brains from algebra.

"I just knew the stuff," Robert said with a smile. "I learned it, slowly but surely."

Honesty carries its own rewards today, just as it did in ancient times.
Psalm 112 talks about many of those rewards.

* How would the phrase "fair in their business" in verse 5 apply to Robert?
* In what ways can honesty keep you "steady" (verse 7) as you go about your business at school, work and home?

Consider . . .

* rewriting this psalm using your own words and applying it to your own circumstances.
* promising God never to cheat at school.

For more, see . . .

* 1 Samuel 12:1–5 (p.264)
* Colossians 3:9–10 (p.1292)
* Isaiah 33:15–17 (p.672)

⁵It is good to be merciful and generous.
  Those who are fair in their business
⁶will never be defeated.
  Good people will always be remembered.
⁷They won't be afraid of bad news;
  their hearts are steady because they trust
    the LORD.
⁸They are confident and will not be afraid;
  they will look down on their enemies.
⁹They give freely to the poor.
  The things they do are right and will
    continue for ever.
  They will be given great honour.

¹⁰The wicked will see this and become
    angry;
  they will grind their teeth in anger and
    then disappear.
  The wishes of the wicked will come to
    nothing.

Praise for the LORD's Kindness

113 Praise the LORD!

Praise him, you servants of the LORD;
  praise the name of the LORD.
²The LORD's name should be praised
  now and for ever.
³The LORD's name should be praised
  from where the sun rises to where
    it sets.

⁴The LORD is supreme over all the nations;
  his glory reaches to the skies.
⁵No one is like the LORD our God,
  who rules from heaven,
⁶who bends down to look
  at the skies and the earth.

⁷The LORD lifts the poor from the ground
  and takes the helpless from the ashes.
⁸He seats them with princes,
  the princes of his people.
⁹He gives children to the woman who has
    none
  and makes her a happy mother.

Praise the LORD!

God Brought Israel from Egypt

114 When the Israelites went out of
        Egypt,
  the people of Jacob left that foreign
    country.
²Then Judah became God's holy place;
  Israel became the land he ruled.

³The Red Sea ᵈ looked and ran away;
  the Jordan River turned back.
⁴The mountains danced like rams
  and the hills like little lambs.

⁵Sea, why did you run away?
  Jordan, why did you turn back?
⁶Mountains, why did you dance like rams?
  Hills, why did you dance like little lambs?

⁷Earth, shake with fear before the Lord,
  before the God of Jacob.
⁸He turned a rock into a pool of water,
  a hard rock into a spring of water.

The One True God

115 It does not belong to us, LORD.
      The glory belongs to you
  because of your love and loyalty.

²Why do the nations ask,
  "Where is their God?"
³Our God is in heaven.
  He does what he pleases.
⁴Their idols are made of silver and gold,
  the work of human hands.
⁵They have mouths, but they cannot speak.
  They have eyes, but they cannot see.
⁶They have ears, but they cannot hear.
  They have noses, but they cannot smell.
⁷They have hands, but they cannot feel.
  They have feet, but they cannot walk.
  No sounds come from their throats.
⁸People who make idols will be like them,
  and so will those who trust them.

⁹Family of Israel, trust the LORD;
  he is your helper and your protection.
¹⁰Family of Aaron, trust the LORD;
  he is your helper and your protection.
¹¹You who respect the LORD should trust him;
  he is your helper and your protection.

¹²The LORD remembers us and will bless us.
  He will bless the family of Israel;
  he will bless the family of Aaron.
¹³The LORD will bless those who respect him,
  from the smallest to the greatest.

¹⁴May the LORD give you success,
  and may he give you and your children
    success.

Sidelight

When Jesus and his disciples sang on the night Judas betrayed Jesus (Matthew 26:30, p.989), they probably sang Psalms 113—114 or Psalms 115—118. These songs were customarily sung during the Passover, which was being celebrated at the time.

¹⁵May you be blessed by the LORD,
    who made heaven and earth.

¹⁶Heaven belongs to the LORD,
    but he gave the earth to people.
¹⁷Dead people do not praise the LORD;
    those in the grave are silent.
¹⁸But we will praise the LORD
    now and for ever.

Praise the LORD!

Thanksgiving for Escaping Death

116 I love the LORD,
    because he listens to my prayers
        for help.
²He paid attention to me,
    so I will call to him for help as long as I live.

³The ropes of death bound me,
    and the fear of the grave took hold of me.
    I was troubled and sad.

⁴Then I called out the name of the LORD.
    I said, "Please, LORD, save me!"

⁵The LORD is kind and does what is right;
    our God is merciful.
⁶The LORD watches over the foolish;
    when I was helpless, he saved me.
⁷I said to myself, "Relax,
    because the LORD takes care of you."

⁸LORD, you saved me from death.
    You stopped my eyes from crying;
    you kept me from being defeated.
⁹So I will walk with the LORD
    in the land of the living.
¹⁰I believed, so I said,
    "I am completely ruined."
¹¹In my distress I said,
    "All people are liars."

¹²What can I give the LORD
    for all the good things he has given to me?

THANKFULNESS

Showered With Blessings

Lily was brought up with good manners. She always said thank you for birthday presents and thanked God when she managed to get out of forgetting to do her homework.

However, Lily didn't feel like she had anything in common with the guy in **Psalm 116**. She'd never had armies approaching against her or been in a life-threatening situation where God had to save her from death. She knew that the Bible says Jesus is her rescuer but how could she be thankful when she'd never felt him save her like this? Lily knew she had it pretty good – so how could this psalm be relevant to her?

She found the answer in verse 7: "Relax, because the Lord takes care of you."

Whether she'd won a major battle or not, Lily realised her life has been showered with blessings. God was not only there for her in tough situations, but had promised her eternal life, happiness in heaven and she had an everlasting saviour in Jesus Christ. Like the writer in verses 1 and 2, Lily knew that God would hear and answer her every call and she should thank him for that, as well as everything else he gives her every day.

She made a vow to show her thankfulness to God in every situation, whether good or bad, for her favourite shoes or for strawberry milkshakes, for blessings that she never realised she had. She decided to live a life that made the most of the gifts God had given her, simply because she is his daughter.

* What does the psalm writer promise to give back to God to say thank you? Should we do the same?
* What do verses 14 and 18 mean? Does this say anything to us about how church should be?

Consider . . .

* whether you have felt like Lily did. Give thanks to God for all he has given you.
* making a list of all the things you love about God? Do you thank him for who he is as well as what he's given to you?

For more, see . . .

* John 3:16 (p.1100)
* 1 Thessalonians 5:16–18 (p.1301)

* Colossians 3:12–17 (p.1293)

13I will lift up the cup of salvation,
and I will pray to the LORD.
14I will give the LORD what I promised
in front of all his people.

15The death of one that belongs to the LORD
is precious in his sight.
16LORD, I am your servant;
I am your servant and the son of your
female servant.
You have freed me from my chains.

17I will give you an offering to show thanks
to you,
and I will pray to the LORD.
18I will give the LORD what I promised
in front of all his people,
19in the Temple *d* courtyards
in Jerusalem.

Praise the LORD!

> **Sidelight** The shortest chapter in
> the Bible – Psalm 117 –
> is long on praise. The psalmist encourages
> the whole world to make music to God, which
> would make the Guinness Book of World
> Records for the Largest Community Sing-a-long.

A Hymn of Praise

117 All you nations, praise the LORD.
All you people, praise him
2because the LORD loves us very much,
and his truth is everlasting.

Praise the LORD!

Thanksgiving for Victory

118 Thank the LORD because he is good.
His love continues for ever.

2Let the people of Israel say,
"His love continues for ever."
3Let the family of Aaron say,
"His love continues for ever."
4Let those who respect the LORD say,
"His love continues for ever."
5I was in trouble, so I called to the LORD.
The LORD answered me and set me free.
6I will not be afraid, because the LORD is
with me.
People can't do anything to me.
7The LORD is with me to help me,
so I will see my enemies defeated.

8It is better to trust the LORD
than to trust people.

9It is better to trust the LORD
than to trust princes.

10All the nations surrounded me,
but I defeated them in the name of the
LORD.
11They surrounded me on every side,
but with the LORD's power I defeated them.
12They surrounded me like a swarm of bees,
but they died as quickly as thorns burn.
By the LORD's power, I defeated them.

13They chased me until I was almost defeated,
but the LORD helped me.
14The LORD gives me strength and a song.
He has saved me.

15Shouts of joy and victory
come from the tents of those who
do right:
"The LORD has done powerful things."
16The power of the LORD has won the victory;
with his power the LORD has done mighty
things.

17I will not die, but live,
and I will tell what the LORD has done.
18The LORD has taught me a hard lesson,
but he did not let me die.

19Open for me the Temple *d* gates.
Then I will come in and thank the LORD.
20This is the LORD's gate;
only those who are good may enter
through it.
21LORD, I thank you for answering me.
You have saved me.

22The stone that the builders rejected
became the cornerstone. *d*
23The LORD did this,
and it is wonderful to us.
24This is the day that the LORD has made.
Let us rejoice and be glad today!

25Please, LORD, save us;
please, LORD, give us success.
26God bless the one who comes in the name of
the LORD.
We bless all of you from the Temple of the
LORD.
27The LORD is God,
and he has shown kindness to us.
With branches in your hands, join the feast.
Come to the corners of the altar.

28You are my God, and I will thank you;
you are my God, and I will praise your
greatness.

29Thank the LORD because he is good.
His love continues for ever.

The Word of God

119 Happy are those who live pure lives,
who follow the LORD's teachings.

Sidelight "Ah, your eyes, your lips, your regulations!" You've probably never written a love song to a book of laws, but the writer of Psalm 119 did. The longest chapter in the Bible serenades God's commandments – probably as written in Genesis through to Deuteronomy.

²Happy are those who keep his rules,
who try to obey him with their whole heart.
³They don't do what is wrong;
they follow his ways.
⁴LORD, you gave your orders
to be obeyed completely.
⁵I wish I were more loyal
in obeying your demands.
⁶Then I would not be ashamed
when I study your commands.
⁷When I learned that your laws are fair,
I praised you with an honest heart.
⁸I will obey your demands,
so please don't ever leave me.

⁹How can a young person live a pure life?
By obeying your word.
¹⁰With all my heart I try to obey you.
Don't let me break your commands.
¹¹I have taken your words to heart
so I would not sin against you.
¹²LORD, you should be praised.
Teach me your demands.
¹³My lips will tell about
all the laws you have spoken.
¹⁴I enjoy living by your rules
as people enjoy great riches.
¹⁵I think about your orders
and study your ways.
¹⁶I enjoy obeying your demands,
and I will not forget your word.

¹⁷Do good to me, your servant, so I can live,
so I can obey your word.
¹⁸Open my eyes to see
the miracles ᵈ in your teachings.
¹⁹I am a stranger on earth.
Do not hide your commands from me.
²⁰I wear myself out with desire
for your laws all the time.
²¹You scold proud people;
those who ignore your commands are cursed.

²²Don't let me be insulted and hated
because I keep your rules.
²³Even if princes speak against me,
I, your servant, will think about your demands.
²⁴Your rules give me pleasure;
they give me good advice.

²⁵I am about to die.
Give me life, as you have promised.
²⁶I told you about my life, and you answered me.
Teach me your demands.
²⁷Help me understand your orders.
Then I will think about your miracles.
²⁸I am sad and tired.
Make me strong again as you have promised.
²⁹Don't let me be dishonest;
have mercy on me by helping me obey your teachings.
³⁰I have chosen the way of truth;
I have obeyed your laws.
³¹I hold on to your rules.
LORD, do not let me be disgraced.
³²I will quickly obey your commands,
because you have made me happy.

³³LORD, teach me your demands,
and I will keep them until the end.
³⁴Help me understand, so I can keep your teachings,
obeying them with all my heart.
³⁵Lead me in the path of your commands,
because that makes me happy.
³⁶Make me want to keep your rules
instead of wishing for riches.
³⁷Keep me from looking at worthless things.
Let me live by your word.
³⁸Keep your promise to me, your servant,
so you will be respected.
³⁹Take away the shame I fear,
because your laws are good.
⁴⁰How I want to follow your orders.
Give me life because of your goodness.

⁴¹LORD, show me your love,
and save me as you have promised.
⁴²I have an answer for people who insult me,
because I trust what you say.
⁴³Never keep me from speaking your truth,
because I depend on your fair laws.
⁴⁴I will obey your teachings
for ever and ever.
⁴⁵So I will live in freedom,
because I want to follow your orders.
⁴⁶I will discuss your rules with kings
and will not be ashamed.

⁴⁷I enjoy obeying your commands,
  which I love.
⁴⁸I praise your commands, which I love,
  and I think about your demands.

⁴⁹Remember your promise to me, your servant;
  it gives me hope.
⁵⁰When I suffer, this comforts me:
  your promise gives me life.
⁵¹Proud people always make fun of me,
  but I do not reject your teachings.
⁵²I remember your laws from long ago,
  and they comfort me, LORD.
⁵³I become angry with wicked people
  who do not keep your teachings.
⁵⁴I sing about your demands
  wherever I live.
⁵⁵LORD, I remember you at night,
  and I will obey your teachings.
⁵⁶This is what I do:
  I follow your orders.

⁵⁷LORD, you are my share in life;
  I have promised to obey your words.
⁵⁸I prayed to you with all my heart.
  Have mercy on me as you have promised.

⁵⁹I thought about my life,
  and I decided to follow your rules.
⁶⁰I hurried and did not wait
  to obey your commands.
⁶¹Wicked people have tied me up,
  but I have not forgotten your teachings.
⁶²In the middle of the night, I get up to
    thank you
  because your laws are right.
⁶³I am a friend to everyone who fears you,
  to anyone who obeys your orders.
⁶⁴LORD, your love fills the earth.
  Teach me your demands.

⁶⁵You have done good things for your servant,
  as you have promised, LORD.
⁶⁶Teach me wisdom and knowledge
  because I trust your commands.
⁶⁷Before I suffered, I did wrong,
  but now I obey your word.
⁶⁸You are good, and you do what is good.
  Teach me your demands.
⁶⁹Proud people have made up lies about me,
  but I will follow your orders with all my
    heart.

JUSTICE

To Live in Freedom

Reward posters offered large sums of money for her capture, dead or alive. She was just over 1.5 metres tall, and used to suffer from fainting spells because of a head injury inflicted by an owner when she was younger, but many people regarded her as extremely dangerous. Some even called her "the devil".

But others, many others, called her "Moses". She had, after all, led more than 200 men, women and children out of slavery to freedom in Canada via the Underground Railway.

Her real name was Harriet Tubman, and in the years just before America's Civil War in the 1800s, she risked her life time and time again, returning to the South to guide escaped slaves to freedom in the North.

In **Psalm 119:33–48**, the psalmist yearns for guidance to "live in freedom", as so many slaves did long ago. Just as the slaves depended on Harriet Tubman, so the psalmist depended on God to show him the way.

- Which verses of the passage would Harriet Tubman have identified with?
- According to this passage, how can God set you free?

Consider . . .

- writing down what total freedom means to you and what you think God would say it means.
- becoming a "Moses" to someone else by helping him or her to overcome an enslaving problem, such as drug abuse or a negative attitude.

For more, see . . .

- Joshua 1:8–9 (p.203)
- Romans 6:15–23 (p.1192)

- John 8:34–47 (p.1110)

⁷⁰Those people have no feelings,
but I love your teachings.
⁷¹It was good for me to suffer
so I would learn your demands.
⁷²Your teachings are worth more to me
than thousands of pieces of gold and silver.

⁷³You made me and formed me with your hands.
Give me understanding so I can learn your
commands.
⁷⁴Let those who respect you rejoice when they
see me,
because I put my hope in your word.
⁷⁵LORD, I know that your laws are right
and that it was right for you to punish me.
⁷⁶Comfort me with your love,
as you promised me, your servant.
⁷⁷Have mercy on me so that I may live.
I love your teachings.
⁷⁸Make proud people ashamed because they
lied about me.
But I will think about your orders.
⁷⁹Let those who respect you return to me,
those who know your rules.
⁸⁰Let me obey your demands perfectly
so I will not be ashamed.

⁸¹I am weak from waiting for you to save me,
but I hope in your word.
⁸²My eyes are tired from looking for your
promise.
When will you comfort me?
⁸³Even though I am like a wine bag going up
in smoke,
I do not forget your demands.
⁸⁴How long will I live?
When will you judge those who are
hurting me?
⁸⁵Proud people have dug pits to trap me.
They have nothing to do with your teachings.
⁸⁶All of your commands can be trusted.
Liars are hurting me. Help me!
⁸⁷They have almost put me in the grave,
but I have not rejected your orders.
⁸⁸Give me life by your love
so I can obey your rules.

⁸⁹LORD, your word is everlasting;
it continues for ever in heaven.
⁹⁰Your loyalty will go on and on;
you made the earth, and it still stands.
⁹¹All things continue to this day because of
your laws,
because all things serve you.
⁹²If I had not loved your teachings,
I would have died from my sufferings.
⁹³I will never forget your orders,
because you have given me life by them.
⁹⁴I am yours. Save me.
I want to obey your orders.

⁹⁵Wicked people are waiting to destroy me,
but I will think about your rules.
⁹⁶Everything I see has its limits,
but your commands have none.

⁹⁷How I love your teachings!
I think about them all day long.
⁹⁸Your commands make me wiser than my
enemies,
because they are mine for ever.
⁹⁹I am wiser than all my teachers,
because I think about your rules.
¹⁰⁰I have more understanding than the older
leaders,
because I follow your orders.
¹⁰¹I have avoided every evil way
so I could obey your word.
¹⁰²I haven't walked away from your laws,
because you yourself are my teacher.
¹⁰³Your promises are sweet to me,
sweeter than honey in my mouth!
¹⁰⁴Your orders give me understanding,
so I hate lying ways.

¹⁰⁵Your word is like a lamp for my feet
and a light for my path.
¹⁰⁶I will do what I have promised
and obey your fair laws.
¹⁰⁷I have suffered for a long time.
LORD, give me life by your word.
¹⁰⁸LORD, accept my willing praise
and teach me your laws.
¹⁰⁹My life is always in danger,
but I haven't forgotten your teachings.
¹¹⁰Wicked people have set a trap for me,
but I haven't strayed from your orders.
¹¹¹I will follow your rules for ever,
because they make me happy.
¹¹²I will try to do what you demand
for ever, until the end.

¹¹³I hate disloyal people,
but I love your teachings.
¹¹⁴You are my hiding place and my shield;
I hope in your word.
¹¹⁵Get away from me, you who do evil,
so I can keep my God's commands.
¹¹⁶Support me as you promised so I can live.
Don't let me be embarrassed because of my
hopes.
¹¹⁷Help me, and I will be saved.
I will always respect your demands.
¹¹⁸You reject those who ignore your demands,
because their lies mislead them.
¹¹⁹You throw away the wicked of the world
like rubbish.
So I will love your rules.
¹²⁰I shake in fear of you;
I respect your laws.

¹²¹I have done what is fair and right.
Don't leave me to those who wrong me.
¹²²Promise that you will help me, your servant.
Don't let proud people wrong me.
¹²³My eyes are tired from looking for your
salvation
and for your good promise.
¹²⁴Show your love to me, your servant,
and teach me your demands.
¹²⁵I am your servant. Give me wisdom
so I can understand your rules.
¹²⁶LORD, it is time for you to do something,
because people have disobeyed your
teachings.
¹²⁷I love your commands
more than the purest gold.
¹²⁸I respect all your orders,
so I hate lying ways.

¹²⁹Your rules are wonderful.
That is why I keep them.
¹³⁰Learning your words gives wisdom
and understanding for the foolish.
¹³¹I am nearly out of breath.
I really want to learn your commands.
¹³²Look at me and have mercy on me
as you do for those who love you.
¹³³Guide my steps as you promised;
don't let any sin control me.
¹³⁴Save me from harmful people
so I can obey your orders.
¹³⁵Show your kindness to me, your servant.
Teach me your demands.
¹³⁶Tears stream from my eyes,
because people do not obey your teachings.

¹³⁷LORD, you do what is right,
and your laws are fair.
¹³⁸The rules you commanded are right
and completely trustworthy.
¹³⁹I am so upset I am worn out,
because my enemies have forgotten your
words.
¹⁴⁰Your promises are proven,
so I, your servant, love them.
¹⁴¹I am unimportant and hated,
but I have not forgotten your orders.
¹⁴²Your goodness continues for ever,
and your teachings are true.
¹⁴³I have had troubles and misery,
but I love your commands.
¹⁴⁴Your rules are always good.
Help me understand so I can live.

¹⁴⁵LORD, I call to you with all my heart.
Answer me, and I will keep your demands.
¹⁴⁶I call to you.
Save me so I can obey your rules.
¹⁴⁷I wake up early in the morning and cry out.
I hope in your word.

¹⁴⁸I stay awake all night
so I can think about your promises.
¹⁴⁹Listen to me because of your love;
LORD, give me life by your laws.
¹⁵⁰Those who love evil are near,
but they are far from your teachings.
¹⁵¹But, LORD, you are also near,
and all your commands are true.
¹⁵²Long ago I learned from your rules
that you made them to continue for ever.

¹⁵³See my suffering and rescue me,
because I have not forgotten your
teachings.
¹⁵⁴Argue my case and save me.
Let me live by your promises.
¹⁵⁵Wicked people are far from being saved,
because they do not want your demands.
¹⁵⁶LORD, you are very kind;
give me life by your laws.
¹⁵⁷Many enemies are chasing me,
but I have not rejected your rules.
¹⁵⁸I see those traitors, and I hate them,
because they do not obey what you say.
¹⁵⁹See how I love your orders.
LORD, give me life by your love.
¹⁶⁰Your words are true from the start,
and all your laws will be fair for ever.

¹⁶¹Leaders attack me for no reason,
but I fear your law in my heart.
¹⁶²I am as happy over your promises
as if I had found a great treasure.
¹⁶³I hate and despise lies,
but I love your teachings.
¹⁶⁴Seven times a day I praise you
for your fair laws.
¹⁶⁵Those who love your teachings will find true
peace,
and nothing will defeat them.
¹⁶⁶I am waiting for you to save me, LORD.
I will obey your commands.
¹⁶⁷I obey your rules,
and I love them very much.
¹⁶⁸I obey your orders and rules,
because you know everything I do.

¹⁶⁹Hear my cry to you, LORD.
Let your word help me understand.
¹⁷⁰Listen to my prayer;
save me as you promised.
¹⁷¹Let me speak your praise,
because you have taught me your
demands.
¹⁷²Let me sing about your promises,
because all your commands are fair.
¹⁷³Give me your helping hand,
because I have chosen your commands.
¹⁷⁴I want you to save me, LORD.
I love your teachings.

¹⁷⁵Let me live so I can praise you,
and let your laws help me.
¹⁷⁶I have wandered like a lost sheep.
Look for your servant, because I have not
forgotten your commands.

A Prayer of Someone Far from Home

A psalm for going up to worship.

120 When I was in trouble, I called to
the LORD,
and he answered me.
²LORD, save me from liars
and from those who plan evil.

³You who plan evil, what will God do to you?
How will he punish you?
⁴He will punish you with the sharp arrows of
a warrior
and with burning coals of wood.

⁵How terrible it is for me to live in the land of
Meshech,
to live among the people of Kedar.
⁶I have lived too long
with people who hate peace.
⁷When I talk peace,
they want war.

The LORD Guards His People

A song for going up to worship.

121 I look up to the hills,
but where does my help come
from?
²My help comes from the LORD,
who made heaven and earth.

³He will not let you be defeated.
He who guards you never sleeps.
⁴He who guards Israel
never rests or sleeps.
⁵The LORD guards you.

The LORD is the shade that protects you
from the sun.
⁶The sun cannot hurt you during the day,
and the moon cannot hurt you at night.

⁷The LORD will protect you from all dangers;
he will guard your life.
⁸The LORD will guard you as you come and go,
both now and for ever.

Happy People in Jerusalem

A song for going up to worship. Of David.

122 I was happy when they said to me,
"Let's go to the Temple ^d of the
LORD."
²Jerusalem, we are standing
at your gates.

³Jerusalem is built as a city
with the buildings close together.
⁴The tribes ^d go up there,
the tribes who belong to the LORD.
It is the rule in Israel
to praise the LORD at Jerusalem.
⁵There the descendants ^d of David
set their thrones to judge the people.
⁶Pray for peace in Jerusalem:
"May those who love her be safe.
⁷May there be peace within her walls
and safety within her strong towers."
⁸To help my relatives and friends,
I say, "Let Jerusalem have peace."
⁹For the sake of the Temple of the LORD
our God,
I wish good for her.

A Prayer for Mercy

A song for going up to worship.

123 LORD, I look upwards to you,
you who live in heaven.
²Slaves depend on their masters,
and a female servant depends on her
mistress.
In the same way, we depend on the LORD
our God;
we wait for him to show us mercy.

³Have mercy on us, LORD. Have mercy
on us,
because we have been insulted.
⁴We have suffered many insults from lazy
people
and much cruelty from the proud.

The LORD Saves His People

A song for going up to worship. Of David.

124 What if the LORD had not been on
our side?
(Let Israel repeat this.)
²What if the LORD had not been on our side
when we were attacked?
³When they were angry with us,
they would have swallowed us alive.
⁴They would have been like a flood
drowning us;
they would have poured over us like a
river.
⁵ They would have swept us away like a
mighty stream.

⁶Praise the LORD,
who did not let them chew us up.
⁷We escaped like a bird
from the hunter's trap.
The trap broke,
and we escaped.

8Our help comes from the LORD,
who made heaven and earth.

God Protects Those Who Trust Him

A song for going up to worship.

125 Those who trust the LORD are like
Mount Zion, *d*
which sits unmoved for ever.
2As the mountains surround Jerusalem,
the LORD surrounds his people
now and for ever.

3The wicked will not rule
over those who do right.
If they did, the people who do right
might use their power to do evil.

4LORD, be good to those who are good,
whose hearts are honest.
5But, LORD, when you remove those who do
evil,
also remove those who stop following
you.

Let there be peace in Israel.

LORD, Bring Your People Back

A song for going up to worship.

126 When the LORD brought the
prisoners back to Jerusalem,
it seemed as if we were dreaming.
2Then we were filled with laughter,
and we sang happy songs.
Then the other nations said,
"The LORD has done great things
for them."
3The LORD has done great things for us,
and we are very glad.

4LORD, return our prisoners again,
as you bring streams to the desert.
5Those who cry as they plant crops
will sing at harvest time.
6Those who cry
as they carry out the seeds
will return singing
and carrying bundles of grain.

All Good Things Come from God

A song for going up to worship. Of Solomon.

127 If the LORD doesn't build the house,
the builders are working for
nothing.
If the LORD doesn't guard the city,
the guards are watching for nothing.
2It is no use for you to get up early
and stay up late,
working for a living.
The LORD gives sleep to those he loves.

3Children are a gift from the LORD;
babies are a reward.
4Children who are born to a young man
are like arrows in the hand of a warrior.
5Happy is the man
who has his bag full of arrows.
They will not be defeated
when they fight their enemies at the city
gate.

The Happy Home

A song for going up to worship.

128 Happy are those who respect the
LORD
and obey him.
2You will enjoy what you work for,
and you will be blessed with good
things.
3Your wife will give you many children,
like a vine that produces much fruit.
Your children will bring you much good,
like olive branches that produce many
olives.
4This is how the man who respects the
LORD
will be blessed.

5May the LORD bless you from Mount Zion; *d*
may you enjoy the good things of Jerusalem
all your life.
6May you see your grandchildren.

Let there be peace in Israel.

A Prayer Against the Enemies

A song for going up to worship.

129 They have treated me badly all my
life.
(Let Israel repeat this.)
2They have treated me badly all my life,
but they have not defeated me.
3Like farmers ploughing, they ploughed over
my back,
making long wounds.
4But the LORD does what is right;
he has set me free from those wicked
people.

5Let those who hate Jerusalem
be turned back in shame.
6Let them be like the grass on the roof
that dries up before it has grown.
7There is not enough of it to fill a hand
or to make into a bundle to fill one's
arms.
8Let those who pass by them not say,
"May the LORD bless you.
We bless you by the power of the LORD."

A Prayer for Mercy

A song for going up to worship.

130 LORD, I am in great trouble,
so I call out to you.
[2]Lord, hear my voice;
listen to my prayer for help.
[3]LORD, if you punished people for all
their sins,
no one would be left, Lord.
[4]But you forgive us,
so we respect you.

[5]I wait for the LORD to help me,
and I trust his word.
[6]I wait for the Lord to help me
more than night-watchmen wait for the
dawn,
more than night-watchmen wait for the
dawn.

[7]People of Israel, put your hope in the
LORD
because he is loving
and able to save.
[8]He will save Israel
from all their sins.

Childlike Trust in the LORD

A song for going up to worship. Of David.

131 LORD, my heart is not proud;
I don't look down on others.
I don't do great things,
and I can't do miracles. *d*
[2]But I am calm and quiet,
like a baby with its mother.
I am at peace, like a baby with its
mother.

[3]People of Israel, put your hope in the
LORD
now and for ever.

In Praise of the Temple

A song for going up to worship.

132 LORD, remember David
and all his suffering.
[2]He made an oath to the LORD,
a promise to the Mighty God of Jacob.
[3]He said, "I will not go home to my house,
or lie down on my bed,
[4]or close my eyes,
or let myself sleep

FAMILY

Happy Families

Is there such thing as a normal family? Marriage, divorce, single parents, stepparents, adoption, living with the grandparents, fostering, alternative lifestyle – just as we individually are all unique, so too are our families. Normality, when it comes to families, is being different.

Families come in all sorts of shapes and sizes. However a family is put together, it is God's desire that we are supported and cared for by people who love us.

The writer of **Psalm 128** believes that children are a sign of blessing from God; that God uses families as a way of showing how he cares for each of us; and that if God is at the heart of the household, the house can become a home.

* Why do you think the writer of this psalm believes families are important?
* What parts of your family are similar to your friends'? How is it different? Is difference a good or bad thing?

Consider . . .

* collecting photos of your extended family or drawing pictures of them, building a collage of your family tree. Join each member together with thread, brothers and sisters, parents and children. See how you all connect. Thank God for the diversity in your family and pray for his blessing on it.
* making a prayer box filled with objects or photos to remind you of family members. Pray for one member of your family each day, asking God to be at the heart of their home.

For more, see . . .

* Joshua 24:14–15 (p.222)
* Ephesians 6:1–4 (p.1276)

⁵until I find a place for the LORD.
   I want to provide a home for the Mighty
      God of Jacob."

⁶We heard about the Ark *d* in Bethlehem.
   We found it at Kiriath Jearim.
⁷Let's go to the LORD's house.
   Let's worship at his footstool.
⁸Rise, LORD, and come to your resting place;
   come with the Ark that shows your
      strength.
⁹May your priests do what is right.
   May your people sing for joy.

¹⁰For the sake of your servant David,
   do not reject your appointed king.

¹¹The LORD made a promise to David,
   a sure promise that he will not
      take back.
He promised, "I will make one of your
      descendants *d*
   rule as king after you.
¹²If your sons keep my agreement
   and the rules that I teach them,
then their sons after them will rule
   on your throne for ever and ever."

¹³The LORD has chosen Jerusalem;
   he wants it for his home.
¹⁴He says, "This is my resting place for ever.
   Here is where I want to stay.

SIN

What Harm?

Sarah knew it was stealing, in a way at least. But what choice did she have? Mr Walker, the Head of Music, had talked her into playing a solo, but her flute was old and unreliable. It sounded more like a tin pipe than a flute when she played it.

Ann, on the other hand, had a new, top-of-the-range flute that made each note sound like liquid silver. Ann didn't like other people playing her instrument, but what harm would it do if Sarah just switched the flutes in their cases the day before the contest?

For days Sarah agonised over her decision but finally decided, right or wrong, she just had to do it. She was nearly sick with nerves as she sneaked into the deserted music room the day before the contest, but the actual switch was easy. There was no one around to see her.

Sarah played her solo for the judges the next day. Ann's flute sounded lovely, but Sarah made lots of stupid mistakes. Her fingers felt like rubber. She couldn't concentrate.

Afterwards, she found Ann warming up for the band's contest number, using, of course, Sarah's old tin-pipe flute. As Sarah sat down in her own place beside Ann's first-flute spot, Ann stopped playing and turned to face her.

"Ann, I'm so sorry," Sarah whispered, her face burning. "I'm so ashamed. I just feel sick, and have all day."

Ann looked at Sarah for a long minute and then smiled. "Let's just forget it happened," she said. "It's OK, really."

But Sarah knew it wasn't OK. Not quite. Ann had forgiven her, but it would be harder for Sarah to forgive herself. She had let herself down.

People like Sarah have always faced temptation, and sometimes they've given in. **Psalm 130** shows the need for forgiveness of these sins.

* What might the psalmist advise Sarah to do next in her situation?
* What temptations do you face that you need to ask God to help you sort out?

Consider . . .

* writing on a slip of paper the main temptations you face today and then asking God each week to help you to overcome them.
* apologising to someone for something you did that hurt him or her.

For more, see . . .

* Isaiah 44:22–23 (p.687)
* 1 Corinthians 15:1–5 (p.1235)
* Jeremiah 31:31–34 (p.753)

15I will bless her with plenty;
I will fill her poor with food.
16I will cover her priests with salvation,
and those who worship me will really sing
for joy.
17"I will make a king come from the family of
David.
I will provide my appointed one
descendants to rule after him.
18I will cover his enemies with shame,
but his crown will shine."

The Love of God's People

A song for going up to worship. Of David.

133 It is good and pleasant
when God's people live together
in peace!
2It is like perfumed oil poured on the priest's
head
and running down his beard.
It ran down Aaron's beard
and on to the collar of his robes.
3It is like the dew of Mount Hermon
falling on the hills of Jerusalem.
There the LORD gives his blessing
of life for ever.

Temple Guards, Praise the LORD

A song for going up to worship.

134 Praise the LORD, all you servants of
the LORD,
you who serve at night in the Temple *d* of
the LORD.
2Raise your hands in the Temple
and praise the LORD.
3May the LORD bless you from Mount Zion, *d*
he who made heaven and earth.

Sidelight　The night servants in the
Temple (Psalm 134:1)
were the security guards of their day. They kept
the keys to the temple gates and made sure
that no one walked off with the valuables stored
there.

The LORD Saves, Idols do Not

135 Praise the LORD!
Praise the name of the LORD;
praise him, you servants of the LORD,
2you who stand in the LORD's Temple *d*
and in the Temple courtyards.
3Praise the LORD, because he is good;
sing praises to him, because it is pleasant.

4The LORD has chosen the people of Jacob for
himself;
he has chosen the people of Israel for his
very own.
5I know that the LORD is great.
Our Lord is greater than all the gods.
6The LORD does what he pleases,
in heaven and on earth,
in the seas and the deep oceans.
7He brings the clouds from the ends of the
earth.
He sends the lightning with the rain.
He brings out the wind from his
storehouses.
8He destroyed the firstborn *d* sons in Egypt
the firstborn of both people and animals.
9He did many signs and miracles *d* in Egypt
against the king and his servants.
10He defeated many nations
and killed powerful kings:
11Sihon king of the Amorites,
Og king of Bashan,
and all the kings of Canaan.
12Then he gave their land as a gift,
a gift to his people, the Israelites.

13LORD, your name is everlasting;
LORD, you will be remembered for ever.
14The LORD defends his people
and has mercy on his servants.

15The idols of other nations are made of silver
and gold,
the work of human hands.
16They have mouths, but they cannot speak.
They have eyes, but they cannot see.
17They have ears, but they cannot hear.
They have no breath in their mouths.
18People who make idols will be like them,
and so will those who trust them.

19Family of Israel, praise the LORD.
Family of Aaron, praise the LORD.
20Family of Levi, praise the LORD.
You who respect the LORD should
praise him.
21You people of Jerusalem, praise the LORD on
Mount Zion. *d*

Praise the LORD!

God's Love Continues For Ever

136 Give thanks to the LORD because he
is good.
His love continues for ever.
2Give thanks to the God of gods.
His love continues for ever.
3Give thanks to the Lord of lords.
His love continues for ever.

⁴Only he can do great miracles. *d*
  His love continues for ever.
⁵With his wisdom he made the skies.
  His love continues for ever.
⁶He spread out the earth on the seas.
  His love continues for ever.
⁷He made the sun and the moon.
  His love continues for ever.
⁸He made the sun to rule the day.
  His love continues for ever.
⁹He made the moon and stars to rule the
    night.
  His love continues for ever.

¹⁰He killed the firstborn *d* sons of the
    Egyptians.
  His love continues for ever.
¹¹He brought the people of Israel out of Egypt.
  His love continues for ever.
¹²He did it with his great power and strength.
  His love continues for ever.

¹³He parted the water of the Red Sea. *d*
  His love continues for ever.
¹⁴He brought the Israelites through the middle
    of it.
  His love continues for ever.
¹⁵But the king of Egypt and his army drowned
    in the Red Sea.
  His love continues for ever.

¹⁶He led his people through the desert.
  His love continues for ever.
¹⁷He defeated great kings.
  His love continues for ever.
¹⁸He killed powerful kings.
  His love continues for ever.
¹⁹He defeated Sihon king of the Amorites.
  His love continues for ever.
²⁰He defeated Og king of Bashan.
  His love continues for ever.
²¹He gave their land as a gift.
  His love continues for ever.
²²It was a gift to his servants, the Israelites.
  His love continues for ever.

²³He remembered us when we were in
    trouble.
  His love continues for ever.
²⁴He freed us from our enemies.
  His love continues for ever.
²⁵He gives food to every living creature.
  His love continues for ever.

²⁶Give thanks to the God of heaven.
  His love continues for ever.

Israelites in Captivity

137 By the rivers in Babylon we sat and
    cried
  when we remembered Jerusalem.

²On the poplar trees nearby
  we hung our harps.
³Those who captured us asked us to sing;
  our enemies wanted happy songs.
  They said, "Sing us a song about
    Jerusalem!"

⁴But we cannot sing songs about the LORD
  while we are in this foreign country!
⁵Jerusalem, if I forget you,
  let my right hand lose its skill.
⁶Let my tongue stick to the roof of my mouth
  if I do not remember you,
  if I do not think about Jerusalem
  as my greatest joy.

⁷LORD, remember what the Edomites did
  on the day Jerusalem fell.
  They said, "Tear it down!
  Tear it down to its foundations!"

⁸People of Babylon, you will be destroyed.
  The people who pay you back for what you
    did to us will be happy.
⁹They will grab your babies
  and throw them against the rocks.

A Hymn of Thanksgiving

A psalm of David.

138 LORD, I will thank you with all my
    heart;
  I will sing to you before the gods.
²I will bow down facing your holy Temple, *d*
  and I will thank you for your love and
    loyalty.
  You have made your name and your word
    greater than anything.
³On the day I called to you, you
    answered me.
  You made me strong and brave.

⁴LORD, let all the kings of the earth praise
    you
  when they hear the words you speak.
⁵They will sing about what the LORD has
    done,
  because the LORD's glory is great.

⁶Though the LORD is supreme,
  he takes care of those who are humble,
  but he stays away from the proud.
⁷LORD, even when I have trouble all
    around me,
  you will keep me alive.
  When my enemies are angry,
  you will reach down and save me by your
    power.
⁸LORD, you do everything for me.
  LORD, your love continues for ever.
  Do not leave us, whom you made.

God Knows Everything

For the director of music. A psalm of David.

139 LORD, you have examined me
and know all about me.
²You know when I sit down and when I
get up.
You know my thoughts before I think
them.
³You know where I go and where I lie down.
You know thoroughly everything I do.
⁴LORD, even before I say a word,
you already know it.

⁵You are all around me—in front and at the
back—
and have put your hand on me.
⁶Your knowledge is amazing to me;
it is more than I can understand.

⁷Where can I go to get away from your
Spirit? *d*
Where can I run from you?
⁸If I go up to the heavens, you are there.
If I lie down in the grave, you are there.
⁹If I rise with the sun in the east
and settle in the west beyond the sea,
¹⁰even there you would guide me.
With your right hand you would
hold me.

¹¹I could say, "The darkness will hide me.
Let the light around me turn into night."
¹²But even the darkness is not dark to you.
The night is as light as the day;
darkness and light are the same to you.

¹³You made my whole being;
you formed me in my mother's body.

ABORTION

Precious

Chelsea had an abortion four years ago. She hadn't planned to, it just sort of happened. She hadn't planned to have sex with Ben or get pregnant either, that just sort of happened too. They were both shocked when they found out. It was too much to take in what with Ben's parents' divorce and their GCSEs. They split up three weeks later and Chelsea was advised to get rid of "It". She was told to move on with her life and forget it ever happened.

But it wasn't so easy to move on and forget. She began counselling sessions at a local church and, over the next two years, Chelsea began to deal with the pain and anger she felt. Each week she talked and prayed with her counsellor.

What did God think of her and what she had done to her baby? How could God forgive her? How could she ever forgive herself? One evening, as she was reading the words of Psalm 139 she felt an incredible sense of peace and it was then she knew: she belonged to God, she was his daughter. All the days of her life were precious and planned by her heavenly Father. She would never forget her past but she knew now that she had a future with the loving arms of God wrapped around her.

Take a look at **Psalm 139:13–16**.

* You're God's greatest invention! He put a lot of time and effort into you. Besides yourself, what's your other favourite invention of God's e.g. sand, guinea pigs, clouds?
* In verse 23, the psalm writer asks God to examine him to see if there is any bad thing in him. Do we make the most of God taking an interest in everything we do?

Consider . . .

* whether you know of anyone who thinks that their birth was "just an accident". How could you use this psalm to let them know they're precious to God?
* whether there are things in your life that you find hard to ask forgiveness for. Find someone in your church or youth group that you trust who will pray with you.

For more, see . . .

* Matthew 7:1–5 (p.949)
* Romans 8:38–39 (p.1197)

¹⁴I praise you because you made me in an
    amazing and wonderful way.
    What you have done is wonderful.
    I know this very well.
¹⁵You saw my bones being formed
    as I took shape in my mother's body.
    When I was put together there,
¹⁶ you saw my body as it was formed.
    All the days planned for me
    were written in your book
    before I was one day old.

¹⁷God, your thoughts are precious to me.
    They are so many!
¹⁸If I could count them,
    they would be more than all the grains of
      sand.
    When I wake up,
    I am still with you.

¹⁹God, I wish you would kill the wicked!
    Get away from me, you murderers!
²⁰They say evil things about you.
    Your enemies use your name
      thoughtlessly.
²¹LORD, I hate those who hate you;
    I hate those who rise up against you.
²²I feel only hate for them;
    they are my enemies.

²³God, examine me and know my heart;
    test me and know my nervous thoughts.
²⁴See if there is any bad thing in me.
    Lead me on the road to everlasting life.

A Prayer for Protection

For the director of music. A psalm of David.

140   LORD, rescue me from evil people;
         protect me from cruel people
²who make evil plans,
    who always start fights.
³They make their tongues sharp as a snake's;
    their words are like snake poison.   *Selah*^d

⁴LORD, guard me from the power of wicked
      people;
    protect me from cruel people
    who plan to trip me up.
⁵The proud hid a trap for me.
    They spread out a net beside the road;
    they set traps for me.   *Selah*

⁶I said to the LORD, "You are my God."
    LORD, listen to my prayer for help.
⁷LORD God, my mighty Saviour,
    you protect me in battle.
⁸LORD, do not give the wicked what they
      want.
    Don't let their plans succeed,
    or they will become proud.   *Selah*

⁹Those around me have planned trouble.
    Now let it come to them.
¹⁰Let burning coals fall on them.
    Throw them into the fire
    or into pits from which they cannot escape.
¹¹Don't let liars settle in the land.
    Let evil quickly hunt down cruel people.

¹²I know the LORD will get justice for the poor
    and will defend the needy in court.
¹³Good people will praise his name;
    honest people will live in his presence.

A Prayer Not to Sin

A psalm of David.

141   LORD, I call to you. Come quickly.
         Listen to me when I call to you.
²Let my prayer be like incense ^d placed
    before you,
    and my praise like the evening sacrifice.

³LORD, help me control my tongue;
    help me be careful about what I say.
⁴Take away my desire to do evil
    or to join others in doing wrong.
    Don't let me eat tasty food
    with those who do evil.

⁵If a good person punished me, that would be
      kind.
    If he corrected me, that would be like
      perfumed oil on my head.
    I shouldn't refuse it.

    But I pray against those who do evil.
⁶ Let their leaders be thrown down the cliffs.
    Then people will know that I have spoken
      correctly:
⁷"The ground is ploughed and broken up.
    In the same way, our bones have been
      scattered at the grave."

⁸GOD, I look to you for help.
    I trust in you, LORD. Don't let me die.
⁹Protect me from the traps they set for me
    and from the net that evil people have
      spread.
¹⁰Let the wicked fall into their own nets,
    but let me pass by safely.

A Prayer for Safety

A maskil ^d of David when he was in the cave.
A prayer.

142   I cry out to the LORD;
         I pray to the LORD for mercy.
²I pour out my problems to him;
    I tell him my troubles.

³When I am afraid,
    you, LORD, know the way out.

In the path where I walk,
a trap is hidden for me.
[4]Look around me and see.
No one cares about me.
I have no place of safety;
no one cares if I live.

[5]LORD, I cry out to you.
I say, "You are my protection.
You are all I want in this life."
[6]Listen to my cry,
because I am helpless.
Save me from those who are chasing me,
because they are too strong for me.
[7]Free me from my prison,
and then I will praise your name.

Then good people will surround me,
because you have taken care of me.

A Prayer Not to be Killed

A psalm of David.

143

LORD, hear my prayer;
listen to my cry for mercy.
Answer me
because you are loyal and good.
[2]Don't judge me, your servant,
because no one alive is right before
you.

[3]My enemies are chasing me;
they crushed me to the ground.
They made me live in darkness
like those long dead.
[4]I am afraid;
my courage is gone.

[5]I remember what happened long ago;
I consider everything you have done.
I think about all you have made.
[6]I lift my hands to you in prayer.
As a dry land needs rain, I thirst for you.

Selah[d]

[7]LORD, answer me quickly,
because I am getting weak.
Don't turn away from me,
or I will be like those who are dead.
[8]Tell me in the morning about your love,
because I trust you.
Show me what I should do,
because my prayers go up to you.
[9]LORD, save me from my enemies;
I hide in you.
[10]Teach me to do what you want,
because you are my God.
Let your good Spirit [d]
lead me on level ground.

[11]LORD, let me live
so people will praise you.

In your goodness
save me from my troubles.
[12]In your love defeat my enemies.
Destroy all those who trouble me,
because I am your servant.

A Prayer for Victory

Of David.

144

Praise the LORD, my Rock, [d]
who trains me for war,
who trains me for battle.
[2]He protects me like a fortified city, and he
loves me.
He is my defender and my Saviour,
my shield and my protection.
He helps me keep my people under
control.

[3]LORD, why are people important to you?
Why do you even think about human
beings?
[4]People are like a breath;
their lives are like passing shadows.

[5]LORD, tear open the sky and come down.
Touch the mountains so they will smoke.
[6]Send the lightning and scatter my enemies.
Shoot your arrows and force them away.
[7]Reach down from above.
Save me and rescue me out of this sea of
enemies,
from these foreigners.
[8]They are liars;
they are dishonest.

[9]God, I will sing a new song to you;
I will play to you on the ten-stringed
harp.
[10]You give victory to kings.
You save your servant David from cruel
swords.

[11]Save me, rescue me from these foreigners.
They are liars; they are dishonest.
[12]Let our sons in their youth
grow like plants.
Let our daughters be
like the decorated stones in the Temple. [d]
[13]Let our barns be filled
with crops of all kinds.
Let our sheep in the fields have
thousands and tens of thousands of lambs.
[14] Let our cattle be strong.
Let no one break in.
Let there be no war,
no screams in our streets.

[15]Happy are those who are like this;
happy are the people whose God is the
LORD.

Praise to God the King

A psalm of praise. Of David.

145 I praise your greatness, my God the
         King;
I will praise you for ever and ever.
[2]I will praise you every day;
I will praise you for ever and ever.
[3]The LORD is great and worthy of our praise;
no one can understand how great he is.

[4]Parents will tell their children what you have
      done.
They will retell your mighty acts,

[5]wonderful majesty and glory.
And I will think about your miracles. *d*
[6]They will tell about the amazing things
      you do,
and I will tell how great you are.
[7]They will remember your great
      goodness
and will sing about your fairness.

[8]The LORD is kind and shows mercy.
He does not become angry quickly but is
      full of love.
[9]The LORD is good to everyone;

ADDICTION

Burning Desire

Lisa and Paula were good friends at work. They shared the same interests and laughed at the same jokes. One day Lisa came in to the office waving two tickets in her hand.

"You'll never guess what!" she smiled at her friend. "I've won two seats for Wembley Arena on Thursday!" Paula jumped out of her chair. "Oh that's fantastic! Who are you going to take?"

Lisa was waiting for this question, because she knew that the band who were playing at the arena, were one of Paula's favourites, and hers too.

"Well, I thought I might ask you . . . " she said lightly, knowing her friend would be thrilled.

The girls spent some time talking about what they were going to wear and then Lisa said, "The only thing is, it's a mid-week concert and we have to be back for work the next day, so I wondered if you should stay at our house for the night and then we could travel back to work together."

The plans were made, the concert was everything they dreamed of, and then the next morning . . .

Lisa found that waking her friend was a real problem. She shook her a few times and finally she roused from sleep.

"Paula! We're going to be late! Please get up!" cried a worried Lisa. Paula looked over the top of the duvet and said, "Give me a minute." With that she groped over the side of the bed and took a cigarette from her bag and lit it.

"Oh Paula! I can't believe you can do that!"

"Do what?" asked her friend.

"Put a cigarette in your mouth before you've even opened your eyes properly, or had a cup of tea or anything!" replied Lisa.

Paula looked at her friend wearily and said, "If you want me to get out of this bed, I need it. Believe me. I need it."

Read **Psalm 143:5–10** to find out what David needed.

- What is the difference between Paula's need and psalm writer David's need according to this passage?
- What are the likely outcomes of pursuing these two needs (addictions) for a long time?

Consider . . .

- Making a list of things you "need" and ask yourself if any of them have a harmful effect on your life.
- Asking the Lord to help you give up smoking, or help a friend who may wish to quit.

For more, see . . .

- Psalm 63:1–5 (p.536)
- 2 Peter 2:19 (p.1367)
- 1 Corinthians 3:16 (p.1218)

Sidelight　If you're looking for
something new to pray
before each meal, try Psalm 145. This psalm is
still recited in the morning, at noon and in the
evening in Jewish synagogues. A fourth-century
rabbi believed that reciting the psalm three times
a day would assure one a place in the world
to come.

he is merciful to all he has made.
¹⁰LORD, everything you have made will
　　praise you;
those who belong to you will bless you.
¹¹They will tell about the glory of your
　　kingdom
and will speak about your power.
¹²Then everyone will know the mighty things
　　you do
and the glory and majesty of your kingdom.

¹³Your kingdom will go on and on,
　　and you will rule for ever.

The LORD will keep all his promises;
　　he is loyal to all he has made.
¹⁴The LORD helps those who have been
　　defeated
and takes care of those who are in trouble.
¹⁵All living things look to you for food,
　　and you give it to them at the right time.
¹⁶You open your hand,
　　and you satisfy all living things.

¹⁷Everything the LORD does is right.
　　He is loyal to all he has made.
¹⁸The LORD is close to everyone who prays
　　to him,
to all who truly pray to him.
¹⁹He gives those who respect him what they
　　want.
He listens when they cry, and he saves
　　them.

HUNGER AND POVERTY

Real Food

Linda's parents tell her that street beggars misuse money, spending it on drugs and alcohol. She sees the Big Issue seller outside the supermarket everyday on her way home from school. She doesn't like buying it, as she never has time to read it.

There is this one guy who sits in the underpass. He hardly looks up as he speaks. "Spare some change please," he says in a sickly, quiet voice. Linda tries to get eye contact.

"Sorry," she says, wanting to chat. She knows her parents would be cross if she gave the man money but perhaps she can make friends with him – bring him a sandwich or something.

After a few weeks, she does manage to sit by the man and chat for a few minutes. His name is Adam. He doesn't do drugs. He drinks sometimes as it makes him happier. He ran away from home aged fifteen when his stepfather threatened to kill him, and not for the first time. He shows Linda some sketches he has done of people who pass by. They are very good. He has a real eye for a mannerism. They are like cartoons. He shows her a picture he did of her. She has a halo round her head. She cries.

One day, at home by herself, Linda reads **Psalm 146**. She notices in particular verse 7 and wonders whether if God feeds the hungry perhaps she should stop worrying and leave it to him.

* What should Linda do?
* How does God feed the hungry today?

Consider . . .

* whether your prayer list is too local. How often do you pray for other parts of the world where there is terrible poverty?
* finding out whether there is a project for the homeless near you that you could volunteer to help with.

For more, see . . .

* Psalm 140:12–13 (p.582)
* Matthew 25:31–46 (p.987)
* Isaiah 61:1–3 (p.705)

²⁰The LORD protects everyone who loves him,
  but he will destroy the wicked.
²¹I will praise the LORD.
  Let everyone praise his holy name for ever.

Praise God Who Helps the Weak

146 Praise the LORD!
  My whole being, praise the LORD.
²I will praise the LORD all my life;
  I will sing praises to my God as long as I live.

³Do not put your trust in princes
  or other people, who cannot save you.
⁴When people die, they are buried.
  Then all of their plans come to an end.

⁵Happy are those who are helped by the God
    of Jacob.
  Their hope is in the LORD their God.
⁶He made heaven and earth,
    the sea and everything in it.
  He remains loyal for ever.

⁷He does what is fair for those who have been
    wronged.
  He gives food to the hungry.
  The LORD sets the prisoners free.
⁸ The LORD gives sight to the blind.
  The LORD lifts up people who are in
    trouble.
  The LORD loves those who do right.
⁹The LORD protects the foreigners.
  He defends the orphans and widows,
  but he blocks the way of the wicked.

¹⁰The LORD will be King for ever.
  Jerusalem, your God is everlasting.

  Praise the LORD!

Praise God Who Helps His People

147 Praise the LORD!

  It is good to sing praises to our God;
  it is good and pleasant to praise him.

WORSHIP

Carrying a Rhythm of Praise

Phil was feeling like a fraud. He was starting to realise that when he was in church, he would sing songs declaring his love for God, making extravagant promises to read his Bible twenty-eight hours a day and to pray for five hours before he went to school. But then in the very next instant, he had forgotten all of his promises and abandoned all of his good intentions, his lifestyle not matching his words. Phil started to wonder if it was all worth it, because at the end of the day, he just felt guilty for not doing the things he said he would. Then a small phrase from a book Phil was reading really struck him: "Saving faith is the confidence that if you sell all you have and forsake all sinful pleasures, the hidden treasure of holy joy will satisfy your deepest desires" (John Piper – *Desiring God*) .

Phil suddenly realised that Jesus is more amazing and more brilliant than anything he could pursue in this world. That's why, when he was in that place of worship, he just wanted to give it all – what else can you do when presented with such beauty? The journey for Phil became about carrying the rhythm of those moments into the rest of his life. When Phil forgot to read his Bible or pray, he didn't feel guilty, he was just gutted that he'd missed out on spending time with his mate, Jesus.
Read **Psalm 150** and see the response of the psalmist as he gets a glimpse of God.

* Have you ever felt like Phil, full of good intentions, but sadly lacking the lifestyle to match?
* How does Phil's story inspire you? Does the psalmist inspire you about what your reaction is when you're face to face with God?

Consider . . .

* your walk with Jesus so far. How much of it has been about you, your failings and issues? How much of it has been about him and who he is?
* making a list of things you're going to do this week to pursue Jesus – not because you have to, but because he's worth it!

For more, see . . .

* Psalm 96 (p.556)
* Isaiah 6:1–8 (p.645)

²The LORD rebuilds Jerusalem;
  he brings back the captured Israelites.
³He heals the broken-hearted
  and bandages their wounds.

⁴He counts the stars
  and names each one.
⁵Our Lord is great and very powerful.
  There is no limit to what he knows.
⁶The LORD defends the humble,
  but he throws the wicked to the ground.

⁷Sing praises to the LORD;
  praise our God with harps.
⁸He fills the sky with clouds
  and sends rain to the earth
  and makes grass grow on the hills.
⁹He gives food to cattle
  and to the little birds that call.

¹⁰He does not enjoy the strength of a horse
  or the strength of a man.

¹¹The LORD is pleased with those who
  respect him,
  with those who trust his love.

¹²Jerusalem, praise the LORD;
  Jerusalem, praise your God.
¹³He makes your city gates strong
  and blesses your children inside.
¹⁴He brings peace to your country
  and fills you with the finest grain.

¹⁵He gives a command to the earth,
  and it quickly obeys him.
¹⁶He spreads the snow like wool
  and scatters the frost like ashes.
¹⁷He throws down hail like rocks.
  No one can stand the cold he sends.
¹⁸Then he gives a command, and it melts.
  He sends the breezes, and the waters flow.
¹⁹He gave his word to Jacob,
  his laws and demands to Israel.

MUSIC

Turn it Up Loud

Jenny did not believe in God. Her best friend Louise, however, was the complete opposite. She was a Christian and she was not shy about telling anyone. Jenny couldn't understand why Louise was so excited about her faith because when she thought of Christians all she could imagine was a bunch of old people, sitting in a huge church not being allowed to talk. Because of this, when Louise invited Jenny to a youth night run by her church Jenny said she'd go, but deep down wasn't looking forward to it. At 8 p.m. that night, Louise knocked on Jenny's door and together they drove to the church. Even before the girls walked through the doors, they could hear the loud music pumping out and the laughing and chattering coming from inside. Louise was smiling but Jenny looked confused.

"I thought churches were supposed to be quiet places where people go to pray," Jenny said.

"They can be," said Louise. "But that's not all church is. We believe we've got something to celebrate and you can't celebrate something that amazing in a quiet way all the time, can you! Imagine it was your birthday and instead of all your friends being upbeat and excited around you, they just handed you your presents with a quick handshake. How would you feel?"

Slowly it started to dawn on Jenny that the way in which Louise expressed her faith was very different to how she had first imagined, not all quiet and timid but actually using music and creating a great party atmosphere.

Louise was right in saying that Christians can praise God in all sorts of ways. Check out **Psalm 150**.

* There are many different ways to praise God. What are some of those mentioned in this psalm?
* When praising God, have you ever experienced the loud, party atmosphere described in this psalm?

Consider . . .

* looking at the way you thank God for things. Try to find new and exciting ways to express your praise.
* having a party with some friends in God's honour. Enjoy it and thank him with that same party atmosphere.

For more, see . . .

* Exodus 15:19–21 (p.73)
* John 12:3 (p.1116)
* Mark 11:8–10 (p.1019)

²⁰He didn't do this for any other nation.
  They don't know his laws.

Praise the LORD!

The World Should Praise the Lord

148 Praise the LORD!

Praise the LORD from the skies.
  Praise him high above the earth.
²Praise him, all you angels.
  Praise him, all you armies of heaven.
³Praise him, sun and moon.
  Praise him, all you shining stars.
⁴Praise him, highest heavens
  and you waters above the sky.
⁵Let them praise the LORD,
  because they were created by his
    command.
⁶He put them in place for ever and ever;
  he made a law that will never change.

⁷Praise the LORD from the earth,
  you large sea animals and all the
    oceans,
⁸lightning and hail, snow and mist
  and stormy winds that obey him,
⁹mountains and all hills,
  fruit trees and all cedars,
¹⁰wild animals and all cattle,
  crawling animals and birds,
¹¹kings of the earth and all nations,
  princes and all rulers of the earth,
¹²young men and women,
  old people and children.

¹³Praise the LORD,
  because he alone is great.
  He is more wonderful than heaven and
    earth.
¹⁴God has given his people a king.
  He should be praised by all who belong
    to him;
  he should be praised by the Israelites, the
    people closest to his heart.

Praise the LORD!

Praise the God of Israel

149 Praise the LORD!

Sing a new song to the LORD;
  sing his praise in the meeting of his people.

²Let the Israelites be happy because of God,
  their Maker.
  Let the people of Jerusalem rejoice because
    of their King.
³They should praise him with dancing.
  They should sing praises to him with
    tambourines *d* and harps.
⁴The LORD is pleased with his people;
  he saves the humble.
⁵Let those who worship him rejoice in his glory.
  Let them sing for joy even in bed!

⁶Let them shout his praise
  with their two-edged swords in their hands.
⁷They will punish the nations
  and defeat the people.
⁸They will put those kings in chains
  and those important men in iron bands.
⁹They will punish them as God has written.
  God is honoured by all who worship him.

Praise the LORD!

Praise the LORD with Music

150 Praise the LORD!

Praise God in his Temple; *d*
  praise him in his mighty heaven.
²Praise him for his strength;
  praise him for his greatness.
³Praise him with trumpet blasts;
  praise him with harps and lyres. *d*
⁴Praise him with tambourines *d* and dancing;
  praise him with stringed instruments and
    flutes.
⁵Praise him with loud cymbals;
  praise him with crashing cymbals.
⁶Let everything that breathes praise the LORD.

Praise the LORD!

Proverbs

Why Read This Book:

* Discover life's basic goal (Proverbs 2:1–15).
* Find clear guidance on right and wrong (Proverbs 3, 10–23).
* Learn how to be wise instead of foolish (Proverbs 4, 6, 8, 9, 24).

When?

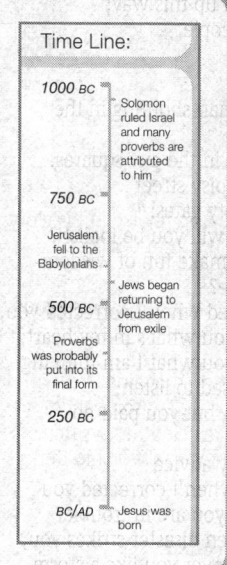

Time Line:

1000 BC — Solomon ruled Israel and many proverbs are attributed to him

750 BC

Jerusalem fell to the Babylonians

Jews began returning to Jerusalem from exile

500 BC

Proverbs was probably put into its final form

250 BC

BC/AD — Jesus was born

Behind the Scenes:

If you like "quotable quotes" or bumper sticker slogans, you'll love Proverbs. Unlike other books of the Bible, Proverbs is mostly a collection of one- and two-line sayings on various everyday subjects – family life, work, money, getting along with others, honesty and many more. These sayings represent the heart of important truths about life and relationships. This is the wisdom of God for every day.

The book is filled with sharp phrases, dramatic contrasts and vivid scenes from everyday life. A chapter may deal with dozens of different subjects (for example, see chapter 14). Because of their short, catchy style, these proverbs are easy to memorise. Other parts of Proverbs are longer, unified poems about wisdom, which is personified as a woman (see Proverbs 1:20–33).

Proverbs is divided into eight main sections. It begins with an introduction on wisdom (Proverbs 1–9), then has six collections of sayings by various "wise men" (Proverbs 10–31:9). It concludes with an acrostic poem on a perfect wife (Proverbs 31:10–31). Many scholars note that the perfect wife at the end of Proverbs is actually a fulfilment of all the virtues described in the rest of the book.

Collected hundreds of years ago to teach young people principles for life, Proverbs can still help guide us to make wise choices. And though many parts of Proverbs don't explicitly mention God, the sayings were gathered to help us to follow God in everything we do.

LIFE FILE LINKS

Investigate the Theme

To find a list of real life stories on this subject turn to the LIFE FILE GUIDE on pages 12 to 22 at the front of the Youth Bible.

1....
2....
3....

PRIORITIES

The Importance of Proverbs

1 These are the wise words of Solomon son of David, king of Israel.

[2]They teach wisdom and self-control;
they will help you understand wise words.

Sidelight   Proverbs – short, catchy sayings – aren't found just in the book of Proverbs. They were a common type of writing in ancient times, and Jesus used them regularly in his teaching. See some examples in Matthew 6:21 (p.948) and Matthew 7:13 (p.950).

---

[3]They will teach you how to be wise and self-controlled
and will teach you to do what is honest
and fair and right.
[4]They make the uneducated clever
and give knowledge and sense to the young.
[5]Wise people can also listen and learn;
even clever people can find good advice in these words.
[6]Then anyone can understand wise words and stories,
the words of the wise and their riddles.

[7]Knowledge begins with respect for the LORD,
but fools hate wisdom and self-control.

Warnings Against Evil

[8]My child, listen to your father's teaching
and do not forget your mother's advice.
[9]Their teaching will be like flowers in your hair
or a necklace around your neck.

[10]My child, if sinners try to lead you into sin,
do not follow them.
[11]They will say, "Come with us.
Let's ambush and kill someone;
let's attack some innocent people just for fun.
[12]Let's swallow them alive, as death does;
let's swallow them whole, as the grave does.
[13]We will take all kinds of valuable things
and fill our houses with stolen goods.
[14]Come and join us,
and we will share with you stolen goods."
[15]My child, do not go along with them;
do not do what they do.

[16]They are eager to do evil
and are quick to kill.
[17]It is useless to spread out a net
right where the birds can see it.
[18]But sinners will fall into their own traps;
they will only catch themselves!
[19]All greedy people end up this way;
greed kills selfish people.

Wisdom Speaks

[20]Wisdom is like a woman shouting in the street;
she raises her voice in the city squares.
[21]She cries out in the noisy street
and shouts at the city gates: [n]
[22]"You fools, how long will you be foolish?
How long will you make fun of wisdom
and hate knowledge?
[23]If only you had listened when I corrected you,
I would have told you what's in my heart;
I would have told you what I am thinking.
[24]I called, but you refused to listen;
I held out my hand, but you paid no attention.
[25]You did not follow my advice
and did not listen when I corrected you.
[26]So I will laugh when you are in trouble.
I will make fun when disaster strikes you,
[27]when disaster comes over you like a storm,
when trouble strikes you like a whirlwind,
when pain and trouble overwhelm you.

[28]"Then you will call to me,
but I will not answer.
You will look for me,
but you will not find me.
[29]It is because you rejected knowledge
and did not choose to respect the LORD.
[30]You did not accept my advice,
and you rejected my correction.
[31]So you will get what you deserve;
you will get what you planned for others.
[32]Fools will die because they refuse to listen;
they will be destroyed because they do not care.
[33]But those who listen to me will live in safety
and be at peace, without fear of injury."

Rewards of Wisdom

2 My child, listen to what I say
and remember what I command you.
[2]Listen carefully to wisdom;
set your mind on understanding.
[3]Cry out for wisdom,
and beg for understanding.

---

city gates   People came here to conduct business. Public meetings and court cases were also held here.

⁴Search for it like silver,
  and hunt for it like hidden treasure.
⁵Then you will understand respect for the LORD,
  and you will find that you know God.
⁶Only the LORD gives wisdom;
  he gives knowledge and understanding.
⁷He stores up wisdom for those who are
    honest.
  Like a shield he protects the innocent.
⁸He makes sure that justice is done,
  and he protects those who are loyal
    to him.

⁹Then you will understand what is honest and
    fair
  and what is the good and right thing to do.
¹⁰Wisdom will come into your mind,
  and knowledge will be pleasing to you.

¹¹Good sense will protect you;
  understanding will guard you.
¹²It will keep you from the wicked,
  from those whose words are bad,
¹³who don't do what is right
  but what is evil.
¹⁴They enjoy doing wrong
  and are happy to do what is crooked and
    evil.
¹⁵What they do is wrong,
  and their ways are dishonest.

¹⁶It will save you from the unfaithful wife
  who tries to lead you into adultery*d* with
    pleasing words.
¹⁷She leaves the husband she married when she
    was young.
  She ignores the promise she made before God.

SCHOOL

Wise Up!

At the end of year 7, Jason was top in his year in all subjects. His favourite subjects were maths and English, but he was also excellent in sports and music. Everyone liked him and would ask him the questions to the homework that no one else could answer! When he finished year 8, the teachers had high hopes that he'd go on to be one of the brightest pupils in the country.

However, by the time Jason reached year 9 he had started to MC with a crew that met near his house. Jason had a quick mind and was brilliant at writing lyrics for raps and soon he learnt how to battle other MCs. He began to make a name for himself with the crews around his area and started hanging out till the early hours of the morning and not going into school. By year 10, he had started getting involved in the drug culture too and began to get violent. His teachers started to get concerned when they saw that Jason's attendance at school was dropping and that his grades were slipping.

One teacher, Mr Mason, turned things around. He showed Jason that he could get into music after he had done his exams and that this was his only shot at the exams. Jason knew he was right and decided to go for it.

When Jason's exam results came through, he had come 10th in the country. Mr Mason came over to congratulate him and offer to help with his music career.

Jason replied, "I should be thanking you. I feel like I can do so much with my life now!"
Read **Proverbs 2:1–10**.

- What are the rewards of hard work and dedication, and what did Jason have to do to get them?
- Do these rewards apply to you? What rewards from learning and education do you want?

Consider . . .

- verse 1 which says – "remember what I command you". Write down some of the commands of God and ask him to help you keep them.
- asking a teacher, youth leader, family member or friend to give you extra help with the subjects at school that you find difficult.

For more, see . . .

- 1 Kings 3:4–15 (p.316)
- James 1:5 (p.1348)
- Colossians 2:1–4 (p.1291)

¹⁸Her house is on the way to death;
those who took that path are now all dead.
¹⁹No one who goes to her comes back
or walks the path of life again.

²⁰But wisdom will help you be good
and do what is right.
²¹Those who are honest will live in the land,
and those who are innocent will remain
in it.
²²But the wicked will be removed from the
land,
and the unfaithful will be thrown out of it.

Advice to Children

3 My child, do not forget my teaching,
but keep my commands in mind.
²Then you will live a long time,
and your life will be successful.

³Don't ever forget kindness and truth.
Wear them like a necklace.
Write them on your heart as if on a tablet.
⁴Then you will be respected
and will please both God and people.

⁵Trust the LORD with all your heart,
and don't depend on your own
understanding.
⁶Remember the LORD in all you do,
and he will give you success.

⁷Don't depend on your own wisdom.
Respect the LORD and refuse to do wrong.
⁸Then your body will be healthy,
and your bones will be strong.

⁹Honour the LORD with your wealth
and the first fruits ^d from all your crops.
¹⁰Then your barns will be full,
and your wine barrels will overflow with
new wine.

¹¹My child, do not reject the LORD's discipline,
and don't get angry when he corrects you.
¹²The LORD corrects those he loves,
just as parents correct the child they
delight in.

¹³Happy is the person who finds wisdom,
the one who gets understanding.
¹⁴Wisdom is worth more than silver;
it brings more profit than gold.
¹⁵Wisdom is more precious than rubies;
nothing you could want is equal to it.
¹⁶With her right hand wisdom offers you a long
life,
and with her left hand she gives you riches
and honour.
¹⁷Wisdom will make your life pleasant
and will bring you peace.

¹⁸As a tree produces fruit, wisdom gives life to
those who use it,
and everyone who uses it will be happy.
¹⁹The LORD made the earth, using his wisdom.
He set the sky in place, using his
understanding.
²⁰With his knowledge, he made springs flow
into rivers
and the clouds drop rain on the earth.

²¹My child, hold on to wisdom and
good sense.
Don't let them out of your sight.
²²They will give you life
and beauty like a necklace around your
neck.
²³Then you will go your way in safety,
and you will not get hurt.
²⁴When you lie down, you won't be afraid;
when you lie down, you will sleep in peace.
²⁵You won't be afraid of sudden trouble;
you won't fear the ruin that comes to the
wicked,
²⁶because the LORD will keep you safe.
He will keep you from being trapped.

²⁷Whenever you are able,
do good to people who need help.
²⁸If you have what your neighbour asks for,
don't say, "Come back later.
I will give it to you tomorrow."
²⁹Don't make plans to hurt your neighbour
who lives nearby and trusts you.
³⁰Don't accuse a person for no good reason;
don't accuse someone who has not
harmed you.

³¹Don't be jealous of those who use violence,
and don't choose to be like them.
³²The LORD hates those who do wrong,
but he is a friend to those who are honest.
³³The LORD will curse the evil person's house,
but he will bless the home of those who do
right.
³⁴The LORD laughs at those who laugh at him,
but he gives grace to those who are not
proud.
³⁵Wise people will receive honour,
but fools will be disgraced.

Wisdom is Important

4 My children, listen to your father's
teaching;
pay attention so you will understand.
²What I am telling you is good,
so do not forget what I teach you.
³When I was a young boy in my father's house
and like an only child to my mother,

⁴my father taught me and said,
  "Hold on to my words with all your heart.
  Keep my commands and you will live.
⁵Get wisdom and understanding.
  Don't forget or ignore my words.
⁶Hold on to wisdom, and it will take care
    of you.
  Love it, and it will keep you safe.
⁷Wisdom is the most important thing; so get
    wisdom.
  If it costs everything you have, get
    understanding.
⁸Treasure wisdom, and it will make you great;
  hold on to it, and it will bring you honour.
⁹It will be like flowers in your hair
  and like a beautiful crown on your head."

¹⁰My child, listen and accept what I say.
  Then you will have a long life.
¹¹I am guiding you in the way of wisdom,
  and I am leading you on the right path.
¹²Nothing will hold you back;
  you will not be overwhelmed.
¹³Always remember what you have been taught,
  and don't let go of it.
  Keep all that you have learned;
  it is the most important thing in life.
¹⁴Don't follow the ways of the wicked;
  don't do what evil people do.
¹⁵Avoid their ways, and don't follow them.
  Stay away from them and keep on going,
¹⁶because they cannot sleep until they do evil.
  They cannot rest until they harm someone.
¹⁷They feast on wickedness and cruelty
  as if they were eating bread and drinking
    wine.
¹⁸The way of the good person is like the light
    of dawn,
  growing brighter and brighter until full
    daylight.
¹⁹But the wicked walk around in the dark;
  they can't even see what makes them
    stumble.

²⁰My child, pay attention to my words;
  listen closely to what I say.
²¹Don't ever forget my words;
  keep them always in mind.
²²They are the key to life for those who find them;
  they bring health to the whole body.
²³Be careful what you think,
  because your thoughts run your life.
²⁴Don't use your mouth to tell lies;
  don't ever say things that are not true.
²⁵Keep your eyes focused on what is right,
  and look straight ahead to what is good.
²⁶Be careful what you do,
  and always do what is right.

²⁷Don't turn off the road of goodness;
  keep away from evil paths.

Warning About Adultery

5 My son, pay attention to my wisdom;
    listen to my words of understanding.
²Be careful to use good sense,
  and watch what you say.
³The words of another man's wife may seem
    sweet as honey;
  they may be as smooth as olive oil.
⁴But in the end she will bring you sorrow,
  causing you pain like a two-edged sword.
⁵She is on the way to death;
  her steps are headed straight to the grave.
⁶She gives little thought to life.
  She doesn't even know that her ways are
    wrong.

⁷Now, my sons, listen to me,
  and don't ignore what I say.
⁸Stay away from such a woman.
  Don't even go near the door of her house,
⁹or you will give your riches to others,
  and the best years of your life will be given
    to someone cruel.
¹⁰Strangers will enjoy your wealth,
  and what you worked so hard for will go to
    someone else.
¹¹You will groan at the end of your life
  when your health is gone.
¹²Then you will say, "I hated being told what
    to do!
  I would not listen to correction!
¹³I would not listen to my teachers
  or pay attention to my instructors.
¹⁴I came close to being completely ruined
  in front of a whole group of people."

¹⁵Be faithful to your own wife,
  just as you drink water from your own well.
¹⁶Don't pour your water in the streets;
  don't give your love to just any woman.
¹⁷These things are yours alone
  and shouldn't be shared with strangers.
¹⁸Be happy with the wife you married when
    you were young.
  She gives you joy, as your fountain gives
    you water.
¹⁹She is as lovely and graceful as a deer.
  Let her love always make you happy;
  let her love always hold you captive.
²⁰My son, don't be held captive by a woman
    who takes part in adultery. *d*
  Don't hold another man's wife.

²¹The LORD sees everything you do,
  and he watches where you go.
²²An evil man will be caught in his wicked ways;
  the ropes of his sins will tie him up.

²³He will die because he does not control
himself,
and he will be held captive by his
foolishness.

Dangers of Being Foolish

6 My child, be careful about giving a
guarantee for somebody else's loan,
about promising to pay what someone else
owes.
²You might get trapped by what you say;
you might be caught by your own words.
³My child, if you have done this and are under
your neighbour's control,
here is how to get free.
Don't be proud. Go to your neighbour
and beg to be free from your promise.
⁴Don't go to sleep
or even rest your eyes,
⁵but free yourself like a deer running from a
hunter,
like a bird flying away from a trapper.

⁶Go and watch the ants, you lazy person.
Watch what they do and be wise.
⁷Ants have no commander,
no leader or ruler,
⁸but they store up food in the summer
and gather their supplies at harvest.
⁹How long will you lie there, you lazy person?
When will you get up from sleeping?
¹⁰You sleep a little; you take a nap.
You fold your hands and lie down to rest.
¹¹So you will be as poor as if you had been
robbed;
you will have as little as if you had been
held up.

> **Sidelight** Sleeping until noon
> was not on for the writer
> of Proverbs (6:6–11). The book of Proverbs
> constantly blasts laziness and warns that lazy
> people will end up poor. He doesn't say that all
> the poor are lazy. Read the other side of the
> story in Proverbs 13:23 (p.601) and Proverbs
> 22:1–2, 22–23 (p.608).

¹²Some people are wicked and no good.
They go around telling lies,
¹³winking with their eyes, signalling with their
feet
and making signs with their fingers.
¹⁴They make evil plans in their hearts
and are always starting arguments.
¹⁵So trouble will strike them in an instant;
suddenly they will be so hurt no one can
help them.

¹⁶There are six things the LORD hates.
There are seven things he cannot stand:
¹⁷   a proud look,
a lying tongue,
hands that kill innocent people,
¹⁸   a mind that thinks up evil plans,
feet that are quick to do evil,
¹⁹   a witness who lies,
and someone who starts arguments
among families.

Warning About Adultery

²⁰My son, keep your father's commands,
and don't forget your mother's
teaching.
²¹Keep their words in mind for ever
as though you had them tied around your
neck.
²²They will guide you when you walk.
They will guard you when you sleep.
They will speak to you when you are
awake.
²³These commands are like a lamp;
this teaching is like a light.
And the correction that comes from them
will help you have life.
²⁴They will keep you from sinful women
and from the pleasing words of another
man's unfaithful wife.
²⁵Don't desire her because she is beautiful.
Don't let her capture you by the way she
looks at you.
²⁶A prostitute *d* will treat you like a loaf of
bread,
and a woman who takes part in adultery *d*
may cost you your life.
²⁷You cannot carry hot coals against
your chest
without burning your clothes,
²⁸and you cannot walk on hot coals
without burning your feet.
²⁹The same is true if you have sexual relations
with another man's wife.
Anyone who does so will be punished.

³⁰People don't hate a thief
when he steals because he is hungry.
³¹But if he is caught, he must pay back seven
times what he stole,
and it may cost him everything he owns.
³²A man who takes part in adultery has no
sense;
he will destroy himself.
³³He will be beaten up and disgraced,
and his shame will never go away.
³⁴Jealousy makes a husband very angry,
and he will have no pity when he gets
revenge.

[35]He will accept no payment for the wrong;
he will take no amount of money.

The Woman of Adultery

7 My son, remember what I say,
and treasure my commands.
[2]Obey my commands, and you will live.
Guard my teachings as you would your
own eyes.
[3]Remind yourself of them;
write them on your heart as if on a tablet.
[4]Treat wisdom as a sister,
and make understanding your closest friend.
[5]Wisdom and understanding will keep you
away from adultery, [d]
away from the unfaithful wife and her
pleasing words.

[6]Once while I was at the window of my
house
I looked out through the shutters
[7]and saw some foolish young men.
I noticed one of them had no wisdom.
[8]He was walking down the street near the
corner
on the road leading to her house.
[9]It was the twilight of the evening;
the darkness of the night was just
beginning.
[10]Then the woman approached him,
dressed like a prostitute [d]
and planning to trick him.
[11]She was loud and stubborn
and never stayed at home.
[12]She was always out in the streets or in the
city squares,
waiting around on the corners of the streets.
[13]She took hold of him and kissed him.
Without shame she said to him,
[14]"I made my fellowship offering and took
some of the meat home.
Today I have kept my special promises.
[15]So I have come out to meet you;
I have been looking for you and have
found you.
[16]I have covered my bed
with coloured sheets from Egypt.
[17]I have made my bed smell sweet
with myrrh, [d] aloes [d] and cinnamon.
[18]Come, let's make love until morning.
Let's enjoy each other's love.
[19]My husband is not home;
he has gone on a long trip.
[20]He took a lot of money with him
and won't be home for weeks."

[21]By her clever words she made him give in;
by her pleasing words she led him into
doing wrong.
[22]All at once he followed her,
like an ox led to the butcher,
like a deer caught in a trap
[23] and shot through the liver with an arrow.
Like a bird caught in a trap,
he didn't know what he did would
kill him.

[24]Now, my sons, listen to me;
pay attention to what I say.
[25]Don't let yourself be tricked by such a
woman;
don't go where she leads you.
[26]She has ruined many good men,
and many have died because of her.
[27]Her house is on the road to death,
the road that leads down to the grave.

Listen to Wisdom

8 Wisdom calls to you like someone
shouting;
understanding raises her voice.
[2]On the hilltops along the road
and at the crossroads, she stands calling.
[3]Beside the city gates, [n]
at the entrances into the city, she calls out:
[4]"Listen, everyone, I'm calling out to you;
I am shouting to all people.
[5]You who are uneducated, be cleverer.
You who are foolish, get understanding.
[6]Listen, because I have important things
to say,
and what I tell you is right.
[7]What I say is true,
I refuse to speak evil.
[8]Everything I say is honest;
nothing I say is crooked or false.
[9]People with good sense know what I say is
true;
and those with knowledge know my words
are right.
[10]Choose my teachings instead of silver,
and knowledge rather than the finest gold.
[11]Wisdom is more precious than rubies.
Nothing you could want is equal to it.

[12]"I am wisdom, and I am clever.
I also have knowledge and good sense.
[13]If you respect the LORD, you will also hate
evil.
I hate pride and boasting,
evil ways and lies.

---

city gates People came here to conduct business. Public meetings and court cases were also held here.

¹⁴I have good sense and advice,
and I have understanding and power.
¹⁵I help kings to govern
and rulers to make fair laws.
¹⁶Princes use me to lead,
and so do all important people who judge
fairly.
¹⁷I love those who love me,
and those who seek me find me.
¹⁸Riches and honour are mine to give.
So are wealth and lasting success.
¹⁹What I give is better than the finest gold,
better than the purest silver.
²⁰I do what is right
and follow the path of justice.
²¹I give wealth to those who love me,
filling their houses with treasures.

²²"I, wisdom, was with the LORD when he
began his work,
long before he made anything else.
²³I was created in the very beginning,
even before the world began.

²⁴I was born before there were oceans,
or springs overflowing with water,
²⁵before the hills were there,
before the mountains were put in place.
²⁶God had not made the earth or fields,
not even the first dust of the earth.
²⁷I was there when God put the skies in place,
when he stretched the horizon over the
oceans,
²⁸when he made the clouds above
and put the deep underground springs in
place.
²⁹I was there when he ordered the sea
not to go beyond the borders he had set.
I was there when he laid the earth's foundation.
³⁰ I was like a child by his side.
I was delighted every day,
enjoying his presence all the time,
³¹enjoying the whole world,
and delighted with all its people.

³²"Now, my children, listen to me,
because those who follow my ways are happy.

CREATION

Moment of Wonder

Waves rolled under Marty's canoe. One crested behind her and broke, spewing foam over her back. Panic gripped her. She leaned into the wind, paddling hard. Her muscles ached. Why had she taken this outdoor pursuits course?

The answer echoed within her, "to get back in touch with God." But where was he?

When she rounded the rocky point, stillness surrounded her. Sunlight broke through the clouds, sparkling into the blue depths of the protected cove. Marty rested her paddle and looked beneath her. Silver fish darted. She leaned back and gazed at the horizon. Sea birds skimmed inches above the water.

Suddenly the sea split beside her. A dolphin arched high, then dived, circling her. She sucked in her breath, overcome with wonder.

"Lord, oh Lord, you're everywhere!"

The voice of wisdom, in Proverbs, speaks about the joy in observing God's creation. Read about it in **Proverbs 8:22–31**.

* What might wisdom's voice say to Marty from this passage?
* Where do you most strongly sense God's presence? Why?

Consider . . .

* searching for the tiny forms of God's creation as you walk across a garden or open space, and thanking God for them.
* finding a special place in nature where you can go regularly to be with God.

For more, see . . .

* Psalm 104:1–35 (p.560)
* Revelation 4:11 (p.1391)

* Luke 8:22–26 (p.1053)

³³Listen to my teaching, and you will be wise;
    do not ignore it.
³⁴Happy are those who listen to me,
    watching at my door every day,
    waiting at my open doorway.
³⁵Those who find me find life,
    and the LORD will be pleased with them.
³⁶Those who do not find me hurt themselves.
    Those who hate me love death."

Being Wise or Foolish

9 Wisdom has built her house;
    she has made its seven columns.
²She has prepared her food and wine;
    she has set her table.
³She has sent out her servant girls,
    and she calls out from the highest place in
    the city.
⁴She says to those who are uneducated,
    "Come in here, you foolish people!
⁵Come and eat my food
    and drink the wine I have prepared.

⁶Stop your foolish ways, and you will live;
    take the road of understanding.

⁷"If you correct someone who makes fun of
    wisdom, you will be insulted.
    If you correct an evil person, you will get
    hurt.
⁸Do not correct those who make fun of
    wisdom, or they will hate you.
    But correct the wise, and they will love you.
⁹Teach the wise, and they will become even
    wiser;
    teach good people, and they will learn even
    more.

¹⁰"Wisdom begins with respect for the LORD,
    and understanding begins with knowing the
    Holy One.
¹¹If you live wisely, you will live a long time;
    wisdom will add years to your life.
¹²The wise person is rewarded by wisdom,
    but whoever makes fun of wisdom will
    suffer for it."

SCHOOL

Crossroads

Paul's cane tapped from side to side, sweeping across the pavement. He approached a crossroad, but veered left. As his cane struck metal, he stopped.

"Mr Kennedy? Where am I?" he asked.

Paul's instructor from the school for the blind stood watching Paul's cane technique.

"What have you hit?" he asked. "Listen to the sound of it. Feel it."

Paul swung his cane again, turning his head as he listened to the metallic ring. "It's a car."

"Good. Get back on the pavement and cross the road." The instructor tensed. Would Paul follow what he had been taught? Or would he step into the path of an oncoming car?

Lorries passed in front of Paul. "I'm scared!"

"Listen for the traffic. You can do it," the instructor said.

Finally Paul stepped onto the crossing. The teacher let out a relieved breath; Paul had chosen the right time.

Proverbs 9:8–12 describes the rewards for a wise student who learns from a good teacher, as Paul did.

* According to this passage, where does the wisdom begin?
* Have you ever been regarded as wise, at school or otherwise as mentioned in verse 12?

Consider . . .

* telling a teacher whom you admire how he or she has helped you in life.
* offering to help classmates who are having trouble at school so that you can pass on to others what your teachers have taught you.

For more, see . . .

* Psalm 16:7–11 (p.508)
* John 7:14–18 (p.1108)
* Daniel 1:3–18 (p.833)

¹³Foolishness is like a loud woman;
  she does not have wisdom or
    knowledge.
¹⁴She sits at the door of her house
  at the highest place in the city.
¹⁵She calls out to those who are passing by,
  who are going along, minding their own
    business.
¹⁶She says to those who are uneducated,
  "Come in here, you foolish people!
¹⁷Stolen water is sweeter,
  and food eaten in secret tastes better."
¹⁸But these people don't know that everyone
  who goes there dies,
    that her guests end up deep in the grave.

The Wise Words of Solomon

10 These are the wise words of Solomon:

A wise son makes his father happy,
  but a foolish son makes his mother sad.

²Riches gained by doing wrong have no value,
  but right living will save you from death.

³The LORD does not let good people go hungry,
  but he keeps evil people from getting what
    they want.

> ### Sidelight
>
> Two sections of Proverbs
> (Proverbs 10:1—22:16
> and 25:1—29:27, p.611) are attributed to
> Solomon, the king who was said to have spoken
> 3,000 wise sayings (1 Kings 4:32–34, p.318).

⁴A lazy person will end up poor,
  but a hard worker will become rich.

⁵Those who gather crops on time are wise,
  but those who sleep through the harvest
    are a disgrace.

⁶Good people will have rich blessings,
  but the wicked will be overwhelmed by
    violence.

⁷Good people will be remembered as a
  blessing,
    but evil people will soon be forgotten.

⁸The wise do what they are told,
  but a talkative fool will be ruined.

⁹The honest person will live in safety,
  but the dishonest will be caught.

¹⁰A wink may get you into trouble,
  and foolish talk will lead to your ruin.

¹¹The words of a good person give life, like a
  fountain of water,
    but the words of the wicked contain
      nothing but violence.

¹²Hatred stirs up trouble,
  but love forgives all wrongs.

¹³Clever people speak wisely,
  but people without wisdom should be
    punished.

¹⁴The wise don't tell everything they know,
  but the foolish talk too much and are
    ruined.

¹⁵Having lots of money protects the rich,
  but having no money destroys the poor.

¹⁶Good people are rewarded with life,
  but evil people are paid with punishment.

¹⁷Whoever accepts correction is on the way to
  life,
    but whoever ignores correction will lead
      others away from life.

¹⁸Whoever hides hate is a liar.
  Whoever tells lies is a fool.

¹⁹If you talk a lot, you are sure to sin;
  if you are wise, you will keep quiet.

²⁰The words of a good person are like pure
  silver,
    but an evil person's thoughts are worth
      very little.

²¹Good people's words will help many others,
  but fools will die because they don't have
    wisdom.

²²The LORD's blessing brings wealth,
  and no sorrow comes with it.

²³A foolish person enjoys doing wrong,
  but a person with understanding enjoys
    doing what is wise.

²⁴Evil people will get what they fear most,
  but good people will get what they want
    most.

²⁵A storm will blow the evil person away,
  but a good person will always be safe.

²⁶A lazy person bothers the one he works for
  like vinegar on the teeth or smoke in the
    eyes.

²⁷Whoever respects the LORD will have a long
  life,
    but the life of an evil person will be cut
      short.

²⁸A good person can look forward to happiness,
  but an evil person can expect nothing.

²⁹The LORD will protect good people
  but will ruin those who do evil.

³⁰Good people will always be safe,
  but evil people will not remain in the land.

³¹A good person says wise things,
  but a liar's tongue will be stopped.

³²Good people know the right thing to say,
  but evil people only tell lies.

11 The LORD hates dishonest scales,
  but he is pleased with honest
  weights.
²Pride leads only to shame;
  it is wise to be humble.

³Good people will be guided by honesty;
  dishonesty will destroy those who are not
  trustworthy.

⁴Riches will not help when it's time to die,
  but right living will save you from death.

⁵The goodness of the innocent makes life
  easier,
  but the wicked will be destroyed by their
  wickedness.

⁶Doing right brings freedom to honest people,
  but those who are not trustworthy will be
  caught by their own desires.

Sidelight

Because they didn't have
digital scales in Bible
times, people had to use stones and metal
objects to work out how heavy something was
before buying or selling it. They probably used
hand-held scales and put the merchandise on
one side and the weight on the other. Proverbs
11:1 warns against using inaccurate scales to
cheat someone.

⁷When the wicked die, hope dies with them;
  their hope in riches will come to nothing.

⁸The good person is saved from trouble;
  it comes to the wicked instead.

⁹With words an evil person can destroy a
  neighbour,
  but a good person will escape by being clever.

¹⁰When good people succeed, the city is happy.
  When evil people die, there are shouts
  of joy.

¹¹Good people bless and build up their city,
  but the wicked can destroy it with their
  words.

¹²People without good sense find fault with
  their neighbours,
  but those with understanding keep quiet.

¹³Gossips can't keep secrets,
  but a trustworthy person can.

¹⁴Without leadership a nation falls,
  but lots of good advice will save it.

¹⁵Whoever guarantees to pay somebody else's
  loan will suffer.
  It is safer to avoid such promises.

¹⁶A kind woman gets respect,
  but cruel men get only wealth.

¹⁷Kind people do themselves a favour,
  but cruel people bring trouble on
  themselves.

¹⁸An evil person really earns nothing,
  but a good person will surely be
  rewarded.

¹⁹Those who are truly good will live,
  but those who chase after evil will die.

²⁰The LORD hates those with evil hearts
  but is pleased with those who are innocent.

²¹Evil people will certainly be punished,
  but those who do right will be set free.

²²A beautiful woman without good sense
  is like a gold ring in a pig's snout.

²³Those who do right only wish for good,
  but the wicked can expect to be defeated
  by God's anger.

²⁴Some people give much but get back even
  more.
  Others don't give what they should and
  end up poor.

²⁵Whoever gives to others will get richer;
  those who help others will themselves be
  helped.

²⁶People curse those who keep all the grain,
  but they bless the one who is willing to
  sell it.

²⁷Whoever looks for good will find kindness,
  but whoever looks for evil will find trouble.

²⁸Those who trust in riches will be ruined,
  but a good person will be healthy like a
  green leaf.

²⁹Whoever brings trouble to his family
  will be left with nothing but the wind.
  A fool will be a servant to the wise.

³⁰A good person gives life to others;
  the wise person teaches others how
  to live.

³¹Good people will be rewarded on earth,
  and the wicked and the sinners will be
  punished.

12

Anyone who loves learning accepts correction,
but a person who hates being corrected is stupid.

2 The LORD is pleased with a good person,
but he will punish anyone who plans evil.

3 Doing evil brings no safety at all,
but a good person has safety and security.

4 A good wife is like a crown for her husband,
but a disgraceful wife is like a disease in his bones.

5 The plans that good people make are fair,
but the advice of the wicked will trick you.

6 The wicked talk about killing people,
but the words of good people will save them.

7 Wicked people die and they are no more,
but a good person's family continues.

8 The wisdom of the wise wins praise,
but there is no respect for the stupid.

9 A person who is not important but has a servant is better off
than someone who acts important but has no food.

10 Good people take care of their animals,
but even the kindest acts of the wicked are cruel.

11 Those who work their land will have plenty of food,
but the one who chases empty dreams is not wise.

12 The wicked want what other evil people have stolen,
but good people want to give what they have to others.

13 Evil people are trapped by their evil talk,
but good people stay out of trouble.

14 People will be rewarded for what they say,
and they will also be rewarded for what they do.

15 Fools think they are doing right,
but the wise listen to advice.

16 Fools quickly show that they are upset,
but the wise ignore insults.

17 An honest witness tells the truth,
but a dishonest witness tells lies.

18 Careless words stab like a sword,
but wise words bring healing.

19 Truth will continue for ever,
but lies are only for a moment.

20 Those who plan evil are full of lies,
but those who plan peace are happy.

21 No harm comes to a good person,
but an evil person's life is full of trouble.

22 The LORD hates those who tell lies
but is pleased with those who keep their promises.

23 Wise people keep what they know to themselves,
but fools can't keep from showing how foolish they are.

24 Hard workers will become leaders,
but those who are lazy will be slaves.

25 Worry is a heavy load,
but a kind word cheers you up.

26 Good people take advice from their friends,
but an evil person is easily led to do wrong.

27 The lazy catch no food to cook,
but a hard worker will have great wealth.

28 Doing what is right is the way to life,
but there is another way that leads to death.

13

Wise children take their parents' advice,
but whoever makes fun of wisdom won't listen to correction.

2 People will be rewarded for what they say,
but those who can't be trusted want only violence.

3 Those who are careful about what they say protect their lives,
but whoever speaks without thinking will be ruined.

4 The lazy will not get what they want,
but those who work hard will.

5 Good people hate what is false,
but the wicked do shameful and disgraceful things.

6 Doing what is right protects the honest person,
but doing evil ruins the sinner.

7 Some people pretend to be rich but really have nothing.
Others pretend to be poor but really are wealthy.

8 The rich may have to pay a ransom for their lives,
but the poor will face no such danger.

⁹Good people can look forward to a bright
future,
but the future of the wicked is like a flame
going out.

¹⁰Pride only leads to arguments,
but those who take advice are wise.

¹¹Money that comes easily disappears quickly,
but money that is gathered little by little
will grow.

¹²It is sad not to get what you hoped for.
But wishes that come true are like eating
fruit from the tree of life.

¹³Those who reject what they are taught will
pay for it,
but those who obey what they are told will
be rewarded.

¹⁴The teaching of a wise person gives life.
It is like a fountain that can save people
from death.

¹⁵People with good understanding will be well
liked,
but the lives of those who are not
trustworthy are hard.

¹⁶Every wise person acts with good sense,
but fools show how foolish they are.

¹⁷A wicked messenger brings nothing but
trouble,
but a trustworthy one makes everything
right.

¹⁸A person who refuses correction will end up
poor and disgraced,
but the one who accepts correction will be
honoured.

¹⁹It is so good when wishes come true,
but fools hate to stop doing evil.

²⁰Spend time with the wise and you will
become wise,
but the friends of fools will suffer.

²¹Trouble always comes to sinners,
but good people enjoy success.

²²Good people leave their wealth to their
grandchildren,
but a sinner's wealth is stored up for good
people.

²³A poor person's field might produce plenty of
food,
but others often steal it away.

²⁴If you do not punish your children, you don't
love them,
but if you love your children, you will
correct them.

²⁵Good people have enough to eat,
but the wicked will go hungry.

14 A wise woman strengthens her family,
but a foolish woman destroys hers by
what she does.

²People who live good lives respect the LORD,
but those who live evil lives don't.

³Fools will be punished for their proud words,
but the words of the wise will protect
them.

⁴When there are no oxen, there is no food in
the barn.
But with a strong ox, much grain can be
grown.

Sidelight In ancient times, oxen
were more valuable to
the Israelites than a music player is to a teenager
(Proverbs 14:4). These great beasts were used
to plough, tread corn, and pull carts. They
even had a day off on the Sabbath (Exodus
23:12, p.83).

---

⁵A truthful witness does not lie,
but a false witness tells nothing but lies.

⁶Those who make fun of wisdom look for it
and do not find it,
but knowledge comes easily to those with
understanding.

⁷Stay away from fools,
because they can't teach you anything.

⁸A wise person will understand what to do,
but a foolish person is dishonest.

⁹Fools don't care if they sin,
but honest people work at being right.

¹⁰No one else can know your sadness,
and strangers cannot share your joy.

¹¹The wicked person's house will be destroyed,
but a good person's tent will still be
standing.

¹²Some people think they are doing right,
but in the end it leads to death.

¹³Someone who is laughing may be sad inside,
and joy may end in sadness.

¹⁴Evil people will be paid back for their evil
ways,
and good people will be rewarded for their
good ones.

¹⁵Fools will believe anything,
but the wise think about what they do.

¹⁶Wise people are careful and stay out of
trouble,
but fools are careless and quick to act.

¹⁷Someone with a quick temper does foolish
things,
but someone with understanding remains
calm.

¹⁸Fools are rewarded with nothing but more
foolishness,
but the wise are rewarded with knowledge.

¹⁹Evil people will bow down to those who are
good;
the wicked will bow down at the door of
those who do right.

²⁰The poor are rejected, even by their
neighbours,
but the rich have many friends.

²¹It is a sin to hate your neighbour,
but being kind to the needy brings
happiness.

²²Those who make evil plans will be ruined,
but those who plan to do good will be
loved and trusted.

²³Those who work hard make a profit,
but those who only talk will be poor.

²⁴Wise people are rewarded with wealth,
but fools only get more foolishness.

²⁵A truthful witness saves lives,
but a false witness is a traitor.

²⁶Those who respect the LORD will have
security,
and their children will be protected.

²⁷Respect for the LORD gives life.
It is like a fountain that can save people
from death.

²⁸A king is honoured when he has many
people to rule,
but a prince is ruined if he has none.

²⁹Patient people have great understanding,
but people with quick tempers show their
foolishness.

³⁰Peace of mind means a healthy body,
but jealousy will rot your bones.

³¹Whoever mistreats the poor insults their
Maker,
but whoever is kind to the needy
honours God.

³²The wicked are ruined by their own evil,
but those who do right are protected even
in death.

³³Wisdom lives in those with understanding,
and even fools recognise it.

³⁴Doing what is right makes a nation great,
but sin will bring disgrace to any people.

³⁵A king is pleased with a wise servant,
but he will become angry with one who
causes him shame.

15 A gentle answer will calm a person's
anger,
but an unkind answer will cause more
anger.

²Wise people use knowledge when they speak,
but fools pour out foolishness.

³The LORD's eyes see everything;
he watches both evil and good people.

⁴As a tree gives fruit, healing words give life,
but dishonest words crush the spirit.

⁵Fools reject their parents' correction,
but anyone who accepts correction is wise.

⁶Much wealth is in the houses of good people,
but evil people get nothing but trouble.

⁷Wise people use their words to spread
knowledge,
but there is no knowledge in the thoughts
of fools.

⁸The LORD hates the sacrifice that the wicked
offer,
but he likes the prayers of honest people.

⁹The LORD hates what evil people do,
but he loves those who do what is right.

¹⁰The person who stops doing what is right
will be punished,
and the one who hates to be corrected
will die.

¹¹The LORD knows what is happening in the
world of the dead,
so he surely knows the thoughts of the
living.

¹²Those who make fun of wisdom don't like to
be corrected;
they will not ask the wise for advice.

¹³Happiness makes a person smile,
but sadness can break a person's spirit.

¹⁴People with understanding want more
knowledge,
but fools just want more foolishness.

¹⁵Every day is hard for those who suffer,
but a happy heart is like a continual feast.

¹⁶It is better to be poor and respect the LORD
than to be wealthy and have much trouble.

¹⁷It is better to eat vegetables with those who
love you
than to eat meat with those who hate you.

¹⁸People with quick tempers cause trouble,
but those who control their tempers stop a
quarrel.

¹⁹A lazy person's life is like a patch of thorns,
but an honest person's life is like a smooth
highway.

²⁰A wise son makes his father happy,
but a foolish son hates his mother.

²¹A person without wisdom enjoys being
foolish,
but someone with understanding does what
is right.

²²Plans fail without good advice,
but they succeed with the advice of many
others.

²³People enjoy giving good advice.
Saying the right word at the right time is so
pleasing.

²⁴Wise people's lives get better and better.
They avoid whatever would cause their
death.

²⁵The LORD will tear down the proud person's
house,
but he will protect the widow's property.

²⁶The LORD hates evil thoughts
but is pleased with kind words.

²⁷Greedy people bring trouble to their
families,
but the person who can't be paid to do
wrong will live.

²⁸Good people think before they answer,
but the wicked simply pour out evil.

²⁹The LORD does not listen to the wicked,
but he hears the prayers of those who do
right.

³⁰Good news makes you feel better.
Your happiness will show in your eyes.

³¹If you listen to correction to improve your life,
you will live among the wise.

³²Those who refuse correction hate themselves,
but those who accept correction gain
understanding.

³³Respect for the LORD will teach you wisdom.
If you want to be honoured, you must be
humble.

16 People may make plans in their minds,
but only the LORD can make them
come true.

²You may believe you are doing right,
but the LORD will judge your reasons.

³Depend on the LORD in whatever you do,
and your plans will succeed.

⁴The LORD makes everything go as he pleases.
He has even prepared a day of disaster for
evil people.

⁵The LORD hates those who are proud.
They will surely be punished.

⁶Love and truth bring forgiveness of sin.
By respecting the LORD you will avoid evil.

⁷When people live so that they please the
LORD,
even their enemies will make peace with
them.

⁸It is better to be poor and right
than to be wealthy and dishonest.

⁹People may make plans in their minds,
but the LORD decides what they will do.

¹⁰The words of a king are like a message
from God,
so his decisions should be fair.

¹¹The LORD wants honest balances and scales;
all the weights are his work.

¹²Kings hate those who do wrong,
because governments only continue if they
are fair.

¹³Kings like honest people;
they value someone who speaks the truth.

¹⁴An angry king can put someone to death,
so a wise person will try to make him
happy.

¹⁵A smiling king can give people life;
his kindness is like a spring shower.

¹⁶It is better to get wisdom than gold,
and to choose understanding rather than
silver!

¹⁷Good people stay away from evil.
By watching what they do, they protect
their lives.

¹⁸Pride will destroy a person;
a proud attitude leads to ruin.

¹⁹It is better to be humble and be with those
who suffer
than to share stolen property with the
proud.

²⁰Whoever listens to what is taught will
succeed,
and whoever trusts the LORD will be happy.

²¹The wise are known for their understanding.
Their pleasant words make them better
teachers.

²²Understanding is like a fountain which gives
life to those who use it,
but foolishness brings punishment to fools.

²³Wise people's minds tell them what to say,
and that helps them be better teachers.

²⁴Pleasant words are like a honeycomb,
making people happy and healthy.

²⁵Some people think they are doing right,
but in the end it leads to death.

²⁶The workers' hunger helps them,
because their desire to eat makes them
work.

²⁷Useless people make evil plans,
and their words are like a burning fire.

²⁸A useless person causes trouble,
and a gossip ruins friendships.

²⁹Cruel people trick their neighbours
and lead them to do wrong.

³⁰Someone who winks is planning evil,
and the one who grins is planning
something wrong.

³¹Grey hair is like a crown of honour;
it is earned by living a good life.

³²Patience is better than strength.
Controlling your temper is better than
capturing a city.

³³People throw lots *d* to make a decision,
but the answer comes from the LORD.

17 It is better to eat a dry crust of bread
in peace
than to have a feast where there is
quarrelling.

²A wise servant will rule over the master's
disgraceful child
and will even inherit a share of what the
master leaves his children.

³A hot furnace tests silver and gold,
but the LORD tests hearts.

⁴Evil people listen to evil words.
Liars pay attention to cruel words.

⁵Whoever mistreats the poor insults their
Maker;
whoever enjoys someone's trouble will be
punished.

⁶Old people are proud of their
grandchildren,
and children are proud of their parents.

⁷Fools should not be proud,
and rulers should not be liars.

⁸Some people think they can pay others to do
anything they ask.
They think it will work every time.

⁹Whoever forgives someone's sin makes a
friend,
but telling about the sin breaks up
friendships.

¹⁰A wise person will learn more from a warning
than a fool will learn from a hundred
lashings.

¹¹Disobedient people look only for trouble,
so a cruel messenger will be sent against
them.

¹²It is better to meet a bear robbed of her
cubs
than to meet a fool doing foolish things.

¹³Whoever gives evil in return for good
will always have trouble at home.

¹⁴Starting a quarrel is like a leak in a dam,
so stop it before a fight breaks out.

¹⁵The LORD hates both of these things:
freeing the guilty and punishing the
innocent.

¹⁶It won't do a fool any good to try to buy
wisdom,
because he doesn't have the ability to be
wise.

¹⁷A friend loves you all the time,
and a brother helps in time of trouble.

¹⁸It is not wise to promise
to pay what your neighbour owes.

¹⁹Whoever loves to argue loves to sin.
Whoever is proud a lot is asking for
trouble.

²⁰A person with an evil heart will find no
success,
and the person whose words are evil will
get into trouble.

²¹It is sad to have a foolish child;
there is no joy in being the parent of a fool.

²²A happy heart is like good medicine,
but a broken spirit drains your strength.

23When the wicked accept money to do wrong
there can be no justice.

24The person with understanding is always
looking for wisdom,
but the mind of a fool wanders everywhere.

25A foolish son makes his father sad
and causes his mother great sorrow.

26It is not good to punish the innocent
or to beat leaders for being honest.

27The clever person says very little,
and one with understanding stays calm.

28Even fools seem to be wise if they keep
quiet;
if they don't speak, they appear to
understand.

18 Unfriendly people are selfish
and hate all good sense.

2Fools do not want to understand anything.
They only want to tell others what they
think.

3Do something evil, and people won't
like you.
Do something shameful, and they will
make fun of you.

4Spoken words can be like deep water,
but wisdom is like a flowing stream.

5It is not good to honour the wicked
or to be unfair to the innocent.

6The words of fools start quarrels.
They make people want to beat them.

7The words of fools will ruin them;
their own words will trap them.

8The words of a gossip are like tasty bits of
food.
People like to take them all up.

9A person who doesn't work hard
is just like someone who destroys things.

10The LORD is like a strong tower;
those who do right can run to him for
safety.

11Rich people trust their wealth to protect
them.
They think it is like the high walls of a
city.

12Proud people will be ruined,
but the humble will be honoured.

13Anyone who answers without listening
is foolish and confused.

14The will to live can get you through sickness,
but no one can live with a broken spirit.

15The mind of a person with understanding
gets knowledge;
the wise person listens to learn more.

16Taking a gift to an important man
will help get you in to see him.

17The person who tells one side of a story
seems right,
until someone else comes and asks
questions.

18Throwing lots *d* can settle arguments
and keep the two sides from fighting.

19A brother who has been insulted is harder to
win back than a walled city,
and arguments separate people like the
barred gates of a palace.

20People will be rewarded for what they say;
they will be rewarded by how they speak.

21What you say can mean life or death.
Those who speak with care will be
rewarded.

22When a man finds a wife, he finds something
good.
It shows that the LORD is pleased
with him.

23The poor beg for mercy,
but the rich give rude answers.

24Some friends may ruin you,
but a real friend will be more loyal than a
brother.

19 It is better to be poor and honest
than to be foolish and tell lies.

2Enthusiasm without knowledge is not good.
If you act too quickly, you might make a
mistake.

3People's own foolishness ruins their lives,
but in their minds they blame the LORD.

4Wealthy people are always finding more
friends,
but the poor lose all theirs.

5A witness who lies will not go free;
liars will never escape.

6Many people want to please a leader,
and everyone is friends with those who
give gifts.

7Poor people's relatives avoid them;
even their friends stay far away.
They run after them, begging,
but they are gone.

8Those who get wisdom do themselves a
favour,
and those who love learning will succeed.

⁹A witness who lies will not go free;
   liars will die.

¹⁰A fool should not live in luxury.
   A slave should not rule over princes.

¹¹Clever people are patient;
   they will be honoured if they ignore
      insults.

¹²An angry king is like a roaring lion,
   but his kindness is like the dew on the
      grass.

¹³A foolish son will ruin his father,
   and a quarrelling wife is like dripping
      water.

Sidelight   When we think of dripping
water, we most often
think of a dripping tap. But the dripping water
of Proverbs 19:13 was much more annoying.
It probably referred to a leaking roof. In Bible
times, houses were made of mud and had flat
roofs. With good care, roofs stayed pretty
watertight, but leaky roofs were a common
problem – and the source of many jokes.

---

¹⁴Houses and wealth are inherited from
      parents,
   but a wise wife is a gift from the LORD.

¹⁵Lazy people sleep a lot,
   and idle people will go hungry.

¹⁶Those who obey the commands protect
      themselves,
   but those who are careless will die.

¹⁷Being kind to the poor is like lending to the
      LORD;
   he will reward you for what you have
      done.

¹⁸Correct your children while there is still
      hope;
   do not let them destroy themselves.

¹⁹People with quick tempers will have to pay
      for it.
   If you help them out once, you will have to
      do it again.

²⁰Listen to advice and accept correction,
   and in the end you will be wise.

²¹People can make all kinds of plans,
   but only the LORD's plan will happen.

²²People want others to be loyal,
   so it is better to be poor than to be a liar.

²³Those who respect the LORD will live
   and be satisfied, unbothered by trouble.

²⁴Though the lazy person puts his hand in the
      dish,
   he won't lift the food to his mouth.

²⁵Whip those who make fun of wisdom, and
      perhaps foolish people will gain some
      wisdom.
   Correct those with understanding, and they
      will gain knowledge.

²⁶A son who robs his father and sends away
      his mother
   brings shame and disgrace on himself.

²⁷Don't stop listening to correction, my child,
   or you will forget what you have already
      learned.

²⁸An evil witness makes fun of fairness,
   and wicked people love what is evil.

²⁹People who make fun of wisdom will be
      punished,
   and the backs of foolish people will be
      beaten.

20 Wine and beer make people loud and
      uncontrolled;
   it is not wise to get drunk on them.

²An angry king is like a roaring lion.
   Making him angry may cost you your life.

³Foolish people are always fighting,
   but avoiding quarrels will bring you
      honour.

⁴Lazy farmers don't plough when they
      should;
   they expect a harvest, but there is none.

⁵People's thoughts can be like a deep well,
   but someone with understanding can find
      the wisdom there.

⁶Many people claim to be loyal,
   but it is hard to find a trustworthy
      person.

⁷The good people who live honest lives
   will be a blessing to their children.

⁸When a king sits on his throne to judge,
   he knows evil when he sees it.

⁹No one can say, "I am innocent;
   I have never done anything wrong."

¹⁰The LORD hates both these things:
dishonest weights and dishonest
measures.

¹¹Even children are known by their
behaviour;
their actions show if they are innocent
and good.

¹²The LORD has made both these things:
ears to hear and eyes to see.

¹³If you love to sleep, you will be poor.
If you stay awake, you will have plenty of
food.

¹⁴Buyers say, "This is bad. It's no good."
Then they go away and boast about what
they bought.

¹⁵There is gold and plenty of rubies,
but only a few people speak with
knowledge.

¹⁶Take the coat of someone who promises to
pay a stranger's debts,
and keep it until he pays what the stranger
owes.

¹⁷Stolen food may taste sweet at first,
but later it will feel like a mouth full of
gravel.

¹⁸Get advice if you want your plans to work.
If you go to war, get the advice of others.

¹⁹Gossips can't keep secrets,
so avoid people who talk too much.

²⁰Those who curse their father or mother
will be like a light going out in darkness.

²¹Wealth inherited quickly in the beginning
will do you no good in the end.

²²Don't say, "I'll pay you back for the wrong
you did."
Wait for the LORD, and he will make things
right.

²³The LORD hates dishonest weights,
and dishonest scales do not please him.

²⁴The LORD decides what a person will do;
no one understands what his life is all
about.

²⁵It's dangerous to promise something to God
too quickly.
After you've thought about it, it may be too
late.

²⁶A wise king separates out the evil people,
and he drives the threshing wheel over
them as they deserve.

²⁷The LORD looks deep inside people
and searches through their thoughts.

²⁸Loyalty and truth keep a king in power;
he continues to rule if he is loyal.

²⁹Young men glory in their strength,
and old men are honoured for their grey
hair.

³⁰Hard punishment will get rid of evil,
and whippings can change an evil heart.

21 The LORD can control a king's mind as
he controls a river;
he can direct it as he pleases.

²You may believe you are doing right,
but the LORD judges your reasons.

³Doing what is right and fair
is more important to the LORD than
sacrifices.

⁴Proud looks, proud thoughts
and evil actions are sin.

⁵The plans of people who work hard earn a
profit,
but those who act too quickly become
poor.

⁶Wealth that comes from telling lies
vanishes like a mist and leads to death.

⁷The violence of the wicked will destroy them,
because they refuse to do what is right.

⁸Guilty people live dishonest lives,
but honest people do right.

⁹It is better to live in a corner on the roof ⁿ
than inside the house with a quarrelling
wife.

¹⁰Evil people only want to harm others.
Their neighbours get no mercy from them.

¹¹If you punish those who make fun of
wisdom, a foolish person may gain
some wisdom.
But if you teach the wise, they will get
knowledge.

¹²God, who is always right, watches the house
of the wicked
and brings ruin on every evil person.

roof In Bible times houses were built with flat roofs. The roof was used for drying things such as flax and fruit. And it was used
as an extra room, as a place for worship and as a place to sleep in the summer.

13Whoever ignores the poor when they cry for
    help
  will also cry for help and not be answered.

14A secret gift will calm an angry person;
  a present given in secrecy will still great
    anger.

15When justice is done, good people are happy,
  but evil people are ruined.

16Whoever does not use good sense
  will end up among the dead.

17Whoever loves pleasure will become poor;
  whoever loves wine and perfume will never
    be rich.

18Wicked people will suffer instead of good
    people,
  and those who cannot be trusted will suffer
    instead of those who do right.

19It is better to live alone in the desert
  than with a quarrelling and complaining wife.

20Wise people's houses are full of the best
    foods and olive oil,
  but fools waste everything they have.

21Whoever tries to live right and be loyal
  finds life, success and honour.

22A wise person can defeat a city full of warriors
  and tear down the defences they trust in.

23Those who are careful about what they say
  keep themselves out of trouble.

24People who act with stubborn pride
  are called "proud", "boaster" and "mocker".

25Lazy people's desire for sleep will kill them,
  because they refuse to work.
26All day long they wish for more,
  but good people give without holding back.

27The LORD hates sacrifices brought by evil
    people,
  particularly when they offer them for the
    wrong reasons.

28A lying witness will be forgotten,
  but a truthful witness will speak on.

29Wicked people are stubborn,
  but good people think carefully about what
    they do.

30There is no wisdom, understanding or advice
  that can succeed against the LORD.

31You can get the horses ready for battle,
  but it is the LORD who gives the victory.

22

Being respected is more important than
  having great riches.
To be well thought of is better than silver
  or gold.

2The rich and the poor are alike
  in that the LORD made them all.

3The wise see danger ahead and avoid it,
  but fools keep going and get into trouble.

4Respecting the LORD and not being proud
  will bring you wealth, honour and life.

5Evil people's lives are like paths covered with
    thorns and traps.
  People who guard themselves don't have
    such problems.

6Train children how to live right,
  and when they are old, they will not
    change.

7The rich rule over the poor,
  and borrowers are servants to those who
    lend.

8Those who plan evil will receive trouble.
  Their cruel anger will come to an end.

9Generous people will be blessed,
  because they share their food with the
    poor.

10Get rid of the one who makes fun of
    wisdom.
  Then fighting, quarrels and insults will stop.

11Whoever loves pure thoughts and kind words
  will have even the king as a friend.

12The LORD guards knowledge,
  but he destroys false words.

13The lazy person says, "There's a lion outside!
  I might get killed out in the street!"

14The words of an unfaithful wife are like a
    deep trap.
  Those who make the LORD angry will get
    caught by them.

15Every child is full of foolishness,
  but punishment can get rid of it.

16Whoever gets rich by mistreating the poor,
  and gives presents to the wealthy, will
    become poor.

Other Wise Sayings
17Listen carefully to what wise people say;
  pay attention to what I am teaching you.
18It will be good to keep these things in mind
  so that you are ready to repeat them.

¹⁹I am teaching them to you now
    so that you will put your trust in
        the LORD.
²⁰I have written thirty sayings for you,
    which give knowledge and good advice.
²¹I am teaching you true and reliable words
    so that you can give true answers to
        anyone who asks.

²²Do not abuse poor people because they are
        poor,
    and do not take away the rights of the
        needy in court.
²³The LORD will defend them in court
    and will take the life of those who take
        away their rights.

²⁴Don't make friends with bad-tempered people
    or spend time with those who have bad
        tempers.
²⁵If you do, you will be like them.
    Then you will be in real danger.

²⁶Don't promise to pay what someone else
        owes,
    and don't guarantee anyone's loan.
²⁷If you cannot pay the loan,
    your own bed may be taken right out from
        under you.

²⁸Don't move an old stone that marks a border,
    because those stones were set up by your
        ancestors.

FAMILY

Trust

The flashing of police lights reflected in the mirror of Eve's car. Oh no, not a speeding fine! At the worst possible time too. Eve pulled over and waited for the police officer to come to her car. Eve felt like crying. She had been planning to drive to an open-air concert at the weekend. However, getting a speeding fine would put her weekend plans at risk – if her parents found out. As the officer asked for her driving licence, she decided it would be better to tell her parents about the fine, after the concert. Then, she returned home and kept silent.

That night Eve tossed and turned. Her parents had always trusted her to tell the truth. Finally, at around midnight, she got up and went to her older brother to ask for his advice. He was still awake, listening to his music.

Eve told him what had happened and then asked what he thought.

"You had better tell them," he said. "They'll find out, and then you really will be in trouble!"

The next morning at breakfast, Eve spilled out the whole story to her parents. She told them about the fine and how sorry she was about it, and how she had struggled with telling them.

Disappointment clouded their eyes.

"I don't like the thought of you speeding," Dad said firmly.

"I know, Dad," Eve said. "I have learned the hard way."

Her parents left the room for a few mintues to talk together. Then they returned.

"You have to pay the fine," Mum said and then paused.

"And you can still go to the concert," Dad added with a smile.

Thrilled, Eve determined never to betray her parents' trust – and she is still keeping to that promise.

Read how **Proverbs 22:1–9** reflect Eve's family values of honesty and generosity.

* Which verse in the passage best summarises Eve's story?
* What would you pay to gain your family's respect and trust? As much as stated in verse 1?

Consider . . .

* talking to your parents about building trust in your relationship.
* writing on a card four things you can do to build your family's trust in you. Put it where only you can see it.

For more, see . . .

* Genesis 4:1–12 (p.7)
* 2 Timothy 3:14–15 (p.1319)
* Genesis 45:1–11 (p.51)

²⁹Do you see people skilled in their work?
  They will work for kings, not for ordinary
    people.

23 If you sit down to eat with a ruler,
    notice the food that is in front
     of you.
²Control yourself
  if you have a big appetite.
³Don't be greedy for his fine foods,
  because that food might be a trick.

⁴Don't wear yourself out trying to get rich;
  be wise enough to control yourself.
⁵Wealth can vanish in the wink of an eye.
  It can seem to grow wings
  and fly away like an eagle.

⁶Don't eat the food of selfish people;
  don't be greedy for their fine foods.
⁷Selfish people are always worrying
  about how much the food costs.
 They tell you, "Eat and drink,"
  but they don't really mean it.
⁸You will throw up the little you have eaten,
  and you will have wasted your kind
    words.

⁹Don't speak to fools;
  they will only ignore your wise words.

¹⁰Don't move an old stone that marks a border,
  and don't take fields that belong to
    orphans.
¹¹God, their defender, is strong;
  he will take their side against you.

¹²Remember what you are taught,
  and listen carefully to words of knowledge.

¹³Don't fail to punish children.
  If you spank them, they won't die.
¹⁴If you spank them,
  you will save them from death.

¹⁵My child, if you are wise,
  then I will be happy.
¹⁶I will be so pleased
  if you speak what is right.

¹⁷Don't envy sinners,
  but always respect the LORD.
¹⁸Then you will have hope for the future,
  and your wishes will come true.

¹⁹Listen, my child, and be wise.
  Keep your mind on what is right.
²⁰Don't drink too much wine
  or eat too much food.
²¹Those who drink and eat too much become
    poor.
  They sleep too much and end up wearing
    rags.

²²Listen to your father, who gave you life,
  and do not forget your mother when she
    is old.
²³Learn the truth and never reject it.
  Get wisdom, self-control and understanding.
²⁴The father of a good child is very happy;
  parents who have wise children are glad
    because of them.
²⁵Make your father and mother happy;
  give your mother a reason to be glad.

²⁶My son, pay attention to me,
  and watch closely what I do.
²⁷A prostitute *d* is as dangerous as a deep pit,
  and an unfaithful wife is like a narrow well.
²⁸They ambush you like robbers
  and cause many men to be unfaithful to
    their wives.

²⁹Who has trouble? Who has pain?
  Who fights? Who complains?
 Who has unnecessary bruises?
  Who has bloodshot eyes?
³⁰It is people who drink too much wine,
  who try out all different kinds of strong
    drinks.
³¹Don't stare at the wine when it is red,
  when it sparkles in the cup,
  when it goes down smoothly.
³²Later it bites like a snake
  with poison in its fangs.
³³Your eyes will see strange sights,
  and your mind will be confused.
³⁴You will feel dizzy as if you're in a storm on
    the ocean,
  as if you're on top of a ship's sails.
³⁵You will think, "They hit me, but I'm not
    hurt.
  They beat me up, but I don't remember it.
 I wish I could wake up.
  Then I would get another drink."

24 Don't envy evil people
    or try to be friends with them.
²Their minds are always planning violence,
  and they always talk about making
    trouble.

³It takes wisdom to have a good family,
  and it takes understanding to make it
    strong.
⁴It takes knowledge to fill a home
  with rare and beautiful treasures.

⁵Wise people have great power,
  and those with knowledge have great
    strength.
⁶So you need advice when you go to war.
  If you have lots of good advice, you
    will win.

7Foolish people cannot understand wisdom.
They have nothing to say in a discussion.

8Whoever makes evil plans
will be known as a troublemaker.
9Making foolish plans is sinful,
and making fun of wisdom is hateful.

10If you give up when trouble comes,
it shows that you are weak.

11Save those who are being led to their death;
rescue those who are about to be killed.
12If you say, "We don't know anything about
this,"
God, who knows what's in your mind, will
notice.
He is watching you, and he will know.
He will reward each person for what he
has done.

13My child, eat honey because it is good.
Honey from the honeycomb tastes sweet.
14In the same way, wisdom is pleasing to you.
If you find it, you have hope for the future,
and your wishes will come true.

15Don't be wicked and attack a good family's
house;
don't rob the place where they live.
16Even though good people may be bothered
by trouble seven times, they are never
defeated,
but the wicked are overwhelmed by
trouble.

17Don't be happy when your enemy is defeated;
don't be glad when he is overwhelmed.
18The LORD will notice and be displeased.
He may not be angry with them any more.

19Don't envy evil people,
and don't be jealous of the wicked.
20An evil person has nothing to hope for;
the wicked will die like a flame that is
put out.

21My child, respect the LORD and the king.
Don't join those people who refuse to obey
them.
22The LORD and the king will quickly destroy
such people.
Those two can cause great disaster!

More Words of Wisdom

23These are also sayings of the wise:

It is not good to take sides when you are the
judge.
24Don't tell the wicked that they are innocent;
people will curse you, and nations will
hate you.

25But things will go well if you punish the
guilty,
and you will receive rich blessings.

26An honest answer is as pleasing
as a kiss on the lips.

27First, finish your outside work
and prepare your fields.
After that, you can build your house.

28Don't testify against your neighbour for no
good reason.
Don't say things that are false.
29Don't say, "I'll get even;
I'll do to him what he did to me."

30I passed by a lazy person's field
and by the vineyard of someone with no
sense.
31Thorns had grown up everywhere.
The ground was covered with weeds,
and the stone walls had fallen down.
32I thought about what I had seen;
I learned this lesson from what I saw.
33You sleep a little; you take a nap.
You fold your hands and lie down to
rest.
34Soon you will be as poor as if you had been
robbed;
you will have as little as if you had been
held up.

More Wise Sayings of Solomon

25 These are more wise sayings of Solomon,
copied by the men of Hezekiah king of
Judah.

2God is honoured for what he keeps secret.
Kings are honoured for what they can
discover.

3No one can measure the height of the skies or
the depth of the earth.
So also no one can understand the mind of
a king.

4Remove the scum from the silver,
so the silver can be used by the
silversmith.

Sidelight Do you need a good
brain teaser to catch
your friends out? Proverbs is filled with ancient
riddles (see Proverbs 25:2–3). Unfortunately,
the punchlines have lost some of their punch
through translation, so they are not as much
fun as they used to be.

⁵Remove wicked people from the king's
    presence;
  then his government will be honest and last
    a long time.

⁶Don't boast to the king
  and act as if you are great.
⁷It is better for him to give you a higher position
  than to bring you down in front of the
    prince.

Because of something you have seen,
⁸ do not quickly take someone to court.
What will you do later
  when your neighbour proves you wrong?

⁹If you have an argument with your
    neighbour,
  don't tell other people what was said.
¹⁰Whoever hears it might shame you,
  and you might not ever be respected
    again.

¹¹The right word spoken at the right time
  is as beautiful as golden apples in a silver
    bowl.

¹²A wise warning to someone who will listen
  is as valuable as gold earrings or fine gold
    jewellery.

¹³Trustworthy messengers refresh those who
    send them,
  like the coolness of snow in the summer-time.

¹⁴People who boast about gifts they never give
  are like clouds and wind that give no rain.

¹⁵With patience you can convince a ruler,
  and a gentle word can get through to the
    hard-headed.

¹⁶If you find honey, don't eat too much,
  or it will make you vomit.
¹⁷Don't go to your neighbour's house too often;
  too much of you will make him hate you.

¹⁸When you lie about your neighbours,
  it hurts them as much as a club, a sword
    or a sharp arrow.

¹⁹Trusting unfaithful people when you are in
    trouble
  is like eating with a broken tooth or walking
    with a crippled foot.

BOASTING

All Puffed Up

Porcupine puffer fish dart in and out of coral reefs as they feed. Their pale brown colour blends magically with the buff coral. But let a predator, such as a barracuda, threaten them, and they immediately become defensive. They pump water into themselves, almost doubling their size. They inflate into spine-covered balls. The attacker usually retreats, unwilling to swallow such large, thorny creatures.

However, when they puff up, predators can spot them. These floating curiosities are worth a lot of money. Once netted and brought to the surface, puffer fish inflate themselves with air. In that condition they die. Then they are dried and eventually hung on walls or heaped on shelves of coastal curio shops.

People who brag and boast are like spiny puffers. Take in what **Proverbs 25:6–7** says about puffed-up people.

* What are the puffer fish and the "boaster" in this passage trying to hide?
* In what situations are you tempted to exaggerate your knowledge, abilities, or material possessions? What might happen to you if you didn't pretend to be "great" as this passage directs?

Consider . . .

* writing on a ribbon three things you're tempted to boast about. Then tie the ribbon to your key-ring or purse as a reminder not to boast.
* writing a note to at least three people you admire for not being "people-pleasers", telling them how you admire that quality in them.

For more, see . . .

* Daniel 4:28–37 (p.837)
* Luke 18:9–14 (p.1078)

* Mark 9:33–35 (p.1015)

20Singing songs to someone who is sad
    is like taking away his coat on a cold day
    or pouring vinegar on soda.

21If your enemy is hungry, feed him.
    If he is thirsty, give him a drink.

22Doing this will be like pouring burning coals
    on his head,
    and the LORD will reward you.

23As the north wind brings rain,
    telling gossip brings angry looks.

24It is better to live in a corner on the roof[n]
    than inside the house with a quarrelling
    wife.

25Good news from a faraway place
    is like a cool drink when you are tired.

26A good person who gives in to evil
    is like a muddy spring or a dirty well.

27It is not good to eat too much honey,
    nor does it bring you honour to boast about
    yourself.

28Those who do not control themselves
    are like a city whose walls are broken
    down.

26

It shouldn't snow in summer or rain at
    harvest.
    Neither should a foolish person ever be
    honoured.

2Curses will not harm someone who is
    innocent;
    they are like sparrows or swallows that fly
    around and never land.

3Whips are for horses, and harnesses are for
    donkeys,
    so paddles are good for fools.

4Don't give fools a foolish answer,
    or you will be just like them.

5But answer fools as they should be answered,
    or they will think they are really wise.

6Sending a message by a foolish person
    is like cutting off your feet or drinking
    poison.

7A wise saying spoken by a fool
    is as useless as the legs of a crippled
    person.

8Giving honour to a foolish person
    is like tying a stone in a catapult.

9A wise saying spoken by a fool
    is like a thorn stuck in the hand of a
    drunkard.

10Employing a foolish person or anyone just
    passing by
    is like an archer shooting at just anything.

11A fool who repeats his foolishness
    is like a dog that goes back to what it has
    vomited.

12There is more hope for a foolish person
    than for those who think they are wise.

13The lazy person says, "There's a lion in the
    road!
    There's a lion in the streets!"

14Like a door turning back and forth on its
    hinges,
    the lazy person turns over and over in bed.

15Lazy people may put their hands in the dish,
    but they are too tired to lift the food to
    their mouths.

16The lazy person thinks he is wiser
    than seven people who give sensible answers.

17Interfering in someone else's quarrel as you
    pass by
    is like grabbing a dog by the ears.

18Like a madman shooting
    deadly, burning arrows
19is the one who tricks a neighbour
    and then says, "I was just joking."

20Without wood, a fire will go out,
    and without gossip, quarrelling will stop.

21Just as charcoal and wood keep a fire going,
    a quarrelsome person keeps an argument
    going.

22The words of a gossip are like tasty bits of
    food;
    people like to take them all up.

23Kind words from a wicked mind
    are like a shiny coating on a clay pot.

24Those who hate you may try to fool you with
    their words,
    but in their minds they are planning evil.
25People's words may be kind, but don't
    believe them,
    because their minds are full of evil thoughts.
26Lies can hide hate,
    but the evil will be plain to everyone.

---

roof In Bible times houses were built with flat roofs. The roof was used for drying things such as flax and fruit. And it was used
    as an extra room, as a place for worship and as a place to sleep in the summer.

27Whoever digs a pit for others will fall into it.
  Whoever tries to roll a boulder down on
    others will be crushed by it.

28Liars hate the people they hurt,
  and false praise can ruin others.

27 Don't boast about tomorrow;
    you don't know what may happen
    then.

2Don't praise yourself. Let someone else do it.
  Let the praise come from a stranger and
    not from your own mouth.

3Stone is heavy, and sand is weighty,
  but a complaining fool is worse than either.

4Anger is cruel and destroys like a flood,
  but no one can put up with jealousy!

5It is better to correct someone openly
  than to have love and not show it.

6The slap of a friend can be trusted to
    help you,
  but the kisses of an enemy are nothing but
    lies.

7When you are full, not even honey tastes
    good,
  but when you are hungry, even something
    bitter tastes sweet.

8A person who leaves his home
  is like a bird that leaves its nest.

9The sweet smell of perfume and oils is
    pleasant,
  and so is good advice from a friend.

Sidelight If you don't like taking
baths, slap on some extra
aftershave or perfume. Water was usually scarce
in Israel in Old Testament times, and that's what
people did. No wonder putting on oil and
perfume made people happy (Proverbs 27:9).
It probably made everyone nearby even happier!

10Don't forget your friend or your parent's
    friend.
  Don't always go to your family for help
    when trouble comes.
  A neighbour close by is better than a family
    far away.

11Be wise, my child, and make me happy.
  Then I can respond to any insult.

12The wise see danger ahead and avoid it,
  but fools keep going and get into trouble.

13Take the coat of someone who promises to
    pay a stranger's loan,
  and keep it until he pays what the stranger
    owes.

14If you loudly greet your neighbour early in the
    morning,
  he will think of it as a curse.

15A quarrelling wife is as bothersome
  as a continual dripping on a rainy day.
16Stopping her is like stopping the wind
  or trying to hold oil in your hand.

17As iron sharpens iron,
  so people can improve each other.

18Whoever tends a fig tree gets to eat its fruit,
  and whoever takes care of his master will
    receive honour.

19As water reflects your face,
  so your mind shows what kind of person
    you are.

20People will never stop dying and being
    destroyed,
  and they will never stop wanting more than
    they have.

21A hot furnace tests silver and gold,
  and people are tested by the praise they
    receive.

22Even if you ground up a foolish person like
    grain in a bowl,
  you couldn't remove the foolishness.

23Be sure you know how your sheep are doing,
  and pay attention to the condition of your
    cattle.
24Riches will not go on for ever,
  nor do governments go on for ever.
25Bring in the hay, and let the new grass appear.
  Gather the grass from the hills.
26Make clothes from the lambs' wool,
  and sell some goats to buy a field.
27There will be plenty of goat's milk
  to feed you and your family
  and to make your servant girls healthy.

28 Evil people run even though no one is
    chasing them,
  but good people are as brave as a lion.

2When a country is disobedient, it has one
    ruler after another;
  but when it is led by a man with
    understanding and knowledge, it
    continues strong.

3Rulers who mistreat the poor
  are like a hard rain that destroys the crops.

⁴Those who disobey what they have been
    taught praise the wicked,
but those who obey what they have been
    taught are against them.

⁵Evil people do not understand justice,
but those who follow the Lord understand
    it completely.

⁶It is better to be poor and innocent
    than to be rich and wicked.

⁷Children who obey what they have been
    taught are clever,
but friends of troublemakers disgrace their
    parents.

⁸Some people get rich by overcharging others,
but their wealth will be given to those who
    are kind to the poor.

⁹If you refuse to obey what you have been
    taught,
your prayers will not be heard.

¹⁰Those who lead good people to do wrong
    will be ruined by their own evil,
but the innocent will be rewarded with
    good things.

¹¹Rich people may think they are wise,
but the poor with understanding will prove
    them wrong.

¹²When good people triumph, there is great
    happiness,
but when the wicked get control,
    everybody hides.

¹³If you hide your sins, you will not succeed.
If you confess and reject them, you will
    receive mercy.

¹⁴Those who are always respectful will be happy,
but those who are stubborn will get into
    trouble.

¹⁵A wicked ruler is as dangerous to poor people
    as a roaring lion or a charging bear.

¹⁶A ruler without wisdom will be cruel,
but the one who refuses to take dishonest
    money will rule a long time.

¹⁷Don't help those who are guilty of murder;
    let them run until they die.

¹⁸Innocent people will be kept safe,
but those who are dishonest will suddenly
    be ruined.

¹⁹Those who work their land will have plenty
    of food,
but the ones who chase empty dreams
    instead will end up poor.

²⁰A truthful person will have many blessings,
but those eager to get rich will be
    punished.

²¹It is not good for a judge to take sides,
but some will sin for only a piece of bread.

²²Selfish people are in a hurry to get rich
and do not realise they soon will be poor.

²³Those who correct others will later be liked
more than those who give false praise.

²⁴Whoever robs his father or mother
and says, "It's not wrong,"
is just like someone who destroys things.

²⁵A greedy person causes trouble,
but the one who trusts the Lord will
    succeed.

²⁶Those who trust in themselves are foolish,
but those who live wisely will be
    kept safe.

²⁷Whoever gives to the poor will have
    everything he needs,
but the one who ignores the poor will
    receive many curses.

²⁸When the wicked get control, everybody
    hides,
but when they die, good people do well.

29 Whoever is stubborn after being
    corrected many times
will suddenly be hurt beyond cure.

²When good people do well, everyone is
    happy,
but when evil people rule, everyone
    groans.

³Those who love wisdom make their parents
    happy,
but friends of prostitutes ᵈ waste their
    money.

⁴If a king is fair, he makes his country strong,
but if he takes gifts dishonestly, he tears his
    country down.

⁵Those who give false praise to their
    neighbours
are setting a trap for them.

⁶Evil people are trapped by their own sin,
but good people can sing and be happy.

⁷Good people care about justice for the poor,
but the wicked are not concerned.

⁸People who make fun of wisdom cause
    trouble in a city,
but wise people calm anger down.

⁹When a wise person takes a foolish person to court,
the fool only shouts or laughs, and there is no peace.

¹⁰Murderers hate an honest person
and try to kill those who do right.

¹¹Foolish people lose their tempers,
but wise people control theirs.

¹²If a ruler pays attention to lies,
all his officers will become wicked.

¹³The poor person and the cruel person are alike
in that the LORD gave eyes to both of them.

¹⁴If a king judges poor people fairly,
his government will continue for ever.

¹⁵Correction and punishment make children wise,
but those left alone will disgrace their mother.

¹⁶When there are many wicked people, there is much sin,
but those who do right will see them destroyed.

¹⁷Correct your children, and you will be proud;
they will give you satisfaction.

¹⁸Where there is no word from God, people are uncontrolled,
but those who obey what they have been taught are happy.

¹⁹Words alone cannot correct a servant,
because even if he understands, he won't respond.

²⁰Do you see people who speak too quickly?
There is more hope for a foolish person than for them.

²¹If you spoil your servants when they are young,
they will bring you grief later on.

²²An angry person causes trouble;
a person with a quick temper sins a lot.

²³Pride will ruin people,
but those who are humble will be honoured.

²⁴Partners of thieves are their own worst enemies.
If they have to testify in court, they are afraid to say anything.

²⁵Being afraid of people can get you into trouble,
but if you trust the LORD, you will be safe.

²⁶Many people want to speak to a ruler,
but justice comes only from the LORD.

²⁷Good people hate those who are dishonest,
and the wicked hate those who are honest.

Wise Words from Agur

30 These are the words of Agur son of Jakeh.

This is his message to Ithiel and Ucal:

²"I am the most stupid person there is,
and I have no understanding.

³I have not learned to be wise,
and I don't know much about God, the Holy One.

⁴Who has gone up to heaven and come back down?
Who can hold the wind in his hand?
Who can gather up the waters in his coat?
Who has set in place the ends of the earth?
What is his name or his son's name?
Tell me, if you know!

⁵"Every word of God is true.
He guards those who come to him for safety.

⁶Do not add to his words,
or he will correct you and prove you are a liar.

⁷"I ask two things from you, LORD.
Don't refuse me before I die.

⁸Keep me from lying and being dishonest.
And don't make me either rich or poor;
just give me enough food for each day.

⁹If I have too much, I might reject you
and say, 'I don't know the LORD.'
If I am poor, I might steal
and disgrace the name of my God.

¹⁰"Do not say bad things about servants to their masters,
or they will curse you, and you will suffer for it.

¹¹"Some people curse their fathers
and do not bless their mothers.

¹²Some people think they are pure,
but they are not really free from evil.

¹³Some people have such a proud look!
They look down on others.

¹⁴Some people have teeth like swords;
their jaws seem full of knives.
They want to remove the poor from the earth
and the needy from the land.

¹⁵"Greed has two daughters
named 'Give' and 'Give'.

There are three things that are never satisfied,
  really four that never say, 'I've had
    enough!':
[16]the cemetery, the childless mother,
  the land that never gets enough rain
  and fire that never says, 'I've had enough!'

[17]"If you make fun of your father
  and refuse to obey your mother,
  the birds of the valley will peck out your eyes,
  and the vultures will eat them.

[18]"There are three things that are too hard
    for me,
  really four I don't understand:
[19]the way an eagle flies in the sky,
  the way a snake slides over a rock,
  the way a ship sails on the sea
  and the way a man and a woman fall in
    love.

[20]"This is the way of a woman who takes part
    in adultery: [d]
  she acts as if she had eaten and washed
    her face;
  she says, 'I haven't done anything wrong.'

[21]"There are three things that make the earth
    tremble,
  really four it cannot stand:
[22]a servant who becomes a king,
  a foolish person who has plenty to eat,
[23]a hated woman who gets married
  and a maid who replaces her mistress.

[24]"There are four things on earth that are
    small,
  but they are very wise:
[25]Ants are not very strong,
  but they store up food in the summer.
[26]Rock badgers are not very powerful,
  but they can live among the rocks.
[27]Locusts [d] have no king,
  but they all go forwards in formation.
[28]Lizards can be caught in the hand,
  but they are found even in kings' palaces.

[29]"There are three things that strut proudly,
  really four that walk as if they were
    important:
[30]a lion, the proudest animal,
  which is strong and runs from nothing,
[31]a rooster, a male goat
  and a king when his army is around him.

[32]"If you have been foolish and proud,
  or if you have planned evil, shut your
    mouth.
[33]Just as stirring milk makes butter,
  and twisting noses makes them bleed,
  so stirring up anger causes trouble."

Wise Words of King Lemuel

31 These are the words of King Lemuel, the
  message his mother taught him:

[2]"My son, I gave birth to you.
  You are the son I prayed for.
[3]Don't waste your strength on women
  or your time on those who ruin kings.

[4]"Kings should not drink wine, Lemuel,
  and rulers should not desire beer.
[5]If they drink, they might forget the law
  and keep the needy from getting their
    rights.
[6]Give beer to people who are dying
  and wine to those who are sad.
[7]Let them drink and forget their need
  and remember their misery no more.

[8]"Speak up for those who cannot speak for
    themselves;
  defend the rights of all those who have
    nothing.
[9]Speak up and judge fairly,
  and defend the rights of the poor and
    needy."

The Good Wife

[10]It is hard to find a good wife,
  because she is worth far more than rubies.
[11]Her husband trusts her completely.
  With her, he has everything he needs.
[12]She does him good and not harm
  for as long as she lives.
[13]She looks for wool and flax
  and likes to work with her hands.
[14]She is like a trader's ship,
  bringing food from far away.
[15]She gets up while it is still dark
  and prepares food for her family
  and feeds her servant girls.
[16]She inspects a field and buys it.
  With money she earned, she plants a
    vineyard.
[17]She does her work with energy,
  and her arms are strong.
[18]She knows that what she makes is good.
  Her lamp burns late into the night.

Sidelight The "good wife" of
  Proverbs 31:10–31
would have been a "supermum" centuries
before that term was invented. Not only did
she do everything around the house, she also
farmed (verse 16), worked in manufacturing
(verse 24), and did volunteer work (verse 20).
The question is, what did the men do?

¹⁹She makes thread with her hands
  and weaves her own cloth.
²⁰She welcomes the poor
  and helps the needy.
²¹She does not worry about her family when it
    snows,
  because they all have fine clothes to keep
    them warm.
²²She makes coverings for herself;
  her clothes are made of linen and other
    expensive material.
²³Her husband is known at the city meetings,
  where he makes decisions as one of the
    elders of the land.
²⁴She makes linen clothes and sells them
  and provides belts for the merchants.

²⁵She is strong and is respected by the people.
  She looks forward to the future with joy.
²⁶She speaks wise words
  and teaches others to be kind.
²⁷She watches over her family
  and never wastes her time.
²⁸Her children speak well of her.
  Her husband also praises her,
²⁹saying, "There are many fine women,
  but you are better than all of them."
³⁰Charm can fool you, and beauty can trick you,
  but a woman who respects the LORD should
    be praised.
³¹Give her the reward she has earned;
  she should be praised in public for what she
    has done.

MARRIAGE

Like Great-Grandmother

Sarah Walker stood in her great-grandmother's wedding dress, watching her mother fit the new sleeves into place. "I'm scared," she said.

"Of what, Sarah?"

"Marriage." Sarah stared into the mirror. "I'm scared of being an adult – of being responsible for building a new life with Ben."

"I know." Her mother pushed back her hair. "But follow your great-grandmother's example; she built a wonderful life for herself and her husband."

Her mother smiled, remembering. "She helped keep the house, bore the babies, worked in the woollen mill, set broken bones, canned and pickled hundreds of jars of food each year, sewed clothes and prayed beside her children's beds each night. And through it all she was a loving lady. She and grandpa really loved each other and they made a great team. As grandpa lay dying, after 66 years of marriage, he said she was still his angel."

"Funny, she seems more like a modern, working woman, besides being a wife and mother," Sarah said.

The good wife in Proverbs also possessed some of the great-grandmother's qualities. Read **Proverbs 31:10–31**.

* In what ways is the great-grandmother like the wife in this passage?
* Which qualities, listed here in these verses, do you most want in your life?

Consider . . .

* looking for qualities of a godly wife or husband at your church, then asking God to help you build these qualities in yourself so that you will be a godly spouse if you marry.
* asking couples you admire for their secret of a successful marriage.

For more, see . . .

* Ruth 3—4 (p.251)
* 1 Peter 3:1–7 (p.1360)
* Ephesians 5:21–33 (p.1275)

Ecclesiastes

When?

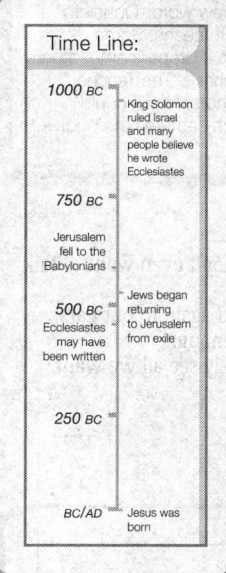

Time Line:

1000 BC — King Solomon ruled Israel and many people believe he wrote Ecclesiastes

750 BC — Jerusalem fell to the Babylonians

500 BC — Jews began returning to Jerusalem from exile / Ecclesiastes may have been written

250 BC

BC/AD — Jesus was born

Why Read This Book:

* See the results of living a variety of lifestyles (Ecclesiastes 1—2).
* Find companionship when bad things happen (Ecclesiastes 4—5).
* Explore the problem of injustice and the mystery of God (Ecclesiastes 9—10).
* Accept and enjoy life as God has given it (Ecclesiastes 3, 6, 11—12).

Behind the Scenes:

What brings happiness? What gives life meaning? People look in all kinds of places for answers to these questions.

Some people spend their lives making money to buy happiness. Then they die feeling empty and lonely.

Other people work hard at a career, hoping to find a way to leave a lasting impression on the world. Then they die, and people forget them.

Some people study and learn all they can in a quest for knowledge and understanding. Yet the world still holds mysteries they can't understand.

Other people spend all their time enjoying themselves, trying to have fun and feel good. But afterwards, life seems hollow and purposeless.

The writer of Ecclesiastes – often called the "Preacher" or the "Teacher" – walked down all these paths looking for happiness. Yet he never found it. Life was too complex and contradictory to understand through simple formulas. Good people suffered. Bad people prospered. It didn't make sense.

The book of Ecclesiastes contains the Teacher's thoughts about life and its meaning. Sometimes he seems cynical, because nothing in life seems meaningful (Ecclesiastes 1:2 and 12:8). Sometimes he says God is so distant we can't know him (Ecclesiastes 5:2).

Yet Ecclesiastes also gives insight and comfort on several levels.

* It is important to explore and reflect on what it means to follow God.

* It is all right to ask questions about life and our place in the universe. In fact, asking questions about ourselves and our relationship with God and the world can often help us to become stronger in our faith.

* We can see that despite having fame, fortune and wisdom, living without knowing God personally is empty and void of all meaning.

* The author believes life is worth living, even with its problems. He urges people to grab onto and enjoy the good things God gives us.

* Finally, God is in control – even when we can't see his work. "Honour God and obey his commands," he urges, "because this is all people must do" (Ecclesiastes 12:13).

1 These are the words of the Teacher, a son of David, king in Jerusalem.

[2] The Teacher says,
  "Useless! Useless!
Completely useless!
  Everything is useless."

[3] What do people really gain
  from all the hard work they do here on earth?

Things Never Change

[4] People live, and people die,
  but the earth continues for ever.
[5] The sun rises, the sun sets,
  and then it hurries back to where it rises again.
[6] The wind blows to the south;
  it blows to the north.
It blows from one direction and then another.
  Then it turns round and repeats the same pattern, going nowhere.

[7] All the rivers flow to the sea,
  but the sea never becomes full.

[8] Everything is boring,
  so boring that you don't even want to talk about it.
Words come again and again to our ears,
  but we never hear enough,
  nor can we ever really see all we want to see.

DISCOURAGEMENT

Nothing Changes Round Here

Sean lay on top of his bed. "I'm bored", he thought. "Nothing ever happens around here any more." He looked round his room and his eyes fell on his skateboard which he hadn't used since the skate park got shut – "lack of funds" is what the council had said.

"Its just pointless – nothing ever changes."

All of Sean's friends had just stopped hanging out when the skate park got locked up. Now they settled for playing skate games in their rooms, on their own.

Sean suddenly sat up. What if, just what if something could change? He began to scribble words into a notebook; he picked up his phone and sent texts to a couple of friends. And then he felt stupid. What was he thinking? Nothing could ever change. He couldn't make a difference. And so he threw his notebook aside, turned off his phone and went back to his PC skate game again.

Sean had a lot in common with the writer of Ecclesiastes. People at the time were pretty discouraged – they didn't think that anything could change. Take a look at **Ecclesiastes 1:2–11**.

* Which of these verses do you think Sean would have most identified with?
* Think about a time when you have felt like nothing will ever change. Which verses best describe how you felt?

Consider . . .

* looking in a local paper or on the Internet to find a story of someone choosing to make a difference.
* whether there is something you could get involved in that will change things where you live.

For more, see . . .

* Joshua 1:1–9 (p.202)
* Psalm 22 (p.512)

* Job 42:1–5 (p.498)

9All things continue the way they have been
　　　since the beginning.
　　What has happened will happen again;
　　　there is nothing new here on earth.
10Someone might say,
　　"Look, this is new,"
　　but really it has always been here.
　　It was here before we were.
11People don't remember what happened
　　　long ago,
　　and in the future people will not remember
　　　what happens now.
　　Even later, other people will not remember
　　　what was done before them.

Does Wisdom Bring Happiness?

12I, the Teacher, was king over Israel in Jerusalem. 13I decided to use my wisdom to learn
about everything that happens on earth. I learned
that God has given us terrible things to face. 14I
looked at everything done on earth and saw that
it is all useless, like chasing the wind.

15If something is crooked,
　　you can't make it straight.
　　If something is missing,
　　you can't say it is there.

16I said to myself, "I have become very wise
and am now wiser than anyone who ruled
Jerusalem before me. I know what wisdom and
knowledge really are." 17So I decided to find out
about wisdom and knowledge and also about
foolish thinking, but this turned out to be like
chasing the wind.

18With much wisdom comes much
　　　disappointment;
　　the person who gains more knowledge also
　　　gains more sorrow.

Does "Having Fun" Bring Happiness?

2 I said to myself, "I will try having fun. I will
enjoy myself." But I found that this is also
useless. 2It is foolish to laugh all the time, and
having fun doesn't accomplish anything. 3I decided to cheer myself up with wine while my
mind was still thinking wisely. I wanted to find a
way to enjoy myself and see what was good for
people to do during their few days of life.

Does Hard Work Bring Happiness?

4Then I did great things: I built houses and
planted vineyards for myself. 5I made gardens and
parks and I planted all kinds of fruit trees in them.
6I made pools of water for myself and used them
to water my growing trees. 7I bought male and
female slaves, and slaves were also born in my
house. I had large herds and flocks, more than
anyone in Jerusalem had ever had before. 8I also
gathered silver and gold for myself, treasures
from kings and other areas. I had male and female
singers and all the women a man could ever
want. 9I became very famous, even greater than
anyone who had lived in Jerusalem before me.
My wisdom helped me in all this.

10Anything I saw and wanted, I got for myself;
　　I did not miss any pleasure I desired.
　　I was pleased with everything I did,
　　　and this pleasure was the reward for all my
　　　hard work.
11But then I looked at what I had done,
　　　and I thought about all the hard work.
　　Suddenly I realised it was useless, like
　　　chasing the wind.
　　There is nothing to gain from anything we
　　　do here on earth.

> ### Sidelight
> The writer could have
> been thinking of people
> in the modern Western world. We suspect that
> there has to be more to life than work and a
> good time. There is. Our purpose can be found
> by following God.

Maybe Wisdom is the Answer

12Then I began to think again about being
　　　wise,
　　and also about being foolish and doing mad
　　　things.
　　But after all, what more can anyone do?
　　He can't do more than what the other king
　　　has already done.
13I saw that being wise is certainly better than
　　　being foolish,
　　just as light is better than darkness.
14Wise people see where they are going,
　　but fools walk around in the dark.
　　Yet I saw that
　　　both wise and foolish people end the
　　　same way.

15I thought to myself,
　　"What happens to a fool will happen to
　　　me too,
　　so what is the reward for being wise?"
　　I said to myself,
　　"Being wise is also useless."
16The wise person and the fool
　　will both die,
　　and no one will remember either one for long.
　　In the future, both will be forgotten.

Is There Real Happiness in Life?

17So I hated life. It made me sad to think that
everything here on earth is useless, like chasing

the wind. [18]I hated all the things I had worked for here on earth, because I must leave them to someone who will live after me. [19]Someone else will control everything for which I worked so hard here on earth, and I don't know if he will be wise or foolish. This is also useless. [20]So I became sad about all the hard work I had done here on earth. [21]People can work hard using all their wisdom, knowledge and skill, but they will die, and other people will get the things for which they worked. They did not do the work, but they will get everything. This is also unfair and useless. [22]What do people get for all their work and struggling here on earth? [23]All of their lives their work is full of pain and sorrow, and even at night their minds don't rest. This is also useless.

[24]The best that people can do is eat, drink and enjoy their work. I saw that even this comes from God, [25]because no one can eat or enjoy life without him. [26]If people please God, God will give them wisdom, knowledge and joy. But sinners will get only the work of gathering and storing wealth that they will have to give to the ones who please God. So all their work is useless, like chasing the wind.

There is a Time for Everything

3 There is a time for everything,
   and everything on earth has its special
      season.
[2]There is a time to be born
   and a time to die.
There is a time to plant
   and a time to pull up plants.
[3]There is a time to kill
   and a time to heal.
There is a time to destroy
   and a time to build.
[4]There is a time to cry
   and a time to laugh.
There is a time to be sad
   and a time to dance.
[5]There is a time to throw away stones
   and a time to gather them.

HAPPINESS

In the Here and Now

At the crack of dawn Rebecca lay in her bed, replaying the county trials in her head. She was running the 1,800 metres, pushing towards the finish. She had to get into the medal positions. She finished fourth.

"Rebecca, breakfast!" her mother called from the kitchen. Her mum had always been there for her, since her father had left. She crawled out of bed and ambled down the stairs.

As Rebecca sat down her mum joined her, saying, "Rebecca, I know you lost what was an important race for you, but then life isn't always fair. Just remember this: God has given you a gift and a body that enjoys it."

"Um," Rebecca grunted into her orange juice. "So?"

"I'm talking about enjoying the moment – the feel of your feet pounding the track, the tingle of adrenaline in your arms and legs, the sheer pleasure of being alive. It's good, even if you do lose a race or two."

Her mother's words fell on deaf ears then, but in the following years, those words helped Rebecca to really live life. Now she finds pleasure in the many things that God has given to her.

The writer of Ecclesiastes tried to find happiness in the middle of loss as well. Read **Ecclesiastes 2:18–26**.

* How does Rebecca's mum's advice compare with the advice in Ecclesiastes?
* How can you apply the advice in the passage to your life this week?

Consider . . .

* focusing only on your body sensations while washing the car, or eating or exercising.
* going for a walk in the woods and then writing in a diary all the good things that you noticed.

For more, see . . .

* Psalm 16:7–11 (p.508)
* 2 Corinthians 4:7–9 (p.1243)
* Luke 12:22–31 (p.1064)

There is a time to embrace
and a time to refrain.
[6]There is a time to look for something
and a time to stop looking for it.
There is a time to keep things
and a time to throw things away.
[7]There is a time to tear apart
and a time to sew together.
There is a time to be silent
and a time to speak.
[8]There is a time to love
and a time to hate.
There is a time for war
and a time for peace.

God Controls His World

[9]Do people really gain anything from their work? [10]I saw the hard work God has given people to do. [11]God has given them a desire to know the future. He does everything just right and on time, but people can never completely understand what he is doing. [12]So I realise that the best thing for them is to be happy and enjoy themselves as long as they live. [13]God wants all people to eat and drink and be happy in their work, which are gifts from God. [14]I know that everything God does will continue for ever. People cannot add anything to what God has done, and they cannot take anything away from it. God does it this way to make people respect him.

[15]What happens now has happened in the past,
and what will happen in the future has
happened before.
God makes the same things happen again
and again.

Unfairness on Earth

[16]I also saw this here on earth:
where there should have been justice, there
was evil;

SADNESS

Death Watch

Derek's grandfather lay quietly in his bed at home, shrivelled to the bone by Parkinson's disease.
Derek held his calloused hand and whispered, "I love you, Grandad."
"I love you too," the old man whispered back, barely able to talk.
Tears sprang to Derek's eyes. "What will I do without you?"
"Remember our good times." The old man closed his eyes. "Enjoy your life . . . and follow God."
"I don't want to let you go," Derek began to cry.
"It's all right," Grandad said. "It's my time to go. God knows what he's doing."
Derek fought back tears as he watched his grandfather struggle to breathe.
"Will you play 'Take My Hand, Precious Lord'?" Grandad asked.
Derek sat at the piano in the next room and played the song Grandad had heard so many times before. Derek's heart broke with each note. But there was also a distant joy for the times he and Grandad had shared and the fact that the pain would finally end.
Even the sadness of death can be seen as a natural part of life, according to
Ecclesiastes 3:1–13.

* Where in these verses are there words like the ones that Derek's grandfather spoke?
* How do these verses help you to cope with sadness?

Consider . . .

* writing an example for each of the times listed in the passage.
* looking through family photos and remembering times like those listed in Ecclesiastes.

For more, see . . .

* Psalm 88 (p.552)
* Philippians 3:4–7 (p.1283)

* Romans 5:3–5 (p.1190)

where there should have been right, there
was wrong.
¹⁷I said to myself,
God has planned a time for everything and
every action,
so he will judge both good people and bad.

¹⁸I decided that God leaves it the way it is to
test people and to show them they are just like
animals. ¹⁹The same thing happens to animals
and to people; they both have the same breath, so
they both die. People are no better off than the
animals, because everything is useless. ²⁰Both
end up the same way; both came from dust and
both will go back to dust. ²¹Who can be sure that
the human spirit goes up to God and that the
spirit of an animal goes down into the ground?
²²So I saw that the best thing people can do is to
enjoy their work, because that is all they have.
No one can help another person see what will
happen in the future.

Is It Better to be Dead?

4 Again I saw all the people who were mistreated here on earth.
I saw their tears
and that they had no one to comfort them.
Cruel people had all the power,
and there was no one to comfort those
they hurt.
²I decided that the dead
are better off than the living.
³But those who have never been born
are better off still;
they have not seen the evil
that is done here on earth.

Why Work So Hard?

⁴I realised the reason people work hard and try
to succeed: they are jealous of each other. This,
too, is useless, like chasing the wind.

⁵Some say it is foolish to fold your hands and
do nothing,
because you will starve to death.
⁶Maybe so, but I say it is better to be content
with what little you have.
Otherwise, you will always be struggling for
more,
and that is like chasing the wind.

⁷Again I saw something here on earth that
was useless:
⁸I saw a man who had no family,
no son or brother.
He always worked hard
but was never satisfied with what he had.
He never asked himself, "For whom am I
working so hard?

Why don't I let myself enjoy life?"
This also is very sad and useless.

Friends and Family Give Strength
⁹Two people are better than one,
because they get more done by working
together.
¹⁰If one falls down,
the other can help him up.
But it is bad for the person who is alone and
falls,
because no one is there to help.
¹¹If two lie down together, they will be warm,
but a person alone will not be warm.
¹²An enemy might defeat one person,
but two people together can defend
themselves;
a rope that is woven of three strings is hard
to break.

Fame and Power are Useless

¹³A poor but wise boy is better than a foolish
but old king who doesn't listen to advice. ¹⁴A boy
became king. He had been born poor in the kingdom and had even gone to prison before becoming king. ¹⁵I watched all the people who live
on earth follow him and make him their king.
¹⁶Many followed him at first, but later, they did
not like him, either. So fame and power are useless, like chasing the wind.

Be Careful About Making Promises

5 Be careful when you go to worship at the
Temple. ᵈ It is better to listen than to offer
foolish sacrifices without even knowing you are
doing wrong.

²Think before you speak,
and be careful about what you say to God.
God is in heaven,
and you are on the earth,
so say only a few words to God.
³The saying is true: bad dreams come from
too much worrying,
and too many words come from foolish
people.

⁴If you make a promise to God, don't be slow
to keep it. God is not happy with fools, so give
God what you promised. ⁵It is better not to promise anything than to promise something and not
do it. ⁶Don't let your words cause you to sin, and
don't say to the priest at the Temple, "I didn't
mean what I promised." If you do, God will become angry with your words and will destroy
everything you have worked for. ⁷Many useless
promises are like so many dreams; they mean
nothing. You should respect God.

Officers Cheat Each Other

8In some places you will see poor people mistreated. Don't be surprised when they are not treated fairly or given their rights. One officer is

cheated by a higher officer who in turn is cheated by even higher officers. 9The wealth of the country is divided up among them all. Even the king makes sure he gets his share of the profits.

Wealth Cannot Buy Happiness

10Whoever loves money
will never have enough money;
Whoever loves wealth
will not be satisfied with it.
This is also useless.
11The more wealth people have,
the more friends they have to help spend it.
So what do people really gain?
They gain nothing except to look at their
riches.
12Those who work hard sleep in peace;
it is not important if they eat little or
much.
But rich people worry about their wealth
and cannot sleep.

13I have seen real misery here on earth:
money saved is a curse to its owners.
14 They lose it all in a bad deal
and have nothing to give to their children.
15People come into this world with nothing,
and when they die they leave with nothing.
In spite of all their hard work,
they leave just as they came.
16This, too, is real misery:
they leave just as they came.
So what do they gain from chasing the
wind?
17All they get are days full of sadness and
sorrow,
and they end up sick, defeated and angry.

Enjoy Your Life's Work

18I have seen what is best for people here on earth. They should eat and drink and enjoy their work, because the life God has given them on earth is short. 19God gives some people the ability to enjoy the wealth and property he gives them,

as well as the ability to accept their area in life and enjoy their work. 20They do not worry about how short life is, because God keeps them busy with what they love to do.

6 I have seen something else wrong here on earth that causes serious problems for people. 2God gives great wealth, riches and honour to some people; they have everything they want. But God does not let them enjoy such things; a stranger enjoys them instead. This is useless and very wrong. 3A man might have 100 children and live a long time, but what good is it if he can't enjoy the good God gives him or have a proper burial? I say a baby born dead is better off than he is. 4A baby born dead is useless. It returns to darkness without even a name. 5That baby never saw the sun and never knew anything, but it finds more rest than that man. 6Even if he lives 2,000 years, he doesn't enjoy the good God gives him. Everyone is going to the same place.

7People work just to feed themselves,
but they never seem to get enough to eat.
8In this way a wise person
is no better off than a fool.
Then, too, it does a poor person little good
to know how to get along in life.
9It is better to see what you have
than to want more.
Wanting more is useless—
like chasing the wind.

Who Can Understand God's Plan?

10Whatever happens was planned long ago.
Everyone knows what people are like.
No one can argue with God,
who is stronger than anyone.
11The more you say,
the more useless it is.
What good does it do?

12People have only a few useless days of life on the earth; their short life passes like a shadow. Who knows what is best for them while they live? Who can tell them what the future will bring?

Some Benefits of Serious Thinking

7 It is better to have respect than good
perfume.
The day of death is better than the day of
birth.
2It is better to go to a funeral
than to a party.
We all must die,
and everyone living should think
about this.
3Sorrow is better than laughter,
and sadness has a good influence on you.

⁴A wise person thinks about death,
    but a fool thinks only about having a good
        time.
⁵It is better to be criticised by a wise person
    than to be praised by a fool.
⁶The laughter of fools
    is like the burning of thorns in a cooking
        fire.
    Both are useless.

⁷Even wise people are fools
    if they let money change their thinking.

⁸It is better to finish something
    than to start it.
    It is better to be patient
    than to be proud.
⁹Don't become angry quickly,
    because getting angry is foolish.
¹⁰Don't ask, "Why was life better in the 'good
        old days?' "
    It is not wise to ask such questions.

¹¹Wisdom is better when it comes with money.
    They both help those who are alive.
¹²Wisdom is like money:
    they both help.
    But wisdom is better,
    because it can save whoever has it.

¹³Look at what God has done:
    no one can straighten what he has made
        crooked.
¹⁴When life is good, enjoy it.
    But when life is hard, remember:
    God gives good times and hard times,
    and no one knows what tomorrow will
        bring.

It is Impossible to be Truly Good

¹⁵In my useless life I have seen both of these:
    I have seen good people die in spite of their
        goodness
    and evil people live a long time in spite of
        their evil.
¹⁶Don't be too right,
    and don't be too wise.
    Why destroy yourself?
¹⁷Don't be too wicked,
    and don't be foolish.
    Why die before your time?
¹⁸It is good to grasp the one and not let go of
        the other;
    those who honour God will hold them both.

¹⁹Wisdom makes a person stronger
    than ten leaders in a city.

²⁰Surely there is not a good person on earth
    who always does good and never sins.

²¹Don't listen to everything people say,
    or you might hear your servant
        insulting you.
²²You know that many times
    you have insulted others.

²³I used wisdom to test all these things.
    I wanted to be wise,
    but it was too hard for me.
²⁴I cannot understand why things are as
        they are.
    It is too hard for anyone to understand.
²⁵I studied and tried very hard to find wisdom,
    to find some meaning for everything.
    I learned that it is foolish to be evil,
    and it is mad to act like a fool.
²⁶I found that some women are worse than
        death
    and are as dangerous as traps.
    Their love is like a net,
    and their arms hold men like chains.
    A man who pleases God will be saved from
        them,
    but a sinner will be caught by them.

²⁷The Teacher says, "This is what I learned:
    I added all these things together
    to find some meaning for everything.
²⁸While I was searching but not finding
    I found one man among the thousands.
    But not one woman among all these.
²⁹One thing I have learned:
    God made people good,
    but they have found all kinds of ways to
        be bad."

Obey the King

8 No one is like the wise person
    who can understand what things mean.
Wisdom brings happiness;
    it makes sad faces happy.

²Obey the king's command, because you made a promise to God. ³Don't be too quick to leave the king. Don't support something that is wrong, because the king does whatever he pleases. ⁴What the king says is law; no one tells him what to do.

⁵Whoever obeys the king's command will be
        safe.
    A wise person does the right thing at the
        right time.
⁶There is a right time and a right way for
        everything,
    yet people often have many troubles.
⁷They do not know what the future holds,
    and no one can tell them what will
        happen.

⁸No one can control the wind
    or stop his own death.
No soldier is released in times of war,
    and evil does not set free those who do
      evil.

Justice, Rewards and Punishment

⁹I saw all of this as I considered all that is done
here on earth. Sometimes men harm those they
control. ¹⁰I saw the funerals of evil people who
used to go in and out of the holy place. They
were honoured in the same towns where they
had done evil. This is useless too.

¹¹When evil people are not punished right
away, it makes others want to do evil too.
¹²Though a sinner might do 100 evil things and
might live a long time, I know it will be better for
those who honour God. ¹³I also know it will not
go well for evil people, because they do not honour God. Like a shadow, they will not last.
¹⁴Sometimes something useless happens on
earth. Bad things happen to good people, and
good things happen to bad people. I say that this
is also useless. ¹⁵So I decided it was more important to enjoy life. The best that people can do here
on earth is to eat, drink and enjoy life, because
these joys will help them do the hard work God
gives them here on earth.

We Cannot Understand All God Does

¹⁶I tried to understand all that happens on
earth. I saw how busy people are, working day
and night and hardly ever sleeping. ¹⁷I also saw
all that God has done. Nobody can understand
what God does here on earth. No matter how
hard people try to understand it, they cannot.
Even if wise people say they understand, they
cannot; no one can really understand it.

Is Death Fair?

9 I thought about all this and tried to understand it. I saw that God controls good people
and wise people and what they do, but no one
knows if they will experience love or hate.

²Good and bad people end up the same—
    those who are right and those who are
      wrong,
those who are good and those who are evil,
    those who are clean and those who are
      unclean,
    those who sacrifice and those who do not.
The same things happen to a good person
    as happen to a sinner,
to a person who makes promises to God
    and to one who does not.

³This is something wrong that happens here
on earth: what happens to one happens to all.

So people's minds are full of evil and foolish
thoughts while they live. After that, they join the
dead. ⁴But anyone still alive has hope; even a live
dog is better off than a dead lion!

⁵The living know they will die,
    but the dead know nothing.
Dead people have no more reward,
    and people forget them.
⁶After people are dead,
    they can no longer love or hate
      or envy.
They will never again share
    in what happens here on earth.

Enjoy Life While You Can

⁷So go and eat your food and enjoy it;
    drink your wine and be happy,
because that is what God wants you to do.
⁸Put on nice clothes
    and make yourself look good.

⁹Enjoy life with the wife you love. Enjoy all the
useless days of this useless life God has given you
here on earth, because it is all you have. So enjoy
the work you do here on earth. ¹⁰Whatever work
you do, do your best, because you are going to
the grave, where there is no working, no planning, no knowledge and no wisdom.

Sidelight   Like most ancient Jews,
the Teacher believed that
death brought only "the grave" (Ecclesiastes
9:10). The Hebrew word "Sheol" referred to
a silent gloomy, mysterious world where the
early Jews believed that departed spirits went.
The idea of heaven is more appealing, don't
you think?

Time and Chance

¹¹I also saw something else here on earth:
    the fastest runner does not always win the
      race,
    the strongest soldier does not always win
      the battle,
the wisest does not always have food,
    the cleverest man does not always become
      wealthy
    and the talented one does not always
      receive praise.
Time and chance happen to everyone.
¹²No one knows what will happen next.
Like a fish caught in a net,
    or a bird caught in a trap,
people are trapped by evil
    when it suddenly falls on them.

Wisdom Does Not Always Win

¹³I also saw something wise here on earth that was very impressive to me. ¹⁴There was a small town with only a few people in it. A great king fought against it and put his armies all around it. ¹⁵Now there was a poor but wise man in the town who used his wisdom to save his town. But later on, everyone forgot about him. ¹⁶I still think wisdom is better than strength. But those people forgot about the poor man's wisdom and stopped listening to what he said.

¹⁷The quiet words of a wise person
    are better
than the shouts of a foolish ruler.
¹⁸Wisdom is better than weapons of war,
    but one sinner can destroy much good.

10 Dead flies can make even perfume
    stink.
In the same way, a little foolishness can
    spoil wisdom.
²The heart of the wise leads to right,
    but the heart of a fool leads to wrong.
³Even in the way fools walk along the road,
    they show they are not wise;
they show everyone how stupid they are.
⁴Don't leave your job
    just because your ruler is angry with you.
Remaining calm solves great problems.

⁵There is something else wrong that happens
    here on earth.
It is the kind of mistake rulers make:
⁶fools are given important positions
    while rich people are given lower ones;
⁷I have seen servants ride horses
    while princes walk like servants on foot.
⁸Anyone who digs a pit might fall into it;
    anyone who knocks down a wall might be
        bitten by a snake;
⁹anyone who moves boulders might be hurt
    by them;
    and anyone who cuts logs might be harmed
        by them.
¹⁰A dull axe means harder work.
    Being wise will make it easier.
¹¹If a snake bites the tamer before it is tamed,
    what good is the tamer?

¹²The words of the wise bring them praise,
    but the words of a fool will destroy them.
¹³A fool begins by saying foolish things
    and ends by saying insane and wicked
        things.
¹⁴A fool talks too much.
    No one knows the future,
    and no one can tell what will happen after
        death.

¹⁵Work wears fools out;
    they don't even know how to get home.

The Value of Work

¹⁶How terrible it is for a country whose king is
    a child
    and whose leaders eat all morning.
¹⁷How happy a country is whose king comes
    from a good family,
    whose leaders eat only at mealtimes
    and for strength, not to get drunk.

¹⁸If someone is lazy, the roof will begin to fall.
    If he doesn't fix it, the house will leak.

¹⁹A party makes you feel good,
    wine makes you feel happy
    and money buys anything.

²⁰Don't make fun of the king,
    and don't make fun of rich people, even in
        your bedroom.
A little bird might carry your words;
    a bird might fly and tell what you said.

Boldly Face the Future

11 Invest what you have,
    because after a while you will get a
        return.
²Invest what you have in several different
    businesses,
    because you don't know what disasters
        might happen.

³If clouds are full of rain,
    they will shower on the earth.
A tree can fall to the north or south,
    but it will stay where it falls.
⁴Those who wait for perfect weather
    will never plant seeds;
those who look at every cloud
    will never harvest crops.
⁵You don't know where the wind will blow,
    and you don't know how a baby grows
        inside the mother.
In the same way, you don't know what God
    is doing,
    or how he created everything.
⁶Plant early in the morning,
    and work until evening,
because you don't know if this or that will
    succeed.
    They might both do well.

Serve God While You are Young

⁷Sunshine is sweet;
    it is good to see the light of day.
⁸People ought to enjoy every day of their lives,
    no matter how long they live.

But they should also remember this:
   you will be dead a long time.
Everything that happens then is useless.
9Young people, enjoy yourselves while you are
   young;
be happy while you are young.
Do whatever your heart desires,
   whatever you want to do.
But remember that God will judge you
   for everything you do.
10Don't worry,
   and forget the troubles of your body,
because youth and childhood are useless.

The Problems of Old Age

12 Remember your Creator
      while you are young,
before the days of trouble come
and the years when you say,
   "I find no pleasure in them."
2When you get old,
   the light from the sun, moon and stars will
      grow dark;
the rain clouds will never seem to go away.
3At that time your arms will shake
   and your legs will become weak.
Your teeth will fall out so you cannot chew,
   and your eyes will not see clearly.
4Your ears will be deaf to the noise in the
      streets,
and you will barely hear the millstone
      grinding grain.
You will wake up when a bird starts singing,
   but you will barely hear the faint singing.
5You will fear high places
   and will be afraid to go for a walk.
Your hair will become white like the flowers
      on an almond tree.
You will limp along like a grasshopper
      when you walk.
Your appetite will be gone.
Then you will go to your everlasting home,
   and people will go to your funeral.

6Soon your life will snap like a silver chain
   or break like a golden bowl.
You will be like a broken pitcher at a spring,
   or a broken wheel at a well.
7You will turn back into the dust of the earth
      again,
but your spirit will return to God who
      gave it.

8Everything is useless!
   The Teacher says that everything is useless.

Conclusion: Honour God

9The Teacher was very wise and taught the people what he knew. He very carefully thought about, studied and set in order many wise teachings. 10The Teacher looked for just the right words to write what is dependable and true.
11Words from wise people are like sharp sticks used to guide animals. They are like nails that have been driven in firmly. Altogether they are wise teachings that come from one Shepherd. 12So be careful, my son, about other teachings. People are always writing books, and too much study will make you tired.

Sidelight

When the homework piles up, quote the last part of Ecclesiastes 12:12. Maybe someone will take pity on you. The words "my son" were a common way for teachers to address pupils in Old Testament times.

13Now, everything has been heard,
   so I give my final advice:
honour God and obey his commands,
   because this is all people must do.
14God will judge everything,
   even what is done in secret,
   the good and the evil.

Song of Solomon

Why Read This Book:

- Identify with lovers' longing for each other (Song of Solomon 1—2).
- Celebrate true love and affection for a lover (Song of Solomon 3—5).
- Watch true love develop into commitment (Song of Solomon 6—8).

When?

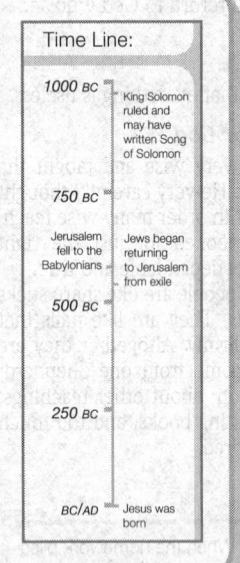

Time Line:

1000 BC — King Solomon ruled and may have written Song of Solomon

750 BC

Jerusalem fell to the Babylonians — Jews began returning to Jerusalem from exile

500 BC

250 BC

BC/AD — Jesus was born

Behind the Scenes:

Romance. People read about it, dream about it and fantasise about it. We each hope that someone wonderful will meet us, marry us, share passionate, lasting love with us. But we don't expect to find much about this kind of romance in the Bible.

That's what's so surprising about the Song of Solomon, also known as Song of Songs. Using graphic imagery and language, this unusual book in the Bible celebrates God's gifts of love and sexuality. It appears to tell about a king and a shepherd both pursuing a beautiful peasant woman. Through poetry, the book shows admiration, yearning for love, physical attractiveness and dedicated commitment.

Scholars have debated the Song of Solomon for centuries – beginning before Jesus was born. They suggest several possible ways to interpret this unusual book:

- Symbolic – the book has a hidden or symbolic religious meaning about the relationship between God and Israel or between Christ and the church. Beneath the pictures of physical love lies the spiritual truth that God loves us completely.

- Literal – the book is what it appears to be: love songs about a beautiful courtship between a man and a woman. So these poems affirm a place for beautiful expressions of human love within our faith.

- Dramatic – the book is a drama about sexual love. The songs were written to be sung or performed by two to four actors and a chorus. The drama may have been performed as entertainment during weddings.

Whatever your view on the book's purpose, Song of Solomon should be treasured, because it gives beautiful images of committed love – both physical and spiritual – and celebrates human love as a gift from God.

LIFE FILE LINKS

Investigate the Theme

To find a list of real life stories on this subject turn to the LIFE FILE GUIDE on pages 12 to 22 at the front of the Youth Bible.

MARRIAGE

1 Solomon's Greatest Song.

The Woman Speaks to the Man She Loves

²Kiss me with the kisses of your mouth,
because your love is better than wine.

> **Sidelight** This book is the ultimate in marriage guidance counselling. The dramatic poetry pictures the love that Solomon has for his bride. In this we can see the importance of physical love within the boundaries of marriage.

³The smell of your perfume is pleasant,
and your name is pleasant like expensive
perfume.
That's why the young women love you.
⁴Take me with you; let's run together.
The king takes me into his rooms.

Friends Speak to the Man

We will rejoice and be happy with you;
we praise your love more than wine.
With good reason, the young women
love you.

The Woman Speaks

⁵I'm dark but lovely,
women of Jerusalem,
dark like the tents of Kedar,
like the curtains of Solomon.
⁶Don't look at how dark I am,
at how dark the sun has made me.
My brothers were angry with me
and made me tend the vineyards,
so I haven't tended my own vineyard!
⁷Tell me, you whom I love,
where do you feed your sheep?
Where do you let them rest at noon?
Why should I look for you near your friend's
sheep,
like a woman who wears a veil? *n*

The Man Speaks to the Woman

⁸You are the most beautiful of women.
Surely you know to follow the sheep
and feed your young goats
near the shepherds' tents.
⁹My darling, you are like a mare
among the king's stallions.
¹⁰Your cheeks are beautiful with ornaments,
and your neck with jewels.
¹¹We will make for you gold earrings
with silver hooks.

The Woman Speaks

¹²The smell of my perfume spreads out
to the king on his couch.
¹³My lover is like a bag of myrrh *d*
that lies all night between my breasts.
¹⁴My lover is like a bunch of flowers
from the vineyards at En Gedi.

> **Sidelight** Ancient lovers didn't have designer perfumes, but they were still into being attractive to others. Women wore sachets of fragrance around their necks (Song of Solomon 1:12–14), while men splashed perfume on their beards and robes.

The Man Speaks

¹⁵My darling, you are beautiful!
Oh, you are beautiful,
and your eyes are like doves.

The Woman Answers the Man

¹⁶You are so handsome, my lover,
and so pleasant!
Our bed is the grass.
¹⁷Cedar trees form our roof;
our ceiling is made of juniper wood.

The Woman Speaks Again

2 I am a rose in the Plain of Sharon,
a lily in the valleys.

The Man Speaks Again

²Among the young women, my darling
is like a lily among thorns!

The Woman Answers

³Among the young men, my lover
is like an apple tree in the woods!
I enjoy sitting in his shadow;
his fruit is sweet to my taste.
⁴He brought me to the banquet room,
and his banner over me is love.
⁵Strengthen me with raisins,
and refresh me with apples,
because I am weak with love.
⁶My lover's left hand is under my head,
and his right arm holds me tight.

The Woman Speaks to the Friends

⁷Women of Jerusalem, promise me
by the gazelles *d* and the deer
not to awaken
or excite my feelings of love
until it is ready.

veil   This was the way a prostitute usually dressed.

The Woman Speaks Again

⁸I hear my lover's voice.
Here he comes jumping across the
mountains,
skipping over the hills.
⁹My lover is like a gazelle *d* or a young deer.
Look, he stands behind our wall
looking through the windows,
looking through the blinds.
¹⁰My lover spoke and said to me,
"Get up, my darling;
let's go away, my beautiful one.
¹¹Look, the winter is past;
the rains are over and gone.
¹²Blossoms appear through all the land.
The time has come to sing;

the cooing of doves is heard in our
land.
¹³There are young figs on the fig trees,
and the blossoms on the vines smell
sweet.
Get up, my darling;
let's go away, my beautiful one."

The Man Speaks

¹⁴My beloved is like a dove hiding in the
cracks of the rock,
in the secret places of the cliff.
Show me your face,
and let me hear your voice.
Your voice is sweet,
and your face is lovely.

LOVE

Walk On By

Vicky would spend hours looking at the poster on her wall. What would it be like to meet him? If only she could, she knew that he would love her . . . they were made for each other . . . if only . . .

Then one day she managed to get tickets for his concert! She was so excited that she arrived hours too early and was rewarded by seeing the whole band arrive at the backstage area. She screamed with the other girls and the musicians politely came over and spoke to them through the wired fence. Vicky got his autograph and was overwhelmed when he smiled at her and said, "Will you be coming to Sheffield?" She nodded wildly and smiled back at him.

After the concert she went home and started to add up her savings. The Sheffield concert was hundreds of miles away from where she lived, but she was convinced that the pop star had personally invited her to be there.

She found out where they would be staying and managed to book a single room there as soon as she arrived. She was only fourteen years old but dressed herself up to look much older.

Then it happened. The dream of all dreams . . . she saw him outside his room and he beckoned her in. Deliriously happy, she allowed him to sleep with her but was a little confused when he wanted her to go. She told herself that it would be different when she saw him the next day. But when she saw him in the morning, he walked straight past her. No hint of recognition. Vicky was devastated as she began to realise what had happened. She'd used all her savings, lost respect . . . and her virginity. It wasn't love after all. It was just being used.

Read Song of **Solomon 2:10 — 3:4**, it talks of "never letting go" (3:4) and "My lover is mine and I am his" (2:16). Don't make Vicky's mistake.

* Where did Vicky go wrong, according to this passage?
* Could you look at the person you love and relate your feelings to this passage?

Consider . . .

* listing the things that you would feel, that would help to you know you are in love.
* talking to a couple you know who have a strong relationship, and asking them what makes their marriage so strong.

For more, see . . .

* Genesis 29:20 (p.34)
* 1 John 4:7–21 (p.1374)

* John 15:9–17 (p.1125)

¹⁵Catch the foxes for us—
 the little foxes that ruin the vineyards
 while they are in blossom.

The Woman Speaks

¹⁶My lover is mine, and I am his.
 He feeds among the lilies
¹⁷until the day dawns
 and the shadows disappear.
 Turn, my lover.
 Be like a gazelle *d* or a young deer
 on the mountain valleys.

The Woman Dreams

3 At night on my bed,
 I looked for the one I love;
 I looked for him, but I could not find him.
²I got up and went around the city,
 in the streets and squares,
looking for the one I love.
 I looked for him, but I could not find him.
³The watchmen found me as they patrolled
 the city,
 so I asked, "Have you seen the one
 I love?"
⁴As soon as I had left them,
 I found the one I love.
I held him and would not let him go
 until I brought him to my mother's house,
 to the room where I was born.

The Woman Speaks to the Friends

⁵Women of Jerusalem, promise me
 by the gazelles *d* and the deer
not to awaken
 or excite my feelings of love
 until it is ready.
⁶Who is this coming out of the desert
 like a cloud of smoke?
Who is this that smells like myrrh, *d*
 incense *d*
 and other spices?
⁷Look, it's Solomon's couch *n*
 with 60 soldiers around it,
 the finest soldiers of Israel.
⁸These soldiers all carry swords
 and have been trained in war.
 Every man wears a sword at his side
 and is ready for the dangers of the night.
⁹King Solomon had a couch made for himself
 of wood from Lebanon.
¹⁰He made its posts of silver
 and its braces of gold.
 The seat was covered with purple cloth
 that the women of Jerusalem wove with
 love.

¹¹Women of Jerusalem, go out and see King
 Solomon.
 He is wearing the crown his mother put on
 his head
on his wedding day,
 when his heart was happy!

The Man Speaks to the Woman

4 How beautiful you are, my darling!
 Oh, you are beautiful!
Your eyes behind your veil are like doves.
 Your hair is like a flock of goats streaming
 down Mount Gilead.
²Your teeth are white like newly sheared
 sheep
 just coming from their bath.
 Each one has a twin,
 and none of them is missing.
³Your lips are like red silk thread,
 and your mouth is lovely.
 Your cheeks behind your veil
 are like slices of a pomegranate. *d*
⁴Your neck is like David's tower,
 built with rows of stones.
 A thousand shields hang on its walls;
 each shield belongs to a strong soldier.
⁵Your breasts are like two fawns,
 like twins of a gazelle, *d*
 feeding among the lilies.
⁶Until the day dawns
 and the shadows disappear,
 I will go to that mountain of myrrh *d*
 and to that hill of incense. *d*
⁷My darling, everything about you is beautiful,
 and there is nothing at all wrong with you.

> **Sidelight** The poem in Song of
> Solomon 4:1–7 contains
> comparisons that may seem quite ridiculous to
> us today, but they were quite appealing in
> ancient times!

⁸Come with me from Lebanon, my bride.
 Come with me from Lebanon,
from the top of Mount Amana,
 from the tops of Mount Senir and Mount
 Hermon.
Come from the lions' dens
 and from the leopards' hills.
⁹My sister, my bride,
 you have thrilled my heart;
you have thrilled my heart
 with a glance of your eyes,
 with one sparkle from your necklace.

---

couch Something like a bed carried by slaves on which the king lay or sat while travelling.

[10]Your love is so sweet, my sister, my bride.
   Your love is better than wine,
   and your perfume smells better than any spice.
[11]My bride, your lips drip honey;
   honey and milk are under your tongue.
   Your clothes smell like the cedars of Lebanon.
[12]My sister, my bride, you are like a garden
      locked up,
   like a walled-in spring, a closed fountain.
[13]Your limbs are like an orchard
   of pomegranates with all the best fruit,
   filled with flowers and nard, [d]
[14]nard and saffron, [d] calamus [d] and cinnamon,
   with trees of incense, myrrh and aloes [d]—
   all the best spices.
[15]You are like a garden fountain—
   a well of fresh water
   flowing down from the mountains of
      Lebanon.

The Woman Speaks

[16]Awake, north wind.
   Come, south wind.
Blow on my garden,
   and let its sweet smells flow out.
Let my lover enter the garden
   and eat its best fruits.

The Man Speaks

5 I have entered my garden, my sister, my
      bride.
   I have gathered my myrrh [d] with my
      spice.
   I have eaten my honeycomb and my honey.
   I have drunk my wine and my milk.

The Friends Speak

Eat, friends, and drink;
   yes, drink deeply, lovers.

SEXUALITY

Warning Signs

Matt had seen the warning signs. Rachel never really seemed that interested in praying with him and she had made some pretty bad choices in her past. Her insecurities had led her into a string of damaging relationships with non-Christian guys who had made her feel "loved" . . . as long as she gave them what they wanted. Matt knew that we all make bad choices and have to live with the consequences, and that God's grace offers forgiveness and a brand new start whatever we've done, but the problem was that Rachel never really seemed sorry for her past, so actually it was still a problem for the present. Was Rachel really the godly girl he had waited for, or was she just "playing at being a Christian" on Sundays?

   Matt had only ever been interested in dating a girl who put Jesus first in her life. The trouble was things were getting complicated now – he had fallen in love! His heart was starting to make excuses. "Sure, Rachel isn't perfect, but none of us are, right?" "Maybe with my influence she'll put God first and deal with her past?" and "I'll never find another girl as nice as her!"

   In the end, the decision to end the relationship was an easy one when Matt found out that Rachel had been cheating on him. Matt was devastated. In time, God healed his broken heart and Matt trusts that God has someone better for him.

   God created the passion and excitement of falling in love. Check out the way it should be in **Song of Solomon 5:2–6**.

* What does this passage tell us about God's attitude to sex?
* Why does the Bible tell us that God's best for us is to marry a Christian and to wait until we're married before we have sex?

Consider . . .

* finding a Christian friend of the same sex to pray with and be accountable to in this area.
   It can be really great to pray together and help each other make good choices.
* any mistakes you may have made in this area. Ask God to forgive you and give you a new start.

For more, see . . .

* 1 Kings 11:1–13 (p.325)
* Proverbs 31:10–31 (p.617)
* Proverbs 7:1–27 (p.595)
* 2 Corinthians 6:14–18 (p.1247)

The Woman Dreams

²I sleep, but my heart is awake.
　I hear my lover knocking.
"Open to me, my sister, my darling,
　my dove, my perfect one.
My head is wet with dew,
　and my hair with the dampness of the
　　night."
³I have taken off my garment
　and don't want to put it on again.
I have washed my feet
　and don't want to get them dirty again.
⁴My lover put his hand through the opening,
　and I felt excited inside.
⁵I got up to open the door for my lover.
　Myrrh ᵈ was dripping from my hands
and flowing from my fingers,
　onto the handles of the lock.
⁶I opened the door for my lover,
　but my lover had left and was gone.
　When he spoke, he took my breath away.
I looked for him, but I could not find him;
　I called for him, but he did not answer.
⁷The watchmen found me
　as they patrolled the city.
They hit me and hurt me;
　the guards on the wall took away my veil.
⁸Promise me, women of Jerusalem,
　if you find my lover,
　tell him I am weak with love.

The Friends Answer the Woman

⁹How is your lover better than other lovers,
　most beautiful of women?
How is your lover better than other lovers?
　Why do you want us to promise this?

The Woman Answers the Friends

¹⁰My lover is healthy and tanned,
　the best of ten thousand men.
¹¹His head is like the finest gold;
　his hair is wavy and black like a raven.
¹²His eyes are like doves
　by springs of water.
They seem to be bathed in cream
　and are set like jewels.
¹³His cheeks are like beds of spices;
　they smell like mounds of perfume.
His lips are like lilies
　flowing with myrrh. ᵈ
¹⁴His hands are like gold hinges,
　filled with jewels.
His body is like shiny ivory
　covered with sapphires.
¹⁵His legs are like large marble posts,
　standing on bases of fine gold.
He is like a cedar of Lebanon,
　like the finest of the trees.

¹⁶His mouth is sweet to kiss,
　and I desire him very much.
Yes, daughters of Jerusalem,
　this is my lover
　and my friend.

The Friends Speak to the Woman

6 Where has your lover gone,
　most beautiful of women?
Which way did your lover turn?
　We will look for him with you.

The Woman Answers the Friends

²My lover has gone down to his garden,
　to the beds of spices,
to feed in the gardens
　and to gather lilies.
³I belong to my lover,
　and my lover belongs to me.
He feeds among the lilies.

The Man Speaks to the Woman

⁴My darling, you are as beautiful as the city
　of Tirzah,
　as lovely as the city of Jerusalem,
　like an army flying flags.
⁵Turn your eyes from me,
　because they excite me too much.
Your hair is like a flock of goats
　streaming down Mount Gilead.
⁶Your teeth are white like sheep
　just coming from their bath;
each one has a twin,
　and none of them is missing.
⁷Your cheeks behind your veil
　are like slices of a pomegranate. ᵈ

> **Sidelight** You wouldn't usually say that your girlfriend has "fruity cheeks", but it was a compliment in Old Testament days! The pomegranate is a small, red fruit that's especially refreshing in a hot climate like Israel's (Song of Solomon 6:7). The round fruit is filled with pulp and seeds, somewhat like the inside of an orange in texture.

⁸There may be sixty queens and eighty slave
　women ᵈ
　and so many girls you cannot count them,
⁹but there is only one like my dove, my
　perfect one.
　She is her mother's only daughter,
　the brightest of the one who gave her birth.
The young women saw her and called her
　happy;
　the queens and the slave women also
　praised her.

The Young Women Praise the Woman

¹⁰Who is that young woman
    that shines out like the dawn?
She is as pretty as the moon,
    as bright as the sun,
    as wonderful as an army flying flags.

The Man Speaks

¹¹I went down into the orchard of nut trees
    to see the blossoms of the valley,
    to look for buds on the vines,
    to see if the pomegranate *d* trees had
       bloomed.
¹²Before I realised it, my desire for you made
    me feel
    like a prince in a chariot.

The Friends Call to the Woman

¹³Come back, come back, woman of Shulam.
    Come back, come back,
    so we may look at you!

The Woman Answers the Friends

Why do you want to look at the woman of
    Shulam
    as you would at the dance of two armies?

The Man Speaks to the Woman

7 Your feet are beautiful in sandals,
    you daughter of a prince.
Your round thighs are like jewels
    shaped by an artist.
²Your navel is like a round drinking cup
    always filled with wine.
Your stomach is like a pile of wheat
    surrounded with lilies.
³Your breasts are like two fawns,
    like twins of a gazelle. *d*
⁴Your neck is like an ivory tower.
Your eyes are like the pools in Heshbon
    near the gate of Bath Rabbim.
Your nose is like the mountain of Lebanon
    that looks down on Damascus.
⁵Your head is like Mount Carmel,
    and your hair is like purple cloth;
    the king is captured in its folds.
⁶You are beautiful and pleasant;
    my love, you are full of delights.
⁷You are tall like a palm tree,
    and your breasts are like its bunches of
       fruit.
⁸I said, "I will climb up the palm tree
    and take hold of its fruit."
Let your breasts be like bunches of grapes,
    the smell of your breath like apples,
⁹   and your mouth like the best wine.

The Woman Speaks to the Man

Let this wine go down sweetly for my lover;
    may it flow gently past the lips and teeth.
¹⁰I belong to my lover,
    and he desires only me.
¹¹Come, my lover,
    let's go out into the country
    and spend the night in the fields.
¹²Let's go early to the vineyards
    and see if the buds are on the vines.
Let's see if the blossoms have already
    opened
    and if the pomegranates *d* have bloomed.
There I will give you my love.
¹³The mandrake flowers give their sweet smell,
    and all the best fruits are at our gates.
I have saved them for you, my lover,
    the old delights and the new.

Sidelight   The mandrake flower
(Song of Solomon 7:13)
not only gave a sweet smell but was also
thought to arouse sexual desire. The yellow-red
fruit was also thought to increase fertility (see
Genesis 30:14–16, p.35). No wonder it was
called the "love apple"!

---

8 I wish you were like my brother
    who fed at my mother's breasts.
If I found you outside,
    I would kiss you,
    and no one would look down on me.
²I would lead you and bring you
    to my mother's house;
    she is the one who taught me.
I would give you a drink of spiced wine
    from my pomegranates.

The Woman Speaks to the Friends

³My lover's left hand is under my head,
    and his right arm holds me tight.
⁴Women of Jerusalem,
    promise not to awaken
    or excite my feelings of love
    until it is ready.

The Friends Speak

⁵Who is this coming out of the desert,
    leaning on her lover?

The Man Speaks to the Woman

I woke you under the apple tree
    where you were born;
    there your mother gave birth to you.
⁶Put me like a seal on your heart,
    like a seal on your arm.

Love is as strong as death;
jealousy is as strong as the grave.
Love bursts into flames
and burns like a hot fire.
[7]Even much water cannot put out the flame
of love;
floods cannot drown love.
If a man offered everything in his house for
love,
people would totally reject it.

The Woman's Brothers Speak

[8]We have a little sister,
and her breasts are not yet grown.
What should we do for our sister
on the day she becomes engaged?
[9]If she is a wall,
we will put silver towers on her.
If she is a door,
we will protect her with cedar boards.

The Woman Speaks

[10]I am a wall,
and my breasts are like towers.
So I was to him,
as one who brings happiness.
[11]Solomon had a vineyard at Baal Hamon.
He rented the vineyards for others to
tend,
and everyone who rented had to pay
a thousand silver pieces for the fruit.
[12]But my own vineyard is mine to give.
Solomon, the thousand silver pieces are
for you,
and two hundred pieces are for those who
tend the fruit.

Sidelight

If girls think their brothers are overprotective today, imagine how they would have felt in biblical times (Song of Solomon 8:8–9). Brothers were responsible for a sister until marriage, so they kept other men from taking advantage of her innocence. They would probably come with her on her dates today!

The Man Speaks to the Woman

[13]You who live in the gardens,
my friends are listening for your voice;
let me hear it.

The Woman Speaks to the Man

[14]Hurry, my lover,
be like a gazelle [d]
or a young deer
on the mountains where spices grow.

Isaiah

When?

Why Read This Book:

- See how God works through world events to bring people to himself (Isaiah 1—3
- Discover what can happen when people trust in things other than God (Isaiah 36—39).
- Be assured that God is working in the world, even when life seems hopeless (Isaiah 40—66).

Behind the Scenes:

Isaiah could have had a simple life in Judah. He was probably well educated and may have been a priest. He knew the top people in Jerusalem, including the king.

But Isaiah saw trouble brewing, and the Lord called him to be a prophet. Though his country had been peaceful and prosperous under King Uzziah's leadership (see 2 Chronicles 26:1–23, p.420), Isaiah could tell that the good situation was changing. God wanted him to speak out!

First, he watched as the Assyrians conquered neighbouring Israel and threatened Judah. The king of Judah was tempted to form military alliances to protect the nation; Isaiah believed Judah should rely on God instead.

Second, while people paid lip service to God, they didn't really follow him. Instead, they took advantage of the poor.

The book of Isaiah has two distinct parts:

Chapters 1—39 deal with events in the eighth century before Christ, when Judah was independent but constantly threatened by the Assyrians. During this time, the prophet blasted the rich and powerful who neglected and oppressed the poor. And he challenged the nation not to rely on military power to defend itself, but to rely on God. ▷

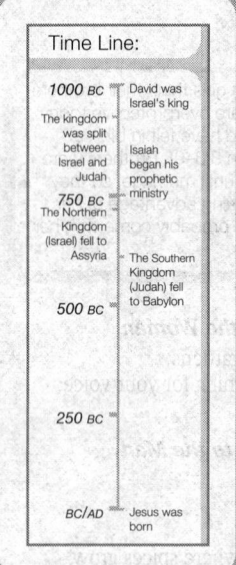

Time Line:

1000 BC	David was Israel's king
The kingdom was split between Israel and Judah	Isaiah began his prophetic ministry
750 BC The Northern Kingdom (Israel) fell to Assyria	
	The Southern Kingdom (Judah) fell to Babylon
500 BC	
250 BC	
BC/AD	Jesus was born

Where?

The Assyrians invaded and eventually captured much of Judah, fulfilling Isaiah's prophecy in Isaiah 7:18–25.

Mediterranean Sea

Samaria, the capital of Israel, was captured by the Assyrians while Isaiah lived (Isaiah 8:4).

ASSYRIA

ARAM

ISRAEL

Samaria •

Jerusalem •

MOAB

Isaiah spoke out against the people of Moab (Isaiah 15—16).

Isaiah lived in Jerusalem, the capital of Judah, the city to which he prophesied (Isaiah 1:1).

JUDAH

ARABIA

EGYPT

Red Sea

Tigris

Persian Gulf

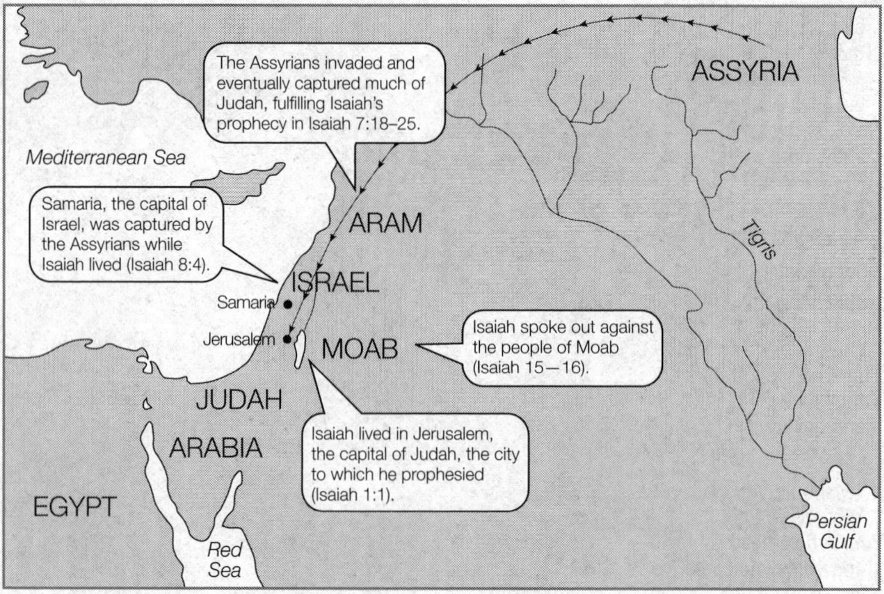

Behind the Scenes (cont.): Chapters 40—66 zoom forward to about two hundred years later, when the Persian Empire controlled Judah. After being in exile, the Jews were trying to rebuild their lives. Through this section, the prophet constantly comforts the people, assuring them that the past, present and future are all in God's hands. God's presence and love gave them hope.

Isaiah's message of hope points to a time when God would deliver his people through God's suffering servant (Isaiah 52—57). Since New Testament times, Christians have believed that these promises were fulfilled in the coming of Jesus Christ, who suffered and died for the sins of the world. (For example, see Isaiah 53.)

---

1 This is the vision Isaiah son of Amoz saw about what would happen to Judah and Jerusalem. Isaiah saw these things while Uzziah, [n] Jotham, Ahaz and Hezekiah were kings of Judah.

Sidelight The book of Isaiah is quoted more in the New Testament than any other book – and more than all the other prophetic books combined. The New Testament refers to Isaiah 150 times and actually quotes it 50 times.

God's Case Against His Children

2Heaven and earth, listen,
    because the LORD is speaking:
"I raised my children and helped them
      grow up,
    but they have turned against me.
3An ox knows its master,
    and a donkey knows where its owner
      feeds it,
but the people of Israel do not know me;
    my people do not understand."

4How terrible! Israel is a nation of sin,
    a people loaded down with guilt,
a group of children doing evil,
    children who are full of evil.
They have left the LORD;
    they hate God, the Holy One of Israel,
    and have turned away from him as if he
      were a stranger.

5Why should you continue to be punished?
    Why do you continue to turn against him?
Your whole head is hurt,
    and your whole heart is sick.

6There is no healthy spot
    from the bottom of your foot to the top of
      your head;
you are covered with wounds, hurts and
      open sores
that are not cleaned and covered,
    and no medicine takes away the pain.

7Your land is ruined;
    your cities have been burnt with fire.
While you watch,
    your enemies are stealing everything from
      your land;
it is ruined like a country destroyed by
      enemies.
8Jerusalem is left alone
    like an empty shelter in a vineyard,
like a hut left in a field of melons,
    like a city surrounded by enemies.
9The LORD All-powerful
    allowed a few of our people to live.
Otherwise we would have been completely
      destroyed
    like the cities of Sodom and Gomorrah.

10Jerusalem, your rulers are like those of
      Sodom,
    and your people are like those of
      Gomorrah.
Hear the word of the LORD;
    listen to the teaching of our God!
11The LORD says,
    "I do not want all these sacrifices.
I have had enough of your burnt
      sacrifices
of rams and fat from fine animals.
I am not pleased
    by the blood of bulls, lambs and goats.
12You come to meet with me,
    but who asked you to do

Uzziah Also called Azariah.

all this running in and out of my Temple's *d* rooms?
[13]Don't continue bringing me worthless sacrifices!
I hate the incense *d* you burn.
I can't stand your New Moons, *d* Sabbaths *d* and other feast days;
I can't stand the evil you do in your holy meetings.
[14]I hate your New Moon feasts
and your other yearly feasts.
They have become a heavy weight on me,
and I am tired of carrying it.
[15]When you raise your arms to me in prayer,
I will refuse to look at you.
Even if you say many prayers,
I will not listen to you,
because your hands are full of blood.
[16]Wash yourselves and make yourselves clean. *d*
Stop doing the evil things I see you do.
Stop doing wrong.
[17] Learn to do good.
Seek justice.
Punish those who hurt others.
Help the orphans.
Stand up for the rights of widows."

[18]The LORD says,
"Come, let us talk about these things.
Though your sins are bright red,
they can be as white as snow.
Though your sins are deep red,
they can be white like wool.
[19]If you become willing and obey me,
you will eat good crops from the land.
[20]But if you refuse to obey and if you turn against me,
you will be destroyed by your enemies' swords."
The LORD himself said these things.

Jerusalem is Not Loyal to God

[21]The city of Jerusalem once followed the LORD,
but she is no longer loyal to him.
She used to be filled with fairness;
people there lived the way God wanted.
But now, murderers live there.
[22]Jerusalem, you have become like the scum left when silver is purified;
you are like wine mixed with water.
[23]Your rulers are rebels
and friends of thieves.

They all accept money for doing wrong,
and they are paid to cheat people.
They don't seek justice for the orphans
or listen to the widows' needs.
[24]So the Lord GOD All-powerful,
the Mighty One of Israel, says:
"You, my enemies, will not cause me any more trouble.
I will pay you back for what you did.
[25]I will turn against you
and clean away all your wrongs as if with soap;
I will take all the worthless things out of you.
[26]I will bring back judges as you had long ago;
your counsellors will be like those you had in the beginning.
Then you will be called the City That Is Right with God,
the Loyal City."

[27]By doing what is fair,
Jerusalem will be free again.
By doing what is right,
her people who come back to the LORD will have freedom.
[28]But sinners and those who turn against him will be destroyed;
those who have left the LORD will die.

[29]"You will be ashamed,
because you have worshipped gods under the oak trees.
You will be disgraced,
because you have worshipped idols in your gardens.
[30]You will be like an oak whose leaves are dying
or like a garden without water.
[31]Powerful people will be like small, dry pieces of wood,
and their works will be like sparks.
They will burn together,
and no one will be able to put out that fire."

The Message About Jerusalem

2 Isaiah son of Amoz saw this message about Judah and Jerusalem:
[2]In the last days
the mountain on which the LORD's Temple *d* stands
will become the most important of all mountains.
It will be raised above the hills,
and people from all nations will come streaming to it.

³Many nations will come and say,
  "Come, let us go up to the mountain of the
    LORD,
  to the Temple of the God of Jacob.
Then God will teach us his ways,
  and we will obey his teachings."
His teachings will go out from Jerusalem;
  the message of the LORD will go out from
    Jerusalem.
⁴He will settle arguments among the nations
  and will make decisions for many nations.
Then they will make their swords into
    ploughs
  and their spears into hooks for trimming
    trees.
Nations will no longer fight other nations,
  nor will they train for war any more.

⁵Come, family of Jacob,
  and let us follow the way of the LORD.

A Terrible Day is Coming

⁶LORD, you have left your people,
  the family of Jacob,
because they have become filled with wrong
    ideas from people in the East.
They try to tell the future like the
    Philistines,
  and they have completely accepted those
    foreign ideas.
⁷Their land has been filled with silver and gold;
  there are a great many treasures there.
Their land has been filled with horses;
  there are many chariots there.
⁸Their land is full of idols.
  The people worship these idols they made
    with their own hands
  and shaped with their own fingers.
⁹People will not be proud any longer
  but will bow low with shame.
  God, do not forgive them.

PEACE

Peace at Any Price

The two boys pulled the cart behind them, up the street towards the depot. Occasionally bits of scrap would fall off and Danny, the smaller one, would have to stop and pile them back on top. They were very pleased with their haul.

They had an old stair rail that they had found in a bus shelter, some pots that they found in their father's shed, and some of his old garden tools too.

They were sure that the scrap metal they had collected would be enough to make a new gun for a soldier. They had seen the government film about turning ordinary objects into items that could be used for war, and they wanted to play their part. They thought that if they could just make enough weapons then Britain would win, and their father would be able to return home.

Sadly, that story from World War II did not bring peace. In fact most of the scrap metal collected was just left to rot – it was just an idea to make people feel like they were involved in the war effort.

The idea of turning ordinary things into weapons may have been one idea to win a war – but that is not God's plan for peace. In **Isaiah 2:1–5** God talks about doing the very opposite thing.

* Why do you think there will be no more war?
* According to this passage, what's the only way in which true peace – at home or in the world – can be achieved?

Consider . . .

* writing a list of what God will do in the last days.
* how we can learn from different countries and their wars in our relationships. Think about one situation that involves you, and one that is a world situation. Pray and ask God what you can do to stop the fighting in both of them.

For more, see . . .

* John 14:25–27 (p.1124)
* Philippians 4:7 (p.1286)
* Ephesians 4:26 (p.1274)

¹⁰Go into the caves of the cliffs;
  dig holes and hide in the ground
from the anger of the LORD
  and from his great power!
¹¹Proud people will be made humble,
  and they will bow low with shame.
At that time only the LORD will still be
    praised.

¹²The LORD All-powerful has a certain day
    planned
  when he will punish the proud and those
    who boast,
  and they will no longer be important.
¹³He will bring down the tall cedar trees from
    Lebanon
  and the great oak trees of Bashan,
¹⁴all the tall mountains
  and the high hills,
¹⁵every tall tower
  and every high, strong wall,
¹⁶all the trading ships
  and the beautiful ships.
¹⁷At that time proud people will be made
    humble,
  and they will bow low with shame.
At that time only the LORD will be praised,
¹⁸ but all the idols will be gone.

¹⁹People will run to caves in the rocky cliffs
  and will dig holes and hide in the ground
from the anger of the LORD
  and his great power,
  when he stands to shake the earth.
²⁰At that time people will throw away
  their gold and silver idols,
which they made for themselves to worship;
  they will throw them away to the bats and
    moles.
²¹Then the people will hide in caves
  and cracks in the rocks
from the anger of the LORD
  and his great power,
  when he stands to shake the earth.

²²You should stop trusting in people to
    save you,
  because people are only human;
  they aren't able to help you.

God Will Punish Judah and Jerusalem

3 Understand this:
    the Lord GOD All-powerful
  will take away everything Judah and
    Jerusalem need—
  all the food and water,
²the heroes and great soldiers,
  the judges and prophets, *d*
people who do magic and older leaders,

³the military leaders and government
    leaders,
  the counsellors, the skilled craftsmen and
    those who try to tell the future.
⁴The LORD says, "I will cause young boys to be
    your leaders,
  and foolish children will rule over you.
⁵People will be against each other; everyone
    will be against his neighbour.
Young people will not respect older
    people,
  and common people will not respect
    important people."
⁶At that time a man will seize one of his
    brothers
  from his own family and say,
"You have a coat, so you will be our leader.
  These ruins will be under your control."
⁷But that brother will stand up and say,
  "I cannot help you,
because I do not have food or clothes in my
    house.
You will not make me your leader."
⁸This will happen because Jerusalem has
    stumbled,
  and Judah has fallen.
The things they say and do are against the
    LORD;
  they turn against him.
⁹The look on their faces shows they are
    guilty;
  like the people of Sodom, they are proud of
    their sin.
They don't care who sees it.
How terrible it will be for them,
  because they have brought much trouble on
    themselves.

¹⁰Tell those who do what is right that things
    will go well for them,
  because they will receive a reward for what
    they do.
¹¹But how terrible it will be for the wicked!
  They will be punished for all the wrong
    they have done.
¹²Children treat my people cruelly,
  and women rule over them.
My people, your guides lead you in the
    wrong way
  and turn you away from what is right.

¹³The LORD takes his place in court
  and stands to judge the people.
¹⁴The LORD presents his case
  against the older leaders and other leaders
    of his people:
"You have burned the vineyard.
  Your houses are full of what you took from
    the poor.

¹⁵What gives you the right to crush my people
and grind the faces of the poor into the
ground?"
The Lord GOD All-powerful says this.

A Warning to Women of Jerusalem

¹⁶The LORD says,
"The women of Jerusalem are proud.
They walk around with their heads held
high,
and they flirt with their eyes.
They take quick, short steps,
making noise with their ankle bracelets."

¹⁷So the Lord will put sores on the heads of
those women in Jerusalem,
and he will make them lose their hair.

¹⁸At that time the Lord will take away everything that makes them proud: their beautiful ankle bracelets, their headbands, their necklaces shaped like the moon, ¹⁹their earrings, bracelets and veils, ²⁰their scarves, ankle chains, the cloth belts worn around their waists, their bottles of perfume and charms, ²¹their signet *d* rings, nose rings, ²²their fine robes, capes, shawls and purses, ²³their mirrors, linen dresses, turbans and long shawls.

IMAGE

Hold Your Head Up!

Thomas had an eye for the girls. He also had an eye for the mirror. Everywhere he went, you could be sure that he found the nearest piece of glass to check his appearance. His friends often teased him about it, but he didn't care.

One day, he was going to church with around half-a-dozen of his mates and when they arrived, the youth leader was unloading his car. He was bringing in all the spare boxes of drinks and crisps from the youth club down the road.

"Give us a hand lads!" he yelled as they went past him.

The boys started to lift the boxes from the car. Just then, a very pretty girl walked into the church. None of the lads could remember seeing her before and they all nudged each other. Thomas immediately started smoothing his hair and said to the youth leader:

"Ermm, which is the heaviest box?"

The leader pointed to a rather huge box in the corner, and Thomas picked it up.

"Be careful Tom" the leader warned. "You won't be able to see over the top properly."

"No problem," he yelled back.

Thomas started trudging up the aisle with his heavy box, feeling every inch the hero, and dying to walk past the new girl and make an impression. Suddenly, his feet seemed to be trudging even more, and he could hear sniggers. Then he felt something on his shins. Then he went head first up the aisle!

Somehow, when he'd walked into the church, he'd managed to catch his feet under the narrow carpet that led down the middle of the church. And as he walked along, it rolled along in front of him, until now it was a huge roll of carpet!

Lying on the floor, he grinned at his mates as he realised what a fool he'd made of himself. Holding your head high can sometimes ruin your image. And it's not only the guys that make a mess of it, look at what **Isaiah 3:16–23** says about some of the women of the day.

* What mistake did Thomas make, that was the same as the women in verse 16?
* What danger do we face by being preoccupied with our appearance?

Consider . . .

* making a spiritual list to challenge the image list in verses 18–22.
* taking a decision to keep your spiritual development and personal appearance on a par.

For more, see . . .

* Mark 10:31 (p.1017)
* 1 Corinthians 4:7 (p.1219)

* Mark 12:38–40 (p.1023)

²⁴Instead of wearing sweet-smelling perfume,
   they will stink.
   Instead of fine cloth belts, they will wear
      the ropes of captives.
   Instead of having their hair fixed in fancy
      ways, they will be bald.
   Instead of fine clothes, they will wear
      clothes of sadness.
   Instead of being beautiful, they will wear
      the brand of a captive.
²⁵At that time your men will be killed with
      swords,
   and your heroes will die in war.
²⁶There will be crying and sadness near the
      city gates.
   Jerusalem will be like a woman who has
      lost everything and sits on the ground.

4 At that time seven women
   will seize one man
and say, "We will eat our own bread
   and make our own clothes,
but please marry us!
   Please, take away our shame."

The Branch of the LORD

²At that time the LORD's branch will be very
beautiful and great. The people still living in Israel
will be proud of what the land grows. ³Those
who are still living in Jerusalem will be called
holy; their names are recorded among the living
in Jerusalem. ⁴The Lord will wash away the filth
from the women of Jerusalem. He will wash the
bloodstains out of Jerusalem and clean the city
with the spirit of fairness and the spirit of fire.
⁵Then the LORD will cover Mount Zion and the
people who meet there with a cloud of smoke
during the day and with a bright, flaming fire at
night. There will be a covering over every person.
⁶This covering will protect the people from the
heat of the sun and will provide a safe place to
hide from the storm and rain.

Israel, the LORD's Vineyard

5 Now I will sing for my friend a song about
   his vineyard.
My friend had a vineyard
   on a hill with very rich soil.
²He dug and cleared the field of stones
   and planted the best grapevines there.
He built a tower in the middle of it
   and cut out a winepress ᵈ as well.
He hoped good grapes would grow there,
   but only bad ones grew.

³My friend says, "You people living in
      Jerusalem,
   and you people of Judah,
   judge between me and my vineyard.

⁴What more could I have done for my
      vineyard
   than I have already done?
Although I expected good grapes to grow,
   why were there only bad ones?
⁵Now I will tell you
   what I will do to my vineyard:
I will remove the hedge,
   and it will be burnt.
I will break down the stone wall,
   and it will be walked on.
⁶I will ruin my field.
   It will not be trimmed or hoed,
   and weeds and thorns will grow there.
I will command the clouds
   not to rain on it."

⁷The vineyard belonging to the LORD
      All-powerful
   is the nation of Israel;
the garden that he loves
   is the people of Judah.
He looked for justice, but there was only
      killing.
He hoped for right living, but there were
      only cries of pain.

⁸How terrible it will be for you who add more
      houses to your houses
   and more fields to your fields
until there is no room left for other people.
   Then you are left alone in the land.

⁹The LORD All-powerful said this to me:
"The fine houses will be destroyed;
   the large and beautiful houses will be left
      empty.
¹⁰At that time a 25-hectare vineyard will make
      only 20 litres of wine,
   and 200 litres of seed will grow only 20
      litres of grain."

¹¹How terrible it will be for people who rise
      early in the morning
   to look for strong drink,
who stay awake late at night,
   becoming drunk with wine.
¹²At their parties they have lyres, ᵈ harps,
   tambourines, ᵈ flutes and wine.
They don't see what the LORD has done
   or notice the work of his hands.
¹³So my people will be captured and taken
      away,
   because they don't really know me.
All the great people will die of hunger,
   and the common people will die of
      thirst.
¹⁴So the place of the dead wants more and
      more people,
   and it opens wide its mouth.

Jerusalem's important people and common
        people will go down into it,
    with their happy and noisy ones.
¹⁵So the common people and the great people
        will be brought down;
    those who are proud will be humbled.
¹⁶The LORD All-powerful will receive glory by
        judging fairly;
    the holy God will show himself holy by
        doing what is right.
¹⁷Then the sheep will go anywhere they want,
    and lambs will feed on the land that rich
        people once owned.

¹⁸How terrible it will be for those people!
    They pull their guilt and sins behind them
        as people pull wagons with ropes.
¹⁹They say, "Let God hurry;
    let him do his work soon
    so we may see it.
    Let the plan of the Holy One of Israel happen
        soon
    so that we will know what it is."

²⁰How terrible it will be for people who call
        good things bad
    and bad things good,
    who think darkness is light
    and light is darkness,
    who think sour is sweet
    and sweet is sour.

²¹How terrible it will be for people who think
        they are wise
    and believe they are clever.

²²How terrible it will be for people who are
        famous for drinking wine
    and are champions at mixing drinks.
²³They take money to set the guilty free
    and don't allow good people to be judged
        fairly.
²⁴They will be destroyed
    just as fire burns straw or dry grass.
    They will be destroyed
    like a plant whose roots rot
    and whose flower dies and blows away like
        dust.
    They have refused to obey the teachings of
        the LORD All-powerful
    and have hated the message from the Holy
        God of Israel.
²⁵So the LORD has become very angry with his
        people,
    and he has raised his hand to punish
        them.
    Even the mountains are frightened.
    Dead bodies lie in the streets like
        rubbish.

But the LORD is still angry;
    his hand is still raised to strike down the
        people.

²⁶He raises a banner for the nations far away.
    He whistles to call those people from the
        ends of the earth.
    Look! The enemy comes quickly!
²⁷Not one of them becomes tired or falls down.
    Not one of them gets sleepy and falls asleep.
    Their weapons are close at hand,
    and their sandal straps are not broken.
²⁸Their arrows are sharp,
    and all of their bows are ready to shoot.
    The horses' hoofs are as hard as rocks,
    and their chariot wheels move like a
        whirlwind.
²⁹Their shout is like the roar of a lion;
    it is loud like a young lion.
    They growl as they capture their captives.
    There is no one to stop them from taking
        their captives away.
³⁰On that day they will roar
    like the waves of the sea.
    And when people look at the land,
    they will see only darkness and pain;
    all light will become dark in this thick
        cloud.

Isaiah Becomes a Prophet

6 In the year that King Uzziah died, I saw the
Lord sitting on a very high throne. His long
robe filled the Temple. *d* ²Heavenly creatures of
fire stood above him. Each creature had six
wings: it used two wings to cover its face, two
wings to cover its feet and two wings for flying.
³Each creature was calling to the others:
    "Holy, holy, holy is the LORD All-powerful.
    His glory fills the whole earth."
⁴Their calling caused the frame around the door
to shake, as the Temple filled with smoke.

⁵I said, "Oh, no! I will be destroyed. I am not
pure, and I live among people who are not pure,
but I have seen the King, the LORD All-powerful."

⁶One of the heavenly creatures used a pair of
tongs to take a hot coal from the altar. Then he
flew to me with the hot coal in his hand. ⁷The
creature touched my mouth with the hot coal
and said, "Look, your guilt is taken away, because
this hot coal has touched your lips. Your sin is
taken away."

⁸Then I heard the Lord's voice, saying, "Whom
can I send? Who will go for us?"

So I said, "Here I am. Send me!"

⁹Then the Lord said, "Go and tell this to the
people:

'You will listen and listen, but you will not
        understand.

You will look and look, but you will not
learn.'
[10]Make the minds of these people dumb.
Shut their ears. Cover their eyes.
Otherwise, they might really understand
what they see with their eyes
and hear with their ears.
They might really understand in their minds
and come back to me and be healed."

[11]Then I asked, "Lord, how long should I do
this?"
He answered,
"Until the cities are destroyed
and the people are gone,
until there are no people left in the houses,
until the land is destroyed and left empty.
[12]The LORD will send the people
far away,
and the land will be left empty.
[13]One-tenth of the people will be left in the
land,

Sidelight Did you know that Isaiah
included 32 references
to fire? Throughout the Bible, fire is a common
symbol of God's presence, action and
judgement. For example, look up Genesis
15:17 (p.18), Exodus 13:21–22 (p.71), Acts
2:3 (p.1138), Hebrews 12:29 (p.1345) and
Revelation 2:18 (p.1390).

WORSHIP

Understanding God's Heart

When John Wesley was rescued from a blazing house as a child, he was convinced that God had saved him
for a purpose. As he grew up in eighteenth-century England, he applied all his energy towards accomplishing
God's will for his life. While studying at Oxford University, John led a group of men known as the "Holy Club".
They met for Bible study and prayer, and cared for the sick, poor and imprisoned. Not long after completing
his work at the university, John and his brother, Charles, sailed to America to spread Christ's message.

John had good intentions but still felt like a failure. He knew God had given him a purpose in life, but he
didn't seem able to carry it out. He needed to know and experience God's heart before he could offer it to
anyone else. John returned to England discouraged and disillusioned. "I went to America to convert the
Indians," John said. "But, oh, who shall convert me?"

Then something wonderful happened. On 24 May 1738, John attended a Christian meeting
in London, and his life was changed. In his journal, John described what happened.

"I felt my heart strangely warmed," he wrote. "I felt I did trust in Christ, Christ alone for
salvation; and an assurance was given to me that he had taken away my sins, even mine,
and saved me from the law of sin and death."

John Wesley became one of the most influential men in the history of Christianity. During the
52 years following that experience in 1738, he preached over 40,000 sermons and travelled over
300,000 kilometres, sharing the message of Christ with hundreds of thousands.

John needed to understand and worship God before trying to serve him. The prophet Isaiah had a
similar experience that launched his ministry. Read about Isaiah's encounter with God in **Isaiah 6:1–8**.

* Why did both John Wesley and Isaiah need to understand God's heart and worship him before they
could adequately serve God?
* According to this passage, what do you know about God's character?

Consider . . .

* asking God to reveal himself to you the way he did to Isaiah or to John Wesley.
* writing a song to God, praising him for the qualities about him that you know are true.

For more, see . . .

* 2 Chronicles 29:18–36 (p.422)
* Revelation 19:1–9 (p.1401)
* Psalm 50 (p.529)

but it will be destroyed again.
These people will be like an oak tree
　　whose stump is left when the tree is
　　chopped down.
The people who remain will be like a
　　stump that will sprout again."

Trouble with Aram

7 Now Ahaz was the son of Jotham, who was
　the son of Uzziah.[n] When Ahaz was king
of Judah, Rezin king of Aram and Pekah son of
Remaliah, the king of Israel, went up to Jerusalem
to fight against it. But they were not able to defeat the city.

[2]Ahaz king of Judah received a message saying,
"The armies of Aram and Israel[n] have joined
together."

When Ahaz heard this, he and the people were
frightened. They shook with fear like trees of the
forest blown by the wind.

[3]Then the LORD told Isaiah, "You and your son
Shear-Jashub[n] should go and meet Ahaz at the
place where the water flows into the upper pool,
on the road where people do their laundry. [4]Tell
Ahaz, 'Be calm and don't worry.
Don't let those two men, Rezin and Pekah son of
Remaliah, scare you. Don't be afraid of their anger or Aram's anger, because they are like two
barely burning sticks that are ready to go out.
[5]They have made plans against you, saying,
[6]"Let's fight against Judah and tear it apart. We
will divide the land for ourselves and make the
son of Tabeel the new king of Judah." [7]But I, the
Lord GOD, say,

" 'Their plan will not succeed;
　　it will not happen,
[8]because Aram is led by the city of Damascus,
　　and Damascus is led by its weak king,
　　　　Rezin.
Within 65 years Israel will no longer be a
　　nation.
[9]Israel is led by the city of Samaria,
　　and Samaria is led by its weak king, the son
　　　　of Remaliah.
If your faith is not strong,
　　you will not have strength enough to
　　　　last.' "

Immanuel—God is With Us

[10]Then the LORD spoke to Ahaz again, saying,
[11]"Ask for a sign from the LORD your God to prove

to yourself that these things are true. It may be a
sign from as deep as the place of the dead or as
high as the heavens."

[12]But Ahaz said, "I will not ask for a sign or test
the LORD."

[13]Then Isaiah said, "Ahaz, descendant[d] of
David, listen carefully! Isn't it bad enough that you
wear out the patience of people? Do you also
have to wear out the patience of my God? [14]The
Lord himself will give you a sign: the virgin[n] will
be pregnant. She will have a son, and she will
name him Immanuel.[n] [15]He will be eating milk
curds and honey when he learns to reject what is
evil and to choose what is good. [16]You are afraid
of the kings of Israel and Aram now. But before
the child learns to choose good and reject evil,
the lands of Israel and Aram will be empty. [17]The
LORD will bring troubled times to you, your people
and to the people of your father's family. They
will be worse than anything that has happened
since Israel separated from Judah. The LORD will
bring the king of Assyria to fight against you.

[18]"At that time the LORD will whistle for the
Egyptians, and they will come like flies from
Egypt's faraway streams. He will call for the
Assyrians, and they will come like bees. [19]These
enemies will camp in the deep ravines and in the
cliffs, by the thorn-bushes and watering holes.
[20]The Lord will hire Assyria and use it like a razor
to punish Judah. It will be as if the Lord is shaving
the hair from Judah's head and legs and removing
Judah's beard.

[21]"At that time a person will be able to keep
only one young cow and two sheep alive. [22]There
will be only enough milk for that person to eat
milk curds. All who remain in the land will go
back to eating just milk curds and honey. [23]In this
land there are now vineyards that have 1,000
grapevines, which are worth about 1,000 pieces
of silver. But these fields will become full of
weeds and thorns. [24]The land will become wild
and useful only as a hunting ground. [25]People
once worked and grew food on these hills, but at
that time people will not go there, because the
land will be filled with weeds and thorns. Only
sheep and cattle will go to those places."

Assyria will Come Soon

8 The LORD told me, "Take a large scroll and
　write on it with an ordinary pen: 'Maher-
Shalal-Hash-Baz'. [2]I will gather some men to be

Uzziah　Also called Azariah.
Israel　Literally, "Ephraim". Isaiah often uses "Ephraim" to mean all of Israel.
Shear-Jashub　This name means "a part of the people will come back".
virgin　The Hebrew word means "a young woman". Often this meant a girl who was not married and had not yet had sexual
　　relations with anyone.
Immanuel　This name means "God is with us".

reliable witnesses: Uriah the priest and Zechariah son of Jeberekiah."

³Then I went to the prophetess, *d* and she became pregnant and had a son. The LORD told me, "Name the boy Maher-Shalal-Hash-Baz, *n* ⁴because the king of Assyria will take away all the wealth and possessions of Damascus and Samaria before the boy learns to say 'my father' or 'my mother'."

⁵Again the LORD spoke to me, saying,

⁶"These people refuse to accept
    the slow-moving waters of the pool of
        Shiloah
and are terrified of Rezin
    and Pekah son of Remaliah.
⁷So I, the Lord, will bring
    the king of Assyria and all his power
        against them,
    like a powerful flood of water from the
        Euphrates River.

The Assyrians will be like water rising over
    the banks of the river,
    flowing over the land.
⁸That water will flow into Judah and pass
    through it,
    rising to Judah's throat.
Immanuel, this army will spread its wings
    like a bird
    until it covers your whole country."

⁹Be broken, all you nations,
    and be smashed to pieces.
Listen, all you faraway countries.
    Prepare for battle and be smashed to pieces!
    Prepare for battle and be smashed to pieces!
¹⁰Make your plans for the fight,
    but they will be defeated.
Give orders to your armies,
    but they will be useless,
because God is with us.

Maher-Shalal-Hash-Baz   This name means "there will soon be looting and stealing".

DOUBT

Having Confidence

Jon had a problem with talking to girls.

While it seemed that all Jon's friends in college had steady girlfriends, he couldn't even approach a girl without breaking out in a cold sweat. It was bad enough being a new student in a new college, without also having to suffer the embarrassment of a glistening forehead and sweaty palms.

One night, Jon sought comfort and advice from his older brother, Mike. "I don't suppose I'll ever have a girlfriend," Jon confessed. "I just don't know what to say to girls. I'm not like the others. They all have girlfriends."

"That's ridiculous," Mike said flatly. "They don't have anything you haven't got. You've just go to believe in yourself. Take a risk."

Jon went to his room to think and pray about what Mike said. That night, he asked God to help him to see himself the way God does. He prayed for God to help him to develop confidence.

Jon needed help from God to ease his doubts and build his confidence. In **Isaiah 7:10–16**, King Ahaz also needed God's help to ease his doubts.

* What do King Ahaz and Jon have in common?
* Why do you sometimes hesitate to ask God for something, even if you feel you really need it?

Consider . . .

* listing ways in which God could help you to ease your doubt about him or any situation in your life and then asking him to give you that help.
* asking your parent or youth leader about ways in which you can overcome specific doubts in your life.

For more, see . . .

* Judges 6:11–24 (p.231)
* James 1:6–8 (p.1348)
* Matthew 14:22–33 (p.966)

Warnings to Isaiah

[11]The LORD spoke to me with his great power and warned me not to follow the lead of the rest of the people. He said,

[12]"People are saying that others make plans
    against them,
    but you should not believe them.
Don't be afraid of what they fear;
    do not dread those things.
[13]But remember that the LORD All-powerful is
    holy.
He is the one you should fear;
    he is the one you should dread.
[14]Then he will be a place of safety for you.
    But for the two families of Israel,
he will be like a stone that causes people to
    stumble,
    like a rock that makes them fall.
He will be like a trap for the people of
    Jerusalem,
    and he will catch them in his trap.
[15]Many people will fall over this rock.
They will fall and be broken;
    they will be trapped and caught."

[16]Make an agreement.
    Seal up the teaching while my followers are
    watching.
[17]I will wait for the LORD to help us,
    the LORD who is ashamed of the family of
    Israel.
I will wait for him.

[18]I am here, and with me are the children the LORD has given me. We are signs and proofs for the people of Israel from the LORD All-powerful, who lives on Mount Zion. *d*

[19]Some people say, "Ask the mediums *d* and fortune-tellers, who whisper and mutter, what to do." But I tell you that people should ask their God for help. Why should people who are still alive ask something from the dead? [20]You should follow the teachings and the agreement with the LORD. The mediums and fortune-tellers do not speak the word of the LORD, so their words are worth nothing.

[21]People will wander through the land troubled and hungry. When they become hungry, they will become angry and will look up and curse their king and their God. [22]They will look around them at their land and see only trouble, darkness and awful gloom. And they will be forced into the darkness.

A New Day is Coming

9 But suddenly there will be no more gloom for the land that suffered. In the past God made the lands of Zebulun and Naphtali hang their heads in shame, but in the future those lands will be made great. They will stretch from the road along the Mediterranean Sea to the land beyond the Jordan River and north to Galilee, the land of people who are not Israelites.

[2]Before those people lived in darkness,
    but now they have seen a great light.
They lived in a dark land,
    but a light has shone on them.
[3]God, you have caused the nation to grow
    and made the people happy.
And they have shown their happiness to you,
    like the joy during harvest time,
like the joy of people
    taking what they have won in war.
[4]Like the time you defeated Midian,
    you have taken away their heavy load
and the heavy pole from their backs
    and the rod the enemy used to punish
    them.
[5]Every boot that marched in battle
    and every uniform stained with blood
    has been thrown into the fire.
[6]A child has been born to us;
    God has given a son to us.
He will be responsible for leading the
    people.
His name will be Wonderful Counsellor,
    Powerful God,
Father Who Lives For Ever, Prince of
    Peace.
[7]Power and peace will be in his kingdom
    and will continue to grow for ever.
He will rule as king on David's throne
    and over David's kingdom.
He will make it strong
    by ruling with justice and goodness
    from now on and for ever.
The LORD All-powerful will do this
    because of his strong love for his people.

God Will Punish Israel

[8]The Lord sent a message against the people
    of Jacob;
    it says that God will judge Israel.
[9]Then everyone in Israel, even the leaders in
    Samaria,
    will know that God has sent it.
Those people are proud and boast by saying,
[10]"These bricks have fallen,
    but we will build again with cut stones.
These small trees have been chopped down,
    but we will put great cedars there."
[11]But the LORD has brought the enemies of
    Rezin against them;
    he has stirred up their enemies against
    them.

¹²The Arameans came from the east
and the Philistines from the west,
and they ate up Israel with their armies.

But the LORD was still angry;
his hand was still raised to punish the people.

¹³But the people did not return to the one who
had struck them;
they did not follow the LORD All-powerful.
¹⁴So the LORD cut off Israel's head and tail,
taking away both the branch and stalk
in one day.
¹⁵The older leaders and important men were
the head,
and the prophets ^d who speak lies were the tail.
¹⁶Those who led the people led them in the
wrong direction,
and those who followed them were
destroyed.

¹⁷So the Lord is not happy with the young
people,
nor will he show mercy to the orphans and
widows.
All the people are separated from God and
are very evil;
they all speak lies.

But the LORD is still angry;
his hand is still raised to strike down the
people.

¹⁸Evil is like a small fire.
First, it burns weeds and thorns.
Next, it burns the larger bushes in the forest,
and they all go up in a column of smoke.
¹⁹The LORD All-powerful is angry,
so the land will be burnt.
The people are like fuel for the fire;
no one will try to save his brother or sister.

JUSTICE

Christmas Truce

The bombs had been falling for weeks now. Rain had soaked into the soil till it could take no more. Puddles had formed and grown until the whole battlefield was a mess of mud and wire. The noise, booming hour on hour and day on day left no one in any doubt – these were dark days.

And yet that night, as soldiers lay in their damp rooms, carved out from the clay soil, something had changed. At first, they didn't notice. The sound was so much part of their daily routine that the soldiers had blocked it out. It took a good couple of hours to really register that the bombing had stopped.

As the sun rose, there was no smoke to hide its power. Day dawned unimpeded for the first time in months. There was light.

Soldiers tentatively put their heads above the trench top and looked over the desolate no-man's-land.

And then they heard singing . . .

Early in World War I, soldiers on both sides stopped their fighting for Christmas – the day remembering the birth of Jesus.

While they stopped only for one day to remember the birth of the Prince of Peace, this passage (**Isaiah 9:1–7**) talks about what Jesus really came to do, making things as they were always supposed to be. It's what we call justice.

* God talks about bringing light to us individually and as a society. What areas of your life do you want God to bring light to (to change for good)?
* What things does the passage say will happen when God moves to bring justice?

Consider . . .

* how God has always used people to help him make the world right. What can you see around you that you think needs God's light? Make a note to pray every day for God to change things.
* what you can get involved in locally that will help make things better for people around you.

For more, see . . .

* Matthew 5:14–16 (p.942)
* John 12:46 (p.1119)
* John 1:1–5 (p.1096)

²⁰People will grab something on the right,
  but they will still be hungry.
They will eat something on the left,
  but they will not be filled.
Then they will each turn and eat their own
  children.
²¹The people of Manasseh will fight against the
    people of Ephraim,
  and Ephraim will fight against Manasseh.
  Then both of them will turn against Judah.

But the LORD is still angry;
  his hand is still raised to strike down the
    people.

10
How terrible it will be for those who
    make unfair laws,
  and those who write laws that make life
    hard for people.
²They are not fair to the poor,
  and they rob my people of their rights.
They allow people to steal from widows
  and to take from orphans what really
    belongs to them.
³How will you explain the things you have
    done?
  What will you do when your destruction
    comes from far away?
Where will you run for help?
  Where will you hide your riches then?
⁴You will have to bow down among the captives
  or fall down among the dead bodies.

But the LORD is still angry;
  his hand is still raised to strike down the
    people.

God Will Punish Assyria

⁵God says, "How terrible it will be for the
    king of Assyria.
  I use him like a rod to show my anger;
  in anger I use Assyria like a club.
⁶I send it to fight against a nation that is
    separated from God.
  I am angry with those people,
    so I command Assyria to fight against them,
  to take their wealth from them,
    to trample them down like mud in the
      streets.
⁷But Assyria's king doesn't understand that I
    am using him;
  he doesn't know he is a tool for me.
He only wants to destroy other people
  and to defeat many nations.
⁸The king of Assyria says to himself,
  'All of my commanders are like kings.
⁹The city Calno is like the city Carchemish.
  The city Hamath is like the city Arpad.
  The city Samaria is like the city Damascus.

¹⁰I defeated those kingdoms that worship idols,
  and those idols were more than the idols of
    Jerusalem and Samaria.
¹¹As I defeated Samaria and her idols,
  I will also defeat Jerusalem and her idols.'"

¹²When the Lord finishes doing what he
planned to Mount Zion*d* and Jerusalem, he will
punish Assyria. The king of Assyria is very proud,
and his pride has made him do these evil things,
so God will punish him. ¹³The king of Assyria
says this:
  "By my own power I have done these things;
    by my wisdom I have defeated many
      nations.
  I have taken their wealth,
    and, like a mighty one, I have taken their
      people.
¹⁴I have taken the riches of all these people,
  like a person reaching into a bird's nest.
I have taken these nations,
  like a person taking eggs.
Not one raised a hand
  or opened its mouth to stop me."

¹⁵An axe is not better than the person who
    swings it.
A saw is not better than the one who
    uses it.
A stick cannot control the person who picks
    it up.
A club cannot pick up the person!
¹⁶So the Lord GOD All-powerful
  will send a terrible disease upon Assyria's
    soldiers.
The strength of Assyria will be burned up
  like a fire burning until everything is gone.

> ### Sidelight
> When the Assyrian army marched into town, the locals could count on problems (Isaiah 10:12–16). The Assyrians were known for flattening cities with battering rams, shooting defenders from mobile archery towers and skinning survivors alive.

¹⁷God, the Light of Israel, will be like a fire;
  the Holy One will be like a flame.
He will be like a fire
  that suddenly burns the weeds and thorns.
¹⁸The fire burns away the great trees and rich
    farmlands,
  destroying everything.
It will be like a sick person who wastes
    away.
¹⁹The trees left standing will be so few
  that even a child could count them.

20At that time some people will be left alive in
  Israel
    from the family of Jacob.
  They will not continue to depend
    on the person who defeated them.
  They will learn truly to depend on the LORD,
    the Holy One of Israel.
21Those who are left alive in Jacob's family
    will again follow the powerful God.
22Israel, your people are many,
    like the grains of sand by the sea.
  But only a few of them will be left alive to
    return to the LORD.
  God has announced that he will destroy the
    land
    completely and fairly.
23The Lord GOD All-powerful will certainly
    destroy this land
    as he has announced.

24This is what the Lord GOD All-powerful says:
  "My people living in Jerusalem,
    don't be afraid of the Assyrians,
  who beat you with a rod
    and raise a stick against you, as Egypt did.
25After a short time my anger against you will
    stop,
    and then I will turn my anger to destroying
    them."

26Then the LORD All-powerful will beat the
    Assyrians with a whip
  as he defeated Midian at the rock of Oreb.
  He will raise his stick over the waters
    as he did in Egypt.
27Then the troubles that Assyria puts on you
    will be removed,
  and the load they make you carry
    will be taken away.

Assyria Invades Israel

28The army of Assyria will enter near Aiath.
  Its soldiers will walk through Migron.
  They will store their food in Michmash.
29The army will go over the pass.
  The soldiers will sleep at Geba.
  The people of Ramah will be afraid,
    and the people of Saul at Gibeah will run
    away.
30Cry out, Bath Gallim!
  Laishah, listen!
  Poor Anathoth!
31The people of Madmenah are running away;
  the people of Gebim are hiding.
32This day the army will stop at Nob.

They will shake their fist at Mount Zion, *d*
  at the hill of Jerusalem.
33Watch! The Lord GOD All-powerful
  with his great power will chop them down
    like a great tree.
  Those who are great will be cut down;
    those who are important will fall to the
    ground.
34He will cut them down
  as a forest is cut down with an axe.
  And the great trees of Lebanon
    will fall by the power of the Mighty One.

The King of Peace is Coming

11 A new branch will grow
    from a stump of a tree;
  so a new king will come
    from the family of Jesse. *n*
2The Spirit *d* of the LORD will rest upon that
    king.
  The Spirit will give him wisdom and
    understanding, guidance and power.
  The Spirit will teach him to know and
    respect the LORD.
3This king will be glad to obey the LORD.
  He will not judge by the way things look
    or decide by what he hears.
4But he will judge the poor honestly;
  he will be fair in his decisions for the poor
    people of the land.
  At his command evil people will be
    punished,
    and by his words the wicked will be put to
    death.
5Goodness and fairness will give him strength,
  like a belt around his waist.

6Then wolves will live in peace with lambs,
  and leopards will lie down to rest with
    goats.
  Calves, lions and young bulls will eat together,
    and a little child will lead them.
7Cows and bears will eat together in peace.
  Their young will lie down to rest together.
  Lions will eat hay as oxen do.

Sidelight   Until God fully sets up the
                   peaceful, new kingdom,
you'll want to steer clear of the cobra (Isaiah
11:8). Some varieties of this snake – which can
grow up to six feet long – spit venom into their
victim's eyes.

Jesse King David's father.

8A baby will be able to play near a cobra's
    hole,
  and a child will be able to put his hand into
    the nest of a poisonous snake.
9They will not hurt or destroy each other
  on all my holy mountain,
because the earth will be full of the
    knowledge of the LORD,
  as the sea is full of water.

10At that time the new king from the family of
Jesse[n] will stand as a banner for all peoples. The
nations will come together around him, and the
place where he lives will be filled with glory. 11At
that time the Lord will again reach out and take
his people who are left alive in Assyria, North
Egypt, South Egypt, Cush, Elam, Babylonia,
Hamath and all the islands of the sea.

12God will raise a banner as a sign for all
    nations,
  and he will gather the people of Israel who
    were forced from their country.

Jesse King David's father.

He will gather the scattered people of Judah
  from all parts of the earth.
13At that time Israel will not be jealous any
    more,
  and Judah will have no more enemies.
Israel will not be jealous of Judah,
  and Judah will not hate Israel.
14But Israel and Judah will attack the
    Philistines on the west.
Together they will take the riches from the
    people of the east.
They will conquer Edom and Moab,
  and the people of Ammon will be under
    their control.
15The LORD will dry up
  the Red Sea[d] of Egypt.
He will wave his arm over the Euphrates
    River
  and dry it up with a scorching wind.
He will divide it into seven small rivers
  so that people can walk across them with
    their sandals on.

FUTURE

Back Again?

Lydia had a life where everything seemed hopeless. Her father was absent – in prison for drugs offences.
Her mother had too many boyfriends calling round. In fact both parents loved Lydia very much but not each
other. They were simply unable to cope. They wanted to, but they had never quite managed to provide her
with clean clothes, a safe home and regular meals. Lydia and her brothers had to leave home and be taken
into care.

    One summer, Lydia went on a holiday with some people from the local church. It painted a picture of
another world – strange, weird and wonderful. Folks took an interest in her, looked out for her, listened to
her, played with her and prayed for her. Someone made sure there were spare clothes if she got wet.
Food arrived three times a day, exactly when the timetable said it would. Every evening someone
told a story from the Bible about things Jesus did.

    Read **Isaiah 11:1–10**. It's about how Isaiah saw hope in the future.

* What will this branch, this king, this new and special leader be like? What will he do?
* Why did the church holiday work for Lydia? Why is it so good to get away from a situation in
  order to reflect upon it?

Consider . . .

* what's going on in the news at the moment that would make you pray for justice and hope for the future.
* praying verse 2 for yourself. Ask God to give you wisdom, understanding, guidance and power. If you have
  hopes and dreams, let him edit them.

For more, see . . .

* Isaiah 9:2–7 (p.649)
* Isaiah 49:22–23 (p.693)

16So God's people who are left alive
    will have a way to leave Assyria,
just like the time the Israelites
    came out of Egypt.

A Song of Praise to God

12 At that time you will say:
    "I praise you, LORD!
You were angry with me,
but you are not angry with me now!
You have comforted me.
2God is the one who saves me;
    I will trust him and not be afraid.
The LORD, the LORD gives me strength and
    makes me sing.
He has saved me."
3You will receive your salvation with joy
    as you would draw water from a well.

4At that time you will say,
"Praise the LORD and worship him.
    Tell everyone what he has done
    and how great he is.
5Sing praise to the LORD, because he has done
    great things.
    Let all the world know what he has done.

6Shout and sing for joy, you people of
    Jerusalem,
because the Holy One of Israel does great
    things before your eyes."

God's Message to Babylon

13 God showed Isaiah son of Amoz this
    message about Babylon:
2Raise a flag on the bare mountain.
    Call out to the men.
Raise your hand to signal them
    to enter through the gates for important
    people.
3I myself have commanded those people
    whom I have separated as mine.
I have called those warriors to carry out my
    anger.
    They rejoice and are glad to do my will.

4Listen to the loud noise in the mountains,
    the sound of many people.
Listen to the noise among the kingdoms,
    the sound of nations gathering
    together.
The LORD All-powerful is calling
    his army together for battle.

ETERNAL LIFE

Safe Under the Falls

From a distance, Niagara Falls is a spectacular sight. But close up, it can be terrifying. Millions of litres of water rush over the cliff, falling 50 metres with tremendous force. Anyone caught in the falls would die instantly from the crushing impact on the jagged rocks below.

But with the help of guides, visitors can put on rubber suits and carefully make their way behind the falls. With water roaring and spraying just a few metres away, they can stand in a particular spot known as the Cave of the Winds and be perfectly safe.

Sometimes life can seem like the crushing pressure of Niagara Falls. But, as **Isaiah 12** promises, we can trust God to save and protect us.

* What similarities are there between the Cave of the Winds and God's promise of eternal life?
* How does reading this passage give you assurance of God's gift when you are surrounded by troubles?

Consider . . .

* blowing up a balloon and writing on it reasons you have to celebrate God's gift of eternal life. Keep the balloon in your room as a reminder.
* following Isaiah 12:4 by telling a non-Christian friend about the joy you have found in God's love, comfort and salvation.

For more, see . . .

* Micah 7:7–9 (p.896)
* 2 Peter 1:3–11 (p.1365)
* John 3:1–16 (p.1099)

⁵This army is coming from a faraway land,
 from the edge of the horizon.
In anger the LORD is using this army like a
  weapon
 to destroy the whole country.

⁶Cry, because the LORD's day of judging is
  near;
 the Almighty is sending destruction.
⁷People will be weak with fear,
 and their courage will melt away.
⁸Everyone will be afraid.
 Pain and hurt will grab them;
 they will hurt like a woman giving birth to
  a baby.
They will look at each other in fear,
 with their faces red like fire.

God's Judgement Against Babylon

⁹Look, the LORD's day of judging is coming—
 a terrible day, a day of God's anger.
He will destroy the land
 and the sinners who live in it.
¹⁰The stars will not show their light;
 the skies will be dark.
The sun will grow dark as it rises,
 and the moon will not give its light.

¹¹The LORD says, "I will punish the world for
  its evil
 and wicked people for their sins.
I will cause proud people to lose their pride,
 and I will destroy the pride of those who are
  cruel to others.
¹²People will be harder to find than pure gold;
 there will be fewer people than there is
  fine gold in Ophir.
¹³I will make the sky shake,
 and the earth will be moved from its place
by the anger of the LORD All-powerful
 at the time of his burning anger.

¹⁴"Then the people from Babylon ᵈ will run
  away like hunted deer
 or like sheep who have no shepherd.
Everyone will turn back to his own people;
 each will run back to his own land.
¹⁵Everyone who is captured will be killed;
 everyone who is caught will be killed with
  a sword.
¹⁶Their little children will be beaten to death in
  front of them.
 Their houses will be robbed
 and their wives raped.

¹⁷"Look, I will cause the armies of Media to
  attack Babylon.
 They do not care about silver
 or delight in gold.

¹⁸Their soldiers will shoot the young men with
  arrows;
 they will show no mercy on children,
 nor will they feel sorry for little ones.
¹⁹Babylon is the most beautiful of all kingdoms,
 and the Babylonians are very proud of it.
But God will destroy it
 like Sodom ᵈ and Gomorrah. ᵈ
²⁰No one will ever live there
 or settle there again.
No Arab will put a tent there;
 no shepherd will bring sheep there.
²¹Only desert animals will live there,
 and their houses will be full of wild dogs.
Owls will live there,
 and wild goats will leap about in the houses.
²²Wolves will howl within the strong walls,
 and wild dogs will bark in the beautiful
  buildings.
The end of Babylon is near;
 its time is almost over."

Israel will Return Home

14 The LORD will show mercy to the people
of Jacob, and he will again choose the
people of Israel. He will settle them in their own
land. Then non-Israelite people will join the
Israelites and will become a part of the family of
Jacob. ²Nations will take the Israelites back to
their land. Then those men and women from the
other nations will become slaves to Israel in the
LORD's land. In the past the Israelites were their
slaves, but now the Israelites will defeat those
nations and rule over them.

The King of Babylon will Fall

³The LORD will take away the Israelites' hard
work and will comfort them. They will no longer
have to work hard as slaves. ⁴On that day Israel
will sing this song about the king of Babylon:
 The cruel king who ruled us is finished;
  his angry rule is finished!
⁵The LORD has broken the sceptre ᵈ of evil
  rulers
 and taken away their power.
⁶The king of Babylon struck people in anger
  again and again.
 He ruled nations in anger
 and continued to hurt them.
⁷But now, the whole world rests and is quiet.
 Now the people begin to sing.
⁸Even the pine trees are happy,
 and the cedar trees of Lebanon rejoice.
They say, "The king has fallen,
 so no one will ever cut us down again."

⁹The place of the dead is excited
 to meet you when you come.

It wakes the spirits of the dead,
　　the leaders of the world.
It makes kings of all nations
　　stand up from their thrones to greet you.
10All these leaders will make fun of you
　　and will say,
"Now you are weak, as we are.
　　Now you are just like us."
11Your pride has been sent down to the place
　　of the dead.
The music from your harps goes with it.
Flies are spread out like your bed
　　beneath you,
　　and worms cover your body like a
　　blanket.

12King of Babylon, morning star, you have
　　fallen from heaven,
even though you were as bright as the
　　rising sun!
In the past all the nations on earth bowed
　　down before you,
but now you have been cut down.
13You told yourself,
"I will go up to heaven.
I will put my throne
　　above God's stars.
I will sit on the mountain of the gods,
　　on the slopes of the sacred mountain.
14I will go up above the tops of the clouds.
　　I will be like God Most High."
15But you were brought down to the grave,
　　to the deep places where the dead are.

16Those who see you stare at you.
　　They think about what has happened to you
and say, "Is this the same man who caused
　　great fear on earth,
who shook the kingdoms,
17who turned the world into a desert,
　　who destroyed its cities,
who captured people in war
　　and would not let them go home?"

18Every king of the earth has been buried with
　　honour,
　　each in his own grave.
19But you are thrown out of your grave,
　　like an unwanted branch.
You are covered by bodies
　　that died in battle,
by bodies to be buried in a rocky pit.
　　You are like a dead body other soldiers
　　walk on.
20 You will not be buried with those bodies,
because you ruined your own country
　　and killed your own people.

The children of evil people
　　will never be mentioned again.
21Prepare to kill his children,
　　because their father is guilty.
They will never again take control of the earth;
　　they will never again fill the world with
　　their cities.
22The LORD All-powerful says this:
"I will fight against those people;
I will destroy Babylon and its people,
　　its children and their descendants," *d* says
　　the LORD.
23"I will make Babylon fit only for owls
　　and for swamps.
I will sweep Babylon as with a broom of
　　destruction,"
　　says the LORD All-powerful.

God will Punish Assyria

24The LORD All-powerful has made this promise:
"These things will happen exactly as I
　　planned them;
they will happen exactly as I set them up.
25I will destroy the king of Assyria in my
　　country;
I will trample him on my mountains.
He placed a heavy load on my people,
　　but that weight will be removed.
26"This is what I plan to do for all the earth.
　　And this is the hand that I have raised over
　　all nations."
27When the LORD All-powerful makes a plan,
　　no one can stop it.
When the LORD raises his hand to punish
　　people,
　　no one can stop it.

God's Message to Philistia

28This message was given in the year that King
Ahaz died:
29Country of Philistia, don't be happy
　　that the king who struck you is now dead.
He is like a snake that will give birth to
　　another dangerous snake.
The new king will be like a quick,
　　dangerous snake to bite you.
30Even the poorest of my people will be able to
　　eat safely,
　　and people in need will be able to lie down
　　in safety.
But I will kill your family with hunger,
　　and all your people who are left will die.

31People near the city gates, *n* cry out!
　　Philistines, be frightened,

city gates   People come here to conduct business. Public meetings and court cases were also held there.

because a cloud of dust comes from the north.
It is an army, full of men ready to fight.
32What shall we tell the messengers from
    Philistia?
Say that the LORD has made Jerusalem
    strong
and that his poor people will go there for
    safety.

God's Message to Moab

15 This is a message about Moab:
    In one night armies took the wealth
       from Ar in Moab,
and it was destroyed.
In one night armies took the wealth from Kir
    in Moab,
    and it was destroyed.

> **Sidelight**
>
> Even though the Moabites (Isaiah 15:1) were distant cousins of the Israelites, the two groups had been enemies ever since Moses tried to enter Canaan about seven hundred years before Isaiah (Judges 11:17, p.238).

2The people of Dibon go to the places of
    worship to cry.
The people of Moab cry for the cities of
    Nebo and Medeba.
Every head and beard has been shaved to
    show how sad Moab is.
3In the streets they wear rough cloth to show
    their sadness.
On the roofs[n] and in the public squares,
they are crying loudly.
4People in the cities Heshbon and Elealeh cry
    out loud.
You can hear their voices far away in the
    city Jahaz.
Even the soldiers are frightened;
    they are shaking with fear.

5My heart cries with sorrow for Moab.
Its people run away to Zoar for safety;
    they run to Eglath Shelishiyah.
People are going up the mountain road to
    Luhith,
    crying as they go.
People are going on the road to Horonaim,
    crying over their destruction.
6But the water of Nimrim has dried up.
The grass has dried up,
and all the plants are dead;
    nothing green is left.

7So the people gather up what they have
    saved
and carry it across the Ravine of the
    Poplars.
8Crying is heard everywhere in Moab.
Their crying is heard as far away as the
    city Eglaim;
it is heard as far away as Beer Elim.
9The water of the city Dibon is full of
    blood,
and I, the LORD, will bring even more
    troubles to Dibon.
A few people living in Moab have escaped
    the enemy,
but I will send lions to kill them.

16 Send the king of the land
    the payment he demands.
Send a lamb from Sela through the
    desert
    to the mountain of Jerusalem.
2The women of Moab
    try to cross the river Arnon
like little birds
    that have fallen from their nest.

3They say: "Help us.
Tell us what to do.
Protect us from our enemies
    as shade protects us from the
    noon sun.
Hide us, because we are running for
    safety!
    Don't give us to our enemies.
4Let those of us who were forced out of Moab
    live in your land.
Hide us from our enemies."

The robbing of Moab will stop.
The enemy will be defeated;
those who hurt others will disappear from
    the land.
5Then a new loyal king will come;
    this faithful king will be from the family of
    David.
He will judge fairly
    and do what is right.

6We have heard that the people of Moab are
    proud
    and very conceited.
They are very proud and angry,
    but their boasting means nothing.
7So the people of Moab will cry;
    they will all be sad.

roofs   In Bible times houses were built with flat roofs. The roof was used for drying things such as flax and fruit. And it was used as an extra room, as a place for worship and as a place to sleep in the summer.

They will moan and groan
  for the raisin cakes they had in
    Kir Hareseth.
⁸But the fields of Heshbon and the vines of
    Sibmah cannot grow grapes;
  foreign rulers have destroyed the
    grapevines.
The grapevines once spread as far as the city
    of Jazer and into the desert;
  they had spread as far as the sea.
⁹I cry with the people of Jazer
  for the grapevines of Sibmah.
I will cry with the people of Heshbon and
    Elealeh.
There will be no shouts of joy,
  because there will be no harvest or ripe
    fruit.
¹⁰There will be no joy and happiness in the
    orchards
  and no songs or shouts of joy in the
    vineyards.
No one makes wine in the winepresses, *d*
  because I have put an end to shouts
    of joy.
¹¹My heart cries for Moab like a harp playing a
    funeral song;
  I am very sad for Kir Hareseth.
¹²The people of Moab will go to their places of
    worship
  and will try to pray.
But when they go to their temple to pray,
  they will not be able.

¹³Earlier the LORD said these things about
Moab. ¹⁴Now the LORD says, "In three years all
those people and what they take pride in will be
hated. (This is three years as a hired helper would
count time.) There will be a few people left, but
they will be weak."

God's Message to Aram

17 This is a message about Damascus:
  "The city of Damascus will be
    destroyed;
  only ruins will remain.
²People will leave the cities of Aroer.
  Flocks will wander freely in those empty
    towns,
  and there will be no one to bother them.
³The fortified cities of Israel will be
    destroyed.
  The government in Damascus will end.
Those left alive of Aram will be
  like the glory of Israel," says the LORD
    All-powerful.

⁴"At that time Israel's wealth will all be gone.
  Israel will be like someone who has lost
    much weight from sickness.

⁵That time will be like the grain harvest in the
    Valley of Rephaim.
  The workers cut the wheat.
Then they cut the heads of grain from the
    plants
  and collect the grain.
⁶That time will also be like the olive
    harvest,
  when a few olives are left.
Two or three olives are left in the top
    branches.
  Four or five olives are left on full branches,"
    says the LORD, the God of Israel.

⁷At that time people will look to God, their
    Maker;
  their eyes will see the Holy One of
    Israel.
⁸They will not trust the altars they
    have made,
  nor will they trust what their hands have
    made,
not even the Asherah *d* idols
  and altars.

⁹In that day all their strong cities will be empty.
They will be like the cities the Hivites and the
Amorites left when the Israelites came to take the
land. Everything will be ruined.

¹⁰You have forgotten the God who
    saves you;
  you have not remembered that God is your
    place of safety.
You plant the finest grapevines
  and grapevines from faraway places.
¹¹You plant your grapevines one day and try to
    make them grow,
  and the next day you make them
    blossom.
But at harvest time everything will
    be dead;
  a sickness will kill all the plants.

¹²Listen to the many people!
  Their crying is like the noise from
    the sea.
Listen to the nations!
  Their crying is like the crashing of great
    waves.
¹³The people roar like the waves,
  but when God speaks harshly to them, they
    will run away.
They will be like chaff *d* on the hills being
    blown by the wind,
  or like tumbleweeds blown away by a
    storm.
¹⁴At night the people will be very
    frightened.
  Before morning, no one will be left.

So our enemies will come to our land,
but they will become nothing.

God's Message to Cush

18
How terrible it will be for the land
beyond the rivers of Cush.
It is filled with the sound of wings.
²That land sends messengers across the sea;
they go on the water in boats made of
reeds.

Go, quick messengers,
to a people who are tall and
smooth-skinned,
who are feared everywhere.
They are a powerful nation that defeats other
nations.
Their land is divided by rivers.

³All you people of the world, look!
Everyone who lives in the world, look!
You will see a banner raised on a
mountain.
You will hear a trumpet sound.
⁴The Lord said to me,
"I will quietly watch from where I live,
like heat in the sunshine,
like the dew in the heat of harvest time."
⁵The time will come, after the flowers have
bloomed and before the harvest,
when new grapes will be budding and
growing.
The enemy will cut the plants with knives;
he will cut down the vines and take them
away.
⁶They will be left for the birds of the
mountains
and for the wild animals.
Birds will feed on them all summer,
and wild animals will eat them that
winter."

⁷At that time a gift will be brought to the
Lord All-powerful
from the people who are tall and
smooth-skinned,
who are feared everywhere.
They are a powerful nation that defeats other
nations.
Their land is divided by rivers.
These gifts will be brought to the place of the
Lord All-powerful,
to Mount Zion. *d*

God's Message to Egypt

19
This is a message about Egypt:
Look, the Lord is coming on a fast
cloud
to enter Egypt.

The idols of Egypt will tremble before him,
and Egypt's courage will melt away.

²The Lord says, "I will cause the Egyptians to
fight against themselves.
People will fight with their relatives;
neighbours will fight neighbours;
cities will fight cities;
kingdoms will fight kingdoms.
³The Egyptians will be afraid,
and I will ruin their plans.
They will ask advice from their idols and
spirits of the dead,
from their mediums *d* and fortune-tellers."
⁴The Lord GOD All-powerful says,
"I will hand Egypt over to a hard master,
and a powerful king will rule over them."

⁵The sea will become dry,
and the water will disappear from the Nile
River.
⁶The canals will stink;
the streams of Egypt will decrease and
dry up.
All the water plants will rot;
⁷ all the plants along the banks of the Nile
will die.
Even the planted fields by the Nile
will dry up, blow away and disappear.
⁸The fishermen, all those who catch fish from
the Nile,
will groan and cry;
those who fish in the Nile will be sad.
⁹All the people who make cloth from flax will
be sad,
and those who weave linen will lose hope.
¹⁰Those who weave cloth will be broken.
All those who work for money will be sad.

¹¹The officers of the city of Zoan are fools;
the wise men who advise the king of Egypt
give wrong advice.
How can you say to him, 'I am wise'?
How can you say, 'I am from the old family
of the kings'?
¹²Egypt, where are your wise men?
Let them show you
what the Lord All-powerful has planned for
Egypt.
¹³The officers of Zoan have been fooled;
the leaders of Memphis have believed false
things.
So the leaders of Egypt
lead that nation the wrong way.
¹⁴The Lord has made the leaders confused.
They have led Egypt to wander in the
wrong ways,
like drunk people stumbling in their own
vomit.

¹⁵There is nothing Egypt can do;
 no one there can help.

¹⁶In that day the Egyptians will be like women. They will be afraid of the LORD All-powerful, because he will raise his hand to strike them down. ¹⁷The land of Judah will bring fear to Egypt. Anyone there who hears the name Judah will be afraid, because the LORD All-powerful has planned terrible things for them. ¹⁸At that time five cities in Egypt will speak Hebrew, the language of Canaan, and they will promise to be loyal to the LORD All-powerful. One of these cities will be named the City of Destruction. ¹⁹At that time there will be an altar for the LORD in the middle of Egypt and a monument to the LORD at the border of Egypt. ²⁰This will be a sign and a witness to the LORD All-powerful in the land of Egypt. When the people cry to the LORD for help, he will send someone to save and defend them. He will rescue them from those who hurt them. ²¹So the LORD will show himself to the Egyptians, and then they will know he is the LORD. They will worship God and offer many sacrifices. They will make promises to the LORD and will keep them. ²²The LORD will punish the Egyptians, but then he will heal them. They will come back to the LORD, and he will listen to their prayers and heal them.

²³At that time there will be a highway from Egypt to Assyria, and the Assyrians will go to Egypt, and the Egyptians will go to Assyria. The Egyptians and Assyrians will worship God together. ²⁴At that time Israel, Assyria and Egypt will join together, which will be a blessing for the earth. ²⁵The LORD All-powerful will bless them, saying, "Egypt, you are my people. Assyria, I made you. Israel, I own you. You are all blessed!"

> ### Sidelight
> Sargon, an Assyrian king during Isaiah's time (Isaiah 20:1), was not only a powerful military leader, but must have also been quite a scholar. He built the oldest library archaeologists have discovered, where twenty-five hundred books were found. Of course, that's a small number compared with modern libraries, which can have several million books.

Assyria will Defeat Egypt and Cush

20 Sargon king of Assyria sent a military commander to Ashdod to attack that city. So the commander attacked and captured it. ²Then the LORD spoke through Isaiah son of Amoz, saying, "Take the rough cloth off your body, and take your sandals off your feet." So Isaiah obeyed and walked around naked and barefoot.

³Then the LORD said, "Isaiah my servant has walked around naked and barefoot for three years as a sign against Egypt and Cush. ⁴The king of Assyria will carry away prisoners from Egypt and Cush. Old people and young people will be led away naked and barefoot, with their buttocks bare. So the Egyptians will be shamed. ⁵People who looked to Cush for help will be afraid, and those who were amazed by Egypt's glory will be shamed. ⁶People who live near the sea will say, 'Look at those countries. We trusted them to help us. We ran to them so they would save us from the king of Assyria. So how will we be able to escape?'"

God's Message to Babylon

21 This is a message about the Desert by the Sea:[n]
Disaster is coming from the desert
 like wind blowing in the south.
 It is coming from a terrible country.
²I have seen a terrible vision.
 I see traitors turning against you
 and people taking your wealth.

Elam, attack the people!
 Media, surround the city and attack it!
 I will bring an end to the pain the city
   causes.
³I saw those terrible things, and now I am in
   pain;
 my pains are like the pains of giving
   birth.
What I hear makes me very afraid;
 what I see causes me to shake with fear.
⁴I am worried,
 and I am shaking with fear.
My pleasant evening
 has become a night of fear.

⁵They set the table;
 they spread the rugs;
 they eat and drink.
Leaders, stand up.
 Prepare the shields for battle!

⁶The Lord said to me,
 "Go, place a lookout for the city
 and have him report what he sees.
⁷If he sees chariots and teams of horses,
 donkeys or camels,
he should pay very close attention."

Desert by the Sea Probably Babylon.

[8]Then the lookout called out,
"My master, each day I stand in the
watchtower watching;
every night I have been on guard.
[9]Look, I see a man coming in a chariot
with a team of horses."
The man gives back the answer,
"Babylon has fallen. It has fallen!
All the statues of her gods
lie broken on the ground."

[10]My people are crushed like grain on the
threshing [d] floor.
My people, I tell you what I have heard
from the LORD All-powerful,
from the God of Israel.

God's Message to Edom

[11]This is a message about Dumah: [n]
Someone calls to me from Edom,
"Watchman, how much of the night is left?
Watchman, how much longer will it be
night?"
[12]The watchman answers,
"Morning is coming, but then night will
come again.
If you have something to ask,
then come back and ask."

God's Message to Arabia

[13]This is a message about Arabia:
A group of traders from Dedan
spent the night near some trees in Arabia.
[14] They gave water to thirsty travellers;
the people of Tema gave food
to those who were escaping.
[15]They were running from swords,
from swords ready to kill,
from bows ready to shoot,
from a hard battle.

[16]This is what the Lord said to me: "In one
year all the glory of the country of Kedar will be
gone. (This is a year as a hired helper counts
time.) [17]At that time only a few of the archers,
the soldiers of Kedar, will be left alive." The
LORD, the God of Israel, has spoken.

God's Message to Jerusalem

22 This is a message about the Valley of
Vision: [n]
What is wrong with you people?
Why are you on your roofs? [n]
[2]This city was a very busy city,
full of noise and wild parties.

Now your people have been killed,
but not with swords,
nor did they die in battle.
[3]All your leaders ran away together,
but they have been captured without using
a bow.
All you who were captured
tried to run away before the enemy
came.
[4]So I say, "Don't look at me.
Let me cry loudly.
Don't hurry to comfort me
about the destruction of Jerusalem."
[5]The Lord GOD All-powerful has chosen a
special day
of riots and confusion.
People will trample each other in the Valley
of Vision.
The city walls will be knocked down,
and the people will cry out to the mountain.
[6]The soldiers from Elam will gather their
arrows
and their chariots and men on horses.
Kir will prepare their shields.
[7]Your nicest valleys will be filled with
chariots.
Horsemen will be ordered to guard the
gates of the city.
[8] The walls protecting Judah will fall.

At that time the people of Jerusalem
depended on
the weapons kept at the Palace of the
Forest.
[9]You saw that the walls of Jerusalem
had many cracks that needed repairing.
You stored up water in the lower pool.
[10]You counted the houses of Jerusalem,
and you tore down houses to repair the
walls with their stones.
[11]You made a pool between the two walls
to save water from the old pool,
but you did not trust the God who made
these things;
you did not respect the One who planned
them long ago.

[12]The Lord GOD All-powerful told the people
to cry and be sad,
to shave their heads and wear rough
cloth.
[13]But look, the people are happy
and are having wild parties.
They kill the cattle and the sheep;
they eat the food and drink the wine.

Dumah Another name for Edom.
Valley of Vision This probably means a valley near Jerusalem.
roofs In Bible times houses were built with flat roofs. The roof was used for drying things such as flax and fruit. And it was
used as an extra room, as a place for worship and as a place to sleep in the summer.

They say, "Let us eat and drink,
  because tomorrow we will die."

¹⁴The LORD All-powerful said to me: "You people will die before this guilt is forgiven." The Lord
GOD All-powerful said this.

God's Message to Shebna

¹⁵This is what the Lord GOD All-powerful says:
"Go to this servant Shebna,
  the manager of the palace.
¹⁶Say to him, 'What are you doing here?
  Who said you could cut out a tomb for
    yourself here?
  Why are you preparing your tomb in a high
    place?
  Why are you carving out a tomb from the
    rock?
¹⁷Look, mighty one! The LORD will throw you
    away.
  He will take firm hold of you
¹⁸and roll you tightly into a ball
  and throw you into another country.
  There you will die,
  and there your fine chariots will remain.
  You are a disgrace to your master's
    house.
¹⁹I will force you out of your important job,
  and you will be thrown down from your
    important place.'

²⁰"At that time I will call for my servant Eliakim
son of Hilkiah. ²¹I will take your robe and put it
on him and give him your belt. I will hand over
to him the important job you have, and he will be
like a father to the people of Jerusalem and the
family of Judah. ²²I will put the key to the house
of David around his neck. If he opens a door, no
one will be able to close it; if he closes a door, no
one will be able to open it. ²³He will be like an
honoured chair in his father's house. I will make
him strong like a peg that is hammered into a
strong board. ²⁴All the honoured and important
things of his family will depend on him; all the
adults and little children will depend on him.
They will be like bowls and jars hanging on him.
²⁵"At that time," says the LORD All-powerful,
"the peg hammered into the strong board will
weaken. It will break and fall, and everything
hanging on it will be destroyed." The LORD says
this.

God's Message to Lebanon

23 This is a message about Tyre:
  You trading ships, cry!
The houses and harbour of Tyre are
  destroyed.
This news came to the ships
  from the land of Cyprus.

²Be silent, you who live on the island
  of Tyre;
  you merchants of Sidon, be silent.
  Sailors have made you rich.
³They travelled the sea to bring grain from
    Egypt;
  the sailors of Tyre brought grain from the
    Nile Valley
  and sold it to other nations.

⁴Sidon, be ashamed.
  Strong city of the sea, be ashamed, because
    the sea says:
  "I have not felt the pain of giving birth;
  I have not reared young men or women."
⁵Egypt will hear the news about Tyre,
  and it will make Egypt hurt with sorrow.

⁶You ships should return to Tarshish.
  You people living near the sea should
    be sad.
⁷Look at your once happy city!
  Look at your old, old city!
People from that city have travelled
  far away to live.
⁸Who planned Tyre's destruction?
  Tyre made others rich.
Its merchants were treated like princes,
  and its traders were greatly respected.
⁹It was the LORD All-powerful who planned
    this.
  He decided to make these proud people
    unimportant;
  he decided to disgrace those who were
    greatly respected.
¹⁰Go through your land, people of Tarshish,
  like the Nile goes through Egypt.
  There is no harbour for you now!
¹¹The LORD has stretched his hand over
    the sea
  and made its kingdoms tremble.
He commands that Canaan's
  fortified cities be destroyed.
¹²He said, "Sidon, you will not rejoice any
    longer,
  because you are destroyed.
Even if you cross the sea to Cyprus,
  you will not find a place to rest."
¹³Look at the land of the Babylonians;
  it is not a country now.
Assyria has made it a place for wild animals.
  Assyria built towers to attack it;
the soldiers took all the treasures from its
    cities,
  and they turned it into ruins.
¹⁴So be sad, you trading ships,
  because your strong city is destroyed.
¹⁵At that time people will forget about Tyre for
70 years, which is the length of a king's life.

After 70 years, Tyre will be like the prostitute *d* in this song:

16"Oh woman, you are forgotten.
    Take your harp and walk through the city.
    Play your harp well. Sing your song often.
    Then people will remember you."

17After 70 years the LORD will deal with Tyre, and it will again have trade. It will be like a prostitute for all the nations of the earth. 18The profits will be saved for the LORD. Tyre will not keep the money she earns but will give them to the people who serve the LORD, so they will have plenty of food and nice clothes.

The LORD will Punish the World

24 Look! The LORD will destroy the earth
        and leave it empty;
    he will ruin the surface of the land and
        scatter its people.
2At that time the same thing will happen to
        everyone:
    to common people and priests,
    to slaves and masters,
    to women slaves and their women masters,
    to buyers and sellers,
    to those who borrow and those who lend,
    to bankers and those who owe the bank.
3The earth will be completely empty.
    The wealth will all be taken,
    because the LORD has commanded it.
4The earth will dry up and die;
    the world will grow weak and die;
    the great leaders in this land will become
        weak.
5The people of the earth have ruined it,
    because they do not follow God's teachings
or obey God's laws
    or keep their agreement with God that was
        to last for ever.
6So a curse will destroy the earth.
    The people of the world are guilty,
so they will be burned up;
    only a few will be left.
7The new wine will be bad, and the
        grapevines will die.
    People who were happy will be sad.
8The happy music of the tambourines *d* will end.
    The happy sounds of wild parties will stop.
    The joyful music from the harps will end.
9People will no longer sing while they drink
        their wine.
    The beer will taste bitter to those who drink it.
10The ruined city will be empty,
    and people will hide behind closed doors.
11People in the streets will ask for wine,
    but joy will have turned to sadness;
    all the happiness will have left.

12The city will be left in ruins,
    and its gates will be smashed to pieces.
13This is what will happen all over the earth
    and to all the nations.
    The earth will be like an olive tree after the
        harvest
    or like the few grapes left on a vine after
        harvest.

14The people shout for joy.
    From the west they praise the greatness of
        the LORD.
15People in the east, praise the LORD.
    People in the islands of the sea,
    praise the name of the LORD, the God of
        Israel.
16We hear songs from every part of the earth
    praising God, the Righteous One.

But I said, "I am dying! I am dying!
    How terrible it will be for me!
Traitors turn against people;
    with their dishonesty, they turn against
        people."
17There are terrors, holes and traps
    for the people of the earth.
18Anyone who tries to escape from the sound
        of terror
    will fall into a hole.
Anyone who climbs out of the hole
    will be caught in a trap.
The clouds in the sky will pour out rain,
    and the foundations of the earth will shake.
19The earth will be broken up;
    the earth will split open;
    the earth will shake violently.
20The earth will stumble around like someone
        who is drunk;
    it will shake like a hut in a storm.
Its sin is like a heavy weight on its back;
    it will fall and never rise again.

21At that time the LORD will punish
    the powers in the sky above
    and the rulers on earth below.
22They will be gathered together
    like prisoners thrown into a pit;
they will be shut up in prison.
    After much time they will be punished.
23The moon will be embarrassed,
    and the sun will be ashamed,
because the LORD All-powerful will rule as
        king
    on Mount Zion *d* in Jerusalem.
Jerusalem's leaders will see his greatness.

A Song of Praise to God

25 LORD, you are my God.
        I honour you and praise you,

because you have done amazing things.
You have always done what you said you
would do;
you have done what you planned long ago.
²You have made the city a pile of rocks
and have destroyed her walls.
The city our enemies built with strong walls
is gone;
it will never be built again.
³People from powerful nations will honour you;
cruel people from strong cities will
fear you.
⁴You protect the poor;
you protect the helpless when they are in
danger.
You are like a shelter from storms,
like shade that protects them from the heat.

The cruel people attack
like a rainstorm beating against the wall,
⁵ like the heat in the desert.
But you, God, stop their violent attack.
As a cloud cools a hot day,
you silence the songs of those who have no
mercy.

God's Banquet for His Servants

⁶The LORD All-powerful will prepare a feast
on this mountain for all people.
It will be a feast with all the best food and
wine,
the finest meat and wine.
⁷On this mountain God will destroy
the veil that covers all nations,
the veil that stretches over all peoples;

DEATH

Welcomed Into Heaven

Anna and Drew were sitting by her bedside, watching, when it happened. They'd seen the moment on TV and in films loads of times before, but this was real, this they were seeing with their own eyes.

Anna's nan was old and had been getting increasingly ill over the last few weeks. The hospital called to say that they expected her to pass away in a matter of days, so Anna's family arranged a rota so that someone would be by Nan's bedside 24 hours a day.

Anna and Drew were on the first night shift. Squeezing Drew's hand tightly, Anna prayed that somehow, even now, Nan would meet Jesus before she died and left this world.

Slowly, Nan's face changed. She had seemed asleep, but now, her eyes opened, looking past Anna and Drew towards the end of the bed. She seemed brighter, and for a second they could only look and stare. They'd never felt God's presence as clearly as they did at that moment. Then Nan relaxed back into the bed, closed her eyes, and gently took her last breath. She died, and slowly the colour drained from her face.

Anna and Drew stayed silent for a moment – but the fear had gone. They had just seen Nan pass away – and it was so obvious that what they saw in the bed before them was now just an empty body . . . the shell of Nan. They prayed again, thanking God that Nan had died peacefully – and they were sure that she had met Jesus before she went.

Read **Isaiah 25:6–9**. When we are sad because someone has died, there are promises that God is still in charge and has everything under control.

* How do you feel about the idea of death?
* What do these verses tell us about how God deals with death?

Consider . . .

* an experience you've had of someone close to you dying. Take some time to thank God for that person and for what they meant to you.
* writing a list of all the happy memories you have of them and remind yourself of them each time you feel sad.

For more, see . . .

* Psalm 23 (p.513)
* 1 Thessalonians 4:13–18 (p.1299)

* 1 Corinthians 15:50–57 (p.1237)

8 he will destroy death for ever.
The Lord GOD will wipe away every tear from
    every face.
  He will take away the shame of his people
    from the earth.
The LORD has spoken.

9 At that time people will say,
  "Our God is doing this!
We have waited for him, and he has come to
    save us.
This is the LORD. We waited for him,
so we will rejoice and be happy when he
    saves us."
10 The LORD will protect Jerusalem,
  but he will crush our enemy Moab
like straw that is trampled down in the
    manure.

Sidelight   Lawn care treatments
may be new, but fertiliser
has been around for a long time. The ancient
Israelite farmers would mix together straw and
manure to make fertiliser (Isaiah 25:10). If they
were around today, they could sell their produce
to organic farmers.

---

11 They will spread their arms in it
  like a person who is swimming.
But God will bring down their pride,
  and all the clever things they have made
    will mean nothing.
12 Moab's high walls protect them,
  but God will destroy these walls.
He will throw them down to the ground,
  even to the dust.

A Song of Praise to God

26 At that time people will sing this song in
Judah:
We have a strong city.
  God protects us with its strong walls and
    defences.
2 Open the gates,
  and the good people will enter,
  those who follow God.
3 You, LORD, give true peace
  to those who depend on you,
  because they trust you.
4 So, trust the LORD always,
  because he is our Rock *d* for ever.
5 He will destroy the proud city,
  and he will punish the people living there.
He will bring that high city down to the
    ground
  and throw it down into the dust.

6 Then those who were hurt by the city will
    walk on its ruins;
  those who were made poor by the city will
    trample it under their feet.
7 The path of life is level for those who are
    right with God;
  LORD, you make the way of life smooth for
    those people.
8 But, LORD, we are waiting
  for your way of justice.
Our souls want to remember
  you and your name.
9 My soul wants to be with you at night,
  and my spirit wants to be with you at the
    dawn of every day.
When your way of justice comes to
    the land,
  people of the world will learn the right way
    of living.
10 Evil people will not learn to do good
  even if you show them kindness.
They will continue doing evil, even if they
    live in a good world;
  they never see the LORD's greatness.
11 LORD, you are ready to punish those people,
  but they do not see that.
Show them your strong love for your people.
  Then those who are evil will be ashamed.
Burn them in the fire
  you have prepared for your enemies.
12 LORD, all our success is because of what you
    have done,
  so give us peace.
13 LORD, our God, other masters besides you
    have ruled us,
  but we honour only you.
14 Those masters are now dead;
  their ghosts will not rise from death.
You punished and destroyed them
  and destroyed any memory of them.
15 LORD, you multiplied the number of your
    people;
  you multiplied them and brought honour to
    yourself.
You made the borders of the land wide.
16 LORD, people remember you when they are in
    trouble;
  they say quiet prayers to you when you
    punish them.
17 LORD, when we are with you,
  we are like a woman giving birth
    to a baby;
  she cries and has pain from the birth.
18 In the same way, we had pain.
  We gave birth, but only to wind.
We don't bring salvation to the land
  or make new people for the world.

¹⁹Your people have died, but they will live
again;
  their bodies will rise from death.
You who lie in the ground,
  wake up and be happy!
The dew covering you is like the dew of a
    new day;
  the ground will give birth to the dead.

Judgement: Reward or Punishment

²⁰My people, go into your rooms
  and shut your doors behind you.
Hide in your rooms for a short time
  until God's anger is finished.
²¹The LORD will leave his place
  to punish the people of the world for their
    sins.
The earth will show the blood of the people
  who have been killed;
  it will not cover the dead any longer.

27 At that time the LORD will punish
Leviathan, *d* the gliding snake.
He will punish Leviathan, the coiled snake,
  with his great and hard and powerful
    sword.
He will kill the monster in the sea.

²At that time
  people will sing about the pleasant vineyard.
³"I, the LORD, will care for that vineyard;
  I will water it at the right time.
No one will hurt it,
  because I will guard it day and night.
⁴I am not angry.
If anyone builds a wall of thorn-bushes
    in war,
  I will march to it and burn it.
⁵But if anyone comes to me for safety
  and wants to make peace with me,
  he should come and make peace with me."
⁶In the days to come, the people of Jacob will
    be like a plant with good roots;
  Israel will grow like a plant beginning to
    bloom.
Then the world will be filled with their
    children.

The LORD will Send Israel Away

⁷The LORD has not hurt his people as he hurt
    their enemies;
  his people have not been killed like those
    who tried to kill them.
⁸He will settle his argument with Israel by
    sending it far away.
Like a hot desert wind, he will drive it
    away.
⁹This is how Israel's guilt will be forgiven;
  this is how its sins will be taken away:

Israel will crush the rocks of the altar
    to dust,
  and no statues or altars will be left standing
    for the Asherah *d* idols.
¹⁰At that time the fortified city will be empty
  like a desert.
Calves will eat grass there.
  They will lie down there
  and eat leaves from the branches.
¹¹The limbs will become dry and break off,
  so women will use them for firewood.
The people refuse to understand,
  so God will not comfort them;
  their Maker will not be kind to them.
¹²At that time the LORD will begin gathering his
people one by one from the Euphrates River to
the brook of Egypt. He will separate them from
others as grain is separated from chaff. *d* ¹³Many
of my people are now lost in Assyria. Some have
run away to Egypt. But at that time a great trumpet will be blown, and all those people will come
and worship the LORD on that holy mountain in
Jerusalem.

Warnings to Israel

28 How terrible it will be for Samaria, the
pride of Israel's drunken people!
That beautiful crown of flowers is just a
    dying plant
  set on a hill above a rich valley where
    drunkards live.
²Look, the Lord has someone who is strong
    and powerful.
  Like a storm of hail and strong wind,
  like a sudden flood of water pouring over the
    country,
  he will throw Samaria down to the ground.
³That city, the pride of Israel's drunken people,
  will be trampled underfoot.
⁴That beautiful crown of flowers is just a
    dying plant
  set on a hill above a rich valley.
That city will be like the first fig of summer.
  Anyone who sees it
  quickly picks it and eats it.

⁵At that time the LORD All-powerful
  will be like a beautiful crown,
  like a wonderful crown of flowers
  for his people who are left alive.
⁶Then he will give wisdom to the judges who
    must decide cases
  and strength to those who battle at the city
    gate.
⁷But now those leaders are drunk with
    wine;
  they stumble from drinking too much
    beer.

The priests and prophets *d* are drunk with
      beer
   and are filled with wine.
They stumble from too much beer.
   The prophets are drunk when they see
      their visions;
   the judges stumble when they make their
      decisions.
[8] Every table is covered with vomit,
   so there is not a clean place anywhere.

[9] The LORD is trying to teach the people a
      lesson;
   he is trying to make them understand his
      teachings.
But the people are like babies too old for
      breast milk,
   like those who no longer nurse at their
      mother's breast.
[10] So they make fun of the LORD's prophet
      and say:
   "A command here, a command there.
   A rule here, a rule there.
   A little lesson here, a little lesson there."
[11] So the LORD will use strange words and
      foreign languages
   to speak to these people.
[12] God said to them,
   "Here is a place of rest;
   let the tired people come and rest.
This is the place of peace."
   But the people would not listen.
[13] So the words of the LORD will be,
   "A command here, a command there.
   A rule here, a rule there.
   A little lesson here, a little lesson there."
They will fall back and be defeated;
   they will be trapped and captured.

[14] So listen to the LORD's message, you who
      boast,
   you leaders in Jerusalem.
[15] You say, "We have made an agreement with
      death;
   we have a contract with death.
When terrible punishment passes by,
   it won't hurt us.
Our lies will keep us safe,
   and our tricks will hide us."

[16] Because of these things, this is what the Lord
GOD says:
   "I will put a stone in the ground in
      Jerusalem,
   a tested stone.
Everything will be built on this important and
      precious rock.
   Anyone who trusts in it will never be
      disappointed.

[17] I will use justice as a measuring line
   and goodness as the standard.
The lies you hide behind will be destroyed as
      if by hail.
   They will be washed away as if in a flood.
[18] Your agreement with death will be erased;
   your contract with death will not help you.
When terrible punishment comes,
   you will be crushed by it.
[19] Whenever punishment comes, it will take
      you away.
   It will come morning after morning;
   it will defeat you by day and by night.
Those who understand this punishment will
   be terrified."
[20] You will be like the person who tried to sleep
      on a bed that was too short
and with a blanket that was too narrow
   to wrap around himself.
[21] The LORD will fight as he did at Mount
      Perazim.
   He will be angry as he was in the Valley of
      Gibeon.
   He will do his work, his strange work.
   He will finish his job, his strange job.
[22] Now, you must not make fun of these things,
   or the ropes around you will become
      tighter.
The Lord GOD All-powerful has told me
   how the whole earth will be destroyed.

The LORD Punishes Fairly

[23] Listen closely to what I tell you;
   listen carefully to what I say.
[24] A farmer does not plough his field all the
      time;
   he does not go on working the soil.
[25] He makes the ground flat and smooth.
   Then he plants the dill and scatters the
      cumin.
He plants the wheat in rows,
   the barley in its special place
   and other wheat as a border around the
      field.
[26] His God teaches him
   and shows him the right way.
[27] A farmer doesn't use heavy boards to crush
      dill;
   he doesn't use a wagon wheel to crush
      cumin.
He uses a small stick to break open the dill,
   and with a stick he opens the cumin.
[28] The grain is ground to make bread.
   People do not ruin it by crushing it for
      ever.
The farmer separates the wheat from the
      chaff *d* with his cart,
   but he does not let his horses grind it.

²⁹This lesson also comes from the LORD All-powerful,
who gives wonderful advice, who is very wise.

Warnings to Jerusalem

29 How terrible it will be for you, Jerusalem,
the city where David camped.
Your festivals have continued
year after year.
²I will attack Jerusalem,
and that city will be filled with sadness and crying.
It will be like an altar to me.
³I will put armies all around you, Jerusalem;
I will surround you with towers
and with devices to attack you.
⁴You will be pulled down and will speak from the ground;
I will hear your voice rising from the ground.
It will sound like the voice of a ghost;
your words will come like a whisper from the dust.

⁵Your many enemies will become like fine dust;
the many cruel people will be like chaff *d*
that is blown away.
Everything will happen very quickly.
⁶ The LORD All-powerful will come
with thunder, earthquakes and great noises,
with storms, strong winds and a fire that destroys.
⁷Then all the nations that fight against Jerusalem
will be like a dream;
all the nations that attack her
will be like a vision in the night.
⁸They will be like a hungry man who dreams he is eating,
but when he awakens, he is still hungry.
They will be like a thirsty man who dreams he is drinking,
but when he awakens, he is still weak and thirsty.
It will be the same way with all the nations
who fight against Mount Zion. *d*

⁹Be surprised and amazed.
Blind yourselves so that you cannot see.
Become drunk, but not from wine.
Trip and fall, but not from beer.
¹⁰The LORD has made you go into a deep sleep.
He has closed your eyes. (The prophets *d* are your eyes.)
He has covered your heads. (The seers *d* are your heads.)

¹¹This vision is like the words of a book that is closed and sealed. You may give the book to someone who can read and tell that person to read it. But he will say, "I can't read the book, because it is sealed." ¹²Or you may give the book to someone who cannot read and tell him to read it. But he will say, "I don't know how to read."

¹³The Lord says:
"These people say they love me;
they show honour to me with words,
but their hearts are far from me.
The honour they show me
is nothing but human rules.
¹⁴So I will continue to amaze these people
by doing more and more miracles. *d*
Their wise men will lose their wisdom;
their wise men will not be able to understand."

Warnings About Other Nations

¹⁵How terrible it will be for those who try
to hide things from the LORD
and who do their work in darkness.
They think no one will see them or know what they do.
¹⁶You are confused.
You think the clay is equal to the potter.
You think that an object can tell the one who made it,
"You didn't make me."
This is like a pot telling its maker,
"You don't know anything."

A Better Time is Coming

¹⁷In a very short time, Lebanon will become rich farmland,
and the rich farmland will seem like a forest.
¹⁸At that time the deaf will hear the words in a book.
Instead of having darkness and gloom, the blind will see.
¹⁹The LORD will make the poor people happy;
they will rejoice in the Holy One of Israel.
²⁰Then the people without mercy will come to an end;
those who do not respect God will disappear.
Those who enjoy doing evil will be gone:
²¹those who lie about others in court,
those who trap people in court,
those who lie and take justice from innocent people in court.

[22]This is what the LORD who set Abraham free says to the family of Jacob:
"Now the people of Jacob will not be
    ashamed
    or disgraced any longer.
[23]When they see all their children,
    the children I made with my hands,
they will say my name is holy.
    They will agree that the Holy One of Jacob
        is holy,
    and they will respect the God of Israel.
[24]People who do wrong will now understand.
    Those who complain will accept being
        taught."

Warnings to the Stubborn Nation

30 The LORD said,
    "How terrible it will be for these
        stubborn children.
They make plans, but they don't ask me to
    help them.
They make agreements with other nations,
    without asking my Spirit. [d]
They are adding more and more sins to
    themselves.
[2]They go down to Egypt for help
    without asking me about it first.
They hope they will be saved by the king of
    Egypt;
    they want Egypt to protect them.
[3]But hiding in Egypt will bring you only
        shame;
    Egypt's protection will only disappoint you.
[4]Your officers have gone to Zoan,
    and your messengers have gone to Hanes,
[5]but they will be put to shame,
    because Egypt is useless to them.
It will give no help and will be of no use;
    it will cause them only shame and
        embarrassment."

God's Message to Judah

[6]This is a message about the animals in southern Judah:
Southern Judah is a dangerous place
    full of lions and lionesses,
    poisonous snakes and darting snakes.
The messengers travel through there with
        their wealth on the backs of donkeys
    and their treasure on the backs of camels.
They carry them to a nation that cannot help
        them,
[7]   to Egypt whose help is useless.
So I call that country Rahab [d] the
        Do-Nothing.

[8]Now write this on a sign for the people,
    write this on a scroll,
so that for the days to come
    this will be a witness for ever.
[9]These people are like children who lie and
        refuse to obey;
    they refuse to listen to the LORD's teachings.
[10]They tell the seers, [d]
    "Don't see any more visions!"
They say to the prophets, [d]
    "Don't tell us the truth!
Say things that will make us feel good;
    see only good things for us.
[11]Stop blocking our path.
    Get out of our way.
Stop telling us
    about God, the Holy One of Israel."

[12]So this is what the Holy One of Israel says:
"You people have refused to accept this message
        and have depended on cruelty and lies to
        help you.
[13]You are guilty of these things.
    So you will be like a high wall with cracks
        in it
    that falls suddenly and breaks into small
        pieces.
[14]You will be like a clay jar that breaks,
    smashed into many pieces.
Those pieces will be too small
    to take coals from the fire
    or to get water from a well."

[15]This is what the Lord GOD, the Holy One of Israel, says:
"If you come back to me and trust me, you
        will be saved.
    If you will be calm and trust me, you will
        be strong."
But you don't want to do that.
[16]You say, "No, we need horses to run
        away on."
    So you will run away on horses.
You say, "We will ride away on fast horses."
    So those who chase you will be fast.
[17]One enemy will make threats,
    and 1,000 of your men will run away.
Five enemies will make threats,
    and all of you will run from them.
You will be left alone like a flagpole on a
        hilltop,
    like a banner on a hill.
[18]The LORD wants to show his mercy to you.
    He wants to rise and comfort you.
The LORD is a fair God,
    and everyone who waits for his help will
        be happy.

The LORD will Help His People

[19]You people who live on Mount Zion [d] in Jerusalem will not cry any more. The LORD will

hear your crying, and he will comfort you. When he hears you, he will help you. [20]The Lord has given you sorrow and hurt like the bread and water you ate every day. He is your teacher; he will not continue to hide from you, but you will see your teacher with your own eyes. [21]If you go the wrong way—to the right or to the left—you will hear a voice behind you saying, "This is the right way. You should go this way." [22]You have statues covered with silver and gold, but you will ruin them for further use. You will throw them away like filthy rags and say, "Go away!"

[23]At that time the LORD will send rain for the seeds you plant in the ground, and the ground will grow food for you. The harvest will be rich and great, and you will have plenty of food in the fields for your animals. [24]Your oxen and donkeys that work the soil will have all the food they need. You will have to use shovels and pitchforks to spread all their food. [25]Every mountain and hill will have streams filled with water. These things will happen after many people are killed and the towers are pulled down. [26]At that time the light from the moon will be bright like the sun, and the light from the sun will be seven times brighter than now, like the light of seven days. These things will happen when the LORD bandages his broken people and heals the hurts he gave them.

[27]Look! The LORD comes from far away.
His anger is like a fire with thick clouds of
     smoke.
His mouth is filled with anger,
     and his tongue is like a burning fire.
[28]His breath is like a rushing river,
     which rises to the throat.
He will judge the nations as if he is sifting
     them through the strainer of
     destruction.
He will place in their mouths a bit that will
     lead them the wrong way.
[29]You will sing happy songs
     as on the nights you begin a festival.
You will be happy like people listening to
     flutes
     as they come to the mountain of the LORD,
     to the Rock *d* of Israel.
[30]The LORD will cause all people to hear his
     great voice
     and to see his powerful arm come down
     with anger,
     like a great fire that burns everything,
     like a great storm with much rain and hail.
[31]Assyria will be afraid when it hears the voice
     of the LORD,
     because he will strike Assyria with a rod.

[32]When the LORD punishes Assyria with a rod,
     he will beat them to the music of
     tambourines *d* and harps;
     he will fight against them with his mighty
     weapons.

[33]Topheth *n* has been made ready for a long
     time;
     it is ready for the king.
It was made deep and wide
     with much wood and fire.
And the LORD's breath will come
     like a stream of burning sulphur and set it
     on fire.

Warnings About Relying on Egypt

31 How terrible it will be for those people
     who go down to Egypt for help.
They think horses will save them.
They think their many chariots
     and strong horsemen will save them.
But they don't trust God, the Holy One of
     Israel,
     or ask the LORD for help.
[2]But he is wise and can bring them disaster.
He does not change his warnings.
He will rise up and fight against the evil
     people
     and against those who try to help evil
     people.
[3]The Egyptians are only people and are
     not God.
Their horses are only animals and are not
     spirit.
The LORD will stretch out his arm,
     and the one who helps will stumble,
     and the people who wanted help will fall.
All of them will be destroyed together.

[4]The LORD says this to me:
"When a lion or a lion's cub kills an animal
     to eat,
     it stands over the dead animal and roars.
A band of shepherds
     may be assembled against it,

Topheth Gehenna; the Valley of Hinnom. Here people burned the bodies of criminals and animals, along with rubbish.

but the lion will not be afraid of their yelling
  or upset by their noise.
So the LORD All-powerful will come down
  to fight on Mount Zion *d* and on its hill.
⁵The LORD All-powerful will defend Jerusalem
  like birds flying over their nests.
He will defend and save it;
  he will 'pass over' and save Jerusalem."

⁶You children of Israel, come back to the God
you fought against. ⁷The time is coming when
each of you will stop worshipping idols of gold
and silver, which you sinned by making.

⁸"Assyria will be defeated by a sword, but not
    the sword of a person;
  Assyria will be destroyed, but not by a
    person's sword.
  Assyria will run away from the sword
    of God,
  but its young men will be caught and made
    slaves.
⁹They will panic, and their protection will be
    destroyed.
  Their commanders will be terrified when
    they see God's battle flag,"
says the LORD,
  whose fire is in Jerusalem
  and whose furnace is in Jerusalem.

A Good Kingdom is Coming

32 A king will rule in a way that brings
    justice,
  and leaders will make fair decisions.
²Then each ruler will be like a shelter from
    the wind,
  like a safe place in a storm,
  like streams of water in a dry land,
  like a cool shadow from a large rock in a
    hot land.

³People will look to the king for help,
  and they will truly listen to what he says.
⁴People who are now worried will be able to
    understand.
  Those who cannot speak clearly now will
    then be able to speak clearly and
    quickly.
⁵Fools will not be called great,
  and people will not respect the wicked.
⁶A fool says foolish things,
  and in his mind he plans evil.
  A fool does things that are wicked,
    and he says wrong things about the LORD.
  A fool does not feed the hungry
    or let thirsty people drink water.
⁷The wicked person uses evil like a tool.
  He plans ways to take everything from the
    poor.

He destroys the poor with lies,
  even when the poor person is in the right.
⁸But a good leader plans to do good,
  and those good things make him a good
    leader.

Hard Times are Coming

⁹You women who are calm now,
  stand up and listen to me.
You women who feel safe now,
  hear what I say.
¹⁰You women feel safe now,
  but after one year you will be afraid.
There will be no grape harvest
  and no summer fruit to gather.
¹¹Women, you are calm now, but you should
    shake with fear.
  Women, you feel safe now, but you should
    tremble.
Take off your nice clothes
  and put rough cloth around your waist to
    show your sadness.
¹²Beat your breasts in grief, because the fields
    that were pleasant are now empty.
  Cry, because the vines that once had fruit
    now have no more grapes.
¹³Cry for the land of my people,
  in which only thorns and weeds
    now grow.
  Cry for the city that once was happy
    and for all the houses that once were filled
    with joy.
¹⁴The palace will be empty;
  people will leave the noisy city.
  Strong cities and towers will be empty.
    Wild donkeys will love to live there, and
    sheep will go there to eat.

Things will Get Better

¹⁵This will continue until God pours his Spirit *d*
  from above upon us.
  Then the desert will be like a fertile field
    and the fertile field like a forest.
¹⁶Justice will be found even in the desert,
  and fairness will be found in the fertile
    fields.
¹⁷That fairness will bring peace,
  and it will bring calm and safety for ever.
¹⁸My people will live in peaceful places
  and in safe homes
  and in calm places of rest.
¹⁹Hail will destroy the forest,
  and the city will be completely
    destroyed.
²⁰But you will be happy as you plant seeds
    near every stream
  and as you let your cattle and donkeys
    wander freely.

Warnings to Assyria and Promises to God's People

33 How terrible it will be for you who
destroy others
but have not been destroyed yet.
How terrible it will be for you, traitor,
whom no one has turned against yet.
When you stop destroying,
others will destroy you.
When you stop turning against others,
they will turn against you.

²LORD, be kind to us.
We have waited for your help.
Give us strength every morning.
Save us when we are in trouble.
³Your powerful voice makes people run away
in fear;
your greatness causes the nations to run away.
⁴Like locusts, *d* your enemies will take away
the things you stole in war.
Like locusts rushing about, they will take
your wealth.
⁵The LORD is very great, and he lives in a high
place.
He fills Jerusalem with fairness and justice.
⁶He will be your safety.
He is full of salvation, wisdom and
knowledge.
Respect for the LORD is the greatest treasure.

⁷See, brave men are crying out in the streets;
those who tried to bring peace are crying
loudly.
⁸There is no one on the roads,
no one walking in the paths.
People have broken the agreements they
made.
They refuse to believe the proof from
witnesses.
No one respects other people.
⁹The land is sick and dying;
Lebanon is ashamed and dying.
The Plain of Sharon is dry like the desert,
and the trees of Bashan and Carmel are
dying.

¹⁰The LORD says, "Now, I will stand up
and show my greatness.
Now, I will become important to the
people.
¹¹You people do useless things
that are like hay and straw.
A destructive wind will burn you
like fire.
¹²People will be burned until their bones
become like lime;
they will burn quickly like dry
thorn-bushes."

¹³You people in faraway lands, hear what I
have done.
You people who are near me, learn about
my power.
¹⁴The sinners in Jerusalem are afraid;
those who are separated from God shake
with fear.
They say, "Can any of us live through this
fire that destroys?
Who can live near this fire that burns on
and on?"
¹⁵A person who does what is right
and speaks what is right,
who refuses to take money unfairly,
who refuses to take money to hurt
others,
who does not listen to plans of murder,
who refuses to think about evil—
¹⁶this is the kind of person who will be safe.
He will be protected as he would be in a
high, walled city.
He will always have bread,
and he will not run out of water.
¹⁷Your eyes will see the king in his beauty.
You will see the land that stretches far away.
¹⁸You will think about the terror of the past:
"Where is that officer?
Where is the one who collected the
taxes?
Where is the officer in charge of our
defence towers?"
¹⁹No longer will you see those proud people
from other countries,
whose strange language you couldn't
understand.

God will Protect Jerusalem

²⁰Look at Jerusalem, the city of our festivals.
Look at Jerusalem, that beautiful place of
rest.
It is like a tent that will never be moved;
the pegs that hold her in place will never
be pulled up,
and her ropes will never be broken.
²¹There the LORD will be our Mighty One.
That land is a place with streams and wide
rivers,
but there will be no enemy boats on those
rivers;
no powerful ship will sail on them.
²²This is because the LORD is our judge.
The LORD makes our laws.
The LORD is our king.
He will save us.
²³You sailors from other lands, hear:
The ropes on your boats hang loose.
The mast is not held firm.
The sails are not spread open.

Then your great wealth will be divided.
　　There will be so much wealth that even
　　　　the crippled people will carry off a
　　　　share.
24No one living in Jerusalem will say, "I am
　　sick."
　　The people who live there will have their
　　　　sins forgiven.

God will Punish His Enemies

34 All you nations, come near and listen.
　　　　Pay attention, you peoples!
The earth and all the people in it should
　　listen,
　　the world and everything in it.
2The LORD is angry with all the nations;
　　he is angry with their armies.
　　He will destroy them and kill them all.
3Their bodies will be thrown outside.
　　The stink will rise from the bodies,
　　and the blood will flow down the
　　　　mountains.
4The sun, moon and stars will dissolve,
　　and the sky will be rolled up like a scroll.
　　The stars will fall
　　like dead leaves from a vine
　　or dried-up figs from a fig tree.
5The LORD's sword in the sky is covered with
　　　　blood.
　　It will cut through Edom
　　and destroy those people as an offering to
　　　　the LORD.
6The LORD's sword will be covered with blood;
　　it will be covered with fat,
　　with the blood from lambs and goats,
　　with the fat from the kidneys of rams.
This is because the LORD decided there will be
　　　　a sacrifice in Bozrah
　　and much killing in Edom.
7The oxen will be killed,
　　and the cattle and the strong bulls.
The land will be filled with their blood,
　　and the earth will be covered with
　　　　their fat.

8The LORD has chosen a time for
　　　　punishment.
　　He has chosen a year when people must
　　　　pay for the wrongs they did to
　　　　Jerusalem.
9Edom's rivers will be like hot tar.
　　Its earth will be like burning sulphur.
　　Its land will be like burning tar.
10The fires will burn night and day;
　　the smoke will rise from Edom for ever.
Year after year that land will be empty;
　　no one will ever travel through that land
　　　　again.

11Birds and small animals will own that land,
　　and owls and ravens will live there.
God will make it an empty wasteland;
　　it will have nothing left in it.
12The important people will have no one left to
　　　　rule them;
　　the leaders will all be gone.
13Thorns will take over the strong towers,
　　and wild bushes will grow in the walled
　　　　cities.
It will be a home for wild dogs
　　and a place for owls to live.
14Desert animals will live with the hyenas,
　　and wild goats will call to their friends.
Night animals will live there
　　and find a place of rest.
15Owls will nest there and lay eggs.
　　When the eggs open, the owls will gather
　　　　their young under their wings.
Hawks will gather
　　with their own kind.

16Look at the LORD's scroll and read what is
written there:
　　None of these will be missing;
　　none will be without its mate.
God has given the command,
　　so his Spirit d will gather them together.
17God has divided the land among them,
　　and he has given them each their
　　　　portion.
So they will own that land for ever
　　and will live there year after year.

God will Comfort His People

35 The desert and dry land will become
　　　　happy;
　　the desert will be glad and will produce
　　　　flowers.
Like a flower, 2it will have many blooms.
　　It will show its happiness, as if it were
　　　　shouting with joy.
It will be beautiful like the forest of
　　　　Lebanon,
　　as beautiful as the hill of Carmel and the
　　　　Plain of Sharon.
Everyone will see the glory of the LORD
　　and the splendour of our God.

3Make the weak hands strong
　　and the weak knees steady.
4Say to people who are frightened,
　　"Be strong. Don't be afraid.
Look, your God will come,
　　and he will punish your enemies.
He will make them pay for the wrongs
　　　　they did,
　　but he will save you."

⁵Then the blind people will see again,
and the deaf will hear.
⁶Crippled people will jump like deer,
and those who can't talk now will shout
with joy.
Water will flow in the desert,
and streams will flow in the dry land.
⁷The burning desert will have pools of water,
and the dry ground will have springs.
Where wild dogs once lived,
grass and water plants will grow.
⁸A road will be there;
this highway will be called "The Road to
Being Holy".
Evil people will not be allowed to walk on
that road;
only good people will walk on it.
No fools will go on it.
⁹No lions will be there,
nor will dangerous animals be on that road.
They will not be found there.
That road will be for the people God saves;

¹⁰ the people the LORD has freed will return
there.
They will enter Jerusalem with joy,
and their happiness will last for ever.
Their gladness and joy will fill them
completely,
and sorrow and sadness will go far away.

The Assyrians Invade Judah

36 During Hezekiah's fourteenth year as king, Sennacherib king of Assyria attacked all the fortified cities of Judah and captured them. ²The king of Assyria sent out his field commander with a large army from Lachish to King Hezekiah in Jerusalem. When the commander came near the waterway from the upper pool on the road where people do their laundry, he stopped. ³Eliakim, Shebna and Joah went out to meet him. Eliakim son of Hilkiah was the palace manager, Shebna was the royal secretary and Joah son of Asaph was the recorder.

DEPRESSION

Positive

"Are you sure you did the test properly?" Jan asked as she gently coaxed the instruction sheet out of Nicola's trembling hand. "Each one of these home kits is different, and you have to make sure you follow the directions." Jan began to read the instructions.

Nicola stood shaking as the tears ran silently down her cheeks. She could barely speak.

"I've taken this test three times, and it's the same every time." Nicola's voice began to crack. "I'm pregnant. I'm going to have a baby. But I don't want a baby . . . not now. I'm only sixteen years old. Jan, I'm so afraid, and so sad. Why did this have to happen to me?"

Nicola walked across the room and collapsed into the old brown chair that had comforted her so many times when she was a little girl. But there was no comfort in that chair now. With no words left, Jan quietly sat down next to Nicola, put her arms round her and began to pray.

Nicola's pregnancy may cause her to face many bouts of depression, but God can help her. Read **Isaiah 35** to discover the comfort that God can bring for Nicola and others who turn to him.

* If you could talk to Nicola, which verses of Isaiah 35 would you use to encourage her?
* Think about how you feel when you're depressed. What does Isaiah 35 say to you about your depression?

Consider . . .

* suggesting that your youth leader put a box marked "Teenage Problems" in your church, and encouraging group members to submit, anonymously, any situations they are having problems with. Spend time each week discussing the problems and finding biblical solutions.
* talking to a trusted friend about the cause of your depression.

For more, see . . .

* Job 19:7–27 (p.481)
* 2 Corinthians 1:3–5 (p.1241)

* Psalm 88 (p.552)

⁴The field commander said to them, "Tell Hezekiah this:

"'The great king, the king of Assyria, says: What can you trust in now? ⁵You say you have battle plans and power for war, but your words mean nothing. Whom are you trusting for help so that you turn against me? ⁶Look, you are depending on Egypt to help you, but Egypt is like a splintered walking stick. If you lean on it for help, it will stab your hand and hurt you. The king of Egypt will hurt all those who depend on him. ⁷You might say, "We are depending on the LORD our God," but Hezekiah destroyed the LORD's altars and the places of worship. Hezekiah told Judah and Jerusalem, "You must worship only at this one altar."

⁸"'Now make an agreement with my master, the king of Assyria: I will give you 2,000 horses if you can find enough men to ride them. ⁹You cannot defeat one of my master's least important officers, so why do you depend on Egypt to give you chariots and horsemen? ¹⁰I have not come to attack and destroy this country without an order from the LORD. The LORD himself told me to come to this country and destroy it.'"

¹¹Then Eliakim, Shebna and Joah said to the field commander, "Please speak to us in the Aramaic language. We understand it. Don't speak to us in Hebrew, because the people on the city wall can hear you."

¹²But the commander said, "My master did not send me to tell these things only to you and your king. He sent me to speak also to those people sitting on the wall who will have to eat their own dung and drink their own urine like you."

¹³Then the commander stood and shouted loudly in the Hebrew language, "Listen to what the great king, the king of Assyria says. ¹⁴The king says you should not let Hezekiah fool you, because he can't save you. ¹⁵Don't let Hezekiah talk you into trusting the LORD by saying, "The LORD will surely save us. This city won't be handed over to the king of Assyria.'

¹⁶"Don't listen to Hezekiah. The king of Assyria says, 'Make peace with me, and come out of the city to me. Then everyone will be free to eat the fruit from his own grapevine and fig tree and to drink water from his own well. ¹⁷After that I will come and take you to a land like your own—a land with grain and new wine, bread and vineyards.'

¹⁸"Don't let Hezekiah fool you, saying, 'The LORD will save us.' Has a god of any other nation saved his people from the power of the king of Assyria? ¹⁹Where are the gods of Hamath and Arpad? Where are the gods of Sepharvaim? They did not save Samaria from my power. ²⁰Not one

of all the gods of these countries has saved his people from me. Neither can the LORD save Jerusalem from my power."

²¹The people were silent. They didn't answer the commander at all, because King Hezekiah had ordered, "Don't answer him."

²²Then Eliakim, Shebna and Joah tore their clothes to show how upset they were. (Eliakim son of Hilkiah was the palace manager, Shebna was the royal secretary and Joah son of Asaph was the recorder.) The three men went to Hezekiah and told him what the field commander had said.

Hezekiah Asks God to Help

37 When King Hezekiah heard the message, he tore his clothes and put on rough cloth to show how sad he was. Then he went into the Temple^d of the LORD. ²Hezekiah sent Eliakim, the palace manager, and Shebna, the royal secretary, and the older priests to Isaiah. They were all wearing rough cloth when they came to Isaiah the prophet,^d the son of Amoz. ³They told Isaiah, "This is what Hezekiah says: Today is a day of sorrow and punishment and disgrace, as when a child should be born, but the mother is not strong enough to give birth to it. ⁴The king of Assyria sent his field commander to make fun of the living God. Maybe the LORD your God will hear what the commander said and will punish him for it. So pray for the few of us who are left alive."

⁵When Hezekiah's officers came to Isaiah, ⁶he said to them, "Tell your master this: The LORD says, 'Don't be afraid of what you have heard. Don't be frightened by the words the servants of the king of Assyria have spoken against me. ⁷Listen! I am going to put a spirit in the king of Assyria. He will hear a report that will make him return to his own country, and I will cause him to die by the sword there.'"

⁸The field commander heard that the king of Assyria had left Lachish. When he went back, he found the king fighting against the city of Libnah.

⁹The king received a report that Tirhakah, the Cushite king of Egypt, was coming to attack him. When the king of Assyria heard this, he sent messengers to Hezekiah, saying, ¹⁰"Tell Hezekiah king of Judah: don't be fooled by the god you trust. Don't believe him when he says Jerusalem will not be handed over to the king of Assyria. ¹¹You have heard what the kings of Assyria have done. They have completely defeated every country, so do not think you will be saved. ¹²Did the gods of those people save them? My ancestors destroyed them, defeating the cities of Gozan, Haran and Rezeph, and the people of

Eden living in Tel Assar. ¹³Where are the kings of Hamath and Arpad? Where are the kings of Sepharvaim, Hena and Ivvah?"

Hezekiah Prays to the LORD

¹⁴When Hezekiah received the letter from the messengers and read it, he went up to the Temple*d* of the LORD. He spread the letter out before the LORD ¹⁵and prayed to the LORD: ¹⁶"LORD All-powerful, you are the God of Israel, whose throne is between the gold creatures with wings, only you are God of all the kingdoms of the earth. You made the heavens and the earth. ¹⁷Hear, LORD, and listen. Open your eyes, LORD, and see. Listen to all the words Sennacherib has said to insult the living God.

¹⁸"It is true, LORD, that the kings of Assyria have destroyed all these countries and their lands. ¹⁹They have thrown the gods of these nations into the fire, but they were only wood and rock statues that people made. So the kings have destroyed them. ²⁰Now, LORD our God, save us from the king's power so that all the kingdoms of the earth will know that you, LORD, are the only God."

The LORD Answers Hezekiah

²¹Then Isaiah son of Amoz sent a message to Hezekiah that said, "This is what the LORD, the God of Israel, says: "You prayed to me about Sennacherib king of Assyria. ²²So this is what the LORD has said against Sennacherib:

The people of Jerusalem
  hate you and make fun of you;
the people of Jerusalem
  laugh at you as you run away.
²³You have insulted me and spoken against me;
  you have raised your voice against me.
You have a proud look on your face,
  which is against me, the Holy One of
    Israel!
²⁴You have sent your messengers to insult the
  Lord.
You have said, "With my many chariots
I have gone to the tops of the mountains,
  to the highest mountains of Lebanon.
I have cut down its tallest cedars
  and its best pine trees.
I have gone to its greatest heights
  and its best forests.
²⁵I have dug wells in foreign countries
  and drunk water there.
By the soles of my feet,
  I have dried up all the rivers of Egypt."

²⁶" 'King of Assyria, surely you have heard.
Long ago I, the LORD, planned these
  things.

Long ago I designed them,
  and now I have made them
    happen.
I allowed you to turn those fortified cities
  into piles of rocks.
²⁷The people in those cities were weak;
  they were frightened and put to shame.
They were like grass in the field,
  like tender, young grass,
like grass on the housetop
  that is burned by the wind before it can
    grow.

²⁸" 'I know when you rest,
  when you come and go,
  and how you rage against me.
²⁹Because you rage against me,
  and because I have heard your proud
    words,
I will put my hook in your nose
  and my bit in your mouth.
Then I will force you to leave my country
  the same way you came.'

³⁰"Then the LORD said, 'Hezekiah, I will give you this sign:
This year you will eat the grain that grows
  wild,
  and the second year you will eat what
    grows wild from that.
But in the third year, plant grain and
  harvest it.
Plant vineyards and eat their fruit.
³¹Some of the people in the family of Judah
  will escape.
Like plants that take root,
  they will grow strong and have many
    children.
³²A few people will come out of Jerusalem
  alive;
  a few from Mount Zion *d* will live.
The strong love of the LORD All-powerful
  will make this happen.'

³³"So this is what the LORD says about the king of Assyria:
'He will not enter this city
  or even shoot an arrow here.
He will not fight against it with shields
  or build a ramp to attack the city walls.
³⁴He will return to his country the same way
  he came,
  and he will not enter this city,'
  says the LORD.
³⁵'I will defend and save this city
  for my sake and for David, my servant.' "

³⁶Then the angel of the LORD went out and killed 185,000 men in the Assyrian camp. When

the people got up early the next morning, they saw all the dead bodies. ³⁷So Sennacherib king of Assyria left and went back to Nineveh and stayed there.

³⁸One day as Sennacherib was worshipping in the temple of his god Nisroch, his sons Adrammelech and Sharezer killed him with a sword. Then they escaped to the land of Ararat. So Sennacherib's son Esarhaddon became king of Assyria.

Hezekiah's Illness

38 At that time Hezekiah became very sick; he was almost dead. The prophet *d* Isaiah son of Amoz went to see him and told him, "This is what the LORD says: Make arrangements, because you are not going to live, but die."

²Hezekiah turned towards the wall and prayed to the LORD, ³"LORD, please remember that I have always obeyed you. I have given myself completely to you and have done what you said was right." Then Hezekiah cried loudly.

⁴Then the LORD spoke his word to Isaiah: ⁵"Go to Hezekiah and tell him: 'This is what the LORD, the God of your ancestor David, says: I have heard your prayer and seen your tears. So I will add fifteen years to your life. ⁶I will save you and this city from the king of Assyria; I will defend this city.

⁷" 'The LORD will do what he says. This is the sign from the LORD to show you: ⁸the sun has made a shadow go down the stairway of Ahaz, but I will make it go back ten steps.' " So the shadow made by the sun went back up the ten steps it had gone down.

⁹After Hezekiah king of Judah got well, he wrote this song:

¹⁰I said, "I am in the middle of my life.
   Do I have to go through the gates of death?
   Will I have the rest of my life taken away
      from me?"
¹¹I said, "I will not see the LORD
   in the land of the living again.

DEATH

Old Before I Die

"I hope I'm old before I die." So sang Robbie Williams in an effort to get away from the old rebel teenage thought of dying before you got too old.

In Isaiah 38:1–9 Hezekiah King of Judah had been having a bad time, he'd been really sick and thought he was about to die. But the Lord had other ideas and sent Isaiah to tell Hezekiah to "make other plans" because God was going to heal him! The king was so overjoyed, that once he was well again, he wrote a song!

There are always times when we feel that life is not worth living. Robbie, who went to numerous detox centres, must have felt the same. But when threatened with death, we cling on and on because we don't want to lose our life.

Hezekiah sang about people he loved, his home, and the fact that he was only in the middle of his life – this was no time to die!

For Robbie, death was a serious threat and to the King of Judah it was a foregone conclusion, but they both recovered.

And they both wanted to sing about it!

Read Hezekiah's lyrics in **Isaiah 38:9–20**.

* What did Hezekiah suggest we do about life, in Isaiah 38:19.
* What different ways can you think of to celebrate life?

Consider . . .

* visiting and giving some encouragement to someone who has a serious illness that may be making them depressed.
* giving some financial help to an organisation helping the desperate, such as the Samaritans.

For more, see . . .

* Proverbs 20:29 (p.607)
* 2 Corinthians 4:16–17 (p.1244)

* 2 Corinthians 1:8–10 (p.1241)

I will not again see the people
who live on the earth.
[12]Like a shepherd's tent,
my home has been pulled down and taken
from me.
I am finished
like the cloth a weaver rolls up and cuts
from the loom [n]
In one day you brought me to this end.
[13]All night I cried loudly.
Like a lion, he crushed all my bones.
In one day you brought me to this end.
[14]I cried like a bird
and moaned like a dove.
My eyes became tired as I looked to the
heavens.
Lord, I have troubles. Please help me."

[15]What can I say?
The Lord told me what would happen and
then made it happen.
I have had these troubles in my soul,
so now I will be humble all my life.
[16]Lord, because of you, people live.
Because of you, my spirit also lives;
you made me well and let me live.
[17]It was for my own good
that I had such troubles.
Because you love me very much,
you did not let me die
but threw my sins
far away.
[18]People in the place of the dead cannot
praise you;
those who have died cannot sing praises
to you;
those who die don't trust you
to help them.
[19]The people who are alive are the ones who
praise you.
They praise you as I praise you today.
A father should tell his children
that you provide help.

[20]The LORD saved me,
so we will play songs on stringed instruments
in the Temple of the LORD
all the days of our lives.

[21]Then Isaiah said, "Make a paste from figs and
put it on Hezekiah's boil. Then he will get well."
[22]Hezekiah then asked Isaiah, "What will be the
sign? What will show that I will go up to the
Temple [d] of the LORD?"

Messengers from Babylon

39 At that time Merodach-Baladan son of
Baladan was king of Babylon. He sent

letters and a gift to Hezekiah, because he had
heard that Hezekiah had been sick and was now
well. [2]Hezekiah was pleased and showed the
messengers what was in his storehouses: the silver, gold, spices, expensive perfumes, his swords
and shields, and all his wealth. He showed them
everything in his palace and in his kingdom.

[3]Then Isaiah the prophet [d] went to King Hezekiah and asked him, "What did these men say?
Where did they come from?"

Hezekiah said, "They came from a faraway
country—from Babylon."

[4]So Isaiah asked him, "What did they see in
your palace?"

Hezekiah said, "They saw everything in my
palace. I showed them all my wealth."

> **Sidelight** Isaiah's vocal challenges
> to the different kings of
> Judah didn't make him popular (see Isaiah
> 39:1–8, for example). According to tradition, the
> evil king Manasseh had Isaiah killed by tying him
> between two planks of wood and sawing him
> in half.

[5]Then Isaiah said to Hezekiah: "Listen to the
words of the LORD All-powerful: [6]'In the future
everything in your palace and everything your
ancestors have stored up until this day will be
taken away to Babylon. Nothing will be left,' says
the LORD. [7]Some of your own children, those who
will be born to you, will be taken away, and they
will become servants in the palace of the king of
Babylon."

[8]Hezekiah told Isaiah, "These words from the
LORD are good." He said this because he thought,
"There will be peace and security in my lifetime."

> **Sidelight** There's an old saying
> "Every cloud has a silver
> lining". The "silver lining" in Isaiah begins at
> chapter 40 – good news after a long series of
> gloomy news bulletins.

Israel's Punishment will End

40 Your God says,
"Comfort, comfort my people.
[2]Speak kindly to the people of Jerusalem
and tell them
that their time of service is finished,
that they have paid for their sins,
that the LORD has punished Jerusalem
twice for every sin they did."

[m] A machine for making cloth from thread.

³This is the voice of one who calls out:
"Prepare in the desert
  the way for the LORD.
Make a straight road in the dry lands
  for our God.
⁴Every valley should be raised up,
  and every mountain and hill should be
    made flat.
The rough ground should be made level,
  and the rugged ground should be made
    smooth.
⁵Then the glory of the LORD will be shown,
  and all people together will see it.
The LORD himself said these things."

⁶A voice says, "Cry out!"
  Then I said, "What shall I cry out?"

"Say all people are like the grass,
  and all their glory is like the flowers of the
    field.

⁷The grass dies and the flowers fall
  when the breath of the LORD blows on them.
  Surely the people are like grass.
⁸The grass dies and the flowers fall,
  but the word of our God will live for ever."
⁹Jerusalem, you have good news to tell.
  Go up on a high mountain.
Jerusalem, you have good news to tell.
  Shout out loud the good news.
Shout it out and don't be afraid.
  Say to the towns of Judah,
  "Here is your God."
¹⁰Look, the Lord GOD is coming with power
  to rule all the people.
Look, he will bring reward for his people;
  he will have their payment with him.
¹¹He takes care of his people like a shepherd.
  He gathers them like lambs in his arms
  and carries them close to him.
He gently leads the mothers of the lambs.

CELEBRATING

Ha!

Need a reason to laugh? Consider these.

* It takes 72 muscles to frown, but only fourteen to smile.
* Laughing relieves stress. After you laugh, your blood pressure briefly falls below normal, breathing slows, and tension subsides.
* A Stanford University doctor says that laughing 100 times each day is about the same amount of exercise as ten minutes of rowing a boat.
* Laughing may release natural painkillers in your body that have been found to combat arthritis and other painful conditions.
* "Happy patients usually work harder to recover," says the humour co-ordinator at a hospital in New York. So the hospital has a "humour room" where patients can benefit from funny books, tapes and music.
* You could get in the *Guinness Book of Records* by smiling longer than the current world record of ten hours and five minutes.

Isaiah 40:1–11 gives an even better reason to celebrate, smile and laugh with joy. Read a promise that will bring a smile to your face!

* What parts of this passage give you a good reason to laugh – or shout – with joyful celebration?
* How does it make you feel to know the promise of God's comfort and love that this passage celebrates?

Consider . . .

* keeping a "celebration first-aid kit" where you can put reminders of God's goodness to you. When you are feeling down, look through the kit to remind yourself that you have something to celebrate every day.
* throwing a party for friends just to have fun together.

For more, see . . .

* Ezra 6:13–22 (p.437)
* Romans 15:8–13 (p.1208)
* Luke 15 (p.1070)

God is Supreme

12Who has measured the oceans in the palm of
his hand?
Who has used his hand to measure
the sky?
Who has used a bowl to measure all the dust
of the earth
and scales to weigh the mountains and hills?
13Who has known the mind of the LORD
or been able to give him advice?
14Whom did he ask for help?
Who taught him the right way?
Who taught him knowledge
and showed him the way to understanding?

15The nations are like one small drop in a bucket;
they are no more than the dust on his
measuring scales.
To him the islands are no more than fine
dust on his scales.
16All the trees in Lebanon are not enough for
the altar fires,
and all the animals in Lebanon are not
enough for burnt offerings.
17Compared to the LORD all the nations are
worth nothing;
to him they are less than nothing.

18Can you compare God to anything?
Can you compare him to an image of
anything?
19An idol is formed by a craftsman,
and a goldsmith covers it with gold
and makes silver chains for it.
20A poor person cannot buy those expensive
statues,
so he finds a tree that will not rot.
Then he finds a skilled craftsman
to make it into an idol that will not fall over.

21Surely you know. Surely you have heard.
Surely from the beginning someone told you.
Surely you understand how the earth was
created.
22God sits on his throne above the circle of the
earth,
and compared to him, people are like
grasshoppers.
He stretches out the skies like a piece of cloth
and spreads them out like a tent to sit
under.
23He makes rulers unimportant
and the judges of this world worth nothing.
24They are like plants that are placed in the
ground,
like seeds that are planted.
As soon as they begin to grow strong,
he blows on them and they die,
and the wind blows them away like chaff. *d*

25God, the Holy One, says, "Can you compare
me to anyone?
Is anyone equal to me?"
26Look up to the skies.
Who created all these stars?
He leads out the army of heaven one by one
and calls all the stars by name.
Because he is strong and powerful,
not one of them is missing.

27People of Jacob, why do you complain?
People of Israel, why do you say,
"The LORD does not see what happens to me;
he does not care if I am treated fairly"?
28Surely you know.
Surely you have heard.
The LORD is the God who lives for ever,
who created all the world.
He does not become tired or need to rest.
No one can understand how great his
wisdom is.
29He gives strength to those who are tired
and more power to those who are weak.
30Even children become tired and need to rest,
and young people trip and fall.
31But the people who trust the LORD will
become strong again.
They will rise up as an eagle in the sky;
they will run and not need rest;
they will walk and not become tired.

The LORD will Help Israel

41 The LORD says, "Faraway countries,
listen to me.
Let the nations become strong.
Come to me and speak;
we will meet together to decide who is
right.

2"Who caused the one to come from
the east?
Who gives him victories everywhere he
goes?
The one who brought him gives nations over
to him
and defeats kings.
He uses his sword, and kings become like
dust.
He uses his bow, and they are blown away
like chaff. *d*
3He chases them and is never hurt,
going places he has never been before.
4Who caused this to happen?
Who has controlled history since the
beginning?
I, the LORD, am the one. I was here at the
beginning,
and I will be here when all things are
finished."

[5]All you faraway places, look and be afraid;
    all you places far away on the earth, shake
        with fear.
Come close and listen to me.
[6] The workers help each other
    and say to each other, "Be strong!"
[7]The craftsman encourages the goldsmith,
    and the workman who smooths the metal
        with a hammer encourages the one
        who shapes the metal.
He says, "This metal work is good."
    He nails the statue to a base so it can't fall
        over.

Only the LORD Can Save Us

[8]The LORD says, "People of Israel, you are my
        servants.
    People of Jacob, I chose you.
    You are from the family of my friend
        Abraham.
[9]I took you from places far away on the
        earth
    and called you from a faraway country.
I said, 'You are my servants.'
    I have chosen you and have not turned
        against you.
[10]So don't worry, because I am with you.
    Don't be afraid, because I am your God.
I will make you strong and will help you;
    I will support you with my right hand that
        saves you.

[11]"All those people who are angry with you
    will be ashamed and disgraced.
Those who are against you
    will disappear and be lost.
[12]You will look for your enemies,
    but you will not find them.
Those who fought against you
    will vanish completely.
[13]I am the LORD your God,
    who holds your right hand,
and I tell you, 'Don't be afraid.
    I will help you.'
[14]You few people of Israel who are left,
        do not be afraid even though you are weak
            as a worm.
    I myself will help you," says the LORD.
    "The one who saves you is the Holy One of
        Israel.
[15]Look, I have made you like a new threshing[d]
        board
    with many sharp teeth.
So you will walk on mountains and crush
        them;
    you will make the hills like chaff. [d]

[16]You will throw them into the air, and the
        wind will carry them away;
    a windstorm will scatter them.
Then you will be happy in the LORD;
    you will be proud of the Holy One
        of Israel.

[17]"The poor and needy people look for water,
    but they can't find any.
    Their tongues are dry with thirst.
But I, the LORD, will answer their prayers;
    I, the God of Israel, will not leave them to
        die.
[18]I will make rivers flow on the dry hills
    and springs flow through the valleys.
I will change the desert into a lake of
        water
    and the dry land into fountains of
        water.
[19]I will make trees grow in the desert—
    cedars, acacia, myrtle and olive trees.
I will put pine, fir and cypress trees
    growing together in the desert.
[20]People will see these things and
        understand;
    they will think carefully about these things
        and learn
    that the LORD's power did this,
    that the Holy One of Israel made these
        things."

The LORD Challenges False Gods

[21]The LORD says, "Present your case."
    The King of Jacob says, "Tell me your
        arguments.
[22]Bring in your idols to tell us
    what is going to happen.
Have them tell us what happened in the
        beginning.
    Then we will think about these things,
    and we will know how they will turn
        out.
Or tell us what will happen in the future.
[23] Tell us what is coming next
    so we will believe that you are gods.
Do something, whether it is good or bad,
    and make us afraid.
[24]You gods are less than nothing;
    you can't do anything.
    Those who worship you should be hated.

[25]"I have brought someone to come out of the
        north. [n]
    I have called by name a man from the east,
        and he knows me.
He walks on kings as if they were mud,
    just as a potter walks on the clay.

---

someone . . . north   This probably means Cyrus, a king of Persia.

²⁶Who told us about this before it happened?
    Who told us ahead of time so we could
        say, 'He was right'?
  None of you told us anything;
    none of you told us before it happened;
    no one heard you tell about it.
²⁷I, the LORD, was the first one to tell Jerusalem
    that the people were coming home.
  I sent a messenger to Jerusalem with the
    good news.
²⁸I look at the idols, but there is not one that
    can answer.
  None of them can give advice;
    none of them can answer my questions.
²⁹Look, all these idols are false.
  They cannot do anything;
  they are worth nothing.

The LORD's Special Servant

42 "Here is my servant, the one I support.
    He is the one I chose, and I am
      pleased with him.
I have put my Spirit *d* upon him,
  and he will bring justice to all
    nations.
²He will not cry out or yell
  or speak loudly in the streets.
³He will not break a crushed blade
    of grass
  or put out even a weak flame.
He will truly bring justice;
⁴ he will not lose hope or give up
  until he brings justice to the world.
  And people far away will trust his
    teachings."

SERVICE

Called to Compassion

Claudia was blind, autistic and in pain. Put in an institution when she was young, Claudia was angry and withdrawn. She would scream, eat her clothes, and refuse to co-operate with others.

When Claudia was fifteen she was still blind, and she was still autistic. She still could not really communicate with people, but she was peaceful, loving and trusting.

What had changed?

When she was nine or ten, Claudia became part of a l'Arche community in Honduras. The love, compassion and care she experienced in this Christian community helped her to discover inner peace.

Founded by Canadian-born Jean Vanier, more than seventy l'Arche (which means "the Ark" in French) communities around the world are home to people with learning disabilities who are forgotten or rejected by their society. For about thirty years, Vanier has given his life to these "little people", as he calls them.

For Vanier, his work is his ministry in Christ's name. "When we love others," Vanier says, "we can walk with them and share their pain . . . I believe that Jesus is calling us to be men and women of compassion, to walk with people in their pain . . . And then we discover how the pain and the cross are intimately linked with the joy of the resurrection."

Through his work with people who have learning disabilities around the world, Jean Vanier lives a life that reflects the spirit of **Isaiah 42:1–9**, which promises a special servant who would lead the people – a promise that was fulfilled in Jesus Christ.

* What parallels are there between the ministry of Jean Vanier and the description in the passage?
* How can you follow in the footsteps of the special servant described in the passage?

Consider . . .

* giving a few hours of your free time to work with people who have learning disabilities in your community. Afterwards, talk to a parent, friend, or trusted adult about the experience.
* reaching out to someone in need even when it may be inconvenient for you.

For more, see . . .

* Deuteronomy 11:13–15 (p.176)
* 1 Corinthians 9:19–23 (p.1227)

* 1 Samuel 3:1–10 (p.258)

⁵God, the LORD, said these things.
He created the skies and stretched them out.
  He spread out the earth and everything
    on it.
He gives life to all people on earth,
  to everyone who walks on the earth.
⁶The LORD says, "I, the LORD, called you to do
    right,
  and I will hold your hand
and protect you.
  You will be the sign of my agreement with
    the people,
  a light to shine for all people.
⁷You will help the blind to see.
  You will free those who are in prison,
  and you will lead those who live in darkness
    out of their prison.

⁸"I am the LORD. That is my name.
  I will not give my glory to another;
  I will not let idols take the praise that
    should be mine.
⁹The things I said would happen have happened,
  and now I tell you about new things.
Before those things happen,
  I tell you about them."

A Song of Praise to the LORD

¹⁰Sing a new song to the LORD;
  sing his praise everywhere on the earth.
Praise him, you people who sail on the seas
    and you animals who live in them.
  Praise him, you people living in faraway
    places.
¹¹The deserts and their cities should
    praise him.
  The settlements of Kedar should praise him.
The people living in Sela should sing for joy;
  they should shout from the mountain tops.
¹²They should give glory to the LORD.
  People in faraway lands should praise him.
¹³The LORD will march out like a strong soldier;
  he will be excited like a man ready to fight
    a war.
He will shout out the battle cry
  and defeat his enemies.

¹⁴The LORD says, "For a long time I have said
    nothing;
  I have been quiet and held myself back.
But now I will cry out
  and strain like a woman giving birth to a
    child.
¹⁵I will destroy the hills and mountains
  and dry up all their plants.
I will make the rivers become dry land
  and dry up the pools of water.
¹⁶Then I will lead the blind along a way they
    never knew;

I will guide them along paths they have not
    known.
I will make the darkness become light for
    them,
  and the rough ground smooth.
These are the things I will do;
  I will not leave my people.
¹⁷But those who trust in idols,
  who say to their statues,
'You are our gods'
  will be rejected in disgrace.

Israel Refused to Listen to the LORD

¹⁸"You who are deaf, hear me.
  You who are blind, look and see.
¹⁹No one is more blind than my servant Israel
  or more deaf than the messenger I send.
No one is more blind than the person I own
  or more blind than the servant of the LORD.
²⁰Israel, you have seen much, but you have not
    obeyed.
  You hear, but you refuse to listen."
²¹The LORD made his teachings wonderful,
  because he is good.
²²These people have been defeated and robbed.
  They are trapped in pits
    or locked up in prison.
Like robbers, enemies have taken them away,
  and there is no one to save them.
Enemies carried them off,
  and no one said, "Bring them back."

²³Will any of you listen to this?
  Will you listen carefully in the future?
²⁴Who let the people of Jacob be carried off?
  Who let robbers take Israel away?
The LORD allowed this to happen,
  because we sinned against him.
We did not live the way he wanted us to live
  and did not obey his teaching.
²⁵So he became very angry with us
  and brought terrible wars against us.
It was as if the people of Israel had fire all
    around them,
  but they didn't know what was happening.
It was as if they were burning,
  but they didn't pay any attention.

God is Always with His People

43 Now this is what the LORD says.
  He created you, people of Jacob;
he formed you, people of Israel.
He says, "Don't be afraid, because I have
    saved you.
  I have called you by name, and you are
    mine.
²When you pass through the waters, I will be
    with you.
  When you cross rivers, you will not drown.

When you walk through fire, you will not be
burnt,
nor will the flames hurt you.
³This is because I, the LORD, am your God,
the Holy One of Israel, your Saviour.
I gave Egypt to pay for you,
and I gave Cush and Seba to make you
mine.
⁴Because you are precious to me,
because I give you honour and
love you,
I will give other people in your place;
I will give other nations to save your life.
⁵Don't be afraid, because I am with you.
I will bring your children from the east
and gather you from the west.
⁶I will tell the north: give my people to me.
I will tell the south: don't keep my people
in prison.
Bring my sons from far away
and my daughters from faraway places.
⁷Bring to me all the people who are mine,
whom I made for my glory,
whom I formed and made."

Judah is God's Witness

⁸Bring out the people who have eyes but
don't see
and those who have ears but don't hear.
⁹All the nations gather together,
and all the people come together.
Which of their gods said this would
happen?
Which of their gods can tell what happened
in the beginning?
Let them bring their witnesses to prove they
were right.
Then others will say, "It is true."
¹⁰The LORD says, "You are my witnesses
and the servant I chose.
I chose you so you would know and
believe me,
so you would understand that I am the
true God.
There was no God before me,
and there will be no God after me.
¹¹I myself am the LORD;
I am the only Saviour.
¹²I myself have spoken to you, saved you and
told you these things.
It was not some foreign god among you.
You are my witnesses, and I am God,"
says the LORD.
¹³ "I have always been God.
No one can save people from my power;
when I do something, no one can
change it."

¹⁴This is what the LORD, who saves you,
the Holy One of Israel, says:
"I will send armies to Babylon for you,
and I will knock down all its locked gates.
The Babylonians will shout their cries of sorrow.
¹⁵I am the LORD, your Holy One,
the Creator of Israel, your King."

God will Save His People Again

¹⁶This is what the LORD says.
He is the one who made a road through
the sea
and a path through rough waters.
¹⁷He is the one who defeated the chariots and
horses
and the mighty armies.
They fell together and will never rise again.
They were destroyed as a flame is put out.
¹⁸The LORD says, "Forget what happened
before,
and do not think about the past.
¹⁹Look at the new thing I am going to do.
It is already happening. Don't you see it?
I will make a road in the desert
and rivers in the dry land.
²⁰Even the wild animals will be thankful
to me—
the wild dogs and owls.
They will honour me when I put water in
the desert
and rivers in the dry land
to give water to my people, the ones I chose.
21 The people I made
will sing songs to praise me.

²²"People of Jacob, you have not called to me;
people of Israel, you have become tired
of me.
²³You have not brought me your sacrifices of
sheep
nor honoured me with your sacrifices.
I did not weigh you down with sacrifices to
offer
or make you tired with incense ᵈ to burn.
²⁴So you did not buy incense for me;
you did not freely bring me fat from your
sacrifices.
Instead you have weighed me down with
your many sins;
you have made me tired of your many
wrongs.

²⁵"I, I am the One who forgives all your sins,
for my sake;
I will not remember your sins.
²⁶But you should remind me.
Let's meet and decide what is right.
Tell what you have done and show you are
right.

27Your first father sinned,
   and your leaders have turned against me.
28So I will make your holy rulers unholy.
   I will bring destruction on the people of
      Jacob,
   and I will let Israel be insulted."

The LORD is the Only God

44 The LORD says, "People of Jacob, you
         are my servants. Listen to me!
      People of Israel, I chose you."
2This is what the LORD says, who made you,
   who formed you in your mother's body,
   who will help you:
"People of Jacob, my servants, don't be afraid.
   Israel, I chose you.
3I will pour out water for the thirsty land
   and make streams flow on dry land.
   I will pour out my Spirit *d* into your children
   and my blessing on your descendants.

4Your children will grow like a tree in the
      grass,
   like poplar trees growing beside streams of
      water.
5One person will say, 'I belong to the LORD,'
   and another will use the name Jacob.
Another will sign his name 'I am the LORD's,'
   and another will use the name Israel."

6The LORD, the king of Israel,
   is the LORD All-powerful, who saves
      Israel.
This is what he says: "I am the beginning
      and the end.
   I am the only God.
7Who is a god like me?
   That god should come and prove it.
Let him tell and explain all that has
      happened since I set up my ancient
      people.

SIN

Taking the Weight Off

Miriam didn't want to be in home group. Lately, she had felt distant from God. As she took her coat off, her home group leader handed her paper and a pencil.

"Write down whatever's bothering you," Sarah said, "mistakes you've made or worries you have."

Miriam watched other people working on their lists. She thought about the party she had gone to two weeks earlier. The whole experience had made her feel cheap: as though she wasn't worthy of anyone's respect. She started writing: "acting wild", "going further than I wanted to".

"When we give our problems to God, he makes the weight lighter," Sarah said, after everyone had finished. She passed a metal wastebasket around the circle, and Miriam dropped her list in quickly. Sarah struck a match and set fire to the lists. As Miriam watched her list of sins burning, she felt God's love within her "burn away" the hurt of the sins she had committed. She took a deep breath and felt relieved for the first time in days. She realised that by admitting her mistakes to God she felt closer to him. Perhaps she could make a new start now.

Sin keeps people from being what God wants them to be. **Isaiah 43:16–25** reminds us that God is willing to forgive sin so that we can be close to him.

* How would Miriam have reacted to reading this passage?
* Which verses in this passage help you to understand God's forgiveness of your sin?

Consider . . .

* making a list of sins you've committed recently. Ask God to forgive you for each sin. Then burn the list in a metal dustbin outside.
* giving God a thank-you present because he forgives you. Choose a gift God would appreciate, such as something for the needy or a time commitment from you.

For more, see . . .

* Psalm 32:1–7 (p.518)   * Micah 7:18–20 (p.897)
* Romans 3:23–26 (p.1187)

He should also tell what will happen in the future.

⁸Don't be afraid! Don't worry!
I have always told you what will happen.
You are my witnesses.
There is no other God but me.
I know of no other Rock; *d* I am the only One."

Idols are Useless

⁹Some people make idols, but they are worth nothing.
People treasure them, but they are useless.
Those people are witnesses for the statues,
but those people cannot see.

They know nothing, so they will be ashamed.

¹⁰Who made these gods?
Who made these useless idols?
¹¹The workmen who made them will be ashamed,
because they are only human.
If they all would come together,
they would all be ashamed and afraid.

¹²One workman uses tools to heat iron,
and he works over hot coals.
With his hammer he beats the metal and makes a statue,
using his powerful arms.

SELF-ESTEEM

Chosen

Luke's self-confidence was low. To be honest, he was not a huge fan of how he looked and he really wished his hair did not do that odd frizzy thing. Though he had friends, he often felt nervous in a group and worried what other people thought of him. There were loads of things that he enjoyed, but he didn't think he was particularly good at any of them. He had never been chosen for anything, so never really volunteered for stuff either.

One thing that he loved was photography. It was something he could do on his own, and he enjoyed the craft of taking great pictures. His bedroom was covered in amazing photos and he had a real talent, though he doubted that was true.

One day his sister saw a leaflet advertising a competition for young photographers. She knew that Luke would never enter himself, so she copied some examples of his work and entered him without his knowledge.

Five weeks later Luke received a letter saying that he had been short-listed to win the competition and that he was invited to exhibit some of his work and attend an awards ceremony. He was deeply confused. Who had entered him, how had this happened and what would he do? His sister owned up and after much discussion, persuaded him to go for it.

The day of the exhibition came. Luke's work looked amazing professionally framed and displayed. There were many people there and he was very nervous. Incredibly, his name was read out as the winner. He was gobsmacked! For the first time in his life he had been chosen; he had won the prize. Instantly, Luke's confidence and belief in himself grew.
Read **Isaiah 44:1–8**. God has chosen his people. He has chosen you!

* Where do you get your confidence from? How you look? Maybe success at school or in sports?
* How does knowing that God has chosen you affect your belief in yourself?

Consider . . .

* flicking through the Bible and writing down as many verses as you can that speak of the fact that God has chosen us, that he loves us, that he delights in us. Pin this list up somewhere in your room.
* starting each day by thanking God that he has chosen you.

For more, see . . .

* Psalm 139 (p.581)
* Ephesians 2:10 (p.1271)

* Romans 8:15–17 (p.1195)

But when he becomes hungry, he loses his
power.
If he does not drink water, he becomes tired.

13Another workman uses a line and a
compass
to draw on the wood.
Then he uses his chisels to cut a statue
and his calipers to measure the statue.
In this way, the workman makes the wood
look exactly like a person,
and this statue of a person sits in the
house.
14He cuts down cedars
or cypress or oak trees.
Those trees grew by their own power in the
forest.
Or he plants a pine tree, and the rain
makes it grow.
15Then he burns the tree.
He uses some of the wood for a fire to
keep himself warm.
He also starts a fire to bake his bread.
But he uses part of the wood to make a god,
and then he worships it!
He makes the idol and bows down to it!
16The man burns half of the wood in the fire.
He uses the fire to cook his meat,
and he eats the meat until he is full.
He also burns the wood to keep himself
warm. He says,
"Good! Now I am warm. I can see because
of the fire's light."
17But he makes a statue from the wood that is
left and calls it his god.
He bows down to it and worships it.
He prays to it and says,
"You are my god. Save me!"
18Those people don't know what they are
doing. They don't understand!
It is as if their eyes are covered so they
can't see.
Their minds don't understand.
19They have not thought about these things;
they don't understand.
They have never thought to themselves,
"I burnt half of the wood in the fire
and used the hot coals to bake my bread.
I cooked and ate my meat.
And I used the wood that was left to make
this hateful thing.
I am worshipping a block of wood!"
20He doesn't know what he is doing;
his confused mind leads him the
wrong way.

He cannot save himself
or say, "This statue I am holding is a
false god."

The LORD is the True God

21"People of Jacob, remember these things!
People of Israel, remember you are my
servants.
I made you, and you are my servants.
So Israel, I will not forget you.
22I have swept away your sins like a big cloud;
I have removed your sins like a cloud that
disappears into the air.
Come back to me because I saved you."

23Skies, sing for joy because the LORD did great
things!
Earth, shout for joy, even in your deepest parts!
Sing, you mountains, with thanks to God.
Sing, too, you trees in the forest!
The LORD saved the people of Jacob!
He showed his glory when he saved Israel.
24This is what the LORD says, who saved you,
who formed you in your mother's body:
"I, the LORD, made everything,
stretching out the skies by myself
and spreading out the earth all alone.
25I show that the lying prophets' [d] signs
are false;
I make fools of those who do magic.
I confuse even wise men;
they think they know much, but I make
them look foolish.
26I make the messages of my servants come true;
I make the advice of my messengers come
true.
I say to Jerusalem,
'People will live in you again!'
I say to the towns of Judah,
'You will be built again!'
I say to Jerusalem's ruins,
'I will repair you.'
27I tell the deep waters, 'Become dry!
I will make your streams become dry!'
28I say of Cyrus, [n] 'He is my shepherd
and will do all that I want him to do.
He will say to Jerusalem, "You will be built
again!"
He will tell the Temple, [d] "Your foundations
will be rebuilt."'"

God Chooses Cyrus to Free Israel

45 This is what the LORD says to Cyrus,
his appointed king:
"I hold your right hand

Cyrus A king of Persia who ruled from about 550 to 530 BC.

and will help you defeat nations
and take away other kings' power.
I will open doors for you
so city gates will not stop you.
²I will go before you
and make the mountains flat.
I will break down the bronze gates of the cities
and cut through their iron bars.
³I will give you the wealth that is stored away
and the hidden riches
so you will know I am the LORD,
the God of Israel, who calls you by name.
⁴I do these things for my servants, the people
of Jacob,
and for my chosen people, the Israelites.
Cyrus, I call you by name,
and I give you a title of honour even though
you don't know me.
⁵I am the LORD. There is no other God;
I am the only God.
I will make you strong,
even though you don't know me,
⁶so that everyone will know
there is no other God.
From the east to the west they will know
I alone am the LORD.
⁷I made the light and the darkness.
I bring peace, and I cause troubles.
I, the LORD, do all these things.

⁸"Sky above, make victory fall like rain;
clouds, pour down victory.
Let the earth receive it,
and let salvation grow,
and let victory grow with it.
I, the LORD, have created it.

⁹"How terrible it will be for those who argue
with the God who made them.
They are like a piece of broken pottery
among many pieces.
The clay does not ask the potter,
'What are you doing?'
The thing that is made doesn't say to its
maker,
'You have no hands.'
¹⁰How terrible it will be for the child who says
to his father,
'Why are you giving me life?'
How terrible it will be for the child who says
to his mother,
'Why are you giving birth to me?'"

¹¹This is what the LORD,
the Holy One of Israel, and its Maker, says:
"You ask me about what will happen.
You question me about my children.
You give me orders about what I have
made.

¹²I made the earth
and all the people living on it.
With my own hands I stretched out the skies,
and I commanded all the armies in the sky.
¹³I will bring Cyrus to do good things,
and I will make his work easy.
He will rebuild my city
and set my people free
without any payment or reward.
The LORD All-powerful says this."

¹⁴The LORD says,
"The goods made in Egypt and Cush
and the tall people of Seba
will come to you
and will become yours.
The Sabeans will walk behind you,
coming along in chains.
They will bow down before you
and pray to you, saying,
'God is with you,
and there is no other God.'"

¹⁵God and Saviour of Israel,
you are a God that people cannot see.
¹⁶All the people who make idols will be put to
great shame;
they will go off together in disgrace.
¹⁷But Israel will be saved by the LORD,
and that salvation will continue for ever.
Never again will Israel be put to shame.

¹⁸The LORD created the heavens.
He is the God who formed the earth and
made it.
He did not want it to be empty,
but he wanted life on the earth.
This is what the LORD says:
"I am the LORD. There is no other God.
¹⁹I did not speak in secret
or hide my words in some dark place.
I did not tell the family of Jacob
to look for me in empty places.
I am the LORD, and I speak the truth;
I say what is right.

²⁰"You people who have escaped from other
nations,
gather together and come before me;
come near together.
People who carry idols of wood don't know
what they are doing.
They pray to a god who cannot save them.
²¹Tell these people to come to me.
Let them talk about these things together.
Who told you long ago that this would
happen?
Who told about it long ago?
I, the LORD, said these things.
There is no other God besides me.

I am the only good God. I am the Saviour.
There is no other God.

22"All people everywhere,
follow me and be saved.
I am God. There is no other God.
23I will make a promise by my own power,
and my promise is true;
what I say will not be changed.
I promise that everyone will bow before me
and will promise to follow me.
24People will say about me, 'Goodness and power
come only from the LORD.'"
Everyone who has been angry with him
will come to him and be ashamed.
25But with the LORD's help, the people of Israel
will be found to be good,
and they will praise him.

False Gods are Useless

46 Bel *d* and Nebo *d* bow down.
Their idols are carried by animals.
The statues are only heavy loads that must be
carried;
they only make people tired.

> **Sidelight** The god Bel wasn't nice
> (Isaiah 46:1). According to
> mythology, Bel killed a dragon-goddess named
> Tiamat, cut her up, and formed the universe
> from her remains.

2These gods will all bow down.
They cannot save themselves
but will all be carried away like prisoners.

3"Family of Jacob, listen to me!
All you people from Israel who are still
alive, listen!
I have carried you since you were born;
I have taken care of you from your birth.
4Even when you are old, I will be the same.
Even when your hair has turned grey, I will
take care of you.
I made you and will take care of you.
I will carry you and save you.

5"Can you compare me to anyone?
No one is equal to me or like me.
6Some people are rich with gold
and weigh their silver on the scales.
They hire a goldsmith, and he makes it into
a god.
Then they bow down and worship it.
7They put it on their shoulders and carry it.
They set it in its place, and there it stands;
it cannot move from its place.
People may yell at it, but it cannot answer.
It cannot save them from their troubles.

8"Remember this, and do not forget it!
Think about these things, you who turn
against God.
9Remember what happened long ago.
Remember that I am God, and there is no
other God.
I am God, and there is no one like me.
10From the beginning I told you what would
happen in the end.
A long time ago I told you things that have
not yet happened.
When I plan something, it happens.
What I want to do, I will do.
11I am calling a man from the east to carry out
my plan;
he will come like a hawk from a country
far away.
I will make what I have said come true;
I will do what I have planned.
12Listen to me, you stubborn people,
who are far from what is right.
13I will soon do the things that are right.
I will bring salvation soon.
I will save Jerusalem
and bring glory to Israel."

God will Destroy Babylon

47 The LORD says, "City of Babylon,
go down and sit in the earth.
People of Babylon, sit on the ground.
You are no longer the ruler.
You will no longer be called
tender or beautiful.
2 You must use large stones to grind grain
into flour.
Remove your veil and your nice skirts.
Uncover your legs and cross the rivers.
3People will see your nakedness;
they will see your shame.
I will punish you;
I will punish every one of you."

4Our Saviour is named the LORD All-powerful;
he is the Holy One of Israel.

5"Babylon, sit in darkness and say nothing.
You will no longer be called the queen of
kingdoms.
6I was angry with my people,
so I rejected those who belonged to me.
I gave them to you,
but you showed them no mercy.
You even made the old people
work very hard.
7You said, 'I will live for ever
as the queen.'
But you did not think about these things
or consider what would happen.

8"Now, listen, you lover of pleasure.
  You think you are safe.
You tell yourself,
  'I am the only important person.
I will never be a widow
  or lose my children.'
9Two things will happen to you suddenly, in a
    single day.
  You will lose your children and your husband.
These things will truly happen to you,
  in spite of all your magic,
  in spite of your powerful tricks.
10You do evil things, but you feel safe
  and say, 'No one sees what I do.'
Your wisdom and knowledge
  have fooled you.
You say to yourself,
  'I am God, and no one is equal to me.'
11But troubles will come to you,
  and you will not know how to stop them.
Disaster will fall on you,
  and you will not be able to keep it away.
You will be destroyed quickly;
  you will not even see it coming.

12"Keep on using your tricks
  and doing all your magic
  that you have used since you were young.
Maybe they will help you;
  maybe you will be able to scare someone.
13You are tired of the advice you have received.
So let those who study the sky—
  those who tell the future by looking at the
    stars and the new moons—
  let them save you from what is about to
    happen to you.
14But they are like straw;
  fire will quickly burn them up.
They cannot save themselves
  from the power of the fire.
They are not like coals that give warmth
  nor like a fire that you may sit beside.
15You have worked with these people,
  and they have been with you since you
    were young,
  but they will not be able to help you.
Everyone will go his own way,
  and there will be no one left to save you."

God Controls the Future

48 The LORD says, "Family of Jacob, listen
        to me.
  You are called Israel,
  and you come from the family of Judah.
You swear by the LORD's name
  and praise the God of Israel,
  but you are not honest or sincere.

2You call yourselves people of the holy city,
  and you depend on the God of Israel,
  who is named the LORD All-powerful.
3Long ago I told you what would happen.
  I said these things and made them known;
  suddenly I acted, and these things happened.
4I knew you were stubborn;
  your neck was like an iron muscle,
  and your head was like bronze.
5So a long time ago I told you about these things;
  I told you about them before they happened
so you couldn't say, 'My idols did this,
  and my wooden and metal statues made
    these things happen.'
6"You heard and saw everything that happened,
  so you should tell this news to others.
Now I will tell you about new things,
  hidden things that you don't know yet.
7These things are happening now, not long ago;
  you have not heard about them before today.
So you cannot say, 'We already knew about that.'
8But you have not heard me; you have not
    understood.
  Even long ago you did not listen to me.
I knew you would surely turn against me;
  you have fought against me since you were
    born.
9But for my own sake I will be patient.
  People will praise me for not becoming angry
    and destroying you.
10I have made you pure, but not by fire, as
    silver is made pure.
  I have purified you by giving you troubles.
11I do this for myself, for my own sake.
  I will not let people speak evil against me,
  and I will not let some god take my glory.

Israel will be Free

12"People of Jacob, listen to me.
  People of Israel, I have called you to be my
    people.
I am God;
  I am the beginning and the end.
13I made the earth with my own hands.
  With my right hand I spread out the skies.
When I call them,
  they come together before me."

14All of you, come together and listen.
  None of the gods said these things would
    happen.
The LORD has chosen someone
  to attack the Babylonians;
  he will carry out his wishes against Babylon.
15"I have spoken; I have called him. [n]
  I have brought him, and I will make him
    successful.

---

him This probably refers to Cyrus king of Persia.

[16]Come to me and listen to this.
  From the beginning I have spoken openly.
  From the time it began, I was there."

Now, the Lord GOD
  has sent me with his Spirit. *d*

[17]This is what the LORD, who saves you,
  the Holy One of Israel, says:
"I am the LORD your God,
  who teaches you to do what is good,
  who leads you in the way you should go.
[18]If you had obeyed me,
  you would have had peace like a
    full-flowing river.
  Good things would have flowed to you like
    the waves of the sea.
[19]You would have had many children,
  as many as the grains of sand.

They would never have died out
  nor been destroyed."

[20]My people, leave Babylon!
  Run from the Babylonians!
Tell this news with shouts of joy to the
    people;
  spread it everywhere on earth.
Say, "The LORD has saved his servants, the
    people of Jacob."
[21]They did not become thirsty when he led
    them through the deserts.
  He made water flow from a rock
    for them.
He split the rock,
  and water flowed out.

[22]"There is no peace for evil people," says the
  LORD.

FOLLOWING GOD

On a Mission

Joan was always a little bit strange. She was pretty religious, and some of her friends thought she was a bit intense. When she started saying that God was talking to her, her friends were even more puzzled. This religious stuff was for older people, monks and nuns, not twelve-year-old girls.

But Joan carried on, saying that she knew what it was she had to do in life, and that she was going to do it. As time went on, her friends thought it was just rubbish – she didn't seem to be doing anything different to them. Until one day, she went missing. Rumours flew around the village.

Then one night a royal herald (messenger) turned up and they got news that Joan had done exactly what she had been saying for years. She had gone to the king and crowned him. She had led an army and was defending her country against attackers.

This story may sound crazy – a seventeen-year-old girl leading an army – but it's true! It's the story of Joan of Arc. She lived in the 1400s, and was convinced that God had given her a mission to defend France (her country) against the English who had invaded. By the age of seventeen, she had led an army, had reinstated a French king, and was widely respected. Two years later, she was burned at the stake by the church who didn't know what to make of her. They thought she was wrong – but later apologised and remembered her as a saint.

Look at Isaiah 49:1–13. It talks of a God who gives people a mission in life – to be "a light for all nations to show people all over the world the way to be saved".

* What are some of the things that God asks of his servant?
* What is the end result?

Consider . . .

* what it is specifically that God might want you to do. It may not be leading an army, but what might it be?
* writing a list of the things you care about and seeing how they compare with the things that God talks about in the passage.

For more, see . . .

* Isaiah: 61:1–4 (p.705)
* Matthew 28:18–20 (p.995)

* Jeremiah 29:11–14 (p.749)

God Calls His Special Servant

49 All of you people in faraway places,
          listen to me.
Listen, all you nations far away.
Before I was born, the LORD called me to
          serve him.
     The LORD named me while I was still in my
          mother's body.
[2]He made my tongue like a sharp sword.
He hid me in the shadow of his hand.
He made me like a sharp arrow.
He hid me in the holder for his arrows.
[3]He told me, "Israel, you are my servant.
I will show my glory through you."
[4]But I said, "I have worked hard for nothing;
I have used all my power, but I did nothing
          useful.
But the LORD will decide what my work is
          worth;
     God will decide my reward."
[5]The LORD made me in the body of my mother
          to be his servant,
to lead the people of Jacob back to him
so that Israel might be gathered to him.
The LORD will honour me,
     and I will get my strength from my God.
[6]Now he told me,
"You are an important servant to me
     to bring back the tribes [d] of Jacob,
     to bring back the people of Israel who are
          left alive.
But, more importantly, I will make you a
          light for all nations
     to show people all over the world the way
          to be saved."

[7]The LORD who saves you
     is the Holy One of Israel.
He speaks to the one who is hated by the
          people,
     to the servant of rulers.
This is what he says: "Kings will see you and
          stand to honour you;
     great leaders will bow down before you,
because the LORD can be trusted.
     He is the Holy One of Israel, who has
          chosen you."

The Day of Salvation

[8]This is what the LORD says:
"At the right time I will hear your prayers.
     On the day of salvation I will help you.
I will protect you,
     and you will be the sign of my agreement
          with the people.
You will bring back the people to the land
     and give the land that is now ruined back
          to its owners.

[9]You will tell the prisoners, 'Come out of your
          prison.'
     You will tell those in darkness, 'Come into
          the light.'
The people will eat beside the roads,
     and they will find food even on bare hills.
[10]They will not be hungry or thirsty.
     Neither the hot sun nor the desert wind
          will hurt them.
The God who comforts them will lead them
     and guide them by springs of water.
[11]I will make my mountains into roads,
     and the roads will be raised up.
[12]Look, people are coming to me from far away,
     from the north and from the west,
     from Aswan in southern Egypt."

[13]Heavens and earth, be happy.
     Mountains, shout with joy,
because the LORD comforts his people
     and will have pity on those who suffer.

Jerusalem and Her Children

[14]But Jerusalem said, "The LORD has left me;
     the Lord has forgotten me."

[15]The LORD answers, "Can a woman forget the
          baby she nurses?
     Can she feel no kindness for the child to
          which she gave birth?
Even if she could forget her children,
     I will not forget you.
[16]See, I have written your name on my hand.
     Jerusalem, I always think about your walls.
[17]Your children will soon return to you,
     and the people who defeated you and
          destroyed you will leave.
[18]Look up and look around you.
     All your children are gathering to return
          to you."
The LORD says, "As surely as I live,
     your children will be like jewels
     that a bride wears proudly.

[19]"You were destroyed and defeated,
     and your land was made useless.
But now you will have more people than the
          land can hold,
     and those people who destroyed you will be
          far away.
[20]Children were born to you while you were sad,
     but they will say to you,
'This place is too small for us.
     Give us a bigger place to live.'
[21]Then you will say to yourself,
'Who gave me all these children?
I was sad and lonely,
     defeated and separated from my people.
So who reared these children?

I was left all alone.
  Where did all these children come from?' "

²²This is what the Lord GOD says:
  "See, I will lift my hand to signal the nations;
  I will raise my banner for all the people
      to see.
Then they will bring your sons back to you
      in their arms,
  and they will carry your daughters on their
      shoulders.
²³Kings will teach your children,
  and daughters of kings will take care of them.
They will bow down before you
  and kiss the ground at your feet.
Then you will know I am the LORD.
  Anyone who trusts in me will not be
      disappointed."

²⁴Can the wealth a soldier wins in war be
      taken away from him?
  Can a prisoner be freed from a powerful
      soldier?
²⁵This is what the LORD says:
  "The prisoners will be taken from the strong
      soldiers.
  What the soldiers have taken will be saved.
I will fight your enemies,
  and I will save your children.
²⁶I will force those who trouble you to eat
      their own flesh.
  Their own blood will be the wine that
      makes them drunk.
Then everyone will know
  I, the LORD, am the One who saves you;
  I am the Powerful One of Jacob who
      saves you."

Israel was Punished for Its Sin

50 This is what the LORD says:
  "People of Israel, you say I divorced
      your mother.
Then where is the paper that proves it?
Or do you think I sold you
  to pay a debt?
Because of the evil things you did, I sold you.
  Because of the times she turned against me,
      your mother was sent away.
²I came home and found no one there;
  I called, but no one answered.
Do you think I am not able to save you?
  Do I not have the power to save you?
Look, I need only to shout and the sea
      becomes dry.
I change rivers into a desert,
and their fish rot because there is no water;
  they die of thirst.
³I can make the skies dark;
  I can make them black like clothes of sadness."

God's Servant Obeys

⁴The Lord GOD gave me the ability to teach
  so that I know what to say to make the
      weak strong.
Every morning he wakes me.
  He teaches me to listen like a student.
⁵The Lord GOD helps me learn,
  and I have not turned against him
  nor stopped following him.
⁶I offered my back to those who beat me.
  I offered my cheeks to those who pulled
      my beard.
I won't hide my face from them
  when they make fun of me and spit at me.
⁷The Lord GOD helps me,
  so I will not be ashamed.
I will be determined,
  and I know I will not be disgraced.
⁸He shows that I am innocent, and he is
      close to me.
  So who can accuse me?
  If there is someone, let us go to court together.
If someone wants to prove I have done wrong,
  he should come and tell me.
⁹Look! It is the Lord GOD who helps me.
  So who can prove me guilty?
Look! All those who try will become useless
      like old clothes;
  moths will eat them.

¹⁰Who among you fears the LORD
  and obeys his servant?
That person may walk in the dark
  and have no light.
Then let him trust in the LORD
  and depend on his God.
¹¹But instead, some of you want to light your
      own fires
  and make your own light.
So, go, walk in the light of your fires,
  and trust your own light to guide you.
But this is what you will receive from me:
  you will lie down in a place of pain.

Jerusalem will be Saved

51 The LORD says, "Listen to me,
  those of you who try to live right
      and follow the LORD.
Look at the rock from which you were cut;
  look at the stone quarry from which you
      were dug.
²Look at Abraham, your ancestor,
  and Sarah, who gave birth to your ancestors.
Abraham had no children when I called him,
  but I blessed him and gave him many
      descendants. ᵈ
³So the LORD will comfort Jerusalem;
  he will show mercy to those who live in
      her ruins.

He will change her deserts into a garden like
        Eden;
    he will make her empty lands like the
        garden of the LORD.
People there will be very happy;
    they will give thanks and sing songs.

⁴"My people, listen to me;
    my nation, pay attention to me.
I will give the people my teachings,
    and my decisions will be like a light to all
        people.
⁵I will soon show that I do what is right.
    I will soon save you.
    I will use my power and judge all nations.
All the faraway places are waiting for me;
    they wait for my power to help them.
⁶Look up to the heavens.
    Look around you at the earth below.
The skies will disappear like clouds of smoke.
    The earth will become useless like old clothes,
    and its people will die like flies.

But my salvation will continue for ever,
    and my goodness will never end.

⁷"You people who know what is right should
        listen to me;
    you people who follow my teachings should
        hear what I say.
Don't be afraid of the evil things people say,
    and don't be upset by their insults.
⁸Moths will eat those people as if they were
        clothes,
    and worms will eat them as if they were wool.
But my goodness will continue for ever,
    and my salvation will continue from now on."

⁹Wake up, wake up, and use your strength,
        powerful LORD.
Wake up as you did in the old times,
    as you did a long time ago.
With your own power, you cut Rahab *d* into
        pieces
    and killed that sea monster.

REVENGE

Payback

Gavin woke up in the morning and, as usual, in his imagination, devised some terrible ways for the Millhouse gang to meet their ends. He rather hoped giant flying rats might eat them very slowly, swooping down to pick off an ear here and a finger there until they were no more, having first cried out for help in immense pain. Gavin was pulled back to reality by his mum's call from downstairs that his breakfast was ready.

Isaiah 50:4–9 does not tell us how to deal with a big bully if we're small or a white bully if we're black. In those cases, you should tell the teacher. Revenge is a blind alley.

It is a good passage to encourage you if you are being bullied, mocked and accused falsely because of your faith. It tells you to be a student of God and to look to him for support. If you are being bullied because you are teaching God's word or a Christian, then you should expect that people may make fun of you, and in some parts of the world even beat you (verse 6).

It is one of the most important passages in the Old Testament about Jesus – a passage Jesus lived out. He offered himself and did not hide.

- To whom do you think this passage applies? The world in general? Teachers of the Word of God? Followers of Jesus?
- Does God speak to you each morning as verse 5 suggests? Let God open your ears every day. Let his voice be the first voice you hear.

Consider . . .

- whether there is anyone on whom you really want revenge. Are you prepared to leave that to God for the sake of the gospel?
- how you would defend your faith with words in the law court mentioned in verse 8. How well would you do?

For more, see . . .

- Leviticus 19:17–18 (p.119)
- Acts 18:5–6 (p.1169)
- Matthew 5:38–42 (p.946)

¹⁰You dried up the sea
  and the waters of the deep ocean.
You made the deepest parts of the sea into a road
  for your people to cross over and be saved.
¹¹The people the LORD has freed will return
  and enter Jerusalem with joy.
Their happiness will last for ever.
They will have joy and gladness,

and all sadness and sorrow will be gone
  far away.
¹²The LORD says, "I am the one who comforts you.
  So why should you be afraid of people,
    who die?
  Why should you fear people who die like
    the grass?
¹³Have you forgotten the LORD who made you,
  who stretched out the skies
  and made the earth?
Why are you always afraid
  of those angry people who trouble you
  and who want to destroy?
But where are those angry people now?
¹⁴ People in prison will soon be set free;
they will not die in prison,
  and they will have enough food.
¹⁵I am the LORD your God,
  who stirs the sea and makes the waves roar.
  My name is the LORD All-powerful.
¹⁶I will give you the words I want you to say.
  I will cover you with my hands and
    protect you.
I made the heavens and the earth,
  and I say to Jerusalem, 'You are my people.'"

God Punished Israel

¹⁷Awake! Awake!
  Get up, Jerusalem.
The LORD was very angry with you;
  your punishment was like wine in a cup.
The LORD made you drink that wine;
  you drank the whole cup until you
    stumbled.
¹⁸Jerusalem had many people,
  but there was not one to lead her.
Of all the people who grew up there,
  no one was there to guide her.

¹⁹Troubles came to you two by two,
  but no one will feel sorry for you.
There was ruin and disaster, great hunger
  and fighting.
No one can comfort you.
²⁰Your people have become weak.
  They fall down and lie on every street
    corner,
  like animals caught in a net.
They have felt the full anger of the LORD
  and have heard God's angry shout.

²¹So listen to me, poor Jerusalem,
  you who are drunk but not from wine.
²²Your God will defend his people.
  This is what the LORD your God says:
  "The punishment I gave you is like a cup
    of wine.
  You drank it and could not walk straight.
But I am taking that cup of my anger away
    from you,
  and you will never be punished by my
    anger again.
²³I will now give that cup of punishment to
    those who gave you pain,
who told you,
  'Bow down so we can walk over you.'
They made your back like dirt for them to
    walk on;
  you were like a street for them to
    travel on."

Jerusalem will be Saved

52 Wake up, wake up, Jerusalem!
      Become strong!
Be beautiful again,
  holy city of Jerusalem.
The people who do not worship God and
    who are not pure
  will not enter you again.
²Jerusalem, you once were a prisoner.
  Now shake off the dust and stand up.
Jerusalem, you once were a prisoner.
  Now free yourself from the chains around
    your neck.
³This is what the LORD says:
"You were not sold for a price,
  so you will be saved without cost."
⁴This is what the Lord GOD says:
"First my people went down to Egypt
  to live.
Later Assyria made them slaves.

⁵"Now see what has happened," says the LORD.
  "Another nation has taken away my people
    for nothing.
This nation who rules them makes fun of
    me," says the LORD.
"All day long they speak against me.

⁶This has happened so my people will know
      who I am,
and so, on that future day, they will know
that I am the one speaking to them.
    It will really be me."

⁷How beautiful is the person
    who comes over the mountains to bring
      good news,
who announces peace
    and brings good news,
    who announces salvation
and says to Jerusalem,
    "Your God is King."
⁸Listen! Your guards are shouting.
    They are all shouting for joy!
They all will see with their own eyes
    when the LORD returns to Jerusalem.
⁹Jerusalem, your buildings are destroyed now,
    but shout and rejoice together,
because the LORD has comforted his people.
    He has saved Jerusalem.

¹⁰The LORD will show his holy power
    to all the nations.
Then everyone on earth
    will see the salvation of our God.

¹¹You people, leave, leave; get out of Babylon!
    Touch nothing that is unclean. *d*
You men who carry the LORD's things used in
      worship,
    leave there and make yourselves pure.
¹²You will not be forced to leave Babylon quickly;
    you will not be forced to run away,
because the LORD will go before you,
    and the God of Israel will guard you from
      behind.

The LORD's Suffering Servant

¹³The LORD says, "See, my servant will act
    wisely.
    People will greatly honour and respect him.
¹⁴Many people were shocked when they
    saw him.

FREEDOM

Chains

Katherine was a forty-year-old American woman, with a huge secret.

One day she threw a party and invited all her friends and relations, she even sent invitations to her husband and her children. Unbeknown to them, this was going to be the biggest day in Katherine's life.

When everyone arrived at the party they were puzzled. It wasn't her birthday, so what were they celebrating? Katherine stepped into the middle of them and began to confess to a horrendous story. She was on the FBI's most wanted list. She had been running from them for twenty-three years. She explained how she couldn't live with the terrible guilt any more. And then, to everyone's amazement, she picked up the phone and called the FBI and gave herself up.

The FBI came around to the house and in front of everyone she loved, Katherine gave herself up. Yet, in the newspaper the next day, there was a photograph of a woman grinning from ear to ear as she was being led away in handcuffs.

She was quoted saying, "I am now learning to live with openness and truth."

It was Katherine's first day of freedom in twenty-three years.

* Look at Isaiah 52:2. How does Katherine's story compare with Isaiah's?
* What are the "chains" that keep you from freedom?

Consider . . .

* writing down things in your life that make you feel guilty and stop you from following Jesus the way you really want to.
* taking a deep breath and confessing to a friend something that has made you feel bad. Then pray about it together.

For more, see . . .

* John 8:31–36 (p.1110)
* 1 John 1:9 (p.1371)

* Romans 6:15–23 (p.1192)

His appearance was so changed he did not
look like a man;

his form was changed so much they could
barely tell he was human.

15But now he will surprise many nations.
Kings will be amazed and shut their mouths.
They will see things they had not been told
about him,

and they will understand things they had
not heard."

53 Who would have believed what we
heard?

Who saw the LORD's power in this?

2He grew up like a small plant before the LORD,
like a root growing in a dry land.

He had no special beauty or form to make us
notice him;

there was nothing in his appearance to
make us desire him.

3He was hated and rejected by people.
He had much pain and suffering.

People would not even look at him.
He was hated, and we didn't even notice him.

4But he took our suffering on him
and felt our pain for us.

We saw his suffering
and thought God was punishing him.

5But he was wounded for the wrong we did;
he was crushed for the evil we did.

The punishment, which made us well, was
given to him,

and we are healed because of his wounds.

6We all have wandered away like sheep;
each of us has gone his own way.

But the LORD has put on him the
punishment

for all the evil we have done.

7He was beaten down and punished,
but he didn't say a word.

He was like a lamb being led to be killed.
He was quiet, as a sheep is quiet while its
wool is being cut;

he never opened his mouth.

8Men took him away roughly and unfairly.
He died without children to continue his
family.

JESUS CHRIST

What Love Looks Like

Robert was an "MK", a missionary kid; his parents served in South Asia. Sitting round a table with American friends one night, he and the others started talking about missions and how to know whether a person was "cut out" to be a missionary. Robert thought about his parents. He knew the commitment and love it took to be effective for Christ.

"It takes love to do missions," Robert stated. "And do you know what love looks like?

"Once I watched my dad hold a man's diseased feet in his hands," Robert continued. "The feet were swollen and full of pus, but he wasn't afraid to touch him, because he cared for that person. His only concern was loving that man like Jesus does. That's the kind of love I want to have."

Because of Jesus' deep love for us, he experienced extreme pain and suffering.
Isaiah 52:13—53:12 is a prophetic picture of this servant of God.

* How was the love of Robert's father for the sick man like the love of God's servant in this passage?
* What kind of suffering could you face as God's servant today?

Consider . . .

* writing a description of how Jesus might live today. What would he wear? How would he spend his time? With whom would he associate? Where would he go?
* adopting a person who serves God through mission work, ministry, or some kind of service by writing a note of appreciation, praying for the work he or she does, or offering your assistance.

For more, see . . .

* Isaiah 11:1–10 (p.652)
* Philippians 2:1–11 (p.1282)
* John 1:1–18 (p.1096)

He was put to death;
  he was punished for the sins of my people.
⁹He was buried with wicked men,
  and he died with the rich.
He had done nothing wrong,
  and he had never lied.

¹⁰But it was the LORD who decided
  to crush him and make him suffer.
The LORD made his life a penalty offering,
but he will still see his descendants *d* and live
  a long life.
He will complete the things the LORD wants
  him to do.
¹¹"After his soul suffers many things,
  he will see life and be satisfied.
My good servant will make many people
  right with God;
  he will carry away their sins.
¹²For this reason I will make him a great man
  among people,
  and he will share in all things with those
  who are strong.
He willingly gave his life
  and was treated like a criminal.
But he carried away the sins of many
  people
  and asked forgiveness for those who
  sinned."

People will Return to Jerusalem

54 The LORD says, "Sing, Jerusalem.
  You are like a woman who never
  gave birth to children.
Start singing and shout for joy.
  You never felt the pain of giving birth,
but you will have more children
  than the woman who has a husband.
²Make your tent bigger;
  stretch it out and make it wider.
Do not hold back.
Make the ropes longer
  and its stakes stronger,
³because you will spread out to the right and
  to the left.
Your children will take over other nations,
  and they will again live in cities that once
  were destroyed.

⁴"Don't be afraid, because you will not be
  ashamed.
Don't be embarrassed, because you will not
  be disgraced.
You will forget the shame you felt earlier;
  you will not remember the shame you felt
  when you lost your husband.
⁵The God who made you is like your
  husband.
His name is the LORD All-powerful.

The Holy One of Israel is the one who
  saves you.
He is called the God of all the earth.
⁶You were like a woman whose husband
  left her,
  and you were very sad.
You were like a wife who married young
  and then her husband left her.
But the LORD called you to be his,"
  says your God.
⁷God says, "I left you for a short time,
  but with great kindness I will bring you
  back again.
⁸I became very angry
  and hid from you for a time,
but I will show you mercy with kindness for
  ever,"
  says the LORD who saves you.

⁹The LORD says, "This day is like the time of
  Noah to me.
I promised then that I would never flood
  the world again.
In the same way, I promise I will not be
  angry with you
  or punish you again.
¹⁰The mountains may disappear,
  and the hills may come to an end,
but my love will never disappear;
  my promise of peace will not come to
  an end,"
  says the LORD who shows mercy to you.

¹¹"You poor city. Storms have hurt you,
  and you have not been comforted.
But I will rebuild you with turquoise stones,
  and I will build your foundations with
  sapphires.
¹²I will use rubies to build your walls
  and shining jewels for the gates
  and precious jewels for all your outer walls.
¹³All your children will be taught by the LORD,
  and they will have much peace.
¹⁴I will build you using fairness.
You will be safe from those who would
  hurt you,
  so you will have nothing to fear.
Nothing will come to make you afraid.
¹⁵I will not send anyone to attack you,
  and you will defeat those who do
  attack you.

¹⁶"See, I made the blacksmith.
He fans the fire to make it hotter,
  and he makes the kind of tool he wants.
In the same way I have made the destroyer
  to destroy.
¹⁷ So no weapon that is used against you will
  defeat you.

You will show that those who speak against
    you are wrong.
These are the good things my servants
    receive.
Their victory comes from me," says the
    LORD.

God Gives What is Good

55 The LORD says, "All you who are
    thirsty,
come and drink.
Those of you who do not have money,
    come, buy and eat!
Come buy wine and milk
    without money and without cost.
²Why spend your money on something that is
    not real food?
Why work for something that doesn't really
    satisfy you?
Listen closely to me, and you will eat what is
    good;
    your soul will enjoy the rich food that
      satisfies.
³Come to me and listen;
    listen to me so you may live.
I will make an agreement with you that will
    last for ever.
I will give you the blessings I promised to
    David.
⁴I made David a witness of my power for all
    nations,
    a ruler and commander of many nations.
⁵You will call for nations that you don't yet
    know.
    And these nations that do not know you
      will run to you
because of the LORD your God,
    because of the Holy One of Israel who
      honours you."

⁶So you should look for the LORD before it is
    too late;
    you should call to him while he is near.
⁷The wicked should stop doing wrong,
    and they should stop their evil thoughts.
They should return to the LORD so he may
    have mercy on them.
    They should come to our God, because he
      will freely forgive them.

⁸The LORD says, "My thoughts are not like
    your thoughts.
    Your ways are not like my ways.
⁹Just as the heavens are higher than the earth,
    so are my ways higher than your ways
    and my thoughts higher than your thoughts.
¹⁰Rain and snow fall from the sky
    and don't return without watering the
      ground.

They cause the plants to sprout and grow,
    making seeds for the farmer
    and bread for the people.
¹¹The same thing is true of the words I speak.
    They will not return to me empty.
They make the things happen that I want to
    happen,
    and they succeed in doing what I send
      them to do.

¹²"So you will go out with joy
    and be led out in peace.
The mountains and hills will burst into song
    before you,
    and all the trees in the fields will clap their
      hands.
¹³Large cypress trees will grow where
    thorn-bushes were.
    Myrtle trees will grow where weeds were.
These things will be a reminder of the LORD's
    promise,
    and this reminder will never be destroyed."

Sidelight Replacing thorn-bushes
with myrtle would require
more than a little plant food (Isaiah 55:13).
Thorn-bushes and weeds (or briars) are scraggly
desert plants that survive with little nourishment.
The myrtle is an evergreen shrub that grows
along rivers and streams, and it symbolises
peace, joy, generosity and justice – which fits
the prophet's vision for the future.

All Nations will Obey the LORD

56 This is what the LORD says:
    "Give justice to all people,
    and do what is right,
because my salvation will come to you soon.
    Soon everyone will know that I do what is
      right.
²The person who obeys the law about the
    Sabbath *d*
will be blessed,
and the person who does no evil
    will be blessed."

³Foreigners who have joined the LORD should
    not say,
    "The LORD will not accept me with his
      people."
The eunuch *d* should not say,
    "Because I cannot have children, the LORD
      will not accept me."
⁴This is what the LORD says:
    "The eunuchs should obey the law about the
      Sabbath

and do what I want
and keep my agreement.
⁵If they do, I will make their names
    remembered
    within my Temple *d* and its walls.
It will be better for them than children.
I will give them a name that will last for
    ever,
    that will never be forgotten.
⁶Foreigners will join the LORD
    to worship him and love him,
    to serve him,
to obey the law about the Sabbath,
    and to keep my agreement.
⁷I will bring these people to my holy
    mountain
    and give them joy in my house of prayer.
The offerings and sacrifices
    they place on my altar will please me,
because my Temple will be called
    a house for prayer for people from all
        nations."
⁸The Lord GOD says—
    he who gathers the Israelites that were
        forced to leave their country:
"I will bring together other people
    to join those who are already gathered."

Israel's Leaders are Evil

⁹All you animals of the field,
    all you animals of the forest, come to eat.
¹⁰The leaders who are to guard the people are
    blind;
    they don't know what they are doing.
All of them are like quiet dogs
    that don't know how to bark.
They lie down and dream
    and love to sleep.
¹¹They are like hungry dogs
    that are never satisfied.
They are like shepherds
    who don't know what they are doing.
They all have gone their own way;
    all they want to do is satisfy themselves.
¹²They say, "Come, let's drink some wine;
    let's drink all the beer we want.
And tomorrow we will do this again,
    or, maybe we will have an even better
        time."

Israel Does Not Follow God

57 Those who are right with God
        may die,
    but no one pays attention.
Good people are taken away,
    but no one understands.
Those who do right are being taken away
    from evil

² and are given peace.
Those who live as God wants
    find rest in death.

³"Come here, you magicians!
    Come here, you sons of prostitutes *d* and
        those who take part in adultery! *d*
⁴Of whom are you making fun?
    Whom are you insulting?
At whom do you stick out your tongue?
You turn against God,
    and you are liars.
⁵You have sexual relations under every green
    tree
    to worship your gods.
You kill children in the ravines
    and sacrifice them in the rocky places.
⁶You take the smooth rocks from the
    ravines
    as your portion.
You pour drink offerings on them to worship
    them,
    and you give grain offerings to them.
Do you think this makes me want to show
    you mercy?
⁷You make your bed on every hill and
    mountain,
    and there you offer sacrifices.
⁸You have hidden your idols
    behind your doors and doorposts.
You have left me, and you have uncovered
    yourself.
You have pulled back the covers and
    climbed into bed.
You have made an agreement with those
    whose beds you love,
    and you have looked at their nakedness.
⁹You use your oils and perfumes
    to look nice for Molech. *d*
You have sent your messengers to faraway
    lands;
    you even tried to send them to the place of
        the dead.
¹⁰You were tired from doing these things,
    but you never gave up.
You found new strength,
    so you did not stop.

¹¹"Whom were you so afraid of
    that you lied to me?
You have not remembered me
    or even thought about me.
I have been quiet for a long time.
    Is that why you are not afraid of me?
¹²I will tell about your 'goodness' and what
    you do,
    and those things will do you no good.
¹³When you cry out for help,
    let the gods you have gathered help you.

The wind will blow them all away;
  just a puff of wind will take them away.
But the person who depends on me will
    receive the land
  and own my holy mountain."

The Lord will Save His People

¹⁴Someone will say, "Build a road! Build a
    road! Prepare the way!
  Make the way clear for my people."
¹⁵And this is the reason: God lives for ever and
    is holy.
  He is high and lifted up.
  He says, "I live in a high and holy place,
    but I also live with people who are sad and
    humble.
  I give new life to those who are humble
    and to those whose hearts are broken.
¹⁶I will not accuse for ever,
    nor will I always be angry,
  because then human life would grow weak.
    Human beings, whom I created, would die.
¹⁷I was angry because they were dishonest in
    order to make money.
  I punished them and turned away from
    them in anger,
    but they continued to do evil.
¹⁸I have seen what they have done, but I will
    heal them.
  I will guide them and comfort them and
    those who felt sad for them.
  They will all praise me.
¹⁹I will give peace, real peace, to those far and
    near,
    and I will heal them," says the Lord.
²⁰But evil people are like the angry sea,
    which cannot rest,
  whose waves toss up waste and mud.
²¹"There is no peace for evil people," says
    my God.

How to Honour God

58 The Lord says, "Shout out loud. Don't
      hold back.
  Shout out loud like a trumpet.
  Tell my people what they have done against
    their God;
    tell the family of Jacob about their sins.
²They still come every day looking for me
    and want to learn my ways.
  They act just like a nation that does what is
    right,
    that obeys the commands of its God.
  They ask me to judge them fairly.
    They want God to be near them.
³They say, 'To honour you we had special
    days when we gave up eating,
    but you didn't see.

We humbled ourselves to honour you,
    but you didn't notice.' "

But the Lord says, "You do what pleases
    yourselves on these special days,
    and you are unfair to your workers.
⁴On these special days when you do not eat,
    you argue and fight
    and hit each other with your fists.
  You cannot do these things as you do now
    and believe your prayers are heard in
    heaven.
⁵This kind of special day is not what I want.
  This is not the way I want people to be
    sorry for what they have done.
  I don't want people just to bow their heads
    like a plant
    and wear rough cloth and lie in ashes to
    show their sadness.
  This is what you do on your special days
    when you do not eat,
    but do you think this is what the Lord
    wants?

⁶"I will tell you the kind of special day
    I want:
  free the people you have put in prison unfairly
    and undo their chains.
  Free those to whom you are unfair
    and stop their hard labour.
⁷Share your food with the hungry
    and bring poor, homeless people into your
    own homes.
  When you see someone who has no clothes,
    give him yours,
    and don't refuse to help your own
    relatives.
⁸Then your light will shine like the dawn,
    and your wounds will quickly heal.
  Your God will walk before you,
    and the glory of the Lord will protect you
    from behind.
⁹Then you will call out, and the Lord will
    answer.
  You will cry out, and he will say, 'Here
    I am.'

"If you stop making trouble for others,
    if you stop using cruel words and pointing
    your finger at others,
¹⁰if you feed those who are hungry
    and take care of the needs of those who
    are troubled,
  then your light will shine in the darkness,
    and you will be bright like sunshine at
    noon.
¹¹The Lord will always lead you.
  He will satisfy your needs in dry lands
    and give strength to your bones.

You will be like a garden that has much
    water,
like a spring that never runs dry.
¹²Your people will rebuild the old cities that
        are now in ruins;
    you will rebuild their foundations.
You will be known for repairing the broken
        places
    and for rebuilding the roads and houses.
¹³"You must obey God's law about the Sabbath *d*
    and not do what pleases yourselves on that
        holy day.
You should call the Sabbath a joyful day
    and honour it as the LORD's holy day.
You should honour it by not doing whatever
        you please
    nor saying whatever you please on that day.
¹⁴Then you will find joy in the LORD,
    and I will carry you to the high places
        above the earth.

I will let you eat the crops of the land your
        ancestor Jacob had."
The LORD has said these things.

The Evil That People Do

59 Surely the LORD's power is enough to
        save you.
He can hear you when you ask him for help.
²It is your evil that has separated
        you from your God.
Your sins cause him to turn away from you,
    so he does not hear you.
³With your hands you have killed others,
    and with your fingers you have done wrong.
With your lips you have lied,
    and with your tongue you say evil things.
⁴People take each other to court unfairly,
    and no one tells the truth in arguing his case.
They accuse each other falsely and tell lies.
    They cause trouble and create more evil.

HYPOCRISY

Meaningless Acts

In the Minster there was a great procession at the start of the Easter Sunday morning communion service. They called it a Eucharist. Up the centre aisle came a line of people dressed in robes and finery – the good and the great. Minor canons, major canons, canons emeriti, archdeacons, deans, suffragan bishops and bishops. Everyone had been looking forward to this celebration for ages, even though most of the guests didn't understand most of the procession's titles.

The staff of the Minster, now processing in a dignified and orderly fashion along with their guests, had been at each other's throats that very morning. They had been arguing about the ceremony. They had been disputing the order of the procession. They had even squabbled about the sausage roll quality for the post-service buffet. Yet all the back-biting was put on hold for the procession. The organ boomed; the choir sang. "Everything is fine" said the service; "I hate your guts," said the people in their hearts.

In the congregation, the people sang the songs and hymns with gusto. They said, "Thanks be to God" at the end of readings, when prompted, affirming God's hatred of poverty and inequality. After a Bank Holiday relaxing, they went back to their regular jobs in the city and continued exploiting others for a little more cash.

Read **Isaiah 58:3–9a**.

* Why do some people pretend to be one way, then behave completely the opposite?
* How does God feel about those people? Is he like that?

Consider . . .

* becoming accountable to a friend for your behaviour as a Christian. Make a deal with each other that you will ask each other the hard questions about your behaviour, use of time and commitment to Jesus?
* whether members of your Christian youth group pretend they are more holy than they are.

For more, see . . .

* Hosea 6:1–10 (p.854)
* James 1:22–27 (p.1348)
* Matthew 7:1–5 (p.949)

5They hatch evil like eggs from poisonous
    snakes.
  If you eat one of those eggs, you will die,
    and if you break one open, a poisonous
    snake comes out.
People tell lies as they would spin a
    spider's web.
6   The webs they make cannot be used for
    clothes;
  you can't cover yourself with those webs.
The things they do are evil,
  and they use their hands to hurt others.
7They eagerly run to do evil,
  and they are always ready to kill innocent
    people.
They think evil thoughts.
  Everywhere they go they cause ruin and
    destruction.
8They don't know how to live in peace,
  and there is no fairness in their lives.
They are dishonest.
  Anyone who lives as they live will never
    have peace.

Israel's Sin Brings Trouble

9Fairness has gone far away;
  goodness is nowhere to be found.
We wait for the light, but there is only
    darkness now.
  We hope for a bright light, but all we have
    is darkness.
10We are like the blind feeling our way along a
    wall.
  We feel our way as if we had no eyes.
In the brightness of day we trip as if it were
    night.
  We are like dead men among the strong.
11All of us growl like the bears.
  We call out sadly like the doves.
We look for justice, but there isn't any.
  We want to be saved, but salvation is far
    away.
12We have done many wrong things against
    our God;
  our sins show we are wrong.
We know we have turned against God;
  we know the evil things we have done:
13sinning and rejecting the LORD,
  turning away from our God,
planning to hurt others and to disobey God,
  planning and speaking lies.
14So we have driven away justice,
  and we have kept away from what is
    right.
Truth is not spoken in the streets;
  what is honest is not allowed to enter the
    city.

15Truth cannot be found anywhere,
  and people who refuse to do evil are attacked.

The LORD looked and could not find any justice,
  and he was displeased.
16He could not find anyone to help the people,
  and he was surprised that there was no one
    to help.
So he used his own power to save the
    people;
  his own goodness gave him strength.
17He covered himself with goodness like
    armour.
  He put the helmet of salvation on his head.
He put on the clothes of punishment
  and wrapped himself in the coat of his
    strong love.
18The LORD will pay back his enemies for what
    they have done.
  He will show his anger to those who were
    against him;
  he will punish the people in faraway places
    as they deserve.
19Then people from the west will fear the LORD,
  and people from the east will fear his glory.
The LORD will come quickly like a fast-flowing
    river,
  driven by the breath of the LORD.

20"Then a Saviour will come to Jerusalem
  and to the people of Jacob who have
    turned from sin,"
  says the LORD.

21The LORD says, "This is my agreement with
these people: My Spirit d and my words that I give
you will never leave you or your children or your
grandchildren, now and for ever."

Jerusalem will be Great

60 "Jerusalem, get up and shine, because
    your light has come,
  and the glory of the LORD shines on you.
2Darkness now covers the earth;
  deep darkness covers her people.
But the LORD shines on you,
  and people see his glory around you.
3Nations will come to your light;
  kings will come to the brightness of your
    sunrise.

4"Look around you.
  People are gathering and coming to you.
Your sons are coming from far away,
  and your daughters are coming with
    them.
5When you see them, you will shine with
    happiness;
  you will be excited and full of joy,

because the wealth of the nations across the
 seas will be given to you;
the riches of the nations will come to you.
⁶Herds of camels will cover your land,
 young camels from Midian and Ephah.
People will come from Sheba
 bringing gold and incense, ^d
and they will sing praises to the LORD.
⁷All the sheep from Kedar will be given to you;

the rams from Nebaioth will be brought
 to you.
They will be pleasing sacrifices on my altar,
 and I will make my beautiful Temple ^d more
 beautiful.

⁸"The people are returning to you like clouds,
 like doves flying to their nests.
⁹People in faraway lands are waiting for me.
 The great trading ships will come first,
bringing your children from faraway lands,
 and with them silver and gold.
This will honour the LORD your God,
 the Holy One of Israel,
who does wonderful things for you.

¹⁰"Jerusalem, foreigners will rebuild your walls,
 and their kings will serve you.
When I was angry, I hurt you,
 but now I want to be kind to you and
 comfort you.

Sidelight

The promise to Jerusalem that people from Sheba would come to Jerusalem to worship was quite an impressive promise (Isaiah 60:6). Sheba was over two thousand kilometres away – across the desert of present-day Saudia Arabia. Years earlier, the queen of Sheba had visited King Solomon and seen all his wealth (1 Kings 10:1–13, p.325).

SHARING FAITH

Take That Opportunity

Adam just didn't know how he was going to tell his friends about Jesus. He thought he'd done pretty well recently. All his friends knew he went to church, because he told them every Monday morning when they asked him what he'd got up to at the weekend. He'd even put his hand up in a religious studies lesson when the teacher asked if anyone in the room followed "the Christian religion". However, he knew that wasn't enough. He knew that Jesus wanted him to talk to his friends about the way he had changed Adam's life. Only problem was how to do it.

Adam decided his best bet was to start off by praying for his friends that they would become interested in Jesus. Imagine his surprise when a few weeks later one of his friends, Jay, started talking about Jesus. He said, "I saw this TV programme on Jesus last night and they said that he was a bit of a hippie and he probably took drugs. But that isn't right is it Adam? Tell me – what's the truth about this Jesus bloke."

Adam couldn't believe it – here was the perfect opportunity, so he took it. He had spent the last three weeks working out what he would say if someone did ask him about Jesus! Jay was really interested. He even started coming along to Adam's youth group to find out more.

Read **Isaiah 60:1–6** to see how God shines on Christians to make them a witness.

* Why do you think Adam wanted to talk about Jesus and not just his "Christian religion"?
* How can we be a light to people, like the one Isaiah talks about?

Consider . . .

* thinking and praying about two people you can show the "light of God" to over the next week.
 Plan how you can do it and then do it!
* what you would say to your friends if they asked you to talk about Jesus for five minutes.

For more, see . . .

* John 6:44 (p.1105)
* 2 Corinthians 5:11–21 (p.1245)

* 2 Corinthians 3:17–18 (p.1242)

11Your gates will always be open;
  they will not be closed day or night
so the nations can bring their wealth to you,
  and their kings will be led to you.
12The nation or kingdom that doesn't serve you
    will be destroyed;
  it will be completely ruined.

13"The great trees of Lebanon will be given
    to you:
  its pine, fir and cypress trees together.
You will use them to make my Temple
    beautiful,
  and I will give much honour to this place
    where I rest my feet.
14The people who have hurt you will bow
    down to you;
  those who hated you will bow down at
    your feet.
They will call you The City of the LORD,
  Jerusalem, city of the Holy One of Israel.

15"You have been hated and left empty
  with no one passing through.
But I will make you great from now on;
  you will be a place of happiness for ever
    and ever.
16You will be given what you need from the
    nations,
  like a child drinking milk from its mother.
Then you will know that it is I, the LORD,
  who saves you.
You will know that the Powerful One of
    Jacob protects you.
17I will bring you gold in place of bronze,
  silver in place of iron,
bronze in place of wood,
  iron in place of rocks.
I will change your punishment into peace,
  and you will be ruled by what is right.
18There will be no more violence in your country;
  it will not be ruined or destroyed.
You will name your walls Salvation
  and your gates Praise.
19The sun will no longer be your light during
    the day
  nor will the brightness from the moon be
    your light,
because the LORD will be your light for ever,
  and your God will be your glory.
20Your sun will never set again,
  and your moon will never be dark,
because the LORD will be your light for ever,
  and your time of sadness will end.
21All of your people will do what is right.
  They will receive the earth for ever.
They are the plant I have planted,
  the work of my own hands
  to show my greatness.

22The smallest family will grow to a thousand.
  The least important of you will become a
    powerful nation.
I am the LORD,
  and when it is time, I will make these
    things happen quickly."

The LORD's Message of Freedom

61 The Lord GOD has put his Spirit *d*
      in me,
  because the LORD has appointed me to tell
    the good news to the poor.
He has sent me to comfort those whose
    hearts are broken,
  to tell the captives they are free
  and to tell the prisoners they are released.
2He has sent me to announce the time when
    the LORD will show his kindness
  and the time when our God will punish
    evil people.
He has sent me to comfort all those who
    are sad
3   and to help the sorrowing people of
      Jerusalem.
I will give them a crown to replace their ashes,
  and the oil of gladness to replace their sorrow,
  and clothes of praise to replace their spirit
    of sadness.
Then they will be called Trees of Goodness,
  trees planted by the LORD to show his
    greatness.

4They will rebuild the old ruins
  and restore the places destroyed long ago.
They will repair the ruined cities
  that were destroyed for so long.

5My people, foreigners will come to tend your
    sheep.
  People from other countries will tend your
    fields and vineyards.
6You will be called priests of the LORD;
  you will be named the servants of our God.
You will have riches from all the nations on
    earth,
  and you will take pride in them.
7Instead of being ashamed, my people will
    receive twice as much wealth.
Instead of being disgraced, they will be
    happy because of what they receive.
They will receive a double share of the land,
  so their happiness will continue for ever.
8"I, the LORD, love justice.
  I hate stealing and everything that is wrong.
I will be fair and give my people what they
    should have,
  and I will make an agreement with them
    that will continue for ever.

⁹Everyone in all nations will know the
    children of my people,
and their children will be known among
    the nations.
Anyone who sees them will know
    that they are people the LORD has blessed."

¹⁰The LORD makes me very happy;
    all that I am rejoices in my God.
He has covered me with clothes of
    salvation
and wrapped me with a coat of goodness,
like a bridegroom dressed for his wedding,
like a bride dressed in jewels.
¹¹The earth causes plants to grow,
    and a garden causes the seeds planted in it
    to grow.

In the same way the Lord GOD will make
    goodness and praise
come from all the nations.

New Jerusalem

62 Because I love Jerusalem, I will
    continue to speak for her;
for Jerusalem's sake I will not stop speaking
until her goodness shines like a bright light,
    until her salvation burns bright like a flame.
²Jerusalem, the nations will see your goodness,
    and all kings will see your glory.
Then you will have a new name,
    which the LORD himself will give you.
³You will be like a beautiful crown in the
    LORD's hand,
like a king's crown in your God's hand.

FREEDOM

The Last Word

The screams could be heard from miles around. Echoes bounced off the surrounding cliffs, as Jo's lungs emptied themselves in agony.

Somewhere in the darkness, the perpetrator scurried away back under a rock, as in an instant Jo discovered that, whilst they may not kill you, Portuguese scorpions cause a great deal of pain.

With a total abandonment of dignity, and tears streaming down her face, Jo floundered around desperately searching for a way to limit the pain searing through her body. Her friends struggled to remain calm in all the confusion and panic.

The situation was not looking good. The friends had been camping in the middle of nowhere. It was now the middle of the night and the mobile phones weren't working. How was help going to come? Jo couldn't focus on anything but the pain. She began to doubt that it would ever stop. Relief was a luxury that might never come.

But help did arrive. An ambulance drove her to the hospital. And with the administration of local anaesthetic and the antidote to the poison, she was freed from the pain, and peace and calm did indeed resume. And within a few weeks, although Jo could think of the pain, she couldn't remember the pain itself. She had been cured.

Isn't it amazing how pain never gets the last word? That even the memory of pain, can't seem to carry with it the pain within it? Peace lasts, pain doesn't.

Read **Isaiah 61:1–11**.

* How many promises does God make in the passage? What does he promise to bring freedom from?
* Have you ever felt like you're in one of those scenarios? What freedom does God promise you?

Consider . . .

* making a promise box full of pictures or objects that will remind you of the promises God makes us.
* how you can help someone who is bound up by one of the situations listed in the passage.

For more, see . . .

* Ezekiel 37:11–14 (p.820)
* Hebrews 2:14–15 (p.1331)

* Ephesians 3:14–21 (p.1271)

⁴You will never again be called the People that
    God Left,
  nor your land the Land that God
    Destroyed.
You will be called the People God Loves,
  and your land will be called the Bride
    of God,
because the LORD loves you.
  And your land will belong to him as a bride
    belongs to her husband.
⁵As a young man marries a woman,
  so your children will marry your
    land.
As a man rejoices over his new wife,
  so your God will rejoice over you.

⁶Jerusalem, I have put guards on the walls to
    watch.
  They must not be silent day or night.
You people who remind the LORD of your
    needs in prayer
  should never be quiet.
⁷You should not stop praying to him until he
    builds up Jerusalem
  and makes it a city all people will praise.

⁸The LORD has made a promise,
  and by his power he will keep his promise.
He said, "I will never again give your grain
    as food to your enemies.
I will not let your enemies drink the new
    wine
  that you have worked to make.
⁹The person who gathers food will eat it,
  and he will praise the LORD.
The person who gathers the grapes will drink
    the wine
  in the courts of my Temple." *d*

¹⁰Go through, go through the gates!
  Make the way ready for the people.
Build up, build up the road!
  Move all the stones off the road.
Raise the banner as a sign for the people.

¹¹The LORD is speaking
    to all the faraway lands:
"Tell the people of Jerusalem,
  'Look, your Saviour is coming.
He is bringing your reward to you;
  he is bringing his payment with him.'"

PATIENCE

Wait On

Gilly is a new Christian. It is the first year of her Christian life. And now she is becoming impatient with her church, her prayer life (individual and at church) and the slow pace of change. She has grown quickly; they move slowly. Frustration follows.

At Gilly's church they don't sing the sort of songs they sang at the summer camp she attended. There are no guitarists in her church. It is full of older people who don't seem very enthusiastic.

One day Gilly talks to one of the older ladies over coffee after church. She discovers that they have been praying for someone like her to join them. Unbeknown to her, they have waited, watched, hoped and prayed for years. She is the answer to their prayers and they can't wait to see how God will use Gilly to bring new life to the church.

Read **Isaiah 62:1–12**.

* How might this passage encourage someone like Gilly?
* How much of this passage appears to be about the immediate (returning to Jerusalem) and how much about the distant future (your Saviour is coming)?

Consider . . .

* how patient you are. What things stretch your patience?
* what God is preparing you for. How is he doing that?

For more, see . . .

* Psalm 37:3–9 (p.521)
* Luke 18:1–8 (p.1078)

* Isaiah 40:3–11 (p.679)

¹²His people will be called the Holy People,
the Saved People of the LORD,
and Jerusalem will be called the City God
Wants,
the City God Has Not Rejected.

The LORD Judges His People

63 Who is this coming from Edom,
from the city of Bozrah, dressed
in red?
Who is this dressed in fine clothes
and marching forwards with his great
power?

He says, "I, the LORD, speak what is right.
I have the power to save you."

²Someone asks, "Why are your clothes
bright red
as if you had walked on the grapes to make
wine?"

³The LORD answers, "I have walked in the
winepress *d* alone,
and no one among the nations
helped me.
I was angry and walked on the nations
and crushed them because of
my anger.
Blood splashed on my clothes,
and I stained all my clothing.
⁴I chose a time to punish people,
and the time has come for me to save.
⁵I looked around, but I saw no one to
help me.
I was surprised that no one supported
me.
So I used my own power to save my
people;
my own anger supported me.
⁶While I was angry, I walked on the nations.
In my anger I punished them
and poured their blood on the ground."

SUFFERING

Feeling What You Feel

She woke in the middle of the night in excruciating pain. She knew something was wrong, very wrong. Emma struggled to get out of bed and downstairs to the phone to call the ambulance. It seemed to take an eternity for the ambulance to arrive and rush her off to hospital. She was in so much pain that she couldn't stand up straight; she was bent over in agony.

She woke up several hours later in a quiet hospital room on her own. A doctor walked past and noticed she was awake, so he came in to talk to her. Emma could tell by the expression on the doctor's face that something was wrong. The doctor sat down and started to tell Emma that there had been a complication with the pregnancy. They had tried everything they could to save the baby, but sadly it wasn't enough and the baby had died.

Emma was devastated. As she lay on her bed alone and in the silence, all she could think to do was to pray.

In the midst of all her sadness, she really felt Jesus alongside her. It was as if he was there with her, crying with her, with his arm around her shoulder.

Read **Isaiah 63:7–9**.

* Why do you think God chooses to feel the pain that we feel?
* When you are suffering how can you know God is there, like Emma did?

Consider . . .

* looking out for those people around you who are suffering and think of ways you can show them you care.
* praying for those Christians around the world who are tortured and suffer because of their faith.

For more, see . . .

* Jeremiah 31:12–13 (p.752)
* Hebrews 13:1–3 (p.1345)
* Romans 8:18 (p.1195)

The LORD's Kindness to His People

⁷I will tell about the LORD's kindness
　and praise him for everything he has
　　done.
I will praise the LORD for the many good
　things he has given us
and for his goodness to the people
　of Israel.
He has shown great mercy to us
　and has been very kind to us.
⁸He said, "These are my people;
　my children will not lie to me."
So he saved them.
⁹When they suffered, he suffered also.
　He sent his own angel to save them.
Because of his love and kindness, he saved
　them.
　Since long ago he has picked them up and
　　carried them.
¹⁰But they turned against him
　and made his Holy Spirit ᵈ very sad.
So he became their enemy,
　and he fought against them.

¹¹But then his people remembered what
　happened long ago,
　in the days of Moses and the Israelites
　　with him.
Where is the LORD who brought the people
　through the sea,
　with the leaders of his people?
Where is the one
　who put his Holy Spirit among them,
¹²who led Moses by the right hand
　with his wonderful power,
who divided the water before them
　to make his name famous for ever,
¹³who led the people through the deep waters?
Like a horse walking through a desert,
　the people did not stumble.
¹⁴Like cattle that go down to the valley,
　the Spirit of the LORD gave the people a
　　place to rest.
LORD, that is the way you led your people,
　and by this you won for yourself wonderful
　　fame.

A Prayer for Help

¹⁵LORD, look down from the heavens and see;
　look at us from your wonderful and holy
　　home in heaven.
Where is your strong love and power?
　Why are you keeping your love and mercy
　　from us?
¹⁶You are our father.
　Abraham doesn't know we are his children,

and Israel doesn't recognise us.
LORD, you are our father.
　You are called "the one who has always
　　saved us".
¹⁷LORD, why are you making us wander from
　your ways?
　Why do you make us stubborn so that we
　　don't honour you?
For our sake come back to us,
　your servants, who belong to you.
¹⁸Your people had your Temple ᵈ for a while,
　but now our enemies have walked on your
　　holy place and crushed it.
¹⁹We have become like people you never ruled
　over,
　like those who have never worn your
　　name.

64 Tear open the skies and come down to
　earth
so that the mountains will tremble
　before you.
²Like a fire that burns twigs,
　like a fire that makes water boil,
let your enemies know who you are.
　Then all nations will shake with fear when
　　they see you.
³You have done amazing things we did not
　expect.
　You came down, and the mountains
　　trembled before you.
⁴From long ago no one has ever heard of a
　God like you.
　No one has ever seen a God besides you,
　who helps the people who trust you.
⁵You help those who enjoy doing good,
　who remember how you want them
　　to live.
But you were angry because we sinned.
　For a long time we disobeyed,
　so how can we be saved?
⁶All of us are dirty with sin.
　All the right things we have done are like
　　filthy pieces of cloth.
All of us are like dead leaves,
　and our sins, like the wind, have carried us
　　away.
⁷No one worships you
　or even asks you to help us.
That is because you have turned away
　from us
and have let our sins destroy us.
⁸But LORD, you are our father.
　We are like clay, and you are the potter;
　your hands made us all.
⁹LORD, don't continue to be angry with us;
　don't remember our sins for ever.
Please, look at us,

because we are your people.

¹⁰Your holy cities are empty like the desert.
Jerusalem is like a desert;
it is destroyed.

¹¹Our ancestors worshipped you
in our holy and wonderful Temple,
but now it has been burned with fire,
and all our precious things have been
destroyed.

¹²When you see these things, will you hold
yourself back from helping us, LORD?
Will you be silent and punish us beyond
what we can stand?

All People will Learn About God

65 The LORD says, "I made myself known
to people who were not looking
for me.
I was found by those who were not asking
me for help.
I said, 'Here I am. Here I am,'

to a nation that was not praying to me.
²All day long I stood ready to accept
people who turned against me,
but the way they continue to live is not
good;
they do anything they want to do.
³Right in front of me
they continue to do things that make me angry.
They offer sacrifices to their gods in their
gardens,
and they burn incense *d* on altars of brick.
⁴They sit among the graves
and spend their nights waiting to get
messages from the dead.
They eat the meat of pigs,
and their pots are full of soup made from
meat that is wrong to eat.
⁵But they tell others, 'Stay away and don't
come near me.
I am too holy for you.'
These people are like smoke in my nose.

FOLLOWING GOD

No Wonder Your Breath Smells

Jack couldn't believe his eyes! He watched in horror as his dog was sick. A worrying sight for any eight-year-old who loves his pet, but what made it truly terrible was when, with a lick of her whiskers, Jack's dog slowly and very happily began to chew and chomp away at the vomit. Jack stood and screamed at her, "Stop it, it's gross, no wonder your breath smells!" But the dog paid no attention, she was simply thinking, "Great! Lunch . . . again."

God knows how disgusting sin is. He knows that it messes up our relationship with him, others and even ourselves. Much of what God said through prophets like Isaiah was, "Stop it, it's gross, it's going to mess your life up!" But like Jack's dog, Israel seemed to love doing the things that God hates. As a result, things had gone downhill. Isaiah was full of regret and disappointment. He could see how his people had stopped living God's way and were doing their own thing. Like a driver who has turned their Sat Nav off, Israel had stopped listening to God and had got themselves seriously lost.

Isaiah 63:16; 64:1–8 tells what it's like to be lost without God.

- How is being physically lost similar to wandering away from God's path for your life?
- According to Isaiah, his people wouldn't even ask for directions. Do you need to ask God for help?

Consider . . .

- the sins that you keep going back to. What could you do to make it more difficult for you to do that? Is there someone you could talk to each time that happens?
- listing the things that help you follow God such as people who help you, music, the Bible. Decide to have at least one of these things as part of your day, every day.

For more, see . . .

- Psalm 25 (p.514)
- James 1:21–25 (p.1348)

- Proverbs 26:11 (p.613)

Like a fire that burns all the time, they
    continue to make me angry.

6"Look, it is written here before me.
    I will not be quiet; instead, I will repay you
        in full.
    I will punish you for what you have done.
7I will punish you for your sins and your
        ancestors' sins,"
    says the LORD.
    "They burned incense to gods on the
        mountains
    and shamed me on those hills.
So I will punish them as they should be
        punished
    for what they did."

8This is what the LORD says:
    "When there is juice left in the grapes,
        people do not destroy them,
    because they know there is good left in
        them.
So I will do the same thing to my servants—
    I will not completely destroy them.
9I will leave some of the children of Jacob,
    and some of the people of Judah will
        receive my mountain.
    I will choose the people who will live there;
        my servants will live there.
10Then the Plain of Sharon will be a field for
        flocks,
    and the Valley of Achor will be a place for
        herds to rest.
    They will be for the people who want to
        follow me.

11"But as for you who left the LORD,
    who forgot about my holy mountain,
who worship the god Luck,
    who hold religious feasts for the god Fate,
12I decide your fate, and I will punish you with
        my sword.
    You will all be killed,
because I called you, but you refused to
        answer.
    I spoke to you, but you wouldn't listen.
You did the things I said were evil
    and chose to do things that displease me."

13So this is what the Lord GOD says:
    "My servants will eat,
        but you evil people will be hungry.
    My servants will drink,
        but you evil people will be thirsty.
    My servants will be happy,
        but you evil people will be shamed.
14My servants will shout for joy
    because of the goodness of their hearts,
but you evil people will cry,

because you will be sad.
    You will cry loudly, because your spirits will
        be broken.
15Your names will be like curses to my servants,
    and the Lord GOD will put you to death.
    But he will call his servants by another
        name.
16People in the land who ask for blessings
    will ask for them from the faithful God.
And people in the land who make a
        promise
    will promise in the name of the
        faithful God,
because the troubles of the past will be
        forgotten.
    I will make those troubles go away.

A New Time is Coming

17"Look, I will make new heavens and a new
        earth,
    and people will not remember the past
    or think about those things.
18My people will be happy for ever
    because of the things I will make.
    I will make a Jerusalem that is full of joy,
    and I will make her people a delight.
19Then I will rejoice over Jerusalem
    and be delighted with my people.
    There will never again be heard in
        that city
    the sounds of crying and sadness.
20There will never be a baby from that city
    who lives only a few days.
And there will never be an older person
    who doesn't have a long life.
A person who lives 100 years will be called
        young,
    and a person who dies before he is 100
        will be thought of as a sinner.
21In that city those who build houses will live
        there.
    Those who plant vineyards will get to eat
        their grapes.
22No more will one person build a house and
        someone else live there.
    One person will not plant a garden and
        someone else eat its fruit.
My people will live a long time,
    as trees live long.
My chosen people will live there
    and enjoy the things they make.
23They will never again work for nothing.
    They will never again give birth to children
        who die young.
All my people will be blessed by the LORD;
    they and their children will be blessed.
24I will provide for their needs before they
        ask,

and I will help them while they are still
asking for help.

25Wolves and lambs will eat together
in peace.
Lions will eat hay like oxen,
and a snake on the ground will not hurt
anyone.
They will not hurt or destroy each other
on all my holy mountain,"
says the LORD.

The LORD will Judge All Nations

66 This is what the LORD says:
"Heaven is my throne,
and the earth is my footstool.
So do you think you can build a house
for me?

Do I need a place to rest?
2My hand made all things.
All things are here because I made them,"
says the LORD.

"These are the people I am pleased with:
those who are not proud or stubborn
and who fear my word.
3But those people who kill bulls as a sacrifice
to me
are like those who kill people.
Those who kill sheep as a sacrifice
are like those who break the necks of
dogs.
Those who give me grain offerings
are like those who offer me the blood of
pigs. *n*

dogs . . . pigs   God did not want his people to offer dogs and pigs as sacrifices because they were unclean animals.

EUTHANASIA

Playing God

Mike decided to get a part time job so he could start saving money towards his first car. It wasn't long before he found himself looking after grumpy old Charlie, a man in his mid-80s who lived just down the street from him. The job was relatively easy, a bit of gardening and tidying up around the house, so Mike set himself the task of spending quality time getting to know Charlie. He quickly discovered that beneath this rough, bitter exterior was a genuine, caring old man with tons of exciting stories from his experiences in the war.

A few months later, Charlie suffered a stroke which left him in a coma, unable to move or communicate. Mike was horrified when he overheard a few hushed conversations in which people kept using the term "euthanasia" (the process of painlessly ending the life of someone in Charlie's state). Surely that was up to God, wasn't it?

For those of us in the twenty-first century, euthanasia is a pretty hot topic, even among Christians. But **Isaiah 65:19–20** promises the people of God that a time is coming when even a 100-year-old will be called young!

* Where would you draw the line on the topic of euthanasia and "playing God"? What is that based upon?
* Do you have any close relationships with people you'd consider to be old? How might you benefit from such a friendship?

Consider . . .

* helping to shape your government's policies on euthanasia by writing to them. Your opinions count!
* taking time out to get to know an old person and even witness to them. They may be closer to their eternal home than you are.

For more, see . . .

* Genesis 21:1–7 (p.24)
* Proverbs 16:31 (p.604)

* Deuteronomy 5:16 (p.170)

Those who burn incense *d*
    are like those who worship idols.
These people choose their own ways, not
    mine,
    and they love the terrible things they do.
⁴So I will choose their punishments,
    and I will punish them with what they fear
    most.
This is because I called to them, but they did
    not listen.
    I spoke to them, but they did not hear me.
They did things I said were evil;
    they chose to do things I did not like."

⁵You people who obey the words of the
    LORD,
    listen to what he says:
"Your brothers hated you
    and turned against you because you
    followed me.
Your brothers said, 'Let the LORD be
    honoured
    so we may see you rejoice,'
    but they will be punished.
⁶Listen to the loud noise coming from
    the city;
    hear the noise from the Temple. *d*
It is the LORD punishing his enemies,
    giving them the punishment they should
    have.

⁷"A woman does not give birth before she feels
    the pain;
    she does not give birth to a son before the
    pain starts.
⁸No one has ever heard of that happening;
    no one has ever seen that happen.
In the same way no one ever saw a country
    begin in one day;
    no one has ever heard of a new nation
    beginning in one moment.
But Jerusalem will give birth to her
    children
    just as soon as she feels the birth pains.
⁹In the same way I will not cause pain
    without allowing something new to be
    born," says the LORD.
"If I cause you the pain,
    I will not stop you from giving birth to
    your new nation," says your God.
¹⁰"Jerusalem, rejoice.
    All you people who love Jerusalem, be
    happy.
Those of you who felt sad for Jerusalem
    should now feel happy with her.
¹¹You will take comfort from her and be
    satisfied,
    as a child is nursed by its mother.

You will receive her good things
    and enjoy her wealth."

¹²This is what the LORD says:

"I will give her peace that will flow to her like
    a river.
The wealth of the nations will come to her
    like a river overflowing its banks.
Like babies you will be nursed and held in
    my arms
    and bounced on my knees.
¹³I will comfort you
    as a mother comforts her child.
You will be comforted in Jerusalem."

¹⁴When you see these things, you will be
    happy
    and you will grow like the grass.
The LORD's servants will see his power,
    but his enemies will see his anger.
¹⁵Look, the LORD is coming with fire
    and his armies with clouds of dust.
He will punish those people with
    his anger;
    he will punish them with flames
    of fire.
¹⁶The LORD will judge the people
    with fire
    and he will destroy many people with his
    sword;
    he will kill many people.

¹⁷"These people make themselves holy and
pure to go to worship their gods in their gardens.

Sidelight Isaiah is the "Bible in
miniature". It has sixty-six
chapters – as compared with sixty-six biblical
books. Both Isaiah and the Bible end with "new
heavens and the new earth" (Isaiah 66:22 and
Revelation 21:1, p.1403).

Following each other into their special gardens,
they eat the meat of pigs and rats and other
hateful things. But they will all be destroyed
together," says the LORD.

¹⁸"I know they have evil thoughts and do evil
things, so I am coming to punish them. I will
gather all nations and all people, and they will
come together and see my glory.

¹⁹"I will put a mark on some of the people,
and I will send some of these saved people to the
nations: to Tarshish, Libya, Lud (the land of
archers), Tubal, Greece and all the faraway
lands. These people have never heard about
what I have done nor seen my glory. So the saved

people will tell the nations about my glory. [20]And they will bring all your fellow Israelites from all nations to my holy mountain in Jerusalem. Your fellow Israelites will come on horses, donkeys and camels and in chariots and wagons. They will be like the grain offerings that the people bring in clean containers to the Temple," says the LORD. [21]"And I will choose even some of these people to be priests and Levites," says the LORD.

[22]"I will make new heavens and the new earth, which will last for ever," says the LORD. "In the same way, your names and your children will always be with me. [23]All people will come to worship me every Sabbath [d] and every New Moon," [d] says the LORD. [24]"They will go out and see the dead bodies of the people who sinned against me. The worms that eat them will never die, and the fires that burn them will never stop, and everyone will hate to see those bodies."

GOD'S LOVE

Like a Mother

She is frequently on the telephone. "Yes, nine-fifteen is fine," she might reply or "I'll try to get there tomorrow morning." Cots, blankets and beds fill her garage.

Susan directs unused and often unwanted clothing and furniture to those families and single parents who have touched "rock bottom". Often in their teens, many young mothers have nothing to put their babies in when they come home from hospital, or are being rapidly moved out of temporary hostel accommodation, with no furniture or money to create a home of their own.

Susan has her own family and home to run, and she often juggles meal-times with crisis callers, spending time and effort to provide basic supplies and a helping hand. Caring practically, she bubbles over with God's caring love and concern.

A new mother and desperate situations often need more than baby prams and furniture. They need the strength that comes from Christ. Susan makes that difference by offering those in need that kind of strength.

God loves his people as much as a mother loves her children. **Isaiah 66:10–14** describes God's love and care for us.

* How does Susan demonstrate the love that this passage describes?
* In what ways does God comfort and care for you?

Consider . . .

* writing a thank-you letter to someone who has shown you the kind of love that this passage describes.
* writing a description of the "perfect" parent and then thanking God for being a perfect parent to you.

For more, see . . .

* Deuteronomy 32:9–12 (p.195)
* 1 John 4:7–10 (p.1374)
* Hosea 11:1–4 (p.858)

Jeremiah

Why Read This Book:

* Learn the responsibilities that come with belonging to God (Jeremiah 1 – 25).
* See God's continuing love for people even when they have sinned (Jeremiah 26 – 36).
* Find hope even in times of suffering (Jeremiah 37 – 45).

Behind the Scenes:

The nation of Judah was like somebody caught in the crossfire between warring inner-city gangs. Three world powers were fighting for control of the area we call the Near East. The Assyrians had been in control for quite a while, but the Egyptians and Babylonians would each take power within Jeremiah's lifetime. And Judah was caught in the middle.

But Judah was not like an innocent victim. Judah had stopped following God and was forming partnerships with pagan nations to try to protect itself. The people needed a word from God, and Jeremiah became the one whom God would use to proclaim that word – a word that Judah did not want to hear.

Jeremiah warned the people of Judah that they needed to obey God and rely on him. He condemned the false prophets and emphasised the need to repent and seek a personal relationship with God.

Jeremiah's tough message wasn't easy to accept – for Jeremiah or for the people of Judah. At first, Jeremiah was reluctant even to take the job (Jeremiah 1:6). He was abused, ridiculed, exiled to Egypt, and, in the end, possibly killed for what he said. ▷

When?

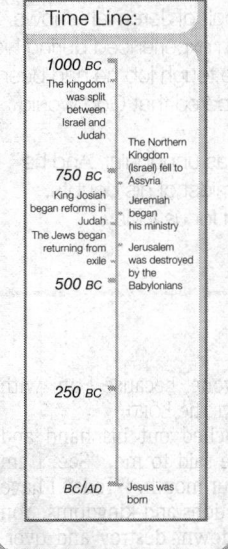

Time Line:

1000 BC
The kingdom was split between Israel and Judah

The Northern Kingdom (Israel) fell to Assyria

750 BC
King Josiah began reforms in Judah
The Jews began returning from exile

Jeremiah began his ministry

Jerusalem was destroyed by the Babylonians

500 BC

250 BC

BC/AD — Jesus was born

Where?

Babylon became the dominant power in the region when it captured the Assyrian capital of Nineveh.

Most of the people of Jerusalem were taken into exile in Babylon when Jerusalem was captured by the Babylonians (Jeremiah 52:1–30).

Mediterranean Sea

Nineveh

Euphrates

Tigris

BABYLON

Jeremiah spent most of his life and ministry in Jerusalem.

Jerusalem

The border of the Babylonian Empire in Jeremiah's time.

Persian Gulf

Jeremiah was taken into exile in Egypt, where he died (Jeremiah 43:4–7).

EGYPT

Red Sea

ARABIAN DESERT

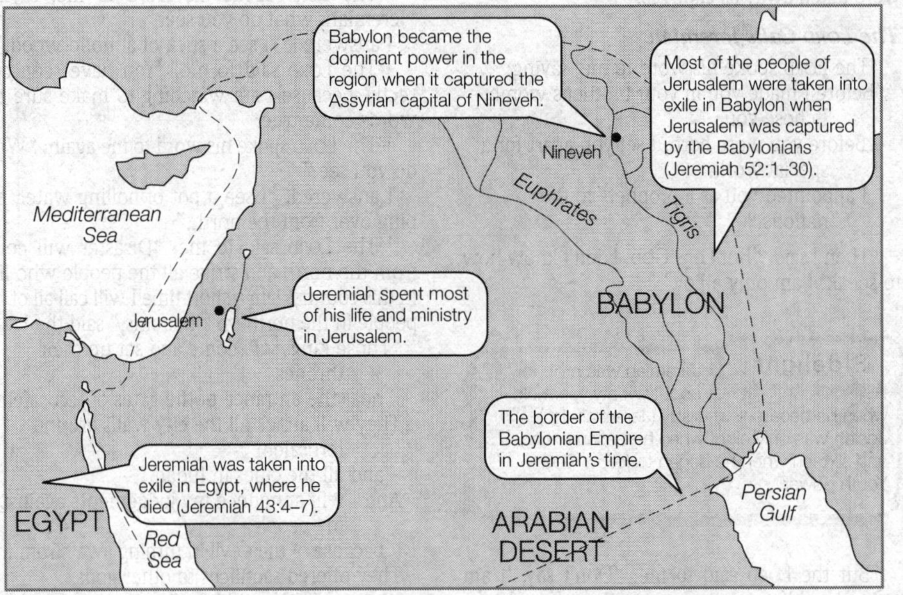

**Behind the
Scenes (cont.):**

The pain he faced and the pain he saw his people experiencing saddened him. His book – which was dictated to his secretary Baruch (Jeremiah 36:4) – is difficult to follow. The poems aren't arranged in logical order. Events jump back and forth in history. To get a better feel for the historical events surrounding the book, read either 2 Kings 23—24 (p.368) or 2 Chronicles 34—36 (p.427).

Through poems, stories, and object lessons, the book of Jeremiah shows the personal struggles, depression and anger Jeremiah experienced during his career. But through it all, Jeremiah continued doing the tough job he had been given. And even when he felt like giving up, he remembered that God would stand by him and comfort him.

Jeremiah was faithful to God's call – even when it was unpopular. And he was honest with God and faithful to God, even in the midst of his doubts, frustrations and anger. His life can be a valuable model for us today.

1 These are the words of Jeremiah son of Hilkiah. He belonged to the family of priests who lived in the town of Anathoth in the land of Benjamin. ²The LORD spoke his word to Jeremiah during the thirteenth year that Josiah son of Amon was king of Judah. ³The LORD also spoke to Jeremiah while Jehoiakim son of Josiah was king of Judah and during the eleven years that Zedekiah son of Josiah was king of Judah. In the fifth month of his last year, the people of Jerusalem were taken away as captives.

The LORD Calls Jeremiah

⁴The LORD spoke his word to me, saying:
⁵"Before I made you in your mother's womb,
     I chose you.
Before you were born, I set you apart for a
     special work.
I appointed you as a prophet_d_ to the
     nations."

⁶Then I said, "But Lord GOD, I don't know how to speak. I am only a boy."

Sidelight Jeremiah was probably about twenty years old when he began his ministry (Jeremiah 1:6). Josiah was only eight when he became king – and sixteen when he began to follow God. Youth power!

---

⁷But the LORD said to me, "Don't say, 'I am only a boy.' You must go everywhere I send you, and you must say everything I tell you to say.

⁸Don't be afraid of anyone, because I am with you to protect you," says the LORD.

⁹Then the LORD reached out his hand and touched my mouth. He said to me, "See, I am putting my words in your mouth. ¹⁰Today I have put you in charge of nations and kingdoms. You will pull up and tear down, destroy and overthrow, build up and plant."

Jeremiah Sees Two Visions

¹¹The LORD spoke his word to me, saying: "Jeremiah, what do you see?"

I answered, "I see a stick of almond wood."

¹²The LORD said to me, "You have seen correctly, because I am watching to make sure my words come true."

¹³The LORD spoke his word to me again: "What do you see?"

I answered, "I see a pot of boiling water, tipping over from the north."

¹⁴The LORD said to me, "Disaster will come from the north and strike all the people who live in this country. ¹⁵In a short time I will call all of the people in the northern kingdoms," said the LORD.
"Those kings will come and set up their
     thrones
  near the entrance of the gates of Jerusalem.
They will attack all the city walls around
     Jerusalem
  and all the cities in Judah.
¹⁶And I will announce my judgements against
     my people
  because of their evil in turning away from me.
They offered sacrifices to other gods
  and worshipped idols they had made with
     their own hands.

¹⁷"Jeremiah, get ready. Stand up and tell them everything I command you to say. Don't be afraid of the people, or I will give you good reason to be afraid of them. ¹⁸Today I am going to make you a strong city, an iron pillar, a bronze wall. You will be able to stand against everyone in the land: Judah's kings, officers, priests and the people of the land. ¹⁹They will fight against you, but they will not defeat you, because I am with you to protect you!" says the LORD.

Israel Turns from God

2 The LORD spoke his word to me, saying: ²"Go and speak to the people of Jerusalem, saying: This is what the LORD says:

'I remember how faithful you were to me
　when you were a young nation.
You loved me like a young bride.
You followed me through the desert,
　a land that had never been planted.

³The people of Israel were holy to the LORD,
　like the first fruits from his harvest.
Those who tried to hurt Israel were judged
　guilty.
　Disasters struck them,' " says the LORD.

⁴Hear the word of the LORD, family of Jacob,
　all you family groups of Israel.
⁵This is what the LORD says:
"I was fair to your ancestors,
　so why did they turn away from me?
Your ancestors worshipped useless idols
　and became useless themselves.
⁶Your ancestors didn't say,
　'Where is the LORD who brought us out of
　　Egypt?
He led us through the desert,
　through a dry and rocky land,
through a dark and dangerous land.
　He led us where no one travels or lives.'

SELF-ESTEEM

The New Kid in the Group

As the newest member of the theatre group, Adam felt a little intimidated. There were good actors in the group. Also, Adam was afraid that friendships had already formed and that he would be an outsider.

On top of that, people in theatre learn to be very honest with their feelings. Adam feared that someone would tell him he was a hopeless actor. What if he didn't measure up?

But Adam's fears evaporated as he got involved. The group realised pretty quickly that Adam was a good actor. People accepted him at first because of his talent, and later they accepted him as a good friend too.

Adam was a little shy about sharing his friendship with God with his new-found friends. Before long, however, he found himself in deep conversations about faith with people who hadn't really given God much thought. He invited them to church, and some went.

Although he started as an intimidated newcomer, with God's help Adam discovered his own value to the group and to God.

Jeremiah was a young man when God first called him. Read how God responded to Jeremiah's fears and lack of self-esteem, in **Jeremiah 1:4–10**.

* Why were both Adam and Jeremiah at first fearful of what they had to do?
* When you sense that God wants you to do something, how do your feelings and thoughts compare to those of young Jeremiah?

Consider . . .

* writing verses 6–8 on a piece of paper and carrying it with you for times when you need a confidence boost.
* giving three friends a self-esteem boost this week by telling them each a reason why you like or respect them.

For more, see . . .

* Isaiah 6:1–8 (p.645)
* 1 Timothy 4:12–16 (p.1311)
* Galatians 1:1–20 (p.1257)

⁷I brought you into a fertile land
    so you could eat its fruit and produce.
But you came and made my land unclean; *d*
    you made it a hateful place.
⁸The priests didn't ask,
    'Where is the LORD?'
The people who know the teachings didn't
    know me.
The leaders turned against me.
The prophets *d* prophesied in the name of
    Baal *d*
and worshipped useless idols.

⁹"So now I will again tell what I have against
    you," says the LORD.
    "And I will tell what I have against your
        grandchildren.
¹⁰Go across the sea to the island of Cyprus
    and see.
    Send someone to the land of Kedar to look
        closely.
    See if there has ever been anything like
        this.
¹¹Has a nation ever exchanged its gods?
    (Of course, its gods are not really gods
        at all.)
But my people have exchanged their
    glorious God
for idols worth nothing.
¹²Skies, be shocked at the things that have
    happened
    and shake with great fear!" says the LORD.
¹³"My people have done two sins:
they have turned away from me,
    the spring of living water.
And they have dug their own wells,
    which are broken wells that cannot hold
        water.
¹⁴Have the people of Israel become slaves?
    Have they become like someone who was
        born a slave?
Why were they taken captive?
¹⁵Enemies have roared like lions at Israel;
    they have growled at Israel.
They have destroyed the land of Israel.
    The cities of Israel lie in ruins,
    and all the people have left.
¹⁶The men from the cities of Memphis and
    Tahpanhes
have disgraced you by shaving the top of
    your head.
¹⁷Haven't you brought this on yourselves
    by turning away from the LORD your God
    when he was leading you in the right way?
¹⁸It did not help to go to Egypt
    and drink from the Shihor River.
It did not help to go to Assyria
    and drink from the Euphrates River.

¹⁹Your evil will bring punishment to you,
    and the wrong you have done will teach
        you a lesson.
Think about it and understand
    that it is a terrible evil to turn away from the
        LORD your God.
It is wrong not to fear me,"
    says the Lord GOD All-powerful.
²⁰"Long ago you refused to obey me as an ox
    breaks its yoke. *d*
You broke the ropes I used to hold you
    and said, 'I will not serve you!'
In fact, on every high hill
    and under every green tree
    you lay down as a prostitute. *d*
²¹But I planted you as a special vine,
    as a very good seed.
How then did you turn
    into a wild vine that grows bad fruit?
²²Although you wash yourself with cleanser
    and use much soap,
    I can still see the stain of your guilt," says
        the Lord GOD.
²³"How can you say to me, 'I am not guilty.
    I have not worshipped the Baal *d* idols'?
Look at the things you did in the valley.
    Think about what you have done.
You are like a she-camel in mating season
    that runs from place to place.
²⁴You are like a wild donkey that lives in the
    desert
and sniffs the wind at mating time.
    At that time who can hold her back?
Any male who chases her will easily
    catch her;
    at mating time, it is easy to find her.
²⁵Don't run until your feet are bare
    or until your throat is dry.
But you say, 'It's no use!
    I love those other gods
    and I must chase them!'

²⁶"A thief is ashamed when someone catches
    him stealing.
    In the same way, the family of Israel is
        ashamed—
they, their kings, their officers,
    their priests and their prophets.
²⁷They say to things of wood, 'You are my
    father,'
    and to idols of stone, 'You gave birth to me.'
Those people won't look at me;
    they have turned their backs to me.
But when they get into trouble, they say,
    'Come and save us!'
²⁸Where are the idols you made for yourselves?
    Let them come and save you
    when you are in trouble!

People of Judah, you have as many idols
as you have towns!

²⁹"Why do you complain to me?
All of you have turned against me," says
the LORD.
³⁰"I punished your people, but it did not
help.
They didn't come back when they were
punished.
With your swords you killed your
prophets
like a hungry lion.

³¹"People of Judah, pay attention to the word
of the LORD:
have I been like a desert to the people of
Israel
or like a dark and dangerous land?
Why do my people say, 'We are free to
wander.
We won't come to you any more'?
³²A young woman does not forget her
jewellery,
and a bride does not forget the decorations
for her dress.
But my people have forgotten me
for more days than can be counted.
³³You really know how to chase after love.
Even the worst women can learn evil ways
from you.
³⁴Even on your clothes you have the blood
of poor and innocent people,
but they weren't thieves you caught
breaking in.
You do all these things,
³⁵ but you say, 'I am innocent.
God is not angry with me.'
But I will judge you guilty of lying,
because you say, 'I have not sinned.'
³⁶It is so easy for you to change your mind.
Even Egypt will let you down,
as Assyria let you down.
³⁷You will eventually leave that place
with your hands on your head, like
captives.
You trusted those countries,
but you will not be helped by them,
because the LORD has rejected them.

Judah is Unfaithful

3 "If a man divorces his wife
and she leaves him and marries
another man,
should her first husband come back to her
again?
If he went back to her, wouldn't the land
become completely unclean? ᵈ

But you have acted like a prostitute ᵈ with
many lovers,
and now you want to come back to me?"
says the LORD.
²"Look up to the bare hilltops, Judah.
Is there any place where you have not
been a prostitute?
You have sat by the road waiting for lovers
like an Arab in the desert.
You made the land unclean,
because you did evil and were like a
prostitute.
³So the rain has not come,
and there have not been any spring
rains.
But your face still looks like the face of a
prostitute.
You refuse even to be ashamed of what
you did.

Sidelight In the Middle East, almost
all of the rain falls during
spring (May) and autumn (October). Since crops
depend on this rain, the weather was often seen
as a sign of God's blessing or cursing (see
Jeremiah 3:3). No rain meant rejection by God,
while a good period of rain meant God's
blessing. Read 1 Kings 17:1–16 (p.332), 1 Kings
18:41–46 (p.335) and Isaiah 30:23–26 (p.670).

---

⁴Now you are calling to me,
'My father, you have been my friend since
I was young.
⁵Will you always be angry at me?
Will your anger last for ever?'
Judah, you said this,
but you did as much evil as you could!"

Judah and Israel are like Sisters

⁶When King Josiah was ruling Judah, the LORD
said to me, "Did you see what unfaithful Israel
did? She was like a prostitute ᵈ with her idols on
every hill and under every green tree. ⁷I said to
myself, 'Israel will come back to me after she
does this evil,' but she didn't come back. And
Israel's wicked sister Judah saw what she did.
⁸Judah saw that I divorced unfaithful Israel because of her adultery, ᵈ but that didn't make
Israel's wicked sister Judah afraid. She also went
out and acted like a prostitute! ⁹And she didn't
care that she was acting like a prostitute. So she
made her country unclean ᵈ and was guilty of
adultery, because she worshipped idols made of
stone and wood. ¹⁰Israel's wicked sister didn't
even come back to me with her whole heart, but
only pretended," says the LORD.

¹¹The LORD said to me, "Unfaithful Israel had a better excuse than wicked Judah. ¹²Go and speak this message towards the north:

'Come back, unfaithful people of Israel,' says
    the LORD.
'I will stop being angry with you,
because I am full of mercy,' says the LORD.
'I will not be angry with you for ever.
¹³All you have to do is admit your sin—
    that you turned against the LORD your God
    and worshipped gods under every green tree
    and didn't obey me,'" says the LORD.

¹⁴"Come back to me, you unfaithful children," says the LORD, "because I am your master. I will take one person from every city and two from every family group, and I will bring you to Jerusalem. ¹⁵Then I will give you new rulers who will be faithful to me, who will lead you with knowledge and understanding. ¹⁶In those days there will be many of you in the land," says the LORD. "At that time people will no longer say, 'I remember the Ark ᵈ of the Agreement.' They won't think about it any more or remember it or miss it or make another one. ¹⁷At that time people will call Jerusalem The Throne of the LORD, and all nations will come together in Jerusalem to show respect to the LORD. They will not follow their stubborn, evil hearts any more. ¹⁸In those days the family of Judah will join the family of Israel. They will come together from a land in the north to the land I gave their ancestors.

¹⁹"I, the LORD, said,

'How happy I would be to treat you as my
    own children
    and give you a pleasant land,
    a land more beautiful than that of any other
    nation.'
I thought you would call me 'My Father'
    and not turn away from me.
²⁰But like a woman who is unfaithful to her
    husband,
    family of Israel, you have been unfaithful to
    me," says the LORD.

²¹You can hear crying on the bare hilltops.
    It is the people of Israel crying and praying
    for mercy.
They have become very evil
    and have forgotten the LORD their God.

²²"Come back to me, you unfaithful children,
    and I will forgive you for being unfaithful."

"Yes, we will come to you,
    because you are the LORD our God.
²³It was foolish to worship idols on the hills
    and on the mountains.
Surely the salvation of Israel
    comes from the LORD our God.

²⁴Since our youth, shameful gods have eaten
    up in sacrifice
    everything our ancestors worked for—
    their flocks and herds,
    their sons and daughters.
²⁵Let us lie down in our shame,
    and let our disgrace cover us like a blanket.
We have sinned against the LORD our God,
    both we and our ancestors.
From our youth until now,
    we have not obeyed the LORD our God."

4 "If you will return, Israel,
    then return to me," says the LORD.
"If you will throw away your idols that I
    hate,
    then don't wander away from me.
²If you say when you make a promise,
    'As surely as the LORD lives,'
    and you can say it in a truthful, honest and
    right way,
then the nations will be blessed by him
    and they will praise him for what he has
    done."

³This is what the LORD says to the people of Judah and to Jerusalem:

"Plough your unploughed fields,
    and don't plant seeds among thorns.
⁴Give yourselves to the service of the LORD
    and decide to obey him,
    people of Judah and people of Jerusalem.
If you don't, my anger will spread among you
    like a fire,
    and no one will be able to put it out,
    because of the evil you have done.

Trouble from the North

⁵"Announce this message in Judah and say it
    in Jerusalem:
'Blow the trumpet throughout the country!'
Shout out loud and say,
'Come together!
Let's all escape to the fortified cities!'
⁶Raise the signal flag towards Jerusalem!
Run for your lives and don't wait,
    because I am bringing disaster from the
    north.
There will be terrible destruction."

⁷A lion has come out of his den;
    a destroyer of nations has begun to march.
He has left his home
    to destroy your land.
Your towns will be destroyed
    with no one left to live in them.
⁸So put on rough cloth,
    show how sad you are and cry loudly.
The terrible anger of the LORD
    has not turned away from us.

[9]"When this happens," says the LORD,
"the king and officers will lose their
courage.
The priests will be terribly afraid
and the prophets [d] will be shocked!"

[10]Then I said, "Lord GOD, you have tricked the
people of Judah and Jerusalem. You said, 'You
will have peace,' but now the sword is pointing
at our throats!"

[11]At that time this message will be given to
Judah and Jerusalem: "A hot wind blows from
the bare hilltops of the desert towards the LORD's
people. It is not a gentle wind to separate grain
from chaff. [d] [12]I feel a stronger wind than that.
Now even I will announce judgements against
the people of Judah."

[13]Look! The enemy rises up like a cloud,
and his chariots come like a windstorm.
His horses are faster than eagles.
How terrible it will be for us! We are
ruined!
[14]People of Jerusalem, clean the evil from your
hearts so that you can be saved.
Don't continue making evil plans.
[15]A voice from Dan makes an announcement
and brings bad news from the mountains of
Ephraim.
[16]"Report this to the nations.
Spread this news in Jerusalem:
'Invaders are coming from a faraway
country,
shouting words of war against the cities of
Judah.
[17]The enemy has surrounded Jerusalem as men
guard a field,
because Judah turned against me,' " says
the LORD.
[18]"The way you have lived and acted
has brought this trouble to you.
This is your punishment.
How terrible it is!
The pain stabs your heart!"

Jeremiah's Cry

[19]Oh, how I hurt! How I hurt!
I am bent over in pain.
Oh, the torture in my heart!
My heart is pounding inside me.
I cannot keep quiet,
because I have heard the sound of the
trumpet.
I have heard the shouts of war.
[20]Disaster follows disaster;
the whole country has been destroyed.
My tents are destroyed in only a moment.
My curtains are torn down quickly.

[21]How long must I look at the war flag?
How long must I listen to the war trumpet?
[22]The LORD says, "My people are foolish.
They do not know me.
They are stupid children;
they don't understand.
They are skilful at doing evil,
but they don't know how to do good."

Disaster is Coming

[23]I looked at the earth
and it was empty and had no shape.
I looked at the sky
and its light was gone.
[24]I looked at the mountains
and they were shaking.
All the hills were trembling.
[25]I looked, and there were no people.
Every bird in the sky had flown away.
[26]I looked, and the good, rich land had become
a desert.
All its towns had been destroyed
by the LORD and his great anger.

[27]This is what the LORD says:
"All the land will be ruined,
but I will not completely destroy it.
[28]So the people in the land will cry loudly
and the sky will grow dark,
because I have spoken and will not change
my mind.
I have made a decision and I will not
change it."

[29]At the sound of the horsemen and the
archers,
all the people in the towns run away.
They hide in the thick bushes
and climb up into the rocks.
All of the cities of Judah are empty;
no one lives in them.
[30]Judah, you destroyed nation, what are you
doing?
Why do you put on your finest dress
and decorate yourself with gold jewellery?
Why do you put colour around your eyes?
You make yourself beautiful, but it is all
useless.
Your lovers hate you;
they want to kill you.
[31]I hear a cry like a woman having a baby,
distress like a woman having her first
child.
It is the sound of Jerusalem gasping for
breath.
She lifts her hands in prayer and says,
"Oh! I am about to faint
before my murderers!"

No One is Right

5 The LORD says, "Walk up and down the streets of Jerusalem.
Look around and discover these things.
Search the public squares of the city.
If you can find one person who does honest things,
who searches for the truth,
I will forgive this city.
²Although the people say, 'As surely as the LORD lives!'
they don't really mean it."

³LORD, don't you look for truth in people?
You struck the people of Judah,
but they didn't feel any pain.
You crushed them,
but they refused to learn what is right.
They became more stubborn than a rock;
they refused to turn back to God.
⁴But I thought,
"These are only the poor, foolish people.
They have not learned the way of the LORD
and what their God wants them to do.
⁵So I will go to the leaders of Judah
and talk to them.
Surely they understand the way of the LORD
and know what God wants them to do."
But even the leaders had all joined together
to break away from the LORD;
they had broken their ties with him.
⁶So a lion from the forest will attack them.
A wolf from the desert will kill them.
A leopard is waiting for them near their towns.
It will tear to pieces anyone who comes out of the city,
because the people of Judah have sinned greatly.
They have wandered away from the LORD many times.

⁷The LORD said, "Tell me why I should forgive you.
Your children have left me
and have made promises to idols that are not gods at all.
I gave your children everything they needed,
but they still were like an unfaithful wife to me.
They spent much time in houses of prostitutes. *d*
⁸They are like well-fed horses filled with sexual desire;
each one wants another man's wife.
⁹Shouldn't I punish the people of Judah for doing these things?" says the LORD.

"Shouldn't I give a nation such as this the punishment it deserves?

¹⁰"Go along and cut down Judah's vineyards,
but do not completely destroy them.
Cut off all her people as if they were branches,
because they do not belong to the LORD.
¹¹The families of Israel and Judah
have been completely unfaithful to me,"
says the LORD.

¹²Those people have lied about the LORD
and said, "He will not do anything to us!
Nothing bad will happen to us!
We will never see war or hunger!
¹³The prophets *d* are like an empty wind;
the word of God is not in them.
Let the bad things they say happen to them."

¹⁴So this is what the LORD God All-powerful says:
"The people said I would not punish them.
So, the words I give you will be like fire,
and these people will be like wood that it burns up.
¹⁵Listen, family of Israel," says the LORD,
"I will soon bring a nation from far away to attack you.
It is an old nation that has lasted a long time.
The people there speak a language you do not know;
you cannot understand what they say.
¹⁶Their arrows bring death.
All their people are strong warriors.
¹⁷They will eat your crops and your food.
They will eat your sons and daughters.
They will eat your flocks and herds.
They will eat your grapes and figs.
They will destroy with their swords
the fortified cities you trust.

¹⁸"Yet even then," says the LORD, "I will not destroy you completely. ¹⁹When the people of Judah ask, "Why has the LORD our God done all these terrible things to us?' then give them this answer: 'You have left the LORD and served foreign idols in your own land. So now you will serve foreigners in a land that does not belong to you.'

²⁰"Announce this message to the family of Jacob,
and tell it to the nation of Judah:
²¹hear this message, you foolish people who have no sense.
They have eyes, but they don't really see.
They have ears, but they don't really listen.
²²Surely you are afraid of me," says the LORD.

"You should shake with fear in my
     presence.
I am the one who made the beaches to be a
     border for the sea,
a border the water can never go past.
The waves may pound the beach, but they
     can't win over it.
They may roar, but they cannot go
     beyond it.
23But the people of Judah are stubborn and
     have turned against me.
They have turned aside and gone away
     from me.
24They do not say to themselves,
     'We should fear the LORD our God,
who gives us autumn and spring rains in
     their seasons,
who makes sure we have the harvest at the
     right time.'
25But your evil has kept away both rain and
     harvest.
Your sins have kept you from enjoying good
     things.
26There are wicked men among my people.
Like those who make nets for catching
     birds,
they set their traps to catch people.
27Like cages full of birds,
     their houses are full of lies.
They have become rich and powerful.
28   They have grown big and fat.
There is no end to the evil things they do.
     They won't plead the case of the orphan
     or help the poor be judged fairly.
29Shouldn't I punish the people of Judah for
     doing these things?" says the LORD.
     "Shouldn't I give a nation such as this the
     punishment it deserves?

30"A terrible and shocking thing
     has happened in the land of Judah:
31the prophets speak lies
     and the priests take power into their own
     hands,
and my people love it this way.
     But what will you do when the end
     comes?

Jerusalem is Surrounded

6   "Run for your lives, people of Benjamin!
     Run away from Jerusalem!
Blow the war trumpet in the town of Tekoa!
     Raise the warning flag over the town of
     Beth Hakkerem!
Disaster is coming from the north;
     terrible destruction is coming to you.
2Jerusalem, I will destroy you,
     you who are fragile and gentle.

3Shepherds with their flocks will come against
     Jerusalem.
They will set up their tents all around her,
     each shepherd taking care of his own
     section."
4They say, "Get ready to fight against
     Jerusalem!
Get up! We will attack at noon!
But it is already getting late;
     the evening shadows are growing long.
5So get up! We will attack at night.
     We will destroy the strong towers of
     Jerusalem!"

6This is what the LORD All-powerful says:
"Cut down the trees around Jerusalem
     and build an attack ramp to the top of its
     walls.
This city must be punished.
     Inside it is nothing but slavery.
7Jerusalem pours out her evil
     as a well pours out its water.
The sounds of violence and destruction are
     heard within her.
I can see the sickness and hurts of
     Jerusalem.
8Listen to this warning, Jerusalem,
     or I will turn my back on you
and make your land an empty desert
     where no one can live."

9This is what the LORD All-powerful says:
"Gather the few people of Israel who are left
     alive,
     as you would gather the last grapes on a
     grapevine.
Check each vine again,
     like someone who gathers grapes."

10To whom can I speak? Whom can I warn?
     Who will listen to me?
The people of Israel have closed ears,
     so they cannot hear my warnings.
They don't like the word of the LORD;
     they don't want to listen to it!
11But I am full of the anger of the LORD
     and I am tired of holding it in.

"Pour out my anger on the children who play
     in the street
and on the young men gathered together.
A husband and his wife will both be caught
     in his anger,
     as will the very old.
12Their houses will be turned over to
     others,
     along with their fields and wives,
because I will raise my hand
     and punish the people of Judah," says the
     LORD.

¹³"Everyone, from the least important to the
greatest,
  is greedy for money.
Even the prophets *d* and priests
  all tell lies.
¹⁴They tried to heal my people's serious
    injuries
  as if they were small wounds.
They said, 'It's all right, it's all right.'
  But really, it is not all right.
¹⁵They should be ashamed of the terrible way
    they act,
  but they are not ashamed at all.
They don't even know how to blush about
    their sins.
So they will fall, along with everyone else.
  They will be thrown to the ground when I
    punish them," says the LORD.

¹⁶This is what the LORD says:
"Stand where the roads cross and look.
  Ask where the old way is,
where the good way is, and walk on it.
  If you do, you will find rest for yourselves.
But they have said, 'We will not walk on
    the good way.'
¹⁷I set watchmen over you
  and told you, 'Listen for the sound of the
    war trumpet!'
But they said, 'We will not listen.'
¹⁸So listen, all you nations,
  and pay attention, you witnesses.
Watch what I will do to the people of
    Judah.
¹⁹Hear this, people of the earth:
  I am going to bring disaster to the people
    of Judah
because of the evil they plan.
They have not listened to my messages
  and have rejected my teachings.
²⁰Why do you bring me offerings of incense *d*
    from the land of Sheba?
Why do you bring me sweet-smelling cane
    from a faraway land?
Your burnt offerings will not be accepted;
  your sacrifices do not please me."

²¹So this is what the LORD says:
"I will put problems in front of Judah.
  Fathers and sons will stumble over them
    together.
Neighbours and friends will die."

²²This is what the LORD says:
"Look, an army is coming
  from the land of the north;
a great nation is coming
  from the far sides of the earth.
²³The soldiers carry bows and spears.
  They are cruel and show no mercy.

They sound like the roaring ocean
  when they ride their horses.
That army is coming lined up for battle,
  ready to attack you, Jerusalem."

²⁴We have heard the news about that army
  and are helpless from fear.
We are trapped by our pain,
  like a woman having a baby.
²⁵Don't go out into the fields
  or walk down the roads,
because the enemy has swords.
  There is terror on every side.
²⁶My people, put on rough cloth
  and roll in the ashes to show how sad
    you are.
Cry loudly for those who are dead,
  as if your only son were dead,
because the destroyer
  will soon come against us.

²⁷"Jeremiah, I have made you like a worker
    who tests metal,
  and my people are like the metal.
You must observe their ways
  and test them.
²⁸All my people have turned against me and
    are stubborn.
  They go around telling lies about others.
They are like bronze and iron
  that became covered with rust.
  They all act dishonestly.
²⁹The fire is fanned to make it hotter,
  but the lead does not melt.
The pure metal does not come out;
  the evil is not removed from my people.
³⁰My people will be called rejected silver,
  because the LORD has rejected them."

Jeremiah's Temple Message

7 This is the word that the LORD spoke to
Jeremiah: ²"Stand at the gate of the Temple *d*
and preach this message there:
  " 'Hear the word of the LORD, all you people of
the nation of Judah! All you who come through
these gates to worship the LORD, listen to this
message! ³This is what the LORD All-powerful, the
God of Israel, says: Change your lives and do
what is right! Then I will let you live in this place.
⁴Don't trust the lies of people who say, "This is
the Temple of the LORD. This is the Temple of the
LORD. This is the Temple of the LORD!" ⁵You must
change your lives and do what is right. Be fair to
each other. ⁶You must not oppress strangers,
orphans and widows. Don't kill innocent people
in this place! Don't follow other gods, or they
will ruin your lives. ⁷If you do these things, I will
let you live in this land that I gave to your ancestors to keep for ever.

8" 'But look, you are trusting lies, which is useless. 9Will you steal and murder and be guilty of adultery? *d* Will you falsely accuse other people? Will you burn incense *d* to the god Baal *d* and follow other gods you have not known? 10If you do that, do you think you can come before me and stand in this place where I have chosen to be worshipped? Do you think you can say, "We are safe!" when you do all these hateful things? 11This place where I have chosen to be worshipped is nothing more to you than a hideout for robbers. I have been watching you, says the LORD.

12" 'You people of Judah, go now to the town of Shiloh, where I first made a place to be worshipped. See what I did to it because of the evil things the people of Israel had done. 13You people of Judah have done all these evil things too, says the LORD. I spoke to you again and again, but you did not listen to me. I called you, but you did not

answer. 14So I will destroy the place where I have chosen to be worshipped in Jerusalem. You trust in that place, which I gave to you and your ancestors, but I will destroy it just as I destroyed Shiloh. 15I will push you away from me just as I pushed away your relatives, the people of Israel!'

16"As for you, Jeremiah, don't pray for these people. Don't cry out for them or ask anything for them or beg me to help them, because I will not listen to you. 17Don't you see what they are doing in the towns of Judah and in the streets of Jerusalem? 18The children gather wood, and the fathers use the wood to make a fire. The women make the dough for cakes of bread, and they offer them to the Queen Goddess. *d* They pour out drink offerings to other gods to make me angry. 19But I am not the one the people of Judah are really hurting, says the LORD. They are only hurting themselves and bringing shame upon themselves.

FOLLOWING GOD

More Than Words

Daniel and Matt were brothers. Their dad was a very busy man. He ran his own business buying, renovating and selling houses, and Daniel and Matt spent many Saturdays working for their old man.

On one particular occasion, their dad was short-staffed and went to his sons to see if they could help. Daniel agreed. He didn't have any other plans so he thought, "Why not?" Matt did have other plans. He didn't want to spend his half-term covered in dust and paint, so he simply said, "No".

Half-term arrived, and Daniel and Matt's dad arrived at the job ready to get going. Unfortunately, Daniel was not there. 9.00 a.m., 10.00 a.m., 11.00 a.m., midday . . . still no Daniel. Though he had promised to turn up and help, he let his dad down and just didn't show. However, Matt was a different story. Though he had initially said no, he thought about it and decided he did want to help his dad. Matt arrived at 8.45 a.m. ready to work and spent the whole week covered in dust and paint.

Jesus tells a similar story to this in Matthew 21. It illustrates a famous phrase that says "actions speak louder than words". In **Jeremiah 7:1–15** the prophet warns the people that true worship is displayed, not by words or duty, but through our lives and in actions.

Following God means that we are more like Matt than Daniel. Daniel's actions did not back up his words. However, Matt's actions spoke much louder than his words.

* Can people see that you are a Christian by the way you live your life or are they left thinking, "You say one thing but do another!"
* If someone said to you, "Change your life and do what is right," what might you change?

Consider . . .

* spending a day making a note of every promise you make – from promising to help with the washing-up to arranging to meet a friend. How many of these commitments do you meet?
* whether there are things you could do (e.g. caring for people or giving to the poor) that demonstrate that your Christian life is more than words.

For more, see . . .

* 1 Kings 9:1–9 (p.324)
* Romans 12:1–2 (p.1203)
* Matthew 21:28–32 (p.978)

20" 'So this is what the Lord GOD says: I will pour out my anger on this place, on people and animals, on the trees in the field and the crops in the ground. My anger will be like a hot fire that no one can put out.

Obedience is More than Sacrifice

21" 'This is what the LORD All-powerful, the God of Israel, says: Offer burnt offerings along with your other sacrifices, and eat the meat yourselves! 22When I brought your ancestors out of Egypt, I did not speak to them and give them commands only about burnt offerings and sacrifices. 23I also gave them this command: obey me, and I will be your God and you will be my people. Do all that I command so that good things will happen to you. 24But your ancestors did not listen or pay attention to me. They were stubborn and did whatever their evil hearts wanted. They went backwards, not forwards. 25Since the day your ancestors left Egypt, I have sent my servants, the prophets, again and again to you. 26But your ancestors did not listen or pay attention to me. They were very stubborn and did more evil than their ancestors.'

27"Jeremiah, you will tell all these things to the people of Judah, but they will not listen to you. You will call to them, but they will not answer you. 28So say to them, 'This is the nation that has not obeyed the LORD its God. These people do nothing when I correct them. They do not tell the truth; it has disappeared from their lips.

The Valley of Killing

29" 'Cut off your hair and throw it away. Go up to the bare hilltop and cry out, because the LORD has rejected these people. He has turned his back on them, and in his anger will punish them. 30The people of Judah have done what I said was evil, says the LORD. They have set up their hateful idols in the place where I have chosen to be worshipped and have made it unclean. *d* 31The people of Judah have built places of worship at Topheth in the Valley of Ben Hinnom. There they burned their own sons and daughters as sacrifices, something I never commanded. It never even entered my mind. 32So, I warn you. The days are coming, says the LORD, when people will not call this place Topheth or the Valley of Ben Hinnom any more. They will call it the Valley of Killing. They will bury the dead in Topheth until there is no room to bury anyone else. 33Then the bodies of the dead will become food for the birds of the sky and for the wild animals. There will be no one left alive to chase them away. 34I will end the happy sounds of the bride and bridegroom. There will be no happy sounds in the cities of Judah or in the streets of Jerusalem, because the land will become an empty desert!

8 " 'The LORD says: At that time they will remove from their tombs the bones of Judah's kings and officers, priests and prophets, *d* and the people of Jerusalem. 2The bones will be spread on the ground under the sun, moon and stars that the people loved and served and went after and searched for and worshipped. No one will gather up the bones and bury them. So they will be like dung thrown on the ground. 3I will force the people of Judah to leave their homes and their land. Those of this evil family who are not dead will wish they were, says the LORD All-powerful.'

Sin and Punishment

4"Say to the people of Judah: 'This is what the LORD says:

When people fall down, don't they get up
     again?
   And when someone goes the wrong way,
     doesn't he turn back?
5Why, then, have the people of Jerusalem gone
     the wrong way
   and not turned back?
They believe their own lies
   and refuse to turn around and come back.
6I have listened to them very carefully,
   but they do not say what is right.
They do not feel sorry about their wicked ways,
   saying, "What have I done?"
Each person goes his own way,
   like a horse charging into a battle.
7Even the birds in the sky
   know the right times to do things.
The storks, doves, swifts and thrushes
   know when it is time to migrate.
But my people don't know
   what the LORD wants them to do.

8" 'You keep saying, "We are wise,
   because we have the teachings of the LORD."
But actually, those who explain the Scriptures
   have written lies with their pens.
9These wise men refused to listen to the word
     of the LORD,
   so they are not really wise at all.
They will be ashamed.
   They will be shocked and trapped.
10So I will give their wives to other men
   and their fields to new owners.
Everyone, from the least important to the
     greatest,
   is greedy for money.
Even the prophets *d* and priests
   all tell lies.
11They tried to heal my people's serious injuries
   as if they were small wounds.
They said, "It's all right, it's all right."
   But really, it is not all right.

¹²They should be ashamed of the terrible way
they act,
but they are not ashamed at all.
They don't even know how to blush about
their sins.
So they will fall, along with everyone else.
They will be thrown to the ground when I
punish them, says the LORD.

¹³" 'I will take away their crops, says the LORD.
There will be no grapes on the vine
and no figs on the fig tree.
Even the leaves will dry up and die.
I will take away what I gave them.' "

¹⁴"Why are we just sitting here?
Let's get together!
We have sinned against the LORD,
so he has given us poisoned water to drink.
Come, let's run to the fortified cities.
The LORD our God has decided that we
must die,
so let's die there.

¹⁵We hoped to have peace,
but nothing good has come.
We hoped for a time when he would heal us,
but only terror has come.

¹⁶From the land of Dan,
the snorting of the enemy's horses is heard.
The ground shakes from the neighing of
their large horses.
They have come and destroyed
the land and everything in it,
the city and all who live there."

¹⁷"Look! I am sending poisonous snakes to
attack you.
These snakes cannot be charmed,
and they will bite you," says the LORD.

Jeremiah's Sadness

¹⁸God, you are my comfort when I am very sad
and when I am afraid.

¹⁹Listen to the sound of my people.
They cry from a faraway land:
"Isn't the LORD still in Jerusalem?
Isn't Jerusalem's king still there?"

But God says, "Why did the people make me
angry by worshipping idols,
useless foreign idols?"

²⁰And the people say, "Harvest time is over;
summer has ended,
and we have not been saved."

²¹Because my people are crushed, I am crushed.
I cry loudly and am afraid for them.
²²Isn't there balm ᵈ in the land of Gilead?
Isn't there a doctor there?
So why aren't the hurts of my people healed?

9 I wish my head were like a spring of
water
and my eyes like a fountain of tears!
Then I could cry day and night
for my people who have been killed.
²I wish I had a place in the desert—
a house where travellers spend the night—
so I could leave my people.
I could go away from them,
because they are all unfaithful to God;
they are all turning against him.

Judah's Failures

³"They use their tongues like a bow,
shooting lies from their mouths like arrows.
Lies, not truth,
have grown strong in the land.
They go from one evil thing to another.
They do not know who I am," says the LORD.
⁴"Watch out for your friends
and don't trust your own relatives,
because every relative is a cheat
and every friend tells lies about you.
⁵Everyone lies to his friend
and no one speaks the truth.
The people of Judah have taught their
tongues to lie.
They have become tired from sinning.
⁶Jeremiah, you live in the middle of lies.
With their lies the people refuse to know
me," says the LORD.

⁷So this is what the LORD All-powerful says:
"I will test the people of Judah as a person
tests metal in a fire.
I have no other choice,
because my people have sinned.
⁸Their tongues are like sharp arrows.
Their mouths speak lies.
Everyone speaks nicely to his neighbour,
but he is secretly planning to attack him.
⁹Shouldn't I punish the people for doing this?"
says the LORD.
"Shouldn't I give a nation like this the
punishment it deserves?"

¹⁰I, Jeremiah, will cry loudly for the mountains
and sing a funeral song for the empty fields.
They are empty, and no one passes through.
The mooing of cattle cannot be heard.

The birds have flown away,
    and the animals are gone.

11"I, the Lord, will make the city of Jerusalem
        a heap of ruins,
    a home for wild dogs.
I will destroy the cities of Judah
    so no one can live there."

12What person is wise enough to understand these things? Is there someone who has been taught by the Lord who can explain them? Why was the land ruined? Why has it been made like an empty desert where no one goes? 13The Lord answered, "It is because Judah has stopped following my teachings that I gave them. They have not obeyed me or done what I told them to do. 14Instead, they were stubborn and followed the Baals,*d* as their ancestors taught them to do." 15So this is what the Lord All-powerful, the God of Israel, says: "I will soon make the people of Judah eat bitter food and drink poisoned water. 16I will scatter them through other nations that they and their ancestors never knew about. I will chase the people of Judah with the sword until they are all killed."

17This is what the Lord All-powerful says:
"Now, think about these things!
    Call for the women who cry at funerals to
        come.
    Send for those women who are good at
        that job.
18Let them come quickly
    and cry loudly for us.
Then our eyes will fill with tears
    and streams of water will flow from our
        eyelids.
19The sound of loud crying is heard from
        Jerusalem:
    'We are truly ruined!
    We are truly ashamed!
We must leave our land,
    because our houses are in ruins.'"

20Now, women of Judah, listen to the word of
        the Lord;
    open your ears to hear the words of his
        mouth.
Teach your daughters how to cry loudly.
    Teach one another a funeral song.
21Death has climbed in through our windows
    and has entered our strong cities.
Death has taken away our children who play
        in the streets
    and the young men who meet in the city
        squares.

22Say, "This is what the Lord says:
'The dead bodies of people will lie
    in the open field like dung.

They will lie like grain a farmer has cut,
    but there will be no one to gather them.'"

23This is what the Lord says:
"The wise must not boast about their
        wisdom.
    The strong must not boast about their
        strength.
    The rich must not boast about their money.
24But if someone wants to boast, let him boast
        that he understands and knows me.
Let him boast that I am the Lord,
    and that I am kind and fair,
    and that I do things that are right on earth.
This kind of boasting pleases me," says the
        Lord.

25The Lord says, "The time is coming when I will punish all those who are circumcised *d* only in the flesh: 26the people of Egypt, Judah, Edom, Ammon and Moab and the desert people who cut their hair short. The men in all those countries are not circumcised. And the whole family of Israel does not give itself to serving me."

The Lord and the Idols

10 Family of Israel, listen to what the Lord says to you. 2This is what he says:
"Don't live like the people from other
        nations,
    and don't be afraid of special signs in
        the sky,
    even though the other nations are afraid of
        them.
3The customs of other people are worth
        nothing.
    Their idols are just wood cut from the
        forest,
    shaped by a worker with his chisel.
4They decorate their idols with silver and
        gold.
    With hammers and nails they fasten them
        down
    so they won't fall over.
5Their idols are like scarecrows in melon
        fields;
    they cannot talk.
Since they cannot walk,
    they must be carried.
Do not be afraid of those idols,
    because they can't hurt you
    and they can't help you either."

6Lord, there is no one like you.
    You are great,
    and your name is great and powerful.
7Everyone should respect you, King of the
        nations;
    you deserve respect.

Of all the wise people among the nations
   and in all the kingdoms,
     none of them is as wise as you.
⁸Those wise people are stupid and foolish.
   Their teachings come from worthless
     wooden idols.
⁹Hammered silver is brought from Tarshish
   and gold from Uphaz,
so the idols are made by craftsmen and
   goldsmiths.
   They put blue and purple clothes on the
     idols.
   All these things are made by skilled
     workers.
¹⁰But the LORD is the only true God.
   He is the only living God, the King for
     ever.
The earth shakes when he is angry
   and the nations cannot stand up to his
     anger.

¹¹"Tell them this message: 'These gods did not make heaven and earth; they will be destroyed and disappear from heaven and earth.' "

¹²God made the earth by his power.
   He used his wisdom to build the world
   and his understanding to stretch out the
     skies.
¹³When he thunders, the waters in the skies
     roar.
   He makes clouds rise in the sky all over the
     earth.
He sends lightning with the rain
   and brings out the wind from his
     storehouses.
¹⁴People are so stupid and know so little.
   Goldsmiths are made ashamed by their
     idols,
because those statues are only false gods.
   They have no breath in them.
¹⁵They are worth nothing; people make fun of
     them.
   When they are judged, they will be
     destroyed.
¹⁶But God, who is Jacob's Portion, *d* is not like
   the idols.
   He made everything
and he chose Israel to be his special people.
   The LORD All-powerful is his name.

Destruction is Coming

¹⁷Get everything you own and prepare to
     leave,
   you people who are trapped by your
     enemies.
¹⁸This is what the LORD says:
   "At this time I will throw out the people
     who live in this land.

I will bring trouble to them
   so that they may be captured."
¹⁹How terrible it will be for me because of my
     injury.
   My wound cannot be healed.
Yet I told myself,
   "This is my sickness; I must suffer
     through it."
²⁰My tent is ruined
   and all its ropes are broken.
My children have gone away and left me.
   No one is left to put up my tent again
   or to set up a shelter for me.
²¹The shepherds are stupid
   and don't ask the LORD for advice.
So they do not have success
   and all their flocks are scattered and lost.
²²Listen! The news is coming.
   A loud noise comes from the north
to make the towns of Judah an empty
     desert
   and a home for wild dogs!

Jeremiah's Prayer

²³LORD, I know that a person's life doesn't
     really belong to him.
   No one can control his own life.
²⁴LORD, correct me, but be fair.
   Don't punish me in your anger,
   or you will destroy me.
²⁵Pour out your anger on other nations
   that do not know you
   and do not pray to you.
Those nations have destroyed Jacob's
     family.
   They have eaten him up completely
   and destroyed his homeland.

The Agreement is Broken

11 These are the words that the LORD spoke to Jeremiah: ²"Listen to the words of this agreement and tell them to the people of Judah and those living in Jerusalem. ³Tell them this is what the LORD, the God of Israel, says: 'Cursed is the person who does not obey the words of this agreement ⁴that I made with your ancestors when I brought them out of Egypt. Egypt was like a furnace for melting iron!' I told them, 'Obey me and do everything I command you. Then you will be my people, and I will be your God. ⁵Then I will keep the promise I made to your ancestors to give them a fertile land.' And you are living in that country today."

I answered, "Amen, LORD."

⁶The LORD said to me, "Announce *d* this message in the towns of Judah and in the streets of Jerusalem: 'Listen to the words of this agreement

and obey them. ⁷I warned your ancestors to obey me when I brought them out of Egypt. I have warned them again and again to this very day: "Obey me!" ⁸But your ancestors did not listen to me. They were stubborn and did what their own evil hearts wanted. So I made all the curses of this agreement come upon them. I commanded them to obey the agreement, but they did not.' "

⁹Then the LORD said to me, "I know the people of Judah and those living in Jerusalem have made secret plans. ¹⁰They have gone back to the same sins their ancestors did. Their ancestors refused to listen to my message and followed and worshipped other gods instead. The families of Israel and Judah have broken the agreement I made with their ancestors. ¹¹So this is what the LORD says: 'I will soon bring a disaster on the people of Judah which they will not be able to escape. They will cry to me for help, but I will not listen to them. ¹²The people living in the towns of Judah and the city of Jerusalem will pray to their idols to whom they burn incense. *d* But those idols will not be able to help when disaster comes. ¹³Look, people of Judah, you have as many idols as there are towns in Judah. You have built as many altars to burn incense to that shameful god Baal *d* as there are streets in Jerusalem.'

¹⁴"As for you, Jeremiah, don't pray for these people or cry out for them or ask anything for them. I will not listen when they call to me in the time of their trouble.

¹⁵"What is my beloved Judah doing in my
   Temple *d*
  when she makes many evil plans?
  Do you think animal sacrifices will stop your
   punishment?
When you do your evil, then you are happy."
¹⁶The LORD called you "a leafy olive tree,
  with beautiful fruit and shape."
But with the roar of a strong storm
  he will set that tree on fire,
  and its branches will be burned up.

¹⁷The LORD All-powerful, who planted you, has announced that disaster will come to you. This is because the families of Israel and Judah have done evil and have made him angry by burning incense to Baal.

Evil Plans Against Jeremiah

¹⁸The LORD showed me that men were making plans against me. Because he showed me what they were doing, I knew they were against me. ¹⁹Before this, I was like a gentle lamb waiting to be slaughtered. I did not know they had made plans against me, saying:

"Let us destroy the tree and its fruit.
Let's kill him so people will forget him."

²⁰But, LORD All-powerful, you are a fair judge.
  You know how to test people's hearts and
   minds.
I have told you what I have against them.
  So let me see you give them the
   punishment they deserve.

²¹So the LORD speaks about the men from Anathoth who plan to kill Jeremiah and say, "Don't prophesy *d* in the name of the LORD, or we will kill you!" ²²So this is what the LORD All-powerful says: "I will soon punish the men from Anathoth. Their young men will die in war. Their sons and daughters will die from hunger. ²³No one from the city of Anathoth will be left alive, because I will cause a disaster to happen to them that year."

Jeremiah's First Complaint

12 LORD, when I bring my case to you,
   you are always right.
But I want to ask you about the justice you
   give.
  Why are evil people successful?
  Why do dishonest people have such easy
   lives?
²You have put the evil people here
  like plants with strong roots.
  They grow and produce fruit.
With their mouths they speak well of you,
  but their hearts are really far away
   from you.
³But you know my heart, LORD.
  You see me and test my thoughts
   about you.
Drag the evil people away like sheep to be
   slaughtered.
  Set them aside for the day of killing.
⁴How much longer will the land stay
   dried up
  and the grass in every field be dead?
The animals and birds in the land have died,
  because the people are evil.
Yes, they are even saying,
  "God does not see what happens to us."

Sidelight   How would you like to have a complaint named after you? Jeremiah's protesting to God (Jeremiah 12:1–4) made its way into the dictionary as "jeremiad" – "a lamentation or tale of woe".

The LORD's Answer to Jeremiah

⁵"If you get tired while racing against people,
  how can you race against horses?
If you stumble in a country that is safe,

what will you do in the thick thorn-bushes
    along the Jordan River?
[6]Even your own brothers and members of your
    own family
  are making plans against you.
  They are crying out against you.
Don't trust them,
  even when they say nice things to you!

[7]"I have left Israel;
  I have left my people.
I have given the people I love
  over to their enemies.
[8]My people have become to me
  like a lion in the forest.
They roar at me,
  so I hate them.
[9]My people have become to me
  like a speckled bird attacked on all sides by
    hawks.
Go, gather the wild animals.
  Bring them to get something to eat.
[10]Many shepherds have ruined my vineyards
  and trampled the plants in my field.
They have turned my beautiful field
  into an empty desert.
[11]They have turned my field into a desert
  that is wilted and dead.
The whole country is an empty desert,
  because no one who lives there cares.
[12]Many soldiers have marched over those
    barren hills.
  The LORD is using the armies to punish that
    land
from one end to the other.
  No one is safe.
[13]The people have planted wheat,
  but they have harvested only thorns.
They have worked hard until they were very
    tired,
  but they have nothing for all their work.
They are ashamed of their poor harvest,
  because the LORD's terrible anger has caused
    this."

[14]This is what the LORD said to me: "Here is
what I will do to all my wicked neighbours who
take the land I gave my people Israel. I will pull
them up and throw them out of their land. And
I will pull up the people of Judah from among
them. [15]But after I pull them up, I will feel sorry
for them again. I will bring each person back to
his own property and to his own land. [16]I want
them to learn their lessons well. In the past they
taught my people to swear by Baal's[d] name. But
if they will now learn to swear by my name,
saying 'As surely as the LORD lives . . .' I will
allow them to rebuild among my people. [17]But if

a nation will not listen to my message, I will pull
it up completely and destroy it," says the LORD.

Jeremiah's Linen Belt

13 This is what the LORD said to me: "Go
and buy a linen belt and put it around
your waist. Don't let the belt get wet."

[2]So I bought a linen belt, just as the LORD told
me, and put it around my waist. [3]Then the LORD
spoke his word to me a second time: [4]"Take
the belt you bought and are wearing, and go to
Perath. Hide the belt there in a crack in the
rocks." [5]So I went to Perath and hid the belt
there, just as the LORD told me.

[6]Many days later the LORD said to me, "Now
go to Perath and get the belt I told you to hide
there." [7]So I went to Perath and dug up the belt
and took it from where I had hidden it. But now
it was ruined; it was good for nothing.

[8]Then the LORD spoke his word to me. [9]This
is what the LORD said: "In the same way I will
ruin the pride of the people of Judah and the
great pride of Jerusalem. [10]These evil people
refuse to listen to my warnings. They stubbornly
do only what they want to do, and they follow
other gods to serve and worship them. So they
will become like this linen belt—good for nothing. [11]As a belt is wrapped tightly around a
person's waist, I wrapped the families of Israel
and Judah around me," says the LORD. "I did
that so they would be my people and bring
fame, praise and honour to me. But my people
would not listen.

Sidelight

The Bible is full of people
who taught in original
ways. Elijah called down fire from heaven
(1 Kings 18:20–39, p.363), and Jesus taught
by parables (Matthew 13, p.961). Read how
Jeremiah taught in Jeremiah 13:1–11 and
19:12–15 (p.738).

Warnings About Leather Wine Bags

[12]"Say to them: 'This is what the LORD, the God
of Israel, says: all leather bags for holding wine
should be filled with wine.' People will say to
you: 'Of course, we know all wine bags should be
filled with wine.' [13]Then you will say to them,
'This is what the LORD says: I will make everyone in this land like a drunken person—the
kings who sit on David's throne, the priests and
the prophets[d] and all the people who live in
Jerusalem. [14]I will make them smash against one
another, fathers and sons alike, says the LORD. I
will not feel sorry or have pity on them or show

mercy that would stop me from destroying them.' "

Threat of Slavery

¹⁵Listen and pay attention.
   Don't be too proud,
   because the LORD has spoken to you.
¹⁶Give glory to the LORD your God
   before he brings darkness
and before you slip and fall
   on the dark hills.
You hope for light,
   but he will turn it into thick darkness;
   he will change it into deep gloom.
¹⁷If you don't listen to him,
   I will cry secretly
   because of your pride.
I will cry painfully,
   and my eyes will overflow with tears,
   because the LORD's people will be captured.

¹⁸Tell this to the king and the queen mother:
   "Come down from your thrones,
because your beautiful crowns
   have fallen from your heads."
¹⁹The cities of southern Judah are locked up
   and no one can open them.
All Judah will be taken as captives to a
      foreign land;
   they will be carried away completely.

²⁰Jerusalem, look up and see
   the people coming from the north.
Where is the flock God gave you to care for,
   the flock you boasted about?
²¹What will you say when they appoint as your
      heads
   those you had thought were your friends?
Won't you have much pain and trouble,
   like a woman giving birth to a baby?
²²You might ask yourself,
   "Why has this happened to me?"
It happened because of your many sins.
   Because of your sins, your skirt was torn off
   and your body has been treated badly.
²³Can a person from Cush change the colour of
      his skin?
   Can a leopard change his spots?
In the same way, Jerusalem, you cannot
      change and do good,
   because you are accustomed to doing evil.

²⁴"I will scatter you like chaff *ᵈ* that is blown
      away by the desert wind.
²⁵This is what will happen to you;
   this is your part in my plans," says the
      LORD.
   "Because you forgot me
   and trusted in false gods,

²⁶I will pull your skirts up over your face
   so everyone will see your shame.
²⁷I have seen the terrible things you have
      done:
   your acts of adultery *ᵈ* and your snorting,
   your prostitution, *ᵈ*
your hateful acts
   on the hills and in the fields.
How terrible it will be for you, Jerusalem.
   How long will you continue being
      unclean?" *ᵈ*

A Time Without Rain

14 These are the words that the LORD spoke to Jeremiah about the time when there was no rain:
²"The nation of Judah cries as if someone has
      died,
   and her cities are very sad.
They are distressed over the land.
   A cry goes up to God from Jerusalem.
³The important men send their servants to get
      water.
   They go to the wells,
   but they find no water.
So they return with empty jars.
   They are ashamed and embarrassed
   and cover their heads in shame.
⁴The ground is dry and cracked open,
   because no rain falls on the land.
The farmers are upset and sad,
   so they cover their heads in shame.
⁵Even the mother deer in the field
   leaves her newborn fawn to die,
   because there is no grass.
⁶Wild donkeys stand on the bare hills
   and sniff the wind like wild dogs.
But their eyes go blind,
   because there is no food."

⁷We know that we suffer because of our
      sins.
   LORD, do something to help us for the good
      of your name.
We have left you many times;
   we have sinned against you.
⁸God, the Hope of Israel,
   you have saved Israel in times of trouble.
Why are you like a stranger in the land,
   or like a traveller who only stays one
      night?
⁹Why are you like someone who has been
      attacked by surprise,
   like a warrior who is not able to save
      anyone?
But you are among us, LORD,
   and we are called by your name
   so don't leave us without help!

¹⁰This is what the LORD says about the people of Judah:

"They really love to wander from me;
   they don't stop themselves from
      leaving me.
So now the LORD will not accept them.
   He will now remember the evil they do
   and will punish them for their sins."

¹¹Then the LORD said, "Don't pray for good things to happen to the people of Judah. ¹²Even if they give up eating, I will not listen to their prayers. Even if they offer burnt offerings and grain offerings to me, I will not accept them. Instead, I will destroy the people of Judah with war, hunger and terrible diseases."

¹³But I said, "Oh, Lord GOD, the prophets *d* keep telling the people, 'You will not suffer from an enemy's sword or from hunger. I, the LORD, will give you peace in this land.'"

¹⁴Then the LORD said to me, "Those prophets are prophesying lies in my name. I did not send them or appoint them or speak to them. They have been prophesying false visions, idolatries, worthless magic and their own wishful thinking. ¹⁵So this is what I say about the prophets who are prophesying in my name. I did not send them. They say, 'No enemy will attack this country with swords. There will never be hunger in this land.' So those prophets will die from hunger and from an enemy's sword. ¹⁶And the people to whom the prophets speak will be thrown into the streets of Jerusalem. There they will die from hunger and from an enemy's sword. And no one will be there to bury them, or their wives, or their sons or their daughters. I will punish them.

¹⁷"Jeremiah, speak this message to the people of Judah:

'Let my eyes be filled with tears
   night and day, without stopping.
My people have received a terrible blow;
   they have been hurt badly.
¹⁸If I go into the country,
   I see people killed by swords.
If I go into the city,
   I see much sickness, because the people
      have no food.
Both the priests and the prophets
   have been taken to a foreign land.'"

¹⁹LORD, have you completely rejected the nation
      of Judah?
   Do you hate Jerusalem?
Why have you hurt us so badly
   that we cannot be made well again?
We hoped for peace,
   but nothing good has come.
We looked for a time of healing,
   but only terror came.

²⁰LORD, we admit that we are wicked
   and that our ancestors did evil things.
   We have sinned against you.
²¹For your sake, do not hate us.
   Do not take away the honour from your
      glorious throne.
Remember your agreement with us,
   and do not break it.
²²Do foreign idols have the power to bring
      rain?
   Does the sky itself have the power to send
      down showers?
No, it is you, LORD our God.
   You are our only hope,
   because you are the one who made all these
      things.

15 Then the LORD said to me: "I would not feel sorry for the people of Judah even if Moses and Samuel prayed for them. Send them away from me! Tell them to go! ²When they ask you, 'Where will we go?' tell them: 'This is what the LORD says:

Those who are meant to die
   will die.
Those who are meant to die in war
   will die in war.
Those who are meant to die from hunger
   will die from hunger.
Those who are meant to be taken captive
   will be taken captive.'

³"I will send four kinds of destroyers against them," says the LORD. "I will send war to kill, dogs to drag the bodies away, and the birds of the air and wild animals to eat and destroy the bodies. ⁴I will make the people of Judah hated by everyone on earth because of what Manasseh did in Jerusalem. (Manasseh son of Hezekiah was king of the nation of Judah.)

⁵"Who will feel sorry for you, Jerusalem?
   Who will be sad and cry for you?
   Who will go out of his way to ask how
      you are?
⁶Jerusalem, you have left me," says the LORD.
   "You keep going further and further away,
so I have taken hold of you and destroyed you.
   I was tired of holding back my anger.
⁷I have separated the people of Judah with my
      pitchfork
   and scattered them at the city gates of the
      land.
My people haven't changed their ways.
   So I have destroyed them
   and taken away their children.
⁸There are more widows than grains of sand
      in the sea.
I brought a destroyer at noontime

against the mothers of the young men of
Judah.
I suddenly brought pain and fear
on the people of Judah.
⁹When the enemy attacked, a woman with
seven sons felt faint because they would
all die.
She became weak and unable to breathe.
Her bright day became dark from sadness.
She felt shame and disgrace.
And everyone else left alive in Judah
I will hand over to the enemies too!" says
the LORD.

Jeremiah's Second Complaint

¹⁰Mother, I am sorry that you gave birth to me
since I must accuse and criticise the whole
land.
I have not loaned or borrowed anything,
but everyone curses me.
¹¹The LORD said,
"I have saved you for a good reason.
I have made your enemies beg you
in times of disaster and trouble.
¹²No one can smash a piece of iron or bronze
that comes from the north.
¹³Your wealth and treasures
I will give to others free of charge,
because the people of Judah have sinned
throughout the country.
¹⁴I will make you slaves to your enemies
in a land you have never known.
My anger is like a hot fire,
and it will burn against you."

¹⁵LORD, you understand.
Remember me and take care of me.
Punish for me those who are hurting me.
Don't destroy me while you remain patient
with them.
Think about the shame I suffer for you.
¹⁶Your words came to me and I listened
carefully to them.
Your words made me very happy,
because I am called by your name,
LORD God All-powerful.
¹⁷I never sat with the crowd
as they laughed and had fun.
I sat by myself, because you were there,
and you filled me with anger at the evil
around me.
¹⁸I don't understand why my pain has no end.
I don't understand why my injury is not
cured or healed.
Will you be like a brook that goes dry?
Will you be like a spring that stops flowing?

¹⁹So this is what the LORD says:

"If you change your heart and return to me, I
will take you back.
Then you may serve me.
And if you speak things that have worth,

> **Sidelight** Reading Jeremiah is like
> stumbling into a room
> and finding someone crying (for example, see
> Jeremiah 15:10–18 and 20:7–18, p.739). No
> wonder Jeremiah became known as "the
> weeping prophet".

not useless words,
then you may speak for me.
Let the people of Judah turn to you,
but you must not change and be
like them.
²⁰I will make you as strong as a wall to this
people,
as strong as a wall of bronze.
They will fight against you,
but they will not defeat you,
because I am with you.
I will rescue you and save you," says the
LORD.
²¹"I will save you from these wicked people
and rescue you from these cruel people."

The Day of Disaster

16 Then the LORD spoke his word to me:
²"You must not get married or have sons
or daughters in this place."

³The LORD says this about the sons and daughters born in this land and their mothers and fathers: ⁴"They will die of terrible diseases, and no
one will cry for them or bury them. Their bodies
will lie on the ground like dung. They will die in
war, or they will starve to death. Their bodies will
be food for the birds of the sky and for the wild
animals."

⁵So this is what the LORD says: "Jeremiah, do
not go into a house where there is a funeral meal.
Do not go there to cry for the dead or to show
your sorrow for them, because I have taken back
my blessing, my love and my pity from these people," says the LORD. ⁶"Important people and common people will die in the land of Judah. No one
will bury them or cry for them or cut himself or
shave his head to show sorrow for them. ⁷No one
will bring food to comfort those who are crying
for the dead. No one will offer a drink to comfort
someone whose mother or father has died.

⁸"Do not go into a house where the people are
having a feast to sit down to eat and drink, ⁹because this is what the LORD All-powerful, the God
of Israel, says: I will soon stop the sounds of joy

and gladness and the happy sounds of brides and bridegrooms in this place. This will happen during your lifetime.

¹⁰"When you tell the people of Judah these things, they will ask you, 'Why has the LORD said these terrible things to us? What have we done wrong? What sin have we done against the LORD our God?'

¹¹"Then say to them: 'This is because your ancestors stopped following me,' says the LORD. 'And they followed other gods and served and worshipped them. Your ancestors left me and stopped obeying my teaching. ¹²But you have done even more evil than your ancestors. You are very stubborn and do only what you want to do; you have not obeyed me. ¹³So I will throw you out of this country and send you into a land that you and your ancestors never knew. There you can serve other gods day and night, because I will not help you or show you any favours.'

¹⁴"People say, 'As surely as the LORD lives, who brought the people of Israel out of Egypt . . .' But the time is coming," says the LORD, "when people will not say this any more. ¹⁵They will say instead, 'As surely as the LORD lives, who brought the Israelites from the northern land and from all the countries where he had sent them . . .' And I will bring them back to the land I gave to their ancestors.

¹⁶"I will soon send for many fishermen to come to this land," says the LORD. "And they will catch the people of Judah. After that, I will send for many hunters to come to this land. And they will hunt the people of Judah on every mountain and hill and in the cracks of the rocks. ¹⁷I see everything they do. They cannot hide from me the things they do; their sin is not hidden from my eyes. ¹⁸I will pay back the people of Judah twice for every one of their sins, because they have made my land unclean. *d* They have filled my country with their hateful idols."

¹⁹LORD, you are my strength and my
    protection,
  my safe place in times of trouble.
The nations will come to you from all over
    the world
  and say, "Our ancestors had only false
    gods,
  useless idols that didn't help them.
²⁰Can people make gods for themselves?
  They will not really be gods!"

²¹The LORD says, "So I will teach those who
    make idols.
  This time I will teach them
  about my power and my strength.
Then they will know
  that my name is the LORD.

Judah's Guilty Heart

17 "The sin of the people of Judah is
    written with an iron tool.
Their sins were cut with a hard point into
    the stone that is their hearts.
Their sins were cut into the corners of their
    altars.
²Even their children remember
  their altars to idols and their Asherah *d*
    idols
beside the green trees
  and on the high hills.
³My mountain in the open country
  and your wealth and treasures
I will give away to other people.
  I will give away the places of worship in
    your country,
  because you sinned by worshipping there.
⁴You will lose the land I gave you
  and it is your own fault.
I will let your enemies take you as their
    slaves
  to a land you have never known.
This is because you have made my anger
    burn like a hot fire,
  and it will burn for ever."

Trusting in Humans or God

⁵This is what the LORD says:
"A curse is placed on those who trust other
    people,
  who depend on humans for strength,
  who have stopped trusting the LORD.
⁶They are like a bush in a desert
  that grows in a land where no one lives,
  a hot and dry land with bad soil.
They don't know about the good things God
    can give.

⁷"But the person who trusts in the LORD will
    be blessed.
  The LORD will show him that he can be
    trusted.
⁸He will be strong, like a tree planted near
    water
  that sends its roots by a stream.
It is not afraid when the days are hot;
  its leaves are always green.
It does not worry in a year when no rain
    comes;
  it always produces fruit.

⁹"More than anything else, a person's mind is
    evil
  and cannot be healed.
  No one truly understands it.
¹⁰But I, the LORD, look into a person's heart
  and test the mind.
So I can decide what each one deserves;

I can give each one the right payment for
    what he does."

[11]Like a bird hatching an egg it did not lay,
    so are the people who get rich by cheating.
When their lives are half finished, they will
    lose their riches.
    At the end of their lives, it will be clear
    they were fools.

[12]From the beginning, our Temple *d* has been
    honoured
    as a glorious throne for God.
[13]LORD, hope of Israel,
    those who leave you will be shamed.
People who stop following the LORD will be
    like a name written in the dust,
because they have left the LORD, the spring
    of living water.

Jeremiah's Third Complaint

[14]LORD, heal me, and I will truly be healed.
Save me, and I will truly be saved.
You are the one I praise.
[15]The people of Judah keep asking me,
    "Where is the word from the LORD?
Let's see that message come true!"

[16]LORD, I didn't run away from being the
    shepherd you wanted.
    I didn't want the terrible day to come.
You know everything I have said;
    you see all that is happening.
[17]Don't be a terror to me.
    I run to you for safety in times of trouble.
[18]Make those who are hurting me be ashamed,
    but don't bring shame to me.
Let them be terrified,
    but keep me from terror.
Bring the day of disaster on my enemies.
    Destroy them, and destroy them again.

Keeping the Sabbath Holy

[19]This is what the LORD said to me: "Go and stand at the People's Gate of Jerusalem, where the kings of Judah go in and out. And then go to all the other gates of Jerusalem. [20]Say to them there: 'Hear the word of the LORD, kings of Judah, all you people of Judah, and all who live in Jerusalem, who come through these gates into the city. [21]This is what the LORD says: be careful not to carry a load on the Sabbath *d* day or bring it through the gates of Jerusalem. [22]Don't take a load out of your houses on the Sabbath or do any

DECISION MAKING

What Do You Believe?

The book *Walden Two* tells about scientists who played a trick on some sheep. First, they fenced them in with an electrified wire. The sheep worked out pretty quickly that they should stay away from the wire.

Then the scientists replaced the wire with a piece of string. Not knowing the difference, the sheep stayed away from the string too. They even taught their young to stay away from the string. The young sheep believed that the string was dangerous because that's what the older sheep taught them.

People may not believe in electrified string, but we surely listen to a lot of things other people tell us. God warns us to put our trust in him, not in other people. He used Jeremiah to warn the people of Israel to trust in him and not be led astray by other people. Read about it in **Jeremiah 17:5–8**.

• How are the sheep in the experiment like the people in this passage?
• According to this passage, how should you evaluate others' advice?

Consider . . .

• listening to your favourite radio station and writing down the messages you hear in several songs. Do you trust those messages?
• keeping a list this week of the messages you hear about yourself from your friends (for example, "you're pretty", "you're a clown", "you're strange") and deciding if you agree with those messages.

For more, see . . .

• Exodus 32:1–35 (p.90)
• 2 Corinthians 11:12–15 (p.1251)
• Psalm 146:3–6 (p.586)

work on that day. But keep the Sabbath as a holy day, as I commanded your ancestors. 23But your ancestors did not listen or pay attention to me. They were very stubborn and did not listen. I punished them, but it didn't do any good. 24But you must be careful to obey me, says the LORD. You must not bring a load through the gates of Jerusalem on the Sabbath, but you must keep the Sabbath as a holy day and not do any work on that day.

25" 'If you obey this command, kings who sit on David's throne will come through the gates of Jerusalem with their officers. They will come riding in chariots and on horses, along with the people of Judah and Jerusalem. And the city of Jerusalem will have people living in it for ever. 26People will come to Jerusalem from the villages around it, from the towns of Judah, from the land of Benjamin, from the western hills, from the mountains and from southern Judah. They will all bring to the Temple d of the LORD burnt offerings, sacrifices, grain offerings, incense d and offerings to show thanks to God. 27But you must obey me and keep the Sabbath day as a holy day. You must not carry any loads into Jerusalem on the Sabbath. If you don't obey me, I will start a fire at the gates of Jerusalem, and it will burn until it burns even the strong towers. And it will not be put out.' "

The Potter and the Clay

18 This is the word the LORD spoke to Jeremiah: 2"Go down to the potter's house, and I will give you my message there." 3So I went down to the potter's house and saw him working at the potter's wheel. 4He was using his hands to make a pot from clay, but something went wrong with it. So he used that clay to make another pot the way he wanted it to be.

Sidelight The potter (Jeremiah 18:1–4) had an important job in the ancient world. Pottery was preferred over leather or baskets, because it lasted longer, held liquids better, and protected things from animals and insects. Even broken pottery was useful. People etched notes on it because leather and papyrus – the paper of the day – were too expensive.

5Then the LORD spoke his word to me: 6"Family of Israel, can't I do the same thing with you?" says the LORD. "You are in my hands like the clay in the potter's hands. 7There may come a time when I will speak about a nation or a kingdom that I will pull up by its roots or that I will pull down to destroy it. 8But if the people of that nation stop doing the evil they have done, I will change my mind and not carry out my plans to bring disaster to them. 9There may come another time when I will speak about a nation that I will build up and plant. 10But if I see it doing evil by not obeying me, I will change my mind and not carry out my plans to do good for them.

11"So, say this to the people of Judah and those who live in Jerusalem: 'This is what the LORD says: I am preparing disaster for you and making plans against you. So stop doing evil. Change your ways and do what is right.' 12But the people of Judah will answer, 'It won't do any good to try! We will continue to do what we want. Each of us will do what his stubborn, evil heart wants!' "

13So this is what the LORD says:
"Ask the people in other nations this
    question:
    'Have you ever heard anything like this?'
    The people of Israel have done a horrible
        thing.
14The snow on the mountains of Lebanon
    never melts from the rocks.
Its cool, flowing streams
    do not dry up.
15But my people have forgotten me.
    They burn incense to worthless idols
and have stumbled in what they do
    and in the old ways of their ancestors.
They walk along back roads
    and on poor highways.
16So Judah's country will become an empty
        desert.
    People will not stop making fun of it.
They will shake their heads as they pass by;
    they will be shocked at how the country
        was destroyed.
17Like a strong east wind,
    I will scatter them before their enemies.
At that awful time they will not see me
        coming to help them;
    they will see me leaving."

Jeremiah's Fourth Complaint

18Then the people said, "Come, let's make plans against Jeremiah. Surely the teaching of the law by the priest will not be lost. We will still have the advice from the wise men and the words of the prophets. d So let's ruin him by telling lies about him. We won't pay attention to anything he says."

19LORD, listen to me.
    Listen to what my accusers are saying!
20Good should not be paid back with evil,
    but they have dug a pit in order to kill me.

Remember that I stood before you
  and asked you to do good things for these
    people
  and to turn your anger away from them.
²¹So now, let their children starve,
  and let their enemies kill them with
    swords.
Let their wives lose their children and
    husbands.
Let the men from Judah be put to death
  and the young men be killed with swords
    in battle.
²²Let them cry out in their houses
  when you bring an enemy against them
    suddenly.
Let all this happen, because my enemies have
    dug a pit to capture me
  and have hidden traps for my feet.
²³LORD, you know
  about all their plans to kill me.
Don't forgive their crimes
  or erase their sins from your mind.
Make them fall from their places;
  punish them while you are angry.

Judah is like a Broken Jar

19 This is what the LORD said to me: "Go and buy a clay jar from a potter. ²Take some of the elders of the people and the priests, and go out to the Valley of Ben Hinnom, near the front of the Potsherd Gate. There speak the words I tell you. ³Say, 'Kings of Judah and people of Jerusalem, listen to this message from the LORD. This is what the LORD All-powerful, the God of Israel, says: I will soon bring a disaster on this place that will amaze and frighten everyone who hears about it. ⁴The people of Judah have stopped following me. They have made this a place for foreign gods. They have burnt sacrifices to other gods that neither they, nor their ancestors, nor the kings of Judah ever knew. They have filled this place with the blood of innocent people. ⁵They have built places on hilltops to worship Baal, *d* where they burn their children in the fire to Baal. That is something I did not command or speak about; it never even entered my mind. ⁶Now people call this place the Valley of Ben Hinnom or Topheth, but the days are coming, says the LORD, when people will call it the Valley of Killing.

⁷"'At this place I will ruin the plans of the people of Judah and Jerusalem. The enemy will chase them, and I will have them killed with swords. I will make their dead bodies food for the birds and wild animals. ⁸I will completely destroy this city. People will make fun of it and shake their heads when they pass by. They will be shocked when they see how the city was destroyed. ⁹An enemy army will surround the city and will not let anyone go out to get food. I will make the people so hungry that they will eat the bodies of their own sons and daughters, and then they will begin to eat each other.'

¹⁰"While the people with you are watching, break that jar. ¹¹Then say this: 'The LORD All-powerful says: I will break this nation and this city just as someone breaks a clay jar that cannot be put back together again. The dead people will be buried here in Topheth, because there is no other place for them. ¹²This is what I will do to these people and to this place, says the LORD. I will make this city like Topheth. ¹³The houses in Jerusalem and the king's palaces will become as unclean *d* as this place, Topheth, because the people worshipped gods on the roofs ⁿ of their houses. They worshipped the stars and burnt incense *d* to honour them and gave drink offerings to gods.'"

¹⁴When Jeremiah left Topheth where the LORD had sent him to prophesy, *d* he went to the LORD's Temple, *d* stood in the courtyard, and said to all the people: ¹⁵"This is what the LORD All-powerful, the God of Israel, says: 'I will soon bring disaster to Jerusalem and the villages around it, as I said I would. This will happen because the people are very stubborn and do not listen at all to what I say.'"

Pashhur will be Captured

20 Pashhur son of Immer was a priest and the highest officer in the Temple *d* of the LORD. When he heard Jeremiah prophesying *d* in the Temple courtyard, ²he had Jeremiah the prophet beaten. And he locked Jeremiah's hands and feet between large blocks of wood at the Upper Gate of Benjamin of the LORD's Temple. ³The next day when Pashhur took Jeremiah out of the blocks of wood, Jeremiah said to him, "The LORD's name for you is not Pashhur. Now his name for you is Terror on Every Side. ⁴This is what the LORD says: 'I will soon make you a terror to yourself and to all your friends. You will watch enemies killing your friends with swords. And I will give all the people of Judah to the king of Babylon, who will take them away as captives to Babylon and then will kill them with swords. ⁵I will give all the wealth of this city to its enemies— its goods, its valuables and the treasures of the kings of Judah. The enemies will carry all those valuables off to Babylon. ⁶And Pashhur, you and

---

roofs   In Bible times houses were built with flat roofs. The roof was used for drying things such as flax and fruit. And it was used as an extra room, as a place for worship and as a place to sleep in the summer.

everyone in your house will be taken captive. You will be forced to go to Babylon, where you will die and be buried, you and your friends to whom you have prophesied lies.'"

Jeremiah's Fifth Complaint

⁷LORD, you tricked me, and I was fooled.
  You are stronger than I am, so you won.
I have become a joke;
  everyone makes fun of me all day long.
⁸Every time I speak, I shout.
  I am always shouting about violence and
    destruction.
I tell the people about the message I received
    from the LORD,
  but this only brings me insults.
The people make fun of me all day long.
⁹Sometimes I say to myself,
  "I will forget about the LORD.
  I will not speak any more in his name."
But then his message becomes like a burning
    fire inside me,
  deep within my bones.
I get tired of trying to hold it inside me,
  and finally, I cannot hold it in.
¹⁰I hear many people whispering about me:
  "Terror on every side!
  Tell on him! Let's tell the rulers about him."
My friends are all just waiting for me to
    make some mistake.
  They are saying,
"Maybe we can trick him
  so we can defeat him
  and pay him back."

¹¹But the LORD is with me like a strong warrior,
  so those who are chasing me will trip and
    fall;
  they will not defeat me.
They will be ashamed because they have
    failed,
  and their shame will never be forgotten.

¹²LORD All-powerful, you test good people;
  you look deeply into the heart and mind of
    a person.
I have told you my arguments against these
    people,
  so let me see you give them the
    punishment they deserve.

¹³Sing to the LORD!
  Praise the LORD!
He saves the life of the poor
  from the power of the wicked.

Jeremiah's Sixth Complaint

¹⁴Let there be a curse on the day I was born;
  let there be no blessing on the day when my
    mother gave birth to me.

¹⁵Let there be a curse on the man
  who brought my father the news:
"You have a son!"
  This made my father very glad.
¹⁶Let that man be like the towns
  the LORD destroyed without pity.
Let him hear loud crying in the morning
  and battle cries at noon,
¹⁷because he did not kill me before I was
    born.
Then my mother would have been my
    grave;
  she would have stayed pregnant for ever.
¹⁸Why did I have to come out of my mother's
    body?
All I have known is trouble and sorrow,
  and my life will end in shame.

God Rejects King Zedekiah's Request

21 This is the word that the LORD spoke to Jeremiah. It came when Zedekiah king of Judah sent Pashhur son of Malkijah and the priest Zephaniah son of Maaseiah to Jeremiah. ²They said, "Ask the LORD for us what will happen, because Nebuchadnezzar king of Babylon is attacking us. Maybe the LORD will do miracles *d* for us as he did in the past so Nebuchadnezzar will stop attacking us and leave."

³But Jeremiah answered them, "Tell King Zedekiah this: ⁴'Here is what the LORD, the God of Israel, says: you have weapons of war in your hands to defend yourselves against the king of Babylon and the Babylonians, who are all around the city wall. But I will make those weapons useless. Soon I will bring them into the centre of this city. ⁵In my anger, my very great anger, I myself will fight against you with my great power and strength. ⁶I will kill everything living in Jerusalem—both people and animals. They will die from terrible diseases. ⁷Then, says the LORD, I will hand over Zedekiah king of Judah, his officers and the people in Jerusalem who do not die from the terrible diseases or battle or hunger, to Nebuchadnezzar king of Babylon. I will let those win who want to kill the people of Judah, so the people of Judah and Jerusalem will be killed in war. Nebuchadnezzar will not show any mercy or pity or feel sorry for them!'

⁸"Also tell this to the people of Jerusalem: 'This is what the LORD says: I will let you choose to live or die. ⁹Anyone who stays in Jerusalem will die in war or from hunger or from a terrible disease. But anyone who goes out of Jerusalem and surrenders to the Babylonians who are attacking you will live. Anyone who leaves the city will save his life as if it were a prize won in war. ¹⁰I have decided to make trouble for this

city and not to help it, says the LORD. I will give it to the king of Babylon, and he will burn it with fire.'

[11] "Say to Judah's royal family: 'Hear the word of the LORD. [12]Family of David, this is what the LORD says:

You must judge people fairly every morning.
Save the person who has been robbed
from the power of his attacker.
If you don't, I will become very angry.
My anger will be like a fire that no one can
put out,
because you have done evil things.

[13] "'Jerusalem, I am against you,
you who live on top of the mountain
over this valley, says the LORD.
You say, "No one can attack us
or come into our strong city."
[14]But I will give you the punishment you
deserve, says the LORD.
I will start a fire in your forests
that will burn up everything around
you!'"

Judgement Against Evil Kings

22 This is what the LORD says: "Go down to the palace of the king of Judah and prophesy[d] this message there: [2]'Hear the word of the LORD, king of Judah, who rules from David's throne. You and your officers, and your people who come through these gates, listen! [3]This is what the LORD says: do what is fair and right. Save the one who has been robbed from the power of his attacker. Don't mistreat or hurt the foreigners, orphans or widows. Don't kill innocent people here. [4]If you carefully obey these commands, kings who sit on David's throne will come through the gates of this palace with their officers and people, riding in chariots and on horses. [5]But if you don't obey these commands, says the LORD, I swear by my own name that this king's palace will become a ruin.'"

[6]This is what the LORD says about the palace where the king of Judah lives:

"You are tall like the forests of Gilead,
like the mountain tops of Lebanon.
But I will truly make you into a desert,
into towns where no one lives.
[7]I will send men to destroy the palace,
each with his weapons.
They will cut up your strong, beautiful cedar
beams
and throw them into the fire.

[8]"People from many nations will pass by this city and ask each other, 'Why has the LORD done such a terrible thing to Jerusalem, this great city?' [9]And the answer will be: 'Because the people of

Judah stopped following the agreement with the LORD their God. They worshipped and served other gods.'"

Judgement Against Jehoahaz

[10]Don't cry for the dead king or be sad
about him.
But cry painfully for the king who is being
taken away,
because he will never return
or see his homeland again.

[11]This is what the LORD says about Jehoahaz son of Josiah who became king of Judah after his father died and who has left this place: "He will never return. [12]He will die where he has been taken captive, and he will not see this land again."

Judgement Against Jehoiakim

[13]"How terrible it will be for one who builds
his palace by doing evil,
who cheats people so he can build its
upper rooms.
He makes his own people work for nothing
and does not pay them.
[14]He says, 'I will build a great palace for
myself
with large upper rooms.'
So he builds it with large windows
and uses cedar wood for the walls,
which he paints red.

[15]"Does having a lot of cedar in your house
make you a great king?
Your father was satisfied to have food and
drink.
He did what was right and fair,
so everything went well for him.
[16]He helped those who were poor and needy,
so everything went well for him.
That is what it means to know God,"
says the LORD.
[17]"But you only look for and think about
what you can get dishonestly.
You are even willing to kill innocent people to
get it.
You feel free to hurt people and to steal
from them."

[18]So this is what the LORD says to Jehoiakim son of Josiah king of Judah:

"The people of Judah will not cry when
Jehoiakim dies,
saying: 'Oh, my brother,' or 'Oh, my sister.'
They will not cry for him, saying:
'Oh, master,' or 'Oh, my king.'
[19]They will bury him like a donkey,
dragging his body away
and throwing it outside the gates of
Jerusalem.

²⁰"Judah, go up to Lebanon and cry out.
  Let your voice be heard in Bashan.
Cry out from Abarim,
  because all your friends are destroyed!
²¹Judah, when you were successful, I
    warned you,
  but you said, 'I won't listen.'
You have acted like this since you were
    young;
  you have not obeyed me.
²²Like a storm, my punishment will blow all
    your shepherds away
  and send your friends into captivity.
Then you will really be ashamed and
    disgraced
  because of all the wicked things you did.
²³King, you live in your palace,
  cosy in your rooms of cedar.
But when your punishment comes, how you
    will groan
  like a woman giving birth to a baby!

Judgement Upon Jehoiachin

²⁴"As surely as I live," says the LORD, "Je-
hoiachin son of Jehoiakim king of Judah, even if
you were a signet^d ring on my right hand, I
would still pull you off. ²⁵I will hand you over to
Nebuchadnezzar king of Babylon and to the
Babylonians—those people you fear because
they want to kill you. ²⁶I will throw you and
your mother into another country. Neither of
you was born there, but both of you will die
there. ²⁷They will want to come back, but they
will never be able to return."

²⁸Jehoiachin is like a broken pot someone
    threw away;
  he is like something no one wants.
Why will Jehoiachin and his children be
    thrown out
  and sent into a foreign land?
²⁹Land, land, land of Judah,
  hear the word of the LORD!
³⁰This is what the LORD says:
"Write this down in the record about
    Jehoiachin:
  He is a man without children,
  a man who will not be successful in his
    lifetime.
And none of his descendants will be
    successful;
  none will sit on the throne of David
  or rule in Judah."

The Evil Leaders of Judah

23 "How terrible it will be for the leaders of
Judah, who are scattering and destroying
my people," says the LORD.

²They are responsible for the people, so the
LORD, the God of Israel, says to them: "You have
scattered my people and forced them away and
not taken care of them. So I will punish you for
the evil things you have done," says the LORD. ³"I
sent my people to other countries, but I will
gather those who are left alive and bring them
back to their own country. Then they will have
many children and grow in number. ⁴I will place
new leaders over my people, who will take care
of them. And my people will not be afraid or
terrified again, and none of them will be lost,"
says the LORD.

The Good Branch will Come

⁵"The days are coming," says the LORD,
  "when I will raise up a good branch in
    David's family.
He will be a king who will rule in a wise way;
  he will do what is fair and right in the
    land.
⁶In his time Judah will be saved
  and Israel will live in safety.
This will be his name:
  The LORD Does What Is Right.
⁷"So the days are coming," says the LORD, "when
people will not say again: 'As surely as the LORD
lives, who brought Israel out of Egypt . . .' ⁸but
people will say something new: 'As surely as
the LORD lives, who brought the descendants of
Israel from the land of the north and from all the
countries where he had sent them away. . .' then
the people of Israel will live in their own land."

False Prophets will be Punished

⁹A message to the prophets: ^d
My heart is broken.
  All my bones shake.
I'm like someone who is drunk,
  like someone who has been overcome with
    wine.
This is because of the LORD
  and his holy words.
¹⁰The land of Judah is full of people who are
    guilty of adultery. ^d
Because of this, the LORD cursed the land.
It has become a very sad place
  and the pastures have dried up.
The people are evil
  and use their power in the wrong way.

¹¹"Both the prophets and the priests live as if
    there were no God.
I have found them doing evil things even in
    my own Temple," ^d says the LORD.
¹²"So they will be in danger.
They will be forced into darkness
  where they will be defeated.

I will bring disaster on them
in the year I punish them," says the LORD.

[13]"I saw the prophets of Samaria
do something wrong.
Those prophets prophesied by Baal [d]
and led my people Israel away.
[14]And I have seen the prophets of Jerusalem
do terrible things.
They are guilty of adultery
and live by lies.
They encourage evil people to keep on doing
evil,
so the people don't stop sinning.
All of those people are like the city of
Sodom.
The people of Jerusalem are like the city of
Gomorrah to me!"

[15]So this is what the LORD All-powerful says
about the prophets:
"I will make those prophets eat bitter food
and drink poisoned water,

because the prophets of Jerusalem spread
wickedness
through the whole country."

[16]This is what the LORD All-powerful says:
"Don't pay attention to what those prophets
are saying to you.
They are trying to fool you.
They talk about visions their own minds
made up,
not about visions from me.
[17]They say to those who hate me:
'The LORD says: you will have peace.'
They say to all those who are stubborn and do
as they please:
'Nothing bad will happen to you.'
[18]But none of these prophets has stood in the
meeting of angels
to see or hear the message of the LORD.
None of them has paid close attention to
his message.
[19]Look, the punishment from the LORD
will come like a storm.

LEADERSHIP

Who'll Pay For It?

Stephanie had nothing to do with the college "joke" that caused damages of about £1,000 to a small garden in the grounds. She didn't destroy the cherry tree, break the branches off another tree, or saw through the split-rail fence. But it was her picture that appeared on the front page of the local paper with the news story of the vandalism.

Why? Because as student union chair, Stephanie was responsible for answering to the press. She and the other union officers also had the responsibility to pay for the damage out of union funds. They had planned to donate those funds to the children's hospital.

Ironically, the garden had been constructed as a memorial to a student who died in 1974. The student's parents spent at least £7,000 of their own money to create the garden. This family, at the very least, deserved an apology. Whose responsibility was that?

Most student leaders consider that position to be an honour. But being a leader, Stephanie found out, also carries responsibility. In Judah, God held the leaders responsible for misguiding his people. See what God has to say to them in **Jeremiah 23:1–6**.

* Why do you think Stephanie and the leaders of Judah were held accountable for the things happening around them?
* What are some ways you can serve as a leader for God's people?

Consider . . .

* helping your family by taking responsibility for a household chore without being asked.
* offering your leadership in your school or church for a project that needs to be done, and then responsibly completing it.

For more, see . . .

* Micah 3:9–12 (p.892)
* 2 Peter 2:1–3 (p.1365)

* Matthew 23:13–36 (p.982)

His anger will be like a hurricane.
It will come swirling down on the heads of
those wicked people.
20The LORD's anger will not stop
until he finishes what he plans to do.
When that day is over,
you will understand this clearly.
21I did not send those prophets,
but they ran to tell their message.
I did not speak to them,
but they prophesied anyway.
22But if they had stood in the meeting of angels,
they would have told my message to my
people.
They would have turned the people from
their evil ways
and from doing evil.

23"I am a God who is near," says the LORD.
"I am also a God who is far away."
24"No one can hide
where I cannot see him," says the LORD.

"I fill all of heaven and earth," says the
LORD.

25"I have heard the prophets who prophesy lies in my name. They say, 'I have had a dream! I have had a dream!' 26How long will this continue in the minds of these lying prophets? They prophesy from their own wishful thinking. 27They are trying to make the people of Judah forget me by telling each other these dreams. In the same way, their ancestors forgot me and worshipped Baal. 28Is straw the same thing as wheat?" says the LORD. "If a prophet wants to tell about his dreams, let him! But let the person who hears my message speak it truthfully! 29Isn't my message like a fire?" says the LORD. "Isn't it like a hammer that smashes a rock?

30"So I am against the false prophets," says the LORD. "They keep stealing words from each other and say they are from me. 31I am against the false prophets," says the LORD. "They use their own words and pretend it is a message from me.

HONESTY

Slow to Heal

After coming second at the regional karate tournament, Dan McCarty got an invitation to a national competition. But one week before the trip, he tore the ligaments in his ankle and ended up in a plaster cast.

Still, nothing would stop Dan. He convinced his parents to let him make the trip anyway, promising just to watch the tournament. Once on his way, he told his karate instructor that the doctor had put him in a cast only as a precaution. He said he had both his doctor's and parents' permission to participate. Since it was a removable cast, he took it off when he got to the tournament and competed. He even won a few matches.

Although the cast was back on when he got home, his parents worked out what he had done by the way he talked about the competition. They felt betrayed!

Dan paid for his scheme: his ankle healed much more slowly than it would have otherwise. Luckily, the ankle wasn't permanently damaged.

Dan falsely used the authority of his doctor and parents to back up his lies to his instructor. In a similar way, false prophets appealed to God's authority to back up their lies in **Jeremiah 23:23–30**.

* Why were Dan's karate instructor and the people in the passage quick to accept lies?
* When people say, "Honest to God!" do you believe their story more than you would have otherwise? Why or why not?

Consider . . .

* tracking down a rumour you've heard at school and finding out how much is true.
* Mark Twain's comment on lying: "If you tell the truth you don't have to remember anything." Think of a time you've lied. Then make a list of all the other lies you had to tell to support it.

For more, see . . .

* Psalm 139:1–18 (p.581)
* Matthew 5:33–37 (p.945)
* 1 John 4:1–6 (p.1374)

32I am against the prophets who prophesy false dreams," says the LORD. "They mislead my people with their lies and false teachings! I did not send them or command them to do anything for me. They can't help the people of Judah at all," says the LORD.

The Sad Message from the LORD

33"Suppose the people of Judah, a prophet *d* or a priest asks you: 'Jeremiah, what is the message from the LORD?' You will answer them and say, 'You are a heavy load to the LORD, and I will throw you down, says the LORD.' 34A prophet or a priest or one of the people might say, 'This is a message from the LORD.' That person has lied, so I will punish him and his whole family. 35This is what you will say to each other: 'What did the LORD answer?' or 'What did the LORD say?' 36But you will never again say, 'The message of the LORD', because the only message you speak is your own words. You have changed the words of our God, the living God, the LORD All-powerful. 37This is how you should speak to the prophets: 'What answer did the LORD give you?' or 'What did the LORD say?' 38But don't say, 'The message from the LORD'. If you use these words, this is what the LORD says: because you called it a 'message from the LORD', though I told you not to use those words, 39I will pick you up and throw you away from me, along with Jerusalem, which I gave to your ancestors and to you. 40And I will make a disgrace of you for ever; your shame will never be forgotten."

The Good and Bad Figs

24 Nebuchadnezzar king of Babylon captured Jehoiachin son of Jehoiakim and king of Judah, his officers and all the craftsmen and metalworkers of Judah. He took them away from Jerusalem and brought them to Babylon. It was then that the LORD showed me two baskets of figs arranged in front of the Temple *d* of the LORD. 2One of the baskets had very good figs in it, like figs that ripen early in the season. But the other basket had figs too rotten to eat.

3The LORD said to me, "What do you see, Jeremiah?"

I answered, "I see figs. The good figs are very good, but the rotten figs are too rotten to eat."

4Then the LORD spoke his word to me: 5"This is what the LORD, the God of Israel, says: 'I sent the people of Judah out of their country to live in the country of Babylon. I think of those people as good, like these good figs. 6I will look after them and bring them back to the land of Judah. I will not tear them down, but I will build them up. I will not pull them up, but I will plant them so they can grow. 7I will make them want to know

me, that I am the LORD. They will be my people, and I will be their God, because they will return to me with their whole hearts.

8" 'But the bad figs are too rotten to eat.' So this is what the LORD says: 'Zedekiah king of Judah, his officers and all the people from Jerusalem who are left alive, even those who live in Egypt, will be like those rotten figs. 9I will make those people hated as an evil people by all the kingdoms of the earth. People will make fun of them and tell jokes about them and point fingers at them and curse them everywhere I scatter them. 10I will send war, hunger and disease against them. I will attack them until they have all been killed. Then they will no longer be in the land I gave to them and their ancestors.' "

> **Sidelight** Just as book reviews in newspapers give a summary of what each book is about, Jeremiah 25 was written as a summary of the prophet's ministry. So if you are feeling a little confused, Jeremiah 25 offers a brief review of the story so far . . .

A Summary of Jeremiah's Preaching

25 This is the message that came to Jeremiah concerning all the people of Judah. It came in the fourth year that Jehoiakim son of Josiah was king of Judah and the first year Nebuchadnezzar was king of Babylon. 2This is the message Jeremiah the prophet *d* spoke to all the people of Judah and Jerusalem:

3The LORD has spoken his word to me again and again for these past 23 years. I have been a prophet since the thirteenth year of Josiah son of Amon king of Judah. I have spoken messages from the LORD to you from that time until today, but you have not listened.

4The LORD has sent all his servants the prophets to you over and over again, but you have not listened or paid any attention to them. 5Those prophets have said, "Stop your evil ways. Stop doing what is wrong so you can stay in the land that the LORD gave to you and your ancestors to live in for ever. 6Don't follow other gods to serve them or to worship them. Don't make me, the LORD, angry by worshipping idols that are the work of your own hands, or I will punish you."

7"But you people of Judah did not listen to me," says the LORD. "You made me angry by worshipping idols that were the work of your own hands, so I punished you."

8So this is what the LORD All-powerful says: "Since you have not listened to my messages, 9I will send for all the peoples of the north," says the LORD, "along with my servant Nebuchadnezzar king of Babylon. I will bring them all against Judah, those who live there, and all the nations around you, too. I will completely destroy all those countries and leave them in ruins for ever. People will be shocked when they see how badly I have destroyed those countries. [10]I will bring an end to the sounds of joy and happiness, the sounds of brides and bridegrooms, and the sound of people grinding meal. And I will take away the light of the lamp. [11]That whole area will be an empty desert, and these nations will be slaves of the king of Babylon for 70 years.

[12]"But when the 70 years have passed, I will punish the king of Babylon and his entire nation for their evil," says the LORD. "I will make that land a desert for ever. [13]I will make happen all the terrible things I said about Babylonia—everything Jeremiah prophesied about all those foreign nations, the warnings written in this book. [14]Even the Babylonians will have to serve many nations and many great kings. I will give them the punishment they deserve for all their own hands have done."

Judgement on the Nations

[15]The LORD, the God of Israel, said this to me: "My anger is like the wine in a cup. Take it from my hand and make all the nations, to whom I am sending you, drink all my anger from this cup. [16]They will drink my anger and stumble about and act like madmen because of the war I am going to send among them."

[17]So I took the cup from the LORD's hand and went to those nations and made them drink from it. [18]I served this wine to the people of Jerusalem and the towns of Judah, and the kings and officers of Judah, so they would become a ruin. Then people would be shocked and would insult them and speak evil of them. And so it has been to this day. [19]I also made these people drink of the LORD's anger: the king of Egypt, his servants, his officers, all his people [20]and all the foreigners there; all the kings of the land of Uz; all the kings of the Philistines (the kings of the cities of Ashkelon, Gaza, Ekron and the people left at Ashdod); [21]the people of Edom, Moab and Ammon; [22]all the kings of Tyre and Sidon; all the kings of the coastal countries to the west; [23]the people of Dedan and Tema and Buz; all who cut their hair short; [24]all the kings of Arabia; and the kings of the people who live in the desert; [25]all the kings of Zimri, Elam and Media; [26]and all the kings of the north, near and far, one after the other. I made all the kingdoms on earth drink from the cup of the LORD's anger, but the king of Babylon will drink from this cup after all the others.

[27]"Then say to them, 'This is what the LORD All-powerful, the God of Israel, says: drink this cup of my anger. Get drunk from it and vomit. Fall down and don't get up because of the war I am sending among you!'

[28]"If they refuse to take the cup from your hand and drink, say to them, 'The LORD All-powerful says this: you must drink from this cup. [29]Look! I am already bringing disaster on Jerusalem, the city that is called by my name. Do you think you will not be punished? You will be punished! I am sending war on all the people of the earth, says the LORD All-powerful.'

[30]"You, Jeremiah, will prophesy *d* against them with all these words. Say to them:

'The LORD will roar from heaven
    and will shout from his Holy Temple. *d*
He will roar loudly against his land.
He will shout like people who walk on
        grapes to make wine;
    he will shout against all who live on the
        earth.
[31]The noise will spread all over the earth,
    because the LORD will accuse all the
        nations.
He will judge and tell what is wrong with all
        people,
    and he will kill the evil people with a
        sword,' " says the LORD.

[32]This is what the LORD All-powerful says:
"Disasters will soon spread
    from nation to nation.
They will come like a powerful storm
    from the faraway places on earth."

[33]At that time those killed by the LORD will reach from one end of the earth to the other. No one will cry for them or gather up their bodies and bury them. They will be left lying on the ground like dung.

[34]Cry, you leaders! Cry out loud!
    Roll around in the dust, leaders of the
        people!
It is now time for you to be killed.
    You will fall and be scattered,
    like pieces of a broken jar.
[35]There will be no place for the leaders to hide;
    they will not escape.
[36]I hear the sound of the leaders shouting.
    I hear the leaders of the people crying
        loudly,
    because the LORD is destroying their land.
[37]Those peaceful pastures will be like an empty
        desert,
    because the LORD is very angry.
[38]Like a lion, he has left his den.
    Their land has been destroyed

because of the terrible war he brought,
because of his fierce anger.

Jeremiah's Lesson at the Temple

26 This message came from the LORD soon after Jehoiakim son of Josiah became king of Judah. [2]This is what the LORD said: "Jeremiah, stand in the courtyard of the Temple *d* of the LORD. Give this message to all the people of the towns of Judah who are coming to worship at the Temple of the LORD. Tell them everything I tell you to say; don't leave out a word. [3]Perhaps they will listen and stop their evil ways. If they will, I will change my mind about bringing on them the disaster that I am planning because of the evil they have done. [4]Say to them: 'This is what the LORD says: you must obey me and follow my teachings that I gave you. [5]You must listen to what my servants the prophets *d* say to you. I have sent them to you again and again, but you did not listen. [6]If you don't obey me, I will destroy my Temple in Jerusalem as I destroyed my Holy Tent *d* at Shiloh. When I do, people all over the world will curse Jerusalem.'"

[7]The priests, the prophets and all the people heard Jeremiah speaking these words in the Temple of the LORD. [8]When Jeremiah finished speaking everything the LORD had commanded him to say, the priests, prophets and all the people grabbed Jeremiah. They said, "You must die! [9]How dare you prophesy in the name of the LORD that this Temple will be destroyed like the one at Shiloh! How dare you say that Jerusalem will become a desert without anyone to live in it!" And all the people crowded around Jeremiah in the Temple of the LORD.

[10]Now when the officers of Judah heard about what was happening, they came out of the king's palace and went up to the Temple of the LORD and took their places at the entrance of the New Gate. [11]Then the priests and prophets said to the officers and all the other people, "Jeremiah should

---

PEER PRESSURE

Quick Comeback

Tim's alcohol and drug abuse started as a simple desire to be "one of the lads". Tim wanted to fit in with his older brother and his brother's friends. Drinking and getting high were ways to do that.

Before long, Tim went from feeling peer pressure to delivering it. "I became the bad influence," he remembers. He would encourage friends to get drunk at parties, and he persuaded people who had never used drugs to get high.

One day, when Tim couldn't obtain any drugs or alcohol, he lost his temper and was beaten up in a fight. Then he saw himself in the mirror – and realised how desperate he was. Tim went for treatment for alcoholism and drug abuse. Thankfully, he's been able to stay clean and sober for ten months. And peer pressure hasn't deterred him.

Tim still sees some of his old friends who drink. But they don't try to get Tim to drink. And if they did, Tim would know how to respond. "You've made your choice to use drugs or alcohol," he'd say. "Please respect my choice."

Jeremiah's peers wanted him to stop preaching God's word to them. They used the ultimate peer pressure threat: stop preaching, or we'll kill you. See how he responded in **Jeremiah 26:8–15**.

* What are the differences between Tim's friends and the people of Jeremiah's time?
* How is peer pressure today different from the peer pressure in this passage?

Consider . . .

* talking to a parent about the negative peer pressure he or she experiences – and how he or she deals with it.
* asking a close friend to form a partnership for positive peer pressure and perhaps writing a "contract" of specific ways you'll help each other.

For more, see . . .

* Daniel 3 (p.835)
* Acts 4:1–22 (p.1143)
* Matthew 5:10–12 (p.942)

be killed. He prophesied against Jerusalem, and you heard him yourselves."

¹²Then Jeremiah spoke these words to all the officers of Judah and all the other people: "The LORD sent me to say everything you have heard about this Temple and this city. ¹³Now change your lives and start doing good and obey the LORD your God. Then he will change his mind and not bring on you the disaster he has told you about. ¹⁴As for me, I am in your power. Do to me what you think is good and right. ¹⁵But be sure of one thing. If you kill me, you will be guilty of killing an innocent person. You will make this city and everyone who lives in it guilty too! The LORD truly sent me to you to give you this message."

¹⁶Then the officers and all the people said to the priests and the prophets, "Jeremiah must not be killed. What he told us comes from the LORD our God."

¹⁷Then some of the elders of Judah stood up and said to all the people, ¹⁸"Micah, from the city of Moresheth, was a prophet during the time Hezekiah was king of Judah. Micah said to all the people of Judah, 'This is what the LORD All-powerful says:

Jerusalem will be ploughed like a field.
It will become a pile of rocks,
and the hill where the Temple stands will
be covered with bushes.'

¹⁹"Hezekiah king of Judah and the people of Judah did not kill Micah. You know that Hezekiah feared the LORD and tried to please the LORD. So the LORD changed his mind and did not bring on Judah the disaster he had promised. If we hurt Jeremiah, we will bring a terrible disaster on ourselves!"

²⁰(Now there was another man who prophesied in the name of the LORD. His name was Uriah son of Shemaiah from the city of Kiriath Jearim. He preached the same things against Jerusalem and the land of Judah that Jeremiah did. ²¹When King Jehoiakim, all his army officers and all the leaders of Judah heard Uriah preach, King Jehoiakim wanted to kill Uriah. But Uriah heard about it and was afraid. So he escaped to Egypt. ²²Then King Jehoiakim sent Elnathan son of Acbor and some other men to Egypt, ²³and they brought Uriah back from Egypt. Then they took him to King Jehoiakim, who had Uriah killed with a sword. His body was thrown into the burial place where poor people are buried.)

²⁴Ahikam son of Shaphan supported Jeremiah. So Ahikam did not hand Jeremiah over to be killed by the people.

Nebuchadnezzar is Made Ruler

27 The LORD spoke his word to Jeremiah soon after Zedekiah son of Josiah was made king of Judah. ²This is what the LORD said to me: "Make a yoke^d out of straps and poles, and put it on the back of your neck. ³Then send messages to the kings of Edom, Moab, Ammon, Tyre and Sidon by their messengers who have come to Jerusalem to see Zedekiah king of Judah. ⁴Tell them to give this message to their masters: 'The LORD All-powerful, the God of Israel, says: "Tell your masters: ⁵I made the earth, its people and all its animals with my great power and strength. I can give the earth to anyone I want. ⁶Now I have given all these lands to Nebuchadnezzar king of Babylon, my servant. I will make even the wild animals obey him. ⁷All nations will serve Nebuchadnezzar and his son and grandson. Then the time will come for Babylon to be defeated, and many nations and great kings will make Babylon their servant.

⁸"'"But if some nations or kingdoms refuse to serve Nebuchadnezzar king of Babylon and refuse to be under his control, I will punish them with war, hunger and terrible diseases, says the LORD. I will use Nebuchadnezzar to destroy them. ⁹So don't listen to your false prophets,^{d} those who use magic to tell the future, those who explain dreams, the mediums^d or magicians. They all tell you, 'You will not be slaves to the king of Babylon.' ¹⁰They are telling you lies that will cause you to be taken far from your homeland. I will force you to leave your homes, and you will die in another land. ¹¹But the nations who put themselves under the control of the king of Babylon and serve him I will let stay in their own country, says the LORD. The people from those nations will live in their own land and farm it."'"

¹²I gave the same message to Zedekiah king of Judah. I said, "Put yourself under the control of the king of Babylon and serve him, and you will live. ¹³Why should you and your people die from war, hunger or disease, as the LORD said would happen to those who do not serve the king of Babylon? ¹⁴But the false prophets are saying, 'You will never be slaves to the king of Babylon.' Don't listen to them because they are prophesying lies to you! ¹⁵'I did not send them,' says the LORD. 'They are prophesying lies and saying the message is from me. So I will send you away, Judah. And you and those prophets who prophesy to you will die.'"

¹⁶Then I, Jeremiah, said to the priests and all the people, "This is what the LORD says: Those false prophets are saying, 'The Babylonians will soon return what they took from the Temple^d of the LORD.' Don't listen to them! They are prophesying lies to you. ¹⁷Don't listen to those prophets. But serve the king of Babylon, and you will live. There is no reason for you to cause Jerusalem to become a ruin. ¹⁸If they are prophets and have the message from the LORD, let them

pray to the LORD All-powerful. Let them ask that the things which are still in the Temple of the LORD and in the king's palace and in Jerusalem not be taken away to Babylon.

¹⁹"This is what the LORD All-powerful says about those things left in Jerusalem, the pillars, the large bronze bowl, which is called the Sea, the stands that can be moved and other things. ²⁰Nebuchadnezzar king of Babylon did not take these away when he took as captives Jehoiachin son of Jehoiakim king of Judah and all the other important people from Judah and Jerusalem to Babylon. ²¹This is what the LORD All-powerful, the God of Israel, says about the things left in the Temple of the LORD and in the king's palace and in Jerusalem: ²²'All of them will also be taken to Babylon. And they will stay there until the day I go to get them,' says the LORD. 'Then I will bring them back and return them to this place.' "

The False Prophet Hananiah

28 It was in that same year, in the fifth month of Zedekiah's fourth year as king of Judah, soon after he began to rule. The prophet ᵈ Hananiah son of Azzur, from the town of Gibeon, spoke to me in the Temple ᵈ of the LORD in front of the priests and all the people. He said: ²"The LORD All-powerful, the God of Israel, says: 'I have broken the yoke ᵈ the king of Babylon has put on Judah. ³Before two years are over, I will bring back everything that Nebuchadnezzar king of Babylon took to Babylon from the LORD's Temple. ⁴I will also bring back Jehoiachin son of Jehoiakim king of Judah and all the other captives from Judah who went to Babylon,' says the LORD. 'So I will break the yoke the king of Babylon put on Judah.' "

⁵Then the prophet Jeremiah spoke to the prophet Hananiah in front of the priests and all the people who were standing in the Temple ᵈ of the LORD. ⁶He said, "Amen! Let the LORD really do that! May the LORD make the message you prophesy come true. May he bring back here everything from the LORD's Temple and all the people who were taken as captives to Babylon.

⁷"But listen to what I am going to say to you and all the people. ⁸There were prophets long before we became prophets, Hananiah. They prophesied that war, hunger and terrible diseases would come to many countries and great kingdoms. ⁹But if a prophet prophesies that we will have peace and that message comes true, he can be recognised as one truly sent by the LORD."

¹⁰Then the prophet Hananiah took the yoke off Jeremiah's neck and broke it. ¹¹Hananiah said in front of all the people, "This is what the LORD says: 'In the same way I will break the yoke of Nebuchadnezzar king of Babylon. He put that

yoke on all the nations of the world, but I will break it before two years are over.' " After Hananiah had said that, Jeremiah left the Temple.

¹²The LORD spoke his word to Jeremiah after the prophet Hananiah had broken the yoke off the prophet Jeremiah's neck. ¹³The LORD said, "Go and tell Hananiah, 'This is what the LORD says: You have broken a wooden yoke, but I will make a yoke of iron in its place! ¹⁴The LORD All-powerful, the God of Israel, says: I will put a yoke of iron on the necks of all these nations to make them serve Nebuchadnezzar king of Babylon, and they will be slaves to him. I will even give Nebuchadnezzar control over the wild animals.' "

¹⁵Then the prophet Jeremiah said to the prophet Hananiah, "Listen, Hananiah! The LORD did not send you, and you have made the people of Judah trust in lies. ¹⁶So this is what the LORD says: 'Soon I will remove you from the earth. You will die this year, because you taught the people to turn against the LORD.' "

¹⁷Hananiah died in the seventh month of that same year.

A Letter to the Captives in Babylon

29 This is the letter that Jeremiah the prophet ᵈ sent from Jerusalem to the elders who were among the captives, the priests and the prophets. He sent it to all the other people Nebuchadnezzar had taken as captives from Jerusalem to Babylon. ²(This letter was sent after all these people were taken away: Jehoiachin the king and the queen mother; the officers and leaders of Judah and Jerusalem; and the craftsmen and metalworkers from Jerusalem.) ³Zedekiah king of Judah sent Elasah son of Shaphan and Gemariah son of Hilkiah to Babylon to Nebuchadnezzar king of Babylon. So Jeremiah gave them this letter to carry to Babylon:

⁴This is what the LORD All-powerful, the God of Israel, says to all those people I sent away from Jerusalem as captives to Babylon: ⁵"Build houses and settle in the land. Plant gardens and eat the food they grow. ⁶Get married and have sons and daughters. Find wives for your sons, and let your daughters be married so they also may have sons and daughters. Have many children in Babylon; don't become fewer in number. ⁷Also do good things for the city where I sent you as captives. Pray to the LORD for the city where you are living, because if good things happen in the city, good things will happen to you also." ⁸The LORD All-powerful, the God of Israel, says: "Don't let the prophets among you and the people who do magic fool you. Don't listen to their dreams.

[9]They are prophesying lies to you, saying that their message is from me. But I did not send them," says the LORD.

[10]This is what the LORD says: "Babylon will be powerful for 70 years. After that time I will come to you, and I will keep my promise to bring you back to Jerusalem. [11]I say this because I know what I am planning for you," says the LORD. "I have good plans for you, not plans to hurt you. I will give you hope and a good future. [12]Then you will call my name. You will come to me and pray to me, and I will listen to you. [13]You will search for me. And when you search for me with all your heart, you will find me! [14]I will let you find me," says the LORD. "And I will bring you back from your captivity. I forced you to leave this place, but I will gather you from all the nations, from the places I have sent you as captives," says the LORD. "And I will bring you back to this place."

[15]You might say, "The LORD has given us prophets here in Babylon."

[16]But the LORD says this about the king who is sitting on David's throne now and all the other people still in Jerusalem, your relatives who did not go as captives to Babylon with you. [17]The LORD All-powerful says: "I will soon send war, hunger and terrible diseases against those still in Jerusalem. I will make them like bad figs that are too rotten to eat. [18]I will chase them with war, hunger and terrible diseases. I will make them hated by all the kingdoms of the earth. People will curse them and be shocked and will use them as a shameful example wherever I make them go. [19]This is because they have not listened to my message," says the LORD. "I sent my message to them again and again through my servants, the prophets, but they did not listen," says the LORD.

[20]You captives, whom I forced to leave Jerusalem and go to Babylon, listen to the message from the LORD. [21]The LORD All-powerful, the God of Israel, says this about Ahab son of Kolaiah and Zedekiah son of Maaseiah: "These two men have been prophesying lies to you, saying that their message is from me. But soon I will hand over those two prophets to Nebuchadnezzar king of Babylon, and he will kill them in front of you. [22]Because of them, all the captives from Judah in Babylon will use this curse: 'May the LORD treat you like Zedekiah and Ahab, whom the king of Babylon burned in the fire.' [23]They have done evil things among the people of Israel. They are guilty of adultery[d] with their neighbours'

wives. They have also spoken lies and said those lies were a message from me. I did not tell them to do that. I know what they have done; I am a witness to it," says the LORD.

[24]Also give a message to Shemaiah from the Nehelamite family. [25]The LORD All-powerful, the God of Israel, says: "Shemaiah, you sent letters in your name to all the people in Jerusalem, to the priest Zephaniah son of Maaseiah, and to all the priests. [26]You said to Zephaniah, 'The LORD has made you priest in place of Jehoiada. You are to be in charge of the Temple[d] of the LORD. You should arrest any madman who acts like a prophet. Lock his hands and feet between wooden blocks, and put iron rings around his neck. [27]Now Jeremiah from Anathoth is acting like a prophet. So why haven't you arrested him? [28]Jeremiah has sent this message to us in Babylon: you will be there for a long time, so build houses and settle down. Plant gardens and eat what they grow.'"

[29]Zephaniah the priest read the letter to Jeremiah the prophet. [30]Then the LORD spoke his word to Jeremiah: [31]"Send this message to all the captives in Babylon: 'This is what the LORD says about Shemaiah the Nehelamite: Shemaiah has prophesied to you, but I did not send him. He has made you believe a lie. [32]So the LORD says, I will soon punish Shemaiah the Nehelamite and his family. He will not see the good things I will do for my people, says the LORD. None of his family will be left alive among the people, because he has taught the people to turn against me.'"

> **Sidelight** Jeremiah pulls no punches in telling the world exactly what God thinks. But at the same time he offers hope for his people (Jeremiah 30 and 33). Because of this, these two chapters have traditionally been called the "Book of Consolation" or the "Little Book of Comfort".

Promises of Hope

30 These are the words that the LORD spoke to Jeremiah. [2]The LORD, the God of Israel, said: "Jeremiah, write in a book all the words I have spoken to you. [3]The days will come when I will bring Israel and Judah back from captivity," says the LORD. "I will return them to the land I gave their ancestors, and they will own it!" says the LORD.

[4]The LORD spoke this message about the people of Israel and Judah: [5]this is what the LORD said:

"We hear people crying from fear.
    They are afraid; there is no peace.

6Ask this question, and consider it:
a man cannot have a baby.
So why do I see every strong man
holding his stomach in pain like a woman
having a baby?
Why is everyone's face turning white like a
dead man's face?
7This will be a terrible day!
There will never be another time like this.
This is a time of great trouble for the people
of Jacob,
but they will be saved from it."

8The LORD All-powerful says, "At that time
I will break the yoke *d* from their necks
and tear off the ropes that hold them.
Foreign people will never again make my
people slaves.
9They will serve the LORD their God
and David their king,
whom I will send to them.

10"So people of Jacob, my servants, don't be
afraid.
Israel, don't be frightened," says the
LORD.
"I will soon save you from that faraway place
where you are captives.
I will save your family from that land.
The people of Jacob will be safe and have
peace again;
there will be no enemy to frighten them.
11I am with you and will save you,"
says the LORD.
"I will completely destroy all those nations
where I scattered you,
but I will not completely destroy you.
I will punish you fairly,
but I will still punish you."

12This is what the LORD says:
"You people have a wound that cannot be
cured;
your injury will not heal.
13There is no one to argue your case
and no cure for your sores.
So you will not be healed.
14All those nations who were your friends have
forgotten you.
They don't care about you.
I have hurt you as an enemy would.
I punished you very hard,
because your guilt was so great
and your sins were so many.
15Why are you crying out about your injury?
There is no cure for your pain.
I did these things to you because of your
great guilt,
because of your many sins.

16But all those nations that destroyed you will
now be destroyed.
All your enemies will become captives in
other lands.
Those who stole from you will have their
own things stolen.
Those who took things from you in war
will have their own things taken.
17I will bring back your health
and heal your injuries," says the LORD,
"because other people forced you away.
They said about you, 'No one cares for
Jerusalem!' "

18This is what the LORD says:
"I will soon make the tents of Jacob's people
as they used to be,
and I will have pity on Israel's houses.
The city will be rebuilt on its hill of ruins,
and the king's palace will stand in its
proper place.
19People in those places will sing songs of
praise.
There will be the sound of laughter.
I will give them many children
so their number will not be small.
I will bring honour to them
so no one will look down on them.
20Their descendants *d* will be as they were in
the old days.
I will set them up as a strong people
before me,
and I will punish the nations who have hurt
them.
21One of their own people will lead them;
their ruler will come from among them.
He will come near to me when I invite him.
Who would dare to come to me
uninvited?" says the LORD.
22"So you will be my people,
and I will be your God."

23Look! It is a storm from the LORD!
He is angry and has gone out to punish the
people.
Punishment will come like a storm
crashing down on the evil people.
24The LORD will stay angry
until he finishes punishing the people.
He will stay angry
until he finishes the punishment he
planned.
When that day comes,
you will understand this.

The New Israel

31 The LORD says, "At that time I will be
God of all Israel's family groups, and they
will be my people."

²This is what the LORD says:
"The people who were not killed by the
    enemy's sword
  found help in the desert.
  I came to give rest to Israel."

³And from far away the LORD appeared to his
people and said,
  "I love you people
    with a love that will last for ever.
  That is why I have continued
    showing you kindness.
⁴People of Israel, I will build you up again
    and you will be rebuilt.
  You will pick up your tambourines *d*
    again
  and dance with those who are joyful.
⁵You will plant vineyards again
  on the hills around Samaria.
  The farmers will plant them
  and enjoy their fruit.

⁶There will be a time when watchmen in the
    mountains of Ephraim shout this
    message:
  'Come, let's go up to Jerusalem to worship
    the LORD our God!' "

⁷This is what the LORD says:
"Be happy and sing for the people of Jacob.
  Shout for Israel, the greatest of the nations.
Sing your praises and shout this:
  'LORD, save your people,
  those who are left alive from the nation of
    Israel!'
⁸Look, I will soon bring Israel from the
    country in the north,
  and I will gather them from the faraway
    places on earth.
Some of the people are blind and crippled.
  Some of the women are pregnant, and
    some are ready to give birth.
A great many people will come back.

CELEBRATING

Remembering Matt

Matt Floyd, seventeen, finished writing his talk for the retreat and attended a planning meeting on Sunday, but he never gave his talk. Three days later, while walking in the mountains, Matt lost his footing and fell to his death.

    Matt's death shocked the other members of the youth group. But over the next few weeks, they pulled together and learned how to celebrate even in the face of tragedy. They attended Matt's funeral and celebrated the seventeen years of life God had granted him.

    Then they went on with the retreat, introducing other teenagers to the God whom Matt knew. Matt's talk was read at the time he was supposed to give it. Kids cried as they listened to his words and remembered his voice. Some of the team members wore friendship bands to remind them of Matt's friendship. At the end of the weekend, they offered those bands to God.

    "When Matt died we thought about cancelling the retreat," said one of the planning team members. "But I'm glad we didn't. God brought us closer together and helped us celebrate the blessings Matt had brought us."

    Matt's friends learned that even in the midst of tragedies, we can celebrate God's goodness. Read how God encourages celebration – in hard times as well as good ones – in **Jeremiah 31:1–17**.

- What role does God play in the celebrations for Matt and the ones described in the passage?
- How do these celebrations compare to your ideas about celebrating?

Consider . . .

- celebrating what God has done for you the next time you are in a tough situation.
- writing your thoughts and memories of a relative or friend who has died, celebrating what that person meant to you.

For more, see . . .

- Nehemiah 8:9–12 (p.450)
- Luke 1:68–79 (p.1038)

- Psalm 150 (p.588)

⁹They will be crying as they come,
  but they will pray as I bring them back.
I will lead those people by streams of
    water
  on an even road where they will not
    stumble.
I am Israel's father,
  and Israel is my firstborn *d* son.

¹⁰"Nations, listen to the message from the
    LORD.
  Tell this message in the faraway lands by
    the sea:
'The one who scattered the people of Israel
    will bring them back,
  and he will watch over his people like a
    shepherd.'
¹¹The LORD will pay for the people of Jacob
  and will buy them back from people
    stronger than they were.
¹²The people of Israel will come to the high
    points of Jerusalem
  and shout for joy.
Their faces will shine with happiness about
    all the good things from the LORD:
  the grain, new wine, oil, young sheep and
    young cows.
They will be like a garden that has plenty of
    water,
  and they will not be troubled any more.
¹³Then young women of Israel will be happy
    and dance,
  the young men and old men also.
I will change their sadness into happiness;
  I will give them comfort and joy instead of
    sadness.
¹⁴The priests will have more than enough
    sacrifices,
  and my people will be filled with the good
    things I give them!" says the LORD.

¹⁵This is what the LORD says:
"A voice was heard in Ramah
  of painful crying and deep sadness:
Rachel crying for her children.
  She refused to be comforted,
  because her children are dead!"

¹⁶But this is what the LORD says:
"Stop crying;
  don't let your eyes fill with tears.
You will be rewarded for your work!" says
    the LORD.
  "The people will return from their enemy's
    land.
¹⁷So there is hope for you in the future," says
    the LORD.
  "Your children will return to their own
    land.

¹⁸"I have heard Israel moaning:
'LORD, you punished me, and I have learned
  my lesson.
I was like a calf that had never been
  trained.
Take me back so that I may come back.
  You truly are the LORD my God.
¹⁹LORD, after I wandered away from you,
  I changed my heart and life.
After I understood,
  I beat my breast with sorrow.
I was ashamed and disgraced,
  because I suffered for the foolish things I
    did when I was young.'

²⁰"You know that Israel is my dear son,
  The child I love.
Yes, I often speak against Israel,
  but I still remember him.
I love him very much
  and I want to comfort him," says the LORD.

²¹"People of Israel, fix the road signs.
  Put up signs to show you the way home.
Watch the road.
  Pay attention to the road on which you
    travel.
People of Israel, come home,
  come back to your towns.
²²You are an unfaithful daughter.
  How long will you wander before you
    come home?
The LORD has made something new happen in
    the land:
  a woman will go seeking a man."

²³The LORD All-powerful, the God of Israel, says: "I will again do good things for the people of Judah. At that time the people in the land of Judah and its towns will again use these words: 'May the LORD bless you, home of what is good, holy mountain.' ²⁴People in all the towns of Judah will live together in peace. Farmers and those who move around with their flocks will live together in peace. ²⁵I will give rest and strength to those who are weak and tired."

²⁶After hearing that, I, Jeremiah, woke up and looked around. My sleep had been very pleasant.

²⁷The LORD says, "The time is coming when I will help the families of Israel and Judah and their children and animals to grow. ²⁸In the past I watched over Israel and Judah, to pull them up and tear them down, to destroy them and bring them disaster. But now I will watch over them to build them up and make them strong," says the LORD. ²⁹"At that time people will no longer say:
'The parents have eaten sour grapes,
  and that caused the children to grind their
    teeth from the sour taste.'

³⁰Instead, each person will die for his own sin; the person who eats sour grapes will grind his own teeth.

The New Agreement

³¹"Look, the time is coming," says the LORD,
"when I will make a new agreement
with the people of Israel
and the people of Judah.
³²It will not be like the agreement
I made with their ancestors
when I took them by the hand
to bring them out of Egypt.
I was a husband to them,
but they broke that agreement," says the
LORD.
³³"This is the agreement I will make
with the people of Israel at that time," says
the LORD:
"I will put my teachings in their minds
and write them on their hearts.

I will be their God,
and they will be my people.
³⁴People will no longer have to teach their
neighbours and relatives
to know the LORD,
because all people will know me,
from the least to the most important," says
the LORD.
"I will forgive them for the wicked things
they did,
and I will not remember their sins any more."

The LORD will Never Leave Israel

³⁵The LORD makes the sun shine in the day
and the moon and stars to shine at night.
He stirs up the sea so that its waves crash on
the shore.
The LORD All-powerful is his name.
This is what the LORD says:
³⁶"Only if these laws should ever fail,"
says the LORD,

PROMISES

Changing Lives

Aristides Alvarado, twenty, is in his second year at university. But when he was in primary school, most people who knew him gave him less than a 50 per cent chance of passing any exams at all. Fortunately, "most people" didn't include Eugene M. Lang.

Lang is a wealthy businessman, in fact, a millionaire. A number of years ago, he returned to his primary school – one of the poorest schools in the United States. He promised 61 pupils, including Aristides, that if they passed the necessary exams he would pay for their college education.

Lang is keeping that promise. He helped those students through the final years of school, paying for trips and even tutors to help them stay on. About a half of the original 61 are in college, and their education is being paid for through Lang's "I Have a Dream" Foundation.

The students, who call themselves "Dreamers" are deeply grateful that Lang is keeping his promise.

"Mr Lang was one of the first people who took an interest in me," says Aristides. "I know I'm going to make it. And someday I'll be big – really big – and pay the tuition for my class of dreamers."

Lang and his friends aren't the only ones keeping promises these days. Read about God's promises in **Jeremiah 31:27–37**.

* What effects might Lang's or God's promises have on the people involved?
* What choices must you make to receive the benefit of God's promises?

Consider . . .

* reading Jesus' teaching in the Beatitudes (Matthew 5:1–12, p.942). Imagine Jesus using your name in his promises for believers.
* keeping a promise you've neglected.

For more, see . . .

* Lamentations 3:22–25 (p.783)
* John 2:18–22 (p.1098)
* Matthew 7:7–11 (p.950)

"will Israel's descendants *d* ever stop
being a nation before me."

37This is what the LORD says:
"Only if people can measure the sky above
and learn the secrets of the earth below,
will I reject all the descendants of Israel
because of what they have done," says the
LORD.

The New Jerusalem

38The LORD says, "The time is coming when
Jerusalem will be rebuilt for me—everything
from the Tower of Hananel to the Corner Gate.
39The measuring line will stretch from the Corner Gate straight to the hill of Gareb. Then it
will turn to the place named Goah. 40The whole
valley where dead bodies and ashes are thrown,
and all the terraces out to the Kidron Valley on
the east as far as the corner of the Horse Gate—
all that area will be holy to the LORD. The city
of Jerusalem will never again be torn down or
destroyed."

Jeremiah Buys a Field

32 This is the word the LORD spoke to
Jeremiah in the tenth year Zedekiah was
king of Judah, which was the eighteenth year of
Nebuchadnezzar. 2At that time the army of the
king of Babylon was surrounding Jerusalem. Jeremiah the prophet was under arrest in the
courtyard of the guard, which was at the palace
of the king of Judah.

3Zedekiah king of Judah had put Jeremiah
in prison there. Zedekiah had asked, "Why
have you prophesied *d* the things you have?"
(Jeremiah had said, "This is what the LORD says:
'I will soon hand the city of Jerusalem over to
the king of Babylon, and he will capture it.
4Zedekiah king of Judah will not escape from the
Babylonian army, but he will surely be handed
over to the king of Babylon. And he will speak to
the king of Babylon face to face and see him with
his own eyes. 5The king will take Zedekiah to
Babylon, where he will stay until I have punished him,' says the LORD. 'If you fight against
the Babylonians, you will not succeed.' ")

6While Jeremiah was in prison, he said,
"The LORD spoke this word to me: 7Your cousin
Hanamel, son of your uncle Shallum, will come
to you soon. Hanamel will say to you, 'Jeremiah,
you are my nearest relative, so buy my field near
the town of Anathoth. It is your right and your
duty to buy that field.'

8"Then it happened just as the LORD had said.
My cousin Hanamel came to me in the courtyard
of the guard and said to me, 'Buy for yourself my
field near Anathoth in the land of Benjamin. It is

your right and duty to buy it and own it.' So I
knew this was a message from the LORD.

9"I bought the field at Anathoth from my
cousin Hanamel, weighing out 17 pieces of silver
for him. 10I signed the record and sealed it and
had some people witness it. I also weighed out
the silver on the scales. 11Then I took both copies
of the record of ownership—the one that was
sealed that had the demands and limits of ownership, and the one that was not sealed. 12And I
gave them to Baruch son of Neriah, the son of
Mahseiah. My cousin Hanamel, the other witnesses who signed the record of ownership, and
many Jews sitting in the courtyard of the guard
saw me give the record of ownership to Baruch.

13"With all the people watching, I told Baruch,
14'This is what the LORD All-powerful, the God of
Israel, says: Take both copies of the record of
ownership—the sealed copy and the copy that
was not sealed—and put them in a clay jar so
they will last a long time. 15This is what the LORD
All-powerful, the God of Israel, says: in the future
my people will once again buy houses and fields
for grain and vineyards in the land of Israel.'

16"After I gave the record of ownership to
Baruch son of Neriah, I prayed to the LORD, 17Oh,
Lord GOD, you made the skies and the earth with
your very great power. There is nothing too hard
for you to do. 18You show love and kindness to
thousands of people, but you also bring punishment to children for their parents' sins. Great
and powerful God, your name is the LORD All-
powerful. 19You plan and do great things. You see
everything that people do, and you reward people
for the way they live and for what they do. 20You
did miracles *d* and wonderful things in the land of
Egypt. You have continued doing them in Israel
and among the other nations even until today. So
you have become well known. 21You brought
your people, the Israelites, out of Egypt using
signs and miracles and your great power and
strength. You brought great terror on everyone.
22You gave them this land that you promised to
their ancestors long ago, a fertile land. 23They
came into this land and took it for their own, but
they did not obey you or follow your teachings.
They did not do everything you commanded.
So you made all these terrible things happen to
them.

24"Look! The enemy has surrounded the city
and has built roads to the top of the walls to
capture it. Because of war, hunger and terrible
diseases, the city will be handed over to the
Babylonians who are attacking it. You said this
would happen and now you see it is happening.
25But now, Lord GOD, you tell me, 'Buy the field
with silver and call in witnesses.' You tell me this

while the Babylonian army is ready to capture the city."

26Then the LORD spoke this word to Jeremiah: 27"I am the LORD, the God of every person on the earth. Nothing is impossible for me. 28So this is what the LORD says: I will soon hand over the city of Jerusalem to the Babylonian army and to Nebuchadnezzar king of Babylon, who will capture it. 29The Babylonian army is already attacking the city of Jerusalem. They will soon enter it and start a fire to burn down the city and its houses. The people of Jerusalem offered sacrifices to Baal *d* on the roofs *n* of those same houses and poured out drink offerings to other idols to make me angry. 30From their youth, the people of Israel and Judah have done only the things I said were wrong. They have made me angry by worshipping idols made with their own hands," says the LORD. 31"From the day Jerusalem was built until now, this city has made me angry, so angry that I must remove it from my sight. 32I will destroy it, because of all the evil the people of Israel and Judah have done. The people, their kings and officers, their priests and prophets, all the people of Judah and the people of Jerusalem have made me angry. 33They turned their backs to me, not their faces. I tried to teach them again and again, but they wouldn't listen or learn. 34They put their hateful idols in the place where I have chosen to be worshipped, so they made it unclean. *d* 35In the Valley of Ben Hinnom they built places to worship Baal so they could burn their sons and daughters as sacrifices to Molech. *d* But I never commanded them to do such a hateful thing. It never entered my mind that they would do such a thing and cause Judah to sin.

36"You are saying, 'Because of war, hunger and terrible diseases, the city will be handed over to the king of Babylon.' But the LORD, the God of Israel, says about Jerusalem: 37I forced the people of Israel and Judah to leave their land, because I was furious and very angry with them. But soon I will gather them from all the lands where I forced them to go, and I will bring them back to this place, where they may live in safety. 38The people of Israel and Judah will be my people, and I will be their God. 39I will make them truly want to be one people with one goal. They will truly want to worship me all their lives, for their own good and for the good of their children after them. 40"I will make an agreement with them that will last for ever. I will never turn away from them; I will always do good to them. I will make them want to respect me so they will never turn

away from me. 41I will enjoy doing good to them. And with my whole being I will surely plant them in this land and make them grow."

42This is what the LORD says: "I have brought this great disaster to the people of Israel and Judah. In the same way I will bring the good things that I promise to do for them. 43You are saying, 'This land is an empty desert, without people or animals. It has been handed over to the Babylonians.' But in the future, people will again buy fields in this land. 44They will use their money to buy fields. They will sign and seal their agreements and call in witnesses. They will again buy fields in the land of Benjamin, in the area around Jerusalem, in the towns of Judah and in the mountains, in the western hills and in southern Judah. I will make everything as good for them as it once was," says the LORD.

The Promise of the LORD

33 While Jeremiah was still locked up in the courtyard of the guards, the LORD spoke his word to him a second time: 2"These are the words of the LORD, who made the earth, shaped it and gave it order, whose name is the LORD: 3'Judah, pray to me, and I will answer you. I will tell you important secrets you have never heard before.' 4This is what the LORD, the God of Israel, says about the houses in Jerusalem and the royal palaces of Judah that have been torn down to be used in defence of the attack by the Babylonian army: 5'Some people will come to fight against the Babylonians. They will fill these houses with the bodies of people I killed in my hot anger. I have turned away from this city because of all the evil its people have done.

6" 'But then I will bring health and healing to the people there. I will heal them and let them enjoy great peace and safety. 7I will bring Judah and Israel back from captivity and make them strong countries as in the past. 8They sinned against me, but I will wash away that sin. They did evil and turned away from me, but I will forgive them. 9Then 'Jerusalem' will be to me a name that brings joy! And people from all nations of the earth will praise it when they hear about the good things I am doing there. They will be surprised and shocked at all the good things and the peace I will bring to Jerusalem.'

10"You are saying, 'Our country is an empty desert, without people or animals.' But this is what the LORD says: It is now quiet in the streets of Jerusalem and in the towns of Judah, without people or animals, but it will be noisy there soon! 11There will be sounds of joy and gladness and

---

roofs   In Bible times houses were built with flat roofs. The roof was used for drying things such as flax and fruit. And it was used as an extra room, as a place for worship and as a place to sleep in the summer.

the happy sounds of brides and bridegrooms. There will be the sounds of people bringing to the Temple *d* of the LORD their offerings of thanks to the LORD. They will say,

'Praise the LORD All-powerful,
  because the LORD is good!
His love continues for ever!'

They will say this because I will again do good things for Judah, as I did in the beginning," says the Lord.

¹²This is what the LORD All-powerful says: "This place is empty now, without people or animals. But there will be shepherds in all the towns of Judah and pastures where they let their flocks rest. ¹³Shepherds will again count their sheep as the sheep walk in front of them. They will count them in the mountains and in the western hills, in southern Judah and the land of Benjamin, and around Jerusalem and the other towns of Judah!" says the LORD.

The Good Branch

¹⁴The LORD says, "The time is coming when I will do the good thing I promised to the people of Israel and Judah.

¹⁵In those days and at that time,
  I will make a good branch sprout from
    David's family.
He will do what is fair and right in the land.
¹⁶At that time Judah will be saved
  and the people of Jerusalem will live in safety.
The branch will be named:
  The LORD Does What Is Right."

¹⁷This is what the LORD says: "Someone from David's family will always sit on the throne of the family of Israel. ¹⁸And there will always be priests from the family of Levi. They will always stand before me to offer burnt offerings and grain offerings and sacrifices to me."

¹⁹The LORD spoke his word to Jeremiah, saying: ²⁰"This is what the LORD says: I have an agreement with day and night that they will always come at the right times. If you could change that agreement, ²¹only then could you change my agreement with David and Levi. Only then would my servant David not have a descendant *d* ruling as king on David's throne. And only then would the family of Levi not be priests serving me in the Temple. *d* ²²But I will give many descendants to my servant David and to the family group of Levi

---

FUTURE

Will Peace Ever Come?

"Nuclear weapons were described as a 'satanic weapon' that can cripple the total nervous system of civilisation." – *Die Zeit* (a German newspaper)

"The atomic age is here to stay – but are we?" – Bennett Cerf (publisher)

"Vast webs of advanced machinery pose danger enough . . . How much worse, then, when we consider another common trait of man: goofing up." – John Wesley White (author)

The future can seem uncertain and dangerous, and the spread of nuclear weapons adds to that uncertainty. But, even in difficult times, God keeps his promises. Read one of God's promises for the future in **Jeremiah 33:14–16**.

* God promises a Saviour in the passage. Do you think that promise includes being saved from nuclear weapons and war? Why or why not?
* How does your future look? How does faith in Christ affect the way you look at your future?

Consider . . .

* each day asking God to guide some part of your future. For example, Monday: Who will I marry? Tuesday: What career should I choose?
* writing one paragraph on how you would like to be remembered after your death. Choose one thing to do this week to help you towards your goals.

For more, see . . .

* Genesis 9:8–17 (p.11)
* Acts 1:6–11 (p.1137)

* Matthew 6:25–34 (p.948)

who serve me in the Temple. They will be as many as the stars in the sky that no one can count. They will be as many as the grains of sand on the seashore that no one can measure."

²³The LORD spoke his word to Jeremiah, saying: ²⁴"Jeremiah, have you heard what the people are saying? They say: 'The LORD turned away from the two families of Israel and Judah that he chose.' Now they don't think of my people as a nation any more!"

²⁵This is what the LORD says: "If I had not made my agreement with day and night, and if I had not made the laws for the sky and earth, ²⁶only then would I turn away from Jacob's descendants. And only then would I not let the descendants of David my servant rule over the descendants of Abraham, Isaac and Jacob. But I will be kind to them and cause good things to happen to them again."

A Warning to Zedekiah

34 The LORD spoke his word to Jeremiah when Nebuchadnezzar king of Babylon was fighting against Jerusalem and all the towns around it. Nebuchadnezzar had with him all his army and the armies of all the kingdoms and peoples he ruled. ²This is what the LORD, the God of Israel, said: "Jeremiah, go to Zedekiah king of Judah and tell him: 'This is what the LORD says: I will soon hand the city of Jerusalem over to the king of Babylon, and he will burn it down! ³You will not escape from the king of Babylon; you will surely be captured and handed over to him. You will see the king of Babylon with your own eyes, and he will talk to you face to face. And you will go to Babylon. ⁴But, Zedekiah king of Judah, listen to the promise of the LORD. This is what the LORD says about you: You will not be killed with a sword. ⁵You will die in a peaceful way. As people made funeral fires to honour your ancestors, the kings who ruled before you, so people will make a funeral fire to honour you. They will cry for you and sadly say, "Ah, master!" I myself make this promise to you, says the LORD.'"

⁶So Jeremiah the prophet*ᵈ* gave this message to Zedekiah in Jerusalem. ⁷This was while the army of the king of Babylon was fighting against Jerusalem and the cities of Judah that had not yet been taken—Lachish and Azekah. These were the only fortified cities left in the land of Judah.

Slaves are Mistreated

⁸The LORD spoke his word to Jeremiah. This was after King Zedekiah had made an agreement with all the people in Jerusalem to free all the Hebrew slaves. ⁹Everyone was supposed to free his Hebrew slaves, both male and female. No one was to keep a fellow Jew as a slave. ¹⁰All the officers and all the people accepted this agreement; they agreed to free their male and female slaves and no longer keep them as slaves. So all the slaves were set free. ¹¹But after that, the people who had slaves changed their minds. So they took back the people they had set free and made them slaves again.

¹²Then the LORD spoke his word to Jeremiah: ¹³"This is what the LORD, the God of Israel, says: I brought your ancestors out of Egypt where they were slaves and made an agreement with them. ¹⁴I said to your ancestors: 'At the end of every seven years, each one of you must set his Hebrew slaves free. If a fellow Hebrew has sold himself to you, you must let him go free after he has served you for six years.' But your ancestors did not listen or pay attention to me. ¹⁵A short time ago you changed your hearts and did what I say is right. Each of you gave freedom to his fellow Hebrews who were slaves. And you even made an agreement before me in the place where I have chosen to be worshipped. ¹⁶But now you have changed your minds. You have shown you do not honour me. Each of you has taken back the male and female slaves you had set free, and you have forced them to become your slaves again.

¹⁷"So this is what the LORD says: You have not obeyed me. You have not given freedom to your fellow Hebrews, neither relatives nor friends. But now I will give freedom, says the LORD, to war, to terrible diseases and to hunger. I will make you hated by all the kingdoms of the earth. ¹⁸I will hand over the men who broke my agreement, who have not kept the promises they made before me. They cut a calf into two pieces before me and walked between the pieces. *ⁿ* ¹⁹These people made the agreement before me by walking between the pieces of the calf: the leaders of Judah and Jerusalem, the officers of the court, the priests and all the people of the land. ²⁰So I will hand them over to their enemies and to everyone who wants to kill them. Their bodies will become food for the birds of the air and for the wild animals of the earth. ²¹I will hand Zedekiah king of Judah and his officers over to their enemies and to everyone who wants to kill them, and to the army of the king of Babylon, even though they have left Jerusalem. ²²I will give the order, says the LORD, to bring the Babylonian army back to Jerusalem. It will fight against Jerusalem, capture it, set it on fire and burn it down. I will destroy the towns in Judah so that they become ruins where no one lives!"

They . . . pieces.   This showed that the men were willing to be killed, like this animal, if they did not keep their agreement.

The Recabite Family Obeys God

35 When Jehoiakim son of Josiah was king of Judah, the LORD spoke his word to Jeremiah, saying: 2"Go to the family of Recab. Invite them to come to one of the side rooms of the Temple d of the LORD, and offer them wine to drink."

3So I went to get Jaazaniah son of Jeremiah, n the son of Habazziniah. And I gathered all of Jaazaniah's brothers and sons and the whole family of the Recabites together. 4Then I brought them into the Temple of the LORD. We went into the room of the sons of Hanan son of Igdaliah, who was a man of God. The room was next to the one where the officers stay and above the room of Maaseiah son of Shallum, the doorkeeper in the Temple. 5Then I put some bowls full of wine and some cups before the men of the Recabite family. And I said to them, "Drink some wine."

6But the Recabite men answered, "We never drink wine. Our ancestor Jonadab son of Recab gave us this command: 'You and your descendants d must never drink wine. 7Also you must never build houses, plant seeds or plant vineyards, or do any of those things. You must live only in tents. Then you will live a long time in the land where you are wanderers.' 8So we Recabites have obeyed everything Jonadab our ancestor commanded us. Neither we nor our wives, sons or daughters ever drink wine. 9We never build houses in which to live, or own fields or vineyards, or plant crops. 10We have lived in tents and have obeyed everything our ancestor Jonadab commanded us. 11But when Nebuchadnezzar king of Babylon attacked Judah, we said to each other, 'Come, we must enter Jerusalem so we can escape the Babylonian army and the Aramean army.' So we have stayed in Jerusalem."

12Then the LORD spoke his word to Jeremiah: 13"This is what the LORD All-powerful, the God of Israel, says: Jeremiah, go and tell the men of Judah and the people of Jerusalem: 'You should learn a lesson and obey my message,' says the LORD. 14'Jonadab son of Recab ordered his descendants not to drink wine, and that command has been obeyed. Until today they have obeyed their ancestor's command; they do not drink wine. But I, the LORD, have given you messages again and again, but you did not obey me. 15I sent all my servants the prophets to you again and again, saying, "Each of you must stop doing evil. You must change and be good. Do not follow other gods to serve them. If you obey me, you will live in the land I have given to you and your ancestors." But you have not listened to me or

paid attention to my message. 16The descendants of Jonadab son of Recab obeyed the commands their ancestor gave them, but the people of Judah have not obeyed me.'

17"So the LORD God All-powerful, the God of Israel, says: 'I will soon bring every disaster I said would come to Judah and to everyone living in Jerusalem. I spoke to those people, but they refused to listen. I called out to them, but they did not answer me.'"

18Then Jeremiah said to the Recabites, "This is what the LORD All-powerful, the God of Israel, says: 'You have obeyed the commands of your ancestor Jonadab and have followed all of his teachings; you have done everything he commanded.' 19So this is what the LORD All-powerful, the God of Israel, says: 'There will always be a descendant of Jonadab son of Recab to serve me.'"

Jehoiakim Burns Jeremiah's Scroll

36 The LORD spoke this word to Jeremiah during the fourth year that Jehoiakim son of Josiah was king of Judah: 2"Get a scroll. Write on it all the words I have spoken to you about Israel and Judah and all the nations. Write everything from when I first spoke to you, when Josiah was king, until now. 3Perhaps the family of Judah will hear what disasters I am planning to bring on them and will stop doing wicked things. Then I would forgive them for the sins and the evil things they have done."

4So Jeremiah called for Baruch son of Neriah. Jeremiah spoke the messages the LORD had given him, and Baruch wrote those messages on the

> **Sidelight** Baruch was Jeremiah's secretary and friend who recorded the prophet's thoughts on scrolls made from treated animal skins (Jeremiah 36:4). Baruch was an important citizen of Jerusalem and probably served as a royal clerk. That made working with Jeremiah an occupational hazard, since Jeremiah was rarely in the king's good books.

scroll. 5Then Jeremiah commanded Baruch, "I cannot go to the Temple d of the LORD. I must stay here. 6So I want you to go to the Temple of the LORD on a day when the people are giving up eating. Read from the scroll to all the people of Judah who come into Jerusalem from their towns. Read the messages from the LORD, which are the words you wrote on the scroll as I spoke them to you. 7Perhaps they will ask the LORD to

---

Jeremiah   Not the prophet Jeremiah, but a different man with the same name.

help them. Perhaps each one will stop doing wicked things, because the LORD has announced that he is very angry with them." [8]So Baruch son of Neriah did everything Jeremiah the prophet [d] told him to do. In the LORD's Temple he read aloud the scroll that had the LORD's messages written on it.

[9]In the ninth month of the fifth year that Jehoiakim son of Josiah was king, a special time to give up eating was announced. All the people of Jerusalem and everyone who had come into Jerusalem from the towns of Judah were supposed to give up eating to honour the LORD. [10]At that time Baruch read to all the people there the scroll containing Jeremiah's words. He read the scroll in the Temple of the LORD in the room of Gemariah son of Shaphan, a royal secretary. That room was in the upper courtyard at the entrance of the New Gate of the Temple.

[11]Micaiah son of Gemariah, the son of Shaphan, heard all the messages from the LORD that were on the scroll. [12]Micaiah went down to the royal secretary's room in the king's palace where all of the officers were sitting: Elishama the royal secretary; Delaiah son of Shemaiah; Elnathan son of Acbor; Gemariah son of Shaphan; Zedekiah son of Hananiah; and all the other officers. [13]Micaiah told those officers everything he had heard Baruch read to the people from the scroll.

[14]Then the officers sent a man named Jehudi son of Nethaniah to Baruch. (Nethaniah was the son of Shelemiah, who was the son of Cushi.) Jehudi said to Baruch, "Bring the scroll that you read to the people and come with me."

So Baruch son of Neriah took the scroll and went with Jehudi to the officers. [15]Then the officers said to Baruch, "Please sit down and read the scroll to us."

So Baruch read the scroll to them. [16]When the officers heard all the words, they became afraid and looked at each other. They said to Baruch, "We must certainly tell the king about these words." [17]Then the officers asked Baruch, "Tell us, please, where did you get all these words you wrote on the scroll? Did you write down what Jeremiah said to you?"

[18]"Yes," Baruch answered. "Jeremiah spoke them all to me, and I wrote them down with ink on this scroll."

[19]Then the officers said to Baruch, "You and Jeremiah must go and hide, and don't tell anyone where you are."

[20]The officers put the scroll in the room of Elishama the royal secretary. Then they went to the king in the courtyard and told him all about the scroll. [21]So King Jehoiakim sent Jehudi to get the scroll. Jehudi brought the scroll from the room of Elishama the royal secretary and read it

to the king and to all the officers who stood around the king. [22]It was the ninth month of the year, so King Jehoiakim was sitting in the winter apartment. There was a fire burning in a small firepot in front of him. [23]After Jehudi had read three or four columns, the king cut those columns off of the scroll with a pen knife and threw them into the firepot. Finally, the whole scroll was burnt in the fire. [24]King Jehoiakim and his servants heard everything that was said, but they were not frightened! They did not tear their clothes to show their sorrow. [25]Elnathan, Delaiah and Gemariah even tried to talk King Jehoiakim out of burning the scroll, but he would not listen to them. [26]Instead, the king ordered Jerahmeel son of the king, Seraiah son of Azriel and Shelemiah son of Abdeel to arrest Baruch the secretary and Jeremiah the prophet. But the LORD had hidden them.

[27]So King Jehoiakim burnt the scroll where Baruch had written all the words Jeremiah had spoken to him. Then the LORD spoke his word to Jeremiah: [28]"Get another scroll. Write all the words on it that were on the first scroll that Jehoiakim king of Judah burnt up. [29]Also say this to Jehoiakim king of Judah: 'This is what the LORD says: you burnt up that scroll and said, "Why, Jeremiah, did you write on it 'the king of Babylon will surely come and destroy this land and the people and animals in it'?" [30]So this is what the LORD says about Jehoiakim king of Judah: Jehoiakim's descendants [d] will not sit on David's throne. When Jehoiakim dies, his body will be thrown out on the ground. It will be left out in the heat of the day and in the cold frost of the night. [31]I will punish Jehoiakim and his children and his servants, because they have done evil things. I will bring disasters upon them and upon all the people in Jerusalem and Judah— everything I promised but which they refused to hear.'"

Sidelight

Imagine how you would feel if you'd spent hours working hard on an essay, only to have someone cut it up and burn it! That's what happened to Jeremiah when the king heard what he had written (Jeremiah 36:20–26). But Jeremiah didn't give up. He wrote an even longer book to replace the burnt one, which was still unpopular (Jeremiah 36:27–32)!

[32]So Jeremiah took another scroll and gave it to Baruch son of Neriah, his secretary. As Jeremiah spoke, Baruch wrote on the scroll the same words that were on the scroll Jehoiakim king of

Judah had burnt in the fire. And many like words were added to the second scroll.

Jeremiah in Prison

37 Nebuchadnezzar king of Babylon had appointed Zedekiah son of Josiah to be king of Judah. Zedekiah took the place of Jehoiachin son of Jehoiakim. [2]But Zedekiah, his servants and the people of Judah did not listen to the words the LORD had spoken through Jeremiah the prophet. *d*

[3]Now King Zedekiah sent Jehucal son of Shelemiah and the priest Zephaniah son of Maaseiah with a message to Jeremiah the prophet. This was the message: "Jeremiah, please pray to the LORD our God for us."

[4]At that time Jeremiah had not yet been put into prison. So he was free to go anywhere he wanted. [5]The army of the king of Egypt had marched from Egypt towards Judah. Now the Babylonian army had surrounded the city of Jerusalem. When they heard about the Egyptian army marching towards them, the Babylonian army left Jerusalem.

[6]The LORD spoke his word to Jeremiah the prophet: [7]"This is what the LORD, the God of Israel, says: Jehucal and Zephaniah, I know Zedekiah king of Judah sent you to seek my help. Tell this to King Zedekiah: 'The army of the king of Egypt came here to help you, but they will go back to Egypt. [8]After that, the Babylonian army will return and attack Jerusalem and capture it and burn it down.'

[9]"This is what the LORD says: People of Jerusalem, do not fool yourselves. Don't say, 'The Babylonian army will surely leave us alone.' They will not! [10]Even if you defeated all of the Babylonian army that is attacking you and there were only a few injured men left in their tents, they would come from their tents and burn down Jerusalem!"

[11]So the Babylonian army left Jerusalem to fight the army of the king of Egypt. [12]Now Jeremiah tried to travel from Jerusalem to the land of Benjamin to get his share of the property that belonged to his family. [13]When Jeremiah got to the Benjamin Gate of Jerusalem, the captain in charge of the guards arrested him. The captain's name was Irijah son of Shelemiah son of Hananiah. Irijah said, "You are leaving us to join the Babylonians!"

[14]But Jeremiah said to Irijah, "That's not true! I am not leaving to join the Babylonians." Irijah refused to listen to Jeremiah, so he arrested Jeremiah and took him to the officers of Jerusalem. [15]Those rulers were very angry with Jeremiah and beat him. Then they put him in jail in the house of Jonathan the royal secretary, which had been made into a prison. [16]So those people put Jeremiah into a cell in a dungeon, and Jeremiah was there for a long time.

[17]Then King Zedekiah sent for Jeremiah and had him brought to the palace. Zedekiah asked him in private, "Is there any message from the LORD?"

Jeremiah answered, "Yes, there is. Zedekiah, you will be handed over to the king of Babylon." [18]Then Jeremiah said to King Zedekiah, "What crime have I done against you or your officers or the people of Jerusalem? Why have you thrown me into prison? [19]Where are your prophets that prophesied this message to you: 'The king of Babylon will not attack you or this land of Judah?' [20]But now, my master, king of Judah, please listen to me, and please do what I ask of you. Do not send me back to the house of Jonathan the royal secretary, or I will die there!"

[21]So King Zedekiah gave orders for Jeremiah to be put under guard in the courtyard of the guard and to be given bread each day from the street of the bakers until there was no more bread in the city. So he stayed under guard in the courtyard of the guard.

Jeremiah is Thrown into a Well

38 Shephatiah son of Mattan, Gedaliah son of Pashhur, Jehucal son of Shelemiah and Pashhur son of Malkijah heard what Jeremiah was telling all the people. He said: [2]"This is what the LORD says: 'Everyone who stays in Jerusalem will die from war, or hunger or terrible diseases. But everyone who surrenders to the Babylonian army will live; they will escape with their lives and live.' [3]And this is what the LORD says: 'This city of Jerusalem will surely be handed over to the army of the king of Babylon. He will capture this city!' "

[4]Then the officers said to the king, "Jeremiah must be put to death! He is discouraging the soldiers who are still in the city, and all the people, by what he is saying to them. He does not want good to happen to us; he wants to ruin us."

[5]King Zedekiah said to them, "Jeremiah is in your control. I cannot do anything to stop you."

[6]So the officers took Jeremiah and put him into the well of Malkijah, the king's son, which was in the courtyard of the guards. The officers used ropes to lower Jeremiah into the well, which did not have any water in it, only mud. And Jeremiah sank down into the mud.

[7]But Ebed-Melech, a Cushite and a servant in the palace, heard that the officers had put Jeremiah into the well. As King Zedekiah was sitting at the Benjamin Gate, [8]Ebed-Melech left the palace and went to the king. Ebed-Melech said to him, [9]"My master and king, these rulers have

acted in an evil way. They have treated Jeremiah the prophet badly. They have thrown him into a well and left him there to die! When there is no more bread in the city, he will starve to death."

> **Sidelight** Originally used as a water supply, the well of Malkijah was used to imprison Jeremiah (Jeremiah 38:6). It was a muddy tank – a plastered hole in the ground – which could have been six metres deep.

¹⁰Then King Zedekiah commanded Ebed-Melech the Cushite, "Take 30 men from the palace and lift Jeremiah the prophet out of the well before he dies."

¹¹So Ebed-Melech took the men with him and went to a room under the storeroom in the palace. He took some old rags and worn-out clothes from that room. Then he let those rags down with some ropes to Jeremiah in the well. ¹²Ebed-Melech the Cushite said to Jeremiah, "Put these old rags and worn-out clothes under your arms to be pads for the ropes." So Jeremiah did as Ebed-Melech said. ¹³The men pulled Jeremiah up with the ropes and lifted him out of the well. And Jeremiah stayed under guard in the courtyard of the guard.

Zedekiah Questions Jeremiah

¹⁴Then King Zedekiah sent someone to get Jeremiah the prophet *d* and bring him to the third entrance to the Temple *d* of the LORD. The king said to Jeremiah, "I am going to ask you something. Do not hide anything from me, but tell me everything honestly."

¹⁵Jeremiah said to Zedekiah, "If I give you an answer, you will surely kill me. And even if I give you advice, you will not listen to me."

¹⁶But King Zedekiah made a secret promise to Jeremiah, "As surely as the LORD lives who has given us breath and life, I will not kill you. And I promise not to hand you over to the officers who want to kill you."

¹⁷Then Jeremiah said to Zedekiah, "This is what the LORD God All-powerful, the God of Israel, says: 'If you surrender to the officers of the king of Babylon, your life will be saved. Jerusalem will not be burnt down, and you and your family will live. ¹⁸But if you refuse to surrender to the officers of the king of Babylon, Jerusalem will be handed over to the Babylonian army, and they will burn it down. And you yourself will not escape from them.' "

¹⁹Then King Zedekiah said to Jeremiah, "I'm afraid of some Jews who have already gone over to the side of the Babylonian army. If the Babylonians hand me over to them, they will treat me badly."

²⁰But Jeremiah answered, "The Babylonians will not hand you over to the Jews. Obey the LORD by doing what I tell you. Then things will go well for you, and your life will be saved. ²¹But if you refuse to surrender to the Babylonians, the LORD has shown me what will happen. ²²All the women left in the palace of the king of Judah will be brought out and taken to the important officers of the king of Babylon. Your women will make fun of you with this song:

'Your good friends misled you
      and were stronger than you.
While your feet were stuck in the mud,
      they left you.'

²³"All your wives and children will be brought out and given to the Babylonian army. You yourself will not even escape from them. You will be taken prisoner by the king of Babylon, and Jerusalem will be burned down."

²⁴Then Zedekiah said to Jeremiah, "Do not tell anyone that I have been talking to you, or you will die. ²⁵If the officers find out I talked to you, they will come to you and say, 'Tell us what you said to King Zedekiah and what he said to you. Don't keep any secrets from us. If you don't tell us everything, we will kill you.' ²⁶If they ask you, tell them, 'I was begging the king not to send me back to Jonathan's house to die.' "

²⁷All the officers did come to question Jeremiah. So he told them everything the king had ordered him to say. Then the officers said no more to Jeremiah, because no one had heard what Jeremiah and the king had discussed.

²⁸So Jeremiah stayed under guard in the courtyard of the guard until the day Jerusalem was captured.

The Fall of Jerusalem

39 This is how Jerusalem was captured: Nebuchadnezzar king of Babylon marched against Jerusalem with his whole army and surrounded the city to attack it. This was during the tenth month of the ninth year in which Zedekiah was king of Judah. ²This lasted until the ninth day of the fourth month in Zedekiah's eleventh year. Then the city wall was broken through. ³And all these officers of the king of Babylon came into Jerusalem and sat down at the Middle Gate: Nergal-Sharezer of the district of Samgar; Nebo-Sarsekim, a chief officer; Nergal-Sharezer, an important leader; and all the other important officers.

⁴When Zedekiah king of Judah and all his soldiers saw them, they ran away. They left Jerusalem at night and went out from the king's garden.

They went through the gate that was between the two walls and then headed towards the Jordan Valley. 5But the Babylonian army chased them and caught up with Zedekiah in the plains of Jericho. They captured him and took him to Nebuchadnezzar king of Babylon, who was at the town of Riblah in the land of Hamath. There Nebuchadnezzar passed his sentence on Zedekiah. 6At Riblah the king of Babylon killed Zedekiah's sons and all the important officers of Judah as Zedekiah watched. 7Then he put out Zedekiah's eyes. He put bronze chains on Zedekiah and took him to Babylon.

8The Babylonians set fire to the palace and to the houses of the people, and they broke down the walls around Jerusalem. 9Nebuzaradan, commander of the king's special guards, took the people left in Jerusalem, those captives who had surrendered to him earlier and the rest of the people of Jerusalem, and he took them all away to Babylon. 10But Nebuzaradan, commander of the guard, left some of the poorest people of Judah behind. They owned nothing, but that day he gave them vineyards and fields.

Sidelight The eighteen-month siege of Jerusalem by the Babylonians was a gruelling experience for Jeremiah (Jeremiah 39:1–10). Lamentations 4 (p.784) describes the horrible conditions, including starvation and cannibalism.

11Nebuchadnezzar king of Babylon had given these orders about Jeremiah through Nebuzaradan, commander of the guard: 12"Find Jeremiah and take care of him. Do not hurt him, but do for him whatever he asks you." 13So Nebuchadnezzar sent these men for Jeremiah: Nebuzaradan, commander of the guards; Nebushazban, a chief officer; Nergal-Sharezer, an important leader; and all the other officers of the king of Babylon. 14They had Jeremiah taken out of the courtyard of the guard. Then they turned him over to Gedaliah son of Ahikam son of Shaphan, who had orders to take Jeremiah back home. So they took him home and he stayed among the people left in Judah.

15While Jeremiah was guarded in the courtyard, the LORD spoke his word to him: 16"Jeremiah, go and tell Ebed-Melech the Cushite this message: 'This is what the LORD All-powerful, the God of Israel, says: very soon I will make my words about Jerusalem come true through disaster, not through good times. You will see everything come true with your own eyes. 17But I will save you on that day, Ebed-Melech, says the LORD.

You will not be handed over to the people you fear. 18I will surely save you, Ebed-Melech. You will not die from a sword, but you will escape and live. This will happen because you have trusted in me, says the LORD.' "

Jeremiah is Set Free

40 The LORD spoke his word to Jeremiah after Nebuzaradan, commander of the guards, had set Jeremiah free at the city of Ramah. He had found Jeremiah in Ramah bound in chains with all the captives from Jerusalem and Judah who were being taken away to Babylon. 2When commander Nebuzaradan found Jeremiah, Nebuzaradan said to him, "The LORD your God announced this disaster would come to this place. 3And now the LORD has done everything he said he would do. This disaster happened because the people of Judah sinned against the LORD and did not obey him. 4But today I am freeing you from the chains on your wrists. If you want to, come with me to Babylon and I will take good care of you. But if you don't want to come, then don't. Look, the whole country is open to you. Go wherever you wish." 5Before Jeremiah turned to leave, Nebuzaradan said, "Or go back to Gedaliah son of Ahikam, the son of Shaphan. The king of Babylon has chosen him to be governor over the towns of Judah. Go and live with Gedaliah among the people, or go anywhere you want."

Then Nebuzaradan gave Jeremiah some food and a present and let him go. 6So Jeremiah went to Gedaliah son of Ahikam at Mizpah and stayed with him there. He lived among the people who were left behind in Judah.

The Short Rule of Gedaliah

7Some officers and their men from the army of Judah were still out in the open country. They heard that the king of Babylon had put Gedaliah son of Ahikam in charge of the people who were left in the land: the men, women and children who were the poorest. They were the ones who were not taken to Babylon as captives. 8So these soldiers came to Gedaliah at Mizpah: Ishmael son of Nethaniah, Johanan and Jonathan sons of Kareah, Seraiah son of Tanhumeth, the sons of Ephai the Netophathite, Jaazaniah son of the Maacathite and their men. 9Gedaliah son of Ahikam, the son of Shaphan, made a promise to them, saying, "Do not be afraid to serve the Babylonians. Stay in the land and serve the king of Babylon. Then everything will go well for you. 10I myself will live in Mizpah and will speak for you before the Babylonians who come to us here. Harvest the wine, the summer fruit and the oil, and put what you harvest in your storage jars. Live in the towns you control."

[11]The Jews in Moab, Ammon, Edom and other countries also heard that the king of Babylon had left a few Jews alive in the land. And they heard the king of Babylon had chosen Gedaliah as governor over them. (Gedaliah was the son of Ahikam, the son of Shaphan.) [12]When the people of Judah heard this news, they came back to Judah from all the countries where they had been scattered. They came to Gedaliah at Mizpah and gathered a large harvest of wine and summer fruit.

[13]Johanan son of Kareah and all the army officers of Judah still in the open country came to Gedaliah at Mizpah. [14]They said to him, "Don't you know that Baalis king of the Ammonite people wants you dead? He has sent Ishmael son of Nethaniah to kill you." But Gedaliah son of Ahikam did not believe them.

[15]Then Johanan son of Kareah spoke to Gedaliah in private at Mizpah. He said, "Let me go and kill Ishmael son of Nethaniah. No one will know anything about it. We should not let Ishmael kill you. Then all the Jews gathered around you would be scattered to different countries again, and the few people of Judah who are left alive would be lost."

[16]But Gedaliah son of Ahikam said to Johanan son of Kareah, "Do not kill Ishmael! The things you are saying about Ishmael are not true."

41 In the seventh month Ishmael son of Nethaniah and ten of his men came to Gedaliah son of Ahikam at Mizpah. (Nethaniah was the son of Elishama.) Now Ishmael was a member of the king's family and had been one of the officers of the king of Judah. While they were eating a meal with Gedaliah at Mizpah, [2]Ishmael and his ten men got up and killed Gedaliah son of Ahikam, the son of Shaphan, with a sword. (Gedaliah was the man the king of Babylon had chosen as governor over Judah.) [3]Ishmael also killed all the Jews and the Babylonian soldiers who were there with Gedaliah at Mizpah.

[4]The day after Gedaliah was murdered, before anyone knew about it, [5]80 men came to Mizpah bringing grain offerings and incense *d* to the Temple*d* of the LORD. Those men from Shechem, Shiloh and Samaria had shaved off their beards, torn their clothes and cut themselves. *n* [6]Ishmael son of Nethaniah went out from Mizpah to meet them, crying as he walked. When he met them, he said, "Come with me to meet Gedaliah son of Ahikam." [7]So they went into Mizpah. Then Ishmael son of Nethaniah and his men killed 70 of them and threw the bodies into a deep well. [8]But the ten men who were left alive said to Ishmael, "Don't kill us! We have wheat and barley and oil

and honey that we have hidden in a field." So Ishmael let them live and did not kill them with the others. [9]Now the well where he had thrown all the bodies had been made by King Asa as a part of his defences against Baasha king of Israel. But Ishmael son of Nethaniah put dead bodies in it until it was full.

[10]Ishmael captured all the other people in Mizpah: the king's daughters and all the other people who were left there. They were the ones whom Nebuzaradan, commander of the guard, had chosen Gedaliah son of Ahikam to take care of. So Ishmael son of Nethaniah captured those people, and he started to cross over to the country of the Ammonites.

[11]Johanan son of Kareah and all his army officers with him heard about all the evil things Ishmael son of Nethaniah had done. [12]So they took their men and went to fight Ishmael son of Nethaniah and caught him near the big pool of water at Gibeon. [13]When the captives Ishmael had taken saw Johanan and the army officers, they were glad. [14]So all the people Ishmael had taken captive from Mizpah turned around and ran to Johanan son of Kareah. [15]But Ishmael son of Nethaniah and eight of his men escaped from Johanan and ran away to the Ammonites.

[16]So Johanan son of Kareah and all his army officers saved the captives that Ishmael son of Nethaniah had taken from Mizpah after he murdered Gedaliah son of Ahikam. Among those left alive were soldiers, women, children and palace officers. And Johanan brought them back from the town of Gibeon.

The Escape to Egypt

[17-18]Johanan and the other army officers were afraid of the Babylonians. Since the king of Babylon had chosen Gedaliah son of Ahikam to be governor of Judah and Ishmael son of Nethaniah had murdered him, Johanan was afraid that the Babylonians would be angry. So they decided to run away to Egypt. On the way they stayed at Geruth Kimham, near the town of Bethlehem.

42 While there, Johanan son of Kareah and Jezaniah son of Hoshaiah went to Jeremiah the prophet. *d* All the army officers and all the people, from the least important to the greatest, went along too. [2]They said to him, "Jeremiah, please listen to what we ask. Pray to the LORD your God for all the people left alive from the family of Judah. At one time there were many of us, but you can see that there are few of us now. [3]So pray that the LORD your God will tell us where we should go and what we should do."

---

shaved . . . themselves   The men did this to show they were sad about the Temple in Jerusalem being destroyed.

[4]Then Jeremiah the prophet answered, "I understand what you want me to do. I will pray to the LORD your God as you have asked. I will tell you everything he says and not hide anything from you."

[5]Then the people said to Jeremiah, "May the LORD be a true and loyal witness against us if we don't do everything the LORD your God sends you to tell us. [6]It does not matter if we like the message or not. We will obey the LORD our God, to whom we are sending you. We will obey what he says so good things will happen to us."

[7]Ten days later the LORD spoke his word to Jeremiah. [8]Then Jeremiah called for Johanan son of Kareah, the army officers with him and all the other people, from the least important to the greatest. [9]Jeremiah said to them, "You sent me to ask the LORD for what you wanted. This is what the God of Israel says: [10]'If you will stay in Judah, I will build you up and not tear you down. I will plant you and not pull you up, because I am sad about the disaster I brought on you. [11]Now you fear the king of Babylon, but don't be afraid of him. Don't be afraid of him,' says the LORD, 'because I am with you. I will save you and rescue you from his power. [12]I will be kind to you, and he will also treat you with mercy and let you stay in your land.'

[13]"But if you say, 'We will not stay in Judah,' you will disobey the LORD your God. [14]Or you might say, 'No, we will go and live in Egypt. There we will not see war, or hear the trumpets of war or be hungry.' [15]If you say that, listen to the message of the LORD, you who are left alive from Judah. This is what the LORD All-powerful, the God of Israel, says: 'If you make up your mind to go and live in Egypt, these things will happen: [16]you are afraid of war, but it will find you in the land of Egypt. And you are worried about hunger, but it will follow you into Egypt, and you will die there. [17]Everyone who goes to live in Egypt will die in war or from hunger or terrible disease. No one who goes to Egypt will live; no one will escape the terrible things I will bring to them.'

[18]"This is what the LORD All-powerful, the God of Israel, says: 'I showed my anger against the people of Jerusalem. In the same way I will show my anger against you when you go to Egypt. Other nations will speak evil of you. People will be shocked by what will happen to you. You will become a curse word, and people will insult you. And you will never see Judah again.'

[19]"You who are left alive in Judah, the LORD has told you, 'Don't go to Egypt.' Be sure you understand this; I warn you today [20]that you are making a mistake that will cause your deaths. You sent me to the LORD your God, saying, 'Pray to the LORD our God for us. Tell us everything the LORD our God says, and we will do it.' [21]So today I have told you, but you have not obeyed the LORD your God in all that he sent me to tell you. [22]So now be sure you understand this: you want to go to live in Egypt, but you will die there by war, hunger or terrible diseases."

43

So Jeremiah finished telling the people the message from the LORD their God; he told them everything the LORD their God had sent him to tell them.

[2]Azariah son of Hoshaiah, Johanan son of Kareah, and some other men were too proud. They said to Jeremiah, "You are lying! The LORD our God did not send you to say, 'You must not go to Egypt to live there.' [3]Baruch son of Neriah is causing you to be against us. He wants you to hand us over to the Babylonians so they can kill us or capture us and take us to Babylon."

[4]So Johanan, the army officers and all the people disobeyed the LORD's command to stay in Judah. [5]But Johanan son of Kareah and the army officers led away those who were left alive from Judah. They were the people who had run away from the Babylonians to other countries but then had come back to live in Judah. [6]They led away the men, women and children, and the king's daughters. Nebuzaradan commander of the guard had put Gedaliah son of Ahikam son of Shaphan in charge of those people. Johanan also took Jeremiah the prophet[d] and Baruch son of Neriah. [7]These people did not listen to the LORD. So they all went to Egypt to the city of Tahpanhes.

> **Sidelight**   Tahpanhes (Jeremiah 43:7) was an Egyptian border fortress in the delta area of the Nile River. It would be the first city that refugees from Israel would reach when they entered Egypt.

[8]In Tahpanhes the LORD spoke his word to Jeremiah: [9]"Take some large stones. Bury them in the clay in the brick pavement in front of the king of Egypt's palace in Tahpanhes. Do this while the Jews are watching you. [10]Then say to them, 'This is what the LORD All-powerful, the God of Israel, says: I will soon send for my servant, Nebuchadnezzar king of Babylon. I will set his throne over these stones I have buried, and he will spread his covering for shade above them. [11]He will come here and attack Egypt. He will bring death to those who are supposed to die. He will make prisoners of those who are to be taken captive, and he will bring war to those who are to be killed with a sword. [12]Nebuchadnezzar will set fire to the temples of the gods of Egypt and

burn them. And he will take the idols away as captives. As a shepherd wraps himself in his clothes, so Nebuchadnezzar will wrap Egypt around him. Then he will safely leave Egypt. ¹³He will destroy the stone pillars in the temple of the sun god in Egypt, and he will burn down the temples of the gods of Egypt.' "

Disaster in Egypt

44 Jeremiah received a message from the LORD for all the Jews living in Egypt—in the cities of Migdol, Tahpanhes, Memphis and in southern Egypt. This was the message: ²"The LORD All-powerful, the God of Israel, says: You saw all the terrible things I brought on Jerusalem and the towns of Judah, which are ruins today with no one living in them. ³It is because the people who lived there did evil. They made me angry by burning incense *d* and worshipping other gods that neither they nor you nor your ancestors ever knew. ⁴I sent all my servants, the prophets, *d* to you again and again. By them I said to you, 'Don't do this terrible thing that I hate.' ⁵But they did not listen or pay attention. They did not stop doing evil things and burning incense to other gods. ⁶So I showed my great anger against them. I poured out my anger in the towns of Judah and the streets of Jerusalem so they are only ruins and piles of stones today.

⁷"Now the LORD All-powerful, the God of Israel, says: Why are you doing such great harm to yourselves? You are cutting off the men and women, children and babies from the family of Judah, leaving yourselves without anyone from the family of Judah. ⁸Why do you want to make me angry by making idols? Why do you burn incense to the gods of Egypt, where you have come to live? You will destroy yourselves. Other nations will speak evil of you and make fun of you. ⁹Have you forgotten about the evil things your ancestors did? And have you forgotten the evil the kings and queens of Judah did? Have you forgotten about the evil you and your wives did? These things were done in the country of Judah and in the streets of Jerusalem. ¹⁰Even to this day the people of Judah are still too proud. They have not learned to respect me or to follow my teachings. They have not obeyed the laws I gave you and your ancestors.

¹¹"So this is what the LORD All-powerful, the God of Israel, says: I am determined to bring disasters on you. I will destroy the whole family of Judah. ¹²The few who were left alive from Judah were determined to go to Egypt and settle there, but they will all die in Egypt. They will be killed in war or die from hunger. From the least important to the greatest, they will be killed in war or die from hunger. Other nations will speak evil

about them. People will be shocked by what has happened to them. They will become a curse word, and people will insult them. ¹³I will punish those people who have gone to live in Egypt, just as I punished Jerusalem, using swords, hunger and terrible diseases. ¹⁴Of the people of Judah who were left alive and have gone to live in Egypt, none will escape my punishment. They want to return to Judah and live there, but none of them will live to return to Judah, except a few people who will escape."

¹⁵A large group of the people of Judah who lived in southern Egypt were meeting together. Among them were many women of Judah who were burning incense to other gods, and their husbands knew it. All these people said to Jeremiah, ¹⁶"We will not listen to the message from the LORD that you spoke to us. ¹⁷We promised to make sacrifices to the Queen Goddess, *d* and we will certainly do everything we promised. We will burn incense and pour out drink offerings to worship her, just as we, our ancestors, kings and officers did in the past. All of us did these things in the towns of Judah and in the streets of Jerusalem. At that time we had plenty of food and were successful, and nothing bad happened to us. ¹⁸But since we stopped making sacrifices to the Queen Goddess and stopped pouring out drink offerings to her, we have had great problems. Our people have also been killed in war and by hunger."

¹⁹The women said, "Our husbands knew what we were doing. We had their permission to burn incense to the Queen Goddess and to pour out drink offerings to her. Our husbands knew we were making cakes that looked like her and were pouring out drink offerings to her."

²⁰Then Jeremiah spoke to all the people—men and women—who answered him. ²¹He said to them, "The LORD remembered that you and your ancestors, kings and officers, and the people of the land burnt incense in the towns of Judah and in the streets of Jerusalem. He remembered and thought about it. ²²Then he could not be patient with you any longer. He hated the terrible things you did. So he made your country an empty desert, where no one lives. Other people curse that country. And so it is today. ²³All this happened because you burnt incense to other gods. You sinned against the LORD. You did not obey him or follow his teachings or the laws he gave you. You did not keep your part of the agreement with him. So this disaster has happened to you. It is there for you to see."

²⁴Then Jeremiah said to all those men and women, "People of Judah who are now in Egypt, hear the word of the LORD: ²⁵The LORD All-powerful, the God of Israel, says: you and your

wives did what you said you would do. You said, 'We will certainly keep the promises we made. We promised to make sacrifices to the Queen Goddess and to pour out drink offerings to her.' So, go ahead. Do the things you promised, and keep your promises. ²⁶But hear the word of the LORD. Listen, all you Jews living in Egypt. The LORD says, 'I have sworn by my great name: the people of Judah now living in Egypt will never again use my name to make promises. They will never again say in Egypt, "As surely as the Lord GOD lives. . ." ²⁷I am watching over them, not to take care of them, but to hurt them. The Jews who live in Egypt will die from swords or hunger until they are all destroyed. ²⁸A few will escape being killed by the sword and will come back to Judah from Egypt. Then, of the people of Judah who came to live in Egypt, those who are left alive will know if my word or their word came true. ²⁹I will give you a sign that I will punish you here in Egypt,' says the LORD. 'When you see it happen, you will know that my promises to hurt you will really happen.' ³⁰This is what the LORD says: 'Hophra king of Egypt has enemies who want to kill him. Soon I will hand him over to his enemies just as I handed Zedekiah king of Judah over to Nebuchadnezzar king of Babylon, who wanted to kill him.' "

A Message to Baruch

45 In the fourth year that Jehoiakim son of Josiah was king of Judah, Jeremiah the prophet ᵈ told these things to Baruch son of Neriah, and Baruch wrote them on a scroll: ²"This is what the LORD, the God of Israel, says to you, Baruch: ³You have said, 'How terrible it is for me! The LORD has given me sorrow along with my pain. I am tired because of my suffering and cannot rest.' "

⁴The LORD said, "Say this to Baruch: 'This is what the LORD says: I will soon tear down what I have built, and I will pull up what I have planted everywhere in Judah. ⁵Baruch, you are looking for great things for yourself. Don't look for them, because I will bring disaster on all the people, says the LORD. You will have to go to many places, but I will let you escape alive wherever you go.' "

Messages to the Nations

46 The LORD spoke this word to Jeremiah the prophet ᵈ about the nations:
²This message is to Egypt. It is about the army of Neco king of Egypt, which was defeated at the city of Carchemish on the Euphrates River by Nebuchadnezzar king of Babylon. This was in the fourth year that Jehoiakim son of Josiah

was king of Judah. This is the LORD's message to Egypt:
³"Prepare your shields, large and small,
  and march out for battle!
⁴Harness the horses
  and get on them!
Go to your places for battle
  and put on your helmets!
Polish your spears.
  Put on your armour!
⁵What do I see?
  That army is terrified,
and the soldiers are running away.
  Their warriors are defeated.
They run away quickly
  without looking back.
There is terror on every side!" says the LORD.
⁶"The fast runners cannot run away;
  the strong soldiers cannot escape.
They stumble and fall
  in the north, by the Euphrates River.
⁷Who is this, rising up like the Nile River,
  like strong, fast rivers?
⁸Egypt rises up like the Nile River,
  like strong, fast rivers.
Egypt says, 'I will rise up and cover the earth.
  I will destroy cities and the people in them!'
⁹Horsemen, charge into battle!
  Chariot drivers, drive hard!
March on, brave soldiers—
  soldiers from the countries of Cush and Put
    who carry shields,
  soldiers from Lydia who use bows.

¹⁰"But that day belongs to the Lord GOD
    All-powerful.
  At that time he will give those people the
    punishment they deserve.
The sword will kill until it is finished,
  until it satisfies its thirst for their blood.
The Lord GOD All-powerful will offer a sacrifice
  in the land of the north, by the Euphrates
    River.

¹¹"Go up to Gilead and get some balm, ᵈ
  people of Egypt!
You have prepared many medicines,
  but they will not work;
  you will not be healed.
¹²The nations have heard of your shame,
  and your cries fill all the earth.
One warrior has run into another;
  both of them have fallen down together!"

¹³This is the message the LORD spoke to Jeremiah the prophet ᵈ about Nebuchadnezzar king of Babylon's coming to attack Egypt:
¹⁴"Announce this message in Egypt, and preach it in Migdol.

Preach it also in the cities of Memphis and
Tahpanhes:
'Get ready for war,
because the battle is all around you.'
¹⁵Egypt, why were your warriors killed?
They could not stand because the LORD
pushed them down.
¹⁶They stumbled again and again
and fell over each other.
They said, 'Get up. Let's go back
to our own people and our homeland.
We must get away from our enemy's
sword!'
¹⁷In their homelands those soldiers called out,
'The king of Egypt is only a lot of noise.
He missed his chance for glory!'"

¹⁸The King's name is the LORD All-powerful.
He says, "As surely as I live,
a powerful leader will come.
He will be like Mount Tabor among the
mountains,
like Mount Carmel by the sea.
¹⁹People of Egypt, pack your things
to be taken away as captives,
because Memphis will be destroyed.
It will be a ruin, and no one will live
there.

²⁰"Egypt is like a beautiful young cow,
but a horsefly is coming
from the north to attack her.
²¹The hired soldiers in Egypt's army
are like fat calves,
because even they all turn and run away
together;
they do not stand strong against the
attack.
Their time of destruction is coming;
they will soon be punished.
²²Egypt is like a hissing snake that is trying to
escape.
The enemy comes closer and closer.
They come against Egypt with axes
like men who cut down trees.
²³They will chop down Egypt's army
as if it were a great forest," says the LORD.
"There are more enemy soldiers than
locusts; ᵈ
there are too many to count.
²⁴The people of Egypt will be ashamed.
They will be handed over to the enemy
from the north."

²⁵The LORD All-powerful, the God of Israel,
says: "Very soon I will punish Amon, the god of
the city of Thebes. And I will punish Egypt, her
kings, her gods and the people who depend on
the king. ²⁶I will hand those people over to their

enemies, who want to kill them. I will give them
to Nebuchadnezzar king of Babylon and his officers. But in the future, Egypt will live in peace as
it once did," says the LORD.

A Message to Israel

²⁷"People of Jacob, my servants, don't be
afraid;
don't be frightened, Israel.
I will surely save you from those faraway
places
and your children from the lands where
they are captives.
The people of Jacob will have peace and
safety again,
and no one will make them afraid.
²⁸People of Jacob, my servants, do not be
afraid,
because I am with you," says the LORD.
"I will completely destroy the many different
nations
where I scattered you.
But I will not completely destroy you.
I will punish you fairly,
but I will not let you escape your
punishment."

A Message to the Philistines

47 Before the king of Egypt attacked the city
of Gaza, the LORD spoke his word to
Jeremiah the prophet. ᵈ This message is to the
Philistine people.
²This is what the LORD says:
"See, the enemy is gathering in the north like
rising waters.
They will become like an overflowing
stream
and will cover the whole country like a flood,
even the towns and the people living in
them.
Everyone living in that country
will cry for help;
the people will cry painfully.
³They will hear the sound of the running
horses
and the noisy chariots
and the rumbling chariot wheels.
Parents will not help their children to safety,
because they will be too weak to help.
⁴The time has come
to destroy all the Philistines.
It is time to destroy all who are left alive
who could help the cities of Tyre and
Sidon.
The LORD will soon destroy the Philistines,
those left alive from the island of Crete.
⁵The people from the city of Gaza will be sad
and shave their heads.

The people from the city of Ashkelon will
  be made silent.
Those left alive from the valley,
  how long will you cut yourselves? [n]

[6]"You cry, 'Sword of the LORD,
  how long will you keep fighting?
Return to your holder.
  Stop and be still.'
[7]But how can his sword rest
  when the LORD has given it a command?
He has ordered it
  to attack Ashkelon and the seacoast."

A Message to Moab

48 This message is to the country of Moab.
  This is what the LORD All-powerful, the
God of Israel, says:
"How terrible it will be for the city of Nebo,
  because it will be ruined.
The town of Kiriathaim will be disgraced and
    captured;
  the strong city will be disgraced and
    shattered.
[2]Moab will not be praised again.
  Men in the town of Heshbon plan Moab's
    defeat.
They say, 'Come, let us put an end to that
    nation!'
Town of Madmen, [n] you will also be silenced.
  The sword will chase you.
[3]Listen to the cries from the town of
    Horonaim,
  cries of much confusion and destruction.
[4]Moab will be broken up.
  Her little children will cry for help.
[5]Moab's people go up the path to the town of
    Luhith,
  crying loudly as they go.
On the road down to Horonaim,
  cries of pain and suffering can be heard.
[6]Run! Run for your lives!
  Go like a bush being blown through the
    desert.
[7]You trust in the things you do and in your
    wealth,
  so you also will be captured.
The god Chemosh [d] will go into captivity
  and his priests and officers with him.
[8]The destroyer will come against every town;
  not one town will escape.
The valley will be ruined,
  and the high plain will be destroyed,
  as the LORD has said.
[9]Give wings to Moab,
  because she will surely leave her land.

Moab's towns will become empty,
  with no one to live in them.
[10]A curse will be on anyone who doesn't do
    what the LORD says,
  and a curse will be on anyone who holds
    back his sword from killing.

[11]"The people of Moab have never known
    trouble.
  They are like wine left to settle;
they have never been poured from one jar to
    another.
  They have not been taken into captivity.
So they taste as they did before,
  and their smell has not changed.
[12]A time is coming," says the LORD,
  "When I will send people to pour you from
    your jars.
They will empty Moab's jars
  and smash her jugs.
[13]The people of Israel trusted that god in the
    town of Bethel,
  and they were ashamed when there was no
    help.
In the same way Moab will be ashamed of
    their god Chemosh.

[14]"You cannot say, 'We are warriors!
  We are brave men in battle!'
[15]The destroyer of Moab and her towns has
    arrived.
  Her best young men will be killed!" says
    the King,
  whose name is the LORD All-powerful.
[16]"The end of Moab is near,
  and she will soon be destroyed.
[17]All you who live around Moab,
  all you who know her, cry for her.
Say, 'The ruler's power is broken;
  Moab's power and glory are gone.'

[18]"You people living in the town of Dibon,
  come down from your place of
    honour
and sit on the dry ground,
  because the destroyer of Moab has come
    against you.
And he has destroyed your fortified cities.
[19]You people living in the town of Aroer,
  stand next to the road and watch.
See the man running away and the woman
    escaping.
  Ask them, 'What happened?'
[20]Moab is filled with shame, because she is
    ruined.
  Cry, Moab, cry out!

---

sad and . . . yourselves The people did these things to show their sadness.
Madmen This name sounds like the Hebrew word for "be silenced".

Announce at the Arnon River
that Moab is destroyed.

²¹People on the high plain have been punished.
Judgement has come to these towns:
Holon, Jahzah and Mephaath;
²² Dibon, Nebo and Beth Diblathaim;
²³ Kiriathaim, Beth Gamul and Beth Meon;
²⁴ Kerioth and Bozrah.
Judgement has come to all the towns of
Moab, far and near.
²⁵Moab's strength has been cut off,
and its arm broken!" says the LORD.

²⁶"The people of Moab thought they were
greater than the LORD,
so punish them until they act as if they are
drunk.
Moab will fall and roll around in its own
vomit,
and people will even make fun of it.
²⁷Moab, you made fun of Israel.
Israel was caught in the middle of a gang of
thieves.
When you spoke about Israel,
you shook your head and acted as if you
were better than it.
²⁸People in Moab, leave your towns empty
and go and live among the rocks.
Be like a dove that makes its nest
at the entrance of a cave.

²⁹"We have heard that the people of Moab are
proud,
very proud.
They are proud, very proud,
and in their hearts they think they are
important."
³⁰The LORD says,
"I know Moab's great pride, but it is
useless.
Moab's boasting accomplishes nothing.
³¹So I cry sadly for Moab,
for everyone in Moab.
I moan for the people from the town of Kir
Hareseth.
³²I cry with the people of the town of Jazer
for you, the grapevines of the town of
Sibmah.
In the past your vines spread all the way to
the sea,
as far as the sea of Jazer.
But the destroyer has taken over
your fruit and grapes.
³³Joy and happiness are gone
from the large, rich fields of Moab.

I have stopped the flow of wine from the
winepresses. ᵈ
No one walks on the grapes with shouts
of joy.
There are shouts,
but not shouts of joy.

³⁴"Their crying can be heard from Moabite
towns,
from Heshbon to Elealeh and Jahaz.
It can be heard from Zoar as far away as
Horonaim and Eglath Shelishiyah.
Even the waters of Nimrim are dried up.
³⁵I will stop Moab
from making burnt offerings at the places of
worship
and from burning incense ᵈ to their gods,"
says the LORD.

³⁶"My heart cries sadly for Moab like a flute
playing a funeral song.
It cries like a flute for the people from Kir
Hareseth.
The money they made has all been taken
away.
³⁷Every head has been shaved
and every beard cut off.
Everyone's hands are cut,
and everyone wears rough cloth around his
waist. ⁿ

> ### Sidelight
> If you wanted to show your sadness for those who had died in the time of Jeremiah 48:37, you would usually shave your head, cut your beard off and wear sackcloth around your waist. Today we simply wear black, but both approaches symbolise mourning.

³⁸People are crying on every roof ⁿ in Moab
and in every public square.
There is nothing but sadness,
because I have broken Moab
like a jar no one wants," says the LORD.
³⁹"Moab is shattered! The people are crying!
Moab turns away in shame!
People all around her make fun of her.
The things that happened fill them with
great fear."

⁴⁰This is what the LORD says:
"Look! Someone is coming, like an eagle
diving down from the sky
and spreading its wings over Moab.

Every head . . . waist. The people did these things to show their sadness for those who had died.
roof In Bible times houses were built with flat roofs. The roof was used for drying things such as flax and fruit. And it was
used as an extra room, as a place for worship and as a place to sleep in the summer.

[41] The towns of Moab will be captured,
and the fortified cities will be defeated.
At that time Moab's warriors will be
frightened,
like a woman who is having a baby.
[42] The nation of Moab will be destroyed,
because they thought they were greater
than the LORD.
[43] Fear, deep pits and traps wait for you,
people of Moab," says the LORD.
[44] "People will run from fear,
but they will fall into the pits.
Anyone who climbs out of the pits
will be caught in the traps.
I will bring the year of punishment to Moab,"
says the LORD.

[45] "People have run from the powerful enemy
and have gone to Heshbon for safety.
But fire started in Heshbon;
a blaze has spread from the home town of
Sihon king of Moab.
It burnt up the leaders of Moab
and destroyed those proud people.
[46] How terrible it is for you, Moab!
The people who worship Chemosh have
been destroyed.
Your sons have been taken captive,
and your daughters have been taken away.

[47] "But in days to come,
I will make good things happen again to
Moab," says the LORD.

This ends the judgement on Moab.

A Message to Ammon

49 This message is to the Ammonite people.
This is what the LORD says:
"Do you think that Israel has no children?
Do you think there is no one to take the
land when the parents die?
If that were true, why did Molech *d* take
Gad's land
and why did Molech's people settle in
Gad's towns?"
[2] The LORD says,
"The time will come when I will make
Rabbah,
the capital city of the Ammonites, hear the
battle cry.
It will become a hill covered with ruins,
and the towns around it will be burnt.
Those people forced Israel out of that land,
but now Israel will force them out!" says
the LORD.
[3] "People in the town of Heshbon, cry sadly
because the town of Ai is destroyed!
Those who live in Rabbah, cry out!

Put on your rough cloth to show your
sadness, and cry loudly.
Run here and there for safety inside the
walls,
because Molech will be taken captive
and his priests and officers with him.
[4] You boast about your valleys
and about the fruit in your valleys.
You are like an unfaithful child
who believes his treasures will save him.
You think, 'Who would attack me?'
[5] I will soon bring terror on you
from everyone around you,"
says the Lord GOD All-powerful.
"You will all be forced to run away,
and no one will be able to gather you.

[6] "But the time will come
when I will make good things happen to
the Ammonites again,"
says the LORD.

A Message to Edom

[7] This message is to Edom. This is what the
LORD All-powerful says:
"Is there no more wisdom in the town of
Teman?
Can the wise men of Edom no longer give
good advice?
Have they lost their wisdom?
[8] You people living in the town of Dedan,
run away and hide in deep caves,
because I will bring disaster on the people of
Esau.
It is time for me to punish them.
[9] If workers came and picked the grapes from
your vines,
they would leave a few grapes behind.
If robbers came at night,
they would steal only enough for
themselves.
[10] But I will strip Edom bare.
I will find all their hiding places,
so they will not be able to hide
from me.
The children, relatives and neighbours
will die,
and Edom will be no more.
[11] Leave the orphans, and I will take care of
them.
Your widows also can trust in me."

[12] This is what the LORD says: "Some people did
not deserve to be punished, but they had to drink
from the cup of suffering anyway. People of
Edom, you deserve to be punished, so you will not
escape punishment. You must certainly drink from
the cup of suffering." [13] The LORD says, "I swear

by my own name that the city of Bozrah will become a pile of ruins! People will be shocked by what happened there. They will insult that city and speak evil of it. And all the towns around it will become ruins for ever."

¹⁴I have heard a message from the LORD.
A messenger has been sent among the nations, saying,
"Gather your armies to attack it!
Get ready for battle!"

¹⁵"Soon I will make you the smallest of nations,
and you will be greatly hated by everyone.
¹⁶Edom, you frightened other nations,
but your pride has fooled you.
You live in the hollow places of the cliff
and control the high places of the hills.
Even if you build your home as high as an eagle's nest,
I will bring you down from there," says the LORD.

¹⁷"Edom will be destroyed.
People who pass by will be shocked to see the destroyed cities,
and they will be amazed at all her injuries.
¹⁸Edom will be destroyed like the cities of Sodom and Gomorrah
and the towns around them," says the LORD.
"No one will live there!
No one will stay in Edom."

¹⁹"Like a lion coming up from the thick bushes near the Jordan River
to attack a strong pen for sheep,
I will suddenly chase Edom from its land.
Who is the one I have chosen to do this?
There is no one like me,
no one who can take me to court.
None of their leaders can stand up against me."

²⁰So listen to what the LORD has planned to do against Edom.
Listen to what he has decided to do to the people in the town of Teman.
He will surely drag away the young ones of Edom.
Their home towns will surely be shocked at what happens to them.
²¹At the sound of Edom's fall, the earth will shake.
Their cry will be heard all the way to the Red Sea.
²²The LORD is like an eagle swooping down and spreading its wings over the city of Bozrah.

At that time Edom's soldiers will become very frightened,
like a woman having a baby.

A Message to Damascus

²³This message is to the city of Damascus:
"The towns of Hamath and Arpad are put to shame,
because they have heard bad news.
They are discouraged.
They are troubled like the tossing sea.
²⁴The city of Damascus has become weak.
The people want to run away;
they are ready to panic.
The people feel pain and suffering,
like a woman giving birth to a baby.
²⁵Damascus was a city of my joy.
Why have the people not left that famous city yet?
²⁶Surely the young men will die in the city squares,
and all her soldiers will be killed at that time," says the LORD All-powerful.
²⁷"I will set fire to the walls of Damascus,
and it will completely burn the strong cities of King Ben-Hadad."

A Message to Kedar and Hazor

²⁸This message is to the tribe ᵈ of Kedar and the kingdoms of Hazor, which Nebuchadnezzar king of Babylon defeated. This is what the LORD says:
"Go and attack the people of Kedar,
and destroy the people of the East.
²⁹Their tents and flocks will be taken away.
Their belongings will be carried off—
their tents, all their goods and their camels.
Men will shout to them,
'Terror on every side!'

³⁰"Run away quickly!
People in Hazor, find a good place to hide!" says the LORD.
"Nebuchadnezzar king of Babylon has made plans against you
and wants to defeat you.

³¹"Get up! Attack the nation that is comfortable,
that is sure no one will defeat it," says the LORD.
"It does not have gates or fences to protect it.
Its people live alone.
³²The enemy will steal their camels
and their large herds of cattle as war prizes.
I will scatter the people who cut their hair short to every part of the earth,
and I will bring disaster on them from everywhere," says the LORD.

33"The city of Hazor will become a home for
     wild dogs;
   it will be an empty desert for ever.
 No one will live there,
     and no one will stay in it."

A Message to Elam

34Soon after Zedekiah became king of Judah,
the LORD spoke this word to Jeremiah the
prophet. *d* This message is to the nation of Elam.
   35This is what the LORD All-powerful says:
 "I will soon break Elam's bow,
     its greatest strength.
36I will bring the four winds against Elam
     from the four corners of the skies.
 I will scatter its people everywhere the four
     winds blow;
     its captives will go to every nation.
37I will terrify Elam in front of their enemies,
     who want to destroy them.
 I will bring disaster to Elam
     and show them how angry I am!" says the
     LORD.
 "I will send a sword to chase Elam
     until I have killed them all.
38I will set up my throne in Elam to show that
     I am king,
     and I will destroy its king and its officers!"
     says the LORD.
39"But I will make good things happen to Elam
     again
   in the future," says the LORD.

A Message to Babylon

50 This is the message the LORD spoke to
     Babylon and the Babylonian people
through Jeremiah the prophet. *d*
   2"Announce this to the nations.
     Lift up a banner and tell them.
   Speak the whole message and say:
   'Babylon will be captured.
     The god Bel *d* will be put to shame,
     and the god Marduk *d* will be afraid.
   Babylon's gods will be put to shame,
     and her idols will be afraid!'
3A nation from the north will attack
     Babylon
     and make it like an empty desert.
 No one will live there;
     both people and animals will run away."

4The LORD says, "At that time
   the people of Israel and Judah will come
     together.
 They will cry and look for the LORD
     their God.
5Those people will ask how to go to Jerusalem
   and will start in that direction.

They will come and join themselves to the
     LORD.
 They will make an agreement with him that
     will last for ever,
   an agreement that will never be forgotten.
6"My people have been like lost sheep.
   Their leaders have led them in the
     wrong way
 and made them wander around in the
     mountains and hills.
 They forgot where their resting place was.
7Whoever saw my people hurt them.
   And those enemies said, 'We did nothing
     wrong.
 Those people sinned against the LORD, their
     true resting place,
   the God their fathers trusted.'
8"Run away from Babylon,
   and leave the land of the Babylonians.
 Be like the goats that lead the flock.
9I will soon bring against Babylon
   many great nations from the north.
 They will take their places for war against it,
   and it will be captured by people from the
     north.
 Their arrows are like trained soldiers
   who do not return from war with empty
     hands.
10The enemy will take all the wealth from the
     Babylonians.
   Those enemy soldiers will get all they
     want," says the LORD.

11"Babylon, you are excited and happy,
   because you took my land.
 You dance around like a young cow in the grain.
   Your laughter is like the neighing of male
     horses.
12Your mother will be very ashamed;
   the woman who gave birth to you will be
     disgraced.
 Soon Babylonia will be the least important of
     all the nations.
   She will be an empty, dry desert.
13Because of the LORD's anger,
   no one will live there.
 She will be completely empty.
 Everyone who passes by Babylon will be
     shocked.
   They will shake their heads when they see
     all her injuries.

14"Take your positions for war against Babylon,
   all you soldiers with bows.
 Shoot your arrows at Babylon! Do not save
     any of them,
   because Babylon has sinned against the
     LORD.

¹⁵Soldiers around Babylon, shout the
　　war cry!
　Babylon has surrendered, her towers have
　　fallen,
　and her walls have been torn down.
　The LORD is giving her people the punishment
　　they deserve.
　You nations should give her what she
　　deserves;
　do to her what she has done to others.
¹⁶Don't let the people from Babylon plant their
　　crops
　or gather the harvest.
　The soldiers treated their captives cruelly.
　Now, let everyone go back home.
　Let everyone run to his own country.

¹⁷"The people of Israel are like a flock of sheep
　　that are scattered
　from being chased by lions.
　The first lion to eat them up
　　was the king of Assyria.
　The last lion to crush their bones
　　was Nebuchadnezzar king of Babylon."

¹⁸So this is what the LORD All-powerful, the
God of Israel, says:
　"I will punish the king of Babylon and his
　　country
　as I punished the king of Assyria.
¹⁹But I will bring the people of Israel back to
　　their own pasture.
　They will eat on Mount Carmel and in
　　Bashan.
　They will eat and be full
　　on the hills of Ephraim and Gilead."
²⁰The LORD says,
　"At that time people will try to find Israel's
　　guilt,
　but there will be no guilt.
　People will try to find Judah's sins,
　　but no sins will be found,
　because I will leave a few people alive from
　　Israel and Judah,
　and I will forgive their sins.

²¹"Attack the land of Merathaim.
　Attack the people who live in Pekod.
　Chase them, kill them, and completely
　　destroy them.
　Do everything I commanded you!" says the
　　LORD.

²²"The noise of battle can be heard all over the
　　country;
　it is the noise of much destruction.
²³Babylon was the hammer of the whole
　　earth,
　but how broken and shattered that hammer
　　is now.

It is truly the most ruined
　of all the nations.
²⁴Babylon, I set a trap for you,
　and you were caught before you knew it.
　You fought against the LORD,
　so you were found and taken prisoner.
²⁵The LORD has opened up his storeroom
　and brought out the weapons of his anger,
　because the Lord GOD All-powerful has work
　　to do
　in the land of the Babylonians.
²⁶Come against Babylon from far away.
　Break open her storehouses of grain.
　Pile up her dead bodies like heaps of grain.
　Completely destroy Babylon
　and do not leave anyone alive.
²⁷Kill all the young men in Babylon;
　let them be killed like animals.
　How terrible it will be for them, because the
　　time has come for their defeat;
　it is time for them to be punished.
²⁸Listen to the people running to escape the
　　country of Babylon!
　They are telling Jerusalem
　how the LORD our God is punishing Babylon
　　as it deserves
　for destroying his Temple. ᵈ

²⁹"Call for the archers
　to come against Babylon.
　Tell them to surround the city,
　and let no one escape.
　Pay her back for what she has done;
　do to her what she has done to other
　　nations.
　Babylon acted with pride against the LORD,
　the Holy One of Israel.
³⁰So her young men will be killed in her streets.
　All her soldiers will die on that day," says
　　the LORD.
³¹"Babylon, you are too proud, and I am
　　against you,"
　says the Lord GOD All-powerful.
　"The time has come
　for you to be punished.
³²Proud Babylon will stumble and fall,
　and no one will help her get up.
　I will start a fire in her towns,
　and it will burn up everything around her."

³³This is what the LORD All-powerful says:
　"The people of Israel
　and Judah are slaves.
　The enemy took them as prisoners
　and won't let them go.
³⁴But God is strong and will buy them back.
　His name is the LORD All-powerful.
　He will surely defend them with power
　so he can give rest to their land.

But he will not give rest to those living in
  Babylon."

35The LORD says,
"Let a sword kill the people living in
    Babylon
  and her officers and wise men!
36Let a sword kill her false prophets, *d*
  and they will become fools.
Let a sword kill her warriors,
  and they will be full of terror.
37Let a sword kill her horses and chariots
  and all the soldiers hired from other
    countries!
Then they will be like frightened women.
Let a sword attack her treasures,
  so they will be taken away.
38Let a sword attack her waters
  so they will be dried up.
She is a land of idols,
  and the people go insane with fear over
    them.

39"Desert animals and hyenas will live there,
  and owls will live there,
but no people will ever live there again.
  She will never be filled with people again.
40God completely destroyed the cities of Sodom
    and Gomorrah
  and the towns around them," says the
    LORD.
"In the same way no people will live in
    Babylon,
  and no human being will stay there.

41"Look! An army is coming from the north.
  A powerful nation and many kings
  are coming together from all around the
    world.
42Their armies have bows and spears.
  The soldiers are cruel and have no
    mercy.
As the soldiers come riding on their horses,
  the sound is loud like the roaring sea.
They stand in their places, ready for battle.
  They are ready to attack you, city of
    Babylon.
43The king of Babylon heard about those
    armies,
  and he became helpless with fear.
Distress has gripped him.
  His pain is like that of a woman giving
    birth to a baby.

44"Like a lion coming up from the thick bushes
    near the Jordan River
  to attack a strong pen for sheep,
I will suddenly chase the people of Babylon
    from their land.
  Who is the one I have chosen to do this?

There is no one like me,
  no one who can take me to court.
None of their leaders can stand up
    against me."

45So listen to what the LORD has planned to do
    against Babylon.
  Listen to what he has decided to do to the
    people in the city of Babylon.
He will surely drag away the young ones of
    Babylon.
  Their home towns will surely be shocked at
    what happens to them.
46At the sound of Babylon's capture, the earth
    will shake.
  People in all nations will hear Babylon's cry
    of distress.

51 This is what the LORD says:
  "I will soon cause a destroying wind
    to blow
  against Babylon and the Babylonian people.
2I will send foreign people to destroy Babylon
  like a wind that blows chaff *d* away.
  They will destroy the land.
Armies will surround the city
  when the day of disaster comes upon her.
3Don't let the Babylonian soldiers prepare their
    bows to shoot.
  Don't even let them put on their armour.
Don't feel sorry for the young men of Babylon,
  but completely destroy her army.
4They will be killed in the land of the
    Babylonians
  and will die in her streets.
5The Lord GOD All-powerful
  did not leave Israel and Judah,
even though they were completely guilty
  in the presence of the Holy One of Israel.

6"Run away from Babylon
  and save your lives!
Don't stay and be killed because of
    Babylon's sins.
It is time for the LORD to punish Babylon;
  he will give Babylon the punishment she
    deserves.
7Babylon was like a gold cup in the LORD's
    hand
  that made the whole earth drunk.
The nations drank Babylon's wine,
  and so they went mad.
8Babylon has suddenly fallen and been broken.
    Cry for her!
Get balm *d* for her pain,
  and perhaps she can be healed.

9"Foreigners in Babylon say, 'We tried to heal
    Babylon,
  but she cannot be healed.

So let us leave her and each go to his own
　　country.
　　Babylon's punishment is as high as the sky;
　　it reaches to the clouds.'

¹⁰"The people of Judah say, 'The LORD has
　　shown us to be right.
　　Come, let us tell in Jerusalem
　　what the LORD our God has done.'

¹¹"Sharpen the arrows!
　　Pick up your shields!
　　The LORD has stirred up the kings of the
　　　Medes,
　　because he wants to destroy Babylon.
　　The LORD will punish them as they deserve
　　for destroying his Temple. ᵈ
¹²Lift up a banner against the walls of
　　Babylon!
　　Bring more guards.
　　Put the watchmen in their places,
　　and get ready for a secret attack!
　　The LORD will certainly do what he has
　　　planned
　　and what he said he would do against the
　　people of Babylon.
¹³People of Babylon, you live near much water
　　and are rich with many treasures,
　　but your end as a nation has come.
　　It is time to stop you from robbing other
　　nations.
¹⁴The LORD All-powerful has promised in his
　　own name:
　　'Babylon, I will surely fill you with so many
　　　enemy soldiers they will be like a
　　　swarm of locusts. ᵈ
　　They will stand over you and shout their
　　victory.'

¹⁵"The LORD made the earth by his power.
　　He used his wisdom to build the world
　　and his understanding to stretch out the
　　skies.
¹⁶When he thunders, the waters in the skies
　　roar.
　　He makes clouds rise in the sky all over the
　　earth.
　　He sends lightning with the rain
　　and brings out the wind from his
　　storehouses.

¹⁷"People are so stupid and know so little.
　　Goldsmiths are made ashamed by their
　　idols,
　　because those statues are only false gods.
　　They have no breath in them.
¹⁸They are worth nothing; people make fun of
　　them.
　　When they are judged, they will be
　　destroyed.

¹⁹But God, who is Jacob's Portion, ᵈ is not like
　　the idols.
　　He made everything,
　　and he chose Israel to be his special people.
　　The LORD All-powerful is his name.

²⁰"You are my war club,
　　my battle weapon.
　　I use you to smash nations.
　　I use you to destroy kingdoms.
²¹I use you to smash horses and riders.
　　I use you to smash chariots and drivers.
²²I use you to smash men and women.
　　I use you to smash old people and young
　　people.
　　I use you to smash young men and young
　　women.
²³I use you to smash shepherds and flocks.
　　I use you to smash farmers and oxen.
　　I use you to smash governors and officers.

²⁴"But I will pay back Babylon and all the
Babylonians for all the evil things they did to
Jerusalem in your sight," says the LORD.

²⁵The LORD says,
　　"Babylon, you are a destroying mountain,
　　and I am against you.
　　You have destroyed the whole land.
　　I will put my hand out against you.
　　I will roll you off the cliffs,
　　and I will make you a burnt out mountain.
²⁶People will not find any rocks in Babylon big
　　enough for cornerstones. ᵈ
　　People will not take any rocks from
　　　Babylon to use for the foundation of a
　　　building,
　　because your city will be just a pile of ruins
　　for ever," says the LORD.

²⁷"Lift up a banner in the land!
　　Blow the trumpet among the nations!
　　Get the nations ready for battle against
　　Babylon.
　　Call these kingdoms of Ararat, Minni and
　　　Ashkenaz to fight against her.
　　Choose a commander to lead the army
　　　against Babylon.
　　Send so many horses that they are like a
　　swarm of locusts.
²⁸Get the nations ready for battle against
　　Babylon—
　　the kings of the Medes,
　　their governors and all their officers,
　　and all the countries they rule.
²⁹The land shakes and moves in pain,
　　because the LORD will do what he has
　　planned to Babylon.
　　He will make Babylon an empty desert,
　　where no one will live.

30Babylon's warriors have stopped fighting.
    They stay in their protected cities.
Their strength is gone,
    and they have become like frightened
        women.
Babylon's houses are burning.
    The bars of her gates are broken.
31One messenger follows another;
    messenger follows messenger.
They announce to the king of Babylon
    that his whole city has been captured.
32The river crossings have been captured,
    and the swamplands are burning.
All of Babylon's soldiers are terribly afraid."

33This is what the LORD All-powerful, the God
of Israel, says:
"The city of Babylon is like a threshing*d*
    floor,
where people crush the grain at harvest
    time.
The time to harvest Babylon is coming
    soon."

34"Nebuchadnezzar king of Babylon has
    defeated and destroyed us.
In the past he took our people away,
    and we became like an empty jar.
He was like a giant snake that swallowed us.
He filled his stomach with our best things.
    Then he spat us out.
35Babylon did terrible things to hurt us.
Now let those things happen to Babylon,"
    say the people of Jerusalem.
"The people of Babylon killed our people.
Now let them be punished for what they
    did," says Jerusalem.

36So this is what the LORD says:
"I will soon defend you, Judah,
    and make sure that Babylon is punished.
I will dry up Babylon's sea
    and make her springs become dry.
37Babylon will become a pile of ruins,
    a home for wild dogs.
People will be shocked by what happened
    there.
No one will live there any more.
38Babylon's people roar like young lions;
    they growl like baby lions.
39While they are stirred up,
    I will give a feast for them
    and make them drunk.
They will shout and laugh.
    And they will sleep for ever and never
        wake up!" says the LORD.
40"I will take the people of Babylon to be killed.
They will be like lambs,
    like rams and goats waiting to be killed.

41"How Babylon has been defeated!
    The pride of the whole earth has been
        taken captive.
People from other nations are shocked at
    what happened to Babylon,
and the things they see make them afraid.
42The sea has risen over Babylon;
    its roaring waves cover her.
43Babylon's towns are ruined and empty.
    It has become a dry, desert land,
a land where no one lives.
People do not even travel through
    Babylon.
44I will punish the god Bel*d* in Babylon.
    I will make him spit out what he has
        swallowed.
Nations will no longer come to Babylon;
    even the wall around the city will fall.

45"Come out of Babylon, my people!
    Run for your lives!
    Run from the LORD's great anger.
46Don't lose courage;
    rumours will spread through the land, but
        don't be afraid.
One rumour comes this year, and another
    comes the next year.
There will be rumours of terrible fighting in
    the country,
of rulers fighting against rulers.
47The time will surely come
    when I will punish the idols of Babylon,
and the whole land will be disgraced.
    There will be many dead people lying all
        around.
48Then heaven and earth and all that is in
    them
    will shout for joy about Babylon.
They will shout because the army comes
    from the north
    to destroy Babylon," says the LORD.

49"Babylon must fall, because she killed people
    from Israel.
She killed people from everywhere on
    earth.
50You who have escaped being killed with
    swords,
    leave Babylon! Don't wait!
Remember the LORD in the faraway land
    and think about Jerusalem."

51"We people of Judah are disgraced,
    because we have been insulted.
We have been shamed,
    because strangers have gone into
        the holy places of the LORD's Temple!"*d*

52So the Lord says, "The time is coming soon
    when I will punish the idols of Babylon.

Wounded people will cry with pain
    all over that land.
[53]Even if Babylon grows until she touches
    the sky,
    and even if she makes her highest cities
        strong,
    I will send people to destroy her," says the
        LORD.

[54]"Sounds of people crying are heard in
    Babylon.
    Sounds of people destroying things
    are heard in the land of the Babylonians.
[55]The LORD is destroying Babylon
    and making the loud sounds of the city
        become silent.
    Enemies come roaring in like ocean waves.
    The roar of their voices is heard all
        around.
[56]The army has come to destroy Babylon.
    Her soldiers have been captured,
    and their bows are broken,
    because the LORD is a God who punishes
        people for the evil they do.
    He gives them the full punishment they
        deserve.
[57]I will make Babylon's rulers and wise men
        drunk,
    and her governors, officers and soldiers too.
    Then they will sleep for ever and never wake
        up," says the King,
    whose name is the LORD All-powerful.

[58]This is what the LORD All-powerful says:
"Babylon's thick wall will be completely
        pulled down
    and her high gates burnt.
    The people will work hard, but it won't
        help;
    their work will only become fuel for the
        flames!"

A Message to Babylon

[59]This is the message that Jeremiah the
prophet [d] gave to the officer Seraiah son of Neriah,
who was the son of Mahseiah. Seraiah went to
Babylon with Zedekiah king of Judah in the
fourth year of Zedekiah's reign. His duty was to
arrange the king's food and housing on the trip.
[60]Jeremiah had written on a scroll all the terrible
things that would happen to Babylon, all these
words about Babylon. [61]Jeremiah said to Seraiah,
"As soon as you come to Babylon, be sure to read
this message so all the people can hear you.
[62]Then say, 'LORD, you have said that you will
destroy this place so that no people or animals
will live in it. It will be an empty ruin for ever.'

[63]After you finish reading this scroll, tie a stone to
it and throw it into the Euphrates River. [64]Then
say, 'In the same way Babylon will sink and will
not rise again because of the terrible things I will
make happen here. Her people will fall.' "
    The words of Jeremiah end here.

The Fall of Jerusalem

52 Zedekiah was 21 years old when he became king, and he was king in Jerusalem
for eleven years. His mother's name was Hamutal
daughter of Jeremiah, [n] and she was from Libnah.
[2]Zedekiah did what the LORD said was wrong,
just as Jehoiakim had done. [3]All this happened
in Jerusalem and Judah because the LORD was
angry with them. Finally, he threw them out of
his presence.
    Zedekiah turned against the king of Babylon.
[4]Then Nebuchadnezzar king of Babylon marched
against Jerusalem with his whole army. They
made a camp around the city and built devices all
around the city walls to attack it. This happened
in Zedekiah's ninth year, tenth month and tenth
day as king. [5]And the city was under attack until
Zedekiah's eleventh year as king.
    [6]By the ninth day of the fourth month, the
hunger was terrible in the city; there was no food
for the people to eat. [7]Then the city wall was
broken through, and the whole army of Judah ran
away at night. They left the city through the gate
between the two walls by the king's garden. Even
though the Babylonians were surrounding the
city, Zedekiah and his men headed towards the
Jordan Valley.
    [8]But the Babylonian army chased King
Zedekiah and caught him in the plains of Jericho.
All of his army was scattered from him. [9]So the
Babylonians captured Zedekiah and took him to
the king of Babylon at the town of Riblah in the
land of Hamath. There he passed sentence on
Zedekiah. [10]At Riblah the king of Babylon killed
Zedekiah's sons as he watched. The king also
killed all the officers of Judah. [11]Then he put
out Zedekiah's eyes, and put bronze chains
on him and took him to Babylon. And the king
kept Zedekiah in prison there until the day
he died.
    [12]Nebuzaradan, commander of the king's spe-
cial guards and servant of the king of Babylon,
came to Jerusalem on the tenth day of the fifth
month. This was in Nebuchadnezzar's nineteenth year as king of Babylon. [13]Nebuzaradan
set fire to the Temple [d] of the LORD, the palace
and all the houses of Jerusalem; every important
building was burnt. [14]The whole Babylonian
army, led by the commander of the king's special

Jeremiah   This is not the prophet Jeremiah but a different man with the same name.

guards, broke down all the walls around Jerusalem. [15]Nebuzaradan, the commander of the king's special guards, took captive some of the poorest people, those who were left in Jerusalem, those who had surrendered to the king of Babylon and the skilled craftsmen who were left in Jerusalem. [16]But Nebuzaradan left behind some of the poorest people of the land to take care of the vineyards and fields.

[17]The Babylonians broke into pieces the bronze pillars, the bronze stands and the large bronze bowl, called the Sea, which were in the Temple of the LORD. Then they carried all the bronze pieces to Babylon. [18]They also took the pots, shovels, wick trimmers, bowls, dishes and all the bronze objects used to serve in the Temple. [19]The commander of the king's special guards took away bowls, pans for carrying hot coals, large bowls, pots, lampstands, pans and bowls used for drink offerings. He took everything that was made of pure gold or silver.

[20]There was so much bronze that it could not be weighed: two pillars, the large bronze bowl called the Sea with the twelve bronze bulls under it and the movable stands, which King Solomon had made for the Temple of the LORD. [21]Each of the pillars was about 9 metres high, 6 metres around and hollow inside. The wall of each pillar was 8 centimetres thick. [22]The bronze capital *d* on top of the one pillar was about 2.5 metres high. It was decorated with a net design and bronze pomegranates *d* all around it. The other pillar also had pomegranates and was like the first pillar. [23]There were 96 pomegranates on the sides of the pillars. There was a total of 100 pomegranates above the net design.

[24]The commander of the king's special guards took as prisoners Seraiah the chief priest, Zephaniah the priest next in rank and the three doorkeepers. [25]He also took from the city the officer in charge of the soldiers, seven people who advised the king, the royal secretary who selected people for the army and 60 other men from Judah who were in the city when it fell. [26]Nebuzaradan, the commander, took these people and brought them to the king of Babylon at the town of Riblah. [27]There at Riblah, in the land of Hamath, the king had them killed.

So the people of Judah were led away from their country as captives. [28]This is the number of the people Nebuchadnezzar took away as captives: in the seventh year, 3,023 Jews; [29]in Nebuchadnezzar's eighteenth year, 832 people from Jerusalem; [30]in Nebuchadnezzar's twenty-third year, Nebuzaradan, commander of the king's special guards, took 745 Jews as captives.

In all 4,600 people were taken captive.

Jehoiachin is Set Free

[31]Jehoiachin king of Judah was in prison in Babylon for 37 years. The year Evil-Merodach became king of Babylon he let Jehoiachin king of Judah out of prison. He set Jehoiachin free on the twenty-fifth day of the twelfth month. [32]Evil-Merodach spoke kindly to Jehoiachin and gave him a seat of honour above the seats of the other kings who were with him in Babylon. [33]So Jehoiachin put away his prison clothes, and for the rest of his life, he ate at the king's table. [34]Every day the king of Babylon gave Jehoiachin an allowance. This lasted as long as he lived, until the day Jehoiachin died.

Lamentations

When?

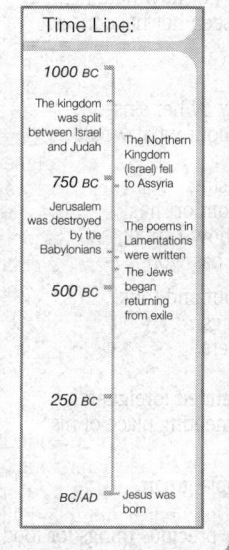

Time Line:

1000 BC

The kingdom was split between Israel and Judah

The Northern Kingdom (Israel) fell to Assyria

750 BC

Jerusalem was destroyed by the Babylonians

The poems in Lamentations were written

500 BC

The Jews began returning from exile

250 BC

BC/AD — Jesus was born

Why Read This Book:

- Find ways to express grief to God (Lamentations 1—2).
- Learn about taking responsibility for choices and consequences (Lamentations 3—4).
- Be encouraged to turn to God in times of trouble (Lamentations 5).

Behind the Scenes:

All of Jerusalem was in ruins.
Babylonians had surrounded the city and then burned it to the ground.
Children, women and men had been killed.
Desolation was everywhere.
Everything the Jews had known and loved was gone.
Full of sorrow, the five poems in Lamentations were written.
Grief is evident in each of the poems.
Hope shines through only towards the end of the book.
In future years, people read the book in times of sorrow.
Jews read it each year in August to remember the Temple's
    destruction and to repent of their sins.
Knowing God's love can help through times of crisis like this.

Like the lines you've just read, each part of the five poems in Lamentations begins with a different consecutive letter of the Hebrew alphabet – 22 letters in all. Of course, we can't see the structure in English, because the translated words are different. But the ancient Hebrews understood that the poems expressed their sorrow from beginning to end, "from A to Z".

Where?

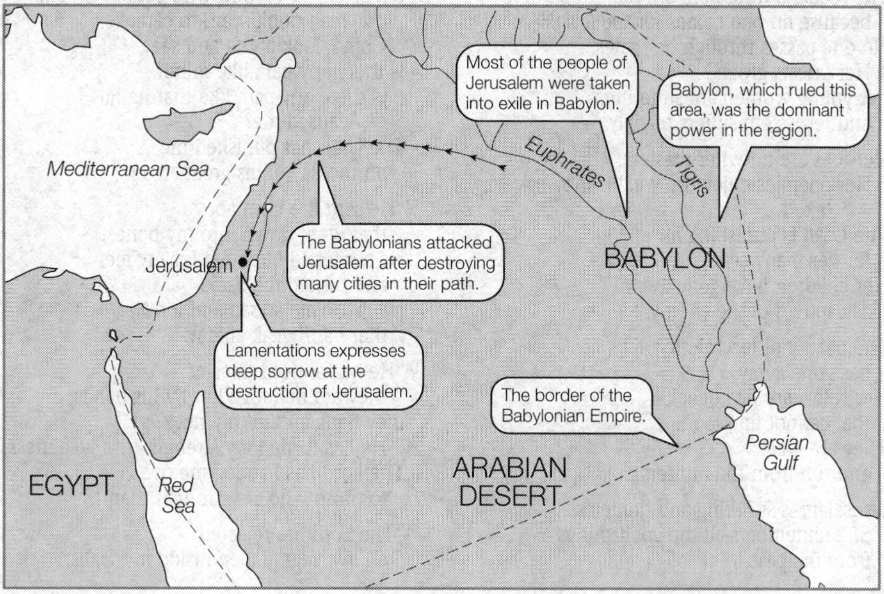

The map shows the region with the following labels:

- Most of the people of Jerusalem were taken into exile in Babylon.
- Babylon, which ruled this area, was the dominant power in the region.
- The Babylonians attacked Jerusalem after destroying many cities in their path.
- Lamentations expresses deep sorrow at the destruction of Jerusalem.
- The border of the Babylonian Empire.

Mediterranean Sea
Euphrates
Tigris
Jerusalem
BABYLON
EGYPT
Red Sea
ARABIAN DESERT
Persian Gulf

Jerusalem Cries over Her Loss

1 Jerusalem once was full of people,
  but now the city is empty.
Jerusalem once was a great city among the
    nations,
  but now she ^{n} is like a widow.
She was like a queen of all the other cities,
  but now she is a slave.

2 She cries loudly at night,
  and tears are on her cheeks.
There is no one to comfort her;
  all who loved her are gone.
All her friends have turned against her
  and are now her enemies.

Sidelight   The "blues" are nothing
new. There are many
books in the Bible which contain songs of
sorrow (such as 2 Samuel 1:17–27, p.284,
and Psalm 74, p.544), but the book of
Lamentations is the only book of the Bible
which is blue all through!

---

3 Judah has gone into captivity
  where she suffers and works hard.
She lives among other nations,
  but she has found no rest.
Those who chased her caught her
  when she was in trouble.

4 The roads to Jerusalem are sad,
  because no one comes for the feasts.
No one passes through her gates.
  Her priests groan,
her young women are suffering,
  and Jerusalem suffers terribly.

5 Her foes are now her masters.
  Her enemies enjoy the wealth they have
    taken.
The LORD is punishing her
  for her many sins.
Her children have gone away
  as captives of the enemy.

6 The beauty of Jerusalem
  has gone away.
Her rulers are like deer
  that cannot find food.
They are weak
  and run from the hunters.

7 Jerusalem is suffering and homeless.
  She remembers all the good things
  from the past.

But her people were defeated by the enemy,
  and there was no one to help her.
When her enemies saw her,
  they laughed to see her ruined.

8 Jerusalem sinned terribly,
  so she has become unclean. ^{d}
Those who honoured her now hate her,
  because they have seen her nakedness.
She groans
  and turns away.

9 She made herself dirty by her sins
  and did not think about what would
    happen to her.
Her defeat was surprising,
  and no one could comfort her.
She says, "LORD, see how I suffer,
  because the enemy has won."

10 The enemy reached out and took
  all her precious things.
She even saw foreigners
  enter her Temple. ^{d}
The LORD had commanded foreigners
  never to enter the meeting place of his
    people.

11 All of Jerusalem's people groan,
  looking for bread.
They are trading their precious things for food
  so they can stay alive.
The city says, "Look, LORD, and see.
  I am hated."

12 Jerusalem says, "You who pass by on the
    road don't seem to care.
  Come, look at me and see.
Is there any pain like mine?
  Is there any pain like that he has
    caused me?
The LORD has punished me
  on the day of his great anger.

13 "He sent fire from above
  that went down into my bones.
He stretched out a net for my feet
  and turned me back.
He made me so sad and lonely
  that I am weak all day.

14 "He has noticed my sins;
  they are tied together by his hands;
they hang around my neck.
  He has turned my strength into weakness.
The Lord has handed me over
  to those who are stronger than I.

15 "The Lord has rejected
  all my mighty men inside my walls.

---

she In this poem the city of Jerusalem is described as a woman.

He brought an army against me
  to destroy my young men.
As if in a winepress, *d* the Lord has crushed
  the capital city of Judah.

¹⁶"I cry about these things;
  my eyes overflow with tears.
There is no one near to comfort me,
  no one who can give me strength again.
My children are left sad and lonely,
  because the enemy has won."

¹⁷Jerusalem reaches out her hands,
  but there is no one to comfort her.
The LORD commanded the people of Jacob
  to be surrounded by their enemies.
Jerusalem is now unclean
  like those around her.

¹⁸Jerusalem says, "The LORD is right,
  but I refused to obey him.
Listen, all you people,
  and look at my pain.
My young women and men
  have gone into captivity.

¹⁹"I called out to my friends,
  but they turned against me.
My priests and my elders
  have died in the city
while looking for food
  to stay alive.

²⁰"Look at me, LORD. I am upset
  and greatly troubled.
My heart is troubled,
  because I have been so stubborn.
Out in the streets, the sword kills;
  inside the houses, death destroys.

²¹"People have heard my groaning,
  and there is no one to comfort me.
All my enemies have heard of my trouble,
  and they are happy you have done this
    to me.
Now bring that day you have announced
  so that my enemies will be like me.

²²"Look at all their evil.
  Do to them what you have done to me
  because of all my sins.
I groan over and over again,
  and I am afraid."

The LORD Destroyed Jerusalem

2 Look how the Lord in his anger
  has brought Jerusalem to shame.
He has thrown down the greatness of Israel
  from the sky to the earth;
he did not remember the Temple, *d* his
    footstool,
  on the day of his anger.

²The Lord swallowed up without mercy
  all the houses of the people of Jacob;
in his anger he pulled down
  the strong places of Judah.
He threw her kingdom and its rulers
  down to the ground in dishonour.

³In his anger he has removed
  all the strength of Israel;
he took away his power from Israel
  when the enemy came.
He burnt against the people of Jacob like a
    flaming fire
  that burns up everything around it.

⁴Like an enemy, he prepared to shoot
    his bow,
  and his hand was against us.
Like an enemy, he killed
  all the good-looking people;
he poured out his anger like fire
  on the tents of Jerusalem.

⁵The Lord was like an enemy;
  he swallowed up Israel.
He swallowed up all her palaces
  and destroyed all her strongholds. *d*
He has caused more moaning and groaning
  for Judah.

⁶He cut down his Temple like a garden;
  he destroyed the meeting-place.
The LORD has made Jerusalem forget
  the set feasts and Sabbath *d* days.
He has rejected the king and the priest
  in his great anger.

⁷The Lord has rejected his altar
  and abandoned his Temple.
He has handed over to the enemy
  the walls of Jerusalem's palaces.
Their uproar in the LORD's Temple
  was like that of a feast day.

⁸The LORD planned to destroy
  the wall around Jerusalem.
He measured the wall
  and did not stop himself from destroying it.
He made the walls and defences sad;
  together they have fallen.

⁹Jerusalem's gates have fallen to the ground;
  he destroyed and smashed the bars of the
    gates.
Her king and her princes are among the
    nations.
The teaching of the LORD has stopped,
and the prophets *d* do not have
  visions from the LORD.

¹⁰The elders of Jerusalem
  sit on the ground in silence.

They throw dust on their heads
  and put on rough cloth to show their
    sadness.
The young women of Jerusalem
  bow their heads to the ground in
    sorrow.

11My eyes have no more tears,
  and I am sick to my stomach.
I feel empty inside,
  because my people have been destroyed.
Children and babies are fainting
  in the streets of the city.

12They ask their mothers,
  "Where is the grain and wine?"
They faint like wounded soldiers
  in the streets of the city
  and die in their mothers' arms.

13What can I say about you, Jerusalem?
  What can I compare you to?
What can I say you are like?
  How can I comfort you, Jerusalem?
Your ruin is as deep as the sea.
  No one can heal you.

14Your prophets saw visions,
  but they were false and worth nothing.
They did not point out your sins
  to keep you from being captured.
They preached what was false
  and led you wrongly.

15All who pass by on the road
  clap their hands at you;
they make fun of Jerusalem
  and shake their heads.
They ask, "Is this the city that people called
  the most beautiful city,
  the happiest place on earth?"

16All your enemies open their mouths
  to speak against you.
They make fun and grind their teeth in
    anger.
  They say, "We have swallowed you up.
This is the day we were waiting for!
  We have finally seen it happen."

17The Lord has done what he planned;
  he has kept his word
  that he commanded long ago.
He has destroyed without mercy,
  and he has let your enemies laugh
    at you.
He has strengthened your enemies.

18The people cry out to the Lord.
  Wall of Jerusalem,
let your tears flow
  like a river day and night.

Do not stop
  or let your eyes rest.

19Get up, cry out in the night,
  even as the night begins.
Pour out your heart like water
  in prayer to the Lord.
Lift up your hands in prayer to him
  for the life of your children
who are fainting with hunger
  on every street corner.

20Jerusalem says: "Look, Lord, and see
  to whom you have done this.
Women eat their own babies,
  the children they have cared for.
Priests and prophets are killed
  in the Temple of the Lord.

21"People young and old
  lie outside on the ground.
My young women and young men
  have been killed by the sword.
You killed them on the day of your anger;
  you killed them without mercy.

22"You invited terrors to come against me on
    every side,
  as if you were inviting them to a feast.
No one escaped or remained alive
  on the day of the Lord's anger.
My enemy has killed
  those I cared for and brought up."

The Meaning of Suffering

3 I am a man who has seen the suffering
  that comes from the rod of the Lord's
    anger.
2He led me
  into darkness, not light.
3He turned his hand against me
  again and again, all day long.

4He wore out my flesh and skin
  and broke my bones.
5He surrounded me with sadness
  and attacked me with grief.
6He made me sit in the dark,
  like those who have been dead a
    long time.

7He shut me in so I could not get out;
  he put heavy chains on me.
8I cry out and beg for help,
  but he ignores my prayer.
9He blocked my way with a stone wall
  and led me in the wrong direction.

10He is like a bear ready to attack me,
  like a lion in hiding.

¹¹He led me the wrong way and let me stray
and left me without help.
¹²He prepared to shoot his bow
and made me the target for his arrows.

¹³He shot me in the kidneys
with the arrows from his bag.
¹⁴I was a joke to all my people,
who make fun of me with songs all day
long.
¹⁵The LORD filled me with misery;
he made me drunk with suffering.

¹⁶He broke my teeth with gravel
and trampled me into the ground.
¹⁷I have no more peace.
I have forgotten what happiness is.
¹⁸I said, "My strength is gone,
and I have no hope in the LORD."

¹⁹LORD, remember my suffering and my
misery,
my sorrow and trouble.
²⁰Please remember me
and think about me.
²¹But I have hope
when I think of this:

²²The LORD's love never ends;
his mercies never stop.
²³They are new every morning;
LORD, your loyalty is great.
²⁴I say to myself, "The LORD is mine,
so I hope in him."

²⁵The LORD is good to those who hope
in him,
to those who seek him.
²⁶It is good to wait quietly
for the LORD to save.
²⁷It is good for someone to work hard
while he is young.

²⁸He should sit alone and be quiet;
the LORD has given him hard work
to do.
²⁹He should bow down to the ground;
perhaps there is still hope.
³⁰He should let anyone slap his cheek;
he should be filled with shame.

³¹The Lord will not reject
his people for ever.
³²Although he brings sorrow,
he also has mercy and great love.

SUFFERING

Letting it All Out

While lots of us go though hard times and difficult experiences, for the most part we don't have to deal with what Christians in other parts of the world go through. For them, being a Christian is a daily risk that may lead to attack, arrest, prison, torture – or worse. They live with suffering and stress that we can't even imagine. We are fortunate to be living in a place where we can express our Christian faith freely. It's important that we remember to pray for our brothers and sisters around the world. History shows us that people like them who stand up for God can find themselves experiencing serious suffering.

Read **Lamentations 3:1–24**, but be warned, it's not one of those bits of the Bible that will give you warm fuzzy feelings. You might have noticed that when it comes to dealing with suffering there are two kinds of people: those who suffer in silence and those who let it all out.

* Look at verses 22–24. What do the writer's thoughts lead him to do?
* What three top tips could you give, from this passage, to help someone who is suffering?

Consider . . .

* finding out more about organisations who work to help Christians around the world who are suffering persecution.
* sending an e-card to someone you know who is having a tough time at the moment.

For more, see . . .

* Isaiah 61:1–3 (p.705)
* 2 Corinthians 4:7–10 (p.1243)
* Romans 8:15–19 (p.1195)

³³He does not like to punish people
    or make them sad.

³⁴He sees if any prisoner of the earth
    is crushed under his feet;
³⁵he sees if someone is treated unfairly
    before the Most High God;
³⁶the Lord sees
    if someone is cheated in his case in court.

³⁷Nobody can speak and have it happen
    unless the Lord commands it.
³⁸Both bad and good things
    come by the command of the Most
        High God.
³⁹No one should complain
    when he is punished for his sins.

⁴⁰Let us examine and see what we have done
    and then return to the Lord.
⁴¹Let us lift up our hands and pray from our
        hearts
    to God in heaven:
⁴²"We have sinned and turned against you,
    and you have not forgiven us.

⁴³"You wrapped yourself in anger and
        chased us;
    you killed us without mercy.
⁴⁴You wrapped yourself in a cloud,
    and no prayer could get through.
⁴⁵You made us like scum and rubbish
    among the other nations.

⁴⁶"All our enemies
    open their mouths and speak against us.
⁴⁷We have been frightened and fearful,
    ruined and destroyed."
⁴⁸Streams of tears flow from my eyes,
    because my people are destroyed.

⁴⁹My tears flow continually,
    without stopping,
⁵⁰until the Lord looks down
    and sees from heaven.
⁵¹I am sad when I see
    what has happened to all the women of my
        city.

⁵²Those who are my enemies for no reason
    hunted me like a bird.
⁵³They tried to kill me in a pit;
    they threw stones at me.
⁵⁴Water came up over my head,
    and I said, "I am going to die."

⁵⁵I called out to you, Lord,
    from the bottom of the pit.
⁵⁶You heard me calling, "Do not close your
        ears
    and ignore my cry and shouts."

⁵⁷You came near when I called to you;
    you said, "Don't be afraid."

⁵⁸Lord, you have taken my case
    and given me back my life.
⁵⁹Lord, you have seen how I have been
        wronged.
    Now judge my case for me.
⁶⁰You have seen how my enemies took revenge
        on me
    and made evil plans against me.

⁶¹Lord, you have heard their insults
    and all their evil plans against me.
⁶²The words and thoughts of my enemies
    are against me all the time.
⁶³Look! In everything they do
    they make fun of me with songs.

⁶⁴Pay them back, Lord,
    for what they have done.
⁶⁵Make them stubborn,
    and put your curse on them.
⁶⁶Chase them in anger, Lord,
    and destroy them from under your
        heavens.

The Attack on Jerusalem

4 See how the gold has lost its shine,
    how the pure gold has lost its shine!
The stones of the Temple ^d are scattered
    at every street corner.

²The precious people of Jerusalem
    were more valuable than gold,
but now they are thought of as clay jars
    made by the hands of a potter.

Sidelight Because only priests were allowed to enter the Most Holy Place in the Temple, the Babylonian trampling of the Temple (Lamentations 4:1) was difficult to cope with. In fact, the Temple's destruction was even more tragic to the devout Jew than the devastation in the rest of Jerusalem.

---

³Even wild dogs give their milk
    to feed their young,
but my people are cruel
    like ostriches in the desert.

⁴The babies are so thirsty
    their tongues stick to the roofs of their
        mouths.
Children beg for bread,
    but no one gives them any.

⁵Those who once ate fine foods
    are now starving in the streets.
People who grew up wearing nice clothes
    now pick through rubbish piles.

⁶My people have been punished
    more than Sodom was.
Sodom was destroyed suddenly,
    and no hands reached out to help her.

⁷Our princes were purer than snow
    and whiter than milk.
Their bodies were redder than rubies;
    they looked like sapphires.

⁸But now they are blacker than coal,
    and no one recognises them in the streets.
Their skin hangs on their bones;
    it is as dry as wood.

⁹Those who were killed in the war were
        better off
    than those killed by hunger.
They starve in pain and die,
    because there is no food from the field.

¹⁰With their own hands kind women
    cook their own children.
They became food
    when my people were destroyed.

¹¹The LORD turned loose all of his anger;
    he poured out his strong anger.
He set fire to Jerusalem,
    burning it down to the foundations.

¹²Kings of the earth and people of the world
    could not believe
that enemies and foes
    could enter the gates of Jerusalem.

¹³It happened because her prophets *d* sinned
    and her priests did evil.
They killed in the city
    those who did what was right.

¹⁴They wandered in the streets
    as if they were blind.
They were dirty with blood,
    so no one would touch their clothes.

¹⁵"Go away! You are unclean," *d* people
        shouted at them.
    "Get away! Get away! Don't touch us!"
So they ran away and wandered.
    Even the other nations said, "Don't stay
        here."

¹⁶The LORD himself scattered them
    and did not look after them any more.
No one respects the priests
    or honours the elders.

¹⁷Also, our eyes grew tired,
    looking for help that never came.
We kept watch from our towers
    for a nation to save us.

¹⁸Our enemies hunted us,
    so we could not even walk in the
        streets.
Our end is near. Our time is up.
    Our end has come.

¹⁹Those who chased us
    were faster than eagles in the sky.
They ran us into the mountains
    and ambushed us in the desert.

²⁰The LORD's appointed king, who was our very
        breath,
    was caught in their traps.
We had said about him, "We will be
        protected by him
    among the nations."

²¹Be happy and glad, people of Edom,
    you who live in the land of Uz.
The cup of God's anger will come to you;
    then you will get drunk and go naked.

²²Your punishment is complete, Jerusalem.
    He will not send you into captivity again.
But the LORD will punish the sins of Edom;
    he will uncover your evil.

A Prayer to the LORD

5 Remember, LORD, what happened to us.
    Look and see our disgrace.
²Our land has been turned over to strangers;
    our houses have been given to foreigners.
³We are like orphans with no father;
    our mothers are like widows.
⁴We have to buy the water we drink;
    we must pay for the firewood.
⁵Those who chase after us want to catch us
        by the neck.
    We are tired and find no rest.
⁶We made an agreement with Egypt
    and with Assyria to get enough food.
⁷Our ancestors sinned against you, but they
        are gone;
    now we suffer because of their sins.
⁸Slaves have become our rulers,
    and no one can save us from them.
⁹We risk our lives to get our food;
    we face death in the desert.
¹⁰Our skin is hot like an oven;
    we burn with starvation.
¹¹The enemy abused the women of
        Jerusalem
    and the girls in the cities of Judah.

¹²Princes were hung by the hands;
  they did not respect our elders.
¹³The young men ground grain at the mill,
  and boys stumbled under loads of wood.
¹⁴The elders no longer sit at the city gates;
  the young men no longer sing.
¹⁵We have no more joy in our hearts;
  our dancing has turned to sadness.
¹⁶The crown has fallen from our head.
  How terrible it is because we sinned.
¹⁷Because of this we are afraid,
  and now our eyes are dim.

¹⁸Mount Zion *d* is empty,
  and wild dogs wander around it.

¹⁹But you rule for ever, LORD.
  You will be King from now on.
²⁰Why have you forgotten us for so long?
  Have you left us for ever?
²¹Bring us back to you, LORD, and we will
  return.
  Make our days as they were before,
²²or have you completely rejected us?
  Are you so angry with us?

Ezekiel

When?

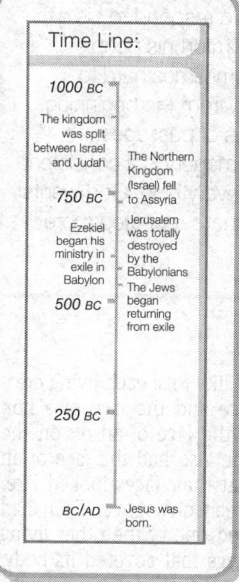

Time Line:

1000 BC

The kingdom was split between Israel and Judah

750 BC

The Northern Kingdom (Israel) fell to Assyria

Ezekiel began his ministry in exile in Babylon

Jerusalem was totally destroyed by the Babylonians

The Jews began returning from exile

500 BC

250 BC

BC/AD — Jesus was born.

Why Read This Book:

- Be encouraged by God's extraordinary efforts to call his people back to himself (Ezekiel 1—24).
- Take comfort in the promises God made through the prophet Ezekiel (Ezekiel 33—48).

Behind the Scenes:

"Prophet Sees UFO!" the headline would have screamed.

The story would reveal how Ezekiel, the prophet, saw the sky opening up, glowing lights in the sky, fire, and something like glowing metal in the middle of a cloud. Then, the story would continue, the prophet saw creatures – creatures who, the writer suggests, were probably aliens.

Finally – and this was the best part – a voice above the creatures boomed out. When Ezekiel looked up, he saw an amazing throne. It was all so powerful he was knocked off his feet.

But the prophet didn't see a UFO. The prophet saw a vision of God.

This unusual book is filled with such stories. Ezekiel lived during the most difficult time in the Old Testament. Jerusalem had been destroyed, and the people – including Ezekiel – had been taken into exile, mostly in Babylon. The people couldn't understand what had happened to their beloved city. Had God abandoned them?

Through visions, strange actions, and symbolic language, the prophet interpreted what had happened to the city and his people. ▷

Where?

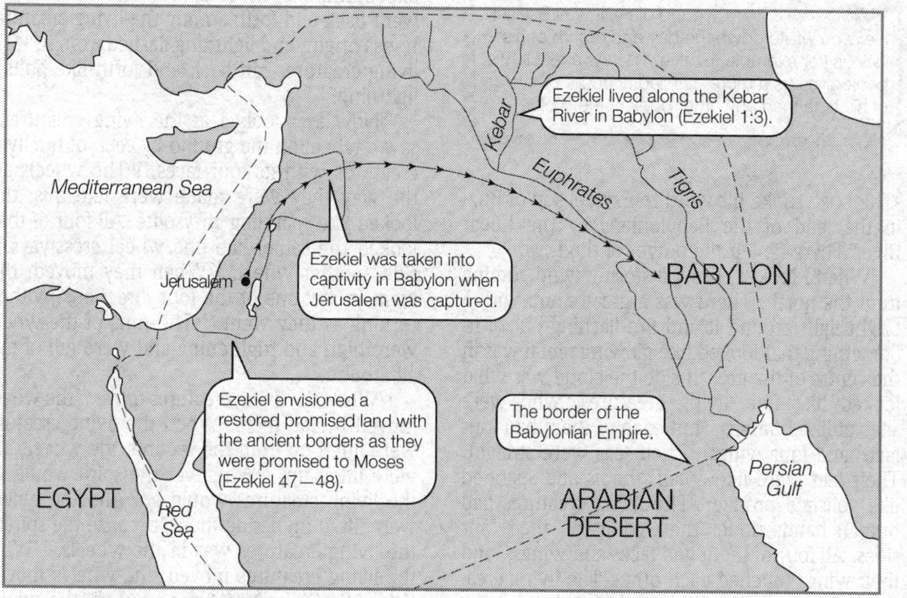

Mediterranean Sea

Kebar

Euphrates

Tigris

Ezekiel lived along the Kebar River in Babylon (Ezekiel 1:3).

BABYLON

Jerusalem

Ezekiel was taken into captivity in Babylon when Jerusalem was captured.

Ezekiel envisioned a restored promised land with the ancient borders as they were promised to Moses (Ezekiel 47—48).

The border of the Babylonian Empire.

Persian Gulf

EGYPT

Red Sea

ARABIAN DESERT

Behind the Scenes (cont.): First, he told how the people of Judah got themselves into trouble by refusing to listen to earlier prophets or to follow God. So God had used the invading Babylonians to punish the people.

Yet God had not abandoned his chosen people, Ezekiel insisted. Because of God's love and trustworthiness, he would restore the city to them and renew his relationship with them. They would respond to his gift by returning to him. At that point, God would again comfort his people.

As Ezekiel describes his dreams and visions, it's sometimes hard to understand the prophet's underlying message. In fact, from the beginning, scholars have been stumped by the specific meanings of passages.

But beneath all the unusual language, poetry, and imagery is a consistent message that still has meaning for us today: through everything, God wants people to "know that I am the Lord God" – a phrase that's repeated more than sixty times through the book.

Ezekiel's Vision of Living Creatures

1 It was the fifth day of the fourth month of the thirtieth year of our captivity. I was by the Kebar River among the people who had been carried away as captives. The sky opened, and I saw visions of God.

²It was the fifth day of the month of the fifth year that King Jehoiachin had been a prisoner.

> **Sidelight** If any prophet kept a good diary, it was Ezekiel. He even wrote down the day and month of his visions (for example, Ezekiel 1:1). As a result, his book gives us a more detailed account of events of his time than any other book in the Bible.

³The LORD spoke his word to Ezekiel son of Buzi in the land of the Babylonians by the Kebar River. There he felt the power of the LORD.

⁴When I looked, I saw a stormy wind coming from the north. There was a great cloud with a bright light around it and fire flashing out of it. Something that looked like glowing metal was in the centre of the fire. ⁵Inside the cloud was what looked like four living creatures, who were shaped like humans, ⁶but each of them had four faces and four wings. ⁷Their legs were straight. Their feet were like a calf's hoofs and sparkled like polished bronze. ⁸The living creatures had human hands under their wings on their four sides. All four of them had faces and wings, ⁹and their wings touched each other. The living creatures did not turn when they moved, but each went straight ahead.

¹⁰Their faces looked like this: each living creature had a human face and the face of a lion on the right side and the face of an ox on the left side. And each one also had the face of an eagle. ¹¹That was what their faces looked like. Their wings were spread out above. Each had two wings that touched one of the other living creatures and two wings that covered its body. ¹²Each went straight ahead. Wherever the spirit would go, the living creatures would also go, without turning. ¹³The living creatures looked like burning coals of fire or like torches. Fire went back and forth among the living creatures. It was bright, and lightning flashed from it. ¹⁴The living creatures ran back and forth like bolts of lightning.

¹⁵Now as I looked at the living creatures, I saw a wheel on the ground by each of the living creatures with its four faces. ¹⁶The wheels and the way they were made were like this: they looked like sparkling chrysolite. All four of them looked the same, like one wheel crossways inside another wheel. ¹⁷When they moved, they went in any one of the four directions, without turning as they went. ¹⁸The rims of the wheels were high and frightening and were full of eyes all around.

¹⁹When the living creatures moved, the wheels moved beside them. When the living creatures were lifted up from the ground, the wheels also were lifted up. ²⁰Wherever the spirit would go, the living creatures would go. And the wheels were lifted up beside them, because the spirit of the living creatures was in the wheels. ²¹When the living creatures moved, the wheels moved. When the living creatures stopped, the wheels stopped. And when the living creatures were

lifted from the ground, the wheels were lifted beside them, because the spirit of the living creatures was in the wheels.

²²Now, over the heads of the living creatures was something like a dome that sparkled like ice and was frightening. ²³And under the dome the wings of the living creatures were stretched out straight towards one another. Each living creature also had two wings covering its body. ²⁴I heard the sound of their wings, like the roaring sound of the sea, as they moved. It was like the voice of God Almighty, a roaring sound like a noisy army. When the living creatures stopped, they lowered their wings.

²⁵A voice came from above the dome over the heads of the living creatures. When the living creatures stopped, they lowered their wings. ²⁶Now above the dome there was something that looked like a throne. It looked like a sapphire gem. And on the throne was a shape like a human. ²⁷Then I noticed that from the waist up the shape looked like glowing metal with fire inside. From the waist down it looked like fire, and a bright light was all around. ²⁸The surrounding glow looked like the rainbow in the clouds on a rainy day. It seemed to look like the glory of the LORD. So when I saw it, I bowed face down on the ground and heard a voice speaking.

The LORD Speaks to Ezekiel

2 He said to me, "Human, stand up on your feet so I may speak with you." ²While he spoke to me, the Spirit*ᵈ* entered me and put me on my feet. Then I heard the LORD speaking to me.

³He said, "Human, I am sending you to the people of Israel. That nation has turned against me and broken away from me. They and their ancestors have sinned against me until this very day. ⁴I am sending you to people who are stubborn and who do not obey. You will say to them, 'This is what the Lord GOD says.' ⁵They may listen, or they may not, since they are a people who have turned against me. But they will know that a prophet*ᵈ* has been among them. ⁶You, human, don't be afraid of the people or their words. Even though they may be like thorny branches and thorns all around you, and though you may feel as if you live with poisonous insects, don't be afraid. Don't be afraid of their words or their looks, because they are a people who rebel against me. ⁷But speak my words to them. They may listen, or they may not, because they turn against me. ⁸But you, human, listen to what I say to you. Don't turn against me as those people do. Open your mouth and eat what I am giving you."

⁹Then I looked and saw a hand stretched out to me, and a scroll was in it. ¹⁰He opened the scroll in front of me. Funeral songs, sad writings and words about troubles were written on the front and back.

3 Then the LORD said to me, "Human, eat what you find; eat this scroll. Then go and speak to the people of Israel." ²So I opened my mouth, and he gave me the scroll to eat.

³He said to me, "Human, eat this scroll which I am giving you, and fill your stomach with it." Then I ate it, and it was as sweet as honey in my mouth.

> **Sidelight** Ever eaten something for a dare? Ezekiel ate stationery and said that it tasted like honey! When God told Ezekiel to eat the scroll (Ezekiel 3:1–3), it symbolised that the prophet had accepted God's mission to tell the news to the Jewish people. It would get people's attention on modern high streets, too.

⁴Then he said to me, "Human, go to the people of Israel, and speak my words to them. ⁵You are not being sent to people whose speech you can't understand, whose language is difficult. You are being sent to Israel. ⁶You are not being sent to many nations whose speech you can't understand and whose language is difficult and whose words you cannot understand. If I had sent you to them, they would have listened to you. ⁷But the people of Israel will not be willing to listen to you, because they are not willing to listen to me. Yes, all the people of Israel are stubborn and will not obey. ⁸See, I now make you as stubborn and as hard as they are. ⁹I am making you as hard as a diamond, harder than stone. Don't be afraid of them or be frightened by them, though they are a people who rebel against me."

¹⁰Also, he said to me, "Human, believe all the words I will speak to you, and listen carefully to them. ¹¹Then go to the captives, your own people, and say to them, 'The Lord GOD says this.' Tell them this whether they listen or not."

¹²Then the Spirit lifted me up, and I heard a loud rumbling sound behind me, saying, "Praise the glory of the LORD in heaven." ¹³I heard the wings of the living creatures touching each other and the sound of the wheels by them. It was a loud rumbling sound. ¹⁴So the Spirit lifted me up and took me away. I was unhappy and angry, and I felt the great power of the LORD. ¹⁵I came to the captives from Judah, who lived by the Kebar River at Tel Abib. I sat there seven days where these people lived, feeling shocked.

Israel's Warning

¹⁶After seven days the LORD spoke his word to me again. He said, ¹⁷"Human, I now make you a watchman for Israel. Any time you hear a word from my mouth, warn them for me. ¹⁸When I say to the wicked, 'You will surely die,' you must warn them so they may live. If you don't speak out to warn the wicked to stop their evil ways, they will die in their sin. But I will hold you responsible for their death. ¹⁹If you warn the wicked and they do not turn from their wickedness or their evil ways, they will die because of their sin. But you will have saved your life.

²⁰"Again, those who do right may turn away from doing good and do evil. If I make something bad happen to them, they will die. Because you have not warned them, they will die because of their sin, and the good they did will not be remembered. But I will hold you responsible for their deaths. ²¹But if you have warned those good people not to sin, and they do not sin, they surely live, because they believed the warning. And you will have saved your life."

²²Then I felt the power of the LORD there. He said to me, "Get up and go out to the plain. There I will speak to you." ²³So I got up and went out to the plain. I saw the glory of the LORD standing there, like the glory I saw by the Kebar River, and I bowed face down on the ground.

²⁴Then the Spirit *d* entered me and made me stand on my feet. He spoke to me and said, "Go, shut yourself up in your house. ²⁵As for you, human, the people will tie you up with ropes so that you will not be able to go out among them. ²⁶Also, I will make your tongue stick to the roof of your mouth so you will be silent. You will not be able to argue with the people, even though they turn against me. ²⁷But when I speak to you, I will open your mouth, and you will say to them, 'The Lord GOD says this.' Those who will listen, let them listen. Those who refuse, let them refuse, because they are a people who rebel against me.

The Map of Jerusalem

4 "Now, human, get yourself a brick, put it in front of you, and draw a map of Jerusalem on it. ²Then surround it with an army. Build battle works against the city and a dirt road to the top of the city walls. Set up camps around it, and

HONESTY

The Whole Truth

Jessica knew she was in trouble when the car skidded on the wet road, hitting the kerb hard enough to ruin a front wheel. Even though no one was hurt, the car would not move.

When she got home, Jessica told her parents what had happened. She admitted having seven people in her mini, and going over the speed limit.

"What I didn't tell them was that a friend was driving my car," she says.

Jessica's paying for the damage now with money from her Saturday job. She's afraid that if she tells her parents the whole truth, she will get into even more trouble. Jessica's parents might appreciate her honesty and not punish her more severely. God, too, appreciates honesty. He expects it even when it may cause more trouble than keeping silent. He demanded that Ezekiel tell the people the whole truth in **Ezekiel 3:16–21**.

* Why might it be difficult for Jessica or Ezekiel to be completely honest?
* How can you be honest with a friend who is doing something wrong and still preserve the friendship?

Consider . . .

* warning a friend about something he or she is doing that's wrong.
* discussing with your friends when, if ever, it's OK to tell white lies.

For more, see . . .

* Genesis 3:1–9 (p.5)
* Acts 5:1–11 (p.1145)
* 2 Samuel 12:1–14 (p.295)

put heavy logs in place to break down the walls. [3]Then get yourself an iron plate and set it up like an iron wall between you and the city. Turn your face towards the city as if to attack it and then attack. This is a sign to Israel.

[4]"Then lie down on your left side, and take the guilt of Israel on yourself. Their guilt will be on you for the number of days you lie on your left side. [5]I have given you the same number of days as the years of the people's sin. So you will have the guilt of Israel's sin on you for 390 days.

[6]"After you have finished these 390 days, lie down for a second time, on your right side. You will then have the guilt of Judah on you. I will give it to you for 40 days, a day for each year of their sin. [7]Then you will look towards Jerusalem, which is being attacked. With your arm bare, you will prophesy [d] against Jerusalem. [8]I will put ropes on you so you cannot turn from one side to the other until you have finished the days of your attack on Jerusalem.

Sidelight
To get God's message across, Ezekiel resorted to dramatic measures. Once he lay on his left side for 390 days to symbolise the siege of Jerusalem (Ezekiel 4:4–8). Another time he burned his hair (Ezekiel 5:1–3) to symbolise military defeat for Jerusalem. You won't see those drama sketches in church!

---

[9]"Take wheat, barley, beans, small peas and millet seeds, put them in one bowl, and make them into bread for yourself. You will eat it for the 390 days you lie on your side. [10]You will eat 220 grammes of food every day at set times. [11]You will drink about ½ a litre of water every day at set times. [12]Eat your food as you would eat a barley cake, baking it over human dung where the people can see." [13]Then the LORD said, "In the same way Israel will eat unclean [d] food among the nations where I force them to go."

[14]But I said, "No, Lord GOD! I have never been made unclean. From the time I was young until now I've never eaten anything that died by itself or was torn by animals. Unclean meat has never entered my mouth."

Sidelight
When God told Ezekiel to cook his food over human excrement (Ezekiel 4:9–14), the prophet refused because human excrement was considered unclean (see Deuteronomy 23:12–14, p.186). But dried cow dung was – and still is – a common fuel in the Near East.

---

[15]"Very well," he said. "Then I will give you cow's dung instead of human dung to use for your fire to bake your bread."

[16]He also said to me, "Human, I am going to cut off the supply of bread to Jerusalem. They will eat the bread that is measured out to them, and they will worry as they eat. They will drink water that is measured out to them, and they will be in shock as they drink it. [17]This is because bread and water will be hard to find. The people will be shocked at the sight of each other, and they will become weak because of their sin.

Ezekiel Cuts His Hair

5 "Now, human, take a sharp sword, and use it like a barber's razor to shave your head and beard. Then take scales and weigh and divide the hair. [2]Burn a third with fire in the middle of the city when the days of the attack on Jerusalem are over. Then take a third and cut it up with the knife all around the city. And scatter a third to the wind. This is how I will chase them with a sword. [3]Also take a few of these hairs and tie them in the folds of your clothes. [4]Take a few more, throw them into the fire and burn them up. From there a fire will spread to all the people of Israel.

[5]"This is what the Lord GOD says: this is Jerusalem. I have put her at the centre of the nations with countries all around her. [6]But she has refused to obey my laws and has been more evil than the nations. She has refused to obey my rules, even more than nations around her. The people of Jerusalem have rejected my laws and have not lived by my rules.

[7]"So this is what the Lord GOD says: you have caused more trouble than the nations around you. You have not followed my rules or obeyed my laws. You have not even obeyed the laws of the nations around you.

[8]"So this is what the Lord GOD says: I myself am against you, and I will punish you as the nations watch. [9]I will do things among you that I have not done before and the like of which I will never do again, because you do the things I hate. [10]So parents among you will eat their children, and children will eat their parents. I will punish you and will scatter to the winds all who are left alive. [11]So the Lord GOD says: you have made my Temple [d] unclean [d] with all your evil idols and the hateful things you do. Because of this, as surely as I live, I will cut you off. I will have no pity, and I will show no mercy. [12]A third of you will die by disease or be destroyed by hunger inside your walls. A third will fall dead by the sword outside your walls. And a third I will scatter in every direction as I chase them with a sword. [13]Then my anger will come to an end. I will use it up against them, and then I will be satisfied. Then they will

know that I, the LORD, have spoken. After I have carried out my anger against them, they will know the strength of my feelings. ¹⁴"I will make you a ruin and a shame among the nations around you, to be seen by all who pass by. ¹⁵Then the nations around you will shame you and make fun of you. You will be a warning and a terror to them. This will happen when I punish you in my great anger. I, the LORD, have spoken. ¹⁶I will send a time of hunger to destroy you, and then I will make your hunger get even worse, and I will cut off your supply of food. ¹⁷I will send a time of hunger and wild animals against you, and they will kill your children. Disease and death will sweep through your people, and I will bring the sword against you to kill you. I, the LORD, have spoken."

Prophecies Against the Mountains

6 Again the LORD spoke his word to me, saying: ²"Human, look towards the mountains of Israel, and prophesy *d* against them. ³Say, 'Mountains of Israel, listen to the word of the Lord GOD. The Lord GOD says this to the mountains, the hills, the ravines and the valleys: I will bring a sword against you, and I will destroy your places of idol worship. ⁴Your altars will be destroyed and your incense *d* altars broken down. Your people will be killed in front of your idols. ⁵I will lay the dead bodies of the Israelites in front of their idols, and I will scatter your bones around your altars. ⁶In all the places you live, cities will become empty. The places of idol worship will be ruined; your altars will become lonely ruins. Your idols will be broken and brought to an end. Your incense altars will be cut down, and the things you made will be wiped out. ⁷Your people will be killed and fall among you. Then you will know that I am the LORD.

⁸"'But I will leave some people alive; some will not be killed by the nations when you are scattered among the foreign lands. ⁹Then those who have escaped will remember me, as they live among the nations where they have been taken as captives. They will remember how I was hurt because they were unfaithful to me and turned away from me and desired to worship their idols. They will hate themselves because of the evil things they did that I hate. ¹⁰Then they will know that I am the LORD. I did not bring this terrible thing on them for no reason.

¹¹"'This is what the Lord GOD says: clap your hands, stamp your feet and groan because of all the hateful, evil things the people of Israel have done. They will die by war, hunger and disease. ¹²The person who is far away will die by disease. The one who is nearby will die in war. The person who is still alive and has escaped these will die from hunger. So I will carry out my anger on them. ¹³Their people will lie dead among their idols around the altars, on every high hill, on all the mountain tops and under every green tree and leafy oak—all the places where they offered sweet-smelling incense to their idols. Then you will know that I am the LORD. ¹⁴I will use my power against them to make the land empty and wasted from the desert to Diblah, wherever they live. Then they will know that I am the LORD.'"

Ezekiel Tells of the End

7 Again the LORD spoke his word to me, saying: ²"Human, the Lord GOD says this to the land of Israel: an end! The end has come on the four

> ### Sidelight
> Why does God repeatedly address Ezekiel as "Human"? (See Ezekiel 7:2, for example.) It was simply to remind the people of the huge difference between God and people.

corners of the land. ³Now the end has come for you, and I will send my anger against you. I will judge you for the way you have lived, and I will make you pay for all your actions that I hate. ⁴I will have no pity on you; I will not hold back punishment from you. Instead, I will make you pay for the way you have lived and for your actions that I hate. Then you will know that I am the LORD.

⁵"This is what the Lord GOD says: disaster on top of disaster is coming. ⁶The end has come! The end has come! It has stirred itself up against you! Look! It has come! ⁷Disaster has come for you who live in the land! The time has come; the day of confusion is near. There will be no happy shouting on the mountains. ⁸Soon I will pour out my anger against you; I will carry out my anger against you. I will judge you for the way you have lived and will make you pay for everything you have done that I hate. ⁹I will show no pity, and I will not hold back punishment. I will pay you back for the way you have lived and the things you have done that I hate. Then you will know that I am the LORD who punishes.

¹⁰"Look, the day is here. It has come. Disaster has come, violence has grown and there is more pride than ever. ¹¹Violence has grown into a weapon for punishing wickedness. None of the people will be left—none of that crowd, none of their wealth and nothing of value. ¹²The time has come; the day has arrived. Don't let the buyer be happy or the seller be sad, because my burning anger is against the whole crowd. ¹³Sellers will not return to the land they have sold as long as

they live, because the vision against all that crowd will not be changed. Because of their sins, they will not save their lives. ¹⁴They have blown the trumpet, and everything is ready. But no one is going to the battle, because my anger is against all that crowd.

¹⁵"The sword is outside, and disease and hunger are inside. Whoever is in the field will die by the sword. Hunger and disease will destroy those in the city. ¹⁶Those who are left alive and who escape will be on the mountains, moaning like doves of the valleys about their own sin. ¹⁷All hands will hang weakly with fear, and all knees will become weak as water. ¹⁸They will put on rough cloth to show how sad they are. They will tremble all over with fear. Their faces will show their shame, and all their heads will be shaved. ¹⁹The people will throw their silver into the streets, and their gold will be like rubbish. Their silver and gold will not save them from the LORD's anger. It will not satisfy their hunger or fill their stomachs, because it caused them to fall into sin. ²⁰They were proud of their beautiful jewellery and used it to make their idols and their evil statues, which I hate. So I will turn their wealth into rubbish. ²¹I will give it to foreigners as treasures from war and to the most evil people in the world as treasure, and they will dishonour it. ²²I will also turn away from the people of Israel, and they will dishonour my treasured place. Then robbers will enter and dishonour it.

²³"Make chains for captives, because the land is full of bloody crimes and the city is full of violence. ²⁴So I will bring the worst of the nations to take over the people's houses. I will also end the pride of the strong, and their holy places will be dishonoured. ²⁵When the people are suffering greatly, they will look for peace, but there will be none. ²⁶Disaster will come on top of disaster, and rumour will be added to rumour. Then they will try to get a vision from a prophet; ᵈ the teachings of God from the priest and the advice from the older leaders will be lost. ²⁷The king will cry greatly, the prince will give up hope and the hands of the people who own land will shake with fear. I will punish them for the way they have lived. The way they have judged others is the way I will judge them. Then they will know that I am the LORD."

Ezekiel's Vision of Jerusalem

8 It was the fifth day of the sixth month of the sixth year of our captivity. I was sitting in my house with the elders of Judah in front of me. There I felt the power of the Lord GOD. ²I looked

and saw something that looked like a human. From the waist down it looked like fire, and from the waist up it looked like bright glowing metal. ³It stretched out the shape of a hand and caught me by the hair on my head. The Spirit ᵈ lifted me up between the earth and the sky. He took me in visions of God to Jerusalem, to the entrance to the north gate of the inner courtyard of the Temple. ᵈ In the courtyard was the idol that caused God to be jealous. ⁴I saw the glory of the God of Israel there, as I had seen on the plain.

⁵Then he said to me, "Human, now look towards the north." So I looked up towards the north, and in the entrance north of the gate of the altar was the idol that caused God to be jealous.

⁶He said to me, "Human, do you see what they are doing? Do you see how many hateful things the people of Israel are doing here that drive me far away from my Temple? But you will see things more hateful than these."

⁷Then he brought me to the entry of the courtyard. When I looked, I saw a hole in the wall. ⁸He said to me, "Human, dig through the wall." So I dug through the wall and saw an entrance.

⁹Then he said to me, "Go in and see the hateful, evil things they are doing here." ¹⁰So I entered and looked, and I saw every kind of crawling thing and hateful beast and all the idols of the people of Israel, carved on the wall all around. ¹¹Standing in front of these carvings and idols were 70 of the elders of Israel and Jaazaniah son of Shaphan. Each man had his pan for burning incense ᵈ in his hand, and a sweet-smelling cloud of incense was rising.

¹²Then he said to me, "Human, have you seen what the elders of Israel are doing in the dark? Have you seen each man in the room of his own idol? They say, 'The LORD doesn't see us. The LORD has left the land.'" ¹³He also said to me, "You will see them doing even more hateful things."

¹⁴Then he brought me to the entrance of the north gate of the Temple of the LORD, where I saw women sitting and crying for Tammuz. ⁿ ¹⁵He said to me, "Do you see, human? You will see things even more hateful than these."

¹⁶Then he brought me into the inner courtyard of the Temple. There I saw about 25 men at the entrance to the Temple of the LORD, between the porch and the altar. With their backs turned to the Temple of the LORD, they faced east and were worshipping the sun in the east.

¹⁷He said to me, "Do you see, human? Is it unimportant that the people of Judah are doing the hateful things they have done here? They have

---

Tammuz Tammuz was a god in Babylon. Every year people thought this god died when the plants died. After they cried for him, they believed he came back to life and the plants lived again.

filled the land with violence and made me continually angry. Look, they are insulting me in every way they can. ¹⁸So I will act in anger. I will have no pity, nor will I show mercy. Even if they shout in my ears, I won't listen to them."

Vision of the Angels

9 Then he shouted with a loud voice in my ears, "You who are chosen to punish this city, come near with your weapon in your hand." ²Then six men came from the direction of the upper gate, which faces north, each with his powerful weapon in his hand. Among them was a man dressed in linen with a writing case at his side. The men went in and stood by the bronze altar.

³Then the glory of the God of Israel went up from above the creatures with wings, where it had been, to the place in the Temple *d* where the door opened. He called to the man dressed in linen who had the writing case at his side. ⁴He said to the man, "Go through Jerusalem and put a mark on the foreheads of the people who groan and cry about all the hateful things being done among them."

> ### Sidelight
> The "mark" in Ezekiel 9:4 was the taw – the last letter of the Hebrew alphabet – and was used to identify the righteous. Failure to have the mark on your forehead meant that you would be killed!

⁵As I listened, he said to the other men, "Go through the city behind the man dressed in linen and kill. Don't pity anyone, and don't show mercy. ⁶Kill and destroy old men, young men and women, little children and older women, but don't touch any who have the mark on them. Start at my Temple." So they started with the elders who were in front of the Temple.

⁷Then he said to the men, "Make the Temple unclean, *d* and fill the courtyards with those who have been killed. Go out!" So the men went out and killed the people in the city. ⁸While the men were killing the people, I was left alone. I bowed face down on the ground and I cried out, "Oh, Lord GOD! Will you destroy everyone left alive in Israel when you turn loose your anger on Jerusalem?"

⁹Then he said to me, "The sin of the people of Israel and Judah is very great. The land is filled with people who murder, and the city is full of people who are not fair. The people say, 'The LORD has left the land, and the LORD does not see.' ¹⁰But I will have no pity, nor will I show mercy. I will bring their evil back on their heads."

¹¹Then the man dressed in linen with the writing case at his side reported, "I have done just as you commanded me."

The Coals of Fire

10 Then I looked and saw in the dome above the heads of the living creatures something like a sapphire gem which looked like a throne. ²The LORD said to the man dressed in linen, "Go in between the wheels under the living creatures, fill your hands with coals of fire from between the living creatures, and scatter the coals over the city."

As I watched, the man with linen clothes went in. ³Now the living creatures were standing on the south side of the Temple *d* when the man went in. And a cloud filled the inner courtyard. ⁴Then the glory of the LORD went up from the living creatures and stood over the door of the Temple. The Temple was filled with the cloud, and the courtyard was full of the brightness from the glory of the LORD. ⁵The sound of the wings of the living creatures was heard all the way to the outer courtyard. It was like the voice of God Almighty when he speaks.

⁶When the LORD commanded the man dressed in linen, "Take fire from between the wheels, from between the living creatures," the man went in and stood by a wheel. ⁷One living creature put out his hand to the fire that was among them, took some of the fire, and put it in the hands of the man dressed in linen. Then the man took the fire and went out.

The Wheels and the Creatures

⁸Something that looked like a human hand could be seen under the wings of the living creatures. ⁹I saw the four wheels by the living creatures, one wheel by each living creature. The wheels looked like shining chrysolite. ¹⁰All four wheels looked alike: each looked like a wheel crossways inside another wheel. ¹¹When the wheels moved, they went in any of the directions that the four living creatures faced. The wheels did not turn about, and the living creatures did not turn their bodies as they went. ¹²All their bodies, their backs, their hands, their wings and the wheels were full of eyes all over. Each of the four living creatures had a wheel. ¹³I heard the wheels being called "whirling wheels". ¹⁴Each living creature had four faces. The first face was the face of a creature with wings. The second face was a human face, the third was the face of a lion and the fourth was the face of an eagle.

¹⁵Then the living creatures flew up. They were the same living creatures I had seen by the Kebar River. ¹⁶When the living creatures moved,

the wheels moved beside them. When the living creatures lifted their wings to fly up from the ground, the wheels did not leave their place beside them. ¹⁷When the living creatures stopped, the wheels stopped. When the creatures went up, the wheels went up also, because the spirit of the living creatures was in the wheels.

¹⁸Then the glory of the Lord left the door of the Temple *d* and stood over the living creatures. ¹⁹As I watched, the living creatures spread their wings and flew up from the ground, with the wheels beside them. They stood where the east gate of the Temple of the Lord opened, and the glory of the God of Israel was over them.

²⁰These were the living creatures I had seen under the God of Israel by the Kebar River. I knew they were called cherubim. *d* ²¹Each one had four faces and four wings, and under their wings were things that looked like human hands. ²²Their faces looked the same as the ones I had seen by the Kebar River. They each went straight ahead.

Prophecies Against Evil Leaders

11 The Spirit *d* lifted me up and brought me to the front gate of the Temple *d* of the Lord, which faces east. I saw 25 men where the gate opens, among them Jaazaniah son of Azzur and Pelatiah son of Benaiah, who were leaders of the people. ²Then the Lord said to me, "Human, these are the men who plan evil and give wicked advice in this city of Jerusalem. ³They say, 'It is almost time for us to build houses. This city is like a cooking pot, and we are like the best meat.' ⁴So prophesy *d* against them, prophesy, human."

⁵Then the Spirit of the Lord entered me and told me to say: "This is what the Lord says: you have said these things, people of Israel, and I know what you are thinking. ⁶You have killed many people in this city, filling its streets with their bodies.

⁷"So this is what the Lord God says: those people you have killed and left in the middle of the city are like the best meat, and this city is like the cooking pot. But I will force you out of the city. ⁸You have feared the sword, but I will bring a sword against you, says the Lord God. ⁹I will force you out of the city and hand you over to strangers and punish you. ¹⁰You will die by the sword. I will punish you at the border of Israel so you will know that I am the Lord. ¹¹This city will not be your cooking pot, and you will not be the best meat in the middle of it. I will punish you at the border of Israel. ¹²Then you will know that I am the Lord. You did not live by my rules or obey my laws. Instead, you did the same things as the nations around you."

¹³As I prophesied, Pelatiah son of Benaiah died. Then I bowed face down on the ground and shouted with a loud voice, "Oh no, Lord God! Will you completely destroy the Israelites who are left alive?"

Promise to Those Remaining

¹⁴The Lord spoke his word to me, saying, ¹⁵"Human, the people still in Jerusalem have spoken about your own relatives and all the people of Israel who are captives with you, saying, 'They are far from the Lord. This land has been given to us as our property.'

¹⁶"So say, 'This is what the Lord God says: I sent the people far away among the nations and scattered them among the countries. But for a little while I have become a Temple *d* to them in the countries where they have gone.'

¹⁷"So say: 'This is what the Lord God says: I will gather you from the nations and bring you together from the countries where you have been scattered. Then I will give you back the land of Israel.'

¹⁸"When they come to this land, they will remove all the evil idols and all the hateful images. ¹⁹I will give them a desire to respect me completely, and I will put inside them a new way of thinking. I will take out the stubborn heart of stone from their bodies, and I will give them an obedient heart of flesh. ²⁰Then they will live by my rules and obey my laws and keep them. They will be my people, and I will be their God. ²¹But those who want to serve their evil statues and hateful idols, I will pay back for their evil ways, says the Lord God."

Ezekiel's Vision Ends

²²Then the living creatures lifted their wings with the wheels beside them, and the glory of the God of Israel was above them. ²³The glory of the Lord went up from inside Jerusalem and stopped on the mountain on the east side of the city. ²⁴The Spirit *d* lifted me up and brought me to the captives who had been taken from Judah to Babylonia. This happened in a vision given by the Spirit of God, and then the vision I had seen ended. ²⁵And I told the captives from Judah all the things the Lord had shown me.

Ezekiel Moves Out

12 Again the Lord spoke his word to me, saying: ²"Human, you are living among a people who refuse to obey. They have eyes to see, but they do not see, and they have ears to hear, but they do not hear, because they are a people who refuse to obey.

³"So, human, pack your things as if you will be taken away captive, and walk away like a captive

in the daytime with the people watching. Move from your place to another with the people watching. Perhaps they will understand, even though they are a people who refuse to obey. ⁴During the day when the people are watching, bring out the things you would pack as captive. At evening, with the people watching, leave your place like those who are taken away as captives from their country. ⁵Dig a hole through the wall while they watch, and bring your things out through it. ⁶Lift them onto your shoulders with the people watching, and carry them out in the dark. Cover your face so you cannot see the ground, because I have made you a sign to the people of Israel."

⁷I did these things as I was commanded. In the daytime I brought what I had packed as if I were being taken away captive. Then in the evening I dug through the wall with my hands. I brought my things out in the dark and carried them on my shoulders as the people watched.

⁸Then in the morning the LORD spoke his word to me, saying: ⁹"Human, didn't Israel, who refuses to obey, ask you, 'What are you doing?' ¹⁰Say to them, 'This is what the Lord GOD says: this message is about the king in Jerusalem and all the people of Israel who live there.' ¹¹Say, 'I am a sign to you.'

"The same things I have done will be done to the people in Jerusalem. They will be taken away from their country as captives. ¹²The king among them will put his things on his shoulder in the dark and will leave. The people will dig a hole through the wall to bring him out. He will cover his face so he cannot see the ground. ¹³But I will spread my net over him, and he will be caught in my trap. Then I will bring him to Babylon in the land of the Babylonians. He will not see that land, but he will die there. ¹⁴All who are around the king—his helpers and all his army—I will scatter in every direction, and I will chase them with a sword.

¹⁵"They will know that I am the LORD when I scatter them among the nations and spread them among the countries. ¹⁶But I will save a few of them from the sword and from hunger and disease. Then they can tell of their hateful actions among the nations where they go. Then they will know that I am the LORD."

The Lesson of Ezekiel's Shaking

¹⁷The LORD spoke his word to me, saying: ¹⁸"Human, tremble as you eat your food, and shake with fear as you drink your water. ¹⁹Then say to the people of the land: 'This is what the Lord GOD says about the people who live in Jerusalem in the land of Israel: they will eat their food with fear and drink their water in shock,

because their land will be stripped bare because of the violence of the people who live in it. ²⁰The cities where people live will become ruins, and the land will become empty. Then you will know that I am the LORD.'"

The Visions will Come True

²¹The LORD spoke his word to me, saying: ²²"Human, what is this saying you have in the land of Israel: 'The days go by and every vision comes to nothing'? ²³So say to them, 'This is what the Lord GOD says: I will make them stop saying this, and nobody in Israel will use this saying any more.' But tell them, 'The time is near when every vision will come true. ²⁴There will be no more false visions or pleasing prophecies d inside the nation of Israel, ²⁵but I, the LORD, will speak. What I say will be done, and it will not be delayed. You refuse to obey, but in your time I will say the word and do it, says the Lord GOD.'"

²⁶The LORD spoke his word to me, saying: ²⁷"Human, the people of Israel are saying, 'The vision that Ezekiel sees is for a time many years from now. He is prophesying about times far away.' ²⁸So say to them: 'The Lord GOD says this: none of my words will be delayed any more. What I have said will be done, says the Lord GOD.'"

Ezekiel Speaks Against False Prophets

13 The LORD spoke his word to me, saying: ²"Human, prophesy d against the prophets d of Israel. Say to those who make up their own prophecies: 'Listen to the word of the LORD. ³This is what the Lord GOD says: how terrible it will be for the foolish prophets who follow their own ideas and have not seen a vision from me! ⁴People of Israel, your prophets have been like wild dogs hunting to kill and eat among ruins. ⁵Israel is like a house in ruins, but you have not gone up into the broken places or repaired the wall. So how can Israel hold back the enemy in the battle on the LORD's day of judging? ⁶Your prophets see false visions and prophesy lies. They say, "This is the message of the LORD," when the LORD has not sent them. But they still hope their words will come true. ⁷You said, "This is the message of the LORD," but that is a false vision. Your prophecies are lies, because I have not spoken.

⁸" 'So this is what the Lord GOD says: because you prophets spoke things that are false and saw visions that do not come true, I am against you, says the Lord GOD. ⁹I will punish the prophets who see false visions and prophesy lies. They will have no place among my people. Their names will not be written on the list of the people of

Israel, and they will not enter the land of Israel. Then you will know that I am the Lord GOD.

¹⁰"'It is because they lead my people the wrong way by saying, "Peace!" when there is no peace. When the people build a weak wall, the prophets cover it with whitewash to make it look strong. ¹¹So tell those who cover a weak wall with whitewash that it will fall down. Rain will pour down, hailstones will fall and a stormy wind will break the wall down. ¹²When the wall has fallen, people will ask you, "Where is the whitewash you used on the wall?"

¹³"'So this is what the Lord GOD says: I will break the wall with a stormy wind. In my anger rain will pour down, and hailstones will destroy the wall. ¹⁴I will tear down the wall on which you put whitewash. I will level it to the ground so that people will see the wall's foundation. And when the wall falls, you will be destroyed under it. Then you will know that I am the LORD. ¹⁵So I will carry out my anger on the wall and against those who covered it with whitewash. Then I will tell you, "The wall is gone, and those who covered it with whitewash are gone. ¹⁶The prophets of Israel who prophesy to Jerusalem and who see visions of peace for the city, when there is no peace, will be gone, says the Lord GOD."'

False Women Prophets

¹⁷"Now, human, look towards the women among your people who make up their own prophecies. *d* Prophesy against them. ¹⁸Say, 'This is what the Lord GOD says: how terrible it will be for women who sew magic charms on their wrists and make veils of every length to trap people! You ruin the lives of my people but try to save your own lives. ¹⁹For handfuls of barley and pieces of bread, you have dishonoured me among my people. By lying to my people, who listen to lies, you have killed people who should not die, and you have kept alive those who should not live.

²⁰"'So this is what the Lord GOD says: I am against your magic charms, by which you trap people as if they were birds. I will tear those charms off your arms, and I will free those people you have trapped like birds. ²¹I will also tear off your veils and save my people from your hands. They will no longer be trapped by your power. Then you will know that I am the LORD. ²²By your lies you have caused those who did right to be sad, when I did not make them sad. And you have encouraged the wicked not to stop being wicked, and so save their lives. ²³So you will not see false visions or prophesy any more, and I will save my people from your power so you will know that I am the LORD.'"

Stop Worshipping Idols

14 Some of the elders of Israel came to me and sat down in front of me. ²Then the LORD spoke his word to me, saying: ³"Human, these men want to worship idols. They put up evil things that cause people to sin. Should I allow them to ask me for help? ⁴So speak to them and tell them, 'This is what the Lord GOD says: when any of the people of Israel want to worship idols and put up evil things that cause people to sin and then come to the prophet, *d* I, the LORD, will answer them myself for worshipping idols. ⁵Then I will win back my people Israel, who have left me because of all their idols.'

⁶"So say to the people of Israel, 'This is what the Lord GOD says: Change your hearts and lives, and stop worshipping idols. Stop doing all the things I hate. ⁷Any of the Israelites or foreigners in Israel can separate themselves from me by wanting to worship idols or by putting up the things that cause people to sin. Then if they come to the prophet to ask me questions, I, the LORD, will answer them myself. ⁸I will reject them. I will make them a sign and an example, and I will separate them from my people. Then you will know that I am the LORD.

⁹"'But if the prophet is tricked into giving a prophecy, it is because I, the LORD, have tricked that prophet to speak. Then I will use my power against him and destroy him from among my people Israel. ¹⁰The prophet will be as guilty as the one who asks him for help; both will be responsible for their guilt. ¹¹Then the nation of Israel will not leave me any more or make themselves unclean*d* any more with all their sins. They will be my people, and I will be their God, says the Lord GOD.'"

Sidelight If you wanted to listen to a "gentle" preacher in Bible times, you wouldn't have enjoyed hearing the prophet Ezekiel speak (Ezekiel 14:1–11). He pulled no punches, and might have been "bleeped" for referring to pagan idols as "dung balls" 39 times! This term is used elsewhere in the Old Testament, but only nine times.

Jerusalem will Not be Spared

¹²The LORD spoke his word to me, saying: ¹³"Human, if the people of a country sin against me by not being loyal, I will use my power against them. I will cut off their supply of food and send a time of hunger, destroying both people and animals. ¹⁴Even if three great men like Noah, Daniel and Job were in that country, their

goodness could save only themselves, says the Lord GOD.

15"Or I might send wild animals into that land, leaving the land empty and without children. Then no one would pass through it because of the animals. 16As surely as I live, says the Lord GOD, even if Noah, Daniel and Job were in the land, they could not save their own sons or daughters. They could save only themselves, but that country would become empty.

17"Or I might bring a war against that country. I might say, 'Let a war be fought in that land,' in this way destroying its people and its animals. 18As surely as I live, says the Lord GOD, even if those three men were in the land, they could not save their sons or daughters. They could save only themselves.

19"Or I might cause a disease to spread in that country. I might pour out my anger against it, destroying and killing people and animals. 20As surely as I live, says the Lord GOD, even if Noah, Daniel and Job were in the land, they could not save their son or daughter. They could save only themselves because they did what was right.

21"This is what the Lord GOD says: my plans for Jerusalem are much worse! I will send my four terrible punishments against it—war, hunger, wild animals and disease—to destroy its people and animals. 22But some people will escape; some sons and daughters will be led out. They will come out to you, and you will see what happens to people who live as they did. Then you will be comforted after the disasters I have brought against Jerusalem, after all the things I have brought against it. 23You will be comforted when you see what happens to them for living as they did, because you will know there was a good reason for what I did to Jerusalem, says the Lord GOD."

Story of the Vine

15 The LORD spoke his word to me, saying: 2"Human, is the wood of the vine better than the wood of any tree in the forest? 3Can wood be taken from the vine to make anything? Can you use it to make a peg on which to hang something? 4If the vine is thrown into the fire for fuel, and the fire burns up both ends and starts to burn the middle, is it useful for anything? 5When the vine was whole, it couldn't be made into anything. When the fire has burnt it completely, it certainly cannot be made into anything."

6So this is what the Lord GOD says: "Out of all the trees in the forest, I have given the wood of the vine as fuel for fire. In the same way I have given up the people who live in Jerusalem 7and will turn against them. Although they came through one fire, fire will still destroy them. When I turn against them, you will know that I am the LORD. 8So I will make the land empty, because the people have not been loyal, says the Lord GOD."

The LORD's Kindness to Jerusalem

16 The LORD spoke his word to me, saying: 2"Human, tell Jerusalem about her hateful actions. 3Say, 'This is what the Lord GOD says to Jerusalem: your beginnings and your ancestors were in the land of the Canaanites. Your father was an Amorite, and your mother was a Hittite. 4On the day you were born, your cord *n* was not cut. You were not washed with water to clean you. You were not rubbed with salt or wrapped in cloths. 5No one felt sorry enough for you to do any of these things for you. No, you were thrown out into the open field, because you were hated on the day you were born.

> **Sidelight**   In the time of Ezekiel 16:4, it was usual to rub a newborn baby with salt. This was believed to have had a medicinal purpose, and may also have symbolised purity (see 2 Kings 2:19–22, p.346).

6" 'When I passed by and saw you kicking about in your blood, I said to you, "Live!" 7I made you grow like a plant in the field. You grew up and became tall and became like a beautiful jewel. Your breasts formed, and your hair grew, but you were naked and without clothes.

8" 'Later when I passed by you and looked at you, I saw that you were old enough for love. So I spread my robe over you and covered your nakedness. I also made a promise to you and entered into an agreement with you so that you became mine, says the Lord GOD.

9" 'Then I bathed you with water, washed all the blood off you, and put oil on you. 10I put beautiful clothes made with needlework on you and put sandals of fine leather on your feet. I wrapped you in fine linen and covered you with silk. 11I put jewellery on you: bracelets on your arms, a necklace around your neck, 12a ring in your nose, earrings in your ears and a beautiful crown on your head. 13So you wore gold and silver. Your clothes were made of fine linen, silk and beautiful needlework. You ate fine flour,

---

cord   The umbilical cord that gives the unborn baby food and air from its mother.

honey and olive oil. You were very beautiful and became a queen. ¹⁴Then you became famous among the nations, because you were so beautiful. Your beauty was perfect, because of the glory I gave you, says the Lord GOD.

Jerusalem Becomes a Prostitute

¹⁵ 'But you trusted in your beauty. You became a prostitute,^d because you were so famous. You had sexual relations with anyone who passed by. ¹⁶You took some of your clothes and made your places of worship colourful. There you carried on your prostitution. These things should not happen; they should never occur. ¹⁷You also took your beautiful jewellery, made from my gold and silver I had given you, and you made for yourselves male idols so you could be a prostitute with them. ¹⁸Then you took your clothes with beautiful needlework and covered the idols. You gave my oil and incense ^d as an offering to them. ¹⁹Also, you took the bread I gave you, the fine flour, oil and honey I gave you to eat, and you offered them before the gods as a pleasing smell. This is what happened, says the Lord GOD.

²⁰" 'But your sexual sins were not enough for you. You also took your sons and daughters who were my children, and you sacrificed them to the idols as food. ²¹You killed my children and offered them up in fire to the idols. ²²While you did all your hateful acts and sexual sins, you did not remember when you were young, when you were naked and had no clothes and were left in your blood.

²³" 'How terrible! How terrible it will be for you, says the Lord GOD. After you did all these evil things, ²⁴you built yourself a place to worship gods. You made for yourself a place of worship in every city square. ²⁵You built a place of worship at the beginning of every street. You made your beauty hateful, offering your body for sex to anyone who passed by, and your sexual sins became worse and worse. ²⁶You also had sexual relations with the Egyptians, who were your neighbours and partners in sexual sin. Your sexual sins became even worse, and they caused me to be angry. ²⁷So then, I used my power against you and took away some of your land. I let you be defeated by those who hate you, the Philistine women, who were ashamed of your evil ways. ²⁸Also, you had sexual relations with the Assyrians, because you could not be satisfied. Even though you had sexual relations with them, you still were not satisfied. ²⁹You did many more sexual sins in Babylonia, the land of traders, but even this did not satisfy you.

³⁰" 'Truly your will is weak, says the Lord GOD. You do all the things a stubborn prostitute does.

³¹You built your place to worship gods at the beginning of every street, and you made places of worship in every city square. But you were not like a prostitute when you refused to accept payment.

³²" 'You are a wife who is guilty of adultery. ^d You desire strangers instead of your husband. ³³Men pay prostitutes, but you pay all your lovers to come to you. And they come from all around for sexual relations. ³⁴So you are different from other prostitutes. No man asks you to be a prostitute, and you pay money instead of having money paid to you. Yes, you are different.

The Prostitute is Judged

³⁵" 'So, prostitute, ^d hear the word of the LORD. ³⁶This is what the Lord GOD says: you showed your nakedness to other countries. You uncovered your body in your sexual sins with them as your lovers and with all your hateful idols. You killed your children and offered their blood to your idols. ³⁷So I will gather all your lovers with whom you found pleasure. Yes, I will gather all those you loved and those you hated. I will gather them against you from all around, and I will strip you naked in front of them so they can see your nakedness. ³⁸I will punish you as women guilty of adultery ^d or as murderers are punished. I will put you to death because I am angry and jealous. ³⁹I will also hand you over to your lovers. They will tear down your places of worship and destroy other places where you worship gods. They will tear off your clothes and take away your jewellery, leaving you naked and bare. ⁴⁰They will bring a crowd against you to throw stones at you and cut you into pieces with their swords. ⁴¹They will burn down your houses and will punish you in front of many women. I will put an end to your sexual sins, and you will no longer pay your lovers. ⁴²Then I will rest from my anger against you, and I will stop being jealous. I will be quiet and not angry any more.

⁴³" 'Because you didn't remember when you were young, but have made me angry in all these ways, I will repay you for what you have done, says the Lord GOD. Didn't you add sexual sins to all your other acts which I hate?

⁴⁴" 'Everyone who uses wise sayings will say this about you: "The daughter is like her mother." ⁴⁵You are like your mother, who hated her husband and children. You are also like your sisters, who hated their husbands and children. Your mother was a Hittite, and your father was an Amorite. ⁴⁶Your older sister is Samaria, who lived north of you with her daughters; your younger sister is Sodom, who lived south of you with her daughters. ⁴⁷You not only followed their ways and did the hateful things they did, but you were

soon worse than they were in all your ways. [48]As surely as I live, says the Lord GOD, this is true. Your sister Sodom and her daughters never did what you and your daughters have done.

[49] 'This was the sin of your sister Sodom: she and her daughters were proud and had plenty of food and lived in great comfort, but she did not help the poor and needy. [50]So Sodom and her daughters were proud and did things I hate in front of me. So I got rid of them when I saw what they did. [51]Also, Samaria did not do half the sins you do; you have done more hateful things than they did. So you make your sisters look good because of all the hateful things you have done. [52]You will suffer disgrace, because you have provided an excuse for your sisters. They are better than you are. Your sins were even more terrible than theirs. Feel ashamed and suffer disgrace, because you made your sisters look good.

[53] 'But I will give back to Sodom and her daughters the good things they once had. I will give back to Samaria and her daughters the good things they once had. And with them I will also give back the good things you once had [54]so you may suffer disgrace and feel ashamed for all the things you have done. You even gave comfort to your sisters in their sins. [55]Your sisters, Sodom with her daughters and Samaria with her daughters, will return to what they were before. You and your daughters will also return to what you were before. [56]You humiliated your sister Sodom when you were proud, [57]before your evil was uncovered. And now the Edomite women and their neighbours say bad things about you. Even the Philistine women humiliate you. Those around you hate you. [58]This is your punishment for your terrible sins and for actions that I hate, says the LORD.

God Keeps His Promises

[59] 'This is what the Lord GOD says: I will do to you what you have done. You hated and broke the agreement you promised to keep. [60]But I will remember my agreement I made with you when you were young, and I will make an agreement that will continue for ever with you. [61]Then you will remember what you have done and feel ashamed when you receive your sisters—both your older and your younger sisters. I will give them to you like daughters, but not because they share in my agreement with you. [62]I will set up my agreement with you, and you will know that I am the LORD. [63]You will remember what you did and feel ashamed. You will not open your mouth again because of your shame, when I forgive you for all the things you have done, says the Lord GOD.' "

The Eagle and the Vine

17 The LORD spoke his word to me, saying: [2]"Human, give a riddle and tell a story to the people of Israel. [3]Say, 'This is what the Lord GOD says: a giant eagle with big wings and long feathers of many different colours came to Lebanon and took hold of the top of a cedar tree. [4]He pulled off the top branch and brought it to a land of traders, where he planted it in a city of traders.

[5] 'The eagle took some seed from the land and planted it in a good field near plenty of water. He planted it to grow like a willow tree. [6]It grew and became a low vine that spread over the ground. The branches turned towards the eagle, but the roots were under the eagle. So the seed became a vine, and its branches grew, sending out leaves.

[7] 'But there was another giant eagle with big wings and many feathers. The vine then bent its roots towards this eagle. It sent out its branches from the area where it was planted towards the eagle so he could water it. [8]It had been planted in a good field by plenty of water so it could grow branches and give fruit. It could have become a fine vine.'

[9]"Say to them, 'This is what the Lord GOD says: the vine will not continue to grow. The first eagle will pull up the vine's roots and strip off its fruit. Then the vine and all its new leaves will dry up and die. It will not take a strong arm or many people to pull the vine up by its roots. [10]Even if it is planted again, it will not continue to grow. It will completely dry up and die when the east wind hits it in the area where it grew.' "

Zedekiah Against Nebuchadnezzar

[11]Then the LORD spoke his word to me, saying: [12]"Say now to the people who refuse to obey: 'Do you know what these things mean?' Say: 'The king of Babylon came to Jerusalem and took the king and important men of Jerusalem and brought them to Babylon. [13]Then he took a member of the family of the king of Judah and made an agreement with him, forcing him to take an oath. The king also took away the leaders of Judah [14]to make the kingdom weak so it would not be strong again. Then the kingdom of Judah could continue only by keeping its agreement with the king of Babylon. [15]But the king of Judah turned against the king of Babylon by sending his messengers to Egypt and asking them for horses and many soldiers. Will the king of Judah succeed? Will the one who does such things escape? He cannot break the agreement and escape.

[16] 'As surely as I live, says the Lord GOD, he will die in Babylon, in the land of the king who made him king of Judah. The king of Judah hated

his promise to the king of Babylon and broke his agreement with him. ¹⁷The king of Egypt with his mighty army and many people will not help the king of Judah in the war. The Babylonians will build devices to attack the cities and to kill many people. ¹⁸The king of Judah showed that he hated the promise by breaking the agreement. He promised to support Babylon, but he did all these things. So he will not escape.

¹⁹" 'So this is what the Lord GOD says: as surely as I live, this is true: I will pay back the king of Judah for hating my promise and breaking my agreement. ²⁰I will spread my net over him, and he will be caught in my trap. Then I will bring him to Babylon, where I will punish him for the unfaithful acts he did against me. ²¹All the best of his soldiers who escape will die by the sword, and those who live will be scattered to every wind. Then you will know that I, the LORD, have spoken.

²²" 'This is what the Lord GOD says: I myself will also take a young branch from the top of a cedar tree, and I will plant it. I will cut off a small twig from the top of the tree's young branches, and I will plant it on a very high mountain. ²³I will plant it on the high mountain of Israel. Then it will grow branches and give fruit and become a great cedar tree. Birds of every kind will build nests in it and live in the shelter of the tree's branches. ²⁴Then all the trees in the countryside will know that I am the LORD. I bring down the high tree and make the low tree tall. I dry up the green tree and make the dry tree grow. I am the LORD. I have spoken, and I will do it.' "

God is Fair

18 The LORD spoke his word to me, saying: ²"What do you mean by using this saying about the land of Israel:

'The parents have eaten sour grapes,
　　and that caused the children to grind their
　　　　teeth from the sour taste'?

³"As surely as I live, says the Lord GOD, this is true: you will not use this saying in Israel any more. ⁴Every living thing belongs to me. The life of the parent is mine, and the life of the child is mine. The person who sins is the one who will die.

⁵"Suppose a person is good and does what is fair and right. ⁶He does not eat at the mountain places of worship. He does not look to the idols of Israel for help. He does not have sexual relations with his neighbour's wife or with a woman during her time of monthly bleeding. ⁷He does not mistreat anyone but returns what was given as a promise for a loan. He does not rob other people. He gives bread to the hungry and clothes to those who have none. ⁸He does not lend

money to get too much interest or profit. He keeps his hand from doing wrong. He judges fairly between one person and another. ⁹He lives by my rules and obeys my laws faithfully. Whoever does these things is good and will surely live, says the Lord GOD.

¹⁰"But suppose this person has a wild son who murders people and who does any of these other things. ¹¹(Though the father himself has not done any of these things.) This son eats at the mountain places of worship. He has sexual relations with his neighbour's wife. ¹²He mistreats the poor and needy. He steals and refuses to return what was promised for a loan. He looks to idols for help. He does things which I hate. ¹³He lends money for too much interest and profit. Will this son live? No, he will not live! He has done all these hateful things, so he will surely be put to death. He will be responsible for his own death.

¹⁴"Now suppose this son has a son who has seen all his father's sins, but after seeing them does not do those things. ¹⁵He does not eat at the mountain places of worship. He does not look to the idols of Israel for help. He does not have sexual relations with his neighbour's wife. ¹⁶He does not mistreat anyone or keep something promised for a loan or steal. He gives bread to the hungry and clothes to those who have none. ¹⁷He keeps his hand from doing wrong. He does not take too much interest or profit when he lends money. He obeys my laws and lives by my rules. He will not die for his father's sin; he will surely live. ¹⁸But his father took other people's money unfairly and robbed his brother and did what was wrong among his people. So he will die for his own sin.

¹⁹"But you ask, 'Why is the son not punished for the father's sin?' The son has done what is fair and right. He obeys all my rules, so he will surely live. ²⁰The person who sins is the one who will die. A child will not be punished for a parent's sin, and a parent will not be punished for a child's sin. Those who do right will enjoy the results of their own goodness; evil people will suffer the results of their own evil.

²¹"But suppose the wicked stop doing all the sins they have done and obey all my rules and do what is fair and right. Then they will surely live; they will not die. ²²Their sins will be forgotten. Because they have done what is right, they will live. ²³I do not really want the wicked to die, says the Lord GOD. I want them to stop their bad ways and live.

²⁴"But suppose good people stop doing good and do wrong and do the same hateful things the wicked do. Will they live? All their good acts will be forgotten, because they became unfaithful.

They have sinned, so they will die because of their sins.

²⁵"But you say, 'What the Lord does isn't fair.' Listen, people of Israel. I am fair. It is what you do that is not fair! ²⁶When good people stop doing good and do wrong, they will die because of it. They will die, because they did wrong. ²⁷When the wicked stop being wicked and do what is fair and right, they will save their lives. ²⁸Because they thought about it and stopped doing all the sins they had done, they will surely live; they will not die. ²⁹But the people of Israel still say, 'What the Lord does isn't fair.' People of Israel, I am fair. It is what you do that is not fair.

³⁰"So I will judge you, people of Israel; I will judge each of you by what you do, says the Lord GOD. Change your hearts and stop all your sinning so sin will not bring your ruin. ³¹Get rid of all the sins you have done, and get for yourselves a new heart and a new way of thinking. Why do you want to die, people of Israel? ³²I do not want anyone to die, says the Lord GOD, so change your hearts and lives so you may live.

A Sad Song for Israel

19 "Sing a funeral song for the leaders of Israel. ²Say:

'Your mother was like a female lion.
She lay down among the young lions.
She had many cubs.
³When she brought up one of her cubs,
he became a strong lion.
He learned to tear the animals he hunted,
and he ate people.
⁴The nations heard about him.
He was trapped in their pit,
and they brought him with hooks
to the land of Egypt.

⁵" 'The mother lion wait d and saw
that there was no hope for her cub.
So she took another one of her cubs
and made him a strong lion.
⁶This cub roamed among the lions.
He was now a strong lion.
He learned to tear the animals he hunted,
and he ate people.
⁷He tore down their strong places
and destroyed their cities.
The land and everything in it
were terrified by the sound of his roar.
⁸Then the nations came against him
from areas all around,
and they spread their net over him.
He was trapped in their pit.
⁹Then they put him into a cage with chains
and brought him to the king of Babylon.
They put him into prison

so his roar could not be heard again
on the mountains of Israel.

¹⁰" 'Your mother was like a vine in your
vineyard,
planted beside the water.
The vine had many branches and gave much
fruit,
because there was plenty of water.
¹¹The vine had strong branches,
good enough for a king's sceptre. d
The vine became tall
among the thick branches.
And it was seen, because it was tall
with many branches.
¹²But it was pulled up by its roots in anger
and thrown down to the ground.
The east wind dried it up.
Its fruit was torn off.
Its strong branches were broken off
and burned up.
¹³Now the vine is planted in the desert,
in a dry and thirsty land.
¹⁴Fire spread from the vine's main branch,
destroying its fruit.
There is not a strong branch left on it
that could become a sceptre for a king.'

This is a funeral song; it is to be used as a funeral song."

Israel Has Refused God

20 It was the tenth day of the fifth month of the seventh year of our captivity. Some of the elders of Israel came to ask about the LORD and sat down in front of me.

²The LORD spoke his word to me, saying: ³"Human, speak to the elders of Israel and say to them: 'This is what the Lord GOD says: did you come to ask me questions? As surely as I live, I will not let you ask me questions.'

⁴"Will you judge them? Will you judge them, human? Let them know the hateful things their ancestors did. ⁵Say to them: 'This is what the Lord GOD says: When I chose Israel, I made a promise to the descendants d of Jacob. I made myself known to them in Egypt, and I promised them, "I am the LORD your God." ⁶At that time I promised them I would bring them out of Egypt into a land I had found for them, a fertile land, the best land in the world. ⁷I said to them, "Each one of you must throw away the hateful idols you have seen and liked. Don't make yourselves unclean d with the idols of Egypt. I am the LORD your God."

⁸" 'But they turned against me and refused to listen to me. They did not throw away the hateful idols which they saw and liked; they did not give up the idols of Egypt. Then I decided to pour out

my anger against them while they were still in Egypt. ⁹But I acted for the sake of my name so it would not be dishonoured in full view of the nations where the Israelites lived. I made myself known to the Israelites with a promise to bring them out of Egypt while the nations were watching. ¹⁰So I took them out of Egypt and brought them into the desert. ¹¹I gave them my rules and told them about my laws, by which people will live if they obey them. ¹²I also gave them my Sabbaths *d* to be a sign between us so they would know that I am the LORD who made them holy.

¹³" But in the desert Israel turned against me. They did not follow my rules, and they rejected my laws, by which people will live if they obey them. They dishonoured my Sabbaths. Then I decided to pour out my anger against them and destroy them in the desert. ¹⁴But I acted for the sake of my name so it would not be dishonoured in full view of the nations who watched as I had brought the Israelites out of Egypt. ¹⁵And in the desert I swore to the Israelites that I would not bring them into the land I had given them. It is a fertile land, the best land in the world. ¹⁶This was because they rejected my laws and did not follow my rules. They dishonoured my Sabbaths and wanted to worship their idols. ¹⁷But I had pity on them. I did not destroy them or put an end to them in the desert. ¹⁸I said to their children in the desert, "Don't live by the rules of your parents, or obey their laws. Don't make yourselves unclean with their idols. ¹⁹I am the LORD your God. Live by my rules, obey my laws and follow them. ²⁰Keep my Sabbaths holy, and they will be a sign between me and you. Then you will know that I am the LORD your God."

²¹" 'But the children turned against me. They did not live by my rules, nor were they careful to obey my laws, by which people will live if they obey them. They dishonoured my Sabbaths. So I decided to pour out my anger against them in the desert. ²²But I held back my anger. I acted for the sake of my name so it would not be dishonoured in full view of the nations who watched as I brought the Israelites out. ²³And in the desert I swore to the Israelites that I would scatter them among the nations and spread them among the countries, ²⁴because they had not obeyed my laws. They had rejected my rules and dishonoured my Sabbaths and worshipped the idols of their parents. ²⁵I also allowed them to follow rules that were not good and laws by which they could not live. ²⁶I let the Israelites make themselves unclean by the gifts they brought to their gods when they sacrificed their first children in the fire. I wanted to terrify them so they would know that I am the LORD.'

²⁷"So, human, speak to the people of Israel. Say to them, 'This is what the Lord GOD says: your ancestors spoke against me by being unfaithful to me in another way. ²⁸When I had brought them into the land I promised to give them, they saw every high hill and every leafy tree. There they offered their sacrifices to gods. They brought offerings that made me angry and burned their incense *d* and poured out their drink offerings. ²⁹Then I said to them: what is this high place where you go to worship?' " (It is still called High Place today.)

³⁰"So say to the people of Israel: 'This is what the Lord GOD says: are you going to make yourselves unclean as your ancestors did? Are you going to be unfaithful and desire their hateful idols? ³¹When you offer your children as gifts and sacrifice them in the fire, you are making yourselves unclean with all your idols even today. So, people of Israel, should I let you ask me questions? As surely as I live, says the Lord GOD, I will not accept questions from you.

³²" 'What you want will not come true. You say, "We want to be like the other nations, like the people in other lands. We want to worship idols made of wood and stone." ³³As surely as I live, says the Lord GOD, I will use my great power and strength and anger to rule over you. ³⁴I will bring you out from the foreign nations. With my great power and strength and anger I will gather you from the lands where you are scattered. ³⁵I will bring you among the nations as I brought your ancestors into the desert with Moses. There I will judge you face to face. ³⁶I will judge you the same way I judged your ancestors in the desert of the land of Egypt, says the Lord GOD. ³⁷I will count you like sheep and will bring you into line with my agreement. ³⁸I will get rid of those who refuse to obey me and who turn against me. I will bring them out of the land where they are now living, but they will never enter the land of Israel. Then you will know that I am the LORD.

³⁹" 'This is what the Lord GOD says: people of Israel, go and serve your idols for now. But later you will listen to me; you will not continue to dishonour my holy name with your gifts and gods. ⁴⁰On my holy mountain, the high mountain of Israel, all Israel will serve me in the land, says the Lord GOD. There I will accept you. There I will expect your offerings, the first harvest of your offerings, and all your holy gifts. ⁴¹I will accept you like the pleasing smell of sacrifices when I bring you out from the foreign nations and gather you from the lands where you are scattered. Then through you I will show how holy I am so the nations will see. ⁴²When I bring you into the land of Israel, the land I promised your ancestors, you will know that I am the LORD. ⁴³There you will remember everything you did that made you

unclean, and then you will hate yourselves for all the evil things you have done. ⁴⁴I will deal with you for the sake of my name, not because of your evil ways or unclean actions. Then you will know I am the LORD, people of Israel, says the Lord GOD.'"

Babylon, the LORD's Sword

⁴⁵Now the LORD spoke his word to me, saying: ⁴⁶"Human, look towards the south. Prophesy*d* against the south and against the forest of the southern area. ⁴⁷Say to that forest: 'Hear the word of the LORD. This is what the Lord GOD says: I am ready to start a fire in you that will destroy all your green trees and all your dry trees. The flames that burn will not be put out. Every face from south to north will feel their heat. ⁴⁸Then all the people will see that I, the LORD, have started the fire. It will not be put out.'"

⁴⁹Then I said, "Ah, Lord GOD! The people are saying about me, 'He is only telling stories.'"

21 Then the LORD spoke his word to me, saying: ²"Human, look towards Jerusalem and speak against the holy place. Prophesy*d* against the land of Israel. ³Say to Israel: 'This is what the LORD says: I am against you. I will pull my sword out of its holder, and I will cut off from you both the wicked and those who do right. ⁴Because I am going to cut off the wicked and those who do right, my sword will come out from its holder and attack all people from south to north. ⁵Then all people will know that I, the LORD, have pulled my sword out from its holder. My sword will not go back in again.'

⁶"So, human, groan with a breaking heart and great sadness. Groan in front of the people. ⁷When they ask you, 'Why are you groaning?' you will say, 'Because of what I have heard is going to happen. When it happens, every heart will melt with fear, and all hands will become weak. Everyone will be afraid; all knees will become weak as water. Look, it is coming, and it will happen, says the Lord GOD.'"

⁸The LORD spoke his word to me, saying: ⁹"Human, prophesy and say, 'This is what the Lord says:

A sword, a sword,
made sharp and polished.
¹⁰It is made sharp for the killing.
It is polished to flash like lightning.

"'You are not happy about this horrible punishment by the sword. But my son Judah, you did not change when you were only beaten with a rod.
¹¹The sword should be polished.
It is meant to be held in the hand.
It is made sharp and polished,
ready for the hand of a killer.

¹²Shout and yell, human,
because the sword is meant for my people,
for all the rulers of Israel.
They will be killed by the sword,
along with my people.
So beat your chest in sadness.

¹³"'The test will come. And Judah, who is hated by the armies of Babylon, will not last, says the Lord GOD.'

¹⁴"So, human, prophesy
and clap your hands.
Let the sword strike
two or three times.
It is a sword meant for killing,
a sword meant for much killing.
This sword surrounds the people to be killed.
¹⁵Their hearts will melt with fear,
and many people will die.
I have placed the killing sword
at all their city gates.
Oh! The sword is made to flash like lightning.
It is held, ready for killing.
¹⁶Sword, cut on the right side;
then cut on the left side.
Cut anywhere your blade is turned.
¹⁷I will also clap my hands
and use up my anger.
I, the LORD, have spoken."

Jerusalem to be Destroyed

¹⁸The LORD spoke his word to me, saying: ¹⁹"Human, mark two roads that the king of Babylon and his sword can follow. Both of these roads will start from the same country. And make signs where the road divides and one way goes towards the city. ²⁰Mark one sign to show the road he can take with his sword to Rabbah in the land of the Ammonites. Mark the other sign to show the road to Judah and Jerusalem, which is protected with strong walls. ²¹The king of Babylon has come to where the road divides, and he is using magic. He throws lots*d* with arrows and asks questions of his family idols. He looks at the liver of a sacrificed animal to learn where he

should go. ²²The lot in his right hand tells him to go to Jerusalem. It tells him to use logs to break down the city gates, to shout the battle cry and give the order to kill, and to build a dirt road to the top of the walls and devices to attack the walls. ²³The people of Jerusalem have made agreements with other nations to help them fight Babylon. So they will think this prediction is wrong, but it is really proof of their sin, and they will be captured.

²⁴"So this is what the Lord GOD says: 'You have shown how sinful you are by turning against the LORD. Your sins are seen in all the things you do. Because of this proof against you, you will be taken captive by the enemy.

²⁵ 'You unclean *d* and evil leader of Israel, you will be killed! The time of your final punishment has come. ²⁶This is what the Lord GOD says: take off the royal turban and remove the crown. Things will change. Those who are important now will be made unimportant, and those who are unimportant now will be made important. ²⁷A ruin! A ruin! I will make it a ruin! This place will not be rebuilt until the one comes who has a right to be king. Then I will give him that right.'

The Punishment of Ammon

²⁸"And you, human, prophesy *d* and say: 'This is what the Lord GOD says about the people of Ammon and their insults:

a sword, a sword
   is pulled out of its holder.
It is polished to kill and destroy,
   to flash like lightning!
²⁹Prophets *d* see false visions about you
   and prophesy lies about you.
The sword will be put on the necks
   of these unclean *d* and evil people.
Their day of judging has come;
   the time of final punishment has come.
³⁰Put the sword back in its holder.
   I will judge you
in the place where you were created,
   in the land where you were born.
³¹I will pour out my anger against you
   and blast you with the fire of my anger.
I will hand you over to cruel men,
   experts in destruction.
³²You will be like fuel for the fire;
   you will die in the land.
You will not be remembered,
   because I, the LORD, have spoken.' "

The Sins of Jerusalem

22 The LORD spoke his word to me, saying: ²"And you, human, will you judge? Will you judge the city of murderers? Then tell her about all her hateful acts. ³You are to say: 'This is what the Lord GOD says: you are a city that kills those who come to live there. You make yourself unclean *d* by making idols. ⁴You have become guilty of murder and have become unclean by your idols which you have made. So you have brought your time of punishment near; you have come to the end of your years. That is why I have made you a shame to the nations and why all lands laugh at you. ⁵Those near and those far away laugh at you with your bad name, you city full of confusion.

⁶ 'Jerusalem, see how each ruler of Israel in you has been trying to kill people. ⁷The people in you hate their fathers and mothers. They mistreat the foreigners in you and wrong the orphans and widows in you. ⁸You hate my holy things and dishonour my Sabbaths. *d* ⁹The men in you tell lies to cause the death of others. The people in you eat food offered to idols at the mountain places of worship, and they take part in sexual sins. ¹⁰The men in you have sexual relations with their fathers' wives and with women who are unclean, during their time of monthly bleeding. ¹¹One man in you does a hateful act with his neighbour's wife, while another has shamefully made his daughter-in-law unclean sexually. And another forces his half-sister to have sexual relations with him. ¹²The people in you take money to kill others. You take unfair interest and profits and make profits by mistreating your neighbour. And you have forgotten me, says the Lord GOD.

¹³"So, Jerusalem, I will shake my fist at you for stealing money and for murdering people. ¹⁴Will you still be brave and strong when I punish you? I, the LORD, have spoken, and I will act. ¹⁵I will scatter you among the nations and spread you through the countries. That is how I will get rid of your uncleanness. ¹⁶But you, yourself, will be dishonoured in the sight of the nations. Then you will know that I am the LORD.' "

Israel is Worthless

¹⁷The LORD spoke his word to me, saying: ¹⁸"Human, the people of Israel have become useless like scum to me. They are like the copper, tin, iron and lead left in the furnace when silver is purified. ¹⁹So this is what the Lord GOD says: 'Because you have become useless like scum, I am going to put you together inside Jerusalem. ²⁰People put silver, copper, iron, lead and tin together inside a furnace to melt them down in a blazing fire. In the same way I will gather you in my hot anger and put you together in Jerusalem and melt you down. ²¹I will put you together and make you feel the heat of my anger. You will be melted down inside Jerusalem. ²²As silver is melted in a furnace, you will be melted inside

the city. Then you will know that I, the Lord, have poured out my anger on you.' "

Sins of the People

23The Lord spoke his word to me, saying: 24"Human, say to the land, 'You are a land that has not had rain or showers when God is angry.' 25Like a roaring lion that tears the animal it has caught, Israel's rulers make evil plans. They have destroyed lives and have taken treasure and valuable things. They have caused many women to become widows. 26Israel's priests do cruel things to my teachings and do not honour my holy things. They make no difference between holy and unholy things, and they teach there is no difference between clean *d* and unclean things. They do not remember my Sabbaths, *d* so I am dishonoured by them. 27Like wolves tearing a dead animal, Jerusalem's leaders have killed people for profit. 28And the prophets *d* try to cover this up by false visions and by lying messages. They say, 'This is what the Lord God says' when the Lord has not spoken. 29The people cheat others and steal. They hurt people who are poor and needy. They cheat foreigners and do not treat them fairly.

30"I looked for someone to build up the walls and to stand before me where the walls are broken to defend these people, so I would not have to destroy them. But I could not find anyone. 31So I let them see my anger. I destroyed them with an anger that was like fire because of all the things they have done, says the Lord God."

Samaria and Jerusalem

23 The Lord spoke his word to me, saying: 2"Human, a woman had two daughters. 3While they were young, they went to Egypt and became prostitutes. *d* They let men touch and hold their breasts. 4The older girl was named Oholah, and her sister was named Oholibah. They became my wives and had sons and daughters. Oholah is Samaria, and Oholibah is Jerusalem. *n*

5"While still my wife, Samaria had sexual relations with other men. She had great sexual desire for her lovers, men from Assyria. The Assyrians were warriors and 6wore blue uniforms. They were all handsome young captains and commanders riding on horseback. 7Samaria became a prostitute for all the important men in Assyria and made herself unclean *d* with all the idols of everyone she desired. 8She continued the prostitution she began in Egypt. When she was young, she

had slept with men, and they touched her breasts and had sexual relations with her.

9"So I handed her over to her lovers, the Assyrians, that she wanted so badly. 10They stripped her naked and took away her sons and daughters. Then they killed her with a sword. Women everywhere began talking about how she had been punished.

11"Her sister Jerusalem saw what happened, but she became worse than her sister in her sexual desire and prostitution. 12She also desired the Assyrians, who were all soldiers in beautiful uniforms—handsome young captains and commanders riding horses. 13I saw that both girls were alike; both were prostitutes.

14"But Jerusalem went even further. She saw carvings of Babylonian men on a wall. They wore red 15and had belts around their waists and turbans on their heads. They all looked like chariot officers born in Babylonia. 16When she saw them, she wanted to have sexual relations with them and sent messengers to them in Babylonia. 17So these Babylonian men came and had sexual relations with her and made her unclean. After that, she became sick of them. 18But she continued her prostitution so openly that everyone knew about it. And I finally became sick of her, as I had her sister. 19But she remembered how she was a young prostitute in Egypt, so she took part in even more prostitution. 20She wanted men who behaved like animals in their sexual desire. 21In the same way you desired to do the sinful things you had done in Egypt. There men touched and held your young breasts.

God's Judgement on Jerusalem

22"So, Jerusalem, this is what the Lord God says: you are tired of your lovers. So now I will make them angry with you and cause them to attack you from all sides. 23Men from Babylon and all Babylonia and men from Pekod, Shoa and Koa will attack you. All the Assyrians will attack you: handsome young captains and commanders, all of them important men and all riding horses. 24Those men will attack you with great armies and with their weapons, chariots and wagons. They will surround you with large and small shields and with helmets. And I will give them the right to punish you, and they will give you their own kind of punishment. 25Then you will see how strong my anger can be when they punish you in their anger. They will cut off your noses and ears. They will take away your sons and daughters, and those who are left will be burned. 26They will take off your clothes and steal

---

Oholah . . . Jerusalem Throughout this chapter Samaria is used in place of Oholah, and Jerusalem is used in place of Oholibah.

your jewellery. ²⁷I will put a stop to the sinful life you began when you were in Egypt so that you will not desire it or remember Egypt any more.

²⁸"This is what the Lord GOD says: you became tired of your lovers, but I am going to hand you over to those men you now hate. ²⁹They will treat you with hate and take away everything you worked for, leaving you empty and naked. Everyone will know about the sinful things you did. Your sexual sins ³⁰have brought this on you. You have had sexual relations with the nations and made yourselves unclean *d* by worshipping their idols. ³¹You did the same things your sister did, so you will get the same punishment, like a bitter cup to drink.

³²"This is what the Lord GOD says:
  you will drink the same cup your sister did,
    and that cup is deep and wide.
  Everyone will make fun of you,
    because the cup is full.
³³It will make you miserable and drunk.
  It is the cup of fear and ruin.
  It is the cup of your sister Samaria.
³⁴You will drink everything in it,
    and then you will smash it
    and tear at your breasts.
I have spoken, says the Lord God.

³⁵"So this is what the Lord GOD says: you have forgotten me and turned your back on me. So you will be punished for your sexual sins."

Judgement on Samaria and Jerusalem

³⁶The LORD said to me: "Human, will you judge Samaria and Jerusalem, showing them their hateful acts? ³⁷They are guilty of adultery *d* and murder. They have taken part in adultery with their idols. They even offered our children as sacrifices in the fire to be food for these idols. ³⁸They have also done this to me: they made my Temple *d* unclean *d* and at the same time they dishonoured my Sabbaths. *d* ³⁹They sacrificed their children to their idols. Then they entered my Temple at that very time to dishonour it. That is what they did inside my Temple!

⁴⁰"They even sent for men from far away, who came after a messenger was sent to them. The two sisters bathed themselves for them, painted their eyes and put on jewellery. ⁴¹They sat on a fine bed with a table set before it, on which they put my incense *d* and my oil.

⁴²"There was the noise of a reckless crowd in the city. Common people gathered, and drunkards were brought from the desert. They put bracelets on the wrists of the two sisters and beautiful crowns on their heads. ⁴³Then I said about the one who was worn out by her acts of adultery, 'Let them continue their sexual sins with her. She is nothing but a prostitute.' *d* ⁴⁴They

kept going to her as they would go to a prostitute. So they continued to go to Samaria and Jerusalem, these shameful women. ⁴⁵But men who do right will punish them as they punish women who take part in adultery and who murder people, because they are guilty of adultery and murder.

⁴⁶"This is what the Lord GOD says: bring together a mob against Samaria and Jerusalem, and hand them over to be frightened and robbed. ⁴⁷Let the mob kill them by throwing stones at them, and let them cut them down with their swords. Let them kill their sons and daughters and burn their houses down.

⁴⁸"So I will put an end to sexual sins in the land. Then all women will be warned, and they will not do the sexual sins you have done. ⁴⁹You will be punished for your sexual sins and the sin of worshipping idols. Then you will know that I am the Lord GOD."

The Pot and the Meat

24 The LORD spoke his word to me on the tenth day of the tenth month of the ninth year of our captivity. He said: ²"Human, write down today's date, this very date. The king of Babylon has surrounded Jerusalem this very day. ³And tell a story to the people who refuse to obey me. Say to them: 'This is what the Lord GOD says:
  put on the pot; put it on
    and pour water in it.
⁴Put in the pieces of meat,
    the best pieces—the legs and the
      shoulders.
  Fill it with the best bones.
⁵ Take the best of the flock,
  and pile wood under the pot.
  Boil the pieces of meat
    until even the bones are cooked.

⁶ 'This is what the Lord GOD says:
  how terrible it will be for the city of
      murderers!
  How terrible it will be for the rusty pot
    whose rust will not come off!
Take the meat out of it, piece by piece.
  Don't choose any special piece.

⁷ 'The blood from her killings is still in the
      city.
  She poured the blood on the bare rock.
  She did not pour it on the ground
    where dust would cover it.
⁸To stir up my anger and revenge,
  I put the blood she spilled on the bare
      rock
  so it will not be covered.

9" 'So this is what the Lord GOD says:
How terrible it will be for the city of
    murderers!
I myself will pile the wood high for
    burning.
¹⁰Pile up the wood
    and light the fire.
Finish cooking the meat.
    Mix in the spices,
    and let the bones burn.
¹¹Then set the empty pot on the coals
    so it may become hot and its copper sides
        glow.
The dirty scum stuck inside it may then melt
    and its rust burn away.
¹²But efforts to clean the pot have failed.
    Its heavy rust cannot be removed,
    even in the fire.

¹³" 'By your sinful action you have become unclean. *d* I wanted to cleanse you, but you are still
unclean. You will never be cleansed from your
sin until my anger against you is carried out.
¹⁴" 'I, the LORD, have spoken. The time has come
for me to act. I will not hold back punishment or
feel pity or change my mind. I will judge you by
your ways and actions, says the Lord GOD.' "

The Death of Ezekiel's Wife

¹⁵Then the LORD spoke his word to me, saying:
¹⁶"Human, I am going to take your wife from
you, the woman you look at with love. She will
die suddenly, but you must not be sad or cry
loudly for her or shed any tears. ¹⁷Groan silently;
do not cry loudly for the dead. Tie on your turban, and put your sandals on your feet. Do not
cover your face, and do not eat the food people
eat when they are sad about a death."
¹⁸So I spoke to the people in the morning, and
my wife died in the evening. The next morning
I did as I had been commanded.
¹⁹Then the people asked me, "Tell us, what do
the things you are doing mean for us?"
²⁰Then I said to them, "The LORD spoke his
word to me. He said, ²¹'Say to the people of
Israel, this is what the Lord GOD says: I am going
to dishonour my Temple. *d* You think it gives you
strength. You are proud of it, and you look at it
with love and tenderness. But your sons and
daughters that you left behind in Jerusalem will
fall dead by the sword. ²²When that happens,
you are to act as I have: you are not to cover
your face, and you are not to eat the food people
eat when they are sad about a death. ²³Your turbans must stay on your heads, and your sandals
on your feet. You must not cry loudly, but you
must rot away in your sins and groan to each
other. ²⁴So Ezekiel is to be an example for you.

You must do all the same things he did. When all
this happens, you will know that I am the Lord
GOD.'
²⁵"And as for you, human, this is how it will
be. I will take away the Temple that gives them

Sidelight   If God had allowed
                    Ezekiel to grieve for his
wife, there would have been no flowers or nice
funeral clothes. Under normal circumstances,
the prophet would have gone barefoot, worn
sackcloth, and sprinkled ashes on his head.
To learn why he did none of them read Ezekiel
24:15–24.

---

strength and joy, that makes them proud. They
look at it with love, and it makes them happy.
And I will take away their sons and daughters
also. ²⁶At that time a person who escapes will
come to you with information for you to hear.
²⁷At that very time your mouth will be opened.
You will speak and be silent no more. So you will
be a sign for them, and they will know that I am
the LORD."

Prophecy Against Ammon

25 The LORD spoke his word to me, saying:
²"Human, look towards the people of
Ammon and prophesy *d* against them. ³Say to
them, 'Hear the word of the Lord GOD. This is
what the Lord GOD says: you were glad when
my Temple *d* was dishonoured, when the land of
Israel was ruined and when the people of Judah
were taken away as captives. ⁴So I am going to
give you to the people of the East to be theirs.
They will set up their camps among you and
make their homes among you. They will eat your
fruit and drink your milk. ⁵I will make the city of
Rabbah a pasture for camels and the land of
Ammon a resting place for sheep. Then you will
know that I am the LORD. ⁶This is what the Lord
GOD says: you have clapped your hands and
stamped your feet; you have laughed about all the
insults you made against the land of Israel. ⁷So I
will use my power against you. I will give you to
the nations as if you were treasures taken in war.
I will wipe you out of the lands so you will no
longer be a nation, and I will destroy you. Then
you will know that I am the LORD.'

Prophecy Against Moab and Edom

⁸"This is what the Lord GOD says: 'Moab and
Edom say, "The people of Judah are like all the
other nations." ⁹So I am going to take away the
cities that protect Moab's borders, the best cities
in that land: Beth Jeshimoth, Baal Meon and
Kiriathaim. ¹⁰Then I will give Moab, along with the

Ammonites, to the people of the East as their possession. Then, along with the Ammonites, Moab will not be a nation any more. [11]So I will punish the people of Moab, and they will know that I am the LORD.'

Prophecy Against Edom

[12]"This is what the Lord GOD says: 'Edom took revenge on the people of Judah, and the Edomites became guilty because of it. [13]So this is what the Lord GOD says: I will use my power against Edom, killing every human and animal in it. And I will destroy Edom all the way from Teman to Dedan as they die in battle. [14]I will use my people Israel to take revenge on Edom. So the Israelites will do to Edom what my hot anger demands. Then the Edomites will know what my revenge feels like, says the Lord GOD.'

Prophecy Against Philistia

[15]"This is what the Lord GOD says: 'The Philistines have taken revenge with hateful hearts. Because of their strong hatred, they have tried to destroy Judah. [16]So this is what the Lord GOD says: I will use my power against the Philistines. I will kill the Kerethites, and I will destroy those people still alive on the coast of the Mediterranean Sea. [17]I will punish them in my anger and do great acts of revenge to them. They will know that I am the LORD when I take revenge on them.'"

Prophecy Against Tyre

26 It was the eleventh year of our captivity, on the first day of the month. The LORD spoke his word to me, saying: [2]"Human, the city of Tyre has spoken against Jerusalem: 'The city that traded with the nations is destroyed. Now we can be the trading centre. Since the city of Jerusalem is ruined, we can make money.' [3]So this is what the Lord GOD says: I am against you, Tyre. I will bring many nations against you, like the sea beating its waves on your island shores. [4]They will destroy the walls of Tyre and pull down her towers. I will also scrape away her ruins and make her a bare rock. [5]Tyre will be an island where fishermen dry their nets. I have spoken, says the Lord GOD. The nations will steal treasures from Tyre. [6]Also, her villages on the shore across from the island will be destroyed by war. Then they will know that I am the LORD.

Nebuchadnezzar to Attack Tyre

[7]"This is what the Lord GOD says: I will bring a king from the north against Tyre. He is Nebuchadnezzar king of Babylon, the greatest king, with his horses, chariots, horsemen and a great army. [8]He will fight a battle and destroy your villages on the shore across from the island. He will set up devices to attack you. He will build a road of earth to the top of the walls. He will raise his shields against you. [9]He will bring logs to pound through your city walls, and he will break down your towers with his iron bars. [10]His horses will be so many that they will cover you with their dust. Your walls will shake at the noise of horsemen, wagons and chariots. The king of Babylon will enter your city gates as men enter a city where the walls are broken through. [11]The hoofs of his horses will run over your streets. He will kill your army with the sword, and your strong pillars will fall down to the ground. [12]Also, his men will take away your riches and will steal the things you sell. They will break down your walls and destroy your nice houses. They will throw your stones, wood and rubbish into the sea. [13]So I will stop your songs; the music of your harps will not be heard any more. [14]I will make you a bare rock, and you will be a place for drying fishing nets. You will not be built again, because I, the LORD, have spoken, says the Lord GOD.

[15]"This is what the Lord GOD says to Tyre: the people who live along the sea coast will shake with fear when they hear about your defeat. Those of you who are injured and dying will groan. [16]Then all the leaders of the sea coast will get down from their thrones, take off their beautiful needlework clothes and show how afraid they are. They will sit on the ground and tremble all the time. When they see you, they will be shocked. [17]They will begin singing a funeral song about you and will say to you:

'Tyre, you famous city, you have been
      destroyed!
   You have lost your sea power!
You and your people
      had great power on the seas.
You made everyone around you
      afraid of you.
[18]Now the people who live by the coast
      tremble,
   now that you have fallen.
The islands of the sea
   are afraid because you have been defeated.'

[19]"This is what the Lord GOD says: I will make you an empty city, like cities that have no people living in them. I will bring the deep ocean waters over you, and the Mediterranean Sea will cover you. [20]At that time I will send you down to the place of the dead to join those who died long ago. I will make you live with the dead below the earth in places that are like old ruins. You will not come back from there or have any place in the world of the living again. [21]Other people will be afraid of what happened to you, and it will be the

end of you. People will look for you, but they will never find you again, says the Lord GOD."

A Funeral Song for Tyre

27 The LORD spoke his word to me, saying: [2]"Human, sing a funeral song for the city

of Tyre. [3]Speak to Tyre, which has ports for the Mediterranean Sea and is a place for trade for the people of many lands along the sea coast. 'This is what the Lord GOD says:

Tyre, you have said,
"I am like a beautiful ship."
[4]You were at home on the high seas.
Your builders made your beauty perfect.
[5]They made all your boards
of fir trees from Mount Hermon.
They took a cedar tree from Lebanon
to make a ship's mast for you.
[6]They made your oars
from oak trees from Bashan.
They made your deck
from cypress trees from the coast of Cyprus
and set ivory into it.
[7]Your sail of linen with designs sewed on it
came from Egypt
and became like a flag for you.
Your cloth shades over the deck were blue
and purple
and came from the island of Cyprus.
[8]Men from Sidon and Arvad used oars to
row you.
Tyre, your skilled men were the sailors on
your deck.
[9]Workers of Byblos were with you,
putting caulk [n] in your ship's seams.
All the ships of the sea and their sailors
came alongside to trade with you.

[10]"Men of Persia, Lydia and Put
were warriors in your army
and hung their shields and helmets on your
sides.
They made you look beautiful.
[11]Men of Arvad and Cilicia
guarded your city walls all around.

Men of Gammad
were in your watchtowers
and hung their shields around your walls.
They made your beauty perfect.

[12]"People of Tarshish became traders for you because of your great wealth. They traded your goods for silver, iron, tin and lead. [13]"People of Greece, Tubal and Meshech became merchants for you. They traded your goods for slaves and things of bronze. [14]"People of Beth Togarmah traded your goods for work horses, war horses and mules. [15]"People of Rhodes became merchants for you, selling your goods on many coastal lands. They brought back ivory tusks and valuable black wood as your payment. [16]"People of Aram became traders for you, because you had so many good things to sell. They traded your goods for turquoise, purple cloth, cloth with designs sewed on, fine linen, coral and rubies. [17]"People of Judah and Israel became merchants for you. They traded your goods for wheat from Minnith, and for honey, olive oil and balm. [d] [18-19]"People of Damascus became traders for you because you have many good things and great wealth. They traded your goods for wine from Helbon, wool from Zahar and barrels of wine from Izal. They received wrought iron, cassia [d] and sugar cane in payment for your good things. [20]"People of Dedan became merchants for you, trading saddle blankets for riding. [21]"People of Arabia and all the rulers of Kedar became traders for you. They received lambs, rams and goats in payment for you. [22]" 'The merchants of Sheba and Raamah became merchants for you. They traded your goods for all the best spices, valuable gems and gold. [23]"People of Haran, Canneh and Eden and the traders of Sheba, Asshur and Kilmad became merchants for you. [24]They were paid with the best clothes, blue cloth, cloth with designs sewed on, carpets of many colours and tightly wound ropes.

[25]" 'Trading ships
carried the things you sold.
You were like a ship full of heavy cargo
in the middle of the sea.
[26]The men who rowed you
brought you out into the high seas,
but the east wind broke you to pieces
in the middle of the sea.
[27]Your wealth, your trade, your goods,
your seamen, your sailors, your workers,

---

caulk   Something like tar put between the boards of a ship to make it waterproof.

your traders, your warriors
and everyone else on board
sank into the sea
on the day your ship was wrecked.
²⁸The people on the shore shake with fear
when your sailors cry out.
²⁹All the men who row
leave their ships;
the seamen and the sailors of other ships
stand on the shore.
³⁰They cry loudly about you;
they cry very much.
They throw dust on their heads
and roll in ashes to show they are sad.
³¹They shave their heads for you,
and they put on rough cloth to show they
are upset.
They cry and sob for you;
they cry loudly.
³²And in their loud crying
they sing a funeral song for you:
"No one was ever destroyed like Tyre,
surrounded by the sea."
³³When the goods you traded went out over
the seas,
you met the needs of many nations.
With your great wealth and goods,
you made kings of the earth rich.
³⁴But now you are broken by the sea
and have sunk to the bottom.
Your goods and all the people on board
have gone down with you.
³⁵All those who live along the shore
are shocked by what happened to you.
Their kings are terribly afraid,
and their faces show their fear.
³⁶The traders among the nations hiss at you.
You have come to a terrible end,
and you are gone for ever.' "

Prophecy Against the King of Tyre

28 The LORD spoke his word to me, saying:
²"Human, say to the ruler of Tyre: 'This
is what the Lord GOD says:
because you are proud,
you say, "I am a god.
I sit on the throne of a god
in the middle of the seas."
You think you are as wise as a god,
but you are a human, not a god.
³You think you are wiser than Daniel.
You think you can find out all secrets.
⁴Through your wisdom and understanding
you have made yourself rich.
You have gained gold and silver
and have saved it in your storerooms.
⁵Through your great skill in trading,
you have made your riches grow.

You are too proud
because of your riches.

⁶" 'So this is what the Lord GOD says:
you think you are wise
like a god,
⁷but I will bring foreign people against you,
the cruellest nation.
They will pull out their swords
and destroy all that your wisdom has built,
and they will dishonour your greatness.
⁸They will kill you;
you will die a terrible death
like those who are killed at sea.
⁹While they are killing you,
you will not be able to say any more, "I am
a god."
You will be only a human, not a god,
when your murderers kill you.
¹⁰You will die like an unclean ᵈ person;
foreigners will kill you.

I have spoken, says the Lord God.' "

¹¹The LORD spoke his word to me, saying:
¹²"Human, sing a funeral song for the king of Tyre.
Say to him: 'This is what the Lord GOD says:
You were an example of what was perfect,
full of wisdom and perfect in beauty.
¹³You had a wonderful life,
as if you were in Eden, the garden of God.
Every valuable gem was on you:
ruby, topaz and emerald,
yellow quartz, onyx and jasper,
sapphire, turquoise and chrysolite.
Your jewellery was made of gold.
It was prepared on the day you were
created.
¹⁴I appointed a living creature to guard you.
I put you on the holy mountain of God.
You walked among the gems that shone
like fire.
¹⁵Your life was right and good
from the day you were created,
until evil was found in you.
¹⁶Because you traded with countries far away,
you learned to be cruel, and you sinned.
So I threw you down in disgrace from the
mountain of God.
And the living creature who guarded you
forced you out from among the gems that
shone like fire.
¹⁷You became too proud
because of your beauty.
You ruined your wisdom
because of your greatness.
I threw you down to the ground.
Your example taught a lesson to other
kings.

18You dishonoured your places of worship
through your many sins and dishonest
trade.
So I set on fire the place where you lived,
and the fire burned you up.
I turned you into ashes on the ground
for all those watching to see.
19All the nations who knew you
are shocked about you.
Your punishment was so terrible,
and you are gone for ever.' "

Prophecy Against Sidon

20The LORD spoke his word to me, saying:
21"Human, look towards the city of Sidon and
prophesy *d* against her. 22Say: 'This is what the
Lord GOD says:

I am against you, Sidon,
and I will show my glory among you.
People will know that I am the LORD
when I have punished Sidon;
I will show my holiness by defeating her.
23I will send diseases to Sidon,
and blood will flow in her streets.
Those who are wounded in Sidon will fall dead,
attacked from all sides.
Then they will know that I am the LORD.

God will Help Israel

24" 'No more will neighbouring nations be like
thorny branches or sharp thorns to hurt Israel.
Then they will know that I am the Lord GOD.
25" 'This is what the Lord GOD says: I will
gather the people of Israel from the nations where
they are scattered. I will show my holiness when
the nations see what I do for my people. Then
they will live in their own land—the land I gave
to my servant Jacob. 26They will live safely in the
land and will build houses and plant vineyards.
They will live in safety after I have punished all
the nations around who hate them. Then they
will know that I am the LORD their God.' "

Prophecy Against Egypt

29 It was the tenth year of our captivity, in
the tenth month, on the twelfth day of
the month. The LORD spoke his word to me,
saying: 2"Human, look towards the king of
Egypt, and prophesy *d* against him and all Egypt.
3Say: 'This is what the Lord GOD says:

I am against you, king of Egypt.
You are like a great crocodile that lies in
the Nile River.
You say, "The Nile is mine;
I made it for myself."
4But I will put hooks in your jaws,
and I will make the fish of the Nile stick to
your sides.

I will pull you up out of your rivers,
with all the fish sticking to your sides.
5I will leave you in the desert,
you and all the fish from your rivers.
You will fall onto the ground;
you will not be picked up or buried.
I have given you to the wild animals
and to the birds of the sky for food.
6Then all the people who live in Egypt will know
that I am the LORD.

" 'Israel tried to lean on you for help, but you
were like a crutch made out of a weak stalk of
grass. 7When their hands grabbed you, you splintered and tore open their shoulders. When they
leaned on you, you broke and made all their
backs twist.

8" 'So this is what the Lord GOD says: I
will cause an enemy to attack you and kill your
people and animals. 9Egypt will become an
empty desert. Then they will know that I am the
LORD.

" 'Because you said, "The Nile River is mine,
and I have made it," 10I am against you and your
rivers. I will destroy the land of Egypt and make
it an empty desert from Migdol in the north to
Aswan in the south, all the way to the border of
Cush. 11No person or animal will walk through it,
and no one will live in Egypt for 40 years. 12I will
make the land of Egypt the most deserted country
of all. Her cities will be the most deserted of all
ruined cities for 40 years. I will scatter the Egyptians among the nations, spreading them among
the countries.

13" 'This is what the Lord GOD says: after 40
years I will gather Egypt from the nations
where they have been scattered. 14I will bring
back the Egyptian captives and make them return to southern Egypt, to the land they came
from. They will become a weak kingdom there.
15It will be the weakest kingdom, and it will
never again rule other nations. I will make it so
weak it will never again rule over the nations.
16The Israelites will never again depend on
Egypt. Instead, Egypt's punishment will remind
the Israelites of their sin in turning to Egypt
for help. Then they will know that I am the
Lord GOD.' "

Egypt is Given to Babylon

17It was the first day of the first month of
the twenty-seventh year of our captivity. The
LORD spoke his word to me, saying: 18"Human,
Nebuchadnezzar king of Babylon made his army
fight hard against Tyre. Every soldier's head was
rubbed bare and every shoulder was rubbed raw.
But Nebuchadnezzar and his army gained nothing from fighting Tyre. 19So this is what the
Lord GOD says: I will give the land of Egypt to

Nebuchadnezzar king of Babylon. He will take away Egypt's people and its wealth and its treasures as pay for his army. ²⁰I am giving Nebuchadnezzar the land of Egypt as a reward for working hard for me, says the Lord GOD.

²¹"At that time I will make Israel grow strong again, and I will let you, Ezekiel, speak to them. Then they will know that I am the LORD."

Egypt will be Punished

30 The LORD spoke his word to me, saying: ²"Human, prophesy^d and say, 'This is what the Lord GOD says:
Cry and say,
  "The terrible day is coming."
³The day is near;
  the LORD's day of judging is near.
It is a cloudy day
  and a time when the nations will be judged.
⁴An enemy will attack Egypt,
  and Cush will tremble with fear.
When the killing begins in Egypt,
  her wealth will be taken away,
  and her foundations will be torn down.

⁵Cush, Put, Lydia, Arabia, Libya and some of my people who had made an agreement with Egypt will fall dead in war.
⁶" 'This is what the LORD says:
  those who fight on Egypt's side will fall.
  The power she is proud of will be lost.
The people in Egypt will fall dead in war
  from Migdol in the north to Aswan in the south,
  says the Lord GOD.
⁷They will be the most deserted lands.
  Egypt's cities will be the worst of cities that lie in ruins.
⁸Then they will know that I am the LORD
  when I set fire to Egypt
  and when all those nations on her side are crushed.
⁹" 'At that time I will send messengers in ships to frighten Cush, which now feels safe. The people of Cush will tremble with fear when Egypt is punished. And that time is sure to come.
¹⁰" 'This is what the Lord GOD says:
I will destroy great numbers of people in Egypt
  through the power of Nebuchadnezzar king of Babylon.
¹¹Nebuchadnezzar and his army,
  the cruellest army of any nation,
  will be brought in to destroy the land.
They will pull out their swords against Egypt
  and will fill the land with those they kill.

¹²I will make the streams of the Nile River become dry land,
  and then I will sell the land to evil people.
I will destroy the land and everything in it
  through the power of foreigners.

I, the LORD, have spoken.

Egypt's Idols are Destroyed

¹³" 'This is what the Lord GOD says:
I will destroy the idols
  and take away the statues of gods from the city of Memphis.
There will no longer be a leader in Egypt,
  and I will spread fear through the land of Egypt.
¹⁴I will make southern Egypt empty
  and start a fire in Zoan
  and punish Thebes.
¹⁵And I will pour out my anger against Pelusium,
  the stronghold of Egypt.
I will destroy great numbers of people in Thebes.
¹⁶I will set fire to Egypt.
  Pelusium will be in great pain.
The walls of Thebes will be broken open,
  and Memphis will have troubles every day.
¹⁷The young men of Heliopolis and Bubastis
  will fall dead in war,
  and the people will be taken away as captives.
¹⁸In Tahpanhes the day will be dark
  when I break Egypt's power.
Then she will no longer be proud of her power.
A cloud will cover Egypt,
  and her villages will be captured and taken away.
¹⁹So I will punish Egypt,
  and they will know I am the LORD.' "

Egypt Becomes Weak

²⁰It was in the eleventh year of our captivity, in the first month, on the seventh day of the month. The LORD spoke his word to me, saying: ²¹"Human, I have broken the powerful arm of the king of Egypt. It has not been tied up, so it will not get well. It has not been wrapped with a bandage, so it will not be strong enough to hold a sword in war. ²²So this is what the Lord GOD says: I am against the king of Egypt. I will break his arms, both the strong arm and the broken arm, and I will make the sword fall from his hand. ²³I will scatter the Egyptians among the nations, spreading them among the countries. ²⁴I will make the arms of the king of Babylon strong and put my sword in his hand. But I will break the arms of

the king of Egypt. Then when he faces the king of Babylon, he will cry out in pain like a dying person. ²⁵So I will make the arms of the king of Babylon strong, but the arms of the king of Egypt will fall. Then people will know that I am the LORD when I put my sword into the hand of the king of Babylon and he uses it in war against Egypt. ²⁶Then I will scatter the Egyptians among the nations, spreading them among the countries. Then they will know that I am the LORD."

A Cedar Tree

31 It was on the first day of the third month of the eleventh year of our captivity. The LORD spoke his word to me, saying: ²"Human, say to the king of Egypt and his people:

'No one is like you in your greatness.
³Assyria was once like a cedar tree in Lebanon
    with beautiful branches that shaded the
        forest.
It was very tall;
    its top was among the clouds.
⁴Much water made the tree grow;
    the deep springs made it tall.
Rivers flowed
    around the bottom of the tree
and sent their streams
    to all other trees in the countryside.
⁵So the tree was taller
    than all the other trees in the countryside.
Its limbs became long and big
    because of so much water.
⁶All the birds of the sky
    made their nests in the tree's limbs.
And all the wild animals
    gave birth under its branches.
All great nations
    lived in the tree's shade.
⁷So the tree was great and beautiful,
    with its long branches,
    because its roots reached down to much
        water.
⁸The cedar trees in the garden of God
    were not as great as it was.
The pine trees
    did not have such great limbs.
The plane trees
    did not have such branches.
No tree in the garden of God
    was as beautiful as this tree.
⁹I made it beautiful
    with many branches,
and all the trees of Eden in the garden
        of God
    wanted to be like it.

¹⁰"So this is what the Lord GOD says: the tree grew tall. Its top reached the clouds, and it

became proud of its height. ¹¹So I handed it over to a mighty ruler of the nations for him to punish it. Because it was evil, I got rid of it. ¹²The cruellest foreign nation cut it down and left it. The tree's branches fell on the mountains and in all the valleys, and its broken limbs were in all the ravines of the land. All the nations of the earth left the shade of that tree. ¹³The birds of the sky live on the fallen tree. The wild animals live among the tree's fallen branches. ¹⁴So the trees that grow by the water will not be proud to be tall; they will not put their tops among the clouds. None of the trees that are watered well will grow that tall, because they all are meant to die and go under the ground. They will be with people who have died and have gone down to the place of the dead.

¹⁵"This is what the Lord GOD says: on the day when the tree went down to the place of the dead, I made the deep springs cry loudly. I covered them and held back their rivers, and the great waters stopped flowing. I dressed Lebanon in black to show her sadness about the great tree, and all the trees in the countryside were sad about it. ¹⁶I made the nations shake with fear at the sound of the tree falling when I brought it down to the place of the dead. It went to join those who have gone down to the grave. Then all the trees of Eden and the best trees of Lebanon, all the well-watered trees, were comforted in the place of the dead below the earth. ¹⁷These trees had also gone down with the great tree to the place of the dead. They joined those who were killed in war and those among the nations who had lived under the great tree's shade.

¹⁸"So no tree in Eden is equal to you, Egypt, in greatness and honour, but you will go down to join the trees of Eden in the place below the earth. You will lie among unclean *ᵈ* people, with those who were killed in war.

"'This is about the king of Egypt and all his people, says the Lord GOD.'"

A Funeral Song

32 It was on the first day of the twelfth month of the twelfth year. The LORD spoke his word to me, saying: ²"Human, sing a funeral song about the king of Egypt. Say to him:

'You are like a young lion among the nations.
    You are like a crocodile in the seas.
You splash around in your streams
    and stir up the water with your feet,
    making the rivers muddy.

³"This is what the Lord GOD says:
I will spread my net over you,
    and I will use a large group of people
        to pull you up in my net.

⁴Then I will throw you on the land
　　dropping you onto the ground.
　I will let the birds of the sky rest on you
　　and all the animals of the earth eat you
　　　until they are full.
⁵I will scatter your flesh on the mountains
　　and fill the valleys with what is left
　　　of you.
⁶I will drench the land with your flowing
　　blood
　　as far as the mountains,
　　and the ravines will be full of your flesh.
⁷When I make you disappear,
　　I will cover the sky and make the stars
　　　dark.
　I will cover the sun with a cloud,
　　and the moon will not shine.
⁸I will make all the shining lights in the sky
　　become dark over you;
　I will bring darkness over your land,
　　says the Lord GOD.
⁹I will cause many people to be afraid
　　when I bring you as a captive into other
　　　nations,
　to lands you have not known.
¹⁰I will cause many people to be shocked
　　about you.
　Their kings will tremble with fear because
　　　of you
　　when I swing my sword in front of them.
　They will shake every moment
　　on the day you fall;
　　each king will be afraid for his own life.

¹¹" 'So this is what the Lord GOD says:
　the sword of the king of Babylon
　　will attack you.
¹²I will cause your people to fall
　　by the swords of mighty soldiers,
　　the most terrible in the world.
　They will destroy the pride of Egypt
　　and all its people.
¹³I will also destroy all Egypt's cattle
　　which live alongside much water.
　The foot of a human will not stir the water,
　　and the hoofs of cattle will not muddy it
　　　any more.
¹⁴So I will let the Egyptians' water become
　　clear.
　I will cause their rivers to run as smoothly
　　as olive oil,
　　says the Lord GOD.
¹⁵When I make the land of Egypt empty
　　and take everything that is in the land,
　when I destroy all those who live in Egypt,
　　then they will know that I am the LORD.'

¹⁶"This is the funeral song people will sing for
Egypt. The women of the nations will sing it; they
will sing a funeral song for Egypt and all its people, says the Lord GOD."

Egypt to be Destroyed

¹⁷It was in the twelfth year of our captivity, on
the fifteenth day of the month. The LORD spoke
his word to me, saying: ¹⁸"Human, cry for the
people of Egypt. Bring down Egypt, together with
the women of the powerful nations; bring them
down to the place of the dead below the earth to
join those who go to the place of the dead. ¹⁹Say
to them: 'Are you more beautiful than others?
Go and lie down in death with those who are unclean.' ᵈ ²⁰The Egyptians will fall among those
killed in war. The sword is ready; the enemy will
drag Egypt and all her people away. ²¹From the
place of the dead the leaders of the mighty ones
will speak about the king of Egypt and the nations
which help him: 'The unclean, those killed in
war, have come down here and lie dead.'

²²"Assyria and all its army lie dead there. The
graves of their soldiers are all around. All were
killed in war, ²³and their graves were put in the
deepest parts of the place of the dead. Assyria's
army lies around its grave. When they lived on
earth, they frightened people, but now all of them
have been killed in war.

²⁴"The nation of Elam is there with all its army
around its grave. All of them were killed in war.
They had frightened people on earth and were
unclean, so they went down to the lowest parts
of the place of the dead. They must carry their
shame with those who have gone down to the
place of the dead. ²⁵A bed has been made for
Elam with all those killed in war. The graves of
her soldiers are all around her. All Elam's people
are unclean, killed in war. They frightened people
when they lived on earth, but now they must
carry their shame with those who have gone
down to the place of the dead. Their graves are
with the rest who were killed.

²⁶"Meshech and Tubal are there with the
graves of all their soldiers around them. All of
them are unclean and have been killed in war.
They also frightened people when they lived on
earth. ²⁷But they are not buried with the other
soldiers who were killed in battle long ago, those
who went with their weapons of war to the place
of the dead. These soldiers had their swords laid
under their heads and their shields on their bodies. These mighty soldiers used to frighten people
when they lived on earth.

²⁸"You, king of Egypt, will be broken and lie
among those who are unclean, who were killed
in war.

²⁹"Edom is there also, with its kings and all its
leaders. They were mighty, but now they lie in
death with those killed in war, with those who

are unclean, with those who have gone down to the place of the dead.

30"All the rulers of the north and all the Sidonians are there. Their strength frightened people, but they have gone down in shame with those who were killed. They are unclean, lying with those killed in war. They carry their shame with those who have gone down to the place of the dead.

31"The king of Egypt and his army will see these who have been killed in war. Then he will be comforted for all his soldiers killed in war, says the Lord GOD. 32I made people afraid of the king of Egypt while he lived on earth. But he and all his people will lie among those who are unclean, who were killed in war, says the Lord GOD."

Ezekiel is Watchman for Israel

33 The LORD spoke his word to me, saying: 2"Human, speak to your people and say to them: 'Suppose I bring a war against a land. The people of the land may choose one of their men and make him their watchman. 3When he sees the enemy coming to attack the land, he will blow the trumpet and warn the people. 4If they hear the sound of the trumpet but do nothing, the enemy will come and kill them. They will be responsible for their own deaths. 5They heard the sound of the trumpet but didn't do anything. So they are to blame for their own deaths. If they had done something, they would have saved their own lives. 6But if the watchman sees the enemy coming to attack and does not blow the trumpet, the people will not be warned. Then if the enemy comes and kills any of them, they have died because of their own sin. But I will punish the watchman for their deaths.'

7"You, human, are the one I have made a watchman for Israel. If you hear a word from my mouth, you must warn them for me. 8Suppose I say to the wicked: 'Wicked people, you will surely die,' but you don't speak to warn the wicked to stop doing evil. Then they will die because they were sinners, but I will punish you for their deaths. 9But if you warn the wicked to stop doing evil and they do not stop, they will die because they were sinners. But you have saved your life.

10"So you, human, say to Israel: 'You have said: surely our law-breaking and sins are hurting us. They will kill us. What can we do so we will live?' 11Say to them: "The Lord GOD says: as surely as I live, I do not want any who are wicked to die. I want them to stop doing evil and live. Stop! Stop your wicked ways! You don't want to die, do you, people of Israel?'

12"Human, say to your people: 'The goodness of those who do right will not save them when

they sin. The evil of wicked people will not cause them to be punished if they stop doing it. If good people sin, they will not be able to live by the good they did earlier.' 13If I tell good people, "You will surely live," they might think they have done enough good and then do evil. Then none of the good things they did will be remembered. They will die because of the evil they have done. 14Or, if I say to the wicked people, "You will surely die," they may stop sinning and do what is right and honest. 15For example, they may return what somebody gave them as a promise to repay a loan, or pay back what they stole. If they live by the rules that give life and do not sin, then they will surely live, and they will not die. 16They will not be punished for any of their sins. They now do what is right and fair, so they will surely live.

17"Your people say: 'The way of the Lord is not fair.' But it is their own ways that are not fair. 18When the good people stop doing good and do evil, they will die for their evil. 19But when the wicked stop doing evil and do what is right and fair, they will live. 20You still say: 'The way of the Lord is not fair.' Israel, I will judge all of you by your own ways."

The Fall of Jerusalem Explained

21It was on the fifth day of the tenth month of the twelfth year. A person who had escaped from Jerusalem came to me and said, "Jerusalem has been captured." 22Now I had felt the power of the LORD on me the evening before. He had made me able to talk again before this person came to me. I could speak; I was not without speech any more.

23Then the LORD spoke his word to me, saying: 24"Human, people who live in the ruins in the land of Israel are saying: 'Abraham was only one person, yet he was given the land as his own. Surely the land has been given to us, who are many, as our very own.' 25So say to them: 'This is what the Lord GOD says: you eat meat with the blood still in it, you ask your idols for help and you murder people. Should you then have the land as your very own? 26You depend on your sword and do terrible things which I hate. Each of you has sexual relations with his neighbour's wife. So should you have the land?'

27"Say to them: 'This is what the Lord GOD says: as surely as I live, those who are among the city ruins in Israel will be killed in war. I will cause those who live in the country to be eaten by wild animals. People hiding in the strongholds *d* and caves will die of disease. 28I will make the land an empty desert. The people's pride in the land's power will end. The mountains of Israel will become empty so that no one will pass through them. [29]They will know that I am the LORD when I make the land an empty desert because of the things they have done that I hate.'

[30]"But as for you, human, your people are talking about you by the walls and in the doorways of houses. They say to each other: 'Come now, and hear the message from the LORD.' [31]So they come to you in crowds as if they were really ready to listen. They sit in front of you as if they were my people and hear your words, but they will not obey them. With their mouths they tell me they love me, but their hearts desire their selfish profits. [32]To your people you are nothing more than a singer who sings love songs and has a beautiful voice and plays a musical instrument well. They hear your words, but they will not obey them.

Sidelight   If Ezekiel were a preacher today, he would probably have a big following. Ezekiel 33:32 tells how people were so attracted to his style and his beautiful voice that they didn't hear his challenging message.

---

[33]"When this comes true, and it surely will happen, then the people will know that a prophet [d] has been among them."

The Leaders are Like Shepherds

34 The LORD spoke his word to me, saying: [2]"Human, prophesy [d] against the leaders of Israel, who are like shepherds. Prophesy and say to them: 'This is what the Lord GOD says: how terrible it will be for the shepherds of Israel who feed only themselves! Why don't the shepherds feed the flock? [3]You eat the milk curds, and you clothe yourselves with the wool. You kill the fat sheep, but you do not feed the flock. [4]You have not made the weak strong. You have not healed the sick or put bandages on those that were hurt. You have not brought back those who strayed away or searched for the lost. But you have ruled the sheep with cruel force. [5]The sheep were scattered, because there was no shepherd, and they became food for every wild animal. [6]My flock wandered over all the mountains and on every high hill. They were scattered all over the face of the earth, and no one searched or looked for them.

[7]"So, you shepherds, hear the word of the LORD. This is what the Lord GOD says: [8]As surely as I live, my flock has been caught and eaten by all the wild animals, because the flock has no shepherd. The shepherds did not search for my flock. No, they fed themselves instead of

my flock. [9]So, you shepherds, hear the word of the LORD. [10]This is what the Lord GOD says: I am against the shepherds. I will blame them for what has happened to my sheep and will not let them tend the flock any more. Then the shepherds will stop feeding themselves, and I will take my flock from their mouths so they will no longer be their food.

[11]"'This is what the Lord GOD says: I, myself, will search for my sheep and take care of them. [12]As a shepherd takes care of his scattered flock when it is found, I will take care of my sheep. I will save them from all the places where they were scattered on a cloudy and dark day. [13]I will bring them out from the nations and gather them from the countries. I will bring them to their own land and pasture them on the mountains of Israel, in the ravines and in all the places where people live in the land. [14]I will feed them in a good pasture, and they will eat grass on the high mountains of Israel. They will lie down on good ground where they eat grass, and they will eat in rich grassland on the mountains of Israel. [15]I will feed my flock and lead them to rest, says the Lord GOD. [16]I will search for the lost, bring back those that strayed away, put bandages on those that were hurt and make the weak strong. But I will destroy those sheep that are fat and strong. I will tend the sheep with fairness.

[17]"'This is what the Lord GOD says: as for you, my flock, I will judge between one sheep and another, between the rams and the male goats. [18]Is it not enough for you to eat grass in the good land? Must you crush the rest of the grass with your feet? Is it not enough for you to drink clear water? Must you make the rest of the water muddy with your feet? [19]Must my flock eat what you crush, and must they drink what you make muddy with your feet?

[20]"'So this is what the Lord GOD says to them: I, myself, will judge between the fat sheep and the thin sheep. [21]You push with your side and with your shoulder, and you knock down all the weak sheep with your horns until you have forced them away. [22]So I will save my flock; they will not be hurt any more. I will judge between one sheep and another. [23]Then I will put over them one shepherd, my servant David. He will feed them and tend them and be their shepherd. [24]Then I, the LORD, will be their God, and my servant David will be a ruler among them. I, the LORD, have spoken.

[25]"'I will make an agreement of peace with my sheep and will remove harmful animals from the land. Then the sheep will live safely in the desert and sleep in the woods. [26]I will bless them and let them live around my hill. I will cause the

rains to come when it is time; there will be showers to bless them. ²⁷Also the trees in the countryside will give their fruit, and the land will give its harvest. And the sheep will be safe on their land. Then they will know that I am the LORD when I break the bars of their captivity and save them from the power of those who made them slaves. ²⁸They will not be led captive by the nations again. The wild animals will not eat them, but they will live safely, and no one will make them afraid. ²⁹I will give them a place famous for its good crops, so they will no longer suffer from hunger in the land. They will not suffer the insults of other nations any more. ³⁰Then they will know that I, the LORD their God, am with them. The nation of Israel will know that they are my people, says the Lord GOD. ³¹You, my human sheep, are the sheep I care for, and I am your God, says the Lord GOD.' "

Prophecy Against Edom

35 The LORD spoke his word to me, saying: ²"Human, look towards Edom and prophesy *d* against it. ³Say to it: 'This is what the Lord GOD says: I am against you, Edom. I will stretch out my hand against you and make you an empty desert. ⁴I will destroy your cities, and you will become empty. Then you will know that I am the LORD.

⁵" 'You have always been an enemy of Israel. You let them be defeated in war when they were in trouble at the time of their final punishment. ⁶So the Lord GOD says, as surely as I live, I will let you be murdered. Murder will chase you. Since you did not hate murdering people, murder will chase you. ⁷I will make Edom an empty ruin and destroy everyone who goes in or comes out of it. ⁸I will fill its mountains with those who are killed. Those killed in war will fall on your hills,

SCHOOL

Abused Privileges

Jenny felt honoured to be selected for the Vocal Ensemble, a special choir at her school. The group was invited to compete at a national music festival, held at a big concert hall. After the performance, the judges gave the group top marks. Jenny felt proud to be a member.

The choir's director gave the singers some free time before returning home. Many of them felt pretty rowdy. How could they have fun?

First, they tried monopolising the lifts and escalators. Jenny joined in.

They began disrupting others who had come for the festival. Jenny did too.

Some invaded the cafeteria, where one member was kicked out after fooling around with some trays. Others dumped ash trays on the floor.

Finally, the manager of the hall demanded to see the teacher in charge. When she learned what was going on, she disbanded the Vocal Ensemble on the spot. "I gave you free time as a reward for performing well," she said angrily, "but you selfishly violated my trust and other people's rights."

Now Jenny is not so proud to have been a part of the Ensemble. "It's a memory that you wish wasn't a memory," she says.

Like the members of the Vocal Ensemble, God's people receive special honours and privileges. When God promised special gifts for his people in **Ezekiel 34:11–24**, he also warned them not to abuse them selfishly.

* What do this passage and Jenny's story have to say about selfishness?
* What gifts has God given to you that you must be careful not to abuse?

Consider . . .

* drawing four circles on a sheet of paper, one each for family, time, money and friends. In each circle, list one way in which you can be less selfish this coming week, and then put all four ideas into action.
* asking forgiveness from someone whose trust you've broken or with whom you've acted selfishly.

For more, see . . .

* Exodus 16:11–21 (p.75)
* 1 Corinthians 11:20–22 (p.1229)
* Mark 12:1–12 (p.1021)

in your valleys and in all your ravines. ⁹I will make you a ruin for ever; no one will live in your cities. Then you will know that I am the LORD.

¹⁰"'You said, "These two nations, Israel and Judah, and these two lands will be ours. We will take them for our own." But the LORD was there. ¹¹So this is what the Lord GOD says: As surely as I live, I will treat you just as you treated them. You were angry and jealous because you hated them. So I will punish you and show the Israelites who I am. ¹²Then you will know that I, the LORD, have heard all your insults against the mountains of Israel. You said, "They have been ruined. They have been given to us to eat." ¹³You have not stopped your proud talk against me. I have heard you. ¹⁴This is what the Lord GOD says: all the earth will be happy when I make you an empty ruin. ¹⁵You were happy when the land of Israel was ruined, but I will do the same thing to you. Mount Seir and all Edom, you will become an empty ruin. Then you will know that I am the LORD.'"

Israel to Come Home

36 "Human, prophesy*d* to the mountains of Israel and say: 'Mountains of Israel, hear the word of the LORD. ²This is what the Lord GOD says: the enemy has said about you, "Now the old places to worship gods have become ours."' ³So prophesy and say: "This is what the Lord GOD says: they have made you an empty ruin and have crushed you from all around. So you became a possession of the other nations. People have talked and whispered against you. ⁴So, mountains of Israel, hear the word of the Lord GOD. The Lord GOD speaks to the mountains, hills, ravines and valleys, to the empty ruins and abandoned cities that have been robbed and laughed at by the other nations. ⁵This is what the Lord GOD says: I speak in hot anger against the other nations. I speak against the people of Edom, who took my land for themselves with joy and with hate in their hearts. They forced out the people and took their pastureland.' ⁶So prophesy about the land of Israel and say to the mountains, hills, ravines and valleys: 'This is what the Lord GOD says: I speak in my jealous anger, because you have suffered the insults of the nations. ⁷So this is what the Lord GOD says: I promise that the nations around you will also have to suffer insults.

⁸"'But you, mountains of Israel, will grow branches and fruit for my people, who will soon come home. ⁹I am concerned about you; I am on your side. You will be ploughed, and seed will be planted in you. ¹⁰I will increase the number of people who live on you, all the people of Israel. The cities will have people living in them, and the

ruins will be rebuilt. ¹¹I will increase the number of people and animals living on you. They will grow and have many young. You will have people living on you as you did before, and I will make you better off than at the beginning. Then you will know that I am the LORD. ¹²I will cause my people Israel to walk on you and own you, and you will belong to them. You will never again take their children away from them.

¹³"'This is what the Lord GOD says: People say about you, "You eat people and take children from your nation." ¹⁴But you will not eat people any more or take away the children, says the Lord GOD. ¹⁵I will not make you listen to insults from the nations any more; you will not suffer shame from them any more. You will not cause your nation to fall any more, says the Lord GOD.'"

The LORD Acts for Himself

¹⁶The LORD spoke his word to me again, saying: ¹⁷"Human, when the nation of Israel was living in their own land, they made it unclean *d* by their ways and the things they did. Their ways were like a woman's uncleanness in her time of monthly bleeding. ¹⁸So I poured out my anger against them, because they murdered in the land and because they made the land unclean with their idols. ¹⁹I scattered them among the nations, and they were spread through the countries. I punished them for how they lived and what they did. ²⁰They dishonoured my holy name in the nations where they went. The nations said about them: 'These are the people of the LORD, but they had to leave the land which he gave them.' ²¹But I had concern for my holy name, which the nation of Israel had dishonoured among the nations where they went.

²²"So say to the people of Israel, 'This is what the Lord GOD says: Israel, I am going to act, but not for your sake. I will do something to help my holy name, which you have dishonoured among the nations where you went. ²³I will prove the holiness of my great name, which has been dishonoured among the nations. You have dishonoured it among these nations, but the nations will know that I am the LORD when I prove myself holy before their eyes, says the Lord GOD. ²⁴"'I will take you from the nations and gather you out of all the lands and bring you back into your own land. ²⁵Then I will sprinkle clean water on you, and you will be clean. I will cleanse you from all your uncleanness and your idols. ²⁶Also, I will teach you to respect me completely, and I will put a new way of thinking inside you. I will take out the stubborn hearts of stone from your bodies, and I will give you obedient hearts of flesh. ²⁷I will put my Spirit *d* inside you and help you live by my rules and carefully obey my laws.

[28]You will live in the land I gave to your ancestors, and you will be my people, and I will be your God. [29]So I will save you from all your uncleanness. I will command the grain to come and grow; I will not allow a time of hunger to hurt you. [30]I will increase the harvest of the field so you will never again suffer shame among the nations because of hunger. [31]Then you will remember your evil ways and actions that were not good, and you will hate yourselves because of your sins and your terrible acts that I hate. [32]I want you to know that I am not going to do this for your sake, says the Lord GOD. Be ashamed and embarrassed about your ways, Israel.

[33]" 'This is what the Lord GOD says: this is what will happen on the day I cleanse you from all your sins: I will cause the cities to have people living in them again, and the destroyed places will be rebuilt. [34]The empty land will be ploughed so it will no longer be a ruin for everyone who passes by to see. [35]They will say, "This land was ruined, but now it has become like the garden of Eden. The cities were destroyed, empty and ruined, but now they are protected and have people living in them." [36]Then those nations still around you will know that I, the LORD, have rebuilt what was destroyed and have planted what was empty. I, the LORD, have spoken, and I will do it.'

[37]"This is what the Lord GOD says: I will let myself be asked by the people of Israel to do this for them again: I will make their people grow in number like a flock. [38]They will be as many as the flocks brought to Jerusalem during her holy feasts. Her ruined cities will be filled with flocks of people. Then they will know that I am the LORD."

The Vision of Dry Bones

37 I felt the power of the LORD on me, and he brought me out by the Spirit[d] of the LORD and put me down in the middle of a valley. It was full of bones. [2]He led me around among the bones, and I saw that there were many bones in the valley and that they were very dry. [3]Then he asked me, "Human, can these bones live?"

I answered, "Lord GOD, only you know."

[4]He said to me, "Prophesy[d] to these bones and say to them, 'Dry bones, hear the word of the LORD. [5]This is what the Lord GOD says to the bones: I will cause breath to enter you so you will come to life. [6]I will put muscles on you and flesh on you and cover you with skin. Then I will put breath in you so you will come to life. Then you will know that I am the LORD.' "

[7]So I prophesied as I was commanded. While I prophesied, there was a noise and a rattling.

The bones came together, bone to bone. [8]I looked and saw muscles come on the bones, and flesh grew and skin covered the bones. But there was no breath in them.

[9]Then he said to me, "Prophesy to the wind.[n] Prophesy, human, and say to the wind, 'This is what the Lord GOD says: wind, come from the four winds, and breathe on these people who were killed so they can come back to life.' " [10]So I prophesied as the LORD commanded me. And the breath came into them, and they came to life and stood on their feet, a very large army.

[11]Then he said to me, "Human, these bones are like all the people of Israel. They say, 'Our bones are dried up, and our hope has gone. We are destroyed.' [12]So, prophesy and say to them, 'This is what the Lord GOD says: my people, I will open your graves and cause you to come up out of your graves. Then I will bring you into the land of Israel. [13]My people, you will know that I am the LORD when I open your graves and cause you to come up from them. [14]And I will put my Spirit inside you, and you will come to life. Then I will put you in your own land. And you will know that I, the LORD, have spoken and done it, says the LORD.' "

Judah and Israel Back Together

[15]The LORD spoke his word to me, saying, [16]"Human, take a stick and write on it, 'For Judah and all the Israelites with him.' Then take another stick and write on it, 'The stick of Ephraim, for Joseph and all the Israelites with him.' [17]Then join them together into one stick so they will be one in your hand.

[18]"When your people say to you, 'Explain to us what you mean by this,' [19]say to them, 'This is what the Lord GOD says: I will take the stick for Joseph and the tribes[d] of Israel with him, which is in the hand of Ephraim, and I will put it with the stick of Judah. I will make them into one stick, and they will be one in my hand.' [20]Hold the sticks on which you wrote these names in your hand so the people can see them. [21]Say to the people, 'This is what the Lord GOD says: I am going to take the people of Israel from among the nations where they have gone. I will gather them from all around and bring them into their own land. [22]I will make them one nation in the land, on the mountains of Israel. One king will rule all of them. They will never again be two nations; they will not be divided into two kingdoms any more. [23]They will not continue to make themselves unclean[d] by their idols, their statues of gods which I hate, or by their sins. I will save them from all the ways they sin and turn against

wind This Hebrew word could also mean "breath" or "spirit".

me, and I will make them clean. Then they will be my people, and I will be their God. ²⁴" 'My servant David will be their king, and they will all have one shepherd. They will live by my rules and obey my laws. ²⁵They will live on the land I gave to my servant Jacob, the land in which your ancestors lived. They will all live on the land for ever: they, their children and their grandchildren. David my servant will be their king for ever. ²⁶I will make an agreement of peace with them, an agreement that continues for ever. I will put them in their land and make them grow in number. Then I will put my Temple *d* among them for ever. ²⁷The place where I live will be with them. I will be their God, and they will be my people. ²⁸When my Temple is among them for ever, the nations will know that I, the LORD, make Israel holy.' "

Prophecy Against Gog

38 The LORD spoke his word to me, saying, ²"Human, look towards Gog of the land of Magog, the chief ruler of the nations of

> **Sidelight**   Ezekiel 38 and 39 give
> a prophecy about Gog
> and Magog, an unknown invading king and
> nation who will attack Israel. In Revelation
> 20:7–10 (p.1403), John continues this prophecy
> by telling of the ultimate defeat of this enemy.

Meshech and Tubal. Prophesy *d* against him ³and say, 'The Lord GOD says this: I am against you, Gog, chief ruler of Meshech and Tubal. ⁴I will turn you around and put hooks in your jaws. And I will bring you out with all your army, horses and horsemen, all of whom will be dressed in beautiful uniforms. They will be a large army with large and small shields and all having swords. ⁵Persia, Cush and Put will be with them, all of them having shields and helmets. ⁶There will also be Gomer with all its troops and the nation of Togarmah from the far north with all its troops— many nations with you.

⁷" 'Be prepared. Be prepared, you and all the armies that have come together to make you their commander. ⁸After a long time you will be called for service. After those years you will come into a land that has been rebuilt from war. The people in the land will have been gathered from many nations to the mountains of Israel, which were empty for a long time. These people were brought out from the nations, and they will all be living in safety. ⁹You will come like a storm. You, all your troops, and the many nations with you will be like a cloud covering the land.

¹⁰" 'This is what the Lord GOD says: at that time ideas will come into your mind, and you will think up an evil plan. ¹¹You will say, "I will march against a land of towns without walls. I will attack those who are at rest and live in safety. All of them live without city walls or gate bars or gates. ¹²I will capture treasures and take valuable things. I will turn my power against the rebuilt ruins that now have people living in them. I will attack these people who have been gathered from the nations, who have become rich with farm animals and property, who live at the centre of the world." ¹³Sheba, Dedan and the traders of Tarshish, with all its villages, will say to you, "Did you come to capture treasure? Did you bring your troops together to take valuable things? Did you bring them to carry away silver and gold and to take away farm animals and property?" '

¹⁴"So prophesy, human, and say to Gog, 'This is what the Lord GOD says: now that my people Israel are living in safety, you will know about it. ¹⁵You will come with many people from your place in the far north. You will have a large group with you, a mighty army, all riding on horses. ¹⁶You will attack my people Israel like a cloud that covers the land. This will happen in the days to come when I bring you against my land. Gog, then the nations will know me when they see me prove how holy I am in what I do through you.

¹⁷" 'This is what the Lord GOD says: You are the one about whom I spoke in past days. I spoke through my servants, the prophets of Israel, who prophesied for many years that I would bring you against them. ¹⁸This is what will happen: on the day Gog attacks the land of Israel, I will become very angry, says the Lord GOD. ¹⁹With jealousy and great anger I tell you that at that time there will surely be a great earthquake in Israel. ²⁰The fish of the sea, the birds of the sky, the wild animals, everything that crawls on the ground and all the people on the earth will shake with fear before me. Also, the mountains will be thrown down, the cliffs will fall and every wall will fall to the ground. ²¹Then I will call for a war against Gog on all my mountains, says the Lord GOD. Everyone's sword will attack the soldier next to him. ²²I will punish Gog with disease and death. I will send a heavy rain with hailstones and burning sulphur on Gog, his army and the many nations with him. ²³Then I will show how great I am. I will show my holiness, and I will make myself known to the many nations that watch. Then they will know that I am the LORD.'

The Death of Gog and His Army

39 "Human, prophesy *d* against Gog and say, 'This is what the Lord GOD says: I am against you, Gog, chief ruler of Meshech and Tubal.

2I will turn you around and lead you. I will bring you from the far north and send you to attack the mountains of Israel. 3I will knock your bow out of your left hand and throw down your arrows from your right hand. 4You, all your troops and the nations with you will fall dead on the mountains of Israel. I will let you be food for every bird that eats meat and for every wild animal. 5You will lie fallen on the ground, because I have spoken, says the Lord GOD. 6I will send fire on Magog and those who live in safety on the coastal lands. Then they will know that I am the LORD.

7" 'I will make myself known among my people Israel, and I will not let myself be dishonoured any more. Then the nations will know that I am the LORD, the Holy One in Israel. 8It is coming! It will happen, says the Lord GOD. The time I talked about is coming.

9" 'Then those who live in the cities of Israel will come out and make fires with the enemy's weapons. They will burn them, both large and small shields, bows and arrows, war clubs and spears. They will use the weapons to burn in their fires for seven years. 10They will not need to take wood from the field or chop firewood from the forests, because they will make fires with the weapons. In this way they will take the treasures of those who took their treasures; they will take the valuable things of those who took their valuable things, says the Lord GOD.

11" 'At that time I will give Gog a burial place in Israel, in the Valley of the Travellers, east of the Dead Sea. d It will block the road for travellers. Gog and all his army will be buried there, so people will call it The Valley of Gog's Army.

12" 'The people of Israel will be burying them for seven months to make the land clean d again. 13All the people in the land will bury them, and they will be honoured on the day of my victory, says the Lord GOD.

14" 'The people of Israel will choose men to work through the land to make it clean. Along with others, they will bury Gog's soldiers still lying dead on the ground. After the seven months are finished, they will still search. 15As they go through the land, anyone who sees a human bone is to put a marker by it. The sign will stay there until the gravediggers bury the bone in The Valley of Gog's Army. 16A city will be there named Hamonah. So they will make the land clean again.'

17"Human, this is what the Lord GOD says: speak to every kind of bird and wild animal: 'Come together, come! Come together from all around to my sacrifice, a great sacrifice which I will prepare for you on the mountains of Israel. Eat flesh and drink blood! 18You are to eat the flesh of the mighty and drink the blood of the rulers of the earth as if they were fat animals from Bashan: rams, lambs, goats and bulls. 19You are to eat and drink from my sacrifice which I have prepared for you, eating fat until you are full and drinking blood until you are drunk. 20At my table you are to eat until you are full of horses and riders, mighty men and all kinds of soldiers,' says the Lord GOD.

21"I will show my glory among the nations. All the nations will see my power when I punish them. 22From that time onwards the people of Israel will know that I am the LORD their God. 23The nations will know Israel was taken away captive because they turned against me. So I turned away from them and handed them over to their enemies until all of them died in war. 24Because of their uncleanness d and their sins, I punished them and turned away from them.

25"So this is what the Lord GOD says: Now I will bring the people of Jacob back from captivity, and I will have mercy on the whole nation of Israel. I will not let them dishonour me. 26The people will forget their shame and how they rejected me when they live again in safety on their own land with no one to make them afraid. 27I will bring the people back from other lands and gather them from the lands of their enemies. So I will use my people to show many nations that I am holy. 28Then my people will know that I am the LORD their God, because I sent them into captivity among the nations, but then I brought them back to their own land, leaving no one behind. 29I will not turn away from them any more, because I will put my Spirit d into the people of Israel, says the Lord GOD."

The New Temple

40 It was the twenty-fifth year of our captivity, at the beginning of the year, on the tenth day of the month. It was in the fourteenth year after Jerusalem was captured. On that same day I felt the power of the LORD, and he brought me to Jerusalem. 2In the visions of God he brought me to the land of Israel and put me down on a very high mountain. On the south of the mountain there were some buildings that looked like a city. 3He took me closer to the buildings, and I saw a man who looked as if he were made of bronze, standing in the gateway. He had a cord made of linen and a stick in his hand, both for measuring. 4The man said to me, "Human, look with your eyes and hear with your ears. Pay attention to all that I will show you, because that's why you have been brought here. Tell the people of Israel all that you see."

The East Gateway

[5]I saw a wall that surrounded the Temple[d] area. The measuring stick in the man's hand was 3 metres long. So the man measured the wall, which was 3 metres thick and 3 metres high.

[6]Then the man went to the east gateway. He went up its steps and measured the opening of the gateway. It was 3 metres deep. [7]The rooms for the guards were 3 metres long and 3 metres wide. The walls that came out between the guards' rooms were about 2.5 metres thick. The opening of the gateway next to the porch that faced the Temple was 3 metres deep. [8]Then the man measured the porch of the gateway. [9]It was about 4.5 metres deep, and its side walls were a metre thick. The porch of the gateway faced the Temple.

[10]On each side of the east gateway were three rooms, which measured the same on each side. The walls between each room were the same thickness. [11]The man measured the width of the entrance to the gateway, which was 5 metres wide. The width of the gate was about 6.5 metres. [12]And there was a low wall about 50 centimetres high in front of each room. The rooms were 3 metres on each side. [13]The man measured the gateway from the roof of one room to the roof of the opposite room. It was about 12.5 metres from one door to the opposite door. [14]The man also measured the porch, which was about 10 metres wide. The courtyard was around the porch. [15]From the front of the outer side of the gateway to the front of the porch of the inner side of the gateway was 25 metres. [16]The rooms and porch had small windows on both sides. The windows were narrower on the side facing the gateway. Carvings of palm trees were on each side wall of the rooms.

The Outer Courtyard

[17]Then the man brought me into the outer courtyard where I saw rooms and a pavement of stones all around the court. Thirty rooms were along the edge of the paved walkway. [18]The pavement ran alongside the gates and was as deep as the gates were wide. This was the lower pavement. [19]Then the man measured from the outer wall to the inner wall. The outer court between these two walls was 50 metres on the east and on the north.

The North Gateway

[20]The man measured the length and width of the north gateway leading to the outer courtyard. [21]Its three rooms on each side, its inner walls and its porch measured the same as the first gateway. It was 25 metres long and 12.5 metres wide. [22]Its windows, porch and carvings of palm trees measured the same as the east gateway. Seven steps went up to the gateway, and the gateway's porch was at the inner end. [23]The inner courtyard had a gateway across from the northern gateway like the one on the east. The man measured it and found it was 50 metres from inner gateway to outer gateway.

The South Gateway

[24]Then the man led me south where I saw a gateway facing south. He measured its inner walls and its porch, and they measured the same as the other gateways. [25]The gateway and its porch had windows all around like the other gateways. It was 25 metres long and 12.5 metres wide. [26]Seven steps went up to this gateway. Its porch was at the inner end, and it had carvings of palm trees on its inner walls. [27]The inner courtyard had a gateway on its south side. The man measured from gate to gate on the south side, which was 50 metres.

The Inner Courtyard

[28]Then the man brought me through the south gateway into the inner courtyard. The inner south gateway measured the same as the gateways in the outer wall. [29]The inner south gateway's rooms, inner walls and porch measured the same as the gateways in the outer wall. There were windows all around the gateway and its porch. The gateway was 25 metres long and 12.5 metres wide. [30]Each porch of each inner gateway was about 15 metres long and about 2.5 metres wide. [31]The inner south gateway's porch faced the outer courtyard. Carvings of palm trees were on its side walls, and its stairway had eight steps.

[32]The man brought me into the inner courtyard on the east side. He measured the inner east gateway, and it was the same as the other gateways. [33]The inner east gateway's rooms, inside walls and porch measured the same as the other gateways. Windows were all around the gateway and its porch. The inner east gateway was 25 metres long and 12.5 metres wide. [34]Its porch faced the outer courtyard. Carvings of palm trees were on its inner walls on each side, and its stairway had eight steps.

35Then the man brought me to the inner north gateway. He measured it, and it was the same as the other gateways. 36Its rooms, inner walls and porch measured the same as the other gateways. There were windows all around the gateway, which was 25 metres long and 12.5 metres wide. 37Its porch faced the outer courtyard. Carvings of palm trees were on its inner walls on each side, and its stairway had eight steps.

Rooms for Preparing Sacrifices

38There was a room with a door that opened onto the porch of the inner north gateway. In this room the priests washed animals for the burnt offerings. 39There were two tables on each side of the porch, on which animals for burnt offerings, sin offerings and penalty offerings were killed. 40Outside, by each side wall of the porch, at the entrance to the north gateway, were two more tables. 41So there were four tables inside the gateway, and four tables outside. In all there were eight tables on which the priests killed animals for sacrifices. 42There were four tables made of cut stone for the burnt offering. These tables were about 75 centimetres long, 75 centimetres wide and about 50 centimetres high. On these tables the priests put their tools which they used to kill animals for burnt offerings and the other sacrifices. 43Double shelves 8 centimetres wide were put up on all the walls. The flesh for the offering was put on the tables.

The Priests' Rooms

44There were two rooms in the inner courtyard. One was beside the north gateway and faced south. The other room was beside the south gateway and faced north. 45The man said to me, "The room which faces south is for the priests who serve in the Temple d area, 46while the room that faces north is for the priests who serve at the altar. This second group of priests are descendants d of Zadok, the only descendants of Levi who can come near the LORD to serve him."

47The man measured the inner courtyard. It was a square—50 metres long and 50 metres wide. The altar was in front of the Temple.

The Temple Porch

48The man brought me to the porch of the Temple d and measured each side wall of the porch. Each was about 2.5 metres thick. The doorway was 7 metres wide. The side walls of the doorway were each about 1.5 metres wide. 49The porch was 10 metres long and 6 metres wide, with ten steps leading up to it. Pillars were by the side walls, one on each side of the entrance.

The Holy Place of the Temple

41 The man brought me to the Holy Place and measured its side walls, which were each 3 metres thick. 2The entrance was 5 metres wide. The walls alongside the entrance were each about 2.5 metres wide. The man measured the Holy Place, which was 25 metres long and 10 metres wide.

3Then the man went inside and measured the side walls of the next doorway. Each was a metre thick. The doorway was 3 metres wide, and the walls next to it were each more than 3.5 metres thick. 4Then the man measured the room at the end of the Holy Place. It was 10 metres long and 10 metres wide. The man said to me, "This is the Most Holy Place."

5Then the man measured the wall of the Temple, d which was 3 metres thick. There were side rooms 2 metres wide all around the Temple. 6The side rooms were on three different storeys, each above the other, with 30 rooms on each storey. All around the Temple walls there were ledges for the side rooms. The upper rooms rested on the ledges but were not attached to the Temple walls. 7The side rooms around the Temple were wider on each higher storey, so rooms were wider on the top storey. A stairway went up from the lowest storey to the highest through the middle storey.

8I also saw that the Temple had a raised base all around. Its edge was the foundation for the side rooms, and it was 3 metres thick. 9The outer wall of the side rooms was about 2.5 metres thick. There was an open area between the side rooms of the Temple 10and some other rooms. It was 10 metres wide and went all around the Temple. 11The side rooms had doors which led to the open area around the outside of the Temple. One door faced north, and the other faced south. The open area was about 2.5 metres wide all around.

12The building facing the private area at the west side was 35 metres wide. The wall around the building was about 2.5 metres thick and 45 metres long.

13Then the man measured the Temple. It was 50 metres long. The private area, including the building and its walls, was in all 50 metres long. 14Also the front of the Temple and the private area on its east side were 50 metres wide.

15The man measured the length of the building facing the private area on the west side, and it was 50 metres from one wall to the other. The Holy Place, the Most Holy Place and the outer porch 16had wood panels on the walls. By the doorway, the Temple had wood panels on the walls. The wood covered all the walls from the floor up to the windows, [17]up to the part of the wall above the entrance.

All the walls inside the Most Holy Place and the Holy Place, and on the outside, in the porch, [18]had carvings of creatures with wings and palm trees. A palm tree was between each carved creature, and every creature had two faces. [19]One was a human face looking towards the palm tree on one side. The other was a lion's face looking towards the palm tree on the other side. They were carved all around the Temple walls. [20]From the floor to above the entrance, palm trees and creatures with wings were carved. The walls of the Holy Place [21]had square doorposts. In front of the Most Holy Place was something that looked like [22]an altar of wood. It was 1.5 metres high and 1 metre wide. Its corners, base and sides were wood. The man said to me, "This is the table that is in the presence of the LORD." [23]Both the Holy Place and the Most Holy Place had double doors. [24]Each of the doors had two pieces that would swing open. [25]Carved on the doors of the Holy Place were palm trees and creatures with wings, like those carved on the walls. And there was a wooden roof over the front Temple porch. [26]There were windows and palm trees on both side walls of the porch. The side rooms of the Temple were also covered by a roof over the stairway.

The Priests' Rooms

42 Then the man led me north out into the outer courtyard and to the rooms across from the private area and the building. [2]These rooms on the north side were 50 metres long and 25 metres wide. [3]There was 10 metres of the inner courtyard between them and the Temple. On the other side, they faced the stone pavement of the outer courtyard. The rooms were built in three storeys like steps and had balconies. [4]There was a path on the north side of the rooms, which was 5 metres wide and 50 metres long. Doors led into the rooms from this path. [5]The top rooms were narrower, because the balconies took more space from them. The rooms on the first and second storeys of the building were wider. [6]The rooms were on three storeys. They did not have pillars like the pillars of the courtyards. So the top rooms were farther back than those on the first and second storeys. [7]There was a wall outside parallel to the rooms and to the outer courtyard. It ran in front of the rooms for 25 metres. [8]The row of rooms along the outer courtyard was 25 metres long, and the rooms that faced the Temple were about 50 metres long. [9]The lower rooms had an entrance on the east side so a person could enter them from the outer courtyard, [10]at the start of the wall beside the courtyard.

There were rooms on the south side, which were across from the private area and the building. [11]These rooms had a path in front of them. They were like the rooms on the north with the same length and width and the same doors. [12]The doors of the south rooms were like the doors of the north rooms. There was an entrance at the open end of a path beside the wall, so a person could enter at the east end.

[13]The man said to me, "The north and south rooms across from the private area are holy rooms. There the priests who go near the LORD will eat the most holy offerings. There they will put the most holy offerings—the grain offerings, sin offerings and penalty offerings—because the place is holy. [14]The priests who enter the Holy Place must leave their serving clothes there before they go into the outer courtyard, because these clothes are holy. After they put on other clothes, they may go to the part of the Temple area which is for the people."

Outside the Temple Area

[15]When the man finished measuring inside the Temple [d] area, he brought me out through the east gateway. He measured the area all around. [16]The man measured the east side with the measuring stick; it was 250 metres by the measuring stick. [17]He measured the north side; it was 250 metres by the measuring stick. [18]He measured the south side; it was 250 metres by the measuring stick. [19]He went around to the west side; it measured 250 metres by the measuring stick. [20]So he measured the Temple area on all four sides. The Temple area had a wall all around it that was 250 metres long and 250 metres wide. It separated what was holy from that which was not holy.

The LORD Among His People

43 Then the man led me to the outer east gateway, [2]and I saw the glory of the God of Israel coming from the east. It sounded like the roar of rushing water, and its brightness made the earth shine. [3]The vision I saw was like the vision I had seen when the LORD came to destroy the city and also like the vision I had seen by the Kebar River. I bowed face down on the ground. [4]The glory of the LORD came into the Temple [d] area through the east gateway. [5]Then the Spirit [d] picked me up and brought me into the inner courtyard. There I saw the LORD's glory filling the Temple. [6]As the man stood at my side, I heard someone speaking to me from inside the Temple. [7]The voice from the Temple said to me, "Human, this is my throne and the place where my feet rest. I will live here among the Israelites for ever. The people of Israel will not make my holy name unclean [d] again. Neither the people nor their kings will make it unclean with their sexual sins or with the dead bodies of their kings. 8The kings made my name unclean by putting their doorway next to my doorway, and their doorpost next to my doorpost so only a wall separated me from them. When they did their acts that I hate, they made my holy name unclean, and so I destroyed them in my anger. 9Now let them stop their sexual sins and take the dead bodies of their kings far away from me. Then I will live among them for ever.

10"Human, tell the people of Israel about the Temple so they will be ashamed of their sins. Let them think about the plan of the Temple. 11If they are ashamed of all they have done, let them know the design of the Temple and how it is built. Show them its exits and entrances, all its designs and also all its rules and teachings. Write the rules as they watch so they will obey all the teachings and rules about the Temple. 12This is the teaching about the Temple: all the area around the top of the mountain is most holy. This is the teaching about the Temple.

The Altar

13"These are the measurements of the altar, using the measuring stick. The altar's rim is 50 centimetres high and 50 centimetres wide, and its rim is about 25 centimetres around its edge. And the altar is this tall: 14from the ground up to the lower ledge, it measures 1 metre. It is 50 centimetres wide. It measures 2 metres from the smaller ledge to the larger ledge and is 50 centimetres wide. 15The place where the sacrifice is burned on the altar is 2 metres high, with its four corners shaped like horns and reaching up above it. 16It is square, 6 metres long and 6 metres wide. 17The upper ledge is also square, 7 metres long and 7 metres wide. The rim around the altar is 25 centimetres wide, and its border is 50 centimetres wide all around. Its steps are on the east side."

18Then the man said to me, "Human, this is what the Lord GOD says: these are the rules for the altar. When it is built, use these rules to offer burnt offerings and to sprinkle blood on it. 19You must give a young bull as a sin offering to the priests, the Levites who are from the family of Zadok and who come near me to serve me, says the Lord GOD. 20Take some of the bull's blood and put it on the four corners of the altar, on the four corners of the ledge, and all around the rim. This is how you will make the altar pure and ready for God's service. 21Then take the bull for the sin offering and burn it in the proper place in the Temple d area, outside the Temple building.

22"On the second day offer a male goat that has nothing wrong with it for a sin offering. The priests will make the altar pure and ready for God's service as they did with the young bull. 23When you finish making the altar pure and ready, offer a young bull and a ram from the flock, both without defect. 24You must offer them in the presence of the LORD, and the priests are to throw salt on them and offer them as a burnt offering to the LORD.

25"You must prepare a goat every day for seven days as a sin offering. Also, the priests must prepare a young bull and ram from the flock, both without defect. 26For seven days the priests are to make the altar pure and ready for God's service. Then they will give the altar to God. 27After these seven days, on the eighth day, the priests must offer your burnt offerings and your fellowship offerings on the altar. Then I will accept you, says the Lord GOD."

The Outer East Gate

44 Then the man brought me back to the outer east gateway of the Temple d area, but the gate was shut. 2The LORD said to me, "This gate will stay shut; it will not be opened. No one may enter through it, because the LORD God of Israel has entered through it. So it must stay shut. 3Only the ruler himself may sit in the gateway to eat a meal in the presence of the LORD. He must enter through the porch of the gateway and go out the same way."

4Then the man brought me through the outer north gate to the front of the Temple. As I looked, I saw the glory of the LORD filling the Temple of the LORD, and I bowed face down on the ground.

5The LORD said to me, "Human, pay attention. Use your eyes to see, and your ears to hear. See and hear everything I tell you about all the rules and teachings of the Temple of the LORD. Pay attention to the entrance to the Temple and to all the exits from the Temple area. 6Then speak to those who refuse to obey. Say to the people of Israel, 'This is what the Lord GOD says: Stop doing all your acts that I hate, Israel! 7You brought foreigners into my Holy Place who were not circumcised d in the flesh and had not given themselves to serving me. You dishonoured my Temple when you offered me food, fat and blood. You broke my agreement by all the things you did that I hate. 8You did not take care of my holy things yourselves but put foreigners in charge of my Temple. 9This is what the Lord GOD says: foreigners who are not circumcised in the flesh and who do not give themselves to serving me may not enter my Temple. Not even a foreigner living among the people of Israel may enter.

¹⁰" 'But the Levites who stopped obeying me when Israel left me and who followed their idols must be punished for their sin. ¹¹These Levites are to be servants in my Holy Place. They may guard the gates of the Temple and serve in the Temple area. They may kill the animals for the burnt offering and the sacrifices for the people. They may stand before the people to serve them. ¹²But these Levites helped the people worship their idols and caused the people of Israel to fall, so I make this promise: they will be punished for their sin, says the Lord GOD. ¹³They will not come near me to serve as priests, nor will they come near any of my holy things or the most holy offerings. But they will be made ashamed of the things they did that I hate. ¹⁴I will put them in charge of taking care of the Temple area, all the work that must be done in it.

¹⁵" 'But the priests who are Levites and descendants *d* of Zadok took care of my Holy Place when Israel left me, so they may come near to serve me. They may stand in my presence to offer me the fat and blood of the animals they sacrifice, says the Lord GOD. ¹⁶They are the only ones who may enter my Holy Place. Only they may come near my table to serve me and take care of the things I gave them to do.

¹⁷" 'When they enter the gates of the inner courtyard, they must wear linen robes. They must not wear wool to serve at the gates of the inner courtyard or in the Temple. ¹⁸They will wear linen turbans on their heads and linen underclothes. They will not wear anything that makes them perspire. ¹⁹When they go out into the outer courtyard to the people, they must take off their serving clothes before they go. They must leave these clothes in the holy rooms and put on other clothes. Then they will not let their holy clothes hurt the people.

²⁰" 'They must not shave their heads or let their hair grow long but must keep the hair of their heads trimmed. ²¹None of the priests may drink wine when they enter the inner courtyard. ²²The priests must not marry widows or divorced women. They may marry only virgins *d* from the people of Israel or widows of priests. ²³They must teach my people the difference between what is holy and what is not holy. They must help my people know what is unclean *d* and what is clean.

²⁴" 'In court they will act as judges. When they judge, they will follow my teachings. They must obey my laws and my rules at all my special feasts and keep my Sabbaths *d* holy.

²⁵" 'They must not go near a dead person, making themselves unclean. *d* But they are allowed to make themselves unclean if the dead person is their father, mother, son, daughter, brother or a sister who has not married. ²⁶After a priest has been made clean again, he must wait seven days. ²⁷Then he may go into the inner courtyard to serve in the Temple, but he must offer a sin offering for himself, says the Lord GOD.

²⁸" 'These are the rules about the priests and their property: they will have me instead of property. You will not give them any land to own in Israel; I am what they will own. ²⁹They will eat the grain offerings, sin offerings and penalty offerings. Everything Israel gives to me will be theirs. ³⁰The best fruits of all the first harvests and all the special gifts offered to me will belong to the priests. You will also give to the priests the first part of your grain that you grind and so bring a blessing on your family. ³¹The priests must not eat any bird or animal that died a natural death or one that has been torn by wild animals.

The Land is Divided

45 " 'When you divide the land for the Israelite tribes *d* by throwing lots, *d* you must give a part of the land to belong to the LORD. It will be about 12 kilometres long and about 10 kilometres wide; all of this land will be holy. ²From this land, an area 250 metres square will be for the Temple. *d* There will be an open space around the Temple that is 250 metres wide. ³In the holy area you will measure a part about 12 kilometres long and 5 kilometres wide, and in it will be the Most Holy Place. ⁴This holy part of the land will be for the priests who serve in the Temple, who come near to the LORD to serve him. It will be a place for the priests' houses and for the Temple. ⁵Another area about 12 kilometres long and more than 5 kilometres wide will be for the Levites, who serve in the Temple area. It will belong to them so they will have cities in which to live.

⁶" 'You must give the city an area that is about 2.5 kilometres wide and about 12 kilometres long, along the side of the holy area. It will belong to all the people of Israel.

⁷" 'The ruler will have land on both sides of the holy area and the city. On the west of the holy area, his land will reach to the Mediterranean Sea. On the east of the holy area, his land will reach to the eastern border. It will be as long as the land given to each tribe. ⁸Only this land will be the ruler's property in Israel. So my rulers will not be cruel to my people any more, but they will let each tribe in the nation of Israel have its share of the land.

⁹" 'This is what the Lord GOD says: You have gone far enough, you rulers of Israel! Stop being cruel and hurting people, and do what is right and fair. Stop forcing my people out of their homes, says the Lord GOD. ¹⁰You must have honest scales, an honest dry measurement and

an honest liquid measurement. [11]The dry measure and the liquid measure will be the same: the liquid measure will always be a tenth of a homer, [n] and the ephah will always be a tenth of a homer. The measurement they follow will be the homer. [12]The shekel [n] will be worth 20 gerahs, and a mina will be worth 60 shekels.

Offerings and Holy Days

[13]" 'This is the gift you should offer: one sixtieth of your harvest of wheat, and one sixtieth of your harvest of barley. [14]The amount of oil you are to offer is one-hundredth of your harvest. (Ten baths make a homer and also make a cor.) [15]You should give one sheep from each flock of 200 from the watering places of Israel. All these are to be offered for the grain offerings, burnt offerings and fellowship offerings to remove sins so you will belong to God, says the Lord GOD. [16]All people in the land will give this special offering to the ruler of Israel. [17]It will be the ruler's responsibility to supply the burnt offerings, grain offerings and drink offerings. These offerings will be given at the feasts, at the New Moons, [d] on the Sabbaths [d] and at all the other feasts of Israel. The ruler will supply the sin offerings, grain offerings and fellowship offerings to pay for the sins of Israel.

[18]" 'This is what the Lord GOD says: on the first day of the first month take a young bull without defect. Use it to make the Temple [d] pure and ready for God's service. [19]The priest will take some of the blood from this sin offering and put it on the doorposts of the Temple, on the four corners of the ledge of the altar and on the posts of the gate to the inner courtyard. [20]You will do the same thing on the seventh day of the month for anyone who has sinned by accident or without knowing it. This is how you make the Temple pure and ready for God's service.

Passover Feast Offerings

[21]" 'On the fourteenth day of the first month you will celebrate the Feast [d] of Passover. It will be a feast of seven days when you eat bread made without yeast. [22]On that day the ruler must offer a bull for himself and for all the people of the land as a sin offering. [23]During the seven days of the feast he must offer seven bulls and seven rams that have nothing wrong with them. They will be burnt offerings to the LORD, which the ruler will offer every day of the seven days of the feast. He must also offer a male goat every day as a sin offering. [24]The ruler must give as a grain offering

20 litres for each bull and 20 litres for each ram. He must give 4 litres of olive oil for each 20 litres.

[25]" 'Beginning on the fifteenth day of the seventh month, when you celebrate the Feast [d] of Shelters, the ruler will supply the same things for seven days: the sin offerings, burnt offerings, grain offerings and the olive oil.

Rules for Worship

46

" 'This is what the Lord GOD says: the east gate of the inner courtyard will stay shut on the six working days, but it will be opened on the Sabbath [d] day and on the day of the New Moon. [d] [2]The ruler will enter from outside through the porch of the gateway and stand by the gatepost, while the priests offer the ruler's burnt offering and fellowship offering. The ruler will worship at the entrance of the gateway, and then he will go out. But the gate will not be shut until evening. [3]The people of the land will worship at the entrance of that gateway in the presence of the LORD on the Sabbaths and New Moons. [4]This is the burnt offering the ruler will offer to the LORD on the Sabbath day: six male lambs all without defect and a ram that has nothing wrong with it. [5]He must give a 20 litre grain offering with the ram, but he may give as much grain offering with the lambs as he pleases. He must also give 4 litres of olive oil for each 20 litres of grain. [6]On the day of the New Moon he must offer a young bull that has nothing wrong with it. He must also offer six lambs and a ram that have nothing wrong with them. [7]The ruler must give a 20 litre grain offering with the bull and 20 litres with the ram. With the lambs, he may give as much grain as he pleases. But he must give 4 litres of olive oil for each 20 litres of grain. [8]When the ruler enters, he must go in through the porch of the gateway, and he must go out the same way.

[9]" 'When the people of the land come into the LORD's presence at the special feasts, those who enter through the north gate to worship must go out through the south gate. Those who enter through the south gate must go out through the north gate. They must not return the same way they entered; everyone must go out the opposite way. [10]The ruler will go in with the people when they go in and go out with them when they go out.

[11]" 'At the feasts and regular times of worship 20 litres of grain must be offered with a young bull, and 20 litres of grain must be offered with a ram. But with an offering of lambs, the ruler

---

homer   The Hebrew word means "donkey-load". It measured about 200 litres. So an ephah was about 20 litres, and a bath was about 20 litres.

shekel   In Ezekiel's time a shekel weighed about 11 grammes.

may give as much grain as he pleases. He should give 4 litres of olive oil for each 20 litres of grain. [12]The ruler may give an offering as a special gift to the Lord; it may be a burnt offering or fellowship offering. When he gives it to the Lord, the inner east gate is to be opened for him. He must offer his burnt offering or his fellowship offering as he does on the Sabbath [d] day. Then he will go out, and the gate will be shut after he has left.

[13]" 'Every day you will give a year-old lamb that has nothing wrong with it for a burnt offering to the Lord. Do it every morning. [14]Also, you must offer a grain offering with the lamb every morning. For this you will give 3 litres of grain and 1 litre of olive oil, to make the fine flour moist, as a grain offering to the Lord. This is a rule that must be kept from now on. [15]So you must always give the lamb, together with the grain offering and the olive oil, every morning as a burnt offering.

Rules for the Ruler

[16]" 'This is what the Lord God says: if the ruler gives a gift from his land to any of his sons, that land will belong to the son and then to the son's children. It is their property passed down from their family. [17]But if the ruler gives a gift from his land to any of his servants, that land will belong to the servant only until the year of freedom. Then the land will go back to the ruler. Only the ruler's sons may keep a gift of land from the ruler. [18]The ruler must not take any of the people's land, forcing them out of their land. He must give his sons some of his own land so my people will not be scattered out of their own land.' "

The Special Kitchens

[19]The man led me through the entrance at the side of the gateway to the priests' holy rooms that face north. There I saw a place at the west end. [20]The man said to me, "This is where the priests will boil the meat of the penalty offering and sin offering and bake the grain offering. Then they will not need to bring these holy offerings into the outer courtyard, because that would hurt the people."

[21]Then the man brought me out into the outer courtyard and led me to its four corners. In each corner of the courtyard was a smaller courtyard. [22]Small courtyards were in the four corners of the courtyard. Each small courtyard was the same size, 20 metres long and 15 metres wide. [23]A stone wall was around each of the four small courtyards, and places for cooking were built in each of the stone walls. [24]The man said to me, "These are the kitchens where those who work

in the Temple[d] will boil the sacrifices offered by the people."

The River from the Temple

47 The man led me back to the door of the Temple, [d] and I saw water coming out from under the doorway and flowing east. (The Temple faced east.) The water flowed down from the south side wall of the Temple and then south of the altar. [2]The man brought me out through the outer north gate and led me around outside to the outer east gate. I found the water coming out on the south side of the gate.

[3]The man went towards the east with a line in his hand and measured about 500 metres. Then he led me through water that came up to my ankles. [4]The man measured about 500 metres again and led me through water that came up to my knees. Then he measured about 500 metres again and led me through water up to my waist. [5]The man measured about 500 metres again, but it was now a river that I could not cross. The water had risen too high; it was deep enough for swimming; it was a river that no one could cross. [6]The man asked me, "Human, do you see this?"

Then the man led me back to the bank of the river. [7]As I went back, I saw many trees on both sides of the river. [8]The man said to me, "This water will flow towards the eastern areas and go down into the Jordan Valley. When it enters the Dead Sea, [d] it will become fresh. [9]Everywhere the river goes, there will be many fish. Wherever this water goes the Dead Sea will become fresh, and so where the river goes there will be many living things. [10]Fishermen will stand by the Dead Sea.

Sidelight   In its current state, the Dead Sea is hardly a healthy habitat for the "many kinds of fish" that Ezekiel sees in his vision (Ezekiel 47:8–10). The surface of this body of water is about 400 metres below sea level, and 25 per cent of the sea is mineral, making it the saltiest and most uninhabitable sea in the world. It will take a true miracle for water to become fresh when it leaves the Dead Sea.

From En Gedi all the way to En Eglaim there will be places to spread fishing nets. There will be many kinds of fish in the Dead Sea, as many as in the Mediterranean Sea. [11]But its swamps and marshes will not become fresh; they will be left for salt. [12]All kinds of fruit trees will grow on both banks of the river, and their leaves will not dry and die. The trees will have fruit every month, because the water for them comes from the

Temple. The fruit from the trees will be used for food, and their leaves for medicine."

Borders of the Land

[13]This is what the Lord GOD says: "These are the borders of the land to be divided among the twelve tribes[d] of Israel. Joseph will have two parts of land. [14]You will divide the land equally. I promised to give it to your ancestors, so this land will belong to you as family property.

[15]"This will be the border line of the land: "On the north side it will start at the Mediterranean Sea. It will go through Hethlon, towards Lebo Hamath and on to the towns of Zedad, [16]Berothah and Sibraim on the border between Damascus and Hamath. Then it will go on to the town of Hazer Hatticon on the border of the country of Hauran. [17]So the border line will go from the Mediterranean Sea east to the town of Hazar Enan, where the land belonging to Damascus and Hamath lies on the north side. This will be the north side of the land.

[18]"On the east side the border runs south from a point between Hauran and Damascus. It will go along the Jordan between Gilead and the land of Israel and will continue to the town of Tamar on the Dead Sea. [d] This will be the east side of the land.

[19]"On the south side the border line will go east from Tamar all the way to the waters of Meribah Kadesh. Then it will run along the brook of Egypt to the Mediterranean Sea. This will be the south side of the land.

[20]"On the west side the Mediterranean Sea will be the border line up to a place across from Lebo Hamath. This will be the west side of your land.

[21]"You will divide this land among the tribes of Israel. [22]You will divide it as family property for yourselves and for the foreigners who live and have children among you. You are to treat these foreigners in the same way as people born in Israel; they are to share the land with the tribes of Israel. [23]In whatever tribe the foreigner lives, you will give him some land," says the Lord GOD.

Dividing the Land

48 "These are the areas of the tribes[d] named here: Dan will have one share at the northern border. It will go from the sea through Hethlon to Lebo Hamath, all the way to Hazar Enan, where Damascus lies to the north. It will stop there next to Hamath. This will be Dan's northern border from the east side to the Mediterranean Sea on the west side.

[2]"South of Dan's border, Asher will have one share. It will go from the east side to the west side.

[3]"South of Asher's border, Naphtali will have one share. It will go from the east side to the west side.

[4]"South of Naphtali's border, Manasseh will have one share. It will go from the east side to the west side.

[5]"South of Manasseh's border, Ephraim will have one share. It will go from the east side to the west side.

[6]"South of Ephraim's border, Reuben will have one share. It will go from the east side to the west side.

[7]"South of Reuben's border, Judah will have one share. It will go from the east side to the west side.

[8]"South of Judah's border will be the holy area which you are to give. It will be about 12 kilometres wide and as long and wide as one of the tribes' shares. It will run from the east side to the west side. The Temple [d] will be in the middle of this area.

[9]"The share which you will give the LORD will be about 12 kilometres long and 10 kilometres wide. [10]The holy area will be divided among these people. The priests will have land about 12 kilometres long on the north and south sides, and 10 kilometres wide on the west and east sides. The Temple of the LORD will be in the middle of it. [11]This land is for the priests who are given the holy duty of serving the LORD. They are the descendants[d] of Zadok who did my work and did not leave me when Israel and the Levites left me. [12]They will have as their share a very holy part of the holy portion of the land. It will be next to the land of the Levites.

[13]"Alongside the land for the priests, the Levites will have a share about 12 kilometres long and 5 kilometres wide; its full length will be about 12 kilometres and its full width about 10 kilometres. [14]The Levites are not to sell or trade any of this land. They are not to let anyone else own any of this best part of the land, because it belongs to the LORD.

City Property

[15]"The rest of the area will be about 2.5 kilometres wide and 12 kilometres long. It will not be holy but will belong to the city and be used for homes and pastures. The city will be in the middle of it. [16]These are the city's measurements: the north side will be about 2 kilometres, the south side about 2 kilometres, the east side about 2 kilometres and the west side about 2 kilometres. [17]The city's land for pastures will be about 125 metres on the north, 125 metres on the south, 125 metres on the east and 125 metres on the west. [18]Along the long side of the holy area there will be left 5 kilometres on the east and 5

kilometres on the west. It will be used to grow food for the city workers. [19]The city workers from all the tribes [d] of Israel will farm this land. [20]This whole area will be square, 12 kilometres by 12 kilometres. You shall give to the LORD the holy share along with the city property.

[21]"Land that is left over on both sides of the holy area and city property will belong to the ruler. That land will extend east of the holy area to the eastern border and west of it to the Mediterranean Sea. Both of these areas run the length of the lands of the tribes, and they belong to the ruler. The holy area with the Holy Place of the Temple [d] will be in the middle. [22]The Levites' land and the city property will be in the middle of the lands belonging to the ruler. Those lands will be between Judah's border and Benjamin's border.

The Other Tribes' Land

[23]"Here is what the rest of the tribes will receive: Benjamin will have one share. It will go from the east side to the Mediterranean Sea on the west side.

[24]"South of Benjamin's land, Simeon will have one share. It will go from the east side to the west side.

[25]"South of Simeon's land, Issachar will have one share. It will go from the east side to the west side.

[26]"South of Issachar's land, Zebulun will have one share. It will go from the east side to the west side.

[27]"South of Zebulun's land, Gad will have one share. It will go from the east side to the west side.

[28]"The southern border of Gad's land will go east from Tamar on the Dead Sea [d] to the waters of Meribah Kadesh. Then it will run along the brook of Egypt to the Mediterranean Sea.

[29]"This is the land you will divide among the tribes of Israel to be their shares," says the Lord GOD.

The Gates of the City

[30]"These will be the outside borders of the city: the north side will measure more than 2 kilometres. [31]There will be three gates facing north: Reuben's Gate, Judah's Gate and Levi's Gate, named after the tribes [d] of Israel.

[32]"The east side will measure more than 2 kilometres. There will be three gates facing east: Joseph's Gate, Benjamin's Gate and Dan's Gate.

[33]"The south side will measure more than 2 kilometres. There will be three gates facing south: Simeon's Gate, Issachar's Gate and Zebulun's Gate.

[34]"The west side will measure more than 2 kilometres. There will be three gates facing west: Gad's Gate, Asher's Gate and Naphtali's Gate.

[35]"The city will measure about 12 kilometres around. From then on the name of the city will be The LORD Is There."

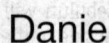

Daniel

Why Read This Book:

- Find courage to stand against pressure to compromise your beliefs (Daniel 1—6).
- Be assured that God works through history to fulfil his purposes (Daniel 7—12).

When?

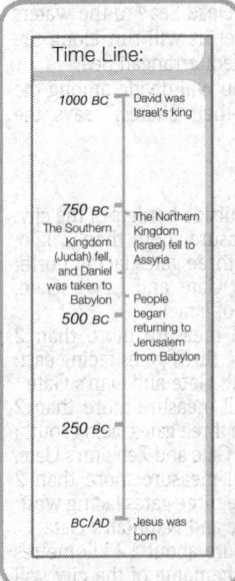

Time Line:

1000 BC	David was Israel's king
750 BC	The Northern Kingdom (Israel) fell to Assyria
The Southern Kingdom (Judah) fell, and Daniel was taken to Babylon	
500 BC	People began returning to Jerusalem from Babylon
250 BC	
BC/AD	Jesus was born

Behind the Scenes:

After moving to a new town, he quickly became popular. People respected him. Then he started getting pressured to do things he knew were wrong. Saying no would have been easier if the people pressuring him weren't so important.

It sounds like something that could happen today, right? But it's a story set 2,500 years ago. Daniel had been dragged off to Babylon (modern-day Iraq) when the empire conquered Judah. Because of Daniel's ability to interpret dreams, the king chose him to be an important adviser.

But Daniel's career took a downward turn when he resisted the pressure to set aside his faith and worship the king. Because he wouldn't give in, he was sent to die in a den of lions, but God's power protected him. Through everything, Daniel remained faithful to God.

The book of Daniel has two parts. In the first part (chapters 1—6), we read the heroic story of Daniel and his friends. Then chapters 7—12 consist of Daniel's unusual visions that include symbols and heavenly messengers that proclaim God's Word. ▷

Where?

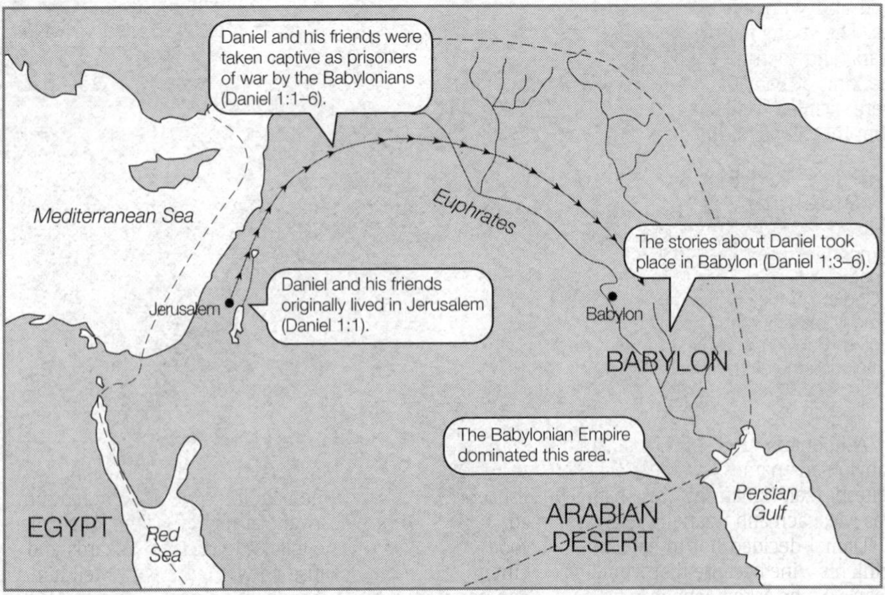

Daniel and his friends were taken captive as prisoners of war by the Babylonians (Daniel 1:1–6).

Mediterranean Sea

Euphrates

The stories about Daniel took place in Babylon (Daniel 1:3–6).

Jerusalem

Daniel and his friends originally lived in Jerusalem (Daniel 1:1).

Babylon

BABYLON

The Babylonian Empire dominated this area.

EGYPT Red Sea

ARABIAN DESERT

Persian Gulf

Behind the Scenes (cont.): Though parts of Daniel are difficult to understand, the book's underlying message is consistent: God is in control of history. Even when things get rough and we are under pressure, we can know that God is working to protect his people and advance his purposes in the world. We, like Daniel, should rely on God and remain faithful to God, no matter what happens.

Daniel Taken to Babylon

1 During the third year that Jehoiakim was king of Judah, Nebuchadnezzar king of Babylon came to Jerusalem and surrounded it with his army. 2The Lord allowed Nebuchadnezzar to capture Jehoiakim king of Judah. Nebuchadnezzar also took some of the things from the Temple *d* of God, which he carried to Babylonia and put in the temple of his gods.

3Then King Nebuchadnezzar ordered Ashpenaz, his chief officer, to bring some of the Israelite men into his palace. He wanted them to be from important families, including the family of the king of Judah. 4King Nebuchadnezzar wanted only young Israelite men who had nothing wrong with them. They were to be handsome and well educated, capable of learning and understanding and able to serve in his palace. Ashpenaz was to teach them the language and writings of the Babylonians. 5The king gave the young men a certain amount of food and wine every day, just like the food he ate. The young men were to be trained for three years, and then they would become servants of the king of Babylon. 6Among those young men were Daniel, Hananiah, Mishael and Azariah from the people of Judah.

> **Sidelight** In Old Testament times, names had important meanings. All four of the Israelites' names in Daniel 1:6 included syllables meaning God (El) or the Lord God (Yah). So these faithful men probably weren't excited when they were given Babylonian names, some of which included the names of false gods.

7Ashpenaz, the chief officer, gave them Babylonian names. Daniel's new name was Belteshazzar, Hananiah's was Shadrach, Mishael's was Meshach and Azariah's was Abednego.

8Daniel decided not to eat the king's food or drink his wine because that would make him unclean. *d* So he asked Ashpenaz for permission not to make himself unclean in this way.

9God made Ashpenaz, the chief officer, want to be kind and merciful to Daniel, 10but Ashpenaz said to Daniel, "I am afraid of my master, the king. He ordered me to give you this food and drink. If you begin to look worse than other young men your age, the king will see this. Then he will cut off my head because of you."

11Ashpenaz had ordered a guard to watch Daniel, Hananiah, Mishael and Azariah. 12Daniel said to the guard, "Please give us this test for ten days: don't give us anything but vegetables to eat and water to drink. 13After ten days compare how we look with how the other young men look who eat the king's food. See for yourself and then decide how you want to treat us, your servants."

14So the guard agreed to test them for ten days. 15After ten days they looked healthier and better fed than all the young men who ate the king's food. 16So the guard took away the king's special food and wine, feeding them vegetables instead.

17God gave these four young men wisdom and the ability to learn many things that people had written and studied. Daniel could also understand visions and dreams.

18At the end of the time set for them by the king, Ashpenaz brought all the young men to King Nebuchadnezzar. 19The king talked to them and found that none of the young men were as good as Daniel, Hananiah, Mishael and Azariah. So those four young men became the king's servants. 20Every time the king asked them about something important, they showed much wisdom and understanding. They were ten times better than all the fortune-tellers and magicians in his kingdom! 21So Daniel continued to be the king's servant until the first year Cyrus was king.

Nebuchadnezzar's Dream

2 During Nebuchadnezzar's second year as king, he had dreams that bothered him and kept him awake at night. 2So the king called for his fortune-tellers, magicians, wizards and wise men, because he wanted them to tell him what he had dreamed. They came in and stood in front of the king.

³Then the king said to them, "I have had a dream that bothers me, and I want to know what it means."

⁴The wise men answered the king in the Aramaic language, "Our king, live for ever! Please tell us, your servants, your dream. Then we will tell you what it means."

⁵King Nebuchadnezzar said to them, "I meant what I said. You must tell me the dream and what it means. If you don't, I will have you torn apart, and I will turn your houses into piles of stones. ⁶But if you tell me my dream and its meaning, I will reward you with gifts and great honour. So tell me the dream and what it means."

⁷Again the wise men said to the king, "Tell us, your servants, the dream, and we will tell you what it means."

⁸King Nebuchadnezzar answered, "I know you are trying to get more time, because you know that I meant what I said. ⁹If you don't tell me my dream, you will be punished. You have all agreed to tell me lies and wicked things, hoping things will change. Now, tell me the dream so that I will know you can tell me what it really means!"

¹⁰The wise men answered the king, saying, "No one on earth can do what the king asks! No great and powerful king has ever asked the fortune-tellers, magicians or wise men to do this; ¹¹the king is asking something that is too hard. Only the gods could tell the king this, but the gods do not live among people."

¹²When the king heard their answer, he became very angry. He ordered that all the wise men of Babylon be killed. ¹³So King Nebuchadnezzar's order to kill the wise men was announced, and men were sent to look for Daniel and his friends to kill them.

¹⁴Arioch, the commander of the king's guards, was going to kill the wise men of Babylon. But Daniel spoke to him with wisdom and skill, ¹⁵saying, "Why did the king order such a terrible punishment?" Then Arioch explained everything to Daniel. ¹⁶So Daniel went to King Nebuchadnezzar and asked for an appointment so that he could tell the king what his dream meant.

¹⁷Then Daniel went to his house and explained the whole story to his friends Hananiah, Mishael and Azariah. ¹⁸Daniel asked his friends to pray that the God of heaven would show them mercy and help them understand this secret so he and his friends would not be killed with the other wise men of Babylon.

¹⁹During the night God explained the secret to Daniel in a vision. Then Daniel praised the God of heaven. ²⁰Daniel said:

"Praise God for ever and ever,
    because he has wisdom and power.

²¹He changes the times and seasons of the
        year.
    He takes away the power of kings
        and gives their power to new kings.
    He gives wisdom to those who are wise
        and knowledge to those who understand.
²²He makes known secrets that are deep and
        hidden;
    he knows what is hidden in darkness,
        and light is all around him.
²³I thank you and praise you, God of my
        ancestors,
    because you have given me wisdom and
        power.
You told me what we asked of you;
    you told us about the king's dream."

The Meaning of the Dream

²⁴Then Daniel went to Arioch, the man King Nebuchadnezzar had chosen to kill the wise men of Babylon. Daniel said to him, "Don't put the wise men of Babylon to death. Take me to the king, and I will tell him what his dream means."

²⁵Very quickly Arioch took Daniel to the king and said, "I have found a man among the captives from Judah who can tell the king what his dream means."

²⁶The king asked Daniel, who was also called Belteshazzar, "Are you able to tell me what I dreamed and what it means?"

²⁷Daniel answered, "No wise man, magician or fortune-teller can explain to the king the secret he has asked about. ²⁸But there is a God in heaven who explains secret things, and he has shown King Nebuchadnezzar what will happen at a later time. This is your dream, the vision you saw while lying on your bed: ²⁹our king, as you were lying there, you thought about things to come. God, who can tell people about secret things, showed you what is going to happen. ³⁰God also told this secret to me, not because I have greater wisdom than any other living person, but so that you may know what it means. In that way you will understand what went through your mind.

³¹"Our king, in your dream you saw a huge, shiny and frightening statue in front of you. ³²The head of the statue was made of pure gold. Its chest and arms were made of silver. Its stomach and the upper part of its legs were made of bronze. ³³The lower part of the legs were made of iron, while its feet were made partly of iron and partly of baked clay. ³⁴While you were looking at the statue, you saw a rock cut free, but no human being touched the rock. It hit the statue on its feet of iron and clay and smashed them. ³⁵Then the iron, clay, bronze, silver and gold broke to pieces at the same time. They became

like chaff[d] on a threshing[d] floor in the summer time; the wind blew them away and there was nothing left. Then the rock that hit the statue became a very large mountain that filled the whole earth.

36"That was your dream. Now we will tell the king what it means. 37Our king, you are the greatest king. God of heaven has given you a kingdom, power, strength and glory. 38Wherever people, wild animals and birds live, God made you ruler over them. King Nebuchadnezzar, you are the head of gold on that statue.

39"Another kingdom will come after you, but it will not be as great as yours. Next a third kingdom, the bronze part, will rule over the earth. 40Then there will be a fourth kingdom, strong as iron. In the same way that iron crushes and smashes things to pieces, the fourth kingdom will smash and crush all the other kingdoms.

41"You saw that the statue's feet and toes were partly baked clay and partly iron. That means the fourth kingdom will be a divided kingdom. It will have some of the strength of iron in it, just as you saw iron was mixed with clay. 42The toes of the statue were partly iron and partly clay. So the fourth kingdom will be partly strong like iron and partly breakable like clay. 43You saw the iron mixed with clay, but iron and clay do not hold together. In the same way the people of the fourth kingdom will be a mixture, but they will not be united as one people.

44"During the time of those kings, the God of heaven will set up another kingdom that will never be destroyed or given to another group of people. This kingdom will crush all the other kingdoms and bring them to an end, but it will continue for ever.

45"King Nebuchadnezzar, you saw a rock cut from a mountain, but no human being touched it. The rock broke the iron, bronze, clay, silver and gold to pieces. In this way the great God showed you what will happen. The dream is true, and you can trust this explanation."

46Then King Nebuchadnezzar fell face down on the ground in front of Daniel. The king honoured him and commanded that an offering and incense[d] be presented to him. 47Then the king said to Daniel, "Truly I know your God is the greatest of all gods, the Lord of all the kings. He tells people about things they cannot know. I know this is true, because you were able to tell these secret things to me."

48Then the king gave Daniel many gifts plus an important position in his kingdom. Nebuchadnezzar made him ruler over the whole area of Babylon and put him in charge of all the wise men of Babylon. 49Daniel asked the king to make Shadrach, Meshach and Abednego leaders over the area of Babylon, so the king did as Daniel asked. Daniel himself became one of the people who stayed at the royal court.

The Gold Idol and Blazing Furnace

3 King Nebuchadnezzar made a gold statue 30 metres high and 3 metres wide and set it up on the plain of Dura in the area of Babylon. 2Then he called for the leaders: the governors, assistant governors, captains of the soldiers, people who advised the king, keepers of the treasury, judges, rulers and all other officers in his kingdom. He wanted them to come to the special service for the statue he had set up. 3So they all came for the special service and stood in front of the statue that King Nebuchadnezzar had set up. 4Then the man who made announcements for the king said in a loud voice, "People, nations and those of every language, this is what you are commanded to do: 5when you hear the sound of the horns, flutes, lyres,[d] zithers,[n] harps, pipes and all the other musical instruments, you must bow down and worship the gold statue that King Nebuchadnezzar has set up. 6Anyone who doesn't bow down and worship will immediately be thrown into a blazing furnace."

7Now people, nations and those who spoke every language were there. When they heard the sound of the horns, flutes, lyres, zithers, pipes and all the other musical instruments they bowed down and worshipped the gold statue King Nebuchadnezzar had set up.

8Then some Babylonians came up to the king and began speaking against the men of Judah. 9They said to King Nebuchadnezzar, "Our king, live for ever! 10Our king, you gave a command that everyone who heard the horns, lyres, zithers, harps, pipes and all the other musical instruments would have to bow down and worship the gold statue. 11Anyone who wouldn't do this was to be thrown into a blazing furnace. 12Our king, there are some men of Judah whom you made officers in the area of Babylon that did not pay attention to your order. Their names are Shadrach, Meshach and Abednego. They do not serve your gods and do not worship the gold statue you have set up."

13Nebuchadnezzar became very angry and called for Shadrach, Meshach and Abednego. When they were brought to the king, 14Nebuchadnezzar said, "Shadrach, Meshach and Abednego, is it true that you do not serve my gods nor worship the gold statue I have set up? 15In a moment you will again hear the sound of

---

zithers Musical instruments with 30 to 40 strings.

the horns, flutes, lyres, zithers, harps, pipes and all the other musical instruments. If you bow down and worship the statue I made, that will be good. But if you do not worship it, you will immediately be thrown into the blazing furnace. What god will be able to save you from my power then?"

16Shadrach, Meshach and Abednego answered the king, saying, "Nebuchadnezzar, we do not need to defend ourselves to you. 17If you throw us into the blazing furnace, the God we serve is able to save us from the furnace. He will save us from your power, Our king. 18But even if God does not save us, we want you, Our king, to know this: we will not serve your gods or worship the gold statue you have set up."

19Then Nebuchadnezzar was furious with Shadrach, Meshach and Abednego, and he changed his mind. He ordered the furnace to be heated seven times hotter than usual. 20Then he commanded some of the strongest soldiers in his army to tie up Shadrach, Meshach and Abednego and throw them into the blazing furnace.

21So Shadrach, Meshach and Abednego were tied up and thrown into the blazing furnace while still wearing their robes, trousers, turbans and other clothes. 22The king's command was very strict, and the furnace was made so hot that the flames killed the strong soldiers who threw Shadrach, Meshach and Abednego into the furnace. 23Firmly tied, Shadrach, Meshach and Abednego fell into the blazing furnace.

24Then King Nebuchadnezzar was so surprised that he jumped to his feet. He asked the men who advised him, "Didn't we tie up only three men and throw them into the fire?"

They answered, "Yes, Our king."

25The king said, "Look! I see four men walking around in the fire. They are not tied up, and they are not burned. The fourth man looks like a son of the gods."

26Then Nebuchadnezzar went to the opening of the blazing furnace and shouted, "Shadrach, Meshach and Abednego, come out! Servants of the Most High God, come here!"

So Shadrach, Meshach and Abednego came out of the fire. 27When they came out, the governors, assistant governors, captains of the soldiers and royal advisers crowded around them and saw that the fire had not harmed their bodies. Their hair was not burned, their robes were not burned and they didn't even smell of smoke!

28Then Nebuchadnezzar said, "Praise the God of Shadrach, Meshach and Abednego. Their God has sent his angel and saved his servants from the fire! These three men trusted their God and refused to obey my command. They were willing to die rather than serve or worship any god other than their own. 29So I now give this command: anyone from any nation or language who says anything against the God of Shadrach, Meshach and Abednego will be torn apart and have his house turned into a pile of stones. No other god

can save his people like this." 30Then the king promoted Shadrach, Meshach and Abednego in the area of Babylon.

Nebuchadnezzar's Dream of a Tree

4 King Nebuchadnezzar sent this letter to the people, nations and those who speak every language in all the world:

I wish you peace and great wealth!

2The Most High God has done miracles *d* and wonderful things for me that I am happy to tell you about.

3His wonderful acts are great,
    and his miracles are mighty.
His kingdom goes on for ever,
    and his rule continues from now on.

4I, Nebuchadnezzar, was happy and successful at my palace, 5but I had a dream that made me afraid. As I was lying on my bed, I saw pictures and visions in my mind that alarmed me. 6So I ordered all the wise men of Babylon to come to me and tell me what my dream meant. 7The fortune-tellers, magicians and wise men came, and I told them about the dream. But they could not tell me what it meant.

8Finally, Daniel came to me. (I called him Belteshazzar to honour my god, because the spirit of the holy gods is in him.) I told my dream to him. 9I said, "Belteshazzar, you are the most important of all the fortune-tellers. I know that the spirit of the holy gods is in you, so there is no secret that is too hard for you to understand. This was what I dreamed; tell me what it means. 10These are the visions I saw while I was lying in my bed: I looked, and there in front of me was a tree standing in the middle of the earth. And it was very tall. 11The tree grew large and strong. The top of the tree touched the sky and could be seen from anywhere on earth. [12]The leaves of the tree were beautiful. It had plenty of good fruit on it, enough food for everyone. The wild animals found shelter under the tree, and the birds lived in its branches. Every animal ate from it.

[13]"As I was looking at those things in the vision while lying on my bed, I saw an observer, a holy angel coming down from heaven. [14]He spoke very loudly and said, 'Cut down the tree and cut off its branches. Strip off its leaves and scatter its fruit. Let the animals under the tree run away, and let the birds in its branches fly away. [15]But leave the stump and its roots in the ground with a band of iron and bronze around it; let it stay in the field with the grass around it.

"'Let the man become wet with dew, and let him live among the animals and plants of the earth. [16]Let him not think like a human any longer, but let him have the mind of an animal for seven years.

[17]"'The observers gave this command; the holy ones declared the sentence. This is so all people may know that the Most High God [d] rules over every kingdom on earth. God gives those kingdoms to anyone he wants, and he chooses people to rule them who are not proud.'

[18]"That is what I, King Nebuchadnezzar, dreamed. Now Belteshazzar, [n] tell me what the dream means. None of the wise men in my kingdom can explain it to me, but you can, because the spirit of the holy gods is in you."

Daniel Explains the Dream

[19]Then Daniel, who was called Belteshazzar, was very quiet for a while, because his understanding of the dream frightened him. So the king said, "Belteshazzar, do not let the dream or its meaning make you afraid."

Then Belteshazzar answered, "My master, I wish the dream were about your enemies, and I wish its meaning were for those who are against you! [20]You saw a tree in your dream that grew large and strong. Its top touched the sky, and it could be seen from all over the earth. [21]Its leaves were beautiful, and it had plenty of fruit for everyone to eat. It was a home for the wild animals, and its branches were nesting places for the birds. [22]Our king, you are that tree! You have become great and powerful, like

the tall tree that touched the sky. Your power reaches to the far parts of the earth.

[23]"Our king, you saw an observer, a holy angel, coming down from heaven who said, 'Cut down the tree and destroy it. But leave the stump and its roots in the ground with a band of iron and bronze around it; leave it in the field with the grass. Let him become wet with dew and live like a wild animal for seven years.'

[24]"This is the meaning of the dream, Our king. The Most High God has commanded these things to happen to my master the king: [25]you will be forced away from people to live among the wild animals. People will feed you grass like an ox, and dew from the sky will make you wet. Seven years will pass, and then you will learn this lesson: the Most High God is ruler over every kingdom on earth, and he gives those kingdoms to anyone he chooses.

[26]"Since the stump of the tree and its roots were left in the ground, your kingdom will be given back to you when you learn that one in heaven rules your kingdom. [27]So, Our king, please accept my advice. Stop sinning and do what is right. Stop doing wicked things and be kind to the poor. Then you might continue to be successful."

The King's Dream Comes True

[28]All these things happened to King Nebuchadnezzar. [29]Twelve months later as he was walking on the roof [n] of his palace in Babylon, [30]he said, "I have built this great Babylon as my royal home. I built it by my power to show my glory and my majesty."

[31]The words were still in his mouth when a voice from heaven said, "King Nebuchadnezzar, these things will happen to you: your royal power has been taken away from you. [32]You will be forced away from people. You will live with the wild animals and will be fed grass like an ox. Seven years will pass before you learn this lesson: the Most High God rules over every kingdom on earth and gives those kingdoms to anyone he chooses."

[33]Immediately the words came true. Nebuchadnezzar was forced to go away from people, and he began eating grass like an ox. He became wet from dew. His hair grew long like the feathers of an eagle, and his nails grew like the claws of a bird.

Belteshazzar Another name for Daniel.
roof In Bible times houses were built with flat roofs. The roof was used for drying things such as flax and fruit. And it was used as an extra room, as a place for worship and as a place to sleep in the summer.

³⁴At the end of that time, I, Nebuchadnezzar, looked up towards heaven, and I could think normally again! Then I gave praise to the Most High God; I gave honour and glory to him who lives for ever.

God's rule is for ever,
    and his kingdom continues for all
        time.
³⁵People on earth
    are not truly important.
God does what he wants
    with the powers of heaven
    and the people on earth.
No one can stop his powerful hand
    or question what he does.

³⁶At that time I could think normally again, and God gave back my great honour and power and returned the glory to my kingdom. The people who advised me and the royal family came to me for help again. I became king again and was even greater and more powerful than before. ³⁷Now I, Nebuchadnezzar, give praise and honour and glory to the King of heaven. Everything he does is right and fair, and he is able to make proud people humble.

The Writing on the Wall

5 King Belshazzar gave a big banquet for 1,000 royal guests and drank wine with them. ²As Belshazzar was drinking his wine, he gave orders to bring the gold and silver cups that his ancestor Nebuchadnezzar had taken from the Temple *d* in Jerusalem. This was so the king, his royal guests, his wives and his slave women *d* could drink from those cups. ³So they brought the gold cups that had been taken from the Temple of God in Jerusalem. And the king and his royal guests, his wives and his slave women drank from them. ⁴As they were drinking, they praised their gods, which were made from gold, silver, bronze, iron, wood and stone.

⁵Suddenly the fingers of a person's hand appeared and began writing on the plaster of the wall, near the lampstand in the royal palace. The king watched the hand as it wrote.

⁶King Belshazzar was very frightened. His face turned white, his knees knocked together and he could not stand up because his legs were too weak. ⁷The king called for the magicians, wise men and wizards of Babylon and said to them, "Anyone who can read this writing and explain it will receive purple clothes fit for a king and a gold chain around his neck. And I will make that person the third highest ruler in the kingdom."

⁸Then all the king's wise men came in, but they could not read the writing or tell the king what it meant. ⁹King Belshazzar became even more afraid, and his face became even whiter. His royal guests were confused.

¹⁰Then the king's mother, who had heard the voices of the king and his royal guests, came into the banquet room. She said, "Our king, live for ever! Don't be afraid or let your face be white with fear! ¹¹There is a man in your kingdom who has the spirit of the holy gods. In the days of your father, this man showed understanding, knowledge and wisdom like the gods. Your father, King Nebuchadnezzar, put this man in charge of all the wise men, fortune-tellers, magicians and wizards. ¹²The man I am talking about is named Daniel, whom the king named Belteshazzar. He was very clever and had knowledge and understanding. He could explain dreams and secrets and could answer very hard problems. Call for Daniel. He will tell you what the writing on the wall means."

¹³So they brought Daniel to the king, and the king asked, "Is your name Daniel? Are you one of the captives my father the king brought from Judah? ¹⁴I have heard that the spirit of the gods is in you, and that you are very clever and have knowledge and extraordinary understanding. ¹⁵The wise men and magicians were brought to me to read this writing and to explain what it means, but they could not explain it. ¹⁶I have heard that you are able to explain what things mean and can find the answers to hard problems. Read this writing on the wall and explain it to me. If you can, I will give you purple clothes fit for a king and a gold chain to wear around your neck. And you will become the third highest ruler in the kingdom."

¹⁷Then Daniel answered the king, "You may keep your gifts for yourself, or you may give those rewards to someone else. But I will read the writing on the wall for you and will explain to you what it means.

¹⁸"Our king, the Most High God made your father Nebuchadnezzar a great, important and powerful king. ¹⁹Because God made him important, all the people, nations and those who spoke every language were very frightened of Nebuchadnezzar. If he wanted someone to die, he killed that person. If he wanted someone to live,

he let that person live. Those he wanted to promote, he promoted. Those he wanted to be less important, he made less important.

20"But Nebuchadnezzar became too proud and stubborn, so he was taken off his royal throne. His glory was taken away. 21He was forced away from people, and his mind became like the mind of an animal. He lived with the wild donkeys and was fed grass like an ox and became wet with dew. These things happened to him until he learned his lesson: the Most High God rules over every kingdom on earth, and he sets anyone he chooses over those kingdoms.

22"Belshazzar, you already knew these things, because you are a descendant d of Nebuchadnezzar. Still you have not been sorry for what you have done. 23Instead, you have set yourself against the Lord of heaven. You ordered the drinking cups from the Temple of the Lord to be brought to you. Then you and your royal guests, your wives and your slave women drank wine from them. You praised the gods of silver, gold, bronze, iron, wood and stone that are not really gods; they cannot see or hear or understand anything. You did not honour God, who has power over your life and everything you do. 24So God sent the hand that wrote on the wall.

25"These are the words that were written on the wall: 'Mene, mene, tekel, parsin'.

26"This is what the words mean: Mene: God has counted the days until your kingdom will end. 27Tekel: you have been weighed on the scales and found not good enough. 28Parsin: your kingdom is being divided and will be given to the Medes and the Persians."

29Then Belshazzar gave an order for Daniel to be dressed in purple clothes and to have a gold chain put around his neck. And it was announced that Daniel was the third highest ruler in the kingdom. 30That very same night Belshazzar, king of the Babylonian people, was killed. 31So Darius the Mede became the new king when he was 62 years old.

Daniel and the Lions

6 Darius thought it would be a good idea to choose 120 governors who would rule his kingdom. 2He chose three men as supervisors over those governors, and Daniel was one of the supervisors. The supervisors were to ensure that the governors did not try to cheat the king. 3Daniel showed that he could do the work better than the other supervisors and governors, so the king planned to put Daniel in charge of the whole kingdom. 4Because of this, the other supervisors and governors tried to find reasons to accuse Daniel about his work in the government. But they could not find anything wrong with him or

any reason to accuse him, because he was trustworthy and not lazy or dishonest. 5Finally these men said, "We will never find any reason to accuse Daniel unless it is about the law of his God."

6So the supervisors and governors went as a group to the king and said: "King Darius, live for ever! 7The supervisors, assistant governors, governors, the people who advise you and the captains of the soldiers have all agreed that you should make a new law for everyone to obey: for the next 30 days no one should pray to any god or human except to you, Our king. Anyone who doesn't obey will be thrown into the lions' den. 8Now, Our king, make the law and sign your name to it so that it cannot be changed, because then it will be a law of the Medes and Persians and cannot be cancelled." 9So King Darius signed the law.

10Even though Daniel knew that the new law had been written, he went to pray in an upstairs room in his house, which had windows that opened towards Jerusalem. Three times each day Daniel would kneel down to pray and thank God, just as he always had done.

> **Sidelight** Daniel really wanted God's attention when he dropped to his knees in prayer (Daniel 6:10). His fellow Jews normally stood when they addressed God.

11Then those men went as a group and found Daniel praying and asking God for help. 12So they went to the king and talked to him about the law he had made. They said, "Didn't you sign a law that says no one may pray to any god or human except you, Our king? Doesn't it say that anyone who disobeys during the next 30 days will be thrown into the lions' den?"

The king answered, "Yes, that is the law, and the laws of the Medes and Persians cannot be cancelled."

13Then they said to the king, "Daniel, one of the captives from Judah, is not paying attention to you, Our king, or to the law you signed. Daniel still prays to his God three times every day." 14The king became very upset when he heard this. He wanted to save Daniel, and he worked hard until sunset trying to think of a way to save him.

15Then those men went as a group to the king. They said, "Remember, Our king, the law of the Medes and Persians says that no law or command given by the king can be changed."

16So King Darius gave the order, and Daniel was brought in and thrown into the lions' den.

The king said to Daniel, "May the God you serve all the time save you!" [17]A big stone was brought and placed over the opening of the lions' den. Then the king used his signet *d* ring and the rings of his royal officers to put special seals *d* on the rock. This showed that no one would move the rock and bring Daniel out. [18]Then King Darius went back to his palace. He did not eat that night, he did not have any entertainment brought to him, and he could not sleep.

[19]The next morning King Darius got up at dawn and hurried to the lions' den. [20]As he came near the den, he was worried. He called out to Daniel, "Daniel, servant of the living God! Has your God that you always worship been able to save you from the lions?"

[21]Daniel answered, "Our king, live for ever! [22]My God sent his angel to close the lions' mouths. They have not hurt me, because my God knows I am innocent. I never did anything wrong to you, Our king."

[23]King Darius was very happy and told his servants to lift Daniel out of the lions' den. So they lifted him out and did not find any injury on him, because Daniel had trusted in his God.

[24]Then the king commanded that the men who had accused Daniel be brought to the lions' den. They, their wives and their children were thrown into the den. The lions grabbed them before they hit the floor of the den and crushed their bones.

[25]Then King Darius wrote a letter to all people and all nations, to those who spoke every language in the world:

I wish you great peace and wealth.

[26]I am making a new law for people in every part of my kingdom. All of you must fear and respect the God of Daniel.

Daniel's God is the living God;
  he lives for ever.
His kingdom will never be destroyed,
  and his rule will never end.
[27]God rescues and saves people
  and does mighty miracles *d*
in heaven and on earth.
He is the one who saved Daniel
  from the power of the lions.

[28]So Daniel was successful during the time Darius was king and when Cyrus the Persian was king.

Daniel's Dream About Four Animals

7 In Belshazzar's first year as king of Babylon, Daniel had a dream. He saw visions as he was lying on his bed, and he wrote down what he had dreamed.

[2]Daniel said: "I saw my vision at night. In the vision the wind was blowing from all four directions, which made the sea very rough. [3]I saw four huge animals come up from the sea, and each animal was different from the others.

[4]"The first animal looked like a lion, but had wings like an eagle. I watched this animal until its wings were torn off. It was lifted from the ground so that it stood up on two feet like a human, and it was given the mind of a human.

[5]"Then I saw a second animal before me that looked like a bear. It was raised up on one of its sides and had three ribs in its mouth between its teeth. It was told, 'Get up and eat all the meat you want!'

[6]"After that, I looked, and there before me was another animal. This animal looked like a leopard with four wings on its back that looked like a bird's wings. This animal had four heads and was given power to rule.

[7]"After that, in my vision at night I saw in front of me a fourth animal that was cruel, terrible and very strong. It had large iron teeth. It crushed and ate what it killed, and then it walked on whatever was left. This fourth animal was different from any animal I had seen before, and it had ten horns.

[8]"While I was thinking about the horns, another horn grew up among them. It was a little horn with eyes like a human's eyes. It also had a mouth, and the mouth was boasting. The little horn pulled out three of the other horns.

[9]"As I looked,
thrones were put in their places,
  and God, who has been alive for ever, sat
    on his throne.
His clothes were white like snow,
  and the hair on his head was white like
    wool.
His throne was made from fire,
  and the wheels of his throne were blazing
    with fire.
[10]A river of fire was flowing
  from in front of him.
Many thousands of angels were serving him,
  and millions of angels stood before him.
Court was ready to begin,
  and the books were opened.

[11]"I kept on looking because the little horn was boasting. I kept watching until finally the fourth animal was killed. Its body was destroyed, and it was thrown into the burning fire. [12](The power and rule of the other animals had been taken from them, but they were permitted to live for a certain period of time.)

[13]"In my vision at night I saw in front of me someone who looked like a human being coming on the clouds in the sky. He came near God,

who has been alive for ever, and he was led to God. [14]He was given authority, glory and the strength of a king. People of every tribe, [d] nation and language will serve him. His rule will last for ever, and his kingdom will never be destroyed.

The Meaning of the Dream

[15]"I, Daniel, was worried. The visions that went through my mind frightened me. [16]I came near one of those standing there and asked what all this meant.

"So he told me and explained to me what these things meant: [17]'The four great animals are four kingdoms that will come from the earth. [18]But the holy people who belong to the Most High God will receive the power to rule and will have the power to rule for ever, from now on.'

[19]"Then I wanted to know what the fourth animal meant, because it was different from all the others. It was very terrible and had iron teeth and bronze claws. It was the animal that crushed and ate what it killed and then walked on whatever was left. [20]I also wanted to know about the ten horns on its head and about the little horn that grew there. It had pulled out three of the other ten horns and looked greater than the others. It had eyes and a mouth that kept boasting. [21]As I watched, the little horn began making war against God's holy people and was defeating them [22]until God, who has been alive for ever, came. He judged in favour of the holy people who belong to the Most High God; then the time came for them to receive the power to rule.

[23]"And he explained this to me: 'The fourth animal is a fourth kingdom that will come on the earth. It will be different from all the other kingdoms and will destroy people all over the world. It will walk on and crush the whole earth. [24]The ten horns are ten kings who will come from this fourth kingdom. After those ten kings are gone, another king will come. He will be different from the kings who ruled before him, and he will

---

PERSISTENCE

What Do You See?

El Salvador suffered a devastating earthquake in 1986. Thousands of people were hurt and killed, and many buildings were destroyed. Carlos, Raphael and Cecilia, like most other people, were initially overwhelmed by the suffering and destruction. Soon, however, they organised their church's youth group to help. They began by sweeping and mopping floors at their church, which sheltered 300 refugees. Then they expanded into day care, tutoring, and health-care programmes. Seeing the amazing results of their work kept the young people going, even when they felt tired or overwhelmed.

They saw their work as the Christian challenge. Although the earthquake disaster eventually passed, they continued to help the victims of their country's civil war. Their belief in Jesus gave them strength to keep going.

"People must be involved together if progress is to be made," Cecilia explains. "We must be informed of needs in today's world and learn to see through the eyes of Jesus." That's where hope begins.

Daniel faced a similar situation that seemed overwhelming. Read about how he found hope in his vision in **Daniel 7:9–14**.

* How did visions of hope motivate the Salvadoran youth group and help Daniel in his troubles?
* Why might hope give you more strength to persist in difficult times?

Consider . . .

* drawing a symbol for one of the obstacles you face and then drawing a large cross through it. Tape it to your mirror to give you strength to persist.
* reading the newspaper and, for one week, asking God to give hope to those who are hurt or discouraged.

For more, see . . .

* Psalm 71 (p.541)
* Romans 8:18–25 (p.1195)
* Matthew 26:62–66 (p.990)

defeat three of the other kings. 25This king will speak against the Most High God, and he will hurt and kill God's holy people. He will try to change times and laws that have already been set. The holy people that belong to God will be in that king's power for three and a half years.

26" 'But the court will decide what should happen. The power of the king will be taken away, and his kingdom will be completely destroyed. 27Then the holy people who belong to the Most High God will have the power to rule. They will rule over all the kingdoms under heaven with power and greatness, and their power to rule will last for ever. People from all the other kingdoms will respect and serve them.'

28"That was the end of the dream. I, Daniel, was very afraid. My face became white from fear, but I kept everything to myself."

Daniel's Vision

8 During the third year of King Belshazzar's rule, I, Daniel, saw another vision, which was like the first one. 2In this vision I saw myself in the capital city of Susa, in the area of Elam. I was standing by the Ulai Canal 3when I looked up and saw a ram standing beside the canal. It had two long horns, but one horn was longer and newer than the other. 4I watched the ram charge to the west, the north and the south. No animal could stand before him, and none could save another animal from his power. He did whatever he wanted and became very powerful.

5While I was watching this, I saw a male goat come from the west. This goat had one large horn between his eyes that was easy to see. He crossed over the whole earth so fast that his feet hardly touched the ground.

6In his anger the goat charged the ram with the two horns that I had seen standing by the canal. 7I watched the angry goat attack the ram and break the sheep's two horns. The ram was not strong enough to stop it. The goat knocked the ram to the ground and then walked all over him. No one was able to save the ram from the goat, 8so the male goat became very great. But when he was strong, his big horn broke off and four horns grew in place of the one big horn. Those four horns pointed in four different directions and were easy to see.

9Then a little horn grew from one of those four horns, and it became very big. It grew to the south, the east and towards the beautiful land of Judah. 10That little horn grew until it reached to the sky. It even threw some of the army of heaven to the ground and walked on them! 11That little horn set itself up as equal to God, the Commander of heaven's armies. It stopped the daily sacrifices that were offered to him, and the Temple,^d the place where people worshipped him, was pulled down. 12Because there was a turning away from God, the people stopped the daily sacrifices. Truth was thrown down to the ground, and the horn was successful in everything it did.

13Then I heard a holy angel speaking. Another holy angel asked the first one, "How long will the things in this vision last—the daily sacrifices, the turning away from God that brings destruction, the Temple^d being pulled down and the army of heaven being walked on?"

14The angel said to me, "This will happen for 2,300 evenings and mornings. Then the holy place will be repaired."

15I, Daniel, saw this vision and tried to understand what it meant. In it I saw someone who looked like a man standing near me. 16And I heard a man's voice calling from the Ulai Canal: "Gabriel, explain the vision to this man."

17Gabriel came to where I was standing. When he came close to me, I was very afraid and bowed face down on the ground. But Gabriel said to me, "Human being, understand that this vision is about the time of the end."

18While Gabriel was speaking, I fell into a deep sleep with my face on the ground. Then he touched me and lifted me to my feet. 19He said, "Now, I will explain to you what will happen in the time of God's anger. Your vision was about the set time of the end.

20"You saw a ram with two horns, which are the kings of Media and Persia. 21The male goat is the king of Greece, and the big horn between its eyes is the first king. 22The four horns that grew in the place of the broken horn are four kingdoms. Those four kingdoms will come from the nation of the first king, but they will not be as strong as the first king.

23"When the end comes near for those kingdoms, a bold and cruel king who tells lies will come. This will happen when many people have turned against God. 24This king will be very powerful, but his power will not come from himself. He will cause terrible destruction and will be successful in everything he does. He will destroy powerful people and even God's holy people. 25This king will succeed by using lies and force. He will think that he is very important. He will destroy many people without warning; he will try to fight even the Prince of princes! But that cruel king will be destroyed, and not by human power.

26"The vision that has been shown to you about these evenings and mornings is true. But seal up the vision, because those things won't happen for a long time."

27I, Daniel, became very weak and was sick for several days after that vision. Then I got up and went back to work for the king, but I was very upset about the vision. I didn't understand what it meant.

Daniel's Prayer

9 These things happened during the first year Darius son of Xerxes was king over Babylon. He was a descendant*d* of the Medes. ²During

> ### Sidelight
> When Daniel was told to seal the vision (Daniel 8:26), it probably involved writing it on a scroll, then rolling up the scroll, tying it shut, and fastening the ties with clay. The clay was then imprinted with a ring or stamp with a special seal or emblem on it. Then all the documents were placed in clay jars for safekeeping.

Darius' first year as king, I, Daniel, was reading the Scriptures. *d* I saw that the Lord told Jeremiah that Jerusalem would be empty ruins for 70 years.

³Then I turned to the Lord God and prayed and asked him for help. I did not eat any food. To show my sadness, I put on rough cloth and sat in ashes. ⁴I prayed to the Lord my God and told him about all of our sins. I said, "Lord, you are a great God who causes fear and wonder. You keep your agreement of love with all who love you and obey your commands.

⁵"But we have sinned and done wrong. We have been wicked and turned against you, your commands and your laws. ⁶We did not listen to your servants, the prophets, who spoke for you to our kings, our leaders, our ancestors and all the people of the land.

⁷"Lord, you are good and right, but we are full of shame today—the people of Judah and Jerusalem, all the people of Israel, those near and far whom you scattered among many nations because they were not loyal to you. ⁸Lord, we are all ashamed. Our kings and leaders and our fathers are ashamed, because we have sinned against you.

⁹"But, Lord our God, you show us mercy and forgive us even though we have turned against you. ¹⁰We have not obeyed the Lord our God or the teachings he gave us through his servants, the prophets. ¹¹All the people of Israel have disobeyed your teachings and have turned away, refusing to obey you. So you brought on us the curses and promises of punishment written in the Teachings of Moses, the servant of God, because we sinned against you.

¹²"You said these things would happen to us and our leaders, and you made them happen; you brought on us a great disaster. Nothing has ever been done on earth like what was done to Jerusalem. ¹³All this disaster came to us just as it is written in the Teachings of Moses. But we have

not pleaded with the Lord our God. We have not stopped sinning. We have not paid attention to your truth. ¹⁴The Lord was ready to bring the disaster on us, and he did it because the Lord our God is right in everything he does. But we still did not obey him.

¹⁵"Lord our God, you used your power and brought us out of Egypt. Because of that, your name is known even today. But we have sinned and have done wrong. ¹⁶Lord, you do what is right, but please do not be angry with Jerusalem, your city on your holy hill. Because of our sins and the evil things done by our ancestors, people all around insult and make fun of Jerusalem and your people.

¹⁷"Now, our God, hear the prayers of your servant. Listen to my prayer for help, and for your sake do good things for your holy place that is in ruins. ¹⁸My God, pay attention and hear me. Open your eyes and see all the terrible things that have happened to us. See how our lives have been ruined and what has happened to the city that is called by your name. We do not ask these things because we are good; instead, we ask because of your mercy. ¹⁹Lord, listen! Lord, forgive! Lord, hear us and do something! For your sake, don't wait, because your city and your people are called by your name."

Gabriel's Explanation

²⁰While I was saying these things in my prayer to the Lord, my God, confessing my sins and the sins of the people of Israel and praying for God's holy hill, ²¹Gabriel came to me. (I had seen him in my last vision.) He came flying quickly to me about the time of the evening sacrifice, while I was still praying. ²²He taught me and said to me, "Daniel, I have come to give you wisdom and to help you understand. ²³When you first started praying, an answer was given, and I came to tell you, because God loves you very much. So think about the message and understand the vision.

²⁴"God has ordered 490 years for your people and your holy city for these reasons: to stop people from turning against God; to put an end to sin; to take away evil; to bring in goodness that continues for ever; to bring about the vision and prophecy; *d* and to appoint a most holy place.

²⁵"Learn and understand these things. A command will come to rebuild Jerusalem. The time from this command until the appointed leader comes will be 49 years and 434 years. Jerusalem will be rebuilt with streets and a trench filled with water around it, but it will be built in times of trouble. ²⁶After the 434 years the appointed leader will be killed; he will have nothing. The people of the leader who is to come will destroy the city and the holy place. The end of the city

will come like a flood, and war will continue until the end. God has ordered that place to be completely destroyed. 27That leader will make firm an agreement with many people for seven years. He will stop the offerings and sacrifices after three and a half years. A destroyer will do terrible things until the ordered end comes to the destroyed city."

Daniel's Vision of a Man

10 During Cyrus' third year as king of Persia, Daniel, whose name was Belteshazzar, received a vision about a great war. It was a true message that Daniel understood.

2At that time I, Daniel, had been very sad for three weeks. 3I did not eat any fancy food or meat, or drink any wine or use any perfumed oil for three weeks.

4On the twenty-fourth day of the first month, I was standing beside the great Tigris River. 5While standing there, I looked up and saw a man dressed in linen clothes with a belt of fine gold wrapped around his waist. 6His body was like shiny yellow quartz. His face was bright like lightning, and his eyes were like fire. His arms and legs were shiny like polished bronze, and his voice sounded like the roar of a crowd.

7I, Daniel, was the only person who saw the vision. The men with me did not see it, because they were so frightened that they ran away and hid. 8So I was left alone, watching this great vision. I lost my strength, my face turned white like a dead person and I was helpless. 9Then I heard the man in the vision speaking. As I listened, I fell into a deep sleep with my face on the ground.

GOD'S GRACE

Backstage Pass

Amber repeated the name of the band, the band that just happened to be Mark's favourite band in the whole world! He had known Amber for years but never realised her cousin who "played drums in a band" was in *that* band!

The following month, Amber sorted Mark out with free tickets. Mark watched the show from the VIP area and then made his way backstage. Hundreds of fans queued up at the stage doors, but their way was barred by two massive bouncers built like tanks. But Mark walked straight past them all with a simple wave of the laminated backstage pass hanging around his neck. Within minutes, he was chatting to the band and having his CD signed at the after-show party.

Mark was no more deserving than any of the other fans, so what made the difference? Grace. Undeserved favour, no strings attached, from someone who cared about him and had the power to help him.

Just like those fans left outside the concert with no way of getting in, none of us can gain entry to heaven without God's grace. All of us have fallen short of God's 100 per cent pass mark because of the wrong things that we've done, and that's enough to separate us from God forever. The fantastic news is that God offers us a free pass into heaven by grace alone, because Jesus has already paid the price for our sin on the cross. We never need to earn God's love – as if we ever could anyway!

Read **Daniel 9:17–19** to see how the writer knows that God is a God of grace and asks for his favour, even though he knows he doesn't deserve it.

* Why does the writer ask for God's forgiveness instead of simply asking God to ignore their sin?
* Why do so many non-Christians think that if God *does* exist, he'll let them into heaven if they've tried to live a good life, or tried to be a bit religious? How does this passage tell us this won't work?

Consider . . .

* ways that you can show grace to someone this week.
* whether you have asked Jesus for his free gift of forgiveness made possible by his death on the cross.

For more, see . . .

* Isaiah 53:4–6, 10–12 (p.697)
* Ephesians 2:1–10 (p.1270)
* Romans 3:21–26 (p.1187)
* Titus 3:3–7 (p.1324)

¹⁰Then a hand touched me and set me on my hands and knees. I was so afraid that I was shaking. ¹¹The man in the vision said to me, "Daniel, God loves you very much. Think carefully about the words I will speak to you, and stand up, because I have been sent to you." When he said this, I stood up, but I was still shaking.

¹²Then the man said to me, "Daniel, do not be afraid. Some time ago you decided to get understanding and to humble yourself before your God. Since that time God has listened to you, and I have come because of your prayers. ¹³But the prince of Persia has been fighting against me for 21 days. Then Michael, one of the most important angels, came to help me, because I had been left there with the king of Persia. ¹⁴Now I have come to explain to you what will happen to your people, because the vision is about a time in the future."

¹⁵While he was speaking to me, I bowed face down and could not speak. ¹⁶Then one who looked like a man touched my lips, so I opened my mouth and started to speak. I said to the one standing in front of me, "Master, I am upset and afraid because of what I saw in the vision. I feel helpless. ¹⁷Master, how can I, your servant, talk with you? My strength is gone, and it is hard for me to breathe."

¹⁸The one who looked like a man touched me again and gave me strength. ¹⁹He said, "Daniel, don't be afraid. God loves you very much. Peace be with you. Be strong now; be courageous."

When he spoke to me, I became stronger and said, "Master, speak, since you have given me strength."

²⁰Then he said, "Daniel, do you know why I have come to you? Soon I must go back to fight against the prince of Persia. When I go, the prince of Greece will come, ²¹but I must first tell you what is written in the Book of Truth. No one stands with me against these enemies except Michael, the angel ruling over your people.

11 In the first year that Darius the Mede was king, I stood up to support Michael in his fight against the prince of Persia.

Kingdoms of the South and North

²"Now then, Daniel, I tell you the truth: three more kings will rule in Persia, and then a fourth king will come. He will be much richer than all the kings of Persia before him and will use his riches to get power. He will stir up everyone against the kingdom of Greece. ³Then a mighty king will come, who will rule with great power and will do anything he wants. ⁴After that king has come, his kingdom will be broken up and divided out towards the four parts of the world. His kingdom will not go to his descendants,ᵈ and it will not have the power that he had, because his kingdom will be pulled up and given to other people.

⁵"The king of the South will become strong, but one of his commanders will become even stronger. He will begin to rule his own kingdom with great power. ⁶Then after a few years, a new friendship will develop. The daughter of the king of the South will marry the king of the North in order to bring peace. But she will not keep her power, and his family will not last. She, her husband, her child and those who brought her to that country will be killed.

⁷"But a person from her family will become king of the South and will attack the armies of the king of the North. He will go into that king's strong, walled city and will fight and win. ⁸He will take their gods, their metal idols and their valuable things made of silver and gold back to Egypt. Then he will not bother the king of the North for a few years. ⁹Next, the king of the North will attack the king of the South, but he will be beaten back to his own country.

¹⁰"The sons of the king of the North will prepare for war. They will get a large army together that will move through the land very quickly, like a powerful flood. Later, that army will come back and fight all the way to the strong, walled city of the king of the South. ¹¹Then the king of the South will become very angry and will march out to fight against the king of the North. The king of the North will have a large army, but he will lose the battle, ¹²and the soldiers will be carried away. The king of the South will then be very proud and will kill thousands of soldiers from the northern army, but he will not continue to be successful. ¹³The king of the North will gather another army, larger than the first one. After several years he will attack with a large army and many weapons.

¹⁴"In those times many people will be against the king of the South. Some of your own people who love to fight will turn against the king of the South, thinking it is time for God's promises to come true. But they will fail. ¹⁵Then the king of the North will come. He will build roads of earth to the tops of the city walls and will capture a strong, walled city. The southern army will not have the power to fight back; even their best soldiers will not be strong enough to stop the northern army. ¹⁶So the king of the North will do whatever he wants; no one will be able to stand against him. He will gain power and control in the beautiful land of Israel and will have the power to destroy it. ¹⁷The king of the North will decide to use all his power to fight against the king of the South, but he will make a peace agreement with the king of the South. The king of the North will give one of his daughters as a wife to the king of the South so that he can defeat him. But those plans will not succeed or help him. ¹⁸Then the king of the North will turn his attention to

cities along the coast of the Mediterranean Sea and will capture them. But a commander will put an end to the pride of the king of the North, turning his pride back on him. ¹⁹After that happens the king of the North will go back to the strong, walled cities of his own country, but he will lose his power. That will be the end of him.

²⁰"The next king of the North will send out a tax collector so he will have plenty of money. In a few years that ruler will be killed, although he will not die in anger or in a battle.

²¹"That ruler will be followed by a very cruel and hated man, who will not have the honour of being from a king's family. He will attack the kingdom when the people feel safe, and he will take power by lying to the people. ²²He will sweep away in defeat large and powerful armies and even a prince who made an agreement. ²³Many nations will make agreements with that cruel and hated ruler, but he will lie to them. He will gain much power, but only a few people will support him. ²⁴The richest areas will feel safe, but that cruel and hated ruler will attack them. He will succeed where his ancestors did not. He will rob the countries he defeats and will give those things to his followers. He will plan to defeat and destroy strong cities, but he will be successful for only a short time.

²⁵"That very cruel and hated ruler will have a large army that he will use to stir up his strength and courage. He will attack the king of the South. The king of the South will gather a large and very powerful army and prepare for war. But the people who are against him will make secret plans, and the king of the South will be defeated. ²⁶People who were supposed to be his good friends will try to destroy him. His army will be swept away in defeat; many of his soldiers will be killed in battle. ²⁷Those two kings will want to hurt each other. They will sit at the same table and lie to each other, but it will not do either one any good, because God has set a time for their end to come. ²⁸The king of the North will go back to his own country with much wealth. Then he will decide to go against the holy agreement. He will take action and then return to his own country.

²⁹"At the right time the king of the North will attack the king of the South again, but this time he will not be successful as he was before. ³⁰Ships from the west will come and fight against the king of the North, so he will be afraid. Then he will return and show his anger against the holy agreement. He will be good to those who have stopped obeying the holy agreement.

³¹"The king of the North will send his army to make the Temple *d* in Jerusalem unclean. *d* They will stop the people from offering the daily sacrifice, and then they will set up the destroying terror.

³²The king of the North will tell lies and cause those who have not obeyed God to be ruined. But those who know God and obey him will be strong and fight back.

³³"Those who are wise will help the others understand what is happening. But they will be killed with swords or burned, or taken captive or robbed of their homes and possessions. These things will continue for many days. ³⁴When the wise ones are suffering, they will get a little help, but many who join the wise ones will not help them in their time of need. ³⁵Some of the wise ones will be killed. But the hard times must come so they can be made stronger and purer and without faults until the time of the end comes. Then, at the right time, the end will come.

The King Who Praises Himself

³⁶"The king of the North will do whatever he wants. He will boast about himself and praise himself and think he is even better than a god. He will say things against the God of gods that no one has ever heard. And he will be successful until all the bad things have happened. Then what God has planned to happen will happen. ³⁷The king of the North will not care about the gods his ancestors worshipped or the god that women worship. He won't care about any god. Instead, he will make himself more important than any god. ³⁸The king of the North will worship power and strength, which his ancestors did not worship. He will honour the god of power with gold and silver, expensive jewels and gifts. ³⁹That king will attack fortified cities with the help of a foreign god. He will give much honour to the people who join him, making them rulers in charge of many other people. And he will make them pay him for the land they rule.

⁴⁰"At the time of the end, the king of the South will fight a battle against the king of the North. The king of the North will attack with chariots, soldiers on horses and many large ships. He will invade many countries and sweep through their lands like a flood. ⁴¹The king of the North will attack the beautiful land of Judah. He will defeat many countries, but Edom, Moab and the leaders of Ammon will be saved from him. ⁴²The king of the North will show his power in many countries; Egypt will not escape. ⁴³The king will get treasures of gold and silver and all the riches of Egypt. The Libyan and Nubian people will obey him. ⁴⁴But the king of the North will hear news from the east and the north that will make him afraid and angry. He will go to destroy completely many nations. ⁴⁵He will set up his royal tents between the sea and the beautiful mountain where the holy Temple *d* is built. But, finally, his end will come, and no one will help him.

The Time of the End

12 "At that time Michael, the great prince who protects your people, will stand up. There will be a time of much trouble, the worst time since nations have been on earth, but your people will be saved. Everyone whose name is written in God's book will be saved. ²Many people who have already died will live again. Some of them will wake up to have life for ever, but some will wake up to find shame and disgrace for ever. ³The wise people will shine like the brightness of the sky. Those who teach others to live right will shine like stars for ever and ever.

⁴"But you, Daniel, close up the book and seal it. These things will happen at the time of the end. Many people will go here and there to find true knowledge."

⁵Then I, Daniel, looked, and saw two other men. One was standing on my side of the river, and the other was standing on the far side. ⁶The man who was dressed in linen was standing over the water in the river. One of the two men spoke to him and asked, "How long will it be before these amazing things come true?"

⁷The man dressed in linen, who stood over the water, raised his hands towards heaven. And I heard him swear by the name of God who lives for ever, "It will be for three and a half years.

> **Sidelight** Daniel 12:2 is the clearest reference in the Old Testament to the resurrection of the dead. Another possible reference is found in Isaiah 26:19 (p.666).

ETERNAL LIFE

Going the Distance

At the age of nineteen, Canadian Terry Fox lost his right leg to cancer. After the amputation, he became a discouraged and bitter young man. He assumed he was stuck in a wheelchair forever and felt cheated out of the "normal" things in life.

Trying to provide some motivation, Terry's former basketball coach showed him an article about a one-legged man who competed in the New York Marathon. The article ignited a sense of challenge in Terry. "If he can do it, so can I," Terry thought.

Gradually, Terry began to set goals for himself and decided to take more control of his life. He began to build his body and find ways to run with an artificial limb. He perfected the stride that came to be called the "Fox Trot". He was soon running frequently and feeling good about his life.

On April 12 1980, Terry started his "Marathon of Hope", a solo run across Canada to raise money for cancer research. Four and a half months later, after covering 5,300 miles and raising $24,000,000, he had to stop. The cancer had spread to his lungs. Terry was hospitalised, and pneumonia set in. He died at the age of twenty-two.

Terry remains a dramatic symbol of hope and courage to Canada and to the world. "I wanted to show people that just because they are disabled, it's not the end," he said.

All of us need more of that kind of hope and courage. Read about the rewards in **Daniel 12:1–3** for those who trust in God for strength to go the distance.

- What hope and encouragement would Terry have found in this passage as he struggled to complete his transcontinental trek?
- If you were to be remembered forever, how would you like to be remembered?

Consider . . .

- completing this sentence as many ways as possible: "When I think of eternal life, I imagine . . ."
- drawing a star and writing the name of a person you respect on it (see verse 3) and then thanking God for that person each day this week.

For more, see . . .

- Ezekiel 37:1–14 (p.820)
- 1 Corinthians 15:12–28 (p.1235)
- Mark 13:1–12 (p.1023)

The power of the holy people will finally be broken, and then all these things will come true."

[8]I heard the answer, but I did not really understand, so I asked, "Master, what will happen after all these things come true?"

[9]He answered, "Go your way, Daniel. The message is closed up and sealed until the time of the end. [10]Many people will be made clean,[d] pure and spotless, but the wicked will continue to be wicked. Those wicked people will not understand these things, but the wise will understand them.

[11]"The daily sacrifice will be stopped. Then, 1,290 days later, the destroying terror will be set up. [12]Those who wait for the end of the 1,335 days will be happy.

[13]"As for you, Daniel, go your way until the end. You will get your rest, and at the end you will rise to receive your reward."

Hosea

Why Read This Book:

- Discover how strong God's love is (Hosea 1—3).
- Learn what can happen when people turn from God (Hosea 6—10).
- Find assurance in God's love and forgiveness (Hosea 11—14).

When?

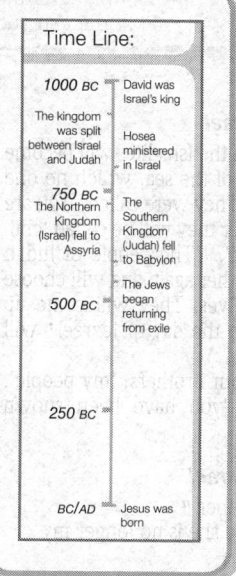

Time Line:

1000 BC	David was Israel's king
The kingdom was split between Israel and Judah	Hosea ministered in Israel
750 BC The Northern Kingdom (Israel) fell to Assyria	The Southern Kingdom (Judah) fell to Babylon
500 BC	The Jews began returning from exile
250 BC	
BC/AD	Jesus was born

Behind the Scenes:

Imagine God telling someone to marry a prostitute. Then imagine that man remaining faithful to his bride even after she returned to her old job.

As improbable as that situation may sound, it is what happened in the book of Hosea. The prophet Hosea married Gomer, a prostitute. She was unfaithful to him, yet he continued to love her and forgive her. Even though her unfaithfulness hurt him, Hosea never stopped loving his unfaithful wife.

Hosea's life symbolised God's relationship to Israel. God had tried to build a relationship with the Israelites. But time after time, the Israelites had turned to other "lovers" – other gods. Yet God's love wouldn't let Israel go.

Hosea preached in the Northern Kingdom (Israel) in the eighth century BC. It was a time of prosperity, so the people didn't listen to him. But years of immorality and unfaithfulness followed, leading to Israel's destruction in 722 BC by the Assyrians. ▷

Where?

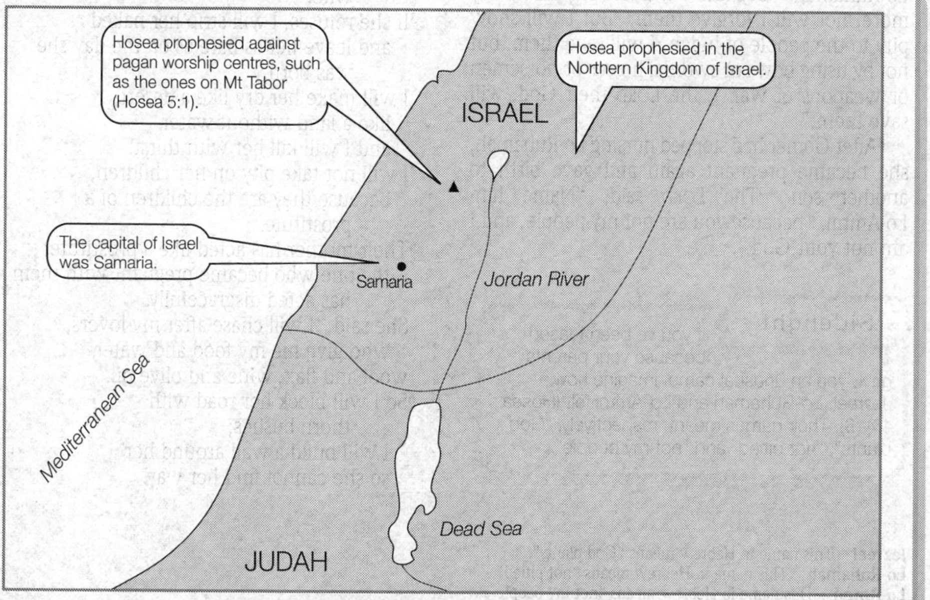

Hosea prophesied against pagan worship centres, such as the ones on Mt Tabor (Hosea 5:1).

Hosea prophesied in the Northern Kingdom of Israel.

ISRAEL

The capital of Israel was Samaria.

Samaria

Jordan River

Mediterranean Sea

Dead Sea

JUDAH

Behind the Scenes (cont.): The book of Hosea tells the story of a prophet's pleading with the people to stop turning away from God and to recognise God's everlasting and tender love. Through the prophet, God says, "I want faithful love . . . I want people to know me . . . " (Hosea 6:6). This central message in Hosea is a message for all time!

---

1 The LORD spoke his word to Hosea son of Beeri during the time that Uzziah, Jotham, Ahaz and Hezekiah were kings of Judah and Jeroboam son of Jehoash was king of Israel.

Hosea's Wife and Children

2When the LORD began speaking through Hosea, the LORD said to him, "Go and marry an unfaithful woman and have unfaithful children, because the people in this country have been completely unfaithful to the LORD." 3So Hosea married Gomer daughter of Diblaim, and she became pregnant and gave birth to Hosea's son.

4The LORD said to Hosea, "Name him Jezreel,[n] because soon I will punish the family of Jehu for the people they killed at Jezreel. In the future I will put an end to the kingdom of Israel 5and break the power of Israel's army in the Valley of Jezreel."

6Gomer became pregnant again and gave birth to a daughter. The LORD said to Hosea, "Name her Lo-Ruhamah,[n] because I will not pity Israel any more, nor will I forgive them. 7But I will show pity to the people of Judah. I will save them, but not by using bows or swords, horses or horsemen or weapons of war. I, the LORD their God, will save them."

8After Gomer had stopped nursing Lo-Ruhamah, she became pregnant again and gave birth to another son. 9The LORD said, "Name him Lo-Ammi,[n] because you are not my people, and I am not your God.

God's Promise to Israel

10"But the number of the Israelites will become like the grains of sand of the sea, which no one can measure or count. They were called, 'You are not my people', but later they will be called 'children of the living God'. 11The people of Judah and Israel will join together again and will choose one leader for themselves. They will come up from the land, because the day of Jezreel[n] will be truly great.

2 "You are to call your brothers, 'my people', and your sisters, 'you have been shown pity'.

God Speaks About Israel

2"Plead with your mother.[n]
  Accuse her, because she is no longer my wife,
    and I am no longer her husband.
  Tell her to stop acting like a prostitute,[d]
    to stop behaving like an unfaithful wife.
3If she refuses, I will strip her naked
    and leave her as bare as on the day she was born.
  I will make her dry like a desert,
    like a land without water,
    and I will kill her with thirst.
4I will not take pity on her children,
    because they are the children of a prostitute.
5Their mother has acted like a prostitute;
    the one who became pregnant with them has acted disgracefully.
  She said, 'I will chase after my lovers,[n]
    who give me my food and water,
  wool and flax, wine and olive oil.'
6So I will block her road with thorn-bushes;
    I will build a wall around her
    so she cannot find her way.

Sidelight If you've been teased because your parents gave you an unusual name, imagine how Jezreel, Lo-Ruhamah and Lo-Ammi felt (Hosea 1:4–9). Their names meant, respectively, "God plants", "not pitied" and "not my people".

Jezreel This name in Hebrew means "God plants".
Lo-Ruhamah This name in Hebrew means "not pitied".
Lo-Ammi This name in Hebrew means "not my people".
mother Refers to the nation of Israel here.
lovers Refers to the nations surrounding Israel, who led Israel to worship false gods.

7She will run after her lovers,
but she won't catch them.
She will look for them,
but she won't find them.
Then she will say, 'I will go back to my first
husband, *n*
because life was better then for me than it
is now.'
8But she does not know that I was the
one
who gave her grain, new wine and oil.
I gave her much silver and gold,
but she used it for Baal. *d*

9"So I will come back and take away my grain
at harvest time
and my new wine when it is ready.
I will take back my wool and linen
that covered her nakedness.
10So I will show her nakedness to her lovers,
and no one will save her from me.

husband   Refers to God here.

11I will put an end to all her celebrations:
her yearly festivals, her New Moon *d*
festivals and her Sabbaths. *d*
I will stop all of her special feasts.
12I will destroy her vines and fig trees,
which she said were her pay from her lovers.
I will turn them into a forest,
and wild animals will eat them.
13I will punish her for all the times
she burned incense *d* to the Baals.
She put on her rings and jewellery
and went chasing after her lovers,
but she forgot me!"
says the LORD.

14"So I am going to attract her;
I will lead her into the desert
and speak tenderly to her.
15There I will give her back her vineyards,
and I will make the Valley of Trouble a
door of hope.

FOLLOWING GOD

Going to the Wilderness

Sometimes it was so difficult to think clearly back home. Danny had grown up in the noise, clamour, and confusion of the inner city. Similar confusion filled his own life. Arrested for a series of minor crimes, Danny was sent to a detention centre.

Now here he was taking part in a survival challenge course – 19 days of mountain living. Feelings of frustration and anger from the inner city followed him. He had snapped at the leaders because of the cold and the rain, the long days of hiking and getting lost. Why couldn't he ever just relax? Why did he always feel angry and out of control?

Sitting out under the stars, Danny tried to sort out his feelings of failure with Bob, his group leader. They talked for a long time. Then Bob said, "If there were just one gift I could give you, it'd be the gift of peace – the peace that begins with accepting yourself as loved by God."

Sometimes following God requires us to leave our usual surroundings and go to a quiet place to hear his message. In **Hosea 2:14–20** read how God would become more real in the wilderness.

* How is God's message to Israel similar to the one that Danny heard?
* How does the passage's theme compare with your own ideas of what it means to follow God?

Consider . . .

* taking a long walk by yourself and listening for ways in which God wants you to serve him.
* serving God through a quiet act of kindness, such as listening to someone without interrupting, or donating your time and money to a ministry you support.

For more, see . . .

* Exodus 3:1–6 (p.61)
* Luke 9:28–36 (p.1055)
* Matthew 4:1–11 (p.941)

There she will respond as when she was
    young,
  as when she came out of Egypt."

[16]The LORD says, "In the future she will call me
  'my husband';
  no longer will she call me 'my baal'. *n*
[17]I will never let her say the names of Baal
  again;
  people won't use their names any more.
[18]At that time I will make an agreement for
  them
  with the wild animals, the birds and the
    crawling things.
I will smash from the land
  the bow and the sword and the weapons
    of war,
  so my people will live in safety.
[19]And I will make you my promised bride for
  ever.
I will be good and fair;
I will show you my love and mercy.
[20]I will be true to you as my promised bride,
  and you will know the LORD.

[21]"At that time I will speak to you," says the
  LORD.
"I will speak to the skies,
  and they will give rain to the earth.
[22]The earth will produce grain, new wine
  and oil;
  much will grow because my people are
    called Jezreel. *n*
[23]I will plant my people in the land,
  and I will show pity to the one I had called
    'not shown pity'.
I will say, 'You are my people'
  to those I had called 'not my people'.
And they will say to me, 'You are
  our God.' "

> **Sidelight**
> Hosea's wife Gomer
> (Hosea 3:1), was a
> prostitute, but God wanted Hosea to love her
> despite her past record of unfaithfulness. In the
> same way, God said that he loved his children
> despite the fact that they were unfaithful to him.
> This is what "unconditional love" really means.

Hosea Buys a Wife

3 The LORD said to me again, "Go and show
your love to a woman loved by someone

else, who has been unfaithful to you. In the same
way the LORD loves the people of Israel, even
though they worship other gods and love to eat
the raisin cakes." *n*
[2]So I bought her for 15 pieces of silver and 150
kilogrammes of barley. [3]Then I told her, "You
must wait for me for many days. You must not be
a prostitute, *d* and you must not have sexual relations with any other man. I will act the same
way towards you."

[4]In the same way Israel will live many days
without a king or leader, without sacrifices or
holy stone pillars, and without the holy robe *d* or
an idol. [5]After this, the people of Israel will return
to the LORD their God and follow him and the
king from David's family. In the last days they
will turn in fear to the LORD, and he will bless
them.

The LORD's Word Against Israel

4 People of Israel, listen to the LORD's
  message.
  The LORD has this
  against you who live in the land:
"The people are not true, not loyal to God,
  nor do those who live in the land even
    know him.
[2]Cursing, lying, killing, stealing and adultery *d*
  are everywhere.
One murder follows another.
[3]Because of this the land dries up,
  and all its people are dying.
Even the wild animals and the birds of
  the air
and the fish of the sea are dying.

God's Case Against the Priests

[4]"No one should accuse
  or blame another person.
Don't blame the people, you priests,
  when they quarrel with you.
[5]You will be ruined in the day,
  and your prophets *d* will be ruined with you
    in the night.
I will also destroy your mother. *n*
[6]My people will be destroyed,
  because they have no knowledge.
You have refused to learn,
  so I will refuse to let you be priests to me.
You have forgotten the teachings of your God,
  so I will forget your children.
[7]The more priests there are,
  the more they sin against me.

---

baal Another Hebrew word for husband, but it was the same word as the god Baal.
Jezreel This name in Hebrew means "God plants".
raisin cakes This food was eaten in the feasts that honoured false gods.
mother Here "mother" refers to the nation of Israel.

I will take away their honour
  and give them shame.
[8]Since the priests live off the sin offerings of
    the people,
  they want the people to sin more and
    more.
[9]The priests are as wrong as the people,
  and I will punish them both for what they
    have done.
  I will repay them for the wrong they have
    done.

[10]"They will eat
  but not have enough;
they will have sexual relations with the
    prostitutes, *d*
but they will not have children,
because they have left the LORD
  to give themselves to [11]prostitution,
to old and new wine,
  which take away their ability to
    understand.

God's Case Against the People

[12]"My people ask wooden idols for advice;
  they ask those sticks of wood to advise them!
Like prostitutes, they have chased after other
    gods
  and have left their own God.
[13]They make sacrifices on the tops of the
    mountains.
  They burn offerings on the hills,
under oaks, poplars and other trees,
  because their shade is nice.
So your daughters become prostitutes,
  and your daughters-in-law are guilty of
    adultery. *d*
[14]"But I will not punish your daughters
  for becoming prostitutes,
nor your daughters-in-law
  for their sins of adultery.
I will not punish them,
  because the men have sexual relations with
    prostitutes

ADDICTION

Sold Out

- There is a boy in Liverpool who was christened with the names of every player in the Liverpool football team.
- There is a girl in Essex who buys tickets for every concert for her favourite artist, regardless of the amount of concerts on the tour, the countries or the expense involved.
- There are loads of people who have every *Star Trek* episode on video and go to every Star Trek Convention, dressed, of course, as their favourite character.
- There are grown male adults who take to the streets in stockings and suspender belts every time the *Rocky Horror Picture Show* comes to town.
- There are people who camp, complete with tents, outside the houses of famous film stars.

OK, some of these things are just fun, but unfortunately some of them are quite serious. The word stalker is defined in our dictionaries as someone who follows, shadows and creeps after people. They have taken their devotion to another level. An unacceptable one.

    These are people who have left their own lives behind them, to take on someone else's. They have almost "sold" themselves. **Hosea 4:12–13** talks of people who have "prostituted themselves to another god".

- What does this passage say is missing in the lives of people such as these?
- What do people today have in common with those of Hosea's time?

Consider . . .

- write down how many things there are in your life that come higher on your list of priorities than your commitment to God.
- if there is anything taking God's place in your life, ask him to help and forgive you.

For more, see . . .

- Matthew 19:16–22 (p.974)
- 2 Peter 2:19 (p.1367)
- 1 Corinthians 6:12 (p.1221)

and offer sacrifices with the temple
  prostitutes.
A foolish people will be ruined.

15"Israel, you act like a prostitute,
  but do not be guilty towards the LORD.
Don't go to Gilgal
  or go up to Beth Aven.*n*
Don't make promises,
  saying, 'As surely as the LORD lives . . .'
16The people of Israel are stubborn
  like a stubborn young cow.
Now the LORD will feed them
  like lambs in the open country.
17The Israelites have chosen to worship idols,
  so leave them alone.
18When they finish their drinking,
  they completely give themselves to being
    prostitutes;
  they love these disgraceful ways.
19They will be swept away as if by a
    whirlwind,
  and their sacrifices will bring them only
    shame.

God's Word Against the Leaders

5 "Listen, you priests.
  Pay attention, people of Israel.
Listen, royal family,
  because you will all be judged.
You have been like a trap at Mizpah
  and like a net spread out at Mount Tabor.
2You have done many evil things,
  so I will punish you all.
3I know all about the people of Israel;
  what they have done is not hidden
    from me.
Now that Israel acts like a prostitute, *d*
  it has made itself unclean. *d*

4"They will not give up their deeds
  and return to their God.
They are determined to be unfaithful
    to me;
  they do not know the LORD.
5Israel's pride testifies against them.
  The people of Israel will stumble because of
    their sin,
  and the people of Judah will stumble with
    them.
6They will come to worship the LORD,
  bringing their flocks and herds,
but they will not be able to find him,
  because he has left them.
7They have not been true to the LORD;
  they are children who do not belong
    to him.

So their false worship
  will destroy them and their land.

8"Blow the horn in Gibeah
  and the trumpet in Ramah.
Give the warning at Beth Aven,
  and be first into battle, people of Benjamin.
9Israel will be ruined
  on the day of punishment.
To the tribes *d* of Israel
  I tell the truth.
10The leaders of Judah are like those
  who steal other people's land.
I will pour my punishment over them
  like a flood of water.
11Israel is crushed by the punishment,
  because it decided to follow idols.
12I am like a moth to Israel,
  like a rot to the people of Judah.
13"When Israel saw its wounds
  and Judah saw its wounds,
Israel went to Assyria for help
  and sent to the great king of Assyria.
But he cannot heal you
  or cure your wounds.
14I will be like a lion to Israel,
  like a young lion to Judah.
I will attack them
  and tear them to pieces.
I will drag them off,
  and no one will be able to save them.
15Then I will go back to my place
  until they suffer for their guilt and turn
    back to me.
In their trouble they will look for me."

The People are Not Faithful

6 "Come, let's go back to the LORD.
  He has hurt us, but he will heal us.
He has wounded us, but he will bandage
    our wounds.
2In two days he will put new life in us;
  on the third day he will raise us up
so that we may live in his presence 3and
    know him.
Let's try to learn about the LORD;
  He will come to us as surely as the dawn
    comes.
He will come to us like rain,
  like the spring rain that waters the
    ground."

4The LORD says, "Israel, what should I do
    with you?
Judah, what should I do with you?
Your faithfulness is like a morning mist,
  like the dew that goes away early in the day.

Gilgal . . . Beth Aven   Cities in Israel where people worshipped false gods.

⁵I have warned you by my prophets *d*
    that I will kill you and destroy you.
    My justice comes out like bright light.
⁶I want faithful love
    more than I want animal sacrifices.
I want people to know me
    more than I want burnt offerings.
⁷But they have broken the agreement as
      Adam did;
    they have been unfaithful to me.

⁸Gilead is a city of people who do evil;
    their footprints are bloody.
⁹The priests are like robbers waiting to attack
      people;
    they murder people on the road to
      Shechem *n*
    and do wicked things.
¹⁰I have seen horrible things in Israel.
    Look at Israel's prostitution; *d*
    Israel has become unclean. *d*

Shechem   A city of safety where people could go for protection.

FOLLOWING GOD

Off Track

"Are you joking?" Richard asked.

The coach shook his head. "No, I'm not joking. You've been selected as a member of this year's national junior athletics team."

Richard took a deep breath to slow down the sudden surge of adrenaline that shot to his brain. Being selected for the national team had always been his ambition, but it had always seemed too far ahead to grasp. Nevertheless, he had trained hard and his ambition was now being fulfilled – he would be competing in the games which were only seven months away.

Curiously, Richard began to get lazy with his training. He began to enjoy talking more about his sport than he did practising it. Before long, he was regularly skipping training sessions in favour of posing in front of his friends.

"It's got to change, Richard," his coach told him four months before the big competition.

"What has?"

"Your attitude," the coach replied. "You're just not training hard enough for a national team member. There are a lot of athletes out there who would train all day long if they had to, just to be in your position."

Richard was shocked. He hadn't realised how much he had been neglecting his training.

This shock sent him back to his roots, back to the regular training which had earned him a position on the team in the first place. Gradually, his time improved, and eventually he was clocking faster times than ever before; but it had taken strong words of warning from the coach to shake him back into action.

In the same way, God is not satisfied with Christians who think they've done all they need to do and can relax until they get to heaven. Read about the burning enthusiasm which God expects in **Hosea 6:1–6**.

- Why did Richard's coach and God become angry with half-hearted efforts?
- How would your life change if you put everything you've got into following God? How could the church be different if every member got "on fire" for God? How would this affect the world?

Consider . . .

- comparing the activities of "routine" Christians with those of "committed" believers. Decide to become "committed" to God and put your decision into action.
- feeding your enthusiasm by getting to know God better through deeper times of daily prayer and studying the Bible.

For more, see . . .

- Micah 6:8 (p.896)
- Colossians 3:12–17 (p.1293)
- Matthew 22:34–40 (p.980)

[11]"Judah, I have set a harvest time for you
    when I will make the lives of my people
      good again.

7

When I heal Israel,
    Israel's sin will go away,
and so will Samaria's evil.

"They cheat a lot!
    Thieves break into houses,
    and robbers are in the streets.
[2]It never enters their minds
    that I remember all their evil deeds.
The bad things they do are all around
      them;
    they are right in front of me.

Israel's Evil Kings

[3]"They make the king happy with their
      wickedness;
    their rulers are glad with their lies.
[4]But all of them are traitors.
    They are like an oven heated by a baker.
  While he mixes the dough,
    he does not need to stir up the fire.
[5]The kings get so drunk they get sick
      every day.
    The rulers become crazy with wine;
    they make agreements with those who do
      not know the true God.
[6]They burn like an oven;
    their hearts burn inside them.
  All night long their anger is low,
    but when morning comes, it becomes a
      roaring fire.
[7]All these people are as hot as an oven;
    they burn up their rulers.
  All their kings fall,
    and no one calls on me.

Sidelight

Political stability was
something that the
Israelites were lacking. In the space of just 25
years, the prophets saw the reign of six kings –
four of whom were assassinated. This is probably
what Hosea was referring to in Hosea 7:7.

Israel and the Other Nations

[8]"Israel mixes with other nations;
    he is like a pancake cooked only on one
      side.
[9]Foreign nations have eaten up his
      strength,
    but he doesn't know it.
  Israel is weak and feeble, like an old man,
    but he doesn't know it.

[10]Israel's pride will cause their defeat;
    they will not turn back to the LORD
      their God
    or look to him for help in all this.
[11]Israel has become like a pigeon—
    easy to fool and stupid.
  First they call to Egypt for help.
    Then they run to Assyria.
[12]When they go, I will catch them in a net,
    I will bring them down like birds from
      the sky;
    I will punish them countless times for their
      evil.
[13]How terrible for them because they left me!
    They will be destroyed, because they
      turned against me.
  I want to save them,
    but they have spoken lies against me.
[14]They do not call to me from their hearts.
    They just lie on their beds and cry.
  They come together to ask for grain and new
      wine,
    but they really turn away from me.
[15]Though I trained them and gave them
      strength,
    they have made evil plans against me.
[16]They did not turn to the Most High God.
    They are like a loose bow that can't shoot.
  Because their leaders boast about their
      strength,
    they will be killed with swords,
  and the people in Egypt
    will laugh at them.

Israel Has Trusted Wrong Things

8

"Put the trumpet to your lips and give the
      warning!
  The enemy swoops down on the LORD's
      people like an eagle.
  The Israelites have broken my agreement
    and have turned against my teachings.
[2]They cry out to me,
    'Our God, we in Israel know you!'
[3]But Israel has rejected what is good,
    so the enemy will chase them.
[4]They chose their own kings
    without asking my permission.
  They chose their own leaders,
    people I did not know.
  They made their silver and gold into idols,
    and for all this they will be destroyed.
[5]I hate the calf-shaped idol of Israel!
    I am very angry with the people.
  How long will they remain unclean? *d*
[6]The idol is something a craftsman made;
    it is not God.
  Israel's calf-shaped idol
    will surely be smashed to pieces.

7"Israel's foolish plans are like planting the
    wind,
  but they will harvest a storm.
Like a stalk with no head of grain,
  it produces nothing.
Even if it produced something,
  other nations would eat it.
8Israel is eaten up;
  the people are mixed among the other
    nations
  and have become useless to me.
9Israel is like a wild donkey all by itself.
  They have run to Assyria;
  They have hired other nations to protect
    them.
10Although Israel is mixed among the nations,
  I will gather them together.
They will become weaker and weaker
  as they suffer under the great king of
    Assyria.

11"Although Israel built more altars to
    remove sin,
  they have become altars for sinning.
12I have written many teachings for them,
  but they think the teachings are strange
    and foreign.
13The Israelites offer sacrifices to me as gifts
  and eat the meat,
but the LORD is not pleased with them.
  He remembers the evil they have done,
and he will punish them for their sins.
  They will be slaves again as they were in
    Egypt.
14Israel has forgotten their Maker and has built
    palaces;
  Judah has built many strong, walled cities.
But I will send fire on their cities
  and destroy their strong buildings."

Israel's Punishment

9 Israel, do not rejoice;
    don't shout for joy as the other
      nations do.
  You have been like a prostitute d against
    your God.
  You love the pay of prostitutes on every
    threshing d floor.
2But the threshing floor and the winepress will
    not feed the people,
  and there won't be enough new wine.
3The people will not stay in the LORD's land.
  Israel will return to being captives as they
    were in Egypt,
  and in Assyria they will eat food that they
    are not allowed to eat.

4The Israelites will not give offerings of wine
    to the LORD;
  they will not give him sacrifices.
Their sacrifices will be like food that is eaten
    at a funeral;
  it is unclean, d and everyone who eats it
    becomes unclean.
Their food will only satisfy their hunger;
  they cannot sacrifice it in the Temple. d
5What will you do then on the day of feasts
  and on the day of the LORD's festival?
6Even if the people are not destroyed,
  Egypt will capture them;
  Memphis n will bury them.
Weeds will grow over their silver treasures,
  and thorns will drive them out of their
    tents.
7The time of punishment has come,
  the time to pay for sins.
  Let Israel know this:
you think the prophet d is a fool,
  and you say the spiritual person is mad.
You have sinned very much,
  and your hatred is great.
8Is Israel a watchman?
  Are God's people prophets?
Everywhere Israel goes, traps are set
    for him.
  He is an enemy in God's house.
9The people of Israel have gone deep into sin
  as the people of Gibeah n did.
The Lord will remember the evil things they
    have done
  and he will punish their sins.

10"When I found Israel,
  it was like finding grapes in the desert.
Your ancestors were like
  finding the first figs on the fig tree.
But when they came to Baal Peor
  they began worshipping an idol,
  and they became as hateful as the thing
    they worshipped.
11Israel's glory will fly away like a bird;
  there will be no more pregnancy, no more
    births, no more getting pregnant.
12But even if the Israelites bring up children,
  I will take them all away.
How terrible it will be for them
  when I go away from them!
13I have seen Israel, like Tyre,
  given a pleasant place.
But the people of Israel will soon bring out
  their children to be killed."
14LORD, give them what they should have.
  What will you give them?

Memphis A city in Egypt famous for its tombs.
Gibeah The sins of the people of Gibeah caused a civil war. See Judges 19—21.

Make their women unable to have
children;
give them dried-up breasts that cannot feed
their babies.

15"The Israelites were very wicked in Gilgal,
so I have hated them there.
Because of the sinful things they have done,
I will force them to leave my land.
I will no longer love them;
their leaders have turned against me.
16Israel is beaten down;
its root is dying, and it has no fruit.
If they have more children,
I will kill the children they love."

17God will reject them,
because they have not obeyed him;
they will wander among the nations.

Israel will Pay for Sin

10 Israel is like a large vine
that produced plenty of fruit.
As the people became richer,
they built more altars for idols.
As their land became better,
they put up better stone pillars to honour
gods.
2Their heart was false,
and now they must pay for their guilt.
The LORD will break down their altars;
he will destroy their holy stone pillars.

3Then they will say, "We have no king,
because we didn't honour the LORD.
As for the king,
he couldn't do anything for us."
4They make many false promises
and agreements which they don't keep.
So people sue each other in court;
they are like poisonous weeds growing in a
ploughed field.
5The people from Israel are worried about
the calf-shaped idol at Beth Aven.
The people will cry about it,
and the priests will cry about it.
They used to shout for joy about its glory,
6but it will be carried off to Assyria
as a gift to the great king.
Israel will be disgraced,
and the people will be ashamed for not
obeying.
7Israel will be destroyed;
its king will be like a chip of wood floating
on the water.
8The places of false worship will be destroyed,
the places where Israel sinned.

Thorns and weeds will grow up
and cover their altars.
Then they will say to the mountains,
"Cover us!"
and to the hills, "Fall on us!"

9"Israel, you have sinned since the time of
Gibeah, *n*
and the people there have continued
sinning.
But war will surely overwhelm them in
Gibeah,
because of the evil they have done there.
10When I am ready,
I will come to punish them.
Nations will come together against them,
and they will be punished for their double
sins.
11Israel is like a well-trained young cow
that likes to thresh *d* grain.
I will put a yoke *d* on her neck
and make her work hard in the field.
Israel will plough,
and Judah will break up the ground.
12I said, 'Plant goodness,
harvest the fruit of loyalty,
plough the new ground of knowledge.
Look for the LORD until he comes
and pours goodness on you like water.'
13But you have ploughed evil
and harvested trouble;
you have eaten the fruit of your lies.
Because you have trusted in your own power
and your many soldiers,
14your people will hear the noise of battle,
and all your strong, walled cities will be
destroyed.
It will be like the time King Shalman
destroyed Beth Arbel in battle,
when mothers and their children were
crushed to death.
15The same will happen to you, people of
Bethel,
because you did so much evil.
When the sun comes up,
the king of Israel will die.

God's Love for Israel

11 "When Israel was a child, I loved him,
and I called my son out of Egypt.
2But when I called the people of Israel,
they went away from me.
They offered sacrifices to the Baals *d*
and burned incense *d* to the idols.
3It was I who taught Ephraim to walk,
and I took them by the arms,

Gibeah   The sins of the people of Gibeah caused a civil war. See Judges 19—21.

but they did not understand
    that I had healed them.
[4]I led them with cords of human kindness,
    with ropes of love.
I lifted the yoke *d* from their neck
    and bent down and fed them.

[5]"The Israelites will become captives again, as
    they were in Egypt,
and Assyria will become their king,
    because they refuse to turn back to God.
[6]War will sweep through their cities
    and will destroy them
and kill them because of their wicked
    plans.
[7]My people have made up their minds
    to turn away from me.
The prophets *d* call them to turn to me,
    but none of them honours me at all.

[8]"Israel, how can I give you up?
    How can I give you away, Israel?
I don't want to make you like Admah
    or treat you like Zeboiim. *n*
My heart beats for you,
    and my love for you stirs up my pity.
[9]I won't punish you in my anger,
    and I won't destroy Israel again.
I am God and not a human;
    I am the Holy One, and I am among you.
I will not come against you in anger.
[10]They will go after the LORD,
    and he will roar like a lion.
When he roars,
    his children will hurry to him from the west.
[11]They will come swiftly
    like birds from Egypt
and like doves from Assyria.
I will settle them again in their homes,"
    says the LORD.

The LORD is Against Israel

[12]Israel has surrounded me with lies;
    the people have made evil plans.
And Judah turns against God,
    the faithful Holy One.

12 What Israel does is as useless as
    chasing the wind;
he chases the east wind all day.
They tell more and more lies
    and do more and more violence.
They make agreements with Assyria,
    and they send a gift of olive oil to Egypt.
[2]The LORD also has some things against Judah.
    He will punish Israel for what they have
    done;

he will give them what they deserve.
[3]Their ancestor Jacob held on to his brother's
    heel
while the two of them were being born.
When he grew to be a man,
    he wrestled with God.
[4]When Jacob wrestled with the angel
    and won,
he cried and asked for his blessing.
Later, God met with him at Bethel
    and spoke with him there.
[5]It was the LORD God All-powerful;
    the LORD is his great name.
[6]You must return to your God;
    love him, do what is just,
    and always trust in him as your God.

[7]The merchants use dishonest scales;
    they like to cheat people.
[8]Israel said, "I am rich! I am someone with
    power!"
All their money will do them no good
    because of the sins they have done.

[9]"But I am the LORD your God,
    who brought you out of Egypt.
I will make you live in tents again
    as you used to do on worship days.
[10]I spoke to the prophets *d*
    and gave them many visions;
through them, I taught my lessons
    to you."

[11]The people of Gilead are evil,
    worth nothing.
Though people sacrifice bulls at Gilgal,
    their altars will become like piles of stone
    in a ploughed field.
[12]Your ancestor Jacob fled to North West
    Mesopotamia
where he worked to get a wife;
    he tended sheep to pay for her.
[13]Later the LORD used a prophet
    to bring Jacob's descendants *d* out of
    Egypt;
he used a prophet
    to take care of the Israelites.
[14]But the Israelites made the Lord angry when
    they killed other people,
and they deserve to die for their crimes.
The Lord will make them pay
    for the disgraceful things they have done.

The Final Word Against Israel

13 People used to fear the tribe *d* of
    Ephraim;
they were important people in Israel.

Admah . . . Zeboiim Two other cities destroyed when God destroyed Sodom and Gomorrah.

But they sinned by worshipping Baal,*d*
 so they must die.
²But they still keep on sinning more and
 more.
They make idols of their silver,
idols that are cleverly made,
 the work of a craftsman.
Yet the people of Israel say to each other,
 "Kiss those calf idols and sacrifice to
 them."
³So those people will be like the morning
 mist;
they will disappear like the morning
 dew.
They will be like chaff*d* blown from the
 threshing*d* floor,
 like smoke going out of a window.

⁴"I, the LORD, have been your God
 since you were in the land of Egypt.
You should have known no other God
 except me.
 I am the only one who saves.
⁵I cared for them in the desert
 where it was hot and dry.
⁶I gave them food, and they became full and
 satisfied.
But then they became too proud and
 forgot me.
⁷That is why I will be like a lion to them,
 like a leopard waiting by the road.
⁸I will attack like a bear robbed of her cubs,
 ripping their bodies open.
 I will devour them like a lion
 and tear them apart like a wild animal.

⁹"Israel, I will destroy you.
 Who will be your helper then?
¹⁰What good is your king?
 Can he save you in any of your towns?
What good are your leaders?
 You said, 'Give us a king and leaders.'
¹¹So I gave you a king, but only in anger,
 and I took him away in my great anger.
¹²The sins of Israel are on record,
 stored away, waiting for punishment.
¹³The pain of birth will come for him,
 but he is like a foolish baby

who won't come out of its mother's womb.
¹⁴Will I save them from the place of the
 dead?
 Will I rescue them from death?
Where is your sickness, death?
 Where is your pain, place of death?
 I will show them no mercy.
¹⁵Israel is doing well among the nations,
 but the LORD will send a wind from
 the east,
coming from the desert,
 that will dry up his springs and wells of
 water.
It will destroy from their treasure houses
 everything of value.
¹⁶The nation of Israel will be ruined,
 because it fought against God.
The people of Israel will die in war;
 their children will be torn to pieces,
 and their pregnant women will be ripped
 open."

Israel Returns to God

14 Israel, return to the LORD your God,
 because your sins have made you
 fall.
²Come back to the LORD
 and say these words to him:
"Take away all our sin
 and kindly receive us,
and we will keep the promises we made
 to you.
³Assyria cannot save us,
 nor will we trust in our horses.
We will not say again, 'Our gods',
 to the things our hands have made.
 You show mercy to orphans."

⁴The LORD says,
"I will forgive them for leaving me
 and will love them freely,
 because I am not angry with them any
 more.
⁵I will be like the dew to Israel,
 and they will blossom like a lily.
Like the cedar trees in Lebanon,
 their roots will be firm.
⁶They will be like spreading branches,
 like the beautiful olive trees
 and the sweet-smelling cedars in Lebanon.
⁷The people of Israel will again live under my
 protection.
 They will grow like the grain,
they will bloom like a vine,
 and they will be as famous as the wine of
 Lebanon.
⁸Israel, have nothing to do with idols.

I, the LORD, am the one who answers your
prayers and watches over you.
I am like a green pine tree;
your blessings come from me."

9A wise person will know these things,
and an understanding person will take
them to heart.
The LORD's ways are right.
Good people live by following them,
but those who turn against God die
because of them.

Joel

Why Read This Book:
- See how forgiveness begins with a change of heart (Joel 2).
- Hear Joel announce a new life for the faithful (Joel 3).

When?

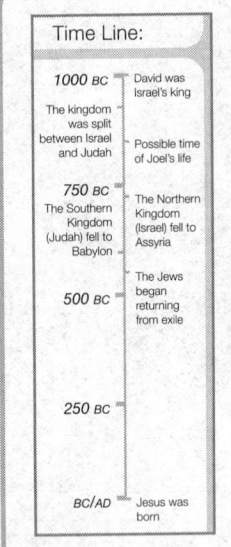

Time Line:

1000 BC	David was Israel's king
The kingdom was split between Israel and Judah	Possible time of Joel's life
750 BC	
The Southern Kingdom (Judah) fell to Babylon	The Northern Kingdom (Israel) fell to Assyria
500 BC	The Jews began returning from exile
250 BC	
BC/AD	Jesus was born

Behind the Scenes:

We seem to be living in an age of worldwide catastrophes.

- Economic recession has resulted in unemployment and homelessness.
- Disregard for God's environment has resulted in worldwide pollution.
- Greed for ornaments and fashion clothing, as well as the need for more land, has led to the extinction of rare animal species.
- Improved technology – whatever it costs – has led to a hole in the ozone layer.
- Selfishness and disobedience have resulted in Third World famines.
- "Easy sex" has led to a worldwide epidemic of AIDS, threatening the lives of millions.
- Modern wars make it easier to kill more people than ever before.

Judah was no stranger to catastrophes either, except that the land was attacked by locusts instead of AIDS. These insects destroyed everything in their paths, including crops of vegetables, fields, trees and vineyards. The swarms turned healthy farmland into barren wastelands. The people of Judah had never seen anything like it before.

In the book of Joel, the prophet saw what was happening as a sign of God's judgement of the people. He warned them that if they did not repent and turn back to God, a plague of locusts would be nothing compared with what would happen. If they repented, however, God would restore his people and bless them.

We don't know much about Joel himself, but the message which he preached is as relevant today as it was in his own time. God will bless those who follow him obediently, and judge those who oppose him.

LIFE FILE LINKS

Investigate the Theme

To find a list of real life stories on this subject turn to the LIFE FILE GUIDE on pages 12 to 22 at the front of the Youth Bible.

SIN

Locusts Destroy the Crops

1 The LORD spoke his word to Joel son of Pethuel:

[2]Elders, listen to this message.
Listen to me, all you who live in the
land.
Nothing like this has ever happened during
your lifetime
or during your ancestors' lifetimes.

[3]Tell your children about these things,
let your children tell their children,
and let your grandchildren tell their
children.
[4]What the cutting locusts have left,
the swarming locusts have eaten;
what the swarming locusts have left,
the hopping locusts have eaten,
and what the hopping locusts have left,
the destroying locusts [n] have eaten.

[5]Drunkards, wake up and cry!
All you people who drink wine, cry!
Cry because your wine
has been taken away from your mouths.
[6]A powerful nation has come into my land
with too many soldiers to count.
It has teeth like a lion,
jaws like a female lion.
[7]It has made my grapevine a waste
and made my fig tree a stump.
It has stripped all the bark off my trees
and left the branches white.

[8]Cry as a young woman cries
when the man she was going to marry has
died.

[9]There will be no more grain or drink
offerings
to offer in the Temple[d] of the LORD.
Because of this, the priests,
the servants of the LORD, are sad.
[10]The fields are ruined;
the ground is dried up.
The grain is destroyed,
the new wine is dried up,
and the olive oil runs out.
[11]Be sad, farmers.
Cry loudly, you who grow grapes.
Cry for the wheat and the barley.
Cry because the harvest of the field is lost.
[12]The vines have become dry,
and the fig trees are dried up.
The pomegranate[d] trees, the date palm trees,
the apple trees—
all the trees in the field have died.
And the happiness of the people has
died, too.
[13]Priests, put on your rough cloth and cry to
show your sadness.
Servants of the altar, cry out loud.
Servants of my God,
keep your rough cloth on all night to show
your sadness.
Cry because there will be no more grain or
drink offerings
to offer in the Temple of your God.
[14]Call for a day when no one eats food!
Tell everyone to stop work!
Bring the elders
and everyone who lives in the land
to the Temple of the LORD your God,
and cry out to the LORD.
[15]What a terrible day it will be!
The LORD's day of judging is near,
when punishment will come
like a destroying attack from the
Almighty.

[16]Our food is taken away
while we watch.
Joy and happiness are gone
from the Temple of our God.
[17]Though we planted fig seeds,
they lie dry and dead in the earth.
The barns are empty and falling down.
The storerooms for grain have been broken
down,
because the grain has dried up.
[18]The animals are groaning!
The herds of cattle wander around
confused,

---

cutting . . . locusts   These are different names for an insect like a large grasshopper. The locust can quickly destroy trees,
plants and crops, and in this destruction, Joel sees a warning. God will cause this type of destruction when he punishes
his people.

because they have no grass to eat;
   even the flocks of sheep suffer.
[19]Lord, I am calling to you for help,
   because fire has burned up the open pastures,
   and flames have burned all the trees in the
     field.
[20]Wild animals also need your help.
   The streams of water have dried up,
   and fire has burned up the open pastures.

The Coming Day of Judgement

2 Blow the trumpet in Jerusalem;
   shout a warning on my holy mountain.
Let all the people who live in the land shake
     with fear,
   because the Lord's day of judging is
     coming;
   it is near.
[2]It will be a dark, gloomy day,
   cloudy and black.

Like the light at sunrise,
   a great and powerful army will spread over
     the mountains.
There has never been anything like it before,
   and there will never be anything like it
     again.

[3]In front of them a fire destroys;
   behind them a flame burns.
The land in front of them is like the garden
     of Eden;
   the land behind them is like an empty
     desert.
   Nothing will escape from them.
[4]They look like horses,
   and they run like war horses.
[5]It is like the noise of chariots
   rumbling over the tops of the mountains,
like the noise of a roaring fire
   burning dry stalks.

GOD'S POWER

The Big Blast

For 123 years Mount St Helens slept quietly. Whenever geologists looked down the throat of the volcano in Washington state, USA, all they found was ash and ice. Then, on 20 March 1980, earthquakes shook the area. Within a week the volcano became active

At first, people were frightened. But as weeks went by and nothing happened, they grew accustomed to living next to an active volcano. They got tired of hearing warnings of possible disaster. In fact, a carnival-like attitude prevailed, and the volcano's small eruptions became a source of entertainment.

On 18 May, Mount St Helens was rattled by another series of earthquakes. This time a huge section of the northern slope came crashing down the mountain. Two minutes later, the mountain exploded. The explosion, heard 300 kilometres away, was louder and more powerful than an atomic bomb. A billowing cloud of ash shot more than 20 kilometres into the air. Nearly 500 square kilometres of forest land were levelled. Hundreds of thousands of trees vaporised, clouds of grey ash filled the air, and the land was left barren.

The predicted eruption had come.

Like many of the people who scoffed at the predictions of Mount St Helens's eruption, most of the people in Joel's time paid little attention to the prophet's warnings that the Lord's judgement was soon to come. Read how the prophet describes God's warnings in **Joel 2:1–2**.

- Why do you think many of the people living near Mount St Helens and those who heard Joel's prophecy of God's power didn't believe the warnings?
- What warning signs should you be paying attention to?

Consider . . .

- going for a bike ride and viewing God's power in nature as you ride.
- reading Revelation (p.1388) and comparing John's visions with the ones in Joel.

For more, see . . .

- Psalm 98 (p.557)
- 2 Peter 3:1–13 (p.1367)
- Matthew 12:33–37 (p.961)

They are like a powerful army lined up for
    battle.
⁶When they see them, nations shake with fear,
    and everyone's face becomes pale.

⁷They charge like soldiers;
    they climb over the wall like warriors.
They all march straight ahead
    and do not move off their path.
⁸They do not run into each other,
    because each walks in line.
They break through all efforts to stop them
    and keep coming.
⁹They run into the city.
    They run at the wall
and climb into the houses,
    entering through windows like thieves.

> **Sidelight** The Israelites couldn't
> keep the locusts out of
> their houses (Joel 2:9), because they didn't have
> glass windows or even shutters. Instead, they
> had wooden lattice-work built into the windows,
> but that didn't stop the "powerful army" (Joel
> 2:5) from "entering . . . like thieves".

¹⁰Before them, earth and sky shake.
The sun and the moon become dark,
    and the stars stop shining.
¹¹The LORD shouts out orders
    to his army.
His army is very large!
    Those who obey him are very strong!
The LORD's day of judging
    is an overwhelming and terrible day.
No one can stand up against it!

Change Your Hearts

¹²The LORD says, "Even now, come back to me
    with all your heart.
Go without food, and cry and be sad."

¹³Tearing your clothes is not enough to show
        you are sad;
    let your heart be broken.
Come back to the LORD your God,
    because he is kind and shows mercy.
He doesn't become angry quickly,
    and he has great love.
He can change his mind about doing harm.
¹⁴Who knows? Maybe he will turn back to you
    and leave behind a blessing for you.
Grain and drink offerings belong to the LORD
    your God.

¹⁵Blow the trumpet in Jerusalem;
    call for a day when no one eats food.

Tell everyone to stop work.
¹⁶Bring the people together
    and make the meeting holy for the LORD.
Bring together the elders,
    as well as the children,
    and even babies that still feed at their
        mothers' breasts.
The bridegroom should come from his
        room,
    the bride from her bedroom.
¹⁷The priests, the LORD's servants, should cry
    between the altar and the entrance to the
        Temple.*d*
They should say, "LORD, have mercy on your
        people.
Don't let them be put to shame;
    don't let other nations make fun of
        them.
Don't let people in other nations ask,
    'Where is their God?' "

The LORD Restores the Land

¹⁸Then the LORD became concerned about his
        land
    and felt sorry for his people.
¹⁹He said to them:
    "I will send you grain, new wine and
        olive oil,
    so that you will have plenty.
No more will I shame you
    among the nations.
²⁰I will force the army from the north to leave
        your land
    and go into a dry, empty land.
Their soldiers in front will be forced into the
        Dead Sea, *d*
    and those in the rear into the
        Mediterranean Sea.
Their bodies will rot and stink.
    The LORD has surely done a wonderful
        thing!"

²¹Land, don't be afraid;
    be happy and full of joy,
    because the LORD has done a wonderful
        thing.
²²Wild animals, don't be afraid,
    because the open pastures have grown
        grass.
The trees have given fruit;
    the fig trees and the grapevines have grown
        much fruit.
²³So be happy, people of Jerusalem;
    be joyful in the LORD your God.
Because he does what is right,
    he has brought you rain;
he has sent the autumn rain
    and the spring rain for you, as before.

²⁴And the threshing^d floors will be full of grain;
  the barrels will overflow with new wine
    and olive oil.

The LORD Speaks

²⁵"Though I sent my great army against you—
  those swarming locusts and hopping
    locusts,
  the destroying locusts and the cutting
    locustsⁿ that ate your crops—
I will pay you back
  for those years of trouble.
²⁶Then you will have plenty to eat
  and be full.
You will praise the name of the LORD your God,
  who has done miracles^d for you.
My people will never again be shamed.

²⁷Then you will know that I am among the
    people of Israel,
  that I am the LORD your God,
  and there is no other God.
My people will never be shamed again.

²⁸"After this,
  I will pour out my Spirit^d on all kinds of
    people.
Your sons and daughters will prophesy,^d
  your old men will dream dreams,
  and your young men will see visions.
²⁹At that time I will pour out my Spirit
  also on male slaves and female slaves.
³⁰I will show miracles
  in the sky and on the earth:
  blood, fire and thick smoke.

swarming . . . locusts   These are different names for an insect like a large grasshopper. The locust can quickly destroy trees, plants and crops, and in this destruction, Joel sees a warning. God will cause this type of destruction when he punishes his people.

FORGIVENESS

Change of Heart

When their only son was killed by a drunk driver, Frank and Elizabeth Morris had just one wish: revenge. "We wanted him dead," Mrs Morris admits, talking about the killer.

Tommy Pigage pleaded guilty to the charge and was sent to prison. The Morrises were angry at the court for not giving him a longer sentence. In time, however, they realised their bitterness stopped them from getting on with their lives. They decided to visit Tommy.

Tommy expressed deep remorse for killing their son and admitted that he deserved his punishment. The Morrises were moved by his sensitivity and honesty. "I didn't want my son's death to be totally vain," Mrs Morris says. "And in my heart I know that if he could, my son would tell us to forgive Tommy."

The Morrises' decision to forgive not only freed them from their bitterness, but also started a change in Tommy's life. He quit drinking and turned to God. The Morrises continue to visit Tommy regularly and support him in his struggle with alcoholism. "The accident already wiped out one very special life. I don't want to see it waste Tommy's life, too," Mrs Morris says.

The giving and receiving of forgiveness is necessary for living in Christ. To change their lives, the Morrises needed to forgive – and Tommy needed their forgiveness. Read **Joel 2:12–19** for God's plea for people to change their hearts.

* How is the Morrises' (and Tommy's) change of heart similar to what God required of the people in Joel's time?
* Is forgiveness the same thing as fairness? Why or why not?

Consider . . .

* making a paper heart and listing on it people you need to forgive. Ask God to help you do it.
* taking the risk of asking forgiveness from someone you've hurt.

For more, see . . .

* Psalm 51 (p.530)
* Luke 13:1–5 (p.1066)

* Matthew 5:21–26 (p.943)

³¹The sun will become dark,
   the moon red as blood,
   before the overwhelming and terrible day of
    the LORD comes.
³²Then anyone who calls on the LORD
   will be saved,
because on Mount Zion ^d and in Jerusalem
   there will be people who will be saved,
just as the LORD has said.
Those left alive after the day of punishment
   are the people whom the LORD called.

Punishment for Judah's Enemies

3   "In those days and at that time,
    when I will make things better for Judah
     and Jerusalem,
²I will gather all the nations together
   and bring them down into the Valley
    Where the LORD Judges.
   There I will judge them,

because those nations scattered my own
    people Israel
   and forced them to live in other nations.
They divided up my land
³ and threw lots ^d for my people.
They traded boys for prostitutes, ^d
   and they sold girls to buy wine to drink.

⁴"Tyre and Sidon and all of you regions of Philistia! What did you have against me? Were you punishing me for something I did, or were you doing something to hurt me? I will very quickly do to you what you have done to me. ⁵You took my silver and gold, and you put my precious treasures in your temples. ⁶You sold the people of Judah and Jerusalem to the Greeks so that you could send them far from their land.

⁷"You sent my people to that faraway place, but I will get them and bring them back, and I will do to you what you have done to them. ⁸I will sell your sons and daughters to the people of

---

CREATION

A Load of Rubbish!

Marion Stoddart and her family watched their nice neighbourhood become a dumping ground for industrial waste and rubbish. Once beautiful, the river bank was scattered with litter, old furniture, and abandoned cars. The river smelled like a sewer.

Finally, Marion realised she could either move away or rescue the river, which was so polluted that people said it was "too thick to pour and too thin to plough". She organised other concerned residents in the community to reclaim the river.

They showed trade unions, business leaders, and politicians how everyone would benefit from making the river "fishable and swimmable". They even got one important politician's attention by giving him a bottle of filthy river water to keep on his desk until the river was clean again. Slowly, the various users of the river did their part to stop polluting and to clean up the mess, due in large part to Mrs Stoddart's group. Mrs Stoddart says it is possible for ordinary people to reclaim their world for good.

"You don't have to be really clever to make a difference," she says. "You just have to persuade the people with power, the people who care, and be really committed, persistent, and honest."

It is not God's will that we rubbish his creation. In **Joel 2:21–27** read of God's desire for the land's health and vitality.

* How does Mrs Stoddart's crusade compare to God's will for the land?
* From your reading of the passage, what do you think is God's will for the way we are to use the earth?

Consider . . .

* choosing one way today to show God's love for creation by reducing the amount of rubbish you create.
* leading a group from your school or church in cleaning up a river bank, a public park or a lake shore where you live.

For more, see . . .

* Genesis 1 (p.2)
* Luke 12:22–31 (p.1064)
* Psalm 104 (p.560)

Judah, and they will sell them to the Sabean people far away." The LORD said this.

God Judges the Nations

⁹Announce this among the nations:
  Prepare for war!
Wake up the soldiers!
  Let all the men of war come near and attack.
¹⁰Make swords from your ploughs,
  and make spears from your hooks for trimming trees.
Let even the weak person say,
  "I am a soldier."
¹¹All of you nations, hurry,
  and come together in that place.
LORD, send your soldiers
  to gather the nations.

¹²"Wake up, nations,
  and come to attack in the Valley Where the LORD Judges.
There I will sit to judge
  all the nations on every side.
¹³Swing the cutting tool,
  because the harvest is ripe.
Come, walk on them as you would walk on
  grapes to get their juice,
because the winepress *d* is full
  and the barrels are spilling over,
because these people are so evil!"

¹⁴There are huge numbers of people
  in the Valley of Decision, *n*
because the LORD's day of judging is near
  in the Valley of Decision.
¹⁵The sun and the moon will become dark,
  and the stars will stop shining.

¹⁶The LORD will roar like a lion from Jerusalem;
  his loud voice will thunder from that city,
  and the sky and the earth will shake.
But the LORD will be a safe place for his
  people,
a strong place of safety for the people of
  Israel.

¹⁷"Then you will know that I, the LORD
  your God,
  live on my holy Mount Zion. *d*
Jerusalem will be a holy place,
  and strangers will never even go through it
  again.

A New Life Promised for Judah

¹⁸"On that day wine will drip from the
  mountains,
milk will flow from the hills,
  and water will run through all the ravines
  of Judah.
A fountain will flow from the Temple *d* of the
  LORD
  and give water to the valley of acacia
  trees.
¹⁹But Egypt will become empty,
  and Edom an empty desert,
because they were cruel to the people of
  Judah.
They killed innocent people in that land.
²⁰But there will always be people living in
  Judah,
  and people will live in Jerusalem from
  now on.
²¹Egypt and Edom killed my people,
  so I will definitely punish them."

The LORD lives in Jerusalem!

Valley of Decision This is like the name Valley Where the LORD Judges in 3:2 and 3:12.

Amos

Why Read This Book:

* Read of the Lord's punishment for injustice (Amos 1—2).
* Be warned about vanity and self-centredness (Amos 6).
* See the Lord's reaction to those who oppress the poor (Amos 8).

When?

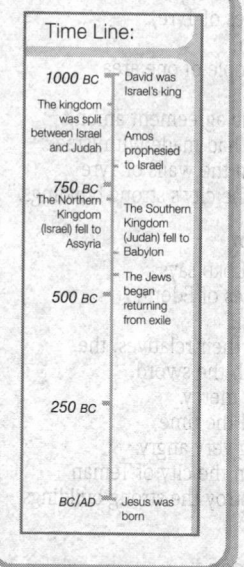

Time Line:

1000 BC	David was Israel's king
The kingdom was split between Israel and Judah	Amos prophesied to Israel
750 BC The Northern Kingdom (Israel) fell to Assyria	The Southern Kingdom (Judah) fell to Babylon
500 BC	The Jews began returning from exile
250 BC	
BC/AD	Jesus was born

Behind the Scenes:

Amos was a very angry farmer! All around him were smug, satisfied people. The nation was prosperous. Surely God was on Israel's side. So why was Amos angry?

Underneath the prosperity was corruption. People had acquired their wealth by stepping on the poor. They relied on military power instead of God. Their worship was superficial. In short, they had forgotten what it meant to follow God.

Though he lived in the Southern Kingdom of Judah, Amos preached to the people of Israel in the Northern Kingdom. He took his uncompromising message straight to the religious authorities of his day. Instead of listening to him, they threw him out.

In the same way that Amos challenged the Israelites to reconsider their priorities, he challenges us. In the climax to his book, he reminds us what God wants: "Let justice flow like a river, and let goodness flow like a stream that never stops" (Amos 5:24).

Where?

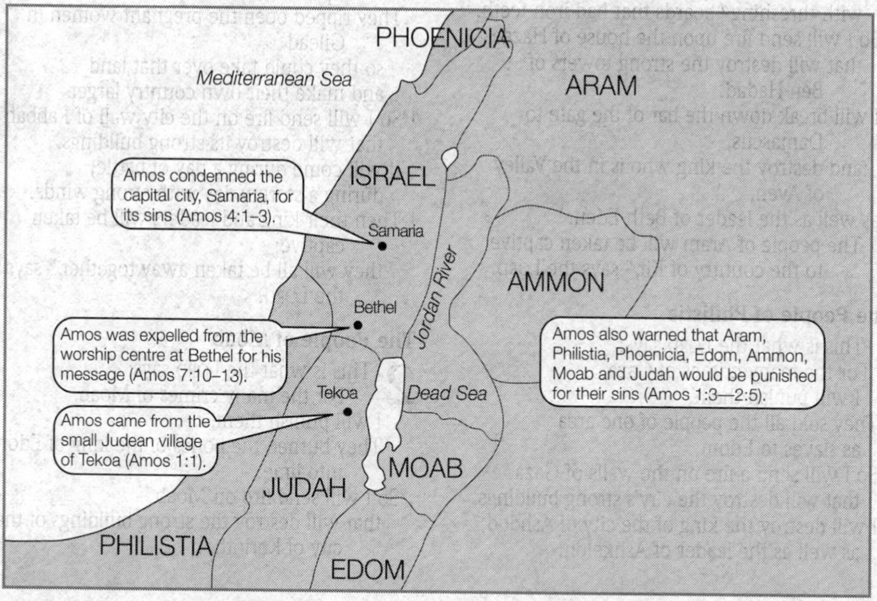

Amos condemned the capital city, Samaria, for its sins (Amos 4:1-3).

Amos was expelled from the worship centre at Bethel for his message (Amos 7:10-13).

Amos came from the small Judean village of Tekoa (Amos 1:1).

Amos also warned that Aram, Philistia, Phoenicia, Edom, Ammon, Moab and Judah would be punished for their sins (Amos 1:3—2:5).

PHOENICIA

Mediterranean Sea

ARAM

ISRAEL

Samaria

Jordan River

Bethel

AMMON

Tekoa

Dead Sea

MOAB

JUDAH

PHILISTIA

EDOM

1 These are the words of Amos, one of the shepherds from the town of Tekoa. He saw this vision about Israel two years before the earthquake. It was at the time Uzziah was king of Judah and Jeroboam son of Jehoash was king of Israel.

²Amos said,

"The LORD will roar from Jerusalem;
he will send his voice from Jerusalem.
The pastures of the shepherds will
become dry,
and even the top of Mount Carmel will
dry up."

Sidelight   The whole region of Israel was shaken by the earthquake mentioned in Amos 1:1. Though no one knows the exact date, it's probably the same earthquake mentioned in Zechariah 14:5 (p.926). Archaeologists believe the city of Hazor was destroyed by an earthquake about the same time.

Israel's Neighbours are Punished

The People of Aram

³This is what the LORD says:
"For the many crimes of Damascus,
I will punish them.
They drove over the people of Gilead
with threshing[d] boards that had iron teeth.
⁴So I will send fire upon the house of Hazael
that will destroy the strong towers of
Ben-Hadad.
⁵I will break down the bar of the gate to
Damascus
and destroy the king who is in the Valley
of Aven,
as well as the leader of Beth Eden.
The people of Aram will be taken captive
to the country of Kir," says the LORD.

The People of Philistia

⁶This is what the LORD says:
"For the many crimes of Gaza,
I will punish them.
They sold all the people of one area
as slaves to Edom.
⁷So I will send a fire on the walls of Gaza
that will destroy the city's strong buildings.
⁸I will destroy the king of the city of Ashdod,
as well as the leader of Ashkelon.

Then I will turn against the people of the city
of Ekron,
and the last of the Philistines will die," says
the Lord GOD.

The People of Phoenicia

⁹This is what the LORD says:
"For the many crimes of Tyre,
I will punish them.
They sold all the people of one area
as slaves to Edom,
and they forgot the agreement among
relatives they had made with Israel.
¹⁰So I will send fire on the walls of Tyre
that will destroy the city's strong buildings."

The People of Edom

¹¹This is what the LORD says:
"For the many crimes of Edom,
I will punish them.
They hunted down their relatives, the
Israelites, with the sword,
showing them no mercy.
They were angry all the time
and kept on being very angry.
¹²So I will send fire on the city of Teman
that will even destroy the strong buildings
of Bozrah." [n]

The People of Ammon

¹³This is what the LORD says:
"For the many crimes of Ammon,
I will punish them.
They ripped open the pregnant women in
Gilead
so they could take over that land
and make their own country larger.
¹⁴So I will send fire on the city wall of Rabbah
that will destroy its strong buildings.
It will come during a day of battle,
during a stormy day with strong winds.
¹⁵Then their king and leaders will be taken
captive;
they will all be taken away together," says
the LORD.

The People of Moab

2 This is what the LORD says:
"For the many crimes of Moab,
I will punish them.
They burned the bones of the king of Edom
into lime.
²So I will send fire on Moab
that will destroy the strong buildings of the
city of Kerioth.

Teman . . . Bozrah   Since Teman was in northern Edom and Bozrah was in southern Edom, this means the whole country will be destroyed.

The people of Moab will die in a great
    noise,
  in the middle of the sounds of war and
    trumpets.
³So I will bring an end to the king of Moab,
  and I will kill all its leaders with him," says
    the LORD.

The People of Judah

⁴This is what the LORD says:
"For the many crimes of Judah,
  I will punish them.
They rejected the teachings of the LORD
  and did not keep his commands;
they followed the same gods
  as their ancestors had followed.
⁵So I will send fire on Judah,
  and it will destroy the strong buildings of
    Jerusalem."

Israel is Punished

⁶This is what the LORD says:
"For the many crimes of Israel,
  I will punish them.
For silver, they sell people who have done
    nothing wrong;
  they sell the poor to buy a pair of sandals.
⁷They walk on poor people as if they were
    nothing,
  and they refuse to be fair to those who are
    suffering.
Fathers and sons have sexual relations with
    the same woman,
  and so they ruin my holy name.
⁸As they worship at their altars,
  they lie down on clothes taken from the
    poor.
They fine people,
  and with that money they buy wine to
    drink in the house of their god.

⁹"But it was I who destroyed the Amorites
    before them,
  who were tall like cedar trees and as strong
    as oaks—
I destroyed them completely.
¹⁰It was I who brought you from the land of
    Egypt
  and led you for 40 years through the
    desert
  so I could give you the land of the
    Amorites.
¹¹I made some of your children prophets ᵈ
  and some of your young people Nazirites. ᵈ
People of Israel, isn't this true?" says the
    LORD.
¹²"But you made the Nazirites drink wine
  and told the prophets not to prophesy.

¹³Now I will make you get stuck,
  as a wagon loaded with grain gets stuck.
¹⁴No one will escape, not even the fastest
    runner.
  Strong people will not be strong enough;
  warriors will not be able to save themselves.
¹⁵Soldiers with bows and arrows will not stand
    and fight,
  and even fast runners will not get away;
  soldiers on horses will not escape alive.
¹⁶At that time even the bravest warriors
  will run away without their armour," says
    the LORD.

Warning to Israel

3 Listen to this word that the LORD has spoken
    against you, people of Israel, against the
whole family he brought out of Egypt.
²"I have chosen only you
  out of all the families of the earth,
so I will punish you
  for all your sins."

³Two people will not walk together
  unless they have agreed to do so.
⁴A lion in the forest does not roar
  unless it has caught an animal;
it does not growl in its den
  when it has caught nothing.
⁵A bird will not fall into a trap
  where there is no bait;
the trap will not spring shut
  if there is nothing to catch.
⁶When a trumpet blows a warning in a city,
  the people tremble.
When trouble comes to a city,
  the LORD has caused it.
⁷Before the Lord GOD does anything,
  he tells his plans to his servants the
    prophets. ᵈ
⁸The lion has roared!
  Who wouldn't be afraid?
The Lord GOD has spoken.
  Who will not prophesy?

⁹Announce this to the strong buildings of
    Ashdod
  and to the strong buildings of Egypt:
"Come to the mountains of Samaria,
  where you will see great confusion
  and people hurting others."

¹⁰"The people don't know how to do what is
    right," says the LORD.
"Their strong buildings are filled with
    treasures they took by force from
    others."

¹¹So this is what the Lord GOD says:
"An enemy will take over the land

and pull down your strongholds; *d*
he will take the treasures out of your strong
   buildings."

¹²This is what the LORD says:
"A shepherd might save from a lion's
   mouth
only two leg bones or a scrap of an ear of
   his sheep.
In the same way only a few Israelites in
   Samaria will be saved—
people who now sit on their beds
   and on their couches."

¹³"Listen and be witnesses against the family of
Jacob," says the Lord GOD, the God All-powerful.

¹⁴"When I punish Israel for their sins,
   I will also destroy the altars at Bethel.
The corners of the altar will be cut off,
   and they will fall to the ground.
¹⁵I will tear down the winter house,
   together with the summer house.
The houses decorated with ivory will be
   destroyed,
   and the great houses will come to an end,"
   says the LORD.

Sidelight   If rich people today
built like the rich people in
Amos's day, elephants would certainly be
extinct. A great sign of wealth was to have ivory
inlays in furniture and panelling in your house
(Amos 3:15). Amos wasn't impressed.

Israel will Not Return

4 Listen to this message, you cows of
   Bashan *n* on the Mountain of Samaria.
You take things from the poor
   and crush people who are in need.
Then you command your husbands,
   "Bring us something to drink!"
²The Lord GOD has promised this:
"Just as surely as I am a holy God,
the time will come
   when you will be taken away by hooks,
   and what is left of you with fish-hooks.
³You will go straight out of the city
   through holes in the walls,
   and you will be thrown on the rubbish
   dump," says the LORD.

⁴"Come to the city of Bethel and sin;
   come to Gilgal and sin even more.

Offer your sacrifices every morning,
   and bring one-tenth of your crops every
   three days.
⁵Offer bread made with yeast as a sacrifice to
   show your thanks,
   and boast about the special offerings you
   bring,
because this is what you love to do,
   Israelites," says the Lord GOD.

⁶"I did not give you any food in your cities,
   and there was not enough to eat in any of
   your towns,
but you did not come back to me," says the
   LORD.
⁷"I held back the rain from you
   three months before harvest time.
Then I let it rain on one city
   but not on another.
Rain fell on one field,
   but another field got none and dried up.
⁸People weak from thirst went from town to
   town for water,
   but they could not get enough to drink.
Still you did not come back to me," says
   the LORD.
⁹"I made your crops die from disease and
   mildew. *d*
When your gardens and your vineyards got
   larger,
locusts *d* ate your fig and olive trees.
   But still you did not come back to me,"
   says the LORD.
¹⁰"I sent disasters against you,
   as I did to Egypt.
I killed your young men with swords,
   and your horses were taken from you.
I made you smell the stink from all the dead
   bodies,
   but still you did not come back to me,"
   says the LORD.
¹¹"I destroyed some of you
   as I destroyed Sodom and Gomorrah.
You were like a burning stick pulled from a fire,
   but still you did not come back to me,"
   says the LORD.

¹²"So this is what I will do to you, Israel;
   because I will do this to you,
   get ready to meet your God, Israel."

¹³He is the one who makes the mountains
   and creates the wind
   and makes his thoughts known to people.
He changes the dawn into darkness
   and walks over the mountains of the earth.
His name is the LORD God All-powerful.

Bashan Amos compares the rich, lazy women of Samaria to well-fed cows from Bashan, a place known for its rich animal
pastures.

Israel Needs to Repent

5 Listen to this funeral song that I sing about
you, people of Israel.
[2]"The young girl Israel has fallen,
and she will not rise up again.
She was left alone in her own land,
and there is no one to help her up."

[3]This is what the Lord GOD says:
"If 1,000 soldiers leave a city,
only 100 will return;
if 100 soldiers leave a city,
only ten will return."

[4]This is what the LORD says to the nation of
Israel:
"Come to me and live.
[5] But do not look in Bethel
or go to Gilgal,
and do not go down to Beersheba.
The people of Gilgal will be taken away as
captives,
and Bethel will become nothing."
[6]Come to the LORD and live,
or he will move like fire against the
descendants [d] of Joseph.
The fire will burn Bethel,
and there will be no one to put it out.
[7]You turn justice upside down,
and you throw on the ground what
is right.

[8]God is the one who made the star groups
Pleiades and Orion;
he changes darkness into the morning
light,
and the day into dark night.
He calls for the waters of the sea
to pour out on the earth.
The LORD is his name.
[9]He destroys the protected city;
he ruins the strong, walled city.

[10]You hate those who speak in court against
evil,
and you can't stand those who tell the
truth.
[11]You walk on poor people,
forcing them to give you grain.
You have built fancy houses of cut stone,
but you will not live in them.
You have planted beautiful vineyards,
but you will not drink the wine from
them.
[12]I know your many crimes,
your terrible sins.
You hurt people who do right,
you take money to do wrong,
and you keep the poor from getting justice
in court.

[13]In such times the wise person will keep
quiet,
because it is a bad time.

[14]Try to do good, not evil,
so that you will live,
and the LORD God All-powerful will be
with you
just as you say he is.
[15]Hate evil and love good;
be fair in the courts.
Perhaps the LORD God All-powerful will be
kind
to the people of Joseph who are left alive.

[16]This is what the Lord, the LORD God All-
powerful, says:
"People will be crying in all the streets;
they will be saying, 'Oh, no!' in the public
places.
They will call the farmers to come and
weep
and will pay people to cry out loud for
them.
[17]People will be crying in all the vineyards,
because I will pass among you to punish
you," says the LORD.

> **Sidelight** The people in Amos's
> time expected "the day
> of the LORD" to be a picnic. Amos painted a
> different picture – of inescapable terror. You
> can run but you can't hide!

The LORD's Day of Judging

[18]How terrible it will be for you who want
the LORD's day of judging to come.
Why do you want that day to come?
It will bring darkness for you, not light.
[19]It will be like someone who runs from a lion
and meets a bear,
or like someone who goes into his house
and puts his hand on the wall,
and then is bitten by a snake.
[20]So the LORD's day of judging will bring
darkness, not light;
it will be very dark, not light at all.

[21]The LORD says, "I completely hate your
feasts;
I cannot stand your religious meetings.
[22]If you offer me burnt offerings and grain
offerings,
I won't accept them.
You bring your best fellowship offerings of
fattened cattle,
but I will ignore them.

23Take the noise of your songs away from
   me!
   I won't listen to the music of your
      harps.
24But let justice flow like a river,
   and let goodness flow like a stream that
      never stops.

25"People of Israel, you did not bring me
      sacrifices and offerings
   while you travelled in the desert for 40
      years.
26You have carried with you
   your king, the god Sakkuth
   and Kaiwan your idol,
   and the star gods you have made.
27So I will send you away as captives beyond
      Damascus,"
   says the LORD, whose name is the God
      All-powerful.

Israel will be Destroyed

6 How terrible it will be for those who have
   an easy life in Jerusalem,
   for those who feel safe living on Mount
      Samaria.
You think you are the important people of
      the best nation in the world;
   the Israelites come to you for help.
2Go and look at the city of Calneh,
   and from there go to the great city Hamath;
   then go down to Gath of the Philistines.
You are no better than these kingdoms.
   Your land is no larger than theirs.
3You put off the day of punishment,
   but you bring near the day when you can
      do evil to others.
4You lie on beds decorated with ivory
   and stretch out on your couches.
You eat tender lambs
   and fattened calves.

HYPOCRISY

Empty Words

In her school, Elaine usually hung around with a close group of five or six girls. One of the fringe members of the group, Anne, was a common topic of conversation when she wasn't around. Even though Anne could be fun, the group didn't really like her.

When Anne was with the other girls, they were always friendly towards her. But after she had gone, they would go back to talking about her. "We all did it," Elaine says. "We were nice to her when she was around but destroyed her behind her back. It was sort of a habit to say bad things about her."

After a while, Elaine realised that the group was being hypocritical. "You really couldn't tell whether or not we liked Anne," she says. "I began to feel funny about the way we were treating her."

Elaine soon realised that she couldn't believe much of what the group said. Their words were often empty. So Elaine left the group. "What do they say about me now that I'm not around?" she wonders.

Just as Elaine's group was hypocritical in saying one thing but doing another, the people in Amos's time participated in Temple worship, but behaved in ways opposite to those that God desires. In **Amos 5:18–24**, the people of Israel are rebuked because their sinful actions didn't match their pious words.

* What was hypocritical about the way the group treated Anne and the way the people worshipped God in the passage?
* How do you think God's desire for justice, as expressed in the passage, applies to your own worship?

Consider . . .

* keeping a list of times when you have been hypocritical – when your actions were different from your beliefs. Pray for integrity and offer the list to God.
* calling your friends' attention to their mistreatment of someone else, but doing so in a Christian manner.

For more, see . . .

* Psalm 62 (p.535)
* Luke 13:10–17 (p.1067)

* Matthew 6:2–6 (p.947)

[9]At that time there might be only ten people left alive in just one house, but they will also die. [10]When the relatives come to get the bodies to take them outside, one of them will call to the other and ask, "Are there any other dead bodies with you?"

That person will answer, "No."

Then the one who asked will say, "Hush! We must not say the name of the LORD."

[11]The LORD has given the command;
    the large house will be broken into
        pieces,
    and the small house into bits.
[12]Horses do not run on rocks,
    and people do not plough rocks with
        oxen.
But you have changed fairness into poison;
    you have changed what is right into a bitter
        taste.
[13]You are happy that the town of Lo Debar
        was captured,
    and you say, "We have taken Karnaim [n] by
        our own strength."
[14]The LORD God All-powerful says,
    "Israel, I will bring a nation against you
    that will make your people suffer from Lebo
        Hamath in the north
    to the valley south of the Dead Sea." [d]

The Vision of Locusts

7 This is what the Lord GOD showed me: he was forming a swarm of locusts, [d] after the king had taken his share of the first crop and the second crop had just begun growing. [2]When the locusts ate all the crops in the country, I said, "Lord GOD, forgive us. How could Israel live through this? It is too small already!"

[3]So the LORD changed his mind about this. "It will not happen," said the LORD.

The Vision of Fire

[4]This is what the Lord GOD showed me: the Lord GOD was calling for fire to come down like rain. It burned up the deep water and was going to burn up the land. [5]Then I cried out, "Lord GOD, stop! How could Israel live through this? It is too small already."

[6]So the LORD changed his mind about this too. "It will not happen," said the Lord GOD.

The Vision of the Plumb Line

[7]This is what he showed me: the Lord stood by a straight wall, with a plumb line [d] in his hand. [8]The LORD said to me, "Amos, what do you see?"

I said, "A plumb line."

Then the Lord said, "See, I will put a plumb line among my people Israel to show how crooked they are. I will not look the other way any longer.

[9]"The places where Isaac's descendants [d]
        worship will be destroyed,
    Israel's holy places will be turned into
        ruins,
    and I will attack King Jeroboam's family
        with the sword."

Amaziah Speaks Against Amos

[10]Amaziah, a priest at Bethel, sent this message to Jeroboam king of Israel: "Amos is making evil plans against you with the people of Israel. He has been speaking so much that this land can't hold all his words. [11]This is what Amos has said:
'Jeroboam will die by the sword,
    and the people of Israel will be taken as
        captives
out of their own country.'"

[12]Then Amaziah said to Amos, "Seer, [d] go back right now to Judah. Do your prophesying [d] and earn your living there, [13]but don't prophesy any more here at Bethel. This is the king's holy place, and it is the nation's temple."

[14]Then Amos answered Amaziah, "I do not make my living as a prophet, nor am I a member of a group of prophets. I make my living as a

> **Sidelight**   When Amos said that he took care of sycamore trees (Amos 7:14) – which bore figs – he did more than pick their fruit once a year. To ensure good fruit from these trees, the farmer had to slit the top of each fig as it grew.

shepherd, and I take care of sycamore trees. [15]But the LORD took me away from tending the flock and said to me, 'Go and prophesy to my people Israel.' [16]So listen to the LORD's word. You tell me,
'Don't prophesy against Israel,
    and stop prophesying against the
        descendants of Isaac.'

[17]"Because you have said this, the LORD says:
'Your wife will become a prostitute [d] in the
        city,
    and your sons and daughters will be killed
        with swords.

Lo Debar . . . Karnaim   These were cities in Israel that the Israelites had captured in war.

⁵You make up songs on your harps,
and, like David, you compose songs on
musical instruments.
⁶You drink wine by the bowlful
and use the best perfumed lotions.
But you are not sad over the ruin of
Israel,
⁷so you will be some of the first ones taken as
slaves.

Your feasting and lying around will come to
an end.

⁸The Lord GOD made this promise; the LORD
God All-powerful says:
"I hate the pride of the Israelites,
and I hate their strong buildings,
so I will let the enemy take the city
and everything in it."

SELF-ESTEEM

Hidden Talent

On the outside Nicolle was very ordinary. She lived on a council estate in the East End of London and had a thick Cockney accent. She was fourteen years old and had just started going to church. Everything was new to her and so she would comment on it.

"Cor! This Jesus stuff's good innit?" she would remark, and several people would raise an eyebrow at her rough approach to Christianity. In fact some members of the church treated her in a very condescending manner, almost as if her accent made her a second-class citizen.

Nicolle never really noticed this, and just went on blissfully enjoying her life as a very new Christian. She enjoyed the services and noticed that people often took part, giving a testimony, or singing a song.

"I wonder if I could do that?" she asked her friend one day, as they were walking to the bus stop.

"Do what?" asked Vicky.

"Well, I dunno. Sing a song I suppose. I think I only know 'Amazing Grace' . . . " she finished lamely.

Vicky looked alarmed . . . 'Amazing Grace' was a notoriously hard song to sing as a solo.

"Why not just give a testimony?" her friend suggested.

"'Cos I could never talk in front of all them people!" laughed Nicolle. Then she added, "But I could sing to 'em . . . "

Whilst waiting for the bus to arrive, Vicky found out that her new friend went to singing classes, and no ordinary singing classes. Nicolle was trained in Italian Opera . . . at the age of fourteen!

"I don't tell many people," she blushed. "Don't s'pose many people like that stuff."

Vicky couldn't wait for the service. When it finally arrived, she could see people looking uncomfortable as Nicolle took the platform. She watched as people nudged each other as her friend announced:

"I'm going to sing 'Amazing Grace'," and then nodded to the pianist.

The silence when she sang was almost as deafening as the applause afterwards!

She was outstanding!

Vicky hugged her friend as she took her seat.

Sometimes we think we are better than we are, and sometimes there is more to a person than we see. Read **Amos 6:1–7** to see why God rebuked Israel for their wrong attitudes.

* Look at verse 1. How are the people in the passage like some of the people in Nicolle's church?
* How close to your own views of materialism and feelings of security are those mentioned in this passage?

Consider . . .

* Listing the values – not the material things – that would improve your self-esteem.
* Joining a group to help others (and yourself) to grow in good self-esteem.

For more, see . . .

* Romans 12:3–16 (p.1204)
* James 4:1–6 (p.1351)

* Philippians 2:1–4 (p.1282)

Other people will measure your land and
    divide it among themselves,
and you will die in a foreign country.
The people of Israel will definitely be taken
    from their own land as captives.' "

The Vision of Ripe Fruit

8 This is what the Lord GOD showed me: a
basket of summer fruit. [2]He said to me,
"Amos, what do you see?"

I said, "A basket of summer fruit."

Then the LORD said to me, "An end [n] has come
for my people Israel, because I will not overlook
their sins any more.

[3]"On that day the palace songs will become
funeral songs," says the Lord GOD. "There will be
dead bodies thrown everywhere! Silence!"

[4]Listen to me, you who walk on helpless
    people,
    you who are trying to destroy the poor
        people of this country, saying,
[5]"When will the New Moon [d] festival be
        over
    so we can sell grain?
When will the Sabbath [d] be over
    so we can bring out wheat to sell?
We can charge them more
    and give them less,
    and we can change the scales to cheat the
        people.
[6]We will buy poor people for silver,
    and needy people for the price of a pair of
        sandals.
    We will even sell the wheat that was swept
        up from the floor."

[7]The LORD has sworn by his name, the Pride of
Jacob, "I will never forget everything that these
people did.
[8]The whole land will shake because of it,
    and everyone who lives in the land will cry
        for those who died.
The whole land will rise like the Nile;
    it will be shaken, and then it will fall
    like the Nile River in Egypt."

[9]The Lord GOD says:
"At that time I will cause the sun to go
    down at noon
and make the earth dark on a bright day.
[10]I will change your festivals into days of crying
    for the dead,
and all your songs will become songs of
    sadness.

I will make all of you wear rough cloth to
    show your sadness;
I will make you shave your heads
    as well.
I will make it like a time of crying for the
    death of an only son,
    and its end like the end of an awful day."

[11]The Lord GOD says: "The days are coming
    when I will cause a time of hunger in the
    land.
The people will not be hungry for bread or
    thirsty for water,
but they will be hungry for words from the
    LORD.
[12]They will wander from the Mediterranean
    Sea to the Dead Sea, [d]
from the north to the east.
They will search for the word of the LORD,
    but they won't find it.
[13]At that time the beautiful young women and
    the young men
will become weak from thirst.
[14]They make promises by the idol in Samaria
    and say, 'As surely as the god of Dan
        lives . . .'
    and, 'As surely as the god of Beersheba [n]
        lives, we promise . . .'
So they will fall
    and never get up again."

Israel will be Destroyed

9 I saw the Lord standing by the altar, and he
said:
"Smash the top of the pillars
    so that even the bottom of the doors will
        shake.
Make the pillars fall on the people's
        heads;
    anyone left alive I will kill with a sword.
Not one person will get away;
    no one will escape.
[2]If they dig down as deep as the place of the
    dead,
    I will pull them up from there.
If they climb up into heaven,
    I will bring them down from there.
[3]If they hide at the top of Mount Carmel,
    I will find them and take them away.
If they try to hide from me at the bottom of
    the sea,
    I will command a snake to bite them.
[4]If they are captured and taken away by their
    enemies,

---

end   The Hebrew word for "end" sounds like the Hebrew word for "summer fruit".
Dan . . . Beersheba   Dan was the city farthest north in Israel, and Beersheba was the city farthest south. So this means all the
    people of Israel.

I will command the sword to kill them.
I will keep watch over them,

but I will keep watch to give them trouble,
not to do them good."

⁵The Lord GOD All-powerful touches the land,
and the land shakes.

Then everyone who lives in the land cries
for the dead.
The whole land rises like the Nile River
and falls like the river of Egypt.
⁶The LORD builds his upper rooms above the
skies;
he sets their foundations on the earth.
He calls for the waters of the sea
and pours them out on the land.
The LORD is his name.

⁷The LORD says,
"Israel, you are no different to me than the
people of Cush.
I brought Israel out of the land of Egypt,
the Philistines from Crete
and the Arameans from Kir.

JUSTICE

Dont Fake It

In the late seventies and eighties, a vicious civil war raged in the central American country of El Salvador. In 1980 alone, the war claimed the lives of 3,000 people every month. One man alone made a public appeal for the world to intervene. His name was Oscar Romero, the Catholic Archbishop of El Salvador.

Oscar Romero was not seen as political protestor. In fact he was appointed to such a high position because many of the bishops in El Salvador were wary of angering the government. They felt that Oscar, famous for being a "bookworm" would keep quiet. But something happened shortly after Oscar's appointment that meant he would stop at nothing to see the war end. The first priest Oscar ordained was ambushed by the army and killed for helping farmers stand up against the government.

On 24 March 1980, Archbishop Romero was shot dead by an army assassin during a mass where he was officiating. The day before his murder, he told a reporter:

"You can tell the people if they succeed in killing me, that I forgive and bless those who do it. Hopefully, they will realise they are wasting their time. A bishop will die, but the church of God, which is the people, will never perish."

God's voice throughout the Old and New Testament has always spoken out against injustice, as in **Amos 8:4–8**. His church and his prophets today still do.

* Would you be willing to speak up when you saw injustice, as Oscar Romero did?
* Look at verse 6. God pays attention to the cries of the poor. Do we pay enough attention to the impact our shopping choices have on poor people in the world?

Consider . . .

* taking time this week to allow God to speak to you through the injustice you see in your town and in the world.
* whether you and your family can buy more products that have been fairly traded, and so help those trying to earn a living in poorer countries.

For more, see . . .

* Psalm 146 (p.586)
* Luke 16:19–31 (p.1075)

* Luke 11:37–42 (p.1062)

⁸I, the Lord God, am watching the sinful
  kingdom Israel.
I will destroy it
  from off the earth,
but I will not completely destroy
  Jacob's descendants," ᵈ says the Lord.
⁹"I am giving the command
  to scatter the nation of Israel among all
    nations.
It will be like someone shaking grain through
  a strainer,
but not even a tiny stone falls through.
¹⁰All the sinners among my people
  will die by the sword—
those who say,
  'Nothing bad will happen to us.'

The Lord Promises to Restore Israel

¹¹"The kingdom of David is like a fallen tent,
  but in that day I will set it up again
  and mend its broken places.
I will rebuild its ruins
  as it was before.

¹²Then Israel will take over what is left of Edom
  and the other nations that belong to me,"
says the Lord,
  who will make it happen.

¹³The Lord says, "The time is coming when
  there will be all kinds of food.
People will still be harvesting crops
  when it's time to plough again.
People will still be taking the juice from grapes
  when it's time to plant again.
Wine will drip from the mountains
  and pour from the hills.
¹⁴I will bring my people Israel back from
  captivity;
they will build the ruined cities again,
  and they will live in them.
They will plant vineyards and drink the wine
  from them;
they will plant gardens and eat their fruit.
¹⁵I will plant my people on their land,
  and they will not be pulled out again
  from the land which I have given them,"
says the Lord your God.

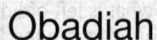

Obadiah

Why Read This Book:
* Learn what can happen to a nation that's filled with false pride (Obadiah 2–8).
* See how the righteous will be victorious (Obadiah 17–21).

When?

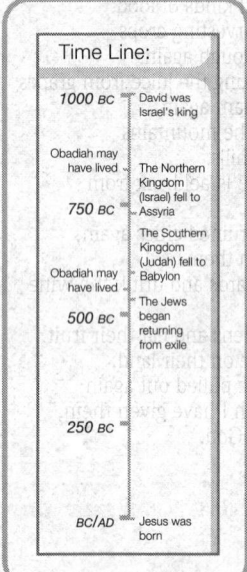

Time Line:

1000 BC	David was Israel's king
Obadiah may have lived	The Northern Kingdom (Israel) fell to Assyria
750 BC	
	The Southern Kingdom (Judah) fell to Babylon
Obadiah may have lived	The Jews began returning from exile
500 BC	
250 BC	
BC/AD	Jesus was born

Behind the Scenes:

If you think you've seen real rivalries on the football pitch, "you ain't seen nothing yet!" Israel vs. Edom – now that's real rivalry!

Even though they were close neighbours, these two countries had been rivals for hundreds of years. They fought over control of trade routes. Then when Israel was raided by major empires, Edom not only didn't help, but actually shared the loot! All this from a nation of people who were actually related to Israel. Esau, the father of the Edomites, was the brother of Jacob (who was also called Israel). (See Genesis 25:30, p.30.)

Into the middle of this rivalry steps the prophet Obadiah. He describes God's anger at Edom for not helping oppressed people and for rejoicing over the Israelites' misfortune. And he predicts that Edom will be destroyed for its sinfulness, and that the nation of Israel will have the final victory.

Obadiah's message was more than a motivational talk at a rally for the Israelites. At times, it was harsh and full of revenge. God will correct the injustice by bringing down the Edomites, Obadiah said. His message reminds us to care for the weak around us and to keep hopeful even when we feel overwhelmed and beaten down. God will be victorious in the end!

Where?

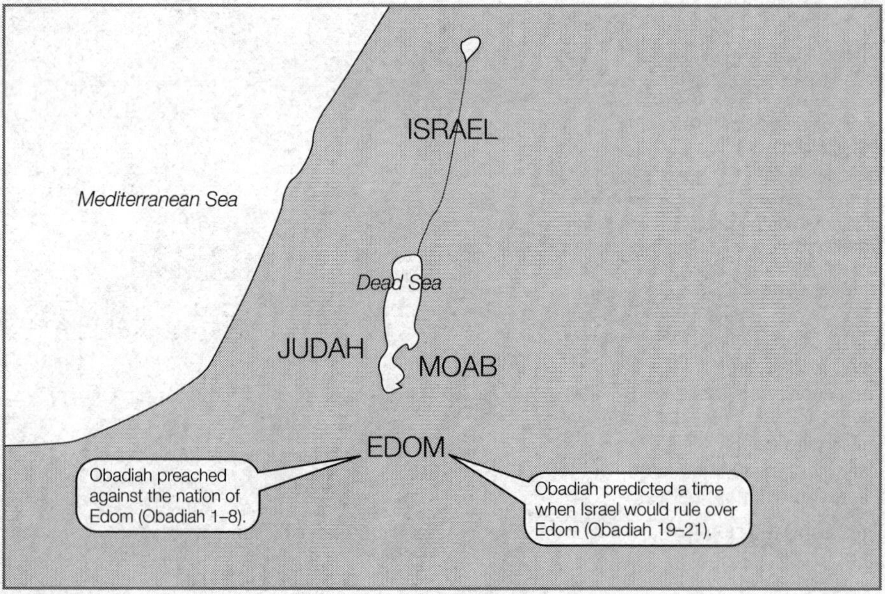

ISRAEL

Mediterranean Sea

Dead Sea

JUDAH

MOAB

EDOM

Obadiah preached against the nation of Edom (Obadiah 1–8).

Obadiah predicted a time when Israel would rule over Edom (Obadiah 19–21).

The LORD will Punish the Edomites

[1]This is the vision of Obadiah.

This is what the Lord GOD says about Edom:[n]
We have heard a message from the LORD.
 A messenger has been sent among the nations, saying,
 "Attack! Let's go and attack Edom!"

The Lord Speaks to the Edomites

[2]"Soon I will make you the smallest of nations.
 You will be greatly hated by everyone.
[3]Your pride has fooled you,
 you who live in the hollow places of the cliff.
 Your home is up high,
 you who say to yourself,
 'No one can bring me down to the ground.'
[4]Even if you fly high like the eagle
 and make your nest among the stars,
 I will bring you down from there," says the LORD.
[5]"You will really be ruined!
 If thieves came to you,
 if robbers came by night,
 they would steal only enough for themselves.
 If workers came and picked the grapes from your vines,
 they would leave a few behind.
[6]But you, Edom, will really lose everything!
 People will find all your hidden treasures!

Sidelight   Some people hide their money under mattresses, but the Edomites hoarded their wealth in the red cliffs, south of the Dead Sea where they lived (Obadiah 6). Obadiah mentions "treasures" on an average of once every seventh verse!

---

[7]All the people who are your friends
 will force you out of the land.
 The people who are at peace with you
 will trick you and defeat you.
 Those who eat your bread with you now
 are planning a trap for you,
 and you will not notice it."

[8]The LORD says, "On that day

I will surely destroy the wise people from Edom,
 and those with understanding from the mountains of Edom.
[9]Then, city of Teman, your best warriors will be afraid
 and everyone from the mountains of Edom will be killed.
[10]You did violence to your relatives, the Israelites,
 so you will be covered with shame
 and destroyed for ever.
[11]You stood aside without helping
 while strangers carried Israel's treasures away.
 When foreigners entered Israel's city gate
 and threw lots[d] to decide what part of Jerusalem they would take,
 you were like one of them.

Commands That Edom Broke

[12]"Edom, do not laugh at your brother Israel in his time of trouble
 or be happy about the people of Judah when they are destroyed.
 Do not boast when cruel things are done to them.
[13]Do not enter the city gate of my people
 in their time of trouble
 or laugh at their problems
 in their time of trouble.
 Do not take their treasures
 in their time of trouble.
[14]Do not stand at the crossroads
 to destroy those who are trying to escape.
 Do not capture those who escape alive and
 turn them over to their enemy
 in their time of trouble.

The Nations will be Judged

[15]"The LORD's day of judging is coming soon
 to all the nations.
 The same evil things you did to other people
 will happen to you;
 they will come back upon your own head.
[16]Because you drank in my Temple,[d]
 all the nations will drink on and on.
 They will drink and drink
 until they disappear.

Edom   The Edomites were the people who came from Esau, Jacob's twin brother. They were enemies of the Israelites.

[17]But on Mount Zion [d] some will escape the
  judgement,
  and it will be a holy place.
The people of Jacob will take back their
  land
from those who took it from them.
[18]The people of Jacob will be like a fire
  and the people of Joseph [n] like a flame.
But the people of Esau [n] will be like dry
  stalks.
The people of Jacob will set them on fire
  and burn them up.

There will be no one left of the people of
  Esau."
This will happen because the LORD has said it.

[19]Then God's people will regain southern Judah
  from Edom;
  they will take back the mountains of Edom.
They will take back the western hills
  from the Philistines.
They will regain the lands of Ephraim and
  Samaria,
  and Benjamin will take over Gilead.

people of Jacob . . . Joseph The people who came from Jacob and Joseph, or the Israelites.
people of Esau The people who came from Esau, or the Edomites.

SIN

What Are We Really Like?

What's the worst thing anyone can do? Kill someone? That's what people generally think.

Murder is probably the worst thing that can happen between human beings. But what about when God comes into the picture?

According to the Bible, sin is really serious. Often we can get away with things that our teachers and parents don't find out about, or we can talk our way out of trouble. But God always knows absolutely everything that we've done, and he knows our attitude to him.

He doesn't just see everything that we *do* – he knows what goes on in our heads as well. So he's well aware of what we're really like. Because God doesn't want his world to contain sin forever, eventually he will come in judgement and wipe it out. Where will we be when this happens? The truth is that we'll be in trouble, because we're all contaminated with this disease of sin. We will be in danger of what the Bible calls hell.

But God hasn't left us in this terrible situation. The good news, or the "Gospel", is that God has sent his son, Jesus, to rescue us. He can take away the sin that is such a massive part of our lives and which has such terrible results. On the cross, he died for our sin so we don't have to face the punishment for it. When we recognise that, we're brought into God's family. God never abandons us because of what we have done – he is much greater and more powerful than even the worst thing we can do. Jesus is always there and will never let us go.

Read **Obadiah 12–14**.

* What is sin against God?
* What happens if we sin even after we've asked God into our lives?

Consider . . .

* writing down everything you can remember doing wrong recently, praying for forgiveness, then tearing up the paper into the tiniest pieces possible!
* telling a friend if you find yourself thinking about your sins even after you've confessed them to God. Get them to pray with you that you would know and accept God's forgiveness and have the strength not to do these things again.

For more, see . . .

* Psalm 51:1–5 (p.530)
* Romans 3:23 (p.1187)

* Acts 2:38 (p.1140)
* Romans 6:23 (p.1193)

20People from Israel who once were forced to
  leave their homes
    will take the land of the Canaanites,
    all the way to Zarephath.
  People from Judah who once were forced
    to leave Jerusalem and live in Sepharad
will take back the cities of southern Judah.
21Powerful warriors will go up on
  Mount Zion,
where they will rule the people living on
  Edom's mountains.
And the kingdom will belong to the LORD.

Jonah

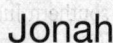

When?

Why Read This Book:

- Discover truth in a story of a prophet who was reluctant to do what God wanted him to do (Jonah 1—2).
- See that God's love and mercy are for all the world (Jonah 3—4).

Behind the Scenes:

Being chosen to be a leader is always a great honour. But you probably wouldn't last long in the position if you simply basked in the glow of being chosen. You would have to fulfil the tasks – some you might not like – that come with the honour.

The Jews had been chosen by God to be his special people. Through history, God had guided and protected them. But what responsibilities for the rest of the world did that honour include? Should God's people shut off the world, focusing on their gifts from God? Or should they take the story of God's love to the rest of the world?

The story of Jonah addressed this dilemma. God called the prophet Jonah to go and preach at Nineveh, the heathen capital of Assyria. Not wanting to preach to non-Jewish people – especially pagans whose cruelty was widely known – Jonah went in the opposite direction. Like many Israelites, he enjoyed God's mercy on Israel but wanted all enemies to be destroyed.

God wouldn't let Jonah off from his mission, though. Through a storm and a big fish, God got Jonah's attention and turned him around. Reluctantly, Jonah went to Nineveh and preached, and the whole city turned to God. But Jonah wasn't happy. He went to sulk about God sparing the Ninevites from destruction.

God responded with a message that's at the heart of the book: "Shouldn't I show concern for the great city Nineveh, which has more than 120,000 people who do not know right from wrong . . .?" (Jonah 4:11). ▷

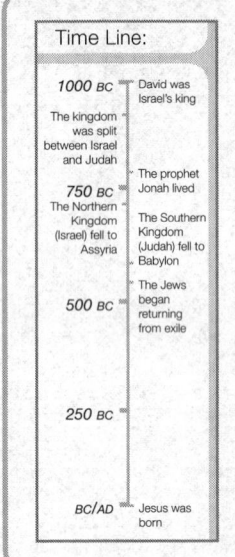

Time Line:

1000 BC	David was Israel's king
The kingdom was split between Israel and Judah	
750 BC	The prophet Jonah lived
The Northern Kingdom (Israel) fell to Assyria	The Southern Kingdom (Judah) fell to Babylon
500 BC	The Jews began returning from exile
250 BC	
BC/AD	Jesus was born

Where?

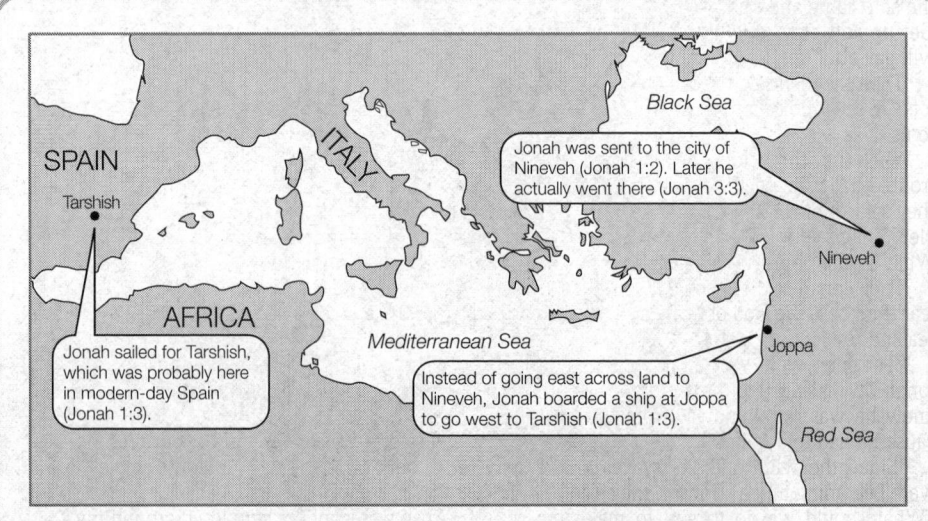

Black Sea

Jonah was sent to the city of Nineveh (Jonah 1:2). Later he actually went there (Jonah 3:3).

SPAIN

ITALY

Tarshish

Nineveh

AFRICA

Mediterranean Sea

Joppa

Jonah sailed for Tarshish, which was probably here in modern-day Spain (Jonah 1:3).

Instead of going east across land to Nineveh, Jonah boarded a ship at Joppa to go west to Tarshish (Jonah 1:3).

Red Sea

Behind the   Jonah's story reminds all God's followers that no one owns God. As Jesus
Scenes (cont.):   said in Luke 5:32 (p.1047), "I have not come to invite good people but sinners
                        to change their hearts and lives."

God Calls and Jonah Runs

1 The LORD spoke his word to Jonah son of Amittai: ²"Get up and go to the great city of Nineveh and preach against it, because I see the evil things they do."

³But Jonah got up to run away from the LORD by going to Tarshish. He went to the city of Joppa, where he found a ship that was going to the city of Tarshish. Jonah paid for the trip and went aboard, planning to go to Tarshish to run away from the LORD.

> **Sidelight**   The name Jonah (Jonah 1:1) means "dove" which may be a traditional symbol for Israel (see Psalm 74:19–21, p.544).

⁴But the LORD sent a great wind on the sea, which made the sea so stormy that the ship was in danger of breaking apart. ⁵The sailors were afraid, and each man cried to his own god. They began throwing the cargo from the ship into the sea to make the ship lighter.

But Jonah had gone down far inside the ship to lie down, and he fell fast asleep. ⁶The captain of the ship came and said, "Why are you sleeping? Get up and pray to your god! Maybe your god will pay attention to us, and we won't die!"

⁷Then the men said to each other, "Let's throw lots *d* to see who caused these troubles to happen to us."

When they threw lots, the lot showed that the trouble had happened because of Jonah. ⁸Then they said to him, "Tell us, who caused our trouble? What is your job? Where do you come from? What is your country? Who are your people?"

⁹Then Jonah said to them, "I am a Hebrew. I fear the LORD, the God of heaven, who made the sea and the land."

¹⁰The men were very afraid, and they asked Jonah, "What terrible thing did you do?" (They knew he was running away from the LORD because he had told them.)

¹¹Since the wind and the waves of the sea were becoming much stronger, they said to him, "What should we do to you to make the sea calm down for us?"

¹²Jonah said to them, "Pick me up and throw me into the sea, and then it will calm down. I know it is my fault that this great storm has come on you."

¹³Instead, the men tried to row the ship back to the land, but they could not, because the sea was becoming more stormy.

Jonah's Punishment

¹⁴So the men cried to the LORD, "LORD, please don't let us die because of this man's life; please don't think we are guilty of killing an innocent person. LORD, you have caused all this to happen; you wanted it this way." ¹⁵So they picked up Jonah and threw him into the sea, and the sea became calm. ¹⁶Then they began to fear the LORD very much; they offered a sacrifice to the LORD and made promises to him.

¹⁷The LORD caused a big fish to swallow Jonah, and Jonah was inside the fish for three days and three nights.

> **Sidelight**   Jonah spent three days and three nights in the belly of an enormous fish before it threw up (Jonah 1:7—2:10). Jesus used this incident to illustrate his own death and resurrection (see Matthew 12:40, p.961).

2 While Jonah was inside the fish, he prayed to the LORD his God and said,
²"When I was in danger,
    I called to the LORD,
    and he answered me.
I was about to die,
    so I cried to you
    and you heard my voice.
³You threw me into the sea,
    down, down into the deep sea.
The water was all around me,
    and your powerful waves flowed
        over me.
⁴I said, 'I was driven out of your presence,
    but I hope to see your Holy Temple *d*
        again.'
⁵The waters of the sea closed around my
        throat.

The deep sea was all around me;
seaweed was wrapped around my head.
⁶When I went down to where the mountains
of the sea start to rise,
I thought I was locked in this prison
for ever,
but you saved me from the pit of death,
LORD my God.

⁷"When my life had almost gone,
I remembered the LORD.
I prayed to you,
and you heard my prayers in your Holy
Temple.

⁸"People who worship useless idols
give up their loyalty to you.
⁹But I will praise and thank you
while I give sacrifices to you,
and I will keep my promises to you.
Salvation comes from the LORD!"

¹⁰Then the LORD spoke to the fish, and the fish
threw up Jonah onto the dry land.

God Calls and Jonah Obeys

3 The LORD spoke his word to Jonah again
and said, ²"Get up and go to the great city
Nineveh and preach to it what I tell you to say."

³So Jonah obeyed the LORD and got up and
went to Nineveh. It was a very large city; just to
walk across it took a person three days. ⁴After
Jonah had entered the city and walked for one
day, he preached to the people, saying, "After 40
days, Nineveh will be destroyed!"

⁵The people of Nineveh believed God. They
announced that they would stop eating for a
while, and they put on rough cloth to show their
sadness. All the people in the city did this, from
the most important to the least important.

⁶When the king of Nineveh heard this news,
he got up from his throne, took off his robe and
covered himself with rough cloth and sat in
ashes to show how upset he was.

⁷He sent this announcement through Nineveh:

By command of the king and his important
men: no person or animal, herd or flock, will

THANKFULNESS

In All Circumstances

Lana came home from a wonderful weekend at her grandparents' to find that burglars had taken everything:
camera, money, and a laptop with some really important work on it. Two windows were smashed, the whole
place ransacked. She walked around the house and discovered more and more damage and mess.

This was when she became aware that she had a choice – she could look at the bad bits and enjoy the
sympathy people would bring to her over the next few days, or she could celebrate in God that she and her
family were safe, the house hadn't burned down, and that the insurance cover would enable them to replace
the items that had been stolen. She realised that material possessions aren't actually that important.
Her heart soared as she felt God's love flow through her, as she realised she'd passed one of God's
biggest tests. She was learning what it means to praise God through the hard times!

Lana learnt that each time something bad happens, we can choose to be victims or we can
choose to learn from it. We can choose to be negative or we can choose to be positive and look
for the good. We can read about Jonah's thankful heart in **Jonah 2:2–9**.

* What did Lana have to do to be able to praise God through the hard times?
* What do you think now about praising God through the hard times?

Consider . . .

* writing a list or a poem about all the good things in your life you can thank God for.
* keeping greetings cards and stamps handy and sending thank-you letters when people do nice
things for you.

For more, see . . .

* 1 Chronicles 29:10–20 (p.399)
* 1 Thessalonians 5:12–18 (p.1301)
* Isaiah 63:7–9 (p.709)

be allowed to taste anything. Do not let them eat food or drink water. [8]But every person and animal should be covered with rough cloth, and people should cry loudly to God. Everyone must turn away from evil living and stop doing harm all the time. [9]Who knows? Maybe God will change his mind. Maybe he will stop being angry and then we will not die.

FORGIVENESS

Personal Peace

By 1938, when eighteen-year-old Joseph Mavsar left home to study for the ministry, he had heard many sermons about forgiveness. In a few years, however, he would know how hard it would become to live out those sermons.

In 1941, Italy invaded Yugoslavia and occupied Joseph's village.

The family's troubles increased when his father, a respected leader, refused to join the local communist resistance.

The family gathered for Christmas, 1942. Two days later, the communists attacked the house and killed Joseph's parents, four of his brothers and his only sister. Joseph and his twelve-year-old brother, Bill, jumped from a second-floor window and fled to the woods. The communists burned the others' bodies and stole the family's property.

Just two brothers of the large family survived the war.

Joseph went to the USA in 1948 as a minister. He amazed some and shocked others as he preached forgiveness for war crimes. Although he wanted the truth of the crimes against his family to be known, he still preached forgiveness.

As the 25th anniversary of his ordination approached, however, Joseph still struggled to forgive personally the people who had killed his family and taken all their possessions. Then a cousin in Yugoslavia wrote to Joseph, telling him that some of the killers were haunted by what they had done. "Come back and make peace with them," the cousin wrote.

Joseph returned to his village and found one of the communists living in his father's house.

"As I shook this man's hand and told him I forgave him," Joseph remembers, "he thanked me over and over, and said it was the best day of his life."

In his old age, Joseph continued to preach forgiveness. "In life we cannot be happy unless we're able to forgive," he said. "We must forgive, no matter how painful the hurt."

He knows what he's talking about.

Sometimes offences seem too great ever to be forgiven. Read in **Jonah 3:1–10** how the Lord forgives the people of Nineveh for their many sins.

* Jonah did not think Nineveh should be forgiven (Jonah 4:1). How do Joseph and Jonah differ in their willingness to forgive?
* Have you ever found it difficult to forgive someone, even though it was necessary for your own peace of mind?

Consider . . .

* forgiving someone who has hurt you, even though it's difficult to do.
* making the first move to restore a damaged relationship within your family or peers.

For more, see . . .

* Joel 2:12–19 (p.865)
* Acts 10:43 (p.1157)
* Luke 23:26–34 (p.1091)

[10]When God saw what the people did, that they stopped doing evil, he changed his mind and did not do what he had warned. He did not punish them.

God's Mercy Makes Jonah Angry

4 But this made Jonah very unhappy, and he became angry. [2]He prayed to the LORD, "When I was still in my own country this is what I said would happen, and that is why I quickly ran away to Tarshish. I knew that you are a God who is kind and shows mercy. You don't become angry quickly, and you have great love. I knew you would choose not to cause harm. [3]So now I ask you, LORD, please kill me. It is better for me to die than to live."

[4]Then the LORD said, "Do you think it is right for you to be angry?"

[5]Jonah went out and sat down east of the city. There he made a shelter for himself and sat in the shade, waiting to see what would happen to the city. [6]The LORD made a plant grow quickly up over Jonah, which gave him shade and helped him to be more comfortable. Jonah was very pleased to have the plant. [7]But the next day when the sun rose, God sent a worm to attack the plant so that it died.

[8]As the sun rose higher in the sky, God sent a very hot east wind to blow, and the sun became so hot on Jonah's head that he became very weak and wished he were dead. He said, "It is better for me to die than to live."

STRESS

Not Going My Way

Debbie was sweating – she had been dancing, singing and acting for the whole morning. She had worked so hard and really wanted that place at stage school. She'd prayed about it so much. She also wanted to stay in the area where she had so many friends.

They were announcing the numbers they had picked to go on to the next stage. Her number was 23 and the numbers went all the way to 50.

. . . 16, 19, 22, 27 . . . Number 23 wasn't called out. She sat with her heart still racing and looked at the floor. Why had it not worked out? Every one said she would make it. Why?

She started walking home, tears slowly rolling down her face. She was so stressed about her future and what to do next, she even wondered whether there was a point in living if she couldn't perform. Her friend Lucy was walking by and saw how upset Debbie was. They both sat on a bench and Lucy decided the best thing to do was pray.

After praying, Debbie felt a lot better and Lucy said to her, "God has got something better than you could ever think, he is in control, it's all good!" Debbie really hoped she was right.

Sometimes we need God to speak to us through a practical lesson in order for us to put our trust in him fully, and in Debbie's case God needed to close off an opportunity in order for her to see the greater plans he had for her.

Read **Jonah 4:5–9**.

* Have you ever felt like Jonah or Debbie?
* What do you think God was showing Jonah by sending the worm?

Consider . . .

* a time where you were really stressed about something. Think about what God taught you through that time.
* any exams or events that are coming up that may get you stressed and pray for wisdom in those circumstances.

For more, see . . .

* Matt 6:25–27 (p.948)
* Luke 10:38–42 (p.1058)
* Matt 10:29–31 (p.956)
* Romans 8:28 (p.1196)

⁹But God said to Jonah, "Do you think it is right for you to be angry about the plant?"

Jonah answered, "It is right for me to be angry! I am so angry I could die!"

¹⁰And the LORD said, "You are so concerned for that plant even though you did nothing to make it grow. It appeared one day, and the next day it died. ¹¹Then shouldn't I show concern for the great city Nineveh, which has more than 120,000 people who do not know right from wrong, and many animals too?"

Micah

Why Read This Book:

• See God's judgement on a nation that didn't follow him (Micah 1—2).
• Find out what happens when leaders' actions are unjust (Micah 3).
• Be encouraged by God's promise for the future (Micah 7).

When?

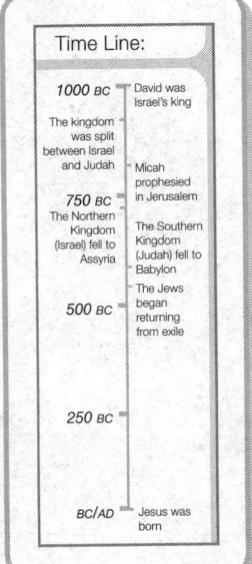

Time Line:

1000 BC — David was Israel's king

The kingdom was split between Israel and Judah

Micah prophesied in Jerusalem

750 BC

The Northern Kingdom (Israel) fell to Assyria

The Southern Kingdom (Judah) fell to Babylon

The Jews began returning from exile

500 BC

250 BC

BC/AD — Jesus was born

Behind the Scenes:

Everything was falling apart, but no one seemed to notice. And when people were confronted with their problems, they just yawned.

That was the prophet Micah's situation. When he started preaching in Judah, Israel was about to be conquered. And, he believed, the same fate awaited Judah because of its injustice to the poor and its immoral leadership.

Yet, Micah said, God would establish a kingdom of eternal peace.

The heart of Micah's message summarised what most of the prophets called people to do: "The Lord has told you, human, what is good; he has told you what he wants from you: to do what is right to other people, love being kind to others, and live humbly, obeying your God" (Micah 6:8). It's a message that's just as relevant today as it was more than 2,500 years ago.

Where?

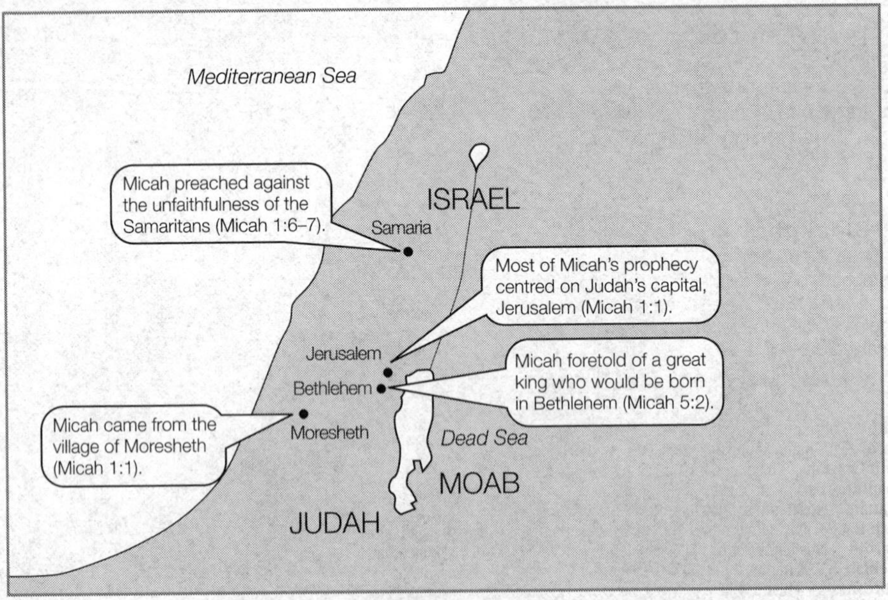

Mediterranean Sea

Micah preached against the unfaithfulness of the Samaritans (Micah 1:6–7).

ISRAEL

Samaria

Most of Micah's prophecy centred on Judah's capital, Jerusalem (Micah 1:1).

Jerusalem

Bethlehem

Micah foretold of a great king who would be born in Bethlehem (Micah 5:2).

Micah came from the village of Moresheth (Micah 1:1).

Moresheth

Dead Sea

MOAB

JUDAH

Samaria and Israel to Be Punished

1 During the time that Jotham, Ahaz and Hezekiah were kings of Judah, the word of the LORD came to Micah, who was from Moresheth. He saw these visions about Samaria and Jerusalem.

² Hear this, all you nations;
    listen, earth and all you who live on it.
The Lord GOD will be a witness against you,
    the Lord from his Holy Temple. *d*
³ See, the LORD is coming out of his place;
    he is coming down to walk on the tops of
        the mountains.
⁴ The mountains will melt under him,
    and the valleys will crack open,
like wax near a fire,
    like water running down a hillside.
⁵ All this is because of Jacob's sin,
    because of the sins of the nation of Israel.
What is the place of Jacob's sin?
    Isn't it Samaria?
What is Judah's place of idol worship?
    Isn't it Jerusalem?

The LORD Speaks

⁶ "So I will make Samaria a pile of ruins in the
        open country,
    a place for planting vineyards.
I will pour her stones down into the valley
    and strip her down to her foundations.
⁷ All her idols will be broken into pieces;
    all the gifts to her idols will be burned with
        fire.
I will destroy all her idols,
    and because Samaria earned her money by
        being unfaithful to me,
    this money will be carried off by others
        who are not faithful to me."

Micah's Great Sadness

⁸ I will moan and cry because of this evil,
    going around barefoot and naked.
I will cry loudly like the wild dogs
    and make sad sounds like the owls do,
⁹ because Samaria's wound cannot be healed.
    It will spread to Judah;
it will reach the city gate of my people,
    all the way to Jerusalem.
¹⁰ Don't tell it in Gath. *n*
    Don't cry in Acco. *n*
Roll in the dust
    at Beth Ophrah. *n*
¹¹ Pass on your way, naked and ashamed,
    you who live in Shaphir. *n*
Those who live in Zaanan *n*
    won't come out.
The people in Beth Ezel *n* will cry,
    but they will not give you any support.
¹² Those who live in Maroth *n*
    will be anxious for good news to come,
because trouble will come from the LORD,
    all the way to the gate of Jerusalem.
¹³ You people living in Lachish, *n*
    harness the fastest horse to the chariot.
Jerusalem's sins started in you;
    yes, Israel's sins were found in you.
¹⁴ So you must give farewell gifts
    to Moresheth *n* in Gath.
The houses in Achzib *n* will be false help
    to the kings of Israel.
¹⁵ I will bring against you people who will take
        your land,
    you who live in Mareshah. *n*
The glory of Israel
    will go in to Adullam.
¹⁶ Cut off your hair to show you are sad
    for the children you love.
Make yourself bald like the eagle,
    because your children will be taken away to
        a foreign land.

The Evil Plans of People

2 How terrible it will be for people who
        plan wickedness,
    who lie on their beds and make evil plans.
When the morning light comes, they do what
        they planned,

Sidelight Micah has sometimes been called the "wailing prophet", based on Micah 1:8. He's not the only one who went "barefoot and naked" to make a point. Isaiah attracted attention the same way, in Isaiah 20:2–4 (p.660).

Gath   This name sounds like the Hebrew word for "tell".
Acco   This name sounds like the Hebrew word for "cry".
Beth Ophrah   This name means "house of dust".
Shaphir   This name means "beautiful".
Zaanan   This name sounds like the Hebrew word for "come out".
Beth Ezel   This name means "house by the side of another", suggesting help or support.
Maroth   This name sounds like the Hebrew word for "sad" or "miserable".
Lachish   This name sounds like the Hebrew word for "horses".
Moresheth   This may be a play on the word "engaged", referring to a farewell gift to a bride.
Achzib   This name means "lie" or "trick".
Mareshah   This name sounds like the Hebrew word for a person who captures other cities and lands.

because they have the power to do so.
²They want fields, so they take them;
    they want houses, so they take them away.
They cheat people to get their houses;
    they rob them even of their property.

³That is why the LORD says:
"Look, I am planning trouble against such
        people,
    and you won't be able to save yourselves.
You will no longer walk proudly,
    because it will be a terrible time.
⁴At that time people will make fun of you
    and sing this sad song about you:
'We are completely ruined;
    the LORD has taken away my people's land.
Yes, he has taken it away from me
    and divided our fields among our
        enemies!' "
⁵So you will have no one from the LORD's
        people
    to throw lots *d* to divide the land.

Micah is Asked Not to Prophesy

⁶The prophets say, "Don't prophesy *d* to us!
    Don't prophesy about these things!
    Nothing to make us feel bad will happen!"
⁷But I must say this, people of Jacob:
    the LORD is becoming angry about what you
        have done.
My words are welcome
    to the person who does what is right.
⁸But you are fighting against my people like an
        enemy.
    You take the coats from people who
        pass by;
    you rob them of their safety;
    you plan war.
⁹You've forced the women of my people
    from their nice houses;
you've taken my glory
    from their children for ever.
¹⁰Get up and leave.
    This is not your place of rest any more.
You have made this place unclean, *d*
    and it is doomed to destruction.
¹¹But you people want a false prophet
    who will tell you nothing but lies.
You want one who promises to prophesy
        good things for you
    if you give him wine and beer.
He's just the prophet for you.

The LORD Promises to Rescue His People

¹²"Yes, people of Jacob, I will bring all of you
        together;
    I will bring together all those left alive in
        Israel.

I will put them together like sheep in a pen,
    like a flock in its pasture;
    the place will be filled with many people.
¹³Someone will open the way and lead the
        people out.
The people will break through the gate and
    leave the city where they were held
    captive.
Their king will go out in front of them,
    and the LORD will lead them."

The Leaders of Israel are Guilty of Evil

3 Then I said,
    "Listen, leaders of the people of Jacob;
    listen, you rulers of the nation of Israel.
You should know how to decide cases fairly,
²   but you hate good and love evil.
You skin my people alive
    and tear the flesh off their bones.
³You eat my people's flesh
    and skin them and break their bones;
you chop them up like meat for the pot,
    like meat in a cooking pan.
⁴They will cry to the LORD,
    but he won't answer them.
At that time he will hide his face from them,
    because what they have done is evil."

⁵The LORD says this about the prophets *d* who
teach his people the wrong way of living:
"If these prophets are given food to eat,
    they shout, 'Peace!'
But if someone doesn't give them what they
        ask for,
    they call for a holy war against that person.
⁶So it will become like night for them,
    without visions.
It will become dark for them, without any
    way to tell the future.
The sun is about to set for the prophets;
    their day will become dark.
⁷The seers *d* will be ashamed;
    the people who see the future will be
        embarrassed.
Yes, all of them will cover their mouths,
    because there will be no answer
        from God."

Micah is an Honest Prophet of God

⁸But I am filled with power,
    with the Spirit *d* of the LORD,
    and with justice and strength,
to tell the people of Jacob how they have
        turned against God,
    and the people of Israel how they have
        sinned.
⁹Leaders of Jacob and rulers of Israel,
    listen to me,

you who hate fairness
and twist what is right.
¹⁰You build Jerusalem by murdering people;
you build it with evil.
¹¹Its judges take money
to decide who wins in court.
Its priests only teach for pay,
and its prophets *d* only look into the future
when they get paid.
But they lean on the LORD and say,
"The LORD is here with us,
so nothing bad will happen to us."
¹²Because of you,
Jerusalem will be ploughed like a field.
The city will become a pile of rocks,
and the hill on which the Temple *d* stands
will be covered with bushes.

The Mountain of the LORD

4 In the last days
the mountain on which the LORD's
Temple *d* stands
will become the most important of all
mountains.
It will be raised above the hills,
and people from other nations will come
streaming to it.
²Many nations will come and say,
"Come, let us go up to the mountain of the
LORD,
to the Temple of the God of Jacob,
so that he can teach us his ways
and we can obey his teachings."
His teachings will go out from Jerusalem,
the word of the LORD from that city.
³The Lord will judge many nations;
he will make decisions about strong nations
that are far away.
They will hammer their swords into plough
blades
and their spears into hooks for trimming
trees.
Nations will no longer raise swords against
other nations;
they will not train for war any more.
⁴Everyone will sit under his own vine and fig
tree,
and no one will make them afraid,
because the LORD All-powerful has said it.
⁵All other nations may follow their own gods,
but we will follow the LORD our God for
ever and ever.

⁶The LORD says, "At that time,
I will gather the crippled;

I will bring together those who were sent
away,
those whom I caused to have trouble.
⁷I will keep alive those who were crippled,
and I will make a strong nation of those
who were sent away.
The LORD will be their king in Mount Zion *d*
from now on and for ever.
⁸And you, watchtower of the flocks, *n* hill of
Jerusalem,
to you will come the kingdom as in the
past.
Jerusalem, the right to rule will come again
to you."

Why the Israelites Must Go to Babylon

⁹Now, why do you cry so loudly?
Is your king gone?
Have you lost your helper,
so that you are in pain, like a woman
trying to give birth?
¹⁰People of Jerusalem, strain and be in pain.
Be like a woman trying to give birth,
because now you must leave the city
and live in the field.
You will go to Babylon,
but you will be saved from that place.
The LORD will go there
and buy you back from your enemies.

¹¹But now many nations
have come to fight against you,
saying, "Let's destroy Jerusalem.
We will look at her and be glad we have
defeated her."
¹²But they don't know
what the LORD is thinking;
they don't understand his plan.
He has gathered them like bundles of grain
to the threshing *d* floor.
¹³"Get up and beat them, people of
Jerusalem.
I will make you strong as if you had horns
of iron
and hoofs of bronze.
You will beat many nations into small
pieces
and give their wealth to the LORD,
their treasure to the Lord of all the earth."

5 So, strong city, gather your soldiers
together,
because we are surrounded and attacked.
They will hit the leader of Israel
in the face with a club.

---

watchtower . . . flocks　This probably means a part of Jerusalem. The leaders would be like shepherds in a tower watching
their sheep.

The Ruler to Be Born in Bethlehem

2"But you, Bethlehem Ephrathah,
  though you are too small to be among the
    army groups from Judah,
from you will come one who will rule Israel
    for me.
He comes from very old times,
from days long ago."

3The LORD will give up his people
  until the one who is having a baby gives birth;
then the rest of his relatives will return
  to the people of Israel.
4At that time the ruler of Israel will stand
  and take care of his people

with the LORD's strength
  and with the power of the name of the
    LORD his God.
The Israelites will live in safety,
  because his greatness will reach all over the
    earth.
5 He will bring peace.

Rescue and Punishment

Assyria will surely come into our country
  and walk over our large buildings.
We will set up seven shepherds,
  eight leaders of the people.
6They will destroy the Assyrians with their
    swords;
  they will conquer the land of Assyria with
    their swords drawn.
They will rescue us from the Assyrians when
    they come into our land,
  when they walk over our borders.

7Then the people of Jacob who are left alive
  will be to other people

LEADERSHIP

It's Not About How You Start . . .

Have you ever found yourself looking at other people and wishing you had their life? Maybe it's someone famous or just the person you sit next to in your maths class. We end up thinking that the rest of our life would be so much better if we had what they have. But your background doesn't have to dictate the rest of your life.

Agnes Gonxha Bojaxhiu was born in Macedonia in 1910. She had a relatively poor upbringing in an area that was being torn apart by religious intolerance and political upheaval. When she was seven, her father was killed. Not the greatest of starts in life! By the time Agnes was twelve she had decided that God wanted her to make a difference with her life and so six years later, when she was only eighteen, she moved into a convent in Ireland and became a nun.

Later, Agnes moved to India. She felt God telling her to "follow Jesus into the slums" and she started a work with the poor that would have a worldwide impact. Agnes became one of the greatest leaders the world has ever seen – motivating thousands of people to reach out to those others wouldn't touch. You might know her better as Mother Teresa.

Read **Micah 5:2–4**.

* What similarities are there between Jesus' background and Mother Teresa's?
* What makes someone like Mother Teresa want to make a difference in the world?

Consider . . .

* talking to God and asking him to show you where he wants you to lead.
* talking to your youth leader about ways in which you can begin to make a difference in your local area.

For more, see . . .

* Joshua 1:1–9 (p.202)
* Titus 1:5–9 (p.1323)

* 1 Timothy 4:12 (p.1311)

like dew from the LORD
  or rain on the grass—
it does not wait for human beings;
  it does not pause for any person.
⁸Those of Jacob's people who are left alive
  will be scattered among many nations and
    peoples.
They will be like a lion among the animals of
    the forest,
  like a young lion in a flock of sheep:
as it goes, it jumps on them
  and tears them to pieces,
  and no one can save them.
⁹So you will raise your fist in victory over
    your enemies,
  and all your enemies will be destroyed.

¹⁰The LORD says, "At that time,
  I will take your horses from you
  and destroy your chariots.
¹¹I will destroy the cities in your country
  and tear down all your defences.

¹²I will take away the magic charms you use
  so you will have no more fortune-tellers.
¹³I will destroy your statues of gods
  and the stone pillars you worship
so that you will no longer worship
  what your hands have made.
¹⁴I will tear down Asherah *d* idols from you
  and destroy your cities.
¹⁵In my anger and rage,
  I will pay back the nations that have not
    listened."

The LORD's Case

6 Now hear what the LORD says:
  "Get up; plead your case in front of the
    mountains;
  let the hills hear your story.
²Mountains, listen to the LORD's legal case.
  Foundations of the earth, listen.
The LORD has a legal case against his people,
  and he will accuse Israel."

³He says, "My people, what did I do to you?
    How did I make you tired of me?
    Tell me.
⁴I brought you from the land of Egypt
    and freed you from slavery;
    I sent Moses, Aaron and Miriam to you.
⁵My people, remember
    the evil plans of Balak king of Moab
    and what Balaam son of Beor told Balak.
    Remember what happened from Acacia to
        Gilgal
    so that you will know the LORD does what
        is right!"

⁶You say, "What can I bring with me
    when I come before the LORD,
    when I bow before God on high?
    Should I come before him with burnt
        offerings,
    with year-old calves?
⁷Will the LORD be pleased with 1,000 rams?
    Will he be pleased with 10,000 rivers
        of oil?
    Should I give my first child for the evil I have
        done?
    Should I give my very own child for
        my sin?"
⁸The LORD has told you, human, what is good;
    he has told you what he wants from you:
    to do what is right to other people,
    love being kind to others,
    and live humbly, obeying your God.

⁹The voice of the LORD calls to the city,
    and the wise person honours him.
    So pay attention to the rod of punishment;
    pay attention to the One who threatens to
        punish.
¹⁰Are there still in the wicked house
    wicked treasures
    and the cursed false measure?
¹¹Can I forgive people who cheat others
    with wrong weights and scales?
¹²The rich people of the city
    do cruel things.
    Its people tell lies;
    they do not tell the truth.
¹³As for me, I will make you sick.
    I will attack you, ruining you because of
        your sins.
¹⁴You will eat, but you won't become full;
    you will still be hungry and empty.
    You will store up, but save nothing,
    and what you store up, the sword will
        destroy.

¹⁵You will plant,
    but you won't harvest.
    You will step on your olives,
    but you won't get any oil from them.
    You will crush the grapes,
    but you will not drink the new wine.
¹⁶This is because you obey the laws of King
        Omri
    and do all the things that Ahab's family
        does;
    you follow their advice.
    So I will let you be destroyed.
    The people in your city will be laughed at,
    and other nations will make fun of you.

The Evil That People Do

7 Poor me! I am like a hungry man,
    and all the summer fruit has been
        picked—
there are no grapes left to eat,
    none of the early figs I love.
²All of the faithful people are gone;
    there is not one good person left in this
        country.
    Everyone is waiting to kill someone;
    everyone is trying to trap someone else.
³With both hands they are doing evil.
    Rulers ask for money,
    and judges' decisions are bought for
        a price.
    Rich people tell what they want,
    and they get it.
⁴Even the best of them is like a thorn-bush;
    the most honest of them is worse than a
        prickly thorn-bush.
    The day that your watchmen ⁿ warned you
        about has come.
    Now they will be confused.
⁵Don't believe your neighbour
    or trust a friend.
    Don't say anything,
    even to your wife.
⁶A son will not honour his father,
    a daughter will turn against her mother
and a daughter-in-law will be against her
        mother-in-law;
    a person's enemies will be members of his
        own family.

The LORD's Kindness

⁷Israel says, "I will look to the LORD for help.
    I will wait for God to save me;
    my God will hear me.
⁸Enemy, don't laugh at me.

---

watchmen Another name for prophets. The prophets were like guards who stood on a city's wall and watched for trouble
    coming from far away.

I have fallen, but I will get up again.
I sit in the shadow of trouble now,
    but the LORD will be a light for me.
⁹I sinned against the LORD,
    so he was angry with me,
but he will defend my case in court.
    He will bring about what is right for me.
Then he will bring me out into the light,
    and I will see him set things right.
¹⁰Then my enemies will see this,
    and they will be ashamed,
those who said to me,
    'Where is the LORD your God?'
I will look down on them.
    They will get walked on, like mud in the
    street."

Israel will Return

¹¹The time will come when your walls will be
        built again,
    when your country will grow.
¹²At that time your people will come back
        to you
    from Assyria and the cities of Egypt,
and from Egypt to the Euphrates River,
    and from sea to sea and mountain to
        mountain.
¹³The earth will be ruined for the people who
        live in it
    because of their deeds.

A Prayer to God

¹⁴So shepherd your people with your stick;
    tend the flock of people who belong to you.
That flock now lives alone in the forest
    in the middle of a garden land.
Let them feed in Bashan and Gilead
    as in days long ago.

¹⁵"As in the days when I brought you out of
        Egypt,
    I will show them miracles." *d*

¹⁶When the nations see those miracles,
    they will no longer boast about their power.
They will put their hands over their mouths,
    refusing to listen.
¹⁷They will crawl in the dust like a snake,
    like insects crawling on the ground.
They will come trembling from their holes to
        the LORD our God
    and will turn in fear before you.
¹⁸There is no God like you.
    You forgive those who are guilty of sin;
you don't look at the sins of your people
    who are left alive.
You will not stay angry for ever,
    because you enjoy being kind.
¹⁹You will have mercy on us again;
    you will conquer our sins.
You will throw away all our sins
    into the deepest part of the sea.

> **Sidelight**
>
> Micah's name means, "Who is like God?" He answers the question in Micah 7:18–19. No one is. In fact, the Lord is so great that he tosses our darkest sins into the ocean. Since the Middle Ages, Orthodox Jews have visited a river or other body of water on the Jewish New Year and repeated verse 19 three times while tossing breadcrumbs on the water.

²⁰You will be true to the people of Jacob,
    and you will be kind to the people of
        Abraham
    as you promised to our ancestors long ago.

Nahum

Why Read This Book:

- Discover how God can become angry when people don't follow him (Nahum 1).
- See how God's justice is victorious in the end (Nahum 2–3).

When?

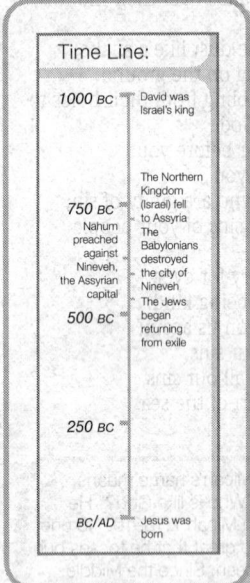

Time Line:

1000 BC — David was Israel's king

750 BC — The Northern Kingdom (Israel) fell to Assyria
Nahum preached against Nineveh, the Assyrian capital
The Babylonians destroyed the city of Nineveh

500 BC — The Jews began returning from exile

250 BC

BC/AD — Jesus was born

Behind the Scenes:

Think of the most powerful force in all the universe. Now imagine that force being angry. Scary, isn't it?

Nineveh – the capital of Assyria – heated God's anger to boiling point. The Assyrians had captured and destroyed Israel. For about 250 years, the brutal Assyrians had attacked and persecuted Israel and Judah. As a result, the city of Nineveh had come to symbolise everything evil.

The prophet Nahum announced the downfall of Nineveh, using a series of poems to convey his message. In these poems, we see God's anger at unrighteousness, and we see the wickedness of this city. Compare the book of Nahum with the book of Jonah (p.884), which also focuses on Nineveh. The comparison gives you a better sense of the many dimensions of God's personality. And in both books, we're reminded that God's strength extends to the whole world.

Where?

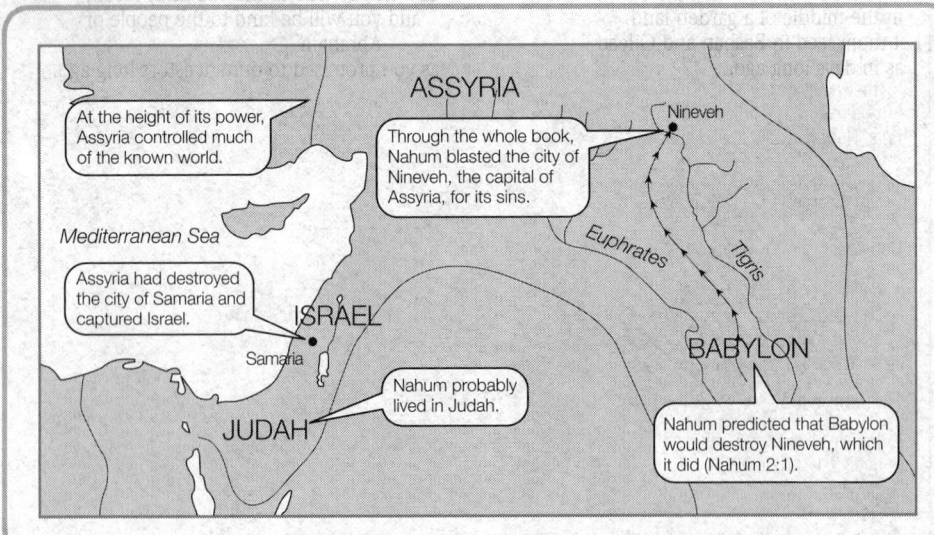

ASSYRIA

Nineveh

At the height of its power, Assyria controlled much of the known world.

Through the whole book, Nahum blasted the city of Nineveh, the capital of Assyria, for its sins.

Mediterranean Sea

Euphrates

Tigris

Assyria had destroyed the city of Samaria and captured Israel.

ISRAEL

Samaria

BABYLON

Nahum probably lived in Judah.

JUDAH

Nahum predicted that Babylon would destroy Nineveh, which it did (Nahum 2:1).

1

This is the message for the city of Nineveh. [n] This is the book of the vision of Nahum, who was from the town of Elkosh.

The LORD is Angry with Nineveh

[2]The LORD is a jealous God who punishes; the LORD punishes and is filled with anger.
The LORD punishes those who are against him, and he stays angry with his enemies.
[3]The LORD does not become angry quickly, and his power is great.

The LORD will not let the guilty go unpunished.
Where the LORD goes, there are whirlwinds and storms, and the clouds are the dust beneath his feet.
[4]He speaks to the sea and makes it dry; he dries up all the rivers.
The areas of Bashan and Carmel dry up, and the flowers of Lebanon dry up.
[5]The mountains shake in front of him, and the hills melt.
The earth trembles when he comes;

Nineveh   The capital city of the country of Assyria. Nahum uses Nineveh to stand for all of Assyria.

JEALOUSY

Jealous Anger

After ten years of marriage and three children, David's commitment to his family began to wane. He started spending more time at the factory, and he was distant whenever he was home. Finally, he told his wife, Carol, that he had been having an affair for more than year. He was confused, he said, and guilt-ridden. He didn't expect Carol to forgive him, and even if she did, he wasn't sure he wanted the marriage to continue.

Carol was crushed. Their marriage had seemed so stable. Although they had fought more lately, David had always seemed to be a good father and husband.

Emotions flooded Carol. Sadness. Fear. Confusion. But, most of all, anger. She wanted to hurt the woman who had intruded into her family. "I hate her," Carol cried. "If I see her, I'll probably kill her – and maybe David too."

But Carol knew that wasn't the answer. So she prayed, and as she prayed, she believed that God wanted her to hold her family together. Carol channelled her anger into saving her family.

She told David that she loved him; she demanded that he cut off contact with the other woman; and she moved out until David could also decide that his family was worth fighting for.

One month later, David went to Carol. He told her that he wanted his family more than anything. He told her that he needed God back in his life. And he told her that the affair was over.

They have spent the past two years rebuilding their family with God's help.

God restored David and Carol's family because Carol channelled her jealous anger for good.
Read **Nahum 1:2–6** to find out how God uses his jealous anger against his enemies.

* How is God's jealous anger like Carol's? How is it different?
* What are some other ways in which jealous anger can have good results? What are its dangers?

Consider . . .

* defining positive jealous anger and negative jealous anger. Include in your definitions the difference between the two.
* asking your parents or other married adults how they have seen jealous anger in their relationship have positive or negative results.

For more, see . . .

* Hosea 11:1–11 (p.858)
* John 2:12–16 (p.1098)
* Jonah 4:1–11 (p.888)

the world and all who live in it shake with
fear.
[6]No one can stay alive when he is angry;
no one can survive his strong anger.
His anger is poured out like fire;
the rocks are smashed by him.

[7]The LORD is good,
giving protection in times of trouble.
He knows who trusts in him.
[8]But like a rushing flood,
he will completely destroy Nineveh;
he will chase his enemies until he kills
them.

> ## Sidelight
>
> Nineveh was one of the oldest cities in
> Mesopotamia, and was situated next to the
> Tigris River, which is in what we now know as
> Iraq. It was a city of palaces and other beautiful
> buildings, and was looked upon as a powerful
> centre of trade and commerce. Today, however,
> Nineveh is only a vague memory – it has existed
> as nothing more than a pile of ruins ever since it
> was destroyed more than 2,500 years ago!

[9]The LORD will completely destroy
anyone making plans against him.
Trouble will not come a second time.
[10]Those people will be like tangled thorns
or like people drunk from their wine;
they will be burned up quickly like dry
weeds.
[11]Someone has come from Nineveh
who makes evil plans against the LORD
and gives wicked advice.

[12]This is what the LORD says:
"Although Assyria is strong and has many
people,
it will be defeated and brought to
an end.
Although I have made you suffer, Judah,
I will make you suffer no more.
[13]Now I will free you from their control
and tear away your chains."

[14]The LORD has given you this command,
Nineveh:
"You will not have descendants [d] to carry
on your name.
I will destroy the idols and metal images
that are in the temple of your gods.
I will make a grave for you,
because you are wicked."

[15]Look, there on the hills,
someone is bringing good news!
He is announcing peace!
Celebrate your feasts, people of Judah,
and give your promised sacrifices to God.
The wicked will not come to attack you
again;
they have been completely destroyed.

Nineveh will be Defeated

2 The destroyer [n] is coming to attack you,
Nineveh.
Guard the defences.
Watch the road.
Get ready.
Gather all your strength!
[2]Destroyers have destroyed God's people
and ruined their vines,
but the LORD will bring back Jacob's greatness
like Israel's greatness.

[3]The shields of his soldiers are red;
the army is dressed in red.
The metal on the chariots flashes like fire
when they are ready to attack;
their horses are excited.
[4]The chariots race through the streets
and rush back and forth through the city
squares.
They look like torches;
they run like lightning.

[5]He [n] calls his officers,
but they stumble on the way.
They hurry to the city wall,
and the shield is put into place.
[6]The river gates are thrown open,
and the palace is destroyed.
[7]It has been announced that the people of
Nineveh
will be captured and carried away.
The slave girls moan like doves
and beat their breasts, because they are sad.
[8]Nineveh is like a pool,
and now its water is draining away.
"Stop! Stop!" the people yell,
but no one turns back.
[9]Take the silver!
Take the gold!
There is no end to the treasure—
piles of wealth of every kind.
[10]Nineveh is robbed, ruined and destroyed.
The people lose their courage, and their
knees knock.
Stomachs ache, and everyone's face grows
pale.

---

destroyer The Babylonians, the Scythians and the Medes destroyed Nineveh.
He This probably means the king of Assyria.

[11]Where is the lions'[n] den
   and the place where they feed their
      young?
Where did the lion, lioness and cubs go
   without being afraid?
[12]The lion killed enough for his cubs,
   enough for his mate.
He filled his cave with the animals he caught;
   he filled his den with meat he had killed.

[13]"I am against you, Nineveh,"
   says the LORD All-powerful.
"I will burn up your chariots in smoke,
   and the sword will kill your young lions.
I will stop you from hunting down others
      on the earth,
   and your messengers' voices
   will no longer be heard."

It will be Terrible for Nineveh

3 How terrible it will be for the city that has
      killed so many.
   It is full of lies
and goods stolen from other countries.
   It is always killing somebody.
[2]Hear the sound of whips
   and the noise of the wheels.
Hear horses galloping
   and chariots bouncing along!
[3]Horses are charging,
   swords are shining,
      spears are gleaming!
Many are dead;
   their bodies are piled up—
too many to count.
   People stumble over the dead bodies.

Sidelight   The wartime cruelty of
the Assyrians (Nahum 3:3)
would have been similar to the terrible things
that happened to the Jewish people in World
War II. One Assyrian King boasted of building
pyramids of chopped-off heads outside the
enemy's city. Other kings stacked corpses like
firewood near the conquered city's gates.

---

[4]The city was like a prostitute;[d]
   she was charming and a lover of magic.
She made nations slaves with her
      prostitution[d]
   and her witchcraft.[d]

[5]"I am against you, Nineveh," says the LORD
      All-powerful.
   "I will pull your dress up over your face

and show the nations your nakedness
   and the kingdoms your shame.
[6]I will throw filthy rubbish on you
   and make a fool of you.
I will make people stare at you.
[7]Everyone who sees you will run away
      and say,
   'Nineveh is in ruins. Who will cry for her?'
Nineveh, where will I find anyone to
      comfort you?"

[8]You are no better than Thebes,[n]
   who sits by the Nile River
   with water all around her.
The river was her defence;
   the waters were like a wall around her.
[9]Cush and Egypt gave her endless strength;
   Put and Libya supported her.
[10]But Thebes was captured
   and went into captivity.
Her small children were beaten to death
   at every street corner.
Lots[d] were thrown for her important men,
   and all of her leaders were put in chains.

[11]Nineveh, you will be drunk too.
   You will hide;
   you will look for a place safe from the
      enemy.
[12]All your defences are like fig trees with ripe
      fruit.
   When the tree is shaken, the figs fall into
      the mouth of the eater.
[13]Look at your soldiers.
   They are all women!
The gates of your land
   are wide open for your enemies;
   fire has burned the bars of your gates.

[14]Get enough water before the long war
      begins.
   Make your defences strong!
Get mud,
   mix clay,
   make bricks!
[15]There the fire will burn you up.
   The sword will kill you;
   like grasshoppers eating crops, the battle
      will completely destroy you.
Grow in number like hopping locusts;[d]
   grow in number like swarming locusts!
[16]Your traders are more than the stars in
      the sky,
   but like locusts, they strip the land and
      then fly away.
[17]Your guards are like locusts.
   Your officers are like swarms of locusts

---

lions'   The symbol of Assyria was the lion.
Thebes   A great city in Egypt.

that hang on the walls on a cold day.
When the sun comes up, they fly away,
  and no one knows where they have gone.
18King of Assyria, your rulers are asleep;
  your important men lie down to rest.
Your people have been scattered on the
  mountains,

and there is no one to bring them
  back.
19Nothing can heal your wound;
  your injury will not heal.
Everyone who hears about you applauds,
  because everyone has felt your endless
  cruelty.

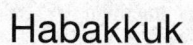

Habakkuk

Why Read This Book:

* Listen to what God says about why wicked people prosper (Habakkuk 1–2).
* Learn the importance of waiting patiently for God (Habakkuk 3).

When?

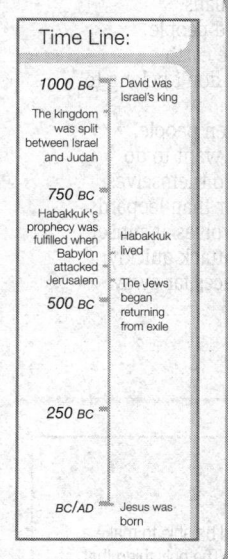

Time Line:

1000 BC — David was Israel's king

The kingdom was split between Israel and Judah

750 BC

Habakkuk's prophecy was fulfilled when Babylon attacked Jerusalem — Habakkuk lived

500 BC — The Jews began returning from exile

250 BC

BC/AD — Jesus was born

Behind the Scenes:

Sometimes it's hard to understand what God is doing in the world. Bad people seem to do well while good people suffer. Is God absent? Isn't he in control? Doesn't he have the power to control things? Or is God not a righteous God?

The prophet Habakkuk had those tough questions, and he wasn't afraid to ask them directly of God. His book takes the form of a question-and-answer session with God. Habakkuk asks the questions, and then God, through visions, gives answers:

Habakkuk: God, why don't you deliver your people from injustice?

God: Be patient. I've got it under control. The evil people will be punished.

Habakkuk: Why do you wait silently while wicked people destroy other people?

God: Justice will come. Live faithfully and you will be rewarded.

This short book is filled with comfort for people who suffer unjustly and for those who have trouble finding meaning in life. Not only does the prophet take honest questions to God, but the answers convince him that God is faithful and powerful.

"I will still be glad in the LORD," Habakkuk concludes. "I will rejoice in God my Saviour. The Lord God is my strength" (Habakkuk 3:18–19a). It's a reassuring message of faith and hope for all people who see life as meaningless or who suffer unjustly.

Where?

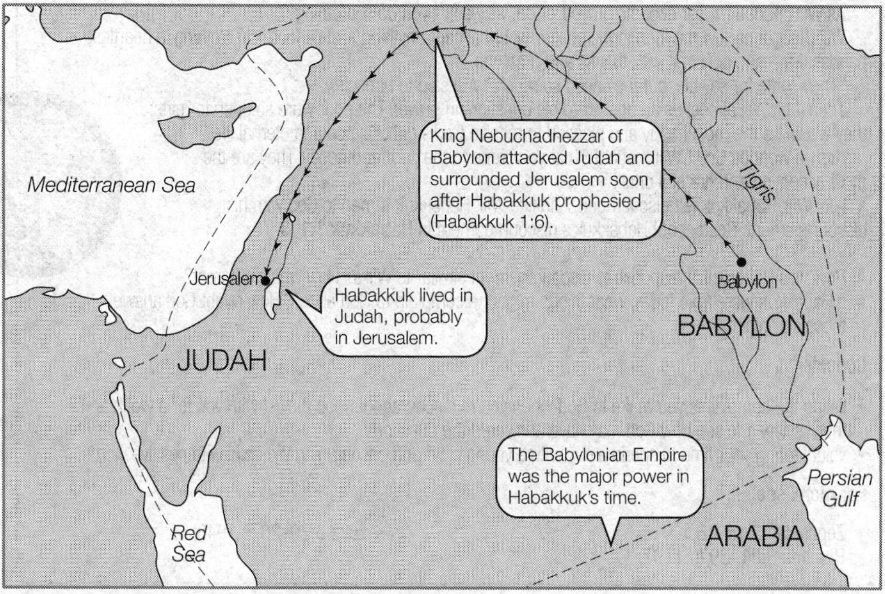

Mediterranean Sea

King Nebuchadnezzar of Babylon attacked Judah and surrounded Jerusalem soon after Habakkuk prophesied (Habakkuk 1:6).

Tigris

Jerusalem

Babylon

BABYLON

Habakkuk lived in Judah, probably in Jerusalem.

JUDAH

The Babylonian Empire was the major power in Habakkuk's time.

Persian Gulf

ARABIA

Red Sea

1
This is the message Habakkuk the prophet received. *d*

Habakkuk Complains

2LORD, how long must I ask for help
  and you ignore me?
I cry out to you about violence,
  but you do not save us!
3Why do you make me see wrong things
  and make me look at trouble?
People are destroying things and hurting
    others in front of me;
  they are arguing and fighting.
4So the teachings are weak,
  and justice never comes.
Evil people gain while good people lose;
  the judges no longer make fair
    decisions.

The LORD Answers

5"Look at the nations!
  Watch them and be amazed and shocked.
I will do something in your lifetime
  that you won't believe even when you are
    told about it.
6I will use the Babylonians,
  those cruel and wild people
who march across the earth
  and take lands that don't belong to
    them.
7They scare and frighten people.
  They do what they want to do
  and are good only to themselves.
8Their horses are faster than leopards
  and quicker than wolves at sunset.
Their horse soldiers attack quickly;
  they come from places far away.

DISCOURAGEMENT

Is There Hope?

Will had volunteered to stay all night at the hostel for the homeless, hoping that he would be able to make a difference, hoping conditions might somehow change, hoping to feel needed and useful. The only thing that Will felt as he left the old building, though, was discouragement. As he left the shelter, he was glad to be free from the smell of old clothes, the sight of loneliness and the sounds of sadness.

He knew one thing: this type of service wasn't for him. He felt that he wasn't helpful and could do no good. Why do anything?

As Will opened his car door, he prayed, "God, why don't you do something?"

Will thought of how the men in the shelter would accept anything – stale food, old clothing, a heartless handshake – and accept it with thanks and gratitude.

"They settle for so little, but they need so much," Will said to himself.

Then it hit Will almost as an answer to his questioning prayer. The poor were so open for gifts; they would be the most happy and pleased to receive God's gift of grace and eternal life.

"It's no wonder, God," Will thought, "that you came to the poor and needy. They are the most accepting and grateful of all."

Like Will, Habakkuk felt discouraged. And like Will, Habakkuk turned to God with his discouragement. Read about Habakkuk's discouragement in **Habakkuk 1:1–3**.

* How was Habakkuk's response to discouragement similar to Will's? How was it different?
* If Habakkuk were alive today, what things might he complain to God about? How might God answer those complaints?

Consider . . .

* listing the complaints you make to God when you're discouraged. Keep the list with you for a week and then review it to see how God may have answered the questions.
* volunteering your time to spend a day with a young child and encouraging the child with positive words.

For more, see . . .

* Zephaniah 3:14–18 (p.914)
* Romans 8:31–39 (p.1197)
* Luke 6:20–26 (p.1048)

They attack quickly, like an eagle swooping
    down for food.
⁹ They all come to fight.
Nothing can stop them.
    Their prisoners are as many as the grains of
      sand.
¹⁰They laugh at kings
    and make fun of rulers.
They laugh at all the fortified cities
    and build mounds of earth to the top of the
      walls to capture them.
¹¹Then they leave like the wind and
    move on.
    They are guilty of worshipping their own
      strength."

Sidelight

The name "Habakkuk" means "embracer" or "wrestler". This book of the Bible reads like a transcript of a telephone conversation – first Habakkuk complains to God, and then God responds. Read Habakkuk 1:1—2:17 for an example of this.

Habakkuk Complains Again

¹²LORD, you live for ever,
    my God, my holy God.
    We will not die.
LORD, you have chosen the Babylonians to
      punish people;
    our Rock, *d* you picked them to punish.
¹³Your eyes are too good to look at evil;
    you cannot stand to see those who do
      wrong.
So how can you put up with those evil
      people?
    How can you be quiet when the wicked
      swallow up people who are better than
      they are?
¹⁴You treat people like fish in the sea,
    like sea creatures without a leader.
¹⁵The enemy brings them in with hooks.
    He catches them in his net
and drags them in his nets.
    So he rejoices and sings for joy.
¹⁶The enemy offers sacrifices to his net
    and burns incense *d* to worship it,
because it lets him live like the rich
    and enjoy the best food.
¹⁷Will he keep on taking riches with his
      net?
    Will he go on destroying people without
      showing mercy?

2 I will stand like a guard to watch
    and place myself at the tower.

I will wait to see what he will say to me;
    I will wait to learn how God will answer
      my complaint.

The LORD Answers

²The LORD answered me:
"Write down the vision;
    write it clearly on clay tablets
    so whoever reads it can run to tell
      others.
³It is not yet time for the message to come
      true,
    but that time is coming soon;
    the message will come true.
It may seem like a long time,
    but be patient and wait for it,
because it will surely come;
    it will not be delayed.
⁴The evil nation is very proud of itself;
    it is not living as it should.
    But those who are right with God will live
      by trusting in him.

⁵"Just as wine can fool a person,
    those who are too proud will not last,
because their desire is like a grave's desire for
      death,
    and like death they always want more.
They gather other nations for themselves
    and collect for themselves all the
      countries.
⁶But all the nations the Babylonians have hurt
    will laugh at them.
    They will make fun of the Babylonians
and say, 'How terrible it will be for the one
      that steals many things.

Sidelight

Wearing nose jewellery may be fashionable at different times, but people probably wouldn't be attracted to the "hooks" mentioned in Habakkuk 1:15. The verse may refer to the Assyrian practice of leading prisoners of war by rope that was attached to a hook pierced through the nose or lower lip.

How long will that nation get rich by
    forcing others to pay them?'

⁷"One day the people from whom you have
    taken money will turn against you.
    They will realise what is happening and
      make you shake with fear.
    Then they will take everything you have.
⁸Because you have stolen from many
      nations,

those who are left will take much
from you.
This is because you have killed many
people,
destroying countries and cities and
everyone in them.

⁹"How terrible it will be for the nation that
becomes rich by doing wrong,
thinking they will live in a safe place
and escape harm.
¹⁰Because you have made plans to destroy
many people,
you have made your own houses ashamed
of you.
Because of it, you will lose your lives.
¹¹The stones of the walls will cry out
against you,
and the boards that support the roof will
agree that you are wrong.

¹²"How terrible it will be for the nation that
kills people to build a city,

that wrongs others just to start a town.
¹³The LORD All-powerful will send fire
to destroy what those people have built;
all the nations' work will be for nothing.
¹⁴Then, just as water covers the sea,
people everywhere will know the LORD's
glory.

¹⁵"How terrible for the nation that makes its
neighbours drink,
pouring from the jug of wine until they are
drunk
so that it can look at their naked bodies.
¹⁶You Babylonians will be filled with disgrace,
not respect.
It's your turn to drink and fall to the
ground like a drunk person.
The cup of anger from the LORD's right hand
is coming around to you.
You will receive disgrace, not respect.
¹⁷You hurt many people in Lebanon,
but now you will be hurt.
You killed many animals there,

PATIENCE

I Want it Now!

It was easily the biggest and best film in the history of the universe. Or at least that is what the trailer, the magazines, film critics, and all the websites had said. Today was the premiere, and Mark was overcome with excitement.

He had rushed out of school on the "B of the bell" and got to the cinema in record time. Thirty minutes later and Mark was still alone in the room, even the adverts hadn't started. He began to get restless.

After a little while, Mark could take it no more. He stood, turned to face the projection room, and yelled out "HURRY UP!"

Read **Habakkuk 2:1–4**. In this passage, Habakkuk is learning to be patient. He finds out that God is in control and the best plan will happen, but in God's timing (which is perfect). Until then, he has to carry on being patient, and trusting in God.

* What are the differences between the way the evil nation and the person right with God are described in verse 4?
* Read chapter 3. It's Habakkuk's final response. He remembers all that he has seen God do in the past. How might this help him to be patient and trust in God again for the future?

Consider . . .

* writing down all the wonderful things God has done in your past, and all the things you want him to do in your future. Thank him for the past and ask for help in trusting him for the future.
* talking to older people around you about things they have had to wait a long time for from God and learning from their experience.

For more, see . . .

* Psalm 37 (p.521)
* Hebrews 6:13–15 (p.1335)

* Galatians 5:22–23 (p.1264)

and now you must be afraid
because of what you did
to that land, those cities and the people
who lived in them.

The Message About Idols

18"An idol does no good, because a human
made it;
it is only a statue that teaches lies.
The one who made it expects his own work
to help him,
but he makes idols that can't even speak!
19How terrible it will be for the one who says
to a wooden statue, 'Come
to life!'
How terrible it will be for the one who
says to a silent stone, 'Get up!'
It cannot tell you what to do.
It is only a statue covered with gold and
silver;
there is no life in it.
20The LORD is in his Holy Temple; *d*
all the earth should be silent in his
presence."

Habakkuk's Prayer

3 This is the prayer of Habakkuk the prophet, *d*
on shigionoth. *d*

2LORD, I have heard the news about you;
I am amazed at what you have done.
LORD, do great things once again in our
time;
make those things happen again in our own
days.
Even when you are angry,
remember to be kind.

3God is coming from Teman;
the Holy One comes from Mount Paran. *n*
                                      Selah *d*

His glory covers the skies,
and his praise fills the earth.
4He is like a bright light.
Rays of light shine from his hand,
and there he hides his power.
5Sickness goes before him,
and disease follows behind him.
6He stands and shakes the earth.
He looks, and the nations shake with fear.
The mountains, which stood for ages, break
into pieces;
the old hills fall down.

God has always done this.

7I saw that the tents of Cushan were in
trouble
and that the tents of Midian trembled.
8LORD, were you angry with the rivers,
or were you angry with the streams?
Were you angry with the sea
when you rode your horses and chariots of
victory? *n*
9You uncovered your bow
and commanded many arrows to be
brought to you.   *Selah*
You split the earth with rivers.
10 The mountains saw you and shook with
fear.
The rushing water flowed.
The sea made a loud noise,
and its waves rose high.
11The sun and moon stood still in the sky;
they stopped when they saw the flash of
your flying arrows
and the gleam of your shining spear.
12In anger you marched on the earth;
in anger you punished the nations.
13You came out to save your people,
to save your chosen one.
You crushed the leader of the wicked
ones
and took everything he had, from head to
toe.   *Selah*
14With the enemy's own spear you stabbed
the leader of his army.
His soldiers rushed out like a storm to
scatter us.
They were happy
as they were robbing the poor people in
secret.
15But you marched through the sea with your
horses,
stirring the great waters.

16I hear these things, and my body
trembles;
my lips tremble when I hear the
sound.
My bones feel weak,
and my legs shake.

But I will wait patiently for the day of
disaster
that will come to the people who
attack us.
17Fig trees may not grow figs,

Teman . . . Paran   God is seen as again coming from the direction of Mount Sinai. He came from Sinai when he rescued his
people from Egypt.
sea . . . victory   This is probably talking about the Israelites crossing the Red Sea.

and there may be no grapes on the
vines.
There may be no olives growing
and no food growing in the
fields.
There may be no sheep in the pens
and no cattle in the barns.
¹⁸But I will still be glad in the LORD;

I will rejoice in God my Saviour.
¹⁹The Lord GOD is my strength.
He makes me like a deer that does not
stumble
so I can walk on the steep mountains.

For the director of music. On my stringed
instruments.

Zephaniah

Why Read This Book:

- Discover what moral corruption can do to people (Zephaniah 1—2).
- Hear the promise of God's comfort for the faithful (Zephaniah 3).

When?

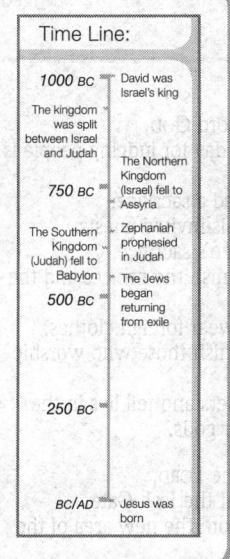

Time Line:

1000 BC	David was Israel's king
The kingdom was split between Israel and Judah	
	The Northern Kingdom (Israel) fell to Assyria
750 BC	
The Southern Kingdom (Judah) fell to Babylon	Zephaniah prophesied in Judah
	The Jews began returning from exile
500 BC	
250 BC	
BC/AD	Jesus was born

Behind the Scenes:

Have you ever had a really lousy day – so lousy that you were glad to go to bed to get it over with? When you woke up the next morning, you were determined to start out afresh, and you did everything to make sure the next day would be better.

In a sense, the people of Judah had just had a lousy hundred years. Their land had been controlled by the Assyrians. But now they had gained independence. They were ready to start a new day – to rebuild their nation and start again. King Josiah would lead them to new political strength.

But the people needed religious renewal as well. Domination by foreign powers had brought with it foreign customs and pagan gods. The Canaanite religion, Baalism, flourished in the country.

The prophet Zephaniah saw the corruption in the land and warned the people to change. As a prophet in Jerusalem, his ministry was probably influential in getting King Josiah to institute widespread religious reform based on the book of Deuteronomy (p.164).

Zephaniah's message to the people was that God would judge Judah for turning away from him. The book is filled with terrifying images of doom and punishment on "the Lord's day of judging" (Zephaniah 1:14). ▷

Where?

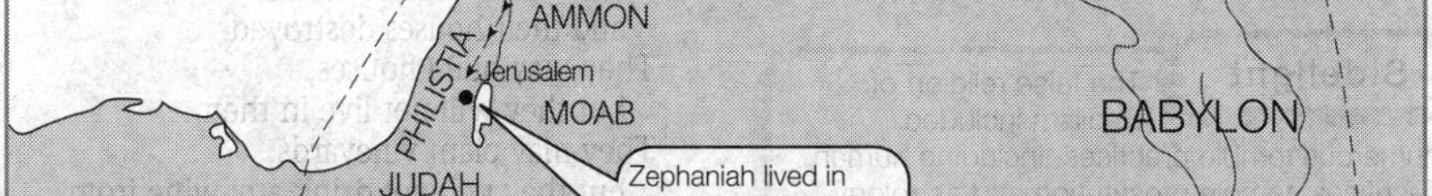

An attack from Scythians from the region where Russia is today may have prompted Zephaniah's prophecy.

Zephaniah lived in Jerusalem, which he condemned for taking part in false religions (Zephaniah 1:4).

Zephaniah predicted doom for Ammon, Assyria, Cush, Philistia and Moab.

Mediterranean Sea

ISRAEL

AMMON

PHILISTIA

Jerusalem

MOAB

JUDAH

BABYLON

Tigris

CUSH

Red Sea

ARABIA

Persian Gulf

Behind the
Scenes (cont.):

But the book ends on a positive note, describing a time when people would return to God and the nation would be restored.

The book of Zephaniah has a message that's similar to that of many prophets: disaster will ultimately come for those who turn away from God. But God will build a new, lasting relationship with those who repent and serve him faithfully.

1 This is the word of the LORD that came through Zephaniah while Josiah son of Amon was king of Judah. Zephaniah was the son of Cushi, who was the son of Gedaliah. Gedaliah was the son of Amariah, who was the son of Hezekiah.

The LORD's Judgement

2"I will sweep away everything
    from the earth," says the LORD.
3"I will sweep away the people and animals;
    I will destroy the birds in the air
    and the fish of the sea.
I will ruin the evil people,
    and I will remove human beings from the
        earth," says the LORD.

The Future of Judah

4"I will punish Judah
    and all the people living in Jerusalem.
I will remove from this place
    all signs of Baal, d the false priests and the
        other priests.
5I will destroy those who worship
    the stars from the roofs, n
and those who worship and make
        promises
    by both the LORD and the god Molech, d

> ### Sidelight
>
> The false religion of Baalism included numerous terrible practices, including human sacrifices, temple prostitution and astrology. Making matters worse, the Israelites often tried to mix these false religions with true religion – and practise them both at the same time (Zephaniah 1:4–5)!

6and those who turn away from the LORD,
    and those who stopped following the LORD
        and praying to him for direction.

7Be silent before the Lord GOD,
    because the LORD's day for judging people is
        coming soon.
The LORD has prepared a sacrifice;
    he has made holy his invited guests.
8On the day of the LORD's sacrifice,
    I, the LORD, will punish the princes and the
        king's sons
    and all those who wear foreign clothes.
9On that day I will punish those who worship
        Dagon, d
    those who hurt others and tell lies in the
        temples of their gods.

10"On that day," says the LORD,
    "a cry will be heard at the Fish Gate.
A wail will come from the new area of the
        city,
    and a loud crash will echo from the
        hills.
11Cry, you people living in the market area,
    because all the merchants will be dead;
    all the silver traders will be gone.
12At that time I, the LORD, will search
        Jerusalem with lamps.
I will punish those who are satisfied with
        themselves,
    who think, 'The LORD won't help us or
        punish us.'
13Their wealth will be stolen
    and their houses destroyed.
They may build houses,
    but they will not live in them.
They may plant vineyards,
    but they will not drink any wine from
        them.

The LORD's Day of Judging

14"The LORD's day of judging is coming soon;
    it is near and coming fast.
The cry will be very sad on the day of the
        LORD;
    even soldiers will cry.

---

roofs   In Bible times houses were built with flat roofs. The roof was used for drying things such as flax and fruit. And it was used as an extra room, as a place for worship and as a place to sleep in the summer.

¹⁵That day will be a day of anger,
  a day of terror and trouble,
a day of destruction and ruin,
  a day of darkness and gloom,
  a day of clouds and blackness,
¹⁶a day of alarms and battle cries.
  'Attack the strong, walled cities!
  Attack the corner towers!'
¹⁷I will make life hard for the people;
  they will walk around like the blind,
  because they have sinned against the LORD.
Their blood will be poured out like dust,
  and their insides will be dumped like
    rubbish.
¹⁸On the day that God will show his anger,
  neither their silver nor gold will save them.
The LORD's anger will be like a fire
  that will burn up the whole world;

suddenly he will bring an end, yes, an end
  to everyone on earth."

The LORD Asks People to Change

2 Gather together, gather,
  you unwanted people.
²Do it before it's too late,
  before you are blown away like chaff, ^d
before the LORD's terrible anger reaches
  you,
  before the day of the LORD's anger comes
    to you.
³Come to the LORD, all you who are not
  proud,
who obey his laws.
Do what is right. Learn to be humble.
  Maybe you will escape
  on the day the LORD shows his anger.

MONEY

Look Where it Got Them

Who, in 1923, was:

* president of the USA's largest steel company?
* president of the largest American gas company?
* president of the New York Stock Exchange?
* the greatest wheat speculator in America?
* the "Great Bear" of Wall Street?

In their day, these people made lots of money. They would have been considered the most successful men in the world. But look at what became of these successful moneybags:

* The president of the largest steel company, Charles Schwab, died penniless.
* The president of the largest gas company, Howard Hopson, went insane.
* The president of the New York Stock Exchange, Richard Whitney, was released from prison to die at home.
* Arthur Cutten, the greatest wheat speculator, died overseas – penniless and homeless.
* Mr C. Rivermore, the "Great Bear" of Wall Street, committed suicide.

Although these men had wealth and worldly success, their "kingdom" fell. They had based their lives and priorities on money, and money couldn't meet all their needs.

God wanted the people in Zephaniah's day to base their lives and priorities on much more than money. Read **Zephaniah 1:7–18** to learn more about God's directions and the limitations of money.

* How are the men in this story like the people in this passage?
* According to the Bible passage, what will happen to those who trust in money and riches?

Consider . . .

* giving some of your money and prized possessions to someone less fortunate.
* keeping track of the money you spend this week and evaluating whether your spending is pleasing to God.

For more, see . . .

* Ecclesiastes 7:11–12 (p.626)
* Mark 10:17–31 (p.1016)
* Matthew 6:19–34 (p.948)

Philistia will be Punished

⁴No one will be left in the city of Gaza,
and the city of Ashkelon will be destroyed.
Ashdod will be empty by noon,
and the people of Ekron will be chased
away.
⁵How terrible it will be for you who live by
the Mediterranean Sea,
you Philistines!
The word of the LORD is against you,
Canaan, land of the Philistines.

"I will destroy you
so that no one will be left."
⁶The land by the Mediterranean Sea, in which
you live,
will become pastures, fields for shepherds
and pens for sheep.
⁷It will belong to the descendants *d* of Judah
who are left alive.
There they will let their sheep eat grass.
At night they will sleep
in the houses of Ashkelon.
The LORD their God will pay attention to
them
and will make their life good again.

Moab and Ammon will be Punished

⁸"I have heard the insults of the country of
Moab
and the threats of the people of Ammon.
They have insulted my people
and have taken their land."
⁹So the LORD All-powerful, the God of Israel,
says,
"As surely as I live,
Moab will be destroyed like Sodom, *d*
and Ammon will be destroyed like
Gomorrah *d*
a heap of weeds, a pit of salt
and a ruin for ever.
Those of my people who are left alive will
take whatever they want from them;
those who are left from my nation will take
their land."

¹⁰This is what Moab and Ammon get for being
proud,
because they insulted and made fun of the
people of the LORD All-powerful.
¹¹The LORD will frighten them,
because he will destroy all the gods of the
earth.
Then everyone in faraway places
will worship him wherever they are.

Cush and Assyria will be Destroyed

¹²"You Cushites also
will be killed by my sword."

¹³Then the LORD will turn against the north
and destroy Assyria.
He will make Nineveh

a ruin as dry as a desert.
¹⁴Flocks and herds will lie down there,
and all wild animals.
The owls and crows will sit
on the stone pillars.
The owl will call through the windows,
rubbish will be in the doorways,
and the wooden boards of the buildings
will be gone.
¹⁵This is the happy and safe city
that thinks there is no one else as strong as
it is.
But what a ruin it will be,
a place where wild animals live.
All those who pass by will make fun
and shake their fists.

Jerusalem will be Punished

3 How terrible for the wicked, stubborn city
of Jerusalem,
which hurts its own people.
²It obeys no voice;
it can't be taught to do right.
It doesn't trust the LORD;
it doesn't worship its God.
³Its officers are like roaring lions.
Its rulers are like hungry wolves that attack
in the evening,
and in the morning nothing is left of those
they attacked.
⁴Its prophets *d* are proud;
they are people who cannot be trusted.
Its priests don't respect holy things;
they break God's teachings.
⁵But the LORD is good, and he is there in that
city.
He does no wrong.
Every morning he governs the people
fairly;
every day he can be trusted.
But evil people are not ashamed of what
they do.

⁶"I have destroyed nations;
their towers were ruined.

I made their streets empty
so no one goes there any more.
Their cities are ruined;
no one lives there at all.
7I said, 'Surely now Jerusalem will respect me
and will accept my teaching.'
Then the place where they lived would not
be destroyed,
and I would not have to punish them.
But they were still eager
to do evil in everything they did.
8Just wait," says the LORD.
"Some day I will stand up as a witness.
I have decided that I will gather nations
and assemble kingdoms.
I will pour out my anger on them,
all my strong anger.

My anger will be like fire
that will burn up the whole world.

A New Day for God's People

9"Then I will give the people of all nations
pure speech
so that all of them will speak the name of
the LORD
and worship me together.
10People will come from where the Nile River
begins;
my scattered people will come with gifts
for me.
11Then Jerusalem will not be ashamed
of the wrongs done against me,
because I will remove from this city
those who like to boast;

HAPPINESS

Singing Your Heart Out

Calvin loved footy and every week he would sing his heart out for his team. Chanting, clapping, singing –
nothing gave Calvin a bigger buzz than watching his team win. And the songs didn't just stay in the stadium,
everyone on the train and on his walk home would get to hear how happy Calvin and his mates were.

Calvin didn't just watch his team though – he played for them too. He had always been a talented player,
but the turning point in Calvin's life was when he got signed at the age of twelve to play for the team he
had always supported. It was a dream come true.

Over the years, Calvin worked hard playing for the youth teams and eventually, when he was eighteen, got
to play for the reserves. Now Calvin was on the books a lot had changed. He was even getting up early in the
mornings for training. One thing didn't change though – he still loved to watch his team play and would stand
with thousands of others to sing and chant with joy at every goal.

When he was nineteen, Calvin played his first game for the first team. As he walked out of the tunnel and
onto the pitch, the noise hit him. Looking up into the stands, Calvin slowly turned 360 degrees and absorbed
the moment. Someone somewhere started a song and all the home fans joined in; it was deafening
and the proudest day of Calvin's life. He had always been the one of the singers, celebrating and
bigging up his team. Now the crowds were singing about him.

In **Zephaniah 3:14–18** the prophet tells Israel that they had got something to shout and
sing about.

* What does the passage say that God's people should be celebrating?
* Like the crowd at Calvin's first game, verse 17 says that God will sing and be joyful about you.
  How does that make you feel?

Consider . . .

* re-reading the passage putting your own name in the place of "Jerusalem", "Israel" and "you".
* most football songs are famous tunes with the lyrics changed. Try rewriting one of your favourite songs
  with lyrics about God's love.

For more, see . . .

* Psalm 146 (p.586)
* 1 Peter 1:8 (p.1357)

there will never be any more proud people
  on my holy mountain in Jerusalem.
12But I will leave in the city
  the humble and those who are not proud,
  and they will trust in the LORD.
13Those who are left alive in Israel won't do
    wrong
  or tell lies;
  they won't trick people with their words.
They will eat and lie down
  with no one to make them afraid."

A Happy Song

14Sing, Jerusalem.
  Israel, shout for joy!
Jerusalem, be happy
  and rejoice with all your heart.
15The LORD has stopped punishing you;
  he has sent your enemies away.
The King of Israel, the LORD, is with you;
  you will never again be afraid of being
    harmed.
16On that day Jerusalem will be told,
  "Don't be afraid, city of Jerusalem.
  Don't give up.

17The LORD your God is with you;
  the mighty One will save you.
He will rejoice over you.
  You will rest in his love;
  he will sing and be joyful about you."

18"I will take away the sadness planned
    for you,
  which would have made you very
    ashamed.
19At that time I will punish
  all those who harmed you.
I will save my people who cannot walk
  and gather my people who have been
    thrown out.
I will give them praise and honour
  in every place where they were
    shamed.
20At that time I will gather you;
  at that time I will bring you back
    home.
I will give you honour and praise
  from people everywhere
when I make things go well again for you,
  as you will see with your own eyes," says
    the LORD.

Haggai

Why Read This Book:

- Understand the importance of focusing on God's priorities instead of our own desires (Haggai 1).
- See the excitement of working together for God's glory (Haggai 2).

When?

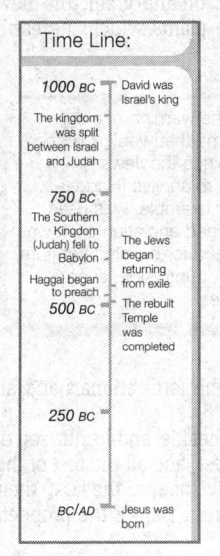

Time Line:

1000 BC	David was Israel's king
The kingdom was split between Israel and Judah	
750 BC	
The Southern Kingdom (Judah) fell to Babylon	The Jews began returning from exile
Haggai began to preach	
500 BC	The rebuilt Temple was completed
250 BC	
BC/AD	Jesus was born

Behind the Scenes:

If you've ever moved, you know what it's like to get settled. You have to find your way around. You have to make new friends. You have to settle into a job or a school. In short, you are busy putting your new life together.

The Jewish people had just returned to Judah after being captives in Babylon. They were caught up in planting crops, repairing homes and earning a living.

But something was missing. While the Jews were enjoying their new freedom in their nice homes, God's Temple lay in ruins. God sent the prophet Haggai to show the Jews that their priorities were wrong: that they were being selfish and materialistic.

Building the Temple was important for the Jews, not so that they would have a place to worship, but as a symbol of God's leadership and lordship in the nation. It was the "place" of God's personal contact with his people. Haggai believed that the Temple would bring hope to a people who were depressed and struggling.

Haggai's ministry involved motivating people to complete God's Temple, which had been started almost twenty years earlier. Within three weeks, the people had started work on the Temple again. And four years later, the Temple was complete.

Though we don't face the challenge of building a Temple in Jerusalem, the book of Haggai still has important reminders for us. It reminds us to keep our priorities straight. And it reminds us to make God the centre of our lives – just as the Temple was the centre of life for the Jewish people.

Where?

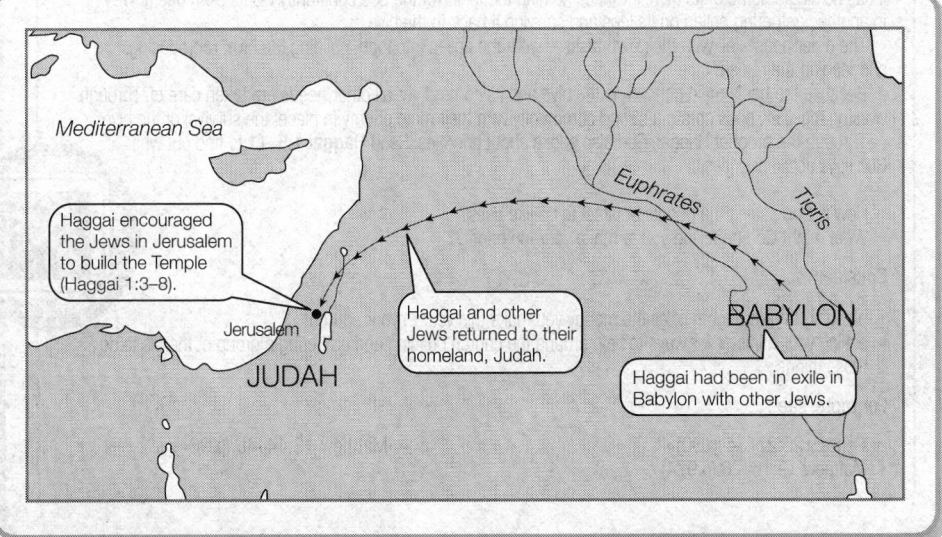

Haggai encouraged the Jews in Jerusalem to build the Temple (Haggai 1:3–8).

Haggai and other Jews returned to their homeland, Judah.

Haggai had been in exile in Babylon with other Jews.

It is Time to Build the Temple

1 The prophet[d] Haggai spoke the word of the LORD to Zerubbabel son of Shealtiel, the governor of Judah, and to Joshua son of Jehozadak, the high priest. This message came in the second year that Darius was king, on the first day of the sixth month:

²"This is what the LORD All-powerful says: 'The people say the right time has not come to rebuild the Temple[d] of the LORD.'"

³Then Haggai the prophet spoke the word of the LORD: ⁴"Is it right for you to be living in fancy houses while the Temple is still in ruins?"

⁵This is what the LORD All-powerful says: "Think about what you have done. ⁶You have planted much, but you harvest little. You eat, but you do not become full. You drink, but you are still thirsty. You put on clothes, but you are not warm enough. You earn money, but then you lose it all as if you had put it into a purse full of holes."

⁷This is what the LORD All-powerful says: "Think about what you have done. ⁸Go up to the mountains, bring back wood and build the Temple. Then I will be pleased with it and be honoured," says the LORD. ⁹"You look for much, but you find little. When you bring it home, I

destroy it. Why?" asks the LORD All-powerful. "Because you all work hard for your own houses while my house is still in ruins! ¹⁰Because of what you have done, the sky holds back its rain and the ground holds back its crops. ¹¹I have called for a time without rain on the land, and on the mountains, and on the grain, the new wine, the olive oil, the plants which the earth

Sidelight

The warning of a dry time that would ruin the harvest was alarming, since the Jews depended on the crops to survive (Haggai 1:11). The olive tree, for example, was used for food, fuel, medicine and anointing oil. It was also used in sacrifices and for building furniture. Olive trees covered the countryside, even growing on rocky hillsides.

produces, the people, the farm animals and all the work of your hands."

¹²Zerubbabel son of Shealtiel and Joshua son of Jehozadak, the high priest, and all the rest of the people who were left alive obeyed the LORD their God and the message from Haggai the prophet,

PRIORITIES

The Way to Bee

It has no single home of its own. It makes nothing for itself. Yet the bee constantly works from one flower to another, gathering pollen on its legs and carrying it back to the hive.

The other bees – all with their own tasks – work the pollen into food, building the hive, reproducing, and feeding the queen.

Because the bee's main concern is the hive and its community, all other needs are taken care of. Through working together, bees create a strong community with their main priority in place: the survival of the hive.

Through the prophet Haggai, God also spoke about priorities. Read **Haggai 1:5–11** to find out what God says about priorities.

* How is God asking the people of Israel to be like bees?
* What might God be telling you to make your top priority?

Consider . . .

* pledging to give a tenth of all the money you make this year to your church.
* asking your minister for ways to help around the church building and gathering a group of friends to do those things.

For more, see . . .

* Genesis 25:27–34 (p.30)
* Matthew 13:44–46 (p.964)
* Matthew 19:16–26 (p.974)

because the LORD their God had sent him. And the people feared the LORD.

¹³Haggai, the LORD's messenger, gave the LORD's message to the people, saying, "The LORD says, 'I am with you.'" ¹⁴The LORD stirred up Zerubbabel son of Shealtiel, the governor of Judah, and Joshua son of Jehozadak, the high priest, and all the rest of the people who were left alive. So they came and worked on the Temple of their God, the LORD All-powerful. ¹⁵They began on the twenty-fourth day of the sixth month in the second year Darius was king.

The Beauty of the Temple

2 On the twenty-first day of the seventh month, the LORD spoke his word through Haggai the prophet,ᵈ saying, ²"Speak to Zerubbabel son of Shealtiel, governor of Judah, and to Joshua son of Jehozadak, the high priest, and to the rest of the people who are left alive. Say, ³'Do any of you remember how great the Temple ᵈ was before it was destroyed? What does it look like now? Doesn't it seem like nothing to you?' ⁴But the LORD says, 'Zerubbabel, be brave. Also, Joshua son of Jehozadak, the high priest, be brave. And all you people who live in the land, be brave,' says the LORD. 'Work, because I am with you,' says the LORD All-powerful. ⁵'I made a promise to you when you came out of Egypt, and my Spirit ᵈ is still with you. So don't be afraid.'

⁶"This is what the LORD All-powerful says: 'In a short time I will once again shake the heavens and the earth, the sea and the dry land. ⁷I will shake all the nations, and they will bring their wealth. Then I will fill this Temple with glory,' says the LORD All-powerful. ⁸'The silver is mine, and the gold is mine,' says the LORD All-powerful. ⁹'The new Temple will be greater than the one before,' says the LORD All-powerful. 'And in this place I will give peace,' says the LORD All-powerful."

¹⁰On the twenty-fourth day of the ninth month in the second year Darius was king, the LORD spoke his word to Haggai the prophet, saying, ¹¹"This is what the LORD All-powerful says: 'Ask the priests for a teaching. ¹²Suppose a person carries in the fold of his clothes some meat made holy for the LORD. If that fold touches bread, cooked food, wine, olive oil or some other food, will that be made holy?'"

The priests answered, "No."

¹³Then Haggai said, "A person who touches a dead body will become unclean. ᵈ If he touches any of these foods, will it become unclean, too?"

The priests answered, "Yes, it would become unclean."

¹⁴Then Haggai answered, "The LORD says, 'This is also true for the people of this nation. They are unclean, and everything they do with their hands is unclean to me. Whatever they offer at the altar is also unclean.

¹⁵"'Think about this from now on! Think about how it was before you started laying stones on top of stones to build the Temple of the LORD. ¹⁶A person used to come to a pile of grain expecting to find 20 basketfuls, but there were only ten. And a person used to come to the wine vat to take out 50 jarfuls, but only 20 were there. ¹⁷I destroyed your work with diseases, mildew ᵈ and hail, but you still did not come back to me,' says the LORD. ¹⁸'It is the twenty-fourth day of the ninth month, the day in which the people finished working on the foundation of the Temple of the LORD. From now on, think about these things: ¹⁹Do you have seeds for crops still in the barn? Your vines, fig trees, pomegranates ᵈ and olive trees have not given fruit yet. But from now on I will bless you!'"

The LORD Makes a Promise to Zerubbabel

²⁰Then the LORD spoke his word a second time to Haggai on the twenty-fourth day of the month. He said, ²¹"Tell Zerubbabel, the governor of Judah, 'I am going to shake the heavens and the earth. ²²I will destroy the foreign kingdoms and take away the power of the kingdoms of the nations. I will destroy the chariots and their riders. The horses will fall with their riders, as people kill each other with swords.' ²³The LORD All-powerful says, 'On that day I will take you, Zerubbabel son of Shealtiel, my servant,' says the LORD, 'and I will make you important like my signet ᵈ ring, because I have chosen you!' says the LORD All-powerful."

Zechariah

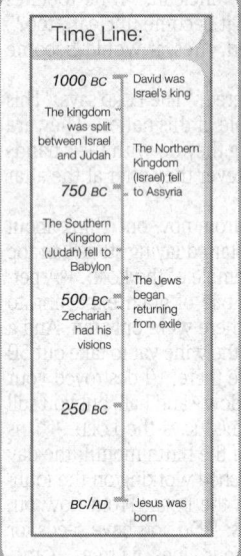

When?

Time Line:

- **1000 BC** — David was Israel's king
- The kingdom was split between Israel and Judah
- **750 BC** — The Northern Kingdom (Israel) fell to Assyria
- The Southern Kingdom (Judah) fell to Babylon
- **500 BC** — Zechariah had his visions — The Jews began returning from exile
- **250 BC**
- **BC/AD** — Jesus was born

Why Read This Book:

- Be challenged to follow God and do his will (Zechariah 1—8).
- Find encouragement in knowing a glorious, peaceful future awaits God's people (Zechariah 9—14).

Behind the Scenes:

When you work on something, you like to see results. You want to know that your hard work will be worth the time and energy you've invested.

The people of Israel also wanted to see results when they started rebuilding their Temple. They wanted to know that they would be blessed for what they were doing.

The prophet Zechariah was there to assure them and encourage them. Like his colleague Haggai (p.915), who ministered at the same time, Zechariah believed that completing the Temple would be the first step towards bringing God's kingdom to earth.

Zechariah's encouragement came in a series of visions about the Temple (Zechariah 1:7—6:8). Each vision in the first part of the book shows activity between heaven and earth. They each show a world that's changing, and they have a universal theme – that God is bigger than the Temple or Judah. Through each vision, Zechariah encourages the people to rebuild the Temple and to focus on following God so that they will be ready for the coming of God's kingdom.

The second part of Zechariah (chapters 9—14) has a different focus. It concentrates on the coming kingdom of God instead of the Temple. In the coming age, the wicked will be destroyed and the righteous will be saved. This new kingdom will focus on justice, kindness and mercy rather than on rituals of religion.

The book of Zechariah has been treasured by Christians because many of its images of the Messiah (such as the Prince of Peace, Zechariah 9:9–10), foreshadow Jesus Christ's life and ministry. Just as Zechariah offered encouragement, hope and joy to the people of his day, so the book offers encouragement, hope and joy to us today.

LIFE FILE LINKS

Investigate the Theme

To find a list of real life stories on this subject turn to the LIFE FILE GUIDE on pages 12 to 22 at the front of the Youth Bible.

LEADERSHIP

The LORD Calls His People Back

1 In the eighth month of Darius' second year as king, the LORD spoke his word to the prophet *d* Zechariah son of Berekiah, who was the son of Iddo. The LORD said, [2]"The LORD was very angry with your ancestors. [3]So tell the people: this is what the LORD All-powerful says: 'Return to me, and I will return to you,' says the LORD

Sidelight   If you were to try and count the names in the phone book that begin with the letter "Z", the chances are that you wouldn't come up with many. But in the Bible, the name Zechariah alone (Zechariah 1:1) was used for more than 30 people! These included a gatekeeper (1 Chronicles 26:2, p.395), a harpist (1 Chronicles 15:20, p.387) and a trumpet-blowing priest (1 Chronicles 15:24, p.387). The Zechariah in this book was a prophet and probably also a priest.

All-powerful. [4]Don't be like your ancestors. In the past the prophets said to them: this is what the LORD All-powerful says: 'Stop your evil ways and evil actions.' But they wouldn't listen or pay attention to me, says the LORD. [5]Your ancestors are dead, and those prophets didn't live for ever. [6]I commanded my words and laws to my servants the prophets, and they preached to your ancestors, who returned to me. They said, 'The LORD All-powerful did as he said he would. He punished us for the way we lived and for what we did.'"

The Vision of the Horses

[7]It was on the twenty-fourth day of the eleventh month, which is the month of Shebat, in Darius' second year as king. The LORD spoke his word to the prophet *d* Zechariah son of Berekiah, who was the son of Iddo.

[8]During the night I had a vision. I saw a man riding a red horse. He was standing among some myrtle trees in a ravine, with red, brown and white horses behind him.

[9]I asked, "What are these, sir?"

The angel who was talking with me answered, "I'll show you what they are."

[10]Then the man standing among the myrtle trees explained, "They are the ones the LORD sent through all the earth."

[11]Then they spoke to the LORD's angel, who was standing among the myrtle trees. They said, "We have gone through all the earth, and everything is calm and quiet."

[12]Then the LORD's angel asked, "LORD All-powerful, how long will it be before you show mercy to Jerusalem and the cities of Judah? You have been angry with them for 70 years now."

[13]So the LORD answered the angel who was talking with me, and his words were comforting and good.

[14]Then the angel who was talking to me said to me, "Announce this: this is what the LORD All-powerful says: 'I have a strong love for Jerusalem. [15]And I am very angry with the nations that feel so safe. I was only a little angry at them, but they made things worse.'

[16]"So this is what the LORD says: 'I will return to Jerusalem with mercy. My Temple *d* will be rebuilt,' says the LORD All-powerful, 'and the measuring line will be used to rebuild Jerusalem.'

[17]"Also announce: this is what the LORD All-powerful says: 'My towns will be rich again. The LORD will comfort Jerusalem again, and I will again choose Jerusalem.'"

The Vision of the Horns

[18]Then I looked up and saw four animal horns. [19]I asked the angel who was talking with me, "What are these?"

He said, "These are the horns that scattered the people of Judah, Israel and Jerusalem."

[20]Then the LORD showed me four craftsmen. [21]I asked, "What are they coming to do?"

He answered, "They have come to scare and throw down the horns. These horns scattered the people of Judah so that no one could even lift up his head. These horns stand for the nations that attacked the people of Judah and scattered them."

The Vision of the Measuring Line

2 Then I looked up and saw a man holding a line for measuring objects. [2]I asked him, "Where are you going?"

He said to me, "I am going to measure Jerusalem, to see how wide and how long it is."

[3]Then the angel who was talking with me left, and another angel came out to meet him. [4]The second angel said to him, "Run and tell that young man, 'Jerusalem will become a city without walls, because there will be so many people and cattle in it. [5]I will be a wall of fire around it,' says the LORD. 'And I will be the glory within it.'

[6]"Oh no! Oh no! Run away from Babylon, because I have scattered you like the four winds of heaven," says the LORD.

[7]"Oh no, Jerusalem! Escape, you who live right in Babylon." [8]This is what the LORD All-powerful says: "After he has honoured me and sent me against the nations who took your possessions— because whoever touches you hurts what is precious to me— [9]I will shake my hand against them so that their slaves will rob them."

Then you will know that the LORD All-powerful sent me.

10"Shout and be glad, Jerusalem. I am coming, and I will live among you," says the LORD. 11"At that time people from many nations will join with the LORD and will become my people. Then I will live among you, and you will know that the LORD All-powerful has sent me to you. 12The LORD will take Judah as his own part of the holy land, and Jerusalem will be his chosen city again. 13Be silent, everyone, in the presence of the LORD. He is coming out of the holy place where he lives."

The Vision of the High Priest

3 Then he showed me Joshua, the high priest, standing in front of the LORD's angel. And Satan was standing by Joshua's right side to accuse him. 2The LORD said to Satan, "The LORD says no to you, Satan! The LORD who has chosen Jerusalem says no to you! This man was like a burning stick pulled from the fire."

3Joshua was wearing dirty clothes and was standing in front of the angel. 4The angel said to those standing in front of him, "Take off those dirty clothes."

Then the angel said to Joshua, "Look, I have taken away your sin from you, and I am giving you beautiful, fine clothes."

5Then I said, "Put a clean turban on his head." So they put a clean turban on his head and dressed him while the LORD's angel stood there.

6Then the LORD's angel said to Joshua, 7"This is what the LORD All-powerful says: 'If you do as I tell you and serve me, you will be in charge of my Temple d and my courtyards. And I will let you be with these angels who are standing here.

8" 'Listen, Joshua, the high priest, and your friends who are sitting in front of you. They stand for what will happen. I am going to bring my servant called the Branch. 9Look, I put this stone in front of Joshua, a stone with seven sides. I will carve a message on it,' says the LORD All-powerful. 'And in one day I will take away the sin of this land.'

10"The LORD All-powerful says, 'In that day, each of you will invite your neighbour to sit under your own grapevine and under your own fig tree.' "

The Vision of the Lampstand

4 Then the angel who was talking with me returned and woke me up as if I had been asleep. 2He asked me, "What do you see?"

I said, "I see a solid gold lampstand with a bowl at the top. And there are seven lamps and also seven places for wicks. 3There are two olive trees by it, one on the right of the bowl and the other on the left."

4I asked the angel who talked with me, "Sir, what are these?"

5The angel said, "Don't you know what they are?"

"No, sir," I said.

6Then he told me, "This is the word of the LORD to Zerubbabel: 'You will not succeed by your own strength or power, but by my Spirit,' d says the LORD All-powerful.

7"Who are you, big mountain? In front of Zerubbabel you will become flat land, and he will bring out the topmost stone, shouting, 'It's beautiful! It's beautiful!' "

8Then the LORD spoke his word to me again, saying, 9"Zerubbabel has laid the foundation of this Temple, d and he will complete it. Then you will know that the LORD All-powerful has sent me to you.

10"The people should not think that small beginnings are unimportant. They will be happy when they see Zerubbabel with tools, building the Temple.

"(These are the seven eyes of the LORD, which look back and forth across the earth.)"

11Then I asked the angel, "What are the two olive trees on the right and left of the lampstand?"

12I also asked him, "What are the two olive branches beside the two gold pipes, from which the olive oil flows to the lamps?"

13He answered, "Don't you know what they are?"

"No, sir," I said.

14So he said, "They stand for the two who have been appointed to serve the LORD of all the earth."

> **Sidelight** Though the flying scroll of Zechariah 5 had impressive dimensions, it doesn't hold the record. Archaeologists have discovered scrolls that would stretch almost half the length of a football field. Try fitting one of those textbooks into your locker!

The Vision of the Flying Scroll

5 I looked up again and saw a flying scroll. 2The angel asked me, "What do you see?"

I answered, "I see a flying scroll, 10 metres long and 5 metres wide."

3And he said to me, "This is the curse that will go all over the land. One side says every thief will be taken away. The other side says everyone who makes false promises will be taken away. 4The LORD All-powerful says, 'I will send it to the houses of thieves and to those who use my name to make false promises. The scroll will stay in that person's house and destroy it with its wood and stones.' "

The Vision of the Woman

5Then the angel who was talking with me came forwards and said to me, "Look up and see what is going out."

6"What is it?" I asked.

He answered, "It is a measuring basket going out." He also said, "It stands for the people's sins in all the land."

7Then the lid made of lead was raised, and there was a woman sitting inside the basket. 8The angel said, "The woman stands for wickedness." Then he pushed her back into the basket and put the lid back down.

9Then I looked up and saw two women going out with the wind in their wings. Their wings were like those of a stork, and they lifted up the basket between earth and the sky.

10I asked the angel who was talking with me, "Where are they taking the basket?"

11"They are going to Babylonia to build a temple for it," he answered. "When the temple is ready, they will set the basket there in its place."

The Vision of the Four Chariots

6 I looked up again and saw four chariots going out between two mountains, mountains of bronze. 2Red horses pulled the first chariot. Black horses pulled the second chariot. 3White horses pulled the third chariot, and strong, spotted horses pulled the fourth chariot. 4I asked the angel who was talking with me, "What are these, sir?"

5He said, "These are the four spirits of heaven. They have just come from the presence of the Lord of the whole world. 6The chariot pulled by the black horses will go to the land of the north. The white horses will go to the land of the west, and the spotted horses will go to the land of the south."

7When the powerful horses went out, they were eager to go through all the earth. So he said, "Go through all the earth," and they did.

8Then he called to me, "Look, the horses that went north have caused my spirit to rest in the land of the north."

A Crown for Joshua

9The Lord spoke his word to me, saying, 10"Take silver and gold from Heldai, Tobijah and Jedaiah, who were captives in Babylon. Go that same day to the house of Josiah son of Zepha-

niah, who came from Babylon. 11Make the silver and gold into a crown, and put it on the head of Joshua son of Jehozadak, the high priest. 12Tell him this is what the Lord All-powerful says: 'A man whose name is the Branch will branch out from where he is, and he will build the Temple d of the Lord. 13One man n will build the Temple of the Lord, and the other n will receive honour. One man will sit on his throne and rule, and the other will be a priest on his throne. And these two men will work together in peace.' 14The crown will be kept in the Temple of the Lord to remind Heldai, Tobijah, Jedaiah and Josiah son of Zephaniah. 15People living far away will come and build the Temple of the Lord. Then you will know the Lord All-powerful has sent me to you. This will happen if you completely obey the Lord your God."

The People Should Show Mercy

7 In Darius' fourth year as king, on the fourth day of the ninth month, which is called Kislev, the Lord spoke his word to Zechariah. 2The city of Bethel sent Sharezer, Regem-Melech and their men to ask the Lord a question. 3They went to the prophets d and priests who were at the Temple d of the Lord All-powerful. The men said, "For years in the fifth month of each year we have shown our sadness and gone without food. Should we continue to do this?"

4The Lord All-powerful spoke his word to

> **Sidelight** In Zechariah 7:4–10, God criticises the prophets and priests for fasting simply to make themselves feel better while failing to love and care for the people around them. Compare Zechariah 7:9–10 with James 1:26–27 (p.1348).

me, saying, 5"Tell the priests and the people in the land: 'For 70 years you went without food and cried in the fifth and seventh months, but that was not really for me. 6And when you ate and drank, it was really for yourselves. 7The Lord used the earlier prophets to say the same thing, when Jerusalem and the surrounding towns were at peace and wealthy, and people settled in the southern area and the western hills.' "

8And the Lord spoke his word to Zechariah again, saying, 9"This is what the Lord All-powerful says: 'Do what is right and true. Be kind

---

One man   This probably refers to Zerubbabel.
other   This probably refers to Joshua.

and merciful to each other. [10]Don't hurt widows and orphans, foreigners or the poor; don't even think of doing evil to somebody else.'

[11]"But they refused to pay attention; they were stubborn and did not want to listen any more. [12]They made their hearts as hard as rock and would not listen to the teachings of the LORD All-powerful. And they would not hear the words he sent by his Spirit through the earlier prophets. So the LORD All-powerful became very angry.

[13]" 'When I called to them, they would not listen. So when they called to me, I would not listen,' says the LORD All-powerful. [14]'I scattered them like a hurricane to other countries which they did not know. This good land was left so ruined behind them that no one could live there. They had made the desired land a ruin.' "

The LORD will Bless Jerusalem

8 The LORD All-powerful spoke his word, saying, [2]this is what the LORD All-powerful says: "I have a very strong love for Jerusalem. My strong love for her is like a fire burning in me."

[3]This is what the LORD says: "I will return to Jerusalem and live in it. Then it will be called the City of Truth, and the mountain of the LORD All-powerful will be called the Holy Mountain."

[4]This is what the LORD All-powerful says: "Old men and old women will again sit along Jerusalem's streets, each carrying a cane because of age. [5]And the streets will be filled with boys and girls playing."

[6]This is what the LORD All-powerful says: "Those who are left alive then may think it is too difficult to happen, but it is not too difficult for me," says the LORD All-powerful. [7]This is what the LORD All-powerful says: "I will save my people from countries in the east and west. [8]I will bring them back, and they will live in Jerusalem. They will be my people, and I will be their good and loyal God."

[9]This is what the LORD All-powerful says: "Work hard, you who are hearing these words today. The prophets spoke these words when the foundation was laid for the house of the LORD All-powerful, for the building of the Temple. [d] [10]Before that time there was no money to hire people or animals. People could not safely come and go because of their enemies; I had turned everyone against his neighbour. [11]But I will not do to these people who are left what I did in the past," says the LORD All-powerful.

[12]"They will plant their seeds in peace, their grapevines will have fruit, the ground will give good crops, and the sky will send rain. I will give all this to the people who are left alive. [13]Judah and Israel, your names have been used as curses

in other nations. But I will save you, and you will become a blessing. So don't be afraid; work hard."

[14]This is what the LORD All-powerful says: "When your ancestors made me angry, I planned to punish you. I did not change my mind," says the LORD All-powerful. [15]"But now I will do something different. I am planning to do good to Jerusalem and Judah. So don't be afraid. [16]These are the things you should do: tell each other the truth. In the courts judge with truth and complete fairness. [17]Do not make plans to hurt your neighbours, and don't love false promises. I hate all these things," says the LORD.

[18]The LORD All-powerful spoke his word to me again. [19]This is what the LORD All-powerful says: "The special days when you give up eating in the fourth, fifth, seventh and tenth months will become good, joyful, happy feasts in Judah. But you must love truth and peace."

[20]This is what the LORD All-powerful says: "Many people from many cities will still come to Jerusalem. [21]People from one city will go and say to those from another city, 'We are going to pray to the LORD and to ask the LORD All-powerful for help. Come and go with us.' [22]Many people and powerful nations will come to worship the LORD All-powerful in Jerusalem and to pray to the LORD for help."

[23]This is what the LORD All-powerful says: "At that time, ten men from different countries will come and take hold of a Judean by his coat. They will say to him, 'Let us go with you, because we have heard that God is with you.' "

Punishment on Israel's Enemies

9 This message is the word of the LORD.

The message is against the land of Hadrach
  and the city of Damascus.
The tribes[d] of Israel and all people
  belong to the LORD.
[2]The message is also against the city of
    Hamath, on the border,
  and against Tyre and Sidon, with their skill.
[3]Tyre has built a strong wall for herself.
  She has piled up silver like dust
  and gold like the mud in the streets.
[4]But the Lord will take away all she has
  and destroy her power on the sea.
  That city will be destroyed by fire.
[5]The city of Ashkelon will see it and be afraid.
  The people of Gaza will shake with fear,
  and the people of Ekron will lose hope.
No king will be left in Gaza,
  and no one will live in Ashkelon any more.
[6]Foreigners will live in Ashdod,
  and I will destroy the pride of the
    Philistines.

⁷I will stop them from drinking blood
    and from eating forbidden food.
Those left alive will belong to God.
    They will be leaders in Judah,
    and Ekron will become like the Jebusites.
⁸I will protect my Temple*d*
    from armies who would come or go.
No one will hurt my people again,
    because now I am watching them.

> ### Sidelight
> In times of peace, royalty would ride on a donkey, rather than on a white horse (which symbolised war). In Zechariah 9:9, the prophet pictures the future king of Jerusalem riding on a donkey, bringing peace and hope with him.

The King is Coming

⁹Rejoice greatly, people of Jerusalem!
    Shout for joy, people of Jerusalem!
Your king is coming to you.
    He does what is right, and he saves.
    He is gentle and riding on a donkey,
    on the colt of a donkey.
¹⁰I will take away the chariots from Ephraim
    and the horses from Jerusalem.
The bows used in war will be broken.
    The king will talk to the nations about peace.
    His kingdom will go from sea to sea,
    and from the Euphrates River to the ends
    of the earth.

¹¹As for you, because of the blood of the
    agreement with you
    I will set your prisoners free from the
    dry pit.
¹²You prisoners who have hope,
    return to your place of safety.
Today I am telling you
    that I will give you back twice as much as
    before.
¹³I will use Judah like a bow
    and Ephraim like the arrows.
Jerusalem, I will use your men
    to fight the men of Greece.
    I will use you like a warrior's sword.

¹⁴Then the LORD will appear above them,
    and his arrows will shoot like lightning.
The Lord GOD will blow the trumpet,
    and he will march in the storms of the
    south.
¹⁵The LORD All-powerful will protect them;
    they will destroy the enemy with catapults.
They will drink and shout like drunkards.
    They will be filled like a bowl

used for sprinkling blood at the corners of
    the altar.
¹⁶On that day the LORD their God will save
    them
    as if his people were sheep.
They will shine in his land
    like jewels in a crown.
¹⁷They will be so pretty and beautiful.
    The young men will grow strong on the
    grain
    and the young women on new wine.

The LORD's Promises

10 Ask the LORD for rain during the
    springtime.
    The LORD is the one who makes the clouds.
He sends the showers
    and gives everyone green fields.
²Idols tell lies;
    fortune-tellers see false visions
and tell about false dreams.
    The comfort they give is worth nothing.
So the people are like lost sheep.
    They are abused, because there is no
    shepherd.

³The LORD says, "I am angry with my
    shepherds,
    and I will punish the leaders.
I, the LORD All-powerful, care
    for my flock, the people of Judah.
I will make them like my proud war
    horses.
⁴From Judah will come the cornerstone, *d*
    and the tent peg,
    the battle bow,
    and every ruler.
⁵Together they will be like soldiers
    marching to battle through muddy streets.
The LORD is with them,
    so they will fight and defeat the horsemen.

⁶"I will strengthen the people of Judah
    and save the people of Joseph.
I will bring them back,
    because I care about them.
It will be as though
    I had never left them,
because I am the LORD their God,
    and I will answer them.
⁷The people of Ephraim will be strong like
    soldiers;
    they will be as glad as when they have
    drunk wine.
Their children will see it and rejoice;
    they will be happy in the LORD.
⁸I will call my people
    and gather them together.
I will save them,

and they will grow in number as they grew
in number before.
[9]I have scattered them among the nations,
but in those faraway places, they will
remember me.
They and their children will live and
return.
[10]I will bring them back from the land of
Egypt
and gather them from Assyria.
I will bring them to Gilead and Lebanon
until there isn't enough room for them all.
[11]They will come through the sea of trouble.
The waves of the sea will be calm,
and the Nile River will dry up.
I will defeat Assyria's pride
and destroy Egypt's power over other
countries.
[12]I will make my people strong,
and they will live as I say," says the LORD.

11 Lebanon, open your gates
so fire may burn your cedar trees. [n]
[2]Cry, pine trees, because the cedar has fallen,
because the tall trees are ruined.
Cry, oaks in Bashan,
because the mighty forest has been cut
down.
[3]Listen to the shepherds crying
because their rich pastures are destroyed.
Listen to the lions roaring
because the lovely land of the Jordan River
is ruined.

The Two Shepherds

[4]This is what the LORD my God says: "Feed the
flock that are about to be killed. [5]Their buyers kill
them and are not punished. Those who sell them
say, 'Praise the LORD, I am rich.' Even the shepherds don't feel sorry for their sheep. [6]I don't feel
sorry any more for the people of this country,"
says the LORD. "I will let everyone be under the
power of his neighbour and king. They will bring
trouble to the country, and I will not save anyone
from them."

[7]So I fed the flock about to be killed, particularly the weakest ones. Then I took two sticks; I
called one Pleasant and the other Union, and I
fed the flock. [8]In one month I got rid of three
shepherds. The flock did not pay attention to me,
and I got impatient with them. [9]I said, "I will no
longer take care of you like a shepherd. Let those
that are dying die, and let those that are to be
destroyed be destroyed. Let those that are left eat
each other."

[10]Then I broke the stick named Pleasant to
break the agreement God made with all the nations. [11]That day it was broken. The weak ones in
the flock who were watching me knew this message was from the LORD.
[12]Then I said, "If you want to pay me, pay me.
If not, then don't." So they paid me 30 pieces of
silver.
[13]The LORD said to me, "Throw the money to
the potter." That is how little they thought I was
worth. [n] So I took the 30 pieces of silver and
threw them to the potter in the Temple [d] of the
LORD.
[14]Then I broke the second stick, named Union,
to break the brotherhood between Judah and
Israel.
[15]Then the LORD said to me, "Get the things
used by a foolish shepherd again, [16]because I am
going to get a new shepherd for the country. He
will not care for the dying sheep, or look for the
young ones, or heal the injured ones or feed the
healthy. But he will eat the best sheep and tear
off their hoofs.

[17]"How terrible it will be for the useless
shepherd
who abandoned the flock.
A sword will strike his arm and his right eye.
His arm will lose all its strength,
and his right eye will go blind."

Jerusalem will be Saved

12 This message is the word of the LORD to
Israel. This is what the LORD says, who
stretched out the skies, and laid the foundations
of the earth, and put the human spirit within: [2]"I
will make Jerusalem like a cup of poison to the
nations around her. They will come and attack
Jerusalem and Judah. [3]One day all the nations on
earth will come together to attack Jerusalem, but
I will make it like a heavy rock; anyone who tries
to move it will get hurt. [4]At that time I will confuse every horse and cause its rider to go mad,"
says the LORD. "I will watch over Judah, but I will
blind all the horses of the enemies. [5]Then the
leaders of Judah will say to themselves, 'The people of Jerusalem are strong, because the LORD
All-powerful is their God.'

[6]"At that time I will make the leaders of Judah
like a fire burning a stack of wood or like a fire
burning straw. They will destroy all the people
around them left and right. But the people of
Jerusalem will remain safe.

[7]"The LORD will save the homes of Judah first
so that the honour given to David's family and to

---

trees In this poem, trees, bushes and animals stand for leaders of countries around Judah.
worth This was a small amount. It was about the price paid for a slave.

the people of Jerusalem won't be greater than the honour given to Judah. ⁸At that time the LORD will protect the people in Jerusalem. Then even the weakest of them will be strong like David. And the family of David will be like God, like an angel of the LORD in front of them. ⁹At that time I will go to destroy all the nations that attack Jerusalem.

Crying for the One They Stabbed

¹⁰"I will pour out on David's family and the people in Jerusalem a spirit of kindness and mercy. They will look at me, the one they have stabbed, and they will cry like someone crying over the death of an only child. They will be as sad as someone who has lost a firstborn ᵈ son. ¹¹At that time there will be much crying in Jerusalem, like the crying for Hadad Rimmon in the plain of Megiddo. ¹²The land will cry, each family by itself: the family of David by itself and their wives by themselves, the family of Nathan by itself and their wives by themselves, ¹³the family of Levi by itself and their wives by themselves,

the family of Shimei by itself and their wives by themselves, ¹⁴and all the rest of the families by themselves and their wives by themselves.

13 "At that time a fountain will be open for David's descendants ᵈ and for the people of Jerusalem to cleanse them of their sin and uncleanness."

²The LORD All-powerful says, "At that time I will get rid of the names of the idols from the land; no one will remember them any more. I will also remove the prophets ᵈ and unclean ᵈ spirits from the land. ³If a person continues to prophesy, his own father and mother, the ones who gave birth to him, will tell him, 'You have told lies using the LORD's name, so you must die.' When he prophesies, his own father and mother who gave birth to him will stab him.

⁴"At that time the prophets will be ashamed of their visions and prophecies. They won't try to trick people by wearing the prophet's clothes made of hair. ⁵Each of them will say, 'I am not a prophet. I am a farmer and have been a farmer

SADNESS

Stabbed in the Back

Youth leader Hannah felt cheated and abused by her youth group. After returning from a recent retreat, she discovered that one of the older teenagers had bought and supplied beer and spirits for the younger kids on the trip.

When the group returned home, the word got out. Parents rang Hannah the next day, asking how such a thing could happen.

Hannah had no idea how it had happened. That was what made it so embarrassing. She thought she knew the group. Now she wasn't so sure. She had trusted the kids. Now she could make no promises.

Hannah spent the next month talking to all the kids who had been on the retreat. She shared her anger, pain and sadness. She also showed the group that she still loved them. Then she worked – against heavy opposition – to plan another youth retreat, one that could be done properly.

When the kids saw how much Hannah cared for them and how they had abused her trust in them, they felt sad and sorry. The sadness they felt was much like the sadness described in **Zechariah 12:7–10**.

* How did Hannah's youth group act like the people described in verse 10?
* According to this passage, how does God feel when we disobey?

Consider . . .

* listening carefully to a friend the next time he or she is sad.
* rewriting Zechariah 12:7–9, substituting your own name for "the people of Judah", "the people in Jerusalem" and "the family of David". Read the passage on bad days.

For more, see . . .

* Job 2:11–13 (p.471)
* Luke 19:41–44 (p.1083)
* Mark 15:33–34 (p.1030)

since I was young.' 6But someone will ask, 'What are the deep cuts on your body?' And each will answer, 'I was hurt at my friend's house.'

The Shepherd is Killed

7"Sword, hit the shepherd.
  Attack the man who is my friend,"
says the LORD All-powerful.

"Kill the shepherd,
  and the sheep will scatter,
  and I will punish the little ones."
8The LORD says, "Two-thirds of the people
  through all the land will die. They will be
    gone,
  and one-third will be left.
9The third that is left I will test with fire,
  purifying them like silver,
  testing them like gold.
Then they will call on me,
  and I will answer them.
I will say, 'You are my people,'
  and they will say, 'The LORD is our God.' "

The Day of Punishment

14 The LORD's day of judging is coming when the wealth you have taken will be divided among you.

2I will bring all the nations together to fight Jerusalem. They will capture the city and rob the houses and attack the women. Half the people will be taken away as captives, but the rest of the people won't be taken from the city. 3Then the LORD will go to war against those nations; he will fight as in a day of battle. 4On that day he will stand on the Mount of Olives, d east of Jerusalem. The Mount of Olives will split in two, forming a deep valley that runs east and west. Half the mountain will move towards the north, and half will move towards the south. 5You will run through this mountain valley to the other side, just as you ran from the earthquake when Uzziah was king of Judah. Then the LORD my God will come and all the holy ones with him.

6On that day there will be no light, cold or frost. 7There will be no other day like it, and the LORD knows when it will come. There will be no day or night; even at evening it will still be light. 8At that time fresh water will flow from Jerusalem. Half of it will flow east to the Dead Sea, d and half will flow west to the Mediterranean Sea. It will flow in summer and winter. 9Then the LORD will be king over the whole world. At that time there will be only one LORD, and his name will be the only name.

10All the land south of Jerusalem from Geba to Rimmon will be turned into a plain. Jerusalem will be raised up, but it will stay in the same place. The city will reach from the Benjamin Gate, to the First Gate, to the Corner Gate, and from the Tower of Hananel to the king's winepresses. d 11People will live there, and it will never be destroyed again. Jerusalem will be safe.

12But the LORD will bring a terrible disease on the nations that fought against Jerusalem. Their flesh will rot away while they are still standing up. Their eyes will rot in their sockets, and their tongues will rot in their mouths. 13At that time the LORD will cause panic. Everybody will grab his neighbour, and they will attack each other. 14The people of Judah will fight in Jerusalem. And the wealth of the nations around them will be collected—much gold, silver and clothes. 15A similar disease will strike the horses, mules, camels, donkeys and all the animals in the camps.

16All of those left alive of the people who came to fight Jerusalem will come back to Jerusalem year after year to worship the King, the LORD All-powerful, and to celebrate the Feast d of Shelters. 17Anyone from the nations who does not go to Jerusalem to worship the King, the LORD All-powerful, will not have rain fall on his land. 18If the Egyptians do not go to Jerusalem, they will have no rain. Then the LORD will send them the same terrible disease he sent the other nations that did not celebrate the Feast of Shelters. 19This will be the punishment for Egypt and any nation which does not go to celebrate the Feast of Shelters.

20At that time the horses' bells will have written on them: HOLY TO THE LORD. The cooking pots in the Temple d of the LORD will be like the holy altar bowls. 21Every pot in Jerusalem and Judah will be holy to the LORD All-powerful, and everyone who offers sacrifices will be able to take food from them and cook in them. At that time there will not be any buyers or sellers in the Temple of the LORD All-powerful.

Malachi

Why Read This Book:

* Learn how to be loyal when things are tough (Malachi 1 – 2).
* Claim God's promise in the midst of discouragement (Malachi 3).

When?

Time Line:

1000 BC	David was Israel's king
The kingdom was split between Israel and Judah	
750 BC	The Northern Kingdom (Israel) fell to Assyria
The Southern Kingdom (Judah) fell to Babylon	
500 BC	The Jews began returning from exile
Malachi ministered in Jerusalem	
250 BC	
BC/AD	Jesus was born

Behind the Scenes:

Everything was supposed to be better now. The Jewish people returned to Jerusalem from exile, excited by the promises of Haggai (p.915) and Zechariah (p.918) about the coming of God's kingdom. But many years had passed, and life seemed about the same as it had always been – if not worse.

The community was still poor. Droughts and locusts continually ruined crops. Families were falling apart through divorce and adultery. The poor were being abused. And, worst of all, people had forgotten their faith. They just went through the motions of worshipping God.

In short, times were hard and God seemed far away. Why even try? the people seemed to say. They were upset and impatient. It seemed that God had not carried through his part of the agreement.

Enter Malachi, whose name means "my messenger". He pointed out how the country's priests were abusing or neglecting their God-given responsibilities. Their failure, the prophet said, was the main reason why things hadn't got any better. The prophet then challenged people to return to their faith. Then, at the time of judgement, the faithful would receive God's blessing.

When things don't go as we expect or hope, it's easy to think that God has let us down. And it's easy to relax our faith. But the book of Malachi urges us to stay strong. God loves us and is faithful, even when we can't see him working. We can have courage and hope in knowing that, in the end, God has a great future for all those that follow him.

LIFE FILE LINKS

Investigate the Theme

To find a list of real life stories on this subject turn to the LIFE FILE GUIDE on pages 12 to 22 at the front of the Youth Bible.

JUSTICE

1

This message is the word of the LORD given to Israel through Malachi.

God Loves Israel

²The LORD said, "I have loved you."

But you ask, "How have you loved us?"

The LORD said, "Esau and Jacob were brothers. I loved Jacob, ³but I hated Esau. I destroyed his mountain country and left his land to the wild dogs of the desert."

⁴The people of Edom might say, "We were destroyed, but we will go back and rebuild the ruins."

But the LORD All-powerful says, "If they rebuild them, I will destroy them. People will say, 'Edom is a wicked country. The LORD is always angry with the Edomites.' ⁵You will see these things with your own eyes. And you will say, 'The LORD is great, even outside the borders of Israel!' "

The Priests Don't Respect God

⁶The LORD All-powerful says, "A child honours his father, and a servant honours his master. I am a father, so why don't you honour me? I am a master, so why don't you respect me? You priests do not respect me.

"But you ask, 'How have we shown you disrespect?'

⁷"You have shown it by bringing unclean*d* food to my altar.

"But you ask, 'What makes it unclean?'

"It is unclean because you don't respect the altar of the LORD. ⁸When you bring blind animals as sacrifices, that is wrong. When you bring crippled and sick animals, that is wrong. Try giving them to your governor. Would he be pleased with you? He wouldn't accept you," says the LORD All-powerful.

⁹"Now ask God to be kind to you, but he won't accept you with such offerings," says the LORD All-powerful.

¹⁰"I wish one of you would close the Temple *d* doors so that you would not light useless fires on my altar! I am not pleased with you and will not accept your gifts," says the LORD All-powerful.

¹¹"From the east to the west I will be honoured among the nations. Everywhere they will bring incense *d* and clean offerings to me, because I will be honoured among the nations," says the LORD All-powerful.

¹²"But you don't honour me. You say about the Lord's altar, 'It is unclean, and the food has no worth.' ¹³You say, 'We are tired of doing this,' and you sniff at it in disgust," says the LORD All-powerful.

"And you bring hurt, crippled and sick animals as gifts. You bring them as gifts, but I won't accept them from you," says the LORD. ¹⁴"The person who cheats will be cursed. He has a male animal in his flock and promises to offer it, but then he offers to the Lord an animal that has something wrong with it. I am a great king," says the LORD All-powerful, "and I am feared by all the nations.

Rules for Priests

2

"Priests, this command is for you. ²Listen to me. Pay attention to what I say. Honour my name," says the LORD All-powerful. "If you don't, I will send a curse on you and on your blessings. I have already cursed them, because you don't pay attention to what I say.

³"I will punish your descendants. *d* I will smear your faces with the animal insides left from your feasts, and you will be thrown away with it. ⁴Then you will know that I am giving you this command so my agreement with Levi will continue," says the LORD All-powerful. ⁵"My agreement for priests was with the tribe *d* of Levi. I promised them life and peace so they would honour me. And they did honour me and fear me. ⁶They taught the true teachings and spoke no lies. With peace and honesty they did what I said they should do, and they kept many people from sinning.

⁷"A priest should teach what he knows, and people should learn the teachings from him, because he is the messenger of the LORD All-powerful. ⁸But you priests have stopped obeying me. With your teachings you have caused many people to do wrong. You have broken the agreement with the tribe *d* of Levi!" says the LORD All-powerful. ⁹"You have not been careful to do what I say, but instead you take sides in court cases. So I have caused you to be hated and disgraced in front of everybody."

Judah was Not Loyal to God

¹⁰We all have the same father; the same God made us. So why do people break their promises to each other and show no respect for the agreement our ancestors made with God? ¹¹The people of Judah have broken their promises. They have done something God hates in Israel and Jerusalem: the people of Judah did not respect the Temple *d* that the LORD loves, and the men of Judah married women who worship foreign gods. ¹²Whoever does this might bring offerings to the LORD All-powerful, but the LORD will still cut that person off from the community of Israel.

¹³This is another thing you do. You cover the Lord's altar with your tears. You cry and moan, because he does not accept your offerings and is not pleased with what you bring. ¹⁴You ask, "Why?" It is because the LORD sees how you treated the wife you married when you

were young. You broke your promise to her, even though she was your partner and you had an agreement with her. [15]God made husbands and wives to become one body and one spirit for his purpose— so they would have children who are true to God.

So be careful, and do not break your promise to the wife you married when you were young.

[16]The LORD God of Israel says, "I hate divorce. And I hate people who do cruel things as easily as they put on clothes," says the LORD All-powerful.

So be careful. And do not break your trust.

The Special Day of Judging

[17]You have tired the LORD with your words.

You ask, "How have we tired him?"

You did it by saying, "The LORD thinks anyone who does evil is good, and he is pleased with them." Or you asked, "Where is the God who is fair?"

3 The LORD All-powerful says, "I will send my messenger, who will prepare the way for me. Suddenly, the Lord you are looking for will come to his Temple; *d* the messenger of the agreement, whom you want, will come." [2]No one can live through that time; no one can survive when he comes. He will be like a purifying fire and like laundry soap. [3]Like someone who heats and purifies silver, he will purify the Levites and make them pure like gold and silver. Then they will bring offerings to the LORD in the right way. [4]And the LORD will accept the offerings from Judah and Jerusalem, as it was in the past. [5]The LORD All-powerful says, "Then I will come to you and judge you. I will be quick to testify against those who take part in evil magic, adultery *d* and lying under oath, those who cheat workers of their pay and who cheat widows and orphans, those who are unfair to foreigners, and those who do not respect me.

GOD'S POWER

The Power of Right

Laura, the Head Girl, had a remarkable power over the school. The school hall could be full, and all Laura needed to do to quieten things down was to stand up, look out over the crowd and wait. Within a minute the whole hall would be quiet.

Where did Laura get her power?

Ask her fellow students:

"I trust her. If she says she's going to do something, she always does her best to do it."

Ask her teachers:

"She's truthful and honest. She owns up to her mistakes and will always try to do better. She even helps others through their mistakes."

Ask her friends' parents:

"I like her sincerity. Laura will listen to my daughter if she has a problem. She's a good friend who's there for others."

People had no reason to doubt Laura and countless reasons to admire her.

As you get to know God, you'll discover a God who has the ultimate powerful qualities of trust, honesty and sincerity. Read **Malachi 3:1–4** about the promised "messenger" of God whose power is like a purifying fire. This "messenger" is the promised Messiah, the Son of God.

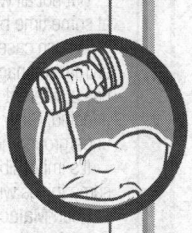

* How much greater is God's power in Malachi than that of Laura?
* What area of your life needs the purifying power of God?

Consider . . .

* choosing one of the symbols of God's power from the passage (matches, laundry soap, silver or gold) and keeping it in your room as a reminder of God's power.
* wearing something gold or silver every day this week to remind you to pray for God's purifying power in your life.

For more, see . . .

* Psalm 51:10–13 (p.530)
* Revelation 21:1–8 (p.1403)
* Isaiah 25:1–5 (p.663)

Stealing from God

[6]"I the LORD do not change. So you descendants [d] of Jacob have not been destroyed. [7]Since the time of your ancestors, you have disobeyed my rules and have not kept them. Return to me, and I will return to you," says the LORD All-powerful.

"But you ask, 'How can we return?'

[8]"Should a person rob God? But you are robbing me.

"You ask, 'How have we robbed you?'

"You have robbed me in your offerings and the tenth of your crops. [9]So a curse is on you, because the whole nation has robbed me. [10]Bring to the storehouse a full tenth of what you earn so there will be food in my house. Test me in this," says the LORD All-powerful. "I will open the windows of heaven for you and pour out all the blessings you need. [11]I will stop the insects so they won't eat your crops. The grapes won't fall from your vines before they are ready to pick," says the LORD All-powerful. [12]"All the nations will call you blessed, because you will have a pleasant country," says the LORD All-powerful.

The LORD's Promise of Mercy

[13]The LORD says, "You have said terrible things about me.

END TIMES

Don't Know When

Just because James had been on a couple of camping trips before, read a few books and seen countless "survival" programmes on TV, he thought he knew everything. He confidently set up the camp fire and threw enough wood on it to last him the night. But as the flames grew higher, a gust of wind suddenly scattered the hot embers and before he knew it, trees all around him were ablaze. He managed to escape and raise the alarm, but by now the damage was done and he could only watch in horror as the fire spread across the hillside.

It is estimated that over two-thirds of forest fires are started – accidentally or on purpose – by humans. Thousands and thousands of acres of forest are destroyed every year and when they burn out of control because of dry conditions and strong winds. Even people's houses caught in the path of the advancing flames go up in smoke too.

But not all wildfires are preventable. Many are inevitable – they will always happen somewhere, at some time because lightning is a common cause of fires, as well.

In such cases, most of the vegetation, trees and plants, is destroyed by the flames, but some animals manage to escape, relying on their instinct and abilities to survive. Every kind of animal has a different strategy. Deer, foxes and bears move quickly, so they can often escape the area affected. Other animals can't move as fast, so mice, snakes and lizards burrow deep into underground nests to escape the fire above.

It's impossible to tell when forest fires are going to happen, but they will. And when they do, some things will be destroyed but some things will survive.

Read **Malachi 4:1–2**. It talks about a day when some people will be destroyed and others will live. But nobody knows when it will be.

* What day are the verses describing?
* How are those who "honour God" (verse 2) protected from the fire that will burn the "proud and evil people" (verse 1)?

Consider . . .

* ways in which you can honour God. Think of three practical things you can do, and share them with a friend so that they can help you do them.
* how you can talk to your non-Christian friends about the day of judgement.

For more, see . . .

* Psalm 68:1–4 (p.538)
* 1 Peter 4:4–5 (p.1360)

* Luke 3:7–9 (p.1042)

"But you ask, 'What have we said about you?'

14"You have said, 'It is useless to serve God. It did no good to obey his laws and to show the LORD All-powerful that we were sorry for what we did. 15So we say that proud people are happy. Evil people succeed. They challenge God and get away with it.'"

16Then those who honoured the LORD spoke with each other, and the LORD listened and heard them. The names of those who honoured the LORD and respected him were written in his presence in a book to be remembered.

17The LORD All-powerful says, "They belong to me; on that day they will be my very own. As a parent shows mercy to his child who serves him, I will show mercy to my people. 18You will again see the difference between good and evil people, between those who serve God and those who don't.

The Day of the LORD's Judging

4 "There is a day coming that will burn like a hot furnace, and all the proud and evil people will be like straw. On that day they will be completely burned up so that not a root or branch will be left," says the LORD All-powerful. 2"But for you who honour me, goodness will shine on you like the sun, with healing in its rays. You will jump around, like well-fed calves. 3Then you will crush the wicked like ashes under your feet on the day I will do this," says the LORD All-powerful.

4"Remember the teaching of Moses my servant, those laws and rules I gave to him on Mount Sinai for all the Israelites.

5"But I will send you Elijah the prophet d before that great and terrifying day of the LORD's judging. 6Elijah will help parents love their children and children love their parents. Otherwise, I will come and put a curse on the land."

NEW
Testament

Matthew

When?

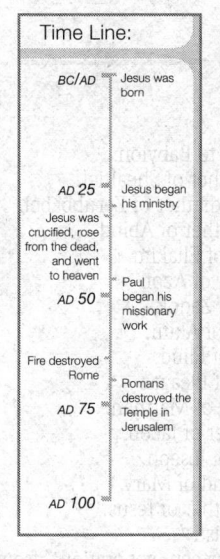

Time Line:

BC/AD	Jesus was born
AD 25	Jesus began his ministry
Jesus was crucified, rose from the dead, and went to heaven	
AD 50	Paul began his missionary work
Fire destroyed Rome	
AD 75	Romans destroyed the Temple in Jerusalem
AD 100	

Where?

Why Read This Book:

- Learn how Jesus filled the role of the Messiah – the Saviour whose coming was anticipated in the Old Testament (Matthew 1—4).
- Find guidelines for living (Matthew 5—7).
- Understand Jesus' power as shown through many miracles and stories (Matthew 8—20).
- See what happened to Jesus that led to his death and resurrection (Matthew 21—28).

Behind the Scenes:

When you go for a job interview, your employers will want to know all about you, particularly if you are to be trusted with people's lives or their money. They will ask questions about your background. Where do you come from? Have you kept your word in the past? Are you honest? Are you reliable?

In the book of Matthew, the author digs into Jesus' background. He starts by listing Jesus' family tree – or genealogy – and then starts telling his life story in a simple yet dynamic style. Matthew quotes the Old Testament more than any of the other three gospels (he uses 53 actual quotations, and many more passing references) in order to prove to us that Jesus is God's promised Messiah to the Jews and Saviour of the Gentiles. Thanks to the author's linking Old Testament prophecies with the life of Jesus, this book acts as a "bridge" for us between the Old and New Testaments.

The Jews expected God to send a political Messiah who would set up a powerful kingdom here on earth, and were shocked that Jesus didn't seem to fit into the role that they had imagined. ▷

GALILEE

Lake Galilee

Nazareth

Gadara

Matthew focuses mainly on Jesus' ministry in the region of Galilee (Matthew 4—18).

In the region of Gadara, Jesus cast out demons and sent them into pigs (Matthew 8:28–34).

Jesus was rejected at his home town of Nazareth (Matthew 13:53–58).

Mediterranean Sea

Jesus went to Jerusalem where he was killed (Matthew 20—28).

Jesus was baptised in the Jordan River (Matthew 3:13–17). Tradition places the event near here.

Jerusalem

Bethlehem

Dead Sea

Jesus was born in Bethlehem (Matthew 1:18–25; 2:1).

Note: Some of the events in Matthew are shown on the maps in Mark, Luke and John.

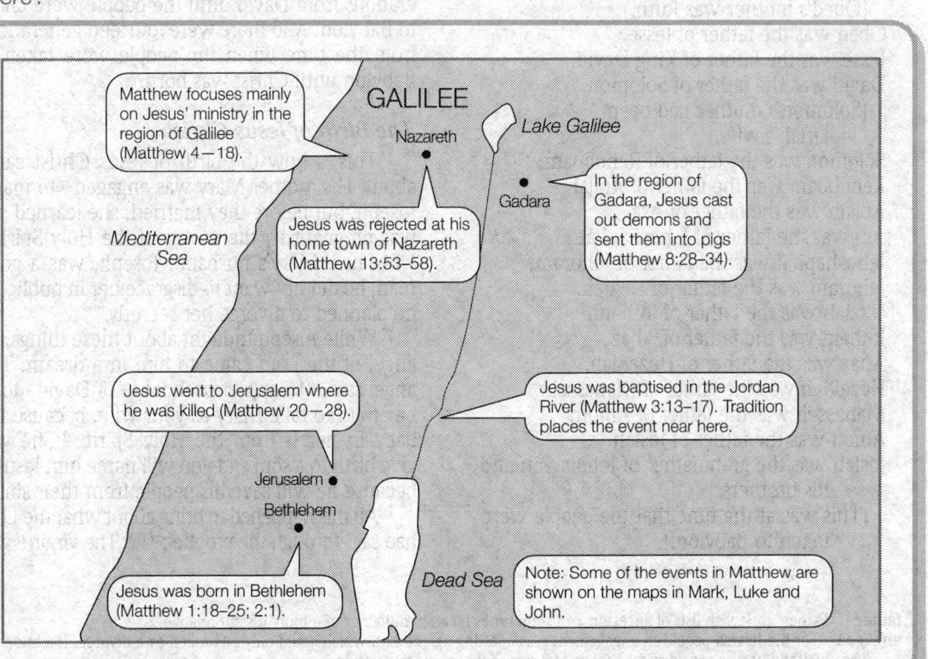

Behind the
Scenes (cont.):

Because of this, Matthew emphasises Jesus' teachings about what his kingdom would really be like, and proclaims him to be not only a king, but the King of Kings – the best of the best!

The grand finale of this book is a moving account of Jesus' last days on earth (Chapters 26–28), ending with his glorious resurrection and return to heaven.

The Family History of Jesus

1 This is the family history of Jesus Christ. He came from the family of David, and David came from the family of Abraham.

[2] Abraham was the father[n] of Isaac.

Isaac was the father of Jacob.

Jacob was the father of Judah and his brothers.

[3] Judah was the father of Perez and Zerah.

(Their mother was Tamar.)

Perez was the father of Hezron.

Hezron was the father of Ram.

[4] Ram was the father of Amminadab.

Amminadab was the father of Nahshon.

Nahshon was the father of Salmon.

[5] Salmon was the father of Boaz.

(Boaz's mother was Rahab.)

Boaz was the father of Obed.

(Obed's mother was Ruth.)

Obed was the father of Jesse.

[6] Jesse was the father of King David.

David was the father of Solomon.

(Solomon's mother had been Uriah's wife.)

[7] Solomon was the father of Rehoboam.

Rehoboam was the father of Abijah.

Abijah was the father of Asa.

[8] Asa was the father of Jehoshaphat.

Jehoshaphat was the father of Jehoram.

Jehoram was the father of Uzziah.

[9] Uzziah was the father of Jotham.

Jotham was the father of Ahaz.

Ahaz was the father of Hezekiah.

[10] Hezekiah was the father of Manasseh.

Manasseh was the father of Amon.

Amon was the father of Josiah.

[11] Josiah was the grandfather of Jehoiachin and his brothers.

(This was at the time that the people were taken to Babylon.)

[12] After they were taken to Babylon:

Jehoiachin was the father of Shealtiel.

Shealtiel was the grandfather of Zerubbabel.

[13] Zerubbabel was the father of Abiud.

Abiud was the father of Eliakim.

Eliakim was the father of Azor.

[14] Azor was the father of Zadok.

Zadok was the father of Akim.

Akim was the father of Eliud.

[15] Eliud was the father of Eleazar.

Eleazar was the father of Matthan.

Matthan was the father of Jacob.

[16] Jacob was the father of Joseph.

Joseph was the husband of Mary,

and Mary was the mother of Jesus.

Jesus is called the Christ. [d]

[17] So there were fourteen generations from Abraham to David. And there were fourteen generations from David until the people were taken to Babylon. And there were fourteen generations from the time when the people were taken to Babylon until Christ was born.

The Birth of Jesus Christ

[18] This is how the birth of Jesus Christ came about. His mother Mary was engaged[n] to marry Joseph, but before they married, she learned she was pregnant by the power of the Holy Spirit. [d] [19] Because Mary's husband, Joseph, was a good man, he did not want to disgrace her in public, so he planned to divorce her secretly.

[20] While Joseph thought about these things, an angel of the Lord came to him in a dream. The angel said, "Joseph, descendant[d] of David, don't be afraid to take Mary as your wife, because the baby in her is from the Holy Spirit. [21] She will give birth to a son, and you will name him Jesus,[n] because he will save his people from their sins." [22] All this happened to bring about what the Lord had said through the prophet:[d] [23] "The virgin[d] will

---

father   "Father" in Jewish lists of ancestors can sometimes mean grandfather or a more distant relative.

engaged   For the Jewish people an engagement was a lasting agreement, which could only be broken by a divorce. If a bride was unfaithful, it was considered adultery, and she could be put to death.

Jesus   The name Jesus means "salvation".

be pregnant. She will have a son, and they will name him Immanuel," [n] which means "God is with us".

[24] When Joseph woke up, he did what the Lord's angel had told him to do. Joseph took Mary as his wife, [25] but he did not have sexual relations with her until she gave birth to the son. And Joseph named him Jesus.

Wise Men Come to Visit Jesus

2 Jesus was born in the town of Bethlehem in Judea during the time when Herod was king. When Jesus was born, some wise men from the east came to Jerusalem. [2] They asked, "Where is the baby who was born to be the king of the Jews? We saw his star in the east and have come to worship him."

[3] When King Herod heard this, he was troubled, as well as all the people in Jerusalem. [4] Herod called a meeting of all the leading priests and teachers of the law and asked them where the Christ [d] would be born. [5] They answered, "In the town of Bethlehem in Judea. The prophet [d] wrote about this in the Scriptures: [d]

[6] 'But you, Bethlehem, in the land of Judah,
   are important among the tribes [d] of Judah.

A ruler will come from you
   who will be like a shepherd for my people Israel.' "

Micah 5:2

"The virgin . . . Immanuel," Quotation from Isaiah 7:14.

FOLLOWING GOD

What's Going On?

Jen had been acting strange for weeks. Up until now, Ian had really been enjoying going out with her, but recently things just hadn't felt right. She seemed to disappear without warning every now and then and Ian never really believed her excuses when she returned. Jen even stopped him from seeing her text messages and emails . . . but she'd never been bothered before.

It was getting Ian down. He still liked her – but why was she acting like this? Why couldn't they just relax with each other like before? She definitely had something on her mind. Maybe he should think about speaking to her, confronting her, perhaps even break up with her? He didn't want to make the wrong decision, so kept quiet and thought about it, to give himself some time.

One evening they were walking back to Ian's house when Jen suddenly suggested they walk a different route. Confused, but too preoccupied with his thoughts to argue, Ian followed. Before long, Jen stopped outside the community centre. "Let's go inside," she said. "But why?" Ian protested as he was dragged inside, "Why on earth do you want to come in here?"

"SURPRISE!" The room exploded into life – lights blinked on and music started up. The streamers finally settled and Ian looked round at the familiar faces. "Now do you understand why I've been acting a bit weird lately?" grinned Jen. "Hope it's worth it!"

Ian sighed and smiled. How had she kept it from him? How had he not guessed?

Read **Matthew 1:18–25**. Joseph, like Ian, was confused about what was going on with his relationship with his fiancée, Mary. And there was a surprise in store for him too!

* What difficult decisions did Joseph face?
* How might other people have viewed Joseph because of what he did?

Consider . . .

* whether you are confused by what God is doing in your life? Talk it through with an older Christian who may be able to advise and pray for you.
* taking time out to be with God and see what he says, before you make any big decisions in your life.

For more, see . . .

* Genesis 15:1–6 (p.16)
* 1 Timothy 4:7–10 (p.1311)

[7]Then Herod had a secret meeting with the wise men and learned from them the exact time they first saw the star. [8]He sent the wise men to Bethlehem, saying, "Look carefully for the child. When you find him, come and tell me so I can worship him too."

[9]After the wise men heard the king, they left. The star that they had seen in the east went before them until it stopped above the place where the child was. [10]When the wise men saw the star, they were filled with joy. [11]They came to the house where the child was and saw him with his mother, Mary, and they bowed down and worshipped him. They opened their gifts and gave him treasures of gold, frankincense *d* and myrrh. *d*

[12]But God warned the wise men in a dream not to go back to Herod, so they returned to their own country by a different way.

Jesus' Parents Take Him to Egypt

[13]After they left, an angel of the Lord came to Joseph in a dream and said, "Get up! Take the child and his mother and escape to Egypt, because Herod is starting to look for the child so he can kill him. Stay in Egypt until I tell you to return."

[14]So Joseph got up and left for Egypt during the night with the child and his mother. [15]And Joseph

WORSHIP

Enjoying God's Gifts

Sean hated Sunday mornings. "Sunday meant church, and that meant boring," he said. He felt boredom start with the first note of the organ, and he steadily suffered as worship went on. The best part to him was walking out of the church on the way home to lunch.

"Much of what happened there just didn't seem important," he said. "We sang a few old songs, read the Bible, listened to somebody talk for 30 minutes – how did any of that really worship God?"

The only thing that kept Sean's interest in church was the youth group. One Sunday evening, the group gathered at a nearby lake. They started a camp fire, and everyone watched a spectacular sunset. Sean sat in silence, enjoying the sunset's reflection on the still lake, until the last pink streak faded in the sky. "That's the most beautiful thing I've ever seen," he said.

Caroline overheard him. She had been sitting so quietly that he hadn't noticed her. She asked him, "Do you think God hears us when we say things like that? Do you think God likes it when we enjoy a sunset?"

"Yes," Sean replied. Then suddenly something "clicked" for Sean about worship. "Perhaps part of worship is enjoying something God has made," he said. "To watch a sunset, or the rain, and to be thankful that God had such good taste. Am I right?"

The next time he worshipped at church, he looked around at the people. Many of their faces wore the same expression of awe Sean had felt at the lake.

"Maybe this feeling of 'Wow!' is worship," he thought. "It isn't the motions you go through. It's when you see or hear or remember things so good that you have to catch your breath, and then thank and praise God for them."

In **Matthew 2:1–12**, read about the "Wow!" the wise men must have felt when they saw and worshipped the infant Jesus.

* In what ways might the wise men have felt as Sean did while he watched the sunset?
* When have you experienced a sense of "Wow!" in worship, either in or out of church?

Consider . . .

* noticing the ways that your church worships God and finding out the meaning of each part of the service.
* visiting a few other churches with your family or friends, and seeing what each church does differently.

For more, see . . .

* Psalm 19:1–6 (p.510)
* Revelation 4:1–11 (p.1391)
* Luke 9:28–36 (p.1055)

stayed in Egypt until Herod died. This happened to bring about what the Lord had said through the prophet: *d* "I called my son out of Egypt." *n*

Herod Kills the Baby Boys

[16]When Herod saw that the wise men had tricked him, he was furious. So he gave an order to kill all the baby boys in Bethlehem and in the surrounding area who were two years old or younger. This was in keeping with the time he learnt from the wise men. [17]So what God had said through the prophet *d* Jeremiah came true:
[18]"A voice was heard in Ramah
    of painful crying and deep sadness:
Rachel crying for her children.
    She refused to be comforted,
    because her children are dead." *Jeremiah 31:15*

"**I called . . . Egypt.**" Quotation from Hosea 11:1.

FREEDOM

Going to a Safe Place

White journalist Donald Woods openly opposed the South African government's cruel policies towards its black people. In the early 1970s, Woods began to publish a newspaper that chronicled the government's repressive actions.

Woods befriended several leaders in the black liberation movement, including Steve Biko, and he grew even more committed to freedom for blacks. In spite of government and police warnings, Woods refused to turn his back on his friends.

The political situation soon worsened in South Africa. The police stepped up arrests of black leaders, who were later found tortured and often dead. In 1977, Steve Biko was arrested. Woods worked furiously for his friend's release, but faced unbending opposition from officials.

When Woods personally discovered the dead body of his tortured friend, he blasted the official explanation that Biko's death was accidental. While questioning the doctor, Woods heard him tearfully admit to falsifying the autopsy report. Woods, in his raging grief, openly accused the government of murdering Biko. South Africa's response was to arrest Woods.

After Woods had been held under house arrest for three months, his friends in the liberation movement devised a plan for him to escape from the country. After escaping the guards, he crossed the country disguised as a priest. Along the way, sympathisers risked their lives to see him safely along. But he finally made it to the bordering country of Lesotho.

Woods' family also escaped and joined him in Lesotho. They moved to England, where Woods wrote the story of South Africa's cruelty. If he had not been able to escape, his story and Steve Biko's would not have been told. Because of changes in South Africa, Woods has been able to return. His story – and others like it – directly influenced these changes.

Joseph, Mary and Jesus also had to flee from their country so that Jesus could grow up and fulfil God's purpose for him. Read their story in **Matthew 2:13–23**.

* Why did Joseph and Mary and Donald Woods temporarily leave their homes instead of facing their persecution?
* Have you ever had to leave a "comfort zone" in your life to follow God? What happened?

Consider . . .

* watching the film *Cry Freedom* (about Donald Woods) and talking about whether God's freedom is similar or different, and why.
* looking up the word "freedom" in the dictionary, and then defining "Christian freedom" in your own words.

For more, see . . .

* Exodus 12:31–50 (p.70)
* John 8:31–36 (p.1110)
* Galatians 5:13–15 (p.1263)

Joseph and Mary Return

[19]After Herod died, an angel of the Lord spoke to Joseph in a dream while he was in Egypt. [20]The angel said, "Get up! Take the child and his mother and go to the land of Israel, because the people who were trying to kill the child are now dead."

> **Sidelight**
>
> The "three kings" traditionally associated with Matthew 2:1–12 were probably neither "three" nor "kings". Some sources suggest that as many as a hundred of these philosophers, doctors and astrologers visited Jesus. Now that would make a Christmas play! The traditional idea of "three" comes from the three gifts they brought – gold, frankincense and myrrh.

[21]So Joseph took the child and his mother and went to Israel. [22]But he heard that Archelaus was now king in Judea since his father Herod had died. So Joseph was afraid to go there. After being warned in a dream, he went to the area of Galilee, [23]to a town called Nazareth, and lived there. And so what God had said through the prophets[d] came true: "He will be called a Nazarene."[n]

The Work of John the Baptist

3 About that time John the Baptist[d] began preaching in the desert area of Judea. [2]John said, "Change your hearts and lives because the kingdom of heaven is near." [3]John the Baptist is the one Isaiah the prophet[d] was talking about when he said:

"This is a voice of one
    who calls out in the desert:
'Prepare the way for the Lord.
    Make the road straight for him.'"   *Isaiah 40:3*

[4]John's clothes were made from camel's hair, and he wore a leather belt around his waist. For food, he ate locusts[d] and wild honey. [5]Many people came from Jerusalem and Judea and all the area around the Jordan River to hear John. [6]They confessed their sins, and he baptised them in the Jordan River.

[7]Many of the Pharisees[d] and Sadducees[d] came to the place where John was baptising people.

When John saw them, he said, "You are all snakes! Who warned you to run away from God's coming punishment? [8]Do the things that show you really have changed your hearts and lives. [9]And don't think you can say to yourselves, 'Abraham is our father.' I tell you that God could make children for Abraham from these rocks. [10]The axe is now ready to cut down the trees,

> **Sidelight**
>
> Many people today talk about eating "organic" foods, but John the Baptist was doing this almost 2,000 years ago! His diet of locusts and wild honey (Matthew 3:4) makes some people think that he might have been part of the desert Qumran community. These were people who lived in caves above the Dead Sea, and it was in these caves that the Dead Sea Scrolls – a selection of some of the earliest manuscripts of the Bible, and other writings – were discovered in 1947.

and every tree that does not produce good fruit will be cut down and thrown into the fire.[n]

[11]"I baptise you with water to show that your hearts and lives have changed. But there is one coming after me who is greater than I am, whose sandals I am not good enough to carry. He will baptise you with the Holy Spirit[d] and fire. [12]He will come ready to clean the grain, separating the good grain from the chaff.[d] He will put the good part of the grain into his barn, but he will burn the chaff with a fire that cannot be put out."[n]

Jesus is Baptised by John

[13]At that time Jesus came from Galilee to the Jordan River and wanted John to baptise him. [14]But John tried to stop him, saying, "Why do you come to me to be baptised? I need to be baptised by you!"

[15]Jesus answered, "Let it be this way for now. We should do all things that are God's will." So John agreed to baptise Jesus.

[16]As soon as Jesus was baptised, he came up out of the water. Then heaven opened, and he saw God's Spirit[d] coming down on him like a dove. [17]And a voice from heaven said, "This is my Son, whom I love, and I am very pleased with him."

Nazarene   A person from the city of Nazareth, a name probably meaning "branch" (see Isaiah 11:1).
The axe . . . fire.   This means that God is ready to punish his people who do not obey him.
He will . . . out.   This means that Jesus will come to separate good people from bad people, saving the good and punishing the bad.

The Temptation of Jesus

4 Then the Spirit *d* led Jesus into the desert to be tempted by the devil. ²Jesus ate nothing for 40 days and nights. After this, he was very hungry. ³The devil came to Jesus to tempt him, saying, "If you are the Son of God, tell these rocks to become bread."

⁴Jesus answered, "It is written in the Scriptures, *d* 'A person does not live by eating only bread, but by everything God says.' " *n*

⁵Then the devil led Jesus to the holy city of Jerusalem and put him on a high place of the Temple. *d* ⁶The devil said, "If you are the Son of God, jump down, because it is written in the Scriptures:

'He has put his angels in charge
    of you.
They will catch you in their hands
so that you will not hit your foot on a
    rock.' "   *Psalm 91:11–12*

⁷Jesus answered him, "It also says in the Scriptures, 'Do not test the Lord your God.' " *n*

⁸Then the devil led Jesus to the top of a very high mountain and showed him all the kingdoms of the world and all their splendour. ⁹The devil said, "If you will bow down and worship me, I will give you all these things."

'A person . . . says.'   Quotation from Deuteronomy 8:3.
'Do . . . God.'   Quotation from Deuteronomy 6:16.

GOD'S WILL

Are You Sure, Lord?

Jon sat in his supervisor's office discussing whether or not he should to stay for a second year as leader of his mission team. It was a hard decision. Jon had laid down his ambition of becoming a rock drummer to do this and the first year had been really tough. After praying about it and asking advice from friends and church leaders, he felt that despite the challenges, it *was* God's will for him to do a second year.

Then a few weeks later, Jon's friend Kate phoned him: "Amazing news, I've just met a band in America that needs a new drummer for their US tour. I told them about you and they want you to join! This *must* be from God! It's everything you've dreamed of!" Jon was stunned – this band was really famous. This was a once in a lifetime opportunity!

Jon knew God would never want him to do something that involved selfishness and broken promises, so he couldn't join the American band with any integrity, even though he wanted to so badly. Kate thought he was crazy to reject the offer, but Jon knew it was the only godly choice.

God really blessed his decision and used the situation to strengthen Jon's character. He and his team's ministry was really successful that year, leading many students to Christ. Years later, God even surprised him with better musical opportunities.

Read **Matthew 3:13–17** to see how John the Baptist also found God's will confusing and yet perfect. He was expecting Jesus to baptise *him* but Jesus insisted it should be the other way round!

- How can this passage help us when we see God act in a surprising way, contrary to what we were expecting?
- Why is it not always God's will for us to be happy and comfortable? Look at John the Baptist's lifestyle in the rest of chapter 3.

Consider . . .

- how you work out what God's will for you is. Do you just go by your feelings or do you also pray, read the Bible and ask for wisdom from older, wiser Christians?
- your ambitions, hopes and dreams? If God asked you to give them up for a different calling, could you?

For more, see . . .

- Isaiah 55:8–11 (p.699)
- Ephesians 2:10 (p.1271)

- Matthew 26:36–42 (p.990)
- 2 Peter 1:3–11 (p.1365)

[10]Jesus said to the devil, "Go away from me, Satan! It is written in the Scriptures, 'You must worship the Lord your God and serve only him.' "[n]

[11]So the devil left Jesus, and angels came and took care of him.

Jesus Begins Work in Galilee

[12]When Jesus heard that John had been put in prison, he went back to Galilee. [13]He left Nazareth and went to live in Capernaum, a town near Lake Galilee, in the area near Zebulun and Naphtali. [14]Jesus did this to bring about what the prophet[d] Isaiah had said:

[15]"Land of Zebulun and land of Naphtali
    along the sea,
 beyond the Jordan River.
    This is Galilee where the non-Jewish people
        live.
[16]These people who live in darkness
    will see a great light.
 They live in a place covered with the
        shadows of death,
    but a light will shine on them."   *Isaiah 9:1–2*

Jesus Chooses Some Followers

[17]From that time Jesus began to preach, saying, "Change your hearts and lives, because the kingdom of heaven is near."

[18]As Jesus was walking by Lake Galilee, he saw two brothers, Simon (called Peter) and his brother Andrew. They were throwing a net into the lake because they were fishermen. [19]Jesus said, "Come follow me, and I will make you fish for people." [20]So Simon and Andrew immediately left their nets and followed him.

[21]As Jesus continued walking by Lake Galilee, he saw two other brothers, James and John, the sons of Zebedee. They were in a boat with their father Zebedee, mending their nets. Jesus told them to come with him. [22]Immediately they left the boat and their father, and they followed Jesus.

Jesus Teaches and Heals People

[23]Jesus went everywhere in Galilee, teaching in the synagogues,[d] preaching the Good News[d] about the kingdom of heaven, and healing all the people's diseases and sicknesses. [24]The news about Jesus spread all over Syria, and people brought all the sick to him. They were suffering from different kinds of diseases. Some were in great pain, some had demons,[d] some were epileptics[n] and some were paralysed. Jesus healed all of them. [25]Many people from Galilee, the Ten Towns,[n] Jerusalem, Judea and the land across the Jordan River followed him.

Jesus Teaches the People

5 When Jesus saw the crowds, he went up on a hill and sat down. His followers came to him, [2]and he began to teach them, saying:
[3]"Those people who know they have great
        spiritual needs are happy,
    because the kingdom of heaven belongs to
        them.
[4]Those who are sad now are happy,
    because God will comfort them.
[5]Those who are humble are happy,
    because the earth will belong
        to them.
[6]Those who want to do right more than
        anything else are happy,
    because God will fully satisfy them.
[7]Those who show mercy to others
        are happy,
    because God will show mercy to them.
[8]Those who are pure in their thinking are
        happy,
    because they will be with God.
[9]Those who work to bring peace are happy,
    because God will call them his children.
[10]Those who are treated badly for doing good
        are happy,
    because the kingdom of heaven belongs to
        them.
[11]"People will insult you and hurt you. They will lie and say all kinds of evil things about you because you follow me. But when they do, you will be happy. [12]Rejoice and be glad, because you have a great reward waiting for you in heaven. People did the same evil things to the prophets[d] who lived before you.

You are like Salt and Light

[13]"You are the salt of the earth. But if the salt loses its salty taste, it cannot be made salty again. It is good for nothing, except to be thrown out and walked on.

[14]"You are the light that gives light to the world. A city that is built on a hill cannot be hidden. [15]And people don't hide a light under a bowl. They put it on a lampstand so the light shines for all the people in the house. [16]In the same way, you should be a light for other people.

'You . . . him.' Quotation from Deuteronomy 6:13.
epileptic A person with a disease that causes them sometimes to lose control of their body and perhaps faint, shake strongly or be unable to move.
Ten Towns In Greek, called "Decapolis". It was an area east of Lake Galilee that once had ten main towns.

Live so that they will see the good things you do and will praise your Father in heaven.

The Importance of the Law

17"Don't think that I have come to destroy the law of Moses or the teaching of the prophets. *d* I have not come to destroy them but to bring about what they said. 18I tell you the truth, nothing will disappear from the law until heaven and earth are gone. Not even the smallest letter or the smallest part of a letter will be lost until everything has happened. 19Whoever refuses to obey any command and teaches other people not to obey that command will be the least important in the kingdom of heaven. But whoever obeys the commands and teaches other people to obey them will be great in the kingdom of heaven. 20I tell you that if you are no more obedient than the teachers of the law and the Pharisees, *d* you will never enter the kingdom of heaven.

Jesus Teaches About Anger

21"You have heard that it was said to our people long ago, 'You must not murder anyone. *n* Anyone who murders another will be judged.' 22But I tell you, if you are angry with a brother or sister, *n* you will be judged. If you say bad things

You . . . anyone.   Quotation from Exodus 20:13; Deuteronomy 5:17.
brother . . . sister   Although the Greek text reads "brother" here and throughout this book, Jesus' words were meant for the entire church, including men and women.

HAPPINESS

Turning it on its Head

Lauren was in two minds about getting along to football practise. She loved the game and she was one of the best players at the club, but training was never much fun. That was down to the coach, David. His favourite thing to shout at the team was, "If you're smiling you're not training hard enough!" He was a football coach but he would never actually use footballs! David would have them doing endless laps of the training field, sit-ups and shuttle runs. Every week was the same, no variety . . . and no footballs! It just wasn't fun any more.

As she got to the ground, there was an unfamiliar figure standing in the middle of the team. Someone else was taking the training session. Lauren sat down with the rest of her team and the new coach introduced herself. Rachel was going to be taking the training from now on. David had moved to another team.

The next two hours were great! Lauren hadn't laughed so much in ages. They trained hard but Rachel made it fun. Relay races, piggyback races and mini competitions between the players . . . they even used footballs! Rachel explained that if the team was going to be a winning team they had to get on together. Next week was going to be a social at the ten-pin bowling alley. Rachel was turning everything they'd learnt about being a team on its head.

As Lauren cycled home, she had a huge smile on her face . . . she just felt sorry for the team that David was now training!
Read through **Matthew 5:1–12**.

* Have you ever had someone teach you in a new way that challenges how you think?
* In this passage, what do you think Jesus says to the crowd that's new?

Consider . . .

* making a list or drawing the things that make you happy. Compare your list to Matthew 5:1–12. What would Jesus' list look like?
* talking to God and asking him to help you understand what real happiness is.

For more, see . . .

* Psalm 1:1–3 (p.500)
* John 15:5–11 (p.1125)
* John 10:10 (p.1114)

to a brother or sister, you will be judged by the council. And if you call someone a fool, you will be in danger of the fire of hell.

23"So when you offer your gift to God at the altar, and you remember that your brother or sister has something against you, 24leave your gift there at the altar. Go and make peace with that person, and then come and offer your gift.

25"If your enemy is taking you to court, become friends quickly, before you go to court. Otherwise, your enemy might turn you over to the judge, and the judge might give you to a guard to put you in jail. 26I tell you the truth, you will not leave there until you have paid everything you owe.

Jesus Teaches About Sexual Sin

27"You have heard that it was said, 'You must not be guilty of adultery.' n 28But I tell you that if anyone looks at a woman and wants to sin sexually with her, in his mind he has already done that sin with the woman. 29If your right eye causes you to sin, take it out and throw it away. It is better to lose one part of your body than to have your whole body thrown into hell. 30If your right hand causes you to sin, cut it off and throw it away. It is better to lose one

'You . . . adultery.' Quotation from Exodus 20:14; Deuteronomy 5:18.

Grain of Truth

Salt is used by humans in more than 14,000 ways. Did you know that:

* adding a pinch of salt to milk will keep it fresh longer.
* if you get stung by a bee, you should wet the spot with water immediately and cover it with salt to relieve the pain.
* sprinkling a little salt in canvas shoes occasionally will take up the moisture and help remove bad smells.

Read **Matthew 5:13–16** and see how Jesus uses salt as an example of how to be a Christian.

Salt used to have a much higher value than it does now. It was incredibly handy to have. Romans even got paid in salt rather than money sometimes! It had so many uses: it kept food fresh (in a time when there were no fridges), it purified food, stopped it from rotting and, just like with the bee sting, it was used for healing wounds.

When we understand how important salt was to the people Jesus was speaking to, we can begin to see what Jesus meant by saying that we should be like salt to the world. Jesus is saying that, as followers of him, we are to be like salt in our society: we are to purify it by our behaviour and keep the good things about it alive and fresh, to stop the rot, be examples of his kingdom, and bring God's healing.

* What do you think Jesus means about salt losing its saltiness?
* Can you think of a time when someone you know has been a really good light – where people have seen the good things they have done, and seen Jesus through them?

Consider . . .

* how you can make sure you don't lose your saltiness, so that you can always demonstrate God's love to people around you.
* getting a sachet of salt and sprinkling it somewhere where you want to be a light for God. As you do so, pray that God will help you as you live for him in that place.

For more, see . . .

* Isaiah 9:2–7 (p.649)
* 1 John 1:5–6 (p.1371)

* 1 Corinthians 13:1–7 (p.1232)

part of your body than for your whole body to go into hell.

Jesus Teaches About Divorce

[31]"It was also said, 'Anyone who divorces his wife must give her a written divorce paper.'[n] [32]But I tell you that anyone who divorces his wife forces her to be guilty of adultery.[d] The only reason for a man to divorce his wife is if she has sexual relations with another man. And anyone who marries that divorced woman is guilty of adultery.

Make Promises Carefully

[33]"You have heard that it was said to our people long ago, "Don't break your promises, but keep the promises you make to the Lord.'[n] [34]But I tell you, never swear an oath. Don't swear an oath using the name of heaven, because heaven is God's throne. [35]Don't swear an oath using the

'Anyone . . . divorce paper.'   Quotation from Deuteronomy 24:1.
'Don't . . . Lord.'   This refers to Leviticus 19:12; Numbers 30:2; Deuteronomy 19:21.

ANGER

Beating the Bully

Life wasn't going well for twelve-year-old Carl. His parents had recently divorced, and he and his mum had moved from their farm to the city. Carl felt alone in his new school, which seemed huge. But now there was another problem. Another student, Darren, had threatened to beat Carl up after school. And he meant it.

After the last bell on Thursday, Carl tried to slip out of school without being seen. He wanted to get home quickly. As he turned a corner, Darren was waiting for him.

Carl's heart pounded with fear. Darren attacked and landed blow after blow. Carl tried to fight back, but Darren was several years older and much stronger. After a few minutes of a one-sided fight, Darren left his victim lying on the pavement. Carl got up slowly and walked the rest of the way home. At the front door, his mother saw his torn clothes, his bloody face and hands. Carl told her what had happened and asked, "Mum, why are people like that? Why does Darren like to hurt other people?"

"I don't know, darling," she answered. "It doesn't make sense. There must be something wrong with him." Carl knew that she was upset, although she was trying to hide her anger towards Darren.

Later that evening, Carl looked at his reflection in the hall mirror. His face was already puffy and purple. He looked at his mum and said, "I look peculiar, don't I?"

She laughed, and then he began to laugh. "You've certainly looked better," she said, with a sad smile. "How do you feel?"

"Sore," he said. "And a bit scared. But you know what? I'm not really cross with Darren. What you said about there being something wrong – I think there is. I thought I'd hate him. But I don't. I feel sort of sorry for him. I don't think anybody likes him. Perhaps that's why he does those things."

Jesus offers several ways for us to respond when we're angered and hurt by others. In **Matthew 5:17–26**, read how Jesus might have reacted.

- Did Carl react in the way Jesus commands? Why or why not?
- If Darren had beaten you up, how would you have handled your anger and hurt? What are some ways to handle the situation, according to the passage?

Consider . . .

- watching how some TV characters handle their anger. What would happen in the real world if people handled their anger in those ways?
- making peace with someone with whom you have a conflict before you next attend church.

For more, see . . .

- Proverbs 15:1 (p.602)
- Ephesians 4:17–32 (p.1273)
- Matthew 5:38–48 (p.946)

name of the earth, because the earth belongs to God. Don't swear an oath using the name of Jerusalem, because that is the city of the great King. [36]Don't even swear by your own head, because you cannot make one hair on your head become white or black. [37]Say only yes if you mean yes, and no if you mean no. If you say more than yes or no, it is from the Evil One.

Don't Fight Back

[38]"You have heard that it was said, 'An eye for an eye, and a tooth for a tooth.' [n] [39]But I tell you, don't stand up against an evil person. If someone slaps you on the right cheek, turn to him the other cheek as well. [40]If someone wants to sue you in court and take your shirt, let him have your coat as well. [41]If someone forces you to go with him a kilometre, go with him 2 kilometres. [42]If a person asks you for something, give it to him. Don't refuse to give to someone who wants to borrow from you.

Love All People

[43]"You have heard that it was said, 'Love your neighbour [n] and hate your enemies.' [44]But I say to you, love your enemies. Pray for those who hurt you. [45]If you do this, you will be true children of your Father in heaven. He causes

---

'An eye . . . tooth.'   Quotation from Exodus 21:24; Leviticus 24:20; Deuteronomy 19:21.
Love your neighbour   Quotation from Leviticus 19:18.

SEXUALITY

How Far's Too Far?

Unlike Gemma, Matt wasn't a Christian but early on in the relationship, Gemma had explained that as a Christian she didn't want to have sex before she got married. Unlike guys before him, Matt seemed to totally understand and told her that was fine.

During their 3-month relationship, Gemma and Matt had grown really close. He was sweet, caring and they were really open and shared everything in their lives. However, as they grew closer, so did their physical relationship. The line got pushed further and further forward.

Searching for answers, Gemma turned to the Bible. She needed to know how far was too far. It was obvious that God created sex for marriage but that just wasn't specific enough! She wanted details – a checklist of "OK" and "not OK". In a flash of revelation Gemma suddenly thought, "What if sex isn't just about my virginity?" In that moment, she understood that she and Matt had experienced things together that God intended for marriage. It all fell into place.

Gemma knew she'd sinned, but now she faced a decision. Did she stay with Matt and finish what she'd started or did she end the relationship and go back to God? This was the tougher option. It involved facing up to her actions, saying sorry, receiving forgiveness and changing the way she lived – with no Matt.
Read **Matthew 5:27–37**.

• Why do you think Jesus feels so strongly about sexual sin?
• Look at what Jesus says in verse 37. Does your body language matter as much as what you say?

Consider . . .

• how far is too far, and how this affects your current and future relationships.
• talking through these issues with someone wise who you trust. Be accountable to them and give them permission to ask how you're doing on your new rules.

For more, see . . .

• 1 Corinthians 6:12–13 (p.1221)
• Hebrews 13:4 (p.1345)

• 1 Thessalonians 4:3–4 (p.1298)

the sun to rise on good people and on evil people, and he sends rain to those who do right and to those who do wrong. ⁴⁶If you love only the people who love you, you will get no reward. Even the tax collectors do that. ⁴⁷And if you are nice only to your friends, you are no better than other people. Even those who don't know God are nice to their friends. ⁴⁸So you must be perfect, just as your Father in heaven is perfect.

Jesus Teaches About Giving

6 "Be careful! When you do good things, don't do them in front of people to be seen by them. If you do that, you will have no reward from your Father in heaven.

²"When you give to the poor, don't be like the hypocrites. *d* They blow trumpets in the synagogues *d* and on the streets so that people will see them and honour them. I tell you the truth, those hypocrites already have their full

---

PEACE

The Second Mile

Tracy Collins pulled her car into the drive and groaned when she saw that the front door was ajar. "Not again!" she fumed. She knew her flat had been burgled for the third time.

When the police arrived, they helped her make a list of what was missing. "Not that there was much left to take," she said. "He really cleaned me out the first time."

The police were virtually positive who the thief was. After the previous burglary, one of the officers had let the name slip: Tim O'Conner. They recognised his style.

Tracy worked in an inner-city mission distributing food and clothing to needy people. Among the volunteers were adults placed on probation. Instead of going to prison, they were required to provide community service.

Several weeks after the third burglary, Tracy interviewed a new probationer, filling out a form that would record the hours worked. "What's your name?" she asked, her pen ready on the correct line.

"Tim O'Conner," he said.

Tracy choked, and looked into the young man's eyes. He sat calmly, waiting for the next question. He was well-dressed, well-groomed, and had good manners. She shook her head as if to clear it, and turned the document back to the first page, searching for the line that would tell her why he had been convicted. "Burglary," it read.

"Is something wrong?" he asked in a polite voice.

"He has no idea I'm one of his victims," she thought angrily. Then her anger turned into compassion as she wondered what made him break into other people's homes. "No," she answered. "Let's finish this form."

After they finished the interview, Tim was given a job. "Thanks," he said. "I'm glad the judge sent me here."

"So am I," Tracy said.

Tracy was surprised when she didn't feel like hitting back at Tim. Then she realised Jesus' words in **Matthew 5:38–48** must have helped her handle her anger in a peaceful manner.

* In light of the passage, do you think Tracy did the right thing?
* Does "turning the other cheek" mean that Jesus wants people to walk all over your rights? Why or why not?

Consider . . .

* listing the "normal" ways for handling conflicts, and then listing the "cheek-turning", peaceful ways next to them. Promise yourself to "turn the other cheek" the next time a conflict arises.
* walking away from a fight or keeping your cool in an argument in the future.

For more, see . . .

* Psalm 37 (p.521)
* Colossians 3:12–13 (p.1293)
* Luke 6:27–36 (p.1048)

reward. ³So when you give to the poor, don't let anyone know what you are doing. ⁴Your giving should be done in secret. Your Father can see what is done in secret, and he will reward you.

Jesus Teaches About Prayer

⁵"When you pray, don't be like the hypocrites. ᵈ They love to stand in the synagogues ᵈ and on the street corners and pray so people will see them. I tell you the truth, they already have their full reward. ⁶When you pray, you should go into your room and close the door and pray to your Father who cannot be seen. Your Father can see what is done in secret, and he will reward you.

⁷"And when you pray, don't be like those people who don't know God. They continue saying things that mean nothing, thinking that God will hear them because of their many words. ⁸Don't be like them, because your Father knows the things you need before you ask him. ⁹So when you pray, you should pray like this:

'Our Father in heaven,
  may your name always be kept holy.
¹⁰May your kingdom come
  and what you want be done,
    here on earth as it is in heaven.
¹¹Give us the food we need for each day.
¹²Forgive us for our sins,

just as we have forgiven those who sinned
  against us.
¹³And do not cause us to be tempted,
  but save us from the Evil One.'
¹⁴Yes, if you forgive others for their sins, your Father in heaven will also forgive you for your sins. ¹⁵But if you don't forgive others, your Father in heaven will not forgive your sins.

Jesus Teaches About Worship

¹⁶"When you give up eating, ⁿ don't put on a sad face like the hypocrites. ᵈ They make their faces look sad to show people they are giving up eating. I tell you the truth, those hypocrites already have their full reward. ¹⁷So when you give up eating, comb your hair and wash your face. ¹⁸Then people will not know that you are giving up eating, but your Father, whom you cannot see, will see you. Your Father sees what is done in secret, and he will reward you.

God is More Important than Money

¹⁹"Don't store treasures for yourselves here on earth where moths and rust will destroy them and thieves can break in and steal them. ²⁰But store your treasures in heaven where they cannot be destroyed by moths or rust and where thieves cannot break in and steal them. ²¹Your heart will be where your treasure is.

²²"The eye is a light for the body. If your eyes are good, your whole body will be full of light. ²³But if your eyes are evil, your whole body will be full of darkness. And if the only light you have is really darkness, then you have the worst darkness.

²⁴"No one can serve two masters. The person will hate one master and love the other, or will follow one master and refuse to follow the other. You cannot serve both God and worldly riches.

Don't Worry

²⁵"So I tell you, don't worry about the food or drink you need to live, or about the clothes you need for your body. Life is more than food, and the body is more than clothes. ²⁶Look at the birds in the air. They don't plant or harvest or store food in barns, but your heavenly Father feeds them. And you know that you are worth much more than the birds. ²⁷You cannot add any time to your life by worrying about it. ²⁸"And why do you worry about clothes? Look at how the lilies in the field grow. They don't

---

give up eating This is called "fasting". The people would give up eating for a special time of prayer and worship to God. It was also done to show sadness and disappointment.

work or make clothes for themselves. ²⁹But I tell you that even Solomon with his riches was not dressed as beautifully as one of these flowers. ³⁰God clothes the grass in the field, which is alive today but tomorrow is thrown into the fire. So you can be even more sure that God will clothe you. Don't have so little faith! ³¹Don't worry and say, 'What will we eat?' or 'What will we drink?' or 'What will we wear?' ³²The people who don't know God keep trying to get these things, and your Father in heaven knows you need them. ³³The thing you should want most is God's kingdom and doing what God wants. Then all these other things you need will be given to you. ³⁴So don't worry about tomorrow, because tomorrow will have its own worries. Each day has enough trouble of its own.

Be Careful About Judging Others

7 "Don't judge other people, or you will be judged. ²You will be judged in the same way that you judge others, and the amount you give to others will be given to you.

³"Why do you notice the little piece of dust in your friend's eye, but you don't notice the big piece of wood in your own eye? ⁴How can you say to your friend, "Let me take that little piece of dust out of your eye'? Look at yourself! You still have that big piece of wood in your own eye. ⁵You hypocrite! *d* First, take the wood out of your

---

PRIORITIES

Where's Your Heart?

Chris loved watching films – so much so that he tried to buy every one ever made. As soon as he had enough money, you'd find him in the local shop rummaging through the DVDs as if his life depended on it!

His films, known simply as "The Collection" took pride of place in Chris's bedroom. Sometimes they were organised alphabetically, sometimes in the order they were released and once, only once, in the order that Chris had bought them.

"The Collection" was the most important thing in Chris's life . . . until Helen started going to his youth group.

Helen was intelligent, funny, pretty and, most importantly, she had great taste in films. Helen was nice! On Thursday evenings, she volunteered at the old people's home and she gave all her old clothes to the local homeless shelter. She made friends with people that no one else liked and always helped out around the house.

The more time that Chris spent with Helen, the less time he spent watching films. He didn't even notice the change at first, until one day he bought a bunch of flowers for an old lady in his church that he hardly even knew. As he handed the florist his ten-pound note he thought about the DVDs he was giving up and "The Collection" sitting at home, sadly neglected . . . but he handed the money over anyway.

In **Matthew 6:19–21** Jesus is asking his disciples where their treasure is and what their priorities are. It wasn't a bad thing that Chris had lots of DVDs, the important thing was where his heart was.

* According to the passage, where should your treasure be?
* Where would making friends with people or giving clothes to a homeless shelter be described as storing treasure?

Consider . . .

* making a list of all the different "treasures" in your life. Make two columns, one for treasures that you can only enjoy here on earth and another for those that have heavenly and eternal value.
* where your treasure is. Ask God to be your treasure and to have your heart.

For more, see . . .

* 1 Corinthians 13:13 (p.1232)
* 1 Timothy 6:17–19 (p.1314)

own eye. Then you will see clearly to take the dust out of your friend's eye.

6"Don't give holy things to dogs, and don't throw your pearls before pigs. Pigs will only trample on them, and dogs will turn to attack you.

Ask God for What You Need

7"Ask, and God will give to you. Search, and you will find. Knock, and the door will open for you. 8Yes, everyone who asks will receive. Everyone who searches will find. And everyone who knocks will have the door opened.

9"If your children ask for bread, which of you would give them a stone? 10Or if your children ask for a fish, would you give them a snake? 11Even though you are bad, you know how to give good gifts to your children. How much more will your heavenly Father give good things to those who ask him!

12"Do to others what you want them to do to you. This is the meaning of the law of Moses and the teaching of the prophets. *d*

The Way to Heaven is Hard

13"Enter through the narrow gate. The gate is wide and the road is wide that leads to hell, and many people enter through that gate. 14But the gate is small and the road is narrow that leads to true life. Only a few people find that road.

People Know You by Your Actions

15"Be careful of false prophets. *d* They come to you looking gentle like sheep, but they are really dangerous like wolves. 16You will know these

---

WORRYING

Baby Blues

Tom's mum had just had another baby.

She'd spent the whole pregnancy worrying – "Will the nursery be ready in time?" "Will I be able to cope with another baby?" "Will we have enough money?" Tom could see she was excited about this new addition but at the same time was scared about the responsibility, about the worry that this new life would bring.

She needn't have worried. Grace was perfect. Unlike her mum, Grace simply didn't have the capacity to worry about anything. When she was cold, Tom put a blanket on her. When she needed feeding, Tom's mum fed her. When times were busy, people from church offered to baby-sit. Everything Grace needed was provided for her by those who loved her.

Even though Tom and his mum were grown up, both needed God in the same way. As children of God, just as they provided for Grace, God provides for their every need.

There was no need for Tom's mum to ever have worried because God has promised to look after them.

Somebody once said, "Worry is like a rocking chair. It gives you something to do but doesn't get you anywhere."

Read **Matthew 6:25–34**.

* What does this passage say we should think about when we are tempted to worry?
* Read Genesis 1:26 and 29–30. Here we are told that humans alone are made in his image and are "very good", when everything else is "good". How does that make you feel?

Consider . . .

* what you could do to help a friend cope with being stressed or worried.
* what you worry about most. Write it down and give it to God.

For more, see . . .

* Exodus 16 (p.74)
* Philippians 4:6 (p.1285)
* Psalm 46 (p.527)

people by what they do. Grapes don't come from thorn-bushes, and figs don't come from thorny weeds. ¹⁷In the same way, every good tree produces good fruit, but a bad tree produces bad fruit. ¹⁸A good tree cannot produce bad fruit, and a bad tree cannot produce good fruit. ¹⁹Every tree that does not produce good fruit is cut down and thrown into the fire. ²⁰In the same way, you will know these false prophets by what they do.

²¹"Not all those who say that I am their Lord will enter the kingdom of heaven. The only people who will enter the kingdom of heaven are those who do what my Father in heaven wants. ²²On the last day many people will say to me, 'Lord, Lord, we spoke for you, and through you we forced out demons *d* and did many miracles.' *d* ²³Then I will tell them clearly, "Get away from me, you who do evil. I never knew you.'

Two Kinds of People

²⁴"Everyone who hears my words and obeys them is like a wise man who built his house on rock. ²⁵It rained hard, the floods came and the winds blew and hit that house. But it did not fall, because it was built on rock. ²⁶Everyone who hears my words and does not obey them is like a foolish man who built his house on sand. ²⁷It rained hard, the floods came and the winds blew and hit that house, and it fell with a big crash."

²⁸When Jesus finished saying these things, the people were amazed at his teaching, ²⁹because he did not teach like their teachers of the law. He taught like a person who had authority.

Jesus Heals a Sick Man

8 When Jesus came down from the hill, great crowds followed him. ²Then a man with a skin disease came to Jesus. The man bowed down before him and said, "Lord, you can heal me if you will."

³Jesus reached out his hand and touched the man and said, "I will. Be healed!" And immediately the man was healed of his disease. ⁴Then Jesus said to him, "Don't tell anyone about this.

CULTS

Deadly Deception

Malaysia is home for a species of praying mantis that's made a career out of looking like a flower. But this "flower" kills unsuspecting bugs.

Pink, petal-like structures flank its spindly legs. Part of its green thorax simulates the stem of an orchid. A few brown markings here and there make it look slightly wilted. When a soft breeze blows, the mantis even simulates the flower's gentle swaying.

But this unusual insect is as deadly as it is beautiful. If a butterfly mistakes the mantis for an orchid, the mantis strikes with frightful speed and captures the butterfly in pink, vice-like forelegs.

Like butterflies, Christians need to be aware that not everything is as it appears. Many cults may look appealing, just as the praying mantis looks like an orchid to an unsuspecting butterfly. Learn how you can watch out for this kind of deception in **Matthew 7:15–29**.

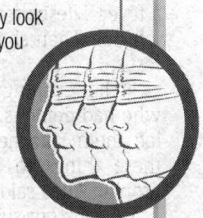

* How is a butterfly being captured by a praying mantis like those who build their houses on the sand?
* Who are some modern-day "false prophets" or groups you have heard of or have been contacted by? How might Jesus react to them?

Consider . . .

* praying for ways to resist the temptations of cults, and then investing time to grow in your faith in Christ.
* praying for those caught in cults, and sharing your faith with non-Christians.

For more, see . . .

* 1 Kings 18:1–40 (p.332)
* 2 Peter 2:1–22 (p.1365)
* Mark 13:14–23 (p.1024)

But go and show yourself to the priest[n] and offer the gift Moses commanded[n] for people who are made well. This will show the people what I have done."

Jesus Heals a Soldier's Servant

[5]When Jesus entered the city of Capernaum, an army officer came to him, begging for help. [6]The officer said, "Lord, my servant is at home in bed. He can't move his body and is in much pain."

[7]Jesus said to the officer, "I will go and heal him."

[8]The officer answered, "Lord, I am not worthy for you to come into my house. You only need to command it, and my servant will be healed. [9]I, too, am a man under the authority of others, and I have soldiers under my command. I tell one soldier, 'Go,' and he goes. I tell another soldier, 'Come,' and he comes. I say to my servant, 'Do this,' and my servant does it."

[10]When Jesus heard this, he was amazed. He said to those who were following him, "I tell you the truth, this is the greatest faith I have found, even in Israel. [11]Many people will come from the east and from the west and will sit and eat with Abraham, Isaac and Jacob in the kingdom of heaven. [12]But those people who should be in the kingdom will be thrown outside into the darkness, where people will cry and grind their teeth with pain."

[13]Then Jesus said to the officer, "Go home. Your servant will be healed just as you believed he would." And his servant was healed that same hour.

Jesus Heals Many People

[14]When Jesus went to Peter's house, he saw that Peter's mother-in-law was sick in bed with a fever. [15]Jesus touched her hand, and the fever left her. Then she stood up and began to serve Jesus.

[16]That evening people brought to Jesus many who had demons.[d] Jesus spoke and the demons left them, and he healed all the sick. [17]He did these things to bring about what Isaiah the prophet[d] had said:

"He took our suffering on him
and carried our diseases."   *Isaiah 53:4*

People Want to Follow Jesus

[18]When Jesus saw the crowd around him, he told his followers to go to the other side of the lake. [19]Then a teacher of the law came to Jesus and said, "Teacher, I will follow you wherever you go."

[20]Jesus said to him, "The foxes have holes to live in, and the birds have nests, but the Son of Man[d] has no place to rest his head."

[21]Another man, one of Jesus' followers, said to him, "Lord, first let me go and bury my father."

[22]But Jesus told him, "Follow me, and let the people who are dead bury their own dead."

Jesus Calms a Storm

[23]Jesus got into a boat, and his followers went with him. [24]A great storm arose on the lake so that waves covered the boat, but Jesus was sleeping. [25]His followers went to him and woke him, saying, "Lord, save us! We will drown!"

[26]Jesus answered, "Why are you afraid? You don't have enough faith." Then Jesus got up and gave a command to the wind and the waves, and it became completely calm.

[27]The men were amazed and said, "What kind of man is this? Even the wind and the waves obey him!"

Jesus Heals Two Men with Demons

[28]When Jesus arrived at the other side of the lake in the area of the Gadarene[n] people, two men who had demons[d] in them met him. These men lived in the burial caves and were so dangerous that people could not use the road by those caves. [29]They shouted, "What do you want with us, Son of God? Did you come here to torture us before the right time?"

[30]Near that place there was a large herd of pigs feeding. [31]The demons begged Jesus, "If you make us leave these men, please send us into that herd of pigs."

[32]Jesus said to them, "Go!" So the demons left the men and went into the pigs. Then the whole herd rushed down the hill into the lake and were drowned. [33]The herdsmen ran away and went into the town, where they told about all of this and what had happened to the men who had demons. [34]Then the whole town went out to see Jesus. When they saw him, they begged him to leave their area.

Jesus Heals a Paralysed Man

9 Jesus got into a boat and went back across the lake to his own town. [2]Some people brought to Jesus a man who was paralysed and

---

show . . . priest   The law of Moses said a priest must say when a Jewish person with a skin disease was well.
Moses commanded   Read about this in Leviticus 14:1–32.
Gadarene   From Gadara, an area south east of Lake Galilee.

lying on a mat. When Jesus saw the faith of these people, he said to the paralysed man, "Be encouraged, young man. Your sins are forgiven."

[3]Some of the teachers of the law said to themselves, "This man speaks as if he were God. That is blasphemy!"[n]

[4]Knowing their thoughts, Jesus said, "Why are you thinking evil thoughts? [5]Which is easier: to say, 'Your sins are forgiven,' or to tell him, 'Stand up and walk'? [6]But I will prove to you that the Son of Man[d] has authority on earth to forgive sins." Then Jesus said to the paralysed man, "Stand up, take your mat and go home." [7]And the man stood up and went home. [8]When the people saw this, they were amazed and praised God for giving power like this to human beings.

blasphemy   Saying things against God or not showing respect for God.

Jesus Chooses Matthew

[9]When Jesus was leaving, he saw a man named Matthew sitting in the tax collector's booth. Jesus said to him, "Follow me," and he stood up and followed Jesus.

> **Sidelight**   Tax collectors in New Testament times were despised because they worked for the hated Roman invaders. Matthew was a tax collector when Jesus chose him (Matthew 9:9–13). Matthew's unpopularity rubbed off on Jesus.

[10]As Jesus was having dinner at Matthew's house, many tax collectors and "sinners" came

NON-CHRISTIANS

From the Problem to the Answer

Damien grew up in a very violent home in Manchester. His father was an abusive alcoholic who regularly beat him and his mother up.

Because he was bullied, he himself, as so often happens, became a bully. He displayed his anger and feelings of rejection through violence and crime. His life also slipped into a dangerous spiral of drugs and alcohol. Before too long, he was sentenced to six years in prison for armed robbery.

In prison, some Christians told him about the love of God and he had a powerful conversion. He came out of prison determined to change his ways, but without any support, he slipped back into his old destructive habits. It was only when some Christians moved into his area of inner-city Manchester and got alongside him that he received the encouragement and help he needed to make a go of his new Christian life.

Damien's life is now altogether different. He is a leader in the church, a positive role model to young people in the area and is bringing up his six-week-old son in a loving, Jesus-filled home. He has gone from being the problem to being the answer in that part of Manchester.

It is clear from reading **Matthew 9:9–13** that Jesus had a big heart for people like Damien. He chose to get alongside the "tax collectors and sinners" rather than condemning them, so that they would get the chance to be the people they were meant to be.

* What does Damien's story and these verses say to you about teaching those who don't know Jesus yet in your world?
* Why do you think the Pharisees were so upset with Jesus for associating with Matthew and his friends?

Consider . . .

* whether there is someone who God has spoken to you about who he wants you to pray for and share your faith with.
* how you could generally be more active in sharing Jesus' "invitation to sinners".

For more, see . . .

* Isaiah 56:1–8 (p.699)
* James 2:14–26 (p.1350)
* Luke 12:8–9 (p.1062)

and ate with Jesus and his followers. [11]When the Pharisees [d] saw this, they asked Jesus' followers, "Why does your teacher eat with tax collectors and sinners?"

[12]When Jesus heard them, he said, "It is not the healthy people who need a doctor, but the sick. [13]Go and learn what this means: 'I want kindness more than I want animal sacrifices.' [n] I did not come to invite good people but to invite sinners."

Jesus' Followers are Criticised

[14]Then the followers of John [n] came to Jesus and said, "Why do we and the Pharisees [d] often give up eating for a certain time, [n] but your followers don't?"

[15]Jesus answered, "The friends of the bridegroom are not sad while he is with them. But the time will come when the bridegroom will be taken from them, and then they will give up eating.

[16]"No one sews a patch of unshrunken cloth over a hole in an old coat. If he does, the patch will shrink and pull away from the coat, making the hole worse. [17]Also, people never pour new wine into old leather bags. Otherwise, the bags will break, the wine will spill and the wine bags will be ruined. But people always pour new wine into new wine bags. Then both will continue to be good."

Jesus Gives Life to a Dead Girl and Heals a Sick Woman

[18]While Jesus was saying these things, a leader of the synagogue [d] came to him. He bowed down before Jesus and said, "My daughter has just died. But if you come and lay your hand on her, she will live again." [19]So Jesus and his followers stood up and went with the leader.

[20]Then a woman who had been bleeding for twelve years came behind Jesus and touched the edge of his coat. [21]She was thinking, "If I can just touch his clothes, I will be healed."

[22]Jesus turned and saw the woman and said, "Be encouraged, dear woman. You are made well because you believed." And the woman was healed from that moment on.

[23]Jesus continued along with the leader and went into his house. There he saw the funeral musicians and many people crying. [24]Jesus said, "Go away. The girl is not dead, only asleep." But the people laughed at him. [25]After the crowd had been thrown out of the house, Jesus went into the girl's room and took hold of her hand, and

she stood up. [26]The news about this spread all around the area.

Jesus Heals More People

[27]When Jesus was leaving there, two blind men followed him. They cried out, "Have mercy on us, Son of David!" [d]

[28]After Jesus went inside, the blind men went with him. He asked the men, "Do you believe that I can make you see again?"

They answered, "Yes, Lord."

[29]Then Jesus touched their eyes and said, "Because you believe I can make you see again, it will happen." [30]Then the men were able to see. But Jesus warned them strongly, saying, "Don't tell anyone about this." [31]But the blind men left and spread the news about Jesus all around that area.

[32]When the two men were leaving, some people brought another man to Jesus. This man could not talk because he had a demon [d] in him. [33]After Jesus forced the demon to leave the man, he was able to speak. The crowd was amazed and said, "We have never seen anything like this in Israel."

[34]But the Pharisees [d] said, "The prince of demons is the one that gives him power to force demons out."

[35]Jesus travelled through all the towns and villages, teaching in their synagogues, [d] preaching the Good News [d] about the kingdom and healing all kinds of diseases and sicknesses. [36]When he saw the crowds, he felt sorry for them because they were hurting and helpless, like sheep without a shepherd. [37]Jesus said to his followers, "There are many people to harvest but only a few workers to help harvest them. [38]Pray to the Lord, who owns the harvest, that he will send more workers to gather his harvest." [n]

Jesus Sends Out His Apostles

10 Jesus called his twelve followers together and gave them authority to drive out evil spirits and to heal every kind of disease and sickness. [2]These are the names of the twelve apostles: [d] Simon (also called Peter) and his brother Andrew; James son of Zebedee, and his brother John; [3]Philip and Bartholomew; Thomas and Matthew, the tax collector; James son of Alphaeus, and Thaddaeus; [4]Simon the Zealot [d] and Judas Iscariot, who turned against Jesus.

[5]Jesus sent out these twelve men with the following order: "Don't go to the non-Jewish people or to any town where the Samaritans [d] live. [6]But go to the people of Israel, who are like

---

'I want . . . sacrifices.'   Quotation from Hosea 6:6.
John   John the Baptist, who preached to people about Christ's coming (Matthew 3, Luke 3).
give up . . . time   This is called "fasting". The people would give up eating for a special time of prayer and worship to God. It was also done to show sadness and disappointment.
"There are . . . harvest."   As a farmer sends workers to harvest the grain, Jesus sends his followers to bring people to God.

lost sheep. [7]When you go, preach this: 'The kingdom of heaven is near.' [8]Heal the sick, raise the dead to life again, heal those who have skin diseases and force demons [d] out of people. I give you these powers freely, so help other people freely. [9]Don't carry any money with you—gold or silver or copper. [10]Don't carry a bag or extra clothes or sandals or a walking stick. Workers should be given what they need.

[11]"When you enter a city or town, find some worthy person there and stay in that home until you leave. [12]When you enter that home, say, 'Peace be with you.' [13]If the people there welcome you, let your peace stay there. But if they don't welcome you, take back the peace you wished for them. [14]And if a home or town refuses to welcome you or listen to you, leave that place and shake its dust off your feet.[n] [15]I tell you the truth, on the Judgement Day it will be better for the towns of Sodom[d] and Gomorrah[d] than for the people of that town.

Jesus Warns His Apostles

[16]"Listen, I am sending you out like sheep among wolves. So be as clever as snakes and as innocent as doves. [17]Be careful of people, because they will arrest you and take you to court and whip you in their synagogues. [d] [18]Because of me

---

shake . . . feet.   A warning. It showed that they had rejected these people.

SICKNESS

Giving the World Friends

Rebecca, a high school student in the USA, can dance, walk and run. Not a huge achievement for most of us – but for Rebecca those abilities prove God's power. For not long ago, she was almost completely paralysed.

In the first year, Rebecca felt her muscles slowly becoming numb. She started avoiding PE lessons. Walking caused excruciating pain. Her mother finally took her to a doctor, and Rebecca was admitted to the hospital the same day.

A spinal tap confirmed that she had Guillain Barr Syndrome, a rare condition in which a virus attacks the nervous system, causing paralysis in all the motor functions. Although she began various drug and physical treatments, Rebecca's condition got worse. "The syndrome spread, and I could no longer sit upright in bed by myself," she recalls.

Doctors gave her little chance for recovery. But they did not count on God! "My spirits have been strengthened because of the love from family and friends," Rebecca says. "Daily I received phone calls, cards and flowers. My room was crowded with friends every day. It was a time for fellowship and support, not only for me, but also for my family and friends."

The doctors continued treatment, and Rebecca slowly recovered.

"Some people say the Lord doesn't give us answers we can see or touch, yet we all see and touch our family and friends," Rebecca says. "The Lord answered my prayers with a family who stroked my hair and sat next to me day and night while I lay motionless.

"The Lord brought me friends who told me, 'You will get better, because I'm praying for you.' I thank God for the answers he's given me."

Rebecca's doctors were amazed at her healing. Yet **Matthew 9:35 – 10:8** tells us how Jesus commissioned the disciples to heal the sick.

* How well did the people who prayed and stayed with Rebecca follow Jesus' commission to the apostles?
* How can you reach out in love and faith?

Consider . . .

* doing one activity this week to better your health and well-being.
* visiting someone in a hospital or nursing home and praying with him or her.

For more, see . . .

* 2 Kings 20:1–11 (p.365)
* Luke 18:35–43 (p.1080)
* Psalm 30:2–3 (p.517)

you will be taken to stand before governors and kings, and you will tell them and the non-Jewish people about me. [19]When you are arrested, don't worry about what to say or how to say it. At that time you will be given the things to say. [20]It will not really be you speaking but the Spirit of your Father speaking through you.

[21]"Brothers will give their own brothers to be killed, and fathers will give their own children to be killed. Children will fight against their own parents and have them put to death. [22]All people will hate you because you follow me, but those people who keep their faith until the end will be saved. [23]When you are treated badly in one city, run to another city. I tell you the truth, you will not finish going through all the cities of Israel before the Son of Man [d] comes.

[24]"A student is not better than his teacher, and a servant is not better than his master. [25]A student should be satisfied to become like his teacher; a servant should be satisfied to become like his master. If the head of the family is called Beelzebul, [d] then the other members of the family will be called worse names!

Fear God, Not People

[26]"So don't be afraid of those people, because everything that is hidden will be shown. Everything that is secret will be made known. [27]I tell you these things in the dark, but I want you to tell them in the light. What you hear whispered in your ear you should shout from the housetops. [28]Don't be afraid of people, who can kill the body but cannot kill the soul. The only one you should fear is the one who can destroy the soul and the body in hell. [29]Two sparrows cost only a penny, but not even one of them can die without your Father's knowing it. [30]God even knows how

---

SELF-ESTEEM

Playing Your Part

The second-period algebra test had been a disaster for Charlene Markham. Then she had slipped and fallen in the hallway in front of two dozen other students. As she sat in sixth-period band practise, her mind was everywhere except on the sheets of music.

"Sometimes I wonder if my being here at Springbrook High makes any difference at all," she thought as the music filled the room. "It's like the flautist's part in this medley. All you can hear are the trumpets and trombones, anyway."

As an experiment, Charlene raised the flute to her lips but only pretended to play. "See," she thought after the piece, "no one even noticed."

Just before the bell rang, Mr Westmore, the music teacher, instructed the students to put away their instruments. Then he asked Charlene to stay after the bell.

"Why didn't you play in the Sousa medley?" he asked.

Charlene was stunned that he knew. She didn't answer him. "Charlene," he said kindly, yet firmly, "we need every part in a piece of music to make it complete. The conductor looks for everyone to be playing his or her part."

Somehow Charlene felt better knowing she had been missed. "Maybe I have a part to play after all," she thought. Learn what Jesus says about your importance in **Matthew 10:24–33**.

- How does the Bible passage speak to Charlene's feelings of worthlessness?
- How does knowing that God loves you affect your feelings about yourself?

Consider . . .

- investing thirty minutes today in an activity for your own growth, health and well-being.
- listing all of the "sections" in God's "band" (the church) you can think of, such as musicians, leaders, helpers and so forth. Pick the one "section" that you're most interested in, and volunteer to "play" in it.

For more, see . . .

- Psalm 8:3–9 (p.503)
- 1 Corinthians 12:12–31 (p.1231)
- Romans 5:1–11 (p.1190)

many hairs are on your head. ³¹So don't be afraid. You are worth much more than many sparrows.

Tell People About Your Faith

³²"All those who stand before others and say they believe in me, I will say before my Father in heaven that they belong to me. ³³But all who stand before others and say they do not believe in me, I will say before my Father in heaven that they do not belong to me.

³⁴"Don't think that I came to bring peace to the earth. I did not come to bring peace, but a sword. ³⁵I have come so that

'a son will be against his father,
   a daughter will be against her mother,
   a daughter-in-law will be against her
      mother-in-law.

³⁶ A person's enemies will be members of his
   own family.'   *Micah 7:6*

³⁷"Those who love their father or mother more than they love me are not worthy to be my followers. Those who love their son or daughter more than they love me are not worthy to be my followers. ³⁸Whoever is not willing to carry the cross and follow me is not worthy of me. ³⁹Those who try to hold on to their lives will give up true life. Those who give up their lives for me will hold on to true life. ⁴⁰Whoever accepts you also accepts me, and whoever accepts me also accepts the One who sent me. ⁴¹Whoever meets a prophet *d* and accepts him will receive the reward of a prophet. And whoever accepts a good person because that person is good will receive the reward of a good person. ⁴²Those who give one of

---

PRIORITIES

Who Comes First?

Jason was enthralled by every word Keith, his new pastor, spoke. He seemed to sell an attractive, yet challenging way of life that went the extra mile. He was getting some opposition within the church – people were beginning to feel uncomfortable because he was so radical – but he seemed to expect it and even thrive on it.

The church grew dramatically, doubling in size in a matter of months. Keith worked hard and seemed to be everywhere.

Jason followed Keith round learning about ministry, public speaking, evangelism and serving, by carrying bags and setting up equipment for meetings.

One day Keith took Jason aside. "You're special and I trust you," he said. "God is calling me to do something even more radical. I am being called to leave here and start a new community. Next week I'm going to move to a special place in the country that God has shown me. It will be a place where people trust God, live on the land and devote their time to worship, prayer and outreach. It will be a completely new type of society – a Jesus one. So are you in or out?"

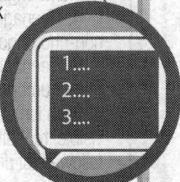

Jason felt all sorts of objections going off in his head and wondered what his friends and family would say. But Keith suggested he read **Matthew 10:34–42**. He did. And as he read, he discovered that Keith was simply doing the Jesus thing. His pastor was calling people to follow Jesus more closely, not to follow him.

* What did Jesus mean when he said (verse 42) that he had not come to bring peace on the earth? Who did Jesus think he was?
* "Who is this man?" is the key question posed by the Gospels about Jesus. Was he mad, bad, good or God? In which direction does this passage point?

Consider . . .

* how you would feel if you were asked to give up everything and follow Jesus.
* what it means to carry Jesus' cross (verse 38).

For more, see . . .

* Luke 10:1–3 (p.1056)
* 1 John 3:1–3 (p.1373)

these little ones a cup of cold water because they are my followers will truly get their reward."

Jesus and John the Baptist

11 After Jesus finished telling these things to his twelve followers, he left there and went to the towns in Galilee to teach and preach.

[2]John the Baptist [d] was in prison, but he heard about what Christ was doing. So John sent some of his followers to Jesus. [3]They asked him, "Are you the One who is to come, or should we wait for someone else?"

[4]Jesus answered them, "Go and tell John what you hear and see: [5]the blind can see, the crippled can walk and people with skin diseases are healed. The deaf can hear, the dead are raised to life and the Good News [d] is preached to the poor. [6]Those who do not stumble in their faith because of me are blessed."

[7]As John's followers were leaving, Jesus began talking to the people about John. Jesus said, "What did you go out into the desert to see? A reed[n] blown by the wind? [8]What did you go out to see? A man dressed in fine clothes? No, those who wear fine clothes live in kings' palaces. [9]So why did you go out? To see a prophet? [d] Yes, and I tell you, John is more than a prophet. [10]This was written about him:

'I will send my messenger ahead of you,
　　who will prepare the way for you.'   *Malachi 3:1*
[11]I tell you the truth, John the Baptist is greater than any other person ever born, but even the least important person in the kingdom of heaven is greater than John. [12]Since the time

---

reed   This means that John was not ordinary or weak like grass blown by the wind.

The Faith Difference

Next time friends ask you, "Does your faith make a difference?" remember these statistics about teenagers:

1. Teenagers who have never used illegal drugs – 61% of regular churchgoers, versus 39% of non-churchgoers.
2. Teenagers who have never had sexual intercourse – 61% of regular churchgoers, versus 35% of non-churchgoers.
3. Teenagers who believe in a personal God – 87% of regular churchgoers, versus 64% of non-churchgoers.
4. Teenagers who read the Bible weekly – 58% of regular churchgoers, versus 17% of non-churchgoers.
5. Teenagers who plan to go to college – 57% of regular churchgoers, versus 33% of non-churchgoers.

Faith isn't an intellectual thing. As the statistics above illustrate, a committed faith makes a visible, real difference in the way we live. Perhaps it should make more. In **Matthew 11:2–11** the followers of John the Baptist asked Jesus whether he was the Christ. Read how he responded.

* Why is faith a powerful force in the miracles of Jesus as well as the behaviour of regular churchgoers?
* What difference does faith make in your own life? Have you seen the signs of God's work that are listed in the passage?

Consider . . .

* surveying your own behaviour in comparison to statistics. How well did you fit?
* drawing up your own survey and interviewing both churchgoers and non-churchgoers. Share your results with others at church and school.

For more, see . . .

* Judges 6:11–24 (p.231)
* James 5:13–18 (p.1353)
* Luke 13:1–9 (p.1066)

John the Baptist came until now, the kingdom of heaven has been going forwards in strength, and people have been trying to take it by force. [13]All the prophets and the law of Moses told about what would happen until the time John came. [14]And if you will believe what they said, you will believe that John is Elijah, whom they said would come. [15]You people who can hear me, listen!

[16]"What can I say about the people of this time? What are they like? They are like children sitting in the market place, who call out to each other,

[17]'We played music for you, but you did not dance;

we sang a sad song, but you did not cry.'

[18]John came and did not eat or drink like other people. So people say, 'He has a demon.' [d] [19]The Son of Man [d] came, eating and drinking, and people say, 'Look at him! He eats too much and drinks too much wine, and he is a friend of tax collectors and sinners.' But wisdom is proved to be right by what it does."

Jesus Warns Unbelievers

[20]Then Jesus criticised the cities where he did most of his miracles, [d] because the people did not change their lives and stop sinning. [21]He said, "How terrible for you, Korazin! How terrible for you, Bethsaida! [n] If the same miracles I did in you

Korazin . . . Bethsaida   Towns by Lake Galilee where Jesus preached to the people.

WORRYING

Driving You Crazy

"Watch out for that hedge! Get off of the pavement! Ellie the brake is the one in the middle!" barked Ellie's dad as he sat rigid with both hands gripping the sides of his passenger seat.

"You're not helping, Dad!" Ellie whined whilst steering back onto the road with a clunk and thud. "You keep shouting at me and telling me what to do – it's stressing me out!"

Later that night, Ellie explained the evening's lesson to her mum over a cup of tea.

Ellie's mum leaned forward across the kitchen table, "Don't worry, you can do it, you just need help. Listen darling, I know it will cost you, but I think you need to start learning with someone else. You need a professional who can help you feel more relaxed."

Ellie's new instructor, Pauline, was amazing. Ellie still found some things about driving difficult and scary but Pauline made it so much easier. She was gentle and fun. And soon Ellie began to believe that she could pass, with Pauline's help.

Many of the Jewish people had difficult lives. What made it worse was that the religious leaders told these people that their problems were because they weren't living right and keeping the rules. They thought God was angry and had abandoned them.

In **Matthew 11:25–30** Jesus turns everything upside down. When times are tough, he doesn't say that God is angry or list all their mistakes, instead he offers help, comfort and new ways of learning how to live.

* Compare Pauline with Jesus. What similarities can you think of?
* Ellie could give up or get help to get through. What are the things in your life that you feel "rubbish" about or want to give up on? Could you go to Jesus for help to get through them?

Consider . . .

* writing the things that are worrying you on separate bits of paper. Pray about each thing and find a different way each day throughout the week to destroy the paper (e.g. make into a paper aeroplane, throw on a fire, shred, paint over the words).
* buying a "well done, you passed" card. Graffiti/decorate the card's front with verses and pictures to help you remember that Jesus will help you. Frame the card.

For more, see . . .

* Psalm 4 (p.501)
* Jude 24–25 (p.1386)

had happened in Tyre and Sidon,[n] those people would have changed their lives a long time ago. They would have worn rough cloth and put ashes on themselves to show they had changed. [22]But I tell you, on the Judgement Day it will be better for Tyre and Sidon than for you. [23]And you, Capernaum,[n] will you be lifted up to heaven? No, you will be thrown down to the depths. If the miracles I did in you had happened in Sodom,[d] its people would have stopped sinning, and it would still be a city today. [24]But I tell you, on the Judgement Day it will be better for Sodom than for you."

Jesus Offers Rest to People

[25]At that time Jesus said, "I praise you, Father, Lord of heaven and earth, because you have hidden these things from the people who are wise and clever. But you have shown them to those who are like little children. [26]Yes, Father, this is what you really wanted.

[27]"My Father has given me all things. No one knows the Son, except the Father. And no one knows the Father, except the Son and those whom the Son chooses to tell.

[28]"Come to me, all of you who are tired and have heavy loads, and I will give you rest. [29]Accept my teachings and learn from me, because I am gentle and humble in spirit, and you will find rest for your lives. [30]The teaching that I ask you to accept is easy; the load I give you to carry is light."

Jesus is Lord of the Sabbath

12 At that time Jesus was walking through some fields of grain on a Sabbath[d] day. His followers were hungry, so they began to pick the grain and eat it. [2]When the Pharisees[d] saw this, they said to Jesus, "Look! Your followers are doing what is unlawful to do on the Sabbath day."

[3]Jesus answered, "Have you not read what David did when he and the people with him were hungry? [4]He went into God's house, and he and those with him ate the holy bread, which was lawful only for priests to eat. [5]And have you not read in the law of Moses that on every Sabbath day the priests in the Temple[d] break this law about the Sabbath day? But the priests are not wrong for doing that. [6]I tell you that there is something here that is greater than the Temple. [7]The Scripture[d] says, 'I want kindness more than I want animal sacrifices.'[n] You don't really know what those words mean. If you understood them, you would not judge those who have done nothing wrong.

[8]"So the Son of Man[d] is Lord of the Sabbath day."

Jesus Heals a Man's Hand

[9]Jesus left there and went into their synagogue,[d] [10]where there was a man with a crippled hand. They were looking for a reason to accuse Jesus, so they asked him, "Is it right to heal on the Sabbath[d] day?"[n]

[11]Jesus answered, "If any of you has a sheep, and it falls into a ditch on the Sabbath day, you will help it out of the ditch. [12]Surely a human being is more important than a sheep. So it is lawful to do good things on the Sabbath day."

[13]Then Jesus said to the man with the crippled hand, "Hold out your hand." The man held out his hand, and it became well again, like the other hand. [14]But the Pharisees[d] left and made plans to kill Jesus.

Jesus is God's Chosen Servant

[15]Jesus knew what the Pharisees[d] were doing, so he left that place. Many people followed him, and he healed all who were sick. [16]But Jesus warned the people not to tell who he was. [17]He did these things to bring about what Isaiah the prophet[d] had said:

[18]"Here is my servant whom I have chosen.
I love him, and I am pleased with him.
I will put my Spirit[d] upon him,
and he will tell of my justice to all people.
[19]He will not argue or cry out;
no one will hear his voice in the streets.
[20]He will not break a crushed blade of grass
or put out even a weak flame
until he makes justice win the victory.
[21] In him will the non-Jewish people find
hope."

Isaiah 42:1–4

Jesus' Power is from God

[22]Then some people brought to Jesus a man who was blind and could not talk, because he had a demon.[d] Jesus healed the man so that he could talk and see. [23]All the people were amazed and said, "Perhaps this man is the Son of David!"[d]

Sidelight If you think that today's society has a lot of rules and regulations, take a look at the Pharisees and think again (Matthew 12:1–8). On the Sabbath, no less than 39 major activities were forbidden, including putting a fire out, lifting something weighing more than two figs, writing and healing someone!

Tyre and Sidon Towns where wicked people lived.
Capernaum A town by Lake Galilee where Jesus preached to the people.
'I . . . sacrifices.' Quotation from Hosea 6:6.
"Is it right . . . day?" It was against Jewish law to work on the Sabbath day.

24When the Pharisees *d* heard this, they said, "Jesus uses the power of Beelzebul, *d* the ruler of demons, to force demons out of people."

25Jesus knew what the Pharisees were thinking, so he said to them, "Every kingdom that is divided against itself will be destroyed. And any city or family that is divided against itself will not continue. 26And if Satan forces out himself, then Satan is divided against himself, and his kingdom will not continue. 27You say that I use the power of Beelzebul to force out demons. If that is true, then what power do your people use to force out demons? So they will be your judges. 28But if I use the power of God's Spirit *d* to force out demons, then the kingdom of God has come to you.

29"If anyone wants to enter a strong person's house and steal his things, he must first tie up the strong person. Then he can steal the things from the house.

30"Whoever is not with me is against me. Whoever does not work with me is working against me. 31So I tell you, people can be forgiven for every sin and everything they say against God. But whoever speaks against the Holy Spirit will not be forgiven. 32Anyone who speaks against the Son of Man *d* can be forgiven, but anyone who speaks against the Holy Spirit will not be forgiven, now or in the future.

People Know You by Your Words

33"If you want good fruit, you must make the tree good. If your tree is not good, it will have bad fruit. A tree is known by the kind of fruit it produces. 34You snakes! You are evil people, so how can you say anything good? The mouth speaks the things that are in the heart. 35Good people have good things in their hearts, and so they say good things. But evil people have evil in their hearts, so they say evil things. 36And I tell you that on the Judgement Day people will be responsible for every careless thing they have said. 37The words you have said will be used to judge you. Some of your words will prove you right, but some of your words will prove you guilty."

The People Ask for a Miracle

38Then some of the Pharisees *d* and teachers of the law answered Jesus, saying, "Teacher, we want to see you work a miracle *d* as a sign."

39Jesus answered, "Evil and sinful people are the ones who want to see a miracle for a sign. But no sign will be given to them, except the sign of the prophet *d* Jonah. 40Jonah was in the stomach of the big fish for three days and three

nights. In the same way, the Son of Man *d* will be in the grave three days and three nights. 41On the Judgement Day the people from Nineveh *n* will stand up with you people who live now, and they will show that you are guilty. When Jonah preached to them, they were sorry and changed their lives. And I tell you that someone greater than Jonah is here. 42On the Judgement Day, the Queen of the South *n* will stand up with you people who live today. She will show that you are guilty, because she came from far away to listen to Solomon's wise teaching. And I tell you that someone greater than Solomon is here.

People Today are Full of Evil

43"When an evil spirit comes out of a person, it travels through barren places, looking for a place to rest, but it doesn't find it. 44So the spirit says, 'I will go back to the house I left.' When the spirit comes back, it finds the house still empty, swept clean and made neat. 45Then the evil spirit goes out and brings seven other spirits even more evil than it is, and they go in and live there. So the person has even more trouble than before. It is the same way with the evil people who live today."

Jesus' True Family

46While Jesus was talking to the people, his mother and brothers stood outside, trying to find a way to talk to him. 47Someone told Jesus, "Your mother and brothers are standing outside, and they want to talk to you."

48He answered, "Who is my mother? Who are my brothers?" 49Then he pointed to his followers and said, "Here are my mother and my brothers. 50My true brother and sister and mother and father are those who do what my Father in heaven wants."

A Story About Planting Seed

13 That same day Jesus went out of the house and sat by the lake. 2Large crowds gathered around him, so he got into a boat and sat down, while the people stood on the shore. 3Then Jesus used stories to teach them many things. He said: "A farmer went out to plant his seed. 4While he was planting, some seed fell by the road, and the birds came and ate it all up. 5Some seed fell on rocky ground, where there wasn't much earth. That seed grew very fast, because the ground was not deep. 6But when the sun rose, the plants dried up, because they did not have deep roots. 7Some other seed fell among thorny weeds, which grew and choked the good

Nineveh   The city where Jonah preached to warn the people. Read Jonah 3.
Queen of the South   The Queen of Sheba. She travelled 1,600 kilometres to learn God's wisdom from Solomon. Read 1 Kings 10:1–13.

plants. [8]Some other seed fell on good ground where it grew and produced a crop. Some plants made 100 times more, some made 60 times more and some made 30 times more. [9]You people who can hear me, listen."

Why Jesus Used Stories to Teach

[10]The followers came to Jesus and asked, "Why do you use stories to teach the people?"

[11]Jesus answered, "You have been chosen to know the secrets about the kingdom of heaven, but others cannot know these secrets. [12]Those who have understanding will be given more, and they will have all they need. But those who do not have understanding, even what they have will be taken away from them. [13]This is why I use stories to teach the people: they see, but they don't really see. They hear, but they don't really hear or understand. [14]So they show that the things Isaiah said about them are true:

'You will listen and listen, but you will not
  understand.
You will look and look, but you will not learn.
[15]For the minds of these people have become
  stubborn.
They do not hear with their ears,
  and they have closed their eyes.
Otherwise they might really understand
  what they see with their eyes
  and hear with their ears.
They might really understand in their minds
  and come back to me and be healed.'

Isaiah 6:9–10

[16]But you are blessed, because you see with your eyes and hear with your ears. [17]I tell you the truth, many prophets [d] and good people wanted

---

FOLLOWING GOD

The Secrets of the Kingdom

English cricket is a mystery to some and an absolute passion to others. What on earth is the strangely named "silly mid wicket", "square leg" or a "googly"? These and lots of other secrets are only made known to those who love the game of cricket and are keen enough to find out.

Even football, which may seem a far simpler game to cricket, has its hidden depths. How many of the millions who sit in the stadiums understand the "offside laws" or know what a "flat back 4" or the "spine" of a team is? Anyone, of course, can play the games but if you want to be exceptional, you need to know this stuff.

Jesus says to his followers (a very ordinary bunch of guys) in Matthew 13 that they have been chosen to know the secrets, not about some game or other, but about the very "kingdom of heaven". Those words, of course, are not just for the disciples but for us as well, two thousand years later. As we get passionate for God and put in the effort required in terms of prayer, Bible study, fellowship and reaching out to our friends, we'll find that more and more we are in tune with God and that he gives us eyes to see and ears to hear what the kingdom is all about.

Read **Matthew 13:1–23** and ask God to help you understand the "secrets of the kingdom".

* Why do you think Jesus compares following God to being the "good ground" for the seed of faith?
* How could you in your situation produce a crop of 30, 60, or 100 times what is being sown into you through the word of God?

Consider . . .

* giving God some extra time this week. Don't just storm in straight away with your requests, but listen and try to tune in to his way of thinking.
* people you know who started really well as Christians but have now stopped growing? Where do you think they have gone wrong? Pray for them and try gently encouraging them back to Jesus.

For more, see . . .

* Deuteronomy 31:11–13 (p.193)
* 2 Corinthians 13:8–13 (p.1254)

* 1 Samuel 3:1–21 (p.258)

to see the things that you now see, but they did not see them. And they wanted to hear the things that you now hear, but they did not hear them.

Jesus Explains the Seed Story

[18]"So listen to the meaning of that story about the farmer. [19]What is the seed that fell by the road? That seed is like the person who hears the message about the kingdom but does not understand it. The Evil One comes and takes away what was planted in that person's heart. [20]And what is the seed that fell on rocky ground? That seed is like the person who hears the teaching and quickly accepts it with joy. [21]But he does not let the teaching go deep into his life, so he keeps it only a short time. When trouble or persecution comes because of the teaching he accepted, he quickly gives up. [22]And what is the seed that fell among the thorny weeds? That seed is like the person who hears the teaching but lets worries about this life and the temptation of wealth stop that teaching from growing. So the teaching does

not produce fruit[n] in that person's life. [23]But what is the seed that fell on the good ground? That seed is like the person who hears the teaching and understands it. That person grows and produces fruit, sometimes 100 times more, sometimes 60 times more and sometimes 30 times more."

A Story About Wheat and Weeds

[24]Then Jesus told them another story: "The kingdom of heaven is like a man who planted good seed in his field. [25]That night, when everyone was asleep, his enemy came and planted weeds among the wheat and then left. [26]Later, the wheat grew and the heads of grain grew, but the weeds also grew. [27]Then the man's servants came to him and said, 'You planted good seed in your field. Where did the weeds come from?' [28]The man answered, 'An enemy planted weeds.' The servants asked, 'Do you want us to pull up the weeds?' [29]The man answered, 'No, because when you pull up the weeds, you might also pull up the wheat. [30]Let the weeds and the wheat

produce fruit   To produce fruit means to have in your life the good things God wants.

SIN

A Crafty Enemy

Life in the Arctic would be pretty safe for the seal if it weren't for its enemy the polar bear.

This crafty predator probably uses more strategies than any other animal in capturing and killing its prey. It may spend 30 minutes in the water approaching a resting seal on an ice floe, surfacing silently to see where the prey is and then submerging again. It may drift like a small, harmless iceberg to within striking distance, and then explode from the water so suddenly and ferociously that the seal has no time to react.

When it's stalking on the ice, the polar bear slithers along on its chest and forelegs. It will build mounds of snow to hide behind while it waits at the edge of a breathing hole. It can surface in the seal's den and catch it sleeping there. Or it can dive so quickly into the den from above that the seal cannot escape.

We, too, must be wary of a crafty enemy. You can read about the enemy in Jesus' parable of the wheat and weeds in **Matthew 13:24–30**.

* How are the polar bear's tactics similar to the enemy's in the passage?
* How can you be prepared for the traps of the enemy in your life?

Consider . . .

* separating the forms of entertainment that you enjoy into categories of "wheat" and "weeds". Consider giving up one (or more) of the "weeds".
* looking up references to "Satan" and "devil" in the "Dictionary and Topical Concordance" at the back of this Bible (p.1406). Share what you learn with friends.

For more, see . . .

* Genesis 3:1–9 (p.5)
* 1 Peter 5:8–9 (p.1363)

* Hebrews 3:12–14 (p.1332)

grow together until the harvest time. At harvest time I will tell the workers, "First gather the weeds and tie them together to be burnt. Then gather the wheat and bring it to my barn."'"

Stories of Mustard Seed and Yeast

31Then Jesus told another story: "The kingdom of heaven is like a mustard seed that a man planted in his field. 32That seed is the smallest of all seeds, but when it grows, it is one of the largest garden plants. It becomes big enough for the wild birds to come and build nests in its branches."

33Then Jesus told another story: "The kingdom of heaven is like yeast that a woman took and hid in a large bowl of flour until it made all the dough rise."

34Jesus used stories to tell all these things to the people; he always used stories to teach them. 35This is as the prophet *d* said:

"I will speak using stories;
    I will tell things that have been secret since
        the world was made." *Psalm 78:2*

Jesus Explains About the Weeds

36Then Jesus left the crowd and went into the house. His followers came to him and said, "Explain to us the meaning of the story about the weeds in the field."

37Jesus answered, "The man who planted the good seed in the field is the Son of Man. *d* 38The field is the world, and the good seeds are all of God's children who belong to the kingdom. The weeds are those people who belong to the Evil One. 39And the enemy who planted the bad seed is the devil. The harvest time is the end of the world, and the workers who gather are God's angels.

40"Just as the weeds are pulled up and burnt in the fire, so it will be at the end of the world. 41The Son of Man will send out his angels, and

---

HAPPINESS

Real Treasure

When seventeen-year-old Derek bought his first car – a "previously owned" model – he expected to hit the road and leave his problems in the dust.

The car, Derek expected, would give him more time to do as he pleased. It would get him out of the house and away from his parents fighting all the time. It would surely improve his standing with girls.

But only a week later, the fan belt broke on the way to a football match.

One month later, he had to buy two new tyres.

Now he discovered, 30 kilometres from home, that the radiator was leaking. As the traffic swished past on the motorway, Derek and his friend Phil sat in the front seat of the car, watching the steam rise from under the bonnet.

"I always looked forward to owning my own car," Derek said. "But sometimes I feel as if the car owns me."

Derek learned an ageless truth that the more things we acquire, the more they use our time and energy. Possessions rarely bring the happiness expected, and often bring just the opposite. The Bible often talks about the spiritual kingdom and the only true happiness. Read three of Jesus' parables on the kingdom in **Matthew 13:44–52**.

* What are the differences between Derek's car and the "treasure hidden in a field" mentioned in the passage?
* What is the true value of the things you treasure?

Consider . . .

* praying that God will help you to value the things in life that truly last.
* interviewing an elderly Christian about what has meant most in his or her lifetime.

For more, see . . .

* Ecclesiastes 3:1–8 (p.622)
* Revelation 3:14–22 (p.1391)

* Philippians 4:4–9 (p.1285)

they will gather out of his kingdom all who cause sin and all who do evil. ⁴²The angels will throw them into the blazing furnace, where the people will cry and grind their teeth with pain. ⁴³Then the good people will shine like the sun in the kingdom of their Father. You people who can hear me, listen.

Stories of a Treasure and a Pearl

⁴⁴"The kingdom of heaven is like a treasure hidden in a field. One day a man found the treasure, and then he hid it in the field again. He was so happy that he went and sold everything he owned to buy that field.

⁴⁵"Also, the kingdom of heaven is like a man looking for fine pearls. ⁴⁶When he found a very valuable pearl, he went and sold everything he had and bought it.

A Story of a Fishing Net

⁴⁷"Also, the kingdom of heaven is like a net that was put into the lake and caught many different kinds of fish. ⁴⁸When it was full, the fishermen pulled the net to the shore. They sat down and put all the good fish in baskets and threw away the bad fish. ⁴⁹It will be this way at the end of the world. The angels will come and separate the evil people from the good people. ⁵⁰The angels will throw the evil people into the blazing furnace, where people will cry and grind their teeth with pain."

⁵¹Jesus asked his followers, "Do you understand all these things?"

They answered, "Yes, we understand."

⁵²Then Jesus said to them, "So every teacher of the law who has been taught about the kingdom of heaven is like the owner of a house. He brings out both new things and old things he has saved."

Jesus Goes to His Home Town

⁵³When Jesus finished teaching with these stories, he left there. ⁵⁴He went to his home town and taught the people in the synagogue, ᵈ and they were amazed. They said, "Where did this man get this wisdom and this power to do miracles? ᵈ ⁵⁵He is just the son of a carpenter. His mother is Mary, and his brothers are James, Joseph, Simon and Judas. ⁵⁶And all his sisters are here with us. Where then does this man get all these things?" ⁵⁷So the people were upset with Jesus.

But Jesus said to them, "A prophet ᵈ is honoured everywhere except in his home town and in his own home."

⁵⁸So he did not do many miracles there because they had no faith.

How John the Baptist Was Killed

14 At that time Herod, the ruler of Galilee, heard the reports about Jesus. ²So he said to his servants, "Jesus is John the Baptist, ᵈ who

has risen from the dead. That is why he can work these miracles." ᵈ

³Some time before this, Herod had arrested John, tied him up, and put him in prison. Herod did this because of Herodias, who had been the wife of Philip, Herod's brother. ⁴John had been telling Herod, "It is not lawful for you to be married to Herodias." ⁵Herod wanted to kill John, but he was afraid of the people, because they believed John was a prophet. ᵈ

⁶On Herod's birthday, the daughter of Herodias danced for Herod and his guests, and she pleased him. ⁷So he promised with an oath to give her anything she wanted. ⁸Herodias told her daughter what to ask for, so she said to Herod, "Give me the head of John the Baptist here on a dish." ⁹Although King Herod was very sad, he had made a promise, and his dinner guests had heard him. So Herod ordered that what she asked for be done. ¹⁰He sent soldiers to the prison to cut off John's head. ¹¹And they brought it on a dish and gave it to the girl, and she took it to her mother. ¹²John's followers came and got his body and buried it. Then they went and told Jesus.

More than 5,000 Fed

¹³When Jesus heard what had happened to John, he left in a boat and went to a lonely place by himself. But the crowds heard about it and followed him on foot from the towns. ¹⁴When he arrived, he saw a great crowd waiting. He felt sorry for them and healed those who were sick.

> **Sidelight** The two fish which were brought to Jesus in Matthew 14:17–21 were probably sardine-sized fish which were plentiful in Lake Galilee. The poor usually ate this fish.

¹⁵When it was evening, his followers came to him and said, "No one lives in this place, and it is already late. Send the people away so they can go to the towns and buy food for themselves."

¹⁶But Jesus answered, "They don't need to go away. You give them something to eat."

¹⁷They said to him, "But we have only five loaves of bread and two fish."

¹⁸Jesus said, "Bring the bread and the fish to me." ¹⁹Then he told the people to sit down on the grass. He took the five loaves and the two fish and, looking up to heaven, he thanked God for the food. Jesus divided the bread and gave it to his followers, who gave it to the people. ²⁰All the people ate and were satisfied. Then the followers

filled twelve baskets with the leftover pieces of food. ²¹There were about 5,000 men there who ate, not counting women and children.

Jesus Walks on the Water

²²Immediately Jesus told his followers to get into the boat and go ahead of him across the lake. He stayed there to send the people home. ²³After he had sent them away, he went by himself up into the hills to pray. It was late, and Jesus was there alone. ²⁴By this time, the boat was already far away from land. It was being hit by waves, because the wind was blowing against it. ²⁵Between three and six o'clock in the morning, Jesus came to them, walking on the water.

²⁶When his followers saw him walking on the water, they were afraid. They said, "It's a ghost!" and cried out in fear.

²⁷But Jesus quickly spoke to them, "Have courage! It is I. Do not be afraid."

²⁸Peter said, "Lord, if it is really you, then command me to come to you on the water."

²⁹Jesus said, "Come."

And Peter left the boat and walked on the water to Jesus. ³⁰But when Peter saw the wind and the waves, he became afraid and began to sink. He shouted, "Lord, save me!"

³¹Immediately Jesus reached out his hand and caught Peter. Jesus said, "Your faith is small. Why did you doubt?"

FEAR

The Handicap

Chris was "cool". Nothing seemed to unnerve him. That's why the youth group was surprised when he objected to the idea of a weekend service retreat at a home for mentally and physically disabled people.

"Why don't you like the idea?" someone asked.

"It's stupid, that's all!" Chris said.

"Are you scared, or what?" someone else asked.

"Yes, sure!" Chris responded sarcastically.

The group decided to go ahead, and planned the retreat. Chris grudgingly went along, and kept up his "cool" veneer. But inside, Chris was afraid of the people at the home. He coped with his fear by avoiding any contact with the residents.

But he couldn't avoid the dance. Chris walked in late and leaned against a wall in a dark corner. Sally, one of the residents, saw him and rushed up in her wheelchair. She tugged at his arm. "Dance with me," she pleaded.

He pretended he had not heard her.

"Please dance with me," she persisted. "Please?"

Reluctantly, Chris agreed. Although he felt awkward at first, Chris's fears soon faded. He discovered that Sally was fun. She had a sharp wit. Sally actually made Chris feel comfortable.

"I was scared," he admitted later. "I didn't know what to expect. Then I saw the love and care these people give. They are just like me. I am the one who was handicapped."

Like Chris's fear of the residents, Peter, one of Jesus' disciples, often suffered from fear. Read how he was afraid in **Matthew 14:22–33**.

* How are Chris's and Peter's reactions to fear similar?
* Would you have stayed in the boat or got out to walk on the water? Why?

Consider . . .

* dividing a piece of paper equally. On the left side list fears. On the right side list ways to overcome fears. Share your lists with a friend. Pray for one another.
* taking a step this week in overcoming one of your fears. For example, if you're shy, go up to someone at school or church and introduce yourself.

For more, see . . .

* Psalm 27 (p.515)
* 1 Corinthians 2:1–5 (p.1215)

* Mark 4:35–41 (p.1005)

32After they got into the boat, the wind became calm. 33Then those who were in the boat worshipped Jesus and said, "Truly you are the Son of God!"

34When they had crossed the lake, they came to shore at Gennesaret. 35When the people there recognised Jesus, they told people in the area there that Jesus had come, and they brought all their sick to him. 36They begged Jesus to let them touch just the edge of his coat, and all who touched it were healed.

Obey God's Law

15 Then some Pharisees *d* and teachers of the law came to Jesus from Jerusalem. They asked him, 2"Why don't your followers obey the unwritten laws which have been handed down to us? They don't wash their hands before they eat."

3Jesus answered, "And why do you refuse to obey God's command so that you can follow your own teachings? 4God said, 'Honour your father and your mother,' *n* and 'Anyone who says cruel things to his father or mother must be put to death.' *n* 5But you say a person can tell his father or mother, 'I have something I could use to help you, but I have given it to God instead.' 6You teach that person not to honour his father or his mother. You rejected what God said for the sake of your own rules. 7You are hypocrites! *d* Isaiah was right when he said about you:

8'These people show honour to me with words,
    but their hearts are far from me.
9Their worship of me is worthless.
    The things they teach are nothing but
    human rules.' "   *Isaiah 29:13*

10After Jesus called the crowd to him, he said, "Listen and understand what I am saying. 11It is not what people put into their mouths that makes them unclean. *d* It is what comes out of their mouths that makes them unclean."

'Honour . . . mother.' Quotation from Exodus 20:12; Deuteronomy 5:16.
'Anyone . . . death.' Quotation from Exodus 21:17.

PERSISTENCE

A Bible on Computer

Jayne Chenery wanted to develop a Bible that could be read by people like herself with cerebral palsy. Eventually she contacted the Bible Society and they agreed to start work. Jayne was determined to make sure that the project was completed. She would frequently ask her mother to telephone to check on progress – often with some new request.

Eventually the special computer edition of the books of Luke and Acts was completed and launched in December 1992. It had a speech synthesiser so that it could be understood by blind people. It also had enlarged type for those with sight problems and it could be operated by a person's head or fist or by blowing down a straw. It even included special helps and advice for people who were seriously disabled, all accessed by computer. Jayne was determined to make Luke's Story happen, even though, as a result of her disabilities, she died at sixteen years old – before it was finally launched.

In a way similar to Jayne's dedication to her dream, a woman pursued Jesus to heal her daughter. Read **Matthew 15:21–28** to see how.

* How is Jayne's persistence similar to the mother's in the passage?
* When have you been persistent like the mother? What happened?

Consider . . .

* looking for examples of persistent people on television. What qualities do they possess? Write five of those qualities on a card. Tape it to your mirror.
* taking a step this week in overcoming one of your fears. For example, if you're shy, go up to someone at school or church and introduce yourself.

For more, see . . .

* Ruth 1:1–18 (p.249)
* Ephesians 6:10–20 (p.1277)
* Mark 5:25–34 (p.1005)

¹²Then his followers came to him and asked, "Do you know that the Pharisees are angry because of what you said?"

¹³Jesus answered, "Every plant that my Father in heaven has not planted himself will be pulled up by the roots. ¹⁴Stay away from the Pharisees; they are blind leaders. And if a blind person leads a blind person, both will fall into a ditch."

¹⁵Peter said, "Explain the example to us."

¹⁶Jesus said, "Do you still not understand? ¹⁷Surely you know that all the food that enters the mouth goes into the stomach and then goes out of the body. ¹⁸But what people say with their mouths comes from the way they think; these are the things that make people unclean. ¹⁹Out of the mind come evil thoughts, murder, adultery, *d* sexual sins, stealing, lying and speaking evil of others. ²⁰These things make people unclean; eating with unwashed hands does not make them unclean."

Jesus Helps a Non-Jewish Woman

²¹Jesus left that place and went to the area of Tyre and Sidon. ²²A Canaanite woman from that area came to Jesus and cried out, "Lord, Son of David, *d* have mercy on me! My daughter has a demon, *d* and she is suffering very much."

²³But Jesus did not answer the woman. So his followers came to Jesus and begged him, "Tell the woman to go away. She is following us and shouting."

²⁴Jesus answered, "God sent me only to the lost sheep, the people of Israel."

²⁵Then the woman came to Jesus again and bowed before him and said, "Lord, help me!"

²⁶Jesus answered, "It is not right to take the children's bread and give it to the dogs."

²⁷The woman said, "Yes, Lord, but even the dogs eat the crumbs that fall from their masters' table."

²⁸Then Jesus answered, "Woman, you have great faith! I will do what you asked." And at that moment the woman's daughter was healed.

Jesus Heals Many People

²⁹After leaving there, Jesus went along the shore of Lake Galilee. He went up on a hill and sat there.

³⁰Great crowds came to Jesus, bringing with them the lame, the blind, the crippled, those who could not speak and many others. They put them at Jesus' feet, and he healed them. ³¹The crowd was amazed when they saw that people who could not speak before were now able to speak. The crippled were made strong. The lame could walk, and the blind could see. And they praised the God of Israel for this.

More than 4,000 Fed

³²Jesus called his followers to him and said, "I feel sorry for these people, because they have already been with me three days, and they have nothing to eat. I don't want to send them away hungry. They might faint while going home."

³³His followers asked him, "How can we get enough bread to feed all these people? We are far away from any town."

³⁴Jesus asked, "How many loaves of bread do you have?"

They answered, "Seven, and a few small fish."

³⁵Jesus told the people to sit on the ground. ³⁶He took the seven loaves of bread and the fish and gave thanks to God. Then he divided the food and gave it to his followers, and they gave it to the people. ³⁷All the people ate and were satisfied. Then his followers filled seven baskets with the leftover pieces of food. ³⁸There were about 4,000 men there who ate, besides women and children. ³⁹After sending the people home, Jesus got into the boat and went to the area of Magadan.

The Leaders Ask for a Miracle

16 The Pharisees *d* and Sadducees *d* came to Jesus, wanting to trick him. So they asked him to show them a miracle *d* from God.

²Jesus answered, "At sunset you say we will have good weather, because the sky is red. ³And in the morning you say that it will be a rainy day, because the sky is dark and red. You see these signs in the sky and know what they mean. In the same way, you see the things that I am doing now, but you don't know their meaning. ⁴Evil and sinful people ask for a miracle as a sign, but they will not be given any sign, except the sign of Jonah." *n* Then Jesus left them and went away.

Guard Against Wrong Teachings

⁵Jesus' followers went across the lake, but they had forgotten to bring bread. ⁶Jesus said to them, "Be careful! Beware of the yeast of the Pharisees *d* and the Sadducees." *d*

⁷His followers discussed the meaning of this, saying, "He said this because we forgot to bring bread."

⁸Knowing what they were talking about, Jesus asked them, "Why are you talking about not

> **Sidelight** The city of Caesarea Philippi (Matthew 16:13) where Peter declared that Jesus was God's Son, was north of Lake Galilee in an area that wasn't Jewish. In fact, it had a pagan shrine to Pan, a Greek and Roman nature god.

---

sign of Jonah   Jonah's three days in the fish are like Jesus' three days in the tomb. The story about Jonah is in the book of Jonah.

having bread? Your faith is small. [9]Do you still not understand? Remember the five loaves of bread that fed the 5,000? And remember that you filled many baskets with the leftovers? [10]Or the seven loaves of bread that fed the 4,000 and the many baskets you then also filled? [11]I was not talking to you about bread. Why don't you understand that? I am telling you to beware of the yeast of the Pharisees and the Sadducees." [12]Then the followers understood that Jesus was not telling them to beware of the yeast used in bread but to beware of the teaching of the Pharisees and the Sadducees.

Peter Says Jesus is the Christ

[13]When Jesus came to the area of Caesarea Philippi, he asked his followers, "Who do people say the Son of Man [d] is?"

[14]They answered, "Some say you are John the Baptist. [d] Others say you are Elijah, and still others say you are Jeremiah or one of the prophets." [d]

[15]Then Jesus asked them, "And who do you say I am?"

[16]Simon Peter answered, "You are the Christ,[d] the Son of the living God."

[17]Jesus answered, "You are blessed, Simon son of Jonah, because no person taught you that. My Father in heaven showed you who I am. [18]So I tell you, you are Peter.[n] On this rock I will build my church, and the power of death will not be able to defeat it. [19]I will give you the keys of the kingdom of heaven; the things you don't allow on earth will be the things that God does not allow, and the things you allow on earth will be the things that God allows." [20]Then Jesus warned his followers not to tell anyone he was the Christ.

Jesus Says that He Must Die

[21]From that time on Jesus began telling his followers that he must go to Jerusalem, where the older Jewish leaders, the leading priests, and

Peter   The Greek name "Peter", like the Aramaic name "Cephas", means "rock".

FAITH

T-e-a-c-h-e-r

A fever left Helen Keller blind and deaf at birth. She was imprisoned in a dark, silent world.

In 1887, when Helen was seven, Anne Sullivan, herself partially blind, became Helen's teacher. Anne had great vision and hope. She believed that Helen held untapped and unseen abilities. Months passed with very little progress, but Anne still believed.

Then, finally, Anne witnessed the results of faith. Helen was playing at the water pump. Anne finger-spelled "w-a-t-e-r" into her free hand. Anne wrote in her journal, "The word coming so close upon the sensation of cold water rushing over her hand seemed to startle her. A new light came into her face. She understood! Then turning around she asked my name. I spelled 'T-e-a-c-h-e-r'."

Thanks to Anne's faith, Helen's dark, lonely life opened wide to the light of communication and learning. Helen graduated with honours from Radcliffe College, and went on to a distinguished career as an educator, speaker and author. Helen and "Teacher" were lifelong companions.

Teacher's faith brought Helen out of darkness and into light. In **Matthew 16:13–20**, read how Jesus had faith in Peter, even when Peter wasn't sure of his own faith.

* How was Anne's and Helen's friendship similar to Jesus' and Peter's?
* Anne's faith enabled her to teach Helen. Peter's faith helped him to become a church leader. What does your faith help you to do?

Consider . . .

* helping young children to grow in their faith by volunteering to help one Sunday in the church crèche, Sunday school or holiday activity group.
* writing a Haiku poem that expresses faith. A Haiku poem has three lines. The first and third lines each have five syllables. The middle line has seven.

For more, see . . .

* Nehemiah 9:6–8 (p.451)
* Hebrews 11 (p.1341)
* Mark 8:27–38 (p.1012)

the teachers of the law would make him suffer many things. He told them he must be killed and then be raised from the dead on the third day.

²²Peter took Jesus aside and told him not to talk like that. He said, "God save you from those things, Lord! Those things will never happen to you!"

²³Then Jesus said to Peter, "Go away from me, Satan!ⁿ You are not helping me! You don't care about the things of God, but only about the things people think are important."

²⁴Then Jesus said to his followers, "If people want to follow me, they must give up the things they want. They must be willing even to give up their lives to follow me. ²⁵Those who want to save their lives will give up true life, and those who give up their lives for me will have true life. ²⁶It is worth nothing for them to have the whole world if they lose their souls. They could never pay enough to buy back their souls. ²⁷The Son of Man ᵈ will come again with his Father's glory and with his angels. At that time, he will reward them for what they have done. ²⁸I tell you the truth, some people standing here will see the Son of Man coming with his kingdom before they die."

Jesus Talks with Moses and Elijah

17 Six days later, Jesus took Peter, James and John, the brother of James, up on a high mountain by themselves. ²While they watched, Jesus' appearance was changed; his face became bright like the sun, and his clothes

> **Sidelight** When Peter suggested building three tents in Matthew 17:4, he may have been thinking about the annual Feast of Shelters. During this feast (which was like a harvest festival), Jews from everywhere would come to Jerusalem and build shelters in the streets and town square – anywhere with a little space.

became white as light. ³Then Moses and Elijah ⁿ appeared to them, talking with Jesus.

⁴Peter said to Jesus, "Lord, it is good that we are here. If you want, I will put up three tents here—one for you, one for Moses and one for Elijah."

⁵While Peter was talking, a bright cloud covered them. A voice came from the cloud and said, "This is my Son, whom I love, and I am very pleased with him. Listen to him!"

⁶When his followers heard the voice, they were so frightened they fell to the ground. ⁷But

Jesus went to them and touched them and said, "Stand up. Don't be afraid." ⁸When they looked up, they saw Jesus was now alone.

⁹As they were coming down the mountain, Jesus commanded them not to tell anyone about what they had seen until the Son of Man ᵈ had risen from the dead.

¹⁰Then his followers asked him, "Why do the teachers of the law say that Elijah must come first?"

¹¹Jesus answered, "They are right to say that Elijah is coming and that he will make everything the way it should be. ¹²But I tell you that Elijah has already come, and they did not recognise him. They did to him whatever they wanted to do. It will be the same with the Son of Man; those same people will make the Son of Man suffer." ¹³Then the followers understood that Jesus was talking about John the Baptist. ᵈ

Jesus Heals a Sick Boy

¹⁴When Jesus and his followers came back to the crowd, a man came to Jesus and bowed before him. ¹⁵The man said, "Lord, have mercy on my son. He has epilepsy ⁿ and is suffering very much, because he often falls into the fire or into the water. ¹⁶I brought him to your followers, but they could not cure him."

¹⁷Jesus answered, "You people have no faith, and your lives are all wrong. How long must I put up with you? How long must I continue to be patient with you? Bring the boy here." ¹⁸Jesus gave a strong command to the demon ᵈ inside the boy. Then the demon came out, and the boy was healed from that time on.

¹⁹The followers came to Jesus when he was alone and asked, "Why couldn't we force the demon out?"

²⁰Jesus answered, "Because your faith is too small. I tell you the truth, if your faith is as big as a mustard seed, you can say to this mountain, 'Move from here to there,' and it will move. All things will be possible for you." ²¹ ⁿ

Jesus Talks About His Death

²²While Jesus' followers were gathering in Galilee, he said to them, "The Son of Man ᵈ will be handed over to people, ²³and they will kill him. But on the third day he will be raised from the dead." And the followers were filled with sadness.

Jesus Talks About Paying Taxes

²⁴When Jesus and his followers came to Capernaum, the men who collected the Temple ᵈ

Satan Name for the devil, meaning "the enemy". Jesus means that Peter was talking like Satan.
Moses and Elijah Two of the most important Jewish leaders in the past. Moses had given them the law, and Elijah was an important prophet.
epilepsy A disease that causes a person sometimes to lose control of their body and perhaps faint, shake strongly or be unable to move.
Verse 21 Some Greek copies add verse 21: "That kind of spirit comes out only if you use prayer and give up eating."

tax came to Peter. They asked, "Does your teacher pay the Temple tax?"

25Peter answered, "Yes, Jesus pays the tax."

Peter went into the house, but before he could speak, Jesus said to him, "What do you think? The kings of the earth collect different kinds of taxes. But who pays the taxes—the king's children or others?"

26Peter answered, "Other people pay the taxes."

Jesus said to Peter, "Then the children of the king don't have to pay taxes. 27But we don't want to upset these tax collectors. So go to the lake and fish. After you catch the first fish, open its mouth and you will find a coin. Take that coin and give it to the tax collectors for you and me."

Who is the Greatest?

18 At that time the followers came to Jesus and asked, "Who is greatest in the kingdom of heaven?"

2Jesus called a little child to him and stood the child before his followers. 3Then he said, "I tell you the truth, you must change and become like little children. Otherwise, you will never enter the kingdom of heaven. 4The greatest person in the kingdom of heaven is the one who makes himself humble like this child.

5"Whoever accepts a child in my name accepts me. 6If one of these little children believes in me, and someone causes that child to sin, it would be better for that person to have a large stone tied

FAITH

Speak Up

"Daddy, Daddy," whispered Nicki, "I need to say something!" Nicki's dad was about to lead an Easter Sunday service in the African village of Mwanza and was trying to listen to his translator – the last thing he needed was his five-year-old daughter interrupting.

"Be quiet," he replied.

Nicki was determined to be heard, so she went and bugged her mum until she listened. During one of the hymns before the sermon, Nicki's mum said to her husband, "I think you need to hear what she has to say."

So Nicki's dad relented. "Quickly Nicki, what is it you want to tell me?"

"Well . . . it's Easter Sunday and no one is smiling, I think someone should say something!"

So after being introduced to the 400 people Nicki stood up, fiddling with her dress and looking at the floor. After a few nervous moments, she looked up at the tall translator and said slowly, "Do you know that today is a very special day, because Jesus died on the cross and rose again for you and for me so we could have a place in heaven with him one day. So I don't really understand why no one is smiling. We should be really happy because Jesus loves us so much." As Nicki went to sit down you could hear a pin drop, and all you could see was a bunch of bright white smiles.

That morning there was no preaching because Nicki had said it all. People gave their lives to Jesus that day – people who went on to lead churches of their own.

Nicki was a little girl who had faith; God chose to use her on that day and the Holy Spirit really moved in that place.

Read **Matthew 17:14–20**.

* How do you think the disciples felt when they were told they could do anything if they had faith?
* Do you think you have faith that can move mountains?

Consider . . .

* next time someone tells you that they're unwell. Will your first thought be that they can be healed? If so, pray for them.
* chatting to someone you know who has been healed or someone who's prayed for another person and they've been healed. Ask them about their experience and about their faith.

For more, see . . .

* Matthew 21:18–22 (p.977)
* Luke 17:5–6 (p.1076)
* Luke 8:22–25 (p.1053)

around the neck and be drowned in the sea. [7]How terrible for the people of the world because of the things that cause them to sin. Such things will happen, but how terrible for the one who causes them to happen! [8]If your hand or your foot causes you to sin, cut it off and throw it away. It is better for you to lose part of your body and live for ever than to have two hands and two feet and be thrown into the fire that burns for ever. [9]If your eye causes you to sin, take it out and throw it away. It is better for you to have only one eye and live for ever than to have two eyes and be thrown into the fire of hell.

A Lost Sheep

[10]"Be careful. Don't think these little children are worth nothing. I tell you that they have angels in heaven who are always with my Father in heaven. [11] *n*

[12]"If a man has 100 sheep but one of the sheep gets lost, he will leave the other 99 on the hill and go to look for the lost sheep. [13]I tell you the truth, he is happier about that one sheep than about the 99 that were never lost. [14]In the same way, your Father in heaven does not want any of these little children to be lost.

When a Person Sins Against You

[15]"If your fellow believer sins against you, go and tell him in private what he did wrong. If he listens to you, you have helped that person to be your brother or sister again. [16]But if he refuses to listen, go to him again and take one or two other people with you. 'Every case may be

Verse 11   Some Greek copies add verse 11: "The Son of Man came to save lost people."

FRIENDS

Communication's What You Need

"I hate her. I can't believe she spoke to me like that, who does she think she is!" Kate had just come home and was livid with Gemma, her manager at work. Kate had been shouted at in front of everyone for taking five minutes extra on her lunch break. She felt embarrassed and hurt and wanted everyone to know how hard done by she was. She'd thought Gemma was a friend.

Kate's mum listened to her getting angrier and stopped her in mid-flow. "Have you spoken to Gemma about how she made you feel?"

Kate paused. "No, why would I do that? It would just bring up the bad situation again and she might even embarrass me further."

"But Gemma might just have had a bad day," explained Kate's mum, "or maybe what she said just came out wrong. You know she is a good friend and wouldn't want you to be unhappy. But you have to tell her what's up."

Kate calmed down and realised that perhaps she was blowing the situation out of proportion and decided to speak to Gemma to resolve the situation.

Read **Matthew 18:15–20** where it specifically talks about friendship in the church. It all comes down to communication.

* What does God promise to us in this passage?
* Do you think this approach works in every situation?

Consider . . .

* how you communicate that you appreciate your friends. Make a list of all your friends and write a letter or note saying something great about them, then send it to them.
* next time you have a conflict with a friend, talking it through with them properly rather than gossiping and complaining about them.

For more, see . . .

* Proverbs 11:13 (p.599)
* Matthew 6:14 (p.948)

* Proverbs 27:6 (p.614)
* Matthew 22:39 (p.980)

proved by two or three witnesses.' [n] [17]If he refuses to listen to them, tell the church. If he refuses to listen to the church, then treat him like a person who does not believe in God or like a tax collector.

[18]"I tell you the truth, the things you don't allow on earth will be the things God does not allow. And the things you allow on earth will be the things that God allows.

[19]"Also, I tell you that if two of you on earth agree about something and pray for it, it will be done for you by my Father in heaven. [20]This is true because if two or three people come together in my name, I am there with them."

An Unforgiving Servant

[21]Then Peter came to Jesus and asked, "Lord, when my fellow believer sins against me, how many times must I forgive him? Should I forgive him as many as seven times?"

[22]Jesus answered, "I tell you, you must forgive him more than seven times. You must forgive him even if he does wrong to you 77 times.

[23]"The kingdom of heaven is like a king who decided to collect the money his servants owed him. [24]When the king began to collect his money, a servant who owed him several thousand pounds was brought to him. [25]But the servant did not have enough money to pay his master, the king. So the master ordered that everything the servant owned should be sold, even the servant's wife and children. Then the money would be used to pay the king what the servant owed.

[26]"But the servant fell on his knees and begged, 'Be patient with me, and I will pay you

'Every . . . witnesses.' Quotation from Deuteronomy 19:15.

FORGIVENESS

So Sorry

Karen was in trouble and she knew it. She hadn't even started to look at the textbook, and the history exam would decide her grade.

She sat behind Mark, who was a bright student. He would help, she thought. "Psst, Mark," she whispered, poking him with her pencil. "Question five. Give me a clue."

Mark shrugged.

Karen poked him again with the pencil. Mark turned. "Stop it," he hissed.

"Mark, come up here and bring your paper," interrupted Ms Miller, the history teacher. As Mark walked to Ms Miller's desk, Karen pretended to work on her exam.

"I won't tolerate cheating," Ms Miller said quietly to Mark. She tossed the exam paper into the waste basket. Mark tried to explain what had happened, but she didn't believe him. "Take your seat and be quiet for the rest of the period," she snapped.

Karen saw Mark's face as he walked back towards his seat. His eyes showed his deep anger and hurt. "Why?" he whispered. Karen looked away.

As school ended, Karen saw Mark in the hall and tried to tell him how sorry she was. But Mark ignored her. At midnight, she still couldn't get Mark's hurt out of her mind. She knew what to do.

"Tomorrow," she thought, "I'll tell Ms Miller what really happened, but will Mark ever forgive me?"

Both Karen and Mark could learn from **Matthew 18:21–35**.

- How is Karen's and Mark's struggle similar to the one in Jesus' story?
- Which character in Jesus' parable do you identify with most? Why?

Consider . . .

- listing the things you find difficult to forgive. Put them in order, from least to most difficult to forgive. What factors make forgiveness difficult?
- thinking of two people: one who has hurt you most, and one you have hurt the most. Pray for strength, and then do one thing to help bring forgiveness to both people.

For more, see . . .

- Jonah 3 (p.886)
- Luke 17:1–4 (p.1076)
- Micah 7:18–20 (p.897)

everything I owe.' [27]The master felt sorry for his servant and told him he did not have to pay it back. Then he let the servant go free.

[28]"Later, that same servant found another servant who owed him a few pounds. The servant grabbed him around the neck and said, 'Pay me the money you owe me!'

[29]"The other servant fell on his knees and begged him, 'Be patient with me, and I will pay you everything I owe.'

[30]"But the first servant refused to be patient. He threw the other servant into prison until he could pay everything he owed. [31]When the other servants saw what had happened, they were very sorry. So they went and told their master all that had happened.

[32]"Then the master called his servant in and said, 'You evil servant! Because you begged me to forget what you owed, I told you that you did not have to pay anything. [33]You should have shown mercy to that other servant, just as I showed mercy to you.' [34]The master was very angry and put the servant in prison to be punished until he could pay everything he owed.

[35]"This king did what my heavenly Father will do to you if you do not forgive your brother or sister from your heart."

Jesus Teaches About Divorce

19 After Jesus said all these things, he left Galilee and went into the area of Judea on the other side of the Jordan River. [2]Large crowds followed him, and he healed them there.

[3]Some Pharisees [d] came to Jesus and tried to trick him. They asked, "Is it right for a man to divorce his wife for any reason he chooses?"

[4]Jesus answered, "Surely you have read in the Scriptures: [d] when God made the world, 'he made them male and female'. [n] [5]And God said, 'So a man will leave his father and mother and be united with his wife, and the two will become one body.' [n] [6]So there are not two, but one. God has joined the two together, so no one should separate them."

[7]The Pharisees asked, "Why then did Moses give a command for a man to divorce his wife by giving her divorce papers?"

[8]Jesus answered, "Moses allowed you to divorce your wives because you refused to accept God's teaching, but divorce was not allowed in the beginning. [9]I tell you that anyone who divorces his wife and marries another woman is guilty of adultery. [d] The only reason for a man to divorce his wife is if his wife has sexual relations with another man."

[10]The followers said to him, "If that is the only reason a man can divorce his wife, it is better not to marry."

[11]Jesus answered, "Not everyone can accept this teaching, but God has made some able to accept it. [12]There are different reasons why some men cannot marry. Some men were born without the ability to become fathers. Others were made that way later in life by other people. And some men have given up marriage because of the kingdom of heaven. But the person who can marry should accept this teaching about marriage." [n]

Jesus Welcomes Children

[13]Then the people brought their little children to Jesus so he could put his hands on them [n] and pray for them. His followers told them to stop, [14]but Jesus said, "Let the little children come to me. Don't stop them, because the kingdom of heaven belongs to people who are like these children." [15]After Jesus put his hands on the children, he left that place.

A Rich Young Man's Question

[16]A man came to Jesus and asked, "Teacher, what good thing must I do to have life for ever?"

[17]Jesus answered, "Why do you ask me about what is good? Only God is good. But if you want to have life for ever, obey the commands."

[18]The man asked, "Which commands?"

Jesus answered, " 'You must not murder anyone; you must not be guilty of adultery; [d] you must not steal; you must not tell lies about your neighbour; [19]honour your father and mother; [n] and love your neighbour as you love yourself.' " [n]

[20]The young man said, "I have obeyed all these things. What else do I need to do?"

[21]Jesus answered, "If you want to be perfect, then go and sell your possessions and give the

---

Sidelight Divorce has always been a controversial subject – even in Jesus' day. While some religious leaders said that someone could only get a divorce because of unfaithfulness, others argued that a husband could divorce a wife for burning supper, wearing the wrong thing in public, or even talking to another man. Jesus entered the debate in Matthew 19:1–12.

'he made . . . female' Quotation from Genesis 1:27 or 5:2.
'So . . . body.' Quotation from Genesis 2:24.
But . . . marriage. This may also mean, "The person who can accept this teaching about not marrying should accept it."
put his hands on them Showing that Jesus gave special blessings to these children.
'You . . . mother.' Quotation from Exodus 20:12–16; Deuteronomy 5:16–20.
'love . . . yourself.' Quotation from Leviticus 19:18.

money to the poor. If you do this, you will have treasure in heaven. Then come and follow me."

[22]But when the young man heard this, he left very sad, because he was rich.

[23]Then Jesus said to his followers, "I tell you the truth, it will be hard for a rich person to enter the kingdom of heaven. [24]Yes, I tell you that it is easier for a camel to go through the eye of a needle than for a rich person to enter the kingdom of God."[25]When Jesus' followers heard this, they were very surprised and asked, "Then who can be saved?"

[26]Jesus looked at them and said, "This is something people cannot do, but God can do all things."

[27]Peter said to Jesus, "Look, we have left everything and followed you. So what will we have?"

[28]Jesus said to them, "I tell you the truth, when the age to come has arrived, the Son of Man[d] will sit on his great throne. All of you who followed me will also sit on twelve thrones, judging the twelve tribes[d] of Israel. [29]And all those who have left houses, brothers, sisters, father, mother, children or farms to follow me will get much more than they left, and they will have life for ever. [30]Many who have the highest place now will have the lowest place in the future. And many who have the lowest place now will have the highest place in the future.

JUSTICE

It's Not Fair

The annual fun-run at Mount Farm had arrived at last. Hundreds of enthusiastic runners gathered at the starting line and prepared themselves for the three-mile race which lay ahead of them. They weren't running to win, but simply to take part. A medal was to be given to every competitor who completed the full three miles.

When the starting pistol was fired, feet pounded against the road in one thunderous roar. Many of the competitors had been sponsored, and were running in order to raise money for charity. Others were running to prove to their children and grandchildren that they were still fit. The children ran to prove that they were still fitter!

As the competitors approached the final half-mile of the race, a young boy of about twelve years of age joined in. He was wearing tracksuit bottoms and a white T-shirt. He ran more slowly than the rest of the runners, but when he finally reached the finishing line, he laughed out loud, thrilled with himself.

Then the medals were handed out. All the competitors who had gone the whole three miles were given their medals, and then the judge gave the young twelve-year-old boy a medal.

"You can't do that! He only ran half a mile!" some of the other competitors shouted.

The judge motioned for those who were making a fuss to come and take a look at something. Then he rolled the boy's trouser-leg up so that they could see his false foot.

"It may only be half a mile to you folks," the judge said, "but since young Robert here lost his foot in an accident, today was a half-mile marathon!"

Jesus tells a similar story in **Matthew 20:1–16**.

* How were the competitors' complaints similar to those of the vineyard workers?
* If you were amongst the first hired, how would you have felt? Would you have felt the same if you were one of the last hired? Why or why not?

Consider . . .

* watching the news on television or reading the newspapers and spotting items where justice is said to have been done. Ask yourself if justice, as taught by Jesus, really has been done.
* asking people that you meet what the word "justice" means. Compare their definitions with that of a dictionary, and then come up with your own definition.

For more, see . . .

* Job 8:3–6 (p.474)
* 2 Thessalonians 1:3–12 (p.1304)
* Luke 14:12–24 (p.1069)

A Story About Workers

20 "The kingdom of heaven is like a person who owned some land. One morning, he went out very early to hire some people to work in his vineyard. ²The man agreed to pay the workers a silver coin*n* for working on that day. Then he sent them into the vineyard to work. ³At about nine o'clock the man went to the market-place and saw some other people standing there, doing nothing. ⁴So he said to them, 'If you go and work in my vineyard, I will pay you what your work is worth.' ⁵So they went to work in the vineyard. The man went out again at about twelve o'clock and three o'clock and did the same thing. ⁶At about five o'clock the man went to the market-place again and saw others standing there. He asked them, 'Why have you stood here all day doing nothing?' ⁷They answered, 'No one has given us a job.' The man said to them, 'Then you can go and work in my vineyard.'

⁸"At the end of the day, the owner of the vineyard said to the foreman of all the workers, 'Call the workers and pay them. Start with the last people I hired and end with those I hired first.'

⁹"When the workers who were hired at five o'clock came to get their pay, each received a silver coin. ¹⁰When the workers who were hired first came to get their pay, they thought they would be paid more than the others. But each one of them also received a silver coin. ¹¹When they got their coin, they complained to the man who owned the land. ¹²They said, 'Those people were hired last and worked only one hour. But you paid them the same as you paid us who worked hard all day in the hot sun.' ¹³But the man who owned the vineyard said to one of those workers, 'Friend, I am being fair to you. You agreed to work for a silver coin. ¹⁴So take your pay and go. I want to give the man who was hired last the same pay that I gave you. ¹⁵I can do what I want with my own money. Are you jealous because I am good to those people?'

¹⁶"So those who have the last place now will have the first place in the future, and those who have the first place now will have the last place in the future."

Jesus Talks About His Own Death

¹⁷While Jesus was going to Jerusalem, he took his twelve followers aside privately and said to them, ¹⁸"Look, we are going to Jerusalem. The Son of Man *d* will be turned over to the leading priests and the teachers of the law, and they will say that he must die. ¹⁹They will give the Son of Man to the non-Jewish people to laugh at him and beat him with whips and crucify him. But on the third day, he will be raised to life again."

A Mother Asks Jesus a Favour

²⁰Then the wife of Zebedee came to Jesus with her sons. She bowed before him and asked him to do something for her.

> **Sidelight** James and John, the sons of Zebedee, were nicknamed "the sons of thunder" (Matthew 20:20–24; see also Mark 3:17, p.1003). The nicknames may have come from their booming voices, or more probably, from the sort of behaviour they displayed in Luke 9:51–55 (p.1055)!

²¹Jesus asked, "What do you want?"

She said, "Promise that one of my sons will sit at your right side and the other will sit at your left side in your kingdom."

²²But Jesus said, "You don't understand what you are asking. Can you drink the cup that I am about to drink?" *n*

The sons answered, "Yes, we can."

²³Jesus said to them, "You will drink from my cup. But I cannot choose who will sit at my right or my left; those places belong to those for whom my Father has prepared them."

²⁴When the other ten followers heard this, they were angry with the two brothers. ²⁵Jesus called all the followers together and said, "You know that the rulers of the non-Jewish people love to show their power over the people. And their important leaders love to use all their authority. ²⁶But it should not be that way among you. Whoever wants to become great among you must serve the rest of you like a servant. ²⁷Whoever wants to become first among you must serve the rest of you like a slave. ²⁸In the same way, the Son of Man *d* did not come to be served. He came to serve others and to give his life as a ransom for many people."

Jesus Heals Two Blind Men

²⁹When Jesus and his followers were leaving Jericho, a great many people followed him. ³⁰Two blind men sitting by the road heard that Jesus was going by, so they shouted, "Lord, Son of David, *d* have mercy on us!"

---

coin Roman denarii. A silver coin was the average pay for one day's work.
drink . . . drink Jesus used the idea of drinking from a cup to ask if they could accept the same terrible things that would happen to him.

³¹The people warned the blind men to be quiet, but they shouted even more, "Lord, Son of David, have mercy on us!"

³²Jesus stopped and said to the blind men, "What do you want me to do for you?"

³³They answered, "Lord, we want to see."

³⁴Jesus felt sorry for the blind men and touched their eyes, and at once they could see. Then they followed Jesus.

Jesus Enters Jerusalem as a King

21 As Jesus and his followers were coming closer to Jerusalem, they stopped at Bethphage at the hill called the Mount of Olives. *d* From there Jesus sent two of his followers ²and said to them, "Go to the town you can see ahead of you. When you enter it, you will quickly find a donkey tied there with its colt. Untie them and bring them to me. ³If anyone asks you why you are taking the donkeys, say that the Master needs them, and he will send them at once."

⁴This was to bring about what the prophet *d* had said:

⁵"Tell the people of Jerusalem,
    'Your king is coming to you.
He is gentle and riding on a donkey,
    on the colt of a donkey.'"   *Zechariah 9:9*

⁶The followers went and did what Jesus told them to do. ⁷They brought the donkey and the colt to Jesus and laid their coats on them, and Jesus sat on them. ⁸Many people spread their coats on the road. Others cut branches from the trees and spread them on the road. ⁹The people were walking ahead of Jesus and behind him, shouting,

"Praise *n* to the Son of David! *d*
God bless the One who comes in the name
    of the Lord!
Praise to God in heaven!"   *Psalm 118:26*

¹⁰When Jesus entered Jerusalem, all the city was filled with excitement. The people asked, "Who is this man?"

¹¹The crowd answered, "This man is Jesus, the prophet from the town of Nazareth in Galilee."

Jesus Goes to the Temple

¹²Jesus went into the Temple*d* and threw out all the people who were buying and selling there. He turned over the tables of those who were exchanging different kinds of money, and he upset the benches of those who were selling doves. ¹³Jesus said to all the people there, "It is written

in the Scriptures, *d* 'My Temple will be called a house for prayer.' *n* But you are changing it into a 'hideout for robbers'." *n*

¹⁴The blind and crippled people came to Jesus in the Temple, and he healed them. ¹⁵The leading priests and the teachers of the law saw that Jesus was doing wonderful things and that the children were praising him in the Temple, saying, "Praise *n* to the Son of David." *d* All these things made the priests and the teachers of the law very angry.

¹⁶They asked Jesus, "Do you hear the things these children are saying?"

Jesus answered, "Yes. Haven't you read in the Scriptures, 'You have taught children and babies to sing praises'?" *n*

¹⁷Then Jesus left and went out of the city to Bethany, where he spent the night.

The Power of Faith

¹⁸Early the next morning, as Jesus was going back to the city, he became hungry. ¹⁹Seeing a fig tree beside the road, Jesus went to it, but there were no figs on the tree, only leaves. So Jesus said to the tree, "You will never again have fruit." The tree immediately dried up.

²⁰When his followers saw this, they were amazed. They asked, "How did the fig tree dry up so quickly?"

²¹Jesus answered, "I tell you the truth, if you have faith and do not doubt, you will be able to do what I did to this tree and even more. You will be able to say to this mountain, 'Go, fall into the sea.' And if you have faith, it will happen. ²²If you believe, you will get anything you ask for in prayer."

Leaders Doubt Jesus' Authority

²³Jesus went to the Temple,*d* and while he was teaching there, the leading priests and the older leaders of the people came to him. They said, "What authority do you have to do these things? Who gave you this authority?"

²⁴Jesus answered, "I also will ask you a question. If you answer me, then I will tell you what authority I have to do these things. ²⁵Tell me: when John baptised people, did that come from God or just from other people?"

They argued about Jesus' question, saying, "If we answer, 'John's baptism was from God', Jesus will say, 'Then why didn't you believe him?' ²⁶But if we say, 'It was from people', we are afraid

---

Praise   Literally, "Hosanna", a Hebrew word used at first in praying to God for help. At this time it was probably a shout of joy used in praising God or his Messiah.
'My Temple . . . prayer.'   Quotation from Isaiah 56:7.
'hideout for robbers.'   Quotation from Jeremiah 7:11.
'You . . . praises'   Quotation from the Septuagint (Greek) version of Psalm 8:2.

of what the crowd will do because they all believe that John was a prophet." *d*

²⁷So they answered Jesus, "We don't know."

Jesus said to them, "Then I won't tell you what authority I have to do these things.

A Story About Two Sons

²⁸"Tell me what you think about this: a man had two sons. He went to the first son and said, 'Son, go and work today in my vineyard.' ²⁹The son answered, 'I will not go.' But later the son changed his mind and went. ³⁰Then the father went to the other son and said, 'Son, go and work today in my vineyard.' The son answered, 'Yes, sir, I will go and work,' but he did not go. ³¹Which of the two sons obeyed his father?"

The priests and leaders answered, "The first son."

Jesus said to them, "I tell you the truth, the tax collectors and the prostitutes *d* will enter the kingdom of God before you do. ³²John came to show you the right way to live. You did not believe him, but the tax collectors and prostitutes believed him. Even after seeing this, you still refused to change your ways and believe him.

A Story About God's Son

³³"Listen to this story: there was a man who owned a vineyard. He put a wall around it and dug a hole for a winepress *d* and built a tower. Then he leased the land to some farmers and left for a trip. ³⁴When it was time for the grapes to be picked, he sent his servants to the farmers to get his share of the grapes. ³⁵But the farmers grabbed the servants, beat one, killed another and then killed a third servant with stones. ³⁶So the man sent some other servants to the farmers, even more than he sent the first time. But the farmers did the same thing to the servants that they had done before. ³⁷So the man decided to send his son to the farmers. He said, 'They will respect my son.' ³⁸But when the farmers saw

HYPOCRISY

Caught on Camera

If you read the little booklets that are inserted into the CD cases of some of the world's most famous music artists, you will often find messages of thanks to God. In fact, some pop celebrities make an even bigger deal out of publicly "giving God all the glory" when they are picking up awards or getting interviewed in magazines.

It's then really sad when a few weeks later they end up splashed all over the front page of the newspapers because they've been caught on camera looking bedraggled on a booze binge, or a having a shifty snog with somebody who isn't their partner! It's not our place to judge them – but we can learn from their mistakes.

Maybe you're not famous enough to have the paparazzi pouncing on you when you're up to no good, but you can ask your mates to watch your back instead. True friends will tell you when you're starting to go off the rails; they'll give you a hard time when you're starting to act like somebody different to the person God's made you to be.

Read **Matthew 21:28–32**.

* People say one thing and do another. Do you ever do that?
* Neither of the brothers in Jesus' story got it 100 per cent right. What would be the best way for them, and for you, to connect your words and actions?

Consider . . .

* asking a friend to point out your three greatest strengths and your three biggest weaknesses.
* writing a letter to yourself describing the kind of person you really want to be. Then sealing it in an envelope and opening it in a year's time.

For more, see . . .

* Genesis 3:8–12 (p.5)
* Matthew 7:4–5 (p.949)
* Psalm 26 (p.514)

the son, they said to each other, 'This son will inherit the vineyard. If we kill him, it will be ours!' [39]Then the farmers grabbed the son, threw him out of the vineyard and killed him. [40]So what will the owner of the vineyard do to these farmers when he comes?"

[41]The priests and leaders said, "He will surely kill those evil men. Then he will lease the vineyard to some other farmers who will give him his share of the crop at harvest time."

[42]Jesus said to them, "Surely you have read this in the Scriptures: *d*

'The stone that the builders rejected
    became the cornerstone. *d*

Verse 44   Some copies do not have verse 44.

The Lord did this,
    and it is wonderful to us.'   *Psalm 118:22–23*
[43]"So I tell you that the kingdom of God will be taken away from you and given to people who do the things God wants in his kingdom. [44]The person who falls on this stone will be broken, and on whomsoever that stone falls, that person will be crushed." *n*

[45]When the leading priests and the Pharisees *d* heard these stories, they knew Jesus was talking about them. [46]They wanted to arrest him, but they were afraid of the people, because the people believed that Jesus was a prophet. *d*

PRIORITIES

Top of the List

Lauren became a Christian after a wonderful week away at the church holiday club. Until then, she'd had no idea how much God loved her and that he wanted a relationship with her. It was incredible! She was thrilled when the leaders presented her with a Bible and she promised God she'd read it every day.

When she got home, Lauren volunteered to help out at Kids' Club and joined the youth group. Being a Christian meant so much to Lauren and she wanted to tell everyone and anyone about Jesus.

The following year Lauren started a new school, and over the next few years, things changed. Lauren made lots of friends and joined the drama group. She got the lead role in the school play but had to give up Kids' Club as she had too many rehearsals. Soon Lauren was missing church, as her boss at the restaurant wanted her to work Sundays. Even reading her Bible was difficult with all the homework she got.

In RE class one day, Lauren's teacher asked if anyone was a Christian. As Lauren raised her hand, her best friend Anna laughed. "Very funny," she said, "there's no way you're a Christian". Lauren was so shocked that she put her hand down and said nothing. She couldn't believe her closest friend had no idea she was a Christian.

At home that night, Lauren took out her Bible. Tears filled her eyes. She realised God wasn't her top priority any more; he wasn't even in the top ten. Friends, school, her job, the play – they had all taken the place that God once had in her life.

In **Matthew 22:1–14** Jesus tells a parable that helps us come to the same conclusions as Lauren: the most important thing in our lives is our relationship with God and how we live.

* How different were Lauren's priorities to that of the wedding guests?
* The king had a guest thrown out of the feast because he wasn't dressed properly. In what way do you think Lauren may not have looked like a Christian to her friends?

Consider . . .

* what your priorities are. Does God come first?
* how you can remind yourself that God is top priority. Try looking at how you spend your time each day. How much is spent on God?

For more, see . . .

* Matthew 22:37–38 (p.980)
* Colossians 3:1–17 (p.1292)
* Luke 10:38–42 (p.1058)

A Story About a Wedding Feast

22 Jesus again used stories to teach the people. He said, [2]"The kingdom of heaven is like a king who prepared a wedding feast for his son. [3]The king invited some people to the feast. When the feast was ready, the king sent his servants to tell the people, but they refused to come.

[4]"Then the king sent other servants, saying, 'Tell those who have been invited that my feast is ready. I have killed my best bulls and calves for the dinner, and everything is ready. Come to the wedding feast.'

[5]"But the people refused to listen to the servants and left to do other things. One went to work in his field, and another went to his business. [6]Some of the other people grabbed the servants, beat them and killed them. [7]The king was furious and sent his army to kill the murderers and burn their city.

[8]"After that, the king said to his servants, 'The wedding feast is ready. I invited those people, but they were not worthy to come. [9]So go to the street corners and invite everyone you find to come to my feast.' [10]So the servants went into the streets and gathered all the people they could find, both good and bad. And the wedding hall was filled with guests.

[11]"When the king came in to see the guests, he saw a man who was not dressed for a wedding. [12]The king said, 'Friend, how were you allowed to come in here? You are not dressed for a wedding.' But the man said nothing. [13]So the king told some servants, 'Tie this man's hands and feet. Throw him out into the darkness, where people will cry and grind their teeth with pain.'

[14]"Yes, many people are invited, but only a few are chosen."

Is It Right to Pay Taxes or Not?

[15]Then the Pharisees [d] left that place and made plans to trap Jesus into saying something wrong. [16]They sent some of their own followers and some people from the group called Herodians. [n] They said, "Teacher, we know that you are an honest man and that you teach the truth about God's way. You are not afraid of what other people think about you, because you pay no attention to who they are. [17]So tell us what you think. Is it right to pay taxes to Caesar [d] or not?"

[18]But knowing that these leaders were trying to trick him, Jesus said, "You hypocrites! [d] Why are you trying to trap me? [19]Show me a coin used for paying the tax." So the men showed him a coin. [n] [20]Then Jesus asked, "Whose image and name are on the coin?"

[21]The men answered, "Caesar's."

Then Jesus said to them, "Give to Caesar the things that are Caesar's, and give to God the things that are God's."

[22]When the men heard what Jesus said, they were amazed and left him and went away.

Some Sadducees Try to Trick Jesus

[23]That same day some Sadducees [d] came to Jesus and asked him a question. (Sadducees believed that people would not rise from the dead.) [24]They said, "Teacher, Moses said if a married man dies without having children, his brother must marry the widow and have children for him. [25]Once there were seven brothers among us. The first one married and died. Since he had no children, his brother married the widow. [26]Then the second brother also died. The same thing happened to the third brother and all the other brothers. [27]Finally, the woman died. [28]Since all seven men had married her, when people rise from the dead, whose wife will she be?"

[29]Jesus answered, "You don't understand, because you don't know what the Scriptures [d] say, and you don't know about the power of God. [30]When people rise from the dead, they will not marry, nor will they be given to someone to marry. They will be like the angels in heaven. [31]Surely you have read what God said to you about rising from the dead. [32]God said, 'I am the God of Abraham, the God of Isaac and the God of Jacob.' [n] God is the God of the living, not the dead."

[33]When the people heard this, they were amazed at Jesus' teaching.

The Most Important Command

[34]When the Pharisees [d] learned that the Sadducees [d] could not argue with Jesus' answers to them, the Pharisees met together. [35]One Pharisee, who was an expert on the law of Moses, asked Jesus this question to test him: [36]"Teacher, which command in the law is the most important?"

[37]Jesus answered, " 'Love the Lord your God with all your heart, all your soul and all your mind.' [n] [38]This is the first and most important command. [39]And the second command is like

---

Herodians   A political group that followed Herod and his family.
coin   Roman denarii. A silver coin was the average pay for one day's work.
'I am . . . Jacob.'   Quotation from Exodus 3:6.
'Love . . . mind.'   Quotation from Deuteronomy 6:5.

the first: 'Love your neighbour as you love yourself.' *n* [40]All the law and the writings of the prophets *d* depend on these two commands."

Jesus Questions the Pharisees

[41]While the Pharisees *d* were together, Jesus asked them, [42]"What do you think about the Christ? *d* Whose son is he?"

They answered, "The Christ is the Son of David." *d*

[43]Then Jesus said to them, "Then why did David call him 'Lord'? David, speaking by the power of the Holy Spirit, *d* said,

[44]'The Lord said to my Lord:

Sit by me at my right side,

until I put your enemies under your

control.'   *Psalm 110:1*

'Love . . . yourself.' Quotation from Leviticus 19:18.

[45]David calls the Christ 'Lord', so how can the Christ be his son?"

[46]None of the Pharisees could answer Jesus' question, and after that day no one was brave enough to ask him any more questions.

Jesus Accuses Some Leaders

23 Then Jesus said to the crowds and to his followers, [2]"The teachers of the law and the Pharisees *d* have the authority to tell you what the law of Moses says. [3]So you should obey and follow whatever they tell you, but their lives are not good examples for you to follow. They tell you to do things, but they themselves don't do them. [4]They make strict rules and try to force people to obey them, but they are unwilling to help those who struggle

---

HYPOCRISY

Watch Me

Matt was always doing something crazy to raise money for charity: sponsored mountain bike rides, shaving his eyebrows, or bungee jumping in a pair of Y-fronts.

"I'm just happy to help a hurting world. I really care about people who aren't as fortunate as me," he would tell the girls, who would all flutter their eyelids at him and tell him what a kind and generous person he was. Matt never seemed embarrassed by the attention.

Jon felt the pressure to be generous towards his classmate, Matt. Jon was a Christian, and felt others were watching him to see how he would react. "Matt is helping people," reasoned Jon, "and that's what Jesus told us to do."

Jon's church youth group were planning their mission week, when they would clean the local area and help people with their gardening and decorating to demonstrate God's love in a practical way. Jon decided to invite Matt to join in, as he always seemed so keen to help people.

But Jon was hurt by Matt's response: "Er no thanks! I don't want to waste my holiday doing the boring kind of work for other people that I usually try to get out of doing in my own home. But I do have a sponsored parachute jump coming up soon – it's going to be wicked fun, and it's for a good cause – maybe you can sponsor me for that?"

It's not a new thing for people's actions to say the opposite to their words. Jesus didn't like it. See what he had to say about it in **Matthew 23:1–12**.

* What are the similarities in behaviour between Matt and the Pharisees?
* What things were both Matt and the Pharisees getting right, and what things were they both getting wrong?

Consider . . .

* whether there are parts of your life where you need to bridge the gap between what you "preach" and what you "practise". What can you do about that this week?
* whether there is a situation where you could better demonstrate God's love through actions rather than words. Pray: "Lord Jesus, show me the situations in my life that require me to act like you, not just to talk like you."

For more, see . . .

* Mark 12:28–44 (p.1022)   * Luke 6:37–42 (p.1048)
* Luke 10:25–37 (p.1058)

under the weight of their rules.

5"They do good things so that other people will see them. They make the boxes [n] of Scriptures [d] that they wear bigger, and they make their special prayer clothes very long. 6Those Pharisees and teachers of the law love to have the most important seats at feasts and in the synagogues. [d] 7They love people to greet them with respect in the market-places, and they love to have people call them 'Teacher'.

8"But you must not be called 'Teacher', because you have only one Teacher, and you are all brothers and sisters together. 9And don't call any person on earth 'Father', because you have one Father, who is in heaven. 10And you should not be called 'Master', because you have only one Master, the Christ. [d] 11Whoever is your servant is the greatest among you. 12Whoever makes himself great will be made humble. Whoever makes himself humble will be made great.

13"How terrible for you, teachers of the law and Pharisees! You are hypocrites! [d] You close the door for people to enter the kingdom of heaven. You yourselves don't enter, and you stop others who are trying to enter. 14 [n]

15"How terrible for you, teachers of the law and Pharisees! You are hypocrites! You travel across land and sea to find one person who will change to your ways. When you find that person, you make him more fit for hell than you are.

16"How terrible for you! You guide the people, but you are blind. You say, 'If people swear by the Temple [d] when they make a promise, that means nothing. But if they swear by the gold that is in the Temple, they must keep that promise.' 17You are blind fools! Which is greater: the gold or the Temple that makes that gold holy? 18And you say, 'If people swear by the altar when they make a promise, that means nothing. But if

they swear by the gift on the altar, they must keep that promise.' 19You are blind! Which is greater: the gift or the altar that makes the gift holy? 20The person who swears by the altar is really using the altar and also everything on the altar. 21And the person who swears by the Temple is really using the Temple and also everything in the Temple. 22The person who swears by heaven is also using God's throne and the One who sits on that throne.

23"How terrible for you, teachers of the law and Pharisees! You are hypocrites! You give to God one-tenth of everything you earn—even your mint, dill and cumin. [n] But you don't obey the really important teachings of the law— justice, mercy and being loyal. These are the things you should do, as well as those other things. 24You guide the people, but you are blind! You are like a person who picks a fly out of a drink and then swallows a camel! [n]

25"How terrible for you, teachers of the law and Pharisees! You are hypocrites! You wash the outside of your cups and dishes, but inside they are full of things you got by cheating others and by pleasing only yourselves. 26Pharisees, you are blind! First make the inside of the cup clean, and then the outside of the cup can be truly clean.

27"How terrible for you, teachers of the law and Pharisees! You are hypocrites! You are like tombs that are painted white. Outside, those tombs look fine, but inside, they are full of the bones of dead people and all kinds of unclean things. 28It is the same with you. People look at you and think you are good, but on the inside you are full of hypocrisy and evil.

29"How terrible for you, teachers of the law and Pharisees! You are hypocrites! You build tombs for the prophets, [d] and you show honour to the graves of those who lived good lives. 30You say, 'If we had lived during the time of our ancestors, we would not have helped them kill the prophets.' 31But you give proof that you are children of those who murdered the prophets. 32And you will complete the sin that your ancestors started.

33"You are snakes! A family of poisonous snakes! How are you going to escape God's judgement? 34So I tell you this: I am sending to you prophets and wise men and teachers. Some of them you will kill and crucify. Some of them

boxes   Small leather boxes containing four important Scriptures. Some Jews tied these to the forehead and left arm, probably to show they were very religious.

Verse 14   Some Greek copies add verse 14: "How terrible for you, teachers of the law and Pharisees. You are hypocrites. You take away widows' houses, and you say long prayers so that people will notice you. So you will have a worse punishment."

mint, dill and cumin   Herbs grown in gardens and used for spices. Only very religious people would be careful enough to give a tenth of these plants.

You . . . camel!   Meaning, "You worry about the smallest mistakes but commit the biggest sin."

you will beat in your synagogues and chase from town to town. [35]So you will be guilty for the death of all the good people who have been killed on earth—from the murder of that good man Abel to the murder of Zechariah[n] son of Berakiah, whom you murdered between the Temple and the altar. [36]I tell you the truth, all of these things will happen to you people who are living now.

Jesus Feels Sorry for Jerusalem

[37]"Jerusalem, Jerusalem! You kill the prophets[d] and stone to death those who are sent to you. Many times I wanted to gather your people as a hen gathers her chicks under her wings, but you did not let me. [38]Now your house will be left completely empty. [39]I tell you, you will not see me again until that time when you will say, 'God bless the One who comes in the name of the Lord.'"[n]

The Temple will Be Destroyed

24 As Jesus left the Temple[d] and was walking away, his followers came up to him to show him the Temple's buildings. [2]Jesus asked, "Do you see all these buildings? I tell you the truth, not one stone will be left on another. Every stone will be thrown down to the ground."

[3]Later, as Jesus was sitting on the Mount of Olives,[d] his followers came to be alone with him. They said, "Tell us, when will these things happen? And what will be the sign that it is time for you to come again and for this age to end?"

[4]Jesus answered, "Be careful that no one fools

Abel . . . Zechariah   In the order of the books of the Hebrew Old Testament, the first and last men to be murdered.
'God . . . Lord.'   Quotation from Psalm 118:26.

LEADERSHIP

Leading a Just Cause

On 1 November 1872, Susan B. Anthony walked into a polling station, demanding to be registered to vote. She voted in the national election. Two weeks later a US marshal arrested her for "voting without lawful right". The judge wouldn't allow a jury trial. Her sentence was to pay a fine and the cost of the trial.

"Your Honour," declared Susan Anthony, "I shall never pay one dollar of your unjust penalty."

Susan had long been familiar with the controversy and conflict of reform movements. Years earlier, she had worked for the American Anti-Slavery Society. She regarded slavery as evil and un-Christian. She published the first women's newspaper and organised the first women's union. Now Susan was at the front of the National Women's Suffrage Movement, working tirelessly for women's voting rights.

The work was often discouraging. The press mocked her. She was denied entry into meetings. She was attacked by angry mobs. But these persecutions didn't stop her. She lectured, lobbied Congress and organised petitions.

In 1920, her efforts helped to change the law, making sure that everyone had the right to vote, regardless of their sex. But Susan never had the chance to vote. She had died fourteen years earlier.

Those who lead movements for justice usually suffer ridicule, persecution, and sometimes death. Read in **Matthew 23:34–39** what Jesus thinks about those who persecute the prophets of God.

* Why do you think people fear and persecute leaders such as Susan B. Anthony and the ones Jesus describes?
* When has your unpopular stance caused you to suffer persecution?

Consider . . .

* reading through one of the prophets of the Old Testament such as Amos (p.870), trying to understand why his messages were ridiculed and rejected.
* listening to leaders who have differing options, keeping your mind open for truth – even if it's uncomfortable.

For more, see . . .

* Jeremiah 3:11–13 (p.720)
* 2 Timothy 3:1–9 (p.1318)
* Ezekiel 20:13–20 (p.803)

you. [5]Many will come in my name, saying, 'I am the Christ',[d] and they will fool many people. [6]You will hear about wars and stories of wars that are coming, but don't be afraid. These things must happen before the end comes. [7]Nations will fight against other nations; kingdoms will fight against other kingdoms. There will be times when there is no food for people to eat, and there will be earthquakes in different places. [8]These things are like the first pains when something new is about to be born.

[9]"Then people will arrest you, hand you over to be hurt and kill you. They will hate you because you believe in me. [10]At that time, many will lose their faith, and they will turn against each other and hate each other. [11]Many false prophets[d] will come and cause many people to believe lies. [12]There will be more and more evil in the world, so most people will stop showing their love for each other. [13]But those people who keep their faith until the end will be saved. [14]The Good News[d] about God's kingdom will be preached in all the world, to every nation. Then the end will come.

[15]"Daniel the prophet spoke about 'the destroying terror'.[n] You will see this standing in the holy place." (You who read this should understand what it means.) [16]"At that time, the people in Judea should run away to the mountains. [17]If people are on the roofs[n] of their houses, they must not go down to get anything out of their houses. [18]If people are in the fields, they must not go back to get their coats. [19]At that time, how terrible it will be for women who are pregnant or have nursing babies! [20]Pray that it will not be winter or a Sabbath[d] day when these things happen and you have to run away, [21]because at that time there will be much trouble. There will be more trouble than there has ever been since the beginning of the world until now, and nothing as bad will ever happen again. [22]God has decided to make that terrible time short. Otherwise, no one would go on living. But God will make that time short to help the people he has chosen. [23]At that time, someone might say to you, 'Look, there is the Christ!' Or another person might say, 'There he is!' But don't believe them. [24]False Christs and false prophets will come and perform great wonders and miracles.[d] They will try to fool even the people God has chosen, if that were possible. [25]Now I have warned you about this before it happens.

[26]"If people tell you, 'The Christ is in the desert', don't go there. If they say, 'The Christ is in the inner room', don't believe it. [27]When the Son of Man[d] comes, he will be seen by everyone, like lightning flashing from the east to the west. [28]Wherever the dead body is, there the vultures will gather.

[29]"Soon after the trouble of those days,

'the sun will grow dark,
    and the moon will not give its light.
The stars will fall from the sky.
    And the powers of the heavens will be
    shaken.'   *Isaiah 13:10; 34:4*

[30]"At that time, the sign of the Son of Man will appear in the sky. Then all the peoples of the world will cry. They will see the Son of Man coming on clouds in the sky with great power and glory. [31]He will use a loud trumpet to send his angels all around the earth, and they will gather his chosen people from every part of the world.

[32]"Learn a lesson from the fig tree: when its branches become green and soft and new leaves appear, you know summer is near. [33]In the same way, when you see all these things happening, you will know that the time is near, ready to come. [34]I tell you the truth, all these things will happen while the people of this time are still living. [35]Earth and sky will be destroyed, but the words I have said will never be destroyed.

When will Jesus Come Again?

[36]"No one knows when that day or time will be, not the angels in heaven, not even the Son. Only the Father knows. [37]When the Son of Man[d] comes, it will be like what happened during Noah's time. [38]In those days before the flood, people were eating and drinking, marrying and giving their children to be married, until the day Noah entered the ark. [39]They knew nothing about what was happening until the flood came and destroyed them. It will be the same when the Son of Man comes. [40]Two men will be in the field. One will be taken, and the other will be left. [41]Two women will be grinding grain with a mill.[n] One will be taken, and the other will be left.

[42]"So always be ready, because you don't know the day your Lord will come. [43]Remember this: if the owner of the house knew what time of night a thief was coming, the owner would watch and not let the thief break in. [44]So you also must be ready, because the Son of Man will come at a time you don't expect him.

'the destroying terror'   Mentioned in Daniel 9:27; 12:11 (see also Daniel 11:31).
roofs   In Bible times houses were built with flat roofs. The roof was used for drying things such as flax and fruit. And it was used as an extra room, as a place for worship and as a place to sleep in the summer.
mill   Two large, round, flat rocks used for grinding grain to make flour.

45"Who is the wise and loyal servant that the master trusts to give the other servants their food at the right time? 46When the master comes and finds the servant doing his work, the servant will be blessed. 47I tell you the truth, the master will choose that servant to take care of everything he owns. 48But suppose that servant is evil, and thinks to himself, 'My master will not come back soon,' 49and he begins to beat the other servants and eat and get drunk with others like him? 50The master will come when that servant is not ready and is not expecting him. 51Then the master will cut him in pieces and send him away to be with the hypocrites, *d* where people will cry and grind their teeth with pain.

A Story About Ten Bridesmaids

25 "At that time the kingdom of heaven will be like ten bridesmaids who took their lamps and went to wait for the bridegroom. 2Five of them were foolish and five were wise. 3The five foolish bridesmaids took their lamps, but they did not take spare oil for the lamps to burn. 4The wise bridesmaids took their lamps and more oil in jars. 5Because the bridegroom was late, they became sleepy and went to sleep.

6"At midnight someone cried out, 'The bridegroom is coming! Come and meet him!' 7Then all the bridesmaids woke up and got their lamps ready. 8But the foolish ones said to the wise, 'Give us some of your oil, because our lamps are going out.' 9The wise bridesmaids answered, 'No, the oil we have might not be enough for all of us. Go to the people who sell oil and buy some for yourselves.'

10"So while the five foolish bridesmaids went to buy oil, the bridegroom came. The bridesmaids who were ready went in with the bridegroom to the wedding feast. Then the door was closed and locked.

FUTURE

The Rock

In San Francisco Bay, USA, an abandoned prison sits on Alcatraz Island. Its prisoners called it "The Rock".

Whitey Thompson was a "hardened criminal". He grew up in an abusive home. He ran away. Whitey seemed to have no future. After a failed bank robbery, Whitey was sent to jail, where he fought with guards and other prisoners. Being sent to "The Rock" seemed logical. It was the end of the line for those considered to be hopeless criminals.

Ironically, Whitey's life turned around at Alcatraz. Whitey began to think about his future, which led him to find hope in Jesus.

Instead of killing time, he learned new skills, including painting. He painted beautiful landscapes. Guards, prisoners and visitors admired his art.

Whitey was released directly from Alcatraz to the streets. It wasn't easy to keep looking towards the future and to build a new life. But Whitey finds strength in Jesus. Now Whitey can return to Alcatraz as a guest of the National Park Service, which runs the former prison as a tourist attraction. His eyes twinkle when tourists ask how he survived. "Here I was on The Rock," he says. "Now I've found the true Rock."

The future lies in Jesus. In **Matthew 24:36–44**, read Jesus' promise to return. This promise not only gives hope for the future, but also a reason for living today, as Whitey discovered.

* What did Whitey discover in Jesus to help him to find hope for his future?
* How does knowing that Christ will return affect your view of your future?

Consider . . .

* making a list of the things you want to achieve. Keep the scripture in mind.
  If Jesus came tomorrow would you be ready?
* telling a cynical friend about the hope for the future you have in Jesus.

For more, see . . .

* Psalm 33:13–22 (p.519)
* 1 Thessalonians 5:1–11 (p.1300)
* Luke 12:35–40 (p.1064)

¹¹"Later the others came back and said, 'Sir, sir, open the door to let us in.' ¹²But the bridegroom answered, 'I tell you the truth, I don't want to know you.'

¹³"So always be ready, because you don't know the day or the hour the Son of Man ᵈ will come.

A Story About Three Servants

¹⁴"The kingdom of heaven is like a man who was going to another place for a visit. Before he left, he called for his servants and told them to take care of his things while he was gone. ¹⁵He gave one servant five bags of gold, another servant two bags of gold and a third servant one bag of gold, to each one as much as he could manage. Then he left. ¹⁶The servant who got five bags went quickly to invest the money and earned five more bags. ¹⁷In the same way, the servant who had two bags invested them and earned two more. ¹⁸But the servant who got one bag went out and dug a hole in the ground and hid the master's money.

¹⁹"After a long time the master came home and asked the servants what they had done with his money. ²⁰The servant who was given five bags of gold brought five more bags to the master and said, 'Master, you trusted me to care for five bags of gold, so I used your five bags to earn five more.' ²¹The master answered, 'You did well. You are a good and loyal servant. Because you were loyal with small things, I will let you care for much greater things. Come and share my joy with me.'

²²"Then the servant who had been given two

DECISION MAKING

Watch the Time

Tim was so excited about the school trip to the theme park. Mrs Hill, his teacher, was always joking with Tim about how bad his timekeeping was, but on the afternoon before the trip, she called Tim to one side: "Tim, I know you'd be late for your own funeral but listen, we've GOT to leave on time tomorrow, so if you're not here at 8.30 a.m., we're leaving without you. OK?"

All the way home, Tim was telling himself over and over again what he needed to do: get everything ready before he went to bed, set the alarm, go to bed early and get a good night's sleep. But as always, when Tim got into the house, he switched on his computer, and got engrossed in some games. Time flew by. When Tim finally fell into bed, he leant over and set his alarm clock for 7.00 a.m.

He woke with a start. Squinting, he looked at the clock – 8.23 a.m! Frantically, he jumped out of bed and raced to get his clothes on. He grabbed his bag and a couple of things he wished he'd got ready the night before and, still half-dressed, ran out of the front door and down the road.

Tim was back at his house just fifteen minutes later. He'd missed the coach. Just as Mrs Hill had warned, they had gone without him. How had it happened? How had he not been ready for something that was so important to him? It must have been a problem with the alarm clock.

Back in his room, Tim grabbed the clock to check he'd set it properly and slumped on his bed. It read 7.00 . . . p.m!

Read **Matthew 25:1–13**. It's a story that Jesus told to explain how some people won't be ready when he comes back.

- Both Tim and the bridesmaids in the story really wanted to be ready. What got in the way?
- Tim was disappointed at missing out on the trip. What did Jesus mean that the consequences were of the bridesmaids missing the wedding?

Consider . . .

- how we can be ready for when Jesus comes back. What does it mean?
- the things that distract you from being "watchful".

For more, see . . .

- Mark 13:32–35 (p.1024)
- Romans 7:15–25 (p.1193)
- Luke 12:35–48 (p.1064)

bags of gold came to the master and said, 'Master, you gave me two bags of gold to care for, so I used your two bags to earn two more.' ²³The master answered, 'You did well. You are a good and loyal servant. Because you were loyal with small things, I will let you care for much greater things. Come and share my joy with me.'

²⁴"Then the servant who had been given one bag of gold came to the master and said, 'Master, I knew that you were a hard man. You harvest things you did not plant. You gather crops where you did not sow any seed. ²⁵So I was afraid and went and hid your money in the ground. Here is your bag of gold.' ²⁶The master answered, 'You are a wicked and lazy servant! You say you knew that I harvest things I did not plant and that I gather crops where I did not sow any seed. ²⁷So

you should have put my gold in the bank. Then, when I came home, I would have received my gold back with interest.'

²⁸"So the master told his other servants, 'Take the bag of gold from that servant and give it to the servant who has ten bags of gold. ²⁹Those who have much will get more, and they will have much more than they need. But those who do not have much will have everything taken away from them.' ³⁰Then the master said, 'Throw that useless servant outside, into the darkness where people will cry and grind their teeth with pain.'

The King will Judge All People

³¹"The Son of Man *d* will come again in his great glory, with all his angels. He will be King and sit on his great throne. ³²All the nations of the

---

SERVICE

Coffee For the Boss

Chris had, without doubt, managed to get the best work experience placement in the whole school. Chris was jammy like that. For the next three weeks, he was going to be the personal assistant to Sir James Mears, an incredibly rich, powerful and influential businessman. Everywhere he went, Chris would go too. So, whilst his classmates were serving customers in shops, Chris would be flying to New York in a private jet with Sir James to attend a meeting. OK, so he would be mainly making tea and coffee all day, but his mates would never know that! Besides, Chris thought he was making quite an impact, and was quietly hopeful he might be given a job at the end of it.

The final day arrived, and Chris was called into Sir James's office for his appraisal.

"Well Chris," began Sir James, "thank you for all you have done here. Although, I have to say I am a little disappointed. You have hardly made any cups of tea and coffee, and haven't done any of the other things I hoped you might."

Chris was stunned. "I made you loads of cups of coffee," he replied.

"Yes, you made me coffee," said Sir James, "but you never made a single cup for anyone else who works here. You ignored each and every one of them, even though you had to walk past them to get to the kitchen. You didn't think they were important enough to serve. In my company, we are all important, and we all serve each other. In fact, a measure of how good an employee you are is how much you serve the people around you, rather than just trying to impress the boss."

Read **Matthew 25:31–46**.

* How does verse 34 describe the reward Jesus has for people who serve others?
* Read the things that God regards as good service in verses 34–36. Do they sound hard things to do or are they things you could easily get involved in?

Consider . . .

* helping out in serving the needy with your church or a local charity.
* praying for people to cross your path who you can demonstrate Jesus' love to.

For more, see . . .

* Isaiah 1:11–17 (p.639)
* John 13:1–17 (p.1119)
* Matthew 20:25–28 (p.976)

world will be gathered before him, and he will separate them into two groups as a shepherd separates the sheep from the goats. 33The Son of Man will put the sheep on his right and the goats on his left.

34"Then the King will say to the people on his right, 'Come, my Father has given you his blessing. Receive the kingdom God has prepared for you since the world was made. 35I was hungry, and you gave me food. I was thirsty, and you gave me something to drink. I was alone and away from home, and you invited me into your house. 36I was without clothes, and you gave me something to wear. I was sick, and you cared for me. I was in prison, and you visited me.'

37"Then the good people will answer, 'Lord, when did we see you hungry and give you food, or thirsty and give you something to drink? 38When did we see you alone and away from home and invite you into our house? When did we see you without clothes and give you something to wear? 39When did we see you sick or in prison and care for you?'

40"Then the King will answer, 'I tell you the truth, anything you did for even the least of my people here, you also did for me.'

41"Then the King will say to those on his left, 'Go away from me. You will be punished. Go into the fire that burns for ever that was prepared for the devil and his angels. 42I was hungry, and you gave me nothing to eat. I was thirsty, and you gave me nothing to drink. 43I was alone and away from home, and you did not invite me into your house. I was without clothes, and you gave me nothing to wear. I was sick and in prison, and you did not care for me.'

44"Then those people will answer, 'Lord, when did we see you hungry or thirsty or alone and away from home or without clothes or sick or in prison? When did we see these things and not help you?'

45"Then the King will answer, 'I tell you the truth, anything you refused to do for even the least of my people here, you refused to do for me.'

46"These people will go off to be punished for ever, but the good people will go to live for ever."

The Plan to Kill Jesus

26 After Jesus finished saying all these things, he told his followers, 2"You know that the day after tomorrow is the day of the Passover d Feast. On that day the Son of Man d will be given to his enemies to be crucified."

3Then the leading priests and the Jewish elders had a meeting at the palace of the high priest, named Caiaphas. 4At the meeting, they planned to set a trap to arrest Jesus and kill him. 5But they said, "We must not do it during the feast, because the people might cause a riot."

Perfume for Jesus' Burial

6Jesus was in Bethany at the house of Simon, who had a skin disease. 7While Jesus was there, a woman approached him with an alabaster d jar filled with expensive perfume. She poured this perfume on Jesus' head while he was eating.

8His followers were upset when they saw the woman do this. They asked, "Why waste that perfume? 9It could have been sold for a great deal of money and the money given to the poor."

10Knowing what had happened, Jesus said, "Why are you troubling this woman? She did an excellent thing for me. 11You will always have the poor with you, but you will not always have me. 12This woman poured perfume on my body to prepare me for burial. 13I tell you the truth, wherever the Good News d is preached in all the world, what this woman has done will be told, and people will remember her."

Judas Becomes an Enemy of Jesus

14Then one of the twelve apostles, Judas Iscariot, went to talk to the leading priests. 15He said, "What will you pay me for giving Jesus to you?" And they gave him 30 silver coins. 16After that, Judas watched for the best time to turn Jesus over.

Jesus Eats the Passover Meal

17On the first day of the Feast d of Unleavened Bread, the followers came to Jesus. They said, "Where do you want us to prepare for you to eat the Passover d meal?"

18Jesus answered, "Go into the city to a certain man and tell him, 'The Teacher says: the chosen time is near. I will have the Passover with my followers at your house.' " 19The followers did what Jesus told them to do, and they prepared the Passover meal.

20In the evening Jesus was sitting at the table with his twelve followers. 21As they were eating, Jesus said, "I tell you the truth, one of you will turn against me."

22This made the followers very sad. Each one began to say to Jesus, "Surely, Lord, I am not the one who will turn against you, am I?"

23Jesus answered, "The man who has dipped his hand with me into the bowl is the one who will turn against me. 24The Son of Man d will die, just as the Scriptures d say. But how terrible it will be for the person who hands the Son of Man over to be killed. It would be better for him if he had never been born."

[25]Then Judas, who would give Jesus to his enemies, said to Jesus, "Teacher, surely I am not the one, am I?"

Jesus answered, "Yes, it is you."

The Lord's Supper

[26]While they were eating, Jesus took some bread and thanked God for it and broke it. Then he gave it to his followers and said, "Take this bread and eat it; this is my body."

[27]Then Jesus took a cup and thanked God for it and gave it to the followers. He said, "Every one of you drink this. [28]This is my blood which is the new agreement that God makes with his people. This blood is poured out for many to forgive their sins. [29]I tell you this: I will not drink of this fruit of the vine [n] again until that day when I drink it new with you in my Father's kingdom."

[30]After singing a hymn, they went out to the Mount of Olives. [d]

Jesus' Followers will Leave Him

[31]Jesus told his followers, "Tonight you will all stumble in your faith on account of me, because it is written in the Scriptures: [d]

'I will kill the shepherd,
    and the sheep will scatter.'   *Zechariah 13:7*

[32]But after I rise from the dead, I will go ahead of you into Galilee."

[33]Peter said, "Everyone else may stumble in their faith because of you, but I will not."

[34]Jesus said, "I tell you the truth, tonight before the cockerel crows you will say three times that you don't know me."

[35]But Peter said, "I will never say that I don't know you! I will even die with you!" And all the other followers said the same thing.

---

fruit of the vine   Product of the grapevine; this may also be translated "wine".

FRIENDS

Don't Drop Me

Have you ever played a trust game in a drama lesson? They're really simple – it's like playing a game of catch, only you're the ball. For example, you might be in a pair, standing in front of your partner. All you have to do is keep your feet still and fall backwards. Your partner promises to catch you. The question is, do you trust them enough to catch you or will you move your feet and catch yourself?

Trust is a tricky thing. You can't live your life without putting your trust in other people every single day: the bus driver not to crash the bus; the teacher to teach you the right information; a friend to keep a confidence. The problem with trust is that it makes us vulnerable. We don't want to have to rely on someone else. And we don't want to get hurt if they let us down.

Imagine someone catching you in a trust game and then, instead of tipping you forward so that you are upright again, they take a step back, dropping you to the floor. That is betrayal: putting your trust in someone and finding them to be unworthy of it; trusting someone who lets you down.

Read **Matthew 26:14–25**.

* Have you ever been betrayed? Have you ever betrayed someone else? How did it make you feel?
* Read on through the story (up to chapter 27:10). What do you think Jesus felt about Judas? How did the disciples feel about Judas? How did Judas feel about himself?

Consider . . .

* whether there is someone who has betrayed you. If so, write down what they did and how it made you feel. Ask Jesus to help you forgive that person and restore trust. Rip up the piece of paper, knowing that you don't hold anything against them anymore.
* whether there someone you have let down. Make them a card, asking them to forgive you.

For more, see . . .

* 2 Samuel 12:1–10 (p.295)
* Matthew 5:43–48 (p.946)

* Psalm 25:1–7 (p.514)

Jesus Prays Alone

36Then Jesus went with his followers to a place called Gethsemane. He said to them, "Sit here while I go over there and pray." 37He took Peter and the two sons of Zebedee with him, and he began to be very sad and troubled. 38He said to them, "My heart is full of sorrow, to the point of death. Stay here and watch with me."

39After walking a little farther away from them, Jesus fell to the ground and prayed, "My Father, if it is possible, do not give me this cup[n] of suffering. But do what you want, not what I want." 40Then Jesus went back to his followers and found them asleep. He said to Peter, "You men, could you not stay awake with me for one hour? 41Stay awake and pray for strength against temptation. The spirit wants to do what is right, but the body is weak."

42Then Jesus went away a second time and prayed, "My Father, if it is not possible for this painful thing to be taken from me, and if I must do it, I pray that what you want will be done."

43Then he went back to his followers, and again he found them asleep, because their eyes were heavy. 44So Jesus left them and went away and prayed a third time, saying the same thing.

45Then Jesus went back to his followers and said, "Are you still sleeping and resting? The time has come for the Son of Man[d] to be handed over to sinful people. 46Get up, we must go. Look, here comes the man who has turned against me."

Jesus is Arrested

47While Jesus was still speaking, Judas, one of the twelve apostles,[d] came up. With him were many people carrying swords and clubs who had been sent from the leading priests and the Jewish elders of the people. 48Judas had planned to give them a signal, saying, "The man I kiss is Jesus. Arrest him." 49At once Judas went to Jesus and said, "Greetings, Teacher!" and kissed him.

50Jesus answered, "Friend, do what you came to do."

Then the people came and grabbed Jesus and arrested him. 51When that happened, one of Jesus' followers reached for his sword and pulled it out. He struck the servant of the high priest and cut off his ear.

52Jesus said to the man, "Put your sword back in its place. All who use swords will be killed with swords. 53Surely you know I could ask my Father, and he would give me more than twelve armies of angels. 54But it must happen this way to bring about what the Scriptures[d] say."

55Then Jesus said to the crowd, "You came to get me with swords and clubs as if I were a criminal. Every day I sat in the Temple[d] teaching, and you did not arrest me there. 56But all these things have happened so that it will come about as the prophets[d] wrote." Then all of Jesus' followers left him and ran away.

Jesus Before the Leaders

57Those people who arrested Jesus led him to the house of Caiaphas, the high priest, where the teachers of the law and the Jewish elders were gathered. 58Peter followed far behind to the courtyard of the high priest's house, and he sat down with the guards to see what would happen to Jesus.

59The leading priests and the whole Jewish council tried to find something false against Jesus so they could kill him. 60Many people came and told lies about him, but the council could find no real reason to kill him. Then two people came and said, 61"This man said, 'I can destroy the Temple[d] of God and build it again in three days.'"

62Then the high priest stood up and said to Jesus, "Aren't you going to answer? Don't you have something to say about their charges against you?" 63But Jesus said nothing.

Again the high priest said to Jesus, "I command you by the power of the living God: tell us if you are the Christ,[d] the Son of God."

64Jesus answered, "Those are your words. But I tell you, in the future you will see the Son of Man[d] sitting at the right hand of God, the Powerful One, and coming on clouds in the sky."

65When the high priest heard this, he tore his clothes and said, "This man has said things that are against God! We don't need any more witnesses; you all heard him say these things against God. 66What do you think?"

The people answered, "He should die."

67Then the people there spat in Jesus' face and beat him with their fists. Others slapped him. 68They said, "Prove to us that you are a prophet,[d] you Christ! Tell us who hit you!"

Peter Says He Doesn't Know Jesus

69At that time, as Peter was sitting in the courtyard, a servant girl came to him and said, "You also were with Jesus of Galilee."

---

cup   Jesus is talking about the terrible things that will happen to him. Accepting these things will be very hard, like drinking a cup of something bitter.

⁷⁰But Peter said to all the people there that he was never with Jesus. He said, "I don't know

what you are talking about."

⁷¹When he left the courtyard and was at the gate, another girl saw him. She said to the people there, "This man was with Jesus of Nazareth."

⁷²Again, Peter said he was never with him, saying, "I swear I don't know this man Jesus!"

⁷³A short time later, some people standing there went to Peter and said, "Surely you are one of those who followed Jesus. The way you talk proves it."

⁷⁴Then Peter began to place a curse on himself and swear, "I don't know the man." At once, a cockerel crowed. ⁷⁵And Peter remembered what Jesus had told him: "Before the cockerel crows, you will say three times that you don't know me." Then Peter went outside and cried bitterly.

Jesus is Taken to Pilate

27 Early the next morning, all the leading priests and elders of the people decided that Jesus should die. ²They tied him, led him away, and turned him over to Pilate, the governor.

Judas Kills Himself

³Judas, the one who had given Jesus to his enemies, saw that they had decided to kill Jesus. Then he was very sorry for what he had done. So he took the 30 silver coins ⁿ back to the priests

coins   Roman denarii. A silver coin was the average pay for one day's work.

STRESS

All Too Much

After school, there was a growing excitement. A steady crescendo of "Fight, fight, fight, FIGHT!" could be heard across the playground. Geoff heard the noise but wasn't interested. Then he heard the horrible half-cry/half-scream of "Geoff, help!"

Geoff's body froze as he turned his head through 180°. His eyes dilated as through the crowd he saw Tony, the new kid, his friend. Geoff gasped as he saw Tony fall under the blows of the bullies. Tony wouldn't hurt anyone but he was a little "different". People often felt threatened by that.

A younger kid began tugging at Geoff's jacket. It took a full five seconds for Geoff's awareness to register the annoyance. "You're Tony's mate, aren't you? Tony with the weird dress sense. Look, he's not even fighting back. He's soft," said the girl as she spat on the ground.

Geoff pulled free, "No, I don't know him. Sorry." Geoff looked back to the scene and held eye contact with Tony for the briefest of moments. In one movement, he turned and pressed play on his MP3 player to drown out the shouts. However, the music couldn't drown out the voice of guilt whispering in his mind. He started to pray.

Geoff knew that he should stand up for his friend, but in times of stress it's often difficult to make the right choices. Read how Peter coped under pressure in **Matthew 26:69–75**.

* Why do you think Peter didn't stand up for Jesus? How is this similar to Geoff's situation?
* In what situations do you find it difficult to make the right choices?

Consider . . .

* talking with a friend about how to make the right choices in times of stress.
* someone you know who needs a friend right now. Pray for an opportunity to show them friendship.

For more, see . . .

* Proverbs 28:13 (p.615)
* Luke 22:55–62 (p.1089)

and the leaders, [4]saying, "I sinned; I handed over to you an innocent man."

The leaders answered, "What is that to us? That's your problem, not ours."

[5]So Judas threw the money into the Temple. [d] Then he went off and hanged himself.

[6]The leading priests picked up the silver coins in the Temple and said, "Our law does not allow us to keep this money with the Temple money, because it has paid for a man's death." [7]So they decided to use the coins to buy Potter's Field as a place to bury strangers who died in Jerusalem. [8]That is why that field is still called the Field of Blood. [9]So what Jeremiah the prophet [d] had said came true: "They took 30 silver coins. That is how little the Israelites thought he was worth. [10]They used those 30 silver coins to buy the potter's field, as the Lord commanded me." [n]

Pilate Questions Jesus

[11]Jesus stood before Pilate the governor, and Pilate asked him, "Are you the king of the Jews?"

Jesus answered, "Those are your words."

[12]When the leading priests and the elders accused Jesus, he said nothing.

[13]So Pilate said to Jesus, "Don't you hear them accusing you of all these things?"

[14]But Jesus said nothing in answer to Pilate, and Pilate was very surprised at this.

Pilate Tries to Free Jesus

[15]Every year at the time of Passover [d] the governor would free one prisoner whom the people chose. [16]At that time there was a man in prison, named Barabbas, who was known to be very bad. [17]When the people gathered at Pilate's house, Pilate said, "Whom do you want me to set free: Barabbas or Jesus who is called the Christ?" [d] [18]Pilate knew that the people had turned Jesus over to him because they were jealous.

[19]While Pilate was sitting there on the judge's seat, his wife sent this message to him: "Don't have anything to do with that man, because he is innocent. Today I had a dream about him, and it troubled me very much."

[20]But the leading priests and elders convinced the crowd to ask for Barabbas to be freed and for Jesus to be killed.

[21]Pilate said, "I have Barabbas and Jesus. Which do you want me to set free for you?"

The people answered, "Barabbas."

[22]Pilate asked, "So what should I do with Jesus, the one called the Christ?"

They all answered, "Crucify him!"

[23]Pilate asked, "Why? What wrong has he done?"

But they shouted louder, "Crucify him!"

[24]When Pilate saw that he could do nothing about this and that a riot was starting, he took some water and washed his hands [n] in front of the crowd. Then he said, "I am not guilty of this man's death. You are the ones who are causing it!"

[25]All the people answered, "We and our children will be responsible for his death."

[26]Then he set Barabbas free. But Jesus was beaten with whips and handed over to the soldiers to be crucified.

[27]The governor's soldiers took Jesus into the governor's palace, and they all gathered around him. [28]They took off his clothes and put a red robe on him. [29]Using thorny branches, they made a crown, put it on his head, and put a stick in his right hand. Then the soldiers bowed before Jesus and made fun of him, saying, "Hail, King of the Jews!" [30]They spat on Jesus. Then they took his stick and began to beat him on the head. [31]After they finished, the soldiers took off the robe and put his own clothes on him again. Then they led him away to be crucified.

Jesus is Crucified

[32]As the soldiers were going out of the city with Jesus, they forced a man from Cyrene, named Simon, to carry the cross for Jesus. [33]They all came to the place called Golgotha, which means the Place of the Skull. [34]The soldiers gave Jesus wine mixed with gall [n] to drink. He tasted the wine but refused to drink it. [35]When the soldiers had crucified him, they threw lots [d] to decide who would get his clothes. [36]The soldiers sat there and continued watching him. [37]They put a sign above Jesus' head with a charge against him. It said: THIS IS JESUS, THE KING OF THE JEWS. [38]Two robbers were crucified beside Jesus, one on the right and the other on the left. [39]People walked by and insulted Jesus and shook their heads, [40]saying, "You said you could destroy the Temple [d] and build it again in three days. So save yourself! Come down from that cross if you are really the Son of God!"

"They . . . commanded me." See Zechariah 11:12–13 and Jeremiah 32:6–9.
washed his hands He did this as a sign to show that he wanted no part in what the people did.
gall Probably a drink of wine mixed with drugs to help a person feel less pain.

[41]The leading priests, the teachers of the law and the Jewish elders were also making fun of Jesus. [42]They said, "He saved others, but he can't save himself! He says he is the king of Israel! If he is the king, let him come down now from the cross. Then we will believe in him. [43]He trusts in God, so let God save him now, if God really wants him. He himself said, 'I am the Son of God.'"

[44]And in the same way, the robbers who were being crucified beside Jesus insulted him.

Jesus Dies

[45]At noon the whole country became dark, and the darkness lasted for three hours. [46]At about three o'clock Jesus cried out in a loud voice, "Eli, Eli, [n] lama sabachthani?" This means, "My God, my God, why have you rejected me?" [47]Some of the people standing there who heard this said, "He is calling Elijah." [48]Quickly one of them ran and got a sponge and filled it with vinegar and tied it to a stick and gave it to Jesus to drink. [49]But the others said, "Don't bother him. We want to see if Elijah will come to save him."

[50]But Jesus cried out again in a loud voice and died. [51]Then the curtain in the Temple [n] was torn into two pieces, from the top to the bottom. Also, the earth shook and rocks broke apart. [52]The graves opened, and many of God's people who had died were raised from the dead. [53]They came out of the graves after Jesus was raised from the dead and went into the holy city, where they appeared to many people.

[54]When the army officer and the soldiers guarding Jesus saw this earthquake and everything else that happened, they were very frightened and said, "He really was the Son of God!"

[55]Many women who had followed Jesus from Galilee to help him were standing at a distance from the cross, watching. [56]Mary Magdalene, and Mary the mother of James and Joseph, and the mother of James and John were there.

Jesus is Buried

[57]That evening a rich man named Joseph, a follower of Jesus from the town of Arimathea, came to Jerusalem. [58]Joseph went to Pilate and asked to have Jesus' body. So Pilate gave orders for the soldiers to give it to Joseph. [59]Then Joseph took the body and wrapped it in a clean linen cloth. [60]He put Jesus' body in a new tomb that he had cut out of a wall of rock, and he rolled a very large stone to block the entrance of the tomb. Then Joseph went away. [61]Mary Magdalene and the other woman named Mary were sitting near the tomb.

The Tomb of Jesus is Guarded

[62]The next day, the day after Preparation [d] Day, the leading priests and the Pharisees [d] went to Pilate. [63]They said, "Sir, we remember that while that liar was still alive he said, 'After three days I will rise from the dead.' [64]So give the order for the tomb to be guarded closely till the third day. Otherwise, his followers might come and steal the body and tell people that he has risen from the dead. That lie would be even worse than the first one."

[65]Pilate said, "Take some soldiers and go and guard the tomb the best way you know." [66]So they all went to the tomb and made it safe from thieves by sealing the stone in the entrance and putting soldiers there to guard it.

Jesus Rises from the Dead

28 The day after the Sabbath [d] day was the first day of the week. At dawn on the first day, Mary Magdalene and another woman named Mary went to look at the tomb.

[2]At that time there was a strong earthquake. An angel of the Lord came down from heaven, went to the tomb and rolled the stone away from the entrance. Then he sat on the stone. [3]He was shining as bright as lightning, and his clothes were white as snow. [4]The soldiers guarding the

> **Sidelight** The stones in front of tombs in Jesus' day were large, disc-shaped boulders (Matthew 28:2). They were placed in grooves so that they would roll down and block the entrance to the cave-like tombs, making them difficult to move.

tomb shook with fear because of the angel, and they became like dead men.

[5]The angel said to the women, "Don't be afraid. I know that you are looking for Jesus, who has been crucified. [6]He is not here. He has risen from the dead as he said he would. Come and see the place where his body was. [7]And then go

---

Eli, Eli   Some Bibles translate this as Eloi, Eloi.
curtain in the Temple   A curtain divided the Most Holy Place from the other part of the Temple. That was the special building in Jerusalem where God commanded the Jewish people to worship him.

quickly and tell his followers, 'Jesus has risen from the dead. He is going into Galilee ahead of you, and you will see him there.'" Then the angel said, "Now I have told you."

[8]The women left the tomb quickly. They were afraid, but they were also very happy. They ran to tell Jesus' followers what had happened. [9]Suddenly, Jesus met them and said, "Greetings." The women came up to him, took hold of his feet, and worshipped him. [10]Then Jesus said to them, "Don't be afraid. Go and tell my followers to go on to Galilee, and they will see me there."

The Soldiers Report to the Leaders

[11]While the women went to tell Jesus' followers, some of the soldiers who had been guarding the tomb went into the city to tell the leading priests everything that had happened. [12]Then the priests met with the Jewish elders and made a plan. They paid the soldiers a large amount of money [13]and said to them, "Tell the people that Jesus' followers came during the night and stole the body while you were asleep. [14]If the governor hears about this, we will satisfy him and save you from trouble." [15]So the soldiers kept the money and did as they were told. And that story is still spread among the Jewish people even today.

Jesus Talks to His Followers

[16]The eleven followers went to Galilee to the mountain where Jesus had told them to go. [17]On the mountain they saw Jesus and worshipped him,

SADNESS

Deeper Than Dewy Eyes

Being sad doesn't really mean what it used to. It can describe someone's dress sense or taste in music! But real sadness is a totally different thing, and it can't necessarily be seen on the outside. Yes, sometimes sadness is visible; we all shed a tear every now and again. But there is a kind of sadness that is much deeper than just getting dewy eyes during a slushy film.

The famous scientist Albert Einstein said, "Learn from yesterday, live for today, hope for tomorrow." Real sadness is the emotion that comes and fills the gap where hope used to live. It gives us the feeling that there's no point to tomorrow — it tells us that the best things in life are behind us and there's nothing left to look forward to.

At some time in our lives, we will all have to endure the bitter taste of this sadness. Some people seem to get off lightly; some people seem to get more than their fair share. Sadness can either creep or crash into our lives. Knowing how to deal with it will mean that we come out stronger instead of being paralysed by it.

Read **Matthew 27:57–61**.

* Think about the hopes and dreams Jesus' friends had in their hearts as they hung out with him. What kind of sadness would they be feeling at this time?
* The Bible talks about how Jesus understood the pain we go through at certain times in our life (see Isaiah 53:4). Isn't it amazing to know a God who shares our sadness as well as our joys?

Consider . . .

* asking your older relatives to tell you stories from their life. Listening is a great gift and they will appreciate your interest.
* whether something you've said or done has made someone else sad. Think about how you can make sure you don't do it again.

For more, see . . .

* Isaiah 35:10 (p.674)
* John 20:10–18 (p.1132)
* Isaiah 53:4–5 (p.697)
* Revelation 21:1–5 (p.1403)

but some of them did not believe it was really Jesus. [18]Then Jesus came to them and said, "All power in heaven and on earth is given to me. [19]So go and make followers of all people in the world. Baptise them in the name of the Father and the Son and the Holy Spirit. [d] [20]Teach them to obey everything that I have taught you, and I will be with you always, even until the end of this age."

FOLLOWING GOD

Not Me, Lord!

"How do I know what God wants me to do?" Beth asked her minister. Beth was in her second year at college, struggling with her future. She was home for the Christmas break, thinking about the summer.

"Obviously, you want to follow God," Reverend Jones said. "Try listening. You'll be surprised at what you hear."

"I don't want to be a minister!" Beth shot back. "I'm not sure I feel called to do that."

"You don't have to be in full-time ministry to follow God," he said quietly. "Following God takes different paths. Why not explore other possibilities?"

Beth stayed open to God's calling. She was offered a job for the summer at a church camp. She accepted. She worked with children, led Bible studies, planned and led worship and music, and camped outdoors. She listened for God and learned what it meant to be a follower.

She returned to college ready for her final year. "I discovered that I'm good at things like teaching. I even like Bible studies," she wrote to Reverend Jones. "I still don't know what I'll do. But I'll keep finding ways to follow God."

Beth learned that following God may seem frightening at first. But after the initial "Yes, send me," serving God brings adventure, growth and true joy. Read **Matthew 28:16–20** to find Jesus' commission and promise for those who agree to follow him.

* What did Beth learn about following God? How is this similar to Jesus' command?
* How do you follow God? How do you seek to make others followers of God?

Consider . . .

* writing a scenario in which you befriend people who have never heard about Jesus. How will you teach them about faith?
* listing the ways in which the careers you're interested in could minister and spread God's kingdom.

For more, see . . .

* Exodus 3 (p.61)
* Acts 1:7–11 (p.1137)

* John 21 (p.1134)

Mark

Why Read This Book:

* Learn about the healings and miracles that Jesus performed (Mark 2—8).
* Listen to Jesus' teachings about following him (Mark 9—12).
* See how Jesus was victorious even though people killed him (Mark 14—16).

When?

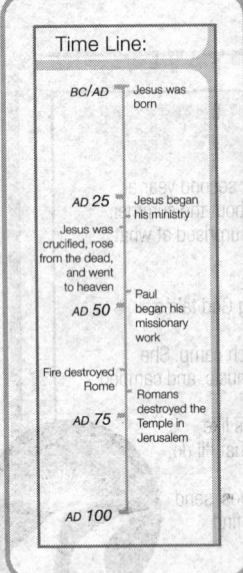

Time Line:

BC/AD	Jesus was born
AD 25	Jesus began his ministry
Jesus was crucified, rose from the dead, and went to heaven	
AD 50	Paul began his missionary work
Fire destroyed Rome	
AD 75	Romans destroyed the Temple in Jerusalem
AD 100	

Behind the Scenes:

The Gospel of Mark is filled with short, quick "news items" about Jesus — moving quickly from scene to scene, and filled with action and drama.

It cuts quickly from one scene to the next — packed with simple, vivid stories. The Greek word translated "immediately" or "then" appears more than forty times in just sixteen chapters!

The book begins with a short section on John the Baptist, who announced Jesus' coming. Then it tells about Jesus' miracles and activities in the region of Lake Galilee. Finally, the action moves to Jerusalem, where Jesus was arrested and killed. Then he rose from the grave.

Unlike the other three gospels, this book was for people who weren't familiar with stories about Jesus, so it's a great place to begin learning the basics!

Where?

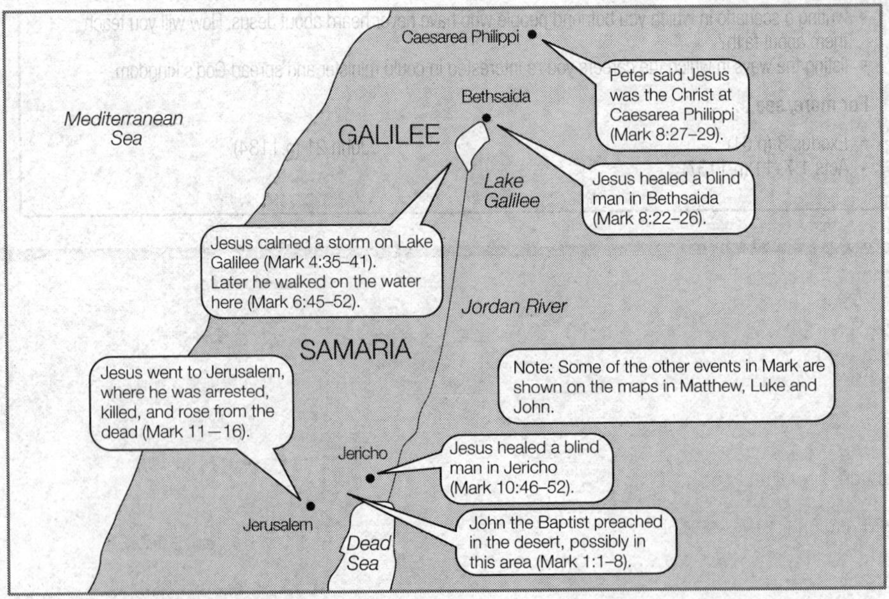

Mediterranean Sea

GALILEE

Lake Galilee

Jordan River

SAMARIA

Jericho

Jerusalem

Dead Sea

Caesarea Philippi

Bethsaida

Peter said Jesus was the Christ at Caesarea Philippi (Mark 8:27–29).

Jesus healed a blind man in Bethsaida (Mark 8:22–26).

Jesus calmed a storm on Lake Galilee (Mark 4:35–41). Later he walked on the water here (Mark 6:45–52).

Jesus went to Jerusalem, where he was arrested, killed, and rose from the dead (Mark 11—16).

Note: Some of the other events in Mark are shown on the maps in Matthew, Luke and John.

Jesus healed a blind man in Jericho (Mark 10:46–52).

John the Baptist preached in the desert, possibly in this area (Mark 1:1–8).

John Prepares for Jesus

1 This is the beginning of the Good News *d* about Jesus Christ, the Son of God,*n* ²as the prophet *d* Isaiah wrote:

"I will send my messenger ahead of you,
    who will prepare your way." *Malachi 3:1*

³"This is a voice of one
    who calls out in the desert:
'Prepare the way for the Lord.
    Make the road straight for him.'" *Isaiah 40:3*

> **Sidelight**   John the Baptist quoted
>   from Isaiah about
> preparing the way for the Lord (Mark 1:2–3), a
> passage of scripture describing an ancient
> practice for travelling oriental kings. Whenever a
> ruler went to places without roads, a crew of
> workers went ahead to smooth out rough places
> for the king's chariot.

⁴John was baptising people in the desert and preaching a baptism of changed hearts and lives for the forgiveness of sins. ⁵All the people from Judea and Jerusalem were going out to him. They confessed their sins and were baptised by him in the Jordan River. ⁶John wore clothes made from camel's hair, had a leather belt around his waist and ate locusts *d* and wild honey. ⁷This is what John preached to the people: "There is one coming after me who is greater than I; I am not good enough even to kneel down and untie his sandals. ⁸I baptise you with water, but he will baptise you with the Holy Spirit." *d*

Jesus is Baptised

⁹At that time Jesus came from the town of Nazareth in Galilee and was baptised by John in the Jordan River. ¹⁰Immediately, as Jesus was coming up out of the water, he saw heaven open. The Holy Spirit *d* came down on him like a dove, ¹¹and a voice came from heaven: "You are my Son, whom I love, and I am very pleased with you."

¹²Then the Spirit sent Jesus into the desert. ¹³He was in the desert for 40 days and was tempted by Satan. He was with the wild animals, and the angels came and took care of him.

Jesus Chooses Some Followers

¹⁴After John was put in prison, Jesus went into Galilee, preaching the Good News *d* from God. ¹⁵He said, "The right time has come. The kingdom of God is near. Change your hearts and lives and believe the Good News!"

¹⁶When Jesus was walking by Lake Galilee, he saw Simon *n* and his brother Andrew throwing a net into the lake because they were fishermen. ¹⁷Jesus said to them, "Come follow me, and I will make you fish for people." ¹⁸So Simon and Andrew immediately left their nets and followed him.

¹⁹Going a little farther, Jesus saw two more brothers, James and John, the sons of Zebedee. They were in a boat, mending their nets. ²⁰Jesus immediately called them, and they left their father in the boat with the hired workers and followed Jesus.

Jesus Forces Out an Evil Spirit

²¹Jesus and his followers went to Capernaum. On the Sabbath *d* day he went to the synagogue *d* and began to teach. ²²The people were amazed at his teaching, because he taught like a person who had authority, not like their teachers of the law. ²³Just then, a man was there in the synagogue who had an evil spirit in him. He shouted, ²⁴"Jesus of Nazareth! What do you want with us? Did you come to destroy us? I know who you are—God's Holy One!"

²⁵Jesus commanded the evil spirit, "Be quiet! Come out of the man!" ²⁶The evil spirit shook the man violently, gave a loud cry and then came out of him.

²⁷The people were so amazed they asked each other, "What is happening here? This man is teaching something new, and with authority. He even gives commands to evil spirits, and they obey him." ²⁸And the news about Jesus spread quickly everywhere in the area of Galilee.

Jesus Heals Many People

²⁹As soon as Jesus and his followers left the synagogue, *d* they went with James and John to the home of Simon *n* and Andrew. ³⁰Simon's mother-in-law was sick in bed with a fever, and the people told Jesus about her. ³¹So Jesus went to her bed, took her hand and helped her up. The fever left her, and she began serving them.

³²That evening, after the sun went down, the people brought to Jesus all who were sick and had demons *d* in them. ³³The whole town gathered at the door. ³⁴Jesus healed many who had different kinds of sicknesses, and he forced many demons to leave people. But he would not allow the demons to speak, because they knew who he was.

³⁵Early the next morning, while it was still dark, Jesus woke and left the house. He went to a lonely place, where he prayed. ³⁶Simon and his friends went to look for Jesus. ³⁷When they found him, they said, "Everyone is looking for you!"

---

the Son of God   Some Greek copies omit these words.
Simon   Simon's other name was Peter.

[38]Jesus answered, "We should go to other towns around here so I can preach there too. That is the reason I came." [39]So he went everywhere in Galilee, preaching in the synagogues and forcing out demons.

Jesus Heals a Sick Man

[40]A man with a skin disease came to Jesus. He fell to his knees and begged Jesus, "You can heal me if you will."

[41]Jesus felt sorry for the man, so he reached out his hand and touched him and said, "I will. Be healed!" [42]Immediately the disease left the man, and he was healed.

[43]Jesus told the man to go away at once, but he warned him strongly, [44]"Don't tell anyone about this. But go and show yourself to the priest. And offer the gift Moses commanded for people who are made well. [n] This will show the people what I have done." [45]The man left there, but he began to tell everyone that Jesus had healed him, and so he spread the news about Jesus. As a result, Jesus could not enter a town if people saw him. He stayed in remote places [where nobody lived], but people came to him from everywhere.

Jesus Heals a Paralysed Man

2 A few days later, when Jesus came back to Capernaum, the news spread that he was at home. [2]Many people gathered together so that there was no room in the house, not even outside the door. And Jesus was teaching them God's message. [3]Four people came, carrying a paralysed man. [4]Since they could not get to Jesus because

---

Moses . . . well   Read about this in Leviticus 14:1–32.

FOLLOWING GOD

Leaving Everything

Li Tang grew up in the Chinese capital of Beijing. All her life, Li's family and friends had taught her that God was not real. Li believed what others told her, but she hoped that some day she would find that there really is a God.

When Li was seventeen years old, she found a Bible in an old library. She opened it and began reading about God loving people and sending his Son to the world.

Li was amazed. Why had she never heard about this before? She wanted to know more about this God and follow him. How could she? She decided that she would leave everything – her family, her friends and even her country – to follow Jesus.

Her parents weren't thrilled with Li's decision to study Christianity, but they wanted her to be happy. Many of her friends couldn't understand why she wanted to leave.

Li moved to England to study and learn more about Jesus so that some day she could return to tell others about him. While in England, she met Christians who helped her to learn and to grow.

"You really experience the change in your life," Li reflected after she had decided to follow Jesus. "It's really a difference."

Jesus asked people to follow him. Often, following meant leaving many things behind. Yet following also meant gaining a friend like Jesus. Read about Jesus' first followers in **Mark 1:14–20**.

* How did what Li had to give up compare with what the disciples had to give up to follow Jesus?
* What have you had to give up to follow Jesus? What do you need to give up now to follow Jesus more fully?

Consider . . .

* making a small, wooden cross as a reminder of what it means to follow Jesus.
* interviewing two Christian friends about what it means to them to follow Jesus.

For more, see . . .

* Ruth 1:11–18 (p.249)
* John 1:35–42 (p.1097)

* Matthew 4:12–22 (p. 942)

of the crowd, they dug a hole in the roof right above where he was speaking. When they got through, they lowered the mat with the paralysed man on it. [5]When Jesus saw the faith of these people, he said to the paralysed man, "Young man, your sins are forgiven."

[6]Some of the teachers of the law were sitting there, thinking to themselves, [7]"Why does this man say things like that? He is speaking as if he were God. Only God can forgive sins."

[8]Jesus knew immediately what these teachers of the law were thinking. So he said to them, "Why are you thinking these things? [9]Which is easier: to tell this paralysed man, 'Your sins are forgiven,' or to tell him, 'Stand up. Take your mat and walk'? [10]But I will prove to you that the Son of Man[d] has authority on earth to forgive sins." So Jesus said to the paralysed man, [11]"I tell you, stand up, take your mat, and go home." [12]Immediately the paralysed man stood up, took his mat and walked out while everyone was watching him.

The people were amazed and praised God. They said, "We have never seen anything like this!"

Sidelight   Most of Jesus' ministry took place around Lake Galilee (for example, see Mark 2:13–14). This lake is the world's lowest freshwater lake, with a surface 207 metres below sea level. Despite the lake's prominence in Jesus' ministry, it's only mentioned three times in the Old Testament (Numbers 34:11, p.161; Joshua 12:3, p.213; and Joshua 13:27, p.214).

FORGIVENESS

The Christmas Gift

"I can't stand him! He's the one who left us. Why should I have to ruin my Christmas by spending it with him?" Jessica shouted at her mother through sobs.

"Darling, that was three years ago," Helen said. She put her hand on her daughter's shoulder. "A lot has happened since then. We're different people now – and happier too."

"That doesn't make it right. He still left us," Jessica countered.

Helen sat down beside Jessica. "Your father needed work, and there was nothing here for him. He had to go somewhere he could feel useful and needed. I never believed he really wanted to leave us."

"But he did leave us," Jessica said. "And he never came back."

"You're right. But that doesn't mean he doesn't love you. Now he wants you to understand, to forgive him, and to get to know him again. Could you please forgive your father and go to his house for a few days for Christmas?" Helen asked sympathetically.

"I suppose I never really understood why he left, Mum." Jessica thought for a moment, then said, "I don't really want to, but I suppose I could spend part of my Christmas holiday with Dad."

As Jessica reached for the phone, Helen smiled and said quietly, "Perhaps forgiveness can be your Christmas gift to your dad."

Forgiveness can bring healing to people and relationships. Read **Mark 2:1–12** to see how Jesus' miracle resulted in forgiveness and healing.

* How did Jesus' and Jessica's forgiveness bring about healing?
* Who needs a healing word of forgiveness from you?

Consider . . .

* phoning someone you've not talked to for a long time because of a misunderstanding.
* listing people you need to forgive, forgiving each person and then performing an act of service for each one to bring about healing.

For more, see . . .

* Psalm 130 (p.577)
* Hebrews 12:14–15 (p.1344)

* Luke 5:17–26 (p.1047)

¹³Jesus went to the lake again. The whole crowd followed him there, and he taught them. ¹⁴While he was walking along, he saw a man named Levi[n] son of Alphaeus, sitting in the tax collector's booth. Jesus said to him, "Follow me," and he stood up and followed Jesus.

¹⁵Later, as Jesus was having dinner at Levi's house, many tax collectors and "sinners" were eating there with Jesus and his followers. Many people like this followed Jesus. ¹⁶When the teachers of the law who were Pharisees[d] saw Jesus eating with the tax collectors and "sinners", they asked his followers, "Why does he eat with tax collectors and sinners?"

¹⁷Jesus heard this and said to them, "It is not the healthy people who need a doctor, but the sick. I did not come to invite good people but to invite sinners."

Jesus' Followers are Criticised

¹⁸Now the followers of John[n] and the Pharisees[d] often gave up eating for a certain time.[n]

Levi   Also known as Matthew.
John   John the Baptist, who preached to people about Christ's coming (Mark 1:4–8; Luke 3:1–22).
gave . . . time   This is called "fasting". The people would give up eating for a special time of prayer and worship to God. It was also done to show sadness and disappointment.

CELEBRATING

Party Blues

Alison's graduation party really drew a crowd. She had invited all her friends, which came to around thirty. On top of that, her parents had invited several relatives and friends.

People filled every nook and corner in the house. A group of boys talked and joked on the patio. Several of the girls gathered in the kitchen and laughed at each other's stories. And a large assortment of other people crammed into the living room, talking about the degree ceremony and laughing at the antics of some of the students.

Everyone was having a great time. Everyone, that is, except Alison. She stood quietly in a corner of the kitchen, only half-listening to the girls' conversation.

"What's wrong, Al?" asked Christine, walking quietly over to Alison. "You seem far away."

"Yes, I suppose I am," Alison said with a weak smile. "It's just that now that I'm out of university, I don't know what's going to happen to my friendships. I love you all so much; it makes me sad to think of you not being in my life any more."

Christine touched Alison on the arm. "Hey, listen, none of us knows what's going to happen from one day to the next. We may all get to stay together for ever, or we may not. We just can't know for sure. But," she added with a smile, "we're here today. So let's go and join the others and have some fun, all right? After all, it is your party."

"OK, OK," Alison said jokingly. Then she reached out and grabbed Christine's hand. "Thanks, Chris. I needed to hear that."

Christine helped Alison to realise the importance of celebrating the good things that come along, even though they may not last. Jesus helped his disciples to understand the same truth. Read the story that Jesus used in **Mark 2:18–22**.

* How was Alison like the Pharisees' followers in this passage?
* How can you celebrate Jesus' presence in your life, as this passage directs?

Consider . . .

* writing down all the ways that Jesus reveals his presence in your life, and then thanking God for being so real to you.
* throwing a party to celebrate friendship and God's love.

For more, see . . .

* Isaiah 62:1–9 (p.706)
* John 3:25–30 (p.1101)
* Matthew 9:14–17 (p.954)

Some people came to Jesus and said, "Why do John's followers and the followers of the Pharisees often give up eating, but your followers don't?"

¹⁹Jesus answered, "The friends of the bridegroom do not give up eating while the bridegroom is still with them. As long as the bridegroom is with them, they cannot give up eating. ²⁰But the time will come when the bridegroom will be taken from them, and then they will give up eating.

²¹"No one sews a patch of unshrunken cloth over a hole in an old coat. Otherwise, the patch will shrink and pull away—the new patch will pull away from the old coat. Then the hole will be worse. ²²Also, no one ever pours new wine into old leather bags. Otherwise, the new wine will break the bags, and the wine will be ruined along with the bags. But new wine should be put into new leather bags."

Jesus is Lord of the Sabbath

²³One Sabbath ᵈ day, as Jesus was walking through some fields of grain, his followers began to pick some grain to eat. ²⁴The Pharisees ᵈ said to Jesus, "Why are your followers doing what is not lawful on the Sabbath day?"

²⁵Jesus answered, "Have you never read what David did when he and those with him were hungry and needed food? ²⁶During the time of Abiathar the high priest, David went into God's house and ate the holy bread, which is lawful only for priests to eat. And David also gave some of the bread to those who were with him."

²⁷Then Jesus said to the Pharisees, "The Sabbath day was made to help people; they were not made to be ruled by the Sabbath day. ²⁸So then, the Son of Man ᵈ is Lord even of the Sabbath day."

Jesus Heals a Man's Hand

3 Another time when Jesus went into a synagogue, ᵈ a man with a crippled hand was there. ²Some people watched Jesus closely to see if he would heal the man on the

FREEDOM

Breathe Easy

Julia's heart was thumping. She was late home again and Dad would be cross. Dad had given her a curfew time of 9.30 p.m. but her watch now said 10.30 p.m. Julia had already been late home twice that week.

Julia wondered what she would say to her dad. She ran over the evening's events in her mind. She had been on her way home when she had heard crying. Her heart tightened and her fingernails cut into her palms. There before her was a boy of no more than six with terror-stricken, puffy eyes. "I'm lost," he said in dismay between sobs. Two thoughts struck her. Firstly, what about the curfew? Secondly, she had to help this poor, lost boy.

Julia reached into her handbag to find her phone and called the police, explaining where she was and who she had found. Julia held the small boy's hand until the police arrived. Mission accomplished.

Now Julia had to face her dad. The door of the house swung open and Julia saw him silhouetted in the entrance. His angry face softened into concern. "You did the right thing. We're so proud," he said.

Julia's dad set a curfew because he loved her but Julia was also given freedom to make her own choice. Read **Mark 2:23 – 3:6** to see how Jesus exercised freedom in love.

* Why do you think Jesus healed a man on the Sabbath day when it angered the religious leaders?
* Have you ever been guilty of having a judging attitude like the Pharisees?

Consider . . .

* the phrase "Love God and do what you please". Take some time to think about what that phrase means.
* praying that God will help you to understand when you judge people in the way the Pharisees judged Jesus. Ask him for forgiveness.

For more, see . . .

* Matthew 11:19 (p.959)
* Galatians 5:1 (p.1263)
* 2 Corinthians 3:17 (p.1242)

Sabbath *d* day so they could accuse him.

³Jesus said to the man with the crippled hand, "Stand up here in the middle of everyone."

⁴Then Jesus asked the people, "Which is lawful on the Sabbath day: to do good or to do evil, to save a life or to kill?" But they said nothing to answer him.

⁵Jesus was angry as he looked at the people, and he felt very sad because they were stubborn. Then he said to the man, "Hold out your hand." The man held out his hand and it was healed. ⁶Then the Pharisees *d* left and began making plans with the Herodians *n* about a way to kill Jesus.

Herodians   A political group that followed Herod and his family.

Many People Follow Jesus

⁷Jesus left with his followers for the lake, and a large crowd from Galilee followed him. ⁸Also many people came from Judea, from Jerusalem, from Idumea, from the lands across the Jordan River and from the area of Tyre and Sidon. When they heard what Jesus was doing, many people came to him. ⁹When Jesus saw the crowds, he told his followers to get a boat ready for him to keep people from crowding against him. ¹⁰He had healed many people, so all the sick were pushing towards him to touch him. ¹¹When evil spirits saw Jesus, they fell down

EVIL

Fearful Escape

Susan was small, tired and afraid. Her troubled eyes continually darted around the crowded bus stop. Everyone looked suspicious to Susan and made her want to run somewhere – anywhere – to get away from those who might find her and take her back.

Susan had a good reason to be afraid. Although she looked like any other teenager, Susan was different from most.

For the past six years, Susan had been involved in a coven that worshipped Satan. It had seemed fun when she started. Now, at eighteen, she wanted to get out.

Susan pulled at the sleeves of her sweater. Her arms must not be seen. They would expose her. Carved into her flesh were Satanic symbols to identify her as a devout Satanist. These marks were only an outward sign of the evil she had witnessed.

Susan had met some Christians a few years earlier. They had tried to tell her the truth about God's love and had offered to help her to escape to a new way of life. She had refused then, but now she was going to find them.

Seeing that no one was following her, she breathed a sigh of relief. As she climbed up the bus steps, Susan thought about how each step she took brought her closer to the freedom that Jesus offered.

Since the beginning of time, Satan has lied to people, telling them that his way is right and God's way is evil.

Mark 3:20–35 shows one instance when Satan convinced people that Jesus himself had an evil spirit.

* Why did Susan and the people in Jesus' day fear Satan?
* What promise do you see in this passage that helps you in the face of evil?

Consider . . .

* praying for your church and family to be united so that they can stand against evil.
* identifying an evil influence in your life and working to get rid of it.

For more, see . . .

* Genesis 3 (p.5)
* John 10:19–21 (p.1114)

* Matthew 9:32–34 (p.954)

before him and shouted, "You are the Son of God!" ¹²But Jesus strongly warned them not to tell who he was.

Jesus Chooses His Twelve Apostles

¹³Then Jesus went up on a mountain and called to him the men he wanted, and they came to him. ¹⁴Jesus chose twelve men and called them apostles. *d* He wanted them to be with him, and he wanted to send them out to preach ¹⁵and to have the authority to force demons *d* out of people. ¹⁶These are the twelve men he chose: Simon (Jesus named him Peter), ¹⁷James and John, the sons of Zebedee (Jesus named them Boanerges, which means "Sons of Thunder"), ¹⁸Andrew, Philip, Bartholomew, Matthew, Thomas, James the son of Alphaeus, Thaddaeus, Simon the Zealot *d* ¹⁹and Judas Iscariot, who later turned against Jesus.

Some People Say Jesus Has a Devil

²⁰Then Jesus went home, but again a crowd gathered. There were so many people that Jesus and his followers could not eat. ²¹When his family heard this, they went to get him because they thought he was out of his mind. ²²But the teachers of the law from Jerusalem were saying, "Beelzebul *d* is living inside him! He uses power from the ruler of demons *d* to force demons out of people."

²³So Jesus called the people together and taught them with stories. He said, "Satan will not force himself out of people. ²⁴A kingdom that is divided cannot continue, ²⁵and a family that is divided cannot continue. ²⁶And if Satan is against himself and fights against his own people, he cannot continue; that is the end of Satan. ²⁷No one can enter a strong person's house and steal his things unless he first ties up the strong person. Then he can steal things from the house. ²⁸I tell you the truth, all sins that people do and all the things people say against God can be forgiven. ²⁹But anyone who speaks against the Holy Spirit *d* will never be forgiven; he is guilty of a sin that continues for ever."

³⁰Jesus said this because the teachers of the law said that he had an evil spirit inside him.

Jesus' True Family

³¹Then Jesus' mother and brothers arrived. Standing outside, they sent someone in to tell him to come out. ³²Many people were sitting around Jesus, and they said to him, "Your mother and brothers are waiting for you outside."

³³Jesus asked, "Who are my mother and my brothers?" ³⁴Then he looked at those sitting around him and said, "Here are my mother and my brothers! ³⁵My true brother and sister and mother and father are those who do what God wants."

A Story About Planting Seed

4 Again Jesus began teaching by the lake. A great crowd gathered around him, so he sat down in a boat near the shore. All the people stayed on the shore close to the water. ²Jesus taught them many things, using stories. He said, ³"Listen! A farmer went out to plant his seed. ⁴While he was planting, some seed fell by the road, and the birds came and ate it up. ⁵Some seed fell on rocky ground where there wasn't much earth. That seed grew very fast, because the ground was not deep. ⁶But when the sun rose, the plants dried up because they did not have deep roots. ⁷Some other seed fell among thorny weeds, which grew and choked the good plants. So those plants did not produce a crop. ⁸Some other seed fell on good ground and began to grow. It got taller and produced a crop. Some

> **Sidelight**
>
> Jesus' story about planting seeds (Mark 4:1–9) not only has spiritual truth, but tells a lot about farming in those days. After ploughing a field, farmers would walk through the field scattering seeds around the field. Then they would go back over the field dragging branches across to cover the seeds and protect them from birds and strong winds.

plants made 30 times more, some made 60 times more, and some made 100 times more."

⁹Then Jesus said, "You people who can hear me, listen!"

Jesus Tells Why He Used Stories

¹⁰Later, when Jesus was alone, the twelve apostles *d* and others around him asked him about the stories.

¹¹Jesus said, "You can know the secret about the kingdom of God. But to other people I tell everything by using stories ¹²so that:

'They will look and look, but they will not
    learn.
They will listen and listen, but they will
    not understand.
If they did learn and understand,
    they would come back to me and be
        forgiven.' "   *Isaiah 6:9–10*

Jesus Explains the Seed Story

¹³Then Jesus said to his followers, "Don't you understand this story? If you don't, how will you

understand any story? [14]The farmer is like a person who plants God's message in people. [15]Sometimes the teaching falls on the road. This is like the people who hear the teaching of God, but Satan quickly comes and takes away the teaching that was planted in them. [16]Others are like the seed planted on rocky ground. They hear the teaching and quickly accept it with joy. [17]But since they don't allow the teaching to go deep into their lives, they keep it only a short time. When trouble or persecution comes because of the teaching they accepted, they quickly give up. [18]Others are like the seed planted among the thorny weeds. They hear the teaching, [19]but the worries of this life, the temptation of wealth and many other evil desires keep the teaching from growing and producing fruit[n] in their lives. [20]Others are like the seed planted in the good ground. They hear the teaching and accept it. Then they grow and produce fruit—sometimes 30 times more,

sometimes 60 times more and sometimes 100 times more."

Use What You Have

[21]Then Jesus said to them, "Do you hide a lamp under a bowl or under a bed? No! You put the lamp on a lampstand. [22]Everything that is hidden will be made clear and every secret thing will be made known. [23]You people who can hear me, listen!

[24]"Think carefully about what you hear. The way you give to others is the way God will give to you, but God will give you even more. [25]Those who have understanding will be given more. But those who do not have understanding, even what they have will be taken away from them."

Jesus Uses a Story About Seed

[26]Then Jesus said, "The kingdom of God is like someone who plants seed in the ground. [27]Night and day, whether the person is asleep or

producing fruit   To produce fruit means to have in your life the good things God wants.

FAITH

It's Alive!

Witness, if you will, one of the most efficient, self-contained structures in nature. It possesses – on its own – almost everything it needs to survive and grow. It has its own coat, its own embryo and its own food supply.

It can even impregnate itself. That's right, each one has the male and female components it needs to create a fertilised egg.

The reproductive system is incredible, but it does need extra help to grow. After fertilisation, it remains dormant until warm, moist conditions promote germination.

Then its coat softens and the metabolism rate in the cells increases. It drinks water and even starts "breathing", while a simple digestion begins. The digested food travels to new areas of growth that emerge when cell division begins.

And congratulations, Mr and Mrs Seed, it's a plant!

The incredible seed is like the kingdom of God. Read **Mark 4:26–34** to see.

* How is a seed's reproductive system like faith's growth process in you?
* According to this passage, what benefits can come from faith's growth in you? What benefits can come from many people growing in faith?

Consider . . .

* working in a garden and drawing other parallels between the plant world and faith. Write your own parable to illustrate those parallels.
* choosing one quality from 2 Peter 1:5–9 (p.1365) to add to your faith. Create one project to help develop that quality.

For more, see . . .

* Ecclesiastes 11:1–6 (p.628)
* Luke 13:18–20 (p.1067)
* Matthew 13:24–32 (p.963)

awake, the seed still grows, but the person does not know how it grows. [28]By itself the earth produces grain. First the plant grows, then the ear and then all the grain in the ear. [29]When the grain is ready, the farmer cuts it, because the harvest time has come."

A Story About Mustard Seed

[30]Then Jesus said, "How can I show you what the kingdom of God is like? What story can I use to explain it? [31]The kingdom of God is like a mustard seed, the smallest seed you plant in the ground. [32]But when planted, this seed grows and becomes the largest of all garden plants. It produces large branches, and the wild birds can make nests in its shade."

[33]Jesus used many stories like these to teach the crowd God's message—as much as they could understand. [34]He always used stories to teach them. But when he and his followers were alone, Jesus explained everything to them.

Jesus Calms a Storm

[35]That evening, Jesus said to his followers, "Let's go across the lake." [36]Leaving the crowd behind, they took him in the boat just as he was. There were also other boats with them. [37]A very strong wind came up on the lake. The waves came over the sides and into the boat so that it was already full of water. [38]Jesus was at the back of the boat, sleeping with his head on a pillow. His followers woke him and said, "Teacher, don't you care that we are drowning!"

[39]Jesus stood up and commanded the wind and said to the waves, "Quiet! Be still!" Then the wind stopped, and it became completely calm.

[40]Jesus said to his followers, "Why are you afraid? Do you still have no faith?"

[41]The followers were very afraid and asked each other, "Who is this? Even the wind and the waves obey him!"

A Man with Demons Inside Him

5 Jesus and his followers went to the other side of the lake to the area of the Gerasene people. [2]When Jesus got out of the boat, instantly a man with an evil spirit came to him from the burial caves. [3]This man lived in the caves, and no one could tie him up, not even with a chain. [4]Many times people had used chains to tie the man's hands and feet, but he always broke them off. No one was strong enough to control him. [5]Day and night he would wander around the burial caves and on the hills, screaming and cutting himself with stones. [6]While Jesus

was still far away, the man saw him, ran to him and fell down before him.

[7]The man shouted in a loud voice, "What do you want with me, Jesus, Son of the Most High God? I command you in God's name not to torture me!" [8]He said this because Jesus was saying to him, "You evil spirit, come out of the man."

[9]Then Jesus asked him, "What is your name?"

He answered, "My name is Legion,[n] because we are many spirits." [10]He begged Jesus again and again not to send them out of that area.

[11]A large herd of pigs was feeding on a hill near there. [12]The demons[d] begged Jesus, "Send us into the pigs; let us go into them." [13]So Jesus allowed them to do this. The evil spirits left the man and went into the pigs. Then the herd of pigs—about 2,000 of them—rushed down the hill into the lake and were drowned.

[14]The herdsmen ran away and went to the town and to the countryside, telling everyone about this. So people went out to see what had happened. [15]They came to Jesus and saw the man who used to have the many evil spirits, sitting, clothed and in his right mind. And they were frightened. [16]The people who saw this told the others what had happened to the man who had the demons living in him, and they told about the pigs. [17]Then the people began to beg Jesus to leave their area.

[18]As Jesus was getting back into the boat, the man who was freed from the demons begged to go with him.

[19]But Jesus would not let him. He said, "Go home to your family and tell them how much the Lord has done for you and how he has had mercy on you." [20]So the man left and began to tell the people in the Ten Towns[n] about what Jesus had done for him. And everyone was amazed.

Jesus Gives Life to a Dead Girl and Heals a Sick Woman

[21]When Jesus went in the boat back to the other side of the lake, a large crowd gathered around him there. [22]A leader of the synagogue,[d] named Jairus, came there, saw Jesus and fell at his feet. [23]He begged Jesus, saying again and again, "My daughter is dying. Please come and put your hands on her so she will be healed and will live." [24]So Jesus went with him.

A large crowd followed Jesus and pushed very close around him. [25]Among them was a woman who had been bleeding for twelve years. [26]She had suffered very much from many doctors and had spent all the money she had, but instead of improving, she was getting worse. [27]When the woman heard about Jesus, she came up behind him in the

---

Legion　Means very many. A legion was about 5,000 men in the Roman army.
Ten Towns　In Greek, called "Decapolis". It was an area east of Lake Galilee that once had ten main towns.

crowd and touched his coat. ²⁸She thought, "If I can just touch his clothes, I will be healed." ²⁹Instantly her bleeding stopped, and she felt in her body that she was healed from her disease.

³⁰At once Jesus felt power go out from him. So he turned around in the crowd and asked, "Who touched my clothes?"

³¹His followers said, "Look at how many people are pushing against you! And you ask, 'Who touched me?'"

³²But Jesus continued looking around to see who had touched him. ³³The woman, knowing that she was healed, came and fell at Jesus' feet. Shaking with fear, she told him the whole truth. ³⁴Jesus said to her, "Dear woman, you are made well because you believed. Go in peace; be healed of your disease."

³⁵While Jesus was still speaking, some people came from the house of the synagogue leader. They said, "Your daughter is dead. There is no need to bother the teacher any more."

³⁶But Jesus paid no attention to what they said. He told the synagogue leader, "Don't be afraid; just believe."

³⁷Jesus let only Peter, James and John the brother of James go with him. ³⁸When they came to the house of the synagogue leader, Jesus found many people there making lots of noise and crying loudly. ³⁹Jesus entered the house and said to them, "Why are you crying and making so much noise? The child is not dead, only asleep." ⁴⁰But they laughed at him. So, after throwing them out of the house, Jesus took the child's father and mother and his three followers into the room where the child was. ⁴¹Taking hold of the girl's hand, he said to her, "Talitha, koum!" (This means, "Young girl, I tell you to stand up!") ⁴²At once the girl stood right up and began walking. (She was twelve years old.) Everyone was completely amazed. ⁴³Jesus gave them strict orders not to tell people about this. Then he told them to give the girl something to eat.

Jesus Goes to His Home Town

6 Jesus left there and went to his home town, and his followers went with him. ²On the Sabbath ᵈ day he taught in the synagogue. ᵈ Many people heard him and were amazed, saying,

SICKNESS

Miracles Happen

Doris's face was streaked with tears. "They say there's no hope," she sobbed, reaching for another tissue. "My granddaughter has a tumour the size of a tennis ball. It has completely surrounded her kidneys."
She continued haltingly, "The doctors aren't sure if other organs are involved. They don't think she'll live long."
Betty placed her hand on Doris's shoulder.
"Miracles do happen, Doris. We need to pray for a miracle."
"I've given up with God. Even he can't heal Wendy now. And besides, I don't think he's listening any more."
Doris was wrong. Even the doctors were wrong. A new medicine was added to Wendy's treatment, and she was healed.
God heals. He can use doctors, nurses and medicine to accomplish his purposes. Often he heals without their help, too – when people pray in faith. Read **Mark 5:21–43** to see how Jesus healed two people.

* How were the three healings – Wendy, the woman (verses 25–34) and the little girl – different from each other?
* Does God still heal in the way that Jesus did in this passage?

Consider . . .

* writing a letter as though you were going to send it to someone who has asked for healing and hasn't received it. Encourage that imaginary person.
* walking down the corridor of a local hospital and silently praying for God's healing for each patient.

For more, see . . .

* Psalm 103:1–5 (p.559)
* James 5:13–18 (p.1353)
* Matthew 9:1–26 (p.952)

"Where did this man get these teachings? What is this wisdom that has been given to him? And where did he get the power to do miracles? *d* ³He is just the carpenter, the son of Mary and the brother of James, Joseph, Judas and Simon. And his sisters are here with us." So the people were upset with Jesus.

⁴Jesus said to them, "A prophet *d* is honoured everywhere except in his home town and with his own people and in his own home." ⁵So Jesus was not able to work any miracles there except to heal a few sick people by putting his hands on them. ⁶He was amazed at how many people had no faith.

Then Jesus went to other villages in that area and taught. ⁷He called his twelve followers together and got ready to send them out two by two and gave them authority over evil spirits. ⁸This is what Jesus commanded them: "Take nothing for your trip except a walking stick. Take no bread, no bag and no money in your pockets. ⁹Wear sandals, but take only the clothes you are wearing. ¹⁰When you enter a house, stay there until you leave that town. ¹¹If the people in a certain place refuse to welcome you or listen to you, leave that place. Shake its dust off your feet *n* as a warning to them."

¹²So the followers went out and preached that people should change their hearts and lives. ¹³They forced many demons *d* out and put olive oil on many sick people and healed them.

How John the Baptist was Killed

¹⁴King Herod heard about Jesus, because he was now well known. Some people said, "He is John the Baptist, *d* who has risen from the dead. That is why he can work these miracles." *d*

¹⁵Others said, "He is Elijah." *n*

Other people said, "Jesus is a prophet, *d* like the prophets who lived long ago."

¹⁶When Herod heard this, he said, "I killed John by cutting off his head. Now he has risen from the dead!"

¹⁷Herod himself had ordered his soldiers to arrest John and put him in prison in order to please his wife, Herodias. She had been the wife of Philip, Herod's brother, but then Herod had married her. ¹⁸John had been telling Herod, "It is not lawful for you to be married to your brother's wife." ¹⁹So Herodias hated John and wanted to kill him. But she couldn't, ²⁰because Herod was afraid of John and protected him. He knew John was a good and holy man. Also, though John's preaching always bothered him, he enjoyed listening to John.

²¹Then the perfect time came for Herodias to cause John's death. On Herod's birthday, he gave a dinner party for the most important government leaders, the commanders of his army and the most important people in Galilee. ²²When the daughter of Herodias came in and danced, she pleased Herod and the people eating with him. So King Herod said to the girl, "Ask me for anything you want, and I will give it to you." ²³He promised her, "Anything you ask for I will give to you—up to half of my kingdom."

²⁴The girl went to her mother and asked, "What should I ask for?"

Sidelight   King Herod wasn't the sort of person who you would like to bump into on a dark night. He was responsible for beheading John the Baptist (Mark 6:14–29) and even murdering his own children!

Her mother answered, "Ask for the head of John the Baptist." *d*

²⁵At once the girl went back to the king and said to him, "I want the head of John the Baptist right now on a dish."

²⁶Although the king was very sad, he had made a promise, and his dinner guests had heard it. So he did not want to refuse what she asked. ²⁷Immediately the king sent a soldier to bring John's head. The soldier went and cut off John's head in the prison ²⁸and brought it back on a dish. He gave it to the girl, and the girl gave it to her mother. ²⁹When John's followers heard this, they came and got John's body and put it in a tomb.

More than 5,000 Fed

³⁰The apostles *d* gathered around Jesus and told him about all the things they had done and taught. ³¹Crowds of people were coming and going so that Jesus and his followers did not even have time to eat. He said to them, "Come away by yourselves, and we will go to a lonely place to get some rest."

³²So they went in a boat by themselves to a lonely place. ³³But many people saw them leave and recognised them. So from all the towns they ran to the place where Jesus was going, and they got there before him. ³⁴When he arrived, he saw a great crowd waiting. He felt sorry for them, because they were like sheep without a shepherd. So he began to teach them many things.

Shake . . . feet   A warning. It showed that they were rejecting these people.
Elijah   A man who spoke for God and who lived hundreds of years before Christ. See 1 Kings 17.

35When it was late in the day, his followers came to him and said, "No one lives in this place, and it is already very late. 36Send the people away so they can go to the countryside and towns around here to buy themselves something to eat."

37But Jesus answered, "You give them something to eat."

They said to him, "We would all have to work a month to earn enough money to buy that much bread!"

38Jesus asked them, "How many loaves of bread do you have? Go and see."

When they found out, they said, "Five loaves and two fish."

39Then Jesus told his followers to have the people sit in groups on the green grass. 40So they sat in groups of 50 or 100. 41Jesus took the five loaves and two fish and, looking up to heaven, he thanked God for the food. He divided the bread and gave it to his followers for them to give to the people. Then he divided the two fish among them all. 42All the people ate and were satisfied. 43The followers filled twelve baskets with the leftover pieces of bread and fish. 44There were 5,000 men who ate.

HUNGER AND POVERTY

The Multiplication Principle

"We have only 3,000 tins. I wanted to collect 10,000," Kristen Green complained to Mr Rossetti, the Head of St Francis De Sales High School.

Mr Rossetti listened but didn't say much. Later that day during school assembly, he surprised Kristen by asking her to speak to the students about the food drive.

Kristen spoke about a man she had met at the local soup kitchen who each night asked for an extra plate of food for his dying wife. Kristen also told them about a hungry woman who shared her orange with the person sitting beside her. She continued, "We think of starving people being in Ethiopia, but these people live three blocks from this school." Kristen challenged the students to meet the goal of 10,000 tins of food in the next week.

After assembly, students asked Kristen how they could help. Suddenly everyone was mobilised. The football team went from door to door in the neighbourhood, asking for donations of tinned goods. The Fellowship of Christian Athletes collected $1,500 worth of food in one night. Kristen and a friend asked area grocers for food donations.

By Wednesday, the goal of 10,000 tins was met – a goal people had thought was unrealistic. (Only 4,000 tins had been collected the year before.) Kristen decided not to tell anyone that the goal had been reached before the deadline. On Friday, people cheered when she announced the total: 17,299 tins!

Kristen and others filled three school buses with the food. As they delivered the food to the soup kitchen, people standing in line thanked them and patted them on the back.

"We knew we were making a difference," Kristen says. "People were going to be able to eat."

Jesus and his disciples were also confronted with the challenge of feeding hungry people.

Read **Mark 6:30–44** to see how Jesus fed a hungry mob.

* How is the multiplication of tinned food at De Sales High similar to Jesus' multiplying food for the multitude? How is it different?
* How have you seen Jesus increase your gifts or resources to help others?

Consider . . .

* giving up eating a meal and spending time in prayer for those who have less to eat than you do. Donate the money you would have spent on the meal to a Christian relief agency.
* organising a tinned food collection at your local church or school.

For more, see . . .

* 2 Kings 4:42–44 (p.349)
* John 6:1–15 (p.1104)
* Matthew 14:13–21 (p.965)

Jesus Walks on the Water

⁴⁵Immediately Jesus told his followers to get into the boat and go ahead of him to Bethsaida across the lake. He stayed behind to send the people home. ⁴⁶After sending them away, he went into the hills to pray.

⁴⁷That night, the boat was in the middle of the lake, and Jesus was alone on the land. ⁴⁸He saw his followers struggling hard to row the boat, because the wind was blowing against them. Between three and six o'clock in the morning, Jesus came to them, walking on the water, and he wanted to walk past the boat. ⁴⁹But when they saw him walking on the water, they thought he was a ghost and cried out. ⁵⁰They all saw him and were afraid. But immediately Jesus spoke to them and said, "Have courage! It is I. Do not be afraid." ⁵¹Then he got into the boat with them, and the wind became calm. The followers were greatly amazed. ⁵²They did not understand about the miracle of the five loaves, because their minds were closed.

⁵³When they had crossed the lake, they came to shore at Gennesaret and tied the boat there. ⁵⁴When they got out of the boat, people immediately recognised Jesus. ⁵⁵They ran everywhere in that area and began to bring sick people on mats wherever they heard he was. ⁵⁶And everywhere he went—into towns, cities or countryside—the people brought the sick to the market-places. They begged him to let them touch just the edge of his coat, and all who touched it were healed.

Obey God's Law

7 When some Pharisees *d* and some teachers of the law came from Jerusalem, they gathered around Jesus. ²They saw some of Jesus' followers eating food with hands that were not clean, *d* that is, they hadn't washed them. ³(The Pharisees and all the Jews never eat before washing their hands in a special way according to their unwritten laws. ⁴And when they buy something in the market, they never eat it until

HYPOCRISY

An Open Letter to God

James was tired of seeing what he called "the Dr Jekyll and Mr Hyde" sides of his father. In his frustration, he wrote this letter to God.

Dear God,

There are a few things I just don't understand about people and the way they act.

Take my dad, for example. Don't get me wrong. He's a nice man; he goes to church with us and everything. But when it comes to his business, he really changes. Dad's always talking about how he really "got the best of that bloke" in a business deal or how he "beat her out of a contract." It just doesn't seem very Christian.

Oh, and another place is on the road. My dad gets really angry with other drivers and sometimes even yells at them.

And, oh well, I suppose I just don't understand. It just doesn't seem very Christian.

Can you help me to understand, God?

James

Hypocrisy is common. Even in Jesus' day, Jesus' followers were troubled by hypocrites. Read **Mark 7:1–23** to learn more about the situation.

* What was hypocritical about James's dad's actions and the Pharisees' actions?
* According to this passage, what's the cure for hypocrisy?

Consider . . .

* evaluating your own life for any hypocrisies and applying the "cure" to get rid of them.
* writing a letter to James that responds to his frustrations.

For more, see . . .

* Isaiah 29:13–14 (p.668)
* Romans 14:13–18 (p.1207)
* Matthew 15:1–20 (p.967)

they have washed themselves in a special way. They also follow many other unwritten laws, such as the washing of cups, pitchers and pots.)

[5]The Pharisees and the teachers of the law said to Jesus, "Why don't your followers obey the unwritten laws which have been handed down to us? Why do your followers eat their food with hands that are not clean?"

[6]Jesus answered, "Isaiah was right when he spoke about you hypocrites. [d] He wrote,

'These people show honour to me with words,
    but their hearts are far from me.
[7]Their worship of me is worthless.
    The things they teach are nothing but
        human rules.'   *Isaiah 29:13*

[8]You have stopped following the commands of God, and you follow only human teachings."

[9]Then Jesus said to them, "You cleverly ignore the commands of God so you can follow your own teachings. [10]Moses said, 'Honour your father and your mother,' [n] and 'Anyone who says cruel things to his father or mother must be put to death.' [n] [11]But you say a person can tell his father or mother, 'I have something I could use to help you, but it is Corban—a gift to God.' [12]You no longer let that person use that money for his father or his mother. [13]By your own rules, which you teach people, you are rejecting what God said. And you do many things like that."

[14]After Jesus called the crowd to him again, he said, "Every person should listen to me and understand what I am saying. [15]There is nothing people put into their bodies that makes them unclean. People are made unclean by the things that come out of them." [16] [n]

[17]When Jesus left the people and went into the house, his followers asked him about this story. [18]Jesus said, "Do you still not understand? Surely you know that nothing that enters someone from the outside can make that person unclean. [19]It does not go into the heart, but into the stomach. Then it goes out of the body." (When Jesus said this, he meant that no longer was any food unclean for people to eat.)

[20]And Jesus said, "The things that come out of people are the things that make them unclean. [21]All these evil things begin inside people, in the heart: evil thoughts, sexual sins, stealing, murder, adultery, [d] [22]greed, evil actions, lying, doing sinful things, jealousy, speaking evil of others, pride and foolish living. [23]All these evil things come from inside and make people unclean."

Jesus Helps a Non-Jewish Woman

[24]Jesus left that place and went to the area around Tyre. When he went into a house, he did not want anyone to know he was there, but he could not stay hidden. [25]A woman whose daughter had an evil spirit in her heard that he was there. So she quickly came to Jesus and fell at his feet. [26]She was Greek, born in Phoenicia, in Syria. She begged Jesus to force the demon[d] out of her daughter.

[27]Jesus told the woman, "It is not right to take the children's bread and give it to the dogs. First let the children eat all they want."

[28]But she answered, "Yes, Lord, but even the dogs under the table can eat the children's crumbs."

[29]Then Jesus said, "Because of your answer, you may go. The demon has left your daughter."

[30]The woman went home and found her daughter lying in bed; the demon was gone.

Jesus Heals a Deaf Man

[31]Then Jesus left the area around Tyre and went through Sidon to Lake Galilee, to the area of the Ten Towns. [n] [32]While he was there, some people brought a man to him who was deaf and could not talk plainly. The people begged Jesus to put his hand on the man to heal him.

[33]Jesus led the man away from the crowd, by himself. He put his fingers in the man's ears and then spat and touched the man's tongue. [34]Looking up to heaven, he sighed and said to the man, "Ephphatha!" (This means, "Be opened.") [35]Instantly the man was able to hear and to use his tongue so that he spoke clearly.

[36]Jesus commanded the people not to tell anyone about what happened. But the more he commanded them, the more they told about it. [37]They were completely amazed and said, "Jesus does everything well. He makes the deaf hear! And those who can't talk he makes able to speak."

More than 4,000 People Fed

8 Another time there was a great crowd with Jesus that had nothing to eat. So Jesus called his followers and said, [2]"I feel sorry for these people, because they have already been with me for three days, and they have nothing to eat. [3]If I send them home hungry, they will faint on the way. Some of them live a long way from here."

[4]Jesus' followers answered, "How can we get enough bread to feed all these people? We are far away from any town."

'Honour . . . mother' Quotation from Exodus 20:12; Deuteronomy 5:16.
'Anyone . . . death.' Quotation from Exodus 21:17.
Verse 16 Some Greek copies add verse 16: "You people who can hear me, listen!"
Ten Towns In Greek, called "Decapolis". It was an area east of Lake Galilee that once had ten main towns.

5Jesus asked, "How many loaves of bread do you have?"

They answered, "Seven."

6Jesus told the people to sit on the ground. Then he took the seven loaves, gave thanks to God, and divided the bread. He gave the pieces to his followers to give to the people, and they did so. 7The followers also had a few small fish. After Jesus gave thanks for the fish, he told his followers to give them to the people as well. 8All the people ate and were satisfied. Then his followers filled seven baskets with the leftover pieces of food. 9There were about 4,000 people who ate. After they had eaten, Jesus sent them home. 10Then right away he got into a boat with his followers and went to the area of Dalmanutha.

The Leaders Ask for a Miracle

11The Pharisees *d* came to Jesus and began to ask him questions. Hoping to trap him, they

Sidelight

Jesus had conflicts with the Pharisees (Mark 8:11) throughout his ministry. These leaders were respected for their accurate interpretations of Jewish law. The historian Josephus estimates that 6,000 Pharisees lived in Palestine during Jesus' years.

asked Jesus for a miracle *d* from God. 12Jesus sighed deeply and said, "Why do you people ask for a miracle as a sign? I tell you the truth, no sign

SICKNESS

She Made a Difference

In the 1940s, more than 500,000 people in the city of Calcutta (5% of the city's population) literally lived and died in the streets. With even winter temperatures hovering in the upper 30s, the city could seem like hell on earth. It was there that the "poorest of the poor" lived, plagued by leprosy, tuberculosis, pneumonia and, most of all, poverty.

What hope was there in such a place? Surely no one could make a difference there. But Agnes thought differently. She believed that God was calling her to bring hope to these poor and downtrodden people.

In her journal, Agnes, better known as Mother Teresa, described her first day in the slums as a day of meeting Christ. She met Christ face to face there – the hungry Christ, the naked Christ, the sick Christ, the homeless Christ. She said that the touch of him in this distressing disguise gave her great joy, peace and strength.

So, clad in a white sari edged with blue, Mother Teresa began her work. She and a group of nuns taught the children of the poor. They provided care for lepers who could not get help anywhere else. They built shelters and hospitals so that the poor would have a place out of the streets. They fed the hungry and loved the unlovable. They literally changed the face of Calcutta.

Jesus' love flowed through Mother Teresa to touch people. Jesus' love always makes a difference. When Jesus touches sick people, their lives are never the same. Read **Mark 7:31–37** and imagine how the sick people who met Jesus must have felt.

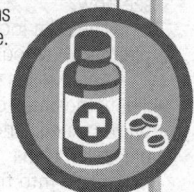

- How is Mother Teresa's approach to ministry like Jesus' approach?
- Which of Jesus' actions are most important to people who are sick?

Consider . . .

- doing a task that you don't like to do (such as cleaning a bathroom) for a housebound member of your church.
- talking to your minister about how your church can minister to people with AIDS.

For more, see . . .

- Leviticus 13 (p.111)
- Luke 17:11–19 (p.1077)

- Matthew 8:1–4 (p.951)

will be given to you." [13]Then Jesus left the Pharisees and went in the boat to the other side of the lake.

Guard Against Wrong Teachings

[14]His followers had only one loaf of bread with them in the boat; they had forgotten to bring more. [15]Jesus warned them, "Be careful! Beware of the yeast of the Pharisees [d] and the yeast of Herod."

[16]His followers discussed the meaning of this, saying, "He said this because we have no bread."

[17]Knowing what they were talking about, Jesus asked them, "Why are you talking about not having bread? Do you still not see or understand? Are your minds closed? [18]You have eyes, but you don't really see. You have ears, but you don't really listen. Remember when [19]I divided five loaves of bread for the 5,000? How many baskets did you fill with leftover pieces of food?"

They answered, "Twelve."

[20]"And when I divided seven loaves of bread for the 4,000, how many baskets did you fill with leftover pieces of food?"

They answered, "Seven."

[21]Then Jesus said to them, "Don't you understand yet?"

Jesus Heals a Blind Man

[22]Jesus and his followers came to Bethsaida. There some people brought a blind man to Jesus and begged him to touch the man. [23]So Jesus took the blind man's hand and led him out of the village. Then he spat on the man's eyes and put his hands on the man and asked, "Can you see now?"

[24]The man looked up and said, "Yes, I see people, but they look like trees walking around."

[25]Again Jesus put his hands on the man's eyes. Then the man opened his eyes wide and they were healed, and he was able to see everything clearly. [26]Jesus told him to go home, saying, "Don't go into the town."

Peter Says Jesus is the Christ

[27]Jesus and his followers went to the towns around Caesarea Philippi. While they were travelling, Jesus asked them, "Who do people say I am?"

[28]They answered, "Some say you are John the Baptist. [d] Others say you are Elijah, [n] and others say you are one of the prophets." [d]

[29]Then Jesus asked, "But who do you say I am?"

Peter answered, "You are the Christ." [d]

[30]Jesus warned his followers not to tell anyone who he was.

[31]Then Jesus began to teach them that the Son of Man [d] must suffer many things and that he would be rejected by the Jewish elders, the leading priests and the teachers of the law. He told them that the Son of Man must be killed and then rise from the dead after three days. [32]Jesus told them plainly what would happen. Then Peter took Jesus aside and began to tell him not to talk like that. [33]But Jesus turned and looked at his followers. Then he told Peter not to talk in that way. He said, "Go away from me, Satan! [n] You don't care about the things of God, but only about things people think are important."

[34]Then Jesus called the crowd to him, along with his followers. He said, "If people want to follow me, they must give up the things they want. They must be willing even to give up their lives to follow me. [35]Those who want to save their lives will give up true life. But those who give up their lives for me and for the Good News [d] will have true life. [36]It is worth nothing for them to have the whole world if they lose their souls. [37]They could never pay enough to buy back their souls. [38]The people who live now are living in a sinful and evil time. If people are ashamed of me and my teaching, the Son of Man [d] will be ashamed of them when he comes with his Father's glory and with the holy angels."

9 Then Jesus said to the people, "I tell you the truth, some people standing here will see the kingdom of God come with power before they die."

Jesus Talks with Moses and Elijah

[2]Six days later, Jesus took Peter, James and John up on a high mountain by themselves. While they watched, Jesus' appearance was changed. [3]His clothes became shining white, whiter than any person could make them. [4]Then Elijah and Moses [n] appeared to them, talking with Jesus.

[5]Peter said to Jesus, "Teacher, it is good that we are here. Let us make three tents—one for you, one for Moses and one for Elijah." [6]Peter did not know what to say, because he and the others were so frightened.

[7]Then a cloud came and covered them, and a voice came from the cloud, saying, "This is my Son, whom I love. Listen to him!"

Elijah A man who spoke for God and who lived hundreds of years before Christ. See 1 Kings 17.
Satan Name for the devil meaning "the enemy". Jesus means that Peter was talking like Satan.
Elijah and Moses Two of the most important Jewish leaders in the past. Moses had given them the law, and Elijah was an important prophet.

⁸Suddenly Peter, James and John looked around, but they saw only Jesus there alone with them.

⁹As they were coming down the mountain, Jesus commanded them not to tell anyone about what they had seen until the Son of Man *d* had risen from the dead.

¹⁰So the followers obeyed Jesus, but they discussed what he meant about rising from the dead.

¹¹Then they asked Jesus, "Why do the teachers of the law say that Elijah must come first?"

¹²Jesus answered, "They are right to say that Elijah must come first and make everything the way it should be. But why does the Scripture *d* say that the Son of Man will suffer much and that people will treat him as if he were nothing? ¹³I tell you that Elijah has already come. And people did to him whatever they wanted to do, just as the Scriptures said it would happen."

Jesus Heals a Sick Boy

¹⁴When Jesus, Peter, James and John came back to the other followers, they saw a great crowd around them and the teachers of the law arguing with them. ¹⁵But as soon as the crowd saw Jesus, the people were surprised and ran to welcome him. ¹⁶Jesus asked, "What are you arguing about?"

¹⁷A man answered, "Teacher, I brought my son to you. He has an evil spirit in him that stops him from talking. ¹⁸When the spirit attacks him, it throws him on the ground. Then my son foams at the mouth, grinds his teeth and becomes very stiff. I asked your followers to force the evil spirit out, but they couldn't."

¹⁹Jesus answered, "You people have no faith. How long must I stay with you? How long must I put up with you? Bring the boy to me."

²⁰So the followers brought him to Jesus. As soon as the evil spirit saw Jesus, it made the boy

---

FAITH

Are You Sure?

The debate had been fierce. After a GCSE Biology lesson, Esther and Livi had begun a discussion with Giles and Kat about how the world began. Esther and Livi were Christians and believed that there was a God behind all of creation and that there was a reason and purpose to it all. Giles and Kat were not Christians and believed that the world existed due to a random sequence of events and that there was no purpose behind it at all. The debate continued long into their lunch break.

Eventually, Mrs Lloyd, the biology teacher, interrupted the discussion and said something that took all four of them by surprise. She said, "Ultimately, even though you disagree, all four of you have some kind of faith."

What? Giles and Kat did not like this at all, so Giles responded, "No, they are making a statement of faith because they believe in religion. We are making a statement of fact because we believe in science."

Mrs Lloyd continued, "But Giles, none of what you are saying can be categorically proven, so the fact is, you have faith in what you are saying, even though your side of the argument does not have all the facts to back up your claim."

In **Mark 9:1–9**, Peter, James and John saw something that was almost beyond belief. Were they hallucinating? Were they dreaming? How could Jesus be standing with two people who were meant to be dead?

- If you were one of the disciples, it would be easier to have faith in Jesus, because you would have spoken and spent time with him. So what helps you have faith in Jesus?
- What things might you do to help build your faith?

Consider . . .

- making a list of all the things people have faith in: money, science, friendships, etc. What are the differences between having faith in these things and having faith in Jesus? How should these differences change your outlook on life?
- reading Hebrews 11:3 whilst staring at the stars. Give God the chance to speak to you whilst doing this.

For more, see . . .

- Mark 11:20–26 (p.1020)   • Hebrews 11:1–3 (p.1341)

lose control of himself, and he fell down and rolled on the ground, foaming at the mouth.

²¹Jesus asked the boy's father, "How long has this been happening?"

The father answered, "Since he was very young. ²²The spirit often throws him into a fire or into water to kill him. If you can do anything for him, please have pity on us and help us."

²³Jesus said to the father, "You said, 'If you can!' All things are possible for the one who believes."

²⁴Immediately the father cried out, "I do believe! Help me to believe more!"

²⁵When Jesus saw that a crowd was quickly gathering, he ordered the evil spirit, saying, "You spirit that makes people unable to hear or speak, I command you to come out of this boy and never enter him again!"

²⁶The evil spirit screamed and caused the boy to fall on the ground again. Then the spirit came out. The boy looked as if he were dead, and many people said, "He is dead!" ²⁷But Jesus took hold of the boy's hand and helped him to stand up.

²⁸When Jesus went into the house, his followers began asking him privately, "Why couldn't we force that evil spirit out?"

²⁹Jesus answered, "That kind of spirit can only be forced out by prayer."

Jesus Talks About His Death

³⁰Then Jesus and his followers left that place and went through Galilee. He didn't want anyone to know where he was, ³¹because he was teaching his followers. He said to them, "The Son of Man *d* will be handed over to people, and they will kill him. After three days, he will rise from the dead." ³²But the followers did not understand what Jesus meant, and they were afraid to ask him.

POPULARITY

Everyone is Going

Sam slammed his locker shut. It was Friday afternoon; the final bell had rung. He needed to catch Stuart and Justin before they got on their bus to check that they were all meeting at the football match that night.

As Sam turned from his locker, his foot caught on a wheel. It was Alex's wheelchair. Alex had broken his neck in a diving accident and was paralysed from the shoulders down.

"Hey, Sam, what are you lot doing tonight?" Alex asked.

"Well, er . . . " Sam hesitated as his eyes searched the cloakroom for the others, but Alex didn't wait for an answer.

"Would you like to come over to my house? My mum said she'd pick up some videos. Could you open my locker and put away the books in my rucksack, please?"

Sam impatiently unloaded the rucksack and deposited the books. As Sam closed the locker, Alex asked again, "Well? What about tonight?"

Sam glanced down the empty hall. The buses were pulling away. It was too late to make plans with Justin and Stuart. Alex needed a friend. But everyone would be going to the match.

Sam thought for a moment and then smiled at Alex. "What time do you want me to come over?"

The disciples also had to make a decision about what it meant to be popular. They were arguing about who was the greatest or the most popular. Read **Mark 9:30–37** to see how Jesus turned the tables on them.

- How would Sam's actions make him important in the kingdom of God?
- When have you had to decide between doing what's popular and what's right? How was that experience like the incident in this passage?

Consider . . .

- having lunch with an unpopular classmate.
- doing a household chore that everyone in your family dislikes doing.

For more, see . . .

- Proverbs 11:24–26 (p.599)
- Philippians 2:5–7 (p.1282)
- Matthew 18:1–5 (p.971)

Who is the Greatest?

[33]Jesus and his followers went to Capernaum. When they went into a house there, he asked them, "What were you arguing about on the road?" [34]But the followers did not answer, because their argument on the road was about which one of them was the greatest.

[35]Jesus sat down and called the twelve apostles [d] to him. He said, "Whoever wants to be the most important must be last of all and servant of all."

[36]Then Jesus took a small child and had him stand among them. Taking the child in his arms, he said, [37]"Whoever accepts a child like this in my name accepts me. And whoever accepts me accepts the One who sent me."

Anyone Not Against Us is For Us

[38]Then John said, "Teacher, we saw someone using your name to force demons [d] out of a person. We told him to stop, because he does not belong to our group."

[39]But Jesus said, "Don't stop him, because anyone who uses my name to do powerful things will not easily say evil things about me. [40]Whoever is not against us is with us. [41]I tell you the truth, whoever gives you a drink of water because you belong to the Christ [d] will truly get his reward.

[42]"If one of these little children believes in me, and someone causes that child to sin, it would be better for that person to have a large stone tied around his neck and be drowned in

---

ENVIRONMENT

Burning Bushes

Anya was on a wonderful holiday in Australia, and while she was there she stayed with some folk in Brisbane who owned land. The scenery was magnificent – everything she'd imagined and more. One very hot day, her host was taking her for a drive around the area and they came across some burnt forestry. It seemed to her that they drove for quite a way before they came across thriving bushland again.

"What happened there?" she asked Darryl. "Was it one of those bush fires we read about?"

He laughed and shook his head. "No, no," he said. "That was done deliberately."

"Deliberately?" she replied looking shocked.

"Yeah," he continued. "It's actually to stop bush fires. That's the reason it's done!"

Anya looked puzzled. "That doesn't make any sense. How can setting something on fire, stop a fire?"

Darryl explained. "When we have a really outrageous fire here, it spreads very quickly for miles and miles. Not just the trees and plants catch fire, but animals and birds as well. It's very sad to see. You know, a bird can be burnt and fly on for metres before it dies, so when it drops from the sky, it can start a fire there too."

"So how does the deliberate fire help?" Anya was confused.

"Well," replied her host. "If you first burn everything in say, a mile radius, before any fires start, then if you do have a fire, it will automatically stop when it gets to the burnt-out spot. You'll see burnt-out places like this all over the country. Safety, see?"

"So, it's better to damage part of the land, to save the rest!" smiled Anya. "What a clever idea!"

"Bonzer!" laughed Darryl.

Read **Mark 9:42–48** and see how the same thing can apply to humans!

* How is Darryl's idea similar to this teaching?
* When have you had to cut something out of your life to bring you back to God?

Consider . . .

* volunteering to help at a local nature reserve, to make it a healthier environment for wildlife.
* writing down something you want to cut out of your life that affects your relationship with others. Then pray that God will help you to deal with it.

For more, see . . .

* John 15:1–2 (p.1124)
* 1 Corinthians 3:11–13 (p.1217)

* Romans 7:14–25 (p.1193)

the sea. [43]If your hand causes you to sin, cut it off. It is better for you to lose part of your body and live for ever than to have two hands and go to hell, where the fire never goes out. [44] n [45]If your foot causes you to sin, cut it off. It is better for you to lose part of your body and to live for ever than to have two feet and be thrown into hell. [46] n [47]If your eye causes you to sin, take it out. It is better for you to enter the kingdom of

> ## Sidelight
>
> The Greek word for "hell" (Mark 9:45–49) is Gehenna, and is based on the Hebrew name for the Hinnom Valley just outside Jerusalem. The valley, which was once used as a site for child sacrifices (see Jeremiah 32:35, p.755) later became a place to burn the bodies of animals and criminals. Jesus uses this word "hell" to describe the place of eternal punishment where all who reject the Good News will go (see also Matthew 13:40–42, p.964).

God with only one eye than to have two eyes and be thrown into hell. [48]In hell the worm does not die; the fire is never put out. [49]Every person will be salted with fire. n

[50]"Salt is good, but if the salt loses its salty taste, you cannot make it salty again. So, be full of salt, and have peace with each other."

Jesus Teaches About Divorce

10 Then Jesus left that place and went into the area of Judea and across the Jordan River. Again, crowds came to him, and he taught them as he usually did.

[2]Some Pharisees d came to Jesus and tried to trick him. They asked, "Is it right for a man to divorce his wife?"

[3]Jesus answered, "What did Moses command you to do?"

[4]They said, "Moses allowed a man to write out divorce papers and send her away." n

[5]Jesus said, "Moses wrote that command for you because you were stubborn. [6]But when God made the world, 'he made them male and female'. n [7]'So a man will leave his father and mother and be united with his wife, [8]and the two will become one body.' n So there are not two, but one. [9]God has joined the two together, so no one should separate them."

[10]Later, in the house, his followers asked Jesus again about the question of divorce. [11]He answered, "Anyone who divorces his wife and marries another woman is guilty of adultery d against her. [12]And the woman who divorces her husband and marries another man is also guilty of adultery."

Jesus Accepts Children

[13]Some people brought their little children to Jesus so he could touch them, but his followers told them to stop. [14]When Jesus saw this, he was upset and said to them, "Let the little children come to me. Don't stop them, because the kingdom of God belongs to people who are like these children. [15]I tell you the truth, you must accept the kingdom of God as if you were a little child, or you will never enter it." [16]Then Jesus took the children in his arms, put his hands on them and blessed them.

A Rich Young Man's Question

[17]As Jesus started to leave, a man ran to him and fell on his knees before Jesus. The man asked, "Good teacher, what must I do to have life for ever?"

[18]Jesus answered, "Why do you call me good? Only God is good. [19]You know the commands: 'You must not murder anyone. You must not be guilty of adultery. d You must not steal. You must not tell lies about your neighbour. You must not cheat. Honour your father and mother.' " n

[20]The man said, "Teacher, I have obeyed all these things since I was a boy."

[21]Jesus, looking at the man, loved him and said, "There is one more thing you need to do. Go and sell everything you have, and give the money to the poor and you will have treasure in heaven. Then come and follow me."

[22]He was very sad to hear Jesus say this, and he left very sad, because he was rich.

[23]Then Jesus looked at his followers and said, "How hard it will be for the rich to enter the kingdom of God!"

[24]The followers were amazed at what Jesus said. But he said again, "My children, it is very hard to enter the kingdom of God! [25]It is easier for a camel to go through the eye of a needle than for a rich person to enter the kingdom of God."

[26]The followers were even more surprised and said to each other, "Then who can be saved?"

[27]Jesus looked at them and said, "This is something people cannot do, but God can. God can do all things."

Verse 44   Some Greek copies of Mark add verse 44, which is the same as verse 48.
Verse 46   Some Greek copies of Mark add verse 46, which is the same as verse 48.
Salted with fire   Purified by fire as with the action of salt.
"Moses . . . away."   Quotation from Deuteronomy 24:1.
'he made . . . female'   Quotation from Genesis 1:27.
'So . . . body.'   Quotation from Genesis 2:24.
'You . . . mother.'   Quotation from Exodus 20:12–16; Deuteronomy 5:16–20.

²⁸Peter said to Jesus, "Look, we have left everything and followed you."

²⁹Jesus said, "I tell you the truth, all those who have left houses, brothers, sisters, mother, father, children or farms for me and for the Good News *d* ³⁰will get more than they left. Here in this world they will have a hundred times more homes, brothers, sisters, mothers, children and fields. And with those things, they will also suffer for their belief. But in the age that is coming they will have life for ever. ³¹Many who have the highest place now will have the lowest place in the future. And many who have the lowest place now will have the highest place in the future."

Jesus Talks About His Death

³²As Jesus and the people with him were on the road to Jerusalem, he was leading the way. His followers were amazed, but others in the crowd who followed were afraid. Again Jesus took the twelve apostles *d* aside and began to tell them what was about to happen in Jerusalem. ³³He said, "Look, we are going to Jerusalem. The Son of Man *d* will be turned over to the leading priests and the teachers of the law. They will say that he must die, and they will turn him over to the non-Jewish people, ³⁴who will laugh at him and spit on him. They will beat him with whips and crucify him. But on the third day, he will rise to life again."

Two Followers Ask Jesus a Favour

³⁵Then James and John, sons of Zebedee, came to Jesus and said, "Teacher, we want to ask you to do something for us."

³⁶Jesus asked, "What do you want me to do for you?"

³⁷They answered, "Let one of us sit at your right side and one of us sit at your left side in your glory in your kingdom."

³⁸Jesus said, "You don't understand what you are asking. Can you drink the cup that I must

FAITH

Christmas in June, July . . .

Corky is unique. He's a real trendsetter. For example, he always wears one red sock and one green sock to remind himself that every day is Christmas. His socks are a perfect reflection of the way he lives his Christian faith with others.

Corky often plays with children and talks with elderly people in his neighbourhood. Once he drove 200 miles to comfort someone whose friend had died suddenly. He is also a gifted photographer who captures the best of each person he photographs.

Corky is a joy to be with. His beaming smile lights up his cheeks as though he were Santa Claus himself. When friends see him, their natural reaction is to smile and give him a hug.

His faith is alive with wonder and joy – much like the excitement of a child who has just discovered that dirt and water make mud.

Jesus, himself, challenges us, no matter how old or young we are, to live the childlike faith and joy that Corky lives each day.

Read **Mark 10:13–16** to see how Jesus requires childlike faith.

* How does Corky reflect the kingdom of God in a childlike way?
* In what ways do you feel challenged to be more childlike in your own faith?

Consider . . .

* listing the questions you had about God as a child, then writing the answers you have discovered as you've grown.
* playing with a little child. Build with blocks, paint with your fingers, read stories. Notice the childlike qualities, such as curiosity, innocence and trust. Then work at applying those qualities to your faith.

For more, see . . .

* Isaiah 11:1–6 (p.652)
* Romans 8:14–17 (p.1195)
* Mark 9:33–37 (p.1015)

drink? And can you be baptised with the same kind of baptism that I must go through?" [n]

39They answered, "Yes, we can."

Jesus said to them, "You will drink the same cup that I will drink, and you will be baptised with the same baptism that I must go through. 40But I cannot choose who will sit at my right or my left; those places belong to those for whom they have been prepared."

41When the other ten followers heard this, they began to be angry with James and John.

42Jesus called them together and said, "The non-Jewish people have rulers. You know that those rulers love to show their power over the people, and their important leaders love to use all their authority. 43But it should not be that way among you. Whoever wants to become great among you must serve the rest of you like a servant. 44Whoever wants to become the first among you must serve all of you like a slave. 45In the same way, the Son of Man [d] did not come to be served. He came to serve others and to give his life as a ransom for many people."

Jesus Heals a Blind Man

46Then they came to the town of Jericho. As Jesus was leaving there with his followers and a great many people, a blind beggar named Bartimaeus son of Timaeus was sitting by the road. 47When he heard that Jesus from Nazareth was walking by, he began to shout, "Jesus, Son of David, [d] have mercy on me!"

48Many people warned the blind man to be quiet, but he shouted even more, "Son of David, have mercy on me!"

49Jesus stopped and said, "Tell the man to come here."

So they called the blind man, saying, "Cheer up! Get to your feet. Jesus is calling you." 50The blind man jumped up, left his coat there, and went to Jesus.

51Jesus asked him, "What do you want me to do for you?"

The blind man answered, "Teacher, I want to see."

52Jesus said, "Go, you are healed because you believed." At once the man could see, and he followed Jesus on the road.

Can you . . . through? Jesus was asking if they could suffer the same terrible things that would happen to him.

MONEY

What's Important?

"I have made many millions, but they have brought me no happiness. I would barter them all for the days I sat on an office stool in Cleveland and counted myself rich on $3 a week." – John Rockefeller, a multi-millionaire.

"The care of $200 million is too great a load for any brain or back to bear. It is enough to kill anyone. There is no pleasure in it." – W. H. Vanderbilt, who inherited a fortune.

"I am the most miserable man on earth." – John Jacob Astor, who died leaving $5 million.

"Millionaires seldom smile." – Andrew Carnegie, a millionaire.

Each of these people, who had lots of money, knew that other things were more important than money. Jesus tried to teach the same lesson to the young man in **Mark 10:17–30**. Read how he responded.

* How is what Jesus said similar to the quotes from these millionaires?
* How does your "wealth" help or hinder your faith?

Consider . . .

* drawing a treasure chest and "filling" it with all the things that are most valuable to you. Evaluate what Jesus would think of your treasure.
* giving someone £5 with no strings attached and for no particular reason – just for the fun of it. How does it make you feel?

For more, see . . .

* Deuteronomy 14:22–29 (p.179)
* Acts 3:1–10 (p.1142)

* Luke 21:1–4 (p.1085)

Jesus Enters Jerusalem as a King

11 As Jesus and his followers were coming closer to Jerusalem, they came to the towns of Bethphage and Bethany near the Mount of Olives. *d* From there Jesus sent two of his followers [2]and said to them, "Go to the town you can see there. When you enter it, you will quickly find a colt tied, which no one has ever ridden. Untie it and bring it here to me. [3]If anyone asks you why you are doing this, tell him its Master needs the colt, and he will send it at once."

[4]The followers went into the town, found a colt tied in the street near the door of a house, and untied it. [5]Some people were standing there and asked, "What are you doing? Why are you untying that colt?" [6]The followers answered the way Jesus told them to answer, and the people let them take the colt.

[7]They brought the colt to Jesus and put their coats on it, and Jesus sat on it. [8]Many people spread their coats on the road. Others cut branches in the fields and spread them on the road. [9]The people were walking ahead of Jesus and behind him, shouting,

"Praise *n* God!
God bless the One who comes in the name
    of the Lord!   *Psalm 118:26*
[10]God bless the kingdom of our father David!
    That kingdom is coming!
Praise to God in heaven!"

[11]Jesus entered Jerusalem and went into the Temple. *d* After he had looked at everything, since it was already late, he went out to Bethany with the twelve apostles. *d*

[12]The next day as Jesus was leaving Bethany, he became hungry. [13]Seeing a fig tree in leaf from far away, he went to see if it had any figs

---

Praise Literally, "Hosanna", a Hebrew word used at first in praying to God for help. At this time it was probably a shout of joy used in praising God or his Messiah.

SERVICE

The Small Things

Caleb was counting the days until he would be off to youth camp – the highlight of the year. Not only would he be playing guitar in the band on stage where everyone would see him, but he'd also get to hang out with his hero Zac, the youth leader. Caleb idolised Zac. He was generous, fun and always put the young people in the youth group first. To top it all, Zac was a fantastic guitarist who did gigs all over the country.

The day finally came when Caleb arrived at the youth camp complete with tent and rucksack. Excitedly, he went in search of Zac in the music tent, but Zac was nowhere to be found. Confused, Caleb started scouring the grounds. Just when he was about to give up, Caleb heard a rustling behind one of the tents. It was Zac, holding a black bin bag and sporting a cheerful smile.

"What are you doing?" exclaimed Caleb, disgusted to see someone like Zac picking up empty crisp packets so cheerfully. Zac beamed, "Well, someone's got to do it haven't they! The last group left rubbish everywhere. Fancy helping me out, Caleb?"

Caleb, like James and John, misunderstood what it meant to be a true servant. Read about James and John's encounter with Jesus in **Mark 10:35–45**.

* How is Zac's attitude similar to Jesus' attitude?
* What are the challenges of being a servant?

Consider . . .

* someone you know who is servant-hearted. Think of something special you could do for them today to show your appreciation.
* next time you're at youth group, looking out for the jobs which need doing and then take a couple of mates and do them.

For more, see . . .

* 1 Samuel 3:1–10 (p.258)
* John 13:1–17 (p.1119)
* Luke 22:24–27 (p.1087)

on it. But he found no figs, only leaves, because it was not the right season for figs. [14]So Jesus said to the tree, "May no one ever eat fruit from you again." And Jesus' followers heard him say this.

Jesus Goes to the Temple

[15]When Jesus returned to Jerusalem, he went into the Temple [d] and began to throw out those who were buying and selling there. He turned over the tables of those who were exchanging different kinds of money, and he upset the benches of those who were selling doves. [16]Jesus refused to allow anyone to carry goods through the Temple courts. [17]Then he taught the people, saying, "It is written in the Scriptures, [d] 'My Temple will be called a house for prayer for people from all nations.' [n] But you are changing God's house into a 'hideout for robbers'." [n]

[18]The leading priests and the teachers of the law heard all this and began trying to find a way to kill Jesus. They were afraid of him, because all the people were amazed at his teaching. [19]That evening, Jesus and his followers left the city.

The Power of Faith

[20]The next morning as Jesus was passing by with his followers, they saw the fig tree dry and dead, even to the roots. [21]Peter remembered the tree and said to Jesus, "Teacher, look! The fig tree you cursed is dry and dead!"

Sidelight
The people that Jesus threw out of the Temple were merchants who took advantage of those in Jerusalem on religious pilgrimages (Mark 11:15–17). They exchanged foreign currency for money to use in the Temple – with an extra charge, of course. Others sold doves to be used in Temple sacrifices.

'My Temple . . . nations.' Quotation from Isaiah 56:7.
'hideout for robbers'. Quotation from Jeremiah 7:11.

PERSISTENCE

The Long Run

"We don't know if your baby will live through the night," the doctors told Pat's new parents. She was born in 1966, weighing only one kilogramme, when few babies born three months premature survived.

But Pat was a fighter from the start.

By the time she reached secondary school, she was an excellent student and a local tennis star. She was also the area track champion in the 3,000 metres. When she finished eighth in her first county athletics meeting, everyone was confident that she had a great running future.

But then a back injury changed her plans. She could no longer run the way she used to. So she found a new way to give of herself – by becoming the track team's manager.

Pat explains why she perseveres: "My persistence comes from making the most of each opportunity I'm given. I wasn't expected to live in the first place, so now I just want to use the gifts I have to the best of my ability."

At one point in Jesus' ministry, he met a blind man who also exhibited Pat's perseverance. Read about the blind man in **Mark 10:46–52**.

* Why did Pat and the blind man persevere?
* How does your faith in Jesus help you to persevere in pursuing your goals?

Consider . . .

* making a plan of action to improve performance in one area of your life. Then spend the time needed to make progress. Evaluate your progress every month.
* setting short- and long-term goals. Write them in a diary, and keep the diary in your bag or wallet.

For more, see . . .

* Isaiah 35:1–10 (p.673)
* Hebrews 10:32–39 (p.1341)
* Luke 5:17–25 (p.1047)

²²Jesus answered, "Have faith in God. ²³I tell you the truth, you can say to this mountain, 'Go, fall into the sea.' And if you have no doubts in your mind and believe that what you say will happen, God will do it for you. ²⁴So I tell you to believe that you have received the things you ask for in prayer, and God will give them to you. ²⁵When you are praying, if you are angry with someone, forgive him so that your Father in heaven will also forgive your sins." ²⁶ *n*

Leaders Doubt Jesus' Authority

²⁷Jesus and his followers went again to Jerusalem. As Jesus was walking in the Temple, *d* the leading priests, the teachers of the law and the elders came to him. ²⁸They said to him, "What authority do you have to do these things? Who gave you this authority?"

²⁹Jesus answered, "I will ask you one question.

If you answer me, I will tell you what authority I have to do these things. ³⁰Tell me: when John baptised people, was that authority from God or just from other people?"

³¹They argued about Jesus' question, saying, "If we answer, 'John's baptism was from God,' Jesus will say, 'Then why didn't you believe him?' ³²But if we say, 'It was from other people,' the crowd will be against us." (These leaders were afraid of the people, because all the people believed that John was a prophet.*d*)

³³So they answered Jesus, "We don't know."

Jesus said to them, "Then I won't tell you what authority I have to do these things."

A Story About God's Son

12 Jesus began to use stories to teach the people. He said, "A man planted a vineyard. He put a wall around it and dug a hole for

---

Verse 26   Some early Greek copies add verse 26: "But if you don't forgive other people, then your Father in heaven will not forgive your sins."

WORSHIP

1964

On 18 August 1964, the Beatles boarded a plane in London and flew to San Francisco to begin their first coast-to-coast concert tour of North America. The "Fab Four" expected to perform before more people in their 31-day tour than any other act in music history. What they didn't expect was "Beatlemania".

When the musicians arrived, they were greeted at the airport by 5,000 screaming fans. At the hotel where they stayed, they were greeted by 4,000 more. And that was just the beginning.

In the months that followed, the Beatles found themselves confronted by mobs raging with excitement. The foursome often had to travel in secret to avoid crowds. At their concerts, the music was often drowned out by excited, screaming fans.

Some people might think that the Beatles loved the attention. But they didn't.

"It wasn't as much fun for us as it was for all of you," commented George Harrison, the band's lead guitarist, when asked about Beatlemania. People worshipped the Beatles – even though they were just human beings and didn't really deserve that kind of adoration.

Everyone longs to worship something, to have a hero to look up to. That was true even in Jesus' time. **Mark 11:1–11** describes a worship scene that resembled Beatlemania – except Jesus actually deserves that much praise.

- How is the story in the passage like Beatlemania?
- If you had been in Jerusalem at the time of the passage, how would you have worshipped Jesus? How do you worship him today?

Consider . . .

- going to a Christian concert to discover a new way to worship.
- writing a song or poem of worship to Jesus, thanking him for what he's done for you.

For more, see . . .

- Psalm 66 (p.537)
- Luke 19:28–40 (p.1083)
- Matthew 21:1–11 (p.977)

a winepress *d* and built a tower. Then he leased the land to some farmers and left for a trip. [2]When it was time for the grapes to be picked, he sent a servant to the farmers to get his share of the grapes. [3]But the farmers grabbed the servant and beat him and sent him away empty-handed. [4]Then the man sent another servant. They hit him on the head and showed no respect for him. [5]So the man sent another servant, whom they killed. The man sent many other servants; the farmers beat some of them and killed others.

[6]"The man had one person left to send, his son whom he loved. He sent him last of all, saying, 'They will respect my son.'

[7]"But the farmers said to each other, 'This son will inherit the vineyard. If we kill him, it will be ours.' [8]So they took the son, killed him and threw him out of the vineyard.

[9]"So what will the owner of the vineyard do? He will come and kill those farmers and will give the vineyard to other farmers. [10]Surely you have read this Scripture: *d*

'The stone that the builders rejected
became the cornerstone. *d*
[11]The Lord did this,
and it is wonderful to us.' "   *Psalm 118:22–23*

[12]The Jewish leaders knew that the story was about them. They wanted to find a way to arrest Jesus, but they were afraid of the people. So the leaders left him and went away.

Is It Right to Pay Taxes or Not?

[13]Later, the Jewish leaders sent some Pharisees *d* and Herodians *n* to Jesus to trap him into saying something wrong. [14]They came to him and said, "Teacher, we know that you are an honest man. You are not afraid of what other people think about you, because you pay no attention to who they are. And you teach the truth about God's way. Tell us: is it right to pay taxes to Caesar *d* or not? [15]Should we pay them, or not?"

But knowing what these men were really trying to do, Jesus said to them, "Why are you trying to trap me? Bring me a coin to look at." [16]They gave Jesus a coin, and he asked, "Whose image and name are on the coin?"

They answered, "Caesar's."

[17]Then Jesus said to them, "Give to Caesar the things that are Caesar's, and give to God the things that are God's." The men were amazed at what Jesus said.

Some Sadducees Try to Trick Jesus

[18]Then some Sadducees *d* came to Jesus and asked him a question. (Sadducees believed that people would not rise from the dead.) [19]They said, "Teacher, Moses wrote that if a man's brother dies, leaving a wife but no children, then that man must marry the widow and have children for his brother. [20]Once there were seven brothers. The first brother married and died, leaving no children. [21]So the second brother married the widow, but he also died and had no children. The same thing happened with the third brother. [22]All seven brothers married her and died, and none of the brothers had any children. Finally the woman died too. [23]Since all seven brothers had married her, when people rise from the dead, whose wife will she be?"

[24]Jesus answered, "Why don't you understand? Don't you know what the Scriptures *d* say, and don't you know about the power of God? [25]When people rise from the dead, they will not marry, nor will they be given to someone to marry. They will be like the angels in heaven. [26]Surely you have read what God said about people rising from the dead. In the book in which Moses wrote about the burning bush, *n* it says that God told Moses, 'I am the God of Abraham, the God of Isaac and the God of Jacob.' *n* [27]God is the God of the living, not the dead. You Sadducees are wrong!"

The Most Important Command

[28]One of the teachers of the law came and heard Jesus arguing with the Sadducees. *d* Seeing that Jesus gave good answers to their questions, he asked Jesus, "Which of the commands is most important?"

[29]Jesus answered, "The most important command is this: 'Listen, people of Israel! The Lord our God is the only Lord. [30]Love the Lord your God with all your heart, all your soul, all your mind and all your strength.' *n* [31]The second command is this: 'Love your neighbour as you love yourself.' *n* There are no commands more important than these."

[32]The man answered, "That was a good answer, Teacher. You were right when you said God is the only Lord and there is no other God besides him. [33]One must love God with all his heart, all his mind and all his strength. And one must love his neighbour as he loves himself. These commands are more important than all the animals and sacrifices we offer to God."

Herodians A political group that followed Herod and his family.
burning bush Read Exodus 3:1–12 in the Old Testament.
'I am . . . Jacob.' Quotation from Exodus 3:6.
'Listen . . . strength.' Quotation from Deuteronomy 6:4–5.
'Love . . . yourself.' Quotation from Leviticus 19:18.

³⁴When Jesus saw that the man answered him wisely, Jesus said to him, "You are close to the kingdom of God." And after that, no one was brave enough to ask Jesus any more questions.

³⁵As Jesus was teaching in the Temple, *d* he asked, "Why do the teachers of the law say that the Christ *d* is the son of David? ³⁶David himself, speaking by the Holy Spirit, *d* said:

'The LORD said to my Lord:
 Sit by me at my right side,
 until I put your enemies under your
     control.'
Psalm 110:1

³⁷David himself calls the Christ 'Lord', so how can the Christ be his son?" The large crowd listened to Jesus with pleasure.

³⁸Jesus continued teaching and said, "Beware of the teachers of the law. They like to walk around wearing fancy clothes, and they love people to greet them with respect in the marketplaces. ³⁹They love to have the most important seats in the synagogues *d* and at feasts. ⁴⁰But they cheat widows and steal their houses and then try to make themselves look good by saying long prayers. They will receive a greater punishment."

True Giving

⁴¹Jesus sat near the Temple *d* money box and watched the people put in their money. Many rich people gave large sums of money. ⁴²Then a poor widow came and put in two very small copper coins, which were not even worth a penny.

⁴³Calling his followers to him, Jesus said, "I tell you the truth, this poor widow gave more than all those rich people. ⁴⁴They gave only what they did not need. This woman is very poor, but she gave all she had; she gave all she had to live on."

The Temple will Be Destroyed

13 As Jesus was leaving the Temple, *d* one of his followers said to him, "Look, Teacher!

GIVING

Cough Up

The Dean of Murchester Cathedral strolls along the covered way to the almshouses. He has the court order in his hand and a solicitor with him. He wears his robes for emphasis; the solicitor wears a gown. In the houses, curtains twitch as people wonder what is going on.

These houses have been for the benefit of the local poor for many years. But now they are to be evicted. Even though some of the residents are very old and have lived in these houses for many years they will have to go. They will have to live in homes for the elderly from now on.

The well-to-do of Murchester, walking in the pretty, well-kept grounds of the Cathedral, see the thermometer marking the amount of money raised so far. They also write out cheques, feeling good that they have participated. Coming soon – new roof. The scaffolding will be ugly for a bit, but then there is always a price to pay for improvement.

Bekki likes popping into the Cathedral on the way home from school. She doesn't know why but it makes her feel peaceful. She sometimes wanders around the cool quiet covered corridors. Other times she sits in a side chapel and thinks for a bit. She feels sad that the roof needs repairing and as she leaves, she drops next week's dinner money into the box. "Hope Mum doesn't find out," she says to herself.
Read **Mark 12:38–44**.

⁕ With which of the characters do you most identify? What should our attitude be towards giving?
⁕ How do you feel about what Bekki did?

Consider . . .

⁕ giving a percentage of your income to your church or charity.
⁕ doing something for someone, without any benefit to yourself.

For more, see . . .

⁕ Luke 18:9–14 (p.1078)   ⁕ 2 Corinthians 8:1–3 (p.1248)
⁕ Philippians 4:10–13 (p.1286)

How beautiful the buildings are! How big the stones are!"

[2]Jesus said, "Do you see all these great buildings? Not one stone will be left on another. Every stone will be thrown down to the ground."

[3]Later, as Jesus was sitting on the Mount of Olives, [d] opposite the Temple, he was alone with Peter, James, John and Andrew. They asked Jesus, [4]"Tell us, when will these things happen? And what will be the sign that they are going to happen?"

[5]Jesus began to answer them, "Be careful that no one fools you. [6]Many people will come in my

Sidelight   Jesus' prediction that the Temple would be destroyed (Mark 13:1–2) came true within about 40 years. In AD 70, the Romans surrounded and sacked Jerusalem, burning the Temple to the ground. Today, the Muslim shrine called the "Dome of the Rock" stands on the Temple site.

name, saying, 'I am the One,' and they will fool many people. [7]When you hear about wars and stories of wars that are coming, don't be afraid. These things must happen before the end comes. [8]Nations will fight against other nations, and kingdoms against other kingdoms. There will be earthquakes in different places, and there will be times when there is no food for people to eat. These things are like the first pains when something new is about to be born.

[9]"You must be careful. People will arrest you and take you to court and beat you in their synagogues. [d] You will be forced to stand before kings and governors, to tell them about me. This will happen to you because you follow me. [10]But before these things happen, the Good News [d] must be told to all people. [11]When you are arrested and judged, don't worry ahead of time about what you should say. Say whatever is given you to say at that time, because it will not really be you speaking; it will be the Holy Spirit. [d]

[12]"Brothers will give their own brothers to be killed, and fathers will give their own children to be killed. Children will fight against their own parents and cause them to be put to death. [13]All people will hate you because you follow me, but those people who keep their faith until the end will be saved.

[14]"You will see 'the destroying terror' [n] standing where it should not be." (You who read this should understand what it means.) "At that

time, the people in Judea should run away to the mountains. [15]If people are on the roofs [n] of their houses, they must not go down or go inside to get anything out of their houses. [16]If people are in the fields, they must not go back to get their coats. [17]At that time, how terrible it will be for women who are pregnant or have nursing babies! [18]Pray that these things will not happen in winter, [19]because those days will be full of trouble. There will be more trouble than there has ever been since the beginning, when God made the world, until now, and nothing as bad will ever happen again. [20]God has decided to make that terrible time short. Otherwise, no one would go on living. But God will make that time short to help the people he has chosen. [21]At that time, someone might say to you, 'Look, there is the Christ!' [d] Or another person might say, 'There he is!' But don't believe them. [22]False Christs and false prophets [d] will come and perform great wonders and miracles. [d] They will try to fool even the people God has chosen, if that were possible. [23]So be careful. I have warned you about all this before it happens.

[24]"During the days after this trouble comes,
    'the sun will grow dark,
    and the moon will not give its light.
[25]The stars will fall from the sky.
    And the powers of the heavens will be
      shaken.'   *Isaiah 13:10; 34:4*

[26]"Then people will see the Son of Man [d] coming in clouds with great power and glory. [27]Then he will send his angels all around the earth to gather his chosen people from every part of the earth and from every part of heaven.

[28]"Learn a lesson from the fig tree: when its branches become green and soft and new leaves appear, you know summer is near. [29]In the same way, when you see these things happening, you will know that the time is near, ready to come. [30]I tell you the truth, all these things will happen while the people of this time are still living. [31]Earth and sky will be destroyed, but the words I have said will never be destroyed.

[32]"No one knows when that day or time will be, not the angels in heaven, not even the Son. Only the Father knows. [33]Be careful! Always be ready, because you don't know when that time will be. [34]It is like a man who goes on a trip. He leaves his house and lets his servants take care of it, giving each one a special job to do. The man tells the servant guarding the door always to be watchful. [35]So always be ready, because you don't know when the owner of the house will come back. It might be in the evening, or at midnight,

---

'the destroying terror'   Mentioned in Daniel 9:27; 12:11 (cf. Daniel 11:31).
roofs   In Bible times houses were built with flat roofs. The roof was used for drying things such as flax and fruit. And it was used as an extra room, as a place for worship and as a place to sleep in the summer.

or in the morning while it is still dark, or when the sun rises. 36Always be ready. Otherwise he might come back suddenly and find you sleeping. 37I tell you this, and I say this to everyone: 'Be ready!'"

The Plan to Kill Jesus

14 It was now only two days before the Passover *d* and the Feast *d* of Unleavened Bread. The leading priests and teachers of the law were trying to find a trick to arrest Jesus and kill him. 2But they said, "We must not do it during the feast, because the people might cause a riot."

A Woman with Perfume for Jesus

3Jesus was in Bethany at the house of Simon, who had a skin disease. While Jesus was eating there, a woman approached him with an alabaster *d* jar filled with very expensive perfume, made of pure nard. *d* She opened the jar and poured the perfume on Jesus' head.

4Some who were there became upset and said to each other, "Why waste that perfume? 5It was worth a full year's work. It could have been sold and the money given to the poor." And they got very angry with the woman.

6Jesus said, "Leave her alone. Why are you troubling her? She did an excellent thing for me. 7You will always have the poor with you, and you can help them any time you want. But you will not always have me. 8This woman did the only thing she could do for me; she poured perfume on my body to prepare me for burial. 9I tell you the truth, wherever the Good News *d* is preached in all the world, what this woman has done will be told, and people will remember her."

FUTURE

Be Prepared

In November 1990, grocery store shelves in New Madrid, Missouri, were cleared and boxes were packed with food, water, first-aid kits, torches and radios. People were frightened. Some people wouldn't even sleep in their own homes; they slept in their cars and pick-up trucks instead. Many even left the area.

"I'm terrified of this," resident Anna Harper said. "I feel like it's some terminal illness. I don't want to believe it, but there is so much talk about it."

Residents of this small town were preparing for the earthquake that Iben Browning, a business consultant from New Mexico, had predicted. He said that tidal forces were unusually high and could trigger an earthquake of 6.5 to 7.5 on the Richter scale 48 hours before or after 3 December, along the New Madrid fault.

While many residents of the small town scurried about to prepare for the catastrophe, others were calm about it. After all, these residents said, it's not as though they didn't already know they were living on a fault line.

The day in question came and went, and there was no earthquake.

In **Mark 13:24–33**, Jesus warns his followers of a certain day that they need to be prepared for in the future.

* According to this passage, no one knows when Jesus will return. To prepare for that day, which people should we be like – the people who prepared at the last minute or those who were ready at all times?
* If Jesus were to return today, would you be ready?

Consider . . .

* deciding what things you would put in an "emergency kit" for the end of the world, for example, faith or courage. Think about what you need to do to have those things ready.
* asking your minister or youth leader to teach on the "last days".

For more, see . . .

* Genesis 9:1–17 (p.10)
* 1 Thessalonians 4:13–5:11 (p.1299)
* Luke 21:25–36 (p.1087)

Judas Becomes an Enemy of Jesus

¹⁰One of the twelve apostles, Judas Iscariot, went to talk to the leading priests to offer to hand Jesus over to them. ¹¹These priests were pleased about this and promised to pay Judas money. So he watched for the best time to turn Jesus over.

Jesus Eats the Passover Meal

¹²It was now the first day of the Feast *d* of Unleavened Bread when the Passover *d* lamb was sacrificed. Jesus' followers said to him, "Where do you want us to go and prepare for you to eat the Passover meal?"

¹³Jesus sent two of his followers and said to them, "Go into the city and a man carrying a jar of water will meet you. Follow him. ¹⁴When he goes into a house, tell the owner of the house, 'The Teacher says: where is my guest room in which I can eat the Passover meal with my followers?' ¹⁵The owner will show you a large room upstairs that is furnished and ready. Prepare the food for us there."

¹⁶So the followers left and went into the city. Everything happened as Jesus had said, so they prepared the Passover meal.

¹⁷In the evening, Jesus went to that house with the twelve. ¹⁸While they were all eating, Jesus said, "I tell you the truth, one of you will turn against me—one of you eating with me now."

¹⁹The followers were very sad to hear this. Each one began to say to Jesus, "I am not the one, am I?"

DEATH

The Greatest Lesson

The common mayfly has a life expectancy of just one day, but is he miserable about it? Not one bit. He fills his day with the things he loves. He soars, he swoops, he savours every moment. Maybe there's a lesson in this for us longer-living creatures. Just think . . . if we embraced life like the mayfly, what a life that would be!

Many people think this is the best way life can be lived – being free with no responsibilities, taking each day as it comes and definitely never thinking about scary stuff like death. And yet we only have to watch the news for five minutes to be brought back down to earth with a bump – death is an unavoidable part of our lives. Similarly, Jesus' disciples had been living the dream. They'd heard him describe a new way of living life (see Matthew 6:25–34, p.948) and they'd watched him as he brought this life to impossible situations (see John 11:38–44, p.1116).

Read **Mark 14:12–26**. Jesus used this mealtime to introduce the greatest lesson he would ever teach. The lesson was this: only when you know that your eternity is secure can you really enjoy the time you have. Jesus knew that death had no power over him, so he could face it without fear. And the amazing thing is that the victory of his resurrection has enabled us to also share his prize – eternal life!

* Can you imagine why the disciples might find the things Jesus said around the meal table confusing?
* Was this Jesus' way of saying goodbye?

Consider . . .

* listening to a worship song about Jesus' death on the cross.
* what you would do with your life if you knew you only had one year left.

For more, see . . .

* Genesis 46:29–30 (p.53)
* Hebrews 2:9 (p.1330)
* Luke 2:28–32 (p.1040)

[20]Jesus answered, "It is one of the twelve—the one who dips his bread into the bowl with me. [21]The Son of Man [d] will die, just as the Scriptures [d] say. But how terrible it will be for the person who hands the Son of Man over to be killed. It would be better for him if he had never been born."

The Lord's Supper

[22]While they were eating, Jesus took some bread and thanked God for it and broke it. Then he gave it to his followers and said, "Take it; this is my body."

[23]Then Jesus took a cup and thanked God for it and gave it to the followers, and they all drank from the cup.

[24]Then Jesus said, "This is my blood which is the new agreement that God makes with his people. This blood is poured out for many. [25]I tell you the truth, I will not drink of this fruit of the vine [n] again until that day when I drink it new in the kingdom of God."

[26]After singing a hymn, they went out to the Mount of Olives. [d]

Jesus' Followers Will Leave Him

[27]Then Jesus told the followers, "You will all stumble in your faith, because it is written in the Scriptures: [d]
'I will kill the shepherd,
    and the sheep will scatter.'   Zechariah 13:7
[28]But after I rise from the dead, I will go ahead of you into Galilee."

[29]Peter said, "Everyone else may stumble in their faith, but I will not."

[30]Jesus answered, "I tell you the truth, tonight before the cockerel crows twice you will say three times you don't know me."

[31]But Peter insisted, "I will never say that I don't know you! I will even die with you!" And all the other followers said the same thing.

Jesus Prays Alone

[32]Jesus and his followers went to a place called Gethsemane. He said to them, "Sit here while I pray." [33]Jesus took Peter, James and John with him, and he began to be very sad and troubled. [34]He said to them, "My heart is full of sorrow, to the point of death. Stay here and watch."

[35]After walking a little farther away from them, Jesus fell to the ground and prayed that, if possible, he would not have this time of suffering. [36]He prayed, "Abba, [n] Father! You can do all things. Take away this cup [n] of suffering. But do what you want, not what I want."

[37]Then Jesus went back to his followers and found them asleep. He said to Peter, "Simon, are you sleeping? Couldn't you stay awake with me for one hour? [38]Stay awake and pray for strength against temptation. The spirit wants to do what is right, but the body is weak."

[39]Again Jesus went away and prayed the same thing. [40]Then he went back to his followers, and again he found them asleep, because their eyes were very heavy. And they did not know what to say to him.

[41]After Jesus prayed a third time, he went back to his followers and said to them, "Are you still sleeping and resting? That's enough. The time has come for the Son of Man [d] to be handed over to sinful people. [42]Get up, we must go. Look, here comes the man who has turned against me."

Jesus is Arrested

[43]At once, while Jesus was still speaking, Judas, one of the twelve apostles, [d] came up. With him were many people carrying swords and clubs who had been sent from the leading priests, the teachers of the law and the Jewish elders.

[44]Judas had planned a signal for them, saying, "The man I kiss is Jesus. Arrest him and guard him while you lead him away." [45]So Judas went straight to Jesus and said, "Teacher!" and kissed him. [46]Then the people grabbed Jesus and arrested him. [47]One of his followers standing nearby pulled out his sword and struck the servant of the high priest and cut off his ear.

[48]Then Jesus said, "You came to get me with swords and clubs as if I were a criminal. [49]Every day I was with you teaching in the Temple, [d] and you did not arrest me there. But all these things have happened to make the Scriptures [d] come true." [50]Then all of Jesus' followers left him and ran away.

[51]A young man, wearing only a linen cloth, was following Jesus, and the people also grabbed him. [52]But the cloth he was wearing came off, and he ran away naked.

Jesus Before the Leaders

[53]The people who arrested Jesus led him to the house of the high priest, where all the leading priests, the Jewish elders and the teachers of the law were gathered. [54]Peter followed far behind and entered the courtyard of the high priest's house. There he sat with the guards, warming himself by the fire.

[55]The leading priests and the whole Jewish council tried to find something that Jesus had

---

fruit of the vine   Product of the grapevine; this may also be translated "wine".
Abba   Name that a child called his father.
cup   Jesus is talking about the terrible things that will happen to him. Accepting these things will be very hard, like drinking a
    cup of something bitter.

done wrong so they could kill him. But the council could find no proof of anything. [56]Many people came and told false things about him, but all said different things—none of them agreed.

[57]Then some people stood up and lied about Jesus, saying, [58]"We heard this man say, 'I will destroy this Temple [d] that people made. And three days later, I will build another Temple not made by people.'" [59]But even the things these people said did not agree.

[60]Then the high priest stood before them and asked Jesus, "Aren't you going to answer? Don't you have something to say about their charges against you?" [61]But Jesus said nothing; he did not answer.

The high priest asked Jesus another question: "Are you the Christ, [d] the Son of the blessed God?"

[62]Jesus answered, "I am. And in the future you will see the Son of Man [d] sitting at the right hand of God, the Powerful One, and coming on clouds in the sky."

[63]When the high priest heard this, he tore his clothes and said, "We don't need any more witnesses! [64]You all heard him say these things against God. What do you think?"

They all said that Jesus was guilty and should die. [65]Some of the people there began to spit at Jesus. They blindfolded him and beat him with their fists and said, "Prove you are a prophet!" [d] Then the guards led Jesus away and beat him.

Peter Says He Doesn't Know Jesus

[66]While Peter was in the courtyard, a servant girl of the high priest came there. [67]She saw Peter warming himself at the fire and looked closely at him.

Then she said, "You also were with Jesus, that man from Nazareth."

[68]But Peter said that he was never with Jesus. He said, "I don't know or understand what you are talking about." Then Peter left and went towards the entrance of the courtyard. And the cockerel crowed. [n]

[69]The servant girl saw Peter there, and again she said to the people who were standing nearby, "This man is one of those who followed Jesus." [70]Again Peter said that it was not true.

A short time later, some people were standing near Peter saying, "Surely you are one of those who followed Jesus, because you are from Galilee, too."

[71]Then Peter began to place a curse on himself and swear, "I don't know this man you're talking about!"

[72]At once, the cockerel crowed the second time. Then Peter remembered what Jesus had told him: "Before the cockerel crows twice, you will say three times that you don't know me." Then Peter lost control of himself and began to cry.

Pilate Questions Jesus

15 Very early in the morning, the leading priests, the older leaders, the teachers of the law and all the Jewish council decided what to do with Jesus. They tied him, led him away and turned him over to Pilate, the governor.

[2]Pilate asked Jesus, "Are you the king of the Jews?"

Jesus answered, "Those are your words."

[3]The leading priests accused Jesus of many things. [4]So Pilate asked Jesus another question, "You can see that they are accusing you of many things. Aren't you going to answer?"

[5]But Jesus still said nothing, so Pilate was very surprised.

Pilate Tries to Free Jesus

[6]Every year at the time of the Passover [d] the governor would free one prisoner whom the people chose. [7]At that time, there was a man named Barabbas in prison who was a rebel and had committed murder during a riot. [8]The crowd came to Pilate and began to ask him to free a prisoner as he always did.

[9]So Pilate asked them, "Do you want me to free the king of the Jews?" [10]Pilate knew that the leading priests had turned Jesus over to him because they were jealous. [11]But the leading priests had persuaded the people to ask Pilate to free Barabbas, not Jesus.

[12]Then Pilate asked the crowd again, "So what should I do with this man you call the king of the Jews?"

[13]They shouted, "Crucify him!"

[14]Pilate asked, "Why? What wrong has he done?"

But they shouted even louder, "Crucify him!"

[15]Pilate wanted to please the crowd, so he freed Barabbas for them. After having Jesus beaten with whips, he handed Jesus over to the soldiers to be crucified.

Sidelight The sort of beating that Jesus experienced (Mark 15:15) was a gruesome practice among the Romans. The whip was made of leather, lead and bone, and could tear out eyes, sever veins and rip open stomachs. It was a customary part of the death sentence.

And . . . crowed. A few, early Greek copies leave out this phrase.

[16]The soldiers took Jesus into the governor's palace (called the Praetorium) and called all the other soldiers together. [17]They put a purple robe on Jesus and used thorny branches to make a crown for his head. [18]They began to call out to him, "Hail, King of the Jews!" [19]The soldiers beat Jesus on the head many times with a stick. They spat on him and made fun of him by bowing on their knees and worshipping him. [20]After they finished, the soldiers took off the purple robe and put his own clothes on him again. Then they led him out of the palace to be crucified.

Jesus is Crucified

[21]A man named Simon from Cyrene, the father of Alexander and Rufus, was coming from the fields to the city. The soldiers forced Simon to carry the cross for Jesus. [22]They led Jesus to the place called Golgotha, which means the Place of the Skull. [23]The soldiers tried to give Jesus wine mixed with myrrh[d] to drink, but he refused. [24]The soldiers crucified Jesus and divided his clothes among themselves, throwing lots[d] to decide what each soldier would get.

[25]It was nine o'clock in the morning when they crucified Jesus. [26]There was a sign with this charge against Jesus written on it: THE KING OF THE JEWS. [27]They also put two robbers on crosses beside Jesus, one on the right, and the other on the left. [28] [n] [29]People walked by and insulted Jesus and shook their heads, saying, "You said you could destroy the Temple[d] and build it again in three days. [30]So save yourself! Come down from that cross!"

[31]The leading priests and the teachers of the law were also making fun of Jesus. They said to each other, "He saved other people, but he can't save himself. [32]If he is really the Christ,[d] the

---

Verse 28   Some Greek copies add verse 28: "And the Scripture came true that says, 'They put him with criminals.'"

PEER PRESSURE

Don't Give In!

Lee was considered the class geek and everyone had decided that this lunchtime they would pick on him. Half of Tom wanted to run in front of Lee and save him from this bullying, but the other half of him was scared that he would end up getting the same treatment. Then someone in the class shouted, "Oi Tom, what have you got to say?" There was a deafening silence as everyone looked at Tom to see whether he would stick up for his friend or join in with the group.

Without thinking, he shouted at Lee. He figured that the group would back off Lee if they thought they'd managed to turn his friend against him. But it didn't happen like that. As soon as Tom had finished shouting, the rest of the group carried on where they had left off and continued punching Lee, as Tom stood there watching helplessly. They only stopped when a teacher turned the corner, at which point they all ran off, Tom included.

Read **Mark 15:1–20**.

* Why did Tom and Pilate give in to pressure?
* Have you ever given in to pressure and then wished you hadn't?

Consider . . .

* times when you have given in to pressure and done something you've regretted. Ask God to forgive you and help you next time to withstand the urge to give in.
* whether the next time your friends are speaking against Jesus you will stand up for him.

For more, see . . .

* Proverbs 1:10–19 (p.590)
* Hebrews 12:1–3 (p.1343)
* Luke 6:22–23 (p.1048)

king of Israel, let him come down now from the cross. When we see this, we will believe in him." The robbers who were being crucified beside Jesus also insulted him.

Jesus Dies

[33]At noon the whole country became dark, and the darkness lasted for three hours. [34]At three o'clock Jesus cried in a loud voice, "Eli, Eli,[n] lama sabachthani." This means, "My God, my God, why have you rejected me?"

[35]When some of the people standing there heard this, they said, "Listen! He is calling Elijah."

[36]Someone there ran and got a sponge, filled it with vinegar, tied it to a stick, and gave it to Jesus to drink. He said, "We want to see if Elijah will come to take him down from the cross."

[37]Then Jesus cried in a loud voice and died.

[38]The curtain in the Temple[n] was torn into two pieces, from the top to the bottom. [39]When the army officer who was standing in front of the cross saw what happened when Jesus died, he said, "This man really was the Son of God!"

[40]Some women were standing at a distance from the cross, watching; among them were Mary Magdalene, Salome and Mary the mother of James and Joseph. (James was her youngest son.) [41]These women had followed Jesus in Galilee and helped him. Many other women were also there who had come with Jesus to Jerusalem.

Jesus is Buried

[42]This was Preparation[d] Day. (That means the day before the Sabbath[d] day.) That evening, [43]Joseph from Arimathea was brave enough to go to Pilate and ask for Jesus' body. Joseph, an important member of the Jewish council, was one of the people who was waiting for the kingdom of God to come. [44]Pilate was amazed that Jesus

---

Eli, Eli   Some Bibles translate this as Eloi, Eloi.

curtain in the Temple   A curtain divided the Most Holy Place from the other part of the Temple. That was the special building in Jerusalem where God commanded the Jewish people to worship him.

JESUS CHRIST

Unexpected Saviour

Jesus painted no pictures. Yet some of the greatest artists were inspired by him to paint their greatest works.
Jesus wrote no poetry. Yet hundreds of the world's greatest poems pay tribute to him.
Jesus composed no music. Yet great musicians wrote some of their greatest music to praise him.
Jesus preached and taught for only three years. Socrates taught for 40 years, Plato for 50 years, and Aristotle for 40 years. Yet hundreds of millions more people follow Jesus than follow the three philosophers combined.
Jesus died on a cross as a criminal. Yet even a guard who helped to put him to death recognised that he was God's Son. Read **Mark 15:33–39** to see how Jesus showed that he was God's Son even in his death.

* What unexpected things do you see in Jesus' life as described by the passage and by the comparisons above?
* How does this passage strengthen your faith in Jesus as God's Son?

Consider . . .

* listing everything that you would expect a king to do. Then compare it to what you read in the Bible about Jesus. Identify similarities and differences.
* rereading the passage, putting yourself in the place of the officer. How would you have responded to this situation? What would you have said?

For more, see . . .

* Isaiah 53 (p.697)
* John 19:28–37 (p.1131)

* Matthew 16:21–28 (p.969)

was already dead, so he called the army officer who had guarded Jesus and asked him if Jesus had already died. [45]The officer told Pilate that he was dead, so Pilate told Joseph he could have the

body. [46]Joseph bought some linen cloth, took the body down from the cross, and wrapped it in the linen. He put the body in a tomb that was cut out of a wall of rock. Then he rolled a very large

stone to block the entrance of the tomb. [47]And Mary Magdalene and Mary the mother of Joseph saw the place where Jesus was laid.

Jesus Rises from the Dead

16 The day after the Sabbath [d] day, Mary Magdalene, Mary the mother of James, and Salome bought some sweet-smelling spices to put on Jesus' body. [2]Very early on that day, the first day of the week, soon after sunrise, the women were on their way to the tomb. [3]They said to each other, "Who will roll away for us the stone that covers the entrance of the tomb?"

[4]Then the women looked and saw that the stone had already been rolled away, even though it was very large. [5]The women entered the tomb and saw a young man wearing a white robe and sitting on the right side, and they were afraid.

LIFE

A Light in the Darkness

Adam was heavily into drugs by the time he was fourteen. After being arrested for helping his friends to steal a radio, he was placed in a young offenders' unit. But he kept slipping further and further downhill.

He became more distant from his family and friends. And he started using drugs daily to try to escape the pain he felt inside.

One day Adam couldn't stand the pain any longer. He hated himself, and he didn't want to go on living. He felt trapped. The darkness was overwhelming, and he just couldn't see a way out.

Finally, he cried out to God. "Please," he pleaded, "please help me." Almost immediately he sensed a peace and calm inside, as if the darkness was replaced with a new hope.

In the following weeks, he began attending drug users' support meetings and joined a Christian fellowship. Adam had a new beginning.

"Turning my life over to God's direction is the toughest decision I've ever made," Adam later explained. "But my faith is beginning to pay off. I'm making new friends. I've found a job. I'm taking art classes. I feel alive. It's a day-to-day struggle to stay free of drugs, but I'm headed in the right direction for the first time in my life."

Adam was beginning to experience the life and power of Jesus' resurrection. Read about the resurrection in **Mark 16:1–8**.

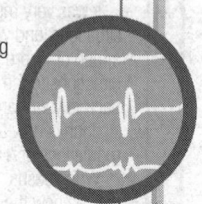

* How was Adam's new life similar to Jesus' resurrection? How was it different?
* How is your response to Jesus' resurrection like or unlike the women's reactions?

Consider . . .

* asking God to "roll away" an obstacle in your life with his resurrection power.
* listing the ways in which you can "stop the pain" you may be experiencing, just as Adam stopped his pain. Ask others for help if you need to.

For more, see . . .

* Exodus 14 (p.71)
* John 20:1–18 (p.1132)

     * Matthew 28:1–10 (p.993)

[6]But the man said, "Don't be afraid. You are looking for Jesus from Nazareth, who has been crucified. He has risen from the dead; he is not here. Look, here is the place where they laid him. [7]Now go and tell his followers and Peter, 'Jesus is going into Galilee ahead of you, and you will see him there as he told you before.'"

[8]The women were confused and shaking with fear, so they left the tomb and ran away. They did not tell anyone about what happened, because they were afraid.

Verses 9–20 are not included in two of the best and oldest Greek copies of Mark.

Some Followers See Jesus

[[9]After Jesus rose from the dead early on the first day of the week, he showed himself first to Mary Magdalene. Once in the past, he had forced seven demons [d] out of her. [10]After Mary saw Jesus, she went and told his followers, who were very sad and were crying. [11]But Mary told them that Jesus was alive. She said that she had seen him, but the followers did not believe her.

[12]Later, Jesus showed himself to two of his followers while they were walking in the country, but he did not look the same as before. [13]These followers went back to the others and told them what had happened, but again, the followers did not believe them.

Jesus Talks to the Apostles

[14]Later Jesus showed himself to the eleven apostles while they were eating, and he criticised them because they had no faith. They were stubborn and refused to believe those who had seen him after he had risen from the dead.

SHARING FAITH

Follow the Leader

As a young boy of five years old, John used to love to look in toyshops. He would daydream at a shop window and watch the working models going round and round.

One day he went out with his parents to a large shopping centre in Cardiff and was thrilled when they turned into the arcade. In actual fact, his mum and dad wanted to look at some furniture, but John knew this was also the place where his favourite toyshop was! So as soon as he had the chance, he let go of his mum's hand and ran off down the arcade to his shop window.

Minutes went by as John stood entranced. Then, thinking it was time to go, he looked up for his parents and they were nowhere to be seen. As a very small boy, all he could see were giants everywhere!

It was very frightening, and a situation we can all sympathise with. Many of us have been in similar situations, and when you are in a situation like that, you don't need some huge person to come up with a map of where you live, and try to explain how to get home. You don't want a list of bus stops, or directions to the nearest train station. You need a kind person to hold out their hand and lead you back to your parents.

John is now an evangelist, but he always remembers that people don't want a set of rules and regulations of "How to Become a Christian", they need someone to take them to Jesus.

When Jesus' followers first went out, they took this Good News everywhere. In **Mark 16:19–20** we see how the Lord helped his followers spread the Good News.

* How do people react when you tell them the Good News of Jesus Christ?
* What's the difference between a "map" and a "helping hand"?

Consider . . .

* telling a non-Christian friend about Jesus.
* asking your minister or youth leader to lead a training course on "How to Tell Others About Christ".

For more, see . . .

* Acts 1:1–14 (p.1137)
* 1 John 1:1–4 (p.1371)

¹⁵Jesus said to his followers, "Go everywhere in the world, and tell the Good News *d* to everyone. ¹⁶Anyone who believes and is baptised will be saved, but anyone who does not believe will be punished. ¹⁷And those who believe will be able to do these things as proof: they will use my name to force out demons. *d* They will speak in new languages. *n* ¹⁸They will pick up snakes and drink poison without being hurt.

They will touch the sick, and the sick will be healed."

¹⁹After the Lord Jesus said these things to his followers, he was carried up into heaven, and he sat at the right side of God. ²⁰The followers went everywhere in the world and told the Good News to people, and the Lord helped them. The Lord proved that the Good News they told was true by giving them power to work miracles. *d*]

---

languages   This can also be translated "tongues".

Luke

When?

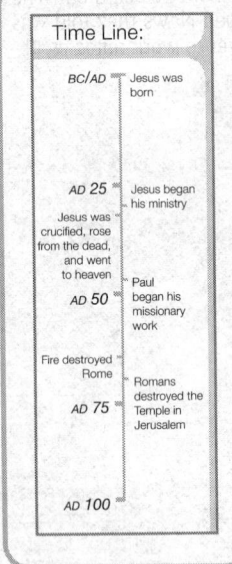

Time Line:

BC/AD — Jesus was born

AD 25 — Jesus began his ministry

Jesus was crucified, rose from the dead, and went to heaven

AD 50 — Paul began his missionary work

Fire destroyed Rome

AD 75 — Romans destroyed the Temple in Jerusalem

AD 100

Why Read This Book:

- Discover the Bible's only stories about Jesus' childhood (Luke 2).
- See how Jesus ministered to all people, especially the poor and the outcast (Luke 4—8).
- Enjoy some of Jesus' most famous stories (Luke 10, 15—16).
- Learn how Jesus gave his life for our sins (Luke 22—24).

Behind the Scenes:

Imagine never hearing that Jesus was laid in a feeding box when he was born (Luke 2:7–11). Imagine not knowing the parable of the Good Samaritan (Luke 10:25–37). Or the parable of the son who left home, who is also known as the Prodigal Son (Luke 15:11–32). Imagine not knowing about Jesus' encounter with Zacchaeus (Luke 19:1–10).

We wouldn't have any of these stories without the Gospel of Luke.

Though the books of Matthew, Mark and John tell many stories about Jesus, they don't include about one-third of the material in Luke. Luke is the most complete account of Jesus' life. It's a detailed, organised picture of Jesus' life and ministry.

As you read the Gospel of Luke, you'll discover some important emphases. First, this book emphasises that Jesus came for all people, not just the Jews. You'll also see Jesus' particular concern for women, the poor and the outcasts of the world. Then the book shows Jesus as God's Spirit-led Son who came to offer eternal life to all people who follow him. ▷

Where?

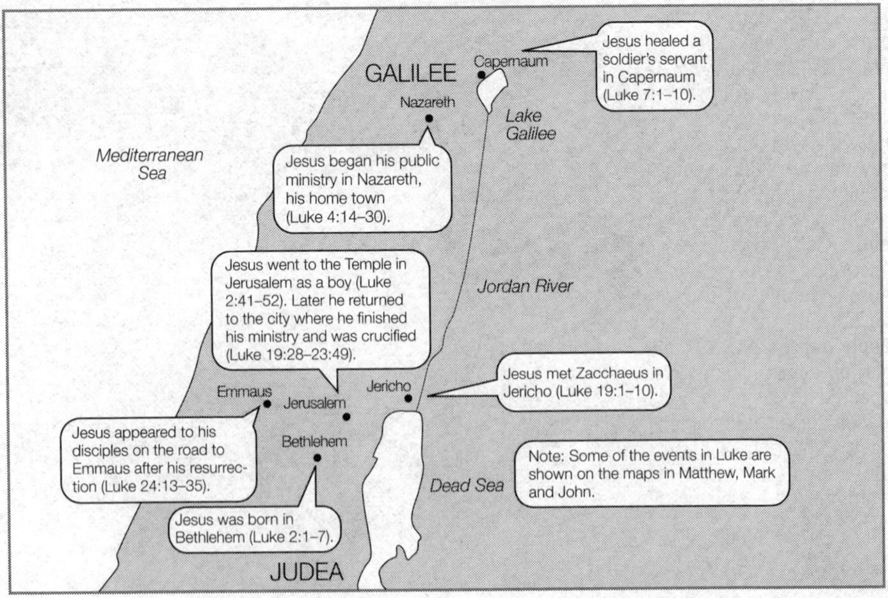

GALILEE

Capernaum — Jesus healed a soldier's servant in Capernaum (Luke 7:1–10).

Nazareth

Lake Galilee

Mediterranean Sea

Jesus began his public ministry in Nazareth, his home town (Luke 4:14–30).

Jesus went to the Temple in Jerusalem as a boy (Luke 2:41–52). Later he returned to the city where he finished his ministry and was crucified (Luke 19:28–23:49).

Jordan River

Jesus met Zacchaeus in Jericho (Luke 19:1–10).

Emmaus   Jericho

Jesus appeared to his disciples on the road to Emmaus after his resurrection (Luke 24:13–35).

Jerusalem

Bethlehem

Note: Some of the events in Luke are shown on the maps in Matthew, Mark and John.

Dead Sea

Jesus was born in Bethlehem (Luke 2:1–7).

JUDEA

**Behind the
Scenes (cont.):** Luke 19:10 says that "the Son of Man came to find lost people and save them". This book tells, in detail, the story of his coming. If you like the Gospel of Luke, try the sequel: the book of Acts (p.1136). It's written by the same author, and continues the story where Luke leaves off.

Luke Writes About Jesus' Life

1 Many have tried to report on the things that happened among us. [2]They have written the same things that we learned from others—the people who saw those things from the beginning and served God by telling people his message. [3]Since I myself have studied everything carefully from the beginning, most excellent[n] Theophilus, it seemed good for me to write it out for you. I arranged it in order [4]to help you know that what you have been taught is true.

> ### Sidelight
> The Gospel of Luke is the longest New Testament book, with 1,151 verses. And the book of Acts – which Luke also wrote – isn't far behind. Since Luke was a doctor, a simple prescription probably took reams of paper!

Zechariah and Elizabeth

[5]During the time Herod ruled Judea, there was a priest named Zechariah who belonged to Abijah's group.[n] Zechariah's wife, Elizabeth, came from the family of Aaron. [6]Zechariah and Elizabeth truly did what God said was good. They did everything the Lord commanded and were without fault in keeping his law. [7]But they had no children, because Elizabeth could not have a baby, and both of them were very old.

[8]One day Zechariah was serving as a priest before God, because his group was on duty. [9]According to the custom of the priests, he was chosen by lot[d] to go into the Temple of the Lord and burn incense.[d] [10]There were a great many people outside praying at the time the incense was offered. [11]Then an angel of the Lord appeared to Zechariah, standing on the right side of the incense table. [12]When he saw the angel, Zechariah was startled and frightened. [13]But the angel said to him, "Zechariah, don't be afraid. God has heard your prayer. Your wife,

Elizabeth, will give birth to a son, and you will name him John. [14]He will bring you joy and gladness, and many people will be happy because of his birth. [15]John will be a great man for the Lord. He will never drink wine or beer, and even from birth, he will be filled with the Holy Spirit.[d] [16]He will help many people of Israel return to the Lord their God. [17]He will go before the Lord in spirit and power like Elijah. He will make peace between parents and their children and will bring those who are not obeying God back to the right way of thinking, to make a people ready for the coming of the Lord."

[18]Zechariah said to the angel, "How can I know that what you say is true? I am an old man, and my wife is old, too."

[19]The angel answered him, "I am Gabriel. I stand before God, who sent me to talk to you and to tell you this good news. [20]Now, listen! You will not be able to speak until the day these things happen, because you did not believe what I told you. But they will really happen."

[21]Outside, the people were still waiting for Zechariah and were surprised that he was staying so long in the Temple. [22]When Zechariah came outside, he could not speak to them, and they knew he had seen a vision in the Temple. He could only make signs to them and remained unable to speak. [23]When his time of service at the Temple was finished, he went home.

[24]Later, Zechariah's wife, Elizabeth, became pregnant and did not go out of her house for five months. Elizabeth said, [25]"Look what the Lord has done for me! My people were ashamed[n] of me, but now the Lord has taken away that shame."

An Angel Appears to Mary

[26]During Elizabeth's sixth month of pregnancy, God sent the angel Gabriel to Nazareth, a town in Galilee, [27]to a virgin.[d] She was engaged to marry a man named Joseph from the family of

---

excellent This word was used to show respect to an important person like a king or ruler.
Abijah's group The Jewish priests were divided into 24 groups. See 1 Chronicles 24.
ashamed The Jewish people thought it was a disgrace for women not to have children.

David. Her name was Mary. 28The angel came to her and said, "Greetings! The Lord has blessed you and is with you."

29But Mary was very startled by what the angel said and wondered what this greeting might mean.

30The angel said to her, "Don't be afraid, Mary; God has shown you his grace. 31Listen! You will become pregnant and give birth to a son, and you will name him Jesus. 32He will be great and will be called the Son of the Most High. The Lord God will give him the throne of King David, his ancestor. 33He will rule over the people of Jacob for ever, and his kingdom will never end."

34Mary said to the angel, "How will this happen since I am a virgin?"

35The angel said to Mary, "The Holy Spirit d will come upon you, and the power of the Most High will cover you. For this reason the baby will be holy and will be called the Son of God. 36Now

Elizabeth, your relative, is also pregnant with a son though she is very old. Everyone thought she could not have a baby, but she has been pregnant for six months. 37God can do anything!"

38Mary said, "I am the servant of the Lord. Let this happen to me as you say!" Then the angel went away.

Mary Visits Elizabeth

39Mary got up and went quickly to a town in the hills of Judea. 40She came to Zechariah's house and greeted Elizabeth. 41When Elizabeth heard Mary's greeting, the unborn baby inside her jumped, and Elizabeth was filled with the Holy Spirit. d 42She cried out in a loud voice, "God has blessed you more than any other woman, and he has blessed the baby to whom you will give birth. 43Why has this good thing happened to me, that the mother of my Lord comes to me? 44When I heard your voice, the baby inside me jumped with joy. 45You are blessed because

GOD'S POWER

Power in Letting Go

Joni Eareckson loved to swim when she was young. She was an excellent diver too, and had even thought about trying out for the Olympics.

When she was seventeen, Joni and her friends went swimming in Chesapeake Bay. Joni dived into the unfamiliar waters, expecting to experience that cool, free-floating feeling she had come to love. Instead, she felt nothing. As her head struck the bottom, her spinal cord snapped – leaving her paralysed from the neck down.

Joni felt depressed and angry at the prospect of spending the rest of her life in a wheelchair. Most of her anger was aimed at God. "Oh God, how can you do this to me?" she prayed. "What have you done to me?"

Though God has never healed her physically, over the years she has grown into a beautiful free spirit. She sums it up like this: "When I had no choice but acceptance, trust and surrender . . . it was as if I had finally gained emotional independence – through complete dependence on God."

Read **Luke 1:26–38** to see how God brought forth life in another teenage girl because she was ready to accept, trust and surrender.

* How was Mary's response to God's actions different from or similar to Joni's?
* In what specific ways would you like to see God's power change your life?

Consider . . .

* underlining the verses in this passage that speak most to you, and memorising them.
* asking God to help you to understand his unlimited power and the ways that he chooses to use (or not to use) it.

For more, see . . .

* Psalm 31:14–24 (p.518)
* James 1:1–5 (p.1348)

* 2 Corinthians 12:7–10 (p.1252)

you believed that what the Lord said to you would really happen."

Mary Praises God

⁴⁶Then Mary said,
"My soul praises the Lord;
⁴⁷ my heart rejoices in God my Saviour,
⁴⁸because he has shown his concern for his
        humble servant girl.
From now on, all people will say that I am
        blessed,
⁴⁹ because the Powerful One has done great
        things for me.
His name is holy.
⁵⁰God will show his mercy for ever and ever
        to those who worship and serve him.
⁵¹He has done mighty deeds by his power.
He has scattered the people who are proud
        and think great things about themselves.
⁵²He has brought down rulers from their
        thrones
and raised up the humble.

⁵³He has filled the hungry with good things
        and sent the rich away with nothing.
⁵⁴He has helped his servant, the people of
        Israel,
        remembering to show them mercy
⁵⁵as he promised to our ancestors,
        to Abraham and to his children for ever."
⁵⁶Mary stayed with Elizabeth for about three months and then returned home.

The Birth of John

⁵⁷When it was time for Elizabeth to give birth, she had a boy. ⁵⁸Her neighbours and relatives heard how good the Lord was to her, and they rejoiced with her.

⁵⁹When the baby was eight days old, they came to circumcise*d* him. They wanted to name him Zechariah because this was his father's name, ⁶⁰but his mother said, "No! He will be named John."

⁶¹The people said to Elizabeth, "But no one in your family has this name." ⁶²Then they made

---

BOASTING

A Tale of Two Teenagers

Ted and Ed were in their final year at school. One was voted most popular; the other most respected. Both passed their exams with excellent grades.

Ed never talked about himself. He never seemed to mind not being in the spotlight.

But Ted had to be the centre of attention. If he thought that others had missed the significance of his accomplishments, he quickly filled them in.

They were two of the county's best cross-country runners. Ted almost always finished first, and Ed almost always came in just behind him. They were both comfortable with that, and always managed to congratulate and praise each other after a race. In their final race meeting, however, Ed finished first. Ted couldn't congratulate or praise him, or even accept congratulations for himself. He was only comfortable with being Number One.

Ted boasted a lot to get attention, but Ed didn't. Read **Luke 1:39–56** to see how God blessed a young girl, who didn't boast or take credit for herself.

* If Mary were around today, what do you think she would be like?
* Are you more like Ed or Ted? How does Mary's prayer apply to you?

Consider . . .

* drawing a line with two endpoints labelled ED and TED. Place a pencil point where you think you fit on the line, and another where you would like to be on the line. Ask God to help you to reach your goal.
* thinking of someone you know who is like Ed, and spending more time with that person.

For more, see . . .

* Jeremiah 9:23–24 (p.728)
* Philippians 2:5–11 (p.1282)

* Romans 12:3–5 (p.1204)

signs to his father to find out what he would like to name him.

⁶³Zechariah asked for a writing tablet and wrote, "His name is John," and everyone was surprised. ⁶⁴Immediately Zechariah could talk again, and he began praising God. ⁶⁵All their neighbours became alarmed, and in all the mountains of Judea people continued talking about all these things. ⁶⁶The people who heard about them wondered, saying, "What will this child be?" because the Lord was with him.

Zechariah Praises God

⁶⁷Then Zechariah, John's father, was filled with the Holy Spirit and prophesied: *d*

⁶⁸"Let us praise the Lord, the God of Israel,
　because he has come to help his people
　　and has given them freedom.
⁶⁹He has given us a powerful Saviour
　from the family of God's servant David.
⁷⁰He said that he would do this
　through his holy prophets*d* who lived
　　long ago:
⁷¹He promised he would save us from our
　　enemies
　and from the power of all those who
　　hate us.
⁷²He said he would give mercy to our fathers
　and that he would remember his holy
　　promise.
⁷³God promised Abraham, our father,
⁷⁴　that he would save us from the power of
　　our enemies
　so we could serve him without fear,
⁷⁵being holy and good before God as long as
　　we live.

WORSHIP

Humble Beginnings

He was born in a simple 2-bedroom house in Tupelo, Mississippi on 8 January 1935. His twin brother, Jesse Garon, was stillborn, leaving him to grow up as an only child. His early years were spent in poverty, with his mum, Gladys, working as a cotton picker and his dad, Vernon, drifting from one job to another.

When he was eleven, his parents couldn't afford the bicycle he really wanted, so his mum persuaded him to have a guitar instead. After he left school, he did a variety of jobs. He also went to night school and studied to be an electrician.

Doesn't sound like a life that would make many people stop and take notice – just a normal, average guy – a nobody. Who would have thought that he would achieve anything special, that he would become so famous that people would recognise him from just his first name?

His name was Elvis Presley. Adored by millions, he went on to star in 33 successful films and sold over one billion records across the world – more than any other artist. He is regarded as one of the most important figures of twentieth-century popular culture. That's quite some nobody!

Luke 2:8–21 tells of Jesus' birth in a very humble setting – when he was born he was put in an animal's feeding trough. And yet, some shepherds were being told about the very special man Jesus was going to grow up to be.

* Imagine you were one of the shepherds. How amazing must the experience have been for them to believe that this boy, born in such poverty would become the man they had been told about?
* Why was the news of Jesus – the Saviour – something to get so excited by?

Consider . . .

* expressing your worship to God for who Jesus is in whatever way you want – singing, dancing, doing some art, etc.
* what God might do with your life! Pray about what you would like to do, write your thoughts down, keep them in a safe place and read them again in a few years' time. See what God has done during that time.

For more, see . . .

* Psalm 98 (p.557)
* Philippians 2:5–11 (p.1282)
* Isaiah 9:6–7 (p.649)

76"Now you, child, will be called a prophet of
the Most High God.

You will go before the Lord to prepare his way.
77You will make his people know that they will
be saved

by having their sins forgiven.
78With the loving mercy of our God,

a new day from heaven will dawn upon us.
79It will shine on those who live in darkness,

in the shadow of death.

It will guide us into the path of peace."

80And so the child grew up and became
strong in spirit. John lived in the desert until the
time when he came out to preach to Israel.

The Birth of Jesus

2 At that time, Augustus Caesar *d* sent an
order that all people in the countries under
Roman rule must list their names in a register.
2This was the first registration;*n* it was taken
while Quirinius was governor of Syria. 3And all
went to their own towns to be registered.

4So Joseph left Nazareth, a town in Galilee,
and went to the town of Bethlehem in Judea,
known as the town of David. Joseph went there
because he was from the family of David.
5Joseph registered with Mary, to whom he was
engaged *n* and who was now pregnant. 6While
they were in Bethlehem, the time came for
Mary to have the baby, 7and she gave birth
to her first son. Because there were no rooms
left in the inn, she wrapped the baby with
pieces of cloth and laid him in a box where
animals are fed.

Sidelight　When Mary wrapped
Jesus with cloths (Luke
2:7), he probably couldn't move his arms
because he was wrapped so tightly. In biblical
times, people believed a good six-month
"wrapping" prevented arms and legs from
becoming crooked.

Shepherds Hear About Jesus

8That night, some shepherds were in the fields
nearby watching their sheep. 9Then an angel of
the Lord stood before them. The glory of the Lord
was shining around them, and they became very
frightened. 10The angel said to them, "Do not be
afraid. I am bringing you good news that will be
a great joy to all the people. 11Today your Saviour
was born in the town of David. He is Christ, *d* the
Lord. 12This is how you will know him: you will
find a baby wrapped in pieces of cloth and lying
in a feeding box."

13Then a very large group of angels from
heaven joined the first angel, praising God and
saying:

14"Give glory to God in heaven,
and on earth let there be peace among the
people who please God."

15When the angels left them and went back to
heaven, the shepherds said to each other, "Let's
go to Bethlehem. Let's see this thing that has
happened which the Lord has told us about."
16So the shepherds went quickly and found
Mary and Joseph and the baby, who was lying in
a feeding box. 17When they had seen him, they
told what the angels had said about this child.
18Everyone was amazed at what the shepherds
said to them. 19But Mary treasured these things
and continued to think about them. 20Then the
shepherds went back to their sheep, praising God
and thanking him for everything they had seen
and heard. It had been just as the angel had told
them.

21When the baby was eight days old, he was
circumcised *d* and was named Jesus, the name
given by the angel before the baby began to grow
in Mary's womb.

Jesus is Presented in the Temple

22When the time came for Mary and Joseph to
do what the law of Moses taught about being
made pure, *n* they took Jesus to Jerusalem to
present him to the Lord. 23(It is written in the law
of the Lord: "Every first-born *d* male shall be given
to the Lord.") *n* 24Mary and Joseph also went
to offer a sacrifice, as the law of the Lord says:
"You must sacrifice two doves or two young
pigeons." *n*

Simeon Sees Jesus

25In Jerusalem lived a man named Simeon who
was a good man and godly. He was waiting for
the time when God would take away Israel's sorrow, and the Holy Spirit *d* was in him. 26Simeon
had been told by the Holy Spirit that he would
not die before he saw the Christ *d* promised by the
Lord. 27The Spirit led Simeon to the Temple. *d*

---

registration　Census. A counting of all the people and the things they own.
engaged　For the Jewish people an engagement was a lasting agreement, which could only be broken by a divorce. If a bride
was unfaithful it was considered adultery and she could be put to death.
pure　The law of Moses said that 40 days after a Jewish woman gave birth to a son, she must be cleansed by a ceremony at the
Temple. Read Leviticus 12:2–8.
"Every . . . Lord."　Quotation from Exodus 13:2.
"You . . . pigeons."　Quotation from Leviticus 12:8.

When Mary and Joseph brought the baby Jesus to the Temple to do what the law said they must do, 28Simeon took the baby in his arms and thanked God:

29"Now, Lord, you can let me, your servant,
    die in peace as you said.
30With my own eyes I have seen your
    salvation,
31 which you prepared before all people.
32It is a light for the non-Jewish people to see
    and an honour for your people, the
    Israelites."

33Jesus' father and mother were amazed at what Simeon had said about him. 34Then Simeon blessed them and said to Mary, "God has chosen this child to cause the fall and rise of many in Israel. He will be a sign from God that many people will not accept 35so that the thoughts of many will be made known. And the things that will happen will make your heart sad, too."

Anna Sees Jesus

36There was a prophetess, d Anna, from the family of Phanuel in the tribe d of Asher. Anna was very old. She had once been married for seven years. 37Then her husband died, and she was a widow for 84 years. Anna never left the Temple but worshipped God, going without food and praying day and night. 38Standing there at that time, she thanked God and spoke about Jesus to all who were waiting for God to free Jerusalem.

Joseph and Mary Return Home

39When Joseph and Mary had done everything the law of the Lord commanded, they went home

---

FAMILY

Faith 'n' Family

It was the last evening at the Christian camp and Ross had loved every minute of it. He had been playing footie, watching DVDs, having water fights and hanging out with his mates. During the camp, there had also been talks about God.

Each day he was getting more interested in what was being said. The final evening's talk was on "Being a Christian at Home". Ross started to realise that the main reason why he didn't want to be a Christian wasn't that he didn't believe in God and want to follow him, it was that he was that scared about what his family would say. He loved his family, and he and his big brothers were always having a laugh and getting into trouble.

One of the youth leaders came up to Ross at the end of the talk and they got chatting. The youth leader listened and then told him that although it might be hard when he got home, God would be with him and would help him.

Ross made a commitment that night to follow God and hasn't looked back since. As he had feared, his brothers teased him, but with God's help it wasn't as difficult as Ross thought it might be. His brothers even began to ask questions, wanting to know more about what he believed in. Ross realised that God was actually helping him love and look out for his family in a way he'd not done before.

Read **Luke 2:22–40.**

* Why did Jesus need his family? Why do we need our families?
* Who are the "Simeons" and "Annas" in your life who help you to see God's work in your life and your family? Why are these people important to you?

Consider . . .

* encouraging a family member, or someone who helps you get closer to God, by telling them why you think they are great and how they've helped you.
* when things get hard at home, finding someone in your church who can pray for you and for your family.

For more, see . . .

* Exodus 20:12 (p.79)   * Mark 5:19 (p.1005)
* 1 Timothy 5:8 (p.1311)

to Nazareth, their own town in Galilee. [40]The little child grew and became strong. He was filled with wisdom, and God's goodness was upon him.

Jesus as a Boy

[41]Every year Jesus' parents went to Jerusalem for the Passover [d] Feast. [42]When he was twelve years old, they went to the feast as they always did. [43]After the feast days were over, they started home. The boy Jesus stayed behind in Jerusalem, but his parents did not know it. [44]Thinking that Jesus was with them in the group, they travelled for a whole day. Then they began to look for him among their family and friends. [45]When they did not find him, they went back to Jerusalem to look for him there. [46]After three days they found Jesus sitting in the Temple [d] with the teachers, listening to them and asking them questions. [47]All who heard him were amazed at his understanding and

answers. [48]When Jesus' parents saw him, they were astonished. His mother said to him, "Son, why did you do this to us? Your father and I were very worried about you and have been looking for you."

[49]Jesus said to them, "Why were you looking for me? Didn't you know that I must be in my Father's house?" [50]But they did not understand the meaning of what he said.

[51]Jesus went with them to Nazareth and was obedient to them. But his mother kept in her mind all that had happened. [52]Jesus became wiser and grew physically. People liked him, and he pleased God.

The Preaching of John

3 It was the fifteenth year of the rule of Tiberius Caesar. [d] These men were under Caesar: Pontius Pilate, the ruler of Judea; Herod, the ruler

SPIRITUAL GROWTH

Who Am I?

When Brian was a boy, he used to love to make mud pies by the outdoor tap at the back of his house. His mum would give him old pie dishes, and he'd fill them with just the right mix of earth and water.

"You had to be careful to mix it properly," Brian recalls. "Too much earth, and your pie would crumble. Too much water, and it would ooze."

As Brian got older, he didn't make mud pies as often. But he still enjoyed working with his hands to create. In art class, Brian learned the basics of sculpture.

"I was hooked from then on," Brian says with a smile. "I loved the idea of taking an image in my head and making it a reality in the clay. It's been fun ever since!"

Brian now works as a sculptor part-time after school. He has already won several awards for his work and plans to attend an art school in London when he leaves school.

"I want to design the sort of sculptures that you see around the big office buildings," says Brian, "and have my own business."

Brian grins. "I never realised you could turn making mud pies into a career."

Brian's interest and skill in sculpting grew as he got older. In the same way, our ability to understand and appreciate God grows as we get older and expose ourselves to more of God's ways. Jesus also experienced this spiritual growth process. Read about it in **Luke 2:41–52**, especially verse 52.

- What do Jesus and Brian have in common based on the passage?
- Have you continued to learn more and more in the past year?

Consider . . .

- thinking about all the ways in which you have changed in the past year, and thanking God for helping you to grow spiritually.
- keeping a prayer journal to help you to log spiritual growth in your life.

For more, see . . .

- 1 Samuel 2:26 (p.257)
- Ephesians 4:4–16 (p.1272)
- 1 Corinthians 13:11–13 (p.1232)

of Galilee; Philip, Herod's brother, the ruler of Iturea and Trachonitis; and Lysanias, the ruler of Abilene. [2]Annas and Caiaphas were the high priests. At this time, the word of God came to John son of Zechariah in the desert. [3]He went all over the area around the Jordan River preaching a baptism of changed hearts and lives for the forgiveness of sins. [4]As it is written in the book of Isaiah the prophet: [d]

This is the voice of one who calls out:
"Prepare in the desert
    the way for the LORD.
Make a straight road in the dry lands
    for our God.
[5]Every valley should be raised up,
    and every mountain and hill should be
    made flat.
The rough ground should be made level,
    and the rugged ground should be made
    smooth.
[6]Then the glory of the LORD will be shown,
    and all people together will see it.
The LORD himself said these things."

Isaiah 40:3–5

[7]To the crowds of people who came to be baptised by John, he said, "You are all snakes! Who warned you to run away from God's coming punishment? [8]Do the things that show you really have changed your hearts and lives. Don't begin to say to yourselves, 'Abraham is our father.' I tell you that God could make children for Abraham from these rocks. [9]The axe is now ready to cut down the trees, and every tree that does not produce good fruit will be cut down and thrown into the fire." [n]

[10]The people asked John, "Then what should we do?"

[11]John answered, "If you have two shirts, share with the person who does not have one. If you have food, share that also."

[12]Even tax collectors came to John to be baptised. They said to him, "Teacher, what should we do?"

[13]John said to them, "Don't take more taxes from people than you have been ordered to take."

[14]The soldiers asked John, "What about us? What should we do?"

John said to them, "Don't force people to give you money, and don't lie about them. Be satisfied with the pay you get."

[15]Since the people were hoping for the Christ [d] to come, they wondered if John might be the one.

The axe . . . fire.   This means that God is ready to punish his people who do not obey him.

JUSTICE

Your Fair Share

The saddest thing about poverty is that it can be stopped; there is enough money and enough resources in the world that everyone could afford to live and no one should have to die of starvation.

The great human rights campaigner, Nelson Mandela, once said, "Overcoming poverty is not a gesture of charity, it is an act of justice. It is the protection of a human right, the right to dignity and a decent life . . . Sometimes it falls on a generation to be great. You can be that great generation. Let your greatness blossom."

In **Luke 3:1–18** John urges the people to be satisfied with what they've got and give to the needy. He warns them that they shouldn't just be concerned with religion but with justice as well.

* What practical things does John suggest that the people do?
* If John were alive today, what do you think he'd say about the injustice in the world? What advice would he give us?

Consider . . .

* simple ways in which you can "let your greatness blossom". How could you help people that suffer from poverty?
* trying to remember the good things that God has given you and being quick to thank him for them.

For more, see . . .

* Amos 5:24 (p.874)
* Matthew 6:1–4 (p.947)
* Micah 6:6–8 (p.896)

[16]John answered everyone, "I baptise you with water, but there is one coming who is greater than I am. I am not good enough to untie his sandals. He will baptise you with the Holy Spirit [d] and fire. [17]He will come ready to clean the grain, separating the good grain from the chaff. [d] He will put the good part of the grain into his barn, but he will burn the chaff with a fire that cannot be put out." [n] [18]And John continued to preach the Good News, [d] saying many other things to encourage the people.

[19]But John spoke against Herod, the governor, because of his sin with Herodias, the wife of Herod's brother, and because of the many other evil things Herod did. [20]So Herod did something even worse: he put John in prison.

Jesus is Baptised by John

[21]When all the people were being baptised by John, Jesus also was baptised. While Jesus was praying, heaven opened [22]and the Holy Spirit [d] came down on him in the form of a dove. Then a voice came from heaven, saying, "You are my Son, whom I love, and I am very pleased with you."

The Family History of Jesus

[23]When Jesus began his ministry, he was about 30 years old. People thought that Jesus was Joseph's son.

Joseph was the son [n] of Heli.
[24]Heli was the son of Matthat.
Matthat was the son of Levi.
Levi was the son of Melki. [n]
Melki was the son of Jannai.
Jannai was the son of Joseph.
[25]Joseph was the son of Mattathias.
Mattathias was the son of Amos.
Amos was the son of Nahum.
Nahum was the son of Esli.
Esli was the son of Naggai.
[26]Naggai was the son of Maath.
Maath was the son of Mattathias.
Mattathias was the son of Semein.
Semein was the son of Josech.
Josech was the son of Joda.
[27]Joda was the son of Joanan.
Joanan was the son of Rhesa.
Rhesa was the son of Zerubbabel.
Zerubbabel was the grandson of Shealtiel.
Shealtiel was the son of Neri.
[28]Neri was the son of Melki. [n]
Melki was the son of Addi.
Addi was the son of Cosam.

Cosam was the son of Elmadam.
Elmadam was the son of Er.
[29]Er was the son of Joshua.
Joshua was the son of Eliezer.
Eliezer was the son of Jorim.
Jorim was the son of Matthat.
Matthat was the son of Levi.
[30]Levi was the son of Simeon.
Simeon was the son of Judah.
Judah was the son of Joseph.
Joseph was the son of Jonam.
Jonam was the son of Eliakim.
[31]Eliakim was the son of Melea.
Melea was the son of Menna.
Menna was the son of Mattatha.
Mattatha was the son of Nathan.
Nathan was the son of David.
[32]David was the son of Jesse.
Jesse was the son of Obed.
Obed was the son of Boaz.
Boaz was the son of Salmon.
Salmon was the son of Nahshon.
[33]Nahshon was the son of Amminadab.
Amminadab was the son of Admin. [n]
Admin was the son of Arni.
Arni was the son of Hezron.
Hezron was the son of Perez.
Perez was the son of Judah.
[34]Judah was the son of Jacob.
Jacob was the son of Isaac.
Isaac was the son of Abraham.
Abraham was the son of Terah.
Terah was the son of Nahor.
[35]Nahor was the son of Serug.
Serug was the son of Reu.
Reu was the son of Peleg.
Peleg was the son of Eber.
Eber was the son of Shelah.
[36]Shelah was the son of Cainan.
Cainan was the son of Arphaxad.
Arphaxad was the son of Shem.
Shem was the son of Noah.
Noah was the son of Lamech.
[37]Lamech was the son of Methuselah.
Methuselah was the son of Enoch.
Enoch was the son of Jared.
Jared was the son of Mahalalel.
Mahalalel was the son of Kenan.
[38]Kenan was the son of Enosh.
Enosh was the son of Seth.
Seth was the son of Adam.
Adam was the son of God.

He will . . . out. This means that Jesus will come to separate good people from bad people, saving the good and punishing the bad.
son "Son" in Jewish lists of ancestors can sometimes mean grandson or more distant relative.
Melki Some manuscripts spell Melki as Melchi.
Admin Some manuscripts say, "Amminadab, the son of Ram, the son of Hezron", other manuscripts vary widely.

Jesus is Tempted by the Devil

4 Jesus, filled with the Holy Spirit, *d* returned from the Jordan River. The Spirit led Jesus into the desert [2]where the devil tempted Jesus for 40 days. Jesus ate nothing during that time, and when those days were ended, he was very hungry.

[3]The devil said to Jesus, "If you are the Son of God, tell this rock to become bread."

[4]Jesus answered, "It is written in the Scriptures: *d* 'A person does not live by eating only bread.' " *n*

[5]Then the devil took Jesus and showed him all the kingdoms of the world in an instant. [6]The devil said to Jesus, "I will give you all these kingdoms and all their power and glory. It has all been given to me, and I can give it to anyone I wish. [7]If you worship me, then it will all be yours."

[8]Jesus answered, "It is written in the Scriptures: 'You must worship the Lord your God and serve only him.' " *n*

[9]Then the devil led Jesus to Jerusalem and put him on a high place of the Temple. *d* He said to Jesus, "If you are the Son of God, jump down. [10]It is written in the Scriptures:

'He has put his angels in charge of you
    to watch over you.'   *Psalm 91:11*

[11]It is also written:

'They will catch you in their hands
    so that you will not hit your foot on a
        rock.' "   *Psalm 91:12*

[12]Jesus answered, "But it also says in the Scriptures: 'Do not test the Lord your God.' " *n*

[13]After the devil had tempted Jesus in every way, he left him to wait until a better time.

'A person . . . bread.'   Quotation from Deuteronomy 8:3.
'You . . . him.'   Quotation from Deuteronomy 6:13.
'Do . . . God.'   Quotation from Deuteronomy 6:16.

SIN

Tempted?

Andrew and Sean were good friends. They went to the same church where they'd both been baptised. When they were a bit older, they started to help lead the youth club on a Friday night.

It was coming up to their eighteenth birthdays and the leaders invited them to go to Africa on a mission for three weeks. They jumped at the chance, and soon they were in Africa serving God. They saw hundreds become Christians and join the church. It was Christmas. Could life get any better?

When they came back from Africa, they started to celebrate their birthdays. Andrew went out for a posh meal with his family and planned to sample the nightlife of Manchester. Sean went to the pub with his mates and got drunk. Then he got a new job and started going out with a girl from work. Two weeks later, he moved in with her. He stopped going to church and seeing his Christian friends. He completely turned his back on God.

Andrew decided to make God the centre of his life. He goes to church and small group, and has nearly finished his college course. He hopes to go back to Africa again one day.

We've always got choices about how to live our lives. We're faced with temptation all the time. The question is, will we give in and be like Sean or resist it and be like Andrew? It is a hard thing to do, and in **Luke 4:1–13** Jesus is tempted by the devil but he doesn't give in for a second. Read it to see what happened.

* How did Jesus and Andrew have the strength to resist the devil and the temptation of sin?
* Do you think that God says it's OK to give in to temptation and sin? Why?

Consider . . .

* next time you're about to give in to sin, trying to stop and asking God to help you not to do it.
* praying for your friends who, like Sean, have given in to sin.

For more, see . . .

* Colossians 3:5–10 (p.1292)
* James 5:19–20 (p.1354)

* James 4:7–8 (p.1351)

Jesus Teaches the People

[14]Jesus returned to Galilee in the power of the Holy Spirit,*d* and stories about him spread throughout all the area. [15]He began to teach in their synagogues,*d* and everyone praised him.

[16]Jesus travelled to Nazareth, where he had grown up. On the Sabbath*d* day he went to the synagogue, as he always did, and stood up to read. [17]The book of Isaiah the prophet*d* was given to him. He opened the book and found the place where this is written:

[18]"The Lord has put his Spirit in me,
> because he appointed me to tell the Good News*d* to the poor.

He has sent me to tell the captives they are free
> and to tell the blind that they can see again.   *Isaiah 61:1*

God sent me to free those who have been
> treated unfairly   *Isaiah 58:6*

[19] and to announce the time when the Lord will show his kindness."   *Isaiah 61:2*

[20]Jesus closed the book, gave it back to the assistant and sat down. Everyone in the synagogue was watching Jesus closely. [21]He began to say to them, "While you heard these words just now, they were coming true!"

[22]All the people spoke well of Jesus and were amazed at the words of grace he spoke. They asked, "Isn't this Joseph's son?"

Sidelight If you don't like being noticed when you visit different churches, you wouldn't have visited many synagogues in Jesus' day. It was customary for the synagogue leader to invite visitors to address the congregation. Jesus took advantage of the opportunity to preach in Luke 4:14–19.

JUSTICE

I'm Not Part of the Problem!

When you look around the world today, it is pretty easy to see injustice. Millions of people die every year simply because they were born into poverty and don't have the same choices as people that live in richer countries. Millions of people are sold as slaves, to be exploited and worked until they are no longer physically able to endure the hardship. Rich countries force poor countries to open up their economies and spend their money paying back debts which drain their budgets dry so they can't spend money on things like health care and education. Where's the justice?

It's very easy to think that we aren't part of the problem. It's easy to blame injustice on people in power, like governments and the really, really rich. But realising justice requires all of us to understand that we all have a part to play. The reality is that every decision we make has an impact on other people. If we choose to buy clothes at the cheapest prices, then someone else will be forced to make those clothes for us and be paid very little for it. Is that fair? Is that justice? If we just sit silent and don't speak out on behalf of the billions of people in our world who are oppressed, can we really say we aren't part of the problem?

The world God created and intended us to live in was one of complete and perfect justice. Every time we make a decision, act or speak out in favour of people whose lives are destroyed by injustice, we bring our world back one step closer to the justice God wants for each and every person he created. Read **Luke 4:16–30**.

* What are some of the choices you make every day that affect the lives of other people?
* Do you react to injustice in the same way that the people Jesus was teaching did?

Consider . . .

* what changes you could make to your choices to ensure that you are not part of "the problem".
* making a commitment to choose to buy ethical and fair-trade products wherever possible.

For more, see . . .

* Exodus 23:1–9 (p.82)
* Amos 5 (p.873)
* Psalm 140:11–13 (p.582)

23Jesus said to them, "I know that you will tell me the old saying: 'Doctor, heal yourself.' You want to say, 'We heard about the things you did in Capernaum. Do those things here in your own town!'" 24Then Jesus said, "I tell you the truth, a prophet is not accepted in his home town. 25But I tell you the truth, there were many widows in Israel during the time of Elijah. It did not rain in Israel for three and a half years, and there was no food anywhere in the whole country. 26But Elijah was sent to none of those widows, only to a widow in Zarephath, a town in Sidon. 27And there were many with skin diseases living in Israel during the time of the prophet Elisha. But none of them were healed, only Naaman, who was from the country of Syria."

28When all the people in the synagogue heard these things, they became very angry. 29They got up, forced Jesus out of town, and took him to the edge of the cliff on which the town was built. They planned to throw him off the edge, 30but Jesus walked through the crowd and went on his way.

Jesus Forces Out an Evil Spirit

31Jesus went to Capernaum, a city in Galilee, and on the Sabbath *d* day, he taught the people. 32They were amazed at his teaching, because he spoke with authority. 33In the synagogue *d* a man who had within him an evil spirit shouted in a loud voice, 34"Jesus of Nazareth! What do you want with us? Did you come to destroy us? I know who you are—God's Holy One!"

35Jesus commanded the evil spirit, "Be quiet! Come out of the man!" The evil spirit threw the man down to the ground before all the people and then left the man without hurting him.

36The people were amazed and said to each other, "What does this mean? With authority and power he commands evil spirits, and they come out." 37And so the news about Jesus spread to every place in the whole area.

Jesus Heals Many People

38Jesus left the synagogue *d* and went to the home of Simon. *n* Simon's mother-in-law was sick with a high fever, and they asked Jesus to help her. 39He came to her side and commanded the fever to leave. It left her, and immediately she got up and began serving them.

40When the sun went down, the people brought those who were sick to Jesus. Putting his hands on each sick person, he healed every one of them. 41Demons *d* came out of many people, shouting, "You are the Son of God." But Jesus commanded the demons and would not allow them to speak, because they knew Jesus was the Christ. *d*

42At daybreak, Jesus went to a lonely place, but the people looked for him. When they found him, they tried to keep him from leaving. 43But Jesus said to them, "I must preach about God's kingdom to other towns, too. This is why I was sent."

44Then he kept on preaching in the synagogues *d* of Judea.

Jesus' First Followers

5 One day while Jesus was standing beside Lake Galilee, many people were pressing all around him to hear the word of God. 2Jesus saw two boats at the shore of the lake. The fishermen had left them and were washing their nets. 3Jesus got into one of the boats, the one that belonged to Simon, *n* and asked him to push off a little from the land. Then Jesus sat down and continued to teach the people from the boat.

4When Jesus had finished speaking, he said to Simon, "Take the boat into deep water, and put your nets in the water to catch some fish."

5Simon answered, "Master, we worked hard all night trying to catch fish, and we caught nothing. But you say to put the nets in the water, so I will." 6When the fishermen did as Jesus told them, they caught so many fish that the nets began to break. 7They called to their partners in the other boat to come and help them. They came and filled both boats so full that they were almost sinking.

8When Simon Peter saw what had happened, he bowed down before Jesus and said, "Go away from me, Lord. I am a sinful man!" 9He and the other fishermen were amazed at the many fish they caught, as were 10James and John, the sons of Zebedee, Simon's partners.

Jesus said to Simon, "Don't be afraid. From now on you will fish for people." 11When the men brought their boats to the shore, they left everything and followed Jesus.

Jesus Heals a Sick Man

12When Jesus was in one of the towns, there was a man covered with a skin disease. When he saw Jesus, he bowed before him and begged him, "Lord, you can heal me if you will."

13Jesus reached out his hand and touched the man and said, "I will. Be healed!" Immediately the disease disappeared. 14Then Jesus said, "Don't tell anyone about this, but go and show yourself to the priest *n* and offer a gift for your healing, as Moses commanded. *n* This will show the people what I have done."

Simon   Simon's other name was Peter.
show . . . priest   The law of Moses said a priest must say when a Jewish person with a skin disease was well.
Moses commanded   Read about this in Leviticus 14:1–32.

[15]But the news about Jesus spread even more. Many people came to hear Jesus and to be healed of their sicknesses, [16]but Jesus often slipped away to be alone so he could pray.

Jesus Heals a Paralysed Man

[17]One day as Jesus was teaching the people, the Pharisees[d] and teachers of the law from every town in Galilee and Judea and from Jerusalem were there. The power of the Lord was present for him to heal the sick. [18]Just then, some men were carrying on a mat a man who was paralysed. They tried to bring him in and put him down before Jesus. [19]But because there were so many people there, they could not find a way in. So they went up on the roof and lowered the man on his mat through the ceiling into the middle of the crowd right before Jesus. [20]Seeing their faith, Jesus said, "Friend, your sins are forgiven."

> **Sidelight**
> If you think access to buildings is a new problem for disabled people, read Luke 5:18–20. The friends probably had to dig through layers of clay, grass and branches to make a hole in the roof, since that's how most roofs were made in Jesus' time. The roofs were supported by wooden beams, which stretched from wall to wall.

[21]The Jewish teachers of the law and the Pharisees thought to themselves, "Who is this man who is speaking as if he were God? Only God can forgive sins."

[22]But Jesus knew what they were thinking and said, "Why are you thinking these things? [23]Which is easier: to say, 'Your sins are forgiven,' or to say, 'Stand up and walk'? [24]But I will prove to you that the Son of Man[d] has authority on earth to forgive sins." So Jesus said to the paralysed man, "I tell you, stand up, take your mat, and go home."

[25]At once the man stood up before them, picked up his mat and went home, praising God. [26]All the people were completely amazed and began to praise God. They were filled with much respect and said, "Today we have seen amazing things!"

Levi Follows Jesus

[27]After this, Jesus went out and saw a tax collector named Levi[n] sitting in the tax collector's booth. Jesus said to him, "Follow me!" [28]So Levi got up, left everything and followed him.

[29]Then Levi gave a big dinner for Jesus at his house. Many tax collectors and other people were eating there, too. [30]But the Pharisees[d] and the men who taught the law for the Pharisees began to complain to Jesus' followers, "Why do you eat and drink with tax collectors and sinners?"

[31]Jesus answered them, "It is not the healthy people who need a doctor, but the sick. [32]I have not come to invite good people but sinners to change their hearts and lives."

Jesus Answers a Question

[33]They said to Jesus, "John's followers often give up eating[n] for a certain time and pray, just as the Pharisees[d] do. But your followers eat and drink all the time."

[34]Jesus said to them, "You cannot make the friends of the bridegroom give up eating while he is still with them. [35]But the time will come when the bridegroom will be taken away from them, and then they will give up eating."

[36]Jesus told them this story: "No one takes cloth off a new coat to cover a hole in an old coat. Otherwise, he ruins the new coat, and the cloth from the new coat will not be the same as the old cloth. [37]Also, no one ever pours new wine into old leather bags. Otherwise, the new wine will break the bags, the wine will spill out and the leather bags will be ruined. [38]New wine must be put into new leather bags. [39]No one after drinking old wine wants new wine, because he says, 'The old wine is better.'"

Jesus is Lord over the Sabbath

6 One Sabbath[d] day Jesus was walking through some fields of grain. His followers picked the heads of grain, rubbed them in their hands and ate them. [2]Some Pharisees[d] said, "Why do you do what is not lawful on the Sabbath day?"

[3]Jesus answered, "Have you not read what David did when he and those with him were hungry? [4]He went into God's house and took and ate the holy bread, which is lawful only for priests to eat. And he gave some to the people who were with him." [5]Then Jesus said to the Pharisees, "The Son of Man[d] is Lord of the Sabbath day."

Jesus Heals a Man's Hand

[6]On another Sabbath[d] day Jesus went into the synagogue[d] and was teaching, and a man with a crippled right hand was there. [7]The teachers of the law and the Pharisees[d] were watching closely

---

Levi   Also known as Matthew.
give up eating   This is called "fasting". The people would give up eating for a special time of prayer and worship to God. It was also done to show sadness and disappointment.

to see if Jesus would heal on the Sabbath day so they could accuse him. [8]But he knew what they were thinking, and he said to the man with the crippled hand, "Stand up here in the middle of everyone." The man got up and stood there. [9]Then Jesus said to them, "I ask you, which is lawful on the Sabbath day: to do good or to do evil, to save a life or to destroy it?" [10]Jesus looked around at all of them and said to the man, "Hold out your hand." The man held out his hand, and it was healed.

[11]But the Pharisees and the teachers of the law were very angry and discussed with each other what they could do to Jesus.

Jesus Chooses His Apostles

[12]At that time Jesus went off to a mountain to pray, and he spent the night praying to God. [13]The next morning, Jesus called his followers to him and chose twelve of them, whom he named apostles: [d] [14]Simon (Jesus named him Peter), his brother Andrew, James, John, Philip, Bartholomew, [15]Matthew, Thomas, James son of Alphaeus, Simon (called the Zealot [d]), [16]Judas son of James and Judas Iscariot, who later turned Jesus over to his enemies.

Jesus Teaches and Heals

[17]Jesus and the apostles [d] came down from the mountain, and he stood on level ground. A large group of his followers were there, as well as many people from all around Judea, Jerusalem, and the sea coast cities of Tyre and Sidon. [18]They all came to hear Jesus teach and to be healed of their sicknesses, and he healed those who were troubled by evil spirits. [19]All the people were trying to touch Jesus, because power was coming from him and healing them all.

[20]Jesus looked at his followers and said,
"Happy you people who are poor,
   because the kingdom of God belongs to
      you.
[21]Happy you people who are now hungry,
   because you will be satisfied.
Happy you people who are now crying,
   because you will laugh with joy.
[22]"People will hate you, shut you out, insult you and say you are evil, because you follow the Son of Man. [d] But when they do, you will be happy. [23]Be full of joy at that time, because you have a great reward waiting for you in heaven. Their ancestors did the same things to the prophets. [d]
[24]"But how terrible it will be for you who are rich,
   because you have had your easy life.
[25]How terrible it will be for you who are
      full now,
   because you will be hungry.

How terrible it will be for you who are
      laughing now,
   because you will be sad and cry.
[26]"How terrible when everyone says only good things about you, because their ancestors said the same things about the false prophets.

Love Your Enemies

[27]"But I say to you who are listening, love your enemies. Do good to those who hate you, [28]bless those who curse you, pray for those who are cruel to you. [29]If anyone slaps you on one cheek, offer him the other cheek, too. If someone takes your coat, do not stop him from taking your shirt. [30]Give to everyone who asks you, and when someone takes something that is yours, don't ask for it back. [31]Do to others what you would want them to do to you. [32]If you love only the people who love you, what praise should you get? Even sinners love the people who love them. [33]If you do good only to those who do good to you, what praise should you get? Even sinners do that! [34]If you lend things to people, always hoping to get something back, what praise should you get? Even sinners lend to other sinners so that they can get back the same amount! [35]But love your enemies, do good to them, and lend to them without hoping to get anything back. Then you will have a great reward and you will be children of the Most High God, because he is kind even to people who are ungrateful and full of sin. [36]Show mercy, just as your Father shows mercy.

Look at Yourselves

[37]"Don't judge other people, and you will not be judged. Don't accuse others of being guilty, and you will not be accused of being guilty. Forgive, and you will be forgiven. [38]Give, and you will receive. You will be given much. Pressed down, shaken together and running over, it will spill into your lap. The way you give to others is the way God will give to you."

[39]Jesus told them this story: "Can a blind person lead another blind person? No! Both of them will fall into a ditch. [40]A student is not better than the teacher, but the student who has been fully trained will be like the teacher.

[41]"Why do you notice the little piece of dust in your friend's eye, but you don't notice the big piece of wood in your own eye? [42]How can you say to your friend, 'Friend, let me take that little piece of dust out of your eye' when you cannot see that big piece of wood in your own eye! You hypocrite! [d] First, take the wood out of your own eye. Then you will see clearly to take the dust out of your friend's eye.

Two Kinds of Fruit

43"A good tree does not produce bad fruit, nor does a bad tree produce good fruit. 44Each tree is known by its own fruit. People don't gather figs from thorn-bushes, and they don't get grapes from bushes. 45Good people bring good things out of the good stored in their hearts. But evil people bring evil things out of the evil stored in their hearts. People speak the things that are in their hearts.

Two Kinds of People

46"Why do you call me, 'Lord, Lord,' but do not do what I say? 47I will show you what everyone is like who comes to me and hears my words and obeys. 48That person is like a man building a house who dug deep and laid the foundation on rock. When the floods came, the water tried to wash the house away, but it could not shake it, because the house was built well. 49But the one who hears my words and does not obey is like a man who built his house on the ground without a foundation. When the floods came, the house quickly fell and was completely destroyed."

Jesus Heals a Soldier's Servant

7 When Jesus finished saying all these things to the people, he went to Capernaum. 2There was an army officer who had a servant who was very important to him. The servant was so sick he was nearly dead. 3When the officer heard about Jesus, he sent some Jewish elders to him to ask Jesus to come and heal his servant. 4The men went to Jesus and begged him, saying, "This officer is worthy of your help. 5He loves our people, and he built us a synagogue." *d*

6So Jesus went with the men. He was getting near the officer's house when the officer sent friends to say, "Lord, don't trouble yourself, because I am not worthy to have you come into my house. 7That is why I did not come to you myself. But you only need to command it, and my servant will be healed. 8I, too, am a man under the authority of others, and I have soldiers under my command. I tell one soldier, 'Go,' and he goes. I tell another soldier, 'Come,' and he comes. I say to my servant, 'Do this,' and my servant does it."

LEADERSHIP

Fish Out of Water

Whales Commit Mass Suicide.

The 1986 newspaper headline alerted the community in Cape Cod to the baffling incident that had happened the night before. A herd, or "pod," of 94 whales had beached themselves on the shores of Cape Cod. They just swam up on to the sand . . . and died.

This wasn't the first or the last time that whales have committed this strange act around the world. Newspapers periodically report stories of whales beaching themselves.

Several theories try to explain why whales do this. One of them is that the whales are following a basic herd instinct. Every pod has a leader. If the leader becomes ill or disoriented, it might react by beaching itself. But since it's the leader, the other whales simply follow, even though it means death.

Sound ridiculous? Perhaps, but it's not so unlike the way that many people act. It's easy to follow leaders who say they have the right answers.

People who pretend to have life's answers but live destructively are called hypocrites. In **Luke 6:39–49**, Jesus was saddened and angered to find hypocrisy in the religious leaders around him.

* How is the lead whale like the blind leaders Jesus talks about in this passage?
* What leaders do young people follow, even though the leaders' lifestyles seem destructive?

Consider . . .

* listing the "good fruits" and "bad fruits" that you see in your own life, then asking God to take away the bad fruit.
* telling people you look to as leaders about the "good fruits" you see in their lives.

For more, see . . .

* Isaiah 29:13 (p.668)
* James 1:19–27 (p.1348)
* Amos 8:4–8 (p.877)

9When Jesus heard this, he was amazed. Turning to the crowd that was following him, he said, "I tell you, this is the greatest faith I have found anywhere, even in Israel."

10Those who had been sent to Jesus went back to the house where they found the servant in good health.

Jesus Brings a Man Back to Life

11Soon afterwards Jesus went to a town called Nain, and his followers and a large crowd travelled with him. 12When he came near the town gate, he saw a funeral. A mother, who was a widow, had lost her only son. A large crowd from the town was with the mother while her son was being carried out. 13When the Lord saw her, he felt very sorry for her and said, "Don't cry." 14He went up and touched the coffin, and the people who were carrying it stopped. Jesus said, "Young man, I tell you, get up!" 15And the son sat up and began to talk. Then Jesus gave him back to his mother.

16All the people were amazed and began praising God, saying, "A great prophet *d* has come to us! God has come to help his people."

> ### Sidelight
> The coffin where the boy lay when Jesus brought him back to life (Luke 7:11–15) wasn't like coffins today. In fact, it was probably just a board on which they laid the body. Just like today, wealthier people sometimes had more elaborate "funeral biers", as they were called.

17This news about Jesus spread through all Judea and into all the places around there.

FAITH

To the Letter

"Do as I say to the letter and you'll be fine. Disobey and it could cost you your life!"

Those were the words which Ruth's parachute instructor had spoken to her at the beginning of her first lesson three weeks ago. Now, her training was almost complete. In minutes she would be leaping out of a plane thousands of feet in the air.

"Obedience," the instructor had continued, "is the essence of success in parachute jumping. Some people, eager to jump, ignore what they consider to be 'boring rules and regulations'. Sadly, a few of those folk have died."

As the plane settled into a steady path and her instructor motioned for her to go with him to the door, Ruth suddenly realised that talking about jumping from a plane and actually doing it were two very different things. But it was too late to go back now. She just had to step out in faith.

Ruth thought the fall was amazing – she couldn't put her excitement into words. The important thing was that she landed safely, just as her instructor had promised she would, and that she had raised over £500 for charity.

Ruth's instructor was teaching her to have faith in him and to obey his words if she wanted to succeed. In **Luke 7:1–10**, a soldier also understood this type of faith and became a success because of it.

* How is the soldier in this passage similar to Ruth? How is he different?
* Is your faith as strong as the officer's in this passage? Why or why not?

Consider . . .

* how your life would be different if you followed God's instructions to the letter. Why not choose to put your faith in him for every area of your life?
* memorising Hebrews 11:1 (p.1341) to learn God's definition of faith.

For more, see . . .

* Genesis 22:1–18 (p.25)
* Hebrews 11 (p.1341)
* Matthew 13:22–35 (p.963)

John Asks a Question

¹⁸John's followers told him about all these things. He called for two of his followers ¹⁹and sent them to the Lord to ask, "Are you the One who is to come, or should we wait for someone else?"

²⁰When the men came to Jesus, they said, "John the Baptist *d* sent us to you with this question: 'Are you the One who is to come, or should we wait for someone else?'"

²¹At that time, Jesus healed many people of their sicknesses, diseases and evil spirits, and he gave sight to many blind people. ²²Then Jesus answered John's followers, "Go and tell John what you saw and heard here. The blind can see, the crippled can walk and people with skin diseases are healed. The deaf can hear, the dead are raised to life and the Good News *d* is preached to the poor. ²³Those who do not stumble in their faith because of me are blessed!"

²⁴When John's followers left, Jesus began talking to the people about John: "What did you go out into the desert to see? A reed *n* blown by the wind? ²⁵What did you go out to see? A man dressed in fine clothes? No, people who have fine clothes and much wealth live in kings' palaces. ²⁶But what did you go out to see? A prophet? *d* Yes, and I tell you, John is more than a prophet. ²⁷This was written about him:

'I will send my messenger ahead of you,
    who will prepare the way for you.' *Malachi 3:1*

²⁸I tell you, John is greater than any other person ever born, but even the least important person in the kingdom of God is greater than John."

²⁹(When the people, including the tax collectors, heard this, they all agreed that God's teaching was good, having been baptised by John. ³⁰But the Pharisees*d* and experts on the law refused to accept God's plan for themselves; they did not let John baptise them.)

³¹Then Jesus said, "What shall I say about the people of this time? What are they like? ³²They are like children sitting in the market-place, calling to one another and saying,

'We played music for you, but you did not
    dance;
we sang a sad song, but you did not cry.'

³³John the Baptist came and did not eat bread or drink wine, and you say, 'He has a demon *d* in him.' ³⁴The Son of Man *d* came eating and drinking, and you say, 'Look at him! He eats too much and drinks too much wine, and he is a friend of tax collectors and sinners!' ³⁵But wisdom is proved to be right by what it does."

A Woman Washes Jesus' Feet

³⁶One of the Pharisees *d* asked Jesus to eat with him, so Jesus went into the Pharisee's house and sat at the table. ³⁷A sinful woman in the town learnt that Jesus was eating at the Pharisee's house. So she brought an alabaster *d* jar of perfume ³⁸and stood behind Jesus at his feet, crying. She began to wash his feet with her tears, and she dried them with her hair, kissing them many times and rubbing them with the perfume. ³⁹When the Pharisee who asked Jesus to come to his house saw this, he thought to himself, "If Jesus were a prophet, *d* he would know that the woman touching him is a sinner!"

⁴⁰Jesus said to the Pharisee, "Simon, I have something to say to you."

Simon said, "Teacher, tell me."

⁴¹Jesus said, "Two people owed money to the same banker. One owed 500 silver coins *n* and the other owed 50 silver coins. ⁴²They had no money to pay what they owed, but the banker told both of them they did not have to pay him. Which person will love the banker more?"

⁴³Simon, the Pharisee, answered, "I think it would be the one who owed him the most money."

Jesus said to Simon, "You are right." ⁴⁴Then Jesus turned towards the woman and said to Simon, "Do you see this woman? When I came into your house, you gave me no water for my feet, but she washed my feet with her tears and dried them with her hair. ⁴⁵You gave me no kiss of greeting, but she has been kissing my feet since I came in. ⁴⁶You did not put oil on my head, but she poured perfume on my feet. ⁴⁷I tell you that her many sins are forgiven, so she showed great love. But the person who is forgiven only a little will love only a little."

⁴⁸Then Jesus said to her, "Your sins are forgiven."

⁴⁹The people sitting at the table began to say among themselves, "Who is this who even forgives sins?"

⁵⁰Jesus said to the woman, "Because you believed, you are saved from your sins. Go in peace."

The Group with Jesus

8 After this, while Jesus was travelling through some cities and small towns, he preached and told the Good News *d* about God's kingdom. The twelve apostles *d* were with him, ²and also some women who had been healed of sicknesses and evil spirits: Mary, called Magdalene, from whom seven demons *d* had gone out; ³Joanna, the

---

reed   It means that John was not ordinary or weak like grass blown by the wind.
coins   Roman denarii. A silver coin was the average pay for one day's work.

wife of Chuza (the manager of Herod's house); Susanna; and many others. These women used their own money to help Jesus and his apostles.

A Story About Planting Seed

4When a great crowd was gathered, and people were coming to Jesus from every town, he told them this story:

5"A farmer went out to plant his seed. While he was planting, some seed fell by the road. People walked on the seed, and the birds ate it up. 6Some seed fell on rock, and when it began to grow, it died because it had no water. 7Some seed fell among thorny weeds, but the weeds grew up with it and choked the good plants. 8And some seed fell on good ground and grew and made 100 times more."

As Jesus finished the story, he called out, "You people who can hear me, listen!"

9Jesus' followers asked him what this story meant.

10Jesus said, "You have been chosen to know the secrets about the kingdom of God. But I use stories to speak to other people so that:

'You will listen and listen, but you will not understand.
You will look and look, but you will not learn.'   Isaiah 6:9

11"This is what the story means: the seed is God's message. 12The seed that fell beside the road is like the people who hear God's teaching, but the devil comes and takes it away from them so they cannot believe it and be saved. 13The seed that fell on rock is like those who hear God's teaching and

NON-CHRISTIANS

The Kickflip Footballer

Carl was sitting in the back of the car listening to the radio. He was just about to drop off to sleep when he heard the DJ mention Carl's favourite football player, Justin Walker. The DJ was talking about a competition. The grand prize was Justin visiting the winner's house for tea. Within seconds Carl had typed the competition's answer into his mobile and was pressing send. Unbelievably, it was Carl's name that the DJ read out! Carl cheered, his mum clapped, narrowly missing a cyclist, and Carl's mates heard about nothing else all day.

Carl spent the next two weeks getting things organised for the visit of a lifetime, and his first job was to make sure his sister Amy stayed away! In Carl's eyes Amy was a complete "skater geek". She knew nothing about football and Carl thought that she would be an embarrassment – after all, he had a reputation to keep up. There was no way he wanted someone as cool as Justin to meet Amy.

Two weeks later, Justin Walker arrived, with a photographer and a producer from the radio station. Carl's mates looked impressed and everything was going well, until Amy walked in. Carl stared at her with anger and embarrassment. What was she doing here? Justin wouldn't want to talk to her?

Carl's train of thought was suddenly interrupted by Justin's laughter. Carl tuned in to Justin and Amy's conversation and couldn't believe what he was hearing.

"Yeah, yeah, he's an awesome skater isn't he," said Justin. "I've got an amazing DVD with him in. I'll send you one if you want." Justin Walker into skateboarding – NO WAY!

Read about the Pharisee that couldn't believe that Jesus would be interested in someone "sinful" in **Luke 7:36–50**.

* Both Jesus and Justin were interested in people that others had rejected. If Jesus was in your school or college, who do you think he would spend most of his time with?
* Carl was convinced that Justin wouldn't want to meet Amy, but he was wrong. Who have you thought wouldn't be interested in Jesus? Could you be wrong?

Consider . . .

* asking God to show you non-Christians that he wants you to spend more time with.
* asking your youth leader to do some sessions on how to tell your friends about Jesus.

For more, see . . .

* Isaiah 61:1–2 (p.705)
* Romans 1:16 (p.1185)

accept it gladly, but they don't allow the teaching to go deep into their lives. They believe for a while, but when trouble comes, they give up. [14]The seed that fell among the thorny weeds is like those who hear God's teaching, but they let the worries, riches and pleasures of this life keep them from growing and producing good fruit. [15]And the seed that fell on the good ground is like those who hear God's teaching with good, honest hearts and obey it and patiently produce good fruit.

Use What You Have

[16]"No one after lighting a lamp covers it with a bowl or hides it under a bed. Instead, the person puts it on a lampstand so those who come in will see the light. [17]Everything that is hidden will become clear, and every secret thing will be made known. [18]So be careful how you listen. Those who have understanding will be given more. But from those who do not have understanding, even what they think they have will be taken away."

Jesus' True Family

[19]Jesus' mother and brothers came to see him, but there was such a crowd they could not get to him. [20]Someone said to Jesus, "Your mother and your brothers are standing outside, wanting to see you."

[21]Jesus answered them, "My mother and my brothers are those who listen to God's teaching and obey it!"

Jesus Calms a Storm

[22]One day Jesus and his followers got into a boat, and he said to them, "Let's go across the lake." And so they started across. [23]While they were sailing, Jesus fell asleep. A very strong wind blew up on the lake, causing the boat to fill with water, and they were in danger.

[24]The followers went to Jesus and woke him, saying, "Master! Master! We will drown!"

Jesus got up and gave a command to the wind and the waves. They stopped, and it became calm. [25]Jesus said to his followers, "Where is your faith?"

The followers were afraid and amazed and said to each other, "Who is this that commands even the wind and the water, and they obey him?"

A Man with Demons Inside Him

[26]Jesus and his followers sailed across the lake from Galilee to the area of the Gerasene people. [27]When Jesus got out on the land, a man from the town who had demons[d] inside him came to

Jesus. For a long time he had worn no clothes and had lived in the burial caves, not in a house. [28]When he saw Jesus, he cried out and fell down before him. He said with a loud voice, "What do you want with me, Jesus, Son of the Most High God? I beg you, don't torture me!" [29]He said this because Jesus was commanding the evil spirit to come out of the man. Many times it had taken hold of him. Though he had been kept under guard and chained hand and foot, he had broken his chains and had been forced by the demon out into a lonely place.

[30]Jesus asked him, "What is your name?"

He answered, "Legion,"[n] because many demons were in him. [31]The demons begged Jesus not to send them into eternal darkness.[n] [32]A large herd of pigs was feeding on a hill, and the demons begged Jesus to allow them to go into the pigs. So Jesus allowed them to do this. [33]When the demons came out of the man, they went into the pigs, and the herd ran down the hill into the lake and was drowned.

[34]When the herdsmen saw what had happened, they ran away and reported this in the town and the countryside. [35]And people went to see what had happened. When they came to Jesus, they found the man sitting at Jesus' feet, clothed and in his right mind, because the demons were gone. But the people were frightened. [36]The people who saw this happen told the others how Jesus had made the man well. [37]All the people of the Gerasene country asked Jesus to leave, because they were all very afraid. So Jesus got into the boat and went back to Galilee.

[38]The man whom Jesus had healed begged to go with him, but Jesus sent him away, saying, [39]"Go back home and tell people how much God has done for you." So the man went all over town telling how much Jesus had done for him.

Jesus Gives Life to a Dead Girl and Heals a Sick Woman

[40]When Jesus got back to Galilee, a crowd welcomed him, because everyone was waiting for him. [41]A man named Jairus, a leader of the synagogue,[d] came to Jesus and fell at his feet, begging him to come to his house. [42]Jairus' only daughter, about twelve years old, was dying.

While Jesus was on his way to Jairus' house, the people were crowding all around him. [43]A woman was in the crowd who had been bleeding for twelve years, but no one was able to heal her. [44]She came up behind Jesus and touched the edge of his coat, and instantly her bleeding stopped. [45]Then Jesus said, "Who touched me?"

When all the people said they had not touched him, Peter said, "Master, the people are all around you and are pushing against you."

⁴⁶But Jesus said, "Someone did touch me, because I felt power go out from me." ⁴⁷When the woman saw she could not hide, she came forwards, shaking, and fell down before Jesus. While all the people listened, she told why she had touched him and how she had been instantly healed. ⁴⁸Jesus said to her, "Dear woman, you are made well because you believed. Go in peace."

⁴⁹While Jesus was still speaking, someone came from the house of the synagogue leader and said to him, "Your daughter is dead. Don't bother the teacher any more."

⁵⁰When Jesus heard this, he said to Jairus, "Don't be afraid. Just believe, and your daughter will be well."

⁵¹When Jesus went to the house, he let only Peter, John, James and the girl's father and mother go inside with him. ⁵²All the people were crying and feeling sad because the girl was dead, but Jesus said, "Stop crying. She is not dead, only asleep."

⁵³The people laughed at Jesus because they knew the girl was dead. ⁵⁴But Jesus took hold of her hand and called to her, "My child, stand up!" ⁵⁵Her spirit came back into her, and she stood up at once. Then Jesus ordered that she be given something to eat. ⁵⁶The girl's parents were amazed, but Jesus told them not to tell anyone what had happened.

Jesus Sends Out the Apostles

9 Jesus called the twelve apostles *d* together and gave them power and authority over all demons *d* and the ability to heal sicknesses. ²He sent the apostles out to tell about God's kingdom and to heal the sick. ³He said to them, "Take nothing for your trip, neither a walking stick, bag, bread, money or extra clothes. ⁴When you enter a house, stay there until it is time to leave. ⁵If people do not welcome you, shake the dust off your feet *n* as you leave the town, as a warning to them."

⁶So the apostles went out and travelled through all the towns, preaching the Good News *d* and healing people everywhere.

Herod is Confused About Jesus

⁷Herod, the governor, heard about all the things that were happening and was confused, because some people said, "John the Baptist *d* has risen from the dead." ⁸Others said, "Elijah has come to us." And still others said, "One of the prophets *d* who lived long ago has risen from the dead." ⁹Herod said, "I cut off John's head, so who is this man I hear such things about?" And Herod kept trying to see Jesus.

More than 5,000 Fed

¹⁰When the apostles *d* returned, they told Jesus everything they had done. Then Jesus took them with him to a town called Bethsaida where they could be alone together. ¹¹But the people learned where Jesus went and followed him. He welcomed them and talked with them about God's kingdom and healed those who needed to be healed.

¹²Late in the afternoon, the twelve apostles came to Jesus and said, "Send the people away. They need to go to the towns and countryside around here and find places to sleep and something to eat, because no one lives in this place."

¹³But Jesus said to them, "You give them something to eat."

They said, "We have only five loaves of bread and two fish, unless we go and buy food for all these people." ¹⁴(There were about 5,000 men there.)

Jesus said to his followers, "Tell the people to sit in groups of about 50 people."

¹⁵So the followers did this, and all the people sat down. ¹⁶Then Jesus took the five loaves of bread and two fish, and, looking up to heaven, he thanked God for the food. Then he divided the food and gave it to the followers to give to the people. ¹⁷They all ate and were satisfied, and what was left over was gathered up, filling twelve baskets.

Jesus is the Christ

¹⁸Once when Jesus was praying alone, his followers were with him, and he asked them, "Who do the people say I am?"

¹⁹They answered, "Some say you are John the Baptist. *d* Others say you are Elijah. *n* And others say you are one of the prophets *d* from long ago who has come back to life."

²⁰Then Jesus asked, "But who do you say I am?"

Peter answered, "You are the Christ *d* from God."

²¹Jesus warned them not to tell anyone, saying, ²²"The Son of Man *d* must suffer many things. He will be rejected by the Jewish elders, the leading priests, and the teachers of the law. He will be killed and after three days will be raised from the dead."

²³Jesus said to all of them, "If people want to follow me, they must give up the things they want.

---

shake . . . feet   A warning. It showed that they had rejected these people.
Elijah   A man who spoke for God and who lived hundreds of years before Christ. See 1 Kings 17.

They must be willing to give up their lives daily to follow me. 24Those who want to save their lives will give up their lives. But those who give up their lives for me will have true life. 25It is worth nothing for them to have the whole world if they themselves are destroyed or lost. 26If people are ashamed of me and my teaching, then the Son of Man*d* will be ashamed of them when he comes in his glory and with the glory of the Father and the holy angels. 27I tell you the truth, some people standing here will see the kingdom of God before they die."

Jesus Talks with Moses and Elijah

28About eight days after Jesus said these things, he took Peter, John and James and went up on a mountain to pray. 29While Jesus was praying, the appearance of his face changed, and his clothes became shining white. 30Then two men, Moses and Elijah,*n* were talking with Jesus. 31They appeared in heavenly glory, talking about his intended departure which he would soon bring about in Jerusalem. 32Peter and the others were very sleepy, but when they awoke fully, they saw the glory of Jesus and the two men standing with him. 33When Moses and Elijah were about to leave, Peter said to Jesus, "Master, it is good that we are here. Let us make three tents—one for you, one for Moses and one for Elijah." (Peter did not know what he was talking about.)

34While he was saying these things, a cloud came and covered them, and they became afraid as the cloud covered them. 35A voice came from the cloud, saying, "This is my Son, whom I have chosen. Listen to him!" 36When the voice finished speaking, only Jesus was there. Peter, John and James said nothing and told no one at that time what they had seen.

Jesus Heals a Sick Boy

37The next day, when they came down from the mountain, a large crowd met Jesus. 38A man in the crowd shouted to him, "Teacher, please come and look at my son, because he is my only child. 39An evil spirit seizes my son, and suddenly he screams. It causes him to lose control of himself and foam at the mouth. The evil spirit keeps on hurting him and almost never leaves him. 40I begged your followers to force the evil spirit out, but they could not do it."

41Jesus answered, "You people have no faith, and your lives are all wrong. How long must I stay with you and put up with you? Bring your son here."

42While the boy was coming, the demon*d* threw him on the ground and made him lose control of himself. But Jesus gave a strong command to the evil spirit and healed the boy and gave him back to his father. 43All the people were amazed at the great power of God.

Jesus Talks About His Death

While everyone was wondering about all that Jesus did, he said to his followers, 44"Don't forget what I tell you now: the Son of Man*d* will be handed over to people." 45But the followers did not understand what this meant; the meaning was hidden from them so they could not understand. But they were afraid to ask Jesus about it.

Who is the Greatest?

46Jesus' followers began to have an argument about which one of them was the greatest. 47Jesus knew what they were thinking, so he took a little child and stood the child beside him. 48Then Jesus said, "Whoever accepts this little child in my name accepts me. And whoever accepts me accepts the One who sent me, because whoever is least among you all is really the greatest."

Anyone Not Against Us is For Us

49John answered, "Master, we saw someone using your name to force demons*d* out of people. We told him to stop, because he does not belong to our group."

50But Jesus said to him, "Don't stop him, because whoever is not against you is for you."

A Town Rejects Jesus

51When the time was coming near for Jesus to depart, he was determined to go to Jerusalem. 52He sent some men ahead of him, who went into a town in Samaria to make everything ready for him. 53But the people there would not welcome him, because he was set on going to Jerusalem. 54When James and John, followers of Jesus, saw this, they said, "Lord, do you want us to call fire down from heaven and destroy those people?"*n* 55But Jesus turned and scolded them. 56Then*n* they went to another town.

Following Jesus

57As they were going along the road, someone said to Jesus, "I will follow you anywhere you go."

Moses and Elijah Two of the most important Jewish leaders in the past. Moses had given them the law, and Elijah was an important prophet.
Verse 54 Here, some Greek copies add: ". . . as Elijah did."
Verses 55–56 Some copies read: "But Jesus turned and scolded them. And Jesus said, 'You don't know what kind of spirit you belong to. 56The Son of Man did not come to destroy the souls of people but to save them.' Then"

58Jesus said to them, "The foxes have holes to live in, and the birds have nests, but the Son of Man[d] has no place to rest his head."

Sidelight

The disciples' reaction to Jesus' not being welcomed in a Samaritan town (Luke 9:51–56) would have been common in Jesus' day, given the hatred between the Jews and Samaritans at that time. A hundred years earlier, Jews had destroyed a Samaritan temple. Then, during the night, Samaritans had strewn human bones on the steps of the Jewish Temple in Jerusalem. To see Jesus' attitude towards the Samaritans, read John 4:5–10 (p.1101).

72 Many Greek copies read 70.

59Jesus said to another man, "Follow me!" But he said, "Lord, first let me go and bury my father."

60But Jesus said to him, "Let the people who are dead bury their own dead. You must go and tell about the kingdom of God."

61Another man said, "I will follow you, Lord, but first let me go and say goodbye to my family."

62Jesus said, "Anyone who begins to plough a field but keeps looking back is of no use in the kingdom of God."

Jesus Sends Out the Seventy-two

10 After this, the Lord chose 72[n] others and sent them out in pairs ahead of him into every town and place where he planned

DECISION MAKING

Moving On

The family looked at each other. Murray's mum and sisters were smiling but he wasn't sure.

"Can we sleep on it?" Murray asked.

His dad smiled. "Of course," he said. "This is going to affect us all so I want the decision to be a family one and not just mine."

His father had been offered a chance of a new business, and that meant a bigger house and nicer cars, as well as his dad finally getting the job that he'd worked so hard for. The problem was that if his dad accepted the promotion, they'd have to live in Devon.

Murray sighed. All his friends were in Surrey.

On the other hand, his father would have the job of his dreams at last. The traffic was quieter and the sea was close by. It seemed that for every good point for staying in Surrey, there was a good point for moving to Devon.

Because of that, Murray thought that he had made up his mind, but he wanted to sleep on it before declaring his decision.

"Well?" his father asked the next morning. "I've already asked your mother and sisters and they've told me what they want. Now it all depends on you."

He took a deep breath. "I'd like to move to Devon!" he said nervously.

In **Luke 9:51–62** Jesus points out that important decisions can involve letting go of the past in order to get to a better place.

* How was Murray unlike those who asked about following Jesus?
* Have you decided to follow Jesus wherever he leads you? If not, why not?

Consider . . .

* the next time you have to make a decision, writing a list of points "for" and "against". Then take advice and pray about the decision before committing yourself.
* having a discussion with your youth group about difficult decisions you've each had to face.

For more, see . . .

* Joshua 24:14–15 (p.222)
* Acts 5:1–11 (p.1145)
* Proverbs 8 (p.595)

to go. ²He said to them, "There are a great many people to harvest, but there are only a few workers. So pray to God, who owns the harvest, that he will send more workers to help gather his harvest. ³Go now, but listen! I am sending you out like sheep among wolves. ⁴Don't carry a purse, a bag or sandals, and don't waste time talking with people on the road. ⁵Before you go into a house, say, 'Peace be with this house.' ⁶If peaceful people live there, your blessing of peace will stay with them, but if not, then your blessing will come back to you. ⁷Stay in the peaceful house, eating and drinking what the people there give you. A worker should be given his pay. Don't move from house to house. ⁸If you go into a town and the people welcome you, eat what they give you. ⁹Heal the sick who live there, and tell them, 'The kingdom of God is near you.' ¹⁰But if you go into a town, and the people don't welcome you, then go into the streets and say, ¹¹'Even the dust from your town that sticks to our feet we wipe off against you. *n* But remember that the kingdom of God is near.' ¹²I tell you, on the Judgement Day it will be better for the people of Sodom *d* than for the people of that town.

Jesus Warns Unbelievers

¹³"How terrible for you, Korazin! How terrible for you, Bethsaida! If the miracles *d* I did in you had happened in Tyre and Sidon, *n* those people would have changed their lives long ago. They would have worn rough cloth and put ashes on

dust . . . you   A warning. It showed that they had rejected these people.
Tyre and Sidon   Towns where wicked people lived.

SHARING FAITH

Inspiring Graffiti

In 1956, while working as a church caretaker, Arthur Stace, a former alcoholic and homeless man, heard a sermon preached at a church in Sydney, Australia, by a man called John Ridley. The preacher passionately expressed how he wished that the word "Eternity" could be written all over the streets and buildings of Sydney to encourage people to choose to live life in all its fullness, now and forever. Arthur was hugely impacted by the simple message, and after the service had finished took some chalk and wrote the word "Eternity" in neat, curved writing on the pavement outside.

For the next forty years, Arthur continued to write that same one-word sermon in chalk on pavements and walls all over Sydney. The word was often in the news, as various other people took the credit for the iconic graffiti. But Arthur didn't write the word for fame or fortune. He wrote it because his life was changed by the gift of eternity he received when he first accepted Christ. He couldn't preach amazing sermons but he could communicate this one life-changing word "Eternity".

In the year 2000, as the world celebrated the new millennium, fireworks exploded in amazing colours and patterns all over the Sydney Harbour Bridge. But the grand finale was the lighting of the word Eternity, written, this time in fire, in the same distinctive style that Arthur had used for decades. A life transformed by a simple message, that had been shared in a simple way to millions of people, was now broadcast to the entire world at one of the most significant celebrations in our modern history.

Read **Luke 10:1–12**.

* What is the one word that describes your life and all you live for?
* What can you do to share and show that word in the life you live?

Consider . . .

* asking God to help you find ways to share your faith everyday in the life that you live for him.
* making your own sign, poster or even T-shirt with the one word you feel God wants you to share with others.

For more, see . . .

* Mark 16:14–16 (p.1032)
* Acts 8:11–13 (p.1151)

themselves to show they had changed. [14]But on the Judgement Day it will be better for Tyre and Sidon than for you. [15]And you, Capernaum,[n] will you be lifted up to heaven? No! You will be thrown down to the depths!

[16]"Whoever listens to you listens to me, and whoever refuses to accept you refuses to accept me. And whoever refuses to accept me refuses to accept the One who sent me."

Satan Falls

[17]When the 72[n] came back, they were very happy and said, "Lord, even the demons[d] obeyed us when we used your name!"

[18]Jesus said, "I saw Satan fall like lightning from heaven. [19]Listen, I have given you power to walk on snakes and scorpions, power that is greater than the enemy has. So nothing will hurt you. [20]But you should not be happy because the spirits obey you but because your names are written in heaven."

Jesus Prays to the Father

[21]Then Jesus rejoiced in the Holy Spirit[d] and said, "I praise you, Father, Lord of heaven and earth, because you have hidden these things from the people who are wise and clever. But you have shown them to those who are like little children. Yes, Father, this is what you really wanted.

[22]"My Father has given me all things. No one knows who the Son is, except the Father. And no one knows who the Father is, except the Son and those whom the Son chooses to tell."

[23]Then Jesus turned to his followers and said privately, "You are blessed to see what you now see. [24]I tell you, many prophets[d] and kings wanted to see what you now see, but they did not, and they wanted to hear what you now hear, but they did not."

The Good Samaritan

[25]Then an expert on the law stood up to test Jesus, saying, "Teacher, what must I do to get eternal life?"

[26]Jesus said, "What is written in the law? What do you read there?"

[27]The man answered, "Love the Lord your God with all your heart, all your soul, all your strength and all your mind."[n] Also, "Love your neighbour as you love yourself."[n]

[28]Jesus said to him, "Your answer is right. Do this and you will live."

[29]But the man, wanting to show the importance of his question, said to Jesus, "And who is my neighbour?"

[30]Jesus answered, "As a man was going down from Jerusalem to Jericho, some robbers attacked him. They tore off his clothes, beat him, and left him lying there, almost dead. [31]It happened that a Jewish priest was going down that road. When he saw the man, he walked by on the other side.

> ### Sidelight
> The Jerusalem-to-Jericho road where the man was robbed in Jesus' story (Luke 10:30) was notoriously dangerous. With a 1,097 metre drop in only 27 kilometres, this narrow, steep, twisting path – nicknamed "The Bloody Way" – was the notorious hangout of robbers.

[32]Next, a Levite[n] came there, and after he went over and looked at the man, he walked by on the other side of the road. [33]Then a Samaritan[n] travelling down the road came to where the hurt man was. When he saw the man, he felt very sorry for him. [34]The Samaritan went to him, poured olive oil and wine[n] on his wounds and bandaged them. Then he put the hurt man on his own donkey and took him to an inn where he cared for him. [35]The next day, the Samaritan brought out two silver coins,[n] gave them to the innkeeper, and said, 'Take care of this man. If you spend more money on him, I will pay it back to you when I come again.'"

[36]Then Jesus said, "Which one of these three men do you think was a neighbour to the man who was attacked by the robbers?"

[37]The expert on the law answered, "The one who showed him mercy."

Jesus said to him, "Then go and do what he did."

Mary and Martha

[38]While Jesus and his followers were travelling, Jesus went into a town. A woman named Martha

---

Korazin . . . Bethsaida . . . Capernaum Towns by Lake Galilee where Jesus preached to the people.
72 Many Greek copies read 70.
"Love . . . mind." Quotation from Deuteronomy 6:5.
"Love . . . yourself." Quotation from Leviticus 19:18.
Levite Levites were members of the tribe of Levi who helped the Jewish priests with their work in the Temple. Read 1 Chronicles 23:24–32.
Samaritan Samaritans were people from Samaria. These people were part Jewish, but the Jews did not accept them as true Jews. Samaritans and Jews disliked each other.
olive oil and wine Oil and wine were used like medicine to soften and clean wounds.
coins Roman denarii. A silver coin was the average pay for one day's work.

let Jesus stay at her house. ³⁹Martha had a sister named Mary, who was sitting at Jesus' feet and listening to him teach. ⁴⁰But Martha was busy with all the work to be done. She went in and said, "Lord, don't you care that my sister has left me alone to do all the work? Tell her to help me."

⁴¹But the Lord answered her, "Martha, Martha, you are worried and upset about many things. ⁴²Only one thing is important. Mary has chosen the better thing, and it will never be taken away from her."

Jesus Teaches About Prayer

11 Once Jesus was praying in a certain place. When he finished, one of his followers said to him, "Lord, teach us to pray as John taught his followers."

²Jesus said to them, "When you pray, say:

'Father, may your name always be kept holy.
  May your kingdom come.
³Give us the food we need for each day.
⁴Forgive us for our sins,
    because we forgive everyone who has done
        wrong to us.
And do not cause us to be tempted.'"

Continue to Ask

⁵Then Jesus said to them, "Suppose one of you went to your friend's house at midnight and said to him, 'Friend, loan me three loaves of bread. ⁶A friend of mine has come into town to visit me, but I have nothing for him to eat.' ⁷Your friend inside the house answers, 'Don't bother me! The door is already locked, and my children and I are in bed. I cannot get up and give you anything.' ⁸I tell you, if friendship is not enough to make him

---

SERVICE

I Cannot Walk Away

In Rwanda in 1994, a massive civil war broke out between two different people groups in the country – it was between the Tutsis and the Hutus.

A Catholic priest called Vjeko Curic watched the horror unfold before his eyes; the situation was growing worse in the village where he lived. A Hutu mob was rising up and many Tutsi people were scared for their lives. He knew he had to do something to save his friends before it was too late. He began to shelter Tutsi families and smuggled others out of the country to safety. He helped provide meals, clothing and did anything he could to display God's love for them in this time of war and horror.

As the situation grew more and more dangerous, UN peacekeepers that were helping Father Curic began to leave the country. The Vatican also advised him to leave with them for his own safety, but Curic would not leave people in trouble, who he knew he could help.

After several years, and a million deaths in Rwanda, the war ended. The country was shattered, but still Father Curic did not walk away. He helped people rebuild their lives, providing housing and medical supplies. He persevered in helping to bring peace back to the country, bringing Hutu and Tutsi people together.

Father Curic did all this in a country that he was not born in, with a people that spoke a different language, had a different skin colour and often saw him as an outsider.

Read **Luke 10:25–37**.

* How can you be like Father Curic where you live? Would you have walked away if you were in his position?
* What qualities do you see in Father Curic and the Good Samaritan? Do you have these?

Consider . . .

* helping someone where you live in a practical way, to show God's love to them, e.g. washing their car, tidying their garden.
* praying for people you know who work around the world helping people who are modern-day Good Samaritans.

For more, see . . .

* Matthew 25:31–46 (p.987)
* 1 John 3:10–23 (p.1374)
* James 2:14–18 (p.1350)

get up to give you the bread, your boldness will make him get up and give you whatever you need. ⁹So I tell you, ask, and God will give to you. Search, and you will find. Knock, and the door will open for you. ¹⁰Yes, everyone who asks will receive. The one who searches will find. And everyone who knocks will have the door opened. ¹¹If your children ask for a fish, which of you would give them a snake instead? ¹²Or, if your children ask for an egg, would you give them a scorpion? ¹³Even though you are bad, you know how to give good things to your children. How much more will your heavenly Father give the Holy Spirit*d* to those who ask him!"

Jesus' Power is from God

¹⁴Once Jesus was sending out a demon *d* that could not talk. When the demon came out, the man who had been unable to speak, then spoke. The people were amazed. ¹⁵But some of them said, "Jesus uses the power of Beelzebul, *d* the ruler of demons, to force demons out of people."

¹⁶Other people, wanting to test Jesus, asked him to give them a sign from heaven. ¹⁷But knowing their thoughts, he said to them, "Every kingdom that is divided against itself will be destroyed. And a family that is divided against itself will not continue. ¹⁸So if Satan is divided against himself, his kingdom will not continue. You say

WORRYING

Fear in Disguise

Did you know that over 133,000 people every year are injured by doors? Apparently, over 400,000 people in the United States suffer injuries every year while relaxing or sleeping in bed!

Hearing statistics like that, does it make you worry about walking through a door or sleeping in bed? Probably not!

So why do we worry about some things and not about others?

Worrying is usually fear in disguise. Imagine someone who was scared about injuring themselves on a door – you can understand them worrying about whether it would happen or not. If you were scared that you were going to fall out of bed and hurt yourself, you'd probably worry about it.

Worrying is a state of mind and we can often find ourselves battling in our own minds, trying desperately not to worry – and yet we can't help it! But how often does what we're worrying about actually happen? One survey revealed that 92 per cent of our worries waste our time and energy and cause stress needlessly. The survey said that 40 per cent of our worries are over things that never happen and 30 per cent are over things in the past that cannot be changed or altered.

By using up time and energy worrying, we're unable to do other things. So next time you're feeling worried, stop, think and pray about how you could be using that time and energy positively.

And just in case you happen to be afraid of spiders or flying in planes – remember the following: by the law of averages, you are more likely to be killed by a flying champagne cork than by a poisonous spider and you have a higher chance of being killed by a donkey than dying in a plane crash.

Read **Luke 10:38–42**. When Jesus meets Mary and Martha, Martha is worried and it stops her from listening to Jesus.

* What do you think Martha might have been worrying about? What was she scared of?
* How does Jesus react to Martha's worrying?

Consider . . .

* whether there is anything you find yourself worrying about regularly. In the light of the passage, what is this worrying preventing you from doing?
* writing the words of Philippians 4:6–7 out on a piece of paper and putting it in a place where you can read it whenever you feel worried.

For more, see . . .

* Psalm 131 (p.577)
* 1 Peter 5:6–7 (p.1362)

* Philippians 4:6–7 (p.1285)

that I use the power of Beelzebul to force out demons. ¹⁹But if I use the power of Beelzebul to force out demons, what power do your people use to force demons out? So they will be your judges. ²⁰But if I use the power of God to force out demons, then the kingdom of God has come to you.

²¹"When a strong person with many weapons guards his own house, his possessions are safe. ²²But when someone stronger comes and defeats him, the stronger one will take away the weapons the first man trusted and will give away the possessions.

²³"Anyone who is not with me is against me, and anyone who does not work with me is working against me.

The Empty Person

²⁴"When an evil spirit comes out of a person, it travels through dry places, looking for a place to rest. But when it finds no place, it says, 'I will go back to the house I left.' ²⁵And when it comes back, it finds that house swept clean and made neat. ²⁶Then the evil spirit goes out and brings seven other spirits more evil than it is, and they go in and live there. So the person has even more trouble than before."

People Who Are Truly Happy

²⁷As Jesus was saying these things, a woman in the crowd called out to Jesus, "Happy is the mother who gave birth to you and nursed you."

²⁸But Jesus said, "No, happy are those who hear the teaching of God and obey it."

The People Want a Miracle

²⁹As the crowd grew larger, Jesus said, "The people who live today are evil. They want to see a miracle *d* for a sign, but no sign will be given them, except the sign of Jonah. *n* ³⁰As Jonah was a sign for those people who lived in Nineveh, the Son of Man *d* will be a sign for the people of this

---

sign of Jonah   Jonah's three days in the fish are like Jesus' three days in the tomb. See Matthew 12:40.

PRAYER

Countdown to Victory

"Oh, I'll never get it right. There's just no cure. It's hopeless."

That's probably what a lot of scientists were thinking in the first part of the twentieth century, when a disease called polio crippled and killed millions of people. Hundreds of researchers looked frantically for a cure. But it seemed like an impossible task. Then, in 1954, Dr Jonas Salk announced that after 200 attempts he had developed a vaccine. This terrible disease disappeared virtually overnight.

Later, a reporter asked Dr Salk how it felt to have had 200 failures and only one success. Salk replied that he had never experienced 200 failures. He had learned 200 lessons. And those lessons enabled him to create a usable vaccine. Rather than viewing each unsuccessful attempt as a tragedy, Dr Salk chose to see it as an opportunity to learn.

Dr Salk saw a need and didn't stop until the need was met. Similarly, persistent prayer is what Jesus recommends as one of the best ways to find answers in life. Read the story that Jesus told in **Luke 11:1–13**.

- How is Dr Salk like the man who needed bread in Jesus' story?
- How should you pray about problems you really care about?

Consider . . .

- writing about seven concerns that are important to you, and praying about a different concern each day this week.
- making a pact with a friend to become your "prayer partner" for the next month. Meet at least once a week to share requests and pray for each other.

For more, see . . .

- Psalm 130 (p.577)
- Luke 18:1–8 (p.1078)

- Matthew 6:1–15 (p.947)

time. [31]On the Judgement Day the Queen of the South[n] will stand up with the people who live now. She will show they are guilty, because she came from far away to listen to Solomon's wise teaching. And I tell you that someone greater than Solomon is here. [32]On the Judgement Day the people of Nineveh will stand up with the people who live now, and they will show that you are guilty. When Jonah preached to them, they were sorry and changed their lives. And I tell you that someone greater than Jonah is here.

Be a Light for the World

[33]"No one lights a lamp and puts it in a secret place or under a bowl, but on a lampstand so the people who come in can see. [34]Your eye is a light for the body. When your eyes are good, your whole body will be full of light. But when your eyes are evil, your whole body will be full of darkness. [35]So be careful not to let the light in you become darkness. [36]If your whole body is full of light, and none of it is dark, then you will shine bright, as when a lamp shines on you."

Jesus Accuses the Pharisees

[37]After Jesus had finished speaking, a Pharisee[d] asked Jesus to eat with him. So Jesus went in and sat at the table. [38]But the Pharisee was surprised when he saw that Jesus did not wash his hands[n] before the meal. [39]The Lord said to him, "You Pharisees clean the outside of the cup and the dish, but inside you are full of greed and evil. [40]You foolish people! The same one who made what is outside also made what is inside. [41]So give what is in your dishes to the poor, and then you will be fully clean. [42]How terrible for you Pharisees! You give God one-tenth of even your mint, your rue[d] and every other plant in your garden. But you fail to be fair to others and to love God. These are the things you should do while continuing to do those other things. [43]How terrible for you Pharisees, because you love to have the most important seats in the synagogues,[d] and you love to be greeted with respect in the market places. [44]How terrible for you, because you are like hidden graves, which people walk on without knowing."

Jesus Talks to Experts on the Law

[45]One of the experts on the law said to Jesus, "Teacher, when you say these things, you are insulting us, too."

[46]Jesus answered, "How terrible for you, you experts on the law! You make strict rules that are very hard for people to obey, but you yourselves don't even try to follow those rules. [47]How terrible for you, because you build tombs for the prophets[d] whom your ancestors killed! [48]And now you show that you approve of what your ancestors did. They killed the prophets, and you build tombs for them! [49]This is why in his wisdom God said, 'I will send prophets and apostles[d] to them. They will kill some, and they will treat others cruelly.' [50]So you who live now will be punished for the deaths of all the prophets who were killed since the beginning of the world— [51]from the killing of Abel to the killing of Zechariah,[n] who died between the altar and the Temple.[d] Yes, I tell you that you who are alive now will be punished for them all.

[52]"How terrible for you, you experts on the law. You have taken away the key to learning about God. You yourselves would not learn, and you stopped others from learning, too."

[53]When Jesus left, the teachers of the law and the Pharisees[d] began to give him trouble, asking him questions about many things and [54]trying to catch him saying something wrong.

Don't Be Like the Pharisees

12 So many thousands of people had gathered that they were stepping on each other. Jesus spoke first to his followers, saying, "Beware of the yeast of the Pharisees,[d] because they are hypocrites.[d] [2]Everything that is hidden will be shown, and everything that is secret will be made known. [3]What you have said in the dark will be heard in the light, and what you have whispered in an inner room will be shouted from the housetops.

[4]"I tell you, my friends, don't be afraid of people who can kill the body but after that can do nothing more to hurt you. [5]I will show you the one to fear. Fear the one who has the power to kill you and also to throw you into hell. Yes, this is the one you should fear.

[6]"Five sparrows are sold for only two pennies, and God does not forget any of them. [7]But God even knows how many hairs you have on your head. Don't be afraid. You are worth much more than many sparrows.

Don't Be Ashamed of Jesus

[8]"I tell you, all those who stand before others and say they believe in me, I, the Son of Man,[d]

Queen of the South   The Queen of Sheba. She travelled 1,600 kilometres to learn God's wisdom from Solomon. Read 1 Kings 10:1–3.
wash his hands   This was a Jewish religious custom that the Pharisees thought was very important.
Abel . . . Zechariah   In the Hebrew Old Testament, the first and last men to be murdered.

will say before the angels of God that they belong to me. [9]But all who stand before others and say they do not believe in me, I will say before the angels of God that they do not belong to me.

[10]"Anyone who speaks against the Son of Man [d] can be forgiven, but anyone who speaks against the Holy Spirit [d] will not be forgiven.

[11]"When you are brought into the synagogues[d] before the leaders and other powerful people, don't worry about how to defend yourselves or what to say. [12]At that time the Holy Spirit will teach you what you must say."

Jesus Warns Against Selfishness

[13]Someone in the crowd said to Jesus, "Teacher, tell my brother to divide with me the property our father left us."

[14]But Jesus said to him, "Who said I should judge or decide between you?" [15]Then Jesus said to them, "Be careful and guard against all kinds of greed. Life is not measured by how much one owns."

[16]Then Jesus told this story: "There was a rich man who had some land, which grew a good crop. [17]He thought to himself, 'What will I do?

ABORTION

What's it Worth?

The phone sounded urgent, even as it rang. Siobhan ran to answer it. She was used to urgent phone calls, as a minister's wife she got quite a few.

"Hello?"

There was silence and then a female voice started to whisper down the phone.

"You probably won't remember me. My name's Natalie, we met last year."

"Natalie? Oh yes, you were the girl I spoke to after the meeting at St Edmunds . . . " Siobhan was puzzled by the whispering voice, but tried not to let it bother her.

"I need to talk to you, but my dad's in the other room," Natalie carried on. "I can't let him hear me."

By now it was obvious that the teenager was in considerable distress.

"What's happened? Just tell me," said the minister's wife.

"I'm pregnant and my dad's found out," she replied simply.

"Oh no." Siobhan's mind was racing. This girl was only fifteen.

"He came home tonight and told me that he has made an appointment for me to have an abortion. I have to go with him to hospital tomorrow." Natalie sounded terrified.

"Oh Natalie, my dear . . . " began Siobhan.

"The problem is," the teenage girl carried on, "the day after the abortion I have my exams! Will I be alright? Will I be able to go to school? You see, I must pass my exams, I've been working so hard."

Siobhan could hear Natalie starting to cry at the other end.

"But Natalie, this is really no time to worry about exams . . . " Siobhan started. "You are about to lose a baby!"

"I don't care about the baby," wailed Natalie. "I want to pass my exams!"

Luke 12:6–7 talks about values.

- What is the difference between Natalie's values and those of the passage?
- Take a moment to think about your own values. Is life the most precious thing to you?

Consider . . .

- making a list of the five most important things in your life. Now put them in the order you feel God would like them to be.
- supporting an organisation like "Care For The Family", that seeks to help young single parents.

For more, see . . .

- Psalm 121 (p.575)
- Luke 9:25 (p.1055)

- Matthew 6:25–27 (p.948)

I have no place to keep all my crops.' ¹⁸Then he said, 'This is what I will do: I will tear down my barns and build bigger ones, and there I will store all my grain and other goods. ¹⁹Then I can say to myself, "I have enough good things stored to last for many years. Rest, eat, drink and enjoy life!" '

²⁰"But God said to him, 'Foolish man! Tonight your life will be taken from you. So who will get those things you have prepared for yourself?'

²¹"This is how it will be for those who store up things for themselves and are not rich towards God."

> **Sidelight** The rich man in Jesus' story (Luke 12:16–21) would probably have been a millionaire today. Most farmers stored their food supply in clay jars of various sizes. To have a barn or grain silo would indicate extreme wealth. Archaeologists have discovered some underground grain silos that are over seven metres wide and more than six metres deep!

Don't Worry

²²Jesus said to his followers, "So I tell you, don't worry about the food you need to live, or about the clothes you need in order for your body. ²³Life is more than food, and the body is more than clothes. ²⁴Look at the birds. They don't plant or harvest, they don't have storerooms or barns, but God feeds them. And you are worth much more than birds. ²⁵You cannot add any time to your life by worrying about it. ²⁶If you cannot do even the little things, then why worry about the big things? ²⁷Consider how the lilies grow; they don't work or make clothes for themselves. But I tell you that even Solomon with his riches was not dressed as beautifully as one of these flowers. ²⁸God clothes the grass in the field, which is alive today but tomorrow is thrown into the fire. So how much more will God clothe you? Don't have so little faith! ²⁹Don't always think about what you will eat or what you will drink, and don't keep worrying. ³⁰All the people in the world are trying to get these things, and your Father knows you need them. ³¹But seek God's kingdom, and all the other things you need will be given to you.

Don't Trust in Money

³²"Don't fear, little flock, because your Father wants to give you the kingdom. ³³Sell your possessions and give to the poor. Get for yourselves

purses that will not wear out, the treasure in heaven that never runs out, where thieves can't steal and moths can't destroy. ³⁴Your heart will be where your treasure is.

Always Be Ready

³⁵"Be dressed, ready for service, and have your lamps shining. ³⁶Be like servants who are waiting for their master to come home from a wedding party. When he comes and knocks, the servants immediately open the door for him. ³⁷They will be blessed when their master comes home, because he sees that they are watching for him. I tell you the truth, the master will dress himself to serve and tell the servants to sit at the table, and he will serve them. ³⁸Those servants will be happy when he comes in and finds them still waiting, even if it is midnight or later.

³⁹"Remember this: if the owner of the house knew what time a thief was coming, he would not allow the thief to enter his house. ⁴⁰So you also must be ready, because the Son of Man ᵈ will come at a time when you don't expect him!"

Who is the Trusted Servant?

⁴¹Peter said, "Lord, did you tell this story to us or to all people?"

⁴²The Lord said, "Who is the wise and trusted servant that the master trusts to give the other servants their food at the right time? ⁴³When the master comes and finds the servant doing his work, the servant will be blessed. ⁴⁴I tell you the truth, the master will choose that servant to take care of everything he owns. ⁴⁵But suppose the servant thinks to himself, 'My master will not come back soon,' and he begins to beat the other servants, men and women, and to eat and drink and get drunk. ⁴⁶The master will come when that servant is not ready and is not expecting him. Then the master will cut him in pieces and send him away to be with the others who don't obey.

⁴⁷"The servant who knows what his master wants but is not ready, or who does not do what the master wants, will be beaten with many blows! ⁴⁸But the servant who does not know what his master wants and does things that should be punished will be beaten with few blows. From everyone who has been given much, much will be demanded. And from the one trusted with much, much more will be expected.

Jesus Causes Division

⁴⁹"I came to set fire to the world, and I wish it were already burning! ⁵⁰I have a baptism ⁿ to undergo and I feel very troubled until it is over. ⁵¹Do you think I came to give peace to the earth?

---

1 ... baptism Jesus was talking about the suffering he would soon go through.

No, I tell you, I came to divide it. [52]From now on, a family with five people will be divided, three against two, and two against three. [53]They will be divided: father against son and son against father, mother against daughter and daughter against mother, mother-in-law against daughter-in-law and daughter-in-law against mother-in-law."

Understanding the Times

[54]Then Jesus said to the people, "When you see clouds coming up in the west, you say, 'It's going to rain,' and it happens. [55]When you feel the wind begin to blow from the south, you say, 'It will be a hot day,' and it happens. [56]Hypocrites![d] You know how to understand the appearance of the earth and sky. Why don't you understand what is happening now?

Settle Your Problems

[57]"Why can't you decide for yourselves what is right? [58]If your enemy is taking you to court, try hard to settle it on the way. If you don't, your

---

MONEY

It's Only Money

By the time he was thirty, Millard Fuller had achieved the American Dream. He was worth more than $1 million and lived a lifestyle that showed it. He drove a fancy car, lived in a huge house, owned lots of land, and generally enjoyed the things his money could buy. He and his wife Linda had just about anything that a young couple could want, except . . .

Except what? Well, they weren't sure. All Millard and Linda did know was that they weren't happy.

"We just thought there must be something more to life," Millard explains.

On the advice of a friend, Millard and Linda turned to God. They spent time reading the Bible and praying with other Christians at Koinonia Farms.

What could they do? What should they do?

"By seeing other Christians' lifestyles," explains Linda, "we quickly saw there was much more to life than the success money can bring. We realised God had a purpose for us. And we were determined to find out what it was."

Finally, they received the answer to their prayers. They believed that God wanted them to start something new. Something big. They believed God wanted them to make a new start.

So they did. They sold off their businesses and their big house, and gave the money away. They sold their land, their boats, their horses, their cattle. In fact, they got rid of just about everything.

After this, they didn't go on tour to boast about how kind they were, or how many points they had earned with God. Instead, they continued to pray about what God was calling them towards. For more than five years, they worked at various mission stations, continuing to pray. Finally, at God's prompting, they formed "Habitat for Humanity", a worldwide group that seeks to eliminate all substandard housing. Because the Fullers were able to give everything away and listen to God, thousands of families go to bed each night in safe, secure homes.

One of the passages that helped the Fullers to make their decision was **Luke 12:32–40**. Read it and see if you can understand their actions.

* How did these verses influence the Fullers?
* What can you do to apply Jesus' words in this passage?

Consider . . .

* deciding to give a specific portion of your money to your church charity.
* keeping a list of all the money you spend in a week. Sit down with your list and see who really determines how you spend it. Then pray for the freedom to give everything to God.

For more, see . . .

* Isaiah 58:6–11 (p.701)
* 2 Corinthians 9:6–9 (p.1248)
* Matthew 6:19–21 (p.948)

enemy might take you to the judge, and the judge might turn you over to the officer, and the officer might throw you into jail. [59]I tell you, you will not get out of there until you have paid everything you owe."

Change Your Hearts

13 At that time some people were there who told Jesus that Pilate[n] had killed some people from Galilee while they were worshipping. He mixed their blood with the blood of the animals they were sacrificing to God. [2]Jesus answered, "Do you think this happened to them because they were more sinful than all others from Galilee? [3]No, I tell you. But unless you change your hearts and lives, you will be destroyed

as they were! [4]What about those eighteen people who died when the tower of Siloam fell on them? Do you think they were more sinful than all the others who live in Jerusalem? [5]No, I tell you. But unless you change your hearts and lives, you will all be destroyed too!"

The Useless Tree

[6]Jesus told this story: "A man had a fig tree planted in his vineyard. He came looking for some fruit on the tree, but he found none. [7]So the man said to his gardener, 'I have been looking for fruit on this tree for three years, but I never find any. Cut it down. Why should it waste the ground?' [8]But the servant answered, 'Master, let the tree have one more year to produce fruit.

Pilate   Pontius Pilate was the Roman governor of Judea from AD 26 to AD 36.

END TIMES

Both Eyes Open

When Jade started working at the shop, everyone noticed the difference. Things were tidied away and everywhere looked brighter.

"It's not your job to dust and tidy," Alan, her boss, said to her one day. Jade smiled. "I know that, but I'm not doing anything else at the moment, so why not?"

Alan shrugged and let her get on with it. During the next few months, the shop almost changed shape. Layouts were rearranged, and orders kept up to date. He even came back from a holiday to find the shelves painted!

Then one day a customer came into the shop determined to cause trouble. Jade did her best to be nice to her, but nothing she did was going to be good enough for this cantankerous old woman.

"Get me the manager!" she yelled. "I demand to see the manager!"

By now, Alan had heard the rumpus at the other end of the shop and came over to see what was wrong. The lady complained bitterly that the "shop girl" was incompetent and should be sacked.

Alan very smoothly said, "I'm very sorry about this, but I stand by my staff. Jade is probably the best girl we've ever had here and is in no way incompetent. Perhaps you would let me serve you instead?"

Jade breathed a sigh of relief as she realised that her service to her boss had paid off at an awkward moment.

Luke 12:42–46 speaks about serving your master whether he's there or not.

* What might have happened to Jade if she hadn't been so watchful?
* What are the rewards for this kind of service, according to this passage?

Consider . . .

* Helping to prepare and clear up the room – or helping with refreshments – at your youth group.
* Ways to keep your life clean and tidy, ready for Christ.

For more see . . .

* Amos 4:12 (p.872)
* 1 Thessalonians 5:1–6 (p.1300)

Let me dig up the earth around it and put on some manure. ⁹If the tree produces fruit next year, good. But if not, you can cut it down.' "

Jesus Heals on the Sabbath

¹⁰Jesus was teaching in one of the synagogues *d* on the Sabbath *d* day. ¹¹A woman was there who, for eighteen years, had an evil spirit in her that made her crippled. Her back was always bent; she could not stand up straight. ¹²When Jesus saw her, he called her over and said, "Woman, you are free from your sickness." ¹³Jesus put his hands on her, and immediately she was able to stand up straight and began praising God.

¹⁴The synagogue leader was angry because Jesus healed on the Sabbath day. He said to the people, "There are six days when one has to work. So come to be healed on one of those days, and not on the Sabbath day."

¹⁵The Lord answered, "You hypocrites! *d* Doesn't each of you untie your work animals and lead them to drink water every day—even on the Sabbath day? ¹⁶This woman that I healed, a daughter of Abraham, has been held by Satan for eighteen years. Surely it is not wrong for her to be freed from her sickness on a Sabbath day!" ¹⁷When Jesus said this, all of those who were criticising him were ashamed, but the entire crowd rejoiced at all the wonderful things Jesus was doing.

Stories of Mustard Seed and Yeast

¹⁸Then Jesus said, "What is God's kingdom like? What can I compare it with? ¹⁹It is like a mustard seed that a man plants in his garden.

SPIRITUAL GROWTH

Every Day Counts

Tim was a friend of mine, in an unusual way. We met by accident and had very little in common. We liked different foods, different sports, different girls, and we each had our own definition of a "good time". We did share two things, though: we had the same birthday and we loved the same God. Sometimes this was all we could agree on, but we usually enjoyed our time together.

When we were eighteen, Tim died suddenly of a heart attack. He said that he wasn't feeling well, and he had passed out by the time the ambulance arrived. He was dead hours later. Through my tears, I realised that I didn't have anyone to share my birthday with. And I wasn't so sure about the God that I loved. Why did this happen? Everybody knows that teenagers aren't supposed to die, surely?

A few days later, Tim's family and friends got together to mourn his death. As we sat around talking, somebody told a story about Tim that brought a smile to our faces. Before long, all of Tim's old jokes were flying, along with stories of how his short life had touched each of us. In that conversation, we saw that Tim had tried to live each day as though it were an important chance to serve God.

I think of my friend Tim often, because his life challenged me. I realised that I don't know what will happen. So I must work to make each day count.

When people asked Jesus about their friends who had died, he gave them a challenge to use their days well. Read about it in **Luke 13:1–9**.

* How is Tim's story like the stories in the passage?
* What can you do to prepare yourself to "bear fruit" and so avoid being like the useless tree in the passage?

Consider . . .

* imagining that you have only two weeks to live. Decide what your priorities would be, then do them.
* buying two small potted plants and taking one to a person who is sick, elderly or shut-in. Keep the other in your room as a reminder to pray for your special friend – and as a reminder to always try to bear fruit for God's kingdom.

For more, see . . .

* Psalm 90 (p.554)
* Galatians 6:7–10 (p.1265)

* Matthew 7:15–23 (p.950)

The seed grows and becomes a tree, and the wild birds build nests in its branches."

20Jesus said again, "What can I compare God's kingdom with? 21It is like yeast that a woman took and hid in a large bowl of flour until it made all the dough rise."

The Narrow Door

22Jesus was teaching in every town and village as he travelled towards Jerusalem. 23Someone said to Jesus, "Lord, will only a few people be saved?"

Jesus said, 24"Try hard to enter through the narrow door, because many people will try to enter there, but they will not be able. 25When the owner of the house gets up and closes the door, you can stand outside and knock on the door and say, 'Sir, open the door for us.' But he will answer, 'I don't know you or where you come from.' 26Then you will say, 'We ate and drank with you, and you taught in the streets of our town.' 27But he will say to you, 'I don't know you or where you come from. Go away from me, all you who do evil!' 28You will cry and grind your teeth with pain when you see Abraham, Isaac, Jacob and all the prophets d in God's kingdom, but you yourselves thrown outside.

ETERNAL LIFE

Lollipop Ladies

It didn't matter whether it was blue sky or raining cats and dogs, whenever Hayley went to pick up her little sister Lucy from school, the lollipop lady was always there, standing in the middle of the road in her day-glo coat, waving a crocodile of tiny children across the road. Most of the traffic was driven by local people – and most of them were afraid of Mary. She ruled with a rod of iron! When she held up that baton, the vehicles came to a standstill.

One day Hayley got out of school earlier than usual and stood by the railings waiting for the bell to go. Mary came along, cheerful as ever:

"Hello darling, how are you today? Looks as if it will rain later, maybe even snow if it gets any colder . . ." The woman was a constant chatterbox.

Hayley smiled and said, "I hope not, our church has got its annual Fun Run tomorrow, we could do without snow!"

The lollipop lady turned towards her in amusement and said, "Well, now, I didn't take you for one of those Holy Joes!"

It was Hayley's turn to look puzzled as she said, "I'm suprised you're not a church-goer yourself, you seem to spend an awful lot of time helping other people."

"Ah well, that's where we are different," Mary replied confidently. "I don't need to go to church. I do my best, give help where it's needed. Look at all these little ones coming out now, yes, I'm sure God will shake my hand when I get to heaven . . ." And with that she ushered the children into single file and saw them safely across the road.

Hayley's heart was heavy as she made her way home. How sad that someone who was so eager to please had dismissed the God who had given her the helpful heart.

Listen to Jesus' words of warning in **Luke 13:22–30**.

* What did Jesus say about people like Mary who thought they were "good enough" to gain entrance to heaven?
* How can you keep on the narrow road to eternal life and avoid the obstacles?

Consider . . .

* taking a few minutes to write down what you imagine heaven to be like.
* selecting five goals that will help you walk the "narrow road". Write them down in your diary. Six months from now, see if you have achieved your goals.

For more, see . . .

* Matthew 7:13–23 (p.950)
* Hebrews 6:7–12 (p.1335)
* Ephesians 2:8–9 (p.1270)

[29]People will come from the east, west, north and south and will sit down at the table in the kingdom of God. [30]There are those who have the lowest place in life now who will have the highest place in the future. And there are those who have the highest place now who will have the lowest place in the future."

Jesus will Die in Jerusalem

[31]At that time some Pharisees[d] came to Jesus and said, "Go away from here! Herod wants to kill you!"

[32]Jesus said to them, "Go and tell that fox Herod, 'Today and tomorrow I am forcing demons[d] out and healing people. Then, on the third day, I will reach my goal.' [33]Yet I must be on my way today and tomorrow and the next day. Surely it cannot be right for a prophet[d] to be killed anywhere except in Jerusalem.

[34]"Jerusalem, Jerusalem! You kill the prophets and stone to death those who are sent to you. Many times I wanted to gather your people as a hen gathers her chicks under her wings, but you would not let me. [35]Now your house is left completely empty. I tell you, you will not see me until that time when you will say, 'God bless the One who comes in the name of the Lord.' "[n]

Healing on the Sabbath

14 On a Sabbath[d] day, when Jesus went to eat at the home of a leading Pharisee,[d] the people were watching Jesus very closely. [2]And in front of him was a man with dropsy.[n] [3]Jesus said to the Pharisees and experts on the law, "Is it right or wrong to heal on the Sabbath day?" [4]But they would not answer his question. So Jesus took the man, healed him and sent him away. [5]Jesus said to the Pharisees and teachers of the law, "If your child or ox falls into a well on the Sabbath day, will you not pull him out quickly?" [6]And they could not answer him.

Don't Make Yourself Important

[7]When Jesus noticed that some of the guests were choosing the best places to sit, he told this story: [8]"When someone invites you to a wedding feast, don't take the most important seat, because someone more important than you may have been invited. [9]The host, who invited both of you, will come to you and say, 'Give this person your seat.' Then you will be embarrassed and will have to move to the last place. [10]So when you are invited, go and sit in a seat that is not important. When the host comes to you, he

may say, 'Friend, move up here to a more important place.' Then all the other guests will respect you. [11]All who make themselves great will be made humble, but those who make themselves humble will be made great."

You will Be Rewarded

[12]Then Jesus said to the man who had invited him, "When you give a lunch or a dinner, don't invite only your friends, your family, your other relatives and your rich neighbours. At another time they will invite you to eat with them, and you will be repaid. [13]Instead, when you give a feast, invite the poor, the crippled, the lame and the blind. [14]Then you will be blessed, because they have nothing and cannot pay you back. But you will be repaid when the good people rise from the dead."

A Story About a Big Banquet

[15]One of those at the table with Jesus heard these things and said to him, "Happy are the people who will share in the meal in God's kingdom."

[16]Jesus said to him, "A man gave a big banquet and invited many people. [17]When it was time to eat, the man sent his servant to tell the guests, 'Come. Everything is ready.'

[18]"But all the guests made excuses. The first one said, 'I have just bought a field, and I must go and look at it. Please excuse me.' [19]Another said, 'I have just bought five pairs of oxen; I must go and try them. Please excuse me.' [20]A third person said, 'I just got married; I can't come.' [21]So the servant returned and told his master what had happened. Then the master became angry and said, 'Go at once into the streets and alleys of the town, and bring in the poor, the crippled, the blind, and the lame.' [22]Later the servant said to him, 'Master, I did what you commanded, but we still have room.' [23]The master said to the servant, 'Go out to the roads and country lanes, and tell the people there to come so my house will be full. [24]I tell you, none of those whom I invited first will eat with me.' "

> **Sidelight** A party invitation in Jesus' day (Luke 14:15–24) included the day but never the hour. When the party was ready, slaves would go and get the guests. To reject an invitation you had earlier accepted was the ultimate insult – as this story illustrates!

'God ... Lord.' Quotation from Psalm 118:26.
dropsy A sickness that causes the body to swell larger and larger.

The Cost of Being Jesus' Follower

²⁵Large crowds were travelling with Jesus, and he turned and said to them, ²⁶"If anyone comes to me but loves his father, mother, wife, children, brothers or sisters—or even life—more than me, he cannot be my follower. ²⁷Whoever is not willing to carry the cross and follow me cannot be my follower. ²⁸If you want to build a tower, you first sit down and decide how much it will cost, to see if you have enough money to finish the job. ²⁹If you don't, you might lay the foundation, but you would not be able to finish. Then all who saw it would make fun of you, ³⁰saying, 'This person began to build but was not able to finish.'

³¹"If a king is going to fight another king, first he will sit down and plan. He will decide if he and his 10,000 soldiers can defeat the other king who has 20,000 soldiers. ³²If he can't, then while the other king is still far away, he will send some people to speak to him and ask for peace. ³³In the same way, you must give up everything you have to be my follower.

Don't Lose Your Influence

³⁴"Salt is good, but if it loses its salty taste, you cannot make it salty again. ³⁵It is no good for the soil or for manure; it is thrown away.

"You people who can hear me, listen."

A Lost Sheep, a Lost Coin

15 The tax collectors and sinners all came to listen to Jesus. ²But the Pharisees ᵈ and the teachers of the law began to complain: "Look, this man welcomes sinners and even eats with them."

³Then Jesus told them this story: ⁴"Suppose one of you has 100 sheep but loses one of them. Then he will leave the other 99 sheep in the open field and go out and look for the lost sheep until

---

FRIENDS

No Such Thing as a Free Lunch?

Janice spent every Saturday cooking lunch for fifty old ladies and gentlemen.

She planned meticulously the week before, trying to add up how many carrots she would need, and borrowing pots and pans. On the day itself, she would get up at 6 a.m. to peel vegetables, heat the oven and lay tables like a 5-star restaurant.

Janice gave every Saturday for at least twenty years of her life to these old people. They were old and ill, she got no payment for cooking so many roast dinners, and very little help. So why did she do it?

Because she realised that God loved her and loved all these people that she cooked for. They had no family nearby, had probably not spoken to anyone that week or had the energy to cook themselves a decent meal. She wanted to show them love and friendship, so that they might see something of God's love for them on earth. She trusted in God and humbly gave her time and talents, knowing that the people she provided for would never be able to return the favour.

She knew that Jesus had died for her in order for her to be his friend, and she'd done nothing to deserve this friendship. So Janice will continue to wash potatoes and watch old ladies dribble, because she knows that for once in their week they feel loved and cared for; they'll know that they have a friend.

Read **Luke 14:7–14**.

- What does this passage tell us about people that we might not like to spend time with?
- What does it tell us about how to be a good friend? What is our reward for this friendship?

Consider . . .

- what friendship with Jesus really means. What does/should he get in return from us?
- making friends with someone who won't be able to repay you for your friendship.

For more, see . . .

- Matthew 25:34–40 (p.988)
- James 2:1–9 (p.1348)
- Philippians 2:1–11 (p.1282)

he finds it. [5]And when he finds it, he happily puts it on his shoulders [6]and goes home. He calls to his friends and neighbours and says, 'Be happy with me because I found my lost sheep.' [7]In the same way, I tell you there is more joy in heaven over one sinner who changes his heart and life, than over 99 good people who don't need to change.

[8]"Suppose a woman has ten silver coins, [n] but loses one. She will light a lamp, sweep the house and look carefully for the coin until she finds it. [9]And when she finds it, she will call her friends and neighbours and say, 'Be happy with me because I have found the coin that I lost.' [10]In the same way, there is joy in the presence of the angels of God when one sinner changes his heart and life."

The Son Who Left Home

[11]Then Jesus said, "A man had two sons. [12]The younger son said to his father, 'Give me my share of the property.' So the father divided the property between his two sons. [13]Then the younger son gathered up all that was his and travelled far away to another country. There he wasted his money in foolish living. [14]After he had spent everything, a time came when there was no food anywhere in the country, and the son was poor

---

coins   Roman denarii. A silver coin was the average pay for one day's work.

PRIORITIES

Too Much to Do

Andrew Bolte is a likeable boy. He's athletic, funny, good-looking and charming. In fact, when Andrew joined the youth group at church, attendance went up. He was eager to learn more about following God and making friends.

Andrew was also eager to please others. So it wasn't long before he agreed to take part in Bible study, Sunday school and other activities. After a few years, you couldn't go to any youth group event without seeing Andrew or hearing how wonderful he was. And he was a great follower of God.

As time passed, Andrew stayed active in the group. But new things came up, too. He started playing sports at school. He joined a couple of academic clubs. He got a new girlfriend. He got a job and a car.

Andrew didn't want his friends to think he had forgotten them, so he kept volunteering for jobs in the group. He got so busy, though, that he began to do them poorly, or just forgot about them.

He still comes along to the youth group occasionally. Not long ago, he came to encourage the younger ones to keep active – "Just like I am," he said.

Afterwards, Michelle commented: "Andrew is all talk and no action. He never does what he says he will. It seems pretty useless to me."

Andrew wanted to follow God, but his overloaded lifestyle got in the way. When people asked Jesus what it takes to truly follow God, he had them make some hard choices. Read Jesus' requirements in **Luke 14:25–33**.

* How is Andrew's situation like that of the king mentioned in the passage?
* What does this passage say about your priorities and following God?

Consider . . .

* listing your top five priorities in life and taping the list to your mirror. Each day, pray for the chance to follow God in those areas of your life.
* keeping a daily diary for the coming week, writing down everything you do and how long it takes. At the end of the week, compare your daily diary with your priorities. What does it say?

For more, see . . .

* Psalm 119:105–115 (p.573)
* Philippians 3:8–11 (p.1283)
* Luke 9:23–26 (p.1054)

and hungry. [15]So he got a job with one of the citizens there who sent the son into the fields to feed pigs. [16]The son was so hungry that he wanted to eat the food the pigs were eating, but no one gave him anything. [17]When he realised what he was doing, he thought, 'All my father's servants have plenty of food. But I am here, almost dying with hunger. [18]I will leave and return to my father and say to him, "Father, I have sinned against God and have done wrong to you. [19]I am no longer worthy to be called your son, but let me be like one of your servants."' [20]So the son left and went to his father.

"While the son was still a long way off, his father saw him and felt sorry for his son. So the father ran to him and hugged and kissed him. [21]The son said, 'Father, I have sinned against God and have done wrong to you. I am no longer worthy to be called your son.' [22]But the father said to his servants, 'Hurry! Bring the best clothes and put them on him. Also, put a ring on his finger and sandals on his feet. [23]And get our fat calf and kill it so we can have a feast and celebrate. [24]My son was dead, but now he is alive again! He was lost, but now he is found!' So they began to celebrate.

FAMILY

Stubborn Love

Stuart sat dumbfounded at the dining room table in Alan's house. For years Alan had told stories about how he hated his mum because she didn't really care about him. Alan had accused her of trying to control him, choose his friends for him, even choose his music.

He didn't really believe that his mother loved him.

Alan's mum had wanted him to stop smoking. She told him how hurtful and addictive it can be. But Alan claimed it was all a front – his mum just wanted to control him. She got her pleasure out of ruling his life, he thought.

But now, Stuart didn't know what to believe. He knew that at least some of Alan's stories must have been true, but a quick glance around the table told him that they weren't true any more. As Alan and his mum laughed and joked, it was obvious that something – no, everything, had changed.

Stuart didn't understand it, but he liked it. Later, when the others were outside working on Alan's eighteen-speed bike, Stuart asked what had changed.

"It was amazing," Alan said. "After one of our battles, Mum and I were both really upset. She started crying, and I yelled something like, 'What do you have to cry about?' She said she was crying because she loved me, and smoking was hurting me."

"At that moment I looked at her and realised she was telling the truth. I don't know how – something just clicked inside. I realised that she really does love me. So we decided to start all over again. It hasn't been easy, but I've given up smoking. Things have got a lot better!"

Alan discovered how God's love can change things for the better. Jesus told stories that show how God's love can change people's lives. Check them out in **Luke 15:1–10**.

* How do you think the love that Jesus talked about in this passage helped Alan's relationship with his mum to change?
* What can you do to help you to feel God's love for you?

Consider . . .

* writing what you think God's love is like, then comparing your ideas with 1 Corinthians 13:4–7 (p.1232).
* reading the words of "Amazing Grace" from a hymn book. Rewrite them to fit your own family. Then sing your own song of thanks to God for his love!

For more, see . . .

* Zephaniah 3:14–17 (p.914)   • John 3:16 (p.1100)
* 1 John 3:1–3 (p.1373)

²⁵"The older son was in the field, and as he came closer to the house, he heard the sound of music and dancing. ²⁶So he called to one of the servants and asked what all this meant. ²⁷The servant said, 'Your brother has come back, and your father killed the fat calf, because your brother came home safely.' ²⁸The older son was angry and would not go in to the feast. So his father went out and begged him to come in. ²⁹But the older son said to his father, 'I have served you like a slave for many years and have always obeyed your commands. But you never gave me even a young goat to have at a feast with my friends. ³⁰But your other son, who wasted all your money on prostitutes, *d* comes home, and you kill the fat calf for him!' ³¹The father said to him, 'Son, you are always with me, and all that I have is yours. ³²We had to

celebrate and be happy because your brother was dead, but now he is alive. He was lost, but now he is found.'"

True Wealth

16 Jesus also said to his followers, "Once there was a rich man who had a manager to take care of his business. This manager was accused of cheating him. ²So he called the manager in and said to him, 'What is this I hear about you? Give me an account of what you have done with my money, because you can't be my manager any longer.' ³The manager thought to himself, 'What will I do since my master is taking my job away from me? I am not strong enough to dig ditches, and I am too proud to beg. ⁴I know what I'll do so that when I lose my job people will welcome me into their homes.'

REBELLION

All is Forgiven

Many years ago in Spain there was a young man called José. He often disagreed with his father's old-fashioned ways. The two had had their differences for some time, but one day it all came to a head and they had a huge row. With much bitterness and hurt, José stormed from the house and fled to Madrid.

Neither of them could stop thinking about the other, and after many years, both José and his father wished that they could see each other, to put aside their differences and start over again, but neither could pluck up the courage to get in contact. Until one day, the father could bear it no longer. Because he didn't know where his son was, he arranged for an advert to go in the *El Liberal* newspaper. It said: "JOSÉ, MEET ME AT THE HOTEL MONTANA, NOON, TUESDAY. ALL IS FORGIVEN, PAPA."

The father hoped desperately that his son would be there, but he couldn't ever have imagined what he saw that day when he arrived. Not only was his son there, but there were 800 other young men waiting!

José is such a common name in Spain that hundreds of men called José had seen the advert in the newspaper and hoped it was for them; 800 young men were desperate for forgiveness and wanted to return home to a place where they knew they were accepted and loved.

Read **Luke 15:11–32**.

* When you have an argument with someone at home, how can you prevent it becoming so severe that you feel like leaving?
* What does the father in the passage teach us that God is like? Write a list of all the characteristics of God you can see through the story.

Consider . . .

* folding a piece of paper in half and making a list on one side of the ways in which you can sometimes be like the Prodigal Son in the story. Write some words on the other side that describe how you would like to behave.
* asking God to help you be more like Jesus in your reactions to conflict and hurt.

For more, see . . .

* Daniel 9:3–19 (p.843)
* 1 John 3:1 (p.1373)
* John 3:16–21 (p.1100)

5"So the manager called in everyone who owed the master any money. He asked the first one, 'How much do you owe?' 6He answered, '3,000 litres of olive oil.' The manager said to him, 'Take your bill, sit down quickly and write 1,500 litres.' 7Then the manager asked another one, 'How much do you owe?' He answered, '18 tonnes of wheat.' Then the manager said to him, 'Take your bill and write 14 tonnes.' 8So, the master praised the dishonest manager for being clever. Yes, worldly people are more clever with their own kind than spiritual people are.

9"I tell you, make friends for yourselves using worldly riches so that when those riches are gone, you will be welcomed in those homes that continue for ever. 10Whoever can be trusted with a little can also be trusted with a lot, and whoever is dishonest with a little is dishonest with a lot. 11If you cannot be trusted with worldly riches, then who will trust you with true riches? 12And if you cannot be trusted with things that belong to someone else, who will give you things of your own?

13"No servant can serve two masters. The servant will hate one master and love the other, or will follow one master and refuse to follow the other. You cannot serve both God and worldly riches."

God's Law Cannot Be Changed

14The Pharisees, [d] who loved money, were listening to all these things and made fun of Jesus. 15He said to them, "You make yourselves look good in front of people, but God knows what is really in your hearts. What is important to people is hateful in God's sight.

16"The law of Moses and the writings of the prophets [d] were preached until John [n] came. Since then the Good News [d] about the kingdom of God has been told, and everyone tries to enter

John John the Baptist, who preached to people about Christ's coming (Matthew 3, Luke 3).

MONEY

Tool or Master?

Money was tight for John Wesley. When he began his ministry in the 1700s, he had to budget to survive. After making careful calculations, he determined that he would need about £40 a year to live on. Remember, this was a long time ago! Because there was little inflation during that time, John stayed on that yearly budget for the rest of his life. When he first made that decision, his annual income was about £44. John was able to give away £4 that first year.

Later in his life, after he had written several books and become a famous minister, his income often exceeded £2,000 per year. But John still held to his budget and lived on £40. He gave the rest of the money to people who needed it or to charities that would help to tell others about God's love for them.

How could John do this? Was it hard? We don't know the answers to those questions. All we do know is that at an early age John Wesley decided to make sure that money would be his servant, not his master.

John Wesley, who started the Methodist Church, understood what Jesus talks about in **Luke 16:1-13**. Read the passage to learn Jesus' view on money.

* How did John Wesley apply Jesus' teaching in this passage to his own life?
* How would heeding these verses change your spending habits?

Consider . . .

* looking through the advertisements of two or three current magazines to see what they reveal about our society's view of money and material goods. How does society's view of money compare with Jesus'?
* making a commitment to give money to a worthwhile organisation, such as Christian Aid.

For more, see . . .

* Proverbs 30:7-9 (p.616)
* James 1:9-11 (p.1348)
* Luke 16:19-31 (p.1075)

it by force. [17]It would be easier for heaven and earth to pass away than for the smallest part of a letter in the law to be changed.

Divorce and Remarriage

[18]"If a man divorces his wife and marries another woman, he is guilty of adultery, *d* and the man who marries a divorced woman is also guilty of adultery."

The Rich Man and Lazarus

[19]Jesus said, "There was a rich man who always dressed in the finest clothes and lived in luxury every day. [20]And a very poor man named Lazarus, whose body was covered with sores, was laid at the rich man's gate. [21]He wanted to eat only the small pieces of food that fell from the rich man's table. And the dogs would come and lick his sores. [22]Later, Lazarus died, and the angels carried him to the arms of Abraham. *d* The rich man died, too, and was buried. [23]In the place of the dead, he was in much pain. The rich man saw Abraham far away with Lazarus at his side.

[24]He called, 'Father Abraham, have mercy on me! Send Lazarus to dip his finger in water and cool my tongue, because I am suffering in this fire!'

DECISION MAKING

But I Didn't Think . . .

Sixteen-year-old Adam was in a daze as he walked out of Mr Lloyd's English class. His friends and classmates swirled by him in a rush to get to their final exam of the day.

"How was I supposed to know all that stuff?" he asked out loud.

"Oh, come on, Adam," said his friend Guy. "You've known for weeks that our whole exam would come from *Moby Dick*. Don't act surprised now."

"Yes, but it all seemed so complicated. There were so many details!"

"Tell the truth, Adam. Have you even read the book?" he asked.

He groaned. "Of course not! You know I watched the film. It's a stupid book anyway. What do I care about Ahab and the *Pequod* or whatever? I didn't have time. I thought all I'd need was the basic plot, not every little detail."

"You know whose fault that is," sighed Guy as he left Adam by the lockers. "See you later."

Adam did know whose fault it was. If only he could turn back the clock, he thought. If only he had made the right decision. Then he could have passed.

Adam made the wrong decision, and suffered for it. Fortunately, Adam's exam was not a life-or-death matter. **Luke 16:19–31** records a story about another man's test. But this man's test had eternal consequences.

- What similarities do you think exist between Adam and the rich man in the passage?
- How was the decision that the rich man faced like the decisions you face in life?

Consider . . .

- using a concordance to find times when Jesus talked about the importance of making wise choices. Look up "wisdom", "choice", "decide" or "decision".
- listing all the decisions you are facing right now, and asking your youth leader for advice on which choices would be best.

For more, see . . .

- Proverbs 8:10–11 (p.595)
- Romans 7:15–25 (p.1193)
- Isaiah 58:3–9 (p.701)

25But Abraham said, 'Child, remember when you were alive you had the good things in life, but bad things happened to Lazarus. Now he is comforted here, and you are suffering. 26Besides, there is a big pit between you and us, so no one can cross over to you, and no one can leave there and come here.' 27The rich man said, 'Father, then please send Lazarus to my father's house. 28I have five brothers, and Lazarus could warn them so that they will not come to this place of pain.' 29But Abraham said, 'They have the law of Moses and the writings of the prophets; *d* let them learn from them.' 30The rich man said, 'No, father Abraham! If someone goes to them from the dead, they would believe and change their hearts and lives.' 31But Abraham said to him, 'If they will not listen to Moses and the prophets, they will not listen to someone who comes back from the dead.' "

Sin and Forgiveness

17 Jesus said to his followers, "Things that cause people to sin will happen, but how terrible for the person who causes them to happen! 2It would be better for you to be thrown into the sea with a large stone around your neck than to cause one of these little ones to sin. 3So be careful!

"If another follower sins, warn him, and if he is sorry and stops sinning, forgive him. 4If he sins against you seven times in one day and says that he is sorry each time, forgive him."

How Big is Your Faith?

5The apostles *d* said to the Lord, "Give us more faith!"

6The Lord said, "If your faith were the size of a mustard seed, you could say to this mulberry

---

FRIENDS

For Better or For Worse

When a man and a woman get married, they make a lot of promises to each other. One of the toughest commitments in the marriage vows is the line "for better or for worse". This promise really takes friendship and relationships to a whole other level.

But is the for-better-or-for-worse approach to relationships just for married couples? This chunk of God's word suggests it isn't!

Great friends are not the mates who agree with everything you say and just let you get on and live your life. Great friends are the people who, even when it is really hard to say it, will challenge you on some of the bad decisions you make and then stick around to help you make the right choices as well.

Martin Luther King Jr once said, "In the end, we will remember not the words of our enemies, but the silence of our friends." If our friends are making bad choices and we say nothing, then we aren't a friend at all. If our friends turn on us and we don't forgive them, then maybe we weren't a friend to begin with.

A real friend will stick with you through the best and the worst life throws at you.
Read **Luke 17:1–10**.

* What are the character qualities you look for in a friend?
* Who are the friends that have challenged you about your choices as well as supported you in the good times?

Consider . . .

* becoming accountability partners with a friend you know you can trust and will ask you tough questions about the choices you make. Someone who you really respect as a strong Christian might be a good choice.
* making a deal to meet regularly and writing a list of challenging questions you can ask each other. Promise to get help from a trusted leader or parent if a situation it is too big for you to deal with on your own.

For more, see . . .

* 1 Samuel 20:1–42 (p.274)
* James 5:19–20 (p.1354)

* Romans 1:11–12 (p.1185)

tree, 'Dig yourself up and plant yourself in the sea,' and it would obey you.

Be Good Servants

[7]"Suppose one of you has a servant who has been ploughing the ground or caring for the sheep. When the servant comes in from working in the field, would you say, 'Come in and sit down to eat'? [8]No, you would say to him, 'Prepare something for me to eat. Then get yourself ready and serve me. After I finish eating and drinking, you can eat.' [9]The servant does not get any special thanks for doing what his master commanded. [10]It is the same with you. When you have done everything you are told to do, you should say, 'We are unworthy servants; we have only done the work we should do.' "

Be Thankful

[11]While Jesus was on his way to Jerusalem, he was going through the area between Samaria and Galilee. [12]As he came into a small town, ten men who had a skin disease met him there. They did not come close to Jesus [13]but called to him, "Jesus! Master! Have mercy on us!"

[14]When Jesus saw the men, he said, "Go and show yourselves to the priests." [n]

As the ten men were going, they were healed. [15]When one of them saw that he was healed, he went back to Jesus, praising God in a loud voice. [16]Then he bowed down at Jesus' feet and thanked him. (And this man was a Samaritan. [d]) [17]Jesus said, "Weren't ten men healed? Where are the other nine? [18]Is this Samaritan the only one who came back to

show . . . priests The law of Moses said a priest must say when a Jewish person with a skin disease became well.

THANKFULNESS

Attitude of Gratitude

Bruce's father shook his head doubtfully. "I don't see how we can do it, son," he said.

Bruce knew his father was right, but it still hurt to think about missing the big trip. All of the players in the jazz orchestra were looking forward to that summer trip. But Bruce's dad had been unemployed for a while, so money was tight – too tight to allow a seventeen-year-old to go touring round Europe for a month.

As Bruce left the room, he asked God to show him a way somehow. He continued to pray about it, and not long afterwards a family in his church asked him to do some gardening. Not much, but it was something. Soon more jobs came in, mostly from families who knew that Bruce was saving his money for the trip.

All spring, Bruce was busier than he had ever been. And that summer, he went to Europe with the band. The families he had worked for had provided the means to get there.

That was a long time ago, but Bruce hasn't forgotten those families. He's a youth minister now, committed to helping kids find their way out of rough spots. "I know I can't go back and thank all those families who helped me," Bruce says. "I don't even remember some of their names. But I feel that I can express my thanks to God for all the good things in my life by helping others."

Sometimes we only think of thankfulness when something really special happens to us. People like Bruce, though, understand what Jesus said about always being thankful. Read Jesus' words in **Luke 17:11–19** to get the best advice on thankfulness.

* How is Bruce like the leper who returned to Jesus?
* What things in your life make you feel like running after Jesus just to say "thanks"?

Consider . . .

* writing a letter to God, thanking him for all the good things in your life.
* keeping stamps and blank postcards handy all the time. When people do something nice for you, send them a note of thanks.

For more, see . . .

* Psalm 100 (p.558)
* 1 Thessalonians 5:15–18 (p.1301)
* Acts 3:1–10 (p.1142)

thank God?" [19]Then Jesus said to him, "Stand up and go on your way. You were healed because you believed."

God's Kingdom is Within You

[20]Some of the Pharisees *d* asked Jesus, "When will the kingdom of God come?"

Jesus answered, "God's kingdom is coming, but not in a way that you will be able to see with your eyes. [21]People will not say, 'Look, here it is!' or, 'There it is!' because God's kingdom is within *n* you."

[22]Then Jesus said to his followers, "The time will come when you will want very much to see one of the days of the Son of Man. *d* But you will not see it. [23]People will say to you, 'Look, there he is!' or, 'Look, here he is!' Stay where you are; don't go away and search.

When Jesus Comes Again

[24]"When the Son of Man *d* comes again, he will shine like lightning, which flashes across the sky and lights it up from one side to the other. [25]But first he must suffer many things and be rejected by the people of this time. [26]When the Son of Man comes again, it will be as it was when Noah lived. [27]People were eating, drinking, marrying and giving their children to be married until the day Noah entered the boat. Then the flood came and killed them all. [28]It will be the same as during the time of Lot. People were eating, drinking, buying, selling, planting and building. [29]But the day Lot left Sodom, *n* fire and sulphur rained down from the sky and killed them all. [30]This is how it will be when the Son of Man comes again.

[31]"On that day, a person who is on the roof and whose belongings are in the house should not go inside to get them. A person who is in the field should not go back home. [32]Remember Lot's wife. *n* [33]Those who try to keep their lives will lose them. But those who give up their lives will save them. [34]I tell you, on that night two people will be sleeping in one bed; one will be taken and the other will be left. [35]There will be two women grinding grain together; one will be taken, and the other will be left." [36]*n*

[37]The followers asked Jesus, "Where will this be, Lord?"

Jesus answered, "Where there is a dead body, there the vultures will gather."

God will Answer His People

18 Then Jesus used this story to teach his followers that they should always pray and never lose hope. [2]"In a certain town there was a judge who did not respect God or care about people. [3]In that same town there was a widow who kept coming to this judge, saying, 'Give me my rights against my enemy.' [4]For a while the judge refused to help her. But afterwards, he thought to himself, 'Even though I don't respect God or care about people, [5]I will see that she gets her rights. Otherwise she will continue to bother me until I am worn out.'"

[6]The Lord said, "Listen to what the unfair judge said. [7]God will always give what is right to his people who cry to him night and day, and he will not be slow to answer them. [8]I tell you, God will help his people quickly. But when the Son of Man *d* comes again, will he find those on earth who believe in him?"

Being Right with God

[9]Jesus told this story to some people who thought they were very good and looked down on everyone else: [10]"A Pharisee *d* and a tax collector both went to the Temple *d* to pray. [11]The Pharisee stood alone and prayed, 'God, I thank you that I am not like other people who steal, cheat or take part in adultery, *d* or even like this tax collector. [12]I give up eating *n* twice a week, and I give one-tenth of everything I earn!'

[13]"The tax collector, standing at a distance, would not even look up to heaven. But he beat on his chest because he was so sad. He said, 'God, have mercy on me, a sinner.' [14]I tell you, when this man went home, he was right with God, but

---

within Or "among".
Sodom A city that God destroyed because the people were so evil.
Lot's wife A story about what happened to Lot's wife is found in Genesis 19:15–17, 26.
Verse 36 A few Greek copies add verse 36: "Two people will be in the field. One will be taken, and the other will be left."
give up eating This is called "fasting". The people would give up eating for a special time of prayer and worship to God. It was also done to show sadness and disappointment.

the Pharisee was not. All who make themselves great will be made humble, but all who make themselves humble will be made great."

Who will Enter God's Kingdom?

[15]Some people brought even their babies to Jesus so he could touch them. When the followers saw this, they told them to stop. [16]But Jesus called for the children, saying, "Let the little children come to me. Don't stop them, because the kingdom of God belongs to people who are like these children. [17]I tell you the truth, you must accept the kingdom of God as if you were a child, or you will never enter it."

A Rich Man's Question

[18]A certain leader asked Jesus, "Good Teacher, what must I do to have life for ever?"

[19]Jesus said to him, "Why do you call me good? Only God is good. [20]You know the commands: 'You must not be guilty of adultery. [d] You must not murder anyone. You must not steal. You must not tell lies about your neighbour. Honour your father and mother.' "[n]

[21]But the leader said, "I have obeyed all these commands since I was a boy."

[22]When Jesus heard this, he said to him, "There is still one more thing you need to do. Sell everything you have and give it to the poor, and you will have treasure in heaven. Then come and

'You . . . mother.'   Quotation from Exodus 20:12–16; Deuteronomy 5:16–20.

END TIMES

If Only . . .

Doug was full of ideas, some of them very good. Unfortunately, most of his ideas stayed in his head and never made it to reality. So, when he had the terrific idea of an outdoor concert in the middle of the park as an outreach to the local people, it sounded great. He got the church youth together and they started making posters and sending letters to other churches asking them to join in. It was exciting. Of course, they needed good weather, but apart from that it was all systems go.

The local park had a great field that sloped, so the idea was that the bands would play in the "dip" end and the audience could then sit almost tiered up the slope end. Ideal.

On the day before the concert, Doug was told that you had to have permission to play in the park, you couldn't just wander in and start setting up stages and equipment all over the place. It was a panic because he hadn't thought of writing for permission. Amazingly, he managed to gain a permit on the day, just as the bands were arriving. He came running up to everyone, holding the important piece of paper in his hand.

"Phew, that was close wasn't it?" He grinned round at everyone and suddenly noticed their grim faces.

"What?" he asked confused. "What's the matter?"

"Doug . . . ?" started one musician.

"Yes?" replied Doug.

"Where's the electricity?"

Sometimes we are so busy planning and organising that we forget the vital things. Read **Luke 17:24–30** and see how the same things happened there.

* How is the lesson that Doug learned similar to one that happened in the time of Lot?

Consider . . .

* how you would change your lifestyle if you knew Christ's return was imminent.
* asking your youth leader to prepare a session on the events that point to Christ's return.

For more, see . . .

* Luke 21:34–36 (p.1087)
* 1 Thessalonians 5:1–6 (p.1300)
* Romans 13:1–14 (p.1206)

follow me." 23But when the man heard this, he became very sad, because he was very rich.

24Jesus looked at him and said, "It is very hard for rich people to enter the kingdom of God. 25It is easier for a camel to go through the eye of a needle than for a rich person to enter the kingdom of God."

Who Can Be Saved?

26When the people heard this, they asked, "Then who can be saved?"

27Jesus answered, "God can do things that are not possible for people to do."

28Peter said, "Look, we have left everything and followed you."

29Jesus said, "I tell you the truth, all those who have left houses, wives, brothers, parents or children for the kingdom of God 30will get much

more in this life. And in the age that is coming, they will have life for ever."

Jesus will Rise from the Dead

31Then Jesus took the twelve apostles *d* aside and said to them, "We are going to Jerusalem. Everything the prophets *d* wrote about the Son of Man *d* will happen. 32He will be turned over to those who are not Jews. They will laugh at him, insult him, spit on him, 33beat him with whips and kill him. But on the third day, he will rise to life again." 34The apostles did not understand this; the meaning was hidden from them, and they did not realise what was said.

Jesus Heals a Blind Man

35As Jesus came near the city of Jericho, a blind man was sitting beside the road, begging. 36When

BOASTING

Maximum Ruler

In October 1989, pictures of General Manuel Noriega shaking his fist at the world made headlines everywhere. As dictator of the country of Panama, he'd just thwarted an attempt to remove him from power. Some reports suggested that he tortured and murdered as many as 75 rebel soldiers after the attempted coup.

Noriega controlled the Panamanian government arrogantly, as though he owned it. He held mock elections in which his people frightened voters away. He reportedly financed his lifestyle through illegal drug trafficking and commonly mocked and belittled his enemies.

In December, his arrogance reached its peak. He boasted that he was Panama's "maximum leader", daring anyone to disagree.

That month the USA invaded Panama and removed Noriega from power. Within days, he was on his way to face drugs charges in a Florida courtroom.

On New Year's Day, the world again saw Manuel Noriega's picture in the headlines. This time, though, the pictures showed a handcuffed man dressed in prison clothes being taken away to prison.

Jesus talked about how God views boastful and conceited people. Read what he said in **Luke 18:9–14**.

* What attitude did both General Noriega and the Pharisee display?
* How can pride interfere in your relationship with Christ?

Consider . . .

* finding "pride" in a dictionary and thinking about what part pride plays in boasting.
* writing the second half of Luke 18:14 on a postcard and placing it on your mirror as an encouragement to avoid arrogance.

For more, see . . .

* Jeremiah 9:23–24 (p.728)
* James 4:13–17 (p.1352)
* 1 Corinthians 4:6–7 (p.1219)

he heard the people coming down the road, he asked, "What is happening?"

37They told him, "Jesus, from Nazareth, is going by."

38The blind man cried out, "Jesus, Son of David, *d* have mercy on me!"

39The people leading the group warned the blind man to be quiet. But the blind man shouted even more, "Son of David, have mercy on me!"

40Jesus stopped and ordered the blind man to be brought to him. When he came near, Jesus asked him, 41"What do you want me to do for you?"

He said, "Lord, I want to see."

42Jesus said to him, "Then see. You are healed because you believed."

43At once the man was able to see, and he followed Jesus, thanking God. All the people who saw this praised God.

Zacchaeus Meets Jesus

19 Jesus was going through the city of Jericho. 2A man was there named Zacchaeus, who was a very important tax collector, and he was wealthy. 3He wanted to see who Jesus was, but he was not able because he was too short to see above the crowd. 4He ran ahead to a place where Jesus would come, and he climbed a sycamore tree so he could see him. 5When Jesus came to that place, he looked up and said to him, "Zacchaeus, hurry and come down! I must stay at your house today."

HOLY SPIRIT

Get Changed!

Christina grew up in a very tough and poor neighbourhood. From a young age, the hardship of her situation and the abuse she endured made Christina very vulnerable to anyone who offered her any kind of attention. In her late teens, she was offered attention by a guy who ended up forcing her to be a prostitute. Long after he had "got rid of her", Christina continued to work as a prostitute because her self-esteem was so low and she thought she didn't have any other way of earning a living. She had also tried to commit suicide and regularly wished she would die.

Then one day Christina met Jesus – "Jesus" in the form of a lady named Sarah. Sarah invited Christina to share a meal at the local café with her. When Christina spoke to her new friend she felt, for the first time, that she was loved and accepted for who she was, not what she could offer. Their friendship grew and Christina quickly realised that Sarah simply wanted to support and love her to a better life.

Christina asked Sarah a lot of questions about her faith and over time realised that Sarah's unconditional friendship was driven by her faith in God. Christina decided she wanted to get to know God as well and so, with Sarah's help, prayed a prayer asking God to change who she was from the inside out. Over time, the Holy Spirit transformed Christina into a woman who had deep confidence and real healing from all the hurts she had experienced.

Christina now teaches Sunday school at her church because she wants to help children to understand that God loves and cares for each of them and can change their lives into a life that is worth living.

Read **Luke 19:1–10**.

• What are the similarities between Zacchaeus and Christina?
• What are the similarities between Jesus and Sarah?

Consider . . .

• writing down some of the things that you do, think and say that you aren't so proud of. Ask the Holy Spirit to change you from the inside out and to help you live a life worth living, then tear up your list and throw it away.
• encouraging someone you know who is trying to change.

For more, see . . .

• Romans 12:1–3 (p.1203)   • 2 Corinthians 3:17–18 (p.1242)
• Hebrews 11:1–3 (p.1341)

⁶Zacchaeus came down quickly and welcomed him gladly. ⁷All the people saw this and began to complain, "Jesus is staying with a sinner!"

⁸But Zacchaeus stood and said to the Lord, "I will give half of my possessions to the poor. And if I have cheated anyone, I will pay back four times more."

⁹Jesus said to him, "Salvation has come to this house today, because this man also belongs to the family of Abraham. ¹⁰The Son of Man ^d came to find lost people and save them."

A Story About Three Servants

¹¹As the people were listening to this, Jesus told them a story because he was near Jerusalem and they thought God's kingdom would appear immediately. ¹²He said: "A very important man went to a country far away to be made a king and then to return home. ¹³So he called ten of his servants and gave a gold coin ⁿ to each servant. He said, 'Do business with this money until I get back.' ¹⁴But the people in the kingdom hated the

coin   A Greek "mina". One mina was enough money to pay a person for three months work.

MONEY

Share and Share Alike

The minister had been giving his sermon as usual on Sunday. It was the story of the three servants, an amusing biblical incident in which a king distributed money to servants and then told them to go away and make more money with it. Graeme was waving his arms about, really getting into the story, happy that his congregation were "with him". They were nodding and agreeing in their seats as he expounded on the results of the servants' money-making escapades.

Then he looked up and said, "Now I would like all the church members to come forward." The members were used to his antics, and thought he was going to get them to act out part of the story. But instead, he came down from the pulpit and proceeded to go along the line giving them all a £10 note! They looked amazed and stupefied as he said,

"OK, now you have your money, I would like you to use it wisely over the next six months and we'll meet again and see how much money you have raised towards the new church building!"

It actually had a stunning effect on everyone, and when they did finally meet up again they had made a serious amount of money!

Some of the older ladies had bought fruit and sugar with their money, and made huge amounts of jam, which they sold in great quantities. Some teenagers had bought ladders, sponges and buckets between them and started up a window-cleaning business. And some of the men had bought shares and watched them go up!

Luke 19:11–27 shows us there is nothing wrong with making money. It's what we do with it that counts.

* What would you do if you had been given £10 in these circumstances?
* What does God expect you to do with the gifts he has given you, according to this passage?

Consider . . .

* evaluating how thoughtfully you spend your money.
* ways you can use what God has given you – be it money or talent – to make the best use of it.

For more, see . . .

* Ecclesiastes 5:10–17 (p.625)
* Acts 4:32–35 (p.1144)

* Matthew 6:31–33 (p.949)

man. So they sent a group to follow him and say, 'We don't want this man to be our king.'

¹⁵"But the man became king. When he returned home, he said, "Call those servants who have my money so I can know how much they earned with it.'

¹⁶"The first servant came and said, 'Sir, I earned ten bags of money with the one you gave me.' ¹⁷The king said to the servant, 'Excellent! You are a good servant. Since I can trust you with small things, I will let you rule over ten of my cities.'

¹⁸"The second servant said, 'Sir, I earned five bags of money with your one.' ¹⁹The king said to this servant, 'You can rule over five cities.'

²⁰"Then another servant came in and said to the king, 'Sir, here is your bag of money which I wrapped in a piece of cloth and hid. ²¹I was afraid of you, because you are a hard man. You even take money that you didn't earn and gather food that you didn't plant.' ²²Then the king said to the servant, 'I will condemn you by your own words, you evil servant. You knew that I am a hard man, taking money that I didn't earn and gathering food that I didn't plant. ²³Why then didn't you put my money in the bank? Then when I came back, my money would have earned some interest.'

²⁴"The king said to the men who were standing by, 'Take the bag of money away from this servant and give it to the servant who earned ten bags of money.' ²⁵They said, 'But sir, that servant already has ten bags of money.' ²⁶The king said, 'Those who have will be given more, but those who do not have anything will have everything taken away from them. ²⁷Now where are my enemies who didn't want me to be king? Bring them here and kill them before me.'"

Jesus Enters Jerusalem as a King

²⁸After Jesus said this, he went on towards Jerusalem. ²⁹As Jesus came near Bethphage and Bethany, towns near the hill called the Mount of Olives, *d* he sent out two of his followers. ³⁰He said, "Go to the town you can see there. When you enter it, you will find a colt tied there, which no one has ever ridden. Untie it and bring it here to me. ³¹If anyone asks you why you are untying it, say that the Master needs it."

³²The two followers went into town and found the colt just as Jesus had told them. ³³As they were untying it, its owners came out and asked the followers, "Why are you untying our colt?"

³⁴The followers answered, "The Master needs it." ³⁵So they brought it to Jesus, threw their coats on the colt's back, and put Jesus on it. ³⁶As Jesus rode towards Jerusalem, others spread their coats on the road before him.

³⁷As he was coming close to Jerusalem, on the way down the Mount of Olives, the whole crowd of followers began joyfully shouting praise to God for all the miracles *d* they had seen. ³⁸They said,

"God bless the king who comes in the name
    of the Lord!   *Psalm 118:26*
There is peace in heaven and glory to God!"

³⁹Some of the Pharisees *d* in the crowd said to Jesus, "Teacher, tell your followers not to say these things."

⁴⁰But Jesus answered, "I tell you, if my followers didn't say these things, then the stones would cry out."

Jesus Cries for Jerusalem

⁴¹As Jesus came near Jerusalem, he saw the city and cried for it, ⁴²saying, "I wish you knew today what would bring you peace. But now it is hidden from you. ⁴³The time is coming when your enemies will build a wall around you and will hold you in on all sides. ⁴⁴They will destroy you and all your people, and not one stone will be left on another. All this will happen because you did not recognise the time when God came to save you."

Jesus Goes to the Temple

⁴⁵Jesus went into the Temple *d* and began to throw out the people who were selling things there. ⁴⁶He said, "It is written in the Scriptures, *d* 'My Temple will be a house for prayer.' *n* But you have changed it into a 'hideout for robbers'!" *n*

⁴⁷Jesus taught in the Temple every day. The leading priests, the experts on the law and some of the leaders of the people wanted to kill Jesus. ⁴⁸But they did not know how they could do it, because all the people were listening closely to him.

Jewish Leaders Question Jesus

20 One day Jesus was in the Temple, *d* teaching the people and telling them the Good News. *d* The leading priests, teachers of the law and Jewish elders came up to talk with him, ²saying, "Tell us what authority you have to do these things? Who gave you this authority?"

³Jesus answered, "I will also ask you a question. Tell me: ⁴when John baptised people, was that authority from God or just from other people?"

⁵They argued about this, saying, "If we answer, 'John's baptism was from God,' Jesus will say, 'Then why did you not believe him?' ⁶But if we say, 'It was from other people,' all the people will stone us to death, because they believe John

---

'My Temple . . . prayer.'   Quotation from Isaiah 56:7.
'hideout for robbers'   Quotation from Jeremiah 7:11.

was a prophet." [d] 7So they answered that they didn't know where it came from.

8Jesus said to them, "Then I won't tell you what authority I have to do these things."

A Story About God's Son

9Then Jesus told the people this story: "A man planted a vineyard and leased it to some farmers. Then he went away for a long time. 10When it was time for the grapes to be picked, he sent a servant to the farmers to get some of the grapes. But they beat the servant and sent him away empty-handed. 11Then he sent another servant. They beat this servant also, and showed no respect for him, and sent him away empty-handed. 12So the man sent a third servant. The farmers wounded him and threw him out. 13The owner of the vineyard said, 'What will I do now? I will send my son whom I love. Maybe they will respect him.' 14But when the farmers saw the son, they said to each other, 'This son will inherit the vineyard. If we kill him, it will be ours.' 15So the farmers threw the son out of the vineyard and killed him.

"What will the owner of this vineyard do to them? 16He will come and kill those farmers and will give the vineyard to other farmers."

When the people heard this story, they said, "Let this never happen!"

17But Jesus looked at them and said, "Then what does this verse mean:

'The stone that the builders rejected
    became the cornerstone'? [d]   *Psalm 118:22*

18Everyone who falls on that stone will be broken, and the person on whom it falls, that person will be crushed!"

19The teachers of the law and the leading priests wanted to arrest Jesus at once, because they knew the story was about them. But they were afraid of what the people would do.

Is It Right to Pay Taxes or Not?

20So they watched Jesus and sent some spies who acted as if they were sincere. They wanted to trap Jesus into saying something wrong so they could hand him over to the authority and power of the governor. 21So the spies asked Jesus, "Teacher,

---

EVIL

Grim Snapshots

A three-year-old is taken from a shopping centre and murdered. Soon after, on the day before Mother's Day, another small child is killed in another shopping centre, this time by an IRA bomb . . .

A "joy rider" kills a ten-year-old girl delivering a birthday card . . .

When Colin discovered that he was adopted, he set about trying to locate his true parents. When at last he finally found his mother, she told him that she hated him and never wanted to see his face again . . .

When two teenage girls got bored, they broke into the home of an elderly lady, tortured and killed her . . .

Let's face it, evil happens. Many people try to sweep it under the rug and pretend that it doesn't exist – but it does.

Jesus never denied that the world is full of evil, but he always pointed out that God is triumphant over it. In **Luke 20:9–19**, Jesus tells a parable about the way God's triumph over evil will come about.

* What motivates people to abuse each other as they did both in the Bible story and in the snapshots above?
* How do you see God's power conquering evil in the passage that you have just read?

Consider . . .

* thanking God that he knows what the world is really like, and that he will one day get rid of evil for ever.
* praying about any situations that you come across which are obvious examples of evil in the world.

For more, see . . .

* Proverbs 24:19–20 (p.611)
* Romans 12:17–21 (p.1205)

* Matthew 21:33–43 (p.978)

we know that what you say and teach is true. You pay no attention to who people are, and you always teach the truth about God's way. ²²Tell us, is it right for us to pay taxes to Caesar *d* or not?"

²³But Jesus, knowing they were trying to trick him, said, ²⁴"Show me a silver coin. *n* Whose image and name are on it?"

They said, "Caesar's."

²⁵Jesus said to them, "Then give to Caesar the things that are Caesar's, and give to God the things that are God's."

²⁶So they were not able to trap Jesus into anything he said in the presence of the people. And being amazed at his answer, they became silent.

> **Sidelight** The Sadducees – who didn't believe in the resurrection of the dead (Luke 20:27) – were major rivals of the Pharisees in Jesus' time. In later years, the Sadducees were often considered heretics by other Jews.

Some Sadducees Try to Trick Jesus

²⁷Some Sadducees, *d* who believed people would not rise from the dead, came to Jesus. ²⁸They asked, "Teacher, Moses wrote that if a man's brother dies and leaves a wife but no children, then that man must marry the widow and have children for his brother. ²⁹Once there were seven brothers. The first brother married and died, but had no children. ³⁰Then the second brother married the widow, and he died. ³¹And the third brother married the widow, and he died. The same thing happened with all seven brothers; they died and had no children. ³²Finally, the woman died also. ³³Since all seven brothers had married her, whose wife will she be when people rise from the dead?"

³⁴Jesus said to them, "On earth, people marry and are given to someone to marry. ³⁵But those who will be worthy to be raised from the dead and live again will not marry, nor will they be given to someone to marry. ³⁶In that life they are like angels and cannot die. They are children of God, because they have been raised from the dead. ³⁷Even Moses clearly showed that the dead are raised to life. When he wrote about the burning bush, *n* he said that the Lord is 'the God of Abraham, the God of Isaac and the God of Jacob.' *n* ³⁸God is the God of the

living, not the dead, because all people are alive to him."

³⁹Some of the teachers of the law said, "Teacher, your answer was good." ⁴⁰No one was brave enough to ask him another question.

Is the Christ the Son of David?

⁴¹Then Jesus said, "Why do people say that the Christ *d* is the Son of David? *d* ⁴²In the book of Psalms, David himself says:

'The LORD said to my Lord:
Sit by me at my right side,
⁴³   until I put your enemies under your control.' *n*
                                        Psalm 110:1

⁴⁴David calls the Christ 'Lord', so how can the Christ be his son?"

Jesus Accuses Some Leaders

⁴⁵While all the people were listening, Jesus said to his followers, ⁴⁶"Beware of the teachers of the law. They like to walk around wearing fancy clothes, and they love people to greet them with respect in the market-places. They love to have the most important seats in the synagogues *d* and at feasts. ⁴⁷But they cheat widows and steal their houses and then try to make themselves look good by saying long prayers. They will receive a greater punishment."

True Giving

21 As Jesus looked up, he saw some rich people putting their gifts into the Temple *d* money box. *n* ²Then he saw a poor widow putting two small copper coins into the box. ³He said, "I tell you the truth, this poor widow gave more than all those rich people. ⁴They gave only what they did not need. This woman is very poor, but she gave all she had to live on."

The Temple will Be Destroyed

⁵Some people were talking about the Temple *d* and how it was decorated with beautiful stones and gifts offered to God.

But Jesus said, ⁶"As for these things you are looking at, the time will come when not one stone will be left on another. Every stone will be thrown down."

⁷They asked Jesus, "Teacher, when will these things happen? What will be the sign that they are about to take place?"

⁸Jesus said, "Be careful so you are not fooled. Many people will come in my name, saying, 'I am

---

coin   Roman denarii. A silver coin was the average pay for one day's work.
burning bush   Read Exodus 3:1–12 in the Old Testament.
'the God of . . . Jacob'   These words are taken from Exodus 3:6.
until . . . control   Literally, "until I make your enemies a footstool for your feet".
money box   A special box in the Jewish place of worship where people put their gifts to God.

the One' and, 'The time has come!' But don't follow them. ⁹When you hear about wars and riots, don't be afraid, because these things must happen first, but the end will come later."

¹⁰Then he said to them, "Nations will fight against other nations, and kingdoms against other kingdoms. ¹¹In various places there will be great earthquakes, sicknesses and a lack of food. Fearful events and great signs will come from heaven.

¹²"But before all these things happen, people will arrest you and treat you cruelly. They will judge you in their synagogues *d* and put you in jail and force you to stand before kings and governors, because you follow me. ¹³But this will give you an opportunity to tell about me. ¹⁴Make up your minds not to worry ahead of time about what you will say. ¹⁵I will give you the wisdom to say things that none of your enemies will be able to stand against or prove wrong. ¹⁶Even your parents, brothers, relatives and friends will turn against you, and they will kill some of you. ¹⁷All people will hate you because you follow me. ¹⁸But none of these things can really harm you. ¹⁹By continuing to have faith you will save your lives.

Jerusalem will Be Destroyed

²⁰"When you see armies all around Jerusalem, you will know it will soon be destroyed. ²¹At that time, the people in Judea should run away to the mountains. The people in Jerusalem must get out, and those who are near the city should not go in. ²²These are the days of punishment to bring about all that is written in the Scriptures. *d* ²³How terrible it will be for women who are pregnant or have nursing babies! Great trouble will come upon this land, and God will be angry with these people. ²⁴They will be killed by the sword and taken as prisoners to all nations. Jerusalem will be crushed by non-Jewish people until their time is over.

PEER PRESSURE

Friends in Deed

Luke was studying for his exams when he learned that he had cancer. He was told that he would have to undergo painful chemotherapy.

For Luke the pain was even harder to take knowing that the treatment would make his hair fall out. Would he fit in at school? What would his friends say? Would they avoid him because they were embarrassed by his baldness? Would he be laughed at and mocked? He knew that his classmates' reactions could make having the awful disease even more unbearable.

What he didn't know – but soon discovered – was that his friends really cared. To make sure that Luke would fit in, his eight best friends all shaved their heads.

A stranger to the area might have wondered why nine students at the college had suddenly become skinheads. But one of those bald heads knew the power of positive peer pressure. That makes all the difference.

Peer pressure can be good or bad. The Bible talks about a negative sort of peer pressure that many Christians will face. Read **Luke 21:5–19**, especially verse 16, to find out more about it.

* Luke faced rejection at school. How will Christians face rejection by the world, according to this passage?
* What encouragement does this passage give you to stand up to pressure from people who try to get you to compromise what you believe?

Consider . . .

* making a list of pressures that challenge your relationships with God and your friends, then asking your youth leader for advice on how to overcome those pressures.
* making a pact with your friends always to encourage each other to follow God.

For more, see . . .

* 1 Samuel 20:28–42 (p.274)
* 1 Corinthians 15:33 (p.1236)
* Matthew 10:16–23 (p.955)

Don't Fear

25"There will be signs in the sun, moon and stars. On earth, nations will be afraid and confused because of the roar and fury of the sea. 26People will be so afraid they will faint, wondering what is happening to the world, because the powers of the heavens will be shaken. 27Then people will see the Son of Man *d* coming in a cloud with power and great glory. 28When these things begin to happen, look up and hold your heads high, because the time when God will free you is near!"

Jesus' Words will Live for Ever

29Then Jesus told this story: "Look at the fig tree and all the other trees. 30When their leaves appear, you know that summer is near. 31In the same way, when you see these things happening, you will know that God's kingdom is near.

32"I tell you the truth, all these things will happen while the people of this time are still living. 33Earth and sky will be destroyed, but the words I have spoken will never be destroyed.

Be Ready All the Time

34"Be careful not to spend your time feasting, drinking or worrying about worldly things. If you do, that day might come on you suddenly, 35like a trap on all people on earth. 36So be ready all the time. Pray that you will be strong enough to escape all these things that will happen and that you will be able to stand before the Son of Man." *d*

37During the day, Jesus taught the people in the Temple, *d* and at night he went out of the city and stayed on the Mount of Olives. *d* 38Every morning all the people got up early to go to the Temple to listen to him.

Judas Becomes an Enemy of Jesus

22 It was almost time for the Feast *d* of Unleavened Bread, called the Passover *d* Feast. 2The leading priests and teachers of the law were trying to find a way to kill Jesus, because they were afraid of the people.

3Satan entered Judas Iscariot, one of Jesus' twelve apostles. *d* 4Judas went to the leading priests and some of the soldiers who guarded the Temple *d* and talked to them about a way to hand Jesus over to them. 5They were pleased and agreed to give Judas money. 6He agreed and watched for the best time to hand Jesus over to them when he was away from the crowd.

Jesus Eats the Passover Meal

7The Day of Unleavened *d* Bread came when the Passover *d* lambs had to be sacrificed. 8Jesus said to Peter and John, "Go and prepare the Passover meal for us to eat."

9They asked, "Where do you want us to prepare it?" 10Jesus said to them, "After you go into the city, a man carrying a jar of water will meet you. Follow him into the house that he enters, 11and tell the owner of the house, 'The Teacher asks where is the guest room in which I may eat the Passover meal with my followers?' 12Then he will show you a large, furnished room upstairs. Prepare the Passover meal there."

13So Peter and John left and found everything as Jesus had said. And they prepared the Passover meal.

The Lord's Supper

14When the time came, Jesus and the apostles *d* were sitting at the table. 15He said to them, "I wanted very much to eat this Passover *d* meal with you before I suffer. 16I will not eat another Passover meal until it is given its true meaning in the kingdom of God."

17Then Jesus took a cup, gave thanks and said, "Take this cup and share it among yourselves. 18I will not drink again from the fruit of the vine *n* until God's kingdom comes."

19Then Jesus took some bread, gave thanks, broke it and gave it to the apostles, saying, "This is my body, which I am giving for you. Do this to remember me." 20In the same way, after supper, Jesus took the cup and said, "This cup is the new agreement that God makes with his people. This new agreement begins with my blood which is poured out for you.

Who will Turn Against Jesus?

21"But one of you will turn against me, and his hand is with mine on the table. 22What God has planned for the Son of Man *d* will happen, but how terrible it will be for that one who turns against the Son of Man."

23Then the apostles *d* asked each other which one of them would do that.

Be like a Servant

24The apostles *d* also began to argue about which one of them was the most important. 25But Jesus said to them, "The kings of the non-Jewish people rule over them, and those who have authority over others like to be called 'friends of the people'. 26But you must not be like that. Instead, the greatest among you should be like the youngest, and the leader should be like the servant. 27Who is more important: the one sitting at the table or the one serving? You think the one at the table is more important, but I am like a servant among you.

28"You have stayed with me through my struggles. 29Just as my Father has given me a kingdom,

---

fruit of the vine   Product of the grapevine; this may also be translated "wine".

I also give you a kingdom [30]so you may eat and drink at my table in my kingdom. And you will sit on thrones, judging the twelve tribes [d] of Israel.

Don't Lose Your Faith!

[31]"Simon, Simon, Satan has asked to test all of you as a farmer tests his wheat. [32]I have prayed that you will not lose your faith! Help your brothers be stronger when you come back to me."

[33]But Peter said to Jesus, "Lord, I am ready to go with you to prison and even to die with you!"

[34]But Jesus said, "Peter, before the cockerel crows this day, you will say three times that you don't know me."

Be Ready for Trouble

[35]Then Jesus said to the apostles, [d] "When I sent you out without a purse, a bag or sandals, did you need anything?"

They said, "No."

[36]He said to them, "But now if you have a purse or a bag, carry that with you. If you don't have a sword, sell your coat and buy one. [37]The Scripture [d] says, 'He was treated like a criminal,' [n] and I tell you this scripture must come true. It was written about me, and it is happening now."

[38]His followers said, "Look, Lord, here are two swords."

He said to them, "That is enough."

Jesus Prays Alone

[39]Jesus left the city and went to the Mount of Olives, [d] as he often did, and his followers went with him. [40]When he reached the place, he said to them, "Pray for strength against temptation." [41]Then Jesus went about a stone's throw away from them. He kneeled down and prayed, [42]"Father, if you are willing, take away this cup [n] of suffering. But do what you want, not what I want." [43]Then an angel from heaven appeared to

---

'He . . . criminal' Quotation from Isaiah 53:12.

cup Jesus is talking about the terrible things that will happen to him. Accepting these things will be hard, like drinking a cup of something bitter.

JEALOUSY

When Others Succeed

"Few men have the strength to honour a friend's success without envy."   — Aeschylus

"Lots of people know a good thing the minute the other fellow sees it first."   — Job E. Hedges

"The man who keeps busy helping the man below him won't have time to envy the man above him — and there may not be anybody above him anyway."   — Henrietta C. Mears

"The greatest among you should be like the youngest, and the leader should be like the servant."   — Jesus Christ

For more about what Jesus said to his jealous disciples — who were arguing about prestige — read **Luke 22:24–30**.

- What similarities and differences are there between what Jesus said and what these famous people said about jealousy?
- How are you like and unlike the disciples in the passage? What would Jesus say to you?

Consider . . .

- stopping yourself next time you feel jealous of someone. Instead, do an act of service for that person.
- setting three goals for the coming week that will help you to overcome jealous feelings you have towards someone you know.

For more, see . . .

- Genesis 37:2–28 (p.42)
- 1 Peter 2:1 (p.1357)
- 1 Samuel 18:6–11 (p.272)

him to strengthen him. [44]Being full of pain, Jesus prayed even harder. His sweat was like drops of blood falling to the ground. [45]When he finished praying, he went to his followers and found them asleep because of their sadness. [46]Jesus said to them, "Why are you sleeping? Get up and pray for strength against temptation."

Jesus is Arrested

[47]While Jesus was speaking, a crowd came up, and Judas, one of the twelve apostles, [d] was leading them. He came close to Jesus so he could kiss him. [48]But Jesus said to him, "Judas, are you using a kiss to give the Son of Man [d] to his enemies?" [49]When those who were standing around him saw what was happening, they said, "Lord, should we strike them with our swords?" [50]And one of them struck the servant of the high priest and cut off his right ear. [51]Jesus said, "Stop! No more of this." Then he touched the servant's ear and healed him.

[52]Those who came to arrest Jesus were the leading priests, the soldiers who guarded the Temple [d] and the older Jewish leaders. Jesus said to them, "You came out here with swords and clubs as though I were a criminal. [53]I was with you every day in the Temple, and you didn't arrest me there. But this is your time—the time when darkness rules."

Peter Says He Doesn't Know Jesus

[54]They arrested Jesus, and led him away, and brought him into the house of the high priest. Peter followed far behind them. [55]After the soldiers started a fire in the middle of the courtyard and sat together, Peter sat with them. [56]A servant girl saw Peter sitting there in the light, and looking closely at him, she said, "This man was also with him."

[57]But Peter said this was not true; he said, "Woman, I don't know him."

[58]A short time later, another person saw Peter and said, "You are also one of them."

GOD'S WILL

Daring to Follow

Bruce Olson believed strongly that God wanted him to live with the savage Motilone Indians in the jungles of South America. So this shy boy set out to find them.

The Motilones were an isolated and fierce group. They hated white people and had killed or wounded all those who tried to contact them. Bruce's first encounter with them came when they shot an arrow through his thigh. Then they captured him and forced him to walk for hours to their village.

The months that followed were filled with pain, hunger and loneliness. But Bruce wouldn't give up. God had sent him. Eventually Bruce learned the Motilones' language and began communicating with his captors. They called him "Bruchko".

The Motilones have now come to love and respect Bruchko. Through him many people have met Jesus and have benefited from Bruchko's medical and agricultural expertise.

Bruce knew what God wanted him to do, and he wouldn't stop until he had accomplished it.

Jesus also refused to give up on God's will. Read about his experience in **Luke 22:39–46**, when he prayed the night before he was to suffer beatings and a cruel death.

* Knowing it would be hard, why do you think both Jesus and Bruchko insisted on following God's leadership?
* Jesus followed God's will all his life. What makes following God's will possible even when it's tough for you?

Consider . . .

* placing an object in your room that will remind you to seek God's desires.
* reading Bruce Olson's autobiography, entitled *Bruchko*.

For more, see . . .

* Psalm 143:8–11 (p.583)
* Mark 14:32–42 (p.1027)
* Matthew 26:36–46 (p.990)

But Peter said, "Man, I am not!"

[59]About an hour later, another man insisted, "Certainly this man was with him, because he is from Galilee, too."

[60]But Peter said, "Man, I don't know what you are talking about!"

At once, while Peter was still speaking, a cockerel crowed. [61]Then the Lord turned and looked straight at Peter. And Peter remembered what the Lord had said: "Before the cockerel crows this day, you will say three times that you don't know me." [62]Then Peter went outside and cried bitterly.

The People Make Fun of Jesus

[63]The men who were guarding Jesus began making fun of him and beating him.

[64]They blindfolded him and said, "Prove that you are a prophet, [d] and tell us who hit you." [65]They said many cruel things to Jesus.

Jesus Before the Leaders

[66]When day came, the council of the elders of the people, both the leading priests and the teachers of the law, came together and led Jesus to their highest court. [67]They said, "If you are the Christ, [d] tell us."

Jesus said to them, "If I tell you, you will not believe me. [68]And if I ask you, you will not answer. [69]But from now on, the Son of Man [d] will sit at the right hand of the powerful God."

[70]They all said, "Then are you the Son of God?"

Jesus said to them, "You say that I am."

[71]They said, "Why do we need witnesses now? We ourselves heard him say this."

Pilate Questions Jesus

23 Then the whole group stood up and led Jesus to Pilate. [n] [2]They began to accuse Jesus, saying, "We caught this man telling things

---

Pilate   Pontius Pilate was the Roman governor of Judea from AD 26 to AD 36.

SUFFERING

The Price of Goals

In West Perrine, Florida, USA, Lee Lawrence had a dream.

"Can you imagine," he said, "all the churches in the neighbourhood . . . marching up Homestead Avenue to let the drug pushers know that we won't take it any more?"

The drug dealers didn't like Lee or his vision. Twice he was shot at while getting out of his car. The grocery shop he owned was vandalised; then someone tried to burn it down. Refusing to give up, Lee got several pushers arrested. His store became a drug-free haven for the neighbourhood kids.

In March 1989, Lee walked outside his shop and was met by a man firing a semi-automatic rifle. The first shot knocked Lee to the ground. A second man shot Lee again as he lay on the pavement. Minutes later he was dead. But his vision was not.

On Lee Lawrence's funeral day, more than 3,000 people from area churches linked arms and marched up Homestead Avenue singing, "We shall overcome: drugs and crime must go!"

It was a dream come true – and the start of big changes in West Perrine.

Lee was willing to face hardship – even death – to see his goal become a reality. Jesus also endured hardship because of his mission to reclaim humanity from sin. Read about it in **Luke 22:63–71**.

- What price were both Lee and Jesus willing to pay to see their goals become reality?
- How was Jesus' response in this passage like the way you respond when others attack your faith? How is your response different from Jesus'?

Consider . . .

- writing down three goals you would be willing to suffer for.
- looking through a newspaper to find three people who are suffering for doing right, and praying for them each day this week.

For more, see . . .

- Exodus 3:6–10 (p.61)
- 1 Peter 2:18–25 (p.1359)
- Mark 14:62–65 (p.1028)

that mislead our people. He says that we should not pay taxes to Caesar, [d] and he calls himself the Christ, [d] a king."

[3]Pilate asked Jesus, "Are you the king of the Jews?"

Jesus answered, "Those are your words."

[4]Pilate said to the leading priests and the people, "I find nothing against this man."

[5]They were insisting, saying, "But Jesus makes trouble with the people, teaching all around Judea. He began in Galilee, and now he is here."

Pilate Sends Jesus to Herod

[6]Pilate heard this and asked if Jesus was from Galilee. [7]Since Jesus was under Herod's authority, Pilate sent Jesus to Herod, who was in Jerusalem at that time. [8]When Herod saw Jesus, he was very glad, because he had heard about Jesus and had wanted to meet him for a long time. He was hoping to see Jesus work a miracle. [d] [9]Herod asked Jesus many questions, but Jesus said nothing. [10]The leading priests and teachers of the law were standing there, strongly accusing Jesus. [11]After Herod and his soldiers had made fun of Jesus, they dressed him in a kingly robe and sent him back to Pilate. [12]In the past, Pilate and Herod had always been enemies, but on that day they became friends.

Jesus Must Die

[13]Pilate called the people together with the leading priests and the Jewish leaders. [14]He said to them, "You brought this man to me, saying he makes trouble among the people. But I have questioned him before you all, and I have not found him guilty of what you say. [15]Also, Herod found nothing wrong with him; he sent him back to us. Look, he has done nothing for which he should die. [16]So, after I punish him, I will let him go free." [17] [n]

[18]But the people shouted together, "Take this man away! Let Barabbas go free!" [19](Barabbas was a man who was in prison for his part in a riot in the city and for murder.)

[20]Pilate wanted to let Jesus go free and told this to the crowd. [21]But they shouted again, "Crucify him! Crucify him!"

[22]A third time Pilate said to them, "Why? What wrong has he done? I can find no reason to kill him. So I will have him punished and set him free."

[23]But they continued to shout, demanding that Jesus be crucified. Their yelling became so loud that [24]Pilate decided to give them what they wanted. [25]He set free the man who was in jail for rioting and murder, and he handed Jesus over to them to do with him as they wished.

Jesus is Crucified

[26]As they led Jesus away, Simon, a man from Cyrene, was coming in from the fields. They forced him to carry Jesus' cross and to walk behind him.

[27]A large crowd of people was following Jesus, including some women who were sad and crying for him. [28]But Jesus turned and said to them, "Women of Jerusalem, don't cry for me. Cry for yourselves and for your children. [29]The time is coming when people will say, 'Happy are the women who cannot have children and who have no babies to nurse.' [30]Then people will say to the mountains, 'Fall on us!' And they will say to the hills, 'Cover us!' [31]If they act like this now when life is good, what will happen when bad times come?" [n]

[32]There were also two criminals led out with Jesus to be put to death. [33]When they came to a place called the Skull, the soldiers crucified Jesus and the criminals—one on his right and

> ### Sidelight
> If Jesus had been crucified the way most Roman prisoners were executed, he was probably nailed to a capital T-shaped (Roman) cross rather than the Italian cross that most churches now display (Luke 23:32–33).

the other on his left. [34]Jesus said, "Father, forgive them, because they don't know what they are doing." [n]

The soldiers threw lots [d] to decide who would get his clothes. [35]The people stood there watching. And the leaders made fun of Jesus, saying, "He saved others. Let him save himself if he is God's Chosen One, the Christ." [d]

[36]The soldiers also made fun of him, coming to Jesus and offering him some vinegar. [37]They said, "If you are the king of the Jews, save yourself!" [38]At the top of the cross these words were written: THIS IS THE KING OF THE JEWS.

[39]One of the criminals on a cross began to shout insults at Jesus: "Aren't you the Christ? Then save yourself and us."

[40]But the other criminal stopped him and said, "You should fear God! You are getting the same punishment as he is. [41]We are punished justly, getting what we deserve for what we did. But this man has done nothing wrong." [42]Then he said, "Jesus, remember me when you come into your kingdom."

Verse 17 A few Greek copies add verse 17: "Every year at the Passover Feast, Pilate had to release one prisoner to the people."
If . . . come? Literally, "If they do these things in the green tree, what will happen in the dry?"
Verse 34 Some early Greek copies do not have this part of the verse.

[43]Jesus said to him, "I tell you the truth, today you will be with me in paradise."[n]

Jesus Dies

[44]It was about noon, and the whole land became dark until three o'clock in the afternoon, [45]because the sun did not shine. The curtain in the Temple [n] was torn in two. [46]Jesus cried out in a loud voice, "Father, I give you my life." After Jesus said this, he died.

[47]When the army officer there saw what happened, he praised God, saying, "Surely this was a good man!"

[48]When all the people who had gathered there to watch saw what happened, they returned home, beating their chests because they were so sad. [49]But those who were close friends of Jesus, including the women who had followed him from Galilee, stood at a distance and watched.

Joseph Takes Jesus' Body

[50]There was a good and religious man named Joseph who was a member of the Jewish council. [51]But he had not agreed to the other leaders' plans and actions against Jesus. He was from the Jewish town of Arimathea and was waiting for the kingdom of God to come. [52]Joseph went to Pilate to ask for the body of Jesus. [53]He took the body down from the cross, wrapped it in cloth, and put it in a tomb that was cut out of a wall of rock. This tomb had never been used before. [54]This was late on Preparation [d] Day, and when the sun went down, the Sabbath [d] day would begin.

---

paradise   A place where people who are obedient to God go when they die.
curtain in the Temple   A curtain divided the Most Holy Place from the other part of the Temple. That was the special building in Jerusalem where God commanded the Jewish people to worship him.

NON-CHRISTIANS

Taking Every Opportunity

Steve and Lisa went on holiday to Indonesia and they were expecting it to be luxurious: sunbathing on the white sandy beach, snorkelling on the coral reef, eating lots of nice food and seeing all the sights. Things turned out very differently.

On the day they arrived, they were talking to some of the locals on the beach. They ended up talking about Jesus and, to their amazement, they all wanted to find out more. They asked Steve and Lisa to come back the next day and share from the Bible with them. They went back the next day and twenty people turned up!

Steve and Lisa spent every afternoon running a Bible study on the beach, and by the end of their holiday eight people had become Christians. They were also asked to speak at the local church in the shanty town. They got on so well that they were asked to return and run three weeks of mission.

Steve and Lisa returned several months later, and during the three weeks saw hundreds of people give their lives to God. They were absolutely blown away by what they saw – and all as a result of talking to people while on holiday!

Read **Luke 23:26–43**.

• How do you think Jesus would have felt about Steve and Lisa spending their holiday talking about him?
• Do you look for opportunities to talk about Jesus and then take them when they come?

Consider . . .

• being bold and talking to your friends about what Jesus has done in your life.
• meeting up with some Christian friends to pray for your other friends to become Christians and see what God does.

For more, see . . .

• Romans 1:16 (p.1185)
• 1 Peter 3:15–18 (p.1360)
• Ephesians 5:13–16 (p.1275)

[55]The women who had come from Galilee with Jesus followed Joseph and saw the tomb and how Jesus' body was laid. [56]Then the women left to prepare spices and perfumes.

On the Sabbath day they rested, as the law of Moses commanded.

Jesus Rises from the Dead

24 Very early on the first day of the week, at dawn, the women came to the tomb, bringing the spices they had prepared. [2]They found the stone rolled away from the entrance of the tomb, [3]but when they went in, they did not find the body of the Lord Jesus. [4]While they were wondering about this, two men in shining clothes suddenly stood beside them. [5]The women were very afraid and bowed their heads to the ground. The men said to them, "Why are you looking for a living person in this place for the dead? [6]He is not here; he has risen from the dead. Do you remember what he told you in Galilee? [7]He said the Son of Man *d* must be handed over to sinful people, be crucified and rise from the dead on the third day." [8]Then the women remembered what Jesus had said.

[9]The women left the tomb and told all these things to the eleven apostles *d* and the other followers. [10]It was Mary Magdalene, Joanna, Mary the mother of James, and some other women who told the apostles everything that had happened at the tomb. [11]But they did not believe the women, because it sounded like nonsense. [12]But Peter got up and ran to the tomb. Bending down and looking in, he saw only the cloth that Jesus' body had been wrapped in. Peter went away to his home, wondering about what had happened.

Jesus on the Road to Emmaus

[13]That same day two of Jesus' followers were going to a town named Emmaus, about eleven kilometres from Jerusalem. [14]They were talking about everything that had happened. [15]While they were talking and discussing, Jesus himself came near and began walking with them, [16]but they were kept from recognising him. [17]Then he said, "What are these things you are talking about while you walk?"

The two followers stopped, looking very sad. [18]The one named Cleopas answered, "Are you the only visitor in Jerusalem who does not know what just happened there?"

LIFE

Good News

Bob Delker's family members mourned the day he died, but they also knew that others would live now because of him. Bob had decided to give his body to medicine. This meant that people who desperately needed organ donations would receive them. For these people, Bob's death brought new life.

A few received badly needed bone transplants. Critically injured burn victims received skin grafts. Corneas from Bob's eyes allowed two people to see.

In all, Bob's final gift helped 34 people. Countless others have been inspired to become organ donors because of Bob's example.

Bob's death brought new life to many people. Similarly, the sad news of Jesus' death meant the possibility of new life for all people everywhere. But unlike Bob Delker, Jesus didn't stay dead. Read **Luke 24:1–11** to discover what happened.

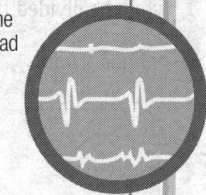

- How is an organ transplant a little like Jesus' coming back from the dead?
- How does Jesus' rising from the dead make a difference in your life?

Consider . . .

- listing the ways in which Christ's death has given you life.
- growing a plant in your room as a reminder of the spiritual life that Jesus gives you.

For more, see . . .

- Psalm 36:7–9 (p.521)
- John 20:1–18 (p.1132)
- Mark 16:1–8 (p.1031)

¹⁹Jesus said to them, "What are you talking about?"

They said, "About Jesus of Nazareth. He was a prophet ᵈ who said and did many powerful things before God and all the people. ²⁰Our leaders and the leading priests handed him over to be sentenced to death, and they crucified him. ²¹But we were hoping that he would free Israel. Besides this, it is now the third day since this happened. ²²And today some women among us amazed us. Early this morning they went to the tomb, ²³but they did not find his body there. They came and told us that they had seen a vision of angels who said that Jesus was alive! ²⁴So some of our group went to the tomb, too. They found it just as the women said, but they did not see Jesus."

²⁵Then Jesus said to them, "You are foolish and slow to believe everything the prophets said. ²⁶They said that the Christ ᵈ must suffer these things before he enters his glory." ²⁷Then starting with what Moses and all the prophets had said about him, Jesus began to explain everything that had been written about himself in the Scriptures. ᵈ

²⁸They came near the town of Emmaus, and Jesus acted as if he were going farther. ²⁹But they begged him, "Stay with us, because it is late; it is almost night." So he went in to stay with them.

³⁰When Jesus was at the table with them, he took some bread, gave thanks, divided it and gave it to them. ³¹And then they were allowed to recognise Jesus. But when they saw who he was, he disappeared. ³²They said to each other, "It felt like a fire burning in us when Jesus talked to us on the road and explained the Scriptures to us."

³³So the two followers got up at once and went back to Jerusalem. There they found the eleven apostles ᵈ and others gathered. ³⁴They were saying, "The Lord really has risen from the dead! He showed himself to Simon."

³⁵Then the two followers told what had happened on the road and how they recognised Jesus when he divided the bread.

Jesus Appears to His Followers

³⁶While the two followers were telling this, Jesus himself stood right in the middle of them and said, "Peace be with you."

³⁷They were fearful and terrified and thought they were seeing a ghost. ³⁸But Jesus said, "Why are you troubled? Why do you doubt what you see? ³⁹Look at my hands and my feet. It is I myself! Touch me and see, because a ghost does not have a living body as you see I have."

⁴⁰After Jesus said this, he showed them his hands and feet. ⁴¹While they still could not believe it because they were amazed and happy, Jesus said to them, "Do you have any food here?" ⁴²They gave him a piece of grilled fish. ⁴³While the followers watched, Jesus took the fish and ate it.

⁴⁴He said to them, "Remember when I was with you before? I said that everything written about me must happen—everything in the law of Moses, the books of the prophets ᵈ and the Psalms."

⁴⁵Then Jesus opened their minds so they could understand the Scriptures. ᵈ ⁴⁶He said to them, "It is written that the Christ ᵈ would suffer and rise from the dead on the third day ⁴⁷and that a change of hearts and lives and forgiveness of sins would be preached in his name to all nations, starting at Jerusalem. ⁴⁸You are witnesses of these things. ⁴⁹I will send you what my Father has promised, but you must stay in Jerusalem until you have received that power from heaven."

Jesus Goes Back to Heaven

⁵⁰Jesus led his followers as far as Bethany, and he raised his hands and blessed them. ⁵¹While he was blessing them, he was separated from them and carried into heaven. ⁵²They worshipped him and returned to Jerusalem very happy. ⁵³They stayed in the Temple ᵈ all the time, praising God.

John

Why Read This Book:
* Be reminded that Jesus Christ is fully human and fully divine (John 1).
* Find stories that reveal Jesus' glory as giver of eternal life (John 2—11).
* Learn the importance of Jesus' death and resurrection (John 13—21).

When?

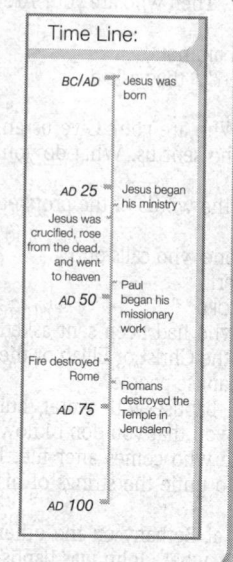

Time Line:

BC/AD — Jesus was born

AD 25 — Jesus began his ministry

Jesus was crucified, rose from the dead, and went to heaven

AD 50 — Paul began his missionary work

Fire destroyed Rome

AD 75 — Romans destroyed the Temple in Jerusalem

AD 100

Behind the Scenes:

Imagine meeting someone for the first time. The conversation begins with "Hi, I'm Emma. I work in the Finance Department. I live down the road." You might go on to talk about hobbies, interests, background and other information.

But you still wouldn't really know that person. If you saw each other regularly, you would begin to understand each other's personality, values and uniqueness.

In some ways, the first three gospels (Matthew, p.935; Mark, p.996; and Luke, p.1034) are like the first part of a relationship with Jesus Christ. Through these books, we get to know stories about Jesus and what he did. But the Gospel of John digs deeper into who Jesus was, why he lived and the meaning of his life.

This fourth gospel is quite different from the other three. Like the others, it tells what Jesus said and did. But it goes a step further by interpreting Jesus' significance as God's Son.

Many new believers turn first to this gospel to discover what it means to be a Christian. That's not surprising, given the book's purpose as stated in John 20:31: "These [things] are written so that you may believe that Jesus is the Christ, the Son of God. Then, by believing, you may have life through his name."

Where?

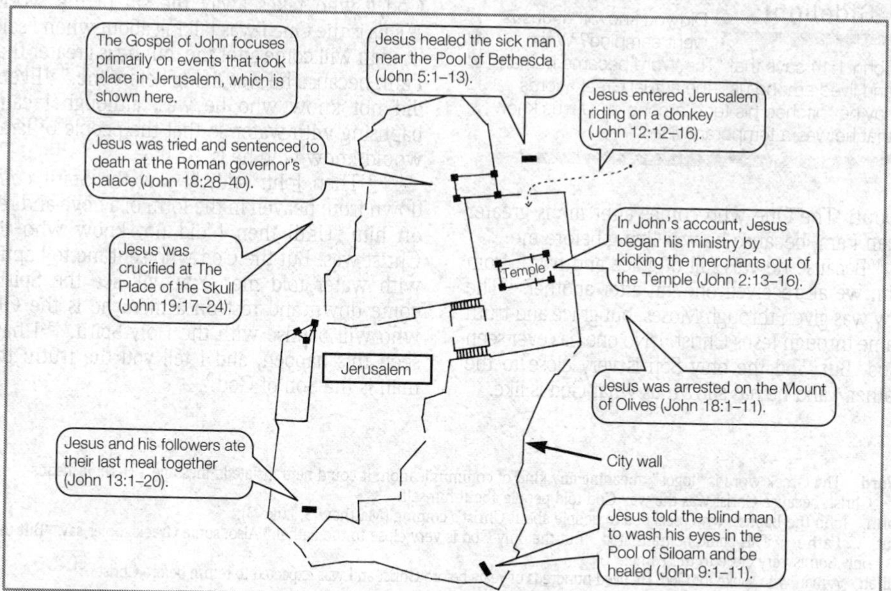

The Gospel of John focuses primarily on events that took place in Jerusalem, which is shown here.

Jesus healed the sick man near the Pool of Bethesda (John 5:1–13).

Jesus entered Jerusalem riding on a donkey (John 12:12–16).

Jesus was tried and sentenced to death at the Roman governor's palace (John 18:28–40).

In John's account, Jesus began his ministry by kicking the merchants out of the Temple (John 2:13–16).

Temple

Jesus was crucified at The Place of the Skull (John 19:17–24).

Jerusalem

Jesus was arrested on the Mount of Olives (John 18:1–11).

City wall

Jesus and his followers ate their last meal together (John 13:1–20).

Jesus told the blind man to wash his eyes in the Pool of Siloam and be healed (John 9:1–11).

Christ Comes to the World

1 In the beginning there was the Word.[n] The Word was with God, and the Word was God. [2]He was with God in the beginning. [3]All things were made by him, and nothing was made without him. [4]In him there was life, and that life was the light of all people. [5]The Light shines in the darkness, and the darkness has not overpowered it.

[6]There was a man named John[n] who was sent by God. [7]He came to tell people the truth about the Light so that through him all people could hear about the Light and believe. [8]John was not the Light, but he came to tell people the truth about the Light. [9]The true Light that gives light to all was coming into the world!

[10]The Word was in the world, and the world was made by him, but the world did not know him. [11]He came to the world that was his own, but his own people did not accept him. [12]But to all who did accept him and believe in him he gave the right to become children of God. [13]They did not become his children in any human way— by any human parents or human desire. They were born of God.

[14]The Word became human and lived among us. We saw his glory—the glory that belongs to the only Son of the Father—and he was full of grace and truth. [15]John tells the truth about him and cries out, saying, "This is the One I told you

---

Sidelight Did you know that Jesus went camping? When John 1:14 says that "The Word became human and lived among us," the actual Greek words say he "pitched his tent" among us. Jesus knew that he was a temporary visitor.

---

about: 'The One who comes after me is greater than I am, because he was living before me.' "

[16]Because he was full of grace and truth, from him we all received one gift after another. [17]The law was given through Moses, but grace and truth came through Jesus Christ. [18]No one has ever seen God. But God the only Son is very close to the Father,[n] and he has shown us what God is like.

John Tells People About Jesus

[19]Here is the truth John[n] told when the Jews in Jerusalem sent priests and Levites to ask him, "Who are you?"

[20]John spoke freely and did not refuse to answer. He said, "I am not the Christ."[d]

[21]So they asked him, "Then who are you? Are you Elijah?"[n]

He answered, "No, I am not."

"Are you the Prophet?"[n] they asked.

He answered, "No."

[22]Then they said, "Who are you? Give us an answer to tell those who sent us. What do you say about yourself?"

[23]John told them in the words of the prophet Isaiah:

"This is the voice of one who calls out:
    'Prepare in the desert
        the way for the LORD.' "   *Isaiah 40:3*

[24]Some Pharisees[d] who had been sent asked John: [25]"If you are not the Christ or Elijah or the Prophet, why do you baptise people?"

[26]John answered, "I baptise with water, but there is one here with you that you don't know about. [27]He is the One who comes after me. I am not good enough to untie the strings of his sandals."

[28]This all happened at Bethany on the other side of the Jordan River, where John was baptising people.

[29]The next day John saw Jesus coming towards him. John said, "Look, the Lamb of God,[n] who takes away the sin of the world! [30]This is the One I was talking about when I said, 'A man will come after me, but he is greater than I am, because he was living before me.' [31]Even I did not know who he was, although I came baptising with water so that the people of Israel would know who he is."

[32-33]Then John said, "I saw the Spirit come down from heaven in the form of a dove and rest on him. Until then I did not know who the Christ was. But the God who sent me to baptise with water told me, 'You will see the Spirit[d] come down and rest on a man; he is the One who will baptise with the Holy Spirit.' [34]I have seen this happen, and I tell you the truth: this man is the Son of God."

Word   The Greek word is "logos", meaning any kind of communication; it could be translated "message". Here, it means Christ, because Christ was the way God told people about himself.

John   John the Baptist, who preached to people about Christ's coming (Matthew 3, Luke 3).

But . . . Father   This could be translated, "But the only God is very close to the Father." Also, some Greek copies say, "But the only Son is very close to the Father."

Elijah   A man who spoke for God. He lived hundreds of years before Christ and was expected to return before Christ (Malachi 4:5–6).

Prophet   They probably meant the prophet that God told Moses he would send (Deuteronomy 18:15–19).

Lamb of God   Name for Jesus. Jesus is like the lambs that were offered for a sacrifice to God.

The First Followers of Jesus

[35]The next day John[n] was there again with two of his followers. [36]When he saw Jesus walking by, he said, "Look, the Lamb of God!"[n]

[37]The two followers heard John say this, so they followed Jesus. [38]When Jesus turned and saw them following him, he asked, "What are you looking for?"

They said, "Rabbi, where are you staying?" ("Rabbi" means "Teacher".)

[39]He answered, "Come and see." So the two men went with Jesus and saw where he was staying and stayed there with him that day. It was about four o'clock in the afternoon.

[40]One of the two men who followed Jesus after they heard John speak about him was Andrew, Simon Peter's brother. [41]The first thing Andrew did was to find his brother Simon and say to him, "We have found the Messiah." ("Messiah" means "Christ". [d])

John John the Baptist, who preached to people about Christ's coming (Matthew 3, Luke 3).
Lamb of God Name for Jesus. Jesus is like the lambs that were offered for a sacrifice to God.

JESUS CHRIST

Where's the Party?

"Do you want to go to the party on Saturday, Annie?" Simon asked.

Annie looked at the floor and said, "No thanks, it's alright."

"What? Why don't you want to come? It'll be fun! It's only at Noel's and his parents will be there," he explained.

"I know, but no thanks," she replied sadly.

Simon could never understand Annie. She was a really nice-looking girl and he was sure she could be a lot of fun, but somehow it seemed that she never joined in anything. Almost as if she was afraid. He knew that she was a Christian, but failed to see how going to a party could be so terrible. He wasn't asking her to sleep with him or anything!

Annie could see that Simon was mystified, and one day she tried to explain her feelings to him.

"It's just that I don't want to be seen doing things that people might think are wrong . . . " she started.

Simon interrupted her straight away.

"No, Annie, you've got it wrong. If you want to be a good Christian then you've got to start being like Jesus. People never pointed at Jesus because he was doing things wrong, they pointed at him because he was doing things right!"

Annie was stunned. She'd never thought of it like that before.

But he was right! Jesus was known for the things he did, not the things he didn't do!

So she went to the party with Simon — taking Jesus with her — and had a great time. She danced and laughed and made new friends that she could influence for Christ, without ever having to compromise her position as a Christian. Gradually Annie became seen as a beautiful, fun-loving Christian girl.

Read **John 1:1–18** and see that John always pointed towards the glory of Jesus. He spoke of his grace and truth.

* How did Annie become like Jesus?
* Can you see your life as a way of pointing people to Jesus?

Consider . . .

* listing the things you can do with your friends without compromising your Christian beliefs.
* praying for a friend you would like to tell about Jesus and the way he has changed your life.

For more, see . . .

* Matthew 11:16–19 (p.959)
* Philippians 2:5–11 (p.1282)
* John 17:13–19 (p.1128)

⁴²Then Andrew took Simon to Jesus. Jesus looked at him and said, "You are Simon son of John. You will be called Cephas." ("Cephas" means "Peter". ⁿ)

⁴³The next day Jesus decided to go to Galilee. He found Philip and said to him, "Follow me."

⁴⁴Philip was from the town of Bethsaida, where Andrew and Peter lived. ⁴⁵Philip found Nathanael and told him, "We have found the man that Moses wrote about in the law, and the prophets ᵈ also wrote about him. He is Jesus, the son of Joseph, from Nazareth."

⁴⁶But Nathanael said to Philip, "Can anything good come from Nazareth?"

Philip answered, "Come and see."

⁴⁷As Jesus saw Nathanael coming towards him, he said, "Here is truly an Israelite. There is nothing false in him."

⁴⁸Nathanael asked, "How do you know me?"

Jesus answered, "I saw you when you were under the fig tree, before Philip told you about me."

⁴⁹Then Nathanael said to Jesus, "Teacher, you are the Son of God; you are the King of Israel."

⁵⁰Jesus said to Nathanael, "Do you believe simply because I told you I saw you under the fig tree? You will see greater things than that."
⁵¹And Jesus said to them, "I tell you the truth, you will all see heaven open and 'angels of God going up and coming down' ⁿ on the Son of Man." ᵈ

The Wedding at Cana

2 Two days later there was a wedding in the town of Cana in Galilee. Jesus' mother was there, ²and Jesus and his followers were also invited to the wedding. ³When all the wine was gone, Jesus' mother said to him, "They have no more wine."

⁴Jesus answered, "Dear woman, why come to me? My time has not yet come."

⁵His mother said to the servants, "Do whatever he tells you to do."

⁶In that place there were six stone water jars that the Jews used in their washing ceremony. ⁿ Each jar held about 100 litres.

⁷Jesus said to the servants, "Fill the jars with water." So they filled the jars to the top.

⁸Then he said to them, "Now take some out and give it to the master of the feast."

So they took the water to the master. ⁹When he tasted it, the water had become wine. He did not know where the wine came from, but the servants who had brought the water knew. The master of the wedding called the bridegroom ¹⁰and said to him, "People always serve the best wine first. Later, after the guests have been drinking awhile, they serve the cheaper wine. But you have saved the best wine till now."

¹¹So in Cana of Galilee Jesus did his first miracle. ᵈ There he showed his glory, and his followers believed in him.

Sidelight The wedding at Cana (John 2:1–11) wouldn't have involved a short ceremony followed by a cold buffet reception. In Jesus' day, weddings usually lasted about a week. On the first day, the couple exchanged vows under a canopy. Then, for the next six days or more, the couple and all the guests celebrated with dancing, games, music, food and wine.

Jesus in the Temple

¹²After this, Jesus went to the town of Capernaum with his mother, brothers and followers. They stayed there for just a few days. ¹³When it was almost time for the Jewish Passover ᵈ Feast, Jesus went to Jerusalem. ¹⁴In the Temple ᵈ he found people selling cattle, sheep and doves. He saw others sitting at tables, exchanging different kinds of money. ¹⁵Jesus made a whip out of cords and forced all of them, both the sheep and cattle, to leave the Temple. He turned over the tables and scattered the money of those who were exchanging it. ¹⁶Then he said to those who were selling pigeons, "Take these things out of here! Don't make my Father's house a place for buying and selling!"

¹⁷When this happened, the followers remembered what was written in the Scriptures: ᵈ "My strong love for your Temple completely controls me." ⁿ

¹⁸The Jews said to Jesus, "Show us a miracle ᵈ to prove you have the right to do these things."

¹⁹Jesus answered them, "Destroy this temple, and I will build it again in three days."

Peter The Greek name "Peter", like the Aramaic name "Cephas", means "rock".
'angels . . . down' These words are from Genesis 28:12.
washing ceremony The Jewish people washed themselves in special ways before eating, before worshipping in the Temple and at other special times.
"My . . . me." Quotation from Psalm 69:9.

20The Jews answered, "It took 46 years to build this Temple! Do you really believe you can build it again in three days?"

21(But the temple Jesus meant was his own body. 22After Jesus was raised from the dead, his followers remembered that Jesus had said this. Then they believed the Scripture *d* and the words Jesus had said.)

23When Jesus was in Jerusalem for the Passover Feast, many people believed in him because they saw the miracles he did. 24But Jesus did not trust himself to them because he knew them all. 25He did not need anyone to tell him about people, because he knew what was in people's minds.

Nicodemus Comes to Jesus

3 There was a man named Nicodemus who was one of the Pharisees *d* and an important Jewish leader. 2One night Nicodemus came to Jesus and said, "Teacher, we know you are a teacher sent from God, because no one can do the miracles *d* you do unless God is with him."

3Jesus answered, "I tell you the truth, unless one is born again, he cannot be in God's kingdom."

4Nicodemus said, "But if a person is already old, how can he be born again? He cannot enter his mother's body again. So how can a person be born a second time?"

5But Jesus answered, "I tell you the truth, unless one is born from water and the Spirit, *d* he cannot enter God's kingdom. 6Human life comes from human parents, but spiritual life comes from the Spirit. 7Don't be surprised when I tell you, 'You must all be born again.' 8The wind blows where it wants to and you hear the sound of it, but you don't know where the wind comes from or where it is going. It is the same with every person who is born from the Spirit."

ANGER

Anger to Action

Ben and Caroline were students when they visited a township primary school in South Africa. The system of Apartheid had meant that the white minority lived much wealthier lives than the black majority. They saw black children sitting three to a desk and struggling to afford even basic pencils and notebooks. This made them angry when they thought of the school they had seen that morning, with its swimming pool, landscaped grounds and fantastic resources, which had been previously only for white children.

It would have been easy for them to feel bitter about the injustice they had seen, but instead Ben and Caroline felt that God was telling them to do something about the township children's situation.

The school had a brilliant choir, and Ben and Caroline thought that if they could bring them to the UK to perform, they would be able to raise money for their school.

They had never done anything like this before, and it took two years of hard fundraising and planning back in the UK to make this dream a reality, but it was their anger at the injustice that they had felt in South Africa that kept them going.

The choir came to the UK and performed around the country, selling CDs of their music and even meeting the Prime Minister. It was an amazing experience for Ben, Caroline and the children, but more importantly, the choir raised enough money to pay for a library and science building at the school in South Africa.

Jesus sometimes became angry too. Read what made him angry in **John 2:12–22**.

* What was the root cause of Jesus', and Ben and Caroline's anger?
* If Jesus and Ben and Caroline had not been angry, how might the outcomes have differed?

Consider . . .

* whether you feel angry about something at the moment. Is it righteous anger?
* asking God to show you how you can use your anger at an injustice to fuel you to demonstrate his love.

For more, see . . .

* Psalm 103:7–13 (p.559)
* James 1:19–20 (p.1348)

* Ephesians 4:26–27 (p.1274)

⁹Nicodemus asked, "How can this happen?"

¹⁰Jesus said, "You are an important teacher in Israel, and you don't understand these things? ¹¹I tell you the truth, we talk about what we know, and we tell about what we have seen, but you don't accept what we tell you. ¹²I have told you about things here on earth, and you do not believe me. So you will not believe me if I tell you about things of heaven. ¹³The only one who has ever gone up to heaven is the One who came down from heaven—the Son of Man. *d*

¹⁴"Just as Moses lifted up the snake in the desert, *n* the Son of Man must also be lifted up. ¹⁵So that everyone who believes can have eternal life in him.

¹⁶"God loved the world so much that he gave his one and only Son so that whoever believes in him may not be lost, but have eternal life. ¹⁷God did not send his Son into the world to judge the world guilty, but to save the world through him. ¹⁸People who believe in God's Son are not judged guilty. Those who do not believe have already been judged guilty, because they have not believed in God's one and only Son. ¹⁹They are judged by this fact: the Light has come into the world, but they did not want light. They wanted darkness, because they were doing evil things. ²⁰All who do evil hate the light and will not come to the light, because it will show all the evil things they do. ²¹But those who follow the true way come to the light, and it shows that the things they do were done through God."

Jesus and John the Baptist

²²After this, Jesus and his followers went into the area of Judea, where he stayed with his followers and baptised people. ²³John was also

---

Moses . . . desert When the Israelites were dying from snake bites, God told Moses to put a brass snake on a pole. The people who looked at the snake were healed (Numbers 21:4–9).

ETERNAL LIFE

The Ultimate Price

Tim had been in New York City before. He loved the annual trip that his family made from Provo, Utah, to watch the US Open together in New York, USA.

One Sunday during the 1990 tournament, Tim was waiting with his parents in a Manhattan underground station when a gang approached them. Surrounding the family, they robbed Tim's father and then attacked Tim's mother.

Tim fought back to defend his mother. The attackers turned from Tim's mother to Tim. In the struggle, one of the robbers pulled a knife and stabbed Tim to death.

Tim paid the ultimate price because he couldn't stand watching the ones he loved get hurt. Jesus, God's son, willingly paid the ultimate price for us because he doesn't want us to get hurt for ever.

In **John 3:1–21**, Jesus talks about the gift of eternal life that his death would provide.

- How were Tim's feelings for his parents like God's desires for us? How were they different?
- According to this passage (especially verses 16–18), what must we do to receive all that God desires for us?

Consider . . .

- writing John 3:16 on paper, putting it in a box, and gift-wrapping the box. Give the box to a friend as a reminder of God's gift of eternal life.
- asking your minister or youth leader what eternal life is, then comparing the answer with what Jesus said in this passage.

For more, see . . .

- Isaiah 12 (p.654)
- 1 John 5:1–12 (p.1375)
- 1 Timothy 1:12–17 (p.1308)

baptising in Aenon, near Salim, because there was plenty of water there. People were going there to be baptised. 24(This was before John was put into prison.)

25Some of John's followers had an argument with a Jew about religious washing. *n* 26So they came to John and said, "Teacher, remember the man who was with you on the other side of the Jordan River, the one you spoke about so much? He is baptising, and everyone is going to him."

27John answered, "A man can get only what God gives him. 28You yourselves heard me say, 'I am not the Christ, *d* but I am the one sent to prepare the way for him.' 29The bride belongs only to the bridegroom. But the friend who helps the bridegroom stands by and listens to him. He is thrilled that he gets to hear the bridegroom's voice. In the same way, I am really happy. 30He must become greater, and I must become less important.

The One Who Comes from Heaven

31"The One who comes from above is greater than all. The one who is from the earth belongs to the earth and talks about things on the earth. But the One who comes from heaven is greater than all. 32He tells what he has seen and heard, but no one accepts what he says. 33Whoever accepts what he says has proven that God is true. 34The One whom God sent speaks the words of God, because God gives him the Spirit *d* fully. 35The Father loves the Son and has given him power over everything. 36Those who believe in the Son have eternal life, but those who do not obey the Son will never have life. God's anger stays on them."

Jesus and a Samaritan Woman

4 The Pharisees *d* heard that Jesus was making and baptising more followers than John, 2although Jesus himself did not baptise people, but his followers did. 3Jesus knew that the Pharisees had heard about him, so he left Judea and went back to Galilee. 4But on the way he had to go through the country of Samaria.

5In Samaria Jesus came to the town called Sychar, which is near the field Jacob gave to his son Joseph. 6Jacob's well was there. Jesus was tired from his long trip, so he sat down beside the well. It was about twelve o'clock noon. 7When a Samaritan *d* woman came to the well to get some water, Jesus said to her, "Please give me a drink."

8(This happened while Jesus' followers were in town buying some food.)

9The woman said, "I am surprised that you ask me for a drink, since you are a Jewish man and I am a Samaritan woman." (Jewish people are not friends with Samaritans. *n*)

10Jesus said, "If you only knew the free gift of God and who it is that is asking you for water, you would have asked him, and he would have given you living water."

11The woman said, "Sir, where will you get this living water? The well is very deep, and you have nothing to get water with. 12Are you greater than Jacob, our father, who gave us this well and drank from it himself along with his sons and flocks?"

13Jesus answered, "Everyone who drinks this water will be thirsty again, 14but whoever drinks the water I give will never be thirsty. The water I give will become a spring of water flowing up inside that person, giving eternal life."

15The woman said to him, "Sir, give me this water so I will never be thirsty again and will not have to come back here to get more water."

16Jesus told her, "Go and get your husband and come back here."

17The woman answered, "I have no husband."

Jesus said to her, "You are right to say you have no husband. 18Really you have had five husbands, and the man you live with now is not your husband. You told the truth."

19The woman said, "Sir, I can see that you are a prophet. *d* 20Our ancestors worshipped on this mountain, but you Jews say that Jerusalem is the place where people must worship."

21Jesus said, "Believe me, woman. The time is coming when neither in Jerusalem nor on this mountain will you actually worship the Father. 22You Samaritans worship something you don't understand. We understand what we worship, because salvation comes from the Jews. 23The time is coming when the true worshippers will worship the Father in spirit and truth, and that time is here already. You see, the Father too is actively seeking such people to worship him. 24God is spirit, and those who worship him must worship in spirit and truth."

25The woman said, "I know that the Messiah is coming." (Messiah is the One called Christ. *d*) "When the Messiah comes, he will explain everything to us."

26Then Jesus said, "I am he—I, the one talking to you."

---

religious washing The Jewish people washed themselves in special ways before eating, before worshipping in the Temple and at other special times.
Jewish people . . . Samaritans. This can also be translated "Jewish people don't use things that Samaritans have used."

²⁷Just then his followers came back from town and were surprised to see him talking with a woman. But none of them asked, "What do you want?" or "Why are you talking with her?"

²⁸Then the woman left her water jar and went back to town. She said to the people, ²⁹"Come and see a man who told me everything I ever did. Do you think he might be the Christ?" ³⁰So the people left the town and went to see Jesus.

³¹Meanwhile, his followers were begging him, "Teacher, eat something."

³²But Jesus answered, "I have food to eat that you know nothing about."

³³So the followers asked themselves, "Has somebody already brought him food?"

³⁴Jesus said, "My food is to do what the One who sent me wants me to do and to finish his work. ³⁵You have a saying, 'Four more months till harvest.' But I tell you, open your eyes and look at the fields ready for harvest now. ³⁶Already, the

Sidelight

Jesus risked getting into a lot of trouble when he spoke with the Samaritan woman (see John 4:1–30). The Jewish law made it illegal for teachers to speak to women, Jews to talk to Samaritans and the "righteous" to mingle with "sinners". Read what Jesus might have said to some of his critics in Matthew 9:10–12 (p.953).

STEREOTYPES

Prejudice

The bell rang. English was over for another day. Sam stared at his short story.

His classmates walked by, some commenting as they passed. "What an imagination you have in there!" Sam wasn't sure if it was a compliment or not. "I'd love to hear you try reading it yourself, spastic!" He was sure that wasn't a compliment.

Sam waited for the classroom to clear, then made his way to his next class: maths.

His teacher greeted him at the doorway. "Hello, Sam!" he yelled. "How are you today?"

Sam just nodded and wondered, once again, why people treated him as though he was deaf.

When Sam moved from his special school, one of the hardest adjustments was learning how to communicate with others. Some people were great. They shared Sam's interest in chess and science fiction, and made special efforts to make him their friend. Others, though, openly insulted him for being different.

Sam learned a lot about prejudice during his time at school. Because of his severe cerebral palsy, some people expected Sam to be stupid. He always took special pleasure in knocking down stereotypes by writing a creative short story or tackling the toughest maths problem.

Sam was different from others in some ways. His speech was often difficult to understand. He communicated by typing with touchsticks strapped to his hands. And he travelled by moving a joystick attached to his wheelchair.

But Sam had a lot more in common with those around him than many people thought. A lot of them refused to see beyond his wheelchair or his inability to speak as they did. And their prejudice was tough on Sam.

Jesus also had to overcome people's prejudice. Read **John 4:5–42** about how Jesus dealt with prejudice towards himself and others.

- How did Sam break down prejudice in the same way that Jesus did?
- What prejudices do you have? How would Jesus respond to those prejudices?

Consider . . .

- writing a letter to the editor of your school or local newspaper concerning a prejudice you see. Describe ways to combat that prejudice.
- regularly eating lunch at school with someone who has been hurt by prejudice.

For more, see . . .

- Psalm 9:7–10 (p.505)
- Galatians 3:26–29 (p.1261)
- Acts 10:1–33 (p.1154)

one who harvests is being paid and is gathering crops for eternal life. So the one who plants and the one who harvests celebrate at the same time. ³⁷Here the saying is true, 'One person plants, and another harvests.' ³⁸I sent you to harvest a crop that you did not work for. Others did the work, and you will finish their work." ⁿ

³⁹Many of the Samaritans in that town believed in Jesus because of what the woman said: "He told me everything I ever did." ⁴⁰When the Samaritans came to Jesus, they begged him to stay with them, so he stayed there two more days. ⁴¹And many more believed because of the things he said.

⁴²They said to the woman, "First we believed in Jesus because of what you told us, but now we believe because we heard him ourselves. We know that this man really is the Saviour of the world."

Jesus Heals an Officer's Son

⁴³Two days later, Jesus left and went to Galilee. ⁴⁴(Jesus had said before that a prophet ^d is not respected in his own country.) ⁴⁵When Jesus arrived in Galilee, the people there welcomed him. They had seen all the things he did at the Passover ^d Feast in Jerusalem, because they had been there, too.

⁴⁶Jesus went again to visit Cana in Galilee where he had changed the water into wine. One of the king's important officers lived in the city of Capernaum, and his son was sick. ⁴⁷When he heard that Jesus had come from Judea to Galilee, he went to Jesus and begged him to come to Capernaum and heal his son, because his son was almost dead. ⁴⁸Jesus said to him, "You people must see signs and miracles ^d before you will believe in me."

⁴⁹The officer said, "Sir, come before my child dies."

⁵⁰Jesus answered, "Go. Your son will live."

The man believed what Jesus told him and went home. ⁵¹On the way the man's servants came and met him and told him, "Your son is alive."

⁵²The man asked, "What time did my son begin to get well?"

They answered, "Yesterday at one o'clock the fever left him."

⁵³The father knew that one o'clock was the exact time that Jesus had said, "Your son will live." So the man and all the people who lived in his house believed in Jesus.

⁵⁴That was the second miracle Jesus did after coming from Judea to Galilee.

Jesus Heals a Man at a Pool

5 Later Jesus went to Jerusalem for a special Jewish feast. ²In Jerusalem there is a pool with five covered porches, which is called Bethesda ⁿ in the Jewish language. ⁿ This pool is near the Sheep Gate. ³Many sick people were lying on the porches beside the pool. Some were blind, some were crippled and some were paralysed. ⁿ ⁵A man was lying there who had been sick for 38 years. ⁶When Jesus saw the man and knew that he had been sick for such a long time, Jesus asked him, "Do you want to be well?"

⁷The sick man answered, "Sir, there is no one to help me get into the pool when the water starts moving. While I am coming to the water, someone else always gets in before me."

⁸Then Jesus said, "Stand up. Pick up your mat and walk." ⁹And immediately the man was well; he picked up his mat and began to walk.

The day this happened was a Sabbath ^d day. ¹⁰So the Jews said to the man who had been healed, "Today is the Sabbath. It is against our law for you to carry your mat on the Sabbath day."

¹¹But he answered, "The man who made me well told me, 'Pick up your mat and walk.'"

¹²Then they asked him, "Who is the man who told you to pick up your mat and walk?"

¹³But the man who had been healed did not know who it was, because there were many people in that place, and Jesus had left.

¹⁴Later, Jesus found the man at the Temple ^d and said to him, "See, you are well now. Stop sinning so that something worse does not happen to you."

¹⁵Then the man left and told the Jews that Jesus was the one who had made him well.

¹⁶Because Jesus was doing this on the Sabbath day, the Jews began to persecute him. ¹⁷But Jesus said to them, "My Father never stops working, and so I keep working, too."

¹⁸This made the Jews try still harder to kill him. They said, "First Jesus was breaking the law about the Sabbath day. Now he says that God is his own Father, making himself equal with God!"

But I . . . their work. As a farmer sends workers to harvest grain, Jesus sends his followers out to bring people to God.
Bethesda Also called Bethsaida or Bethzatha, a pool of water north of the Temple in Jerusalem.
Jewish language Hebrew or Aramaic, the languages of the Jewish people in the first century.
Verse 3 Some Greek copies add "and they waited for the water to move". A few later copies add verse 4: "Sometimes an angel of the Lord came down to the pool and stirred up the water. After the angel did this, the first person to go into the pool was healed from any sickness he had."

Jesus Has God's Authority

[19]But Jesus said, "I tell you the truth, the Son can do nothing alone. The Son does only what he sees the Father doing, because the Son does whatever the Father does. [20]The Father loves the Son and shows the Son all the things he himself does. But the Father will show the Son even greater things than this so that you can all be amazed. [21]Just as the Father raises the dead and gives them life, so also the Son gives life to those he wants to. [22]In fact, the Father judges no one, but he has given the Son power to do all the judging [23]so that all people will honour the Son as much as they honour the Father. Anyone who does not honour the Son does not honour the Father who sent him.

[24]"I tell you the truth, whoever hears what I say and believes in the One who sent me has eternal life. That person will not be judged guilty but has already left death and entered life. [25]I tell you the truth, the time is coming and is already here when the dead will hear the voice of the Son of God, and those who hear will have life. [26]Life comes from the Father himself, and he has allowed the Son to have life in himself as well. [27]And the Father has given the Son the power to judge, because he is the Son of Man. [d] [28]Don't be surprised at this: a time is coming when all who are dead and in their graves will hear his voice. [29]Then they will come out of their graves. Those who did good will rise and have life for ever, but those who did evil will rise to be judged guilty.

Jesus is God's Son

[30]"I can do nothing alone. I judge only the way I am told, so my judgement is fair. I don't try to please myself, but I try to please the One who sent me.

[31]"If only I tell people about myself, what I say does not count. [32]But there is another who tells about me, and I know that the things he says about me are true.

[33]"You have sent people to John, and he has told you the truth. [34]It is not that I accept such human telling; I tell you this so you can be saved. [35]John was like a burning and shining lamp, and you were happy to enjoy his light for a while.

[36]"But I have a proof about myself that is greater than that of John. The things I do, which are the things my Father gave me to do, prove that the Father sent me. [37]And the Father himself who sent me has given proof about me. You have never heard his voice or seen what he looks like. [38]His teaching does not live in you, because you don't believe in the One the Father sent. [39]You carefully study the Scriptures [d] because you think they give you eternal life. They do in

fact tell about me, [40]but you refuse to come to me to have that life.

[41]"I don't need praise from people. [42]But I know you—I know that you don't have God's love in you. [43]I have come from my Father and speak for him, but you don't accept me. But when another person comes, speaking only for himself, you will accept him. [44]You try to get praise from each other, but you do not try to get the praise that comes from the only God. So how can you believe? [45]Don't think that I will stand before the Father and say you are wrong. The one who says you are wrong is Moses, the one you hoped would save you. [46]If you really believed Moses, you would believe me, because Moses wrote about me. [47]But if you don't believe what Moses wrote, how can you believe what I say?"

More than 5,000 Fed

6 After this, Jesus went across Lake Galilee (or, Lake Tiberias). [2]Many people followed him because they saw the miracles [d] he did to heal the sick. [3]Jesus went up on a hill and sat down there with his followers. [4]It was almost the time for the Jewish Passover [d] Feast.

[5]When Jesus looked up and saw a large crowd coming towards him, he said to Philip, "Where can we buy enough bread for all these people to eat?" [6](Jesus asked Philip this question to test him, because Jesus already knew what he planned to do.)

[7]Philip answered, "We would all have to work a month to buy enough bread for each person to have only a little piece."

[8]Another one of his followers, Andrew, Simon Peter's brother, said, [9]"Here is a boy with five loaves of barley bread and two little fish, but that is not enough for so many people."

[10]Jesus said, "Tell the people to sit down." This was a very grassy place, and about 5,000 men sat down there. [11]Then Jesus took the loaves of bread, thanked God for them and gave them to the people who were sitting there. He did the same with the fish, giving as much as the people wanted.

[12]When they had all had enough to eat, Jesus said to his followers, "Gather the leftover pieces

---

Sidelight There were three types of bread in Jesus' day: small loaves (that would look similar to our rolls), round loaves (about the size of a football) and flat loaves (large, bread-like pancakes). The boy who gave loaves to Jesus (John 6:9) probably gave the first type, and they were made from barley, which suggests that he was poor.

of fish and bread so that nothing is wasted." [13]So they gathered up the pieces and filled twelve baskets with the pieces left from the five barley loaves.

[14]When the people saw this miracle [d] that Jesus did, they said, "He must truly be the Prophet [n] who is coming into the world."

[15]Jesus knew that the people planned to come and take him by force and make him their king, so he left and went into the hills alone.

Jesus Walks on the Water

[16]That evening Jesus' followers went down to Lake Galilee. [17]It was dark now, and Jesus had not yet come to them. The followers got into a boat and started across the lake to Capernaum. [18]By now a strong wind was blowing, and the waves on the lake were getting bigger. [19]When they had rowed the boat about five or six kilometres, they saw Jesus walking on the water, coming towards the boat. The followers were afraid, [20]but Jesus said to them, "It is I. Do not be afraid." [21]Then they were glad to take him into the boat. At once the boat came to land at the place where they wanted to go.

The People Seek Jesus

[22]The next day the people who had stayed on the other side of the lake knew that Jesus had not gone in the boat with his followers but that they had left without him. And they knew that only one boat had been there. [23]But then some boats came from Tiberias and landed near the place where the people had eaten the bread after the Lord had given thanks. [24]When the people saw that Jesus and his followers were not there now, they got into boats and went to Capernaum to find Jesus.

Jesus, the Bread of Life

[25]When the people found Jesus on the other side of the lake, they asked him, "Teacher, when did you come here?"

[26]Jesus answered, "I tell you the truth, you aren't looking for me because you saw me do miracles. [d] You are looking for me because you ate the bread and were satisfied. [27]Don't work for the food that spoils. Work for the food that stays good always and gives eternal life. The Son of Man [d] will give you this food, because on him God the Father has put his power."

[28]The people asked Jesus, "What are the things God wants us to do?"

[29]Jesus answered, "The work God wants you to do is this: believe the One he sent."

[30]So the people asked, "What miracle will you do? If we see a miracle, we will believe you. What will you do? [31]Our fathers ate the manna [d] in the desert. This is written in the Scriptures: [d] 'He rained manna [d] down on them to eat.'" [n]

[32]Jesus said, "I tell you the truth, it was not Moses who gave you bread from heaven; it is my Father who is giving you the true bread from heaven. [33]God's bread is the One who comes down from heaven and gives life to the world."

[34]The people said, "Sir, give us this bread always."

[35]Then Jesus said, "I am the bread that gives life. Whoever comes to me will never be hungry, and whoever believes in me will never be thirsty. [36]But as I told you before, you have seen me and still don't believe. [37]The Father gives me my people. Every one of them will come to me, and I will always accept them. [38]I came down from heaven to do what God wants me to do, not what I want to do. [39]Here is what the One who sent me wants me to do: I must not lose even one whom God gave me, but I must raise them all on the last day. [40]Those who see the Son and believe in him have eternal life, and I will raise them on the last day. This is what my Father wants."

[41]The Jews began to complain about Jesus because he said, "I am the bread that comes down from heaven." [42]They said, "This is Jesus, the son of Joseph. We know his father and mother. How can he say, 'I came down from heaven'?"

[43]But Jesus answered, "Stop complaining to each other. [44]The Father is the One who sent me. No one can come to me unless the Father draws him to me, and I will raise that person up on the last day. [45]It is written in the prophets, [d] 'They will all be taught by God.' [n] Everyone who listens to the Father and learns from him comes to me. [46]No one has seen the Father except the One who is from God; only he has seen the Father. [47]I tell you the truth, whoever believes has eternal life. [48]I am the bread that gives life. [49]Your ancestors ate the manna in the desert, but still they died. [50]Here is the bread that comes down from heaven. Anyone who eats this bread will never die. [51]I am the living bread that came down from heaven. Anyone who eats this bread will live for ever. This bread is my flesh, which I will give up so that the world may have life."

Prophet   They probably meant the prophet that God told Moses he would send (Deuteronomy 18:15–19).
'He gave . . . eat.'   Quotation from Psalm 78:24.
'They . . . God.'   Quotation from Isaiah 54:13.

52Then the Jews began to argue among themselves, saying, "How can this man give us his flesh to eat?"

53Jesus said, "I tell you the truth, you must eat the flesh of the Son of Man and drink his blood. Otherwise, you won't have real life in you. 54Those who eat my flesh and drink my blood have eternal life, and I will raise them up on the last day. 55My flesh is true food, and my blood is true drink. 56Those who eat my flesh and drink my blood live in me, and I live in them. 57The living Father sent me, and I live because of the Father. So whoever eats me will live because of me. 58I am not like the bread your ancestors ate. They ate that bread and still died. I am the bread that came down from heaven, and whoever eats this bread will live for ever." 59Jesus said all these things while he was teaching in the synagogue *d* in Capernaum.

The Words of Eternal Life

60When the followers of Jesus heard this, many of them said, "This teaching is hard. Who can accept it?"

61Knowing that his followers were complaining about this, Jesus said, "Does this teaching bother you? 62Then will it also bother you to see the Son of Man *d* going back to the place where he came from? 63It is the Spirit that gives life. The flesh doesn't give life. The words I told you are spirit, and they give life. 64But some of you don't believe." (Jesus knew from the beginning who did not believe and who would turn against him.) 65Jesus said, "That is the reason

PRIORITIES

One Man Down

"I'll do it!" one guy told Tony.

Tony looked at the volunteer and shook his head. "You're too fat."

"Then what about me?" another asked hopefully.

He shook his head again. "Too skinny."

"And me?" Yet another asked enthusiastically.

Tony shook his head again. "You must be joking! You're scared of the ball."

Tony was captain of the five-a-side indoor football team, and one player was ill. Some of the others had heard about the temporary vacancy and had volunteered to stand in for that evening. "Why weren't they any good?" Noel asked his friend. "We're one man down and there's less than two hours before the match! How can we play five-a-side with four men?"

Tony shrugged. "But they weren't what I was looking for. I want someone who's good, athletic . . . and fits with the image of my team!"

As the evening approached, Tony began to panic. In desperation, he located the boys who had earlier volunteered to play. "Do you still want to play?" he asked them – almost begged them.

"No thanks, Tony," they replied. "We've been asked to play on the basketball team tonight."

So with one man down, Tony's team played their five-a-side match. Predictably, they lost . . .

Tony placed more emphasis on how the boys looked than on finding a player. In **John 6:24–51**, some people put more emphasis on Jesus' miracles than on the Saviour himself.

- What similarities do you see between Tony and the people in this passage?
- What do you think this passage says about what God wants your priorities to be?

Consider . . .

- whether you are guilty of seeing people for what they are instead of who they are. How can you put this right?
- becoming friends with someone in your school that everyone else ignores. Show them that you are interested in their personality and not their looks.

For more, see . . .

- 1 Samuel 16:6–13 (p.269)
- James 2:1–9 (p.1348)
- Matthew 6:25–34 (p.948)

I said, 'If the Father does not bring a person to me, that one cannot come.'"

⁶⁶After Jesus said this, many of his followers left him and stopped following him.

⁶⁷Jesus asked the twelve followers, "Do you want to leave, too?"

⁶⁸Simon Peter answered him, "Lord, where would we go? You have the words that give eternal life. ⁶⁹We believe and know that you are the Holy One from God."

⁷⁰Then Jesus answered, "I chose all twelve of you, but one of you is a devil."

⁷¹Jesus was talking about Judas, the son of Simon Iscariot. Judas was one of the twelve, but later he was going to turn against Jesus.

Jesus' Brothers Don't Believe

7 After this, Jesus travelled around Galilee. He did not want to travel in Judea, because the Jews there wanted to kill him. ²It was time for the Jewish Feast *d* of Shelters. ³So Jesus' brothers said to him, "You should leave here and go to Judea so your followers there can see the miracles *d* you do. ⁴Anyone who wants to be well known does not hide what he does. If you are doing these things, show yourself to the world." ⁵(Even Jesus' brothers did not believe in him.)

⁶Jesus said to his brothers, "The right time for me has not yet come, but any time is right for you. ⁷The world cannot hate you, but it hates me, because I tell it the evil things it does. ⁸So you go to the feast. I will not go yet to this feast, because the right time for me has not yet come." ⁹After saying this, Jesus stayed in Galilee.

¹⁰But after Jesus' brothers had gone to the feast, Jesus went also. But he did not let people see him. ¹¹At the feast the Jews were looking for him and saying, "Where is that man?"

LIFE

Along For the Ride

Amy had kept quiet about her heart problem for so long that even the memories of operations and long spells in hospital didn't seem real to her.

So when her youth group took a trip, Amy reluctantly delivered her mother's note to their group leader. The note said that Amy shouldn't go on the "white-knuckle" rides.

At first, Amy refused to join her boyfriend on one of the theme park's best rides. She kept quiet about her heart while he teased her about being chicken.

Amy finally gave in. The initial ride left her short of breath, but she wasn't feeling too bad at the end of it.

Just as her second attempt was beginning, Amy passed out. The ride operator stopped the ride, got Amy out, and called an ambulance.

Three hours later, Amy was having another heart operation. In the middle of surgery, her heart stopped for 20 seconds. Amy might have died if she had not been plugged into life-support equipment.

Amy has fully recovered, but her brush with death has made her more aware of how fragile life can be. And she's more open about her heart.

Life is a wonderful gift. Read **John 6:59–69** to see how Jesus said that he was the only one who could give life.

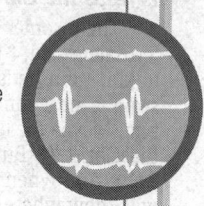

* What words of assurance would Amy find in the passage?
* What do you appreciate most about the life that Jesus has given you?

Consider . . .

* buying or picking a flower to display in your room as a reminder of the gift of life.
* spending an afternoon taking pictures of the things you enjoy most about life, then creating a photo arrangement.

For more, see . . .

* Leviticus 17:10–14 (p.116)
* Hebrews 9:11–15 (p.1337)
* Psalm 104:33–35 (p.561)

[12]Within the large crowd there, many people were whispering to each other about Jesus. Some said, "He is a good man."

Others said, "No, he fools the people." [13]But no one was brave enough to talk about Jesus openly, because they were afraid of the Jews.

Jesus Teaches at the Feast

[14]When the feast was about half over, Jesus went to the Temple [d] and began to teach. [15]The Jews were amazed and said, "This man has never studied. How did he learn so much?"

[16]Jesus answered, "The things I teach are not my own, but they come from him who sent me. [17]If people choose to do what God wants, they will know that my teaching comes from God and not from me. [18]Those who teach their own ideas are trying to get honour for themselves. But those who try to bring honour to the one who sent them speak the truth, and there is nothing false in them. [19]Moses gave you the law, [n] but none of you obeys that law. Why are you trying to kill me?"

[20]The people answered, "A demon [d] has come into you. We are not trying to kill you."

[21]Jesus said to them, "I did one miracle, [d] and you are all amazed. [22]Moses gave you the law about circumcision. [d] (But really Moses did not give you circumcision; it came from our ancestors.) And yet you circumcise a baby on a Sabbath [d] day. [23]If a baby can be circumcised on a Sabbath day to obey the law of Moses, why are you angry at me for healing a person's whole body on the Sabbath day? [24]Stop judging by the way things look, but judge by what is really right."

Is Jesus the Christ?

[25]Then some of the people who lived in Jerusalem said, "This is the man they are trying to kill. [26]But he is teaching where everyone can see and hear him, and no one is trying to stop him. Maybe the leaders have decided he really is the Christ. [d] [27]But we know where this man is from. And when the real Christ comes, no one will know where he comes from."

[28]Jesus, teaching in the Temple, [d] cried out, "Yes, you know me, and you know where I am from. But I have not come by my own authority. I was sent by the One who is true, whom you don't know. [29]But I know him, because I am from him, and he sent me."

[30]When Jesus said this, the people tried to take him. But no one was able to touch him, because it was not yet the right time. [31]But many of the people believed in Jesus. They said, "When the Christ comes, will he do more miracles [d] than this man has done?"

The Leaders Try to Arrest Jesus

[32]The Pharisees [d] heard the crowd whispering these things about Jesus. So the leading priests and the Pharisees sent some Temple [d] guards to arrest him. [33]Jesus said, "I will be with you a little while longer. Then I will go back to the One who sent me. [34]You will look for me, but you will not find me. And you cannot come where I am."

[35]The Jews said to each other, "Where will this man go so we cannot find him? Will he go to the Greek cities where our people live and teach the Greek people there? [36]What did he mean when he said, 'You will look for me, but you will not find me,' and 'You cannot come where I am'?"

Jesus Talks About the Spirit

[37]On the last and most important day of the feast Jesus stood up and said in a loud voice, "Let anyone who is thirsty come to me and drink. [38]If anyone believes in me, rivers of living water will flow out from that person's heart, as the Scripture [d] says." [39]Jesus was talking about the Holy Spirit. [d] The Spirit had not yet been given, because Jesus had not yet been raised to glory. But later, those who believed in Jesus would receive the Spirit.

The People Argue About Jesus

[40]When the people heard Jesus' words, some of them said, "This man really is the Prophet." [n]
[41]Others said, "He is the Christ." [d]

Still others said, "The Christ will not come from Galilee. [42]The Scripture [d] says that the Christ will come from David's family and from Bethlehem, the town where David lived." [43]So the people did not agree with each other about Jesus. [44]Some of them wanted to arrest him, but no one was able to touch him.

Some Leaders Won't Believe

[45]The Temple [d] guards went back to the leading priests and the Pharisees, [d] who asked, "Why didn't you bring Jesus?"

[46]The guards answered, "The words he says are greater than the words of any other person who has ever spoken!"

[47]The Pharisees answered, "So Jesus has fooled you also! [48]Have any of the leaders or the Pharisees believed in him? No! [49]But these people,

---

law Moses gave God's people the law that God gave him on Mount Sinai (Exodus 34:29–32).
Prophet They probably meant the prophet God told Moses he would send (Deuteronomy 18:15–19).

who know nothing about the law, are under God's curse."

⁵⁰Nicodemus, who had gone to see Jesus before, was in that group.ⁿ He said, ⁵¹"Our law does not judge a man without hearing him and knowing what he has done."

⁵²They answered, "Are you from Galilee, too? Study the Scriptures,ᵈ and you will learn that no prophetᵈ comes from Galilee."

Some early Greek manuscripts do not contain 7:53—8:11.

[⁵³And everyone left and went home.

Nicodemus . . . group. The story about Nicodemus going and talking to Jesus is in John 3:1–21.

The Woman Caught in Adultery

8 Jesus went to the Mount of Olives.ᵈ ²But early in the morning he went back to the Temple,ᵈ and all the people came to him, and he sat and taught them. ³The teachers of the law and the Phariseesᵈ brought a woman who had been caught in adultery.ᵈ They forced her to stand before the people. ⁴They said to Jesus, "Teacher, this woman was caught having sexual relations with a man who is not her husband. ⁵The law of Moses commands that we stone to death every woman who does this. What do you say we should do?" ⁶They were asking this to trick Jesus so that they could have some charge against him.

Once Forgiven, What Then?

Stephanie silently wept as Ross sat next to her on the settee, buttoning his shirt. The silence seemed to swallow them.

"Ross, we said we'd never do this again," she finally said through her tears.

"Well, we didn't mean to . . . It just happened," Ross responded.

"That's what you always say."

The two sat silently for a long time, and then Stephanie finally spoke, "I don't think we should see each other any more."

Ross didn't say anything. He just stared out of the window. But Stephanie knew by his sniffling that he was crying.

Stephanie reached across and touched his arm. "I'm sorry, Ross, but I just can't keep doing this to us – or to God. We just keep doing it and then asking God to forgive us."

Ross jerked his head around and looked at Stephanie. "But God does forgive us, Steph," Ross argued. "We won't do it again."

Stephanie started crying even harder. "No, Ross, we say that every time. I'm serious this time. We can't keep sinning and expect God to forgive us. I love you, but this hurts too much. Please take me home."

In **John 8:1–11**, Jesus faced a woman caught in sexual sin. Read what he said to her.

* How are Ross and Stephanie similar to the woman caught in adultery? How are they different?
* What does this passage tell us about Jesus' perspective on sexual sin and the person who commits it? What is there in your life that needs to hear his "don't sin any more".

Consider . . .

* evaluating the videos you watch and deciding what view of sexuality they promote.
* acting on one area of your life where Jesus is telling you to go and not sin any more. Tell a friend or parent about it, and ask that person to support you in your decision.

For more, see . . .

* Psalm 51:1–19 (p.530)
* Ephesians 6:10–18 (p.1277)
* 1 Corinthians 6:12–20 (p.1221)

But Jesus bent down and started writing on the ground with his finger. [7]When they continued to ask Jesus their question, he rose up and said, "Anyone here who has never sinned can throw the first stone at her." [8]Then Jesus bent over again and wrote on the ground.

[9]Those who heard Jesus began to leave one by one, first the older men and then the others. Jesus was left there alone with the woman standing before him. [10]Jesus rose up again and asked her, "Woman, where are they? Has no one judged you guilty?"

[11]She answered, "No one, sir."

Then Jesus said, "I also don't judge you guilty. You may go now, but don't sin any more."]

Jesus is the Light of the World

[12]Later, Jesus talked to the people again, saying, "I am the light of the world. The person who follows me will never live in darkness but will have the light that gives life."

[13]The Pharisees[d] said to Jesus, "When you talk about yourself, you are the only one to say these things are true. We cannot accept what you say."

[14]Jesus answered, "Yes, I am saying these things about myself, but they are true. I know where I came from and where I am going. But you don't know where I came from or where I am going. [15]You judge by human standards. I am not judging anyone. [16]But when I do judge, my judgement is true, because I am not alone. The Father who sent me is with me. [17]Your own law says that when two witnesses say the same thing, you must accept what they say. [18]I am one of the witnesses who speaks about myself, and the Father who sent me is the other witness."

[19]They asked, "Where is your father?"

Jesus answered, "You don't know me or my Father. If you knew me, you would know my Father, too." [20]Jesus said these things while he was teaching in the Temple,[d] near where the money is kept. But no one arrested him, because the right time for him had not yet come.

The People Misunderstand Jesus

[21]Again, Jesus said to the people, "I will leave you, and you will look for me, but you will die in your sins. You cannot come where I am going."

[22]So the Jews asked, "Will Jesus kill himself? Is that why he said, 'You cannot come where I am going'?"

[23]Jesus said, "You people are from here below, but I am from above. You belong to this world, but I don't belong to this world. [24]So I told you that you would die in your sins. Yes, you will die in your sins if you don't believe that I am he."

[25]They asked, "Then who are you?"

Jesus answered, "I am what I have told you from the beginning. [26]I have many things to say and decide about you. But I tell people only the things I have heard from the One who sent me, and he speaks the truth."

[27]The people did not understand that he was talking to them about the Father. [28]So Jesus said to them, "When you lift up the Son of Man,[d] you will know that I am he. You will know that these things I do are not by my own authority but that I say only what the Father has taught me. [29]The One who sent me is with me. I always do what is pleasing to him, so he has not left me alone." [30]While Jesus was saying these things, many people believed in him.

Freedom from Sin

[31]So Jesus said to the Jews who believed in him, "If you continue to obey my teaching, you are truly my followers. [32]Then you will know the truth, and the truth will make you free."

[33]They answered, "We are Abraham's children, and we have never been anyone's slaves. So why do you say we will be free?"

[34]Jesus answered, "I tell you the truth, everyone who lives in sin is a slave to sin. [35]A slave does not stay with a family for ever, but a son belongs to the family for ever. [36]So if the Son makes you free, you will be truly free. [37]I know you are Abraham's children, but you want to kill me because you don't accept my teaching. [38]I am telling you what my Father has shown me, but you do what your own father has told you."

[39]They answered, "Our father is Abraham."

Jesus said, "If you were really Abraham's children, you would do the things Abraham did. [40]I am a man who has told you the truth which I heard from God, but you are trying to kill me. Abraham did nothing like that. [41]So you are doing the things your own father did."

But they said, "We are not like children who never knew who their father was. God is our Father; he is the only Father we have."

[42]Jesus said to them, "If God were really your Father, you would love me, because I came from God and now I am here. I did not come by my own authority; God sent me. [43]You don't understand what I say, because you cannot accept my teaching. [44]You belong to your father the devil, and you want to do what he wants. He was a murderer from the beginning and was against the truth, because there is no truth in him. When he tells a lie, he shows what he is really like, because he is a liar and the father of lies. [45]But because I speak the truth, you don't believe me. [46]Can any of you prove that I am guilty of sin? If I am telling the truth, why don't you believe me? [47]The person who belongs to God accepts what God says. But you don't accept what God says, because you don't belong to God."

Jesus is Greater than Abraham

[48]The Jews answered, "We say you are a Samaritan *d* and have a demon *d* in you. Are we not right?"

[49]Jesus answered, "I have no demon in me. I give honour to my Father, but you dishonour me. [50]I am not trying to get honour for myself. There is One who wants this honour for me, and he is the judge. [51]I tell you the truth, whoever obeys my teaching will never die."

[52]The Jews said to Jesus, "Now we know that you have a demon in you! Even Abraham and the prophets *d* died. But you say, 'Whoever obeys my teaching will never die.' [53]Do you think you are greater than our father Abraham, who died? And the prophets died, too. Who do you think you are?"

[54]Jesus answered, "If I give honour to myself, that honour is worth nothing. The One who gives me honour is my Father, and you say he is your God. [55]You don't really know him, but I know him. If I said I did not know him, I would be a liar like you. But I do know him, and I obey what he says. [56]Your father Abraham was very happy that he would see my day. He saw that day and was glad."

[57]The Jews said to him, "You have never seen Abraham! You are not even 50 years old."

[58]Jesus answered, "I tell you the truth, before Abraham was even born, I am!" [59]When Jesus said this, the people picked up stones to throw at him. But Jesus hid himself, and then he left the Temple. *d*

Jesus Heals a Man Born Blind

9 As Jesus was walking along, he saw a man who had been born blind. [2]His followers asked him, "Teacher, whose sin caused this man to be born blind—his own sin or his parents' sin?"

[3]Jesus answered, "It is not this man's sin or his parents' sin that made him be blind. This man was born blind so that God's power could be shown in him. [4]While it is daytime, we must continue doing the work of the One who sent me. Night is coming, when no one can work. [5]While I am in the world, I am the light of the world."

[6]After Jesus said this, he spat on the ground and made some mud with it and put the mud on the man's eyes. [7]Then he told the man, "Go and wash in the Pool of Siloam." (Siloam means Sent.) So the man went, washed and came back seeing.

> **Sidelight** Sending the blind man to wash in the Pool of Siloam would clearly have been symbolic for the people in Jesus' day (John 9:7). This pool was the source of water used for religious ceremonies. It was also Jerusalem's main water supply.

[8]The neighbours and some people who had earlier seen this man begging said, "Isn't this the same man who used to sit and beg?"

[9]Some said, "He is the one," but others said, "No, he only looks like him."

The man himself said, "I am the man."

[10]They asked, "How did you get your sight?"

[11]He answered, "The man named Jesus made some mud and put it on my eyes. Then he told me to go to Siloam and wash. So I went and washed, and then I could see."

[12]They asked him, "Where is this man?"

"I don't know," he answered.

Pharisees Question the Healing

[13]Then the people took to the Pharisees *d* the man who had been blind. [14]The day Jesus had made mud and healed his eyes was a Sabbath *d* day. [15]So now the Pharisees asked the man, "How did you get your sight?"

He answered, "He put mud on my eyes, I washed, and now I see."

[16]So some of the Pharisees were saying, "This man does not keep the Sabbath day, so he is not from God."

But others said, "A man who is a sinner can't do miracles *d* like these." So they could not agree with one another.

[17]They asked the man again, "What do you say about him since it was your eyes he opened?"

The man answered, "He is a prophet." *d*

¹⁸The Jews did not believe that he had been blind and could now see again. So they sent for the man's parents ¹⁹and asked them, "Is this your son who you say was born blind? Then how does he now see?"

²⁰His parents answered, "We know that this is our son and that he was born blind. ²¹But we don't know how he can now see. We don't know who opened his eyes. Ask him. He is old enough to speak for himself." ²²His parents said this because they were afraid of the Jews, who had already decided that anyone who said Jesus was the Christ *d* would be put out of the synagogue. *d* ²³That is why his parents said, "He is old enough. Ask him."

²⁴So for the second time, they called the man who had been blind. They said, "You should give God the glory by telling the truth. We know that this man is a sinner."

²⁵He answered, "I don't know if he is a sinner. One thing I do know: I was blind, and now I see."

²⁶They asked, "What did he do to you? How did he make you see again?"

²⁷He answered, "I have already told you, and you didn't listen. Why do you want to hear it again? Do you want to become his followers, too?"

²⁸Then they insulted him and said, "You are his follower, but we are followers of Moses. ²⁹We know that God spoke to Moses, but as for this man we don't even know where he comes from."

³⁰The man answered, "This is a very strange thing. You don't know where he comes from, and yet he opened my eyes. ³¹We all know that God does not listen to sinners, but he listens to anyone who worships and obeys him. ³²Nobody has ever heard of anyone giving sight to a man born blind. ³³If this man were not from God, he could do nothing."

³⁴They answered, "You were born full of sin! Are you trying to teach us?" And they threw him out.

SIN

Blind Side

"I actually thought no one could tell I was drinking." Joe studied his hands for a moment before he looked up at the group. "I got caught the first time I got drunk. I thought about giving it up then. But my friends were into it, so I kept drinking with them."

Joe paused and took a deep breath. Then he continued, "Before long, I didn't need them as an excuse to drink. I enjoyed it so much, I drank whenever I got the chance." A few other teenagers in the group nodded knowingly. Joe relaxed a bit.

"I thought I was keeping up pretty well. I kept my position on the football team and my school results hadn't slipped too far. I tried to be careful with getting in on time and covering the alcohol on my breath."

"One day, my dad made some comment to me about how I was going to end up just like him. That shocked me! Dad's an alcoholic. And it scared me.

"So I talked to my youth leader, and he suggested that I join this support group," Joe said as his eyes swept over the teenagers seated in a circle. "I really thought I had everyone fooled. I suppose the only one blind to my drinking problem was me."

Jesus encountered blind people of all kinds. Read **John 9:1–41** to see the key to true sight.

* What are the similarities and differences between Joe's blindness and the Pharisees' blindness? Between Joe's blindness and that of the blind man?
* What does this Bible passage tell us about being blind to sin?

Consider . . .

* asking God to open your eyes to areas where you are blind to sin.
* asking a good friend to tell you about a blind spot in your life, then working to change it.

For more, see . . .

* Isaiah 6:9–10 (p.645)
* Ephesians 5:6–15 (p.1275)
* Matthew 15:1–20 (p.967)

Spiritual Blindness

³⁵When Jesus heard that they had thrown him out, Jesus found him and said, "Do you believe in the Son of Man?" *d*

³⁶He asked, "Who is the Son of Man, sir, so that I can believe in him?"

³⁷Jesus said to him, "You have seen him. The Son of Man is the one talking with you."

³⁸He said, "Lord, I believe!" Then the man worshipped Jesus.

³⁹Jesus said, "I came into this world so that the world would be judged. I came so that the blind *n* will see and so that those who see will become blind."

⁴⁰Some of the Pharisees *d* who were nearby heard Jesus say this and asked, "Are you saying we are blind, too?"

⁴¹Jesus said, "If you were blind, you would not be guilty of sin. But since you keep saying you see, your guilt remains."

The Shepherd and His Sheep

10 Jesus said, "I tell you the truth, the person who does not enter the sheepfold by the door, but climbs in by some other way, is a thief and a robber. ²The one who enters by the door is the shepherd of the sheep. ³The one who guards the door opens it for him. And the sheep listen to the voice of the shepherd. He calls his own sheep by name and leads them out. ⁴When he brings all his sheep out, he goes ahead of them, and they follow him because they know his voice. ⁵But they will never follow a stranger. They will run away from him because they don't know his voice." ⁶Jesus told the people this story, but they did not understand what it meant.

Jesus is the Good Shepherd

⁷So Jesus said again, "I tell you the truth, I am the door for the sheep. ⁸All the people who came before me were thieves and robbers. The sheep

---

blind   Jesus is talking about people who are spiritually blind, not physically blind.

JESUS CHRIST

Shepherds and Sheep

Shepherds have been around for thousands of years – and they're still going strong.

In Bible times, a shepherd could often be seen sitting alone on the hills, watching carefully for any wolves that might come and attack his flock.

Often, the shepherds of old would have a name for each of their sheep. They could tell the difference between each one and saw them as individual animals rather than just "one of my flock".

Even as night fell, the shepherds would remain with their sheep, and it wasn't unusual for them to sleep in the same field as their flock!

Occasionally, one of the sheep would get the idea of wandering away from the rest of the flock, and very often fell into a ditch or got its wool tangled in thorn bushes. In cases like this, the shepherd would leave the rest of his flock and go to help the one that had got itself into trouble.

Jesus seemed to know all about the shepherds of his day. In **John 10:1–30**, he identified himself as the Good Shepherd, and all his followers as his sheep.

* How is Jesus' care for his followers similar to the way that a shepherd takes care of his flock?
* How easily do you identify yourself as a sheep? Do you find it easy to follow Jesus the Shepherd or are you inclined to "wander off" and get into trouble?

Consider . . .

* why Jesus identified himself as the Good Shepherd, and ask yourself if you are a good sheep.
* identifying areas in your life where you tend to wander. How can you follow Jesus closely?

For more, see . . .

* Psalm 23 (p.513)
* Luke 15:1–7 (p.1070)
* Ezekiel 34:11–31 (p.817)

did not listen to them. 9I am the door, and the person who enters through me will be saved and will be able to come in and go out and find pasture. 10A thief comes to steal and kill and destroy, but I came to give life—life in all its fullness.

Sidelight When Jesus describes a sheepfold in John 10:1–6 his listeners would have understood immediately, since sheep were the most common animals around. Sheepfolds were low buildings to protect the flock in bad weather with an outdoor pen and a wall. The wall was covered with thorny bushes to keep out wild animals.

11"I am the good shepherd. The good shepherd gives his life for the sheep. 12The worker who is paid to keep the sheep is different from the shepherd who owns them. When the worker sees a wolf coming, he runs away and leaves the sheep alone. Then the wolf attacks the sheep and scatters them. 13The man runs away because he is only a paid worker and does not really care about the sheep.

14-15"I am the good shepherd. I know my sheep, as the Father knows me. And my sheep know me, as I know the Father. I give my life for the sheep. 16I have other sheep that are not in this flock, and I must bring them also. They will listen to my voice, and there will be one flock and one shepherd. 17The Father loves me because I give my life so that I can take it back again. 18No one takes it away from me; I give my own life freely. I have the right to give my life, and I have the right to take it back. This is what my Father commanded me to do."

19Again the Jews did not agree with each other because of these words of Jesus. 20Many of them said, "A demon d has come into him and made him crazy. Why listen to him?"

21But others said, "A man who is crazy with a demon does not say things like this. Can a demon open the eyes of the blind?"

Jesus is Rejected

22The time came for the Feast d of Dedication at Jerusalem. It was winter, 23and Jesus was walking in the Temple d in Solomon's Porch. d 24The Jews gathered around him and said, "How long will you make us wonder about you? If you are the Christ, d tell us plainly."

25Jesus answered, "I have already told you, but you did not believe. The miracles d I do in my Father's name show who I am. 26But you don't believe, because you are not my sheep. 27My sheep listen to my voice; I know them, and they follow me. 28I give them eternal life, and they will never die, and no one can steal them out of my hand. 29My Father gave my sheep to me. He is greater than all, and no person can steal my sheep out of my Father's hand. 30The Father and I are one."

31Again the Jews picked up stones to kill Jesus. 32But he said to them, "I have done many good works from the Father. Which of these good works are you killing me for?"

33The Jews answered, "We are not killing you because of any good work you have done, but because you speak against God. You are only a human, but you say you are the same as God!"

34Jesus answered, "It is written in your law that God said, 'I said, you are gods.' n 35This Scripture d called those people gods who received God's message, and Scripture is always true. 36So why do you say that I speak against God because I said, 'I am God's Son'? I am the one God chose and sent into the world. 37If I don't do what my Father does, then don't believe me. 38But if I do what my Father does, even though you don't believe in me, believe what I do. Then you will know and understand that the Father is in me and I am in the Father."

39They tried to take Jesus again, but he escaped from them.

40Then he went back across the Jordan River to the place where John had first baptised. Jesus stayed there, 41and many people came to him and said, "John never did a miracle, but everything John said about this man is true." 42And in that place many believed in Jesus.

The Death of Lazarus

11 A man named Lazarus was sick. He lived in the town of Bethany, where Mary and her sister Martha lived. 2Mary was the woman who later put perfume on the Lord and wiped his feet with her hair. Mary's brother was Lazarus, the man who was now sick. 3So Mary and Martha sent someone to tell Jesus, "Lord, the one you love is sick."

4When Jesus heard this, he said, "This sickness will not end in death. It is for the glory of God, to bring glory to the Son of God." 5Jesus loved Martha and her sister and Lazarus. 6But when he heard that Lazarus was sick, he stayed where he was for two more days. 7Then Jesus said to his followers, "Let's go back to Judea."

'I . . . gods.' Quotation from Psalm 82:6.

[8]The followers said, "But Teacher, the Jews there tried to stone you to death only a short time ago. Now you want to go back there?"

[9]Jesus answered, "Are there not twelve hours in the day? If anyone walks in the daylight, he will not stumble, because he can see by this world's light. [10]But if anyone walks at night, he stumbles because there is no light to help him see."

[11]After Jesus said this, he added, "Our friend Lazarus has fallen asleep, but I am going there to wake him."

[12]The followers said, "But Lord, if he is only asleep, he will be all right."

[13]Jesus meant that Lazarus was dead, but his followers thought he meant Lazarus was really sleeping. [14]So then Jesus said plainly, "Lazarus is dead. [15]And I am glad for your sakes I was not there so that you may believe. But let's go to him now."

[16]Then Thomas (the one called Didymus) said to the other followers, "Let us also go so that we can die with him."

Jesus in Bethany

[17]When Jesus arrived, he learned that Lazarus had already been dead and in the tomb for four days. [18]Bethany was about three kilometres from Jerusalem. [19]Many of the Jews had come there to comfort Martha and Mary about their brother.

[20]When Martha heard that Jesus was coming, she went out to meet him, but Mary stayed at home. [21]Martha said to Jesus, "Lord, if you had been here, my brother would not have died. [22]But I know that even now God will give you anything you ask."

[23]Jesus said, "Your brother will rise and live again."

[24]Martha answered, "I know that he will rise and live again in the resurrection [n] on the last day."

resurrection   Being raised from the dead to live again.

DEATH

Sharing Sadness

They made their way through the church doors to a back pew. Neither of them knew Polly's father, but they had decided to go to his funeral because Polly was in their class.

It wasn't a comfortable situation for Stephen or Dan, but they couldn't begin to imagine how hard it must have been for Polly. As they followed the coffin out to the graveyard after the service, Polly looked round at them and sort of smiled and cried at the same time.

The next Thursday Polly came back to school and made a point of talking to Dan and Stephen before class. "I really want to thank you for being at my dad's funeral last Saturday. It means a lot to me," Polly said.

"We didn't know what else we could do to help," Dan offered.

"That was enough," Polly said. "Just knowing I had friends there made a difference. I didn't feel so alone. Your being around made the service easier to take. It was as if you were sharing some of the pain."

Jesus understood what it was like to grieve with friends. Read **John 11:1–45** to see how Jesus shared his friends' grief and how Jesus' presence made a difference.

* How did Stephen and Dan's actions compare with Jesus' actions?
* What does Jesus' reaction teach us about dealing with sadness?

Consider . . .

* telling a trusted friend about the death of someone who was important to you. Openly express your emotions.
* asking your minister or youth leader to help you and a group of friends to devise things that you can do when a friend's family member dies.

For more, see . . .

* Isaiah 61:1–3 (p.705)
* Revelation 21:1–4 (p.1403)

* Romans 12:9–15 (p.1205)

25Jesus said to her, "I am the resurrection and the life. Those who believe in me will have life even if they die. 26And everyone who lives and believes in me will never die. Martha, do you believe this?"

27Martha answered, "Yes, Lord. I believe that you are the Christ, d the Son of God, the One who was to come into the world."

Jesus Cries

28After Martha said this, she went back and talked to her sister Mary alone. Martha said, "The Teacher is here and he is asking for you." 29When Mary heard this, she got up quickly and went to Jesus. 30Jesus had not yet come into the town but was still at the place where Martha had met him. 31The Jews were with Mary in the house, comforting her. When they saw her stand and leave quickly, they followed her, thinking she was going to the tomb to cry there.

32But Mary went to the place where Jesus was. When she saw him, she fell at his feet and said, "Lord, if you had been here, my brother would not have died."

33When Jesus saw Mary crying and the Jews who came with her also crying, he was upset and was deeply troubled. 34He asked, "Where did you bury him?"

"Come and see, Lord," they said.

35Jesus cried.

36So the Jews said, "See how much he loved him."

37But some of them said, "If Jesus opened the eyes of the blind man, why couldn't he keep Lazarus from dying?"

Jesus Raises Lazarus

38Again feeling very upset, Jesus came to the tomb. It was a cave with a large stone covering the entrance. 39Jesus said, "Move the stone away."

Martha, the sister of the dead man, said, "But, Lord, it has been four days since he died. There will be a bad smell."

> **Sidelight** Lazarus had been dead four days before Jesus arrived (John 11:39). That would have made bringing him back to life particularly miraculous to people in Jesus' day. They believed that a soul stayed with a body for three days and then left.

40Then Jesus said to her, "Didn't I tell you that if you believed you would see the glory of God?"

41So they moved the stone away from the entrance. Then Jesus looked up and said, "Father, I thank you that you heard me. 42I know that you always hear me, but I said these things because of the people here around me. I want them to believe that you sent me." 43After Jesus said this, he cried out in a loud voice, "Lazarus, come out!" 44The dead man came out, his hands and feet wrapped with pieces of cloth, and a cloth around his face.

Jesus said to them, "Take the cloth off him and let him go."

The Plan to Kill Jesus

45Many of the Jews, who had come to visit Mary and saw what Jesus did, believed in him. 46But some of them went to the Pharisees d and told them what Jesus had done. 47Then the leading priests and Pharisees called a meeting of the Jewish council. They asked, "What should we do? This man is doing many miracles. d 48If we let him continue doing these things, everyone will believe in him. Then the Romans will come and take away our Temple d and our nation."

49One of the men there was Caiaphas, the high priest that year. He said, "You people know nothing! 50You don't realise that it is better for one man to die for the people than for the whole nation to be destroyed."

51Caiaphas did not think of this himself. As high priest that year, he was really prophesying d that Jesus would die for the Jewish nation 52and for God's scattered children to bring them all together and make them one.

53That day they started planning to kill Jesus. 54So Jesus no longer travelled openly among the Jews. He left there and went to a place near the desert, to a town called Ephraim and stayed there with his followers.

55It was almost time for the Jewish Passover d Feast. Many from the country went up to Jerusalem before the Passover to do the special things to make themselves pure. 56The people looked for Jesus and stood in the Temple asking each other, "Is he coming to the Feast? What do you think?" 57But the leading priests and the Pharisees had given orders that if anyone knew where Jesus was, he must tell them. Then they could arrest him.

Jesus with Friends in Bethany

12 Six days before the Passover d Feast, Jesus went to Bethany, where Lazarus lived, whom Jesus had raised from the dead. 2There they had a dinner for Jesus. Martha served the food, and Lazarus was one of the people eating with Jesus. 3Mary brought in half a litre of very expensive perfume made from pure nard. d She poured the perfume on Jesus' feet, and then she wiped his feet with her hair. And the sweet smell from the perfume filled the whole house.

[4]Judas Iscariot, one of Jesus' followers, who would later turn against him, was there. Judas said, [5]"This perfume was worth 300 silver coins.[n] Why wasn't it sold and the money given to the poor?" [6]But Judas did not really care about the poor; he said this because he was a thief. He was the one who kept the money bag, and he often stole from it.

[7]Jesus answered, "Leave her alone. It was right for her to save this perfume for today, the day for me to be prepared for burial. [8]You will always have the poor with you, but you will not always have me."

The Plot Against Lazarus

[9]A large crowd of Jews heard that Jesus was in Bethany. So they went there to see not only Jesus but Lazarus, whom Jesus raised from the dead. [10]So the leading priests made plans to kill Lazarus, too. [11]Because of Lazarus many of the Jews were leaving them and believing in Jesus.

Jesus Enters Jerusalem

[12]The next day a great crowd who had come to Jerusalem for the Passover[d] Feast heard that Jesus was coming there. [13]So they took branches of palm trees and went out to meet Jesus, shouting,
"Praise[n] God!
God bless the One who comes in the name of the Lord!
God bless the King of Israel!"   *Psalm 118:25–26*
[14]Jesus found a colt and sat on it. This was as the Scripture[d] says,
[15]"Don't be afraid, people of Jerusalem!
Your king is coming,
sitting on the colt of a donkey."   *Zechariah 9:9*

coins A silver Roman denarii coin was the average pay for one day's work.
Praise Literally, "Hosanna", a Hebrew word used at first in praying to God for help. At this time it was probably a shout of joy used in praising God or his Messiah.

SERVICE

Poured Out

On 9 October 2001, the BBC reported this story: "It's official – 'Jedi Knight' is ON the list of religions for the 2001 UK census." That year, in the lead up to the government census, emails were being excitedly passed around stating that if 10,000 people or more wrote in the census that their religious persuasion was Jedi Knight, it would become an official religion! How does a 1977 sci-fi B-movie influence over 10,000 people's supposed religious stance more than twenty-four years later? The reality is, sticking your name on a form doesn't make you a Jedi Knight, but at the same time, something caught the imagination of the country.

The struggle between good and evil is championed by heroes of courage, honour, dignity, courtesy and nobleness. We love those stories of old, with knights rescuing fair maidens, honouring their king, fighting for justice, taking up the charge to serve and protect the weak in humility, with no thought of reward. For these guys, to die for their king wasn't a matter of sacrifice, rather, it was considered an honour.

Mary of Bethany (the same Mary who sat at Jesus' feet and believed in him for the resurrection of her brother Lazarus) is someone who seems to have grasped the value of Jesus. She was ready to not only sign her name next to his, but to literally pour out an offering which was not just a sacrifice, but also an honour, because it was for Jesus. Check out **John 12:1–11**.

* Have you ever found yourself feeling a bit like Judas, as if things just aren't worth your time?
* If Jesus were in your house today, how might you serve him?

Consider . . .

* you and Jesus. Is he your king? Is he worth being poured out for?
* whether sometimes it can be as if we've shoved our name down to be a Christian, but not followed it through. Serving God is a privilege and begins with making a decision to become his constant student, to learn to serve the way he served. Is today the day to take things further?

For more, see . . .

* Genesis 22:1–19 (p.25)
* Luke 22:39–46 (p.1088)
* 2 Samuel 23:13–17 (p.308)
* Luke 23:26–46 (p.1091)

16The followers of Jesus did not understand this at first. But after Jesus was raised to glory, they remembered that this had been written about him and that they had done these things to him.

People Tell About Jesus

17There had been many people with Jesus when he raised Lazarus from the dead and told him to come out of the tomb. Now they were telling others about what Jesus did. 18Many people went out to meet Jesus, because they had heard about this miracle. *d* 19So the Pharisees *d* said to each other, "You can see that nothing is going right for us. Look! The whole world is following him."

Jesus Talks About His Death

20There were some Greek people, too, who came to Jerusalem to worship at the Passover *d* Feast. 21They went to Philip, who was from Bethsaida in Galilee, and said, "Sir, we would like to see Jesus." 22Philip told Andrew, and then Andrew and Philip told Jesus.

23Jesus said to them, "The time has come for the Son of Man *d* to receive his glory. 24I tell you the truth, a grain of wheat must fall to the ground and die to make many seeds. But if it never dies, it remains only a single seed. 25Those who love their lives will lose them, but those who hate their lives in this world will keep true life for ever. 26Whoever serves me must follow me. Then my servant will be with me everywhere I am. My Father will honour anyone who serves me.

27"Now I am very troubled. Should I say, 'Father, save me from this time'? No, I came to this time in order to suffer. 28Father, bring glory to your name!"

Then a voice came from heaven, "I have brought glory to it, and I will do it again."

29The crowd standing there, who heard the voice, said it was thunder.

But others said, "An angel has spoken to him." 30Jesus said, "That voice was for your sake, not mine. 31Now is the time for the world to be

LIFE

Life From the Ashes

In the summer of 1988, forest fires swept through nearly half of Yellowstone National Park's 1 million hectares in the USA. At first, it seemed as though life in the park could never be the same. The fire seemed to be a total disaster.

But it wasn't. Foresters pointed out that lodgepole pine trees had cones on them that would only open under intense heat – almost as though they were designed to respond to a forest fire. Yellowstone's dry climate kept dead wood from decaying quickly, so the ashes from the fire provided nutrients to the ground that could actually mean better growth for years to come. Bluebirds and woodpeckers would benefit from the open areas that the fire had created. Other animals would flourish with the nearly tenfold increase in plant species that the newly fortified and uncovered earth could offer.

No one at Yellowstone looks forward to forest fires. But it is known that fires, however devastating they seem, don't mean the end of things.

The devastation of death can be sudden and tragic – like the devastation of a forest fire. But new life can result. Read **John 12:20–36** to discover what Jesus said about life and new growth.

* How might an ecologist's attitude towards forest fires be like Jesus' attitude towards new life?
* What does the Bible passage say to you about life?

Consider . . .

* writing on a sheet of paper about an area of your life in which you need to give something up and then burying the paper in your garden. A week later, dig it up and evaluate your progress in letting go.
* walking through a park or forest to notice how death gives way to new growth.

For more, see . . .

* Ecclesiastes 3:1–8 (p.622)
* 1 John 1:5–7 (p.1371)
* 2 Corinthians 4:16—5:10 (p.1244)

judged; now the ruler of this world will be thrown down. ³²If I am lifted up from the earth, I will draw all people towards me." ³³Jesus said this to show how he would die.

³⁴The crowd said, "We have heard from the law that the Christ *d* will live for ever. So why do you say, 'The Son of Man must be lifted up'? Who is this 'Son of Man'?"

³⁵Then Jesus said, "The light will be with you for a little longer, so walk while you have the light. Then the darkness will not catch you. If you walk in the darkness, you will not know where you are going. ³⁶Believe in the light while you still have it so that you will become children of light." When Jesus had said this, he left and hid himself from them.

Some People Won't Believe in Jesus

³⁷Though Jesus had done many miracles *d* in front of the people, they still did not believe in him. ³⁸This was to bring about what Isaiah the prophet *d* had said:

"Who would have believed what we heard?
Who saw the Lord's power in this?"

Isaiah 53:1

³⁹This is why the people could not believe: Isaiah had also said,

⁴⁰Make the minds of these people dumb.
Shut their ears. Cover their eyes.
Otherwise, they might really understand
what they see with their eyes
and hear with their ears.
They might really understand in their
minds
and come back to me and be healed."

Isaiah 6:10

⁴¹Isaiah said this because he saw Jesus' glory and spoke about him.

⁴²But many believed in Jesus, even many of the leaders. But because of the Pharisees, *d* they did not say they believed in him for fear they would be put out of the synagogue. *d* ⁴³They loved praise from people more than praise from God.

⁴⁴Then Jesus cried out, "Whoever believes in me is really believing in the One who sent me. ⁴⁵Whoever sees me sees the One who sent me. ⁴⁶I have come as light into the world so that whoever believes in me would not stay in darkness.

⁴⁷"Anyone who hears my words and does not obey them, I do not judge, because I did not come to judge the world, but to save the world. ⁴⁸There is a judge for those who refuse to believe in me and do not accept my words. The word I have taught will be their judge on the last day. ⁴⁹The things I taught were not from myself. The Father who sent me told me what

to say and what to teach. ⁵⁰And I know that eternal life comes from what the Father commands. So whatever I say is what the Father told me to say."

Jesus Washes His Followers' Feet

13 It was almost time for the Jewish Passover *d* Feast. Jesus knew that it was time for him to leave this world and go back to the Father. He had always loved those who were his own in the world, and he loved them all the way to the end.

²Jesus and his followers were at the evening meal. The devil had already persuaded Judas Iscariot, the son of Simon, to turn against Jesus. ³Jesus knew that the Father had given him power over everything and that he had come from God and was going back to God. ⁴So during the meal Jesus stood up and took off his outer clothing. Taking a towel, he wrapped it around his waist. ⁵Then he poured water into a bowl and began to wash the followers' feet, drying them with the towel that was wrapped around him.

⁶Jesus came to Simon Peter, who said to him, "Lord, are you going to wash my feet?"

⁷Jesus answered, "You don't understand now what I am doing, but you will understand later."

⁸Peter said, "No, you will never wash my feet."

Jesus answered, "If I don't wash your feet, you are not one of my people."

⁹Simon Peter answered, "Lord, then wash not only my feet, but wash my hands and my head, too!"

¹⁰Jesus said, "After a person has had a bath, his whole body is clean. He needs only to wash his feet. And you men are clean, *d* but not all

---

Sidelight   Washing your hands before a meal is OK. But feet? They quickly became sore and dirty in New Testament times because people wore open sandals. Washing feet was an important sign of hospitality. Jesus washed the feet of his disciples as though he were a servant (John 13:1–20), showing his disciples how to serve one another. (See also Philippians 2:3–11, p.1282.)

---

of you." ¹¹Jesus knew who would turn against him, and that is why he said, "Not all of you are clean."

¹²When he had finished washing their feet, he put on his clothes and sat down again. He asked, "Do you understand what I have just done for you? ¹³You call me 'Teacher' and 'Lord', and you are right, because that is what I am. ¹⁴If I,

Lord and Teacher, have washed your feet, you also should wash each other's feet. [15]I did this as an example so that you should do as I have done for you. [16]I tell you the truth, a servant is not greater than his master. A messenger is not greater than the one who sent him. [17]If you know these things, you will be happy if you do them.

[18]"I am not talking about all of you. I know those I have chosen. But this is to bring about what the Scripture [d] said: 'The man who ate at my table has turned against me.' [n] [19]I am telling you this now before it happens so that when it happens, you will believe that I am he. [20]I tell you the truth, whoever accepts anyone I send also accepts me. And whoever accepts me also accepts the One who sent me."

Jesus Talks About His Death

[21]After Jesus said this, he was very troubled. He said openly, "I tell you the truth, one of you will turn against me."

[22]The followers all looked at each other, because they did not know whom Jesus was

---

'The man . . . me.' Quotation from Psalm 41:9.

CHURCH

Servants

Meet three men who each have 10 years of professional training behind them and yet are happy to do caretaking duties for no pay.

John is a Consultant Pathologist at a large hospital. He controls the work of a large department and often speaks at international conferences.

Alan is a manager and an engineer with responsibility for 300 staff and essential supplies to part of a large city.

Peter is an architect. He makes decisions involving millions of pounds and travels first-class to the sites where he is working.

Each man has responsibility, power and status, leading a large team. They are used to being in charge.

But each is part of another team, a serving team in their local church. They hire school halls for Sunday meetings, writing letters and making sure that they are posted. They stack chairs and sweep up afterwards. If somebody needs a lift to church, they make arrangements or do it themselves. They will even help church members with mowing the lawn or decorating if necessary.

Other people take the key management decisions in the church and not everybody in the church is happy to be involved in doing the humble tasks. But these men see their service as a way of meeting real needs.

John, Alan and Peter humble themselves without thinking too much about it, though the leaders of the church recognise their servant roles. They try to make sure that everyone in the church understands that in God's eyes setting out chairs is as important as preaching. In **John 13:1–17**, Jesus humbled himself and washed his disciples' feet.

- How is the men's help similar to Jesus' act of washing the feet of his disciples?
- The disciples felt uncomfortable as Jesus began to wash their feet. How would you have felt in their position and why?

Consider . . .

- how you could humble yourself and serve someone in your church.
- helping someone in church to do something which is boring but needs doing.

For more, see . . .

- Nehemiah 5:1–13 (p.447)
- Galatians 5:13–15 (p.1264)
- Matthew 20:20–28 (p.976)

talking about. [23]One of the followers sitting [n] next to Jesus was the follower Jesus loved. [24]Simon Peter made signs to him to ask Jesus whom he was talking about.

[25]That follower leaned closer to Jesus and asked, "Lord, who is it?"

[26]Jesus answered, "I will dip this bread into the dish. The man I give it to is the man who will turn against me." So Jesus took a piece of bread, dipped it, and gave it to Judas Iscariot, the son of Simon. [27]As soon as Judas took the bread, Satan entered him. Jesus said to him, "The thing that you will do—do it quickly." [28]No one at the table understood why Jesus said this to Judas. [29]Since

he was the one who kept the money bag, some of the followers thought Jesus was telling him to buy what was needed for the feast or to give something to the poor.

[30]Judas took the bread Jesus gave him and immediately went out. It was night.

[31]When Judas was gone, Jesus said, "Now the Son of Man [d] receives his glory, and God receives glory through him. [32]If God receives glory through him, then God will give glory to the Son through himself. And God will give him glory quickly."

[33]Jesus said, "My children, I will be with you only a little longer. You will look for me, and

---

sitting   Literally, "lying". The people of that time ate lying down and leaning on one arm.

LOVE

Tough Love

Amie was furious. "But Dad, Rachel has the exact same skirt! And I know for a fact that her father doesn't think it's too short."

Amie's dad remained calm, yet firm. "Sweetheart, I simply cannot allow you to leave this house wearing that." Amie stomped back to her room and reluctantly changed into some jeans. Later on, at the party, she found Rachel surrounded by boys, all of them blatantly attracted by the skirt *she* should've been wearing. "My dad hates me," she thought . . .

In reality, Amie's dad didn't hate her at all. In fact, it was quite the opposite. Her father was simply exercising tough love. He knew, like Amie, that the skirt would achieve its purpose of grabbing all the guys' attention. Not only was he protecting her, but he also knew something that Amie wasn't ready to admit to herself yet. She really needed someone to like her for more than just the skirt she was wearing. Amie's dad was willing to trade his short-term discomfort for her long-term happiness.

Tough love is when your friend whispers, "You've got something between your teeth," without laughing at you. Tough love is when your teacher continues to show up for work each day, despite finding no respect in the classroom. It chooses honesty over popularity; sacrifice over fame.

In **John 13:31–35** Jesus showed his friends tough love when he told them, "Where I am going, you cannot come." He knew that the only way for them to truly understand how they should love each other, was if he exemplified the toughest love of all. Jesus *died* for his friends, and then he told them to do the same.

- How is Amie's dad's tough love for her like our Heavenly Father's tough love for us?
- Look at verse 34. Is Jesus' call to tough love a suggestion or a command? Would you be willing to die for your faith?

Consider . . .

- spending some time thinking about the people who show you tough love. Thank them, and show them the same kind of love.
- asking your heavenly dad for the same sacrificial heart Jesus had – one that was willing to die, in order that others could live.

For more, see . . .

- 1 Samuel 20 (p.274)
- John 15:12–17 (p.1125)

- Proverbs 27:6 (p.614)

what I told the Jews, I tell you now: where I am going you cannot come.

³⁴"I give you a new command: love each other. You must love each other as I have loved you. ³⁵All people will know that you are my followers if you love each other."

Peter will Say He Doesn't Know Jesus

³⁶Simon Peter asked Jesus, "Lord, where are you going?"

Jesus answered, "Where I am going you cannot follow now, but you will follow later."

³⁷Peter asked, "Lord, why can't I follow you now? I am ready to die for you!"

³⁸Jesus answered, "Are you ready to die for me? I tell you the truth, before the cockerel crows, you will say three times that you don't know me."

Jesus Comforts His Followers

14 Jesus said, "Don't let your hearts be troubled. Trust in God, and trust in me. ²There are many rooms in my Father's house; I would not tell you this if it were not true. I am going there to prepare a place for you. ³After I go and prepare a place for you, I will come back and take you to be with me so that you may be where I am. ⁴You know the way to the place where I am going."

⁵Thomas said to Jesus, "Lord, we don't know where you are going. So how can we know the way?"

⁶Jesus answered, "I am the way, and the truth, and the life. The only way to the Father is through me. ⁷If you really knew me, you would know my Father, too. But now you do know him, and you have seen him."

DOUBT

Riding Out the Storm

Robin Graham is one of the youngest people in history to sail round the world alone. But success didn't come easily for him. He left on his three-year odyssey as a sixteen-year-old thrill-seeker. Adventure was like a drug to him.

His trip changed something deep inside him. A violent storm almost capsized his little sloop, the *Dove*. In the midst of the torrent, the *Dove's* mast snapped in two, and Robin barely survived a waterspout – a water-filled tornado.

But that wasn't the worst of it. When his boat entered the doldrums, a windless, currentless part of the ocean near the equator, Robin almost went mad with despair and doubt. At one point, he completely gave up hope that he would ever make it out of the doldrums, so he splashed paraffin all over his boat and set it on fire. Fortunately, Robin came to his senses and doused the fire before it did serious damage.

Three years after his departure, Robin sailed into the Los Angeles harbour to cheering crowds, honking cars and blasting steam whistles. He had made it. And, more importantly, he had wrestled with two great enemies – doubt and despair – and found himself stronger as a result.

Robin Graham is a courageous hero. But he had crippling doubts about himself, just like the "heroes of faith" in **John 14:1–14**.

* How were Robin's doubts like the doubts the disciples experienced after Jesus told them that he was leaving them?
* What doubts have you had that seem impossible for God to solve?

Consider . . .

* writing on paper, "The one thing I doubt the most is . . ." and finishing the sentence. Then ask a friend to pray with you about your doubt.
* writing out one nagging doubt you have about God. Then tape your "doubt" to a specific date on a calendar at least a week from today. Ask God to give you insight into your doubt by that date.

For more, see . . .

* Jonah (p.885)
* James 1:2–8 (p.1348)

* Matthew 14:22–33 (p.965)

[8]Philip said to him, "Lord, show us the Father. That is all we need."

[9]Jesus answered, "I have been with you a long time now. Do you still not know me, Philip? Whoever has seen me has seen the Father. So why do you say, "Show us the Father"? [10]Don't you believe that I am in the Father and the Father is in me? The words I say to you don't come from me, but the Father lives in me and does his own work. [11]Believe me when I say that I am in the Father and the Father is in me. Or believe because of the miracles [d] I have done. [12]I tell you the truth, whoever believes in me will do the same things that I do. Those who believe will do even greater things than these, because I am going to the Father. [13]And if you ask for anything in my name, I will do it for you so that the Father's glory will be shown through the Son. [14]If you ask me for anything in my name, I will do it.

The Promise of the Holy Spirit

[15]"If you love me, you will obey my commands. [16]I will ask the Father, and he will give you another Helper [n] to be with you for ever— [17]the Spirit [d] of truth. The world cannot accept him, because it does not see him or know him. But you know him, because he lives with you and he will be in you.

Helper "Counsellor" or "Comforter". Jesus is talking about the Holy Spirit.

PEACE

The True Champion

Four decades after his death, an obscure Scottish sprinter named Eric Liddell became a household name when the Oscar-winning film *Chariots of Fire* profiled his heroics in the 1924 Olympic Games. The film told of Liddell's strong Christian convictions and his decision to drop out of the Olympic 100-metre dash because the race was scheduled for Sunday, a day which he believed was to be a day of rest for Christians.

Later, Liddell shocked the sports world by competing in and winning the Olympic 400-metre race – an event he had not intended to enter. The actor who played Liddell in the film, Ian Charleson, said, "What I admired about him was his serenity. My whole personality changed during the time I was doing the part. I became very slow and laconic."

After his Olympic victory, Liddell returned to China where he continued his work as a Christian missionary. When war broke out, he and other Westerners were rounded up by Japanese troops and held as "civil internees". During Liddell's two years in the camp, he was cut off from his wife and children. Liddell worked long hours – with little complaint – to organise a sports and recreation programme for teenagers. He also helped people in any way he could and tutored students at night.

Towards the end of the war, Liddell died fighting a brain tumour. He died the same way he always ran – fighting for every inch but at peace inside.

Annie Buchan, a close friend, was with him when he died. Before slipping into a coma from which he would never recover, Eric told his friend, "Annie, it's complete surrender."

Eric Liddell knew by experience the sort of peace that Jesus promises to those who follow him. Read about that peace in **John 14:15–29**.

* Have you experienced the sort of peace that Eric Liddell knew and Jesus talked about?
* What does the passage tell you about how to know God's peace? What's one thing in your life that you feel you need peace about?

Consider . . .

* watching for times when you don't feel at peace, and stopping to pray for fifteen seconds.
* planning to take few hours or even a day or two for a "personal retreat" with God. Spend the time reading the Bible, praying and worshipping.

For more, see . . .

* Psalm 119:162–165 (p.574)
* James 3:13–18 (p.1351)
* Philippians 4:6–9 (p.1285)

18"I will not leave you all alone like orphans; I will come back to you. 19In a little while the world will not see me any more, but you will see me. Because I live, you will live, too. 20On that day you will know that I am in my Father, and that you are in me and I am in you. 21Those who know my commands and obey them are the ones who love me, and my Father will love those who love me. I will love them and will show myself to them."

22Then Judas (not Judas Iscariot) said, "But, Lord, why do you plan to show yourself to us and not to the rest of the world?"

23Jesus answered, "If people love me, they will obey my teaching. My Father will love them, and we will come to them and make our home with them. 24Those who do not love me do not obey my teaching. This teaching that you hear is not really mine; it is from my Father, who sent me.

25"I have told you all these things while I am with you. 26But the Helper will teach you everything and will cause you to remember all that I told you. This Helper is the Holy Spirit whom the Father will send in my name.

27"I leave you peace; my peace I give you. I do not give it to you as the world does. So don't let your hearts be troubled or afraid. 28You heard me say to you, 'I am going, but I am coming back to you.' If you loved me, you would be happy that I am going back to the Father, because he is greater than I am. 29I have told you this now, before it happens, so that when it happens, you will believe. 30I will not talk with you much longer, because the ruler of this world is coming. He has no power over me, 31but the world must know that I love the Father, so I do exactly what the Father told me to do.

"Come now, let us go.

Jesus is Like a Vine

15 "I am the true vine; my Father is the gardener. 2He cuts off every branch of

SPIRITUAL GROWTH

Stick to Your Roots

Farzana's grandad was an avid gardener. He liked nothing better than going down to his allotment and tending to his award-winning roses. In fact, Farzana's grandma used to say that he liked plants more than people!

Farzana loved going to visit him and watch him care for his plants. He knew what was best for each and every one of them in order for them to reach their full potential. He faithfully visited each plant, as he knew that they would grow to be beautiful and all his hard work would be worthwhile.

In John 15:1–17 we are told that the Lord is like a gardener, tending to us and giving us all we need. We are told that if we remain in him – if we learn about him, spend time with him and rely upon him for our every need – then God will give us everything we need in order to reach our full potential.

In Farzana's Christian life it sometimes felt like it was all too much hard work. She kept asking herself why she should cut off a bad habit if it wasn't harming anyone else, or why she should read the Bible when it seemed so out of date.

However, through her grandad's example, she could see how God was working with her, being a faithful gardener, having full confidence that she will produce beautiful fruit when she trusts in his way.

* Why does Jesus want to tell us this?
* We are told that, as part of the vine, God wants us to bear fruit. What do you think he means by this fruit (see also Galatians 5:22–23)?

Consider . . .

* which parts of your life need to be pruned in order for you to bear fruit.
* what practical things you think you need to do in order to remain in the vine and live in Jesus.

For more, see . . .

* Galatians 5:22–23 (p.1264)
* Hebrews 12:1 (p.1343)

* Philippians 1:6 (p.1280)

mine that does not produce fruit. And he trims and cleans every branch that produces fruit so that it will produce even more fruit. ³You are already clean *d* because of the words I have spoken to you. ⁴Remain in me, and I will remain in you. A branch cannot produce fruit alone but must remain in the vine. In the same way, you cannot produce fruit alone but must remain in me.

⁵"I am the vine, and you are the branches. If any remain in me and I remain in them, they produce much fruit. But without me they can do nothing. ⁶If any do not remain in me, they are like a branch that is thrown away and then dies. People pick up dead branches, throw them into the fire and burn them. ⁷If you remain in me and follow my teachings, you can ask anything you want, and it will be given to you. ⁸You should produce much fruit and show that you are my followers, which brings glory to my Father. ⁹I loved you as the Father loved me. Now remain in my love. ¹⁰I have obeyed my Father's commands, and I remain in his love. In the same way, if you obey my commands, you will remain in my love. ¹¹I have told you these things so that you can have the same joy I have and so that your joy will be the fullest possible joy.

Sidelight

Jesus' listeners would have immediately understood the comparison he made with himself and the vine in John 15:1–11. Vineyards were common in Israel, and people knew that to get a good harvest, the dead branches must be cut off from the vine and burned. This gave the other branches a better chance to grow and bear fruit. Without this painful care the grapes would be small and bitter.

¹²"This is my command: love each other as I have loved you. ¹³The greatest love a person can show is to die for his friends. ¹⁴You are my friends if you do what I command you. ¹⁵I no longer call you servants, because a servant does not know what his master is doing. But I call you friends, because I have made known to you everything I heard from my Father. ¹⁶You did not choose me; I chose you. And I gave you this work: to go and produce fruit, fruit that will last. Then the Father will give you anything you ask for in my name. ¹⁷This is my command: love each other.

Jesus Warns His Followers

¹⁸"If the world hates you, remember that it hated me first. ¹⁹If you belonged to the world, it would love you as it loves its own. But I have chosen you out of the world, so you don't belong to it. That is why the world hates you. ²⁰Remember what I told you: a servant is not greater than his master. If people did wrong to me, they will do wrong to you, too. And if they obeyed my teaching, they will obey yours, too. ²¹They will do all this to you on account of me, because they do not know the One who sent me. ²²If I had not come and spoken to them, they would not be guilty of sin, but now they have no excuse for their sin. ²³Whoever hates me also hates my Father. ²⁴I did works among them that no one else has ever done. If I had not done these works, they would not be guilty of sin. But now they have seen what I have done, and yet they have hated both me and my Father. ²⁵But this happened so that what is written in their law would be true: 'They hated me for no reason.' *n*

²⁶"I will send you the Helper *n* from the Father; he is the Spirit of truth who comes from the Father. When he comes, he will tell about me, ²⁷and you also must tell people about me, because you have been with me from the beginning.

16 "I have told you these things to keep you from giving up. ²People will put you out of their synagogues. *d* Yes, the time is coming when those who kill you will think they are offering service to God. ³They will do this because they have not known the Father and they have not known me. ⁴I have told you these things now so that when the time comes you will remember that I warned you.

The Work of the Holy Spirit

"I did not tell you these things at the beginning, because I was with you then. ⁵Now I am going back to the One who sent me. But none of you asks me, 'Where are you going?' ⁶Your hearts are filled with sadness because I have told you these things. ⁷But I tell you the truth, it is better for you that I go away. When I go away, I will send the Helper *n* to you. If I do not go away, the Helper will not come. ⁸When the Helper comes, he will prove to the people of the world the truth about sin, about being right with God and about judgement. ⁹He will prove to them that sin is not believing in me. ¹⁰He will prove to them that being right with God comes through my going to the Father and not being seen by you any more. ¹¹And the Helper will prove to them that judgement happened when the ruler of this world was judged.

¹²"I have many more things to say to you, but they are too much for you now. ¹³But when the Spirit *d* of truth comes, he will lead you into

---

'They . . . reason.'   These words could be from Psalm 35:19 or Psalm 69:4.
Helper   "Counsellor" or "Comforter". Jesus is talking about the Holy Spirit.

all truth. He will not speak his own words, but he will speak only what he hears, and he will tell you what is to come. ¹⁴The Spirit of truth will bring glory to me, because he will take what I have to say and tell it to you. ¹⁵All that the Father has is mine. That is why I said that the Spirit will take what I have to say and tell it to you.

Sadness will Become Happiness

¹⁶"After a little while you will not see me, and then after a little while you will see me again."

¹⁷Some of the followers said to each other, "What does Jesus mean when he says, 'After a little while you will not see me, and then after a little while you will see me again'? And what does he mean when he says, 'Because I am going to the Father'?" ¹⁸They also asked, "What does he mean by 'a little while'? We don't understand what he is saying."

¹⁹Jesus saw that the followers wanted to ask him about this, so he said to them, "Are you asking each other what I meant when I said, 'After a little while you will not see me, and then after a little while you will see me again'? ²⁰I tell you the truth, you will cry and be sad, but the world will be happy. You will be sad, but your sadness will become joy. ²¹When a woman gives birth to a baby, she has pain, because her time has come. But when her baby is born, she forgets the pain, because she is so happy that a child has been

---

HOLY SPIRIT

The Improbable Disciple

Nicky Cruz was a murderous, uncontrollable gang leader who had killed before and would probably kill again. Without overstating the truth, Cruz was the most unlikely prospect for Christian conversion. He was also one of the first gang members whom David Wilkerson, a rural minister, met on the rough streets of New York City.

Wilkerson left his comfortable surroundings and started a missionary outreach to gang members in New York during the late 1950s. He was idealistic, and sometimes his efforts to gain a foothold for Christ among the vicious gang culture failed miserably.

Time after time, Nicky rejected David's pleas to seek God's forgiveness – once threatening the thin, quaking minister with a knife to his throat. But David replied, "You can cut me to pieces, Nicky, but every piece will still cry out, 'I love you'."

David invited Nicky to attend a city-wide meeting he was organising for gang members. Impressed by the man's courage, Nicky told David that he and his gang would be there.

Nicky did show up, and David invited him to collect the offering. Nicky and his gang did and then headed for the backstage exit, sniggering at the gullible preacher.

But on the way out, Nicky felt a heavy, almost overpowering weight on his shoulders. He stopped. He couldn't escape the fearful truth: the Jesus about whom David had spoken required something of him. Nicky and his gang returned to meet David on stage. At the end of the meeting, Nicky told David, "I've given my heart to God."

Today Nicky works with tough, inner-city teenagers. Jesus said one of the Holy Spirit's main responsibilities is to prove the truth to people who are like Nicky Cruz used to be. Read about the Holy Spirit in **John 16:4–15**.

* According to verse 8, how did the Holy Spirit influence Nicky Cruz?
* When have you felt the Holy Spirit working with you? Explain.

Consider . . .

* listing ten words that could replace the word "Holy" and ten words that could replace the word "Spirit". Mix and match the words to come up with combinations such as "Perfect Presence" or "Pure Companion".
* spending five minutes at the end of each day, thinking of ways in which the Holy Spirit was with you throughout the day.

For more, see . . .

* Psalm 51:10–13 (p.530)
* Acts 2:1–36 (p.1138)

* Luke 11:5–13 (p.1059)

born into the world. [22]It is the same with you. Now you are sad, but I will see you again and you will be happy, and no one will take away your joy. [23]In that day you will not ask me for anything. I tell you the truth, my Father will give you anything you ask for in my name. [24]Until now you have not asked for anything in my name. Ask and you will receive, so that your joy will be the fullest possible joy.

Victory Over the World

[25]"I have told you these things, using stories that hide the meaning. But the time will come when I will not use stories like that to tell you things; I will speak to you in plain words about the Father. [26]In that day you will ask the Father for things in my name. I mean, I will not need to ask the Father for you. [27]The Father himself loves you. He loves you because you have loved me and believed that I came from God. [28]I came from the Father into the world. Now I am leaving the world and going back to the Father."

[29]Then the followers of Jesus said, "You are speaking clearly to us now and are not using stories that are hard to understand. [30]We can see now that you know all things. You can answer a person's question even before it is asked. This makes us believe you came from God."

[31]Jesus answered, "So now you believe? [32]Listen to me; a time is coming when you will be scattered, each to his own home. That time is now here. You will leave me alone, but I am never really alone, because the Father is with me.

[33]"I told you these things so that you can have peace in me. In this world you will have trouble, but be brave! I have defeated the world."

PRAYER

God on the Streets

As I stood waiting, a Mancunian lad who looked familiar ran up to me with an excitement that belied his cool-bloke image. Clapping his hands together he blurted, "We've gotta get you to pray some stuff for us! You sorted Daz's hand right out so . . ."

"Where is he?" I interrupted. I *had* to see this . . . I'd prayed for Daz in the street two days before. He told me how he'd punched through a glass window because he lost his phone. Daz had severed two tendons in his hand, and his mate had then described in gruesome detail how the hand had been cut to the bone. Talking through it on the streets a few nights ago, Daz had been sceptical, but trusted enough to let me hold his hand in front of his mates and pray for him right there.

"It's tingling," he'd said, looking carefully at it. "I know there are some things in the world I don't understand."

"Daz!" his mate called him over. Daz wandered over looking a bit sheepish, a coy smile on his face. I reckon he was trying to work out how he was gonna explain himself. He looked down at his hand.

"I could move it a bit again," he showed me his wiggling little finger, "so I took the cast off and I could move it properly," he smiled. God had totally healed his hand.

This story is told by someone who had gone out of his way to offer to pray for people in the street. He is convinced that when we pray God does things. Are you?

John 17:1–26 gives us a record of some of the things Jesus prayed for his followers.

* What did Jesus pray?
* Why do you think he prayed for these things? How do they compare with your priorities in prayer?

Consider . . .

* getting some of your friends together regularly to pray for each other. You could set up a phone chain of people to pray.
* whether you have any friends like Daz. They may not know Jesus but you can be praying for them. Pick three or four friends to pray for – keep a note of what happens when you pray.

For more, see . . .

* Matthew 6:5–15 (p.948)   * Ephesians 3:14–21 (p.1271)
* Philippians 4:6 (p.1285)

Jesus Prays for His Followers

17 After Jesus said these things, he looked towards heaven and prayed, "Father, the time has come. Give glory to your Son so that the Son can give glory to you. [2]You gave the Son power over all people so that the Son could give eternal life to all those you gave him. [3]And this is eternal life: that people know you, the only true God, and that they know Jesus Christ, the One you sent. [4]Having finished the work you gave me to do, I brought you glory on earth. [5]And now, Father, give me glory with you; give me the glory I had with you before the world was made.

[6]"I showed what you are like to those you gave me from the world. They belonged to you, and you gave them to me, and they have obeyed your teaching. [7]Now they know that everything you gave me comes from you. [8]I gave them the teachings you gave me, and they accepted them. They knew that I truly came from you, and they believed that you sent me. [9]I am praying for them. I am not praying for people in the world but for those you gave me, because they are yours. [10]All I have is yours, and all you have is mine. And my glory is shown through them. [11]I am coming to

> ### Sidelight
> Jesus' prayer in John 17 is the longest prayer in the New Testament. But Nehemiah holds the record for the longest Bible prayer with his prayer of praise, confession and covenant in Nehemiah 9:5–37 (p.451).

you; I will not stay in the world any longer. But they are still in the world. Holy Father, keep them safe by the power of your name, the name you gave me, so that they will be one, just as you and I are one. [12]While I was with them, I kept them safe by the power of your name, the name you gave me. I protected them, and only one of them, the one worthy of destruction, was lost so that the Scripture [d] would come true.

[13]"I am coming to you now. But I pray these things while I am still in the world so that these followers can have all my joy in them. [14]I have given them your teaching. And the world has hated them, because they don't belong to the world, just as I don't belong to the world. [15]I am not asking you to take them out of the world but to keep them safe from the Evil One. [16]They don't belong to the world, just as I don't belong to the world. [17]Make them ready for your service through your truth; your teaching is truth. [18]I have sent them into the world, just as you sent me into the world. [19]For their sake, I am making myself ready to serve so that they can be ready for their service of the truth.

[20]"I pray for these followers, but I am also praying for all those who will believe in me because of their teaching. [21]Father, I pray that they can be one. As you are in me and I am in you, I pray that they can also be one in us. Then the world will believe that you sent me. [22]I have given these people the glory that you gave me so that they can be one, just as you and I are one. [23]I will be in them and you will be in me so that they will be completely one. Then the world will know that you sent me and that you loved them just as much as you loved me.

[24]"Father, I want these people that you gave me to be with me where I am. I want them to see my glory, which you gave me because you loved me before the world was made. [25]Father, you are the One who is good. The world does not know you, but I know you, and these people know you sent me. [26]I showed them what you are like, and I will show them again. Then they will have the same love that you have for me, and I will live in them."

Jesus is Arrested

18 When Jesus finished praying, he went with his followers across the Kidron Valley. On the other side there was a garden, and Jesus and his followers went into it.

[2]Judas knew where this place was, because Jesus often met his followers there. Judas was the one who turned against Jesus. [3]So Judas came there with a group of soldiers and some guards from the leading priests and the Pharisees. [d] They were carrying torches, lanterns and weapons.

[4]Knowing everything that would happen to him, Jesus went out and asked, "Who is it you are looking for?"

[5]They answered, "Jesus from Nazareth."

"I am he," Jesus said. (Judas, the one who turned against Jesus, was standing there with them.) [6]When Jesus said, "I am he," they moved back and fell to the ground.

[7]Jesus asked them again, "Who is it you are looking for?"

They said, "Jesus of Nazareth."

[8]"I told you that I am he," Jesus said. "So if you are looking for me, let the others go." [9]This happened so that the words Jesus said before would come true: "I have not lost any of the ones you gave me."

> ### Sidelight
> The sword that Simon Peter used in John 18:10–11 was probably similar to a modern machete. Roman soldiers of this time used lightweight, well-balanced swords that were usually just over half a metre long for close-range combat. The sword is the most common weapon mentioned in the Bible, appearing more than 400 times from Genesis to Revelation.

¹⁰Simon Peter, who had a sword, pulled it out and struck the servant of the high priest, cutting off his right ear. (The servant's name was Malchus.) ¹¹Jesus said to Peter, "Put your sword back. Shouldn't I drink the cup *n* the Father gave me?"

Jesus is Brought Before Annas

¹²Then the soldiers with their commander and the Jewish guards arrested Jesus. They tied him ¹³and led him first to Annas, the father-in-law of Caiaphas, the high priest that year. ¹⁴Caiaphas was the one who had told the Jews that it would be better if one man died for all the people.

Peter Says He Doesn't Know Jesus

¹⁵Simon Peter and another one of Jesus' followers went along after Jesus. This follower knew the high priest, so he went with Jesus into the high priest's courtyard. ¹⁶But Peter waited outside near the door. The follower who knew the high priest came back outside, spoke to the girl at the door, and brought Peter inside. ¹⁷The girl at the door said to Peter, "Aren't you also one of that man's followers?"

Peter answered, "No, I am not!"

¹⁸It was cold, so the servants and guards had built a fire and were standing around it, warming

---

cup Jesus is talking about the terrible things that will happen to him. Accepting these things will be very hard, like drinking a cup of something bitter.

FEAR

All That You Can't Leave Behind

Nathan had developed a reputation for being a bad lad. He was proud of it because it meant that he got respect from his crew. Nathan and the guys were tight. What had been going round having a bit of a laugh in an attempt to evade boredom, had become carrying knives and looking for fights. Nathan was getting in deep.

Then something happened. The geeky Christians who ran the youth club had persuaded him to go along to a camp for the weekend, with the promise of abseiling, canoeing and some "God stuff" too. So Nathan went, thinking he'd do the activities, find a couple of girls to snog round the campfire, and catch forty winks while the Christians went on about God.

That weekend, he met God in a way that was inescapable and he found out that God loved him and accepted him – words that Nathan seldom heard. All the things he had been doing with his mates faded to grey when he held them against the promise of this new life with God.

It wasn't until the journey home in the minibus that his fears hit him. They approached his home town and Nathan saw the old streets where he lived out his old life. It had been so easy being a Christian away from home, away from his mates.

He worried that he would have no mates, no respect. What would his family say? He remembered what he used to call the Christians and dreaded to think what his mates would call him. As well as all this, he knew the dealers that supplied him wouldn't be happy about him pulling out of the game. As the minibus pulled up outside his house, he thought to himself, "Wouldn't it be easier if I just pretended this weekend had never happened?"

Read **John 18:1–27**.

* How is Peter's situation similar to Nathan's? How is it different?
* How do you think Jesus was able to overcome the fears he had about going to the cross?

Consider . . .

* writing down some of the things you would be fearful to give up so that you could follow Jesus. Pause and ask God what plans and adventures he has for your life as you choose to follow him.
* asking God to give you the strength to overcome your fears.

For more, see . . .

* Esther 4:1–17 (p.462)
* 1 John 4:18 (p.1374)
* Psalm 118:5–9 (p.570)

themselves. Peter also was standing with them, warming himself.

The High Priest Questions Jesus

[19]The high priest asked Jesus questions about his followers and his teaching. [20]Jesus answered, "I have spoken openly to everyone. I have always taught in synagogues [d] and in the Temple, [d] where all the Jews come together. I never said anything in secret. [21]So why do you question me? Ask the people who heard my teaching. They know what I said."

[22]When Jesus said this, one of the guards standing there hit him. The guard said, "Is that the way you answer the high priest?"

[23]Jesus answered him, "If I said something wrong, then say what it was. But if what I said is true, why do you hit me?"

[24]Then Annas sent Jesus, who was still tied, to Caiaphas the high priest.

Peter Says Again He Doesn't Know Jesus

[25]As Simon Peter was standing and warming himself, they said to him, "Aren't you one of that man's followers?"

Peter said it was not true; he said, "No, I am not."

[26]One of the servants of the high priest was there. This servant was a relative of the man whose ear Peter had cut off. The servant said, "Didn't I see you with him in the garden?"

[27]Again Peter said it wasn't true. At once a cockerel crowed.

Jesus is Brought Before Pilate

[28]Early in the morning they led Jesus from Caiaphas' house to the Roman governor's palace. They would not go inside the palace, because they did not want to make themselves unclean; [n] they wanted to eat the Passover [d] meal. [29]So Pilate went outside to them and asked, "What charges do you bring against this man?"

[30]They answered, "If he were not a criminal, we wouldn't have brought him to you."

[31]Pilate said to them, "Take him yourselves and judge him by your own law."

"But we are not allowed to put anyone to death," the Jews answered. [32](This happened so that what Jesus said about how he would die would come true.)

[33]Then Pilate went back inside the palace and called Jesus to him and asked, "Are you the king of the Jews?"

[34]Jesus said, "Is that your own question, or did others tell you about me?"

[35]Pilate answered, "I am not Jewish. It was your own people and their leading priests who handed you over to me. What have you done wrong?"

[36]Jesus answered, "My kingdom does not belong to this world. If it belonged to this world, my servants would fight so that I would not be given over to the Jews. But my kingdom is from another place."

[37]Pilate said, "So you are a king!"

Jesus answered, "You are the one saying I am a king. This is why I was born and came into the world: to tell people the truth. And everyone who belongs to the truth listens to me."

[38]Pilate said, "What is truth?" After he said this, he went out to the Jews again and said to them, "I find nothing against this man. [39]But it is your custom that I free one prisoner to you at Passover time. Do you want me to free the 'king of the Jews'?"

[40]They shouted back, "No, not him! Let Barabbas go free!" (Barabbas was a robber.)

19 Then Pilate ordered that Jesus be taken away and whipped. [2]The soldiers made a crown from some thorny branches and put it on Jesus' head and put a purple robe around him. [3]Then they came to him many times and said, "Hail, King of the Jews!" and hit him in the face.

[4]Again Pilate came out and said to them, "Look, I am bringing Jesus out to you. I want you to know that I find nothing against him." [5]So Jesus came out, wearing the crown of thorns and the purple robe. Pilate said to them, "Here is the man!"

[6]When the leading priests and the guards saw Jesus, they shouted, "Crucify him! Crucify him!"

But Pilate answered, "Crucify him yourselves, because I find nothing against him."

[7]The Jews answered, "We have a law that says he should die, because he said he is the Son of God."

[8]When Pilate heard this, he was even more afraid. [9]He went back inside the palace and asked Jesus, "Where do you come from?" But Jesus did not answer him. [10]Pilate said, "You refuse to speak to me? Don't you know I have power to set you free and power to have you crucified?"

[11]Jesus answered, "The only power you have over me is the power given to you by God. The man who betrayed me to you is guilty of a greater sin."

[12]After this, Pilate tried to let Jesus go. But the Jews cried out, "Anyone who makes himself king is against Caesar. If you let this man go, you are no friend of Caesar."

[13]When Pilate heard what they were saying, he brought Jesus out and sat down on the judge's

---

unclean   Going into a non-Jewish place would make them unfit to eat the Passover Feast, according to Jewish law.

seat at the place called The Stone Pavement. (In the Jewish language[n] the name is Gabbatha.) [14]It was about noon on Preparation[d] Day of Passover[d] week. Pilate said to the Jews, "Here is your king!"

[15]They shouted, "Take him away! Take him away! Crucify him!"

Pilate asked them, "Do you want me to crucify your king?"

The leading priests answered, "The only king we have is Caesar."

[16]So Pilate handed Jesus over to them to be crucified.

Jesus is Crucified

The soldiers took charge of Jesus. [17]Carrying his own cross, Jesus went out to a place called The Place of the Skull, which in the Jewish language[n] is called Golgotha. [18]There they crucified Jesus. They also crucified two other men, one on each side, with Jesus in the middle. [19]Pilate wrote a sign and put it on the cross. It read: JESUS OF NAZARETH, THE KING OF THE JEWS. [20]The sign was written in the Jewish language, in Latin and in Greek. Many of the Jews read the sign, because the place where Jesus was crucified was near the city. [21]The leading Jewish priests said to Pilate, "Don't write, 'The King of the Jews'. But write, 'This man said, "I am the King of the Jews."'"

[22]Pilate answered, "What I have written, I have written."

[23]After the soldiers crucified Jesus, they took his clothes and divided them into four parts, with each soldier getting one part. They also took his long shirt, which was all one piece of cloth, woven from top to bottom. [24]So the soldiers said to each other, "We should not tear this into parts. Let's throw lots[d] to see who will get it." This happened so that this Scripture would come true:[d]

"They divided my clothes among them,
and they threw lots[d] for my clothing."

Psalm 22:18

So the soldiers did this.

[25]Standing near his cross were Jesus' mother, his mother's sister, Mary the wife of Clopas, and Mary Magdalene. [26]When Jesus saw his mother and the follower he loved standing nearby, he said to his mother, "Dear woman, here is your son." [27]Then he said to the follower, "Here is your mother." From that time on, the follower took her to live in his home.

Jesus Dies

[28]After this, Jesus knew that everything had been done. So that the Scripture[d] would come true, he said, "I am thirsty."[n] [29]There was a jar

> ### Sidelight
> The "long shirt" that the soldiers gambled for (John 19:23–24) was, in reality, like Jesus' undergarment. Crucifixions were often done with the criminals naked to make the execution even more humiliating.

full of vinegar there, so the soldiers soaked a sponge in it, put the sponge on a branch of a hyssop plant and lifted it to Jesus' mouth. [30]When Jesus tasted the vinegar, he said, "It is finished." Then he bowed his head and died.

[31]This day was Preparation[d] Day, and the next day was a special Sabbath[d] day. Since the Jews did not want the bodies to stay on the cross on the Sabbath day, they asked Pilate to order that the legs of the men be broken[n] and the bodies be taken away. [32]So the soldiers came and broke the legs of the first man on the cross beside Jesus. Then they broke the legs of the man on the other cross beside Jesus. [33]But when the soldiers came to Jesus and saw that he was already dead, they did not break his legs. [34]But one of the soldiers stuck his spear into Jesus' side, and at once blood and water came out. [35](The one who saw this happen is the one who told us this, and whatever he says is true. And he knows that he tells the truth, and he tells it so that you might believe.) [36]These things happened to make the Scripture come true: "Not one of his bones will be broken."[n] [37]And another Scripture says, "They will look at the one they stabbed."[n]

Jesus is Buried

[38]Later, Joseph from Arimathea asked Pilate if he could take the body of Jesus. (Joseph was a secret follower of Jesus, because he was afraid of the Jews.) Pilate gave his permission, so Joseph came and took Jesus' body away. [39]Nicodemus, who earlier had come to Jesus at night, went with Joseph. He brought about 30 kilogrammes of myrrh[d] and aloes.[d] [40]These two men took Jesus' body and wrapped it with the spices in pieces of linen cloth, which is how the Jewish people bury the dead. [41]In the place where Jesus was crucified,

---

Jewish language   Hebrew or Aramaic, the languages of the Jewish people in the first century.
"I am thirsty."   Read Psalms 22:15; 69:21.
broken   The breaking of their bones would make them die sooner.
"Not one . . . broken."   Quotation from Psalm 34:20. The idea is from Exodus 12:46; Numbers 9:12.
"They . . . stabbed."   Quotation from Zechariah 12:10.

there was a garden. In the garden was a new tomb that had never been used before. [42]The men laid Jesus in that tomb because it was nearby, and the Jews were preparing to start their Sabbath *d* day.

Jesus' Tomb is Empty

20 Early on the first day of the week, Mary Magdalene went to the tomb while it was still dark. When she saw that the large stone had been moved away from the tomb, [2]she ran to Simon Peter and the follower whom Jesus loved. Mary said, "They have taken the Lord out of the tomb, and we don't know where they have put him."

[3]So Peter and the other follower started for the tomb. [4]They were both running, but the other follower ran faster than Peter and reached the tomb first. [5]He bent down and looked in and saw the strips of linen cloth lying there, but he did not go in. [6]Then, following him, Simon Peter arrived and went into the tomb and saw the strips of linen lying there. [7]He also saw the cloth that had been around Jesus' head, which was folded up and laid in a different place from the strips of linen. [8]Then the other follower, who had reached the tomb first, also went in. He saw and believed. [9](They did not yet understand from the Scriptures *d* that Jesus must rise from the dead.)

Jesus Appears to Mary Magdalene

[10]Then the followers went back home. [11]But Mary stood outside the tomb, crying. As she was crying, she bent down and looked inside

---

DEATH

Questions Unanswered

Jo was full of life. She'd been working for a Christian charity for several months now, but unlike the others, Jo didn't believe in God. At first, Jo was quiet; she kept her head down and found her new environment a bit strange. Naturally outgoing, it didn't take long before she was laughing, joking and having a ball with all her colleagues.

Without any faith in God, Jo found it amusing to see her new friends on their knees praying in the money for the bills. Much to her surprise, Jo witnessed the answers to the prayers, as every month every penny came in. Again and again she witnessed miracles as a God she didn't believe in kept doing amazing things!

Over a year down the line, Jo had seen God at work in her own life as well as all around her. Her colleagues challenged her. For the first time Jo was serious. She admitted she believed in God, she understood what Jesus did, but she wasn't ready to give up living the way she wanted, not just yet. Shortly after this, Jo got her dream job, one she'd always wanted. She'd regularly pop back to her old office, say hello and bring her enormous grin and even bigger personality!

A few weeks after one of these visits, the office received a phone call. Jo had been sent home from work ill. That night she had a pulmonary aneurysm, her heart stopped instantly, without warning; Jo had died. There was no way anyone could have known; she was only young. The whole office was shaken by the sad loss but more than that, one unspoken question hung in their minds, "Did she know Jesus?"

Read **John 19:38–42**.

* If you'd been there, how would you have reacted to the death of Jesus?
* What could Joseph of Arimathea have in common with Jo?

Consider . . .

* spending more time praying for those close to you who don't know Jesus.
* looking for ways to share Jesus with friends who don't know him – there's not always as much time as we think.

For more, see . . .

* John 14:6 (p.1122)
* Revelation 21:3–4 (p.1403)

* 2 Corinthians 5:1 (p.1244)

the tomb. [12]She saw two angels dressed in white, sitting where Jesus' body had been, one at the head and one at the feet.

[13]They asked her, "Woman, why are you crying?"

She answered, "They have taken away my Lord, and I don't know where they have put him." [14]When Mary said this, she turned around and saw Jesus standing there, but she did not know it was Jesus.

[15]Jesus asked her, "Woman, why are you crying? Whom are you looking for?"

Thinking he was the gardener, she said to him, "Did you take him away, sir? Tell me where you put him, and I will get him."

[16]Jesus said to her, "Mary."

Mary turned towards Jesus and said in the Jewish language,[n] "Rabboni." (This means Teacher.)

[17]Jesus said to her, "Don't hold on to me, because I have not yet gone up to the Father. But go to my brothers and tell them, 'I am going back to my Father and your Father, to my God and your God.'"

[18]Mary Magdalene went and said to the followers, "I saw the Lord!" And she told them what Jesus had said to her.

Jesus Appears to His Followers

[19]When it was evening on the first day of the week, the followers were together. The doors

Jewish language Hebrew or Aramaic, the languages of the Jewish people in the first century.

DOUBT

The Death of Doubt

Rob and his brothers had fought with their dad through the years. He was a quiet man and a strong disciplinarian. He expected a lot from his four sons; his standards were high and generally inflexible. Going to church wasn't an option; it was expected.

Rob loved his dad, but it had always been a fearful, distant love. He had never really known, deep inside, whether his dad loved him. He saw God the same way – as a fearful, distant ruler he was forced to obey. So he wasn't sure if God loved him either. Until one cold November day.

Rob's dad had asked Rob to go for a walk with him – just the two of them. Rob didn't know what to think. What have I done? he wondered.

So Rob and his dad climbed up the hill together. They didn't say much and Rob could see that his dad had something important to tell him.

After a tense, awkward hour, his dad stopped, looked at Rob and said, "I know we haven't always seen eye to eye. And I know I've made life tough for you. But I don't ever want you to forget what I'm about to say to you. I love you as much as a father can love his son. And nothing will ever change that."

The words came with a power and a peace that enveloped Rob. Something changed between him and his dad in that moment. And something changed between Rob and God in that moment.

Rob felt, for the first time, the assurance of God's love for him.

Like Rob, the disciples sometimes had a hard time believing God. They doubted many of the promises Jesus had told them. And the chief doubter among them was Thomas. Read about Thomas's doubt in **John 20:19–31**.

* How did Rob's doubts about his father's love for him compare to Thomas's doubts about Jesus rising from the dead?
* When have you doubted the love of someone close to you?

Consider . . .

* taking a twenty-minute walk and asking God to demonstrate his love for you in something you see.
* reaffirming your love to a friend or family member who may be doubting your love.

For more, see . . .

* Job 40 – 41 (p.496)
* Romans 14:14–23 (p.1207)
* Luke 24:13–53 (p.1093)

were locked, because they were afraid of the Jews. Then Jesus came and stood right in the middle of them and said, "Peace be with you." 20After he said this, he showed them his hands and his side. The followers were thrilled when they saw the Lord.

21Then Jesus said again, "Peace be with you. As the Father sent me, I now send you." 22After he said this, he breathed on them and said, "Receive the Holy Spirit. *d* 23If you forgive anyone his sins, they are forgiven. If you don't forgive them, they are not forgiven."

Jesus Appears to Thomas

24Thomas (called Didymus), who was one of the twelve, was not with them when Jesus came. 25The other followers kept telling Thomas, "We saw the Lord."

But Thomas said, "I will not believe it until I see the nail marks in his hands and put my finger where the nails were and put my hand into his side."

26A week later the followers were in the house again, and Thomas was with them. The doors were locked, but Jesus came in and stood right in the middle of them. He said, "Peace be with you." 27Then he said to Thomas, "Put your finger here, and look at my hands. Put your hand here in my side. Stop being an unbeliever and believe."

28Thomas said to him, "My Lord and my God!"

29Then Jesus told him, "You believe because you see me. Those who believe without seeing me will be truly happy."

Why John Wrote this Book

30Jesus did many other miracles *d* in the presence of his followers that are not written in this book. 31But these are written so that you may believe that Jesus is the Christ, *d* the Son of God. Then, by believing, you may have life through his name.

Jesus Appears to Seven Followers

21 Later, Jesus showed himself to his followers again—this time at Lake Galilee. *n* This is how he showed himself: 2some of the followers were together—Simon Peter, Thomas (called Didymus), Nathanael from Cana in Galilee, the two sons of Zebedee and two other followers. 3Simon Peter said, "I am going out to fish."

The others said, "We will go with you." So they went out and got into the boat. They fished that night but caught nothing.

4Early the next morning Jesus stood on the shore, but the followers did not know it was Jesus. 5Then he said to them, "Friends, did you catch any fish?"

They answered, "No."

6He said, "Throw your net on the right side of the boat, and you will find some." So they did, and they caught so many fish they could not pull the net back into the boat.

7The follower whom Jesus loved said to Peter, "It is the Lord!" When Peter heard him say this, he wrapped his coat around himself. (Peter had taken his clothes off.) Then he jumped into the water. 8The other followers went ashore in the boat, dragging the net full of fish. They were not very far from shore, only about a hundred yards. 9When the followers stepped out of the boat and onto the shore, they saw a fire of hot coals. There were fish on the fire, and there was bread.

10Then Jesus said, "Bring some of the fish you have just caught."

11Simon Peter went into the boat and pulled the net to the shore. It was full of big fish, 153 in all, but even though there were so many, the net did not tear. 12Jesus said to them, "Come and eat." None of the followers dared ask him, "Who are you?" because they knew it was the Lord. 13Jesus came and took the bread and gave it to them, along with the fish.

14This was now the third time Jesus showed himself to his followers after he was raised from the dead.

Sidelight   Barbecued fish for breakfast, anyone? That's what Jesus served when he appeared to his disciples (see John 21:4–13). Cooking fish on an open, charcoal fire was common in Jesus' day. He may have served them musht fish (now known as St Peter's fish), which is one of the most common fish in Lake Galilee.

Jesus Talks to Peter

15When they finished eating, Jesus said to Simon Peter, "Simon son of John, do you love me more than these?"

He answered, "Yes, Lord, you know that I love you."

Jesus said, "Feed my lambs."

16Again Jesus said, "Simon son of John, do you love me?"

He answered, "Yes, Lord, you know that I love you."

Jesus said, "Take care of my sheep."

Lake Galilee   Literally, "Sea of Tiberias".

¹⁷A third time he said, "Simon son of John, do you love me?"

Peter was hurt because Jesus asked him the third time, "Do you love me?" Peter said, "Lord, you know everything; you know that I love you!"

He said to him, "Feed my sheep. ¹⁸I tell you the truth, when you were younger, you tied your own belt and went where you wanted. But when you are old, you will put out your hands and someone else will tie you and take you where you don't want to go." ¹⁹(Jesus said this to show how Peter would die to give glory to God.) Then Jesus said to Peter, "Follow me!"

²⁰Peter turned and saw that the follower Jesus loved was walking behind them. (This was the follower who had leaned against Jesus at the supper and had said, "Lord, who will turn against you?") ²¹When Peter saw him behind them, he asked Jesus, "Lord, what about him?"

²²Jesus answered, "If I want him to live until I come back, that is not your business. You follow me."

²³So a story spread among the followers that this one would not die. But Jesus did not say he would not die. He only said, "If I want him to live until I come back, that is not your business."

²⁴That follower is the one who is telling these things and who has now written them down. We know that what he says is true.

²⁵There are many other things Jesus did. If every one of them were written down, I suppose the whole world would not be big enough for all the books that would be written.

CELEBRATING

Tears of Joy

Alison watched as her grandfather was carried into the ambulance. She had been with him when he had the heart attack, and now it was doubtful that she would ever see him alive again. As she watched the ambulance drive away with its sirens wailing and lights flashing, she began to sob.

Alison visited her grandfather that evening at the hospital. He was still alive, but only just. Alison was only allowed to see him for two minutes, and was then asked to leave him so he could try and recover in peace.

She telephoned the hospital several times each day to find out how her grandfather was getting on. Every time the answer was the same – stable but still critical.

Alison found herself imagining life without her grandfather. It would seem so empty. He had been her closest friend ever since she could remember, and now that friend was going to die.

It was one long, painful week later when the hospital telephoned Alison's house. Her mum was out, so Alison answered the phone.

It was the hospital. A lump rose in Alison's throat and threatened to explode. She almost knew what they were going to say . . .

"Your grandfather is now stable and out of danger," the nurse told her.

Alison replaced the telephone and sat down, stunned. She didn't know whether to laugh or cry, so she did both at the same time.

The disciples must have felt a similar sort of joyful relief when Jesus rose from the dead. You can read about their experience in **John 21:1–14**.

* How did Alison's up and down emotions compare with those of the disciples, both before and after they had heard the good news?
* Have you ever felt the sort of joy that the disciples experienced on the shores of Lake Galilee? When?

Consider . . .

* organising a special "celebration of Jesus" party with your church youth group. Why not make it a type of Christmas celebration?
* having a mini-celebration first thing every morning. Sing a song of praise and thank God that Jesus is alive!

For more, see . . .

* Psalm 126 (p.576)
* James 1:2–4 (p.1348)

* Luke 15:1–7 (p.1070)

Acts

When?

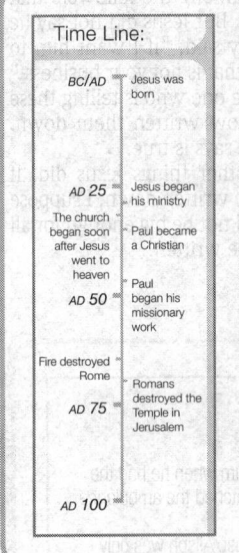

Time Line:

BC/AD	Jesus was born
AD 25	Jesus began his ministry
The church began soon after Jesus went to heaven	Paul became a Christian
AD 50	Paul began his missionary work
Fire destroyed Rome	Romans destroyed the Temple in Jerusalem
AD 75	
AD 100	

Why Read This Book:

- Discover how the Christian church was born (Acts 1—9).
- Recognise that God wants all people to have faith in him (Acts 10—12).
- Be encouraged to tell others about your faith, as the early Christians did (Acts 13—28).

Behind the Scenes:

It looked like everything was over. Jesus was dead – executed by the Romans. After three years with Jesus, the disciples weren't sure what to do next. Maybe go back to fishing and tax-collecting and the other things they did before Jesus came along.

But three days later, Jesus rose from the dead, and the world has never been the same. The book of Acts tells how that event began changing the world.

Written by Luke, Acts picks up where the Gospel of Luke (p.1034) ends. It tells how Jesus went up into heaven, then sent his Holy Spirit fifty days later (Acts 2). The rest of the book tells how the Good News of Jesus Christ spread rapidly throughout the world. Most of the book focuses on two people: Peter and Paul. Peter had been Jesus' disciple, and his life was completely changed by the coming of the Spirit.

Unlike Peter, Paul began as an enemy of Christians. But through a miraculous conversion (Acts 9), he became a devout Christian and great church leader. Acts tells about his travels to spread the Good News and about many of the churches to which he later wrote letters.

Acts tells about a time Christians were in danger. Many churches had to meet in hiding, and Christian leaders were regularly thrown in jail – or killed – for what they believed and taught. Yet the early Christians didn't back down. Their determination can encourage us to live out our faith and tell others about it – even when we are tempted to hide it.

Where?

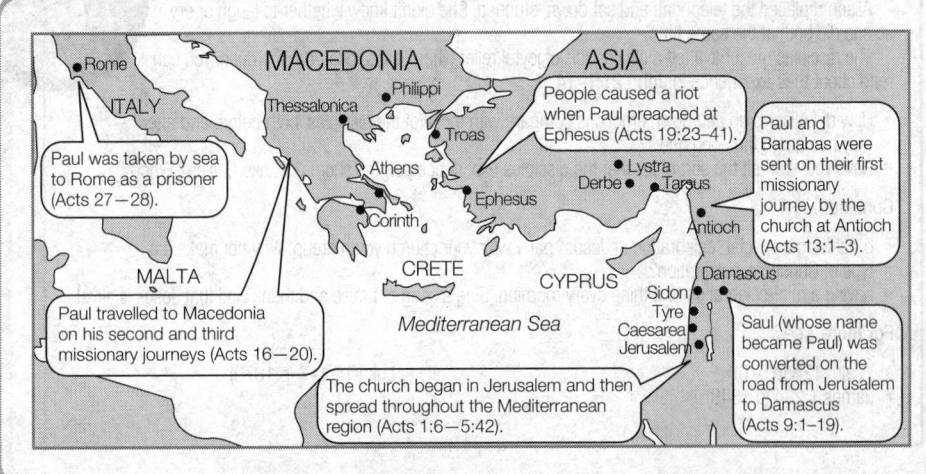

Rome
ITALY
MACEDONIA
Philippi
Thessalonica
Troas
ASIA

People caused a riot when Paul preached at Ephesus (Acts 19:23–41).

Paul and Barnabas were sent on their first missionary journey by the church at Antioch (Acts 13:1–3).

Paul was taken by sea to Rome as a prisoner (Acts 27—28).

Athens
Lystra
Derbe
Tarsus
Corinth
Ephesus
Antioch

MALTA
CRETE
CYPRUS
Damascus

Saul (whose name became Paul) was converted on the road from Jerusalem to Damascus (Acts 9:1–19).

Paul travelled to Macedonia on his second and third missionary journeys (Acts 16—20).

Mediterranean Sea
Sidon
Tyre
Caesarea
Jerusalem

The church began in Jerusalem and then spread throughout the Mediterranean region (Acts 1:6—5:42).

Luke Writes Another Book

1 To Theophilus.

The first book I wrote was about everything Jesus began to do and teach ²until the day he was taken up into heaven. Before this, with the help of the Holy Spirit, *d* Jesus told the apostles *d* he had chosen what they should do. ³After his death, he showed himself to them and proved in many ways that he was alive. The apostles saw Jesus during the 40 days after he was raised from the dead, and he spoke to them about the kingdom of God. ⁴Once when he was eating with them, he told them not to leave Jerusalem. He said, "Wait here to receive the promise from the Father which I told you about. ⁵John baptised people with water, but in a few days you will be baptised with the Holy Spirit."

Jesus is Taken Up into Heaven

⁶When the apostles *d* were all together, they asked Jesus, "Lord, are you now going to give the kingdom back to Israel?"

⁷Jesus said to them, "The Father is the only One who has the authority to decide dates and times. These things are not for you to know. ⁸But when the Holy Spirit *d* comes to you, you will receive power. You will be my witnesses—in Jerusalem, in all of Judea, in Samaria and in every part of the world."

⁹After he said this, as they were watching, he was lifted up, and a cloud hid him from their sight. ¹⁰As he was going, they were looking into the sky. Suddenly, two men wearing white clothes stood beside them. ¹¹They said, "Men of Galilee, why are you standing here looking into

---

SHARING FAITH

Taking to the Streets

In an effort to turn the youth weekend into a more practical event, the young people at the church in Kent were going to take a survey onto the high streets. They had spent most of their time inside the church building, having great fun with videos, music and Bible studies, but now it was time to "get real".

The survey was good, it was based on general questions like: Have you ever been to church? What do you think the church should be doing for young people? If you could get to know Jesus as a real person, would you be interested?

The 35-strong youth group had split up into small groups and were ready to go out.

"Who's going to ask the questions?" Lisa was talking to her group.

"Let's take it in turns," suggested Aaron.

"Now, remember . . ." began Hazel their youth leader, "as there are so many of you, it would be good to find groups of young people hanging around the town – shouldn't be too difficult on a Saturday afternoon! Right, you have exactly one hour. Go!"

Later when they came back, they were all talking and yelling excitedly.

"I can't believe you asked that bloke!" giggled Rosie.

"Well, what about the guys in McDonald's? They were a scream!" yelled Lisa.

"I just can't believe everyone was so great about it. I've filled in loads of surveys!" said Aaron.

"I've got at least six people who want to come back and watch the film tonight," related Jo.

Michael flopped into the nearest armchair. "Who would have thought talking about being a Christian could be so easy?"

Read **Acts 1:6–8** and see how the apostles were sent out.

* How does verse 8 compare to the youth weekend?
* How did the Holy Spirit help the apostles to witness?

Consider . . .

* praying seriously that the Holy Spirit would give you the power to be an effective witness.
* asking your minister or youth leader to plan a special event that can be used alongside a survey, as a witness in your area.

For more, see . . .

* Matthew 28:19–20 (p.995)
* Romans 10:13–15 (p.1200)
* Luke 24:46–49 (p.1094)

the sky? Jesus, whom you saw taken up from you into heaven, will come back in the same way you saw him go."

A New Apostle Is Chosen

12Then they went back to Jerusalem from the Mount of Olives. *d* (This mountain is about a kilometre from Jerusalem.) 13When they entered the city, they went to the upstairs room where they were staying. Peter, John, James, Andrew, Philip, Thomas, Bartholomew, Matthew, James son of Alphaeus, Simon (known as the Zealot *d*) and Judas son of James were there. 14They all continued praying together with some women, including Mary the mother of Jesus, and Jesus' brothers.

15During this time there was a meeting of the believers (about 120 in all). Peter stood up and said, 16-17"Brothers and sisters, *n* in the Scriptures *d* the Holy Spirit *d* said through David something that must happen involving Judas. He was one of our own group and served together with us. He led those who arrested Jesus." 18(Judas bought a field with the money he got for his evil act. But he fell to his death, his body burst open, and all his intestines poured out. 19Everyone in Jerusalem learned about this so they named this place Akeldama. In their language Akeldama means "Field of Blood".) 20"In the Book of Psalms," Peter said, "this is written:

'May his place be empty;
    leave no one to live in it.'   *Psalm 69:25*

And it is also written:

'Let another man replace him as leader.'
                                           Psalm 109:8

21-22"So now a man must become a witness with us of Jesus' being raised from the dead. He must be one of the men who were part of our group during all the time the Lord Jesus was among us—from the time John was baptising people until the day Jesus was taken up from us to heaven."

23They put the names of two men before the group. One was Joseph Barsabbas, who was also called Justus. The other was Matthias. 24-25The apostles prayed, "Lord, you know the thoughts of everyone. Show us which one of these two you have chosen to do this work. Show us who should be an apostle *d* in place of Judas, who turned away and went where he belongs." 26Then they used lots *d* to choose between them, and the lots showed that Matthias was the one. So he became an apostle with the other eleven.

The Coming of the Holy Spirit

2 When the day of Pentecost *d* came, they were all together in one place. 2Suddenly a noise like a strong, blowing wind came from heaven and filled the whole house where they were sitting. 3They saw something like flames of fire that were separated and stood over each person there. 4They were all filled with the Holy Spirit, *d* and they began to speak different languages *n* by the power the Holy Spirit was giving them.

> **Sidelight**   Before the birth of the church, Pentecost (Acts 2:1–4) was a major time of celebration among Jews. This festival celebrated the wheat harvest with religious ceremonies, eating, drinking, and music. The festivities surrounding the event may be why people thought the disciples were drunk (Acts 2:13).

5There were some religious Jews staying in Jerusalem who were from every country in the world. 6When they heard this noise, a crowd came together. They were all surprised, because each one heard them speaking in his own language. 7They were completely amazed at this. They said, "Look! Aren't all these people that we hear speaking from Galilee? 8Then how is it possible that we each hear them in our own languages? We are from different places: 9Parthia, Media, Elam, Mesopotamia, Judea, Cappadocia, Pontus, Asia, 10Phrygia, Pamphylia, Egypt, the areas of Libya near Cyrene, Rome 11(both Jews and those who had become Jews), Crete and Arabia. But we hear them telling in our own languages about the great things God has done!" 12They were all amazed and confused, asking each other, "What does this mean?"

13But others were making fun of them, saying, "They have had too much wine."

Peter Speaks to the People

14But Peter stood up with the eleven apostles, *d* and in a loud voice he spoke to the crowd: "My fellow Jews, and all of you who are in Jerusalem, listen to me. Pay attention to what I have to say. 15These people are not drunk, as you think; it is only nine o'clock in the morning! 16But Joel the prophet *d* wrote about what is happening here today:

17'God says: In the last days
    I will pour out my Spirit *d* on all kinds of
        people.

Brothers and sisters   Although the Greek text says "brothers" here and throughout this book, these words of the speakers were meant for the entire church, both men and women.
languages   This can also be translated "tongues".

Your sons and daughters will prophesy. *d*
  Your old men will dream dreams,
  and your young men will see visions.
¹⁸At that time I will pour out my Spirit
  also on my male slaves and female slaves.
¹⁹I will show miracles *d*
  in the sky and on the earth:
  blood, fire and thick smoke.
²⁰The sun will become dark,
  the moon red as blood,
  before the overwhelming and terrible day of
    the LORD comes.
²¹Then anyone who calls on the LORD
  will be saved.'   *Joel 2:28–32*

²²"People of Israel, listen to these words: Jesus from Nazareth was a very special man. God clearly showed this to you by the miracles, wonders and signs he did through Jesus. You all know this, because it happened right here among you. ²³Jesus was given to you, and with the help of those who don't know the law, you put him to death by nailing him to a cross. But this was God's plan which he had made long ago; he knew all this would happen. ²⁴God raised Jesus from the dead and set him free from the pain of death, because death could not hold him. ²⁵For David said this about him:

  'I keep the LORD before me always.
  Because he is close by my side,
    I will not be hurt.
²⁶So I rejoice and am glad.
  Even my body has hope,
²⁷because you will not leave me in the grave.
  You will not let your holy one rot.
²⁸You will teach me how to live a holy life.
  Being with you will fill me with joy.'
                                         Psalm 16:8–11

²⁹"Brothers and sisters, I can tell you truly that David, our ancestor, died and was buried. His grave is still here with us today. ³⁰He was a prophet and knew God had promised him that he would make a person from David's

---

HOLY SPIRIT

Power Up

On 15 June 1752, American politician and scientist, Benjamin Franklin went outside to fly a kite. Instead of choosing a nice, sunny afternoon, Franklin chose a stormy one in the hope that the dark clouds overhead could become a lightning storm. The scientist successfully extracted sparks from the clouds proving his theory that lightning was electricity. He survived his dangerous experiment unhurt, unlike other famous scientists who have since died from lightning strikes while performing similar experiments.

Electricity has immense power, capable of both lightning storms and boiling kettles, powering an entire city and giving light to a torch. Electrical power is everywhere – it's just there, meeting our every need, every time we turn on a light switch or open the fridge, use our mobile phone or watch a film. It's even there when we make a friend's hair stand on end with a balloon we've just rubbed on a jumper.

In **Acts 2:1–21** we read about the day of Pentecost when the Holy Spirit came and filled the disciples, giving them power, courage and amazing gifts. Just as electricity is everywhere, ready to power the things we need, so the Holy Spirit is with us whenever we need him as a source of power and comfort. As we invite the Holy Spirit into our lives, we are given the power we need to live the Christian life.

* Electricity powers many different things in different ways. How does the Holy Spirit give power to Christians?
* In what ways do we see the Holy Spirit's power in the passage?

Consider . . .

* asking God to fill you with his Holy Spirit and to use you.
* telling one person about Jesus. Depend on the Holy Spirit to help you communicate clearly.

For more, see . . .

* Joel 2:28 (p.866)
* 1 Corinthians 12:1–11 (p.1230)

* John 14:15–26 (p.1123)

family a king just as he was.[n] [31]Knowing this before it happened, David talked about the Christ[d] rising from the dead. He said:

'He was not left in the grave.
  His body did not rot.'

[32]So Jesus is the One whom God raised from the dead. And we are all witnesses to this. [33]Jesus was lifted up to heaven and is now at God's right side. The Father has given the Holy Spirit to Jesus as he promised. So Jesus has poured out that Spirit, and this is what you now see and hear. [34]David was not the one who was lifted up to heaven, but he said:

'The LORD said to my Lord,

"Sit by me at my right side,
35 until I put your enemies under your
      control." '[n]
                                    Psalm 110:1

[36]"So, all the people of Israel should know this truly: God has made Jesus—the man you nailed to the cross—both Lord and Christ."

[37]When the people heard this, they felt guilty and asked Peter and the other apostles, "What shall we do?"

[38]Peter said to them, "Change your hearts and lives and be baptised,[d] each one of you, in the name of Jesus Christ for the forgiveness of your sins. And you will receive the gift of the Holy Spirit. [39]This promise is for you, for your

God . . . was   See 2 Samuel 7:13; Psalm 132:11.
until . . . control   Literally, "until I make your enemies a footstool for your feet".

SHARING FAITH

Say What You See

Toby turned up at youth group with a massive grin on his face. The other lads knew he would have some amazing news and were soon swarming round him with their questions.

"What was it like?"
"What did you see?"
"Did you get to demo stuff?"

Toby's dad worked for a magazine that reviewed computer games and consoles. Every year his dad would go to an international conference where the big companies launched their new games and hardware. This year, the magazine wanted to do an article about fathers and sons who both loved to game. So not only did Toby get to go to the conference but his dad interviewed him about everything they had seen and played.

"It was awesome," he told his mates. "Dad has been telling me about some of these games that have been in development for months but it was amazing to see them for myself." Then he started to explain everything he had seen, which games looked good, what the graphics were like, the playability . . . He went into every tiny detail and his mates were loving it.

A month or so later, he strolled in with his dad's magazine tucked under his arm, for the first time ever his words had been printed.

"How did you know what to say?" one of his friends asked.

"It was easy," Toby smiled, "I just said what I saw."

Read **Acts 2:29–32** to find out about someone else who "just said what he saw".

* What difference does it make that both Peter and Toby talked about things that they had seen for themselves?
* Do you like to hear about the things that have happened in people's lives? Why?

Consider . . .

* writing down what you have seen and know that God has done in your own life?
* ways that you can focus on your own story and personal experience of God when you talk to people about Christianity.

For more, see . . .

* 2 Peter 1:16–18 (p.1365)
* 1 John 1:1–3 (p.1371)

children and for all who are far away. It is for everyone the Lord our God calls to himself."

⁴⁰Peter warned them with many other words. He begged them, "Save yourselves from the evil of today's people!" ⁴¹Then those people who accepted what Peter said were baptised. About 3,000 people were added to the number of believers that day. ⁴²They spent their time learning the apostles' teaching, sharing, breaking bread[n] and praying together.

The Believers Share

⁴³The apostles[d] were doing many miracles[d] and signs, and everyone felt great respect for God. ⁴⁴All the believers were together and shared everything. ⁴⁵They would sell their land and the things they owned and then divide the money and give it to anyone who needed it. ⁴⁶The believers met together in the Temple[d] every day. They ate together in their homes, happy to share their food with joyful hearts. ⁴⁷They praised God and were liked

breaking bread This may mean a meal as in verse 46, or the Lord's Supper, the special meal that Jesus told his followers to eat to remember him (Luke 22:14–20).

CHURCH

The Place to Belong

Rebecca longed to fit in. She wanted people to like her and be her friend. That's why she joined every organisation she could at school. She still didn't feel as though she fitted in, but at least she was busy.

During Science Club meeting one day, Lee invited Rebecca to church. She was not interested, remembering the church she had attended with her mother years before. Each service had been one long, boring sermon with her mum telling her to be quiet. That was not Rebecca's idea of fun. She was "busy", she lied to Lee.

But Lee persisted. Finally Rebecca agreed to endure one service – just to get him to leave her alone.

She didn't say much to him. When Lee and Rebecca arrived for church the next Sunday evening, the kids were standing around talking and laughing. Several of them recognised Rebecca and welcomed her. During the group time, people spoke to Rebecca and asked her opinion. Several people invited Rebecca to sit with them during the worship. And during the sermon, the minister told interesting stories. Rebecca never felt bored.

After church, all the kids went to Jason's house to complete plans for their fundraising project. Rebecca helped to make posters.

All the way home, Rebecca couldn't stop talking about how much she had liked Lee's church.

"It just seems as though I fit in there; know what I mean?" she commented.

"Yes, I know," Lee smiled. "So, I suppose we'll see you next week?"

Rebecca laughed and asked, "What do you think?"

People are attracted to places where people really care and teach God's Word. Read **Acts 2:36–47** to see how the first church attracted people by the way its people lived and worshipped together.

* How does the church in Acts compare with Lee's church?
* Which qualities does the Acts church have in common with your church and which qualities of this church are different from your church's?

Consider . . .

* befriending visitors who come to your church. Ask them to sit with you or invite them to other church activities.
* doing a specific job in your church, such as greeting visitors or writing for the newsletter. Become one of the people who makes church more of what God wants it to be.

For more, see . . .

* Isaiah 2:2–5 (p.640)
* Romans 12 (p.1203)

* Acts 4:32–35 (p.1144)

by all the people. Every day the Lord added those who were being saved to the group of believers.

Peter Heals a Crippled Man

3 One day Peter and John went to the Temple*d* at three o'clock, the time set each day for the afternoon prayer service. ²There, at the Temple gate called Beautiful Gate, was a man who had been crippled all his life. Every day he was carried to this gate to beg for money from the people going into the Temple. ³The man saw Peter and John going into the Temple and asked them for money. ⁴Peter and John looked straight at him and said, "Look at us!" ⁵The man looked at them, thinking they were going to give him some money. ⁶But Peter said, "I don't have any silver or gold, but I do have something else I can give you. By the power of Jesus Christ from Nazareth, stand up and walk!" ⁷Then Peter took the man's right hand and lifted him up.

Immediately the man's feet and ankles became strong. ⁸He jumped up, stood on his feet and began to walk. He went into the Temple with them, walking and jumping and praising God. ⁹⁻¹⁰All the people recognised him as the crippled man who always sat by the Beautiful Gate begging for money. Now they saw this same man walking and praising God, and they were amazed. They wondered how this could happen.

Peter Speaks to the People

¹¹While the man was holding on to Peter and John, all the people were amazed and ran to them at Solomon's Porch. *d* ¹²When Peter saw this, he said to them, "People of Israel, why are you surprised? You are looking at us as if it were our own power or goodness that made this man walk. ¹³The God of Abraham, Isaac and Jacob, the God of our ancestors, gave glory to Jesus, his servant. But you handed him over to be killed. Pilate

SICKNESS

The Hospital Proved It

"Dad . . . I was healed at one of the meetings," said the voice on the phone.

"Were you? Are you sure?"

Sue was sixteen years old – bright and popular. She was fit and working on her Silver Award for outdoor pursuits. Few people knew that she had a heart murmur which was picked up by the doctor's stethoscope. A hospital scanner showed that it was caused by a defective heart valve. The problem made little difference to her lifestyle but it was always in the background. Any infection – however small – had to be taken seriously and treated with antibiotics.

One week of the summer was spent at a Christian camp where a nationally known rock band – 65dba – led the youth work. High on the agenda was learning to respond to God in faith. During a time of worship, Ray – the leader – called for people with heart problems to go forward for prayer. Sue knew she had been healed and told her Christian parents. A month later she went for a regular hospital check up confident that she was now well.

"That's funny," said the technician operating the echocardiogram. "I thought you had a bicuspid heart valve." She looked at the records. "We must have made a mistake."

Healings through the power of Jesus are often difficult to cope with. Read **Acts 3:11–19** to see.

* Why do you think Sue's father was uncertain about her healing? Should Sue have explained to the hospital staff about being prayed for?
* What does the passage say was the key factor in the man's healing?

Consider . . .

* talking to people who have been healed by faith in Jesus about how it happened.
* asking non-Christians about how they feel about healing through faith in Jesus.

For more, see . . .

* 2 Kings 4 (p.347)
* Luke 10:1–12 (p.1056)
* Mark 1:29–39 (p.997)

decided to let him go free, but you told Pilate you did not want Jesus. [14]You did not want the One who is holy and good but asked Pilate to give you a murderer[n] instead. [15]And so you killed the One who gives life, but God raised him from the dead. We are witnesses to this. [16]It was faith in Jesus that made this crippled man well. You can see this man, and you know him. He was made completely well because of trust in Jesus, and you all saw it happen!

[17]"Brothers and sisters,[n] I know you did those things to Jesus because neither you nor your leaders understood what you were doing. [18]God said through the prophets[d] that his Christ[d] would suffer and die. And now God has made these things come true in this way. [19]So you must change your hearts and lives! Come back to God, and he will forgive your sins. Then the Lord will give you times of spiritual rest. [20]And he will send Jesus, the One he chose to be the Christ. [21]But Jesus must stay in heaven until the time comes when all things will be made right again. God told about this time long ago when he spoke through his holy prophets. [22]Moses said, 'The Lord your God will give you a prophet like me, who is one of your own people. You must listen to everything he tells you. [23]Anyone who does not listen to that prophet will die, cut off from God's people.'[n] [24]Samuel, and all the other prophets who spoke for God after Samuel, told about this time now. [25]You are descendants[d] of the prophets. You have received the agreement God made with your ancestors. He said to your father Abraham, 'Through your descendants all the nations on the earth will be blessed.'[n] [26]God has raised up his servant Jesus and sent him to you first to bless you by turning each of you away from doing evil."

Peter and John at the Council

4 While Peter and John were speaking to the people, Jewish priests, the captain of the soldiers that guarded the Temple[d] and Sadducees[d] came up to them. [2]They were upset because the two apostles[d] were teaching the people and were preaching that people will rise from the dead through the power of Jesus. [3]The Jewish leaders grabbed Peter and John and put them in jail. Since it was already night, they kept them in jail until the next day. [4]But many of those who had heard Peter and John preach believed the things they said. There were now about 5,000 in the group of believers.

[5]The next day the Jewish rulers, the Jewish elders and the teachers of the law met in Jerusalem. [6]Annas the high priest, Caiaphas, John and Alexander were there, as well as everyone from the high priest's family. [7]They made Peter and John stand before them and then asked them, "By what power or authority did you do this?"

[8]Then Peter, filled with the Holy Spirit,[d] said to them, "Rulers of the people and you elders, [9]are you questioning us about a good thing that was done to a crippled man? Are you asking us who made him well? [10]We want all of you and all the Jewish people to know that this man was made well by the power of Jesus Christ from Nazareth. You crucified him, but God raised him from the dead. This man was crippled, but he is now well and able to stand here before you because of the power of Jesus. [11]Jesus is

'the stone[n] that you builders rejected,
  which has become the cornerstone.'[d]

Psalm 118:22

[12]Jesus is the only One who can save people. His name is the only power in the world that has been given to save people. We must be saved through him."

[13]The Jewish leaders saw that Peter and John were not afraid to speak, and they understood that these men had no special training or education. So they were amazed. Then they realised that Peter and John had been with Jesus. [14]Because they saw the healed man standing there beside the two apostles, they could say nothing against them. [15]After the Jewish leaders ordered them to leave the meeting, they began to talk to each other. [16]They said, "What shall we do with these men? Everyone in Jerusalem knows they have done a great miracle,[d] and we cannot say it is not true. [17]But to keep it from spreading among the people, we must warn them not to talk to people any more using that name."

[18]So they called Peter and John in again and told them not to speak or to teach at all in the

---

murderer   Barabbas, the man the crowd asked Pilate to set free instead of Jesus (Luke 23:18).
Brothers and sisters   Although the Greek text says "brothers" here and throughout this book. Paul's words were meant for the entire church, including men and women.
'The Lord . . . people.'   Quotation from Deuteronomy 18:15,19.
'Through . . . blessed.'   Quotation from Genesis 22:18; 26:4.
stone   A symbol meaning Jesus.

name of Jesus. ¹⁹But Peter and John answered them, "You decide what God would want. Should we obey you or God? ²⁰We cannot keep quiet. We must speak about what we have seen and heard." ²¹The Jewish leaders warned the apostles again and let them go free. They could not find a way to punish them, because all the people were praising God for what had been done. ²²The man who received the miracle of healing was more than 40 years old.

The Believers Pray

²³After Peter and John left the meeting of Jewish leaders, they went to their own group and told them everything the leading priests and the Jewish elders had said to them. ²⁴When the believers heard this, they prayed to God together, "Lord, you are the One who made the sky, the earth, the sea and everything in them. ²⁵By the Holy Spirit, ᵈ through our father David your servant, you said:

'Why are the nations so angry?

Why are the people making useless plans?

²⁶The kings of the earth prepare to fight,

and their leaders make plans together

against the LORD

and his appointed one.'   *Psalm 2:1–2*

²⁷These things really happened when Herod, Pontius Pilate, those who are not Jews and the Jewish people all came together against Jesus here in Jerusalem. Jesus is your holy servant, the One you made to be the Christ. ᵈ ²⁸These people made your plan happen because of your power and your will. ²⁹And now, Lord, listen to their threats. Lord, help us, your servants, to speak your word without fear. ³⁰Help us to be brave by showing us your power to heal. Give proofs and make miracles ᵈ happen by the power of Jesus, your holy servant."

³¹After they had prayed, the place where they were meeting was shaken. They were all filled with the Holy Spirit, and they spoke God's word without fear.

The Believers Share

³²The group of believers were united in their hearts and spirit. All those in the group acted as

---

SHARING FAITH

Responding to Opportunities

"Come on, Matt. Don't let me down! Mrs Reece trusts you," Sean pleaded. "She would let you into the classroom to use the lab at night, and you could copy the test answers while you're there. She'd never know."

"I can't abuse Mrs Reece's trust that way," Matt said. "And besides, it's wrong to cheat."

"Why can't you do it just this once? No one will know!" Sean persisted.

"I'll know and so will Jesus," Matt answered.

"But Jesus wants you to get good results, doesn't he?" Sean challenged.

"Yes, he does. This just isn't the way to get those good results."

Sean finally gave up pressuring Matt to compromise his faith. In fact, over time Sean even started asking about "this Jesus who runs your life".

Caught in a difficult situation, Matt shared his faith by showing how it influenced his actions. Read how Peter and John took advantage of an opportunity to talk about Jesus in **Acts 4:1–13**.

• What obstacles did Matt and Peter have to overcome to talk about their faith?
• What basic facts about Jesus did Peter consider essential in discussing his faith?

Consider . . .

• writing down ways in which you could share your faith with a non-Christian. Use one of these ways with someone this week.
• enlisting a friend to role-play faith-sharing situations, role-play talking to people who are sceptical, open, rebellious or interested.

For more, see . . .

• Daniel 1:3–16 (p.833)
• Colossians 4:5–6 (p.1294)

• Matthew 10:16–20 (p.955)

though their private property belonged to everyone in the group. In fact, they shared everything. [33]With great power the apostles[d] were telling people that the Lord Jesus was truly raised from the dead. And God blessed all the believers very much. [34]No one in the group needed anything. From time to time those who owned fields or houses sold them, brought the money, [35]and gave it to the apostles. Then the money was given to anyone who needed it.

[36]One of the believers was named Joseph, a Levite born in Cyprus. The apostles called him Barnabas (which means "one who encourages"). [37]Joseph owned a field, sold it, brought the money and gave it to the apostles.

Ananias and Sapphira Die

5 But a man named Ananias and his wife Sapphira sold some land. [2]He kept back part of the money for himself; his wife knew about this and agreed to it. But he brought the rest of the money and gave it to the apostles.[d] [3]Peter said, "Ananias, why did you let Satan rule your thoughts to lie to the Holy Spirit[d] and to keep for yourself part of the money you received for the land? [4]Before you sold the land, it belonged to you. And even after you sold it, you could have used the money in any way you wanted. Why did you think of doing this? You lied to God, not to us!" [5-6]When Ananias heard this, he fell down and died. Some young men came in, wrapped up his body, carried it out and buried it. And everyone who heard about this was filled with fear.

[7]About three hours later his wife came in, but she did not know what had happened. [8]Peter said to her, "Tell me, was the money you got for your field this much?"

Sapphira answered, "Yes, that was the price." [9]Peter said to her, "Why did you and your husband agree to test the Spirit of the Lord? Look! The men who buried your husband are at the door, and they will carry you out." [10]At that moment Sapphira fell down by his feet and died. When the young men came in and saw that she was dead, they carried her out and buried her beside her husband. [11]The whole church and all the others who heard about these things were filled with fear.

The Apostles Heal Many

[12]The apostles[d] did many signs and miracles[d] among the people. And they would all meet together on Solomon's Porch.[d] [13]None of the others dared to join them, but all the people respected them. [14]More and more men and women believed in the Lord and were added to the group of believers. [15]The people placed their sick on beds and mats in the streets, hoping that when Peter passed by at least his shadow might fall on them. [16]Crowds

came from all the towns around Jerusalem, bringing their sick and those who were bothered by evil spirits, and all of them were healed.

Leaders Try to Stop the Apostles

[17]The high priest and all his friends (a group called the Sadducees[d]) became very jealous. [18]They took the apostles and put them in jail. [19]But during the night, an angel of the Lord opened the doors of the jail and led the apostles outside. The angel said, [20]"Go and stand in the Temple[d] and tell the people everything about this new life." [21]When the apostles heard this, they obeyed and went into the Temple early in the morning and continued teaching.

When the high priest and his friends arrived, they called a meeting of the Jewish leaders and all the important Jewish elders. They sent some men to the jail to bring the apostles to them. [22]But, upon arriving, the officers could not find the apostles. So they went back and reported to the Jewish leaders. [23]They said, "The jail was closed and locked, and the guards were standing at the doors. But when we opened the doors, the jail was empty!" [24]Hearing this, the captain of the Temple guards and the leading priests were confused and wondered what was happening.

[25]Then someone came and told them, "Listen! The men you put in jail are standing in the Temple teaching the people." [26]Then the captain and his men went out and brought the apostles back. But the soldiers did not use force, because they were afraid the people would stone them to death.

[27]The soldiers brought the apostles to the meeting and made them stand before the Jewish leaders. The high priest questioned them, [28]saying, "We gave you strict orders not to continue teaching in that name. But look, you have filled Jerusalem with your teaching and are trying to make us responsible for this man's death."

[29]Peter and the other apostles answered, "We must obey God, not human authority! [30]You killed Jesus by hanging him on a cross. But God, the God of our ancestors, raised Jesus up from the dead! [31]Jesus is the One whom God raised to be on his right side, as Leader and Saviour. Through him, all Jewish people can change their hearts and lives and have their sins forgiven. [32]We saw all these things happen. The Holy Spirit,[d] whom God has given to all who obey him, also proves these things are true."

[33]When the Jewish leaders heard this, they became angry and wanted to kill them. [34]But a Pharisee[d] named Gamaliel stood up in the meeting. He was a teacher of the law, and all the people respected him. He ordered the apostles to leave the meeting for a little while. [35]Then he said, "People of Israel, be careful what you are planning to do to these men. [36]Remember when

Theudas appeared? He said he was a great man, and about 400 men joined him. But he was killed, and all his followers were scattered; they were able to do nothing. [37]Later, a man named Judas came from Galilee at the time of the registration.[n] He also led a group of followers and was killed, and all his followers were scattered.

[38]And so now I tell you: stay away from these men, and leave them alone. If their plan comes from human authority, it will fail. [39]But if it is from God, you will not be able to stop them. You might even be fighting against God himself!"

The Jewish leaders agreed with what Gamaliel said. [40]They called the apostles in, beat them and

registration Census. A counting of all the people and the things they own.

PRIORITIES

Who's the Boss?

Richard Wurmbrand fidgeted in his chair as he listened to Gheorghe Gheorghiu-Dej, the Communist Party boss. Gheorghe promised the post-World War II clergy of Romania that his government would pay the clergy out of tax revenues if communism and Christianity would work together. Most of the audience cheered, and one church leader promised that the clergy would co-operate with the state.

But Richard didn't cheer. He had already been imprisoned and beaten several times for his faith. He knew that speaking out could again cost him his freedom.

Richard's wife, Sabina, sat beside him. "Go and wash this shame from the face of Christ!" she demanded.

Richard pleaded that he would be taken away if he spoke out against the communists.

"I don't need a coward," Sabina replied.

Gathering his courage, Richard asked permission to speak and was welcomed forward by the organisers, who apparently anticipated a unity speech. Instead, Richard began by saying it was the duty of ministers to glorify God, not earthly powers. He encouraged the clergy to support the eternal kingdom of God, not the powers of Romania.

As he continued, someone suddenly began to clap. And another person also clapped. Soon, the clapping erupted into waves of applause.

"Stop! Your right to speak has been withdrawn," ordered the Minister of Cults ("cults" included religious bodies of all kinds in Romania).

"My right to speak comes from God," Richard declared. He kept speaking until his microphone was disconnected.

Richard was imprisoned and the Ministry of Cults ran the church.

The situation has changed in Romania but in many other parts of the world, people face serious trouble if they stand up for Christ.

Like Richard, the apostles recognised the priority of obeying God and speaking out for him. Read **Acts 5:17–32** to see how they spoke out for Jesus even when threatened by imprisonment.

- Based on the story and the Bible passage, what were the top priorities for Richard Wurmbrand and the apostles?
- When have you faced opposition for your faith? How was that experience like and unlike the scripture passage?

Consider . . .

- making a poster of Acts 5:29 and writing around the border five priorities which you believe God wants you to follow. Then make a weekly schedule that reflects those priorities.
- talking to a friend about times when you have had to do something unpopular to make your faith your top priority.

For more, see . . .

- Psalm 119:17–24 (p.571)
- 2 Corinthians 11:23–29 (p.1252)
- Matthew 10:32–36 (p.957)

told them not to speak in the name of Jesus again. Then they let them go free. [41]The apostles left the meeting full of joy because they were given the honour of suffering disgrace for Jesus. [42]Every day in the Temple and in people's homes they continued teaching the people and telling the Good News *d*—that Jesus is the Christ. *d*

Seven Leaders are Chosen

6 The number of followers was growing. But during this same time, the Greek-speaking followers had an argument with the other Jewish followers. The Greek-speaking widows were not getting their share of the food that was given out every day. [2]The twelve apostles *d* called the whole group of followers together and said, "It is not right for us to stop our work of teaching

---

Sidelight

Relationships between Jews and non-Jewish people were strained in Bible times. This prejudice shows up in Acts 6:1 where Greek (non-Jewish) Christians complained that their widows weren't receiving a fair share of the church's distributions. The book of Acts is filled with other stories that highlight the tensions between Jewish and non-Jewish Christians.

God's word in order to serve tables. [3]So, brothers and sisters, choose seven of your own men who are good, full of the Spirit *d* and full of wisdom. We will put them in charge of this work. [4]Then we can continue to pray and to teach the word of God."

[5]The whole group liked the idea, so they chose these seven men: Stephen (a man with great faith and full of the Holy Spirit), Philip, *n* Procorus, Nicanor, Timon, Parmenas and Nicolas (a man from Antioch who had become a Jew). [6]Then they put these men before the apostles, who prayed and laid their hands *n* on them.

[7]The word of God was continuing to spread. The group of followers in Jerusalem increased, and a great number of the Jewish priests believed and obeyed.

Stephen is Accused

[8]Stephen was richly blessed by God who gave him the power to do great miracles *d* and signs among the people. [9]But some Jewish people were against him. They belonged to the

synagogue *d* of Free Men *n* (as it was called), which included Jewish people from Cyrene, Alexandria, Cilicia and Asia. They all came and argued with Stephen.

[10]But the Spirit *d* was helping him to speak with wisdom, and his words were so strong that they could not argue with him. [11]So they secretly urged some men to say, "We heard Stephen speak against Moses and against God."

[12]This upset the people, the Jewish elders and the teachers of the law. They came and grabbed Stephen and brought him to a meeting of the Jewish leaders. [13]They brought in some people to tell lies about Stephen, saying, "This man is always speaking against this holy place and the law of Moses. [14]We heard him say that Jesus from Nazareth will destroy this place and that Jesus will change the customs Moses gave us." [15]All the people in the meeting were watching Stephen closely and saw that his face looked like the face of an angel.

Stephen's Speech

7 The high priest said to Stephen, "Are these things true?"

[2]Stephen answered, "Brothers and fathers, listen to me. Our glorious God appeared to Abraham, our ancestor, in Mesopotamia before he lived in Haran. [3]God said to Abraham, 'Leave your country and your relatives, and go to the land I will show you.' *n* [4]So Abraham left the country of Chaldea and went to live in Haran. After Abraham's father died, God sent him to this place where you now live. [5]God did not give Abraham any of this land, not even a foot of it. But God promised that he would give this land to him and his descendants, *d* even before Abraham had a child. [6]This is what God said to him: 'Your descendants will be strangers in a land they don't own. The people there will make them slaves and will mistreat them for 400 years. [7]But I will punish the nation where they are slaves. Then your descendants will leave that land and will worship me in this place.' *n* [8]God made an agreement with Abraham, the sign of which was circumcision. *d* And so when Abraham had his son, Isaac, Abraham circumcised him when he was eight days old. Isaac also circumcised his son, Jacob, and Jacob did the same for his sons, the twelve ancestors *n* of our people.

[9]"Jacob's sons became jealous of Joseph and sold him to be a slave in Egypt. But God was with

---

Philip Not the apostle named Philip.

laid their hands on The laying on of hands had many purposes, including the giving of a blessing, power or authority.

Free Men Jewish people who had been slaves or whose fathers had been slaves, but who were now free.

'Leave . . . you.' Quotation from Genesis 12:1.

'Your descendants . . . place.' Quotation from Genesis 15:13–14 and Exodus 3:12.

twelve ancestors Important ancestors of the Jewish people; the leaders of the twelve Jewish tribes.

him [10]and saved him from all his troubles. The king of Egypt liked Joseph and respected him because of the wisdom God gave him. The king made him governor of Egypt and put him in charge of all the people in his palace.

[11]"Then all the land of Egypt and Canaan became so dry that nothing would grow, and the people suffered very much. Jacob's sons, our ancestors, could not find anything to eat. [12]But when Jacob heard there was grain in Egypt, he sent his sons there. This was their first trip to Egypt. [13]When they went there a second time, Joseph told his brothers who he was, and the king learned about Joseph's family. [14]Then Joseph sent messengers to invite Jacob, his father, to come to Egypt along with all his relatives (75 persons altogether).

[15]So Jacob went down to Egypt, where he and his sons died. [16]Later their bodies were moved to Shechem and put in a grave there. (It was the same grave Abraham had bought for a sum of money from the sons of Hamor in Shechem.)

[17]"The promise God made to Abraham was soon to come true, and the number of people in Egypt grew large. [18]Then a new king, who did not know who Joseph was, began to rule Egypt. [19]This king tricked our people and was cruel to our ancestors, forcing them to leave their babies outside to die. [20]At this time Moses was born, and he was very beautiful. For three months Moses was cared for in his father's house. [21]When they put Moses outside, the king's daughter adopted him and raised him as if he

HONESTY

Rumours

"Shhhhh! There she is."

The girls at the back of the room stopped giggling and whispering when Zoë arrived for her history class on Monday morning.

"What's going on?" Zoë asked uncomfortably as she sat next to her best friend, Mary.

Mary shot a dirty look at the girls in the back of the room. "Someone is saying you're 'easy'," she said.

"There's a note in the boys' toilets that says 'Zoë's fine, so get in line'."

Zoë couldn't believe it. She felt as though someone had just kicked her in the chest.

Just then, Mark leaned across the aisle and asked, "Hey, Zoë, can I be next in line?"

Zoë burst into tears and ran from the room. Her mind raced as she stumbled along the empty corridor. Where could such a false rumour have come from? Who could say such ugly things?

Then she remembered what Ben, her ex-boyfriend, had said. After begging her not to break up, he warned that she would be sorry if she did.

"This must be what he meant," Zoë thought as she leaned against a locker and slid down to sit on the floor.

Zoë knew it would take a long time to clear her reputation. But she was determined that, no matter what, it would be cleared.

"Lord," she prayed, "help me to be strong." Zoë maintained her high standards in relationships with boys and in time the rumours died down.

Stephen was also a victim of lies and rumours, but he remained faithful to God, as we read in **Acts 6:8–15**.

* How could Zoë and Stephen be strong in the face of lies and rumours?
* When has someone told lies about you the way these people did about Stephen? How did you respond?

Consider . . .

* thinking of a tactful way to respond to people who spread rumours. Always talk to the person who is being talked about rather than spread rumours.
* what you would do to clear your reputation if someone spread dishonest rumours about you.

For more, see . . .

* Leviticus 19:16–19 (p.119)
* James 3:1–12 (p.1351)
* Matthew 26:57–68 (p.990)

were her own son. ²²The Egyptians taught Moses everything they knew, and he was a powerful man in what he said and did.

²³"When Moses was about 40 years old, he thought it would be good to visit his own people, the people of Israel. ²⁴Moses saw an Egyptian mistreating an Israelite, so he defended the Israelite and punished the Egyptian by killing him. ²⁵Moses thought his own people would understand that God was using him to save them, but they did not. ²⁶The next day when Moses saw two men of Israel fighting, he tried to make peace between them. He said, 'Men, you are brothers. Why are you hurting each other?' ²⁷The man who was hurting the other pushed Moses away and said, 'Who made you our ruler and judge? ²⁸Are you going to kill me as you killed the Egyptian yesterday?' *n* ²⁹When Moses heard him say this, he left Egypt and went to live in the land of Midian where he was a stranger. While Moses lived in Midian, he had two sons.

³⁰"Forty years later an angel appeared to Moses in the flames of a burning bush as he was in the desert near Mount Sinai. ³¹When Moses saw this, he was amazed and went near to look closer. Moses heard the Lord's voice say, ³²'I am the God of your ancestors, the God of Abraham, Isaac and Jacob.' *n* Moses began to shake with fear and was afraid to look. ³³The Lord said to him, 'Take off your sandals, because you are standing on holy ground. ³⁴I have seen the troubles my people have suffered in Egypt. I have heard their cries and have come down to save them. And now, Moses, I am sending you back to Egypt.' *n*

³⁵"This Moses was the same man the two men of Israel rejected, saying, 'Who made you a ruler and judge?' *n* Moses is the same man God sent to be a ruler and saviour, with the help of the angel that Moses saw in the burning bush. ³⁶So Moses led the people out of Egypt. He worked miracles *d* and signs in Egypt, at the Red Sea *d* and then in the desert for 40 years. ³⁷This is the same Moses that said to the people of Israel, 'God will give you a prophet *d* like me, who is one of your own people.' *n* ³⁸This is the Moses who was with the gathering of the Israelites in the desert. He was with the angel that spoke to him at Mount Sinai, and he was with our ancestors. He received commands from God that give life, and he gave those commands to us.

³⁹"But our ancestors did not want to obey Moses. They rejected him and wanted to go back to Egypt. ⁴⁰They said to Aaron, 'Make us gods who will lead us. Moses led us out of Egypt, but we don't know what has happened to him.' *n* ⁴¹So the people made an idol that looked like a calf. Then they brought sacrifices to it and were proud of what they had made with their own hands. ⁴²But God turned against them and did not try to stop them from worshipping the sun, moon and stars. This is what is written in the book of the prophets: God says,

'People of Israel, you did not bring me
    sacrifices and offerings
    while you travelled in the desert for 40
      years.
⁴³You have carried with you
    your king, the god Sakkuth,
    and Kaiwan your idol
    and the star gods you have made.
So I will send you away as captives beyond
    Damascus.'   *Amos 5:25–27*

⁴⁴"The Holy Tent *d* where God spoke to our ancestors was with them in the desert. God told Moses how to make this Tent, and he made it like the plan God showed him. ⁴⁵Later, Joshua led our ancestors to capture the lands of the other nations. Our people went in, and God forced the other people out. When our people went into this new land, they took with them this same Tent they had received from their ancestors. They kept it until the time of David, ⁴⁶who pleased God and asked God to let him build a house for him, the God of Jacob. ⁴⁷But Solomon was the one who built the Temple. *d*

⁴⁸"But the Most High does not live in houses that people build with their hands. As the prophet says:
⁴⁹'Heaven is my throne,
    and the earth is my footstool.
So do you think you can build a house for
    me? says the Lord.
    Do I need a place to rest?
⁵⁰Remember, my hand made all these things!' "
          Isaiah 66:1–2

⁵¹Stephen continued speaking: "You stubborn people! You have not given your hearts to God, nor will you listen to him! You are always against what the Holy Spirit *d* is trying to tell you, just as your ancestors were. ⁵²Your ancestors tried to hurt every prophet who ever lived. Those prophets said long ago that the One who is good

---

'Who . . . yesterday?'   Quotation from Exodus 2:14.
'I am . . . Jacob.'   Quotation from Exodus 3:6.
'Take . . . Egypt.'   Quotation from Exodus 3:5–10.
'Who . . . judge?'   Quotation from Exodus 2:14.
'God . . . people.'   Quotation from Deuteronomy 18:15.
'Make . . . him.'   Quotation from Exodus 32:1.

would come, but your ancestors killed them. And now you have turned against and killed the One who is good. [53]You received the law of Moses, which God gave you through his angels, but you haven't obeyed it."

Stephen is Killed

[54]When the leaders heard this, they became furious. They were so cross they were grinding their teeth at Stephen. [55]But Stephen was full of the Holy Spirit. [d] He looked up to heaven and saw the glory of God and Jesus standing at God's right side. [56]He said, "Look! I see heaven open and the Son of Man [d] standing at God's right side."

[57]Then they shouted loudly and covered their ears and all ran at Stephen. [58]They took him out of the city and began to throw stones at him to kill him. And those who told lies against Stephen left their coats with a young man named Saul. [59]While they were throwing stones, Stephen prayed, "Lord Jesus, receive my spirit." [60]He fell

---

Philip Not the apostle named Philip.

---

on his knees and cried in a loud voice, "Lord, do not hold this sin against them." After Stephen said this, he died.

8 Saul agreed that the killing of Stephen was good.

Troubles for the Believers

On that day the church of Jerusalem began to be persecuted, [d] and all the believers, except the apostles, [d] were scattered throughout Judea and Samaria.

[2]And some religious people buried Stephen and cried loudly for him. [3]Saul was also trying to destroy the church, going from house to house, dragging out men and women and putting them in jail. [4]And wherever they were scattered, they told people the Good News. [d]

Philip Preaches in Samaria

[5]Philip [n] went to the city of Samaria and preached about the Christ. [d] [6]When the people

---

ANGER

Rage

Ann, thirteen, appeared to be a model student and a devoted daughter. But one night, Ann brought two boys into her bedroom and called her father to come upstairs. Using a knife and a length of pipe, the three teenagers slashed and beat him to death. Ann had been psychologically abused by her father.

Alan, fourteen, was the school punchbag. Gangling and clumsy, with few friends, he was the target of daily harassment and beatings. One morning in late January, Alan headed for school carrying one of his father's high-power rifles and ammunition. When he got there, he opened fire, killing the school's headmaster and wounding two teachers and one student. He thought his actions might win his harsh father's approval.

A group of Jewish leaders, religious and proper, faithfully practised the regulations of their faith. When Stephen, a Christian disciple, started preaching about Jesus, the Jewish leaders went berserk. They carried Stephen out of the city and hurled stones at him until he was dead.

Read **Acts 7:51–60** to get the full story of how these Jewish leaders let their anger lead to destruction.

- What caused Ann's, Alan's and the Jewish leaders' rage?
- Why was Stephen able to respond to his killers the way he did?

Consider . . .

- praying before expressing your anger so that you won't do something you'll regret later.
- seeking help from Christian friends if your anger turns to rage. Protect yourself and others by learning how to handle anger.

For more, see . . .

- Deuteronomy 13:6–11 (p.178)
- James 1:19–20 (p.1348)
- Ephesians 4:26–32 (p.1274)

there heard Philip and saw the miracles *d* he was doing, they all listened carefully to what he said. [7]Many of these people had evil spirits in them, but Philip made the evil spirits leave. The spirits made a loud noise when they came out. Philip also healed many weak and crippled people there. [8]So the people in that city were very happy.

[9]But there was a man named Simon in that city. Before Philip came there, Simon had practised magic and amazed all the people of Samaria. He boasted and called himself a great man. [10]All the people—the least important to the most important—paid attention to Simon, saying, "This man has the power of God, called 'the Great Power!' " [11]Simon had amazed them with his magic so long that the people became his followers. [12]But when Philip told them the Good News *d* about the kingdom of God and the power of Jesus Christ, men and women believed Philip and were baptised. *d* [13]Simon himself believed, and after he was baptised, he stayed very close to Philip. When he saw the miracles and the powerful things Philip did, Simon was amazed.

[14]When the apostles *d* who were still in Jerusalem heard that the people of Samaria had accepted the word of God, they sent Peter and John to them. [15]When Peter and John arrived, they prayed that the Samaritan believers might receive the Holy Spirit. *d* [16]These people had been baptised in the name of the Lord Jesus, but the Holy Spirit had not yet come upon any of them. [17]Then, when the two apostles began laying their hands on *n* the people, they received the Holy Spirit.

[18]Simon saw that the Spirit was given to people when the apostles laid their hands on them. So he offered the apostles money, [19]saying, "Give me also this power so that anyone on whom I lay my hands will receive the Holy Spirit."

[20]Peter said to him, "You and your money should both be destroyed, because you thought you could buy God's gift with money. [21]You cannot share with us in this work since your heart is not right before God. [22]Change your heart! Turn away from this evil thing you have done, and pray to the Lord. Maybe he will forgive you for thinking this. [23]I see that you are full of bitter jealousy and ruled by sin."

[24]Simon answered, "Both of you pray for me to the Lord so the things you have said will not happen to me."

[25]After Peter and John told the people what they had seen Jesus do and after they had spoken the message of the Lord, they went back to Jerusalem. On the way, they went through many Samaritan towns and preached the Good News to the people.

Philip Teaches an Ethiopian

[26]An angel of the Lord said to Philip, *n* "Get ready and go south to the road that leads down to Gaza from Jerusalem—the desert road." [27]So Philip got ready and went. On the road he saw a man from Ethiopia, a eunuch. *d* He was an important officer in the service of Candace, the queen of the Ethiopians; he was responsible for taking care of all her money. He had gone to Jerusalem to worship. [28]Now, as he was on his way home, he was sitting in his chariot reading from the Book of Isaiah, the prophet. *d* [29]The Spirit *d* said to Philip, "Go to that chariot and stay near it."

[30]So when Philip ran towards the chariot, he heard the man reading from Isaiah the prophet. Philip asked, "Do you understand what you are reading?"

[31]He answered, "How can I understand unless someone explains it to me?" Then he invited Philip to climb in and sit with him. [32]The portion of Scripture *d* he was reading was this:

"He was like a sheep being led to be killed.
He was quiet, as a lamb is quiet while its
    wool is being cut;
he never opened his mouth.
[33]　He was shamed and was treated unfairly.
He died without children to continue his
        family.
His life on earth has ended."　　*Isaiah 53:7–8*

[34]The officer said to Philip, "Please tell me, who is the prophet talking about—himself or someone else?" [35]Philip began to speak, and starting with this same Scripture, he told the man the Good News *d* about Jesus.

Sidelight　Acts 8:26–40 tells of what is probably the conversion of the first African. He came from an area south of Egypt called Nubia. Philip had travelled about 80 kilometres from Jerusalem to witness to this man.

---

[36]While they were travelling down the road, they came to some water. The officer said, "Look, here is water. Why shouldn't I be baptised?" *d*

---

laying their hands on　The laying on of hands had many purposes, including the giving of a blessing, power or authority.
Philip　Not the apostle named Philip.

[37] *n* [38]Then the officer commanded the chariot to stop. Both Philip and the officer went down into the water, and Philip baptised him. [39]When they came up out of the water, the Spirit of the Lord took Philip away; the officer never saw him again. And the officer continued on his way home, full of joy. [40]But Philip appeared in a city called Azotus and preached the Good News in all the towns on the way from Azotus to Caesarea.

Saul is Converted

9 In Jerusalem Saul was still threatening the followers of the Lord by saying he would kill them. So he went to the high priest [2]and asked him to write letters to the synagogues *d* in the city of Damascus. Then if Saul found any followers of Christ's Way, men or women, he would arrest them and bring them back to Jerusalem.

[3]So Saul headed towards Damascus. As he came near the city, a bright light from heaven suddenly flashed around him. [4]Saul fell to the ground and heard a voice saying to him, "Saul, Saul! Why are you persecuting *d* me?"

[5]Saul said, "Who are you, Lord?"

The voice answered, "I am Jesus, whom you are persecuting. [6]Get up now and go into the city. Someone there will tell you what you must do."

[7]The people travelling with Saul stood there but said nothing. They heard the voice, but they saw no one. [8]Saul got up from the ground and opened his eyes, but he could not see. So those with Saul took his hand and led him into

Verse 37 Some late copies of Acts add verse 37: "Philip answered, 'If you believe with all your heart, you can.' The officer said, 'I believe that Jesus Christ is the Son of God.'"

BIBLE STUDY

Creative Questions

"I've begun wondering if there really is a God," Kevin said and looked down at his shoes. "I mean, how do I know Christianity isn't just wishful thinking?"

Kevin looked round the room. Everyone was silent.

Finally, Jeremy spoke up. "I like to tackle it from the opposite point of view. I try to prove that there isn't a God."

Then everyone started talking at once.

"That leads to even harder questions," said someone in the corner. "How can you explain everything in this world if there isn't a Creator?"

"And why do people get angry at things like murder and child abuse if there isn't a God who shows the difference between right and wrong?"

"Yes! And what about people's need for religion? Why should they want to worship God if there is no God?"

The questions went on and on. Finally, the kids were silent. Jeremy looked round and smiled. "Believing there is no God takes more faith than realising there is one," he said. "Thanks for stretching my faith."

There's nothing wrong with sincere questions because they lead to real answers. An Ethiopian asked questions that led to faith in Jesus in **Acts 8:26–40**.

* How do you think his questions led Kevin to deeper faith? How did the Ethiopian's questions lead him to God's salvation?
* What questions would you ask about the passage which the Ethiopian had read?

Consider . . .

* listing the questions you have about God and searching for answers to those questions.
* writing down questions as you read the Bible. Ask these questions during youth group.

For more, see . . .

* Isaiah 53:7–8 (p.697)
* Hebrews 6:1–3 (p.1335)
* John 20:24–29 (p.1134)

Damascus. [9]For three days Saul could not see and did not eat or drink.

[10] There was a follower of Jesus in Damascus named Ananias. The Lord spoke to Ananias in a vision, "Ananias!"

Ananias answered, "Here I am, Lord."

[11]The Lord said to him, "Get up and go to Straight Street. Find the house of Judas, [n] and ask for a man named Saul from the city of Tarsus. He is there now, praying. [12]Saul has seen a vision in which a man named Ananias comes to him and lays his hands on him. Then he is able to see again."

[13]But Ananias answered, "Lord, many people have told me about this man and the terrible things he did to your holy people in Jerusalem. [14]Now he has come here to Damascus, and the leading priests have given him the power to arrest everyone who worships you."

[15]But the Lord said to Ananias, "Go! I have chosen Saul for an important work. He must tell about me to those who are not Jews, to kings and to the people of Israel. [16]I will show him how much he must suffer for my name."

[17]So Ananias went to the house of Judas. He laid his hands on [n] Saul and said, "Brother Saul, the Lord Jesus sent me. He is the one you saw on the road on your way here. He sent me so that you can see again and be filled with the Holy Spirit." [d] [18]Immediately, something that looked like fish scales fell from Saul's eyes, and he was able to see again! Then Saul got up and was baptised. [d] [19]After he ate some food, his strength returned.

Saul Preaches in Damascus

Saul stayed with the followers of Jesus in Damascus for a few days. [20]Soon he began to

Judas   This is not either of the apostles named Judas.
laid his hands on   The laying on of hands had many purposes, including the giving of a blessing, power or authority.

NON-CHRISTIANS

Show and Tell

Charles Blondin stretched a 330-metre tightrope across Niagara Falls on 30 June 1859. About 25,000 spectators gathered to watch the incredible stunt. Charles stood in front of the crowd and asked, "How many believe I can walk across Niagara Falls?"

"We believe," the crowd roared. And Charles walked safely across Niagara Falls, 50 metres up.

Five days later, he asked, "How many believe I can walk across Niagara Falls blindfolded and pushing a wheelbarrow?"

The crowd cheered. And Charles did it again.

Two weeks later, the crowd gathered again. "How many believe I can walk across with a person on my back?" he asked.

The crowd screamed: "Of course! We believe!"

Charles looked straight at a person in the front. "You, sir. Climb on!" The man refused.

There's a big difference between talking about faith and acting on that faith. In **Acts 9:1–20**, Saul and Ananias both learned what it meant to act on their faith.

* Which was most difficult to act on: Charles's challenge or Jesus' instructions to Saul and Ananias? Why?
* What did Ananias's actions communicate to Saul?

Consider . . .

* becoming an "Ananias" to a friend who is struggling with his or her faith. Provide encouragement and support as that person searches for what it means to follow God.
* writing the story of a time when you have experienced God's love. Then tell your story to a friend.

For more, see . . .

* Exodus 4:1–17 (p.63)
* James 2:14–18 (p.1350)

* Acts 22:1–16 (p.1174)

preach about Jesus in the synagogues, *d* saying, "Jesus is the Son of God."

²¹All the people who heard him were amazed. They said, "This is the man who was in Jerusalem trying to destroy those who trust in this name! He came here to arrest the followers of Jesus and take them back to the leading priests."

²²But Saul grew more powerful. His proofs that Jesus is the Christ *d* were so strong that the Jewish people in Damascus could not argue with him.

²³After many days, some Jewish people made plans to kill Saul. ²⁴They were watching the city gates day and night, but Saul learned about their plan. ²⁵One night some followers of Saul helped him leave the city by lowering him in a basket through an opening in the city wall.

Saul Preaches in Jerusalem

²⁶When Saul went to Jerusalem, he tried to join the group of followers, but they were all afraid of him. They did not believe he was really a follower. ²⁷But Barnabas accepted Saul and took him to the apostles. *d* Barnabas explained to them that Saul had seen the Lord on the road and the Lord had spoken to Saul. Then he told them how boldly Saul had preached in the name of Jesus in Damascus.

²⁸And so Saul stayed with the followers, going everywhere in Jerusalem, preaching boldly in the name of the Lord. ²⁹He would often talk and argue with the Jewish people who spoke Greek, but they were trying to kill him. ³⁰When the followers learned about this, they took Saul to Caesarea and from there sent him to Tarsus.

³¹The church everywhere in Judea, Galilee and Samaria had a time of peace and became stronger. Respecting the Lord by the way they lived, and being encouraged by the Holy Spirit, *d* the group of believers continued to grow.

Peter Heals Aeneas

³²As Peter was travelling through all the area, he visited God's people who lived in Lydda. ³³There he met a man named Aeneas, who was paralysed and had not been able to leave his bed for the past eight years. ³⁴Peter said to him, "Aeneas, Jesus Christ heals you. Stand up and make your bed." Aeneas stood up immediately. ³⁵All the people living in Lydda and on the Plain of Sharon saw him and turned to the Lord.

Peter Heals Tabitha

³⁶In the city of Joppa there was a follower named Tabitha (whose Greek name was Dorcas). She was always doing good deeds and kind acts. ³⁷While Peter was in Lydda, Tabitha became sick

and died. Her body was washed and put in a room upstairs. ³⁸Since Lydda is near Joppa and the followers in Joppa heard that Peter was in Lydda, they sent two messengers to Peter. They begged him, "Hurry, please come to us!" ³⁹So Peter got ready and went with them. When he arrived, they took him to the upstairs room where all the widows stood around Peter, crying. They showed him the shirts and coats Tabitha had made when she was still alive. ⁴⁰Peter sent everyone out of the room and kneeled and prayed. Then he turned to the body and said, "Tabitha, stand up." She opened her eyes, and when she saw Peter, she sat up. ⁴¹He gave her his hand and helped her up. Then he called the saints *d* and the widows into the room and showed them that Tabitha was alive. ⁴²People everywhere in Joppa learned about this, and many believed in the Lord. ⁴³Peter stayed in Joppa for many days with a man named Simon who was a leatherworker.

Peter Teaches Cornelius

10 At Caesarea there was a man named Cornelius, an officer in the Italian group of the Roman army. ²Cornelius was a religious man. He and all the other people who lived in his house worshipped the true God. He gave much of his money to the poor and prayed to God often. ³One afternoon about three o'clock, Cornelius clearly saw a vision. An angel of God came to him and said, "Cornelius!"

⁴Cornelius stared at the angel. He became afraid and said, "What do you want, Lord?"

The angel said, "God has heard your prayers. He has seen that you give to the poor, and he remembers you. ⁵Send some men now to Joppa to bring back a man named Simon who is also called Peter. ⁶He is staying with a man, also named Simon, who is a leatherworker and has a house beside the sea." ⁷When the angel who spoke to Cornelius left, Cornelius called two of his servants and a soldier, a religious man who worked for him. ⁸Cornelius explained everything to them and sent them to Joppa.

⁹About noon the next day as they came near Joppa, Peter was going up to the roof[n] to pray. ¹⁰He was hungry and wanted to eat, but while the food was being prepared, he had a vision. ¹¹He saw heaven opened and something coming down that looked like a big sheet being lowered to earth by its four corners. ¹²In it were all kinds of animals, reptiles and birds. ¹³Then a voice said to Peter, "Get up, Peter; kill and eat."

¹⁴But Peter said, "No, Lord! I have never eaten food that is unholy or unclean." *d*

---

roof   In Bible times houses were built with flat roofs. The roof was used for drying things such as flax and fruit. And it was used as an extra room, as a place for worship and as a place to sleep in the summer.

¹⁵But the voice said to him again, "God has made these things clean so don't call them 'unholy'!" ¹⁶This happened three times, and at once the sheet was taken back to heaven.

¹⁷While Peter was wondering what this vision meant, the men Cornelius sent had found Simon's house and were standing at the gate. ¹⁸They asked, "Is Simon Peter staying here?"

¹⁹While Peter was still thinking about the vision, the Spirit *d* said to him, "Listen, three men are looking for you. ²⁰Get up and go downstairs. Go with them without doubting, because I have sent them to you."

²¹So Peter went down to the men and said, "I am the one you are looking for. Why did you come here?"

²²They said, "A holy angel spoke to Cornelius, an army officer and a good man; he worships God. All the Jewish people respect him. The angel told Cornelius to ask you to come to his house so that he can hear what you have to say." ²³So Peter asked the men to come in and spend the night.

The next day Peter got ready and went with them, and some of the followers from Joppa joined him. ²⁴On the following day they came to Caesarea. Cornelius was waiting for them and had called together his relatives and close friends. ²⁵When Peter entered, Cornelius met him, fell at his feet and worshipped him. ²⁶But Peter helped him up, saying, "Stand up. I too am only a human." ²⁷As he talked with Cornelius, Peter went inside where he saw many people gathered. ²⁸He said, "You people understand that it is against our Jewish law for Jewish people to associate with or visit anyone who is not Jewish. But God has shown me that I should not call any person 'unholy' or 'unclean'. ²⁹That is why I did not argue when I was asked to come here. Now, please tell me why you sent for me."

EUTHANASIA

I'm Coming Home

Geoff's life stretched out in front of him. Young, intelligent, handsome, popular, he had everything going for him. To look at him you would never have thought that something was wrong. But a whisper began to circulate the church. Geoff had been diagnosed with cancer.

It was almost as if the diagnosis made him sick. Over the course of a few short weeks, Geoff turned from a young, healthy, active teenager, to someone greying and old before his time. His weight dropped dramatically, his hair thinned. His body looked all out of proportion. Although nobody wanted to say it, everybody knew that Geoff was dying.

The prospect of death raises a whole host of uneasy questions and emotions. Will God heal him? What should we do about watching him suffer? When do we pray, comfort, act? How do we do any of these things?

Out of all those involved in Geoff's last few months, it was he who led everyone through the maze of knowing what to do. His wisdom: God is in control; if God wants to change this he can do, but he will take me home when he wants.

Read **Acts 9:36–42**.

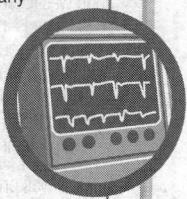

* How could Geoff trust that God knew best?
* How would this passage be an encouragement to Geoff?

Consider . . .

* making a list of things you find it hard to trust God with. Things that you like to be in control of. Put them in a box and bury them in the ground. Hold a funeral service as the things you are in control of die, so God can take control.
* prayer-walking around your local park. Look at how God looks after everything growing around you. God is in control of the natural world. Ask God to be in control of your life too.

For more see . . .

* Ecclesiastes 3:1–8 (p.622)
* Hebrews 12:1–3 (p.1343)
* Daniel 3:13–27 (p.835)

³⁰Cornelius said, "Four days ago, I was praying in my house at this same time—three o'clock in the afternoon. Suddenly, there was a man standing before me wearing shining clothes. ³¹He said, 'Cornelius, God has heard your prayer and has seen that you give to the poor and remembers you. ³²So send some men to Joppa and ask Simon Peter to come. Peter is staying in the house of a man, also named Simon, who is a leatherworker and has a house beside the sea.' ³³So I sent for you immediately, and it was very good of you to come. Now we are all here before God to hear everything the Lord has commanded you to tell us."

³⁴Peter began to speak: "I really understand now that to God every person is the same. ³⁵In every country God accepts anyone who worships him and does what is right. ³⁶You know the message that God has sent to the people of Israel is the Good News ᵈ that peace has come through Jesus Christ. Jesus is the Lord of all people! ³⁷You know what has happened all over Judea, beginning in Galilee after John ⁿ preached to the people about baptism. ³⁸You know about Jesus from Nazareth, that God gave him the Holy Spirit ᵈ and power. You know how Jesus went everywhere doing good and healing those who were ruled by the devil, because God was with him. ³⁹We saw what Jesus did in Judea and in Jerusalem, but the Jews in Jerusalem killed him by hanging him on a cross. ⁴⁰Yet, on the third day, God raised Jesus to life and caused him to be seen, ⁴¹not by all the people, but only by the witnesses God had already chosen. And we are those witnesses who ate and drank with him after he was raised from the dead. ⁴²He told us to

John   John the Baptist, who preached to people about Christ's coming (Matthew 3, Luke 3).

STEREOTYPES

The Colour of Hatred

"It's not that blacks are bad," John says. "There are quite a few, well, not quite a few, but a sizeable number of non-whites who are intelligent."

John is a racist. He believes that whites are the "chosen people" – that all non-white races should live in their own territories, away from whites. He is also a leader of the Aryan Youth Movement.

John doesn't look like a skinhead. His blond hair is cut conservatively. He has a respectable job and dresses like most people his age.

But John's racist beliefs are deeply ingrained. His father leads a group of adult racists called the White Aryan Resistance. When other children were growing up with stories about Goldilocks and the three bears, John was listening to stories of hatred and prejudice.

Skinheads in John's Aryan Youth Movement have been linked to such brutalities as beating people to death, terrorising people of non-white origin, and even nailing a former skinhead to a cross. And they have done all these things in the name of preserving their race.

Prejudice has blinded John and other racists to the fact that God loves all people the same. In **Acts 10:34–48**, Peter challenges the people of his day to see others from God's perspective and to lay their prejudices aside.

* How was prejudice in Peter's day different from John's prejudice? How was it similar?
* According to this passage, what is the cure for prejudice?

Consider . . .

* observing people in a shopping centre. Evaluate which people you do or don't have prejudices towards. Then ask God to remove your prejudices.
* getting to know someone you have prejudged. Think about the ways in which that person is different from what you had expected.

For more, see . . .

* Genesis 3:20 (p.7)
* Acts 11:1–18 (p.1157)
* John 4:1–27 (p.1101)

preach to the people and to tell them that he is the one whom God chose to be the judge of the living and the dead. ⁴³All the prophets say it is true that all who believe in Jesus will be forgiven their sins through Jesus' name."

⁴⁴While Peter was still saying this, the Holy Spirit *d* came down on all those who were listening. ⁴⁵The Jewish believers who came with Peter were amazed that the gift of the Holy Spirit had been given even to those who were not Jews. ⁴⁶These Jewish believers heard them speaking in different languages *n* and praising God. Then Peter said, ⁴⁷"Can anyone keep these people from being baptised *d* with water? They have received the Holy Spirit just as we did!" ⁴⁸So Peter ordered that they be baptised in the name of Jesus Christ. Then they asked Peter to stay with them for a few days.

Peter Returns to Jerusalem

11 The apostles *d* and the believers in Judea heard that some who were not Jewish had accepted God's teaching too. ²But when Peter came to Jerusalem, some Jewish believers argued with him. ³They said, "You went into the homes of people who are not circumcised *d* and ate with them!"

⁴So Peter explained the whole story to them. ⁵He said, "I was in the city of Joppa, and while I was praying, I had a vision. I saw something that looked like a big sheet being lowered from heaven by its four corners. It came very close to me. ⁶I looked inside it and saw animals, wild beasts, reptiles and birds. ⁷I heard a voice say to me, 'Get up, Peter; kill and eat.' ⁸But I said, 'No, Lord! I have never eaten anything that is unholy or unclean.' *d* ⁹But the voice from heaven spoke again, 'God has made these things clean, so don't call them unholy.' ¹⁰This happened three times. Then the whole thing was taken back to heaven. ¹¹Just then three men who were sent to me from Caesarea came to the house where I was staying. ¹²The Spirit *d* told me to go with them without doubting. These six believers here also went with me, and we entered the house of Cornelius. ¹³He told us about the angel he saw standing in his house. The angel said to him, 'Send some men to Joppa and invite Simon Peter to come. ¹⁴By the words he will say to you, you and all your family will be saved.' ¹⁵When I began my speech, the Holy Spirit came upon them just as he came upon us at the beginning. ¹⁶Then I remembered the words of the Lord. He said, 'John baptised *d* with water, but you will be baptised with the Holy Spirit.' ¹⁷Since God gave them the same gift he gave us who believed in the Lord Jesus Christ, how could I stop the work of God?"

¹⁸When the Jewish believers heard this, they stopped arguing. They praised God and said, "So God is allowing even those who are not Jewish to turn to him and live."

The Good News Comes to Antioch

¹⁹Many of the believers were scattered when they were persecuted *d* after Stephen was killed. Some of them went as far as Phoenicia, Cyprus and Antioch telling the message to others, but only to Jews. ²⁰Some of these believers were people from Cyprus and Cyrene. When they came to Antioch, they spoke also to Greeks, telling them the Good News *d* about the Lord Jesus. ²¹The Lord was helping the believers, and a large group of people believed and turned to the Lord.

²²The church in Jerusalem heard about all of this, so they sent Barnabas to Antioch. ²³⁻²⁴Barnabas was a good man, full of the Holy Spirit *d* and full of faith. When he reached Antioch and saw how God had blessed the people, he was glad. He encouraged all the believers in Antioch always to obey the Lord with all their hearts, and many people became followers of the Lord.

²⁵Then Barnabas went to the city of Tarsus to look for Saul, ²⁶and when he found Saul, he brought him to Antioch. For a whole year Saul and Barnabas met with the church and taught many people there. In Antioch the followers were called Christians for the first time.

> **Sidelight** The name "Christian" (Acts 11:26) may have originally been an insult. It meant "devotees of the Anointed One" or "followers of Christ". The term was widely used by the end of the first century.

²⁷About that time some prophets *d* came from Jerusalem to Antioch. ²⁸One of them, named Agabus, stood up and spoke with the help of the Holy Spirit. He said, "A very hard time is coming to the whole world. There will be no food to eat." (This happened when Claudius ruled.) ²⁹The believers all decided to help the followers who lived in Judea, as much as each one could. ³⁰They gathered the money and gave it to Barnabas and Saul, who brought it to the elders *d* in Judea.

Herod Agrippa Hurts the Church

12 During that same time King Herod began to mistreat some who belonged to the church. ²He ordered James, the brother of John, to be killed by the sword. ³Herod saw that the

languages This can also be translated "tongues".

Jewish people liked this, so he decided to arrest Peter, too. (This happened during the time of the Feast *d* of Unleavened Bread.)

⁴After Herod arrested Peter, he put him in jail and handed him over to be guarded by sixteen soldiers. Herod planned to bring Peter before the people for trial after the Passover *d* Feast. ⁵So Peter was kept in jail, but the church prayed earnestly to God for him.

Peter Leaves the Jail

⁶The night before Herod was to bring him to trial, Peter was sleeping between two soldiers, bound with two chains. Other soldiers were guarding the door of the jail. ⁷Suddenly, an angel of the Lord stood there, and a light shone in the cell. The angel struck Peter on the side and woke him up. "Hurry! Get up!" the angel said. And the chains fell off Peter's hands. ⁸Then the angel told him, "Get dressed and put on your sandals." And Peter did. Then the angel said, "Put on your coat and follow me." ⁹So Peter followed him out, but he did not know if what the angel was doing was real; he thought he might be seeing a vision. ¹⁰They went past the first and second guards and came to the iron gate that separated them from the city. The gate opened by itself for them, and they went through it. When they had walked down one street, the angel suddenly left him.

¹¹Then Peter realised what had happened. He thought, "Now I know that the Lord really sent his angel to me. He rescued me from Herod and from all the things the Jewish people thought would happen."

¹²When he considered this, he went to the home of Mary, the mother of John Mark. Many people were gathered there, praying. ¹³Peter knocked on the outside door, and a servant girl named Rhoda came to answer it. ¹⁴When she recognised Peter's voice, she was so happy she forgot to open the door. Instead, she ran inside and told the group, "Peter is at the door!"

¹⁵They said to her, "You are mad!" But she kept on saying it was true, so they said, "It must be Peter's angel."

¹⁶Peter continued to knock, and when they opened the door, they saw him and were amazed. ¹⁷Peter made a sign with his hand to tell them to be quiet. He explained how the Lord led him out of the jail, and he said, "Tell James and the other believers what happened." Then he left to go to another place.

¹⁸The next day the soldiers were very upset and wondered what had happened to Peter.

¹⁹Herod looked everywhere for him but could not find him. So he questioned the guards and ordered that they be killed.

The Death of Herod Agrippa

Later Herod moved from Judea and went to the city of Caesarea, where he stayed. ²⁰Herod was very angry with the people of Tyre and Sidon, but the people of those cities all came in a group to him. After convincing Blastus, the king's personal servant, to be on their side, they asked Herod for peace, because their country got its food from his country.

²¹On a chosen day Herod put on his royal robes, sat on his throne and made a speech to the people. ²²They shouted, "This is the voice of a god, not a human!" ²³Because Herod did not give the glory to God, an angel of the Lord immediately caused him to become sick, and he was eaten by worms and died.

²⁴God's message continued to spread and reach people.

²⁵After Barnabas and Saul finished their task in Jerusalem, they returned to Antioch, taking John Mark with them.

Barnabas and Saul are Chosen

13 In the church at Antioch there were these prophets *d* and teachers: Barnabas, Simeon (also called Niger), Lucius (from the city of Cyrene), Manaen (who had grown up with Herod, the ruler) and Saul. ²They were all worshipping the Lord and gave up eating for a certain time. *n* During this time the Holy Spirit *d* said to them, "Set apart for me Barnabas and Saul to do a special work for which I have chosen them."

³So after they had given up eating and prayed, they laid their hands on *n* Barnabas and Saul and sent them out.

Barnabas and Saul in Cyprus

⁴Barnabas and Saul, sent out by the Holy Spirit, *d* went to the city of Seleucia. From there they sailed to the island of Cyprus. ⁵When they came to Salamis, they preached the Good News *d* of God in the Jewish synagogues. *d* John Mark was with them to help.

⁶They went across the whole island to Paphos where they met a Jewish magician named Bar-Jesus. He was a false prophet *d* ⁷who always stayed close to Sergius Paulus, the governor and a clever man. He asked Barnabas and Saul to come to him, because he wanted to hear the message of God. ⁸But Elymas, the magician, was against them. (Elymas is the name for Bar-Jesus

---

gave up . . . time   This is called "fasting". The people would give up eating for a special time of prayer and worship to God. It was also done to show sadness and disappointment.

laid their hands on   The laying on of hands had many purposes, including the giving of a blessing, power or authority.

in the Greek language.) He tried to stop the governor from believing in Jesus. [9]But Saul, who was also called Paul, was filled with the Holy Spirit. He looked straight at Elymas [10]and said, "You son of the devil! You are an enemy of everything that is right! You are full of evil tricks and lies, always trying to change the Lord's truths into lies. [11]Now the Lord will touch you, and you will be blind. For a time you will not be able to see anything—not even the light from the sun."

Then everything became dark for Elymas, and he walked around, trying to find someone to lead him by the hand. [12]When the governor saw this, he believed because he was amazed at the teaching about the Lord.

Paul and Barnabas Leave Cyprus

[13]Paul and those with him sailed from Paphos and came to Perga, in Pamphylia. There John Mark left them to return to Jerusalem. [14]They continued their trip from Perga and went to Antioch, a city in Pisidia. On the Sabbath[d] day they went into the synagogue[d] and sat down. [15]After the law of Moses and the writings of the prophets[d] were read, the leaders of the synagogue sent a message to Paul and Barnabas: "Brothers, if you have any message that will encourage the people, please speak."

[16]Paul stood up, raised his hand and said, "You Israelites and you who worship God, please listen! [17]The God of the Israelites chose our ancestors. He made the people great during the time they lived in Egypt, and he brought them out of that country with great power. [18]And he was patient with them for 40 years in the desert. [19]God destroyed seven nations in the land of Canaan and gave the land to his people. [20]All this happened in about 450 years.

"After this, God gave them judges until the time of Samuel the prophet. [21]Then the people asked for

BIBLE STUDY

The Maker's Instructions

As Luke ripped open the packaging to his new laptop, he knew that his dad was going to say it. Even as he held it in his hands and grappled with the power lead to plug it in, he was just waiting for his dad to say those same words that he said every time he got something new . . . "Don't lose the instructions!"

"Luke, don't rush. Take your time. Sit down. Let me read the instructions through with you. You'll only regret it later when you don't know how to use it properly!"

Luke hated it! It was always the same. His dad always seemed to be putting a downer on getting something new. It was same when he got his new phone, and his new sound system. Luke even remembered his dad doing the same when he got his first bike! It had 3 wheels – what could go wrong?

No one reads the instructions to anything! His dad was so frustrating. And what annoyed him most was that Luke knew his dad was right! Luke took a deep breath and let his dad help him. They read through how to set up the laptop. An hour later they had got on the Internet, set up some user profiles and found out how to make it secure online.

Read through **Acts 13:22–33**.

* In this passage, Paul shows that he really knows his stuff when it comes to Jesus. How easy do you find it to understand the Bible? When we take time to understand the Bible we will understand more about Jesus.
* Have you ever taken the time to make sure you really understood something you were trying to do? Did you get more out of it?

Consider . . .

* chatting with someone in your church about how they can help you understand the Bible better.
* setting yourself a challenge to spend a week researching different ways to read the Bible and understand it better. At the end of the week, decide on your strategy to get into the Bible.

For more, see . . .

* Psalm 119:105 (p.573)
* 2 Timothy 3:13–17 (p.1319)
* John 8:31–32 (p.1110)

a king, so God gave them Saul son of Kish. Saul was from the tribe *d* of Benjamin and was king for 40 years. ²²After God took him away, God made David their king. God said about him: 'I have found in David son of Jesse the kind of man I want. He will do all I want him to do.' ²³So God has brought Jesus, one of David's descendants, *d* to Israel to be its Saviour, *d* as he promised. ²⁴Before Jesus came, John *n* preached to all the people of Israel about a baptism *d* of changed hearts and lives. ²⁵When he was finishing his work, he said, 'Who do you think I am? I am not the Christ. *d* He is coming later, and I am not worthy to untie his sandals.'

²⁶"Brothers, sons of the family of Abraham, and those of you who are not Jews who worship God, listen! The news about this salvation has been sent to us. ²⁷Those who live in Jerusalem and their leaders did not realise that Jesus was the Saviour. They did not understand the words that the prophets wrote, which are read every Sabbath day. But they made them come true when they said Jesus was guilty. ²⁸They could not find any real reason for Jesus to be put to death, but they asked Pilate to have him killed. ²⁹When they had done to him all that the Scriptures *d* had said, they took him down from the cross and laid him in a tomb. ³⁰But God raised him up from the dead! ³¹After this, for many days, those who had gone with Jesus from Galilee to Jerusalem saw him. They are now his witnesses to the people. ³²We tell you the Good News *d* about the promise God made to our ancestors. ³³God has made this promise come true for us, his children, by raising Jesus from the dead. We read about this also in Psalm 2:

'You are my son.

Today I have become your father.' *Psalm 2:7*

³⁴God raised Jesus from the dead, and he will never go back to the grave and become dust. So God said:

'I will give you the blessings
I promised to David.' *Isaiah 55:3*

³⁵But in another place God says:

'You will not let your holy one rot.' *Psalm 16:10*

³⁶David did God's will during his lifetime. Then he died and was buried beside his ancestors, and his body did rot in the grave. ³⁷But the One God raised from the dead did not rot in the grave. ³⁸⁻³⁹Brothers, understand what we are telling you: you can have forgiveness of your sins through Jesus. The law of Moses could not free you from your sins. But through Jesus everyone who believes is free from all sins. ⁴⁰Be careful! Don't let what the prophets said happen to you:

⁴¹'Look at the nations!

Watch them and be amazed and shocked.
I will do something in your lifetime

that you won't believe even when you are
told about it.' " *Habakkuk 1:5*

⁴²While Paul and Barnabas were leaving the synagogue, the people asked them to tell them more about these things on the next Sabbath. ⁴³When the meeting was over, many Jews and those who had changed to the Jewish religion and who worshipped God followed Paul and Barnabas from that place. Paul and Barnabas were persuading them to continue trusting in God's grace.

⁴⁴On the next Sabbath day, almost everyone in the city came to hear the word of the Lord. ⁴⁵Seeing the crowd, the Jewish people became very jealous and said insulting things and argued against what Paul said. ⁴⁶But Paul and Barnabas spoke very boldly, saying, "We must speak the message of God to you first. But you refuse to listen. You are judging yourselves not worthy of having eternal life! So we will now go to the people of other nations. ⁴⁷This is what the Lord told us to do, saying:

'I have made you a light for the nations;
you will show people all over the world the
way to be saved.' " *Isaiah 49:6*

⁴⁸When those who were not Jewish heard Paul say this, they were happy and gave honour to the message of the Lord. And the people who were chosen to have life for ever believed the message. ⁴⁹So the message of the Lord was spreading through the whole country. ⁵⁰But the Jewish people stirred up some of the important religious women and the leaders of the city. They started trouble against Paul and Barnabas and forced them out of their area. ⁵¹So Paul and Barnabas shook the dust off their feet *n* and went to Iconium. ⁵²But the followers were filled with joy and the Holy Spirit. *d*

Paul and Barnabas in Iconium

14 In Iconium, Paul and Barnabas went as usual to the Jewish synagogue. *d* They spoke so well that a great many Jews and Greeks believed. ²But some of the Jews who did not believe excited the non-Jewish people and turned them against the believers. ³Paul and Barnabas stayed in Iconium a long time and spoke bravely for the Lord. He showed that their message about his grace was true by giving them the power to work miracles *d* and signs. ⁴But the city was divided. Some of the people agreed with the Jews, and others believed the apostles. *d*

⁵Some who were not Jews, some Jews and some of their rulers wanted to mistreat Paul and Barnabas and to stone them to death. ⁶When Paul and Barnabas learned about this, they ran away to Lystra and Derbe, cities in Lycaonia, and

---

John John the Baptist, who preached to people about Christ's coming (Matthew 3, Luke 3).
shook . . . feet A warning. It showed that they had rejected these people.

to the areas around those cities. ⁷They announced the Good News *d* there, too.

Paul in Lystra and Derbe

⁸In Lystra there sat a man who had been born crippled; he had never walked. ⁹As this man was listening to Paul speak, Paul looked straight at him and saw that he believed God could heal him. ¹⁰So he cried out, "Stand up on your feet!" The man jumped up and began walking around. ¹¹When the crowds saw what Paul did, they shouted in the Lycaonian language, "The gods have become like humans and have come down to us!" ¹²Then the people began to call Barnabas "Zeus" *n* and Paul "Hermes", *n* because he was the main speaker.

¹³The priest in the temple of Zeus, which was near the city, brought some bulls and flowers to the city gates. He and the people wanted to offer a sacrifice to Paul and Barnabas. ¹⁴But when the apostles, *d* Barnabas and Paul, heard about it, they tore their clothes. They ran in among the people, shouting, ¹⁵"Friends, why are you doing these things? We are only human beings like you. We are bringing you the Good News *d* and are telling you to turn away from these worthless things and turn to the living God. He is the One who made the sky, the earth, the sea and everything in them. ¹⁶In the past, God let all the nations do what they wanted. ¹⁷Yet he proved he is real by showing kindness, by giving you rain from heaven and

---

"Zeus"　The Greeks believed in many gods, of whom Zeus was the most important.
"Hermes"　The Greeks believed he was a messenger for the other gods.

JEALOUSY

A Door to Greater Evil

School report day. David dreaded walking into his house. He reckoned that his parents had already seen Sarah's report, and he knew that his would never compare to hers.

"They'll probably give her a new CD or something for every A," David thought.

As David opened the front door, he heard his parents talking in the living room.

"Sarah, this is an outstanding report – as usual," his dad gushed.

"We're so proud of you, darling. You've worked so hard," his mother added.

David tried to sneak past his parents, but just as he turned the corner his mother called out, "David, come here. Let's see how you did this term."

"Oh great," David thought, "here comes World War III." David walked into the living room and handed his mother his crumpled report from his back pocket.

She unfolded it and said, "Well, these are good grades, David."

"Hmmm," his dad mused. "You seem to have improved your grade in biology. Good work."

"Yes, right," David fumed. "I know it's not as good as Sarah's. Nothing I do is ever as good as her."

He stormed out of the room, leaving his family in shock.

David let his jealousy of Sarah affect his response to his parents. In **Acts 13:44–52**, some Jewish leaders allowed their jealousy to affect the way they treated Paul and Barnabas.

* Why were David and the Jewish leaders jealous? What were the consequences of David's and the Jewish leaders' jealousy?
* When have you been jealous of someone? What were the consequences?

Consider . . .

* making a list of your talents and things you are good at, then reading the list when you are tempted to be jealous of someone else.
* thanking God for someone you are jealous of. Be excited when that person does well.

For more, see . . .

* Genesis 37 (p.42)
* Acts 17:5–9 (p.1167)
* Psalm 37:1–8 (p.521)

crops at the right times, by giving you food and filling your hearts with joy." [18]Even with these words, they were barely able to keep the crowd from offering sacrifices to them.

[19]Then some Jewish people came from Antioch and Iconium and persuaded the people to turn against Paul. So they threw stones at him and dragged him out of town, thinking they had killed him. [20]But the followers gathered around him, and he got up and went back into the town. The next day he and Barnabas left and went to the city of Derbe.

The Return to Antioch in Syria

[21]Paul and Barnabas told the Good News [d] in Derbe, and many became followers. Paul and Barnabas returned to Lystra, Iconium and Antioch, [22]making the followers of Jesus stronger and helping them stay in the faith. They said, "We must suffer many things to enter God's kingdom." [23]They chose elders [d] for each church, by praying and giving up eating for a certain time. [n] These elders had trusted the Lord, so Paul and Barnabas put them in the Lord's care.

[24]Then they went through Pisidia and came to Pamphylia. [25]When they had preached the

> ### Sidelight
> Paul and Barnabas faced a real case of mistaken identity when they visited Lystra, a town in the centre of modern-day Turkey (Acts 14:8–18). The people in the region believed a myth that the Greek gods Zeus and Hermes had previously visited the area. When Paul and Barnabas healed a cripple, the people thought the gods had returned, putting the Christian missionaries in an awkward situation.

giving up . . . time   This is called "fasting". The people would give up eating for a special time of prayer and worship to God. It was also done to show sadness and disappointment.

HEROES

Admire, Don't Worship

Mandy admired everything about her minister. When he first came to her church, she was immediately drawn to his dynamic personality, his warm smile and his genuine concern for people.

The minister always had time to listen. He always talked about how great the young people of the church were. Mandy believed that God must be just like her minister.

Whenever the youth group had a controversial discussion, Mandy would go to her minister later and ask what he thought. Mandy would explain what he said in the next meeting.

Eleven months after coming to Mandy's church, her minister left suddenly to go to another church. He never answered any of Mandy's letters, and didn't return her phone calls. He never even said goodbye.

Mandy was crushed and heartbroken. How could he treat her church like this? How could he treat her like this when she had respected him so much? Mandy felt betrayed. Could she ever trust a minister again?

Worshipping a person always leads to disappointment. Her minister turned out to be human – with human faults and inconsistencies. In **Acts 14:8–18**, God used Paul and Barnabas to work miracles, but even they weren't worthy of worship.

* What led Mandy to worship her minister, and the people to worship Paul and Barnabas?
* Based on Paul and Barnabas's words, what are appropriate ways to treat spiritual leaders?

Consider . . .

* thanking God for the good qualities of people you admire. Ask God to help you to keep your admiration in proper perspective.
* getting to know someone you admire and learning about his or her human and less admirable qualities as well.

For more, see . . .

* Exodus 20:2–6 (p.79)
* 1 Corinthians 4:1–7 (p.1218)

* Daniel 3 (p.835)

message in Perga, they went down to Attalia. 26And from there they sailed away to Antioch where the believers had put them into God's care and had sent them out to do this work. Now they had finished.

27When they arrived in Antioch, Paul and Barnabas gathered the church together. They told the church all about what God had done with them and how God had made it possible for those who were not Jewish to believe. 28And they stayed there a long time with the followers.

The Meeting at Jerusalem

15 Then some people came to Antioch from Judea and began teaching the non-Jewish believers: "You cannot be saved if you are not circumcised *d* as Moses taught us." 2Paul and Barnabas were against this teaching and argued with them about it. So the church decided to send Paul, Barnabas and some others to Jerusalem where they could talk more about this with the apostles *d* and elders. *d*

3The church helped them leave on the trip, and they went through the countries of Phoenicia and Samaria, telling all about how those who were not Jewish had turned to God. This made all the believers very happy. 4When they arrived in Jerusalem, they were welcomed by the apostles, the elders and the church. Paul, Barnabas and the others told about everything God had done with them. 5But some of the believers who belonged to the Pharisee *d* group came forwards and said, "The non-Jewish believers must be circumcised. They must be told to obey the law of Moses."

6The apostles and the elders gathered to consider this problem. 7After a long debate, Peter stood up and said to them, "Brothers, you know that in the early days God chose me from among you to preach the Good News *d* to those who are not Jewish. They heard the Good News from me, and they believed. 8God, who knows the thoughts of everyone, accepted them. He showed this to us by giving them the Holy Spirit, *d* just as he did to us. 9To God, those people are not different from us. When they believed, he made their hearts pure. 10So now why are you testing God by putting a heavy load around the necks of the non-Jewish believers? It is a load that neither we nor our ancestors were able to carry. 11But we believe that we and they too will be saved by the grace of the Lord Jesus."

12Then the whole group became quiet. They listened to Paul and Barnabas tell about all the miracles *d* and signs that God did through them among the non-Jewish people. 13After they finished speaking, James said, "Brothers, listen to me. 14Simon has told us how God showed his love for the non-Jewish people. For the first time

he is accepting from among them a people to be his own. 15The words of the prophets *d* agree with this too:

16'After these things I will return.
   The kingdom of David is like a fallen tent.
   But I will rebuild its ruins,
      and I will set it up.
17Then those people who are left alive may ask
      the Lord for help,
   and the other nations that belong to me,
says the Lord,
   who will make it happen.
18 And these things have been known for a
      long time.' *Amos 9:11–12*

19"So I think we should not bother the non-Jewish people who are turning to God. 20Instead, we should write a letter to them telling them these things: stay away from food that has been offered to idols (which makes it unclean *d*), any kind of sexual sin, eating animals that have been strangled, and blood. 21They should do these things, because for a long time in every city the law of Moses has been taught. And it is still read in the synagogue *d* every Sabbath *d* day."

Letter to Non-Jewish Believers

22The apostles, *d* the elders *d* and the whole church decided to send some of their men with Paul and Barnabas to Antioch. They chose Judas Barsabbas and Silas, who were respected by the believers. 23They sent the following letter with them:

From the apostles and elders, your brothers.
To all the non-Jewish believers in Antioch, Syria and Cilicia:
Greetings!
24We have heard that some of our group have come to you and said things that trouble and upset you. But we did not tell them to do this. 25We have all agreed to choose some messengers and send them to you with our dear friends Barnabas and Paul— 26people who have given their lives to serve our Lord Jesus Christ. 27So we are sending Judas and Silas, who will tell you the same things. 28It has pleased the Holy Spirit *d* that you should not have a heavy load to carry, and we agree. You need to do only these things: 29stay away from any food that has been offered to idols, any animals that have been strangled, blood and any kind of sexual sin. If you stay away from these things, you will do well.
Goodbye.

30So they left Jerusalem and went to Antioch where they gathered the church and gave them the letter. [31]When they read it, they were very happy because of the encouraging message. [32]Judas and Silas, who were also prophets, *d* said many things to encourage the believers and make them stronger. [33]After some time Judas and Silas were sent off in peace by the believers, and they went back to those who had sent them. [34] *n*

[35]But Paul and Barnabas stayed in Antioch and, along with many others, preached the Good News *d* and taught the people the message of the Lord.

Paul and Barnabas Separate

[36]After some time, Paul said to Barnabas, "We should go back to all those towns where we preached the message of the Lord. Let's visit the believers and see how they are doing."

[37]Barnabas wanted to take John Mark with them, [38]but he had left them at Pamphylia; he did not continue with them in the work. So Paul did not think it was a good idea to take him. [39]Paul and Barnabas had such a serious argument about this that they separated and went different ways. Barnabas took Mark and sailed to Cyprus, [40]but Paul chose Silas and left. The believers in Antioch put Paul into the Lord's care, [41]and he went through Syria and Cilicia, giving strength to the churches.

Timothy Goes with Paul

16 Paul came to Derbe and Lystra, where a follower named Timothy lived. Timothy's mother was Jewish and a believer, but his father was a Greek. [2]The believers in Lystra and Iconium respected Timothy and said good things about him. [3]Paul wanted Timothy to travel with him, but all the Jews living in that area knew that Timothy's father was Greek. So Paul circumcised *d* Timothy to please the Jews. [4]Paul and those with him travelled from town to town and gave the decisions made by the apostles *d* and elders *d* in Jerusalem for the people to obey. [5]So the churches became stronger in the faith and grew larger every day.

Paul is Called Out of Asia

[6]Paul and those with him went through the areas of Phrygia and Galatia since the Holy Spirit *d* did not let them preach the Good News *d* in the country of Asia. [7]When they came near the country of Mysia, they tried to go into Bithynia, but the Spirit of Jesus did not let them. [8]So they passed by Mysia and went to Troas. [9]That night Paul saw in a vision a man from Macedonia. The man stood and begged, "Come over to Macedonia and help us." [10]After Paul had seen the vision, we immediately prepared to leave for Macedonia, understanding that God had called us to tell the Good News to those people.

Lydia Becomes a Christian

[11]We left Troas and sailed straight to the island of Samothrace. The next day we sailed to Neapolis. *n* [12]Then we went by land to Philippi, a Roman colony *n* and the leading city in that part of Macedonia. We stayed there for several days. [13]On the Sabbath *d* day we went outside the city gate to the river where we thought we would find a special place for prayer. Some women had gathered there, so we sat down and talked with them. [14]One of the listeners was a woman named Lydia from the city of Thyatira whose job was selling purple cloth. She worshipped God, and he opened her mind to pay attention to what Paul was saying. [15]She and all the people in her house were baptised. *d* Then she invited us to her home, saying, "If you think I am truly a believer in the Lord, then come and stay in my house." And she persuaded us to stay with her.

Paul and Silas in Jail

[16]Once, while we were going to the place for prayer, a servant girl met us. She had a special spirit *n* in her, and she earned a lot of money for her owners by telling fortunes. [17]This girl followed Paul and us, shouting, "These men are servants of the Most High God. They are telling you how you can be saved."

[18]She kept this up for many days. This bothered Paul, so he turned and said to the spirit, "By the power of Jesus Christ, I command you to come out of her!" Immediately, the spirit came out.

[19]When the owners of the servant girl saw this, they knew that now they could not use her to make money. So they grabbed Paul and Silas and dragged them before the city rulers in the market place. [20]They brought Paul and Silas to the Roman rulers and said, "These men are Jews and are making trouble in our city. [21]They are teaching things that are not right for us as Romans to do."

[22]The crowd joined the attack against them. The Roman officers tore the clothes of Paul and

---

Verse 34 Some Greek copies add verse 34: ". . . but Silas decided to remain there."
Neapolis City in Macedonia. It was the first city Paul visited on the continent of Europe.
Roman colony A town begun by Romans with Roman laws, customs and privileges.
spirit This was a spirit from the devil, which caused her to have special knowledge.

Silas and had them beaten with rods. ²³Then Paul and Silas were thrown into jail, and the jailer was ordered to guard them carefully. ²⁴When he heard this order, he put them far inside the jail and pinned their feet down between large blocks of wood.

²⁵About midnight Paul and Silas were praying and singing songs to God as the other prisoners listened. ²⁶Suddenly, there was a strong earthquake that shook the foundation of the jail. Then all the doors of the jail broke open, and all the prisoners were freed from their chains. ²⁷The jailer woke up and saw that the jail doors were open. Thinking that the prisoners had already escaped, he got his sword and was about to kill himself. *n* ²⁸But Paul shouted, "Don't hurt yourself! We are all here."

²⁹The jailer told someone to bring a light. Then he ran inside and, shaking with fear, fell down before Paul and Silas. ³⁰He brought them outside and said, "Men, what must I do to be saved?"

kill himself He thought the leaders would kill him for letting the prisoners escape.

GOD'S WILL

Close to Your Heart

Sandra Graham was one term away from leaving school and she had no idea what she would do with her life. She had been praying for God to show her his will, but still there were no answers.

One Sunday after church, Ted Holt, the youth leader, asked Sandra to come home with his family of eight for dinner.

All through the meal, they talked about Sandra's plans after school.

"What do you think God wants you to do, Sandra?" Ted asked as they picked up their coffee cups.

"I've been praying about it, but God just doesn't seem to answer," Sandra lamented.

Ted's voice softened. "What do you want to do?" he asked.

"God's will," she answered.

Again, Ted asked, "But what do you want to do?"

Sandra was confused. "That's it. I want to do God's will."

Ted smiled. "Sandra, I have six kids, and I want nothing more than for each of my kids to be happy. I'll do almost anything to make that happen."

Sandra nodded, not sure what this had to do with her decision.

Ted laughed heartily when he saw her confusion. "Sandra, God is your father, and he wants you to be happy. He's probably been showing you all the time what his will is."

"He has?" Sandra asked incredulously.

"Yes, he has. Look into your heart. I'll bet your desires will point you towards God's will."

Sandra did find God's will. She went to college and after she graduated, she used her love for drama to teach others how to communicate their faith. In **Acts 16:6–10**, Paul also found God's will.

* What was Ted trying to help Sandra learn about finding God's will? In the passage, how did God show his will to Paul and the others?
* Do you think God still reveals his will to people as he did in the passage? In what other ways do people learn God's will?

Consider . . .

* keeping track of what happens to you in the coming week. See if any patterns emerge that show God leading you in a particular direction.
* interviewing an older person in your church about discovering God's will.

For more, see . . .

* Psalm 32:6–11 (p.518)
* Luke 22:41–43 (p.1088)
* Matthew 6:9–13 (p.948)

[31]They said to him, "Believe in the Lord Jesus and you will be saved—you and all the people in your house." [32]So Paul and Silas told the message of the Lord to the jailer and all the people in his house. [33]At that hour of the night the jailer took Paul and Silas and washed their wounds. Then he and all his people were baptised *d* immediately. [34]After this the jailer took Paul and Silas home and gave them food. He and his family were very happy because they now believed in God.

[35]The next morning, the Roman officers sent the police to tell the jailer, "Let these men go free."

[36]The jailer said to Paul, "The officers have sent an order to let you go free. You can leave now. Go in peace."

[37]But Paul said to the police, "They beat us in public without a trial, even though we are Roman citizens. [n] And they threw us in jail. Now they want to make us go away quietly. No! Let them come themselves and bring us out."

[38]The police told the Roman officers what Paul said. When the officers heard that Paul and Silas were Roman citizens, they were afraid. [39]So they came and told Paul and Silas they were sorry and took them out of jail and asked them to leave the city. [40]So when they came out of the jail,

Roman citizens   Roman law said that Roman citizens must not be beaten before they had a trial.

SHARING FAITH

Take Me Instead

Maximilian Kolbe was born in Poland in 1894 and ordained as a priest in 1918. In 1941, he was transported in a trainload of prisoners to the Nazi concentration camp in Auschwitz.

During his time in the camp, one of the prisoners escaped from his block and as a deterrent, the commandant sentenced ten prisoners to death by starvation. No food, no water, no hope, no return.

One of the prisoners sentenced to death was Francis Gajowniczek. When he heard he had been picked to be the tenth man to die, he exclaimed in a panic-stricken voice, "I have a wife and family, please don't take me!"

When Maximilian Kolbe heard Francis, he spoke loudly and clearly, "I will die in his place. I am old, and as a younger man, Francis can be more useful. He has a wife and child. I have no family. Take me instead of him."

This was unheard of, but his request was granted. Maximilian Kolbe spent the rest of his time in Auschwitz praying for the other prisoners and talking to them about God. He was eventually killed by lethal injection.

Francis was later freed and dedicated his life to telling the story of Maximilian Kolbe.

Read **Acts 16:25–34** which is an account of how Paul and disciples acted as God's witnesses whilst in prison, just like Maximilian Kolbe.

* Why do you think Paul and the disciples weren't afraid to share their faith in Jesus whilst they were in prison?
* What things stop you from telling others about Jesus?

Consider . . .

* writing down the names of two friends who you want to speak to about Jesus in the next month. Meet with a friend to pray for them.
* asking your youth leader to recommend some books about inspiring figures from history who have shared their faith in Jesus.

For more, see . . .

* Luke 12:8–9 (p.1062)
* 1 John 4:13–18 (p.1374)
* Romans 10:9–11 (p.1200)

they went to Lydia's house where they saw some of the believers and encouraged them. Then they left.

Paul and Silas in Thessalonica

17 Paul and Silas travelled through Amphipolis and Apollonia and came to Thessalonica where there was a Jewish synagogue. *d* ²Paul went into the synagogue as he always did, and on each Sabbath *d* day for three weeks, he talked with the Jews about the Scriptures. *d* ³He explained and proved that the Christ *d* must die and then rise from the dead. He said, "This Jesus I am telling you about is the Christ." ⁴Some of the Jews were convinced and joined Paul and Silas, along with many of the Greeks who worshipped God and many of the important women.

⁵But the Jews became jealous. So they got some evil men from the market-place, formed a mob and started a riot. They ran to Jason's house, looking for Paul and Silas, wanting to bring them out to the people. ⁶But when they did not find them, they dragged Jason and some other believers to the leaders of the city. The people were yelling, "These people have made trouble everywhere in the world, and now they have come here too! ⁷Jason is keeping them in his house. All of them do things against the laws of Caesar, *d* saying there is another king, called Jesus."

⁸When the people and the leaders of the city heard these things, they became very upset. ⁹They made Jason and the others put up a sum of money. Then they let the believers go free.

FRIENDS

Loyalty Card

Joe and Dan were really good friends. Dan was clever, but had very bad dyslexia. Joe understood. His eldest brother Steve had had similar problems. Besides, nothing would stop Joe and Dan being friends.

One day a new family came to live in the flat upstairs from Dan. Almost immediately, there was trouble. Billy was big for his age and started making his presence felt in the estate. He took to calling Dan names and trying to get other kids to gang up on him. Joe consistently stood up for him, and one night stood in front of Dan as if to protect him and confronted Billy.

"I want you to leave Dan alone," he shouted. "He's done nothing to you."

"But he can't even spell his own name," laughed back Billy cruelly.

Dan went red and kept silent. Joe's brother Steve came out of the flat at that moment. He was a rugby player, a big guy, and glared at Billy.

"I don't think we've met," Steve said to Billy without a smile. "But like our Joe said, if you mess with Dan here, I won't be too pleased. I have dyslexia too and it's not stopped me doing anything I've set my mind to. Stay away from him, yeah!"

Billy was stunned and quickly made his way home.

Steve smiled at Dan, "Come on mate, let's have a go on that computer of yours and see if I can beat you again!"

Take a look at **Acts 17:1–15**.

* How is Steve like Jason in the Bible passage?
* Paul and Silas had each other for encouragement when they had a tough time – how do you think Dan felt about having Joe (and Steve) standing up for him?

Consider . . .

* what makes a friendship great. Can you think of a few ways that you could show your friends this week what they mean to you?
* encouraging a Christian friend who is in a difficult situation to be strong and keep going.

For more, see . . .

* Proverbs 17:9 (p.604)
* John 15:13 (p.1125)

* Proverbs 18:24 (p.605)

Paul and Silas Go to Berea

[10]That same night the believers sent Paul and Silas to Berea where they went to the Jewish synagogue. [d] [11]These Jews were more willing to listen than the Jews in Thessalonica. The Jews in Berea were eager to hear what Paul and Silas said and studied the Scriptures [d] every day to find out if these things were true. [12]So, many of them believed, as well as many important Greek women and men. [13]But the Jews in Thessalonica learned that Paul was preaching the word of God in Berea, too. So they came there, upsetting the people and making trouble. [14]The believers quickly sent Paul away to the coast, but Silas and Timothy stayed in Berea. [15]The people leading Paul went with him to Athens. Then they carried a message from Paul back to Silas and Timothy for them to come to him as soon as they could.

Paul Preaches in Athens

[16]While Paul was waiting for Silas and Timothy in Athens, he was troubled because he saw that the city was full of idols. [17]In the synagogue, [d] he talked with the Jews and the Greeks who worshipped God. He also talked every day with people in the market-place. [18]Some of the Epicurean and Stoic philosophers [n] argued with him, saying, "This man doesn't know what he is talking about. What is he trying to say?" Others said, "He seems to be telling us about some other gods," because Paul was telling them about Jesus and his rising from the dead. [19]They got Paul and took him to a meeting of the Areopagus, [n] where they said, "Please explain to us this new idea you have been teaching. [20]The things you are saying are new to us, and we want to know what this teaching means." [21](All the people of Athens and those from other countries who lived there always used their time to talk about the newest ideas.)

[22]Then Paul stood before the meeting of the Areopagus and said, "People of Athens, I can see you are very religious in all things. [23]As I was going through your city, I saw the objects you worship. I found an altar that had these words written on it: TO A GOD WHO IS NOT KNOWN. You worship a god that you don't know, and this is the God I am telling you about! [24]The God who made the whole world and everything in it is the Lord of the land and the sky. He does not live in temples [d] built by human hands.

[25]This God is the One who gives life, breath and everything else to people. He does not need any help from them; he has everything he needs. [26]God began by making one person, and from him came all the different people who live everywhere in the world. God decided exactly when and where they must live. [27]God wanted them to look for him and perhaps search all around for him and find him, though he is not far from any of us: [28]'We live in him. We walk in him. We are in him.' Some of your own poets have said: 'For we are his children.' [29]Since we are God's children, you must not think that God is like something that people imagine or make from gold, silver or rock. [30]In the past, people did not understand God, and he ignored this. But now, God tells all people in the world to change their hearts and lives. [31]God has set a day that he will judge all the world with fairness, by the man he chose long ago. And God has proved this to everyone by raising that man from the dead!"

[32]When the people heard about Jesus being raised from the dead, some of them laughed. But others said, "We will hear more about this from you later." [33]So Paul went away from them. [34]But some of the people believed Paul and joined him. Among those who believed was Dionysius, a member of the Areopagus, a woman named Damaris and some others.

Paul in Corinth

18 Later Paul left Athens and went to Corinth. [2]Here he met a Jew named Aquila who had been born in the country of Pontus. But Aquila and his wife, Priscilla, had recently moved to Corinth from Italy, because Claudius [n] commanded that all Jews must leave Rome. Paul went to visit Aquila and Priscilla. [3]Because they were tentmakers, just as he was,

---

Sidelight Claudius (Acts 18:2) ruled Rome for thirteen years and was partially paralysed. He kicked Christians out of Rome for allegedly starting riots that threatened the Roman peace – a common charge against early Christians.

---

he stayed with them and worked with them. [4]Every Sabbath [d] day he talked with the Jews and Greeks in the synagogue, [d] trying to persuade

---

Epicurean and Stoic philosophers Philosophers were those who searched for truth. Epicureans believed that pleasures, especially pleasures of the mind, were the goal of life. Stoics believed that life should be without feelings of joy or grief.
Areopagus A council or group of important leaders in Athens. They were like judges.
Claudius The emperor (ruler) of Rome, AD 41–54.

them to believe in Jesus.

⁵Silas and Timothy came from Macedonia and joined Paul in Corinth. After this, Paul spent all his time telling people the Good News,*d* showing the Jews that Jesus is the Christ.*d* ⁶But they would not accept Paul's teaching and said some evil things. So he shook off the dust from his clothes*n* and said to them, "If you are not saved, it will be your own fault! I have done all I can do! After this, I will go only to those who are not Jewish." ⁷Paul left the synagogue and moved into the home of Titius Justus, next to the synagogue. This man worshipped God. ⁸Crispus was the leader of that synagogue, and he and all the people living in his house believed in the Lord. Many others in Corinth also listened to Paul and believed and were baptised. *d*

⁹During the night, the Lord told Paul in a vision: "Don't be afraid. Continue talking to people and don't be quiet. ¹⁰I am with you, and no one will hurt you because many of my people are in this city." ¹¹Paul stayed there for a year and a half, teaching God's word to the people.

Paul is Brought Before Gallio

¹²When Gallio was the governor of the country of Southern Greece, some of the Jews came together against Paul and took him to the court. ¹³They said, "This man is teaching people to worship God in a way that is against our law."

¹⁴Paul was about to say something, but Gallio spoke to the Jews, saying, "I would listen to you Jews if you were complaining about a crime or some wrong. ¹⁵But the things you are saying are only questions about words and names—arguments about your own law. So you must solve this problem yourselves. I don't want to be a judge of these things." ¹⁶And Gallio made them leave the court.

¹⁷Then they all grabbed Sosthenes, the leader of the synagogue, *d* and beat him there before the court. But this did not bother Gallio.

Paul Returns to Antioch

¹⁸Paul stayed with the believers for many more days. Then he left and sailed for Syria, with Priscilla and Aquila. At Cenchrea Paul cut off his hair, *n* because he had made a promise to God. ¹⁹Then they went to Ephesus, where Paul left

---

shook . . . clothes   This was a warning to show that Paul would no longer talk to the Jews in that city.
cut . . . hair   Jews did this to show that the time of a special promise to God was finished.

NON-CHRISTIANS

A Starting Place

Jay Dugan is a talented musician. His friend explained God as a director who "conducts" every element of life to move in harmony.

Amanda Reddy has moved nine times in eleven years. Her friend explained God as the friend who goes with us no matter where we move or what new situation we face.

Jason Gaddy is a soccer star. His friend explained God as a coach who insists on practise, works to tone our life muscles, teaches strategy for difficult experiences, and cheers every games from the sidelines.

Some Greek leaders thought there must be a god they did not know. In **Acts 17:22–31**, Paul focused on their understanding of that god to guide them to a full knowledge of the true God.

* Why is it effective to explain God by using things people already understand?
* What images did Paul use to describe God in this passage?

Consider . . .

* underlining phrases about God in Acts 17:22–31 that someone who has never been in church could understand. Use these phrases to explain God to your non-Christian friends.
* thinking of a way to explain Jesus to a non-Christian friend. Begin with an image your friend will relate to.

For more, see . . .

* Exodus 3:12–15 (p.61)
* 1 Corinthians 9:19–23 (p.1227)

* John 4:5–25 (p.1101)

Priscilla and Aquila. While Paul was there, he went into the synagogue *d* and talked with the Jews. [20]When they asked him to stay with them longer, he refused. [21]But as he left, he said, "I will come back to you again if God wants me to." And so he sailed away from Ephesus.

[22]When Paul landed at Caesarea, he went and gave greetings to the church in Jerusalem. After that, Paul went to Antioch. [23]He stayed there for a while and then left and went through the regions of Galatia and Phrygia. He travelled from town to town in these regions, giving strength to all the followers.

Apollos in Ephesus and Corinth

[24]A Jew named Apollos came to Ephesus. He was born in the city of Alexandria and was a good speaker who knew the Scriptures *d* well. [25]He had been taught about the way of the Lord and was always very excited when he spoke and taught the truth about Jesus. But the only baptism *d* Apollos knew about was the baptism that John *n* taught. [26]Apollos began to speak very boldly in the synagogue, *d* and when Priscilla and Aquila heard him, they took him to their home and helped him better understand the way of God. [27]Now Apollos wanted to go to the country of Southern Greece. So the believers helped him and wrote a letter to the followers there, asking them to accept him. These followers had believed in Jesus because of God's grace, and when Apollos arrived, he helped them very much. [28]He argued very strongly with the Jews before all the people, clearly proving with the Scriptures that Jesus is the Christ. *d*

Paul in Ephesus

19 While Apollos was in Corinth, Paul was visiting some places on the way to Ephesus. There he found some followers [2]and asked them, "Did you receive the Holy Spirit *d* when you believed?"

They said, "We have never even heard of a Holy Spirit."

[3]So he asked, "What kind of baptism did you have?"

They said, "It was the baptism *d* that John *n* taught."

[4]Paul said, "John's baptism was a baptism of changed hearts and lives. He told people to believe in the One who would come after him, and that One is Jesus."

[5]When they heard this, they were baptised in the name of the Lord Jesus. [6]Then Paul laid his hands on them, *n* and the Holy Spirit came upon them. They began speaking different languages *n* and prophesying. *d* [7]There were about twelve people in this group.

[8]Paul went into the synagogue *d* and spoke out boldly for three months. He talked with the Jews and persuaded them to accept the things he said about the kingdom of God. [9]But some of the Jews became stubborn. They refused to believe and said evil things about the Way of Jesus before all the people. So Paul left them, and, taking the followers with him, he went to the school of a man named Tyrannus. There Paul talked with people every day [10]for two years. Because of his work, every Jew and Greek in the country of Asia heard the word of the Lord.

The Sons of Sceva

[11]God used Paul to do some very special miracles. *d* [12]Some people took handkerchiefs and clothes that Paul had used and put them on the sick. When they did this, the sick were healed and evil spirits left them.

[13]But some Jews also were travelling around and making evil spirits go out of people. They tried to use the name of the Lord Jesus to force the evil spirits out. They would say, "By the same Jesus that Paul talks about, I order you to come out!" [14]Seven sons of Sceva, a leading Jewish priest, were doing this.

[15]But on one occasion an evil spirit said to them, "I know Jesus, and I know about Paul, but who are you?"

[16]Then the man who had the evil spirit jumped on them. Because he was so much stronger than all of them, they ran away from the house naked and hurt. [17]All the people in Ephesus—Jews and Greeks—learned about this and were filled with fear and gave great honour to the Lord Jesus. [18]Many of the believers began to confess openly and tell all the evil things they had done. [19]Some of them who had used magic brought their magic books and burned them before everyone. Those books were worth about 50,000 silver coins. *n*

[20]So in a powerful way the word of the Lord kept spreading and growing.

[21]After these things, Paul decided to go to Jerusalem, planning to go through the countries of Macedonia and Southern Greece and then on to Jerusalem. He said, "After I have been to Jerusalem, I must also visit Rome." [22]Paul sent

---

John   John the Baptist, who preached to people about Christ's coming (Matthew 3, Luke 3).
laid his hands on them   The laying on of hands had many purposes, including the giving of a blessing, power or authority.
languages   This can also be translated "tongues".
50,000 silver coins   Probably drachmas. A silver coin was enough to pay a worker for one day's labour.

Timothy and Erastus, two of his helpers, ahead to Macedonia, but he himself stayed in Asia for a while.

Trouble in Ephesus

23And during that time, there was some serious trouble in Ephesus about the Way of Jesus. 24A man named Demetrius, who worked with silver, made little silver models that looked like the temple *d* of the goddess Artemis. *n* Those who did this work made much money. 25Demetrius had a meeting with them and some others who did the same kind of work. He told them, "Men, you know that we make a lot of money from our business. 26But look at what this man Paul is doing. He has convinced and turned away many people in Ephesus and in almost all of Asia! He says the gods made by human hands are not real. 27There is a danger that our business will lose its good name, but there is also another danger: people will begin to think that the temple of the great goddess Artemis is not important. Her greatness will be destroyed, but Artemis is the goddess that everyone in Asia and the whole world worships."

28When the others heard this, they became very angry and shouted, "Artemis, the goddess of Ephesus, is great!" 29The whole city became confused. The people grabbed Gaius and Aristarchus,

Artemis   A Greek goddess that the people of Asia Minor worshipped.

FAITH

Growing Up

Tick the items that are true of your relationship with God.
☐ I understand God better now than when I first started learning about him. ☐ I genuinely enjoy being involved in activities related to my faith. ☐ God helps me to love and care for people. ☐ My relationships are better as a result of my faith in God. ☐ I understand scripture better than I used to. ☐ I ask God to help me to solve problems. ☐ My friends and family know that I'm a Christian. ☐ I take time each day to pray. ☐ I know that God loves me. ☐ I ask God to forgive me when I have done something wrong. ☐ I am honest with God about my feelings. ☐ I tell people about Jesus. ☐ My relationship with God deeply influences my actions.

Now rate yourself:

* 6 to 13 ticks – Your faith is definitely growing. You are experiencing the type of growth described in Acts 19:1–7.
* 3 to 5 ticks – Be careful that your faith is not stagnating. Read the items you didn't tick, and begin building those things into your life. Be encouraged by Acts 19:1–7.
* 0 to 2 ticks – Your faith is wilting. Water it with the Word of God and get involved with other Christians soon – before your faith withers.

In **Acts 19:1–7**, Paul explained truth that the followers did not know. When they heard all that God had done for them, they were changed – and their faith could grow.

* How did Paul help people's faith to grow? What items in the checklist would be true for the people in the passage?
* How did the people in this passage express their faith?

Consider . . .

* pretending it's New Year resolution time. Write a letter to Jesus describing ways your relationship has grown, what you appreciate about him and how you hope your relationship will grow in the next year.
* choosing one item from the list to begin building into your life.

For more, see . . .

* Psalm 15 (p.506)
* Colossians 1:9–14 (p.1289)
* 1 Corinthians 3:1–9 (p.1216)

who were from Macedonia and were travelling with Paul, and ran to the theatre. 30Paul wanted to go in and talk to the crowd, but the followers did not let him. 31Also, some leaders of Asia who were friends of Paul sent him a message, begging him not to go into the theatre. 32Some people were shouting one thing, and some were shouting another. The meeting was completely confused; most of them did not know why they had come together. 33The Jews put a man named Alexander in front of the people, and some of them told him what to do. Alexander waved his hand so he could explain things to the people. 34But when they saw that Alexander was a Jew, they all shouted the same thing for two hours: "Great is Artemis of Ephesus!"

35Then the city clerk made the crowd be quiet. He said, "People of Ephesus, everyone knows that Ephesus is the city that keeps the temple of the great goddess Artemis and her holy stone *n* that fell from heaven. 36Since no one can say this is not true, you should be quiet. Stop and think before you do anything. 37You brought these men here, but they have not said anything evil against our goddess or stolen anything from her temple. 38If Demetrius and those who work with him have a charge against anyone they should go to the courts and judges where they can argue with each other. 39If there is something else you want to talk about, it can be decided at the legal town meeting of the people. 40I say this because some people might see this trouble today and say that we are rioting. We could not explain this, because there is no real reason for this meeting." 41After the city clerk said these things, he told the people to go home.

Paul in Macedonia and Greece

20 When the trouble stopped, Paul sent for the followers to come to him. After he had encouraged them and said goodbye, he left and went to the country of Macedonia. 2He said many things to strengthen the followers in the different places on his way through Macedonia. Then he went to Greece, 3where he stayed for three months. He was ready to sail for Syria, but some Jews were planning something against him. So Paul decided to go back through Macedonia to Syria. 4The men who went with him were Sopater son of Pyrrhus, from the city of Berea; Aristarchus and Secundus, from the city of Thessalonica; Gaius, from Derbe; Timothy; and Tychicus and Trophimus, two men from the country of Asia. 5These men went on ahead and waited for us at Troas. 6We sailed from Philippi after the Feast *d* of

Unleavened Bread. Five days later we met them in Troas, where we stayed for seven days.

Paul's Last Visit to Troas

7On the first day of the week, *n* we all met together to break bread, *n* and Paul spoke to the group. Because he was planning to leave the next day, he kept on talking until midnight. 8We were all together in a room upstairs, and there were many lamps in the room. 9A young man named Eutychus was sitting in the window. As Paul continued talking, Eutychus was falling into a deep sleep. Finally, he went sound asleep and fell to the ground from the third floor. When they picked him up, he was dead. 10Paul went down to Eutychus, knelt down and put his arms around him. He said, "Don't worry. He is alive now." 11Then Paul went upstairs again, broke bread and ate. He spoke to them for a long time, until it was early morning, and then he left. 12They took the young man home alive and were greatly comforted.

The Trip from Troas to Miletus

13We went on ahead of Paul and sailed for the city of Assos, where he wanted to join us on the ship. Paul had planned this because he wanted to go to Assos by land. 14When he met us there, we took him aboard and went to Mitylene. 15We sailed from Mitylene and the next day came to a place near Chios. The following day we sailed to Samos, and the next day we reached Miletus. 16Paul had already decided not to stop at Ephesus, because he did not want to stay too long in the country of Asia. He was hurrying to be in Jerusalem on the day of Pentecost, *d* if that were possible.

The Elders from Ephesus

17Now from Miletus Paul sent to Ephesus and called for the elders *d* of the church. 18When they came to him, he said, "You know about my life from the first day I came to Asia. You know the way I lived all the time I was with you. 19The Jews made plans against me, which troubled me very much. But you know I always served the Lord unselfishly, and I often cried. 20You know I preached to you and did not hold back anything that would help you. You know that I taught you in public and in your homes. 21I warned both Jews and Greeks to change their lives and turn to God and believe in our Lord Jesus. 22But now I must obey the Holy Spirit *d* and go to Jerusalem. I don't know what will happen to me there. 23I know only that in every city the Holy Spirit tells

---

holy stone   Probably a meteorite or stone that the people thought looked like Artemis.
first day of the week   Sunday, which for the Jews began at sunset on our last day of the week. But if in this part of Asia a
  different system of time was used, then the meeting was on our Sunday night.
break bread   Probably the Lord's Supper, the special meal that Jesus told his followers to eat to remember him (Luke
  22:14–20).

me that troubles and even jail wait for me. 24I don't care about my own life. The most important thing is that I complete my mission, the work that the Lord Jesus gave me—to tell people the Good News *d* about God's grace.

25"And now, I know that none of you among whom I was preaching the kingdom of God will ever see me again. 26So today I tell you that if any of you should be lost, I am not responsible, 27because I have told you everything God wants you to know. 28Be careful for yourselves and for all the people the Holy Spirit has given to you to care for. You must be like shepherds to the church of God, *n* which he bought with the death of his own Son. 29I know that after I leave, some people will come like wild wolves and try to destroy the flock. 30Also, some from your own group will rise up and twist the truth and will lead away followers after them. 31So be careful! Always remember that for three years, day and night, I never stopped warning each of you, and I often cried over you.

32"Now I am putting you in the care of God and the message about his grace. It is able to give you strength, and it will give you the blessings God has for all his holy people. 33When I was with you, I never wanted anyone's money or fine clothes. 34You know I always worked to take care of my own needs and the needs of those who were with me. 35I showed you in all things that you should work as I did and help the weak. I taught you to remember the words Jesus said: 'It is more blessed to give than to receive.' "

36When Paul had said this, he knelt down with all of them and prayed. 37-38And they all cried because Paul had said they would never see him again. They put their arms around him and kissed him. Then they went with him to the ship.

Paul Goes to Jerusalem

21 After we all said goodbye to them, we sailed straight to the island of Cos. The next day we reached Rhodes, and from there we went to Patara. 2There we found a ship going to Phoenicia, so we went aboard and sailed away. 3We sailed near the island of Cyprus, seeing it to the north, but we sailed on to Syria. We stopped at Tyre because the ship needed to unload its cargo there. 4We found some followers in Tyre and stayed with them for seven days. Through the Holy Spirit *d* they warned Paul not to go to Jerusalem. 5When we finished our visit, we left and continued our trip. All the followers, even the women and children, came outside the city

with us. After we all knelt on the beach and prayed, 6we said goodbye and got on the ship, and the followers went back home.

7We continued our trip from Tyre and arrived at Ptolemais, where we greeted the believers and stayed with them for a day. 8The next day we left Ptolemais and went to the city of Caesarea. There we went into the home of Philip the preacher, *d* one of the seven helpers, *n* and stayed with him. 9He had four unmarried daughters who had the gift of prophesying. *d* 10After we had been there for some time, a prophet named Agabus arrived from Judea. 11He came to us and borrowed Paul's belt and used it to tie his own hands and feet. He said, "The Holy Spirit says, 'This is how the Jews in Jerusalem will tie up the man who wears this belt. Then they will give him to those who are not Jews.' "

12When we all heard this, we and the people there begged Paul not to go to Jerusalem. 13But he said, "Why are you crying and making me so sad? I am not only ready to be tied up in Jerusalem, I am ready to die for the Lord Jesus!"

14We could not persuade him to stay away from Jerusalem. So we stopped begging him and said, "We pray that what the Lord wants will be done."

15After this, we got ready and started on our way to Jerusalem. 16Some of the followers from Caesarea went with us and took us to the home of Mnason, where we would stay. He was from Cyprus and was one of the first followers.

Paul Visits James

17In Jerusalem the believers were glad to see us. 18The next day Paul went with us to visit James, and all the elders *d* were there. 19Paul greeted them and told them everything God had done among the non-Jewish people through him. 20When they heard this, they praised God. Then they said to Paul, "Brother, you can see that many thousands of Jews have become believers. And they think it is very important to obey the law of Moses. 21They have heard about your teaching, that you tell the Jews who live among those who are not Jews to leave the law of Moses. They have heard that you tell them not to circumcise *d* their children and not to obey Jewish customs. 22What should we do? They will learn that you have come. 23So we will tell you what to do: four of our men have made a promise to God. 24Take these men with you and share in their cleansing ceremony. *n* Pay their expenses so they can shave their heads. *n* Then it will prove to everyone that what they have heard about

---

of God   Some Greek copies say, "of the Lord".
helpers   The seven men chosen for a special work described in Acts 6:1–6.
cleansing ceremony   The special things Jews did to end the Nazirite promise.
shave their heads   The Jews did this to show that their promise was finished.

you is not true and that you follow the law of Moses in your own life. 25We have already sent a letter to the non-Jewish believers. The letter said: 'Do not eat food that has been offered to idols, or blood or animals that have been strangled. Do not take part in sexual sin.' "

26The next day Paul took the four men and shared in the cleansing ceremony with them. Then he went to the Temple[d] and announced the time when the days of the cleansing ceremony would be finished. On the last day an offering would be given for each of the men.

27When the seven days were almost over, some Jews from Asia saw Paul at the Temple. They upset all the people and grabbed Paul. 28They shouted, "People of Israel, help us! This is the man who goes everywhere teaching against the law of Moses, against our people and against this Temple. Now he has brought some Greeks into the Temple and has made this holy place unclean!"[d] 29(The Jews said this because they had seen Trophimus, a man from Ephesus, with Paul in Jerusalem. The Jews thought that Paul had brought him into the Temple.)

Sidelight When Paul was accused of making the Temple unclean, he was being accused of a crime punishable by death (Acts 21:28). Archaeologists have found a temple inscription that says: "No foreigner is to enter . . . Whoever is caught will render himself liable to the consequent penalty of death."

30All the people in Jerusalem became upset. Together they ran, took Paul and dragged him out of the Temple. The Temple doors were closed immediately. 31While they were trying to kill Paul, the commander of the Roman army in Jerusalem learned that there was trouble in the whole city. 32Immediately he took some officers and soldiers and ran to the place where the crowd was gathered. When the people saw them, they stopped beating Paul. 33The commander went to Paul and arrested him. He told his soldiers to tie Paul with two chains. Then he asked who he was and what he had done wrong. 34Some in the crowd were yelling one thing, and some were yelling another. Because of all this confusion and shouting, the commander could not learn what had happened. So he ordered the soldiers to take Paul to the army building. 35When Paul came to the steps, the soldiers had

to carry him because the people were ready to hurt him. 36The whole mob was following them, shouting, "Kill him!"

37As the soldiers were about to take Paul into the army building, he spoke to the commander, "May I say something to you?"

The commander said, "Do you speak Greek? 38I thought you were the Egyptian who started some trouble against the government not long ago and led 4,000 killers out to the desert."

39Paul said, "No, I am a Jew from Tarsus in the country of Cilicia. I am a citizen of that important city. Please, let me speak to the people."

40The commander gave permission, so Paul stood on the steps and waved his hand to quiet the people. When there was silence, he spoke to them in the Jewish language.[n]

Paul Speaks to the People

22 Paul said, "Friends, fellow Jews, listen to my defence to you." 2When the Jews heard him speaking the Jewish language,[n] they became very quiet. Paul said, 3"I am a Jew, born in Tarsus in the country of Cilicia, but I grew up in this city. I was a student of Gamaliel,[n] who carefully taught me everything about the law of our ancestors. I was very serious about serving God, just as are all of you here today. 4I persecuted the people who followed the Way of Jesus, and some of them were even killed. I arrested men and women and put them in jail. 5The high priest and the whole council of Jewish elders can tell you this is true. They gave me letters to the Jewish brothers in Damascus. So I was going there to arrest these people and bring them back to Jerusalem to be punished.

6"At about noon when I came near Damascus, a bright light from heaven suddenly flashed all around me. 7I fell to the ground and heard a voice saying, 'Saul, Saul, why are you persecuting me?' 8I asked, 'Who are you, Lord?' The voice said, 'I am Jesus from Nazareth whom you are persecuting.' 9Those who were with me did not hear the voice, but they saw the light. 10I said, 'What shall I do, Lord?' The Lord answered, 'Get up and go to Damascus. There you will be told about all the things I have planned for you to do.' 11I could not see, because the bright light had made me blind. So my companions led me into Damascus.

12"There a man named Ananias came to me. He was a religious man; he obeyed the law of Moses, and all the Jews who lived there respected him. 13He stood by me and said, 'Brother

---

Jewish language Hebrew or Aramaic, the languages of the Jews in the first century.
Gamaliel A very important teacher of the Pharisees, a Jewish religious group (Acts 5:34).

Saul, see again!' Immediately I was able to see him. ¹⁴He said, 'The God of our ancestors chose you long ago to know his plan, to see the Righteous One and to hear words from him. ¹⁵You will be his witness to all people, telling them about what you have seen and heard. ¹⁶Now, why wait any longer? Get up, be baptised *d* and wash your sins away, trusting in him to save you.'

¹⁷"Later, when I returned to Jerusalem, I was praying in the Temple, *d* and I saw a vision. ¹⁸I saw the Lord saying to me, 'Hurry! Leave Jerusalem now! The people here will not accept the truth about me.' ¹⁹But I said, 'Lord, they know that in every synagogue *d* I put the believers in jail and beat them. ²⁰They also know I was there when Stephen, your witness, was killed. I stood there agreeing and holding the coats of those who were killing him!' ²¹But the Lord said to me, 'Leave now. I will send you far away to the non-Jewish people.' "

²²The crowd listened to Paul until he said this. Then they began shouting, "Kill him! Get him out of the world! He should not be allowed to live!" ²³They shouted, threw off their coats *n* and threw dust into the air. *n*

threw off their coats   This showed that the Jews were very angry with Paul.
threw dust into the air   This showed even greater anger.

SHARING FAITH

It Happened to Me

Did you know that it is against the law to go into a school and tell kids that they should become Christians? There is a good reason for it, you see kids have to be in school, they don't have an option, therefore anyone could go in and tell them anything and they would have to accept it as the truth. Schools would be wide open to people preaching all sorts of weird and perverted ideas, so this law is in place to prevent that happening.

However, Christians are welcomed in to many Religious Education lessons to give a testimony – basically, the story of their life and how they became Christians. That way, you are saying "This is what happened to me," and that's fine.

When Joel was asked to give his testimony at his local school (it was only two years after leaving!) he was very nervous, especially as his Christian testimony was only one year old! He was known at his school for all the bad things he did. But as his old teacher gave him a warm introduction with reminders of his wayward escapades, he began to relax.

He told the students how he'd left school with not much hope of a job, even though he was good at woodwork, and how he'd met up with a girl who was a Christian. She introduced him to her church and he gradually started to do odd jobs for them. He was soon indispensable and the more time he spent with these "Christians" the more he listened and liked what he heard. He told the pupils how he had asked questions about the life of Jesus, and how people at the church had explained things to him.

He didn't realise how excited and interesting his talk was, until kids started to ask questions at the end. He answered everything by starting off with, "I can only tell you what happened to me, but . . ."

Read **Acts 22:12–16** to see how important a testimony is.

* How were Joel's actions like the instructions given to Paul in this passage?
* What did Paul need to do before telling others about Jesus?

Consider . . .

* asking your minister to approach a local headmaster to see if he would let your church help with Christian assemblies.
* being baptised or confirmed, as a public witness to others of your Christian beliefs.

For more see . . .

* Isaiah 43:10 (p.684)
* 2 Peter 1:16 (p.1365)

* Acts 10:39–42 (p.1156)

[24]Then the commander ordered the soldiers to take Paul into the army building and beat him. He wanted to make Paul tell why the people were shouting against him like this. [25]But as the soldiers were tying him up, preparing to beat him, Paul said to an officer nearby, "Do you have the right to beat a Roman citizen [n] who has not been proven guilty?"

[26]When the officer heard this, he went to the commander and reported it. The officer said, "Do you know what you are doing? This man is a Roman citizen."

[27]The commander came to Paul and said, "Tell me, are you really a Roman citizen?"

He answered, "Yes."

[28]The commander said, "I paid a lot of money to become a Roman citizen."

But Paul said, "I was born a citizen."

[29]The men who were preparing to question Paul moved away from him immediately. The commander was frightened because he had already tied Paul, and Paul was a Roman citizen.

Paul Speaks to Jewish Leaders

[30]The next day the commander decided to learn why the Jews were accusing Paul. So he ordered the leading priests and the Jewish council to meet. The commander took Paul's chains off. Then he brought Paul out and stood him before their meeting.

23 Paul looked at the Jewish council and said, "Brothers, I have lived my life with a clear conscience before God up to this day." [2]Ananias, [n] the high priest, heard this and told the men who were standing near Paul to hit him on the mouth. [3]Paul said to Ananias, "God will hit you, too! You are like a wall that has been painted white. You sit there and judge me, using the law of Moses, but you are telling them to hit me, and that is against the law."

[4]The men standing near Paul said to him, "You cannot insult God's high priest like that!"

[5]Paul said, "Brothers, I did not know this man was the high priest. It is written in the Scriptures, [d] 'You must not curse a leader of your people.' " [n]

[6]Some of the men in the meeting were Sadducees, [d] and others were Pharisees. [d] Knowing this, Paul shouted to them, "My brothers, I am a Pharisee, and my father was a Pharisee. I am on trial here because I believe that people will rise from the dead."

[7]When Paul said this, there was an argument between the Pharisees and the Sadducees, and the group was divided. [8](The Sadducees do not believe in angels or spirits or that people will rise from the dead. But the Pharisees believe in them all.) [9]So there was a great uproar. Some of the teachers of the law, who were Pharisees, stood up and argued, "We find nothing wrong with this man. Maybe an angel or a spirit did speak to him."

[10]The argument was beginning to turn into such a fight that the commander was afraid the Jews would tear Paul to pieces. So he told the soldiers to go down and take Paul away and put him in the army building.

[11]The next night the Lord came and stood by Paul. He said, "Be brave! You have told people in Jerusalem about me. You must do the same in Rome."

[12]In the morning some of the Jews made a plan to kill Paul, and they took an oath not to eat or drink anything until they had killed him. [13]There were more than 40 Jews who made this plan. [14]They went to the leading priests and the Jewish elders and said, "We have taken an oath not to eat or drink until we have killed Paul. [15]So this is what we want you to do: send a message to the commander to bring Paul out to you as though you want to ask him more questions. We will be waiting to kill him while he is on the way here."

[16]But Paul's nephew heard about this plan and went to the army building and told Paul. [17]Then Paul called one of the officers and said, "Take this young man to the commander. He has a message for him."

[18]So the officer brought Paul's nephew to the commander and said, "The prisoner, Paul, asked me to bring this young man to you. He wants to tell you something."

[19]The commander took the young man's hand and led him to a place where they could be alone. He asked, "What do you want to tell me?"

[20]The young man said, "The Jews have decided to ask you to bring Paul down to their council meeting tomorrow. They want you to think they are going to ask him more questions. [21]But don't believe them! More than 40 men are hiding and waiting to kill Paul. They have all taken an oath not to eat or drink until they have killed him. Now they are waiting for you to agree."

[22]The commander sent the young man away, ordering him, "Don't tell anyone that you have told me about their plan."

Roman citizen   Roman law said that Roman citizens must not be beaten before they had a trial.
Ananias   This is not the man named Ananias in Acts 22:12.
'You . . . people.'   Quotation from Exodus 22:28.

Paul is Sent to Caesarea

23Then the commander called two officers and said, "I need some men to go to Caesarea. Get 200 soldiers, 70 horsemen and 200 men with spears ready to leave at nine o'clock tonight. 24Get some horses for Paul to ride so he can be taken to Governor Felix safely." 25And he wrote a letter that said:

26From Claudius Lysias.
To the Most Excellent Governor Felix: Greetings.
27The Jews had taken this man and planned to kill him. But I learned that he is a Roman citizen, so I went with my soldiers and saved him. 28I wanted to know why they were accusing him, so I brought him before their council meeting. 29I learned that the Jews said Paul did some things that were wrong by their own laws, but no charge was worthy of jail or death. 30When I was told that some of the Jews were planning to kill Paul, I sent him to you at once. I also told those Jews to tell you what they have against him.

31So the soldiers did what they were told and took Paul and brought him to the city of Antipatris that night. 32The next day the horsemen went with Paul to Caesarea, but the other soldiers went back to the army building in Jerusalem. 33When the horsemen came to Caesarea and gave the letter to the governor, they turned Paul over to him. 34The governor read the letter and asked Paul, "What area are you from?" When he learned that Paul was from Cilicia, 35he said, "I will hear your case when those who are against you come here, too." Then the governor gave orders for Paul to be kept under guard in Herod's palace.

Paul is Accused

24 Five days later Ananias, the high priest, went to the city of Caesarea with some of the Jewish elders and a lawyer named Tertullus. They had come to make charges against Paul before the governor. 2Paul was called into the meeting, and Tertullus began to accuse him, saying, "Most Excellent Felix! Our people enjoy much peace because of you, and many wrong things in our country are being made right through your wise help. 3We accept these things always and in every place, and we are thankful for them. 4But not wanting to take any more of your time, I beg you to be kind and listen to our few words. 5We have found this man to be a troublemaker, stirring up the Jews everywhere in

the world. He is a leader of the Nazarene *d* group. 6Also, he was trying to make the Temple *d* unclean, *d* but we stopped him. *n* 8By asking him questions yourself, you can decide if all these things are true." 9The other Jews agreed and said that all of this was true.

10When the governor made a sign for Paul to speak, Paul said, "Governor Felix, I know you have been a judge over this nation for a long time. So I am happy to defend myself before you. 11You can learn for yourself that I went to worship in Jerusalem only twelve days ago. 12Those who are accusing me did not find me arguing with anyone in the Temple or stirring up the people in the synagogues *d* or in the city. 13They cannot prove the things they are saying against me now. 14But I will tell you this: I worship the God of our ancestors as a follower of the Way of Jesus. The Jews say that the Way of Jesus is not the right way. But I believe everything that is taught in the law of Moses and that is written in the books of the Prophets. *d* 15I have the same hope in God that they have—the hope that all people, good and bad, will surely be raised from the dead. 16This is why I always try to do what I believe is right before God and people.

17"After being away from Jerusalem for several years, I went back to bring money to my people and to offer sacrifices. 18I was doing this when they found me in the Temple. I had finished the cleansing ceremony and had not made any trouble; no people were gathering around me. 19But there were some Jews from the country of Asia who should be here, standing before you. If I have really done anything wrong, they are the ones who should accuse me. 20Or ask these Jews here if they found any wrong in me when I stood before the Jewish council in Jerusalem. 21But I did shout one thing when I stood before them: 'You are judging me today because I believe that people will rise from the dead!' "

22Felix already understood much about the Way of Jesus. He stopped the trial and said, "When commander Lysias comes here, I will decide your case." 23Felix told the officer to keep Paul guarded but to give him some freedom and to let his friends bring what he needed.

Paul Speaks to Felix and His Wife

24After some days Felix came with his wife, Drusilla, who was Jewish, and asked for Paul to be brought to him. He listened to Paul talk about believing in Christ Jesus. 25But Felix became afraid when Paul spoke about living right, self-control and the time when God will judge the

---

Verse 6   Some Greek copies add verses 6b–8a: "And we wanted to judge him by our own law. 7But the officer Lysias came and used much force to take him from us. 8And Lysias commanded those who wanted to accuse Paul to come to you."

world. He said, "Go away now. When I have more time, I will call for you." ²⁶At the same time Felix hoped that Paul would give him some money, so he often sent for Paul and talked with him.

²⁷But after two years, Felix was replaced by Porcius Festus as governor. But Felix had left Paul in prison to please the Jews.

Paul Asks to See Caesar

25 Three days after Festus became governor, he went from Caesarea to Jerusalem.

> ### Sidelight
> The Judean governor Felix was greedy, brutal and incompetent. He once killed 400 men suspected of terrorist activities – without a trial. When Paul wouldn't pay him a bribe, Felix left the apostle in jail for two years, until Felix was succeeded in office (Acts 24:1–27).

²There the leading priests and the important Jewish leaders made charges against Paul before Festus. ³They asked Festus to do them a favour. They wanted him to send Paul back to Jerusalem, because they had a plan to kill him on the way. ⁴But Festus answered that Paul would be kept in Caesarea and that he himself was returning there soon. ⁵He said, "Some of your leaders should go with me. They can accuse the man there in Caesarea, if he has really done something wrong."

⁶Festus stayed in Jerusalem another eight or ten days and then went back to Caesarea. The next day he told the soldiers to bring Paul before him. Festus was seated on the judge's seat ⁷when Paul came into the room. The Jewish people who had come from Jerusalem stood around him, making serious charges against him, which they could not prove. ⁸This is what Paul said to defend himself: "I have done nothing wrong against the Jewish law, against the Temple ᵈ or against Caesar." ᵈ

⁹But Festus wanted to please the Jews. So he asked Paul, "Do you want to go to Jerusalem for me to judge you there on these charges?"

¹⁰Paul said, "I am standing at Caesar's judgement seat now, where I should be judged. I have done nothing wrong to the Jews; you know this is true. ¹¹If I have done something wrong and the law says I must die, I do not ask to be saved from death. But if these charges are not true, then no

one can give me to them. I want Caesar to hear my case!"

¹²Festus talked about this with his advisors. Then he said, "You have asked to see Caesar, so you will go to Caesar!"

Paul Before King Agrippa

¹³A few days later King Agrippa and Bernice came to Caesarea to visit Festus. ¹⁴They stayed there for some time, and Festus told the king about Paul's case. Festus said, "There is a man that Felix left in prison. ¹⁵When I went to Jerusalem, the leading priests and the Jewish elders there made charges against him, asking me to sentence him to death. ¹⁶But I answered, 'When a man is accused of a crime, Romans do not hand him over until he has been allowed to face his accusers and defend himself against their charges.' ¹⁷So when these Jews came here to Caesarea for the trial, I did not waste time. The next day I sat on the judge's seat and commanded that the man be brought in. ¹⁸The Jews stood up and accused him, but not of any serious crime as I thought they would. ¹⁹The things they said were about their own religion and about a man named Jesus who died. But Paul said that he is still alive. ²⁰Not knowing how to find out about these questions, I asked Paul, 'Do you want to go to Jerusalem and be judged there?' ²¹But he asked to be kept in Caesarea. He wants a decision from the emperor. ⁿ So I ordered that he be held until I could send him to Caesar." ᵈ

²²Agrippa said to Festus, "I would also like to hear this man myself."

Festus said, "Tomorrow you will hear him."

²³The next day Agrippa and Bernice appeared with great show, acting like very important people. They went into the judgement room with the army leaders and the important men of Caesarea. Then Festus ordered the soldiers to bring Paul in. ²⁴Festus said, "King Agrippa and all who are gathered here with us, you see this man. All the Jewish people, here and in Jerusalem, have complained to me about him, shouting that he should not live any longer. ²⁵When I judged him, I found no reason to order his death. But since he asked to be judged by Caesar, I decided to send him. ²⁶But I have nothing definite to write to the emperor about him. So I have brought him before all of you—especially you, King Agrippa. I hope you can question him and give me something to write. ²⁷I think it is foolish to send a prisoner to Caesar without telling what charges are against him."

---

emperor   The ruler of the Roman Empire, which was almost all the known world.

Paul Defends Himself

26 Agrippa said to Paul, "You may now speak to defend yourself."

Then Paul raised his hand and began to speak. [2]He said, "King Agrippa, I am very happy to stand before you and will answer all the charges the Jewish people make against me. [3]You know so much about all the Jewish customs and the things the Jews argue about, so please listen to me patiently.

[4]"All the Jewish people know about my whole life, how I lived from the beginning in my own country and later in Jerusalem. [5]They have known me for a long time. If they want to, they can tell you that I was a good Pharisee. [d] And the Pharisees obey the laws of the Jewish religion more carefully than any other group. [6]Now I am on trial because I hope for the promise that God made to our ancestors. [7]This is the promise that the twelve tribes [d] of our people hope to receive as they serve God day and night. My king, the Jews have accused me because I hope for this same promise! [8]Why do any of you people think it is impossible for God to raise people from the dead?

[9]"I, too, thought I ought to do many things against Jesus from Nazareth. [10]And that is what I did in Jerusalem. The leading priests gave me the power to put many of God's people in jail, and when they were being killed, I agreed it was a good thing. [11]In every synagogue, [d] I often punished them and tried to make them speak against Jesus. I was so angry against them I even went to other cities to find them and punish them.

[12]"On one occasion the leading priests gave me permission and the power to go to Damascus. [13]On the way there, at noon, I saw a light from heaven. It was brighter than the sun and flashed all around me and those who were travelling with me. [14]We all fell to the ground. Then I heard a voice speaking to me in the Jewish language, [n] saying, 'Saul, Saul, why are you persecuting me? You are only hurting yourself by fighting me.' [15]I said, 'Who are you, Lord?' The Lord said, 'I am Jesus, the one you are persecuting. [16]Stand up! I have chosen you to be my servant and my witness—you will tell people the things that you have seen and the things that I will show you. This is why I have come to you today. [17]I will keep you safe from your own people and also from those who are not Jewish. I am sending you to them [18]to open their eyes so that they may turn away from darkness to the light, away from the power of Satan and to God. Then their sins can be forgiven, and they can have a place with those people who have been made holy by believing in me.'

[19]"King Agrippa, after I had this vision from heaven, I obeyed it. [20]I began telling people that they should change their hearts and lives and turn to God and do things to show they really had changed. I told this first to those in Damascus, then in Jerusalem and in every part of Judea, and also to those who are not Jewish. [21]This is why the Jews took me and were trying to kill me in the Temple. [d] [22]But God has helped me, and so I stand here today, telling all people, small and great, what I have seen. But I am saying only what Moses and the prophets [d] said would happen— [23]that the Christ [d] would die, and as the first to rise from the dead, he would bring light to the Jewish and non-Jewish people."

Paul Tries to Persuade Agrippa

[24]While Paul was saying these things to defend himself, Festus said loudly, "Paul, you are out of your mind! Too much study has driven you insane!"

[25]Paul said, "Most excellent Festus, I am not mad. My words are true and sensible. [26]King Agrippa knows about these things, and I can speak freely to him. I know he has heard about all these things, because they did not happen in a corner. [27]King Agrippa, do you believe what the prophets [d] wrote? I know you believe."

[28]King Agrippa said to Paul, "Do you think you can persuade me to become a Christian in such a short time?"

[29]Paul said, "Whether it is a short or a long time, I pray to God that not only you but every person listening to me today would be saved and be like me—except for these chains I have."

[30]Then King Agrippa, Governor Festus, Bernice and all the people sitting with them stood up [31]and left the room. Talking to each other, they said, "There is no reason why this man should die or be put in jail." [32]And Agrippa said to Festus, "We could let this man go free, but he has asked Caesar [d] to hear his case."

Paul Sails for Rome

27 It was decided that we would sail for Italy. An officer named Julius, who served in the emperor's [n] army, guarded Paul and some other prisoners. [2]We got on a ship that was from the city of Adramyttium and was about to sail to different ports in the country of Asia. Aristarchus, a man from the city of Thessalonica in Macedonia, went with us. [3]The next day we came to Sidon. Julius was very good to Paul and

---

Jewish language Hebrew or Aramaic, the languages of the Jews in the first century.
emperor The ruler of the Roman Empire, which was almost all the known world.

gave him freedom to go and visit his friends, who took care of his needs. [4]We left Sidon and sailed close to the island of Cyprus, because the wind was blowing against us. [5]We went across the sea by Cilicia and Pamphylia and landed at the city of Myra, in Lycia. [6]There the officer found a ship from Alexandria that was going to Italy, so he put us on it.

[7]We sailed slowly for many days. We had a hard time reaching Cnidus because the wind was blowing against us, and we could not go any further. So we sailed by the south side of the island of Crete near Salmone. [8]Sailing past it was hard. Then we came to a place called Fair Havens, near the city of Lasea.

[9]We had lost much time, and it was now dangerous to sail, because it was already after the Day of Cleansing.[n] So Paul warned them, [10]"Men, I can see there will be a lot of trouble on this trip. The ship, the cargo and even our lives may be lost." [11]But the captain and the owner of the ship did not agree with Paul, and the officer believed what the captain and owner of the ship said. [12]Since that harbour was not a good place for the ship to stay for the winter, most of the men decided that the ship should leave. They hoped we could go to Phoenix and stay there for the winter. Phoenix, a city on the island of Crete, had a harbour which faced south-west and north-west.

The Storm

[13]When a good wind began to blow from the south, the men on the ship thought, "This is the wind we wanted, and now we have it." So they pulled up the anchor, and we sailed very close to the island of Crete. [14]But then a very strong wind named the "northeaster" came from the island. [15]The ship was caught in it and could not sail against it. So we stopped trying and let the wind carry us. [16]When we went below a small island named Cauda, we were barely able to bring in the lifeboat. [17]After the men took the lifeboat in, they tied ropes around the ship to hold it together. The men were afraid that the ship would hit the sandbanks of Syrtis,[n] so they lowered the sail and let the wind carry the ship. [18]The next day the storm was blowing us so hard that the men threw out some of the cargo. [19]A day later with their own hands they threw out the ship's equipment. [20]When we could not see the sun or the stars for many days, and the storm was very bad, we lost all hope of being saved.

[21]After the men had gone without food for a long time, Paul stood up before them and said, "Men, you should have listened to me. You should not have sailed from Crete. Then you would not have had all this trouble and loss. [22]But now I tell you to cheer up because none of you will die. Only the ship will be lost. [23]Last night an angel came to me from the God I belong to and worship. [24]The angel said, 'Paul, do not be afraid. You must stand before Caesar.[d] And God has promised you that he will save the lives of everyone sailing with you.' [25]So men, have courage. I trust in God that everything will happen as his angel told me. [26]But we will run aground on an island."

[27]On the fourteenth night we were still being carried around in the Adriatic Sea.[n] About midnight the sailors thought we were close to land, [28]so they lowered a rope with a weight on the end of it into the water. They found that the water was 20 fathoms deep. They went a little further and lowered the rope again. It was 15 fathoms deep. [29]The sailors were afraid that we would hit the rocks, so they threw four anchors into the water and prayed for daylight to come. [30]Some of the sailors wanted to leave the ship, and they lowered the lifeboat, pretending they were throwing more anchors from the front of the ship. [31]But Paul told the officer and the other soldiers, "If these men do not stay in the ship, your lives cannot be saved." [32]So the soldiers cut the ropes and let the lifeboat fall into the water.

[33]Just before dawn Paul began persuading all the people to eat something. He said, "For the past fourteen days you have been waiting and watching and not eating. [34]Now I beg you to eat something. You need it to stay alive. None of you will lose even one hair of your heads." [35]After he said this, Paul took some bread and thanked God for it before all of them. He broke off a piece and began eating. [36]They all felt better and started eating, too. [37]There were 276 people on the ship. [38]When they had eaten all they wanted, they began making the ship lighter by throwing the grain into the sea.

The Ship is Destroyed

[39]When daylight came, the sailors saw land. They did not know what land it was, but they saw a bay with a beach and wanted to sail the ship to the beach if they could. [40]So they cut the ropes to the anchors and left the anchors in the sea. At the same time, they untied the ropes that were holding the rudders. Then they raised the front sail into the wind and sailed towards

---

Day of Cleansing   An important Jewish holy day in the autumn of the year. Bad storms arose on the sea at this time of year.
Syrtis   Shallow area in the sea near the Libyan coast.
Adriatic Sea   The sea between Greece and Italy, including the central Mediterranean.

the beach. [41]But the ship hit a sandbank. The front of the ship stuck there and could not move, but the back of the ship began to break up from the big waves.

[42]The soldiers decided to kill the prisoners so none of them could swim away and escape. [43]But Julius, the officer, wanted to let Paul live and did not allow the soldiers to kill the prisoners. Instead he ordered everyone who could swim to jump into the water first and swim to land. [44]The rest were to follow using wooden boards or pieces of the ship. And this is how all the people made it safely to land.

Sidelight Paul often experienced rough waters while sailing (Acts 27:13–44). Storms, a common occurrence in the Mediterranean Sea, made travel hazardous for wooden trading ships. Today, one Greek island, only fourteen and a half kilometres long, has 400 churches that were built by sailors who were fulfilling vows they made to God in the midst of perilous storms.

Paul on the Island of Malta

28 When we were safe on land, we learned that the island was called Malta. [2]The people who lived there were very good to us. Because it was raining and very cold, they made a fire and welcomed all of us. [3]Paul gathered a pile of sticks and was putting them on the fire when a poisonous snake came out because of the heat and bit him on the hand. [4]The people living on the island saw the snake hanging from Paul's hand and said to each other, "This man must be a murderer! He did not die in the sea, but Justice[n] does not want him to live." [5]But Paul shook the snake off into the fire and was not hurt. [6]The people thought that Paul would swell up or fall down dead. They waited and watched him for a long time, but nothing bad happened to him. So they changed their minds and said, "He is a god!"

[7]There were some fields around there owned by Publius, an important man on the island. He welcomed us into his home and was very good to us for three days. [8]Publius' father was sick with a fever and dysentery.[n] Paul went to him, prayed and put his hands on the man and healed him. [9]After this, all the other sick people on the island came to Paul, and he healed them, too. [10-11]The people on the island gave us many honours.

When we were ready to leave, three months later, they gave us the things we needed.

Paul Goes to Rome

We got on a ship from Alexandria that had stayed on the island during the winter. On the front of the ship was the sign of the twin gods.[n] [12]We stopped at Syracuse for three days. [13]From there we sailed to Rhegium. The next day a wind began to blow from the south, and a day later we came to Puteoli. [14]We found some believers there who asked us to stay with them for a week. Finally, we came to Rome. [15]The believers in Rome heard that we were there and came out as far as the Market of Appius[n] and the Three Inns[n] to meet us. When Paul saw them, he was encouraged and thanked God.

Paul in Rome

[16]When we arrived at Rome, Paul was allowed to live alone, with the soldier who guarded him.

[17]Three days later Paul sent for the Jewish leaders there. When they came together, he said, "Brothers, I have done nothing against our people or the customs of our ancestors. But I was arrested in Jerusalem and given to the Romans. [18]After they asked me many questions, they could find no reason why I should be killed. They wanted to let me go free, [19]but the Jewish people there argued against that. So I had to ask to come to Rome to have my trial before Caesar.[d] But I have no charge to bring against my own people. [20]That is why I wanted to see you and talk with you. I am bound with this chain because I believe in the hope of Israel."

[21]They answered Paul, "We have received no letters from Judea about you. None of our Jewish brothers who have come from there brought news or told us anything bad about you. [22]But we want to hear your ideas, because we know that people everywhere are speaking against this religious group."

[23]Paul and the Jewish people chose a day for a meeting and on that day many more of the Jews met with Paul at the place he was staying. He spoke to them all day long. Using the law of Moses and the prophets'[d] writings, he explained the kingdom of God, and he tried to persuade them to believe these things about Jesus. [24]Some believed what Paul said, but others did not. [25]So they argued and began leaving after Paul said one

---

Justice The people thought there was a god named Justice who would punish bad people.
dysentery A sickness like diarrhoea.
twin gods Statues of Castor and Pollux, gods in old Greek tales.
Market of Appius A town about 44 kilometres from Rome.
Three Inns A town about 48 kilometres from Rome.

more thing to them: "The Holy Spirit *d* spoke the truth to your ancestors through Isaiah the prophet, saying,

[26]'Go and tell this people:
You will listen and listen, but you will not
  understand.
You will look and look, but you will not learn.
[27]Make the minds of these people dumb.
  Shut their ears. Cover their eyes.
Otherwise, they might really understand
  what they see with their eyes
  and hear with their ears.

They might really understand in their
  minds
  and come back to me and be healed.'

Isaiah 6:9–10

[28]"I want you to know that God has also sent his salvation to those who are not Jewish, and they will listen!" [29] *n*

[30]Paul stayed two full years in his own rented house and welcomed all people who came to visit him. [31]He boldly preached about the kingdom of God and taught about the Lord Jesus Christ, and no one tried to stop him.

Verse 29 Some late Greek copies add verse 29: "After Paul said this, the Jews left. They were arguing very much with one another."

Romans

Why Read This Book:

- Understand that all people have sinned (Romans 1—3).
- Learn how Jesus Christ pays for our sins (Romans 4—8).
- Be challenged to live the Christian life (Romans 12—15).

When?

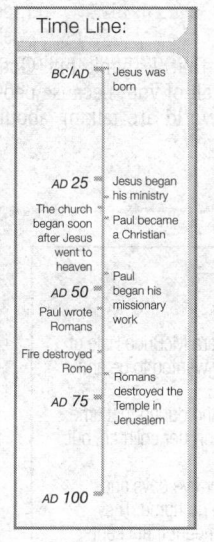

Time Line:

BC/AD	Jesus was born
AD 25	Jesus began his ministry
The church began soon after Jesus went to heaven	Paul became a Christian
AD 50	Paul began his missionary work
Paul wrote Romans	
Fire destroyed Rome	Romans destroyed the Temple in Jerusalem
AD 75	
AD 100	

Behind the Scenes:

Suppose a friend sat down with you at lunchtime and asked, out of the blue, "What do you believe?" What would you say?

Romans is the apostle Paul's answer to that question: What do you believe? For more than twenty years, he had been a missionary, spreading the good news about Jesus Christ. He wanted to visit the Roman church, but before he went, he wanted the Roman Christians to understand what he believed.

So he wrote them this letter, which many people believe is the best, most powerful summary of Christian beliefs in the Bible. It reads like a text book as it sets out to explain important principles. The letter explains how all people have sinned and how God sent Jesus to pay for those sins and make people right with God (Romans 3:22–28).

But don't think that Romans is all theory. Right from the beginning Paul highlights the real-life impact of the principles. Later in the book he deals with issues like:

- baptism
- overcoming sin
- spiritual gifts
- government
- relating to unbelievers

Romans is packed with powerful statements about God and faith. From this book we can learn how God's love for us overcomes the power of sin in our lives and how we can live lives that please God.

Where?

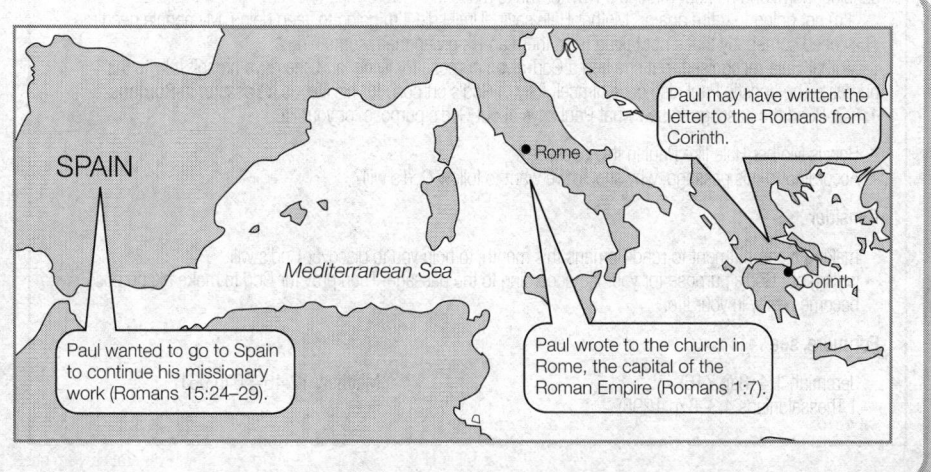

Paul may have written the letter to the Romans from Corinth.

SPAIN

Mediterranean Sea

Rome

Corinth

Paul wanted to go to Spain to continue his missionary work (Romans 15:24–29).

Paul wrote to the church in Rome, the capital of the Roman Empire (Romans 1:7).

1 From Paul, a servant of Christ Jesus. God called me to be an apostle *d* and chose me to tell the Good News. *d*

²God promised this Good News long ago through his prophets, *d* as it is written in the Holy Scriptures. *d* ³⁻⁴The Good News is about God's Son, Jesus Christ our Lord. As a man, he was born from the family of David. But through the Spirit *d* of holiness he was appointed to be God's Son with great power by rising from the dead. ⁵Through Christ, God gave me the special work of an apostle, which was to lead people of all nations to believe and obey. I do this work for him. ⁶And you who are in Rome are also called to belong to Jesus Christ.

⁷To all of you in Rome whom God loves and has called to be his holy people:

Grace and peace to you from God our Father and the Lord Jesus Christ.

A Prayer of Thanks

⁸First I want to say that I thank my God through Jesus Christ for all of you, because people everywhere in the world are talking about

GOD'S WILL

Mother Hale

"My husband and I had dreams of what we were going to do with our children," recalls Clara McBride Hale of her life in the early part of the 1900s. "We dreamed that they'd grow up and be what they wanted to be and have a good life."

But Clara's husband died when their children, Lorraine and Nathan, were five and six. And during that time, untrained women could only do domestic jobs, such as house cleaning. Clara had to support her children, but she didn't want to leave them alone while she went to work.

"So I decided to take in other people's children," Clara continues. "They were coming for five days and going home on Saturday and Sunday. But then they started saying that they didn't want to go home. They wanted to stay with me all the time. So the parents would give me extra money, and that meant that I kept them all the time."

What started as a "survival" business bloomed into a lifetime ministry for Clara, who came to be known by the children and their parents as "Mother Hale".

"I raised 40," Mother Hale recalls. "Every one of them went to college, every one of them graduated, and they all have lovely jobs. I have singers, dancers, preachers and things like that. No big names or anything, but they're happy."

In 1969, when Mother Hale was 64 years old, she decided to retire. She had raised 40 children and felt ready for someone else to take over.

"Then my daughter sent me a girl with an addict baby. Within two months, I had 22 babies living in a five-room flat. My decision to stop didn't mean anything. It seemed as though God wanted them. He kept sending them, and he kept making a way for me to make it.

"I'm not going to retire again," Mother Hale says. "Until I die, I'm going to keep doing. My people need me. They need somebody that's not taking from them and is giving them something."

Mother Hale recognised that she had a God-given purpose for living, and she gave herself fully to that purpose. The apostle Paul also gave himself fully to God's purpose for his life, as he asserts in **Romans 1:1–7**. Read the passage to see what Paul says about God's purpose for your life.

* How is Mother Hale like Paul in this passage?
* According to this passage, why should we want to follow God's will?

Consider . . .

* making a commitment to read Romans this month, to help you to discover God's will.
* writing out God's purpose for your life according to the passage. Then pray for God to make his purpose become reality in your life.

For more, see . . .

* Jeremiah 1:4–8 (p.716)
* 1 Thessalonians 4:3–8 (p.1298)

* Matthew 12:46–50 (p.961)

your faith. ⁹God, whom I serve with my whole heart by telling the Good News *d* about his Son, knows that I always mention you ¹⁰every time I pray. I pray that I will be allowed to come to you,

and this will happen if God wants it. ¹¹I want very much to see you, to give you some spiritual gift to make you strong. ¹²I mean that I want us to help each other with the faith we have. Your faith will help me, and my faith will help you. ¹³Brothers and sisters, *n* I want you to know that I planned many times to come to you, but this has not been possible. I wanted to come so that I could help you grow spiritually as I have helped the other non-Jewish people.

¹⁴I have a duty to all people—Greeks and those who are not Greeks, the wise and the foolish. ¹⁵That is why I want so much to preach the Good News to you in Rome.

¹⁶I am proud of the Good News, because it is the power God uses to save everyone who believes—to save the Jews first, and also to save those who are not Jews. ¹⁷The Good News shows how God makes people right with himself—that it begins and ends with faith. As the Scripture *d* says, "But those who are right with God will live by trusting in him." *n*

All People Have Done Wrong

¹⁸God's anger is shown from heaven against all the evil and wrong things people do. By their own evil lives they hide the truth. ¹⁹God shows his anger because some knowledge of him has been made clear to them. Yes, God has shown himself to them. ²⁰There are things about him that people cannot see—his eternal power and all the things that make him God. But since the beginning of the world those things have been easy to understand by what God has made. So people have no excuse for the bad things they do. ²¹They knew God, but they did not give glory to God or thank him. Their thinking became useless. Their foolish minds were filled with darkness. ²²They

said they were wise, but they became fools. ²³They traded the glory of God who lives for ever for the worship of idols made to look like earthly people, birds, animals and snakes.

²⁴Because they did these things, God left them and let them go their sinful way, wanting only to do evil. As a result, they became full of sexual sin, using their bodies wrongly with each other. ²⁵They traded the truth of God for a lie. They worshipped and served what had been created instead of the God who created those things, who should be praised for ever. Amen.

²⁶Because people did those things, God left them and let them do the shameful things they wanted to do. Women stopped having natural sex and started having sex with other women. ²⁷In the same way, men stopped having natural sex and began wanting each other. Men did shameful things with other men, and in their bodies they received the punishment for those wrongs.

²⁸People did not think it was important to have a true knowledge of God. So God left them and allowed them to have their own worthless thinking and to do things they should not do. ²⁹They are filled with every kind of sin, evil, selfishness and hatred. They are full of jealousy, murder, fighting, lying and thinking the worst about each other. They gossip ³⁰and say evil things about each other. They hate God. They are rude and conceited and boast about themselves. They invent ways of doing evil. They do not obey their parents. ³¹They are foolish, they do not keep their promises, and they show no kindness or mercy to others. ³²They know God's law says that those who live like this should die. But they themselves not only continue to do these evil things, they applaud others who do them.

You People Also are Sinful

2 If you think you can judge others, you are wrong. When you judge them, you are really judging yourself guilty, because you do the same things they do. ²God judges those who do wrong things, and we know that his judging is right. ³You judge those who do wrong, but you do wrong yourselves. Do you think you will be able to escape the judgement of God? ⁴He has been very kind and patient, waiting for you to change, but you think nothing of his kindness. Perhaps you do not understand that God's kindness is meant to lead you to change your hearts and lives. ⁵But you are stubborn and refuse to change,

Brothers and sisters Although the Greek text says "brothers" here and throughout this book, Paul's words were meant for the entire church, both men and women.
"But those . . . him." Quotation from Habakkuk 2:4.

so you are making your own punishment even greater on the day he shows his anger. On that day everyone will see God's right judgements. ⁶God will reward or punish every person for what that person has done. ⁷Some people, by always continuing to do good, live for God's glory, for honour and for life that has no end. God will give them life for ever. ⁸But other people are selfish. They refuse to follow truth and, instead, follow evil. God will give them his punishment and anger. ⁹He will give trouble and suffering to everyone who does evil—to the Jews first and also to those who are not Jews. ¹⁰But he will give glory, honour and peace to everyone who does good— to the Jews first and also to those who are not Jews. ¹¹For God judges all people in the same way.

¹²People who do not have the law *d* and who are sinners will be lost, although they do not have the law. And, in the same way, those who have the law and are sinners will be judged by the law. ¹³Hearing the law does not make people right with God. It is those who obey the law who will be right with him. ¹⁴(Those who are not Jews do not have the law, but when they freely do what the law commands, they are the law for themselves. This is true even though they do not have the law. ¹⁵They show that in their hearts they know what is right and wrong, just as the law commands. And they show this by their thoughts. Sometimes their thoughts tell them they did wrong, and sometimes their thoughts tell them they did right.) ¹⁶All these things will happen on the day when God, through Christ Jesus, will judge people's secret thoughts. The Good News *d* that I preach says this.

PARENTS

Funny Folks

Tom needed an excuse to use his parents' car to take his friends for a spin. "Dad, can I borrow your car to pick up some school notes from my mate's house?"

His dad said no, so he moved on to his mum but, "Sorry son, your dad said no so I need to stand by his decision."

Furious that he didn't get his own way, Tom waited until his mum and dad were settled in front of the TV, then sneaked out, took the car and picked up his friends.

Later, there was a knock on the door. As Tom's parents looked into the face of a policeman they learned that he'd pulled Tom over for reckless driving and wanted to confirm that the car wasn't stolen. Tom was in BIG trouble!

Looking back on it, Tom admitted he had known his parents were right to say no, and he wished he'd listened. Instead of resenting the way they made decisions together, he became happy and relieved that they were a team he could trust in.

Tom learned a big lesson about obeying your parents even if you're angry at their decision. If they love you, they want the best for you, and you don't need to keep questioning or fighting against their decisions.

Read **Romans 1:28–32**.

- How could Tom have better dealt with the dilemma he faced?
- Why does the Bible tell us that we should obey our parents?

Consider . . .

- talking to your parents about taking on a little more responsibility in certain areas, for example, managing your money or time.
- your reactions towards your parents and try making a bigger effort to listen to their point of view.

For more see . . .

- Exodus 20:12 (p.79)
- Colossians 3:20 (p.1294)
- Ephesians 6:1 (p.1276)

The Jews and the Law

[17]What about you? You call yourself a Jew. You trust in the law of Moses and boast that you are close to God. [18]You know what he wants you to do and what is important, because you have learned the law. [19]You think you are a guide for the blind and a light for those who are in darkness. [20]You think you can show foolish people what is right and teach those who know nothing. You have the law; so you think you know everything and have all truth. [21]You teach others, so why don't you teach yourself? You tell others not to steal, but you steal. [22]You say that others must not take part in adultery, [d] but you are guilty of that sin. You hate idols, but you steal from temples. [23]You boast about having God's law, but you bring shame to God by breaking his law, [24]just as the Scriptures [d] say: "Those who are not Jews speak against God's name because of you." [n]

[25]If you follow the law, your circumcision [d] has meaning. But if you break the law, it is as if you were never circumcised. [26]People who are not Jews are not circumcised, but if they do what the law says, it is as if they were circumcised. [27]You Jews have the written law and circumcision, but you break the law. So those who are not circumcised in their bodies, but still obey the law, will show that you are guilty. [28]They can do this because a person is not a true Jew if he is only a Jew in his physical body; true circumcision is not only on the outside of the body. [29]A person is a Jew only if he is a Jew inside; true circumcision is done in the heart by the Spirit, [d] not by the works of the written law. Such a person gets praise from God rather than from people.

3 So, do Jews have anything that other people do not have? Is there anything special about being circumcised? [d] [2]Yes, of course, there is in every way. The most important thing is this: God trusted the Jews with his teachings. [3]If some Jews were not faithful to him, will that stop God from doing what he promised? [4]No! God will continue to be true even when every person is false. As the Scriptures [d] say:

"So you will be shown to be right when you
        speak,
    and you will win your case."   Psalm 51:4

[5]When we do wrong, that shows more clearly that God is right. So can we say that God is wrong to punish us? (I am talking as people might talk.) [6]No! If God could not punish us, he could not judge the world.

[7]A person might say, "When I lie, it really gives him glory, because my lie shows God's truth. So why am I judged a sinner?" [8]It would be the same to say, "We should do evil so that good will come." Some people find fault with us and say we teach this, but they are wrong and deserve the punishment they will receive.

All People are Guilty

[9]So are we Jews better than others? No! We have already said that Jews and those who are not Jews are all guilty of sin. [10]As the Scriptures [d] say:

"There is no one who always does what is
        right,
    not even one.
[11] There is no one who understands.
    There is no one who looks to God for help.
[12]All have turned away.
    Together, everyone has become useless.
    There is no one who does anything good;
        there is not even one."   Psalm 14:1–3
[13]"Their throats are like open graves;
    they use their tongues for telling lies."
                                        Psalm 5:9
"Their words are like snake poison."   Psalm 140:3
[14] "Their mouths are full of cursing and hate."
                                        Psalm 10:7
[15]They are always ready to kill people.
[16] Everywhere they go they cause ruin and
        misery.
[17]They don't know how to live in peace."
                                        Isaiah 59:7–8
[18] "They have no fear of God."   Psalm 36:1

[19]We know that the law's commands are for those who have the law. [d] This stops all excuses and brings the whole world under God's judgement, [20]because no one can be made right with God by following the law. The law only shows us our sin.

How God Makes People Right

[21]But God has a way to make people right with him without the law, and he has now shown us that way which the law and the prophets [d] told us about. [22]God makes people right with himself through their faith in Jesus Christ. This is true for all who believe in Christ, because all people are the same: [23]all have sinned and are not good enough for God's glory, [24]and all need to be made right with God by his grace, which is a free gift. They need to be made free from sin through Jesus Christ. [25]God gave him as a way to forgive sin through faith in the blood of Jesus' death. This showed that God always does what is right and fair, as in the past when he was patient and did not punish people for their sins. [26]And God gave Jesus to show today that he does what is right. God did this so he could judge rightly and so he could make right any person who has faith in Jesus.

"Those . . . you."   Quotation from Isaiah 52:5; Ezekiel 36:20.

²⁷So do we have a reason to boast about ourselves? No! And why not? It is the way of faith that stops all boasting, not the way of trying to obey the law. ²⁸A person is made right with God through faith, not through obeying the law. ²⁹Is God only the God of the Jews? Is he not also the God of those who are not Jews? ³⁰Of course he is, because there is only one God. He will make Jews right with him by their faith, and he will also make those who are not Jews right with him through their faith. ³¹So do we destroy the law by following the way of faith? No! Faith causes us to be what the law truly wants.

The Example of Abraham

4 So what can we say that Abraham,ⁿ the father of our people, learned about faith? ²If Abraham was made right by the things he did, he had a reason to boast. But this is not God's view, ³because the Scripture ᵈ says, "Abraham believed God, and God accepted Abraham's faith, and that faith made him right with God." ⁿ

⁴When people work, their pay is not given as a gift, but as something earned. ⁵But people cannot do any work that will make them right with God. So they must trust in him, who makes even evil people right in his sight. Then God accepts their faith, and that makes them right with him. ⁶David said the same thing. He said that people are truly blessed when God, without paying attention to good deeds, makes people right with himself.
⁷"Happy are they
　　whose sins are forgiven,
　　whose wrongs are pardoned.

Abraham　Most respected ancestor of the Jews. Every Jew hoped to see Abraham.
"Abraham . . . God."　Quotation from Genesis 15:6.

FORGIVENESS

Only a Car

Uncle Charles let Dean borrow his new, red Mazda MX5 for the New Year Disco. It was less than two weeks old.

The magical night ended much too early for Dean, about 3 a.m., when he dropped off his partner at her house and started the long drive across town to home. The next thing he knew, he was waking up, skidding madly across the deserted suburban road, scraping the side of the car against a crash barrier before he could come to a stop.

He drove home, parked the car against the kerb, and sat on the front steps, waiting for morning to come. His stomach was in a knot. He didn't even try to sleep.

At 8 a.m., Dean stood next to his uncle as he silently examined the wide scar that now marred the door of his new car. Uncle Charles's breathing was slow and measured. The silence seemed to go on for ever.

How could Dean ever make this up to him? How could he pay for the damage or heal the hurt he saw in his face?

Finally, the older man placed his hand on Dean's shoulder and gave it a reassuring squeeze. He shrugged, smiled and said, "It's only a car."

At that moment, Dean knew something of the sort of forgiveness Paul was talking about when he wrote **Romans 3:21–28**.

• How is Uncle Charles's act of forgiveness like the forgiveness that Paul talks about in this passage?
• According to the passage, how do we receive God's forgiveness?

Consider . . .

• writing about a way someone has hurt you recently and then tearing up the paper and forgiving the hurt.
• talking to a friend you've hurt and asking for forgiveness.

For more, see . . .

• Psalm 103:10–13 (p.559)
• Hebrews 8:10–13 (p.1337)
• Luke 6:27–36 (1048)

[8]Happy is the person
    whom the Lord does not consider guilty."

Psalm 32:1–2

[9]Is this blessing only for those who are circumcised [d] or also for those who are not circumcised? We have already said that God accepted Abraham's faith and that faith made him right with God. [10]So how did this happen? Did God accept Abraham before or after he was circumcised? It was before his circumcision. [11]Abraham was circumcised to show that he was right with God through faith before

he was circumcised. So Abraham is the father of all those who believe but are not circumcised; he is the father of all believers who are accepted as being right with God. [12]And Abraham is also the father of those who have been circumcised and who live following the faith that our father Abraham had before he was circumcised.

God Keeps His Promise

[13]Abraham [n] and his descendants [d] received the promise that they would get the whole world.

Abraham   Most respected ancestor of the Jews. Every Jew hoped to see Abraham.

FAITH

Free Approval

Ed really liked Julie. In fact, he was totally crazy about her.

Julie was funny, clever, beautiful – everything Ed wanted in a girl. For weeks, Ed watched Julie as she went from office to office. He watched her while she ate lunch. He watched her as she walked home from work.

Finally, after weeks of planning, he worked up the courage to ask her out.

"Hello, Ed. What's up?" Julie asked with that smile Ed loved so much.

"Er, I was wondering . . ." he said, clearing his throat. "I was wondering if you'd like to go out on Friday night." Ed couldn't believe that his heart could pound so hard.

"Certainly, I'd love to," Julie responded without missing a beat.

That was the first of many evenings together. Julie really liked Ed. He was funny and sensitive. And, of course, Ed liked Julie, but he couldn't believe that she could be interested in him.

As they continued to go out together, Ed kept doing things for Julie to keep her interested. He bought her gifts. He offered to run errands for her. One day, he even offered her his car so that she wouldn't have to walk to work.

"Ed, I don't want your car," Julie said.

"It's OK, really," Ed assured her. "I want you to have it."

"No, Ed, you don't understand." Julie took a deep breath. "You don't need to try so hard. I already like you. You really don't need to do anything to win my love. So just relax, all right? You're starting to drive me mad."

Ed felt embarrassed. "It's just that it's hard to believe," he said.

"Well, believe it," Julie said, grinning, and she kissed him.

Ed had a difficult time believing that Julie could love him unless he did things to earn her affection.
Romans 4:1–12 tells a similar story about Abraham, who discovered that God's favour is also based on believing. Read the passage to see why we can't earn God's approval through our actions.

* How does Ed's response to Julie differ from Abraham's response to God?
* According to the passage, what does God require for you to have a relationship with him?

Consider . . .

* thinking of ways in which you might try to earn God's love and then asking God to help you to accept his love by faith.
* writing out how you think God sees you, and having your youth leader do the same. Compare the two descriptions, and ask God to increase your faith to believe the truth about how he sees you.

For more, see . . .

* Genesis 15:1–6 (p.16)
* Ephesians 2:8–9 (p.1270)
* Galatians 3:6–27 (p.1260)

He did not receive that promise through the law, *d* but through being right with God by his faith. [14]If people could receive what God promised by following the law, then faith is worthless. And God's promise to Abraham is worthless, [15]because the law can only bring God's anger. But if there is no law, there is nothing to disobey.

[16]So people receive God's promise by having faith. This happens so the promise can be a free gift. Then all of Abraham's children can have that promise. It is not only for those who live under the law of Moses but for anyone who lives with faith like that of Abraham, who is the father of us all. [17]As it is written in the Scriptures: *d* "I am making you a father of many nations." *n* This is true before God, the God Abraham believed, the God who gives life to the dead and who creates something out of nothing.

[18]There was no hope that Abraham would have children. But Abraham believed God and continued hoping, and so he became the father of many nations. As God told him, "Your descendants also will be too many to count."*n* [19]Abraham was almost 100 years old, much past the age for having children, and Sarah could not have children. Abraham thought about all this, but his faith in God did not become weak. [20]He never doubted that God would keep his promise, and he never stopped believing. He grew stronger in his faith and gave praise to God. [21]Abraham felt sure that God was able to do what he had promised. [22]So, "God accepted Abraham's faith, and that faith made him right with God." *n* [23]Those words ("God accepted Abraham's faith") were written not only for Abraham [24]but also for us. God will accept us also because we believe in the One who raised Jesus our Lord from the dead. [25]Jesus was given to die for our sins, and he was raised from the dead to make us right with God.

Right with God

5 Since we have been made right with God by our faith, we have peace with God. This happened through our Lord Jesus Christ, [2]who has brought us into that blessing of God's grace that we now enjoy. And we are happy because of the hope we have of sharing God's glory. [3]We also have joy with our troubles, because we know that these troubles produce patience. [4]And patience produces character, and character produces hope. [5]And this hope will never disappoint us, because God has poured out his love to fill our hearts. He gave us his love through the Holy Spirit, *d* whom God has given to us.

[6]When we were unable to help ourselves, at the moment of our need, Christ died for us, although we were living against God. [7]Very few people will die to save the life of someone else although perhaps for a good person someone might possibly die. [8]But God shows his great love for us in this way: Christ died for us while we were still sinners.

[9]So through Christ we will surely be saved from God's anger, because we have been made right with God by the blood of Christ's death. [10]While we were God's enemies, he made friends with us through the death of his Son. Surely, now that we are his friends, he will save us through his Son's life. [11]And not only that, now we are also very happy in God through our Lord Jesus Christ. Through him we are now God's friends again.

Adam and Christ Compared

[12]Sin came into the world because of what one man did, and with sin came death. This is why everyone must die—because everyone sinned. [13]Sin was in the world before the law of Moses, *d* but sin is not counted against us as breaking a command when there is no law. [14]But from the time of Adam to the time of Moses, everyone had to die, even those who had not sinned by breaking a command, as Adam had.

Adam was like the One who was coming in the future. [15]But God's free gift is not like Adam's sin. Many people died because of the sin of that one man. But the grace from God was much greater; many people received God's gift of life by the grace of the one man, Jesus Christ. [16]After Adam sinned once, he was judged guilty. But the gift of God is different. God's free gift came after many sins, and it makes people right with God. [17]One man sinned, and so death ruled all people because of that one man. But now those people who accept God's full grace and the great gift of being made right with him will surely have true life and rule through the one man, Jesus Christ.

[18]So as one sin of Adam brought the punishment of death to all people, one good act that

---

Sidelight　Adam – the man in the Garden of Eden (Genesis 1—4, p.2) – seems to get blamed for more than his share of sin in Romans 5:12–21. But don't feel too sorry for him. Paul uses Adam to represent all people. That's not surprising when you know that "adam" means "human".

"I . . . nations."　Quotation from Genesis 17:5.
"Your . . . count."　Quotation from Genesis 15:5.
"God . . . God."　Quotation from Genesis 15:6.

Christ did makes all people right with God. And that brings true life for all. [19]One man disobeyed God, and many became sinners. In the same way, one man obeyed God, and many will be made right. [20]The law came to make sin worse. But when sin grew worse, God's grace increased. [21]Sin once used death to rule us, but God gave people more of his grace so that grace could rule by making people right with him. And this brings life for ever through Jesus Christ our Lord.

Dead to Sin but Alive in Christ

6 So do you think we should continue sinning so that God will give us even more grace? [2]No! We died to our old sinful lives, so how can we continue living with sin? [3]Did you forget that all of us became part of Christ when we were baptised? [d] We shared his death in our baptism. [4]When we were baptised, we were buried with Christ and shared his death. So, just as Christ was

raised from the dead by the wonderful power of the Father, we also can live a new life.

[5]Christ died, and we have been joined with him by dying too. So we will also be joined with him by rising from the dead as he did. [6]We know that our old life died with Christ on the cross so that our sinful selves would have no power over us and we would not be slaves to sin. [7]Anyone who has died is made free from sin's control.

[8]If we died with Christ, we know we will also live with him. [9]Christ was raised from the dead, and we know that he cannot die again. Death has no power over him now. [10]Yes, when Christ died, he died to defeat the power of sin just once— enough for all time. He now has a new life, and his new life is with God. [11]In the same way, you should see yourselves as being dead to the power of sin and alive with God through Christ Jesus.

[12]So, do not let sin control your life here on earth so that you do what your sinful self wants

FRIENDS

What Are Friends For?

Sometimes Liz got frustrated with her friends. It seemed as though she was always having to bail them out of something.

Take Christine for example. She was bottom in algebra. And Nancy had just broken up with her boyfriend and was depressed all the time. Linda was gaining weight like mad, and all she did was complain about it and go on eating.

As if that weren't enough, last week all three of these friends had gone to a party and had got drunk. Liz had to drive them home to make sure that they got home safely.

Sometimes it seemed as though Liz's friends were trying to cause her problems. It was all getting to be too much. Too much concern, too much pain.

Perhaps she should just find new friends. It would certainly make her life easier. But . . .

"Hello, Liz!" Christine said, setting her tray down beside Liz's at the cafeteria table. "This algebra is impossible. Can you help me?"

This was it. The true test. Was Liz strong enough? She gathered her courage, took a deep breath, paused and said, "Sure, Christine. What are friends for?" And she meant it.

Liz learned that friendship means commitment, even when friends disappoint you.

Romans 5:1–19 calls God our friend. Read the passage to discover how committed he is to us.

* How is Liz's friendship with her friends like God's friendship with us in Jesus Christ?
* How can you model your friendship with God in human friendships?

Consider . . .

* writing down the names of three friends and praying for them each day this week.
* writing a card, buying flowers or doing a favour for a friend, just to say "I'm committed to you".

For more, see . . .

* Job 2:11–13 (p.471)
* John 15:13–16 (p.1125)

* Proverbs 17:17 (p.604)

to do. [13]Do not offer the parts of your body to serve sin, as things to be used in doing evil. Instead, offer yourselves to God as people who have died and now live. Offer the parts of your body to God to be used in doing good. [14]Sin will not be your master, because you are not under law but under God's grace.

Be Slaves of Righteousness

[15]So what should we do? Should we sin because we are under grace and not under law? No! [16]Surely you know that when you give yourselves like slaves to obey someone, then you are really slaves of that person. The person you obey is your master. You can follow sin, which brings spiritual death, or you can obey God, which makes you right with him. [17]In the past you were slaves to sin—sin controlled you. But thank God, you fully obeyed the things that you were taught. [18]You were made free from sin, and now you are slaves to goodness. [19]I use this example because this is hard for you to understand. In the past you offered the parts of your body to be slaves to sin and evil; you lived only for evil. In the same way now you must give yourselves to be slaves of goodness. Then you will live only for God.

[20]In the past you were slaves to sin, and goodness did not control you. [21]You did evil things, and now you are ashamed of them. Those things only bring death. [22]But now you are free from sin

FREEDOM

With Freedom Comes Responsibility

It seemed like every time something good came along Paul's parents would tell him he couldn't do it, as he was "too young". He was too young to stay out late, too young to drink at parties, too young to have a girlfriend. But as Paul got older, his parents were running out of excuses to tell him what he could and couldn't do.

Opportunities were coming his way – parties every weekend where alcohol was on tap. If he dressed right, Paul found he could pass for eighteen and get into a nightclub. Some of his mates were driving now – they didn't have to leave early for parents to pick them up or even get the last bus home – they could stay out all night!

If he was honest, Paul knew that his parents didn't like the way he was living. And he also knew that people at his church would struggle with it too. But he'd decided to get the most out of life – he'd show his mates that being a Christian meant he could still do everything they did!

After a particularly heavy session, Paul was struggling to stay awake at his youth group. They were reading through Romans and his youth leader said something that got through his headache.

"As you get older you will get more freedom from your parents and you're going to face choices. Will you decide to push the boundaries God has given us? With freedom comes responsibility. Will you abuse the freedom you get or will you take responsibility for how you live?" Paul knew that he needed to decide.

Read **Romans 6:1–12**.

* What does this passage say about the freedom God has given us? What responsibilities do Christians have?
* What decision has Paul got to make?

Consider . . .

* writing the words "I AM FREE TO DO GOOD" right across the middle of a piece of paper. Around it write about the freedom that you're going to get as you get older – driving, drinking, staying out later, college, etc. With a different-coloured pen, write next to each freedom how you can use it for some good, e.g. drinking responsibly to set an example for your mates.
* making a promise with a friend to pray for each other that as you get older you'll take your responsibilities seriously and live life God's way.

For more, see . . .

* Proverbs 4:20–27 (p.593)
* Romans 12:2 (p.1204)

and have become slaves of God. This brings you a life that is only for God, and this gives you life for ever. [23]When people sin, they earn what sin pays—death. But God gives us a free gift—life for ever in Christ Jesus our Lord.

An Example from Marriage

7 Brothers and sisters, all of you understand the law of Moses. *d* So surely you know that the law rules over people only while they are alive. [2]For example, a woman must stay married to her husband as long as he is alive. But if her husband dies, she is free from the law of marriage. [3]But if she marries another man while her husband is still alive, the law says she is guilty of adultery. *d* But if her husband dies, she is free from the law of marriage. Then if she marries another man, she is not guilty of adultery.

[4]In the same way, my brothers and sisters, your old selves died, and you became free from the law through the body of Christ. This happened so that you might belong to someone else—the One who was raised from the dead—and so that we might be used in service to God. [5]In the past, we were ruled by our sinful selves. The law made us want to do sinful things that controlled our bodies, so the things we did were bringing us death. [6]In the past, the law held us like prisoners, but our old selves died and we were made free from the law. So now we serve God in a new way with the Spirit, *d* and not in the old way with written rules.

Our Fight Against Sin

[7]You might think I am saying that sin and the law *d* are the same thing. That is not true. But the law was the only way I could learn what sin meant. I would never have known what it means to want to take something belonging to someone else if the law had not said, "You must not want to take your neighbour's things." *n* [8]And sin found a way to use that command and cause me to want all kinds of things I should not want. But without the law, sin has no power. [9]I was alive before I knew the law. But when the law's command came to me, then sin began to live, [10]and I died. The command was meant to bring life, but for me it brought death. [11]Sin found a way to fool me by using the command to make me die.

[12]So the law is holy, and the command is holy and right and good. [13]Does this mean that something that is good brought death to me? No! Sin used something that is good to bring death to me. This happened so that I could see what sin is really like; the command was used to show that sin is very evil.

The War Within Us

[14]We know that the law is spiritual, but I am not spiritual since sin rules me as if I were its slave. [15]I do not understand the things I do. I do not do what I want to do, and I do the things I hate. [16]And if I do not want to do the hated things I do, that means I agree that the law is good. [17]But I am not really the one who is doing these hated things; it is sin living in me that does them. [18]Yes, I know that nothing good lives in me—I mean nothing good lives in the part of me that is earthly and sinful. I want to do the things that are good, but I do not do them. [19]I do not do the good things I want to do, but I do the bad things I do not want to do. [20]So if I do things I do not want to do, then I am not the one doing them. It is sin living in me that does those things.

[21]So I have learned this rule: when I want to do good, evil is there with me. [22]In my mind, I am happy with God's law. [23]But I see another law working in my body, which makes war against the law that my mind accepts. That other law working in my body is the law of sin, and it makes me its prisoner. [24]What a miserable man I am! Who will save me from this body that brings me death? [25]I thank God for saving me through Jesus Christ our Lord!

So in my mind I am a slave to God's law, but in my sinful self I am a slave to the law of sin.

Be Ruled by the Spirit

8 So now, those who are in Christ Jesus are not judged guilty. [2]Through Christ Jesus the law of the Spirit *d* that brings life made me free from the law that brings sin and death. [3]The law was without power, because the law was made weak by our sinful selves. But God did what the law could not do. He sent his own Son to earth with the same human life that others use for sin. By sending his Son to be an offering to pay for sin, God used a human life to destroy sin. [4]He did this so that we could be the kind of people the law correctly wants us to be. Now we do not live following our sinful selves, but we live following the Spirit.

[5]Those who live following their sinful selves think only about things that their sinful selves want. But those who live following the Spirit are thinking about the things the Spirit wants them to do. [6]If people's thinking is controlled by the sinful self, there is death. But if their thinking is controlled by the Spirit, there is life and peace. [7]When people's thinking is controlled by the sinful self, they are against God, because they refuse to obey God's law and really are not even able to

---

"You . . . things." Quotation from Exodus 20:17.

obey God's law. [8]Those people who are ruled by their sinful selves cannot please God.

[9]But you are not ruled by your sinful selves. You are ruled by the Spirit, if that Spirit of God really lives in you. But the person who does not have the Spirit of Christ does not belong to Christ. [10]Your body will always be dead because of sin. But if Christ is in you, then the Spirit gives you life, because Christ made you right with God.

[11]God raised Jesus from the dead, and if God's Spirit is living in you, he will also give life to your bodies that die. God is the One who raised Christ from the dead, and he will give life through his Spirit that lives in you.

[12]So, my brothers and sisters, we must not be ruled by our sinful selves or live the way our sinful selves want. [13]If you use your lives to do the wrong things your sinful selves want, you

DRUGS AND ALCOHOL

Not Alone . . .

Seven years, five months, three days. That's how long Sharon had been sober. Counting today. And she didn't mind talking about it to her fellow Alcoholics Anonymous members. It helped her to stick at recovering.

"I started drinking when I was still at school," she explained. "But I didn't start abusing it until I was in college. By the time I was out of education and starting a career, I was an alcoholic."

Sharon went on to tell how a marriage and the addition of two children didn't change her drinking habits much. "I managed to keep up with my responsibilities, both at home and at work," she said. "As long as I did that, I convinced myself that I had it under control."

But then things changed. A messy divorce. Trouble at work. And a daughter who almost died from rheumatic fever.

"I began to drink more often – for comfort, and sometimes, to forget. Eventually, events in my life began to blur together. I was never sober.

"And the worse I felt about myself the more I drank. Finally, I just wanted to die. So I tried to drink myself to death. Five days later I woke up in a hospital room attached to a load of machines. The doctors say that I didn't even know who I was. I lay there and cried. I couldn't eat. I couldn't sleep. I was a failure. I couldn't even kill myself properly." Sharon pulled a tissue from the box beside her. The session leader motioned her to continue.

"Then," she went on, "the hospital chaplain walked in, and there was this woman with him. They both just sat down. And the woman asked, 'Do you want to give up drinking?'"

Now Sharon's tears came in full flood. "I just cried like a baby. I wanted to give up, but I didn't know how! Then she said, 'You don't have to do it alone. You've got me and the chaplain here and a whole flock of people willing to help. And you've got God, too, love. Don't forget about God'."

Sharon blew her nose on a tissue and looked around at the faces of her friends. "For the first time I realised that I wasn't alone. And I haven't had a drink since that day – all because you, and God, are keeping me sober."

Sharon learned that she wasn't alone in her struggle. And God made a difference in her life. The apostle Paul made a similar discovery. Read about it in **Romans 7:14–25**.

* How is Sharon's addiction like the "battle" that Paul describes?
* In what ways does God show that he is with you when you're pressured to use alcohol or drugs?

Consider . . .

* encouraging a friend who is dealing with issues like Sharon's to seek skilled help.
* finding an appropriate support group in your community if you struggle with a drinking or drug problem. Your minister or a church leader can help you.

For more, see . . .

* Proverbs 23:29–32 (p.610)
* Luke 21:34–36 (p.1087)
* Isaiah 5:11–12 (p.644)

will die spiritually. But if you use the Spirit's help to stop doing the wrong things you do with your body, you will have true life.

¹⁴The true children of God are those who let God's Spirit lead them. ¹⁵The Spirit we received does not make us slaves again to fear: it makes us children of God. With that Spirit we cry out, "Father". *n* ¹⁶And the Spirit himself joins with our spirits to say we are God's children. ¹⁷If we are God's children, we will receive blessings from God together with Christ. But we must suffer as Christ suffered so that we will have glory as Christ has glory.

Our Future Glory

¹⁸The sufferings we have now are nothing compared to the great glory that will be shown to us. ¹⁹Everything God made is waiting with excitement for God to show his children's glory completely. ²⁰Everything God made was changed to become useless, not by its own wish but because God wanted it and because all along there was this hope: ²¹that everything God made would be set free from ruin to have the freedom and glory that belong to God's children.

²²We know that everything God made has been waiting until now in pain, like a woman

"Father"   Literally, "Abba, Father". Jewish children called their fathers "Abba".

SPIRITUAL GROWTH

Power to Change

Rick was a young guy who had always been self-centred and rude. Many people found him hard to get on with and even a little scary. He hung around with friends who encouraged him to be a bully and together they would torment the other pupils at their school. He even terrified members of his own family, who walked on eggshells to keep the peace.

One day his parents sent him on a Christian camp. He was furious at having to go and threatened to leave home and never come back again. But despite all the threats, he went to the camp, as they wanted. At least, he thought, he didn't have to be with his family for a whole week . . . and who knows what trouble he could get himself into without them around!

Whilst Rick was at the camp, he was surprised to meet people who loved Jesus but were still funny, cool and interesting. One night, he went to one of the meetings and a huge transformation occurred. He gave his life to God. Rick instantly felt different on the inside – all the hate and anger he'd felt for so long suddenly weren't there!

When he came home, his family couldn't believe the immediate change in him. They could even see that something was different about him before he'd got down the garden path! At school he was sometimes tempted to fall back into old habits and behave in ways he knew were wrong. But he could feel something had altered inside and he knew that everything that was happening in him was good.

Read **Romans 8:6–17**. The passage explains how – just like Rick – when we become Christians, some amazing changes can take place in our lives.

* According to the passage, what changes take place in us when we become Christians?
* Can you tell when other people have the Spirit of God "living" in them (verse 11) as people could with Rick?

Consider . . .

* what changes you have noticed in yourself or in other people since you or they became Christians.
* what areas of your life still need the Holy Spirit's work. If you don't already pray regularly with someone, ask someone to be a prayer partner with you so you can help each other be changed by God's power.

For more, see . . .

* Psalm 1:1–3 (p.500)
* Hebrews 12:1–13 (p.1343)
* Colossians 3:1–10 (p.1292)

ready to give birth. [23]Not only the world, but we also have been waiting with pain inside us. We have the Spirit [d] as the first part of God's promise. So we are waiting for God to finish making us his own children, which means our bodies will be made free. [24]We were saved, and we have this hope. If we see what we are waiting for, that is not really hope. People do not hope for something they already have. [25]But we are hoping for something we do not have yet, and we are waiting for it patiently.

[26]Also, the Spirit helps us with our weakness. We do not know how to pray as we should. But the Spirit himself speaks to God for us, even begs God for us with deep feelings that words cannot explain. [27]God can see what is in people's hearts. And he knows what is in the mind of the Spirit, because the Spirit speaks to God for his people in the way God wants.

[28]We know that in everything God works for the good of those who love him. They are the people he called, because that was his plan. [29]God knew them before he made the world, and he decided that they would be like his Son so that Jesus would be the firstborn [n] of many brothers. [30]God planned for them to be like

firstborn   Here this probably means that Christ was the first in God's family to share God's glory.

PATIENCE

Looking Back

Patrick had been a Christian for about six months before the problems started.

What problems? "Well, I lost my job," Patrick recalls. "Then the transmission on my car packed up, and I had no money to repair it. But that wasn't the real problem. My girlfriend broke up with me. I really wanted to marry this girl, but she said that I wasn't what she wanted in a husband. That really hurt."

Before he had become a Christian at the age of eighteen, Patrick had lived a wild lifestyle, filled with drinking and taking drugs and sleeping with girlfriends.

"I came to Christ to get away from all that," he recalls. "But when all these problems started, I began to feel really insecure. It was all I could do not to go out and get drunk or call up one of my old girlfriends. I felt gross inside. I began to wonder whether I was really a Christian."

But Patrick didn't go back to his old lifestyle. Even though he didn't understand why all these things were happening to him, he knew that God was in control. So he waited.

"Things didn't get better right away," Patrick says, "but I knew I had made the right decision. And that helped me to believe even more that, if I was patient, God would come through for me. And he did!"

Patrick and his girlfriend got back together, and he got a new job – better than the other one. Now Patrick knows the value of obeying God even when you don't know what God is doing.

Patrick learned that becoming like Christ takes patience. Paul talked about how all creation is waiting patiently for us to become like Christ. Read why in **Romans 8:22–30**.

* How does Patrick demonstrate the patience that the passage describes?
* According to the passage, what is God's ultimate purpose for you? Why do we need patience to wait for his purpose to be fulfilled?

Consider . . .

* dreaming about the kind of person you want to be ten years from now, then asking God to give you the patience to let him make you into the person he wants you to be.
* working on a project that takes a long time to finish, such as a quilt or a model ship. Use the experience to learn more about patience.

For more, see . . .

* Lamentations 3:25–26 (p.783)
* James 5:7–11 (p.1352)
* Hebrews 11:8–16 (p.1342)

his Son; and those he planned to be like his Son, he also called; and those he called, he also made right with him; and those he made right, he also glorified.

God's Love in Christ Jesus

³¹So what should we say about this? If God is with us, no one can defeat us. ³²He did not spare his own Son but gave him for us all. So with Jesus, God will surely give us all things. ³³Who can accuse the people God has chosen? No one, because God is the One who makes them right. ³⁴Who can say God's people are guilty? No one, because Christ Jesus died, but he was also raised from the dead, and now he is on God's right side, begging God for us. ³⁵Can anything separate us from the love Christ has for us? Can troubles or problems or sufferings or hunger or nakedness or danger or violent death? ³⁶As it is written in the Scriptures: ᵈ

"For you we are in danger of death all the
        time.
    People think we are worth no more than
        sheep to be killed."   *Psalm 44:22*

³⁷But in all these things we have full victory through God who showed his love for us. ³⁸Yes, I am sure that neither death, nor life, nor angels, nor ruling spirits, nothing now, nothing in the future, nor powers, ³⁹nothing above us, nothing below us, nor anything else in the whole world will ever be able to separate us from the love of God that is in Christ Jesus our Lord.

LOVE

You Can't Break the Unbreakable

Gary had listened to his parents arguing for many months. He knew they were going through a tough patch, and he'd even heard the "D" word mentioned. But surely not – *his* parents wouldn't end their marriage, would they?

When Gary's parents divorced in 2004, they were one of 167,116 divorces granted in the UK. That's 334,232 individuals choosing to break off a relationship they had been committed to. How many children and family members would have been affected by those broken relationships too?

We're not used to relationships that are completely permanent. Thousands of people promise to stay with each other forever but marriages frequently break up, and even the strongest friendships sometimes fade away. Pop group members who seem inseparable often try their luck with a solo career.

It's very easy for us to think of our relationship with God in the same way. At times, we may feel really close to him, but during tough times we may feel that the relationship is breaking. Sometimes, when people attack us for our belief and trust in God, we can feel threatened and distanced from God, as if our relationship has become fragile and could break any minute.

But we need to think of our relationship with God as being like concrete. Once you mix sand, water and cement powder together to make concrete, there's no way of getting it back to its component parts. Not your bare hands, a hammer, nor even a pneumatic drill will be able to break concrete up and turn it back into sand, water and cement. When we become Christians there's *nothing* that can separate us from God! **Romans 8:31–39** explains how we should trust that our relationship with God is unbreakable.

* Is there anything that can separate us from the love of God?
* What role does Jesus play in our unbreakable relationship with God?

Consider . . .

* writing out this passage and putting it up on your bedroom wall as a reminder that even when you *feel* distant from God, you'll never be separated from him.
* telling God that you intend to stick with him through all circumstances.

For more, see . . .

* Matthew 6:25–34 (p.948)   * Ephesians 2:1–10 (p.1270)
* Ephesians 6:10–18 (p.1277)

God and the Jewish People

9 I am in Christ, and I am telling you the truth; I do not lie. My feelings are ruled by the Holy Spirit,[d] and they tell me I am not lying. [2]I have great sorrow and always feel much sadness. [3]I wish I could help my Jewish brothers and sisters, my people. I would even wish that I were cursed and cut off from Christ if that would help them. [4]They are the people of Israel, God's chosen children. They have seen the glory of God, and they have the agreements that God made between himself and his people. God gave them the law of Moses[d] and the right way of worship and his promises. [5]They are the descendants[d] of our great ancestors, and they are the earthly family into which Christ was born, who is God over all. Praise him for ever![n] Amen.

[6]It is not that God failed to keep his promise to them. But only some of the people of Israel are truly God's people,[n] [7]and only some of Abraham's[n] descendants are true children of Abraham. But God said to Abraham: "The descendants I promised you will be from Isaac."[n] [8]This means that not all of Abraham's descendants are God's true children. Abraham's true children are those who become God's children because of the promise God made to Abraham. [9]God's promise to Abraham was this: "At the right time I will return, and Sarah will have a son."[n] [10]And that is not all. Rebekah's sons had

born . . . for ever!   This can also mean, "born. May God, who rules over all things, be praised for ever!"
God's people   Literally, "Israel", the people God chose to bring his blessings to the world.
Abraham   Most respected ancestor of the Jews. Every Jew hoped to see Abraham.
"The descendants . . . Isaac."   Quotation from Genesis 21:12.
"At . . . son."   Quotation from Genesis 18:10,14.

GOD'S GRACE

Undeserving

There were only 14 places on the trip and everyone wanted to go. The school football team had been invited to go on a two-week tour to play other school teams in France and Germany.

The day came to announce the squad and there was no surprise when Tom Bannister's name was read out first. He was the Captain and everyone knew that he was bound to be chosen. One by one the names were read out and, to be honest, the list was as everyone had expected.

Eventually the coach came to read out the 14th member of the squad. There were three possibilities for this final place and everyone waited in eager anticipation to see which one of three were in. But something then happened that shocked the listening crowd that had gathered. A complete outsider, Will Arnold, got the place.

Will Arnold! Nobody could believe it. Why him? He didn't deserve a place in the squad. He had never played for the first team and he hadn't even turned up to one of the trials. There was uproar and disbelief as the coach stood by his decision and said it was *his* choice and his choice was Will Arnold.

The story sounds hard to believe. But in **Romans 9:10–16** we have a similar situation.

The passage talks about the fact that God chose Jacob because "he was the one God wanted to call, not because of anything he did" (verse 12). It goes on to say that God chooses who he wants to choose and it is not based on what we want or try to do. This is grace!

* Do you still think that you need to do things in order to earn God's approval?
* God chose Jacob because Jacob was the one that he wanted to call. What might God be calling you to?

Consider . . .

* how God includes us even though we don't deserve it. How might this affect how you include other people and give them a second chance?
* starting each day by thanking God that he has shown kindness to you even though you don't deserve it.

For more, see . . .

* Jeremiah 1:4–10 (p.716)
* 1 Timothy 1:12–14 (p.1308)
* 1 Corinthians 1:26–31 (p.1215)

the same father, our father Isaac. [11–12]But before the two boys were born, God told Rebekah, "The older will serve the younger." [n] This was before the boys had done anything good or bad. God said this so that the one chosen would be chosen because of God's own plan. He was chosen because he was the one God wanted to call, not because of anything he did. [13]As the Scripture [d] says, "I loved Jacob, but I hated Esau." [n]

[14]So what should we say about this? Is God unfair? In no way. [15]God said to Moses, "I will show kindness to anyone to whom I want to show kindness, and I will show mercy to anyone to whom I want to show mercy." [n] [16]So God will choose the one to whom he decides to show mercy; his choice does not depend on what people want or try to do. [17]The Scripture says to the king of Egypt: "I made you king for this reason: to show my power in you so that my name will be talked about in all the earth." [n] [18]So God shows mercy where he wants to show mercy, and he makes stubborn the people he wants to make stubborn.

[19]So one of you will ask me: "Then why does God blame us for our sins? Who can fight his will?" [20]You are only human, and human beings have no right to question God. An object should not ask the person who made it, "Why did you make me like this?" [21]The potter can make anything he wants to make. He can use the same clay to make one thing for special use and another thing for daily use.

[22]It is the same way with God. He wanted to show his anger and to let people see his power. But he patiently stayed with those people he was angry with—people who were due to be destroyed. [23]He waited with patience so that he could make known his rich glory to the people who receive his mercy. He has prepared these people to have his glory, [24]and we are those people whom God called. He called us not from the Jews only but also from those who are not Jews. [25]As the Scripture says in Hosea:

"I will say, 'You are my people'

to those I had called 'not my people'.
And I will show my love
　　to those people I did not love." *Hosea 2:1, 23*
[26]"They were called,
　'You are not my people',
but later they will be called
　'children of the living God'." *Hosea 1:10*
　　[27]And Isaiah cries out about Israel:
"Israel, your people are many,
　like the grains of sand by the sea.
But only a few of them will be left alive to
　　return to the Lord.
[28]　God has announced that he will destroy the
　　land completely and fairly." *Isaiah 10:22*
[29]It is as Isaiah said:
"The Lord All-powerful
　allowed a few of our people to live.
Otherwise we would have been completely
　　destroyed
like the cities of Sodom [d] and Gomorrah." [d]
Isaiah 1:9

[30]So what does all this mean? Those who are not Jews were not trying to make themselves right with God, but they were made right with God because of their faith. [31]The people of Israel tried to follow a law to make themselves right with God. But they did not succeed, [32]because they tried to make themselves right by the things they did instead of trusting in God to make them right. They stumbled over the stone that causes people to stumble. [33]As it is written in the Scripture:
"I will put in Jerusalem a stone that causes
　　people to stumble,
　a rock that makes them fall.
Anyone who trusts in it will never be
　　disappointed." *Isaiah 8:14; 28:16*

10

Brothers and sisters, the thing I want most is for all the Jews to be saved. That is my prayer to God. [2]I can say this about them: they really try to follow God, but they do not know the right way. [3]Because they did not know the way that God makes people right with him, they tried to make themselves right in their own way. So they did not accept God's way of making people right. [4]Christ ended the law [d] so that everyone who believes in him may be right with God.

[5]Moses describes how to be made right by following the law. He says, "A person who obeys these things will live because of them." [n] [6]But this is what the Scripture says about being made right through faith: "Don't say to yourself, 'Who will go up into heaven?'" (That means, "Who

---

"The older . . . younger."　Quotation from Genesis 25:23.
"I . . . Esau."　Quotation from Malachi 1:2–3.
"I . . . mercy."　Quotation from Exodus 33:19.
"I . . . earth."　Quotation from Exodus 9:16.
"A person . . . them."　Quotation from Leviticus 18:5.

will go up to heaven and bring Christ down to earth?") [7]"And do not say, 'Who will go down into the world below?'" (That means, "Who will go down and bring Christ up from the dead?") [8]This is what the Scripture says: "The word is near you; it is in your mouth and in your heart." [n] That is the teaching of faith that we are telling. [9]If you use your mouth to say, "Jesus is Lord," and if you believe in your heart that God raised Jesus from the dead, you will be saved. [10]We believe with our hearts, and so we are made right with God. And we use our mouths to say that we believe and so we are saved. [11]As the Scripture says, "Anyone who trusts in him will never be disappointed." [n]

[12]That Scripture says "anyone" because there is no difference between those who are Jews and those who are not. The same Lord is the Lord of all and gives many blessings to all who trust in him, [13]as the Scripture says, "Anyone who calls on the Lord will be saved." [n]

[14]But before people can ask the Lord for help, they must believe in him; and before they can believe in him, they must hear about him; and for them to hear about the Lord, someone must tell them; [15]and before someone can go and tell them, that person must be sent. It is written, "How beautiful is the person who comes to bring good news." [n]

Verses 6–8 Quotations from Deuteronomy 30:12–14.
"Anyone . . . disappointed." Quotation from Isaiah 28:16.
"Anyone . . . saved." Quotation from Joel 2:32.
"How . . . news." Quotation from Isaiah 52:7.

SHARING FAITH

You Don't Say

Every Monday at school, Olivia's best friend Hannah would ask her about her weekend.

"Um, just saw some friends, spent some time with the family," she'd reply, even though she had been at youth group, heard about some amazing miracles, prayed, worshipped and then had a fantastic time at a church picnic which had felt like a big family party.

Hannah felt sorry for Olivia. She knew she went to church at weekends, but Olivia never seemed to have anything very exciting happen in her life. Week after week, the pattern was the same. Olivia felt as if she came alive during her "God time" at the weekends, and yet the best thing in her life was the hardest thing in her life to share with her friend.

Hannah started to feel that Olivia was losing interest in their friendship. Hannah didn't keep any secrets from her mates, but she felt that Olivia was keeping a lot back from her. One Monday Hannah confronted Olivia.

"Liv, I was really fed up this weekend and texted you to see if we could meet up. You didn't get back to me, and then I saw you with a gang of other guys having a great time playing rounders in the park . . . but you'd said you didn't have anything much planned for the weekend." Tears welled up in Hannah's eyes.

Olivia didn't know what to say. She had been afraid to share the biggest and best part of her life with a friend who really cared about her.

Read **Romans 10:8–18** which explains the importance of telling others of your faith in Christ, and not assuming that they won't want to know.

- Why was Olivia so afraid of sharing her faith, and were her fears justified?
- In the Bible passage, why are you told to tell others about your faith in Jesus?

Consider . . .

- how you would explain to someone what being a Christian means. Try writing your response down.
- praying for someone you know who doesn't know the good news of Jesus. Ask God for wisdom to know how to share your faith with them.

For more, see . . .

- Matthew 5:13–16 (p.942)
- Acts 2 (p.1138)
- Matthew 10:32–33 (p.957)

16But not all the Jews accepted the good news. As Isaiah said, "Lord, who believed what we told them?" *n* 17So faith comes from hearing the Good News, *d* and people hear the Good News when someone tells them about Christ.

18But I ask: Didn't people hear the Good News? Yes, they heard—as the Scripture says:

"Their message went out through all the
    world;
  their words go everywhere on earth."

Psalm 19:4

"Lord, . . . them?"   Quotation from Isaiah 53:1.

19Again I ask: Didn't the people of Israel understand? Yes, they did understand. First, Moses says:

"So I will use those who are not a nation to
    make them jealous;
  I will use a nation that does not understand
    to make them angry."   *Deuteronomy 32:21*

20Then Isaiah is bold enough to say:

"I was found by those who were not asking
    me for help.
  I said, 'Here I am. Here I am,' to a nation
    that was not praying to me."   *Isaiah 65:1*

GOD'S GRACE

Pockets of People

Everywhere they looked, it seemed to Paul and Katie that people were building empires. The Christians they knew were all part of some organisation, and even their church had a sister building.

"How come we're not part of someone's set up?" asked Paul one day.

"I don't really know," said Katie. "It's never felt right has it? We've always been here by ourselves."

They had a ministry with young people and it was growing, but every time someone asked them to join their organisation, they felt that God was saying "No".

"It's just the opposite to what everyone else is doing . . . can it be right?" they kept asking themselves. But the more offers they had, the more they felt adamant about turning them down. Even a chance to become pastors in a massive youth church in America didn't sway them.

After one particularly enticing offer, they decided to go and talk the situation over with a well-respected national leader.

"Do you think we should come and join you?" they asked him, knowing that he would like the idea.

"No," came the bold reply.

Paul and Katie were quite shocked. They expected to be ushered into the Christian Ministry team with open arms.

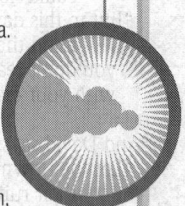

"Why ever not?" they asked in unison.

"Because," replied the leader, "I firmly believe that God has pockets of people all over the world, and he wants them on their own, in that place. You are two of those people."

The couple were so pleased with his honest reply. It would have been so easy for him to use them, and yet he saw God's grace at work in them and realised it was a "no-go" area.

The leader knew that God had chosen Paul and Katie. Read **Romans 11:1–6** to see how God sets people aside by his grace.

- How important was the couple's own ability according to this passage?
- According to this passage, how important is it to prepare yourself should God choose you?

Consider . . .

- where you place your trust. Is it in your own abilities or in God's strength?
- listing a few Christians in places of influence (politicians, musicians . . .). Pray regularly that God will give them grace and strength to make a stand for Christian values.

For more, see . . .

- Romans 5:15 (p.1190)
- Titus 3:5–7 (p.1324)
- Romans 9:10–16 (p.1198)

[21]But about Israel God says,
"All day long I stood ready to accept
people who turned against me."   *Isaiah 65:2*

God Shows Mercy to All People

11 So I ask: Did God throw out his people? No! I myself am an Israelite from the family of Abraham, from the tribe *d* of Benjamin. [2]God chose the Israelites to be his people before they were born, and he has not thrown his people out. Surely you know what the Scripture *d* says about Elijah, how he prayed to God against the people of Israel. [3]"Lord," he said, "they have killed your prophets, *d* and they have destroyed your altars. I am the only prophet left, and now they are trying to kill me too." *n* [4]But what answer did God give Elijah? He said, "But I have left 7,000 people in Israel who have never bowed down before Baal." *n* [5]It is the same now. There are a few people that God has chosen by his grace. [6]And if he chose them by grace, it is not for the things they have done. If they could be made God's people by what they did, God's gift of grace would not really be a gift.

[7]So this is what has happened: although the Israelites tried to be right with God, they did not succeed, but the ones God chose did become right with him. The others were made stubborn and refused to listen to God. [8]As it is written in the Scriptures:

"God gave the people a dull mind so they
could not understand."   *Isaiah 29:10*
"But to this day the Lord has not given you a
mind that understands;
you don't really understand what you see
with your eyes or hear with your ears."
Deuteronomy 29:4

[9]And David says:
"Let their own feasts trap them and cause
their ruin;
let their feasts cause them to stumble and
be paid back.
[10]Let their eyes be closed so they cannot see
and their backs be for ever weak from
troubles."   *Psalm 69:22–23*

[11]So I ask: when the Jews fell, did that fall destroy them? No! But their mistake brought salvation to those who are not Jews, in order to make the Jews jealous. [12]The Jews' mistake brought rich blessings for the world, and the Jews' loss brought rich blessings for the non-Jewish people. So surely the world will receive much richer blessings when enough Jews become the kind of people God wants.

[13]Now I am speaking to you who are not Jews. I am an apostle *d* to those who are not Jews, and

since I have that work, I will make the most of it. [14]I hope I can make my own people jealous and, in that way, help some of them to be saved. [15]When God turned away from the Jews, he became friends with other people in the world. So when God accepts the Jews, surely that will bring them life after death.

[16]If the first piece of bread is offered to God, then the whole loaf is made holy. If the roots of a tree are holy, then the tree's branches are holy too.

[17]It is as if some of the branches from an olive tree have been broken off. You non-Jewish people are like the branch of a wild olive tree that has been joined to that first tree. You now share the strength and life of the first tree, the Jews. [18]So do not boast about those branches that were broken off. If you boast, remember that you do not support the root, but the root supports you. [19]You will say, "Branches were broken off so that I could be joined to their tree." [20]That is true. But those branches were broken off because they did not believe, and you continue to be part of the tree only because you believe. Do not be proud, but be afraid. [21]If God did not let the natural branches of that tree stay, then he will not let you stay if you don't believe.

[22]So you see that God is kind and also very strict. He punishes those who stop following him. But God is kind to you, if you continue following in his kindness. If you do not, you will be cut off from the tree. [23]And if the Jews will believe in God again, he will accept them back. God is able to put them back where they were. [24]It is not natural for a wild branch to be part of a good tree. And you who are not Jews are like a branch cut from a wild olive tree and joined to a good olive tree. But since those Jews are like a branch that grew from the good tree, surely they can be joined to their own tree again.

[25]I want you to understand this secret, brothers and sisters, so you will understand that you do not know everything: part of Israel has been made stubborn, but that will change when many who are not Jews have come to God. [26]And that is how all Israel will be saved. It is written in the Scriptures:

"Then a Saviour will come to Jerusalem
and to the people of Jacob *n* who have
turned from sin.
[27]This is how Israel's guilt will be forgiven;
this is how its sins will be taken away."
Isaiah 59:20–21; 27:9

[28]The Jews refuse to accept the Good News, *d* so they are God's enemies. This has happened to help you who are not Jews. But the Jews are

---

"Lord . . . too."   Quotation from 1 Kings 19:10,14.
"But . . . Baal."   Quotation from 1 Kings 19:18.
Jacob   Father of the twelve family groups of Israel, the people God chose to be his own.

still God's chosen people, and he loves them very much because of the promises he made to their ancestors. ²⁹God never changes his mind about the people he calls and the things he gives them. ³⁰At one time you refused to obey God. But now you have received mercy, because those people refused to obey. ³¹And now the Jews refuse to obey, because God showed mercy to you. But this happened so that they also can receive mercy from him. ³²God has given all people over to their stubborn ways so that he can show mercy to all.

Praise to God

³³Yes, God's riches are very great, and his wisdom and knowledge have no end! No one can explain the things God decides or understand his ways. ³⁴As the Scripture *d* says,

> "Who has known the mind of the Lord
>   or been able to give him
>   advice?"   *Isaiah 40:13*

³⁵"No one has ever given God anything
   that he must pay back."   *Job 41:11*

³⁶Yes, God made all things, and everything continues through him and for him. To him be the glory for ever! Amen.

Give Your Lives to God

12 So brothers and sisters, since God has shown us great mercy, I beg you to offer your lives as a living sacrifice to him. Your offering must be only for God and pleasing to him, which is the spiritual way for you to worship. ²Do not change yourselves to be like the people of this world, but be changed within by a new way of thinking. Then you will be able

---

GOD'S LOVE

Free Gifts

James volunteered to help in an inner-city community shop, where he sorted used clothing and helped people to pick out things they needed for free.

One Friday, while James was walking to the bus stop near the shop, he passed a market stall. He recognised one of the kids as the child of a woman who often came to the free shop. After a few moments of talking to the child, he began to recognise more than just the little boy.

There, piled on the old card tables, were stacks of blue jeans, sweatshirts, socks, shoes and mittens that James had seen earlier that week at the free shop. He was outraged! These people didn't take the clothing from the shop because they needed it. They took it so that they could sell it! What a rip-off!

"It just doesn't seem right," James complained to Jim, the shop manager. "We gave them those clothes so that they'd have something to wear, not so that they could sell them."

"Well, it seems they needed the clothes either way," responded Jim. "They needed the clothes to sell for cash so that they could buy other things. Besides, we help these people because we care about them, not because they always respond the way we want them to."

"It sounds risky," James said.

"Love always is," answered Jim.

Jim helped James to see that their love wasn't something people should have to earn. God's love is like that too. Read **Romans 11:29–36** to find a description of God's merciful gift of love for us.

* How is the free shop like God's love for us?
* What would happen to your relationship with God if his love depended on your doing what he wanted?

Consider . . .

* writing down five reasons why God's love can never be taken away from you. Read Romans 8:31–39 (p.1197) for a few hints.
* giving a pound to someone you meet who is in need – without knowing how that person will use the money.

For more, see . . .

* Psalm 103:6–14 (p.559)   * Ephesians 2:4–7 (p.1270)
* 1 John 4:7–12 (p.1374)

to decide what God wants for you; you will know what is good and pleasing to him and what is perfect. ³Because God has given me a special gift, I have something to say to everyone among you. Do not think you are better than you are. You must decide what you really are by the amount of faith God has given you. ⁴Each one of us has a body with many parts, and these parts all have different uses. ⁵In the same way, we are many, but in Christ we are all one body. Each one is a part of that body, and each part belongs to all the other parts. ⁶We all have different gifts, each of which came because of the grace God gave us. The person who has the gift of prophecy *d* should use that gift in agreement with the faith. ⁷Anyone who has the gift of serving should serve. Anyone who has the gift of teaching should teach. ⁸Whoever has the gift of encouraging others should encourage. Whoever has the gift of giving to others should give freely. Anyone who has the gift of being a leader should try hard when he leads. Whoever has the gift of showing mercy to others should do so with joy.

FOLLOWING GOD

Bouncing Betties

The Bouncing Betty was the worst sort of land mine in the Vietnam War. It was loaded with a spring so that when you stepped on it, it flew into the air, about waist high, and then exploded. It was designed to blow people apart and to strike terror into the hearts of young soldiers.

The plan worked on Craig.

He was on patrol one day with five other soldiers and a Vietnamese man who was supposed to be their guide. They had been out for about three hours, walking quietly through the bush, just looking and listening and trying not to get shot.

Then they came to a clearing, perhaps thirty metres across. The situation had "Bouncing Betty" written all over it. And Craig just knew that snipers were hiding in the jungle on the other side, waiting for him and his buddies to step into that clearing. But the bush was too thick to go around the clearing, so they had no choice but to go through.

The Vietnamese guide signalled for quiet and pointed to his feet, then spread his fingers on both hands. "Stay quiet," he whispered. "Follow me. Put your feet where I put mine. Stay ten metres behind the man in front of you."

Craig had never been so scared in his life. The guide went ten metres out into the clearing and then motioned for Craig to follow. Slowly now, despite his fears, he managed to keep putting his feet in the impressions left by the guide. He kept his head down, waiting for a sniper's bullet.

And then it was over. He took a deep breath and realised that he had made it across. Shaking violently, he looked up and saw the Vietnamese guide smiling at him. It was nice to have someone in whose steps you could walk.

Craig learned that to get through rough times he had to deny his own desires and follow someone he could trust, someone who knew the way. **Romans 12:1–16** talks about God as the one who knows the way for our lives. Read the passage to see how we can walk in his steps.

- How is the way that Craig followed the guide similar to the way that you follow God?
- According to the passage, why should you follow God (see verses 1–2)?

Consider . . .

- asking your youth leader to read Romans 12:6–8. Ask the leader to tell you which gifts he thinks you have. Then ask God to give you more opportunities to use your gifts.
- writing down how your life would change if you walked each day in Christ's steps by following his instructions in this passage.

For more, see . . .

- Psalm 119:9–16 (p.571)
- Luke 14:25–33 (p.1070)
- Luke 9:23–26 (p.1054)

9Your love must be real. Hate what is evil, and hold on to what is good. 10Love each other like brothers and sisters. Give each other more honour than you want for yourselves. 11Do not be lazy but work hard, serving the Lord with all your heart. 12Be joyful because you have hope. Be patient when trouble comes, and pray at all times. 13Share with God's people who need help. Bring strangers in need into your homes.

14Wish good for those who harm you; wish them well and do not curse them. 15Be happy with those who are happy, and be sad with those who are sad. 16Live in peace with each other. Do not be proud, but make friends with those who seem unimportant. Do not think how clever you are.

17If someone does wrong to you, do not pay him back by doing wrong to him. Try to do what

GOVERNMENT

An Inch is as Good as a Mile

Daniel used to write a column for his school newspaper. It wasn't a big column, but it was fun. He wrote humorously about school food, class workload, or the latest bungle of the notoriously bad football team. He had been given the job because his best friend, Sam, was the editor. And much to their surprise, the column had become one of the paper's most popular features, even among kids who attended other schools.

One Monday on the way to class, Daniel saw a student in a wheelchair and an older woman trying – unsuccessfully – to push the wheelchair over the kerb.

When Daniel stopped to help, he noticed a wheelchair ramp cut into the kerb just a few yards away. But the yellow paint that marked it off had faded, and someone had parked in front of it.

"Unbelievable," Daniel said, shaking his head.

"Believe it," said the student in the wheelchair, whose name was Bruce. "It happens all the time. That's why my mum has to come with me. More than half the ramps haven't been painted for five years. People just ignore them."

Daniel smelled a story. He agreed to meet Bruce and his mum the next day. They would bring their extra wheelchair, and Daniel would spend the day trying to get around school in it.

That's how Daniel discovered that the main lift stopped two inches below the floor level (as good as two miles when you're in a wheelchair). He had trouble negotiating the super-narrow doors in the music room. And he discovered high water fountains everywhere and over a hundred obstacles all over the school. And that was in just six hours!

The next day, Daniel wrote about his experiences, but somehow that just didn't seem enough. He also attended student council meetings and talked to the headmaster about it.

A few months later, Daniel talked to Bruce again. But this time his mum wasn't with him. "She doesn't need to come with me any more," he said. "For some reason, the head just seemed to wake up."

"Perhaps somebody tapped him on the shoulder," Daniel said.

Romans 13:1–10 encourages us to do what's right in serving our government. In Paul's day, that meant carefully following the laws laid out by Rome. But in today's democracy, it can mean helping to shape policy – just as Daniel did. Read the passage to see what else Paul said about your relationship with the government.

* Would Paul have approved of Daniel's actions? Why or why not?
* What's one thing that you can do to apply this passage to your situation?

Consider . . .

* standing for a place on your school or college's student council.
* writing a letter to your member of parliament, relating your concerns about the disabled, education, or some other issue that you care about.

For more, see . . .

* 1 Samuel 8:1–22 (p.261)
* Matthew 22:17–21 (p.980)
* 1 Peter 2:13–17 (p.1358)

everyone thinks is right. [18]Do your best to live in peace with everyone. [19]My friends, do not try to punish others when they wrong you, but wait for God to punish them with his anger. It is written: "I will punish those who do wrong; I will repay them," [n] says the Lord. [20]But you should do this:

"If your enemy is hungry, feed him.
     If he is thirsty, give him a drink.
     Doing this will be like pouring burning coals
         on his head."
                       Proverbs 25:21–22

[21]Do not let evil defeat you, but defeat evil by doing good.

Christians Should Obey the Law

13 All of you must yield to the government rulers. No one rules unless God has given him the power to rule, and no one rules now without that power from God. [2]So those who are against the government are really against what God has commanded. And they will bring punishment on themselves. [3]Those who do right do not have to fear the rulers; only those who do wrong fear them. Do you want to be unafraid of the rulers? Then do what is right, and they will praise you. [4]The ruler is God's servant to help you. But if you do wrong, then be afraid. He has the power to punish; he is God's servant to punish those who do wrong. [5]So you must yield to the government, not only because you might be punished, but because you know it is right.

[6]This is also why you pay taxes. Rulers are working for God and give their time to their work. [7]Pay everyone, then, what you owe. If you owe any kind of tax, pay it. Show respect and honour to them all.

"I . . . them,"   Quotation from Deuteronomy 32:35.

DRUGS AND ALCOHOL

Just Trying to Fit In?

Despite hearing horror stories about drugs, Carly thought she thought could handle it. When she moved schools in year 9 she didn't want to get bullied again and tried her hardest to fit in with the popular crowd at her new school. At first she thought it was just a bit of fun, she thought she could get away with it. Just as long as she didn't take any "really bad" drugs, she thought she'd be OK. Carly thought wrong. Her life went completely downhill. She hit rock bottom and even attempted suicide.

Talking to a friend some time later Carly said, "I tried everything just to be popular. I only wanted to be liked. Since then God has come into my life and shown me that he loves me. And if the creator of the universe loves me then I don't need to do anything to fit in, I already fit in to God's amazing family."

It's unbelievable to see how much the people we hang around with can influence us. You can choose to be influenced by them or let God influence your life.

Romans 13:11–14 talks about leaving the world of darkness and living in God's light instead. If you know and have accepted what Jesus has done for you it means you can and should live in God's light, not in the darkness of sin.

* How do you think Carly's life changed?
* Are there any areas of your life you're living in darkness? If so, ask God to help you live for him.

Consider . . .

* if you haven't done already or you feel you need to again, asking God to forgive you and come into your life and help you to live in the light.
* praying for any friends you have who are living in darkness and ask God to show you a way of bringing them to his light.

For more, see . . .

* Proverbs 23:31–35 (p.610)
* Ephesians 5:17–18 (p.1275)
* Ephesians 2:1–4 (p.1270)
* 1 Peter 4:2–5 (p.1360)

Loving Others

[8]Do not owe people anything, except always owe love to each other, because the person who loves others has obeyed all the law. [9]The law says, "You must not be guilty of adultery. [d] You must not murder anyone. You must not steal. You must not want to take your neighbour's things." [n] All these commands and all others are really only one rule: "Love your neighbour as you love yourself." [n] [10]Love never hurts a neighbour, so loving is obeying all the law.

[11]Do this because we live in an important time. It is now time for you to wake up from your sleep, because our salvation is nearer now than when we first believed. [12]The "night" [n] is almost finished, and the "day" [n] is almost here. So we should stop doing things that belong to darkness and take up the weapons used for fighting in the light. [13]Let us live in a right way, like people who belong to the day. We should not have wild parties or get drunk. There should be no sexual sins of any kind, no fighting or jealousy. [14]But clothe yourselves with the Lord Jesus Christ and forget about satisfying your sinful self.

Do Not Criticise Other People

14 Accept into your group someone who is weak in faith, and do not argue about opinions. [2]One person believes it is right to eat all kinds of food. [n] But another, who is weak, believes it is right to eat only vegetables. [3]The one who knows that it is right to eat any kind of food must not reject the one who eats only vegetables. And the person who eats only vegetables must not think that the one who eats all foods is wrong, because God has accepted that person. [4]You cannot judge another person's servant. The master decides if the servant is doing well or not. And the Lord's servant will do well because the Lord helps him do well.

[5]Some think that one day is more important than another, and others think that every day is the same. Let all be sure in their own mind. [6]Those who think one day is more important than other days are doing that for the Lord. And those who eat all kinds of food are doing that for the Lord, and they give thanks to God. Others who refuse to eat some foods do that for the Lord, and they give thanks to God. [7]We do not

live or die for ourselves. [8]If we live, we are living for the Lord, and if we die, we are dying for the Lord. So living or dying, we belong to the Lord.

> **Sidelight** Relations with the government were important to Roman Christians, since they lived in the capital city. When Paul wrote Romans 13:1–7, about obeying the government, Christians were tolerated – sometimes even protected – by the state. Within a few years, though, Christians would face the constant threat of torture and execution.

[9]The reason Christ died and rose from the dead to live again was so he would be Lord over both the dead and the living. [10]So why do you judge your brothers or sisters in Christ? And why do you think you are better than they are? We will all stand before God to be judged, [11]because it is written in the Scriptures: [d]

> "'As surely as I live,' says the Lord,
> 'Everyone will bow before me and will
> promise to follow me.'" *Isaiah 45:23*

[12]So each of us will have to answer to God.

Do Not Cause Others to Sin

[13]For that reason we should stop judging each other. We must make up our minds not to do anything that will make another Christian sin. [14]I am in the Lord Jesus, and I know that there is no food that is wrong to eat. But if a person believes something is wrong, that thing is wrong for him. [15]If you hurt your brother's or sister's faith because of something you eat, you are not really following the way of love. Do not destroy someone's faith by eating food he thinks is wrong, because Christ died for him. [16]Do not allow what you think is good to become what others say is evil. [17]In the kingdom of God, eating and drinking are not important. The important things are living right with God, peace, and joy in the Holy Spirit. [d] [18]Anyone who serves Christ by living this way is pleasing God and will be accepted by other people.

[19]So let us try to do what makes for peace and help one another. [20]Do not let the eating of food destroy the work of God. All foods are all right to

---

"You . . . things." Quotation from Exodus 20:13–15,17.
"Love . . . yourself." Quotation from Leviticus 19:18.
"night" This is used as a symbol of the sinful world we live in. This world will soon end.
"day" This is used as a symbol of the good time that is coming, when we will be with God.
all . . . food The Jewish law said there were some foods Jews should not eat. When Jews became Christians, some of them did not understand they could now eat all foods.

eat, but it is wrong to eat food that causes someone else to sin. ²¹It is better not to eat meat or drink wine or do anything that will cause your brother or sister to sin.

²²Your beliefs about these things should be kept secret between you and God. People are happy if they can do what they think is right without feeling guilty. ²³But those who eat something without being sure it is right are wrong because they did not believe it was right. Anything that is done without believing it is right is a sin.

15 We who are strong in faith should help the weak with their weaknesses, and not please only ourselves. ²Let each of us please our neighbours for their good, to help them be stronger in faith. ³Even Christ did not live to please himself. It was as the Scriptures *d* said: "When people insult you, it hurts me." *n* ⁴Everything that was written in the past was written to teach us. The Scriptures give us patience and encouragement so that we can have hope. ⁵Patience and encouragement come from God. And I pray that God will help you all agree with each other the way Christ Jesus wants. ⁶Then you will all be joined together, and you will give glory to God the Father of our Lord Jesus Christ. ⁷Christ accepted you, so you should accept each other, which will bring glory to God. ⁸I tell you that Christ became a servant of the Jews to show that God's promises to the Jewish ancestors

"When . . . me."   Quotation from Psalm 69:9.

DECISION MAKING

Different is OK!

Katie studied languages at university, so when she got married just after graduating she and her new husband, Rob, chose to go to Italy for their honeymoon. On Sunday they managed to find a church much like their own back home.

Once the service started Rob and Katie enjoyed themselves, even though Katie noticed that one or two women were looking at her quite oddly. After the service, the questioning began to find out whether Katie and Rob were Christians, what church they came from and whether they believed the Bible was God's Word. Eventually their new Italian friends were satisfied, even though they still looked puzzled.

"Tell us," they asked, "do many Christian women wear trousers and make-up in Britain?"

"Yes. It's not a problem," said Katie, surprised but glad to know what the issue had been.

Later that week Katie, Rob and their new friends had a meal together and laughed over the misunderstanding, as they passed around several bottles of wine and discussed differences between Christian groups they each knew.

"Did you know," teased Rob, "that there are some Christians in Britain and North America who believe that you can't be a Christian and drink wine."

"No," said the Italians. "That's impossible. How could anybody believe that?" Eventually they agreed that each person should make honest decisions based on their own convictions, even if others would disagree.

Romans 14:5–12 challenges us all to make decisions based on our faith.

- How are the Christians Rob and Katie met like the people in the passage?
- How might this passage affect the way you make comparisons between groups of Christians?

Consider . . .

- talking to your youth leader about your church's beliefs. Ask how your church came to believe the things it does.
- making lifestyle decisions based on what the Bible teaches. Work towards making sure that your lifestyle matches your beliefs.

For more, see . . .

- 1 Kings 12:1–20 (p.327)
- Acts 5:12–32 (p.1145)
- Matthew 7:13–14 (p.950)

are true. ⁹And he also did this so that those who are not Jews could give glory to God for the mercy he gives to them. It is written in the Scriptures:

"So I will praise you, LORD, among the
nations.
I will sing praises to your name."   *Psalm 18:49*

¹⁰The Scripture also says,

"Be happy, you who are not Jews, together
with his people."   *Deuteronomy 32:43*

¹¹Again the Scripture says,

"All you nations, praise the LORD.
All you people, praise him."   *Psalm 117:1*

¹²And Isaiah says,

"The new king from the family of Jesse *n*
will stand as a banner for all peoples;

Jesse   Jesse was the father of David, king of Israel. Jesus was from their family.

FRIENDS

Hey Grunge!

It was on a cold Sunday morning in December that Peter first came to church. He arrived halfway through the pastor's message and sat quietly at the back. He felt more than a little out of place, to say the least. What made him feel even more uncomfortable was the fact that everyone seemed to be staring at him . . .

"I wonder who that is?" Belinda asked her mum when she saw the visitor.

"I'd have nothing to do with him if I were you, Belinda," her mum said.

Belinda looked at Peter's haircut and the many earrings he wore – and the stud in his nose. "Well, I know he doesn't look like the usual sort of person who comes to church, but shouldn't we make him feel welcome anyway?"

Belinda's mum shook her head. "His name's Peter," she said. "His dad's in prison for beating up a security guard and his sister's a prostitute, or so they say."

"What difference does that make? Jesus became a friend of prostitutes didn't he?"

"You're not Jesus," her mum replied.

Belinda soon discovered that a lot of other people in the church felt the same way. It wasn't that they were trying to be nasty, but they were careful not to talk to him.

Peter continued to visit the church for several weeks, but still no one had spoken to him. He began to feel as though he wasn't welcome, despite the fact that he'd accepted Jesus as his Lord and Saviour just a few weeks ago.

Belinda had been praying for Peter every day since she had first seen him. She had resisted the urge to go and say "Hello", but now that seemed to be ridiculous. How could the church claim to be a true representative of Jesus Christ if it didn't make a guy like Peter feel welcome? Surely Jesus would have been the first to go and sit next to him?

Although she knew her mum wouldn't approve, Belinda approached Peter after the service and invited him to tea.

Belinda's mum soon got to know Peter for the person he was, rather than for the reputation he had been branded with. Within weeks, Belinda's family were good friends of Peter, and before long his mum was coming to church and discovering the good news of Jesus!

Belinda started the ball rolling by accepting Peter when everyone else was too scared to go near him. Read what the apostle Paul said about accepting others in **Romans 15:4–13**.

* Based on this passage, what might Paul have said to Belinda?
* How does the fact that Christ has accepted someone help you to accept them too?

Consider . . .

* getting to know someone who is often neglected because of the way he or she dresses.
* asking God to help you to accept others just as he has accepted them – unconditionally.

For more, see . . .

* 1 Samuel 18:1–4 (p.272)
* John 13:20 (p.1120)
* Job 2:11–13 (p.471)

the nations will come together
    around him
and the place where he lives will be filled
    with glory."   *Isaiah 11:10*

[13]I pray that the God who gives hope will fill you with much joy and peace while you trust in him. Then your hope will overflow by the power of the Holy Spirit. *d*

Paul Talks About His Work

[14]My brothers and sisters, I am sure that you are full of goodness. I know that you have all the knowledge you need and that you are able to teach each other. [15]But I have written to you very openly about some things I wanted you to remember. I did this because God gave me this special gift: [16]to be a minister of Christ Jesus to those who are not Jews. I served God by teaching his Good News, *d* so that the non-Jewish people could be an offering that God would accept—an offering made holy by the Holy Spirit. *d*

[17]So I am proud of what I have done for God in Christ Jesus. [18]I will not talk about anything except what Christ has done through me in leading those who are not Jews to obey God. They have obeyed God because of what I have said and done, [19]because of the power of miracles *d* and the great things they saw, and because of the power of the Holy Spirit. I preached the Good News from Jerusalem all the way around to Illyricum, and so I have finished that part of my work. [20]I always want to preach the Good News in places where people have never heard of Christ, because I do not want to build on the work someone else has already started. [21]But it is written in the Scriptures: *d*

"Those who were not told about him
    will see,
and those who have not heard about him
    will understand."   *Isaiah 52:15*

Paul's Plan to Visit Rome

[22]This is the reason I was stopped many times from coming to you. [23]Now I have finished my work here. Since for many years I have wanted to come to you, [24]I hope to visit you on my way to Spain. After I enjoy being with you for a while, I hope you can help me on my trip. [25]Now I am going to Jerusalem to help God's people. [26]The believers in Macedonia and Southern Greece were happy to give their money to help the poor among God's people at Jerusalem. [27]They were happy to do this, and really they owe it to them. These who are not Jews have shared in the Jews' spiritual blessings, so they should use their material possessions to help the Jews. [28]After I am sure the poor in Jerusalem get the money that has been given for them, I will leave for Spain and visit you on the way. [29]I know that when I come to you I will bring Christ's full blessing.

[30]Brothers and sisters, I beg you to help me in my work by praying to God for me. Do this because of our Lord Jesus and the love that the Holy Spirit *d* gives us. [31]Pray that I will be saved from the non-believers in Judea and that this help I bring to Jerusalem will please God's people there. [32]Then, if God wants me to, I will come to you with joy, and together you and I will have a time of rest. [33]The God who gives peace be with you all. Amen.

Greetings to the Christians

16 I recommend to you our sister Phoebe, who is a helper *n* in the church in Cenchrea. [2]I ask you to accept her in the Lord in the way God's people should. Help her with anything she needs, because she has helped me and many other people also.

[3]Give my greetings to Priscilla and Aquila, who work together with me in Christ Jesus [4]and who risked their own lives to save my life. I am thankful to them, and all the non-Jewish churches are thankful as well. [5]Also, greet for me the church that meets at their house.

Greetings to my dear friend Epenetus, who was the first person in the country of Asia to follow Christ. [6]Greetings to Mary, who worked very hard for you. [7]Greetings to Andronicus and Junias, my relatives, who were in prison with me. They are very important apostles. *d* They were believers in Christ before I was. [8]Greetings to Ampliatus, my dear friend in the Lord. [9]Greetings to Urbanus, a worker together with me for Christ. And greetings to my dear friend Stachys. [10]Greetings to Apelles, who was

> **Sidelight** Since the early Christians didn't have any church buildings, they usually met in each others' homes (Romans 16:3–5). Priscilla and Aquila were quite wealthy and they had a large house where Christians could gather for worship. Even today, meeting in a house has a different atmosphere from a church meeting!

---

helper   Literally, "deaconess". This might mean the same as one of the special women helpers in 1 Timothy 3:11.

tested and proved that he truly loves Christ. Greetings to all those who are in the family of Aristobulus. [11]Greetings to Herodion, my fellow citizen. Greetings to all those in the family of Narcissus who belong to the Lord. [12]Greetings to Tryphena and Tryphosa, women who work very hard for the Lord. Greetings to my dear friend Persis, who also has worked very hard for the Lord. [13]Greetings to Rufus, who is a special person in the Lord, and to his mother, who has been like a mother to me also. [14]Greetings to Asyncritus, Phlegon, Hermes, Patrobas, Hermas and all the brothers who are with them. [15]Greetings to Philologus and Julia, Nereus and his sister, and Olympas, and to all God's people with them. [16]Greet each other with a holy kiss. All of Christ's churches send greetings to you.

BIBLE STUDY

Recipe

Chas had baked bread before. Hundreds of times.

Well, twice, anyway.

"It's a simple loaf of white bread. That shouldn't be too hard," Chas thought aloud. "A little yeast, a little oil, a little flour – nothing to it."

Chas put all the ingredients into the big bowl that his mother always used, added more flour until the mixture was a big ball, and then dumped it on to the worktop.

As Chas kneaded the dough he imagined how surprised his parents would be when he presented his bread for breakfast the next morning. It was their 25th wedding anniversary.

Chas covered the big ball of dough with a light coating of butter, flipped it into the bowl, covered it with clingfilm, and set it aside in a warm corner of the room to rise.

"See, nothing to it," he said smugly. "Didn't even have to look at the recipe."

Now all he had to do was wait for it to rise. Thirty minutes. Nothing. An hour. Nothing.

"It's just sitting there in the bowl like a . . . like a big lump of dough. Why isn't it rising?" Chas asked himself.

He checked the expiry date on the yeast packed. No problem – it wouldn't expire for another three months. So what could it be?

Reluctantly, he went to the cookery book.

"Let's see," he mused. "Flour, oil, yeast, sugar . . .

"Sugar! Of course!"

Without sugar, the yeast couldn't do its job. No wonder the bread wasn't rising! He had left out a small but vital ingredient.

Chas's bread couldn't rise without sugar. In the same way, Paul says that a Christian can't reach a mature faith without having the right ingredients in his or her life. Read **Romans 16:22–27** to see what those ingredients are.

* What, according to Paul, is the effect of God's message on people's lives?
* According to this passage, what ingredients might you be lacking to bring you to Christian maturity?

Consider . . .

* asking your parent or youth leader to give you a recipe for Bible study. Ask what steps you should follow in studying the Bible.
* regularly attending your youth group's weekly Bible study. If you don't have one, ask your youth leader to start one.

For more, see . . .

* Joshua 1:8 (p.203)
* Revelation 1:1–3 (p.1388)
* Psalm 19:7–11 (p.510)

[17]Brothers and sisters, I ask you to look out for those who cause people to be against each other and who upset other people's faith. They are against the true teaching you learned, so stay away from them. [18]Such people are not serving our Lord Christ but are only doing what pleases themselves. They use fancy talk and fine words to fool the minds of those who do not know about evil. [19]All the believers have heard that you obey, so I am very happy because of you. But I want you to be wise in what is good and innocent in what is evil.

[20]The God who brings peace will soon defeat Satan and give you power over him.

The grace of our Lord Jesus be with you.

[21]Timothy, a worker together with me, sends greetings, as well as Lucius, Jason and Sosipater, my relatives.

[22]I am Tertius, and I am writing this letter from Paul. I send greetings to you in the Lord.

[23]Gaius is letting me and the whole church here use his home. He also sends greetings to you, as do Erastus, the city treasurer, and our brother Quartus. [24] [n]

[25]Glory to God who can make you strong in faith by the Good News [d] that I tell people and by the message about Jesus Christ. The message about Christ is the secret that was hidden for long ages past but is now made known. [26]It has been made clear through the writings of the prophets. [d] And by the command of the eternal God it is made known to all nations that they might believe and obey.

[27]To the only wise God be glory for ever through Jesus Christ! Amen.

1 Corinthians

Why Read This Book:

- Hear down-to-earth advice about dealing with church problems (1 Corinthians 1—10).
- Learn the importance of working together as Christians (1 Corinthians 11—13).
- Discover the promise of Christ's victory over death (1 Corinthians 14—16).

Behind the Scenes:

When Bob went on a trip with his friends, he thought that it would be a riot with no adults around.

For the first few days everything was great. But as the week wore on, everyone got on everyone else's nerves. With no set regulations to keep everyone in line, chaos ruled. By the end of the week Bob couldn't wait to get home and return to a normal routine.

The Corinthian church faced a similar situation. It was made up of people from a whole variety of backgrounds and income levels, and appears to have been weak on leadership. They began arguing about sex, marriage, leaders and worship, and before long, the church was divided.

That's where the apostle Paul comes in. He had started the church himself around two years before these problems arose and so, naturally, he was concerned that it was destroying itself. He wrote 1 Corinthians, and made a point of answering the major questions that had started the arguments in the church – marriage and being single, food offered to idols, what life in the church should be like, the role of spiritual gifts including tongues. Then he challenged the church to follow Christ in everything.

Maybe you think that the problems we face nowadays are unique and that life nearly 2,000 years ago was vastly different? Read 1 Corinthians and think again.

When?

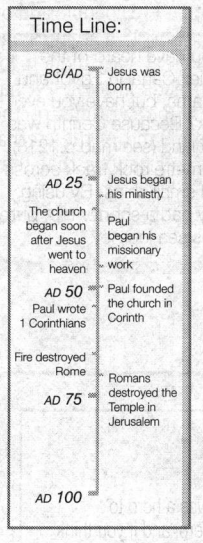

Time Line:

BC/AD	Jesus was born
AD 25	Jesus began his ministry
The church began soon after Jesus went to heaven	Paul began his missionary work
AD 50 Paul wrote 1 Corinthians	Paul founded the church in Corinth
Fire destroyed Rome	
AD 75	Romans destroyed the Temple in Jerusalem
AD 100	

Where?

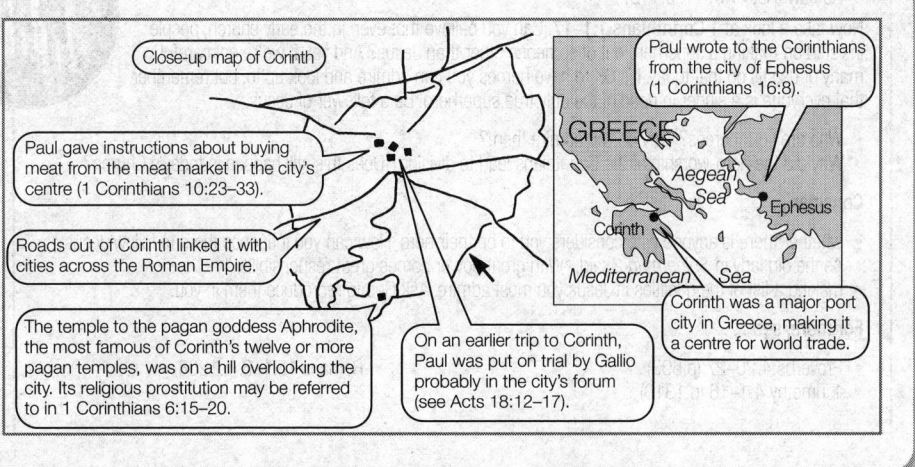

Close-up map of Corinth

Paul gave instructions about buying meat from the meat market in the city's centre (1 Corinthians 10:23–33).

Roads out of Corinth linked it with cities across the Roman Empire.

The temple to the pagan goddess Aphrodite, the most famous of Corinth's twelve or more pagan temples, was on a hill overlooking the city. Its religious prostitution may be referred to in 1 Corinthians 6:15–20.

On an earlier trip to Corinth, Paul was put on trial by Gallio probably in the city's forum (see Acts 18:12–17).

Paul wrote to the Corinthians from the city of Ephesus (1 Corinthians 16:8).

GREECE

Aegean Sea

Ephesus

Corinth

Mediterranean Sea

Corinth was a major port city in Greece, making it a centre for world trade.

1 From Paul. God called me to be an apostle*d* of Christ Jesus because that is what God wanted. Also from Sosthenes, our brother in Christ.

²To the church of God in Corinth, to you who have been made holy in Christ Jesus. You were called to be God's holy people with all people everywhere who pray in the name of the Lord Jesus Christ—their Lord and ours:

³Grace and peace to you from God our Father and the Lord Jesus Christ.

Paul Gives Thanks to God

⁴I always thank my God for you because of the grace God has given you in Christ Jesus. ⁵I thank God because in Christ you have been made rich in every way, in all your speaking and in all your knowledge. ⁶Just as our witness about Christ has been proved to you, ⁷so you have every gift from God while you wait for our Lord Jesus Christ to come again. ⁸Jesus will keep you strong until the end so that there will be no wrong in you on the day our Lord Jesus Christ comes again. ⁹God, who has called you to share everything with his Son, Jesus Christ our Lord, is faithful.

Sidelight You have heard of the Suez Canal in Egypt and the Panama Canal in Panama, but have you ever heard of the Corinth Track? Because Corinth was located on a small strip of land (see map p.1213), the city built an eight-kilometre rock track across the land to roll cargo and small ships. By using this track, sailors not only had a shorter trip, but they avoided a dangerous sea journey.

HEROES

Superhero

The Bible is full of heroes. Moses was a hero to Joshua, Elijah was a hero to Elisha, Paul was a hero to Timothy, and David was a hero to his entire nation. But there is really only one true superhero, and if you think about it long enough, you'll know exactly who that is. Philippians 2:8–9 tells us that God the Father was so impressed with his Son's humility, that he raised him to the highest place, and made his name greater than any other name. Let's take a minute to consider some of Jesus' superhero qualities:

* He controlled the weather (Matthew 8:23–27, p.952)
* He forgave sins (Matthew 9:1–8, p.952)
* He multiplied stuff (Mark 6:30–44, p.1007)
* He walked on water (Mark 6:45–51, p. 1009)
* He healed people (Mark 6:53–56, p.1009)
* He raised the dead (John 11:1–44, p.1114)
* He rose from the dead (John 20:1–9, p.1132)
* He flew (Acts 1:9–11, p.1137)

Now take a look at **1 Corinthians 1:1–17**. Can you believe that even in the early church, people insisted on making a superhero out of someone other than Jesus? And yet, if we're not careful, many of us still do that today. It's OK to have heroes you can admire and look up to, but remember that everyone is a sinner in need of the only true superhero. Be a follower of Jesus.

* Who are your heroes? Why do you admire them?
* Why did the hero-worship of the Corinthians lead to division? Does this still happen in today's Church?

Consider . . .

* whether there is anyone who considers you to be their hero. How can you influence them to follow Jesus? As the old lady in *Spiderman 2* said, "With great power comes great responsibility."
* making a list of the qualities in Jesus you most admire. Ask God to reproduce them in you.

For more, see . . .

* Proverbs 4:20–27 (p.593)
* 1 Timothy 4:1–16 (p.1310)
* Romans 15:1–6 (p.1208)

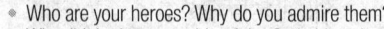

Problems in the Church

[10]I beg you, brothers and sisters, [n] by the name of our Lord Jesus Christ that all of you agree with each other and not be split into groups. I beg that you be completely joined together by having the same kind of thinking and the same purpose. [11]My brothers and sisters, some people from Chloe's family have told me quite plainly that there are quarrels among you. [12]This is what I mean: one of you says, "I follow Paul"; another says, "I follow Apollos"; another says, "I follow Peter"; and another says, "I follow Christ." [13]Christ has been divided up into different groups! Did Paul die on the cross for you? No! Were you baptised [d] in the name of Paul? No! [14]I thank God I did not baptise any of you except Crispus and Gaius [15]so that now no one can say you were baptised in my name. [16](I also baptised the family of Stephanas, but I do not remember that I baptised anyone else.) [17]Christ did not send me to baptise people but to preach the Good News. [d] And he sent me to preach the Good News without using words of human wisdom so that the cross of Christ [n] would not lose its power.

Christ is God's Power and Wisdom

[18]The teaching about the cross is foolishness to those who are being lost, but to us who are being saved it is the power of God. [19]It is written in the Scriptures: [d]

"Their wise men will lose their wisdom;
　their wise men will not be able to
　　understand."
　　　　　　　　　　　　Isaiah 29:14

[20]Where is the wise person? Where is the educated person? Where is the skilled talker of this world? God has made the wisdom of the world foolish. [21]Because of the wisdom of God the world did not know God through its own wisdom. So God chose to use the message that sounds foolish to save those who believe. [22]The Jews ask for miracles, [d] and the Greeks want wisdom. [23]But we preach a crucified Christ. This is a big problem to the Jews, and it is foolishness to those who are not Jews. [24]But Christ is the power of God and the wisdom of God to those people God has called—Jews and Greeks. [25]Even the foolishness of God is wiser than human wisdom, and the weakness of God is stronger than human strength.

[26]Brothers and sisters, look at what you were when God called you. Not many of you were wise in the way the world judges wisdom. Not many of you had great influence. Not many of you came from important families. [27]But God chose the foolish things of the world to shame the wise, and he chose the weak things of the world to shame the strong. [28]He chose what the world thinks is unimportant and what the world looks down on and thinks is nothing in order to destroy what the world thinks is important. [29]God did this so that no one can boast in his presence. [30]Because of God you are in Christ Jesus, who has become for us wisdom from God. In Christ we are put right with God, and have been made holy, and have been set free from sin. [31]So, as the Scripture says, "If someone wants to boast, he should boast only about the Lord." [n]

The Message of Christ's Death

2 Dear brothers and sisters, when I came to you, I did not come preaching God's secret with fancy words or a show of human wisdom. [2]I decided that while I was with you I would forget about everything except Jesus Christ and his death on the cross. [3]So when I came to you, I was weak and fearful and trembling. [4]My teaching and preaching were not with words of human wisdom that persuade people but with proof of the power that the Spirit [d] gives. [5]This was so that your faith would be in God's power and not in human wisdom.

God's Wisdom

[6]However, I speak a wisdom to those who are mature. But this wisdom is not from this world or from the rulers of this world, who are losing their power. [7]I speak God's secret wisdom, which he has kept hidden. Before the world began, God planned this wisdom for our glory. [8]None of the rulers of this world understood it. If they had, they would not have crucified the Lord of glory. [9]But as it is written in the Scriptures: [d]

"From long ago no one
　has ever heard of a God like you.
No one has ever seen
　a God besides you,
　who helps the people who trust you."
　　　　　　　　　　　　Isaiah 64:4

[10]But God has shown us these things through the Spirit. [d]

The Spirit searches out all things, even the deep secrets of God. [11]Who knows the thoughts

---

brothers and sisters　Although the Greek text says "brothers" here and throughout this book, Paul's words were meant for the entire church, both men and women.
cross of Christ　Paul uses the cross as a picture of the gospel, the story of Christ's death and rising from the dead to pay for our sins. The cross, or Christ's death, was God's way to save us.
"If . . . Lord."　Quotation from Jeremiah 9:24.

that another person has? Only a person's spirit that lives within him knows his thoughts. It is the same with God. No one knows the thoughts of God except the Spirit of God. [12]Now we did not receive the spirit of the world, but we received the Spirit that is from God so that we can know all that God has given us. [13]And we speak about these things, not with words taught us by human wisdom but with words taught us by the Spirit. And so we explain spiritual truths to spiritual people. [14]A person who does not have the Spirit does not accept the truths that come from the Spirit of God. That person thinks they are foolish and cannot understand them, because they can only be judged to be true by the Spirit. [15]The spiritual person is able to judge all things, but no one can judge him. The Scripture says:

[16]"Who has known the mind of the LORD
　　or been able to give him advice?"　*Isaiah 40:13*
But we have the mind of Christ.

Following People is Wrong

3 Brothers and sisters, in the past I could not talk to you as I talk to spiritual people. I had to talk to you as I would to people without the Spirit*d*—babies in Christ. [2]The teaching I gave you was like milk, not solid food, because you were not able to take solid food. And even now you are not ready. [3]You are still not spiritual, because there is jealousy and quarrelling among you, and this shows that you are not spiritual. You are acting like people of the world. [4]One of you says, "I belong to Paul," and another says, "I belong to Apollos." When you say things like this, you are acting like people of the world.

[5]Is Apollos important? No! Is Paul important? No! We are only servants of God who helped you believe. Each one of us did the work God gave us to do. [6]I planted the seed, and Apollos watered it. But God is the One who made it grow. [7]So the one who plants is not important,

PRIORITIES

Is This All There Is?

When Howard Hughes was 45, he was one of the most glamorous men in America. He owned an airline and hotels around the world. He dated actresses, flew exotic test aircraft, and worked on top-secret CIA contracts.

Twenty years later, Howard Hughes was the world's richest man – with $2.3 billion. But he was also one of the world's most pathetic. He lived in small, dark rooms in his hotels. He preferred to keep his life without sun and without joy. He had a straggly beard down to his waist and two-inch-long fingernails. His body had wasted away to a mere 50 kilogrammes.

He spent most of his time watching films over and over again – sometimes watching the same film 150 times. He lay naked in bed, deathly afraid of germs. Life had lost its meaning for him.

Finally, hooked on drugs, Howard Hughes died at the age of 67, because he didn't have a medical device his company had helped to develop.

Howard Hughes had it all – worldly wisdom, wealth, power, fame. He had all the things the world considers important. But they weren't enough. Read **1 Corinthians 1:18–31** to see what Paul says is really important in life.

* How was Howard Hughes's life an illustration of this passage?
* According to this passage, what does God say is the most important thing for Christians?

Consider . . .

* doing something "foolish" – such as helping someone who doesn't deserve it – as a sign of your faith.
* tearing out words and pictures from a magazine that show what the world says is important and what God says is important. Make a separate pile for each category.

For more, see . . .

* Psalm 139:1–18 (p.581)
* 1 John 3:1–3 (p.1373)
* 2 Corinthians 11:16–31 (p.1251)

and the one who waters is not important. Only God, who makes things grow, is important. [8]The one who plants and the one who waters have the same purpose, and each will be rewarded for his own work. [9]We are God's workers, working together; you are like God's farm, God's house.

[10]Using the gift God gave me, I laid the foundation of that house like an expert builder. Others are building on that foundation, but all people should be careful how they build on it. [11]The foundation that has already been laid is Jesus Christ, and no one can lay down any other foundation. [12]But if people build on that

foundation, using gold, silver, jewels, wood, grass or straw, [13]their work will be clearly seen, because the Day of Judgement [n] will make it seen. That Day will appear with fire, and the fire will test everyone's work to show what sort of work it was. [14]If the building that has been put

Day of Judgement   The day Christ will come to judge all people and take his people to live with him.

SCHOOL

The Powerful Way

It was disgusting! While Scott was at the evening soccer practise, someone had smeared animal guts all over his bike. Scott just stood in the car park looking shocked.

Things had not been the same since he had seriously committed his life to Christ. Many of his friends didn't understand. They thought that Scott was snubbing them when he wouldn't go drinking with them. The abuse came first. Then a few flattened tyres. Then rumours.

But this? This was sick!

Scott's best friend, Geoff, walked up behind him. When he saw the bike, Geoff blew up.

"I can't believe . . . the nerve of those . . . " Geoff was so angry that he couldn't even finish his sentences. "We know who's behind this," he fumed. "Let's go and kick some heads!"

Scott shook his head and began to smile. "No way. Two quid and some elbow grease, and we'll never know it happened. Besides, aren't we supposed to act more like Jesus? Do you think Jesus would bash heads now?"

Geoff looked at his friend and began to smile. "You're something else. You're also right. OK. To the jet wash we go!"

Scott had plenty of reasons to take revenge. But, instead, Scott prayed for those people and treated them as he would anyone else. People noticed. During his final months at school, people who knew what Scott had been through asked what his secret was.

It was hard for Scott to live the Christian life at school. But because he didn't fight back, Scott's actions demonstrated God's power. To find out more about demonstrating God's power at school, read **1 Corinthians 2:1–11**.

* How do Scott's actions show the difference between God's wisdom and the world's wisdom?
* According to this passage, what should our attitude be as we talk about and demonstrate our faith?

Consider . . .

* imagining that you were with Paul when he was experiencing some of the feelings he talks about in this passage. Write what you would say to encourage him.
* demonstrating God's power at school by not getting angry if people ridicule your faith.

For more, see . . .

* Joshua 6 (p.205)
* 2 Timothy 1:6–8 (p.1316)
* Ephesians 3:14–21 (p.1271)

on the foundation still stands, the builder will get a reward. [15]But if the building is burned up, the builder will suffer loss. The builder will be saved, but it will be as one who escaped from a fire.

[16]Don't you know that you are God's temple and that God's Spirit lives in you? [17]If anyone destroys God's temple, God will destroy that person, because God's temple is holy and you are that temple.

[18]Do not fool yourselves. If you think you are wise in this world, you should become a fool so that you can become truly wise, [19]because the wisdom of this world is foolishness with God. It is written in the Scriptures, [d] "He catches those who are wise in their own clever traps." [n] [20]It is also written in the Scriptures, "The Lord knows what wise people think. He knows their thoughts are just a puff of wind." [n] [21]So you should not boast about human leaders. All things belong to you: [22]Paul, Apollos and Peter; the world, life, death, the present and the future—all these belong to you. [23]And you belong to Christ, and Christ belongs to God.

Apostles are Servants of Christ

4 People should think of us as servants of Christ, the ones God has trusted with his secrets. [2]Now in this way those who are trusted with something valuable must show they are worthy of that trust. [3]As for myself, I do not care if I am judged by you or by any human court. I do not even judge myself. [4]I know of no wrong I

"He . . . traps."　Quotation from Job 5:13.
"The Lord . . . wind."　Quotation from Psalm 94:11.

POPULARITY

Pop Idols and Popularity

Mark was a pretty average kid at school and had lots of friends, but like so many people, he wanted to be one of the "in crowd". The popular kids had it so easy – everyone wanted to be *like* them and the opposite sex wanted to be *with* them! Never was this truer than for the lads in the year 11 rock band as they sang the classic rock song "It's so easy, when everybody's tryin' to please me" to a star-struck crowd of teenage girls. So Mark did what any self-respecting wannabe would do – he learned to play the electric guitar and joined a band!

After a few years, he had become a fine guitarist, graduated from music college and enjoyed the popularity and prestige of touring the UK with a band. At his peak, God challenged Mark to serve him with his music and give up his ambitions of fame and fortune. Over the next few years, Mark took the Gospel into schools, colleges and universities all over Europe as part of a band who gave their testimonies and preached the Gospel at shows.

Mark never earned much money, never achieved the fame he'd once dreamt of and never gained any critical acclaim for his music, but had the far greater joy of knowing that God had used him to bring many young people to Jesus and encouraged countless others in their faith.

Read **1 Corinthians 3:1–23**.

* The Corinthians were arguing over who was a better leader and evangelist, Paul or Apollos. How does this passage show us that this is foolish?
* What does this passage tell us is more important than popularity?

Consider . . .

* whether you have any special talents or skills that you could use for God rather than your own popularity. Why not chat to a church leader or youth leader about how you could use them in church?
* whether you try hard to be popular. Ask God to show you that he created you to be uniquely you, not to try and be someone you're not.

For more, see . . .

* Proverbs 23:15–21 (p.610)
* 1 Corinthians 12:12–27 (p.1231)
* Daniel 1:1–21 (p.833)
* Philippians 2:1–11 (p.1282)

have done, but this does not make me right before the Lord. The Lord is the One who judges me. [5]So do not judge before the right time; wait until the Lord comes. He will bring to light things that are now hidden in darkness, and will make known the secret purposes of people's hearts. Then God will praise each one of them.

[6]Brothers and sisters, I have used Apollos and myself as examples so you could learn through us the meaning of the saying, "Follow only what is written in the Scriptures." [d] Then you will not be more proud of one person than another. [7]Who says you are better than others? What do you have that was not given to you? And if it was given to you, why do you boast as if you did not receive it as a gift?

[8]You think you already have everything you need. You think you are rich. You think you have become kings without us. I wish you really were kings so we could be kings together with you. [9]But it seems to me that God has put us apostles [d] in last place, like those sentenced to die. We are like a show for the whole world to see—angels and people. [10]We are fools for Christ's sake, but you are very wise in Christ. We are weak, but you are strong. You receive honour, but we are shamed. [11]Even to this very hour we do not have enough to eat or drink or to wear. We are often beaten, and we have no homes in which to live. [12]We work hard with our own hands for our food. When people curse us, we bless them. When they hurt us, we put up with it. [13]When they tell evil lies about

SERVICE

Worthy of the Trust

"Son, please don't go."

Bill Dukes's eyes met his father's. "Dad, I believe God wants me in Brazil this year. We've been waiting on the missionary board for a long time. Now the appointment is here. I've got to go."

Bill nearly broke down as he watched his dad's eyes fill with tears. The doctors didn't think Bill's dad had long to live. If Bill left for Brazil, his father might die before Bill could come home.

"Look, Dad, I know you want me to stay. I want to be with you too. But I have to ask what God wants. And as far as I can tell now, he wants me in Brazil."

As Bill drove away from his parents' house, his mind replayed doubts that others had expressed about his decision.

"A wife, one boy, and a baby on the way. You're crazy!"

"Do you really think God would call you away from your father now?"

"We need priests in this country. Why don't you stay?"

Bill weighed his options.

For eight years, Bill and his family worked in South America. And, against all predictions by doctors and the expectations of Bill's family, Bill's father was alive to welcome him home.

"I'm convinced that God is faithful," Bill says, "especially in those times when someone has to make a hard choice to be faithful in serving God."

The Corinthian Christians needed to be reminded of the same thing. Read how Paul makes the point clear in **1 Corinthians 4:1–5**.

* How would Bill's feelings about his life compare with Paul's feelings?
* How do you feel about God knowing and judging the secrets of your heart?

Consider . . .

* thanking God for a servant whose faithfulness has helped you in some way. Ask God to help you to do the same for someone else.
* evaluating any commitments to serve that you have made and haven't kept. Begin fulfilling those commitments this week.

For more, see . . .

* Joshua 24:14–15 (p.222)
* Ephesians 4:11–16 (p.1273)
* Luke 16:10–12 (p.1074)

us, we speak nice words about them. Even today, we are treated as though we were the rubbish of the world—the scum of the earth.

¹⁴I am not trying to make you feel ashamed. I am writing this to give you a warning as my own dear children. ¹⁵For though you may have 10,000 teachers in Christ, you do not have many fathers. Through the Good News *d* I became your father in Christ Jesus, ¹⁶so I beg you, please follow my example. ¹⁷That is why I am sending to you Timothy, my son in the Lord. I love Timothy, and he is faithful. He will help you remember my way of life in Christ Jesus, just as I teach it in all the churches everywhere.

¹⁸Some of you have become proud, thinking that I will not come to you again. ¹⁹But I will come to you very soon if the Lord wishes. Then I will know what the proud ones do, not what they say, ²⁰because the kingdom of God is present not in talk but in power. ²¹Which do you want: that I come to you with punishment or with love and gentleness?

Wickedness in the Church

5 It is actually being said that there is sexual sin among you. And it is a kind that does not happen even among people who do not know God. A man there has his father's wife. ²And you are proud! You should have been filled with sadness so that the man who did this should be put out of your group. ³I am not there with you in person, but I am with you in spirit. And I have already judged the man who did that sin as if I were really there. ⁴When you meet together in the name of our Lord Jesus, and I meet with you in spirit with the power of our Lord Jesus, ⁵then hand this man over to Satan. So his sinful self *n* will be destroyed, and his spirit will be saved on the day of the Lord.

⁶Your boasting is not good. You know the saying, "Just a little yeast makes the whole batch of dough rise." ⁷Take out all the old yeast so that you will be a new batch of dough without yeast, which you really are. For Christ, our Passover *d* lamb, has been sacrificed. ⁸So let us celebrate this feast, but not with the bread that has the old yeast—the yeast of sin and wickedness. Let us celebrate this feast with the bread that has no yeast—the bread of goodness and truth.

⁹I wrote to you in my earlier letter not to associate with those who sin sexually. ¹⁰But I did not mean you should not associate with those of this world who sin sexually, or with the greedy, or robbers, or those who worship idols. To get away from them you would have to leave this world.

¹¹I am writing to tell you that you must not associate with those who call themselves believers in Christ but who sin sexually, or are greedy, or worship idols, or abuse others with words, or get drunk, or cheat people. Do not even eat with people like that.

¹²⁻¹³It is not my business to judge those who are not part of the church. God will judge them. But you must judge the people who are part of the church. The Scripture *d* says, "You must get rid of the evil person among you." *n*

> ### Sidelight
> Corinth was known for lawsuits (1 Corinthians 6:1). Trials were social events, and sitting on the jury was a privilege. One record tells of a jury with 6,000 people on it.

Judging Problems Among Christians

6 When you have something against another Christian, how can you bring yourself to go before judges who are not right with God? Why do you not let God's people decide who is right? ²Surely you know that God's people will judge the world. So if you are to judge the world, are you not able to judge small cases as well? ³You know that in the future we will judge angels, so surely we can judge the ordinary things of this life. ⁴If you have ordinary cases that must be judged, are you going to appoint people as judges who mean nothing to the church? ⁵I say this to shame you. Surely there is someone among you wise enough to judge a complaint between believers. ⁶But now one believer goes to court against another believer—and you do this in front of unbelievers!

⁷The fact that you have lawsuits against each other shows that you are already defeated. Why not let yourselves be wronged? Why not let yourselves be cheated? ⁸But you yourselves do wrong and cheat, and you do this to other believers!

⁹⁻¹⁰Surely you know that the people who do wrong will not inherit God's kingdom. Do not be fooled. Those who sin sexually, worship idols, take part in adultery, *d* those who are male prostitutes *d* or men who have sexual relations with other men, those who steal, are greedy, get drunk, lie about others or rob—these people will not inherit God's kingdom. ¹¹In the past, some of you were like that, but you were washed clean. You were made holy, and you were made right with God in the name of the Lord Jesus Christ and in the Spirit *d* of our God.

---

sinful self　Literally, "flesh". This could also mean his body.
"You . . . you."　Quotation from Deuteronomy 17:7; 19:19; 22:21,24; 24:7.

Use Your Bodies for God's Glory

[12]"I am allowed to do all things," but all things are not good for me to do. "I am allowed to do all things," but I will not let anything make me its slave. [13]"Food is for the stomach, and the stomach for food," but God will destroy them both. The body is not for sexual sin but for the Lord, and the Lord is for the body. [14]By his power God has raised the Lord from the dead and will also raise us from the dead. [15]Surely you know that your bodies are parts of Christ himself. So I must never take the parts of Christ and join them to a prostitute! [d] [16]It is written in the Scriptures, [d] "The two will become one body." [n] So you should know that anyone who joins with a prostitute becomes one body with the prostitute. [17]But the one who joins with the Lord is one spirit with the Lord.

[18]So run away from sexual sin. Every other sin people do is outside their bodies, but those who sin sexually sin against their own bodies. [19]You should know that your body is a temple for the Holy Spirit [d] who is in you. You have received the Holy Spirit from God. So you do not belong to yourselves, [20]because you were bought by God for a price. So honour God with your bodies.

About Marriage

7 Now I will discuss the things you wrote to me about. It is good for a man not to have sexual relations with a woman. [2]But because sexual sin is a danger, each man should have his own wife, and each woman should have her own husband. [3]The husband should give his wife all that he owes her as his wife. And the wife should give her husband all that she owes him as her husband. [4]The wife does not have full rights over her own body; her husband shares them. And the husband does not have full rights over his own body; his wife shares them. [5]Do not refuse to give your bodies to each other, unless you both agree to stay

"The two . . . body." Quotation from Genesis 2:24.

BOASTING

Honest to God!

Nothing ordinary ever seemed to happen to Rob. His stories of extravagant family holidays, chance meetings with famous people and doing unbelievable feats were too amazing to be true. When Tim McCormick questioned the facts of his stories, Rob would get defensive. He would insist he was being truthful by saying, "Honest to God!"

Finally, Tim caught Rob in a blatant lie. One Saturday morning he phoned to tell Tim that he had got a ticket to a rock concert that had been sold out for more than two months. He wouldn't show Tim the ticket for fear of losing it, he said, nor would he explain how he got it. Yet he tried to make Tim believe that he had an "inside" source. He promised to tell him all about the concert the next day.

But that night, during the very hour of the concert, Tim spotted Rob with his family at a superstore more than fifty kilometres from the concert site! Tim confronted Rob the next day, and he still insisted that he had been at the concert. When Tim told him he had seen him at the superstore, he finally admitted that he had exaggerated a little – but he had bought the group's latest album, he said.

Tim's friendship with Rob crumbled after that. Read **1 Corinthians 5:6–8** to see what Paul thought about boasting.

* How was Rob's boasting like the yeast that Paul writes about?
* What effects has boasting had in your relationships?

Consider . . .

* listing specific ways in which people can keep themselves from boasting.
* asking God to show you if you have been boasting. If so, tell the modest truth to the people you boasted to.

For more, see . . .

* Isaiah 10:8–15 (p.651)
* James 4:13–17 (p.1352)
* Jeremiah 9:23–24 (p.728)

away from sexual relations for a time so you can give your time to prayer. Then come together again so Satan cannot tempt you because of a lack of self-control. ⁶I say this to give you permission to stay away from sexual relations for a time. It is not a command to do so. ⁷I wish that everyone were like me, but each person has his own gift from God. One has one gift, another has another gift.

⁸Now for those who are not married and for the widows I say this: it is good for them to stay unmarried as I am. ⁹But if they cannot control themselves, they should marry. It is better to marry than to burn with sexual desire.

¹⁰Now I give this command for the married people. (The command is not from me; it is from the Lord.) A wife should not leave her husband. ¹¹But if she does leave, she must not marry again, or she should make up with her husband. Also the husband should not divorce his wife.

¹²For all the others I say this (I am saying this, not the Lord): if a Christian man has a wife who is not a believer, and she is happy to live with him, he must not divorce her. ¹³And if a Christian woman has a husband who is not a believer, and he is happy to live with her, she must not divorce him. ¹⁴The husband who is not a believer is made holy through his believing wife. And the wife who is not a believer is made holy through her believing husband. If this were not true, your children would not be clean, *d* but now your children are holy.

¹⁵But if those who are not believers decide to leave, let them leave. When this happens, the Christian man or woman is free. But God called us to live in peace. ¹⁶Wife, you don't know; maybe you will save your husband. And husband, you don't know; maybe you will save your wife.

HOMOSEXUALITY

Step Up For the Prize

The moment of truth had arrived. After months of exhausting rehearsals and fierce competitions, the final ten contestants stood before the judges. Only five of them would be chosen to make the band, the others would be sent home empty-handed. As they stood waiting silently, their hearts seemed to beat very loudly.

Five names were called out. One by one, the judges gave a list of reasons why each one of them would not be in the band. They were sent home. And the other five then stepped up and claimed their prize.

Read **1 Corinthians 6:9–11**. In this passage, Paul, like the competition judges, gives us a list of some of the characteristics of people who will not win the prize of inheriting God's kingdom.

It causes arguments today, but homosexuality is clearly stated here as something that does not please God. Homosexuality has been around for ages, it is found in Genesis, but people are still unsure as to what makes a person "gay" (is it in the genes or is it a conscious decision?). Despite its history and mystery, it's on the list.

If, as you read this, you are thinking that you may be gay, you need first to know that Jesus loves you. Then you need to spend some time with him, working out how you can live the life you were created to live, walking with Jesus the whole time.

* How do you react to people who fail God's test for levels of sexual purity? How does Jesus react to them? Read John 8:1–11 (p.1109) to find out more.
* "If I follow what Paul is saying, I am able to do whatever I want, because I will just be forgiven again, right?" Read Paul's answer in Romans 6:1–14 (p.1191).

Consider . . .

* whether your attitude towards homosexuality is one that might not please Jesus? Maybe you could spend some time saying sorry to God and asking him to change your attitude.
* making a list of characteristics you want to display in your life. For help, check out Matthew 5:1–12 (p.942).

For more, see . . .

* Genesis 2:4–25 (p.3)
* John 8:1–11 (p.1109)

* Genesis 19:1–29 (p.23)

Live as God Called You

[17]But in any case each one of you should continue to live the way God has given you to live— the way you were when God called you. This is a rule I make in all the churches. [18]If a man was already circumcised *d* when he was called, he should not undo his circumcision. If a man was without circumcision when he was called, he should not be circumcised. [19]It is not important if a man is circumcised or not. The important thing is obeying God's commands. [20]Each one of you should stay the way you were when God called you. [21]If you were a slave when God called you, do not let that bother you. But if you can be free, then make good use of your freedom. [22]Those who were slaves when the Lord called them are free persons who belong to the Lord. In the same way, those who were free when they were called are now Christ's slaves. [23]You all were bought at a great price, so do not become slaves of people. [24]Brothers and sisters, each of you should stay as you were when you were called, and stay there with God.

Questions About Getting Married

[25]Now I write about people who are not married. I have no command from the Lord about this; I give my opinion. But I can be trusted, because the Lord has shown me mercy. [26]The present time is a time of trouble, so I think it is good for you to

DRUGS AND ALCOHOL

God's Temple is Your Body!

Penny went to a party on a Friday night with a whole load of her mates. After a while, some of the group got bored and decided to go to the corner shop to see if they would get served if they tried to buy a bottle of vodka. A little bit later, they came back with two bottles which were quickly opened and passed around. Penny didn't really feel comfortable about this and at first managed to ignore the bottle and carry on her conversation. However, after a while, some of the group started teasing her about not drinking and she gave in and had a large swig. While not really liking the taste, she felt pressured and carried on drinking throughout the evening. She ended up feeling really dizzy and was sick in the toilet. The next morning she felt rather ill and embarrassed.

It is easy to come into contact with illegal substances. A survey of over 9,000 English school pupils aged eleven to fifteen found that:

* 11 per cent had taken drugs in the last month
* 19 per cent had taken drugs in the last year
* 9 per cent were regular smokers (10 per cent of girls, compared with 7 per cent of boys)
* 22 per cent had drunk alcohol in the last week

How do Penny's actions and the statistics of school pupils compare with people you know of that age?

Read **1 Corinthians 6:12–20.** Paul warns of the dangers of becoming focused on or addicted to worldly things. In our culture these might include food, sex, computer gaming, drugs and alcohol.

* Why should you listen to what the Bible says about these temptations?
* What are the things that you do that damage your "temple for the Holy Spirit" (verse 19)?

Consider . . .

* thinking about everything linked to parties you go to. Write them down on a piece of paper under three columns: things which God would take delight in; things which are not wrong in themselves but open to abuse; things which God would forbid.
* developing an accountability group with a couple of your mates where you check up on each other, including how you act on a party night.

For more, see . . .

* Proverbs 1:10 (p.590)
* Romans 12:2 (p.1203)
* Proverbs 23:29–35 (p.610)

stay the way you are. [27]If you have a wife, do not try to become free from her. If you are not married, do not try to find a wife. [28]But if you decide to marry, you have not sinned. And if a girl who has never married decides to marry, she has not sinned. But those who marry will have trouble in this life, and I want you to be free from trouble.

[29]Brothers and sisters, this is what I mean: we do not have much time left. So starting now, those who have wives should live as if they had no wives. [30]Those who are crying should live as if they were not crying. Those who are happy should live as if they were not happy. Those who buy things should live as if they own nothing. [31]Those who use the things of the world should live as if they were not using them, because this world in its present form will soon be gone.

[32]I want you to be free from worry. A man who is not married is busy with the Lord's work, trying to please the Lord. [33]But a man who is married is busy with things of the world, trying to please his wife. [34]He must think about two things—pleasing his wife and pleasing the Lord. A woman who is not married or a girl who has never married is busy with the Lord's work. She wants to be holy in body and spirit. But a married woman is busy with things of the world, as to how she can please her husband. [35]I am saying this to help you, not to limit you. But I want you to live in the right way, to give yourselves fully to the Lord without concern for other things.

[36]If a man thinks he is not doing the right thing with the girl he is engaged to, if she is almost past the best age to marry and he feels he should marry her, he should do what he wants. They should get married. It is no sin. [37]But if a man is sure in his mind that there is no need for marriage, and has his own desires under control, and has decided not to marry the one to whom he is engaged, he is doing the right thing. [38]So the man who marries his girl does right, but the man who does not marry will do better.

[39]A woman must stay with her husband as long as he lives. But if her husband dies, she is free to marry any man she wants, but she must

LOVE

Give God the No.1 Spot

Dave first saw Dawn when he was leaving church and she was in a coffee shop opposite. He knew her from school, and had always liked her, but for the first time their eyes met and she smiled! Instantly, Dave melted.

As time went by, they got to know each other better. To begin with, Dave was worried that Dawn wasn't a Christian, but he thought that maybe if he prayed hard enough it would only be a matter of time before she met God. Time went by and whilst they got to know each other much better – and fell in love – Dawn had not yet met God. Dave still really wanted to be involved in the church and help run the percussion group he'd set up, but increasingly he found himself phoning at the last minute to say he couldn't come. He knew he was putting Dawn before God.

However much he tried, he couldn't seem to change the priorities in his life. The love he had for Dawn was really strong, and he knew deep down that it was pulling him further from a deeper love, the love of his Father God.

Read **1 Corinthians 7:29–35**. Paul gives some advice about people in this kind of situation.

* What do you think Paul would say to Dave?
* What are the things in verse 35 that Paul says we should do?

Consider . . .

* spending some time thinking and praying about how you can live for God fully and not let other things get in the way.
* whether you have asked Jesus into your life. If not, why not ask him to forgive you and give you new life today.

For more, see . . .

* Matthew 10:37 (p.957)
* 1 John 3:16 (p.1374)
* 1 John 5:1–5 (p.1375)

marry in the Lord. [40]The woman is happier if she does not marry again. This is my opinion, but I believe I also have God's Spirit. *d*

About Food Offered to Idols

8 Now I will write about meat that is sacrificed to idols. We know that "we all have knowledge." Knowledge puffs you up with pride, but love builds up. [2]If you think you know something, you do not yet know anything as you should. [3]But if any person loves God, that person is known by God.

[4]So this is what I say about eating meat sacrificed to idols: we know that an idol is really nothing in the world, and we know there is only one God. [5]Even though there are things called gods, in heaven or on earth (and there are many "gods" and "lords"), [6]for us there is only one God—our Father. All things came from him, and we live for him. And there is only one Lord—Jesus Christ. All things were made through him, and we also were made through him.

[7]But not all people know this. Some people are still so used to idols that when they eat meat, they still think of it as being sacrificed to an idol. Because their conscience is weak, when they eat it, they feel guilty. [8]But food will not bring us closer to God. Refusing to eat does not make us less pleasing to God, and eating does not make us better in God's sight.

[9]But be careful that your freedom does not cause those who are weak in faith to fall into sin. [10]You have "knowledge", so you have freedom to eat in an idol's temple. *n* But someone who is weak in faith might see you eating there and be encouraged to eat meat sacrificed to idols while thinking it is wrong to do so. [11]This weak believer for whom Christ died is ruined because of your "knowledge". [12]When you sin against your brothers and sisters in Christ like this and cause them to do what they feel is wrong, you are also sinning against Christ. [13]So if the food I eat causes them to fall into sin, I will never eat meat again so that I will not cause any of them to sin.

idol's temple   Building where a god is worshipped.

FREEDOM

Free to Do Good

Holly was overweight. All the kids made fun of her when she tried to play games with them. And when refreshments were served, they would say things such as "Quick! Hide the food. Here comes Holly."

One night after youth group, youth leader Max found Holly crying in an empty room. She told Max about how much it hurt when the others made fun of her, and how she wanted to lose weight but couldn't. Max couldn't relate to Holly's weight problem; he was a runner and never seemed to put on weight. But he could empathise with the pain that she felt.

"I'll tell you what, Holly," he offered. "You give up sweets and so will I. And why don't you start running with me?"

Holly agreed. The two ran together three times a week. And at youth group meetings, while the kids were eating biscuits and sweets, Max and Holly chewed on raw carrot.

In four months, Holly had lost 15 kilogrammes. She felt better about herself. Holly told Max that she couldn't have done it without him.

Max could have eaten whatever he wanted, but he gave up his freedom to help Holly. Read **1 Corinthians 8:1–13** to see how Paul encourages Christians to use their freedom to help others.

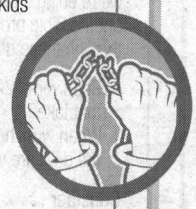

* How do Max's actions demonstrate the principles of this passage?
* How would your friends describe your use of the freedom you have in Jesus?

Consider . . .

* changing an area of your life if your freedom is hurting others.
* talking to a new Christian and asking what he or she thinks about how Christians use their freedom.

For more, see . . .

* Deuteronomy 30:11–20 (p.192)
* 1 Timothy 4:10–12 (p.1311)

* 1 Corinthians 10:23–24 (p.1228)

Paul is like the Other Apostles

9 I am a free man. I am an apostle. *d* I have seen Jesus our Lord. You people are all an example of my work in the Lord. [2]If others do not accept me as an apostle, surely you do, because you are proof that I am an apostle in the Lord.

[3]This is the answer I give people who want to judge me: [4]do we not have the right to eat and drink? [5]Do we not have the right to bring a believing wife with us when we travel as do the other apostles and the Lord's brothers and Peter? [6]Are Barnabas and I the only ones who must work to earn our living? [7]No soldier ever serves in the army and pays his own salary. No one ever plants a vineyard without eating some of the grapes. No person takes care of a flock without drinking some of the milk.

[8]I do not say this by human authority; God's law also says the same thing. [9]It is written in the law of Moses: "When an ox is working in the grain, do not cover its mouth to keep it from eating."*n* When God said this, was he thinking only about oxen? No. [10]He was really talking about us. Yes, that Scripture *d* was written for us, because it goes on to say: "The one who ploughs and the one who works in the grain should hope to get some of the grain for their work." [11]Since we planted spiritual seed among you, is it too much if we should harvest from you some things for this life? [12]If others have the right to get something from you, surely we have this right, too. But we do not use it. No, we put up with everything ourselves so that we will not keep anyone from believing the Good News *d* of Christ. [13]Surely you know that those who work at the Temple *d* get their food from the Temple, and

"When an ox . . . eating."   Quotation from Deuteronomy 25:4.

SHARING FAITH

Just Doin' My Job Sir

A paperboy drops a newspaper outside a house on one of his regular rounds. The homeowner opens the door and calls after him, "Thanks for bringing me my paper this morning!"

"Just doin' my job, sir."

A doctor finishes a routine check-up with one of his oldest patients. Before leaving the room, the old lady turns and says, "Thank you for fitting me into your busy schedule."

"Just doin' my job, ma'am."

A missionary is mocked and ridiculed by the very people he's sacrificed everything for. His family is kidnapped, his home is torched, and he's beaten to within an inch of his life and left bleeding in the gutter.

"Just doin' my job, sir."

In **1 Corinthians 9:16–27**, the apostle Paul reminds us that as Christians it is our *duty* to share our faith. We're *all* meant to be missionaries – people willing to set aside our own precious ambitions for the most important job entrusted to mankind this side of heaven – telling the Good News. And if we're doing it properly, we will definitely face tough times. We want health, wealth and happiness, but the Bible promises trials, tests and temptations! Like a good athlete, we must grow stronger through these difficult situations, using self-control to win the prize.

* Read verse 22. Who have you become like, in order to win them to Christ? How much effort did that take?
* When was the last time you were mocked for sharing your faith in Jesus? How much of a threat to the devil are you?

Consider . . .

* disciplining yourself to memorise Bible verses that will come in handy when you're sharing your faith.
* teaming up with other young Christians for the purpose of going out and witnessing together. Why not do it right now?

For more, see . . .

* Isaiah 61:1–3 (p.705)
* Matthew 10:1–15 (p.954)

those who serve at the altar get part of what is offered at the altar. ¹⁴In the same way, the Lord has commanded that those who tell the Good News should get their living from this work.

¹⁵But I have not used any of these rights. And I am not writing this now to get anything from you. I would rather die than have my reason for boasting taken away. ¹⁶Telling the Good News does not give me any reason for boasting. Telling the Good News is my duty—something I must do. And how terrible it will be for me if I do not tell the Good News. ¹⁷If I preach because it is my own choice, I have a reward. But if I preach and it is not my choice to do so, I am only doing the duty that was given to me. ¹⁸So what reward do I get? This is my reward: that when I tell the Good News I can offer it freely. I do not use my full rights in my work of preaching the Good News.

¹⁹I am free and belong to no one. But I make myself a slave to all people to win as many as I can. ²⁰To the Jews I became like a Jew to win the Jews. I myself am not ruled by the law. But to those who are ruled by the law I became like a person who is ruled by the law. I did this to win those who are ruled by the law. ²¹To those who are without the law I became like a person who is without the law. I did this to win those people who are without the law. (But really, I am not without God's law—I am ruled by Christ's law.) ²²To those who are weak, I became weak so I could win the weak. I have become all things to all people so I could save some of them in any way possible. ²³I do all this because of the Good News and so I can share in its blessings.

²⁴You know that in a race all the runners run, but only one gets the prize. So run to win! ²⁵All those who compete in the games use self-control so they can win a crown. That crown is an earthly thing that lasts only a short time, but our crown will never be destroyed. ²⁶So I do not run without a goal. I fight like a boxer who is hitting something—not just the air. ²⁷I treat my body hard and make it my slave so that I myself will not be rejected after I have preached to others.

Warnings from Israel's Past

10 Brothers and sisters, I want you to know what happened to our ancestors who followed Moses. They were all under the cloud and all went through the sea. ²They were all

Exit Strategy

There were a few battered chairs and a dartboard in the corner. A group of lads Alex recognised from school were huddled together on one of the sofas in the youth club, flicking through a magazine and laughing. As Alex and Joe approached them, Alex could see they were looking at a "top-shelf" magazine. One of the guys looked up, "Here you go Alex, I found a pile of these in a skip." And he chucked one at him.

"Nah mate, not interested," said Alex. "Come on Joe, let's go and play some pool." But Joe wanted to hang around with the guys. "Come on Joe, let's go."

"It's alright *little boy,* we know you're not quite grown up enough for this yet?" teased one of the boys, Alex could tell that Joe wanted to stay and join in with them. Alex nearly gave in. He was about to sit down and look at the mags when he realised the pool table had just become free.

"Come on Joe, let's see who the little boy is! See if you can beat me at pool, best out of five."

"All right," said Joe, "you're on!"
Read **1 Corinthians 10:1–13**.

* Why is Paul keen to warn the Corinthians not to sin sexually?
* What are the best ways of avoiding temptation to sin sexually?

Consider . . .

* designing an "exit strategy" for times when you are tempted by sexual sin.
* listing situations when you might be tempted sexually. Then decide how you will avoid them.

For more, see . . .

* John 8:31–38 (p.1110)
* Ephesians 5:1–5 (p.1274)
* Galatians 6:7–10 (p.1265)

baptised *d* as followers of Moses in the cloud and in the sea. ³They all ate the same spiritual food, ⁴and all drank the same spiritual drink. They drank from that spiritual rock that followed them, and that rock was Christ. ⁵But God was not pleased with most of them, so they died in the desert.

⁶And these things happened as examples for us, to stop us from wanting evil things as those people did. ⁷Do not worship idols, as some of them did. Just as it is written in the Scriptures: *d* "They sat down to eat and drink, and then they got up and sinned sexually." *n* ⁸We must not take part in sexual sins, as some of them did. In one day 23,000 of them died because of their sins. ⁹We must not test Christ as some of them did; they were killed by snakes. ¹⁰Do not complain as some of them did; they were killed by the angel that destroys.

¹¹The things that happened to those people are examples. They were written down to teach us, because we live in a time when all these things of the past have reached their goal. ¹²If you think you are strong, you should be careful not to fall. ¹³The only temptation that has come to you is that which everyone has. But you can trust God, who will not let you be tempted more than you can stand. But when you are tempted, he will also give you a way to escape so that you will be able to stand it.

¹⁴So, my dear friends, run away from the worship of idols. ¹⁵I am speaking to you as to intelligent people; judge for yourselves what I say. ¹⁶We give thanks for the cup of blessing, *n* which is a sharing in the blood of Christ. And the bread that we break is a sharing in the body of Christ. ¹⁷Because there is one loaf of bread, we who are many are one body, because we all share that one loaf.

¹⁸Think about the Israelites: do not those who eat the sacrifices share in the altar? ¹⁹I do not mean that the food sacrificed to an idol is important. I do not mean that an idol is anything at all. ²⁰But I say that what is sacrificed to idols is offered to demons, *d* not to God. And I do not want you to share anything with demons. ²¹You cannot drink the cup of the Lord and the cup of demons also. You cannot share in the Lord's table and the table of demons. ²²Are we trying to make the Lord jealous? We are not stronger than he is, are we?

How to Use Christian Freedom

²³"We are allowed to do all things," but all things are not good for us to do. "We are allowed to do all things," but not all things help others grow stronger. ²⁴Do not look out only for yourselves. Look out for the good of others also.

²⁵Eat any meat that is sold in the meat market. Do not ask questions to see if it is meat you think is wrong to eat. ²⁶You may eat it, "because the earth belongs to the Lord, and everything in it." *n* ²⁷Those who are not believers may invite you to eat with them. If you want to go, eat anything that is put before you. Do not ask questions to see if you think it might be wrong to eat. ²⁸But if anyone says to you, "That food was offered to idols," do not eat it. Do not eat it because of that person who told you and because eating it might be thought to be wrong. ²⁹I don't mean you think it is wrong, but the other person might. But why, you ask, should my freedom be judged by someone else's conscience? ³⁰If I eat the meal with thankfulness, why am I criticised because of something for which I thank God?

³¹The answer is, if you eat or drink, or if you do anything, do it all for the glory of God. ³²Never do anything that might hurt others—Jews, Greeks or God's church— ³³just as I, also, try to please everybody in every way. I am not trying to do what is good for me but what is good for most people so they can be saved.

11 Follow my example, as I follow the example of Christ.

Being Under Authority

²I praise you because you remember me in everything, and you follow closely the teachings just as I gave them to you. ³But I want you to understand this: the head of every man is Christ, the head of a woman is the man *n* and the head of Christ is God. ⁴Every man who prays or prophesies *d* with his head covered brings shame to his head. ⁵But every woman who prays or prophesies with her head uncovered brings shame to her head. She is the same as a woman who has her head shaved. ⁶If a woman does not cover her head, she should have her hair cut off. But since it is shameful for a woman to cut off her hair or to shave her head, she should cover her head. ⁷But a man should not cover his head, because he is the

---

"They . . . sexually." Quotation from Exodus 32:6.
cup of blessing The cup of the fruit of the vine that Christians thank God for and drink at the Lord's Supper.
"because . . . it." Quotation from Psalms 24:1; 50:12; 89:11.
the man This could also mean "her husband".

likeness and glory of God. But woman is man's glory. [8]Man did not come from woman, but woman came from man. [9]And man was not made for woman, but woman was made for man. [10]So that is why a woman should have a symbol of authority on her head, because of the angels.

[11]But in the Lord women are not independent of men, and men are not independent of women. [12]This is true because woman came from man, but also man is born from woman. But everything comes from God. [13]Decide this for yourselves: is it right for a woman to pray to God with her head uncovered? [14]Even nature itself teaches you that wearing long hair is shameful for a man. [15]But long hair is a woman's glory. Long hair is given to her as a covering. [16]Some people may still want to argue about this, but I would add that neither we nor the churches of God have any other practice.

The Lord's Supper

[17]In the things I tell you now I do not praise you, because when you come together you do more harm than good. [18]First, I hear that when you meet together as a church you are divided, and I believe some of this. [19](It is necessary to have differences among you so that it may be clear which of you really have God's approval.) [20]When you come together, you are not really eating the Lord's Supper. [n] [21]This is because when you eat, each person eats without waiting for the others. Some people do not get enough to eat, while others have too much to drink. [22]You can eat and drink in your own homes! You seem to think God's church is not important, and you embarrass those who are poor. What should I tell you? Should I praise you? I do not praise you for doing this.

Lord's Supper   The special meal that Jesus told his followers to eat to remember him (Luke 22:14–20).

WORSHIP

Remember Me?

The second Sunday in March is a special day for Sharon's family. Each year on this date, her family gathers for a meal. When the table has been cleared, the family photo albums are brought out and passed round.

Everyone smiles to see how each family member has changed from picture to picture over the years. The giggles sometimes erupt into laughter when the pictures prompt funny stories. Sharon's favourite is the one about her dad being chased by a bull when he was a teenager.

And there are always tears when the family sees the photos of its absent members. No eye is dry when photos of Jonathan, Sharon's younger brother, are passed around. He died of cystic fibrosis when he was five.

Some of Sharon's friends think her family's habit is a bit strange. A few have even wondered if it isn't like worshipping the dead.

But Sharon shrugs off their comments. "It's just how we remember the people who've been important to our family. I never met my grandparents, but I feel as if I know them. I've seen their pictures and heard stories about them at least once a year for as long as I can remember," she explains. "I don't think we worship our dead relatives; we just celebrate their lives."

As Christians, we don't worship the dead. But we do worship one who died and rose from the dead. Read **1 Corinthians 11:23–26** to see how Paul explains one way in which Christians can celebrate Jesus' life and work.

* How is the celebration which Paul describes similar to the celebration in Sharon's family? How is it different?
* What do you do in your church and life to remember Jesus?

Consider . . .

* creating other celebrations to remember Jesus. For example, a candlelit dinner could remind you that Jesus is the light of the world.
* talking to your minister about the ways in which your church follows this scripture.

For more, see . . .

* Exodus 12:14–20 (p.70)
* Luke 22:14–20 (p.1087)

* Exodus 16:31–36 (p.75)

23The teaching I gave you is the same teaching I received from the Lord: on the night when the Lord Jesus was handed over to be killed, he took bread 24and gave thanks for it. Then he broke the bread and said, "This is my body; it is for you. Do this to remember me." 25In the same way, after they ate, Jesus took the cup. He said, "This cup is the new agreement that is sealed with the blood of my death. When you drink this, do it to remember me." 26Every time you eat this bread and drink this cup you are telling others about the Lord's death until he comes.

27So a person who eats the bread or drinks the cup of the Lord in a way that is not worthy of it will be guilty of sinning against the body and the blood of the Lord. 28Look into your own hearts before you eat the bread and drink the cup, 29because all who eat the bread and drink the cup without recognising the body eat and drink judgement against themselves. 30That is why many in your group are sick and weak, and many have died. 31But if we judged ourselves in the right way, God would not judge us. 32But when the Lord judges us, he punishes us so that we will not be destroyed along with the world.

33So my brothers and sisters, when you come together to eat, wait for each other. 34Anyone who is too hungry should eat at home so that in meeting together you will not bring God's judgement on yourselves. I will tell you what to do about the other things when I come.

Gifts from the Holy Spirit

12 Now, brothers and sisters, I want you to understand about spiritual gifts. 2You know

---

SELF-ESTEEM

A Reassuring Gift

People have differing views about spiritual gifts today. This true story shows how important the issue was for one person.

Debbie was a normal twelve-year-old, apart from one invisible but serious problem. She suffered from dyslexia. People like Debbie lack the ability to work out how words should be spelled and often have poor handwriting, as well as finding difficulty with reading and spelling – even when they are very intelligent. Debbie's problem meant that she often felt left out – that God had not given her one very important gift and that she was worth less than other people.

One day Debbie was in a church meeting where people of her age were asked whether they wanted to know the Holy Spirit's power in their lives. During that meeting as she prayed, Debbie received the gift of speaking in different languages – that have never been learned. It is sometimes called the "gift of tongues". The best thing about it was that this new gift made her feel so much closer to her Heavenly Father. Now she felt that God had included her and that she was just as important as everybody else.

Debbie still uses her prayer language to speak to God and still finds spelling a problem. But she found the confidence to apply to university when she was about twenty-two years old. The course was ideal for her because she was sometimes allowed to present her work audiovisually instead of writing essays.

Today Debbie is a qualified social worker, helping families who feel worthless and unwanted.

Read **1 Corinthians 12:1–11** to find out what Paul says about gifts.

* According to the passage what are the important things about spiritual gifts? Are they different from natural abilities?
* How do you feel about gifts like tongues, prophecy and healing?

Consider . . .

* meeting with friends to discuss how you each feel about spiritual gifts (including those mentioned in other parts of the Bible).
* identifying people like Debbie and reassuring them that they are important to God and to you.

For more, see . . .

* 1 Samuel 16:1–13 (p.269)
* 1 Corinthians 14:1–5 (p.1232)
* Romans 12:1–8 (p.1203)

the way you lived before you were believers. You let yourselves be influenced and led away to worship idols—things that could not speak. ³So I want you to understand that no one who is speaking with the help of God's Spirit*d* says, "Jesus be cursed." And no one can say, "Jesus is Lord," without the help of the Holy Spirit.

⁴There are different kinds of gifts, but they are all from the same Spirit. ⁵There are different ways to serve but the same Lord to serve. ⁶And there are different ways that God works through people but the same God. God works in all of us in everything we do. ⁷Something from the Spirit can be seen in each person, for the common good. ⁸The Spirit gives one person the ability to speak with wisdom, and the same Spirit gives another the ability to speak with knowledge. ⁹The same Spirit gives faith to one person. And, to

another, that one Spirit gives gifts of healing. ¹⁰The Spirit gives to another person the power to do miracles, *d* to another the ability to prophesy. *d* And he gives to another the ability to know the difference between good and evil spirits. The Spirit gives one person the ability to speak in different kinds of languages*n* and to another the ability to interpret those languages. ¹¹One Spirit, the same Spirit, does all these things, and the Spirit decides what to give each person.

The Body of Christ Works Together

¹²A person's body is only one thing, but it has many parts. Though there are many parts to a body, all those parts make only one body. Christ is like that also. ¹³Some of us are Jews, and some are Greeks. Some of us are slaves, and some are free. But we were all baptised *d* into one body

languages   This can also be translated "tongues".

CHURCH

Watching Every Detail

Michelangelo spent four years painting the 40-metre-long by 13-metre-wide ceiling of the Sistine Chapel. Every day for hours, Michelangelo would lie on his back on the scaffolding, perfecting the details of hundreds of figures from the book of Genesis.

The colour. The curves of the lines. The facial expressions. The shadows. The hair. The noses. The fingers. Every detail was important.

But the ceiling was nearly twenty metres from the floor. Those admiring Michelangelo's work could see the mastery of his work, but they couldn't see the details from so far away.

One day one of Michelangelo's friends asked Michelangelo why he spent so many hours painstakingly perfecting each detail – details no one would ever be able to see. "After all, who will know whether it is perfect or not?" he asked.

"I shall," Michelangelo replied.

Michelangelo saw the many possibilities of detail for the ceiling of the Sistine Chapel. And he knew that when all those details came together, they would make a masterpiece.

That's what **1 Corinthians 12:12–27** is all about. Read what Paul says about the importance of many parts making one body – the church.

* According to the passage, why are details so important?
* How can this passage help you see to the important gifts that each person brings to your church?

Consider . . .

* asking a teenager, a middle-aged adult, and a senior citizen about the ways in which they contribute to church and why those contributions are important. Then evaluate your own contributions.
* getting involved in the church and using your talents. If you sing, join the choir. If you're good at art, make posters to publicise events.

For more, see . . .

* 1 Kings 5:5–18 (p.318)
* 1 Peter 4:7–11 (p.1360)
* Colossians 3:11–17 (p.1292)

through one Spirit. *d* And we were all made to share in the one Spirit.

[14]The human body has many parts. [15]The foot might say, "Because I am not a hand, I am not part of the body." But saying this would not stop the foot from being a part of the body. [16]The ear might say, "Because I am not an eye, I am not part of the body." But saying this would not stop the ear from being a part of the body. [17]If the whole body were an eye, it would not be able to hear. If the whole body were an ear, it would not be able to smell. [18–19]If each part of the body were the same part, there would be no body. But truly God put all the parts, each one of them, in the body as he wanted them. [20]So then there are many parts, but only one body.

[21]The eye cannot say to the hand, "I don't need you!" And the head cannot say to the foot, "I don't need you!" [22]No! Those parts of the body that seem to be the weaker are really necessary. [23]And the parts of the body we think are less are the parts to which we give the most honour. We give special respect to the parts we want to hide. [24]The more beautiful parts of our body need no special care. But God put the body together and gave more honour to the parts that need it [25]so our body would not be divided. God wanted the different parts to care the same for each other. [26]If one part of the body suffers, all the other parts suffer with it. Or if one part of our body is honoured, all the other parts share its honour.

[27]Together you are the body of Christ, and each one of you is a part of that body. [28]In the church God has given a place first to apostles, *d* second to prophets *d* and third to teachers. Then God has given a place to those who do miracles, *d* those who have gifts of healing, those who can help others, those who are able to govern, and those who can speak in different languages. *n* [29]Not all are apostles. Not all are prophets. Not all are teachers. Not all do miracles. [30]Not all have gifts of healing. Not all speak in different languages. Not all interpret those languages. [31]But you should truly want to have the greater gifts.

Love is the Greatest Gift

And now I will show you the best way of all.

13 I may speak in different languages *n* of people or even angels. But if I do not have love, I am only a noisy bell or a crashing cymbal. [2]I may have the gift of prophecy. *d* I may

understand all the secret things of God and have all knowledge, and I may have faith so great I can move mountains. But even with all these things, if I do not have love, then I am nothing. [3]I may give away everything I have, and I may even give my body as an offering to be burnt. *n* But I gain nothing if I do not have love.

[4]Love is patient and kind. Love is not jealous, it does not boast, and it is not proud. [5]Love is not rude, is not selfish, and does not get upset with others. Love does not count up wrongs that have

Sidelight   The Bible's famous "love chapter" (1 Corinthians 13) stands in sharp contrast to the kind of "love" for which Corinth was infamous. Above Corinth on the hill of Acropolis was the temple of Aphrodite, who was the Greek goddess of love. Prostitute-priestesses worked in that temple, supposedly "cleansing" men of sin through weird sexual acts.

been done. [6]Love is not happy with evil but is happy with the truth. [7]Love patiently accepts all things. It always trusts, always hopes, and always remains strong.

[8]Love never ends. There are gifts of prophecy, but they will be ended. There are gifts of speaking in different languages, but those gifts will stop. There is the gift of knowledge, but it will come to an end. [9]The reason is that our knowledge and our ability to prophesy are not perfect. [10]But when perfection comes, the things that are not perfect will end. [11]When I was a child, I talked like a child, I thought like a child, I reasoned like a child. When I became a man, I stopped those childish ways. [12]It is the same with us. Now we see a dim reflection, as if we were looking into a mirror, but then we shall see clearly. Now I know only a part, but then I will know fully, as God has known me. [13]So these three things continue for ever: faith, hope and love. And the greatest of these is love.

Desire Spiritual Gifts

14 You should seek after love, and you should truly want to have the spiritual gifts, especially the gift of prophecy. *d* [2]I will explain why. Those who have the gift of speaking in different languages *n* are not speaking to people; they are speaking to God. No one understands them; they are speaking secret things through the Spirit. *d* [3]But those who prophesy

---

languages   This can also be translated "tongues".
Verse 3   Other Greek copies read: "hand over my body in order that I may boast."

are speaking to people to give them strength, encouragement and comfort. [4]The ones who speak in different languages are helping only themselves, but those who prophesy are helping the whole church. [5]I wish all of you had the gift of speaking in different kinds of languages, but more, I wish you would prophesy. Those who prophesy are greater than those who can only speak in different languages—unless someone is there who can explain what is said so that the whole church can be helped.

[6]Brothers and sisters, will it help you if I come to you speaking in different languages? No! It will help you only if I bring you a new truth or some new knowledge, or prophecy, or teaching. [7]It is the same as with lifeless things that make sounds—like a flute or a harp. If they do not make clear musical notes, you will not know what is being played. [8]And in a war, if the trumpet does not give a clear sound, who will prepare for battle? [9]It is the same with you. Unless you speak clearly with your tongue, no one can understand what you are saying. You will be talking into the air! [10]It may be true that there are all kinds of sounds in the world, and none is without meaning. [11]But unless I understand the meaning of what someone says to me, I will be a foreigner to him, and he will be a foreigner to me. [12]It is the same with you. Since you want spiritual gifts very much, seek most of all to have the gifts that help the church grow stronger.

[13]The one who has the gift of speaking in a different language should pray for the gift to interpret what is spoken. [14]If I pray in a different language, my spirit is praying, but my mind does

LOVE

All or Nothing?

Scott and Charlotte were Christians. They went to the same church youth group. They both really liked each other and eventually Scott asked her out on a date.

Charlotte's friends came round to help her get ready and soon it came to 7.30 p.m., when Scott would be arriving to pick her up.

When the doorbell rang, Charlotte ran down the stairs and flung the door open . . . all she could see was roses. Scott had brought her a dozen red roses and a box of her favourite chocolates!

"I just want everything to be perfect tonight," Scott explained. They left for the date and Charlotte was continually surprised by Scott's generosity. He gave her compliments all night and paid for a lovely meal and for tickets to a film she really wanted to see.

On the way out of the cinema, Charlotte thanked Scott for such a great time.

"It wasn't difficult," Scott said, "you're easy to do nice things for. I really like you!"

Just as he said that, they passed a homeless man on the street who was asking for money.

"Should we give him anything?" Charlotte asked Scott.

Begrudgingly, Scott said, "Er, well I guess we ought to give him a little something because we're Christians."

Read **1 Corinthians 13:1–13**.

* Why was it easy for Scott to be loving towards Charlotte but not the homeless man?
* Verses 4–8 talk about the gifts or qualities of love that we should show. Which ones do you find the easiest and which are the hardest?

Consider . . .

* making a list of the people you find difficult to love and copy out verses 4–8 alongside it. Pray for them each week that God would help you to love them more and to show it.
* hanging on with a friend or relative you are about to give up on. Keep loving this person through a difficult time.

For more, see . . .

* Matthew 5:43–48 (p.946)
* Luke 6:27–36 (p.1048)

nothing. [15]So what should I do? I will pray with my spirit, but I will also pray with my mind. I will sing with my spirit, but I will also sing with my mind. [16]If you praise God with your spirit, those persons there without understanding cannot say amen [n] to your prayer of thanks, because they do not know what you are saying. [17]You may be thanking God in a good way, but the other person is not helped.

[18]I thank God that I speak in different kinds of languages more than all of you. [19]But in the church meetings I would rather speak five words I understand in order to teach others than thousands of words in a different language.

[20]Brothers and sisters, do not think like children. In evil things be like babies, but in your thinking you should be like adults. [21]It is written in the Scriptures: [d]

"With people who use strange words and
  foreign languages

The LORD will speak to these people.
But people would not listen to me,"

Isaiah 28:11–12

says the Lord.
[22]So the gift of speaking in different kinds of languages is a proof for those who do not believe, not for those who do believe. And prophecy is for people who believe, not for those who do not believe. [23]Suppose the whole church meets together and everyone speaks in different languages. If some people come in who do not understand or do not believe, they will say you are mad. [24]But suppose everyone is prophesying and some people come in who do not believe or do not understand. If everyone is prophesying, their sin will be shown to them, and they will be judged by all that they hear. [25]The secret things in their hearts will be made known. So they will bow down and worship God saying, "Truly, God is with you."

---

amen   To say amen means to agree with the things that were said.

HOLY SPIRIT

A New Dimension

Knowing how to pray can sometimes be a real problem.

Richard was at his church prayer meeting and was praying quietly for each of the people in the college Christian group where he was one of the student leaders.

Even though he was just an average teenage Christian he did want to see each of the people he was involved with developing their relationship with God. Prayer was going well until he came to one particular girl – Sarah. Was she a Christian or was she not? She probably was but he was unsure. How should he pray?

Richard chose to pray in different languages (or tongues) as Paul suggested in **1 Corinthians 14:13–20**.

Richard prayed quietly for some minutes and stopped when he knew that God had answered his prayers, even though he did not understand what he was praying.

Several days later, at a special meeting attended by the college group, Sarah decided to become a Christian. As she explained to her friends, "I knew that I needed to be sure." Richard was glad that the Holy Spirit had helped him pray effectively.

* According to this passage, what does Paul think about speaking in different languages given by the Spirit?
* Are there the same dangers with other spiritual gifts?

Consider . . .

* getting together with your friends and discussing ways in which you need the Holy Spirit's help in praying.
* thumbing through your address book and asking the Holy Spirit how you might pray for each person listed.

For more, see . . .

* Jonah 4 (p.888)
* Romans 8:26–27 (p.1196)

* Matthew 6:5–15 (p.948)
* 1 Timothy 2:1–4 (p.1308)

Meetings Should Help the Church

[26]So, brothers and sisters, what should you do? When you meet together, one person has a song, and another has a teaching. Another has a new truth from God. Another speaks in a different language,[n] and another person interprets that language. The purpose of all these things should be to help the church grow strong. [27]When you meet together, if anyone speaks in a different language, it should be only two, or not more than three, who speak. They should speak one after the other, and someone else should interpret. [28]But if there is no interpreter, then those who speak in a different language should be quiet in the church meeting. They should speak only to themselves and to God.

[29]Only two or three prophets[d] should speak, and the others should judge what they say. [30]If a message from God comes to another person who is sitting, the first speaker should stop. [31]You can all prophesy one after the other. In this way all the people can be taught and encouraged. [32]The spirits of prophets are under the control of the prophets themselves. [33]God is not a God of confusion but a God of peace.

As is true in all the churches of God's people, [34]women should keep quiet in the church meetings. They are not allowed to speak, but they must yield to this rule as the law says. [35]If they want to learn something, they should ask their own husbands at home. It is shameful for a woman to speak in the church meeting. [36]Did God's teaching come from you? Or are you the only ones to whom it has come?

[37]Those who think they are prophets or spiritual persons should understand that what I am writing to you is the Lord's command. [38]Those who ignore this will be ignored by God.

[39]So my brothers and sisters, you should truly want to prophesy. But do not stop people from using the gift of speaking in different kinds of languages. [40]But let everything be done in a right and orderly way.

The Good News About Christ

15 Now, brothers and sisters, I want you to remember the Good News[d] I brought to you. You received this Good News and continue strong in it. [2]And you are being saved by it if you continue believing what I told you. If you do not, then you believed for nothing.

[3]I passed on to you what I received, of which this was most important: that Christ died for our sins, as the Scriptures[d] say; [4]that he was buried

and was raised to life on the third day as the Scriptures say; [5]and that he was seen by Peter and then by the twelve apostles.[d] [6]After that, Jesus was seen by more than 500 of the believers at the same time. Most of them are still living today, but some have died. [7]Then he was seen by James and later by all the apostles. [8]Last of all he was seen by me—as by a person not born at the normal time. [9]All the other apostles are greater than I am. I am not even good enough to be called an apostle, because I persecuted the church of God. [10]But God's grace has made me what I am, and his grace to me was not wasted. I worked harder than all the other apostles. (But it was not I really; it was God's grace that was with me.) [11]So if I preached to you or the other apostles preached to you, we all preach the same thing, and this is what you believed.

We will be Raised from the Dead

[12]Now since we preached that Christ was raised from the dead, why do some of you say that people will not be raised from the dead? [13]If no one is ever raised from the dead, then Christ has not been raised. [14]And if Christ has not been raised, then our preaching is worth nothing, and your faith is worth nothing. [15]And also, we are guilty of lying about God, because we testified of him that he raised Christ from the dead. But if people are not raised from the dead, then God never raised Christ. [16]If the dead are not raised, Christ has not been raised either. [17]And if Christ has not been raised, then your faith has nothing to it; you are still guilty of your sins. [18]And those in Christ who have already died are lost. [19]If our hope in Christ is for this life only, we should be pitied more than anyone else in the world.

[20]But Christ has truly been raised from the dead—the first one, and proof that those who sleep in death will also be raised. [21]Death has come because of what one man did, but the rising from death also comes because of one man. [22]In Adam all of us die. In the same way, in Christ all of us will be made alive again. [23]But everyone will be raised to life in the right order. Christ was first to be raised. When Christ comes again, those who belong to him will be raised to life, [24]and then the end will come. At that time Christ will destroy all rulers, authorities and powers, and he will hand over the kingdom to God the Father. [25]Christ must rule until he puts all enemies under his control. [26]The last enemy to be destroyed will be death. [27]The Scripture[d] says that God put all things under his control.[n]

---

language   This can also be translated "tongue".
God put . . . control.   From Psalm 8:6.

When it says "all things" are under him, it is clear this does not include God himself. God is the One who put everything under his control. [28]After everything has been put under the Son, then he will put himself under God, who had put all things under him. Then God will be the complete ruler over everything.

[29]If the dead are never raised, what will people do who are being baptised [d] for the dead? If the dead are not raised at all, why are people being baptised for them?

[30]And what about us? Why do we put ourselves in danger every hour? [31]I die every day. That is true, brothers and sisters, just as it is true that I boast about you in Christ Jesus our Lord. [32]If I fought wild animals in Ephesus only with human hopes, I have gained nothing. If the dead are not raised, "Let us eat and drink, because tomorrow we will die." [n]

[33]Do not be fooled: "Bad friends will ruin good habits." [34]Come back to your right way of

"Let us . . . die." Quotation from Isaiah 22:13; 56:12.

thinking and stop sinning. Some of you do not know God—I say this to shame you.

What Kind of Body will We Have?

[35]But someone may ask, "How are the dead raised? What kind of body will they have?" [36]Foolish person! When you sow a seed, it must

Sidelight   Though Paul probably didn't fight wild animals himself (1 Corinthians 15:32), he is probably referring to the Roman "sport" of putting prisoners in an arena, then releasing wild animals to maul the prisoners while huge crowds watched. Animals used in this activity included lions, bears, leopards, rhinoceroses, crocodiles, tigers and elephants. A decade after Paul wrote this letter, Christians faced this kind of persecution.

FAITH

Stick With It

It's not easy to become an emperor moth. To emerge into the world, the moth must force its way through the neck of a flask-shaped cocoon. Getting through this opening takes hours of intense struggle. The insect must squirm and wriggle to push its way through.

If you watched an emperor moth's struggle, you might feel sorry for the struggling insect and snip the confining threads to make an easier exit. But if you did, the moth would never develop its wings. Instead, it would spend most of its life crawling, never able to spread its wings and fly.

Scientists who study this moth believe that the pressure on the insect's body forces the essential juices into the wings, thus preparing the wings for flight. Without the pressure, the wings would never become strong.

Sometimes having faith is difficult. Like the emperor moth, we struggle. We feel overwhelmed – tested. And we wish someone would step in and take the struggle away.

But our faith grows through those struggles, as Paul reminds us in **1 Corinthians 15:1–11**.

* According to this passage, what are we to continue to believe in?
* How can the example of the people's faith in this passage encourage you when you struggle with your faith?

Consider . . .

* phoning an older person in your congregation to ask about his or her journey of faith – including the ups and downs.
* talking to a friend about the ways in which you have grown after a difficult time.

For more, see . . .

* Genesis 22 (p.25)
* Hebrews 11 (p.1341)
* Daniel 3 (p.835)

die in the ground before it can live and grow. [37]And when you sow it, it does not have the same "body" it will have later. What you sow is only a bare seed, maybe wheat or something else. [38]But God gives it a body that he has planned for it, and God gives each kind of seed its own body. [39]All things made of flesh are not the same: people have one kind of flesh, animals have another, birds have another and fish have another. [40]Also there are heavenly bodies and earthly bodies. But the beauty of the heavenly bodies is one kind, and the beauty of the earthly bodies is another. [41]The sun has one kind of beauty, the moon has another beauty and the stars have another. And each star is different in its beauty.

[42]It is the same with the dead who are raised to life. The body that is "planted" will ruin and decay, but it is raised to a life that cannot be destroyed. [43]When the body is "planted", it is without honour, but it is raised in glory. When the body is "planted", it is weak, but when it is raised, it is powerful. [44]The body that is "planted" is a physical body. When it is raised, it is a spiritual body.

There is a physical body, and there is also a spiritual body. [45]It is written in the Scriptures: [d] "The first man, Adam, became a living person." [n] But the last Adam became a spirit that gives life. [46]The spiritual did not come first, but the physical and then the spiritual. [47]The first man came from the dust of the earth. The second man came from heaven. [48]People who belong to the earth are like the first man of earth. But those people who belong to heaven are like the man of heaven. [49]Just as we were made like the man of earth, so we will also be made like the man of heaven.

[50]I tell you this, brothers and sisters: flesh and blood cannot have a part in the kingdom of God. Something that will ruin cannot have a part in something that never ruins. [51]But look! I tell you this secret: we will not all sleep in death, but we will all be changed. [52]It will take only a second— as quickly as an eye blinks—when the last trumpet sounds. The trumpet will sound, and those who have died will be raised to live for ever, and we will all be changed. [53]This body that can be destroyed must clothe itself with something that can never be destroyed. And this body that dies

"The first . . . person." Quotation from Genesis 2:7.

DEATH

Life After Death

What do teenagers think about death? According to a Gallup poll, two-thirds of teenagers believe in life after death. But while most teenagers believe in life after death, most teenagers also fear death. According to a Youth Monitor poll:

* Three out of four teenagers worry that one of their parents will die.
* Half worry about themselves dying.
* Two other major worries – being in a car accident or a plane crash – also hint at this fear of death.

Fearing death is natural for most people. But Paul says that death isn't final for Christians. Read about the other side of death in **1 Corinthians 15:12–28**.

* Why does Paul talk about Christ when explaining being raised from the dead?
* How does this passage help you to deal with your fears about death?

Consider . . .

* going to a church cemetery and reading the epitaphs on gravestones. Decide how you can develop the faith and hope indicated by the sayings.
* having coffee with your youth leader and talking about your fears concerning death.

For more, see . . .

* Isaiah 57:1–2 (p.700)
* Hebrews 2:14–15 (p.1331)

* John 5:24–29 (p.1104)

must clothe itself with something that can never die. [54]So this body that can be destroyed will clothe itself with that which can never be destroyed, and this body that dies will clothe itself with that which can never die. When this happens, this Scripture will be made true:

"Death is destroyed for ever."   *Isaiah 25:8*
[55]"Death, where is your victory?
    Where is your pain, place of death?"

Hosea 13:14

[56]Death's power to hurt is sin, and the power of sin is the law. *d* [57]But we thank God! He gives us the victory through our Lord Jesus Christ.

[58]So my dear brothers and sisters, stand strong. Do not let anything change you. Always give yourselves fully to the work of the Lord, because you know that your work in the Lord is never wasted.

The Gift for Other Believers

16 Now I will write about the collection of money for God's people. Do the same thing I told the Galatian churches to do: [2]on the first day of every week, each one of you should put aside money as you have been blessed. Save

it up so you will not have to collect money after I come. [3]When I arrive, I will send whomever you approve to take your gift to Jerusalem. I will send them with letters of introduction, [4]and if it seems good for me to go also, they will go along with me.

Paul's Plans

[5]I plan to go through Macedonia, so I will come to you after I go through there. [6]Perhaps I will stay with you for a time or even all winter. Then you can help me on my trip, wherever I go. [7]I do not want to see you now just in passing. I hope to stay a longer time with you if the Lord allows it. [8]But I will stay at Ephesus until Pentecost, *d* [9]because a good opportunity for a great and growing work has been given to me now. And there are many people working against me.

[10]If Timothy comes to you, see to it that he has nothing to fear with you, because he is working for the Lord just as I am. [11]So none of you should treat Timothy as unimportant, but help him on his way in peace so that he can come back to me. I am expecting him to come with the brothers.

ETERNAL LIFE

We Shall All Be Changed

Coal, buried deep within the earth, sometimes encounters intense pressure and heat. When it does, over time, a diamond results. Under the right conditions, the mineral beryl transforms into an emerald, another precious stone. But if beryl contains impurities and undergoes the same conditions, the result is aquamarine – which is only a semi-precious stone. When rocks with specks of gold are melted, the weighty gold deposits sink to the bottom, and the impurities are scraped from the top. After the process has been repeated several times, only pure gold remains.

Just as minerals change under the right conditions, so our bodies will change at death. In **1 Corinthians 15:35–58**, Paul talks about the transformation and refining that will occur in our bodies.

* How will the change in our bodies be similar to what happens to rocks? How will it be different?
* How does the value of eternal life compare with the value of precious stones?

Consider . . .

* drawing a picture of what you think heaven will be like.
* hanging a "We Shall All Be Changed" sign in your wardrobe to remind you of how our earthly bodies will change.

For more, see . . .

* Job 19:25–27 (p.481)
* Revelation 22:1–5 (p.1404)

* Psalm 73:23–28 (p.544)

¹²Now about our brother Apollos: I strongly encouraged him to visit you with the other brothers. He did not at all want to come now; he will come when he has the opportunity.

Paul Ends His Letter

¹³Be careful. Continue strong in the faith. Have courage, and be strong. ¹⁴Do everything in love.

¹⁵You know that the family of Stephanas were the first believers in Southern Greece and that they have given themselves to the service of God's people. I ask you, brothers and sisters, ¹⁶to follow the leading of people like these and anyone else who works and serves with them.

¹⁷I am happy that Stephanas, Fortunatus and Achaicus have come. You are not here, but they have filled your place. ¹⁸They have refreshed my spirit and yours. You should recognise the value of people like these.

¹⁹The churches in the country of Asia send greetings to you. Aquila and Priscilla greet you in the Lord, as does the church that meets in their house. ²⁰All the brothers and sisters here send greetings. Give each other a holy kiss when you meet.

²¹I, Paul, am writing this greeting with my own hand.

²²If anyone does not love the Lord, let him be separated from God—lost for ever!

Come, O Lord!

²³The grace of the Lord Jesus be with you.

²⁴My love be with all of you in Christ Jesus.

2 Corinthians

Why Read This Book:
* Explore what it means to be a minister for Christ (2 Corinthians 1—7).
* Be challenged to give generously to God's work (2 Corinthians 8—9).
* See what Christians have to brag about (2 Corinthians 10—13).

When?

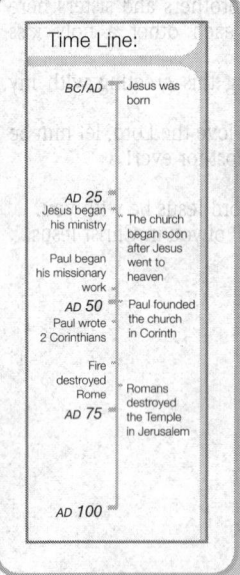

Time Line:

BC/AD	Jesus was born
AD 25 Jesus began his ministry	The church began soon after Jesus went to heaven
Paul began his missionary work	
AD 50 Paul wrote 2 Corinthians	Paul founded the church in Corinth
Fire destroyed Rome	Romans destroyed the Temple in Jerusalem
AD 75	
AD 100	

Behind the Scenes:

Paul frequently had to handle people problems. In 1 Corinthians, Paul urged the Christians of Corinth to stop arguing and start working together as they followed Christ. They listened, and the divisions in the church were healed. But then, about a year later, word gets back to him that they are heading for trouble once again . . .

The problem was that some people had started spreading rumours about Paul. They said that he was unqualified, unstable, boastful and a liar. Even worse, the Corinthians believed these lies, and turned to false teachers for guidance.

Paul was obviously upset that the people he loved were turning against him, but he was more concerned with the fact that they were being led away from following Jesus by these false teachers. He had been forced into defending his ministry, and he did so by writing a blunt letter to the Corinthians (which unfortunately has been lost), being careful not to pull any punches (see 2 Corinthians 2:3–4). In this letter, he demanded that the people stop following the false teachers and turn back to Christ. The church followed his advice and told him how much they cared for him. Paul breathed a sigh of relief and thanked God that the crisis was over.

In 2 Corinthians, Paul begins to rebuild his damaged relationship with the Corinthians by explaining why he wrote the letter (see 2 Corinthians 7:6–16), and telling them how much he loves them (see 2 Corinthians 12:11–21).

This letter shows us that being a Christian leader isn't easy. Leaders are just as human as the next person, and they have feelings that can be hurt. Read 2 Corinthians and see for yourself how a Christian leader feels when faced with difficulties in the church.

Where?

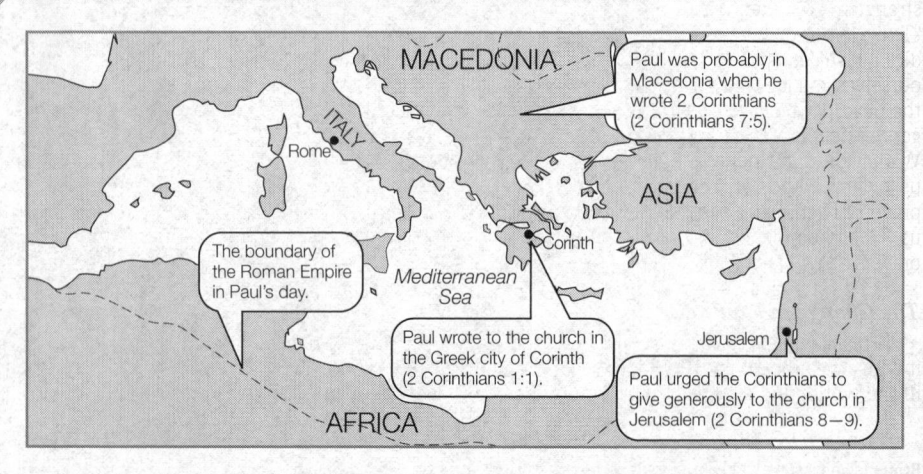

Paul was probably in Macedonia when he wrote 2 Corinthians (2 Corinthians 7:5).

The boundary of the Roman Empire in Paul's day.

Paul wrote to the church in the Greek city of Corinth (2 Corinthians 1:1).

Paul urged the Corinthians to give generously to the church in Jerusalem (2 Corinthians 8—9).

MACEDONIA

ITALY

Rome

ASIA

Corinth

Mediterranean Sea

Jerusalem

AFRICA

1

From Paul, an apostle[d] of Christ Jesus. I am an apostle because that is what God wanted. Also from Timothy our brother in Christ.

To the church of God in Corinth, and to all of God's people everywhere in Southern Greece: [2]Grace and peace to you from God our Father and the Lord Jesus Christ.

> ## Sidelight
> The Corinthian church was made up of a varied group of people who came to this major city from around the world. Paul hints at this when he addresses them in 2 Corinthians 1:2 with "grace", a Greek greeting, and "peace", a Hebrew greeting.

Paul Gives Thanks to God

[3]Praise be to the God and Father of our Lord Jesus Christ. God is the Father who is full of mercy and all comfort. [4]He comforts us every time we have trouble, so when others have trouble, we can comfort them with the same comfort God gives us. [5]We share in the many sufferings of Christ. In the same way, much comfort comes to us through Christ. [6]If we have troubles, it is for your comfort and salvation, and if we have comfort, you also have comfort. This helps you to accept patiently the same sufferings we have. [7]Our hope for you is strong, knowing that you share in our sufferings and also in the comfort we receive.

[8]Brothers and sisters,[n] we want you to know about the trouble we suffered in Asia. We had great burdens there that were beyond our own strength. We even gave up hope of living. [9]Truly, in our own hearts we believed we would die. But this happened so we would not trust in ourselves but in God, who raises people from the dead. [10]God saved us from these great dangers of death, and he will continue to save us. We have put our hope in him, and he will save us again. [11]And you can help us with your prayers. Then many people will give thanks for us—that God blessed us because of their many prayers.

The Change in Paul's Plans

[12]This is what we are proud of, and I can say it with a clear heart: in everything we have done in the world, and especially with you, we have

had an honest and sincere heart from God. We did this by God's grace, not by the kind of wisdom the world has. [13-14]We write to you only what you can read and understand. And I hope that as you have understood some things about us, you may come to know everything about us. Then you can be proud of us, as we will be proud of you on the day our Lord Jesus Christ comes again.

[15]I was so sure of all this that I made plans to visit you first so you could be blessed twice. [16]I planned to visit you on my way to Macedonia and again on my way back. I wanted to get help from you for my trip to Judea. [17]Do you think that I made these plans without really meaning it? Or maybe you think I make plans as the world does, so that I say "yes, yes" and at the same time "no, no."

[18]But if you can believe God, you can believe that what we tell you is never both "yes" and "no". [19]The Son of God, Jesus Christ, that Silas and Timothy and I preached to you, was not "yes" and "no". In Christ it has always been "yes". [20]The "yes" to all of God's promises is in Christ, and through Christ we say "yes" to the glory of God. [21]Remember, God is the One who makes you and us strong in Christ. God made us his chosen people. [22]He put his mark on us to show that we are his, and he put his Spirit[d] in our hearts to be a guarantee for all he has promised.

[23]I tell you this, and I ask God to be my witness that this is true: the reason I did not come back to Corinth was to keep you from being punished or hurt. [24]We are not trying to control your faith. You are strong in faith. But we are workers with you for your own joy.

2

So I decided that my next visit to you would not be another one to make you sad. [2]If I make you sad, who will make me glad? Only you can make me glad—particularly the person whom I made sad. [3]I wrote you a letter for this reason: that when I came to you I would not be made sad by the people who should make me happy. I felt sure of all of you, that you would share my joy. [4]When I wrote to you before, I was very troubled and unhappy in my heart, and I wrote with many tears. I did not write to make you sad, but to let you know how much I love you.

Forgive the Sinner

[5]Someone there among you has caused sadness, not to me, but to all of you. I mean he

caused sadness to all in some way. (I do not want to make it sound worse than it really is.) [6]The punishment that most of you gave him is enough for him. [7]But now you should forgive him and comfort him to keep him from having too much sadness and giving up completely. [8]So I beg you to show that you love him. [9]I wrote to you to test you and to see if you obey in everything. [10]If you forgive someone, I also forgive him. And what I have forgiven—if I had anything to forgive—I forgave it for you, as if Christ were with me. [11]I did this so that Satan would not win anything from us, because we know very well what Satan's plans are.

Paul's Concern in Troas

[12]When I came to Troas to preach the Good News [d] of Christ, the Lord gave me a good opportunity there. [13]But I had no peace, because I did not find my brother Titus. So I said goodbye to them at Troas and went to Macedonia.

Victory Through Christ

[14]But thanks be to God, who always leads us in victory through Christ. God uses us to spread his knowledge everywhere like a sweet-smelling perfume. [15]Our offering to God is this: we are the sweet smell of Christ among those who are being saved and among those who are being lost. [16]To those who are lost, we are the smell of death that brings death, but to those who are being saved, we are the smell of life that brings life. So who is able to do this work? [17]We do not sell the word of God for a profit as many other people do. But in Christ we speak the truth before God, as messengers of God.

Servants of the New Agreement

3 Are we starting to boast about ourselves again? Do we need letters of introduction to you or from you, like some other people? [2]You yourselves are our letter, written on our hearts, known and read by everyone. [3]You show that you are a letter from Christ sent through us. This letter is not written with ink but with the Spirit [d] of the living God. It is not written on stone tablets [n] but on human hearts.

[4]We can say this, because through Christ we feel certain before God. [5]We are not saying that we can do this work ourselves. It is God who makes us able to do all that we do. [6]He made us

able to be servants of a new agreement from himself to his people. This new agreement is not a written law, but it is of the Spirit. The written law brings death, but the Spirit gives life.

[7]The law that brought death was written in words on stone. It came with God's glory, which made Moses' face so bright that the Israelites could not continue to look at it. But that glory later disappeared. [8]So surely the new way that brings the Spirit has even more glory. [9]If the law that judged people guilty of sin had glory, surely the new way that makes people right with God has much greater glory. [10]That old law had glory, but it really loses its glory when it is compared to the much greater glory of this new way. [11]If that law which disappeared came with glory, then this new way which continues for ever has much greater glory.

[12]We have this hope, so we are very bold. [13]We are not like Moses, who put a covering over his face so the Israelites would not see it. The glory was disappearing, and Moses did not want them to see it fade. [14]But their minds were closed, and even today that same covering hides the meaning when they read the old agreement. That covering is taken away only through Christ. [15]Even today, when they read the law of Moses, there is a covering over their minds. [16]But when a person changes and follows the Lord, that covering is taken away. [17]The Lord is the Spirit, and where the Spirit of the Lord is, there is freedom. [18]Our faces, then, are not covered. We all show the Lord's glory, and we are being changed to be like him. This change in us brings ever greater glory, which comes from the Lord, who is the Spirit.

Preaching the Good News

4 God, with his mercy, gave us this work to do, so we don't give up. [2]But we have turned away from secret and shameful ways. We use no trickery, and we do not change the teaching of God. We teach the truth plainly, showing everyone who we are. Then they can know in their hearts what kind of people we are in God's sight. [3]If the Good News [d] that we preach is hidden, it is hidden only to those who are lost. [4]The devil who rules this world has blinded the minds of those who do not believe. They cannot see the light of the Good News—the Good News about the glory of Christ, who is exactly like God. [5]We do not preach about ourselves, but we preach

---

stone tablets   Meaning the law of Moses that was written on stone tablets (Exodus 24:12; 32:16).

that Jesus Christ is Lord and that we are your servants for Jesus. [6]God once said, "Let the light shine out of the darkness!" This is the same God who made his light shine in our hearts by letting us know the glory of God that is in the face of Christ.

Spiritual Treasure in Clay Jars

[7]We have this treasure from God, but we are like clay jars that hold the treasure. This shows that the great power is from God, not from us.

[8]We have troubles all around us, but we are not defeated. We do not know what to do, but we do not give up the hope of living. [9]We are

---

Sidelight Hiding treasures in clay jars was a common practice in biblical times, because people didn't suspect anything valuable would be kept in such a container (2 Corinthians 4:7). It's like hiding your money in a sock.

NON-CHRISTIANS

Trying Too Hard

David tried to live a perfect life. He went to church and was active in his youth group. He faithfully read the Bible and shared his faith with others.

David's problem was that he got carried away.

At school David constantly talked about his beliefs. In history lessons he challenged everything his teacher said. In science lessons he blasted theories and ideas as un-Christian. During lunch he commented on other people's food, telling them that God wanted them to treat their bodies like a temple. Between classes he witnessed in the halls.

At first, teachers and students listened to him. But soon, people around him grew irritated. Teachers began to cut him off, and students just laughed. The more they laughed or ignored him the harder he tried. Finally, even other Christians began to sneer. They started calling him "the preacher" and "super Christian".

Holly was also a Christian. Although she, too, was tired of David's style, she felt sorry when others put him down. One day David complained to Holly that no one ever listened.

"Perhaps you're trying too hard," Holly suggested. "After all, we don't have to be preaching all the time. We just need to let God's love shine through."

Over the next few weeks, whenever Holly saw David she just smiled. For a long time David didn't seem to have heard her. He just kept on preaching and witnessing, and students kept on making fun of him.

Slowly, David began following Holly's advice. He still lived out his faith, but instead of being obnoxious, he expressed it with a smile, a kind word or an offer of help. And, for the first time, people began responding positively to David's efforts.

Sometimes we get so tied up in trying to convert others that we don't let God's love show through us to non-Christians. Read **2 Corinthians 4:3–12** to discover more about the treasure of God's love and how to share your faith with the world.

* How does David's discovery relate to Paul's belief that we are clay jars holding the treasure of God's love?
* How have you shared God's treasure with a non-Christian?

Consider . . .

* asking God to teach you how to respect others while you share your beliefs with them.
* inviting a friend who doesn't go to church to come with you to worship. Introduce him or her to your Christian friends.

For more, see . . .

* Genesis 18:16–33 (p.21)
* Colossians 3:12–17 (p.1293)
* Matthew 28:16–20 (p.994)

persecuted, but God does not leave us. We are hurt sometimes, but we are not destroyed. [10]We carry the death of Jesus in our own bodies so that the life of Jesus can also be seen in our bodies. [11]We are alive, but for Jesus we are always in danger of death so that the life of Jesus can be seen in our bodies that die. [12]So death is working in us, but life is working in you.

[13]It is written in the Scriptures, [d] "I believed, so I spoke." [n] Our faith is like this too. We believe, and so we speak. [14]God raised the Lord Jesus from the dead, and we know that God will also raise us with Jesus. God will bring us together with you, and we will stand before him. [15]All these things are for you. And so the grace of God that is being given to more and more people will bring increasing thanks to God for his glory.

Living by Faith

[16]So we do not give up. Our physical body is becoming older and weaker, but our spirit inside us is made new every day. [17]We have small troubles for a while now, but they are helping us gain an eternal glory that is much greater than the troubles. [18]We set our eyes not on what we see but on what we cannot see. What we see will last only a short time, but what we cannot see will last for ever.

5 We know that our body—the tent we live in here on earth—will be destroyed. But when

---

"I . . . spoke." Quotation from Psalm 116:10.

FAITH

Unseen Water

Frank Zeigler's ranch in Wyoming, USA, had been in his family for years, but had never been used. It was full of cacti and rocks. Surely the land could be used for something, Frank thought. He thought of raising sheep, but sheep couldn't live there without water. He thought of mining the minerals that had been discovered long ago, but there was no water to process the ore.

"I know there is more," he told his wife. "I just know there is. God is always giving us gifts, but half the time we don't see them."

One day as he rode across the barren range, he suddenly stopped. He piled up five or six rocks then went home and phoned a drilling company. Frank told them to drill a deep water well where he had piled the rocks.

At first the owners laughed. "There's no water on that land. You know that," they teased.

But he insisted. "I just have a feeling it's there," he said. Finally they agreed to drill. Months later, they hit water almost one mile underground.

Astonished, the drilling crew asked how he knew water was down there. Frank shrugged. "I guess I had the faith that there was more there than my eyes could see."

As Frank did, it's important for us to have faith not just in things seen but in things unseen as well.

To learn more, read **2 Corinthians 4:13–18**.

* How does Frank's search for water parallel the faith described in the passage? How does it differ?
* Which part of this passage gives you the greatest sense of hope in your faith?

Consider . . .

* thinking about things that you know exist even though you can't see them, such as air and electricity. List ways in which you know that God exists even though you can't see him.
* stepping out in faith in an area where you may not have all the "facts" but still believe that what you're doing is God's will.

For more, see . . .

* Psalm 116 (p.569)
* Colossians 3:1–4 (p.1292)
* Romans 8:18–28 (p.1195)

that happens, God will have a house for us. It will not be a house made by human hands; instead, it will be a home in heaven that will last for ever. ²But now we groan in this tent. We want God to give us our heavenly home, ³because it will clothe us so we will not be naked. ⁴While we live in this body, we have burdens, and we groan. We do not want to be naked, but we want to be clothed with our heavenly home. Then this body that dies will be fully covered with life. ⁵This is what God made us for, and he has given us the Spirit *d* to be a guarantee for this new life.

⁶So we always have courage. We know that while we live in this body, we are away from the Lord. ⁷We live by what we believe, not by what we can see. ⁸So I say that we have courage. We really want to be away from this body and be at home with the Lord. ⁹Our only goal is to please God whether we live here or there, ¹⁰because we must all stand before Christ to be judged. Each of us will receive what we should get—good or bad—for the things we did in the earthly body.

Becoming Friends with God

¹¹Since we know what it means to fear the Lord, we try to help people accept the truth about us. God knows what we really are, and I hope that in your hearts you know too. ¹²We are not trying to prove ourselves to you again, but we are telling you about ourselves so you will be proud of us. Then you will have an answer for those who are proud about things that can be seen rather than what is in the heart. ¹³If we are out of our minds, it is for God. If we have our right

FOLLOWING GOD

Daring to Believe

Christopher Wren's big opportunity as an architect came after the Great Fire of London in 1666. It was the chance of a lifetime: still in his twenties, he was commissioned to rebuild not only 51 churches but also St Paul's Cathedral. He prayed and worked to design a cathedral with a magnificently arched ceiling stretching towards heaven.

But when the church was almost finished, other architects in London claimed that the building was flawed. They said that six additional pillars were needed or else the roof would fall.

Wren genuinely believed that God was guiding him in building the cathedral. Still, the other architects were older and more experienced. So, instead of reacting angrily, he listened and prayed. After much discussion he agreed to add the pillars.

At least that's what everyone thought.

After the cathedral was finished in 1710, Wren left London. Fifty years later, after his death, workers were repainting the ceiling when they discovered something strange. Each of the six additional pillars was a few inches short of the vaulted ceiling.

Like Christopher Wren we are called to follow God as best we know how, which often requires courage and creativity.

To learn more about following God read **2 Corinthians 5:6–17**.

* How does Christopher Wren's decision to follow God's call in his heart relate to Paul's advice to live by believing in Christ?
* How have you made choices that reflect the challenge of verse 9? What happened?

Consider . . .

* choosing a creative way to follow God this week, such as writing, drawing or singing.
* interviewing your minister, a teacher, or a friend about times when he or she struggled with decisions to follow God, and what happened.

For more, see . . .

* Isaiah 65:17–25 (p.711)
* Philippians 1:19–20 (p.1281)
* John 14:1–7 (p.1122)

minds, it is for you. ¹⁴The love of Christ controls us, because we know that One died for all, so all have died. ¹⁵Christ died for all so that those who live would not continue to live for themselves. He died for them and was raised from the dead so that they would live for him.

¹⁶From this time on we do not think of anyone as the world does. In the past we thought of Christ as the world thinks, but we no longer think of him in that way. ¹⁷If anyone belongs to Christ, there begins a new creation. The old things have gone: everything is made new! ¹⁸All this is from God. Through Christ, God made peace between us and himself, and God gave us the work of telling everyone about the peace we can have with him. ¹⁹God was in Christ, making peace between the world and himself. In Christ, God did not hold the world guilty of its sins. And he gave us this message of peace. ²⁰So we have been sent to speak for Christ. It is as if God is calling to you through us. We speak for Christ when we beg you to be at peace with God. ²¹Christ had no sin, but God made him become sin so that in Christ we could become right with God.

6 We are workers together with God, so we beg you: do not let the grace that you received from God be for nothing. ²God says,

"At the right time I will hear your prayers.
On the day of salvation I will help you."

Isaiah 49:8

I tell you that the "right time" is now, and the "day of salvation" is now.

³We do not want anyone to find fault with our work, so nothing we do will be a problem for anyone. ⁴But in every way we show we are servants of God: in accepting many hard things, in troubles, in difficulties and in great problems. ⁵We are beaten and thrown into

SUFFERING

Trying to Stand Strong

Sanjeev, a church minister working in Gampaha district in Sri Lanka, had to suspend church services because he was in fear of physical attack on his church members.

One Sunday, as the congregation attempted to gather at their church in Yakkala in Gampaha, a group of at least fifty people blocked the road leading to the church. The mob was armed with clubs and hurled verbal abuse at the Christians. They had also put up posters featuring anti-Christian slogans around the town.

Sanjeev was warned to stop holding services and told that Yakkala had no need of a Christian church. He was also accused of doing and saying certain things – all of which were lies – in an attempt to ruin his reputation.

The church had been attacked just a few weeks before. He had asked for police protection but no action had been taken. So this second incident led Sanjeev to make the reluctant decision to cancel services so as not to endanger his people and risk a riot and the destruction of the church.

Paul faced similar persecution all his life. Read **2 Corinthians 6:3–10** and see Paul's attitude to what was happening.

* Not all persecution stories have a happy ending. How might Sanjeev apply what Paul writes in Corinthians to his own situation?
* What gave Paul such hope despite all the attacks and opposition he faced?

Consider . . .

* whether you have ever been persecuted because you are a Christian. How did it make you feel?
* how many people around the world suffer merely because of their faith in Jesus. Why not find an organisation that supports persecuted Christians and commit to praying regularly for God's protection and peace.

For more, see . . .

* Psalm 57 (p.533)
* 1 Peter 5:8–11 (p.1363)
* Jeremiah 1:4–8 (p.716)

prison. We meet those who become upset with us and start riots. We work hard, and sometimes we get no sleep or food. [6]We show we are servants of God by our pure lives, our understanding, patience and kindness, by the Holy Spirit,[d] by true love, [7]by speaking the truth and by God's power. We use our right living to defend ourselves against everything. [8]Some people honour us, but others blame us. Some people say evil things about us, but

---

Sidelight Paul knew what the inside of a prison looked like and not just as a visitor. He was beaten up and thrown into prison for his faith (2 Corinthians 6:5) at least seven times in places like Jerusalem, Philippi and Rome before being executed by the Roman government (see 2 Timothy 4:6–8, p.1320).

---

others say good things. Some people say we are liars, but we speak the truth. [9]We are not known, yet we are well known. We seem to be dying, but we continue to live. We are punished, but we are not killed. [10]We have much sadness, but we are always rejoicing. We are poor, but we are making many people rich in faith. We have nothing, but really we have everything.
[11]We have spoken freely to you in Corinth and have opened our hearts to you. [12]Our feelings of love for you have not stopped, but you have stopped your feelings of love for us. [13]I speak to you as if you were my children. Do to us as we have done—open your hearts to us.

Warning About Those Who Do Not Believe

[14]You are not the same as those who do not believe. So do not join yourselves to them. Good and bad do not belong together. Light and darkness cannot share together. [15]How can Christ and Belial, the devil, have any agreement? What can a believer have together with a non-believer? [16]The temple of God cannot have any agreement with idols, and we are the temple of the living God. As God said: "I will live with them and walk with them. And I will be their God, and they will be my people." [n]

[17]"You people, leave, leave,
    get out of Babylon!
Touch nothing that is unclean." [d]   *Isaiah 52:11;*
                                            Ezekiel 20:34,41

[18]"I will be your father,
    and you will be my sons and daughters,
    says the Lord Almighty."   *2 Samuel 7:14; 7:8*

7 Dear friends, we have these promises from God, so we should make ourselves pure— free from anything that makes body or soul unclean. We should try to become holy in the way we live, because we respect God.

Paul's Joy

[2]Open your hearts to us. We have not done wrong to anyone, we have not ruined the faith of anyone, and we have not cheated anyone. [3]I do not say this to blame you. I told you before that we love you so much we would live or die with you. [4]I feel very sure of you and am very proud of you. You give me much comfort, and in all of our troubles I have great joy.

[5]When we came into Macedonia, we had no rest. We found trouble all around us. We had fighting on the outside and fear on the inside. [6]But God, who comforts those who are troubled, comforted us when Titus came. [7]We were comforted, not only by his coming but also by the comfort you gave him. Titus told us about your wish to see me and that you are very sorry for what you did. He also told me about your great care for me, and when I heard this, I was much happier.

[8]Even if my letter made you sad, I am not sorry I wrote it. At first I was sorry, because it made you sad, but you were sad only for a short time. [9]Now I am happy, not because you were made sad, but because your sorrow made you change your lives. You became sad in the way God wanted you to, so you were not hurt by us in any way. [10]The kind of sorrow God wants makes people change their hearts and lives. This leads to salvation, and you cannot be sorry for that. But the kind of sorrow the world has brings death. [11]See what this sorrow—the sorrow God wanted you to have—has done to you: it has made you very serious. It made you want to prove you were not wrong. It made you angry and afraid. It made you want to see me. It made you care. It made you want the right thing to be done. You proved you were innocent in the problem. [12]I wrote that letter, not because of the one who did the wrong or because of the person who was hurt. I wrote the letter so you could see, before God, the great care you have for us. [13]That is why we were comforted.

Not only were we very comforted, we were even happier to see that Titus was so happy.

"I . . . people." Quotation from Leviticus 26:11–12; Jeremiah 32:38; Ezekiel 37:27.

All of you made him feel much better. [14]I boasted to Titus about you, and you showed that I was right. Everything we said to you was true, and you have proved that what we boasted about to Titus is true. [15]And his love for you is stronger when he remembers that you were all ready to obey. You welcomed him with respect and fear. [16]I am very happy that I can trust you fully.

Christian Giving

8 And now, brothers and sisters, we want you to know about the grace God gave the churches in Macedonia. [2]They have been tested by great troubles, and they are very poor. But they gave much because of their great joy. [3]I can tell you that they gave as much as they were able and even more than they could afford. No one told them to do it. [4]But they begged and pleaded with us to let them share in this service for God's people. [5]And they gave in a way we did not expect: they first gave themselves to the Lord and to us. This is what God wants. [6]So we asked Titus to help you finish this special work of grace since he is the one who started it. [7]You are rich in everything—in faith, in speaking, in knowledge, in truly wanting to help, and in the love you learned from us. In the same way, be strong also in the grace of giving.

[8]I am not commanding you to give. But I want to see if your love is true by comparing you with others that really want to help. [9]You know the grace of our Lord Jesus Christ. You know that Christ was rich, but for you he became poor so that by his becoming poor you might become rich.

[10]This is what I think you should do: last year you were the first to want to give, and you were the first who gave. [11]So now finish the work you started. Then your "doing" will be equal to your "wanting to do". Give from what you have. [12]If you want to give, your gift will be accepted. It will be judged by what you have, not by what you do not have. [13]We do not want you to have troubles while other people are at ease, but we want everything to be equal. [14]At this time you have plenty. What you have can help others who are in need. Then later, when they have plenty, they can help you when you are in need, and all will be equal. [15]As it is written in the Scriptures, [d] "The person who gathered more did not have too much, nor did the person who gathered less have too little." [n]

Titus and His Companions Help

[16]I thank God because he gave Titus the same love for you that I have. [17]Titus accepted what we asked him to do. He wanted very much to go to you, and this was his own idea. [18]We are sending with him the brother who is praised by all the churches because of his service in preaching the Good News. [d] [19]Also, this brother was chosen by the churches to go with us when we deliver this gift of money. We are doing this service to bring glory to the Lord and to show that we really want to help.

[20]We are being careful so that no one will criticise us for the way we are handling this large gift. [21]We are trying hard to do what the Lord accepts as right and also what people think is right.

[22]Also, we are sending with them our brother, who is always ready to help. He has proved this to us in many ways, and he wants to help even more now, because he has much faith in you.

[23]Now about Titus—he is my partner who is working with me to help you. And about the other brothers—they are sent from the churches, and they bring glory to Christ. [24]So show these men the proof of your love and the reason we are proud of you. Then all the churches can see it.

Help for Fellow Christians

9 I really do not need to write to you about this help for God's people. [2]I know you want to help. I have been boasting about this to the people in Macedonia, telling them that you in Southern Greece have been ready to give since last year. And your desire to give has made most of them ready to give also. [3]But I am sending the brothers to you so that our boasting about you in this will not be empty words. I want you to be ready, as I said you would be. [4]If any of the people from Macedonia come with me and find that you are not ready, we will be ashamed that we were so sure of you. (And you will be ashamed too!) [5]So I thought I should ask these brothers to go to you before we do. They will finish getting in order the generous gift you promised so it will be ready when we come. And it will be a generous gift—not one that you did not want to give.

[6]Remember this: the person who plants a little will have a small harvest, but the person who plants a lot will have a big harvest. [7]Each

one should give as he has decided in his heart to give. You should not be sad when you give, and you should not give because you feel forced to give. God loves the person who gives happily. ⁸And God can give you more blessings than you need. Then you will always have plenty of everything—enough to give to every good work. ⁹It is written in the Scriptures: *d*

"He gives freely to the poor.
  The things he does are right and will
    continue for ever."   *Psalm 112:9*
¹⁰God is the One who gives seed to the farmer and bread for food. He will give you all the seed you need and make it grow so there will be a great harvest from your goodness. ¹¹He will make you rich in every way so that you can always give freely. And your giving through us

Just For the Record

When Amanda started her new job, she found some of the staff at the shop a little difficult to get on with. One boy called Luke particularly shied away from her.

Then one day during a coffee break, they were all discussing their musical tastes.

"I don't think rock music will ever die," remarked one lad.

"Personally, I prefer dance stuff," replied Amanda.

A scoffing noise came from Luke, who said: "You've just got no taste! You've got to go back to the sixties and pure Bob Dylan to hear anything really decent."

The rest of the staff were surprised to hear that Luke, who probably wasn't born when Dylan was around, was such a big fan. It turned out that he had a huge collection of his vinyl records.

At this point, Amanda remarked, "Strange, because I have a rare Bob Dylan record in my collection."

Luke hooted with laughter. "You? You've got a rare record? No you haven't!" he carried on. "You can't have!"

Amanda started to look puzzled. "OK, maybe it's not. But I used to work for a record company and I got it from there. I'll bring it in tomorrow."

The next day she walked into the shop carrying a brown paper bag.

"Here you are Luke," she said.

He opened the bag slowly, and inside was one of the rarest of all Bob Dylan vinyls. He was shocked to the core and started to turn very pale.

"You have got a rare record . . ." he whispered, stating the obvious. Then he cleared his throat. "Um. OK . . . so how much will you sell it for?"

"Oh, I don't want to sell it . . . have it," she said simply.

"You can't give this away!" yelled Luke. "Have you any idea what it's worth?"

"Luke. You're the fan. I have something that means more to you than me, so it makes sense that you should have it," she replied.

There was a silence, then Luke looked at her and said very seriously: "I know you're a Christian. I'll come and try your church out this Sunday."

Amanda laughed. "It's not a bribe! You don't have to do that!"

But he did.

In a world that gives to receive, Amanda showed kindness. She took **2 Corinthians 8:5–15** to heart.

* Why did Amanda give away a collector's item?
* In what way does this passage challenge you to give to others?

Consider . . .

* doing an unexpected task around the house as a way of giving of yourself.
* organising a fundraising event to help a Christian mission or Third World project.

For more, see . . .

* Acts 20:32–35 (p.1173)
* Philippians 2:5–7 (p.1282)

will cause many to give thanks to God. [12]This service you do not only helps the needs of God's people, it also brings much more thanks to God. [13]It is a proof of your faith. Many people will praise God because you obey the Good News [d] of Christ—the gospel you say you believe—and because you freely share with them and with all others. [14]And when they pray, they will wish they could be with you because of the great grace that God has given you. [15]Thanks be to God for his gift that is too wonderful for words.

Paul Defends His Ministry

10 I, Paul, am begging you with the gentleness and the kindness of Christ. Some people say that I am easy on you when I am with you and bold when I am away. [2]They think we live in a worldly way, and I plan to be very bold with them when I come. I beg you that when I come I will not need to use that same boldness with you. [3]We do live in the world, but we do not fight in the same way the world fights. [4]We fight with weapons that are different from those the world uses. Our weapons have power from God that can destroy the enemy's strong places. We destroy people's arguments [5]and every proud thing that raises itself against the knowledge of God. We capture every thought and make it give up and obey Christ. [6]We are ready to punish anyone there who does not obey, but first we want you to obey fully.

[7]You must look at the facts before you. If you feel sure that you belong to Christ, you must remember that we belong to Christ just as you do. [8]It is true that we boast freely about the authority the Lord gave us. But this authority is

SHARING FAITH

Doing the Right Thing

Indra was always aware of the homeless people she saw on the street, huddled in shop doorways, as she walked home on cold winter nights. She didn't want to stare, but occasionally she glanced over the scarf tightly wrapped round her neck to catch a glimpse of their faces.

There was one person in particular that grabbed her attention – a girl who couldn't have been much older than her. Indra remembered this girl and prayed for her often, though she didn't see her again for some time.

One day, Indra was walking home with a couple of friends when up ahead she saw some of the homeless people, and instantly recognised the girl she had seen before. She felt a nudge deep in her heart to do something for this girl, and as they got closer, Indra was already reaching into her bag to get some money. But she stopped to think and pray, and asked God to show her the best way to help the girl.

The girl looked nervously at Indra. Never before had someone actually stopped to talk to her – at most, people threw the odd coin in her direction as they went past. Indra introduced herself and asked the girl if she was hungry. Then she invited her to come with her to a café to have something to eat.

At first, the other people in the café gave Indra and the girl funny looks, thinking they were going to cause trouble. But when everyone saw what Indra was doing, most people smiled warmly, knowing that she was doing a very kind thing.

Read **2 Corinthians 8:20–21**. Paul and Titus knew that it took a lot of effort to do what was good in God's eyes as well as the eyes of those around them.

* How had Indra been careful to do what was right?
* What effect do you think it had on the people in the café to see what Indra had done?

Consider . . .

* how you can make sure that what you decide to do in your life is seen as good by God *and* other people.
* praying that people would see God through your actions.

For more, see . . .

* Romans 14:13–23 (p.1207)
* 1 Peter 2:11–12 (p.1358)

to build you up, not to tear you down. So I will not be ashamed. [9]I do not want you to think I am trying to scare you with my letters. [10]Some people say, "Paul's letters are powerful and sound important, but when he is with us, he is weak. And his speaking is nothing." [11]They should know this: we are not there with you now, so we say these things in letters. But when we are there with you, we will show the same authority that we show in our letters.

[12]We do not dare to compare ourselves with those who think they are very important. They use themselves to measure themselves, and

> ### Sidelight
>
> Paul may have been a superstar missionary but he would never have made it to the front cover of a fashion magazine. A book, around at the same time as the New Testament was written, described him as "a man small of stature, with bald head and crooked legs . . . with eyebrows meeting and nose somewhat hooked". His critics described him as " . . . weak. And his speaking is nothing" (2 Corinthians 10:10).

they judge themselves by what they themselves are. This shows that they know nothing. [13]But we will not boast about things outside the work that was given us to do. We will limit our boasting to the work that God gave us, and this includes our work with you. [14]We are not boasting too much, as we would be if we had not already come to you. But we have come to you with the Good News [d] of Christ. [15]We limit our boasting to the work that is ours, not what others have done. We hope that as your faith continues to grow, you will help our work to grow much larger. [16]We want to tell the Good News in the areas beyond your city. We do not want to boast about work that has already been done in another person's area. [17]But, "If someone wants to boast, he should boast only about the Lord." [n] [18]It is not those who say they are good who are accepted but those whom the Lord thinks are good.

Paul and the False Apostles

11 I wish you would be patient with me even when I am a little foolish, but you are already doing that. [2]I am jealous over you with a jealousy that comes from God. I promised

to give you to Christ, as your only husband. I want to give you as his pure bride. [3]But I am afraid that your minds will be led away from your true and pure following of Christ just as Eve was tricked by the snake with his evil ways. [4]You are very patient with anyone who comes to you and preaches a different Jesus from the one we preached. You are very willing to accept a spirit or good news that is different from the Spirit [d] and Good News [d] you received from us.

[5]I do not think that those "great apostles" are any better than I am. [6]I may not be a trained speaker, but I do have knowledge. We have shown this to you clearly in every way.

[7]I preached God's Good News to you without pay. I made myself unimportant to make you important. Do you think that was wrong? [8]I accepted pay from other churches, taking their money so I could serve you. [9]If I needed something when I was with you, I did not trouble any of you. The brothers who came from Macedonia gave me all that I needed. I did not allow myself to depend on you in any way, and I will never depend on you. [10]No one in Southern Greece will stop me from boasting about that. I say this with the truth of Christ in me. [11]And why do I not depend on you? Do you think it is because I do not love you? God knows that I love you.

[12]And I will continue doing what I am doing now, because I want to stop those people from having a reason to boast. They would like to say that the work they boast about is the same as ours. [13]Such men are not true apostles [d] but are workers who lie. They change themselves to look like apostles of Christ. [14]This does not surprise us. Even Satan changes himself to look like an angel of light. [n] [15]So it does not surprise us if Satan's servants also make themselves look like servants who work for what is right. But in the end they will be punished for what they do.

Paul Tells About His Sufferings

[16]I tell you again: no one should think I am a fool. But if you think so, accept me as you would accept a fool. Then I can boast a little, too. [17]When I boast because I feel sure of myself, I am not talking as the Lord would talk but as a fool. [18]Many people are boasting about their lives in the world. So I will boast too. [19]You are wise, so you will gladly be patient with fools! [20]You are

---

"If . . . Lord."   Quotation from Jeremiah 9:24.
angel of light   Messenger from God. The devil fools people so that they think he is from God.

even patient with those who order you around, or use you, or trick you, or think they are better than you, or hit you in the face. [21]It is shameful to me to say this, but we were too "weak" to do those things to you!

But if anyone else is brave enough to boast, then I also will be brave and boast. (I am talking as a fool.) [22]Are they Hebrews?[n] So am I. Are they Israelites? So am I. Are they from Abraham's family? So am I. [23]Are they serving Christ? I am serving him more. (I am mad to talk like this.) I have worked much harder than they. I have been in prison more often. I have been hurt more in beatings. I have been near death many times. [24]Five times the Jews have given me their punishment of 39 lashes with a whip. [25]Three different times I was beaten with rods. One time I was almost stoned to death. Three times I was in ships that were wrecked, and one of those times I spent a night and a day in the sea. [26]I have gone on many travels and have been in danger from rivers, thieves, my own people, the Jews and those who are not Jews. I have been in danger in cities, in places where no one lives and on the sea. And I have been in danger with false Christians. [27]I have done hard and tiring work, and many times I did not sleep. I have been hungry and thirsty, and many times I have been without food. I have been cold and without clothes. [28]Besides all this, there is on me every day the load of my concern for all the churches. [29]I feel weak every time someone is weak, and I feel upset every time someone is led into sin.

[30]If I must boast, I will boast about the things that show I am weak. [31]God knows I am not lying. He is the God and Father of the Lord Jesus Christ, and he is to be praised for ever. [32]When I was in Damascus, the governor under King Aretas wanted to arrest me, so he put guards around the city. [33]But my friends lowered me in a basket through a hole in the city wall. So I escaped from the governor.

A Special Blessing in Paul's Life

12 I must continue to boast. It will do no good, but I will talk now about visions and revelations[n] from the Lord. [2]I know a man in Christ who was taken up to the third heaven fourteen years ago. I do not know whether the man was in his body or out of his body, but God knows. [3-4]And I know that this man was taken

up to paradise.[n] I don't know if he was in his body or away from his body, but God knows. He heard things he is not able to explain, things that no human is allowed to tell. [5]I will boast about a man like that, but I will not boast about myself, except about my weaknesses. [6]But if I wanted to boast about myself, I would not be a fool, because I would be telling the truth. But I will not boast about myself. I do not want people to think more of me than what they see me do or hear me say.

[7]So that I would not become too proud of the wonderful things that were shown to me, a painful problem[n] was given to me. This problem was a messenger from Satan, sent to beat me and keep me from being too proud. [8]I begged the Lord three times to take this problem away from me. [9]But he said to me, "My grace is enough for you. When you are weak, my power is made perfect in you." So I am very happy to boast about my weaknesses. Then Christ's power can live in me. [10]For this reason I am happy when I have weaknesses, insults, hard times, sufferings and all kinds of troubles for Christ. Because when I am weak, then I am truly strong.

Paul's Love for the Christians

[11]I have been talking like a fool, but you made me do it. You are the ones who should say good things about me. I am worth nothing, but those "great apostles" are not worth any more than I am! [12]When I was with you, I patiently did the things that prove I am an apostle[d]—signs, wonders and miracles.[d] [13]So you received everything that the other churches have received. Only one thing was different: I was not a burden to you. Forgive me for this!

[14]I am now ready to visit you the third time, and I will not be a burden to you. I want nothing from you, except you. Children should not have to save up to give to their parents. Parents should save to give to their children. [15]So I am happy to give everything I have for you, even myself. If I love you more, will you love me less?

[16]It is clear I was not a burden to you, but you think I was sly and lied to catch you. [17]Did I cheat you by using any of the messengers I sent to you? No, you know I did not. [18]I asked Titus to go to you, and I sent our brother with him. Titus did not cheat you, did he? No, you know

---

Hebrews   A name for the Jews that some Jews were very proud of.
revelation   Making known truth that has been hidden.
paradise   A place where good people go when they die.
painful problem   Literally, "thorn in the flesh".

that Titus and I did the same thing and with the same spirit.

¹⁹Do you think we have been defending ourselves to you all this time? We have been speaking in Christ and before God. You are our dear friends, and everything we do is to make you stronger. ²⁰I am afraid that when I come, you will not be what I want you to be, and I will not be what you want me to be. I am afraid that among you there may be arguing, jealousy, anger, selfish fighting, evil talk, gossip, pride and confusion. ²¹I am afraid that when I come to you again, my God will make me

ashamed before you. I may be saddened by many of those who have sinned because they have not changed their hearts or turned from their sexual sins and the shameful things they have done.

Final Warnings and Greetings

13 I will come to you for the third time. "Every case must be proved by two or three witnesses." *n* ²When I was with you the second time, I gave a warning to those who had sinned. Now I am away from you, and I give a warning to all the others. When I come to you

"**Every . . . witnesses.**" Quotation from Deuteronomy 19:15.

PARENTS

Open House

Any night of the week you would find friends around Joel's house. Weekends were a speciality.

"It's so much better round here than at my place," remarked Andy, one of his best friends.

"Why's that?" asked Joel.

"Well, your mum's so cool. Here we are up in your room, making a noise, playing music and the only thing your mum does is bring us food!" He grinned as he tucked into his third cake.

"Why? What does your mum do?" asked Joel, puzzled.

"She'd kick us all out for a start!" he replied. "There's no way she'd let me have my friends upstairs – and absolutely no way she'd make food for them!"

Joel thought about this after his friend had left, and later spoke to his parents about what Andy had said.

"I thought all parents were like you," he smiled. "So, why do you do all these things for me?"

His mother Cheryl laughed.

"Joel, you're our son, we love seeing you happy and having fun. If your friends want to come round that's great. We get to meet them and talk to them, and the house is full of life, what could be better? Plus of course, we know where you are and who you are with."

"Yes," put in his father. "So, if you go to a football game with Andy, we know he's the one with dyed orange hair who likes chocolate cake and computer games!"

Joel pondered this for a while and then asked, "But things get spilt on the carpet and sometimes you have to come and remind us of the time; don't you mind?"

"I can easily clean things up," his mother replied. "So, you'd better get it through your head that we like having you around, it's your house too you know."

2 Corinthians 12:14–15 reminds us that children are not the providers of a household.

* Why, according to these verses, does the system of parents providing work so well?
* What does Paul ask for in return for his visit?

Consider . . .

* getting up early one Saturday morning and treating your parents to a cooked breakfast in bed!
* asking God to help you to be patient during times of family tension.

For more, see . . .

* Luke 15:20 (p.1072)
* 2 Timothy 1:5 (p.1316)

* Ephesians 6:4 (p.1276)

again, I will not be easy with them. ³You want proof that Christ is speaking through me. My proof is that he is not weak among you, but he is powerful. ⁴It is true that he was weak when he was killed on the cross, but he lives now by God's power. It is true that we are weak in Christ, but for you we will be alive in Christ by God's power.

⁵Look closely at yourselves. Test yourselves to see if you are living in the faith. You know that Jesus Christ is in you—unless you fail the test. ⁶But I hope you will see that we ourselves have not failed the test. ⁷We pray to God that you will not do anything wrong. It is not important to see that we have passed the test, but it is important that you do what is right, even if it seems we have failed. ⁸We cannot do anything against the truth, but only for the truth. ⁹We are happy to be weak, if you are strong, and we pray that you will become complete. ¹⁰I am writing this while I am away from you so that when I come I will not have to be harsh in my use of authority. The Lord gave me this authority to build you up, not to tear you down.

¹¹Now, brothers and sisters, I say goodbye.

IMAGE

On a Personal Level

Joe went into church humming cheerfully to himself. The older man at the door muttered "Good morning" to him and Joe responded by patting his back.

Joe quickly found his friends and waved at them as he made his way across to where they were sitting. "How's it going everyone?" he grinned as he took his seat.

During the service it was noticeable that Joe always gave it his all. He sang with great gusto and prayed seriously. His friends always felt encouraged when he was around.

After the service, he was stopped by the usher at the door.

"Young man," he said. "Do you think your clothes are appropriate for the House of God?"

Joe blinked twice and smiled. "How do you mean?" He looked down at himself, at his scruffy T-shirt and his favourite jeans.

"Well . . . " started the usher. "If you were going to meet the Queen, would you wear those clothes?"

"No," stated Joe.

"And why not?" asked the old man.

"Because I don't know her and I've never been to Buckingham Palace. I'd probably have to spruce up a bit," he explained.

"Then don't you think that Jesus deserves the same treatment?" the usher asked cunningly.

"Not on your life mate!" came the shocked reply. "Jesus is my friend, a really good friend. I know him really well, just like I know my mates here," Joe said, pointing to them. "If I went round my mates' houses all done up like that, they'd think I'd gone mad!"

And with that Joe left the church, still humming happily.

Paul's advice to the people in **2 Corinthians 13:5–10** was to test themselves, to see if Jesus was living in them.

* How can you know if your image as a Christian is right, according to 2 Corinthians 13:7?
* If you look closely at yourself – beyond the clothes – what do you find?

Consider . . .

* whether you are ever guilty of judging people on the clothes that they wear, rather than the person they are.
* discussing with your youth group what sort of statement your clothes make to other people.

For more, see . . .

* 1 Samuel 16:7 (p.269)
* 1 John 2:5 (p.1372)

* 2 Corinthians 5:12 (p.1245)

Try to be perfect. Do what I have asked you to do. Agree with each other, and live in peace. Then the God of love and peace will be with you.

¹²Greet each other with a holy kiss. ¹³All of God's holy people send greetings to you.

¹⁴The grace of the Lord Jesus Christ, the love of God, and the fellowship of the Holy Spirit*d* be with you all.

Galatians

Why Read This Book:
* See the dangers of listening to false teachers (Galatians 1—2).
* Discover the freedom we have through faith in Christ (Galatians 3).
* Find out how Christians should use their freedom (Galatians 5—6).

When?

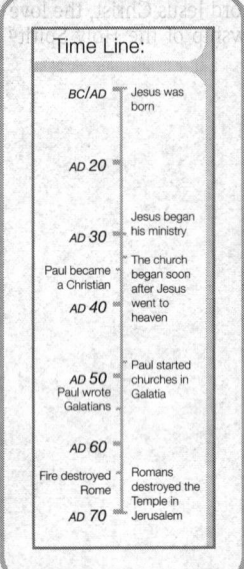

Time Line:

BC/AD	Jesus was born
AD 20	
AD 30	Jesus began his ministry
Paul became a Christian	The church began soon after Jesus went to heaven
AD 40	
AD 50 Paul wrote Galatians	Paul started churches in Galatia
AD 60	
Fire destroyed Rome	Romans destroyed the Temple in Jerusalem
AD 70	

Behind the Scenes:

What do you have to do to be a Christian? Do you have to practise certain rituals? Do you have to follow certain rules?

Those were controversial questions in the early church, as we discover in Paul's letter to the Galatians. Not long before, Paul had started the churches in Galatia. But soon after he left, people began questioning his beliefs and authority. They said that non-Jewish people who became Christians also had to follow Jewish laws and rituals to be true Christians – a view that was splitting the early church (see Acts 15, p.1163).

When Paul heard what was happening, he wrote this letter to confront the problem. "You have already accepted the Good News. If anyone is preaching something different to you, he should be judged guilty!" he blasts in Galatians 1:9. Then Paul gets to the heart of the Christian faith. He explains that people can't do anything to earn God's promises. Those promises are free gifts for all people, to be received by faith in Christ. Instead of being the law's prisoners, Christians live in freedom.

Someone always seems to be telling us that serving God means following a long list of dos and don'ts. Paul's letter to the Galatians reminds us that being a Christian isn't a matter of what we do or don't do; it's a matter of accepting what Jesus Christ did for us. Now that's Good News!

Where?

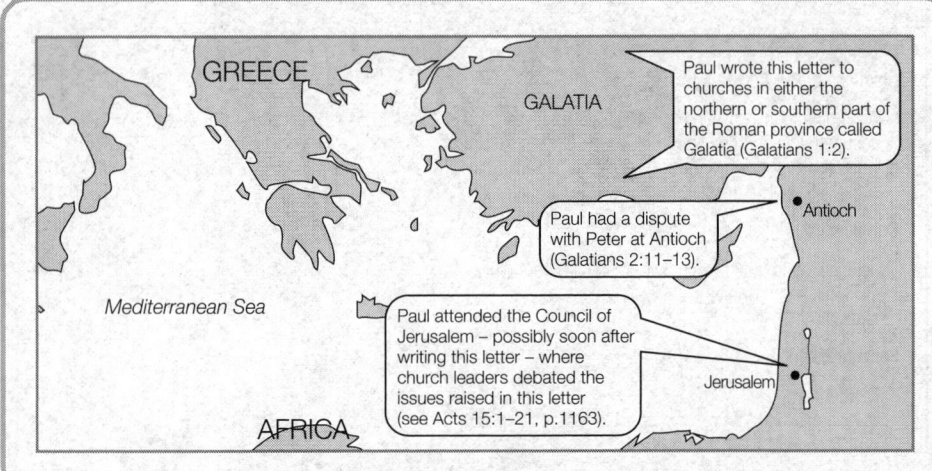

GREECE

GALATIA

Paul wrote this letter to churches in either the northern or southern part of the Roman province called Galatia (Galatians 1:2).

Paul had a dispute with Peter at Antioch (Galatians 2:11–13).

• Antioch

Paul attended the Council of Jerusalem – possibly soon after writing this letter – where church leaders debated the issues raised in this letter (see Acts 15:1–21, p.1163).

Mediterranean Sea

Jerusalem •

AFRICA

1 From Paul, an apostle.[d] I was not chosen to be an apostle by human beings, nor was I sent from human beings. I was made an apostle through Jesus Christ and God the Father who raised Jesus from the dead. [2]This letter is also from all those of God's family[n] who are with me.

To the churches in Galatia:[n]

[3]Grace and peace to you from God our Father and the Lord Jesus Christ. [4]Jesus gave himself for our sins to free us from this evil world we live in, as God the Father planned. [5]The glory belongs to God for ever and ever. Amen.

The Only Good News

[6]God, by his grace through Christ, called you to become his people. So I am amazed that you are turning away so quickly and believing something different from the Good News.[d] [7]Really, there is no other Good News. But some people

---

those . . . family The Greek text says "brothers".
Galatia Probably the same country where Paul preached and began churches on his first missionary trip. Read the book of Acts, chapters 13 and 14.

CULTS

Good News, Bad News

Daniel had gone to church on and off since he was little, but he had never felt that he really needed God. That is, until last summer. Nearly everything Daniel did seemed to go wrong. He was fired from his summer job, and then he wrote his car off. Now his dad had moved out. Daniel began to think that perhaps he needed some help with his life.

He immediately thought of Phil. Nothing seemed to throw him. He seemed to be into the supernatural.

So Daniel started talking to Phil during lunch. Phil had an answer for every question Daniel asked. He made everything seem so simple and clear-cut. Phil talked about what it took to be one of the "Chosen Ones" – a new religious group that he was involved with. "Wow," Daniel thought, "he really knows his stuff!"

Of course, Phil explained the Bible differently from anything Daniel had ever heard, but Phil seemed to know what he was talking about. It all seemed so simple. All you had to do was follow a list of rules and requirements, and you would be fine.

The more Daniel talked to Phil and read Phil's books, the more he began to feel as if he, too, might finally be on the home straight to God. After all, wasn't he learning new things every day? Wasn't he trying to do everything he was supposed to do to be one of the Chosen Ones?

But still Daniel wondered. Sometimes he would wake up in the middle of the night, afraid he had not done everything he was supposed to do. He would thumb through the books, studying the requirements and trying to shake the feeling that he wasn't good enough. Daniel wanted to talk to Phil about his doubts, but he was afraid that if he said anything, he might lose his place among the Chosen Ones.

Daniel wished he could know that he was right with God. Read **Galatians 1:1–10** to see how the Galatians made the same mistake.

* According to this passage (especially verses 4–6), how is the Good News very different from the requirements of groups like the Chosen Ones?
* Have you ever found yourself being attracted by the promises of a cult? What made the promises attractive? How did you resist the pull?

Consider . . .

* asking God to teach you how to respect others while you share your beliefs with them.
* inviting a friend who doesn't go to church to come with you to worship. Introduce him or her to your Christian friends.

For more, see . . .

* Deuteronomy 13:1–4 (p.178)
* 1 John 4:1–6 (p.1374)
* Matthew 7:13–20 (p.950)

are confusing you; they want to change the Good News of Christ. [8]We preached to you the Good News. So if we ourselves, or even an angel from heaven, should preach to you something different, we should be judged guilty! [9]I said this before, and now I say it again: you have already accepted the Good News. If anyone is preaching something different to you, he should be judged guilty!

Sidelight

If Paul wrote Galatians early in his career – as some scholars believe – it may have been the first New Testament book written, dated less than 20 years after Jesus lived. Other scholars think that either 1 Thessalonians (p.1295) or James (p.1347) was the first book to be written.

---

[10]Do you think I am trying to make people accept me? No, God is the One I am trying to please. Am I trying to please people? If I still wanted to please people, I would not be a servant of Christ.

Paul's Authority is from God

[11]Brothers and sisters,[n] I want you to know that the Good News[d] I preached to you was not made up by human beings. [12]I did not get it from humans, nor did anyone teach it to me, but Jesus Christ showed it to me.

[13]You have heard about my past life in the Jewish religion. I attacked the church of God and tried to destroy it. [14]I was becoming a leader in the Jewish religion, doing better than most other Jews of my age. I tried harder than anyone else to follow the teachings handed down by our ancestors.

[15]But God had special plans for me and set me apart for his work even before I was born. He called me through his grace [16]and showed his Son to me so that I might tell the Good News about him to those who are not Jewish. When God called me, I did not get advice or help from any person. [17]I did not go to Jerusalem to see those who were apostles[d] before I was. But, without waiting, I went away to Arabia and later went back to Damascus.

[18]After three years I went to Jerusalem to meet Peter and stayed with him for fifteen days. [19]I met no other apostles, except James, the brother of

the Lord. [20]God knows that these things I write are not lies. [21]Later, I went to the areas of Syria and Cilicia.

[22]In Judea the churches in Christ had never met me. [23]They had only heard it said, "This man who was attacking us is now preaching the same faith that he once tried to destroy." [24]And these believers praised God because of me.

Other Apostles Accepted Paul

2 After fourteen years I went to Jerusalem again, this time with Barnabas. I also took Titus with me. [2]I went because God showed me I should go. I met with the believers there, and in private I told their leaders the Good News[d] that I preach to the non-Jewish people. I did not want my past work and the work I am now doing to be wasted. [3]Titus was with me, but he was not forced to be circumcised,[d] even though he was a Greek. [4]We talked about this problem because some false believers had come into our group secretly. They came in like spies to overturn the freedom we have in Christ Jesus. They wanted to make us slaves. [5]But we did not give in to those false believers for a minute. We wanted the truth of the Good News to continue for you.

[6]Those leaders who seemed to be important did not change the Good News that I preach. (It doesn't matter to me if they were "important" or not. To God everyone is the same.) [7]But these leaders saw that I had been given the work of telling the Good News to those who are not Jewish, just as Peter had the work of telling the Jews. [8]God gave Peter the power to work as an apostle[d] for the Jewish people. But he also gave me the power to work as an apostle for those who are not Jews. [9]James, Peter and John, who seemed to be the leaders, understood that God had given me this special grace, so they accepted Barnabas and me. They agreed that they would go to the Jewish people and that we should go to those who are not Jewish. [10]The only thing they asked us was to remember to help the poor—something I really wanted to do.

Paul Shows that Peter was Wrong

[11]When Peter came to Antioch, I challenged him to his face, because he was wrong. [12]Peter ate with the non-Jewish people until some Jewish people sent from James came to Antioch. When they arrived, Peter stopped eating with those

---

Brothers and sisters Although the Greek text says "brothers" here and throughout this book, Paul's words were meant for the entire church, both men and women.

who weren't Jewish, and he separated himself from them. He was afraid of the Jews. [13]So Peter was a hypocrite, [d] as were the other Jewish believers who joined with him. Even Barnabas was influenced by what these Jewish believers did. [14]When I saw they were not following the truth of the Good News, [d] I spoke to Peter in front of them all. I said, "Peter, you are a Jew, but you are not living like a Jew. You are living like those who are not Jewish. So why do you now try to force those who are not Jewish to live like Jews?"

[15]We were not born as non-Jewish "sinners", but as Jews. [16]Yet we know that a person is made right with God not by following the law, [d] but by trusting in Jesus Christ. So we, too, have put our faith in Christ Jesus, that we might be made right with God because we trusted in Christ. It is not because we followed the law, because no one can be made right with God by following the law.

[17]We Jews came to Christ, trying to be made right with God, and it became clear that we are sinners too. Does this mean that Christ encourages sin? No! [18]But I would really be wrong to begin teaching again those things that I gave up. [19]It was the law that put me to death, and I died to the law so that I can now live for God. [20]I was put to death on the cross with Christ, and I do not live any more—it is Christ who lives in me. I still live in my body, but I live by faith in the Son of God who loved me and gave himself to save me. [21]By saying these things I am not going against God's grace. Just the opposite, if the law could make us right with God, then Christ's death would be useless.

FAITH

It's Not About Rules

Hassan cannot believe the stories his father tells him, Hassan's life is so different to his dad's childhood. Hassan's father speaks of being forced to pray many times in the day, not being allowed to listen to music or the radio, eating only certain food and everyone wearing white robes to show they are all equal in the sight of Allah.

Hassan's life is very different. He comes home, listens to the music charts and, generally, he wears what he likes.

Hassan is confused as to why some people live under such strict rules.

Hassan's father tells of the first time he watched the film telling the story of Jesus. After moving to England, he became friends with a Christian who explained Jesus' love – how Jesus loved him regardless of whether he kept certain rules and laws. Hassan's father found this difficult to understand; he had been brought up to believe that only people who kept all the rules of their religion would enter paradise. He was amazed by this man Jesus – his love, his death and his words of freedom. Could this story be true, that Jesus died to set him free, that there was nothing he could do to earn his place in God's family? Later that night Hassan's father said a short prayer and felt for the first time an overwhelming sense of peace.

Read **Galatians 2:11–21**.

* Hassan's dad and Peter were confused when they heard that salvation is by faith and cannot be earned. How do you understand this?
* How did Hassan's father change when he understood that faith in Jesus is important?

Consider . . .

* writing a "Faith" list of all the things that you need faith to believe in.
* reading more about religions where they believe you have to earn salvation. Pray for the people you read about that, like Hassan's dad, they would hear about Jesus.

For more, see . . .

* Romans 3:21–31 (p.1187)
* Hebrews 11 (p.1341)
* Ephesians 2:4–10 (p.1270)

Sidelight

The Greek word translated "guardian" in Galatians 3:24 could almost be translated "babysitter". It refers to the person – usually a slave – who was responsible for taking care of young children (see also Galatians 4:1–7, p.1261). Possibly half of the population of the Roman Empire were slaves during the New Testament times.

Blessing Comes Through Faith

3 You people in Galatia were told very clearly about the death of Jesus Christ on the cross. But you were foolish; you let someone trick you. ²Tell me this one thing: how did you receive the Holy Spirit? *d* Did you receive the Spirit by following the law? *d* No, you received the Spirit because you heard the Good News *d* and believed it. ³You began your life in Christ by the Spirit. Now are you trying to make it complete by your own power? That is foolish. ⁴Were all your experiences wasted? I hope not! ⁵Does God give you the Spirit and work miracles *d* among you because you follow the law? No, he does these things because you heard the Good News and believed it.

⁶The Scriptures *d* say the same thing about Abraham: "Abraham believed God, and God accepted Abraham's faith, and that faith made him right with God." *n* ⁷So you should know that the true children of Abraham are those who have faith. ⁸The Scriptures, telling what would happen in the future, said that God would make the non-Jewish people right through their faith. This Good News was told to Abraham beforehand, as the Scripture says: "All nations will be blessed through you." *n* ⁹So all who believe as Abraham believed are blessed just as Abraham was. ¹⁰But those who depend on following the law to make them right are under a curse, because the Scriptures say, "Anyone will be cursed who does not always obey what is written in the Book of the Law." *n* ¹¹Now it is clear that no one can be made right with God by the law, because the Scriptures say, "Those who are right with God

will live by trusting in him." *n* ¹²The law is not based on faith. It says, "A person who obeys these things will live because of them." *n* ¹³Christ took away the curse the law put on us. He changed places with us and put himself under that curse. It is written in the Scriptures, "Anyone whose body is displayed on a tree *n* is cursed." ¹⁴Christ did this so that God's blessing promised to Abraham might come through Jesus Christ to those who are not Jews. Jesus died so that by our believing we could receive the Spirit that God promised.

The Law and the Promise

¹⁵Brothers and sisters, *n* let us think in human terms: even an agreement made between two persons is firm. After that agreement is accepted by both people, no one can stop it or add anything to it. ¹⁶God made promises both to Abraham and to his descendant. *d* God did not say, "and to your descendants". That would mean many people. But God said, "and to your descendant". That means only one person; that person is Christ. ¹⁷This is what I mean: God had an agreement with Abraham and promised to keep it. The law, which came 430 years later, cannot change that agreement and so destroy God's promise to Abraham. ¹⁸If the law could give us Abraham's blessing, then the promise would not be necessary. But that is not possible, because God freely gave his blessings to Abraham through the promise he had made.

¹⁹So what was the law for? It was given to show that the wrong things people do are against God's will. And it continued until the special descendant, who had been promised, came. The law was given through angels who used Moses for a mediator *n* to give the law to people. ²⁰But a mediator is not needed when there is only one side, and God is only one.

The Purpose of the Law of Moses

²¹Does this mean that the law is against God's promises? Never! That would be true only if the law could make us right. But God did not give a law that can bring life. ²²Instead, the Scriptures *d* showed that the whole world is

---

"Abraham . . . God."   Quotation from Genesis 15:6.
"All . . . you."   Quotation from Genesis 12:3; 18:18.
"Anyone . . . Law."   Quotation from Deuteronomy 27:26.
"Those . . . him."   Quotation from Habakkuk 2:4.
"A person . . . them."   Quotation from Leviticus 18:5.
displayed on a tree   Deuteronomy 21:22–23 says that when a person was killed for doing wrong, the body was hung on a tree to show shame. Paul means that the cross of Jesus was like that.
brothers and sisters   Although the Greek text says "brothers" here and throughout this book, the words of Paul were meant for the entire church, both men and women.
mediator   A person who helps one person talk to or give something to another person.

bound by sin. This was so the promise would be given through faith to people who believe in Jesus Christ.

²³Before this faith came, we were all held prisoners by the law. We had no freedom until God showed us the way of faith that was coming. ²⁴In other words, the law was our guardian leading us to Christ so that we could be made right with God through faith. ²⁵Now the way of faith has come, and we no longer live under a guardian.

²⁶⁻²⁷You were all baptised ᵈ into Christ, and so you were all clothed with Christ. This means that you are all children of God through faith in Christ Jesus. ²⁸In Christ, there is no difference between Jew and Greek, slave and free person, male and female. You are all the same in Christ Jesus. ²⁹You belong to Christ, so you are Abraham's descendants. You will inherit all of God's blessings because of the promise God made to Abraham.

4 I want to tell you this: while those who will inherit their fathers' property are still children, they are no different from slaves. It does not matter that the children own everything. ²While they are children, they must obey those who are chosen to care for them. But when the children reach the age set by their fathers, they are free. ³It is the same for us. We were once like children, slaves to the

---

STEREOTYPES

Inside Out

In this corner: Harold, church warden, board member, businessman. Grey suit and tie, starched shirt, thick glasses.

In that corner: Josh, would-be radical, always off on some wild project to save the world, usually involving loud music. Out of date mohican haircut, ripped jeans, T-shirt, earring.

Mohican sizes up Suit: "He'll turn me down before I even ask. Old people are like that. Narrow-minded, afraid of anything new."

Suit sizes up Mohican: "Oh dear. Here we go. Another daft idea. And if I say no, he'll call me old-fashioned."

"Hello, Josh. What's up?"

"We want to fix up the old scout hut for a place to have a weekly Bible study." Suit frowns.

So does Mohican. "I knew it," he thinks. "You think we can't be trusted."

"Hmmm," Suit muses. "These kids' clothes are certainly peculiar, but their hearts are in the right place."

"Sounds like an excellent idea to me," Suit finally says. "What's your first topic?"

Mohican is down for the count. "Er, the importance of prayer," he manages to get out.

"Now that's a subject I always need help with," Suit says.

"Well," Mohican grins, "why don't you join us some time?"

Though people may be different on the outside, they are the same in Jesus Christ. Read this truth in **Galatians 3:23–29.**

* How are Suit and Mohican – or as it says in this passage, a Jew and a Greek – no different in Christ?
* What criteria have you used to judge another Christian?

Consider . . .

* tearing out pictures of five different types of people from a magazine. On each picture, write five ideas that you have about people like that person. Check your ideas by getting to know people in each category.
* visiting a church with a different culture. For example, if you are from an Anglican church, visit a Pentecostal church.

For more, see . . .

* 1 Samuel 16:1–13 (p.269)
* 2 Corinthians 5:11–12 (p.1245)
* Romans 2:28–29 (p.1187)

useless rules of this world. [4]But when the right time came, God sent his Son who was born of a woman and lived under the law. [5]God did this so he could buy freedom for those who were under the law and so we could become his children.

[6]Since you are God's children, God sent the Spirit of his Son into your hearts, and the Spirit [d] cries out, "Father". [n] [7]So now you are not a slave; you are God's child, and God will give you the blessing he promised, because you are his child.

Paul's Love for the Christians

[8]In the past you did not know God. You were slaves to gods that were not real. [9]But now you know the true God. Really, it is God who knows you. So why do you turn back to those weak and useless rules you followed before? Do you want to be slaves to those things again? [10]You still follow teachings about special days, months, seasons and years. [11]I am afraid for you, that my work for you has been wasted.

[12]Brothers and sisters, I became like you, so I beg you to become like me. You were very good

"Father"   Literally, "Abba, Father". Jewish children called their fathers "Abba".

GOD'S LOVE

Too Good to be True?

"Yours Free! Just Ring and Claim Your Prize! No Obligation!" It was a once-in-a-lifetime offer that Jackie couldn't refuse when it arrived in the post.

Of course, Jackie had heard that some of these offers were cons. But this one looked like a safe bet. It guaranteed that she would get "a luxurious fur coat" or a "limited edition Mercedes sports car with all the extras".

"Everyone's a winner," the card boasted. "Ring now to learn what you have won!"

"What harm can it do," Jackie thought to herself, picking up the phone.

Sure enough, she had won! The fur coat was being packed for her. And the contest's agent asked if she would also consider another special offer. For only £99 (on credit card, if you like), she could receive beauty tips from "the nation's foremost beauty experts" in an exclusive newsletter for teenage girls called "Looking Good".

In addition, she would have access to a freephone "Looks Line". She could ring the number at any time, day or night, and receive personal consultations on anything from shoes to eye shadow – for the rest of her life. It was just a one-off fee, Jackie told herself. And it was good for a lifetime. So she placed her order with her mum's credit card.

Jackie's excitement turned to displeasure when she received the genuine dyed rabbit fur coat. She knew she had been taken in when the one-page "Looking Good" newsletter arrived, complete with revolutionary beauty tips such as "wash your face thoroughly each night before going to bed".

Something that had seemed like a dream just a few days earlier now seemed like a nightmare. It had sounded too good to be true. And it was.

Galatians 4:4–7 tells about an offer of God's love that seems too good to be true, but really is true!

* What differences do you see between the once-in-a-lifetime offer that Jackie fell for and the once-for-all-times offer of God's love that's described in the passage?
* What parts of God's offer of love are most appealing to you? How have you responded to that offer?

Consider . . .

* using the form and style of a direct-mail offer to write a postcard about God's offer of love. Send it to a friend who needs some encouragement.
* talking to a friend who was adopted about what it feels like to be specially chosen by parents. Discuss similarities between that and the experience of being a child of God.

For more, see . . .

* Isaiah 64:8–9 (p.709)
* Romans 8:31–39 (p.1197)
* Matthew 7:7–11 (p.950)

to me before. [13]You remember that it was because of sickness that I came to you the first time, preaching the Good News. [d] [14]Though my sickness was a trouble for you, you did not hate me or make me leave. But you welcomed me as an angel from God, as if I were Jesus Christ himself! [15]You were very happy then, but where is that joy now? I am ready to testify that you would have taken out your eyes and given them to me if that were possible. [16]Now am I your enemy because I tell you the truth?

[17]Those people [n] are working hard to persuade you, but this is not good for you. They want to persuade you to turn against us and follow only them. [18]It is good for people to show interest in you, but only if their purpose is good. This is always true, not just when I am with you. [19]My little children, again I feel the pain of childbirth for you until you truly become like Christ. [20]I wish I could be with you now and could change the way I am talking to you, because I do not know what to think about you.

The Example of Hagar and Sarah

[21]Some of you still want to be under the law. Tell me, do you know what the law says? [22]The Scriptures [d] say that Abraham had two sons. The mother of one son was a slave woman, and the mother of the other son was a free woman. [23]Abraham's son from the slave woman was born in the normal human way. But the son from the free woman was born because of the promise God made to Abraham.

[24]This story teaches something else: the two women are like the two agreements between God and his people. One agreement is the law that God made on Mount Sinai, [n] and the people who are under this agreement are like slaves. The mother named Hagar is like that agreement. [25]She is like Mount Sinai in Arabia and is a picture of the earthly Jewish city of Jerusalem. This city and its people, the Jews, are slaves to the law. [26]But the heavenly Jerusalem, which is above, is like the free woman. She is our mother. [27]It is written in the Scriptures:

"Be happy, Jerusalem.
You are like a woman who never gave
    birth to children.
Start singing and shout for joy.
You never felt the pain of giving birth,
but you will have more children
    than the woman who has a husband."

Isaiah 54:1

[28]My brothers and sisters, you are God's children because of his promise, as Isaac was then. [29]The son who was born in the normal way treated the other son badly. It is the same today. [30]But what does the Scripture say? "Throw out the slave woman and her son. The son of the slave woman should not inherit anything. The son of the free woman should receive it all." [n] [31]So, my brothers and sisters, we are not children of the slave woman, but of the free woman.

Keep Your Freedom

5 We have freedom now, because Christ made us free. So stand strong. Do not change and go back into the slavery of the law. [d] [2]Listen, I, Paul, tell you that if you go back to the law by being circumcised, [d] Christ does you no good. [3]Again, I warn every man: if you allow yourselves to be circumcised, you must follow all the law. [4]If you try to be made right with God through the law, your life with Christ is over—you have left God's grace. [5]But we have the true hope that comes from being made right with God, and by the Spirit [d] we wait eagerly for this hope. [6]When we are in Christ Jesus, it is not important if we are circumcised or not. The important thing is faith—the kind of faith that works through love.

[7]You were running a good race. Who stopped you from following the true way? [8]This change did not come from the One who chose you. [9]Be

> **Sidelight**   Circumcision (Galatians 5:2–6) was an important ritual for Jews, symbolising bringing a baby boy into God's family. A festive occasion marked each circumcision, which was usually performed by the boy's father.

careful! "Just a little yeast makes the whole batch of dough rise." [10]But I trust in the Lord that you will not believe those different ideas. Whoever is confusing you with such ideas will be punished. [11]My brothers and sisters, I do not teach that a man must be circumcised. If I teach circumcision, why am I still being attacked? If I still taught circumcision, my preaching about the cross would not be a problem. [12]I wish the people who are bothering you would castrate [n] themselves! [13]My brothers and sisters, God called you to be free, but do not use your freedom as an excuse to do what pleases your sinful self. Serve each other

---

Those people   They are the false teachers who were bothering the believers in Galatia (Galatians 1:7).
Mount Sinai   Mountain in Arabia where God gave his laws to Moses (Exodus 19 and 20).
"Throw . . . all."   Quotation from Genesis 21:10.
castrate   To cut off part of the male sex organ. Paul wanted to show that he was very upset with the false teachers.

with love. [14]The whole law is made complete in this one command: "Love your neighbour as you love yourself." [n] [15]If you go on hurting each other and tearing each other apart, be careful, or you will completely destroy each other.

The Spirit and Human Nature

[16]So I tell you: live by following the Spirit. [d] Then you will not do what your sinful selves want. [17]Our sinful selves want what is against the Spirit, and the Spirit wants what is against our sinful selves. The two are against each other, so you cannot do just what you please. [18]But if the Spirit is leading you, you are not under the law.

[19]The wrong things the sinful self does are

"Love . . . yourself."   Quotation from Leviticus 19:18.

clear: being sexually unfaithful, not being pure, taking part in sexual sins, [20]worshipping gods, doing witchcraft, [d] hating, making trouble, being jealous, being angry, being selfish, making people angry with each other, causing divisions among people, [21]feeling envy, being drunk, having wild and wasteful parties, and doing other things like these. I warn you now as I warned you before: those who do these things will not inherit God's kingdom. [22]But the Spirit produces the fruit of love, joy, peace, patience, kindness, goodness, faithfulness, [23]gentleness, self-control. There is no law that says these things are wrong. [24]Those who belong to Christ Jesus have crucified their own sinful selves. They have given up their old

SERVICE

Free to Serve

The 1970s. Afro hair, flares, the Bee Gees.
    And Watergate.
    The scandal of Watergate led to the first resignation by an American president since the nation was founded. It was a turbulent time, full of suspicion, intrigue, distrust and power-hungry leaders. In the middle of it was Charles W. Colson.
    Chuck Colson was a presidential aide for Richard Nixon. He was one of several White House staff who were put in prison for the Watergate scandal. Colson served seven months.
    Before he was sent to prison, Colson became a Christian. And while in prison, he saw at first hand the tremendous obstacles facing prisoners, ex-prisoners and their families. "Rather than rehabilitating, prisons have become breeding grounds for crime," he says.
    After his release from prison, Colson could have done like many people. He could have forgotten about his prison experience and got on with his life. But he chose not to forget. He founded Prison Fellowship, a Christian outreach to inmates. Today, Colson regularly visits prisons and works for prison reform in countries around the world, including Britain.
    Because of Colson's organisation, nearly 40,000 volunteers work in more than 600 prisons in the USA alone. His dedicated concern has resulted in the changed lives of thousands of inmates and families.
    Chuck Colson turned his freedom into an opportunity to help those in prison. **Galatians 5:13–26** talks about the relationship between freedom and service. Read the passage to discover why God sets people free.

• How does Colson's choice to serve prisoners reflect this passage?
• How have you used your freedom in Christ as an avenue to serve others?

Consider . . .

• using some of your "free time" to serve other people.
• becoming a pen pal with a prison inmate, or contacting Prison Fellowship whose address can be obtained through your church.

For more, see . . .

• Leviticus 19:17–18 (p.119)
• Philippians 2:4–7 (p.1282)
• 1 Corinthians 10:23–24 (p.1228)

selfish feelings and the evil things they wanted to do. ²⁵We get our new life from the Spirit, so we should follow the Spirit. ²⁶We must not be proud or make trouble with each other or be jealous of each other.

Help Each Other

6 Brothers and sisters, if someone in your group does something wrong, you who are spiritual should go to that person and gently help make him right again. But be careful, because you might be tempted to sin too. ²By helping each other with your troubles, you truly obey the law of Christ. ³If anyone thinks he is important when he really is not, he is only fooling himself. ⁴Each person should judge his own actions and not compare himself with others. Then he can be proud for what he himself has done. ⁵Each person must be responsible for himself.

⁶Anyone who is learning the teaching of God should share all the good things he has with his teacher.

Life is like Planting a Field

⁷Do not be fooled: you cannot cheat God. People harvest only what they plant. ⁸If they plant to satisfy their sinful selves, their sinful selves will bring them ruin. But if they plant to please the Spirit, *d* they will receive eternal life from the Spirit. ⁹We must not become tired of doing good. We will receive our harvest of eternal life at the right time if we do not give up. ¹⁰When we have the opportunity to help anyone, we should do it. But we should give special attention to those who are in the family of believers.

Paul Ends His Letter

¹¹See what large letters I use to write this myself. ¹²Some people are trying to force you to be circumcised *d* so the Jews will accept them. They

---

FRIENDS

Bringing Someone Back

Dan and Josh had been best mates since they were little. They'd gone to the same school and were in the same church youth group.

Just lately, Dan had started hanging around with a group of his other friends from school. He'd started going to their parties instead of youth group. Then he started going out with a girl from school and slowly stopped coming to church.

Josh was gutted. He and Dan had been such strong Christians and they did everything together. But now things had changed. Dan didn't seem to want to be around Josh any more. It was as if Dan knew that what he was doing was wrong and didn't want to be around Josh because he felt guilty or ashamed.

Josh had a choice to make. He could either be like some of the others in the youth group who bad-mouthed Dan and said things like, "I always knew he wasn't really a Christian," or he could choose to remain friends with Dan and try to show him the way back to Jesus.

It wasn't always easy, and often Josh felt like giving up, but after years of patiently praying and putting up with him, Dan re-committed his life to God.

Galatians 6:1–10 reminds us that none of us is immune to struggling as a Christian and gives us some great advice on how to deal with our friends who are finding it hard to follow Jesus.

* How do you think Josh would have felt seeing Dan turn his back on God?
* How do you react to Christian friends who are finding it hard to stay on the right track?

Consider . . .

* whether there is one of your friends who has turned away from God. Perhaps you could meet up regularly with other friends to pray for them until they come back to Jesus.
* meeting up with another Christian regularly so that they can challenge you when you go in the wrong direction.

For more, see . . .

* Colossians 2:6–10 (p.1292)
* James 5:19–20 (p.1354)
* Hebrews 10:24–25 (p.1339)

are afraid they will be attacked if they follow only the cross of Christ. [n] [13]Those who are circumcised do not obey the law themselves, but they want you to be circumcised so they can boast

about what they forced you to do. [14]I hope I will never boast about things like that. The cross of our Lord Jesus Christ is my only reason for boasting. Through the cross of Jesus my world was crucified, and I died to the world. [15]It is not important if a man is circumcised or uncircumcised. The important thing is being the new people God has made. [16]Peace and mercy to those who follow this rule—and to all of God's people.

[17]So do not give me any more trouble. I have scars on my body that show [n] I belong to Christ Jesus.

[18]My brothers and sisters, the grace of our Lord Jesus Christ be with your spirit. Amen.

---

cross of Christ   Paul uses the cross as a picture of the gospel, the story of Christ's death and rising from the dead to pay for our sins. The cross, or Christ's death, was God's way to save us.

that show   Many times Paul was beaten and whipped by people who were against him because he was teaching about Christ. The scars were from these beatings.

Ephesians

Why Read This Book:

* Discover the blessings we have because we belong to Christ (Ephesians 1—3).
* Learn how to be united in our relationships with others (Ephesians 4—6:4).
* Gather the armour that you need to follow God (Ephesians 6:10–20).

When?

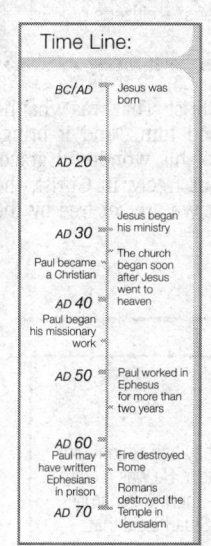

Time Line:

BC/AD	Jesus was born
AD 20	
AD 30	Jesus began his ministry
	The church began soon after Jesus went to heaven
Paul became a Christian	
AD 40	
Paul began his missionary work	
AD 50	Paul worked in Ephesus for more than two years
AD 60	
Paul may have written Ephesians in prison	Fire destroyed Rome
	Romans destroyed the Temple in Jerusalem
AD 70	

Behind the Scenes:

Sometimes it's easy to forget exactly where we fit into God's plan.

* "What is the meaning of my life?"
* "What am I meant to be doing with it?"
* "Where is the world going?"

This letter (addressed to the Ephesian church but passed around several Asian churches) answers such questions. It tells us about the spiritual blessings that Christians have in Jesus, about the fact that we have a brand new life, and how all Christians form one gigantic, powerful, united church.

The letter goes on to give us some guidelines as to how we should live our lives to God's glory. The writer talks about why we should always tell the truth, and he even includes sections about how children and parents, wives and husbands, and slaves and masters should relate to each other.

The final section of Ephesians tells us that we are involved in a very real spiritual battle against the powers of darkness, and describes the armour of God that we can wear at all times.

So there you have it – as Christians, we are brand new people who have been chosen to follow God and stand against evil. Read Ephesians for quick-start instructions on living the life you were made for!

Where?

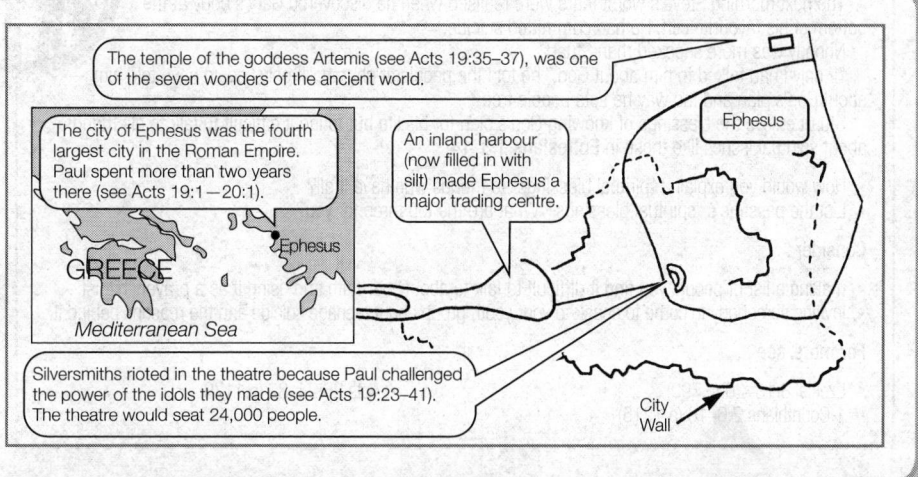

The temple of the goddess Artemis (see Acts 19:35–37), was one of the seven wonders of the ancient world.

The city of Ephesus was the fourth largest city in the Roman Empire. Paul spent more than two years there (see Acts 19:1 — 20:1).

An inland harbour (now filled in with silt) made Ephesus a major trading centre.

GREECE

Ephesus

Mediterranean Sea

Ephesus

Silversmiths rioted in the theatre because Paul challenged the power of the idols they made (see Acts 19:23–41). The theatre would seat 24,000 people.

City Wall

1 From Paul, an apostle *d* of Christ Jesus. I am an apostle because that is what God wanted.
To God's holy people living in Ephesus, believers in Christ Jesus:

²Grace and peace to you from God our Father and the Lord Jesus Christ.

Spiritual Blessings in Christ

³Praise be to the God and Father of our Lord Jesus Christ. In Christ, God has given us every spiritual blessing in the heavenly world. ⁴That is, in Christ, he chose us before the world was made so that we would be his holy people—people without blame before him. ⁵Because of his love, God had already decided to make us his own

children through Jesus Christ. That was what he wanted and what pleased him, ⁶and it brings praise to God because of his wonderful grace. God gave that grace to us freely, in Christ, the One he loves. ⁷In Christ we are set free by the

NON-CHRISTIANS

I May be Gone Some Time

Gary had everything going for him. Money was no problem. His parents had pots of it. They had bought him a car – a convertible with a good turn of speed – as soon as he had passed his driving test. He was a good sportsman and was heavily into outdoor pursuits. Potholing, mountaineering, canoeing – there was hardly a weekend when he didn't have some breathtaking project on. His one Christian friend, Stuart, said that Gary was somebody who was difficult to talk to about needing God because he had got it together so well.

One morning Gary was missing from class. He was due to be playing in a match that afternoon so Stuart tried to ring his home. It was strange that there was no answer to the call. If he was ill why wasn't he answering? However, Gary's whereabouts were soon forgotten in the panic to put the team together.

Late that evening, Steve, Gary's older brother, had gone into his room wondering why Gary had not come in. On his bed was a note which said, "I've gone to our favourite place. I may be gone some time."

The favourite place was a cliff near their home. But it was the last sentence of the note which filled Steve with fear. Both Steve and Gary had often heard the story of Scott's fatal expedition to the South Pole. They both knew that a note which said, "I may be gone some time", had been left by Captain Oates, who had purposely walked out to die in a sub-zero blizzard.

The next morning Steve's worst fears were realised when he discovered Gary's body at the bottom of his favourite cliff. He had committed suicide.

Nobody was more shocked than Stuart.

"If only I had talked to him about God," he told the people at church. "If only I could have told him about God's plan and the way he sets people free."

Stuart enjoys the blessings of knowing God's plan for his life but found it difficult to talk to his friends about spiritual issues like those in **Ephesians 1:3–14**.

* How would you explain "spiritual blessings" to friends who have it all?
* List the passage's "spiritual blessings". What are the top three for you?

Consider . . .

* making a list of people you find it difficult to talk to about your faith and using it as a prayer "hit list".
* inviting somebody to come to speak to your youth group about teenage suicide and the reasons behind it.

For more, see . . .

* Ezekiel 3:16–20 (p.790)
* 1 Corinthians 2:6–16 (p.1215)
* Acts 26:24–32 (p.1179)

blood of his death, and so we have forgiveness of sins. How rich is God's grace, [8]which he has given to us so fully and freely. God, with full wisdom and understanding, [9]let us know his secret purpose. This was what God wanted, and he planned to do it through Christ. [10]His goal was to carry out his plan, when the right time came, that all things in heaven and on earth would be joined together in Christ as the head.

[11]In Christ we were chosen to be God's people, because from the very beginning God had decided this in keeping with his plan. And he is the One who makes everything agree with what he decides and wants. [12]We are the first people who hoped in Christ, and we were chosen so that we would bring praise to God's glory. [13]So it is with you. When you heard the true teaching—the Good News [d] about your salvation—you believed in Christ. And in Christ, God put his special mark of ownership on you by giving you the Holy Spirit [d] that he had promised. [14]That Holy Spirit is the guarantee that we will receive what God promised for his people until God gives full freedom to those who are his—to bring praise to God's glory.

Paul's Prayer

[15]That is why since I heard about your faith in the Lord Jesus and your love for all God's people, [16]I have not stopped giving thanks to God for you. I always remember you in my prayers, [17]asking the God of our Lord Jesus Christ, the glorious Father, to give you a spirit of wisdom and revelation [d] so that you will know him better. [18]I pray also that you will have greater understanding in your heart so you will know the hope to which he has called us and that you will know how rich

GOD'S POWER

Touch From Heaven

Maria stepped onto the stage. She shared how she was born deaf. The preacher asked if he could pray for her. He did, then spoke into one ear, "Do you hear me?"

"Yes!" she replied.

He spoke into the other ear. Again she replied, "Yes!" the excitement in her voice growing.

He returned to the first ear, "Do you hear me now?" he asked in a whisper barely audible to others around. She whispered back, "Yes!"

As the crowd laughed at the amazing events unfolding, Maria couldn't contain her excitement any more. She jumped up and down declaring, "God has healed me; Jesus has healed me!"

This story is an incredible testimony of God's power but it doesn't stop there. Maria actually has a twin sister who was also born deaf. That night the preacher felt God telling him to pray out loud for the sister too, and a day or two later he received a call to say that the sister's ears had also suddenly popped open and she also could hear for the first time!

God is a powerful God. He can bring change in many ways to many people at the same time. He chooses when to visit people, sometimes when we least expect it, and even if our prayers seem to go unanswered, God actually has a way of using our struggles to help others in need.

We are a bit like a vacuum cleaner, if we are not plugged in to the power source we are useless; without God's power we will never see the kind of changes in our lives that we dream of. This power is available to all who ask for it as we read in **Ephesians 1:15–23**.

* How is God's power different from earthly power?
* Are there any areas in your life where you'd like to see more of God's power?

Consider . . .

* making a list of names of people or things in your life you want to see changed by God's power, then commit to praying for them.
* praying for people in other parts of the world who need to depend on God in their struggles.

For more, see . . .

* 1 Chronicles 29:11–12 (p.399)
* 2 Peter 1:3–4 (p.1365)
* Acts 1:7–8 (p.1137)

and glorious are the blessings God has promised his holy people. ¹⁹And you will know that God's power is very great for us who believe. That power is the same as the great strength ²⁰God used to raise Christ from the dead and put him at his right side in the heavenly world. ²¹God has put Christ over all rulers, authorities, powers and kings, not only in this world but also in the next. ²²God put everything under his power and made him the head over everything for the church, ²³which is Christ's body. The church is filled with Christ, and Christ fills everything in every way.

We Now Have Life

2 In the past you were spiritually dead because of your sins and the things you did against God. ²Yes, in the past you lived the way the world lives, following the ruler of the evil powers that are above the earth. That same spirit is now working in those who refuse to obey God. ³In the past all of us lived like them, trying to please our sinful selves and doing all the things our bodies and minds wanted. We should have suffered God's anger because of the way we were. We were the same as all other people.

⁴But God's mercy is great, and he loved us very much. ⁵Though we were spiritually dead because of the things we did against God, he gave us new life with Christ. You have been saved by God's grace. ⁶And he raised us up with Christ and gave us a seat with him in the heavens. He did this for those in Christ Jesus ⁷so that for all future time he could show the very great riches of his grace by being kind to us in Christ Jesus. ⁸I mean that you

PEACE

Enemy in My House

Elaine and her father were best friends. She had always run to him when she was hurt. But as Elaine got older, everything changed. Her father spent more time away from home. And when he was at home, he and Elaine's mother fought all the time.

One day after school, Elaine found her mother lying across her bed, crying. The wardrobe doors were open, and her father's clothes had gone. Elaine's father had been having an affair and had moved out. Elaine couldn't believe it. How could her dad walk out on her like this?

Within three months, Elaine's parents were together, trying to restore their marriage. But Elaine couldn't see herself loving her father again. She avoided him. She even put a "No Men Allowed" sign on her bedroom door.

When Elaine went away to university, she was relieved to get away from the tense relationship with her dad. But during her first year, she heard the gospel and decided to follow Christ.

Her life began to change. She realised that God wanted to rebuild her relationship with her dad. While home one weekend, Elaine cried as she told her dad she forgave him and asked him to forgive her.

From that point on, there was peace in Elaine's home – the kind of peace that made her homesick for time with her father.

God's love brought peace between Elaine and her dad. Read **Ephesians 2:4–22** to see how Christ also broke down the walls and established peace between the Jews and those who were not Jews.

* How was Elaine's broken relationship with her dad like the broken relationship between Jewish and non-Jewish people? How was it different?
* How can Christ break down walls of hatred between you and other people that you know?

Consider . . .

* asking God to reveal any walls in your relationships that need to be broken down.
* making peace with someone from whom you feel separated by giving that person a brick or rock and explaining that you want to break down the "wall" between you.

For more, see . . .

* Psalm 120:6–7 (p.575)
* Hebrews 12:14–15 (p.1344)
* Romans 9 (p.1198)

have been saved by grace through believing. You did not save yourselves: it was a gift from God. [9]It was not the result of your own work, so you cannot boast about it. [10]God has made us what we are. In Christ Jesus, God made us to do good works, which God planned in advance for us to live our lives doing.

One in Christ

[11]You were not born Jewish. You are the people the Jews call "uncircumcised". Those who call you "uncircumcised" call themselves "circumcised". (Their circumcision is only something they themselves do on their bodies.) [12]Remember that in the past you were without Christ. You were not citizens of Israel, and you had no part in the agreements[n] with the promise that God made to his people. You had no hope, and you did not know God. [13]But now in Christ Jesus, you who were far away from God are brought near through the blood of Christ's death. [14]Christ himself is our peace. He made both Jewish people and those who are not Jews one people. They were separated as if there were a wall between them, but Christ broke down that wall of hate by giving his own body. [15]The Jewish law had many commands and rules, but Christ ended that law. His purpose was to make the two groups of people become one new people in him and in this way make peace. [16]It was also Christ's purpose to end the hatred between the two groups, to make them into one body, and to bring them back to God. Christ did all this with his death on the cross. [17]Christ came and preached peace to you who were far away from God, and to those who were near to God. [18]Yes, it is through Christ we all have the right to come to the Father in one Spirit.[d]

[19]Now you who are not Jewish are not foreigners or strangers any longer, but are citizens together with God's holy people. You belong to God's family. [20]You are like a building that was built on the foundation of the apostles[d] and prophets.[d] Christ Jesus himself is the most important stone[n] in that building, [21]and that whole building is joined together in Christ. He makes it grow and become a holy temple in the Lord. [22]And in Christ you, too, are being built together with the Jews into a place where God lives through the Spirit.

Paul's Work in Telling the Good News

3 So I, Paul, am a prisoner of Christ Jesus for you who are not Jews. [2]Surely you have heard that God gave me this work through his grace to help you. [3]He let me know his secret by showing it to me. I have already written a little about this. [4]If you read what I wrote then, you can see that I truly understand the secret about the Christ.[d] [5]People who lived in other times were not told that secret. But now, through the Spirit,[d] God has shown that secret to his holy apostles[d] and prophets.[d] [6]This is that secret: that through the Good News[d] those who are not Jews will share with the Jews in God's blessing. They belong to the same body, and they share together in the promise that God made in Christ Jesus.

[7]By God's special gift of grace given to me through his power, I became a servant to tell that Good News. [8]I am the least important of all God's people, but God gave me this gift—to tell those who are not Jews the Good News about the riches of Christ, which are too great to understand fully. [9]And God gave me the work of telling all people about the plan for his secret, which has been hidden in him since the beginning of time. He is the One who created everything. [10]His purpose was that through the church all the rulers and powers in the heavenly world will now know God's wisdom, which has so many forms. [11]This agrees with the purpose God had since the beginning of time, and he carried out his plan through Christ Jesus our Lord. [12]In Christ we can come before God with freedom and without fear. We can do this through faith in Christ. [13]So I ask you not to become discouraged because of the sufferings I am having for you. My sufferings are for your glory.

The Love of Christ

[14]So I bow in prayer before the Father [15]from whom every family in heaven and on earth gets its true name. [16]I ask the Father in his great glory to give you the power to be strong inwardly through his Spirit.[d] [17]I pray that Christ will live in your hearts by faith and that your lives will be strong in love and be built on love. [18]And I pray that you and all God's holy people will have the power to understand the greatness of Christ's love—how wide and how long and how high

---

Sidelight To describe Jesus as the "most important stone" or cornerstone (Ephesians 2:20) makes him essential for the "building". When workers started building, they would first place one stone – the cornerstone – and then line up all the walls based on this stone to make sure everything was straight.

---

agreements   The agreements that God gave to his people in the Old Testament.
most important stone   Literally, "cornerstone". The first and most important stone in a building.

and how deep that love is. ¹⁹Christ's love is greater than anyone can ever know, but I pray that you will be able to know that love. Then you can be filled with the fullness of God.

²⁰With God's power working in us, God can do much, much more than anything we can ask or imagine. ²¹To him be glory in the church and in Christ Jesus for all time, for ever and ever. Amen.

The Unity of the Body

4 I am in prison because I belong to the Lord. God chose you to be his people, so I tell you now to live the life to which God called you. ²Always be humble, gentle and patient, accepting each other in love. ³You are joined together with peace through the Spirit, *d* so do all you can to continue together in this way. ⁴There is one body and one Spirit, and God called you to have one hope. ⁵There is one Lord, one faith and one baptism. *d* ⁶There is one God and Father of everything. He rules everything and is everywhere and is in everything.

⁷Christ gave each one of us the special gift of grace, showing how generous he is. ⁸That is why it says in the Scriptures, *d*

"When he went up to the heights,
he led a parade of captives,
and he gave gifts to all peoples."   *Psalm 68:18*

GOD'S LOVE

Can You Feel It?

Katie was seventeen years old and thought she was a bad witness for Jesus. It wasn't that she didn't try, it was just that she was never quite sure that she was doing the right thing.

One day she had the opportunity to talk to a TV personality (her father worked for a large TV station and sometimes she was allowed to go and watch a show). This particular day, she found herself drinking coffee in the hospitality suite with her father and the show's host, Peter. He was politely asking her questions and she was so engrossed in her answers that she didn't notice her dad slip away.

Somehow, she'd managed to tell Peter that she was a Christian and how it had totally changed her life. Unknown to her, Peter was very impressed.

Three months later, Katie found herself back in her dad's TV studio watching the rehearsals for a new programme. Her eyebrows lifted in surprise when she saw Peter walk in. He'd been working on another "set" and dropped in unexpectedly. She turned and smiled at him, not in the least expecting him to acknowedge her, but he grinned and walked over.

"Hi Katie!" he said.

"Oh! I didn't think you'd remember me!" she gasped.

Peter laughed and said, "Oh I would always remember you. I meet thousands and thousands of people, but rarely do I meet anyone who has such strong convictions as you." Katie was taken aback as he continued:

"I don't know what it is about you Christians . . . but you always bring a fantastic sense of peace with you. I can honestly say that I don't find it with anyone else." He looked at her earnestly and said, "Do you know, I can almost feel it?"

It reminded Katie that God's love in her life was much stronger than she realised.

Read **Ephesians 3:14–21** to see that God's great love and power is at work in Christians.

* What ways do you show God's love in your life?
* Verse 20 says that God's power works in us. What ways does God work in your life?

Consider . . .

* making a sign about God's love for you. Hang it where you can see it each morning, and remember that God's love for you has no limits.
* thanking God for a way in which he has shown his love for you.

For more, see . . .

* Psalm 36:5–10 (p.521)
* Romans 8:35–39 (p.1197)
* John 13:34–35 (p.1122)

⁹When it says, "He went up," what does it mean? It means that he first came down to the

earth. ¹⁰So Jesus came down, and he is the same One who went up above all the sky. Christ did that to fill everything with his presence. ¹¹And Christ gave gifts to people—he made some to be apostles, ᵈ some to be prophets, ᵈ some to go and tell the Good News, ᵈ and some to have the work of caring for and teaching God's people. ¹²Christ gave those gifts to prepare God's holy people for the work of serving, to make the body of Christ stronger. ¹³This work must continue until we are all joined together in the same faith and in the same knowledge of the Son of God. We must become like a mature person, growing until we become like Christ and have his perfection.

¹⁴Then we will no longer be babies. We will not be tossed about like a ship that the waves carry one way and then another. We will not be influenced by every new teaching we hear from people who are trying to fool us. They make plans and try any kind of trick to fool people into following the wrong path. ¹⁵No! Speaking the truth with love, we will grow up in every way into Christ, who is the head. ¹⁶The whole body depends on Christ, and all the parts of the body are joined and held together. Each part does its own work to make the whole body grow and be strong with love.

The Way You Should Live

¹⁷In the Lord's name, I tell you this. Do not continue living like those who do not believe. Their thoughts are worth nothing. ¹⁸They do not understand, and they know nothing, because they refuse to listen. So they cannot have the life that God gives. ¹⁹They have lost all feeling of

CHURCH

Friends or Foes?

After several months of fighting among Westside Church members, the "get-rid-of-the-minister" side won. The Reverend Howard fought back tears as he announced his resignation on Sunday morning. He moved away within a month.

Many church members on the "keep-the-minister" side were angry and disillusioned; most of them left the Westside Church within six months. Some went to other churches. But some stayed away from the church for years.

Those who stayed at Westside Church chose a new minister – one they were sure they would like much better than the Reverend Howard. But in less than two years, the church members were fighting again.

After watching the church destroy itself for the second time, one of the young people commented, "I don't think you can even call this place a church – anyway, I don't think it's what God meant the church to be."

This teenager's perception fits the description of the church in **Ephesians 4:1–6**. Read this scripture to see what God wants the church to be like.

- If Westside Church members had applied these verses to their situation, how would the outcome have been different?
- How can you use this passage to promote unity within your church?

Consider . . .

- encouraging your youth group to pray weekly for your church to be united.
- talking to your minister about creating an annual "Unity Award" for church members who consistently promote unity in your church.

For more, see . . .

- Psalm 133 (p.579)
- 1 Peter 3:8–12 (p.1360)
- Titus 3:9–11 (p.1324)

shame, and they use their lives for doing evil. They continually want to do all kinds of evil. [20]But what you learned in Christ was not like this. [21]I know that you heard about him, and you are in him, so you were taught the truth that is in Jesus. [22]You were taught to leave your old self— to stop living the evil way you lived before. That old self becomes worse, because people are fooled by the evil things they want to do. [23]But you were taught to be made new in your hearts, [24]to become a new person. That new person is made to be like God—made to be truly good and holy.

[25]So you must stop telling lies. "Tell each other the truth," [n] because we all belong to each other in the same body. [26]When you are angry, do not sin, and be sure to stop being angry before the end of the day. [27]Do not give the devil a way to defeat you. [28]Those who are stealing must stop stealing and start working. They should earn an honest living for themselves. Then they will have something to share with those who are poor.

[29]When you talk, do not say harmful things, but say what people need—words that will help others become stronger. Then what you say will do good to those who listen to you. [30]And do not make the Holy Spirit[d] sad. The Spirit is God's proof that you belong to him. God gave you the Spirit to show that God will make you free when the final day comes. [31]Do not be bitter or angry or cross. Never shout angrily or say things to hurt others. Never do anything evil. [32]Be kind and loving to each other, and forgive each other just as God forgave you in Christ.

Living in the Light

5 You are God's children whom he loves, so try to be like him. [2]Live a life of love just as Christ loved us and gave himself for us as a sweet-smelling offering and sacrifice to God.

"Tell . . . truth," Quotation from Zechariah 8:16.

CULTS

Hazardous to Your Health

Jim Jones was an ordained minister who thought he was the Messiah. Jones demanded total allegiance from his followers, telling them that he was going to create the perfect society – free from hate, crime, and lack of anything.

People sold everything they had and gave it to Jones. Nearly 1,000 people followed Jones to Guyana in South America, where he established a settlement called Jonestown.

In 1978, Leo Ryan, a US representative from California, travelled to Jonestown to investigate rumours that Jones was holding some people against their will. In fear of being caught, Jones had Ryan and three journalists who accompanied Ryan killed. Then, to destroy all evidence of his lies and deceit, Jones ordered his followers to take poison in a religious ceremony. More than 900 people – including Jones himself – died in what is now called the "Jonestown Massacre".

The people in Jonestown didn't recognise Jim Jones's lies. **Ephesians 4:11–16** warns us to be mature so that we can recognise false teachings.

* How were the people in Jim Jones's church like the babies described here?
* Has anyone ever tried to lead you down the wrong path? How did the truth help you to stay on God's path?

Consider . . .

* talking to your minister or other church leader about the elements of truth that your own church emphasises.
* asking your minister or youth leader to lead a study on a new "religious movement" to discover whether or not it is founded on the truth.

For more, see . . .

* Proverbs 4 (p.592)
* Philippians 4:8–9 (p.1286)
* Romans 1:18–32 (p.1185)

³But there must be no sexual sin among you, or any kind of evil or greed. Those things are not right for God's holy people. ⁴Also, there must be no evil talk among you, and you must not speak foolishly or tell evil jokes. These things are not right for you. Instead, you should be giving thanks to God. ⁵You can be sure of this: no one will have a place in the kingdom of Christ and of God who sins sexually, or does evil things, or is greedy. Anyone who is greedy is serving a false god.

⁶Do not let anyone fool you by telling you things that are not true, because these things will bring God's anger on those who do not obey him. ⁷So have nothing to do with them. ⁸In the past you were full of darkness, but now you are full of light in the Lord. So live like children who belong to the light. ⁹Light brings every kind of goodness, right living and truth. ¹⁰Try to learn what pleases the Lord. ¹¹Have nothing to do with the things done in darkness, which are not worth anything. But show that they are wrong. ¹²It is shameful even to talk about what those people do in secret. ¹³But the light makes all things easy to see, ¹⁴and everything that is made easy to see can become light. This is why it is said:

"Wake up, sleeper!
Rise from death,
and Christ will shine on you."

¹⁵So be very careful how you live. Do not live like those who are not wise, but live wisely. ¹⁶Use every chance you have for doing good, because these are evil times. ¹⁷So do not be foolish but learn what the Lord wants you to do. ¹⁸Do not be drunk with wine, which will ruin you, but be filled with the Spirit. ᵈ ¹⁹Speak to each other with psalms, hymns and spiritual songs, singing and making music in your hearts to the Lord. ²⁰Always give thanks to God the Father for everything, in the name of our Lord Jesus Christ.

Wives and Husbands

²¹Yield to obey each other because you respect Christ.

²²Wives, yield to your husbands, as you do to the Lord, ²³because the husband is the head of the wife, as Christ is the head of the church. And he is the Saviour ᵈ of the body, which is the church.

ANGER

Handle With Care

Clare wasn't having a good day. Her boyfriend broke up with her before her first lesson. She got her maths exam back and knew that her parents would not be pleased with her marks. She missed lunch. And then she mouthed off at her PE teacher.

She shook her head as she recalled the incident.

"Come on, Clare," Mrs Eaton had yelled. "You can't do press-ups with your bottom in the air. Try 50 more, and do them properly this time!"

"I'd like to see you do 50 press-ups, you fat slob," Clare mumbled – a little louder than she intended. Now she was sitting in the detention room while everyone else in the school was on their way home.

"If only I'd kept my mouth shut," Clare moaned.

Sometimes our anger can get us into trouble. Read the warning about anger in **Ephesians 4:25 – 5:2.**

* According to this passage, did Clare's anger lead to sin or not?
* How can you be angry, and yet not sin?

Consider . . .

* listing three things that make you angry. Beside each one, write a brief description of how you can handle the situation without sinning.
* resolving to deal quickly with things that make you angry.

For more, see . . .

* Psalm 4 (p.501)
* James 1:19–20 (p.1348)
* Proverbs 22:24–25 (p.609)

24As the church yields to Christ, so you wives should yield to your husbands in everything.

25Husbands, love your wives as Christ loved the church and gave himself for it 26to make it belong to God. Christ used the word to make the church clean by washing it with water. 27He died so that he could give the church to himself like a bride in all her beauty. He died so that the church could be pure and without fault, with no evil or sin or any other wrong thing in it. 28In the same way, husbands should love their wives as they love their own bodies. The man who loves his wife loves himself. 29No one ever hates his own body, but feeds and takes care of it. And that is what Christ does for the church, 30because we are parts of his body. 31The Scripture says, "So a man will leave his father and mother and be united with his wife, and the two will become one body." n 32That secret is very important—I am talking about Christ and the church. 33But each one of you must love his wife as he loves himself, and a wife must respect her husband.

Children and Parents

6 Children, obey your parents as the Lord wants, because this is the right thing to do. 2The command says, "Honour your father and mother." n This is the first command that has a promise with it— 3"Then everything will be well with you, and you will have a long life on the earth." n

4Fathers, do not make your children angry, but raise them with the training and teaching of the Lord.

Slaves and Masters

5Slaves, obey your masters here on earth with fear and respect and from a sincere heart, just as you obey Christ. 6You must do this not only while they are watching you, to please them. With all your heart you must do what God wants as people who are obeying Christ. 7Do your work with enthusiasm. Work as if you were serving the Lord, not as if you were serving only men and women. 8Remember that the Lord will give a reward to everyone, slave or free, for doing good.

"So . . . body."   Quotation from Genesis 2:24.
"Honour . . . mother."   Quotation from Exodus 20:12; Deuteronomy 5:16.
"Then . . . earth."   Quotation from Exodus 20:12; Deuteronomy 5:16.

DECISION MAKING

Who's Going to Know?

Rob was having the time of his life on tour in Germany with his community orchestra – and no parents! There were adults, of course, but Rob was making his own decisions and loving every minute of it.

On Saturday night, Rob's friends went out to get their first taste of Germany. Most band members wanted to take advantage of Germany's sex shows.

Rob wasn't sure. He didn't feel quite right about going but it seemed to be something everybody did when they were away from home.

He thought, "Anyway. Who's going to know?"

"I'd know," Rob finally told himself, after remembering the advice in **Ephesians 5:6–20**. See how this passage can help you to make difficult decisions.

* What principles do you find in this passage that Rob may have used in making his decision?
* How can you use the passage's advice in a decision that you face now?

Consider . . .

* praying and writing about what God wants you to do with your life.
* writing a letter to a friend who's facing a difficult decision. Include the passage's advice on decision making.

For more, see . . .

* 1 Kings 18:1–40 (p.332)
* James 1:5–8 (p.1348)
* Romans 12:1–2 (p.1203)

⁹Masters, in the same way, be good to your slaves. Do not threaten them. Remember that the One who is your Master and their Master is in heaven, and he treats everyone alike.

Wear the Full Armour of God

¹⁰Finally, be strong in the Lord and in his great power. ¹¹Put on the full armour of God so that you can fight against the devil's evil tricks. ¹²Our fight is not against people on earth but against the rulers and authorities and the powers of this world's darkness, against the spiritual powers of evil in the heavenly world. ¹³That is why you need to put on God's full armour. Then on the day of evil you will be able to stand strong. And when you have finished the whole fight, you will still be standing. ¹⁴So stand strong, with the belt of truth tied around your waist and the protection of right living on your chest. ¹⁵On your feet wear the Good News *d* of peace to help you stand strong. ¹⁶And also use the shield of faith with which you can stop all the burning arrows of the

Evil One. ¹⁷Accept God's salvation as your helmet, and take the sword of the Spirit, *d* which is the word of God. ¹⁸Pray in the Spirit at all times with all kinds of prayers, asking for everything you need. To do this you must always be ready and never give up. Always pray for all God's people.

¹⁹Also pray for me that when I speak, God will give me words so that I can tell the secret

> ### Sidelight
> The "shield of faith" in Ephesians 6:16 is a comparison to the large Roman shield used by heavily armed soldiers. This shield was designed to protect against burning darts, one of the most dangerous weapons of the time. When the dart hit the shield, it sank into wood, and the flame was extinguished.

of the Good News without fear. ²⁰I have been sent to preach this Good News, and I am doing

WORSHIP

Guitar Man

Matthew bought his first guitar at a junk sale. Once he could play three chords without looking at his hands, he sometimes played with a rock band – the others in the band were just a little better than him. They really enjoyed themselves, practising, writing songs and playing at parties and school events. They may not have been good – but they were loud and their audiences loved them. Matthew took lessons from a professional rock guitarist and over the next year his skills improved immensely. He practised hard, playing and singing along to CDs in his room.

When he went to university, with all his books and clothes, Matthew took an amplifier and brand new solid guitar. He was hoping to find a place in a college rock band.

But Matthew got deeply involved in the growing Christian Union and soon found himself playing in worship meetings and outreach events – needing to practise every week and learn a lot of new material.

He still enjoys playing rock music and jamming with friends whenever he gets a chance. But now his priority is making music to the Lord and he realises that to lead others into the freedom of real worship requires more than skill on the guitar. Read about it in **Ephesians 5:15–20**.

* What is the difference between playing music and "making music in your hearts to the Lord"?
* Look at the things mentioned in the passage. How might they affect the way you do music?

Consider . . .

* making a list of songs which are important to you and asking your worship leader if they can be included on the church programme.
* starting to collect Christian contemporary or praise music and using it to help you praise God.

For more, see . . .

* 1 Chronicles 25:1–8 (p.393)
* Colossians 3:15–17 (p.1293)
* Psalm 33 (p.519)

that now, here in prison. Pray that when I preach the Good News I will speak without fear, as I should.

Final Greetings

[21]I am sending to you Tychicus, our brother whom we love and a faithful servant of the Lord's work. He will tell you everything that is happening with me. Then you will know how I am and what I am doing. [22]I am sending him to you for this reason—so that you will know how we are, and he can encourage you.

[23]Peace and love with faith to you from God the Father and the Lord Jesus Christ. [24]Grace to all of you who love our Lord Jesus Christ with love that never ends.

HOLY SPIRIT

A New Super-Power

Should I do what my friends want me to? Why should I bother with God? Why care what my family says?

Every day we make decisions – dozens of them – and try to work things out for the best, even though it's a struggle. But there's another even bigger struggle going on: we're caught up in a spiritual war with all the forces of evil in the world. This is terrifying when we realise what it involves – evil spiritual powers trying to influence us to do what we often know is wrong. They help us convince ourselves that we should do something even though it's going to be a bad move. But how can we stop ourselves?

If we believe in Jesus, God gives us the most amazing power that we could have – a power much stronger than the spiritual forces which talk us into doing evil. This power from God is called the "Holy Spirit". Unfortunately, we often think that the Holy Spirit is a bit of a weird, ghostly thing, but that's all wrong. The Holy Spirit is a person: he is God, alongside God the Father and God the Son, Jesus. Although this is a really deep mystery that it's hard to get our heads round, it's true. He's a person who we can know and have a relationship with. When we do things that he doesn't like, the Bible says we upset him. But when we put our trust in God, he leads us and shows us the way we should live.

Often our lives are full of doubts and confused ideas – but if we pray to God, the Holy Spirit will show us what to do. **Ephesians 6:10–20** teaches about the spiritual armour God has given us to help us.

* What wrong ideas might we have about the Holy Spirit?
* What does this passage tell us the Holy Spirit does?

Consider . . .

* how there's much more to life than what we see. Ask God that you would be able to "pray in the Spirit" and know him leading you.
* as you read your Bible, being aware of how the Holy Spirit is speaking to you through it. Share what you feel with someone who has been a Christian for a while.

For more, see . . .

* John 14:26 (p.1124)
* Romans 8:26 (p.1196)
* Acts 2:38 (p.1140)
* Galatians 5:16–26 (p.1264)

Philippians

Why Read This Book:

- Discover how serving other people serves Christ (Philippians 1—2).
- Learn why growing in faith is so important (Philippians 3).
- Learn Paul's secret of having joy amidst suffering (Philippians 4).

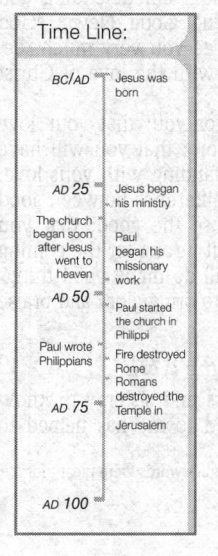

Time Line:

BC/AD	Jesus was born
AD 25	Jesus began his ministry
The church began soon after Jesus went to heaven	Paul began his missionary work
AD 50	Paul started the church in Philippi
Paul wrote Philippians	Fire destroyed Rome
	Romans destroyed the Temple in Jerusalem
AD 75	
AD 100	

Behind the Scenes:

Paul spent his life telling the Good News of Jesus Christ and starting new churches. But what did he get for it? He was put on trial, run out of town, stoned, beaten with rods and thrown in prison several times. In addition, other Christians misunderstood and opposed him.

In short, Paul had plenty of reasons to be gloomy and depressed. But, as we learn in Philippians, Paul felt just the opposite. In fact, this short letter from Paul is probably the most upbeat, cheerful book in the Bible.

Part of the reason he was happy was that the Christians in Philippi had heard about his imprisonment and had taken up a collection for him. Their love and concern made Paul deeply grateful, and Paul thanks them in this letter.

But the most important reason for Paul's happiness is clear in the letter. "To me the only important thing about living is Christ," he writes, "and dying would be profit for me" (Philippians 1:21).

The Romans could chain Paul's body, but they couldn't chain Paul's heart. And in this letter to his friends at Philippi, the apostle shares his secret for facing difficult circumstances with a song on his lips and joy in his heart.

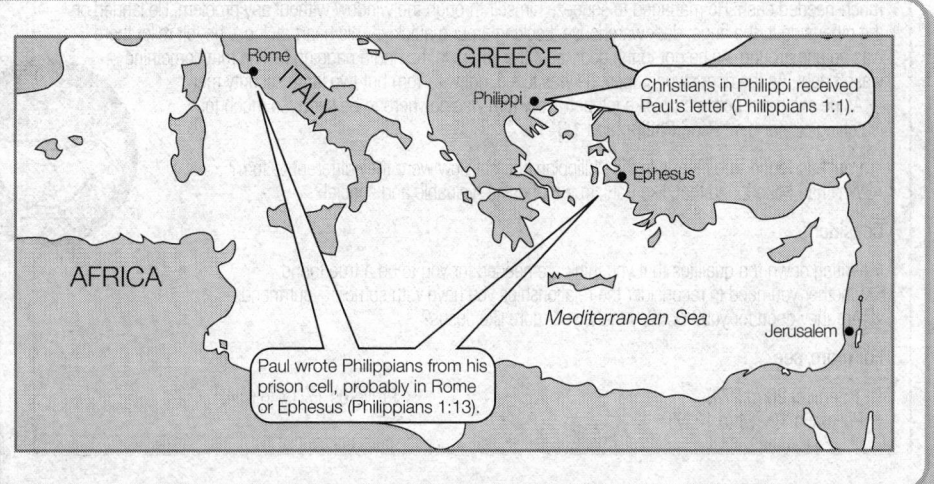

Christians in Philippi received Paul's letter (Philippians 1:1).

Paul wrote Philippians from his prison cell, probably in Rome or Ephesus (Philippians 1:13).

1 From Paul and Timothy, servants of Christ Jesus.

To all of God's holy people in Christ Jesus who live in Philippi, including your elders *d* and deacons: *d*

2Grace and peace to you from God our Father and the Lord Jesus Christ.

> ### Sidelight
> A woman, Lydia, was the first person baptised in Europe. She was probably a leader in the early Philippian church (see Acts 16:11–15, p.1164), but she may not have stayed there long, since she made a living as a travelling merchant who sold purple-dyed cloth.

Paul's Prayer

3I thank my God every time I remember you, 4always praying with joy for all of you. 5I thank God for the help you gave me while I preached the Good News *d*—help you gave from the first day you believed until now. 6God began doing a good work in you, and I am sure he will continue it until it is finished when Jesus Christ comes again.

7And I know that I am right to think like this about all of you, because I have you in my heart. All of you share in God's grace with me while I am in prison and while I am defending and proving the truth of the Good News. 8God knows that I want to see you very much, because I love all of you with the love of Christ Jesus.

9This is my prayer for you: that your love will grow more and more; that you will have knowledge and understanding with your love; 10that you will see the difference between good and bad and will choose the good; that you will be pure and without wrong for the coming of Christ; 11that you will do many good things with the help of Christ to bring glory and praise to God.

Paul's Troubles Help the Work

12I want you brothers and sisters *n* to know that what has happened to me has helped to

brothers and sisters Although the Greek text says "brothers" here and throughout this book, Paul's words were meant for the entire church, both men and women.

FRIENDS

Pick Your Friends Carefully

Mike was smaller than other kids in his class. This made him a bit insecure and he found himself getting into fights. That's when he got friendly with Tom. Tom was someone who everyone feared and it made Mike feel good inside when Tom had asked him to join his gang.

The night was perfect, no one was about and Mike felt a kind of buzz that he would be getting hold of some much-needed cash. He managed to squeeze himself through the window without any problem. He landed on the other side in the huge, dark warehouse. Looking around quickly – his heart racing – he felt relief there was no one around. As he got to the door to let the others in, he had a nagging feeling that something wasn't right. As the door swung open, he was faced, not with Tom but two large security men.

As he sat in the police car, Mike felt betrayed. Tom was nowhere to be seen. So much for watching out for him! Read **Philippians 1:3–11**.

* Paul had found true friends in the Philippian church. How were they different to Tom?
* Why had Mike found that, like Paul, true friends are valuable and special?

Consider . . .

* writing down ten qualities that you think are needed for you to be a true friend.
* whether you need to reconsider the relationships you have with some of your friends. Are they good for you? Do they make you more like Jesus?

For more, see . . .

* 1 Samuel 20 (p.274)
* Philemon 10–14 (p.1327)

* Proverbs 17:17 (p.604)

spread the Good News. *d* [13]All the palace guards and everyone else knows that I am in prison because I am a believer in Christ. [14]Because I am in prison, most of the believers have become more bold in Christ and are not afraid to speak the word of God.

[15]It is true that some preach about Christ because they are jealous and ambitious, but others preach about Christ because they want to help. [16]They preach because they have love, and they know that God gave me the work of defending the Good News. [17]But the others preach about Christ for selfish and wrong reasons, wanting to make trouble for me in prison.

[18]But it doesn't matter. The important thing is that in every way, whether for right or wrong reasons, they are preaching about Christ. So I am happy, and I will continue to be happy. [19]Because you are praying for me and the Spirit of Jesus Christ is helping me, I know this trouble will bring my freedom. [20]I expect and hope that I will not fail Christ in anything but that I will have the courage now, as

DEATH

After AIDS

For Daniel, a childhood filled with rejection became a life of rejection. His parents' failed marriage contributed to his own broken marriages.

A need to escape problems led to drug and alcohol addictions. A desire for some kind of acceptance led to homosexuality. And homosexuality led to AIDS.

Abandoned by family and friends, Daniel faced death alone. He was ready to end his life when Jean, a Christian friend, invited Daniel into her home. Through Jean's caring, Daniel eventually decided to follow Christ.

What changes occurred in the heart of this beaten, lonely man! He experienced the release of forgiveness from his past. For the first time in his life, he felt genuine acceptance and unconditional love. And he had a place to belong, with people who cared for him.

As his body weakened, Daniel's spirit grew stronger and stronger. He was revitalised by his new-found hope in Christ.

Daniel directed his energy to reaching out with the love of Jesus to those who needed it most. He visited AIDS patients at a local hospital and shared his story with many dying people who had also been rejected. He spoke at churches and support groups, and he explained how God's love reaches even those whom some find unlovable. He spent his time eagerly giving and receiving love.

"I don't know how long I'm going to live, but I want to live the rest of my days for the Lord," Daniel told his friends.

After several months, Daniel died. Those who were touched by Daniel's life felt a tremendous loss. But at the same time, they rejoiced because they knew Daniel was at peace and happy to be with Jesus.

Paul faced death peacefully under different circumstances. Read **Philippians 1:21–27** to see Paul's attitude towards living and dying.

- How were Daniel's and Paul's attitudes about life affected by what they thought about death?
- According to this passage, what is the purpose of life and death?

Consider . . .

- thinking of the top reason you have to live, then putting more energy into that activity.
- discussing your feelings about death with a Christian friend. Think about the way your priorities look from a heavenly perspective.

For more, see . . .

- Psalm 42 (p.525)
- Galatians 2:20–21 (p.1259)
- Romans 14:7–8 (p.1207)

always, to show the greatness of Christ in my life here on earth, whether I live or die. ²¹To me the only important thing about living is Christ, and dying would be profit for me. ²²If I continue living in my body, I will be able to work for the Lord. I do not know what to choose—living or dying. ²³It is hard to choose between the two. I want to leave this life and be with Christ, which is much better, ²⁴but you need me here in my body. ²⁵Since I am sure of this, I know I will stay with you to help you grow and have joy in your faith. ²⁶You will be very happy in Christ Jesus when I am with you again.

²⁷Only one thing concerns me: be sure that you live in a way that brings honour to the Good News of Christ. Then whether I come and visit you or am away from you, I will hear that you are standing strong with one purpose, that you work together as one for the faith of the Good News, ²⁸and that you are not afraid of those who are against you. All of this is proof that your enemies will be destroyed but that you will be saved by God. ²⁹God gave you the honour not only of believing in Christ but also of suffering for him, both

of which bring glory to Christ. ³⁰When I was with you, you saw the struggles I had, and you hear about the struggles I am having now. You yourselves are having the same kind of struggles.

2 Does your life in Christ give you strength? Does his love comfort you? Do we share together in the Spirit? Do you have mercy and kindness? ²If so, make me very happy by having the same thoughts, sharing the same love, and having one mind and purpose. ³When you do things, do not let selfishness or pride be your guide. Instead, be humble and give more honour to others than to yourselves. ⁴Do not be interested only in your own life, but be interested in the lives of others.

Be Unselfish like Christ

⁵In your lives you must think and act like Christ Jesus.
⁶Christ himself was like God in everything.
> But he did not think that being equal with God was something to be used for his own benefit.

⁷But he gave up his place with God and made himself nothing.

CHURCH

Sticking Together

When a flock of geese fly south for the winter, they fly in a V-shaped formation. If they didn't, they would never reach their destination.

Researchers have found that the V-shaped formation helps geese to fly at least 71 per cent further than they could fly alone, because each bird creates an updraught for the one behind it, making flying easier.

If one goose falls out of formation, the wind resistance slows the bird down. If it doesn't act quickly, it will not be able to keep up with its flock. So, it quickly gets back into formation.

Like geese, Christians need to work together in the church. Read **Philippians 2:1–11** to learn how.

* How is the geese's V-shaped formation like the passage's description of Christians working together?
* How does being with other Christians encourage you in your faith?

Consider . . .

* writing your name and the names of other people in a V-shaped pattern to symbolise how you support each other. Thank God for people in the church who lead and support you.
* talking to your youth leader or a Sunday school teacher about how you can create an "updraught" to support and encourage others in your church.

For more, see . . .

* Psalm 133:1–3 (p.579)
* Acts 2:44–47 (p.1141)
* Mark 9:33–37 (p.1015)

He was born to be a man
and became like a servant.
[8]And when he was living as a man,
he humbled himself and was fully obedient
to God,
even when that caused his death—death
on a cross.
[9]So God raised him to the highest place.
God made his name greater than every
other name
[10]so that every knee will bow to the name of
Jesus—
everyone in heaven, on earth and under
the earth.
[11]And everyone will confess that Jesus Christ is
Lord
and bring glory to God the Father.

Be the People God Wants You to Be

[12]My dear friends, you have always obeyed
God when I was with you. It is even more important that you obey now while I am away from
you. Keep on working to complete your salvation
with fear and trembling, [13]because God is working in you to help you want to do and be able to
do what pleases him.

[14]Do everything without complaining or arguing. [15]Then you will be innocent and without any
wrong. You will be God's children without fault.
But you are living with crooked and evil people
all around you, among whom you shine like stars
in the dark world. [16]You offer the teaching that
gives life. So when Christ comes again, I can be
happy because my work was not wasted. I ran
the race and won.

[17]Your faith makes you offer your lives as a
sacrifice in serving God. If I have to offer my own
blood with your sacrifice, I will be happy and full
of joy with all of you. [18]You also should be happy
and full of joy with me.

Timothy and Epaphroditus

[19]I hope in the Lord Jesus to send Timothy to
you soon. I will be happy to learn how you are.
[20]I have no one else like Timothy, who truly cares
for you. [21]Other people are interested only in
their own lives, not in the work of Jesus Christ.
[22]You know the kind of person Timothy is. You
know he has served with me in telling the Good
News,[d] as a son serves his father. [23]I plan to send
him to you quickly when I know what will happen to me. [24]I am sure that the Lord will help me
to come to you soon.

[25]Epaphroditus, my brother in Christ, works
and serves with me in the army of Christ. When

I needed help, you sent him to me. I think now
that I must send him back to you, [26]because he
wants very much to see all of you. He is worried
because you heard that he was sick. [27]Yes, he was
sick, and nearly died, but God had mercy on him
and me too so that I would not have more
sadness. [28]I want very much to send him to you
so that when you see him you can be happy, and

> **Sidelight** If the sickness that
> Epaphroditus suffered
> from had been a fever (see Philippians 2:26–27),
> the common treatment in New Testament times
> would have been to hang a bag around his
> neck. The bag would have contained, among
> other items, seven hairs from seven old dogs!

I can stop worrying about you. [29]Welcome him
in the Lord with much joy. Give honour to people like him, [30]because he almost died for the
work of Christ. He risked his life to give me the
help you could not give in your service to me.

The Importance of Christ

3 My brothers and sisters, be full of joy in the
Lord. It is no trouble for me to write the
same things to you again, and it will help you to
be more ready. [2]Watch out for those who do
evil, who are like dogs, who insist on cutting[n]
the body. [3]We are the ones who are truly
circumcised.[d] We worship God through his
Spirit,[d] and our pride is in Christ Jesus. We do
not put trust in ourselves or anything we can
do, [4]although I might be able to put trust in myself. If anyone thinks he has a reason to trust in
himself, he should know that I have greater reason for trusting in myself. [5]I was circumcised
eight days after my birth. I am from the people
of Israel and the tribe[d] of Benjamin. I am a
Hebrew,[n] and my parents were Hebrews. I
had a strict view of the law, which is why I became a Pharisee. [d] [6]I was so enthusiastic I tried
to hurt the church. No one could find fault
with the way I obeyed the law of Moses.
[7]Those things were important to me, but now I
think they are worth nothing because of Christ.
[8]Not only those things, but I think that all
things are worth nothing compared with the
greatness of knowing Christ Jesus my Lord.
Because of him, I have lost all those things, and
now I know they are worthless rubbish. This allows me to have Christ [9]and to belong to him.

---

cutting The word in Greek is like the word "circumcise", but it means "to cut completely off".
Hebrew A name for the Jews that some Jews were very proud of.

Now I am right with God, not because I followed the law, but because I believed in Christ. God uses my faith to make me right with him. [10]I want to know Christ and the power that raised him from the dead. I want to share in his sufferings and become like him in his death. [11]Then I have hope that I myself will be raised from the dead.

Continuing Towards Our Goal

[12]I do not mean that I am already as God wants me to be. I have not yet reached that goal, but I continue trying to reach it and to make it mine. Christ wants me to do that, which is the reason he made me his. [13]Brothers and sisters, I know that I have not yet reached that goal, but there is one thing I always do. Forgetting the past and straining towards what is ahead, [14]I keep trying to reach the goal and

get the prize for which God called me through Christ to the life above.

[15]All of us who are spiritually mature should think this way too. And if there are things you do not agree with, God will make them clear to you. [16]But we should continue following the truth we already have.

[17]Brothers and sisters, all of you should try to follow my example and to copy those who live the way we showed you. [18]Many people live like enemies of the cross of Christ. I have often told you about them, and it makes me cry to tell you about them now. [19]In the end, they will be destroyed. They do whatever their bodies want, they are proud of their shameful acts, and they think only about earthly things. [20]But our homeland is in heaven, and we are waiting for our Saviour, *d* the Lord Jesus Christ, to come from heaven. [21]By his power

POPULARITY

The Right Thing

Michelle had two passions in life: singing and people! As a youth worker, she'd spent the last year working really hard to start a youth club that was now flourishing. She loved the fact that she was able to build up great friendships with those who came.

In her spare time she practised her other passion, singing, in a band. When her band started to get gigs all over the country, she loved it.

Over the next few years, she got to experience many different countries and cultures with the band, and they built up a large fan base. They'd get letters from people all over the world saying how cool their songs were and how they couldn't wait to see the band in concert.

With all the touring that was going on Michelle was spending more and more time away from home, her family and the youth club that she led. Deep down she knew that she wasn't giving as much time and attention to those things as she felt she should be. How could she lead a youth club without being there? The dilemma played on her mind for months before she finally made a decision. In the end, she felt that the calling on her life for the youth project was so strong that she needed to give up the band and concentrate more on those relationships that God had blessed her with back home.

Michelle considered doing what God wanted of her to be more important than the enticing fame and fortune that came with being in a successful band. In **Philippians 3:8–11** Paul is describing a similar situation.

* What was it that Paul gave up in order to focus his attention fully on God?
* Why do you think Paul is so passionate about being right with God?

Consider . . .

* what you would be prepared to give up if God asked you to. Is there anything you wouldn't give up?
* writing a list of priorities in your life and chatting to a friend about them.

For more, see . . .

* Genesis 22:6–13 (p.25)
* Philippians 2:3–11 (p.1282)

to rule all things, he will change our simple bodies and make them like his own glorious body.

What the Christians are to Do

4 My dear brothers and sisters, I love you and want to see you. You bring me joy and make me proud of you, so stand strong in the Lord as I have told you.

2I ask Euodia and Syntyche to agree in the Lord. 3And I ask you, my faithful friend, to help these women. They served with me in telling the Good News, *d* together with Clement and others who worked with me, whose names are written in the book of life. *n*

4Be full of joy in the Lord always. I will say again, be full of joy.

5Let everyone see that you are gentle and kind. The Lord is coming soon. 6Do not worry about anything, but pray and ask God for everything

book of life　God's book that has the names of all God's chosen people (Revelation 3:5; 21:27).

PERSISTENCE

Sticking With It

Wilma Rudolph dreamed of competing in the Olympics. But she had everything stacked against her.

She was born prematurely in a Tennessee shack, weighing only 2 kilogrammes. Scarlet fever and polio struck, forcing her to wear a steel brace on her leg.

Wilma remembers: "My father was the one who sort of babied me and was sympathetic . . . my mother was the one who made me work, made me believe that one day it would be possible for me to walk without braces." Wilma's mother told her that, with persistence, she could follow her dreams in life.

So at the age of nine, Wilma did away with the braces. Four years later she developed a rhythmic stride and entered her first race. She came in last. But she didn't give up.

"I worked very hard for the next four years," Wilma recalls. "I was self-motivated and motivated by my family. It took sheer determination to be able to run 100 metres and remember all of the mechanics that go along with it. It takes steady nerves and being a fighter to stay out there."

In the 1960 Olympics, Wilma Rudolph set the world record in the 100-metre dash. She also won the 200-metre sprint and ran the anchor leg for the US 400-metre relay team. She was the first American woman to win three gold medals in track and field at a single Olympiad.

Wilma Rudolph learned the lesson of **Philippians 3:12–21**. Read the passage to discover the key to persistence.

* In the light of the passage, why was Wilma persistent?
* What was Paul's spiritual goal, according to this passage? How can this passage help you to persist in reaching such a goal?

Consider . . .

* watching part of a sports event on television. Look for evidences of persistence, then apply what you learn to a challenge you face.
* setting a specific goal to help you to grow in your faith and persisting to meet that goal this week.

For more, see . . .

* Psalm 37:23–24 (p.522)
* 1 Timothy 6:11–16 (p.1313)
* Luke 9:57–62 (p.1055)

you need, always giving thanks. ⁷And God's peace, which is so great we cannot understand it, will keep your hearts and minds in Christ Jesus.

⁸Brothers and sisters, think about the things that are good and worthy of praise. Think about the things that are true and honourable and right and pure and beautiful and respected. ⁹Do what you learned and received from me, what I told you, and what you saw me do. And the God who gives peace will be with you.

Paul Thanks the Christians

¹⁰I am very happy in the Lord that you have shown your care for me again. You continued to care about me, but there was no way for you to show it. ¹¹I am not telling you this because I need anything. I have learned to be satisfied with the things I have and with everything that happens. ¹²I know how to live when I am poor, and I know how to live when I have plenty. I have learned the secret of being happy at any time in everything that happens, when I have enough to eat and when I go hungry, when I have more than I need and when I do not have enough. ¹³I can do all things through Christ, because he gives me strength.

¹⁴But it was good that you helped me when I needed it. ¹⁵You Philippians remember when I first preached the Good News ᵈ there. When I left

PEACE

Beyond Understanding

The ringing telephone pierced the night. "Hello, Mrs Gibson? This is the police."

Naomi's throat tightened, but she managed to gulp, "Yes, what is it?"

"It's your daughter, Caroline. There's been an accident." Shocked, Naomi sobbed uncontrollably and dropped the phone. Her husband, Neil, grabbed it and learned that Caroline was still alive, but that she had extensive head injuries and was unconscious. A police helicopter was flying her to hospital.

When Neil and Naomi arrived at the hospital, Caroline was in a coma. Her head was bruised and swollen. Her back was broken, and her body lay lifeless. Her heart had stopped once in the helicopter, but the paramedics had restarted it. Surgeons were inserting a catheter into Caroline's skull to relieve the pressure on her brain.

During the operation, Naomi prayed in the hospital chapel. As she read her Bible, an overwhelming peace filled her. She couldn't explain what she felt, especially with her daughter so close to death. All she knew was that God seemed near and that he would take care of Caroline.

For days, Neil and Naomi rarely left Caroline's side. Naomi's prayers surprised even her, because they were filled with thanksgiving rather than questioning or pleading. Her heart was filled with God's peace.

It took a long time for Caroline to recover, and much of what happened in the weeks after the accident is now a blur to her. But every hour is vivid to Neil and Naomi. They were joyful that their daughter was alive.

In **Philippians 4:1–9**, Paul describes the secret of having a joy that is greater than life's difficulties. Read it to understand Naomi's experience.

* Which actions or attitudes from this passage did Naomi have that resulted in peace?
* Which ones can most help you to experience God's peace?

Consider . . .

* listing the nine steps to peace – one step from each verse in this passage. Choose one step which you can take to experience God's peace.
* planning with a friend to pray together during difficult times.

For more, see . . .

* Psalm 25 (p.514)
* John 14:27–29 (p.1124)
* Luke 6:17–23 (p.1048)

Macedonia, you were the only church that gave me help. ¹⁶Several times you sent me things I needed when I was in Thessalonica. ¹⁷Really, it is not that I want to receive gifts from you, but I want you to have the good that comes from giving. ¹⁸And now I have everything, and more.

Sidelight The words "joy" and "rejoice" occur in some form sixteen times in Philippians (for example, Philippians 4:4). Even in prison, Paul's thoughts were focused on joy!

I have all I need, because Epaphroditus brought your gift to me. It is like a sweet-smelling sacrifice offered to God, who accepts that sacrifice and is pleased with it. ¹⁹My God will use his wonderful riches in Christ Jesus to give you everything you need. ²⁰Glory to our God and Father for ever and ever! Amen.

²¹Greet each of God's people in Christ. Those who are with me send greetings to you. ²²All of God's people greet you, particularly those from the palace of Caesar. *d*

²³The grace of the Lord Jesus Christ be with you all.

Colossians

Why Read This Book:
- Learn the importance of following only Jesus Christ (Colossians 1).
- Discover how to respond to false teachers (Colossians 2).
- Find guidelines for living a Christian life (Colossians 3—4).

When?

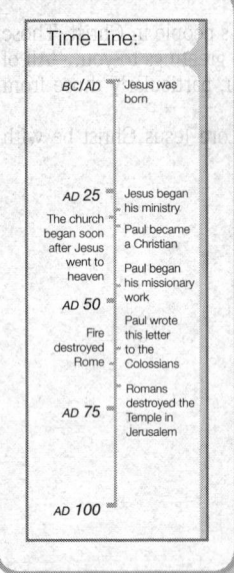

Time Line:

BC/AD	Jesus was born
AD 25	Jesus began his ministry
The church began soon after Jesus went to heaven	Paul became a Christian
	Paul began his missionary work
AD 50	Paul wrote this letter to the Colossians
Fire destroyed Rome	
AD 75	Romans destroyed the Temple in Jerusalem
AD 100	

Behind the Scenes:

Astrology. Witchcraft. Ghosts. UFOs. Tarot cards. Ouija boards. The Loch Ness monster. Mysterious things can intrigue and attract us.

We are not the only people who can be fascinated with these kinds of things. Early Christians in Colosse were attracted to the same kinds of mysterious or supernatural things. Someone apparently came into the church and began teaching people to worship angels and cosmic powers. Jesus is fine, they argued, but these other mysterious powers controlled human destiny and gave secret knowledge (Colossians 2:16–23).

This letter to the Colossians challenges these false teachers. But instead of picking apart their arguments, the letter goes on the offensive, telling the Colossians the truth about Jesus Christ. "He ranks higher than everything that has been made," the letter states. "Christ is all that is important" (Colossians 1:15; 3:11).

The letter's advice to the Colossians is good advice for today, too. When we feel tempted to look for power in other, mysterious things, this book reminds us of the source of true power. And when someone suggests that we need to do something else for salvation, Colossians assures us that Jesus is all we need.

Where?

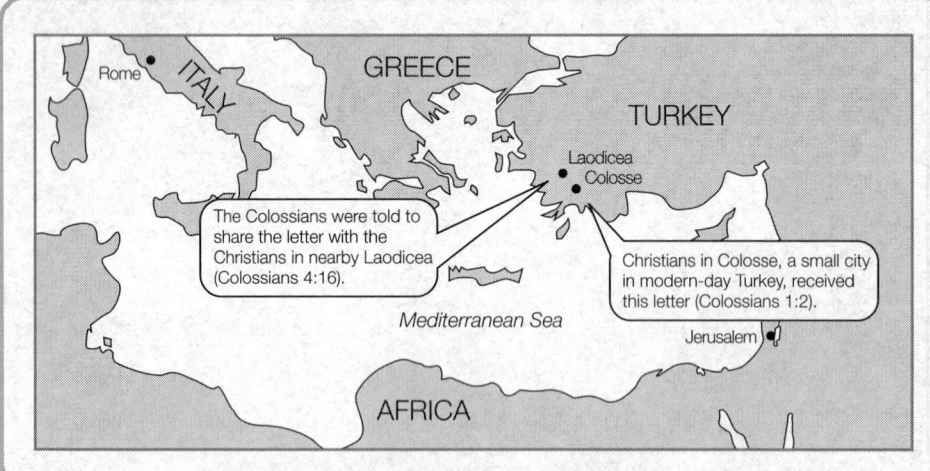

The Colossians were told to share the letter with the Christians in nearby Laodicea (Colossians 4:16).

Christians in Colosse, a small city in modern-day Turkey, received this letter (Colossians 1:2).

1 From Paul, an apostle [d] of Christ Jesus. I am an apostle because that is what God wanted. Also from Timothy, our brother.

[2] To the holy and faithful brothers and sisters [n] in Christ that live in Colosse:

Grace and peace to you from God our Father. [3] In our prayers for you we always thank God, the Father of our Lord Jesus Christ, [4] because we have heard about the faith you have in Christ Jesus and the love you have for all of God's people. [5] You have this faith and love because of your hope, and what you hope for is kept safe for you in heaven. You learned about this hope when you heard the message about the truth, the Good News [d] [6] that was told to you. Everywhere in the world that Good News is bringing blessings and is growing. This has happened with you too, since you heard the Good News and understood the truth about the grace of God. [7] You learned about God's grace from Epaphras, whom we love. He works together with us and is a faithful servant of Christ for us. [8] He also told us about the love you have from the Holy Spirit. [d]

[9] Because of this, since the day we heard about you, we have continued praying for you, asking God that you will know fully what he wants. We pray that you will also have great wisdom and understanding in spiritual things [10] so that you will live the kind of life that honours and pleases the Lord in every way. You will produce fruit in

brothers and sisters   Although the Greek text says "brothers" here and throughout this book, Paul's words were meant for the entire church, both men and women.

GOD'S WILL

A Life Pleasing God

From childhood, Robert Beck knew that he wanted to be a missionary to Africa. Every day he kept his goal foremost in his mind. He read magazine articles and books and watched TV news reports and documentaries on Africa. At school he wrote stories and reports about the African people.

After leaving school, Robert studied for a theology degree, then completed a course at theological college.

After almost 20 years of education, Robert was finally ready to start on his goal. He started a church in Africa.

Robert preached regularly at the mission church. He taught children about God's love. He befriended the people when they were sick and lonely, and cheerfully devoted all his time to his vision of God's will.

But after only one year in Africa, Robert contracted malaria and died of complications.

Some of Robert's friends and relatives wondered if he had wasted his life. "How can it be fair that this should happen to such a promising young man?" they asked bitterly. "Can this really be God's will?"

Back at Robert's college, the news of his death shocked and saddened the whole community. The tutors asked whether any graduating student would consider serving the church that Robert had started.

Eight signed up to serve.

Although Robert died young, he lived "the kind of life that honours and pleases the Lord in every way" and produced "fruit in every good work" (Colossians 1:10). He followed God's will, just as Paul urged his readers to do in **Colossians 1:1–14.**

* In the light of this passage, how was God's will accomplished with Robert?
* How can this passage help you to discover God's will for your life?

Consider . . .

* praying that God will let you "know fully what he wants" for your future (Colossians 1:9).
* keeping a journal about God's will for your life. Read Bible verses about God's will (see below) and write your thoughts as you apply those verses to decisions that you are facing.

For more, see . . .

* Psalm 40:8–10 (p.524)
* Mark 3:31–35 (p.1003)

* Matthew 6:9–13 (p.948)

every good work and grow in the knowledge of God. ¹¹God will strengthen you with his own great power so that you will not give up when troubles come, but you will be patient. ¹²And you

will joyfully give thanks to the Father who has made you able to have a share in all that he has prepared for his people in the kingdom of light. ¹³God has freed us from the power of darkness and brought us into the kingdom of his dear Son.

¹⁴The Son paid for our sins, and in him we have forgiveness.

The Importance of Christ

¹⁵No one can see God, but Jesus Christ is exactly like him. He ranks higher than everything that has been made. ¹⁶Through his power all things were made—things in heaven and on earth, things seen and unseen, all powers, authorities, lords and rulers. All things were made through Christ and for Christ. ¹⁷He was there before anything was made, and all things continue because of him. ¹⁸He is the head of the body, which is the church. Everything comes from him. He is the first one who was raised from the dead. So in all things Jesus has first place. ¹⁹God was pleased for all of himself to live in Christ. ²⁰And through Christ, God has brought all things back to himself again—things on earth and things in heaven. God made peace through the blood of Christ's death on the cross.

²¹At one time you were separated from God. You were his enemies in your minds, and the evil

FORGIVENESS

The Face of Hatred

Just before Leonardo da Vinci began painting "The Last Supper", he argued bitterly with a fellow painter. Da Vinci was so enraged that he decided to paint the face of his enemy as the face of Judas Iscariot. In this way the hated painter's face would be preserved for ages in the face of the disciple who betrayed Jesus.

Da Vinci painted the face of Judas quickly. At first he took delight as everyone who came past recognised the face of the other painter in Judas.

Work on the other disciples' portraits continued. Da Vinci tried several times to start Jesus' face, but couldn't make any progress. Something seemed to baffle him, frustrating his best efforts.

In time, da Vinci saw his hatred of the other painter as the problem holding him back from finishing his work. Only after repainting the face of Judas was he able to paint Jesus' face and complete his masterpiece.

In his work on "The Last Supper", da Vinci learned something important about forgiveness. **Colossians 1:15–29** has a similar lesson as it explains how Christ came to forgive – to end the separation between God and people.

* How was Leonardo da Vinci's separation from his fellow painter like humanity's separation from God as described in the passage?
* How do you feel when you are forgiven? How do you feel when you forgive someone else?

Consider . . .

* confessing your sin to God, and if you can, to an adult you trust. It may help you to feel God's forgiveness.
* closing your eyes and thinking about the face of someone that you need to forgive. Then imagine the face of Jesus next to that person's, and ask God to help you to forgive them.

For more, see . . .

* Psalm 79:8–9 (p.548)
* Romans 5:1–11 (p.1190)
* Luke 6:37–38 (p.1048)

things you did were against God. ²²But now God has made you his friends again. He did this through Christ's death in the body so that he might bring you into God's presence as people who are holy, with no wrong, and with nothing of which God can judge you guilty. ²³This will happen if you continue strong and sure in your faith. You must not be moved away from the hope brought to you by the Good News *d* that you heard. That same Good News has been told to everyone in the world, and I, Paul, help in preaching that Good News.

Paul's Work for the Church

²⁴I am happy in my sufferings for you. There are things that Christ must still suffer through his body, the church. I am accepting, in my body, my part of these things that must be suffered.

²⁵I became a servant of the church because God gave me a special work to do that helps you, and that work is to tell fully the message of God. ²⁶This message is the secret that was hidden from everyone since the beginning of time, but now it is made known to God's holy people. ²⁷God decided to let his people know this rich and glorious secret which he has for all people. This secret is Christ himself, who is in you. He is our only hope for glory. ²⁸So we continue to preach Christ to each person, using all wisdom to warn and to teach everyone, in order to bring each one into God's presence as a mature person in Christ. ²⁹To do this, I work and struggle, using Christ's great strength that works so powerfully in me.

2 I want you to know how hard I work for you, those in Laodicea, and others who have

CULTS

Fatal Attraction

Anne was an average schoolgirl. Her grades were average: Bs and Cs in most subjects. Her interest in school was average: she thought school was OK, but she would much rather play tennis or watch television. Her social life was average: an occasional date or evening out with some friends.

Anne couldn't wait to leave school and get on with life. She didn't know what she wanted, but she knew that it had to be more interesting than what she was doing.

One day after school, Anne went to the shops. There, some members of a religious group approached her. Anne had never heard of the group. But because they offered her a chance to belong, to take part in something greater than herself, she joined them.

After two years, Anne decided that the cult had manipulated her for its own ends. The group had offered "answers" to tough questions, but then told her to stop asking questions – to "just believe". It used her to raise money by selling flowers, sweets, and other things, but when she asked where all the money was going, she was told it wasn't her concern.

Finally, she dropped out. She felt sick about the two years she had wasted. "Why was I attracted to that group?" she later asked herself. "I was a typical youngster with a comfortable lifestyle. Why did I change my life so drastically? I wasn't that unhappy."

The Colossian Christians experienced a similar attraction to false beliefs. **Colossians 2:1–15** warns the early Christians not to be fooled by empty teachings.

* How might Anne's response to the cult have been different if she had listened to the warnings in this passage?
* How can you recognise false teachers today, according to the passage?

Consider . . .

* making a list of Paul's warnings about false teachers. Refer to it when someone offers you quick, appealing answers to tough questions.
* asking your minister or youth leader to get literature from cult groups and asking for his help in evaluating the groups' claims in the light of scripture.

For more, see . . .

* Deuteronomy 13:1–5 (p.178)
* 2 Peter 2:17–22 (p.1367)
* Matthew 24:23–25 (p.984)

never seen me. [2]I want them to be strengthened and joined together with love so that they may be rich in their understanding. This leads to their knowing fully God's secret, that is, Christ himself. [3]In him all the treasures of wisdom and knowledge are safely kept.

[4]I say this so that no one can fool you by arguments that seem good, but are false. [5]Though I am absent from you in my body, my heart is with you, and I am happy to see your good lives and your strong faith in Christ.

Sidelight

Although Paul never visited the Colossian church, it is believed that the fellowship was started by people who heard the gospel in Ephesus (see Acts 19:10, p.1170). Because the population of Colosse was largely a "mixed bag" of different races and creeds, it was easy for crazy (and dangerous) ideas to spring up.

Continue to Live in Christ

[6]As you received Christ Jesus the Lord, so continue to live in him. [7]Keep your roots deep in him and have your lives built on him. Be strong in the faith, just as you were taught, and always be thankful.

[8]Be sure that no one leads you away with false and empty teaching that is only human, which comes from the ruling spirits of this world, and not from Christ. [9]All of God lives in Christ fully (even when Christ was on earth), [10]and you have a full and true life in Christ, who is ruler over all rulers and powers.

[11]Also in Christ you had a different kind of circumcision, [d] a circumcision not done by hands. It was through Christ's circumcision, that is, his death, that you were made free from the power of your sinful self. [12]When you were baptised, [d] you were buried with Christ, and you were raised up with him through your faith in God's power that was shown when he raised Christ from the dead. [13]When you were spiritually dead because of your sins and because you were not free from the power of your sinful self, God made you alive with Christ, and he forgave all our sins. [14]He cancelled the debt, which listed all the rules we failed to follow. He took away that record with its rules and nailed it to the cross. [15]God stripped the spiritual rulers and powers of their authority. With the cross, he won the victory and showed the world that they were powerless.

Don't Follow People's Rules

[16]So do not let anyone make rules for you about eating and drinking or about a religious feast, a New Moon [d] Festival or a Sabbath [d] day. [17]These things were like a shadow of what was to come. But what is true and real has come and is found in Christ. [18]Do not let anyone disqualify you by making you humiliate yourself and worship angels. Such people enter into visions, which fill them with foolish pride because of their human way of thinking. [19]They do not hold tightly to Christ, the head. It is from him that all the parts of the body are cared for and held together. So it grows in the way God wants it to grow.

[20]Since you died with Christ and were made free from the ruling spirits of the world, why do you act as if you still belong to this world by following rules like these: [21]"Don't eat this", "Don't taste that", "Don't even touch that thing"? [22]These rules refer to earthly things that are gone as soon as they are used. They are only man-made commands and teachings. [23]They seem to be wise, but they are only part of a man-made religion. They make people pretend not to be proud and make them punish their bodies, but they do not really control the evil desires of the sinful self.

Your New Life in Christ

3 Since you were raised from the dead with Christ, aim at what is in heaven, where Christ is sitting at the right hand of God. [2]Think only about the things in heaven, not the things on earth. [3]Your old sinful self has died, and your new life is kept with Christ in God. [4]Christ is our life, and when he comes again, you will share in his glory.

[5]So put all evil things out of your life: sexual sinning, doing evil, letting evil thoughts control you, wanting things that are evil and greed. This is really serving a false god. [6]These things make God angry. [n] [7]In your past, evil life you also did these things.

[8]But now also put these things out of your life: anger, bad temper, doing or saying things to hurt others and using evil words when you talk. [9]Do not lie to each other. You have left your old sinful life and the things you did before. [10]You have begun to live the new life, in which you are being made new and are becoming like the One who made you. This new life brings you the true knowledge of God. [11]In the new life there is no difference between Greeks and Jews, those who are circumcised [d] and those who are not circumcised, or people who are foreigners,

---

These . . . angry　Some Greek copies add: "against the people who do not obey God".

or Scythians.[n] There is no difference between slaves and free people. But Christ is in all believers, and Christ is all that is important.

[12]God has chosen you and made you his holy people. He loves you. So always do these things: show mercy to others, be kind, humble, gentle and patient. [13]Get along with each other, and forgive each other. If someone does wrong to you, forgive that person because the Lord forgave you. [14]Do all these things; but most important, love each other. Love is what holds you all together in perfect unity. [15]Let the peace that Christ gives control your thinking, because you were all called together in one body[n] to have peace. Always be thankful. [16]Let the teaching of Christ live in you richly. Use all wisdom to teach and instruct each other by singing psalms, hymns and spiritual songs with thankfulness in your hearts to God. [17]Everything you do or say should be done to obey Jesus your Lord. And in all you do, give thanks to God the Father through Jesus.

Sidelight

If you feel as though you have read some of Colossians somewhere else, you might be right. The book is filled with passages that closely parallel Ephesians (for example, compare Colossians 3:16–17 with Ephesians 5:19–20, p.1275). In fact, about half of Ephesians' 155 verses also have similarities to verses in Colossians.

Scythians   The Scythians were known as very wild and cruel people.
body   The spiritual body of Christ, meaning the church or his people.

FOLLOWING GOD

Wake Up!

At school, George shyly kept to himself. His few friends thought he was nice enough, but nobody, including himself, thought he had much talent or potential. In fact, they rarely seemed to think anything of him. That was all right with George, since he rarely thought about anything anyway. He was content just to exist without any goals, dreams, or ideas.

About the only thing George enjoyed was driving around town in his car. It seemed a way to pass empty hours. But one day another car slammed into George's, sending his car off the road towards a tree. George was thrown from the car just before it smashed into the tree.

When George regained consciousness, he kept hearing the police say how lucky he was. George suffered minor injuries, but the car was a write-off.

George's near tragedy awakened him to the reality of his empty life. Deciding that he wanted to live for more than driving his car, he poured himself into many new interests, including film-making. A few years after his accident, George Lucas entertained millions with *American Graffiti*, the *Star Wars* trilogy, and the *Indiana Jones* films.

George Lucas was lucky: he lost his car, but gained a new purpose in life. **Colossians 3:1–10** tells Christians to "wake up" to a whole, new life that is far more important than any new career.

* How does George Lucas's awakening to life illustrate Paul's challenge to live a different way in Christ? How is it different?
* In the light of this passage, how is your "old life" different from your "new life in Christ"?

Consider . . .

* writing on one side of a sheet of paper things that are different because of your "new life in Christ". On the other side, write out temptations that you can avoid because of this new life. Thank God for giving you strength.
* trying a new skill or interest that might help you to follow God's will. Focus your attention on the gifts that you believe God has given to you.

For more, see . . .

* Habakkuk 3:2 (p.907)
* Revelation 21:1–5 (p.1403)
* Luke 9:24 (p.1055)

Your New Life with Other People

¹⁸Wives, yield to the authority of your husbands, because this is the right thing to do in the Lord.

¹⁹Husbands, love your wives and be gentle with them.

²⁰Children, obey your parents in all things, because this pleases the Lord.

²¹Fathers, do not nag your children. If you are too hard to please, they may want to stop trying.

²²Slaves, obey your masters in all things. Do not obey just when they are watching you, to gain their favour, but serve them honestly, because you respect the Lord. ²³In all the work you are doing, work the best you can. Work as if you were doing it for the Lord, not for people. ²⁴Remember that you will receive your reward from the Lord, which he promised to his people. You are serving the Lord Christ. ²⁵But remember that anyone who does wrong will be punished for that wrong, and the Lord treats everyone the same.

4 Masters, give what is good and fair to your slaves. Remember that you have a Master in heaven.

What the Christians are to Do

²Continue praying, keeping alert and always thanking God. ³Also pray for us that God will give us an opportunity to tell people his message. Pray that we can preach the secret that God has made known about Christ. This is why I am in prison. ⁴Pray that I can speak in a way that will make it clear, as I should.

⁵Be wise in the way you act with people who are not believers, making the most of every opportunity. ⁶When you talk, you should always be kind and pleasant so you will be able to answer everyone in the way you should.

News About the People with Paul

⁷Tychicus is my dear brother in Christ and a faithful minister and servant with me in the Lord. He will tell you all the things that are happening to me. ⁸This is why I am sending him: so you may know how we are and he may encourage you. ⁹I send him with Onesimus, a faithful and dear brother in Christ, and one of your group. They will tell you all that has happened here.

¹⁰Aristarchus, a prisoner with me, and Mark, the cousin of Barnabas, greet you. (I have already told you what to do about Mark. If he comes, welcome him.) ¹¹Jesus, who is called Justus, also greets you. These are the only Jewish believers who work with me for the kingdom of God, and they have been a comfort to me.

¹²Epaphras, a servant of Jesus Christ, from your group, also greets you. He always prays for you that you will grow to be spiritually mature and have everything God wants for you. ¹³I know he has worked hard for you and the people in Laodicea and in Hierapolis. ¹⁴Demas and our dear friend Luke, the doctor, greet you.

¹⁵Greet the brothers in Laodicea. And greet Nympha and the church that meets in her house. ¹⁶After this letter is read to you, be sure it is also read to the church in Laodicea. And you read the letter that I wrote to Laodicea. ¹⁷Tell Archippus, "Be sure to finish the work the Lord gave you."

¹⁸I, Paul, greet you and write this with my own hand. Remember me in prison. Grace be with you.

1 Thessalonians

Why Read This Book:

- Be encouraged to stand up for your faith even when those around you make fun of you (1 Thessalonians 2—3).
- See the importance of growing strong in faith (1 Thessalonians 4—5).

When?

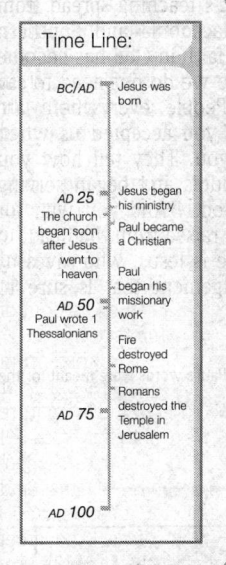

Time Line:

BC/AD	Jesus was born
AD 25	Jesus began his ministry
The church began soon after Jesus went to heaven	Paul became a Christian
	Paul began his missionary work
AD 50 Paul wrote 1 Thessalonians	
	Fire destroyed Rome
AD 75	Romans destroyed the Temple in Jerusalem
AD 100	

Behind the Scenes:

Remember what it was like when you first decided to follow Jesus? You may have thought that all your troubles would be over. You probably felt really good on the inside, and if anyone had warned you that life was still going to be difficult, you might have laughed.

But then it happens. It's Monday morning and you feel bad. Where did that happy feeling get to? Why don't I feel wonderful like I did last week? Will I be able to live out my new faith now that I'm back in the "real world"?

The Thessalonians might have felt the same way. They had just been visited by the apostle Paul, and after listening to him preach, they had become Christians. But now Paul had been forced to leave town, and they were left alone – new Christians in an unfriendly city with nobody to care for them.

Paul wrote this letter to the people of Thessalonica and encouraged them to "hang on in there" and develop their new faith despite their situation. He explained why he had to leave town so suddenly, and then told them to look forward to the day when Christ would return.

Being a Christian isn't easy – no one ever said it would be. This letter was made for new Christians. It can encourage you just as it did the Thessalonians. Read it as if Paul were speaking directly to you, then take up his challenge and decide to develop your faith whatever the world throws at you! Then fix your eyes on Jesus and stay with it because he is coming back again.

Where?

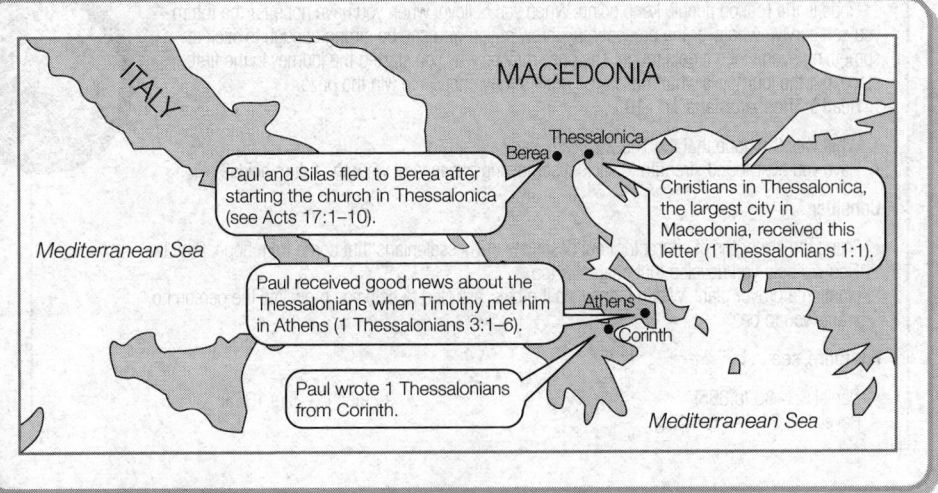

Paul and Silas fled to Berea after starting the church in Thessalonica (see Acts 17:1–10).

Christians in Thessalonica, the largest city in Macedonia, received this letter (1 Thessalonians 1:1).

Paul received good news about the Thessalonians when Timothy met him in Athens (1 Thessalonians 3:1–6).

Paul wrote 1 Thessalonians from Corinth.

1 From Paul, Silas and Timothy.
To the church in Thessalonica, the church in God the Father and the Lord Jesus Christ:
Grace and peace to you.

The Faith of the Thessalonians

[2]We always thank God for all of you and mention you when we pray. [3]We continually recall before God our Father the things you have done because of your faith and the work you have done because of your love. And we thank him that you continue to be strong because of your hope in our Lord Jesus Christ.

[4]Brothers and sisters,[n] God loves you, and we know he has chosen you, [5]because the Good News[d] we brought to you came not only with words, but with power, with the Holy Spirit[d] and with sure knowledge that it is true. Also you know how we lived when we were with you in order to help you. [6]And you became like us and like the Lord. You suffered much, but still you accepted the teaching with the joy that comes from the Holy Spirit. [7]So you became an example to all the believers in Macedonia and Southern Greece. [8]And the Lord's teaching spread from you not only into Macedonia and Southern Greece, but now your faith in God has become known everywhere. So we do not need to say anything about it. [9]People everywhere are telling about the way you accepted us when we were there with you. They tell how you stopped worshipping idols and began serving the living and true God. [10]And you wait for God's Son, whom God raised from the dead, to come from heaven. He is Jesus, who saves us from God's angry judgement that is sure to come.

Brothers and sisters Although the Greek text says "brothers" here and throughout this book, Paul's words were meant for the entire church, both men and women.

SPIRITUAL GROWTH

Those Who Wait

Why do people go on reality TV shows? Fame? Fortune? The dream job? The perfect partner? Just to get on the telly?

Whatever the prize they are competing for, they will go through anything to achieve it.

The prize may be the reason why people go on the show, but it's the drama itself that keeps the viewers watching. These shows make good television because they reveal what a person is really like. The prize is the incentive; the journey is the drama. How much do they want the prize on offer? Will they fight for it? How will they handle setbacks, failures, unforeseen challenges? Will they last the distance? Do they truly believe that the prize is theirs for the taking? "Can they win?" becomes "Will they win?"

Hope is the reason people keep going. When you believe, when you have hope for the future you can survive whatever the present may throw at you. You can be strong enough to stick at something even when it gets tough. The prize may be why you started the journey in the first place, but the journey is what makes you grow strong enough to win the prize.

Read **1 Thessalonians 1:1–10**.

- What was the hope that the Thessalonians had?
- Have you ever found strength to stick at something because of what the future holds?

Consider . . .

- listing the strengths of character Paul describes in Thessalonians that come from hope. Pray that God will help you develop that character too.
- planting a prayer plant. Watch it grow. As it grows, ask God to help you grow into the person he wants you to be.

For more, see . . .

- Daniel 3:1–30 (p.835)
- Revelation 21:1–4 (p.1403)
- 2 Peter 1:3–8 (p.1365)

Paul's Work in Thessalonica

2 Brothers and sisters, you know our visit to you was not a failure. ²Before we came to you, we suffered in Philippi. People there insulted us, as you know, and many people were against us. But our God helped us to be brave and to tell you his Good News. *d* ³Our appeal does not come from lies or wrong reasons, nor were we trying to trick you. ⁴But we speak the Good News because God tested us and trusted us to do it. When we speak, we are not trying to please people, but God, who tests our hearts. ⁵You know that we never tried to influence you by saying nice things about you. We were not trying to get your money; we had no selfishness to hide from you. God knows that this is true. ⁶We were not looking for human praise, from you or anyone else, ⁷even though

---

Sidelight   If all the New Testament books were to appear in the Bible in the order in which they were actually written, 1 Thessalonians might come first (with the possible exception of Galatians, p.1256 or James, p.1347). It is believed to have been written only twenty years after Jesus was crucified and rose from the dead.

Sidelight   Most Christian leaders are not in it for the money. Paul certainly wasn't (1 Thessalonians 2:5–9). To support himself, Paul worked as a tent-maker (see Acts 18:3, p.1168) so that he wouldn't have to take any money away from the churches he started.

LEADERSHIP

Single Minded

Smith Wigglesworth was an amazing man, often referred to as "The Apostle of Faith". He was born in Yorkshire in 1859 and, initially, had a career as a plumber. He did not have great wealth or education and for many years was unable to read. When he was forty-eight he began preaching, and over the next forty years, he achieved awesome things for God around the world. He preached hundreds of times and saw many people saved and many people healed.

His methods were, at times, unconventional and many established Christians, churches and leaders rejected him as being too controversial and, to be honest, slightly odd. But other people's opinions did not seem to bother him – he was completely single-minded. He was only interested in doing what God wanted him to do and because of this, his identity was not based on what other people thought of him. Once, when receiving criticism for what he was doing he simply said, "You people that are judging me, please leave your judgement outside, for I obey God."

What amazing leadership!

In **1 Thessalonians 2:1–13** Paul talks about some of his experiences of leadership. Leadership is not an easy task. It's full of hard work and self-sacrifice and may mean that, at times, you are unpopular. But what is more important – doing what God wants or what other people want?

- What are the leadership qualities that Paul describes in these verses?
- What matters most to you: what God thinks of you and wants you to do or what other people think of you and want you to do?

Consider . . .

- making a list of all the people who influence the decisions you make: teachers, friends, parents, celebrities. Put them in order of those who have most influence through to those who have least. Where does God come in the list?
- how you could display in your life some of the character traits that Paul lists in these verses.

For more, see . . .

- John 13:1–17 (p.1119)
- Philippians 2:1–13 (p.1282)
- 2 Corinthians 6:3–11 (p.1246)

as apostles*d* of Christ we could have used our authority over you.

But we were very gentle with you, like a mother caring for her little children. ⁸Because we loved you, we were happy to share not only God's Good News with you, but even our own lives. You had become so dear to us! ⁹Brothers and sisters, I know you remember our hard work and difficulties. We worked night and day so we would not burden any of you while we preached God's Good News to you.

¹⁰When we were with you, we lived in a holy and honest way, without fault. You know this is true, and so does God. ¹¹You know that we treated each of you as a father treats his own children. ¹²We encouraged you, we told you and we insisted that you live good lives for God, who calls you to his glorious kingdom.

¹³Also, we always thank God because when you heard his message from us, you accepted it as the word of God, not the words of humans. And it really is God's message which works in you who believe. ¹⁴Brothers and sisters, your experiences have been like those of God's churches in Christ that are in Judea.*n* You suffered from the people of your own country, as they suffered from the Jews, ¹⁵who killed both the Lord Jesus and the prophets*d* and forced us to leave that country. They do not please God and are against all people. ¹⁶They try to stop us from teaching those who are not Jews so they may be saved. By doing this, they are increasing their sins to the limit. The anger of God has come to them at last.

Paul Wants to Visit Them Again

¹⁷Brothers and sisters, though we were separated from you for a short time, our thoughts were still with you. We wanted very much to see you and tried hard to do so. ¹⁸We wanted to come to you. I, Paul, tried to come more than once, but Satan stopped us. ¹⁹You are our hope, our joy and the crown we will take pride in when our Lord Jesus Christ comes. ²⁰Truly you are our glory and our joy.

3 When we could not wait any longer, we decided it was best to stay in Athens alone ²and send Timothy to you. Timothy, our brother, works with us for God and helps us tell people the Good News*d* about Christ. We sent him to strengthen and encourage you

in your faith ³so none of you would be upset by these troubles. You yourselves know that we must face these troubles. ⁴Even when we were with you, we told you we all would have to suffer, and you know it has happened. ⁵Because of this, when I could wait no longer, I sent Timothy to you so I could learn about your faith. I was afraid the devil had tempted you, and then our hard work would have been wasted.

⁶But Timothy now has come back to us from you and has brought us good news about your faith and love. He told us that you always remember us in a good way and that you want to see us just as much as we want to see you. ⁷So, brothers and sisters, while we have much trouble and suffering, we are encouraged about you because of your faith. ⁸Our life is really full if you stand strong in the Lord. ⁹We have so much joy before our God because of you. We cannot thank him enough for all the joy we feel. ¹⁰Night and day we continue praying with all our heart that we can see you again and give you all the things you need to make your faith strong.

¹¹Now may our God and Father himself and our Lord Jesus prepare the way for us to come to you. ¹²May the Lord make your love grow more and multiply for each other and for all people so that you will love others as we love you. ¹³May your hearts be made strong so that you will be holy and without fault before our God and Father when our Lord Jesus comes with all his holy ones.

A Life that Pleases God

4 Brothers and sisters, we taught you how to live in a way that will please God, and you are living that way. Now we ask and encourage you in the Lord Jesus to live that way even more. ²You know what we told you to do by the authority of the Lord Jesus. ³God wants you to be holy and to stay away from sexual sins. ⁴He wants each of you to learn to control your own body*n* in a way that is holy and honourable. ⁵Don't use your body for sexual sin like the people who do not know God. ⁶Also, do not wrong or cheat another Christian in this way. The Lord will punish people who do those things as we have already told you and warned you. ⁷God called us to be holy and does not want us to live in sin. ⁸So the person who refuses to obey this teaching is

---

Judea The Jewish land where Jesus lived and taught and where the church first began.
learn . . . body This might also mean "learn to live with your own wife."

disobeying God, not simply a human teaching. And God is the One who gives us his Holy Spirit. *d*

⁹We do not need to write to you about having love for your Christian family, because God has already taught you to love each other. ¹⁰And truly you do love the Christians in all of Macedonia. Brothers and sisters, now we encourage you to love them even more.

¹¹Do all you can to live a peaceful life. Take care of your own business, and do your own work as we have already told you. ¹²If you do, then people who are not believers will respect you, and you will not have to depend on others for what you need.

Sidelight The church in Thessalonica would have been in an excellent position to love all the "Christians in all of Macedonia" (1 Thessalonians 4:10). The city was the capital of its province, so its residents had contact with people from all over the province.

The Lord's Coming

¹³Brothers and sisters, we want you to know about those Christians who have died so you will not be sad, as others who have no hope. ¹⁴We believe that Jesus died and that

HAPPINESS

Piece of Cake

Amy sat in a busy teashop with her mum in Belfast munching on a delicious cake full of cream and chocolate. She watched the many people go by the shop window, while she was nice and warm, away from the cold outside. She loved this teashop, it was her favourite, and spending time with her mum was always special.

After a while, Amy's attention was drawn to a little girl outside the shop, her nose pressed up to the glass of the window, looking in at the lovely cakes. Amy noticed that the little girl did not have any shoes on. On such a cold winter's day, she wore a ragged dress and looked very thin and cold. The little girl licked her lips – she was dreaming of having one of the cakes that Amy was busy munching on. Amy's happiness turned to a feeling of deep sadness.

Sitting by the fire, Amy wrote in large letters on a scrap of paper, "When I grow up and money I have, I know what I will do, I'll build a great big lovely palace, for little girls like you."

Years later, what Amy had written in that short poem came true. Amy Carmichael went on to help hundreds of children in India. She built an orphanage that housed hundreds of children who had no homes or future. The orphanages were not palaces, as she wrote in her childhood poem, but for the children she rescued they were more than palaces – they were homes. Many of the children she rescued were hungry, ill and had nothing, yet in Amy's care experienced a happiness they had only dreamt of.

Read **1 Thessalonians 3:9–13**.

* How was Amy affected by seeing someone who did not have a happy life like she had? Would you have reacted like this?
* Paul states that his true happiness is found in helping others. How is that true of Amy in this story? Do you think this is true for you?

Consider . . .

* asking God to fill you with that deep joy, happiness and security that can only be found in him.
* writing a "Happy" list of ways you can make others happy this week. Make someone else smile!

For more, see . . .

* Psalm 126:1–6 (p.576)
* Proverbs 14:21 (p.602)
* Proverbs 3:1–18 (p.592)

he rose again. So, because of him, God will raise with Jesus those who have died. [15]What we tell you now is the Lord's own message. We who are living when the Lord comes again will not go before those who have already died. [16]The Lord himself will come down from heaven with a loud command, with the voice of the archangel[n] and with the trumpet call of God. And those who have died believing in Christ will rise first. [17]After that, we who are still alive will be gathered up with them in the clouds to meet the Lord in the air. And we will be with the Lord for ever. [18]So encourage each other with these words.

Be Ready for the Lord's Coming

5 Now, brothers and sisters, we do not need to write to you about times and dates. [2]You know very well that the day the Lord comes again will be a surprise, like a thief that comes in the night. [3]While people are saying, "We have peace and we are safe," they will be destroyed quickly. It is like pains that come quickly to a woman having a baby. Those people will not escape. [4]But you, brothers and sisters, are not living in darkness, and so that day will not surprise you like a thief. [5]You are all people who belong to the light and to the day. We do not belong to the night or to darkness. [6]So we should not be like other people who are sleeping, but we should be awake and have self-control. [7]Those who sleep, sleep at night. Those who get drunk, get drunk at night. [8]But we belong to the day, so we should control ourselves. We should wear faith and love to protect us, and the hope of salvation should be our helmet. [9]God did not choose us to suffer his anger but to have salvation through our Lord

archangel   The leader among God's angels or messengers.

DEATH

We Have Hope

Jonathan Harwell was thirteen when his parents had a baby girl. The birth was a major cause for celebration, because Jonathan's parents had wanted another child since he was four years old. Years of trying, years of crying, years of suffering through three miscarriages, had finally produced Jonathan's baby sister, whom they named Sarah.

Jonathan and his parents were overjoyed with the new addition to their family. They redecorated one bedroom as a nursery and designed a playroom. They planned a special outing each weekend. They thoroughly enjoyed their new family member.

Their joy lasted six short months. One morning they woke up to discover that Sarah had died in her sleep. The doctors labelled the cause of death as sudden infant death syndrome – a cot death. They told the family not to blame themselves – it was virtually impossible to prevent a cot death at that time.

Although Jonathan and his parents felt a bit comforted by the doctors, they were still devastated by Sarah's death.

As Jonathan tried to work through his grief, he read **1 Thessalonians 4:13–14**. Jonathan shared the passage with his parents, and they were all comforted by its words of hope.

* How were Jonathan and his family comforted by this passage?
* How does it feel to know that some day you will see Christian loved ones who have died?

Consider . . .

* writing a memorial letter to someone you loved who has died. Keep the letter as a reminder.
* thinking of someone who has recently lost a loved one. Phone, write to, or visit that person, or take them out for a meal. Offer a little comfort.

For more, see . . .

* Isaiah 25:7–8 (p.664)
* 2 Timothy 1:9–10 (p.1316)
* Romans 8:37–39 (p.1197)

Jesus Christ. [10]Jesus died for us so that we can live together with him, whether we are alive or dead when he comes. [11]So encourage each other and give each other strength, just as you are doing now.

Final Instructions and Greetings

[12]Now, brothers and sisters, we ask you to appreciate those who work hard among you, who lead you in the Lord and teach you. [13]Respect them with a very special love because of the work they do.

Live in peace with each other. [14]We ask you, brothers and sisters, to warn those who do not work. Encourage the people who are afraid. Help those who are weak. Be patient with everyone. [15]Be sure that no one pays back wrong for wrong, but always try to do what is good for each other and for all people.

[16]Always be joyful. [17]Pray continually, [18]and give thanks whatever happens. That is what God wants for you in Christ Jesus.

[19]Do not hold back the work of the Holy Spirit. *d* [20]Do not treat prophecy *d* as if it were unimportant. [21]But test everything. Keep what is good, [22]and stay away from everything that is evil.

[23]Now may God himself, the God of peace, make you pure, belonging only to him. May your

ETERNAL LIFE

Be Prepared!

Pete is an evangelist. He's stayed with people in just about every country in the world. Sometimes he's dined with princes, other times he's sat on the ground and eaten rice with his hands. His life is a whirlwind of planes, boats and cars. It doesn't matter to him what the circumstance is, he's just happy preaching. But he also loves to get home and spend some time relaxing with his friends. Going out for meals, listening to music and laughing.

His life "on the road" has given him a great understanding for people in similar situations. He knows what it's like to arrive at someone's house and find that they haven't prepared a meal for him. Or to come in from an exhausting journey and have his hosts talk to him into the early hours, when all he wanted to do was go to bed.

So Pete decided this would never happen to anyone who came to stay with him!

He enjoyed having guests at his house, especially fellow-itinerants (people who spent all their time travelling up and down the country telling people the Good News of Jesus Christ). He had a real understanding of the needs of folk in this situation. So, he made sure that his guest room had everything he could think of.

A very comfortable bed, a TV, books, writing material . . . even a well-stocked fridge!

Regardless of whether he knew there was anyone coming to stay or not, the fridge was full of coke, chocolate bars and other snacks. The date wasn't important to him, if he wasn't home then he knew that a neighbour had the key and could let anyone in.

He was just ready! Ready for anyone at any time. Some people laughed at him for this, but Pete knew how important it was to be prepared.

1 Thessalonians 5:1–11 is all about being prepared and ready for the Lord's coming.

* What qualities did Pete have that are written about in this passage?
* What can you do to "be prepared" for the Lord's return?

Consider . . .

* going through your day's activities as if it were the day Jesus were coming back. Did you act differently or the same?
* hanging a "Maybe Today" sign in your room, to remind you to live each day to the fullest and be ready for Christ's return.

For more, see . . .

* Daniel 12:1–13 (p.847)
* 2 Peter 3:8–13 (p.1368)

* Matthew 21:1–14 (p.977)

whole self—spirit, soul and body—be kept safe and without fault when our Lord Jesus Christ comes. [24]You can trust the One who calls you to do that for you.

[25]Brothers and sisters, pray for us.

[26]Give each other a holy kiss when you meet. [27]I tell you by the authority of the Lord to read this letter to all the believers.

[28]The grace of our Lord Jesus Christ be with you.

2 Thessalonians

Why Read This Book:

- Learn how God is with us now and in the future (2 Thessalonians 1).
- Find hope and comfort in God's love in the midst of life's tough times (2 Thessalonians 2—3).

When?

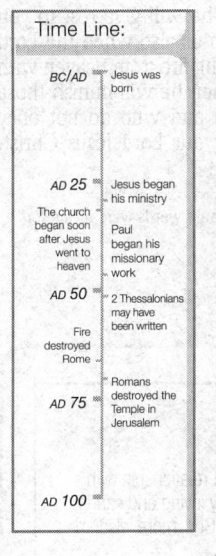

Time Line:	
BC/AD	Jesus was born
AD 25	Jesus began his ministry
The church began soon after Jesus went to heaven	Paul began his missionary work
AD 50	2 Thessalonians may have been written
Fire destroyed Rome	
AD 75	Romans destroyed the Temple in Jerusalem
AD 100	

Behind the Scenes:

You are about to graduate. You have passed all your exams, but you still have one final test left to go. You don't think the test will make any difference to your grade or the job you will get. How hard will you study?

The Thessalonian Christians were in a similar situation. They had been told that "the day of the Lord" (Christ's Second Coming) had already come, and some believed it. As a result, they didn't think they had anything to worry about, since they would all go to heaven soon. So they left work, sat around doing nothing, interfered in other people's business, and depended on the church for charity. Worst of all, people decided they didn't really have to worry about growing spiritually.

2 Thessalonians challenged this outlook, saying the day of the Lord had not come and would not come for some time. Instead of sitting around, waiting for the end, Christians should be working hard and seeking to grow in their faith.

Sometimes we can be so excited about God's gift of eternal life that it makes everything else seem like a waste of time. 2 Thessalonians reminds us that God has a purpose for us on earth, and we are called to do God's work in this world. We are called to keep growing in our faith whatever happens.

LIFE FILE LINKS

Investigate the Theme

To find a list of real life stories on this subject turn to the LIFE FILE GUIDE on pages 12 to 22 at the front of the Youth Bible.

FAITH

1 From Paul, Silas and Timothy.
To the church in Thessalonica in God our Father and the Lord Jesus Christ:
²Grace and peace to you from God the Father and the Lord Jesus Christ.

Paul Talks About God's Judgement

³We must always thank God for you, brothers and sisters. *n* This is only right, because your faith is growing more and more, and the love that every one of you has for each other is increasing. ⁴So we boast about you to the other churches of God. We tell them about the way you continue to be strong and have faith even though you are being treated badly and are suffering many troubles.

⁵This is proof that God is right in his judgement. He wants you to be counted worthy of his kingdom for which you are suffering. ⁶God will do what is right. He will give trouble to those who trouble you. ⁷And he will give rest to you who are troubled and to us also when the Lord Jesus appears with burning fire from heaven with his powerful angels. ⁸Then he will punish those who do not know God and who do not obey the Good News *d* about our Lord Jesus Christ.

---

brothers and sisters Although the Greek text says "brothers" here and throughout this book, Paul's words were meant for the entire church, both men and women.

SUFFERING

When Silence Falls

Susie had been a Christian most of her life. She had a lovely family and home, and a great relationship with God. She was the kind of girl that everyone loved to be around. She was funny, sweet, very loving and caring and the best friend you could ask for. As Susie grew older, she was desperate for more of God, more wisdom, more love and more understanding.

Unlike her friends, Susie had a daily quiet time. God always met with her, until one day.

"That's strange," she thought. "Must be me."

On the days that followed, God seemed to stay quiet. She had no words, no pictures, no good thoughts, no tingle down her spine and no joy. Her days got dryer, so she tried even harder.

Around the same time, Susie realised her boyfriend was acting very strangely towards her. She confronted him and he told her he'd realised he no longer loved her. Susie was devastated and turned to God for comfort, but still he appeared to stay silent.

Shortly afterwards, Susie received a phone call. Her best friend had been in a serious accident, she was lying in intensive care.

Lost and alone, Susie opened her Bible. Desperate, and crying out to God, her quiet time became a very loud time – but still she heard nothing.

Susie began to blame God. "Why are you doing this? Why are you ignoring me? Do you care? Are you even there?" As Susie cried, she remembered in the past telling God that no matter what the circumstances he was still God and deserved her worship. She realised that it's easy to pray when God feels really close and things are good, but as soon as he'd tested her to see if she really meant it about worshipping him in *all* circumstances, she had struggled. Read **2 Thessalonians 1:1–12**.

- What should our response be when suffering comes our way?
- How might knowing that you will have peace with God in the future help you through troubles right now?

Consider . . .

- the troubles you may be experiencing at the moment. Think about what God may be teaching you.
- getting hold of some books by people who have suffered for Jesus. How did they keep going?

For more, see . . .

- Romans 8:17–18 (p.1195)
- 1 Peter 3:8–22 (p.1360)
- 2 Corinthians 1:3–7 (p.1241)

[9]Those people will be punished with a destruction that continues for ever. They will be kept away from the Lord and from his great power. [10]This will happen on the day when the Lord Jesus comes to receive glory because of his holy people. And all the people who have believed will be amazed at Jesus. You will be in that group, because you believed what we told you.

> **Sidelight** Being a Christian in the first century could be dangerous (2 Thessalonians 1:4). The Roman Emperor Nero was notorious for torturing Christians by covering them with tar and setting them on fire, then holding chariot races as they burned.

[11]That is why we always pray for you, asking our God to help you live the kind of life he called you to live. We pray that with his power God will help you do the good things you want and perform the works that come from your faith. [12]We pray all this so that the name of our Lord Jesus Christ will have glory in you, and you will have glory in him. That glory comes from the grace of our God and the Lord Jesus Christ.

Evil Things will Happen

2 Brothers and sisters, we have something to say about the coming of our Lord Jesus Christ and the time when we will meet together with him. [2]Do not become easily upset in your thinking or afraid if you hear that the day of the Lord has already come. Someone may say this in a prophecy[d] or in a message or in a letter as if it came from us. [3]Do not let anyone fool you in any way. That day of the Lord will not come until the turning away[n] from God happens and the Man of Evil, who is on his way to hell, appears. [4]He will be against and put himself above anything called God or anything that people worship. And that Man of Evil will even go into God's Temple[d] and sit there and say that he is God.

[5]I told you when I was with you that all this would happen. Do you not remember? [6]And now you know what is stopping that Man of Evil so he will appear at the right time. [7]The secret power of evil is already working in the world, but there is one who is stopping that power. And he will continue to stop it until he is taken out of the way. [8]Then that Man of Evil will appear, and

the Lord Jesus will kill him with the breath that comes from his mouth and will destroy him with the glory of his coming. [9]The Man of Evil will come by the power of Satan. He will have great power, and he will do many different false miracles,[d] signs and wonders. [10]He will use every kind of evil to trick those who are lost. They will die, because they refused to love the truth. (If they loved the truth, they would be saved.) [11]For this reason God sends them something powerful that leads them away from the truth so they will believe a lie. [12]So all those will be judged guilty who did not believe the truth, but enjoyed doing evil.

You are Chosen for Salvation

[13]Brothers and sisters, whom the Lord loves, God chose you from the beginning to be saved. So we must always thank God for you. You are saved by the Spirit[d] that makes you holy and by your faith in the truth. [14]God used the Good News[d] that we preached to call you to be saved so you can share in the glory of our Lord Jesus Christ. [15]So, brothers and sisters, stand strong and continue to believe the teachings we gave you in our speaking and in our letter.

[16-17]May our Lord Jesus Christ himself and God our Father encourage you and strengthen you in every good thing you do and say. God loved us, and through his grace he gave us a good hope and encouragement that continues for ever.

Pray for Us

3 And now, brothers and sisters, pray for us that the Lord's teaching will continue to spread quickly and that people will give honour to that teaching, just as you did. [2]And pray that we will be protected from stubborn and evil people, because not all people believe. [3]But the Lord is faithful and will give you strength and will protect you from the Evil One. [4]The Lord makes us feel sure that you are doing and will continue to do the things we told you. [5]May the Lord lead your hearts into God's love and Christ's patience.

The Duty to Work

[6]Brothers and sisters, by the authority of our Lord Jesus Christ we command you to stay away from any believer who refuses to work and does not follow the teaching we gave you. [7]You yourselves know that you should live as we live. We were not lazy when we were with you. [8]And when we ate another person's food, we always

turning away Or "the rebellion".

paid for it. We worked very hard night and day so we would not be an expense to any of you. ⁹We had the right to ask you to help us, but we worked to take care of ourselves so we would be an example for you to follow. ¹⁰When we were with you, we gave you this rule: "Anyone who refuses to work should not eat."

¹¹We hear that some people in your group refuse to work. They do nothing but busy themselves in other people's lives. ¹²We command those people and beg them in the Lord Jesus Christ to work quietly and earn their own food. ¹³But you, brothers and sisters, never become tired of doing good.

¹⁴If some people do not obey what we tell you in this letter, then take note of them. Have nothing to do with them so they will feel ashamed. ¹⁵But do not treat them as enemies. Warn them as fellow believers.

Final Words

¹⁶Now may the Lord of peace give you peace at all times and in every way. The Lord be with all of you.

¹⁷I, Paul, end this letter now in my own handwriting. All my letters have this to show they are from me. This is the way I write.

¹⁸The grace of our Lord Jesus Christ be with you all.

Sidelight

Lazy people spent their time interfering in other people's lives instead of working, so Paul told them that if someone didn't work when he was capable of doing so, he shouldn't eat either (2 Thessalonians 3:11–13)! This principle is also taught in Proverbs 19:15 (p.606).

GOD'S LOVE

Difficult Times

The Smith family experienced the pits of despair. Mr Smith, a fantastic engineer, loving husband and father, was killed in a car accident. He left a wife, an eighteen-year-old daughter, and a sixteen-year-old son. How would the family survive this difficult time?

Their church rallied round them. People volunteered to mow their lawn and repair their house. Church members cooked and served meals every day right after the death and once a week throughout the following year. The church collected a special offering for their immediate expenses and found a job for Mrs Smith. Church friends supported the family throughout that difficult first year with phone calls, visits, cards and gifts.

The Smiths wrote this thank-you to their congregation: "Through your prayers, dear friends, we have been comforted. Through your kind acts we have been soothed. We experienced God's love through you and your love. You made an unbearable experience bearable."

As the church comforted the Smiths, **2 Thessalonians 2:13 — 3:5** promises that God's love will comfort Christians who suffer.

* How is the love shown to the Smiths by their congregation like the love that comforted the early Christians?
* How does God's love comfort you through tough times?

Consider . . .

* circling the word "love" each time you read your Bible over the next several days. Count the number of "loves". Notice how God's love for you is stressed throughout the Bible. Start with the passages listed below.
* letting God's love shine through you. Think of someone who is sad or lonely (for example, a new person at school or an elderly church member who has lost a spouse). Surprise that person with a present or a card.

For more, see . . .

* Psalm 89:1–2 (p.553)
* Romans 5:6–8 (p.1190)
* Matthew 11:28–30 (p.960)

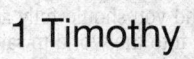

1 Timothy

Why Read This Book:

- Learn how to guard against false teaching (1 Timothy 1).
- Find out what to look for in a good church leader (1 Timothy 2—5).
- See what is really important in life (1 Timothy 6).

When?

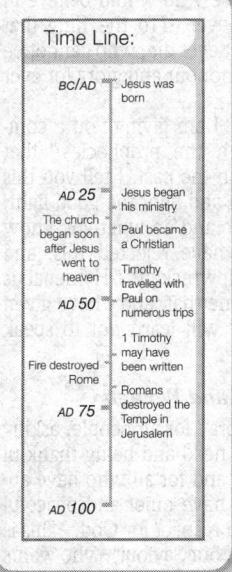

Time Line:

BC/AD — Jesus was born

AD 25 — Jesus began his ministry

The church began soon after Jesus went to heaven — Paul became a Christian

Timothy travelled with Paul on numerous trips

AD 50 —

1 Timothy may have been written

Fire destroyed Rome — Romans destroyed the Temple in Jerusalem

AD 75 —

AD 100 —

Behind the Scenes:

When you begin using a computer, you could just turn it on and start pressing keys, hoping you will hit the right ones to make something happen. But some people begin by reading the machine's manual. There you will find step-by-step things to do to use the machine correctly.

The first Christians didn't have experience of running a church. Many times they tried different things, hoping they were right. But they also needed a "practical handbook".

1 Timothy was just what they needed. It gives church leaders specific guidance on running a church: choosing leaders, dealing with false teachings, and order in worship, for example. It's called a "pastoral letter" because it focuses on the work of pastors. The two other pastoral letters in the Bible are 2 Timothy (p.1315) and Titus (p.1322).

Just because 1 Timothy was originally written about church leaders doesn't mean they are the only ones who can benefit from reading it. The book helps all Christians to learn the differences between true and false teachings. And it gives practical guidance on how to live as Christians.

Where?

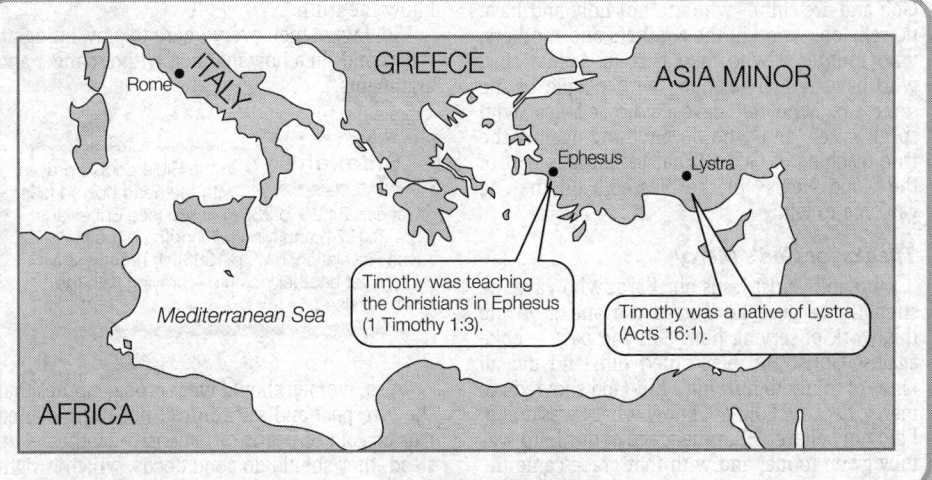

ITALY
Rome
GREECE
ASIA MINOR
Ephesus
Lystra
Mediterranean Sea
AFRICA

Timothy was teaching the Christians in Ephesus (1 Timothy 1:3).

Timothy was a native of Lystra (Acts 16:1).

1 From Paul, an apostle *d* of Christ Jesus, by the command of God our Saviour *d* and Christ Jesus our hope.

²To Timothy, a true child to me because you believe:

Grace, mercy and peace from God the Father and Christ Jesus our Lord.

Warning Against False Teaching

³I asked you to stay longer in Ephesus when I went into Macedonia so you could command some people there to stop teaching false things. ⁴Tell them not to spend their time on stories that are not true and on long lists of names in family histories. These things only bring arguments; they do not help God's work, which is done in

> **Sidelight** Genealogies were popular in Bible times (1 Timothy 1:4). Even Alexander the Great made up his own family tree, and linked himself with the Greek gods Hercules and Achilles!

faith. ⁵The purpose of this command is for people to have love, a love that comes from a pure heart and a good conscience and a true faith. ⁶Some people have missed these things and turned to useless talk. ⁷They want to be teachers of the law, but they do not understand either what they are talking about or what they are sure about.

⁸But we know that the law is good if someone uses it correctly. ⁹We also know that the law is not made for good people but for those who are against the law and for those who refuse to follow it. It is for people who are against God and are sinful, who are not holy and have no religion, who kill their fathers and mothers, who murder, ¹⁰who take part in sexual sins, who have sexual relations with people of the same sex, who sell slaves, who tell lies, who speak falsely and who do anything against the true teaching of God. ¹¹That teaching is part of the Good News *d* of the blessed God that he gave me to tell.

Thanks for God's Mercy

¹²I thank Christ Jesus our Lord, who gave me strength, because he trusted me and gave me this work of serving him. ¹³In the past I spoke against Christ and persecuted him and did all kinds of things to hurt him. But God showed me mercy, because I did not know what I was doing. I did not believe. ¹⁴But the grace of our Lord was fully given to me, and with that grace came the faith and love that are in Christ Jesus.

¹⁵What I say is true, and you should fully accept it: Christ Jesus came into the world to save sinners, of whom I am the worst. ¹⁶But I was given mercy so that in me, the worst of all sinners, Christ Jesus could show that he has patience without limit. His patience with me made me an example for those who would believe in him and have life for ever. ¹⁷To the King that rules for ever, who will never die, who cannot be seen, the only God, be honour and glory for ever and ever. Amen.

¹⁸Timothy, my child, I am giving you a command that agrees with the prophecies *d* that were given about you in the past. I tell you this so you can follow them and fight the good fight. ¹⁹Continue to have faith and do what you know is right. Some people have rejected this, and their faith has been shipwrecked. ²⁰Hymenaeus and Alexander have done that, and I have given them to Satan so they will learn not to speak against God.

Some Rules for Men and Women

2 First, I tell you to pray for all people, asking God for what they need and being thankful to him. ²Pray for rulers and for all who have authority so that we can have quiet and peaceful lives full of worship and respect for God. ³This is good, and it pleases God our Saviour, ⁴who wants all people to be saved and to know the truth. ⁵There is one God and one way human beings can reach God. That way is through Christ Jesus, who is himself human. ⁶He gave himself as a payment to free all people. He is proof that came at the right time. ⁷That is why I was chosen to tell the Good News *d* and to be an apostle. *d* (I am telling the truth; I am not lying.) I was chosen to teach those who are not Jews to believe and to know the truth.

⁸So, I want men everywhere to pray, lifting up their hands in a holy manner, without anger and arguments.

> **Sidelight** In the Bible people prayed with the head bowed (see Genesis 24:26, p.28), kneeling (see Ephesians 3:4, p.1271) and lying full-length on the floor (see Revelation 1:17, p.1389). 1 Timothy 2:8 offers yet another posture – praying with the hands raised.

⁹Also, women should wear proper clothes that show respect and self-control, not using plaited hair or gold or pearls or expensive clothes. ¹⁰Instead, they should do good deeds, which is right for women who say they worship God.

¹¹Let a woman learn by listening quietly and being ready to co-operate in everything. ¹²But I do not allow a woman to teach or to have authority over a man, but to listen quietly, ¹³because Adam was formed first and then Eve. ¹⁴And Adam was not tricked, but the woman was tricked and became a sinner. ¹⁵But she will be saved through having children if they continue in faith, love and holiness, with self-control.

Elders in the Church

3 What I say is true: anyone wanting to become an elder *d* desires a good work. ²An elder must not give people a reason to criticise him, and he must have only one wife. He must be self-controlled, wise, respected by others, ready to welcome guests and able to teach. ³He must not drink too much wine or like to fight, but rather be gentle and peaceful, not loving money. ⁴He must be a good family leader, having children who co-operate with full respect. ⁵(If someone does not know how to lead the family, how can that person take care of God's church?) ⁶But an elder must not be a new believer, or he might be too proud of himself and be judged guilty just as the devil was. ⁷An elder must also have the respect of people who are not in the church so he will not be criticised by others and caught in the devil's trap.

FORGIVENESS

Oops!

Jon had cycled home from school since the age of twelve. Every day he sped out of the school gates and along the road. He passed the butchers and the newsagents, then turned a corner and continued until the driveway of his house was in sight.

After all these years, Jon didn't really need to think about cycling home – it seemed to take care of itself almost automatically. He'd become quite skilful at swerving into the drive and avoiding his father's small saloon car by inches. Fortunately, his dad always parked the car in the same place, so Jon had no trouble in navigating his way around it.

But today he did and it was too late to do anything by the time he realised that the saloon car had been replaced with a brand new estate. He crashed into the side of the car then sat, dazed, staring at the spinning wheel of his bicycle.

"What have you done?" he heard his dad cry in pain. "My car!"

"Oops!" Jon sighed to himself.

"Sorry Dad, I haven't done any damage, have I?"

His dad inspected the door of his new pride and joy and saw a long, deep scratch in the paintwork. "Yes," he murmured.

Jon felt sick. "I didn't expect it," he said.

"I bought it this afternoon. I've been planning to surprise the family for weeks with it . . . It looks like I certainly surprised you."

"I'm sorry," Jon said again.

His dad nodded. "Apology accepted. Just remember to be a bit more careful in future, eh?"

Jon sighed with relief. He didn't expect to be forgiven as easily as that, but he was glad that he had been. Jon's dad showed mercy towards his son. **1 Timothy 1:12–17** also talks about mercy.

* Why were Jon and the writer of 1 Timothy thankful for the forgiveness they received?
* How might God's forgiveness help you to deal with the sins you've committed?

Consider . . .

* asking God to forgive you for anything you have done wrong.
* showing someone mercy the next time they do something wrong to you. Tell them that you have forgiven them and don't bear any grudge.

For more, see . . .

* Genesis 50:15–21 (p.57)
* 2 Corinthians 2:5–10 (p.1241)
* Matthew 6:14–15 (p.948)

Deacons in the Church

⁸In the same way, deacons *d* must be respected by others, not saying things they do not mean. They must not drink too much wine or try to get rich by cheating others. ⁹With a clear conscience they must follow the secret of the faith that God made known to us. ¹⁰Test them first. Then let them serve as deacons if you find nothing wrong in them. ¹¹In the same way, women *n* must be respected by others. They must not speak evil of others. They must be self-controlled and trustworthy in everything. ¹²Deacons must have only one wife and be good leaders of their children and their own families. ¹³Those who serve well as deacons are making an honourable place for themselves, and they will be very bold in their faith in Christ Jesus.

The Secret of Our Life

¹⁴Although I hope I can come to you soon, I am writing these things to you now. ¹⁵Then, even if I am delayed, you will know how to live in the family of God. That family is the church of the living God, the support and foundation of the truth. ¹⁶Without doubt, the secret of our life of worship is great:

He was shown to us in a human body,
    proved right in spirit, *d*
and seen by angels.
    He was preached to those who are not
        Jews,
    believed in by the world,
        and taken up in glory.

A Warning About False Teachers

4 Now the Holy Spirit *d* clearly says that in the later times some people will stop believing the faith. They will follow spirits that lie and teachings of demons. *d* ²Such teachings come from the false words of liars whose understanding is destroyed as if by a hot iron. ³They forbid people to marry and tell them not to eat certain foods

---

women   This might mean the wives of the deacons, or it might mean women who serve in the same way as deacons.

PRAYER

Pray For All People

"I'm sailing tonight to Saudi Arabia. I'll see you when I get back."

Diane put the phone down. Saudi Arabia? Her boyfriend Gary was going to Saudi Arabia with the army. She didn't even really know where Saudi Arabia was!

She said a quick prayer, asking God to keep Gary safe.

Diane swallowed the lump in her throat and searched for a world atlas. She was terrified that something could happen to Gary, but she at least wanted to know where he was going.

During the worship service on Sunday, her minister said, "Let's pray for all people," and then listed different parts of the world, including Saudi Arabia. Diane's mind usually wandered during those prayers, since the places seemed so far away and irrelevant to her life. But this time she paid attention.

What happened in Saudi Arabia really did affect her life.

When Diane's boyfriend suddenly went overseas, she understood the importance of praying for all people. **1 Timothy 2:1–4** expands our prayer concerns beyond ourselves and reminds us that God cares for the whole world.

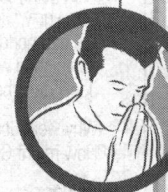

* How does praying for a country such as Saudi Arabia fit the message?
* Which countries and rulers should you pray for today?

Consider . . .

* reading the international section of your newspaper. Ask members of your church to pray for the people mentioned there.
* looking at a world atlas, and praying for people in different parts of the world. Pray for them each evening.

For more, see . . .

* Psalm 46 (p.527)
* James 5:13–18 (p.1353)

* Ephesians 6:18–20 (p.1277)

which God created to be eaten with thanks by people who believe and know the truth. ⁴Everything God made is good, and nothing should be refused if it is accepted with thanks, ⁵because it is made holy by what God has said and by prayer.

Be a Good Servant of Christ

⁶By telling these things to the brothers and sisters, *n* you will be a good servant of Christ Jesus. You will be made strong by the words of the faith and the good teaching which you have been following. ⁷But do not follow foolish stories that disagree with God's truth, but train yourself to serve God. ⁸Training your body helps you in some ways, but serving God helps you in every way by bringing you blessings in this life and in

the future life too. ⁹What I say is true, and you should fully accept it. ¹⁰This is why we work and struggle: we hope in the living God who is the Saviour *d* of all people, especially of those who believe.

¹¹Command and teach these things. ¹²Do not let anyone treat you as if you are unimportant because you are young. Instead, be an example to the believers with your words, your actions, your love, your faith, and your pure life. ¹³Until I come, continue to read the Scriptures *d* to the people, strengthen them, and teach them. ¹⁴Use the gift you have, which was given to you through prophecy *d* when the group of elders *d* laid their hands on *n* you. ¹⁵Continue to do those things; give your life to doing them so your progress may be seen by everyone. ¹⁶Be careful in your life and in your teaching. If you continue to live and teach rightly, you will save both yourself and those who listen to you.

Rules for Living with Others

5 Do not speak angrily to an older man, but plead with him as if he were your father.

Treat younger men like brothers, ²older women like mothers and younger women like sisters. Always treat them in a pure way.

³Take care of widows who are truly widows. ⁴But if a widow has children or grandchildren, let them first learn to do their duty to their own family and to repay their parents or grandparents. That pleases God. ⁵The true widow, who is all alone, puts her hope in God and continues to pray night and day for God's help. ⁶But the widow who uses her life to please herself is really dead while she is alive. ⁷Tell the believers to do these things so that no one can criticise them. ⁸Whoever does not care for his own relatives, especially his own family members, has turned against the faith and is worse than someone who does not believe in God.

⁹To be on the list of widows, a woman must be at least 60 years old. She must have been faithful to her husband. ¹⁰She must be known for her good works—works such as raising her children, accepting strangers, washing the feet of God's people, helping those in trouble and giving her life to do all kinds of good deeds.

¹¹But do not put younger widows on that list. After they give themselves to Christ, they may be pulled away from him by their physical needs, and then they will want to marry again. ¹²They will be judged for not doing what they first promised to do. ¹³Besides that, they would learn to waste their time, going from house to house. And they not only waste their time but also may begin to gossip and busy themselves with other people's lives, saying things they should not say. ¹⁴So I want the younger widows to marry, have children and take care of their homes. Then no enemy will have any reason to criticise them. ¹⁵But some have already turned away to follow Satan.

¹⁶If any woman who is a believer has widows in her family, she should care for them herself. The church should not have to care for them. Then it will be able to take care of those who are truly widows.

¹⁷The elders *d* who lead the church well should receive double honour, especially those who work hard by speaking and teaching, ¹⁸because the Scripture *d* says: "When an ox is working in the grain, do not cover its mouth to keep it from eating," *n* and "A worker should be given his pay." *n*

---

brothers and sisters Although the Greek text says "brothers" here and throughout this book, Paul's words were meant for the entire church, both men and women.
laid their hands on The laying on of hands had many purposes, including the giving of a blessing, power or authority.
"When . . . eating," Quotation from Deuteronomy 25:4.
"A worker . . . pay." Quoted in Luke 10:7.

[19]Do not listen to someone who accuses an elder, without two or three witnesses. [20]Tell those who continue sinning that they are wrong. Do this in front of the whole church so that the others will have a warning.

[21]Before God and Christ Jesus and the chosen angels, I command you to do these things without showing favour of any kind to anyone.

[22]Think carefully before you lay your hands on [n] anyone, and don't share in the sins of others. Keep yourself pure.

[23]Stop drinking only water, but drink a little wine to help your stomach and your frequent sicknesses.

[24]The sins of some people are easy to see even before they are judged, but the sins of others are seen only later. [25]So also good deeds are easy to see, but even those that are not easily seen cannot stay hidden.

6 All who are slaves under a yoke [d] should show full respect to their masters so no one will speak against God's name and our teaching. [2]The slaves whose masters are believers should not show their masters any less respect because they are believers. They should serve their masters even better, because they are helping believers they love.

You must teach and preach these things.

False Teaching and True Riches

[3]Anyone who has a different teaching does not agree with the true teaching of our Lord Jesus Christ and the teaching that shows the true way to serve God. [4]This person is full of pride and understands nothing, but is sick with a love for arguing and fighting about words. This brings jealousy, fighting, speaking against others, evil mistrust [5]and constant quarrels from those who

---

lay your hands on   The laying on of hands had many purposes, including the giving of a blessing, power or authority.

MONEY

The Root of All Evil

We can do whatever we want with our own money, can't we? That's what we usually think. If anyone steals money from us, we want it back. If someone asks us for money on the street, we feel that we should keep the cash deep in our pockets. If we go to church and the collection comes to us, we might put some change in to make sure that people see it and possibly hear a clinking of coins, but we're not going to put much in – it would be like throwing it away.

But God has a totally different view of our money. Like everything else we have, it really belongs to him. Because it's really his, we should be careful about how we spend it. It hasn't just come to us because we've got it as a present from a relative, as an allowance, or because we've earned it – it's actually a gift from God.

A little bit of money can go a long way when God uses it. It could be used to feed hungry people in the Third World. Or it might end up buying Bibles for a country where there's a shortage of them. Or it could be used to buy a Christian book that would help us to follow Jesus better.

God cares about our money: he can use it to change people's lives. Let's ask God to help us resist the temptation just to buy another DVD or pair of trainers or computer game, and think about something different we can do with our cash instead.

Read **1 Timothy 6:6–16**.

* What makes us spend our money as we do?
* What do verses 10 and 11 tell us we should be concentrating on?

Consider . . .

* ways of using some of your money to help people who need it more than you do.
* buying something for yourself that will help you follow Jesus better.

For more, see . . .

* Psalm 24:1 (p.514)
* 1 Corinthians 4:7 (p.1219)
* Luke 21:1–4 (p.1085)

have evil minds and have lost the truth. They think that serving God is a way to get rich.

⁶Serving God does make us very rich, if we are satisfied with what we have. ⁷We brought nothing into the world, so we can take nothing out. ⁸But, if we have food and clothes, we will be satisfied with that. ⁹Those who want to become rich bring temptation to themselves and are caught in a trap. They want many foolish and harmful things that ruin and destroy people. ¹⁰The love of money causes all kinds of evil. Some people have left the faith, because they wanted to get more money, but they have caused themselves much sorrow.

Some Things to Remember

¹¹But you, man of God, run away from all those things. Instead, live in the right way,

serve God, have faith, love, patience and gentleness. ¹²Fight the good fight of faith, grabbing hold of the life that continues for ever. You were called to have that life when you confessed the good confession before many witnesses. ¹³In the sight of God, who gives life to everything, and of Christ Jesus, I give you a command. Christ Jesus made the good confession when he stood before Pontius Pilate. ¹⁴Do what you were commanded to do without wrong or blame until our Lord Jesus Christ comes again. ¹⁵God will make that happen at the right time. He is the blessed and only Ruler, the King of all kings and the Lord of all lords. ¹⁶He is the only One who never dies. He lives in light so bright no one can go near it. No one has ever seen God, or can see him.

FAITH

Knowing it All

Professor Cooper was a very intelligent man. His academic work had won him many awards and prizes. The professor was greatly respected in his community, which was why the local primary school asked him if he would come to speak at one of their morning assemblies.

The professor gave a talk about how important it was to study hard at school, and told the children how hard he had worked and the great things that had happened in his life because of his successful studying. He finished his talk by asking the children what the best thing was that they had ever learnt.

A little boy from the youngest class put his hand up. In a squeaky, yet confident voice the boy said, "Jesus loves me and Jesus loves you."

The professor was stunned; tears welled in his eyes. It was something that he had last heard many years ago at Sunday school when he himself was little; it was something that he had once believed, and yet had ignored for all these years. Suddenly everything that he had learnt and achieved seemed worthless compared to this wonderful faith of a six-year-old.

In the early days of the church, some people were losing sight of the simple message that Jesus had brought, and were being sucked into a false religion called "Gnosticism". This told people that the way to be saved by God was to gain lots of knowledge. Read **1 Timothy 6:20–21** to see what advice Paul gave to the Christians.

* What does this story and the Bible passage tell us is the most important thing to understand?
* According to both the passage and the story, what is in our care that needs to be "looked after" or it will be lost?

Consider . . .

* asking God to make clearer those parts of the gospel that you find difficult to understand, and if you can, ask a good Christian friend to help you too.
* praying that as you learn more about Jesus, you will never lose sight of the very simple message of love that he brought.

For more, see . . .

* 2 Chronicles 1:7–12 (p.402)
* Ephesians 3:16–19 (p.1271)
* Matthew 25:14–30 (p.986)

May honour and power belong to God for ever. Amen.

¹⁷Command those who are rich with things of this world not to be proud. Tell them to hope in God, not in their uncertain riches. God richly gives us everything to enjoy. ¹⁸Tell the rich people to do good, to be rich in doing good deeds, to be generous and ready to share. ¹⁹By doing that, they will be saving a treasure for themselves as a strong foundation for the future. Then they will be able to have the life that is true life.

²⁰Timothy, guard what God has trusted to you. Stay away from foolish, useless talk and from the arguments of what is falsely called "knowledge".

²¹By saying they have that "knowledge", some have missed the true faith.

Grace be with you.

Sidelight

Saying that Jesus Christ is "King of all kings and the Lord of all lords" (1 Timothy 6:15) was a bold statement in the midst of the persecution that the early Christians faced. Near the end of the first century, the Roman emperor Domitian demanded that his subjects address him as "Lord and God". Christians who refused were threatened, exiled and put to death.

2 Timothy

Why Read This Book:

- Be encouraged to keep following God, even when you face danger for doing it (2 Timothy 1—2).
- Find out how to make it through tough times (2 Timothy 3—4).

When?

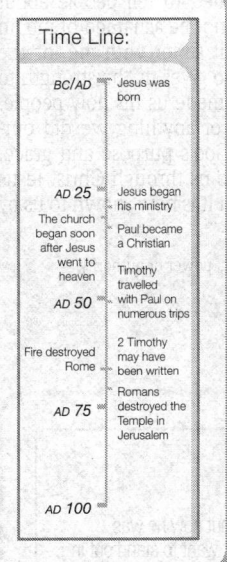

Time Line:

BC/AD	Jesus was born
AD 25	Jesus began his ministry
The church began soon after Jesus went to heaven	Paul became a Christian
AD 50	Timothy travelled with Paul on numerous trips
Fire destroyed Rome	2 Timothy may have been written
AD 75	Romans destroyed the Temple in Jerusalem
AD 100	

Behind the Scenes:

People who know they are soon to die often divide up their belongings and ask those around them to finish the jobs they have started. Paul knew he was facing death (2 Timothy 4:6–8), so – just like a relay runner – he wrote this letter to hand over the baton of ministry for Timothy to carry on.

2 Timothy captures what a retiring leader would say to a new leader. It gives lots of encouragement. It gives advice on how to become a leader. And it says that the road will be rocky and rough at times, but that we should remain strong anyway.

While 1 Timothy gives instructions on how to run a church, 2 Timothy is a personal letter – like one you would write to a close friend. It encourages Christians facing tough times, since the Roman government was persecuting Christians. And it can encourage us to stick to our faith today, even when people try to pull us away.

Where?

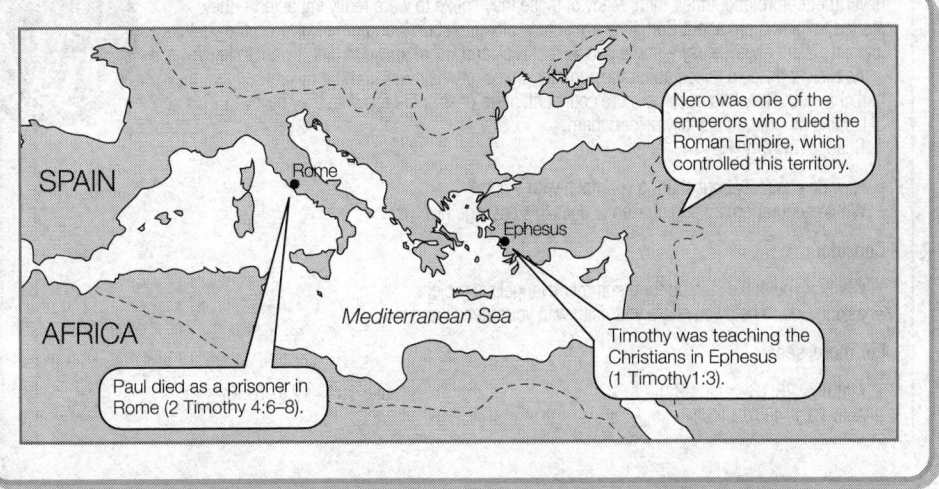

Nero was one of the emperors who ruled the Roman Empire, which controlled this territory.

SPAIN

Rome

Ephesus

Mediterranean Sea

AFRICA

Timothy was teaching the Christians in Ephesus (1 Timothy 1:3).

Paul died as a prisoner in Rome (2 Timothy 4:6–8).

1 From Paul, an apostle *d* of Christ Jesus by the will of God. God sent me to tell about the promise of life that is in Christ Jesus.

[2]To Timothy, a dear child to me:

Grace, mercy and peace to you from God the Father and Christ Jesus our Lord.

Encouragement for Timothy

[3]I thank God as I always mention you in my prayers, day and night. I serve him, doing what I know is right as my ancestors did. [4]Remembering that you cried for me, I want very much to see you so I can be filled with joy. [5]I remember your true faith. That faith first lived in your grandmother Lois and in your mother Eunice, and I know you now have that same faith. [6]This is why I remind you to keep using the gift God gave you when I laid my hands on *n* you. Now let it grow, as a small flame grows into a fire. [7]God did not give us a spirit that makes us afraid but a spirit of power and love and self-control.

[8]So do not be ashamed to tell people about our Lord Jesus, and do not be ashamed of me, in prison for the Lord. But suffer with me for the Good News. *d* God, who gives us the strength to do that, [9]saved us and made us his holy people. That was not because of anything we did ourselves but because of God's purpose and grace. That grace was given to us through Christ Jesus before time began, [10]but it is now shown to us by

---

laid my hands on   The laying on of hands had many purposes, including the giving of a blessing, power or authority.

SHARING FAITH

Stand Out or Sit Down?

Nick signed up to a summer evangelism project. It seemed like a good idea at the time, but now he was beginning to question whether it was "him" or not. Nick was quite a shy person, he didn't want to stand out in the crowd, he just wanted to be like everybody else. People would often say that to be a Christian was to be distinctive, to be different. This was the last thing that Nick wanted – he wanted to be normal. Just as Nick was about to pull out of the summer team, Robin, a friend from his youth group told Nick how he had encouraged him to think about sharing his faith too. Robin wanted to sign up to go on the summer team with Nick. What was Nick to do now? He could pull out and let Robin go on his own, or they could both go together.

It seemed a bit easier for Nick, knowing that Robin was going to be with him for this summer project. The two friends talked about what they expected to happen over the summer, they shared their hopes and their fears together. Nick was glad that Robin was going on the team – he wouldn't have made it otherwise.

The two friends went off on their summer project. It was a great time: challenging at times, fun at times and also terrifying at times. Nick and Robin found themselves talking to people they had never met before about their faith. Many of those they spoke to were really impacted – they started to think more about God, they even came along to church and got involved in the youth club. It wasn't always easy – some people that Nick and Robin spoke to didn't want to know.

As Nick and Robin talked about the summer project on their way home they realised that they had changed. They had become more confident, more passionate for what they believed. This act of helping others had actually helped them.

Read **2 Timothy 1:3–14**.

* How do you feel about sharing your faith with others?
* What encouragement and challenge does this passage give you?

Consider . . .

* whether you could sign up for a summer evangelism project.
* asking God to help you share your faith with your friends and family.

For more, see . . .

* Matthew 28:16–20 (p.994)
* Acts 10:1–48 (p.1154)
* Luke 10:1–12 (p.1056)

the coming of our Saviour [d] Christ Jesus. He destroyed death, and through the Good News he showed us the way to have life that cannot be destroyed. [11]I was chosen to tell that Good News

and to be an apostle and a teacher. [12]I am suffering now because I tell the Good News, but I am not ashamed, because I know Jesus, the One in whom I have believed. And I am sure he is able to protect what he has trusted me with until that day. [n] [13]Follow the pattern of true teachings that you heard from me in faith and love, which are in Christ Jesus. [14]Protect the truth that you were given; protect it with the help of the Holy Spirit [d] who lives in us.

[15]You know that everyone in the country of Asia has left me, even Phygelus and Hermogenes. [16]May the Lord show mercy to the family of Onesiphorus, who has often helped me and was not ashamed that I was in prison. [17]When he came to Rome, he looked eagerly for me until he found me. [18]May the Lord allow him to find mercy from the Lord on that day. You know how many ways he helped me in Ephesus.

A Loyal Soldier of Christ Jesus

2 You then, Timothy, my child, be strong in the grace we have in Christ Jesus. [2]You should teach people whom you can trust the things you and many others have heard me say. Then they will be able to teach others. [3]Share in the troubles we have like a good soldier of Christ Jesus. [4]A soldier wants to please the enlisting officer, so no one serving in the army wastes time with everyday matters. [5]Also an athlete who takes part in a contest must obey all the rules in order to win. [6]The farmer who works hard should be the first person to get some of the food that was grown. [7]Think about what I am saying, because the Lord will give you the ability to understand everything.

[8]Remember Jesus Christ, who was raised from the dead, who is from the family of David. This is the Good News [d] I preach, [9]and I am suffering because of it to the point of being bound with chains like a criminal. But God's teaching is not in chains. [10]So I patiently accept all these troubles so that those whom God has chosen can have the salvation that is in Christ Jesus. With that salvation comes glory that never ends. [11]This teaching is true:

If we died with him, we will also live with him.
[12] If we accept suffering, we will also rule with him.
If we refuse to accept him, he will refuse to accept us.
[13] If we are not faithful, he will still be faithful,
because he cannot be false to himself.

A Worker Pleasing to God

[14]Continue teaching these things, warning people in God's presence not to argue about words. It does not help anyone, and it ruins those who listen. [15]Do the best you can to give yourself to God as the kind of person he will accept. Be a worker who is not ashamed and who uses the true teaching in the right way. [16]Stay away from foolish, useless talk, because that will lead people further away from God. [17]Their evil teaching will spread like a sickness inside the body. Hymenaeus and Philetus are like that. [18]They have left the true teaching, saying that the rising from the dead has already taken place, and so they are destroying the faith of some people. [19]But God's strong foundation continues to stand. These words are written on the seal: "The Lord knows those who belong to him," [n] and "Everyone who wants to belong to the Lord must stop doing wrong."

[20]In a large house there are not only things made of gold and silver, but also things made of wood and clay. Some things are used for special purposes, and others are made for ordinary jobs. [21]All who make themselves clean [d] from evil will be used for special purposes. They will be made holy, useful to the Master, ready to do any good work.

[22]But run away from the evil young people like to do. Try hard to live right and to have faith, love and peace, together with those who trust in the Lord from pure hearts. [23]Stay away from foolish and stupid arguments, because you know they grow into quarrels. [24]And a servant of the Lord must not quarrel but must be kind to everyone, a good teacher and patient. [25]The Lord's servant must gently teach those who disagree. Then maybe God will let them change their minds so they can accept the truth. [26]And they may wake

---

day The day Christ will come to judge all people and take his people to live with him.
"The Lord . . . him", Quotation from Numbers 16:5.

up and escape from the trap of the devil, who catches them to do what he wants.

The Last Days

3 Remember this! In the last days there will be many troubles, ²because people will love themselves, love money, boast and be proud. They will say evil things against others and will not obey their parents or be thankful or be the kind of people God wants. ³They will not love others, will refuse to forgive, will gossip and will not control themselves. They will be cruel, will hate what is good, ⁴will turn against their friends and will do foolish things without thinking. They will be conceited, will love pleasure instead of God, ⁵and will act as if they serve God but will not have his power. Stay away from those people. ⁶Some of them go into homes and get control of weak women who are full of sin and are led by many evil desires. ⁷These women are always learning new teachings, but they are never able to understand the truth fully. ⁸Just as Jannes and

PATIENCE

Worth the Wait

For 30 years, Rosa Parks bristled at the inequalities all around her. Because she was black, she had to ride at the back of the bus. Her skin colour made everything more difficult for her in the segregated South of the USA.

On her way home from work in 1955, in Montgomery, Alabama, Rosa boarded a bus and filled a vacant seat. She was exhausted. Her neck, shoulders and back ached from sewing alterations all day. A few white people boarded the bus after Rosa, and they all found seats, except for one white man.

The bus driver asked someone to give up a seat, meaning that a black person was to give up a seat for the white person. Since Rosa was sitting in a seat closest to the front and closest to the aisle, everyone looked at her. But Rosa would not budge. Finally, two police officers arrested her.

Rosa's arrest stirred an uproar in the black community. People were furious at the unfairness of forcing a black woman to give up her seat on a bus to a white man just because of her skin colour.

People gathered at Dexter Avenue Baptist Church to organise a bus boycott that made history and brought Martin Luther King Jr to national attention. The 381-day boycott required intense patience and endurance as the organisers set up car pools to take workers who relied on the buses. The boycott succeeded when Montgomery buses were made desegregated in 1956. No longer would blacks be forced to give up their seats for whites.

Because of Rosa Parks's patience and the patience of the boycott leaders, the civil rights movement of the 1950s and 1960s was born. By refusing to budge, Rosa showed the patience reflected in **2 Timothy 2:8–13**.

* How are the patience and suffering mentioned in this passage like the patience and suffering of blacks in the boycott?
* How could this passage help you to be more patient during difficult times?

Consider . . .

* asking God for patience to deal with a problem that you are facing, and then being patient.
* talking with your family about creating a rule for silently counting to fifteen when someone tries a family member's patience.

For more, see . . .

* Numbers 11:4–20 (p.139)
* 1 Peter 4:12–19 (p.1361)
* Romans 8:16–18 (p.1195)

Jambres were against Moses, these people are against the truth. Their thinking has been ruined, and they have failed in trying to follow the faith. ⁹But they will not be successful in what they do, because as with Jannes and Jambres, everyone will see that they are foolish.

Obey the Teachings

¹⁰But you have followed what I teach, the way I live, my goal, faith, patience and love. You know I never give up. ¹¹You know how I have been hurt and have suffered, as in Antioch, Iconium and Lystra. I have suffered, but the Lord saved me from all those troubles. ¹²Everyone who wants to live as God desires, in Christ Jesus, will be hurt. ¹³But people who are evil and cheat others will go from bad to worse. They will fool others, but they will also be fooling themselves. ¹⁴But you should continue following the teachings you learned. You know they are true,

because you trust those who taught you. ¹⁵Since you were a child you have known the Holy Scriptures*d* which are able to make you wise. And that wisdom leads to salvation through faith in Christ Jesus. ¹⁶All Scripture is given by God and is useful for teaching, for showing people what is wrong in their lives, for correcting faults and for teaching how to live right. ¹⁷Using the Scriptures, the person who serves God will be capable, having all that is needed to do every good work.

4 I give you a command in the presence of God and Christ Jesus, the One who will judge the living and the dead, and by his coming and his kingdom: ²preach the Good News. *d* Be ready at all times, and tell people what they need to do. Tell them when they are wrong. Encourage them with great patience and careful teaching, ³because the time will come when people will not listen to the true teaching but will find many more teachers who please them by saying

BIBLE STUDY

Take Time to Learn

Reading the Bible is important, isn't it? But do you do it? Many American Christian teenagers don't, said *Teenage* magazine:

* 13 per cent of Christian teenagers say they never read their Bible.
* Only 8 per cent say they read the Bible every day.
* 44 per cent say they read the Bible only when they feel like it.
* And the rest, 35 per cent, read the Bible a few times a week, or less.

The evidence shows that the same is probably true for Britain and Australia as well.
Teenagers say the top five reasons for not reading the Bible are:

1. They are too busy.
2. They would rather do something else.
3. They think the Bible is boring.
4. They don't know how to study the Bible.
5. They forget to read it.

The Bible has been called the most printed and the least read of all books. Teenagers might get a lot from the Bible if they read it knowing the value of Scripture as described in **2 Timothy 3:14—4:5**.

* According to this passage, of what value is Bible study to the Christian's life?
* What can you do to make Bible study an important part of your life?

Consider . . .

* asking your youth minister or pastor for tips on how to make Bible study easier and more effective.
* spending one week reading through one of the Gospels (Matthew, Mark, Luke or John) with a friend, meeting every day at lunch to discuss what you have learned in your reading.

For more, see . . .

* Psalm 119:97–104 (p.573)
* 2 Timothy 1:13–14 (p.1317)
* John 5:39 (p.1104)

the things they want to hear. [4]They will stop listening to the truth and will begin to follow false stories. [5]But you should control yourself at all times, accept troubles, do the work of telling the Good News and complete all the duties of a servant of God.

[6]My life is being given as an offering to God, and the time has come for me to leave this life. [7]I have fought the good fight, I have finished the race, I have kept the faith. [8]Now, a crown is being held for me—a crown for being right with God. The Lord, the judge who judges rightly, will give the crown to me on that day [n]—not only to me but to all those who have waited with love for him to come again.

Personal Words

[9]Do your best to come to me as soon as you can, [10]because Demas, who loved this world, left me and went to Thessalonica. Crescens went to Galatia, and Titus went to Dalmatia. [11]Luke is the only one still with me. Get Mark and bring him with you when you come, because he can help me in my work here. [12]I sent Tychicus to Ephesus. [13]When I was in Troas, I left my coat there with Carpus. So when you come, bring it to me, along with my books, particularly the ones written on parchment. [n]

[14]Alexander the metalworker did many harmful things against me. The Lord will punish him for what he did. [15]You also should be careful that

day   The day Christ will come to judge all people and take his people to live with him.
parchment   A writing paper made from the skins of sheep.

PERSISTENCE

Practise Makes Perfect

Jeff often went to a big Christian festival and loved the times of worship. He dreamed of one day being able to play in a worship band but there was just one problem – he couldn't play!

But on his fourteenth birthday, sporting a big red bow, tied neatly round the neck was his first guitar. For hours, Jeff strutted around his bedroom, imagining he was playing at a huge venue – thousands of people gasping in awe as he thumped out his guitar solos.

Jeff, like every other person when they start playing an instrument, was . . . rubbish. His music teacher told him he would probably fail his GCSE music and shouldn't bother. Without much subtlety, his parents bought him a pair of headphones, and Jeff started to wonder if he was really cut out to be a musician.

One thing kept him going. Every lunchtime, he met up with the other bad guitarists in Room 3, which was always empty, and played each other the "riff of the week", the thing they'd been pouring over every night in their rooms with their guitars, amps . . . and headphones. It was like a kind of self-help group!

After some time, this group became a band. The band did gigs at school, played at the youth club . . . and Jeff got an A for GCSE music.

There was far more at stake for Paul as he considered what it meant to persist through hard times to reach his life goal. Check it out in **2 Timothy 4:6–18**.

* How does Paul's persistence inspire us?
* What was the thing that kept him going?

Consider . . .

* whether there's stuff you're dealing with right now that seems impossible. Ask God to inspire you and give you the strength to persist.
* whether you know anyone who is struggling at the moment. Encourage them to hang in there and keep going.

For more, see . . .

* Daniel 6 (p.839)
* Philippians 3:12–21 (p.1284)

* Romans 5:1–5 (p.1190)

he does not hurt you, because he fought strongly against our teaching.

[16]The first time I defended myself, no one helped me; everyone left me. May they be forgiven. [17]But the Lord stayed with me and gave me strength so I could fully tell the Good News[d] to all those who are not Jews. So I was saved from the lion's mouth. [18]The Lord will save me when anyone tries to hurt me, and he will bring me safely to his heavenly kingdom. Glory for ever and ever be the Lord's. Amen.

Final Greetings

[19]Greet Priscilla and Aquila and the family of Onesiphorus. [20]Erastus stayed in Corinth, and I left Trophimus sick in Miletus. [21]Try as hard as you can to come to me before winter.

Eubulus sends greetings to you. Also Pudens, Linus, Claudia and all the brothers and sisters in Christ greet you.

[22]The Lord be with your spirit. Grace be with you.

Sidelight Have trouble misplacing things? Take heart. So did the apostle Paul. He left his coat in Troas (2 Timothy 4:13), which was more than a hundred miles from Ephesus, and close to a thousand miles from Rome – the two places he might have been when he asked the people to send the coat to him. This coat was probably a heavy cloak that would have kept Paul warmer in a damp prison cell.

Titus

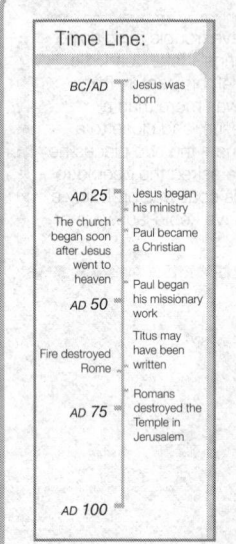

Time Line:

BC/AD	Jesus was born
AD 25	Jesus began his ministry
The church began soon after Jesus went to heaven	Paul became a Christian
AD 50	Paul began his missionary work
Fire destroyed Rome	Titus may have been written
AD 75	Romans destroyed the Temple in Jerusalem
AD 100	

Why Read This Book:

* Find out what it takes to be a Christian leader (Titus 1).
* Discover how to live as a Christian (Titus 2—3).

Behind the Scenes:

Hypocrites – everyone has met them at some time or another. Imagine meeting someone who tells you that they are a Christian, then goes around stealing, cheating other people and spreading lies and rumours about someone. How would you react? Chances are that you wouldn't have anything to do with them if you could possibly help it!

Titus encountered the same sort of people during his visit to Crete. The locals had a reputation for being lazy, telling lies and doing nothing but eating (Titus 1:2). Instead of writing them off, however, he went to work with them, and helped them to grow as Christians.

As you can imagine, it wasn't an easy job, particularly for somebody who was quite young. So Paul encourages Titus to keep up the good work, and gives him some tips about how he can help the Cretans to overcome their past way of life and launch out into living brand new Christian lives.

This letter to Titus is jam-packed with practical, down-to-earth advice, including how Christians should relate to political leaders, those who quarrel about the law and people who start arguments. Like 1 Timothy (p.1307) this letter includes all sorts of practical instructions about Christian leadership mixed in with the basics of belief and help for quality living.

Where?

Before going to Crete, Titus had travelled with Paul in Macedonia (2 Corinthians 7:5–16).

Later in life, Titus ministered in Dalmatia, which is in the former Yugoslavia (2 Timothy 4:10).

Titus was working on the island of Crete (Titus 1:5).

1 From Paul, a servant of God and an apostle *d* of Jesus Christ. I was sent to help the faith of God's chosen people and to help them know the truth that shows people how to serve God. ²That faith and that knowledge come from the hope of life for ever, which God promised to us before time began. And God cannot lie. ³At the right time God let the world know about that life through preaching. He trusted me with that work, and I preached by the command of God our Saviour.

⁴To Titus, my true child in the faith which we share:

Grace and peace from God the Father and Christ Jesus our Saviour.

Titus' Work in Crete

⁵I left you in Crete so you could finish doing the things that still needed to be done and so you could appoint elders *d* in every town, as I directed you. ⁶An elder must not be guilty of doing wrong, must have only one wife, and must have believing children. They must not be known as children who are wild and do not obey. ⁷As a manager of God's work, an elder must not be guilty of doing wrong, being selfish or becoming angry quickly. He must not drink too much wine, like to fight or try to get rich by cheating others. ⁸An elder must be ready to welcome guests, love what is good, be wise,

> **Sidelight** When Titus 1:8 says that elders must accept others into their homes, it means more than just giving them a cup of tea. If a stranger stopped at the door, a hospitable person was expected to feed, lodge, protect and clothe the stranger, if necessary. The Greek word for hospitality literally means "lover of strangers".

live right and be holy and self-controlled. ⁹By holding on to the trustworthy word just as we teach it, an elder can help people by using true teaching, and he can show those who are against the true teaching that they are wrong.

¹⁰There are many people who refuse to obey, who talk about worthless things and lead others into the wrong way—mainly those who say all who are not Jews must be circumcised. *d* ¹¹These people must be stopped, because they are upsetting whole families by teaching things they should not teach, which they do to get rich by cheating people. ¹²Even one of their own prophets said, "Cretan people are always liars, evil animals and lazy people who do nothing but eat." ¹³The words that prophet said are

true. So firmly tell those people they are wrong so they may become strong in the faith, ¹⁴not accepting Jewish false stories and the commands of people who reject the truth. ¹⁵To those who are pure, all things are pure, but to those who are full of sin and do not believe, nothing is pure. Both their minds and their thinking have been ruined. ¹⁶They say they know God, but their actions show they do not accept him. They are hateful people, they refuse to obey and they are useless for doing anything good.

Following the True Teaching

2 But you must tell everyone what to do to follow the true teaching. ²Teach older men to be self-controlled, serious, wise, strong in faith, in love and in patience.

³In the same way, teach older women to be holy in their behaviour, not speaking against others or having the habit of too much wine, but teaching what is good. ⁴Then they can teach the young women to love their husbands, to love their children, ⁵to be wise and pure, to be good workers at home, to be kind and to yield to their husbands. Then no one will be able to criticise the teaching God gave us.

⁶In the same way, encourage young men to be wise. ⁷In every way be an example of doing good deeds. When you teach, do it with honesty and seriousness. ⁸Speak the truth so that you cannot be criticised. Then those who are against you will be ashamed because there is nothing bad to say about us.

⁹Slaves should yield to their own masters at all times, trying to please them and not arguing with them. ¹⁰They should not steal from them but should show their masters they can be fully trusted so that in everything they do they will make the teaching of God our Saviour attractive.

¹¹That is the way we should live, because God's grace that can save everyone has come. ¹²It teaches us not to live against God nor to do the evil things the world wants to do. Instead, that grace teaches us to live now in a wise and right way and in a way that shows we serve God. ¹³We should live like that while we wait for our great hope and the coming of the glory of our great God and Saviour Jesus Christ. ¹⁴He gave himself for us so he might pay the price to free us from all evil and to make us pure people who belong only to him—people who are always wanting to do good deeds.

¹⁵Say these things and encourage the people and tell them what is wrong in their lives, with all authority. Do not let anyone treat you as if you were unimportant.

The Right Way to Live

3 Remind the believers to yield to the authority of rulers and government leaders, to obey them, to be ready to do good, ²to speak no evil about anyone, to live in peace and to be gentle and polite to all people.

³In the past we also were foolish. We did not obey, we were wrong, and we were slaves to many things our bodies wanted and enjoyed. We spent our lives doing evil and being jealous. People hated us, and we hated each other. ⁴But when the kindness and love of God our Saviour was shown, ⁵he saved us because of his mercy. It was not because of good deeds we did to be right with him. He saved us through the washing that made us new people through the Holy Spirit. *d* ⁶God poured out richly upon us that

Holy Spirit through Jesus Christ our Saviour. ⁷Being made right with God by his grace, we could have the hope of receiving the life that never ends.

⁸This teaching is true, and I want you to be sure the people understand these things. Then those who believe in God will be careful to use their lives for doing good. These things are good and will help everyone.

⁹But stay away from those who have foolish arguments and talk about useless family histories and argue and quarrel about the law. *d* Those things are worth nothing and will not help anyone. ¹⁰After a first and second warning, avoid someone who causes arguments. ¹¹You can know that such people are evil and sinful; their own sins prove them wrong.

NON-CHRISTIANS

The Wonder Drug

Alexander Fleming was a brilliant but careless scientific researcher, whose lab was scattered with unfinished experiments. After a long holiday, he found that one of his experiments which had been sitting in the sunlight had gone mouldy. He started experimenting with the mould and found that it could cure illnesses such as meningitis and pneumonia. He had discovered penicillin.

At first, no one took any notice of this remarkable invention, but we now know it as a miracle drug which has saved millions of lives.

Imagine that was you. You've been searching all your life for this cure, and then one day, all of a sudden, it appears. You've done nothing to discover it — it's just been given to you. This drug has the potential to save thousands of lives and cure millions of people — you'd tell the world!

Now imagine it's gone one step further — this drug gives eternal life. It ends unhappiness, it's an invitation to the biggest party ever known, it's a relationship with a guy who loves you so much he died for you, it's a chance to escape all the things that hurt us and make us feel ashamed. It's a fresh start, a new beginning, a cure for every illness and a chance to become perfect. It urges you to practise godliness, to have a pure heart and a desire to do right — qualities that are really attractive to people around you. And the even better news — it's available to everyone.

Despite the initial rebukes and statements of disbelief, you know that people need this drug — and without you, they will never hear about it. Like Alexander Fleming's discovery, only a thousand times better, this is good news! We need to shout it from the rooftops — we've found Jesus!

Read **Titus 2:11 – 3:7**.

* What practical things does this passage tell us about following Jesus?
* How would we respond to those who think this passage implies that God is a killjoy?

Consider . . .

* what we find hard about telling people about Jesus. Why not practise in your head, ways of telling people the Good News, then write them down so that you don't forget them.
* whether you realise how important it is to be open about your faith.

For more, see . . .

* Matthew 28:19–20 (p.995)   • 1 Peter 3:14–16 (p.1360)

Some Things to Remember

¹²When I send Artemas or Tychicus to you, try hard to come to me at Nicopolis, because I have decided to stay there this winter. ¹³Do all you can to help Zenas the lawyer and Apollos on their journey so that they have everything they need. ¹⁴Our people must learn to use their lives for doing good deeds to provide what is necessary so that their lives will not be useless.

¹⁵All who are with me greet you. Greet those who love us in the faith.

Grace be with you all.

Sidelight The reason Paul says he plans to spend the winter in Nicopolis (Titus 3:12) was that ships stopped sailing during the stormy winter months. It made it difficult to get home for Christmas!

Philemon

Why Read This Book:
* Learn how to treat fellow Christians (Philemon 4–7).
* Discover how to see others as friends in Christ (Philemon 8–21).

When?

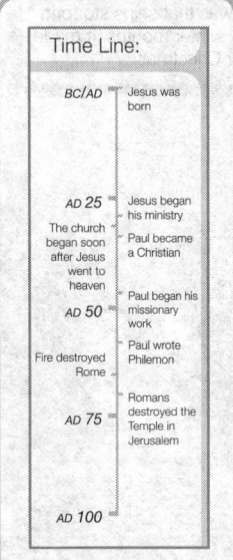

Time Line:

BC/AD	Jesus was born
AD 25	Jesus began his ministry
The church began soon after Jesus went to heaven	Paul became a Christian
AD 50	Paul began his missionary work
Fire destroyed Rome	Paul wrote Philemon
AD 75	Romans destroyed the Temple in Jerusalem
AD 100	

Behind the Scenes:

Life in Roman times could be very hard. Although the Romans were very clever planners and builders and had good laws for the upper classes, they could be very cruel. Onesimus was not one of the privileged people. He was a slave and could be executed. He had stolen from his master, then run away. Under Roman law, a runaway slave had no rights. Disobedience meant possible beatings, branding on the face with a red hot iron and even crucifixion.

But something had happened since Onesimus had left his master. He had become a Christian through Paul's influence. And, making the matter even more complicated, his master Philemon was also a Christian. Onesimus knew he should return to his master, but he also knew that he could die if he went back.

So Paul wrote this letter to persuade Philemon to forgive Onesimus and welcome him back as a Christian friend. Instead of telling Philemon to punish Onesimus, Paul asked that the wrongdoing be charged to Paul.

Though we no longer live with slavery, we, like Philemon, may be tempted to look down on people because of the colour of their skin, the amount of money they have, or what they wear. And we may treat them as second class citizens and think we are first class. In Philemon, Paul challenges all of us to rethink those prejudices.

Where?

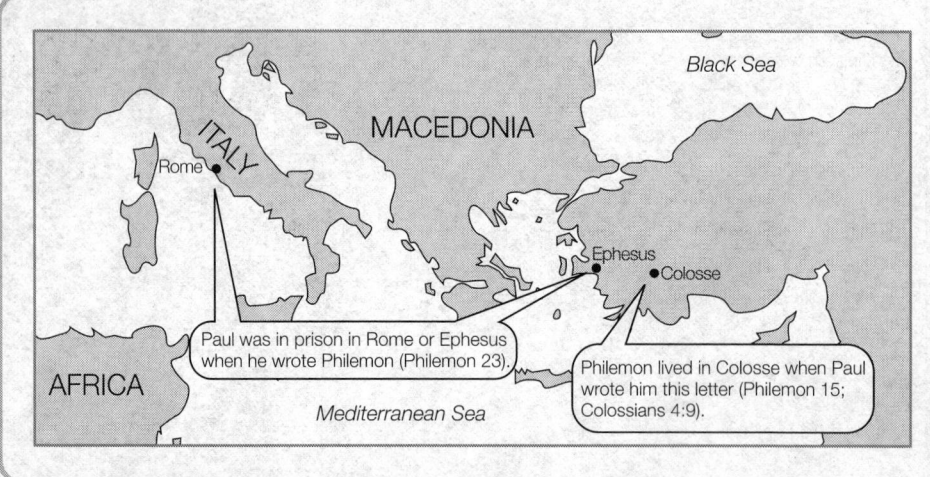

Black Sea

MACEDONIA

ITALY

Rome

Ephesus

Colosse

AFRICA

Mediterranean Sea

Paul was in prison in Rome or Ephesus when he wrote Philemon (Philemon 23).

Philemon lived in Colosse when Paul wrote him this letter (Philemon 15; Colossians 4:9).

¹From Paul, a prisoner of Christ Jesus, and from Timothy, our brother.

To Philemon, our dear friend and worker with us; ²to Apphia, our sister; to Archippus, a worker with us; and to the church that meets in your home:

³Grace and peace to you from God our Father and the Lord Jesus Christ.

Philemon's Love and Faith

⁴I always thank my God when I mention you in my prayers, ⁵because I hear about the love you have for all God's holy people and the faith you have in the Lord Jesus. ⁶I pray that the faith you share may make you understand every blessing we have in Christ. ⁷I have great joy and comfort, my brother, because the love you have shown to God's people has refreshed them.

Accept Onesimus as a Brother

⁸So, in Christ, I could be bold and order you to do what is right. ⁹But because I love you, I am pleading with you instead. I, Paul, an old man now and also a prisoner for Christ Jesus, ¹⁰am pleading with you for my child Onesimus, who became my child while I was in prison. ¹¹In the past he was useless to you, but now he has become useful for both you and me.

¹²I am sending him back to you, and with him I am sending my own heart. ¹³I wanted to keep him with me so that in your place he might help me while I am in prison for the Good News. *d* ¹⁴But I did not want to do anything without asking you first so that any good you do for me will be because you want to do it, not because I forced you. ¹⁵Maybe Onesimus was separated from you for a short time so you could have him back for ever— ¹⁶no longer as a slave, but better

FRIENDS

When Friends Let You Down

Mr Green was one of those cool teachers that everyone loved. Every term he would set an assignment that involved a presentation in front of the class. For most students, this was the highlight of the term. Everyone wanted to do well. Everyone except Simon.

Simon, Jess and Ryan were best friends, and thought it would be great to work together on Mr Green's project. Unfortunately, Simon suffered from an extreme case of full-on laziness. If he could avoid work of any kind, he would.

Jess and Ryan worked hard, preparing their bits of the presentation, doing extra work at home and giving up their lunchtimes to do research. But rather than gathering materials, Simon played football; instead of researching . . . well, who knows what he did!

As Jess and Ryan realised that Simon hadn't done any of the things he'd said he was going to do for the project, their relationship got more and more strained and they stopped hanging out with him.

With one day to go, Jess and Ryan went to Simon and explained to him how what he had done had made them feel. He was gutted, but determined to make amends. They stayed up all night and finished the presentation.

The next day, they did the presentation and Mr Green was amazed, it was so good. Simon got the chance to redeem himself – an A grade won, a friendship restored.

Read **Philemon 4–21** and see what Paul says to Philemon after Onesimus has let him down.

* How does Paul prepare a way for Onesimus and Philemon's friendship?
* How easy would you find it to be a friend to the friendless?

Consider . . .

* whether a friend has ever let you down. How did you deal with it?
* whether there is anyone you know who could do with a friend right now?

For more, see . . .

* Job 42:7–12 (p.498)   * John 21:15–19 (p.1134)
* Romans 3:23–24 (p.1187)

than a slave, as a loved brother. I love him very much, but you will love him even more, both as a person and as a believer in the Lord.

[17]So if you consider me your partner, welcome

Onesimus as you would welcome me. [18]If he has done anything wrong to you or if he owes you anything, charge that to me. [19]I, Paul, am writing

this with my own hand. I will pay it back, and I will say nothing about what you owe me for your own life. [20]So, my brother, I ask that you do this for me in the Lord: refresh my heart in Christ. [21]I write this letter, knowing that you will do what I ask you and even more.

[22]One more thing—prepare a room for me in which to stay, because I hope God will answer your prayers and I will be able to come to you.

Final Greetings

[23]Epaphras, a prisoner with me for Christ Jesus, sends greetings to you. [24]And also Mark, Aristarchus, Demas and Luke, workers together with me, send greetings.

[25]The grace of our Lord Jesus Christ be with your spirit.

Hebrews

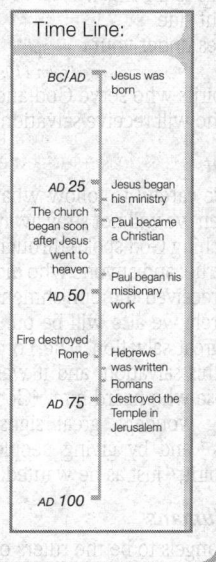

When?

Time Line:

BC/AD	Jesus was born
AD 25	Jesus began his ministry
The church began soon after Jesus went to heaven	Paul became a Christian
AD 50	Paul began his missionary work
Fire destroyed Rome	Hebrews was written
AD 75	Romans destroyed the Temple in Jerusalem
AD 100	

Why Read This Book:

• Discover how Jesus Christ fulfilled God's promises (Hebrews 1—7).
• Learn about the sacrifice Jesus made for us (Hebrews 8—10).
• Be challenged to stay strong in your faith (Hebrews 11—13).

Behind the Scenes:

Imagine a courtroom scene. The jury has heard persuasive testimony from many different people. Now the jury is about to go behind closed doors to come to a verdict about whether Christianity does hold the truth. But first the lawyers will present their closing arguments.

The book of Hebrews is like a closing argument in defence of Christianity. Using careful logic and referring often to testimony, the writer shows that Jesus Christ is the Son of God and worthy of our faith. The book compares and contrasts Jesus with all of Old Testament history and argues that Jesus is the climax of everything in the past.

So, the author concludes, "Let us look only to Jesus, the One who began our faith and who makes it perfect. . . . Think about Jesus' example. . . . So do not get tired and stop trying" (Hebrews 12:2–3).

We don't know how the original readers responded to the convincing argument in Hebrews. But we do know that the book has become a treasured source of encouragement and hope for Christians through the centuries. Just as this letter encouraged its first readers to hold strong to their faith, it can do the same for us today.

LIFE FILE LINKS

Investigate the Theme

To find a list of real life stories on this subject turn to the LIFE FILE GUIDE on pages 12 to 22 at the front of the Youth Bible.

JESUS CHRIST

God Spoke Through His Son

1 In the past God spoke to our ancestors through the prophets *d* many times and in many different ways. ²But now in these last days God has spoken to us through his Son. God has chosen his Son to own all things, and through him he made the world. ³The Son reflects the glory of God and shows exactly what God is like. He holds everything together with his powerful word. When the Son made people clean from their sins, he sat down at the right side of God, the Great One in heaven. ⁴The Son became much greater than the angels, and God gave him a name that is much greater than theirs.

> **Sidelight**   We don't know who wrote Hebrews. Its goal was to show Christ's superiority to the Old Testament laws. Because of this, many people find it useful to read Hebrews alongside Leviticus, because of the connections (for example, read Hebrews 9:11—10:18, p.1337, alongside Leviticus 4, p.103).

⁵This is because God never said to any of the angels,

"You are my Son.
Today I have become your Father." *Psalm 2:7*

Nor did God say of any angel,

"I will be his father,
and he will be my son." *2 Samuel 7:14*

⁶And when God brings his firstborn Son into the world, he says,

"All the gods should worship him." *n* *Psalm 97:7*

⁷This is what God said about the angels:

"God makes his angels become like winds.
He makes his servants become like flames
of fire." *Psalm 104:4*

⁸But God said this about his Son:

"God, your throne will last for ever and
ever.
You will rule your kingdom with fairness.
⁹You love right and hate evil,
so God has chosen you from among your
friends;
he has set you apart with much joy." *Psalm 45:6–7*

¹⁰God also says,

"In the beginning you made the earth,
and your hands made the skies.

¹¹They will be destroyed, but you will remain.
They will all wear out like clothes.
¹²And, like clothes, you will change them and
throw them away.
But you never change,
and your life will never end." *Psalm 102:25–27*

¹³And God never said this to an angel:

"Sit by me at my right side
until I put your enemies under your
control." *n* *Psalm 110:1*

¹⁴All the angels are spirits who serve God and are sent to help those who will receive salvation.

Our Salvation is Great

2 So we must be more careful to follow what we were taught. Then we will not stray away from the truth. ²The teaching God spoke through angels was shown to be true, and anyone who did not follow it or obey it received the punishment that was earned. ³So surely we also will be punished if we ignore this great salvation. The Lord himself first told about this salvation, and it was proven true to us by those who heard him. ⁴God also proved it by using wonders, great signs, many kinds of miracles *d* and by giving people gifts through the Holy Spirit, *d* just as he wanted.

Christ Became like Humans

⁵God did not choose angels to be the rulers of the new world that was coming, which is what we have been talking about. ⁶It is written in the Scriptures, *d*

"But why are people important to you?
Why do you take care of human beings?
⁷You made them a little lower than the angels
and crowned them with glory and honour.
You put them in charge of everything
you made.
⁸ You put all things under their control."
  Psalm 8:4–6

When God put everything under their control, there was nothing left that they did not rule. Still, we do not yet see them ruling over everything. ⁹But we see Jesus, who for a short time was made lower than the angels. And now he is wearing a crown of glory and honour because he suffered and died. And by God's grace, he died for everyone.

¹⁰God is the One who made all things, and all things are for his glory. He wanted to have many children share his glory, so he made the One who leads people to salvation perfect through suffering.

"All . . . him."   These words are found in Deuteronomy 32:43 in the Septuagint, the Greek version of the Old Testament, and in a Hebrew copy among the Dead Sea Scrolls.

until . . . control   Literally, "until I make your enemies a footstool for your feet."

[11]Jesus, who makes people holy, and those who are made holy are from the same family. So he is not ashamed to call them his brothers and sisters. [n] [12]He says,

"Then, I will tell my fellow Israelites
    about you;
I will praise you in the public meeting."

Psalm 22:22

[13]He also says,

"I will trust in God."   *Isaiah 8:17*

And he also says,

"I am here, and with me are the children
    God has given me."   *Isaiah 8:18*

[14]Since these children are people with physical bodies, Jesus himself became like them. He did this so that, by dying, he could destroy the one who has the power of death—the devil— [15]and free those who were like slaves all their lives because of their fear of death. [16]Clearly, it is not angels that Jesus helps, but the people who are from

Abraham. [n] [17]For this reason Jesus had to be made like his brothers in every way so he could be their merciful and faithful high priest in service to God. Then Jesus could bring forgiveness for their sins. [18]And now he can help those who are tempted, because he himself suffered and was tempted.

Jesus is Greater than Moses

3 So all of you holy brothers and sisters, who were called by God, think about Jesus, who was sent to us and is the high priest of our faith. [2]Jesus was faithful to God as Moses was in God's family. [3]Jesus has more honour than Moses, just as the builder of a house has more honour than the house itself. [4]Every house is built by someone, but the builder of everything is God himself. [5]Moses was faithful in God's family as a servant, and he told what God would say in the future. [6]But Christ is faithful as a Son over God's house. And we are God's house if we keep on

---

brothers and sisters   Although the Greek text says "brothers" here and throughout this book, the writer's words refer to the entire church, both men and women.
Abraham   Most respected ancestor of the Jews. Every Jew hoped to see Abraham.

Created by Design

Michael loved designer labels. It was his thing. He really enjoyed going out on a Saturday with his hard-earned cash and coming back home with carrier bags with designer names on them. And like he always said, there's nothing wrong with that, it was his money.

The only trouble was, that Michael worked in a place where oil and grease were the order of the day. He would spend many hours beneath leaking engines and machinery. The firm he worked for provided overalls, but there was no way Michael was ever going to be seen in them! So, each day he dressed for work in designer shirts, trousers and shoes. And each night he would come home with his clothes covered in dirt. When this was pointed out to him, he would shrug his shoulders and say, "It's OK, I'll get some more at the end of the month." His friends thought he was crazy, but that's just the way he was. He couldn't bear to be caught in plain clothes.

Hebrews 1:10–14 talks about how throw-away our lifestyle is.

* What is the difference between God and the "disposable" world?
* How is Michael's attitude to clothes similar to God's view of creation? How is it different?

Consider . . .

* taking care over your appearance just as God took care in creating a beautiful world.
* your financial priorities, is there a good balance in the way you use your money?

For more, see . . .

* Esther 8:15–17 (p.465)
* Matthew 6:28–33 (p.948)
* Psalm 45 (p.526)

being very sure about our great hope.

We Must Continue to Follow God

[7]So it is as the Holy Spirit[d] says:
"Today listen to what he says.
[8]Do not be stubborn as in the past
    when you turned against God,
when you tested God in the desert.
[9]There your ancestors tried me and tested me
    and saw the things I did for 40 years.
[10]I was angry with them.
    I said, 'They are not loyal to me
    and have not understood my ways.'
[11]I was angry and made a promise,
    'They will never enter my rest.'"[n]

Psalm 95:7–11

[12]So brothers and sisters, be careful that none of you has an evil, unbelieving heart that will turn you away from the living God. [13]But encourage each other every day while it is "today".[n] Help each other so none of you will become hardened because sin has tricked you. [14]We all share in Christ if we keep till the end the sure faith we had in the beginning. [15]This is what the Scripture[d] says:
"Today listen to what he says.
    Do not be stubborn as in the past
    when you turned against God." *Psalm 95:7–8*

Sidelight If Hebrews had been submitted as a project, it would probably have been given top marks for research and documentation. The book quotes from the Old Testament more than 80 times, including Psalm 95:7–11 (p.556), in Hebrews 3:7–11.

---

[16]Who heard God's voice and was against him? It was all those people Moses led out of Egypt. [17]And with whom was God angry for 40 years?

---

rest A place in which to rest that God promised to give his people.
"today" This word is taken from verse 7. It means that it is important to do these things now.

SHARING FAITH

Can You Tell the Difference?

When she graduated from college, Bev Johnson became a short-term missionary at a school in Japan. Each day she led a Bible study and taught English to the Japanese.

Each day an elderly woman came to the Bible study. She sat quietly at the back of the room and rushed out when the study ended. And each day Bev grew more curious.

One day after the Bible study, Bev walked quickly to the woman and began a conversation. The woman spoke excellent English. She told Bev that she had heard of Jesus since she was a young girl. The woman owned a Bible and knew much of it by heart.

"Are you a Christian?" Bev asked.

"No, no I'm not," the woman said, "but I've seen Christians, and I'm watching to see if Jesus makes any difference in their lives."

From that incident, Bev learned how people need to see Jesus in Christians. Read how Jesus can shine through us in **Hebrews 2:9–18**.

* How does the older woman's statement to Bev relate to this passage?
* Why do you think God, in Jesus, became a person for us to know?

Consider . . .

* listing all the ways in which Jesus showed what God is like, such as loving all people, and so on. Choose one of those ways to show how you follow Christ.
* letting at least one other person know this week how Christ has made a difference to you.

For more, see . . .

* Isaiah 57:14–21 (p.701)
* John 11:28–43 (p.1116)
* Matthew 20:29–34 (p.976)

He was angry with those who sinned, who died in the desert. [18]And to whom was God talking when he promised that they would never enter his rest? He was talking to those who did not obey him. [19]So we see they were not allowed to enter and have God's rest, because they did not believe.

4 Now, since God has left us the promise that we may enter his rest, let us be very careful so none of you will fail to enter. [2]The Good News *d* was preached to us just as it was to them. But the teaching they heard did not help them, because they heard it but did not accept it with faith. [3]We who have believed are able to enter and have God's rest. As God has said,

"I was angry and made a promise,

'They will never enter my rest.'" *Psalm 95:11*
But God's work was finished from the time he made the world. [4]In the Scriptures he talked about the seventh day of the week: "And on the seventh day God rested from all his works." *n* [5]And again in the Scripture God said, "They will never enter my rest."

[6]It is still true that some people will enter God's rest, but those who first heard the way to be saved did not enter, because they did not obey. [7]So God planned another day, called "today". He spoke about that day through David a long time later in the same Scripture used before:

"Today listen to what he says.

"And . . . works." Quotation from Genesis 2:2.

FOLLOWING GOD

When the Going Gets Tough . . .

Isabella Baumfree was an American slave born to a Dutch owner in Ulster County, New York, USA, about 1797. She was separated from her family and sold twice before she was twelve. Even after she was set free in 1827, she barely survived as a servant in New York City.

After the Civil War began, Isabella left New York to "travel up an' down the land showin' the people their sins an' bein' a sign unto them." She even changed her name to Sojourner Truth.

Sojourner Truth became famous for her unique style of preaching. Although she couldn't read or write, she preached a message of freedom for slaves, women and the poor. She spoke in a heavy Dutch accent, knew the Bible well, and drew stares wearing a turban.

Because blacks – especially black women – were routinely oppressed, Sojourner Truth found the going difficult. But she kept at it, hardened by her life of slavery and struggle. Her fame spread; she even met President Lincoln in 1864.

Fame doesn't always equal popularity, as Sojourner Truth found out. She often preached and lectured before hostile audiences. Many times she was told her mission was hopeless. "I don't care any more for your talk than I do for the bite of a flea," someone told her.

"Perhaps not," she replied, "but the Lord willing, I'll keep you scratchin'."

Sojourner Truth knew that following God requires commitment and endurance. So did the writer of Hebrews. And, in **Hebrews 4:1–13**, the writer promises that endurance and commitment will not go unrewarded.

* How was Sojourner Truth's persistence in her mission like the challenge of the passage to stay obedient to God? How did she embody the theme of verses 12–13?
* What does the passage say about those who truly follow God versus those who just say they do?

Consider . . .

* taking an unpopular stand on an issue because you believe it's what God wants you to do.
* listing things that you would honestly die for. Decide how to follow those priorities better this week.

For more, see . . .

* Deuteronomy 33:26–29 (p.200)
* Acts 7:51–60 (p.1149)
* Luke 10:25–37 (p.1058)

Do not be stubborn." *Psalm 95:7–8*

[8]We know that Joshua[n] did not lead the people into that rest,[n] because God spoke later about another day. [9]This shows that the rest for God's people is still coming. [10]Anyone who enters God's rest will rest from his work as God did. [11]Let us try as hard as we can to enter God's rest so that no one will fail by following the example of those who refused to obey.

[12]God's word is alive and working and is sharper than a double-edged sword. It cuts all the way into us, where the soul and the spirit are joined, to the centre of our joints and bones. And it judges the thoughts and feelings in our hearts. [13]Nothing in all the world can be hidden from God. Everything is clear and lies open before him, and to him we must explain the way we have lived.

Jesus is Our High Priest

[14]Since we have a great high priest, Jesus the Son of God, who has gone into heaven, let us hold

---

Joshua   After Moses died, Joshua became leader of the Jewish people and led them into the land that God promised to give them.

rest   Literally, "sabbath rest", meaning a sharing in the rest that God began after he created the world.

GOD'S LOVE

Mayday!

"Mayday! Mayday!" The international distress message crackled on the coastguard's radio.

The crew, all volunteers, left their day jobs, and leapt onto bicycles and into cars as the siren on the lifeboat house went off. They quickly climbed into their waterproof overalls and lifejackets as the coxswain listened to the coastguard. Within minutes, the doors of the lifeboat house rattled open and the lifeboat was sliding down the ramps into the foaming waves.

The weather was terrible. Torrential rain beat against the surface of the writhing ocean, making visibility a very dangerous problem. The small fishing boat which had sent out the Mayday call had struck rocks in the storm, and the lifeboat crew had to be careful not to do the same thing.

When the crew had located the floundering fishing boat, they managed to get a line across the heaving water and helped the two relieved fishermen onto their lifeboat.

"The skipper's in the water!" one of the fishermen told them.

Without hesitating, one of the crew sent a distress flare into the sky.

By now, an RAF helicopter was hovering over the waters. The pilot managed to find the floating man and sent a winch down to rescue him. For a while it seemed as though the airman on the end of the line would drown, too. But eventually he was able to grab the shivering sailor.

Thirty minutes later the three fishermen were safely ashore. They couldn't thank the sea rescue team enough for saving their lives.

The lifeboat crew are not paid – they are volunteers. Yet many times a year they risk their own lives to save those of others. Jesus Christ carried out an even deadlier mission – he *gave* his life in order to pay for our sins! Read about this amazing love in **Hebrews 4:14 – 5:10**.

- How does the sea rescue team illustrate the kind of self-sacrificing love that this passage describes?
- How does knowing about God's endless love for you affect your everyday life?

Consider . . .

- looking for examples of sacrificial love in the news and on television. Let their stories remind you of Christ's love for mankind.
- thanking God for sending his Son to die for you, then share this good news with those around you.

For more, see . . .

- Daniel 9:1–9 (p.843)
- Romans 3:21–26 (p.1187)
- Matthew 7:7–11 (p.950)

on to the faith we have. [15]For our high priest is able to understand our weaknesses. When he lived on earth, he was tempted in every way that we are, but he did not sin. [16]Let us, then, feel very sure that we can come before God's throne where there is grace. There we can receive mercy and grace to help us when we need it.

5 Every high priest is chosen from among other people. He is given the work of going before God for them to offer gifts and sacrifices for sins. [2]Since he himself is weak, he is able to be gentle with those who do not understand and who are doing wrong things. [3]Because he is weak, the high priest must offer sacrifices for his own sins and also for the sins of the people.

[4]To be a high priest is an honour, but no one chooses himself for this work. He must be called by God as Aaron [n] was. [5]So also Christ did not choose himself to have the honour of being a high priest, but God chose him. God said to him,

"You are my Son.
    Today I have become your Father."   *Psalm 2:7*

[6]And in another Scripture [d] God says,

"You are a priest for ever,
    a priest like Melchizedek." [n]   *Psalm 110:4*

[7]While Jesus lived on earth, he prayed to God and asked God for help. He prayed with loud cries and tears to the One who could save him from death, and his prayer was heard because he trusted God. [8]Even though Jesus was the Son of God, he learned obedience by what he suffered. [9]And because his obedience was perfect, he was able to give eternal salvation to all who obey him. [10]In this way God made Jesus a high priest, a priest like Melchizedek.

Warning Against Falling Away

[11]We have much to say about this, but it is hard to explain because you are so slow to understand. [12]By now you should be teachers, but you need someone to teach you again the first lessons of God's message. You still need the teaching that is like milk. You are not ready for solid food. [13]Anyone who lives on milk is still a baby and knows nothing about right teaching. [14]But solid food is for those who are grown up. They have practised in order to know the difference between good and evil.

6 So let us go on to grown-up teaching. Let us not go back over the beginning lessons we learned about Christ. We should not again start teaching about faith in God and about turning away from those acts that lead to death. [2]We should not return to the teaching about baptisms, [n] about laying on of hands, [n] about the raising of the dead and eternal judgement. [3]And we will go on to grown-up teaching if God allows.

[4]Some people cannot be brought back again to a changed life. They were once in God's light, and enjoyed heaven's gift, and shared in the Holy Spirit. [d] [5]They found out how good God's word is, and they received the powers of his new world. [6]But they fell away from Christ. It is impossible to bring them back to a changed life again, because they are nailing the Son of God to a cross again and are shaming him in front of others.

[7]Some people are like land that gets plenty of rain. The land produces a good crop for those who work it, and it receives God's blessings. [8]Other people are like land that grows thorns and weeds and is worthless. It is in danger of being cursed by God and will be destroyed by fire.

[9]Dear friends, we are saying this to you, but we really expect better things from you that will lead to your salvation. [10]God is fair; he will not forget the work you did and the love you showed for him by helping his people. And

> ### Sidelight
> Many scholars believe that the book of Hebrews may have originally been a sermon, partly because the author mentions speaking in several places (for example, in Hebrews 6:9). If it was originally a sermon, it would have taken about 50 minutes to read aloud. The services often included "breaking of bread" (communion), teaching, preaching, singing, praying, prophesying and reading letters.

he will remember that you are still helping them. [11]We want each of you to go on with the same hard work all your lives so you will surely get what you hope for. [12]We do not want you to become lazy. Be like those who through faith and patience will receive what God has promised.

[13]God made a promise to Abraham. [n] And as there is no one greater than God, he used himself when he swore to Abraham, [14]saying, "I will

---

Aaron   Aaron was Moses' brother and the first Jewish high priest.
Melchizedek   A priest and king who lived in the time of Abraham. (Read Genesis 14:17–24.)
baptisms   The word here may refer to Christian baptism, or it may refer to the Jewish ceremonial washings.
laying on of hands   The laying on of hands had many purposes, including the giving of a blessing, power or authority.
Abraham   Most respected ancestor of the Jews. Every Jew hoped to see Abraham.

surely bless you and give you many descendants." *n* 15Abraham waited patiently for this to happen, and he received what God promised.

16People always use the name of someone greater than themselves when they swear. The oath proves that what they say is true, and this ends all arguing. 17God wanted to prove that his promise was true to those who would get what he promised. And he wanted them to understand clearly that his purposes never change, so he made an oath. 18These two things cannot change: God cannot lie when he makes a promise, and he cannot lie when he makes an oath. These things encourage us who came to God for safety. They give us strength to hold on to the hope we have been given. 19We have this hope as an anchor for the soul, sure and strong. It enters behind the curtain in the Most Holy Place in heaven, 20where Jesus has gone ahead of us and for us. He has become the high priest for ever, a priest like Melchizedek. *n*

Sidelight   If you think Melchizedek (Hebrews 7:1) is a hard name to say, try the Bible's longest name: Maher-Shalal-Hash-Baz, the name of Isaiah's son (Isaiah 8:1, p.647).

The Priest Melchizedek

7 Melchizedek *n* was the king of Salem and a priest for God Most High. He met Abraham when Abraham was coming back after defeating the kings. When they met, Melchizedek blessed Abraham, 2and Abraham gave him a tenth of everything he had brought back from the battle. First, Melchizedek's name means "king of goodness", and he is king of Salem, which means "king of peace". 3No one knows who Melchizedek's father or mother was, *n* where he came from, when he was born, or when he died. Melchizedek is like the Son of God; he continues being a priest for ever.

4You can see how great Melchizedek was. Abraham, the great father, gave him a tenth of everything that he won in battle. 5Now the law says that those in the tribe *d* of Levi who become priests must collect a tenth from the people— their own people—even though the priests and the people are from the family of Abraham. 6Melchizedek was not from the tribe of Levi, but

he collected a tenth from Abraham. And he blessed Abraham, the man who had God's promises. 7Now everyone knows that the more important person blesses the less important person. 8Priests receive a tenth, even though they are only men who live and then die. But Melchizedek, who received a tenth from Abraham, continues living, as the Scripture *d* says. 9We might even say that Levi, who receives a tenth, also paid it when Abraham paid Melchizedek a tenth. 10Levi was not yet born, but he was in the body of his ancestor when Melchizedek met Abraham.

11The people were given the law *n* based on a system of priests from the tribe of Levi, but they could not be made perfect through that system. So there was a need for another priest to come, a priest like Melchizedek, not Aaron. 12And when a different kind of priest comes, the law must be changed, too. 13We are saying these things about Christ, who belonged to a different tribe. No one from that tribe ever served as a priest at the altar. 14It is clear that our Lord came from the tribe of Judah, and Moses said nothing about priests belonging to that tribe.

Jesus is like Melchizedek

15And this becomes even more clear when we see that another priest comes who is like Melchizedek. 16He was not made a priest by human rules and laws but through the power of his life, which continues for ever. 17It is said about him,
   "You are a priest for ever,
   a priest like Melchizedek."   *Psalm 110:4*
18The old rule is now set aside, because it was weak and useless. 19The law of Moses could not make anything perfect. But now a better hope has been given to us, and with this hope we can come near to God. 20It is important that God did this with an oath. Others became priests without an oath, 21but Christ became a priest with God's oath. God said:
   "The Lord has made a promise
   and will not change his mind.
   'You are a priest for ever.' "   *Psalm 110:4*
22This means that Jesus is the guarantee of a better agreement *n* from God to his people.

23When one of the other priests died, he could not continue being a priest. So there were many priests. 24But because Jesus lives for ever, he will never stop serving as priest. 25So he is able always to save those who come to God through him because he always lives, asking God to help them.

"I . . . descendants." Quotation from Genesis 22:17.
Melchizedek A priest and king who lived in the time of Abraham. (Read Genesis 14:17–24.)
No one . . . was Literally, "Melchizedek was without father, without mother, without genealogy."
The . . . law This refers to the people of Israel who were given the law of Moses.
agreement God gives a contract or agreement to his people. For the Jews, this agreement was the law of Moses. But now God has given a better agreement to his people through Christ.

[26]Jesus is the kind of high priest we need. He is holy, sinless, pure, not influenced by sinners and he is raised above the heavens. [27]He is not like the other priests who had to offer sacrifices every day, first for their own sins, and then for the sins of the people. Christ offered his sacrifice only once and for all time when he offered himself. [28]The law chooses high priests who are people with weaknesses, but the word of God's oath came later than the law. It made God's Son to be the high priest, and that Son has been made perfect for ever.

Jesus is Our High Priest

8 Here is the point of what we are saying: we have a high priest who sits on the right side of God's throne in heaven. [2]Our high priest serves in the Most Holy Place, the true place of worship that was made by God, not by humans.

[3]Every high priest has the work of offering gifts and sacrifices to God. So our high priest must also offer something to God. [4]If our high priest were now living on earth, he would not be a priest, because there are already priests here who follow the law by offering gifts to God. [5]The work they do as priests is only a copy and a shadow of what is in heaven. This is why God warned Moses when he was ready to build the Holy Tent: [d] "Be very careful to make everything by the plan I showed you on the mountain." [n] [6]But the priestly work that has been given to Jesus is much greater than the work that was given to the other priests. In the same way, the new agreement that Jesus brought from God to his people is much greater than the old one. And the new agreement is based on promises of better things.

[7]If there had been nothing wrong with the first agreement, [n] there would have been no need for a second agreement. [8]But God found something wrong with his people. He says:

"Look, the time is coming, says the LORD,
    when I will make a new agreement
with the people of Israel
    and the people of Judah.
[9]It will not be like the agreement
    I made with their ancestors
when I took them by the hand
    to bring them out of Egypt.
But they broke that agreement,
    and I turned away from them, says the
        LORD.
[10]This is the agreement I will make
    with the people of Israel at that time, says
        the LORD.

I will put my Teachings in their minds
    and write them on their hearts.
I will be their God,
    and they will be my people.
[11]People will no longer have to teach their
        neighbours and relatives
    to know the LORD,
because all people will know me,
    from the least to the most important.
[12]I will forgive them for the wicked things
        they did,
    and I will not remember their sins any
        more." *Jeremiah 31:31-34*

[13]God called this a new agreement, and so he has made the first agreement old. And anything that is old and worn out is ready to disappear.

The Old Agreement

9 The first agreement [n] had rules for worship and a man-made place for worship. [2]The Holy Tent [d] was set up for this. The first area in the Tent was called the Holy Place. In it were the lamp and the table with the bread that was made holy for God. [3]Behind the second curtain was a room called the Most Holy Place. [4]In it was a golden altar for burning incense [d] and the Ark [d] covered with gold that held the old agreement. Inside this Ark was a golden jar of manna, [d] Aaron's rod that once grew leaves, and the stone tablets [n] of the old agreement. [5]Above the Ark were the creatures that showed God's glory, whose wings reached over the lid. But we cannot tell everything about these things now.

[6]When everything in the Tent was made ready in this way, the priests went into the first room every day to worship. [7]But only the high priest could go into the second room, and he did that only once a year. He could never enter the inner room without taking blood with him, which he offered to God for himself and for sins the people did without knowing they did them. [8]The Holy Spirit [d] uses this to show that the way into the Most Holy Place was not open while the system of the old Holy Tent was still being used. [9]This is an example for the present time. It shows that the gifts and sacrifices offered cannot make the conscience of the worshipper perfect. [10]These gifts and sacrifices were only about food and drink and special washings. They were rules for the body, to be followed until the time of God's new way.

The New Agreement

[11]But when Christ came as the high priest of the good things we now have, he entered the

---

"Be . . . mountain." Quotation from Exodus 25:40.
first agreement The contract God gave the Jewish people when he gave them the law of Moses.
stone tablets They were the two stone tablets on which God wrote the Ten Commandments.

greater and more perfect tent. It is not made by humans and does not belong to this world. [12]Christ entered the Most Holy Place only once—and for all time. He did not take with him the blood of goats and calves. His sacrifice was his own blood, and by it he set us free from sin for ever. [13]The blood of goats and bulls and the ashes of a cow are sprinkled on the people who are unclean,[d] and this makes their bodies clean again. [14]How much more is done by the blood of Christ! He offered himself through the eternal Spirit[n] as a perfect sacrifice to God. His blood will make our consciences pure from useless acts so we may serve the living God.

[15]For this reason Christ brings a new agreement from God to his people. Those who are called by God can now receive the blessings he has promised, blessings that will last for ever. They can have those things because Christ died so that the people who lived under the first agreement could be set free from sin.

[16]When there is a will,[n] it must be proven that the one who wrote that will is dead. [17]A will means nothing while the person is alive; it can be used only after the person dies. [18]This is why even the first agreement could not begin without blood to show death. [19]First, Moses told all the people every command in the law. Next he took the blood of calves and mixed it with water. Then he used red wool and a branch of the hyssop plant to sprinkle it on the Book of the law and on all the people. [20]He said, "This is the blood that begins the Agreement that God commanded you to obey."[n] [21]In the same way, Moses sprinkled

---

Spirit   This refers to the Holy Spirit, to Christ's own spirit, or to the spiritual and eternal nature of his sacrifice.
will   A legal document that shows how a person's money and property are to be distributed at the time of death. This is the same word in Greek as "agreement" in verse 15.
"This . . . obey."   Quotation from Exodus 24:8.

SIN

Unexpected Forgiveness

Diane and Chris had been going out for about a year. Both were sixteen. When Diane stopped coming to youth group meetings, Donna, her youth leader, dropped by after school to see if she was OK.

Diane confessed that her relationship with Chris had got very physical. "I think I'm pregnant," she said.

She and Chris had had sex on a date four weeks earlier. "It just happened. We didn't plan it," she kept saying.

"Have you told your parents?" Donna asked.

"No!" she screamed. "They would absolutely die if they knew!"

"That's not the main issue," Donna said. "They need to know, and you need their help."

Donna promised to stay with Diane until her parents came home from work. When Diane told them the news, they were upset at first, but they assured Diane that they loved her. What she had done was wrong, but it didn't change the way they felt about her. She was their daughter.

Diane learned a hard lesson about sex before marriage. She also learned a lot about the kind of forgiveness and acceptance written about in **Hebrews 9:11–28**.

* How was forgiveness by Diane's parents like and unlike the forgiveness described in this passage? How did the price that Diane's parents paid in the story differ from the price that Christ paid in the passage?
* How are our sins forgiven, according to the passage?

Consider . . .

* talking to a trusted adult about a sin that you're struggling with.
* defining the word "sin", using this passage and the ones listed in "For More, See . . ." for guidance. Find out whether your friends and minister agree with your definition.

For more, see . . .

* Genesis 4:1–12 (p.7)
* Romans 3:21–26 (p.1187)
* Romans 6:12–14 (p.1191)

the blood on the Holy Tent[d] and over all the things used in worship. ²²The law says that almost everything must be made clean by blood, and sins cannot be forgiven without blood to show death.

Christ's Death Takes Away Sins

²³So the copies of the real things in heaven had to be made clean[d] by animal sacrifices. But the real things in heaven need much better sacrifices. ²⁴Christ did not go into the Most Holy Place made by humans, which is only a copy of the real one. He went into heaven itself and is there now before God to help us. ²⁵The high priest enters the Most Holy Place once every year with blood that is not his own. But Christ did not offer himself many times. ²⁶Then he would have had to suffer many times since the world was made. But Christ came only once and for all time at just the right time to take away all sin by sacrificing himself. ²⁷Just as everyone must die once and be judged, ²⁸so Christ was offered as a sacrifice once to take away the sins of many people. And he will come a second time, not to offer himself for sin, but to bring salvation to those who are waiting for him.

10 The law is only an unclear picture of the good things coming in the future; it is not the real thing. The people under the law offer the same sacrifices every year, but these sacrifices can never make perfect those who come near to worship God. ²If the law could make them perfect, the sacrifices would have already stopped. The worshippers would be made clean, and they would no longer have a sense of sin. ³But these sacrifices remind them of their sins every year, ⁴because it is impossible for the blood of bulls and goats to take away sins.

Sidelight

When Hebrews 10:1 talks about making "the same sacrifices every year", it refers to the annual Jewish holiday of Yom Kippur. On this day, the high priest would symbolically transfer the sins of Israel to a goat (known as a scapegoat). Then the goat would be carried away to the desert where it – along with the sins – would be lost and forgotten (see Leviticus 16:7–10, 20–22, p.115).

---

⁵So when Christ came into the world, he said:
"You do not want sacrifices and offerings,
    but you have prepared a body for me.

⁶You do not ask for burnt offerings
    and sacrifices to take away sins.
⁷Then I said, 'Look, I have come.
    It is written about me in the book.
My God, I want to do what you want.' "

Psalm 40:6–8

⁸In this Scripture[d] he first said, "You do not want sacrifices and offerings. You do not ask for burnt offerings and offerings to take away sins." (These are all sacrifices that the law commands.) ⁹Then he said, "Look, I have come to do what you want." God ends the first system of sacrifices so he can set up the new system. ¹⁰And because of this, we are made holy through the sacrifice Christ made in his body once and for all time.

¹¹Every day the priests stand and do their religious service, often offering the same sacrifices. Those sacrifices can never take away sins. ¹²But after Christ offered one sacrifice for sins, for ever, he sat down at the right side of God. ¹³And now Christ waits there for his enemies to be put under his power. ¹⁴With one sacrifice he made perfect for ever those who are being made holy.

¹⁵The Holy Spirit[d] also tells us about this. First he says:
¹⁶"This is the agreement[n] I will make
    with them at that time, says the LORD.
I will put my teachings in their minds
    and write them on their hearts." *Jeremiah 31:33*
¹⁷Then he says:
"Their sins and the evil things they do—
    I will not remember any more." *Jeremiah 31:34*
¹⁸Now when these have been forgiven, there is no more need for a sacrifice for sins.

Continue to Trust God

¹⁹So, brothers and sisters, we are completely free to enter the Most Holy Place without fear because of the blood of Jesus' death. ²⁰We can enter through a new and living way that Jesus opened for us. It leads us through the curtain[d]— Christ's body. ²¹And since we have a great priest over God's house, ²²let us come near to God with a sincere heart and a sure faith, because we have been made free from a guilty conscience, and our bodies have been washed with pure water. ²³Let us hold firmly to the hope that we have confessed, because we can trust God to do what he promised.

²⁴Let us think about each other and help each other to show love and do good deeds. ²⁵You should not stay away from the church meetings, as some are doing, but you should meet together

---

agreement   God gives a contract or agreement to his people. For the Jews, this agreement was the law of Moses. But now God has given a better agreement to his people through Christ.

and encourage each other. Do this even more as you see the day[n] coming.

[26]If we decide to go on sinning after we have learnt the truth, there is no longer any sacrifice for sins. [27]There is nothing but fear in waiting for the judgement and the terrible fire that will destroy all those who live against God. [28]Anyone who refused to obey the law of Moses was found guilty from the proof given by two or three witnesses. He was put to death without mercy. [29]So what do you think should be done to those who do not respect the Son of God, who look at the blood of the agreement that made them holy as no different from others' blood, who insult the Spirit [d] of God's grace? Surely they should have a much worse punishment. [30]We know that God said, "I will punish those who do wrong; I will repay them." [n] And he also said, "The Lord will judge his people." [n] [31]It is a terrible thing to fall into the hands of the living God.

day   The day Christ will come to judge all people and take his people to live with him.
"I . . . them."   Quotation from Deuteronomy 32:35.
"The Lord . . . people."   Quotation from Deuteronomy 32:36; Psalm 135:14.

CHURCH

Family of Friends

Jeremy had had a rough life. His parents were divorced, and he had bounced between one parent and the other. When he signed up for summer youth camp, everyone was surprised, since he had shown little interest in church until then.

When they arrived at the camp, the campers were split into groups of ten, each including an adult leader. The group would stay together for a week.

Jeremy started acting up immediately. His leader and the other campers tried to include him, but he ignored their kind gestures. His behaviour was rude and selfish.

Finally the camp leader, Cheryl, sat down with him after supper. When she asked Jeremy what he didn't like, he said, "All they do is sit around and talk about their problems. I'm bored."

Cheryl explained to Jeremy that they were trying to build relationships, and that he was choosing not to be a part. "You don't have to participate, but you must respect other people's feelings," she said.

Jeremy spent the next day listening. He watched the group care for each other. Before he knew it, he was telling the group about his family and how much he hated moving back and forth between parents.

The group listened. Then one of the boys spoke. "We will be family for you, if you'll let us," he offered Jeremy, and the others agreed.

Jeremy couldn't believe it at first. But through the week, the campers' concern and their openness to him convinced him.

On the last day of camp, Jeremy thanked the group. "I've never known what it meant to have a real family, until this week," he said. "I know things still won't be easy at home, but I know at least ten people who care."

Fortunately for Jeremy, he experienced the love of a group of committed Christians who wouldn't give up on him. In **Hebrews 10:19–39**, the writer talks about this kind of commitment to the family of God.

* How well did Jeremy's group live up to this passage's message?
* According to this passage, why do we need the church?

Consider . . .

* praying for someone at church who you think is incredibly rude or obnoxious. Then pray for help in understanding that person.
* accepting the care and concern of others if they invite you to church youth group meetings or outings. You may find new friends there.

For more, see . . .

* Isaiah 65:1–2 (p.710)
* Acts 2:43–47 (p.1141)
* Matthew 16:13–20 (p.969)

[32]Remember those days in the past when you first learnt the truth. You had a hard struggle with many sufferings, but you continued strong. [33]Sometimes you were hurt and attacked before crowds of people, and sometimes you shared with those who were being treated that way. [34]You helped the prisoners. You even had joy when all that you owned was taken from you, because you knew you had something better and more lasting.

[35]So do not lose the courage you had in the past, which has a great reward. [36]You must hold on, so you can do what God wants and receive what he has promised. [37]For in a very short time,

"The One who is coming will come
    and will not be delayed.
[38]The person who is right with me
    will live by trusting in me.
But if he turns back with fear,
    I will not be pleased with him." *Habakkuk 2:3–4*

[39]But we are not those who turn back and are lost. We are people who have faith and are saved.

What is Faith?

11 Faith means being sure of the things we hope for and knowing that something is real even if we do not see it. [2]Faith is the reason we remember great people who lived in the past.

[3]It is by faith we understand that the whole world was made by God's command so what we see was made by something that cannot be seen.

[4]It was by faith that Abel offered God a better sacrifice than Cain did. God said he was pleased with the gifts Abel offered and called Abel a good man because of his faith. Abel died, but through his faith he is still speaking.

[5]It was by faith that Enoch was taken to heaven so he would not die. He could not be found, because God had taken him away. Before he was taken, the Scripture [d] says that he was a man who truly pleased God. [6]Without faith no one can please God. Anyone who comes to God must believe that he is real and that he rewards those who truly want to find him.

FAITH

Not by Sight

After living with perfect sight for twelve years, Michelle became blind in a matter of seconds. A bad fall caused her to knock the back of her head and her sight was lost forever.

Suddenly, Michelle found herself in a strange world where images of her surroundings didn't exist. She had to learn to read Braille with her fingertips and to get around the house largely by memory.

Then the clinic told Michelle that they were going to give her a guide dog. When they did so, it took her a long time to get used to following an animal instead of her own two eyes.

"It was weird," she says. "All my life I'd been so independent, and now I have to walk not by sight, but by putting my faith in Elli, my guide dog."

In a similar way, the writer of Hebrews wanted Christians to understand how faith sometimes requires us to believe in things that we can't see or hear. He goes on to give some examples of people who lived not by sight, but by faith, in **Hebrews 11:1–16**.

* How is Michelle like the people that the writer of Hebrews uses as examples?
* When have you ever trusted God in "blind faith"? What happened? How would you describe your experience to others?

Consider . . .

* developing an area of your faith that you know is weak, such as witnessing, or serving others.
* how you often trust other people even when you don't realise it (such as having faith in the bus driver to get you safely to a destination), then compare how often you put your faith in God alone.

For more, see . . .

* Genesis 12:1–5 (p.14)
* Romans 4:13–25 (p.1189)
* Mark 4:35–41 (p.1005)

[7]It was by faith that Noah heard God's warnings about things he could not yet see. He obeyed God and built a large boat to save his family. By his faith, Noah showed that the world was wrong, and he became one of those who are made right with God through faith.

[8]It was by faith Abraham obeyed God's call to go to another place God promised to give him. He left his own country, not knowing where he was to go. [9]It was by faith that he lived like a foreigner in the country God promised to give him. He lived in tents with Isaac and Jacob, who had received that same promise from God. [10]Abraham was waiting for the city[n] that has real foundations—the city planned and built by God.

[11]He was too old to have children, and Sarah could not have children. It was by faith that Abraham was made able to become a father, because he trusted God to do what he had promised. [12]This man was so old he was almost dead, but from him came as many descendants[d] as there are stars in the sky. Like the sand on the seashore, they could not be counted.

[13]All these great people died in faith. They did not get the things that God promised his people, but they saw them coming far in the future and were glad. They said they were like visitors and strangers on earth. [14]When people say such things, they show they are looking for a country that will be their own. [15]If they had been thinking about the country they had left, they could have gone back. [16]But they were waiting for a better country—a heavenly country. So God is not ashamed to be called their God, because he has prepared a city for them.

[17]It was by faith that Abraham, when God tested him, offered his son Isaac as a sacrifice. God made the promises to Abraham, but Abraham was ready to offer his own son as a sacrifice. [18]God had said, "The descendants I promised you will be from Isaac."[n] [19]Abraham believed that God could raise the dead, and really, it was as if Abraham got Isaac back from death.

[20]It was by faith that Isaac blessed the future of Jacob and Esau. [21]It was by faith that Jacob, as he was dying, blessed each one of Joseph's sons. Then he worshipped as he leaned on the top of his walking stick.

[22]It was by faith that Joseph, while he was dying, spoke about the Israelites leaving Egypt and told about what to do with his body.

[23]It was by faith that Moses' parents hid him for three months after he was born. They saw that Moses was a beautiful baby, and they were not afraid to disobey the king's order.

[24]It was by faith that Moses, when he grew up, refused to be called the son of the king of Egypt's daughter. [25]He chose to suffer with God's people instead of enjoying sin for a short time. [26]He thought it was better to suffer for the Christ[d] than to have all the treasures of Egypt, because he was looking for God's reward. [27]It was by faith that Moses left Egypt and was not afraid of the king's anger. Moses continued strong as if he could see the God that no one can see. [28]It was by faith that Moses prepared the Passover[d] and spread the blood on the doors so the one who brings death would not kill the firstborn[d] sons of Israel.

[29]It was by faith that the people crossed the Red Sea as if it were dry land. But when the Egyptians tried it, they were drowned.

[30]It was by faith that the walls of Jericho fell after the people had marched around them for seven days.

[31]It was by faith that Rahab, the prostitute,[d] welcomed the spies and was not killed with those who refused to obey God.

[32]Do I need to give more examples? I do not have time to tell you about Gideon, Barak, Samson, Jephthah, David, Samuel and the prophets.[d] [33]Through their faith they defeated kingdoms. They did what was right, received God's promises and shut the mouths of lions. [34]They stopped great fires and were saved from being killed with swords. They were weak, and yet were made strong. They were powerful in battle and defeated other armies. [35]Women received their dead relatives raised back to life. Others were tortured and refused to accept their freedom so they could be raised from the dead to a better life. [36]Some were laughed at and beaten. Others were put in chains and thrown into prison. [37]They were stoned to death, they were cut in half and they were killed with swords. Some wore the skins of sheep and goats. They were poor, abused and treated badly. [38]The world was not good enough for them! They wandered in deserts

---

Sidelight   If you think you have had a hard life, read Hebrews 11:32–38. When verse 37 talks about being "cut in half", it may refer to the prophet Isaiah (p.638), who, according to tradition, met this fate.

---

city   The spiritual "city" where God's people live with him. Also called "the heavenly Jerusalem". (See Hebrews 12:22.)
"The descendants . . . Isaac."   Quotation from Genesis 21:12.

and mountains, living in caves and holes in the earth.

³⁹All these people are known for their faith, but none of them received what God had promised. ⁴⁰God planned to give us something better so that they would be made perfect, along with us.

Follow Jesus' Example

12 We have around us many people whose lives tell us what faith means. So let us run the race that is before us and never give up. We should remove from our lives anything that would get in the way and the sin that so easily holds us back. ²Let us look only to Jesus, the One who began our faith and who makes it perfect. He suffered death on the cross. But he accepted the shame as if it were nothing because of the joy that God put before him. And now he is sitting at the right side of God's throne. ³Think about Jesus' example. He held on while wicked people were doing evil things to him. So do not get tired and stop trying.

God is Like a Father

⁴You are struggling against sin, but your struggles have not yet caused you to be killed.

PERSISTENCE

Worth the Effort

They'd been told that the "Adventure Breaks" were tough, but this weekend was more than they had bargained for.

In order to reach the small huts where they were staying for the weekend, the small group of adventurers had hiked for five miles in the simmering, humid heat of a July heatwave. They'd been given an hour to unpack their rucksacks and have something to eat, then they went canoeing for three hours.

They returned to their huts tired and wet. After just two hours of free time, the group again ventured into the wilderness and spent that first Friday evening learning a little about how to survive in the wild.

Saturday morning had seen the group on the assault course. The various obstacles were designed to push the young teenagers to the limit . . . and beyond.

Having completed the gruelling course, the 30 youngsters were now hiking back to their huts for a brief rest.

"I can't go on!" Tony wheezed as he climbed the hill.

Will knew what his friend meant. It was only Saturday lunchtime and they still had almost a day and a half to go. The rest of the programme included cross-country running, climbing, abseiling and various other strenuous activities.

Tony stopped to catch his breath. "I wish I'd never come."

Will smiled. "You'll feel different when it's over," he said. "The key to making the whole weekend worthwhile is *persistence*."

Tony shook his head and continued.

On Sunday afternoon, Tony had decided that Will was right. The weekend *had* been worth the effort after all. The simple fact that he'd managed to stick out the whole course made him feel good.

Read **Hebrews 12:1–13** and discover the importance of being persistent in our lives as Christians.

* Why is persistence important according to the passage?
* Have you ever felt like Tony and wanted to give up? What made you feel that way?

Consider . . .

* completing a project which you have started and put to one side.
* being persistent where your Bible reading is concerned. Set yourself a target for the coming week and stick with it.

For more, see . . .

* Isaiah 42:1–4 (p.682)
* Ephesians 6:10–18 (p.1277)

* Luke 18:1–5 (p.1078)

[5]You have forgotten the encouraging words that call you his children:

"My child, don't think the Lord's discipline is worth nothing,
and don't get angry when he corrects you.
[6]The Lord corrects those he loves,
and he punishes everyone he accepts as his child."

Proverbs 3:11–12

[7]So hold on through your sufferings, because they are like a father's discipline. God is treating you as children. All children are disciplined by their fathers. [8]If you are never disciplined (and every child must be disciplined), you are not true children. [9]We have all had fathers here on earth who disciplined us, and we respected them. So it is even more important that we accept discipline from the Father of our spirits so we will have life. [10]Our fathers on earth disciplined us for a short time in the way they thought was best. But God disciplines us to help us, so we can become holy as he is. [11]We do not enjoy being disciplined. It is painful, but later, after we have learned from it, we have peace, because we start living in the right way.

Be Careful How You Live

[12]You have become weak, so make yourselves strong again. [13]Live in the right way so that you will be saved and your weakness will not cause you to be lost.

[14]Try to live in peace with all people, and try to live free from sin. Anyone whose life is not holy will never see the Lord. [15]Be careful that no one fails to receive God's grace and begins to cause trouble among you. A person like that can ruin many of you. [16]Be careful that no one takes part in sexual sin or is like Esau and never thinks

WORSHIP

No Matter What

On Wednesday evening, Kerrie and Sam went for a meal to catch up on each other's news. Sam was really enjoying uni life, doing whatever she wanted – sleeping with loads of guys, getting drunk, smoking and having a good time. Kerrie was listening to all of her stories thinking what a change had taken place. The girls used to pray for their school and pray for people who were making the kind of choices Sam was making.

Confused by what she heard, Kerrie asked Sam how her walk with God was going. Sam's reply was simple: "Look I've done so much stuff in my life that's wrong, how can I worship God or even talk to him? I've sinned so many times that I can't get my life back to what it was before."

Kerrie explained to Sam that we don't need to come to God with our lives totally sorted. We need to go to him and be in his presence and ask him about our lives, ask him to forgive us. Running away from God and looking to things that don't give us true joy and even harm us is not the answer.

As time went on, Sam got back into a real relationship with God and worked through the habits of her daily life. She discovered that God doesn't want perfect people, he wants people with broken hearts, confused lives and with imperfections to come to him and to worship him through the hard times as well as the good.

Read **Hebrews 12:18–25**. It talks of the complete forgiveness Jesus has to offer and that we don't have to come to him perfect, but with a heart that lifts him up no matter what.

- Have you ever felt that it's too hard or that you are unworthy to worship God?
- Worship is so much more than just singing. What ways other than singing can we worship God?

Consider . . .

- whether you are feeling that you've sinned beyond repair. It is not uncommon. Remember that God loves you and forgives everything that you've done if you just ask him. You have been saved from your sins by Jesus' death on the cross.
- whether you know anyone who is trying to run away from God. Rather than telling them what they're doing wrong, remind them of his never-ending love and forgiveness.

For more, see . . .

- Psalm 24:3–5 (p.514)
- Luke 15:11–32 (p.1071)

- Psalm 51:10–17 (p.530)

about God. As the elder son, Esau would have received everything from his father, but he sold all that for a single meal. ¹⁷You remember that after Esau did this, he wanted to get his father's blessing, but his father refused. Esau could find no way to change what he had done, even though he wanted the blessing so much that he cried.

¹⁸You have not come to a mountain that can be touched and that is burning with fire. You have not come to darkness, sadness and storms. ¹⁹You have not come to the noise of a trumpet or to the sound of a voice like the one the people of Israel heard and begged not to hear another word. ²⁰They did not want to hear the command: "If anything, even an animal, touches the mountain, it must be put to death with stones." *n* ²¹What they saw was so terrible that Moses said, "I am shaking with fear." *n*

²²But you have come to Mount Zion, to the city of the living God, the heavenly Jerusalem. You have come to thousands of angels gathered together with joy. ²³You have come to the meeting of God's first-born *n* children whose names are written in heaven. You have come to God, the judge of all people, and to the spirits of good people who have been made perfect. ²⁴You have come to Jesus, the One who brought the new agreement from God to his people, and you have come to the sprinkled blood *n* that has a better message than the blood of Abel. *n*

²⁵So be careful and do not refuse to listen when God speaks. Others refused to listen to him when he warned them on earth, and they did not escape. So it will be worse for us if we refuse to listen to God who warns us from heaven. ²⁶When he spoke before, his voice shook the earth, but now he has promised, "Once again I will shake not only the earth but also the heavens." *n* ²⁷The words "once again" clearly show us that everything that was made—things that can be shaken—will be destroyed. Only the things that cannot be shaken will remain.

²⁸So let us be thankful, because we have a kingdom that cannot be shaken. We should worship God in a way that pleases him with respect and fear, ²⁹because our God is like a fire that burns things up.

13 Keep on loving each other as brothers and sisters. ²Remember to welcome strangers, because some who have done this have welcomed angels without knowing it. ³Remember those who are in prison as if you were in prison with them. Remember those who are suffering as if you were suffering with them.

⁴Marriage should be honoured by everyone, and husband and wife should keep their marriage pure. God will judge as guilty those who take part in sexual sins. ⁵Keep your lives free from the love of money, and be satisfied with what you have. God has said,

"I will never leave you;
    I will never forget you."   *Deuteronomy 31:6*
⁶So we can be sure when we say,

"I will not be afraid, because the Lord is my
    helper.
People can't do anything to me."   *Psalm 118:6*

⁷Remember your leaders who taught God's message to you. Remember how they lived and died, and copy their faith. ⁸Jesus Christ is the same yesterday, today and for ever.

⁹Do not let all kinds of strange teachings lead you into the wrong way. Your hearts should be strengthened by God's grace, not by obeying rules about foods, which do not help those who obey them.

¹⁰We have a sacrifice, but the priests who serve in the Holy Tent *d* cannot eat from it. ¹¹The high priest carries the blood of animals into the Most Holy Place where he offers this blood for sins. But the bodies of the animals are burnt outside the camp. ¹²So Jesus also suffered outside the city to make his people holy with his own blood. ¹³So let us go to Jesus outside the camp, holding on as he did when he bore our disgrace.

¹⁴Here on earth we do not have a city that lasts for ever, but we are looking for the city that we will have in the future. ¹⁵So through Jesus let us always offer to God our sacrifice of praise, coming from lips that speak his name. ¹⁶Do not forget to do good to others, and share with them, because such sacrifices please God.

¹⁷Obey your leaders and act under their authority. They are watching over you, because they are responsible for your souls. Obey them so that they will do this work with joy, not sadness. It will not help you to make their work hard.

¹⁸Pray for us. We are sure that we have a clear conscience, because we always want to do the right thing. ¹⁹I especially beg you to pray so that God will send me back to you soon.

"If . . . stones."   Quotation from Exodus 19:12–13.
"I . . . fear."   Quotation from Deuteronomy 9:19.
first-born   The first son born in a Jewish family was given the most important place in the family and received special
    blessings. All of God's children are like that.
sprinkled blood   The blood of Jesus' death.
Abel   The son of Adam and Eve, who was killed by his brother Cain (Genesis 4:8).
"Once . . . heavens."   Quotation from Haggai 2:6,21.

20-21I pray that the God of peace will give you every good thing you need so you can do what he wants. God raised from the dead our Lord Jesus, the Great Shepherd of the sheep, because of the blood of his death. His blood began the eternal agreement that God made with his people. I pray that God will do in us what pleases him, through Jesus Christ, and to him be glory for ever and ever. Amen.

22My brothers and sisters, I beg you to listen patiently to this message I have written to encourage you, because it is not very long. 23I want you to know that our brother Timothy has been let out of prison. If he arrives soon, we will both come to see you.

24Greet all your leaders and all of God's people. Those from Italy send greetings to you.

25Grace be with you all.

SERVICE

Seeing is Believing

James and Lucy were just married. They didn't have their own place, but were renting half of a house. They didn't have a lot, but were thrilled with the carpet and furnishings provided by their friends.

One day they came home to find the lounge flooded. Water was pouring through the ceiling where the people upstairs had left a tap on. The new carpet was ruined and they just stood in despair. A Christian friend chose that moment to call round and see how they were doing. He took one look at the situation and said, "Get your coats, we're going out for a meal!"

"We can't leave this mess!" they both wailed. But he insisted, and took them to a good restaurant and they gradually relaxed in his company. By the time he paid the bill, they were feeling much better.

He turned to them and said, "OK, let's go and tackle the problem!"

Between the three of them, they dragged the carpet onto the lawn outside and dried it out.

Afterwards, James said to Lucy, "I think we've just seen a sermon in action!"

Hebrews 13:1–8 reminds us to care for each other in many different ways.

- How did the Christian friend's attitude compare with this passage?
- Which of these teachings apply to your own life?

Consider . . .

- phoning someone who has done something for you lately to let them know you appreciate what they have done.
- doing something for someone in need, such as gardening, or running an errand.

For more, see . . .

- Matthew 6:1–4 (p.947)
- Acts 4:32–35 (p.1144)
- Luke 7:1–10 (p.1049)

James

Why Read This Book:

* Learn how to handle temptation, testing and trouble (James 1).
* Understand the connection between what you believe and what you do (James 2—3).
* See what can happen when you let God be in charge of your life (James 4—5).

When?

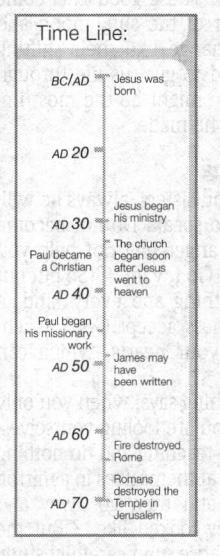

Time Line:

BC/AD — Jesus was born

AD 20 —

AD 30 — Jesus began his ministry

Paul became a Christian — The church began soon after Jesus went to heaven

AD 40 —

Paul began his missionary work

AD 50 — James may have been written

AD 60 —

Fire destroyed Rome

AD 70 — Romans destroyed the Temple in Jerusalem

Behind the Scenes:

If someone says, "Would you mind taking out the rubbish?" it's easy to forget or find some excuse for not doing it. But suppose someone says, "Take out the rubbish!" It's hard to ignore the demand or find an excuse not to do it.

The book of James is like the second example. Its guidance is so clear that it is hard to ignore. "Do not become angry easily" (James 1:19). "Never think some people are more important than others (James 2:1). "Do not tell evil lies about each other" (James 4:11). In fact, James has more than 50 direct commands in just five chapters!

While much of the New Testament focuses on what Christians believe, James focuses on how Christians behave. Some early Christians apparently thought they could do whatever they wanted because God would forgive them anyway. But James warns them that "if people say they have faith, but do nothing, their faith is worth nothing" (James 2:14).

This short book is loaded with advice on putting our faith into action. It covers many areas of life that we continue to struggle with: handling money, relations between the rich and poor, boasting, judging others, being patient. The book is as practical today as when it was written almost 2,000 years ago.

Where?

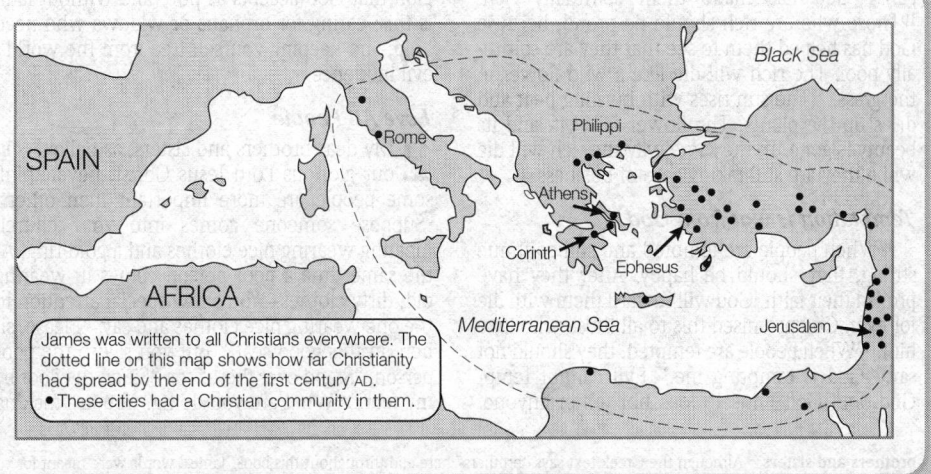

Black Sea

SPAIN

Rome

Philippi

Athens

Corinth

Ephesus

AFRICA

Mediterranean Sea

Jerusalem

James was written to all Christians everywhere. The dotted line on this map shows how far Christianity had spread by the end of the first century AD.

• These cities had a Christian community in them.

1 From James, a servant of God and of the Lord Jesus Christ.

To all of God's people who are scattered everywhere in the world:

Greetings.

Faith and Wisdom

²My brothers and sisters,ⁿ when you have many kinds of troubles, you should be full of joy, ³because you know that these troubles test your

> **Sidelight** James was a common name in the first century, so we are not sure who wrote this letter. One theory is that the author was a brother of Jesus. This James became the leader of the Jerusalem church and later was put to death because of his faith.

faith, and this will give you patience. ⁴Let your patience show itself perfectly in what you do. Then you will be perfect and complete and will have everything you need. ⁵But if any of you needs wisdom, you should ask God for it. He is generous and enjoys giving to all people, so he will give you wisdom. ⁶But when you ask God, you must believe and not doubt. Anyone who doubts is like a wave in the sea, blown up and down by the wind. ⁷⁻⁸Such who doubt are thinking two different things at the same time, and they cannot decide about anything they do. They should not think they will receive anything from the Lord.

True Riches

⁹Believers who are poor should be proud, because God has made them spiritually rich. ¹⁰Those who are rich should be proud, because God has helped them to see that they are spiritually poor. The rich will die like a wild flower in the grass. ¹¹The sun rises with burning heat and dries up the plants. The flower falls off, and its beauty is gone. In the same way the rich will die while they are still taking care of business.

Temptation is Not from God

¹²When people are tempted and still continue strong, they should be happy. After they have proved their faith, God will reward them with life for ever. God promised this to all those who love him. ¹³When people are tempted, they should not say, "God is tempting me." Evil cannot tempt God, and God himself does not tempt anyone.

¹⁴But people are tempted when their own evil desire leads them away and traps them. ¹⁵This desire leads to sin, and then the sin grows and brings death.

¹⁶My dear brothers and sisters, do not be fooled about this. ¹⁷Every good action and every perfect gift is from God. These good gifts come down from the Creator of the sun, moon and stars, who does not change like their shifting shadows. ¹⁸God decided to give us life through the word of truth so we might be the most important of all the things he made.

Listening and Obeying

¹⁹My dear brothers and sisters, always be willing to listen and slow to speak. Do not become angry easily, ²⁰because anger will not help you live the right kind of life God wants. ²¹So put out of your life every evil thing and every kind of wrong. Then in gentleness accept God's teaching that is planted in your hearts, which can save you.

²²Do what God's teaching says; when you only listen and do nothing, you are fooling yourselves. ²³Those who hear God's teaching and do nothing are like people who look at themselves in a mirror. ²⁴They see their faces and then go away and quickly forget what they looked like. ²⁵But the truly happy people are those who carefully study God's perfect law that makes people free, and they continue to study it. They do not forget what they heard, but they obey what God's teaching says. Those who do this will be made happy.

The True Way to Worship God

²⁶People who think they are religious but say things they should not say are just fooling themselves. Their "religion" is worth nothing. ²⁷Religion that God accepts as pure and without fault is this: caring for orphans or widows who need help, and keeping yourself free from the world's evil influence.

Love All People

2 My dear brothers and sisters, as believers in our glorious Lord Jesus Christ, never think some people are more important than others. ²Suppose someone comes into your church meeting wearing nice clothes and a gold ring. At the same time a poor person comes in wearing old, dirty clothes. ³You show special attention to the one wearing nice clothes and say, "Please, sit here in this good seat." But you say to the poor person, "Stand over there," or, "Sit on the floor by my feet." ⁴What are you doing? You are making

brothers and sisters Although the Greek text says "brothers" here and throughout this book, James' words were meant for the entire church, both men and women.

some people more important than others, and with evil thoughts you are deciding that one person is better.

⁵Listen, my dear brothers and sisters! God chose the poor in the world to be rich with faith and to receive the kingdom God promised to those who love him. ⁶But you show no respect to the poor. The rich are always trying to control your lives. They are the ones who take you to court. ⁷And they are the ones who speak against Jesus, who owns you.

⁸This royal law is found in the Scriptures: *d* "Love your neighbour as you love yourself." *n* If you obey this law, you are doing right. ⁹But if you

treat one person as being more important than another, you are sinning. You are guilty of breaking God's law. ¹⁰A person who follows all of

Sidelight

Wearing a gold ring (James 2:2) was a sign of great wealth in New Testament times. People who wanted to show off their wealth would cover their fingers with rings, often several on each finger. They would even rent rings when they particularly wanted to impress people. Imagine the car they would hire to go to the prom!

"Love . . . yourself."   Quotation from Leviticus 19:18.

BIBLE STUDY

Happy People

How many times have you been listening to someone talk and then realised that your mind has been a thousand miles away? And just how embarrassed have you felt when someone has asked you a question relating to that talk? Sometimes it's not even that you didn't want to hear it, but your mind just wandered!

James 1:25 tells us that people who remember what they heard are "happy people" – but it also says that they studied and memorised too!

Here's something to think about:

* You remember 10 per cent of what you hear.
* You remember 30 per cent of what you write down.
* You remember 45 per cent of what you study . . . and . . .
* 100 per cent of what you memorise!

When Ruth went on a youth weekend, she was told that there would be a big prize for whoever could memorise the most of part of the Bible. Some kids were going for 50 words (that's three or four verses), some decided to get together and test each other on a whole parable (word perfect!). Ruth went for Genesis chapter 1. On the final night of the holiday, ten kids had learnt more scripture than they'd ever learnt before. The guy that came third had learnt 230 words! The guy that came second could remember 340 words! Ruth won, she doggedly kept going until she could recite over 500 words of the story of creation!

Sometimes we just need a little incentive, but each of these kids was thrilled to realise that God's word could be fun to learn and then easy to use!

Read **James 1:17–27** to discover what James says about studying the Bible.

* What happens if you hear and do nothing?
* How might your life change if you accepted James's challenge?

Consider . . .

* memorising a few important verses of scripture and repeating them daily.
* taking notes the next time you hear a sermon in church. You'll be amazed how much you will remember.

For more, see . . .

* Psalm 119:9–16 (p.571)   * Luke 11:27–28 (p.1061)
* Acts 17:11 (p.1168)

God's law but fails to obey even one command is guilty of breaking all the commands in that law. [11]The same God who said, "You must not be guilty of adultery," [d,n] also said, "You must not murder anyone." [n] So if you do not take part in adultery but you murder someone, you are guilty of breaking all of God's law. [12]In everything you say and do, remember that you will be judged by the law that makes people free. [13]So you must show mercy to others, or God will not show mercy to you when he judges you. But the person who shows mercy can stand without fear at the judgement.

Faith and Good Works

[14]My brothers and sisters, if people say they have faith, but do nothing, their faith is worth nothing.

Can faith like that save them? [15]A brother or sister in Christ might need clothes or food. [16]If you say to that person, "God be with you! I hope you stay warm and get plenty to eat," but you do not give what that person needs, your words are worth nothing. [17]In the same way, faith that is alone—that does nothing—is dead.

[18]Someone might say, "You have faith, but I have deeds." Show me your faith without doing anything, and I will show you my faith by what I do. [19]You believe there is one God. Good! But the demons [d] believe that too, and they tremble with fear.

[20]You foolish person! Must you be shown that faith that does nothing is worth nothing? [21]Abraham, our ancestor, was made right with God by

"You . . . adultery,"   Quotation from Exodus 20:14; Deuteronomy 5:18.
"You . . . anyone."   Quotation from Exodus 20:13; Deuteronomy 5:17.

STEREOTYPES

A Perfect Ten?

Pat and her friends moved down the food queue. Two boys serving food watched Pat and the other girls, and grinned. When she got near them, they reached under the counter, pulled out two cardboard signs with numbers, and put them on a high ledge behind them. "9" and "5", Pat thought, reading the cards. "I wonder what they mean?"

When Pat's friend Mary got to the same place in the queue, the boys changed the numbers to an "8" and a "6". By now everybody had stopped eating to watch. When the next girl in the queue received a "9" and a "7", people cheered. "They're rating us," Pat suddenly realised. Her face turned red.

Pat and her friends laughed uncomfortably as the two boys continued to rate girls as they passed in line. Then Debbie joined the queue. She wasn't "perfect-looking" and was a bit overweight. Pat dreaded how the boys might rate Debbie. But as she passed along the queue, the boys just ignored her. They didn't rate her at all. Then, when other "better-looking" girls came up in the line, the boys resumed their rating game. But the game wasn't funny to Pat. She felt judged, and imagined how hurt Debbie probably felt.

Sometimes it may seem like fun to judge other people, but being judged is rarely funny. Read in **James 2:1–17** what James wrote about treating people as though they are more important than others.

- What does James say is wrong with judging people the way the boys were rating the girls in the food queue?
- When have you judged someone unfairly because of clothes or grades or skill at sports? What makes us fall into doing things like that?

Consider . . .

- thinking about one person that you have judged. The next time you see this person, say, "Hello".
- watching this week how often you put people down. Whenever you realise that you have put someone down, quickly say something that builds the person up too.

For more, see . . .

- 1 Samuel 16:7 (p.269)
- Romans 12:14–16 (p.1205)
- Matthew 7:1–5 (p.949)

what he did when he offered his son Isaac on the altar. ²²So you see that Abraham's faith and the things he did worked together. His faith was made perfect by what he did. ²³This shows the full meaning of the Scripture *d* that says: "Abraham believed God, and God accepted Abraham's faith, and that faith made him right with God." *n* And Abraham was called God's friend. *n* ²⁴So you see that people are made right with God by what they do, not by faith only.

²⁵Another example is Rahab, a prostitute, *d* who was made right with God by something she did. She welcomed the spies into her home and helped them escape by a different road.

²⁶Just as a person's body that does not have a spirit is dead, so faith that does nothing is dead!

Controlling the Things We Say

3 My brothers and sisters, not many of you should become teachers, because you know that we who teach will be judged more strictly. ²We all make many mistakes. If people never said anything wrong, they would be perfect and able to control their entire selves too. ³When we put bits into the mouths of horses to make them obey us, we can control their whole bodies. ⁴Also a ship is very big, and it is pushed by strong winds. But a very small rudder controls that big ship, making it go wherever the person wants. ⁵It is the same with the tongue. It is a small part of the body, but it boasts about great things.

A big forest fire can be started with only a little flame. ⁶And the tongue is like a fire. It is a whole world of evil among the parts of our bodies. The tongue spreads its evil through the whole body. The tongue is set on fire by hell, and it starts a fire that influences all of life. ⁷People can tame every kind of wild animal, bird, reptile and fish, and they have tamed them, ⁸but no one can tame the tongue. It is wild and evil and full of deadly poison. ⁹We use our tongues to praise our Lord and Father, but then we curse people, whom God made like himself. ¹⁰Praises and curses come from the same mouth! My brothers and sisters, this should not happen. ¹¹Do good and bad water flow from the same spring? ¹²My brothers and sisters, can a fig tree make olives, or can a grapevine make figs? No! And a well full of salty water cannot give good water.

True Wisdom

¹³Are there those among you who are truly wise and understanding? Then they should show it by living right and doing good things with a gentleness that comes from wisdom. ¹⁴But if you

are selfish and have bitter jealousy in your hearts, do not boast. Your boasting is a lie that hides the truth. ¹⁵That kind of "wisdom" does not come from God but from the world. It is not spiritual; it is from the devil. ¹⁶Where jealousy and selfishness are, there will be confusion and every kind of evil. ¹⁷But the wisdom that comes from God is first of all pure, then peaceful, gentle and easy to please. This wisdom is always ready to help those who are troubled and to do good for others. It is always fair and honest. ¹⁸People who work for peace in a peaceful way plant a good crop of good living.

Give Yourselves to God

4 Do you know where your fights and arguments come from? They come from the selfish desires that war within you. ²You want things, but you do not have them. So you are ready to kill and are jealous of other people, but you still cannot get what you want. So you argue and fight. You do not get what you want, because you do not ask God. ³Or when you ask, you do not receive because the reason you ask is wrong. You want things so you can use them for your own pleasures.

⁴So, you are not loyal to God! You should know that loving the world is the same as hating God. Anyone who wants to be a friend of the world becomes God's enemy. ⁵Do you think the Scripture *d* means nothing that says, "The Spirit *d* that God made to live in us wants us for himself alone." *n* ⁶But God gives us even more grace, as the Scripture says,

"God is against the proud,
but he gives grace to the humble."

Proverbs 3:34

⁷So give yourselves completely to God. Stand against the devil, and the devil will run from you. ⁸Come near to God, and God will come near to you. You sinners, clean sin out of your lives. You who are trying to follow God and the world at the same time, make your thinking pure. ⁹Be sad, cry and weep! Change your laughter into crying and your joy into sadness. ¹⁰Don't be too proud in the Lord's presence, and he will make you great.

You Are Not the Judge

¹¹Brothers and sisters, do not tell evil lies about each other. If you speak against your fellow believers or judge them, you are judging and speaking against the law they follow. And when you are judging the law, you are no longer a follower of the law. You have become a judge. ¹²God is

"Abraham . . . God."   Quotation from Genesis 15:6.
God's friend   These words about Abraham are found in 2 Chronicles 20:7 and Isaiah 41:8.
"The Spirit . . . alone."   These words may be from Exodus 20:5.

the only Lawmaker and Judge. He is the only One who can save and destroy. So it is not right for you to judge your neighbour.

Let God Plan Your Life

¹³Some of you say, "Today or tomorrow we will go to some city. We will stay there a year, do business and make money." ¹⁴But you do not know what will happen tomorrow! Your life is like a mist. You can see it for a short time, but then it goes away. ¹⁵So you should say, "If the Lord wants, we will live and do this or that." ¹⁶But now you are proud and you boast. All of this boasting is wrong. ¹⁷Anyone who knows the right thing to do, but does not do it, is sinning.

A Warning to the Rich

5 You rich people, listen! Cry and be very sad because of the troubles that are coming to you. ²Your riches have rotted, and your clothes have been eaten by moths. ³Your gold and silver have rusted, and that rust will be a proof that you were wrong. It will eat your bodies like fire. You saved your treasure for the last days. ⁴The pay

you did not give the workers who harvested your fields cries out against you, and the cries of the workers have been heard by the Lord All-powerful. ⁵Your life on earth was full of rich living and pleasing yourselves with everything you wanted. You made yourselves fat, like an animal ready to be killed. ⁶You have judged guilty and then murdered innocent people, who were not against you.

Be Patient

⁷Brothers and sisters, be patient until the Lord comes again. A farmer patiently waits for his valuable crop to grow from the earth and for it to receive the autumn and spring rains. ⁸You, too, must be patient. Do not give up hope, because the Lord is coming soon. ⁹Brothers and sisters, do not complain against each other or you will be judged guilty. And the Judge is ready to come! ¹⁰Brothers and sisters, follow the example of the prophets *d* who spoke for the Lord. They suffered many hard things, but they were patient. ¹¹We say they are happy because they did not give up. You have heard about Job's patience, and you

---

BOASTING

Spain's Greatest Matador . . . Almost

Though only twenty-one years old, José Cubero had leaped to fame as one of Spain's most spectacular matadors. In bullfight after bullfight, he had dodged his way to triumph.

It was no surprise, then, when he made especially quick work of a bull during a routine bullfight. Thrusting his sword one last time, José watched the bull collapse on to the dirt of the arena. José had performed well, and he knew it. He turned to bask in the applause.

Enjoying the roaring cheers, José was unaware that the bull behind him was not dead. The bull suddenly rose and lunged, one of its horns piercing the matador from the back. José Cubero, a rising young star, was dead.

When we have done well, we like to get people's attention. We like to listen to the cheers. But James reminds us in **James 3:13–18** to do "good things with a gentleness that comes from wisdom." Boasting of our actions is a dangerous practice.

* What else might James have told José Cubero about boasting?
* What makes people eager to boast? Why might Christians have less need to boast?

Consider . . .

* noticing, as you watch television today, which characters boast. How do you feel about these characters?
* writing on a card this saying: "There's no limit to the amount of good you can do if you don't care who gets the credit." Place it where you will see it.

For more, see . . .

* Daniel 4:28–37 (p.837)
* Philippians 2:3–11 (p.1282)

* Luke 14:7–11 (p.1069)

know the Lord's purpose for him in the end. You know the Lord is full of mercy and is kind.

Be Careful What You Say

[12]My brothers and sisters, above all, do not use an oath when you make a promise. Don't use the name of heaven, earth or anything else to prove what you say. When you mean yes, say only "yes", and when you mean no, say only "no" so you will not be judged guilty.

The Power of Prayer

[13]Anyone who is having troubles should pray. Anyone who is happy should sing praises.

[14]Anyone who is sick should call the church's elders. [d] They should pray for and pour oil on the person [n] in the name of the Lord. [15]And the prayer that is said with faith will make the

---

Sidelight

Using oil as medicine was a common practice in Bible times (James 5:14). The good Samaritan in Jesus' parable poured oil on the victim's wounds (Luke 10:34, p.1058). People who had headaches probably had the greasiest heads in town!

---

pour oil on the person Oil was used in the name of the Lord as a sign that the person was now set apart for God's special attention and care.

GOD'S WILL

Thy Will be Done

It's so easy to fantasise about what you would do if you were all of a sudden struck down by some fatal disease. How you would react, how you would be a martyr and accept it. But most of us know that deep down, we would be terrified and yell at God about the unfairness of it all.

Mark was twenty-one years old. Good looking, athletic, he had a host of admirers. One day he had a headache, and by the evening he was feeling really bad. By the next morning he was in intensive care with a suspected brain tumour. His close friends came to see him at the hospital and nobody knew what to say.

"Don't worry lads," he said. "God knows what he's doing."

His friends left the ward devastated. These things just didn't happen to someone like him.

Mark was released from hospital after an operation that was only half-successful. It left him knowing that he had maybe only a few months to live. His mother wanted him to stay at home and be looked after. His church wanted to help him. His friends wanted him to do whatever he felt he should do.

So Mark went into schools, telling kids about his faith in Jesus and the fact that life was precious. He told them about his own life and how it would shortly end, but he knew that God had planned it this way, and he was adamant about it.

Finally, Mark became paralysed and his friends rushed to his bedside where he asked to take communion with them.

As the wine was held to his lips, he whispered, "Isn't it wonderful what Jesus did for us?" and smiled.

He died shortly afterwards.

James 4:13–17 reminds us that our future is in God's hands.

* How was Mark's faith relevant to this passage?
* What plans have you got for your future? How does God fit in to them?

Consider . . .

* evaluating your dreams for the future in the light of this passage on God's will.
* having an "In God's Hands" file. Write down those things that you have to face in the future that you cannot control . . . and commit them to God.

For more, see . . .

* Psalm 139 (p.581)
* Matthew 6:25–34 (p.948)

* Proverbs 16:1–9 (p.603)

sick person well; the Lord will heal that person. And if the person has sinned, the sins will be forgiven. [16]Confess your sins to each other and pray for each other so God can heal you. When a believing person prays, great things happen. [17]Elijah was a human being just like us. He prayed that it would not rain, and it did not rain on the land for three and a half years! [18]Then Elijah prayed again, and the rain came down from the sky, and the land produced crops again.

Saving a Soul

[19]My brothers and sisters, if one of you wanders away from the truth, and someone helps that person come back, [20]remember this: anyone who brings a sinner back from the wrong way will save that sinner's soul from death and will cause many sins to be forgiven.

PATIENCE

What Are You Waiting For?

Connor and Gaz had been friends since year 7. They were both really into skateboarding and spent many hours at the local skate park hanging out with the older lads, perfecting their moves.

Gaz emailed Connor to say that they should meet up back at the skate park. The meeting was set and Gaz arrived early. It was a hot day, so he plonked himself down on a bench and waited for his friend. An hour went by and still Connor didn't show.

Gaz began to walk round the park to check other areas: maybe Connor had forgotten where to go. Just then, he got a text from Connor. "Sorry I'm late. Took the wrong bus. Wait by the skate park. I'll be there soon." Gaz smiled to himself. Connor had never been great at timekeeping, but he was happy to wait. He knew Connor would arrive soon.

Read **James 5:7–11**.

* Gaz was beginning to lose hope that Connor would ever show up. Have you ever felt that you had to wait a long time for God to answer your prayer? Why do you think this is?
* Can you think of someone who has persevered in the face of suffering but who, when the time of pain and difficulty was over, praised God for being good to them? How does that make you feel about issues you're facing?

Consider . . .

* what things you are *really* waiting for. Why don't you pray for God to give you patience?
* how we often have to be patient when we're trying to get good at something – we're not usually great straight away! Why not try learning a new skill to teach you patience and perseverance?

For more, see . . .

* 2 Corinthians 4:16–18 (p.1244)
* Hebrews 10:35–39 (p.1341)
* Galatians 5:22 (p.1264)

1 Peter

Why Read This Book:

- See the benefits of the salvation that God offers you (1 Peter 1:3—2:10).
- Discover how Christians should live (1 Peter 2:11—4:11).
- Learn how to grow even when suffering (1 Peter 4:12—5:11).

When?

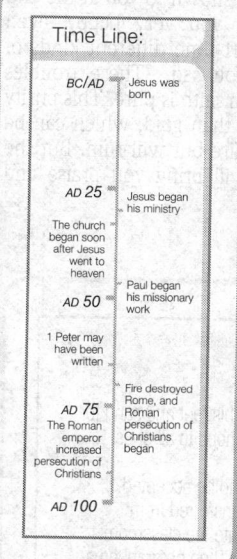

Time Line:

BC/AD	Jesus was born
AD 25	Jesus began his ministry
The church began soon after Jesus went to heaven	
AD 50	Paul began his missionary work
1 Peter may have been written	
AD 75	Fire destroyed Rome, and Roman persecution of Christians began
The Roman emperor increased persecution of Christians	
AD 100	

Behind the Scenes:

Living the Christian life at school or work doesn't always make us popular. Our friends might laugh at us, or make fun of us because of what we believe. Let's face it, living it out in the real world can be tough sometimes. It was certainly tough for the Christians of Asia Minor (modern-day Turkey). They lived in a pagan society, and were laughed at and even beaten and killed because of their faith. Some of them might have felt that living the Christian life was too difficult, or too painful. Some may even have been tempted to get rid of their Christian "label" altogether, and return to living comfortable lives as pagans.

It was to these people that the apostle Peter wrote this letter. It encouraged the Christians of Asia Minor to stick with their faith, despite the suffering to which they were being subjected. It offered practical advice about how they could cope with the pressures they faced and how to live with the pain – reminding them that in everything, no matter how bad things got, God was still in control, and he cared for them with all of his heart.

Maybe you are having a tough time as a Christian. Maybe those around you are making your life uncomfortable, or even painful. Maybe you too are tempted to shake off your Christian "label". Don't give up! Read 1 Peter and apply what he says to your life, and no matter what your life's circumstances are, you too can feel good about the fact that God is in control, and that he will make sure that you are on the winning side in the long term.

Where?

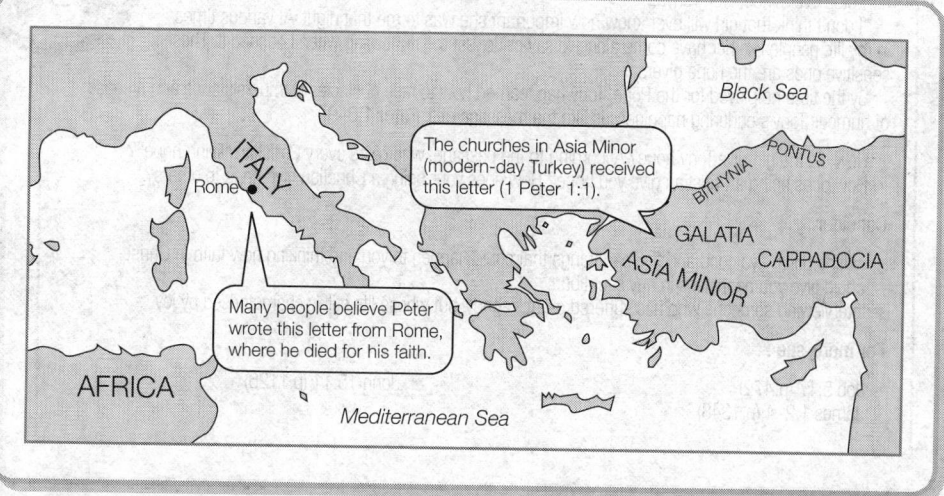

Black Sea

PONTUS

BITHYNIA

GALATIA

CAPPADOCIA

ASIA MINOR

ITALY

Rome

AFRICA

Mediterranean Sea

The churches in Asia Minor (modern-day Turkey) received this letter (1 Peter 1:1).

Many people believe Peter wrote this letter from Rome, where he died for his faith.

1 From Peter, an apostle *d* of Jesus Christ.
To God's chosen people who are away from their homes and are scattered all around the countries of Pontus, Galatia, Cappadocia, Asia and Bithynia. ²God planned long ago to choose you by making you his holy people, which is the Spirit's *d* work. God wanted you to obey him and to be made clean by the blood of the death of Jesus Christ.

Grace and peace be yours more and more.

We Have a Living Hope

³Praise be to the God and Father of our Lord Jesus Christ. In God's great mercy he has caused us to be born again into a living hope, because Jesus Christ rose from the dead. ⁴Now we hope for the blessings God has for his children. These blessings, which cannot be destroyed or be spoiled or lose their beauty, are kept in heaven for you. ⁵God's power protects you through your faith until salvation *d* is shown to you at the end of time. ⁶This makes you very happy, even though now for a short time different kinds of troubles may make you sad. ⁷These troubles come to prove that your faith is pure. This purity of faith is worth more than gold, which can be proved to be pure by fire but will ruin. But the purity of your faith will bring you praise and

HAPPINESS

The Hope Giver

Tony Melendez amazed 100 million US TV viewers in 1987 as he played the guitar with his feet and sang for Pope John Paul II. "Tony," the Pope said, after embracing the performer, "you are giving hope to all of us. My wish to you is to continue giving this hope to all the people."

Born without arms, Tony is normal in every other way. But he had struggled for years to be accepted. Without persistence, Tony might never have graduated from high school. When he transferred from special education into a "normal" English class, all eyes watched him when he walked into the classroom. He shrugged off his rucksack, pulled out a notebook with his toes and put it on the floor. Then he grabbed a pencil between his two biggest toes and began taking notes. Even the teacher had stopped the discussion of *Moby Dick* to watch. Everyone stared in silence.

"Somebody had to break the silence," Tony recalled. "Hope the floor is clean," he said with a grin. "If it isn't, I'll have to turn in a dirty paper." The students and teacher laughed, and then the lesson continued. It was one of the many awkward times when he had to show his strength.

Still, Tony was afraid to go to school dances – afraid he would be rejected by girls. But he finally faced his fears and went alone. He stood along the side watching, wondering if everyone was watching him. Then all of a sudden a girl from his English class walked up, looked him in the eye, and said, "Go!" Seconds later the couple were tearing up the floor. "I've been dancing almost non-stop ever since," Tony says.

"I don't think that girl will ever know how important she was to me that night. At various times in my life people like her have come along to say or do just the right thing when I needed it. These sensitive ones are the hope givers."

By the time he played for the Pope, Tony had learned how to face obstacles with persistence and a sense of humour. Tony's enduring happiness is like the message of **1 Peter 1:3–9**.

* How did the girl give Tony hope? According to the passage, who gives every Christian "living hope"?
* How does being a Christian give you hope? How does your being a Christian give hope to others?

Consider . . .

* writing down five good and five bad things that could happen to you and thinking how faith in Christ could give you happiness in any situation.
* interviewing someone who has suffered great tragedy, but whose life still is characterised by joy.

For more, see . . .

* Job 5:17 (p.472)
* James 1:2–4 (p.1348)
* John 15:11 (p.1125)

glory and honour when Jesus Christ is shown to you. [8]You have not seen Christ, but still you love him. You cannot see him now, but you believe in him. So you are filled with a joy that cannot be explained, a joy full of glory. [9]And you are receiving the goal of your faith—the salvation of your souls.

[10]The prophets [d] searched carefully and tried to learn about this salvation. They prophesied about the grace that was coming to you. [11]The Spirit [d] of Christ was in the prophets, telling in advance about the sufferings of Christ and about the glory that would follow those sufferings. The prophets tried to learn about what the Spirit was showing them, when those things would happen, and what the world would be like at that time. [12]It was shown them that their service was not for themselves but for you, when they told about the truths you have now heard. Those who preached the Good News [d] to you told you those things with the help of the Holy Spirit who was sent from heaven—things into which angels desire to look.

A Call to Holy Living

[13]So prepare your minds for service and have self-control. All your hope should be for the gift of grace that will be yours when Jesus Christ is shown to you. [14]Now that you are obedient children of God do not live as you did in the past. You did not understand, so you did the evil things you wanted. [15]But be holy in all you do, just as God, the One who called you, is holy. [16]It is written in the Scriptures: [d] "You must be holy, because I am holy." [n]

[17]You pray to God and call him Father, and he judges each person's work equally. So while you are here on earth, you should live with respect for God. [18]You know that in the past you were living in a worthless way, a way passed down from the people who lived before you. But you were saved from that useless life. You were bought, not with something that ruins like gold or silver, [19]but with the precious blood of Christ, who was like a pure and perfect lamb. [20]Christ was chosen before the world was made, but he was shown to the world in these last times for your sake. [21]Through Christ you believe in God, who raised Christ from the dead and gave him glory. So your faith and your hope are in God.

[22]Now that you have made your souls pure by obeying the truth, you can have true love for your Christian brothers and sisters. [n] So love each other deeply with all your heart. [23]You have been born again, and this new life did not come from something that dies, but from something that cannot die. You were born again through God's living message that continues for ever. [24]The Scripture says,

"All people are like the grass,
    and all their glory is like the flowers of the
        field.
The grass dies and the flowers fall,
[25]   but the word of the Lord will live for
        ever."   *Isaiah 40:6–8*
And this is the word that was preached to you.

Jesus is the Living Stone

2 So then, rid yourselves of all evil, all lying, hypocrisy, [d] jealousy and evil speech. [2]As newborn babies want milk, you should want the pure and simple teaching. By it you can grow up and be saved, [3]because you have already examined and seen how good the Lord is.

[4]Come to the Lord Jesus, the "stone" [n] that lives. The people of the world did not want this stone, but he was the stone God chose, and he was precious. [5]You also are like living stones, so let yourselves be used to build a spiritual temple—to be holy priests who offer spiritual sacrifices to God. He will accept those sacrifices through Jesus Christ. [6]The Scripture [d] says:

"I will put a stone in the ground in
    Jerusalem.
Everything will be built on this important
    and precious rock.
Anyone who trusts in him
    will never be disappointed."   *Isaiah 28:16*
[7]This stone is worth much to you who believe. But to the people who do not believe,

"the stone that the builders rejected
    has become the cornerstone." [d]   *Psalm 118:22*
[8]Also, he is

"a stone that causes people to stumble,
    a rock that makes them fall."   *Isaiah 8:14*
They stumble because they do not obey what God says, which is what God planned to happen to them.

[9]But you are a chosen people, royal priests, a holy nation, a people for God's own possession. You were chosen to tell about the wonderful acts of God, who called you out of darkness into his wonderful light. [10]At one time you were not a people, but now you are God's people. In the

---

"You must be . . . holy."   Quotation from Leviticus 11:45; 19:2; 20:7.
brothers and sisters   Although the Greek text says "brothers" here and throughout this book, Peter's words refer to the entire church, both men and women.
"stone"   The most important stone in God's spiritual temple or house (his people).

past you had never received mercy, but now you have received God's mercy.

Live for God

[11]Dear friends, you are like foreigners and strangers in this world. I beg you to avoid the evil things your bodies want to do that fight against your soul. [12]People who do not believe are living all around you and might say that you are doing wrong. Live such good lives that they will see the good things you do and will give glory to God on the day when Christ comes again.

Yield to Every Human Authority

[13]For the Lord's sake, yield to the people who have authority in this world: the king, who is the highest authority, [14]and the leaders who are sent by him to punish those who do wrong and to praise those who do right. [15]It is God's desire that by doing good you should stop foolish people from saying stupid things about you. [16]Live as free people, but do not use your freedom as an excuse to do evil. Live as servants of God. [17]Show respect for all people: love the brothers and sisters of God's family, respect God, honour the king.

LOVE

Given, Not Earned

The argument was brutal. Rachel's parents didn't want her to go to the party. They didn't know the boy throwing it, didn't know his parents, didn't know who was going to be there, and didn't know what the teenagers would be doing.

"You're eighteen years old, Rachel," her father said. "We won't forbid you to go. But if you ignore our wishes on this, don't expect us to honour your wishes on other things . . . including the use of the car."

They thought that withholding the car would stop her.

But it didn't. "I'm tired of you using the car to force me to do what you want," she shot back. "Just keep the car! I don't need it! I've got friends who'll take me to parties!"

With that, she stormed out, called her friends, and headed for the party. Rachel savoured her apparent victory.

But then she arrived at the party. It was wild. Heavy drinking. Too many people. No adults around.

She wanted to leave but her "friends" had left without her. She was left to walk 10 kilometres home.

She stood alone outside, wondering what to do.

"Hey, Beautiful! Want a lift?" a voice said from a car pulling up behind her. Rachel felt a surge of fear, and looked for somewhere to run. But when she glanced over her shoulder at the car, she saw her dad's smiling face.

She got in. Dad spoke first. "Diana phoned," he explained. "She said that they tried to find you before they left but it was too crowded. They wanted to get out of there before their car got blocked in."

"I didn't think you'd be willing to come and get me," Rachel said. "Not after the things I said and did."

Dad pulled the car over and turned to look at her. "Hey," he said. "You're my daughter. I love you. Nothing you say or do can ever change that."

Rachel learned something about true love that night. **1 Peter 1:17–23** talks about the kind of love that Rachel felt from her dad.

- According to the passage, how is Rachel's dad's love for her like God's love?
- How might your life change if you trusted and accepted God's love as described in 1 Peter?

Consider . . .

- comparing your parents' love with God's love. Share your observations with your mum or dad.
- talking with a grandparent, aunt, or uncle about times when someone had to discipline your mum or dad. How was that person's love like God's love for you?

For more, see . . .

- Deuteronomy 7:7–9 (p.172)
- 1 John 4:7–10 (p.1374)
- Romans 4:1–8 (p.1188)

Follow Christ's Example

18Slaves, yield to the authority of your masters with all respect, not only those who are

good and kind, but also those who are dishonest. 19A person might have to suffer even when it is unfair, but if he thinks of God and stands the pain, God is pleased. 20If you are beaten for doing wrong, there is no reason to praise you for being patient in your punishment. But if you suffer for doing good, and you are patient, then God is pleased. 21This is what you were called to do, because Christ suffered for you and gave you an example to follow. So you should do as he did.

22"He had never sinned,
    and he had never lied."   *Isaiah 53:9*

23People insulted Christ, but he did not insult them in return. Christ suffered, but he did not threaten. He let God, the One who judges rightly, take care of him. 24Christ carried our sins in his body on the cross so we would stop living for sin and start living for what is right. And you are healed because of his wounds. 25You were like sheep that wandered away, but now you have come back to the Shepherd and Protector of your souls.

SELF-ESTEEM

Bully Boy

For as long as he could remember, Ben had been teased because he was thin. The other boys of his age who were more muscular enjoyed shoving him around and making him feel small, and if there was one thing that Ben hated, it was feeling small.

Like many people who get bullied, instead of doing something positive to deal with the problem, Ben became a bully too.

Obviously, he couldn't bully the boys who were the same age as him because he was the smallest, so he decided to pick on the boys who were younger. He would wait for them to come out of school and then begin to tease them for being so young and weak. Bullying other people made him feel strong and powerful, and that's how he had always wanted to feel.

As the months passed, the boys that Ben bullied decided to continue the chain and bully those who were even younger. Before long there weren't many boys in the school who weren't being bullied by someone or other, and that was all because Ben had decided to try and build his self-esteem at any cost.

1 Peter 2:2–10 tells how Jesus offers a different foundation for building self-esteem.

* If Ben had read this passage, how might he have reacted differently in the situation?
* Whenever your self-esteem takes a knock, how can this passage help you to regain it?

Consider . . .

* what lengths you would go to in order to gain your self-esteem. How do these lengths compare with the teaching contained in this passage?
* making a list of five people you know who have a poor self-esteem.

For more, see . . .

* Isaiah 8:12–14 (p.649)
* 2 Corinthians 6:3–10 (p.1246)
* Hosea 2:23 (p.852)

Wives and Husbands

3 In the same way, you wives should yield to your husbands. Then, if some husbands do not obey God's teaching, they will be persuaded to believe without anyone saying a word to them. They will be persuaded by the way their wives live. [2]Your husbands will see the pure lives you live with your respect for God. [3]It is not fancy hair, gold jewellery or fine clothes that should make you beautiful. [4]No, your beauty should come from within you—the beauty of a gentle and quiet spirit that will never be destroyed and is very precious to God. [5]In this same way the holy women who lived long ago and followed God made themselves beautiful, yielding to their own husbands. [6]Sarah obeyed Abraham, her husband, and called him her master. And you women are true children of Sarah if you always do what is right and are not afraid.

Sidelight When 1 Peter 3:3–4 says true beauty comes from the inside, it would not have made the jewellery merchants happy. In those times, women would decorate their hair with elaborate combs and hairpins, some of which were made of gold and all of which were expensive to buy.

---

[7]In the same way, you husbands should live with your wives in an understanding way, since being answered they are weaker than you. But show them respect, because God gives them the same blessing he gives to you—the grace that gives true life. Do this so that nothing will stop your prayer.

Suffering for Doing Right

[8]Finally, all of you should be in agreement, understanding each other, loving each other as family, being kind and humble. [9]Do not do wrong to repay a wrong, and do not insult to repay an insult. But repay with a blessing, because you yourselves were called to do this so that you might receive a blessing. [10]The Scripture [d] says,

"You must do these things
    to enjoy life and have many happy days.
You must not say evil things,
    and you must not tell lies.
[11]Stop doing evil and do good.
    Look for peace and work for it.
[12]The Lord sees the good people
    and listens to their prayers.
But the Lord is against
    those who do evil."   *Psalm 34:12–16*

[13]If you are trying hard to do good, no one can really hurt you. [14]But even if you suffer for doing right, you are blessed.

"Don't be afraid of what they fear;
    do not dread those things."   *Isaiah 8:12–13*

[15]But respect Christ as the holy Lord in your hearts. Always be ready to answer everyone who asks you to explain about the hope you have, [16]but answer in a gentle way and with respect. Keep a clear conscience so that those who speak evil of your good life in Christ will be made ashamed. [17]It is better to suffer for doing good than for doing wrong if that is what God wants. [18]Christ himself suffered for sins once. He was not guilty, but he suffered for those who are guilty to bring you to God. His body was killed, but he was made alive in the spirit. [19]And in the spirit he went and preached to the spirits in prison [20]who refused to obey God long ago in the time of Noah. God was waiting patiently for them while Noah was building the boat. Only a few people—eight in all—were saved by water. [21]And that water is like baptism [d] that now saves you—not the washing of dirt from the body, but the promise made to God from a good conscience. And this is because Jesus Christ was raised from the dead. [22]Now Jesus has gone into heaven and is at God's right side ruling over angels, authorities and powers.

Change Your Lives

4 Since Christ suffered while he was in his body, strengthen yourselves with the same way of thinking Christ had. The person who has suffered in the body is finished with sin. [2]Strengthen yourselves so that you will live here on earth doing what God wants, not the evil things people want. [3]In the past you wasted too much time doing what non-believers enjoy. You were guilty of sexual sins, evil desires, getting drunk, wild and drunken parties, and hateful idol worship. [4]Non-believers think it is strange that you do not do the many wild and wasteful things they do, so they insult you. [5]But they will have to explain this to God, who is ready to judge the living and the dead. [6]For this reason the Good News [d] was preached to those who are now dead. Even though they were judged like all people, the Good News was preached to them so they could live in the spirit as God lives.

Use God's Gifts Wisely

[7]The time is near when all things will end. So think clearly and control yourselves so that you will be able to pray. [8]Most importantly, love each other deeply, because love will cause

many sins to be forgiven. ⁹Open your homes to each other, without complaining. ¹⁰Each of you has received a gift to use to serve others. Be good servants of God's various gifts of grace. ¹¹Anyone who speaks should speak words from God. Anyone who serves should serve with the strength God gives so that in everything God will be praised through Jesus Christ. Power and glory belong to him for ever and ever. Amen.

Suffering as a Christian

¹²My friends, do not be surprised at the terrible trouble which now comes to test you. Do not think that something strange is happening to you. ¹³But be happy that you are sharing in Christ's sufferings so that you will be happy and full of joy when Christ comes again in glory.

¹⁴When people insult you because you follow Christ, you are blessed, because the glorious Spirit, ^{d} the Spirit of God, is with you. ¹⁵Do not suffer for murder, theft or any other crime, nor because you trouble other people. ¹⁶But if you suffer because you are a Christian, do not be ashamed. Praise God because you wear that name. ¹⁷It is time for judgement to begin with God's family. And if that judging begins with us, what will happen to those people who do not obey the Good News ^{d} of God?

¹⁸"If it is very hard for a good person to be saved,

the wicked person and the sinner will surely be lost!" ^{n}

¹⁹So those who suffer as God wants should trust their souls to the faithful Creator as they continue to do what is right.

"If . . . lost!"   Quotation from Proverbs 11:31 in the Septuagint, the Greek version of the Old Testament.

SUFFERING

The Cost of Faith

"Listen," said Jason to his friend Baz. "I don't want to hear about your Jesus! Leave me alone!"

The words broke Baz's heart. Jason had been his best friend since they moved up to middle school. But now, three years later, their friendship was in jeopardy because Baz had become a Christian and had let his friends know.

Jason had confronted Baz at a friend's party, accusing him of "thinking you're better than everyone else" because Baz had chosen not to drink any more.

"Let me know when you get over this religion stuff," Jason had said. "Maybe then we can be friends again."

At that, Jason left Baz standing alone. Baz feared that he had just lost his best friend.

"No one ever told me that being a Christian could hurt like this or cost so much," Baz muttered to himself as he went home. "Perhaps it's just not worth it. I thought being a Christian meant that life got better, not more painful."

As we grow in faith, we change. Sometimes friends change with us. Sometimes they don't. This change may cause some pain. **1 Peter 4:12–19** reminds us that being a Christian does not insulate us from pain and suffering. In fact, Peter lets us know that we can expect it as we grow in Christ. He also reminds us that some things are worth suffering for.

- What comfort or understanding might this passage give to Baz in the loss of his friendship with Jason?
- When have you paid for your faith? How did you grow from that experience?

Consider . . .

- praying for a friend that you know is suffering at present.
- reading about the life of a Christian martyr. Your minister can help you to find such a story.

For more, see . . .

- Psalm 56:1–4 (p.532)
- 1 Peter 2:19–25 (p.1359)
- John 15:18–21 (p.1125)

The Flock of God

5 Now I have something to say to the elders*d* in your group. I also am an elder. I have seen Christ's sufferings, and I will share in the glory that will be shown to us. I beg you to ²shepherd God's flock, for whom you are responsible. Watch over them because you want to, not because you are forced. That is how God wants it. Do it because you are happy to serve, not because you want money. ³Do not be like a ruler over people you are responsible for, but be good examples to them. ⁴Then when Christ, the Chief Shepherd, comes, you will get a glorious crown that will never lose its beauty.

⁵In the same way, younger people should be willing to be under older people. And all of you should be very humble with each other.

"God is against the proud,
    but he gives grace to the humble."

Proverbs 3:34

⁶Be humble under God's powerful hand so he will lift you up when the right time comes. ⁷Give all your worries to him, because he cares about you.

DRUGS AND ALCOHOL

Out of Control

Sue worried a lot about Mandy. She was such a great outgoing sort of girl, but always on the lookout for something new to try. She got bored fairly easily and was always suggesting outrageous things to do. When she got her first job in the West End of London, she soon found a crowd of friends who smoked pot. She came home on the train with wide empty eyes, to tell Sue of her new-found hobby.

"It's just great, and it doesn't do you any harm at all!" she laughed.

Sue was not so sure. She'd seen people on drugs before and it hadn't looked so great to her. "Mandy, are you sure about this?" she asked. "Be careful!"

Over the next few months, Mandy progressed from pot to pills. Uppers, downers and speed.

"Hey Sue, take some of these, but be sure not to fall asleep, OK?" she would say.

Her friend always refused, and when Mandy asked why, she would always say, "I don't like being out of control." Mandy would just shrug her shoulders and carry on regardless.

Then one day Sue came across Mandy surrounded by a group of "friends". They seemed to be looking closely at something.

"What is it?" asked Sue, breaking through the group.

Mandy held out her arm. "It's my very first track!" She gave a slightly dazed smile. There on the inside of her arm was a small red vein. Mandy was shooting stuff. Very soon, she was out of control, no turning back. Sue watched two of Mandy's best friends die from overdoses.

1 Peter 5:6–11 states very boldy that if you're out of control, then you're the devil's fodder.

* How was Sue's behaviour like verse 9?
* How could this passage help people you know who may be into drugs?

Consider . . .

* praying seriously for any friends you know who are into drugs.
* being totally honest with yourself if you have a drugs or alcohol problem, and then seeking help from your church or local substance abuse programme.

For more, see . . .

* Psalm 10:6 (p.505)
* 2 Peter 2:18–20 (p.1367)

* Proverbs 5:21–23 (p.593)

[8]Control yourselves and be careful! The devil, your enemy, goes around like a roaring lion looking for someone to eat. [9]Refuse to give in to him, by standing strong in your faith. You know that your Christian family all over the world is having the same kinds of suffering.

[10]And after you suffer for a short time, God, who gives all grace, will make everything right. He will make you strong and support you and keep you from falling. He called you to share in his glory in Christ, a glory that will continue for ever. [11]All power is his for ever and ever. Amen.

Final Greetings

[12]I wrote this short letter with the help of Silas, who I know is a faithful brother in Christ. I wrote to encourage you and to tell you that this is the true grace of God. Stand strong in that grace.

Sidelight

When 1 Peter 5:13 mentions Babylon, it probably refers to Rome, the capital of the Roman Empire. (The comparison comes from the common practice of using Babylon as a "code name" for Rome.) By the time 1 Peter was written, the historic city of Babylon was just a small, insignificant village.

[13]The church in Babylon, chosen like you, sends you greetings. Mark, my son in Christ, also greets you. [14]Give each other a kiss of Christian love when you meet.

Peace to all of you who are in Christ.

2 Peter

When?

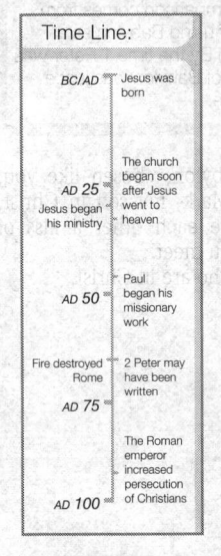

Time Line:

BC/AD	Jesus was born
AD 25 Jesus began his ministry	The church began soon after Jesus went to heaven
AD 50	Paul began his missionary work
Fire destroyed Rome	2 Peter may have been written
AD 75	
AD 100	The Roman emperor increased persecution of Christians

Why Read This Book:

- Be certain that the Christian faith is true (2 Peter 1).
- Learn how to respond to false teaching (2 Peter 2).
- Anticipate Christ's return (2 Peter 3).

Behind the Scenes:

Opinions! Everybody has them and many Christians find it hard to sort them out, but in today's society, it's an issue that crops up again and again. The fact is that there are a lot of different voices in the world telling us entirely different things. Some people claim that Christianity is out of date and useless in the twenty-first century. Others tell us that *they* have a better way of life. A lot of people think that any one religion is as good as another. When it comes down to the bottom line, many Christians ask themselves, "How do I know that I'm right when there are so many other faiths in the world?"

The early Christians probably asked themselves the same thing when false teachers started entering the church. They knew that society had its false teachers, but now they were coming to church! How could they know once and for all that theirs was the true faith?

In 2 Peter, the writer puts their minds at rest. He assures them that the Christian faith is true, and then goes on to tell them all about false teachers, and how they operate. Having said all of that, and having settled any doubts which the Christians had, Peter ends his short letter by reminding them that Christ will come again, and encourages them to concentrate on building up their faith in preparation.

Most Christians have doubts at one time or another. If you have doubts about the Christian faith, read 2 Peter and be certain that the faith is true. If you are already certain, then read 2 Peter and help someone you know who is having doubts.

LIFE FILE LINKS

Investigate the Theme

To find a list of real life stories on this subject turn to the LIFE FILE GUIDE on pages 12 to 22 at the front of the Youth Bible.

FUTURE

1

From Simon Peter, a servant and apostle *d* of Jesus Christ.

To you who have received a faith as valuable as ours, because our God and Saviour *d* Jesus Christ does what is right.

²Grace and peace be given to you more and more, because you truly know God and Jesus our Lord.

Sidelight If you want to read a short version of 2 Peter, look at Jude (p.1384). About nineteen of the twenty-five verses in Jude are similar to verses in 2 Peter.

God Has Given Us Blessings

³Jesus has the power of God, by which he has given us everything we need to live and to serve God. We have these things because we know him. Jesus called us by his glory and goodness. ⁴Through these he gave us the very great and precious promises. With these gifts you can share in being like God, and the world will not ruin you with its evil desires.

⁵Because you have these blessings, do your best to add these things to your lives: to your faith, add goodness; and to your goodness, add knowledge; ⁶and to your knowledge, add self-control; and to your self-control, add patience; and to your patience, add service for God; ⁷and to your service for God, add kindness for your brothers and sisters *n* in Christ; and to this kindness, add love. ⁸If all these things are in you and are growing, they will help you to be useful and productive in your knowledge of our Lord Jesus Christ. ⁹But anyone who does not have these things cannot see clearly. He is blind and has forgotten that he was made clean from his past sins.

¹⁰My brothers and sisters, try hard to be certain that you really are called and chosen by God. If you do all these things, you will never fall. ¹¹And you will be given a very great welcome into the eternal kingdom of our Lord and Saviour Jesus Christ.

¹²You know these things, and you are very strong in the truth, but I will always help you remember them. ¹³I think it is right for me to help you remember as long as I am in this body. ¹⁴I know I must soon leave this body, as our Lord Jesus Christ has shown me. ¹⁵I will try my best so that you may be able to remember these things even after I am gone.

We Saw Christ's Glory

¹⁶When we told you about the powerful coming of our Lord Jesus Christ, we were not telling just clever stories that someone invented. But we saw the greatness of Jesus with our own eyes. ¹⁷Jesus heard the voice of God, the Greatest Glory, when he received honour and glory from God the Father. The voice said, "This is my Son, whom I love, and I am very pleased with him." ¹⁸We heard that voice from heaven while we were with Jesus on the holy mountain.

¹⁹This makes us more sure about the message the prophets *d* gave. It is good for you to follow closely what they said as you would follow a light shining in a dark place, until the day begins and the morning star rises in your hearts. ²⁰Most of all, you must understand this: no prophecy in the Scriptures *d* ever comes from the prophet's own interpretation. ²¹No prophecy ever comes from what a person wanted to say, but people led by the Holy Spirit *d* spoke words from God.

False Teachers

2

There used to be false prophets *d* among God's people, just as you will have some false teachers in your group. They will secretly teach things that are wrong—teachings that will cause people to be lost. They will even refuse to accept the Master, Jesus, who bought their freedom. So they will bring quick ruin on themselves. ²Many will follow their evil ways and say evil things about the way of truth. ³Those false teachers only want your money, so they will use you by telling you lies. Their judgement spoken against them long ago is still coming, and their ruin is certain.

⁴When angels sinned, God did not let them go free without punishment. He sent them to hell and put them in caves of darkness where they are being held for judgement. ⁵And God punished the world long ago when he brought a flood to the world that was full of people who were against him. But God saved Noah, who preached about being right with God, and seven other people with him. ⁶And God also destroyed the evil cities of Sodom *d* and Gomorrah by burning them until they were ashes. He made those cities an example of what will happen to those who are against God. ⁷But he saved Lot from those cities. Lot, a good man, was troubled because of the dirty lives of evil people. ⁸(Lot was a good man, but because he lived with evil people every day, his good heart was hurt by the evil things he saw and heard.) ⁹So the Lord knows how to save

---

brothers and sisters   Although the Greek text says "brothers" here and throughout this book, Peter's words were meant for the entire church, both men and women.

those who serve him when troubles come. He will hold evil people and punish them, while waiting for the Judgement Day. [10]That punishment is especially for those who live by doing the evil things their sinful selves want and who hate authority.

These false teachers are bold and do anything they want. They are not afraid to speak against the angels. [11]But even the angels, who are much stronger and more powerful than false teachers, do not accuse them with insults before the Lord. [12]But these people speak against things they do not understand. They are like animals that act without thinking, animals born to be caught and killed. And, like animals, these false teachers will be destroyed. [13]They have caused many people to suffer, so they themselves will suffer. That is their pay for what they have done. They take pleasure in openly doing evil, so they are like dirty spots and stains among you. They delight in trickery while eating meals with you. [14]Every time they look at a woman they want her, and their desire for sin is never satisfied. They lead weak people into the trap of sin, and they have taught their hearts to be greedy. God will punish them! [15]These false teachers left the right road and lost their way, following the way Balaam went. Balaam was the son of Beor, who loved being paid for doing wrong. [16]But a donkey, which cannot talk, told Balaam he was sinning.

ADDICTION

Twice is Enough

When Caroline saw she was putting on weight she was mortified. This was the kind of thing that happened to her friends. She'd heard them talking about diets and waistlines but had never taken much notice.

So, at the age of eighteen, she decided to go to the gym. It was a great place, not how she'd imagined it at all. The instructors were quite jolly and gave her a good fitness test before they let her do any exercises.

"You're not overweight, Caroline," one of them told her. "You just need to keep fit. If you just tone your muscles up, you'll look and feel loads better."

The first week, she went to the gym on Tuesday and Thursday. The second and third week she did the same. Already Caroline was beginning to see the difference in her appearance, and she liked it!

"Maybe if I went to the gym more often, I'd look even better!" she thought. And so stepped it up to three times a week. By the end of a few months, Caroline was going to the gym every day. Her physique was terrific, but she found she had little time for anything else.

Then one day she was too busy to go. She felt a small panic inside her and the next day she tried to do her fitness programme twice, to make up for it. Suddenly, she felt light-headed and the next thing she knew, she was coming round after fainting.

"Caroline, you're doing far too much," her instructor told her. "You're not an athlete, you're not in training, so twice a week at a gym is sufficient."

"But I was looking so good!" she wailed.

"There won't be much difference in how you look, but if you carry on like this you'll get addicted. We've seen it happen to people and trust me, you're on your way to all sorts of problems," the instructor warned.

Caroline learned a big lesson just in time. Many people become obsessed with exercising and dieting, when all they need is to control their lifestyle. Read **2 Peter 2:19** where we are warned about getting too involved with any one thing.

- What words of warning could Caroline have paid attention to from this passage?
- Why does this passage use the word "slave"?

Consider . . .

- listing some advertisements you have seen that trap you with false words.
- seeking help from your youth leader if you feel addicted or enslaved.

For more, see . . .

- John 8:34–36 (p.1110)
- 1 Peter 2:16 (p.1358)

It spoke with a man's voice and stopped the prophet's mad thinking.

[17] Those false teachers are like springs without water and clouds blown by a storm. A place in the blackest darkness has been kept for them. [18] They boast with words that mean nothing. By their evil desires they lead people into the trap of sin—people who are just beginning to escape from others who live in error. [19] They promise them freedom, but they themselves are not free. They are slaves of things that will be destroyed. For people are slaves of anything that controls them. [20] They were made free from the evil in the world by knowing our Lord and Saviour [d] Jesus Christ. But if they return to evil things and those things control them, then it is worse for them than it was before. [21] Yes, it would be better for them to have never known the right way than to know it and to turn away from the holy teaching that was given to them. [22] What they did is like this true saying: "A dog goes back to what it has thrown up," [n] and, "After a pig is washed, it goes back and rolls in the mud."

Jesus will Come Again

3 My friends, this is the second letter I have written you to help your honest minds remember. [2] I want you to think about the words the holy prophets [d] spoke in the past, and remember the command our Lord and Saviour [d] gave us through your apostles. [d] [3] It is most

"A dog . . . up"   Quotation from Proverbs 26:11.

IMAGE

Who Do You Think You Are?

Luis Palau was enjoying a very successful mission in Cardiff. The mission posters were on all the buses, and his face had been on TV.

The week had gone well, and the evenings at Cardiff Castle were tremendous. Thousands of people came along to hear him preach, and on this particular night, several local VIPs and famous faces too.

Then the thunderstorm started. The sky turned a thick black and the lightning streaked across the castle grounds. The peacocks in the grounds started screaming, and the thunder crashed through the PA.

The singers kept on singing and Luis kept on preaching. He finally reached his appeal, and people started to flock forward, wanting to know more about this Jesus. Wanting him in their lives.

Suddenly, a man appeared from nowhere. He stood in the middle of the swelling crowd at the front of the grounds. He walked until he stood just a few feet from the preacher and he started to laugh. The sound was evil, and the man stood there, wearing a grey raincoat and a crown of thorns. He laughed and he jeered and he pointed to his head.

The platform party started to pray and Luis prayed for the crowd.

The man disappeared as suddenly as he had arrived.

2 Peter 3:3 says we should expect such things.

* Why is it important that we understand these things, according to this passage?
* How can looking forward to Jesus coming back help you in an image crisis?

Consider . . .

* what positive things you might say the next time your faith is challenged or ridiculed.
* planning with your youth group some projects that will improve the image of Christianity in your school or college, such as the Christian Union organising the Christmas party, or fundraising for Third World issues.

For more, see . . .

* Luke 16:14–15 (p.1074)
* Acts 17:32 (p.1168)
* Acts 2:12–13 (p.1138)

important for you to understand what will happen in the last days. People will laugh at you. They will live doing the evil things they want to do. ⁴They will say, "Jesus promised to come again. Where is he? Our fathers have died, but the world continues the way it has been since it was made." ⁵But they do not want to remember what happened long ago. By the word of God heaven was made, and the earth was made from water and with water. ⁶Then the world was flooded and destroyed with water. ⁷And that same word of God is keeping heaven and earth that we now have in order to be destroyed by fire. They are being kept for the Judgement Day and the destruction of all who are against God.

⁸But do not forget this one thing, dear friends: to the Lord one day is as a thousand years, and a thousand years is as one day. ⁹The Lord is not slow in doing what he promised—the way some people understand slowness. But God is being patient with you. He does not want anyone to be lost, but he wants all people to change their hearts and lives.

¹⁰But the day of the Lord will come like a thief. The skies will disappear with a loud noise. Everything in them will be destroyed by fire, and the earth and everything in it will be burnt up. ⁿ

will be burnt up Many Greek copies say, "will be found". One copy says, "will disappear".

School's Out

The school caretaker was annoyed. This was nothing new, he always found something to complain about, but today he was doubly upset. He was opening the top windows during assembly when he heard a man talking to the pupils about Jesus. The pupils listened attentively to the Christian and applauded at the end of his entertaining talk. Fuming, the caretaker went to the headmaster's office and said, "If you are going to allow Christians into your school, then you should invite other people to share their beliefs in assembly."

"Who were you thinking of?" asked the head.

"Me," he replied. "I think I have the right to stand up there and tell them about MY faith!"

The headmaster realised he was being put on the spot and made a snap decision.

"Alright, Harry. You can take assembly next week, it'll do the children good to hear someone they know."

Unfortunately, the head didn't check up on the caretaker's faith and forgot all about it until the day of his assembly.

The caretaker stood on the stage and told the children in no uncertain terms that the world was going to end tomorrow. He told them of signs in the sky and many mathematical equations. He waved his arms about and spoke extremely loudly.

The next day . . . hardly any pupils came to school.

This is a true story, and a sad one. We can be easily led and look whichever way people point. **2 Peter 3:14–18** warns about people such as these.

* How is the school caretaker like the ignorant people Peter writes about?
* How is it best to keep away from false teachings?

Consider . . .

* getting involved in a course such as "Alpha", which would help you to understand the Christian faith better.
* discussing any doubts you may have about the Christian faith with a trusted Christian friend.

For more, see . . .

* Matthew 24:26–31 (p.984)
* Revelation 3:11 (p.1390)
* Colossians 2:6–8 (p.1292)

[11]In that way everything will be destroyed. So what kind of people should you be? You should live holy lives and serve God, [12]as you wait for and look forward to the coming of the day of God. When that day comes, the skies will be destroyed with fire, and everything in them will melt with heat. [13]But God made a promise to us, and we are waiting for a new heaven and a new earth where goodness lives.

Sidelight   According to 2 Peter 3:15–16, you are in good company if you sometimes have trouble understanding Romans (p.1183) or other books that Paul wrote. Peter did too. This passage is a rare example of a New Testament author giving another New Testament book the authority of scripture.

[14]Dear friends, since you are waiting for this to happen, do your best to be without sin and without fault. Try to be at peace with God. [15]Remember that we are saved because our Lord is patient. Our dear brother Paul told you the same thing when he wrote to you with the wisdom that God gave him. [16]He writes about this in all his letters. Some things in Paul's letters are hard to understand, and people who are ignorant and weak in faith explain these things falsely. They also falsely explain the other Scriptures,[d] but they are destroying themselves by doing this.

[17]Dear friends, since you already know about this, be careful. Do not let those evil people lead you away by the wrong they do. Be careful so you will not fall from your strong faith. [18]But grow in the grace and knowledge of our Lord and Saviour Jesus Christ. Glory be to him now and for ever! Amen.

1 John

Why Read This Book:
* Find out how to grow closer to God (1 John 1—2).
* See what it's like to be part of God's family (1 John 3—4).
* Be certain of life with God after death (1 John 5).

When?

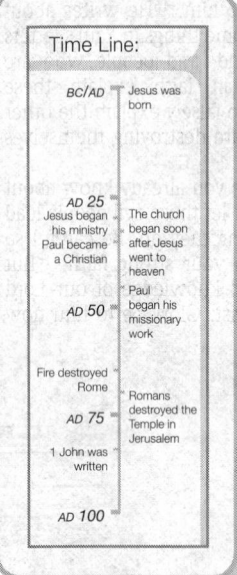

Time Line:

BC/AD	Jesus was born
AD 25 Jesus began his ministry Paul became a Christian	The church began soon after Jesus went to heaven
AD 50	Paul began his missionary work
Fire destroyed Rome	Romans destroyed the Temple in Jerusalem
AD 75	
1 John was written	
AD 100	

Behind the Scenes:

When you read the book of 1 John, you almost have the feeling that a grandfather has gathered his grandchildren around a fire to talk. You can see his love for them and you know from the way they look at him that they respect him a great deal.

As he talks to his "children", as he calls them, you can feel the warmth. He reassures them of God's love for them. He gently coaxes them to believe in and follow God.

But he also has another purpose. He is worried that the younger Christians are hearing mixed messages about Jesus Christ. People – known as gnostics – are saying that Jesus wasn't really human, he was only divine. Furthermore, they were arguing that they could do whatever they wanted to do with their bodies, because the physical body was separate from the spiritual nature.

The grandfather knows that these ideas are wrong. Jesus was both fully human and fully divine. And what the body does certainly affects the spirit – for better or worse. So the grandfather challenges the false teaching and urges his children to stick to the truth.

Of course, 1 John isn't really a fireside chat between a grandfather and his grandchildren. It's a letter or sermon written to Christians to help them to grow in their faith and to counteract the false teaching that was gaining influence.

Yet the true spirit of the letter comes through when we imagine the love and warmth that comes when we sit around a fireplace, listening to the advice of a wise grandfather. Not only did the words encourage and challenge the original hearers to keep following God, but they challenge and encourage us today.

Where?

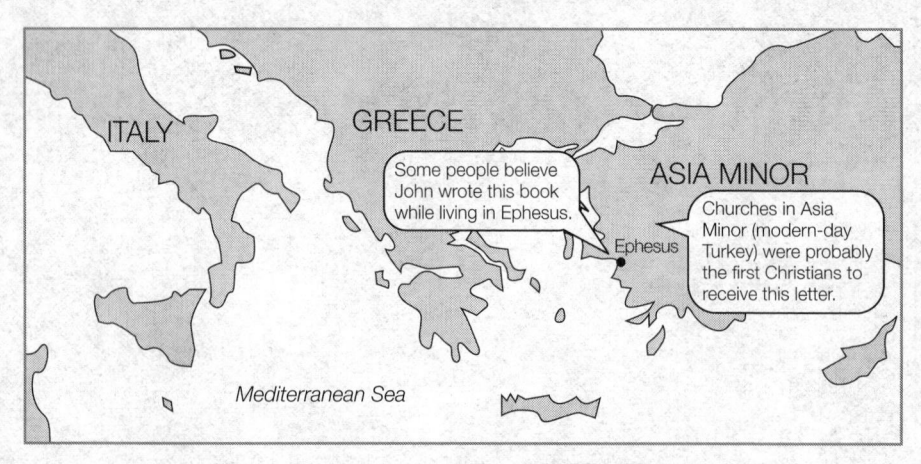

ITALY

GREECE

ASIA MINOR

Some people believe John wrote this book while living in Ephesus.

Churches in Asia Minor (modern-day Turkey) were probably the first Christians to receive this letter.

Ephesus

Mediterranean Sea

1

We write to you now about what has always existed, which we have heard, we have seen with our own eyes, we have looked at, and we have touched with our hands. We write to you about the Word [n] that gives life. [2]He who gives life was shown to us. We saw him and can give proof about it. And now we announce to you that he has life that continues for ever. He was with God the Father and was shown to us. [3]We announce to you what we have seen and heard, because we want you also to have fellowship with us. Our fellowship is with God the Father and with his Son, Jesus Christ. [4]We write this to you so you can be full of joy with us.

God Forgives our Sins

[5]Here is the message we have heard from Christ and now announce to you: God is light, [n] and in him there is no darkness at all. [6]So if we say we have fellowship with God, but we continue living in darkness, we are liars and do not follow the truth. [7]But if we live in the light, as God is in the light, we can share fellowship with each other. Then the blood of Jesus, God's Son, cleanses us from every sin.

[8]If we say we have no sin, we are fooling ourselves, and the truth is not in us. [9]But if we confess our sins, he will forgive our sins, because we can trust God to do what is right. He will

---

Word   The Greek word is "logos", meaning any kind of communication. Here, it means Christ, who was the way God told people about himself.

light   Here, this word is used as a symbol of God's goodness or truth.

HONESTY

No Excuses

Laura remembers the first time that she lied to her mum about where she was going. "Janet, Kate and I are going to see a film," she lied without looking straight into her mum's eyes.

Could her mum tell she was lying? Laura couldn't tell, so she quickly left the house.

The party was well underway when the three girls arrived.

"See, it wasn't so hard to fool your mum," Janet teased Laura.

Still, Laura was tense the whole evening. When she got home, her mum asked about the film.

"It was OK," Laura replied. "Well, good night."

Laura felt relieved as she closed her bedroom door. "I got away with it," she thought.

Each lie became easier. Soon Laura lied with ease. "What Mum doesn't know won't hurt her," she reasoned.

One evening she came home and found her mum waiting for her.

"Your life's a lie!" her mum shouted.

"It's not my fault," Laura cried. "You never let me out of the house unless I lie. Besides, other kids do it. It's no big deal."

"I don't think I know you now," Mum said. "And I can't trust you any more. What has happened to you . . . to us?"

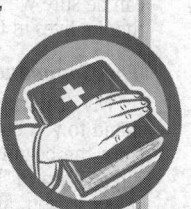

Laura didn't know the answer. Instead, she blamed her mum for her lies and excused her behaviour by comparing herself to her friends. Yet **1 John 1:1 – 2:2** shows that excuses don't eliminate sin.

* How is Laura's situation similar to the sin described in these verses?
* Why do you think John so strongly emphasises confessing sin?

Consider . . .

* apologising to someone who has been hurt by your sins.
* selecting a verse from the passage that conveys the "no excuses" idea. Write the verse on a small card and memorise it.

For more, see . . .

* Genesis 3:1–13 (p.5)
* Luke 15:11–24 (p.1071)

* Psalm 51:1–13 (p.530)

cleanse us from all the wrongs we have done. [10]If we say we have not sinned, we make God a liar, and we do not accept God's teaching.

Jesus is our Helper

2 My dear children, I write this letter to you so you will not sin. But if anyone does sin, we have a helper in the presence of the Father— Jesus Christ, the One who does what is right. [2]He is the way our sins are taken away, and not only our sins but the sins of all people.

> ### Sidelight
>
> Perhaps the biggest heresy (wrong doctrine) that the early church faced involved the gnostic understanding of evil. Gnostics – whose name came from the word for "knowledge" – believed evil was simply an error that grew out of ignorance; the person who did wrong was not really responsible. There are lots of people around today who think the same way. 1 John responded that people are responsible for their sins and must be forgiven to be right with God (1 John 1:9; 2:2).

[3]We can be sure that we know God if we obey his commands. [4]Anyone who says, "I know God," but does not obey God's commands is a liar, and the truth is not in that person. [5]But if someone obeys God's teaching, then in that person God's love has truly reached its goal. This is how we can be sure we are living in God: [6]whoever says that he lives in God must live as Jesus lived.

The Command to Love Others

[7]My dear friends, I am not writing a new command to you but an old command you have had from the beginning. It is the teaching you have already heard. [8]But also I am writing a new command to you, and you can see its truth in Jesus and in you, because the darkness is passing away, and the true light is already shining. [9]Anyone who says, "I am in the light," [n] but hates a brother or sister, [n] is still in the darkness. [10]Whoever loves a brother or sister lives in the light and will not cause anyone to stumble in their faith. [11]But whoever hates a brother or sister is in darkness, lives in darkness and does not know where to go, because the darkness has made that person blind.

[12]I write to you, dear children,
because your sins are forgiven through Christ.
[13]I write to you, parents,
because you know the One who existed
from the beginning.
I write to you, young people,
because you have defeated the Evil One.
[14]I write to you, children,
because you know the Father.
I write to you, parents,
because you know the One who existed
from the beginning.
I write to you, young people,
because you are strong;
the teaching of God lives in you,
and you have defeated the Evil One.

[15]Do not love the world or the things in the world. If you love the world, the love of the Father is not in you. [16]These are the ways of the world: wanting to please our sinful selves, wanting the sinful things we see and being too proud of what we have. None of these come from the Father, but all of them come from the world. [17]The world and everything that people want in it are passing away, but the person who does what God wants lives for ever.

Reject the Enemies of Christ

[18]My dear children, these are the last days. You have heard that the enemy of Christ [d] is coming, and now many enemies of Christ are already here. This is how we know that these are the last days. [19]These enemies of Christ were in our fellowship, but they left us. They never really belonged to us; if they had been a part of us, they would have stayed with us. But they left, and this shows that none of them really belonged to us. [20]You have the gift [n] that the Holy One gave you, so you all know the truth. [21]I do not write to you because you do not know the truth but because you do know the truth. And you know that no lie comes from the truth.

[22]Who is the liar? It is the person who does not accept Jesus as the Christ. This is the enemy of Christ: the person who does not accept the Father and his Son. [23]Whoever does not accept the Son does not have the Father. But whoever confesses the Son has the Father, too.

[24]Be sure you continue to follow the teaching you heard from the beginning. If you continue to follow what you heard from the beginning, you will stay in the Son and in the Father. [25]And this is what the Son promised to us—life for ever.

[26]I am writing this letter about those people who are trying to lead you the wrong way. [27]Christ gave you a special gift that is still in you,

---

light   Here, this word is used as a symbol of God's goodness or truth.
brother or sister   Although the Greek text says "brother" here and throughout this book, John's words were meant for the entire church, both men and women.
gift   This might mean the Holy Spirit, or it might mean teaching or truth as in verse 24.

so you do not need any other teacher. His gift teaches you about everything, and it is true, not false. So continue to live in Christ, as his gift taught you.

28Yes, my dear children, live in him so that when Christ comes back, we can be without fear and not be ashamed in his presence. 29If you know that Christ is all that is right, you know that all who do right are God's children.

We are God's Children

3 The Father has loved us so much that we are called children of God. And we really are his children. The reason the people in the world do not know us is that they have not known him. 2Dear friends, now we are children of God, and we have not yet been shown what we will be in the future. But we know that when Christ comes again, we will be like him, because we will see

him as he really is. 3Christ is pure, and all who have this hope in Christ keep themselves pure like Christ.

4The person who sins breaks God's law. Yes, sin is living against God's law. 5You know that Christ came to take away sins and that there is no sin in Christ. 6So anyone who lives in Christ does not go on sinning. Anyone who goes on sinning has never really understood Christ and has never known him.

7Dear children, do not let anyone lead you the wrong way. Christ is all that is right. So to be like Christ a person must do what is right. 8The devil has been sinning since the beginning, so anyone who continues to sin belongs to the devil. The Son of God came for this purpose: to destroy the devil's work.

9Those who are God's children do not continue sinning, because the new life from God

FOLLOWING GOD

Life at the Top

Lynn Hill has always been at the top of everything. When she was a child, she was at the top of trees, telegraph poles, even street lights. Now she is on top of cliffs and mountains as one of the world's leading rock climbers. She is one of the few people who has defied gravity and scaled cliffs that are "steeper" than vertical.

Lynn has become so good because she dedicates her life to her climbing. A picture taken the day after her wedding shows how important climbing is to her. It shows her and her new husband – also a climber, of course – in full wedding dress hanging from a rope.

Lynn knows how important it is not to become lax in her climbing techniques. Once she fell more than twenty metres down a cliff because she had forgotten to tie a simple knot on her safety rope. A tree branch slowed her fall and saved her life, although she was injured.

"The rock is a tool for learning and understanding," she says. "When you get to the top, you've conquered something inside as well."

Lynn's dedication to climbing illustrates the kind of dedication that Christians should have in following God. 1 John 3:1–24 encourages Christians not to be distracted from following God.

* What parallels do you see between Lynn's dedication to rock climbing and the passage's guidance about being a Christian?
* How have other Christians encouraged and kept you following God?

Consider . . .

* thinking about everything you have done in the past 24 hours. Decide which things helped you to follow God and which ones did not.
* asking a Christian friend to help you overcome a sin that keeps you from following God, with the kind of dedication Lynn has for rock climbing.

For more, see . . .

* Psalm 95:1–11 (p.556)
* Ephesians 5:1–11 (p.1274)
* Romans 7:14–25 (p.1193)

remains in them. They are not able to go on sinning, because they have become children of God. [10]So we can see who God's children are and who the devil's children are: those who do not do what is right are not God's children, and those who do not love their brothers and sisters are not God's children.

We Must Love Each Other

[11]This is the teaching you have heard from the beginning: we must love each other. [12]Do not be like Cain who belonged to the Evil One and killed his brother. And why did he kill him? Because the things Cain did were evil, and the things his brother did were good.

[13]Brothers and sisters, do not be surprised when the people of the world hate you. [14]We know we have left death and have come into life because we love each other. Whoever does not love is still dead. [15]Everyone who hates a brother or sister is a murderer, [n] and you know that no murderers have eternal life in them. [16]This is how we know what real love is: Jesus gave his life for us. So we should give our lives for our brothers

Sidelight

When 1 John 3:13 told believers not to be surprised that the world hates them, it was speaking to an everyday reality for Christians at that time in Asia Minor. Even the Roman historian Tacitus, who lived during that time, wrote that Romans hated the Christians.

and sisters. [17]Suppose someone has enough to live on and sees a brother or sister in need, but does not help. Then God's love is not living in that person. [18]My children, we should love people not only with words and talk, but by our actions and true caring.

[19-20]This is the way we know that we belong to the way of truth. When our hearts make us feel guilty, we can still have peace before God. God is greater than our hearts, and he knows everything. [21]My dear friends, if our hearts do not make us feel guilty, we can come without fear into God's presence. [22]And God gives us what we ask for because we obey God's commands and do what pleases him. [23]This is what God commands: that we believe in his Son, Jesus Christ, and that we love each other, just as he commanded. [24]The people who obey God's commands live in God, and God lives in them.

We know that God lives in us because of the Spirit [d] God gave us.

Warning Against False Teachers

4 My dear friends, many false prophets [d] have gone out into the world. So do not believe every spirit, but test the spirits to see if they are from God. [2]This is how you can know God's Spirit: [d] every spirit who confesses that Jesus Christ came to earth as a human is from God. [3]And every spirit who refuses to say this about Jesus is not from God. It is the spirit of the enemy of Christ, [d] which you have heard is coming, and now he is already in the world.

[4]My dear children, you belong to God and have defeated them, because God's Spirit, who is in you, is greater than the devil, who is in the world. [5]And they belong to the world, so what they say is from the world, and the world listens to them. [6]But we belong to God, and those who know God listen to us. But those who are not from God do not listen to us. That is how we know the Spirit that is true and the spirit that is false.

Love Comes from God

[7]Dear friends, we should love each other, because love comes from God. Everyone who loves has become God's child and knows God. [8]Whoever does not love does not know God, because God is love. [9]This is how God showed his love to us: he sent his one and only Son into the world so that we could have life through him. [10]This is what real love is: it is not our love for God; it is God's love for us in sending his Son to be the way to take away our sins.

[11]Dear friends, if God loved us that much we also should love each other. [12]No one has ever seen God, but if we love each other, God lives in us, and his love is made perfect in us.

[13]We know that we live in God and he lives in us, because he gave us his Spirit. [d] [14]We have seen and can testify that the Father sent his Son to be the Saviour [d] of the world. [15]Whoever confesses that Jesus is the Son of God has God living inside, and that person lives in God. [16]And so we know the love that God has for us, and we trust that love.

God is love. Those who live in love live in God, and God lives in them. [17]This is how love is made perfect in us: that we can be without fear on the day God judges us, because in this world we are like him. [18]Where God's love is, there is no fear, because God's perfect love drives

---

Everyone . . . murderer   If one person hates a brother or sister, then in the heart that person has killed that brother or sister. Jesus taught about this sin to his followers (Matthew 5:21–26).

out fear. It is punishment that makes a person fear, so love is not made perfect in the person who fears.

[19]We love because God first loved us. [20]If people say, "I love God," but hate their brothers or sisters, they are liars. Those who do not love their brothers and sisters, whom they have seen, cannot love God, whom they have never seen. [21]And God gave us this command: those who love God must also love their brothers and sisters.

Faith in the Son of God

5 Everyone who believes that Jesus is the Christ[d] is God's child, and whoever loves the Father also loves the Father's children. [2]This is how we know we love God's children: when we love God and obey his commands. [3]Loving God means obeying his commands. And God's commands are not too hard for us, [4]because everyone who is a child of God conquers the world. And this is the victory that conquers the world— our faith. [5]So the one who wins against the world is the person who believes that Jesus is the Son of God.

[6]Jesus Christ is the One who came by water[n] and blood. [n] He did not come by water only, but by water and blood. And the Spirit[d] says that this is true, because the Spirit is the truth. [7]So there are three witnesses that tell us about Jesus: [8]the Spirit, the water and the blood; and these three witnesses agree. [9]We believe people when they

water   This probably means the water of Jesus' baptism.
blood   This probably means the blood of Jesus' death.

LOVE

Called to the Streets

Kelly had grown up in a nice home and had always struggled with "poor" people. She had been taught to get a job, work hard, and keep a nice home. But Kelly was obedient to God when he called her to move long-term onto an infamous deprived inner-city estate. Kelly believed that if God had called her to work with the poor, he would give her a heart for them.

After a number of weeks, Kelly was beginning to worry. God hadn't changed her heart – in fact, she hated it! She desperately wanted to love these people, but she simply didn't. She continued to pray about the situation.

A few days later, Kelly was sitting on a bench watching the world go by as, with a huge cheeky grin, one of her little neighbours came towards her.

Ruby had filthy hands, disgusting clothes, dirt all over her face and a single finger wedged up her nose. Trying not to pull a face, Kelly forced a smile at Ruby. Reacting to the smile, Ruby walked up to Kelly, went around behind her, pulled her finger out of her nose and went to play with Kelly's flowing hair. Kelly's first reaction was to jump up screaming, "Get your hands off me you disgusting child!" However, she didn't. In that moment, something inside Kelly broke. In an instant, she was filled with the love of Jesus for Ruby. She saw her through a new pair of eyes.

From that day on, Kelly was transformed – her heart was changed and a deep love for the people of the estate flowed through her veins.

Read **1 John 4:7–12**.

* What does the passage teach us about how we should feel about other people?
* Did Kelly do the right thing, according to the passage?

Consider . . .

* how much love you have for people. Make a list of things you could do to increase that love.
* whether there are any people who you're struggling to love. Ask God to change your heart towards them.

For more, see . . .

* Matthew 10:42 (p.957)
* 1 Corinthians 13:4–7 (p.1232)

* John 13:34–35 (p.1122)

say something is true. But what God says is more important, and he has told us the truth about his own Son. [10]Anyone who believes in the Son of God has the truth that God told us. Anyone who does not believe makes God a liar, because that person does not believe what God told us about his Son. [11]This is what God told us: God has given us eternal life, and this life is in his Son. [12]Whoever has the Son has life, but whoever does not have the Son of God does not have life.

We Have Eternal Life Now

[13]I write this letter to you who believe in the Son of God so you will know you have eternal life. [14]And this is the boldness we have in God's presence: that if we ask God for anything that agrees with what he wants, he hears us. [15]If we know he hears us every time we ask him, we know we have what we ask from him.

[16]If anyone sees a brother or sister sinning (sin that does not lead to eternal death), that person

DISCOURAGEMENT

Hope Breakers and Makers

Have you ever had a day when everything went wrong? Sometimes the day seems to consist of one disappointing event after another. These disappointments can be called "hope breakers". Hope breakers can lead to outright discouragement if they persist. Which of these hope breakers seem familiar to you?

- threats of war in the world
- fights with your parents
- an accident in the family car
- breaking up with a girlfriend/boyfriend
- getting a poor result in an exam
- doubting your Christian beliefs
- too much homework
- criticism from others
- feeling alone

Hope can overcome discouragement. Hope reminds you of a brighter future. Which of the events below are "hope makers" for you?

- feeling good about your life
- getting good marks in a difficult exam
- giving and receiving Christian love from others
- getting into the team
- enjoying a beautiful day
- knowing that God loves you
- getting a fantastic job
- having a great time with friends
- renewing a broken friendship

John offered reassurance and hope to Christians who had experienced too many hope breakers. Read John's hope-making ideas in **1 John 5:1–15**.

- How do the breakers and makers above compare with the passage?
- What phrases in this passage offer you the most hope?

Consider . . .

- writing out the promises and assurances in this passage. Stick the list up on your door.
- acting as a hope maker to a discouraged friend by offering encouragement, time or help.

For more, see . . .

- Psalm 42 (p.525)
- Romans 8:35–39 (p.1197)
- John 15:18–27 (p.1125)

should pray, and God will give the sinner life. I am talking about people whose sin does not lead to eternal death. There is sin that leads to death. I do not mean that a person should pray about that sin. ¹⁷Doing wrong is always sin, but there is sin that does not lead to eternal death.

¹⁸We know that those who are God's children do not continue to sin. The Son of God keeps them safe, and the Evil One cannot touch them.

¹⁹We know that we belong to God, but the Evil One controls the whole world. ²⁰We also know that the Son of God has come and has given us understanding so that we can know the True One. And our lives are in the True One and in his Son, Jesus Christ. He is the true God and the eternal life.

²¹So, dear children, keep yourselves away from gods.

2 John

Why Read This Book:
- Learn ways to show Christian love (2 John 1–6).
- Examine the danger of listening to false teachers (2 John 7–11).

When?

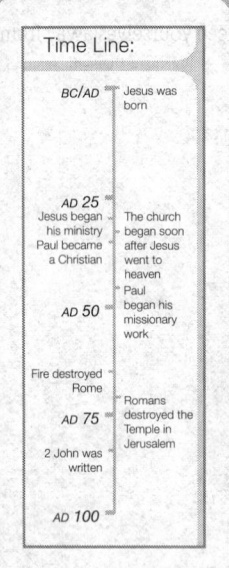

Time Line:

BC/AD	Jesus was born
AD 25 Jesus began his ministry Paul became a Christian	The church began soon after Jesus went to heaven
AD 50	Paul began his missionary work
Fire destroyed Rome	
AD 75	Romans destroyed the Temple in Jerusalem
2 John was written	
AD 100	

Behind the Scenes:

Salesmen use every trick they can to con us into buying things that we don't need. Television advertisements try and tell us that a certain soft drink will make us more popular and will generate friends out of thin air. Newspapers twist facts when reporting stories so that they fit in with their viewpoint. It seems as if there is always someone who is out to pull the wool over our eyes.

The early Christians also knew what it was like to be tricked. Because of their famous generosity and hospitality towards strangers, some false teachers took advantage of them and began teaching false doctrine in the church.

2 John was written to warn churches to be on their guard. It encouraged the Christians to continue being loving towards one another, but told them to make sure that what was taught in the churches didn't contradict the gospel they had first heard. They should stay as far away from false teachers as possible.

While 2 John urges Christians to be on their guard, 3 John reminds them that they shouldn't stop being hospitable to others. In short, the message of 2 John is, "Don't believe the hype!"

LIFE FILE LINKS

Investigate the Theme

To find a list of real life stories on this subject turn to the LIFE FILE GUIDE on pages 12 to 22 at the front of the Youth Bible.

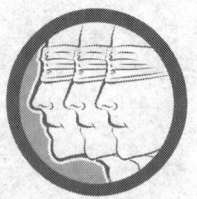

CULTS

[1]From the Elder. [n]

To the chosen lady [n] and her children:

I love all of you in the truth, [n] and all those who know the truth love you. [2]We love you because of the truth that lives in us and will be with us for ever.

[3]Grace, mercy and peace from God the Father and his Son, Jesus Christ, will be with us in truth and love.

[4]I was very happy to learn that some of your children are following the way of truth, as the Father commanded us. [5]And now, dear lady, this is not a new command but is the same command we have had from the beginning. I ask you that we all love each other. [6]And love means living the way God commanded us to live. As you have heard from the beginning, his command is this: live a life of love.

[7]Many false teachers are in the world now who do not confess that Jesus Christ came to earth as a human. Anyone who does not confess

---

Sidelight If other books in the New Testament are letters (such as 1 Corinthians, p.1213), then 2 John is more like a postcard. With only thirteen verses, it is the shortest book in the Bible. One reason why it may have been short is so that it could fit on a single sheet of papyrus, the paper of the day (2 John 12).

Elder "Elder" means an older person. It can also mean a special leader in the church (as in Titus 1:5).
lady This might mean a woman, or in this letter it might mean a church. If it is a church, then "her children" would be the people of the church.
truth The truth or "Good News" about Jesus Christ that joins all believers together.

CULTS

Knock Knock . . .

They're just weird, aren't they? This probably sums up what we really think about cults and what's wrong with them. We don't really bother with what they actually think because it's easy to write them off, just like everyone else does. But what do they think?

The most well known of the "cults" are probably the Jehovah's Witnesses. Like Christians, they believe that the Bible is the inspired word of God. So if they believe in the Bible, then what's the problem with them? The Jehovah's Witnesses' big mistake is that they don't think Jesus is God. This is a complete misunderstanding of the Bible. After all, it calls Jesus "God", and says that he forgives people's sins – something only God can do.

Another group, known as the Mormons, also believes in the Bible. But they get Jesus wrong as well. They teach that we need both Jesus *and* the "new revelation" about God that came in America in the 1800s. But Christians have always believed that Jesus is enough for our salvation. We just need to believe in him – we don't need anything extra. So we don't need "Another Testament of Jesus Christ", as the *Book of Mormon* calls itself on the front cover.

People may get Christianity and these kinds of cults mixed up, but **2 John:7–11** tells us how we can recognise false teaching.

* What attitude does Jesus want us to have to cults?
* How can we be ready to answer their questions?

Consider . . .

* seeking to understand more of Christ's teachings so that you will know when a false teacher "goes beyond" them (verse 9).
* becoming aware of cults operating in your area and learning more about what they believe. Make a list, comparing your findings with Christianity.

For more, see . . .

* John 1:1 (p.1096)
* John 14:5–7 (p.1122)
* 2 Timothy 4:3–4 (p.1319)

this is a false teacher and an enemy of Christ.*d* [8] Be careful yourselves that you do not lose everything you have worked for, but that you receive your full reward.

[9] Anyone who goes beyond Christ's teaching and does not continue to follow only his teaching does not have God. But whoever continues to follow the teaching of Christ has both the Father and the Son. [10] If someone comes to you

and does not bring this teaching, do not welcome or accept that person into your house. [11] If you welcome such a person, you share in the evil work.

[12] I have many things to write to you, but I do not want to use paper and ink. Instead, I hope to come to you and talk face to face so we can be full of joy.

[13] The children of your chosen sister *n* greet you.

---

sister Sister of the "lady" in verse 1. This might be another woman or another church.

3 John

Why Read This Book:

* Consider how Christians can support one another (3 John 1–8).
* See how much damage one negative leader can do (3 John 9–11).

When?

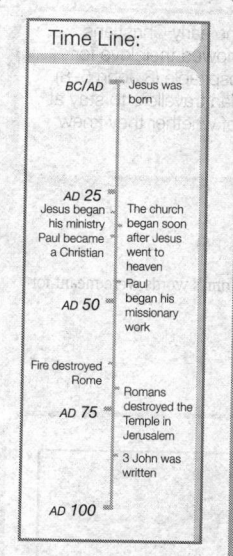

Time Line:

BC/AD	Jesus was born
AD 25 Jesus began his ministry Paul became a Christian	The church began soon after Jesus went to heaven
AD 50	Paul began his missionary work
Fire destroyed Rome AD 75	Romans destroyed the Temple in Jerusalem
	3 John was written
AD 100	

Behind the Scenes:

Suppose a visitor walked into your church. Would you welcome him or her? Would you invite the visitor home for dinner? And suppose the visitor expressed different views from yours during discussion. Would you be open to those views? Or would you cut the person off?

The two central characters in 3 John would answer those questions quite differently. Gaius (3 John 1) would probably welcome the visitor and listen closely to his or her views. Diotrephes (3 John 9) would probably shun the visitor and squelch his or her opinions.

The situation in 3 John was different from your church, of course. Gaius was welcoming missionaries sent by "the Elder" (3 John 1), and the writer thanks him for it. Diotrephes refused to welcome these missionaries. In fact, he tried to kick out of the church anyone who did welcome them.

Like 2 John (p.1378), 3 John focuses on welcoming and showing love to fellow Christians. Taken together, these two letters tell a lot about the church. Christians are called to love, accept and serve one another in Christ. But at the same time, Christians are to be on guard against false teachers. These two themes are as relevant to Christians today as they were back then.

LIFE FILE LINKS

Investigate the Theme

To find a list of real life stories on this subject turn to the LIFE FILE GUIDE on pages 12 to 22 at the front of the Youth Bible.

CHURCH

¹From the Elder. [n]

To my dear friend Gaius, whom I love in the truth: [n]

²My dear friend, I know your soul is doing fine, and I pray that you are doing well in every way and that your health is good. ³I was very happy when some brothers and sisters [n] came and told me about the truth in your life and how you are following the way of truth. ⁴Nothing gives me greater joy than to hear that my children are following the way of truth.

⁵My dear friend, it is good that you help the brothers and sisters, even those you do not know. ⁶They told the church about your love. Please help them to continue their trip in a way worthy of God. ⁷They started out in service to Christ, and they have been accepting nothing from non-believers. ⁸So we should help such people; when we do, we share in

> **Sidelight**　　The early Christians showed their love for one another by being hospitable (3 John 5–8). They would invite Christian travellers to stay at their homes regardless of whether they knew them personally or not.

Elder　"Elder" means an older person. It can also mean a special leader in the church (as in Titus 1:5).
truth　The truth or "Good News" about Jesus Christ that joins all believers together.
brothers and sisters　Although the Greek text says "brothers" here and throughout this book, John's words were meant for the entire church, both men and women.

SERVICE

Every Little Helps

Helena and Darren were fairly new to their church.

One Sunday, an appeal was made from the front that if anyone had specific prayer requests they should make them known. They looked at each other, smiled, and agreed it was time to bite the bullet and let the church know that they had been trying for a baby for years, without success.

From that Sunday onwards, Helena and Darren were astounded by how supportive the church were – praying for them and encouraging them to remain positive.

When, finally, their prayers were answered and they were able to introduce new baby Elizabeth to everyone in the congregation, Helena and Darren were beaming with excitement.

Very soon, both Helena and Darren became increasingly tired because of the sleepless nights. One night, as they slouched exhausted on the couch at the end of another long day, they heard a knock at the door. It was a young couple from their church holding a piping hot casserole dish. Some friends from church had decided to take it in turns to cook and deliver the new parents evening meals for the next month.

Helena and Darren were so grateful for the support their church was giving them that they told friends in other parts of the country all about it. As a result, churches all over the country did similar things for new parents in their church families.

Read **3 John:5–8**.

- Would you be prepared to help anyone – even someone you didn't know?
- What does John consider as the privilege of helping others that makes serving so rewarding?

Consider . . .

- helping out more around the house or helping out someone at your church who is struggling to cope.
- praying that God would open your eyes to the needs of people around you and that you'd know how to respond.

For more, see . . .

- Matthew 25:35–40 (p.988)
- John 13:12–17 (p.1119)
- Luke 10:27–37 (p.1058)

their work for the truth.

[9]I wrote something to the church, but Diotrephes, who loves to be their leader, will not listen to us. [10]So if I come, I will talk about what Diotrephes is doing, about how he lies and says evil things about us. But more than that, he refuses to accept the other brothers and sisters; he even stops those who do want to accept them and puts them out of the church.

[11]My dear friend, do not follow what is bad; follow what is good. The one who does good belongs to God. But the one who does evil has never known God.

[12]Everyone says good things about Demetrius, and the truth agrees with what they say. We also speak well of him, and you know what we say is true.

[13]I have many things I want to write you, but I do not want to use pen and ink. [14]I hope to see you soon and talk face to face.

[15]Peace to you. The friends here greet you. Please greet each friend there by name.

Jude

When?

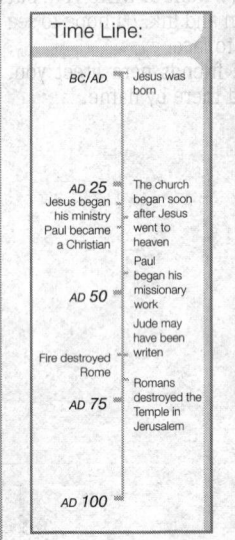

Time Line:

BC/AD	Jesus was born
AD 25 Jesus began his ministry Paul became a Christian	The church began soon after Jesus went to heaven
AD 50	Paul began his missionary work
	Jude may have been writen
Fire destroyed Rome	
AD 75	Romans destroyed the Temple in Jerusalem
AD 100	

Why Read This Book:

* Test others' beliefs against the truth of Jesus Christ (Jude 1—4).
* Focus on the dangers of listening to false teachers (Jude 5—16).
* Be challenged to stay strong in your faith (Jude 17—24).

Behind the Scenes:

Not many people enjoy visiting the dentist, but the fact is that it's necessary. Eating sugary foods can create small holes in the surface of teeth, and if they aren't dealt with, the tooth will eventually go rotten and start to hurt. At that point, it's too late to do anything about it – you either have the tooth filled or pulled out! Eat less sugar and your teeth are less likely to rot.

The early church had to deal with another type of rotting. False teachers had sneaked into the church and started telling lies about Jesus and how to be saved. If the false teachers were allowed to stay then, like a tooth, the whole church would soon be rotten – eaten away by false teaching.

Jude wrote this letter to the Christians and urged them to get rid of the false teachers before the whole church rotted! Their false teaching and low standards were infecting the church and threatening its existence.

Jude encourages the Christians to grow strong in their own faith, so that they won't be influenced by any false teachers who appear on the scene in the future. He tells them to pray, to keep their eyes fixed on God's love for them, and to continue preaching the Good News of Jesus to non-Christians.

LIFE FILE LINKS

Investigate the Theme

To find a list of real life stories on this subject turn to the LIFE FILE GUIDE on pages 12 to 22 at the front of the Youth Bible.

NON-CHRISTIANS

¹From Jude, a servant of Jesus Christ and a brother of James.

To all who have been called by God. God the Father loves you, and you have been kept safe in Jesus Christ:

²Mercy, peace and love be yours richly.

God will Punish Sinners

³Dear friends, I wanted very much to write to you about the salvation *d* we all share. But I felt the need to write to you about something else: I want to encourage you to fight hard for the faith that was given the holy people of God once and for all time. ⁴Some people have secretly entered your group. Long ago the prophets *d* wrote about these people who will be judged guilty. They are against God and have changed the grace of our God into a reason for sexual sin. They also refuse to accept Jesus Christ, our only Master and Lord.

⁵I want to remind you of some things you already know: remember that the Lord saved his people by bringing them out of the land of Egypt. But later he destroyed all those who did not believe. ⁶And remember the angels who did not keep their place of power but left their proper home. The Lord has kept these angels in darkness, bound with everlasting chains, to be judged on the great day. ⁷Also remember the cities of

PERSISTENCE

In the Swim

Charlie had been an asthmatic since birth. He often had to sit out of school sports because he would get out of breath very quickly.

As he sat on the sidelines watching the other kids enjoy themselves, he felt sad. If only there was something that he could do that might make him feel better. If only there was some sport which he could excel in.

On the next visit to his doctor, Charlie asked if there was any sport which he could concentrate on without damaging his health. The doctor suggested swimming as one of the best sports and so within a week Charlie was in his local pool.

At first he could only manage a few strokes before he got breathless, but he persevered and soon he was able to swim from one side of the pool to the other. By now he had decided that his goal was to compete in a 100-metre breaststroke race — and win.

Every day he could be found in the pool, either swimming or exercising his legs or arms on their own. He figured that the stronger his limbs were, the less his body would have to fight for breath.

His theory proved right. Over several months Charlie developed his muscles and felt fitter than ever before. When the date of the 100-metre breaststroke race was announced, Charlie was the first to enter his name.

On the day of the race, his friends came to the pool to cheer him on. None of them really expected Charlie to win; they simply admired his guts and determination.

But the determination paid off, and when Charlie left the pool that day, he was holding a medal for coming first.

It's this kind of determination and faith that **Jude 17–25** urges all Christians to have as they follow God.

* How does Charlie's brave determination compare with the sort that Jude advised Christians to have?
* How can this passage encourage you to "keep going" when the going gets tough?

Consider . . .

* what are the weakest points of your faith? Be determined to strengthen them and so be able to follow God without "losing your breath".
* practising sharing your faith with a Christian friend, then sharing it with a non-Christian friend.

For more, see . . .

* Psalm 113 (p.568)
* 1 Peter 2:4–10 (p.1357)
* 1 Thessalonians 5:12–22 (p.1301)

Sodom *d* and Gomorrah *d* and the other towns around them. In the same way they were full of sexual sin and people who desired sexual relations that God does not allow. They suffer the punishment of eternal fire, as an example for all to see.

[8]It is the same with these people who have entered your group. They are guided by dreams and make themselves dirty with sin. They reject God's authority and speak against the angels. [9]Not even the archangel *n* Michael, when he argued with the devil about who would have the body of Moses, dared to judge the devil guilty. Instead, he said, "The Lord punish you." [10]But these people speak against things they do not understand. And what they do know, by feeling, as dumb animals know things, are the very things that destroy them. [11]It will be terrible for them. They have followed the way of Cain, and for money they have given themselves to doing the wrong that Balaam did. They have fought against God as Korah did, and like Korah, they surely will be destroyed. [12]They are like dirty spots in your special Christian meals you share. They eat with you and have no fear, caring only for themselves. They are clouds without rain, which the wind blows around. They are autumn trees without fruit that are pulled out of the ground. So they are twice dead. [13]They are like wild waves of the sea, tossing up their own shameful actions like foam. They are like stars that wander in the sky. A place in the blackest darkness has been kept for them for ever.

[14]Enoch, the seventh descendant *d* from Adam, said about these people: "Look, the Lord is coming with many thousands of his holy angels to [15]judge every person. He is coming to punish all who are against God for all the evil they have done against him. And he will punish the sinners who are against God for all the evil they have said against him."

[16]These people complain and blame others, doing the evil things they want to do. They boast about themselves, and they flatter others to get what they want.

A Warning and Things to Do

[17]Dear friends, remember what the apostles *d* of our Lord Jesus Christ said before. [18]They said to you, "In the last times there will be people who laugh about God, following their own evil desires which are against God." [19]These are the people who divide you, people whose thoughts are only of this world, who do not have the Spirit. *d*

[20]But dear friends, use your most holy faith to build yourselves up, praying in the Holy Spirit. [21]Keep yourselves in God's love as you wait for the Lord Jesus Christ with his mercy to give you life for ever.

[22]Show mercy to people who have doubts. [23]Take others out of the fire, and save them. Show mercy mixed with fear to others, hating even their clothes which are dirty from sin.

Praise God

[24]God is strong and can keep you from falling. He can bring you before his glory without any wrong in you and can give you great joy. [25]He is the only God, the One who saves us. To him be glory, greatness, power and authority through Jesus Christ our Lord for all time past, now and for ever. Amen.

---

archangel The leader among God's angels or messengers.

Revelation

When?

Why Read This Book:

- Hear warnings about problems in churches (Revelation 1—3).
- See God's power against the forces of evil (Revelation 4—11).
- Be comforted by God's promise of hope for all his people (Revelation 12—22).

Behind the Scenes:

A blood-red moon. A lamb with seven horns and seven eyes. Locusts with golden crowns. White, red, black and pale horses. A giant, red dragon. A sea of glass mixed with fire. All straight out of a science-fiction movie? No! They are from the book of Revelation, the last book of the Bible – exciting, mysterious . . . and confusing.

This book can be so difficult to understand because it is "apocalyptic". Most often, this kind of literature was written during tough times, when the church was being persecuted. One reason for using the images was to have symbols that Christians would understand, but others would not.

That's certainly true of the book of Revelation. At the time, Christians were under attack by the Roman authorities who demanded that all people worship the emperor. Many Christians refused, and many were executed.

Scholars view the symbols, events and visions in Revelation in different ways. Some of the major views include:

- The book describes the first-century situation, and all the events described in it have taken place.
- The book predicts a long chain of events, concluding with Christ's Second Coming.
- The visions describe the final days before the end of the world, and do not relate directly to biblical times.
- The book does not predict the future; rather it uses symbolic language to teach religious truth about God's victory over evil.

Whatever your viewpoint, the main themes are clear. God is powerful. Jesus Christ reigns forever. Those who suffer for Christ will ultimately share his victory.

Where?

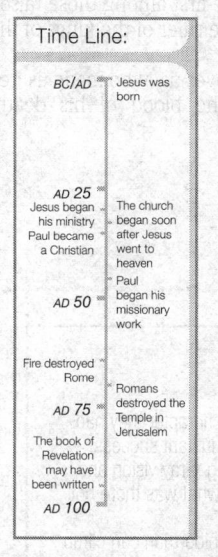

Time Line:

BC/AD — Jesus was born

AD 25 — Jesus began his ministry
Paul became a Christian

The church began soon after Jesus went to heaven

Paul began his missionary work

AD 50

Fire destroyed Rome

Romans destroyed the Temple in Jerusalem

AD 75

The book of Revelation may have been written

AD 100

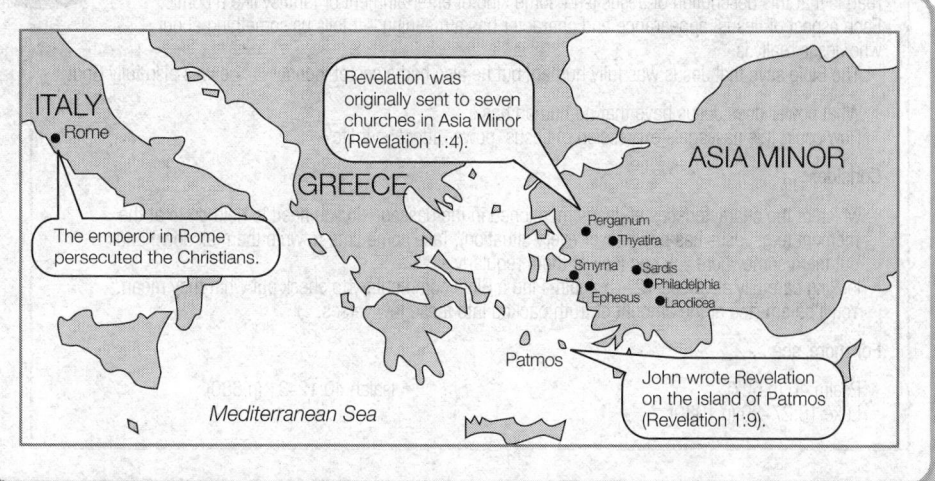

ITALY
• Rome

The emperor in Rome persecuted the Christians.

GREECE

Revelation was originally sent to seven churches in Asia Minor (Revelation 1:4).

ASIA MINOR

Pergamum
• Thyatira
Smyrna • Sardis
• Philadelphia
Ephesus • Laodicea

Patmos

John wrote Revelation on the island of Patmos (Revelation 1:9).

Mediterranean Sea

John Tells About this Book

1 This is the revelation[n] of Jesus Christ, which God gave to him, to show his servants what must soon happen. And Jesus sent his angel to show it to his servant John, [2]who has told everything he has seen. It is the word of God; it is the message from Jesus Christ. [3]Happy is the one who reads the words of God's message, and happy are the people who hear this message and do what is written in it. The time is near when all of this will happen.

revelation   A making known of truth that has been hidden.

Jesus' Message to the Churches

[4]From John.

To the seven churches in the country of Asia:

Grace and peace to you from the One who is and was and is coming, and from the seven spirits before his throne, [5]and from Jesus Christ. Jesus is the faithful witness, the first among those raised from the dead. He is the ruler of the kings of the earth.

He is the One who loves us, who made us free from our sins with the blood of his death.

GOD'S POWER

Is It a Bird?

In a comic book in 1938, writer Jerry Siegel and illustrator Joe Shuster introduced a character they had created when they were growing up together. He was called "Superman" and was an instant success. With a secret identity (he was really called Clark Kent), super-human powers (including x-ray vision and amazing strength), plus a colourful costume (pants on the outside of his trousers?) – what was there not to admire?!

If you could be a superhero and have super-human powers, what would you be? Spiderman can climb up walls and swing through cities . . . Batman has a sidekick, Robin, and the Batmobile. Would you want to have the ability to become invisible or have a special weapon of some kind? And what would your costume be?

Everyone loves a hero.

The reason Superman was so popular was because he did amazing things that no other person could, and he fought evil to make the world a better place. The comic-book readers could easily engross themselves in the story and imagine what it would be like to be the superhero or be rescued by him.

Read **Revelation 1:4–18**. It's an amazing description of Jesus which John saw in a vision that makes Jesus seem like a comic-book superhero. But what we need to remember as we read is that this description of Jesus isn't some kind of entertainment or fantasy like a comic. Each aspect of Jesus' appearance and character has a meaning – it tells us something about who Jesus really is.

The Bible says that Jesus was fully human, but he also had a secret identity . . . he was also fully God!

- What power does Jesus have that no human has?
- How could this passage's expression of Jesus' power affect your life?

Consider . . .

- which of the characteristics of Jesus mentioned in the passage do you need to hold on to at the moment (e.g. Jesus has power over every situation). Take some time to write them all down and put them somewhere you can look at them regularly.
- looking carefully at verses 12–15 again. Find a Bible commentary to check out what they mean. You'll be amazed at the amount of truth packed into these few verses.

For more, see . . .

- Psalm 46 (p.527)
- Luke 18:27–39 (p.1080)
- Isaiah 40:12–31 (p.680)

⁶He made us to be a kingdom of priests who serve God his Father. To Jesus Christ be glory and power for ever and ever! Amen.

⁷Look, Jesus is coming with the clouds, and everyone will see him, even those who stabbed him. And all peoples of the earth will cry loudly because of him. Yes, this will happen! Amen.

⁸The Lord God says, "I am the Alpha and the Omega. *n* I am the One who is and was and is coming. I am the Almighty."

⁹I, John, am your brother. All of us share with Christ in suffering, in the kingdom and in patience to continue. I was on the island of Patmos, *n* because I had preached the word of God and the message about Jesus. ¹⁰On the Lord's day I was in

> **Sidelight**   The island of Patmos, where John wrote Revelation (Revelation 1:9), was the Alcatraz of the Roman Empire. Religious and political prisoners were banished to this island "prison", which is only about sixteen kilometres long.

the Spirit, *d* and I heard a loud voice behind me that sounded like a trumpet. ¹¹The voice said, "Write what you see in a book and send it to the seven churches: to Ephesus, Smyrna, Pergamum, Thyatira, Sardis, Philadelphia and Laodicea."

¹²I turned to see who was talking to me. When I turned, I saw seven golden lampstands ¹³and someone among the lampstands who was "like a Son of Man". *n* He was dressed in a long robe and had a gold band around his chest. ¹⁴His head and hair were white like wool, as white as snow, and his eyes were like flames of fire. ¹⁵His feet were like bronze that glows hot in a furnace, and his voice was like the noise of flooding water. ¹⁶He held seven stars in his right hand, and a sharp two-edged sword came out of his mouth. He looked like the sun shining at its brightest time.

¹⁷When I saw him, I fell down at his feet like a dead man. He put his right hand on me and said, "Do not be afraid. I am the First and the Last. ¹⁸I am the One who lives; I was dead, but look, I am alive for ever and ever! And I hold the keys to death and to the place of the dead. ¹⁹So write the things you see, what is now and what will happen later. ²⁰Here is the secret of the seven stars that you saw in my right hand and the seven golden lampstands: the seven lampstands are the seven churches, and the seven stars are the angels of the seven churches.

To the Church in Ephesus

2 "Write this to the angel of the church in Ephesus:

"The One who holds the seven stars in his right hand and walks among the seven golden lampstands says this: ²I know what you do, how you work hard and never give up. I know you do not put up with the false teachings of evil people. You have tested those who say they are apostles *d* but really are not, and you found they are liars. ³You have patience and have suffered troubles for my name and have not given up.

⁴"But I have this against you: you have left the love you had in the beginning. ⁵So remember where you were before you fell. Change your hearts and do what you did at first. If you do not change, I will come to you and will take away your lampstand from its place. ⁶But there is something you do that is right: you hate what the Nicolaitans *n* do, as much as I.

⁷"Every person who has ears should listen to what the Spirit *d* says to the churches. To those who win the victory I will give the right to eat the fruit from the tree of life, which is in the garden of God.

To the Church in Smyrna

⁸"Write this to the angel of the church in Smyrna:

"The One who is the First and the Last, who died and came to life again, says this: ⁹I know your troubles and that you are poor, but really you are rich! I know the bad things some people say about you. They say they are Jews, but they are not true Jews. They are a synagogue *d* that belongs to Satan. ¹⁰Do not be afraid of what you are about to suffer. I tell you, the devil will put some of you in prison to test you, and you will suffer for ten days. But be faithful, even if you have to die, and I will give you the crown of life.

¹¹"Everyone who has ears should listen to what the Spirit *d* says to the churches. Those who win the victory will not be hurt by the second death.

To the Church in Pergamum

¹²"Write this to the angel of the church in Pergamum:

"The One who has the sharp, two-edged sword says this: ¹³I know where you live. It is where Satan has his throne. But you are true to me. You did not refuse to tell about your faith in me even during the time of Antipas, my faithful witness who was killed in your city, where Satan lives.

Alpha and the Omega   The first and last letters of the Greek alphabet. This means "the beginning and the end".
Patmos   A small island in the Aegean Sea, near the coast of Asia Minor (modern Turkey).
"like . . . Man"   "Son of Man" is a name Jesus called himself. See dictionary.
Nicolaitans   This is the name of a religious group that followed false beliefs and ideas.

¹⁴"But I have a few things against you: you have some there who follow the teaching of Balaam. He taught Balak how to cause the people of Israel to sin by eating food offered to idols and by taking part in sexual sins. ¹⁵You also have some who follow the teaching of the Nicolaitans.ⁿ ¹⁶So change your hearts and lives. If you do not, I will come to you quickly and fight against them with the sword that comes out of my mouth.

¹⁷"Everyone who has ears should listen to what the Spiritᵈ says to the churches.

"I will give some of the hidden mannaᵈ to everyone who wins the victory. I will also give to each one who wins the victory a white stone with a new name written on it. No one knows this new name except the one who receives it.

To the Church in Thyatira

¹⁸"Write this to the angel of the church in Thyatira:

"The Son of God, who has eyes that blaze like fire and feet like shining bronze, says this: ¹⁹I know what you do. I know about your love, your faith, your service and your patience. I know that you are doing more now than you did at first. ²⁰"But I have this against you: you let that woman Jezebel spread false teachings. She says she is a prophetess,ᵈ but by her teaching she leads my people to take part in sexual sins and to eat food that is offered to idols. ²¹I have given her time to change her heart and turn away from her sin, but she does not want to change. ²²So I will throw her on a bed of suffering. And all those who take part in adulteryᵈ with her will suffer greatly if they do not turn away from the wrongs she does. ²³I will also kill her followers. Then all the churches will know I am the One who searches hearts and minds, and I will repay each of you for what you have done.

²⁴"But others of you in Thyatira have not followed her teaching and have not learned what some call Satan's deep secrets. I say to you that I will not put any other load on you. ²⁵Only continue in your loyalty until I come.

²⁶"I will give power over the nations to everyone who wins the victory and continues to be obedient to me until the end.
²⁷'You will rule over them with an iron rod,
    as when pottery is broken into pieces.'
Psalm 2:9
²⁸This is the same power I received from my Father. I will also give him the morning star. ²⁹Everyone who has ears should listen to what the Spiritᵈ says to the churches.

Sidelight Mathematicians, arise! Numbers have an important role in Revelation, with many having symbolic significance. For example, seven (Revelation 3:1) symbolises completeness; four signifies the created universe (Revelation 7:1, p.1393); and twelve symbolises the church or Israel (Revelation 21:12–14, p.1404).

To the Church in Sardis

3 "Write this to the angel of the church in Sardis:

"The One who has the seven spirits and the seven stars says this: I know what you do. People say that you are alive, but really you are dead. ²Wake up! Make yourselves stronger before what you have left dies completely. I have found that what you are doing is less than what my God wants. ³So do not forget what you have received and heard. Obey it, and change your hearts and lives. So you must wake up, or I will come like a thief, and you will not know when I will come to you. ⁴But you have a few there in Sardis who have kept their clothes clean, so they will walk with me and will wear white clothes, because they are worthy. ⁵Those who win the victory will be dressed in white clothes like them. And I will not erase their names from the book of life, but I will say they belong to me before my Father and before his angels. ⁶Everyone who has ears should listen to what the Spiritᵈ says to the churches.

To the Church in Philadelphia

⁷"Write this to the angel of the church in Philadelphia:

"This is what the One who is holy and true, who holds the key of David, says. When he opens a door, no one can close it. And when he closes it, no one can open it. ⁸I know what you do. I have put an open door before you, which no one can close. I know you have a little strength, but you have obeyed my teaching and were not afraid to speak my name. ⁹Those in the synagogueᵈ that belongs to Satan say they are Jews, but they are not true Jews; they are liars. I will make them come before you and bow at your feet, and they will know that I have loved you. ¹⁰You have obeyed my teaching about not giving up your faith. So I will keep you from the time of trouble that will come to the whole world to test those who live on earth.

¹¹"I am coming soon. Continue strong in your faith so no one will take away your crown. ¹²I will

Nicolaitans This is the name of a religious group that followed false beliefs and ideas.

make those who win the victory to become pillars in the temple of my God, and they will never have to leave it. I will write on them the name of my God and the name of the city of my God, the new Jerusalem, *n* that comes down out of heaven from my God. I will also write on them my new name. [13]Everyone who has ears should listen to what the Spirit *d* says to the churches.

To the Church in Laodicea

[14]"Write this to the angel of the church in Laodicea:

"The Amen, *n* the faithful and true witness, the beginning of all God has made, says this: [15]I know what you do, that you are neither hot nor cold. I wish that you were either hot or cold! [16]But because you are warm—neither hot, nor cold—I am ready to spit you out of my mouth. [17]You say, 'I am rich, and I have become wealthy and do not need anything.' But you do not know that you are really miserable, pitiful, poor, blind and naked. [18]I advise you to buy from me gold made pure in fire so you can be truly rich. Buy from me white clothes so you can be clothed and so you can cover your shameful nakedness. Buy from me medicine to put on your eyes so you can truly see.

[19]"I correct and punish those whom I love. So be eager to do right, and change your hearts and lives. [20]Here I am! I stand at the door and knock. If you hear my voice and open the door, I will come in and eat with you, and you will eat with me.

[21]"Those who win the victory will sit with me on my throne in the same way that I won the victory and sat down with my Father on his throne. [22]Everyone who has ears should listen to what the Spirit *d* says to the churches."

John Sees Heaven

4 After the vision of these things I looked, and there before me was an open door in heaven. And the same voice that spoke to me before, that sounded like a trumpet, said, "Come up here, and I will show you what must happen after this." [2]Immediately I was in the Spirit, *d* and before me was a throne in heaven, and someone was sitting on it. [3]The One who sat on the throne looked like precious stones, like jasper and carnelian. All around the throne was a rainbow the colour of an emerald. [4]Around the throne there were 24 other thrones with 24 elders sitting on them. They were dressed in white and had golden crowns on their heads. [5]Lightning flashes and noises and thundering came

from the throne. Before the throne seven lamps were burning, which are the seven spirits of God. [6]Also before the throne there was something that looked like a sea of glass, clear like crystal.

In the centre and around the throne were four living creatures with eyes all over them, in front and behind. [7]The first living creature was like a lion. The second was like a calf. The third had a face like a man. The fourth was like a flying eagle. [8]Each of these four living creatures had six wings and was covered all over with eyes, inside and out. Day and night they never stop saying:

"Holy, holy, holy is the Lord God Almighty.
He was, he is, and he is coming."

[9]These living creatures give glory, honour and thanks to the One who sits on the throne, who lives for ever and ever. [10]Then the 24 elders bow down before the One who sits on the throne, and they worship him who lives for ever and ever. They put their crowns down before the throne and say:

[11]"You are worthy, our Lord and God,
to receive glory and honour and power,
because you made all things.
Everything existed and was made,
because you wanted it."

5 Then I saw a scroll in the right hand of the One sitting on the throne. The scroll had writing on both sides and was kept closed with seven seals. [2]And I saw a powerful angel calling in a loud voice, "Who is worthy to break the seals and open the scroll?" [3]But there was no one in heaven or on earth or under the earth who could open the scroll or look inside it. [4]I cried hard because there was no one who was worthy to

---

Sidelight Ancient scrolls (Revelation 5:1) were created by beating papyrus (a reed found in the Nile River) into sheets (often about 20 cm x 25 cm) and sewing them together. A scroll of Revelation – written on both sides to save money – would have been about 4½ metres long!

---

open the scroll or look inside. [5]But one of the elders said to me, "Do not cry! The Lion *n* from the tribe *d* of Judah, David's descendant, *d* has won the victory so that he is able to open the scroll and its seven seals."

[6]Then I saw a Lamb standing in the centre of the throne and in the middle of the four living creatures and the elders. The Lamb looked as if

---

Jerusalem This name is used to mean the spiritual city God built for his people. See Revelation 21—22.
Amen Used here as a name for Jesus; it means to agree fully that something is true.
Lion Here refers to Christ.

he had been killed. He had seven horns and seven eyes, which are the seven spirits of God that were sent into all the world. [7]The Lamb came and took the scroll from the right hand of the One sitting on the throne. [8]When he took the scroll, the four living creatures and the 24 elders bowed down before the Lamb. Each one of them had a harp and golden bowls full of incense, *d* which are the prayers of God's holy people. [9]And they all sang a new song to the Lamb:

"You are worthy to take the scroll
    and to open its seals,
because you were killed,
    and with the blood of your death you
        bought people for God
    from every tribe, language, people and
        nation.
[10]You made them to be a kingdom of priests
        for our God,
    and they will rule on the earth."

[11]Then I looked, and I heard the voices of many angels around the throne, and the four living creatures, and the elders. There were thousands and thousands of angels, [12]saying in a loud voice:

"The Lamb who was killed is worthy
    to receive power, wealth, wisdom and strength,
    honour, glory and praise!"

[13]Then I heard all creatures in heaven and on earth and under the earth and in the sea saying:

"To the One who sits on the throne
    and to the Lamb
be praise and honour and glory and power
    for ever and ever."

[14]The four living creatures said, "Amen," and the elders bowed down and worshipped.

6 Then I watched while the Lamb opened the first of the seven seals. I heard one of the four living creatures say with a voice like thunder, "Come!" [2]I looked, and there before me was a white horse. The rider on the horse held a bow, and he was given a crown, and he rode out, determined to win the victory.

[3]When the Lamb opened the second seal, I heard the second living creature say, "Come!"

WORSHIP

Heaven Download

Nathan removed his headphones and handed them back to his friend Isaac. "That last song you downloaded had a weird ending."

"I know," Isaac replied. "But hey, maybe that's just the music of tomorrow!" They both proceeded to play air guitars and scrunch their faces.

"Rock and roll, baby, yeah!"

Strangely, the last book of the Bible is full of all sorts of weird things. Living creatures that talk and sing, a lamb with seven horns and seven eyes, periodic bursts of huge crowds shouting and then remaining completely silent . . . and that's just a handful of them! The reason is because the whole book was "downloaded" to the world thousands of years ago through a man who could only describe his glimpse of heaven in images he was familiar with.

Revelation 5:11–14 paints a beautiful picture of all God's creation worshipping him together in perfect unison. The elders are so overloaded by this incredible insight into the character of God, that (like Isaac's computer) they literally "crash" down to their knees, bowing before him.

* What are some ways that you really connect with God?
* What was the last thing you "downloaded" from heaven while spending time worshipping God? When will you tap into eternity again?

Consider . . .

* meditating and thinking about the characteristics of God mentioned in this passage.
* taking the time to find a secret place to connect with God. Let him even give you *new* expressions of worship.

For more, see . . .

* Psalm 100 (p.558)
* Ezekiel 1:1–28 (p.788)
* Isaiah 6:1–8 (p.645)
* Revelation 22:1–5 (p.1404)

4Then another horse came out, a red one. Its rider was given power to take away peace from the earth and to make people kill each other, and he was given a big sword.

5When the Lamb opened the third seal, I heard the third living creature say, "Come!" I looked, and there before me was a black horse, and its rider held a pair of scales in his hand. 6Then I heard something that sounded like a voice coming from the middle of the four living creatures. The voice said, "A litre of wheat for a day's pay, and 3 litres of barley for a day's pay, and do not damage the olive oil and wine!"

7When the Lamb opened the fourth seal, I heard the voice of the fourth living creature say, "Come!" 8I looked, and there before me was a pale horse. Its rider was named death, and Hades[n] was following close behind him. They were given power over a quarter of the earth to kill people by war, by starvation, by disease and by the wild animals of the earth.

9When the Lamb opened the fifth seal, I saw under the altar the souls of those who had been killed because they were faithful to the word of God and to the message they had received. 10These souls shouted in a loud voice, "Holy and true Lord, how long until you judge the people of the earth and punish them for killing us?" 11Then each one of them was given a white robe and was told to wait a short time longer. There were still some of their fellow servants and brothers and sisters[n] in the service of Christ who must be killed as they were. They had to wait until all of this was finished.

12Then I watched while the Lamb opened the sixth seal, and there was a great earthquake. The sun became black like rough black cloth, and the whole moon became red like blood. 13And the stars in the sky fell to the earth like figs falling from a fig tree when the wind blows. 14The sky disappeared as a scroll when it is rolled up, and every mountain and island was moved from its place.

15Then the kings of the earth, the rulers, the generals, the rich people, the powerful people, the slaves and the free people hid themselves in caves and in the rocks on the mountains. 16They called to the mountains and the rocks, "Fall on us. Hide us from the face of the One who sits on the throne and from the anger of the Lamb! 17The great day for their anger has come, and who can stand against it?"

The 144,000 People of Israel

7 After the vision of these things I saw four angels standing at the four corners of the earth. The angels were holding the four winds of the earth to keep them from blowing on the land or on the sea or on any tree. 2Then I saw another angel coming up from the east who had the seal of the living God. And he called out in a loud voice to the four angels to whom God had given power to harm the earth and the sea. 3He said to them, "Do not harm the land or the sea or the trees until we mark with a sign the foreheads of the people who serve our God." 4Then I heard how many people were marked with the sign. There were 144,000 from every tribe[d] of the people of Israel.

5From the tribe of Judah 12,000 were marked with the sign,
from the tribe of Reuben 12,000,
from the tribe of Gad 12,000,
6from the tribe of Asher 12,000,
from the tribe of Naphtali 12,000,
from the tribe of Manasseh 12,000,
7from the tribe of Simeon 12,000,
from the tribe of Levi 12,000,
from the tribe of Issachar 12,000,
8from the tribe of Zebulun 12,000,
from the tribe of Joseph 12,000,
and from the tribe of Benjamin 12,000 were marked with the sign.

The Great Crowd Worships God

9After the vision of these things I looked, and there was a great number of people, so many that no one could count them. They were from every nation, tribe,[d] people and language of the earth. They were all standing before the throne and before the Lamb, wearing white robes and holding palm branches in their hands. 10They were shouting in a loud voice, "Salvation belongs to our God, who sits on the throne, and to the Lamb." 11All the angels were standing around the throne and the elders and the four living creatures. They all bowed down on their faces before the throne and worshipped God, 12saying, "Amen! Praise, glory, wisdom, thanks, honour, power and strength belong to our God for ever and ever. Amen!"

13Then one of the elders asked me, "Who are these people dressed in white robes? Where did they come from?"

14I answered, "You know who they are, sir."

And the elder said to me, "These are the people who have come out of the great distress. They have washed their robes and made them white in the blood of the Lamb.[n] 15Because of this, they are before the throne of God. They worship him day and night in his temple.[d] And the One who sits on the throne will be present with them.

Hades The unseen world of the dead.
brothers and sisters Although the Greek text says "brothers" here and throughout this book, John's words refer to the entire church, both men and women.
washed ... Lamb This means they believed in Jesus so that their sins could be forgiven through Christ's blood.

[16]Those people will never be hungry again, and they will never be thirsty again. The sun will not hurt them, and no heat will burn them, [17]because the Lamb at the centre of the throne will be their shepherd. He will lead them to springs of water that give life. And God will wipe away every tear from their eyes."

The Seventh Seal

8 When the Lamb opened the seventh seal, there was silence in heaven for about half an hour. [2]And I saw the seven angels who stand before God and to whom were given seven trumpets.

[3]Another angel came and stood at the altar, holding a golden pan for incense. [d] He was given

> **Sidelight** The seals which secured the documents in Revelation (see Revelation 8:1) meant: that the message was one of authority, that it belonged to the person named on the seal (in this case God) and that the message was not a fake. The seal also served to make sure that the documents were secure – a kind of biblical "For Your Eyes Only" message!

SADNESS

The Worst Year of Her Life

Lisa had looked forward to her first year in college. She did not know it would be her life's worst.

Early in the autumn her mother was diagnosed as having cancer. Her dad gave up his job to help care for her mum. Money, time and energy were scarce. And Lisa was carrying a heavy workload at college.

"I had to take care of the house, feed everyone, and plough through my work," she recalls. "It was tough, but I got along somehow."

One day, however, her mother entered the hospital for one final, risky operation to fight the cancer. "When the surgeons came out of the operating theatre, I could tell by the way they looked at me that she was gone," she says.

After the funeral, Lisa's life changed dramatically. Her father, in deep grief, wandered about the house. One day Lisa found a "For Sale" sign in their front garden. "It's too painful for me to live here," her father said.

Unable to find work and desperately lonely, her father returned to his home town. Lisa faced the difficult choice: either live with her older sister or go with her father. Even though she missed her dad, Lisa stayed with her sister.

What sustained her through this sad time? "Christian friends and a caring church got me through the experience," she says. "I couldn't pray, because I was mad at God. All I'd do was cry. These friends just kept loving me, even when I was unlovely."

Lisa carried on with college, studying engineering. Her father, in time, overcame his grief and went on with his life.

"My world fell apart when I was sixteen," Lisa reflects. "Our family suffered a lot. But with God's help, we got through it all, and that's what matters."

Everyone experiences pain, disappointment and uncontrollable events. When those sad times seem overwhelming, Christians can turn to passages such as **Revelation 7:9–17** for a message of hope.

* What hope could Lisa gain from these verses?
* How could these verses help you to deal with sadness in your life?

Consider . . .

* doing something positive to help get you out of the blues. Try visiting a friend, watching a comedy film or exercising.
* visiting someone who is having a sad time. Take a small gift to show you care.

For more, see . . .

* Psalm 40:1–3 (p.523)
* Hebrews 10:23–25 (p.1339)
* Ecclesiastes 3:1–8 (p.622)

much incense to offer with the prayers of all God's holy people. The angel put this offering on the golden altar before the throne. [4]The smoke from the incense went up from the angel's hand to God with the prayers of God's people. [5]Then the angel filled the incense pan with fire from the altar and threw it on the earth, and there were flashes of lightning, thunder and loud noises, and an earthquake.

The Seven Angels and Trumpets

[6]Then the seven angels who had the seven trumpets prepared to blow them.

[7]The first angel blew his trumpet, and hail and fire mixed with blood were poured down on the earth. And a third of the earth, and all the green grass, and a third of the trees were burnt up.

[8]Then the second angel blew his trumpet, and something that looked like a big mountain, burning with fire, was thrown into the sea. And a third of the sea became blood, [9]a third of the living things in the sea died, and a third of the ships were destroyed.

[10]Then the third angel blew his trumpet, and a large star, burning like a torch, fell from the sky. It fell on a third of the rivers and on the springs of water. [11]The name of the star is Wormwood. [n] And a third of all the water became bitter, and many people died from drinking the water that was bitter.

[12]Then the fourth angel blew his trumpet, and a third of the sun, and a third of the moon, and a third of the stars were struck. So a third of them became dark, and a third of the day was without light, and also the night.

[13]While I watched, I heard an eagle that was flying high in the air cry out in a loud voice, "Trouble! Trouble! Trouble for those who live on the earth because of the remaining sounds of the trumpets that the other three angels are about to blow!"

9 Then the fifth angel blew his trumpet, and I saw a star fall from the sky to the earth. The star was given the key to the deep hole that leads to the bottomless pit. [2]Then it opened up the hole that leads to the bottomless pit, and smoke came up from the hole like smoke from a big furnace. Then the sun and sky became dark because of the smoke from the hole. [3]Then locusts [d] came down to the earth out of the smoke, and they were given the power to sting like scorpions. [n] [4]They were told not to harm the grass on the earth or any plant or tree. They could harm only the people who did not have the sign of God on their foreheads. [5]These locusts were not given the power to kill anyone, but to cause pain to the

people for five months. And the pain they felt was like the pain a scorpion gives when it stings someone. [6]During those days people will look for a way to die, but they will not find it. They will want to die, but death will run away from them.

[7]The locusts looked like horses prepared for battle. On their heads they wore what looked like crowns of gold, and their faces looked like human faces. [8]Their hair was like women's hair, and their teeth were like lions' teeth. [9]Their chests looked like iron breastplates, and the sound of their wings was like the noise of many horses and chariots hurrying into battle. [10]The locusts had tails with stingers like scorpions, and in their tails was their power to hurt people for five months. [11]The locusts had a king who was the angel of the bottomless pit. His name in the Hebrew language is Abaddon and in the Greek language is Apollyon. [n]

[12]The first trouble is past; there are still two other troubles that will come.

[13]Then the sixth angel blew his trumpet, and I heard a voice coming from the horns on the golden altar that is before God. [14]The voice said to the sixth angel who had the trumpet, "Free the four angels who are tied at the great river Euphrates." [15]And they let loose the four angels who had been kept ready for this hour and day and month and year so they could kill a third of all people on the earth. [16]I heard how many troops on horses were in their army—200,000,000.

[17]The horses and their riders I saw in the vision looked like this: they had breastplates that were fiery red, dark blue and yellow like sulphur. The heads of the horses looked like heads of lions, with fire, smoke and sulphur coming out of their mouths. [18]A third of all the people on earth were killed by these three terrible disasters coming out of the horses' mouths: the fire, the smoke and the sulphur. [19]The horses' power was in their mouths and in their tails; their tails were like snakes with heads, and with them they hurt people.

[20]The other people who were not killed by these terrible disasters still did not change their hearts and turn away from what they had made with their own hands. They did not stop worshipping demons [d] and idols made of gold, silver, bronze, stone and wood—things that cannot see or hear or walk. [21]These people did not change their hearts and turn away from murder or evil magic, from their sexual sins or stealing.

The Angel and the Small Scroll

10 Then I saw another powerful angel coming down from heaven dressed in a cloud

---

Wormwood　Name of a very bitter plant; used here to give the idea of bitter sorrow.
scorpions　A scorpion is an insect-like creature with a poisonous sting.
Abaddon, Apollyon　Both names mean "Destroyer".

with a rainbow over his head. His face was like the sun, and his legs were like pillars of fire. [2]The angel was holding a small scroll open in his hand. He put his right foot on the sea and his left foot on the land. [3]Then he shouted loudly like the roaring of a lion. And when he shouted, the voices of seven thunders spoke. [4]When the seven thunders spoke, I started to write. But I heard a voice from heaven say, "Keep hidden what the seven thunders said, and do not write them down."

[5]Then the angel I saw standing on the sea and on the land raised his right hand to heaven, [6]and he made a promise by the power of the One who lives for ever and ever. He is the One who made the skies and all that is in them, the earth and all that is in it, and the sea and all that is in it. The angel promised, "There will be no more waiting! [7]In the days when the seventh angel is ready to blow his trumpet, God's secret will be finished. This secret is the Good News [d] God told to his servants, the prophets." [d]

[8]Then I heard the same voice from heaven again, saying to me: "Go and take the open scroll that is in the hand of the angel that is standing on the sea and on the land."

[9]So I went to the angel and told him to give me the small scroll. And he said to me, "Take the scroll and eat it. It will be sour in your stomach, but in your mouth it will be sweet as honey." [10]So I took the small scroll from the angel's hand and ate it. In my mouth it tasted sweet as honey, but after I ate it, it was sour in my stomach. [11]Then I was told, "You must prophesy [d] again about many peoples, nations, languages and kings."

The Two Witnesses

11 I was given a measuring stick like a rod, and I was told, "Go and measure the temple [d] of God and the altar, and count the people worshipping there. [2]But do not measure the yard outside the temple. Leave it alone, because it has been given to those who are not God's people. And they will trample on the holy city for 42 months. [3]And I will give power to my two witnesses to prophesy [d] for 1,260 days, and they will be dressed in rough cloth to show their sadness."

[4]These two witnesses are the two olive trees and the two lampstands that stand before the Lord of the earth. [5]And if anyone tries to hurt them, fire comes from their mouths and kills their enemies. And if anyone tries to hurt them in whatever way, in that same way that person will die. [6]These witnesses have the power to stop the sky from raining during the time they are prophesying. And they have power to make the waters become blood, and they have power to send every kind of trouble to the earth as many times as they want.

[7]When the two witnesses have finished telling their message, the beast that comes up from the bottomless pit will fight a war against them. He will defeat them and kill them. [8]The bodies of the two witnesses will lie in the street of the great city where the Lord was killed. This city is named Sodom [n] and Egypt, which has a spiritual meaning. [9]Those from every race of people, tribe, [d] language and nation will look at the bodies of the two witnesses for three and a half days, and they will refuse to bury them. [10]People who live on the earth will rejoice and be happy because these two are dead. They will send each other gifts, because these two prophets brought much suffering to those who live on the earth.

[11]But after three and a half days, God put the breath of life into the two prophets again. They stood on their feet, and everyone who saw them became very afraid. [12]Then the two prophets heard a loud voice from heaven saying, "Come up here!" And they went up into heaven in a cloud as their enemies watched.

[13]In the same hour there was a great earthquake, and a tenth of the city was destroyed. 7,000 people were killed in the earthquake, and those who did not die were very afraid and gave glory to the God of heaven.

[14]The second trouble is finished. Pay attention: the third trouble is coming soon.

The Seventh Trumpet

[15]Then the seventh angel blew his trumpet. And there were loud voices in heaven, saying:
"The power to rule the world
    now belongs to our Lord and his Christ, [d]
and he will rule for ever and ever."
[16]Then the 24 elders, who sit on their thrones before God, bowed down on their faces and worshipped God. [17]They said:
"We give thanks to you, Lord God Almighty,
    who is and who was,
because you have used your great power
    and have begun to rule!
[18]The people of the world were angry,
    but your anger has come.
The time has come to judge the dead
and to reward your servants the prophets [d]
    and your holy people,
    all who respect you, great and small.
The time has come to destroy those who
    destroy the earth!"
[19]Then God's temple [d] in heaven was opened. The Ark [d] that holds the agreement God gave to his people could be seen in his temple. Then there

Sodom City that God destroyed because the people were so evil.

were flashes of lightning, noises, thunder, an earthquake and a great hailstorm.

The Woman and the Dragon

12 And then a great wonder appeared in heaven: a woman was clothed with the sun, and the moon was under her feet, and a crown of twelve stars was on her head. [2]She was pregnant and cried out with pain, because she was about to give birth. [3]Then another wonder appeared in heaven: there was a giant red dragon with seven heads and seven crowns on each head. He also had ten horns. [4]His tail swept a third of the stars out of the sky and threw them down to the earth. He stood in front of the woman who was ready to give birth so he could eat her baby as soon as it was born. [5]Then the woman gave birth to a son who will rule all the nations with an iron rod. And her child was taken up to God and to his throne. [6]The woman ran away into the desert to a place God prepared for her where she would be taken care of for 1,260 days.

[7]Then there was a war in heaven. Michael[n] and his angels fought against the dragon, and the dragon and his angels fought back. [8]But the dragon was not strong enough, and he and his angels lost their place in heaven. [9]The giant dragon was thrown down out of heaven. (He is that old snake called the devil or Satan, who tricks the whole world.) The dragon with his angels was thrown down to the earth.

[10]Then I heard a loud voice in heaven saying:
"The salvation and the power and the
　　kingdom of our God
　and the authority of his Christ[d] have now
　　　come.
The accuser of our brothers and sisters,
　who accused them day and night before
　　our God,
　has been thrown down.
[11]And our brothers and sisters defeated him
　by the blood of the Lamb's death
　and by the message they preached.
They did not love their lives so much
　that they were afraid of death.
[12]So rejoice, you heavens
　and all who live there!
But it will be terrible for the earth and the sea,
　because the devil has come down to you!
He is filled with anger,
　because he knows he does not have much
　　time."

[13]When the dragon saw he had been thrown down to the earth, he hunted for the woman who had given birth to the son. [14]But the woman was given the two wings of a great eagle so she could fly to the place prepared for her in the desert. There she would be taken care of for three and a half years, away from the snake. [15]Then the snake poured water out of its mouth like a river towards the woman so the flood would carry her away. [16]But the earth helped the woman by opening its mouth and swallowing the river that came from the mouth of the dragon. [17]Then the dragon was very angry at the woman, and he went off to make war against all her other children—those who obey God's commands and who have the message Jesus taught.

[18]And the dragon stood on the seashore.

The Two Beasts

13 Then I saw a beast coming up out of the sea. It had ten horns and seven heads, and there was a crown on each horn. A name against God was written on each head. [2]This beast looked like a leopard, with feet like a bear's feet and a mouth like a lion's mouth. And the dragon gave the beast all of his power and his throne and great authority. [3]One of the heads of the beast looked as if it had been killed by a wound, but this death wound was healed. Then the whole world was amazed and followed the beast. [4]People worshipped the dragon because he had given his power to the beast. And they also worshipped the beast, asking, "Who is like the beast? Who can make war against it?"

> **Sidelight** The reign of the Roman Emperor Nero (often paralleled with the first beast in Revelation 13) was marked by terrible crimes, destruction, and persecution of Christians. When he sent someone to murder his own mother, she bared her body and cried, "Strike my womb because it bore a Nero!"

[5]The beast was allowed to say proud words and words against God, and it was allowed to use its power for 42 months. [6]It used its mouth to speak against God, against God's name, against the place where God lives, and against all those who live in heaven. [7]It was given power to make war against God's holy people and to defeat them. It was given power over every tribe,[d] people, language and nation. [8]And all who live on earth will worship the beast—all the people since the beginning of the world whose names are not written in the Lamb's book of life. The Lamb is the One who was killed.

[9]Anyone who has ears should listen:
[10]If you are to be a prisoner,
　　then you will be a prisoner.

Michael The archangel – leader among God's angels or messengers (Jude 9).

If you are to be killed with the sword,
   then you will be killed with the sword.
This means that God's holy people must have patience and faith.

[11]Then I saw another beast coming up out of the earth. It had two horns like a lamb, but it spoke like a dragon. [12]This beast stands before the first beast and uses the same power the first beast has. By this power it makes everyone living on earth worship the first beast, who had the death wound that was healed. [13]And the second beast does great miracles [d] so that it even makes fire come down from heaven to earth while people are watching. [14]It fools those who live on earth by the miracles it has been given the power to do. It does these miracles to serve the first beast. The second beast orders people to make an idol to honour the first beast, the one that was wounded by the deadly sword but sprang to life again. [15]The second beast was given power to give life to the idol of the first one so that the idol could speak. And the second beast was given power to command all who will not worship the image of the beast to be killed. [16]The second beast also forced all people, small and great, rich and poor, free and slave, to have a mark on their right hand or on their forehead. [17]No one could buy or sell without this mark, which is the name of the beast or the number of its name. [18]This takes wisdom. Let the one who has understanding find the meaning of the number, which is the number of a person. Its number is 666.

The Song of the Saved

14 Then I looked, and there before me was the Lamb standing on Mount Zion. [n] With him were 144,000 people who had his name and his Father's name written on their foreheads. [2]And I heard a sound from heaven like the noise of flooding water and like the sound of loud thunder. The sound I heard was like people playing harps. [3]And they sang a new song before the throne and before the four living creatures and the elders. No one could learn the new song except the 144,000 who had been bought from the earth. [4]These are the ones who did not do sinful things with women, because they kept themselves pure. They follow the Lamb everywhere he goes. These 144,000 were bought from among the people of the earth as people to be offered to God and the Lamb. [5]They were not guilty of telling lies; they are without fault.

The Three Angels

[6]Then I saw another angel flying high in the air. He had the eternal Good News [d] to preach to those who live on earth—to every nation, tribe, [d] language and people. [7]He preached in a loud voice, "Fear God and give him praise, because the time has come for God to judge all people. So worship God who made the heavens, and the earth, and the sea, and the springs of water."

[8]Then the second angel followed the first angel and said, "Ruined, ruined is the great city of Babylon! She made all the nations drink the wine of the anger of her adultery." [d]

[9]Then a third angel followed the first two angels, saying in a loud voice: "If anyone worships the beast and his idol and gets the beast's mark on the forehead or on the hand, [10]that one also will drink the wine of God's anger, which is prepared with all its strength in the cup of his anger. And that person will be put in pain with burning sulphur before the holy angels and the Lamb. [11]And the smoke from their burning pain will rise for ever and ever. There will be no rest, day or night, for those who worship the beast and his idol or who get the mark of his name." [12]This means God's holy people must be patient. They must obey God's commands and keep their faith in Jesus.

[13]Then I heard a voice from heaven saying, "Write this: happy are the dead who die from now on in the Lord."

The Spirit [d] says, "Yes, they will rest from their hard work, and the reward of all they have done stays with them."

The Earth is Harvested

[14]Then I looked, and there before me was a white cloud, and sitting on the white cloud was One who looked like a Son of Man. [n] He had a gold crown on his head and a sharp sickle [n] in his hand. [15]Then another angel came out of the temple [d] and called out in a loud voice to the One who was sitting on the cloud, "Take your sickle and harvest the earth, because the time to harvest has come, and the fruit of the earth is ripe." [16]So the One who was sitting on the cloud swung his sickle over the earth, and the earth was harvested.

[17]Then another angel came out of the temple in heaven, and he also had a sharp sickle. [18]And then another angel, who has power over the fire, came from the altar. This angel called to the angel with the sharp sickle, saying, "Take your sharp sickle and gather the bunches of grapes from the

---

Mount Zion   Another name for Jerusalem; here meaning the spiritual city of God's people.
Son of Man   "Son of Man" is a name Jesus called himself. See dictionary.
sickle   A farming tool with a curved blade. It was used to harvest grain.

earth's vine, because its grapes are ripe." ¹⁹Then the angel swung his sickle over the earth. He gathered the earth's grapes and threw them into the great winepress *d* of God's anger. ²⁰They were trampled in the winepress outside the city, and blood flowed out of the winepress as high as horses' bridles for a distance of about 300 kilometres.

The Last Troubles

15 Then I saw another wonder in heaven that was great and amazing. There were seven angels bringing seven disasters. These are the last disasters, because after them, God's anger is finished.

²I saw what looked like a sea of glass mixed with fire. All of those who had won the victory over the beast and his idol and over the number of his name were standing by the sea of glass. They had harps that God had given them. ³They sang the song of Moses, the servant of God, and the song of the Lamb:

"You do great and wonderful things,   *Psalm 111:2*
  Lord God Almighty.   *Amos 3:13*
Everything the LORD does is right and true,
                                        Psalm 145:17
  King of the nations.
⁴Everyone will respect you, Lord,   *Jeremiah 10:7*
  and will honour you.
Only you are holy.
All the nations will come
  and worship you,   *Psalm 86:9–10*
because the right things you have
      done
  are now made known."   *Deuteronomy 32:4*

⁵After this I saw that the temple *d* (the Tent *d* of the Agreement) in heaven was opened. ⁶And the seven angels bringing the seven disasters came out of the temple. They were dressed in clean, shining linen and wore golden bands tied around their chests. ⁷Then one of the four living creatures gave to the seven angels seven golden bowls filled with the anger of God, who lives for ever and ever. ⁸The temple was filled with smoke from the glory and the power of God, and no one could enter the temple until the seven disasters of the seven angels were finished.

The Bowls of God's Anger

16 Then I heard a loud voice from the temple saying to the seven angels, "Go and pour out the seven bowls of God's anger on the earth."

²The first angel left and poured out his bowl on the land. Then ugly and painful sores came upon all those who had the mark of the beast and who worshipped his idol.

³The second angel poured out his bowl on the sea, and it became blood like that of a dead man, and every living thing in the sea died.

⁴The third angel poured out his bowl on the rivers and the springs of water, and they became blood. ⁵Then I heard the angel of the waters saying:
"Holy One, you are the One who is and
      who was.
  You are right to decide to punish these evil
      people.
⁶They have poured out the blood of your holy
      people and your prophets. *d*
  So now you have given them blood to drink
      as they deserve."

⁷And I heard a voice coming from the altar saying:
"Yes, Lord God Almighty,
  the way you punish evil people is right and
      fair."

⁸The fourth angel poured out his bowl on the sun, and he was given power to burn the people with fire. ⁹They were burned by the great heat, and they cursed the name of God, who had control over these disasters. But the people refused to change their hearts and lives and give glory to God.

¹⁰The fifth angel poured out his bowl on the throne of the beast, and darkness covered its kingdom. People bit their tongues because of the pain. ¹¹They also cursed the God of heaven because of their pain and the sores they had, but they refused to change their hearts and turn away from the evil things they did.

¹²The sixth angel poured out his bowl on the great river Euphrates so that the water in the river was dried up to prepare the way for the kings from the east to come. ¹³Then I saw three evil spirits that looked like frogs coming out of the mouth of the dragon, out of the mouth of the beast and out of the mouth of the false prophet. ¹⁴These evil spirits are the spirits of demons, *d* which have power to do miracles. *d* They go out to the kings of the whole world to gather them together for the battle on the great day of God Almighty.

¹⁵"Listen! I will come as a thief comes! Happy are those who stay awake and keep their clothes on so that they will not walk around naked and have people see their shame."

¹⁶Then the evil spirits gathered the kings together to the place that is called Armageddon in the Hebrew language.

¹⁷The seventh angel poured out his bowl into the air. Then a loud voice came out of the temple *d* from the throne, saying, "It is finished!" ¹⁸Then there were flashes of lightning, noises, thunder, and a big earthquake—the worst earthquake that has ever happened since people have

been on earth. ¹⁹The great city split into three parts, and the cities of the nations were destroyed. And God remembered the sins of Babylon the Great, so he gave that city the cup filled with

the wine of his terrible anger. ²⁰Then every island ran away, and mountains disappeared. ²¹Giant hailstones, each weighing up to 50 kilogrammes, fell from the sky upon people. People cursed God for the disaster of the hail, because this disaster was so terrible.

The Woman on the Animal

17 Then one of the seven angels who had the seven bowls came and spoke to me. He said, "Come, and I will show you the punishment that will be given to the great prostitute, *d* the one sitting over many waters. ²The kings of the earth sinned sexually with her, and the people of the earth became drunk from the wine of her sexual sin."

³Then the angel carried me away by the Spirit *d* to the desert. There I saw a woman sitting on a red beast. It was covered with names insulting to God written on it, and it had seven heads and ten horns. ⁴The woman was dressed in purple and red and was shining with the gold, precious jewels and pearls she was wearing. She had a golden cup in her hand, a cup filled with evil things and the uncleanness of her sexual sin. ⁵On her forehead a title was written that was secret. This is what was written:

THE GREAT BABYLON
MOTHER OF PROSTITUTES
AND OF THE EVIL THINGS OF THE EARTH

⁶Then I saw that the woman was drunk with the blood of God's holy people and with the blood of those who were killed because of their faith in Jesus.

When I saw the woman, I was very amazed. ⁷Then the angel said to me, "Why are you amazed? I will tell you the secret of this woman and the beast she rides—the one with seven heads and ten horns. ⁸The beast you saw was once alive but is not alive now. But soon it will

come up out of the bottomless pit and go away to be destroyed. There are people who live on earth whose names have not been written in the book of life since the beginning of the world. They will be amazed when they see the beast, because he was once alive, is not alive now, but will come again.

⁹"You need a wise mind to understand this. The seven heads on the beast are seven mountains where the woman sits. ¹⁰And they are seven kings. Five of the kings have already been destroyed, one of the kings lives now, and another has not yet come. When he comes, he must stay a short time. ¹¹The beast that was once alive, but is not alive now, is also an eighth king. He belongs to the first seven kings, and he will go away to be destroyed.

¹²"The ten horns you saw are ten kings who have not yet begun to rule, but they will receive power to rule with the beast for one hour. ¹³All ten of these kings have the same purpose, and they will give their power and authority to the beast. ¹⁴They will make war against the Lamb, but the Lamb will defeat them, because he is Lord of lords and King of kings. He will defeat them with his called, chosen and faithful followers."

¹⁵Then the angel said to me, "The waters that you saw, where the prostitute sits, are peoples, races, nations and languages. ¹⁶The ten horns and the beast you saw will hate the prostitute. They will take everything she has and leave her naked. They will eat her body and burn her with fire. ¹⁷God made the ten horns want to carry out his purpose by agreeing to give the beast their power to rule, until what God has said comes about. ¹⁸The woman you saw is the great city that rules over the kings of the earth."

Babylon is Destroyed

18 After the vision of these things, I saw another angel coming down from heaven. This angel had great power, and his glory made the earth bright. ²He shouted in a powerful voice:

"Ruined, ruined is the great city of
    Babylon!
  She has become a home for demons *d*
and a prison for every evil spirit,
  and a prison for every unclean *d* bird and
    unclean beast.
³She has been ruined, because all the peoples
    of the earth
  have drunk the wine of the desire of her
    sexual sin.
She has been ruined also because the kings of
    the earth
  have sinned sexually with her,

and the merchants of the earth
　　have grown rich from the great wealth of
　　　her luxury."

[4]Then I heard another voice from heaven
saying:
　"Come out of that city, my people,
　　so that you will not share in her sins,
　　so that you will not receive the disasters
　　　that will come to her.
[5]Her sins have piled up as high as the sky,
　　and God has not forgotten the wrongs she
　　　has done.
[6]Give that city the same as she gave to others.
　　Pay her back twice as much as she did.
　Prepare wine for her that is twice as strong
　　as the wine she prepared for others.
[7]She gave herself much glory and rich living.
　　Give her the same amount of suffering and
　　　sadness.
　She says to herself, 'I am a queen sitting on
　　my throne.
　I am not a widow; I will never be sad.'
[8]So these disasters will come to her in one day:
　　death, and crying, and great hunger,
　and she will be destroyed by fire,
　　because the Lord God who judges her is
　　　powerful."
[9]The kings of the earth who sinned sexually
with her and shared her wealth will see the
smoke from her burning. Then they will cry and
be sad because of her death. [10]They will be afraid
of her suffering and stand far away and say:
　"Terrible! How terrible for you, great city,
　　powerful city of Babylon,
　because your punishment has come in one
　　　hour!"
　[11]And the merchants of the earth will cry and
be sad about her, because now there is no one to
buy their cargoes— [12]cargoes of gold, silver, jewels, pearls; fine linen, purple cloth, silk, red cloth;
all kinds of citron wood and all kinds of things
made from ivory, expensive wood, bronze, iron
and marble; [13]cinnamon, spice, incense, [d]myrrh, [d]
frankincense; [d] wine, olive oil, fine flour, wheat;
cattle, sheep, horses, carriages; slaves and human
lives.
　[14]The merchants will say,
　"Babylon, the good things you wanted are
　　gone from you.
　All your rich and fancy things have
　　disappeared.
　You will never have them again."
[15]The merchants who became rich from selling
to her will be afraid of her suffering and will

stand far away. They will cry and be sad [16]and
say:
　"Terrible! How terrible for the great city!
　　She was dressed in fine linen, purple and
　　　red cloth,
　　and she was shining with gold, precious
　　　jewels and pearls!
[17]All these riches have been destroyed in one
　　hour!"
　Every sea captain, all those who travel, the
sailors, and all those who earn their living from
the sea stood far away from Babylon. [18]As they
saw the smoke from her burning, they cried out
loudly, "There was never a city like this great
city!" [19]And they threw dirt on their heads and
cried, weeping and were sad. They said:
　"Terrible! How terrible for the great city!
　All the people who had ships on the sea
　　became rich because of her wealth!
　But she has been destroyed in one hour!
[20]Be happy because of this, heaven!
　　Be happy, God's holy people and apostles [d]
　　　and prophets! [d]
　God has punished her because of what she
　　　did to you."
　[21]Then a powerful angel picked up a large stone,
like one used for grinding grain, and threw it
into the sea. He said:
　"In the same way, the great city of Babylon
　　will be thrown down,
　　and it will never be found again.
[22]The music of people playing harps and other
　　　instruments, flutes and trumpets,
　　will never be heard in you again.
　No workman doing any job
　　will ever be found in you again.
　The sound of grinding grain
　　will never be heard in you again.
[23]The light of a lamp
　　will never shine in you again,
　and the voices of a bridegroom and bride
　　will never be heard in you again.
　Your merchants were the world's great people,
　　and all the nations were tricked by your
　　　magic.
[24]You are guilty of the death of the prophets
　　and God's holy people
　　and all who have been killed on earth."

People in Heaven Praise God

19 After this vision and announcement I
heard what sounded like a great many
people in heaven saying:
　"Hallelujah! [n]
　Salvation, glory and power belong to our God,

Hallelujah　This means "praise God!"

2 because his judgements are true and right.
He has punished the prostitute *d*
who made the earth evil with her
sexual sin.
He has paid her back for the death of his
servants."
3Again they said:
"Hallelujah!
She is burning, and her smoke will rise for
ever and ever."
4Then the 24 elders and the four living creatures bowed down and worshipped God, who
sits on the throne. They said:
"Amen, Hallelujah!"

Sidelight   In the same way that we
shake hands today to
greet someone, in Bible times people would bow
(Revelation 19:4). Depending on whom you were
greeting, you would either nod your head politely
or give a more elaborate bend-at-the-waist bow.

5Then a voice came from the throne, saying:
"Praise our God, all you who serve him
and all you who honour him, both small
and great!"
6Then I heard what sounded like a great
many people, like the noise of flooding water
and like the noise of loud thunder. The people
were saying:
"Hallelujah!
Our Lord God, the Almighty, rules.
7Let us rejoice and be happy
and give God glory,
because the wedding of the Lamb has come,
and the Lamb's bride has made herself
ready.
8Fine linen, bright and clean, was given to her
to wear."
(The fine linen means the good things done by
God's holy people.)
9And the angel said to me, "Write this: happy
are those who have been invited to the wedding
meal of the Lamb!" And the angel said, "These
are the true words of God."
10Then I bowed down at the angel's feet to
worship him, but he said to me, "Do not worship me! I am a servant like you and your brothers and sisters who have the message of Jesus.
Worship God, because the message about Jesus
is the spirit that gives all prophecy." *d*

The Rider on the White Horse

11Then I saw heaven opened, and there before
me was a white horse. The rider on the horse is
called Faithful and True, and he is right when he

judges and makes war. 12His eyes are like burning
fire, and on his head are many crowns. He has a
name written on him, which no one but himself
knows. 13He is dressed in a robe dipped in blood,
and his name is the Word of God. 14The armies
of heaven, dressed in fine linen, white and clean,
were following him on white horses. 15Out of the
rider's mouth comes a sharp sword that he will
use to defeat the nations, and he will rule them
with a rod of iron. He will crush out the wine in
the winepress *d* of the terrible anger of God the
Almighty. 16On his robe and on his upper leg was
written this name: KING OF KINGS AND LORD OF LORDS.

17Then I saw an angel standing in the sun, and
he called with a loud voice to all the birds flying
in the sky: "Come and gather together for the
great feast of God 18so that you can eat the bodies of kings, generals, mighty people, horses and
their riders, and the bodies of all people—free,
slave, small and great."

19Then I saw the beast and the kings of the
earth. Their armies were gathered together to
make war against the rider on the horse and his
army. 20But the beast was captured and with him
the false prophet *d* who did the miracles *d* for the
beast. The false prophet had used these miracles
to trick those who had the mark of the beast and
worshipped his idol. The false prophet and the
beast were thrown alive into the lake of fire that
burns with sulphur. 21And their armies were
killed with the sword that came out of the mouth
of the rider on the horse, and all the birds ate the
bodies until they were full.

The 1,000 Years

20 I saw an angel coming down from
heaven. He had the key to the bottomless pit and a large chain in his hand. 2The angel
grabbed the dragon, that old snake who is the
devil and Satan, and tied him up for 1,000 years.
3Then he threw him into the bottomless pit,
closed it and locked it over him. The angel did
this so he could not trick the people of the earth
any more until the 1,000 years were ended. After
1,000 years he must be set free for a short time.

4Then I saw some thrones and people sitting
on them who had been given the power to judge.
And I saw the souls of those who had been killed
because they were faithful to the message of Jesus
and the message from God. They had not worshipped the beast or his idol, and they had not
received the mark of the beast on their foreheads
or on their hands. They came back to life and ruled
with Christ for 1,000 years. 5(The others that were
dead did not live again until the 1,000 years
were ended.) This is the first raising of the dead.
6Happy and holy are those who share in this first
raising of the dead. The second death has no power

over them. They will be priests for God and for Christ and will rule with him for 1,000 years.

[7]When the 1,000 years are over, Satan will be set free from his prison. [8]Then he will go out to trick the nations in all the earth—Gog and Magog—to gather them for battle. There are so many people they will be like sand on the seashore. [9]And Satan's army marched across the earth and gathered around the camp of God's people and the city God loves. But fire came down from heaven and burnt them up. [10]And Satan, who tricked them, was thrown into the lake of burning sulphur with the beast and the false prophet. [d] There they will be punished day and night for ever and ever.

People of the World are Judged

[11]Then I saw a great white throne and the One who was sitting on it. Earth and sky ran away from him and disappeared. [12]And I saw the dead, great and small, standing before the throne. Then books were opened, and the book of life was opened. The dead were judged by what they had done, which was written in the books. [13]The sea gave up the dead who were in it, and Death and Hades [n] gave up the dead who were in them. Each person was judged by what he had done. [14]And Death and Hades were thrown into the lake of fire. The lake of fire is the second death. [15]And anyone whose name was not found written in the book of life was thrown into the lake of fire.

The New Jerusalem

21 Then I saw a new heaven and a new earth. The first heaven and the first earth had disappeared, and there was no sea any more. [2]And I saw the holy city, the new Jerusalem, [n] coming down out of heaven from God. It was prepared like a bride dressed for her husband. [3]And I heard a loud voice from the throne, saying, "Now God's presence is with people, and he will live with them, and they will be his people. God himself will be with them and will be their God. [4]He will wipe away every tear from their eyes, and there will be no more death, sadness,

---

Hades　The unseen world of the dead.
new Jerusalem　The spiritual city where God's people live with him.

DEATH

Fear of Dying

"Thank you for flying with us," crackled the steward's voice over the intercom after the jet had landed. "And we encourage you to be extra careful on the most dangerous part of your journey: driving to your final destination in a car."

Many people fear flying, yet the odds of dying in a commercial aeroplane crash are only about 1 in 800,000. You're more likely to die by choking on food than in a plane crash.

In fact, all of the following are more dangerous than flying, based on the number of fatalities for each: car accidents, falls, fires and burns, drownings, shootings, poisonings.

Many people fear the way they will die more than they fear death itself.

The Bible, however, promises Christians that God has overcome death. **Revelation 21:1–6** offers a description of life with God beyond death.

* What does this picture of heaven say to people's many fears about dying?
* How does the passage speak to your own fears about death?

Consider . . .

* selecting a story about death from the newspaper and using it to discuss your feelings about death with a friend or trusted adult.
* imagining what someone who has died might be experiencing in heaven. Thank God for his gift of eternal life that overcomes death.

For more, see . . .

* Psalm 23 (p.513)
* 1 Corinthians 15:12–23 (p.1235)

* Luke 23:32–43 (p.1091)

crying or pain, because all the old ways are gone."

[5]The One who was sitting on the throne said, "Look! I am making everything new!" Then he

said, "Write this, because these words are true and can be trusted."

[6]The One on the throne said to me, "It is finished. I am the Alpha and the Omega,[n] the Beginning and the End. I will give free water from the spring of the water of life to anyone who is thirsty. [7]Those who win the victory will receive this, and I will be their God, and they will be my children. [8]But cowards, those who refuse to believe, who do evil things, who kill, who sin sexually, who do evil magic, who worship idols and who tell lies—all these will have a place in the lake of burning sulphur. This is the second death."

[9]Then one of the seven angels who had the seven bowls full of the seven last troubles came to me, saying, "Come with me, and I will show you the bride, the wife of the Lamb." [10]And the angel carried me away by the Spirit[d] to a very large and high mountain. He showed me the holy city, Jerusalem, coming down out of heaven from God. [11]It was shining with the glory of God and was bright like a very expensive jewel, like a jasper, clear as crystal. [12]The city had a great high wall with twelve gates with twelve angels at the gates, and on each gate was written the name of one of the twelve tribes[d] of Israel. [13]There were three gates on the east, three on the north, three on the south and three on the west. [14]The walls of the city were built on twelve foundation stones, and on the stones were written the names of the twelve apostles[d] of the Lamb.

[15]The angel who talked with me had a measuring rod made of gold to measure the city, its gates and its wall. [16]The city was built in a square, and its length was equal to its width. The angel measured the city with the rod. The city was 2,200 kilometres long, 2,200 kilometres wide and 2,200 kilometres high. [17]The angel also measured the wall. It was 80 metres high, by human measurements, which the angel was using. [18]The wall was made of jasper, and the city was made of pure gold, as pure as glass. [19]The foundation stones of the city walls were decorated with every kind of jewel. The first foundation was jasper, the second was sapphire, the third was chalcedony, the fourth was emerald, [20]the fifth was onyx, the sixth was carnelian, the seventh was chrysolite, the eighth was beryl, the ninth was topaz, the tenth was chrysoprase, the eleventh was jacinth, and the twelfth was amethyst. [21]The twelve gates were twelve pearls, each gate having been made from a single pearl. And the street of the city was made of pure gold as clear as glass.

[22]I did not see a temple[d] in the city, because the Lord God Almighty and the Lamb are the city's temple. [23]The city does not need the sun or the moon to shine on it, because the glory of God is its light, and the Lamb is the city's lamp. [24]By its light the people of the world will walk, and the kings of the earth will bring their glory into it. [25]The city's gates will never be shut on any day, because there is no night there. [26]The glory and the honour of the nations will be brought into it. [27]Nothing unclean[d] and no one who does shameful things or tells lies will ever go into it. Only those whose names are written in the Lamb's book of life will enter the city.

22 Then the angel showed me the river of the water of life. It was shining like crystal and was flowing from the throne of God and of the Lamb [2]down the middle of the street of the city. The tree of life was on each side of the river. It produces fruit twelve times a year, once each month. The leaves of the tree are for the healing of all the nations. [3]Nothing that God judges guilty will be in that city. The throne of God and of the Lamb will be there, and God's servants will worship him. [4]They will see his face, and his name will be written on their foreheads. [5]There will never be night again. They will not need the light of a lamp or the light of the sun, because the Lord God will give them light. And they will rule as kings for ever and ever.

[6]The angel said to me, "These words can be trusted and are true." The Lord, the God of the spirits of the prophets,[d] sent his angel to show his servants the things that must happen soon.

[7]"Listen! I am coming soon! Happy is the one who obeys the words of prophecy in this book."

[8]I, John, am the one who heard and saw these things. When I heard and saw them, I bowed down to worship at the feet of the angel who showed these things to me. [9]But the angel said to me, "Do not worship me! I am a servant like you,

---

Alpha and the Omega   The first and last letters of the Greek alphabet. This means "the beginning and the end".

your brothers the prophets and all those who obey the words in this book. Worship God!"

[10]Then the angel told me, "Do not keep secret the words of prophecy in this book, because the time is near for all this to happen. [11]Let whoever is doing evil continue to do evil. Let whoever is unclean continue to be unclean. Let whoever is doing right continue to do right. Let whoever is holy continue to be holy."

[12]"Listen! I am coming soon! I will bring my reward with me, and I will repay each one of you for what you have done. [13]I am the Alpha and the Omega, [n] the First and the Last, the Beginning and the End.

[14]"Happy are those who wash their robes [n] so that they will receive the right to eat the fruit from the tree of life and may go through the gates into the city. [15]Outside the city are the evil people, those who do evil magic, who sin sexually, who murder, who worship idols, and who love lies and tell lies.

[16]"I, Jesus, have sent my angel to tell you these things for the churches. I am the descendant [d] from the family of David, and I am the bright morning star."

[17]The Spirit [d] and the bride say, "Come!" Let the one who hears this say, "Come!" Let whoever is thirsty come; whoever wishes may have the water of life as a free gift.

[18]I warn everyone who hears the words of the prophecy of this book: if anyone adds anything to these words, God will add to that person the disasters written about in this book. [19]And if anyone takes away from the words of this book of prophecy, God will take away that one's share of the tree of life and of the holy city, which are written about in this book.

[20]Jesus, the One who says these things are true, says, "Yes, I am coming soon."

Amen. Come, Lord Jesus!

[21]The grace of the Lord Jesus be with all. Amen.

Alpha and the Omega   The first and last letters of the Greek alphabet. This means "the beginning and the end".
wash their robes   This means they believed in Jesus so that their sins could be forgiven through Christ's blood.

ETERNAL LIFE

A Bit of Heaven

Three hundred teenage tourists gathered in the Swiss Alps, 2,200 metres above sea level. Rising even higher on one side were craggy, snow-capped peaks. A huge glacier stretched out on the other side, seemingly unaffected by the warm July day.

The group gathered for outdoor worship, which began with a trio of alpine horns echoing hymns across the valley. The minister shared the Good News of Christ. Then voices joined together to close the service with familiar choruses of praise to God.

The day passed quickly, filled with hugs, songs, shouts of pleasure, helping hands, huge smiles and incredible sights. As the teenagers waited to return to Grindelwald on Europe's longest chair lift, several girls talked.

"I hope heaven's like this," said one of the girls.

"Heaven's going to be even better!" said another.

God's promise of eternal life in heaven is even better! Read the promise in **Revelation 22:12–21**.

* What do you think made the girls think of heaven during their outing in Switzerland? How do you think the mountain experience compares with heaven itself?
* What difference does God's promise of eternal life make in your everyday living?

Consider . . .

* remembering a time when you felt overwhelmed by nature as a reminder of God's greatness.
* asking yourself what you need to do to respond to the invitation in verse 17: "Let whoever is thirsty come; whoever wishes may have the water of life as a free gift."

For more, see . . .

* Psalm 16:9–11 (p.508)
* John 4:5–42 (p.1101)

* Matthew 19:16–30 (p.974)

A

Aaron (AIR-on) *older brother of Moses.*
* before the king of Egypt, Exodus 4:14–16; 5:1–5; 7:1–2
* death of, Numbers 20:22–29

Abba (AB-uh) *word for "father" in Aramaic.*
* Jesus called God "Abba", Mark 14:36
* we can call God "Abba", Romans 8:15; Galatians 4:6

Abednego (a-BED-nee-go) *one of the three friends of Daniel whom God protected from the fiery furnace.*
* refused the king of Babylon's food, Daniel 1:3–17
* thrown into the fiery furnace, Daniel 3

Abel (AY-bul) *the second son of Adam and Eve.*
* born to Adam and Eve, Genesis 4:2
* approved by God, Genesis 4:3–4; Hebrews 11:4
* murdered by Cain, Genesis 4:8; 1 John 3:12

Abib (ah-BEEB) *first month of the Jewish calendar, about the same time of year as our March or April; also called "Nisan"; means "young ears of grain".*
* the time the Israelites left Egypt, Exodus 13:3–4
* the time for the feast of Unleavened Bread, Exodus 23:15; 34:18

Abigail, sister of David (AB-ee-gale) 1 Chronicles 2:13–17

Abigail, wife of Nabal
* brought food to David, 1 Samuel 25:14–35
* became David's wife, 1 Samuel 25:36–42

Abijah, king of Judah (a-BY-jah) 1 Kings 15:1–8; 2 Chronicles 13:1 — 14:1

Abijah, son of Jeroboam
* death of, 1 Kings 14:1–18

Abijah, son of Samuel, 1 Samuel 8:1–3

ability
* given by God, 2 Corinthians 3:5–6
* through Christ, Philippians 4:13
* differing abilities, 1 Corinthians 12:7–11

Abimelech, king of Gerar (a-BIM-eh-lek)
* tried to take Sarah as his wife, Genesis 20

Abimelech, king of the Philistines
* tried to take Rebekah as his wife, Genesis 26:6–11

Abimelech, son of Gideon
* birth of, Judges 8:29–31
* murdered his brothers, Judges 9:1–6
* defeated the people of Shechem, Judges 9:22–45
* burned the Tower of Shechem, Judges 9:46–49
* death of, Judges 9:50–55

Abishai (a-BISH-eye) *nephew of King David.*
* served in David's army, 2 Samuel 23:18–19; 1 Chronicles 18:12–13
* saved David's life, 2 Samuel 21:15–17

Abner (AB-nur) *commander of Saul's army.*
* at Goliath's defeat, 1 Samuel 17:55–57
* made Ish-Bosheth king of Israel, 2 Samuel 2:8–10
* later loyal to David, 2 Samuel 3:6–21
* killed by Joab, 2 Samuel 3:22–27

Abraham (AY-bra-ham) *father of the Jewish nation.*
* called from Ur by God, Genesis 12:1–4
* lied about Sarai, Genesis 12:10–20
* separated from Lot, Genesis 13

* God's agreement with, Genesis 15; 17
* name changed, Genesis 17:3–6
* father of Isaac, Genesis 21:1–7
* offered Isaac as a sacrifice, Genesis 22:1–19
* father of the faithful, Romans 4
* God's friend, James 2:23

Absalom (AB-suh-lum) *one of David's sons.*
* turned against David, 2 Samuel 15 — 18:8
* killed by Joab, 2 Samuel 18:9–15

abstain (ab-STAIN) *to keep from doing something.*
* from food offered to idols, Acts 15:20
* from evil, 1 Thessalonians 5:22
* from lust, 1 Peter 2:11

abyss (uh-BISS) See "bottomless pit".

accept
* a prophet not accepted, Luke 4:24
* accepted by God, Acts 10:35; 15:7–8; Romans 14:3
* each other, Romans 14:1; 15:7
* Jesus, John 12:48

accuse
* Jesus accused by the Jews, Matthew 27:12–13; Mark 15:3; Luke 6:7
* Paul accused by the Jews, Acts 23:27–29; 26:7
* the devil, as the accuser, Revelation 12:10

Achaia (a-KA-yuh) See "Greece".

Achan (AY-can) *an Israelite who disobeyed God during the battle of Jericho,* Joshua 7

Achish (AY-kish) *king of the Philistine city of Gath.*
* David pretends to be insane, 1 Samuel 21:10–15
* David in his army, 1 Samuel 27; 29

actions
* judged by, Proverbs 20:11; Matthew 11:19; Galatians 6:4
* of love, 1 John 3:18
* of goodness, Matthew 5:16

Adam (AD-um) *the first man.*
* created by God, Genesis 1:26 — 2:25
* disobeyed God, Genesis 3
* compared to Christ, 1 Corinthians 15:21–22, 45–49

adder, *a poisonous snake.* See "snake".

Adonijah (ad-oh-NY-jah) *David's fourth son.*
* son of Haggith, 2 Samuel 3:4
* tried to become king, 1 Kings 1
* killed by Solomon, 1 Kings 2:12–25

Adoni-Zedek (a-DOH-ny-ZEE-dek) *an Amorite king of Jerusalem.*
* defeated by Joshua, Joshua 10:1–28

Adullam (a-DULL-am) *a city about twenty-one kilometres from Bethlehem.*
* David hid in a cave there, 2 Samuel 23:13

adultery (ah-DULL-ter-ee) *breaking a marriage promise by having sexual relations with someone other than your husband or wife.*
* "You must not be guilty of adultery", Exodus 20:14
* Christ teaches about, Matthew 5:27–32; Luke 16:18
* woman caught in adultery, John 8:1–11

advice
* given by Ahithophel, 2 Samuel 15:30 — 17:23
* given to Rehoboam, 1 Kings 12:1–15

* teachings about, Proverbs 11:14; 12:5,15; 19:20

Agabus (AG-uh-bus) *a Christian prophet.*
* warned the people, Acts 11:27–30
* warned Paul about going to Jerusalem, Acts 21:10–11

Agag (AY-gag) *king of the Amalekites.*
* captured by Saul, 1 Samuel 15

agreement *a contract, promise, or covenant.*
* with Noah, Genesis 9:1–17
* with Abraham, Genesis 15; 17:1–14
* Ark of the Agreement, Exodus 25:10–22; 1 Samuel 4 — 5; 2 Samuel 6:1–15
* with the Israelites, Exodus 19:3–8,24; Deuteronomy 29
* new agreement, 2 Corinthians 2:12 — 3:18
* difference between the old and new agreements, Hebrews 8 — 10

Agrippa (uh-GRIP-pah) See "Herod Agrippa".

Ahab (AY-hab) *evil king of Israel who was married to Jezebel.*
* worshipped Baal, 1 Kings 16:29–33
* had Naboth killed, 1 Kings 21
* death of, 1 Kings 22:1–40

Ahasuerus (ah-HAZ-oo-rus) *Hebrew word for the Greek name Xerxes. See "Xerxes".*

Ahaz (AY-haz) *twelfth king of Judah,* 2 Kings 16; 2 Chronicles 28

Ahaziah, king of Judah (ay-ha-ZY-uh) 2 Chronicles 22:1–9

Ahaziah, son of Ahab
* king of Israel, 1 Kings 22:40–53

Ahijah, great-grandson of Eli (a-HY-jah) 1 Samuel 14:1–23

Ahijah, the prophet
* told Jeroboam the kingdom would be divided, 1 Kings 11:29–39
* told that Jeroboam's son would die, 1 Kings 14:1–18

Ahimelech, the high priest (a-HIM-eh-lek)
* helped David, 1 Samuel 21:1–9

Ahimelech, the Hittite warrior, 1 Samuel 26:6

Ahithophel (a-HITH-oh-fel) *gave advice to King David.*
* helped Absalom rebel against David, 1 Samuel 15:31; 16:15 — 17:23

Ai (AY-eye) *a city completely destroyed by the Israelites,* Joshua 7 — 8:28

Akeldama (a-KEL-dah-mah) *field bought with the money Judas received for betraying Jesus,* Matthew 27:3–10; Acts 1:18–19

alabaster (ala-BAS-ter) *light-coloured stone with streaks or stripes through it,* Matthew 26:7; Mark 14:3; Luke 7:37

alamoth (AL-a-moth) *a musical word, which may mean "like a flute" or "high-pitched",* Psalm 46

All-Powerful, *a name for God,* 1 Chronicles 11:9; Psalm 24:10; Isaiah 6:3–5; Malachi 3:1–17

Almighty, *a name for God.*
* "I am God Almighty", Genesis 17:1
* "I appeared to Abraham . . . by the name, God Almighty", Exodus 6:3
* "Holy, holy, holy is the Lord God Almighty", Revelation 4:8

almond
* design of the lampstands in Holy Tent, Exodus 25:31–36

* Aaron's stick produced, Numbers 17:8

aloes (AL-ohs) *oils from sweet-smelling sap of certain trees; used to make perfume and medicine and to prepare bodies for burial,* Psalm 45:8; Proverbs 7:17
* used to prepare Jesus' body for burial, John 19:39

Alpha and Omega (AL-fah and oh-MAY-guh) *the first and last letters of the Greek alphabet, like our A and Z.*
* used to describe Jesus, Revelation 1:8; 21:6; 22:13

altar (ALL-ter) *a place where sacrifices, gifts, or prayers were offered to a god.*
* built by Noah, Genesis 8:20
* built by Abraham, Genesis 22:9
* for burnt offerings, Exodus 27:1–8
* for incense, Exodus 30:1–10
* corners of, Exodus 27:2; 30:10; 1 Kings 1:50
* for the Temple, 2 Chronicles 4:1

Amalekites (a-MAL-ek-ites) *fierce, fighting people who descended from Esau; they were enemies of Israel and were finally wiped out during the time of Hezekiah.*
* enemies of Israel, Exodus 17:8–16; 1 Samuel 15
* destroyed by King Hezekiah, 1 Chronicles 4:43

Amasa (AM-a-sa) *leader of Absalom's army when he rebelled against David,* 2 Samuel 17:25
* made leader of David's army, 2 Samuel 19:13
* killed by Joab, 2 Samuel 20:1–10

Amaziah (am-ay-ZY-uh) *the ninth king of Judah,* 2 Kings 14; 2 Chronicles 25

amen (AH-MEN) *Hebrew word for "that is right",* 1 Chronicles 16:36; Psalm 106:48; 1 Corinthians 14:16
* "Amen Come, Lord Jesus!" Revelation 22:20

Ammonites (AM-on-ites) *descendants of Lot's son, Ben-Ammi,* Genesis 19:36–38
* enemies of Israel, Judges 10:6 — 11:33; 1 Samuel 11; 2 Samuel 10:1–14
* worshipped Molech, 1 Kings 11:5

Amon (AM-on) *the fifteenth king of Judah,* 2 Kings 21:18–26; 2 Chronicles 33:20–25
* an ancestor of Jesus, Matthew 1:10

Amorites (AM-or-ites) *a group of wicked people who worshipped false gods and lived in Canaan when the Israelites arrived.*
* defeated by Israel, Numbers 21:21–32; Joshua 10:1 — 11:14

Amos (AY-mos) *a prophet who warned Israel of God's punishment for disobedience.*
* a shepherd from Tekoa, Amos 1:1
* his visions, Amos 7 — 9:10

Anak/Anakites (A-nak/AN-uh-kites) *a group of large, fighting people who lived in Canaan when the Israelites arrived.*
* feared by the twelve spies, Numbers 13:22,28,33; Deuteronomy 1:26–28
* defeated by Joshua, Joshua 11:21–23

Ananias, husband of Sapphira (an-uh-NY-us)
* killed for lying to the Holy Spirit, Acts 5:1–6

Ananias, a Christian in Damascus
* helped Saul of Tarsus, Acts 9:10–19; 22:12–16

Ananias, the high priest
* at Paul's trial, Acts 23:1–5

Andrew, *a fisherman and brother of the apostle Peter.*
* chosen by Jesus to be an apostle, Mark 1:16–18; 3:13–19

- brought Peter to Jesus, John 1:40–42
- waited with the apostles in Jerusalem, Acts 1:13

angel (AIN-jel) *a heavenly being.*
- rescued Lot from Sodom, Genesis 19:1–22
- led Israel to Canaan, Exodus 23:20–23; 32:34
- announced Jesus' birth, Matthew 1:20–21; Luke 1:26–37; 2:8–15
- helped Jesus, Matthew 4:11; Luke 22:43
- helped the apostles, Acts 5:19–20; 12:6–10
- will bring judgement, Matthew 13:24–50; 24:31
- archangel, 1 Thessalonians 4:16; Jude 9
- less than Christ, Hebrews 1:4–14; 1 Peter 3:22
- rebellious angels, 2 Peter 2:4; Jude 6
- serving in heaven, Revelation 7 — 10

anger, *wrath.*
- of God toward people, John 3:36; Romans 1:18; 2:5–6; Colossians 3:5–6
- saved from God's anger by Christ, Romans 5:9; 1 Thessalonians 1:10; 5:9
- warnings against, Matthew 5:21–22; Ephesians 4:26,31; James 1:19–20

animal
- created by God, Genesis 1:20–25
- to be ruled by people, Genesis 1:26
- named by Adam, Genesis 2:19–20
- saved by Noah, Genesis 6:19–20
- clean, Leviticus 11:1–3,9; Deuteronomy 14:3–6
- unclean, Leviticus 11:4–8,10–12,26–44; Deuteronomy 14:7–8

Annas (AN-us) *a high priest of the Jews during Jesus' lifetime,* Luke 3:2; John 18:13
- questioned Peter and John, Acts 4:5–22

anoint (a-NOINT) *to pour oil on.*
- to appoint a priest, Exodus 28:41; 40:13
- to appoint a king, 1 Samuel 10:1; 16:12–13; 2 Kings 9:6
- the Holy Tent, Numbers 7:1
- to heal sickness, Mark 6:13; James 5:14

Anti-Christ (AN-tee KRYST) See "enemy of Christ".

Antioch in Pisidia (AN-tee-ok) *a small city in the country of Pisidia.*
- Paul preached there, Acts 13:14–15

Antioch in Syria, *third largest city in the Roman Empire.*
- Saul and Barnabas preached there, Acts 11:19–26
- followers first called "Christians" there, Acts 11:26
- Peter in Antioch, Galatians 2:11–12
- Paul preached there, Acts 13:14–15

Antipas (AN-ti-pas) *the father of Herod the great and the ruler of Judea 55–43 BC,* Revelation 2:13

Apollos (a-POL-us) *an educated Jew from Alexandria.*
- taught by Aquila and Priscilla, Acts 18:24–28
- preached to the Corinthians, 1 Corinthians 1:12; 3:4–6
- friend of Paul, Titus 3:13

apostle (uh-POS-'l) *someone who is sent off. Jesus chose these twelve special followers and sent them to tell the Good News about him to the whole world.*
- twelve chosen by Jesus, Mark 3:14–19
- Matthias chosen, Acts 1:12–26
- Paul chosen, 1 Corinthians 15:3–11; 2 Corinthians 12:11–12
- duties and powers of, Luke 9:1–6; Acts 5:12–16; 8:18
- leaders of the church, Acts 15; 16:4; 1 Corinthians 12:28
- false apostles, 2 Corinthians 11:13; Revelation 2:2

appearance
- not to judge by, 1 Samuel 16:7; John 7:24
- deceiving, Matthew 23:27–28

- of Jesus, Isaiah 53:2; Philippians 2:7

Aquila (AK-wi-lah) *a Jewish Christian from Rome.*
- friend of Paul, Acts 18:2–3; Romans 16:3–5
- taught Apollos, Acts 18:24–28

Arabah (AR-uh-bah) *the Hebrew word for the Jordan Valley.* See "Jordan Valley".

Arabah, Sea of, See "Dead Sea".

Aram (AR-um) *a country northeast of Israel,* 1 Kings 11:25; 15:18; 2 Kings 5:1; Isaiah 7:1
- known as "Syria" in the New Testament, Matthew 4:24; Acts 15:23

Aramaic (AR-uh-MAY-ik) *the language of the people in the nation of Aram.*
- common language of the Jews, 2 Kings 18:26; John 19:13,17,20; Acts 21:40

Ararat (AR-uh-rat) *a group of mountains located in what is now Turkey and the Soviet Union.*
- Noah's boat landed there, Genesis 8:14

Araunah (a-RAW-nah) *a Jebusite who was also called Ornan.*
- sold his threshing floor to King David, 2 Samuel 24:15–25; 1 Chronicles 21:18–28

archangel (ark-AIN-jel) *the leader of God's angels,* 1 Thessalonians 4:16; Jude 9

Areopagus (AR-ee-OP-uh-gus) *a council or group of important leaders in Athens.*
- Paul spoke there, Acts 17:16–34

argue
- the apostles argued, Mark 9:33–37; Luke 9:46–48
- avoid arguments, Philippians 2:14; 2 Timothy 2:23–26; Titus 3:9
- Michael argued with the devil, Jude 9

Aristarchus (ar-i-STAR-kus) *a man from Thessalonica who often travelled with Paul,* Acts 27:2; Colossians 4:10; Philemon 24

ark, Noah's, *the huge boat that Noah built to save his family from the flood God sent to cover the earth.* See "boat".

Ark of the Agreement, *a special box made of acacia wood and gold. Inside were the stone tablets on which the Ten Commandments were written. Later, a pot of manna and Aaron's walking stick were also put into the Ark. It was to remind the people of Israel of God's promise to be with them.*
- building of, Exodus, 25:10–22; 37:1–9
- crossing the Jordan River, Joshua 3:1–17
- captured by the Philistines, 1 Samuel 4 — 7:1
- touched by Uzzah, 2 Samuel 6:1–8; 1 Chronicles 13
- placed in the Temple, 2 Chronicles 5:2–10
- contents of, Hebrews 9:4–5

Ark of the Covenant, See "Ark of the Agreement".

armour
- of Saul, 1 Samuel 17:38–39; 31:9–10
- of God, Ephesians 6:10–17

arrest
- John the Baptist arrested, Matthew 14:3; Mark 6:17
- Jesus arrested, Matthew 26:50–57; Mark 14:44–50; John 18:1–14
- Peter arrested, Acts 12:1–4
- Paul arrested, Acts 28:17–20

Artaxerxes (ar-tah-ZERK-sees) *the title or name of Persian kings,* Ezra 4:7; Nehemiah 2:1
* letter to Ezra, Ezra 7:11–26

Artemis (AR-tuh-mis) *a goddess that many Greeks worshipped,* Acts 19:23–41

Asa (AY-sah) *the third king of Judah,* 1 Kings 15:9–24; 2 Chronicles 14—16

Asaph (AY-saf) *a leader of singers when David was king,* 1 Chronicles 16:5,7; 25:1–2; 2 Chronicles 5:12
* songs of, Psalms 73—83

ascension (uh-SEN-shun) *lifted up; used to describe Jesus' return to heaven,* Acts 1:2–11; 2:32–33

ashamed
* of Jesus, Mark 8:38; Luke 9:26; 2 Timothy 1:8
* for suffering as a Christian, 1 Peter 4:16

Ashdod (ASH-dod) *one of the five strong, walled cities of the Philistines; called Azotus in the New Testament.*
* Ark of the Agreement there, 1 Samuel 5:1–8
* later called "Azotus", Acts 8:40

Asherah (ah-SHIR-ah) *a Canaanite goddess thought to be the wife of the god Baal.*
* worshipped by Israelites, 1 Kings 14:14–15,22–23; 15:13
* worship forbidden, Exodus 34:13–14; Deuteronomy 16:21–22

Ashkelon (ASH-keh-lon) *one of the five important cities of the Philistines,* Judges 1:18; Zephaniah 2:4,7
* thirty of its men killed by Samson, Judges 14:19

Ashtoreth (ASH-toh-reth) *a goddess of the people of Assyria and Canaan. At times the Israelites forgot God and built idols to worship her.* Judges 2:13; 1 Samuel 7:3–4; 12:10
* worshipped by Solomon, 1 Kings 11:5,33

Asia (AY-zhuh) *the western part of the country now called "Turkey".*
* Paul preached there, Acts 19:10,26
* seven churches of, Revelation 1:4

assembly (a-SEM-blee) *a meeting; a group of people gathered for a purpose.*
* of the church, Hebrews 10:24–25
* conduct in, James 2:1–4

assurance (uh-SHURE-ans) *with confidence; without doubts.*
* about the Gospel, 1 Thessalonians 1:5
* before God, Hebrews 10:22–23; 1 John 5:14–15
* faith as, Hebrews 11:1

Assyria (a-SEER-ee-uh) *a powerful nation north and east of Israel.*
* enemy of Israel, 2 Kings 15:19–20; 17:3–6
* enemy of Judah, 2 Kings 18:13—19:36; Isaiah 36—37:37

Astarte (ah-STAR-tay) *another name for the goddess Ashtoreth.* See "Ashtoreth".

Athaliah (ath-uh-LY-uh) *the only woman who ruled over Judah,* 2 Kings 11; 2 Chronicles 22:10—23:21

Athens (ATH-enz) *the leading city of the country of Greece.*
* Paul preached there, Acts 17:16–34

atonement (a-TONE-ment) *to remove or forgive sins.*
* through animal sacrifices, Exodus 30:10; Leviticus 17:11; Numbers 25:13
* through faith in the blood of Jesus' death, Romans 3:25; Hebrews 2:17; 9:22; 10:11–12

Atonement, Day of, See "Cleansing, Day of".

Augustus (aw-GUS-tus) *the title meaning "honoured" that the Romans gave to Octavian when he began ruling the Roman world in 27 BC. He was Emperor when Jesus was born,* Luke 2:1

Augustus Caesar (aw-GUS-tus SEE-zer) *or Caesar Augustus, the first Roman emperor,* Luke 2:1

authority (aw-THOR-ee-tee) *power or right to control.*
* proper use of, Matthew 20:25–26; Luke 22:24–30; Titus 2:15
* respect for, Luke 20:20–26; Romans 13:1–7; 1 Timothy 2:2; 1 Peter 2:13–17; Hebrews 13:17
* Jesus' authority, Matthew 7:29; 9:6; Mark 11:27–33; Luke 5:24; John 5:19–29

B

Baal (BAY-el) *a god of the Canaanites; "Baal" was the common word for "master, lord". He was known as the son of Dagon, or the son of El, who was known as the father of the false gods.*
* worshipped by Israelites, Judges 2:10–11; Jeremiah 11:13
* Elijah defeated prophets of Baal, 1 Kings 18:1–40
* Baal worship destroyed by Jehu, 2 Kings 10:18–28

Baal-Zebub, See "Beelzebul".

Baasha (Baa-shah) *the third king of Israel,* 1 Kings 15:27—16:7; 2 Chronicles 16:1–6; Jeremiah 41:9

Babel (BAY-bel) *a tower built to reach the sky,* Genesis 11:1–9

baby
* Moses as, Exodus 2:1–10
* Solomon determined mother of, 1 Kings 3:16–28
* Elizabeth's, Luke 1:39–44
* Jesus as, Luke 2:6–21
* as a symbol of new Christians, 1 Peter 2:2

Babylon (BAB-ee-lon) *city on the Euphrates River; capital of Babylonia.*
* captives in Babylon, Psalm 137:1; Jeremiah 29:10
* destruction predicted, Jeremiah 51:36–37
* as a symbol of evil, Revelation 14:8; 17:5

Babylonians (bab-e-LONE-e-unz) *people of the country Babylonia. Also called "Chaldeans".*
* capture warned by Jeremiah, Jeremiah 21; 25
* captured the people of Judah, 2 Kings 20:12–18; 24—25; Jeremiah 39:1–10
* Daniel in Babylon, Daniel 1—4
* released Israelite captives, Ezra 2

Balaam (BAY-lum) *a prophet from Midian.*
* asked by Balak to prophesy, Numbers 22—24; 2 Peter 2:15–16; Revelation 2:14
* death of, Numbers 31:8

balm, *oil from a plant used as medicine,* Genesis 37:25; Jeremiah 8:22; 51:8; Ezekiel 27:17

Baptist, John the (BAP-tist) *someone who baptises. John, a relative of Jesus, was called this because he baptised many people.* Matthew 3:1–6
* condemned Pharisees and Sadducees, Matthew 3:7–10
* preached about Jesus, Matthew 3:11–12
* baptised Jesus, Matthew 3:13–17
* in prison, Matthew 11:1–6; Luke 7:18–23
* described by Jesus, Matthew 11:7–12; 17:10–13; Luke 7:24–28
* death of, Matthew 14:1–12; Mark 6:14–29

- baptism of, Matthew 21:25–26; Acts 10:37; 18:25; 19:3–4
- Jesus mistaken for, Matthew 16:13–14; Mark 8:27–28; Luke 9:18–19

baptism (BAP-tiz-em) *dipping or immersing.*

- by John, Matthew 3:6; Mark 1:4; Luke 3; Acts 19:3
- of Jesus, Matthew 3:13–17
- examples of, Acts 2:38–41; 8:36–38; 16:15,33
- with fire, Matthew 3:11; Luke 3:16
- with the Holy Spirit, Mark 1:8; Acts 1:5; 11:16

Barabbas (bah-RAB-us) *a robber who had murdered someone in Jerusalem. He was freed instead of Jesus.* Matthew 27:15–26; Mark 15:6–11

Barak (BA-rak) *a leader of Israel's army when Deborah was judge,* Judges 4 — 5

Bar-Jesus, See "Elymas".

barley (BAR-lee) *a type of grain used to make bread.*

- harvest of, Ruth 1:22; 2:17,23; 2 Samuel 21:9
- loaves of, John 6:9–13

barn

- storing in, Matthew 6:26
- rich man's, Luke 12:16–20

Barnabas (BAR-nah-bus) *an encourager who helped the apostles,* Acts 4:36; 11:23

- worked with Paul, Acts 11:26; 13 — 15
- influenced by hypocrites, Galatians 2:13

Bartholomew (bar-THOL-oh-mew) *one of the twelve apostles of Jesus,* Matthew 10:3; Mark 3:18; Luke 6:14; Acts 1:13

Bartimaeus (bar-teh-MAY-us) *a blind man who was healed by Jesus,* Mark 10:46–52

Baruch (BAH-rook) *a friend of the prophet Jeremiah,* Jeremiah 36

Bathsheba (bath-SHE-buh) *the mother of Solomon and wife of David,* 2 Samuel 11 — 12:25; 1 Kings 1 — 2:22

beatitude (bee-A-ti-tyood) *blessed or happy; often used for Jesus' teaching in Matthew 5:3–12; Luke 6:20–22*

Beelzebul (bee-EL-ze-bull) *false god of the Philistines; in the New Testament it often refers to the devil.*

- name for Satan, Matthew 12:24; Mark 3:22; Luke 11:15

Beersheba (beer-SHE-buh) *the town farthest south in the land of Judah,* 2 Samuel 3:10; 2 Chronicles 30:5

- Abraham made an agreement there, Genesis 21:14–34

beg

- Jesus begged by demons, Matthew 8:28–34; Mark 5:1–13; Luke 8:26–33
- Jesus begged by people, Matthew 14:36; Mark 7:24–26,32; 8:22

beggar

- Bartimaeus, Mark 10:46–52
- Lazarus, Luke 16:19–31
- at Beautiful Gate, Acts 3:1–10
- man born blind, John 9:1–12

Bel, *a false god of the Babylonians,* Jeremiah 50:2; 51:44

believe

- in God, Acts 16:34; Romans 4:24
- in Jesus, Matthew 18:6; John 12:44; 14:11–12; 1 John 5:10
- in the Good News, Mark 1:15; 11:24; Acts 15:7
- rewards of believing, Matthew 21:22; John 20:31; 1 Thessalonians 2:13

- a lie, 2 Thessalonians 2:11

believers (be-LEE-vers) *the followers of Jesus,* John 3:16; Acts 4:32; 5:14; Galatians 6:10

Belshazzar (bell-SHAZ-er) *a ruler of Babylon,* Daniel 5

Belteshazzar (BELL-teh-SHAZ-er) *the Babylonian name that Nebuchadnezzar gave to Daniel,* Daniel 4:8; 5:12

Benaiah (bee-NAY-uh) *the captain of David's bodyguard,* 2 Samuel 23:20–23

- commander of Solomon's army, 1 Kings 2:34–35

Ben-Hadad (ben-HAY-dad) *two or three Syrian kings who often fought against Israel,* 1 Kings 20:1–34; 2 Kings 6:24 — 8:15

Benjamin (BEN-jah-min) *the youngest son of Jacob and Rachel.*

- birth of, Genesis 35:16–20
- reunited with Joseph, Genesis 42 — 45

Bernice (Bur-nees) *the oldest daughter of Herod Agrippa I,* Acts 25:13 — 26:32

Bethany (BETH-a-nee) *a small town about three kilometres from Jerusalem.*

- home of Mary, Martha, and Lazarus, John 11:1; 12:1
- home of Simon, Mark 14:3

Bethel (BETH-el) *a town about nineteen kilometres north of Jerusalem.*

- named by Jacob, Genesis 28:10–19
- Jeroboam built idols there, 1 Kings 12:26–33

Bethesda (be-THES-da) See "Bethzatha, pool of".

Bethlehem (BETH-le-hem) *a small town eight kilometres from Jerusalem.*

- hometown of King David, 1 Samuel 16:1,13
- birthplace of Jesus, Matthew 2:1; Luke 2:15–17

Bethsaida (beth-SAY-ih-duh) *a city in Galilee and home of Peter, Andrew, and Philip,* John 1:44; 12:21

- rejected Jesus, Matthew 11:20–21; Luke 10:13

Bethzatha, pool of (beth-ZA-tha) *a pool in Jerusalem near the Sheep Gate.*

- Jesus healed a man there, John 5:1–18

betray (be-TRAY) *to turn against.*

- families against each other, Mark 13:12–13
- Jesus betrayed, Matthew 26:20–25; Mark 14:18–46; John 13:2–30

birds

- created by God, Genesis 1:20–21
- saved by Noah, Genesis 6:19–20; 7:1–3
- unclean, Leviticus 11:13–19
- cared for by God, Matthew 6:25–27; Luke 12:24

birth

- spiritual birth, John 1:13; 3:3–8; 1 Peter 1:23

bishop, See "elder".

bitter

- water, Exodus 15:22–25; Numbers 5:18–27; Revelation 8:11
- herbs, Exodus 12:8

bitterness (BIT-er-nes) *sorrow or pain; anger or hatred.*

- warning against, Acts 8:23; Ephesians 4:31; James 3:14

blasphemy (BLAS-feh-mee) *saying things against God or not showing respect for God.*

* examples of, 1 Timothy 1:13; Revelation 13:6
* warnings against, Matthew 12:31–32; Mark 3:28–29
* Jesus accused of, Matthew 9:3; 26:65; Mark 2:6–7; John 10:36

blessing (BLES-ing) *a gift from God; asking God's favour on.*
* promised to Abraham, Genesis 12:1–3
* Isaac blessed Jacob, Genesis 27:1–41
* from God, Acts 3:25; Romans 10:12; 15:27; Hebrews 6:7
* by Jesus, Mark 10:16; Luke 24:50; John 1:16
* by each other, Luke 6:28; 1 Corinthians 4:12; 1 Peter 3:9

blind
* the blind healed, Matthew 9:27–31; 15:30; Mark 8:22–26; John 9
* Saul struck blind, Acts 9:8–9
* spiritually blind, Matthew 23:16–26; John 9:35–41; 2 Peter 1:5–9

blood, *sometimes used to mean "death".*
* water turned into, Exodus 7:14–24
* used in the Passover, Exodus 12:13–23
* not to be eaten, Leviticus 3:17; Deuteronomy 12:16; 1 Samuel 14:31–34
* of animal sacrifices, Leviticus 1; 3; 4; Hebrews 9:12–13; 10:4
* of Christ, Matthew 26:28; Romans 5:9; Hebrews 9:14; 1 John 1:7

boasting
* warnings against, Proverbs 27:1; 2 Corinthians 10:12–18; James 4:16; Jude 16
* about the Lord, 1 Corinthians 1:31; 2 Corinthians 10:17; Galatians 6:14

boat, *ark.*
* built by Noah, Genesis 6:11–21
* of the apostles, Matthew 4:21–22; John 21:3–11
* used by Jesus, Matthew 8:23; 13:2; 14:13–34

body
* made of dust, Genesis 2:7; 3:19
* health of, Proverbs 3:7–8; 4:20–22; 14:30
* attitudes toward, Matthew 6:25; Romans 6:13; Ephesians 5:29
* warnings against misuse, Romans 8:13; 1 Corinthians 6:18–20; 1 Thessalonians 4:5

body of Christ, *sometimes means Jesus' human body; also a way of describing Christians.*
* Christ's physical body, John 2:19–21; 19:38; Acts 2:31; 1 Corinthians 11:24; 1 Timothy 3:16; 1 Peter 3:18
* the Church as Christ's spiritual body, Romans 12:5; 1 Corinthians 12:12–31; Ephesians 1:23; 4:4; 5:23

bone
* "whose bones came from my bones", Genesis 2:23
* Ezekiel's vision of, Ezekiel 37:1–14
* none of Jesus' bones to be broken, John 19:36

book, *parchments, scroll.*
* Book of the Jashar, *a book of songs celebrating the glory of Israel,* Joshua 10:13; 2 Samuel 1:18
* Book of the Teachings, Deuteronomy 30:10; Joshua 1:8; 2 Chronicles 34:14–32; Ezra 8
* book of life, Philippians 4:3; Revelation 3:5; 13:8; 20:12; 21:27
* "Jesus did many other miracles . . . not written in this book", John 20:30
* "the whole world would not be big enough for all the books", John 21:25

bottomless pit, *the place where the devil and his demons live,* Luke 8:31; Revelation 9:1–11; 11:7; 17:8; 20:1–3

box of Scriptures, *small leather boxes that some Jews tied to their foreheads and left arms; also called "phylacteries"* or "frontlets".
* held the Law of Moses, Deuteronomy 6:6–8
* Jesus criticised misuse of, Matthew 23:5

bread, *the most important food in New Testament times; usually made of barley or wheat.*
* to feed 5,000 people, Matthew 14:13–21; Mark 6:30–44; Luke 9:10–17; John 6:1–13
* to feed 4,000 people, Matthew 15:32–39; Mark 8:1–10
* Jesus, the bread of life, John 6:25–59
* "A person does not live by eating only bread", Matthew 4:4; Luke 4:4
* "Give us the food we need for each day", Luke 11:3
* in the Lord's Supper, Luke 22:19; Acts 20:7; 1 Corinthians 10:16; 11:17–34

bread that shows we are in God's presence, *twelve loaves of bread that were kept on the table in the Holy Tent and later in the Temple; also called "Bread of the Presence" or "showbread", Leviticus 24:5–9*
* eaten by David, Matthew 12:3–4; Mark 2:25–26; Luke 6:4

bride, Song of Solomon 4:8–12
* belongs to the bridegroom, John 3:29
* of Christ, Revelation 21:2,9

bridegroom
* sun compared to, Psalm 19:5
* Jesus compared to, Matthew 9:15; Mark 2:19–20; Luke 5:34
* Jesus' story of, Matthew 25:1–13
* at Jesus' first miracle, John 2:9

brother, *a family member; people from the same country; or Christians.*
* physical brothers, Proverbs 18:24; Matthew 19:29; Mark 12:18–23
* Jesus' brothers, Matthew 13:55; Mark 3:31; John 2:12; 7:3; Acts 1:14; 1 Corinthians 9:5
* spiritual brothers, Romans 8:29; 12:10; 1 Timothy 6:2; Hebrews 2:11; 1 Peter 2:17

burn
* sacrifices, Exodus 29:10–42; Leviticus 1—4
* incense, Exodus 30:7–8; Numbers 16:40; Jeremiah 48:35; Luke 1:9
* Jericho burned by Israelites, Joshua 6:24
* idols burned by Josiah, 2 Kings 23:4–20
* jealousy like a fire, Psalm 79:5
* chaff, Matthew 3:12; Luke 3:17
* lake of burning sulphur, Revelation 21:8

burnt offerings, *a whole animal sacrificed as a gift to God.*
* rules about, Leviticus 1; 6:8–13; Numbers 28—29
* less important than obedience, 1 Samuel 15:22; Psalm 51:16–19
* less important than love, Hosea 6:6; Mark 12:32–33

bury, Matthew 8:21–22; Luke 9:59–60
* Abraham buried Sarah, Genesis 23
* Jacob not to be buried in Egypt, Genesis 47:29–30; 50:1–14
* strangers, Matthew 27:7
* in baptism, Romans 6:4

C

Caesar (SEE-zer) *a famous Roman family; used as the title of the Roman emperors.*
* Augustus, Luke 2:1
* Tiberius, Luke 3:1; 20:22; John 19:12
* Claudius, Acts 11:28; 17:7; 18:2
* Nero, Acts 25:8; 27:24; Philippians 4:22

Caesarea (SES-uh-REE-uh) *a city on the Mediterranean Sea,* Acts 10:1; 21:8; 23:32

Caesarea Philippi (SES-uh-REE-uh fih-LIP-eye) *a city at the base of Mount Hermon,* Matthew 16:13; Mark 8:27

Caiaphas (KAY-uh-fus) *the Jewish high priest from AD 18 to 36.*
* plotted to kill Jesus, Matthew 26:3–5; John 11:45–54
* father-in-law to Annas, John 18:13
* at Jesus' trial, Matthew 26:57–67
* questioned Peter and John, Acts 4:5–22

Cain, *the first son of Adam and Eve.*
* killed his brother Abel, Genesis 4:1–24; 1 John 3:12

Caleb (KAY-leb) *one of the twelve men Moses sent to spy out Canaan.*
* explored Canaan, Numbers 13—14
* given the city of Hebron, Joshua 14:6–15

calf
* gold idol, Exodus 32:1–20; 1 Kings 12:26–30; 2 Kings 10:28–29
* fatted, Luke 15:23,27,30

camel, Genesis 37:25; 1 Samuel 30:17; 1 Kings 10:2
* Rebekah watered Abraham's camels, Genesis 24:10–20
* "easier for a camel to go through the eye of a needle", Matthew 19:24; Mark 10:25; Luke 18:25
* "swallows a camel", Matthew 23:24

Cana (KAY-nah) *a small town near the city of Nazareth in Galilee.*
* place of Jesus' first miracle, John 2:1–11

Canaan (KAY-nan) *land God promised to the Israelites,* Leviticus 25:38; Numbers 13:2; 33:51; Psalm 105:11

Capernaum (kay-PUR-nee-um) *a city on the western shore of Lake Galilee.*
* Jesus lived there, Matthew 4:12–13
* Jesus healed there, Matthew 8:5–13; Luke 4:31–41
* rejected Jesus, Matthew 11:23–24

capital, *the top of a pillar, usually decorated with beautiful carvings.*
* in the Temple, 1 Kings 7:16–20; 2 Kings 25:17

captive
* Israelites as captives, Deuteronomy 28:41; 2 Kings 25:21; Jeremiah 30:3

cassia (cass-EE-uh) *a pleasant-smelling powder. Its odour is like the bark of the cinnamon plant,* Exodus 30:23–24; Psalm 45:8

census (SEN-sus) *a count of the number of people who live in an area.*
* the Israelites counted, Numbers 1:2; 26:2
* ordered by David, 1 Chronicles 21:1–2
* ordered by Augustus Caesar, Luke 2:1–3

centurion (sen-TYUR-ree-un) *a Roman army officer who commanded a hundred soldiers.*
* centurion's servant healed by Jesus, Matthew 8:5–13; Luke 7:1–10
* at Jesus' death, Matthew 27:54; Mark 15:39; Luke 23:47
* Cornelius, Acts 10

Cephas (SEE-fuss) *the Aramaic word for "rock"; in Greek, "Peter". Jesus gave this name to the apostle Simon.* John 1:42

chaff (CHAF) *the husk of a head of grain. Farmers would toss the* grain and chaff into the air. Since the chaff is lighter, the wind would blow it away, and the good grain would fall back to the threshing floor.
* sinners to be destroyed like chaff, Psalms 1:4; 35:5; Matthew 3:12; Luke 3:17

Chaldeans, See "Babylonians".

change of heart and life, *repentance.*
* commanded, Matthew 3:2; Mark 1:15; Luke 13:3; Acts 3:19; 17:30
* causes of, Romans 2:4; 2 Corinthians 7:9–10
* examples of, Matthew 12:41; Luke 11:32

chariot
* Egyptians' chariots destroyed, Exodus 14:5–28
* of fire, 2 Kings 2:11; 6:17
* Ethiopian taught in a chariot, Acts 8:27–31

Chemosh (KEE-mosh) *a god of the Moabites,* Jeremiah 48:13
* worshipped by Solomon, 1 Kings 11:7

cherubim (CHAIR-uh-bim) *heavenly beings with wings and the faces of men and animals.*
* guarded the garden of Eden, Genesis 3:24
* on the Ark of the Agreement, Exodus 25:18–22; 1 Kings 6:23–28
* seen by Ezekiel, Ezekiel 10:1–20

children
* of God, John 1:12; Romans 8:14; 1 Peter 1:14; 1 John 3:1–10
* training of, Ephesians 6:4; Colossians 3:21
* obedience of, Ephesians 6:1; Colossians 3:20; 1 Timothy 3:4
* become like, Matthew 18:3–4
* "Let the little children come to me", Matthew 19:14; Mark 10:14; Luke 18:16

chosen
* Israelites chosen by God, Deuteronomy 7:7–8; 9:4–5; Isaiah 44:1
* people chosen by God, Romans 8:33; Ephesians 1:4–5; 2 Timothy 2:10; 1 Peter 1:2; 2:9
* Jesus chosen by God, Hebrews 1:2; 1 Peter 2:4

Christ (KRYST) *anointed (or chosen) one. Jesus is the Christ, chosen by God to save people from their sins.*
* active in creation, John 1:1–3; Colossians 1:15–17; Hebrews 1:2,10
* equal with God, John 5:23; 10:30; Philippians 2:6; Colossians 2:9; Hebrews 1:3
* purpose of his death, Romans 5:6; 14:9; Hebrews 9:28; 1 Peter 3:18
* gives life, John 5:21; 6:35; 10:28; 11:25; 14:6
* as Saviour, Matthew 1:21; John 12:47
* as judge, Matthew 10:32–33; 25:31–46; John 5:22; Acts 17:31
* living in Christians, John 17:23; Romans 8:10; 2 Corinthians 1:21; Ephesians 3:17
* his return, Acts 1:11; 1 Thessalonians 5:1–11; Hebrews 9:28; 2 Peter 3:10
* enemy of, 1 John 2:18,22; 4:3; 2 John 7

Christians (KRIS-chuns) *Christ's followers,* Acts 11:26; 26:28; 1 Peter 4:16

church
* established by Christ, Matthew 16:18
* Christ as its head, Ephesians 1:22; 5:23; Colossians 1:18
* Christ died for, Ephesians 5:25
* activities of, Acts 12:5; 1 Corinthians 14:26–40; 1 Timothy 5:16; Hebrews 10:24–25

circumcision (SIR-kum-SIH-zhun) *the cutting off of the foreskin of the male sex organ; each Jewish boy was circumcised on the eighth day after he was born; this was done as a sign of the agreement God had made with his people, the Jews.*
* commanded by God, Genesis 17; Leviticus 12:1–3
* spiritual circumcision, Philippians 3:3; Colossians 2:11

city of refuge, See "safety, city of".

Claudius (CLAW-dee-us) *the fourth Roman emperor. He ruled from AD 41 to 54.* Acts 11:28; 17:7; 18:2

clean, *the state of a person, animal, or action that is pleasing to God. Under the Teachings of Moses, unclean animals could not be eaten. People who were considered clean could live and serve God normally.*
* clean and unclean animals, Deuteronomy 14:1–21; Mark 7:19; Acts 10
* clean and unclean people, Leviticus 13
* spiritually clean, Ephesians 5:26; Hebrews 9:14; 2 Peter 1:9

Cleansing, Day of, *the Day of Atonement; the most special day of the year for the Israelites when the high priest could go into the Most Holy Place. Animals were sacrificed for the sins of the people as a sign that people were cleansed of their sins for a year.*
* rules about, Leviticus 23:26–32; 25:9

cloud
* Israel led by pillar of cloud, Exodus 13:21
* cloud as small as a fist, 1 Kings 18:44
* Jesus leaves and will return in clouds, Luke 21:27; Acts 1:9; 1 Thessalonians 4:17; Revelation 1:7

Colossae (kol-OSS-ee) *a city in the country of Turkey,* Colossians 1:1–2

comfort, *to help ease someone's pain, grief, or trouble.*
* bad comforters, Job 16:2
* by shepherd's rod, Psalm 23:4
* from God, Isaiah 49:13; Matthew 5:4; 2 Corinthians 1:3–4
* from the Holy Spirit, John 14:16–18

commands
* to be taught, Deuteronomy 6:1–7; Matthew 5:19
* to be obeyed, Deuteronomy 8:6; Proverbs 19:16; John 15:10
* a new command, John 13:34
* to love, Galatians 5:14; 1 Timothy 1:5; 2 John 6

communion (KUH-myu-nyun) See "Lord's Supper".

complain
* Pharisees complained, Luke 5:30
* disciples complained, John 6:61
* warnings against, Philippians 2:14

concubine (KON-kyu-bine) See "slave woman".

condemn (kon-DEM) *to judge someone guilty of doing wrong,* John 3:16–18; Romans 2:1; 8:1

coney, See "rock badger".

confess
* admitting sin, Psalm 32:5; Proverbs 28:13; James 5:16; 1 John 1:9
* admitting Christ is Lord, Romans 10:9–10; Philippians 2:11; 1 Timothy 6:12; 1 John 4:2–3

confidence (KON-fih-dens) *a feeling of assurance; trust.*
* from the Lord, 2 Thessalonians 3:4; 2 Timothy 1:7
* in Christ, Philippians 4:13
* before God, 1 John 3:21

conscience (KON-shunts) *a person's belief about what is right and wrong.*
* Paul's good conscience, Acts 23:1
* commanded to have a good conscience, 1 Timothy 3:9; Hebrews 9:14
* a troubled conscience, Hebrews 10:22; 1 John 3:20
* a corrupt conscience, 1 Timothy 4:2; Titus 1:15

contentment, *satisfaction.*
* Paul learned, Philippians 4:11
* with possessions, Luke 3:14; 1 Timothy 6:6; Hebrews 13:5

conversion (kon-VER-zhun) *a person's turning toward God and becoming a Christian.*
* examples of, Acts 9:1–22; 11:19–21; 1 Thessalonians 1:9

coral (KOR-al) *a type of limestone that forms in the ocean,* Job 28:18; Ezekiel 27:16

Corinth (KOR-inth) *a large seaport in the country of Greece.*
* Paul preached there, Acts 18:1–11
* Paul's letters to the church there, 1 and 2 Corinthians

Cornelius (kor-NEEL-yus) *a Roman army officer in charge of a hundred soldiers,* Acts 10

cornerstone, *the most important stone at the corner of the base of a building; Jesus is called the cornerstone of the new law.*
* Christ as the cornerstone, Ephesians 2:20; 1 Peter 2:4–8

council (KOWN-s'l) *or meeting; the highest Jewish court in the days of the Jesus.*
* Jesus before the council, Matthew 26:57–68; Mark 14:53–65
* apostles before the council, Acts 4:1–22; 22:30 – 23:10
* Stephen before the council, Acts 6:8–7

courage
* need for, Joshua 1:6–9; Psalm 27:14; 1 Corinthians 16:13; Philippians 1:20
* examples of, Acts 4:13; 5:17–32; 20:22–24

court, courtyard, *part of a building that has walls, but no roof. The Temple had four courts:*
* the Court of the Non-Jews (Gentiles), a large open area just inside the walls of Herod's Temple, Mark 11:15–17; John 10:23; Acts 3:11
* the Court of Women, the next area, where both men and women were allowed, Mark 12:41–44
* the Court of Israel, the inner area of the Temple, where only Jewish men were allowed
* the Court of the Priests, the innermost court in the Temple, where only priests were allowed, Matthew 23:35

covenant (KUV-eh-nant) See "agreement".

covet (KUV-et) *to want strongly something that belongs to someone else.*
* forbidden by God, Exodus 20:17; Romans 13:9; Hebrews 13:5

creation
* of the world, Genesis 1 — 2; Job 38 — 41; Psalm 8; Isaiah 40:21–26; John 1:1–3; Hebrews 11:3

creator, *one who makes something out of nothing.*
* God as our Maker, Deuteronomy 32:6
* "Remember your Creator", Ecclesiastes 12:1

Crete (KREET) *an island in the Mediterranean Sea.*
* Paul visited there, Acts 27:7; Titus 1:5

cross, *two rough beams of wood nailed together, criminals were killed on crosses.*

* Jesus died on a cross, Matthew 27:31–50; Mark 15:20–37; Luke 23:26–46; John 19:16–30
* importance of, 1 Corinthians 1:18; 2:2; Galatians 6:14; Ephesians 2:16; Colossians 2:13–14
* as a symbol of death to oneself, Matthew 10:38; Luke 9:23; Romans 6:6; Galatians 5:24

crown, *a special band worn around the head.*
* a king's crown, Psalm 21:2–3; Song of Solomon 3:11; Revelation 12:3
* of thorns, Matthew 27:29; Mark 15:17; John 19:2
* of victory, 1 Corinthians 9:25; 2 Timothy 4:8; 1 Peter 5:4

crucifixion (kroo-see-FIK-shun) *to be killed on a cross.* See "cross".

cubit (KU-bit) *a measurement in Bible times; about forty centimetres,* Revelation 21:17

cud, *an animal's food that is chewed slightly, swallowed, brought up, then chewed more completely a second time,* Leviticus 11; Deuteronomy 14

cumin (QU-min) *a plant with small seeds used for seasoning food,* Matthew 23:23

cup
* of the king of Egypt, Genesis 40:11
* of Joseph, Genesis 44:1–17
* of Lord's Supper, Matthew 26:27–29; Mark 14:22–25; Luke 22:17–20; 1 Corinthians 11:25–29
* of anger, Isaiah 51:17–23
* of water, Matthew 10:42; Mark 9:41

cupbearer, *the officer who tasted and served the king his wine.*
* to the king of Egypt, Genesis 40
* Nehemiah, cupbearer to Artaxerxes, Nehemiah 1:11

curse
* from God, Deuteronomy 11:26–29; John 7:49; Galatians 3:10–13
* forbidden to people, Matthew 15:4; Romans 12:14; James 3:9–10
* response to, Luke 6:28; 1 Corinthians 4:12

curtain
* of the Holy Tent, Exodus 26:1–2; 36:9
* of the Temple, Matthew 27:51; Mark 15:38; Luke 23:45

Cush, a country in Africa, Genesis 2:13; Psalm 68:31; Isaiah 18; 20

Cush, grandson of Noah, Genesis 10

Cyprus (SY-prus) *an island in the Mediterranean Sea,* Acts 11:19–20; 13:4; 15:39

Cyrene (sy-REE-nee) *a city in North Africa,* Acts 2:10; 6:9
* Simon of, Matthew 27:32; Mark 15:21; Luke 23:26

Cyrus (SY-rus) *a king of Persia,* Daniel 1:21
* sent captives home, Ezra 1; 6
* chosen by God, Isaiah 44:28 — 45:13

D

Dagon (DAY-gon) *a false god of the Philistines,* Judges 16:23; 1 Samuel 5:2–7; 1 Chronicles 10:10

Damascus (dah-MAS-kus) *a city sixty-four kilometres east of Lake Galilee.*
* a chief city of Syria, 1 Kings 15:18; 2 Chronicles 24:23
* condemned by Amos, Amos 1:3,5
* Paul converted there, Acts 9:1–22

Dan, a city
* Israel's most northern city, Judges 20:1; 2 Samuel 16:11

Dan, son of Jacob, Genesis 30:6; 49:16–17; Joshua 19:40–48

Daniel (DAN-yel) *a Hebrew captive taken to Babylon as a young man.*
* taken to Babylon, Daniel 1:1–6
* became king's servant, Daniel 1:7–21
* explained Nebuchadnezzar's dreams, Daniel 2; 4
* read the writing on the wall, Daniel 5
* thrown into lion's den, Daniel 6
* his visions, Daniel 7; 8; 10
* a prophet, Matthew 24:15

Darius Hystaspes (dah-REE-us his-TAHS-peez) *a ruler of Persia who allowed the Jews to finish rebuilding the Temple,* Ezra 5 — 6

Darius the Mede, *the king of Persia who made Daniel an important ruler under him,* Daniel 5:31 — 6:28; Haggai 1:1; Zechariah 1:1

darkness, *having no light; a symbol of evil.*
* before creation, Genesis 1:2
* as a plague, Exodus 10:21–23
* at Jesus' death, Matthew 27:45; Mark 15:33; Luke 23:44–45
* spiritual, John 1:5; Romans 13:12; Colossians 1:13
* as punishment, Matthew 8:12; 2 Peter 2:17; Jude 6,13

David (DAY-vid) *Israel's greatest king.*
* son of Jesse, 1 Samuel 16:13–23
* played harp for Saul, 1 Samuel 16:14–23
* killed Goliath, 1 Samuel 17
* friend of Jonathan, 1 Samuel 18:1–4; 19:1–7; 20
* chased by Saul, 1 Samuel 18 — 19; 23:7–29
* protected Saul, 1 Samuel 24; 26
* became king, 2 Samuel 2:1–7; 5:1–14
* married Bathsheba, 2 Samuel 11 — 12:25
* reign of, 2 Samuel 5 — 1 Kings 1
* not allowed to build the Temple, 2 Samuel 7:1–17
* death of, 1 Kings 2:1–11
* Jesus as son of David, Matthew 22:42–45; Luke 1:27; 20:41–44

deacon (DEE-kun) *a person chosen to serve the church in special ways,* Philippians 1:1; 1 Timothy 3:8–13

Dead Sea, *large lake at the south end of the Jordan River. Several small streams flow into it, but it has no outlet. It is so salty that nothing lives in it. It is also called the "Sea of Arabah", "Salt Sea", and the "Eastern Sea".* Genesis 14:3; Numbers 34:3,12; Joshua 3:16

deaf, *unable or unwilling to hear.*
* healed, Matthew 11:5; Luke 7:22
* and dumb spirit, Mark 9:25

death
* a result of sin, Genesis 2:16–17; Romans 5:12; 6:23; 1 Corinthians 15:21
* Christ's victory over, 1 Corinthians 15:24–26,54–57; 2 Timothy 1:10; Hebrews 2:14; Revelation 1:18
* spiritual death, Ephesians 2:1; Colossians 2:13

Deborah (DEB-oh-rah) *the only woman judge over Israel,* Judges 4 — 5

Decapolis (dee-KAP-oh-lis) *ten towns in an area southeast of Lake Galilee,* Matthew 4:25; Mark 5:20; 7:31

Delilah (dee-LYE-luh) *an evil Philistine woman whom Samson loved,* Judges 16:4–20

Demas (DEE-mus) *a Christian who helped the apostle Paul when Paul was in prison.*

* worked with Paul, Colossians 4:14; Philemon 24
* left Paul, 2 Timothy 4:10

Demetrius (deh-MEE-tree-us) *a silver worker in Ephesus,* Acts 19:23–27,38

demon, *an evil spirit from the devil. Sometimes demons lived in people, but Jesus could force them out.*
* people possessed by, Matthew 8:28–32; 9:32–33; Mark 7:24–30; 9:17–29
* Jesus accused of demon possession, Mark 3:22; John 7:20; 8:48; 10:20–21
* demons recognised Jesus, Mark 1:23–26; 3:11–12; 5:7–8; Acts 19:15; James 2:19

deny (di-NY) *refusing to believe the truth.*
* denying Christ, Matthew 10:32–33; 2 Timothy 2:12; 1 John 2:22–23
* Peter denied Christ, Matthew 26:34–35,69–75

descendants (de-SEN-dants) *family members who are born to a person or his children; grandchildren, great-grandchildren, great-great-grandchildren and so on,* Genesis 13:14–16; 15:12–16

devil (DEV-'l) *Satan; a spirit and the enemy of God and humans.*
* Jesus tempted by, Matthew 4:1–11; Luke 4:1–13
* children of, John 8:41–44; Acts 13:10; 1 John 3:7–10
* people to oppose, Ephesians 4:27; 6:11; James 4:7

Didymus (DID-ee-mus) *another name for Thomas, one of Jesus' apostles,* John 11:16; 20:24; 21:2

disciple (dih-SYE-p'l) See "follower".

disease
* a result of sin, Exodus 15:26; Deuteronomy 7:15; 28:60–61
* healed by Jesus, Matthew 4:23–24; 15:30–31; 21:14; Luke 7:21
* healed by apostles, Acts 5:12–16; 9:32–35; 14:8–10; 19:11–12; 28:8–9

disobedience
* brought sin, Romans 5:19
* to be punished, 2 Corinthians 10:6; Hebrews 4:11

divide
* heavens and earth, Genesis 1:6–8
* Red Sea, Exodus 14:16,21
* family against itself, Matthew 12:25; Mark 3:25; Luke 11:17

divorce
* teachings about, Deuteronomy 22:13–19,28–29; 24:1–4; Matthew 5:31–32; 19:1–12; 1 Corinthians 7:10–16

dog
* drinking water like a dog, Judges 7:5–6
* returns to its vomit, Proverbs 26:11; 2 Peter 2:22
* licked Ahab's blood, 1 Kings 22:38
* licked Lazarus's sores, Luke 16:20–21

door
* Jesus at the door, John 10:1
* "Knock, and the door will open", Luke 11:9–10
* "I stand at the door and knock", Revelation 3:20

donkey
* Balaam's, Numbers 22:21–30
* jawbone of, Judges 15:15–17
* ridden by Jesus, Matthew 21:1–7

Dorcas (DOR-kus) *Tabitha; a Christian woman known for helping the poor.*

* raised from the dead, Acts 9:36–43

dove, *a small bird similar to a pigeon; often a symbol for love, peace, and the Holy Spirit.*
* sent out by Noah, Genesis 8:8–12
* form taken by the Spirit of God, Matthew 3:16; Mark 1:10
* sellers of, John 2:14–16

dreams
* Joseph's, Genesis 37:1–11
* the king of Egypt's, Genesis 41:1–36
* Nebuchadnezzar's, Daniel 2; 4
* angel appeared to Joseph, Matthew 1:20–21; 2:13,19
* "your old men will dream dreams", Acts 2:17

drunkenness
* Noah became drunk, Genesis 9:20–23
* warnings against, Romans 13:13; 1 Corinthians 6:10; Ephesians 5:18; 1 Peter 4:3

E

eagle
* "to rise up as an eagle", Isaiah 40:31

earth
* creation of, Genesis 1:9–10; Jeremiah 51:15
* belongs to God, Exodus 19:5; Psalm 24:1

earthquake
* experienced by Elijah, 1 Kings 19:11–12
* at the death of Jesus, Matthew 27:51–54
* at Jesus' resurrection, Matthew 28:2
* experienced by Paul and Silas, Acts 16:25–26

Ebal (EE-buhl) *a mountain in Samaria next to Mount Gerizim.*
* place to announce curses, Deuteronomy 11:29; 27:12–13; Joshua 8:30–35

Eden, garden of (EE-den) *the home God created for Adam and Eve,* Genesis 2:8 — 3:24; Ezekiel 36:35; Joel 2:3

Edom (EE-dum) *Esau; the land where Esau's descendants lived.*
* the land of Esau, Genesis 36:8–9
* refused to let Israelites pass through, Numbers 20:14–21; Judges 1:17–18
* broke away from Judah, 2 Kings 8:20–22
* to be punished, Jeremiah 49:7–22; Ezekiel 25:12–14; Obadiah

education
* of Moses, Acts 7:22
* of children, Deuteronomy 6:1–7
* brings wisdom, Proverbs 8:33; 22:6

Eglon (EGG-lon) *a king of Moab,* Judges 3:12–25

Egypt (EE-jipt) *a country in the northeast part of Africa.*
* Joseph there, Genesis 39 — 50
* Israelites there, Genesis 46:5–34; Exodus 1; Acts 7:9–38
* Israelites left, Exodus 12:31–51
* Jesus there, Matthew 2:13–15

Ehud (EE-hud) *the second judge of Israel,* Judges 3:12–30

elder (EL-der) *older men who led God's people; appointed leaders in the church.*
* leaders of the Jews, Numbers 11:16–25; Deuteronomy 19:11–12; Matthew 21:23; Acts 4:5–7
* leaders of the church, Acts 11:30; 14:23; 15:2; 16:4
* duties and qualities, Acts 20:28; 1 Timothy 3:1–7; Titus 1:6–9; 1 Peter 5:1–3

Eleazar (el-ee-AY-zar) *son of Aaron.*

- birth of, Exodus 6:23–25
- Moses became angry with, Leviticus 10:16–20
- a high priest, Numbers 3:32
- divided the promised land, Numbers 34:17

election, *process of selecting.* See "chosen".

Eli (EE-lye) *a priest and the next-to-last judge of Israel.*
- trained Samuel, 1 Samuel 1:9–28; 2:11; 3
- didn't discipline his sons, 1 Samuel 2:12–36
- death of, 1 Samuel 4:1–18

Elihu (ee-LYE-hew) *the fourth of Job's friends to try to explain Job's troubles,* Job 32–37

Elijah (ee-LIE-juh) *a prophet who spoke for God.*
- fed by ravens, 1 Kings 17:1–6
- brought boy to life, 1 Kings 17:7–24
- against prophets of Baal, 1 Kings 18:1–40
- condemned Ahab, 1 Kings 21:17–29
- taken to heaven, 2 Kings 2:1–12
- appeared with Jesus, Matthew 17:1–13; Mark 9:2–13; Luke 9:28–36

Elisha (ee-LYE-shuh) *the prophet who took Elijah's place as God's messenger.*
- received Elijah's spirit, 2 Kings 2:9–14
- helped a Shunammite woman, 2 Kings 4:1–36
- miracles of, 2 Kings 2:19–22; 4:38–44; 6:1–7
- healed Naaman, 2 Kings 5
- death of, 2 Kings 13:14–20

Elizabeth (ee-LIZ-uh-beth) *the wife of Zechariah, a priest.*
- mother of John the Baptist, Luke 1:5–25,57–66
- visited by Mary, Luke 1:39–45

Elkanah (el-KAY-nuh) *the father of Samuel,* 1 Samuel 1 — 2:11

Elymas (EL-ih-mus) *Bar-Jesus; a magician in the city of Paphos in Cyprus,* Acts 13:4–12

Emmaus (ee-MAY-us) *a town twelve kilometres from Jerusalem.*
- Jesus appeared to disciples near there, Luke 24:13–39

encourage
- encouragement from God, Romans 15:4–5
- Christians to encourage each other, 1 Thessalonians 5:14; 2 Timothy 4:2; Hebrews 3:13; 10:24–25
- examples of encouragement, Acts 11:23; 13:15; 15:31–32

endurance, See "patience".

enemy
- attitude toward, Exodus 23:4–5; Matthew 5:43–48; Luke 6:27–36; Romans 12:20
- God's enemies, Romans 5:10; Philippians 3:18–19; James 4:4

enemy of Christ, *the anti-Christ,* 1 John 2:18,22; 4:3; 2 John 7

Enoch (EE-nok) *a man who walked with God,* Genesis 5:21–24; Hebrews 11:5

enrolment, See "census".

envy, See "jealousy".

Epaphras (EP-ah-fruss) *a Christian who started the church at Colossae,* Colossians 1:7–8; 4:12–13; Philemon 23

Epaphroditus (ee-PAF-ro-DYE-tus) *a Christian in the church at Philippi,* Philippians 2:25–30; 4:18

ephah (EE-fah) *a common measurement for dry materials, about twenty litres,* Exodus 16:36

Ephesus (EF-eh-sus) *the capital city in the Roman state of Asia.*
- Paul's work there, Acts 18:18–20; 1 Corinthians 16:8–9
- church there, Ephesians 1:1; Revelation 2:1–7

ephod (EF-ahd) See "robe, holy".

Ephraim (EE-frah-im) *Joseph's younger son,* Genesis 41:50–52; 48:8–20
- descendants of, Numbers 26:35; Joshua 16:5–10

Epicureans (EPI-cure-ee-ans) *people who followed the teachings of a man named Epicurus, who taught that happiness should be a person's goal in life,* Acts 17:18

equality (ee-KWOL-eh-tee) *being identical in value.*
- in death, Ecclesiastes 3:19–20
- of Jewish and non-Jewish people, Romans 10:12
- in Christ, Galatians 3:26–28

Esau (EE-saw) See "Edom".

Esther (ES-ter) *a Jewish girl who became the wife of Ahasuerus, King of Persia,* Esther 1 — 10
- became queen, Esther 1 — 2:18
- learned of the plan to kill the Jews, Esther 3 — 4
- saved the Jews, Esther 5 — 8

eternal, See "forever".

eternal life, *the new kind of life promised to those who follow Jesus, and which never ends.*
- conditions for, Mark 10:17–31; John 3:14–15; 12:25; 17:3; Galatians 6:7–8
- source of, John 6:27–29; 10:28; Titus 1:2; 1 John 5:11–12

Ethiopia (EE-thee-o-pee-uh) *earlier called "Cush".* See "Cush".

eunuch (YOU-nuk) *a man who cannot have sexual relations. In Bible times, eunuchs were often high officers in royal palaces or armies.* 2 Kings 9:32; Esther 2:3; Isaiah 56:3–5; Acts 8:26–40

Euphrates (you-FRAY-teez) *a long, important river in Bible lands.*
- in the garden of Eden, Genesis 2:10–14
- a boundary, Genesis 15:18; 1 Kings 4:21,24; 2 Kings 24:7

Eutychus (YOU-ti-cus) *a young man in the city of Troas who was brought back to life,* Acts 20:7–12

evangelist (ee-VAN-juh-list) *someone who tells the Good News.*
- Philip, the evangelist, Acts 21:8
- as a gift from Christ, Ephesians 4:11

Eve (EEV) *the first woman.*
- created by God, Genesis 2:18–25
- tricked by Satan, Genesis 3; 2 Corinthians 11:3; 1 Timothy 2:13–14

everlasting, *living forever, eternal.*
- God, Genesis 21:33; Nehemiah 9:5; Isaiah 40:28
- Christ, Isaiah 9:6
- kingdom, Daniel 4:3; 2 Peter 1:11
- fire, Matthew 18:8,25,41
- gospel, Revelation 14:6

evil
- warnings against, Amos 5:15; Romans 12:9; 1 Thessalonians 5:22
- to be punished, Proverbs 24:20; Isaiah 13:11

evil spirit, See "demon".

eye
- "eye for eye", Exodus 21:23–24; Matthew 5:38

* wood in, Matthew 7:3–5; Luke 6:41–42

eyewitness, *one who sees an occurrence and reports on it.*
* of Jesus' life, Luke 1:2; 2 Peter 1:16; 1 John 1:1

Ezekiel (ee-ZEEK-yel) *a prophet during the time the Jews were captured by the Babylonians,* Ezekiel 1:3
* his vision of dry bones, Ezekiel 37:1–14

Ezra (EZ-ra) *the leader of a group of Israelites who were allowed to return to Jerusalem from Babylon,* Ezra 7:10; Nehemiah 8

F

faith (FAYTH) *belief and trust.*
* definition of, Hebrews 11:1
* sources of, Romans 1:20; 10:17
* examples of, Matthew 8:5–10; 15:21–28; Hebrews 11
* power of, Matthew 17:20–21; Ephesians 6:16
* made right with God by, Romans 4:3; 5:1; Philippians 3:9
* salvation by, Mark 16:15–16; John 5:24; 20:31; Romans 10:9; Galatians 2:16
* blessings by, Galatians 3:1–14; Ephesians 3:12; 1 Peter 1:5
* continue in, 2 Corinthians 13:5; Colossians 1:23; 1 Timothy 1:19; 2 Timothy 2:22
* lack of, Matthew 8:26; 14:31; 16:8

faithful (FAYTH-ful) *honest, loyal, true.*
* God is faithful, Deuteronomy 32:3–4; Isaiah 49:7; 2 Timothy 2:13; Hebrews 3:6; Revelation 19:11
* God's people must be faithful, Matthew 25:21; Revelation 2:10; 14:12; 17:14

fall, *sometimes used to describe the first sin.*
* Adam and Eve sinned, Genesis 3

false
* gods, Exodus 20:3; Deuteronomy 4:28; 1 Chronicles 16:26
* prophets, Deuteronomy 13:1–11; 18:22; Jeremiah 14:13–16; Matthew 7:15
* Christs, Matthew 24:24; Mark 13:22
* apostles, 2 Corinthians 11:13
* brothers, Galatians 2:4
* teachers, 2 Peter 2:1

family
* of believers, Galatians 6:10; Hebrews 2:11; 1 Peter 4:17

famine (FAM-in) *a time of hunger when there is very little food.*
* in Egypt, Genesis 41:30–31, 53–57
* in Moab, Ruth 1:1
* in Israel, 1 Kings 17:1
* in Jerusalem during Claudius' rule, Acts 11:27–28

fasting (FAST-ing) *giving up food for a while.*
* to show sorrow, 1 Samuel 1:11–12; 2 Samuel 12:15–22
* of Jesus, Matthew 4:1–2
* how to fast, Matthew 6:16–18
* combined with prayer, Ezra 8:23; Luke 5:33; Acts 13:1–3

father
* to be honoured, Exodus 20:12; Ephesians 6:2
* commands to, Colossians 3:21
* God as Father, Matthew 6:9; 23:9; 2 Corinthians 6:18; Galatians 4:6; Hebrews 12:4–11

fear, *a feeling of being afraid, or one of deep respect.*
* of God, Matthew 10:26–31; Luke 23:40
* overcoming, 2 Timothy 1:7; Hebrews 13:6; 1 John 4:18
* "your salvation . . . with fear and trembling", Philippians 2:12

feast (FEEST) *a special meal and celebration for a certain purpose.*

* Feast of Dedication, an eight-day celebration for the Jews that showed they were thankful that the Temple had been cleansed again, John 10:22
* Feast of Harvest, see "Feast of Weeks".
* Feast of Purim (PURE-rim) reminded the Israelites of how they were saved from death during the time of Queen Esther, Esther 9:18–32
* Feast of Shelters, "Feast of Booths" or "Feast of Tents", reminded the Israelites of how God had taken care of them when they left Egypt and lived in tents in the wilderness, Exodus 23:16; Deuteronomy 16:13–17
* Feast of Unleavened Bread, or "Passover"; reminded the Israelites how God brought them out of Egyptian slavery, Exodus 12:1–30; Numbers 28:16–25; Deuteronomy 16:1–8
* Feast of Weeks, or "Pentecost", the "Feast of Harvest", or the "Day of Firstfruits"; a feast of thanksgiving for the summer harvest, Exodus 34:22; Leviticus 23:15–22; Numbers 28:26–31

Felix (FEE-lix) *the Roman governor of Judea from AD 52 to 54.*
* put Paul on trial, Acts 23:23–24; 24

fellowship (FEL-o-ship) *sharing friendship and love with others.*
* with Christ, Matthew 18:20; 1 Corinthians 1:9; 1 John 1:3
* with the Holy Spirit, 2 Corinthians 13:14; Philippians 2:1
* with believers, Acts 2:42; 1 John 1:7

Festus (FES-tus) *governor of Judea after Felix.*
* put Paul on trial, Acts 25 — 26

fighting
* against evil, 2 Corinthians 10:3–6; Ephesians 6:12
* "fight the good fight", 1 Timothy 1:18
* "I have fought the good fight", 2 Timothy 4:7

fire, *used by God as a sign of his presence and power.*
* the burning bush, Exodus 3:1–6
* pillar of, Exodus 13:21–22
* chariot of, 2 Kings 2:11
* wrong kind of, Numbers 26:61
* fiery furnace, Daniel 3:25
* baptism of, Matthew 3:11
* of punishment, Matthew 5:22; 13:41–42; Mark 9:43; 2 Thessalonians 1:8; Hebrews 10:27
* everything destroyed by fire, 2 Peter 3:10
* evidence of the Holy Spirit, Acts 2:3

firstborn (FIRST-born) *the oldest child in a family; the firstborn son in a Jewish family received a double share of his father's wealth and became the leader of the family when his father died.*
* Esau sold his rights, Genesis 25:27–34
* Israelites as God's firstborn, Exodus 4:22; Jeremiah 31:9
* death of, Exodus 11:1–8
* given to God, Exodus 13:1–16

firstfruits (FIRST-fruits) *the first and best crops and animals the Israelites raised and gave to God at harvest time,* Exodus 34:26; Numbers 28:26; Deuteronomy 18:3–4

fish
* clean and unclean, Deuteronomy 14:9–10
* used in miracles, Matthew 14:17; Luke 5:1–7; John 21:1–13

flax (FLAKS) *a plant used to make clothing and ropes,* Exodus 9:31; Isaiah 19:9
* used by Rahab, Joshua 2:6

flood, Genesis 6:9–8; Matthew 24:37–39; 2 Peter 3:5–6

follower (FOLL-o-wer) *a person who is learning from someone else; a "disciple".*

- of John, Matthew 9:14; 11:2; Mark 2:18
- of Christ, Matthew 11:1; 28:18–20; John 19:38;
  Acts 6:1–7; 11:26

fool, *someone who is not wise,* Proverbs 10:8–23; 17:7–28;
26:1–12
- examples of, Matthew 7:24–27; 25:1–13
- rejects God, Psalms 14:1; 53:1; Romans 1:20–23

footwashing, *done as an act of hospitality in Bible times because people wore sandals.*
- examples of, 1 Samuel 25:41; Luke 7:44; John 13:1–17

forever
- God's love continues forever, 1 Chronicles 16:34; Psalm 136
- praise God forever, Psalm 44:8; Romans 9:5
- be with God forever, 1 Thessalonians 4:7; 1 John 2:17
- Jesus lives forever, Hebrews 7:24
- "word of the Lord will live forever", 1 Peter 1:25

forgiveness
- of others, Matthew 6:14–15; 18:21–35; Mark 11:25;
  Luke 17:3–4
- by God, Luke 24:47–48; Acts 10:43; Ephesians 1:7; 1 John 1:9
- not given, Matthew 12:31–32; Mark 3:28–29; Luke 12:10;
  John 20:19–23
- "Father, forgive them", Luke 23:34

fornication (for-ni-KAY-shun) *having sexual relations with someone to whom you are not married.* See "adultery".

fountain, Proverbs 10:11; 13:14; 14:27; 16:22

frankincense (FRANK-in-sens) *a very expensive, sweet-smelling perfume,* Exodus 30:34; Revelation 18:13
- given to Jesus, Matthew 2:11

freedom, *having liberty; not being a slave.*
- given to Jesus, Matthew 2:11
- in Christ, 2 Corinthians 3:17; Galatians 5:1; Hebrews 2:15
- from sin, Romans 6; 8:2; Hebrews 9:15
- to be used wisely, 1 Corinthians 8:9; Galatians 5:13;
  1 Peter 2:16
- "truth will make you free", John 8:32

friend
- characteristics of, Proverbs 17:17; 18:24
- of Jesus, John 15:13–15
- Abraham, as a friend of God, James 2:23

frontlet, See "box of Scriptures".

fruit, *often used to mean "result".*
- spiritual, Matthew 7:15–20; John 15:1–17; Colossians 1:10
- of the Spirit, Galatians 5:22

fulfil (full-FILL) *to give the full meaning or to cause something to come true.*
- prophecy fulfilled, Matthew 2:14–15,17–18; Luke 4:16–21;
  24:44–46; John 19:24

furnace
- Shadrach, Meshach, and Abednego thrown into, Daniel 3
- hell compared to, Matthew 13:42

G

Gabriel (GAY-bree-el) *an angel of God.*
- seen in a vision, Daniel 8:16; 9:21–27
- announced Jesus' birth, Luke 1:8–20,26–38

Gad, *a prophet.*
- David's seer, 1 Samuel 22:5; 2 Samuel 24:11–19

Gad, son of Jacob
- birth of, Genesis 30:9–11
- land of, Deuteronomy 33:20–21; Joshua 22:1–4
- tribe of, Numbers 26:15

Gadarenes (gad-ah-REENZ) *people who lived in Gadara, southeast of Lake Galilee,* Matthew 8:28–34

Galatia (guh-LAY-shuh) *a district of Asia,* Acts 16:6; 18:23;
Galatians 1:2; 1 Corinthians 16:1

Galilee (GAL-i-lee) *the country between the Jordan River and the Mediterranean Sea,* 2 Kings 15:29; Matthew 4:23; 21:11;
John 7:1

Galilee, Lake (GAL-i-lee) *or "Sea of Galilee", "Sea of Kinnereth", "Lake of Gennesaret", "Sea of Tiberias"; a lake twenty kilometres long and thirteen kilometres wide.*
- Jesus preached there, Matthew 4:12–22; 8:23–27;
  John 6:1–2,16–21

Gallio (GAL-ee-oh) *a Roman governor in the country of Achaia.*
- refused to punish Paul, Acts 18:12–17

Gamaliel (guh-MAY-lee-el) *a Pharisee and Jewish teacher of the Law of Moses.*
- prevented deaths of Peter and John, Acts 5:17–40
- Paul's teacher, Acts 22:1–3

gate
- Samson removed, Judges 16:3
- narrow, Matthew 7:13–14
- of heaven, Revelation 21:21

Gath, *one of the Philistines' five strong cities,* Joshua 13:3;
1 Samuel 21:10–12
- captured Ark taken there, 1 Samuel 5:1–10
- home of Goliath, 1 Samuel 17:4

Gaza (GAR-zuh) *one of the Philistines' five strong cities,*
Joshua 13:3; Judges 1:18; 1 Samuel 6:17; Amos 1:6;
Acts 8:26
- Samson in prison there, Judges 16

gazelle (gah-ZEL) *an animal of the antelope family; known for its beauty and speed,* Deuteronomy 12:15; 1 Chronicles 12:8

Gedaliah (ged-ah-LYE-uh) *made governor of Judah by Nebuchadnezzar after capturing Jerusalem,*
2 Kings 25:22–26; Jeremiah 39:14—41:18

Gehazi (geh-HAY-zye) *a servant of the prophet Elisha.*
- and the Shunammite woman, 2 Kings 4:8–37
- and Naaman, 2 Kings 5:1–27

Gehenna, See "Hinnom".

genealogy (jee-nee-AHL-o-jee) *a list of the descendants in a family.*
- of Jesus, Matthew 1:1–17; Luke 3:23–38

generosity (jen-uh-ROSS-et-ee) *unselfishness.*
- shown to Ruth, Ruth 2:14–16
- to the needy, Nehemiah 8:10
- rewarded, Proverbs 11:25; Matthew 7:11

Gennesaret, Lake of (geh-NEZ-a-ret) See "Galilee, Lake".

Gentiles (JEN-tiles) *anyone not Jewish.*
- received the Good News, Acts 10:44–45; 11:18;
  Romans 11:11–15; Ephesians 3:6–8
- conflict with the Jews, Acts 15:5–11; Galatians 2:11–14

Gerasenes (GER-uh-seenz) *or "Gadarenes".* See "Gadarenes".

Gerizim (GER-i-zim) *a mountain next to Mount Ebal about*

forty-eight kilometres north of Jerusalem.
* blessings announced from there, Deuteronomy 11:29; 27:12; Joshua 8:33

Gethsemane (geth-SEM-uh-nee) *a garden of olive trees just outside Jerusalem.*
* Jesus arrested there, Matthew 26:36–56; Mark 14:32–50

Gibeah (GIB-ee-uh) *a city about four kilometres north of Jerusalem,* Judges 19:12 — 20:43; 1 Samuel 10:26

Gibeon (GIB-ee-uhn) *a town about ten kilometres northwest of Jerusalem.*
* Joshua defeated Amorites there, Joshua 9 — 10

Gideon (GID-ee-on) *the judge who led Israel to defeat the Midianites,* Judges 6:1 — 8:35
* angel appeared to, Judges 6:11–24
* destroyed Baal idol, Judges 6:25–32
* defeated Midianites, Judges 6:33 — 8:21
* the sign of the fleece, Judges 6:36–40
* built an idol, Judges 8:22–27
* death of, Judges 8:28–32
* hero of faith, Hebrews 11:32–34

gifts, *talents or abilities.*
* spiritual, Romans 12:6–8; 1 Corinthians 7:7; 12; 14:1–25; Ephesians 4:7

Gihon (GYE-hohn) *a spring outside the walls of Jerusalem,* 1 Kings 1:38–39; 2 Chronicles 32:30; 33:14

Gilead (GIL-ee-ad) *the area that Israel owned east of the Jordan River,* Numbers 32; Deuteronomy 3:10–16

Gilgal (GIL-gal) *the first place the Israelites camped after entering the promised land,* Joshua 4:19 — 5:12

gittith (GIT-tith) *probably a musical word and a musical instrument,* Psalms 8; 81; 84

giving
* examples of generous giving, Mark 12:43; Acts 10:2; 11:29–30; 2 Corinthians 8:3–5
* proper attitude towards, Matthew 6:3–4; Romans 12:8; 1 Corinthians 13:3; 2 Corinthians 9:7

gleaning (GLEEN-ing) *to gather grain left in the field after harvest,* Ruth 2

glory, *visible sign of God's greatness.*
* appeared in a cloud, Exodus 16:10; 24:16–17
* seen by Moses, Exodus 33:18–23
* "The heavens tell the glory of God", Psalm 19:1
* seen by Ezekiel, Ezekiel 1:26–28; 3:23; 8:4
* at Jesus' birth, Luke 2:8–14
* of Jesus, Luke 9:28–32
* seen by Stephen, Acts 7:55
* in the temple in heaven, Revelation 15:8

gluttony (GLUH-tun-ee) *eating too much.*
* warnings against, Deuteronomy 21:20; Proverbs 23:20–21
* Jesus accused of, Matthew 11:19; Luke 7:34

goat
* for a sin offering, Leviticus 9:3
* divided from sheep, Matthew 25:32–33
* blood of, Hebrews 9:12–13; 10:4

God, *the One who made the world and everything in it.* See also "glory".
* the creator, Genesis 1; Acts 17:24; Romans 1:25

* nearness of, Acts 17:27–28; James 4:8
* goodness of, Matthew 19:17; Acts 14:17; Romans 2:4; 1 John 4:7–11
* eternal nature of, Psalm 102:24–28; 1 Timothy 1:17; 6:16
* names of, Exodus 3:13–14; 1 Timothy 6:15; Hebrews 12:9; James 1:17; 5:4
* power of, Job 9:4–19; Isaiah 40:12–31; Matthew 19:26
* mercy of, Exodus 20:6; Numbers 14:18; Ephesians 2:4
* justice of, Psalm 67:4; Acts 17:31; Romans 2:2

golden calf, *an idol made to worship false gods.*
* made by Aaron, Exodus 32:1–24
* made by Jeroboam, 1 Kings 12:26–33

golden rule, *a name often used for Jesus' command: "Do to others what you want them to do to you",* Matthew 7:12; Luke 6:31

Golgotha (GOL-goh-thuh) *Calvary; the hill where Jesus was crucified,* Matthew 27:33; Mark 15:22; John 19:17

Goliath (go-LYE-eth) *the giant from Gath whom David killed,* 1 Samuel 17

Gomorrah (goh-MOR-ruh) *an evil city near Sodom.*
* destroyed by God, Genesis 18:17 — 19:29; Matthew 10:11–15; 2 Peter 2:6

Good News, *also called the "gospel". Jesus died on the cross, was buried, and came back to life so people can be saved.* Mark 1:1; Acts 5:42; 13:26–39
* power of, Romans 1:16–17; Colossians 1:5–6; 1 Corinthians 15:2
* preached by the apostles, Luke 9:6; Acts 8:25; Philippians 1:5,12–14

Goshen (GO-shen) *an area in the Nile delta of Egypt.*
* home for Joseph's family, Genesis 45:9–10; 47:1–6,27

gospel (GOS-p'l) *"good news". The first four books of the New Testament are called the gospels because they tell the good news of what Jesus has done for us.* See "Good News".

gossip
* to be avoided, Romans 1:28–32; 2 Corinthians 12:20; 1 Timothy 5:13

government (GUV-ern-ment) *group of people in charge of managing and making laws for people in a country or city.*
* to be obeyed, Matthew 22:15–21; Romans 13:1–7; Titus 3:1; 1 Peter 2:13–17

governor
* Joseph, governor of Egypt, Genesis 42:6
* Nehemiah, governor of Judah, Nehemiah 5:14
* Pilate, governor of Judea, Matthew 27:2
* Felix, governor of Judea, Acts 23:26

grace, *God's kindness and love shown to us, even though we do not deserve them.*
* source of, Ephesians 3:7; Hebrews 4:14–16
* saved by, Acts 15:11, Romans 3:24; Ephesians 2:5–8; 2 Timothy 1:9
* misuse of, Romans 6; Galatians 5:4; Jude 4

grandchildren
* a blessing, Ruth 4:15; Proverbs 17:6
* inherit grandparents' wealth, Proverbs 13:22

grave, See "tomb".

Great Sea, See "Mediterranean Sea".

Greece, *once the most powerful nation in southeast Europe. Northern Greece was called "Macedonia". Southern Greece was called "Achaia".*
* Paul preached there, Acts 16:11–12; 20:1–6

greed, *selfish desire for more than one's share of something.*
* never satisfied, Proverbs 27:20
* beware of, Luke 12:15
* love of money, 1 Timothy 6:10

Greek, *the language of the New Testament.*
* the language of Greece, John 19:20; Acts 21:37; Revelation 9:11
* the people from Greece, Acts 14:1; 16:1; Colossians 3:11

grief
* of David for Absalom, 2 Samuel 18:33
* of the disciples, Matthew 17:23; John 16:6

guidance (GYD-ns) *direction.*
* by God, Exodus 13:21
* of the humble, Psalm 25:9
* of the Holy Spirit, John 16:15

guilt, *fact of having done wrong; regret, shame.*
* for improper worship, 1 Corinthians 11:27
* for breaking the Law, James 2:10
* cleansed of, Job 33:9; Isaiah 6:7; Hebrews 10:22

H

Habakkuk (HA-ba-kuk) *a prophet who wrote about the same time as Jeremiah,* Habakkuk 1 — 3

Hades (HAY-deez) *the world of the dead,* Revelation 6:8; 20:13–14

Hagar (HAY-gar) *Sarah's slave-girl.*
* gave birth to Ishmael, Genesis 16
* sent away by Sarah, Genesis 21:8–21

Haggai (HAG-ay-eye) *a prophet in Jerusalem when the Israelites came back from Babylon,* Ezra 5:1, 6:14; Haggai 1 — 2

half-tribe, *one of the two parts of the tribe of Manasseh. One half-tribe settled east of the Jordan and the other settled west of the Jordan.* Joshua 1:12–15; 13:8–9; 22

Ham, *the son of Noah,* Genesis 6:10; 9:18–19; 10:6

Haman (HAY-man) *the chief officer under Ahasuerus, King of Persia.*
* planned to kill the Jews, Esther 3 — 6
* hanged, Esther 7

hands, laying on, *a ceremony where a person places his hands upon another.*
* for healing, Mark 5:23; 6:5; Luke 4:40
* to receive the Holy Spirit, Acts 8:17–19; 19:6
* for blessing, Mark 10:16; Acts 13:3

Hannah (HAN-uh) *the mother of Samuel,* 1 Samuel 1 — 2:21

happiness
* of the people of God, Psalms 144:15; 146:5; Proverbs 16:20; Matthew 5:3–12
* comes from wisdom, Proverbs 3:13

Haran (HA-ran)
* Abraham's brother, Genesis 11:26–31
* home of Abraham, Genesis 11:31 — 12:5

harlot, See "prostitute".

harp, *the favourite musical instrument of the Jews.*
* first played, Genesis 4:21
* played by David, 1 Samuel 16:23; 18:10–11
* to praise God, Psalms 33:2; 71:22; 150:3

harvest
* of the poor, Ruth 2
* as a symbol, Matthew 9:37–38; 13:24–30,39; Revelation 14:14–16

hate
* seven things God hates, Proverbs 6:16–19
* a time to, Ecclesiastes 3:8
* of the world toward Jesus, John 15:18
* equal to murder, 1 John 3:15
* commands against, Galatians 5:19–21; 1 John 4:19–21

head
* a part of the body, Genesis 3:15; Psalm 23:5; Matthew 8:20; 1 Corinthians 12:21; Revelation 14:14
* a leader, Ephesians 1:22; Colossians 1:18

heal
* a time to, Ecclesiastes 3:3
* by faith, Matthew 9:21–22; James 5:15
* "Doctor, heal yourself." Luke 4:23

heart, *the mind or feelings; not the physical heart that pumps blood,* Deuteronomy 6:5; Matthew 22:37

heaven
* the home of God, Matthew 5:34; Mark 16:19; John 3:13; Revelation 4
* angel spoke from, Genesis 21:17; 22:11
* opened, Matthew 3:16; Acts 7:56; 10:11
* fire from, 2 Kings 1:10–14; 1 Chronicles 21:26
* third heaven, 2 Corinthians 12:2
* the new heaven, Revelation 21:1–4
* kingdom of, Matthew 3:2; 5:3,19–20

Hebrew (HEE-broo) *the language used by the people of Israel and for the writing of most of the Old Testament,* Acts 21:40

Hebrews (HEE-brooz) *another name for the Jewish people,* Exodus 7:16; 2 Corinthians 11:22; Philippians 3:5

Hebron (HEH-bron) *a city about thirty-three kilometres southwest of Jerusalem,* Genesis 13:18; Numbers 13:22; 2 Samuel 2:1–11

heir (AIR) *the person who inherits what belongs to a relative. Because through Christ we can be adopted children of God, Christians are heirs to God's riches*
* Abraham's heir, Genesis 15:3–4
* heir of God, Romans 8:17; Galatians 4:7

hell
* home of the devil and his angels, 2 Peter 2:4
* future home of sinners, Matthew 10:28; 23:33; Revelation 21:8
* descriptions of, Matthew 13:42; Mark 9:47–48; James 3:6; Revelation 14:11

helmet
* worn in battle, 1 Samuel 17:5; Ezekiel 23:24
* a symbol of salvation, Isaiah 59:17; Ephesians 6:17; 1 Thessalonians 5:8

help
* the stone of help, 1 Samuel 7:12
* the Holy Spirit as helper, Romans 8:26; Philippians 1:19
* from God, Psalms 46:1; 121:1–2; Isaiah 41:10

* commanded, 1 Thessalonians 5:14; Hebrews 6:10

Hermes (HER-meez) *the Greek god of skilful speaking and the messenger of the other Greek gods,* Romans 16:14

Herod I (HEH-rud) *"Herod the Great"; king of Palestine from 40 to 4 BC,* Matthew 2:1; Luke 1:5

Herod Agrippa I (uh-GRIP-a) *king of Palestine from AD 41 to 44,* Acts 12:1

Herod Agrippa II, *king of Palestine from AD 52 to 70,* Acts 25:13 — 26:32

Herod Antipas (AN-ti-pus) *king of Palestine from 4 BC to about AD 39,* Matthew 14:1; Mark 6:14; Luke 23:7

Herodias (heh-ROW-dee-us) *the granddaughter of Herod I.*
* asked for John's head, Matthew 14:3–12; Mark 6:17–28; Luke 3:19

Hezekiah (hez-eh-KY-uh) *one of the good kings of Judah.*
* destroyed idols, 2 Kings 18:1–8; 2 Chronicles 29 — 31
* attacked by Assyria, 2 Kings 18:9 — 19:37; 2 Chronicles 32:1–23; Isaiah 36 — 37
* life extended by God, 2 Kings 20:1–11; Isaiah 38
* death of, 2 Kings 20:12–21; 2 Chronicles 32:24–33

higgaion (hig-GI-on) *probably a time to think quietly during a song,* Psalm 9:16

high place, *a place to worship gods,* 1 Kings 14:23; 2 Chronicles 31:1; 33:3

high priest, *the most important religious leader of the Jewish people.*
* rules for, Leviticus 21:10–15
* of the Jews, Exodus 29:30; Numbers 35:25; Matthew 26:3; Acts 23:2
* Jesus as, Hebrews 2:17; 3:1; 4:14 — 5:10; 8:1–6

Hilkiah (hil-KY-ah) *high priest when Josiah was King,* 2 Kings 22 — 23; 2 Chronicles 34

Hinnom, Valley of (HIN-num) *an area where rubbish was burned just outside of Jerusalem; also called "Gehenna",* Joshua 15:8; 18:16; Nehemiah 11:30

Hiram (HY-rum) *king of Tyre when David and Solomon were kings over Israel.*
* supplied trees for Solomon's Temple, 2 Samuel 5:11; 1 Kings 5:1–18; 9:11–27; 10:22

Hittites (HIT-tites) *people who lived in what is now Turkey,* Genesis 23:1–16; Exodus 3:8; Joshua 1:4; 1 Samuel 11:3

Holy (HO-lee) *pure, belonging to and willing to serve God.*
* holiness of God, Leviticus 11:45; Isaiah 6:3; Hebrews 12:10; Revelation 4:8
* holy kiss, Romans 16:16
* people to be holy, Ephesians 1:4; Colossians 1:22–23; 3:2; 1 Peter 1:15–16

Holy of Holies, See "Most Holy Place".

Holy Place, *a room in the Holy Tent and the Temple,* Exodus 26:31–35; 28:29; Leviticus 6:30; 1 Kings 8:10–11

Holy Spirit (HO-lee SPIH-rit) *one of the three persons of God. The Holy Spirit helped the apostles do miracles and led men to write God's word; he lives in Christians today.*
* in creation, Genesis 1:2
* living in Christians, John 14:15–17; 1 Corinthians 6:19; Galatians 4:6
* as a helper, John 14:25–26; 16:7–15; Romans 8:1–27;

Galatians 5:22–25
* filled with, Luke 1:15; Acts 2:4; 7:55; 11:23–24
* sin against, Matthew 12:31; Acts 5:3; 1 Thessalonians 5:19; Hebrews 10:29

Holy Tent, See "Meeting Tent".

honest (ON-ist)
* heart, Luke 8:15
* people, 2 Kings 12:15
* answer, Proverbs 24:26
* commanded, Mark 10:19; Philippians 4:8

honour (ON-uh)
* for the old, Leviticus 19:32
* from God, 1 Samuel 2:30
* comes from humility, Proverbs 15:33
* to the deserving, Romans 13:7
* shown to parents, Exodus 20:12; Matthew 15:4
* shown to God, Proverbs 3:9; John 5:23; Revelation 4:9
* not shown to a prophet in his own town, Matthew 13:57

hope, *looking forward to something you really expect to happen.*
* reason for, Romans 5:3–5; 15:4; 2 Thessalonians 2:16; 1 Peter 1:13
* nature of, Romans 8:24–25
* results of, Colossians 1:5; Hebrews 6:18

Hophni (HOF-nee) *an evil son of Eli the priest,* 1 Samuel 2:12–34; 3:11 — 4:18

Horeb, Mount, (HOR-rebb) See "Sinai".

horses, Exodus 14:9; 1 Kings 10:26–29; Psalm 33:16–17; James 3:3

Hosanna (ho-ZAN-ah) *a shout of joy in praising God,* Matthew 21:9,15; Mark 11:9; John 12:13

Hosea (ho-ZEE-uh) *a prophet who lived about seven hundred years before Christ.*
* his unfaithful wife, Hosea 1
* his warnings to Israel, Hosea 2:4–14

hospitality
* of Abraham, Genesis 18:1–16
* teachings about, Romans 12:13; 1 Timothy 3:2; 5:9–10; 1 Peter 4:9

hosts, *armies; God is called the "Lord of hosts".* See "Lord of hosts".

Huldah (HUL-duh) *a woman prophet,* 2 Kings 22:14–20; 2 Chronicles 34:22–28

humble (HUM-bul) *not boasting or calling attention to yourself.*
* Moses as example of, Numbers 12:3
* humility commanded, Luke 14:7–11; 22:24–27; Ephesians 4:2; Philippians 2:3
* Jesus' humility, Philippians 2:5–8

hunger
* feeding the hungry, Matthew 25:34–35; Romans 12:20
* spiritual, John 6:35; 1 Peter 2:2

husband
* responsibilities of, 1 Corinthians 7:3–5; Ephesians 5:25–33; Colossians 3:19; 1 Peter 3:7

hymn (HIM) *a song that teaches us about God or praises him,* Matthew 26:30; Ephesians 5:19; Colossians 3:16
* Jesus and apostles sang, Matthew 26:30; Mark 14:26
* teachings about, Ephesians 5:19; Colossians 3:16

hypocrisy (hi-POK-ri-see) *acting as if one is good when that is not true,* Matthew 23:28; 1 Peter 2:1

hypocrite (HIP-oh-krit) *a person who acts as if he is good but isn't.*
* warnings about, Matthew 6:2,5,16; 7:3–5; Luke 13:15–17
* Pharisees as hypocrites, Matthew 15:1–9; 23:13–32

hyssop (HIS-op) *a small bushy plant; marjoram,* Exodus 12:22; Leviticus 14:4,6; John 19:29

I

Iconium (eye-KOH-nee-um) *a city in Galatia where Paul preached,* Acts 14:1–7,19–23

idol (EYE-d'l) *a statue of a false god.* See also "Baal", "Chemosh", "Molech".
* worship of, 2 Kings 17:12–17; Acts 17:16–23; 19:24; Romans 1:25
* warnings against worship of, Leviticus 19:4; Deuteronomy 6:14–15; 1 Corinthians 5:10–11; 6:9–10
* Baal, 1 Kings 18:17–40
* Chemosh, Numbers 21:29
* Molech, Jeremiah 32:35

ignorance (IG-nor-rance) *a lack of knowledge.*
* not an excuse, Leviticus 5:17

image, *likeness.*
* God's, Genesis 1:26–27
* Caesar's, Luke 20:24
* the Lord's, 2 Corinthians 3:18
* Jesus in God's image, Hebrews 1:3

immorality (IM-mor-RAL-i-tee) *evil; sinfulness.* See also "sin".
* warnings against, 1 Corinthians 5:9–11; 6:9–10; Galatians 5:19–21; Ephesians 5:5

immortality (IM-mor-TAL-i-tee) *life after death,* Job 14:1–14; Daniel 12:1–2; 1 Corinthians 15:12–58; 2 Timothy 1:10 See also "eternal life".

impossible
* people cannot do, Matthew 19:26
* for God to lie, Hebrews 6:18
* without faith to please God, Hebrews 11:6

incense (IN-sense) *a spice burned to make a sweet smell.*
* altar of, Exodus 30:1–10,34–38; Revelation 8:3–5
* used in worship, Psalm 141:2
* as a gift, Matthew 2:11

inheritance (In-HEH-ri-tence) *something valuable that is handed down within a family.*
* of land, Numbers 36:8; Deuteronomy 3:28; Psalm 25:13

iniquity, (in-I-kwi-tee) See "sin".

inn, *a place for travellers to spend the night,* Luke 2:7; 10:34

innocence (IN-oh-sense) *not guilty of sin.*
* of Adam and Eve, Genesis 2:25
* declared by Job, Job 34:5
* declared by Pilate, Matthew 27:24

inspiration (IN-spi-RAY-shun) *"God-breathed". It is used to mean that the Bible writers wrote what God wanted them to write,* 2 Timothy 3:16; 2 Peter 1:20–21

Isaac (EYE-zak) *the son of Abraham and Sarah.*
* birth of, Genesis 21:1–4
* offered as a sacrifice, Genesis 22:1–19
* married Rebekah, Genesis 24

* tricked by Jacob, Genesis 27
* hero of faith, Hebrews 11:20

Isaiah (eye-ZY-uh) *prophet who lived about seven hundred years before Christ.*
* became a prophet, Isaiah 6:1–8
* prophesied to Hezekiah, 2 Kings 19 — 20
* prophecies fulfilled, Matthew 3:3; 4:14; 13:14–15

Ish-Bosheth (ish-BOW-sheth) *son of Saul,* 2 Samuel 2:8–4

Ishmael (ISH-may-el) *son of Abraham and Hagar.*
* birth of, Genesis 16:2–16
* sent away from Abraham's camp, Genesis 21:8–21

Israel, kingdom of (IZ-ray-el) *the northern kingdom which had ten tribes.*
* beginning of, 1 Kings 11:27–12
* fall of, 2 Kings 17:1–18
* rulers of, 1 Kings 15:25–16; 22:51–53; 2 Kings 13; 14:23 — 17:6

Israel, son of Isaac, *Hebrew for "he who wrestles with God". Jacob's name was changed to Israel when he struggled with an angel at Bethel.* Genesis 32:22–28; 35:9–10. See also "Jacob".
* name given to Jacob's descendants, Genesis 49:28; Exodus 4:22; Psalm 22:23; Romans 9:3–5

Issachar (IS-uh-car) *a son of Jacob and Leah,* Genesis 30:18
* his descendants, Numbers 1:28–29; 26:23

ivory (EYE-voh-ree) *a creamy white bone that comes from elephant tusks,* 1 Kings 10:18; 22:39; Psalm 45:8

J

Jabbok River (JAB-ok) *a stream about eighty kilometres long that runs into the Jordan River,* Numbers 21:24; Joshua 12:2; Judges 11:13

Jabesh Gilead (JAY-besh GIL-ee-ad) *a small town on the east side of the Jordan River,* Judges 21:6–14; 2 Samuel 2:4–7

Jabin, king of Hazor (JAY-bin) *led a group of kings against the Israelites,* Joshua 11:1–11

Jabin, king of Canaan, *defeated by Israel when Deborah was judge,* Judges 4

Jacob (JAY-cub) *one of the sons of Isaac.*
* cheated Esau, Genesis 25:29–34
* tricked Isaac, Genesis 27:1–29
* his dream of a ladder to heaven, Genesis 28:10–22
* tricked by his sons, Genesis 37:10–22
* moved to Egypt, Genesis 45:25 — 47:12
* hero of faith, Hebrews 11:20–21

Jacob's Portion (JAY-cubs POR-shun) *a name for God, meaning he cares for Jacob's people,* Jeremiah 10:16; 51:19

jailer, *a keeper of a jail.*
* Paul and Silas, Acts 16:23

Jairus (JEYE-rus) *a ruler of the synagogue.*
* Jesus brought his daughter back to life, Matthew 9:18–26; Mark 5:21–43; Luke 8:40–56

James, brother of Jesus, Matthew 13:55; Acts 12:17; 21:18
* later an apostle, Galatians 1:19

James, son of Alphaeus, *an apostle,* Matthew 10:3; Mark 3:18; Luke 6:15; Acts 1:13

James, son of Zebedee, *an apostle of Jesus and a brother of the apostle John,* Matthew 10:2; Mark 10:35; Acts 12:2

Japheth (JAY-fith) *one of Noah's three sons,* Genesis 5:32; 7:13; 9:18–27; 10:1–5

Jashar, Book of (JA-shar) *a book mentioned in the Bible, but not part of it,* Joshua 10:12–13; 2 Samuel 1:17–27

Jason (JAY-son) *a Christian in Thessalonica,* Acts 17:5–9

jealousy (JEH-luh-see)
* to describe God, Exodus 20:5; 34:14; Deuteronomy 5:9
* examples of, Genesis 37:11; 1 Samuel 18:19; Matthew 27:18; Acts 5:17
* warnings against, Romans 13:13; 1 Corinthians 13:4; 1 Timothy 6:4; 1 Peter 2:1

Jebusites (JEB-you-sites) *people who lived around Jerusalem before the time of David,* Joshua 15:63; Judges 19:10–11; 2 Samuel 4:6–8

Jehoahaz, son of Jehu (jeh-HO-uh-haz) *king of Israel who lived about eight hundred years before Christ,* 2 Kings 13:1–9

Jehoahaz, son of Josiah, *king of Judah for only three months,* 2 Kings 23:31–34; 2 Chronicles 36:1–4

Jehoash (jeh-HO-ash) *a king of Israel,* 2 Kings 13:10 – 14:16

Jehoiachin (jeh-HO-uh-kin) *the next-to-last king of Judah.*
* surrendered to Babylon, 2 Kings 24:8–17
* in Babylon, 2 Kings 25:27–30

Jehoiada (jah-HO-yah-duh) *the chief priest in Jerusalem during Joash's rule,* 2 Kings 11 – 12; 2 Chronicles 22:11–24

Jehoiakim (jeh-HO-uh-kim) *king of Judah about 600 BC,* 2 Kings 23:34 – 24:6
* tried to kill Jeremiah, Jeremiah 26:1–23
* burned Jeremiah's scroll, Jeremiah 36:1–23

Jehoram (jeh-HOR-am) *or "Joram"; the fifth king of Judah,* 2 Kings 8:16-29; 2 Chronicles 21:4–20

Jehoshaphat (jeh-HOSH-uh-fat) *one of the good kings of Judah.*
* faithful to God, Chronicles 17:1–9
* appointed judges, 2 Chronicles 19:4–11
* defeated Moab and Ammon, 2 Chronicles 20

Jehovah (jeh-HOVE-uh) *a name for God; also translated "Lord",* Exodus 3:15; 6:3; Deuteronomy 28:58; Psalm 83:18

Jehu (JAY-hew) *an army captain who became king of Israel.*
* appointed as king, 2 Kings 9:1–13
* killed Joram and Ahaziah, 2 Kings 9:14–29
* stopped Baal worship, 2 Kings 10:18–35

Jephthah (JEF-thuh) *one of the judges of Israel.*
* fought the Ammonites, Judges 11:1–29,32–33
* his vow, Judges 11:30–31,34–39
* fought the people of Ephraim, Judges 12:2–7

Jeremiah (jer-eh-MY-ah) *a prophet who warned the people of Judah,* Jeremiah 1 – 52
* became a prophet, Jeremiah 1:1–10
* songs of, 2 Chronicles 35:25
* his prophecies fulfilled, 2 Chronicles 36:21–22; Matthew 2:17; 27:9
* wrote a scroll, Jeremiah 36

Jericho (JEHR-ih-ko) *probably the oldest city in the world,* Mark 10:46; Luke 10:30; 19:1
* fall of, Joshua 2 – 6
* rebuilt, 1 Kings 16:34

Jeroboam, son of Jehoash (jeh-ro-BO-am) *a king of Israel,* 2 Kings 14:23–29; Amos 7:7–17

Jeroboam, son of Nebat, *first ruler of the northern kingdom of Israel.*
* given ten tribes by God, 1 Kings 11:26–40
* built idols, 1 Kings 12:26–33
* warned by God, 1 Kings 13:1–34
* death of his son, 1 Kings 14:1–20

Jerusalem (jeh-ROO-suh-lem) *"Zion" or "City of David"; the greatest city of Palestine.*
* the City of David, 2 Samuel 5:6–7
* captured by Babylonians, 2 Chronicles 36:15–23
* Jews returned to, Ezra 1 – 2
* the new Jerusalem, Galatians 4:26; Hebrews 12:22; Revelation 3:12; 21 – 22

Jesse (JEH-see) *father of King David,* 1 Samuel 16 – 17; 1 Chronicles 2:13–15; Luke 3:32; Romans 15:12

Jesus (JEE-zus) *"Saviour"; the son of God.* See also "Christ", "Son of David", "Son of Man".
* birth and childhood of, Matthew 1 – 2; Luke 1 – 2
* temptation of, Matthew 4:1–11; Mark 1:12–13; Luke 4:1–13
* miracles of, Matthew 8 – 9; Mark 6:30–56; Luke 17:11; 22:50–51; John 2:1; 11
* appeared with Moses and Elijah, Matthew 17:1–13; Mark 9:2–13; Luke 9:28–36
* forced men from the Temple, Matthew 21:12–13; John 2:13–17
* the Last Supper, Matthew 26:17–30; Luke 22:1–20; John 13
* trial and death of, Matthew 26:57 – 27:66; Mark 15; Luke 22:66 – 23:56; John 18 – 19
* appearances after resurrection, Matthew 28; Mark 16; Luke 24: John 20 – 21; 1 Corinthians 15:5–8
* Son of God, Matthew 3:16–17; 26:63–64; John 1:14

Jethro (JETH-row) *father of Moses' wife,* Exodus 2:16–21
* advised Moses, Exodus 18

Jews (JOOZ) *first, the tribe of Judah; later, any of the twelve tribes,* Ezra 4:12; Esther 3 – 10; Acts 2:5
* against Jesus, John 5:16–18; 7:1,32–36; 10:25–42
* Jesus, king of, Matthew 2:2; 27:11–14,29; John 19:17–22
* and non-Jewish people, 1 Corinthians 12:13; Galatians 3:28; Colossians 3:11

Jezebel (JEZ-eh-bell) *the evil wife of King Ahab.*
* married Ahab, 1 Kings 16:31
* killed the Lord's prophets, 1 Kings 18:4–14
* killed Naboth, 1 Kings 21:1–23
* death of, 2 Kings 9:30–37

Jezreel (JEZ-reel) *the name of a town and a valley near the Jordan River,* Judges 6:33; 1 Kings 21:1; 2 Kings 8:29

Joab (JO-ab) *the commander of King David's army,* 2 Samuel 2:12–3; 10 – 11; 14; 18 – 20; 24; 1 Kings 1 – 2

Joanna (jo-ANN-uh) *a woman Jesus healed,* Luke 8:2–3; 23:55 – 24:11

Joash, Gideon's father (JO-ash)
* protected Gideon, Judges 6:28–32

Joash, son of Ahaziah, *became king of Judah when he was seven,* 2 Kings 11 – 12; 2 Chronicles 22:10–14

Job (JOBE) *a wealthy man who honoured God.*
* ruined by Satan, Job 1 – 2:10
* wealth restored, Job 42:7
* example of patience, James 5:11

Joel (JO-el) *a prophet who wrote the book of Joel,* Joel 1 – 3; Acts 2:16

Johanan (jo-HAN-an) *a Jewish army captain,* Jeremiah 40:8 — 43

John, the apostle, *one of the sons of Zebedee.*
* called by Jesus, Mark 1:19–20
* at Jesus' transfiguration, Mark 9:2
* with Jesus in Gethsemane, Mark 14:33–42
* in the early church, Acts 3 — 4
* writer of Revelation, Revelation 1:1–4,9

John the Baptist, *Jesus' relative and the son of Elizabeth and Zechariah the priest.*
* birth of, Luke 1:5–25,57–80
* preached at the Jordan River, Matthew 3:1–12
* baptised Jesus, Matthew 3:13–17
* killed by Herod, Matthew 14:1–12

John Mark, See "Mark".

Jonah (JO-nah) *a prophet whom God told to preach to the city of Nineveh.*
* ran from God, Jonah 1:1–3
* swallowed by a fish, Jonah 1:4 — 2:10
* went to Nineveh, Jonah 3
* complained to God, Jonah 4
* the sign of, Matthew 12:38–41; 16:4; Luke 11:29–32

Jonathan (JON-a-thun) *the oldest son of King Saul.*
* David's friend, 1 Samuel 18:1–4
* saved David's life, 1 Samuel 19:1–7; 20
* death of, 1 Samuel 31:2

Joppa (JOP-uh) *a city on the coast of Palestine,* Jonah 1:3
* Peter preached there, Acts 9:36–42; 10:9–36

Joram (JO-ram) *son of Ahab; also a king of Israel,* 2 Kings 3:1–3; 8:29; 9:14–29

Jordan (JOR-d'n) *the only large river in Palestine.*
* Israelites crossed, Joshua 3
* Jesus baptised in, Matthew 3:13–17; Mark 1:9–11

Jordan Valley, *the valley along the Jordan River,* Deuteronomy 1:1; 3:17; Joshua 11:2

Joseph of Arimathea (JOZ-if) *took the body of Jesus down from the cross and buried it in a tomb Joseph had dug for himself,* Matthew 27:57–60; Mark 15:42–46; Luke 23:50–54

Joseph of Nazareth, *husband of Mary, Jesus' mother.*
* angel appeared to, Matthew 1:18–24
* went to register in Bethlehem, Luke 2:4–7
* took Jesus to the Temple, Luke 2:21–52

Joseph, son of Jacob, *one of the twelve sons of Israel.*
* sold into slavery, Genesis 37
* put into prison, Genesis 39
* interpreted dreams, Genesis 40 — 41
* reunited with family, Genesis 42 — 50

Joshua (JOSH-yoo-ah) *leader of the Israelites into the promised land.*
* spied out Canaan, Numbers 13
* chosen to replace Moses, Numbers 27:12–23; Deuteronomy 34:9–10
* conquered Canaan, Joshua 1; 3 — 12
* death of Joshua 23 — 24

Josiah (jo-SY-uh) *king of Judah about 640 to 609 BC*
* became king, 2 Kings 22:1–2
* found the lost laws of God, 2 Kings 22:3–20
* gave the law to the people, 2 Kings 23:1–30

Jotham, youngest son of Gideon (JO-than) Judges 9:1–21,57

Jotham, son of Uzziah, *a king of Judah,* 2 Kings 15:32–38; 2 Chronicles 27

joy, Psalm 43:4; John 15:11; 17:13; 1 Thessalonians 1:6
* a fruit of the Holy Spirit, Galatians 5:22
* God as the source, Psalms 43:4; 45:7; Romans 15:13
* joy from the Holy Spirit, Luke 10:21; Romans 14:17; Galatians 5:22; 1 Thessalonians 1:6

Jubilee (JOO-bih-lee) *a Jewish celebration that took place once every fifty years. Israelites were to let the soil rest, to free their slaves, and to return land and houses to their first owners or their descendants.* Leviticus 25; 27:17–24; Numbers 36:4

Judah, son of Jacob (JOO-dah) Genesis 29:35
* saved Joseph, Genesis 37:26–27
* deceived by Tamar, Genesis 38
* reunited with Joseph, Genesis 43 — 44
* tribe of, Numbers 1:26–27; 26:20–22; Joshua 15
* Jesus, a descendant of, Matthew 1:2–3; Luke 3:33–34; Revelation 5:5

Judah, kingdom of, *the southern kingdom when Israel split in two.*
* beginning of, 1 Kings 11:27 — 12:20
* rules of, 1 Kings 14:21 — 15:24; 22:41–50; 2 Kings 8:16–29; 11 — 12; 14 — 16; 18 — 24
* fall of, 2 Kings, 24:18 — 25:22

Judas Iscariot (JOO-dus is-KA-ree-ut) *apostle who handed Jesus over to be killed.*
* chosen by Jesus, Matthew 10:4; Mark 3:19
* apostles' treasurer, John 12:4–6; 13:27–29
* betrayed Jesus, Matthew 26:14–16, 47–50; Luke 22:1–6; John 6:70–71; 13:2,21–30
* death of, Matthew 27:3–5

Judas, brother of Jesus, Matthew 13:55; Mark 6:3

Judas, son of James
* an apostle, Luke 6:16; Acts 1:13

Jude (JOOD) *brother of James,* Jude 1

Judea (joo-DEE-uh) *the land of the Jews,* Matthew 2:1; 3:1; Luke 1:5; 3:1; Acts 1:8

judges (JUJ-ez) *leaders of Israel after Joshua and before the kings,* Judges 2:16–19; 3:7–4; 10 — 12; 1 Samuel 8:1–5

judging
* warnings against, Matthew 7:1–5; 1 Corinthians 4:5; James 4:11–12
* good kinds of judging, 1 Corinthians 5:12; 6:2; 10:15
* God's judging of people, Matthew 11:22; Acts 17:31; 2 Peter 2:9; 3:7

Judgement Day (JUJ-ment) *the day Christ will judge all people,* Matthew 11:20–24; 12:33–37; 2 Peter 2:9–10; 3:7–13

Julius (JOOL-yus) *a Roman soldier in charge of Paul while Paul was taken to Rome,* Acts 27:1–3

justify (JUS-teh-fy) *to make someone right with God,* Romans 3:24; 5:1; Galatians 2:16; Titus 3:7

K

Kadesh/Kadesh Barnea (KAY-desh BAR-nee-uh) *a town in the Desert of Zin,* Numbers 20:1–21; Joshua 10:41

Kenites (KEN-ites) *a tribe of early metal workers,* Genesis 15:19; Judges 1:16; 4:11; 1 Samuel 27:10

Kerethites (KAIR-uh-thites) *King David's bodyguards,*
2 Samuel 8:18; 1 Kings 1:38

Keturah (keh-TOO-rah) *Abraham's second wife,* Genesis 25:1–4;
1 Chronicles 1:32–33

key, *something that solves or explains.*
* to God's kingdom, Matthew 16:19
* to death, Revelation 1:18

Kidron Valley (KID-ron) *a valley between Jerusalem and the Mount
of Olives,* 2 Samuel 15:23; John 18:1
* idols burned there, 1 Kings 15:13; 2 Kings 23:4

kill
* Cain killed, Genesis 4:10–11
* laws against, Exodus 20:13
* of baby boys, Exodus 1:16; Matthew 2:16
* Jesus killed, Matthew 27:31–50; Mark 15:20–37;
Luke 23:25–46; John 19:16–30

kindness
* of God, Exodus 34:6–7; Jeremiah 9:24; Romans 2:4;
Ephesians 2:4–7
* commanded, 2 Corinthians 6:6; Ephesians 4:32;
Colossians 3:12; 2 Peter 1:5–7

king
* King of kings, 1 Timothy 6:15; Revelation 17:14

Kingdom (KING-d'm) *the kingdom of heaven is God ruling in the
lives of his people.*
* the nature of, Matthew 5:19–20; 19:14; Luke 17:20–21;
Romans 14:17
* parables of, Matthew 13:24–52; 18:23–35; 20:1–16;
25:1-30; Mark 4:30–33; Luke 13:18–21
* belongs to, Matthew 5:3,10; 19:14

Kiriath Jearim (KEER-yath JEE-ah-rim) *a town in the hills about
nineteen kilometres west of Jerusalem,* 1 Samuel 6:20 —
7:20; 1 Chronicles 13:5–6; 2 Chronicles 1:4

Kish, *father of Saul,* 1 Samuel 9:1–2

Kishon (KI-shon) *the name of a valley and a stream,* Judges 4:13;
5:21; Kings 18:40

kiss, *a greeting of friendship, love, or respect.*
* of Judas, Matthew 26:48–49; Mark 14:44–45; Luke 22:47–48
* holy kiss, Romans 16:16; 1 Corinthians 16:20; 1 Peter 5:14

Kittim (KIH-tim) *the island of Cyprus,* Genesis 10:4;
Numbers 24:24; 1 Chronicles 1:7; Isaiah 23:1,12

kneel (NEEL)
* Solomon kneeled before God, 1 Kings 8:54
* Daniel kneeled before God, Daniel 6:10
* everyone to kneel before Jesus, Philippians 2:10

knock (NOK)
* "knock, and the door will open", Matthew 7:7
* at the door, Luke 13:25
* Peter knocked, Acts 12:13,16
* Jesus knocks, Revelation 3:20

knowledge (NOHL-ij)
* tree of, Genesis 2:9,17
* value of, Proverbs 1:7; 8:10; 18:15; 24:5; 2 Peter 1:5–6
* lack of, Hosea 4:6; Romans 1:28
* limitations of, 1 Corinthians 8:1–2; 13:2, 8–10

Kohath (KO-hath) *a son of Levi,* Exodus 6:16–20;
Numbers 3:17–19

Kohathites (KO-hath-ites) *descendants of Kohath.*
* worked in the Holy Tent and Temple, Numbers 3:27–31; 4:1–20;
1 Chronicles 9:17–32

Korah (KO-rah) *the musician,* Psalms 42; 44 — 49; 84

Korah, son of Izhar, *rebelled against Moses,* Numbers 16:1–40

L

Laban (LAY-ban) *father of Leah and Rachel.*
* Jacob worked for, Genesis 29:13–30
* divided his flocks with Jacob, Genesis 30:29–43
* chased Jacob, Genesis 31:19–55

Lachish (LAK-ish) *a city about fifty kilometres southwest of
Jerusalem*
* Joshua defeated, Joshua 10

lake
* of Galilee, Luke 5:1–2; 8:22–23,33
* of fire, Revelation 19:20
* of sulphur, Revelation 20:10; 21:8

lamb (LAM) *an animal that the Jews often offered as a gift to God.*
* as sacrifice, Genesis 4:4; Exodus 12:3–10; Leviticus 3:6–11;
4:32–35; 5:6; 14:24–25
* Jesus, the lamb of God, John 1:29,36; 1 Corinthians 5:7;
1 Peter 1:19; Revelation 5 — 7

Lamech, a descendant of Cain (LAY-mek) Genesis 4:18–24

Lamech, son of Methuselah, *the father of Noah,*
Genesis 5:28–31

lamp, *a small bowl that held a wick and burned olive oil, thus giving
light,* Matthew 25:1–13; Luke 8:16–18
* "Your word is like a lamp for my feet", Psalm 119:105

lampstand, *a holder for a lamp.*
* in the Holy Tent, Exodus 25:31–40; Numbers 8:1–4
* in the Temple, 1 Kings 7:49
* symbol of the church, Revelation 1:12–13,20

language (LAN-gwij)
* world spoke only one, Genesis 11:1,6
* confused at Babel, Genesis 11:7,9
* Aramaic, 2 Kings 18:26; Ezra 4:7; John 19:20
* Latin, John 19:20
* Greek, John 19:20; Acts 21:37

Laodicea (lay-oh-dih-SEE-uh) *a town in what is now Turkey,*
Colossians 4:13–16; Revelation 3:14–22

Last Supper, *the meal Jesus ate with his followers the night before
his death,* Matthew 26:17–30; Mark 14:12–26;
Luke 22:7–20; 1 Corinthians 11:23–26

Latin (LAT-in) *the language spoken by the Romans during New
Testament times,* John 19:20

laughter (LARF-ter)
* Sarah laughed, Genesis 18:12
* mouths filled with, Psalm 126:2
* sorrow better than, Ecclesiastes 7:3
* changed into crying, James 4:9

law
* as rules, Romans 4:15; 6:14–15; Galatians 5:18
* as God's rules or teachings, Psalm 119; Romans 7:22; 8:7;
James 1:25; 1 John 3:4

Law of Moses, See "Teachings of Moses".

laying on of hands, See "hands, laying on".

Lazarus of Bethany (LAZ-uh-rus) *a brother to Mary and Martha and a friend of Jesus,* John 11:1–45; 12:1–11

Lazarus, *the beggar,* Luke 16:19–31

laziness
* brings poverty, Proverbs 10:4
* not to be fed, 2 Thessalonians 3:10

leadership
* blind, Matthew 15:14
* of own family, 1 Timothy 3:5
* elders worthy of honour, 1 Timothy 5:17

Leah *(LEE-uh) a wife of Jacob,* Genesis 29:15–35; 30:9–21; 49:31

leather, Leviticus 13:47–59; Matthew 3:4

leaven, See "yeast".

Lebanon (LEH-boh-nun) *a country north of Israel.*
* cedars of, 1 Kings 5:1–11; Ezra 3:7
* prophecy of Lebanon's fall, Isaiah 10:34

Legion (LEE-jun) *a man who had many evil spirits in him,* Mark 5:9; Luke 8:30

lend
* money, Exodus 22:25
* borrower, a servant to lender, Proverbs 22:7
* sinners to sinners, Luke 6:34
* to enemies, Luke 6:35

leprosy (LEH-proh-see) *bad skin disease. A person with leprosy was called a leper and had to live outside the city.* Leviticus 13:45–46
* disease of Naaman, 2 Kings 5:1–27
* healed by Jesus, Matthew 8:2–3; Luke 7:11–19

Leviathan (lee-VI-ah-than) *a sea monster; possibly a crocodile,* Job 3:8; 41:1; Psalm 74:14; Isaiah 27:1

Levites (LEE-vites) *descendants of Levi, one of Jacob's sons.*
* served as priests, Numbers 1:47–53; 8:5–26; Deuteronomy 10:8–9; 18:1–8
* towns assigned to, Joshua 21

liar
* better to be poor, Proverbs 19:22
* Satan as a, John 8:44
* Cretans as, Titus 1:12
* to be punished, Revelation 21:8

lid on the Ark of the Agreement, *the mercy seat; the gold lid on the Ark of the Agreement,* Exodus 25:17–22; Hebrews 9:5

life
* breath of, Genesis 2:7
* book of, Philippians 4:3; Revelation 3:5; 21:27
* in the blood, Leviticus 17:14
* length of, Psalm 90:10
* true life, John 12:25
* "I am the . . . life", John 14:6
* eternal, John 5:24–29; 6:35–51

light
* creation of, Genesis 1:3–4
* of the world, Matthew 5:14
* God is, 1 Timothy 6:16; 1 John 1:5
* Jesus is, John 1:4–9; 3:19–20; 8:12; 12:46
* God's word is light, Psalm 119:105
* symbol of God's presence, 2 Corinthians 4:6;

Ephesians 5:8–9; 1 Peter 2:9

linen (LIH-nin) *a type of cloth made from the flax plant.*
* used for priests' clothes, Exodus 28:39–42; Leviticus 6:10
* used for royal clothes, Esther 8:15
* Jesus' body wrapped in, Matthew 27:59

lion
* killed by Samson, Judges 14:5–18
* killed by David, 1 Samuel 17:34–37
* devil like a lion, 1 Peter 5:8

lips
* touched by hot coal, Isaiah 6:5–7

loaves
* used to feed five thousand, Matthew 14:17–19
* used to feed four thousand, Matthew 15:34–38

locust (LO-cust) *an insect that looks like a grasshopper. They travel in large groups and can destroy crops.*
* as a plague, Exodus 10:3–19; Deuteronomy 28:38–42; Joel 1:1–4; Nahum 3:15–17
* food for John the Baptist, Matthew 3:4; Mark 1:6

Lord, *master or one who is in control; ruler of all the world and universe.*
* God as Lord, Exodus 3:15; 7:16; Psalms 31:5; 106:48
* Jesus as Lord, Acts 2:36; 1 Corinthians 8:6; Philippians 2:11; 2 Peter 3:15
* Holy Spirit as Lord, 2 Corinthians 3:18

LORD, *personal name of God, the Hebrew translation of God, Yahweh,* Genesis 4:1

Lord All-powerful, *one of the names used for God, refers to his relationship withe the angelic hosts of heaven,* 1 Samuel 1:3

LORD God, *the Hebrew translation of the name of God, Yahweh Elohim,* Genesis 2:4

Lord GOD, *the Hebrew translation of the name of God, Adonai Yahweh ,* Genesis 15:2

Lord of hosts, *one of the names used for God; also called "Lord All-powerful" and "Lord Sabaoth",* 1 Chronicles 11:9; Psalm 24:10; Isaiah 6:3–5; Malachi 3:1–17

Lord's day
* the first day of the week, Acts 20:7; Revelation 1:10
* as the Judgement Day, 1 Corinthians 5:5; 2 Corinthians 1:14; 1 Thessalonians 5:2; 2 Peter 3:10

Lord's Prayer, *the name often give to the model prayer Jesus taught his followers,* Matthew 6:9–13; Luke 11:1–4

Lord's Supper, *the meal Jesus' followers eat to remember how he died for them; also called "communion".*
* beginning of, Matthew 26:26–29; Mark 14:22–25; Luke 22:14–20
* examples of, Acts 20:7; 1 Corinthians 10:16; 11:17–34

Lot, *Abraham's nephew,* Genesis 11:27–30
* divided land with Abram, Genesis 13
* captured, Genesis 14:1–16
* escaped destruction of Sodom, Genesis 19:1–29
* death of wife, Genesis 19:15–26

lots, *sticks, stones, or pieces of bone thrown like dice to decide something. Often God controlled the result of the lots to let people know what he wanted them to do.*
* Canaan divided by, Numbers 26:55–56
* Jonah found guilty by, Jonah 1:7
* Jesus' clothes divided by, Luke 23:34

* Matthias chosen by, Acts 1:26

love, *a strong feeling of affection, loyalty and concern for someone.*

* love of God commanded, Deuteronomy 6:5; 11:1; Matthew 22:36–38
* of God for people, Psalm 36; John 3:16; Romans 5:8; 8:39; Ephesians 1:4; 1 John 4:10–11
* of people for God, 1 Corinthians 8:3; 1 John 5:3
* of Christ for people, John 13:1; 15:9; Romans 8:35; Galatians 2:20; 1 John 3:16
* of people for Christ, Matthew 10:37; 1 Corinthians 16:22; 1 Peter 1:8
* of people for each other, Leviticus 19:18; Luke 6:27–35; John 13:34–35; 1 Corinthians 13; 1 John 4:7

Luke, *a non-Jewish doctor who often travelled with the apostle Paul,* Colossians 4:14; 2 Timothy 4:11

lust, *wanting something evil.*

* to be avoided, Proverbs 6:25; Matthew 5:28; Colossians 3:5; 1 Thessalonians 4:5
* typical of the ungodly, Romans 1:26; 1 Peter 4:3

Lydia (LID-ee-uh) *a woman from the city of Thyatira who sold purple cloth,* Acts 16:13–15,40

lying

* warnings against, Ephesians 4:25; Colossians 3:9; Revelation 21:8
* devil as a liar, John 8:44
* to the Holy Spirit, Acts 5:1–6

lyre (LIRE) *a musical instrument with strings, similar to a harp,* 1 Chronicles 15:16; Psalms 33:2; 81:2

Lystra (LIS-tra) *a city of Lycaonia.*

* Paul preached there, Acts 14:6–20; 16:1; 2 Timothy 3:11

M

Macedonia (mas-eh-DOH-nee-uh) *the northern part of Greece.*

* Paul preached there, Acts 16:6–10; 20:1–6; 1 Corinthians 16:5–9; Philippians 4:15

Machpelah (mack-PEE-luh) *the land Abraham bought from Ephron, the Hittite.*

* Sarah buried there, Genesis 23:7–19
* Abraham buried there, Genesis 25:7–10
* Jacob buried there, Genesis 49:29–33; 50:12–13

magic (MAJ-ik) *trying to use the power of evil spirits to make unnatural things happen.*

* magicians of Egypt, Genesis 41:8; Exodus 7:11–12
* condemned, Leviticus 19:26; 20:27; Deuteronomy 18:10–12
* Simon the magician, Acts 8:9–24
* Elymas the magician, Acts 13:6–11
* Ephesian magicians burn their books, Acts 19:17–19

mahalath (mah-HAY-lath) *probably a musical word; may be the name of a tune or may mean to dance and shout,* Psalms 53; 88

Malachi (MAL-uh-ky) *a prophet who lived about the time of Nehemiah. He wrote the last book of the Old Testament.* Malachi 1:1

man, *humankind; a male.*

* created by God, Genesis 1:26–27; 2:7–23
* born of woman, Job 14:1
* important to God, Psalm 8:4–8
* woman created for, 1 Corinthians 11:9

Manasseh, son of Hezekiah (mah-NASS-uh) *a king of Judah for fifty-five years,* 2 Kings 21:1–17; 2 Chronicles 33:1–20

Manasseh, son of Joseph, *older brother of Ephraim. His descendants were the tribe of Manasseh.* Genesis 41:51; 46:20; 48:1–20

* descendants of, Numbers 1:34; 26:29–34; Joshua 13:8–13; 17
* eastern half-tribe, Joshua 1:12–17; 22
* western half-tribe, Joshua 21:5,25; 22:7

manger (MAIN-jur) *a box where animals are fed,* Luke 2:6–17

manna (MAN-uh) *the white, sweet-tasting food God gave the people of Israel in the wilderness. It appeared on the ground during the night so they could gather it in the morning.*

* God sent to Israel, Exodus 16:11–36; Joshua 5:10–12
* kept in the Ark, Exodus 16:31–34; Hebrews 9:1–4

Manoah (man-NO-uh) *the father of Samson,* Judges 13

Marduk (MAR-dook) *a god of the Babylonians. The Babylonians believed that people were evil because Marduk had created them from the blood of an evil god.* Jeremiah 50:2

Mark, *John Mark; a cousin to Barnabas; travelled with Paul and Barnabas and wrote the Gospel of Mark,* Acts 12:12,25; 13:5; Colossians 4:10; 2 Timothy 4:11

* left Paul, Acts 13:13
* travelled with Barnabas, Acts 15:36–41

marketplace, *usually a large open area inside a city where people came to buy and sell goods,* Matthew 20:3; Mark 7:4; 12:38; Luke 7:32; Acts 16:19

marriage

* teachings about, Mark 10:6–9; 1 Corinthians 7:1–16; Hebrews 13:4; 1 Timothy 5:14
* authority in, Ephesians 5:21; Colossians 3:18

Mars Hill, See "Areopagus".

Martha (MAR-thuh) *the sister of Mary and Lazarus who lived in Bethany.*

* criticised Mary, Luke 10:38–42
* at death of Lazarus, John 11:17–44

martyr (MAR-ter) *"witness"; one who knows about something. Later, martyr came to mean a person who was killed for being a witness.*

* Stephen, first Christian martyr, Acts 7:54–60
* James killed, Acts 12:2
* heroes of faith killed, Hebrews 11:32–37

Mary Magdalene (MAG-duh-lin) *a follower of Jesus from the town of Magdala; the first person to see Jesus after he came back to life.*

* at Jesus' death, Matthew 27:55–56,61
* saw Jesus after his resurrection, Matthew 28:1–10; Mark 16:1–11; John 20:10–18

Mary, mother of Jesus

* engaged to marry Joseph, Matthew 1:18–25; Luke 2:4–5
* angel appeared to, Luke 1:26–45
* birth of Jesus, Luke 2:6–21
* with Jesus in Jerusalem, Luke 2:41–52
* at wedding in Cana, John 2:1–10
* at Jesus' death, John 19:25–27
* with the apostles, Acts 1:14

Mary of Bethany, *sisters of Martha and Lazarus, and a friend of Jesus.*

* sat at Jesus' feet, Luke 10:38–42
* at death of Lazarus, John 11:1–45
* poured oil on Jesus' feet, John 12:1–8

maskil (MAS-kil) *probably a description of the kind of song that some of the Psalms were,* Psalms 32; 42; 44; 45

master, *lord; ruler.*
* "No one can serve two masters." Matthew 6:24
* not to be called, Matthew 23:10
* to be obeyed, Ephesians 6:5
* how to treat slaves, Ephesians 6:9
* in heaven, Ephesians 6:9; Colossians 4:1
* Jesus as, Luke 5:5; 8:24; 17:13

Matthew (MATH-you) *also called Levi; a tax collector; wrote the Gospel of Matthew,* Matthew 9:9–10; 10:3; Acts 1:13

Matthias (ma-THY-us) *chosen to be an apostle after Judas Iscariot killed himself,* Acts 1:15–26

meat
* given by God in the wilderness, Exodus 16:1–15; Numbers 11:4–34; Psalm 78:27
* eating meat sacrificed to idols, Acts 15:20; 1 Corinthians 8; 10:25–32

Medes (MEEDS) *the people who lived in Media, which is called "Iran" today,* 2 Kings 17:6; Ezra 6:2; Esther 1:3–19; Daniel 5:28; 6:8–15

mediator (MEE-dee-ay-ter) *a go-between.*
* Jesus as, 1 Timothy 2:5

medicine
* happy heart as, Proverbs 17:22

Mediterranean Sea (med-ih-teh-RANE-ee-un) *a large sea west of Canaan; also called the "Great Sea" or the "Western Sea",* Numbers 34:6–7; Joshua 1:4

medium (MEED-ee-um) *a person who tries to help living people talk to the spirits of the dead.*
* condemned, Leviticus 19:31; Deuteronomy 18:11–13; Isaiah 8:19–20
* of Endor, 1 Samuel 28
* Josiah destroyed mediums, 2 Kings 23:24

Meeting Tent, *"Tabernacle" or "Holy Tent"; a special tent where the Israelites worshipped God. It was used from the time they left Egypt until Solomon built the Temple in Jerusalem.*
* description of, Exodus 25 — 27
* set up, Exodus 39:32 — 40:36

Megiddo (meh-GID-oh) *important town in northern Israel where many battles were fought. The book of Revelation tells about a great battle between good and evil at "Armageddon", which means "the hill of Megiddo".* Joshua 12:8–21; 2 Kings 23:29–30; Revelation 16:16

Melchizedek (mel-KIZ-ih-dek) *priest and king who worshipped God in the time of Abraham,* Genesis 14:17–24
* Christ compared to, Hebrews 5:4–10; 7

Mene, mene, tekel, parsin (MEE-nee, TEH-kul, PAR-sun) *the words written on the wall by a mysterious hand at Belshazzar's feast,* Daniel 5

Mephibosheth (me-FIB-o-sheth) *crippled son of Jonathan,* 2 Samuel 4:4
* David's agreement with, 2 Samuel 9
* tricked by Ziba, 2 Samuel 16:1–4; 19:24–30

Merab (ME-rab) *daughter of King Saul,* 1 Samuel 14:49; 18:17–19

Merarites (meh-RA-rites) *descendants of Merari, a son of Levi; they were responsible for caring for the frame of the Holy Tent,* Numbers 3:17,33–37; 4:29–33

mercy (MUR-see) *kindness and forgiveness.*
* God's mercy to people, Exodus 34:6; Deuteronomy 4:31; Luke 1:50; Ephesians 2:4
* people's mercy to each other, Matthew 5:7; James 2:13

mercy seat, See "lid on the Ark of the Agreement".

Mesha (MEE-shuh) *an evil king of Moab,* 2 Kings 3:4–27

Meshach (MEE-shack) *friend of Daniel who was put in the fiery furnace,* Daniel 1 — 3

messenger, 1 Samuel 23:27; 1 Kings 19:2
* John the Baptist as, Matthew 11:10; Mark 1:2; Luke 7:27
* of Satan, 2 Corinthians 12:7

Messiah (meh-SYE-uh) *"anointed one"; the Greek word for Messiah is "Christ". Christians believe that Jesus is the Messiah or the Christ.* John 1:40–41; 4:25–26

Methuselah (meh-THOO-zeh-lah) *lived 969 years, longer than anyone else in the Bible; the son of Enoch and the grandfather of Noah,* Genesis 5:21–27

Micah (MY-cuh) *a prophet who told the people of Israel and Judah about their sins,* Micah 1 — 7

Micaiah (my-KAY-uh) *a prophet of God,* 1 Kings 22:8–28; 2 Chronicles 18

Michael (MY-kul) *the archangel of God,* Jude 9; Revelation 12:7

Michal (MY-kul) *a daughter of Saul and wife of David,* 1 Samuel 18:20–29; 19:11–17; 2 Samuel 3:13–16
* criticised David, 2 Samuel 6:16–23

Michmash (MIK-mash) *a hilly area about ten kilometres northeast of Jerusalem,* 1 Samuel 13:23 — 14:23; Isaiah 10:28

Midian (MID-ee-un) *a son of Abraham; his descendants were called "Midianites",* Genesis 25:1–6
* Joseph sold to, Genesis 37:18–36
* Jethro, a descendant of, Exodus 2:15–21
* enemy of Israel, Judges 6 — 7

midnight
* when the firstborn of Egypt died, Exodus 12:29
* Paul and Silas freed from jail, Acts 16:25–26
* Paul preached until, Acts 20:7

miktam (MIK-tam) *a kind of song that may describe some of the Psalms. It may mean that it is a sad song or a song about danger.* Psalms 16; 56 — 60

mildew (MIL-dyu) *a growth that appears on things that have been damp for a long time,* Leviticus 13:47–59; 14:33–54

milk, 1 Peter 2:2

millstones, *huge stones used for grinding grain into flour or meal,* Deuteronomy 24:6; Matthew 18:6; Luke 17:1–2
* used to kill Abimelech, Judges 9:53; 2 Samuel 11:21

minister (MIN-i-ster) *servant; one who lives serving God and others,* Romans 15:15–16; Colossians 4:7

miracle (MIR-ik-'l) *"wonderful thing"; a great event which can be done only by God's help. Miracles are special signs to show God's power.*
* purpose of, Exodus 10:1–2; Mark 2:8–12; John 2:11; Acts 3:1–10
* over nature, Exodus 14:21–22; Joshua 10:12–13; Matthew 8:23–27; 14:22–32; 21:18–22
* of healing, Matthew 8:14–17; 9:27–31; Mark 7:31–37; Acts 14:3
* of bringing people back to life, Mark 5:21–43; John 11:1–44; Acts 9:36–43

Miriam (MIR-ee-um) *the sister of Moses and Aaron.*
* watched over Moses, Exodus 2:1–8
* song of, Exodus 15:19–21
* punished, Numbers 12:1–15
* death of, Numbers 20:1

mistress (MISS-tres) *a female head of the household,* Proverbs 30:21–23
* Hagar as, Genesis 16:4–9

Mizpah (MIZ-par) *the place where Jacob and Laban made a pile of stones to remind them of their agreement not to be angry with each other,* Genesis 31:44–49

Mizpah, the city, *a few kilometres north of Jerusalem,* Judges 11:29–34; 1 Samuel 7:5–16; 2 Kings 25:23

Moab (MO-ab) *the country on the east side of the Dead Sea.*
* fought with Israel, Numbers 22:1 — 25:9; Judges 3:12–30
* home of Ruth, Ruth 1:2,4
* rebelled against Israel, 2 Kings 3:4–27

mob
* against Paul, Acts 17:5; 21:30–36

Molech (MO-lek) *a god of the Canaanite people. Those who worshipped Molech often sacrificed their own children to him by burning them on altars.* Leviticus 18:21; 20:1–5; 2 Kings 23:10; Jeremiah 32:35

money, *many kinds of money were used in Bible days – gold, silver and copper.*
* proper attitudes toward, Luke 16:13; Hebrews 13:5; 1 Timothy 3:3; 6:10

moneychangers, *people who traded money from other countries for Jewish money.*
* of the Temple, Matthew 21:12–13; Mark 11:15–17; Luke 19:45–46; John 2:13–16

Mordecai (MOR-deh-kay-eye) *a man who helped Esther to save the Jews from death.*
* discovered a plot, Esther 2:19–23
* asked Esther to help, Esther 4
* honoured by the king, Esther 6

Moriah (moh-RYE-uh) *the land where Abraham went to sacrifice Isaac,* Genesis 22:2
* site of the Temple, 2 Chronicles 3:1

mortar (MORE-tar) *a stone bowl where grain is ground into flour by pounding; also, the stick material that holds bricks together,* Genesis 11:3; Exodus 1:14

Moses (MO-zez) *the man who led God's people out of the land of Egypt; the author of the first five books of the Old Testament.*
* birth of, Exodus 2:1–10
* in Midian, Exodus 2:11 — 4:17
* led Israel out of Egypt, Exodus 4:18 — 12:51; 13:17–31
* received the law, Exodus 20 — 31
* struck the rock, Numbers 20:1–13
* death of, Deuteronomy 31:14 — 34:12

Most High God, *translation for the name of the one true God, maker of Heaven and Earth,* Daniel 4:17

Most Holy Place, *the inner and most special room in the Holy Tent and the Temple.*
* rules about, Leviticus 16:2–20
* in the Temple, 1 Kings 6:16–35
* entered by Christ, Hebrews 9:3–25

mother-in-law
* law about, Deuteronomy 27:23
* of Ruth, Ruth 1:3–4
* Peter's, Matthew 8:14–15; Luke 4:38–39
* family against, Matthew 10:35; Luke 12:53

mothers
* treatment of, Exodus 20:12; 21:15,17; Leviticus 19:3; Proverbs 1:8; 13:1; 23:22,25; Matthew 15:4; 1 Timothy 5:2,4

Mount of Olives, *a hill covered with olive trees near Jerusalem; site of the garden of Gethsemane,* Matthew 21:1; 24:3; John 8:1
* David cried there, 2 Samuel 15:30
* Jesus prayed there, Luke 22:39–53
* Jesus ascended from there, Acts 1:6–12

Mount Sinai (SYE-nee-eye) *a mountain in the Sinai Peninsula.*
* Lord spoke with Moses there, Exodus 24:16; Acts 7:30,38
* law given on, Exodus 31:18

Mount Zion (ZY-on) *one of the hills on which Jerusalem was built; later it became another name for the whole city of Jerusalem; also a name for heaven.*
* hill of Jerusalem, 2 Kings 19:31; Psalm 48:2,11; Isaiah 24:23
* as heaven, Hebrews 12:22; Revelation 14:1

mourning (MORN-ing) *showing sadness, especially when someone has died.*
* examples of, Genesis 50:3; Deuteronomy 34:8; 1 Samuel 31:11–13

murder
* laws against, Exodus 20:13; Deuteronomy 5:17; Matthew 5:21
* committed by Barabbas, Mark 15:7
* devil as a murderer, John 8:44
* full of, Romans 1:29

music
* to the Lord, Judges 5:3; Ephesians 5:19
* in the Temple, 1 Chronicles 25:6–7

myrrh (MUR) *sweet-smelling liquid taken from certain trees and shrubs; used as a perfume and a painkiller,* Genesis 37:25; 43:11; Proverbs 7:17
* given to Jesus, Matthew 2:11; Mark 15:23
* used in Jesus' burial, John 19:39–40

mystery (MIH-ster-ee) *a secret.*
* revealed by God, Daniel 2:28
* of the message of Christ, Romans 16:25–26; Colossians 2:2; 4:3
* of Gentiles also being saved, Ephesians 3:1–6; Colossians 1:25–27
* of life after death, 1 Corinthians 15:51

N

Naaman (NAY-uh-mun) *a commander of the Aramean army; healed by Elisha of a skin disease,* 2 Kings 5; Luke 4:27

Nabal (NAY-bal) *husband of Abigail.*
* refused to help David, 1 Samuel 25:2–13
* saved by Abigail, 1 Samuel 25:14–35
* death of, 1 Samuel 25:36–38

Naboth (NAY-both) *killed by Jezebel so she could steal his vineyard,* 1 Kings 21

Nadab (NAY-dab) *son of Aaron.*
* saw God, Exodus 24:1–11
* death of, Leviticus 10:1; Numbers 3:4; 26:61

Nahum (NAY-hum) *a prophet of God; wrote the book of Nahum,*
Nahum 1—3

naked
* Adam and Eve, Genesis 2:25
* realisation of nakedness, Genesis 3:7–10
* born, Job 1:21

Naomi (nay-OH-mee) *mother-in-law of Ruth,* Ruth 1:1–5
* returned to Bethlehem, Ruth 1:6–22
* encouraged Ruth, Ruth 2:19 — 3:4
* became a grandmother, Ruth 4:13–17

Naphtali (NAF-tah-lee) *the sixth son of Jacob; his descendants
were the tribe of Naphtali,* Genesis 30:7–8;
Numbers 26:48–50; Joshua 19:32–39

nard, *an expensive perfume which was imported from India,*
Song of Solomon 4:13; Mark 14:3; John 12:3

Nathan (NAY-thun) *a prophet during the time of David and
Solomon,* 1 Kings 1
* told David not to build the Temple, 2 Samuel 7:1–17
* told David the parable of the lamb, 2 Samuel 12:1–25

Nathanael (nuh-THAN-yul) *one of Jesus' twelve apostles; probably
also called "Bartholomew",* John 1:43–51

nation
* formed and spread, Genesis 10:32
* against nation, Mark 13:8
* Good News preached to every one, Revelation 14:6

Nazarene (NAZ-uh-reen) *a person from the town of Nazareth.
Jesus was called a Nazarene, so his followers sometimes
were also called Nazarenes.* Matthew 2:21–23; Acts 24:5

Nazareth (NAZ-uh-reth) *the city in Galilee where Jesus grew up,*
Matthew 2:21–23; Luke 4:16–30; John 1:45–46

Nazirite (NAZ-e-rite) *a special promise made to God, which had
rules about eating certain foods and cutting the hair.*
* rules for, Numbers 6:1–21
* made by Samson, Judges 13:2–7; 16:17

Nebo, god of the Babylonians (NEE-boh) Isaiah 46:1

Nebo, the mountain
* Moses died there, Deuteronomy 34:1–5

Nebuchadnezzar (neb-you-kud-NEZ-zur) *a Babylonian king.*
* conquered Jerusalem, 2 Kings 24 — 25; 2 Chronicles 36
* his dreams, Daniel 2; 4
* and fiery furnace, Daniel 3

Nebuzaradan (NEB-you-ZAR-ah-dan) *the commander of
Nebuchadnezzar's army.*
* captured Jerusalem, 2 Kings 25:8–12;
Jeremiah 39:8–14; 40:1–6

Neco (NECK-o) *king of Egypt from 609 to 594 BC.*
* killed King Josiah, 2 Kings 23:29–37; 2 Chronicles 35:20–27
* captured Jehoahaz, 2 Chronicles 36:1–4
* defeated by Nebuchadnezzar, Jeremiah 46:2

Nehemiah (NEE-uh-MY-uh) *led the first group of Israelites back to
Jerusalem from Babylon.*
* sent to Jerusalem, Nehemiah 2
* rebuilt walls of Jerusalem, Nehemiah 3 — 4; 6
* as governor, Nehemiah 8:9; 10:1

neighbour (NAY-bur)
* teachings about, Exodus 20:16–17; Leviticus 19:13–18;
Proverbs 3:27–29; Matthew 19:19; Luke 10:25–37

Nephilim (NEF-eh-lim) *people who were famous for being large and
strong. The ten spies who were afraid to enter Canaan had
seen the Nephilim who lived there.* Genesis 6:4;
Numbers 13:30–33

Ner (NUR) *father of Kish,* 1 Chronicles 8:33; 9:36,39

net
* fishing with, Matthew 4:18; Luke 5:5,6; John 21:6–11
* kingdom of heaven like, Matthew 13:47

new
* a new song, Psalms 40:3; 98:1
* a new name, Isaiah 62:2; Revelation 2:17
* new mercies every morning, Lamentations 3:22–23
* a new heart, Ezekiel 18:31; 36:26
* a new life, Romans 6:4; Ephesians 4:23–24; Colossians 3:10;
1 Peter 1:3
* a new agreement, Jeremiah 31:31; 1 Corinthians 11:25;
Hebrews 8:8; 9:15; 12:24
* a new heaven and earth, 2 Peter 3:13; Revelation 21:1

New Moon, *a Jewish feast held on the first day of the month. It was
celebrated with animal sacrifices and the blowing of
trumpets. It was to dedicate the month to the Lord.*
Numbers 10:10; 2 Chronicles 2:4; 8:13; Psalm 81:3;
Isaiah 1:11–17

Nicodemus (nick-oh-DEE-mus) *an important Jewish ruler and
teacher. Jesus taught him about spiritual life.*
John 3:1–21; 7:45–53; 19:38–42

night, *can refer to ordinary darkness or be a symbol of distress,
judgement, or evil.*
* created by God, Genesis 1:5; Psalm 19:1–2
* time of distress, Psalms 30:5; 42:8; 77:6
* time of judgement, John 9:4
* symbol of evil, 1 Thessalonians 5:5
* no night in heaven, Revelation 21:25

Nile River, *a river in Africa more than four thousand kilometres long.*
* baby Moses placed there, Exodus 2:1–10
* turned to blood, Exodus 7:14–25
* produced plague of frogs, Exodus 8:1–15

Nineveh (NIN-uh-vuh) *one of the oldest and most important
cities in the world. For many years it was the capital of
Assyria.* Genesis 10:8–11
* Jonah preached there, Jonah 1:1–2; 3 — 4; Matthew 12:41
* Nahum prophesied against, Nahum 1 — 3

Noah (NO-uh) *saved his family and the animals from the flood.*
* built the boat, Genesis 6:8–22
* saved from the flood, Genesis 7 — 8
* agreement with God, Genesis 9:1–17

Nob, *a town where priests lived during the days of King Saul,*
1 Samuel 21:1

noise
* joyful, Psalm 66:1
* of many people, Isaiah 17:12
* skies will disappear with, 2 Peter 3:10

noon
* sun to go down at, Amos 8:9
* bright light at, Acts 22:6

O

oath, *a promise or vow.*
* rules about, Matthew 5:33–37; 23:16–22; James 5:12
* God's oath, Hebrews 6:16–18
* examples of, 1 Samuel 14:24–28; 1 Kings 1:29–30; Psalm 132:1–12

Obadiah (oh-bah-DYE-uh) *a prophet of God who warned the Edomites they would be punished,* Obadiah 1–21

obedience
* to God, Leviticus 25:18; Deuteronomy 27:10; Acts 5:29
* to parents, Ephesians 6:1; Colossians 3:20
* to government, Romans 13:1–7; Titus 3:1–2; Matthew 22:17–21
* punishment for disobedience, Ephesians 5:6; 2 Thessalonians 1:8; 1 Timothy 1:9

offering *a gift or sacrifice. See "sacrifice".*
* brought by Cain, Genesis 4:3–5
* of non-Jewish people, Romans 15:16
* of Christ, Hebrews 10:5–18

Og (OHG) *the king of Bashan who was defeated by the Israelites,* Numbers 21:33–35; Deuteronomy 3:1–11

oil, *in Bible times usually means olive oil; used for cooking, medicine, burning in lamps, and anointing. See "anoint".*
* for lamps, Exodus 25:5–6; Matthew 25:1–10
* as medicine, Luke 10:34
* in offerings, Leviticus 2; 14:12–31
* in cooking, 1 Kings 17:10–16

ointment, See "perfume".

olive (OL-iv) *a small fruit; its oil was used in anointing ceremonies and as medicine. See "oil".*
* leaf, Genesis 8:11
* trees, Deuteronomy 6:11; 1 Samuel 8:14; Habakkuk 3:17; John 18:1

Omega, See "Alpha and Omega".

Omri (OM-ree) *an evil king of Israel,* 1 Kings 16:15–28

Onesimus (oh-NES-ih-mus) *the slave of a Christian named Philemon,* Colossians 4:9; Philemon

Onesiphorus (OH-nes-if-FOR-us) *a Christian friend of Paul who lived in Ephesus,* 2 Timothy 1:16–18; 4:19

onyx (ON-ix) *a precious stone with layers of black and white running through it,* Genesis 2:12; Job 28:16
* used in the holy vest, Exodus 25:7; 28:9–14; 39:6–7,13

Orpah (OR-pah) *the sister-in-law of Ruth,* Ruth 1:3–14

Ophir (OH-fur) *a land known for its gold and beautiful trees. Its location is uncertain.* Psalm 45:9; Isaiah 13:12
* Solomon traded with Ophir, 1 Kings 9:28; 10:11; 1 Chronicles 29:4

oven, *fire was built in the bottom of a clay barrel to bake bread,* Exodus 8:3; Leviticus 2:4; Hosea 7:4

oxen
* not to be coveted, Exodus 20:17
* as offering, Numbers 7:12–83
* not to be denied food, Deuteronomy 25:4; 1 Corinthians 9:9
* Elisha ploughed with, 1 Kings 19:19–21
* pulled the cart containing the Ark, 1 Chronicles 13:9

P

pain
* of a woman in childbirth, Genesis 3:16; Isaiah 13:8; Romans 8:22; Galatians 4:19,27
* not found in the new Jerusalem, Revelation 21:4

palace
* of David, 2 Samuel 5:11–12
* of Solomon, 1 Kings 7:1–12

palm tree, *a tall tree with long, fan-shaped branches growing out of the top; gives dates for food and wood for building,* Exodus 15:27; Nehemiah 8:15
* Jericho, city of, Deuteronomy 34:3; Judges 1:16; 3:13
* branches spread before Jesus, John 12:12–13

papyrus (pa-PY-rus) *a tall reed that grows in swampy places; used to make paper,* Job 8:11; 9:26

parable (PAR-uh-b'l) *a story that teaches a lesson by comparing two things.*
* of the kingdom of God, Matthew 13; 20:1–16
* of the lost sheep, coin, and son, Luke 15:1–31
* of the Judgement Day, Matthew 25

Paradise (PAR-uh-dice) *"garden"; a place where God's people go when they die,* Luke 23:43; 2 Corinthians 12:3–4

Paran (PAH-ran) *a desert area between Egypt and Canaan,* Genesis 21:20; Numbers 10:12; 12:16; 13:1–26

parchment (PARCH-ment) *a writing material made from the skin of sheep or goats,* 2 Timothy 4:13

parents
* responsibilities of, Ephesians 6:4; Colossians 3:21

Passover Feast (PASS-o-ver FEEST) *an important holy day for the Jews in the spring of each year. They ate a special meal on this day to remind them that God had freed them from being slaves in Egypt.*
* first Passover, Exodus 12:1–30
* commanded, Numbers 9:1–14
* celebrated by Jesus, Matthew 26:2, 17–19

patience (PAY-shentz) *to handle pain or difficult times calmly and without complaining.*
* of God, Romans 2:4; 2 Peter 3:9
* teachings about, 1 Corinthians 13:4,7; Hebrews 6:12
* comes from the Holy Spirit, Galatians 5:22
* commanded, Romans 12:12; Ephesians 4:2; 1 Thessalonians 5:14; James 5:7–8

Patmos (PAT-moss) *a small, rocky island in the Aegean Sea between Greece and Turkey,* Revelation 1:9

Paul, *the Roman name for "Saul". Saul was a Jew, born in the city of Tarsus. He became an apostle and a great servant of God.*
* conversion of, Acts 9:1–22
* name changed from "Saul", Acts 13:9
* healings by, Acts 14:8–10; 19:11–12; 20:7–12; 28:1–11
* imprisoned, Acts 23:35–28:31
* death of, 2 Timothy 4:6–8

peace
* from God, Psalm 29:11; John 14:27; Romans 5:1
* commanded, Romans 12:18; 14:17–19; Colossians 3:15
* Prince of Peace, Isaiah 9:6
* from the Holy Spirit, Galatians 5:22

pearl (PURL), Matthew 7:6; 1 Timothy 2:9; Revelation 21:21

- parable of, Matthew 13:45–46

Pekah (PEE-kuh) *an evil king of Israel,* 2 Kings 15:25–16:9; Isaiah 7:1–10

Pekahiah (peck-uh-HI-uh) *an evil king of Israel,* 2 Kings 15:22–26

Pelethites (PELL-eh-thites) *King David's bodyguards,* 2 Samuel 15:18; 20:6–7,23

Peninnah (pe-NIN-uh) *a wife of Elkanah,* 1 Samuel 1:2–6

Pentecost (PEN-tee-cost) *a Jewish feast day celebrating the summer harvest. The apostles began telling the Good News on Pentecost after Jesus died.* Acts 2:1–41; 20:16; 1 Corinthians 16:8

perfect
- describing Jesus, Hebrews 2:10; 5:9; 7:28
- describing God, Psalm 18:30; Matthew 5:48
- God's perfect law, James 1:25
- will of God, Romans 12:2
- love, 1 John 4:18
- people made perfect, 2 Corinthians 13:11; Hebrews 10:1–14; 11:40; 12:23

perfume
- used in idol worship, Isaiah 57:9
- poured on Jesus' feet, Mark 14:3–9; Luke 7:36–39; John 12:3

Pergamum (PER-guh-mum) *a town in the Roman province of Asia in what is now Turkey,* Revelation 2:12–17

Persecution (PUR-seh-CUE-shun) *trying to hurt people. Christians in the New Testament times were often persecuted by being put in jail or killed.*
- blessings with, Matthew 5:11–12; 1 Peter 3:8–17
- examples of, Acts 8:1–4; 1 Peter 3:13–15
- response to, Matthew 5:44; Romans 12:14; 1 Corinthians 4:12; 2 Corinthians 12:2
- of Christians, Matthew 13:21; 2 Timothy 3:12

Persia (PUR-zhuh) *a powerful country during the last years of the Old Testament; now called "Iran".*
- defeated Babylon, 2 Chronicles 36:20–23
- let captives return to Jerusalem, Ezra 1:1–11

Peter, *a fisherman; he and his brother, Andrew, were the first two apostles Jesus chose. First called "Simon", Jesus changed his name to "Cephas" or "Peter", which means "rock".*
- called to follow Jesus, Matthew 4:18–20
- walked on water, Matthew 14:22–33
- at the Last Supper, John 13:1–11
- defended Jesus, John 18:10–11
- denied Jesus, Mark 14:66–72; Luke 22:54–62
- preached the Good News, Acts 2:14–40
- an elder in the church, 1 Peter 5:1

pharaoh (FAIR-row) *the title given to the kings of Egypt.*
- made Joseph ruler of Egypt, Genesis 40–47
- made Israelites slaves, Exodus 1–14

Pharisees (FA-rih-seez) *"the separate people"; they followed the Jewish religious laws and customs very strictly. Jesus often spoke against them for their religious teachings and traditions.*
- practices of, Matthew 9:14; 15:1–9; Mark 7:1–13; Luke 7:30
- against Jesus, Matthew 12:14; 22:15; John 8:1–6
- criticised by Jesus, Matthew 5:20; Matthew 23

Philadelphia (fill-uh-DEL-fee-uh) *a city in the country now called "Turkey",* Revelation 3:7–13

Philemon (fy-LEE-mun) *a Christian in the city of Colossae,* Philemon 1–25

Philip, the apostle (FIL-ip) *friend of Peter and Andrew.*
- called by Jesus, John 1:43
- brought Nathanael to Jesus, John 1:44–50
- brought Greeks to Jesus, John 12:21–22

Philip, *the evangelist, a Greek-speaking Jew chosen to serve in the church in Jerusalem.*
- preached in Samaria, Acts 8:5–13
- preached to the Ethiopian, Acts 8:26–39
- his daughters prophesied, Acts 21:8–9

Philip, the tetrarch, *son of Herod I and Cleopatra.*
- ruler of Iturea and Trachonitis, Luke 3:1

Philippi (FIL-ip-eye) *a city in northeastern Greece,* Philippians 1:1; 4:15
- Paul in jail there, Acts 16:11–40

Philistines (FIL-ih-steyens) *people who were Israel's enemy for many years; worshipped false gods.*
- Samson defeated, Judges 15–16
- captured the Ark of the Agreement, 1 Samuel 4–6
- David defeated, 1 Samuel 17–18; 2 Samuel 5:17–25; 21:15–22

Phinehas, son of Eleazar (FIN-ee-us) *a priest and grandson of Aaron,* Numbers 25:1–13

Phinehas, son of Eli, *an evil priest,* 1 Samuel 1:3; 2:34; 4:4–11

Phoebe (FEE-bee) *a woman in the church in Cenchrea,* Romans 16:1

Phoenicia (foh-NEE-shuh) *an early name for the land on the east coast of the Mediterranean Sea; called "Lebanon" today,* Mark 7:26; Acts 11:19; 15:3

phylactery (fil-LAK-tur-ee) See "box of Scriptures".

pigs
- considered unclean, Leviticus 11:7
- snout of, Proverbs 11:22
- "don't throw your pearls before pigs", Matthew 7:6
- demons sent into, Matthew 8:30–33; Mark 5:11–13; Luke 8:32–33
- fed by prodigal son, Luke 15:15–16

Pilate, Pontius (PIE-lut, PON-shus) *the Roman governor of Judea from AD 26 to 36,* Luke 3:1; 13:1
- handed Jesus over to be killed, Matthew 27; Mark 15; Luke 23; John 18:28–19:38

pillar (PILL-ur) *a large stone that is set upright; also a tall column of stone that supports the roof of a building.*
- of Jacob, Genesis 28:18–22
- to worship false gods, 2 Kings 17:9–12
- in the Temple, 1 Kings 7:6,15–22
- of cloud and fire, Exodus 13:21–22; 14:19–24; 33:8–10

Pisgah, Mount (PIS-guh) *one of the high spots on Mount Nebo where Moses stood to see into the promised land,* Numbers 23:14; Deuteronomy 3:27; 34:1

plague (PLAYG) *a disaster. God sent ten plagues on the land of Egypt so the Egyptians would set the Israelites free.*
- on the Egyptians, Exodus 7–11
- on the Israelites, Exodus 32:35; Numbers 11:31–33; 16:41–50; 25:1–9

plumb line (PLUM LINE) *a string with a rock or other weight on*

one end. People used it to see if a wall was straight.
* symbol for God's judging, 2 Kings 21:10–13; Amos 7:7–8

pomegranate (POM-ee-gran-it) *a reddish fruit about the size of an apple*, Numbers 13:23; Joel 1:12
* design on priests' clothing, Exodus 28:33–34
* design of Temple decorations, 1 Kings 7:18–20

poor
* God's care for, Psalm 140:12; Proverbs 22:22–23; Matthew 11:5; James 2:5
* treatment of, Leviticus 19:9–10; Matthew 25:34–36; Luke 14:12–14

possessions
* promised land given to Israelites, Genesis 17:8; Numbers 32:22; Joshua 1:11
* proper attitudes toward, Ecclesiastes 5:10 — 6:6; Luke 12:13–21; Acts 2:45; 1 John 3:17
* danger of, Matthew 19:22
* sold by Christians, Acts 2:45

Potiphar (POT-ih-fur) *an officer for the king of Egypt. He put Joseph in charge of his household.* Genesis 39

pottage (POT-edge) *a thick vegetable soup or stew,* Genesis 25:29–34; 2 Kings 4:38–41

potter (POT-ur) *a person who makes pots and dishes out of clay.*
* as a symbol of God, Jeremiah 18:1–6

power
* of Jesus, Matthew 24:30; 28:18; Luke 6:19
* of the Spirit, Luke 4:14; Acts 1:8; Romans 15:19
* of Satan, Acts 26:18
* of the apostles, Luke 9:1; Acts 4:33

praetorium (pray-TORE-ee-um) *the governor's palace in New Testament times,* Matthew 27:27; Acts 23:35

praise (PRAYZ) *to say good things about someone or something. God's people can praise him by singing, praying, and by living the way he tells us to live.* 1 Chronicles 16:4–7; Psalms 103; 104; 145 — 150

prayer
* teachings about, Matthew 5:44–45; 21:18–22; Philippians 4:6; James 5:15–16
* Jesus' model prayer, Matthew 6:5–15

preach, *to give a talk on a religious subject; to tell the Good News.*
* Jonah preached to Nineveh, Jonah 3:2–4
* John preached, Matthew 3:1; Mark 1:4; Luke 3:3
* Jesus preached, Matthew 4:17; Mark 2:2; Luke 4:43–44
* Good News preached, Acts 8:25,40; Galatians 2:7; 1 Thessalonians 2:9
* preaching commanded, 2 Timothy 4:2

Preparation Day (prep-a-RAY-shun DAY) *the day before the Sabbath day. On that day the Jews prepared for the Sabbath.* Luke 23:54; John 19:14,31

pride
* warnings against, Romans 12:3; 1 Corinthians 13:4; Philippians 2:3; James 4:6

priest (PREEST) *in the Old Testament, a servant of God who worked in the Holy Tent or Temple. See also "high priest".*
* clothes for, Exodus 28
* appointing of, Exodus 29:1–37
* rules for, Leviticus 21 — 22:16

Priscilla (prih-SIL-uh) *a friend of Paul,* Acts 18:1–4,18–19; Romans 16:3–4
* taught Apollos, Acts 18:24–26

prison
* Joseph in prison, Genesis 39:20 — 41:40
* Peter in prison, Acts 5:17–20
* Paul in prison, Acts 16:23–34

prodigal (PROD-ee-gul) *careless and wasteful.*
* the prodigal son, Luke 15:11–32

promise
* from God, Joshua 1:3; 1 Kings 8:20; Galatians 3:14; Ephesians 3:6
* first commandment with, Ephesians 6:2
* Lord is not slow in keeping, 2 Peter 2:9

prophecy (PROF-es-see) *a message; God speaking through chosen people called "prophets",* Ezekiel 14:9; 1 Thessalonians 5:20; 2 Peter 1:20–21

prophesy (PROF-es-sy) *to speak a prophecy,* Acts 2:17–18. See "prophecy".
* a spiritual gift, 1 Corinthians 14:1–5

prophet (PROF-it) *a messenger; one who is able, with God's help, to tell God's message correctly. Sometimes prophets told what would happen in the future.* Matthew 11:13–14
* how to judge, Deuteronomy 13:1–5; 18:21–22
* examples of, Ezra 5:1; Jeremiah 1:1–9; Matthew 3:3
* false prophets, Deuteronomy 13:1–5

prophetess (prof-it-ESS) *a female prophet,* Exodus 15:20; Judges 4:4; 2 Kings 22:14; Luke 2:36. See "prophet".

prostitute (PROSS-ti-tyoot) *a person who sells his or her body for sex.*
* warnings against, 1 Corinthians 6:15
* examples of, Genesis 38:15–16; Jeremiah 3:1–3; Hosea 3:2–3; Matthew 21:32

proverbs (PROV-erbs) *wise sayings. The book of Proverbs contains many wise sayings that tell how to live a good and happy life.* 1 Kings 4:32; Proverbs

psalm (SAHM) *a song. The book of Psalms is like a songbook.* Ephesians 5:19; Colossians 3:16

publican (PUB-leh-kun) See "tax collector".

Publius (PUB-lee-uss) *an important man of the island of Malta,* Acts 28:7–8

Pul (PULL) See "Tiglath-Pileser".

punishment
* of Cain, Genesis 4:13
* everlasting, Matthew 25:46; 2 Thessalonians 1:8–9
* for rejecting Jesus, Hebrews 10:29
* by government, Romans 13:4; 1 Peter 2:14

pure
* gold, Exodus 25:11–39; 37; 1 Kings 6:20–21
* heart, Psalm 51:10; Matthew 5:8
* describing Jesus, Hebrews 7:26
* describing people, Job 4:17; 15:14; Philippians 1:10; Titus 1:15
* water, Hebrews 10:22

Purim, See "Feast of Purim".

purple, *a colour that, in Bible times, was worn by kings, queens, and other rich people. Purple cloth was expensive because the purple dye came from special shellfish.* Exodus 25:1–4; Judges 8:26; Mark 15:17; Acts 16:14

Q

quail (KWAYL) *a brownish-white bird.*
* given by God to Israel, Exodus 16:11–13; Numbers 11:31–34; Psalm 105:40

quarrel
* Israelites quarrelled with Moses, Exodus 17:1–7

Queen Goddess, *Ishtar; a goddess of the Babylonians,* Jeremiah 7:18; 44:15–29

Queen of Heaven, See "Queen Goddess".

queen of Sheba, See "Sheba, queen of".

question
* Solomon questioned by queen of Sheba, 1 Kings 10:1–3
* Jesus questioned, Mark 8:11; Luke 23:9; John 8:6
* asked by Jesus, Matthew 21:24
* apostles questioned by Jews, Acts 4:7; 5:27

quiet
* words, Ecclesiastes 9:17
* riot quieted, Acts 19:35–36
* life, 1 Thessalonians 4:11; 1 Timothy 2:2

Quirinius (kwy-RIN-ee-us) *the Roman governor of Syria when Jesus was born,* Luke 2:1–3

quiver (KWIH-vur) *a bag to hold arrows,* Psalm 127:5; Isaiah 49:2

R

Rabbah (RAB-ah) *the capital city of the Ammonites,* 2 Samuel 11:1; 12:26–29; Ezekiel 25:5

rabbi/rabboni (RAB-eye/rah-BONE-eye) *teacher. Jesus' followers often called him "rabbi" as a sign of respect.* John 1:38; 20:16

Rachel (RAY-chel) *a wife of Jacob and the mother of Benjamin and Joseph.*
* married Jacob, Genesis 29:1–30
* gave birth to Joseph, Genesis 30:22–24
* stole Laban's idols, Genesis 31:19–35
* death of, Genesis 35:16–20

Rahab, the dragon (RAY-hab) *In a well-known story, Rahab was defeated. Egypt was sometimes called Rahab to show that it would be defeated.* Job 9:13; Isaiah 30:7

Rahab, the prostitute, *a woman in Jericho. She hid the Israelite spies and helped them escape.*
* hid the spies, Joshua 2:1–21
* rescued from Jericho, Joshua 6:16–25
* an example of faith, Hebrews 11:31; James 2:25

rainbow
* a sign of God's agreement with people, Genesis 9:8–17

raisin, 1 Samuel 25:18; 30:12; 1 Chronicles 12:40

ram, *a male sheep.*
* offered instead of Isaac, Genesis 22:13
* used for burnt offerings, Exodus 29; Leviticus 8:18–29; Numbers 28:11–29:37
* with two horns, Daniel 8:3–22

Ramah (RAY-muh) *a town about eight kilometres north of Jerusalem,* Jeremiah 31:15; Matthew 2:18

Rameses (RAM-eh-seez) *one of the cities built by the Israelites when they were slaves in Egypt,* Exodus 1:11; 12:37; Numbers 33:3

Ramoth Gilead (RAY-moth GIL-ee-ad) *one of the cities of safety on the east side of the Jordan River,* Joshua 20:8; 1 Kings 4:13; 2 Kings 8:28–9:14

ransom, *payment that frees a captive.*
* Jesus as a ransom for sins, Matthew 20:28; 1 Timothy 2:6; Hebrews 9:15

Rapha (RAY-fa) *a leader of a group of people in Canaan who may have been giants. The descendants of Rapha are called "Rephaites".* 2 Samuel 21:15–22; Joshua 13:12

raven, *a large black bird similar to a crow which eats dead things.*
* sent out by Noah, Genesis 8:7
* fed Elijah, 1 Kings 17:4–6

read
* the Book of the Teachings, Joshua 8:34–35; Nehemiah 8:2–9
* reading the teachings commanded, Deuteronomy 17:18–19; 31:9–13
* brings happiness, Revelation 1:3

Rebekah (ree-BEK-uh) *the wife of Isaac and the mother of Jacob and Esau.*
* married Isaac, Genesis 24
* gave birth to Jacob and Esau, Genesis 25:19–26
* helped deceive Isaac, Genesis 27
* buried at Machpelah, Genesis 49:31

redeem (ree-DEEM) *to buy something back or to buy a slave's freedom.*
* property, Leviticus 25:23–34; Ruth 4:3–6
* slave, Leviticus 25:47–49
* redeemed by God, 1 Corinthians 6:20; Galatians 4:5; Titus 2:14

Red Sea, *Sea of Reeds; a large body of water between Africa and Arabia.*
* Israelites crossed, Exodus 13:17–14:31

refuge, *a place of safety or protection.*
* God as our refuge, Deuteronomy 33:27; 2 Samuel 22:3; Psalms 18:2; 31:2; 71:3; 91:2
* city of, Numbers 35:6–34; Joshua 20

Rehoboam (ree-ho-BO-um) *son of Solomon who took his place as king.*
* became king, 1 Kings 11:41–43
* Israel rebelled against, 1 Kings 12:1–24
* strengthened Judah, 2 Chronicles 11:5–17
* disobeyed God, 2 Chronicles 12

rejoice
* commanded to, Matthew 5:11–12; Romans 12:15; Philippians 4:4; 1 Peter 4:13
* examples of, 1 Samuel 6:13; Nehemiah 12:43

remissions (rih-MISH-un) See "forgiveness".

remnant (REM-nant) *a small part that is left; a name used for the Jews who were left alive after their captivity in Babylon.*
* of Israelites who returned to Jerusalem, Ezra 9:15; Nehemiah 1:2; Isaiah 10:20–22

repent (ree-PENT) *being sorry for doing something wrong and not continuing to do that wrong.* See "change of heart and life".

Rephaites, See "Rapha".

respect
* to parents, Leviticus 19:3; 1 Timothy 3:4
* between husbands and wives, Ephesians 5:33; 1 Peter 3:7
* to all people, 1 Peter 2:17; 3:16

rest
* on the seventh day, Genesis 2:2; Exodus 31:15; Hebrews 4:4
* given by the Lord, Psalm 95:11; Jeremiah 6:16; Matthew 11:28
* heaven as a place of rest, Revelation 14:13

resurrection (REZ-uh-REK-shun) *a dead person's coming back to life.*
* of Jesus, Matthew 28:1–10; Mark 16; Luke 24; John 20 — 21; Acts 2:24–32; Romans 1:4
* of God's people, John 6:39; Acts 24:15; 1 Corinthians 15; Philippians 3:10–11; Hebrews 11:35

Reuben (ROO-ben) *oldest of Jacob's twelve sons.*
* birth of, Genesis 29:32
* tried to save Joseph, Genesis 37:18–29
* descendants of, Exodus 6:14; Numbers 1:20; Joshua 13:15–23

revelation (rev-uh-LAY-shun) *showing plainly something that has been hidden,* 2 Corinthians 12:1; Revelation 1:1–3

revenge
* warnings against, Leviticus 19:18; Romans 12:19; 1 Thessalonians 5:15; 1 Peter 3:9

reward
* in heaven, Matthew 5:12
* for obedience, Psalm 19:11
* for what a person does, Matthew 6:1–18; 10:42; 16:27; Colossians 3:24
* children as a reward, Psalm 127:3

Rhoda (ROAD-uh) *a servant girl in the home of John Mark's mother,* Acts 12:6–17

righteousness (RY-chuss-ness) *being right with God and doing what is right.*
* explained, Romans 3:19–26; 2 Corinthians 5:21; 6:4–7; Philippians 3:8–9
* Abraham as an example of, Romans 4:3
* right living, 2 Corinthians 6:7; Ephesians 5:9; 1 Timothy 6:11; 1 Peter 2:24

robber
* Temple as a hideout for, Jeremiah 7:11; Matthew 21:13
* attacked man on road to Jericho, Luke 10:30
* killed with Jesus, Matthew 27:38–44; John 18:40

robe, holy, *"ephod"; a special type of clothing for the priests in the Old Testament. The holy robe for the high priest had gold and gems on it.*
* description of, Exodus 25:7; 28:6–14; 39:2–7
* one made by Micah, Judges 17:1–5; 18:14–20
* worn by David, 2 Samuel 6:14

Rock, *often used as a name for God. As a large rock is strong and provides a hiding place, so God is strong and protects us from our enemies.* Genesis 49:24; 2 Samuel 22:32–49; Psalm 19:14

rock badger (ROK-BAD-jur) *a coney; a small, tailless animal like a rabbit that hides among the mountain gorges and rocky areas of Arabia,* Psalm 104:18; Proverbs 30:26

Rome, *the capital city of the Roman Empire at the time of Christ,* Acts 2:10; 18:2; Romans 1:7
* Paul sent there, Acts 23:11; 28:14–15

roof
* spies hid there, Joshua 2:6
* David saw Bathsheba from there, 2 Samuel 11:2
* built room for Elisha there, 2 Kings 4:8–10
* man lowered through, Mark 2:3–4

* Peter prayed there, Acts 10:9

rue (roo) *a garden plant used for seasoning and medicine,* Luke 11:42

Ruth (ROOTH) *a widow from Moab.*
* moved to Judah, Ruth 1
* worked in Boaz's field, Ruth 2
* married Boaz, Ruth 3 — 4
* birth of Obed, Ruth 4:13–22

S

Sabbath (SAB-uth) *means "rest"; the seventh day of the Jewish week; the Jews' day to worship God. They were not allowed to work on this day.*
* commands about, Exodus 20:8–11; 31:12–17
* Jesus is Lord of, Matthew 12:1–13; Mark 2:23–28; Luke 6:1–11

sackcloth (SAK-cloth) *a type of clothing made from rough cloth; worn by people to show their sadness,* Genesis 37:33–35; Esther 4:1; Matthew 11:21

sacrifice (SAK-rih-fice) *to give something valuable to God.*
* burnt sacrifices, Leviticus 6:8–13
* drink sacrifices, Leviticus 23:13; Numbers 15:5; 28:7
* penalty sacrifices, Leviticus 7:1–10
* fellowship sacrifices, Leviticus 3; 7:11–27
* sin sacrifices, Leviticus 4
* limits of, Hebrews 9; 10
* living sacrifice, Romans 12:1

Sadducees (SAD-you-seez) *a Jewish religious group that didn't believe in angels or resurrection; they believed only the first five books of the Old Testament were true.*
* challenged Jesus, Matthew 22:23–33
* arrested Peter and John, Acts 4:1–3
* arrested the apostles, Acts 5:17–42
* Paul spoke to the council, Acts 23:1–9

safety, city of, *city of refuge. In Bible times, someone who had accidentally killed another person could go to a city of safety for protection. As long as he was there, the dead person's relative could not punish him.*
* rules about, Numbers 35:6–34; Joshua 20

saffron (SAF-ron) *a purple flower; parts of it are used as a spice,* Song of Solomon 4:14

saint, *holy person; another word for "Christian",* Acts 9:41; Romans 1:7; 1 Corinthians 14:33

Salem (SAY-lem) *means "peace"; an old name for Jerusalem.*
* home of Melchizedek, Genesis 14:18; Hebrews 7:1–2

Salome, daughter of Herodias (sah-LO-mee)
* had John the Baptist killed, Matthew 14:3–12; Mark 6:17–29

Salome, wife of Zebedee, *the mother of the apostles James and John,* Mark 15:40; 16:1

salt
* used to preserve foods, Job 6:6; Mark 9:50
* Lot's wife turned into salt, Genesis 19:15–26
* "You are the salt of the earth", Matthew 5:13

Salt Sea, See "Dead Sea".

salvation (sal-VAY-shun) *being rescued from danger; being saved from sin and its punishment.*
* as God's gift, John 3:16; Ephesians 2:8; Titus 2:11
* through Christ, Acts 4:12; 1 Thessalonians 5:9; 1 Timothy 1:15; Hebrews 5:7–9

- as a helmet, Ephesians 6:17; 1 Thessalonians 5:8
- urgency of, 2 Corinthians 6:2; Hebrews 2:3
- rejoice in, Psalms 9:14; 13:5; 51:12; Isaiah 25:9

Samaritan (sah-MAH-rih-tun) *a person from the area of Samaria in Palestine. These people were only partly Jewish, so the Jews hated them.* John 4:9
- Jesus taught a Samaritan woman, John 4:1–42
- story of the good Samaritan, Luke 10:25–37

Samson (SAM-son) *one of Israel's judges; he was famous for his great strength.*
- birth of, Judges 13
- married a Philistine, Judges 14 — 15
- tricked by Delilah, Judges 16:4–22
- death of, Judges 16:23–31
- hero of faith, Hebrews 11:32

Samuel (SAM-u-el) *the last judge in Israel.*
- birth of, 1 Samuel 1:1–20
- worked in the Temple, 1 Samuel 1:21 — 2:26
- became a prophet, 1 Samuel 3
- appointed Saul as king, 1 Samuel 10
- appointed David as king, 1 Samuel 16:1–13
- death of, 1 Samuel 25:1

Sanballat (san-BAL-lat) *governor of Samaria who tried to stop Nehemiah from rebuilding the walls of Jerusalem,* Nehemiah 4 — 6

sanctify (SANK-teh-fy) *to make holy or ready for service to God,* John 17:17–19; 1 Corinthians 6:11; 1 Peter 1:2

sanctuary (SANK-choo-air-ee) See "Holy Place".

sand
- Abraham's descendants as numerous as, Genesis 22:17; 32:12
- Job's days as numerous as, Job 29:18
- house built on, Matthew 7:26–27

Sanhedrin (san-HEE-drin) See "council".

Sapphira (sah-FY-ruh) *wife of Ananias.*
- lied to the Holy Spirit, Acts 5:1–11

Sarah (SAIR-uh) *wife of Abraham,* Genesis 11:29–30
- gave Hagar to Abraham, Genesis 16:1–6
- name changed from "Sarai", Genesis 17:15–16
- gave birth to Isaac, Genesis 21:1–7
- death of, Genesis 23

Satan (SAY-tun) *means "enemy"; the devil; the enemy of God and man.*
- encouraged David to sin, 1 Chronicles 21:1
- tested Job, Job 1:6–12; 2:1–7
- tempted Jesus, Luke 4:1–13
- a fallen angel, Luke 10:18–19
- to be thrown into lake of fire, Revelation 20:10

Saul, king of Israel
- appointed king, 1 Samuel 9 — 10
- disobeyed God, 1 Samuel 15
- tried to kill David, 1 Samuel 19; 23:7–29
- death of, 1 Samuel 31

Saul of Tarsus, Acts 13:9. See "Paul".

saviour, (SAY-vee-ur) *a rescuer*
- God as Saviour, Psalm 25:5; Isaiah 45:21; Luke 1:47; 1 Timothy 1:1
- Christ as Saviour, Luke 2:11; John 4:42; Ephesians 5:23; Titus 2:13

scarlet (SCAR-let) *a bright red colour,* Exodus 26:1; Joshua 2:18; Isaiah 1:18; Matthew 27:28

sceptre (SEP-tur) *a wand or a rod that the king holds; a sign of his power,* Esther 4:11; Psalm 60:7

scourge (SKURJ) *to beat someone with a whip or stick,* 1 Kings 12:11
- Jesus scourged, Matthew 27:26; Mark 15:15
- Paul scourged, Acts 21:32; 2 Corinthians 11:24

scribe, *to write, to count, and to put in order. In New Testament times scribes were men who wrote copies of the Scriptures.*
- Ezra as scribe, Nehemiah 8:1
- against Jesus, Matthew 15:1–9
- condemned by Jesus, Matthew 23:13–36

Scriptures (SCRIP-churs) *special writings of God's word for people. When the word Scriptures is used in the New Testament, it usually means the Old Testament. Later, it came to mean the whole Bible.*
- fulfilled, Matthew 26:52–54; John 19:24,28,36
- given by God, 2 Timothy 3:16

scroll, *a long roll of paper used for writing,* Deuteronomy 17:18; Jeremiah 36; Revelation 5:1–5

Scythians (SITH-ee-unz) *a group of wandering people who lived near the Black Sea,* Colossians 3:11

Sea of Galilee, See "Galilee, Lake".

Sea of Reeds, See "Red Sea".

seal, *a tool with a design or picture carved on it. Kings pressed this seal into wax and used it like a signature. Sometimes these seals were worn as rings.*
- examples of, 1 Kings 21:8; Esther 8:8

seed
- created by God, Genesis 1:11,12,29
- parables of, Matthew 13:1–43

seer, *another name for prophet.* See "prophet".

selah (SEE-lah) *probably a musical direction; used in the Psalms. It may mean to pause. The word was not intended to be spoken when reading the psalm.* Psalms 3:2,4,8;89:4,37, 45,48

Sennacherib (sen-AK-ur-ib) *king of Assyria from 705 to 681 BC*
- attacked Jerusalem, 2 Kings 18:13–19; 2 Chronicles 32:1–23; Isaiah 36 — 37

Sermon on the Mount, *a sermon Jesus preached as he was sitting on the side of a mountain near Lake Galilee,* Matthew 5 — 7

serpent, See "snake".

servant
- of the Lord, Deuteronomy 34:5; Joshua 2:8; 1 Kings 11:32; Luke 1:38
- Jesus as a, Philippians 2:7
- parable of, Matthew 25:14–30
- Jesus' followers to be, Matthew 20:25–27

Seth, *the third son of Adam and Eve,* Genesis 4:25–26; 5:6–8; Luke 3:38

Shadrach (SHAD-rak) *a friend of Daniel.*
- taken into captivity, Daniel 1
- became a leader, Daniel 2:49

* saved from the furnace, Daniel 3

Shallum (SHAL-um) *king of Israel who ruled for only one month in 752 BC,* 2 Kings 15:10–15

Shalmaneser (shal-mah-NEE-zer) *a king of Assyria,* 2 Kings 17:1–6; 18:9

Shaphan (SHAY-fan) *an assistant to King Josiah,* 2 Kings 22:3–14; 2 Chronicles 34:8–21

sharing
* commanded, Luke 3:11; Romans 12:13; 1 Timothy 6:18
* examples of, Acts 2:42–47; 4:32; 2 Corinthians 8:1–4

Sharon (SHAR-un) *the plain in Palestine along the coast of the Mediterranean Sea,* 1 Chronicles 5:16; 27:29; Song of Solomon 2:1; Isaiah 33:9

sheaf (SHEEF) *a bundle of grain stalks that have been cut and tied together,* Genesis 37:7; Leviticus 23:10; Job 24:10

Sheba, queen of (SHE-buh) *a queen who came to visit Solomon and see his wealth,* 1 Kings 10:1–13

Shebna (SHEB-nuh) *the manager of the palace for King Hezekiah,* 2 Kings 18:17 — 19:4; Isaiah 36:1 — 37:4

sheep
* God's people compared to, Ezekiel 34; John 10:1–18; 1 Peter 2:25
* parable of, Luke 15:1–7

Shem, *Noah's oldest son,* Genesis 6:10; 7:13; 10:21–31

sheminith (SHEM-ih-nith) *a musical term in the Psalms that means an octave (eight notes); may mean to use an instrument with eight strings,* Psalms 6; 12

shepherd
* David as, 1 Samuel 17:15,34–36
* Lord as, Psalm 23
* Jesus, the good shepherd, John 10:1–18
* elders as, 1 Peter 5:1–4

Sheshbazzar (shesh-BAZ-ur) *governor of the Jews in 538 BC,* Ezra 1:7–11; 5:13–16

shiggaion (shi-GY-on) *probably a musical term; used in the Psalms; may mean that the psalm is a sad song,* Psalm 7

shigionoth (shi-GY-o-noth) *probably a musical term,* Habakkuk 3:1

Shiloh (SHY-low) *a town north of Jerusalem.*
* location of the Holy Tent, Joshua 18:1,8; Judges 18:31; Jeremiah 7:12

Shimei (SHIM-ee-eye) *a relative of King Saul.*
* cursed David, 2 Samuel 16:5–14
* asked forgiveness, 2 Samuel 19:16–23
* death of, 1 Kings 2:36–46

ship, 1 Kings 9:26–28; 22:48; Acts 27

Shishak (SHY-shak) *king of Egypt during the time of Solomon and Rehoboam.*
* attacked Jerusalem, 1 Kings 14:25–28; 2 Chronicles 12:1–9

showbread, See "bread that shows we are in God's presence".

Shunammite (SHOO-nah-mite) *a person from Shunem, a town in northern Israel.*
* Shunammite woman took care of Elisha, 2 Kings 4:8–17
* her son raised from the dead, 2 Kings 4:18–37
* given back her land, 2 Kings 8:1–6

sickle (SICK-ul) *a tool for cutting grain,* Revelation 14:14–19

Sidon (SY-don) *a Phoenician city on the coast of the Mediterranean Sea,* Genesis 10:19; Matthew 11:21–22; Mark 7:31; Acts 27:3–4

siege mound (SEEJ) *earth piled against a city wall to make it easier for attackers to climb up and attack the city,* 2 Samuel 20:15; Isaiah 37:33; Jeremiah 6:6

signet ring (SIG-net RING) *a ring worn by a king or other important person. It had his seal on it.* Genesis 41:42; Esther 3:10; 8:2–10; Daniel 6:17. See "seal".

Sihon (SY-hon) *a king of the Amorites when the Israelites came out of Egypt.*
* refused to let Israelites pass, Numbers 21:21–31; Deuteronomy 2:24–37

Silas (SY-lus) *also "Silvanus"; a teacher in the church in Jerusalem, who often travelled with Paul.*
* sent to the Gentiles, Acts 15:22–23; 17:16
* joined Paul in Corinth, Acts 18:5
* helped with Peter's letter, 1 Peter 5:12

Siloam, pool of (sy-LO-um) *a pool of water in Jerusalem,* John 9:1–12

Silvanus (sil-VAN-us) See "Silas".

Simeon of Jerusalem (SIM-ee-un) *a godly man who saw baby Jesus in the Temple,* Luke 2:25–35

Simeon of Israel, *one of the twelve sons of Israel,* Genesis 29:33; 42:23–36
* descendants of, Numbers 1:22–23; 26:12–14

Simon, brother of Jesus (SY-mun) Matthew 13:55

Simon of Cyrene (sy-REE-nee) *carried the cross of Jesus,* Matthew 27:32; Mark 15:21; Luke 23:26

Simon Peter, See "Peter".

Simon, the magician, *tried to buy the power of the Holy Spirit,* Acts 8:9–24

Simon, the Zealot, *an apostle of Jesus,* Matthew 10:4; Mark 3:18; Luke 6:15; Acts 1:13

sin, *a word, thought, or act against the law of God.*
* offering for, Leviticus 4; 6:24–30; Hebrews 7:27; 10:4–12
* committed by everyone, Romans 3:23; 1 John 1:8–10
* Christ died for, Romans 4:25; 1 Corinthians 15:3; 1 Peter 2:24; 1 John 2:2; 3:5
* results of, Isaiah 59:2; Romans 6:23; Ephesians 2:1; Hebrews 12:1

Sinai (SYE-nee-eye) *a mountain in the desert between Egypt and Canaan.*
* Moses received the Ten Commandments there, Exodus 19–20

singing, *a way of praising God and teaching each other,* Judges 5:3; Psalm 30:4; Ephesians 5:19; Colossians 3:16

Sisera (SIS-er-uh) *captain of a Canaanite army,* Judges 4

slave
* rules about, Exodus 21:1–11,16,26–32; Ephesians 6:5–9; 1 Timothy 6:1–2

slave woman, *concubine; she bore children for her master, but was not considered equal to a wife.*
* Hagar as, Genesis 16:1–3
* of Solomon, 1 Kings 11:2–3

sleep
* God never sleeps, Psalm 121:4
* danger of, Proverbs 6:10–11
* Eutychus fell asleep, Acts 20:9
* to awake from, Romans 13:11
* a gift from the Lord, Psalm 127:2

sling, *a weapon for throwing rocks,* Judges 20:16; 1 Samuel 17:39–50; 2 Kings 3:24–25

slothful (SLOTH-ful) *lazy and undependable,* Proverbs 6:6–11; 13:4; Matthew 25:26; Hebrews 6:12

sluggard, See "slothful".

snake
* sticks became snakes, Exodus 7:8–13
* bronze snake made by Moses, Numbers 21:4–9; John 3:14
* Paul bitten by, Acts 28:1–6

Sodom (SOD-um) *a town known for its evil people.*
* destroyed, Genesis 18:17 — 19:29
* symbol of evil, Matthew 10:11–15; 11:20–24; Revelation 11:8

soldier
* arrested Jesus, John 18:12–13
* made fun of Jesus, Matthew 27:27–31; Luke 23:11
* at Jesus' death, Matthew 27:32–37; Luke 23:26–38,47; John 19:1–3,16–24,28–35
* lied about Jesus' resurrection, Matthew 28:11–15
* Cornelius, Acts 10:1
* guarded Peter, Acts 12:6
* Christian compared to, 2 Timothy 2:3–4

Solomon (SOL-o-mon) *a son of David; famous for his wisdom.*
* became king, 1 Kings 1:28–53
* wisdom of, 1 Kings 3:1–15; 4:29–34
* made a wise decision, 1 Kings 3:16–28
* built the Temple, 1 Kings 6; 7:13–51
* visited by the queen of Sheba, 1 Kings 10:1–13; Matthew 12:42
* married many women, 1 Kings 11:1–8
* death of, 1 Kings 11:40–41

Solomon's Porch (SOL-o-mon's PORCH) *a covered courtyard on the east side of the Temple,* 1 Kings 7:6; John 10:23; Acts 3:11; 5:12

Son of David, *a name the Jews used for the Christ because the Saviour was to come from the family of King David,* Matthew 1:1; 9:27; 15:22; 21:9

Son of Man, *a name Jesus called himself. It showed that he was God's Son, but he was also a human being.* Matthew 24:30; Mark 13:26; Luke 21:27; 22:69–70

sorcery (SOR-sir-ee) *trying to put magical spells on people or harming them by magic,* Acts 8:9–25; 19:18–19
* warnings against, Leviticus 19:26; Deuteronomy 18:14–15; 2 Kings 17:17

soul (SOLE) *what makes a person alive. Sometimes the Bible writers used words like "heart" and "soul" to mean a person's whole being or the person himself.*
* "destroy the soul and the body", Matthew 10:28
* losing, Matthew 16:26
* "all your heart and all your soul", Matthew 22:37
* joined with the spirit, Hebrews 4:12

sower, *someone who plants seeds to grow into crops,* Matthew 13:1–43; 2 Corinthians 9:6

Spirit (SPIH-rit) See "Holy Spirit".

spirit, *the part of humans that was made to be like God because God is spirit. The New Testament also talks about evil spirits.* Isaiah 26:9; 1 Thessalonians 5:23; James 2:26
* evil spirit, Matthew 12:43; Mark 1:23; 5:2; Luke 4:33

spiritual gifts, *special talents or abilities that God gives his people,* Romans 12:6–8; 1 Corinthians 12:1–11; 14; Ephesians 4:7–13

spring, *a natural fountain,* Genesis 7:11; Exodus 15:27

staff, *a shepherd's walking stick,* Exodus 4:1–5; 7:8–12; Numbers 20:6–11; Psalm 23:4

steal, See also "robber".
* commands against, Exodus 20:15; Matthew 19:18; Romans 13:9; Ephesians 4:28

Stephen (STEE-ven) *one of the seven men chosen to serve the church in Jerusalem; the first martyr for Christ.*
* chosen to serve the church, Acts 6:5–6
* killed by the Jews, Acts 6:8—7:60

Stoics (STOW-ics) *followers of a man named Zero, who believed that nature was controlled by the gods and who taught that people should learn self-control,* Acts 17:18

stoning, *a way of killing someone by throwing rocks at him.*
* commanded, Deuteronomy 17:2–7
* Naboth stoned, 1 Kings 21:13
* Stephen stoned, Acts 7:54–60
* Paul stoned, Acts 14:19

strength
* love God with all your strength, Deuteronomy 6:5; Mark 12:30
* God as the source, Psalms 18:1; 73:26; Philippians 4:13; 1 Peter 4:11

stronghold, *a fortress, a well protected place,* 1 Samuel 22:4; 2 Samuel 5:17

suffering
* proper attitude toward, 2 Corinthians 1:3–7; James 5:10
* value of, Romans 8:17–18; 1 Peter 3:8–17
* of Jesus, Isaiah 53:3–10; Luke 24:26,46; Philippians 3:10; Hebrews 2:18

swaddling clothes, *pieces of cloth that were wrapped around a newborn baby in Jesus' time,* Luke 2:7–12

sword
* of fire, Genesis 3:24
* a weapon, Joshua 5:13; 1 Samuel 17:45; Matthew 26:51–52
* the word of God, Ephesians 6:17; Hebrews 4:12

Sychar (SY-kar) *a small town in Samaria near Jacob's well,* John 4:5–6

synagogue (SIN-uh-gog) *"a meeting". By the first century, the Jews met in synagogues to read and study the Scriptures. The building was also used as the Jewish court and as a school.*
* Jesus taught in, Matthew 4:23; Mark 1:21; Luke 4:16–17
* Paul spoke there, Acts 17:1,10

Syria (SEER-ee-uh) *an area north of Galilee and east of the Mediterranean Sea; called "Aram" in Old Testament times. See "Aram".*
* enemy of Israel, 1 Kings 11:25; 20:1–34; 2 Kings 13:22–25
* learned about Jesus, Matthew 4:24

T

tabernacle (TAB-er-NAK-'l) See "Meeting Tent".

tablets of the agreement, *two flat stones on which God wrote the Ten Commandments.*
* given to Moses, Exodus 19—20; 24:12–18
* broken by Moses, Exodus 32:15–19
* the second tablets, Exodus 34:1–4
* in the Most Holy Place, Hebrews 9:4

Tabitha (TAB-eh-thuh) See "Dorcas".

Tabor, Mount (TAY-bor) *in the Valley of Jezreel about twenty kilometres from Lake Galilee,* Judges 4:6–16; Psalm 89:12

tambourine (tam-bah-REEN) *a musical instrument that is beaten to keep rhythm,* Exodus 15:20; 1 Samuel 18:6; Psalm 81:2

Tarshish (TAR-shish) *a city somewhere on the western side of the Mediterranean Sea,* Jonah 1:3; 4:2

Tarsus (TAR-sus) *the most important city in Cilicia, which is now the country of Turkey,* Acts 9:30; 11:25–26
* home of Paul, Acts 9:11; 21:39; 22:3

tax collector, *a Jew hired by the Romans to collect taxes,* Matthew 9:10–11
* Matthew, Matthew 10:3; Luke 5:27
* Zacchaeus, Luke 19:1–10

teacher
* Jesus called a, Matthew 8:19; Mark 10:17; John 1:38; 3:2
* in the church, Romans 12:7; Ephesians 4:11; 1 Timothy 4:13
* false, 1 Timothy 4:1–5; 2 Peter 2:1
* to be judged more strictly, James 3:1

teaching
* commanded, Deuteronomy 6:1–7; Matthew 28:20; 2 Timothy 2:2,14–15; Titus 2

Teachings of Moses, *or the "Law of Moses",* Deuteronomy 31:24–26; Joshua 23:6; Nehemiah 8
* purpose of, Romans 3:20; 5:20; Galatians 3:21–25
* limitations of, Romans 8:3; Galatians 2:19; Hebrews 10:1

temple (TEM-p'l) *a building where people worship. God told the Jewish people to worship him at the Temple in Jerusalem.*
* Solomon's Temple, 1 Kings 6—8; 2 Chronicles 2—7
* the Temple rebuilt, Ezra 3
* the body as a temple, John 2:19–22; 1 Corinthians 3:16–17; 6:19–20; 2 Corinthians 6:16

temptation (temp-TAY-shun) *the devil's attempt to get us to do something wrong.*
* Jesus tempted, Matthew 4:1–11; Luke 4:1–13; Hebrews 4:15–16
* a way of escape from, 1 Corinthians 10:13
* source of, James 1:13–15

Ten Commandments, *the rules God gave Moses on Mount Sinai,* Exodus 20:1–20; 31:18; 34:1–28; Deteronomy 5:1–22

tent
* Abram's tents, Genesis 13:18
* peg, Judges 4:21–22
* makers of, Acts 18:3

Tent, See "Meeting Tent".

Thaddaeus (THAD-ee-us) *one of the twelve apostles,* Matthew 10:3; Mark 3:18

thankfulness, Psalm 107:1; 1 Thessalonians 5:8; Hebrews 12:28

Theophilus (thee-OFF-ih-lus) *the person to whom the books of Luke and Acts were written,* Luke 1:1–4; Acts 1:1

Thessalonica (THES-ah-loh-nik-ah) *the capital of the country of Macedonia, which is now northern Greece,* 1 Thessalonians 1:1; 2 Thessalonians 1:1
* Paul preached there, Acts 17:1–9

Thomas (TOM-us) *Didymus; one of the twelve apostles,* Matthew 10:2–3
* questioned Jesus, John 14:5–7
* saw Jesus after resurrection, John 20:24–29; 21:2

thorn, *sharp points on a branch or stem of a plant.*
* as a curse on Adam, Genesis 3:17–18
* crown of, Matthew 27:29; Mark 15:17; John 19:2–5

threshing floor, *a place where farmers separated grain from chaff. This was done by beating the stalks on the hard ground, throwing them in the air, and letting the wind blow the chaff away.*
* angel visited Gideon there, Judges 6:11
* David bought, 2 Samuel 24:16–25

throne
* king's throne, 1 Kings 10:18–19
* God's throne, Matthew 5:34; Hebrews 4:16; Revelation 3:21; 4

Thummim (THUM-im) *the Urim and Thummim may have been gems. They were attached to the holy robe of the high priest and were used to learn God's will.* Exodus 28:29–30; Leviticus 8:8; Deuteronomy 33:8

Thyatira (THY-ah-TY-rah) *an important city in Asia famous for its purple cloth,* Acts 16:13–14; Revelation 1:11; 2:18–29

Tiberius Caesar (tie-BEER-ee-us SEE-zur) *Roman emperor during the last half of Jesus' life,* Luke 3:1

Tiglath-Pileser (TIG-lath-peh-LEE-zur) *king of Assyria who helped Ahaz; also called "Pul".*
* attacked Israel, 2 Kings 15:19–20
* rescued Ahaz, 2 Kings 16:7–10

Tigris (TY-gris) *a great river in the eastern part of the Bible lands,* Genesis 2:14; Daniel 10:4

Timothy (TIM-oh-thee) *close friend and helper of the apostle Paul.*
* helped Paul, Acts 16:1–3; 17:13–16; 1 Corinthians 4:17; 2 Corinthians 1:19
* instructed by Paul, 1 and 2 Timothy

tithe (TYTH) *"tenth". The Jews were told to give one tenth of what they earned to God.* Leviticus 27:30–32; Deuteronomy 12:1–6; Luke 11:42; 18:12

Titus (TY-tus) *trusted friend and helper of the apostle Paul.*
* helped Corinthians, 2 Corinthians 7:6–7,13–15;8:6,16,23
* appointed elders, Titus 1:4–5
* Paul's instructions to, Titus 1—3

Tobiah (toe-BY-uh) *tried to keep Nehemiah from rebuilding the walls of Jerusalem,* Nehemiah 2:10–20; 6:10–19; 13:4–9

tomb (TOOM)
* of Lazarus, John 11:38–44
* of Jesus, Matthew 27:57—28:15; Mark 15:42—16:30; Luke 23:50—24:12; John 19:38—20:9

tongue (TUNG)
* lying tongue hated by God, Proverbs 6:16–17
* cannot be tamed, James 3:2–12

tower of Babel, See "Babel".

transfiguration (tranz-fig-you-RAY-shun) *"to change".*
Jesus was transfigured in front of Peter, James, and John when his face and clothes began to shine brightly.
Matthew 17:1–9; Mark 9:2–9; Luke 9:28–36

tree
* of knowledge of good and evil, Genesis 2:9; 3:3
* of life, Genesis 2:9; Revelation 2:7; 22:2,14
* people compared to, Psalms 1:3; 92:12; Jeremiah 17:8; Matthew 3:10; 12:33
* cross described as a tree, Galatians 3:13

trespass, (TRESS-pass) See "sin".

tribe, *all descendants of a certain person. The twelve tribes of Israel were descendants of the twelve sons of Jacob, who was later named "Israel".* Numbers 1 — 2
* Canaan divided among, Joshua 13:7–33; 15 —19

triumphal entry (try-UM-ful) *the time Jesus entered Jerusalem just before his death,* Matthew 21:1–11; Mark 11:1–19; Luke 19:28–44; John 12:12–15

Troas (TRO-az) *one of the most important cities in northwest Asia,* Acts 16:8–10; 20:5–12; 2 Corinthians 2:12

Trophimus (TROF-eh-mus) *non-Jewish Christian who travelled with Paul,* Acts 20:3–4; 21:27–29; 2 Timothy 4:20

trumpet (TRUM-pet) *in Bible times it was made from animal horns; used to call an army together or announce something important,* Numbers 10:2–10; Joshua 6:4–20; 1 Corinthians 15:52

trust
* a duty, Luke 16:11; 1 Corinthians 4:2; Titus 2:10
* in God, Psalm 20:7; Proverbs 3:5; 16:20; Romans 4:5;10:11; 1 Peter 2:6
* in lesser things, Psalms 49:13–14; 118:9; Proverbs 11:28; Isaiah 2:22

truth
* speaking honestly, Psalm 15:2; Proverbs 16:13
* God's message, John 17:17; Romans 1:25; Ephesians 1:13; 1 John 1:6

tunic (TYOU-nik) *a kind of coat,* Exodus 28:39–40; John 19:23

Tychicus (TYK-ih-kus) *Christian from Asia who did important jobs for Paul,* Acts 20:4; Ephesians 6:21–22; Colossians 4:7–9

Tyre (TIRE) *large, important city in Phoenicia, which is now part of the country of Lebanon,* Mark 7:24–31; Acts 12:20
* Hiram, king of, 2 Samuel 5:11; 1 Kings 9:10–14; 2 Chronicles 2
* a wicked city, Matthew 11:21–22; Luke 10:13–14

U

uncircumcised, See "circumcision".

unclean, *the state of a person, animal or action that was not pleasing to God. In the Old Testament God said certain animals were unclean and were not to be eaten. If a person disobeyed the rules about being clean, he was called unclean and could not serve God until he was made clean again.* See "clean".
* unclean animals, Leviticus 11; Acts 10:9–15
* unclean people, Leviticus 12—15
* God declared everyone to be clean, Acts 10

unleavened bread (un-LEV-'nd BREAD) *bread made without yeast.*
* used in the Passover Feast, Exodus 12:20; Deuteronomy 16:1–4

Unleavened Bread, Day of, *the first day of the Feast of Unleavened Bread or Passover,* Matthew 26:17; Luke 22:7

upper room, *upstairs room in a house.*
* Jesus and his followers met there, Mark 14:14–15; Luke 22:9–12

Ur (ERR) *a great city thousands of years ago; today in the country of Iraq.*
* home of Abram, Genesis 11:28–31

Uriah (you-RY-uh) *a soldier in King David's army.*
* killed by David, 2 Samuel 11

Urim (YOUR-im) See "Thummim".

Uzzah (UZ-uh) *touched the Ark of the Agreement and died,* 2 Samuel 6:1–8; 1 Chronicles 13:1–14

Uzziah (uh-ZY-uh) *a king of Judah,* 2 Kings 15:13–15; 2 Chronicles 26; Isaiah 6:1

V

Vashti (VASH-tee) *the wife of Ahasuerus, king of Persia,* Esther 1:1–20

veil (VALE) *a head covering usually worn by women; also, a curtain in the Temple.*
* worn by women, Genesis 24:65; Song of Solomon 4:1; Isaiah 3:19
* the Temple veil, Matthew 27:51; Mark 15:38; Luke 23:45

vine
* fruit of the, Matthew 26:29; Mark 14:25; Luke 22:18
* Jesus as the, John 15:1–11

vineyard (VIN-yard)
* Naboth's, 1 Kings 21
* parables of, Matthew 20:1–16; 28:46; Mark 12:1–12; Luke 20:9–19

virgin (VUR-jin) *person who has not had sexual relations,* Deuteronomy 22:13–29; Isaiah 7:14; Matthew 1:23; Luke 1:34

vision (VIH-shun) *like a dream. God often spoke to his people in visions.*
* of Abram, Genesis 15:1
* of Daniel, Daniel 2:19
* of Peter and Cornelius, Acts 10:1–16
* of Paul, Acts 16:9

vow, *a special and serious promise often made to God.*
* rules about, Numbers 30; Deuteronomy 23:21–23
* the Nazirite, Numbers 6:1–21
* of Jephthah, Judges 11:29–40
* of Paul, Acts 18:18

W

war
* rumours of, Matthew 24:6–7; Mark 13:7–8; Luke 21:9–10
* spiritual, 2 Corinthians 10:3–4
* will end, Micah 4:1–3

watchman
* examples of, 2 Samuel 18:24–27; Psalm 130:6
* prophets as watchmen, Ezekiel 3:17; Micah 7:4

water
* in creation, Genesis 1:1–2,6–10
* bitter, Exodus 15:22–27
* from a rock, Exodus 17:1–7

- for David, 2 Samuel 23:15–17
- drink of, Matthew 10:42; Mark 9:41
- Jesus walked on, Matthew 14:22–36
- turned to wine, John 2:1–11
- living water, John 4:1–15

"Way, the", *one of the earliest names given to Christians. Jesus said he was "the way" to reach God.* Acts 9:1–2; 19:9,23; 22:4; 24:14,22

wedding, Matthew 22:1–14; Luke 14:8; John 2:1–11

Western Sea, See "Mediterranean Sea".

widow
- examples of, Ruth 4:10; 1 Kings 17:8–24; Luke 21:2–4
- care for, Deuteronomy 24:17–22; 1 Timothy 5:3–16; James 1:27

wife
- man united with, Genesis 2:24
- the good wife, Proverbs 31:10–31
- teachings about, 1 Corinthians 7:1–16
- responsibility of, Ephesians 5:21–24,33; Colossians 3:18; 1 Peter 3:1

wine
- danger of, Proverbs 20:1; Ephesians 5:18
- at wedding in Cana, John 2:1–11
- for the stomach, 1 Timothy 5:23

winepress, *a pit where grapes were mashed to get the juice out. The winepress is sometimes used to describe how enemy armies will defeat people as if they were grapes crushed in a winepress.*
- examples of, Judges 6:11; Matthew 21:33
- as a symbol of punishment, Lamentations 1:15; Revelation 14:19–20; 19:15

wisdom (WIZ-d'm) *understanding what is really important in life. This wisdom comes from God.* Proverbs 1:1–2,7; 2; 4
- Solomon asked for, 1 Kings 4:29–34
- source of, James 1:5
- a parable about, Matthew 25:1–13

wise men, *"magi"; men who studied the stars,* Genesis 41:8; Exodus 7:11; Matthew 2:1–12

witchcraft, *using the power of the devil to do magic.*
- warnings against, Deuteronomy 18:10–12; Galatians 5:19–21
- examples of, 2 Kings 9:22; 2 Chronicles 33:6

witness, Acts 1:8,22; 2:32; 22:14–15

woman
- created by God, Genesis 2:22–23
- how to treat a, 1 Timothy 5:2,14

word, *in the Bible often means God's message to us in the Scriptures. Jesus is called the "Word" because he shows us what God is like.*
- like a lamp, Psalm 119:105
- like a sword, Hebrews 4:12
- living in God's people, John 15:7; Colossians 3:16; 1 John 2:14
- lasts forever, Matthew 24:35; 1 Peter 1:25
- people's words, Proverbs 12:25; 25:11; Matthew 12:36–37
- as a message, 1 Peter 1:24–25; 1 John 2:14
- Jesus as the "Word", John 1:1–5,14; 1 John 1:1–2

world, *the planet Earth; also the people on this earth who follow Satan.*

- as the Earth, 2 Samuel 22:16; Psalm 18:15
- as a symbol of wickedness, Romans 12:2; Ephesians 2:2

worship, *to praise and serve God.*
- commanded, Exodus 34:14; Luke 4:8; John 4:20–24

X-Y

Xerxes (ZERK-sees) *a king of Persia; also called "Ahasuerus",* Esther 1 — 10

yeast *an ingredient used to make breads and cakes rise; used in the New Testament to stand for a person's influence over others. See also "unleavened bread".*
- as a symbol for influence, Mark 8:15; Luke 13:21

yoke, *a wooden frame that fits on the necks of animals to hold them together while working.*
- examples of, Deuteronomy 21:3; 1 Kings 19:19–21

youth
- "Remember your Creator", Ecclesiastes 12:1
- teachings about, 1 Timothy 4:12

Z

Zacchaeus (za-KEE-us) *Jewish tax collector in the city of Jericho,* Luke 19:1–8

Zadok (ZAY-dok) *priest who helped King David,* 2 Samuel 15:24–36; 17:15–21; 1 Kings 1:18–45

Zarephath (ZA-reh-fath) *a Canaanite town where the prophet Elijah helped a widow,* 1 Kings 17:8–24; Luke 4:25–26

Zealots (ZEL-ots) *a group of Jewish men also called "Enthusiasts". They hated the Romans for controlling their home country, and they planned to force the Romans out.*
- Simon, the Zealot, Matthew 10:4; Mark 3:18; Luke 6:15; Acts 1:13

Zebedee (ZEB-uh-dee) *a fisherman on Lake Galilee,* Matthew 4:21–22; 20:20; Mark 1:19–20; Luke 5:10; John 21:2

Zechariah, father of John the Baptist (ZEK-uh-RY-uh) *a Jewish priest,* Luke 1:5–25,57–80.

Zechariah, king of Israel, *ruled for only six months; killed by Shallum,* 2 Kings 14:29; 15:8–11

Zechariah, son of Berekiah, *a prophet who wrote the next-to-last book in the Old Testament,* Ezra 5:1; Zechariah 1 — 14

Zechariah, son of Jehoiada, *a priest who taught the people to serve God,* 2 Chronicles 24:20–25

Zedekiah, son of Josiah, (zed-eh-KY-uh) *the last king of Judah,* 2 Kings 24:16 — 25:7

Zedekiah, son of Kenaanah, *a false prophet during the time of King Ahab,* 1 Kings 22:1–24

Zedekiah, son of Maaseiah, *a false prophet in Babylon during the time of Jeremiah,* Jeremiah 29:21–23

Zephaniah (zef-uh-NY-uh) *a prophet who lived when Josiah was king of Judah; wrote the short book of Zephaniah,* Zephaniah 1:1

Zerubbabel (zeh-RUB-uh-bull) *governor of Jerusalem after the Jews had been in captivity in Babylon for seventy years.*
- returned from exile, Ezra 2:2
- built the altar of God, Ezra 3:1–6
- rebuilt the Temple, Ezra 3:7–10; 5:2

Zeus (ZOOSS) *the chief of the Greek gods,* Acts 14:12–14

Ziba (ZY-buh) *a servant of Saul,* 2 Samuel 9:1–11; 16:1–4; 19:24–30

Zimri (ZIM-rye) *a king of Israel,* 1 Kings 16:11–20

Zion (ZY-on) *a hill inside the city of Jerusalem.* See "Mount Zion".

Ziph (ZIF) *a city about forty kilometres south of Jerusalem,* 1 Samuel 23:14–28; 26:1–25

Zipporah (zih-POR-uh) *the wife of Moses,* Exodus 2:15–22; 4:24–26; 18:1–3

zither (ZITH-ur) *a type of musical instrument that had about forty strings on it,* Ezekiel 3:5,7,10,15